S0-AFB-756

• Bloomsbury Treasury of Quotations

•BLOOMSBURY TREASURY OF QUOTATIONS

First published 1994

Bloomsbury Publishing Plc,
2 Soho Square,
London W1V 5DE

A CIP catalogue record for this book is available from the British Library
ISBN 0 7475 1813 0

Compiled and typeset by
Market House Books, Ltd, Aylesbury

Printed in Britain by Richard Clay Ltd., St Ives plc.

• Contents

• Acknowledgments

Editors

John Daintith
Anne Stibbs

Contributors

Fran Alexander
Graham Betts
Elizabeth Bonham
Deborah Chapman
Sue Cope
Eve Daintith
Hazel Egerton
Rosalind Fergusson
Marie Fitzpatrick
Joan Gallagher
Patrick Gallagher
Joanna Gosling
Jock Graham
Lawrence Holden
Valerie Illingworth
Alan Isaacs
Amanda Isaacs
Stephen Jones
Jonathan Law
Elizabeth Martin
Sandra McQueen
Jennifer Monk
Owen Morris
David Pickering
Megan Remmer
Kathy Rooney
Mark Salad
Ruth Salomon
Jessica Scholes
Gwen Shaw
Mary Shields
Kate Smith
Tracey Smith
Barbara Standen
Gwendoline Stibbs
Leonard Stibbs
Lynn Thomson
Brenda Tomkins
Philip Turner
Linda Wells
Edmund Wright
Jean Wright

• Introduction

The *Bloomsbury Treasury of Quotations* is a compilation of over 20,000 quotations by over 3000 people. It has been produced using the unique Bloomsbury quotations database, created and continuously updated over the last 10 years by a team of more than 40 people. It includes two extensive indexes: a keyword index of over 55,000 separate references and a name index of some 10,000 references. In producing the book, we have given a wide coverage to the people quoted and the sources.

Anyone who sets out to compile a collection of quotations has first to consider the question, 'What is a quotation?' The answer is not clear cut – one is reminded of Dr Johnson's remark about the nature of light: 'Anyone knows what light is but it is not so easy to say what it is.' As a working definition we have adopted the idea that a quotation is a phrase or passage from speech or writing, remembered and recounted or reproduced, especially to illustrate a point or support an argument. Quotations are necessarily fairly short – this is not an anthology of prose or poetry. They are interesting, pithy, and revealing. Some give us an insight into a topic and some reveal something about the speaker. Characteristically, quotations have become separated from the work in which they originally appeared, and can be used in a variety of circumstances. They become part of the language – indeed, as Dr Johnson also said, 'Every quotation contributes something to the stability of the language.'

We have not, however, always adhered strictly to these criteria. There is a fuzzy boundary between sayings that are quotations and sayings that are not quite quotations. For a start, not all quotations are well known, even when they are extracts from the writings or speech of well-known people. How does one deal with profound or significant utterances by unknown or obscure people? Also, how does one classify such things as catch phrases, song titles, graffiti, proverbs, and common idiomatic phrases? What about repartee and anecdotes? In compiling this book we have taken a fairly relaxed view on these matters – our main concern has been to include things that might be of use or interest to the reader.

The needs of the reader have also influenced our approach to the organization of the book. Compilers of books of quotations also have to ask the question, 'Why do people use dictionaries of quotations?' There seems to be several possible reasons:

- To check the details about a familiar quotation, or to find a quotation that is only half-remembered.
- To find unfamiliar quotations about a particular topic – love, death, marriage, feminism, football, etc.
- To find out something about an author through their sayings or writings.
- To browse through to find unexpected and interesting quotations.

Traditionally, there are two main ways in which alphabetical dictionaries of quotations can be arranged. One is biographical, with entries arranged under the name of the speaker or writer. The other is thematic, with quotations given under topics. Both have their advantages and disadvantages and both are equally useful for finding details about a quotation through a keyword index. A biographical arrangement is clearly better for finding the quotations by a particular person. It is, however, difficult and often impossible to locate a selection of quotations about a particular topic. A thematic arrangement overcomes this problem. It is also perhaps better for browsing and has the additional advantage that it allows the inclusion of many people who might not normally be found in biographical compilations. It is, however, not useful for finding the sayings of an individual.

A unique feature of the *Bloomsbury Treasury of Quotations* is that it combines the two approaches. This book is a large collection of quotations selected for their interest, relevance, or wit. It combines, in a single volume, biographical entries – quotations by people – and thematic entries – quotations about topics.

Most of the thematic entries are on the subjects that one would expect – life, death, love, hate, sex, etc. Perhaps less predictable are the more topical themes, including pollution, healthy living, and feminism. These entries also have cross-references to related topics – a reader interested in adultery may find extra guidance by reading the entries on sex, unfaithfulness, and even marriage.

The thematic quotations are largely about the topic under which they are listed. In choosing these quotations we have included things that are familiar – the quotations that many people know – or, at least, half remember. We have also included many writings or sayings that are probably not familiar, but perhaps ought to be. In this we have been guided by Anatole France: 'When a thing has been said, and said well, have no scruple. Take it and copy it.' However, we have made no judgments about what is being said. Indeed, one of the interesting features of this method of organization is the juxtaposition of different opinions.

As well as quotations about subjects we have included a number of quotations that are examples of the theme. Under epitaphs for instance, quotations about epitaphs are given together with examples of epitaphs. Similar themes include last words, execution, boasts, telegrams, misquotations, insults, compliments, and repartee. A reader wishing to insult or compliment someone can look up the relevant theme and be guided by experts.

There are about 450 biographical entries. The main criterion for inclusion has been 'quotability', irrespective of any other merit. This accounts for the appearance of Woody Allen and Dorothy Parker as well as Shakespeare, Byron, and Wordsworth. In general, the quotations under a given entry are quotations by the person. In many cases, for interest, we have added quotations made by others about the person concerned. In addition to the thematic and biographical entries there are entries for Biblical quotations, Proverbs, Nursery Rhymes, and quotations by that productive author known as 'Anon' (see Anonymous).

As far as possible, we have tried to give sources for all the quotations in the book. This has not always been possible; many quotations, which we have labelled 'Attrib.', are sayings or remarks generally ascribed to a person but without an identifiable source. There are also problems in attributing some quotations. Some are widely ascribed to two or more people. For these we have included explanatory notes after the quotation. Another problem is that of co-authors, such as Lennon and McCartney. In these cases the quotations are included under the first named, with a cross reference from the second. This does not, of course, imply that one is in any way more important.

The example of Mae West typifies another difficulty. Many of her sayings are lines from films; therefore the author should, strictly speaking, be the script writer. However, remarks such as 'Come up and see me (sometime)' are so closely associated with her that it would be perverse not to include them under her name.

Yet another problem involves such quotations as those of Goldwyn, Spooner, and Dan Quayle, who almost certainly never made some of the remarks attributed to them. We decided to include these, if only because they are too good to leave out. Some indication of the difficulties in attributing quotations is given by the reaction of one person we telephoned about a quotation. 'Yes,' she said, 'it is often said to be by me, but I was only repeating something I heard years ago.' And the difficulty in selection is illustrated by her next remark. 'But I have said lots of other clever things that nobody has noticed.'

Lists of the thematic and biographical entries included are given in the front of the book. In addition, there are two indexes at the back of the book. One is a key word index to help the reader to locate particular quotations. The other is an author index to help locate quotations by particular speakers and writers.

We hope that the *Bloomsbury Treasury of Quotations* is an enjoyable and informative book to read and browse through. Many people have helped in the preparation of this dictionary – their names are listed on the Acknowledgments page.

The Editors

• Guide to the Book

Biographical Entries

These are arranged in the main section of the book in their normal alphabetical position according to surname. The person's dates are given, followed by a brief biographical entry about the subject's life and work. In many cases, the biographical entry has two sections. The first is a short selection of quotations about the subject – remarks made by other people about the author's character or work. Each quotation is followed by the name of the speaker or writer with dates and a brief biographical note. The source, if known, is also given, sometimes accompanied by an explanatory note. The second, and main, section contains quotations by the subject. In this section, the entries are arranged according to the references. First come the subject's own works, arranged in alphabetical order (but ignoring the 'A' and 'The'). Then follow works by other people in which the subject is quoted, again listed in alphabetical order. Next come speeches, letters, etc., which are generally arranged in date order. These are followed by quotations referenced as Attrib. which are sayings or remarks that are widely and generally attributed to the person involved.

We have broken these rules when it seemed logical to do so – for example by putting 'last words' at the end of the entries.

ENTRY —— **ACHESON, DEAN GOODERHAM**

BIOGRAPHY —— (1893–1971) US lawyer and statesman. Noted for his strong stance against Soviet expansionism, he was prominent in the development of the Truman Doctrine, the Marshall Plan, and NATO.

QUOTATIONS ABOUT THE AUTHOR ——

Quotations about Acheson

1 Washington's number 1 number 2 man.

Anonymous

2 Not only did he not suffer fools gladly; he did not suffer them at all.

Lester Pearson (1897–1972) Canadian statesman. *Time*, 25 Oct 1971

QUOTATIONS BY THE AUTHOR ——

Quotations by Acheson

3 It hasn't taken Winston long to get used to American ways. He hadn't been an American citizen for three minutes before attacking an ex-secretary of state!

At a ceremony in 1963 to make Churchill an honorary American citizen, Churchill obliquely attacked Acheson's reference to Britain losing an empire. *Randolph Churchill* (K. Halle)

CROSS-REFERENCE (to other author) ——

4 It is worse than immoral, it's a mistake.

Describing the Vietnam war. *See also* BOULAY DE LA MEURTHE. Quoted by Alistair Cooke in his radio programme *Letter from America*

Thematic Entries

Within a thematic entry itself, the quotations are arranged alphabetically by author; for the first appearance of an author within an entry, the author's dates and brief biographical note are given. This is followed by any explanatory note that may be required and the source, if it is known. Anonymous quotations come at the beginning of a thematic entry and biblical quotations will be found alphabetized under Bible within the entry.

ENTRY

CROSS-REFERENCE

QUOTATION

QUOTATION NUMBER

EXPLANATORY NOTE

REFERENCE

ABSTINENCE

See also alcohol, self-denial, sex, smoking

1 He neither drank, smoked, nor rode a bicycle. Living frugally,saving his money, he died early, surrounded by greedy relatives. It was a great lesson to me.

John Barrymore (1882–1942) US actor. *The Stage*, Jan 1941 (J. P. McEvoy)

2 If someone asks for a soft drink at a party, we no longer think he is a wimp.

Edwina Currie (1946–) British politician. Speech, Dec 1988

3 Teetotallers lack the sympathy and generosity of men that drink.

W. H. Davies (1871–1940) British poet. *Shorter Lyrics of the 20th Century*, Introduction

4 It was a brilliant affair; water flowed like champagne.

William M. Evarts (1818–1901) US lawyer and statesman. Describing a dinner given by US President Rutherford B. Hayes (1877–81), an advocate of temperance. Attrib.

5 If you resolve to give up smoking, drinking and loving, you don't actually live longer; it just seems longer.

Clement Freud (1924–) British Liberal politician and broadcaster. *The Observer*, 27 Dec 1964

6 Mr Mercaptan went on to preach a brilliant sermon on that melancholy sexual perversion known as continence.

Aldous Huxley (1894–1964) British novelist. *Antic Hay*, Ch. 18

7 My experience through life has convinced me that, while moderation and temperance in all things are commendable and beneficial, abstinence from spirituous liquors is the best safeguard of morals and health.

Robert E. Lee (1807–70) US general. Letter, 9 Dec 1869

8 The few bad poems which occasionally are created during abstinence are of no great interest.

Wilhelm Reich (1897–1957) Austrian-born US psychiatrist. *The Sexual Revolution*

9 The people who are regarded as moral luminaries are those who forego ordinary pleasures themselves and find compensation in interfering with the pleasures of others.

Bertrand Russell (1872–1970) British philosopher. *Sceptical Essays*

10 Lastly (and this is, perhaps, the golden rule), no woman should marry a teetotaller, or a man who does not smoke.

Robert Louis Stevenson (1850–94) Scottish writer. *Virginibus Puerisque*

Keyword Index

This lists in alphabetical order keywords that the user may look up to verify a quotation. Who, for example, said, 'I am dying with the help of too many physicians.' Here, a possible keyword is 'physicians', which appears in the index along with the key phrase

'd. with the help of too many p.'

The references in the keyword index are to the main entry headword followed by the number of the quotation (note that the numbers are not page numbers).

KEYWORD

KEY PHRASE

Trojans Do not trust the horse, T. MISTRUST, 12; VIRGIL, 9
troops t. of unrecording friends LIFE, 93; TENNYSON, 77
trot I don't t. it out and about COLETTE, S, 3; VIRTUE, 12
trouble a lot of t. in his life CHURCHILL, W, 29; WORRY, 12
A t. shared PROVERBS, 70; WORRY, 1
a woman is on a…hunt for t. MARRIAGE, 65
if you're on drugs then you're in t. DRUGS, 4
it saves me the t. of liking them AUSTEN, J, 30; NASTINESS, 2
man…is…full of t. BIBLE, 230; HUMAN CONDITION, 3
'normal' people…cause no t. either to themselves TAYLOR, A, 6
One stops being a child when…telling one's t. DISILLUSION, 5
Our progress…/Is t. and care LIFE, 58; LONGFELLOW, H, 15
Prostitution…keeps her out of t. HELLER, J, 7; SEX, 49
troubled let not your heart be t. PEACE, 4
troubles Don't meet t. half-way PROVERBS, 118; WORRY, 2
I have had t. enough BROWNING, R, 38; MISFORTUNE, 6
pack up your t. in your old kit-bag OPTIMISM, 13
take arms against a sea of t. SHAKESPEARE, 90; SUICIDE, 35
Yesterday, all my t. NOSTALGIA, 15; PAST, 8
troublesome t.…bondage of Rhyming MILTON, J, 29; POETRY, 44
trousers bottoms of my t. rolled ELIOT, T, 14; OLD AGE, 44
I shall wear white flannel t. ELIOT, T, 15; OLD AGE, 45
man should never put on his best t. FREEDOM, 26; IBSEN, H, 4
She is trying to wear the t. of Winston Churchill

Names Index

This lists in alphabetical order the names of all the people who have quotations in the book. Those in bold type also have main biographical entries. As with the keyword index, the reference is to the quotation number (not the page).

AUTHOR
(quoted in thematic entries)

AUTHOR
(with main biographical entry
and quotations in thematic entries)

Abbott, Berenice PHOTOGRAPHY, 1
Abel, Niels Henrik EXPERTS, 1
Aberdare, Lord YOUTH, 1
Abernethy, John CHARITY, 2; DISEASE, 2; FASHION, 1
Abraham, Gerald BLAKE, 1
Accius, Lucius RESPECT, 1
Acheson, Dean BRITAIN, 1; BUREAUCRACY, 1; CHURCHILL, 1; GOVERNMENT, 1; MISTAKES, 2; REPARTEE, 1; TRUMAN, 1
Ackerley, J. R. ILLEGITIMACY, 1
Acland, Richard PUBLISHING, 1
Acton, Harold HOSPITALITY, 8
Acton, Lord GOVERNMENT, 2; MAJORITY, 1; POWER, 3
Acton, W. SEX, 1
Adamov, Arthur THEATRE, 1
Adams, Abigail LETTER-WRITING, 1
Adams, Douglas LIFE, 4; SCIENCE FICTION, 1; SPACE, 1
Adams, F. P. ENVY, 2, 3
Adams, Franklin P. AGE, 3; POLITICS, 1
Adams, Henry Brooks EDUCATION, 2; POLITICS, 2, 3; POWER, 4
Adams, John Quincy JEFFERSON, 1; LAST WORDS, 2; POSTERITY, 1

List of Entries

A

ABILITY

1 One should oblige everyone to the extent of one's ability. One often needs someone smaller than oneself.

Jean de La Fontaine (1621–95) French poet. *Fables*, II, 'Le Lion et le Rat'

2 Intelligence is quickness to apprehend as distinct from ability, which is capacity to act wisely on the thing apprehended.

A. N. Whitehead (1861–1947) British philosopher. *Dialogues*, 35

ABORTION

1 A million women abort every year in France. They do it under dangerous conditions because they are condemned to clandestinity, although, when done under medical supervision, this operation is extremely simple. No-one ever mentions these millions of women. I declare that I am one of them. I declare that I have had an abortion. Just as we demand free access to contraception, we demand freedom of abortion.

A statement, signed by 343 French women, and headed by Simone de Beauvoir, marking the beginning of the campaign for free legal abortion on demand in France. *Le Nouvel Observateur*, 5 Apr 1971

2 Until that day when women, and only women, shall determine which American males must, by law, have vasectomies, then – and only then – will you or any man have the right to determine which American women can have abortions.

Betty Beale *Ms*, Mar 1982

3 Abortions will not let you forget. You remember the children you got that you did not get...

Gwendolyn Brooks (1917–) US poet and writer. *A Street in Bronzeville*, 'The Mother'

4 Abortion leads to an appalling trivialization of the act of procreation.

Donald Coggan, Archbishop of York (1909–) British churchman. Speech to the Shaftesbury Society, 2 Oct 1973

5 The 'immorality' of women, favourite theme of misogynists, is not to be wondered at; how could they fail to feel an inner mistrust of the presumptuous principles that men publicly proclaim and secretly disregard? They learn to believe no longer in what men say when they exalt woman or exalt man: the one thing they are sure of is this rifled and bleeding womb, the shreds of crimson life, this child that is not there. It is at her first abortion that woman begins to 'know'.

Simone de Beauvoir (1908–86) French writer. *Le Deuxième Sexe* (The Second Sex)

6 Contrary to the folklore of abortion as life-long trauma, it is not necessarily a profoundly scarring one either.

Helen Dudar US writer. *Saturday Review of the Society*, 'Abortion for the Asking', Apr 1973

7 The wait seemed interminable, but finally Justice Blackmun read: 'This right of privacy...is broad enough to encompass a woman's decision whether or not to terminate her pregnancy.' This privacy right to abortion...was grounded in either the 'Fourteenth Amendment's concept of personal liberty or...in the Ninth Amendment's reservation of rights to the people'...The Court had ruled that a woman's right to abortion was constitutionally protected.

Marian Faux US writer. Referring to a Supreme Court decision in the Roe v. Wade case concerning the right to abortion.

8 I'm opposed to abortion because I happen to believe that life deserves the protection of society.

Ella Grasso (1919–81) US politician. *Ms*, Oct 1974

9 If men could get pregnant, abortion would be a sacrament.

Florynce R. Kennedy (1916–) US lawyer, civil rights activist, and feminist. *Ms*, 'The Verbal Karate of Florynce R. Kennedy, Esq.' Gloria Steinem, Mar 1973

10 We can't deny that we are destroying a life, because we are, but an unwanted pregnancy destroys two lives.

Mary, sister-in-charge at an abortion clinic. *The Independent*, 2 Apr 1993

11 It serves me right for putting all my eggs in one bastard.

Dorothy Parker (1893–1967) US writer and wit. On going into hospital for an abortion. *You Might As Well Live* (J. Keats)

12 Most women decide to have abortions reluctantly, and with trepidation, as the lesser of two evils. No woman has an abortion for *fun*. They do not see why they should take on the responsibility of an unwanted child after their method of contraception has let them down...their circumstances – bad housing, lack of money, ill health – are such that they cannot cope with a new baby.

Joan Smith (1953–) British writer and journalist. *Misogynies*

13 The greatest destroyer of peace is abortion because if a mother can kill her own child what is left for me to kill you and you to kill me? There is nothing between.

Mother Teresa (1910–) Yugoslavian missionary in Calcutta. Nobel Peace Prize Lecture

ABSENCE

See also separation

1 Long absent, soon forgotten.

Proverb

2 Out of sight, out of mind.

Proverb

3 When the cat's away, the mice will play.

Proverb

4 Absence makes the heart grow fonder,
Isle of Beauty, Fare thee well!

Thomas Haynes Bayly (1797–1839) British writer. *Isle of Beauty*

5 What's become of Waring
Since he gave us all the slip?

Robert Browning (1812–89) British poet. *Waring*

6 Absence is to love what wind is to fire; it extinguishes the small, it inflames the great.

Bussy-Rabutin (Roger de Rabutin, Comte de Bussy; 1618–93) French soldier and writer. *Histoire amoureuse des Gaules*

7 What's the good of a home, if you are never in it?

George Grossmith (1847–1912) British singer and comedian. *The Diary of a Nobody*, Ch. 1

8 Has anybody here seen Kelly?
Kelly from the Isle of Man?

C. W. Murphy (19th century) British songwriter. *Has Anybody Here Seen Kelly?*

9 We seek him here, we seek him there,
Those Frenchies seek him everywhere.
Is he in heaven? – Is he in hell?
That damned elusive Pimpernel?

Baroness Orczy (1865–1947) British novelist. *The Scarlet Pimpernel*, Ch. 12

10 Why art thou silent! Is thy love a plant
Of such weak fibre that the treacherous air
Of absence withers what was once so fair?

William Wordsworth (1770–1850) British poet. *Miscellaneous Sonnets*, III

ABSTINENCE

See also alcohol, self-denial, sex, smoking

1 He neither drank, smoked, nor rode a bicycle. Living frugally,saving his money, he died early, surrounded by greedy relatives. It was a great lesson to me.

John Barrymore (1882–1942) US actor. *The Stage*, Jan 1941 (J. P. McEvoy)

2 If someone asks for a soft drink at a party, we no longer think he is a wimp.

Edwina Currie (1946–) British politician. Speech, Dec 1988

3 Teetotallers lack the sympathy and generosity of men that drink.

W. H. Davies (1871–1940) British poet. *Shorter Lyrics of the 20th Century*, Introduction

4 It was a brilliant affair; water flowed like champagne.

William M. Evarts (1818–1901) US lawyer and statesman. Describing a dinner given by US President Rutherford B. Hayes (1877–81), an advocate of temperance. Attrib.

5 If you resolve to give up smoking, drinking and loving, you don't actually live longer; it just seems longer.

Clement Freud (1924–) British Liberal politician and broadcaster. *The Observer*, 27 Dec 1964

6 Mr Mercaptan went on to preach a brilliant sermon on that melancholy sexual perversion known as continence.

Aldous Huxley (1894–1964) British novelist. *Antic Hay*, Ch. 18

7 My experience through life has convinced me that, while moderation and temperance in all things are commendable and beneficial, abstinence from spirituous liquors is the best safeguard of morals and health.

Robert E. Lee (1807–70) US general. Letter, 9 Dec 1869

8 The few bad poems which occasionally are created during abstinence are of no great interest.

Wilhelm Reich (1897–1957) Austrian-born US psychiatrist. *The Sexual Revolution*

9 The people who are regarded as moral luminaries are those who forego ordinary pleasures themselves and find compensation in interfering with the pleasures of others.

Bertrand Russell (1872–1970) British philosopher. *Sceptical Essays*

10 Lastly (and this is, perhaps, the golden rule), no woman should marry a teetotaller, or a man who does not smoke.

Robert Louis Stevenson (1850–94) Scottish writer. *Virginibus Puerisque*

11 She belongs to a Temperance Society and wears one of those badges in the shape of a bow of ribbon to show that she would never take a drink, not even brandy if she were dying. Of course by temperance they all mean the opposite – total abstinence.

Elizabeth Taylor (1912–75) British writer. *Angel*

12 Though in silence, with blighted affection, I pine,
Yet the lips that touch liquor must never touch mine!

G. W. Young (19th century) British writer. *The Lips That Touch Liquor*

ACADEMICS

See also education, intellectuals

1 A professor is one who talks in someone else's sleep.

W. H. Auden (1907–73) British poet. Attrib.

2 First come I; my name is Jowett.
There's no knowledge but I know it.
I am Master of this college:
What I don't know isn't knowledge.

H. C. Beeching (1859–1919) British academic. Referring to Benjamin Jowett, master of Balliol College, Oxford. *The Masque of Balliol*

3 A professor is a gentleman who has a different opinion.

August Bier (1861–1949) Aphorism

4 If there weren't so many professors, medicine would be much easier.

August Bier Aphorism

5 It's no use trying to be *clever* – we are all clever here; just try to be *kind* – a little kind.

F. J. Foakes Jackson (1855–1941) British academic. Advice given to a new don at Jesus College, Cambridge. Noted in A. C. Benson's *Commonplace Book*

6 Like so many ageing college people, Pnin had long ceased to notice the existence of students on the campus.

Vladimir Nabokov (1899–1977) Russian-born US novelist. *Pnin*, Ch. 3

7 The successful teacher is no longer on a height,

pumping knowledge at high pressure into passive receptacles…He is a senior student anxious to help his juniors.

William Osler (1849–1919) Canadian physician. *The Student Life*

8 I am the Dean of Christ Church, Sir:
There's my wife; look well at her.
She's the Broad and I'm the High;
We are the University.

Cecil Arthur Spring-Rice (1859–1918) British diplomat. *The Masque of Balliol*

9 We landed outside the university, where the dons, whose arguments had so thickly populated the ether that they had seen neither sun nor rain for the past five years…

Jeanette Winterson (1959–) British author. *Sexing the Cherry*

ACCIDENTS

See also chance, disaster, misfortune

1 ACCIDENT n. An inevitable occurrence due to the action of immutable natural laws.

Ambrose Bierce (1842–c. 1914) US writer and journalist. *The Devil's Dictionary*

2 The Act of God designation on all insurance policies; which means, roughly, that you cannot be insured for the accidents that are most likely to happen to you.

Alan Coren (1938–) British humorist and writer. *The Lady from Stalingrad Mansions*, 'A Short History of Insurance'

3 Accidents will occur in the best-regulated families.

Charles Dickens (1812–70) British novelist. *David Copperfield*, Ch. 28

4 My good man, I'm not a strawberry.

Edward VII (1841–1910) King of the United Kingdom. Rebuking a footman who had spilt cream on him. *The Last Country Houses* (C. Aslat)

5 Here's another fine mess you've gotten me into.

Oliver Hardy (1892–1957) US film comedian. Catchphrase; said to Stan Laurel

6 Heard there was a party. Came.

Beatrice Lillie (Constance Sylvia Munston, Lady Peel; 1898–1989) Canadian-born British actress. On arriving breathlessly at a friend's house seeking help after a car crash. Attrib.

7 now and then
there is a person born
who is so unlucky
that he runs into accidents
which started out to happen
to somebody else

Don Marquis (1878–1937) US journalist. *archy's life of mehitabel*, 'archy says'

8 O Diamond! Diamond! thou little knowest the mischief done!

Isaac Newton (1642–1727) British scientist. Said to a dog that set fire to some papers, representing several years' work, by knocking over a candle. *Wensley-Dale…a Poem* (Thomas Maude)

9 Knocked down a doctor? With an ambulance? How could she? It's a contradiction in terms.

N. F. Simpson (1919–) British dramatist. *One-Way Pendulum*, I

10 The chapter of accidents is the longest chapter in the book.

John Wilkes (1725–97) British politician. Attrib. in *The Doctor* (Southey), Vol. IV

ACCUSATION

See also responsibility

1 …a disciple and limb of the fiend, called the Pucelle, that used false enchantments and sorcery.

John of Lancaster, Duke of Bedford (1389–1435) Brother of Henry V. Referring to Joan of Arc. *Proceeding and Ordinances of the Privy Council* (ed. N. H. Nicolas), Vol. IV

2 I do not know the method of drawing up an indictment against an whole people.

Edmund Burke (1729–97) British politician. *Speech on Conciliation with America* (House of Commons, 22 Mar 1775)

3 Never make a defence or apology before you be accused.

Charles I (1600–49) King of England. Letter to Lord Wentworth, 3 Sept 1636

4 *J'accuse.*
I accuse.

Émile Zola (1840–1902) French novelist. Title of an open letter to the French president, denouncing the French army's conduct in the Dreyfus affair. *L'Aurore*, 13 Jan 1898

ACHESON, DEAN GOODERHAM

(1893–1971) US lawyer and statesman. Noted for his strong stance against Soviet expansionism, he was prominent in the development of the Truman Doctrine, the Marshall Plan, and NATO.

Quotations about Acheson

1 Washington's number 1 number 2 man.

Anonymous

2 Not only did he not suffer fools gladly; he did not suffer them at all.

Lester Pearson (1897–1972) Canadian statesman. *Time*, 25 Oct 1971

Quotations by Acheson

3 It hasn't taken Winston long to get used to American ways. He hadn't been an American citizen for three minutes before attacking an ex-secretary of state!

At a ceremony in 1963 to make Churchill an honorary American citizen, Churchill obliquely attacked Acheson's reference to Britain losing an empire. *Randolph Churchill* (K. Halle)

4 It is worse than immoral, it's a mistake.

Describing the Vietnam war. *See also* BOULAY DE LA MEURTHE. Quoted by Alistair Cooke in his radio programme *Letter from America*

5 I will undoubtedly have to seek what is happily known as gainful employment, which I am glad to say does not describe holding public office.

Remark made on leaving his post as secretary of state, 1952; he subsequently returned to private legal practice

6 Great Britain has lost an Empire and has not yet found a role.

Speech, Military Academy, West Point, 5 Dec 1962

7 A memorandum is written not to inform the reader but to protect the writer.

Wall Street Journal, 8 Sept 1977

ACHIEVEMENT

See also effort, success

1 Every man who is high up likes to feel that he has done it himself; and the wife smiles, and lets it go at that. It's our only joke. Every woman knows that.

J. M. Barrie (1860–1937) British playwright. *Peter Pan*

2 It is all very well to be able to write books, but can you waggle your ears?

J. M. Barrie Speaking to H. G. Wells. *Barrie: The Story of A Genius* (J. A. Hamerton)

3 Ye shall know them by their fruits. Do men gather grapes of thorns, or figs of thistles?
Even so every good tree bringeth forth good fruit; but a corrupt tree bringeth forth evil fruit.
A good tree cannot bring forth evil fruit, neither can a corrupt tree bring forth good fruit.
Every tree that bringeth not forth good fruit is hewn down, and cast into the fire.
Wherefore by their fruits ye shall know them.

Bible: Matthew 7:16–20

4 Be not afraid of growing slowly, be afraid only of standing still.

Chinese Proverb

5 Our greatest glory is not in never falling, but in rising every time we fall.

Confucius (K'ung Fu-tzu; 551–479 BC) Chinese philosopher. *Analects*

6 One never notices what has been done; one can only see what remains to be done.

Marie Curie (1867–1934) Polish chemist. Letter to her brother, 18 Mar 1894

7 Now my heart turns to and fro,
In thinking what will the people say.
They who shall see my monument in after years,
And shall speak of what I have done.

Hatshepsut (fl. 1503–1482 BC) Egyptian queen. Inscription on her obelisk. *Ancient Egyptian Literature*, Vol. II, 'The New Kingdom' (ed. Miriam Lichtheim)

8 We never do anything well till we cease to think about the manner of doing it.

William Hazlitt (1778–1830) British essayist. *On Prejudice*

9 Well, we knocked the bastard off!

Edmund Hillary (1919–) New Zealand mountaineer. On first climbing Mount Everest (with Tenzing Norgay), 29 May 1953. *Nothing Venture, Nothing Win*

10 Anybody can be Pope; the proof of this is that I have become one.

John XXIII (1881–1963) Italian-born pope. Attrib.

11 I do not want to die...until I have faithfully made the most of my talent and cultivated the seed that was placed in me until the last small twig has grown.

Käthe Kollwitz (1867–1945) German sculptor and graphic artist. *Diaries and Letters*, 15 Feb 1915

12 For, as I suppose, no man in this world hath lived better than I have done, to achieve that I have done.

Thomas Malory (1400–71) English writer. *Morte d'Arthur*, Bk. XVII, Ch. 16

13 Log-cabin to White House.

W. M. Thayer (1820–98) US writer. The title of his biography of James Garfield, US president

14 To achieve great things we must live as though we were never going to die.

Marquis de Vauvenargues (1715–47) French soldier and writer. *Réflexions et maximes*

ACTING

See also action, actors, cinema, criticism, plays, theatre

1 Theatre director: a person engaged by the management to conceal the fact that the players cannot act.

James Agate (1877–1947) British theatre critic. Attrib.

2 Never work with animals or children.

Anonymous Show business maxim.

3 Can't act, can't sing, slightly bald. Can dance a little.

Anonymous Report on Fred Astaire's first screen test.

4 It's not whether you really cry. It's whether the audience thinks you are crying.

Ingrid Bergman (1915–1982) Swedish film and stage actress. *Halliwell's Filmgoer's and Video Viewer's Companion*

5 Acting is the expression of a neurotic impulse. It's a bum's life. Quitting acting, that's the sign of maturity.

Marlon Brando (1924–) US film star. *Halliwell's Filmgoer's and Video Viewer's Companion*

6 For the theatre one needs long arms; it is better to have them too long than too short. An *artiste* with short arms can never, never make a fine gesture.

Sarah Bernhardt (Sarah Henriette Rosine Bernard; 1844–1923) French actress. *Memories of My Life*, Ch. 6

7 Just know your lines and don't bump into the furniture.

Noël Coward (1899–1973) British dramatist. Advice for actors. Attrib.

8 Nothing to be fixed except your performance.

Noël Coward Replying to a telegram from the actress Gertrude Lawrence – 'Nothing wrong that can't be fixed' – referring to her part in Coward's play *Private Lives*. *Noël Coward and his Friends*

9 Pray to God and say the lines.

Bette Davis (Ruth Elizabeth Davis; 1908–89) US film star. Advice to the actress Celeste Holm. Attrib.

10 Acting in English...I'm like a blind man. When you can't see, you develop other senses. In one sense I am blind, but other faculties develop by way of compensation: the sense of hearing, of morbid curiosity, of tolerance. These are the ways you communicate if you don't speak the language.

Gérard Depardieu (1948–) French film actor. *The Observer Life Magazine*, 10 Apr 1994

11 Acting engenders and harbours qualities that are best left way behind in adolescence. People-pleasing, going on those interviews and jamming your whole personality into getting the job, ingratiating yourself to people you wouldn't fucking spit on if they were on fire.

Carrie Fisher (1956–) US film star. *Vanity Fair*, Aug 1990

12 It is easier to get an actor to be a cowboy than to get a cowboy to be an actor.

John Ford (Sean O'Feeney; 1895–1973) US film director. Attrib.

13 It is. But not as hard as farce.

Edmund Gwenn (1875–1959) British actor. On his deathbed, in reply to the comment 'It must be very hard'. *Time*, 30 Jan 1984

14 Blank face is fine. The computer works faster than the brain, don't forget. The art of acting is not to act. Once you show them more, what you show them, in fact, is bad acting.

Anthony Hopkins (1937–) Welsh actor. *Knave*, Nov 1980

15 At school I was quite sure I was a talentless bastard, but at 15 I got my first part in a school play and learnt the art of upstaging.

Eddie Izzard British comedian. *The Independent*, 14 June 1994

16 The part never calls for it. And I've never ever used that excuse. The box office calls for it.

Helen Mirren (1945–) British actress. Referring to nudity. *The Observer*, 'Sayings of the Week', 27 Mar 1994

17 Acting is therefore the lowest of the arts, if it is an art at all.

George Moore (1852–1933) Irish writer and art critic. *Mummer-Worship*

18 The art of acting consists in keeping people from coughing.

Ralph Richardson (1902–83) British actor. *The Observer*

19 In music, the punctuation is absolutely strict, the bars and the rests are absolutely defined. But our punctuation cannot be quite strict, because we have to relate it to the audience. In other words, we are continually changing the score.

Ralph Richardson *The Observer Magazine*, 'Tynan on Richardson', 18 Dec 1977

20 Speak the speech, I pray you, as I pronounced it to you, trippingly on the tongue; but if you mouth it, as many of your players do, I had as lief the town-crier spoke my lines. Nor do not saw the air too much with your hand, thus; but use all gently: for in the very torrent, tempest, and – as I may say – whirlwind of passion, you must acquire and beget a temperance, that may give it smoothness. O! it offends me to the soul to hear a robustious periwig-pated fellow tear a passion to tatters, to very rags, to split the ears of the groundlings, who for the most part are capable of nothing but inexplicable dumb-shows and noise: I would have such a fellow whipped for o'erdoing Termagant; it out-herods Herod: pray you, avoid it.

William Shakespeare (1564–1616) English dramatist. *Hamlet*, III:2

21 Acting, of course, is a good way to keep fit as you are on your feet walking around the rehearsal room all day.

Anthony Sher (1949–) British actor. *The Sunday Times*, 8 July 1990

22 Imagination! imagination! I put it first years ago, when I was asked what qualities I thought necessary for success upon the stage.

Ellen Terry (1847–1928) British actress. *The Story of My Life*, Ch. 2

23 Ladies, just a little more virginity, if you don't mind.

Herbert Beerbohm Tree (1853–1917) British actor and theatre manager. Directing a group of sophisticated actresses. *Smart Aleck* (H. Teichmann)

24 There are those who say I cannot act. And they are right. I cannot act. I am too real.

Nicol Williamson (1938–) British actor. *The Independent on Sunday*, 5 June 1994

ACTION

See also acting

1 Barking dogs seldom bite.

Proverb

2 Doing is better than saying.

Proverb

3 Easier said than done.

Proverb

4 Footprints on the sands of time are not made by sitting down.

Proverb

5 Saying is one thing, and doing another.

Proverb

6 Let's meet, and either do, or die.

Francis Beaumont (1584–1616) English dramatist. *The Island Princess*, II:2

7 He who desires but acts not, breeds pestilence.

William Blake (1757–1827) British poet. *The Marriage of Heaven and Hell*, 'Proverbs of Hell'

8 Liberty's in every blow!
Let us do or die!

Robert Burns (1759–96) Scottish poet. *Scots, Wha Hae*

9 Deliberation is the work of many men. Action, of one alone.

Charles De Gaulle (1890–1970) French general and statesman. *War Memoirs*, Vol. 2

10 No action is in itself good or bad, but only such according to convention.

W. Somerset Maugham (1874–1965) British novelist. *A Writer's Notebook*

11 Suit the action to the word, the word to the action; with this special observance, that you o'erstep not the modesty of nature.

William Shakespeare (1564–1616) English dramatist. *Hamlet*, III:2

12 Thy wish was father, Harry, to that thought.

William Shakespeare *Henry IV, Part Two*, IV:5

13 If to do were as easy as to know what were good to do, chapels had been churches, and poor men's cottages princes' palaces.

William Shakespeare *The Merchant of Venice*, I:2

14 So many worlds, so much to do,
So little done, such things to be.

Alfred, Lord Tennyson (1809–92) British poet. *In Memoriam A.H.H.*, LXXIII

15 It's dogged as does it. It ain't thinking about it.

Anthony Trollope (1815–82) British novelist. *Last Chronicle of Barset*, Ch. 61

ACTORS

General quotes

See also acting, cinema, criticism, plays, theatre

1 I didn't think they gave awards to short ill-tempered megalomaniacs.

Kenneth Branagh (1961–) British actor and director. Receiving an award for 'Outstanding British Contribution to Cinema'.

2 I don't go around saying: 'Hello, did you know I'm the new Olivier?'

Kenneth Branagh *Newsweek*, 9 Oct 1989

3 It's very hard for an actor to open his gob without whatever he says sounding risible. If you even whisper a murmur of complaint, you're labelled a po-faced git who can't see the funny side of things.

Kenneth Branagh Attrib.

4 An actor's a guy who, if you ain't talking about him, ain't listening.

Marlon Brando (1924–) US film star. *The Observer*, 'Sayings of the Year', Jan 1956

5 An actor is something less than a man, while an actress is something more than a woman.

Richard Burton (Richard Jenkins; 1925–84) British actor. *Halliwell's Filmgoer's and Video Viewer's Companion*

6 Never meddle with play-actors, for they're a favoured race.

Miguel de Cervantes (1547–1616) Spanish novelist. *Don Quixote*, Pt. II, Ch. 11

7 Remember you are a star. Never go across the alley even to dump garbage unless you are dressed to the teeth.

Cecil B. de Mille (1881–1959) US film producer and director. *Halliwell's Filmgoer's and Video Viewer's Companion*

8 Actors should be treated like cattle.

Alfred Hitchcock (1889–1980) British film director. Said in clarification of a remark attributed to him, 'Actors are like cattle'. *Quote, Unquote* (N. Rees)

9 At one time I thought he wanted to be an actor. He had certain qualifications, including no money and a total lack of responsibility.

Hedda Hopper (1890–1966) US writer. *From Under My Hat*

10 They didn't act like people and they didn't act like actors. It's hard to explain. They acted more like they knew they were celebrities and all. I mean they were good, but they were *too* good.

J. D. Salinger (1919–) US novelist. *The Catcher in the Rye*, Ch. 17

Specific quotes

11 Can't act. Can't sing. Can dance a little.

Anonymous Studio report after Fred Astaire's first screen test

12 John Wayne is dead.
The hell I am.

Anonymous Inscription on a wall in Bermondsey Antique Market, together with a ghostly denial. *Evening Standard*, 1980

13 If she was a victim of any kind, she was a victim of her friends.

George Cukor (1899–1983) US film director. Referring to Marilyn Monroe. *On Cukor* (Gavin Lambert)

14 Garrick was pure gold beat out into thin leaf.

James Boswell (1740–95) Scottish lawyer and writer. Referring to David Garrick.

15 I remember Sarah Bernhardt's funeral perfectly. I have never had to wait so long to cross the street.

Eric Dunstan *Ego* 9, 14 Oct 1946

16 You look at Harrison Ford and you *listen*. He looks like he's carrying a gun, even if he isn't.

Carrie Fisher (1956–) US film star. *Vanity Fair*, Aug 1990

17 I'm just a lucky slob from Ohio who happened to be in the right place at the right time.

Clark Gable (1901–60) US film actor. Attrib.

18 Olivier's was, to my mind, the definitive Macbeth. Olivier had murder in his heart from the moment he came on the stage.

John Gielgud (1904–) British actor. *An Actor and His Time*

19 He was a star who had no pretensions, something rare in an actor...He was a generous man and he had beautiful manners. He was also Bohemian and wild, which was fun.

John Gielgud Referring to Trevor Howard. Attrib.

20 Chaplin is no business man – all he knows is that he can't take anything less.

Samuel Goldwyn (Samuel Goldfish; 1882–1974) Polish-born US film producer. Attrib.

21 You can't direct a Laughton picture. The best you can hope for is to referee.

Alfred Hitchcock (1889–1980) British film director.

22 Whether the film is good or bad Brando is always compulsive viewing, like Sydney Greenstreet, the vulgarian of all time, or Peter Lorre, or even Bette Davis daring to do *Baby Jane*.

Anthony Hopkins (1937–) Welsh actor. Referring to Marlon Brando. Attrib.

23 He'll put himself out on a limb, totally out on a limb. In fact he'll put himself out on a twig of a tree; if it snaps off and falls, then the fall is very big. He'll risk being appalling. He'll risk being very bad. His portrayal in *The Entertainer* is an example of how far he will go. He dares.

Anthony Hopkins Referring to Laurence Olivier. Attrib.

24 She looked as though butter wouldn't melt in her mouth – or anywhere else.

Elsa Lanchester (1902–86) British-born US actress. Referring to Maureen O'Hara. Attrib.

25 Carole Lombard, Judy Holliday, Marilyn Monroe – just incredibly funny, silly and sweet. I just saw myself in them. My knowingness and my innocence.

Madonna (Madonna Louise Veronica Ciccone; 1958–) US pop singer and film star.

26 Goodbye Norma Jean
Though I never knew you at all
You had the grace to hold yourself

While those around you crawled.
They crawled out of the woodwork
And they whispered into your brain
Set you on the treadmill
And made you change your name.

Bernie Taupin (1950–) British songwriter. Lyrics for a song by Elton John. *Candle in the Wind*; referring to Marilyn Monroe.

27 I don't pretend to be an ordinary housewife.

Elizabeth Taylor (1932–) British-born US actress. Interview

28 As Romeo Irving reminded me of a pig who has been taught to play the fiddle. He did it cleverly, but would be better employed in squealing.

Ellen Terry (1847–1928) British actress. *Notes on Irving*

29 I brought a lot of tranquillisers and my mother.

Emma Thompson (1959–) British actress. Receiving an Oscar for Best Actress, 1993.

30 This whole thing is like a cross between a very severe virus and getting married.

Emma Thompson Receiving an Oscar for Best Actress, 1993.

31 Ah, every day dear Herbert becomes *de plus en plus Oscarié*. It is a wonderful case of nature imitating art.

Oscar Wilde (1854–1900) Irish-born British dramatist. Referring to Beerbohm Tree's unconscious adoption of some of the mannerisms of a character he was playing in one of Wilde's plays. *Great Theatrical Disasters* (G. Brandreth)

ADAMS, DOUGLAS

(1952–) British novelist and scriptwriter. His works include *The Hitch Hiker's Guide to the Galaxy* (1979), *Life, the Universe and Everything* (1982), *The Long Dark Tea-Time of the Soul* (1988), and *Mostly Harmless* (1992).

1 'Its all right, it's just a horse in the bathroom,' he said quietly.

Dirk Gently's Holistic Detective Agency, Ch. 8

2 The idea of walking through walls frankly revolted him. It was something he had been trying strenuously to avoid all night.

Dirk Gently's Holistic Detective Agency, Ch. 15

3 'Good grief,' said Arthur, 'is this really the interior of a flying saucer?'

The Hitch Hiker's Guide to the Galaxy, Ch. 5

4 Mostly harmless.

Description of the Earth. *The Hitch Hiker's Guide to the Galaxy*, Ch. 6

5 Here I am, brain the size of a planet and they ask me to take you down the bridge.

The Hitch Hiker's Guide to the Galaxy, Ch. 11

6 On the planet Earth, man had always assumed that he was more intelligent than dolphins because he had achieved so much – the wheel, New York, wars and so on – whilst all the dolphins had ever done was muck about in the water having a good time. But conversely, the dolphins had always believed that they were far more intelligent than man – for precisely the same reasons.

The Hitch Hiker's Guide to the Galaxy, Ch. 23

7 'Forty-two,' said Deep Thought, with infinite majesty and calm.

The answer to Life, the Universe and Everything. *The Hitch Hiker's Guide to the Galaxy*, Ch. 27

8 What god would be hanging around Terminal Two of Heathrow Airport trying to catch the 15.37 flight to Oslo?

The Long Dark Tea-Time of the Soul, Ch. 6

9 I don't go to mythical places with strange men.

The Long Dark Tea-Time of the Soul, Ch. 22

10 Anything that, in happening, causes itself to happen, happens again.

Mostly Harmless

11 There was an accident with a contraceptive and a time machine.

The Restaurant at the End of the Universe, Ch. 3

12 He's spending a year dead for tax reasons.

The Restaurant at the End of the Universe, Ch. 17

ADAPTABILITY

See also change

1 Remember that to change your mind and follow him who sets you right is to be none the less free than you were before.

Marcus Aurelius (121–180 AD) Roman emperor. *Meditations*, Bk. VIII, Ch. 16

2 Mahomet made the people believe that he would call a hill to him…when the hill stood still, he was never a whit abashed, but said, 'If the hill will not come to Mahomet, Mahomet will go to the hill.'

Francis Bacon (1561–1626) English philosopher. Often misquoted as 'If the mountain will not come to Mohammed'. *Essays*, 'Of Boldness'

3 President Robbins was so well adjusted to his environment that sometimes you could not tell which was the environment and which was President Robbins.

Randall Jarrell (1914–65) US author. *Pictures from an Institution*, Pt. I, Ch. 4

4 As time requireth, a man of marvellous mirth and pastimes, and sometimes of as sad gravity, as who say: a man for all seasons.

Robert Whittington (16th century) English writer. Referring to Sir Thomas More; after Erasmus. *Vulgaria*, Pt. II, 'De constructione nominum'

ADDICTION

1 Cocaine isn't habit-forming. I should know – I've been using it for years.

Tallulah Bankhead (1903–68) US actress. *Pentimento* (Lillian Hellman), 'Theatre'

2 Every form of addiction is bad, no matter whether the narcotic be alcohol or morphine or idealism.

Carl Gustav Jung (1875–1961) Swiss psychoanalyst. *Memories, Dreams, Reflections*, Ch. 12

ADDISON, JOSEPH

(1672–1719) British essayist. A Whig politician, he entered parliament in 1708. Addison contributed numerous essays to the *Tatler* and was cofounder (with Richard Steele) of *The Spectator* (1711).

Quotations about Addison

1 Whoever wishes to attain an English style, familiar but not coarse and elegant but not ostentatious, must give his days and nights to the volumes of Addison.

Samuel Johnson (1709–84) British lexicographer. *Lives of the Poets*

2 A parson in a tye-wig.

Bernard Mandeville (?1670–1733) Dutch-born British doctor, writer, and wit. Remark

Quotations by Addison

3 Pray consider what a figure a man would make in the republic of letters.

Ancient Medals

4 'Tis not in mortals to command success,
But we'll do more, Sempronius; we'll deserve it.

Cato, I:2

5 And if the following day, he chance to find
A new repast, or an untasted spring,
Blesses his stars, and thinks it luxury.

Cato, I:4

6 The woman that deliberates is lost.

Cato, IV:1

7 Content thyself to be obscurely good.
When vice prevails, and impious men bear sway,
The post of honour is a private station.

Cato, IV:1

8 What pity is it
That we can die but once to serve our country!

See also Nathan HALE. *Cato*, IV:1

9 A reader seldom peruses a book with pleasure until he knows whether the writer of it be a black man or a fair man, of a mild or choleric disposition, married or a bachelor.

The Spectator, 1

10 Thus I live in the world rather as a Spectator of mankind, than as one of the species, by which means I have made myself a speculative statesman, soldier, merchant, and artisan, without ever meddling with any practical part of life.

The Spectator, 1

11 Nothing is capable of being well set to music that is not nonsense.

The Spectator, 18

12 The infusion of a China plant sweetened with the pith of an Indian cane.

Referring to tea. *The Spectator*, 69

13 *Sir Roger* told them, with the air of a man who would not give his judgment rashly, that 'much might be said on both sides'.

Sir Roger de Coverley was a fictional archetype of the old-fashioned and eccentric country squire. *The Spectator*, 122

14 I have often thought, says Sir Roger, it happens very well that Christmas should fall out in the Middle of Winter.

The Spectator, 269

15 The Hand that made us is divine.

The Spectator, 465

16 A woman seldom asks advice until she has bought her wedding clothes.

The Spectator, 475

17 We are always doing something for posterity, but I would fain see posterity do something for us.

The Spectator, 583

18 I have but ninepence in ready money, but I can draw for a thousand pounds.

Comparing his ability to make conversation and to write. *Life of Johnson* (Boswell)

19 See in what peace a Christian can die.

Last words

ADMIRATION

See also compliments, love, praise, respect, wonder

1 Miss J. Hunter Dunn, Miss J. Hunter Dunn,
Furnish'd and burnish'd by Aldershot sun.

John Betjeman (1906–84) British poet. *A Subaltern's Love Song*

2 Here's looking at you, kid.

Humphrey Bogart (1899–1957) US film star. *Casablanca*

3 A fool always finds a greater fool to admire him.

Nicolas Boileau (1636–1711) French writer. *L'Art poétique*, I

4 There is a garden in her face,
Where roses and white lilies grow;
A heav'nly paradise is that place,
Wherein all pleasant fruits do flow.
There cherries grow, which none may buy
Till 'Cherry ripe' themselves do cry.

Thomas Campion (1567–1620) English poet. *Fourth Book of Airs*

5 Pretty amazing.

Diana, Princess of Wales (1961–) Wife of Prince Charles. When asked what her first impression was of Prince Charles. Remark, 1981

6 No, it did a lot of other things, too.

James Joyce (1882–1941) Irish novelist. When a young man asked, 'May I kiss the hand that wrote Ulysses?' *James Joyce* (R. Ellman)

7 I do think better of womankind than to suppose they care whether Mister John Keats five feet high likes them or not.

John Keats (1795–1821) British poet. Letter to Benjamin Bailey, 18 July 1818

8 'There is a report that Piso is dead; it is a great loss; he was an honest man, who deserved to live longer; he was intelligent and agreeable, resolute and courageous, to be depended upon, generous and faithful.' Add: 'provided he is really dead'.

Jean de La Bruyère (1645–96) French satirist. *Les Caractères*

9 On Richmond Hill there lives a lass,
More sweet than May day morn,
Whose charms all other maids surpass,
A rose without a thorn.

Leonard MacNally (1752–1820) Irish dramatist and poet. *The Lass of Richmond Hill*

10 Many a man has been a wonder to the world, whose wife and valet have seen nothing in him that was even remarkable. Few men have been admired by their servants.

Michel de Montaigne (1533–92) French essayist. *Essais*, III

11 Charlie is my darling, my darling, my darling,
Charlie is my darling, the young Chevalier.

Carolina Nairne (1766–1845) Scottish songwriter. Referring to Bonnie Prince Charlie. *Charlie is my Darling*

12 Not to admire, is all the art I know
To make men happy, and to keep them so.

Alexander Pope (1688–1744) British poet. *Imitations of Horace*, 'To Mr. Murray'

13 Where'er you walk, cool gales shall fan the glade,
Trees, where you sit, shall crowd into a shade:
Where'er you tread, the blushing flow'rs shall rise,
And all things flourish where you turn your eyes.

Alexander Pope *Pastorals*, 'Summer'

14 But search the land of living men,
Where wilt thou find their like agen?

Walter Scott (1771–1832) Scottish novelist. *Marmion*, I

15 The barge she sat in, like a burnish'd throne,
Burn'd on the water. The poop was beaten gold;
Purple the sails, and so perfumed that
The winds were love-sick with them; the oars were silver,
Which to the tune of flutes kept stroke and made
The water which they beat to follow faster,
As amorous of their strokes. For her own person,
It beggar'd all description.

William Shakespeare (1564–1616) English dramatist. *Antony and Cleopatra*, II:2

16 Age cannot wither her, nor custom stale
Her infinite variety. Other women cloy
The appetites they feed, but she makes hungry
Where most she satisfies.

William Shakespeare *Antony and Cleopatra*, II:2

17 'A was a man, take him for all in all,
I shall not look upon his like again.

William Shakespeare *Hamlet*, I:2

18 Who is Silvia? What is she,
That all our swains commend her?
Holy, fair, and wise is she.

William Shakespeare *The Two Gentlemen of Verona*, IV:2

19 He was a great patriot, a humanitarian, a loyal friend – provided, of course, that he really is dead.

Voltaire (François-Marie Arouet; 1694–1778) French writer. Giving a funeral oration. Attrib.

20 The sweetest thing that ever grew
Beside a human door!

William Wordsworth (1770–1850) British poet. *Lucy Gray*

ADULTERY

See also marriage, sex, unfaithfulness

1 What men call gallantry, and gods adultery,
Is much more common where the climate's sultry.

Lord Byron (1788–1824) British poet. *Don Juan*, I

2 I have looked on a lot of women with lust. I've committed adultery in my heart many times. God recognises I will do this and forgives me.

Jimmy Carter (1924–) US statesman and president. Remark

3 Sara could commit adultery at one end and weep for her sins at the other, and enjoy both operations at once.

Joyce Cary (1888–1957) British novelist. *The Horse's Mouth*, Ch. 8

4 I say I don't sleep with married men, but what I mean is that I don't sleep with happily married men.

Britt Ekland (1942–) Swedish film actress. Attrib.

5 You know, of course, that the Tasmanians, who never committed adultery, are now extinct.

W. Somerset Maugham (1874–1965) British novelist. *The Bread-Winner*

6 A father will have compassion on his son. A mother will never forget her child. A brother will cover the sin of his sister. But what husband ever forgave the faithlessness of his wife?

Margaret of Navarre (1492–1549) French poet, writer, and patron of literature. *Mirror of the Sinful Soul*

7 Lady, lady, should you meet,
One whose ways are all discreet,
One who murmurs that his wife
Is the lodestar of his life,
One who keeps assuring you
That he never was untrue,
Never loved another one...
Lady, lady, better run!

Dorothy Parker (1893–1967) US writer. 'Social note'

8 Madame, you must really be more careful. Suppose it had been someone else who found you like this.

Duc de Richelieu (1766–1822) French statesman. Discovering his wife with her lover. *The Book of Lists* (D. Wallechinsky)

9 The peculiar importance attached, at present, to adultery is quite irrational. It is obvious that many forms of misconduct are more fatal to married happiness than an occasional infidelity.

Bertrand Russell (1872–1970) British philosopher. *Why I am Not a Christian*

10 With all my heart. Whose wife shall it be?

John Horne Tooke (1736–1812) British clergyman, politician, and etymologist. Replying to the suggestion that he take a wife. Attrib.

ADVERTISING

1 Any publicity is good publicity.

Proverb

2 It pays to advertise.

Anonymous Already current by c. 1912 when Cole Porter used it as the title of an early song.

3 Advertising is the most fun you can have with your clothes on.

Jerry Della Femina (1936–) Advertising executive. *From those wonderful folks who gave you Pearl Harbor*

4 Half the money I spend on advertising is wasted, and the trouble is I don't know which half.

Viscount Leverhulme (1851–1925) British industrialist. *Confessions of an Advertising Man* (D. Ogilvy)

5 The consumer isn't a moron; she is your wife. You insult her intelligence if you assume that a mere slogan and a few vapid adjectives will persuade her to buy anything.

David Ogilvy (1911–) British businessman. *Confessions of an Advertising Man*, Ch. 5

6 Freedom of the press in Britain is freedom to print such of the proprietor's prejudices as the advertisers don't object to.

Hannen Swaffer (1879–1962) British journalist. Attrib.

ADVICE

1 A good scare is worth more than good advice.

Proverb

2 Advice is seldom welcome; and those who want it the most always like it the least.

Earl of Chesterfield (1694–1773) English statesman. Letter to his son, 29 Jan 1748

3 I intended to give you some advice but now I remember how much is left over from last year unused.

George Harris (1844–1922) US congressman. Said when addressing students at the start of a new academic year. *Braude's Second Encyclopedia* (J. Braude)

4 On my twenty-first birthday my father said, 'Son, here's a million dollars. Don't lose it.'

Larry Niven (1938–) US science-fiction writer. When asked 'What is the best advice you have ever been given?' Attrib.

5 One gives nothing so freely as advice.

Duc de la Rochefoucauld (1613–80) French writer. *Maximes*, 110

6 Don't tell your friends their social faults, they will cure the fault and never forgive you.

Logan Pearsall Smith (1865–1946) US writer. *Afterthoughts*

7 No one wants advice – only corroboration.

John Steinbeck (1902–68) US novelist. Attrib.

8 It's queer how ready people always are with advice in any real or imaginary emergency, and no matter how many times experience has shown them to be wrong, they continue to set forth their opinions, as if they had received them from the Almighty!

Annie Sullivan (1866–1936) US teacher of the handicapped. Letter, 12 June 1887

AESOP

(6th century BC) Reputed Greek writer of fables said by Herodotus to have been a slave from the island of Samos. Aesop's fables, popularized by the Roman poet Phaedrus (1st century AD), use animal characters to portray human frailties.

1 Beware that you do not lose the substance by grasping at the shadow.

Fables, 'The Dog and the Shadow'

2 I am sure the grapes are sour.

Fables, 'The Fox and the Grapes'

3 Thinking to get at once all the gold that the goose could give, he killed it, and opened it only to find – nothing.

Fables, 'The Goose with the Golden Eggs'

4 The gods help them that help themselves.

Fables, 'Hercules and the Waggoner'

5 It is not only fine feathers that make fine birds.

Fables, 'The Jay and the Peacock'

6 While I see many hoof-marks going in, I see none coming out.

Fables, 'The Lion, the Fox, and the Beasts'

7 I will have nothing to do with a man who can blow hot and cold with the same breath.

Fables, 'The Man and the Satyr'

8 Don't count your chickens before they are hatched.

Fables, 'The Milkmaid and her Pail'

9 The boy cried 'Wolf, wolf!' and the villagers came out to help him.

Fables, 'The Shepherd's Boy'

10 The lamb that belonged to the sheep whose skin the wolf was wearing began to follow the wolf in the sheep's clothing.

Fables, 'The Wolf in Sheep's Clothing'

AFFECTATION

See also ostentation

1 We have become a grandmother.

Margaret Thatcher (1925–) British politician and prime minister. Remark, Mar 1989

2 Don't you sit there and sigh gal like you was Lady Nevershit.

Arnold Wesker (1932–) British dramatist. *Roots*, III

3 She keeps on being Queenly in her own room with the door shut.

Edith Wharton (1862–1937) US novelist. *The House of Mirth*, Bk. II, Ch. 1

AFTERLIFE

See also death, heaven

1 CLOV. Do you believe in the life to come?
HAMM. Mine was always that.

Samuel Beckett (1906–89) Irish novelist and dramatist. *Endgame*

2 That which is the foundation of all our hopes and of all our fears; all our hopes and fears which are of any consideration: I mean a Future Life.

Joseph Butler (1692–1752) British churchman. *The Analogy of Religion*, Introduction

3 We have no reliable guarantee that the afterlife will be any less exasperating than this one, have we?

Noël Coward (1899–1973) British dramatist. *Blithe Spirit*, I

4 We sometimes congratulate ourselves at the moment of waking from a troubled dream; it may be so the moment after death.

Nathaniel Hawthorne (1804–64) US novelist and writer. *American Notebooks*

5 Work and pray, live on hay,
You'll get pie in the sky when you die.

Joe Hill (1879–1915) Swedish-born US songwriter. *The Preacher and the Slave*

6 Death is nothing at all. I have only slipped away into the next room. I am I and you are you. Whatever we were to each other, that we are still.... What is death but negligible accident? Why should I be out of mind because I am out of sight? I am waiting for you, for an interval, somewhere very near just around the corner. All is well.

Henry Scott Holland (1847–1918) British Anglican clergyman. Attrib.

7 Is there another life? Shall I awake and find all this a dream? There must be, we cannot be created for this sort of suffering.

John Keats (1795–1821) British poet. Letter, 1820

8 My doctrine is: Live that thou mayest desire to live again – that is thy duty – for in any case thou wilt live again!

Friedrich Wilhelm Nietzsche (1844–1900) German philosopher. *Eternal Recurrence*

9 After your death you will be what you were before your birth.

Arthur Schopenhauer (1788–1860) German philosopher. *Parerga and Paralipomena*

10 The dread of something after death –
The undiscover'd country, from whose bourn
No traveller returns.

William Shakespeare (1564–1616) English dramatist. *Hamlet*, III:1

11 I am going a long way
With these thou seest – if indeed I go
(For all my mind is clouded with a doubt) –
To the island-valley of Avilion;
Where falls not hail, or rain, or any snow,
Nor ever wind blows loudly; but it lies
Deep-meadow'd, happy, fair with orchard lawns
And bowery hollows crown'd with summer sea,
Where I will heal me of my grievous wound.

Alfred, Lord Tennyson (1809–92) British poet. *Idylls of the King*, 'The Passing of Arthur'

12 One world at a time.

Henry David Thoreau (1817–62) US writer. On being asked his opinion of the hereafter. Attrib.

AGE

See also longevity, old age, youth

1 Never too late to learn.

Proverb

2 There's many a good tune played on an old fiddle.

Proverb

3 Years ago we discovered the exact point the dead center of middle age. It occurs when you are too young to take up golf and too old to rush up to the net.

Franklin P. Adams (1881–1960) US journalist and humorist. *Nods and Becks*

4 An adult is one who has ceased to grow vertically but not horizontally.

Anonymous

5 You've reached middle age when all you exercise is caution.

Anonymous

6 All evil comes from the old. They grow fat on ideas and young men die of them.

Jean Anouilh (1910–87) French dramatist. *Catch as Catch Can*

7 I am past thirty, and three parts iced over.

Matthew Arnold (1822–88) British poet and critic. Letter to A. H. Clough, 12 Feb 1853

8 I refuse to admit that I am more than fifty-two, even if that does make my sons illegitimate.

Nancy Astor (1879–1964) US-born British politician. Attrib.

9 I think your whole life shows in your face and you should be proud of that.

Lauren Bacall (1924–) US actress. Remark, Mar 1988

10 Age will not be defied.

Francis Bacon (1561–1626) English philosopher. *Essays*, 'Of Regiment of Health'

11 A man that is young in years may be old in hours, if he have lost no time.

Francis Bacon *Essays*, 'Of Youth and Age'

12 The only thing I regret about my past life is the length of it. If I had my past life over again I'd make all the same mistakes – only sooner.

Tallulah Bankhead (1903–68) US actress. *The Times*, 28 July 1981

13 You grew old first not in your own eyes, but in other people's eyes; then, slowly, you agreed with their opinion of you.

Julian Barnes (1946–) British novelist. *Staring at the Sun*

14 What is an adult? A child blown up by age.

Simone de Beauvoir (1908–86) French writer. *La Femme rompue*

15 If thou hast gathered nothing in thy youth, how canst thou find any thing in thine age?

Bible: Ecclesiasticus 25:3

16 And all the days of Methuselah were nine hundred sixty and nine years: and he died.

Bible: Genesis 5:27

17 No man also having drunk old wine straightway desireth new: for he saith, The old is better.

Bible: Luke 5:39

18 If I'd known I was gonna live this long, I'd have taken better care of myself.

Eubie Blake (1883–1983) US jazz musician. *The Observer*, 'Sayings of the Week', 13 Feb 1983

19 Old age is ... a lot of crossed off names in an address book.

Ronald Blythe (1922–) British author. *The View in Winter*

20 Being now come to the years of discretion.

The Book of Common Prayer *Order of Confirmation*

21 Therefore I summon age
To grant youth's heritage.

Robert Browning (1812–89) British poet. *Rabbi ben Ezra*, XIII

22 Ah well, perhaps one has to be very old before one learns how to be amused rather than shocked.
Pearl Buck (1892–1973) US novelist. *China, Past and Present*, Ch. 6

23 There's many a good tune played on an old fiddle.
Samuel Butler (1835–1902) British novelist. *The Way of All Flesh*, Ch. 61

24 A lady of a 'certain age', which means
Certainly aged.
Lord Byron (1788–1824) British poet. *Don Juan*, VI

25 It is the misfortune of an old man that though he can put things out of his head he can't put them out of his feelings.
Joyce Carey (1888–1957) British novelist. *To be a Pilgrim*, Ch. 8

26 Man arrives as a novice at each age of his life.
Nicolas Chamfort (1741–94) French writer and wit. *Caractères et anecdotes*, 576

27 A man is as old as he's feeling,
A woman as old as she looks.
Mortimer Collins (1827–76) British writer. *The Unknown Quantity*

28 Pushing forty? She's clinging on to it for dear life.
Ivy Compton-Burnett (1884–1969) British novelist. Attrib.

29 When a middle-aged man says in a moment of weariness that he is half dead, he is telling the literal truth.
Elmer Davis (1890–1958) US journalist. *By Elmer Davis*, 'On not being Dead, as Reported'

30 Middle age is youth without its levity,
And age without decay.
Daniel Defoe (1660–1731) English journalist and writer.

31 You don't have the same resistance to alcohol. You lose the arrogance you have when you are 20. Thank God.
Gérard Depardieu (1948–) French film actor. *Life*, 10 Apr 1994

32 The years that a woman subtracts from her age are not lost. They are added to the ages of other women.
Diane de Poitiers (1499–1566) Attrib.

33 Youth is a blunder; manhood a struggle; old age a regret.
Benjamin Disraeli (1804–81) British statesman. *Coningsby*, Bk. III, Ch. 1

34 I am resolved to grow fat and look young till forty, and then slip out of the world with the first wrinkle and the reputation of five-and-twenty.
John Dryden (1631–1700) British poet and dramatist. *The Maiden Queen*, III

35 Men are but children of a larger growth;
Our appetites as apt to change as theirs,
And full as craving too, and full as vain.
John Dryden *All for Love*, IV

36 Ah, but I was so much older then
I'm younger than that now.
Bob Dylan (Robert Allen Zimmerman; 1941–) US popular singer. *My Back Pages*

37 The years between fifty and seventy are the hardest. You are always being asked to do things, and you are not yet decrepit enough to turn them down.
T. S. Eliot (1888–1965) US-born British poet and dramatist. *Time*, 23 Oct 1950

38 Here I am, an old man in a dry month,
Being read to by a boy, waiting for rain.
T. S. Eliot *Gerontion*

39 *Si jeunesse savait; si vieillesse pouvait.*
If only youth knew, if only age could.
Henri Estienne (1528–98) French scholar. *Les Prémices*

40 At sixteen I was stupid, confused, insecure and indecisive. At twenty-five I was wise, self-confident, prepossessing and assertive. At forty-five I am stupid, confused, insecure and indecisive. Who would have supposed that maturity is only a short break in adolescence?
Jules Feiffer (1929–) US writer, cartoonist, and humorist. *The Observer*, 3 Feb 1974

41 According to the doctors, I'm only suffering from a light form of premature baldness.
Federico Fellini (1920–93) Italian film director. After spending four days in a clinic in Rome. *Variety*, 1986

42 Though the Jazz Age continued, it became less and less an affair of youth. The sequel was like a children's party taken over by the elders.
F. Scott Fitzgerald (1896–1940) US novelist. *The Crack-Up*

43 At twenty years of age, the will reigns; at thirty, the wit; and at forty, the judgement.
Benjamin Franklin (1706–90) US scientist and statesman. *Poor Richard's Almanack*

44 A diplomat is a man who always remembers a woman's birthday but never remembers her age.
Robert Frost (1875–1963) US poet. Attrib.

45 When you're my age, you just never risk being ill – because then everyone says: Oh, he's done for.
John Gielgud (1904–) British actor. *Sunday Express* Magazine, 17 July 1988

46 I never accept lengthy film roles nowadays, because I am always so afraid I will die in the middle of shooting and cause such awful problems.
John Gielgud *The Independent*, 26 Mar 1994

47 She may very well pass for forty-three
In the dusk, with a light behind her!
W. S. Gilbert (1836–1911) British dramatist. *Trial by Jury*

48 'Old Cary Grant fine. How you?'
Cary Grant (Archibald Leach; 1904–86) British-born US film star. Replying to a telegram sent to his agent inquiring: 'How old Cary Grant?' *The Filmgoer's Book of Quotes* (Leslie Halliwell)

49 I find I am not as closely in touch with modern life as I once was; I no longer seem to meet ladies in antique shops who are besotted about antlers.
Joyce Grenfell (1910–79) British entertainer. Said at the age of 60

50 We do not necessarily improve with age: for better or worse we become more like ourselves.
Peter Hall (1930–) British theatre director. *The Observer*, 'Sayings of the Week', 24 Jan 1988

51 You will recognize, my boy, the first sign of old

age: it is when you go out into the streets of London and realize for the first time how young the policemen look.

Seymour Hicks (1871–1949) British actor-manager. *They Were Singing* (C. Pulling)

52 Middle age is when your age starts to show around the middle.

Bob Hope (1904–) British-born US comedian.

53 What do the ravages of time not injure? Our parents' age (worse than our grandparents') has produced us, more worthless still, who will soon give rise to a yet more vicious generation.

Horace (Quintus Horatius Flaccus; 65–8 BC) Roman poet. *Odes*, III

54 I think middle age is the best time, if we can escape the fatty degeneration of the conscience which often sets in at about fifty.

W. R. Inge (1860–1954) British churchman and writer. *The Observer*, 8 June 1930

55 Whenever a man's friends begin to compliment him about looking young, he may be sure that they think he is growing old.

Washington Irving (1783–1859) US writer. *Bracebridge Hall*, 'Bachelors'

56 It is sobering to consider that when Mozart was my age he had already been dead for a year.

Tom Lehrer (1928–) US university teacher and songwriter. *An Encyclopedia of Quotations about Music* (N. Shapiro)

57 Will you still need me, will you still feed me
When I'm sixty-four?

John Lennon (1940–80) British rock musician. *When I'm Sixty-Four* (with Paul McCartney)

58 The four stages of man are infancy, childhood, adolescence and obsolescence.

Art Linkletter (1912–) Canadian-born US radio and television personality. *A Child's Garden of Misinformation*, 8

59 I am just turning forty and taking my time about it.

Harold Lloyd (1893–1971) US silent-film comedian. Reply when, aged 77, he was asked his age. *The Times*, 23 Sept 1970

60 Growth is a greater mystery than death. All of us can understand failure, we all contain failure and death within us, but not even the successful man can begin to describe the impalpable elations and apprehensions of growth.

Norman Mailer (1923–) US writer. *Advertisements for Myself*

61 But at my back I always hear
Time's wingèd chariot hurrying near;
And yonder all before us lie
Deserts of vast eternity.

Andrew Marvell (1621–78) English poet. *To His Coy Mistress*

62 A man is only as old as the woman he feels.

Groucho Marx (Julius Marx; 1895–1977) US comedian. Attrib.

63 I am old enough to be – in fact am – your mother.

A. A. Milne (1882–1956) British writer. *Belinda*

64 How soon hath Time, the subtle thief of youth,
Stolen on his wing my three-and-twentieth year!

John Milton (1608–74) English poet. *Sonnet*: 'On Being Arrived at the Age of Twenty-three'

65 Do you think my mind is maturing late,
Or simply rotted early?

Ogden Nash (1902–71) US poet. *Lines on Facing Forty*

66 At 50, everyone has the face he deserves.

George Orwell (Eric Blair; 1903–50) British novelist. Last words in his manuscript notebook, 17 Apr 1949.

67 Each generation imagines itself to be more intelligent than the one that went before it, and wiser than the one that comes after it.

George Orwell Book Review

68 From forty to fifty a man is at heart either a stoic or a satyr.

Arthur Pinero (1855–1934) British dramatist. *The Second Mrs Tanqueray*, I

69 Life Begins At Forty.

W. B. Pitkin (1878–1953) US writer. Book title

70 One of the pleasures of middle age is to *find out* that one WAS right, and that one was much righter than one knew at say 17 or 23.

Ezra Pound (1885–1972) US poet. *ABC of Reading*, Ch. 1

71 Inexperience is what makes a young man do what an older man says is impossible.

Herbert V. Prochnow (1897–) US writer. *Satuday Evening Post*, 4 Dec 1948

72 You know, by the time you reach my age, you've made plenty of mistakes if you've lived your life properly.

Ronald Reagan (1911–) US politician and president. *The Observer*, 'Sayings of the Week', 8 Mar 1987

73 As we get older we do not get any younger.
Seasons return, and today I am fifty-five,
And this time last year I was fifty-four,
And this time next year I shall be sixty-two.

Henry Reed (1914–86) British poet and dramatist. *A Map of Verona*, 'Chard Whitlow'

74 It is fun to be in the same decade with you.

Franklin D. Roosevelt (1882–1945) US Democratic president. After Churchill had congratulated him on his 60th birthday. *The Hinge of Fate* (Winston S. Churchill), Ch. 4

75 Don't trust anyone over thirty.

Jerry Rubin (1938–) US 'yippie' leader. *Listening to America* (S. B. Flexner)

76 I have always felt that a woman has the right to treat the subject of her age with ambiguity until, perhaps, she passes into the realm of over ninety. Then it is better she be candid with herself and with the world.

Helena Rubinstein (1882–1965) Polish-born US cosmetics manufacturer. *My Life for Beauty*, Pt. I, Ch. 1

77 The young have aspirations that never come to pass, the old have reminiscences of what never happened.

Saki (Hector Hugh Munro; 1870–1916) British writer. *Reginald at the Carlton*

78 The young man who has not wept is a savage, and the old man who will not laugh is a fool.

George Santayana (1863–1952) US philosopher. *Dialogues in Limbo*, Ch. 3

79 When I was young, I was told: 'You'll see, when you're fifty.' I am fifty and I haven't seen a thing.

Erik Satie (1866–1925) French composer. From a letter to his brother. *Erik Satie* (Pierre-Daniel Templier), Ch. 1

80 Thou hast nor youth nor age;
But, as it were, an after-dinner's sleep,
Dreaming on both.

William Shakespeare (1564–1616) English dramatist. *Measure for Measure*, III:1

81 Doth not the appetite alter? A man loves the meat in his youth that he cannot endure in his age.

William Shakespeare *Much Ado About Nothing*, II:3

82 Crabbed age and youth cannot live together:
Youth is full of pleasure, age is full of care;
Youth like summer morn, age like winter weather;
Youth like summer brave, age like winter bare.

William Shakespeare *The Passionate Pilgrim*, XII

83 All that the young can do for the old is to shock them and keep them up to date.

George Bernard Shaw (1856–1950) Irish dramatist and critic. *Fanny's First Play*

84 It's a funny thing about that bust. As time goes on it seems to get younger and younger.

George Bernard Shaw Referring to a portrait bust sculpted for him by Rodin. *More Things I Wish I'd Said* (K. Edwards)

85 There is more felicity on the far side of baldness than young men can possibly imagine.

Logan Pearsall Smith (1865–1946) US writer. *Afterthoughts*

86 One's prime is elusive. You little girls, when you grow up, must be on the alert to recognize your prime at whatever time of your life it may occur. You must then live it to the full.

Muriel Spark (1918–) British novelist. *The Prime of Miss Jean Brodie*, Ch. 1

87 There are so few who can grow old with a good grace.

Richard Steele (1672–1729) English essayist. *The Spectator*

88 I learned that falsifying this one fact about my life made me feel phoney, ridiculous, complicit, and, worst of all, undermined by my own hand.

Gloria Steinem (1934–) US writer and feminist. Referring to a time when she lied about her age. *Moving Beyond Words*, 'Doing Sixty'

89 The mark of the immature man is that he wants to die nobly for a cause, while the mark of the mature man is that he wants to live humbly for one.

Wilhelm Stekel (1868–1940) Viennese psychiatrist. *The Catcher in the Rye* (J. D. Salinger), Ch. 24

90 Men come of age at sixty, women at fifteen.

James Stephens (1882–1950) Irish novelist. *The Observer*, 'Sayings of the Week', 1 Oct 1944

91 Having wrinkles is at once strange and exciting.

Meryl Streep (1949–) US actress. On being asked whether she would have plastic surgery. *The Independent*, 26 Mar 1994

92 The British loathe the middle-aged and I await rediscovery at 65, when one is too old to be in anyone's way.

Roy Strong (1935–) British art critic. Remark, Jan 1988

93 I was born old and get younger every day. At present I am sixty years young.

Herbert Beerbohm Tree (1853–1917) British actor and theatre manager. *Beerbohm Tree* (Hesketh Pearson)

94 Life begins at forty.

Sophie Tucker (Sophia Abuza; 1884–1966) Russian-born US singer. Attrib.

95 From birth to age eighteen, a girl needs good parents. From eighteen to thirty-five, she needs good looks. From thirty-five to fifty-five, she needs a good personality. From fifty-five on, she needs good cash.

Sophie Tucker Attrib.

96 There are no old men any more. *Playboy* and *Penthouse* have between them made an ideal of eternal adolescence, sunburnt and saunaed, with the grey dorianed out of it.

Peter Ustinov (1921–) British actor. *Dear Me*, Ch. 18

97 It is charming to totter into vogue.

Horace Walpole (1717–97) British writer. Letter to G. A. Selwyn, 1765

98 In a man's middle years there is scarcely a part of the body he would hesitate to turn over to the proper authorities.

E. B. White (1899–1985) US journalist and humorist. *The Second Tree from the Corner*, 'A Weekend with the Angels'

99 No woman should ever be quite accurate about her age. It looks so calculating.

Oscar Wilde (1854–1900) Irish-born British dramatist. *The Importance of Being Earnest*, III

100 One should never trust a woman who tells one her real age. A woman who would tell one that, would tell one anything.

Oscar Wilde *A Woman of No Importance*, I

101 The older one grows the more one likes indecency.

Virginia Woolf (1882–1941) British novelist. *Monday or Tuesday*

102 My heart leaps up when I behold
A rainbow in the sky:
So was it when my life began;
So is it now I am a man;
So be it when I shall grow old,
Or let me die!
The Child is Father of the Man;
And I could wish my days to be
Bound each to each by natural piety.

William Wordsworth (1770–1850) British poet. *My Heart Leaps Up*

103 One that is ever kind said yesterday:
'Your well-belovèd's hair has threads of grey,
And little shadows come about her eyes.'

W. B. Yeats (1865–1939) Irish poet. *The Folly of Being Comforted*

104 Where, where but here have Pride and Truth,
That long to give themselves for wage,
To shake their wicked sides at youth
Restraining reckless middle age?

W. B. Yeats *On hearing that the Students of our New University have joined the Agitation against Immoral Literature*

105 Though leaves are many, the root is one;
Through all the lying days of my youth
I swayed my leaves and flowers in the sun;
Now I may wither into the truth.

W. B. Yeats *The Coming of Wisdom with Time*

106 Wine comes in at the mouth
And love comes in at the eye;

That's all we shall know for truth
Before we grow old and die.

W. B. Yeats *A Drinking Song*

107 Be wise with speed,
A fool at forty is a fool indeed.

Edward Young (1683–1765) British poet. *Love of Fame*, II

AGREEMENT

1 My cousin Francis and I are in perfect accord – he wants Milan, and so do I.

Charles V (1500–58) Holy Roman Emperor. Referring to his dispute with Francis I of France over Italian territory. *The Story of Civilization* (W. Durant), Vol. 5

2 I am always of the opinion with the learned, if they speak first.

William Congreve (1670–1729) British Restoration dramatist. *Incognita*

3 We seldom attribute common sense except to those who agree with us.

Duc de la Rochefoucauld (1613–80) French writer. *Maximes*, 347

4 Our agenda is now exhausted. The secretary general is exhausted. All of you are exhausted. I find it comforting that, beginning with our very first day, we find ourselves in such complete unanimity.

Paul Henri Spaak (1899–1972) Belgian statesman. Concluding the first General Assembly meeting of the United Nations

5 Ah! don't say you agree with me. When people agree with me I always feel that I must be wrong.

Oscar Wilde (1854–1900) Irish-born British dramatist. *The Critic as Artist*, Pt. 2

6 If two men on the same job agree all the time, then one is useless. If they disagree all the time, then both are useless.

Darryl F. Zanuck (1902–79) US film producer. *The Observer*, 'Sayings of the Week', 23 Oct 1949

AGRICULTURE

See also countryside

1 We plough the fields, and scatter
The good seed on the land,
But it is fed and watered
By God's Almighty Hand.
He sends the snow in winter,
The warmth to swell the grain,
The breezes and the sunshine,
And soft refreshing rain.

Jane Montgomery Campbell (1817–78) British hymn writer. Hymn

2 Three acres and a cow.

Jesse Collings (1831–1920) British politician. Slogan used in his land-reform propaganda

3 Is my team ploughing,
That I was used to drive?

A. E. Housman (1859–1936) British scholar and poet. *A Shropshire Lad*, 'Bredon Hill'

4 'O Mary, go and call the cattle home,
And call the cattle home,
And call the cattle home,
Across the sands of Dee.'
The western wind was wild and dank with foam,
And all alone went she.

Charles Kingsley (1819–75) British writer. *The Sands of Dee*

5 This bread I break was once the oat,
This wine upon a foreign tree
Plunged in its fruit;
Man in the day or wind at night
Laid the crops low, broke the grape's joy.

Dylan Thomas (1914–53) Welsh poet. *This bread I break*

AIDS

1 Everywhere I go I see increasing evidence of people swirling about in a human cesspit of their own making.

James Anderton (1932–) British Chief Constable of Greater Manchester. Referring to AIDS

2 It could be said that the Aids pandemic is a classic own-goal scored by the human race against itself.

Princess Anne (1950–) The Princess Royal, only daughter of Elizabeth II. Remark, Jan 1988

3 My message to the businessmen of this country when they go abroad on business is that there is one thing above all they can take with them to stop them catching Aids, and that is the wife.

Edwina Currie (1946–) British politician. *The Observer*, 'Sayings of the Week', 15 Feb 1987

4 The vicious circle of fear, prejudice and ignorance has increased the spread of Aids to an alarming level. Due to fear and prejudice, many still do not want to listen. After all, Aids is a killer.

Diana, Princess of Wales (1961–) Wife of Prince Charles. *The Independent*, 17 Feb 1993

5 It's not affected my work – how healthy do you have to be to play Da Do Ron Ron?

Kenny Everett British disc jockey. Confirming that he is HIV positive. *The Sun*, 1992

6 When you have AIDS, you're judged on how much sex you've had and what kind. But *there's nothing wrong with having had a lot of sex*, with putting your arms around someone, holding them, feeling great.

Harvey Fierstein (1954–) US actor. *Playboy*, Aug 1988

7 Every time you sleep with a boy you sleep with all hisold girlfriends.

Government-sponsored AIDS advertisement, 1987

8 These are fantasies I have dreamed up. Like most human beings, when I let my mind go, I rarely think of condoms. My fantasies take place in a perfect world, a place without Aids. Unfortunately, the world is not perfect and I know that condoms are not only necessary but mandatory.

Madonna (Madonna Louise Veronica Ciccone; 1958–) US pop singer and film star. *Sex*

9 Sex is on the up. All this hooplah about Aids is rubbish. People I know rarely wear condoms. If it was true that Aids was a threat, swingers would be dropping like flies.

Robert McGinley US president of North America Swing Clubs Association. *The Sunday Times*, 14 June 1992

10 The way to stop the spread of HIV is not to make sex illegal, but to make it safe.
Ian McKellen (1939–) British stage and film actor. *The Times*, 5 Dec 1991

11 It is far more likely that it was spread in Africa (and Haiti) as the result of injections administered by evangelical 'medical missionaries' – either on purpose (as part of 'God's Republican Plan for The Advancement of Rich American White People') or through incompetence (using dirty needles for multiple injections without sterilization). How did it get back to the US? Is it possible that some of those nice little missionaries share Jim Bakker's blessed sexual preferences?
Frank Zappa (1940–93) US rock musician. Jim Bakker is a US evangelist who was jailed for fraud in 1990, and was involved in a sex scandal. *The Real Frank Zappa Book*

ALCOHOL

See also abstinence, drinks, drunkenness, public houses

1 A cask of wine works more miracles than a church full of saints.
Proverb

2 Adam's ale is the best brew.
Proverb

3 A good drink makes the old young.
Proverb

4 He who drinks a little too much drinks much too much.
Proverb

5 Take a hair of the dog that bit you.
Proverb

6 There's many a slip 'twixt the cup and the lip.
Proverb

7 When the wine is in, the wit is out.
Proverb

8 First the man takes a drink, then the drink takes a drink, then the drink takes the man.
Proverb

9 The brewery is the best drugstore.
Proverb

10 If all be true that I do think,
There are five reasons we should drink;
Good wine – a friend – or being dry –
Or lest we should be by and by –
Or any other reason why.
Dean Aldrich (1647–1710) English poet. *Reasons for Drinking*

11 I feel no pain, dear mother, now
But oh, I am so dry!
O take me to a brewery
And leave me there to die.
Anonymous Shanty

12 Mona Lisa cocktail – two of them and you can't get the silly grin off your face.
Anonymous

13 Punch cures the gout, the colic, and the 'tsick
And is by all agreed the very best of physic.
Anonymous English rhyme (18th Century)

14 So who's in a hurry?
Robert Benchley (1889–1945) US humorist. When asked whether he knew that drinking was a slow death. Attrib.

15 He is believed to have liked port, but to have said of claret that 'it would be port if it could'.
Richard Bentley (1662–1742) English academic. *Bentley* (R. C. Jebb)

16 Woe unto them that rise up early in the morning, that they may follow strong drink; that continue until night, till wine inflame them!
Bible: Isaiah 5:11

17 When the ruler of the feast had tasted the water that was made wine, and knew not whence it was: (but the servants which drew the water knew;) the governor of the feast called the bridegroom,
And saith unto him, Every man at the beginning doth set forth good wine; and when men have well drunk, then that which is worse: but thou hast kept the good wine until now.
Bible: John 2:9–10

18 No man also having drunk old wine straightway desireth new: for he saith, The old is better.
Bible: Luke 5:39

19 Look not thou upon the wine when it is red, when it giveth his colour in the cup, when it moveth itself aright.
At the last it biteth like a serpent, and stingeth like an adder.
Bible: Proverbs 23:31–32

20 Wine is a mocker, strong drink is raging: and whosoever is deceived thereby is not wise.
Bible: Proverbs 20:1

21 Drink no longer water, but use a little wine for thy stomach's sake and thine often infirmities.
Bible: I Timothy 5:23

22 ...while there is more drinking, there is less drunkenness than formerly, and that the increase in drinking is to be laid mainly to the account of the female sex. This latter phase seems to be one of the unexpected results of the emancipation of women.
Charles Booth (1840–1916) British sociologist. *Life and Labour in London*

23 There's nought, no doubt, so much the spirit calms
As rum and true religion.
Lord Byron (1788–1824) British poet.

24 The heart which grief hath cankered
Hath one unfailing remedy – the Tankard.
C. S. Calverley (1831–84) British poet. *Beer*

25 Alcohol is like love: the first kiss is magic, the second is intimate, the third is routine. After that you just take the girl's clothes off.
Raymond Chandler (1888–1959) US novelist. *The Long Goodbye*

26 So was hir joly whistle wel y-wet.
Geoffrey Chaucer (c. 1342–1400) English poet. *The Canterbury Tales*, 'The Reve's Tale'

27 I must point out that my rule of life prescribed as an absolutely sacred rite smoking cigars and also the drinking of alcohol before, after, and if need be during all meals and in the intervals between them.

Winston Churchill (1874–1965) British statesman. Said during a lunch with the Arab leader Ibn Saud, when he heard that the king's religion forbade smoking and alcohol. *The Second World War*

28 Apart from cheese and tulips, the main product of the country is advocaat, a drink made from lawyers.

Alan Coren (1938–) British humorist and writer. Referring to Holland. *The Sanity Inspector*, 'All You Need to Know about Europe'

29 Then trust me, there's nothing like drinking
So pleasant on this side the grave;
It keeps the unhappy from thinking,
And makes e'en the valiant more brave.

Charles Dibdin (1745–1814) British actor and dramatist. *Nothing like Grog*

30 'Did you ever taste beer?' 'I had a sip of it once,' said the small servant. 'Here's a state of things!' cried Mr Swiveller… 'She *never* tasted it – it can't be tasted in a sip!'

Charles Dickens (1812–70) British novelist. *The Old Curiosity Shop*, Ch. 57

31 First you take a drink, then the drink takes a drink, then the drink takes you.

F. Scott Fitzgerald (1896–1940) US novelist. *Ackroyd* (Jules Feiffer), '1964, May 7'

32 A good gulp of hot whisky at bedtime – it's not very scientific, but it helps.

Alexander Fleming (1881–1955) British microbiologist. When asked about a cure for colds. News summary, 22 Mar 1954

33 Best while you have it use your breath,
There is no drinking after death.

John Fletcher (1579–1625) English dramatist. With Jonson and others. *The Bloody Brother*, II:2

34 And he that will go to bed sober,
Falls with the leaf still in October.

John Fletcher *The Bloody Brother*, II:2

35 A taste for drink, combined with gout,
Had doubled him up for ever.

W. S. Gilbert (1836–1911) British dramatist. *The Gondoliers*, I

36 Let schoolmasters puzzle their brain,
With grammar, and nonsense, and learning,
Good liquor, I stoutly maintain,
Gives genius a better discerning.

Oliver Goldsmith (1728–74) Irish-born British writer. *She Stoops to Conquer*, I

37 He that goes to bed thirsty rises healthy.

George Herbert (1593–1633) English poet. *Jacula Prudentum*

38 Who could have foretold, from the structure of the brain, that wine could derange its functions?

Hippocrates (c. 460–c. 377 BC) Greek physician.

39 Our country has deliberately undertaken a great social and economic experiment, noble in motive and far-reaching in purpose.

Herbert Hoover (1874–1964) US president. Referring to Prohibition. Letter to W.H. Borah, 28 Feb 1928

40 Malt does more than Milton can
To justify God's ways to man.

A. E. Housman (1859–1936) British scholar and poet. *A Shropshire Lad*, 'The Welsh Marches'

41 The sway of alcohol over mankind is unquestionably due to its power to stimulate the mystical faculties of human nature.

William James (1842–1910) US philosopher and psychologist. *The Varieties of Religious Experience*, 'Mysticism'

42 Claret is the liquor for boys; port for men; but he who aspires to be a hero must drink brandy.

Samuel Johnson (1709–84) British lexicographer. *Life of Johnson* (J. Boswell), Vol. III

43 No, Sir; there were people who died of dropsies, which they contracted in trying to get drunk.

Samuel Johnson Scornfully criticizing the strength of the wine in Scotland before the Act of Union in response to Boswell's claim that there had been a lot of drunkenness. *Tour to the Hebrides* (J. Boswell)

44 Come, let me know what it is that makes a Scotchman happy!

Samuel Johnson Ordering for himself a glass of whisky. *Tour to the Hebrides* (J. Boswell)

45 My friends should drink a dozen of Claret on my Tomb.

John Keats (1795–1821) British poet. Letter to Benjamin Bailey, 14 Aug 1819

46 O, for a draught of vintage! that hath been
Cool'd a long age in the deep-delved earth.

John Keats *Ode to a Nightingale*

47 O for a beaker full of the warm South,
Full of the true, the blushful Hippocrene,
With beaded bubbles winking at the brim,
And purple-stained mouth.

John Keats *Ode to a Nightingale*

48 Even though a number of people have tried, no one has yet found a way to drink for a living.

Jean Kerr (1923–) US dramatist. *Poor Richard*

49 I'm so holy that when I touch wine, it turns into water.

Aga Khan III (1877–1957) Muslim leader. Defending drinking alcohol. *Who's Really Who* (Compton Miller)

50 If we heard it said of Orientals that they habitually drank a liquor which went to their heads, deprived them of reason and made them vomit, we should say: 'How very barbarous!'

Jean de La Bruyère (1645–96) French satirist. *Les Caractères*

51 Frenchmen drink wine just like we used to drink water before Prohibition.

Ring Lardner Jnr (1885–1933) American humorist. *Wit's End* (R. E. Drennan)

52 It takes a good deal of physical courage to ride a horse. This, however, I have. I get it at about forty cents a flask, and take it as required.

Stephen Leacock (1869–1944) British-born Canadian economist and humorist. *Literary Lapses*, 'Reflections on Riding'

53 Long quaffing maketh a short lyfe.

John Lyly (1554–1606) English dramatist and novelist. *Euphues*

54 If die I must, let me die drinking in an inn.

Walter Map (c. 1140–c. 1209) Welsh clergyman and writer. *De Nugis Curialium*

55 The tranquilizer of greatest value since the early history of man, and which may never become outdated, is alcohol, when administered in moderation. It possesses the distinct advantage of being especially pleasant to the taste buds.

Nathan Masor (1913–) Attrib.

56 I've made it a rule never to drink by daylight and never to refuse a drink after dark.

H. L. Mencken (1880–1956) US journalist. *New York Post*, 18 Sept 1945

57 No man is genuinely happy, married, who has to drink worse gin than he used to drink when he was single.

H. L. Mencken *Prejudices*, 'Reflections on Monogamy'

58 Then to the spicy nut-brown ale.

John Milton (1608–74) English poet. *L'Allegro*

59 Candy
Is dandy
But liquor
Is quicker.

Ogden Nash (1902–71) US poet. *Hard Lines*, 'Reflection on Ice-Breaking'

60 A torchlight procession marching down your throat.

John L. O'Sullivan (1813–95) US writer. Referring to whisky. *Collections and Recollections* (G. W. E. Russell), Ch. 19

61 Wine is the most healthful and most hygienic of beverages.

Louis Pasteur (1822–95) French scientist. *Études sur le vin*, Pt. I, Ch. 2

62 *In vino veritas.*
Truth comes out in wine.

Pliny the Elder (Gaius Plinius Secundus; 23–79 AD) Roman scholar. *Natural History*, XIV

63 It is WRONG to do what everyone else does – namely, to hold the wine list just out of sight, look for the second cheapest claret on the list, and say, 'Number 22, please'.

Stephen Potter (1900–69) British writer. *One-Upmanship*, Ch. 14

64 A good general rule is to state that the bouquet is better than the taste, and vice versa.

Stephen Potter *One-Upmanship*, Ch. 14

65 It is the unbroken testimony of all history that alcoholic liquors have been used by the strongest, wisest, handsomest, and in every way best races of all times.

George Edward Bateman Saintsbury (1845–1933) British writer and critic. *Notes on a Cellar-Book*

66 People may say what they like about the decay of Christianity; the religious system that produced green Chartreuse can never really die.

Saki (Hector Hugh Munro; 1870–1916) British writer. *Reginald on Christmas Presents*

67 By insisting on having your bottle pointing to the north when the cork is being drawn, and calling the waiter Max, you may induce an impression on your guests which hours of laboured boasting might be powerless to achieve. For this purpose, however, the guests must be chosen as carefully as the wine.

Saki *The Chaplet*

68 What will you drink if you stop drinking?
I shall drink water. It's a mixer Patsy.

Jennifer Saunders (1958–) British comedy writer and actress. *Absolutely Fabulous*

69 It provokes the desire, but it takes away the performance. Therefore much drink may be said to be an equivocator with lechery.

William Shakespeare (1564–1616) English dramatist. *Macbeth*, II:3

70 MACDUFF. What three things does drink especially provoke?
PORTER. Marry, sir, nose-painting, sleep, and urine.

William Shakespeare *Macbeth*, II:3

71 Come, come; good wine is a good familiar creature if it be well used; exclaim no more against it.

William Shakespeare *Othello*, II:3

72 I am only a beer teetotaller, not a champagne teetotaller.

George Bernard Shaw (1856–1950) Irish dramatist and critic. *Candida*

73 Alcohol is a very necessary article...It enables Parliament to do things at eleven at night that no sane person would do at eleven in the morning.

George Bernard Shaw *Major Barbara*, II

74 Gin was mother's milk to her.

George Bernard Shaw *Pygmalion*, III

75 Well, then, my stomach must just digest in its waistcoat.

Richard Brinsley Sheridan (1751–1816) British dramatist. On being warned that his drinking would destroy the coat of his stomach. *The Fine Art of Political Wit* (L. Harris)

76 Another little drink wouldn't do us any harm.

Edith Sitwell (1887–1964) British poet and writer. *Façade*, 'Scotch Rhapsody'

77 Selwyn Macgregor, the nicest boy who ever committed the sin of whisky.

Muriel Spark (1918–) British novelist. *The Go-Away Bird*, 'A Sad Tale's Best for Winter'

78 Fifteen men on the dead man's chest
Yo-ho-ho, and a bottle of rum!
Drink and the devil had done for the rest –
Yo-ho-ho, and a bottle of rum!

Robert Louis Stevenson (1850–94) Scottish writer. *Treasure Island*, Ch. 1

79 There are two things that will be believed of any man whatsoever, and one of them is that he has taken to drink.

Booth Tarkington (1869–1946) US novelist. *Penrod*, Ch. 10

80 An alcoholic is someone you don't like who drinks as much as you do.

Dylan Thomas (1914–53) Welsh poet. Attrib.

81 I've had eighteen straight whiskies. I think that's the record...After thirty-nine years, this is all I've done.

Dylan Thomas Attrib.

82 It's a Naive Domestic Burgundy, Without Any Breeding. But I think you'll be Amused by its Presumption.

James Thurber (1894–1961) US humorist. *Men, Women and Dogs*

83 'Joe,' I said, 'was perhaps the first great nonstop literary drinker of the American nineteenth century. He made the indulgences of Coleridge and De

Quincey seem like a bit of mischief in the kitchen with the cooking sherry.'

James Thurber *Alarms and Diversions*, 'The Moribundant Life...'

84 Whiskey is the most popular of all the remedies that won't cure a cold.

Jerry Vale *Bartlett's Unfamiliar Quotations* (Leonard Louis Levinson)

85 I prefer temperance hotels – although they sell worse kinds of liquor than any other kind of hotels.

Artemus Ward (Charles Farrar Browne; 1834–67) US humorous writer. *Artemus Ward's Lecture*

86 Across the Street and Into the Bar.

E. B. White (1899–1985) US humorist. Alluding to Hemingway's book *Across the River and into the Trees*. Title of satire on Ernest Hemingway

87 I hadn't the heart to touch my breakfast. I told Jeeves to drink it himself.

P. G. Wodehouse (1881–1975) British humorous novelist. *My Man Jeeves*

88 It was my Uncle George who discovered that alcohol was a food well in advance of modern medical thought.

P. G. Wodehouse *The Inimitable Jeeves*, Ch. 16

89 I must get out of these wet clothes and into a dry Martini.

Alexander Woollcott (1887–1943) US journalist. *Reader's Digest*

90 Father, dear father, come home with me now,
The clock in the steeple strikes one.

Henry Clay Work (1832–84) US songwriter. A temperance song. *Come Home, Father*

ALLEN, WOODY

(Allen Stewart Konigsberg; 1935–) US film actor and director. His films include *Play It Again, Sam* (1972), *Annie Hall* (1977), *The Purple Rose of Cairo* (1985), *Hannah and Her Sisters* (1986), *September* (1988), and *Husbands and Wives* (1992).

1 Is sex dirty? Only if it's done right.

All You've Ever Wanted to Know About Sex

2 It was the most fun I ever had without laughing.

Referring to sex. *Annie Hall*

3 Don't knock it, it's sex with someone you love.

Referring to masturbation. *Annie Hall*

4 I'm short enough and ugly enough to succeed on my own.

Play It Again Sam

5 I'm really a timid person – I was beaten up by Quakers.

Sleeper

6 My brain? It's my second favourite organ.

Sleeper

7 It's not that I'm afraid to die. I just don't want to be there when it happens.

Without Feathers, 'Death (A Play)'

8 The lion and the calf shall lie down together but the calf won't get much sleep.

Without Feathers, 'The Scrolls'

9 And my parents finally realize that I'm kidnapped and they snap into action immediately: they rent out my room.

Woody Allen and His Comedy (E. Lax)

10 I don't want to achieve immortality through my work...I want to achieve it through not dying.

Woody Allen and His Comedy (E. Lax)

11 I want to tell you a terrific story about oral contraception. I asked this girl to sleep with me and she said 'no'.

Woody Allen: Clown Prince of American Humor (Adler and Feinman), Ch. 2

AMBITION

See also desire

1 He who rides a tiger is afraid to dismount.

Proverb

2 *Per ardua ad astra.*
Through endeavour to the stars.

Anonymous Motto of the Royal Air Force.

3 Room at the Top.

John Braine (1922–86) British novelist. From Daniel Webster's remark 'There is always room at the top'. Book title

4 Ah, but a man's reach should exceed his grasp,
Or what's a heaven for?

Robert Browning (1812–89) British poet. *Andrea del Sarto*

5 Man partly is and wholly hopes to be.

Robert Browning *A Death in the Desert*

6 You seem to have no real purpose in life and won't realize at the age of twenty-two that for a man life means work, and hard work if you mean to succeed.

Jennie Jerome Churchill (1854–1921) US-born British hostess and writer. Letter to her son Winston Churchill, 26 Feb 1897. *Jennie* (Ralph G. Martin), Vol. II

7 I have found some of the best reasons I ever had for remaining at the bottom simply by looking at the men at the top.

Frank More Colby (1865–1925) US editor. *Essays*, II

8 If thy heart fails thee, climb not at all.

Elizabeth I (1533–1603) Queen of England. Written on a window in reply to Walter RALEIGH's line. *Worthies of England* (Fuller), Vol. I

9 Hitch your wagon to a star.

Ralph Waldo Emerson (1803–82) US poet and essayist. *Society and Solitude*, 'Civilization'

10 I would like to throw an egg into an electric fan.

Oliver Herford (1863–1935) British-born US humorist. When asked if he really had no ambition beyond making people laugh. Attrib.

11 With a suitcase full of clothes and underwear in my hand and an indomitable will in my heart, I set out for Vienna...I too hope to become 'something'.

Adolf Hitler (1889–1945) German dictator. *Mein Kampf*

12 I am going to build the kind of nation that President Roosevelt hoped for, President Truman worked for and President Kennedy died for.

Lyndon B. Johnson (1908–73) US statesman. *The Sunday Times*, 27 Dec 1964

13 A slave has but one master; an ambitious man has as many masters as there are people who may be useful in bettering his position.

Jean de La Bruyère (1645–96) French satirist. *Les Caractères*

14 The shades of night were falling fast,
As through an Alpine village passed
A youth, who bore, 'mid snow and ice,
A banner with the strange device,
Excelsior!

Henry Wadsworth Longfellow (1807–82) US poet. Opening of a poem best known as a Victorian drawing-room ballad, and the butt of many music-hall jokes. Excelsior means 'higher' (Latin). *Excelsior*

15 If you would hit the mark, you must aim a little above it;
Every arrow that flies feels the attraction of earth.

Henry Wadsworth Longfellow *Elegiac Verse*

16 If men could regard the events of their own lives with more open minds they would frequently discover that they did not really desire the things they failed to obtain.

André Maurois (Émile Herzog; 1885–1967) French writer. *The Art of Living*

17 I grew up with a lot of brothers and sisters. I did all I could do to really stand out and that nurtured a lot of confidence and drive and ambition.

Madonna (Madonna Louise Veronica Ciccone; 1958–) *Rolling Stone*, 9 May 1985

18 I lost my virginity as a career move.

Madonna *Film Yearbook*, 1989

19 Ambition is the grand enemy of all peace.

John Cowper Powys (1872–1963) British novelist. *The Meaning of Culture*

20 Fain would I climb, yet fear I to fall.

Walter Raleigh (1554–1618) English explorer. Written on a window pane. For the reply *see* ELIZABETH I. Attrib.

21 'Tis a common proof,
That lowliness is young ambition's ladder,
Whereto the climber-upward turns his face;
But when he once attains the upmost round,
He then unto the ladder turns his back,
Looks in the clouds, scorning the base degrees
By which he did ascend.

William Shakespeare (1564–1616) English dramatist. *Julius Caesar*, II:1

22 Ambition should be made of sterner stuff.

William Shakespeare *Julius Caesar*, III:2

23 I have no spur
To prick the sides of my intent, but only
Vaulting ambition, which o'er-leaps itself,
And falls on th' other.

William Shakespeare *Macbeth*, I:7

24 LADY MACBETH. I have given suck, and know
How tender 'tis to love the babe that milks me:
I would, while it was smiling in my face,
Have plucked my nipple from his boneless gums,
And dash'd the brains out, had I so sworn as you
Have done to this.
MACBETH. If we should fail, –
LADY MACBETH. We fail!
But screw your courage to the sticking-place,
And we'll not fail.

William Shakespeare *Macbeth*, I:7

25 Who would not make her husband a cuckold to make him a monarch?

William Shakespeare *Othello*, IV:3

26 And he that strives to touch the stars,
Oft stumbles at a straw.

Edmund Spenser (1552–99) English poet. *The Shepherd's Calendar*, 'July'

27 There is always room at the top.

Daniel Webster (1782–1852) US statesman. When advised not to become a lawyer because the profession was overcrowded. Attrib.

28 Well, good luck to you, kid! I'm going to write the Great Australian Novel.

Patrick White (1912–90) British-born Australian novelist. *The Vivisector*, 112

AMERICA

See also Americans

1 Our society distributes itself into Barbarians, Philistines, and Populace; and America is just ourselves, with the Barbarians quite left out, and the Populace nearly.

Matthew Arnold (1822–88) British poet and critic. *Culture and Anarchy*, Preface

2 God bless the USA, so large,
So friendly, and so rich.

W. H. Auden (1907–73) British poet. *On the Circuit*

3 Yankee Doodle came to town
Riding on a pony;
Stuck a feather in his cap
And called it Macaroni.

Edward Bangs (fl. 1775) US songwriter. *Yankee Doodle; or Father's Return to Camp*

4 O beautiful for spacious skies,
For amber waves of grain,
For purple mountain majesties
Above the fruited plain!
America! America!
God shed His grace on thee
And crown thy good with brotherhood
From sea to shining sea!

Katharine Lee Bates (1859–1929) US writer and poet. *America the Beautiful*

5 The United States is the best and fairest and most decent nation on the face of the earth.

George Bush (1924–) US president. Speech, May 1988

6 I called the New World into existence to redress the balance of the Old.

George Canning (1770–1827) British statesman. Speech, 12 Dec 1826

7 This is virgin territory for whorehouses.

Al Capone (1899–1947) Italian-born US gangster. Talking about suburban Chicago. *The Bootleggers* (Kenneth Allsop), Ch. 16

8 How beautiful it would be for someone who could not read.

G. K. Chesterton (1874–1936) British writer. Referring to the lights on Broadway. Attrib.

9 America is the only nation in history which miraculously has gone directly from barbarism to degeneration without the usual interval of civilization.

Georges Clemenceau (1841–1929) French statesman. Attrib.

10 Nothing means anything here. When they pull down an outstanding building, no one objects. Oh, maybe there's a wee protest from some collectors or something who take a picture of it before it vanishes.

Billy Connolly (1942–) Scottish comedian. *The Times*, 15 Dec 1990

11 Patriotism is easy to understand in America; it means looking out for yourself while looking out for your country.

Calvin Coolidge (1872–1933) US president. Attrib.

12 The business of America is business.

Calvin Coolidge Speech, Washington, 17 Jan 1925

13 Poor Mexico, so far from God and so near to the United States!

Porfirio Díaz (1830–1915) Mexican general and statesman. Attrib.

14 Whatever America hopes to bring to pass in this world must first come to pass in the heart of America.

Dwight D. Eisenhower (1890–1969) US general and statesman. Inaugural address, 1953

15 America is a country of young men.

Ralph Waldo Emerson (1803–82) US poet and essayist. *Society and Solitude*, 'Old Age'

16 Our country is the world – our countrymen are all mankind.

William Lloyd Garrison (1805–79) US abolitionist. *The Liberator*, 15 Dec 1837

17 When I first went to America in 1928, there were spittoons everywhere. I remember avoiding spit as it flew past me in Times Square. Very unattractive.

John Gielgud (1904–) British actor. *Time*, 15 Aug 1983

18 New York...that unnatural city where every one is an exile, none more so than the American.

Charlotte Perkins Gilman (1860–1935) US writer. *The Living of Charlotte Perkins Gilman*

19 The United States is like a gigantic boiler. Once the fire is lighted under it there is no limit to the power it can generate.

Lord Grey (1862–1933) British statesman. *Their Finest Hour* (Winston S. Churchill), Ch. 32

20 The United States, I believe, are under the impression that they are twenty years in advance of this country; whilst, as a matter of actual verifiable fact, of course, they are just about six hours behind it.

Harold Hobson (1904–92) British theatre critic and writer. *The Devil in Woodford Wells*, Ch. 8

21 The American system of rugged individualism.

Herbert Clark Hoover (1874–1964) US statesman. Speech, New York, 22 Oct 1928

22 It created in me a yearning for all that is wide and open and expansive. Something that will never allow me to fit in in my own country, with its narrow towns and narrow roads and narrow kindnesses and narrow reprimands.

Anthony Hopkins (1937–) Welsh actor. *The Independent*, 12 Feb 1994

23 America is not a blanket woven from one thread, one color, one cloth.

Jesse Jackson (1941–) US politician. Speech, Democratic Party Convention, Atlanta, July 1988

24 The United States has to move very fast to even stand still.

John Fitzgerald Kennedy (1917–63) US statesman. *The Observer*, 'Sayings of the Week', 21 July 1963

25 'Tis the star-spangled banner; O long may it wave
O'er the land of the free, and the home of the brave!

Francis Scott Key (1779–1843) US lawyer. *The Star-Spangled Banner*

26 Give me your tired, your poor,
Your huddled masses yearning to breathe free,
The wretched refuse of your teeming shore,
Send these, the homeless, tempest-tossed to me,
I lift my lamp beside the golden door!

Emma Lazarus (1849–87) US poet and philanthropist. Used as an inscription on the Statue of Liberty. *The New Colossus*

27 In other countries, art and literature are left to a lot of shabby bums living in attics and feeding on booze and spaghetti, but in America the successful writer or picture-painter is indistinguishable from any other decent business man.

Sinclair Lewis (1885–1951) US novelist. *Babbitt*, Ch. 14

28 In an English ship, they say, it is poor grub, poor pay, and easy work; in an American ship, good grub, good pay, and hard work. And this is applicable to the working populations of both countries.

Jack London (1876–1916) US novelist. *The People of the Abyss*, Ch. 20

29 First the sweetheart of the nation, then the aunt, woman governs America because America is a land of boys who refuse to grow up.

Salvador de Madariaga y Rogo (1886–1978) Spanish diplomat and writer. *The Perpetual Pessimist* (Sagitarius and George)

30 If there is any country on earth where the course of true love may be expected to run smooth, it is America.

Harriet Martineau (1802–76) British writer. *Society in America*, Vol. III, 'Marriage'

31 The immense popularity of American movies abroad demonstrates that Europe is the unfinished negative of which America is the proof.

Mary McCarthy (1912–89) US novelist. *On the Contrary*

32 I believe the US is a truly monstrous force in the world, now off the leash for obvious reasons.

Harold Pinter (1930–) British dramatist. *The Independent*, 20 Sept 1993

33 The national dish of America is menus.

Robert Robinson (1927–) British writer and broadcaster. BBC TV programme, *Robinson's Travels*, Aug 1977

34 I pledge you, I pledge myself, to a new deal for the American people.

Franklin D. Roosevelt (1882–1945) US Democratic president.

Speech accepting nomination for presidency, Chicago, 2 July 1932

35 America...where law and customs alike are based on the dreams of spinsters.

Bertrand Russell (1872–1970) British philosopher. *Marriage and Morals*

36 In the United States there is more space where nobody is than where anybody is. That is what makes America what it is.

Gertrude Stein (1874–1946) US writer. *The Geographical History of America*

37 I like to walk around Manhattan, catching glimpses of its wild life, the pigeons and cats and girls.

Rex Todhunter Stout (1886–1975) US writer. *Three Witnesses*, 'When a Man Murders'

38 I found there a country with thirty-two religions and only one sauce.

Talleyrand (Charles Maurice de Talleyrand-Périgord; 1754–1838) French politician. *Autant en apportent les mots* (Pedrazzini)

39 America is a large, friendly dog in a very small room. Every time it wags its tail it knocks over a chair.

Arnold Toynbee (1889–1975) British historian. Broadcast news summary, 14 July 1954

40 By the waters of Babylon we sit down and weep, when we think of thee, O America!

Horace Walpole (1717–97) British writer. On the eve of the American Revolution. Letter to Mason, 12 June 1775

41 Up from the meadows rich with corn,
Clear in the cool September morn,

The clustered spires of Frederick stand
Green-walled by the hills of Maryland.

John Greenleaf Whittier (1807–92) US poet. *Barbara Frietchie*

42 We're Americans, we're a simple people but if you piss us off we'll bomb your cities.

Robin Williams (1952–) US actor. *Live*

43 There exists in the world today a gigantic reservoir of good will toward us, the American people.

Wendell Lewis Willkie (1892–1944) US lawyer and businessman. *One World*, Ch. 10

44 Sometimes people call me an idealist. Well, that is the way I know I am an American. America is the only idealistic nation in the world.

Woodrow Wilson (1856–1925) US statesman. Speech, Sioux Falls, 8 Sept 1919

45 America...is the prize amateur nation of the world. Germany is the prize professional nation.

Woodrow Wilson Speech, Aug 1917. *Mr Wilson's War* (John Dos Passos), Pt. III, Ch. 13

46 New York is a small place when it comes to the part of it that wakes up just as the rest is going to bed.

P. G. Wodehouse (1881–1975) British humorous novelist. *My Man Jeeves*, 'The Aunt and the Sluggard'

47 America is God's Crucible, the great Melting-Pot where all the races of Europe are melting and re-forming!

Israel Zangwill (1864–1926) British writer. *The Melting Pot*, I

AMERICANS

1 Good Americans, when they die, go to Paris.

Thomas Gold Appleton (1812–84) US writer. *Autocrat of the Breakfast Table* (O. W. Holmes), Ch. 6

2 If Kuwait and Saudi Arabia sold bananas or oranges, the Americans would not go there. They are there because Kuwait is an oil monarchy.

Julius Nyerere (1922–) Tanzanian statesman. Referring to the international response to the Iraqi invasion of Kuwait (Aug 1990). *The Independent*, 28 Sept 1990

3 The Americans don't really understand what's going on in Bosnia. To them it's the unspellables killing the unpronouncables.

P. J. O'Rourke *The Sun*, 1993

ANALOGY

See also similarity

1 Though analogy is often misleading, it is the least misleading thing we have.

Samuel Butler (1835–1902) British writer. *Notebooks*

2 She, and comparisons are odious.

John Donne (1573–1631) English poet. *Elegies*, 8, 'The Comparison'

3 She has the smile of a woman who has just dined off her husband.

Lawrence Durrell (1912–90) British writer. Referring to the Mona Lisa. Attrib.

4 My mistress' eyes are nothing like the sun;
Coral is far more red than her lips' red.

William Shakespeare (1564–1616) English dramatist. *Sonnet 130*

5 And yet, by heaven, I think my love as rare
As any she belied with false compare.

William Shakespeare *Sonnet 130*

6 Jeeves coughed one soft, low, gentle cough like a sheep with a blade of grass stuck in its throat.

P. G. Wodehouse (1881–1975) British humorous novelist. *The Inimitable Jeeves*, Ch. 13

ANCESTRY

See also aristocracy, family

1 I am my own ancestor.

Duc d'Abrantes (1771–1813) French general. Said on being made a duke. Attrib.

2 I can trace my ancestry back to a protoplasmal primordial atomic globule. Consequently, my family pride is something in-conceivable. I can't help it. I was born sneering.

W. S. Gilbert (1836–1911) British dramatist. *The Mikado*, I

3 The difference between us is that my family begins with me, whereas yours ends with you.

Iphicrates (d. 353 BC) Athenian general. Reply to a descendant of Harmodius (an Athenian hero), who had derided Iphicrates for being the son of a cobbler. Attrib.

4 Being Southerners, it was a source of shame to some members of the family that we had no recorded ancestors on either side of the Battle of Hastings.

Harper Lee (1926–) US writer. *To Kill a Mockingbird*, Pt. I, Ch. 1

5 I don't know who my grandfather was; I am much more concerned to know what his grandson will be.

Abraham Lincoln (1809–65) US statesman. Taking part in a discussion on ancestry. Attrib.

ANGER

1 He could enrage his antagonists by making them feel their own impotence to enrage him.

Anonymous Referring to Henry Cabot Lodge the US Republican politician (1850–1924).

2 The man who gets angry at the right things and with the right people, and in the right way and at the right time and for the right length of time, is commended.

Aristotle (384–322 BC) Greek philosopher. *Nicomachean Ethics*, Bk. IV

3 When they heard these things, they were cut to the heart, and they gnashed on him with their teeth.

Bible: Acts 7:54

4 Never go to bed mad. Stay up and fight.

Phyllis Diller (1917–) US writer and comedienne. *Phyllis Diller's Housekeeping Hints*

5 Anger is one of the sinews of the soul.

Thomas Fuller (1608–61) English historian. *The Holy State and the Profane State*

6 Spleen can subsist on any kind of food.

William Hazlitt (1778–1830) British essayist. *On Wit and Humour*

7 I feel angry that the righteous anger I did manage to express in the past was denigrated as unprofessional or self-defeating, or more subtly suppressed when others praised me as calm, reasonable, not one of those 'angry feminists'.

Gloria Steinem (1934–) US writer and feminist. *The Observer Life Magazine*, 15 May 1994

8 Anger supplies the arms.

Virgil (Publius Vergilius Maro; 70–19 BC) Roman poet. *Aeneid*, Bk. I

ANIMALISM

See also evolution, lust, mankind, sex

1 My brain: it's my second favourite organ.

Woody Allen (Allen Stewart Konigsberg; 1935–) US film actor. *Sleeper*

2 But oh, the farmyard world of sex!

Harley Granville-Barker (1877–1946) British actor and dramatist. *The Madras House*, IV

3 Be a good animal, true to your animal instincts.

D. H. Lawrence (1885–1930) British novelist. *The White Peacock*, Pt. II, Ch. 2

4 It's all this cold-hearted fucking that is death and idiocy.

D. H. Lawrence *Lady Chatterley's Lover*, Ch. 14

5 The soul started at the knee-cap and ended at the navel.

Wyndham Lewis (1882–1957) British novelist. *The Apes of God*, Pt. XII

6 – 'Do you come here often?'
'Only in the mating season.'

Spike Milligan (1918–) British comic actor and author. *The Goon Show*

7 The wren goes to't, and the small gilded fly
Does lecher in my sight.

William Shakespeare (1564–1616) English dramatist. *King Lear*, IV:6

ANIMALS

See also cats, dogs, horses, rabbits

1 There was a young lady of Riga,
Who went for a ride on a tiger;
They returned from the ride
With the lady inside,
And a smile on the face of the tiger.

Anonymous

2 The fox knows many things – the hedgehog one *big* one.

Archilochus (c. 680–c. 640 BC) Greek poet. Attrib.

3 And God said, Let the earth bring forth the living creature after his kind, cattle, and creeping thing, and beast of the earth after his kind: and it was so.

Bible: Genesis 1:24

4 Now the serpent was more subtil than any beast of the field which the Lord God had made.

Bible: Genesis 3:1

5 But the poor man had nothing, save one little ewe lamb, which he had bought and nourished up: and it grew up together with him, and with his children; it did eat of his own meat, and drank of his own cup, and lay in his bosom, and was unto him as a daughter.

Bible: II Samuel 12:3

6 Tiger! Tiger! burning bright
In the forests of the night,
What immortal hand or eye
Could frame thy fearful symmetry?

William Blake (1757–1827) British poet. *Songs of Experience*, 'The Tiger'

7 Rats!
They fought the dogs and killed the cats,
And bit the babies in the cradles.

Robert Browning (1812–89) British poet. *The Pied Piper of Hamelin*

8 And the muttering grew to a grumbling;
And the grumbling grew to a mighty rumbling;
And out of the houses the rats came tumbling.

Robert Browning *The Pied Piper of Hamelin*

9 Wee, sleekit, cow'rin', tim'rous beastie,
O what a panic's in thy breastie!

Robert Burns (1759–96) Scottish poet. *To a Mouse*

10 Whenever you observe an animal closely, you

feel as if a human being sitting inside were making fun of you.

Elias Canetti (1905–) Bulgarian-born novelist. *The Human Province*

11 The devil's walking parody
On all four-footed things.

G. K. Chesterton (1874–1936) British writer. *The Donkey*

12 Fools! For I also had my hour;
One far fierce hour and sweet;
There was a shout about my ears,
And palms before my feet.

G. K. Chesterton *The Donkey*

13 Animals are such agreeable friends – they ask no questions, they pass no criticisms.

George Eliot (Mary Ann Evans; 1819–80) British novelist. *Scenes of Clerical Life*, 'Mr Gilfil's Love Story', Ch. 7

14 Mary had a little lamb,
Its fleece was white as snow,
And everywhere that Mary went
The lamb was sure to go.

Sarah Josepha Hale (1788–1879) US writer. *Poems for Our Children*, 'Mary's Little Lamb'

15 'Twould ring the bells of Heaven
The wildest peal for years,
If Parson lost his senses
And people came to theirs,
And he and they together
Knelt down with angry prayers
For tamed and shabby tigers
And dancing dogs and bears,
And wretched, blind, pit ponies,
And little hunted hares.

Ralph Hodgson (1871–1962) British poet. *The Bells of Heaven*

16 The stars grew bright in the winter sky,
The wind came keen with a tang of frost,
The brook was troubled for new things lost,
The copse was happy for old things found,
The fox came home and he went to ground.

John Masefield (1878–1967) British poet. *Reynard the Fox*

17 I never nurs'd a dear gazelle,
To glad me with its soft black eye
But when it came to know me well,
And love me, it was sure to die!

Thomas Moore (1779–1852) Irish poet. *Lalla Rookh*

18 Dogs, like horses, are quadrupeds. That is to say, they have four rupeds, one at each corner, on which they walk.

Frank Muir (1920–) British writer and broadcaster. *You Can't Have Your Kayak and Heat It* (Frank Muir and Denis Norden), 'Ta-ra-ra-boom-de-ay!'

19 The cow is of the bovine ilk;
One end is moo, the other, milk.

Ogden Nash (1902–71) US poet. *The Cow*

20 Nothing can be more obvious than that all animals were created solely and exclusively for the use of man.

Thomas Love Peacock (1785–1866) British novelist. *Headlong Hall*, Ch. 2

21 Don't go into Mr McGregor's garden: your Father had an accident there; he was put in a pie by Mrs McGregor.

Beatrix Potter (1866–1943) British children's writer. *The Tale of Peter Rabbit*

22 Irish dolphin, swift and single,
Dwelling off the coast of Dingle
Choosing now and then to mingle
With the flipperless and glum.

Vikram Seth (1952–) Indian writer. Dedicated to Funghie the Irish dolphin. *Arion and the Dolphin*, prefatory poem from the libretto

23 *Exit, pursued by a bear.*

William Shakespeare (1564–1616) English dramatist. Stage direction. *The Winter's Tale*, III:3

24 There are two things for which animals are to be envied: they know nothing of future evils, or of what people say about them.

Voltaire (François-Marie Arouet; 1694–1778) French writer. Letter, 1739

25 Let dogs delight to bark and bite,
For God hath made them so;
Let bears and lions growl and fight,
For 'tis their nature too.

Isaac Watts (1674–1748) English theologian and hymn writer. *Divine Songs for Children*, 'Against Quarrelling'

26 Feather-footed through the plashy fen passes the questing vole.

Evelyn Waugh (1903–66) British novelist. *Scoop*, Bk. I, Ch. 1

27 I think I could turn and live with animals, they're so placid and self-contained,
I stand and look at them long and long.

Walt Whitman (1819–92) US poet. *Song of Myself*, 32

ANONYMOUS

This includes a selection of sayings, rhymes, epitaphs, ballads, mottoes, etc., for which the author is unknown. They are arranged in alphabetical order of the first line. Further anonymous quotations are given under the entries for Nursery Rhymes and Proverbs.

1 Adieu, adieu, kind friends, adieu, adieu, adieu,
I can no longer stay with you, stay with you.
I'll hang my harp on a weeping willow-tree.
And may the world go well with thee.

There is a Tavern in the Town

2 *Ad majorem Dei gloriam.*
To the greater glory of God.

Motto of the Jesuits

3 All human beings are born free and equal in dignity and rights.

Universal Declaration of Human Rights (1948), Article 1

4 All present and correct.

Report by the orderly sergeant to the officer of the day. *King's Regulations (Army)*.

5 All who come my grave to see
Avoid damp beds and think of me.

Epitaph of Lydia Eason, St Michael's, Stoke

6 Any officer who shall behave in a scandalous manner, unbecoming the character of an officer and a gentleman shall…be cashiered.

The words 'conduct unbecoming the character of an officer' are a direct quotation from the Naval Discipline Act (10 Aug 1860), Article 24. *Articles of War* (1872), *Disgraceful Conduct*, 79

7 Are we downhearted? No!

A favourite expression of the British soldiers during World War I. Attrib.

8 As I sat on a sunny bank,
On Christmas Day in the morning,
I spied three ships come sailing by.
As I sat on a Sunny Bank

9 *Ave Caesar, morituri te salutant.*
Hail Caesar; those who are about to die salute you.
Greeting to the Roman Emperor by gladiators

10 Begone, dull care! I prithee begone from me!
Begone, dull care, you and I shall never agree.
Begone Dull Care

11 Beneath this stone, in hope of Zion,
Doth lie the landlord of the 'Lion'.
His son keeps on the business still,
Resign'd unto the Heavenly will.
Epitaph, Upton-on-Severn churchyard

12 Come landlord, fill the flowing bowl,
Until it doth run over...
For tonight we'll merry, merry be,
Tomorrow we'll be sober.
Come, Landlord, Fill the Flowing Bowl

13 Come lasses and lads, get leave of your dads,
And away to the Maypole hie,
For every he has got him a she,
And the fiddler's standing by.
Come Lasses and Lads

14 Conduct...to the prejudice of good order and military discipline.
Army Discipline and Regulation Act, Section 40

15 Dear Sir, Your astonishment's odd:
I am always about in the Quad.
And that's why the tree
Will continue to be,
Since observed by Yours faithfully, God.
The response to EWER's limerick

16 Early one morning, just as the sun was rising.
I heard a maid singing in the valley below:
'Oh, don't deceive me; Oh, never leave me!
How could you use a poor maiden so?'
Early One Morning

17 Everyman, I will go with thee, and be thy guide.
In thy most need to go by thy side.
Spoken by Knowledge. *Everyman*, Pt. 1

18 Farewell and adieu to you,
Fair Spanish Ladies,
Farewell and adieu to you, Ladies of Spain.
Spanish Ladies

19 From ghoulies and ghosties and long-leggety beasties
And things that go bump in the night,
Good Lord, deliver us!
Cornish prayer

20 God be in my head,
And in my understanding;
God be in my eyes,
And in my looking;
God be in my mouth,
And in my speaking;
God be in my heart,
And in my thinking;
God be at my end,
And at my departing.
Sarum Missal

21 God rest you merry, gentlemen,
Let nothing you dismay.
God Rest you Merry

22 Greensleeves was all my joy,
Greensleeves was my delight,
Greensleeves was my heart of gold,
And who but Lady Greensleeves.
Greensleeves

23 Ha, ha, ha, you and me,
Little brown jug, don't I love thee!
The Little Brown Jug

24 Hail Mary, full of grace, the Lord is with thee:
Blessed art thou among women, and blessed is the fruit of thy womb, Jesus.
Ave Maria, 11th century

25 Here lie I and my four daughters,
Killed by drinking Cheltenham waters.
Had we but stick to Epsom salts,
We wouldn't have been in these here vaults.
Cheltenham Waters

26 Here lie I by the chancel door;
They put me here because I was poor.
The further in, the more you pay,
But here lie I as snug as they.
Epitaph, Devon churchyard

27 Here lies a man who was killed by lightning;
He died when his prospects seemed to be brightening.
He might have cut a flash in this world of trouble,
But the flash cut him, and he lies in the stubble.
Epitaph, Torrington, Devon

28 Here lies a valiant warrior
Who never drew a sword;
Here lies a noble courtier
Who never kept his word;
Here lies the Earl of Leicester
Who governed the estates
Whom the earth could never living love,
And the just heaven now hates.
Attrib. to Ben Jonson in *Collection of Epitaphs* (Tissington), 1857.

29 Here lies father and mother and sister and I,
We all died within the space of one short year;
They all be buried at Wimble, except I,
And I be buried here.
Epitaph, Staffordshire churchyard

30 Here lies Fred,
Who was alive and is dead:
Had it been his father,
I had much rather;
Had it been his brother,
Still better than another;
Had it been his sister,
No one would have missed her;
Had it been the whole generation,
Still better for the nation:
But since 'tis only Fred,
Who was alive and is dead, –
There's no more to be said.
Referring to Frederick, Prince of Wales, eldest son of George II and father of George III. *Memoirs of George II* (Horace Walpole)

31 Here lies my wife,

Here lies she;
Hallelujah!
Hallelujee!
Epitaph, Leeds churchyard

32 Here lies the body of Mary Ann Lowder,
She burst while drinking a seidlitz powder.
Called from the world to her heavenly rest,
She should have waited till it effervesced.
Epitaph

33 Here lies the body of Richard Hind,
Who was neither ingenious, sober, nor kind.
Epitaph

34 Here lies Will Smith – and, what's something rarish,
He was born, bred, and hanged, all in the same parish.
Epitaph

35 Here's a health unto his Majesty...
Confusion to his enemies...
And he that will not drink his health,
I wish him neither wit nor wealth,
Not yet a rope to hang himself.
Here's a Health unto his Majesty

36 Here's tae us wha's like us?
Gey few, and they're a' deid.
Scottish toast

37 Here we come gathering nuts in May
Nuts in May,
...
On a cold and frosty morning.
Children's song

38 He that fights and runs away
May live to fight another day.
Musarum Deliciae

39 *Honi soit qui mal y pense.*
Evil be to him who evil thinks.
Motto for the Order of the Garter

40 How different, how very different from the home life of our own dear Queen!
Comparing the character of Cleopatra, as performed by Sarah Bernhardt, with that of Queen Victoria. Remark

41 I always eat peas with honey
I've done it all my life,
They do taste kind of funny,
But it keeps them on the knife.
Peas

42 If all the world were paper,
And all the sea were ink,
And all the trees were bread and cheese,
What should we do for drink?
If All the World were Paper

43 I feel no pain, dear mother, now
But oh, I am so dry!
O take me to a brewery
And leave me there to die.
Shanty

44 I know two things about the horse,
And one of them is rather coarse.
The Horse

45 I'll sing you twelve O.
Green grow the rushes O.
What is your twelve O?
Twelve for the twelve apostles,
Eleven for the eleven who went to heaven,
Ten for the ten commandments,
Nine for the nine bright shiners,
Eight for the eight bold rangers,
Seven for the seven stars in the sky,
Six for the six proud walkers,
Five for the symbol at your door,
Four for the Gospel makers,
Three for the rivals,
Two, two, the lily-white boys,
Clothed all in green O,
One is one and all alone
And ever more shall be so.
The Dilly Song

46 I met wid Napper Tandy, and he took me by the hand,
And he said, 'How's poor ould Ireland, and how does she stand?'
She's the most disthressful country that iver yet was seen,
For they're hangin' men an' women there for the wearin' o' the Green.
The Wearin' o' the Green

47 In Dublin's fair city, where the girls are so pretty,
I first set my eyes on sweet Molly Malone,
As she wheeled her wheelbarrow, through streets broad and narrow,
Crying, Cockles and mussels! alive, alive, O!

She was a fishmonger, but sure 'twas no wonder,
For so were her father and mother before.
Cockles and Mussels

48 In good King Charles's golden days,
When loyalty no harm meant,
A zealous High Churchman was I,
And so I got preferment.

And this is law, that I'll maintain,
Unto my dying day, Sir,
That whatsoever King shall reign,
I'll be the Vicar of Bray, Sir.
The Vicar of Bray

49 In Scarlet town, where I was born,
There was a fair maid dwellin',
Made every youth cry *Well-a-way!*
Her name was Barbara Allen.

All in the merry month of May,
When green buds they were swellin',
Young Jemmy Grove on his death-bed lay,
For love of Barbara Allen.

So slowly, slowly rase she up,
And slowly she came nigh him,
And when she drew the curtain by –
'Young man, I think you're dyin'!'.
Barbara Allen's Cruelty

50 *Liberté! Égalité! Fraternité!*
Freedom! Equality! Brotherhood!
Motto for French Revolutionaries

51 Little Willy from his mirror

Licked the mercury right off,
Thinking in his childish error,
It would cure the whooping cough.
At the funeral his mother
Smartly said to Mrs Brown:
'Twas a chilly day for Willie
When the mercury went down'.

Willie's Epitaph

52 Lizzie Borden took an axe
And gave her mother forty whacks;
When she saw what she had done
She gave her father forty-one!

On 4 Aug 1892 in Fall River, Massachusetts, Lizzie Borden was acquitted of the murder of her stepmother and her father.

53 Lo, Hudled up, together Lye
Gray Age, Grene youth, White Infancy.
If Death doth Nature's Laws dispence,
And reconciles All Difference
Tis Fit, One Flesh, One House Should have
One Tombe, One Epitaph, One Grave:
And they that Liv'd and Lov'd Either,
Should Dye and Lye and Sleep together.

Good Reader, whether go or stay
Thou must not hence be Long Away

Epitaph, of William Bartholomew (died 1662), his wife and some of their children, St John the Baptist, Burford

54 Love is blind; friendship closes its eyes.

Proverb

55 Mary Ann has gone to rest,
Safe at last on Abraham's breast,
Which may be nuts for Mary Ann,
But is certainly rough on Abraham.

Epitaph

56 Miss Buss and Miss Beale
Cupid's darts do not feel.
How different from us,
Miss Beale and Miss Buss.

Written about the headmistresses of North London Collegiate School and Cheltenham Ladies' College, respectively

57 My Bonnie lies over the ocean,
My Bonnie lies over the sea,
My Bonnie lies over the ocean,
Oh, bring back my Bonnie to me.

My Bonnie

58 My Love in her attire doth show her wit,
It doth so well become her:
For every season she hath dressings fit,
For winter, spring, and summer.
No beauty she doth miss,
When all her robes are on;
But beauty's self she is,
When all her robes are gone.

Madrigal

59 My name is George Nathaniel Curzon,
I am a most superior person.
My face is pink, my hair is sleek,
I dine at Blenheim once a week.

The Masque of Balliol

60 My sledge and anvil lie declined
My bellows too have lost their wind
My fire's extinct, my forge decayed,
And in the Dust my Vice is laid
My coals are spent, my iron's gone
My Nails are Drove, My Work is done.

An epitaph to William Strange, blacksmith, died 6 June 1746 and buried in Nettlebed churchyard

61 Nation shall speak peace unto nation.

Motto of the British Broadcasting Corporation

62 No one provokes me with impunity.

Motto of the Crown of Scotland

63 Now I am a bachelor, I live by myself and I work at the weaving trade,
And the only only thing that I ever did wrong
Was to woo a fair young maid.

She sighed, she cried, she damned near died: she said 'What shall I do?'
So I took her into bed and covered up her head
Just to save her from the foggy, foggy dew.

Weaver's Song

64 Now I lay me down to sleep,
I pray the Lord my soul to keep.
If I should die before I wake,
I pray the Lord my soul to take.

New England Primer, 1781

65 O Death, where is thy sting-a-ling-a-ling,
O Grave, thy victoree?
The bells of hell go ting-a-ling-a-ling
For you but not for me.

Song of World War I

66 O, Shenandoah, I long to hear you
Away, you rolling river.

Shenandoah

67 O ye'll tak' the high road, and I'll tak' the low road,
And I'll be in Scotland afore ye,
But me and my true love will never meet again,
On the bonnie, bonnie banks o' Loch Lomon'.

The Bonnie Banks o' Loch Lomon'

68 *Per ardua ad astra.*
Through endeavour to the stars.

Motto of the Royal Air Force.

69 Please to remember the Fifth of November,
Gunpowder Treason and Plot.
We know no reason why gunpowder treason
Should ever be forgot.

Traditional

70 Sacred to the memory of
Captain Anthony Wedgwood
Accidentally shot by his gamekeeper
Whilst out shooting
"Well done thou good and faithful servant"

Epitaph

71 She was poor but she was honest
Victim of a rich man's game.
First he loved her, then he left her,
And she lost her maiden name.

See her on the bridge at midnight,
Saying 'Farewell, blighted love.'
Then a scream, a splash and goodness,
What is she a-doin' of?

It's the same the whole world over,

It's the poor wot gets the blame,
It's the rich wot gets the pleasure.
Ain't it all a bleedin' shame?

She was Poor but she was Honest

72 Since wars begin in the minds of men, it is in the minds of men that the defences of peace must be constructed.

Constitution of UNESCO

73 Some talk of Alexander, and some of Hercules,
Of Hector and Lysander, and such great names as these;
But of all the world's brave heroes there's none that can compare
With a tow, row, row, row, row, row for the British Grenadiers.

The British Grenadiers

74 Stranger! Approach this spot with gravity!
John Brown is filling his last cavity.

Epitaph of a dentist

75 Sumer is icumen in,
Lhude sing cuccu!
Groweth sed, and bloweth med,
And springth the wude nu.

Cuckoo Song, c. 1250

76 Swing low sweet chariot,
Comin' for to carry me home,
I looked over Jordan an' what did I see?
A band of Angels coming after me,
Comin' for to carry me home.

Swing Low, Sweet Chariot

77 That this house will in no circumstances fight for its King and country.

Motion passed at the Oxford Union, 9 Feb 1933

78 The animals went in one by one,
There's one more river to cross.

One More River

79 The Campbells are comin', oho, oho.

The Campbells are Comin'

80 The fault is great in man or woman
Who steals a goose from off a common;
But what can plead that man's excuse
Who steals a common from a goose?

The Tickler Magazine, 1 Feb 1821

81 The holly and the ivy,
When they are both full grown,
Of all the trees that are in the wood,
The holly bears the crown.
The rising of the sun
And the running of the deer,
The playing of the merry organ,
Sweet singing in the choir.

The Holly and the Ivy

82 The King over the Water.

Jacobite toast

83 The king sits in Dunfermline town
Drinking the blude-red wine.

'I saw the new moon late yestreen
Wi' the auld moon in her arm;
And if we gang to sea master,
I fear we'll come to harm.'

O lang, lang may the ladies sit,
Wi' their fans into their hand,
Before they see Sir Patrick Spens
Come sailing to the strand!

Sir Patrick Spens

84 The rabbit has a charming face;
Its private life is a disgrace.
I really dare not name to you
The awful things that rabbits do.

The Rabbit, 20th century

85 There are twelve months in all the year,
As I hear many men say,
But the merriest month in all the year
Is the merry month of May.

Robin Hood and the Widow's Three Sons

86 There is a lady sweet and kind,
Was never face so pleased my mind;
I did but see her passing by,
And yet I love her till I die.

Sometimes attrib. to Thomas Forde. *Passing By*

87 There is a tavern in the town,
And there my dear love sits him down,
And drinks his wine 'mid laughter free,
And never, never thinks of me.

Fare thee well, for I must leave thee,
Do not let this parting grieve thee,
And remember that the best of friends must part.

There is a Tavern in the Town

88 There is so much good in the worst of us,
And so much bad in the best of us,
That it hardly becomes any of us
To talk about the rest of us.

Good and Bad

89 There's a wonderful family called Stein,
There's Gert and there's Epp and there's Ein;
Gert's poems are bunk,
Epp's statues are junk,
And no one can understand Ein.

90 There was a faith-healer of Deal,
Who said, 'Although pain isn't real,
If I sit on a pin
And it punctures my skin,
I dislike what I fancy I feel.'

91 There was an old man from Darjeeling,
Who boarded a bus bound for Ealing,
He saw on the door:
'Please don't spit on the floor',
So he stood up and spat on the ceiling.

92 There was an old man of Boulogne
Who sang a most topical song.
It wasn't the words
That frightened the birds,
But the horrible double-entendre.

93 There was a young lady of Riga,
Who went for a ride on a tiger;
They returned from the ride
With the lady inside,
And a smile on the face of the tiger.

94 There was a young man of Japan
Whose limericks never would scan;

When they said it was so,
He replied, 'Yes, I know,
But I always try to get as many words into the last line as ever I possibly can.'

95 There was a young woman called Starkie,
Who had an affair with a darky.
The result of her sins
Was quadruplets, not twins –
One black, and one white, and two khaki.

96 There were three ravens sat on a tree,
They were as black as they might be.
The one of them said to his mate,
'Where shall we our breakfast take?'
The Three Ravens

97 There were twa sisters sat in a bour;
Binnorie, O Binnorie!
There came a knight to be their wooer,
By the bonnie milldams o' Binnorie.
Binnorie

98 The sons of the prophet were brave men and bold,
And quite unaccustomed to fear,
But the bravest by far in the ranks of the Shah
Was Abdul the Bulbul Amir.
Abdul the Bulbul Amir

99 Thirty days hath September,
April, June, and November;
All the rest have thirty-one,
Excepting February alone,
And that has twenty-eight days clear
And twenty-nine in each leap year.
Stevins Manuscript, c. 1555

100 This animal is very bad; when attacked it defends itself.
La Ménagerie (P. K. Théodore), 1828

101 This is a rotten argument, but it should be good enough for their lordships on a hot summer afternoon.
A note on a ministerial brief read out by mistake in the House of Lords. *The Way the Wind Blows* (Lord Home), 1976

102 This the grave of Mike O'Day
Who died maintaining his right of way.
His right was clear, his will was strong.
But he's just as dead as if he'd been wrong.
Epitaph

103 'Tom Pearse, Tom Pearse, lend me your grey mare,
All along, down along, out along, lee
For I want for to go to Widdicombe Fair,
Wi' Bill Brewer, Jan Stewer, Peter Gurney, Peter Davey, Dan'l Whiddon, Harry Hawk;
Old Uncle Tom Cobbleigh and all.
Old Uncle Tom Cobbleigh and all.'
Widdicombe Fair

104 Warm summer sun shine kindly here:
Warm summer wind blow softly here:
Green sod above lie light, lie light:
Good-night, Dear Heart: good-night, good-night.
Memorial to Clorinda Haywood, St Bartholomew's, Edgbaston

105 What shall we do with the drunken sailor
Early in the morning?
Hoo-ray and up she rises
Early in the morning.
What shall we do with the Drunken Sailor?

106 When I am dead, and laid in grave,
And all my bones are rotten,
By this may I remembered be
When I should be forgotten.
On a girl's sampler, 1736

107 When Israel was in Egypt land,
Let my people go,
Oppressed so hard they could not stand,
Let my people go.
Go down, Moses,
Way-down in Egypt land,
Tell old Pharaoh
To let my people go.
Negro spiritual

108 Whose Finger do you want on the Trigger
When the World Situation Is So Delicate?
Headline from the *Daily Mirror* on the day before the General Election, Oct 1951 *Publish and Be Damned* (Hugh Cudlipp), 1953

109 Ye Highlands and ye Lawlands,
O where hae ye been?
They hae slain the Earl of Murray,
And hae laid him on the green.

He was a braw gallant,
And he rid at the ring;
And the bonny Earl of Murray,
O he might hae been a king!

O lang will his Lady
Look owre the Castle Downe,
Ere she see the Earl of Murray
Come sounding through the town!
The Bonny Earl of Murray

ANOUILH, JEAN

(1910–87) French dramatist, whose plays have enjoyed considerable success on the English stage. His most famous works include *Antigone* (1944), *Ring Round the Moon* (1950), *The Lark* (1953), and *Becket* (1959).

1 Oh, love is real enough, you will find it some day, but it has one arch-enemy – and that is life.
Ardèle

2 Love is, above all, the gift of oneself.
Ardèle

3 All evil comes from the old. They grow fat on ideas and young men die of them.
Catch as Catch Can

4 Every man thinks God is on his side. The rich and powerful know that he is.
The Lark

5 The object of art is to give life a shape.
The Rehearsal

6 What fun it would be to be poor, as long as one was *excessively* poor! Anything in excess is most exhilarating.
Ring Round the Moon

7 When you are forty, half of you belongs to the past...And when you are seventy, nearly all of you.
Attrib.

ANTHONY, SUSAN B.

(1820–1906) US editor and campaigner for women's suffrage.

Quotations about Anthony

1 Who does not feel sympathy for Susan Anthony? She has striven long and earnestly to become a man. She has met with some rebuffs, but has never succumbed. She has never done any good in the world, but then she doesn't think so.
Ida Husted Harper *Life and Work of Susan B. Anthony*, Vol. I

2 We touch our caps, and place to night
The visitor's wreath upon her,
The woman who outranks us all
In courage and honor.
Ida Husted Harper *Life and Work of Susan B. Anthony*, Vol. I

Quotations by Anthony

3 Men their rights and nothing more; women their rights and nothing less.
The Revolution, Motto

4 ...there never will be complete equality until women themselves help to make laws and elect lawmakers.
The Arena, May 1897, 'The Status of Women, Past, Present and Future'

5 And yet, in the schoolroom more than any other place, does the difference of sex, if there is any, need to be forgotten.
Elizabeth Cady Stanton (ed. Theodore Stanton and Harriot Stanton Blatch), Vol. II

6 ...and I shall earnestly and persistently continue to urge all women to the practical recognition of the old Revolutionary maxim, 'Resistance to tyranny is obedience to God.'
Speech in court, 18 June 1873. *Jailed for Freedom* (Doris Stevens)

ANTICIPATION

See also expectation

1 A stitch in time saves nine.
Proverb

2 Don't cross the bridge till you get to it.
Proverb

3 The early bird catches the worm.
Proverb

4 Don't count your chickens before they are hatched.
Aesop (6th century BC) Reputed Greek writer of fables. *Fables*, 'The Milkmaid and her Pail'

5 To swallow gudgeons ere they're catched,
And count their chickens ere they're hatched.
Samuel Butler (1612–80) English satirist. *Hudibras*, Pt. II

6 He told me never to sell the bear's skin before one has killed the beast.
Jean de La Fontaine (1621–95) French poet. *Fables*, V, 'L'Ours et les deux Compagnons'

7 To travel hopefully is a better thing than to arrive, and the true success is to labour.
Robert Louis Stevenson (1850–94) Scottish writer. *Virginibus Puerisque*

APARTHEID

See South Africa

APOLOGIES

See also regret

1 Very sorry can't come. Lie follows by post.
Charles Beresford (1846–1919) British naval officer. Reply, by telegram, to a dinner invitation issued at short notice by Edward, Prince of Wales. *The World of Fashion 1837–1922* (R. Nevill), Ch. 5

2 I should never be allowed out in private.
Randolph Churchill (1911–68) British political journalist. Apologizing to a hostess whose dinner party he had ruined. *Randolph* (B. Roberts)

3 I have two huge lions tearing at my flanks, the so-called Emperor Otto and John, King of England. Both try with all their might to upset the Kingdom of France. I cannot leave the country myself or do without my son here.
Philip II (1165–1223) King of France. Explaining, to Pope Innocent III, his refusal to crusade against the Albigensian heretics.

4 Miss Otis regrets she's unable to lunch today.
Cole Porter (1893–1964) US songwriter. *Hi Diddle Diddle*, Miss Otis Regrets

5 Love means never having to say you're sorry.
Erich Segal (1937–) US writer. *Love Story*

6 When a man holds you round the throat, I don't think he has come to apologise.
Ayrton Senna (1960–94) Brazilian motor racing driver. Referring to Nigel Mansell after a collision in the 1987 Belgian Grand Prix. *The Times*, 3 May 1994

7 Mr. Speaker, I said the honorable member was a liar it is true and I am sorry for it. The honourable member may place the punctuation where he pleases.
Richard Brinsley Sheridan (1751–1816) British dramatist. On being asked to apologize for calling a fellow MP a liar. Attrib.

8 It is a good rule in life never to apologize. The right sort of people do not want apologies, and the wrong sort take a mean advantage of them.
P. G. Wodehouse (1881–1975) British humorous novelist. *The Man Upstairs and Other Stories*

APPEARANCE

See also appearances, beauty, clothes, cosmetics, eyes

1 Fine feathers make fine birds.
Proverb

2 Handsome is as handsome does.
Proverb

3 A man need not look in your mouth to know how old you are.

Proverb

4 You're phoney. Everything about you is phoney. Even your hair – which looks false – is real.

Anonymous US diplomat to the British politician Brendan Bracken during World War II.

5 A homely face and no figure have aided many women heavenward.

Minna Antrim (1861–?) US writer. *Naked Truth and Veiled Allusions*

6 Take a close-up of a woman past sixty! You might as well use a picture of a relief map of Ireland!

Nancy Astor (1879–1964) American-born British politician. When asked for a close-up photograph. Attrib.

7 Your cameraman might enjoy himself, because my face looks like a wedding cake left out in the rain.

W. H. Auden (1907–73) British-born poet. *W. H. Auden* (H. Carpenter)

8 I think your whole life shows in your face and you should be proud of that.

Lauren Bacall (1924–) US actress. Remark, Mar 1988

9 Like the skins of some small mammal just not large enough to be used as mats.

Max Beerbohm (1872–1956) British writer. Referring to the dramatist Sir Arthur Pinero's eyebrows. *Edward Marsh* (C. Hassall)

10 But if a woman have long hair, it is a glory to her: for her hair is given her for a covering.

Bible: I Corinthians 11:15

11 I take a different approach to the 'fat is sexy' view. I would rather people just left us alone.

Jo Brand (1958–) British comic. *The Observer*, 10 Apr 1994

12 It's sad that women are encouraged to be obsessed with the triviality of their appearance. There are more important things in life than appearance.

Jo Brand *The Observer*, 10 Apr 1994

13 It is the common wonder of all men, how among so many million of faces, there should be none alike.

Thomas Browne (1605–82) English physician and writer. *Religio Medici*, Pt. II

14 Alas, after a certain age every man is responsible for his face.

Albert Camus (1913–60) French existentialist writer. *The Fall*

15 She never had the looks to lose so she never lost them.

Angela Carter (1940–92) British novelist. *Wise Children*

16 Ears like bombs and teeth like splinters:
A blitz of a boy is Timothy Winters.

Charles Causley (1917–) British poet and broadcaster. *Timothy Winters*

17 It was a blonde. A blonde to make a bishop kick a hole in a stained-glass window.

Raymond Chandler (1888–1959) US novelist. *Farewell, My Lovely*, Ch. 13

18 Mirrors should think longer before they reflect.

Jean Cocteau (1889–1963) French poet and artist. *The Sunday Times*, 20 Oct 1963

19 It's nothing to be born ugly. Sensibly, the ugly woman comes to terms with her ugliness and exploits it as a grace of nature.

Colette (Sidonie-Gabrielle C.; 1873–1954) French novelist. *Journey for Myself*

20 Sunburn is very becoming – but only when it is even – one must be careful not to look like a mixed grill.

Noël Coward (1899–1973) British dramatist. *The Lido Beach*

21 The ring so worn, as you behold,
So thin, so pale, is yet of gold.

George Crabbe (1754–1832) British poet. *His Mother's Wedding Ring*

22 The most delightful advantage of being bald – one can hear snowflakes.

R. G. Daniels (1916–) British magistrate. *The Observer*, 'Sayings of the Week', 11 July 1976

23 He had but one eye, and the popular prejudice runs in favour of two.

Charles Dickens (1812–70) British novelist. Said by Mr Squeers. *Nicholas Nickleby*, Ch. 4

24 It was not a bosom to repose upon, but it was a capital bosom to hang jewels upon.

Charles Dickens Describing Mrs Merdle. *Little Dorrit*, Bk. I, Ch. 21

25 A woman can look both moral and exciting – if she also looks as if it was quite a struggle.

Edna Ferber (1887–1968) US writer and scenarist. *Reader's Digest*, Dec 1954

26 I am so changed that my oldest creditors would hardly know me.

Henry Stephen Fox (1791–1846) British diplomat. Remark after an illness. Letter from Byron to John Murray, 8 May 1817

27 There is a great difference between painting a face and not washing it.

Thomas Fuller (1608–61) English historian. *Church History*, Bk. VII

28 The flowers that bloom in the spring,
Tra la,
Have nothing to do with the case.
I've got to take under my wing,
Tra la,
A most unattractive old thing,
Tra la,
With a caricature of a face.

W. S. Gilbert (1836–1911) British dramatist. *The Mikado*, II

29 There was always something in her voice that made you think of lorgnettes.

O. Henry (William Sidney Porter; 1862–1910) US short-story writer. *The Defeat of the City*

30 There's one thing about baldness – it's neat.

Don Herold Attrib.

31 If it's a boy I'll call him John. If it's a girl I'll call her Mary. But if, as I suspect, it's only wind, I'll call it F. E. Smith.

Gordon Hewart (1870–1943) British lawyer. When F. E. Smith commented on the size of his stomach, saying 'What's it to be – a boy or a girl?' Attrib.

32 We tolerate shapes in human beings that would horrify us if we saw them in a horse.

W. R. Inge (1860–1954) British churchman and writer. Attrib.

33 It is in my family on my father's side. I use make-up to even out the blotches. When people make up stories that I don't want to be who I am it hurts me…what about all the millions of people who sit out in the sun to become darker, to become other than what they are? No one says anything about that.

Michael Jackson (1958–) US pop singer. Referring to vitiligo, a skin pigmentation disorder. Interview with Oprah Winfrey, 1993

34 That white horse you see in the park could be a zebra synchronized with the railings.

Ann Jellicoe (1927–) British dramatist. *The Knack*, III

35 Where's the cheek that doth not fade,
Too much gaz'd at? Where's the maid
Whose lip mature is ever new?

John Keats (1795–1821) British poet. *Fancy*, I

36 It always seemed to me that men wore their beards, like they wear their neckties, for show. I shall always remember Lewis for saying his beard was part of him.

D. H. Lawrence (1885–1930) British novelist. *St Mawr*

37 There was an Old Man with a beard,
Who said, 'It is just as I feared! –
Two Owls and a Hen,
Four Larks and a Wren,
Have all built their nests in my beard!'

Edward Lear (1812–88) British artist and writer. *Book of Nonsense*

38 A smile that snapped back after using, like a stretched rubber band.

Sinclair Lewis (1885–1951) US novelist. Attrib.

39 The Lord prefers common-looking people. That is why he makes so many of them.

Abraham Lincoln (1809–65) US statesman. *Our President* (James Morgan), Ch. 6

40 He looks as if he had been weaned on a pickle.

Alice Roosevelt Longworth (1884–1980) US hostess. Referring to John Calvin Coolidge, US president 1923–29. *Crowded Hours*

41 Dewey looks like the bridegroom on the wedding cake.

Alice Roosevelt Longworth Referring to Thomas E. Dewey, US Republican leader. *New York Times*, 25 Feb 1980

42 Gentlemen always seem to remember blondes.

Anita Loos (1891–1981) US novelist. *Gentlemen Prefer Blondes*, Ch. 1

43 In high school and college my sister Mary was very popular with the boys, but I had braces on my teeth and got high marks.

Betty MacDonald (1908–58) US writer. *The Egg and I*, Ch. 2

44 The huge laughing cockroaches on his top lip.

Osip Mandelstam (1891–1938) Russian poet. *Poems* (Stalin Epigram)

45 Smiling encouragement like a clumsy dentist.

Katherine Mansfield (1888–1923) New-Zealand-born British writer. *Bank Holiday*

46 There's a man outside with a big black moustache.
– Tell him I've got one.

Groucho Marx (Julius Marx; 1895–1977) US comedian. *Horse Feathers*

47 I eat like a vulture. Unfortunately the resemblance doesn't end there.

Groucho Marx Attrib.

48 To Crystal, hair was the most important thing on earth. She would never get married because you couldn't wear curlers in bed.

Edna O'Brien (1936–) Irish novelist. *Winter's Tales*, 8, 'Come into the Drawing Room, Doris'

49 At fifty everyone has the face he deserves.

George Orwell (Eric Blair; 1903–50) British novelist. Final entry in his notebook

50 …reminds me of nothing so much as a recently dead fish before it has had time to stiffen.

George Orwell Referring to Clement Attlee. Diary, 19 May 1942

51 Men seldom make passes
At girls who wear glasses.

Dorothy Parker (1893–1967) US writer. Attrib.

52 All I say is, nobody has any business to go around looking like a horse and behaving as if it were all right. You don't catch horses going around looking like people, do you?

Dorothy Parker *Horsie*

53 His voice was intimate as the rustle of sheets.

Dorothy Parker *Dusk before Fireworks*

54 If people think I'm a dumb blonde because of the way I look, then they're dumber than they think I am. If people think I'm not very deep because of my wigs and outfits, then they're not very deep.

Dolly Parton (1946–) US singer and songwriter. *Ms*, June 1979

55 Had Cleopatra's nose been shorter, the whole face of the world would have changed.

Blaise Pascal (1623–62) French philosopher and mathematician. *Pensées*, II

56 To church; and with my mourning, very handsome, and new periwig, make a great show.

Samuel Pepys (1633–1703) English diarist. *Diary*, 31 Mar 1667

57 A smile that floated without support in the air.

Marcel Proust (1871–1922) French novelist. *Remembrance of Things Past*

58 My nose is huge! Vile snub-nose, flat-nosed ass, flat-head, let me inform you that I am proud of such an appendage, since a big nose is the proper sign of a friendly, good, courteous, witty, liberal, and brave man, such as I am.

Edmond Rostand (1868–1918) French poet and dramatist. *Cyrano de Bergerac*, I:1

59 In the spring…your lovely Chloë lightly turns to one mass of spots.

Ronald Searle (1920–) British cartoonist. *The Terror of St Trinian's*, Ch. 7

60 Your face, my thane, is as a book where men
May read strange matters. To beguile the time,
Look like the time; bear welcome in your eye,
Your hand, your tongue: look like the innocent
flower,
But be the serpent under't.

William Shakespeare (1564–1616) English dramatist. *Macbeth*, I:5

61 Grim-visag'd war hath smooth'd his wrinkl'd front;
And now, instead of mounting barbed steeds,
To fright the souls of fearful adversaries, –
He capers nimbly in a lady's chamber
To the lascivious pleasing of a lute.
But I, that am not shap'd for sportive tricks,
Nor made to court an amorous looking-glass;
I, that am rudely stamp'd, and want love's majesty
To strut before a wanton ambling nymph;
I, that am curtail'd of this fair proportion,
Cheated of feature by dissembling nature,
Deform'd, unfinish'd, sent before my time
Into this breathing world, scarce half made up,
And that so lamely and unfashionable
That dogs bark at me, as I halt by them;
Why, I, in this weak piping time of peace,
Have no delight to pass away the time.

William Shakespeare *Richard III*, I:1

62 Poor soul, the centre of my sinful earth,
Fool'd by these rebel powers that thee array,
Why dost thou pine within and suffer dearth,
Painting thy outward walls so costly gay!
Why so large cost, having so short a lease,
Dost thou upon thy fading mansion spend?

William Shakespeare *Sonnets*, 146

63 For I have sworn thee fair, and thought thee bright,
Who art as black as hell, as dark as night.

William Shakespeare *Sonnets*, 147

64 LORD NORTHCLIFFE. The trouble with you, Shaw, is that you look as if there were famine in the land.
G.B.S. The trouble with you, Northcliffe, is that you look as if you were the cause of it.

George Bernard Shaw (1856–1950) Irish dramatist and critic. Attrib.

65 Why not be oneself? That is the whole secret of a successful appearance. If one is a greyhound why try to look like a Pekinese?

Edith Sitwell (1887–1964) British poet and writer. *Why I Look As I Do*

66 There is more felicity on the far side of baldness than young men can possibly imagine.

Logan Pearsall Smith (1865–1946) US-born British writer. *Afterthoughts*, 2

67 A short neck denotes a good mind...You see, the messages go quicker to the brain because they've shorter to go.

Muriel Spark (1918–) British novelist. *The Ballad of Peckham Rye*, Ch. 7

68 But Shelley had a hyper-thyroid face.

John Collings Squire (1884–1958) British journalist. *Ballade of the Glandular Hypothesis*

69 ...his nicotine eggyellow weeping walrus Victorian moustache worn thick and long in memory of Doctor Crippen.

Dylan Thomas (1914–53) Welsh poet. *Under Milk Wood*

70 Very hard for a man with a wig to keep order.

Evelyn Waugh (1903–66) British novelist. *Decline and Fall*, Pt. I, Ch. 3

71 Enclosing every thin man, there's a fat man demanding elbow-room.

Evelyn Waugh *Officers and Gentlemen*, Interlude

72 He smiled bunching his fat cheeks like twin rolls of smooth pink toilet paper.

Nathaniel West (Nathan Weinstein; 1903–40) US novelist. *Miss Lonelyhearts*

73 But there are other things than dissipation that thicken the features. Tears, for example.

Rebecca West (Cicely Isabel Fairfield; 1892–1983) British novelist and journalist. *Black Lamb and Grey Falcon*, 'Serbia'

74 Grief has turned her fair.

Oscar Wilde (1854–1900) Irish-born British dramatist. Referring to the fact that a recently bereaved lady friend had dyed her hair blonde. Attrib.

75 Big chap with a small moustache and the sort of eye that can open an oyster at sixty paces.

P. G. Wodehouse (1881–1975) British humorous novelist. *The Code of the Woosters*

76 The stationmaster's whiskers are of a Victorian bushiness and give the impression of having been grown under glass.

P. G. Wodehouse *Wodehouse at Work to the End* (Richard Usborne), Ch. 2

77 The affluent, educated, liberated women of the First World...do not feel as free as they want to... This lack of freedom has something to do with – with apparently frivolous issues, things that really should not matter. Many are ashamed to admit that such trivial concerns – to do with physical appearance, bodies, faces, hair, clothes – matter so much.

Naomi Wolf US writer. *The Beauty Myth*

APPEARANCES

See also appearance, deception, hypocrisy

1 All that glitters is not gold.
Proverb

2 Appearances are deceptive.
Proverb

3 Never judge from appearances.
Proverb

4 Still waters run deep.
Proverb

5 Things are not always what they seem.
Proverb

6 Vice is often clothed in virtue's habit.
Proverb

7 You can't tell a book by its cover.
Proverb

8 The lamb that belonged to the sheep whose skin the wolf was wearing began to follow the wolf in the sheep's clothing.

Aesop (6th century BC) Reputed Greek writer of fables. *Fables*, 'The Wolf in Sheep's Clothing'

9 The French are wiser than they seem, and the Spaniards seem wiser than they are.

Francis Bacon (1561–1626) English philosopher. *Essays*, 'Of Seeming Wise'

10 The loveliest face in all the world will not please you if you see it suddenly eye to eye, at a distance of half an inch from your own.

Max Beerbohm (1872–1956) British writer. *Zuleika Dobson*

11 No-wher so bisy a man as he ther nas,
And yet he semed bisier than he was.

Geoffrey Chaucer (c. 1342–1400) English poet. Referring to the man of law. *The Canterbury Tales*, Prologue

12 Keep up appearances; there lies the test
The world will give thee credit for the rest.

Charles Churchill (1731–64) British poet. *Night*

13 I may not hope from outward forms to win
The passion and the life, whose fountains are within.

Samuel Taylor Coleridge (1772–1834) British poet. *Dejection: An Ode*

14 Appearances are not held to be a clue to the truth. But we seem to have no other.

Ivy Compton-Burnett (1892–1969) British novelist. *Manservant and Maidservant*

15 Outside, among your fellows, among strangers, you must preserve appearances, a hundred things you cannot do, but inside, the terrible freedom!

Ralph Waldo Emerson (1803–82) US poet and essayist.

16 No man could be so wise as Thurlow looked.

Charles James Fox (1749–1806) British Whig politician. *Lives of the Lord Chancellors* (Campbell), Vol. V

17 Before I applied the pressure bandages to prevent swelling, I took a final look at my work. The woman before me was no longer forty-five but a lovely person with the taut firm beauty of youth.

Dr. Robert Alyn Franklyn *Beauty Surgeon*

18 Mirrors are the windows of the devil,
overlooking nothing but a landscape of lies!

Leon Garfield (1921–) British writer. *The Prisoners of September*, Ch. 2

19 Ah, pray make no mistake,
We are not shy;
We're very wide awake,
The moon and I.

W. S. Gilbert (1836–1911) British dramatist. *The Mikado*, II

20 She's genuinely bogus.

Christopher Hassall (1912–63) British writer. Referring to Edith Sitwell. Attrib.

21 An' for all 'is dirty 'ide
'E was white, clear white, inside
When 'e went to tend the wounded under fire!

Rudyard Kipling (1865–1936) Indian-born British writer. *Gunga Din*

22 Strip the phoney tinsel off Hollywood and you'll find the real tinsel underneath.

Oscar Levant (1906–72) US pianist and actor. Attrib.

23 Ugliness is a point of view: an ulcer is wonderful to a pathologist.

Austin O'Malley (1858–1932)

24 And you cannot tell by the way a party looks or how he lives in this town, if he has any scratch, because many a party who is around in automobiles, and wearing good clothes, and chucking quite a swell is nothing but a phonus bolonus and does not have any real scratch whatever.

Damon Runyon (1884–1946) US writer. *More than Somewhat*, 'The Snatching of Bookie Bob'

25 Things are entirely what they appear to be and *behind them*...there is nothing.

Jean-Paul Sartre (1905–80) French writer. *Nausea*

26 Care I for the limb, the thews, the stature, bulk, and big assemblance of a man! Give me the spirit.

William Shakespeare (1564–1616) English dramatist. *Henry IV, Part Two*, III:2

27 Fairest Cordelia, that art most rich, being poor;
Most choice, forsaken; and most lov'd, despis'd!

William Shakespeare *King Lear*, I:1

28 A man may see how this world goes with no eyes. Look with thine ears: see how yond justice rails upon yond simple thief. Hark, in thine ear: change places; and, handy-dandy, which is the justice, which is the thief?

William Shakespeare *King Lear*, IV:6

29 Through tatter'd clothes small vices do appear;
Robes and furr'd gowns hide all.

William Shakespeare *King Lear*, IV:6

30 Fair is foul, and foul is fair;
Hover through the fog and filthy air.

William Shakespeare *Macbeth*, I:1

31 ...if ill,
Why hath it given me earnest of success,
Commencing in a truth? I am Thane of Cawdor:
If good, why do I yield to that suggestion
Whose horrid image doth unfix my hair
And make my seated heart knock at my ribs,
Against the use of nature? Present fears
Are less than horrible imaginings;
My thought, whose murder yet is but fantastical,
Shakes so my single state of man that function
Is smother'd in surmise, and nothing is
But what is not.

William Shakespeare *Macbeth*, I:3

32 But I will wear my heart upon my sleeve
For daws to peck at: I am not what I am.

William Shakespeare *Othello*, I:1

33 I am not merry, but I do beguile
The thing I am by seeming otherwise.

William Shakespeare *Othello*, II:1

34 And thus I clothe my naked villany
With odd old ends stol'n forth of holy writ,
And seem a saint when most I play the devil.

William Shakespeare *Richard III*, I:3

35 So may the outward shows be least themselves:
The world is still deceived with ornament.
In law, what plea so tainted and corrupt
But, being season'd with a gracious voice,
Obscures the show of evil? In religion,
What damned error, but some sober brow
Will bless it and approve it with a text,
Hiding the grossness with fair ornament?
There is no vice so simple but assumes
Some mark of virtue on his outward parts.

William Shakespeare *The Merchant of Venice*, III:2

36 Ornament is but the guiled shore
To a most dangerous sea; the beauteous scarf
Veiling an Indian beauty; in a word,
The seeming truth which cunning times put on
To entrap the wisest.

William Shakespeare *The Merchant of Venice*, III:2

37 Our purses shall be proud, our garments poor;
For 'tis the mind that makes the body rich;
And as the sun breaks through the darkest clouds,
So honour peereth in the meanest habit.

William Shakespeare *The Taming of the Shrew*, IV:3

38 Ladies and gentlemen, I stand before you tonight in my green chiffon evening gown, my face softly made up, my fair hair gently waved…the Iron Lady of the Western World. Me? A cold war warrior? Well, yes – if that is how they wish to interpret my defence of values, and freedoms fundamental to our way of life.

Margaret Thatcher (1925–) British politician and prime minister. Referring to the nickname 'The Iron Lady' used by the Soviet paper *Red Star*. Speech, Dorking, 31 Jan 1976

39 It is only shallow people who do not judge by appearances.

Oscar Wilde (1854–1900) Irish-born British dramatist. *The Picture of Dorian Gray*, Ch. 2

ARCHITECTURE

See also houses, stately homes

1 Sir Christopher Wren
Said, 'I am going to dine with some men.
If anybody calls
Say I am designing St Paul's.'

Edmund Clerihew Bentley (1875–1956) British writer. *Biography for Beginners*

2 A very stately palace before him, the name of which was Beautiful.

John Bunyan (1628–88) English writer. *The Pilgrim's Progress*, Pt. I

3 You have to give this much to the Luftwaffe – when it knocked down our buildings it did not replace them with anything more offensive than rubble. We did that.

Charles, Prince of Wales (1948–) Eldest son of Elizabeth II. *See also* Osbert SITWELL. *The Observer*, 'Sayings of the Week', 6 Dec 1987

4 Like a carbuncle on the face of an old and valued friend.

Charles, Prince of Wales Referring to a proposed modern extension to the National Gallery. Speech, 1986

5 …a jostling scrum of office buildings so mediocre that the only way you ever remember them is by the frustration they induce – like a basketball team standing shoulder to shoulder between you and the Mona Lisa.

Charles, Prince of Wales Referring to the buildings surrounding St Paul's Cathedral. Speech, London, 1 Dec 1987

6 A modern, harmonic and lively architecture is the visible sign of an authentic democracy.

Walter Gropius (1883–1969) German architect. *The Observer*, 'Sayings of the Week', 8 Dec 1968

7 'Fan vaulting'…an architectural device which arouses enormous enthusiasm on account of the difficulties it has all too obviously involved but which from an aesthetic standpoint frequently belongs to the 'Last-supper-carved-on-a-peach-stone' class of masterpiece.

Osbert Lancaster (1908–86) British cartoonist. *Pillar to Post*, 'Perpendicular'

8 What has happened to architecture since the second world war that the only passers-by who can contemplate it without pain are those equipped with a white stick and a dog?

Bernard Levin (1928–) British journalist. *The Times*, 1983 can contemplate it a white stick and a dog

9 Sculpture to me is like poetry, and architecture like prose.

Maya Lin Architect and sculptor. *The Observer*, 'Sayings of the Week', 14 May 1994

10 Less is more.

Ludwig Mies Van Der Rohe (1886–1969) German-born architect. *New York Herald Tribune*, 1959

11 I declare this thing open – whatever it is.

Prince Philip (1921–) The consort of Queen Elizabeth II. Opening a new annex at Vancouver City Hall. Attrib.

12 When you think of some of the high flats around us, it can hardly be an accident that they are as near as one can get to an architectural representation of a filing cabinet.

Jimmy Reid Leader of the UCS shop stewards. In his address as new Rector of Glasgow University. *The Observer*, 'Sayings of the Week', 30 Apr 1972

13 No person who is not a great sculptor or painter can be an architect. If he is not a sculptor or painter, he can only be a *builder*.

John Ruskin (1819–1900) British art critic and writer. *Lectures on Architecture and Painting*

14 When we build let us think that we build for ever.

John Ruskin *The Seven Lamps of Architecture*, Ch. 6, 'The Lamp of Memory'

15 Architecture in general is frozen music.

Friedrich Wilhelm Joseph von Schelling (1775–1854) German philosopher. *Philosophie der Kunst*

16 Many of my buildings are condemned now in advance.

Richard Seifert (1910–) British architect. He designed Centre Point, London and other office block schemes. *The Observer*, 'Sayings of the Week', 6 Aug 1972

17 When we mean to build,
We first survey the plot, then draw the model;
And when we see the figure of the house,
Then we must rate the cost of the erection;
Which if we find outweighs ability,
What do we then but draw anew the model
In fewer offices, or at last desist
To build at all?

William Shakespeare (1564–1616) English dramatist. *Henry IV, Part Two*, I:3

18 How simple-minded of the Germans to imagine that we British could be cowed by the destruction of our ancient monuments! As though any havoc of the German bombs could possibly equal the things we have done ourselves!

Osbert Sitwell (1892–1969) British writer. *See also* CHARLES, PRINCE OF WALES. *The Collected Essays, Journalism and Letters of George Orwell*, Vol. III

19 The architect is a servant, a tailor, who cuts and measures the thin chap or the fat chap and tries to make him comfortable. He is not a reformer.

Basil Spence (1907–76) British architect. *The Observer*, 'Sayings of the Week', 25 Oct 1970

20 It's beige! My color!

Elsie De Wolfe (1865–1950) US designer. On first sighting the Acropolis. *Elsie de Wolfe* (J. Smith)

21 In *Architecture* as in all other *Operative* Arts, the *end* must direct the *Operation*. The *end* is to build well. Well building hath three Conditions. *Commodity, Firmness,* and *Delight.*

Henry Wotton (1568–1639) English poet and diplomat. *Elements of Architecture*, Pt. I

22 Architecture has its political use; publick buildings being the ornament of a country; it establishes a nation, draws people and commerce; makes the people love their native country, which passion is the original of all great actions in a commonwealth.

Christopher Wren (1632–1723) English architect and scientist. *Parentalia*

ARGUMENTS

1 It takes two to make a quarrel.

Proverb

2 There is only one way under high heaven to get the best of an argument – and that is to avoid it.

Dale Carnegie (1888–1955) US lecturer and writer. *Dale Carnegie's Scrapbook*

3 It takes in reality only one to make a quarrel. It is useless for the sheep to pass resolutions in favour of vegetarianism while the wolf remains of a different opinion.

Dean Inge (1860–1954) British churchman. *Outspoken Essays*

4 Though a quarrel in the streets is a thing to be hated, the energies displayed in it are fine; the commonest man shows a grace in his quarrel.

John Keats (1795–1821) British poet. Letter

5 When men understand what each other mean, they see, for the most part, that controversy is either superfluous or hopeless.

Cardinal Newman (1801–90) British theologian. Sermon, Oxford, Epiphany 1839

6 Quarrels would not last so long if the fault were on only one side.

Duc de la Rochefoucauld (1613–80) French writer. *Maximes*, 496

7 The most savage controversies are those about matters as to which there is no good evidence either way.

Bertrand Russell (1872–1970) British philosopher. *Unpopular Essays*

8 I love argument, I love debate. I don't expect anyone just to sit there and agree with me, that's not their job.

Margaret Thatcher (1925–) British politician and prime minister. *The Times*, 1980

ARISTOCRACY

See also ancestry, class, Houses of Parliament, nobility, stately homes, titles

1 There are only two kinds of people in the world. Those who are nice to their servants and those who aren't.

Duke of Argyll (1937–) Attrib.

2 One has often wondered whether upon the whole earth there is anything so unintelligent, so unapt to perceive how the world is really going, as an ordinary young Englishman of our upper class.

Matthew Arnold (1822–88) British poet and critic. *Culture and Anarchy*, Ch. 2

3 I was obviously destined to go down and down when in 1958 my father and brother died within ten days of each other and I became an Earl...Life is much easier, being an Earl. It has changed me a lot. I'm much nastier now.

Earl of Arran (1938–) British publisher. *The Sunday Times*, 15 Jan 1967

4 Like many of the upper class
He liked the sound of broken glass.

Hilaire Belloc (1870–1953) French-born British poet. *See also* Evelyn WAUGH. *New Cautionary Tales*, 'About John'

5 The nobility of England, my lord, would have snored through the Sermon on the Mount.

Robert Bolt (1924–) British playwright. *A Man for All Seasons*

6 ...for the most part the worst instructed, and the least knowing of any of their rank, I ever went amongst.

Gilbert Burnet (1643–1715) Scottish-born English bishop. Referring to the English gentry. *History of My Own Times*, Conclusion

7 Lord Salisbury constitutes himself the spokesman of a class, of the class to which he himself belongs, who 'toil not neither do they spin'

Joseph Chamberlain (1836–1914) British politician. Referring to the aristocracy. Speech, Birmingham, 30 Mar 1883

8 We, my lords, may thank heaven that we have something better than our brains to depend upon.

Earl of Chesterfield (1694–1773) English statesman. Speech, House of Lords. *The Story of Civilization* (W. Durant), Vol. 9

9 Democracy means government by the uneducated, while aristocracy means government by the badly educated.

G. K. Chesterton (1874–1936) British writer. *New York Times*, 1 Feb 1931

10 In the eighteenth century he would have become Prime Minister before he was thirty; as it was he appeared honourably ineligible for the struggle of life.

Cyril Connolly (1903–74) British writer. Referring to the British prime minister Sir Alec Douglas-Home at Eton. *Enemies of Promise*

11 The Stately Homes of England
How beautiful they stand,
To prove the upper classes
Have still the upper hand.

Noël Coward (1899–1973) British dramatist. *Operette*, 'The Stately Homes of England'

12 *Honi soit qui mal y pense.*
Evil be to him who evil thinks.

Edward III (1312–77) King of England. Reputedly said on retrieving the Countess of Salisbury's garter, which had fallen off. Attrib. in later tradition; associated with the foundation of the Order of the Garter (1344)

13 If human beings could be propagated by cutting, like apple trees, aristocracy would be biologically sound.

J. B. S. Haldane (1892–1964) British geneticist. *The Inequality of Man*, title essay

14 There are no credentials. They do not even need a medical certificate. They need not be sound either in body or mind. They only require a certificate of birth – just to prove that they are first of the litter. You would not choose a spaniel on these principles.

David Lloyd George (1863–1945) British Liberal statesman. Budget Speech, 1909

15 A fully equipped Duke costs as much to keep up as two Dreadnoughts, and Dukes are just as great a terror, and they last longer.

David Lloyd George Speech, Limehouse, 30 July 1909

16 An aristocracy in a republic is like a chicken whose head has been cut off: it may run about in a lively way, but in fact it is dead.

Nancy Mitford (1904–73) British writer. *Noblesse Oblige*

17 He is without strict doubt a Hoorah Henry, and he is generally figured as nothing but a lob as far as doing anything useful in this world is concerned.

Damon Runyon (1884–1946) US writer. *Short Takes*, 'Tight Shoes'

18 Kind hearts are more than coronets,
And simple faith than Norman blood.

Alfred, Lord Tennyson (1809–92) British poet. *Lady Clara Vere de Vere*, VI

19 If the French noblesse had been capable of playing cricket with their peasants, their chateaux would never have been burnt.

George Macaulay Trevelyan (1876–1962) British historian. *English Social History*, Ch. XIII

20 My Lord Bath, you and I are now two as insignificant men as any in England.

Robert Walpole (1676–1745) British statesman. Said to William Pulteney, Earl of Bath, when they were promoted to the peerage (1742). *Political & Literary Anecdotes* (W. King)

21 The sound of the English county families baying for broken glass.

Evelyn Waugh (1903–66) British novelist. *See also* Hilaire BELLOC. *Decline and Fall*, Prelude

22 Unlike the male codfish which, suddenly finding itself the parent of three million five hundred thousand little codfish, cheerfully resolves to love them all, the British aristocracy is apt to look with a somewhat jaundiced eye on its younger sons.

P. G. Wodehouse (1881–1975) British humorous novelist. *Wodehouse at Work to the End* (Richard Usborne), Ch. 5

ARISTOTLE

(384–322 BC) Greek philosopher and scientist. A former pupil of Plato and tutor to Alexander the Great, he founded a school at the Lyceum in Athens.

1 What we have to learn to do, we learn by doing.

Nicomachean Ethics, Bk. II

2 The man who gets angry at the right things and with the right people, and in the right way and at the right time and for the right length of time, is commended.

Nicomachean Ethics, Bk. IV

3 Obstinate people can be divided into the opinionated, the ignorant, and the boorish.

Nicomachean Ethics, Bk. VII

4 Now a whole is that which has a beginning, a middle, and an end.

Referring specifically to the dramatic form of tragedy. *Poetics*, Ch. 7

5 For this reason poetry is something more philosophical and more worthy of serious attention than history.

Poetics, Ch. 9

6 Man is by nature a political animal.

Politics, Bk. I

7 Either a beast or a god.

Politics, Bk. I

8 Where some people are very wealthy and others have nothing, the result will be either extreme democracy or absolute oligarchy, or despotism will come from either of those excesses.

Politics, Bk. IV

9 Inferiors revolt in order that they may be equal and equals that they may be superior. Such is the state of mind which creates revolutions.

Politics, Bk. V

10 Plato is dear to me, but dearer still is truth.

Attrib.

ARMY

See also officers, soldiers, war, weapons

1 Oh! the grand old Duke of York
He had ten thousand men;
He marched them up to the top of the hill,
And he marched them down again.
And when they were up they were up,
And when they were down they were down,
And when they were only half way up,
They were neither up nor down.

Anonymous Traditional

2 Conduct...to the prejudice of good order and military discipline.

Anonymous Army Act, 40

3 You get to shout at people. It was very useful material for later.

Michael Palin (1943–) British actor and writer. Referring to his time in the army as a colour sergeant. *The Times*, 24 Feb 1990

4 The chief attraction of military service has consisted and will consist in this compulsory and irreproachable idleness.

Leo Tolstoy (1828–1910) Russian writer. *War and Peace*, Bk. VII, Ch. 1

5 An army is a nation within a nation; it is one of the vices of our age.

Alfred de Vigny (1797–1863) French writer. *Servitude et grandeur militaire*, 1

6 I have got an infamous army, very weak and ill-equipped, and a very inexperienced staff.

Duke of Wellington (1769–1852) British general and statesman. Written at the beginning of the Waterloo campaign. Letter to Lord Stewart, 8 May 1815

7 Ours is composed of the scum of the earth.

Duke of Wellington Of the British army. Remark, 4 Nov 1831

8 The army ages men sooner than the law and philosophy; it exposes them more freely to germs, which undermine and destroy, and it shelters them more completely from thought, which stimulates and preserves.

H. G. Wells (1866–1946) British writer. *Bealby*, Pt. VIII, Ch. 1

ARNOLD, MATTHEW

(1822–88) British poet and critic, who served for 35 years as inspector of schools.

Quotations about Arnold

1 He is not as handsome as his photographs – or his poetry.

Henry James (1843–1916) US novelist. Letter to Charles Eliot Norton, 31 Mar 1873

2 Arnold is a dandy Isaiah, a poet without passion...

George Meredith (1829–1909) British novelist. *Fortnightly Review*, July 1909

Quotations by Arnold

3 Culture being a pursuit of our total perfection by means of getting to know, on all the matters which most concern us, the best which has been thought and said in the world.

Culture and Anarchy, Preface

4 Our society distributes itself into Barbarians, Philistines, and Populace; and America is just ourselves, with the Barbarians quite left out, and the Populace nearly.

Culture and Anarchy, Preface

5 The pursuit of perfection, then, is the pursuit of sweetness and light...He who works for sweetness and light united, works to make reason and the will of God prevail.

Culture and Anarchy, Ch. 1

6 One has often wondered whether upon the whole earth there is anything so unintelligent, so unapt to perceive how the world is really going, as an ordinary young Englishman of our upper class.

Culture and Anarchy, Ch. 2

7 For this class we have a designation which now has become pretty well known, and which we may as well still keep for them, the designation of Philistines.

Referring to the middle class. *Culture and Anarchy*, Ch. 3

8 I often, therefore, when I want to distinguish clearly the aristocratic class from the Philistines proper, or middle class, name the former, in my own mind *the Barbarians.*

Culture and Anarchy, Ch. 3

9 But that vast portion, lastly, of the working-class which, raw and half-developed, has long lain half-hidden amidst its poverty and squalor, and is now issuing from its hiding-place to assert an Englishman's heaven-born privilege of doing as he likes, and is beginning to perplex us by marching where it likes, meeting where it likes, bawling what it likes, breaking what it likes – to this vast residuum we may with great propriety give the name of Populace.

Culture and Anarchy, Ch. 3

10 The sea is calm to-night,
The tide is full, the moon lies fair
Upon the Straits.

Dover Beach

11 And we are here as on a darkling plain
Swept with confused alarms of struggle and flight,
Where ignorant armies clash by night.

Dover Beach

12 Is it so small a thing
To have enjoy'd the sun,
To have lived light in the spring,
To have loved, to have thought, to have done?

Empedocles on Etna

13 Home of lost causes, and forsaken beliefs, and unpopular names, and impossible loyalties!

Referring to Oxford. *Essays in Criticism*, First Series, Preface

14 I am bound by my own definition of criticism: a disinterested endeavour to learn and propagate the best that is known and thought in the world.

Essays in Criticism, First Series, 'Functions of Criticism at the Present Time'

15 A criticism of life under the conditions fixed for such a criticism by the laws of poetic truth and poetic beauty.

Essays in Criticism, Second Series, 'The Study of Poetry'

16 Come, dear children, let us away;
Down and away below.

The Forsaken Merman

17 She left lonely for ever
The kings of the sea.

The Forsaken Merman

18 A wanderer is man from his birth.
He was born in a ship
On the breast of the river of Time.

The Future

19 Wandering between two worlds, one dead,
The other powerless to be born.

The Grande Chartreuse

20 Years hence, perhaps, may dawn an age,
More fortunate, alas! than we,
Which without hardness will be sage,
And gay without frivolity.

The Grande Chartreuse

21 The great apostle of the Philistines, Lord Macaulay.

Joubert

22 Culture, the acquainting ourselves with the best that has been known and said in the world, and thus with the history of the human spirit.

Literature and Dogma, Preface

23 Culture is the passion for sweetness and light, and (what is more) the passion for making them prevail.
Literature and Dogma, Preface

24 The eternal *not ourselves* that makes for righteousness.
Literature and Dogma, Ch. 8

25 It always seems to me that the right sphere for Shelley's genius was the sphere of music, not of poetry.
Maurice de Guérin, Footnote

26 When Byron's eyes were shut in death,
We bow'd our head and held our breath.
He taught us little: but our soul
Had *felt* him like the thunder's roll.
Memorial Verses

27 He spoke, and loos'd our heart in tears.
He laid us as we lay at birth
On the cool flowery lap of earth.
Referring to Wordsworth. *Memorial Verses*

28 Time may restore us in his course
Goethe's sage mind and Byron's force:
But where will Europe's latter hour
Again find Wordsworth's healing power?
Memorial Verses

29 We cannot kindle when we will
The fire which in the heart resides,
The spirit bloweth and is still,
In mystery our soul abides.
Morality

30 Now he is dead! Far hence he lies
In the lorn Syrian town;
And on his grave, with shining eyes,
The Syrian stars look down.
Obermann Once More

31 He will find one English book and one only, where, as in the *Iliad* itself, perfect plainness of speech is allied with perfect nobleness; and that book is the Bible.
On Translating Homer

32 I think it will be found that the grand style arises in poetry, when a noble nature, poetically gifted, treats with simplicity or with severity a serious subject.
Closing words. *On Translating Homer*

33 Cruel, but composed and bland,
Dumb, inscrutable and grand,
So Tiberius might have sat,
Had Tiberius been a cat.
Poor Matthias

34 Go, for they call you, Shepherd, from the hill.
The Scholar Gipsy

35 All the live murmur of a summer's day.
The Scholar Gipsy

36 Tired of knocking at Preferment's door.
The Scholar Gipsy

37 Before this strange disease of modern life,
With its sick hurry, its divided aims.
The Scholar Gipsy

38 Still nursing the unconquerable hope,
Still clutching the inviolable shade.
The Scholar Gipsy

39 Resolve to be thyself: and know, that he
Who finds himself, loses his misery.
Self-Dependence

40 Others abide our question, Thou art free,
We ask and ask: Thou smilest and art still,
Out-topping knowledge.
Referring to Shakespeare. *Shakespeare*

41 Truth sits upon the lips of dying men.
Sohrab and Rustum

42 Who saw life steadily, and saw it whole:
The mellow glory of the Attic stage.
Sonnets to a Friend

43 And see all sights from pole to pole,
And glance, and nod, and bustle by;
And never once possess our soul
Before we die.
A Southern Night

44 The difference between genuine poetry and the poetry of Dryden, Pope, and all their school, is briefly this: their poetry is conceived and composed in their wits, genuine poetry is conceived and composed in the soul.
Thomas Gray

45 That sweet City with her dreaming spires
She needs not June for beauty's heightening.
Referring to Oxford. *Thyrsis*

46 And sigh that one thing only has been lent
To youth and age in common – discontent.
Youth's Agitations

47 I am past thirty, and three parts iced over.
Letter to A. H. Clough, 12 Feb 1853

ARROGANCE

See also conceit, egotism, pride

1 The need to be right – the sign of a vulgar mind.
Albert Camus (1913–60) French existentialist writer. *Notebooks*, 1935–42

2 I am sure no man in England will take away my life to make you King.
Charles II (1630–85) King of England. To his brother James following revelation of the Popish Plot fabricated by Titus Oates. Attrib.

3 He was like a cock who thought the sun had risen to hear him crow.
George Eliot (Mary Ann Evans; 1819–80) British novelist. *Adam Bede*

4 If this young man expresses himself in terms too deep for *me*,
Why, what a very singularly deep young man this deep young man must be!
W. S. Gilbert (1836–1911) British dramatist. *Patience*, I

5 There, but for the Grace of God, goes God.

Herman J. Mankiewicz (1897–1953) US journalist and screenwriter. Said of Orson Welles in the making of *Citizen Kane*. Also attributed to others. *The Citizen Kane Book*

6 The bullet that is to kill me has not yet been moulded.

Napoleon I (Napoleon Bonaparte; 1769–1821) French emperor. In reply to his brother Joseph, King of Spain, who had asked whether he had ever been hit by a cannonball. Attrib.

7 What His Royal Highness most particularly prides himself upon, is the excellent harvest.

Richard Brinsley Sheridan (1751–1816) British dramatist. Lampooning George IV's habit of taking credit for everything good in England. *The Fine Art of Political Wit* (L. Harris)

8 A LADY. This landscape reminds me of your work.
WHISTLER. Yes madam, Nature is creeping up.

James Whistler (1834–1903) US painter. *Whistler Stories* (D. Seitz)

9 Well, not bad, but there are decidedly too many of them, and they are not very well arranged. I would have done it differently.

James Whistler His reply when asked if he agreed that the stars were especially beautiful one night. Attrib.

10 The Admiral of the Atlantic salutes the Admiral of the Pacific.

Wilhelm II (1859–1941) King of Prussia and Emperor of Germany. Telegram sent to Czar Nicholas II during a naval exercise. *The Shadow of the Winter Palace* (E. Crankshaw)

11 All men think all men mortal, but themselves.

Edward Young (1683–1765) British poet. *Night Thoughts*

ART

See also artists, arts, painting, design

1 The works of art, by being publicly exhibited and offered for sale, are becoming articles of trade, following as such the unreasoning laws of markets and fashion; and public and even private patronage is swayed by their tyrannical influence.

Prince Albert (1819–61) The consort of Queen Victoria. Referring to the Great Exhibition. Speech, Royal Academy Dinner, 3 May 1851

2 The object of art is to give life a shape.

Jean Anouilh (1910–87) French dramatist. *The Rehearsal*

3 The lower one's vitality, the more sensitive one is to great art.

Max Beerbohm (1872–1956) British writer. *Seven Men*, 'Enoch Soames'

4 It would follow that 'significant form' was form behind which we catch a sense of ultimate reality.

Clive Bell (1881–1964) British art critic. *Art*, Pt. I, Ch. 3

5 Art is the only thing that can go on mattering once it has stopped hurting.

Elizabeth Bowen (1899–1973) Irish novelist. *The Heat of the Day*, Ch. 16

6 It's a spot, which I hang on a white wall.

David Bowie (David Jones; 1947–) British pop singer. Referring to a Damien Hirst painting that he owns. *The Times*, 10 June 1994

7 Art is not a pastime, but a priesthood.

Jean Cocteau (1889–1963) French poet and artist. *New York Times*

8 Art for art's sake.

Victor Cousin (1792–1867) French philosopher. Lecture, Sorbonne, 1818

9 Art is vice, you don't marry it legitimately, you ravish it!

Edgar Degas (1834–1917) French artist. *Degas by himself* (ed. R. Kendall)

10 Art is a jealous mistress.

Ralph Waldo Emerson (1803–82) US poet and essayist. *Conduct of Life*, 'Wealth'

11 Works of art, in my opinion, are the only objects in the material universe to possess internal order, and that is why, though I don't believe that only art matters, I do believe in Art for Art's sake.

E. M. Forster (1879–1970) British novelist. *Art for Art's Sake*

12 No artist is ahead of his time. He *is* his time; it is just that others are behind the times.

Martha Graham (1894–1991) US dancer and choreographer. *The Observer Magazine*, 8 July 1979

13 I rarely draw what I see. I draw what I feel in my body.

Barbara Hepworth (1903–75) British sculptor. *World of Art Series* (A. M. Hammersmith)

14 Art has to move you and design does not, unless it's a good design for a bus.

David Hockney (1937–) British painter, draughtsman and printmaker. Remark, Oct 1988

15 In free society art is not a weapon...Artists are not engineers of the soul.

John Fitzgerald Kennedy (1917–63) US statesman. Address at Dedication of the Robert Frost Library, 26 Oct 1963

16 But the Devil whoops, as he whooped of old: 'It's clever, but is it art?'

Rudyard Kipling (1865–1936) Indian-born British writer. *The Conundrum of the Workshops*

17 You're not meant to understand – they're bloody works of art.

Sonia Lawson Royal Academy Hanging Committee. *The Observer*, 6 June 1993

18 Art is not a special sauce applied to ordinary cooking; it is the cooking itself if it is good.

W. R. Lethaby (1857–1931) British architect. *Form in Civilization*, 'Art and Workmanship'

19 In other countries, art and literature are left to a lot of shabby bums living in attics and feeding on booze and spaghetti, but in America the successful writer or picture-painter is indistinguishable from any other decent business man.

Sinclair Lewis (1885–1951) US novelist. *Babbitt*, Ch. 14

20 I do not know whether he draws a line himself. But I assume that his is the direction...It makes Disney the most significant figure in graphic art since Leonardo.

David Low (1871–1963) New-Zealand-born newspaper cartoonist. *Walt Disney* (R. Schickel), Ch. 20

21 In England, pop art and fine art stand resolutely back to back.

Colin MacInnes (1914–76) British novelist. *England, Half English*, 'Pop Songs and Teenagers'

22 Art is not a mirror to reflect the world, but a hammer with which to shape it.

Vladimir Mayakovsky (1893–1930) Soviet poet. *The Guardian*, 11 Dec 1974

23 Nothing unites the English like war. Nothing divides them like Picasso.

Hugh Mills (1913–71) British screenwriter. *Prudence and the Pill*

24 To be aristocratic in Art one must avoid polite society.

George Moore (1852–1933) Irish writer and art critic. *Enemies of Promise* (Cyril Connolly), Ch. 15

25 All art deals with the absurd and aims at the simple. Good art speaks truth, indeed *is* truth, perhaps the only truth.

Iris Murdoch (1919–) Irish-born British novelist. *The Black Prince*, 'Bradley Pearson's Foreword'

26 All art constantly aspires towards the condition of music.

Walter Pater (1839–94) British critic. *The Renaissance*, 'The School of Giorgione'

27 When I was their age, I could draw like Raphael, but it took me a lifetime to learn to draw like them.

Pablo Picasso (1881–1973) Spanish painter. Visiting an exhibition of drawings by children. *Picasso: His Life and Work* (Ronald Penrose)

28 The pain passes, but the beauty remains.

Pierre Auguste Renoir (1841–1919) French impressionist painter. Explaining why he still painted when his hands were twisted with arthritis. Attrib.

29 Burnings of people and (what was more valuable) works of art.

A. L. Rowse (1903–) British historian and critic. *Historical Essays* (H. R. Trevor-Roper)

30 Life without industry is guilt, and industry without art is brutality.

John Ruskin (1819–1900) British art critic and writer. *Lectures on Art*, 3, 'The Relation of Art to Morals', 23 Feb 1870

31 Fine art is that in which the hand, the head, and the heart of man go together.

John Ruskin *The Two Paths*, Lecture II

32 The trouble, Mr Goldwyn, is that you are only interested in art and I am only interested in money.

George Bernard Shaw (1856–1950) Irish dramatist and critic. Turning down Goldwyn's offer to buy the screen rights of his plays. *The Movie Moguls* (Philip French), Ch. 4

33 A portrait is a picture in which there is something wrong with the mouth.

Eugene Speicher (1883–1962) US painter. Attrib.

34 Skill without imagination is craftsmanship and gives us many useful objects such as wickerwork picnic baskets. Imagination without skill gives us modern art.

Tom Stoppard (1937–) Czech-born British dramatist. *Artist Descending a Staircase*

35 Art is not a handicraft, it is the transmission of feeling the artist has experienced.

Leo Tolstoy (1828–1910) Russian writer. *What is Art?*, Ch. 19

36 What a delightful thing this perspective is!

Paolo Uccello (1397–1475) Italian painter. *Men of Art* (T. Craven)

37 ...any authentic work of art must start an argument between the artist and his audience.

Rebecca West (Cicely Isabel Fairfield; 1892–1983) British novelist and journalist. *The Court and the Castle*, Pt. I, Ch. 1

38 Art is the imposing of a pattern on experience, and our aesthetic enjoyment is recognition of the pattern.

A. N. Whitehead (1861–1947) British philosopher. *Dialogues*, 228

39 Art never expresses anything but itself.

Oscar Wilde (1854–1900) Irish-born British dramatist. *The Decay of Lying*

40 All Art is quite useless.

Oscar Wilde *The Picture of Dorian Gray*, Preface

41 Art is the most intense mode of individualism that the world has known.

Oscar Wilde *The Soul of Man Under Socialism*

ARTISTS

General quotes

See also art, painting

1 The artist who makes himself accessible is self-destructive.

Howard Barker (1946–) British playwright. *The Times*, 31 Jan 1990

2 Poets and painters are outside the class system, or rather they constitute a special class of their own, like the circus people and the gipsies.

Gerald Brenan (Edward Fitzgerald Brenan; 1894–1987) British writer. *Thoughts in a Dry Season*, 'Writing'

3 Remember I'm an artist. And you know what that means in a court of law. Next worst to an actress.

Joyce Cary (1888–1957) British novelist. *The Horse's Mouth*, Ch. 14

4 Beware of the artist who's an intellectual also. The artist who doesn't fit.

F. Scott Fitzgerald (1896–1940) US novelist. *This Side of Paradise*, Bk. II, Ch. 5

5 I don't advise any one to take it up as a business proposition, unless they really have talent, and are crippled so as to deprive them of physical labor.

Grandma Moses (Anna Mary Robertson Moses; 1860–1961) US primitive painter. Referring to painting. *New York Times*, 'How Do I Paint?', 11 May 1947

6 An amateur is an artist who supports himself with outside jobs which enable him to paint. A professional is someone whose wife works to enable him to paint.

Ben Shahn (1898–1969) US artist. Attrib.

7 What is an artist? For every thousand people there's nine hundred doing the work, ninety doing well, nine doing good, and one lucky bastard who's the artist.

Tom Stoppard (1937–) Czech-born British dramatist. *Travesties*, I

8 A painter should not paint what he sees, but what will be seen.

Paul Valéry (1871–1945) French poet and writer. *Mauvaises Pensées et autres*

9 An artist is someone who produces things that people don't need to have but that he – for *some* reason – thinks it would be a good idea to give them.

Andy Warhol (Andrew Warhola; 1926–87) US pop artist. *From A to B and Back Again*, 'Atmosphere'

10 A living is made, Mr Kemper, by selling something that everybody needs at least once a year. Yes, sir! And a million is made by producing something that everybody needs every day. You artists produce something that nobody needs at any time.

Thornton Wilder (1897–1975) US novelist and dramatist. *The Matchmaker*, II

Specific quotes

11 It is comparatively easy to achieve a certain unity in a picture by allowing one colour to dominate, or by muting all the colours. Matisse did neither. He clashed his colours together like cymbals and the effect was like a lullaby.

John Berger (1926–) British author and art critic. *Toward Reality*

12 When Sir Joshua Reynolds died
All Nature was degraded;
The King dropped a tear in the Queen's ear,
And all his pictures faded.

William Blake (1757–1827) British poet. *On Art and Artists*

13 One of the reasons why medieval and renaissance architecture is so much better than our own is that the architects were artists. Bernini, one of the great artists of seventeenth-century Rome, was a sculptor.

Kenneth Clark (1903–83) British art historian. *Civilisation*

14 I do not paint a portrait to look like the subject, rather does the person grow to look like his portrait.

Salvador Dali (1904–89) Spanish painter. *Diary of a Genius*

15 I marry? Oh, I could never bring myself to do it. I would have been in mortal misery all my life for fear my wife might say, 'That's a pretty little thing,' after I had finished a picture.

Edgar Degas (1834–1917) French artist. *Degas by himself* (ed. R. Kendall)

16 The Epstein makes me feel physically sick. The wretched woman has two sets of breasts and a hip joint like a merry thought.

John Galsworthy (1867–1933) British novelist. Letter to Edward Garnett, 14 June 1925

17 His subjects are softened and sentimentalised too much. It is not simple unaffected nature that we see, but nature sitting for her picture.

William Hazlitt (1778–1830) British essayist. Referring to Thomas Gainsborough's pictures.

18 We live in an age where the artist is forgotten. He is a researcher. I see myself that way.

David Hockney (1937–) British painter. June 1991

19 If people dug up the remains of this civilization a thousand years hence, and found Epstein's statues and that man Ellis, they would think we were just savages.

Doris Lessing (1919–) British novelist. *Martha Quest*, Pt. I, Ch. 1

20 I paint objects as I think them, not as I see them.

Pablo Picasso (1881–1973) Spanish painter. *Cubism* (John Golding)

21 I should desire that the last words which I should pronounce in this Academy, and from this place, might be the name of – Michael Angelo.

Joshua Reynolds (1723–92) British portrait painter. Discourse to Students of the Royal Academy, 10 Dec 1790

22 See what will happen to you if you don't stop biting your fingernails.

Will Rogers (1879–1935) US actor and humorist. Message written on a postcard of the Venus de Milo that he sent to his young niece

23 Nobody cares much at heart about Titian, only there is a strange undercurrent of everlasting murmur about his name, which means the deep consent of all great men that he is greater than they.

John Ruskin (1819–1900) British art critic and writer. *The Two Paths*, Lecture II

24 If Botticelli were alive today he'd be working for *Vogue*.

Peter Ustinov (1921–) British actor. *The Observer*, 'Sayings of the Week', 21 Oct 1962

25 No I ask it for the knowledge of a lifetime.

James Whistler (1834–1903) US painter. Replying to the taunt, during the Ruskin trial, that he was asking a fee of 200 guineas for two days' painting. *Lives of the Wits* (H. Pearson)

ARTS

1 Every man's work, whether it be literature or music or pictures or architecture or anything else, is always a portrait of himself.

Samuel Butler (1835–1902) British writer. *The Way of All Flesh*, Ch. 14

2 Everything is dying of art-attacks. Everyone is so busy being artistic – especially directors. They dehydrate the simplicity of it. I just like to get on with it. Do it! Rehearse it! Shoot the damned thing! Don't talk about it, stumbling round for a needle in the haystack when it's right there under his butt end. Shoot it!

Anthony Hopkins (1937–) Welsh actor. *Films Illustrated*, Dec 1980

3 The excellence of every art is its intensity, capable of making all disagreeables evaporate, from their being in close relationship with beauty and truth.

John Keats (1795–1821) British poet. Letter to G. and T. Keats, 21 Dec 1817

4 The whole of art is an appeal to a reality which is not without us but in our minds.

Desmond MacCarthy (1877–1952) British writer and theatre critic. *Theatre*, 'Modern Drama'

5 Music begins to atrophy when it departs too far from the dance…poetry begins to atrophy when it gets too far from music.

Ezra Pound (1885–1972) US poet. *ABC of Reading* 'Warning'

6 The secret of the arts is to correct nature.

Voltaire (François-Marie Arouet; 1694–1778) French writer. *Épitres*, 'À. M. de Verrière'

ASHDOWN, PADDY

(Jeremy John Dunham Ashdown; 1941–) British politician. He became leader of the Social and Liberal Democratic Party in 1988.

1 I have made it clear that the period of coalitions, necessary though it was, is now over. We are on our own.
The Observer, 'Sayings of the Eighties', 31 July 1988

2 We are not rootless vagabonds. We are on our way to power.
Speech, SLD annual conference, Blackpool, Sept 1988

3 I do not believe that our place is at the comfortable mid-point between the extremes of left and right.
Speech, SLD annual conference, Brighton, Sept 1989

4 That's only fair – it is, after all, their turn.
Remark, Mar 1992, on hearing that David Owen announced his support for the Conservative Party at the coming general election.

ASSASSINATION

See also killing, murder

1 If His Majesty shall come by any violent death, it shall be revenged to the utmost upon all Papists.
Anonymous Resolution, House of Commons, 1679

2 They really are bad shots.
Charles De Gaulle (1890–1970) French general and statesman. Remark after narrowly escaping death in an assassination attempt. *Ten First Ladies of the World* (Pauline Frederick)

3 Assassination has never changed the history of the world.
Benjamin Disraeli (1804–81) British statesman. Speech, House of Commons, 1 May 1865

4 My fellow citizens, the President is dead, but the Government lives and God Omnipotent reigns.
James A. Garfield (1831–81) US statesman. Speech following the assassination of Lincoln.

5 Will no one rid me of this turbulent priest?
Henry II (1133–89) King of England. Referring to Thomas Becket, Archbishop of Canterbury; four of Henry's household knights took these words literally, hurried to Canterbury, and killed Becket in the cathedral (Dec 1170). Attrib.

6 A piece of each of us died at that moment.
Michael J. Mansfield (1903–) US senator. Referring to the assassination (22 Nov 1963) of President Kennedy. Speech, Senate, 24 Nov 1963

7 Assassination is the extreme form of censorship.
George Bernard Shaw (1856–1950) Irish dramatist and critic. *The Shewing-Up of Blanco Posnet*, 'The Limits of Toleration'

8 This was the day I was meant not to see.
Margaret Thatcher (1925–) British politician and prime minister. On her feelings the Sunday after she had escaped death in the IRA bomb explosion at the Grand Hotel, Brighton. TV interview, Oct 1984

ASTRONOMY

See also moon, space, stars, sun, universe

1 There is one glory of the sun, and another glory of the moon, and another glory of the stars: for one star differeth from another star in glory.
Bible: I Corinthians 15:41–42

2 ...in my studies of astronomy and philosophy I hold this opinion about the universe, that the Sun remains fixed in the centre of the circle of heavenly bodies, without changing its place; and the Earth, turning upon itself, moves round the Sun.
Galileo Galilei (1564–1642) Italian scientist. Letter to Cristina di Lorena, 1615

3 *Eppur si muove.*
Yet it moves.
Galileo Galilei Referring to the Earth. Remark supposedly made after his recantation (1632) of belief in the Copernican system. Attrib.

4 Astronomy teaches the correct use of the sun and the planets.
Stephen Leacock (1869–1944) English-born Canadian economist and humorist. *Literary Lapses*, 'A Manual of Education'

ATHEISM

See also God, religion

1 An atheist is one point beyond the devil.
Proverb

2 God never wrought miracle to convince atheism, because his ordinary works convince it.
Francis Bacon (1561–1626) English philosopher. *Essays*, 'Of Atheism'

3 For none deny there is a God, but those for whom it maketh that there were no God.
Francis Bacon *Essays*, 'Of Atheism'

4 I am an atheist still, thank God.
Luis Buñuel (1900–83) Spanish film director. *Luis Buñuel: an Introduction* (Ado Kyrou)

5 Wandering in a vast forest at night, I have only a faint light to guide me. A stranger appears and says to me: 'My friend, you should blow out your candle in order to find your way more clearly.' This stranger is a theologian.
Denis Diderot (1713–84) French writer. *Addition aux pensées philosophiques*

6 An atheist is a man who has no invisible means of support.
Harry Emerson Fosdick (1878–1969) US baptist minister. Attrib.

7 Perhaps if I wanted to be understood or to understand I would bamboozle myself into belief, but I am a reporter; God exists only for leader-writers.
Graham Greene (1904–91) British novelist. *The Quiet American*

8 If you don't find a God by five o'clock this afternoon you must leave the college.
Benjamin Jowett (1817–93) British theologian. Responding to a conceited young student's assertion that he could find no evidence for a God. Attrib.

9 I have no need of that hypothesis.

Marquis de Laplace (1749–1827) French mathematician and astronomer. On being asked by Napoleon why he had made no mention of God in his book about the universe, *Mécanique céleste. Men of Mathematics* (E. Bell)

10 He was an embittered atheist (the sort of atheist who does not so much disbelieve in God as personally dislike Him).

George Orwell (Eric Blair; 1903–50) British novelist. *Down and Out in Paris and London*, Ch. 30

11 It has been said that the highest praise of God consists in the denial of Him by the atheist, who finds creation so perfect that he can dispense with a creator.

Marcel Proust (1871–1922) French novelist. *À la recherche du temps perdu: Le Côté de Guermantes*

12 The worst moment for an atheist is when he feels grateful and doesn't know who to thank.

Wendy Ward Attrib.

13 By night an atheist half believes a God.

Edward Young (1683–1765) British poet. *Night Thoughts*

14 'Tisn't beauty, so to speak, nor good talk necessarily. It's just IT.

Rudyard Kipling (1865–1936) Indian-born British writer. *Traffics and Discoveries*, 'Mrs Bathurst'

AUDEN, W. H.

(1907–73) British poet; professor of poetry at Oxford University (1956–61). Auden made his name in the 1930s with such volumes as *Poems* (1930) and *Look, Stranger* (1936); later works included verse dramas and opera libretti.

Quotations about Auden

1 We have one poet of genius in Auden who is able to write prolifically, carelessly and exquisitely, nor does he seem to have to pay any price for his inspiration.

Cyril Connolly (1903–74) British journalist. *Enemies of Promise*

2 The high watermark, so to speak, of Socialist literature is W. H. Auden, a sort of gutless Kipling.

George Orwell (Eric Blair; 1903–50) British novelist. *The Road to Wigan Pier*

Quotations by Auden

3 Yet no one hears his own remarks as prose.

At a Party

4 Political history is far too criminal and pathological to be a fit subject of study for the young. Children should acquire their heroes and villains from fiction.

A Certain World

5 All sin tends to be addictive, and the terminal point of addiction is what is called damnation.

A Certain World

6 Happy the hare at morning, for she cannot read
The Hunter's waking thoughts.

The Dog Beneath the Skin (with Christopher Isherwood)

7 The true men of action in our time, those who transform the world, are not the politicians and statesmen, but the scientists. Unfortunately, poetry cannot celebrate them, because their deeds are concerned with things, not persons and are, therefore, speechless.

The Dyer's Hand, 'The Poet and the City'

8 When I find myself in the company of scientists, I feel like a shabby curate who has strayed by mistake into a drawing-room full of dukes.

The Dyer's Hand, 'The Poet and the City'

9 Man is a history-making creature who can neither repeat his past nor leave it behind.

The Dyer's Hand, 'D. H. Lawrence'

10 Some books are undeservedly forgotten; none are undeservedly remembered.

The Dyer's Hand, 'Reading'

11 No poet or novelist wishes he were the only one who ever lived, but most of them wish they were the only one alive, and quite a number fondly believe their wish has been granted.

The Dyer's Hand, 'Writing'

12 Let us honour if we can
The vertical man
Though we value none
But the horizontal one.

Epigraph for Poems

13 To save your world you asked this man to die:
Would this man, could he see you now, ask why?

Epitaph for an Unknown Soldier

14 Alone, alone, about the dreadful wood
Of conscious evil runs a lost mankind,
Dreading to find its Father.

For the Time Being, 'Chorus'

15 To us he is no more a person
Now but a climate of opinion.

In Memory of Sigmund Freud

16 Now Ireland has her madness and her weather still,
For poetry makes nothing happen.

In Memory of W. B. Yeats, II

17 Earth, receive an honoured guest:
William Yeats is laid to rest.
Let the Irish vessel lie
Emptied of its poetry.

In Memory of W. B. Yeats, III

18 It is time for the destruction of error.
The chairs are being brought in from the garden,
The summer talk stopped on that savage coast
Before the storms.

It is time

19 Look, stranger, at this island now
The leaping light for your delight discovers.

Look, Stranger

20 Lay your sleeping head, my love,
Human on my faithless arm.

Lullaby

21 To the man-in-the-street, who, I'm sorry to say
Is a keen observer of life,
The word Intellectual suggests straight away
A man who's untrue to his wife.

Note on Intellectuals

22 God bless the USA, so large,
So friendly, and so rich.

On the Circuit

23 Only those in the last stage of disease could believe that children are true judges of character.

The Orators, 'Journal of an Airman'

24 My Dear One is mine as mirrors are lonely.

The Sea and the Mirror

25 Their fate must always be the same as yours,
To suffer the loss they were afraid of, yes,
Holders of one position, wrong for years.

Since you are going to begin today

26 When it comes, will it come without warning
Just as I'm picking my nose?
Will it knock on my door in the morning,
Or tread in the bus on my toes?
Will it come like a change in the weather?
Will its greeting be courteous or rough?
Will it alter my life altogether?
O tell me the truth about love.

Twelve Songs, XII

27 Our researchers into Public Opinion are content
That he held the proper opinions for the time of year;
When there was peace, he was for peace; when there was war, he went.

The Unknown Citizen

28 If there are any of you at the back who do not hear me, please don't raise your hands because I am also nearsighted.

Starting a lecture in a large hall. *Book of the Month Club News*, Dec 1946

29 A professor is one who talks in someone else's sleep.

Attrib.

AUDIENCES

1 Long experience has taught me that in England nobody goes to the theatre unless he or she has bronchitis.

James Agate (1877–1947) British theatre critic. *See also* Artur SCHNABEL. *Ego*, 6

2 Audiences should feel encouraged to come in and wade about in complexity. Our world is highly contradictory, so art should reflect that. The artist's duty is to think hard, not shallowly.

Howard Barker (1946–) British playwright. *The Times*, 3 Jan 1990

3 Ladies and gentlemen, unless the play is stopped, the child cannot possibly go on.

John Philip Kemble (1757–1823) British tragic actor. Announcement to the audience when the play he was in was continually interrupted by a child crying *A Book of Anecdotes* (D. George)

4 Those people on the stage are making such a noise I can't hear a word you're saying.

Henry Taylor Parker (1867–1934) US music critic. Rebuking some talkative members of an audience, near whom he was sitting *The Humor of Music* (L. Humphrey)

5 A nice respectable, middle-class, middle-aged maiden lady, with time on her hands and the money to help her pass it...Let us call her Aunt Edna... Aunt Edna is universal, and to those who feel that all the problems of the modern theatre might be saved by her liquidation, let me add that...She is also immortal.

Terence Rattigan (1911–77) British dramatist. *Collected Plays*, Vol II, Preface

6 I know two kinds of audience only – one coughing and one not coughing.

Artur Schnabel (1882–1951) Austrian concert pianist. *See also* James AGATE *My Life and Music*, Pt. II, Ch. 10

7 I quite agree with you, sir, but what can two do against so many?

George Bernard Shaw (1856–1950) Irish dramatist and critic. Responding to a solitary hiss heard amongst the applause at the first performance of *Arms and the Man* in 1894 *Oxford Book of Literary Anecdotes*

8 I always think of the audience when I'm directing – because I am the audience.

Steven Spielberg (1946–) US film director. *Film Yearbook*, 1988

9 I like the audience to feel just a bit guilty about laughing.

John Waters (1946–) US film director. *The Times Magazine*, 11 June 1994

AUSTEN, JANE

(1775–1817) British novelist. Her novels of middle-class life combine humour with perceptive characterization; her six major works were *Sense and Sensibility* (1811), *Pride and Prejudice* (1813), *Mansfield Park* (1814), *Emma* (1815–16), *Northanger Abbey* (1818), and *Persuasion* (1818).

Quotations about Austen

1 More can be learnt from Miss Austen about the nature of the novel than from almost any other writer.

Walter Allen (1911–) British author and literary journalist. *The English Novel*

2 That young lady has a talent for describing the involvements and feelings and characters of ordinary life which is to me the most wonderful thing I ever met with.

Walter Scott (1771–1832) Scottish novelist. *Journals*, 14 Mar 1826

3 Jane Austen's books, too, are absent from this library. Just that one omission alone would make a fairly good library out of a library that hadn't a book in it.

Mark Twain (Samuel Langhorne Clemens; 1835–1910) US writer. *Following the Equator*, Pt. II

Quotations by Austen

4 One half of the world cannot understand the pleasures of the other.

Emma, Ch. 9

5 Nobody is healthy in London, nobody can be.

Emma, Ch. 12

6 A man...must have a very good opinion of himself when he asks people to leave their own fireside, and encounter such a day as this, for the

sake of coming to see him. He must think himself a most agreeable fellow.
Emma, Ch. 13

7 Human nature is so well disposed towards those who are in interesting situations, that a young person, who either marries or dies, is sure to be kindly spoken of.
Emma, Ch. 22

8 The sooner every party breaks up the better.
Emma, Ch. 25

9 Business, you know, may bring money, but friendship hardly ever does.
Emma, Ch. 34

10 One has no great hopes from Birmingham. I always say there is something direful in the sound.
Emma, Ch. 36

11 One of Edward's Mistresses was Jane Shore, who has had a play written about her, but it is a tragedy and therefore not worth reading.
The History of England

12 She was nothing more than a mere good-tempered, civil and obliging young woman; as such we could scarcely dislike her – she was only an Object of Contempt.
Love and Friendship

13 Let other pens dwell on guilt and misery.
Mansfield Park, Ch. 48

14 But are they all horrid, are you sure they are all horrid?
Northanger Abbey, Ch. 6

15 Oh! who can ever be tired of Bath?
Northanger Abbey, Ch. 10

16 A woman, especially if she have the misfortune of knowing anything, should conceal it as well as she can.
Northanger Abbey, Ch. 14

17 One does not love a place the less for having suffered in it unless it has all been suffering, nothing but suffering.
Persuasion, Ch. 20

18 It is a truth universally acknowledged, that a single man in possession of a good fortune must be in want of a wife.
The opening words of the book. *Pride and Prejudice*, Ch. 1

19 She was a woman of mean understanding, little information, and uncertain temper.
Pride and Prejudice, Ch. 1

20 A lady's imagination is very rapid; it jumps from admiration to love, from love to matrimony in a moment.
Pride and Prejudice, Ch. 6

21 Happiness in marriage is entirely a matter of chance.
Pride and Prejudice, Ch. 6

22 It is happy for you that you possess the talent of flattering with delicacy. May I ask whether these pleasing attentions proceed from the impulse of the moment, or are the result of previous study?
Pride and Prejudice, Ch. 14

23 You have delighted us long enough.
Pride and Prejudice, Ch. 18

24 Next to being married, a girl likes to be crossed in love a little now and then.
Pride and Prejudice, Ch. 24

25 One cannot be always laughing at a man without now and then stumbling on something witty.
Pride and Prejudice, Ch. 40

26 For what do we live, but to make sport for our neighbours, and laugh at them in our turn?
Pride and Prejudice, Ch. 57

27 I have been a selfish being all my life, in practice, though not in principle.
Pride and Prejudice, Ch. 58

28 What dreadful hot weather we have! It keeps me in a continual state of inelegance.
Letter, 18 Sept 1796

29 Mrs Hall of Sherbourne was brought to bed yesterday of a dead child, some weeks before she expected, owing to a fright. I suppose she happened unawares to look at her husband.
Letter, 27 Oct 1798

30 I do not want people to be very agreeable, as it saves me the trouble of liking them a great deal.
Letter, 24 Dec 1798

31 We met...Dr Hall in such very deep mourning that either his mother, his wife, or himself must be dead.
Letter to Cassandra Austen, 17 May 1799

32 The little bit (two inches wide) of ivory on which I work with so fine a brush as produces little effect after much labour.
Letter to J. Edward Austen, 16 Dec 1816

AUTHORITARIANISM

See also tyranny

1 *Roma locuta est; causa finita est.*
Rome has spoken; the case is concluded.
St Augustine of Hippo (354–430) Bishop of Hippo. *Sermons*, Bk. I

2 Then cometh the end, when he shall have delivered up the kingdom to God, even the Father; when he shall have put down all rule and all authority and power.
For he must reign, till he hath put all enemies under his feet.
The last enemy that shall be destroyed is death.
Bible: I Corinthians 15:24–26

3 And the Lord said unto Moses, Come up to me into the mount, and be there: and I will give thee tables of stone, and a law, and commandments which I have written; that thou mayest teach them.
Bible: Exodus 24:12

4 Dictators ride to and fro upon tigers which they

dare not dismount. And the tigers are getting hungry.

Winston Churchill (1874–1965) British statesman. *While England Slept*

5 I will have this done, so I order it done; let my will replace reasoned judgement.

Juvenal (Decimus Junius Juvenalis; 60–130 AD) Roman satirist. *Satires*, VI

6 Big Brother is watching you.

George Orwell (Eric Blair; 1903–50) British novelist. *Nineteen Eighty-Four*

7 I am painted as the greatest little dictator, which is ridiculous – you always take some consultations.

Margaret Thatcher (1925–) British politician and prime minister. *The Times*, 1983

8 I don't mind how much my ministers talk – as long as they do what I say.

Margaret Thatcher *The Times*, 1987

9 As for being a General, well, at the age of four with paper hats and wooden swords we're all Generals. Only some of us never grow out of it.

Peter Ustinov (1921–) British actor and dramatist. *Romanoff and Juliet*, I

AYCKBOURN, ALAN

(1939–) British playwright and director whose works include *Absurd Person Singular* (1973), *A Chorus of Disapproval* (1985), and *Wildest Dreams* (1993).

1 I've never to this day really known what most women think about anything.

Absurd Person Singular, III

2 My mother used to say, Delia, if S-E-X ever rears its ugly head, close your eyes before you see the rest of it.

Bedroom Farce, II

3 The greatest feeling in the world...Revenge. Pure, unadulterated revenge. Not weedy little jealousy. Not some piddling little envy. But good, old-fashioned, bloodcurdling revenge.

Revengers' Comedies, I:1

4 When you've been married a few years – you can't help window shopping.

Round and Round the Garden, I:1

5 If you gave Ruth a rose, she'd peel all the petals off to make sure there weren't any greenfly. And when she'd done that, she'd turn round and say, do you call that a rose? Look at it, it's all in bits.

Table Manners, I:2

6 Nevertheless – you know, in life, you get moments – just occasionally which you can positively identify as being among the happy moments.

Time of My Life, II

B

BABIES

See also birth, children

1 There is no finer investment for any community than putting milk into babies.

Winston Churchill (1874–1965) British statesman. Radio broadcast, 21 Mar 1943

2 There is no more sombre enemy of good art than the pram in the hall.

Cyril Connolly (1903–74) British journalist. *Enemies of Promise*, Ch. 3

3 Every baby born into the world is a finer one than the last.

Charles Dickens (1812–70) British novelist. *Nicholas Nickleby*, Ch. 36

4 These wretched babies don't come until they are ready.

Queen Elizabeth II (1926–) Queen of the United Kingdom. Remark, Aug 1988

5 Infants do not cry without some legitimate cause.

Ferrarius (16th century) *The Advancement of Child Health* (A. V. Neale)

6 Other people's babies –
That's my life!
Mother to dozens,
And nobody's wife.

A. P. Herbert (1890–1971) British writer and politician. *A Book of Ballads*, 'Other People's Babies'

7 A loud noise at one end and no sense of responsibility at the other.

Ronald Knox (1888–1957) British Roman Catholic priest. Attrib.

8 We all of us wanted babies – but did we want children?

Eda J. Leshan *How to Survive Children* (Katherine Whitehorn)

9 Sweetes' li'l' feller,
Everybody knows;
Dunno what to call 'im,
But he's mighty lak' a rose!

Frank L. Stanton (1857–1927) US journalist and poet. *Sweetes' Li'l' Feller*

BACON, FRANCIS

(1st Baron Verulam, Viscount St Albans; 1561–1626) English philosopher, lawyer, and politician. While lord chancellor (1618–21) he was charged with corruption and dismissed from public office. His writings include *Novum Organum* (1620), advocating the inductive method of logical reasoning.

1 For all knowledge and wonder (which is the seed of knowledge) is an impression of pleasure in itself.

The Advancement of Learning, Bk. I, Ch. 1

2 If a man will begin with certainties, he shall end in doubts, but if he will be content to begin with doubts, he shall end in certainties.

The Advancement of Learning, Bk. I, Ch. 5

3 They are ill discoverers that think there is no land, when they can see nothing but sea.

The Advancement of Learning, Bk. II, Ch. 7

4 Just as it is always said of slander that something always sticks when people boldly slander, so it might be said of self-praise (if it is not entirely shameful and ridiculous) that if we praise ourselves fearlessly, something will always stick.

The Advancement of Learning

5 One of the Seven was wont to say: 'That laws were like cobwebs; where the small flies were caught, and the great brake through.'

Apothegms

6 I have often thought upon death, and I find it the least of all evils.

An Essay on Death

7 I do not believe that any man fears to be dead, but only the stroke of death.

An Essay on Death

8 Prosperity doth best discover vice; but adversity doth best discover virtue.

Essays, 'Of Adversity'

9 God never wrought miracle to convince atheism, because his ordinary works convince it.

Essays, 'Of Atheism'

10 For none deny there is a God, but those for whom it maketh that there were no God.

Essays, 'Of Atheism'

11 Virtue is like a rich stone, best plain set.

Essays, 'Of Beauty'

12 There is no excellent beauty that hath not some strangeness in the proportion.

Essays, 'Of Beauty'

13 There is in human nature generally more of the fool than of the wise.

Essays, 'Of Boldness'

14 Mahomet made the people believe that he would call a hill to him…when the hill stood still, he was never a whit abashed, but said, 'If the hill will not come to Mahomet, Mahomet will go to the hill.'

Often misquoted as 'If the mountain will not come to Mohammed…'. *Essays*, 'Of Boldness'

15 Houses are built to live in and not to look on; therefore let use be preferred before uniformity, except where both may be had.

Essays, 'Of Building'

16 A wise man will make more opportunities than he finds.

Essays, 'Of Ceremonies and Respects'

17 When he wrote a letter, he would put that which was most material in the postscript, as if it had been a by-matter.

Essays, 'Of Cunning'

18 Men fear death, as children fear to go in the dark; and as that natural fear in children is increased with tales, so is the other.
Essays, 'Of Death'

19 It is as natural to die as to be born; and to a little infant, perhaps, the one is as painful as the other.
Essays, 'Of Death'

20 To choose time is to save time.
Essays, 'Of Dispatch'

21 It is a miserable state of mind to have few things to desire and many things to fear.
Essays, 'Of Empire'

22 Nothing destroyeth authority so much as the unequal and untimely interchange of power pressed too far, and relaxed too much.
Essays, 'Of Empire'

23 Riches are for spending.
Essays, 'Of Expense'

24 Whosoever is delighted in solitude is either a wild beast or a god.
Essays, 'Of Friendship'

25 Cure the disease and kill the patient.
Essays, 'Of Friendship'

26 God Almighty first planted a garden. And indeed it is the purest of human pleasures.
Essays, 'Of Gardens'

27 In charity there is no excess.
Essays, 'Of Goodness, and Goodness of Nature'

28 If a man be gracious and courteous to strangers, it shows he is a citizen of the world.
Essays, 'Of Goodness and Goodness of Nature'

29 As in nature things move violently to their place and calmly in their place, so virtue in ambition is violent, in authority settled and calm.
Essays, 'Of Great Place'

30 He that will not apply new remedies must expect new evils: for time is the greatest innovator.
Essays, 'Of Innovations'

31 The place of justice is a hallowed place.
Essays, 'Of Judicature'

32 Nuptial love maketh mankind; friendly love perfecteth it; but wanton love corrupteth and embaseth it.
Essays, 'Of Love'

33 He that hath wife and children hath given hostages to fortune; for they are impediments to great enterprises, either of virtue or mischief.
See also LUCAN. *Essays*, 'Of Marriage and the Single Life'

34 Wives are young men's mistresses, companions for middle age, and old men's nurses.
Essays, 'Of Marriage and the Single Life'

35 He was reputed one of the wise men, that made answer to the question, when a man should marry? A young man not yet, an elder man not at all.
Essays, 'Of Marriage and the Single Life'

36 Nature is often hidden, sometimes overcome, seldom extinguished.
Essays, 'Of Nature in Men'

37 A man's nature runs either to herbs, or to weeds; therefore let him seasonably water the one, and destroy the other.
Essays, 'Of Nature in Men'

38 The joys of parents are secret, and so are their griefs and fears.
Essays, 'Of Parents and Children'

39 Children sweeten labours, but they make misfortunes more bitter.
Essays, 'Of Parents and Children'

40 Fame is like a river, that beareth up things light and swollen, and drowns things weighty and solid.
Essays, 'Of Praise'

41 Dreams and predictions ought to serve but for winter talk by the fireside.
Essays, 'Of Prophecies'

42 Age will not be defied.
Essays, 'Of Regimen of Health'

43 Revenge is a kind of wild justice; which the more man's nature runs to, the more ought law to weed it out.
Essays, 'Of Revenge'

44 A man that studieth revenge keeps his own wounds green.
Essays, 'Of Revenge'

45 Money is like muck, not good except it be spread.
Essays, 'Of Seditions and Troubles'

46 The remedy is worse than the disease.
Essays, 'Of Seditions and Troubles'

47 The French are wiser than they seem, and the Spaniards seem wiser than they are.
Essays, 'Of Seeming Wise'

48 Nakedness is uncomely as well in mind, as body.
Essays, 'Of Simulation and Dissimulation'

49 Studies serve for delight, for ornament, and for ability.
Essays, 'Of Studies'

50 Some books are to be tasted, others to be swallowed, and some few to be chewed and digested.
Essays, 'Of Studies'

51 Reading maketh a full man; conference a ready man; and writing an exact man.
Essays, 'Of Studies'

52 It were better to have no opinion of God at all, than such an opinion as is unworthy of him.
Essays, 'Of Superstition'

53 Suspicions amongst thoughts are like bats amongst birds, they ever fly by twilight.
Essays, 'Of Suspicion'

54 Travel, in the younger sort, is a part of education; in the elder, a part of experience.
Essays, 'Of Travel'

55 Let diaries, therefore, be brought in use.
Essays, 'Of Travel'

56 What is truth? said jesting Pilate, and would not stay for an answer.
Essays, 'Of Truth'

57 All colours will agree in the dark.
Essays, 'Of Unity in Religion'

58 It was prettily devised of Aesop, 'The fly sat upon the axletree of the chariot-wheel and said, what a dust do I raise.'
Essays, 'Of Vain-Glory'

59 Be so true to thyself, as thou be not false to others.
Essays, 'Of Wisdom for a Man's Self'

60 It is the wisdom of the crocodiles, that shed tears when they would devour.
Essays, 'Of Wisdom for a Man's Self'

61 A man that is young in years may be old in hours, if he have lost no time.
Essays, 'Of Youth and Age'

62 Nature, to be commanded, must be obeyed.
Novum Organum

63 Books must follow sciences, and not sciences books.
Proposition touching Amendment of Laws

64 *Nam et ipsa scientia potestas est.*
Knowledge itself is power.
Religious Meditations, 'Of Heresies'

65 Universities incline wits to sophistry and affectation.
Valerius Terminus of the Interpretation of Nature, Ch. 26

66 The house is well, but it is you, Your Majesty, who have made me too great for my house.
Reply when Elizabeth I remarked on the smallness of his house.
After-dinner Stories and Anecdotes (L. Meissen)

67 I have taken all knowledge to be my province.
Letter to Lord Burleigh, 1592

68 For my name and memory, I leave it to men's charitable speeches, and to foreign nations, and the next ages.
Will, 19 Dec 1625

BAGEHOT, WALTER

(1826–77) British economist and journalist; editor of *The Economist* (1860–77).

1 *The Times* has made many ministries.
The English Constitution, 'The Cabinet'

2 A severe though not unfriendly critic of our institutions said that 'the cure for admiring the House of Lords was to go and look at it.'
The English Constitution, 'The House of Lords'

3 The best reason why Monarchy is a strong government is that it is an intelligible government. The mass of mankind understand it, and they hardly anywhere in the world understand any other.
The English Constitution, 'The Monarchy'

4 It has been said that England invented the phrase, 'Her Majesty's Opposition'.
The English Constitution, 'The Monarchy'

5 Women – one half the human race at least – care fifty times more for a marriage than a ministry.
The English Constitution, 'The Monarchy'

6 But of all nations in the world the English are perhaps the least a nation of pure philosophers.
The English Constitution, 'The Monarchy'

7 The Sovereign has, under a constitutional monarchy such as ours, three rights – the right to be consulted, the right to encourage, the right to warn.
The English Constitution, 'The Monarchy (continued)'

8 Writers, like teeth, are divided into incisors and grinders.
Estimates of some Englishmen and Scotchmen, 'The First Edinburgh Reviewers'

9 No man has come so near our definition of a constitutional statesman – the powers of a first-rate man and the creed of a second-rate man.
Historical Essays, 'The Character of Sir Robert Peel'

10 He believes, with all his heart and soul and strength, that there *is* such a thing as truth; he has the soul of a martyr with the intellect of an advocate.
Historical Essays, 'Mr Gladstone'

11 Poverty is an anomaly to rich people. It is very difficult to make out why people who want dinner do not ring the bell.
Literary Studies, II

BAINBRIDGE, BERYL

(1934–) British author and journalist, whose works include *The Bottle Factory Outing* (1974), *Injury Time* (1977), and *An Awfully Big Adventure* (1990).

1 Joseph seemed the arch-conformer of all time, stereotyped, well-bred, unemotional.
Another Part of the Wood

2 Clothes do matter.
Another Part of the Wood

3 I like funerals. All those flowers – a full life coming to a close.
The Bottle Factory Outing, Ch. 1

4 Time was when you could go on an outing to a town barely thirty miles distant from your own and it was like visiting another country.
Forever England

5 My own family were split down the middle, politically, as in every other way.
Forever England

6 She supposed that basically she was an unhappy person who was happy.
Forever England

7 Prejudice is planted in childhood, learnt like table manners and cadences of speech, nurtured through fictions like *Uncle Tom's Cabin* and *Gone With the Wind.*
Forever England

BALDWIN, JAMES ARTHUR

(1924–87) US writer. A Harlem-born black, he made his name with the novel *Go Tell It on the Mountain* (1953). Later books include *Just Above My Head* (1979) and *The Price of The Ticket* (1985).

1 If the concept of God has any validity or any use, it can only be to make us larger, freer, and more loving. If God cannot do this, then it is time we got rid of Him.
The Fire Next Time

2 Money, it turned out, was exactly like sex, you thought of nothing else if you didn't have it and thought of other things if you did.
Nobody Knows My Name

3 The price one pays for pursuing any profession or calling is an intimate knowledge of its ugly side.
Nobody Knows My Name

4 The future is…black.
The Observer, 'Sayings of the Week', 25 Aug 1963

5 I am a witness. In the church in which I was raised you were supposed to be a witness to the truth.
The Times, review of a biography, 16 June 1994

6 The trick is to love somebody…If you love one person, you see everybody else differently.
Interview

7 It comes as a great shock around the age of 5, 6, or 7 to discover that the flag to which you have pledged allegiance, along with everybody else, has not pledged allegiance to you. It comes as a great shock to see Gary Cooper killing off the Indians and, although you are rooting for Gary Cooper, that the Indians are you.
Speech, Cambridge Union, 17 Feb 1965

BALDWIN, STANLEY

(1st Earl Baldwin of Bewdley; 1867–1947) British statesman; Conservative prime minister (1923–24, 1924–29, 1935–37). He was criticized for his failure to re-arm in the face of German militarism.

1 A lot of hard-faced men who look as if they had done very well out of the war.
Referring to the first House of Commons elected after World War I (1918). *Economic Consequences of the Peace* (J. M. Keynes), Ch. 5

2 Then comes Winston with his hundred-horse-power mind and what can I do?
Stanley Baldwin (G. M. Young), Ch. 11

3 What the proprietorship of these papers is aiming at is power, and power without responsibility – the prerogative of the harlot through the ages.
Attacking the press barons Lords Rothermere and Beaverbrook. It was first used by KIPLING. *See also* DEVONSHIRE (10th Duke). Speech, election rally, 18 Mar 1931

4 The only defence is in offence, which means that you have to kill more women and children more quickly than the enemy if you want to save yourselves.
Speech, Nov 1932

5 I met Curzon in Downing Street, from whom I got the sort of greeting a corpse would give to an undertaker.
After he became prime minister in 1933. Attrib.

6 When you think of the defence of England you no longer think of the chalk cliffs of Dover. You think of the Rhine. That is where our frontier lies to-day.
Speech, House of Commons, 30 July 1934

7 There is a wind of nationalism and freedom blowing round the world, and blowing as strongly in Asia as elsewhere.
Speech, London, 4 Dec 1934

8 I have seldom spoken with greater regret, for my lips are not yet unsealed. Were these troubles over I would make a case, and I guarantee that not a man would go into the Lobby against us.
Referring to the Abyssinian crisis; usually misquoted as 'My lips are sealed'. Speech, House of Commons, 10 Dec 1935

9 God grant him peace and happiness but never understanding of what he has lost.
Referring to Edward VIII's abdication.

10 I would rather be an opportunist and float than go to the bottom with my principles round my neck.
Attrib.

11 The intelligent are to the intelligentsia what a gentleman is to a gent.
Attrib.

12 There are three groups that no British Prime Minister should provoke: the Vatican, the Treasury and the miners.
A similar remark is often attributed to Harold MACMILLAN. Attrib.

13 A platitude is simply a truth repeated till people get tired of hearing it.
Speech, 29 May 1924

BALFOUR, ARTHUR JAMES

(1st Earl of Balfour; 1848–1930) British statesman; Conservative prime minister (1902–05). As foreign secretary (1916–19) he issued the Balfour Declaration supporting a Jewish national state in Palestine.

1 I rather think of having a career of my own.
When asked whether he was going to marry Margot Tennant. *Autobiography* (Margot Asquith), Ch. 9

2 'Christianity, of course but why journalism?'
In reply to Frank Harris's remark, '…all the faults of the age come from Christianity and journalism'. *Autobiography* (Margot Asquith), Ch. 10

3 I thought he was a young man of promise; but it appears he was a young man of promises.
Said of Winston Churchill on his entry into politics, 1899. *Winston Churchill* (Randolph Churchill), Vol. I

4 His Majesty's Government views with favour

the establishment in Palestine of a national home for the Jewish people…

The so-called 'Balfour Declaration'. Letter to Lord Rothschild, 2 Nov 1917

5 It is unfortunate, considering that enthusiasm moves the world, that so few enthusiasts can be trusted to speak the truth.

Letter to Mrs Drew, 19 May 1891

6 Nothing matters very much, and very few things matter at all.

Attrib.

BALZAC, HONORE DE

(1799–1850) French novelist. After several popular novels written under pseudonyms, his first success came with *Les Chouans* (1829). Later novels include *Le Père Goriot* (1834) and *La Cousine Bette* (1846). His entire output – over 40 novels – was organized under the title *La Comédie humaine*.

1 Equality may perhaps be a right, but no power on earth can ever turn it into a fact.

La Duchesse de Langeais

2 There is no such thing as a great talent without great will-power.

La Muse du département

3 The majority of husbands remind me of an orangutang trying to play the violin.

La Physiologie du mariage

4 I am laughing to think what risks you take to try to find money in a desk by night where the legal owner can never find any by day.

Said on waking to find a burglar in the room. Attrib.

5 I should like one of these days to be so well known, so popular, so celebrated, so famous, that it would permit me…to break wind in society, and society would think it a most natural thing.

Attrib.

6 It is easier to be a lover than a husband, for the same reason that it is more difficult to show a ready wit all day long than to produce an occasional *bon mot*.

Attrib.

BANKHEAD, TALLULAH

(1903–68) US actress, famous for her extravagant lifestyle.

Quotations about Bankhead

1 More of an act than an actress.

Anonymous

2 She was always a star, but only intermittently a good actress.

Brendan Gill *The Times*, 4 Aug 1973

3 She was an open, wayward, free, cosmopolitan, liberated, sensuous human being. In thus systematically invading her own privacy she was the first of the modern personalities.

Lee Israel *Miss Tallulah Bankhead*

Quotations by Bankhead

4 I have three phobias which, could I mute them, would make my life as slick as a sonnet, but as dull as ditch water: I hate to go to bed, I hate to get up, and I hate to be alone.

Tallulah, Ch. 1

5 It's one of the tragic ironies of the theatre that only one man in it can count on steady work – the night watchman.

Tallulah, Ch. 1

6 I've been called many things, but never an intellectual.

Tallulah, Ch. 15

7 Cocaine isn't habit-forming. I should know – I've been using it for years.

Pentimento (Lillian Hellman), 'Theatre'

8 There is less in this than meets the eye.

Referring to a revival of a play by Maeterlink. *Shouts and Murmurs* (A. Woollcott), 'Capsule Criticism'

9 Don't bother to thank me. I know what a perfectly ghastly season it's been for you Spanish dancers.

Said on dropping fifty dollars into a tambourine held out by a Salvation Army collector. *With Malice Toward All* (D. Hermann)

10 I'm as pure as the driven slush.

The Observer, 'Sayings of the Week', 24 Feb 1957

11 I'll come and make love to you at five o'clock. If I'm late start without me.

Somerset Maugham (E. Morgan)

12 I thought I told you to wait in the car.

When greeted by a former admirer after many years. Attrib.

13 Only good girls keep diaries. Bad girls don't have the time.

Attrib.

BARRIE, SIR J. M.

(1860–1937) British novelist and dramatist, born in Scotland; author of *Peter Pan* (1904). His other works include *The Admirable Crichton* (1902) and *Dear Brutus* (1917).

1 If it's heaven for climate, it's hell for company.

The Little Minister, Ch. 3

2 It's grand, and ye canna expect to be baith grand and comfortable.

The Little Minister, Ch. 10

3 When the first baby laughed for the first time, the laugh broke into a thousand pieces and they all went skipping about, and that was the beginning of fairies.

Peter Pan, I

4 Every time a child says 'I don't believe in fairies' there is a little fairy somewhere that falls down dead.

Peter Pan, I

5 To die will be an awfully big adventure.

Peter Pan, III

6 What is algebra exactly; is it those three-cornered things?
Quality Street, II

7 One's religion is whatever he is most interested in, and yours is Success.
The Twelve-Pound Look

8 It's a sort of bloom on a woman. If you have it, you don't need to have anything else; and if you don't have it, it doesn't much matter what else you have.
Referring to charm. *What Every Woman Knows*, I

9 A young Scotsman of your ability let loose upon the world with £300, what could he not do? It's almost appalling to think of; especially if he went among the English.
What Every Woman Knows, I

10 You've forgotten the grandest moral attribute of a Scotsman, Maggie, that he'll do nothing which might damage his career.
What Every Woman Knows, II

11 There are few more impressive sights in the world than a Scotsman on the make.
What Every Woman Knows, II

12 I have always found that the man whose second thoughts are good is worth watching.
What Every Woman Knows, III

13 Never ascribe to an opponent motives meaner than your own.
Speech, St Andrews, 3 May 1922

14 Some of my plays peter out, and some pan out.
Attrib.

BEAUMONT, FRANCIS

(1584–1616) English dramatist, who wrote a number of plays in collaboration with John Fletcher. These include *Philaster* (1609) and *A King and No King* (1611).

1 You are no better than you should be.
The Coxcomb, IV:3

2 But what is past my help is past my care.
With John Fletcher. *The Double Marriage*, I:1

3 It is always good
When a man has two irons in the fire.
The Faithful Friends, I:2

4 Let's meet, and either do, or die.
The Island Princess, II:2

5 I'll put a spoke among your wheels.
The Mad Lover, III:6

6 Those have most power to hurt us that we love.
The Maid's Tragedy, V:6

7 Nothing's so dainty sweet as lovely melancholy.
The Nice Valour, III:3

8 All your better deeds
Shall be in water writ, but this in marble.
The Nice Valour, V:3

9 Mortality, behold and fear!
What a change of flesh is here!
On the Tombs in Westminster Abbey

10 As men
Do walk a mile, women should talk an hour,
After supper. 'Tis their exercise.
Philaster, II:4

11 I'll have a fling.
Rule a Wife and have a Wife, III:5

12 Kiss till the cow comes home.
Scornful Lady, II:2

13 Whistle and she'll come to you.
Wit Without Money, IV:4

BEAUTY

See also admiration, appearance, compliments

1 A wife is sought for her virtue, concubine for her beauty.
Chinese proverb

2 A good face is a letter of recommendation.
Proverb

3 Beauty is only skin-deep.
Proverb

4 Beauty is potent but money is omnipotent.
Proverb

5 Small is beautiful.
Proverb

6 My Love in her attire doth show her wit,
It doth so well become her:
For every season she hath dressings fit,
For winter, spring, and summer.
No beauty she doth miss,
When all her robes are on;
But beauty's self she is,
When all her robes are gone.
Anonymous Madrigal

7 You know, you can only perceive real beauty in a person as they get older.
Anouk Aimée (1932–) French actress. Remark, Aug 1988

8 There is no excellent beauty that hath not some strangeness in the proportion.
Francis Bacon (1561–1626) English philosopher. *Essays*, 'Of Beauty'

9 Beauty and the lust for learning have yet to be allied.
Max Beerbohm (1872–1956) British writer. *Zuleika Dobson*, Ch. 7

10 Exuberance is Beauty.
William Blake (1757–1827) British poet. *The Marriage of Heaven and Hell*, 'Proverbs of Hell'

11 For beauty being the best of all we know
Sums up the unsearchable and secret aims
Of nature.
Robert Bridges (1844–1930) British poet. *The Growth of Love*

12 Beauty sat with me all the summer day,
Awaiting the sure triumph of her eye;

Nor mark'd I till we parted, how, hard by,
Love in her train stood ready for his prey.

Robert Bridges *The Growth of Love*

13 Incredibly, inordinately, devastatingly, immortally, calamitously, hearteningly, adorably beautiful.

Rupert Brooke (1887–1915) British) poet. Referring to the actress Cathleen Nesbitt. *Rupert Brooke* (C. Hassall)

14 It is better to be first with an ugly woman than the hundredth with a beauty.

Pearl Buck (1892–1973) US novelist. *The Good Earth*, Ch. 1

15 Beauty in distress is much the most affecting beauty.

Edmund Burke (1729–97) British politician. *On the Sublime and Beautiful*, Pt. III

16 She walks in beauty, like the night
Of cloudless climes and starry skies;
And all that's best of dark and bright
Meet in her aspect and her eyes.

Lord Byron (1788–1824) British poet. *She Walks in Beauty*

17 SONYA. I'm not beautiful.
HELEN. You have lovely hair.
SONYA. No, when a woman isn't beautiful, people always say, 'You have lovely eyes, you have lovely hair.'

Anton Chekhov (1860–1904) Russian dramatist. *Uncle Vanya*, III

18 There is nothing ugly; *I never saw an ugly thing in my life:* for let the form of an object be what it may, – light, shade, and perspective will always make it beautiful.

John Constable (1776–1837) British landscape painter. Letter to John Fisher, 23 Oct 1821

19 There is nothing so lovely as to be beautiful. Beauty is a gift of God and we should cherish it as such.

Marie de Sévigné (1626–96) French letter writer and salonist. *Letters of Madame de Sévigné to her daughters and friends*

20 Love built on beauty, soon as beauty, dies.

John Donne (1573–1631) English poet. *Elegies*, 2, 'The Anagram'

21 Our feeling for beauty is inspired by the harmonious arrangement of order and disorder as it occurs in natural objects – in clouds, trees, mountain ranges, or snow crystals.

Gert Eilenberger German physicist. *Schönheit im Chaos* 'Freedom, Science, and Aesthetics'

22 One girl can be pretty – but a dozen are only a chorus.

F. Scott Fitzgerald (1896–1940) US novelist. *The Last Tycoon*

23 Beauty is a social necessity.

James Goldsmith (1933–) British businessman. *The Times*, 10 June 1994

24 Against the beautiful and the clever and the successful, one can wage a pitiless war, but not against the unattractive.

Graham Greene (1904–91) British novelist. *The Heart of the Matter*

25 Glory be to God for dappled things –
For skies of couple-colour as a brindled cow;
For rose-moles all in stipple upon trout that swim.

Gerard Manley Hopkins (1844–99) British Jesuit and poet. *Pied Beauty*

26 Beauty in things exists in the mind which contemplates them.

David Hume (1711–76) Scottish philosopher. *Essays*, 'Of Tragedy'

27 Beauty is altogether in the eye of the beholder.

Margaret Wolfe Hungerford (c. 1855–97) Irish novelist. Also attributed to the US soldier and writer Lew Wallace (1827–1905). *Molly Bawn*

28 A thing of beauty is a joy for ever:
Its loveliness increases; it will never
Pass into nothingness; but still will keep
A bower quiet for us, and a sleep
Full of sweet dreams, and health, and quiet breathing.

John Keats (1795–1821) British poet. *Endymion*, I

29 'Beauty is truth, truth beauty,' – that is all
Ye know on earth, and all ye need to know.

John Keats *Ode on a Grecian Urn*

30 Was this the face that launch'd a thousand ships
And burnt the topless towers of Ilium?
Sweet Helen, make me immortal with a kiss.

Christopher Marlowe (1564–93) English dramatist. *Doctor Faustus*, V:1

31 Oh, thou art fairer than the evening air
Clad in the beauty of a thousand stars.

Christopher Marlowe *Doctor Faustus*, V:1

32 You're the most beautiful woman I've ever seen, which doesn't say much for you.

Groucho Marx (Julius Marx; 1895–1977) US comedian. *Animal Crackers*

33 Beauty stands
In the admiration only of weak minds
Led captive.

John Milton (1608–74) English poet. *Paradise Regained*, Bk. II

34 I hate that aesthetic game of the eye and the mind, played by these connoisseurs, these mandarins who 'appreciate' beauty. What *is* beauty, anyway? There's no such thing. I never 'appreciate', any more than I 'like'. I love or I hate.

Pablo Picasso (1881–1973) Spanish painter. *Life with Picasso* (Françoise Gilot and Carlton Lake), Ch. 2

35 And when I told them how beautiful you are
They didn't believe me! They didn't believe me!

M. E. Rourke (20th century) US songwriter and lyricist. *They Didn't Believe Me* (song)

36 There are no ugly women, only lazy ones.

Helena Rubinstein (1882–1965) Polish-born US cosmetics manufacturer. *My Life for Beauty*, Pt. II, Ch. 1

37 All she has to do is to walk around and about Georgie White's stage with only a few light bandages on, and everybody considers her very beautiful, especially from the neck down.

Damon Runyon (1884–1946) US writer. *Furthermore*, 'A Very Honourable Guy'

38 Remember that the most beautiful things in the world are the most useless, peacocks and lilies for instance.

John Ruskin (1819–1900) British art critic and writer. *The Stones of Venice*, Vol. I, Ch. 2

39 I always say beauty is only sin deep.

Saki (Hector Hugh Munro; 1870–1916) British writer. *Reginald's Choir Treat*

40 Beauty too rich for use, for earth too dear.

William Shakespeare (1564–1616) English dramatist. *Romeo and Juliet*, I:5

41 Beauty itself doth of itself persuade
The eyes of men without an orator.

William Shakespeare *The Rape of Lucrece*, I

42 From fairest creatures we desire increase,
That thereby beauty's rose might never die.

William Shakespeare *Sonnet 1*

43 For she was beautiful – her beauty made
The bright world dim, and everything beside
Seemed like the fleeting image of a shade.

Percy Bysshe Shelley (1792–1822) British poet. *The Witch of Atlas*, XII

44 Health is beauty, and the most perfect health is the most perfect beauty.

William Shenstone (1714–63) English poet. *Essays on Men and Manners*, 'On Taste'

45 Half light, half shade,
She stood, a sight to make an old man young.

Alfred, Lord Tennyson (1809–92) British poet. *The Gardener's Daughter*

46 But Lancelot mused a little space;
He said, 'She has a lovely face;
God in his mercy lend her grace,
The Lady of Shalott.'

Alfred, Lord Tennyson *The Lady of Shalott*, Pt. IV

47 The more legal and material hindrances women have broken through, the more strictly and heavily and cruelly images of female beauty have come to weigh upon us.

Naomi Wolf US writer. *The Beauty Myth*

48 A woman of so shining loveliness
That men threshed corn at midnight by a tress,
A little stolen tress.

W. B. Yeats (1865–1939) Irish poet. *The Secret Rose*

49 All changed, changed utterly:
A terrible beauty is born.

W. B. Yeats *Easter 1916*

BEAUVOIR, SIMONE DE

(1908–86) French writer. A lifelong companion of Jean-Paul Sartre, she wrote novels on existentialist themes, including *The Mandarins* (1954) and *The Coming of Age* (1973). Her most influential work remains *The Second Sex* (1949) in which she argued for the liberation of women from their traditional roles.

1 What is an adult? A child blown up by age.

La Femme rompue

2 A man would never get the notion of writing a book on the peculiar situation of the human male.

Le Deuxième Sexe (trans. *The Second Sex*)

3 One is not born a woman, one becomes one.

Le Deuxième Sexe (trans. *The Second Sex*)

4 Between women love is contemplative. There is no struggle, no victory, no defeat; in exact reciprocity each is at once subject and object, sovereign and slave; duality becomes mutuality.

Le Deuxième Sexe (trans. *The Second Sex*)

5 For him she is sex – absolute sex, no less. She is defined and differentiated with reference to man and not he with reference to her; she is the incidental, the inessential as opposed to the essential. He is the Subject, he is the Absolute – she is the Other.

Le Deuxième Sexe (trans. *The Second Sex*)

6 If you live long enough, you'll see that every victory turns into a defeat.

Tous les hommes sont mortels

7 If you haven't been happy very young, you can still be happy later on, but it's much harder. You need more luck.

The Observer, 'Sayings of the Week', 19 May 1975

8 I cannot be angry at God, in whom I do not believe.

The Observer, 7 Jan 1979

BEAVERBROOK, LORD

(1879–1964) Canadian-born British newspaper proprietor and politician. He owned the *Daily Express* and *Evening Standard*. In World War I he was minister of information and in World War II he became minister of aircraft production.

1 I am the cat that walks alone.

Beaverbrook (A. J. P. Taylor)

2 He did not care in which direction the car was travelling, so long as he remained in the driver's seat.

Referring to Lloyd George, British Liberal prime minister. *New Statesman*, 14 June 1963

3 If you want to make mischief come and work on my papers.

Inviting the journalist Anthony Howard to join his staff. *Radio Times*, 27 June 1981

4 Go out and speak for the inarticulate and the submerged.

Somerset Maugham (E. Morgan)

5 Our cock won't fight.

Said during the abdication crisis.
Attrib.

6 Buy old masters. They fetch a better price than old mistresses.

Attrib.

BECKETT, SAMUEL

(1906–89) Irish novelist, dramatist, and poet. Having settled in Paris in 1937, he wrote in both English and French. His best-known work is *Waiting for Godot* (1952).

1 CLOV. Do you believe in the life to come?
HAMM. Mine was always that.

Endgame

2 Nothing happens, nobody comes, nobody goes, it's awful!
Waiting for Godot, I

3 VLADIMIR. That passed the time.
ESTRAGON. It would have passed in any case.
VLADIMIR. Yes, but not so rapidly.
Waiting for Godot, I

4 ESTRAGON. ... Let's go.
VLADIMIR. We can't.
ESTRAGON. Why not?
VLADIMIR. We're waiting for Godot.
Waiting for Godot, I

5 We all are born mad. Some remain so.
Waiting for Godot, II

6 Habit is a great deadener.
Waiting for Godot, III

BED

See also idleness, rest, sleep

1 Early to bed and early to rise, makes a man healthy, wealthy and wise.
Proverb

2 Go to bed with the lamb, and rise with the lark.
Proverb

3 It isn't the ecstatic leap across that I deplore, it's the weary trudge home.
Anonymous Referring to single beds.

4 The cool kindliness of sheets, that soon
Smooth away trouble; and the rough male kiss of blankets.
Rupert Brooke (1887–1915) British) poet. *The Great Lover*

5 I'm Burlington Bertie:
I rise at ten-thirty.
W. F. Hargreaves (1846–1919) British songwriter. *Burlington Bertie*

6 I have, all my life long, been lying till noon; yet I tell all young men, and tell them with great sincerity, that nobody who does not rise early will ever do any good.
Samuel Johnson (1709–84) British lexicographer. *Tour to the Hebrides* (J. Boswell)

7 O! it's nice to get up in the mornin',
But it's nicer to stay in bed.
Harry Lauder (Hugh MacLennon; 1870–1950) Scottish music-hall artist. Song

8 Believe me, you have to get up early if you want to get out of bed.
Groucho Marx (Julius Marx; 1895–1977) US comedian. *The Cocoanuts*

9 It was such a lovely day I thought it was a pity to get up.
W. Somerset Maugham (1874–1965) British novelist. *Our Betters*, II

10 And so to bed.
Samuel Pepys (1633–1703) English diarist. *Diary*, 6 May 1660 and *passim*

11 Not to be abed after midnight is to be up betimes.
William Shakespeare (1564–1616) English dramatist. *Twelfth Night*, II:3

12 Early to rise and early to bed makes a male healthy and wealthy and dead.
James Thurber (1894–1961) US humorist. *Fables for Our Time*, 'The Shrike and the Chipmunks'

BEECHAM, SIR THOMAS

(1879–1961) British conductor. Using his inherited wealth, he popularized the works of Richard Strauss and Delius in Britain as well as founding the London Philharmonic Orchestra (1932) and the Royal Philharmonic Orchestra (1947).

1 A musicologist is a man who can read music but can't hear it.
Beecham Remembered (H. Procter-Gregg)

2 There are two golden rules for an orchestra: start together and finish together. The public doesn't give a damn what goes on in between.
Beecham Stories (H. Atkins and A. Newman)

3 Ball...how very singular.
To a man called Ball. *Sir Thomas Beecham* (N. Cardus)

4 The English may not like music – but they absolutely love the noise it makes.
The Wit of Music (L. Ayre)

5 I have recently been all round the world and have formed a very poor opinion of it.
Speech at the Savoy. *The News Review*, 22 Aug 1946

6 Too much counterpoint; what is worse, Protestant counterpoint.
Said of J. S. Bach. *The Guardian*, 8 Mar 1971

7 The sound of the harpsichord resembles that of a bird-cage played with toasting-forks.
Attrib.

8 When we sing 'All we, like sheep, have gone astray', might we please have a little more regret and a little less satisfaction?
To a choir rehearsing Handel's *Messiah*. Attrib.

9 Brass bands are all very well in their place – outdoors and several miles away.
Attrib.

BEERBOHM, SIR MAX

(1872–1956) British writer and caricaturist. His only novel, *Zuleika Dobson* (1911), is set in Oxford.

Quotations about Beerbohm

1 The Incomparable Max.
George Bernard Shaw (1856–1950) Irish dramatist and critic. *Dramatic Opinions and Essays*, Vol. II.

2 He has the most remarkable and seductive genius – and I should say about the smallest in the world.
Lytton Strachey (1880–1932) British writer. Letter to Clive Bell, 4 Dec 1917

Quotations by Beerbohm

3 There is always something rather absurd about the past.
1880

4 To give an accurate and exhaustive account of that period would need a far less brilliant pen than mine.
1880

5 Great men are but life-sized. Most of them, indeed, are rather short.
And Even Now

6 I believe the twenty-four hour day has come to stay.
A Christmas Garland, 'Perkins and Mankind'

7 Anything that is worth doing has been done frequently. Things hitherto undone should be given, I suspect, a wide berth.
Mainly on the Air

8 It is Oxford that has made me insufferable.
More, 'Going back to School'

9 The lower one's vitality, the more sensitive one is to great art.
Seven Men, 'Enoch Soames'

10 Most women are not so young as they are painted.
The Yellow Book

11 The dullard's envy of brilliant men is always assuaged by the suspicion that they will come to a bad end.
Zuleika Dobson

12 It needs no dictionary of quotations to remind me that the eyes are the windows of the soul.
Zuleika Dobson, Ch. 4

13 Women who love the same man have a kind of bitter freemasonry.
Zuleika Dobson, Ch. 4

14 You will find that the woman who is really kind to dogs is always one who has failed to inspire sympathy in men.
Zuleika Dobson, Ch. 6

15 Beauty and the lust for learning have yet to be allied.
Zuleika Dobson, Ch. 7

16 You will think me lamentably crude: my experience of life has been drawn from life itself.
Zuleika Dobson, Ch. 7

17 You cannot make a man by standing a sheep on its hind legs. But by standing a flock of sheep in that position you can make a crowd of men.
Zuleika Dobson, Ch. 9

18 She was one of the people who say, 'I don't know anything about music really, but I know what I like'.
Zuleika Dobson, Ch. 16

19 It's not in support of cricket but as an earnest protest against golf.
Said when giving a shilling towards W. G. Grace's testimonial. *Carr's Dictionary of Extraordinary English Cricketers*

20 Of course we all know that Morris was a wonderful all-round man, but the act of walking round him has always tired me.
Referring to William Morris. *Conversations with Max* (S. N. Behrman)

21 They were a tense and peculiar family, the Oedipuses, weren't they?
Max: A Biography (D. Cecil)

22 What were they going to do with the Grail when they found it, Mr Rossetti?
Caption to a cartoon

BEGINNING

See also prophecy

1 A journey of a thousand leagues begins with a single step.
Chinese Proverb

2 Fingers were made before forks, and hands before knives.
Proverb

3 From small beginnings come great things.
Proverb

4 Great oaks from little acorns grow.
Proverb

5 The first step is the hardest.
Proverb

6 No task is a long one but the task on which one dare not start. It becomes a nightmare.
Charles Baudelaire (1821–67) French poet. *My Heart Laid Bare*

7 She looked at him, as one who awakes:
The past was a sleep, and her life began.
Robert Browning (1812–89) British poet. *The Statue and the Bust*

8 The distance doesn't matter; it is only the first step that is difficult.
Marquise du Deffand (Marie de Vichy-Chamrond; 1697–1780) French noblewoman. Referring to the legend of St Denis, who is traditionally believed to have carried his severed head for six miles after his execution. Letter to d'Alembert, 7 July 1763

9 In my beginning is my end.
T. S. Eliot (1888–1965) US-born poet. *Four Quartets*, 'East Coker'

10 With the possible exception of the equator, everything begins somewhere.
Peter Fleming (1907–71) British travel writer. *One's Company*, 1934

11 From today and from this place there begins a new epoch in the history of the world.
Goethe (1749–1832) German poet and dramatist. On witnessing the victory of the French at the battle of Valmy. *The Story of Civilization* (W. Durant), Vol. II

12 'Tis always morning somewhere in the world.
Richard Henry Horne (1803–84) English writer. *Orion*, Bk. III, Ch. 2

13 There is an old saying 'well begun is half done' – 'tis a bad one. I would use instead – Not begun at all until half done.

John Keats (1795–1821) British poet. Letter, 1817

14 We stand today on the edge of a new frontier.

John Fitzgerald Kennedy (1917–63) US statesman. Said on his nomination as presidential candidate. Speech, Democratic Party Convention, 15 July 1960

15 Are you sitting comfortably? Then I'll begin.

Julia S. Lang (1921–) British broadcaster. Introduction to the story in *Listen with Mother.*

16 If you really want to hear about it, the first thing you'll probably want to know is where I was born and what my lousy childhood was like, and how my parents were occupied and all before they had me, and all that David Copperfield kind of crap.

J. D. Salinger (1919–) US novelist. The opening words of the book. *The Catcher in the Rye*

BEHAN, BRENDAN

(1923–64) Irish playwright. His best-known works are *The Quare Fellow* (1954), the autobiographical *Borstal Boy* (1958), and *The Hostage* (1958). Behan's alcoholism led to his premature death.

1 He was born an Englishman and remained one for years.

The Hostage, I

2 PAT. He was an Anglo-Irishman.
MEG. In the blessed name of God, what's that?
PAT. A Protestant with a horse.

The Hostage, I

3 When I came back to Dublin, I was courtmartialled in my absence and sentenced to death in my absence, so I said they could shoot me in my absence.

The Hostage, I

4 I wish I'd been a mixed infant.

The Hostage, II

5 I am a sociable worker.

The Hostage, II

6 I think weddings is sadder than funerals, because they remind you of your own wedding. You can't be reminded of your own funeral because it hasn't happened. But weddings always make me cry.

Richard's Cork Leg, I

7 Other people have a nationality. The Irish and the Jews have a psychosis.

Richard's Cork Leg, I

8 The English and Americans dislike only *some* Irish – the same Irish that the Irish themselves detest, Irish writers – the ones that *think.*

Richard's Cork Leg, I

9 Come in, you Anglo-Saxon swine
And drink of my Algerian wine.
'Twill turn your eyeballs black and blue,
And damn well good enough for you.

Painted as an advert on the window of a Paris café (the owner of which could not speak English). *My Brother Brendan* (Dominic Behan)

10 I am married to Beatrice Salkeld, a painter. We have no children, except me.

Attrib.

11 Thank you, sister. May you be the mother of a bishop!

Said to a nun nursing him on his deathbed. Attrib.

BEHN, APHRA

(1640–89) English novelist and dramatist. Her writings include the novel *Oroonoko* (1688) and the play *The Rover* (1677–81).

Quotations about Behn

1 Mrs Behn is still be to be found here and there in the dusty worm eaten libraries of old country houses, but as a rule we imagine she has been ejected from all *decent* society for more than a generation or two.

Anonymous *Saturday Review*, 'Literary Garbage', 27 Jan 1862

2 She was involved in an insurrection of slaves, thus going one better than Harriet Beecher Stowe, who merely preached abolitionism.

Anthony Burgess (John Burgess Wilson; 1917–93) British novelist. *The Observer*, 30 Dec 1980

3 Mrs Behn was the first woman in history to earn her living as an author and her remains were appropriately entombed in the cloisters of Westminster Abbey.

Frank Muir (1920–) British writer and broadcaster. *The Frank Muir Book*

Quotations by Behn

4 Since Man with that inconstancy was born,
To love the absent, and the present scorn,
Why do we deck, why do we dress
For a short-liv'd happiness?

Poems on Several Occasions, 'To Alexis'

5 Who is't that to women's beauty would submit,
And yet refuse the fetters of their wit?

The Forced Marriage, Prologue

6 The Devil's in her tongue, and so 'tis in most women's of her age; for when it has quitted the tail, it repairs to the upper tier.

The Town Fop

7 Love ceases to be a pleasure, when it ceases to be a secret.

The Lover's Watch, 'Four o'clock'

8 Faith, Sir, we are here to-day, and gone tomorrow.

The Lucky Chance, IV

BELIEF

See also faith, religion

1 Believe nothing of what you hear, and only half of what you see.

Proverb

2 Seeing is believing.

Proverb

3 A cause is like champagne and high heels – one must be prepared to suffer for it.

Arnold Bennett (1867–1931) British novelist. *The Title*

4 Vain are the thousand creeds
That move men's hearts: unutterably vain;
Worthless as wither'd weeds.

Emily Brontë (1818–48) British novelist. *Last Lines*

5 If Jesus Christ were to come to-day, people would not even crucify him. They would ask him to dinner, and hear what he had to say, and make fun of it.

Thomas Carlyle (1795–1881) Scottish historian and essayist. *Carlyle at his Zenith* (D. A. Wilson)

6 *Action will furnish belief*, – but will that belief be the true one?
This is the point, you know.

Arthur Hugh Clough (1819–61) British poet. *Amours de voyage*, V

7 I believe firmly what I read in the holy Scriptures, and the Creed, called the Apostles', and I don't trouble my head any farther: I leave the rest to be disputed and defined by the clergy, if they please; and if any Thing is in common use with Christians that is not repugnant to the holy Scriptures, I observe it for this Reason, that I may not offend other people.

Erasmus (c. 1467–1536) Dutch humanist. Commenting on the teachings of John Colet, the English theologian (?1467–1519). *The Colloquies of Erasmus*, Vol. I

8 The true believer is in a high degree protected against the danger of certain neurotic afflictions; by accepting the universal neurosis he is spared the task of forming a personal neurosis.

Sigmund Freud (1856–1939) Austrian psychoanalyst. *The Future of an Illusion*, Ch. 8

9 There seems to be a terrible misunderstanding on the part of a great many people to the effect that when you cease to believe you may cease to behave.

Louis Kronenberger (1904–80) US writer and literary critic. *Company Manners*

10 Believe it or not.

R. L. Ripley (1893–1949) US writer. Title of newspaper column

11 I believe because it is impossible.

Tertullian (c. 160–225 AD) Carthaginian father of the church. The usual misquotation of 'It is certain because it is impossible.' *De Carne Christi*, V

12 All right, have it your way – you heard a seal bark.

James Thurber (1894–1961) US humorist. Cartoon caption, 'The Seal in the Bedroom'

13 If there were a verb meaning 'to believe falsely', it would not have any significant first person, present indicative.

Ludwig Wittgenstein (1889–1951) Austrian philosopher. *A Certain World* (W. H. Auden)

BELLOC, HILAIRE

(1870–1953) French-born British poet, essayist, and historian; Liberal MP for Salford (1906–10). Publications include *Cautionary Tales* (1907) and biographies of major historical figures. He was an ardent Roman Catholic.

Quotations about Belloc

1 He cannot bear isolation or final ethical responsibility; he clings to the Roman Catholic Church; he clung to his French nationality because one nation was not enough for him.

George Bernard Shaw (1856–1950) Irish dramatist and critic. *Lives of the Wits* (H. Pearson)

2 He is conscious of being decrepit and forgetful, but not of being a bore.

Evelyn Waugh (1903–66) British novelist. Diary, 1 May 1945

Quotations by Belloc

3 Child! do not throw this book about;
Refrain from the unholy pleasure
Of cutting all the pictures out!
Preserve it as your chiefest treasure.

The Bad Child's Book of Beasts, 'Dedication'

4 And always keep a hold of Nurse
For fear of finding something worse.

Bad Child's Book of Beasts, 'Jim'

5 I shoot the Hippopotamus
With bullets made of platinum,
Because if I use leaden ones
His hide is sure to flatten 'em.

Bad Child's Book of Beasts, 'The Hippopotamus'

6 Matilda told such dreadful lies,
It made one gasp and stretch one's eyes.

Bad Child's Book of Beasts, 'Matilda'

7 I am a sundial, and I make a botch
Of what is done far better by a watch.

Bad Child's Book of Beasts, 'On a Sundial'

8 Alas! That such affected tricks
Should flourish in a child of six!

Cautionary Tales, 'Godolphin Horne'

9 The Chief Defect of Henry King
Was chewing little bits of String.

Cautionary Tales, 'Henry King'

10 'Oh, my Friends, be warned by me,
That Breakfast, Dinner, Lunch and Tea
Are all the Human Frame requires…'
With that the Wretched Child expires.

Cautionary Tales, 'Henry King'

11 A trick that everyone abhors
In little girls is slamming doors.

Cautionary Tales, 'Rebecca'

12 They died to save their country and they only saved the world.

The English Graves

13 The accursed power which stands on Privilege
(And goes with Women, and Champagne, and Bridge)
Broke – and Democracy resumed her reign:
(Which goes with Bridge, and Women and Champagne).

Epigrams, 'On a Great Election'

14 When I am dead, I hope it may be said:
'His sins were scarlet, but his books were read.'
Epigrams, 'On His Books'

15 I'm tired of Love: I'm still more tired of Rhyme.
But Money gives me pleasure all the Time.
'Fatigued'

16 Whatever happens, we have got
The Maxim Gun, and they have not.
Referring to African natives. *The Modern Traveller*

17 The Microbe is so very small
You cannot make him out at all.
More Beasts for Worse Children, 'The Microbe'

18 Like many of the upper class
He liked the sound of broken glass.
New Cautionary Tales, 'About John'

19 The fleas that tease in the high Pyrenees.
Tarantella

20 I always like to associate with a lot of priests because it makes me understand anti-clerical things so well.
Letter to E. S. P. Haynes, 9 Nov 1909

21 I am a Catholic. As far as possible I go to Mass every day. As far as possible I kneel down and tell these beads every day. If you reject me on account of my religion, I shall thank God that he has spared me the indignity of being your representative.
Said in his first election campaign. Speech, Salford, 1906

22 Candidates should not attempt more than six of these.
Suggested addition to the Ten Commandments. Attrib.

BENNETT, ALAN

(1934–) British playwright and actor in comic reviews, such as *Beyond the Fringe* (1960). His plays include *Forty Years On* (1968), *An Englishman Abroad* (1982), *Single Spies* (1988), and *The Madness of George III* (1991).

1 Life is rather like a tin of sardines – we're all of us looking for the key.
Beyond the Fringe

2 I have never understood this liking for war. It panders to instincts already catered for within the scope of any respectable domestic establishment.
Forty Years On, I

3 It's the one species I wouldn't mind seeing vanish from the face of the earth. I wish they were like the White Rhino – six of them left in the Serengeti National Park, and all males.
Referring to dogs. *Getting On*, I

4 Your whole life is on the other side of the glass. And there is nobody watching.
The Old Country, I

5 We were put to Dickens as children but it never quite took. That unremitting humanity soon had me cheesed off.
The Old Country, II

6 I'm not good at precise, coherent argument. But plays are suited to incoherent argument, put into the mouths of fallible people.
The Sunday Times, 24 Nov 1991

BENNETT, ARNOLD

(1867–1931) British novelist. His novels, set in his native Staffordshire, include *Anna of the Five Towns* (1902) and *Clayhanger* (1910).

Quotations about Bennett

1 Bennett – a sort of pig in clover.
D. H. Lawrence (1885–1930) British novelist. Letter to Aldous Huxley, 27 Mar 1928

2 I remember that once, beating his knee with his clenched fist to force the words through his writhing lips, he said, 'I am a nice man.' He was.
W. Somerset Maugham (1874–1965) British novelist. *The Vagrant Mood*

Quotations by Bennett

3 'Ye can call it influenza if ye like,' said Mrs Machin. 'There was no influenza in my young days. We called a cold a cold.'
The Card, Ch. 8

4 The people who live in the past must yield to the people who live in the future. Otherwise the world would begin to turn the other way round.
Milestones

5 Pessimism, when you get used to it, is just as agreeable as optimism.
Things that have Interested Me, 'The Slump in Pessimism'

6 Well, my deliberate opinion is – it's a jolly strange world.
The Title, I

7 Being a husband is a whole-time job. That is why so many husbands fail. They cannot give their entire attention to it.
The Title, I

8 Journalists say a thing that they know isn't true, in the hope that if they keep on saying it long enough it will be true.
The Title, II

9 Good taste is better than bad taste, but bad taste is better than no taste.
The Observer, 'Sayings of the Week', 24 Aug 1930

BEQUESTS

1 When you have told anyone you have left him a legacy the only decent thing to do is to die at once.
Samuel Butler (1835–1902) British writer. *Samuel Butler: A Memoir* (Festing Jones), Vol. 2

2 The man who leaves money to charity in his will is only giving away what no longer belongs to him.
Voltaire (François-Marie Arouet; 1694–1778) French writer. Letter, 1769

BETJEMAN, SIR JOHN

(1906–84) British poet; poet laureate (1972–84). Publications include *Collected Poems* (1958), *High and*

Low (1976), and a verse autobiography, *Summoned by Bells* (1960).

Quotations about Betjeman

1 By appointment: Teddy Bear to the Nation.
Alan Bell *The Times*, 20 Sept 1982

2 You've no idea how original it was to write like Tennyson in the 1930s, rather than Eliot or Auden.
Lord David Cecil (1902–86) British writer and critic. Remark

3 We invite people like that to tea, but we don't marry them.
Lady Chetwode. Lady Chetwode later became Betjeman's mother-in-law. Remark

Quotations by Betjeman

4 Spirits of well-shot woodcock, partridge, snipe
Flutter and bear him up the Norfolk sky.
Death of King George V

5 You ask me what it is I do. Well actually, you know,
I'm partly a liaison man and partly P.R.O.
Essentially I integrate the current export drive
And basically I'm viable from ten o'clock till five.
Executive

6 Phone for the fish knives Norman,
As Cook is a little unnerved;
You kiddies have crumpled the serviettes
And I must have things daintily served.
How to get on in Society

7 I know what I wanted to ask you;
Is trifle sufficient for sweet?
How to get on in Society

8 Oh wasn't it naughty of Smudges?
Oh, Mummy, I'm sick with disgust.
She threw me in front of the judges
And my silly old collarbone's bust.
Hunter Trials

9 Rumbling under blackened girders, Midland, bound for Cricklewood,
Puffed its sulphur to the sunset where the Land of Laundries stood.
Rumble under, thunder over, train and tram alternate go.
Parliament Hill Fields

10 I have a vision of the future, chum.
The workers' flats in fields of soya beans
Tower up like silver pencils.
The Planster's Vision

11 Come, friendly bombs, and fall on Slough
It isn't fit for humans now.
There isn't grass to graze a cow
Swarm over, Death!
...
Come, friendly bombs, and fall on Slough
To get it ready for the plough.
The cabbages are coming now:
The earth exhales.
Slough

12 Miss J. Hunter Dunn, Miss J. Hunter Dunn,
Furnish'd and burnish'd by Aldershot sun.
A Subaltern's Love Song

BETRAYAL

See also treason

1 And he answered and said, He that dippeth his hand with me in the dish, the same shall betray me.
The Son of man goeth as it is written of him: but woe unto that man by whom the Son of man is betrayed! it had been good for that man if he had not been born.
Then Judas, which betrayed him, answered and said, Master, is it I? He said unto him, Thou hast said.
Bible: Matthew 26:23–25

2 Jesus said unto him, Verily I say unto thee, That this night, before the cock crow, thou shalt deny me thrice.
Peter said unto him, Though I should die with thee, yet will I not deny thee. Likewise also said all the disciples.
Bible: Matthew 26:34–35

3 And forthwith he came to Jesus, and said, Hail, master; and kissed him.
And Jesus said unto him, Friend, wherefore art thou come? Then came they, and laid hands on Jesus, and took him.
Bible: Matthew 26:49–50

4 Then Judas, which had betrayed him, when he saw that he was condemned, repented himself, and brought again the thirty pieces of silver to the chief priests and elders,
Saying, I have sinned in that I have betrayed the innocent blood. And they said, What is that to us? see thou to that.
Bible: Matthew 27:3–4

5 Just for a handful of silver he left us,
Just for a riband to stick in his coat.
Robert Browning (1812–89) British poet. *The Lost Leader*

6 It is all right to rat, but you can't re-rat.
Winston Churchill (1874–1965) British statesman. Attrib.

7 I hate the idea of causes, and if I had to choose between betraying my country and betraying my friend, I hope I should have the guts to betray my country.
E. M. Forster (1879–1970) British novelist. *Two Cheers for Democracy*, 'What I Believe'.

8 I'm waiting for the cock to crow.
William Morris Hughes (1864–1952) Australian statesman. Said in parliament, after being viciously critized by a member of his own party. *The Fine Art of Political Wit* (L. Harris)

9 He...felt towards those whom he had deserted that peculiar malignity which has, in all ages, been characteristic of apostates.
Lord Macaulay (1800–59) British historian. *History of England*, Vol. I, Ch. 1

10 I owe you everything, Sire, but I believe I can pay some of my debt with this gift – Colbert.
Cardinal Mazarin (1602–61) Italian-born French statesman. Remark to Louis XIV, shortly before Mazarin's death; referring to Jean-Baptiste Colbert.

11 I let down my friends, I let down my country. I let down our system of government.
Richard Milhous Nixon (1913–94 US president. *The Observer*, 'Sayings of the Week', 8 May 1977

12 *Et tu, Brute?*
You too, Brutus?

William Shakespeare (1564–1616) English dramatist. Said by Julius Caesar. *Julius Caesar*, III:1

13 That pig of a Henry VIII committed such sacrilege by profaning so many ecclesiastical benefices in order to give their goods to those who being so rewarded might stand firmly for the King in the Lower House; and now the King's greatest enemies are those who are enriched by these benefices.

Francis Windebank (1582–1646) English politician. Remark to the Papal envoy, Apr 1635

BEVAN, ANEURIN

(1897–1960) British Labour politician and editor of the left-wing *Tribune* (1940–45). As minister of health (1945–51) he introduced the National Health Service.

1 Its relationship to democratic institutions is that of the death watch beetle – it is not a Party, it is a conspiracy.

Referring to the Communist Party. *Tribune*

2 The language of priorities is the religion of Socialism.

Speech, Labour Party Conference, Blackpool, 8 June 1941

3 He is a man suffering from petrified adolescence.

Referring to Winston Churchill. *Aneurin Bevan* (Vincent Brome), Ch. 11

4 I know that the right kind of political leader for the Labour Party is a desiccated calculating machine.

Usually regarded as a gibe at Hugh Gaitskell. Speech during Labour Party Conference, 29 Sept 1954

5 We know what happens to people who stay in the middle of the road. They get run over.

The Observer, 6 Dec 1953

6 I read the newspapers avidly. It is my one form of continuous fiction.

The Times, 29 Mar 1960

7 This island is almost made of coal and surrounded by fish. Only an organizing genius could produce a shortage of coal and fish in Great Britain at the same time.

Speech, Blackpool, 18 May 1945

8 No amount of cajolery, and no attempts at ethical or social seduction, can eradicate from my heart a deep burning hatred for the Tory Party...So far as I am concerned they are lower than vermin.

Speech, Manchester, 4 July 1948

9 There is no reason to attack the monkey when the organ-grinder is present.

The 'monkey' was Selwyn Lloyd; the 'organ-grinder' was Harold Macmillan. Speech, House of Commons

10 If you carry this resolution and follow out all its implications and do not run away from it, you will send a Foreign Secretary, whoever he may be, naked into the conference chamber.

Referring to unilateral disarmament. Speech, Labour Party Conference, 2 Oct 1957

11 Fascism is not itself a new order of society. It is the future refusing to be born.

Attrib.

12 I stuffed their mouths with gold!

Explaining how he persuaded doctors not to oppose the introduction of the National Health Service. Attrib.

BIBLE

Quotations are taken from the Authorized Version (1611) of the Bible unless otherwise stated. The Books of the Bible are arranged in a single alphabetical order (not all books are represented). *See also* Book of Common Prayer, Psalms.

Acts

1 And when he had spoken these things, while they beheld, he was taken up; and a cloud received him out of their sight.

1:9

2 And when the day of Pentecost was fully come, they were all with one accord in one place.
And suddenly there came a sound from heaven as of a rushing mighty wind, and it filled all the house where they were sitting.
And there appeared unto them cloven tongues like as of fire, and it sat upon each of them.
And they were all filled with the Holy Ghost, and began to speak with other tongues, as the Spirit gave them utterance.

2:1–4

3 Others mocking said, These men are full of new wine.

2:13

4 Then Peter said, Silver and gold have I none; but such as I have give I thee: In the name of Jesus Christ of Nazareth rise up and walk.

3:6

5 When they heard these things, they were cut to the heart, and they gnashed on him with their teeth.

7:54

6 And as he journeyed, he came near Damascus: and suddenly there shined round about him a light from heaven:
And he fell to the earth, and heard a voice saying unto him, Saul, Saul, why persecutest thou me?
And he said, Who art thou, Lord? And the Lord said, I am Jesus whom thou persecutest: it is hard for thee to kick against the pricks.

9:3–5

7 And the Lord said unto him, Arise, and go into the street which is called Straight, and enquire in the house of Judas for one called Saul, of Tarsus: for, behold, he prayeth.

9:11

8 But the Lord said unto him, Go thy way: for he is a chosen vessel unto me, to bear my name before the Gentiles, and kings, and the children of Israel.

9:15

9 But Peter took him up, saying, Stand up; I myself also am a man.

10:26

10 Then Peter opened his mouth, and said, Of a truth I perceive that God is no respecter of persons.
10:34

11 And the people gave a shout, saying, It is the voice of a god, and not of a man.
And immediately the angel of the Lord smote him, because he gave not God the glory: and he was eaten of worms, and gave up the ghost.
12:22–23

12 God that made the world and all things therein, seeing that he is Lord of heaven and earth, dwelleth not in temples made with hands.
17:24

13 For in him we live, and move, and have our being; as certain also of your own poets have said, For we are also his offspring.
17:28

14 And now, behold, I go bound in the spirit unto Jerusalem, not knowing the things that shall befall me there.
20:22

15 And the chief captain answered, With a great sum obtained I this freedom. And Paul said, But I was free born.
22:28

16 Then said Paul unto him, God shall smite thee, thou whited wall: for sittest thou to judge me after the law, and commandest me to be smitten contrary to the law?
23:3

17 Then Festus, when he had conferred with the council, answered, Hast thou appealed unto Caesar? Unto Caesar shalt thou go.
25:12

Amos

18 Seek him that maketh the seven stars and Orion, and turneth the shadow of death into the morning, and maketh the day dark with night: that calleth for the waters of the sea, and poureth them out upon the face of the earth: The Lord is his name.
5:8

Colossians

19 Beware lest any man spoil you through philosophy and vain deceit, after the tradition of men, after the rudiments of the world, and not after Christ.
2:8

20 Where there is neither Greek nor Jew, circumcision nor uncircumcision, Barbarian, Scythian, bond nor free; but Christ is all, and in all.
3:11

21 Husbands, love your wives, and be not bitter against them.
3:19

22 Fathers, provoke not your children to anger, lest they be discouraged.
3:21

23 Let your speech be alway with grace, seasoned with salt, that ye may know how ye ought to answer every man.
4:6

I Corinthians

24 For after that in the wisdom of God the world by wisdom knew not God, it pleased God by the foolishness of preaching to save them that believe.
For the Jews require a sign, and the Greeks seek after wisdom:
But we preach Christ crucified, unto the Jews a stumblingblock, and unto the Greeks foolishness.
1:21–23

25 But as it is written, Eye hath not seen, nor ear heard, neither have entered into the heart of man, the things which God hath prepared for them that love him.
2:9

26 For the kingdom of God is not in word, but in power.
4:20

27 Meats for the belly, and the belly for meats: but God shall destroy both it and them. Now the body is not for fornication, but for the Lord; and the Lord for the body.
6:13

28 What? know ye not that your body is the temple of the Holy Ghost which is in you, which ye have of God, and ye are not your own?
6:19

29 Let the husband render unto the wife due benevolence: and likewise also the wife unto the husband.
7:3

30 But if they cannot contain, let them marry: for it is better to marry than to burn.
7:9

31 But he that is married careth for the things that are of the world, how he may please his wife.
7:33

32 Now as touching things offered unto idols, we know that we all have knowledge. Knowledge puffeth up, but charity edifieth.
8:1

33 Know ye not that they which run in a race run all, but one receiveth the prize? So run, that ye may obtain.
And every man that striveth for the mastery is temperate in all things. Now they do it to obtain a corruptible crown; but we an incorruptible.
9:24–25

34 All things are lawful for me, but all things are not expedient: all things are lawful for me, but all things edify not.
10:23

35 For the earth is the Lord's, and the fulness thereof.
10:26

36 Conscience, I say, not thine own, but of the

other: for why is my liberty judged of another man's conscience?
10:29

37 But if a woman have long hair, it is a glory to her: for her hair is given her for a covering.
11:15

38 Though I speak with the tongues of men and of angels, and have not charity, I am become as sounding brass, or a tinkling cymbal.
And though I have the gift of prophecy, and understand all mysteries, and all knowledge; and though I have all faith, so that I could remove mountains, and have not charity, I am nothing.
And though I bestow all my goods to feed the poor, and though I give my body to be burned, and have not charity, it profiteth me nothing.
Charity suffereth long, and is kind; charity envieth not; charity vaunteth not itself, is not puffed up,
Doth not behave itself unseemly, seeketh not her own, is not easily provoked, thinketh no evil;
Rejoiceth not in iniquity, but rejoiceth in the truth;
Beareth all things, believeth all things, hopeth all things, endureth all things.
Charity never faileth: but whether there be prophecies, they shall fail; whether there be tongues, they shall cease; whether there be knowledge, it shall vanish away.
For we know in part, and we prophesy in part.
But when that which is perfect is come, then that which is in part shall be done away.
When I was a child, I spake as a child, I understood as a child, I thought as a child: but when I became a man, I put away childish things.
For now we see through a glass, darkly; but then face to face: now I know in part; but then shall I know even as also I am known.
And now abideth faith, hope, charity, these three; but the greatest of these is charity.
13:1–13

39 Let all things be done decently and in order.
14:40

40 If after the manner of men I have fought with beasts at Ephesus, what advantageth it me, if the dead rise not? let us eat and drink; for tomorrow we die.
Be not deceived: evil communications corrupt good manners.
15:32–33

41 There is one glory of the sun, and another glory of the moon, and another glory of the stars: for one star differeth from another star in glory.
So also is the resurrection of the dead. It is sown in corruption; it is raised in incorruption.
15:41–42

42 Behold, I shew you a mystery; We shall not all sleep, but we shall all be changed,
In a moment, in the twinkling of an eye, at the last trump: for the trumpet shall sound, and the dead shall be raised incorruptible, and we shall be changed.
For this corruptible must put on incorruption, and this mortal must put on immortality.
So when this corruptible shall have put on incorruption, and this mortal shall have put on immortality, then shall be brought to pass the saying that is written, Death is swallowed up in victory.
O death, where is thy sting? O grave, where is thy victory?
15:51–55

43 If any man love not the Lord Jesus Christ, let him be Anathema Maranatha.
The grace of our Lord Jesus Christ be with you.
16:22–23

II Corinthians

44 For we walk by faith, not by sight.
5:7

45 Every man according as he purposeth in his heart, so let him give; not grudgingly, or of necessity: for God loveth a cheerful giver.
9:7

46 For ye suffer fools gladly, seeing ye yourselves are wise.
11:19

47 And lest I should be exalted above measure through the abundance of the revelations, there was given to me a thorn in the flesh, the messenger of Satan to buffet me, lest I should be exalted above measure.
12:7

Daniel

48 That at what time ye hear the sound of the cornet, flute, harp, sackbut, psaltery, dulcimer, and all kinds of musick, ye fall down and worship the golden image that Nebuchadnezzar the king hath set up:
And whoso falleth not down and worshippeth shall the same hour be cast into the midst of a burning fiery furnace.
3:5–6

49 Then was Nebuchadnezzar full of fury, and the form of his visage was changed against Shadrach, Meshach, and Abed-nego: therefore he spake, and commanded that they should heat the furnace one seven times more than it was wont to be heated.
3:19

50 The same hour was the thing fulfilled upon Nebuchadnezzar: and he was driven from men, and did eat grass as oxen, and his body was wet with the dew of heaven, till his hairs were grown like eagles' feathers, and his nails like birds' claws.
4:33

51 In the same hour came forth fingers of a man's hand, and wrote over against the candlestick upon the plaister of the wall of the king's palace: and the king saw the part of the hand that wrote.
5:5

52 And this is the writing that was written, MENE, MENE, TEKEL, UPHARSIN.
This is the interpretation of the thing: MENE; God hath numbered thy kingdom, and finished it.
TEKEL; Thou art weighed in the balances, and art found wanting.
PERES; Thy kingdom is divided, and given to the Medes and Persians.
5:25–28

53 Then the king commanded, and they brought

Daniel, and cast him into the den of lions. Now the king spake and said unto Daniel, Thy God whom thou servest continually, he will deliver thee.
6:16

Deuteronomy

54 For the Lord thy God bringeth thee into a good land, a land of brooks of water, of fountains and depths that spring out of valleys and hills;
A land of wheat, and barley, and vines, and fig trees, and pomegranates; a land of oil olive, and honey;
A land wherein thou shalt eat bread without scarceness, thou shalt not lack any thing in it; a land whose stones are iron, and out of whose hills thou mayest dig brass.
When thou hast eaten and art full, then thou shalt bless the Lord thy God for the good land which he hath given thee.
8:7–10

55 Take heed to yourselves, that your heart be not deceived, and ye turn aside, and serve other gods, and worship them.
11:16

56 Thou shalt not hearken unto the words of that prophet, or that dreamer of dreams.
13:3

57 I call heaven and earth to record this day against you, that I have set before you life and death, blessing and cursing: therefore choose life, that both thou and thy seed may live.
30:19

58 Be strong and of a good courage, fear not, nor be afraid of them: for the Lord thy God, he it is that doth go with thee; he will not fail thee, nor forsake thee.
31:6

59 He found him in a desert land, and in the waste howling wilderness; he led him about, he instructed him, he kept him as the apple of his eye.
32:10

60 And there arose not a prophet since in Israel like unto Moses, whom the Lord knew face to face.
34:10

Ecclesiastes

61 Vanity of vanities, saith the Preacher, vanity of vanities; all is vanity.
What profit hath a man of all his labour which he taketh under the sun?
One generation passeth away, and another generation cometh: but the earth abideth for ever.
1:2–4

62 All the rivers run into the sea; yet the sea is not full; unto the place from whence the rivers come, thither they return again.
All things are full of labour; man cannot utter it: the eye is not satisfied with seeing, nor the ear filled with hearing.
The thing that hath been, it is that which shall be; and that which is done is that which shall be done: and there is no new thing under the sun.
1:7–9

63 There is no remembrance of former things; neither shall there be any remembrance of things that are to come with those that shall come after.
1:11

64 And I gave my heart to seek and search out by wisdom concerning all things that are done under heaven: this sore travail hath God given to the sons of man to be exercised therewith.
I have seen all the works that are done under the sun; and, behold, all is vanity and vexation of spirit.
1:13–14

65 For in much wisdom is much grief: and he that increaseth knowledge increaseth sorrow.
1:18

66 The wise man's eyes are in his head; but the fool walketh in darkness: and I myself perceived also that one event happeneth to them all.
2:14

67 To every thing there is a season, and a time to every purpose under the heaven:
A time to be born, and a time to die; a time to plant, and a time to pluck up that which is planted;
A time to kill, and a time to heal; a time to break down, and a time to build up;
A time to weep, and a time to laugh; a time to mourn, and a time to dance;
A time to cast away stones, and a time to gather stones together; a time to embrace, and a time to refrain from embracing;
A time to get, and a time to lose; a time to keep, and a time to cast away;
A time to rend, and a time to sew; a time to keep silence, and a time to speak;
A time to love, and a time to hate; a time of war, and a time of peace.
3:1–8

68 Wherefore I praised the dead which are already dead more than the living which are yet alive.
Yea, better is he than both they, which hath not yet been, who hath not seen the evil work that is done under the sun.
4:2–3

69 Two are better than one; because they have a good reward for their labour.
For if they fall, the one will lift up his fellow: but woe to him that is alone when he falleth; for he hath not another to help him up.
4:9–10

70 And if one prevail against him, two shall withstand him; and a threefold cord is not quickly broken.
4:12

71 Better is a poor and a wise child than an old and foolish king, who will no more be admonished.
4:13

72 Then I commended mirth, because a man hath no better thing under the sun, than to eat, and to drink, and to be merry: for that shall abide with him of his labour the days of his life, which God giveth him under the sun.
8:15

73 Whatsoever thy hand findeth to do, do it with thy might; for there is no work, nor device, nor

knowledge, nor wisdom, in the grave, whither thou goest.
9:10

74 I returned, and saw under the sun, that the race is not to the swift, nor the battle to the strong, neither yet bread to the wise, nor yet riches to men of understanding, nor yet favour to men of skill; but time and chance happeneth to them all.
9:11

75 The words of wise men are heard in quiet more than the cry of him that ruleth among fools.
9:17

76 A feast is made for laughter, and wine maketh merry: but money answereth all things.
10:19

77 Cast thy bread upon the waters: for thou shalt find it after many days.
11:1

78 And further, by these, my son, be admonished: of making many books there is no end; and much study is a weariness of the flesh.
12:12

79 Let us hear the conclusion of the whole matter: Fear God, and keep his commandments: for this is the whole duty of man.
12:13

Ecclesiasticus

80 My son, if thou come to serve the Lord, prepare thy soul for temptation.
2:1

81 Be not curious in unnecessary matters: for more things are shewed unto thee than men understand.
3:23

82 Miss not the discourse of the elders: for they also learned of their fathers, and of them thou shalt learn understanding, and to give answer as need requireth.
8:9

83 Forsake not an old friend; for the new is not comparable to him: a new friend is as new wine; when it is old, thou shalt drink it with pleasure.
9:10

84 The physician cutteth off a long disease; and he that is today a king tomorrow shall die.
10:10

85 Desire not a multitude of unprofitable children, neither delight in ungodly sons.
16:1

86 Be not made a beggar by banqueting upon borrowing, when thou hast nothing in thy purse: for thou shalt lie in wait for thine own life, and be talked on.
18:33

87 If thou hast gathered nothing in thy youth, how canst thou find any thing in thine age?
25:3

88 Leave off first for manners' sake: and be not unsatiable, lest thou offend.
31:17

89 Let thy speech be short, comprehending much in few words; be as one that knoweth and yet holdeth his tongue.
32:8

90 The wisdom of a learned man cometh by opportunity of leisure: and he that hath little business shall become wise.
How can he get wisdom that holdeth the plough, and that glorieth in the goad, that driveth oxen, and is occupied in their labours, and whose talk is of bullocks?
38:24–25

91 Let us now praise famous men, and our fathers that begat us.
44:1

92 And some there be, which have no memorial; who are perished, as though they had never been; and are become as though they had never been born; and their children after them.
44:9

93 Their bodies are buried in peace; but their name liveth for evermore.
44:14

Ephesians

94 Wherefore putting away lying, speak every man truth with his neighbour: for we are members one of another.
Be ye angry, and sin not: let not the sun go down upon your wrath:
Neither give place to the devil.
Let him that stole steal no more: but rather let him labour, working with his hands the thing which is good, that he may have to give to him that needeth.
4:25–28

95 Children, obey your parents in the Lord: for this is right.
6:1

96 Finally, my brethren, be strong in the Lord, and in the power of his might.
Put on the whole armour of God, that ye may be able to stand against the wiles of the devil.
For we wrestle not against flesh and blood, but against principalities, against powers, against the rulers of the darkness of his world, against spiritual wickedness in high places.
6:10–12

II Esdras

97 Then had I pity upon your mournings, and gave you manna to eat; so ye did eat angels' bread.
1:19

98 Then were the entrances of this world made narrow, full of sorrow and travail: they are but few and evil, full of perils, and very painful.
For the entrances of the elder world were wide and sure, and brought immortal fruit.
7:12–13

99 For the world hath lost his youth, and the times begin to wax old.
14:10

100 And come hither, and I shall light a candle of understanding in thine heart, which shall not be put out, till the things be performed which thou shalt begin to write.
14:25

Esther

101 And the king loved Esther above all the women, and she obtained grace and favour in his sight more than all the virgins; so that he set the royal crown upon her head, and made her queen instead of Vashti.
2:17

Exodus

102 Now there arose up a new king over Egypt, which knew not Joseph.
1:8

103 And when she could not longer hide him, she took for him an ark of bulrushes, and daubed it with slime and with pitch, and put the child therein; and she laid it in the flags by the river's brink.
2:3

104 He called his name Gershom: for he said, I have been a stranger in a strange land.
2:22

105 And the angel of the Lord appeared unto him in a flame of fire out of the midst of a bush: and he looked, and, behold, the bush burned with fire, and the bush was not consumed.
3:2

106 And I am come down to deliver them out of the hand of the Egyptians, and to bring them up out of that land unto a good land and a large, unto a land flowing with milk and honey; unto the place of the Canaanites, and the Hittites, and the Amorites, and the Perizzites, and the Hivites, and the Jebusites.
3:8

107 And God said unto Moses, I AM THAT I AM: and he said, Thus shalt thou say unto the children of Israel, I AM hath sent me unto you.
3:14

108 For they cast down every man his rod, and they became serpents: but Aaron's rod swallowed up their rods.
7:12

109 Your lamb shall be without blemish, a male of the first year: ye shall take it out from the sheep, or from the goats.
12:5

110 And thus shall ye eat it; with your loins girded, your shoes on your feet, and your staff in your hand; and ye shall eat it in haste: it is the Lord's passover.
For I will pass through the land of Egypt this night, and will smite all the firstborn in the land of Egypt, both man and beast; and against all the gods of Egypt I will execute judgment: I am the Lord.
12:11–12

111 And the Lord went before them by day in a pillar of a cloud, to lead them the way; and by night in a pillar of fire, to give them light; to go by day and night.
13:21

112 And the children of Israel went into the midst of the sea upon the dry ground: and the waters were a wall unto them on their right hand, and on their left.
14:22

113 The Lord is a man of war: the Lord is his name.
15:3

114 And mount Sinai was altogether on a smoke, because the Lord descended upon it in fire: and the smoke thereof ascended as the smoke of a furnace, and the whole mount quaked greatly.
19:18

115 I am the Lord thy God, which have brought thee out of the land of Egypt, out of the house of bondage.
Thou shalt have no other gods before me.
Thou shalt not make unto thee any graven image, or any likeness of any thing that is in heaven above, or that is in the earth beneath, or that is in the water under the earth:
Thou shalt not bow down thyself to them, nor serve them: for Lord thy God am a jealous God, visiting the iniquity of the fathers upon the children unto the third and fourth generation of them that hate me;
And shewing mercy unto thousands of them that love me, and keep my commandments.
Thou shalt not take the name of the Lord thy God in vain; for the Lord will not hold him guiltless that taketh his name in vain.
Remember the sabbath day, to keep it holy.
Six days shalt thou labour, and do all thy work:
But the seventh day is the sabbath of the Lord thy God: in it thou shalt not do any work, thou, nor thy son, nor thy daughter, thy manservant, nor thy maidservant, nor thy cattle, nor thy stranger that is within thy gates:
For in six days the Lord made heaven and earth, the sea, and all that in them is, and rested the seventh day: wherefore the Lord blessed the sabbath day, and hallowed it.
Honour thy father and thy mother: that thy days may be long upon the land which the Lord thy God giveth thee.
Thou shalt not kill.
Thou shalt not commit adultery.
Thou shalt not steal.
Thou shalt not bear false witness against thy neighbour.
Thou shalt not covet thy neighbour's house, thou shalt not covet thy neighbour's wife, nor his manservant, nor his maidservant, nor his ox, nor his ass, nor any thing that is thy neighbour's.
20:2–17

116 And if any mischief follow, then thou shalt give life for life,
Eye for eye, tooth for tooth, hand for hand, foot for foot,

Burning for burning, wound for wound, stripe for stripe.
21:23–25

117 Thou shalt not suffer a witch to live.
22:18

118 The first of the firstfruits of thy land thou shalt bring into the house of the Lord thy God. Thou shalt not seethe a kid in his mother's milk.
23:19

119 And the Lord said unto Moses, Come up to me into the mount, and be there: and I will give thee tables of stone, and a law, and commandments which I have written; that thou mayest teach them.
24:12

120 And he received them at their hand, and fashioned it with a graving tool, after he had made it a molten calf: and they said, These be thy gods, O Israel, which brought thee up out of the land of Egypt.
32:4

121 And he said, Thou canst not see my face: for there shall no man see me, and live.
33:20

122 And it shall come to pass, while my glory passeth by, that I will put thee in a clift of the rock, and will cover thee with my hand while I pass by.
33:22

Ezekiel

123 And thou, son of man, be not afraid of them, neither be afraid of their words, though briers and thorns be with thee, and thou dost dwell among scorpions: be not afraid of their words, nor be dismayed at their looks, though they be a rebellious house.
2:6

124 Son of man, thou dwellest in the midst of a rebellious house, which have eyes to see, and see not; they have ears to hear, and hear not: for they are a rebellious house.
12:2

125 Behold, every one that useth proverbs shall use this proverb against thee, saying, As is the mother, so is her daughter.
16:44–45

126 What mean ye, that ye use this proverb concerning the land of Israel, saying, The fathers have eaten sour grapes, and the children's teeth are set on edge?
18:2

127 Again, when the wicked man turneth away from his wickedness that he hath committed, and doeth that which is lawful and right, he shall save his soul alive.
18:27

128 And he said unto me, Son of man, can these bones live? And I answered, O Lord God, thou knowest.
Again he said unto me, Prophesy upon these bones, and say unto them, O ye dry bones, hear the word of the Lord.
37:3–4

129 So I prophesied as I was commanded: and as I prophesied, there was a noise, and behold a shaking, and the bones came together, bone to his bone.
37:7

Ezra

130 The people could not discern the noise of the shout of joy from the noise of the weeping of the people: for the people shouted with a loud shout, and the noise was heard afar off.
3:13

Galatians

131 O foolish Galatians, who hath bewitched you, that ye should not obey the truth, before whose eyes Jesus Christ hath been evidently set forth, crucified among you?
3:1

132 There is neither Jew nor Greek, there is neither bond nor free, there is neither male nor female: for ye are all one in Christ Jesus.
3:28

133 But Jerusalem which is above is free, which is the mother of us all.
4:26

134 For the flesh lusteth against the Spirit, and the Spirit against the flesh: and these are contrary the one to the other: so that ye cannot do the things that ye would.
5:17

135 But the fruit of the Spirit is love, joy, peace, longsuffering, gentleness, goodness, faith, Meekness, temperance: against such there is no law.
5:22–23

136 Be not deceived: God is not mocked: for whatsoever a man soweth, that shall he also reap.
6:7

Genesis

137 In the beginning God created the heaven and the earth.
And the earth was without form, and void; and darkness was upon the face of the deep. And the Spirit of God moved upon the face of the waters.
And God said, Let there be light: and there was light.
And God saw the light, that it was good: and God divided the light from the darkness.
And God called the light Day, and the darkness he called Night. And the evening and the morning were the first day.
1:1–5

138 Fiat lux.
Vulgate 1:3

139 And God called the dry land Earth; and the gathering together of the waters called he Seas: and God saw that it was good.
And God said, Let the earth bring forth grass, the herb yielding seed, and the fruit tree yielding fruit

after his kind, whose seed is in itself, upon the earth: and it was so.
1:10–11

140 And God made two great lights: the greater light to rule the day, and the lesser light to rule the night: he made the stars also.
1:16

141 And God said, Let the earth bring forth the living creature after his kind, cattle, and creeping thing, and beast of the earth after his kind: and it was so.
1:24

142 And God said, Let us make man in our image, after our likeness: and let them have dominion over the fish of the sea, and over the fowl of the air, and over the cattle, and over all the earth, and over every creeping thing that creepeth upon the earth.
So God created man in his own image, in the image of God created he him; male and female created he them.
And God blessed them, and God said unto them, Be fruitful, and multiply, and replenish the earth, and subdue it: and have dominion over the fish of the sea, and over the fowl of the air, and over every living thing that moveth upon the earth.
1:26–28

143 And on the seventh day God ended his work which he had made; and he rested on the seventh day from all his work which he had made.
2:2

144 But there went up a mist from the earth, and watered the whole face of the ground.
And the Lord God formed man of the dust of the ground, and breathed into his nostrils the breath of life; and man became a living soul.
And the Lord God planted a garden eastward in Eden; and there he put the man whom he had formed.
And out of the ground made the Lord God to grow every tree that is pleasant to the sight, and good for food; the tree of life also in the midst of the garden, and the tree of knowledge of good and evil.
And a river went out of Eden to water the garden.
2:6–10

145 And the Lord God took the man, and put him into the garden of Eden to dress it and to keep it.
And the Lord God commanded the man, saying, Of every tree of the garden thou mayest freely eat:
But of the tree of the knowledge of good and evil, thou shalt not eat of it: for in the day that thou eatest thereof thou shalt surely die.
2:15–17

146 And the Lord God said, It is not good that the man should be alone; I will make him an help meet for him.
And out of the ground the Lord God formed every beast of the field, and every fowl of the air; and brought them unto Adam to see what he would call them: and whatsoever Adam called every living creature, that was the name thereof.
2:18–19

147 And the Lord God caused a deep sleep to fall upon Adam, and he slept: and he took one of his ribs, and closed up the flesh instead thereof;
And the rib, which the Lord God had taken from man, made he a woman, and brought her unto the man.
And Adam said, This is now bone of my bones, and flesh of my flesh: she shall be called Woman, because she was taken out of Man.
Therefore shall a man leave his father and his mother, and shall cleave unto his wife: and they shall be one flesh.
And they were both naked, the man and his wife, and were not ashamed.
2:21–25

148 Now the serpent was more subtil than any beast of the field which the Lord God had made.
3:1

149 God doth know that in the day ye eat thereof, then your eyes shall be opened, and ye shall be as gods, knowing good and evil.
And when the woman saw that the tree was good for food, and that it was pleasant to the eyes, and a tree to be desired to make one wise, she took of the fruit thereof, and did eat, and gave also unto her husband with her; and he did eat.
And the eyes of them both were opened, and they knew that they were naked; and they sewed fig leaves together; and made themselves aprons.
And they heard the voice of the Lord God walking in the garden in the cool of the day: and Adam and his wife hid themselves from the presence of the Lord God amongst the trees of the garden.
3:5–8

150 And he said, I heard thy voice in the garden, and I was afraid, because I was naked; and I hid myself.
And he said, Who told thee that thou wast naked?
3:10–11

151 And the man said, The woman whom thou gavest to be with me, she gave me of the tree, and I did eat.
And the Lord God said unto the woman, What is this that thou hast done? And the woman said, The serpent beguiled me, and I did eat.
And the Lord God said unto the serpent, Because thou hast done this, thou art cursed above all cattle, and above every beast of the field; upon thy belly shalt thou go, and dust shalt thou eat all the days of thy life.
3:12–14

152 In the sweat of thy face shalt thou eat bread, till thou return unto the ground; for out of it wast thou taken: for dust thou art and unto dust shalt thou return.
And Adam called his wife's name Eve; because she was the mother of all living.
3:19–20

153 Abel was a keeper of sheep, but Cain was a tiller of the ground.
4:2

154 And the Lord said unto Cain, Where is Abel thy brother? And he said, I know not: Am I my brother's keeper?
4:9

155 And the Lord said unto him, Therefore whosoever slayeth Cain, vengeance shall be taken

on him sevenfold. And the Lord set a mark upon Cain, lest any finding him should kill him.
And Cain went out from the presence of the Lord, and dwelt in the land of Nod, on the east of Eden.
4:15–16

156 And all the days of Methuselah were nine hundred sixty and nine years: and he died.
5:27

157 And it repented the Lord that he had made man on the earth, and it grieved him at his heart.
6:6

158 And they went in unto Noah into the ark, two and two of all flesh, wherein is the breath of life.
And they that went in, went in male and female of all flesh, as God had commanded him: and the Lord shut him in.
And the flood was forty days upon the earth; and the waters increased, and bare up the ark, and it was lift up above the earth.
7:15–17

159 And the dove came in to him in the evening; and, lo, in her mouth was an olive leaf plucked off: so Noah knew that the waters were abated from off the earth.
8:11

160 Who so sheddeth man's blood, by man shall his blood be shed: for in the image of God made he man.
9:6

161 I do set my bow in the cloud, and it shall be for a token of a covenant between me and the earth.
9:13

162 He was a mighty hunter before the Lord: wherefore it is said, Even as Nimrod the mighty hunter before the Lord.
10:9

163 And the whole earth was of one language, and of one speech.
11:1

164 Therefore is the name of it called Babel; because the Lord did there confound the language of all the earth: and from thence did the Lord scatter them abroad upon the face of all the earth.
11:9

165 Now the Lord had said unto Abram, Get thee out of thy country, and from thy kindred, and from thy father's house, unto a land that I will shew thee:
And I will make of thee a great nation, and I will bless thee, and make thy name great; and thou shalt be a blessing:
And I will bless them that bless thee, and curse him that curseth thee: and in thee shall all families of the earth be blessed.
12:1–3

166 But the men of Sodom were wicked and sinners before the Lord exceedingly.
13:13

167 Then the Lord rained upon Sodom and upon Gomorrah brimstone and fire from the Lord out of heaven.
19:24

168 But his wife looked back from behind him, and she became a pillar of salt.
19:26

169 And Abraham said, My son, God will provide himself a lamb for a burnt offering: so they went both of them together.
22:8

170 And Abraham lifted up his eyes, and looked, and behold behind him a ram caught in a thicket by his horns: and Abraham went and took the ram, and offered him up for a burnt offering in the stead of his son.
22:13

171 And Jacob said to Rebekah his mother, Behold, Esau my brother is a hairy man, and I am a smooth man.
27:11

172 And he dreamed, and behold a ladder set up on the earth, and the top of it reached to heaven: and behold the angels of God ascending and descending on it.
28:12

173 Leah was tender eyed; but Rachel was beautiful and well favoured.
29:17

174 Now Israel loved Joseph more than all his children, because he was the son of his old age: and he made him a coat of many colours.
37:3

175 And they said one to another, Behold, this dreamer cometh.
Come now therefore, and let us slay him, and cast him into some pit, and we will say, Some evil beast hath devoured him: and we shall see what will become of his dreams.
37:19–20

176 And all his sons and all his daughters rose up to comfort him; but he refused to be comforted; and he said, For I will go down into the grave unto my son mourning. Thus his father wept for him.
37:35

177 And Judah said unto Onan, Go in unto thy brother's wife, and marry her, and raise up seed to thy brother.
And Onan knew that the seed should not be his; and it came to pass, when he went in unto his brother's wife, that he spilled it on the ground, lest that he should give seed to his brother.
38:8–9

178 And the seven thin ears devoured the seven rank and full ears. And Pharaoh awoke, and, behold, it was a dream.
41:7

179 And the famine was sore in the land.
43:1

180 And take your father and your households, and come unto me: and I will give you the good of the land of Egypt, and ye shall eat the fat of the land.
45:18

181 Issachar is a strong ass couching down

between two burdens:
And he saw that rest was good, and the land that it was pleasant; and bowed his shoulder to bear, and became a servant unto tribute.
49:14–15

182 Benjamin shall ravin as a wolf: in the morning he shall devour the prey, and at night he shall divide the spoil.
49:27

Habakkuk

183 But the Lord is in his holy temple: let all the earth keep silence before him.
2:20

Haggai

184 Now therefore thus saith the Lord of hosts; Consider your ways.
Ye have sown much, and bring in little; ye eat, but ye have not enough; ye drink, but ye are not filled with drink; ye clothe you, but there is none warm; and he that earneth wages earneth wages to put it into a bag with holes.
1:5–6

Hebrews

185 For the word of God is quick, and powerful, and sharper than any two-edged sword, piercing even to the dividing asunder of soul and spirit, and of the joints and marrow, and is a discerner of the thoughts and intents of the heart.
4:12

186 And almost all things are by the law purged with blood; and without shedding of blood is no remission.
9:22

187 Now faith is the substance of things hoped for, the evidence of things not seen.
11:1

188 By faith the walls of Jericho fell down, after they were compassed about seven days.
11:30

189 Let brotherly love continue.
Be not forgetful to entertain strangers: for thereby some have entertained angels unawares.
13:1–2

Hosea

190 For they have sown the wind, and they shall reap the whirlwind: it hath no stalk: the bud shall yield no meal: if so be it yield, the strangers shall swallow it up.
8:7

Isaiah

191 Come now, and let us reason together, saith the Lord: though your sins be as scarlet, they shall be as white as snow; though they be red like crimson, they shall be as wool.
1:18

192 How is the faithful city become an harlot! it was full of judgment; righteousness lodged in it; but now murderers.
1:21

193 And it shall come to pass in the last days, that the mountain of the Lord's house shall be established in the top of the mountains, and shall be exalted above the hills; and all nations shall flow unto it.
2:2

194 And he shall judge among the nations, and shall rebuke many people: and they shall beat their swords into plowshares, and their spears into pruning-hooks: nation shall not lift up sword against nation, neither shall they learn war any more.
2:4

195 Woe unto them that rise up early in the morning, that they may follow strong drink; that continue until night, till wine inflame them!
5:11

196 Woe unto them that call evil good, and good evil; that put darkness for light, and light for darkness; that put bitter for sweet, and sweet for bitter!
5:20

197 In the year that king Uzziah died I saw also the Lord sitting upon a throne, high and lifted up, and his train filled the temple.
Above it stood the seraphims: each one had six wings; with twain he covered his face, and with twain he covered his feet, and with twain he did fly.
And one cried unto another, and said, Holy, holy, holy, is the Lord of hosts: the whole earth is full of his glory.
6:1–3

198 Therefore the Lord himself shall give you a sign; Behold, a virgin shall conceive, and bear a son, and shall call his name Immanuel.
Butter and honey shall he eat, that he may know to refuse the evil, and choose the good.
7:14–15

199 And he shall be for a sanctuary; but for a stone of stumbling and for a rock of offence to both the houses of Israel, for a gin and for a snare to the inhabitants of Jerusalem.
8:14

200 The people that walked in darkness have seen a great light: they that dwell in the land of the shadow of death, upon them hath the light shined.
9:2

201 For unto us a child is born, unto us a son is given: and the government shall be upon his shoulder: and his name shall be called Wonderful, Counsellor, The mighty God, The everlasting Father, The Prince of Peace.
9:6

202 And there shall come forth a rod out of the stem of Jesse, and a Branch shall grow out of his roots:
And the spirit of the Lord shall rest upon him, the spirit of wisdom and understanding, the spirit of counsel and might, the spirit of knowledge and of the fear of the Lord.
11:1–2

203 The wolf also shall dwell with the lamb, and the leopard shall lie down with the kid; and the calf and the young lion and the fatling together: and a little child shall lead them.
And the cow and the bear shall feed; their young ones shall lie down together: and the lion shall eat straw like the ox.
And the sucking child shall play on the hole of the asp, and the weaned child shall put his hand on the cockatrice' den.
They shall not hurt nor destroy in all my holy mountain: for the earth shall be full of the knowledge of the Lord, as the waters cover the sea.
11:6–9

204 He calleth to me out of Seir, Watchman, what of the night? Watchman, what of the night?
The watchman said, The morning cometh, and also the night: if ye will enquire, enquire ye: return, come.
21:11–12

205 And behold joy and gladness, slaying oxen, and killing sheep, eating flesh, and drinking wine: let us eat and drink; for tomorrow we shall die.
22:13

206 They shall not drink wine with a song; strong drink shall be bitter to them that drink it.
24:9

207 In that day the Lord with his sore and great and strong sword shall punish leviathan the piercing serpent, even leviathan that crooked serpent; and he shall slay the dragon that is in the sea.
27:1

208 For precept must be upon precept, precept upon precept; line upon line, line upon line; here a little, and there a little.
28:10

209 Then the eyes of the blind shall be opened, and the ears of the deaf shall be unstopped.
Then shall the lame man leap as an hart, and the tongue of the dumb sing: for in the wilderness shall waters break out, and streams in the desert.
And the parched ground shall become a pool, and the thirsty land springs of water: in the habitation of dragons, where each lay, shall be grass with reeds and rushes.
35:5–7

210 The voice of him that crieth in the wilderness, Prepare ye the way of the Lord, make straight in the desert a highway for our God.
Every valley shall be exalted, and every mountain and hill shall be made low: and the crooked shall be made straight, and the rough places plain.
40:3–4

211 He shall feed his flock like a shepherd: he shall gather the lambs with his arm, and carry them in his bosom, and shall gently lead those that are with young.
40:11

212 The isles saw it, and feared; the ends of the earth were afraid, drew near, and came.
They helped every one his neighbour; and every one said to his brother, Be of good courage.
41:5–6

213 There is no peace, saith the Lord, unto the wicked.
48:22

214 All we like sheep have gone astray; we have turned every one to his own way; and the Lord hath laid on him the iniquity of us all.
He was oppressed, and he was afflicted, yet he opened not his mouth: he is brought as a lamb to the slaughter, and as a sheep before her shearers is dumb, so he openeth not his mouth.
53:6–7

215 The righteous perisheth, and no man layeth it to heart: and merciful men are taken away, none considering that the righteous is taken away from the evil to come.
57:1

James

216 Blessed is the man that endureth temptation: for when he is tried, he shall receive the crown of life, which the Lord hath promised to them that love him.
1:12

217 Wherefore, my beloved brethren, let every man be swift to hear, slow to speak, slow to wrath:
For the wrath of man worketh not the righteousness of God.
1:19–20

218 Submit yourselves therefore to God. Resist the devil, and he will flee from you.
Draw nigh to God, and he will draw nigh to you. Cleanse your hands, ye sinners; and purify your hearts, ye double minded.
4:7–8

219 Grudge not one against another, brethren, lest ye be condemned: behold, the judge standeth before the door.
5:9

220 Let him know, that he which converteth the sinner from the error of his way shall save a soul from death, and shall hide a multitude of sins.
5:20

Jeremiah

221 Can the Ethiopian change his skin, or the leopard his spots? then may ye also do good, that are accustomed to do evil.
13:23

Job

222 And the Lord said unto Satan, Hast thou considered my servant Job, that there is none like him in the earth, a perfect and an upright man, one that feareth God, and escheweth evil?
Then Satan answered the Lord, and said, Doth Job fear God for nought?
1:8–9

223 Naked came I out of my mother's womb, and naked shall I return thither: the Lord gave, and the Lord hath taken away; blessed be the name of the Lord.
1:21

224 Then said his wife unto him, Dost thou still retain thine integrity? curse God, and die.
2:9

225 Let the day perish wherein I was born, and the night in which it was said, There is a man child conceived.
3:3

226 The eye of him that hath seen me shall see me no more: thine eyes are upon me, and I am not.
7:8

227 Wherefore then hast thou brought me forth out of the womb? Oh that I had given up the ghost, and no eye had seen me!
10:18

228 With the ancient is wisdom; and in length of days understanding.
12:12

229 They grope in the dark without light, and he maketh them to stagger like a drunken man.
12:25

230 Man that is born of a woman is of few days, and full of trouble.
14:1

231 Then Job answered and said, I have heard many such things: miserable comforters are ye all.
16:1–2

232 I have said to corruption, Thou art my father: to the worm, Thou art my mother, and my sister.
17:14

233 For I know that my redeemer liveth, and that he shall stand at the latter day upon the earth:
And though after my skin worms destroy this body, yet in my flesh shall I see God.
19:25–26

234 No mention shall be made of coral, or of pearls: for the price of wisdom is above rubies.
28:18

235 I was eyes to the blind, and feet was I to the lame.
29:15

236 Then the Lord answered Job out of the whirlwind, and said,
Who is this that darkeneth counsel by words without knowledge?
Gird up now thy loins like a man; for I will demand of thee, and answer thou me.
Where wast thou when I laid the foundations of the earth? declare, if thou hast understanding.
Who hath laid the measures thereof, if thou knowest? or who hath stretched the line upon it?
Whereupon are the foundations thereof fastened? or who laid the corner stone thereof;
When the morning stars sang together, and all the sons of God shouted for joy?
38:1–7

237 Canst thou draw out leviathan with an hook? or his tongue with a cord which thou lettest down?
41:1

John

238 In the beginning was the Word, and the Word was with God, and the Word was God.
The same was in the beginning with God.
All things were made by him; and without him was not any thing made that was made.
In him was life; and the life was the light of men.
And the light shineth in darkness; and the darkness comprehended it not.
1:1–5

239 He it is, who coming after me is preferred before me, whose shoe's latchet I am not worthy to unloose.
1:27

240 The next day John seeth Jesus coming unto him, and saith, Behold the Lamb of God, which taketh away the sin of the world.
1:29

241 Jesus saith unto her, Woman, what have I to do with thee? mine hour is not yet come.
2:4

242 When the ruler of the feast had tasted the water that was made wine, and knew not whence it was: (but the servants which drew the water knew;) the governor of the feast called the bridegroom,
And saith unto him, Every man at the beginning doth set forth good wine; and when men have well drunk, then that which is worse: but thou hast kept the good wine until now.
2:9–10

243 Jesus answered and said unto him, Verily, verily, I say unto thee, Except a man be born again, he cannot see the kingdom of God.
3:3

244 Jesus answered, Verily, verily, I say unto thee, Except a man be born of water and of the Spirit, he cannot enter into the kingdom of God.
That which is born of the flesh is flesh; and that which is born of the Spirit is spirit.
3:5–6

245 For God so loved the world, that he gave his only begotten Son, that whosoever believeth in him should not perish, but have everlasting life.
3:16

246 And this is the condemnation, that light is come into the world, and men loved darkness rather than light, because their deeds were evil.
3:19

247 Afterward Jesus findeth him in the temple, and said unto him, Behold, thou art made whole: sin no more, lest a worse thing come unto thee.
5:14

248 Verily, verily, I say unto you, He that heareth my word, and believeth on him that sent me, hath everlasting life, and shall not come into condemnation; but is passed from death unto life.
Verily, verily, I say unto you, The hour is coming, and now is, when the dead shall hear the voice of the Son of God: and they that hear shall live.
5:24–25

249 There is a lad here, which hath five barley

loaves, and two small fishes: but what are they among so many?
And Jesus said, Make the men sit down. Now there was much grass in the place. So the men sat down, in number about five thousand.
6:9–10

250 And Jesus said unto them, I am the bread of life: he that cometh to me shall never hunger; and he that believeth on me shall never thirst.
6:35

251 So when they continued asking him, he lifted up himself, and said unto them, He that is without sin among you, let him first cast a stone at her.
8:7

252 She said, No man, Lord. And Jesus said unto her, Neither do I condemn thee: go, and sin no more.
8:11

253 Then spake Jesus again unto them, saying, I am the light of the world: he that followeth me shall not walk in darkness, but shall have the light of life.
8:12

254 And ye shall know the truth, and the truth shall make you free.
8:32

255 He answered and said, Whether he be a sinner or no, I know not: one thing I know, that, whereas I was blind, now I see.
9:25

256 Jesus said unto her, I am the resurrection, and the life: he that believeth in me, though he were dead, yet shall he live.
11:25

257 When Jesus therefore saw her weeping, and the Jews also weeping which came with her, he groaned in the spirit, and was troubled,
And said, Where have ye laid him? They said unto him, Lord, come and see.
Jesus wept.
11:33–35

258 In my Father's house are many mansions: if it were not so, I would have told you. I go to prepare a place for you.
14:2

259 Jesus saith unto him, I am the way, the truth, and the life: no man cometh unto the Father, but by me.
14:6

260 Greater love hath no man than this, that a man lay down his life for his friends.
15:13

261 But now I go my way to him that sent me; and none of you asketh me, Whither goest thou?
16:5

262 Quo vadis?
Vulgate 16:5

263 A woman when she is in travail hath sorrow, because her hour is come: but as soon as she is delivered of the child, she remembereth no more the anguish, for joy that a man is born into the world.
16:21

264 Now Caiaphas was he, which gave counsel to the Jews, that it was expedient that one man should die for the people.
18:14

265 Pilate saith unto him, What is truth? And when he had said this, he went out again unto the Jews, and saith unto them, I find in him no fault at all.
18:38

266 Then cried they all again, saying, Not this man, but Barabbas. Now Barabbas was a robber.
18:40

267 Then came Jesus forth, wearing the crown of thorns, and the purple robe. And Pilate saith unto them, Behold the man!
19:5

268 Ecce homo.
Vulgate 19:5

269 Pilate answered, What I have written I have written.
19:22

270 When Jesus therefore saw his mother, and the disciple standing by, whom he loved, he saith unto his mother, Woman, behold thy son!
Then saith he to the disciple, Behold thy mother! And from that hour that disciple took her unto his own home.
19:26–27

271 When Jesus therefore had received the vinegar, he said, It is finished: and he bowed his head, and gave up the ghost.
19:30

272 Consummatum est.
Vulgate 19:30

273 Now in the place where he was crucified there was a garden; and in the garden a new sepulchre, wherein was never man yet laid.
19:41

274 The first day of the week cometh Mary Magdalene early, when it was yet dark, unto the sepulchre, and seeth the stone taken away from the sepulchre.
Then she runneth, and cometh to Simon Peter, and to the other disciple, whom Jesus loved, and saith unto them, They have taken the Lord out of the sepulchre, and we know not where they have laid him.
20:1–2

275 Jesus saith unto her, Woman, why weepest thou? whom seekest thou? She, supposing him to be the gardener, saith unto him, Sir, if thou have borne him hence, tell me where thou hast laid him, and I will take him away.
Jesus saith unto her, Mary. She turned herself, and saith unto him, Rabboni; which is to say, Master.
Jesus saith unto her, Touch me not; for I am not yet ascended to my Father: but go to my brethren, and say unto them, I ascend unto my Father, and your Father; and to my God, and your God.
20:15–17

276 Noli me tangere.
Vulgate 20:17

277 The other disciples therefore said unto him, We have seen the Lord. But he said unto them, Except I shall see in his hands the print of the nails, and put my finger into the print of the nails, and thrust my hand into his side, I will not believe.
20:25

278 Then saith he to Thomas, Reach hither thy finger, and behold my hands; and reach hither thy hand, and thrust it into my side: and be not faithless, but believing.
And Thomas answered and said unto him, My Lord and my God.
Jesus saith unto him, Thomas, because thou hast seen me, thou hast believed: blessed are they that have not seen, and yet have believed.
20:27–29

279 So when they had dined, Jesus saith to Simon Peter, Simon, son of Jonas, lovest thou me more than these? He saith unto him, Yea, Lord; thou knowest that I love thee. He saith unto him, Feed my lambs.
21:15

280 He saith unto him the third time, Simon, son of Jonas, lovest thou me? Peter was grieved because he said unto him the third time, Lovest thou me? And he said unto him, Lord, thou knowest all things; thou knowest that I love thee. Jesus saith unto him, Feed my sheep.
21:17

I John

281 If we say that we have no sin, we deceive ourselves, and the truth is not in us.
If we confess our sins, he is faithful and just to forgive us our sins, and to cleanse us from all unrighteousness.
1:8–9

282 Beloved, let us love one another: for love is of God; and every one that loveth is born of God, and knoweth God.
He that loveth not knoweth not God; for God is love.
4:7–8

283 There is no fear in love; but perfect love casteth out fear: because fear hath torment. He that feareth is not made perfect in love.
4:18

284 If a man say, I love God, and hateth his brother, he is a liar: for he that loveth not his brother whom he hath seen, how can he love God whom he hath not seen?
4:20

Jonah

285 So the shipmaster came to him, and said unto him, What meanest thou, O sleeper? arise, call upon thy God, if so be that God will think upon us, that we perish not.
And they said every one to his fellow, Come, and let us cast lots, that we may know for whose cause this evil is upon us. So they cast lots, and the lot fell upon Jonah.
1:6–7

286 Now the Lord had prepared a great fish to swallow up Jonah. And Jonah was in the belly of the fish three days and three nights.
1:17

Joshua

287 And the priests that bare the ark of the covenant of the Lord stood firm on dry ground in the midst of Jordan, and all the Israelites passed over on dry ground, until all the people were passed clean over Jordan.
3:17

288 So the people shouted when the priests blew with the trumpets: and it came to pass, when the people heard the sound of the trumpet, and the people shouted with a great shout, that the wall fell down flat, so that the people went up into the city, every man straight before him, and they took the city.
6:20

289 And the princes said unto them, Let them live; but let them be hewers of wood and drawers of water unto all the congregation; as the princes had promised them.
9:21

Jude

290 Mercy unto you, and peace, and love, be multiplied.
1:2

Judges

291 And when he shewed them the entrance into the city, they smote the city with the edge of the sword; but they let go the man and all his family.
1:25

292 They fought from heaven; the stars in their courses fought against Sisera.
5:20

293 Blessed above women shall Jael the wife of Heber the Kenite be, blessed shall she be above women in the tent.
He asked water, and she gave him milk; she brought forth butter in a lordly dish.
She put her hand to the nail, and her right hand to the workmen's hammer; and with the hammer she smote Sisera, she smote off his head, when she had pierced and stricken through his temples.
At her feet he bowed, he fell, he lay down: at her feet he bowed, he fell: where he bowed, there he fell down dead.
The mother of Sisera looked out at a window, and cried through the lattice, Why is his chariot so long in coming? why tarry the wheels of his chariots?
5:24–28

294 And he said unto them, Out of the eater came forth meat, and out of the strong came forth sweetness. And they could not in three days expound the riddle.
14:14

295 And the men of the city said unto him on the seventh day before the sun went down, What is sweeter than honey? and what is stronger than a lion? And he said unto them, If ye had not plowed with my heifer, ye had not found out my riddle.
14:18

296 In those days there was no king in Israel, but every man did that which was right in his own eyes.
17:6

I Kings

297 So David slept with his fathers, and was buried in the city of David.
2:10

298 Then the king answered and said, Give her the living child, and in no wise slay it: she is the mother thereof.
And all Israel heard of the judgment which the king had judged; and they feared the king: for they saw that the wisdom of God was in him, to do judgment.
3:27–28

299 And when the queen of Sheba heard of the fame of Solomon concerning the name of the Lord, she came to prove him with hard questions.
10:1

300 And he said, Go forth, and stand upon the mount before the Lord. And, behold, the Lord passed by, and a great and strong wind rent the mountains, and brake in pieces the rocks before the Lord; but the Lord was not in the wind: and after the wind an earthquake; but the Lord was not in the earthquake:
And after the earthquake a fire; but the Lord was not in the fire: and after the fire a still small voice.
19:11–12

II Kings

301 And it came to pass, as they still went on, and talked, that, behold, there appeared a chariot of fire, and horses of fire, and parted them both asunder; and Elijah went up by a whirlwind into heaven.
And Elisha saw it, and he cried, My father, my father, the chariot of Israel, and the horsemen thereof. And he saw him no more: and he took hold of his own clothes, and rent them in two pieces.
2:11–12

302 And when Jehu was come to Jezreel, Jezebel heard of it; and she painted her face, and tired her head, and looked out at a window.
9:30

303 And they went to bury her: but they found no more of her than the skull, and the feet, and the palms of her hands.
9:35

304 In those days was Hezekiah sick unto death. And the prophet Isaiah the son of Amoz came to him, and said unto him, Thus saith the Lord, Set thine house in order; for thou shalt die, and not live.
Then he turned his face to the wall.
20:1–2

Lamentations

305 And I said, My strength and my hope is perished from the Lord:
Remembering mine affliction and my misery, the wormwood and the gall.
3:18–19

306 It is good for a man that he bear the yoke in his youth.
3:27

307 Waters flowed over mine head; then I said, I am cut off.
3:54

Luke

308 And the angel came in unto her, and said, Hail, thou that art highly favoured, the Lord is with thee: blessed art thou among women.
And when she saw him, she was troubled at his saying, and cast in her mind what manner of salutation this should be.
1:28–29

309 And Mary said, My soul doth magnify the Lord,
And my spirit hath rejoiced in God my Saviour.
For he hath regarded the low estate of his handmaiden: for, behold, from henceforth all generations shall call me blessed.
1:46–48

310 He hath shewed strength with his arm; he hath scattered the proud in the imagination of their hearts.
He hath put down the mighty from their seats, and exalted them of low degree.
He hath filled the hungry with good things; and the rich he hath sent empty away.
1:51–53

311 And the child grew, and waxed strong in spirit, and was in the deserts till the day of his shewing unto Israel.
1:80

312 And it came to pass in those days, that there went out a decree from Caesar Augustus, that all the world should be taxed.
2:1

313 And she brought forth her firstborn son, and wrapped him in swaddling clothes, and laid him in a manger; because there was no room for them in the inn.
2:7

314 And there were in the same country shepherds abiding in the field, keeping watch over their flock by night.
And, lo, the angel of the Lord came upon them, and the glory of the Lord shone round about them: and they were sore afraid.
And the angel said unto them, Fear not: for, behold, I bring you good tidings of great joy, which shall be to all people.
2:8–10

315 Glory to God in the highest, and on earth peace, good will toward men.
2:14

316 But Mary kept all these things, and pondered them in her heart.
2:19

317 Lord, now lettest thou thy servant depart in peace, according to thy word:
For mine eyes have seen thy salvation,
Which thou hast prepared before the face of all people;
A light to lighten the Gentiles, and the glory of thy people Israel.
2:29–32

318 And it came to pass, that after three days they found him in the temple, sitting in the midst of the doctors, both hearing them, and asking them questions.
And all that heard him were astonished at his understanding and answers.
2:46–47

319 And the devil, taking him up into an high mountain, shewed unto him all the kingdoms of the world in a moment of time.
4:5

320 And he said unto them, Ye will surely say unto me this proverb, Physician, heal thyself: whatsoever we have heard done in Capernaum, do also here in thy country.
4:23

321 No man also having drunk old wine straightway desireth new: for he saith, The old is better.
5:39

322 And he said to the woman, Thy faith hath saved thee; go in peace.
7:50

323 Go your ways: behold, I send you forth as lambs among wolves.
Carry neither purse, nor scrip, nor shoes: and salute no man by the way.
And into whatsoever house ye enter, first say, Peace be to this house.
10:3–5

324 And Jesus answering said, A certain man went down from Jerusalem to Jericho, and fell among thieves, which stripped him of his raiment, and wounded him, and departed, leaving him half dead.
And by chance there came down a certain priest that way: and when he saw him, he passed by on the other side.
10:30–31

325 But a certain Samaritan, as he journeyed, came where he was: and when he saw him, he had compassion on him,
And went to him, and bound up his wounds, pouring in oil and wine, and set him on his own beast, and brought him to an inn, and took care of him.
And on the morrow when he departed, he took out two pence, and gave them to the host, and said unto him, Take care of him; and whatsoever thou spendest more, when I come again, I will repay thee.
10:33–35

326 And he said, He that shewed mercy on him. Then said Jesus unto him, Go, and do thou likewise.
10:37

327 Woe unto you, lawyers! for ye have taken away the key of knowledge: ye entered not in yourselves, and them that were entering in ye hindered.
11:52

328 Are not five sparrows sold for two farthings, and not one of them is forgotten before God?
12:6

329 And they all with one consent began to make excuse. The first said unto him, I have bought a piece of ground, and I must needs go and see it: I pray thee have me excused.
And another said, I have bought five yoke of oxen, and I go to prove them: I pray thee have me excused.
And another said, I have married a wife, and therefore I cannot come.
So that servant came, and shewed his lord these things. Then the master of the house being angry said to his servant, Go out quickly into the streets and lanes of the city, and bring in hither the poor, and the maimed, and the halt, and the blind.
14:18–21

330 What man of you, having an hundred sheep, if he lose one of them, doth not leave the ninety and nine in the wilderness, and go after that which is lost until he find it?
And when he hath found it, he layeth it on his shoulders, rejoicing.
And when he cometh home, he calleth together his friends and neighbours, saying unto them, Rejoice with me; for I have found my sheep which was lost.
I say unto you, that likewise joy shall be in heaven over one sinner that repenteth, more than over ninety and nine just persons, which need no repentance.
15:4–7

331 And he would fain have filled his belly with the husks that the swine did eat: and no man gave unto him.
And when he came to himself, he said, How many hired servants of my father's have bread enough and to spare, and I perish with hunger!
I will arise and go to my father, and will say unto him, Father, I have sinned against heaven, and before thee,
And am no more worthy to be called thy son: make me as one of thy hired servants.
And he arose, and came to his father. But when he was yet a great way off, his father saw him, and had compassion, and ran, and fell on his neck, and kissed him.
15:16–20

332 And bring hither the fatted calf, and kill it; and let us eat, and be merry:
For this my son was dead, and is alive again; he was lost, and is found. And they began to be merry.
15:23–24

333 There was a certain rich man, which was clothed in purple and fine linen, and fared sumptuously every day:
And there was a certain beggar named Lazarus, which was laid at his gate, full of sores,

And desiring to be fed with the crumbs which fell from the rich man's table: moreover the dogs came and licked his sores.
And it came to pass, that the beggar died, and was carried by the angels into Abraham's bosom: the rich man also died, and was buried;
16:19–22

334 And when he was demanded of the Pharisees, when the kingdom of God should come, he answered them and said, The kingdom of God cometh not with observation:
Neither shall they say, Lo here! or, lo there! for, behold, the kingdom of God is within you.
17:20–21

335 Remember Lot's wife.
17:32

336 And he saith unto him, Out of thine own mouth will I judge thee, thou wicked servant. Thou knewest that I was an austere man, taking up that I laid not down, and reaping that I did not sow.
19:22

337 And he answered and said unto them, I tell you that, if these should hold their peace, the stones would immediately cry out.
19:40

338 And when they were come to the place, which is called Calvary, there they crucified him, and the malefactors, one on the right hand, and the other on the left.
23:33

339 Then said Jesus, Father, forgive them; for they know not what they do. And they parted his raiment, and cast lots.
23:34

340 And when Jesus had cried with a loud voice, he said, Father, into thy hands I commend my spirit: and having said thus, he gave up the ghost.
23:46

I Maccabees

341 I perceive therefore that for this cause these troubles are come upon me, and, behold, I perish through great grief in a strange land.
6:13

Malachi

342 Have we not all one father? hath not one God created us? why do we deal treacherously every man against his brother, by profaning the covenant of our fathers?
2:10

343 But unto you that fear my name shall the Sun of righteousness arise with healing in his wings; and ye shall go forth, and grow up as calves of the stall.
4:2

Mark

344 And he said unto them, The sabbath was made for man, and not man for the sabbath: Therefore the Son of man is Lord also of the sabbath.
2:27–28

345 And he asked him, What is thy name? And he answered, saying. My name is Legion: for we are many.
5:9

346 And forthwith Jesus gave them leave. And the unclean spirits went out, and entered into the swine: and the herd ran violently down a steep place into the sea, (they were about two thousand;) and were choked in the sea.
5:13

347 For what shall it profit a man, if he shall gain the whole world, and lose his own soul? Or what shall a man give in exchange for his soul?
8:36–37

348 But when Jesus saw it, he was much displeased, and said unto them. Suffer the little children to come unto me, and forbid them not: for of such is the kingdom of God.
10:14

349 And there came a certain poor widow, and she threw in two mites, which make a farthing. And he called unto him his disciples, and saith unto them, Verily I say unto you, That this poor widow hath cast more in, than all they which have cast into the treasury: For all they did cast in of their abundance; but she of her want did cast in all that she had, even all her living.
12:42–44

350 And he said unto them, Go ye into all the world, and preach the gospel to every creature.
16:15

Matthew

351 Now when Jesus was born in Bethlehem of Judaea in the days of Herod the king, behold, there came wise men from the east to Jerusalem,
Saying, Where is he that is born King of the Jews? for we have seen his star in the east, and are come to worship him.
When Herod the king had heard these things, he was troubled, and all Jerusalem with him.
2:1–3

352 And when they were come into the house, they saw the young child with Mary his mother, and fell down, and worshipped him: and when they had opened their treasures, they presented unto him gifts; gold, and frankincense, and myrrh.
And being warned of God in a dream that they should not return to Herod, they departed into their own country another way.
2:11–12

353 For this is he that was spoken of by the prophet Esaias, saying, The voice of one crying in the wilderness, Prepare ye the way of the Lord, make his paths straight.
And the same John had his raiment of camel's hair, and a leathern girdle about his loins; and his meat was locusts and wild honey.
3:3–4

354 But when he saw many of the Pharisees and Sadducees come to his baptism, he said unto them,

O generation of vipers, who hath warned you to flee from the wrath to come?
3:7

355 And Jesus answering said unto him, Suffer it to be so now: for thus it becometh us to fulfil all righteousness. Then he suffered him.
And Jesus, when he was baptized, went up straightway out of the water: and, lo, the heavens were opened unto him, and he saw the Spirit of God descending like a dove, and lighting upon him:
And lo a voice from heaven, saying, This is my beloved Son, in whom I am well pleased.
3:15–17

356 Then was Jesus led up of the Spirit into the wilderness to be tempted of the devil.
And when he had fasted forty days and forty nights, he was afterward an hungred.
And when the tempter came to him, he said, If thou be the Son of God, command that these stones be made bread.
But he answered and said, It is written, Man shall not live by bread alone, but by every word that proceedeth out of the mouth of God.
4:1–4

357 Jesus said unto him, It is written again, Thou shalt not tempt the Lord thy God.
Again, the devil taketh him up into an exceeding high mountain, and sheweth him all the kingdoms of the world, and the glory of them.
4:7–8

358 From that time Jesus began to preach, and to say, Repent: for the kingdom of heaven is at hand.
4:17

359 And he saith unto them, Follow me, and I will make you fishers of men.
4:19

360 Blessed are the poor in spirit: for theirs is the kingdom of heaven.
Blessed are they that mourn: for they shall be comforted.
Blessed are the meek: for they shall inherit the earth.
Blessed are they which do hunger and thirst after righteousness: for they shall be filled.
Blessed are the merciful: for they shall obtain mercy.
Blessed are the pure in heart: for they shall see God.
Blessed are the peacemakers: for they shall be called the children of God.
Blessed are they which are persecuted for righteousness' sake: for theirs is the kingdom of heaven.
5:3–10

361 Ye are the salt of the earth: but if the salt have lost his savour, wherewith shall it be salted? it is thenceforth good for nothing, but to be cast out, and to be trodden under foot of men.
Ye are the light of the world. A city that is set on an hill cannot be hid.
Neither do men light a candle, and put it under a bushel, but on a candlestick; and it giveth light unto all that are in the house.
Let your light so shine before men, that they may see your good works, and glorify your Father which is in heaven.
5:13–16

362 For verily I say unto you, Till heaven and earth pass, one jot or one tittle shall in no wise pass from the law, till all be fulfilled.
5:18

363 And if thy right eye offend thee, pluck it out, and cast it from thee: for it is profitable for thee that one of thy members should perish, and not that thy whole body should be cast into hell.
5:29

364 But I say unto you, That ye resist not evil: but whosoever shall smite thee on thy right cheek, turn to him the other also.
And if any man will sue thee at the law, and take away thy coat, let him have thy cloke also.
And whosoever shall compel thee to go a mile, go with him twain.
5:39–41

365 But I say unto you, Love your enemies, bless them that curse you, do good to them that hate you, and pray for them which despitefully use you, and persecute you;
That ye may be the children of your Father which is in heaven: for he maketh his sun to rise on the evil and on the good, and sendeth rain on the just and on the unjust.
For if ye love them which love you, what reward have ye? do not even the publicans the same?
5:44–46

366 Be ye therefore perfect, even as your Father which is in heaven is perfect.
5:48

367 But when ye pray, use not vain repetitions, as the heathen do: for they think that they shall be heard for their much speaking.
Be not ye therefore like unto them: for your Father knoweth what things ye have need of, before ye ask him.
After this manner therefore pray ye: Our Father which art in heaven, Hallowed be thy name.
Thy kingdom come. Thy will be done in earth, as it is in heaven.
Give us this day our daily bread.
And forgive us our debts, as we forgive our debtors.
And lead us not into temptation, but deliver us from evil: For thine is the kingdom, and the power, and the glory, for ever. Amen.
6:7–13

368 Lay not up for yourselves treasures upon earth, where moth and rust doth corrupt, and where thieves break through and steal:
But lay up for yourselves treasures in heaven, where neither moth nor rust doth corrupt, and where thieves do not break through nor steal:
For where your treasure is, there will your heart be also.
6:19–21

369 No man can serve two masters: for either he will hate the one, and love the other; or else he will hold to the one, and despise the other. Ye cannot serve God and mammon.
6:24

370 Behold the fowls of the air: for they sow not, neither do they reap, nor gather into barns; yet your heavenly Father feedeth them. Are ye not much better than they?
Which of you by taking thought can add one cubit unto his stature?
And why take ye thought for raiment? Consider the lilies of the field, how they grow; they toil not, neither do they spin:
And yet I say unto you, That even Solomon in all his glory was not arrayed like one of these.
Wherefore, if God so clothe the grass of the field, which today is, and tomorrow is cast into the oven, shall he not much more clothe you, O ye of little faith?
6:26–30

371 Take therefore no thought for the morrow: for the morrow shall take thought for the things of itself. Sufficient unto the day is the evil thereof.
6:34

372 Judge not, that ye be not judged.
7:1

373 And why beholdest thou the mote that is in thy brother's eye, but considerest not the beam that is in thine own eye?
7:3

374 Give not that which is holy unto the dogs, neither cast ye your pearls before swine, lest they trample them under their feet, and turn again and rend you.
7:6

375 Ask, and it shall be given you; seek, and ye shall find; knock, and it shall be opened unto you:
For every one that asketh receiveth; and he that seeketh findeth; and to him that knocketh it shall be opened.
7:7–8

376 Or what man is there of you, whom if his son ask bread, will he give him a stone?
7:9

377 Enter ye in at the strait gate: for wide is the gate, and broad is the way, that leadeth to destruction, and many there be which go in thereat:
Because strait is the gate, and narrow is the way, which leadeth unto life, and few there be that find it.
7:13–14

378 Beware of false prophets, which come to you in sheep's clothing, but inwardly they are ravening wolves.
7:15

379 Ye shall know them by their fruits. Do men gather grapes of thorns, or figs of thistles?
Even so every good tree bringeth forth good fruit; but a corrupt tree bringeth forth evil fruit.
A good tree cannot bring forth evil fruit, neither can a corrupt tree bring forth good fruit.
Every tree that bringeth not forth good fruit is hewn down, and cast into the fire.
Wherefore by their fruits ye shall know them.
7:16–20

380 Therefore whosoever heareth these sayings of mine, and doeth them, I will liken him unto a wise man, which built his house upon a rock:
And the rain descended, and the floods came, and the winds blew, and beat upon that house; and it fell not: for it was founded upon a rock.
And every one that heareth these sayings of mine, and doeth them not, shall be likened unto a foolish man, which built his house upon the sand:
And the rain descended, and the floods came, and the winds blew, and beat upon that house; and it fell: and great was the fall of it.
7:24–27

381 But the children of the kingdom shall be cast out into outer darkness: there shall be weeping and gnashing of teeth.
8:12

382 But Jesus said unto him, Follow me; and let the dead bury their dead.
8:22

383 And his disciples came to him, and awoke him, saying, Lord, save us: we perish.
And he saith unto them, Why are ye fearful, O ye of little faith? Then he arose, and rebuked the winds and the sea; and there was a great calm.
But the men marvelled, saying, What manner of man is this, that even the winds and the sea obey him!
8:25–27

384 Neither do men put new wine into old bottles: else the bottles break, and the wine runneth out, and the bottles perish: but they put new wine into new bottles, and both are preserved.
9:17

385 Heal the sick, cleanse the lepers, raise the dead, cast out devils: freely ye have received, freely give.
10:8

386 And ye shall be hated of all men for my name's sake: but he that endureth to the end shall be saved.
10:22

387 Think not that I am come to send peace on earth: I came not to send peace, but a sword.
10:34

388 He that hath ears to hear, let him hear.
11:15

389 O generation of vipers, how can ye, being evil, speak good things? for out of the abundance of the heart the mouth speaketh.
12:34

390 For whosoever shall do the will of my Father which is in heaven, the same is my brother, and sister, and mother.
12:50

391 And he spake many things unto them in parables, saying, Behold, a sower went forth to sow;
And when he sowed, some seeds fell by the way side, and the fowls came and devoured them up:
Some fell upon stony places, where they had not much earth: and forthwith they sprung up, because they had no deepness of earth:
And when the sun was up, they were scorched; and because they had no root, they withered away.
And some fell among thorns; and the thorns sprung

up, and choked them:
But other fell into good ground, and brought forth fruit, some an hundredfold, some sixtyfold, some thirtyfold.
13:3–8

392 And they were offended in him. But Jesus said unto them, A prophet is not without honour, save in his own country, and in his own house.
13:57

393 But when Herod's birthday was kept, the daughter of Herodias danced before them, and pleased Herod.
Whereupon he promised with an oath to give her whatsoever she would ask.
And she, being before instructed of her mother, said, Give me John Baptist's head in a charger.
14:6–8

394 And in the fourth watch of the night Jesus went unto them, walking on the sea.
And when the disciples saw him walking on the sea, they were troubled, saying, It is a spirit; and they cried out for fear.
But straightway Jesus spake unto them, saying, Be of good cheer; it is I; be not afraid.
14:25–27

395 And immediately Jesus stretched forth his hand, and caught him, and said unto him, O thou of little faith, wherefore didst thou doubt?
14:31

396 And besought him that they might only touch the hem of his garment: and as many as touched were made perfectly whole.
14:36

397 And I say also unto thee, That thou art Peter, and upon this rock I will build my church; and the gates of hell shall not prevail against it.
And I will give unto thee the keys of the kingdom of heaven: and whatsoever thou shalt bind on earth shall be bound in heaven: and whatsoever thou shalt loose on earth shall be loosed in heaven.
16:18–19

398 Then said Jesus unto his disciples, If any man will come after me, let him deny himself, and take up his cross, and follow me.
16:24

399 And said, Verily I say unto you, Except ye be converted, and become as little children, ye shall not enter into the kingdom of heaven.
18:3

400 And whoso shall receive one such little child in my name receiveth me.
But whoso shall offend one of these little ones which believe in me, it were better for him that a millstone were hanged about his neck, and that he were drowned in the depth of the sea.
18:5–6

401 For where two or three are gathered together in my name, there am I in the midst of them.
18:20

402 Then came Peter to him, and said, Lord, how oft shall my brother sin against me, and I forgive him? till seven times?
Jesus saith unto him, I say not unto thee, Until seven times: but, Until seventy times seven.
18:21–22

403 Wherefore they are no more twain, but one flesh. What therefore God hath joined together, let not man put asunder.
19:6

404 Jesus said unto him, If thou wilt be perfect, go and sell that thou hast, and give to the poor, and thou shalt have treasure in heaven: and come and follow me.
But when the young man heard that saying, he went away sorrowful: for he had great possessions.
19:21–22

405 Then said Jesus unto his disciples, Verily I say unto you, That a rich man shall hardly enter into the kingdom of heaven.
And again I say unto you, It is easier for a camel to go through the eye of a needle, than for a rich man to enter into the kingdom of God.
19:23–24

406 But many that are first shall be last; and the last shall be first.
19:30

407 And a very great multitude spread their garments in the way; others cut down branches from the trees, and strawed them in the way.
And the multitudes that went before, and that followed, cried, saying, Hosanna to the Son of David: Blessed is he that cometh in the name of the Lord; Hosanna in the highest.
21:8–9

408 And said unto them, It is written, My house shall be called the house of prayer; but ye have made it a den of thieves.
21:13

409 For many are called, but few are chosen.
22:14

410 And he saith unto them, Whose is this image and superscription?
They say unto him, Caesar's. Then saith he unto them, Render therefore unto Caesar the things which are Caesar's; and unto God the things that are God's.
22:20–21

411 Jesus said unto him, Thou shalt love the Lord thy God with all thy heart, and with all thy soul, and with all thy mind.
This is the first and great commandment.
And the second is like unto it, Thou shalt love thy neighbour as thyself.
On these two commandments hang all the law and the prophets.
22:37–40

412 Woe unto you, scribes and Pharisees, hypocrites! for ye are like unto whited sepulchres, which indeed appear beautiful outward, but are within full of dead men's bones, and of all uncleanness.
23:27

413 And ye shall hear of wars and rumours of wars: see that ye be not troubled: for all these things must

come to pass, but the end is not yet.
For nation shall rise against nation, and kingdom against kingdom: and there shall be famines, and pestilences, and earthquakes, in divers places.
All these are the beginning of sorrows.
24:6–8

414 Immediately after the tribulation of those days shall the sun be darkened, and the moon shall not give her light, and the stars shall fall from heaven, and the powers of the heavens shall be shaken:
And then shall appear the sign of the Son of man in heaven: and then shall all the tribes of the earth mourn, and they shall see the Son of man coming in the clouds of heaven with power and great glory.
And he shall send his angels with a great sound of a trumpet, and they shall gather together his elect from the four winds, from one end of heaven to the other.
24:29–31

415 Heaven and earth shall pass away, but my words shall not pass away.
24:35

416 And at midnight there was a cry made, Behold, the bridegroom cometh; go ye out to meet him.
Then all those virgins arose, and trimmed their lamps.
And the foolish said unto the wise, Give us of your oil; for our lamps are gone out.
25:6–8

417 And unto one he gave five talents, to another two, and to another one; to every man according to his several ability; and straightway took his journey.
25:15

418 His lord said unto him, Well done, thou good and faithful servant: thou hast been faithful over a few things, I will make thee ruler over many things: enter thou into the joy of thy lord.
25:21

419 For unto every one that hath shall be given, and he shall have abundance: but from him that hath not shall be taken away even that which he hath.
And cast ye the unprofitable servant into outer darkness: there shall be weeping and gnashing of teeth.
25:29–30

420 And before him shall be gathered all nations: and he shall separate them one from another, as a shepherd divideth his sheep from the goats:
And he shall set the sheep on his right hand, but the goats on the left.
25:32–33

421 For I was an hungred, and ye gave me meat: I was thirsty, and ye gave me drink: I was a stranger, and ye took me in:
Naked, and ye clothed me: I was sick, and ye visited me: I was in prison, and ye came unto me.
25:35–36

422 And the King shall answer and say unto them, Verily I say unto you, Inasmuch as ye have done it unto one of the least of these my brethren, ye have done it unto me.
25:40

423 And he answered and said, He that dippeth his hand with me in the dish, the same shall betray me.
The Son of man goeth as it is written of him: but woe unto that man by whom the Son of man is betrayed! it had been good for that man if he had not been born.
Then Judas, which betrayed him, answered and said, Master, is it I? He said unto him, Thou hast said.
26:23–25

424 And as they were eating, Jesus took bread, and blessed it, and brake it, and gave it to the disciples, and said, Take, eat; this is my body.
And he took the cup, and gave thanks, and gave it to them, saying, Drink ye all of it;
For this is my blood of the new testament, which is shed for many for the remission of sins.
26:26–28

425 Jesus said unto him, Verily I say unto thee, That this night, before the cock crow, thou shalt deny me thrice.
26:34

426 Watch and pray, that ye enter not into temptation: the spirit indeed is willing, but the flesh is weak.
26:41

427 And forthwith he came to Jesus, and said, Hail, master; and kissed him.
And Jesus said unto him, Friend, wherefore art thou come? Then came they, and laid hands on Jesus, and took him.
26:49–50

428 Then said Jesus unto him, Put up again thy sword into his place: for all they that take the sword shall perish with the sword.
26:52

429 Then Judas, which had betrayed him, when he saw that he was condemned, repented himself, and brought again the thirty pieces of silver to the chief priests and elders,
Saying, I have sinned in that I have betrayed the innocent blood. And they said, What is that to us? see thou to that.
27:3–4

430 When Pilate saw that he could prevail nothing, but that rather a tumult was made, he took water, and washed his hands before the multitude, saying, I am innocent of the blood of this just person: see ye to it.
Then answered all the people, and said, His blood be on us, and on our children.
27:24–25

431 And about the ninth hour Jesus cried with a loud voice, saying, Eli, Eli, lama sabachthani? that is to say, My God, my God, why hast thou forsaken me?
27:46

432 Jesus, when he had cried again with a loud voice, yielded up the ghost.
And, behold, the veil of the temple was rent in twain from the top to the bottom; and the earth did quake, and the rocks rent;

And the graves were opened; and many bodies of the saints which slept arose.
27:50–52

433 Teaching them to observe all things whatsoever I have commanded you: and, lo, I am with you alway, even unto the end of the world. Amen.
28:20

Micah

434 Trust ye not in a friend, put ye not confidence in a guide: keep the doors of thy mouth from her that lieth in thy bosom.
7:5

Nehemiah

435 And I said, Should such a man as I flee? and who is there, that, being as I am, would go into the temple to save his life? I will not go in.
6:11

Numbers

436 The Lord bless thee, and keep thee:
The Lord make his face shine upon thee, and be gracious unto thee:
The Lord lift up his countenance upon thee, and give thee peace.
6:24–26

437 And Moses lifted up his hand, and with his rod he smote the rock twice: and the water came out abundantly, and the congregation drank, and their beasts also.
20:11

438 And the Lord opened the mouth of the ass, and she said unto Balaam, What have I done unto thee, that thou hast smitten me these three times?
22:28

439 But if ye will not do so, behold, ye have sinned against the Lord: and be sure your sin will find you out.
32:23

I Peter

440 Being born again, not of corruptible seed, but of incorruptible, by the word of God, which liveth and abideth for ever.
For all flesh is as grass, and all the glory of man as the flower of grass. The grass withereth, and the flower thereof falleth away.
1:23–24

441 Honour all men. Love the brotherhood. Fear God. Honour the king.
2:17

442 Even as Sara obeyed Abraham, calling him lord: whose daughters ye are, as long as ye do well, and are not afraid with any amazement.
Likewise, ye husbands, dwell with them according to knowledge, giving honour unto the wife, as unto the weaker vessel, and as being heirs together of the grace of life; that your prayers be not hindered.
3:6–7

Philippians

443 That at the name of Jesus every knee should bow, of things in heaven, and things in earth, and things under the earth.
2:10

444 Rejoice in the Lord alway: and again I say, Rejoice.
4:4

445 And the peace of God, which passeth all understanding, shall keep your hearts and minds through Christ Jesus.
4:7

446 Finally, brethren, whatsoever things are true, whatsoever things are honest, whatsoever things are just, whatsoever things are pure, whatsoever things are lovely, whatsoever things are of good report; if there be any virtue; and if there be any praise, think on these things.
4:8

Proverbs

447 For the lips of a strange woman drop as an honeycomb, and her mouth is smoother than oil: But her end is bitter as wormwood, sharp as a two-edged sword.
5:3–4

448 Wisdom hath builded her house, she hath hewn out her seven pillars.
9:1

449 Stolen waters are sweet, and bread eaten in secret is pleasant.
9:17

450 He that spareth his rod hateth his son: but he that loveth him chasteneth him betimes.
13:24

451 Pride goeth before destruction, and an haughty spirit before a fall.
16:18

452 He that is slow to anger is better than the mighty; and he that ruleth his spirit than he that taketh a city.
16:32

453 Wine is a mocker, strong drink is raging: and whosoever is deceived thereby is not wise.
20:1

454 For thou shalt heap coals of fire upon his head, and the Lord shall reward thee.
25:22

455 As cold waters to a thirsty soul, so is good news from a far country.
25:25

456 Answer a fool according to his folly, lest he be wise in his own conceit.
26:5

457 Boast not thyself of tomorrow; for thou knowest not what a day may bring forth.
27:1

458 Who can find a virtuous woman? for her price is far above rubies
The heart of her husband doth safely trust in her, so that he shall have no need of spoil.
She will do him good and not evil all the days of her life.
31:10–12

Revelations

459 Behold, he cometh with clouds; and every eye shall see him, and they also which pierced him: and all kindreds of the earth shall wail because of him. Even so, Amen.
I am Alpha and Omega, the beginning and the ending, saith the Lord, which is, and which was, and which is to come, the Almighty.
1:7–8

460 And I saw in the right hand of him that sat on the throne a book written within and on the backside, sealed with seven seals.
And I saw a strong angel proclaiming with a loud voice, Who is worthy to open the book, and to loose the seals thereof?
5:1–2

461 Saying with a loud voice, Worthy is the Lamb that was slain to receive power, and riches, and wisdom, and strength, and honour, and glory, and blessing.
5:12

462 And I looked, and behold a pale horse: and his name that sat on him was Death, and Hell followed with him. And power was given unto them over the fourth part of the earth, to kill with sword, and with hunger, and with death, and with the beasts of the earth.
6:8

463 And one of the elders answered, saying unto me, What are these which are arrayed in white robes? and whence came they?
And I said unto him, Sir, thou knowest. And he said to me, These are they which came out of great tribulation, and have washed their robes, and made them white in the blood of the Lamb.
7:13–14

464 And the name of the star is called Wormwood: and the third part of the waters became wormwood; and many men died of the waters, because they were made bitter.
8:11

465 And there was war in heaven: Michael and his angels fought against the dragon; and the dragon fought and his angels,
And prevailed not; neither was their place found any more in heaven.
And the great dragon was cast out, that old serpent, called the Devil, and Satan, which deceiveth the whole world: he was cast out into the earth, and his angels were cast out with him.
12:7–9

466 And that no man might buy or sell, save he that had the mark, or the name of the beast, or the number of his name.
Here is wisdom. Let him that hath understanding count the number of the beast: for it is the number of a man; and his number is Six hundred threescore and six.
13:17–18

467 Behold, I come as a thief. Blessed is he that watcheth, and keepeth his garments, lest he walk naked, and they see his shame.
And he gathered them together into a place called in the Hebrew tongue Armageddon.
16:15–16

468 And there came one of the seven angels which had the seven vials, and talked with me, saying unto me, Come hither; I will shew unto thee the judgment of the great whore that sitteth upon many waters.
17:1

469 And the woman was arrayed in purple and scarlet colour, and decked with gold and precious stones and pearls, having a golden cup in her hand full of abominations and filthiness of her fornication:
And upon her forehead was a name written, MYSTERY, BABYLON THE GREAT, THE MOTHER OF HARLOTS AND ABOMINATIONS OF THE EARTH.
And I saw the woman drunken with the blood of the saints, and with the blood of the martyrs of Jesus: and when I saw her, I wondered with great admiration.
17:4–6

470 And I saw heaven opened, and behold a white horse; and he that sat upon him was called Faithful and True, and in righteousness he doth judge and make war.
19:11

471 Blessed and holy is he that hath part in the first resurrection: on such the second death hath no power, but they shall be priests of God and of Christ, and shall reign with him a thousand years.
And when the thousand years are expired, Satan shall be loosed out of his prison,
And shall go out to deceive the nations which are in the four quarters of the earth, Gog and Magog, to gather them together to battle: the number of whom is as the sand of the sea.
20:6–8

472 And I saw a great white throne, and him that sat on it, from whose face the earth and the heaven fled away; and there was found no place for them.
And I saw the dead, small and great, stand before God; and the books were opened: and another book was opened, which is the book of life: and the dead were judged out of those things which were written in the books, according to their works.
And the sea gave up the dead which were in it; and death and hell delivered up the dead which were in them: and they were judged every man according to their works.
20:11–13

473 And I saw a new heaven and a new earth: for the first heaven and the first earth were passed away; and there was no more sea.
And I John saw the holy city, new Jerusalem, coming down from God out of heaven, prepared as a bride adorned for her husband.
21:1–2

474 And he shewed me a pure river of water of life, clear as crystal, proceeding out of the throne of God and of the Lamb.
In the midst of the street of it, and on either side of the river, was there the tree of life, which bare twelve manner of fruits, and yielded her fruit every month: and the leaves of the tree were for the healing of the nations.
22:1–2

Ruth

475 And Ruth said, Intreat me not to leave thee, or to return from following after thee: for whither thou goest, I will go; and where thou lodgest, I will lodge: thy people shall be my people, and thy God my God:
Where thou diest, will I die, and there will I be buried: the Lord do so to me, and more also, if ought but death part thee and me.
1:16–17

476 And he shall be unto thee a restorer of thy life and a nourisher of thine old age: for thy daughter in law, which loveth thee, which is better to thee than seven sons, hath born him.
4:15

I Samuel

477 Therefore Eli said unto Samuel, Go, lie down: and it shall be, if all thee, that thou shalt say, Speak, Lord; for thy servant heareth. So Samuel went and lay down in his place.
3:9

478 But now thy kingdom shall not continue: the Lord hath sought him a man after his own heart, and the Lord hath commanded him to be captain over his people, because thou hast not kept that which the Lord commanded thee.
13:14

479 And the people said unto Saul, Shall Jonathan die, who hath wrought this great salvation in Israel? God forbid: as the Lord liveth, there shall not one hair of his head fall to the ground; for he hath wrought with God this day. So the people rescued Jonathan, that he died not.
14:45

480 And he took his staff in his hand, and chose him five smooth stones out of the brook, and put them in a shepherd's bag which he had, even in a scrip; and his sling was in his hand: and he drew near to the Philistine.
17:40

481 And the women answered one another as they played, and said, Saul hath slain his thousands, and David his ten thousands.
18:7

II Samuel

482 Saul and Jonathan were lovely and pleasant in their lives, and in their death they were not divided: they were swifter than eagles, they were stronger than lions.
1:23–24

483 I am distressed for thee, my brother Jonathan: very pleasant hast thou been unto me: thy love to me was wonderful, passing the love of women.
How are the mighty fallen, and the weapons of war perished!
1:26–27

484 And a certain man saw it, and told Joab, and said, Behold, I saw Absalom hanged in an oak.
18:10

485 And the king was much moved, and went up to the chamber over the gate, and wept: and as he went, thus he said, O my son Absalom, my son, my son Absalom! would God I had died for thee, O Absalom, my son, my son!
18:33

Song of Solomon

486 I am the rose of Sharon, and the lily of the valleys.
As the lily among thorns, so is my love among the daughters.
2:1–2

487 He brought me to the banqueting house, and his banner over me was love.
Stay me with flagons, comfort me with apples: for I am sick of love.
His left hand is under my head, and his right hand doth embrace me.
2:4–6

488 The voice of my beloved! behold, he cometh leaping upon the mountains, skipping upon the hills.
2:8

489 My beloved spake, and said unto me, Rise up, my love, my fair one, and come away.
For, lo, the winter is past, the rain is over and gone;
The flowers appear on the earth; the time of the singing of birds is come, and the voice of the turtle is heard in our land.
2:10–12

490 Take us the foxes, the little foxes, that spoil the vines: for our vines have tender grapes.
2:15

491 My beloved is mine, and I am his: he feedeth among the lilies.
Until the day break, and the shadows flee away, turn, my beloved, and be thou like a roe or a young hart upon the mountains of Bether.
2:16–17

492 A fountain of gardens, a well of living waters, and streams from Lebanon.
4:15

493 I am come into my garden, my sister, my spouse: I have gathered my myrrh with my spice; I have eaten my honeycomb with my honey; I have drunk my wine with my milk: eat, O friends; drink, yea, drink abundantly, O beloved.
I sleep, but my heart waketh: it is the voice of my beloved that knocketh, saying, Open to me, my sister, my love, my dove, my undefiled: for my head is filled with dew, and my locks with the drops of the night.
5:1–2

494 My beloved put in his hand by the hole of the door, and my bowels were moved for him.
5:4

495 My beloved is gone down into his garden, to the beds of spices, to feed in the gardens, and to gather lilies.
I am my beloved's, and my beloved is mine: he feedeth among the lilies.
6:2–3

496 Who is she that looketh forth as the morning, fair as the moon, clear as the sun, and terrible as an army with banners?
6:10

497 Return, return, O Shulamite; return, return, that we may look upon thee. What will ye see in the Shulamite? As it were the company of two armies.
6:13

498 How fair and how pleasant art thou, O love, for delights!
7:6

499 I am my beloved's, and his desire is toward me.
7:10

500 Who is this that cometh up from the wilderness, leaning upon her beloved? I raised thee up under the apple tree: there thy mother brought thee forth: there she brought thee forth that bare thee.
8:5

501 Make haste, my beloved, and be thou like to a roe or to a young hart upon the mountains of spices.
8:14

I Thessalonians

502 Remembering without ceasing your work of faith, and labour of love, and patience of hope in our Lord Jesus Christ, in the sight of God and our Father.
1:3

503 For yourselves know perfectly that the day of the Lord so cometh as a thief in the night.
5:2

504 Prove all things; hold fast that which is good.
5:21

II Thessalonians

505 For even when we were with you, this we commanded you, that if any would not work, neither should he eat.
3:10

I Timothy

506 This is a faithful saying, and worthy of all acceptation, that Christ Jesus came into the world to save sinners; of whom I am chief.
1:15

507 This is a true saying, If a man desire the office of a bishop, he desireth a good work.
A bishop then must be blameless, the husband of one wife, vigilant, sober, of good behaviour, given to hospitality, apt to teach;
Not given to wine, no striker, not greedy of filthy lucre; but patient, not a brawler, not covetous.
3:1–3

508 For every creature of God is good, and nothing to be refused, if it be received with thanksgiving.
4:4

509 Drink no longer water, but use a little wine for thy stomach's sake and thine often infirmities.
5:23

510 For we brought nothing into this world, and it is certain we carry nothing out.
6:7

511 For the love of money is the root of all evil: which while some coveted after, they have erred from the faith, and pierced themselves through with many sorrows.
6:10

512 Fight the good fight of faith, lay hold on eternal life, whereunto thou art also called, and hast professed a good profession before many witnesses.
6:12

II Timothy

513 But evil men and seducers shall wax worse and worse, deceiving, and being deceived.
3:13

514 For I am now ready to be offered, and the time of my departure is at hand.
I have fought a good fight, I have finished my course, I have kept the faith:
Henceforth there is laid up for me a crown of righteousness, which the Lord, the righteous judge, shall give me at that day: and not to me only, but unto all them also that love his appearing.
4:6–8

Titus

515 One of themselves, even a prophet of their own, said, The Cretians are alway liars, evil beasts, slow bellies.
1:12

Tobit

516 Be not greedy to add money to money: but let it be as refuse in respect of our child.
5:18

517 Be of good comfort, my daughter; the Lord of heaven and earth give thee joy for this thy sorrow: be of good comfort, my daughter.
7:18

Wisdom

518 For the ear of jealousy heareth all things: and the noise of murmurings is not hid.
1:10

519 For the bewitching of naughtiness doth obscure things that are honest; and the wandering of concupiscence doth undermine the simple mind.

He, being made perfect in a short time, fulfilled a long time.
4:12–13

520 For all men have one entrance into life, and the like going out.
7:6

521 Wisdom reacheth from one end to another mightily: and sweetly doth she order all things.
8:1

522 For thou hast power of life and death: thou leadest to the gates of hell, and bringest up again.

Quotations about the Bible

See also religion

523 He will find one English book and one only, where, as in the *Iliad* itself, perfect plainness of speech is allied with perfect nobleness; and that book is the Bible.

Matthew Arnold (1822–88) British poet and critic. *On Translating Homer*

524 Candidates should not attempt more than six of these.

Hilaire Belloc (1870–1953) French-born British poet. Suggested addition to the Ten Commandments. Attrib.

525 There's a great text in Galatians,
Once you trip on it, entails
Twenty-nine distinct damnations,
One sure, if another fails.

Robert Browning (1812–89) British poet. *Soliloquy of the Spanish Cloister*

526 Isn't God a shit.

Randolph Churchill (1911–68) British political journalist. Evelyn Waugh discovered that Churchill had never read the Bible and persuaded him to do so; this is Churchill's reaction when asked what he thought of it. *Diaries* (E. Waugh)

527 It's just called 'The Bible' now. We dropped the word 'Holy' to give it a more mass-market appeal.

The Daily Telegraph, 30 Dec 1989

528 I have spent a lot of time searching through the Bible for loopholes.

W. C. Fields (1880–1946) US actor. Said during his last illness. Attrib.

529 The Bible demands suspension of belief, to have a story in which man produces woman at the very beginning is a reversal of nature from the very start.

Marilyn French (1929–) US author and critic. *The Observer*, 'Sayings of the Week', 24 Apr 1994

530 Had the Bible been in clear straightforward language, had the ambiguities and contradictions been edited out, and had the language been constantly modernised to accord with contemporary taste it would almost certainly have been, or become, a work of lesser influence.

John Kenneth Galbraith (1908–) US economist. *Economics, Peace and Laughter*

531 I am very sorry to know and hear how unreverently that most precious jewel, the Word of God, is disputed, rhymed, sung and jangled in every ale-house and tavern, contrary to the true meaning and doctrine of the same.

Henry VIII (1491–1547) King of England. Commenting on the translation of the Bible into English. Speech, Parliament, 24 Dec 1545

532 We have used the Bible as if it was a constable's handbook – an opium-dose for keeping beasts of burden patient while they are being overloaded.

Charles Kingsley (1819–75) British writer. *Letters to the Chartists*, 2

533 The English Bible, a book which, if everything else in our language should perish, would alone suffice to show the whole extent of its beauty and power.

Lord Macaulay (1800–59) British historian. *Essays and Biographies*, 'John Dryden', *Edinburgh Review*

534 The number one book of the ages was written by a committee, and it was called The Bible.

Louis B. Mayer (1885–1957) Russian-born US film producer. Comment to writers who had objected to changes in their work. *The Filmgoer's Book of Quotes* (Leslie Halliwell)

535 There's a Bible on that shelf there. But I keep it next to Voltaire – poison and antidote.

Bertrand Russell (1872–1970) British philosopher. *Kenneth Harris Talking To:* 'Bertrand Russell' (Kenneth Harris)

536 The Bible is literature, not dogma.

George Santayana (1863–1952) US philosopher. *Introduction to the Ethics of Spinoza*

537 As society is now constituted, a literal adherence to the moral precepts scattered throughout the Gospels would mean sudden death.

A. N. Whitehead (1861–1947) British philosopher. *Adventures in Ideas*

538 LORD ILLINGWORTH. The Book of Life begins with a man and a woman in a garden.
MRS ALLONBY. It ends with Revelations.

Oscar Wilde (1854–1900) Irish-born British dramatist. *A Woman of No Importance*, I

BIERCE, AMBROSE GWINNETT

(1842–?1914) US writer and journalist. His short stories were published in such collections as *In the Midst of Life* (1892). He also compiled *The Devil's Dictionary* (1906).

Quotations about Bierce

1 There was nothing of the milk of human kindness in old Ambrose.

H. L. Mencken (1880–1956) US journalist. *Prejudices*, 'Ambrose Bierce'

2 I have heard one young woman declare, 'I can feel him ten feet away!'

George Sterling *American Mercury*, Sept 1925

Quotations by Bierce

3 BORE, n. A person who talks when you wish him to listen.

The Devil's Dictionary

4 BRAIN, n. An apparatus with which we think that we think.

The Devil's Dictionary

5 DEBAUCHEE, n. One who has so earnestly

pursued pleasure that he has had the misfortune to overtake it.
The Devil's Dictionary

6 EGOTIST, n. A person of low taste, more interested in himself than in me.
The Devil's Dictionary

7 FUTURE, n. That period of time in which our affairs prosper, our friends are true and our happiness is assured.
The Devil's Dictionary

8 MARRIAGE, n. The state or condition of a community consisting of a master, a mistress and two slaves, making in all two.
The Devil's Dictionary

9 PATIENCE, n. A minor form of despair, disguised as a virtue.
The Devil's Dictionary

10 PEACE, n. In international affairs, a period of cheating between two periods of fighting.
The Devil's Dictionary

BIOGRAPHY

1 The Art of Biography
Is different from Geography.
Geography is about Maps,
But Biography is about Chaps.

Edmund Clerihew Bentley (1875–1956) British writer. *Biography for Beginners*

2 An autobiography is an obituary in serial form with the last instalment missing.
Quentin Crisp (?1910–) British writer. *The Naked Civil Servant*, Ch. 29

BIRDS

1 One for sorrow, two for mirth; three for a wedding, four for a birth; five for silver, six for gold; seven for a secret, not to be told; eight for heaven, nine for hell; and ten for the devil's own sel.
Referring to magpies or crows; there are numerous variants.
Proverb

2 The simple bird that thinks two notes a song.
W. H. Davies (1871–1940) British poet. Referring to the cuckoo. *April's Charms*

BIRTH

See also babies, life and death

1 It is natural to die as to be born; and to a little infant, perhaps, the one is as painful as the other.
Francis Bacon (1561–1626) English philosopher. *Essays*, 'Of Death'

2 Hanging head downwards between cliffs of bone, was the baby, its arms all but clasped about its neck, its face aslant upon its arms, hair painted upon its skull, closed, secret eyes, a diver poised in albumen, ancient and epic, shot with delicate spasms, as old as a Pharaoh in its tomb.
Enid Bagnold (1889–1981) British writer. *The Door of Life*, Ch. 2

3 A woman when she is in travail hath sorrow, because her hour is come: but as soon as she is delivered of the child, she remembereth no more the anguish, for joy that a man is born into the world.
Bible: John 16:21

4 For all men have one entrance into life, and the like going out.
Bible: Wisdom 7:6

5 My mother groan'd, my father wept,
Into the dangerous world I leapt;
Helpless, naked, piping loud,
Like a fiend hid in a cloud.

William Blake (1757–1827) British poet. *Songs of Experience*, 'Infant Sorrow'

6 For man's greatest crime is to have been born.
Pedro Calderón de la Barca (1600–81) Spanish dramatist. *La Vida es Sueño*, I

7 Parturition is a physiological process – the same in the countess and in the cow.
W. W. Chipman (1866–1950)

8 The history of man for the nine months preceding his birth would, probably, be far more interesting and contain events of greater moment than all the three-score and ten years that follow it.
Samuel Taylor Coleridge (1772–1834) British poet. *Miscellanies, Aesthetic and Literary*

9 If men had to have babies they would only ever have one each.
Diana, Princess of Wales (1961–) Wife of Prince Charles. *The Observer*, 'Sayings of the Week', 29 July 1984

10 Man's main task in life is to give *birth* to himself.
Erich Fromm (1900–80) German-born US psychologist. *Man for Himself*, Ch. 4

11 Birth may be a matter of a moment. But it is a unique one.
Frédérick Leboyer (1918–) French obstetrician. *Birth Without Violence*

12 I'll simply say here that I was born Beatrice Gladys Lillie at an extremely tender age because my mother needed a fourth at meals.
Beatrice Lillie (Constance Sylvia Munston, Lady Peel; 1898–1989) Canadian-born British actress. *Every Other Inch a Lady*, Ch. 1

13 In men nine out of ten abdominal tumors are malignant; in women nine out of ten abdominal swellings are the pregnant uterus.
Rutherford Morison (1853–1939) *The Practitioner*, Oct 1965

14 When we are born we cry that we are come
To this great stage of fools.

William Shakespeare (1564–1616) English dramatist. *King Lear*, IV:6

15 MACBETH. I bear a charmed life, which must not yield
To one of woman born.
MACDUFF. Despair thy charm;
And let the angel whom thou still hast serv'd
Tell thee Macduff was from his mother's womb
Untimely ripp'd.

William Shakespeare *Macbeth*, V:8

16 The explanation is quite simple. I wished to be near my mother.

James Whistler (1834–1903) US painter. Explaining to a snobbish lady why he had been born in such an unfashionable place as Lowell, Massachusetts. Attrib.

17 Our birth is but a sleep and a forgetting.

William Wordsworth (1770–1850) British poet. *Ode: Intimations of Immortality*

BITTERNESS

1 The dupe of friendship, and the fool of love; have I not reason to hate and to despise myself? Indeed I do; and chiefly for not having hated and despised the world enough.

William Hazlitt (1778–1830) British essayist. *On the Pleasure of Hating*

BLACKSTONE, SIR WILLIAM

(1723–80) British jurist; author of the classic *Commentaries on the Laws of England* (1765–69).

1 Man was formed for society.

Commentaries on the Laws of England, Introduction

2 The king never dies.

Commentaries on the Laws of England, Bk. I, Ch. 7

3 Time whereof the memory of man runneth not to the contrary.

Commentaries on the Laws of England, Bk. I, Ch. 18

4 That the king can do no wrong, is a necessary and fundamental principle of the English constitution.

Commentaries on the Laws of England, Bk. III, Ch. 17

5 It is better that ten guilty persons escape than one innocent suffer.

Commentaries on the Laws of England, Bk. IV, Ch. 27

BLAKE, WILLIAM

(1757–1827) British poet, painter, engraver, and visionary. Blake's mystical engravings and watercolours illustrate such works as *Songs of Innocence* (1789) and the poem *Jerusalem* (1804–20).

Quotations about Blake

1 William Blake's insanity was worth more than the sanity of any number of artistic mediocrities.

Gerald Abraham *Radio Times*, 10 Dec 1937

2 Where other poets use reality as a springboard into space, he uses it as a foothold when he returns from flight.

Arthur Symons (1865–1945) British poet. *William Blake*

Quotations by Blake

3 For everything that lives is holy, life delights in life.

America

4 The strongest poison ever known
Came from Caesar's laurel crown.

Auguries of Innocence

5 Every wolf's and lion's howl
Raises from Hell a human soul.

Auguries of Innocence

6 A truth that's told with bad intent
Beats all the lies you can invent.

Auguries of Innocence

7 Every tear from every eye
Becomes a babe in Eternity.

Auguries of Innocence

8 He who shall teach the child to doubt
The rotting grave shall ne'er get out.

Auguries of Innocence

9 To see a World in a grain of sand,
And a Heaven in a wild flower,
Hold Infinity in the palm of your hand,
And Eternity in an hour.

Auguries of Innocence

10 A robin redbreast in a cage
Puts all Heaven in a rage.

Auguries of Innocence

11 Does the Eagle know what is in the pit
Or wilt thou go ask the Mole?
Can Wisdom be put in a silver rod,
Or love in a golden bowl?

The Book of Thel, 'Thel's Motto'

12 'What,' it will be questioned, 'when the sun rises, do you not see a round disc of fire somewhat like a guinea?' 'O no, no, I see an innumerable company of the heavenly host crying, "Holy, Holy, Holy is the Lord God Almighty!"'

Descriptive Catalogue, 'The Vision of Judgment'

13 Humility is only doubt,
And does the sun and moon blot out.

The Everlasting Gospel

14 Great things are done when men and mountains meet;
This is not done by jostling in the street.

Gnomic Verses

15 He who bends to himself a Joy
Doth the wingèd life destroy;
But he who kisses the Joy as it flies
Lives in Eternity's sunrise.

Gnomic Verses

16 He who would do good to another must do it in Minute Particulars.
General Good is the plea of the scoundrel, hypocrite, and flatterer.

Jerusalem

17 I care not whether a man is Good or Evil; all that I care
Is whether he is a Wise Man or a Fool. Go! put off Holiness,
And put on Intellect.

Jerusalem

18 Without Contraries is no progression. Attraction and Repulsion, Reason and Energy, Love and Hate, are necessary to Human existence.

The Marriage of Heaven and Hell, 'The Argument'

19 If the doors of perception were cleansed everything would appear to man as it is, infinite.
The Marriage of Heaven and Hell, 'A Memorable Fancy'

20 Prisons are built with stones of Law, brothels with bricks of Religion.
The Marriage of Heaven and Hell, 'Proverbs of Hell'

21 Sooner murder an infant in its cradle than nurse unacted desires.
The Marriage of Heaven and Hell, 'Proverbs of Hell'

22 In seed time learn, in harvest teach, in winter enjoy.
The Marriage of Heaven and Hell, 'Proverbs of Hell'

23 The cut worm forgives the plough.
The Marriage of Heaven and Hell, 'Proverbs of Hell'

24 What is now proved was once only imagined.
The Marriage of Heaven and Hell, 'Proverbs of Hell'

25 The road of excess leads to the palace of Wisdom.
The Marriage of Heaven and Hell, 'Proverbs of Hell'

26 He who desires but acts not, breeds pestilence.
The Marriage of Heaven and Hell, 'Proverbs of Hell'

27 A fool sees not the same tree that a wise man sees.
The Marriage of Heaven and Hell, 'Proverbs of Hell'

28 Damn braces. Bless relaxes.
The Marriage of Heaven and Hell, 'Proverbs of Hell'

29 Exuberance is Beauty.
The Marriage of Heaven and Hell, 'Proverbs of Hell'

30 Those who restrain Desire, do so because theirs is weak enough to be restrained.
The Marriage of Heaven and Hell, 'Those who restrain Desire...'

31 Man has no Body distinct from his Soul; for that called Body is a portion of Soul discerned by the five Senses, the chief inlets of Soul in this age.
The Marriage of Heaven and Hell, 'The Voice of the Devil'

32 Energy is Eternal Delight.
The Marriage of Heaven and Hell, 'The Voice of the Devil'

33 And did those feet in ancient time
Walk upon England's mountains green?
And was the holy lamb of God
On England's pleasant pastures seen?
...
I will not cease from mental fight,
Nor shall my sword sleep in my hand,
Till we have built Jerusalem
In England's green and pleasant land.
Better known as the hymn 'Jerusalem', with music by Sir Hubert Parry; not to be confused with Blake's longer poem *Jerusalem*.
Milton, Preface

34 Mock on, mock on, Voltaire, Rousseau;
Mock on, mock on; 'tis all in vain!
You throw the sand against the wind,
And the wind blows it back again.
Mock on, mock on, Voltaire, Rousseau

35 When Sir Joshua Reynolds died
All Nature was degraded;
The King dropped a tear in the Queen's ear,
And all his pictures faded.
On Art and Artists

36 Love seeketh not itself to please,
Nor for itself hath any care,
But for another gives its ease,
And builds a Heaven in Hell's despair.
Songs of Experience, 'The Clod and the Pebble'

37 Love seeketh only Self to please,
To bind another to its delight,
Joys in another's loss of ease,
And builds a Hell in Heaven's despite.
Songs of Experience, 'The Clod and the Pebble'

38 My mother groan'd, my father wept,
Into the dangerous world I leapt;
Helpless, naked, piping loud,
Like a fiend hid in a cloud.
Songs of Experience, 'Infant Sorrow'

39 Tiger! Tiger! burning bright
In the forests of the night,
What immortal hand or eye
Could frame thy fearful symmetry?
Songs of Experience, 'The Tiger'

40 When the stars threw down their spears,
And watered heaven with their tears,
Did he smile his work to see?
Did he who made the Lamb make thee?
Songs of Experience, 'The Tiger'

41 Piping down the valleys wild,
Piping songs of pleasant glee,
On a cloud I saw a child.
Songs of Innocence, Introduction

42 'Pipe a song about a Lamb!'
So I piped with merry cheer.
Songs of Innocence, Introduction

43 To Mercy, Pity, Peace, and Love
All pray in their distress.
Songs of Innocence, 'The Divine Image'

44 For Mercy has a human heart,
Pity a human face,
And Love, the human form divine,
And Peace, the human dress.
Songs of Innocence, 'The Divine Image'

45 'Twas on a Holy Thursday, their innocent faces clean,
The children walking two and two, in red and blue and green.
Songs of Innocence, 'Holy Thursday'

46 Little Lamb, who made thee?
Dost thou know who made thee?
Songs of Innocence, 'The Lamb'

47 When the green woods laugh with the voice of joy.
Songs of Innocence, 'Laughing song'

48 My mother bore me in the southern wild.
And I am black, but O! my soul is white;
White as an angel is the English child,
But I am black, as if bereav'd of light.
Songs of Innocence, 'The Little Black Boy'

49 Man's Desires are limited by his Perceptions; none can desire what he has not perceived.
There is no Natural Religion

50 The Desire of Man being Infinite, the possession is Infinite, and himself Infinite.
There is no Natural Religion

51 I mock thee not, though I by thee am mockèd;
Thou call'st me madman, but I call thee blockhead.
To Flaxman

52 To generalize is to be an idiot.
Life of Blake (Gilchrist)

BLEASDALE, ALAN

(1946–) British playwright who has written many works for radio and television. His plays include *Boys from the Blackstuff* (1982), *Having a Ball* (1986), *Are You Lonesome Tonight* (1988), and *On the Ledge* (1993).

1 Gizza job, go on, gizzit.
Boys from the Blackstuff, 'Yosser's Story'

2 All the names under the sun and my mother picked Doreen. I mean, how can you go to a Hunt Ball or a dinner at the Town Hall and be announced as…'Doreen'.
Having a Ball, I

3 I have all the usual male problems – my breath smells, I fart in bed, I come too early, or I don't come at all, sometimes I even come and no one notices…it took me six years to find my wife's clitoris.
Having a Ball, I

4 Oh dear, not another Greta Garbo, that'll be four we've got now.
It's a Madhouse, I

5 Seen better heads on a mop.
It's a Madhouse, II

BLESSING

See also prayer

1 Matthew, Mark, Luke and John,
The bed be blest that I lie on.
Thomas Ady (17th century) English poet. *A Candle in the Dark*

2 I see the moon,
And the moon sees me;
God bless the moon,
And God bless me.
Anonymous *Gammer Gurton's Garland*

3 Thank you, sister. May you be the mother of a bishop!
Brendan Behan (1923–64) Irish playwright. Said to a nun nursing him on his deathbed. Attrib.

4 The Lord bless thee, and keep thee:
The Lord make his face shine upon thee, and be gracious unto thee:
The Lord lift up his countenance upon thee, and give thee peace.
Bible: Numbers 6:24–26

5 And the peace of God, which passeth all understanding, shall keep your hearts and minds through Christ Jesus.
Bible: Philippians 4:7

6 I'm worst at what I do best and for this gift I feel blest.
Kurt Cobain (1967–94) US rock musician. *Nevermind*

7 O happy living things! no tongue
Their beauty might declare:
A spring of love gushed from my heart,
And I blessed them unaware:
Since my kind saint took pity on me,
And I blessed them unaware.
Samuel Taylor Coleridge (1772–1834) British poet. *The Rime of the Ancient Mariner*, IV

8 'God bless us every one!' said Tiny Tim, the last of all.
Charles Dickens (1812–70) British novelist. *A Christmas Carol*

BLINDNESS

See also disability

1 A nod is as good as a wink to a blind horse.
Proverb

2 Men are blind in their own cause.
Proverb

3 My eyes are dim
I cannot see
I have not brought my specs with me.
Anonymous *The Quartermaster's Stores*

4 …for three years I have been deprived of my sight. I wish you to learn from my own hand that thanks to the Divine Goodness I have recovered it. I see but as one sees after an operation, that is to say very dimly. Even this is a blessing for one who has had the misfortune to become blind. When I was sightless I cared for nothing, now I want to see everything….
Rosalba Carriera (1675–1757) Letter, 23 Aug 1749

5 My soul is full of whispered song;
My blindness is my sight;
The shadows that I feared so long
Are all alive with light.
Alice Cary (1820–71) *Dying Hymn*

6 How reconcile this world of fact with the bright world of my imagining? My darkness has been filled with the light of intelligence, and behold, the outer day-light world was stumbling and groping in social blindness.
Helen Keller (1880–1968) US writer and lecturer. *The Cry for Justice* (ed. Upton Sinclair)

7 Ask for this great deliverer now, and find him
Eyeless in Gaza at the mill with slaves.
John Milton (1608–74) English poet. *Samson Agonistes*

8 O dark, dark, dark, amid the blaze of noon,
Irrecoverably dark, total eclipse,
Without all hope of day!
John Milton *Samson Agonistes*

9 When I consider how my light is spent
Ere half my days in this dark world and wide,
And that one talent which is death to hide
Lodged with me useless.
John Milton *Sonnet*: 'On his Blindness'

10 Doth God exact day-labour, light deny'd,
I fondly ask.

John Milton *Sonnet*, 'When I Consider How my Light is Spent'

11 I have only one eye: I have a right to be blind sometimes: I really do not see the signal.

Lord Nelson (1758–1805) British admiral. Remark, Battle of Copenhagen, 2 Apr 1801; Nelson ignored Admiral Parker's order to disengage by placing his telescope to his blind eye; an hour later, he was victorious. *Life of Nelson* Ch. 7 (Robert Southey)

12 He clapped the glass to his sightless eye,
And 'I'm damned if I see it', he said.

Henry John Newbolt (1862–1938) British poet. Referring to Lord Nelson at the Battle of Copenhagen. *Admirals All*

13 And so I betake myself to that course, which is almost as much as to see myself go into my grave – for which, and all the discomforts that will accompany my being blind, the good God prepare me!

Samuel Pepys (1633–1703) English diarist. The closing words of Pepys's *Diary*; he lived another 34 years and did not go blind. *Diary*, 31 May 1669

BOASTS

1 I have done almost every human activity inside a taxi which does not require main drainage.

Alan Brien (1925–) British critic. *Punch*, 5 July 1972

BOATS

See also navy, sea

1 There's something wrong with our bloody ships today.

Earl Beatty (1871–1936) British admiral. Remark during Battle of Jutland, 30 May 1916. Attrib.

2 All rowed fast but none so fast as stroke.

Desmond Coke (1879–1931) British writer. Popular misquotation, derived from the passage: 'His blade struck the water a full second before any other…until…as the boats began to near the winning post, his own was dipping into the water *twice* as often as any other.' *Sandford of Merton*

3 As idle as a painted ship
Upon a painted ocean.

Samuel Taylor Coleridge (1772–1834) British poet. *The Rime of the Ancient Mariner*, I

4 Jolly boating weather,
And a hay harvest breeze,
Blade on the feather,
Shade off the trees
Swing, swing together
With your body between your knees.

William Johnson Cory (1823–92) British schoolmaster and poet. *Eton Boating Song*

5 Fair stood the wind for France
When we our sails advance.

Michael Drayton (1563–1631) English poet. *Agincourt*

6 For you dream you are crossing the Channel, and tossing about in a steamer from Harwich
Which is something between a large bathing machine and a very small second-class carriage.

W. S. Gilbert (1836–1911) British dramatist. *Iolanthe*, II

7 There is nothing – absolutely nothing – half so much worth doing as simply messing about in boats.

Kenneth Grahame (1859–1932) Scottish writer. *The Wind in the Willows*, Ch. 1

8 The little ships, the unforgotten Homeric catalogue of *Mary Jane* and *Peggy IV*, of *Folkestone Belle*, *Boy Billy*, and *Ethel Maud*, of *Lady Haig* and *Skylark*…the little ships of England brought the Army home.

Philip Guedalla (1889–1944) British writer. Referring to the evacuation of Dunkirk. *Mr. Churchill*

9 Well: while was fashioning
This creature of cleaving wing,
The Immanent Will that stirs and urges everything

Prepared a sinister mate
For her – so gaily great –
A Shape of Ice, for the time far and dissociate.

And as the smart ship grew
In stature, grace, and hue,
In shadowy silent distance grew the Iceberg too.

Thomas Hardy (1840–1928) British novelist. Referring to the 'Titanic', a luxury passenger ship, thought to be unsinkable because of its special design. It struck an iceberg on its maiden voyage and sank, causing the loss of 1513 lives. *The Convergence of the Twain*

10 No man will be a sailor who has contrivance enough to get himself into a jail; for being in a ship is being in a jail, with the chance of being drowned…A man in a jail has more room, better food, and commonly better company.

Samuel Johnson (1709–84) British lexicographer. *Life of Johnson* (J. Boswell), Vol. I

11 I'd like to get you
On a slow boat to China.

Frank Loesser (1910–69) US songwriter. *Slow Boat to China*

12 It was the schooner Hesperus,
That sailed the wintry sea;
And the skipper had taken his little daughter,
To bear him company.

Henry Wadsworth Longfellow (1807–82) US poet. *The Wreck of the Hesperus*

13 Quinquireme of Nineveh from distant Ophir
Rowing home to haven in sunny Palestine,
With a cargo of ivory,
And apes and peacocks,
Sandalwood, cedarwood, and sweet white wine.

John Masefield (1878–1967) British poet. *Cargoes*

14 Dirty British coaster with a salt-caked smoke stack,
Butting through the Channel in the mad March days,
With a cargo of Tyne coal,
Road-rail, pig-lead,
Firewood, iron-ware, and cheap tin trays.

John Masefield *Cargoes*

15 Now the sunset breezes shiver,
And she's fading down the river,
But in England's song for ever
She's the Fighting Téméraire.

Henry John Newbolt (1862–1938) British poet. *The Fighting Téméraire*

16 Only fools and passengers drink at sea.

Alan John Villiers (1903–) Australian naval commander. *The Observer*, 'Sayings of the Week', 28 Apr 1957

BOCCACCIO, GIOVANNI

(1313–75) Italian writer and poet. He is chiefly known for the *Decameron*: a hundred stories told by young people escaping from the plague in Florence in 1348. Other works include *Filostrato*, which provided the plot for Chaucer's *Troilus and Criseyde*, and *Teseida* which formed the basis of *The Knights' Tale*.

1 It is annoying and impossible to suffer proud women, because in general Nature has given men proud and high spirits, while it has made women humble in character and submissive, more apt for delicate things than for ruling.
Concerning Famous Women, 'Niobe'

2 It often happens, that he who endeavours to ridicule other people, especially in things of a serious nature, becomes himself a jest, and frequently to his great cost.
Decameron, The Second Day, I

3 There are some people so indiscreet in appearing to know what they had better be unacquainted with, that they think, by reproving other people's inadvertencies, to lessen their own shame: whereas they make that vastly greater.
Decameron, The Third Day, II

4 Although love dwells in gorgeous palaces, and sumptuous apartments, more willingly than in miserable and desolate cottages, it cannot be denied but that he sometimes causes his power to be felt in the gloomy recesses of forests, among the most bleak and rugged mountains, and in the dreary caves of a desert.
Decameron, The Third Day, X

5 Whoever rightly considers the order of things may plainly see the whole race of woman-kind is by nature, custom, and the laws, made subject to man, to be governed according to his discretion: therefore it is the duty of every one of us that desires to have ease, comfort, and repose, with those men to whom we belong, to be humble, patient, and obedient, as well as chaste…
Decameron, The Ninth Day, IX

BOOK OF COMMON PRAYER, THE

See also Bible, Psalms.

1 O all ye Works of the Lord, bless ye the Lord.
Benedicite

2 Man that is born of a woman hath but a short time to live, and is full of misery.
Burial of the Dead, First anthem

3 In the midst of life we are in death.
Burial of the Dead, First anthem

4 Almighty God, give us the grace that we may cast away the works of darkness, and put upon us the armour of light, now in the time of this mortal life.
Collect, 1st Sunday in Advent

5 Read, mark, learn and inwardly digest.
Collect, 2nd Sunday in Advent

6 Increase and multiply upon us they mercy; that, thou being our ruler and guide, we may so pass through things temporal, that we finally lose not the things eternal.
Collect, 4th Sunday after Trinity

7 Grant that those things which we ask faithfully we may obtain effectually.
Collect, 23rd Sunday after Trinity

8 All our doings without charity are nothing worth.
Collect, Quinquagesima Sunday

9 Lighten our darkness, we beseech thee, O Lord; and by thy great mercy defend us from all perils and dangers of this night.
Evening Prayer, Third Collect

10 Ye that do truly and earnestly repent you of your sins, and are in love and charity with your neighbours, and intend to lead a new life, following the commandments of God, and walking from henceforth in his holy ways; Draw near with faith, and take this holy Sacrament to your comfort; and make your humble confession to Almighty God, meekly kneeling upon your knees.
Holy Communion, The Invitation

11 The blessing of God Almighty, the Father, the Son, and the Holy Ghost, be amongst you and remain with you always.
Holy Communion, The Blessing

12 All the deceits of the world, the flesh, and the devil.
The Litany

13 In the hour of death, and in the day of judgement.
The Litany

14 We have erred, and strayed from thy ways like lost sheep.
Morning Prayer, General Confession

15 We have left undone those things which we ought to have done; and we have done those things we ought not to have done.
Morning Prayer, General Confession

16 As it was in the beginning, is now, and ever shall be: world without end.
Morning Prayer, Gloria

17 When two or three are gathered together in thy Name thou wilt grant their requests.
Morning Prayer, Prayer of St Chrysostom

18 Grant that this day we fall into no sin, neither run into any kind of danger.
Morning Prayer, Third Collect, for Grace

19 Being now come to the years of discretion.
Order of Confirmation

20 Defend, O Lord, this thy Child with thy heavenly grace, that he may continue thine for ever; and daily increase in thy holy Spirit more and more, until he come unto thy everlasting kingdom.

Order of Confirmation

21 O merciful God, grant that the old Adam in this Child may be so buried, that the new man may be raised up in him.

Public Baptism of Infants, Invocation of blessing on the child.

22 Renounce the devil and all his works.

Public Baptism of Infants

23 If any of you know cause, or just impediment, why these two persons should not be joined together in holy Matrimony, ye are to declare it.

Solemnization of Matrimony, The Banns

24 First, It was ordained for the procreation of children, to be brought up in the fear and nurture of the Lord, and to the praise of his holy Name.

Solemnization of Matrimony, Exhortation

25 Let him now speak, or else hereafter for ever hold his peace.

Solemnization of Matrimony, Exhortation

26 Wilt thou love her, comfort her, honour, and keep her in sickness and in health; and, forsaking all other, keep thee only unto her, so long as ye both shall live?

Solemnization of Matrimony, Betrothal

27 To have and to hold from this day forward, for better for worse, for richer for poorer, in sickness and in health, to love and to cherish, till death us do part.

Solemnization of Matrimony, Betrothal

28 With this Ring I thee wed, with my body I thee worship, and with all my wordly goods I thee endow.

Solemnization of Matrimony, Wedding

29 Those whom God hath joined together let no man put asunder.

Solemnization of Matrimony, Wedding

BOOKS

See also criticism, fiction, literature, novels, publishing, reading, writing

1 Books and friends should be few but good.

Proverb

2 The true system of the World has been recognized, developed and perfected...Everything has been discussed and analysed, or at least mentioned.

Jean d'Alembert (1717–83) French philosopher and mathematician. Referring to the *Encyclopédie* (1751–80), which he helped to edit. *Elements of Philosophy*

3 Some books are undeservedly forgotten; none are undeservedly remembered.

W. H. Auden (1907–73) British poet. *The Dyer's Hand*, 'Reading'

4 Some books are to be tasted, others to be swallowed, and some few to be chewed and digested.

Francis Bacon (1561–1626) English philosopher. *Essays*, 'Of Studies'

5 Books must follow sciences, and not sciences books.

Francis Bacon *Proposition touching Amendment of Laws*

6 It is all very well to be able to write books, but can you waggle your ears?

J. M. Barrie (1860–1937) British novelist and dramatist. Speaking to H. G. Wells. *Barrie: The Story of A Genius* (J. A. Hamerton)

7 When I am dead, I hope it may be said:
'His sins were scarlet, but his books were read.'

Hilaire Belloc (1870–1953) French-born British poet. *Epigrams*, 'On His Books'

8 Child! do not throw this book about;
Refrain from the unholy pleasure
Of cutting all the pictures out!
Preserve it as your chiefest treasure.

Hilaire Belloc *The Bad Child's Book of Beasts*, 'Dedication'

9 And further, by these, my son, be admonished: of making many books there is no end; and much study is a weariness of the flesh.

Bible: Ecclesiastes 12:12

10 I keep my books at the British Museum and at Mudie's.

Samuel Butler (1835–1902) British writer. *The Humour of Homer*, 'Ramblings in Cheapside'

11 'Tis pleasant, sure, to see one's name in print;
A book's a book, although there's nothing in't.

Lord Byron (1788–1824) British poet. *English Bards and Scotch Reviewers*

12 A good book is the purest essence of a human soul.

Thomas Carlyle (1795–1881) Scottish historian and essayist. Speech made in support of the London Library. *Carlyle and the London Library* (F. Harrison)

13 'What is the use of a book,' thought Alice, 'without pictures or conversation?'

Lewis Carroll (Charles Lutwidge Dodgson; 1832–98) British writer. *Alice's Adventures in Wonderland*, Ch. 1

14 Go, litel book, go litel myn tragedie.
O moral Gower, this book I directe To thee.

Geoffrey Chaucer (c. 1342–1400) English poet. *Troilus and Criseyde*, 5

15 A best-seller was a book which somehow sold well simply because it was selling well.

Daniel J. Boorstin *The Image*, 'From Shapes to Shadows: Dissolving Forms'

16 Due attention to the inside of books, and due contempt for the outside, is the proper relation between a man of sense and his books.

Earl of Chesterfield (1694–1773) English statesman. Letter to his son, 10 Jan 1749

17 Books cannot always please, however good;
Minds are not ever craving for their food.

George Crabbe (1754–1832) British poet. *The Borough*, 'Schools'

18 Books, we are told, propose to *instruct* or to *amuse*. Indeed!...The true antithesis to knowledge, in this case, is not *pleasure,* but *power.* All that is literature seeks to communicate power; all that is not literature, to communicate knowledge.

Thomas De Quincey (1785–1859) British writer. *Letters to a Young Man*

19 A book is not harmless merely because no one is consciously offended by it.

T. S. Eliot (1888–1965) US-born British poet and dramatist. *Religion and Literature*

20 Books are made not like children but like pyramids...and they're just as useless! and they stay in the desert!...Jackals piss at their foot and the bourgeois climb up on them.

Gustave Flaubert (1821–80) French novelist. Letter to Ernest Feydeau, 1857

21 Men of power have not time to read; yet men who do not read are unfit for power.

Michael Foot (1913–) British politician. *Debts of Honour*

22 Learning hath gained most by those books by which the printers have lost.

Thomas Fuller (1608–61) English historian. *The Holy State and the Profane State*

23 A book may be amusing with numerous errors, or it may be very dull without a single absurdity.

Oliver Goldsmith (1728–74) Irish-born British writer. *The Vicar of Wakefield*, Advertisement

24 Few books today are forgivable.

R. D. Laing (1927–89) British psychiatrist. *The Politics of Experience*, Introduction

25 Borrowers of books – those mutilators of collections, spoilers of the symmetry of shelves, and creators of odd volumes.

Charles Lamb (1775–1834) British essayist. *Essays of Elia*, 'The Two Races of Men'

26 Get stewed:
Books are a load of crap.

Philip Larkin (1922–85) British poet. *A Study of Reading Habits*

27 To every man who struggles with his own soul in mystery, a book that is a book flowers once, and seeds, and is gone.

D. H. Lawrence (1885–1930) British novelist. *Phoenix*, 'A Bibliography of D.H.L.'

28 Never judge a cover by its book.

Fran Lebowitz (1950–) US writer. *Metropolitan Life*

29 There can hardly be a stranger commodity in the world than books. Printed by people who don't understand them; sold by people who don't understand them; bound, criticized and read by people who don't understand them; and now even written by people who don't understand them.

Georg Christoph Lichtenberg (1742–99) German physicist and writer. *Aphorisms*

30 He felt about books as doctors feel about medicines, or managers about plays – cynical but hopeful.

Dame Rose Macaulay (1881–1958) British writer. *Crewe Train*, Ch. 8, Pt. 2

31 In recommending a book to a friend the less said the better. The moment you praise a book too highly you awaken resistance in your listener.

Henry Miller (1891–1980) US novelist. *The Books In My Life*

32 Who kills a man kills a reasonable creature, God's image; but he who destroys a good book, kills reason itself, kills the image of God, as it were in the eye.

John Milton (1608–74) English poet. *Areopagitica*

33 A good book is the precious life-blood of a master spirit, embalmed and treasured up on purpose to a life beyond life.

John Milton *Areopagitica*

34 The books one reads in childhood, and perhaps most of all the bad and good bad books, create in one's mind a sort of false map of the world, a series of fabulous countries into which one can retreat at odd moments throughout the rest of life, and which in some cases can even survive a visit to the real countries which they are supposed to represent.

George Orwell (Eric Blair; 1903–50) British novelist. *Riding Down from Bangor*

35 At last, an unprintable book that is readable.

Ezra Pound (1885–1972) US poet. Referring to *Tropic of Cancer* by Henry Miller.

36 An anthology is like all the plums and orange peel picked out of a cake.

Walter Raleigh (1861–1922) British scholar. Letter to Mrs Robert Bridges, 15 Jan 1915

37 I have known her pass the whole evening without mentioning a single book, or *in fact anything unpleasant* at all.

Henry Reed (1914–86) British poet and dramatist. *A Very Great Man Indeed*

38 When a new book is published, read an old one.

Samuel Rogers (1763–1855) British poet. Attrib.

39 We all know that books burn – yet we have the greater knowledge that books cannot be killed by fire. People die, but books never die. No man and no force can abolish memory...In this war, we know, books are weapons.

Franklin D. Roosevelt (1882–1945) US Democratic president. Message to American Booksellers Association, 23 Apr 1942

40 If a book is worth reading, it is worth buying.

John Ruskin (1819–1900) British art critic and writer. *Sesame and Lilies*, 'Of Kings' Treasuries'

41 All books are divisible into two classes, the books of the hour, and the books of all time.

John Ruskin *Sesame and Lilies*, 'Of Kings' Treasuries'

42 How long most people would look at the best book before they would give the price of a large turbot for it!

John Ruskin *Sesame and Lilies*, 'Of Kings' Treasuries'

43 A library is thought in cold storage.

Herbert Samuel (1870–1963) British Liberal statesman. *A Book of Quotations*

44 Children...have no use for psychology. They detest sociology. They still believe in God, the family, angels, devils, witches, goblins, logic, clarity, punctuation, and other such obsolete stuff...When a book is boring, they yawn openly. They don't expect their writer to redeem humanity, but leave to adults such childish illusions.

Isaac Bashevis Singer (1904–91) Polish-born US writer. Speech on receiving the Nobel Prize for Literature. *The Observer*, 17 Dec 1978

45 A best-seller is the gilded tomb of a mediocre talent.

Logan Pearsall Smith (1865–1946) US writer. *Afterthoughts*, 'Art and Letters'

46 No furniture so charming as books.

Sydney Smith (1771–1845) British clergyman and essayist. *Memoir* (Lady Holland)

47 Books are good enough in their own way, but they are a mighty bloodless substitute for life.

Robert Louis Stevenson (1850–94) Scottish writer. *Virginibus Puerisque*

48 My brother-in-law wrote an unusal murder story. The victim got killed by a man from another book.

Robert Sylvester (1907–75) US writer.

49 Not with blinded eyesight poring over miserable books.

Alfred, Lord Tennyson (1809–92) British poet. *Locksley Hall*

50 A good book is the best of friends, the same to-day and for ever.

Martin Farquhar Tupper (1810–89) British writer. *Proverbial Philosophy*, 'Of Reading'

51 Books, I don't know what you see in them…I can understand a person reading them, but I can't for the life of me see why people have to write them.

Peter Ustinov (1921–) British actor. *Photo-Finish*

52 God forbid that any book should be banned. The practice is as indefensible as infanticide.

Rebecca West (Cicely Isabel Fairfield; 1892–1983) British novelist and journalist. *The Strange Necessity*, 'The Tosh Horse'

53 There is no such thing as a moral or an immoral book. Books are well written, or badly written.

Oscar Wilde (1854–1900) Irish-born British dramatist. *The Picture of Dorian Gray*, Preface

BOREDOM

See also bores

1 Nothing happens, nobody comes, nobody goes, it's awful!

Samuel Beckett (1906–89) Irish novelist and dramatist. *Waiting for Godot*, I

2 I'm so bored with it all.

Winston Churchill (1874–1965) British statesman. Said to be his last words. *Clementine* (M. Soames)

3 I wanted to be bored to death, as good a way to go as any.

Peter De Vries (1910–93) US novelist. *Comfort me with Apples*, Ch. 17

4 Millions long for immortality who do not know what to do with themselves on a rainy Sunday afternoon.

Susan Ertz British novelist and playwright. *Anger in the Sky*

5 You ought not to be ashamed of being bored. What you ought to be ashamed of is being boring.

Lord Hailsham (1907–) British Conservative politician. *The Observer*, 'Sayings of the Week', 12 Oct 1975

6 Symmetry is tedious, and tedium is the very basis of mourning. Despair yawns.

Victor Hugo (1802–85) French writer. *Les Misérables*, Vol. II, Bk. IV, Ch. 1

7 The effect of boredom on a large scale in history is underestimated. It is a main cause of revolutions, and would soon bring to an end all the static Utopias and the farmyard civilization of the Fabians.

Dean Inge (1860–1954) British churchman. *The End of an Age*, Ch. 6

8 By his very success in inventing labor-saving devices modern man has manufactured an abyss of boredom that only the privileged classes in earlier civilisations have ever fathomed.

Lewis Mumford (1895–1990) US social philosopher. *The Conduct of Life*

9 Is not life a hundred times too short for us to bore ourselves?

Friedrich Wilhelm Nietzsche (1844–1900) German philosopher. *Jenseits von Gut und Böse*

10 When you're bored with yourself, marry and be bored with someone else.

David Pryce-Jones (1936–) British author and critic. *Owls and Satyrs*

11 Boredom provides a stronger inclination to write than anything.

Vikram Seth (1952–) Indian writer. *The Observer*, 'Sayings of the Week', 1 May 1994

BORES

See also boredom

1 *Bore*, n. A person who talks when you wish him to listen.

Ambrose Bierce (1842–?1914) US writer and journalist. *The Devil's Dictionary*

2 Society is now one polish'd horde,
Form'd of two mighty tribes, the *Bores* and *Bored*.

Lord Byron (1788–1824) British poet. *Don Juan*, XIII

3 Sir, you are like a pin, but without either its head or its point.

Douglas William Jerrold (1803–57) British dramatist. Speaking to a small thin man who was boring him. Attrib.

4 He is not only a bore but he bores for England.

Malcolm Muggeridge (1903–90) British writer. Referring to Sir Anthony Eden, Conservative prime minister (1955–57). In *Newstatesmanship* (E. Hyams), 'Boring for England'

5 A bore is a man who, when you ask him how he is, tells you.

Bert Leston Taylor (1866–1921) US journalist. Attrib.

6 Somebody's boring me, I think it's me.

Dylan Thomas (1914–53) Welsh poet. Remark made after he had been talking continuously for some time. *Four Absentees* (Rayner Heppenstall)

7 He is an old bore; even the grave yawns for him.

Herbert Beerbohm Tree (1853–1917) British actor and theatre manager. Referring to Israel Zangwill (1864–1926) British novelist, playwright, and Zionist. *Beerbohm Tree* (Hesketh Pearson)

8 A healthy male adult bore consumes each year one and a half times his own weight in other people's patience.

John Updike (1932–) US novelist. *Assorted Prose*, 'Confessions of a Wild Bore'

9 Dear Frank, we believe you; you have dined in every house in London – *once*.

Oscar Wilde (1854–1900) Irish-born British dramatist. Interrupting Frank Harris's interminable account of the houses he had dined at. Attrib.

BORROWING

1 Borrowed garments never fit well.
Proverb

2 Be not made a beggar by banqueting upon borrowing, when thou hast nothing in thy purse: for thou shalt lie in wait for thine own life, and be talked on.
Bible: Ecclesiasticus 18:33

3 The human species, according to the best theory I can form of it, is composed of two distinct races, the men who borrow, and the men who lend.
Charles Lamb (1775–1834) British essayist. *Essays of Elia*, The Two Races of Men

4 Borrowers of books – those mutilators of collections, spoilers of the symmetry of shelves, and creators of odd volumes.
Charles Lamb *Essays of Elia*, 'The Two Races of Men'

5 Neither a borrower nor a lender be;
For loan oft loses both itself and friend,
And borrowing dulls the edge of husbandry.
This above all: to thine own self be true,
And it must follow, as the night the day,
Thou canst not then be false to any man.
William Shakespeare (1564–1616) English dramatist. *Hamlet*, 1:3

6 Let us all be happy, and live within our means, even if we have to borrer the money to do it with.
Artemus Ward (Charles Farrar Browne; 1834–67) US humorous writer. *Science and Natural History*

BRADBURY, MALCOLM

(1932–) British academic, novelist, and critic. Novels include *Eating People is Wrong* (1954), *Rates of Exchange* (1983), *Cuts* (1988), and *Doctor Criminale* (1992). His *The Social Context of Modern English Literature* (1972) is widely read.

1 Sympathy – for all these people, for being foreigners – lay over the gathering like a woolly blanket; and no one was enjoying it at all.
Eating People is Wrong, Ch. 2

2 I like the English. They have the most rigid code of immorality in the world.
Eating People is Wrong, Ch. 5

3 'We stay together, but we distrust one another.'
'Ah, yes…but isn't that a definition of marriage?'
The History Man

4 I've noticed your hostility towards him…I ought to have guessed you were friends.
The History Man

5 He goes from the light and air of humanities to the dark mass of social science.
The History Man

6 Reading someone else's newspaper is like sleeping with someone else's wife. Nothing seems to be precisely in the right place, and when you find what you are looking for, it is not clear then how to respond to it.
Stepping Westward, Bk. I, Ch. 1

7 The English are polite by telling lies. The Americans are polite by telling the truth.
Stepping Westward, Bk. II, Ch. 5

8 If God had meant us to have group sex, I guess he'd have given us all more organs.
Who Do You Think You Are?, 'A Very Hospitable Person'

9 God put us on this earth to read *Ulysses* and to try to find the time to get started on *Finnegan's Wake*…He did not intend us to pole-vault or bungy-jump, do aerobics or go white-water rafting.
The Independent Magazine, 'Physicality', 22 May 1993

BRECHT, BERTOLT

(1898–1956) German dramatist and poet. A Marxist, he lived in exile from 1933 to 1949. His best-known works are *The Threepenny Opera* (1928), in collaboration with Kurt Weil, *Mother Courage* (1941), and *The Caucasian Chalk Circle* (1949).

1 Those who have had no share in the good fortunes of the mighty often have a share in their misfortunes.
The Caucasian Chalk Circle

2 ANDREA. Unhappy the land that has no heroes.
GALILEO. No, unhappy the land that needs heroes.
Galileo, 13

3 What they could do with round here is a good war.
Mother Courage, I

4 When he told men to love their neighbour, their bellies were full. Nowadays things are different.
Mother Courage, II

5 I don't trust him. We're friends.
Mother Courage, III

6 The finest plans have always been spoiled by the littleness of those that should carry them out. Even emperors can't do it all by themselves.
Mother Courage, VI

7 A war of which we could say it left nothing to be desired will probably never exist.
Mother Courage, VI

8 What happens to the hole when the cheese is gone?
Mother Courage, VI

9 War is like love, it always finds a way.
Mother Courage, VI

10 Don't tell me peace has broken out.
Mother Courage, VIII

11 The wickedness of the world is so great you have to run your legs off to avoid having them stolen from under you.
The Threepenny Opera, I:3

BREVITY

See also sermons, speeches, verbosity

1 You lose.

Calvin Coolidge (1872–1933) US President. When a lady at a dinner told him that someone had bet her that she would not get more than two words out of him. Attrib.

2 Good things, when short, are twice as good.

Baltasar Gracián (1601–58) Spanish writer. *The Art of Worldly Wisdom*

3 I strive to be brief, and I become obscure.

Horace (Quintus Horatius Flaccus; 65–8 BC) Roman poet. *Ars Poetica*

4 ?

Victor Hugo (1802–85) French writer. The entire contents of a telegram sent to his publishers asking how *Les Misérables* was selling; the reply was '!' *The Literary Life* (R. Hendrickson)

5 But the shortest works are always the best.

Jean de La Fontaine (1621–95) French poet. *Fables*, X, 'Les Lapins'

6 Brevity is the soul of lingerie.

Dorothy Parker (1893–1967) US writer. *While Rome Burns* (Alexander Woollcott)

7 Trust the man who hesitates in his speech and is quick and steady in action, but beware of long arguments and long beards.

George Santayana (1863–1952) US philosopher. *Soliloquies in England*, 'The British Character'

8 Brevity is the soul of wit.

William Shakespeare (1564–1616) English dramatist. *Hamlet*, II:2

9 Men of few words are the best men.

William Shakespeare *Henry V*, III:2

10 Nurse unupblown.

Evelyn Waugh (1903–66) British novelist. Cable sent after he had failed, while a journalist serving in Ethiopia, to substantiate a rumour that an English nurse had been blown up in an Italian air raid. *Our Marvelous Native Tongue* (R. Claiborne)

BRIBERY

See also corruption

1 When their lordships asked Bacon
How many bribes he had taken
He had at least the grace
To get very red in the face.

Edmund Clerihew Bentley (1875–1956) British writer. *Baseless Biography*

2 I stuffed their mouths with gold!

Aneurin Bevan (1897–1960) British Labour politician. Explaining how he persuaded doctors not to oppose the introduction of the National Health Service. Attrib.

3 To a shower of gold most things are penetrable.

Thomas Carlyle (1795–1881) Scottish historian and essayist. *History of the French Revolution*, Pt. I, Bk. III, Ch. 7

4 I have often noticed that a bribe…has that effect – it changes a relation. The man who offers a bribe gives away a little of his own importance; the bribe once accepted, he becomes the inferior, like a man who has paid for a woman.

Graham Greene (1904–91) British novelist. *The Comedians*, Pt. I, Ch. 4

5 Though authority be a stubborn bear, yet he is oft led by the nose with gold.

William Shakespeare (1564–1616) English dramatist. *The Winter's Tale*, IV:3

BRITAIN

See also British, British Empire, England, Ireland, patriotism, Scotland, Wales

1 Great Britain has lost an Empire and has not yet found a role.

Dean Acheson (1893–1971) US lawyer and statesman. Speech, Military Academy, West Point, 5 Dec 1962

2 A nation of shop-keepers are very seldom so disinterested.

Samuel Adams (1722–1803) US revolutionary leader. Referring to Britain, following the Declaration of Independence, 4 July 1776. Speech, Philadelphia, 1 Aug 1776

3 You must not miss Whitehall. At one end you will find a statue of one of our kings who was beheaded; at the other the monument to the man who did it. This is just an example of our attempts to be fair to everybody.

Edward Appleton (1892–1965) British physicist. Referring to Charles I and Cromwell. Speech, Stockholm, 1 Jan 1948

4 Land of Hope and Glory, Mother of the Free,
How shall we extol thee, who are born of thee?
Wider still and wider shall thy bounds be set;
God who made thee mighty, make thee mightier yet.

A. C. Benson (1862–1925) British writer. *Land of Hope and Glory*

5 Britain has lived for too long on borrowed time, borrowed money and even borrowed ideas.

James Callaghan (1912–) British politician and prime minister. *The Observer*, 'Sayings of the Week', 3 Oct 1976

6 God save our Gracious King,
Long live our noble King,
God save the King.
Send him victorious,
Happy and glorious.

Henry Carey (c. 1690–1743) English poet and musician. *God Save the King*

7 When the British warrior queen,
Bleeding from the Roman rods,
Sought, with an indignant mien,
Counsel of her country's gods.

William Cowper (1731–1800) British poet. *Boadicea*

8 Britain is not a country that is easily rocked by revolution…In Britain our institutions evolve. We are a Fabian Society writ large.

William Hamilton (1917–) Scottish MP. *My Queen and I*, Ch. 9

9 We may be a small island, but we are not a small people.

Edward Heath (1916–) British politician and prime minister. *The Observer*, 'Sayings of the Week', 21 June 1970

10 We are unable to influence events in the way we want because we do not have the power or will to do so.

Nicholas Henderson (1919–) British diplomat. Referring to

Britain; written on ceasing to be ambassador to France. Letter to the foreign secretary, David Owen, 1979

11 Sir, it is not so much to be lamented that Old England is lost, as that the Scotch have found it.

Samuel Johnson (1709–84) British lexicographer. *Life of Johnson* (J. Boswell), Vol. III

12 This is a very fine country to be acutely ill or injured in, but take my advice and do not be old and frail or mentally ill here – at least not for a few years. This is definitely not a good country to be deaf or blind in either.

Keith Joseph (1918–) British politician. *The Observer*, 'Sayings of the Week', 1 July 1973

13 Once, when a British Prime Minister sneezed, men half a world away would blow their noses. Now when a British Prime Minister sneezes nobody else will even say 'Bless You'.

Bernard Levin (1928–) British journalist. *The Times*, 1976

14 Everything that is most beautiful in Britain has always been in private hands.

Malcolm Rifkind (1946–) British politician. *The Observer*, 'Sayings of the Week', 17 Jan 1988

15 When Britain first, at heaven's command,
Arose from out the azure main,
This was the charter of the land,
And guardian angels sung this strain:
'Rule, Britannia, rule the waves;
Britons never will be slaves.'

James Thomson (1700–48) British poet. *Alfred: a Masque*, Act II

16 I should like to help Britain to become a Third Programme country.

Ellen Cicely Wilkinson (1891–1947) British feminist and politician. *The Observer*, 'Sayings of the Week', 2 Feb 1947

BRITISH

See also Britain, English, Irish, Scots, Welsh

1 I cannot believe that the great British people, in order to protect their identity, would now be cowering on the very island from which they set sail to travel the world.

Edouard Balladur (1929–) French politician. *The Observer*, 'Sayings of the Week', 8 May 1994

2 A young Scotsman of your ability let loose upon the world with £300, what could he not do? It's almost appalling to think of; especially if he went among the English.

J. M. Barrie (1860–1937) British novelist and dramatist. *What Every Woman Knows*, I

3 There are no countries in the world less known by the British than these selfsame British Islands.

George Henry Borrow (1803–81) British writer. *Lavengro*, Preface

4 The British love permanence more than they love beauty.

Hugh Casson (1910–) British architect. *The Observer*, 'Sayings of the Week', 14 June 1964

5 It must be owned, that the Graces do not seem to be natives of Great Britain; and I doubt, the best of us here have more of rough than polished diamond.

Earl of Chesterfield (1694–1773) English statesman. Letter to his son, 18 Nov 1748

6 The maxim of the British people is 'Business as usual'.

Winston Churchill (1874–1965) British statesman. Speech, Guildhall, 9 Nov 1914

7 They are the only people who like to be told how bad things are – who like to be told the worst.

Winston Churchill Speech, 1921

8 Courtesy is not dead – it has merely taken refuge in Great Britain.

Georges Duhamel (1884–1966) French writer. *The Observer*, 'Sayings of Our Times', 31 May 1953

9 The British won't fight.

Leopoldo Galtieri (1924–) President of Argentina. Referring to the Falklands crisis. Remark to Alexander Haig, US Secretary of State, 10 Apr 1982

10 Of all noxious animals, too, the most noxious is a tourist. And of all tourists the most vulgar, ill-bred, offensive and loathsome is the British tourist.

Francis Kilvert (1840–79) British diarist and clergyman. *Diary*, 5 Apr 1870

11 The spread of personal ownership is in harmony with the deepest instincts of the British people. Few changes have done more to create one nation.

Nigel Lawson (1932–) British Conservative politician. Speech, Jan 1988

12 I would rather be British than just.

Ian Paisley (1926–) Northern Irish politician. *The Sunday Times*, 12 Dec 1971

13 It is beginning to be hinted that we are a nation of amateurs.

Lord Rosebery (1847–1929) British statesman. Rectorial Address, Glasgow, 16 Nov 1900

14 Other nations use 'force'; we Britons alone use 'Might'.

Evelyn Waugh (1903–66) British novelist. *Scoop*, Bk. II, Ch. 5

BRITISH EMPIRE

1 The British flag has never flown over a more powerful or a more united empire…Never did our voice count for more in the councils of nations; or in determining the future destinies of mankind.

George Nathaniel Carson (1859–1925) British politician. Speech, House of Lords, 18 Nov 1918

2 The loss of India would mark and consummate the downfall of the British Empire. That great organism would pass at a stroke out of life into history. From such a catastrophe there could be no recovery.

Winston Churchill (1874–1965) British statesman. Speech to Indian Empire Society, London, 12 Dec 1930

3 I have not become the King's First Minister in order to preside over the liquidation of the British Empire.

Winston Churchill Speech, Mansion House, 10 Nov 1942

4 'Can't' will be the epitaph of the British Empire – unless we wake up in time.

Oswald Mosley (1896–1980) British politician. Speech, Manchester, 9 Dec 1937

5 His Majesty's dominions, on which the sun never sets.

Christopher North (John Wilson; 1785–1854) Scottish writer. *Noctes Ambrosianae*, 20 Apr 1829

6 The Empire is a Commonwealth of Nations.

Lord Rosebery (1847–1929) British statesman. Speech, Adelaide, 18 Jan 1884

BRITTAIN, VERA

(1893–1970) British writer and feminist. Her best-known book, *Testament of Youth* (1933), relates her experiences as an army nurse in World War I.

Quotation about Brittain

1 And in retrospect, my mother was not essentially a novelist, but a chronicler of her times...a promoter of causes rather than a women of creative imagination.

John Catlin *Family Quartet*

Quotations by Brittain

2 It is probably true to say that the largest scope for change still lies in men's attitude to women, and in women's attitude to themselves.

Lady into Woman, Ch. 15

3 The idea that it is necessary to go to a university in order to become a successful writer, or even a man or woman of letters (which is by no means the same thing), is one of those phantasies that surround authorship.

On Being an Author, Ch. 2

4 Meek wifehood is no part of my profession;
I am your friend, but never your possession.

Poems of the War and After, 'Married Love'

5 Politics are usually the executive expression of human immaturity.

The Rebel Passion

BRONOWSKI, JACOB

(1908–74) British scientist and writer, born in Poland. His television series *The Ascent of Man* (1973) was highly successful. His critical works on William Blake are also well-known.

1 Every animal leaves traces of what it was; man alone leaves traces of what he created.

The Ascent of Man, Ch. 1

2 That is the essence of science: ask an impertinent question, and you are on the way to a pertinent answer.

The Ascent of Man, Ch. 4

3 Physics becomes in those years the greatest collective work of science – no, more than that, the great collective work of art of the twentieth century.

Referring to the period around the turn of the century marked by the elucidation of atomic structure and the development of the quantum theory. *The Ascent of Man*, Ch. 10

4 The wish to hurt, the momentary intoxication with pain, is the loophole through which the pervert climbs into the minds of ordinary men.

The Face of Violence, Ch. 5

5 The world is made of people who never quite get into the first team and who just miss the prizes at the flower show.

The Face of Violence, Ch. 6

BRONTE, ANNE

(1820–49) British novelist and poet. She was the younger sister of Charlotte and Emily; her first novel was published under the pseudonym Acton Bell. She wrote *Agnes Grey* (1847) and *The Tenant of Wildfell Hall* (1848).

Quotations about Anne Brontë

1 A sort of literary Cinderella.

George Moore (1852–1933) Irish writer and art critic. *Conversations in Ebury Street*

2 Her gentle and delicate presence, her sad short, short story, her hard life and early death entered deeply into the poetry and tragedy that have always been entwined with the memory of the Brontës, as women and as writers.

Mrs Humphrey Ward (1851–1920) British writer and philanthropist. Preface to the collected edition of the Brontës' work.

Quotations by Anne Brontë

3 But he that dares not grasp the thorn
Should never crave the rose.

The Complete Poems of Anne Brontë (ed. Clement Shorter), 'The Narrow Way'

4 Well, but you affirm that virtue is only elicited by temptation; – and you think that a woman cannot be too little exposed to temptation, or too little acquainted with vice, or anything connected therewith. It must be either that you think she is essentially so vicious, or so feeble-minded, that she cannot withstand temptation.

The Tenant of Wildfell Hall, Ch. 3

5 What is it that constitutes virtue, Mrs. Graham? Is it the circumstance of being able and willing to resist temptation; or that of having no temptations to resist.

The Tenant of Wildfell Hall, Ch. 3

6 Keep a guard over your eyes and ears as the inlets of your heart, and over your lips as the outlet, lest they betray you in a moment of unwariness.

The Tenant of Wildfell Hall, Ch. 16

BRONTE, CHARLOTTE

(1816–55) British novelist. She was the elder sister of Emily and Anne; her first works were published under the pseudonym Currer Bell. Her novels include *Jane Eyre* (1847), *Shirley* (1849), and *Villette* (1853).

Quotations about Charlotte Brontë

1 If these remarkable works are the productions of a woman we shall only say she must be a woman pretty nearly unsexed; and Jane Eyre strikes us as a personage much more likely to have sprung ready-armed from the head of a man and that head a pretty hard one, than to have experienced, in any shape, the softening influence of a female creation.

James Lorimer (1818–90) British jurist and philosopher. *North British Review*, Aug 1849

2 Two gentlemen came in leading a tiny, delicate, serious little lady with fair straight hair and steady eyes. This then is the authoress, the unknown power whose books have set all London talking, reading, speculating.

Anne, Lady Ritchie (1837–1919) British writer. *Chapters From Some Memoirs*

Quotations by Charlotte Brontë

3 Vain favour! coming, like most other favours long deferred and often wished for, too late!

Jane Eyre, Ch. 3

4 I grant an ugly *woman* is a blot on the fair face of creation; but as to the *gentlemen*, let them be solicitous to possess only strength and valour: let their motto be:– Hunt, shoot, and fight: the rest is not worth a fillip.

Jane Eyre, Ch. 17

5 The soul fortunately, has an interpreter – often an unconscious, but still a truthful interpreter – in the eye.

Jane Eyre, Ch. 28

6 Reader, I married him.

Jane Eyre, Ch. 38

7 An abundant shower of curates has fallen upon the north of England.

Shirley, Ch. 1

BRONTE, EMILY

(1818–48) British novelist and poet. She was the sister of Anne and Charlotte; her first works were published under the pseudonym Ellis Bell. Her romantic novel *Wuthering Heights* (1847) was published one year before her death from tuberculosis.

Quotations about Emily Brontë

1 Posterity has paid its debt to her too generously, and with too little understanding.

Ivy Compton-Burnett (1892–1969) British novelist. Letter to Anthony Powell

2 Emily Brontë remains the sphinx of literature.

W. Robertson Nicoll (1851–1923) British writer. *Chambers Encyclopedia of English Literature*

Quotations by Emily Brontë

3 No coward soul is mine,
No trembler in the world's storm-troubled sphere:
I see Heaven's glories shine,
And faith shines equal, arming me from fear.

Last Lines

4 Vain are the thousand creeds
That move men's hearts: unutterably vain;
Worthless as wither'd weeds.

Last Lines

5 O! dreadful is the check – intense the agony –
When the ear begins to hear, and the eye begins to see;
When the pulse begins to throb – the brain to think again –
The soul to feel the flesh, and the flesh to feel the chain.

The Prisoner

6 Once drinking deep of that divinest anguish,
How could I seek the empty world again?

Remembrance

7 A good heart will help you to a bonny face, my lad…and a bad one will turn the bonniest into something worse than ugly.

Wuthering Heights, Ch. 7

BROOKE, RUPERT

(1887–1915) British poet, who became a national hero after the publication of his war poems *1914 and Other Poems* (1915). He died of blood poisoning in the Aegean before seeing action.

1 The cool kindliness of sheets, that soon
Smooth away trouble; and the rough male kiss of blankets.

The Great Lover

2 For England's the one land, I know,
Where men with Splendid Hearts may go;
And Cambridgeshire, of all England,
The shire for Men who Understand.

The Old Vicarage, Grantchester

3 Just now the lilac is in bloom
All before my little room.

The Old Vicarage, Grantchester

4 Unkempt about those hedges blows
An unofficial English rose.

The Old Vicarage, Grantchester

5 Stands the Church clock at ten to three?
And is there honey still for tea?

The Old Vicarage, Grantchester

6 War knows no power. Safe shall be my going,
Secretly armed against all death's endeavour;
Safe though all safety's lost; safe where men fall;
And if these poor limbs die, safest of all.

Safety

7 If I should die, think only this of me:
That there's some corner of a foreign field
That is forever England.

The Soldier

BROOKNER, ANITA

(1938–) British novelist and art historian. Her novels include *Hotel du Lac* (1984), *Family and Friends* (1985), *Friends from England* (1987), *Latecomers* (1988), *Brief Lives* (1990), and *A Closed Eye* (1991).

1 I see that if a woman has it in mind to bring a man to heel she may have to play a part which runs counter to her own instincts.

Brief Lives, Ch. 4

2 When young one can still aspire to sublimity. Old age knows that this is, and probably always was, in devastatingly short supply.

Brief Lives, Ch. 17

3 Young women have a duty to flirt, to engage in heartless and pointless stratagems, to laugh, pretend, tease, have moods, enslave and discard. The purpose of these manoeuvres is to occupy their time, the time that women of later generations are to give to their careers.
Family and Friends, Ch. 1

4 In real life, of course, it is the hare who wins. Every time. Look around you. And in any case it is my contention that Aesop was writing for the tortoise market...Hares have no time to read. They are too busy winning the game.
Hotel du Lac, Ch. 1

5 The company of their own sex, Edith reflected, was what drove many women into marriage.
Hotel du Lac, Ch. 6

6 She was seen as obstinate, unassimilable, refusing to join groups of people like herself for purposes of travel or instruction, in which activities she might be supposed to involve herself honourably, thus leaving the world with no obligations towards her.
A Misalliance, Ch. 3

7 It was clear that wealth had rendered her helpless.
A Misalliance, Ch. 9

BROWNE, SIR THOMAS

(1605–82) English physician and writer. The reflective *Religio Medici* (1642), not originally intended for publication, established his reputation as a writer. Later works included *Pseudodoxia Epidemia* (1646).

1 He who discommendeth others obliquely commendeth himself.
Christian Morals, Pt. I

2 They do most by Books, who could do much without them, and he that chiefly owes himself unto himself, is the substantial Man.
Christian Morals, Pt. II

3 All things are artificial, for nature is the art of God.
Religio Medici, Pt. I

4 Thus the devil played at chess with me, and yielding a pawn, thought to gain a queen of me, taking advantage of my honest endeavours.
Religio Medici, Pt. I

5 For my part, I have ever believed, and do now know, that there are witches.
Religio Medici, Pt. I

6 It is the common wonder of all men, how among so many million of faces, there should be none alike.
Religio Medici, Pt. II

7 No man can justly censure or condemn another, because indeed no man truly knows another.
Religio Medici, Pt. II

8 Charity begins at home, is the voice of the world.
Religio Medici, Pt. II

9 Lord, deliver me from myself.
Religio Medici, Pt. II

10 For the world, I count it not an inn, but an hospital, and a place, not to live, but to die in.
Religio Medici, Pt. II

11 There is surely a piece of divinity in us, something that was before the elements, and owes no homage unto the sun.
Religio Medici, Pt. II

12 Man is a noble animal, splendid in ashes, and pompous in the grave.
Urn Burial, Ch. 5

BROWNING, ELIZABETH BARRETT

(1806–61) British poet. A semi-invalid, she married the poet Robert Browning in 1846 and lived with him in Italy. Her books include *Sonnets from the Portuguese* (1850), *Aurora Leigh* (1856), and *Poems Before Congress* (1860).

Quotation about Elizabeth Browning

1 Fate has not been kind to Mrs Browning. Nobody reads her, nobody discusses her, nobody troubles to put her in her place.
Virginia Woolf (1882–1941) British novelist. *Second Common Reader*

Quotations by Elizabeth Browning

2 Since when was genius found respectable?
Aurora Leigh, Bk. VI

3 Do you hear the children weeping, O my brothers,
Ere the sorrow comes with years?
The Cry of the Children

4 God's gifts put man's best gifts to shame.
Sonnets from the Portuguese, XXVI

5 How do I love thee? Let me count the ways.
I love thee to the depth and breadth and height
My soul can reach, when feeling out of sight
For the ends of Being and idea Grace.
Sonnets from the Portuguese, XLIII

6 I love thee with a love I seemed to lose
With my lost saints – I love thee with the breath,
Smiles, tears, of all my life! – and, if God choose,
I shall but love thee better after death.
Sonnets from the Portuguese, XLIII

BROWNING, ROBERT

(1812–89) British poet. *Men and Women* (1855), *Dramatis Personae* (1864), and *The Ring and the Book* (1868–69), were written after his marriage to the poet Elizabeth Barrett, with whom he eloped to Italy in 1846.

Quotations about Robert Browning

1 Browning used words with the violence of a horse-breaker, giving out the scent of a he-goat. But he got them to do their work.

Ford Madox Ford (1873–1939) British novelist. *The March of Literature*

2 He might have passed for a politician, or a financier, or a diplomatist or, indeed, for anything but a poet.

George William Russell (1867–1965) Irish poet and dramatist. *Portraits of the Seventies*

Quotations by Robert Browning

3 So free we seem, so fettered fast we are!

Andrea del Sarto

4 Ah, but a man's reach should exceed his grasp,
Or what's a heaven for?

Andrea del Sarto

5 Why need the other women know so much?

Any Wife to any Husband

6 No, at noonday in the bustle of man's worktime
Greet the unseen with a cheer!

Asolando, 'Epilogue'

7 My sun sets to rise again.

At the 'Mermaid'

8 Best be yourself, imperial, plain and true!

Bishop Blougram's Apology

9 We mortals cross the ocean of this world
Each in his average cabin of a life.

Bishop Blougram's Apology

10 Just when we are safest, there's a sunset-touch,
A fancy from a flower-bell, some one's death,
A chorus-ending from Euripides, –
And that's enough for fifty hopes and fears
As old and new at once as Nature's self,
To rap and knock and enter in our soul.

Bishop Blougram's Apology

11 The grand Perhaps!

Bishop Blougram's Apology

12 All we have gained then by our unbelief
Is a life of doubt diversified by faith,
For one of faith diversified by doubt:
We called the chess-board white, – we call it black.

Bishop Blougram's Apology

13 No, when the fight begins within himself,
A man's worth something.

Bishop Blougram's Apology

14 He said true things, but called them by wrong names.

Bishop Blougram's Apology

15 'Tis the Last Judgment's fire must cure this place,
Calcine its clods and set my prisoners free.

Childe Roland to the Dark Tower Came, XI

16 As for the grass, it grew as scant as hair
In leprosy.

Childe Roland to the Dark Tower Came, XIII

17 I never saw a brute I hated so;
He must be wicked to deserve such pain.

Childe Roland to the Dark Tower Came, XIV

18 Dauntless the slug-horn to my lips I set,
And blew. *Childe Roland to the Dark Tower came.*

Childe Roland to the Dark Tower Came, XXXIV

19 Though Rome's gross yoke
Drops off, no more to be endured,
Her teaching is not so obscured
By errors and perversities,
That no truth shines athwart the lies.

Christmas Eve, XI

20 Such ever was love's way; to rise, it stoops.

A Death in the Desert

21 For I say, this is death, and the sole death,
When a man's loss comes to him from his gain,
Darkness from light, from knowledge ignorance,
And lack of love from love made manifest.

A Death in the Desert

22 Man partly is and wholly hopes to be.

A Death in the Desert

23 How very hard it is
To be a Christian!

Easter-Day, I

24 At last awake
From life, that insane dream we take
For waking now.

Easter-Day, XIV

25 Oh, to be in England
Now that April's there.

Home Thoughts from Abroad

26 And after April, when May follows,
And the whitethroat builds, and all the swallows!

Home Thoughts from Abroad

27 That's the wise thrush; he sings each song twice over,
Lest you should think he never could recapture
The first fine careless rapture!

Home Thoughts from Abroad

28 I sprang to the stirrup, and Joris, and he;
I galloped, Dirck galloped, we galloped all three.

How they brought the Good News from Ghent to Aix

29 Oh, good gigantic smile o' the brown old earth.

James Lee's Wife, VII

30 And, Robert Browning, you writer of plays,
Here's a subject made to your hand!

A Light Woman, XIV

31 Just for a handful of silver he left us,
Just for a riband to stick in his coat.

The Lost Leader

32 Blot out his name, then, record one lost soul more,
One task more declined, one more footpath untrod,
One more devils'-triumph and sorrow for angels,
One wrong more to man, one more insult to God!

The Lost Leader

33 Then let him receive the new knowledge and wait us,
Pardoned in heaven, the first by the throne!

The Lost Leader

34 Where the quiet-coloured end of evening smiles,
Miles and miles.
Love among the Ruins, I

35 She had
A heart – how shall I say? – too soon made glad,
Too easily impressed.
My Last Duchess

36 Never the time and the place
And the loved one all together!
Never the Time and the Place

37 What's come to perfection perishes.
Things learned on earth, we shall practise in heaven.
Works done least rapidly, Art most cherishes.
Old Pictures in Florence, XVII

38 There remaineth a rest for the people of God:
And I have had troubles enough, for one.
Old Pictures in Florence, XVII

39 Suddenly, as rare things will, it vanished.
One Word More, IV

40 God be thanked, the meanest of his creatures
Boasts two soul-sides, one to face the world with,
One to show a woman when he loves her!
One Word More, XVII

41 Hamelin Town's in Brunswick,
By famous Hanover city;
The river Weser, deep and wide,
Washes its wall on the southern side;
A pleasanter spot you never spied.
The Pied Piper of Hamelin

42 Rats!
They fought the dogs and killed the cats,
And bit the babies in the cradles.
The Pied Piper of Hamelin

43 And the muttering grew to a grumbling;
And the grumbling grew to a mighty rumbling;
And out of the houses the rats came tumbling.
The Pied Piper of Hamelin

44 'You threaten us, fellow? Do your worst,
Blow your pipe there till you burst!'
The Pied Piper of Hamelin

45 The year's at the spring,
And day's at the morn;
Morning's at seven;
The hill-side's dew-pearled;
The lark's on the wing;
The snail's on the thorn;
God's in His heaven –
All's right with the world.
Pippa Passes, Pt. I

46 A king lived long ago,
In the morning of the world,
When earth was nigher heaven than now.
Pippa Passes, Pt. I

47 Such grace had kings when the world begun!
Pippa Passes, Pt. I

48 All service ranks the same with God –
With God, whose puppets, best and worst,
Are we: there is no last or first.
Pippa Passes, Pt. I

49 Therefore I summon age
To grant youth's heritage.
Rabbi ben Ezra, XIII

50 How good is man's life, the mere living! how fit to employ
All the heart and the soul and the senses for ever in joy!
Saul, IX

51 Leave the flesh to the fate it was fit for! the spirit be thine!
Saul, XIII

52 Gr-r-r- there go, my heart's abhorrence!
Water your damned flower-pots, do!
Soliloquy of the Spanish Cloister

53 I the Trinity illustrate,
Drinking watered orange-pulp –
In three sips the Arian frustrate;
While he drains his at one gulp.
Soliloquy of the Spanish Cloister

54 There's a great text in Galatians,
Once you trip on it, entails
Twenty-nine distinct damnations,
One sure, if another fails.
Soliloquy of the Spanish Cloister

55 My scrofulous French novel
On grey paper with blunt type!
Soliloquy of the Spanish Cloister

56 She looked at him, as one who awakes:
The past was a sleep, and her life began.
The Statue and the Bust

57 What of soul was left, I wonder, when the kissing had to stop?
A Toccata of Galuppi's

58 What's become of Waring
Since he gave us all the slip?
Waring

BUCK, PEARL S.

(1892–1973) US novelist. Winner of the Nobel Prize in 1938, her novels include *The Good Earth* (1931) and *The Three Daughters of Madame Liang* (1969).

1 In this unbelievable universe in which we live there are no absolutes. Even parallel lines, reaching into infinity, meet somewhere yonder.
A Bridge for Passing

2 Euthanasia is a long, smooth-sounding word, and it conceals its danger as long, smooth words do, but the danger is there, nevertheless.
The Child Who Never Grew, Ch. 2

3 Nothing and no one can destroy the Chinese people. They are relentless survivors. They are the oldest civilized people on earth. Their civilization passes through phases but its basic characteristics remain the same. They yield, they bend to the wind, but they never break.

China, Past and Present, Ch. 1

4 Ah well, perhaps one has to be very old before one learns how to be amused rather than shocked.
China, Past and Present, Ch. 6

5 No one really understood music unless he was a scientist, her father had declared, and not just a scientist, either, oh, no, only the real ones, the theoreticians, whose language was mathematics.
The Goddess Abides, Pt. I

6 It is better to be first with an ugly woman than the hundredth with a beauty.
The Good Earth, Ch. 1

7 I feel no need for any other faith than my faith in human beings.
I Believe

BUDDHA

(Gautama Siddhartha; c. 563–c. 483 BC) Indian prince, who at the age of about 20 renounced his family and his rich indolent life to search for enlightenment, which he traditionally achieved beneath a banyan tree. The rest of his life was spent teaching his findings and formulating the principles of Buddhism.

1 All things, oh priests, are on fire...The eye is on fire; forms are on fire; eye-consciousness is on fire; impressions received by the eye are on fire.
The Fire Sermon

2 I have never yet met with anything that was dearer to anyone than his own self. Since to others, to each one for himself, the self is dear, therefore let him who desires his own advantage not harm another.
Buddhism (Edward Conze)

3 I do not fight with the world but the world fights with me.
Buddhism (Edward Conze)

4 This Aryan Eightfold Path, that is to say: Right view, right aim, right speech, right action, right living, right effort, right mindfulness, right contemplation.
Some Sayings of the Buddha (F. L. Woodward)

5 Ye must leave righteous ways behind, not to speak of unrighteous ways.
Some Sayings of the Buddha (F. L. Woodward)

BUNYAN, JOHN

(1628–88) English writer and preacher. During imprisonment for illegal preaching (1660–72) he wrote the autobiographical *Grace Abounding* (1666) and began work on his allegory *The Pilgrim's Progress* (1684).

1 As I walked through the wilderness of this world.
The Pilgrim's Progress, Pt. I

2 The name of the slough was Despond.
The Pilgrim's Progress, Pt. I

3 The gentleman's name that met him was Mr Worldly Wiseman.
The Pilgrim's Progress, Pt. I

4 A very stately palace before him, the name of which was Beautiful.
The Pilgrim's Progress, Pt. I

5 It beareth the name of Vanity Fair, because the town where 'tis kept is lighter than vanity.
The Pilgrim's Progress, Pt. I

6 So soon as the man overtook me, he was but a word and a blow.
The Pilgrim's Progress, Pt. I

7 A castle called Doubting Castle, the owner whereof was Giant Despair.
The Pilgrim's Progress, Pt. I

8 So I awoke, and behold it was a dream.
The Pilgrim's Progress, Pt. I

9 One Great-heart.
The Pilgrim's Progress, Pt. II

10 He that is down needs fear no fall;
He that is low, no pride.
The Pilgrim's Progress, 'Shepherd Boy's Song'

BUREAUCRACY

1 A memorandum is written not to inform the reader but to protect the writer.
Dean Acheson (1893–1971) US lawyer and statesman. Attrib.

2 I'm surprised that a government organization could do it that quickly.
Jimmy Carter (1924–) US statesman and president. Visting Egypt, when told that it took twenty years to build the Great Pyramid. *Presidential Anecdotes* (P. Boller)

3 A committee is a cul-de-sac down which ideas are lured and then quietly strangled.
Barnett Cocks (1907–) British political writer. *New Scientist*, 1973

4 Whatever was required to be done, the Circumlocution Office was beforehand with all the public departments in the art of perceiving – HOW NOT TO DO IT.
Charles Dickens (1812–70) British novelist. *Little Dorrit*, Bk. I, Ch. 10

5 A Royal Commission is a broody hen sitting on a china egg.
Michael Foot (1913–) British Labour politician and journalist. Speech, House of Commons, 1964

6 A difficulty for every solution.
Herbert Samuel (1870–1963) British Liberal statesman. Referring to the Civil Service. Attrib.

7 The working of great institutions is mainly the result of a vast mass of routine, petty malice, self interest, carelessness, and sheer mistake. Only a residual fraction is thought.
George Santayana (1863–1952) US philosopher. *The Crime of Galileo*

8 My life's been a meeting, Dad, one long meeting. Even on the few committees I don't yet belong to, the agenda winks at me when I pass.
Gwyn Thomas (1913–81) British writer. *The Keep*, I

9 The British civil service...is a beautifully designed and effective braking mechanism.
Shirley Williams (1930–) British politician. Speech, Royal Institute of Public Administration, 11 Feb 1980

BURGESS, ANTHONY

(John Burgess Wilson; 1917–93) British novelist and critic. His books include *A Clockwork Orange* (1962), *Earthly Powers* (1980), and *Any Old Iron* (1989).

1 A perverse nature can be stimulated by anything. Any book can be used as a pornographic instrument, even a great work of literature if the mind that so uses it is off-balance. I once found a small boy masturbating in the presence of the Victorian steel-engraving in a family Bible.
A Clockwork Orange

2 Not a future. At least not in Europe. America's different, of course, but America's really only a kind of Russia. You've no idea how pleasant it is not to have any future. It's like having a totally efficient contraceptive.
Honey for the Bears, Pt. II, Ch. 6

3 Laugh and the world laughs with you; snore and you sleep alone.
Inside Mr. Enderby

4 Bath twice a day to be really clean, once a day to be passably clean, once a week to avoid being a public menace.
Mr Enderby, Pt. I, Ch. 2

5 Rome's just a city like anywhere else. A vastly overrated city, I'd say. It trades on belief just as Stratford trades on Shakespeare.
Mr Enderby, Pt. II, Ch. 2

6 The possession of a book becomes a substitute for reading it.
New York Times Book Review

7 Without class differences, England would cease to be the living theatre it is.
The Observer, 'Sayings of the Week', 26 May 1985

BURKE, EDMUND

(1729–97) British politician and political philosopher. He entered parliament as a Whig in 1765. In *Reflections on the Revolution in France* (1790) he condemned the French Revolution.

Quotations about Burke

1 Burke was a damned wrong-headed fellow, through his whole life jealous and obstinate.
Charles James Fox (1749–1806) British Whig politician. Attrib.

2 If a man were to go by chance at the same time with Burke under a shed, to shun a shower, he would say – 'this is an extraordinary man.'
Samuel Johnson (1709–84) British lexicographer. *Life of Johnson* (J. Boswell), Vol. IV

Quotations by Burke

3 Example is the school of mankind, and they will learn at no other.
Letters on a Regicide Peace, letter 1

4 The only infallible criterion of wisdom to vulgar minds – success.
Letter to a Member of the National Assembly

5 There is, however, a limit at which forbearance ceases to be a virtue.
Observations on a Late Publication, 'The Present State of the Nation'

6 I am convinced that we have a degree of delight, and that no small one, in the real misfortunes and pains of others.
On the Sublime and Beautiful, Pt. I

7 Beauty in distress is much the most affecting beauty.
On the Sublime and Beautiful, Pt. III

8 Vice itself lost half its evil, by losing all its grossness.
Reflections on the Revolution in France

9 But the age of chivalry is gone. That of sophisters, economists, and calculators, has succeeded; and the glory of Europe is extinguished for ever.
Reflections on the Revolution in France

10 That chastity of honour, that felt a stain like a wound.
Reflections on the Revolution in France

11 Man is by his constitution a religious animal.
Reflections on the Revolution in France

12 Superstition is the religion of feeble minds.
Reflections on the Revolution in France

13 The concessions of the weak are the concessions of fear.
Speech on Conciliation with America (House of Commons, 22 Mar 1775)

14 All government, indeed every human benefit and enjoyment, every virtue, and every prudent act, is founded on compromise and barter.
Speech on Conciliation with America (House of Commons, 22 Mar 1775)

15 The use of force alone is but *temporary*. It may subdue for a moment; but it does not remove the necessity of subduing again: and a nation is not governed, which is perpetually to be conquered.
Speech on Conciliation with America (House of Commons, 22 Mar 1775)

16 I do not know the method of drawing up an indictment against an whole people.
Speech on Conciliation with America (House of Commons, 22 Mar 1775)

17 Kings are naturally lovers of low company.
Speech on the Economical Reform (House of Commons, 11 Feb 1780)

18 The people are the masters.
Speech on the Economical Reform (House of Commons, 11 Feb 1780)

19 And having looked to government for bread, on the very first scarcity they will turn and bite the hand that fed them.
Thoughts and Details on Scarcity

20 When bad men combine, the good must associate; else they will fall one by one, an unpitied sacrifice in a contemptible struggle.

Thoughts on the Cause of the Present Discontents

21 Liberty, too, must be limited in order to be possessed.

Letter to the Sherrifs of Bristol, 1777

22 Among a people generally corrupt, liberty cannot long exist.

Letter to the Sherrifs of Bristol, 1777

23 Nothing is so fatal to religion as indifference, which is, at least, half infidelity.

Letter to William Smith, 29 Jan 1795

24 Somebody has said, that a king may make a nobleman, but he cannot make a gentleman.

Letter to William Smith, 29 Jan 1795

25 The greater the power, the more dangerous the abuse.

Speech, House of Commons, 7 Feb 1771

26 Your representative owes you, not his industry only, but his judgement; and he betrays instead of serving you if he sacrifices it to your opinion.

Speech to the electors of Bristol, 3 Nov 1774

27 He was not merely a chip off the old block, but the old block itself.

Referring to William Pitt the Younger's first speech in the House of Commons, 26 Feb 1781. Remark

28 A thing may look specious in theory, and yet be ruinous in practice; a thing may look evil in theory, and yet be in practice excellent.

Impeachment of Warren Hastings, 19 Feb 1788

29 Dangers by being despised grow great.

Speech, House of Commons, 11 May 1792

BURNS, ROBERT

(1759–96) Scottish poet. A farmer's son, Burns established his reputation with *Poems, Chiefly in the Scottish Dialect* (1786). He subsequently wrote many songs, notably *Auld Lang Syne*, and the narrative poem *Tam o' Shanter*, all of which made him the national poet of Scotland.

Quotations about Burns

1 The largest soul of all the British lands came among us in the shape of a hard-handed Scottish peasant.

Thomas Carlyle (1795–1881) Scottish historian and poet. *On Heroes, Hero-Worship and the Heroic in History*, Lecture V

2 If you can imagine a Scotch commercial traveller in a Scotch commercial hotel leaning on the bar and calling the barmaid 'Dearie' then you will know the keynote of Burns' verse.

A. E. Housman (1859–1936) British scholar and poet. *Electric Delights* (William Plumer)

Quotations by Burns

3 O Thou! Whatever title suit thee –
Auld Hornie, Satan, Nick, or Clootie.

Address to the Devil

4 Should auld acquaintance be forgot,
And never brought to min'?

Auld Lang Syne

5 We'll tak a cup o' kindness yet,
For auld lang syne.

Auld Lang Syne

6 Gin a body meet a body
Coming through the rye;
Gin a body kiss a body,
Need a body cry?

Coming through the Rye

7 I wasna fou, but just had plenty.

Death and Doctor Hornbrook

8 On ev'ry hand it will allow'd be,
He's just – nae better than he should be.

A Dedication to Gavin Hamilton

9 Here lie Willie Michie's banes;
O Satan, when ye tak him,
Gie him the schoolin' of your weans,
For clever deils he'll mak them!

Epitaph on a Schoolmaster

10 A man's a man for a' that.

For a' that and a' that

11 Green grow the rashes O,
Green grow the rashes O,
The sweetest hours that e'er I spend,
Are spent amang the lasses O!

Green Grow the Rashes

12 John Anderson my jo, John,
When we were first acquent,
Your locks were like the raven,
Your bonnie brow was brent.

John Anderson My Jo

13 Let them cant about decorum
Who have characters to lose.

The Jolly Beggars

14 Man's inhumanity to man
Makes countless thousands mourn!

Man was Made to Mourn

15 My heart's in the Highlands, my heart is not here;
My heart's in the Highlands a-chasing the deer;
Chasing the wild deer, and following the roe,
My heart's in the Highlands, wherever I go.

My Heart's in the Highlands

16 My luve's like a red red rose
That's newly sprung in June:
My luve's like the melodie
That's sweetly play'd in tune.

A Red, Red Rose

17 Scots, wha hae wi' Wallace bled,
Scots, wham Bruce has aften led,
Welcome to your gory bed,
Or to victorie.

Scots, Wha Hae

18 Liberty's in every blow!
Let us do or die!

Scots, Wha Hae

19 Some hae meat, and canna eat,
And some wad eat that want it,
But we hae meat and we can eat,
And sae the Lord be thankit.
The Selkirk Grace

20 Ah, gentle dames! It gars me greet
To think how mony counsels sweet,
How mony lengthen'd sage advices,
The husband frae the wife despises!
Tam o' Shanter

21 Wee, sleekit, cow'rin', tim'rous beastie,
O what a panic's in thy breastie!
To a Mouse

22 The best laid schemes o' mice an' men
Gang aft a-gley,
An' lea'e us nought but grief an' pain
For promis'd joy.
To a Mouse

23 But yet the light that led astray
Was light from Heaven.
The Vision

24 Ye banks and braes o' bonnie Doon,
How can ye bloom sae fresh and fair?
How can ye chant, ye little birds,
And I sae weary fu' o' care?
Ye Banks and Braes

BUSH, GEORGE

(1924–) US statesman; vice president (1981–88) and president (1989–93). In 1991 he authorized military action against Iraq in the Gulf War.

Quotations about Bush

1 Reagan can portray a real macho guy. Bush can't. He comes off looking like Liberace.
Carl Parker US senator. Attrib.

2 Bush had two faults. He didn't care for domestic politics, and he didn't care for people.
Charles Wheeler (1923–) British journalist and broadcaster. Newsnight, BBC television, 1992

Quotations by Bush

3 America's freedom is the example to which the world expires.
Campaign speech, Detroit, 1988

4 For 7½ years I have worked alongside him, and I am proud to be his partner. We have had triumphs, we have made mistakes, we have had sex...
Referring to Ronald Reagan. Speech at Republican rally, Twin Falls, Idaho, 1988

5 The United States is the best and fairest and most decent nation on the face of the earth.
Speech, May 1988

6 Learning is good in and of itself...the mothers of the Jewish ghettoes of the east would pour honey on a book so the children would know that learning is sweet. And the parents who settled hungry Kansas would take their children in from the fields when a teacher came.
Accepting his nomination as presidential candidate. Speech, Republican Party Convention, New Orleans, Aug 1988

7 The Congress will push me to raise taxes and I'll say no, and they'll push, and I'll say no, and they'll push again. And I'll say to them, read my lips, no new taxes.
Often misquoted as 'Watch my lips'. Speech, Republican Party Convention, New Orleans, 19 Aug 1988

8 It's not whether people like you but whether they share the bright dreams...and understand the heartbeat of the country.
The Sunday Times, 'Quotes of the Week', 16 Oct 1988

9 A new breeze is blowing – and a nation refreshed by freedom stands ready to push on: there is new ground to be broken, and new action to be taken.
Inaugural speech, 20 Jan 1989

10 Fluency in English is something that I'm not often accused of.
Address to Pakistani prime minister Benazir Bhutto, 1989

11 I will draw a line in the sand.
Referring to the defence of Saudi Arabia by US forces following the Iraqi invasion of Kuwait (1990). Speech, 1990

12 I know what I've told you I'm going to say, I'm going to say. And what else I say, well, I'll take some time to figure out – figure that out.
Press conference, 4 Dec 1990

13 Our goal is not the conquest of Iraq. It is the liberation of Kuwait.
Referring to the Gulf War (1991). *The Times*, 16 Jan 1991

14 War is never cheap or easy.
Referring to the Gulf War (1991). *The Observer*, 20 Jan 1991

15 The war wasn't fought about democracy in Kuwait.
The Observer, 14 July 1991

16 My dog Millie knows more about foreign policy than these two bozos.
Referring to Bill Clinton and Al Gore, his Democratic opponents in the 1992 US presidential election. Al Gore replied: 'It must have been Millie that taught him to roll over and play dead.' Speech, Oct 1992

BUSINESS

See also capitalism

1 In Dublin's fair city, where the girls are so pretty,
I first set my eyes on sweet Molly Malone,
As she wheeled her wheelbarrow, through streets broad and narrow,
Crying, Cockles and mussels! alive, alive, O!

She was a fishmonger, but sure 'twas no wonder,
For so were her father and mother before.
Anonymous *Cockles and Mussels*

2 Today's sales should be better than yesterday's – and worse than tomorrow's.
Anonymous

3 Who will change old lamps for new ones?...new lamps for old ones?

The Arabian Nights (c. 1500) A collection of tales from the East. *The History of Aladdin*

4 You ask me what it is I do. Well actually, you know,
I'm partly a liaison man and partly P.R.O.
Essentially I integrate the current export drive
And basically I'm viable from ten o'clock till five.

John Betjeman (1906–84) British poet. *Executive*

5 I have acquired a deep and abiding respect for all those engaged in the difficult business of commerce.

Kenneth Clarke (1940–) British politician. *The Observer*, 'Sayings of the Week', 20 June 1993

6 Pile it high, sell it cheap.

Jack Cohen (1898–1979) British supermarket trader. Business motto

7 The business of America is business.

Calvin Coolidge (1872–1933) US president. Speech, Washington, 17 Jan 1925

8 Here's the rule for bargains: 'Do other men, for they would do you.' That's the true business precept.

Charles Dickens (1812–70) British novelist. *Martin Chuzzlewit*, Ch. 11

9 Whenever you see a successful business, someone once made a courageous decision.

Peter F. Drucker (1929–) US writer and management consultant.

10 The longest word in the English language is the one following the phrase: 'And now a word from our sponsor.'

Hal Eaton

11 A business that makes nothing but money is a poor kind of business.

Henry Ford (1863–1947) US car manufacturer. Interview

12 No nation was ever ruined by trade.

Benjamin Franklin (1706–90) US scientist and statesman. *Essays*, 'Thoughts on Commercial Subjects'

13 Remember that time is money.

Benjamin Franklin *Advice to a Young Tradesman*

14 There's no such thing as a free lunch.

Milton Friedman (1912–) US economist. Used before Friedman but popularized by him.

15 The salary of the chief executive of the large corporation is not a market award for achievement. It is frequently in the nature of a warm personal gesture by the individual to himself.

John Kenneth Galbraith (1908–) US economist. *Annals of an Abiding Liberal*

16 If you pay peanuts, you get monkeys.

James Goldsmith (1933–) British businessman. Attrib.

17 Where wealth and freedom reign, contentment fails,
And honour sinks where commerce long prevails.

Oliver Goldsmith (1728–74) Irish-born British writer. *The Traveller*

18 Cherry ripe, ripe, ripe, I cry.
Full and fair ones; come and buy.

Robert Herrick (1591–1674) English poet. *Hesperides*, 'Cherry Ripe'

19 When you are skinning your customers, you should leave some skin on to grow so that you can skin them again.

Nikita Khrushchev (1894–1971) Soviet statesman. Said to British businessmen. *The Observer*, 'Sayings of the Week', 28 May 1961

20 ...content to follow mechanically the lead given by their fathers. They worked shorter hours, and they exerted themselves less to obtain new practical ideas than their fathers had done, and thus a part of England's leadership was destroyed rapidly. In the 'nineties it became clear that in the future Englishmen must take business as seriously as their grandfathers had done, and as their American and German rivals were doing: that their training for business must be methodical, like that of their new rivals, and not merely practical, on lines that had sufficed for the simpler world of two generations ago: and lastly that the time had passed at which they could afford merely to teach foreigners and not learn from them in return.

Alfred Marshall (1842–1924) British economist. Referring to British manufacturers. Memorandum; White Paper, 1908

21 He is the only man who is for ever apologizing for his occupation.

H. L. Mencken (1880–1956) US journalist. Referring to the businessman. *Prejudices*, 'Types of Men'

22 If Sony reject my work, it will never see the light of day. There is no such thing as resignation for an artiste in the music industry. Effectively, you sign a piece of paper at the beginning of your career and you are expected to live with that decision, good or bad, for the rest of your professional life.

George Michael (1963–) British pop singer. *The Times*, 22 May 1994

23 He's a businessman. I'll make him an offer he can't refuse.

Mario Puzo (1920–) US novelist. *The Godfather*

24 A friendship founded on business is better than a business founded on friendship.

John D. Rockefeller (1839–1937) US industrialist.

25 A dinner lubricates business.

William Scott (1745–1836) British jurist. *Life of Johnson* (J. Boswell), 1791

26 The customer is always right.

H. Gordon Selfridge (1857–1947) US-born businessman. Slogan adopted at his shops

27 He lends out money gratis, and brings down
The rate of usance here with us in Venice.
If I can catch him once upon the hip,
I will feed fat the ancient grudge I bear him.
He hates our sacred nation, and he rails,
Even there where merchants most do congregate,
On me, my bargains, and my well-won thrift,
Which he calls interest.

William Shakespeare (1564–1616) English dramatist. *The Merchant of Venice*, I:3

28 A snapper-up of unconsidered trifles.

William Shakespeare *The Winter's Tale*, IV:2

29 The big print giveth and the fine print taketh away.

J. Fulton Sheen (1895–1979) US Roman Catholic archbishop. Referring to his contract for a television appearance. Attrib.

30 People of the same trade seldom meet together but the conversation ends in a conspiracy against the public, or in some diversion to raise prices.

Adam Smith (1723–90) Scottish economist. *The Wealth of Nations*

31 You never expected justice from a company, did you? They have neither a soul to lose nor a body to kick.

Sydney Smith (1771–1845) British clergyman and essayist. *Memoir* (Lady Holland)

32 I have heard of a man who had a mind to sell his house, and therefore carried a piece of brick in his pocket, which he shewed as a pattern to encourage purchasers.

Jonathan Swift (1667–1745) Irish-born Anglican priest and writer. *The Drapier's Letters*, 2 (4 Aug 1724)

33 It's just like having a licence to print your own money.

Lord Thomson of Fleet (1894–1976) Canadian-born British newspaper proprietor. Speaking about commercial television. Attrib.

34 All business sagacity reduces itself in the last analysis to a judicious use of sabotage.

Thorstein Bunde Veblen (1857–1929) US social scientist. *The Nature of Peace*

35 The best sun we have is made of Newcastle coal.

Horace Walpole (1717–97) British writer. Letter to Montagu, 15 June 1768

36 If Max gets to Heaven he won't last long. He will be chucked out for trying to pull off a merger between Heaven and Hell...after having secured a controlling interest in key subsidiary companies in both places, of course.

H. G. Wells (1866–1946) British writer. Referring to Lord Beaverbrook. *Beaverbrook* (A. J. P. Taylor)

37 The trouble with the profit system has always been that it was highly unprofitable to most people.

Elwyn Brooks White (1899–1985) US journalist and humorist. Attrib.

38 For many years I thought what was good for our country was good for General Motors, and vice versa.

Charles Erwin Wilson (1890–1961) US engineer. Said in testimony to the Senate Armed Services Committee, Jan 1953. Attrib.

39 Business underlies everything in our national life, including our spiritual life. Witness the fact that in the Lord's Prayer the first petition is for daily bread. No one can worship God or love his neighbour on an empty stomach.

Woodrow Wilson (1856–1925) US statesman. Speech, New York, 1912

40 If two men on the same job agree all the time, then one is useless. If they disagree all the time, then both are useless.

Darryl F. Zanuck (1902–79) US film producer. *The Observer*, 'Sayings of the Week', 23 Oct 1949

BUTLER, SAMUEL

(1612–80) English satirist, secretary to George Villiers, 2nd Duke of Buckingham. The satirical poem *Hudibras* (1663–78), a mock romance, is his most famous work.

1 When civil fury first grew high,
And men fell out they knew not why.

Hudibras, Pt. I

2 For every why he had a wherefore.

Hudibras, Pt. I

3 To swallow gudgeons ere they're catched,
And count their chickens ere they're hatched.

Hudibras, Pt. II

4 Love is a boy, by poets styl'd,
Then spare the rod, and spoil the child.

Hudibras, Pt. II

5 Through perils both of wind and limb,
Through thick and thin she follow'd him.

Hudibras, Pt. II

6 Oaths are but words, and words but wind.

Hudibras, Pt. II

7 What makes all doctrines plain and clear?
About two hundred pounds a year.

Hudibras, Pt. III

8 He that complies against his will,
Is of his own opinion still.

Hudibras, Pt. III

9 The souls of women are so small,
That some believe they've none at all.

Miscellaneous Thoughts

BUTLER, SAMUEL

(1835–1902) British writer. *Erewhon*, a satirical novel published anonymously in 1872, established his reputation; subsequent works include the autobiographical *The Way of All Flesh* (1903).

1 Some who had received a liberal education at the Colleges of Unreason, and taken the highest degrees in hypothetics, which are their principal study.

Erewhon, Ch. 9

2 Straighteners, managers and cashiers of the Musical Banks.

Erewhon, Ch. 9

3 While to deny the existence of an unseen kingdom is bad, to pretend that we know more about it than its bare existence is no better.

Erewhon, Ch. 15

4 The wish to spread those opinions that we hold conducive to our own welfare is so deeply rooted in the English character that few of us can escape its influence.

Erewhon, Ch. 20

5 An art can only be learned in the workshop of those who are winning their bread by it.

Erewhon, Ch. 20

6 It has been said that the love of money is the root of all evil. The want of money is so quite as truly.

Erewhon, Ch. 20

7 Spontaneity is only a term for man's ignorance of the gods.

Erewhon, Ch. 25

8 I keep my books at the British Museum and at Mudie's.

The Humour of Homer, 'Ramblings in Cheapside'

9 Life is one long process of getting tired.

Notebooks

10 Life is the art of drawing sufficient conclusions from insufficient premises.

Notebooks

11 All progress is based upon a universal innate desire on the part of every organism to live beyond its income.

Notebooks

12 When a man is in doubt about this or that in his writing, it will often guide him if he asks himself how it will tell a hundred years hence.

Notebooks

13 An apology for the Devil – it must be remembered that we have only heard one side of the case. God has written all the books.

Notebooks

14 God is Love – I dare say. But what a mischievous devil Love is!

Notebooks

15 The public buys its opinions as it buys its meat, or takes in its milk, on the principle that it is cheaper to do this than to keep a cow. So it is, but the milk is more likely to be watered.

Notebooks

16 The healthy stomach is nothing if not conservative. Few radicals have good digestions.

Notebooks

17 Though analogy is often misleading, it is the least misleading thing we have.

Notebooks

18 Some men love truth so much that they seem to be in continual fear lest she should catch a cold on overexposure.

Notebooks

19 Marriage is distinctly and repeatedly excluded from heaven. Is this because it is thought likely to mar the general felicity?

Notebooks

20 Man is the only animal that can remain on friendly terms with the victims he intends to eat until he eats them.

Notebooks

21 To be at all is to be religious more or less.

Notebooks

22 A client is fain to hire a lawyer to keep from the injury of other lawyers – as Christians that travel in Turkey are forced to hire Janissaries, to protect them from the insolencies of other Turks.

Prose Observations

23 Every man's work, whether it be literature or music or pictures or architecture or anything else, is always a portrait of himself.

The Way of All Flesh, Ch. 14

24 That vice pays homage to virtue is notorious; we call it hypocrisy.

The Way of All Flesh, Ch. 19

25 Pleasure after all is a safer guide than either right or duty.

The Way of All Flesh, Ch. 19

26 The advantage of doing one's praising for oneself is that one can lay it on so thick and exactly in the right places.

The Way of All Flesh, Ch. 34

27 'Tis better to have loved and lost than never to have lost at all.

The Way of All Flesh, Ch. 77

28 When you have told anyone you have left him a legacy the only decent thing to do is to die at once.

Samuel Butler: A Memoir (Festing Jones), Vol. 2

29 Brigands demand your money or your life; women require both.

Attrib.

BYRON, LORD

(George Gordon, 6th Baron Byron; 1788–1824) British poet. The melancholy *Childe Harold's Pilgrimage* (1812) brought him to the attention of literary society. After scandalizing London with his sexual exploits, he lived abroad, largely in Italy; his later works include the poetic drama *Manfred* (1817) and the epic satire *Don Juan* (1819–24).

Quotations about Byron

1 When Byron's eyes were shut in death,
We bow'd our head and held our breath.
He taught us little: but our soul
Had *felt* him like the thunder's roll.

Matthew Arnold (1822–88) British poet and critic. *Memorial Verses*

2 If they had said the sun and the moon was gone out of the heavens it could not have struck me with the idea of a more awful and dreary blank in the creation than the words: Byron is dead.

Jane Welsh Carlyle (1801–66) The wife of the historian Thomas Carlyle. Letter to Thomas Carlyle, 1824

3 Mad, bad, and dangerous to know.

Lady Caroline Lamb (1785–1828) The wife of William Lamb, Viscount Melbourne, the Whig prime minister. Said of Byron in her *Journal*.

Quotations by Byron

4 The 'good old times' – all times when old are good –
Are gone.

The Age of Bronze, I

5 The land self-interest groans from shore to shore,
For fear that plenty should attain the poor.

The Age of Bronze, XIV

6 In short, he was a perfect cavaliero,
And to his very valet seem'd a hero.

Beppo

7 I like the weather, when it is not rainy,
That is, I like two months of every year.
Beppo

8 Maidens, like moths, are ever caught by glare,
And Mammon wins his way where Seraphs might despair.
Childe Harold's Pilgrimage, I

9 Adieu, adieu! my native shore
Fades o'er the waters blue.
Childe Harold's Pilgrimage, I

10 My native Land – Good Night!
Childe Harold's Pilgrimage, I

11 War, war is still the cry, 'War even to the knife!'
Childe Harold's Pilgrimage, I

12 Hereditary bondsmen! know ye not
Who would be free themselves must strike the blow?
Childe Harold's Pilgrimage, I

13 There was a sound of revelry by night,
And Belgium's capital had gather'd then
Her Beauty and her Chivalry, and bright
The lamps shone o'er fair women and brave men.
Childe Harold's Pilgrimage, III

14 On with the dance! let joy be unconfined;
No sleep till morn, when Youth and Pleasure meet
To chase the glowing Hours with flying feet.
Childe Harold's Pilgrimage, III

15 While stands the Coliseum, Rome shall stand;
When falls the Coliseum, Rome shall fall;
And when Rome falls – the World.
Childe Harold's Pilgrimage, IV

16 There is a pleasure in the pathless woods,
There is a rapture on the lonely shore,
There is society, where none intrudes,
By the deep Sea, and music in its roar:
I love not Man the less, but Nature more.
Childe Harold's Pilgrimage, IV

17 The spirit burning but unbent,
May writhe, rebel – the weak alone repent!
The Corsair, II

18 'Tis sweet to hear the watch-dog's honest bark
Bay deep-mouthed welcome as we draw near home;
'Tis sweet to know there is an eye will mark
Our coming, and look brighter when we come.
Don Juan, I

19 What men call gallantry, and gods adultery,
Is much more common where the climate's sultry.
Don Juan, I

20 Man's love is of man's life a thing apart,
'Tis woman's whole existence.
Don Juan, I

21 Man, being reasonable, must get drunk;
The best of life is but intoxication.
Don Juan, II

22 All tragedies are finish'd by a death,
All comedies are ended by a marriage.
The future states of both are left to faith.
Don Juan, III

23 Cost his enemies a long repentance,
And made him a good friend, but bad acquaintance.
Don Juan, III

24 Though sages may pour out their wisdom's treasure,
There is no sterner moralist than Pleasure.
Don Juan, III

25 Agree to a short armistice with truth.
Don Juan, III

26 The isles of Greece, the isles of Greece!
Where burning Sappho loved and sung,
Where grew the arts of war and peace,
Where Delos rose, and Phoebus sprung!
Eternal summer gilds them yet,
But all, except their sun, is set.
Don Juan, III

27 The mountains look on Marathon –
And Marathon looks on the sea:
And musing there an hour alone,
I dream'd that Greece might still be free.
Don Juan, III

28 Nothing so difficult as a beginning
In poesy, unless perhaps the end.
Don Juan, IV

29 I thought it would appear
That there had been a lady in the case.
Don Juan, V

30 The women pardoned all except her face.
Don Juan, V

31 There is a tide in the affairs of women,
Which, taken at the flood, leads – God knows where.
Don Juan, VI

32 A lady of a 'certain age', which means
Certainly aged.
Don Juan, VI

33 Now hatred is by far the longest pleasure;
Men love in haste, but they detest at leisure.
Don Juan, XIII

34 Society is now one polish'd horde,
Form'd of two mighty tribes, the *Bores* and *Bored*.
Don Juan, XIII

35 'Tis strange – but true; for truth is always strange;
Stranger than fiction: if it could be told,
How much would novels gain by the exchange!
Don Juan, XIV

36 I'll publish, right or wrong:
Fools are my theme, let satire be my song.
English Bards and Scotch Reviewers

37 'Tis pleasant, sure, to see one's name in print;
A book's a book, although there's nothing in't.
English Bards and Scotch Reviewers

38 A man must serve his time to every trade
Save censure – critics all are ready made.
English Bards and Scotch Reviewers

39 With death doomed to grapple,

Beneath this cold slab, he
Who lied in the chapel
Now lies in the Abbey.

Epitaph for William Pitt

40 She walks in beauty, like the night
Of cloudless climes and starry skies;
And all that's best of dark and bright
Meet in her aspect and her eyes.

She Walks in Beauty

41 So, we'll go no more a roving
So late into the night,
Though the heart be still as loving,
And the moon be still as bright.

So, we'll go no more a roving

42 Though the night was made for loving,
And the day returns too soon,
Yet we'll go no more a roving
By the light of the moon.

So, we'll go no more a roving

43 A better farmer ne'er brushed dew from lawn,
A worse king never left a realm undone!

Referring to George III. *The Vision of Judgment*, VIII

44 If I should meet thee
After long years,
How should I greet thee? –
With silence and tears.

When we two parted

45 I awoke one morning and found myself famous.

Remark made after the publication of *Childe Harold's Pilgrimage* (1812). Entry in Memoranda

C

CAESAR, JULIUS

(100–44 BC) Roman general and statesman. A member of the first Triumvirate (60 BC) with Pompey and Crassus, his military campaigns in Gaul and Britain won adulation. After the death of Crassus, conflict with Pompey led to civil war, from which Caesar emerged as dictator of Rome. He was assassinated by republican conspirators.

1 All Gaul is divided into three parts.
De Bello Gallico, Vol. I, Ch. 1

2 Caesar's wife must be above suspicion.
Said in justification of his divorce from Pompeia, after she was unwittingly involved in a scandal. *Lives*, 'Julius Caesar' (Plutarch)

3 The die is cast.
Said on crossing the Rubicon (49 BC) at the start of his campaign against Pompey. Remark

4 *Veni, vidi, vici.*
I came, I saw, I conquered.
The Twelve Caesars (Suetonius)

5 *Et tu, Brute?*
You too, Brutus?
Last words

CAMBRIDGE

See also England, Oxford

1 Oxford is on the whole more attractive than Cambridge to the ordinary visitor; and the traveller is therefore recommended to visit Cambridge first, or to omit it altogether if he cannot visit both.
Karl Baedeker (1801–59) German publisher. *Baedeker's Great Britain*, 'From London to Oxford'

2 For Cambridge people rarely smile,
Being urban, squat, and packed with guile.
Rupert Brooke (1887–1915) British poet. *The Old Vicarage, Grantchester*

3 The King to Oxford sent a troop of horse,
For Tories own no argument but force:
With equal skill to Cambridge books he sent,
For Whigs admit no force but argument.
William Browne (1692–1774) English physician. A reply to Joseph TRAPP. *Literary Anecdotes* (Nichols), Vol. III

4 Spring and summer did happen in Cambridge almost every year.
Vladimir Nabokov (1899–1977) Russian-born US novelist. *The Real Life of Sebastian Knight*, Ch. 5

5 This is the city of perspiring dreams.
Frederic Raphael (1931–) British author. *The Glittering Prizes: An Early Life*, III

6 The King, observing with judicious eyes
The state of both his universities,
To Oxford sent a troop of horse, and why?
That learned body wanted loyalty;
To Cambridge books, as very well discerning
How much that loyal body wanted learning.
Joseph Trapp (1679–1747) English churchman and academic. Written after George I donated the Bishop of Ely's library to Cambridge; for a reply see William BROWNE. *Literary Anecdotes* (Nichols), Vol. III

CAMPBELL, ROY

(1901–57) South African poet. His works include *The Flaming Terrapin* (1924); *The Georgiad* (1931), satirizing the Bloomsbury group; and the autobiographical *Broken Record* (1934) and *Light on a Dark Horse* (1951).

1 This mast new-shaved, through whom I rive the ropes,
Says she was once an oread of the slopes,
Graceful and tall upon the rocky highlands,
A slender tree as vertical as noon...
Choosing a Mast

2 Now Spring, sweet laxative of Georgian strains,
Quickens the ink in literary veins,
The Stately Homes of England ope their doors
To piping Nancy-boys and Crashing Bores.
The Georgiad

3 Camões, alone, of all the lyric race,
Born in the black aurora of disaster,
Can look a common soldier in the face.
Luis de Camões

4 Translations (like wives) are seldom faithful if they are in the least attractive.
Poetry Review

5 Far out on the grey silence of the flood
They watch the dawn in smouldering gyres expand
Beyond them: and the day burns through their blood
Like a white candle through a shuttered hand.
The Sisters

CAMPION, THOMAS

(1567–1620) English poet, composer, and physician. In *Observations in the Art of English Poesie* (1602) he attacked the use of rhyme.

1 Follow thy fair sun, unhappy shadow.
Follow Thy Fair Sun

2 There is a garden in her face,
Where roses and white lilies grow;
A heav'nly paradise is that place,
Wherein all pleasant fruits do flow.
There cherries grow, which none may buy
Till 'Cherry ripe' themselves do cry.
See also Robert HERRICK. *Fourth Book of Airs*

3 The man of life upright,
Whose guiltless heart is free
From all dishonest deeds
Or thought of vanity.
The Man of Life Upright

4 Good thoughts his only friends,
His wealth a well-spent age,
The earth his sober inn
And quiet pilgrimage.
The Man of Life Upright

5 The Summer hath his joys,
And Winter his delights.
Though Love and all his pleasures are but toys,
They shorten tedious nights.
Now Winter Nights Enlarge

CAMUS, ALBERT

(1913–60) French existentialist novelist, essayist, and dramatist, born in Algiers. His works include the novels *The Outsider* (1942) and *The Plague* (1947); the play *Caligula* (1944); and *The Myth of Sisyphus* (1942), an essay on the absurd.

Quotations about Camus

1 His work presents the feeling of the *Absurd*, the plight of man's need for clarity and rationality in confrontation with the unreasonable silence of the universe.
William Benét *The Reader's Encyclopedia*

2 His refusal to take solace in a concept of divine or cosmic meaning for human life did not conflict with Camus' humanistic attitude that man is capable of a certain degree of dignity in honestly facing his solitary condition.
William Benét *The Reader's Encyclopedia*

3 The Humphrey Bogart of Absurdism.
Herbert Lottmann *Albert Camus*

Quotations by Camus

4 Alas, after a certain age every man is responsible for his face.
The Fall

5 Style, like sheer silk, too often hides eczema.
The Fall

6 A single sentence will suffice for modern man: he fornicated and read the papers.
The Fall

7 How many crimes committed merely because their authors could not endure being wrong!
The Fall

8 No man is a hypocrite in his pleasures.
The Fall

9 Don't wait for the Last Judgement. It takes place every day.
The Fall

10 Politics and the fate of mankind are shaped by men without ideals and without greatness. Men who have greatness within them don't go in for politics.
Notebooks, 1935–42

11 An intellectual is someone whose mind watches itself.
Notebooks, 1935–42

12 The future is the only kind of property that the masters willingly concede to slaves.
The Rebel

13 One cannot be a part-time nihilist.
The Rebel

14 What is a rebel? A man who says no.
The Rebel

15 All modern revolutions have ended in a reinforcement of the power of the State.
The Rebel

16 He who despairs over an event is a coward, but he who holds hopes for the human condition is a fool.
The Rebel

CANNIBALISM

1 Eating people is wrong.
Michael Flanders (1922–75) British comedian and songwriter. *The Reluctant Cannibal*

2 The better sort of Ishmaelites have been Christian for many centuries and will not publicly eat human flesh uncooked in Lent, without special and costly dispensation from their bishop.
Evelyn Waugh (1903–66) British novelist. *Scoop*, Bk. II, Ch. 1

CAPITALISM

See also business

1 Capitalism is the exploitation of man by man. Communism is the complete opposite.
Anonymous

2 What mean ye that ye beat my people to pieces, and grind the faces of the poor? saith the Lord God of hosts.
Bible: Isaiah 3:15

3 Pile it high, sell it cheap.
Jack Cohen (1898–1979) British supermarket trader. Business motto

4 It is closing time in the gardens of the West.
Cyril Connolly (1903–74) British journalist. *The Condemned Playground*

5 Property has its duties as well as its rights.
Thomas Drummond (1797–1840) British engineer and statesman. Letter to the Earl of Donoughmore, 22 May 1838

6 If I had to give a definition of capitalism I would say: the process whereby American girls turn into American women.
Christopher Hampton (1946–) British writer and dramatist. *Savages*, Sc. 16

7 It is the unpleasant and unacceptable face of capitalism but one should not suggest that the whole of British industry consists of practices of this kind.
Edward Heath (1916–) British politician and prime minister. Referring to the Lonrho Affair. Speech, House of Commons, 15 May 1973

8 If you want to see the acceptable face of capitalism, go out to an oil rig in the North Sea.
Edward Heath Speech, Edinburgh, 18 Feb 1974

9 …militarism…is one of the chief bulwarks of capitalism, and the day that militarism is undermined, capitalism will fail.
Helen Keller (1880–1968) US writer and lecturer. *The Story of My Life*

10 We cannot remove the evils of capitalism without taking its source of power: ownership.

Neil Kinnock (1942–) British politician. *Tribune*, 1975

11 Under capitalism we have a state in the proper sense of the word, that is, a special machine for the suppression of one class by another.

Lenin (Vladimir Ilich Ulyanov; 1870–1924) Russian revolutionary leader. *The State and Revolution*, Ch. 5

12 Not every problem someone has with his girlfriend is necessarily due to the capitalist mode of production.

Herbert Marcuse (1898–1979) German-born US philosopher. *The Listener*

13 Capitalist production begets, with the inexorability of a law of nature, its own negation.

Karl Marx (1818–83) German philosopher and revolutionary. *Das Kapital*, Ch. 15

14 Man is the only creature that consumes without producing.

George Orwell (Eric Blair; 1903–50) British novelist. *Animal Farm*, Ch. 1

15 I have gone to war too…I am going to fight capitalism even if it kills me. It is wrong that people like you should be comfortable and well fed while all around you people are starving.

Sylvia Pankhurst (1882–1960) British suffragette. *The Fighting Pankhursts* (David Mitchell)

16 Property is theft.

Pierre Joseph Proudhon (1809–65) French socialist. *Qu'est-ce que la Propriété?*, Ch. 1

17 Property is organised robbery.

George Bernard Shaw (1856–1950) Irish dramatist and critic. *Major Barbara*, Preface

18 Lenin was the first to discover that capitalism 'inevitably' caused war; and he discovered this only when the First World War was already being fought. Of course he was right. Since every great state was capitalist in 1914, capitalism obviously 'caused' the First World War; but just as obviously it had 'caused' the previous generation of Peace.

A. J. P. Taylor (1906–90) British historian. *The Origins of the Second World War*, Ch. 6

19 In a country economically backward, the proletariat can take power earlier than in countries where capitalism is advanced.

Leon Trotsky (Lev Davidovich Bronstein; 1879–1940) Russian revolutionary. *Permanent Revolution*

20 The public be damned. I am working for my stockholders.

William Henry Vanderbilt (1821–85) US railway chief. Refusing to speak to a reporter, who was seeking to find out his views on behalf of the public.

CARLYLE, JANE WELSH

(1801–66) The wife of Thomas Carlyle. Clearly a writer of some talent, her output was restricted by her difficult life with her husband. Her letters and journal are often witty and stringent.

1 When one has been threatened with a great injustice, one accepts a smaller as a favour.

Journal, 21 Nov 1855

2 He has his talents, his vast and cultivated mind, his vivid imagination, his independence of soul and his high-souled principles of honour. But then – ah, these Buts! Saint Preux never kicked the fireirons, nor made puddings in his tea cup.

Referring to her husband, Thomas Carlyle. Letter to a friend, July 1821

3 If they had said the sun and the moon was gone out of the heavens it could not have struck me with the idea of a more awful and dreary blank in the creation than the words: Byron is dead.

Letter to Thomas Carlyle, 1824

4 Medical men all over the world having merely entered into a tacit agreement to call all sorts of maladies people are liable to, in cold weather, by one name; so that one sort of treatment may serve for all, and their practice thereby be greatly simplified.

Letter to John Welsh, 4 Mar 1837

CARLYLE, THOMAS

(1795–1881) Scottish historian and essayist. *Sartor Resartus*, a philosophical work, appeared in 1836; his subsequent writings include *The French Revolution* (1837) and *Heroes, Hero-Worship and the Heroic in History* (1841).

Quotations about Carlyle

1 It was very good of God to let Carlyle and Mrs Carlyle marry one another and so make only two people miserable instead of four.

Samuel Butler (1835–1902) British writer. Attrib.

2 Carlyle is a poet to whom nature has denied the faculty of verse.

Alfred, Lord Tennyson (1809–92) British poet. Letter to W. E. Gladstone

Quotations by Carlyle

3 A poet without love were a physical and metaphysical impossibility.

Critical and Miscellaneous Essays, 'Burns'

4 A witty statesman said, you might prove anything by figures.

Critical and Miscellaneous Essays, 'Chartism'

5 All reform except a moral one will prove unavailing.

Critical and Miscellaneous Essays, 'Corn Law Rhymes'

6 History is the essence of innumerable biographies.

Critical and Miscellaneous Essays, 'History'

7 A well-written Life is almost as rare as a well-spent one.

Critical and Miscellaneous Essays, 'Richter'

8 Literary men are…a perpetual priesthood.

Critical and Miscellaneous Essays, 'The State of German Literature'

9 The three great elements of modern civilization, Gunpowder, Printing, and the Protestant Religion.

Critical and Miscellaneous Essays, 'The State of German Literature'

10 Genius (which means transcendent capacity of taking trouble, first of all).
Frederick the Great, Vol. IV, Ch. 3

11 No great man lives in vain. The history of the world is but the biography of great men.
Heroes and Hero-Worship, 'The Hero as Divinity'

12 The true University of these days is a collection of books.
Heroes and Hero-Worship, 'The Hero as Man of Letters'

13 Burke said that there were Three Estates in Parliament; but, in the Reporters' Gallery yonder, there sat a *Fourth Estate*, more important far than they all.
Heroes and Hero-Worship, 'The Hero as Man of Letters'

14 France was a long despotism tempered by epigrams.
The French Revolution, Pt. I, Bk. I, Ch. 1

15 To a shower of gold most things are penetrable.
The French Revolution, Pt. I, Bk. III, Ch. 7

16 A whiff of grapeshot.
Describing how Napoleon, early in his career, quelled a minor riot in Paris. *The French Revolution*, Pt. I, Bk. V, Ch. 3

17 The difference between Orthodoxy or My-doxy and Heterodoxy or Thy-doxy.
The French Revolution, Pt. II, Bk. IV, Ch. 2

18 The seagreen Incorruptible.
Referring to the revolutionary Jacobin leader Robespierre. *The French Revolution*, Pt. II, Bk. IV, Ch. 4

19 The Public is an old woman. Let her maunder and mumble.
Journal, 1835

20 Respectable Professors of the Dismal Science.
Referring to economics. *Latter-Day Pamphlets*, 1

21 Nature admits no lie.
Latter-Day Pamphlets, 5

22 Captains of industry.
Past and Present, Bk. IV, Ch. 4

23 No man who has once heartily and wholly laughed can be altogether irreclaimably bad.
Sartor Resartus, Bk. I, Ch. 4

24 Be not the slave of Words.
Sartor Resartus, Bk. I, Ch. 8

25 Lives there the man that can figure a naked Duke of Windlestraw addressing a naked House of Lords?
Sartor Resartus, Bk. I, Ch. 9

26 Sarcasm I now see to be, in general, the language of the devil.
Sartor Resartus, Bk. II, Ch. 4

27 A good book is the purest essence of a human soul.
Speech made in support of the London Library. *Carlyle and the London Library* (F. Harrison)

28 If Jesus Christ were to come to-day, people would not even crucify him. They would ask him to dinner, and hear what he had to say, and make fun of it.
Carlyle at his Zenith (D. A. Wilson)

29 Macaulay is well for a while, but one wouldn't *live* under Niagara.
Referring to the historian and statesman Lord Macaulay (1800–59). *Notebook* (R. M. Milnes)

30 The crash of the whole solar and stellar systems could only kill you once.
Letter to John Carlyle, 1831

31 Work is the grand cure of all the maladies and miseries that ever beset mankind.
Speech, Edinburgh, 2 Apr 1886

32 I never heard tell of any clever man that came of entirely stupid people.
Speech, Edinburgh, 2 Apr 1886

33 I don't pretend to understand the Universe – it's a great deal bigger than I am...People ought to be modester.
Attrib.

34 There they are cutting each other's throats, because one half of them prefer hiring their servants for life, and the other by the hour.
Referring to the American Civil War. Attrib.

35 MARGARET FULLER. I accept the universe.
CARLYLE. Gad! she'd better!
Attrib.

36 Thirty millions, mostly fools.
When asked what the population of England was. Attrib.

CARROLL, LEWIS

(Charles Lutwidge Dodgson; 1832–98) British writer and mathematician; author of the children's classics *Alice's Adventures in Wonderland* (1865) and *Through the Looking-Glass* (1872).

Quotations about Carroll

1 Carroll's ego, a Humpty Dumpty (egg), was in perpetual peril of falling, never to be put together again....His defensive hypersensitivity to a little girl's curiosity is a reflection of a boy too long exposed to feminine eyes. It is the anguished cry of a little boy forced to spend the first years of his life in the almost exclusive company of sisters (of which Carroll ultimately had seven).
Judith Bloomingdale *Aspects of Alice* (Robert Phillips)

2 ...Carroll was not selfish, but a liberal-minded, liberal-handed egotist, but his egotism was all but second childhood.
Harry Furniss *Confessions of a Caricaturist*

3 Carroll's special genius, perhaps, lies in his ability to disguise charmingly the seriousness of his own concern, to make the most playful quality of his work at the same time its didactic crux.
Patricia Spacks *Logic and Language in Through the Looking-Glass*

Quotations by Carroll

4 'What is the use of a book,' thought Alice, 'without pictures or conversation?'
Alice's Adventures in Wonderland, Ch. 1

5 'Curiouser and curiouser!' cried Alice.
Alice's Adventures in Wonderland, Ch. 2

6 'You are old, Father William,' the young man said,
'And your hair has become very white;
And yet you incessantly stand on your head –
Do you think at your age, it is right?'
Alice's Adventures in Wonderland, Ch. 5

7 'If everybody minded their own business,' the Duchess said in a hoarse growl, 'the world would go round a deal faster than it does.'
Alice's Adventures in Wonderland, Ch. 6

8 This time it vanished quite slowly, beginning with the end of the tail, and ending with the grin, which remained some time after the rest of it had gone.
Describing the Cheshire Cat. *Alice's Adventures in Wonderland*, Ch. 6

9 'Then you should say what you mean,' the March Hare went on. 'I do,' Alice hastily replied; 'at least – at least I mean what I say – that's the same thing, you know.'
'Not the same thing a bit!' said the Hatter. 'Why, you might just as well say that 'I see what I eat' is the same thing as 'I eat what I see!"
Alice's Adventures in Wonderland, Ch. 7

10 Twinkle, twinkle, little bat!
How I wonder what you're at!
Up above the world you fly!
Like a teatray in the sky.
Alice's Adventures in Wonderland, Ch. 7

11 'Take some more tea,' the March Hare said to Alice, very earnestly.
'I've had nothing yet,' Alice replied in an offended tone, 'so I can't take more.'
'You mean you can't take *less*,' said the Hatter: 'it's very easy to take *more* than nothing.'
Alice's Adventures in Wonderland, Ch. 7

12 'Off with his head!'
Alice's Adventures in Wonderland, Ch. 8

13 Everything's got a moral, if you can only find it.
Alice's Adventures in Wonderland, Ch. 9

14 Take care of the sense, and the sounds will take care of themselves.
Alice's Adventures in Wonderland, Ch. 9

15 'Reeling and Writhing, of course, to begin with,' the Mock Turtle replied; 'and then the different branches of Arithmetic – Ambition, Distraction, Uglification, and Derision.'
Alice's Adventures in Wonderland, Ch. 9

16 'Will you walk a little faster?' said a whiting to a snail,
'There's a porpoise close behind us, and he's treading on my tail.'
Alice's Adventures in Wonderland, Ch. 10

17 Will you, won't you, will you, won't you, will you join the dance?
Alice's Adventures in Wonderland, Ch. 10

18 Soup of the evening, beautiful Soup!
Said by the Mock Turtle. *Alice's Adventures in Wonderland*, Ch. 10

19 The Queen of Hearts, she made some tarts,
All on a summer day:
The Knave of Hearts, he stole those tarts,
And took them quite away!
Alice's Adventures in Wonderland, Ch. 11

20 'Where shall I begin, please your Majesty?' he asked.
'Begin at the beginning' the King said, gravely, 'and go on till you come to the end: then stop.'
Alice's Adventures in Wonderland, Ch. 11

21 'No, no!' said the Queen. 'Sentence first – verdict afterwards.'
Alice's Adventures in Wonderland, Ch. 12

22 For the Snark *was* a Boojum, you see.
The Hunting of the Snark

23 'Twas brillig, and the slithy toves
Did gyre and gimble in the wabe;
All mimsy were the borogoves,
And the mome raths outgrabe.
Through the Looking-Glass, Ch. 1

24 Now, *here,* you see, it takes all the running *you* can do, to keep in the same place. If you want to get somewhere else, you must run at least twice as fast as that!
Through the Looking-Glass, Ch. 2

25 Tweedledum and Tweedledee
Agreed to have a battle;
For Tweedledum said Tweedledee
Had spoiled his nice new rattle.
Through the Looking-Glass, Ch. 4

26 'Contrariwise,' continued Tweedledee, 'if it was so, it might be; and if it were so, it would be: but as it isn't, it ain't. That's logic.'
Through the Looking-Glass, Ch. 4

27 The Walrus and the Carpenter
Were walking close at hand;
They wept like anything to see
Such quantities of sand:
'If this were only cleared away,'
They said, 'it *would* be grand!'
Through the Looking-Glass, Ch. 4

28 'The time has come,' the Walrus said,
'To talk of many things:
Of shoes – and ships – and sealing-wax –
Of cabbages – and kings –
And why the sea is boiling hot –
And whether pigs have wings.'
Through the Looking-Glass, Ch. 4

29 But answer came there none –
And this was scarcely odd because
They'd eaten every one.
Through the Looking-Glass, Ch. 4

30 The rule is, jam tomorrow and jam yesterday – but never jam today.

Through the Looking-Glass, Ch. 5

31 'They gave it me,' Humpty Dumpty continued thoughtfully,...'for an un-birthday present.'
Through the Looking-Glass, Ch. 6

32 'When *I* use a word,' Humpty Dumpty said in rather a scornful tone, 'it means just what I choose it to mean – neither more nor less.'
Through the Looking-Glass, Ch. 6

33 He's an Anglo-Saxon Messenger – and those are Anglo-Saxon attitudes.
Through the Looking-Glass, Ch. 7

34 It's as large as life, and twice as natural!
Through the Looking-Glass, Ch. 7

35 The Lion looked at Alice wearily. 'Are you animal – or vegetable – or mineral?' he said, yawning at every other word.
Through the Looking-Glass, Ch. 7

36 'Speak when you're spoken to!' the Red Queen sharply interrupted her.
Through the Looking-Glass, Ch. 9

37 'You look a little shy; let me introduce you to that leg of mutton,' said the Red Queen. 'Alice – Mutton; Mutton – Alice.'
Through the Looking-Glass, Ch. 9

CARSON, RACHEL

(1907–64) US biologist. *The Sea Around Us* (1951) and *Silent Spring* (1962) warned of the dangers of polluting the environment.

1 The ocean is a place of paradoxes.
Atlantic Monthly, Under Sea', Sept 1937

2 For all at last return to the sea – to Oceanus, the ocean river, like the ever-flowing stream of time, the beginning and the end.
The closing words of the book. *The Sea Around Us*

3 As cruel a weapon as the cave man's club, the chemical barrage has been hurled against the fabric of life.
The Silent Spring

4 Over increasingly large areas of the United States, spring now comes unheralded by the return of the birds, and the early mornings are strangely silent where once they were filled with the beauty of bird song.
The Silent Spring

CARTER, ANGELA

(1940–92) British novelist, critic, and journalist. Her works include the novels *The Magic Toyshop* (1967), *Nights at the Circus* (1984), *Wise Children* (1991), and the collections of essays *Nothing Sacred* (1982) and *Expletives Deleted* (1992).

Quotations about Carter

1 A true witness of her times, an artist in the here and now of both life and art, Bloody Chamber though it may be.
Robert Coover (1932–) British journalist. *The Independent*, 'Obituary', Feb 1992

2 The boldest of English women writers.
Lorna Sage (1943–) British journalist and critic

Quotations by Carter

3 ...The desert, the abode of enforced sterility, the dehydrated sea of infertility, the post-menopausal part of the earth.
The Passion of New Eve, Ch. 3

4 Solitude and melancholy, that is a woman's life.
The Passion of New Eve, Ch. 9

5 The destination of all journeys is their beginning.
The Passion of New Eve, Ch. 11

6 My anatomy is only part of an infinitely complex organisation, my self.
The Sadeian Woman, 'Polemical Preface'

7 Myth deals in false universals, to dull the pain of particular circumstances.
The Sadeian Woman, 'Polemical Preface'

8 Pornographers are the enemies of women only because our contemporary ideology of pornography does not encompass the possibility of change.
The Sadeian Woman, Ch. 1

9 Welcome to the wrong side of the tracks.
Wise Children, Ch. 1

10 She had, I kid you not, left lipstick on every pair of underpants further up the hierarchy than assistant director on her way to the top.
Wise Children, Ch. 3

11 'If the child is father of the man,' she asked, 'then who is the mother of the woman?'
Wise Children, Ch. 5

CATHOLICISM

See also Christianity, Protestantism, religion

1 A priest is a man who is called Father by everyone except his own children who are obliged to call him Uncle.
Italian proverb

2 *Ad majorem Dei gloriam.*
To the greater glory of God.
Anonymous Motto of the Jesuits

3 I expect you know my friend Evelyn Waugh, who, like you, your Holiness, is a Roman Catholic.
Randolph Churchill (1911–68) British political journalist. Remark made during an audience with the Pope

4 I have a Catholic soul, but a Lutheran stomach.
Erasmus (1466–1536) Dutch humanist, scholar, and writer. Replying to criticism of his failure to fast during Lent. *Dictionnaire Encyclopédique*

5 It is the custom of the Roman Church which I unworthily serve with the help of God, to tolerate some things, to turn a blind eye to some, following the spirit of discretion rather than the rigid letter of the law.

Gregory VII (c. 1020–85) Pope and saint. Letter, 9 Mar 1078

6 We're tripping over each other. Most of us seem to spend most of our time answering invitations to social functions, playing golf, breeding horses, training juveniles, celebrating jubilees, pricing cars and reading the death notices in desperation in case we can't find a funeral to attend.

Father Brendan Hoban Director of communications for Killala diocese. On the surplus of Catholic priests and their resulting lifestyle. *The Times*, 26 Aug 1993

7 The Papacy is not other than the Ghost of the deceased Roman Empire, sitting crowned upon the grave thereof.

Thomas Hobbes (1588–1679) English philosopher. *Leviathan*, Pt. IV, Ch. 37

8 There is no idolatry in the Mass. They believe God to be there, and they adore him.

Samuel Johnson (1709–84) British lexicographer. *Life of Johnson* (J. Boswell), Vol. II

9 We know these new English Catholics. They are the last words in Protest. They are Protestants protesting against Protestantism.

D. H. Lawrence (1885–1930) British novelist. *Phoenix*, 'Review of Eric Gill, *Art Nonsense*'

10 Since God has given us the papacy, let us enjoy it.

Leo X (Giovanni de' Medici; 1475–1521) Pope (1513–21). *Men of Art* (T. Craven)

11 I've always known that Catholicism is a completely sexist, repressed, sin-and-punishment-based religion.

Madonna (1958–) US pop singer and film actress. June 1991

12 One cannot really be a Catholic and grown-up.

George Orwell (Eric Blair; 1903–50) British novelist. *Collected Essays*

13 I was fired from there, finally, for a lot of things, among them my insistence that the Immaculate Conception was spontaneous combustion.

Dorothy Parker (1893–1967) US writer. *Writers at Work, First Series* (Malcolm Cowley)

14 The Pope! How many divisions has *he* got?

Joseph Stalin (J. Dzhugashvili; 1879–1953) Soviet statesman. When urged by Pierre Laval, the prime minister of France, to tolerate Catholicism in the USSR to appease the Pope, 13 May 1935. *The Second World War* (W. S. Churchill), Vol. I, Ch. 8

15 Becoming an Anglo-Catholic must surely be a sad business – rather like becoming an amateur conjurer.

John St Loe Strachey (1901–63) British politician. *The Coming Struggle for Power*, Pt. III, Ch. 11

16 'God knows how you Protestants can be expected to have any sense of direction,' she said. 'It's different with us. I haven't been to mass for years, I've got every mortal sin on my conscience, but I know when I'm doing wrong. I'm still a Catholic.

Angus Wilson (1913–91) British novelist. *The Wrong Set*, 'Significant Experience'

CATS

See also animals

1 Cruel, but composed and bland,
Dumb, inscrutable and grand,
So Tiberius might have sat,
Had Tiberius been a cat.

Matthew Arnold (1822–88) British poet and critic. *Poor Matthias*

2 We must fight against animal overpopulation. I call on all cat and dog owners to have their pets sterilized.

Brigitte Bardot (1934–) French film actress. *France-Soir*, June 1991

3 We're all of us proud to be nodded or bowed to
By Buster Jones in white spats!

T. S. Eliot (1888–1965) US-born British poet and dramatist. *Bustopher Jones: The Cat about Town*

4 Macavity, Macavity, there's no one like Macavity,
There never was a Cat of such deceitfulness and suavity.
He always has an alibi, and one or two to spare:
At whatever time the deed took place – MACAVITY WASN'T THERE!

T. S. Eliot *Macavity: The Mystery Cat*

5 OH!
Well I never!
Was there ever
A Cat so clever
As Magical Mr Mistoffelees!

T. S. Eliot *Mr Mistoffelees*

6 The Naming of Cats is a difficult matter,
It isn't just one of your holiday games.

T. S. Eliot *The Naming of Cats*

7 Old Deuteronomy's lived a long time;
He's a Cat who has lived many lives in succession.

T. S. Eliot *Old Deuteronomy*

8 I have noticed that what cats most appreciate in a human being is not the ability to produce food which they take for granted – but his or her entertainment value.

Geoffrey Household (1900–88) British writer. *Rogue Male*

9 When I observed he was a fine cat, saying, 'why yes, Sir, but I have had cats whom I liked better than this'; and then as if perceiving Hodge to be out of countenance, adding, 'but he is a very fine cat, a very fine cat indeed.'

Samuel Johnson (1709–84) British lexicographer. *Life of Johnson* (J. Boswell), Vol. IV

10 He walked by himself, and all places were alike to him.

Rudyard Kipling (1865–1936) Indian-born British writer. *Plain Tales from the Hills*, 'The Cat That Walked by Himself'

11 If a fish is the movement of water embodied, given shape, then cat is a diagram and pattern of subtle air.

Doris Lessing (1919–) British novelist. *Particularly Cats*, Ch. 2

12 When I play with my cat, who knows whether she is not amusing herself with me more than I with her?

Michel de Montaigne (1533–92) French essayist. *Essais*, II

13 If a dog jumps onto your lap it is because he is fond of you; but if a cat does the same thing it is because your lap is warmer.

A. N. Whitehead (1861–1947) British philosopher. *Dialogues*

CAUTION

See also prudence

1 Better be safe than sorry.

Proverb

2 Don't put all your eggs in one basket.

Proverb

3 He that fights and runs away, may live to fight another day.

Proverb

4 He who sups with the devil should have a long spoon.

Proverb

5 If you trust before you try, you may repent before you die.

Proverb

6 Keep your mouth shut and your eyes open.

Proverb

7 Keep your weather-eye open.

Proverb

8 Look before you leap.

Proverb

9 And all should cry, Beware! Beware!
His flashing eyes, his floating hair!
Weave a circle round him thrice,
And close your eyes with holy dread,
For he on honey-dew hath fed,
And drunk the milk of Paradise.

Samuel Taylor Coleridge (1772–1834) British poet. *Kubla Khan*

10 Chi Wen Tzu always thought three times before taking action. Twice would have been quite enough.

Confucius (K'ung Fu-tzu; 551–479 BC) Chinese philosopher. *Analects*

11 Take example by your father, my boy, and be very careful o' vidders all your life.

Charles Dickens (1812–70) British novelist. *Pickwick Papers*, Ch. 13

12 Don't go into Mr McGregor's garden: your Father had an accident there; he was put in a pie by Mrs McGregor.

Beatrix Potter (1866–1943) British children's writer. *The Tale of Peter Rabbit*

13 The only way to be absolutely safe is never to try anything for the first time.

Magnus Pyke (1908–92) British scientist, television personality, and writer. BBC radio programme

CENSORSHIP

See also pornography, prudery

1 More to the point, would you allow your gamekeeper to read it?

Anonymous Referring to Mervyn Griffiths-Jones's (*see* PRUDERY) remark during the *Lady Chatterley's Lover* trial.

2 To defend society from sex is no one's business. To defend it from officiousness is the duty of everyone who values freedom – or sex.

Brigid Brophy (1929–) British novelist and critic. *The Observer*, 'Sayings of the Week', 9 Aug 1970

3 My English text is chaste, and all licentious passages are left in the decent obscurity of a learned language.

Edward Gibbon (1737–94) British historian. *Autobiography*

4 Whenever books are burned men also in the end are burned.

Heinrich Heine (1797–1856) German poet and writer. *Almansor*

5 It isn't what they put in that bothers me but what they left out. It's as if they took the family to the laundry. Still, I expected worse.

John Irving (1942–) US author. Referring to the film of his *World According To Garp*. *International Herald Tribune*, 22 Oct 1982

6 PBS are engaging in a very serious game of self-censorship. Because they are publicly funded, they're desperately afraid their life's blood will be taken from them for making homosexuals look like regular human beings…I'm making personal pleas to everyone I know who can write a cheque.

Armistead Maupin (1944–) US author. Referring to the banning of the television version of *Tales of the City* by the US television network PBS. *The Times*, 15 June 1994

7 Mahound shakes his head. 'Your blasphemy, Salman, can't be forgiven. Did you think I wouldn't work it out? To set your words against the Words of God.'

Salman Rushdie (1947–) Indian-born British novelist. *The Satanic Verses*

8 The author of the Satanic Verses book, which is against Islam, the Prophet and the Koran, and all those involved in its publication who were aware of its content, are sentenced to death. I ask all Moslems to execute them wherever they find them.

Ayatolla Ruholla Khomeini (1900–89) Iranian Shiite Muslim leader. Speech, 14 Feb 1989

9 I call upon the intellectual community in this country and abroad to stand up for freedom of the imagination, an issue much larger than my book or indeed my life.

Salman Rushdie (1947–) Indian-born British novelist. Press statement, 14 Feb 1989

10 There is in our hands as citizens an instrument to mould the minds of the young and to create great and good and noble citizens for the future.

Edward Shortt (1862–1935) Home Secretary (1919–22); President of the British Board of Film Censors (1929–35). Referring to the British Board of Film Censors. Remark, 1929

11 I strongly believe there's no subject you can't tackle on television. I'm as moral as Mary Whitehouse. The difference between us is that I think people should know about the world they're living in, but she thinks it should be swept under the carpet.

Julia Smith British television producer. *TV Times*, July 1992

12 Censorship is more depraving and corrupting than anything pornography can produce.

Tony Smythe (1938–) Chairman of the National Council for Civil Liberties, Great Britain. *The Observer*, 'Sayings of the Week', 18 Sept 1972

13 God forbid that any book should be banned. The practice is as indefensible as infanticide.

Rebecca West (Cicely Isabel Fairfield; 1892–1983) British novelist and journalist. *The Strange Necessity*, 'The Tosh Horse'

14 If you are a songwriter did anyone ask you if you wanted to spend the rest of your career modifying your lyric content to suit the spiritual needs of an imaginary eleven-year-old?

Frank Zappa (1940–93) US rock musician. *The Real Frank Zappa Book*

CERTAINTY

See also self-confidence

1 If a man will begin with certainties, he shall end in doubts, but if he will be content to begin with doubts, he shall end in certainties.

Francis Bacon (1561–1626) English philosopher. *The Advancement of Learning*, Bk. I, Ch. 5

2 The mind longs for certainty, and perhaps it longs most for a certainty which clubs it down. What the mind can understand, what it can ploddingly prove and approve, might be what it most despises.

Julian Barnes (1946–) British novelist. *Staring at the Sun*

3 Of that there is no manner of doubt –
No probable, possible shadow of doubt –
No possible doubt whatever.

W. S. Gilbert (1836–1911) British dramatist. *The Gondoliers*, I

CERVANTES, MIGUEL DE

(1547–1616) Spanish novelist and dramatist; creator of *Don Quixote* (1605; 1615), a satirical romance of chivalry.

Quotations about Cervantes

1 Casting my mind's eye over the whole of fiction, the only absolutely original creation that I can think of is Don Quixote.

W. Somerset Maugham (1874–1965) British novelist. *10 Novels and their Authors*, Ch. 1

2 Cervantes laughed chivalry out of fashion.

Horace Walpole (1717–97) British writer. Letter to Sir Horace Mann, 19 July 1774

Quotations by Cervantes

3 A silly remark can be made in Latin as well as in Spanish.

The Dialogue of the Dogs

4 Take care, your worship, those things over there are not giants but windmills.

Don Quixote, Pt. I, Ch. 8

5 Didn't I tell you, Don Quixote, sir, to turn back, for they were not armies you were going to attack, but flocks of sheep?

Don Quixote, Pt. I, Ch. 18

6 The Knight of the Doleful Countenance.

Sancho Panza describing Don Quixote; sometimes translated as 'knight of the sad countenance'. *Don Quixote*, Pt. I, Ch. 19

7 Fear has many eyes and can see things underground.

Don Quixote, Pt. I, Ch. 20

8 A leap over the hedge is better than good men's prayers.

Don Quixote, Pt. I, Ch. 21

9 I have always heard, Sancho, that doing good to base fellows is like throwing water into the sea.

Don Quixote, Pt. I, Ch. 23

10 Let them eat the lie and swallow it with their bread. Whether the two were lovers or no, they'll have accounted to God for it by now. I have my own fish to fry.

Don Quixote, Pt. I, Ch. 25

11 A knight errant who turns mad for a reason deserves neither merit nor thanks. The thing is to do it without cause.

Don Quixote, Pt. I, Ch. 25

12 One shouldn't talk of halters in the hanged man's house.

Don Quixote, Pt. I, Ch. 25

13 She isn't a bad bit of goods, the Queen! I wish all the fleas in my bed were as good.

Don Quixote, Pt. I, Ch. 30

14 In me the need to talk is a primary impulse, and I can't help saying right off what comes to my tongue.

Don Quixote, Pt. I, Ch. 30

15 Every man is as Heaven made him, and sometimes a great deal worse.

Don Quixote, Pt. II, Ch. 4

16 The best sauce in the world is hunger.

Don Quixote, Pt. II, Ch. 5

17 Well, now, there's a remedy for everything except death.

Don Quixote, Pt. II, Ch. 10

18 Never meddle with play-actors, for they're a favoured race.

Don Quixote, Pt. II, Ch. 11

19 He's a muddle-headed fool, with frequent lucid intervals.

Sancho Panza describing Don Quixote. *Don Quixote*, Pt. II, Ch. 18

20 There are only two families in the world, my old grandmother used to say, The *Haves* and the *Have-Nots*.

Don Quixote, Pt. II, Ch. 20

21 A private sin is not so prejudicial in the world as a public indecency.

Don Quixote, Pt. II, Ch. 22

22 Tell me what company thou keepest, and I'll tell thee what thou art.

Don Quixote, Pt. II, Ch. 23

23 Good painters imitate nature, bad ones spew it up.
El Licenciado Vidriera

CHAMBERLAIN, NEVILLE

(1869–1940) British statesman; son of the Conservative statesman Joseph Chamberlain. As Conservative prime minister (1937–40) his negotiations with Hitler preceding World War II led him finally to abandon his policy of appeasement and to declare war on Germany. He died shortly after resigning in favour of Churchill.

Quotations about Chamberlain

1 The people of Birmingham have a specially heavy burden for they have given the world the curse of the present British Prime Minister.
Sir Stafford Cripps (1889–1952) British politician. Speech, 18 Mar 1938

2 Well, he seemed such a nice old gentleman, I thought I would give him my autograph as a souvenir.
Adolf Hitler (1889–1945) German dictator. Attrib.

3 He was a meticulous housemaid, great at tidying up.
A. J. P. Taylor (1906–90) British historian. *English History 1914–1945*

Quotations by Chamberlain

4 In war, whichever side may call itself the victor, there are no winners, but all are losers.
Speech, Kettering, 3 July 1938

5 How horrible, fantastic, incredible, it is that we should be digging trenches and trying on gas-masks here because of a quarrel in a far-away country between people of whom we know nothing.
Referring to Germany's annexation of the Sudetenland. Radio broadcast, 27 Sept 1938

6 I believe it is peace for our time...peace with honour.
Broadcast after Munich Agreement, 1 Oct 1938

7 Hitler has missed the bus.
Speech, House of Commons, 4 Apr 1940

CHANCE

See also accident, luck, opportunity

1 Throw out a sprat to catch a mackerel.
Proverb

2 I returned, and saw under the sun, that the race is not to the swift, nor the battle to the strong, neither yet bread to the wise, nor yet riches to men of understanding, nor yet favour to men of skill; but time and chance happeneth to them all.
For man also knoweth not his time: as the fishes that are taken in an evil net, and as the birds that are caught in the snare; so are the sons of men snared in an evil time, when it falleth suddenly upon them.
Bible: Ecclesiastes 9:11–12

3 Of all the gin joints in all the towns in all the world, she walks into mine!
Humphrey Bogart (1899–1957) US film star. *Casablanca*

4 I shot an arrow into the air,
It fell to earth, I knew not where.
Henry Wadsworth Longfellow (1807–82) US poet. *The Arrow and the Song*

5 Accidental and fortuitous concurrence of atoms.
Lord Palmerston (1784–1865) British statesman. Speech, House of Commons, 1857

6 When you take the bull by the horns... what happens is a toss up.
William Pett Ridge (1860–1930) British novelist. *Love at Paddington Green*, Ch. 4

7 I have set my life upon a cast,
And I will stand the hazard of the die.
William Shakespeare (1564–1616) English dramatist. *Richard III*, V:4

CHANEL, COCO

(1883–1971) French fashion designer who revolutionized women's clothing.

Quotations about Chanel

1 Coco Chanel has been distinguished in a business overburdened with chi-chi by the simplicity of her approach to everything concerning fashion.
Meriel McCooey *1000 Makers of the 20th Century*

2 In her own life, Chanel epitomised the New Woman, free and independent in every sense.
Kaori O'Connor *Makers of Modern Culture* (ed. J. Wintle)

Quotations by Chanel

3 There goes a woman who knows all the things that can be taught and none of the things that cannot be taught.
Coco Chanel, Her Life, Her Secrets (Marcel Haedrich)

4 Youth is something very new: twenty years ago no one mentioned it.
Coco Chanel, Her Life, Her Secrets (Marcel Haedrich)

5 Wherever one wants to be kissed.
When asked where one should wear perfume. *Coco Chanel, Her Life, Her Secrets* (Marcel Haedrich)

6 Fashion is architecture: it is a matter of proportions.
Coco Chanel, Her Life, Her Secrets (Marcel Haedrich)

CHANGE

See also conservatism, constancy, progress, transience

1 Can the Ethiopian change his skin, or the leopard his spots? then may ye also do good, that are accustomed to do evil.
Bible: Jeremiah 13:23

2 All reform except a moral one will prove unavailing.
Thomas Carlyle (1795–1881) Scottish historian and essayist. *Critical and Miscellaneous Essays*, 'Corn Law Rhymes'

3 The time's come: there's a terrific thunder-cloud advancing upon us, a mighty storm is coming to freshen us up....It's going to blow away all this idleness and indifference, and prejudice against work....I'm going to work, and in twenty-five or thirty years' time every man and woman will be working.

Anton Chekhov (1860–1904) Russian dramatist. *Three Sisters*, I

4 Variety's the very spice of life
That gives it all its flavour.

William Cowper (1731–1800) British poet. *The Task*

5 Most women set out to try to change a man, and when they have changed him they do not like him.

Marlene Dietrich (Maria Magdalene von Losch; 1904–92) German-born film star. Attrib.

6 The Times They Are A-Changin'.

Bob Dylan (Robert Allen Zimmerman; 1941–) US popular singer and songwriter. Song title

7 Come mothers and fathers
Throughout the land
And don't criticize
What you can't understand.

Bob Dylan *The Times They Are A-Changin'*

8 Man is so made that he can only find relaxation from one kind of labour by taking up another.

Anatole France (Jacques Anatole François Thibault; 1844–1924) French writer. *The Crime of Sylvestre Bonnard*

9 One must never lose time in vainly regretting the past nor in complaining about the changes which cause us discomfort, for change is the very essence of life.

Anatole France Attrib.

10 Most of the change we think we see in life
Is due to truths being in and out of favor.

Robert Frost (1875–1963) US poet. *The Black Cottage*

11 Very often we support change, and then are swept away by the change. I think that...you just make your own response to your own generation. A response adequate to your time.

Nadine Gordimer (1923–) South African novelist. *The Times*, 1 June 1990

12 Everything flows and nothing stays.

Heraclitus (c. 535–c. 475 BC) Greek philosopher. *Cratylus* (Plato), 402a

13 You can't step into the same river twice.

Heraclitus *Cratylus* (Plato), 402a

14 Change is not made without inconvenience, even from worse to better.

Richard Hooker (c. 1554–1600) English theologian. *English Dictionary* (Johnson), Preface

15 There is a certain relief in change, even though it be from bad to worse; as I have found in travelling in a stage-coach, that it is often a comfort to shift one's position and be bruised in a new place.

Washington Irving (1783–1859) US writer. *Tales of a Traveller*, 'To the Reader'

16 An old Dutch farmer, who remarked to a companion once that it was not best to swap horses in mid-stream.

Abraham Lincoln (1809–65) US statesman. Speech, 9 June 1864

17 Well, I find that a change of nuisances is as good as a vacation.

David Lloyd George (1863–1945) British Liberal statesman. On being asked how he maintained his cheerfulness when beset by numerous political obstacles. Attrib.

18 The wind of change is blowing through the continent. Whether we like it or not, this growth of national consciousness is a political fact.

Harold Macmillan (1894–1986) British politician and prime minister. Speech, South African Parliament, 3 Feb 1960

19 At last he rose, and twitched his mantle blue:
To-morrow to fresh woods, and pastures new.

John Milton (1608–74) English poet. *Lycidas*

20 Poor old Daddy – just one of those sturdy old plants left over from the Edwardian Wilderness, that can't understand why the sun isn't shining any more.

John Osborne (1929–) British dramatist. *Look Back in Anger*, II.2

21 We meant to change a nation, and instead, we changed a world.

Ronald Reagan (1911–) US president. Farewell address, 11 Jan 1989

22 Every reform movement has a lunatic fringe.

Theodore Roosevelt (1858–1919) US Republican president. Comment, 1913

23 That which is now a horse, even with a thought
The rack dislimns, and makes it indistinct,
As water is in water.

William Shakespeare (1564–1616) English dramatist. *Antony and Cleopatra*, IV:12

24 Through all the changing scenes of life.

Nahum Tate (1652–1715) Irish-born English poet. *New Version of the Psalms*, 'Through all the Changing'

25 And slowly answer'd Arthur from the barge:
'The old order changeth, yielding place to new,
And God fulfils himself in many ways.'

Alfred, Lord Tennyson (1809–92) British poet. *Idylls of the King*, 'The Passing of Arthur'

CHAPLIN, CHARLIE

(Sir Charles Spencer C.; 1889–1977) British film actor. He developed the character of the pathetic tramp – with baggy trousers, bowler hat, and walking stick – in such films as *The Kid* (1921), *The Gold Rush* (1925), and *Modern Times* (1936)

Quotations about Chaplin

1 Chaplin is no business man. All he knows is that he can't take less.

Samuel Goldwyn (Samuel Goldfish; 1882–1974) Polish-born US film producer. *My Autobiography* (Chaplin)

2 The Zulus know Chaplin better than Arkansas knows Garbo.

Will Rogers (1879–1935) US actor and humorist. *Atlantic Monthly*, Aug 1939

3 ...somehow importing to the peeling of a banana the elegant nonchalance of a duke drawing a monogrammed cigarette from a platinum case.

Alexander Woolcott (1887–1943) US journalist. *While Rome Burns*

Quotations by Chaplin

4 Wars, conflict, it's all business. One murder makes a villain. Millions a hero. Numbers sanctify.

Monsieur Verdoux

5 All I need to make a comedy is a park, a policeman and a pretty girl.

My Autobiography

6 The saddest thing I can imagine is to get used to luxury.

My Autobiography

7 I am for people. I can't help it.

The Observer, 'Sayings of the week', 28 Sept 1952

8 I remain just one thing, and one thing only – and that is a clown.
It places me on a far higher plane than any politician.

The Observer, 'Sayings of the Week', 17 June 1960

9 Life is a tragedy when seen in close-up, but a comedy in long-shot.

The Guardian, Obituary, 28 Dec 1977

CHARACTER

1 Monday's child is fair of face, Tuesday's child is full of grace; Wednesday's child is full of woe, Thursday's child has far to go; Friday's child is loving and giving, Saturday's child works hard for its living; and the child that's born on the Sabbath day, is fair and wise and good and gay.

Proverb

2 If you wish to know what a man is, place him in authority.

Yugoslav Proverb

3 Every man is as Heaven made him, and sometimes a great deal worse.

Miguel de Cervantes (1547–1616) Spanish novelist. *Don Quixote*, Pt. II, Ch. 4

4 He was as fresh as is the month of May.

Geoffrey Chaucer (c. 1342–1400) English poet. Referring to the squire. *The Canterbury Tales*, Prologue

5 Souninge in moral vertu was his speche,
And gladly wolde he lerne, and gladly teche.

Geoffrey Chaucer Referring to the clerk. *The Canterbury Tales*, Prologue

6 From a timid, shy girl I had become a woman of resolute character, who could not longer be frightened by the struggle with troubles.

Anna Dostoevsky (1846–1918) Russian diarist and writer. *Dostoevsky Portrayed by His Wife*

7 What e'r he did was done with so much ease,
In him alone, 'twas Natural to please.

John Dryden (1631–1700) British poet and dramatist. *Absalom and Achitophel*, I

8 A patronizing disposition always has its meaner side.

George Eliot (Mary Ann Evans; 1819–80) British novelist. *Adam Bede*

9 I am a man for whom the outside world exists.

Théophile Gautier (1811–72) French poet and critic. *Journal des Goncourt*, 1 May 1857

10 Talent develops in quiet places, character in the full current of human life.

Goethe (1749–1832) German poet and dramatist. *Torquato Tasso*, I

11 Strong enough to answer back to desires, to despise distinctions, and a whole man in himself, polished and well-rounded.

Horace (Quintus Horatius Flaccus; 65–8 BC) Roman poet. *Satires*, II

12 A tart temper never mellows with age, and a sharp tongue is the only edged tool that grows keener with constant use.

Washington Irving (1783–1859) US writer. *The Sketch Book*, 'Rip Van Winkle'

13 What is character but the determination of incident? What is incident but the illustration of character?

Henry James (1843–1916) US novelist. *Partial Portraits*, 'The Art of Fiction'

14 He was a vicious man, but very kind to me. If you call a dog *Hervey*, I shall love him.

Samuel Johnson (1709–84) British lexicographer. *Life of Johnson* (J. Boswell), Vol. I

15 A very unclubable man.

Samuel Johnson Referring to Sir John Hawkins. *Life of Johnson* (J. Boswell), Vol. I

16 I recognize that I am made up of several persons and that the person that at the moment has the upper hand will inevitably give place to another. But which is the real one? All of them or none?

W. Somerset Maugham (1874–1965) British novelist. *A Writer's Notebook*

17 It is with narrow-souled people as with narrow-necked bottles: the less they have in them, the more noise they make in pouring it out.

Alexander Pope (1688–1744) British poet. *Thoughts on Various Subjects*

18 Children with Hyacinth's temperament don't know better as they grow older; they merely know more.

Saki (Hector Hugh Munro; 1870–1916) British writer. *Hyacinth*

19 There is no such thing as psychological. Let us say that one can improve the biography of the person.

Jean-Paul Sartre (1905–80) French writer. *The Divided Self* (R. D. Laing), Ch. 8

20 A certain person may have, as you say, a wonderful presence: I do not know. What I do know is that he has a perfectly delightful absence.

Idries Shah (1924–) British author. *Reflections*, 'Presence and Absence'

21 His life was gentle; and the elements
So mix'd in him that Nature might stand up
And say to all the world 'This was a man!'

William Shakespeare (1564–1616) English dramatist. Referring to Brutus. *Julius Caesar*, V:5

22 A man of great common sense and good taste, – meaning thereby a man without originality or moral courage.

George Bernard Shaw (1856–1950) Irish dramatist and critic. Referring to Julius Caesar. *Caesar and Cleopatra*, Notes

23 I'm not hard – I'm frightfully soft. But I will not be hounded.

Margaret Thatcher (1925–) British politician and prime minister. *Daily Mail*, 1972

24 He is a man of brick. As if he was born as a baby literally of clay and decades of exposure have baked him to the colour and hardness of brick.

John Updike (1932–) US novelist. *Rabbit, Run*

25 There aren't many left like him nowadays, what with education and whisky the price it is.

Evelyn Waugh (1903–66) British novelist. *Decline and Fall*, Pt. I, Ch. 7

26 I've met a lot of hardboiled eggs in my time, but you're twenty minutes.

Billy Wilder (Samuel Wilder; 1906–) Austrian-born US film director. *Ace in the Hole*

CHARITY

See also generosity, help, parasites

1 Charity begins at home.

Proverb

2 Private patients, if they do not like me, can go elsewhere; but the poor devils in the hospital I am bound to take care of.

John Abernethy (1764–1831) English surgeon. *Memoirs of John Abernethy*, Ch. 5 (George Macilwain)

3 The living need charity more than the dead.

George Arnold (1834–65) US poet and humorist. *The Jolly Old Pedagogue*

4 In charity there is no excess.

Francis Bacon (1561–1626) English philosopher. *Essays*, 'Of Goodness, and Goodness of Nature'

5 Feed the World
Let them know it's Christmas.

Band Aid Song written to raise money for the relief of famine in Ethiopia. *Do They Know It's Christmas?*

6 Don't bother to thank me. I know what a perfectly ghastly season it's been for you Spanish dancers.

Tallulah Bankhead (1903–68) US actress. Said on dropping fifty dollars into a tambourine held out by a Salvation Army collector. *With Malice Toward All* (D. Hermann)

7 Though I speak with the tongues of men and of angels, and have not charity, I am become as sounding brass, or a tinkling cymbal.
And though I have the gift of prophecy, and understand all mysteries, and all knowledge; and though I have all faith, so that I could remove mountains, and have not charity, I am nothing.
And though I bestow all my goods to feed the poor, and though I give my body to be burned, and have not charity, it profiteth me nothing.
Charity suffereth long, and is kind; charity envieth not; charity vaunteth not itself, is not puffed up,
Doth not behave itself unseemly, seeketh not her own, is not easily provoked, thinketh no evil;
Rejoiceth not in iniquity, but rejoiceth in the truth;
Beareth all things, believeth all things, hopeth all things, endureth all things.
Charity never faileth: but whether there be prophecies, they shall fail; whether there be tongues, they shall cease; whether there be knowledge, it shall vanish away.
For we know in part, and we prophesy in part.
But when that which is perfect is come, then that which is in part shall be done away.
When I was a child, I spake as a child, I understood as a child, I thought as a child: but when I became a man, I put away childish things.
For now we see through a glass, darkly; but then face to face: now I know in part; but then shall I know even as also I am known.
And now abideth faith, hope, charity, these three; but the greatest of these is charity.

Bible: I Corinthians 13:1–13

8 Now as touching things offered unto idols, we know that we all have knowledge. Knowledge puffeth up, but charity edifieth.

Bible: I Corinthians 8:1

9 But a certain Samaritan, as he journeyed, came where he was: and when he saw him, he had compassion on him,
And went to him, and bound up his wounds, pouring in oil and wine, and set him on his own beast, and brought him to an inn, and took care of him.
And on the morrow when he departed, he took out two pence, and gave them to the host, and said unto him, Take care of him; and whatsoever thou spendest more, when I come again, I will repay thee.

Bible: Luke 10:33–35

10 Or what man is there of you, whom if his son ask bread, will he give him a stone?

Bible: Matthew 7:9

11 All our doings without charity are nothing worth.

The Book of Common Prayer *Collect, Quinquagesima Sunday*

12 Charity begins at home, is the voice of the world.

Thomas Browne (1605–82) English physician and writer. *Religio Medici*, Pt. II

13 I have always heard, Sancho, that doing good to base fellows is like throwing water into the sea.

Miguel de Cervantes (1547–1616) Spanish novelist. *Don Quixote*, Pt. I, Ch. 23

14 Charity is the power of defending that which we know to be indefensible. Hope is the power of being cheerful in circumstances which we know to be desperate.

G. K. Chesterton (1874–1936) British writer. *Heretics*, Ch. 12

15 No people do so much harm as those who go about doing good.

Mandell Creighton (1843–1901) British churchman. *Life*

16 Lady Bountiful.

George Farquhar (1678–1707) Irish dramatist. *The Beaux' Strategem*, I:1

17 I'm not interested in the bloody system! Why has he no food? Why is he starving to death?

Bob Geldof (1952–) Irish rock musician. *The Observer*, 'Sayings of the Week', 27 Oct 1985

18 In medicine, charity offers to the poor the gains in medical skill, not the leavings.

Alan Gregg (1890–1957) *The Bampton Lectures*

19 She's the sort of woman who lives for others – you can always tell the others by their hunted expression.

C. S. Lewis (1898–1963) British academic and writer. *The Screwtape Letters*

20 In the field of world policy; I would dedicate this nation to the policy of the good neighbor.

Franklin D. Roosevelt (1882–1945) US Democratic president. First Inaugural Address, 4 Mar 1933

21 When they will not give a doit to relieve a lame beggar, they will lay out ten to see a dead Indian.

William Shakespeare (1564–1616) English dramatist. *The Tempest*, II:2

22 If you see anybody fallen by the wayside and lying in the ditch, it isn't much good climbing into the ditch and lying by his side.

H. R. L. Sheppard (1880–1937) British clergyman. *Dick Sheppard* (Carolyn Scott)

23 The white man knows how to make everything, but he does not know how to distribute it.

Sitting Bull (c. 1834–90) US Sioux Indian chief. Attrib.

24 You find people ready enough to do the Samaritan, without the oil and twopence.

Sydney Smith (1771–1845) British clergyman and essayist. *Memoir* (Lady Holland)

25 The house which is not opened for charity will be opened to the physician.

The Talmud

26 To keep a lamp burning we have to keep putting oil in it.

Mother Teresa (Agnes Gonxha Bojaxhui; 1910–) Yugoslavian-born Indian missionary. *Time*, 'Saints Among Us', 29 Dec 1975

27 As for doing good, that is one of the professions which are full.

Henry David Thoreau (1817–62) US writer. *Walden*, 'Economy'

28 I have always depended on the kindness of strangers.

Tennessee Williams (1911–83) US dramatist. *A Streetcar Named Desire*, II:3

CHARLES II

(1630–85) King of England, Scotland, and Ireland (1660–85); son of Charles I. Exiled during Cromwell's Protectorate (1653–59), he returned to England at the Restoration of the monarchy in 1660. Charles's Roman Catholic sympathies led to conflict with parliament; anti-Catholic feeling intensified after the Popish Plot of 1678.

1 Brother, I am too old to go again to my travels.

Referring to his exile, 1651–60. *History of Great Britain* (Hume), Vol. II, Ch. 7

2 Not a religion for gentlemen.

Referring to Presbyterianism. *History of My Own Time* (Burnet), Vol. I, Bk. II, Ch. 2

3 This is very true: for my words are my own, and my actions are my ministers'.

Replying to Lord ROCHESTER's suggested epitaph. *King Charles II* (A. Bryant)

4 I am sure no man in England will take away my life to make you King.

To his brother James following revelation of the Popish Plot fabricated by Titus Oates. Attrib.

5 Better than a play.

Referring to House of Lords debate on the Divorce Bill. Attrib.

6 Let not poor Nelly starve.

Referring to his mistress Nell Gwynne. Said on his death bed

7 He had been, he said, a most unconscionable time dying; but he hoped that they would excuse it.

History of England (Macaulay), Vol. I, Ch. 4

CHARLES, PRINCE OF WALES

(1948–) Eldest son of Elizabeth II and heir to the throne of the United Kingdom. He is noted for his controversial views on architecture and the environment.

1 All the faces here this evening seem to be bloody Poms.

Remark at Australia Day dinner, 1973

2 British management doesn't seem to understand the importance of the human factor.

Speech, Parliamentary and Scientific Committee lunch, 21 Feb 1979

3 Like a carbuncle on the face of an old and valued friend.

Referring to a proposed modern extension to the National Gallery. Speech, 1986

4 You have to give this much to the Luftwaffe – when it knocked down our buildings it did not replace them with anything more offensive than rubble. We did that.

The Observer, 'Sayings of the Week', 6 Dec 1987

5 I am afraid I believe we delude ourselves if we think that humanity is becoming ever more civilised, ever more sophisticated and ever more reasonable. It's simply not the case.

ITV TV programme *Charles: The Private Man, the Public Role*, 29 June 1994

6 I personally would much rather see my title as Defender of Faith, not the Faith, because it means just one interpretation of the faith, which I think is sometimes something that causes a great deal of a problem.

ITV TV programme *Charles: The Private Man, the Public Role*, 29 June 1994

7 I can't describe to you the horror of it – you see your life being set in concrete…It is very much a feeling of being constantly observed. I just do, I hope, the best I can to put people at their ease and try and make it as nice for them as possible.

ITV TV programme *Charles: The Private Man, the Public Role*, 29 June 1994

8 I'm not very good at being a performing monkey.

Referring to his relationship with the media. ITV TV programme *Charles: The Private Man, the Public Role*, 29 June 1994

9 Well, frankly, the problem as I see it at this

moment in time is whether I should just lie down under all this hassle and let them walk all over me, or whether I should just say OK, I get the message, and do myself in.
I mean, let's face it, I'm in a no-win situation, and quite honestly, I'm so stuffed up to here with the whole stupid mess that I can tell you I've just got a good mind to take the easy way out. That's the bottom line. The only problem is, what happens if I find, when I've bumped myself off, there's some kind of...ah, you know, all that mystical stuff about when you die, you might find you're still – know what I mean?

At the presentation of the Thomas Cranmer Schools Prize (1989), suggesting a possible modern English version of Hamlet's soliloquy. The original version is:

To be, or not to be: that is the question:
Whether 'tis nobler in the mind to suffer
The slings and arrows of outrageous fortune,
Or to take arms against a sea of troubles,
And by opposing end them? To die: to sleep;
No more; and, by a sleep to say we end
The heartache and the thousand natural shocks
That flesh is heir to, 'tis a consummation
Devoutly to be wish'd. To die, to sleep; To sleep: perchance to dream: aye, there's the rub;
For in that sleep of death what dreams may come
When we have shuffled off this mortal coil,
Must give us pause.

CHARM

1 Charm is a delusion and beauty fleeting;
it is the God-fearing woman who is honoured.
Extol her for the fruit of her toil,
and let her labours bring her honour in the city gate.

Bible: Proverbs 31:30–31

2 On Richmond Hill there lives a lass,
More sweet than May day morn,
Whose charms all other maids surpass,
A rose without a thorn.

Leonard MacNally (1752–1820) Irish dramatist and poet. *The Lass of Richmond Hill*

3 It's a sort of bloom on a woman. If you have it, you don't need to have anything else; and if you don't have it, it doesn't much matter what else you have.

J. M. Barrie (1860–1937) British novelist and dramatist. *What Every Woman Knows*, I

CHAUCER, GEOFFREY

(c. 1342–1400) English poet. *The Canterbury Tales* is a collection of stories told by pilgrims on their way to Canterbury. His other works include the poem *The Book of the Duchess* and *Troilus and Criseyde*.

Quotations about Chaucer

1 Chaucer, notwithstanding the praises bestowed on him, I think obscene and contemptible; he owes his celebrity merely to his antiquity.

Lord Byron (1788–1824) British poet. Attrib.

2 I read Chaucer still with as much pleasure as any of our poets. He is a master of manners and of description and the first tale-teller in the true enlivened, natural way.

Alexander Pope (1688–1744) British poet. Attrib.

Quotations by Chaucer

3 Whan that Aprille with his shoures sote
The droghte of Marche hath perced to the rote.

The Canterbury Tales, Prologue

4 He was a verray parfit gentil knight.

Referring to the knight. *The Canterbury Tales*, Prologue

5 He was as fresh as is the month of May.

Referring to the squire. *The Canterbury Tales*, Prologue

6 Ful wel she song the service divyne,
Entuned in hir nose ful semely.

Referring to the prioress. *The Canterbury Tales*, Prologue

7 A Clerk ther was of Oxenford also,
That un-to logik hadde longe y-go.

The Canterbury Tales, Prologue

8 As lene was his hors as is a rake.

The Canterbury Tales, Prologue

9 Souninge in moral vertu was his speche,
And gladly wolde he lerne, and gladly teche.

Referring to the clerk. *The Canterbury Tales*, Prologue

10 No-wher so bisy a man as he ther nas,
And yet he semed bisier than he was.

Referring to the man of law. *The Canterbury Tales*, Prologue

11 For gold in phisik is a cordial,
Therfore he lovede gold in special.

Referring to the doctor. *The Canterbury Tales*, Prologue

12 She was a worthy womman al hir lyve,
Housbondes at chirche-dore she hadde fyve,
Withouten other companye in youthe.

Referring to the wife of Bath. *The Canterbury Tales*, Prologue

13 The smyler with the knyf under the cloke.

The Canterbury Tales, 'The Knight's Tale'

14 This world nis but a thurghfare ful of wo,
And we ben pilgrimes, passinge to and fro;
Deeth is an ende of every worldly sore.

The Canterbury Tales, 'The Knight's Tale'

15 Tragedie is to seyn a certeyn storie,
As olde bokes maken us memorie,
Of him that stood in greet prosperitee
And is y-fallen out of heigh degree
Into miserie, and endeth wrecchedly.

The Canterbury Tales, 'The Monk's Prologue'

16 Whan that the month in which the world bigan,
That highte March, whan God first maked man.

The Canterbury Tales, 'The Nun's Priest's Tale'

17 Mordre wol out, that see we day by day.

The Canterbury Tales, 'The Nun's Priest's Tale'

18 So was hir joly whistle wel y-wet.

The Canterbury Tales, 'The Reve's Tale'

19 That lyf so short, the craft so long to lerne,
Th' assay so hard, so sharp the conqueryinge.

See also HIPPOCRATES. *The Parliament of Fowls*

20 For of fortunes sharp adversitee
The worst kinde of infortune is this,
A man to have ben in prosperitee,
And it remembren, what is passed is.

Troilus and Criseyde, 3

CHEKHOV, ANTON

(1860–1904) Russian dramatist and writer. Plays include *The Seagull* (1896), *Uncle Vanya* (1897), *The Three Sisters* (1901), and *The Cherry Orchard* (1904).

Quotations about Chekhov

1 Politically speaking, he might as well have been living on the moon as in Imperial Russia.

Ronald Hingley (1920–) Scottish writer. *A New Life of Anton Chekhov*

2 We are certainly entitled to deduce that he was somewhat undersexed.

Ronald Hingley (1920–) Scottish writer. *A New Life of Anton Chekhov*

3 When I had read this story to the end, I was filled with awe. I could not remain in my room and went out of doors. I felt as if I were locked up in a ward too.

On reading *Ward Number Six* (1892). **Lenin** (Vladimir Ilich Ulyanov; 1870–1924) Russian revolutionary leader. *Anton Chekhov* (W. H. Bruford)

Quotations by Chekhov

4 LIBOV ANDREEVNA. Are you still a student?
TROFIMOV. I expect I shall be a student to the end of my days.

The Cherry Orchard, I

5 When a lot of remedies are suggested for a disease, that means it can't be cured.

The Cherry Orchard, I

6 Before the cherry orchard was sold everybody was worried and upset, but as soon as it was all settled finally and once for all, everybody calmed down, and felt quite cheerful.

The Cherry Orchard, IV

7 MEDVEDENKO. Why do you wear black all the time?
MASHA. I'm in mourning for my life, I'm unhappy.

The Seagull, I

8 NINA. Your play's hard to act, there are no living people in it.
TREPLEV. Living people! We should show life neither as it is nor as it ought to be, but as we see it in our dreams.

The Seagull, I

9 The time's come: there's a terrific thunder-cloud advancing upon us, a mighty storm is coming to freshen us up.…It's going to blow away all this idleness and indifference, and prejudice against work.…I'm going to work, and in twenty-five or thirty years' time every man and woman will be working.

Three Sisters, I

10 Man has been endowed with reason, with the power to create, so that he can add to what he's been given. But up to now he hasn't been a creator, only a destroyer. Forests keep disappearing, rivers dry up, wild life's become extinct, the climate's ruined and the land grows poorer and uglier every day.

Uncle Vanya, I

11 A woman can become a man's friend only in the following stages – first an acquaintance, next a mistress, and only then a friend.

Uncle Vanya, II

12 SONYA. I'm not beautiful.
HELEN. You have lovely hair.
SONYA. No, when a woman isn't beautiful, people always say, 'You have lovely eyes, you have lovely hair.'

Uncle Vanya, III

13 When all is said and done, no literature can outdo the cynicism of real life; you won't intoxicate with one glass someone who has already drunk up a whole barrel.

Letter, 1887

CHESTERFIELD, PHILIP DORMER STANHOPE

(4th Earl of Chesterfield; 1694–1773) English statesman and diplomat; author of the famous *Letters* (1774) to his illegitimate son. Appointed ambassador to The Hague in 1728, he subsequently served in Ireland and as secretary of state (1746–48).

Quotations about Chesterfield

1 This man I thought had been a Lord among wits; but, I find, he is only a wit among Lords.

Samuel Johnson (1709–84) British lexicographer. *Life of Johnson* (J. Boswell), Vol. I

2 They teach the morals of a whore, and the manners of a dancing master.

Samuel Johnson *Life of Johnson* (J. Boswell), Vol. I, Referring to Lord Chesterfield's letters

3 The only Englishman who ever maintained that the art of pleasing was the first duty in life.

Voltaire (François-Marie Arouet; 1694–1778) French writer. Letter to Frederick the Great, 16 Aug 1774

4 He was a man of much wit, middling sense, and some learning; but as absolutely void of virtue as any Jew, Turk or Heathen that ever lived.

John Wesley (1703–91) British religious leader. *Journal*, 11 Oct 1775

Quotations by Chesterfield

5 Be wiser than other people if you can, but do not tell them so.

Letter to his son, 19 Nov 1745

6 Whatever is worth doing at all is worth doing well.

Letter to his son, 10 Mar 1746

7 An injury is much sooner forgotten than an insult.

Letter to his son, 9 Oct 1746

8 Take the tone of the company that you are in.

Letter to his son, 16 Oct 1747

9 Do as you would be done by is the surest method that I know of pleasing.

Letter to his son, 16 Oct 1747

10 I knew once a very covetous, sordid fellow, who

used to say, 'Take care of the pence, for the pounds will take care of themselves.'
Letter to his son, 6 Nov 1747

11 I recommend you to take care of the minutes: for hours will take care of themselves.
Letter to his son, 6 Nov 1747

12 Advice is seldom welcome; and those who want it the most always like it the least.
Letter to his son, 29 Jan 1748

13 It must be owned, that the Graces do not seem to be natives of Great Britain; and I doubt, the best of us here have more of rough than polished diamond.
Letter to his son, 18 Nov 1748

14 Due attention to the inside of books, and due contempt for the outside, is the proper relation between a man of sense and his books.
Letter to his son, 10 Jan 1749

15 Idleness is only the refuge of weak minds.
Letter to his son, 20 July 1749

16 Women are much more like each other than men: they have, in truth, but two passions, vanity and love; these are their universal characteristics.
Letter to his son, 19 Dec 1749

17 Every woman is infallibly to be gained by every sort of flattery, and every man by one sort or other.
Letter to his son, 16 Mar 1752

18 The chapter of knowledge is very short, but the chapter of accidents is a very long one.
Letter to his son, 16 Feb 1753

19 Religion is by no means a proper subject of conversation in a mixed company.
Letter to his godson, Solomon Dayrolles

20 We, my lords, may thank heaven that we have something better than our brains to depend upon.
Speech, House of Lords. *The Story of Civilization* (W. Durant), Vol. 9

21 Make him a bishop, and you will silence him at once.
When asked what steps might be taken to control the evangelical preacher George Whitefield. Attrib.

22 When your ladyship's faith has removed them, I will go thither with all my heart.
Said to his sister, Lady Gertrude Hotham, when she suggested he go to a Methodist seminary in Wales to recuperate, recommending the views. Attrib.

23 Give Dayrolles a chair.
Said on his deathbed when visited by his godson, Solomon Dayrolles. Last words

CHESTERTON, G.K.

(1874–1936) British essayist, novelist, and poet. His detective stories feature the priest Father Brown and his novels include *The Napoleon of Notting Hill* (1904). After conversion to Roman Catholicism (1933) much of his writing was religious.

Quotations about Chesterton

1 Chesterton is like a vile scum on a pond....All his slop – it is really modern catholicism to a great extent, the *never* taking a hedge straight, the mumbo-jumbo of superstition dodging behind clumsy fun and paradox...I believe he creates a milieu in which art is impossible. He and his kind.
Ezra Pound (1885–1972) US poet. Letter to John Quinn, 21 Aug 1917

2 Chesterton's resolute conviviality is about as genial as an *auto da fé* of teetotallers.
George Bernard Shaw (1856–1950) Irish dramatist and critic. *Pen Portraits and Reviews*

3 Here lies Mr Chesterton,
Who to heaven might have gone,
But didn't when he heard the news
That the place was run by Jews.
Humbert Wolfe (1886–1940) British poet. *Lampoons*

Quotations by Chesterton

4 A great deal of contemporary criticism reads to me like a man saying: 'Of course I do not like green cheese: I am very fond of brown sherry.'
All I Survey

5 The modern world...has no notion except that of simplifying something by destroying nearly everything.
All I Survey

6 Talk about the pews and steeples
And the cash that goes therewith!
But the souls of Christian peoples...
Chuck it, Smith!
Antichrist, or the Reunion of Christendom

7 The strangest whim has seized me...After all I think I will not hang myself today.
A Ballade of Suicide

8 'My country, right or wrong' is a thing that no patriot would thing of saying, except in a desperate case. It is like saying 'My mother, drunk or sober.'
The Defendant

9 There is a road from the eye to the heart that does not go through the intellect.
The Defendant

10 The one stream of poetry which is continually flowing is slang.
The Defendant

11 All slang is metaphor, and all metaphor is poetry.
The Defendant

12 The devil's walking parody
On all four-footed things.
The Donkey

13 Fools! For I also had my hour;
One far fierce hour and sweet;
There was a shout about my ears,
And palms before my feet.
The Donkey

14 They died to save their country and they only saved the world.

The English Graves

15 The rich are the scum of the earth in every country.
The Flying Inn

16 One sees great things from the valley; only small things from the peak.
The Hammer of God

17 The word 'orthodoxy' not only no longer means being right; it practically means being wrong.
Heretics, Ch. 1

18 There is no such thing on earth as an uninteresting subject; the only thing that can exist is an uninterested person.
Heretics, Ch. 1

19 As enunciated today, 'progress' is simply a comparative of which we have not settled the superlative.
Heretics, Ch. 2

20 We ought to see far enough into a hypocrite to see even his sincerity.
Heretics, Ch. 5

21 Happiness is a mystery like religion, and should never be rationalized.
Heretics, Ch. 7

22 Charity is the power of defending that which we know to be indefensible. Hope is the power of being cheerful in circumstances which we know to be desperate.
Heretics, Ch. 12

23 Carlyle said that men were mostly fools. Christianity, with a surer and more reverend realism, says that they are all fools.
Referring to the historian, Thomas Carlyle. *Heretics*, Ch. 12

24 A good novel tells us the truth about its hero; but a bad novel tells us the truth about its author.
Heretics, Ch. 15

25 The artistic temperament is a disease that afflicts amateurs.
Heretics, Ch. 17

26 To be clever enough to get all that money, one must be stupid enough to want it.
The Innocence of Father Brown

27 Evil comes at leisure like the disease; good comes in a hurry like the doctor.
The Man who was Orthodox

28 You can only find truth with logic if you have already found truth without it.
The Man who was Orthodox

29 And they think we're burning witches when we're only burning weeds.
Me Heart

30 The human race, to which so many of my readers belong.
The Napoleon of Notting Hill, Vol. I, Ch. 1

31 The madman is not the man who has lost his reason. The madman is the man who has lost everything except his reason.
Orthodoxy, Ch. 1

32 The cosmos is about the smallest hole that a man can hide his head in.
Orthodoxy, Ch. 1

33 Reason is itself a matter of faith. It is an act of faith to assert that our thoughts have any relation to reality at all.
Orthodoxy, Ch. 3

34 Mr Shaw is (I suspect) the only man on earth who has never written any poetry.
Referring to George Bernard Shaw. *Orthodoxy*, Ch. 3

35 All conservatism is based upon the idea that if you leave things alone you leave them as they are. But you do not. If you leave a thing alone you leave it to a torrent of change.
Orthodoxy, Ch. 7

36 Angels can fly because they take themselves lightly.
Orthodoxy, Ch. 7

37 Before the Roman came to Rye or out to Severn strode,
The rolling English drunkard made the rolling English road.
The Rolling English Road

38 Smile at us, pay us, pass us; but do not quite forget.
For we are the people of England, that never have spoken yet.
The Secret People

39 Is ditchwater dull? Naturalists with microscopes have told me that it teems with quiet fun.
The Spice of Life

40 He could not think up to the height of his own towering style.
Speaking of Tennyson. *The Victorian Age in Literature*, Ch. 3

41 Compromise used to mean that half a loaf was better than no bread. Among modern statesmen it really seems to mean that half a loaf is better than a whole loaf.
What's Wrong with the World

42 Mankind is not a tribe of animals to which we owe compassion. Mankind is a club to which we owe our subscription.
Daily News, 10 Apr 1906

43 Just the other day in the Underground I enjoyed the pleasure of offering my seat to three ladies.
Suggesting that fatness had its consolations. *Das Buch des Lachens* (W. Scholz)

44 There is nothing the matter with Americans except their ideals. The real American is all right; it is the ideal American who is all wrong.
New York Times, 1 Feb 1931

45 Democracy means government by the uneducated, while aristocracy means government by the badly educated.
New York Times, 1 Feb 1931

46 Education is simply the soul of a society as it passes from one generation to another.

The Observer, 'Sayings of the Week', 6 July 1924

47 I want to reassure you I am not this size, really – dear me no, I'm being amplified by the mike.

At a lecture in Pittsburgh. *The Outline of Sanity: A Life of G. K. Chesterton* (S. D. Dale)

48 Am in Birmingham. Where ought I to be?

Telegram to his wife during a lecture tour. *Portrait of Barrie* (C. Asquith)

49 The only way to be sure of catching a train is to miss the one before it.

Vacances à tous prix, 'Le Supplice de l'heure' (P. Daninos)

50 How beautiful it would be for someone who could not read.

Referring to the lights on Broadway. Attrib.

51 A puritan's a person who pours righteous indignation into the wrong things.

Attrib.

52 New roads: new ruts.

Attrib.

CHILDREN

See also babies, family, innocence of childhood, youth

1 Spare the rod and spoil the child.

Proverb

2 There's only one pretty child in the world, and every mother has it.

Proverb

3 If this was adulthood the only improvement she could detect in her situation was that she could now eat dessert without eating her vegetables.

Lisa Alther (1944–) US writer. *Kinflicks*

4 It was no wonder that people were so horrible when they started life as children.

Kingsley Amis (1922–) British novelist. *One Fat Englishman*, Ch. 14

5 Only those in the last stage of disease could believe that children are true judges of character.

W. H. Auden (1907–73) British poet. *The Orators*, 'Journal of an Airman'

6 Children sweeten labours, but they make misfortunes more bitter.

Francis Bacon (1561–1626) English philosopher. *Essays*, 'Of Parents and Children'

7 Children have never been very good at listening to their elders, but they have never failed to imitate them. They must, they have no other models.

James Baldwin (1924–87) US writer. *Nobody Knows My Name*

8 I am married to Beatrice Salkeld, a painter. We have no children, except me.

Brendan Behan (1923–64) Irish playwright. Attrib.

9 I wish I'd been a mixed infant.

Brendan Behan *The Hostage*, II

10 Alas! That such affected tricks
Should flourish in a child of six!

Hilaire Belloc (1870–1953) French-born British poet. *Cautionary Tales*, 'Godolphin Horne'

11 A trick that everyone abhors
In little girls is slamming doors.

Hilaire Belloc *Cautionary Tales*, 'Rebecca'

12 Were we closer to the ground as children or is the grass emptier now?

Alan Bennett (1934–) British playwright. *Forty Years On*, II

13 Having no children had been a kind of choice up to the moment when, from a choice, it became a sadness.

Bernardo Bertolucci (1940–) Italian film director. *The Observer*, 'Sayings of the Week', 1 May 1994

14 Desire not a multitude of unprofitable children, neither delight in ungodly sons.

Bible: Ecclesiasticus 16:1

15 Unto the woman he said, I will greatly multiply thy sorrow and thy conception; in sorrow thou shalt bring forth children.

Bible: Genesis 3:16

16 But when Jesus saw it, he was much displeased, and said unto them. Suffer the little children to come unto me, and forbid them not: for of such is the kingdom of God.

Bible: Mark 10:14

17 Verily I say unto you, Except ye be converted, and become as little children, ye shall not enter into the kingdom of heaven.

Bible: Matthew 18:3

18 And whoso shall receive one such little child in my name receiveth me.
But whoso shall offend one of these little ones which believe in me, it were better for him that a millstone were hanged about his neck, and that he were drowned in the depth of the sea.

Bible: Matthew 18:5–6

19 He that spareth his rod hateth his son: but he that loveth him chasteneth him betimes.

Bible: Proverbs 13:24

20 You can do anything with children if you only play with them.

Bismarck (1815–98) German statesman. Attrib.

21 'Twas on a Holy Thursday, their innocent faces clean,
The children walking two and two, in red and blue and green.

William Blake (1757–1827) British poet. *Songs of Innocence*, 'Holy Thursday'

22 I guess that'll hold the little bastards.

Don Carney (1897–1954) US broadcaster. Carney was ending a children's radio show and thought that he was off the air. Attrib.

23 Sometimes when I look at my children I say to myself, 'Lillian, you should have stayed a virgin.'

Mrs Lillian Carter (1898–1983) mother of US president Carter. Remark

24 There is no finer investment for any community than putting milk into babies.

Winston Churchill (1874–1965) British statesman. Radio Broadcast, 21 Mar 1943

25 Boys do not grow up gradually. They move forward in spurts like the hands of clocks in railway stations.

Cyril Connolly (1903–74) British journalist. *Enemies of Promise*, Ch. 18

26 Two things should be cut: the second act and the child's throat.

Noël Coward (1899–1973) British dramatist. Referring to a play featuring a child actor. *The Wit of Noël Coward* (D. Richards)

27 It is only rarely that one can see in a little boy the promise of a man, but one can almost always see in a little girl the threat of a woman.

Alexandre Dumas, fils (1824–95) French writer. Attrib.

28 Anybody who hates children and dogs can't be all bad.

W. C. Fields (1880–1946) US actor. Attrib.

29 To bear many children is considered not only a religious blessing but also an investment. The greater their number, some Indians reason, the more alms they can beg.

Indira Gandhi (1917–84) Indian stateswoman. *New York Review of Books*, 'Indira's Coup' (Oriana Fallaci)

30 You may give them your love but not your thoughts.
For they have their own thoughts.
You may house their bodies but not their souls,
For their souls dwell in the house of tomorrow, which you cannot visit, not even in your dreams.

Kahlil Gibran (1883–1931) Lebanese mystic and poet. *The Prophet*, 'On Children'

31 Three little maids from school are we,
Pert as a school-girl well can be,
Filled to the brim with girlish glee.

W. S. Gilbert (1836–1911) British dramatist. *The Mikado*, I

32 Common morality now treats childbearing as an aberration. There are practically no good reasons left for exercising one's fertility.

Germaine Greer (1939–) Australian-born British writer and feminist.

33 The four eaglets are my four sons who cease not to persecute me even unto death. The youngest of them, whom I now embrace with so much affection, will sometime in the end insult me more grievously and more dangerously than any of the others.

Henry II (1133–89) King of England. Describing a painting of four eaglets preying on their parent. 'The youngest' refers to the future King John. *De Principis Instructione* (Gerald of Wales)

34 Look at little Johnny there,
Little Johnny Head-in-Air.

Heinrich Hoffman (1809–74) German writer. *Struwwelpeter*, 'Johnny Head-in-Air'

35 Anything to me is sweeter
Than to see Shock-headed Peter.

Heinrich Hoffman *Struwwelpeter*, 'Shock-headed Peter'

36 The business of being a child interests a child not at all. Children very rarely play at being other children.

David Holloway (1924–) Literary editor. *The Daily Telegraph*, 15 December 1966

37 Oh, for an hour of Herod!

Anthony Hope (1863–1933) British novelist. Said at the children's play *Peter Pan* (J. M. Barrie). *J. M. Barrie and the Lost Boys* (A. Birkin)

38 One of the most obvious facts about grown-ups to a child is that they have forgotten what it is like to be a child.

Randall Jarrell (1914–65) US author. *Third Book of Criticism*

39 It is easier for a father to have children than for children to have a real father.

Pope John XXIII (Angelo Roncalli; 1881–1963) Italian churchman. Attrib.

40 A child deserves the maximum respect; if you ever have something disgraceful in mind, don't ignore your son's tender years.

Juvenal (Decimus Junius Juvenalis; 60–130 AD) Roman satirist. *Satires*, XIV

41 The real menace in dealing with a five-year-old is that in no time at all you begin to sound like a five-year-old.

Jean Kerr (1923–) US dramatist. *Please Don't Eat the Daisies*

42 At every step the child should be allowed to meet the real experiences of life; the thorns should never be plucked from his roses.

Ellen Key (Karolina Sofia Key; 1849–1926) Swedish writer. *The Century of the Child*, Ch. 3

43 It is...sometimes easier to head an institute for the study of child guidance than it is to turn one brat into a decent human being.

Joseph Wood Krutch (1893–1970) US essayist, critic, and teacher. *If You Don't Mind My Saying*, 'Whom Do We Picket Tonight?'

44 Boys are capital fellows in their own way, among their mates; but they are unwholesome companions for grown people.

Charles Lamb (1775–1834) British essayist. *Essays of Elia*, 'The Old and the New Schoolmaster'

45 A child's a plaything for an hour.

Mary Lamb (1764–1847) Sister of Charles Lamb. *Parental Recollections*

46 Man hands on misery to man.
It deepens like a coastal shelf.
Get out as early as you can,
And don't have any kids yourself.

Philip Larkin (1922–85) British poet. *High Windows*, 'This Be the Verse'

47 Kids haven't changed much, but parents seem increasingly unhappy with the child raising phase of their lives.

Penelope Leach British writer and child-care specialist. Remark, Oct 1988

48 Literature is mostly about having sex and not much about having children; life is the other way round.

David Lodge (1935–) British author. *The British Museum is Falling Down*, Ch. 4

49 Where are the children I might have had? You may suppose I might have wanted them. Drowned to the accompaniment of the rattling of a thousand douche bags.

Malcolm Lowry (1909–57) British novelist. *Under the Volcano*, Ch. 10

50 Monday's child is fair of face,
Tuesday's child is full of grace,
Wednesday's child is full of woe,
Thursday's child has far to go,
Friday's child is loving and giving,

Saturday's child works hard for his living,
And the child that is born on the Sabbath day
Is bonny and blithe, and good and gay.

Nursery Rhyme *Traditions of Devonshire* (A. E. Bray)

51 Part of the reason for the ugliness of adults, in a child's eyes, is that the child is usually looking upwards, and few faces are at their best when seen from below.

George Orwell (Eric Blair; 1903–50) British novelist. *Essays*

52 But at three, four, five, and even six years the childish nature will require sports; now is the time to get rid of self-will in him, punishing him, but not so as to disgrace him.

Plato (c. 427 BC–347 BC) Greek philosopher. *Laws*, VII, 794

53 The nice thing about having relatives' kids around is that they go home.

Cliff Richard (1940–) British pop singer. Remark, Nov 1988

54 Woe to the land that's govern'd by a child!

William Shakespeare (1564–1616) English dramatist. *Richard III*, II:3

55 Thou cam'st on earth to make the earth my hell.
A grievous burden was thy birth to me;
Tetchy and wayward was thy infancy;
Thy school-days frightful, desperate, wild and furious;
Thy prime of manhood daring, bold, and venturous;
Thy age confirm'd, proud, subtle, sly, and bloody,
More mild, but yet more harmful, kind in hatred;
What comfortable hour canst thou name
That ever grac'd me in thy company?

William Shakespeare *Richard III*, IV:4

56 Parents learn a lot from their children about coping with life.

Muriel Spark (1918–) British novelist. *The Comforters*, Ch. 6

57 There are only two things a child will share willingly – communicable diseases and his mother's age.

Dr Benjamin Spock (1903–) US pediatrician and psychiatrist. Attrib.

58 I have a big house – and I hide a lot.

Mary Ure (1933–75) British actress. Explaining how she coped with her large family of children. Attrib.

59 Parents are the bones on which children sharpen their teeth.

Peter Ustinov (1921–) British actor. *Dear Me*

60 Never have children, only grandchildren.

Gore Vidal (1925–) US novelist. *Two Sisters*

61 The English are growing demented about children. When I was a boy the classroom had icicles inside every window at this time of year. We were savagely beaten three times a week...

Auberon Waugh (1939–) British novelist. *The Diaries of Auberon Waugh 1976–1985*, 'January 25, 1979'

62 A food is not necessarily essential just because your child hates it.

Katherine Whitehorn (1926–) British journalist. *How to Survive Children*

CHINA

1 Nothing and no one can destroy the Chinese people. They are relentless survivors. They are the oldest civilized people on earth. Their civilization passes through phases but its basic characteristics remain the same. They yield, they bend to the wind, but they never break.

Pearl Buck (1892–1973) US novelist. *China, Past and Present*, Ch. 1

2 All diplomacy is a continuation of war by other means.

Chou En Lai (1898–1976) Chinese statesman.

3 The tension here is very high, the Chinese are enormously brave and they keep telling me they are not afraid to die for democracy but the students know that they will be the Army's first target.

Alex Woodhatch British student in Peking. *The Times*, 5 June 1989

4 Students were sitting down and tanks were running over them. Other students had tanks run over them as they ran. Flame throwers are said to have been used afterwards on some of those who were run over so that the bodies could not be identified.

Alex Woodhatch *The Times*, 5 June 1989

5 In spring 1989...I saw the buildup of demonstrations from Chengdu to Tiananmen Square. It struck me that fear had been forgotten to such an extent that few of the millions of demonstrators perceived danger. Most seemed to be taken by surprise when the army opened fire.

Jung Chang *Wild Swans*, Epilogue

6 They fired first above the heads and then at the heads. They were laughing wildly as if it was not serious.

Anonymous Chinese student Referring to the soldiers who opened fire on pro-democracy demonstrators in Tiananmen Square. *The Times*, 6 June 1989

7 The worst fears of the Hong Kong people have been confirmed by the events in Peking.

Selina Chow British member of the Legislative Council of Hong Kong. Referring to the massacre in Tiananmen Square. *The Times*, 4 June 1989

8 Even if they're functioning out of ignorance, they are still participating and must be suppressed. In China, even one million people can be considered a small sum.

Deng Xiaoping (1904–) Chinese communist statesman. Referring to the pro-democracy demonstrators in Tiananmen Square. *The Times*, 5 June 1989

9 By relying on the heroic struggle of the officers and men of the units enforcing martial law, the officers and men of the armed police force, public security personnel and by relying on the active coordination and support of the vast number of the masses and revolutionary students, we have won the initial triumph in putting down the riot...a resolute struggle against the extremely small number of people who created the riot.

The Chinese Communist Party Central Committee and State Council Referring to the massacre in Tiananmen Square. *Letter to the People*, June 1989

10 History shows that anything conducive to our national stability is good.

Jiang Zemin (1926–) Chinese party and government official. Referring to the massacre in Tiananmen Square in 1989. *The Times*, 14 May 1994

11 My grandmother's feet had been bound when she was two years old. Her mother...first wound a piece of white cloth about twenty feet long round her feet, bending all the toes except the big toe inward and under the sole. Then she placed a large stone on top to crush the arch.

Jung Chang (1952–) Chinese writer and lecturer. *Wild Swans*, Ch. 1

12 My father said he was going to write to the Jinzhou City Party Committee asking for permission to 'talk about love'...My mother supposed it was a bit like asking permission from the head of the family...the Communist Party was the new patriarch.

Jung Chang *Wild Swans*, Ch. 6

13 Gentleness was considered 'bourgeois'...Over the years of the Cultural Revolution, I was to witness people being attacked for saying 'thank you' too often, which was branded as 'bourgeois hypocrisy'.

Jung Chang *Wild Swans*, Ch. 16

14 Like spring, I treat my comrades warmly.
Like summer, I am full of ardor for my revolutionary work.
I eliminate my individualism as an autumn gale sweeps away fallen leaves
And to the class enemy, I am cruel and ruthless like harsh winter.

Lei Feng (1940–62) Chinese soldier. *The Four Seasons*

15 Since China has a population of 1.1 billion, it won't feel lonely even if it becomes the only socialist country.

Li Peng (1928–) Chinese prime minister. On the world's dwindling number of socialist governments.

16 If some Western politician claims he is in a position to use the normal Western methods to feed and clothe 1.2 billion Chinese, we would be happily prepared to elect him president of China.

Li Peng *The Independent*, 6 July 1994

17 The Chinese do not draw any distinction between food and medicine.

Lin Yutang (1895–1976) *The Importance of Living*, Ch. 9, Sect. 7

18 We are advocates of the abolition of war, we do not want war; but war can only be abolished through war, and in order to get rid of the gun it is necessary to take up the gun.

Mao Tse-Tung (1893–1976) Chinese communist leader. *Quotations from Chairman Mao Tse-Tung*, Ch. 5

19 Letting a hundred flowers blossom and a hundred schools of thought contend is the policy for promoting the progress of the arts and the sciences.

Mao Tse-Tung *Quotations from Chairman Mao Tse-Tung*, Ch. 32

20 Every Communist must grasp the truth, 'Political power grows out of the barrel of a gun.'

Mao Tse-Tung *Selected Works*, Vol II, 'Problems of War and Strategy', 6 Nov 1938.

21 The government burns down whole cities while the people are forbidden to light lamps.

Mao Tse-Tung Attrib.

22 We can soar to heaven, and pierce the earth, because our Great Leader Chairman Mao is our supreme commander.

Red Guard slogan

23 Ever since the foundation of the dynasty, foreigners coming to China have been kindly treated...At first they were amenable to Chinese control, but for the past thirty years they...trample on Chinese people and...absorb the wealth of the Empire.

Tz'u-Lsi (1835–1908) Empress Dowager of China. The start of the Boxer Rising. Declaration of war, 21 June 1900

24 I wonder if Deng Xiaoping is actually watching this right now with his children and grandchildren? And with the knowledge what a horrendous, horrendous human rights situation there is in China, and not only towards their own people but to Tibet as well...if we could all send love and truth and some kind of sanity to Deng Xiaoping right now, that he will take his troops and take the Chinese away from Tibet and allow these people to live as free and independent people again.

Richard Gere (1949–) US actor. Speech, Academy Awards ceremony, May 1993

CHIVALRY

See also courtesy

1 But there is another side to chivalry. If it dispenses leniency, it may with equal justification invoke control.

Freda Adler (1934–) US educator. *Sisters in Crime*, Ch. 4

2 A gentleman is any man who wouldn't hit a woman with his hat on.

Fred Allen (1894–1956) US comedian. Attrib.

3 Even nowadays a man can't step up and kill a woman without feeling just a bit unchivalrous.

Robert Benchley (1889–1945) US humorist. *Chips off the Old Benchley*, 'Down in Front'

4 Somebody has said, that a king may make a nobleman, but he cannot make a gentleman.

Edmund Burke (1729–97) British politician. Letter to William Smith, 29 Jan 1795

5 A Knyght ther was and that a worthy man,
That fro the tyme that he first bigan
To riden out, he loved chivalrie,
Trouthe and honour, fredom and curteisie.
...
He was a verray parfit, gentil knyght.

Geoffrey Chaucer (c. 1342–1400) English poet. *The Canterbury Tales*, Prologue

6 Madame, I would have given you another!

Alfred Jarry (1873–1907) French surrealist dramatist. On being reprimanded by a woman for firing his pistol in the vicinity of her child, who might have been killed. *Recollections of a Picture Dealer* (A. Vollard)

7 Some say that the age of chivalry is past, that the spirit of romance is dead. The age of chivalry is never past, so long as there is a wrong left unredressed on earth.

Charles Kingsley (1819–75) British writer. *Life* (Mrs C. Kingsley), Vol. II, Ch. 28

8 For he's one of Nature's Gentlemen, the best of every time.

W. J. Linton (1812–97) British writer. *Nature's Gentleman*

9 Remember, men, we're fighting for this woman's honour; which is probably more than she ever did.

Groucho Marx (Julius Marx; 1895–1977) US comedian. *Duck Soup*

10 It is almost a definition of a gentleman to say that he is one who never inflicts pain.

Cardinal Newman (1801–90) British theologian. *The Idea of a University*, 'Knowledge and Religious Duty'

11 O, young Lochinvar is come out of the west,
Through all the wide Border his steed was the best.

Walter Scott (1771–1832) Scottish novelist. *Marmion*, V

12 So faithful in love, and so dauntless in war,
There never was knight like the young Lochinvar.

Walter Scott *Marmion*, V

13 I have a truant been to chivalry.

William Shakespeare (1564–1616) English dramatist. *Henry IV, Part One*, V:1

14 Love of honour and honour of love.

Philip Sidney (1554–86) English poet and courtier. Referring to the ideal of chivalry. *English Literature: Mediaeval* (W. P. Ker)

15 A bow-shot from her bower-eaves,
He rode between the barley-sheaves,
The sun came dazzling thro' the leaves
And flamed upon the brazen graves
Of bold Sir Lancelot.

Alfred, Lord Tennyson (1809–92) British poet. *The Lady of Shalott*, Pt. III

16 Every man I meet wants to protect me. I can't figure out what from.

Mae West (1892–1980) US actress.

CHOICE

1 Any colour, so long as it's black.

Henry Ford (1863–1947) US car manufacturer. Referring to the colour options offered for the Model-T Ford car. Attrib.

2 Two roads diverged in a wood, and I –
I took the one less traveled by,
And that has made all the difference.

Robert Frost (1875–1963) US poet. *The Road Not Taken*

3 More ways of killing a cat than choking her with cream.

Charles Kingsley (1819–75) British writer. *Westward Ho!*, Ch. 20

4 We have to believe in free will. We've got no choice.

Isaac Bashevis Singer (1904–91) Polish-born US writer. *The Times*, 21 June 1982

5 The American Standard translation *orders* men to triumph over sin, and you can call sin ignorance. The King James translation makes a promise in 'Thou shalt', meaning that men will surely triumph over sin. But the Hebrew word, the word *timshel* – 'Thou mayest' – that gives a choice. It might be the most important word in the world. That says the way is open.…For if 'Thou mayest' – it is also true that 'Thou mayest not'.

John Steinbeck (1902–68) US novelist Referring to Genesis, 4:7. *East of Eden*, Ch. 24

CHRISTIANITY

See also Catholicism, Protestantism, religion

1 There is a green hill far away,
Without a city wall,
Where the dear Lord was crucified,
Who died to save us all.

C. F. Alexander (1818–95) British hymn writer. *There is a Green Hill Far Away*

2 'Christianity, of course but why journalism?'

Arthur Balfour (1848–1930) British statesman. In reply to Frank Harris's remark, '…all the faults of the age come from Christianity and journalism'. *Autobiography* (Margot Asquith), Ch. 10

3 Onward, Christian soldiers,
Marching as to war,
With the Cross of Jesus
Going on before.

Sabine Baring-Gould (1834–1924) British author and hymn writer. *Onward Christian Soldiers*

4 Jesus picked up twelve men from the bottom ranks of business and forged them into an organization that conquered the world.

Bruce Barton (1886–1967) US advertising executive. *The Man Nobody Knows: A Discovery of the Real Jesus*

5 The Christian glories in the death of a pagan because thereby Christ himself is glorified.

St Bernard (1090–1153) French monk and theologian. *Richard the Lionheart* (J. Gillingham), Ch. 9

6 Oh mighty soldier, O man of war, at last you have a cause for which you can fight without endangering your soul; a cause in which to win is glorious and for which to die is but gain. Are you a shrewd businessman, quick to see the profits of this world? If you are, I can offer you a bargain which you cannot afford to miss. Take the sign of the cross. At once you will have an indulgence for all the sins which you confess with a contrite heart. The cross is cheap and if you wear it with humility you will find that you have obtained the Kingdom of Heaven.

St Bernard Referring in particular to the second Crusade. *Richard the Lionheart* (J. Gillingham), Ch. 6

7 Beware lest any man spoil you through philosophy and vain deceit, after the tradition of men, after the rudiments of the world, and not after Christ.

Bible: Colossians 2:8

8 Where there is neither Greek nor Jew, circumcision nor uncircumcision, Barbarian, Scythian, bond nor free; but Christ is all, and in all.

Bible: Colossians 3:11

9 Take heed to yourselves, that your heart be not deceived, and ye turn aside, and serve other gods, and worship them.

Bible: Deuteronomy 11:16

10 There is neither Jew nor Greek, there is neither

bond nor free, there is neither male nor female: for ye are all one in Christ Jesus.
Bible: Galatians 3:28

11 But the fruit of the Spirit is love, joy, peace, longsuffering, gentleness, goodness, faith, Meekness, temperance: against such there is no law.
Bible: Galatians 5:22–23

12 Therefore the Lord himself shall give you a sign; Behold, a virgin shall conceive, and bear a son, and shall call his name Immanuel.
Butter and honey shall he eat, that he may know to refuse the evil, and choose the good.
Bible: Isaiah 7:14–15

13 He shall feed his flock like a shepherd: he shall gather the lambs with his arm, and carry them in his bosom, and shall gently lead those that are with young.
Bible: Isaiah 40:11

14 He it is, who coming after me is preferred before me, whose shoe's latchet I am not worthy to unloose.
Bible: John 1:27

15 The next day John seeth Jesus coming unto him, and saith, Behold the Lamb of God, which taketh away the sin of the world.
Bible: John 1:29

16 Jesus answered and said unto him, Verily, verily, I say unto thee, Except a man be born again, he cannot see the kingdom of God.
Bible: John 3:3

17 For God so loved the world, that he gave his only begotten Son, that whosoever believeth in him should not perish, but have everlasting life.
Bible: John 3:16

18 Then spake Jesus again unto them, saying, I am the light of the world: he that followeth me shall not walk in darkness, but shall have the light of life.
Bible: John 8:12

19 I am the good shepherd: the good shepherd giveth his life for the sheep.
Bible: John 10:11

20 Jesus said unto her, I am the resurrection, and the life: he that believeth in me, though he were dead, yet shall he live.
Bible: John 11:25

21 Jesus saith unto him, I am the way, the truth, and the life: no man cometh unto the Father, but by me.
Bible: John 14:6

22 But unto you that fear my name shall the Sun of righteousness arise with healing in his wings; and ye shall go forth, and grow up as calves of the stall.
Bible: Malachi 4:2

23 And he said unto them, Go ye into all the world, and preach the gospel to every creature.
Bible: Mark 16:15

24 And Jesus, when he was baptized, went up straightway out of the water: and, lo, the heavens were opened unto him, and he saw the Spirit of God descending like a dove, and lighting upon him:
And lo a voice from heaven, saying, This is my beloved Son, in whom I am well pleased.
Bible: Matthew 3:16–17

25 And he saith unto them, Follow me, and I will make you fishers of men.
Bible: Matthew 4:19

26 Come unto me, all ye that labour and are heavy laden, and I will give you rest.
Take my yoke upon you, and learn of me; for I am meek and lowly in heart: and ye shall find rest unto your souls.
For my yoke is easy, and my burden is light.
Bible: Matthew 11:28–30

27 Then said Jesus unto his disciples, If any man will come after me, let him deny himself, and take up his cross, and follow me.
Bible: Matthew 16:24

28 And said unto them, It is written, My house shall be called the house of prayer; but ye have made it a den of thieves.
Bible: Matthew 21:13

29 And as they were eating, Jesus took bread, and blessed it, and brake it, and gave it to the disciples, and said, Take, eat; this is my body.
And he took the cup, and gave thanks, and gave it to them, saying, Drink ye all of it;
For this is my blood of the new testament, which is shed for many for the remission of sins.
Bible: Matthew 26:26–28

30 But made himself of no reputation, and took upon him the form of a servant, and was made in the likeness of men:
And being found in fashion as a man, he humbled himself, and became obedient unto death, even the death of the cross.
Wherefore God also hath highly exalted him, and given him a name which is above every name:
That at the name of Jesus every knee should bow, of things in heaven, and things in earth, and things under the earth.
Bible: Philippians 2:7–10

31 How very hard it is
To be a Christian!
Robert Browning (1812–89) British poet. *Easter-Day*, I

32 It was just one of those parties which got out of hand.
Lenny Bruce (1925–66) US comedian. Referring to the Crucifixion. *The Guardian*, 10 May 1979

33 If Jesus Christ were to come to-day, people would not even crucify him. They would ask him to dinner, and hear what he had to say, and make fun of it.
Thomas Carlyle (1795–1881) Scottish historian and essayist. *Carlyle at his Zenith* (D. A. Wilson)

34 The Christian ideal has not been tried and found wanting; it has been found difficult and left untried.
G. K. Chesterton (1874–1936) British writer. *What's Wrong with the World*, 'The Unfinished Temple'

35 He who begins by loving Christianity better

than Truth will proceed by loving his own sect or church better than Christianity, and end by loving himself better than all.

Samuel Taylor Coleridge (1772–1834) British poet. *Aids to Reflection: Moral and Religious Aphorisms*

36 We should easily convert even the Turks to the obedience of our gospel, if only we would agree among ourselves and unite in some holy confederacy.

Thomas Cranmer (1489–1556) English churchman. Letter to the Swiss scholar, Joachim Vadian, 1537

37 His Christianity was muscular.

Benjamin Disraeli (1804–81) British statesman. *Endymion*, Bk. 1, Ch. 14

38 Christianity has done a great deal for love by making a sin of it.

Anatole France (Jacques Anatole François Thibault; 1844–1924) French writer. *The Garden of Epicurus*

39 What about it? Do you want to crucify the boy?

Lew Grade (Lewis Winogradsky; 1906–) British film and TV producer. Referring to the revelation that an actor portraying Christ on television was living with a woman to whom he was not married. Attrib.

40 Christianity is part of the Common Law of England.

Matthew Hale (1609–76) English judge. *Historia Placitorum Coronae* (ed. Sollom Emlyn)

41 Tell me the old, old story
Of unseen things above,
Of Jesus and His glory
Of Jesus and His love.

Katherine Hankey (1834–1911) British hymn writer. *Tell Me the Old, Old Story*

42 A local cult called Christianity.

Thomas Hardy (1840–1928) British novelist. *The Dynasts*, I:6

43 The Christian religion not only was at first attended with miracles, but even at this day cannot be believed by any reasonable person without one. Mere reason is insufficient to convince us of its veracity: and whoever is moved by faith to assent to it, is conscious of a continued miracle in his own person, which subverts all the principles of his understanding, and gives him a determination to believe what is most contrary to custom and experience.

David Hume (1711–76) Scottish philosopher. *Essays*, 'Of Miracles' without one all the principles of his understanding

44 Christianity accepted as given a metaphysical system derived from several already existing and mutually incompatible systems.

Aldous Huxley (1894–1964) British novelist. *Grey Eminence*, Ch. 3

45 There must be several young women who would render the Christian life intensely difficult to him if only you could persuade him to marry one of them.

C. S. Lewis (1898–1963) British academic and writer. *The Screwtape Letters*

46 Ride on! ride on in majesty!
In lowly pomp ride on to die.

Henry Hart Milman (1791–1868) British poet and historian. *Ride On*

47 Fight the good fight with all thy might,
Christ is thy strength and Christ thy right,
Lay hold on life, and it shall be
Thy joy and crown eternally.

John Monsell (1811–75) British hymn writer. Hymn

48 No kingdom has ever had as many civil wars as the kingdom of Christ.

Baron de Montesquieu (1689–1755) French writer. *Lettres persanes*

49 I call Christianity the one great curse, the one enormous and innermost perversion, the one great instinct of revenge, for which no means are too venomous, too underhand, too underground and too petty – I call it the one immortal blemish of mankind.

Friedrich Wilhelm Nietzsche (1844–1900) German philosopher. *The Antichrist*

50 As with the Christian religion, the worst advertisement for Socialism is its adherents.

George Orwell (Eric Blair; 1903–50) British novelist. *The Road to Wigan Pier*, Ch. 11

51 Christianity has made of death a terror which was unknown to the gay calmness of the Pagan.

Ouida (Marie Louise de la Ramée; 1839–1908) British novelist. *The Failure of Christianity*

52 All hail, the power of Jesus' name!
Let angels prostrate fall.

Edward Perronet (1726–92) British hymn writer. Hymn

53 People may say what they like about the decay of Christianity; the religious system that produced green Chartreuse can never really die.

Saki (Hector Hugh Munro; 1870–1916) British writer. *Reginald on Christmas Presents*

54 If a Jew is fascinated by Christians it is not because of their virtues, which he values little, but because they represent anonymity, humanity without race.

Jean-Paul Sartre (1905–80) French writer. *Anti-Semite and Jew*

55 Whether you think Jesus was God or not, you must admit that he was a first-rate political economist.

George Bernard Shaw (1856–1950) Irish dramatist and critic. *Androcles and the Lion*, Preface, 'Jesus as Economist'

56 Who dreamed that Christ has died in vain?
He walks again on the Seas of Blood,
He comes in the terrible Rain.

Edith Sitwell (1887–1964) British poet and writer. *The Shadow of Cain*

57 The Church's one foundation
Is Jesus Christ her Lord;
She is His new creation
By water and the Word.

Samuel. J. Stone (1839–1901) US hymn writer. Hymn

58 Well, you might try getting crucified and rising again on the third day.

Talleyrand (Charles Maurice de Talleyrand-Périgord; 1754–1838) French politician. Giving his opinion upon what action might impress the French peasantry. Attrib.

59 Christianity is the most materialistic of all great religions.

William Temple (1881–1944) British churchman. *Reading in St John's Gospel*, Vol. I, Introduction

60 And so the Word had breath, and wrought
With human hands the creed of creeds
In loveliness of perfect deeds,
More strong than all poetic thought.

Alfred, Lord Tennyson (1809–92) British poet. *In Memoriam A.H.H.*, XXXVI

61 The blood of the martyrs is the seed of the Church.

Tertullian (c. 160–225 AD) Carthaginian father of the Church. Traditional misquotation: more accurately, 'Our numbers increase as often as you cut us down: the blood of Christians is the seed.' *Apologeticus*, L

62 See how these Christians love one another.

Tertullian *Apologeticus*, XXXIX

63 Fraser...left his children unbaptized – his wife did it secretly in the washing basin.

Virginia Woolf (1882–1941) British novelist. *Jacob's Room*, Ch. 9

64 A Christian is a man who feels
Repentance on a Sunday
For what he did on Saturday
And is going to do on Monday.

Thomas Russell Ybarra (b. 1880) Venezuelan-born US writer. *The Christian*

CHRISTIE, DAME AGATHA

(1890–1976) British detective-story writer. Her detective Hercule Poirot first appeared in *The Mysterious Affair at Styles* (1920). Among her 50 or so other stories are *Murder on the Orient Express* (1934) and *Death on the Nile* (1937). Her play *The Mousetrap* (1952) has had the longest run of any London play (over 35 years).

1 One doesn't recognize in one's life the really important moments – not until it's too late.

Endless Night, Bk. II, Ch. 14

2 Where large sums of money are concerned, it is advisable to trust nobody.

Endless Night, Bk. II, Ch. 15

3 Hercule Poirot tapped his forehead. 'These little grey cells, It is 'up to them' – as you say over here.'

The Mysterious Affair at Styles

4 If one sticks too rigidly to one's principles one would hardly see anybody.

Toward's Zero, I

5 Curious things, habits. People themselves never knew they had them.

Witness for the Prosecution

6 An archaeologist is the best husband any woman can have: the older she gets, the more interested he is in her.

Attrib.

CHRISTMAS

See also Christianity

1 I have often thought, says Sir Roger, it happens very well that Christmas should fall out in the Middle of Winter.

Joseph Addison (1672–1719) British essayist. *The Spectator*, 269

2 Once in royal David's city
Stood a lowly cattle shed,
Where a Mother laid her Baby
In a manger for His bed:
Mary was that Mother mild,
Jesus Christ her little Child.

C. F. Alexander (1818–95) British hymn writer. *Once in Royal David's City*

3 As I sat on a sunny bank,
On Christmas Day in the morning,
I spied three ships come sailing by.

Anonymous *As I sat on a Sunny Bank*

4 God rest you merry, gentlemen,
Let nothing you dismay.

Anonymous *God Rest you Merry*

5 The holly and the ivy,
When they are both full grown,
Of all the trees that are in the wood,
The holly bears the crown.
The rising of the sun
And the running of the deer,
The playing of the merry organ,
Sweet singing in the choir.

Anonymous *The Holly and the Ivy*

6 I'm dreaming of a white Christmas.

Irving Berlin (1888–1989) US composer and lyricist. *Holiday Inn*, 'White Christmas'

7 For unto us a child is born, unto us a son is given: and the government shall be upon his shoulder: and his name shall be called Wonderful, Counsellor, The mighty God, The everlasting Father, The Prince of Peace.
Of the increase of his government and peace there shall be no end, upon the throne of David, and upon his kingdom, to order it, and to establish it with judgment and with justice from henceforth even for ever. The zeal of the Lord of hosts will perform this.

Bible: Isaiah 9:6–7

8 And she brought forth her firstborn son, and wrapped him in swaddling clothes, and laid him in a manger; because there was no room for them in the inn.

Bible: Luke 2:7

9 And there were in the same country shepherds abiding in the field, keeping watch over their flock by night.
And, lo, the angel of the Lord came upon them, and the glory of the Lord shone round about them: and they were sore afraid.
And the angel said unto them, Fear not: for, behold, I bring you good tidings of great joy, which shall be to all people.

Bible: Luke 2:8–10

10 Now when Jesus was born in Bethlehem of Judaea in the days of Herod the king, behold, there came wise men from the east to Jerusalem,
Saying, Where is he that is born King of the Jews? for we have seen his star in the east, and are come to worship him.
When Herod the king had heard these things, he was troubled, and all Jerusalem with him.

Bible: Matthew 2:1–3

11 And when they were come into the house, they saw the young child with Mary his mother, and fell

down, and worshipped him: and when they had opened their treasures, they presented unto him gifts; gold, and frankincense, and myrrh.
And being warned of God in a dream that they should not return to Herod, they departed into their own country another way.

Bible: Matthew 2:11–12

12 O little town of Bethlehem,
How still we see thee lie;
Above thy deep and dreamless sleep
The silent stars go by.

Phillips Brooks (1835–93) US Episcopal bishop. *O Little Town of Bethlehem*

13 Christians awake, salute the happy morn,
Whereon the Saviour of the world was born.

John Byrom (1692–1763) British poet and hymn writer. *Hymn for Christmas Day*

14 Fortified in their front parlours, at Yuletide men are the more murderous. Drunk, they defy battle-axes, bellow of whale-bone and dung.

Geoffrey Hill (1932–) British poet. Mercian Hymns, XXVI, 'Offa's Bestiary'

15 'Twas the night before Christmas, when all through the house
Not a creature was stirring, not even a mouse;
The stockings were hung by the chimney with care,
In hopes that St Nicholas soon would be there.

Clement Clarke Moore (1779–1863) US writer. In *Troy Sentinel*, 23 Dec 1823, 'A Visit from St. Nicholas'

16 Good King Wenceslas looked out,
On the Feast of Stephen;
When the snow lay round about,
Deep and crisp and even.

John Mason Neale (1818–66) British churchman. *Good King Wenceslas*

17 The first day of Christmas,
My true love sent to me
A partridge in a pear tree.

Nursery Rhyme *Mirth without Mischief*

18 The twelfth day of Christmas,
My true love sent to me
Twelve lords a-leaping,
Eleven ladies dancing,
Ten pipers piping,
Nine drummers drumming,
Eight maids a-milking,
Seven swans a-swimming,
Six geese a-laying,
Five gold rings,
Four colly birds,
Three French hens,
Two turtle doves, and
A partridge in a pear tree.

Nursery Rhyme *Mirth without Mischief*

19 O come all ye faithful,
Joyful and triumphant,
O come ye, O come ye to Bethlehem.

Frederick Oakeley (1802–80) British churchman. Translated from the Latin hymn, *Adeste Fideles. O Come All Ye Faithful*

20 It came upon the midnight clear,
That glorious song of old,
From Angels bending near the earth
To touch their harps of gold;
'Peace on the earth; good will to man
From Heaven's all gracious King.'
The world in solemn stillness lay
To hear the angels sing.

E. H. Sears (1810–76) US clergyman. *That Glorious Song of Old*

21 It is Christmas Day in the Workhouse.

George R. Sims (1847–1922) British writer. *The Dagonet and Other Poems*

22 While shepherds watch'd their flocks by night,
All seated on the ground,
The Angel of the Lord came down,
And Glory shone around.

Nahum Tate (1652–1715) Irish-born English poet. *Supplement to the New Version of the Psalms*, 'While Shepherds Watched'

23 At Christmas play and make good cheer,
For Christmas comes but once a year.

Thomas Tusser (1524–80) English farmer. *Five Hundred Points of Good Husbandry*, 'The Farmer's Daily Diet'

24 To perceive Christmas through its wrapping becomes more difficult with every year.

Elwyn Brooks White (1899–1985) US journalist and humorist. *The Second Tree from the Corner*

CHURCH

See also clergy, religion

1 And I say also unto thee, That thou art Peter, and upon this rock I will build my church; and the gates of hell shall not prevail against it.
And I will give unto thee the keys of the kingdom of heaven: and whatsoever thou shalt bind on earth shall be bound in heaven: and whatsoever thou shalt loose on earth shall be loosed in heaven.

Bible: Matthew 16:18–19

2 For where two or three are gathered together in my name, there am I in the midst of them.

Bible: Matthew 18:20

3 The Vatican is an oppressive regime which, like a bat, fears the light.

Leonardo Boff (1938–) Brazilian theologian. Said on leaving the Roman Catholic Church. *The Observer*, 5 July 1992

4 I see it as an elderly lady, who mutters away to herself in a corner, ignored most of the time.

George Carey (1935–) British churchman; Archbishop of Canterbury. Referring to the Church of England. *Reader's Digest*, Mar 1991

5 And of all plagues with which mankind are curst,
Ecclesiastic tyranny's the worst.

Daniel Defoe (1660–1731) British journalist and writer. *The True-Born Englishman*, Pt. II

6 No Bishop, no King.

James I (1566–1625) King of England. An expression, at a conference on doctrinal reform, of his belief that a non-episcopal form of church government was incompatible with monarchy. Remark, Hampton Court, 14 Jan 1604; reported by William Barlow

7 I laboured nothing more than that the external public worship of God, too much slighted in most parts of this kingdom, might be preserved.

William Laud (1573–1645) Archbishop of Canterbury. Remark at his trial, 12 Mar 1644

8 To arrive at the truth in all things, we ought

always to be ready to believe that what seems to us white is black if the hierarchical Church so defines it.

St Ignatius Loyola (1491–1556) Spanish priest. *Spiritual Exercises*

9 We Italians then owe to the Church of Rome and to her priests our having become irreligious and bad, but we owe her a still greater debt, and one that will be the cause of our ruin, namely that the Church has kept and still keeps our country divided.

Machiavelli (1469–1527) Italian statesman. *Discourses on First Ten Books of Livy*

10 It is hard to tell where MCC ends and the Church of England begins.

J. B. Priestley (1894–1984) British novelist. *New Statesman*, 20 July 1962, 'Topside Schools'

11 The Church should be no longer satisfied to represent only the Conservative Party at prayer.

Agnes Maude Royden (1887–1967) British Congregationalist minister. Speech, London, 16 July 1917

12 The Church exists for the sake of those outside it.

William Temple (1881–1944) British churchman. Attrib.

13 Whatever you think of the church, it does provide a coherence. It is better to have a framework to fight against than no framework at all.

Jeanette Winterson (1959–) British author. *The Guardian*, 18 June 1994

CHURCHILL, SIR WINSTON

(1874–1965) British statesman and writer, prime minister (1940–45, 1951–55). After service as a war correspondent in the Boer War, he became first Lord of the Admiralty in World War I and led a coalition government in World War II. He was celebrated for his skill as an orator and was the author of several historical books.

Quotations about Churchill

1 It hasn't taken Winston long to get used to American ways. He hadn't been an American citizen for three minutes before attacking an ex-secretary of state!

Dean Acheson (1893–1971) US lawyer and statesman. At a ceremony in 1963 to make Churchill an honorary American citizen, Churchill obliquely attacked Acheson's reference to Britain losing an empire. *Randolph Churchill* (K. Halle)

2 Then comes Winston with his hundred-horse-power mind and what can I do?

Stanley Baldwin (1867–1947) British statesman. *Stanley Baldwin* (G. M. Young), Ch. 11

3 I thought he was a young man of promise; but it appears he was a young man of promises.

Arthur Balfour (1848–1930) British statesman. Said of Winston Churchill on his entry into politics, 1899. *Winston Churchill* (Randolph Churchill), Vol. I

4 He is a man suffering from petrified adolescence.

Aneurin Bevan (1897–1960) British Labour politician. *Aneurin Bevan* (Vincent Brome), Ch. 11

5 The first time you meet Winston you see all his faults and the rest of your life you spend in discovering his virtues.

Lady Constance Lytton (1869–1923) British suffragette. *Edward Marsh* (Christopher Hassall), Ch. 7

6 Winston had devoted the best years of his life to preparing his impromptu speeches.

F. E. Smith (1872–1930) British lawyer and politician. Attrib.

7 Simply a radio personality who outlived his prime.

Evelyn Waugh (1903–66) British novelist. *Evelyn Waugh* (Christopher Sykes)

Quotations by Churchill

8 Well, the principle seems the same. The water still keeps falling over.

When asked whether the Niagara Falls looked the same as when he first saw them. *Closing the Ring*, Ch. 5

9 I said that the world must be made safe for at least fifty years. If it was only for fifteen to twenty years then we should have betrayed our soldiers.

Closing the Ring, Ch. 20

10 We must have a better word than 'prefabricated'. Why not 'ready-made'?

Closing the Ring, Appendix C

11 The redress of the grievances of the vanquished should precede the disarmament of the victors.

The Gathering Storm, Ch. 3

12 I felt as if I were walking with destiny, and that all my past life had been but a preparation for this hour and this trial.

The Gathering Storm, Ch. 38

13 I have only one purpose, the destruction of Hitler, and my life is much simplified thereby. If Hitler invaded Hell I would make at least a favourable reference to the Devil in the House of Commons.

The Grand Alliance

14 When you have to kill a man it costs nothing to be polite.

Justifying the fact that the declaration of war against Japan was made in the usual diplomatic language. *The Grand Alliance*

15 Before Alamein we never had a victory. After Alamein we never had a defeat.

The Hinge of Fate, Ch. 33

16 By being so long in the lowest form I gained an immense advantage over the cleverest boys...I got into my bones the essential structure of the normal British sentence – which is a noble thing.

My Early Life, Ch. 2

17 Headmasters have powers at their disposal with which Prime Ministers have never yet been invested.

My Early Life, Ch. 2

18 So they told me how Mr Gladstone read Homer for fun, which I thought served him right.

My Early Life, Ch. 2

19 Which brings me to my conclusion upon Free Will and Predestination, namely – let the reader mark it – that they are identical.

My Early Life, Ch. 3

20 It is a good thing for an uneducated man to read books of quotations.
My Early Life, Ch. 9

21 Everyone threw the blame on me. I have noticed that they nearly always do. I suppose it is because they think I shall be able to bear it best.
My Early Life, Ch. 17

22 Those who can win a war well can rarely make a good peace and those who could make a good peace would never have won the war.
My Early Life, Ch. 26

23 I have never seen a human being who more perfectly represented the modern conception of a robot.
Referring to the Soviet statesman Molotov. *The Second World War*

24 I must point out that my rule of life prescribed as an absolutely sacred rite smoking cigars and also the drinking of alcohol before, after, and if need be during all meals and in the intervals between them.
Said during a lunch with the Arab leader Ibn Saud, when he heard that the king's religion forbade smoking and alcohol. *The Second World War*

25 In Franklin Roosevelt there died the greatest American friend we have ever known and the greatest champion of freedom who has ever brought help and comfort from the New World to the Old.
The Second World War

26 In war, resolution; in defeat, defiance; in victory, magnanimity; in peace, goodwill.
Epigram used by Sir Edward Marsh after World War II; used as 'a moral of the work' in Churchill's book. *The Second World War*

27 No one can guarantee success in war, but only deserve it.
Their Finest Hour

28 Wars are not won by evacuations.
Referring to Dunkirk. *Their Finest Hour*

29 When I look back on all these worries I remember the story of the old man who said on his deathbed that he had had a lot of trouble in his life, most of which had never happened.
Their Finest Hour

30 Peace with Germany and Japan on our terms will not bring much rest....As I observed last time, when the war of the giants is over the wars of the pygmies will begin.
Triumph and Tragedy, Ch. 25

31 Dictators ride to and fro upon tigers which they dare not dismount. And the tigers are getting hungry.
While England Slept

32 In defeat unbeatable; in victory unbearable.
Referring to Viscount Montgomery, who had commanded the victorious 8th Army in North Africa and led the invasion of Normandy (1944). *Ambrosia and Small Beer* (E. Marsh), Ch. 5

33 You may take the most gallant sailor, the most intrepid airman, or the most audacious soldier, put them at a table together – what do you get? *The sum of their fears.*
Talking about the Chiefs of Staffs system, 16 Nov 1943. *The Blast of War* (H. Macmillan), Ch. 16

34 Don't talk to me about naval tradition. It's nothing but rum, sodomy, and the lash.
Former Naval Person (Sir Peter Gretton), Ch. 1

35 Jellicoe was the only man on either side who could lose the war in an afternoon.
The Observer, 'Sayings of the Week', 13 Feb 1927

36 Everybody has a right to pronounce foreign names as he chooses.
The Observer, 'Sayings of the Week', 5 Aug 1951

37 This is the sort of English up with which I will not put.
The story is that Churchill wrote the comment in the margin of a report in which a civil servant had used an awkward construction to avoid ending a sentence with a preposition. An alternative version substitutes 'bloody nonsense' for 'English'. *Plain Words* (E. Gowers), Ch. 9

38 Men will forgive a man anything except bad prose.
Election speech, Manchester, 1906

39 It cannot in the opinion of His Majesty's Government be classified as slavery in the extreme acceptance of the word without some risk of terminological inexactitude.
Speech, House of Commons, 22 Feb 1906

40 *The Times* is speechless and takes three columns to express its speechlessness.
Referring to Irish Home Rule. Speech, Dundee, 14 May 1908

41 He is one of those orators of whom it was well said, 'Before they get up they do not know what they are going to say; when they are speaking, they do not know what they are saying; and when they sit down, they do not know what they have said'.
Referring to the politician Lord Charles Beresford. Speech, House of Commons, 20 Dec 1912

42 The maxim of the British people is 'Business as usual'.
Speech, Guildhall, 9 Nov 1914

43 Labour is not fit to govern.
Election speech, 1920

44 I remember, when I was a child, being taken to the celebrated Barnum's circus, which contained an exhibition of freaks and monstrosities, but the exhibit...which I most desired to see was the one described as 'The Boneless Wonder'. My parents judged that that spectacle would be too revolting and demoralising for my youthful eyes, and I have waited 50 years to see the boneless wonder sitting on the Treasury Bench.
Referring to the Labour prime minister, Ramsey MacDonald. Speech, House of Commons, 28 Jan 1931

45 India is a geographical term. It is no more a united nation than the Equator.
Speech, Royal Albert Hall, 18 Mar 1931

46 We have sustained a defeat without a war.
Speech, House of Commons, 5 Oct 1938

47 I cannot forecast to you the action of Russia. It is a riddle wrapped in a mystery inside an enigma.
Broadcast talk, 1 Oct 1939

48 I have nothing to offer but blood, toil, tears and sweat.
On becoming prime minister. Speech, House of Commons, 13 May 1940

49 Victory at all costs, victory in spite of all terror, victory however long and hard the road may be; for without victory there is no survival.
Speech, House of Commons, 13 May 1940

50 We shall not flag or fail. We shall fight in France, we shall fight on the seas and oceans, we shall fight with growing confidence and growing strength in the air, we shall defend our island, whatever the cost may be, we shall fight on the beaches, we shall fight on the landing grounds, we shall fight in the fields and in the streets, we shall fight in the hills; we shall never surrender.
Speech, House of Commons, 4 June 1940

51 This was their finest hour.
Referring to the Dunkirk evacuation. Speech, House of Commons, 18 June 1940

52 The battle of Britain is about to begin.
Speech, House of Commons, 1 July 1940

53 Never in the field of human conflict was so much owed by so many to so few.
Referring to the Battle of Britain pilots. Speech, House of Commons, 20 Aug 1940

54 We are waiting for the long-promised invasion. So are the fishes.
Radio broadcast to the French people, 21 Oct 1940

55 Give us the tools, and we will finish the job.
Referring to Lend-lease, which was being legislated in the USA, whereby Congress provided equipment and services for the Allies fighting Germany. Radio Broadcast, 9 Feb 1941

56 You do your worst, and we will do our best.
Addressed to Hitler. Speech, 14 July 1941

57 Do not let us speak of darker days; let us rather speak of sterner days. These are not dark days: these are great days – the greatest days our country has ever lived.
Address, Harrow School, 29 Oct 1941

58 When I warned them that Britain would fight on alone whatever they did, their Generals told their Prime Minister and his divided Cabinet: 'In three weeks England will have her neck wrung like a chicken.'
Some chicken! Some neck!
Referring to the French government. Speech, Canadian Parliament, 30 Dec 1941

59 This is not the end. It is not even the beginning of the end. But it is, perhaps, the end of the beginning.
Referring to the Battle of Egypt. Speech, Mansion House, 10 Nov 1942

60 I have not become the King's First Minister in order to preside over the liquidation of the British Empire.
Speech, Mansion House, 10 Nov 1942

61 The Almighty in His infinite wisdom did not see fit to create Frenchmen in the image of Englishmen.
Speech, House of Commons, 10 Dec 1942

62 There is no finer investment for any community than putting milk into babies.
Radio Broadcast, 21 Mar 1943

63 There are few virtues which the Poles do not possess and there are few errors they have ever avoided.
Speech, House of Commons, 1945

64 An iron curtain has descended across the Continent.
Address, Westminster College, Fulton, USA, 5 Mar 1946

65 We must build a kind of United States of Europe.
Speech, Zurich, 19 Sept 1946

66 Perhaps it is better to be irresponsible and right than to be responsible and wrong.
Party Political Broadcast, London, 26 Aug 1950

67 To jaw-jaw is better than to war-war.
Speech, Washington, 26 June 1954

68 They are the only people who like to be told how bad things are – who like to be told the worst.
Referring to the British. Speech, 1921

69 An appeaser is one who feeds a crocodile – hoping that it will eat him last.
Attrib.

70 The nation had the lion's heart. I had the luck to give the roar.
Said on his 80th birthday

CINEMA

See also Goldwynisms

1 Hollywood – a place where people from Iowa mistake themselves for movie stars.
Fred Allen (1894–1956) US comedian. Attrib.

2 To make a film is to create a world.
Lindsay Anderson (1923–) British film and theatre director. *Halliwell's Filmgoer's and Video Viewer's Companion*

3 Garbo Talks!
Anonymous Promotional slogan.

4 What's up, Doc?
Anonymous Used in 'Bugs Bunny' cartoons.

5 If my books had been any worse I should not have been invited to Hollywood, and if they had been any better I should not have come.
Raymond Chandler (1888–1959) US novelist. *The Life of Raymond Chandler* (F. MacShane)

6 Hollywood is a world with all the personality of a paper cup.
Raymond Chandler Attrib.

7 There's a big trend in Hollywood of taking very good European films and turning them into very bad American films. I've been offered a few of those, but it's really a perverse activity. I'd rather go on the dole.

Roddy Doyle (1958–) Irish novelist and playwright. *The Independent*, 25 Apr 1994

8 For *Star Wars*, they had me tape down my breasts because there are no breasts in space. I have some. I have two.

Carrie Fisher (1956–) US film star. *Playboy*, July 1983

9 I was born at the age of twelve on a Metro-Goldwyn-Mayer lot.

Judy Garland (Frances Gumm; 1922–69) US film star. *The Observer*, 'Sayings of the Week', 18 Feb 1951

10 Film people find it difficult to *place* me. The number of films that deal with crowned heads of Europe is rather limited.

John Gielgud (1904–) British actor. *Radio Times*, 4 Nov 1971

11 The only thing I liked about films was looking at the back of my head which otherwise I could only see at the tailor's.

John Gielgud *Time*, 15 Aug 1983

12 I like a film to have a beginning, a middle and an end, but not necessarily in that order.

Jean-Luc Godard (1930–) French film director. Attrib.

13 Photography is truth. And cinema is truth twenty-four times a second.

Jean-Luc Godard *Le Petit Soldat*

14 Why should people go out and pay money to see bad films when they can stay at home and see bad television for nothing?

Samuel Goldwyn (Samuel Goldfish; 1882–1974) Polish-born US film producer. *The Observer*, 'Sayings of the Week', 9 Sept 1956

15 A wide screen just makes a bad film twice as bad.

Samuel Goldwyn Attrib.

16 The cinema is not a slice of life but a piece of cake.

Alfred Hitchcock (1899–1980) British film director. *The Sunday Times*, 6 Mar 1977

17 The very meaninglessness of life forces man to create his own meaning. If it can be written or thought, it can be filmed.

Stanley Kubrick (1928–) US film director. *Halliwell's Filmgoer's and Video Viewer's Companion*

18 Strip the phoney tinsel off Hollywood and you'll find the real tinsel underneath.

Oscar Levant (1906–72) US pianist and actor. Attrib.

19 Film throws up an enormous amount of dust and heat and noise, urgent meetings and so on, which have nothing to do with making a film, but to do with people who are not creatively involved guarding their investments. I suppose its what you should expect when people are spending the GNP of small countries to make other people less bored for 100 minutes.

Ian McEwan (1948–) British novelist and short-story writer. *The Independent*, 19 Aug 1993

20 Working for Warner Bros is like fucking a porcupine; it's a hundred pricks against one.

Wilson Mizner (1876–1933) US writer and wit. *Bring on the Empty Horses* (David Niven)

21 In Hollywood, if you don't have happiness you send out for it.

Rex Reed (1938–) US columnist and actor. *Colombo's Hollywood*, 'Hollywood the Bad' (J. R. Colombo)

22 When I grow up I still want to be a director.

Steven Spielberg (1946–) US film director. *Time*, 15 July 1985

23 Movies for me are a heightened reality. Making reality fun to live with, as opposed to something you run from and protect yourself from.

Steven Spielberg Comment, 1978

24 The most expensive habit in the world is celluloid not heroin and I need a fix every two years.

Steven Spielberg *OM*, Dec 1984

25 I love *Rambo* but I think it's potentially a very dangerous movie. It changes history in a frightening way.

Steven Spielberg *Rolling Stone*, 24 Oct 1985

26 They only got two things right, the camels and the sand.

Lowell Thomas (1892–1981) US author and broadcaster. Referring to the film *Lawrence of Arabia*. Obituary, *The Times*, 29 Aug 1981

27 Take that black box away. I can't act in front of it.

Herbert Beerbohm Tree (1853–1917) British actor and theatre manager. Objecting to the presence of the camera while performing in a silent film. *Hollywood: The Pioneers* (K. Brownlow)

28 Thanks to the movies, gunfire has always sounded unreal to me, even when being fired at.

Peter Ustinov (1921–) British actor. *Dear Me*, Ch. 7

29 Westerns are closer to art than anything else in the motion picture business.

John Wayne (Marion Michael Morrison; 1907–79) US film actor. *Halliwell's Filmgoer's and Video Viewer's Companion*

30 Me? Tarzan?

Johnny Weissmuller (1904–84) US swimmer and film actor. Reacting to an invitation to play Tarzan. Attrib.

31 When you get the personality, you don't need the nudity.

Mae West (1892–1980) US actress. *The Observer*, 'Sayings of the Week', 4 Aug 1968

32 My first film will be a very simple one. I'll need only $10 million. The film will be about a boy, his dog and his budget.

Robin Williams (1952–) US actor. *Playboy*, Oct 1982

CIVILIZATION

See also culture

1 Civilization is a method of living, an attitude of equal respect for all men.

Jane Addams (1860–1935) US social worker. Speech, Honolulu, 1933

2 I wish I could bring Stonehenge to Nyasaland to show there was a time when Britain had a savage culture.

Hastings Banda (1906–) Malawi statesman. *The Observer*, 'Sayings of the Week', 10 Mar 1963

3 The three great elements of modern civilization, Gunpowder, Printing, and the Protestant Religion.

Thomas Carlyle (1795–1881) Scottish historian and essayist. *Critical and Miscellaneous Essays*, 'The State of German Literature'

4 The modern world...has no notion except that of simplifying something by destroying nearly everything.

G. K. Chesterton (1874–1936) British writer. *All I Survey*

5 In essence the Renaissance was simply the green end of one of civilization's hardest winters.

John Fowles (1926–) British novelist. *The French Lieutenant's Woman*, Ch. 10

6 I think it would be a good idea.

Mahatma Gandhi (Mohandas Karamchand Gandhi; 1869–1948) Indian national leader. On being asked for his view on Western civilization. Attrib.

7 There is precious little in civilization to appeal to a Yeti.

Edmund Hillary (1919–) New Zealand mountaineer. *The Observer*, 'Sayings of the Week', 3 June 1960

8 In your time we have the opportunity to move not only toward the rich society and the powerful society but upward to the Great Society.

Lyndon B. Johnson (1908–73) US Democratic president. Speech, University of Michigan, May 1964

9 As civilization advances, poetry almost necessarily declines.

Lord Macaulay (1800–59) British historian. *Literary Essays Contributed to the 'Edinburgh Review'*, 'Milton'

10 The degree of a nation's civilization is marked by its disregard for the necessities of existence.

W. Somerset Maugham (1874–1965) British novelist. *Our Betters*, I

11 I regard everything that has happened since the last war as a decline in civilization.

A. L. Rowse (1903–) British historian and critic. *The Observer*, 'Sayings of the Week', 15 June 1975

CLARITY

See also communication, confusion

1 Oh! rather give me commentators plain,
Who with no deep researches vex the brain;
Who from the dark and doubtful love to run,
And hold their glimmering tapers to the sun.

George Crabbe (1754–1832) British poet. *The Parish Register*, 'Baptisms'

2 It's odd how people waiting for you stand out far less clearly than people you are waiting for.

Jean Giraudoux (1882–1944) French dramatist. *Tiger at the Gates*, I

3 When man's whole frame is obvious to a flea.

Alexander Pope (1688–1744) British poet. *The Dunciad*, IV

CLASS

See also aristocracy, equality, public, snobbery

1 There's one law for the rich, and another for the poor.

Proverb

2 Let the cobbler stick to his last.

Proverb

3 You can measure the social caste of a person by the distance between the husband's and wife's apartments.

Alfonso XIII (1886–1941) Spanish monarch. Attrib.

4 I often, therefore, when I want to distinguish clearly the aristocratic class from the Philistines proper, or middle class, name the former, in my own mind *the Barbarians.*

Matthew Arnold (1822–88) British poet and critic. *Culture and Anarchy*, Ch. 3

5 When Adam delved and Eve span,
Who was then the gentleman?

John Ball (d. 1381) English priest. Text of sermon

6 His Lordship may compel us to be equal upstairs, but there will never be equality in the servants' hall.

J. M. Barrie (1860–1937) British novelist and dramatist. *The Admirable Crichton*, I

7 I love the people with their straightforward minds. It's just that their smell brings on my migraine.

Bertolt Brecht (1898–1956) German dramatist. *The Caucasian Chalk Circle*

8 Yet it is better to drop thy friends, O my daughter, than to drop thy 'H's'.

C. S. Calverley (1831–84) British poet. *Proverbial Philosophy*, 'Of Friendship'

9 One of those refined people who go out to sew for the rich because they cannot bear contact with the poor.

Colette (1873–1954) French novelist. *The Other One*

10 Servants should not be ill. We have quite enough illnesses of our own without them adding to the symptoms.

Lady Diana Cooper (1892–1986) British actress and writer. *Diana Cooper* (Philip Ziegler)

11 I never knew the lower classes had such white skins.

George Nathaniel Curzon (1859–1925) British politician. On seeing soldiers bathing. Attrib.

12 He bade me observe it, and I should always find, that the calamities of life were shared among the upper and lower part of mankind; but that the middle station had the fewest disasters.

Daniel Defoe (1660–1731) British journalist and writer. *Robinson Crusoe*, Pt. I

13 O let us love our occupations,
Bless the squire and his relations,
Live upon our daily rations,
And always know our proper stations.

Charles Dickens (1812–70) British novelist. *The Chimes*, '2nd Quarter'

14 He differed from the healthy type that was essentially middle-class – he never seemed to perspire.

F. Scott Fitzgerald (1896–1940) US novelist. *This Side of Paradise*, Bk. I, Ch. 2

15 All shall equal be.
The Earl, the Marquis, and the Dook,

The Groom, the Butler, and the Cook,
The Aristocrat who banks with Coutts,
The Aristocrat who cleans the boots.

W. S. Gilbert (1836–1911) British dramatist. *The Gondoliers*, I

16 He combines the manners of a Marquis with the morals of a Methodist.

W. S. Gilbert *Ruddigore*, I

17 Bow, bow, ye lower middle classes!
Bow, bow, ye tradesmen, bow, ye masses!

W. S. Gilbert *Iolanthe*, I

18 All the world over, I will back the masses against the classes.

William Ewart Gladstone (1809–98) British statesman. Speech, Liverpool, 28 June 1886

19 Dialect words – those terrible marks of the beast to the truly genteel.

Thomas Hardy (1840–1928) British novelist. *The Mayor of Casterbridge*, Ch. 20

20 '*Bourgeois*,' I observed, 'is an epithet which the riff-raff apply to what is respectable, and the aristocracy to what is decent'.

Anthony Hope (Sir Anthony Hope Hawkins; 1863–1933) British novelist. *The Dolly Dialogues*

21 You may be the most liberal Liberal Englishman, and yet you cannot fail to see the categorical difference between the responsible and the irresponsible classes.

D. H. Lawrence (1885–1930) British novelist. *Kangaroo*, Ch. 1

22 A Social-Democrat must never forget that the proletariat will inevitably have to wage a class struggle for Socialism even against the most democratic and republican bourgeoisie and petty bourgeoisie.

Lenin (Vladimir Ilich Ulyanov; 1870–1924) Russian revolutionary leader. *The State and Revolution*, Ch. 10

23 An Englishman's way of speaking absolutely classifies him
The moment he talks he makes some other Englishman despise him.

Alan Jay Lerner (1918–86) US songwriter. *My Fair Lady*, I:1

24 I'm not interested in classes...Far be it from me to foster inferiority complexes among the workers by trying to make them think they belong to some special class. That has happened in Europe but it hasn't happened here yet.

John Llewellyn Lewis (1880–1969) US labour leader. *The Coming of the New Deal* (A. M. Schlesinger, Jnr), Pt. 7, Ch. 25

25 Said Marx: 'Don't be snobbish, we seek to abolish
The 3rd Class, not the 1st.'

Christopher Logue (1926–) British poet and dramatist. *Christopher Logue's ABC*, 'M'

26 The history of all hitherto existing society is the history of class struggles.

Karl Marx (1818–83) German philosopher and revolutionary. *The Communist Manifesto*, 1

27 Mrs. Carey thought there were only four professions for a gentleman, the Army, the Navy, the Law, and the Church. She had added medicine...but did not forget that in her young days no one ever considered the doctor a gentleman.

W. Somerset Maugham (1874–1965) British writer and doctor. *Of Human Bondage*, Ch. 33

28 Britain is the society where the ruling class does not rule, the working class does not work and the middle class is not in the middle.

George Mikes (1912–87) Hungarian-born British writer. *English Humour for Beginners*

29 The one class you do *not* belong to and are not proud of at all is the lower-middle class. No one ever describes himself as belonging to the lower-middle class.

George Mikes *How to be Inimitable*

30 Only on the third class tourist class passengers' deck was it a sultry overcast morning, but then if you do things on the cheap you must expect these things.

Spike Milligan (1918–) British comic actor and author. *A Dustbin of Milligan*

31 The worst fault of the working classes is telling their children they're not going to succeed, saying: 'There is a life, but it's not for you'.

John Mortimer (1923–) British lawyer and dramatist. *The Observer*, 'Sayings of the Week', 5 June 1988

32 Actually I vote Labour, but my butler's a Tory.

Lord Mountbatten (1900–79) British admiral. Said to a Tory canvasser during the 1945 election

33 We have nothing to lose but our aitches.

George Orwell (Eric Blair; 1903–50) British novelist. Referring to the middle classes. *The Road to Wigan Pier*, Ch. 13

34 I don't think one 'comes down' from Jimmy's university. According to him, it's not even red brick, but white tile.

John Osborne (1929–) British dramatist. *Look Back in Anger*, II:1

35 Prison will not work until we start sending a better class of people there.

Laurence J. Peter (1919–90) Canadian writer. Attrib.

36 You can be in the Horse Guards and still be common, dear.

Terence Rattigan (1911–77) British dramatist. *Separate Tables*: 'Table Number Seven'

37 U and Non-U, An Essay in Sociological Linguistics.

Alan Strode Campbell Ross (1907–78) British professor of linguistics. Essay title, *Noblesse Oblige*, 1956

38 The Englishman...always has in his hands an accurate pair of scales in which he scrupulously weighs up the birth, the rank, and above all, the wealth of the people he meets, in order to adjust his behaviour towards them accordingly.

Jean Rouquet *The Reign of George III* (J. Steven Watson), Ch. 3

39 Since every Jack became a gentleman
There's many a gentle person made a Jack.

William Shakespeare (1564–1616) English dramatist. *Richard III*, I:3

40 There are two classes in good society in England. The equestrian classes and the neurotic classes.

George Bernard Shaw (1856–1950) Irish dramatist and critic. *Heartbreak House*

41 We must be thoroughly democratic and patronise everybody without distinction of class.
George Bernard Shaw *John Bull's Other Island*

42 I am a gentleman. I live by robbing the poor.
George Bernard Shaw *Man and Superman*

43 Common people do not pray; they only beg.
George Bernard Shaw *Misalliance*

44 The English have no respect for their language, and will not teach their children to speak it...It is impossible for an Englishman to open his mouth, without making some other Englishman despise him.
George Bernard Shaw *Pygmalion*, Preface

45 He's a gentleman: look at his boots.
George Bernard Shaw *Pygmalion*

46 I have to live for others and not for myself; that's middle class morality.
George Bernard Shaw *Pygmalion*

47 The British Bourgeoisie
Is not born,
And does not die,
But, if it is ill,
It has a frightened look in its eyes.
Osbert Sitwell (1892–1969) British writer. *At the House of Mrs Kinfoot*

48 It is impossible for one class to appreciate the wrongs of another.
Elizabeth Stanton (1815–1902) US suffragette. *History of Woman Suffrage* (with Susan B. Anthony and Mathilda Gage), Vol. I

49 The charm of Britain has always been the ease with which one can move into the middle class.
Margaret Thatcher (1925–) British politician and prime minister. *The Observer*, 'Sayings of the Week', 27 Oct 1974

50 The ship follows Soviet custom: it is riddled with class distinctions so subtle, it takes a trained Marxist to appreciate them.
Paul Theroux (1941–) US-born writer. *The Great Railway Bazaar*, Ch. 30

51 For generations the British bourgeoisie have spoken of themselves as gentlemen, and by that they have meant, among other things, a self-respecting scorn of irregular perquisites. It is the quality that distinguishes the gentleman from both the artist and the aristocrat.
Evelyn Waugh (1903–66) British novelist. *Decline and Fall*, Pt. I, Ch. 6

52 No writer before the middle of the 19th century wrote about the working classes other than as grotesque or as pastoral decoration. Then when they were given the vote certain writers started to suck up to them.
Evelyn Waugh Interview. *Paris Review*, 1963

53 Bricklayers kick their wives to death, and dukes betray theirs; but it is among the small clerks and shopkeepers nowadays that it comes most often to the cutting of throats.
H. G. Wells (1866–1946) British writer. *Short Stories*, 'The Purple Pileus'

54 Margaret Thatcher's great strength seems to be the better people know her, the better they like her. But, of course, she has one great disadvantage – she is a daughter of the people and looks trim, as the daughters of the people desire to be. Shirley Williams has such an advantage over her because she's a member of the upper-middle class and can achieve that kitchen-sink-revolutionary look that one cannot get unless one has been to a really good school.
Rebecca West (Cicely Isabel Fairfield; 1892–1983) British novelist and journalist. Said in an interview with Jilly Cooper. *The Sunday Times*, 25 July 1976

55 Really, if the lower orders don't set us a good example, what on earth is the use of them?
Oscar Wilde (1854–1900) Irish-born British dramatist. *The Importance of Being Earnest*, I

56 A very large part of English middle-class education is devoted to the training of servants... In so far as it is, by definition, the training of upper servants, it includes, of course, the instilling of that kind of confidence which will enable the upper servants to supervise and direct the lower servants.
Raymond Henry Williams (1921–88) British academic and writer. *Culture and Society*, Ch. 3

57 The constitution does not provide for first and second class citizens.
Wendell Lewis Willkie (1892–1944) US lawyer and businessman. *An American Programme*, Ch. 2

CLASSICS

1 They were a tense and peculiar family, the Oedipuses, weren't they?
Max Beerbohm (1872–1956) British writer. *Max: A Biography* (D. Cecil)

2 So they told me how Mr Gladstone read Homer for fun, which I thought served him right.
Winston Churchill (1874–1965) British statesman. *My Early Life*, Ch. 2

3 Nor can I do better, in conclusion, than impress upon you the study of Greek literature which not only elevates above the vulgar herd, but leads not infrequently to positions of considerable emolument.
Thomas Gaisford (1799–1855) British classicist. Christmas Day Sermon at Oxford. *Reminiscences of Oxford* (Revd W. Tuckwell)

4 To the Greeks the Muse gave native wit, to the Greeks the gift of graceful eloquence.
Horace (Quintus Horatius Flaccus; 65–8 BC) Roman poet. *Ars Poetica*

5 Thou hadst small Latin, and less Greek.
Ben Jonson (1573–1637) English dramatist. *To the Memory of William Shakespeare*

6 The classics are only primitive literature. They belong in the same class as primitive machinery and primitive music and primitive medicine.
Stephen Leacock (1869–1944) English-born Canadian economist and humorist. *Homer and Humbug*

7 Every man with a belly full of the classics is an enemy of the human race.
Henry Miller (1891–1980) US novelist. *Tropic of Cancer*, 'Dijon'

8 Nobody can say a word against Greek: it stamps a man at once as an educated gentleman.

George Bernard Shaw (1856–1950) Irish dramatist and critic. *Major Barbara*, I

9 We were taught as the chief subjects of instruction Latin and Greek. We were taught very badly because the men who taught us did not habitually use either of these languages.

H. G. Wells (1866–1946) British writer. *The New Machiavelli*, Bk. I., Ch. 3

CLASSIFICATION

See also generalizations

1 One of the unpardonable sins, in the eyes of most people, is for a man to go about unlabelled. The world regards such a person as the police do an unmuzzled dog, not under proper control.

T. H. Huxley (1825–95) British biologist. *Evolution and Ethics*

2 The young Cambridge group, the group that stood for 'freedom' and flannel trousers and flannel shirts open at the neck, and a well-bred sort of emotional anarchy, and a whispering, murmuring sort of voice, and an ultra-sensitive sort of manner.

D. H. Lawrence (1885–1930) British novelist. *Lady Chatterley's Lover*, Ch. 1

3 Decades have a delusive edge to them. They are not, of course, really periods at all, except as any other ten years would be. But we, looking at them, are caught by the different name each bears, and give them different attributes, and tie labels on them, as if they were flowers in a border.

Rose Macaulay (1889–1958) British writer. *Told by an Idiot*, Pt. II, Ch. 1

CLEANNESS

1 Bathe early every day and sickness will avoid you.

Hindustani proverb

2 Bath twice a day to be really clean, once a day to be passably clean, once a week to avoid being a public menace.

Anthony Burgess (John Burgess Wilson; 1917–93) British novelist. *Mr Enderby*, Pt. I, Ch. 2

3 MR PRITCHARD. I must dust the blinds and then I must raise them.

MRS OGMORE-PRITCHARD. And before you let the sun in, mind it wipes its shoes.

Dylan Thomas (1914–53) Welsh poet. *Under Milk Wood*

4 Have you ever taken anything out of the clothes basket because it had become, relatively, the cleaner thing?

Katherine Whitehorn (1926–) British journalist. *The Observer*, 'On Shirts', 1964

CLERGY

See also Church, religion

1 I always like to associate with a lot of priests because it makes me understand anti-clerical things so well.

Hilaire Belloc (1870–1953) French-born British poet. Letter to E. S. P. Haynes, 9 Nov 1909

2 This is a true saying, If a man desire the office of a bishop, he desireth a good work.
A bishop then must be blameless, the husband of one wife, vigilant, sober, of good behaviour, given to hospitality, apt to teach;
Not given to wine, no striker, not greedy of filthy lucre; but patient, not a brawler, not covetous.

Bible: I Timothy 3:1–3

3 As for the British churchman, he goes to church as he goes to the bathroom, with the minimum of fuss and no explanation if he can help it.

Ronald Blythe (1922–) British author. *The Age of Illusion*

4 Make him a bishop, and you will silence him at once.

Earl of Chesterfield (1694–1773) English statesman. When asked what steps might be taken to control the evangelical preacher George Whitefield. Attrib.

5 It is no accident that the symbol of a bishop is a crook, and the sign of an archbishop is a double-cross.

Dom Gregory Dix (1901–52) British monk. Letter to *The Times*, 3 Dec 1977 (Francis Bown)

6 For clergy are men as well as other folks.

Henry Fielding (1707–54) British novelist. *Joseph Andrews*, Bk. II, Ch. 6

7 That whisky priest, I wish we had never had him in the house.

Graham Greene (1904–91) British novelist. *The Power and the Glory*, Pt. I

8 In old time we had treen chalices and golden priests, but now we have treen priests and golden chalices.

John Jewel (1522–71) English bishop. *Certain Sermons Preached Before the Queen's Majesty*

9 A man who is good enough to go to heaven, is good enough to be a clergyman.

Samuel Johnson (1709–84) British lexicographer. *Life of Johnson* (J. Boswell), Vol. II

10 Damn it all, another Bishop dead, – I verily believe they die to vex me.

Lord Melbourne (1779–1848) British statesman. Attrib.

11 How can a bishop marry? How can he flirt? The most he can say is, 'I will see you in the vestry after service.'

Sydney Smith (1771–1845) British clergyman and essayist. *Memoir* (Lady Holland)

12 I never saw, heard, nor read, that the clergy were beloved in any nation where Christianity was the religion of the country. Nothing can render them popular, but some degree of persecution.

Jonathan Swift (1667–1745) Irish-born Anglican priest and writer. *Thoughts on Religion*

13 There is a certain class of clergyman whose mendicity is only equalled by their mendacity.

Frederick Temple (1821–1902) British churchman. Remark at a meeting of the Ecclesiastical Commissioners. *Years of Endeavour* (Sir George Leveson Gower)

14 But the churchmen fain would kill their church,
As the churches have kill'd their Christ.

Alfred, Lord Tennyson (1809–92) British poet. *Maud*, V

15 If I were a cassowary
On the plains of Timbuctoo,
I would eat a missionary,
Cassock, band, and hymn-book too.

Samuel Wilberforce (1805–73) British churchman. Also attrib. to W. M. Thackeray. Attrib.

16 The idea that only a male can represent Christ at the altar is a most serious heresy.

George Carey (1935–) British churchman; Archbishop of Canterbury. *Reader's Digest*, Apr 1991

17 If women in the priesthood has come as a result of women's liberation, then I think it is satanic.

William Pwaisiho *Daily Telegraph*, Aug 1988

18 I would burn the bloody bitches.

Anthony Kennedy British churchman; vicar of Lutton with Gedney. Referring to women priests. *The Times*

CLINTON, BILL

(William Jefferson C.; 1946–) US statesman; governor of Arkansas (1979–81, 1983–92) and president (1993–)

Quotations about Clinton

1 We're not running against the comeback kids, we're running against the Karaoke Kids – they'd sing any tune to get elected.

George Bush (1924–) US president. Said in the closing stages of the 1992 presidential election campaign. 'Comeback Kid' was Clinton's nickname chosen by himself

2 We have never said to the press that Clinton is a philandering, pot-smoking draft dodger.

Mary Matalin George Bush's campaign director. In the 1992 US presidential election campaign

3 If he runs the country as well as he ran his campaign, we'll be all right.

Dan Quayle (1946–) US statesman. After being defeated in the 1992 US presidential election campaign

Quotations by Clinton

4 When I was in England, I experimented with marijuana a time or two and I didn't like it. I didn't inhale.

Remark during the 1992 US presidential election campaign. Replying to Republican accusations that he had taken drugs and played a leading role in the movement against the Vietnam War

5 Sure enough at Oxford, I was another Yank half a step behind.

The Observer, 'Sayings of the Week', 12 June 1994

6 If you'll be my voice today, I'll be yours for the next four years.

On polling day in the 1992 presidential elections – Clinton was suffering from laryngitis. Speech, 3 Nov 1992

7 Throughout the Middle East, there is a great yearning for the quiet miracle of a normal life.

Referring to the IsraelPLO peace signing. *The Times*, 14 Sept 1993

8 We must not let the iron curtain be replaced with a veil of indifference.

Speech to NATO, 10 Jan 1994

CLOTHES

See also appearance, beauty, fashion, nakedness

1 Woollen clothing keeps the skin healthy.

Venetian proverb

2 It is not only fine feathers that make fine birds.

Aesop (6th century BC) Reputed Greek writer of fables. *Fables*, 'The Jay and the Peacock'

3 She had a womanly instinct that clothes possess an influence more powerful over many than the worth of character or the magic of manners.

Louisa May Alcott (1832–88) US writer and editor. *Little Women*, Pt. II

4 Gentlemen, it was necessary to abolish the fez, which sat on the heads of our nation as an emblem of ignorance, negligence, fanaticism and hatred of progress and civilization, to accept in its place the hat, the headgear worn by the whole civilized world.

Kemal Ataturk (1880–1938) Founder of the Turkish Republic. Speech, Turkish Assembly, Oct 1927

5 To a woman, the consciousness of being well-dressed gives a sense of tranquility which religion fails to bestow.

Helen Olcott Bell (1839–1918) US writer. *Letters and Social Aims: R. W. Emerson*

6 She just wore
Enough for modesty – no more.

Robert Williams Buchanan (1841–1901) British poet and writer. *White Rose and Red*, I

7 An after-dinner speech should be like a lady's dress – long enough to cover the subject and short enough to be interesting.

R. A. Butler (1902–82) British Conservative politician. Remark made at an Anglo-Jewish dinner

8 I go to a better tailor than any of you and pay more for my clothes. The only difference is that you probably don't sleep in yours.

Clarence Seward Darrow (1857–1938) US lawyer. Reply when teased by reporters about his appearance. *2500 Anecdotes* (E. Fuller)

9 'Good heavens!' said he, 'if it be our clothes alone which fit us for society, how highly we should esteem those who make them.'

Marie Ebner von Eschenbach (1830–1916) Austrian writer. *The Two Countesses*

10 Would you be shocked if I put on something more comfortable?

Jean Harlow (1911–37) US film actress. *Hell's Angels*

11 Those who make their dress a principal part of themselves, will, in general, become of no more value than their dress.

William Hazlitt (1778–1830) British essayist. *On the Clerical Character*

12 A sweet disorder in the dress
Kindles in clothes a wantonness.

Robert Herrick (1591–1674) English poet. *Hesperides*, 'Delight in Disorder'

13 Whenas in silks my Julia goes
Then, then (methinks) how sweetly flows
That liquefaction of her clothes.

Robert Herrick *Hesperides*, 'Upon Julia's Clothes'

14 Fine clothes are good only as they supply the want of other means of procuring respect.

Samuel Johnson (1709–84) British lexicographer. *Life of Johnson* (J. Boswell), Vol. II

15 The uniform 'e wore
Was nothin' much before,
An' rather less than 'arf o' that be'ind.

Rudyard Kipling (1865–1936) Indian-born British writer. *Gunga Din*

16 How do you look when I'm sober?

Ring Lardner Jnr (1885–1933) American humorist. Speaking to a flamboyantly dressed stranger who walked into the club where he was drinking. *Ring* (J. Yardley)

17 Is anything worn beneath the kilt? No, it's all in perfect working order.

Spike Milligan (1918–) British comic actor and author. *The Great McGonagall Scrapbook*

18 Brevity is the soul of lingerie.

Dorothy Parker (1893–1967) US writer. *While Rome Burns* (Alexander Woollcott)

19 Where did you get that hat?
Where did you get that tile?

James Rolmaz (19th century) British songwriter. *Where Did You Get That Hat?*

20 Not a gentleman; dresses too well.

Bertrand Russell (1872–1970) British philosopher. Referring to Sir Anthony Eden, the Conservative statesman. *Six Men* (A. Cooke)

21 His socks compelled one's attention without losing one's respect.

Saki (Hector Hugh Munro; 1870–1916) British writer. *Ministers of Grace*

22 Her frocks are built in Paris but she wears them with a strong English accent.

Saki *Reginald on Women*

23 All my clothes have stretch marks, darling.

Jennifer Saunders (1958–) British comedy writer and actress. *Absolutely Fabulous*

24 Costly thy habit as thy purse can buy,
But not express'd in fancy; rich, not gaudy;
For the apparel oft proclaims the man.

William Shakespeare (1564–1616) English dramatist. *Hamlet*, I:3

25 Thou art the thing itself; unaccommodated man is no more but such a poor, bare, forked animal as thou art. Off, off, you lendings! Come; unbutton here.

William Shakespeare *King Lear*, III:4

26 The only man who really needs a tail coat is a man with a hole in his trousers.

John Taylor (20th century) The editor of the *Tailor and Cutter*. *The Observer*, 'Shouts and Murmurs'

27 You can say what you like about long dresses, but they cover a multitude of shins.

Mae West (1892–1980) US actress. *Peel Me a Grape* (J. Weintraub)

28 Hats divide generally into three classes: offensive hats, defensive hats, and shrapnel.

Katherine Whitehorn (1926–) British journalist. *Shouts and Murmurs*, 'Hats'

29 Then the little man wears a shocking bad hat.

Duke of York and Albany (1763–1827) The second son of George III. Referring to the writer Horace Walpole. Attrib.

COLD WAR

1 Let us not be deceived – we are today in the midst of a cold war.

Bernard Baruch (1870–1965) US financier and presidential adviser. Speech, South Carolina Legislature, 16 Apr 1947

2 An iron curtain has descended across the Continent.

Winston Churchill (1874–1965) British statesman. The phrase 'iron curtain' was originally coined by Joseph Goebbels. Address, Westminster College, Fulton, USA, 5 Mar 1946

COLERIDGE, SAMUEL TAYLOR

(1772–1834) British poet, chiefly remembered for such works as *Kubla Khan* (composed in 1797, under the influence of opium) and *The Rime of the Ancient Mariner* (1798). His *Lyrical Ballads* (1798), written with William Wordsworth, was extremely influential.

Quotations about Coleridge

1 A weak, diffusive, weltering, ineffectual man.

Thomas Carlyle (1795–1881) Scottish historian and essayist. Attrib.

2 His face when he repeats his verses hath its ancient glory, an Archangel a little damaged.

Charles Lamb (1775–1834) British essayist. Letter, 26 Apr 1816

Quotations by Coleridge

3 He who begins by loving Christianity better than Truth will proceed by loving his own sect or church better than Christianity, and end by loving himself better than all.

Aids to Reflection: Moral and Religious Aphorisms,

4 If a man could pass through Paradise in a dream, and have a flower presented to him as a pledge that his soul had really been there, and if he found that flower in his hand when he awoke – Aye, and what then?

Anima Poetae

5 The primary imagination I hold to be the living power and prime agent of all human perception, and as a repetition in the finite mind of the eternal act of creation in the infinite I AM.

Biographia Literaria, Ch. 13

6 The Fancy is indeed no other than a mode of memory emancipated from the order of time and space.

Biographia Literaria, Ch. 13

7 Nothing can permanently please, which does not contain in itself the reason why it is so, and not otherwise.

Biographia Literaria, Ch. 14

8 That willing suspension of disbelief for the moment, which constitutes poetic faith.

Biographia Literaria, Ch. 14

9 Our myriad-minded Shakespeare.
Biographia Literaria, Ch. 15

10 A sight to dream of, not to tell!
Christabel, I

11 I may not hope from outward forms to win
The passion and the life, whose fountains are within.
Dejection: An Ode

12 Swans sing before they die – 'twere no bad thing,
Did certain persons die before they sing.
Epigram on a Volunteer Singer

13 On awaking he…instantly and eagerly wrote down the lines that are here preserved. At this moment he was unfortunately called out by a person on business from Porlock.
Kubla Khan (preliminary note)

14 In Xanadu did Kubla Khan
A stately pleasure-dome decree:
Where Alph, the sacred river, ran
Through caverns measureless to man
Down to a sunless sea.
Kubla Khan

15 It was a miracle of rare device,
A sunny pleasure-dome with caves of ice!
Kubla Khan

16 A savage place! as holy and enchanted
As e'er beneath a waning moon was haunted
By woman wailing for her demon-lover!
Kubla Khan

17 And all should cry, Beware! Beware!
His flashing eyes, his floating hair!
Weave a circle round him thrice,
And close your eyes with holy dread,
For he on honey-dew hath fed,
And drunk the milk of Paradise.
Kubla Khan

18 Poetry is not the proper antithesis to prose, but to science. Poetry is opposed to science, and prose to metre.
Lectures and Notes of 1818, I

19 Reviewers are usually people who would have been poets, historians, biographers,…if they could; they have tried their talents at one or at the other, and have failed; therefore they turn critics.
Lectures on Shakespeare and Milton, I

20 The faults of great authors are generally excellences carried to an excess.
Miscellanies, 149

21 With Donne, whose muse on dromedary trots,
Wreathe iron pokers into true-love knots.
On Donne's Poetry

22 The most happy marriage I can picture or imagine to myself would be the union of a deaf man to a blind woman.
Recollections (Allsop)

23 If men could learn from history, what lessons it might teach us! But passion and party blind our eyes and the light which experience gives is a lantern on the stern, which shines only on the waves behind us!
Recollections (Allsop)

24 It is an ancient Mariner,
And he stoppeth one of three.
'By thy long grey beard and glittering eye,
Now wherefore stopp'st thou me?'
The Rime of the Ancient Mariner, I

25 The Sun came up upon the left,
Out of the sea came he!
And he shone bright, and on the right
Went down into the sea.
The Rime of the Ancient Mariner, I

26 The ice was here, the ice was there,
The ice was all around:
It cracked and growled, and roared and howled,
Like noises in a swound!
The Rime of the Ancient Mariner, I

27 With my cross-bow
I shot the albatross.
The Rime of the Ancient Mariner, I

28 The fair breeze blew, the white foam flew,
The furrow followed free;
We were the first that ever burst
Into that silent sea.
The Rime of the Ancient Mariner, II

29 As idle as a painted ship
Upon a painted ocean.
The Rime of the Ancient Mariner, II

30 Water, water, every where,
And all the boards did shrink;
Water, water, every where,
Nor any drop to drink.
The Rime of the Ancient Mariner, II

31 Alone, alone, all, all alone,
Alone on a wide wide sea!
And never a saint took pity on
My soul in agony.
The Rime of the Ancient Mariner, IV

32 The many men, so beautiful!
And they all dead did lie:
And a thousand thousand slimy things
Lived on; and so did I.
The Rime of the Ancient Mariner, IV

33 The moving Moon went up the sky,
And no where did abide:
Softly she was going up,
And a star or two beside.
The Rime of the Ancient Mariner, IV

34 Oh sleep! it is a gentle thing,
Beloved from pole to pole!
The Rime of the Ancient Mariner, V

35 Quoth he, 'The man hath penance done,
And penance more will do.'
The Rime of the Ancient Mariner, V

36 Like one, that on a lonesome road
Doth walk in fear and dread,
And having once turned round walks on,

And turns no more his head;
Because he knows, a frightful fiend
Doth close behind him tread.

The Rime of the Ancient Mariner, VI

37 No voice; but oh! the silence sank
Like music on my heart.

The Rime of the Ancient Mariner, VI

38 He prayeth well, who loveth well
Both man and bird and beast.

The Rime of the Ancient Mariner, VII

39 He prayeth best, who loveth best
All things both great and small;
For the dear God who loveth us,
He made and loveth all.

The Rime of the Ancient Mariner, VII

40 A sadder and a wiser man,
He rose the morrow morn.

The Rime of the Ancient Mariner, VII

41 I wish our clever young poets would remember my homely definitions of prose and poetry; that is, prose = words in their best order; – poetry = the best words in the best order.

Table Talk

42 No mind is thoroughly well organized that is deficient in a sense of humour.

Table Talk

43 What comes from the heart, goes to the heart.

Table Talk

44 The misfortune is, that he has begun to write verses without very well understanding what metre is.

Referring to Tennyson. *Table Talk*

45 To see him act, is like reading Shakespeare by flashes of lightning.

Referring to Kean. *Table Talk*

46 Summer has set in with its usual severity.

Quoted in Lamb's letter to V. Novello, 9 May 1826

47 I believe the souls of five hundred Sir Isaac Newtons would go to the making up of a Shakespeare or a Milton.

Letter to Thomas Poole, 23 Mar 1801

COLETTE, SIDONIE GABRIELLE

(1873–1954) French novelist. Colette's early works, the 'Claudine' stories, were published under her first husband's pen-name; her later independent novels include *La Vagabonde* (1910), *Chéri* (1920), and *Gigi* (1944).

1 Total absence of humour renders life impossible.

Chance Acquaintances

2 When she raises her eyelids it's as if she were taking off all her clothes.

Claudine and Annie

3 My virtue's still far too small, I don't trot it out and about yet.

Claudine at School

4 Don't ever wear artistic jewellery; it wrecks a woman's reputation.

Gigi

5 Don't eat too many almonds; they add weight to the breasts.

Gigi

COMFORT

See also endurance, sympathy

1 And always keep a hold of Nurse
For fear of finding something worse.

Hilaire Belloc (1870–1953) British writer. *Cautionary Tales*, 'Jim'

2 The crash of the whole solar and stellar systems could only kill you once.

Thomas Carlyle (1795–1881) Scottish historian and essayist. Letter to John Carlyle, 1831

3 When pain and anguish wring the brow,
A ministering angel thou!

Walter Scott (1771–1832) Scottish novelist. *Marmion*, VI: 30

4 For this relief much thanks. 'Tis bitter cold,
And I am sick at heart.

William Shakespeare (1564–1616) English dramatist. *Hamlet*, I:1

5 I beg cold comfort.

William Shakespeare *King John*, V:7

6 Like a bridge over troubled water,
I will ease your mind.

Paul Simon (1942–) US singer. *Bridge Over Troubled Water*

COMMERCIALISM

See also business, economics, money

1 I never will consent to having my name or my face used in any merchandizing context beyond advertising the actual artistic work I've done. I have said no even when I was tempted with regular earnings for Ziggy Stardust dolls.

David Bowie (David Jones; 1947–) British pop singer. *Variety*, 17 May 1983

2 My fear will be that in 15 years time Jerusalem, Bethlehem, once centres of strong Christian presence, might become a kind of Walt Disney Theme Park.

George Carey (1935–) British churchman; Archbishop of Canterbury. *The Observer*, 12 Jan 1992

3 This town was made to make money in and it has no other function. It has no pretence to longevity because it was never designed like that in the first place.

Billy Connolly (1942–) Scottish comedian. Referring to Los Angeles. *The Times*, 15 Dec 1990

4 Our democratic capitalist society has converted Eros into an employee of Mammon.

Octavio Paz (1914–) Mexican poet, critic, and diplomat. *The Observer*, 'Sayings of the Week', 19 June 1994

5 ...everyone in Hollywood is looking for the blockbuster. They tell you their last movie 'only grossed $70 million', as if that were some kind of crime...

Neil Simon (1927–) US playwright. *The Times*, 4 Aug 1990

6 The large print giveth, but the small print taketh away.

Tom Waits (1949–) US rock musician. *Small Change*

COMMITMENT

1 In for a penny, in for a pound.

Proverb

2 In for a penny, in for a pound.

Proverb

3 Never do things by halves.

Proverb

4 One cannot be a part-time nihilist.

Albert Camus (1913–60) French existentialist writer. *The Rebel*

5 Total commitment to family and total commitment to career is possible, but fatiguing.

Muriel Fox (1928–) US business executive and feminist. *New Woman*, Oct 1971

6 Catholics and Communists have committed great crimes, but at least they have not stood aside, like an established society, and been indifferent. I would rather have blood on my hands than water like Pilate.

Graham Greene (1904–91) British novelist. *The Comedians*, Pt. III, Ch. 4

7 It isn't until you begin to fight in your own cause that you (a) become really committed to winning, and (b) become a genuine ally of other people struggling for their freedom.

Robin Morgan (1941–) US writer. *Sisterhood Is Powerful*, Introduction

8 Miss Brodie said: 'Pavolova contemplates her swans in order to perfect her swan dance, she studies them. This is true dedication. You must all grow up to be dedicated women as I have dedicated myself to you.'

Muriel Spark (1918–) British writer and poet. *The Prime of Miss Jean Brodie*, Ch. 3

9 I love being at the centre of things.

Margaret Thatcher (1925–) British politician and prime minister. *Reader's Digest*, 1984

10 Miss Madeleine Philips was making it very manifest to Captain Douglas that she herself was a career; that a lover with any other career in view need not – as the advertisements say – apply.

H. G. Wells (1866–1946) British writer. *Bealby*, Pt. V, Ch. 5

COMMUNICATION

See also clarity, conversation, language, letter-writing, speech

1 Only connect!

E. M. Forster (1879–1970) British novelist. *Howards End*, Epigraph

2 Unless one is a genius, it is best to aim at being intelligible.

Anthony Hope (Sir Anthony Hope Hawkins; 1863–1933) British novelist. *The Dolly Dialogues*

3 The medium is the message. This is merely to say that the personal and social consequences of any medium...result from the new scale that is introduced into our affairs by each extension of ourselves or by any new technology.

Marshall McLuhan (1911–81) Canadian sociologist. *Understanding Media*, Ch. 1

4 And this certainly has to be the most historic phone call ever made.

Richard Milhous Nixon (1913–94) US President. Telephone call to astronauts on moon, 20 July 1969.

5 What have we to say to India?

John Ruskin (1819–1900) British art critic and writer. Referring to the completion of the British-Indian cable. Attrib.

COMMUNISM

See also Marxism, Russia, socialism

1 Are you now or have you ever been a member of a godless conspiracy controlled by a foreign power?

Richard Arens (1913–69) US lawyer. Question put to people appearing at hearings of the House of Representatives Committee on Un-American Activities (1947–c. 1957). *The Fifties* (P. Lewis)

2 Russian communism is the illegitimate child of Karl Marx and Catherine the Great.

Clement Atlee (1883–1967) British statesman and Labour prime minister. Speech, 11 Apr 1956

3 Its relationship to democratic institutions is that of the death watch beetle – it is not a Party, it is a conspiracy.

Aneurin Bevan (1897–1960) British Labour politician. Referring to the Communist Party. *Tribune*

4 Socialism with a human face.

Alexander Dubček (1921–92) Czechoslovak statesman. A resolution by the party group in the Ministry of Foreign Affairs, in 1968, referred to Czechoslovak foreign policy acquiring 'its own defined face'. Attrib.

5 The state is not 'abolished', it withers away.

Friedrich Engels (1820–95) German communist. *Anti-Dühring*

6 Every year humanity takes a step towards Communism. Maybe not you, but at all events your grandson will surely be a Communist.

Nikita Khrushchev (1894–1971) Soviet statesman. Said to Sir William Hayter, June 1956

7 Those who wait for that must wait until a shrimp learns to whistle.

Nikita Khruschev Referring to the chances of the Soviet Union rejecting communism. Attrib.

8 Communism is Soviet power plus the electrification of the whole country.

Lenin (Vladimir Ilich Ulyanov; 1870–1924) Russian revolutionary leader. Political slogan of 1920, promoting the programme of electrification.

9 In a state worthy of the name there is no liberty. The people want to exercise power but what on earth would they do with it if it were given to them?

Lenin *The State and Revolution*

10 It looks like a duck, walks like a duck, and quacks like a duck.

Joseph R. McCarthy (1908–57) US senator. Suggested method of identifying a communist. Attrib.

11 There's no such thing in Communist countries as a load of old cod's wallop, the cod's wallop is always fresh made.

Robert Morley (1908–92 British actor. *Punch*, 20 Feb 1974

12 Between complete Socialism and Communism there is no difference whatever in my mind. Communism is in fact the completion of Socialism; when that ceases to be militant and becomes triumphant, it will be communism.

William Morris (1834–96) English Utopian socialist. Lecture to the Hammersmith Socialist Society, 1893

13 Communism is like prohibition, it's a good idea but it won't work.

Will Rogers (1879–1935) US actor and humorist. *Autobiography*, Nov 1927

14 Nature has no cure for this sort of madness, though I have known a legacy from a rich relative work wonders.

F. E. Smith (1872–1930) British lawyer and politician. Referring to Communism. *Law, Life and Letters* (1927), Vol. II

15 For us in Russia communism is a dead dog, while, for many people in the West, it is still a living lion.

Alexander Solzhenitsyn (1918–) Soviet novelist. *The Listener*, 15 Feb 1979

16 Every communist has a fascist frown, every fascist a communist smile.

Muriel Spark (1918–) British novelist. *The Girls of Slender Means*, Ch. 4

17 The party is the rallying-point for the best elements of the working class.

Joseph Stalin (J. Dzhugashvili; 1879–1953) Soviet statesman. Attrib.

18 Communism continued to haunt Europe as a spectre – a name men gave to their own fears and blunders. But the crusade against Communism was even more imaginary than the spectre of Communism.

A. J. P. Taylor (1906–) British historian. *The Origins of the Second World War*, Ch. 2

19 Lenin's method leads to this: the party organization at first substitutes itself for the party as a whole. Then the central committee substitutes itself for the party organization, and finally a single dictator substitutes himself for the central committee.

Leon Trotsky (Lev Davidovich Bronstein; 1879–1940) Russian revolutionary. *The Communist Parties of Western Europe* (N. McInnes), Ch. 3

COMPLAINTS

1 We have first raised a dust and then complain we cannot see.

Bishop Berkeley (1685–1753) Irish churchman and philosopher. *Principles of Human Knowledge*, Introduction

2 The world is disgracefully managed, one hardly knows to whom to complain.

Ronald Firbank (1886–1926) British novelist. *Vainglory*

3 If you are foolish enough to be contented, don't show it, but grumble with the rest.

Jerome K. Jerome (1859–1927) British humorist. *Idle Thoughts of an Idle Fellow*

4 Nay, Madam, when you are declaiming, declaim; and when you are calculating, calculate.

Samuel Johnson (1709–84) British lexicographer. Commenting on Mrs Thrales's discourse on the price of children's clothes. *Life of Johnson* (J. Boswell), Vol. III

5 I want to register a complaint. Do you know who sneaked into my room at three o'clock this morning?
– Who?
Nobody, and that's my complaint.

Groucho Marx (Julius Marx; 1895–1977) US comedian. *Monkey Business*

6 There are so many things to complain of in this household that it would never have occurred to me to complain of rheumatism.

Saki (Hector Hugh Munro; 1870–1916) British writer. *The Quest*

COMPLIMENTS

See also admiration, beauty, flattery, love, praise

1 Nature made him, and then broke the mould.

Ludovico Ariosto (1474–1533) Italian poet. Referring to Charlemagne's paladin, Roland. *Orlando furioso*

2 It's a sort of bloom on a woman. If you have it, you don't need to have anything else; and if you don't have it, it doesn't much matter what else you have.

J. M. Barrie (1860–1937) British novelist and dramatist. *What Every Woman Knows*, I

3 Miss J. Hunter Dunn, Miss J. Hunter Dunn,
Furnish'd and burnish'd by Aldershot sun.

John Betjeman (1906–84) British poet. *A Subaltern's Love Song*

4 Here's looking at you, kid.

Humphrey Bogart (1899–1957) US film star. *Casablanca*

5 Incredibly, inordinately, devastatingly, immortally, calamitously, hearteningly, adorably beautiful.

Rupert Brooke (1887–1915) British poet. Referring to the actress Cathleen Nesbitt. *Rupert Brooke* (C. Hassall)

6 She walks in beauty, like the night
Of cloudless climes and starry skies;
And all that's best of dark and bright
Meet in her aspect and her eyes.

Lord Byron (1788–1824) British poet. *She Walks in Beauty*

7 There is a garden in her face,
Where roses and white lilies grow;
A heav'nly paradise is that place,
Wherein all pleasant fruits do flow.
There cherries grow, which none may buy
Till 'Cherry ripe' themselves do cry.

Thomas Campion (1567–1620) English poet. *Fourth Book of Airs*

8 She isn't a bad bit of goods, the Queen! I wish all the fleas in my bed were as good.

Miguel de Cervantes (1547–1616) Spanish novelist. *Don Quixote*, Pt. I, Ch. 30

9 It was a blonde. A blonde to make a bishop kick a hole in a stained-glass window.

Raymond Chandler (1888–1959) US novelist. *Farewell, My Lovely*, Ch. 13

10 If you weren't the best light comedian in the country, all you'd be fit for would be the selling of cars in Great Portland Street.

Noël Coward (1899–1973) British dramatist. To Rex Harrison. Attrib.

11 Here with a Loaf of Bread beneath the Bough,
A Flask of Wine, a Book of Verse – and Thou
Beside me singing in the Wilderness –
And Wilderness is Paradise enow.

Edward Fitzgerald (1809–83) British poet. *The Rubáiyát of Omar Khayyám*

12 His worst is better than any other person's best.

William Hazlitt *English Literature*, Ch. XIV, 'Sir Walter Scott'

13 He talked on for ever; and you wished him to talk on for ever.

William Hazlitt (1778–1830) British essayist. Referring to the poet Coleridge. *Lectures on the English Poets*, Lecture VIII, 'On the Living Poets'

14 Whenever a man's friends begin to compliment him about looking young, he may be sure that they think he is growing old.

Washington Irving (1783–1859) US writer. *Bracebridge Hall*, 'Bachelors'

15 She is Venus when she smiles;
But she's Juno when she walks,
And Minerva when she talks.

Ben Jonson (1573–1637) English dramatist. *The Underwood*, 'Celebration of Charis, V. His Discourse with Cupid'

16 On Richmond Hill there lives a lass,
More sweet than May day morn,
Whose charms all other maids surpass,
A rose without a thorn.

Leonard MacNally (1752–1820) Irish dramatist and poet. *The Lass of Richmond Hill*

17 Oh, thou art fairer than the evening air
Clad in the beauty of a thousand stars.

Christopher Marlowe *Doctor Faustus*, V:1

18 Your eyes shine like the pants of my blue serge suit.

Groucho Marx (Julius Marx; 1895–1977) US comedian. *The Cocoanuts*

19 Most people are such fools that it is really no great compliment to say that a man is above the average.

W. Somerset Maugham (1874–1965) British novelist. *A Writer's Notebook*

20 Charlie is my darling, my darling, my darling,
Charlie is my darling, the young Chevalier.

Baroness Nairne (1766–1845) Scottish songwriter. Referring to Bonnie Prince Charlie. *Charlie is my Darling*

21 Pretty witty Nell.

Samuel Pepys (1633–1703) English diarist. Referring to Charles II's mistress Nell Gwynne. *Diary*, 3 Apr 1665

22 Where'er you walk, cool gales shall fan the glade,
Trees, where you sit, shall crowd into a shade:
Where'er you tread, the blushing flow'rs shall rise,
And all things flourish where you turn your eyes.

Alexander Pope (1688–1744) British poet. *Pastorals*, 'Summer'

23 I get no kick from champagne.
Mere alcohol doesn't thrill me at all,
So tell me why should it be true
That I get a kick out of you?

Cole Porter (1891–1964) US composer and lyricist. *Anything Goes*, 'I Get a Kick Out of You'

24 It is fun to be in the same decade with you.

Franklin D. Roosevelt (1882–1945) US Democratic president. After Churchill had congratulated him on his 60th birthday. *The Hinge of Fate* (Winston S. Churchill), Ch. 4

25 My doctor said to me afterwards, 'When you were ill you behaved like a true philosopher. Every time you came to yourself you made a joke.' I never had a compliment that pleased me more.

Bertrand Russell (1872–1970) British philosopher. Letter to Jean Nichol, 2 Oct 1921

26 His vocal cords were kissed by God.

Harold Schoenberg (1915–) US music critic. Referring to Luciano Pavarotti. *The Times*, 30 June 1981

27 But search the land of living men,
Where wilt thou find their like agen?

Walter Scott (1771–1832) Scottish novelist. *Marmion*, I

28 The barge she sat in, like a burnish'd throne,
Burn'd on the water. The poop was beaten gold;
Purple the sails, and so perfumed that
The winds were love-sick with them; the oars were silver,
Which to the tune of flutes kept stroke and made
The water which they beat to follow faster,
As amorous of their strokes. For her own person,
It beggar'd all description.

William Shakespeare (1564–1616) English dramatist. *Antony and Cleopatra*, II:2

29 Age cannot wither her, nor custom stale
Her infinite variety. Other women cloy
The appetites they feed, but she makes hungry
Where most she satisfies.

William Shakespeare *Antony and Cleopatra*, II:2

30 'A was a man, take him for all in all,
I shall not look upon his like again.

William Shakespeare *Hamlet*, I:2

31 Shall I compare thee to a summer's day?
Thou art more lovely and more temperate.
Rough winds do shake the darling buds of May,
And summer's lease hath all too short a date.

William Shakespeare *Sonnet 18*

32 Who is Silvia? What is she,
That all our swains commend her?
Holy, fair, and wise is she.

William Shakespeare *The Two Gentlemen of Verona*, IV:2

33 For she was beautiful – her beauty made
The bright world dim, and everything beside
Seemed like the fleeting image of a shade.

Percy Bysshe Shelley (1792–1822) British poet. *The Witch of Atlas*, XII

34 Won't you come into the garden? I would like my roses to see you.

Richard Brinsley Sheridan (1751–1816) British dramatist. Said to a young lady. Attrib. in *The Perfect Hostess*

35 She would rather light candles than curse the darkness, and her glow has warmed the world.

Adlai Stevenson (1900–65) US statesman. Referring to the writer and diplomat Eleanor Roosevelt. Address, United Nations General Assembly, 9 Nov 1962

36 What, when drunk, one sees in other women, one sees in Garbo sober.

Kenneth Tynan (1927–80) British theatre critic. *The Sunday Times*, 25 Aug 1963

37 Of this blest man, let his just praise be given,
Heaven was in him, before he was in heaven.

Izaak Walton (1593–1683) English writer. Referring to Dr Richard Sibbes. Written in a copy of *Returning Backslider* by Richard Sibbes

38 Roses are flowering in Picardy,
But there's never a rose like you.

Frederic Edward Weatherly (1848–1929) British lawyer and songwriter. *Roses of Picardy*

39 The sweetest thing that ever grew
Beside a human door!

William Wordsworth (1770–1850) British poet. *Lucy Gray*

COMPROMISE

1 It takes two to tango.

Proverb

2 We know what happens to people who stay in the middle of the road. They get run over.

Aneurin Bevan (1897–1960) British Labour politician. *The Observer*, 9 Dec 1953

3 For the flesh lusteth against the Spirit, and the Spirit against the flesh: and these are contrary the one to the other: so that ye cannot do the things that ye would.

Bible: Galatians 5:17

4 All government, indeed every human benefit and enjoyment, every virtue, and every prudent act, is founded on compromise and barter.

Edmund Burke (1729–97) British politician. *Speech on Conciliation with America* (House of Commons, 22 Mar 1775)

5 A cockroach world of compromise.

Angela Carter (1940–92) British novelist. *Wise Children*

6 Compromise used to mean that half a loaf was better than no bread. Among modern statesmen it really seems to mean that half a loaf is better than a whole loaf.

G. K. Chesterton (1874–1936) British writer. *What's Wrong with the World*

CONCEIT

See also arrogance, boasts, egotism, pride

1 I'm the greatest!

Muhammad Ali (Cassius Clay; 1942–) US boxer. Remark, often said after his fights

2 A man…must have a very good opinion of himself when he asks people to leave their own fireside, and encounter such a day as this, for the sake of coming to see him. He must think himself a most agreeable fellow.

Jane Austen (1775–1817) British novelist. *Emma*, Ch. 13

3 It was prettily devised of Aesop, 'The fly sat upon the axletree of the chariot-wheel and said, what a dust do I raise.'

Francis Bacon (1561–1626) English philosopher. *Essays*, 'Of Vain-Glory'

4 To give an accurate and exhaustive account of that period would need a far less brilliant pen than mine.

Max Beerbohm (1872–1956) British writer. *1880*

5 If ever he went to school without any boots it was because he was too big for them.

Ivor Bulmer-Thomas (1905–) British writer and politician. Referring to the Labour politician Harold Wilson. Remark, Conservative Party Conference, 1949

6 Vanity plays lurid tricks with our memory.

Joseph Conrad (Teodor Josef Konrad Korzeniowski; 1857–1924) Polish-born British novelist. *Lord Jim*

7 I know he is, and he adores his maker.

Benjamin Disraeli (1804–81) British statesman. Replying to a remark made in defence of John Bright that he was a self-made man; often also attrib. to Bright referring to Disraeli. *The Fine Art of Political Wit* (L. Harris)

8 We are so vain that we even care for the opinion of those we don't care for.

Marie Ebner von Eschenbach (1830–1916) Austrian writer. *Aphorism*

9 I am the Captain of the *Pinafore*;
And a right good captain too!

W. S. Gilbert (1836–1911) British dramatist. *HMS Pinafore*, I

10 I have a left shoulder-blade that is a miracle of loveliness. People come miles to see it. My right elbow has a fascination that few can resist.

W. S. Gilbert *The Mikado*, II

11 All my shows are great. Some of them are bad. But they are all great.

Lew Grade (Lewis Winogradsky; 1906–) British film and TV producer. *The Observer*, 'Sayings of the Week', 14 Sept 1975

12 Conceit is the finest armour a man can wear.

Jerome K. Jerome (1859–1927) British humorist. *Idle Thoughts of an Idle Fellow*

13 He fell in love with himself at first sight and it is a passion to which he has always remained faithful. Self-love seems so often unrequited.

Anthony Powell (1905–) British novelist. *A Dance to the Music of Time: The Acceptance World*, Ch. 1

14 Self-love is the greatest of all flatterers.

Duc de la Rochefoucauld (1613–80) French writer. *Maximes*, 2

15 Besides Shakespeare and me, who do you think there is?

Gertrude Stein (1874–1946) US writer. Speaking to a friend she considered knew little about literature. *Charmed Circle* (J. Mellow)

16 The Jews have produced only three originative geniuses: Christ, Spinoza, and myself.

Gertrude Stein *Charmed Circle* (J. Mellow)

17 Vanity dies hard; in some obstinate cases it outlives the man.

Robert Louis Stevenson (1850–94) Scottish writer. *Prince Otto*

18 I think, historically, the term 'Thatcherism' will be seen as a compliment.

Margaret Thatcher (1925–) British politician and prime minister. Remark, Oct 1985

19 I think I have become a bit of an institution – you know, the sort of thing people expect to see around the place.

Margaret Thatcher Remark, July 1987

20 He would like to destroy his old diaries and to appear before his children and the public only in his patriarchal robes. His vanity is immense!

Sophie Tolstoy (1844–1919) Russian writer. *A Diary of Tolstoy's Wife, 1860–1891*

21 Isn't it? I know in my case I would grow intolerably conceited.

James Whistler (1834–1903) US painter. Replying to the pointed observaton that it was as well that we do not not see ourselves as others see us. *The Man Whistler* (H. Pearson)

22 A LADY. I only know of two painters in the world: yourself and Velasquez.
WHISTLER. Why drag in Velasquez?

James Whistler *Whistler Stories* (D. Seitz)

23 No, no, Oscar, you forget. When you and I are together we never talk about anything except me.

James Whistler Cable replying to Oscar Wilde's message: 'When you and I are together we never talk about anything except ourselves'. *The Gentle Art of Making Enemies*

24 I cannot tell you that, madam. Heaven has granted me no offspring.

James Whistler Replying to a lady who had inquired whether he thought genius hereditary. *Whistler Stories* (D. Seitz)

25 Nothing, except my genius.

Oscar Wilde (1854–1900) Irish-born British dramatist. Replying to a US customs official on being asked if he had anything to declare. Attrib.

26 To love oneself is the beginning of a lifelong romance.

Oscar Wilde *An Ideal Husband*, III

27 Who am I to tamper with a masterpiece?

Oscar Wilde Refusing to make alterations to one of his own plays. Attrib.

CONFLICT

See also opposites

1 Attack is the best form of defence.

Proverb

2 Fight fire with fire.

Proverb

3 He who lives by the sword dies by the sword.

Proverb

4 Without Contraries is no progression. Attraction and Repulsion, Reason and Energy, Love and Hate, are necessary to Human existence.

William Blake (1757–1827) British poet. *The Marriage of Heaven and Hell*, 'The Argument'

5 No, when the fight begins within himself,
A man's worth something.

Robert Browning (1812–89) British poet. *Bishop Blougram's Apology*

6 Two souls dwell, alas! in my breast.

Goethe (1749–1832) German poet and dramatist. *Faust*, Pt. I

7 Two loves I have, of comfort and despair,
Which like two spirits do suggest me still;
The better angel is a man right fair,
The worser spirit a woman colour'd ill.

William Shakespeare (1564–1616) English dramatist. *Sonnet 144*

CONFORMITY

See also orthodoxy

1 Who spits against the wind, it falls in his face.

Proverb

2 When in Rome, live as the Romans do: when elsewhere, live as they live elsewhere.

St Ambrose (c. 339–397) Bishop of Milan. Advice to St Augustine

3 Take the tone of the company you are in.

Earl of Chesterfield (1694–1773) English statesman. Letter to his son, 9 Oct 1747

4 Whoso would be a man must be a nonconformist.

Ralph Waldo Emerson (1803–82) US poet and essayist. *Essays*, 'Self-Reliance'

5 Uniformity isn't bad, as some people still think, because if the quality is good, it satisfies. People are never happy who want change.

L. P. Hartley (1895–1972) British novelist. *Facial Justice*, Ch. 13

6 Why do you have to be a nonconformist like everybody else?

James Thurber (1894–1961) US humorist. Attrib. Actually a cartoon caption by Stan Hunt in the *New Yorker*

CONFUCIUS

(K'ung Fu-tzu; 551–479 BC) Chinese philosopher, whose sayings are collected in the *Analects*.

1 When you meet someone better than yourself, turn your thoughts to becoming his equal. When you meet someone not as good as you are, look within and examine your own self.

Analects

2 Chi Wen Tzu always thought three times before taking action. Twice would have been quite enough.

Analects

3 Men's natures are alike; it is their habits that carry them far apart.

Analects

4 Study the past, if you would divine the future.

Analects

5 Learning without thought is labour lost; thought without learning is perilous.

Analects

6 Fine words and an insinuating appearance are seldom associated with true virtue.

Analects

7 Have no friends not equal to yourself.

Analects

8 When you have faults, do not fear to abandon them.
Analects

9 To be able to practise five things everywhere under heaven constitutes perfect virtue...gravity, generosity of soul, sincerity, earnestness, and kindness.
Analects

10 The superior man is satisfied and composed; the mean man is always full of distress.
Analects

11 The people may be made to follow a course of action, but they may not be made to understand it.
Analects

12 Recompense injury with justice, and recompense kindness with kindness.
Analects

13 The superior man is distressed by his want of ability.
Analects

14 What you do not want done to yourself, do not do to others.
Analects

CONFUSION

1 Anyone who isn't confused here doesn't really understand what's going on.
Anonymous Referring to the sectarian problems in Northern Ireland.

2 Well, my deliberate opinion is – it's a jolly strange world.
Arnold Bennett (1867–1931) British novelist. *The Title*, I

3 I can't say I was ever lost, but I was bewildered once for three days.
Daniel Boone (1734–1820) US pioneeer. Reply when asked if he had ever been lost. Attrib.

4 'Curiouser and curiouser!' cried Alice.
Lewis Carroll (Charles Lutwidge Dodgson; 1832–98) British writer. *Alice's Adventures in Wonderland*, Ch. 2

5 I believe that I have created a lot of cognitive dissonance in the minds of people who are comfortable with stereotypes.
Hillary Clinton (1947–) US lawyer and First Lady. *The Observer*, 'Sayings of the Week', 15 May 1994

6 This world is very odd we see,
We do not comprehend it;
But in one fact we all agree,
God won't, and we can't mend it.
Arthur Hugh Clough (1819–61) British poet. *Dipsychus*, Bk. II

7 Bewitched, Bothered and Bewildered.
Lorenz Hart (1895–1943) US songwriter. From the musical *Babes in Arms.* Song title

8 I had nothing to offer anybody except my own confusion.
Jack Kerouac (1922–69) US novelist. *On the Road*, Pt. II

9 I don't want you to think I'm not incoherent.
Harold W. Ross (1892–1951) US journalist. *The Years with Ross* (James Thurber)

10 For mine own part, it was Greek to me.
William Shakespeare (1564–1616) English dramatist. *Julius Caesar*, I:2

11 That blessed mood,
In which the burthen of the mystery,
In which the heavy and the weary weight
Of all this unintelligible world,
Is lightened.
William Wordsworth (1770–1850) British poet. *Lines composed a few miles above Tintern Abbey*

CONGREVE, WILLIAM

(1670–1729) British Restoration dramatist, whose comedies include *Love for Love* (1695) and *The Way of the World* (1700). He also wrote a tragedy, *The Mourning Bride* (1697).

Quotations about Congreve

1 William Congreve is the only sophisticated playwright England has produced; and like Shaw, Sheridan, and Wilde, his nearest rivals, he was brought up in Ireland.
Kenneth Tynan (1927–80) British theatre critic. *Curtains*, 'The Way of the World'

2 He spoke of his works as trifles that were beneath him.
Voltaire (François-Marie Arouet; 1694–1778) French writer. *Letters Concerning the English Nation*

Quotations by Congreve

3 She lays it on with a trowel.
The Double Dealer, III:10

4 See how love and murder will out.
The Double Dealer, IV:6

5 I am always of the opinion with the learned, if they speak first.
Incognita

6 O fie miss, you must not kiss and tell.
Love for Love, II:10

7 I know that's a secret, for it's whispered every where.
Love for Love, III:3

8 Music has charms to soothe a savage breast.
The Mourning Bride, I

9 Heaven has no rage like love to hatred turned,
Nor hell a fury like a woman scorned.
The Mourning Bride, III

10 SHARPER. Thus grief still treads upon the heels of pleasure:
Marry'd in haste, we may repent at leisure.
SETTER. Some by experience find those words mis-plac'd:
At leisure marry'd, they repent in haste.
The Old Bachelor, V:8

11 Courtship to marriage, as a very witty prologue to a very dull Play.
The Old Bachelor, V:10

12 Alack he's gone the way of all flesh.
Squire Bickerstaff Detected, attrib.

13 Say what you will, 'tis better to be left than never to have been loved.
The Way of the World, II:1

14 Lord, what is a lover that it can give? Why one makes lovers as fast as one pleases, and they live as long as one pleases, and they die as soon as one pleases: and then if one pleases one makes more.
The Way of the World, II:4

15 I nauseate walking; 'tis a country diversion, I loathe the country and everything that relates to it.
The Way of the World, IV:4

16 I hope you do not think me prone to any iteration of nuptials.
The Way of the World, IV:12

17 O, she is the antidote to desire.
The Way of the World, IV:14

CONNOLLY, CYRIL

(1903–74) British journalist and writer. A contributor to the *New Statesman*, *The Sunday Times*, and other papers, he published several collections of essays, such as *Enemies of Promise* (1938).

Quotations about Connolly

1 Writers like Connolly gave pleasure a bad name.
E. M. Forster (1879–1970) British novelist. Attrib.

2 The key to his behaviour was self-indulgence, which he made almost a rule of life.
Stephen Spender (1909–) British poet. *The Observer*, 10 July 1983

Quotations by Connolly

3 It is closing time in the gardens of the West.
The Condemned Playground

4 A great writer creates a world of his own and his readers are proud to live in it. A lesser writer may entice them in for a moment, but soon he will watch them filing out.
Enemies of Promise, Ch. 1

5 The ape-like virtues without which no one can enjoy a public school.
Enemies of Promise, Ch. 1

6 Literature is the art of writing something that will be read twice; journalism what will be grasped at once.
Enemies of Promise, Ch. 3

7 An author arrives at a good style when his language performs what is required of it without shyness.
Enemies of Promise, Ch. 3

8 As repressed sadists are supposed to become policemen or butchers so those with irrational fear of life become publishers.
Enemies of Promise, Ch. 3

9 Whom the gods wish to destroy they first call promising.
Enemies of Promise, Ch. 3

10 There is no more sombre enemy of good art than the pram in the hall.
Enemies of Promise, Ch. 3

11 All charming people have something to conceal, usually their total dependence on the appreciation of others.
Enemies of Promise, Ch. 16

12 I have always disliked myself at any given moment; the total of such moments is my life.
Enemies of Promise, Ch. 18

13 Boys do not grow up gradually. They move forward in spurts like the hands of clocks in railway stations.
Enemies of Promise, Ch. 18

14 The only way for writers to meet is to share a quick pee over a common lamp-post.
The Unquiet Grave

15 Life is a maze in which we take the wrong turning before we have learnt to walk.
The Unquiet Grave

16 In the sex-war thoughtlessness is the weapon of the male, vindictiveness of the female.
The Unquiet Grave

17 There is no fury like an ex-wife searching for a new lover.
The Unquiet Grave

18 Imprisoned in every fat man a thin one is wildly signalling to be let out.
Similar sentiments have been stated by others. *See* Kingsley AMIS, George ORWELL. *The Unquiet Grave*

19 Better to write for yourself and have no public, than write for the public and have no self.
Turnstile One (ed. V. S. Pritchett)

20 The man who is master of his passions is Reason's slave.
Turnstile One (ed. V. S. Pritchett)

CONRAD, JOSEPH

(Teodor Josef Konrad Korzeniowski; 1857–1924) Polish-born British novelist. His 20 years at sea provided the background for most of his novels and stories, notably *The Nigger of the Narcissus* (1897) and *Lord Jim* (1900).

1 Exterminate all the brutes.
Heart of Darkness, Ch. 2

2 The horror! The horror!
Heart of Darkness, Ch. 3

3 Mistah Kurtz – he dead.
Heart of Darkness, Ch. 3

4 You shall judge of a man by his foes as well as by his friends.
Lord Jim, Ch. 34

5 A work that aspires, however humbly, to the

condition of art should carry its justification in every line.

The Nigger of the Narcissus, Preface

6 The terrorist and the policeman both come from the same basket.

The Secret Agent, Ch. 4

7 A belief in a supernatural source of evil is not necessary; men alone are quite capable of every wickedness.

Under Western Eyes, Part 2

8 I remember my youth and the feeling that will never come back any more – the feeling that I could last for ever, outlast the sea, the earth, and all men; the deceitful feeling that lures us on to joys, to perils, to love, to vain effort – to death...

Youth

9 This could have occurred nowhere but in England, where men and sea interpenetrate, so to speak.

Youth

CONSCIENCE

See also integrity

1 Conscience, I say, not thine own, but of the other: for why is my liberty judged of another man's conscience?

Bible: I Corinthians 10:29

2 All a man can betray is his conscience.

Joseph Conrad *Under Western Eyes*

3 Conscience is the internal perception of the rejection of a particular wish operating within us.

Sigmund Freud (1856–1939) Austrian psychoanalyst. *Totem and Taboo*

4 Conscience is a coward, and those faults it has not strength enough to prevent it seldom has justice enough to accuse.

Oliver Goldsmith (1728–74) Irish-born British writer. *The Vicar of Wakefield*, Ch. 13

5 Those who follow their conscience directly are of my religion; and, for my part, I am of the same religion as all those who are brave and true.

Henri IV (1533–1610) King of France. Henri had become a Roman Catholic, as a political move, in 1576. Letter to M. de Batz, 1577

6 Conscience is the inner voice that warns us somebody may be looking.

H. L. Mencken (1880–1956) US journalist. *A Mencken Chrestomathy*

7 Thus conscience does make cowards of us all;
And thus the native hue of resolution
Is sicklied o'er with the pale cast of thought.

William Shakespeare (1564–1616) English dramatist. *Hamlet*, III:1

8 A peace above all earthly dignities,
A still and quiet conscience.

William Shakespeare *Henry VIII*, III:2

9 Foul whisperings are abroad. Unnatural deeds
Do breed unnatural troubles; infected minds
To their deaf pillows will discharge their secrets;
More needs she the divine than the physician.

William Shakespeare *Macbeth*, V:1

10 Give me another horse! bind up my wounds!
Have mercy, Jesu! Soft! I did but dream.
O coward conscience, how dost thou afflict me!

William Shakespeare *Richard III*, V:3

11 My conscience hath a thousand several tongues,
And every tongue brings in several tale,
And every tale condemns me for a villain.

William Shakespeare *Richard III*, V:3

12 Conscience is but a word that cowards use,
Devis'd at first to keep the strong in awe.

William Shakespeare *Richard III*, V:3

CONSERVATION

See also ecology, environment

1 I gave my beauty and my youth to men. I am going to give my wisdom and experience to animals.

Brigitte Bardot (1934–) French film actress. Referring to her animal-rights campaign. *The Guardian*, 1987

2 As cruel a weapon as the cave man's club, the chemical barrage has been hurled against the fabric of life.

Rachel Carson (1907–64) US marine biologist and writer. *The Silent Spring*

3 Contrary to popular mythology, it is not my Department's mission in life to tarmac over the whole of England.

Paul Channon (1935–) British politician. Speech, Sept 1988

4 Population growth is the primary source of environmental damage.

Jacques Cousteau (1910–) French naval officer and underwater explorer. Remark, Jan 1989

5 Trees are poems that the earth writes upon the sky. We fell them down and turn them into paper that we may record our emptiness.

Kahil Gibran (1833–1931) Lebanese mystic and poet. *Sand and Foam*

6 Green politics is not about being far left or far right, but far-sighted.

David Icke (1952–) Green Party spokesman. Speech, Green Party conference, Sept 1989

7 We are living beyond our means. As a people we have developed a life-style that is draining the earth of its priceless and irreplaceable resources without regard for the future of our children and people all around the world.

Margaret Mead (1910–78) US anthropologist, writer, editor, and museum curator. *Redbook*, 'The Energy Crises – Why Our World Will Never Again Be the Same', Apr 1974

8 The biggest waste of water in the country by far is when you spend half a pint and flush two gallons.

Prince Philip (1921–) The consort of Queen Elizabeth II. Speech, 1965

9 Simply having a convention which says you must not make species extinct does not make a blind bit of difference.

Prince Philip Referring to the UN treaty on world conservation, Mar 1989. *The Sunday Correspondent*, 31 Dec, 1989

10 Our English countryside is one of the most heavily man-made habitats in Europe. To make it into a green museum would be to belie its whole history.

Nicholas Ridley (1929–) British politician. Speech, Nov 1988

11 Small is Beautiful.

E. F. Schumacher (1911–77) German-born economist. Book title.

CONSERVATISM

See also change

1 The most conservative man in the world is the British Trade Unionist when you want to change him.

Ernest Bevin (1881–1951) British trade-union leader and politician. Speech, Trade Union Congress, 8 Sept 1927

2 All conservatism is based upon the idea that if you leave things alone you leave them as they are. But you do not. If you leave a thing alone you leave it to a torrent of change.

G. K. Chesterton (1874–1936) British writer. *Orthodoxy*, Ch. 7

3 I love everything that's old: old friends, old times, old manners, old books, old wine.

Oliver Goldsmith (1728–74) Irish-born British writer. *She Stoops to Conquer*, I

4 You can't teach the old maestro a new tune.

Jack Kerouac (1922–69) US novelist. *On the Road*, Pt. I

5 I do not know which makes a man more conservative – to know nothing but the present, or nothing but the past.

John Maynard Keynes (1883–1946) British economist. *The End of Laisser-Faire*, I

6 What is conservatism? Is it not adherence to the old and tried, against the new and untried?

Abraham Lincoln (1809–65) US statesman. Speech, 27 Feb 1860

7 You can't teach an old dogma new tricks.

Dorothy Parker (1893–1967) US writer. *Wit's End* (R. E. Drennan)

8 The radical invents the views. When he has worn them out, the conservative adopts them.

Mark Twain (Samuel Langhorne Clemens; 1835–1910) US writer. *Notebooks*

CONSTANCY

See also change, conservatism

1 A foolish consistency is the hobgoblin of little minds, adored by little statesmen and philosophers and divines. With consistency a great soul has simply nothing to do.

Ralph Waldo Emerson (1803–82) US poet and essayist. *Essays*, 'Self-reliance'

2 Consistency is contrary to nature, contrary to life. The only completely consistent people are the dead.

Aldous Huxley (1894–1964) British novelist. *Do What you Will*

3 *Plus ça change, plus c'est la même chose.*
The more things change, the more they stay the same.

Alphonse Karr (1808–90) French writer. *Les Guêpes*, Jan 1849

4 For men may come and men may go
But I go on for ever.

Alfred, Lord Tennyson (1809–92) British poet. *The Brook*

5 Still glides the Stream, and shall for ever glide;
The Form remains, the Function never dies.

William Wordsworth (1770–1850) British poet. *The River Duddon*, 'After-Thought'

CONTEMPT

See also ridicule

1 She was nothing more than a mere good-tempered, civil and obliging young woman; as such we could scarcely dislike her – she was only an Object of Contempt.

Jane Austen (1775–1817) British novelist. *Love and Friendship*

2 'You threaten us, fellow? Do your worst,
Blow your pipe there till you burst!'

Robert Browning (1812–89) British poet. *The Pied Piper of Hamelin*

3 He looked at me as if I was a side dish he hadn't ordered.

Ring Lardner Jnr (1885–1933) American humorist. Referring to W. H. Taft, US president (1909–13). *The Home Book of Humorous Quotations* (A. K. Adams)

CONTENTMENT

See also happiness, satisfaction

1 Live with the gods. And he does so who constantly shows them that his soul is satisfied with what is assigned to him.

Marcus Aurelius (121–180 AD) Roman emperor. *Meditations*, Bk. V, Ch. 27

2 Sweet Stay-at-Home, sweet Well-content.

W. H. Davies (1871–1940) British poet. *Sweet Stay-at-Home*

3 Here with a Loaf of Bread beneath the Bough,
A Flask of Wine, a Book of Verse – and Thou
Beside me singing in the Wilderness –
And Wilderness is Paradise enow.

Edward Fitzgerald (1809–83) British poet. *The Rubáiyát of Omar Khayyám*

4 I got rhythm,
I got music,
I got my man –
Who could ask for anything more.

Ira Gershwin (1898–1937) US composer. *Girl Crazy*

5 Notwithstanding the poverty of my outside experience, I have always had a significance for myself, and every chance to stumble along my straight and narrow little path, and to worship at the feet of my Deity, and what more can a human soul ask for?

Alice James (1848–92) US diarist. *The Diary of Alice James* (ed. Leon Edel)

6 If I had not been born Perón, I would have liked to be Perón.

Juan Perón (1895–1974) Argentine statesman. *The Observer*, 'Sayings of the Week', 21 Feb 1960

7 Who doth ambition shun
And loves to live i' the sun,
Seeking the food he eats,
And pleas'd with what he gets.

William Shakespeare (1564–1616) English dramatist. *As You Like It*, II:5

8 I earn that I eat, get that I wear, owe no man hate, envy no man's happiness, glad of other men's good, content with my harm.

William Shakespeare *As You Like It*, III:2

9 O, this life
Is nobler than attending for a check,
Richer than doing nothing for a bribe,
Prouder than rustling in unpaid-for silk.

William Shakespeare *Cymbeline*, III:3

10 Nought's had, all's spent,
Where our desire is got without content.
'Tis safer to be that which we destroy,
Than by destruction dwell in doubtful joy.

William Shakespeare *Macbeth*, III:2

CONTRACEPTION

See also sex

1 Vasectomy means not ever having to say you're sorry.

Larry Adler (1914–) US harmonica player and entertainer. Attrib.

2 I want to tell you a terrific story about oral contraception. I asked this girl to sleep with me and she said 'no'.

Woody Allen (Allen Stewart Konigsberg; 1935–) US film actor. *Woody Allen: Clown Prince of American Humor* (Adler and Feinman), Ch. 2

3 The best contraceptive is a glass of cold water: not before or after, but instead.

Anonymous

4 He no play-a da game. He no make-a da rules!

Earl Butz (1909–) US politician. Referring to the Pope's strictures against contraception. Remark, 1974

5 Accidents will occur in the best-regulated families.

Charles Dickens (1812–70) British novelist. *David Copperfield*, Ch. 28

6 If we had spent £167 million on condoms we wouldn't have had these problems in the first place.

Nicholas Fairbairn (1933–) British politician. Referring to food aid for Africa. *The Observer*, 12 May 1991

7 The command 'Be fruitful and multiply was promulgated according to our authorities, when the population of the world consisted of two people.

Dean Inge (1860–1954) British churchman. *More Lay Thoughts of a Dean*

8 Where are the children I might have had? You may suppose I might have wanted them. Drowned to the accompaniment of the rattling of a thousand douche bags.

Malcolm Lowry (1909–57) British novelist. *Under the Volcano*, Ch. 10

9 I would not like to leave contraception on the long finger too long.

Jack Lynch (1917–) Irish statesman. *Irish Times*, 23 May 1971

10 It is now quite lawful for a Catholic woman to avoid pregnancy by a resort to mathematics, though she is still forbidden to resort to physics and chemistry.

H. L. Mencken (1880–1956) US journalist. *Notebooks*, 'Minority Report'

11 Contraceptives should be used on every conceivable occasion.

Spike Milligan (1918–) British comic actor and author. *The Last Goon Show of All*

12 The Pill has so much bad press because we collectively feel guilty about sexual enjoyment.

David Paintin British chairman of the Birth Control Trust. *The Times*, 18 Feb 1993

13 More people die from pregnancy than from the effect of the Pill.

David Paintin *The Times*, 18 Feb 1993

14 We want far better reasons for having children than not knowing how to prevent them.

Dora Russell (1894–1986) *Hypatia*, Ch. 4

15 Skullion had little use for contraceptives at the best of times. Unnatural, he called them, and placed them in the lower social category of things along with elastic-sided boots and made-up bow ties. Not the sort of attire for a gentleman.

Tom Sharpe (1928–) British novelist. *Porterhouse Blue*, Ch. 9

16 Protestant women may take the Pill. Roman Catholic women must keep taking the *Tablet*.

Irene Thomas (1920–) British writer. *The Tablet* is a British Roman Catholic newspaper. Attrib.

17 Marriages are not normally made to avoid having children.

Rudolf Virchow (1821–1902) German pathologist. *Bulletin of the New York Academy of Medicine*, 4:995, 1928 (F. H. Garrison)

CONVERSATION

See also speech

1 Although there exist many thousand subjects for elegant conversation, there are persons who cannot meet a cripple without talking about feet.

Chinese proverb.

2 I have but ninepence in ready money, but I can draw for a thousand pounds.

Joseph Addison (1672–1719) British essayist. Comparing his ability to make conversation and to write. *Life of Johnson* (Boswell)

3 JOHNSON. Well, we had a good talk.
BOSWELL. Yes, Sir; you tossed and gored several persons.

James Boswell (1740–95) Scottish lawyer and writer. *Life of Johnson*, Vol. II

4 Questioning is not the mode of conversation among gentlemen.

Samuel Johnson (1709–84) British lexicographer. *Life of Johnson* (J. Boswell), Vol. II

5 That is the happiest conversation where there is

no competition, no vanity but a calm quiet interchange of sentiments.

Samuel Johnson *Life of Johnson* (J. Boswell), Vol. II

6 Beware of the conversationalist who adds 'in other words'. He is merely starting afresh.

Robert Morley (1908–92) British actor. *The Observer*, 'Sayings of the Week', 6 Dec 1964

7 Ideal conversation must be an exchange of thought, and not, as many of those who worry most about their shortcomings believe, an eloquent exhibition of wit or oratory.

Emily Post (1873–1960) US writer. *Etiquette*, Ch. 6

8 Conversation has a kind of charm about it, an insinuating and insidious something that elicits secrets from us just like love or liquor.

Seneca (c. 4 BC–65 AD) Roman author. *Epistles*

9 Teas,
Where small talk dies in agonies.

Percy Bysshe Shelley (1792–1822) British poet. *Peter Bell the Third*

10 There is no such thing as conversation. It is an illusion. There are intersecting monologues, that is all.

Rebecca West (Cicely Isabel Fairfield; 1892–1983) British novelist and journalist. *There Is No Conversation*, Ch. 1

11 A good listener is not someone who has nothing to say. A good listener is a good talker with a sore throat.

Katherine Whitehorn (1926–) British journalist. Attrib.

CORRUPTION

See also bribery, decline

1 Among a people generally corrupt, liberty cannot long exist.

Edmund Burke (1729–97) British politician. Letter to the Sheriffs of Bristol, 1777

2 We have a cancer within, close to the Presidency, that is growing. It is growing daily.

John Dean (1938–) US presidential counsel. Referring to the Watergate scandal. *The White House Transcripts*, 1974

3 …no one before Anselm became a bishop or abbot who did not first become the king's man and from his hand receive investiture by the gift of the pastoral staff.

Eadmer (c. 1055–c. 1124) English cleric and historian. *Historia Novorum in Anglia*

4 Corruption, the most infallible symptom of constitutional liberty.

Edward Gibbon (1737–94) British historian. *Decline and Fall of the Roman Empire*, Ch. 21

5 I order you to hold a free election, but forbid you to elect anyone but Richard my clerk.

Henry II (1133–89) King of England. Writ to the electors of the See of Winchester regarding the election of a new bishop; Richard d'Ilchester was one of the king's trusted servants. *Recueil des historiens des Gaules et de la France*, XIV

6 We no longer choose people who are qualified and capable in terms of party leadership calibre. We choose people who offer us money or gifts or other things.

Mahathir bin Mohamed (1925–) Malaysian prime minister. He cut off public sector trade with Britain accusing the press of spreading lies about political corruption in Malaysia. Speech, *The Times*, 20 June 1994

7 The hungry sheep look up, and are not fed,
But, swoln with wind and the rank mist they draw,
Rot inwardly, and foul contagion spread.

John Milton (1608–74) English poet. *Lycidas*

8 As killing as the canker to the rose.

John Milton *Lycidas*

9 There will be no whitewash in the White House.

Richard Milhous Nixon (1913–94) US president. Referring to the Watergate scandal. Statement, 17 Apr 1973

10 All things can corrupt perverted minds.

Ovid (Publius Ovidius Naso; 43 BC–17 AD) Roman poet. *Tristia*, Bk. II

11 Any institution which does not suppose the people good, and the magistrate corruptible is evil.

Robespierre (1758–94) French lawyer and revolutionary. *Déclaration des droits de l'homme*, 24 Apr 1793

12 Something is rotten in the state of Denmark.

William Shakespeare (1564–1616) English dramatist. *Hamlet*, I:4

13 For sweetest things turn sourest by their deeds:
Lilies that fester smell far worse than weeds.

William Shakespeare *Sonnet 94*

14 Let none presume
To wear an undeserved dignity.
O! that estates, degrees, and offices
Were not deriv'd corruptly, and that clear honour
Were purchased by the merit of the wearer.
How many then should cover that stand bare;
How many be commanded that command;
How much low peasantry would then be glean'd
From the true seed of honour; and how much honour
Pick'd from the chaff and ruin of the times
To be new varnish'd!

William Shakespeare *The Merchant of Venice*, II:9

15 A reformer is a guy who rides through a sewer in a glass-bottomed boat.

James J. Walker (1881–1946) US politician. Speech, New York, 1928

16 All those men have their price.

Robert Walpole (1676–1745) British statesman. *Memoirs of Sir Robert Walpole* (W. Coxe)

COSMETICS

See also appearance

1 Most women are not so young as they are painted.

Max Beerbohm (1872–1956) British writer. *A Defence of Cosmetics*

2 Wherever one wants to be kissed.

Coco Chanel (1883–1971) French dress designer. When asked where one should wear perfume. *Coco Chanel, Her Life, Her Secrets* (Marcel Haedrich)

3 All the cosmetics names seemed obscenely obvious to me in their promise of sexual bliss. They were all firming or uplifting or invigorating. They made you *tingle*. Or *glow*. Or feel *young*.

Erica Jong (1942–) US poet and writer. *How to Save your Own Life*

4 Waits at the window wearing the face that she keeps in a jar by the door.

John Lennon (1940–80) British rock musician. *Eleanor Rigby* (with Paul McCartney)

5 In the factory we make cosmetics. In the store we sell hope.

Charles Revson (1906–75) US business tycoon. *Fire and Ice* (A. Tobias)

6 The feminine vanity-case is the grave of masculine illusions.

Helen Rowland (1876–1950) US writer, journalist, and humorist. Personally Speaking', *The Book of Diversion*

COUNTRYSIDE

See also agriculture, ecology, flowers, Nature, trees

1 I nauseate walking; 'tis a country diversion, I loathe the country and everything that relates to it.

William Congreve (1670–1729) British Restoration dramatist. *The Way of the World*, IV:4

2 God made the country, and man made the town.

William Cowper (1731–1800) British poet. *The Task*

3 Ever charming, ever new,
When will the landscape tire the view?

John Dyer (1700–58) British poet. *Grongar Hill*

4 ...the sanctuary and special delight of kings, where, laying aside their cares, they withdraw to refresh themselves with a little hunting; there, away from the turmoils inherent in a court, they breathe the pleasure of natural freedom.

Richard FitzNigel (d. 1198) Treasurer of England and Bishop of London. Referring to the royal forests. *Dialogus de Scaccario*, Bk. I, Ch. 11

5 There is nothing good to be had in the country, or, if there is, they will not let you have it.

William Hazlitt (1778–1830) British essayist. *Observations on Wordsworth's* 'Excursion'

6 When I am in the country I wish to vegetate like the country.

William Hazlitt *On Going a Journey*

7 Here of a Sunday morning
My love and I would lie,
And see the coloured counties,
And hear the larks so high
About us in the sky.

A. E. Housman (1859–1936) British scholar and poet. *A Shropshire Lad*, 'Bredon Hill'

8 Learn from the beasts the physic of the field.

Alexander Pope (1688–1744) English poet. *Essay on Man*

9 It must be generations since anyone but highbrows lived in this cottage...I imagine most of the agricultural labourers round here commute from London.

Anthony Powell (1905–) British novelist. *A Dance to the Music of Time: The Kindly Ones*, Ch. 2

10 O, Brignal banks are wild and fair,
And Gretna woods are green,
And you may gather garlands there
Would grace a summer queen.

Walter Scott (1771–1832) Scottish novelist. *Rokeby*, III

11 Hath not old custom made this life more sweet
Than that of painted pomp? Are not these woods
More free from peril than the envious court?
Here feel we but the penalty of Adam,
The seasons' difference; as, the icy fang
And churlish chiding of the winter's wind,
Which, when it bites and blows upon my body,
Even till I shrink with cold, I smile and say,
'This is no flattery.'

William Shakespeare (1564–1616) English dramatist. *As You Like It*, II:1

12 Under the greenwood tree
Who loves to lie with me,
And turn his merry note
Unto the sweet bird's throat,
Come hither, come hither, come hither.
Here shall he see
No enemy
But winter and rough weather.

William Shakespeare *As You Like It*, II:5

13 Anybody can be good in the country.

Oscar Wilde (1854–1900) Irish-born British dramatist. *The Picture of Dorian Gray*, Ch. 19

14 One impulse from a vernal wood
May teach you more of man,
Of moral evil and of good,
Than all the sages can.

William Wordsworth (1770–1850) British poet. *The Tables Turned*

COURAGE

See also endurance, heroism, patriotism

1 Because of my title, I was the first to enter here. I shall be the last to go out.

Duchesse d'Alençon (d. 1897) Bavarian-born duchess. Refusing help during a fire, 4 May 1897, at a charity bazaar in Paris. She died along with 120 others. Attrib.

2 The sons of the prophet were brave men and bold,
And quite unaccustomed to fear,
But the bravest by far in the ranks of the Shah
Was Abdul the Bulbul Amir.

Anonymous *Abdul the Bulbul Amir*

3 Who dares, wins.

Anonymous Motto of the British Special Air Service regiment

4 No coward soul is mine,
No trembler in the world's storm-troubled sphere:
I see Heaven's glories shine,
And faith shines equal, arming me from fear.

Emily Brontë (1818–48) British novelist. *Last Lines*

5 Perhaps your fear in passing judgement is greater than mine in receiving it.

Giordano Bruno (1548–1600) Italian philosopher. Said to the cardinals who excommunicated him, 8 Feb 1600. Attrib.

6 And though hard be the task,
'Keep a stiff upper lip.'

Phoebe Cary (1824–71) US poet. *Keep a Stiff Upper Lip*

7 Down these mean streets a man must go who is

not himself mean; who is neither tarnished nor afraid.

Raymond Chandler (1888–1959) US novelist. *The Simple Art of Murder*

8 The Red Badge of Courage.

Stephen Crane (1871–1900) US writer. *Title of novel*

9 Take a step forward, lads. It will be easier that way.

Erskine Childers (1870–1922) British-born author and Irish patriot. Last words before being executed by firing squad, 24 Nov 1922. *The Riddle of Erskine Childers* (A. Boyle)

10 Boldness, and again boldness, and always boldness!

Georges Jacques Danton (1759–94) French political activist. Speech, French Legislative Committee, 2 Sept 1792

11 Oliver Twist has asked for more.

Charles Dickens (1812–70) British novelist. *Oliver Twist*, Ch. 2

12 I'll bell the cat.

Archibald Douglas (1449–1514) Scottish nobleman. Of his proposed capture of Robert Cochrane (executed 1482); the phrase 'bell the cat' was earlier used by Eustache Deschamps in his *Ballade: Le Chat et les souris*

13 None but the Brave deserves the Fair.

John Dryden (1631–1700) British poet and dramatist. *Alexander's Feast*

14 The ability to get to the verge without getting into the war is the necessary art. If you cannot master it, you inevitably get into war. If you try to run away from it, if you are scared to go to the brink, you are lost.

John Foster Dulles (1888–1959) US politician. The origin of the term 'brinkmanship'. *Life*, 16 Jan 1956

15 Courage is the price that Life exacts for granting peace.

Amelia Earhart (1898–1937) US flyer. *Courage*

16 I am not belittling the brave pioneer men, but the sunbonnet as well as the sombrero has helped to settle this glorious land of ours.

Edna Ferber (1887–1968) US writer and scenarist. *Cimarron*, Ch. 23

17 Come cheer up, my lads! 'tis to glory we steer,
To add something more to this wonderful year;
To honour we call you, not press you like slaves,
For who are so free as the sons of the waves?
Heart of oak are our ships,
Heart of oak are our men:
We always are ready;
Steady, boys, steady;
We'll fight and we'll conquer again and again.

David Garrick (1717–79) British actor and manager. *Heart of Oak*

18 The boy stood on the burning deck
Whence all but he had fled;
The flame that lit the battle's wreck
Shone round him o'er the dead.

Felicia Dorothea Hemans (1793–1835) British poet. *Casabianca*

19 It is better to be the widow of a hero than the wife of a coward.

Dolores Ibarruri (1895–1989) Spanish politician. Speech, Valencia, 1936

20 It is better to die on your feet than to live on your knees.

Dolores Ibarruri Speech, Paris, 3 Sept 1936

21 ...we could never learn to be brave and patient, if there were only joy in the world.

Helen Keller (1880–1968) US writer and lecturer. *Atlantic Monthly* (May 1890)

22 If the creator had a purpose in equipping us with a neck, he surely meant us to stick it out.

Arthur Koestler (1905–83) Hungarian-born British writer. *Encounter*, May 1970

23 Then out spake brave Horatius,
The Captain of the Gate:
'To every man upon this earth
Death cometh soon or late.
And how can man die better
Than facing fearful odds,
For the ashes of his fathers,
And the temples of his Gods?'

Lord Macaulay (1800–59) British historian. *Lays of Ancient Rome*, 'Horatius', 27

24 They dashed on towards that thin red line tipped with steel.

William Howard Russell (1820–1907) British journalist. *The British Expedition to the Crimea*

25 The stubborn spear-men still made good
Their dark impenetrable wood,
Each stepping where his comrade stood,
The instant that he fell.

Walter Scott (1771–1832) Scottish novelist. *Marmion*, VI

26 And dar'st thou then
To beard the lion in his den,
The Douglas in his hall?

Walter Scott *Marmion*, VI

27 Once more unto the breach, dear friends, once more;
Or close the wall up with our English dead.

William Shakespeare (1564–1616) English dramatist. *Henry V*, III:1

28 I dare do all that may become a man;
Who dares do more is none.

William Shakespeare *Macbeth*, I:7

29 Lay on, Macduff;
And damn'd be him that first cries, 'Hold, enough!'

William Shakespeare *Macbeth*, V:5

30 The camps had taught him that people who say nothing carry something within themselves.

Alexander Solzhenitsyn (1918–) Russian novelist. *Cancer Ward*, Pt. II, Ch. 10

31 And as she look'd about, she did behold,
How over that same door was likewise writ,
Be bold, be bold, and everywhere Be bold.

Edmund Spenser (1552–99) English poet. *The Faerie Queene*, 3:11:54

32 He was a bold man that first eat an oyster.

Jonathan Swift (1667–1745) Irish-born Anglican priest and writer. *Polite Conversation*, Dialogue 2

33 Half a league, half a league,
Half a league onward,
All in the valley of Death
Rode the six hundred.

Alfred, Lord Tennyson (1809–92) British poet. *The Charge of the Light Brigade*

34 Into the jaws of Death,
Into the mouth of Hell.

Alfred, Lord Tennyson *The Charge of the Light Brigade*

35 Fortune favours the brave.

Terence (Publius Terentius Afer; c. 190–159 BC) Roman poet. *Phormio*

36 The three-o'-clock in the morning courage, which Bonaparte thought was the rarest.

Henry David Thoreau (1817–62) US writer. *Walden*, 'Sounds'

COURTESY

See also chivalry, etiquette, manners, respect

1 Civility costs nothing.

Proverb

2 If a man be gracious and courteous to strangers, it shews he is a citizen of the world.

Francis Bacon (1561–1626) English philosopher. *Essays*, 'Of Goodness and Goodness of Nature'

3 The English are polite by telling lies. The Americans are polite by telling the truth.

Malcolm Bradbury (1932–) British academic and novelist. *Stepping Westward*, Bk. II, Ch. 5

4 Courtesy is not dead – it has merely taken refuge in Great Britain.

Georges Duhamel (1884–1966) French writer. *The Observer*, 'Sayings of Our Times', 31 May 1953

COWARD, SIR NOEL

(1899–1973) British actor, dramatist, and songwriter. After his first success, *The Vortex* (1924), he wrote a number of comedies, including *Blithe Spirit* (1941) and *Brief Encounter* (1946), both made into films. His songs include *Mad Dogs and Englishmen.*

Quotations about Coward

1 He was his own greatest invention.

John Osborne (1929–) British dramatist. Attrib.

2 He was once Slightly in *Peter Pan,* and has been wholly in Peter Pan ever since.

Kenneth Tynan (1927–80) British theatre critic. Attrib.

Quotations by Coward

3 We have no reliable guarantee that the afterlife will be any less exasperating than this one, have we?

Blithe Spirit, I

4 Never mind, dear, we're all made the same, though some more than others.

The Café de la Paix

5 There's always something fishy about the French.

Conversation Piece, I:6

6 Dance, dance, dance little lady.

Song title

7 Don't let's be beastly to the Germans.

Song title

8 Don't put your daughter on the stage, Mrs Worthington.

Song title

9 Everybody was up to something, especially, of course, those who were up to nothing.

Future Indefinite

10 Sunburn is very becoming – but only when it is even – one must be careful not to look like a mixed grill.

The Lido Beach

11 Mad about the boy.

Song title

12 Mad dogs and Englishmen go out in the mid-day sun.

Song title

13 And though the Van Dycks have to go
And we pawn the Bechstein grand,
We'll stand by the Stately Homes of England.

Operette, 'The Stately Homes of England'

14 The Stately Homes of England
How beautiful they stand,
To prove the upper classes
Have still the upper hand.

Operette, 'The Stately Homes of England'

15 Poor Little Rich Girl.

Song title

16 Very flat, Norfolk.

Private Lives

17 Extraordinary how potent cheap music is.

Private Lives

18 Certain women should be struck regularly, like gongs.

Private Lives

19 She refused to begin the 'Beguine'
Tho' they besought her to
And with language profane and obscene
She curs'd the man who taught her to
She curs'd Cole Porter too!

Sigh No More, 'Nina'

20 Twentieth-Century Blues.

Song title

21 I've over-educated myself in all the things I shouldn't have known at all.

Wild Oats

22 Work is much more fun than fun.

The Observer, 'Sayings of the Week', 21 June 1963

23 Dear 338171 (May I call you 338?).

Starting a letter to T. E. Lawrence who had retired from public life to become Aircraftsman Brown, 338171. *Letters to T. E. Lawrence*

24 I never realized before that Albert married beneath him.

After seeing a certain actress in the role of Queen Victoria. *Tynan on Theatre* (K. Tynan)

25 Dear Mrs A., hooray hooray,
At last you are deflowered
On this as every other day
I love you. Noël Coward.

Telegram to Gertrude Lawrence on her marriage to Richard S. Aldrich

COWARDICE

See also self-preservation

1 Probably a fear we have of facing up to the real issues. Could you say we were guilty of Noël Cowardice?

Peter De Vries (1910–93) US novelist. *Comfort me with Apples*, Ch. 8

2 If you are scared to go to the brink, you are lost.

John Foster Dulles (1888–1959) US politician. *Life*, 16 Jan 1956

3 None but a coward dares to boast that he has never known fear.

Marshal Foch (1851–1929) French soldier. Attrib.

4 He led his regiment from behind
He found it less exciting.

W. S. Gilbert (1836–1911) British dramatist. *The Gondoliers*, I

5 When the foeman bares his steel,
Tarantara! tarantara!
We uncomfortable feel.

W. S. Gilbert *The Pirates of Penzance*, II

6 To a surprising extent the war-lords in shining armour, the apostles of the martial virtues, tend not to die fighting when the time comes. History is full of ignominious getaways by the great and famous.

George Orwell (Eric Blair; 1903–50) British novelist. *Who Are the War Criminals?*

7 The summer soldier and the sunshine patriot will, in this crisis, shrink from the service of their country.

Thomas Paine (1737–1809) British writer. *Pennsylvania Journal*, 'The American Crisis'

8 Thus conscience does make cowards of us all;
And thus the native hue of resolution
Is sicklied o'er with the pale cast of thought.

William Shakespeare (1564–1616) English dramatist. *Hamlet*, III:1

9 Some craven scruple
Of thinking too precisely on th' event.

William Shakespeare *Hamlet*, IV:4

10 I dare not fight; but I will wink and hold out mine iron.

William Shakespeare *Henry V*, II:1

11 Cowards die many times before their deaths:
The valiant never taste of death but once.

William Shakespeare *Julius Caesar*, II:2

COWPER, WILLIAM

(1731–1800) British poet. A lawyer and commissioner of bankrupts, his life was dogged by depression, bouts of insanity, and suicide attempts. His ballad *John Gilpin's Ride* (1783) and the long poem *The Task* (1785) established his reputation; he also translated Homer.

Quotations about Cowper

1 His taste lay in smiling, colloquial, good-natured humour; his melancholy was a black and diseased melancholy, not a grave and rich contemplativeness.

E. Brydges *Recollection of Foreign Travel*

2 That maniacal Calvinist and coddled poet.

Lord Byron (1788–1824) British poet. Attrib.

Quotations by Cowper

3 Regions Caesar never knew
Thy posterity shall sway,
Where his eagles never flew,
None invincible as they.

Boadicea

4 When the British warrior queen,
Bleeding from the Roman rods,
Sought, with an indignant mien,
Counsel of her country's gods.

Boadicea

5 Rome shall perish – write that word
In the blood that she has spilt.

Boadicea

6 We perish'd, each alone:
But I beneath a rougher sea,
And whelm'd in deeper gulphs than he.

The Castaway

7 He found it inconvenient to be poor.

Charity

8 Absence from whom we love is worse than death.

'Hope, like the Short-lived Ray'

9 John Gilpin was a citizen
Of credit and renown,
A train-band captain eke was he
Of famous London town.

John Gilpin

10 To-morrow is our wedding-day,
And we will then repair
Unto the Bell at Edmonton,
All in a chaise and pair.

John Gilpin

11 Now let us sing, Long live the king,
And Gilpin, long live he;
And when he next doth ride abroad,
May I be there to see!

John Gilpin

12 My hat and wig will soon be here,
They are upon the road.

John Gilpin

13 Says John, It is my wedding-day,
And all the world would stare,
If wife should dine at Edmonton,
And I should dine at Ware.

John Gilpin

14 What peaceful hours I once enjoyed!
How sweet their memory still!
But they have left an aching void
The world can never fill.

Olney Hymns, 1

15 Prayer makes the Christian's armour bright;
And Satan trembles when he sees
The weakest saint upon his knees.
Olney Hymns, 29

16 I seem forsaken and alone,
I hear the lion roar;
And every door is shut but one,
And that is Mercy's door.
Olney Hymns, 33

17 God moves in a mysterious way
His wonders to perform;
He plants his footsteps in the sea,
And rides upon the storm.
Olney Hymns, 35

18 The bud may have a bitter taste,
But sweet will be the flower.
Olney Hymns, 35

19 The poplars are felled, farewell to the shade,
And the whispering sound of the cool colonnade!
The Poplar Field

20 Mortals, whose pleasures are their only care,
First wish to be imposed on, and then are.
The Progress of Error

21 For 'tis a truth well known to most,
That whatsoever thing is lost –
We seek it, ere it come to light,
In every cranny but the right.
The Retired Cat

22 God made the country, and man made the town.
The Task

23 England, with all thy faults, I love thee still,
My country.
The Task

24 Variety's the very spice of life
That gives it all its flavour.
The Task

25 While the bubbling and loud-hissing urn
Throws up a steamy column, and the cups,
That cheer but not inebriate, wait on each,
So let us welcome peaceful evening in.
The Task

26 Nature is but a name for an effect
Whose cause is God.
The Task

27 Oh for a lodge in some vast wilderness,
Some boundless contiguity of shade,
Where rumour of oppression and deceit,
Of unsuccessful or successful war,
Might never reach me more!
The Task

28 Mountains interposed
Make enemies of nations, who had else,
Like kindred drops, been mingled into one.
The Task

29 Slaves cannot breathe in England; if their lungs
Receive our air, that moment they are free;
They touch our country, and their shackles fall.
A situation resulting from a judicial decision in 1772. *The Task*

30 Riches have wings, and grandeur is a dream.
The Task

31 Detested sport,
That owes its pleasures to another's pain.
The Task

32 Knowledge dwells
In heads replete with thoughts of other men;
Wisdom in minds attentive to their own.
The Task

33 Society, friendship, and love,
Divinely bestowed upon man,
Oh, had I the wings of a dove,
How soon would I taste you again!
Verses supposed to be written by Alexander Selkirk

34 I am monarch of all I survey,
My right there is none to dispute;
From the centre all round to the sea
I am lord of the fowl and the brute.
Oh, solitude! where are the charms
That sages have seen in thy face?
Better dwell in the midst of alarms,
Than reign in this horrible place.
Verses supposed to be written by Alexander Selkirk

CREATION

1 The Hand that made us is divine.
Joseph Addison (1672–1719) British essayist. *The Spectator*, 465

2 In the beginning God created the heaven and the earth.
And the earth was without form, and void; and darkness was upon the face of the deep. And the Spirit of God moved upon the face of the waters.
And God said, Let there be light: and there was light.
And God saw the light, that it was good: and God divided the light from the darkness.
And God called the light Day, and the darkness he called Night. And the evening and the morning were the first day.
Bible: Genesis 1:1–5

3 And God called the dry land Earth; and the gathering together of the waters called he Seas: and God saw that it was good.
And God said, Let the earth bring forth grass, the herb yielding seed, and the fruit tree yielding fruit after his kind, whose seed is in itself, upon the earth: and it was so.
Bible: Genesis 1:10–11

4 And God made two great lights: the greater light to rule the day, and the lesser light to rule the night: he made the stars also.
Bible: Genesis 1:16

5 And God said, Let the earth bring forth the living creature after his kind, cattle, and creeping thing, and beast of the earth after his kind: and it was so.
Bible: Genesis 1:24

6 And God said, Let us make man in our image, after our likeness: and let them have dominion over

the fish of the sea, and over the fowl of the air, and over the cattle, and over all the earth, and over every creeping thing that creepeth upon the earth.
So God created man in his own image, in the image of God created he him; male and female created he them.
And God blessed them, and God said unto them, Be fruitful, and multiply, and replenish the earth, and subdue it: and have dominion over the fish of the sea, and over the fowl of the air, and over every living thing that moveth upon the earth.

Bible: Genesis 1:26–28

7 When the stars threw down their spears,
And watered heaven with their tears,
Did he smile his work to see?
Did he who made the Lamb make thee?

William Blake (1757–1827) British poet. *Songs of Experience*, 'The Tiger'

8 Little Lamb, who made thee?
Dost thou know who made thee?

William Blake *Songs of Innocence*, 'The Lamb'

9 Whan that the month in which the world bigan,
That highte March, whan God first maked man.

Geoffrey Chaucer (c. 1342–1400) English poet. *The Canterbury Tales*, 'The Nun's Priest's Tale'

10 'Who *is* the Potter, pray, and who the Pot?'

Edward Fitzgerald (1809–83) British poet. *The Rubáiyát of Omar Khayyám*

11 It took the whole of Creation
To produce my foot, my each feather:
Now I hold creation in my foot.

Ted Hughes (1930–) British poet. *Hawk Roosting*

12 I cannot forgive Descartes; in all his philosophy he did his best to dispense with God. But he could not avoid making Him set the world in motion with a flip of His thumb; after that he had no more use for God.

Blaise Pascal (1623–62) French philosopher and mathematician. *Pensées*, II

13 For suddenly it was clear to me that virtue in the creator is not the same as virtue in the creature. For the creator, if he should love his creature, would be loving only a part of himself; but the creature, praising the creator, praises an infinity beyond himself.

Olaf Stapledon (1886–1950) British philosopher and science-fiction writer. *Star Maker*, Ch. 13

14 'Do you know who made you?' 'Nobody, as I knows on,' said the child, with a short laugh… 'I 'spect I grow'd.'

Harriet Beecher Stowe (1811–96) US novelist. *Uncle Tom's Cabin*, Ch. 20

15 Which beginning of time according to our Chronologie, fell upon the entrance of the night preceding the twenty third day of *Octob.*, in the year of the Julian Calendar, 710.

James Ussher (1581–1656) Irish churchman. Referring to the Creation, as described in Genesis, which, he had calculated, took place on 22 Oct 4004 BC. *The Annals of the World*

16 God made everything out of nothing. But the nothingness shows through.

Paul Valéry (1871–1945) French poet and writer. *Mauvaises Pensées et autres*

17 The art of creation
is older than the art of killing.

Andrei Voznesensky (1933–) Russian poet. *Poem with a Footnote*

CRICKET

See also sport and games

1 It's not in support of cricket but as an earnest protest against golf.

Max Beerbohm (1872–1956) British writer. Said when giving a shilling towards W. G. Grace's testimonial. *Carr's Dictionary of Extraordinary English Cricketers*

2 I do love cricket – it's so very English.

Sarah Bernhardt (Sarah Henriette Rosine Bernard; 1844–1923) French actress. On seeing a game of football. *Nijinsky* (R. Buckle)

3 They came to see me bat not to see you bowl.

W. G. Grace (1848–1915) British doctor and cricketer. Refusing to leave the crease after being bowled first ball in front of a large crowd. Attrib.

4 It's more than a game. It's an institution.

Thomas Hughes (1822–96) British novelist. Referring to cricket. *Tom Brown's Schooldays*, Pt. II, Ch. 7

5 If anyone in the side needs a shoulder to cry on in the dressing room then they shouldn't be playing for England.

Ray Illingworth (1932–) British cricketer; chairman of the English cricket team selectors. *The Observer*, 'Sayings of the Week', 12 June 1994

6 I've always wanted to be one of the top cricketers in the world and I wouldn't want to be in any other situation. I've worked hard and given myself to the game, and this is the result.

Brian Lara (1970–) Trinidadian cricketer. Arriving at Edgbaston, to play for Warwickshire. *The Independent*, 28 Apr 1994

7 I've proved it's not just a gentleman's game. I was born in Yorkshire and I'm available if they want me.

Kathryn Leng England under-19 women's cricket captain. *The Times*, 30 Dec 1993

8 There's a breathless hush in the Close tonight –
Ten to make and the match to win –
A bumping pitch and a blinding light,
An hour to play and the last man in.

Henry John Newbolt (1862–1938) British poet. *Vitaï Lampada*

9 I tend to believe that cricket is the greatest thing that God ever created on earth…certainly greater than sex, although sex isn't too bad either.

Harold Pinter (1930–) British dramatist. *The Observer*, 5 Oct 1980

10 We are honoured when we pull on our shirts to play for England. It costs us a lot of money to play top class women's cricket. Men have things easier and if you have things easier you are not used to setbacks.

Karen Smithies Captain of the England women's cricket team. On why the women's team was more successful than the men's. *The Times*, 3 May 1994

11 I have always looked upon cricket as organised loafing.

William Temple (1881–1944) British churchman. Address to parents when headmaster of Repton School

12 If the French noblesse had been capable of playing cricket with their peasants, their chateaux would never have been burnt.

George Macaulay Trevelyan (1876–1962) British historian. *English Social History*, Ch. XIII

13 It requires one to assume such indecent postures.

Oscar Wilde (1854–1900) Irish-born British dramatist. Explaining why he did not play cricket. Attrib.

CRIME

See also murder, theft

1 And surely your blood of your lives will I require; at the hand of every beast will I require it, and at the hand of man; at the hand of every man's brother will I require the life of man.
Whoso sheddeth man's blood, by man shall his blood be shed: for in the image of God made he man.

Bible: Genesis 9:5–6

2 How many crimes committed merely because their authors could not endure being wrong!

Albert Camus (1913–60) French existentialist writer. *The Fall*

3 Thieves respect property; they merely wish the property to become their property that they may more perfectly respect it.

G. K. Chesterton (1874–1936) British writer. Attrib.

4 He is the Napoleon of crime.

Arthur Conan Doyle (1856–1930) British writer. Referring to Professor Moriarty. *The Final Problem*

5 A burglar who respects his art always takes his time before taking anything else.

O. Henry (1862–1910) US writer. *Makes the Whole World Kin*

6 If poverty is the mother of crime, stupidity is its father.

Jean de La Bruyère (1645–96) French satirist. *Les Caractères*

7 Crime, like virtue, has its degrees.

Jean Racine (1639–99) French dramatist. *Phèdre*, IV:2

8 A man who has never gone to school may steal from a freight car, but if he has a university education he may steal the whole railroad.

Franklin D. Roosevelt (1882–1945) US Democratic president. Attrib.

9 We're barking mad about crime in this country. We have an obsession with believing the worst, conning ourselves that there was a golden age – typically 40 years before the one we're living in.

Nick Ross (1947–) British broadcaster. *Radio Times*, 26 June–2 July 1993

10 I came to the conclusion many years ago that almost all crime is due to the repressed desire for aesthetic expression.

Evelyn Waugh (1903–66) British novelist. *Decline and Fall*, Pt. III, Ch. 1

CRITICISM

See also actors, compliments, insults, poets, writers

1 As a contribution to natural history, the work is negligible.

Anonymous Review of Kenneth Grahame's *The Wind in the Willows* in *The Times Literary Supplement*. *The Life of Kenneth Grahame* (Green)

2 I am bound by my own definition of criticism: a disinterested endeavour to learn and propagate the best that is known and thought in the world.

Matthew Arnold (1822–88) British poet and critic. *Essays in Criticism*, First Series, 'Functions of Criticism at the Present Time'

3 There is less in this than meets the eye.

Tallulah Bankhead (1903–68) US actress. Referring to a revival of a play by Maeterlinck. *Shouts and Murmurs* (A. Woollcott), 'Capsule Criticism'

4 Too much counterpoint; what is worse, Protestant counterpoint.

Thomas Beecham (1879–1961) British conductor. Said of J. S. Bach. *The Guardian*, 8 Mar 1971

5 The musical equivalent of the towers of St Pancras station – neo-Gothic, you know.

Thomas Beecham Referring to Elgar's A Flat Symphony. *Sir Thomas Beecham* (N. Cardus)

6 What can you do with it? – it's like a lot of yaks jumping about.

Thomas Beecham Referring to Beethoven's 7th Symphony. *Beecham Stories* (H. Atkins and A. Newman)

7 I will try to account for the degree of my aesthetic emotion. That, I conceive, is the function of the critic.

Clive Bell (1881–1964) British art critic. *Art*, Pt. II, Ch. 3

8 Of all fatiguing, futile, empty trades, the worst, I suppose, is writing about writing.

Hilaire Belloc (1870–1953) French-born British poet. *The Silence of the Sea*

9 See Hebrews 13:8.

Robert Benchley (1889–1945) US humorist. Criticism of a long-running play; the text is: 'Jesus Christ the same yesterday, and today, and for ever'. Attrib.

10 And why beholdest thou the mote that is in thy brother's eye, but considerest not the beam that is in thine own eye?

Bible: Matthew 7:3

11 Tallulah Bankhead barged down the Nile last night and sank. As the Serpent of the Nile she proves to be no more dangerous than a garter snake.

John Mason Brown (1900–69) US critic. Referring to her performance as Shakespeare's Cleopatra. *Current Biography*

12 He who discommendeth others obliquely commendeth himself.

Thomas Browne (1605–82) English physician and writer. *Christian Morals*, Pt. I

13 A great deal of contemporary criticism reads to me like a man saying: 'Of course I do not like green cheese: I am very fond of brown sherry.'

G. K. Chesterton (1874–1936) British writer. *All I Survey*

14 To see him act, is like reading Shakespeare by flashes of lightning.

Samuel Taylor Coleridge (1772–1834) British poet. Referring to Kean. *Table Talk*

15 I never realized before that Albert married beneath him.

Noël Coward (1899–1973) British dramatist. After seeing a certain actress in the role of Queen Victoria. *Tynan on Theatre* (K. Tynan)

16 Two things should be cut: the second act and the child's throat.

Noël Coward Referring to a play featuring a child actor. *The Wit of Noël Coward* (D. Richards)

17 This paper will no doubt be found interesting by those who take an interest in it.

John Dalton (1766–1844) British scientist. Said on many occasions when chairing scientific meetings. Attrib.

18 If you hear that someone is speaking ill of you, instead of trying to defend yourself you should say: 'He obviously does not know me very well, since there are so many other faults he could have mentioned'.

Epictetus (c. 60–110 AD) Stoic philosopher. *Enchiridion*

19 He played the King as though under momentary apprehension that someone else was about to play the ace.

Eugene Field (1850–95) US poet and journalist. Referring to Creston Clarke's performance in the role of King Lear. Attrib.

20 It is not good enough to spend time and ink in describing the penultimate sensations and physical movements of people getting into a state of rut, we all know them too well.

John Galsworthy (1867–1933) British novelist. Referring to D. H. Lawrence's *Sons and Lovers*. Letter to Edward Garnett, 13 Apr 1914

21 Funny without being vulgar.

W. S. Gilbert (1836–1911) British dramatist. Referring to Sir Henry Irving's *Hamlet*. Attrib.

22 My dear chap! Good isn't the word!

W. S. Gilbert Speaking to an actor after he had given a poor performance. Attrib.

23 We were as nearly bored as enthusiasm would permit.

Edmund Gosse (1849–1928) British writer and critic. Referring to a play by Swinburne. *Biography of Edward Marsh* (C. Hassall)

24 There are two things which I am confident I can do very well: one is an introduction to any literary work, stating what it is to contain, and how it should be executed in the most perfect manner; the other is a conclusion, shewing from various causes why the execution has not been equal to what the author promised to himself and to the public.

Samuel Johnson (1709–84) British lexicographer. *Life of Johnson* (J. Boswell), Vol. I

25 It is burning a farthing candle at Dover, to shew light at Calais.

Samuel Johnson Referring to the impact of Sheridan's works upon the English language. *Life of Johnson* (J. Boswell), Vol. I

26 You *may* abuse a tragedy, though you cannot write one. You may scold a carpenter who has made you a bad table, though you cannot make a table. It is not your trade to make tables.

Samuel Johnson Referring to the qualifications needed to indulge in literary criticism. *Life of Johnson* (J. Boswell), Vol. I

27 This man I thought had been a Lord among wits; but, I find, he is only a wit among Lords.

Samuel Johnson Referring to Lord Chesterfield. *Life of Johnson* (J. Boswell), Vol. I

28 They teach the morals of a whore, and the manners of a dancing master.

Samuel Johnson Referring to Lord Chesterfield's *Letters*. *Life of Johnson* (J. Boswell), Vol. I

29 Yes, Sir, many men, many women, and many children.

Samuel Johnson When asked by Dr Blair whether any man of their own time could have written the poems of Ossian. *Life of Johnson* (J. Boswell), Vol. I

30 Difficult do you call it, Sir? I wish it were impossible.

Samuel Johnson On hearing a famous violinist. *Johnsonian Miscellanies* (ed. G. B. Hill), Vol. II

31 They are forced plants, raised in a hot-bed; and they are poor plants; they are but cucumbers after all.

Samuel Johnson Referring to Gray's *Odes*. *Life of Johnson* (J. Boswell), Vol. IV

32 The pleasure of criticizing robs us of the pleasure of being moved by some very fine things.

Jean de La Bruyère (1645–96) French satirist. *Les Caractères*

33 They are great parables, the novels, but false art. They are only parables. All the people are *fallen angels* – even the dirtiest scrubs. This I cannot stomach. People are not fallen angels, they are merely people.

D. H. Lawrence (1885–1930) British novelist. Referring to the novels of Dostoyevsky. Letter to J. Middleton Murry and Katherine Mansfield, 17 Feb 1916

34 Nothing but old fags and cabbage-stumps of quotations from the Bible and the rest, stewed in the juice of deliberate, journalistic dirty-mindedness.

D. H. Lawrence Referring to James Joyce. Letter to Aldous Huxley, 15 Aug 1928

35 His verse exhibits…something that is rather like Keats's vulgarity with a Public School accent.

F. R. Leavis (1895–1978) British literary critic. Referring to Rupert Brooke. *New Bearings in English Poetry*, Ch. 2

36 I cried all the way to the bank.

Liberace (Wladzin Valentino Liberace; 1919–87) US pianist and showman. Said when asked whether he minded being criticized. *Liberace: An Autobiography*, Ch. 2

37 People who like this sort of thing will find this is the sort of thing they like.

Abraham Lincoln (1809–65) US statesman. A comment on a book. Attrib.

38 His writing bears the same relation to poetry which a Turkey carpet bears to a picture. There are colours in the Turkey carpet out of which a picture might be made. There are words in Mr Montgomery's writing which, when disposed in certain orders and combinations, have made, and will make again, good poetry. But, as they now stand, they seem to be put together on principle in such a manner as to give no image of anything 'in the heavens above, or in the earth beneath, or in the waters under the earth'.

Lord Macaulay (1800–59) British historian. *Literary Essays Contributed to the 'Edinburgh Review'*, 'Mr. Robert Montgomery's Poems'

39 His imagination resembled the wings of an ostrich. It enabled him to run, though not to soar.

Lord Macaulay *Essays and Biographies*, 'John Dryden'

40 It was a book to kill time for those who like it better dead.

Rose Macaulay (1889–1958) British writer. Attrib.

41 I was so long writing my review that I never got around to reading the book.

Groucho Marx (Julius Marx; 1895–1977) US comedian. Attrib.

42 People ask you for criticism, but they only want praise.

W. Somerset Maugham (1874–1965) British novelist. *Of Human Bondage*, Ch. 50

43 I could eat alphabet soup and *shit* better lyrics.

Johnny Mercer (1909–76) US lyricist and composer. Describing a British musical. Attrib.

44 There are passages in *Ulysses* which can be read only in the toilet – if one wants to extract the full flavor of their content.

Henry Miller (1891–1980) US novelist. *Black Spring*

45 Yea, marry, now it is somewhat, for now it is rhyme; before, it was neither rhyme nor reason.

Thomas More (1478–1535) English lawyer and scholar. On reading an unremarkable book recently rendered into verse by a friend of his. *Apophthegms* (Bacon), 287

46 Prolonged, indiscriminate reviewing of books involves constantly *inventing* reactions towards books about which one has no spontaneous feelings whatever.

George Orwell (Eric Blair; 1903–50) British novelist. *Confessions of a Book Reviewer*

47 Mr Blunden is no more able to resist a quotation than some people are to refuse a drink.

George Orwell Reviewing a book by Edmund Blunden. *Manchester Evening News*, 20 Apr 1944

48 She ran the whole gamut of the emotions from A to B.

Dorothy Parker (1893–1967) US writer. Referring to a performance by Katharine Hepburn on Broadway. Attrib.

49 This is not a novel to be tossed aside lightly. It should be thrown with great force.

Dorothy Parker Book review. *Wit's End* (R. E. Dremman)

50 'Tis hard to say, if greater want of skill
Appear in writing or in judging ill.

Alexander Pope (1688–1744) British poet. *An Essay on Criticism*

51 Damn with faint praise, assent with civil leer,
And, without sneering, teach the rest to sneer.

Alexander Pope *Epistle to Dr. Arbuthnot*

52 I never read anything concerning my work. I feel that criticism is a letter to the public which the author, since it is not directed to him, does not have to open and read.

Rainer Maria Rilke (1875–1926) Austrian poet. *Letters*

53 Very good, but it has its *longueurs*.

Antoine de Rivarol (1753–1801) French writer and wit. Giving his opinion of a couplet by a mediocre poet. *Das Buch des Lachens* (W. Scholz)

54 The Stealthy School of Criticism.

Dante Gabriel Rossetti (1828–82) British painter and poet. Letter to the *Athenaeum*, 1871

55 Wagner has lovely moments but awful quarters of an hour.

Gioacchino Rossini (1792–1868) Italian operatic composer. Remark made to Emile Naumann, April 1867. *Italienische Tondichter* (Naumann)

56 I have seen, and heard, much of Cockney impudence before now; but never expected to hear a coxcomb ask two hundred guineas for flinging a pot of paint in the public's face.

John Ruskin (1819–1900) British art critic and writer. On Whistler's painting 'Nocturne in Black and Gold'. Letter, 18 June 1877

57 For I am nothing if not critical.

William Shakespeare (1564–1616) English dramatist. *Othello*, II:1

58 It does not follow…that the right to criticize Shakespeare involves the power of writing better plays. And in fact…I do not profess to write better plays.

George Bernard Shaw (1856–1950) Irish dramatist and critic. *Three Plays for Puritans*, Preface

59 It is disappointing to report that George Bernard Shaw appearing as George Bernard Shaw is sadly miscast in the part. Satirists should be heard and not seen.

Robert E. Sherwood (1896–1955) US writer and dramatist. Reviewing a Shaw play

60 It had only one fault. It was kind of lousy.

James Thurber (1894–1961) US humorist. Remark made about a play. Attrib.

61 A strange, horrible business, but I suppose good enough for Shakespeare's day.

Victoria (1819–1901) Queen of the United Kingdom. Giving her opinion of *King Lear*. *Living Biographies of Famous Rulers* (H. Thomas)

62 I do not think this poem will reach its destination.

Voltaire (François-Marie Arouet; 1694–1778) French writer. Reviewing Rousseau's poem 'Ode to Posterity'. Attrib.

63 As far as criticism is concerned, we don't resent that unless it is absolutely biased, as it is in most cases.

John Vorster (Balthazar Johannes Vorster; 1915–83) South African politician. *The Observer*, 'Sayings of the Week', 9 Nov 1969

64 You have riches and freedom here but I feel no sense of faith or direction. You have so many computers, why don't you use them in the search for love?

Lech Walesa (1943–) Polish statesman. Speech, Dec 1988

65 My dear fellow a unique evening! I wouldn't have left a turn unstoned.

Arthur Wimperis (1874–1953) British screenwriter. Replying when asked his opinion of a vaudeville show. *Fifty Years of Vaudeville* (E. Short)

66 I saw it at a disadvantage – the curtain was up.

Walter Winchell (1879–1972) US journalist. Referring to a show starring Earl Carroll. *Come to Judgment* (A. Whiteman)

67 Trivial personalities decomposing in the eternity of print.

Virginia Woolf (1882–1941) British novelist. *The Common Reader*, 'Jane Eyre'

68 *Middlemarch*, the magnificent book which with all its imperfections is one of the few English novels for grown up people.

Virginia Woolf *The Common Reader*, 'George Eliot'

69 He is all blood, dirt and sucked sugar stick.

W. B. Yeats (1865–1939) Irish poet. Referring to Wilfred Owen. *Letters on Poetry to Dorothy Wellesley*, Letter, 21 Dec 1936

CRITICS

1 I will try to account for the degree of my aesthetic emotion. That, I conceive, is the function of the critic.

Clive Bell (1881–1964) British art critic. *Art*, Pt. II, Ch. 3

2 A man must serve his time to every trade
Save censure – critics all are ready made.

Lord Byron (1788–1824) British poet. *English Bards and Scotch Reviewers*

3 Reviewers are usually people who would have been poets, historians, biographers,...if they could; they have tried their talents at one or at the other, and have failed; therefore they turn critics.

Samuel Taylor Coleridge (1772–1834) British poet. *Lectures on Shakespeare and Milton*, I

4 I make my pictures for people, not for critics.

Cecil B. de Mille (1881–1959) US film producer and director. *Halliwell's Filmgoer's and Video Viewer's Companion*

5 A good critic is one who narrates the adventures of his mind among masterpieces.

Anatole France (Jacques Anatole François Thibault; 1844–1924) French writer. *The Literary Life*, Preface

6 I sometimes think
His critical judgement is so exquisite
It leaves us nothing to admire except his opinion.

Christopher Fry (1907–) British dramatist. *The Dark is Light Enough*, II

7 Asking a working writer what he thinks about critics is like asking a lamp-post how it feels about dogs.

Christopher Hampton (1946–) British writer and dramatist. *The Sunday Times Magazine*, 16 Oct 1977

8 What is a modern poet's fate?
To write his thoughts upon a slate;
The critic spits on what is done,
Gives it a wipe – and all is gone.

Thomas Hood (1799–1845) British poet. *Alfred Lord Tennyson, A Memoir* (Hallam Tennyson), Vol. II, Ch. 3

9 Critics are more malicious about poetry than about other books – maybe because so many manqué poets write reviews.

Elizabeth Jennings (1926–) British poet. Remark, Dec 1987

10 There is a certain race of men that either imagine it their duty, or make it their amusement, to hinder the reception of every work of learning or genius, who stand as sentinels in the avenues of fame, and value themselves upon giving Ignorance and Envy the first notice of a prey.

Samuel Johnson (1709–84) British lexicographer. *The Rambler*

11 A fly, Sir, may sting a stately horse and make him wince; but one is but an insect, and the other is a horse still.

Samuel Johnson *Life of Johnson* (J. Boswell), Vol. I

12 Dear Roger Fry whom I love as a man but detest as a movement.

Edward Howard Marsh (1872–1953) British civil servant and writer. Roger Fry (1866–1934) was an artist and art critic, who championed the postimpressionists. *Edward Marsh* (Christopher Hassall), Ch. 11

13 Insects sting, not from malice, but because they want to live. It is the same with critics – they desire our blood, not our pain.

Friedrich Wilhelm Nietzsche (1844–1900) German philosopher. *Miscellaneous Maxims and Reflections*

14 Nor in the critic let the man be lost.

Alexander Pope (1688–1744) British poet. *An Essay on Criticism*

15 They will review a book by a writer much older than themselves as if it were an over-ambitious essay by a second-year student...It is the little dons I complain about, like so many corgis trotting up, hoping to nip your ankles.

J. B. Priestley (1894–1984) British novelist. *Outcries and Asides*

16 The greater part of critics are parasites, who, if nothing had been written, would find nothing to write.

J. B. Priestley *Outcries and Asides*

17 Pay no attention to what the critics say; no statue has ever been put up to a critic.

Jean Sibelius (1865–1957) Finnish composer. Attrib.

18 I never read a book before reviewing it; it prejudices a man so.

Sydney Smith (1771–1845) British clergyman and essayist. *The Smith of Smiths* (H. Pearson), Ch. 3

19 I doubt that art needed Ruskin any more than a moving train needs one of its passengers to shove it.

Tom Stoppard (1937–) Czech-born British dramatist. *Times Literary Supplement*, 3 June 1977

20 I had another dream the other day about music critics. They were small and rodent-like with padlocked ears, as if they had stepped out of a painting by Goya.

Igor Stravinsky (1882–1971) Russian-born US composer. *The Evening Standard*, 29 Oct 1969

21 A whipper-snapper of criticism who quoted dead languages to hide his ignorance of life.

Herbert Beerbohm Tree (1853–1917) British actor and theatre manager. Referring to A. B. Walkley. *Beerbohm Tree* (Hesketh Pearson)

22 A critic is a man who knows the way but can't drive the car.

Kenneth Tynan (1927–80) British theatre critic. *New York Times Magazine*, 9 Jan 1966

23 A good drama critic is one who perceives what is happening in the theatre of his time. A great drama critic also perceives what is not happening.

Kenneth Tynan *Tynan Right and Left*, Foreword

CROMWELL, OLIVER

(1599–1658) English soldier and statesman. As a leader of the parliamentary army, he was largely responsible for Charles I's defeat in the Civil War. After the king's execution, as Lord Protector of England (1653–58), he failed to find a constitutional basis for ruling the country.

Quotations about Cromwell

1 Cromwell was a man in whom ambition had not wholly suppressed, but only suspended, the sentiments of religion.

Edmund Burke (1729–97) British politician. Letter, 1791

2 He will be looked upon by posterity as a brave, bad man.

Earl of Clarendon *History of the rebellion* 1704

3 Whilst he was cautious of his own words, (not putting forth too many lest they should betray his thoughts) he made others talk until he had, as it were, sifted them, and known their most intimate designs.

Sir William Waller *Recollections*

Quotations by Cromwell

4 Mr Lely, I desire you would use all your skill to paint my picture truly like me, and not flatter me at all; but remark all these roughnesses, pimples, warts, and everything as you see me, otherwise I will never pay a farthing for it.

The origin of the expression 'warts and all'. *Anecdotes of Painting* (Horace Walpole), Ch. 12

5 I beseech you, in the bowels of Christ, think it possible you may be mistaken.

Letter to the General Assembly of the Church of Scotland, 3 Aug 1650

6 What shall we do with this bauble? There, take it away.

Speech dismissing Parliament, 20 Apr 1653

7 It is not fit that you should sit here any longer!...you shall now give place to better men.

Speech to the Rump Parliament, 22 Jan 1655

8 The State, in choosing men to serve it, takes no notice of their opinions. If they be willing faithfully to serve it, that satisfies.

Said before the Battle of Marston Moor, 2 July 1644

9 The people would be just as noisy if they were going to see me hanged.

Referring to a cheering crowd.

CRUELTY

See also hurt, nastiness, violence

1 The wish to hurt, the momentary intoxication with pain, is the loophole through which the pervert climbs into the minds of ordinary men.

Jacob Bronowski (1908–74) British scientist and writer. *The Face of Violence*, Ch. 5

2 Man's inhumanity to man
Makes countless thousands mourn!

Robert Burns (1759–96) Scottish poet. *Man was Made to Mourn*

3 Fear is the parent of cruelty.

J. A. Froude (1818–94) British historian. *Short Studies on Great Subjects*, 'Party Politics'

4 A cruel story runs on wheels, and every hand oils the wheels as they run.

Ouida (Marie Louise de la Ramée; 1839–1908) British novelist. *Wisdom, Wit and Pathos*, 'Moths'

5 I must be cruel only to be kind.

William Shakespeare (1564–1616) English dramatist. *Hamlet*, III:4

6 Whipping and abuse are like laudanum: You have to double the dose as the sensibilities decline.

Harriet Beecher Stowe (1811–96) US novelist. *Uncle Tom's Cabin*, Ch. 20

CULTURE

See also civilization, philistinism

1 Culture, the acquainting ourselves with the best that has been known and said in the world, and thus with the history of the human spirit.

Matthew Arnold (1822–88) British poet and critic. *Literature and Dogma*, Preface

2 Culture is the passion for sweetness and light, and (what is more) the passion for making them prevail.

Matthew Arnold *Literature and Dogma*, Preface

3 Culture is an instrument wielded by professors to manufacture professors, who when their turn comes will manufacture professors.

Simone Weil (1909–43) French philosopher. *The Need for Roots*

4 Mrs Ballinger is one of the ladies who pursue Culture in bands, as though it were dangerous to meet it alone.

Edith Wharton (1862–1937) US novelist. *Xingu*, Ch. 1

CUMMINGS, E. E.

(1894–1962) US poet. His verse relied to some extent on typographical devices. Collections include *Tulips and Chimneys* (1923) and *Eimi* (1933).

1 who knows if the moon's
a balloon, coming out of a keen city
in the sky – filled with pretty people?

Used for the title and epigraph of David Niven's first volume of autobiography, *The Moon's a Balloon*, about his experiences in the film industry. &

2 anyone lived in a pretty how town
(with up so floating many bells down)
spring summer autumn winter
he sang his didn't he danced his did.

anyone lived in a pretty how town

3 Jesus
he was a handsome man
and what i want to know is
how do you like your blueeyed boy
Mister Death

Buffalo Bill's

4 a pretty girl who naked is
is worth a million statues

Collected Poems, 133

5 i remember we all cried like the Missouri
when my Uncle Sol's coffin lurched because
somebody pressed a button
(and down went
my Uncle
Sol

and started a worm farm)

nobody loses all the time

6 a politician is an arse upon which everyone has sat except a man

1 × 1

CURIE, MARIE

(1867–1934) Polish chemist, who emigrated to France in 1891 and pioneered research into radioactivity. With her husband Pierre Curie she also discovered radium and polonium; she won the Nobel Prize in 1903 and 1911.

Quotations about Marie Curie

1 Women cannot be part of the Institute of France.

Emile Hilaire Amagat (1841–1915) French physicist. Comment following the rejection of Marie Curie by the Académie des Sciences, for which she had been nominated in 1910. She was rejected by one vote, and refused to allow her name to be submitted again or, for ten years, to allow her work to be published by the Académie.

2 Marie Curie is, of all celebrated beings, the only one whom fame has not corrupted.

Albert Einstein (1879–1955) German-born US physicist. *Madame Curie* (Eve Curie)

3 That one must do some work seriously and must be independent and not merely amuse oneself in life – this our mother has told us always, but never that science was the only career worth following.

Irene Joliot-Curie (1897–1956) French scientist. Recalling the advice of her mother, Marie Curie *A Long Way from Missouri* (Mary Margaret McBride), Ch. 10.

Quotations by Marie Curie

4 After all, science is essentially international, and it is only through lack of the historical sense that national qualities have been attributed to it.

Memorandum, 'Intellectual Co-operation'

5 All my life through, the new sights of Nature made me rejoice like a child.

Pierre Curie

6 I have no dress except the one I wear every day. If you are going to be kind enough to give me one, please let it be practical and dark so that I can put it on afterwards to go to the laboratory.

Referring to a wedding dress. Letter to a friend, 1849

7 One never notices what has been done; one can only see what remains to be done....

Letter to her brother, 18 Mar 1894

CURIOSITY

See also interfering, wonder

1 Ask no questions and hear no lies.

Proverb

2 Curiosity killed the cat.

Proverb

3 Be not curious in unnecessary matters: for more things are shewed unto thee than men understand.

Bible: Ecclesiasticus 3:23

4 'If everybody minded their own business,' the Duchess said in a hoarse growl, 'the world would go round a deal faster than it does.'

Lewis Carroll (Charles Lutwidge Dodgson; 1832–98) British writer. *Alice's Adventures in Wonderland*, Ch. 6

5 There is no such thing on earth as an uninteresting subject; the only thing that can exist is an uninterested person.

G. K. Chesterton (1874–1936) British writer. *Heretics*, Ch. 1

6 The world is but a school of inquiry.

Michel de Montaigne (1533–92) French essayist. *Essais*, III

7 I ofen looked up at the sky an' assed meself the question – what is the stars, what is the stars?

Sean O'Casey (1884–1964) Irish dramatist. *Juno and the Paycock*, I

8 Curiosity will conquer fear even more than bravery will.

James Stephens (1882–1950) Irish novelist. *The Crock of Gold*

9 Disinterested intellectual curiosity is the life blood of real civilisation.

George Macaulay Trevelyan (1876–1962) British historian. *English Social History*, Preface

CURSES

1 Then said his wife unto him, Dost thou still retain thine integrity? curse God, and die.

Bible: Job 2:9

2 A plague o' both your houses!
They have made worms' meat of me.

William Shakespeare (1564–1616) English dramatist. *Romeo and Juliet*, III:1

3 Curses are like young chickens, they always come home to roost.

Robert Southey (1774–1843) British poet. *The Curse of Kehama*, Motto

4 'The curse is come upon me,' cried
The Lady of Shalott.

Alfred, Lord Tennyson (1809–92) British poet. *The Lady of Shalott*, Pt. III

5 She has heard a whisper say,
A curse is on her if she stay
To look down to Camelot.

Alfred, Lord Tennyson *The Lady of Shalott*, Pt. II

CUSTOM

See also habit

1 *O tempora! O mores!*
What times! What customs!

Cicero (106–43 BC) Roman orator and statesman. *In Catilinam*, I

2 Custom, then, is the great guide of human life.

David Hume (1711–76) Scottish philosopher. *An Enquiry Concerning Human Understanding*

3 Custom calls me to't.
What custom wills, in all things should we do't,
The dust on antique time would lie unswept,
And mountainous error be too highly heap'd
For truth to o'erpeer.

William Shakespeare (1564–1616) English dramatist. *Coriolanus*, II:3

4 But to my mind, though I am native here
And to the manner born, it is a custom
More honour'd in the breach than the observance.

William Shakespeare *Hamlet*, I:4

CYNICISM

1 One is not superior merely because one sees the world in an odious light.

Vicomte de Chateaubriand (1768–1848) French diplomat and writer. Attrib.

2 Cynicism is an unpleasant way of saying the truth.

Lillian Hellman (1905–84) US dramatist. *The Little Foxes*, I

3 A cynic is a man who, when he smells flowers, looks around for a coffin.

H. L. Mencken (1880–1956) US journalist. Attrib.

4 Cynicism is humour in ill-health.

H. G. Wells (1866–1946) British writer. *Short Stories*, 'The Last Trump'

5 A man who knows the price of everything and the value of nothing.

Oscar Wilde (1854–1900) Irish-born British dramatist. A cynic. *Lady Windermere's Fan*, III

D

DAMNATION

See also devil, hell

1 Blot out his name, then, record one lost soul more,
One task more declined, one more footpath untrod,
One more devils'-triumph and sorrow for angels,
One wrong more to man, one more insult to God!

Robert Browning (1812–89) British poet. *The Lost Leader*

2 You will be damned if you do – And you will be damned if you don't.

Lorenzo Dow (1777–1834) British churchman. Speaking of Calvinism. *Reflections on the Love of God*

3 Now hast thou but one bare hour to live,
And then thou must be damn'd perpetually!
Stand still, you ever-moving spheres of heaven,
That time may cease, and midnight never come.

Christopher Marlowe (1564–93) English dramatist. *Doctor Faustus*, V:2

4 Ugly hell, gape not! come not, Lucifer!
I'll burn my books!

Christopher Marlowe *Doctor Faustus*, V:2

DANCING

1 On with the dance! let joy be unconfined;
No sleep till morn, when Youth and Pleasure meet
To chase the glowing Hours with flying feet.

Lord Byron (1788–1824) British poet. *Childe Harold's Pilgrimage*, III

DANGER

1 Any port in a storm.

Proverb

2 If you play with fire you get burnt.

Proverb

3 Defend us from all perils and dangers of this night.

The Book of Common Prayer *Morning Prayer, Prayer of St Chrysostom*

4 Dangers by being despised grow great.

Edmund Burke (1729–97) British politician. Speech, House of Commons, 11 May 1792

5 Of course I realized there was a measure of danger. Obviously I faced the possibility of not returning when first I considered going. Once faced and settled there really wasn't any good reason to refer to it.

Amelia Earhart (1898–1937) US flyer. Referring to her flight in the 'Friendship'. *20 Hours: 40 Minutes – Our Flight in the Friendship*, Ch. 5

6 Believe me! The secret of reaping the greatest fruitfulness and the greatest enjoyment from life is to *live dangerously!*

Friedrich Wilhelm Nietzsche (1844–1900) German philosopher. *Die Fröhliche Wissenschaft*, Bk. IV

7 There's a snake hidden in the grass.

Virgil (Publius Vergilius Maro; 70–19 BC) Roman poet. *Eclogue*, Bk. III

DANTE ALIGHIERI

(1265–1321) Italian poet. Born into a Guelf family, he was involved in the political struggles of the time, which forced him to leave his native Florence; he finally settled in Ravenna. His major works include *La vita nuova* (c. 1292) and *The Divine Comedy* (1307).

1 Midway along the path of our life.

Divine Comedy, 'Inferno', I

2 Abandon all hope, all ye who enter here.

The inscription at the entrance to Hell. *Divine Comedy*, 'Inferno', III

3 There is no greater pain than to remember a happy time when one is in misery.

Divine Comedy, 'Inferno', V

4 The dear and kindly paternal image.

Divine Comedy, 'Inferno', XV

5 Pure and ready to mount to the stars.

Divine Comedy, 'Purgatorio', XXXIII

6 In His will is our peace.

Divine Comedy, 'Paradiso', III

7 The love that moves the sun and the other stars.

Divine Comedy, 'Paradiso', XXXIII

DARWIN, CHARLES

(1809–82) British life scientist, who originated the theory of evolution based on natural selection. The publication of his *Origin of Species by Means of Natural Selection* (1859) caused great controversy because it conflicted with the biblical account of creation. In *The Descent of Man* (1871), Darwin applied his theory to mankind.

Quotations about Darwin

1 I have no patience whatever with these gorilla damnifications of humanity.

Thomas Carlyle (1795–1881) Scottish historian and essayist. *Famous Sayings* (Edward Latham)

2 It is no secret that...there are many to whom Mr. Darwin's death is a wholly irreparable loss. And this not merely because of his wonderfully genial, simple, and generous nature; his cheerful and animated conversation, and the infinite variety and accuracy of his information; but because the more one knew of him, the more he seemed the incorporated ideal of a man of science.

T. H. Huxley (1825–95) British biologist. *Nature*, 1882

3 What Galileo and Newton were to the seventeenth century, Darwin was to the nineteenth.

Bertrand Russell (1872–1970) British philosopher. *History of Western Philosophy*

4 I never know whether to be more surprised at

Darwin himself for making so much of natural selection, or at his opponents for making so little of it.

Robert Louis Stevenson (1850–94) Scottish writer.

Quotations by Darwin

5 I have tried lately to read Shakespeare, and found it so intolerably dull that it nauseated me.

Autobiography

6 The highest possible stage in moral culture is when we recognize that we ought to control our thoughts.

Descent of Man, Ch. 4

7 We must, however, acknowledge, as it seems to me, that man with all his noble qualities, still bears in his bodily frame the indelible stamp of his lowly origin.

Closing words. *Descent of Man*, Ch. 21

8 I have called this principle, by which each slight variation, if useful, is preserved, by the term of Natural Selection.

Origin of Species, Ch. 3

9 We will now discuss in a little more detail the struggle for existence.

Origin of Species, Ch. 3

10 The expression often used by Mr Herbert Spencer of the Survival of the Fittest is more accurate, and is sometimes equally convenient.

Origin of Species, Ch. 3

DAY

1 Now the day is over,
Night is drawing nigh,
Shadows of the evening
Steal across the sky.

Sabine Baring-Gould (1834–1924) British author and hymn writer. *The Evening Hymn*

2 The day begins to droop, –
Its course is done:
But nothing tells the place
Of the setting sun.

Robert Bridges (1844–1930) British poet. *Winter Nightfall*

3 Where the quiet-coloured end of evening smiles,
Miles and miles.

Robert Browning (1812–89) British poet. *Love among the Ruins*, I

4 The day Thou gavest, Lord, is ended,
The darkness falls at Thy behest.

John Ellerton (1826–93) British churchman. *A Liturgy for Missionary Meetings*

5 Awake! for Morning in the Bowl of Night
Has flung the Stone that puts the Stars to Flight:
And Lo! the Hunter of the East has caught
The Sultan's Turret in a Noose of Light.

Edward Fitzgerald (1809–83) British poet. *The Rubáiyát of Omar Khayyám*

6 The Curfew tolls the knell of parting day,
The lowing herd winds slowly o'er the lea,
The plowman homeward plods his weary way,
And leaves the world to darkness and to me.

Thomas Gray (1716–71) British poet. *Elegy Written in a Country Churchyard*

7 Oh, what a beautiful morning!
Oh, what a beautiful day!

Oscar Hammerstein (1895–1960) US lyricist. From the musical *Oklahoma*. *Oh, What a Beautiful Morning*

8 Sweet day, so cool, so calm, so bright,
The bridal of the earth and sky.

George Herbert (1593–1633) English poet. *Virtue*

9 The candles burn their sockets,
The blinds let through the day,
The young man feels his pockets
And wonders what's to pay.

A. E. Housman (1859–1936) British scholar and poet. *Last Poems*, 'Eight O'Clock'

10 Under the opening eye-lids of the morn.

John Milton (1608–74) English poet. *Lycidas*

11 Now came still Evening on, and Twilight grey
Had in her sober livery all things clad.

John Milton *Paradise Lost*, Bk. IV

12 Midnight brought on the dusky hour
Friendliest to sleep and silence.

John Milton *Paradise Lost*, Bk. V

13 Three o'clock is always too late or too early for anything you want to do.

Jean-Paul Sartre (1905–80) French writer. *Nausea*

DEATH

See also afterlife, assassination, drowning, epitaphs, equality in death, execution, funerals, killing, last words, life and death, love and death, memorials, mortality, mourning, murder, obituaries, posterity, suicide

1 After death the doctor.

Proverb

2 A man can die but once.

Proverb

3 A piece of churchyard fits everybody.

Proverb

4 As soon as man is born he begins to die.

Proverb

5 Dead men tell no tales.

Proverb

6 Death defies the doctor.

Proverb

7 Death is the great leveller.

Proverb

8 Death is the poor man's best physician.

Proverb

9 Ever since dying came into fashion, life hasn't been safe.

Proverb

10 Fear of death is worse than death itself.

Proverb

11 Never speak ill of the dead.
Proverb

12 Nothing is certain but death and taxes.
Proverb

13 The good die young.
Proverb

14 The old man has his death before his eyes; the young man behind his back.
Proverb

15 There will be sleeping enough in the grave.
Proverb

16 It's not that I'm afraid to die. I just don't want to be there when it happens.
Woody Allen (Allen Stewart Konigsberg; 1935–) US film actor. *Without Feathers*, 'Death (A Play)'

17 Death is an acquired trait.
Woody Allen *Woody Allen and His Comedy* (E. Lax)

18 God grants an easy death only to the just.
Svetlana Alliluyeva (1926–) Russian writer; daughter of Joseph Stalin. *Twenty Letters to a Friend*

19 Death has got something to be said for it:
There's no need to get out of bed for it;
Wherever you may be,
They bring it to you, free.
Kingsley Amis (1922–) British writer. 'Delivery Guaranteed'

20 As Amr lay on his death-bed a friend said to him: 'You have often remarked that you would like to find an intelligent man at the point of death, and to ask him what his feelings were. Now I ask *you* that question. Amr replied, 'I feel as if heaven lay close upon the earth and I between the two, breathing through the eye of a needle.'
Amr Ibn Al-As (d. 664) Arab conqueror of Egypt. *The Harvest of a Quiet Eye* (Alan L. Mackay)

21 O Death, where is thy sting-a-ling-a-ling,
O Grave, thy victoree?
The bells of hell go ting-a-ling-a-ling
For you but not for me.
Anonymous Song of World War I

22 Swing low sweet chariot,
Comin' for to carry me home,
I looked over Jordan an' what did I see?
A band of Angels coming after me,
Comin' for to carry me home.
Anonymous *Swing Low, Sweet Chariot*

23 There is a dignity in dying that doctors should not dare to deny.
Anonymous

24 He's gone to join the majority.
Petronius Arbiter (1st century AD) Roman satirist. Referring to a dead man. *Satyricon: Cena Trimalchionis*, 42

25 Death must simply become the discreet but dignified exit of a peaceful person from a helpful society that is not torn, not even overly upset by the idea of a biological transition without significance, without pain or suffering, and ultimately without fear.
Philippe Ariès *The Hour of Our Death*

26 Now he is dead! Far hence he lies
In the lorn Syrian town;
And on his grave, with shining eyes,
The Syrian stars look down.
Matthew Arnold (1822–88) British poet and critic. *Obermann Once More*

27 I have often thought upon death, and I find it the least of all evils.
Francis Bacon (1561–1626) English philosopher. *An Essay on Death*

28 I do not believe that any man fears to be dead, but only the stroke of death.
Francis Bacon *An Essay on Death*

29 Men fear death, as children fear to go in the dark; and as that natural fear in children is increased with tales, so is the other.
Francis Bacon *Essays*, 'Of Death'

30 It is natural to die as to be born; and to a little infant, perhaps, the one is as painful as the other.
Francis Bacon *Essays*, 'Of Death'

31 To die will be an awfully big adventure.
J. M. Barrie (1860–1937) British novelist and dramatist. *Peter Pan*, III

32 Graveyards have a morbid reputation. Many people associate them with death.
Bishop of Bath and Wells (1935–) British churchman. Remark, Apr 1988

33 What I like about Clive
Is that he is no longer alive.
There is a great deal to be said
For being dead.
Edmund Clerihew Bentley (1875–1956) British writer. *Biography for Beginners*

34 The physician cutteth off a long disease; and he that is today a king tomorrow shall die.
Bible: Ecclesiasticus 10:10

35 Behold, I shew you a mystery; We shall not all sleep, but we shall all be changed,
In a moment, in the twinkling of an eye, at the last trump: for the trumpet shall sound, and the dead shall be raised incorruptible, and we shall be changed.
For this corruptible must put on incorruption, and this mortal must put on immortality.
So when this corruptible shall have put on incorruption, and this mortal shall have put on immortality, then shall be brought to pass the saying that is written, Death is swallowed up in victory.
O death, where is thy sting? O grave, where is thy victory?
Bible: I Corinthians 15:51–55

36 For all flesh is as grass, and all the glory of man as the flower of grass. The grass withereth, and the flower thereof falleth away.
Bible: I Peter 1:23–24

37 Lord, now lettest thou thy servant depart in peace, according to thy word:
For mine eyes have seen thy salvation,
Which thou hast prepared before the face of all people;
A light to lighten the Gentiles, and the glory of thy people Israel.

Bible: Luke 2:29–32

38 And I looked, and behold a pale horse: and his name that sat on him was Death, and Hell followed with him. And power was given unto them over the fourth part of the earth, to kill with sword, and with hunger, and with death, and with the beasts of the earth.

Bible: Revelations 6:8

39 Its visits,
Like those of angels, short, and far between.

Robert Blair (1699–1746) Scottish poet. *The Grave*

40 In the hour of death, and in the day of judgement.

The Book of Common Prayer *Morning Prayer, Prayer of St Chrysostom*

41 Any amusing deaths lately?

Maurice Bowra (1898–1971) British scholar. Attrib.

42 We all labour against our own cure, for death is the cure of all diseases.

Thomas Browne (1605–82) English physician and writer. *Religio Medici*

43 I am not so much afraid of death, as ashamed thereof, 'tis the very disgrace and ignominy of our natures.

Thomas Browne *Religio Medici*

44 With what shift and pains we come into the World we remember not; but 'tis commonly found no easy matter to get out of it.

Thomas Browne *Christian Morals*, Pt. II

45 For I say, this is death, and the sole death,
When a man's loss comes to him from his gain,
Darkness from light, from knowledge ignorance,
And lack of love from love made manifest.

Robert Browning (1812–89) British poet. *A Death in the Desert*

46 It is important what a man still plans at the end. It shows the measure of injustice in his death.

Elias Canetti (1905–) Bulgarian-born novelist. *The Human Province*

47 Days and moments quickly flying,
Blend the living with the dead;
Soon will you and I be lying
Each within our narrow bed.

Edward Caswall (1814–78) British hymn writer. Hymn

48 He had been, he said, a most unconscionable time dying; but he hoped that they would excuse it.

Charles II (1630–85) King of England. *History of England* (Macaulay), Vol. I, Ch. 4

49 I am ready to meet my Maker. Whether my Maker is ready for the ordeal of meeting me is another matter.

Winston Churchill On his 75th birthday. Speech, 30 Nov 1949

50 Death…a friend that alone can bring the peace his treasures cannot purchase, and remove the pain his physicians cannot cure.

Charles C. Colton (c. 1780–1843) *Lacon*, Vol. II, Ch. 110

51 Alack he's gone the way of all flesh.

William Congreve (1670–1729) British Restoration dramatist. *Squire Bickerstaff Detected*, attrib.

52 We perish'd, each alone:
But I beneath a rougher sea,
And whelm'd in deeper gulphs than he.

William Cowper (1731–1800) British poet. *The Castaway*

53 There is only one ultimate and effectual preventive for the maladies to which flesh is heir, and that is death.

Harvey Cushing (1869–1939) US surgeon. *The Medical Career and Other Papers*, 'Medicine at the Crossroads'

54 He'd make a lovely corpse.

Charles Dickens (1812–70) British novelist. *Martin Chuzzlewit*, Ch. 25

55 Because I could not stop for Death,
He kindly stopped for me;
The carriage held but just ourselves
And Immortality.

Emily Dickinson (1830–86) US poet. *The Chariot*

56 Our journey had advanced;
Our feet were almost come
To that odd fork in Being's road,
Eternity by term.

Emily Dickinson *Our Journey had Advanced*

57 I learned early to keep death in my line of sight, keep it under surveillance, keep it on cleared ground and away from any brush where it might coil unnoticed.

Joan Didion (1935–) US journalist and writer. *The Book of Common Prayer*

58 Death be not proud, though some have called thee
Mighty and dreadful, for, thou art not so.

John Donne (1573–1631) English poet. *Holy Sonnets*, 10

59 Any man's death diminishes me, because I am involved in Mankind; And therefore never send to know for whom the bell tolls; it tolls for thee.

John Donne *Devotions*, 17

60 Sin brought death, and death will disappear with the disappearance of sin.

Mary Baker Eddy (1821–1910) US religious leader. *Science and Health, with Key to the Scriptures*

61 So death, the most terrifying of ills, is nothing to us, since so long as we exist, death is not with us; but when death comes, then we do not exist. It does not then concern either the living or the dead, since for the former it is not, and the latter are no more.

Epicurus (341–270 BC) Greek philosopher. *Letter to Menoeceus*

62 Death is my neighbour now.

Edith Evans (1888–1976) British actress. Said a week before her death. BBC radio interview, 14 Oct 1976

63 It hath been often said, that it is not death, but dying, which is terrible.

Henry Fielding (1707–54) British novelist. *Amelia*, Bk. III, Ch. 4

64 Strange, is it not? that of the myriads who
Before us pass'd the door of Darkness through,
Not one returns to tell us of the Road,
Which to discover we must travel too.

Edward Fitzgerald (1809–83) British poet. *The Rubáiyát of Omar Khayyám*

65 In vain we shall penetrate more and more deeply the secrets of the structure of the human body, we shall not dupe nature; we shall die as usual.

Bernard de Fontenelle (1657–1757) French philosopher. *Dialogues des morts*, Dialogue V

66 He hath shook hands with time.

John Ford (c. 1586–c. 1640) English dramatist. *The Broken Heart*, V:2

67 Death destroys a man, the idea of Death saves him.

E. M. Forster (1879–1970) British novelist. *Howards End*, Ch. 27

68 Dere's no more work for poor old Ned,
He's gone whar de good niggers go.

Stephen Foster (1826–64) US composer of popular songs. *Uncle Ned*

69 If Mr Selwyn calls again, shew him up: if I am alive I shall be delighted to see him; and if I am dead he would like to see me.

Henry Fox (1705–74) British politician. Said during his last illness. George Selwyn was known for his morbid fascination for dead bodies. *George Selwyn and his Contemporaries* (J. H. Jesse), Vol. III

70 Why fear death? It is the most beautiful adventure in life.

Charles Frohman (1860–1915) US theatre producer. Said before going down with the liner *Lusitania*, alluding to 'To die will be an awfully big adventure' from Barrie's *Peter Pan*, which Frohman had produced. *J. M. Barrie and the Lost Boys* (A. Birkin)

71 Something lingering, with boiling oil in it, I fancy.

W. S. Gilbert (1836–1911) British dramatist. *The Mikado*, II

72 I am told he makes a very handsome corpse, and becomes his coffin prodigiously.

Oliver Goldsmith (1728–74) Irish-born British writer. *The Good-Natured Man*, I

73 The doctors found, when she was dead –
Her last disorder mortal.

Oliver Goldsmith *Elegy on Mrs. Mary Blaize*

74 Can storied urn or animated bust
Back to its mansion call the fleeting breath?
Can honour's voice provoke the silent dust,
Or flatt'ry soothe the dull cold ear of death?

Thomas Gray (1716–71) British poet. *Elegy Written in a Country Churchyard*

75 Here rests his head upon the lap of Earth
A youth to fortune and to fame unknown.
Fair Science frown'd not on his humble birth,
And Melancholy mark'd him for her own.

Thomas Gray *Elegy Written in a Country Churchyard*

76 My friend, the artery ceases to beat.

Albrecht von Haller *The Harvest of a Quiet Eye* (Alan L. Mackay)

77 Grieve not that I die young. Is it not well
To pass away ere life hath lost its brightness?

Lady Flora Hastings (1806–39) British poet. *Swan Song*

78 Once you're dead, you're made for life.

Jimi Hendrix (1942–70) US rock musician. Attrib.

79 Death is still working like a mole,
And digs my grave at each remove.

George Herbert (1593–1633) English poet. *Grace*

80 Anno domini – that's the most fatal complaint of all in the end.

James Hilton (1900–54) British novelist. *Good-bye, Mr Chips*, Ch. 1

81 Death is nothing at all. I have only slipped away into the next room. I am I and you are you. Whatever we were to each other, that we are still. Call me by my old familiar name, speak to me in the easy way you always use. Put no difference into your tone, wear no forced air of solemnity or sorrow... What is death but negligible accident? Why should I be out of mind because I am out of sight? I am waiting for you, for an interval, somewhere very near just around the corner. All is well.

Henry Scott Holland (1847–1918) British Anglican clergyman. Attrib.

82 It is the duty of a doctor to prolong life. It is not his duty to prolong the act of dying.

Lord Thomas Horder (1871–1955) Speech, House of Lords, Dec 1936

83 Death...It's the only thing we haven't succeeded in completely vulgarizing.

Aldous Huxley (1894–1964) British novelist. *Eyeless in Gaza*, Ch. 31

84 You mean what everybody means nowadays... Ignore death up to the last moment; then, when it can't be ignored any longer, have yourself squirted full of morphia and shuffle off in a coma.

Aldous Huxley *Time Must Have a Stop*, Ch. 26

85 Our civilization is founded on the shambles, and every individual existence goes out in a lonely spasm of helpless agony.

William James (1842–1910) US psychologist and philosopher. *Varieties of Religious Experience*

86 Who doesn't regret Lazarus was not
Questioned about after-lives? Of course
He only reached death's threshold. I fear what
Dark exercises may with cunning powers
Do when I am brought
To my conclusion.

Elizabeth Jennings (1926–) British poet and writer. *The Fear of Death*

87 I die because I do not die.

St John of the Cross (Juan de Yepes y Alvarez; 1542–91) Spanish churchman and poet. *Coplas del alma que pena por ver a dios*

88 It matters not how a man dies, but how he lives. The act of dying is not of importance, it lasts so short a time.

Samuel Johnson (1709–84) British lexicographer. *Life of Johnson* (J. Boswell), Vol. II

89 I am able to follow my own death step by step. Now I move softly towards the end.

Pope John XXIII (Angelo Roncalli; 1881–1963) Italian churchman. Remark made two days before he died. *The Guardian*, 3 June 1963

90 Above ground I shall be food for kites; below I shall be food for mole-crickets and ants. Why rob one to feed the other?

Juang-zu (4th century BC) Chinese Taoist philosopher. When asked on his deathbed what his wishes were regarding the disposal of his body. *Famous Last Words* (B. Conrad)

91 All right, my lord creator, Don Miguel, you too will die and return to the nothing whence you came. God will cease to dream you!

Miguel de Unamuno y Jugo (1864–1936) Spanish writer. *Mist*

92 Darkling I listen; and, for many a time
I have been half in love with easeful Death,
Call'd him soft names in many a mused rhyme,
To take into the air my quiet breath;
Now more than ever seems it rich to die,
To cease upon the midnight with no pain,
While thou art pouring forth thy soul abroad
In such an ecstasy!

John Keats (1795–1821) British poet. *Ode to a Nightingale*

93 I shall soon be laid in the quiet grave – thank God for the quiet grave – O! I can feel the cold earth upon me – the daisies growing over me – O for this quiet – it will be my first.

John Keats In a letter to John Taylor by Joseph Severn, 6 Mar 1821

94 Teach me to live, that I may dread
The grave as little as my bed.

Thomas Ken (1637–1711) English bishop. *An Evening Hymn*

95 In the long run we are all dead.

John Maynard Keynes (1883–1946) British economist. *Collected Writings*, 'A Tract on Monetary Reform'

96 That is the road we all have to take – over the Bridge of Sighs into eternity.

Søren Kierkegaard (1813–55) Danish philosopher. *Kierkegaard Anthology* (Auden)

97 O pity the dead that are dead, but cannot make
the journey, still they moan and beat
against the silvery adamant walls of life's exclusive city.

D. H. Lawrence (1885–1930) British novelist. *The Houseless Dead*

98 The dead don't die. They look on and help.

D. H. Lawrence Letter

99 I detest life-insurance agents. They always argue that I shall some day die, which is not so.

Stephen Leacock (1869–1944) English-born Canadian economist and humorist. *Literary Lapses*

100 Death is better than disease.

Henry Wadsworth Longfellow (1807–82) US poet. *Christus: A Mystery*, Pt. II, Sect. 1

101 There is a Reaper whose name is Death,
And, with his sickle keen,
He reaps the bearded grain at a breath,
And the flowers that grow between.

Henry Wadsworth Longfellow *The Reaper and the Flowers*

102 There is...no death...There is only...*me... me...who is going to die...*

André Malraux (1901–76) French writer and statesman. *The Royal Way*

103 It is the only disease you don't look forward to being cured of.

Herman J. Mankiewicz (1897–1953) US journalist and screenwriter. Referring to death. *Citizen Kane*

104 Cut is the branch that might have grown full straight,
And burned is Apollo's laurel-bough,
That sometime grew within this learned man.

Christopher Marlowe (1564–93) English dramatist. *Doctor Faustus*, Epilogue

105 The grave's a fine and private place,
But none, I think, do there embrace.

Andrew Marvell (1621–78) English poet. *To His Coy Mistress*

106 Either he's dead or my watch has stopped.

Groucho Marx (Julius Marx; 1895–1977) US comedian. *A Day at the Races*

107 My husband is dead.
– I'll bet he's just using that as an excuse.
I was with him to the end.
– No wonder he passed away.
I held him in my arms and kissed him.
– So it was murder!

Groucho Marx *Duck Soup*

108 Dying is a very dull, dreary affair. And my advice to you is to have nothing whatever to do with it.

W. Somerset Maugham (1874–1965) British novelist. *Escape from the Shadows* (Robin Maugham)

109 Alas! Lord and Lady Dalhousie are dead, and buried at last,
Which causes many people to feel a little downcast.

William McGonagall (1830–1902) Scottish poet. *The Death of Lord and Lady Dalhousie*

110 Dying is the most hellishly boresome experience in the world! Particularly when it entails dying of 'natural causes'.

W. Somerset Maugham *The Two Worlds of Somerset Maugham* (Wilmon Menard), Ch. 22

111 Whom the gods love dies young.

Menander (c. 341–c. 290 BC) Greek dramatist. *Dis Exapaton*

112 One dies only once, and it's for such a long time!

Molière (Jean Baptiste Poquelin; 1622–73) French dramatist. *Le Dépit amoureux*, V:3

113 It's not pining, it's passed on. This parrot is no more. It's ceased to be. It's expired. It's gone to meet its maker. This is a late parrot. It's a stiff. Bereft of life it rests in peace. It would be pushing up the daisies if you hadn't nailed it to the perch. It's rung down the curtain and joined the choir invisible. It's an ex-parrot.

Monty Python's Flying Circus (1969–74) British TV series written by Graham Chapman, John Cleese, Terry Gilliam, Eric Idle, Terry Jones, and Michael Palin. *Sketch*, 14 Dec 1969

114 Oh well, no matter what happens, there's always death.

Napoleon I (Napoleon Bonaparte; 1769–1821) French emperor. Attrib.

115 Christianity has made of death a terror which was unknown to the gay calmness of the Pagan.

Ouida (Marie Louise de la Ramée; 1839–1908) British novelist. *The Failure of Christianity*

116 And in the happy no-time of his sleeping
Death took him by the heart.

Wilfred Owen (1893–1918) British poet. *Asleep*

117 The thought of death came and stayed with her and lent her a sort of drowsy cheer. It would be nice, nice and restful, to be dead.

Dorothy Parker (1893–1967) US writer, poet, and humorist. *Laments for the Living*

118 It costs me never a stab nor squirm
To tread by chance upon a worm.
'Aha, my little dear,' I say,
'Your clan will pay me back one day.'

Dorothy Parker *Sunset Gun*, 'Thought for a Sunshiny Morning'

119 Many men on the point of an edifying death would be furious if they were suddenly restored to life.

Cesare Pavese (1908–50) Italian writer.

120 She closed her eyes; and in sweet slumber lying
her spirit tiptoed from its lodging-place.
It's folly to shrink in fear, if this is dying;
for death looked lovely in her lovely face.

Petrarch (Francesco Petrarca; 1304–74) Italian poet. *Triumphs*

121 Dying
is an art, like everything else.
I do it exceptionally well.

Sylvia Plath (1932–63) US writer. *Lady Lazarus*

122 The surgeon is quiet, he does not speak.
He has seen too much death, his hands are full of it.

Sylvia Plath *Winter Trees*, 'The Courage of Shutting-Up'

123 I mount! I fly!
O grave! where is thy victory?
O death! where is thy sting?

Alexander Pope (1688–1744) British poet. *The Dying Christian to his Soul*

124 Here am I, dying of a hundred good symptoms.

Alexander Pope *Anecdotes by and about Alexander Pope* (Joseph Spence)

125 How often are we to die before we go quite off this stage? In every friend we lose a part of ourselves, and the best part.

Alexander Pope Letter to Jonathan Swift, 5 Dec 1732

126 Death is the greatest kick of all, that's why they save it for last.

Robert Raisner British writer. *Graffiti*, 'Death'

127 The hero is strangely akin to those who die young.

Rainer Maria Rilke (1875–1926) Austrian poet. *Duineser Elegien*, VI

128 I shall have more to say when I am dead.

Edwin Arlington Robinson (1869–1935) US poet. *John Brown*

129 When I am dead, my dearest,
Sing no sad songs for me;
Plant thou no roses at my head,
Nor shady cypress tree:
Be the green grass above me
With showers and dewdrops wet;
And if thou wilt, remember,
And if thou wilt, forget.

Christina Rossetti (1830–74) British poet. *When I am Dead*

130 He who pretends to look on death without fear lies. All men are afraid of dying, this is the great law of sentient beings, without which the entire human species would soon be destroyed.

Jean Jacques Rousseau (1712–78) French philosopher. *Julie, or the New Eloise*

131 Death is the privilege of human nature,
And life without it were not worth our taking.

Nicholas Rowe (1674–1718) English dramatist. *The Fair Penitent*, V:1

132 In the post-mortem room we witness the final result of disease, the failure of the body to solve its problems, and there is an obvious limit to what one can learn about normal business transactions from even a daily visit to the bankruptcy court.

W. Russell, Lord Brain *Canadian Medical Association Journal*, 83:349, 1960

133 Ain't It Grand to Be Bloomin' Well Dead?

Leslie Sarony (1897–1985) British entertainer and writer. Song title

134 To that dark inn, the grave!

Walter Scott (1771–1832) Scottish novelist. *The Lord of the Isles*, VI

135 His morning walk was beneath the elms in the churchyard; 'for death,' he said, 'had been his next-door neighbour for so many years, that he had no apology for dropping the acquaintance.'

Walter Scott *The Legend of Montrose*, Introduction

136 I have a rendezvous with Death
At some disputed barricade.

Alan Seeger (1888–1916) US poet. *I Have a Rendezvous with Death*

137 Death is a punishment to some, to some a gift, and to many a favour.

Seneca (c. 4 BC–AD 65) Roman writer. *Hercules Oetaeus*

138 I will be
A bridegroom in my death, and run into 't
As to a lover's bed.

William Shakespeare (1564–1616) English dramatist. *Antony and Cleopatra*, IV:12

139 If thou and nature can so gently part,
The stroke of death is as a lover's pinch,
Which hurts, and is desir'd.

William Shakespeare *Antony and Cleopatra*, V:2

140 He had rather
Groan so in perpetuity, than be cured
By the sure physician, death.

William Shakespeare *Cymbeline*

141 The rest is silence.

William Shakespeare *Hamlet*, V:2

142 But thoughts, the slaves of life, and life, time's fool,
And time, that takes survey of all the world,
Must have a stop.

William Shakespeare *Henry IV, Part One*, V:4

143 I care not; a man can die but once; we owe God a death.

William Shakespeare *Henry IV, Part Two*, III:2

144 His nose was as sharp as a pen, and 'a babbl'd of green fields.

William Shakespeare Referring to Falstaff on his deathbed. *Henry V*, II:3

145 Why, he that cuts off twenty years of life
Cuts off so many years of fearing death.

William Shakespeare *Julius Caesar*, III:1

146 O mighty Caesar! dost thou lie so low?
Are all thy conquests, glories, triumphs, spoils,
Shrunk to this little measure?
William Shakespeare *Julius Caesar*, III:1

147 Nothing in his life
Became him like the leaving it: he died
As one that had been studied in his death
To throw away the dearest thing he ow'd
As 'twere a careless trifle.
William Shakespeare *Macbeth*, I:4

148 Dar'st thou die?
The sense of death is most in apprehension,
And the poor beetle, that we tread upon,
In corporal sufferance finds a pang as great
As when a giant dies.
William Shakespeare *Measure for Measure*, III:1

149 If I must die,
I will encounter darkness as a bride,
And hug it in mine arms.
William Shakespeare *Measure for Measure*, III:1

150 Ay, but to die, and go we know not where;
To lie in cold obstruction, and to rot;
This sensible warm motion to become
A kneaded clod; and the delighted spirit
To bathe in fiery floods or to reside
In thrilling region of thick-ribbed ice.
William Shakespeare *Measure for Measure*, III:1

151 Be not afraid, though you do see me weapon'd;
Here is my journey's end, here is my butt,
And very sea-mark of my utmost sail.
William Shakespeare *Othello*, V:2

152 The worst is death, and death will have his day.
William Shakespeare *Richard II*, III:2

153 Of comfort no man speak:
Let's talk of graves, of worms, and epitaphs;
Make dust our paper, and with rainy eyes
Write sorrow on the bosom of the earth.
Let's choose executors, and talk of wills.
William Shakespeare *Richard II*, III:3

154 Full fathom five thy father lies;
Of his bones are coral made;
Those are pearls that were his eyes;
Nothing of him that doth fade
But doth suffer a sea-change
Into something rich and strange.
William Shakespeare *The Tempest*, I:2

155 He that dies pays all debts.
William Shakespeare *The Tempest*, III:2

156 After all, what *is* death? Just nature's way of telling us to slow down.
Dick Sharples *In Loving Memory*, Yorkshire Television, 1979

157 Death is the veil which those who live call life:
They sleep, and it is lifted.
Percy Bysshe Shelley (1792–1822) British poet. *Prometheus Unbound*, III

158 It is a modest creed, and yet
Pleasant if one considers it,
To own that death itself must be,
Like all the rest, a mockery.
Percy Bysshe Shelley *The Sensitive Plant*, III

159 I cannot forgive my friends for dying: I do not find these vanishing acts of theirs at all amusing.
Logan Pearsall Smith (1865–1946) US writer. *Trivia*

160 I do really think that death will be marvellous...If there wasn't death, I think you couldn't go on.
Stevie Smith (Florence Margaret Smith; 1902–71) British poet. *The Observer*, 9 Nov 1969

161 Death must be distinguished from dying, with which it is often confused.
Sydney Smith (1771–1845) British clergyman, essayist, and wit. *The Smith of Smiths* (Pearson)

162 The whole of his life had prepared Podduyev for living, not for dying.
Alexander Solzhenitsyn (1918–) Russian novelist. *Cancer Ward*, Pt. I, Ch. 8

163 My name is death; the last best friend am I.
Robert Southey (1774–1843) British poet. *Carmen Nuptiale: The Lay of the Laureate*, 'The Dream'

164 Sleep after toil, port after stormy seas,
Ease after war, death after life does greatly please.
Edmund Spenser (1552–99) English poet. *The Faerie Queene*, I:9

165 Poor soul, very sad; her late husband, you know, a very sad death – eaten by missionaries – poor soul!
William Archibald Spooner (1844–1930) British churchman and academic. *Spooner* (Sir W. Hayter)

166 Under the wide and starry sky
Dig the grave and let me lie.
Glad did I live and gladly die,
– And I laid me down with a will.
This is the verse you grave for me:
'Here he lies where he longed to be;
Home is the sailor, home from sea,
And the hunter home from the hill.'
Robert Louis Stevenson (1850–94) Scottish writer. *Underwoods*, Bk. I, 'Requiem'

167 It is impossible that anything so natural, so necessary, and so universal as death, should ever have been designed by Providence as an evil to mankind.
Jonathan Swift (1667–1745) Irish-born Anglican priest and writer. 'Thoughts on Religion'

168 Even so, in death the same unknown will appear as ever known to me. And because I love this life, I know I shall love death as well.
The child cries out when from the right breast the mother takes it away, in the very next moment to find in the left one its consolation.
Rabindranath Tagore (1861–1941) Indian poet and philosopher. *Gitanjali*

169 Row upon row with strict impunity
The headstones yield their names to the element.
Allen Tate (1899–1979) US poet. *Ode to the Confederate Dead*

170 A day less or more
At sea or ashore,
We die – does it matter when?
Alfred, Lord Tennyson (1809–92) British poet. *The Revenge*, XI

171 I, born of flesh and ghost, was neither
A ghost nor man, but mortal ghost.
And I was struck down by death's feather.

Dylan Thomas (1914–53) Welsh poet. *Before I knocked*

172 After the first death, there is no other.

Dylan Thomas *A Refusal to Mourn the Death, by Fire, of a Child in London*

173 Do not go gentle into that good night,
Old age should burn and rave at close of day;
Rage, rage, against the dying of the light.

Dylan Thomas *Do not go gentle into that good night*

174 And Death Shall Have No Dominion.

Dylan Thomas Title of poem

175 There is not any book
Or face of dearest look
That I would not turn from now
To go into the unknown
I must enter, and leave, alone,
I know not how.

Edward Thomas (1878–1917) British poet. *Lights Out*

176 Death is the price paid by life for an enhancement of the complexity of a live organism's structure.

Arnold Toynbee (1889–1975) British historian. *Life After Death*

177 Go and try to disprove death. Death will disprove you, and that's all!

Ivan Turgenev (1818–83) Russian novelist. *Fathers and Sons*, Ch. 27

178 While I thought that I was learning how to live, I have been learning how to die.

Leonardo da Vinci (1452–1519) Italian artist. *Notebooks*

179 The human race is the only one that knows it must die, and it knows this only through its experience. A child brought up alone and transported to a desert island would have no more idea of death than a cat or a plant.

Voltaire (François-Marie Arouet; 1694–1778) French writer and philosopher. *The Oxford Book of Death* (D. J. Enright)

180 There's no repentance in the grave.

Isaac Watts (1674–1748) English theologian and hymn writer. *Divine Songs for Children*, 'Solemn Thoughts of God and Death'

181 For he who lives more lives than one
More deaths than one must die.

Oscar Wilde (1854–1900) Irish-born British dramatist. *The Ballad of Reading Gaol*, III:37

182 Dead! and…never called me mother.

Mrs Henry Wood (1814–87) British novelist. *East Lynne* (dramatized version; the words do not occur in the novel)

183 Three years she grew in sun and shower,
Then Nature said, 'A lovelier flower
On earth was never sown;
This child I to myself will take;
She shall be mine, and I will make
A Lady of my own.

William Wordsworth (1770–1850) British poet. *Three Years she Grew*

184 We are laid asleep
In body, and become a living soul:
While with an eye made quiet by the power
Of harmony, and the deep power of joy,
We see into the life of things.

William Wordsworth *Lines composed a few miles above Tintern Abbey*

DEBAUCHERY

See also animalism, lust, pleasure, sex

1 A fool bolts pleasure, then complains of moral indigestion.

Minna Antrim (b. 1861) US writer. *Naked Truth and Veiled Allusions*

2 A great many people have come up to me and asked how I manage to get so much work done and still keep looking so dissipated.

Robert Benchley (1889–1945) US humorist. *Chips off the Old Benchley*, 'How to Get Things Done'

3 DEBAUCHEE, n. One who has so earnestly pursued pleasure that he has had the misfortune to overtake it.

Ambrose Bierce (1842–?1914) US writer and journalist. *The Devil's Dictionary*

4 So, we'll go no more a roving
So late into the night,
Though the heart be still as loving,
And the moon be still as bright.

Lord Byron (1788–1824) British poet. *So, we'll go no more a roving*

5 I've over-educated myself in all the things I shouldn't have known at all.

Noël Coward (1899–1973) British dramatist. *Wild Oats*

6 My problem lies in reconciling my gross habits with my net income.

Errol Flynn (1909–59) Australian actor. Attrib.

7 No one ever suddenly became depraved.

Juvenal (Decimus Junius Juvenalis; 60–130 AD) Roman satirist. *Satires*, II

8 We're poor little lambs who've lost our way,
Baa! Baa! Baa!
We're little black sheep who've gone astray,
Baa-aa-aa!
Gentleman-rankers out on the spree,
Damned from here to Eternity,
God ha' mercy on such as we,
Baa! Yah! Bah!

Rudyard Kipling (1865–1936) Indian-born British writer. *Gentleman-Rankers*

9 Some things can't be ravished. You can't ravish a tin of sardines.

D. H. Lawrence (1885–1930) British novelist. *Lady Chatterley's Lover*

10 Home is heaven and orgies are vile
But you need an orgy, once in a while.

Ogden Nash (1902–71) US poet. *Home, 99.44100% Sweet Home*

11 Once: a philosopher; twice: a pervert!

Voltaire (François-Marie Arouet; 1694–1778) French writer. Turning down an invitation to an orgy, having attended one the previous night for the first time. Attrib.

DECEPTION

See also appearances, hypocrisy, insincerity, lying

1 To deceive oneself is very easy.

Proverb

2 Beware of false prophets, which come to you in

sheep's clothing, but inwardly they are ravening wolves.

Bible: Matthew 7:15

3 Almost every man wastes part of his life in attempts to display qualities which he does not possess, and to gain applause which he cannot keep.

Samuel Johnson (1709–84) British lexicographer. *The Rambler*

4 You can fool some of the people all the time and all the people some of the time; but you can't fool all the people all the time.

Abraham Lincoln (1809–65) US statesman. Attrib.

5 Lord, Lord, how this world is given to lying! I grant you I was down and out of breath; and so was he; but we rose both at an instant, and fought a long hour by Shrewsbury clock.

William Shakespeare (1564–1616) English dramatist. *Henry IV, Part One*, V:4

6 I want that glib and oily art
To speak and purpose not; since what I well intend,
I'll do't before I speak.

William Shakespeare *King Lear*, I:1

7 False face must hide what the false heart doth know.

William Shakespeare *Macbeth*, I:7

8 Sigh no more, ladies, sigh no more,
Men were deceivers ever;
One foot in sea, and one on shore,
To one thing constant never.
Then sigh not so,
But let them go,
And be you blithe and bonny,
Converting all your sounds of woe
Into Hey nonny, nonny.

William Shakespeare *Much Ado About Nothing*, II:3

9 If she be false, O! then heaven mocks itself.
I'll not believe it.

William Shakespeare *Othello*, III:3

10 You can fool too many of the people too much of the time.

James Thurber (1894–1961) US humorist. *Fables for Our Time*, 'The Owl Who Was God'

11 I have invented an invaluable permanent invalid called Bunbury, in order that I may be able to go down into the country whenever I choose.

Oscar Wilde (1854–1900) Irish-born British dramatist. *The Importance of Being Earnest*, I

DECISION

See also determination

1 I'm Gonna Wash That Man Right Out of My Hair.

Oscar Hammerstein II (1895–1960) US lyricist. *South Pacific*, Song title

2 Tender-handed stroke a nettle,
And it stings you for your pains;
Grasp it like a man of mettle,
And it soft as silk remains.

Aaron Hill (1685–1750) British poet and dramatist. *Verses Written on Window*

3 Like all weak men he laid an exaggerated stress on not changing one's mind.

W. Somerset Maugham (1874–1965) British novelist. *Of Human Bondage*, Ch. 37

4 If someone tells you he is going to make 'a realistic decision', you immediately understand that he has resolved to do something bad.

Mary McCarthy (1912–89) US novelist. *On the Contrary*

5 This is the night
That either makes me or fordoes me quite.

William Shakespeare (1564–1616) English dramatist. *Othello*, V:1

DECLINE

1 More will mean worse.

Kingsley Amis (1922–) British novelist. *Encounter*, July 1960

2 And though the Van Dycks have to go
And we pawn the Bechstein grand,
We'll stand by the Stately Homes of England.

Noël Coward (1899–1973) British dramatist. *Operette*, 'The Stately Homes of England'

3 That's Why the Lady Is a Tramp.

Lorenz Hart (1895–1943) US songwriter. From the musical *Babes in Arms*. Song title

4 It is the logic of our times,
No subject for immortal verse –
That we who lived by honest dreams
Defend the bad against the worse.

C. Day Lewis (1904–72) British poet. *Where are the War Poets?*

5 From morn
To noon he fell, from noon to dewy eve,
A summer's day, and with the setting sun
Dropped from the zenith, like a falling star.

John Milton (1608–74) English poet. *Paradise Lost*, Bk. I

6 Macmillan seemed, in his very person, to embody the national decay he supposed himself to be confuting. He exuded a flavour of moth-balls.

Malcolm Muggeridge (1903–90) British writer. *Tread Softly For You Tread on My Jokes*, 'England, whose England'

7 It is only a step from the sublime to the ridiculous.

Napoleon I (Napoleon Bonaparte; 1769–1821) French emperor. Remark following the retreat from Moscow, 1812. Attrib.

8 We have on our hands a sick man – a very sick man.

Nicholas I (1796–1855) Tsar of Russia. Referring to Turkey, the 'sick man of Europe'; said to Sir G. H. Seymour, British envoy to St Petersburg, Jan 1853. Attrib.

9 Now there are fields where Troy once was.

Ovid (Publius Ovidius Naso; 43 BC–17 AD) Roman poet. *Heroides*, Bk. I

10 There may have been disillusionments in the lives of the medieval saints, but they would scarcely have been better pleased if they could have foreseen that their names would be associated nowadays chiefly with racehorses and the cheaper clarets.

Saki (Hector Hugh Munro; 1870–1916) British writer. *Reginald at the Carlton*

11 I shall be like that tree; I shall die from the top.

Jonathan Swift (1667–1745) Irish-born Anglican priest and writer. Predicting his own mental decline on seeing a tree with a withered crown. *Lives of the Wits* (H. Pearson)

12 I dreamed there would be Spring no more,
That Nature's ancient power was lost.

Alfred, Lord Tennyson (1809–92) British poet. *In Memoriam A.H.H.*, LXIX

13 The difference between our decadence and the Russians' is that while theirs is brutal, ours is apathetic.

James Thurber (1894–1961) US humorist. *The Observer*, 'Sayings of the Week', 5 Feb 1961

14 I started at the top and worked my way down.

Orson Welles (1915–85) US film actor. *The Filmgoer's Book of Quotes* (Leslie Halliwell)

15 Plain living and high thinking are no more.

William Wordsworth (1770–1850) British poet. *Sonnets*, 'O friend! I know not'

16 Milton! thou shouldst be living at this hour:
England hath need of thee; she is a fen
Of stagnant waters: altar, sword, and pen,
Fireside, the heroic wealth of hall and bower,
Have forfeited their ancient English dower
Of inward happiness.

William Wordsworth *Sonnets*, 'Milton! thou shouldst'

DEFEAT

See also loss

1 If it is a blessing, it is certainly very well disguised.

Winston Churchill (1874–1965) British statesman. Said to his wife after his defeat in the 1945 general election, when she said that it was a blessing in disguise. *Memoirs of Richard Nixon* (R. Nixon)

2 As always, victory finds a hundred fathers, but defeat is an orphan.

Count Galeazzo Ciano (1903–44) Italian Foreign Minister. Diary entry, 9 Sept 1942

3 'Tis better to have fought and lost,
Than never to have fought at all.

Arthur Hugh Clough (1819–61) British poet. *Peschiera*

4 Of all I had, only honour and life have been spared.

Francis I (1494–1547) King of France. Referring to his defeat at the Battle of Pavia, 24 Feb 1525; usually misquoted as 'All is lost save honour.' Letter to Louise of Savoy (his mother), 1525

5 Sire you no longer have an army.

Wilhelm Groener (1867–1939) German general. Said to the Emperor Wilhelm II of Germany, 9 Nov 1918

6 A man can be destroyed but not defeated.

Ernest Hemingway (1899–1961) US novelist. *The Old Man and the Sea*

7 As an English General has very truly said, 'The German army was stabbed in the back'.

Paul von Hindenburg (1847–1934) German Field Marshal and President. Referring to Germany's defeat in World War I; it is not known whom Hindenburg was quoting. Statement to a Reichstag Committee, 18 Nov 1918

8 The war situation has developed not necessarily to Japan's advantage.

Hirohito (1901–89) Japanese head of state. Announcing Japan's surrender, 15 Aug 1945

9 We wuz robbed – We should have stood in bed.

Joe Jacobs (1896–1940) US boxing manager. After Max Schmeling's defeat by Jack Sharkey. *Strong Cigars and Lovely Women* (J. Lardner)

10 Woe to the vanquished.

Livy (Titus Livius; 59 BC–17 AD) Roman historian. *History*, V:48

11 When I am dead and opened, you shall find
'Calais' lying in my heart.

Mary I (1516–58) Queen of England. *Chronicles* (Holinshed), III

12 I brought myself down. I gave them a sword and they stuck it in and they twisted it with relish. And I guess if I'd been in their position I'd have done the same thing.

Richard Milhous Nixon (1913–94) US President. TV interview, 19 May 1977

13 Every man meets his Waterloo at last.

Wendell Phillips (1811–84) US reformer. Speech, Brooklyn, 1 Nov 1859

14 Of the two lights of Christendom, one has been extinguished.

Aeneas Silvius (1405–64) Bishop of Trieste. Remark on hearing of the fall of Constantinople to the Turks (29 May 1453)

15 Well, I have one consolation, No candidate was ever elected ex-president by such a large majority!

William Howard Taft (1857–1930) US statesman. Referring to his disastrous defeat in the 1912 presidential election. Attrib.

16 It is the beginning of the end.

Talleyrand (Charles Maurice de Talleyrand-Périgord; 1754–1838) French politician. Referring to Napoleon's defeat at Borodino, 1813. Attrib.

17 Please understand that there is no one depressed in *this* house; we are not interested in the possibilities of defeat; they do not exist.

Victoria (1819–1901) Queen of the United Kingdom. Referring to the Boer War; said to Balfour. *Life of Salisbury* (Lady G. Cecil)

18 Another year! – another deadly blow!
Another mighty empire overthrown!
And we are left, or shall be left, alone.

William Wordsworth (1770–1850) British poet. Napoleon defeated Prussia at the Battles of Jena and Anerstädt, 14 Oct 1806. *Sonnets*, 'Another year!'

DEFOE, DANIEL

(1660–1731) British journalist and writer. Imprisoned for writing seditious pamphlets, he turned late in his life to fiction, achieving success with *Robinson Crusoe* (1719) and *Moll Flanders* (1722).

1 The good die early, and the bad die late.

Character of the late Dr. Annesley

2 Nature has left this tincture in the blood,
That all men would be tyrants if they could.

The History of the Kentish Petition, Addenda

3 He bade me observe it, and I should always find, that the calamities of life were shared among the upper and lower part of mankind; but that the middle station had the fewest disasters.

Robinson Crusoe, Pt. I

4 I takes my man Friday with me.
Robinson Crusoe, Pt. I

5 Wherever God erects a house of prayer,
The Devil always builds a chapel there;
And 'twill be found, upon examination,
The latter has the largest congregation.
The True-Born Englishman, Pt. I

6 And of all plagues with which mankind are curst,
Ecclesiastic tyranny's the worst.
The True-Born Englishman, Pt. II

DE GAULLE, CHARLES

(1890–1970) French general and statesman. President (1958–69), he became an international figure after World War II. He advocated mechanized warfare in the 1930s, and became leader of the Free French in London after the fall of France, taking over as head of the provisional government after Germany's defeat.

Quotations about de Gaulle

1 Intelligent – brilliant – resourceful – he spoils his undoubted talents by his excessive assurance, his contempt for other people's point of view, and his attitude of a king in exile.
Report, French War College, 1922

2 Just look at him! He might be Stalin with 200 divisions.
Winston Churchill (1874–1965) British statesman. Attrib.

3 An improbable creature, like a human giraffe, sniffing down his nostril at mortals beneath his gaze.
Richard Wilson *The Second Book of Insults* (Nancy McPhee)

Quotations by de Gaulle

4 Deliberation is the work of many men. Action, of one alone.
War Memoirs, Vol. 2

5 I myself have become a Gaullist only little by little.
The Observer, 'Sayings of the Year', 29 Dec 1963

6 Now at last our child is just like all children.
On the death of his daughter Anne, who had Down's Syndrome. *Ten First Ladies of the World* (Pauline Frederick)

7 They really are bad shots.
Remark after narrowly escaping death in an assassination attempt. *Ten First Ladies of the World* (Pauline Frederick)

8 The French will only be united under the threat of danger. Nobody can simply bring together a country that has 265 kinds of cheese.
Speech, 1951

9 *Changez vos amis.*
Change your friends.
Replying to the complaint by Jacques Soustelle (French anthropologist and politician) that he was being attacked by his own friends. Attrib.

10 One does not arrest Voltaire.
Explaining why he had not arrested Jean-Paul Sartre for urging French soldiers in Algeria to desert. Attrib.

11 Since a politician never believes what he says, he is surprised when others believe him.
Attrib.

12 Treaties are like roses and young girls – they last while they last.
Speech at Elysée Palace, 2 July 1967

13 In order to become the master, the politician poses as the servant.
Attrib.

14 Politics is too important to be left to the politicians.
Attrib.

15 I have come to the conclusion that politics are too serious a matter to be left to the politicians.
Replying to Clement Attlee's remark that 'de Gaulle is a very good soldier and a very bad politician'. *A Prime Minister Remembers* (Attlee) (1961)

DELUSION

1 But yet the light that led astray
Was light from Heaven.
Robert Burns (1759–96) Scottish poet. *The Vision*

2 Take care, your worship, those things over there are not giants but windmills.
Miguel de Cervantes (1547–1616) Spanish novelist. *Don Quixote*, Pt. I, Ch. 8

3 Didn't I tell you, Don Quixote, sir, to turn back, for they were not armies you were going to attack, but flocks of sheep?
Miguel de Cervantes *Don Quixote*, Pt. I, Ch. 18

4 Take the life-lie away from the average man and straight away you take away his happiness.
Henrik Ibsen (1828–1906) Norwegian dramatist. *The Wild Duck*, V

5 Many people have delusions of grandeur but you're deluded by triviality.
Eugène Ionesco (1912–94) French dramatist. *Exit the King*

DEMOCRACY

See also class, government, majority, public, republic

1 Democracy means government by discussion but it is only effective if you can stop people talking.
Clement Attlee (1883–1967) British statesman and Labour prime minister. *Anatomy of Britain* (Anthony Sampson)

2 A democracy must remain at home in all matters which affect the nature of her institutions... We do not want the racial antipathies or national antagonisms of the Old World translated to this continent, as they will should we become a part of European politics. The people of this country are overwhelmingly for a policy of neutrality.
William Edgar Borah (1865–1940) US senator. Radio broadcast, 22 Feb 1936

3 A committee is an animal with four back legs.
John Le Carré (1931–) British writer. *Tinker, Tailor, Soldier, Spy*

4 One man shall have one vote.

John Cartwright (1740–1824) British writer. *People's Barrier Against Undue Influence*

5 Democracy means government by the uneducated, while aristocracy means government by the badly educated.

G. K. Chesterton (1874–1936) British writer. *The New York Times*, 1 Feb 1931

6 Populism is on the increase – a populism that rejects anything different, anyone with a different-coloured skin, or a different race or religion. This is the real danger and unspoken risk that threatens to pollute democracy.

Jacques Delors (1925–) French politician and European statesman. *The Independent*, 19 May 1994

7 Democracy is the wholesome and pure air without which a socialist public organisation cannot live a full-blooded life.

Mickhail Gorbachov (1931–) Soviet statesman. Report to 27th Party Congress. Speech, 25 Feb 1986

8 Some comrades apparently find it hard to understand that democracy is just a slogan.

Mikhail Gorbachov *The Observer*, 'Sayings of the Week', 1 Feb 1987

9 Democracy can't work. Mathematicians, peasants, and animals, that's all there is – so democracy, a theory based on the assumption that mathematicians and peasants are equal, can never work. Wisdom is not additive; its maximum is that of the wisest man in a given group.

Robert Heinlein (1907–88) US science-fiction writer. *Glory Road*, Ch. 20

10 Democracy is only an experiment in government, and it has the obvious disadvantage of merely counting votes instead of weighing them.

Dean Inge (1860–1954) British churchman. *Possible Recovery?*

11 The vote is the most powerful instrument ever devised by man for breaking down injustice and destroying the terrible walls which imprison men because they are different from other men.

Lyndon B. Johnson (1908–73) US statesman. Address on signing Voting Rights Bill, Washington, DC, 6 Aug 1965

12 A democracy is a state which recognises the subjecting of the minority to the majority.

Lenin (Vladimir Ilich Ulyanov; 1870–1924) Russian revolutionary leader. *The State and The Revolution*

13 No man is good enough to govern another man without that other's consent.

Abraham Lincoln (1809–65) US statesman. Speech, 1854

14 The ballot is stronger than the bullet.

Abraham Lincoln Speech, 19 May 1856

15 This country, with its institutions, belongs to the people who inhabit it. Whenever they shall grow weary of the existing government, they can exercise their constitutional right of amending it, or their revolutionary right to dismember or overthrow it.

Abraham Lincoln First Inaugural Address, 4 Mar 1861

16 ...that government of the people, by the people, and for the people, shall not perish from the earth.

Abraham Lincoln Speech, 19 Nov 1863, dedicating the national cemetery on the site of the Battle of Gettysburg

17 To have good government, you often need less, not more, democracy.

Kishore Mahbubani (1948–) Singaporean diplomatist. *The Observer*, 'Sayings of the Week', 17 Apr 1994

18 Man's capacity for evil makes democracy necessary and man's capacity for good makes democracy possible.

Reinhold Niebuhr (1892–1971) US churchman. Quoted by Anthony Wedgwood Benn in *The Times*, 18 Jul 1977

19 Democracy passes into despotism.

Plato (429–347 BC) Greek philosopher. *Republic*, Bk. 8

20 I think if the people of this country can be reached with the truth, their judgment will be in favor of the many, as against the privileged few.

Eleanor Roosevelt (1884–1962) US writer and lecturer. *Ladies' Home Journal*

21 We must be the great arsenal of democracy.

Franklin D. Roosevelt (1882–1945) US Democratic president. Broadcast address to Forum on Current Problems, 29 Dec 1940

22 We must be thoroughly democratic and patronise everybody without distinction of class.

George Bernard Shaw (1856–1950) Irish dramatist and critic. *John Bull's Other Island*

23 Democracy substitutes election by the incompetent many for appointment by the corrupt few.

George Bernard Shaw *Man and Superman*, 'Maxims for Revolutionists'

24 You won the elections, but I won the count.

Anastasio Somoza (1925–80) Nicaraguan dictator. *The Guardian*, 17 June 1977

25 It's not the voting that's democracy; it's the counting.

Tom Stoppard (1937–) Czech-born British dramatist. *Jumpers*

26 A committee should consist of three men, two of whom are absent.

Herbert Beerbohm Tree (1853–1917) British actor and theatre manager. *Beerbohm Tree* (H. Pearson)

27 I shall not vote because I do not aspire to advise my sovereign on the choice of her servants.

Evelyn Waugh (1903–66) British novelist. *A Little Order*

28 Democracy means simply the bludgeoning of the people by the people for the people.

Oscar Wilde (1854–1900) Irish-born British dramatist. *The Soul of Man under Socialism*

29 The world must be made safe for democracy.

Woodrow Wilson (1856–1925) US statesman. Address to Congress, asking for a declaration of war 2 Apr 1917

DEPARTURE

See also dismissal, parting

1 Come, dear children, let us away;
Down and away below.

Matthew Arnold (1822–88) British poet and critic. *The Forsaken Merman*

2 She left lonely for ever
The kings of the sea.

Matthew Arnold *The Forsaken Merman*

3 Once I leave, I leave. I am not going to speak to the man on the bridge, and I am not going to spit on the deck.

Stanley Baldwin (1867–1947) British statesman. Statement to the Cabinet, 28 May 1937

4 Adieu, adieu! my native shore
Fades o'er the waters blue.

Lord Byron (1788–1824) British poet. *Childe Harold's Pilgrimage*, I

5 My native Land – Good Night!

Lord Byron *Childe Harold's Pilgrimage*, I

6 Let us go then, you and I,
When the evening is spread out against the sky
Like a patient etherized upon a table.

T. S. Eliot (1888–1965) US-born British poet and dramatist. *The Love Song of J. Alfred Prufrock*

7 And they are gone: aye, ages long ago
These lovers fled away into the storm.

John Keats (1795–1821) British poet. *The Eve of Saint Agnes*, XLII

8 She's leaving home after living alone for so many years.

John Lennon (1940–80) British rock musician. *She's Leaving Home* (with Paul McCartney)

9 When I leave it I never dare look back lest I turn into a pillar of salt and the conductor throw me over his left shoulder for good luck.

Frank Sullivan (1892–) US humorist. Attrib.

DESIGN

See also art

1 Art has to move you and design does not, unless it's a good design for a bus.

David Hockney (1937–) British painter. *The Observer*, 'Sayings of the Week', 30 Oct 1988

2 Demand bare walls in your bedroom, your living room and your dining room. Built-in furniture takes the place of much of the furniture which is expensive to buy...Demand concealed or diffused lighting. Demand a vacuum cleaner. Buy only practical furniture and never buy 'decorative' pieces. If you want to see bad taste, go into the houses of the rich. Put only a few pictures on your walls and none but good ones.

Le Corbusier (Charles-Édouard Jeanneret; 1887–1965) French architect.

3 A machine for living in.

Le Corbusier Referring to a house. *Towards a New Architecture*

4 The materials of city planning are: sky, space, trees, steel and cement; in that order and that hierarchy.

Le Corbusier Attrib.

5 It is not this or that tangible steel or brass machine which we want to get rid of, but the great intangible machine of commercial tyranny which oppresses the lives of us all.

William Morris (1834–96) British designer, artist, and poet.

6 Nothing should be made by man's labour which is not worth making or which must be made by labour degrading to the makers.

William Morris

7 Art will make our streets as beautiful as the woods, as elevating as the mountain-side: it will be a pleasure and a rest, and not a weight upon the spirits to come from the open country into a town. Every man's house will be fair and decent, soothing to his mind and helpful to his work.

William Morris

8 Today industrial design has put murder on a mass-production basis.

Victor Papanek *Design for the Real World*

9 It is all about technique. The great mistake of this century is to put inspiration and creativity first.

Vivienne Westwood British fashion designer. *The Observer*, 'Sayings of the Week', 15 May 1994

10 It will be a great day when cutlery and furniture designs (to name but two) swing like the Supremes.

Michael Wolff

11 The tall modern office building is the machine pure and simple...the engine, the motor and the battleship the works of the century.

Frank Lloyd Wright (1869–1959) US architect.

DESIRE

See also hunger, lust, thirst

1 Give me my golf clubs, fresh air and a beautiful partner, and you can keep my golf clubs and the fresh air.

Jack Benny (Benjamin Kublesky; 1894–1974) US actor. Attrib.

2 Those who restrain Desire, do so because theirs is weak enough to be restrained.

William Blake (1757–1827) British poet. *The Marriage of Heaven and Hell*, 'Those who restrain Desire...'

3 Sooner murder an infant in its cradle than nurse unacted desires.

William Blake *The Marriage of Heaven and Hell*, 'Proverbs of Hell'

4 Man's Desires are limited by his Perceptions; none can desire what he has not perceived.

William Blake *There is no Natural Religion*

5 A sight to dream of, not to tell!

Samuel Taylor Coleridge (1772–1834) British poet. *Christabel*, I

6 O, she is the antidote to desire.

William Congreve (1670–1729) British Restoration dramatist. *The Way of the World*, IV:14

7 Someday I'll wish upon a star.

E. Y. Harburg (1896–1981) US songwriter. From the musical *The Wizard of Oz. Over the Rainbow*

8 Somewhere over the rainbow,
Way up high:
There's a land that I heard of
Once in a lullaby.

E. Y. Harburg From the musical *The Wizard of Oz. Over the Rainbow*

9 Ship me somewheres east of Suez, where the best is like the worst,
Where there aren't no Ten Commandments, an' a

man can raise a thirst:
For the temple-bells are callin', an' it's there that I would be –
By the old Moulmein Pagoda, looking lazy at the sea.

Rudyard Kipling (1865–1936) Indian-born British writer. *The Road to Mandalay*

10 All I want is a room somewhere,
Far away from the cold night air;
With one enormous chair…
Oh, wouldn't it be loverly?

Alan Jay Lerner (1918–86) US songwriter. *My Fair Lady*, I:1

11 There is wishful thinking in Hell as well as on earth.

C. S. Lewis (1898–1963) British academic and writer. *The Screwtape Letters*, Preface

12 There is nothing like desire for preventing the thing one says from bearing any resemblance to what one has in mind.

Marcel Proust (1871–1922) French novelist. *À la recherche du temps perdu: Le Côté de Guermantes*

13 Appetite comes with eating.

François Rabelais (1483–1553) French satirist. *Gargantua*, Bk. I, Ch. 5

14 That she belov'd knows nought that knows not this:
Men prize the thing ungain'd more than it is.

William Shakespeare (1564–1616) English dramatist. *Troilus and Cressida*, I:2

15 There are two tragedies in life. One is to lose your heart's desire. The other is to gain it.

George Bernard Shaw (1856–1950) Irish dramatist and critic. *Man and Superman*, IV

16 Desire is the very essence of man.

Benedict Spinoza (Baruch de Spinoza; 1632–77) Dutch philosopher. *Ethics*

17 As soon as you stop wanting something you get it. I've found that to be absolutely axiomatic.

Andy Warhol (Andrew Warhola; 1926–87) US pop artist. Attrib.

18 And pluck till time and times are done
The silver apples of the moon
The golden apples of the sun.

W. B. Yeats (1865–1939) Irish poet. *The Song of Wandering Aengus*

DESPAIR

See also sorrow

1 Despair is better treated with hope, not dope.

Richard Asher (1912–) *Lancet*, I:954, 1958

2 And about the ninth hour Jesus cried with a loud voice, saying, Eli, Eli, lama sabachthani? that is to say, My God, my God, why hast thou forsaken me?

Bible: Matthew 27:46

3 The name of the slough was Despond.

John Bunyan (1628–88) English writer. *The Pilgrim's Progress*, Pt. I

4 A castle called Doubting Castle, the owner whereof was Giant Despair.

John Bunyan *The Pilgrim's Progress*, Pt. I

5 Not, I'll not, carrion comfort, Despair, not feast on thee;
Not untwist – slack they may be – these last strands of man
In me or, most weary, cry *I can no more*. I can;
Can something, hope, wish day come, not choose not to be.

Gerard Manley Hopkins (1844–99) British Jesuit and poet. *Carrion Comfort*

6 Don't despair, not even over the fact that you don't despair.

Franz Kafka (1883–1924) Czech novelist. *Diary*

7 O! that I were as great
As is my grief, or lesser than my name,
Or that I could forget what I have been,
Or not remember what I must be now.

William Shakespeare (1564–1616) English dramatist. *Richard II*, III:3

8 I shall despair. There is no creature loves me;
And if I die, no soul will pity me:
Nay, wherefore should they, since that I myself
Find in myself no pity to myself?

William Shakespeare *Richard III*, V:3

9 The mass of men lead lives of quiet desperation.

Henry David Thoreau (1817–62) US writer. *Walden*, 'Economy'

DESTINY

See also purpose

1 What must be, must be.

Proverb

2 Whatever may happen to you was prepared for you from all eternity; and the implication of causes was from eternity spinning the thread of your being.

Marcus Aurelius (121–180 AD) Roman emperor. *Meditations*, Bk. X, Ch. 5

3 Everything that happens happens as it should, and if you observe carefully, you will find this to be so.

Marcus Aurelius *Meditations*, Bk. IV, Ch. 10

4 …it was ordained that the winding ivy of a Plantagenet should kill the true tree itself.

Francis Bacon (1561–1626) English philosopher. Referring to the execution (1499) of Perkin Warbeck, who claimed to be Edward V's brother, and the Earl of Warwick, the true heir of the house of York. *The Life of Henry VII*

5 I felt as if I were walking with destiny, and that all my past life had been but a preparation for this hour and this trial.

Winston Churchill (1874–1965) British statesman. *The Gathering Storm*, Ch. 38

6 Which brings me to my conclusion upon Free Will and Predestination, namely – let the reader mark it – that they are identical.

Winston Churchill *My Early Life*, Ch. 3

7 'Tis all a Chequer-board of Nights and Days
Where Destiny with Men for Pieces plays:
Hither and thither moves, and mates, and slays,
And one by one back in the Closet lays.

Edward Fitzgerald (1809–83) British poet. *The Rubáiyát of Omar Khayyám*, XLIX

8 The Moving Finger writes; and, having writ,
Moves on: nor all thy Piety nor Wit
Shall lure it back to cancel half a Line,
Nor all thy Tears wash out a Word of it.

Edward Fitzgerald *The Rubáiyát of Omar Khayyám*, LI

9 And that inverted Bowl we call The Sky,
Whereunder crawling coop't we live and die,
Lift not thy hands to *It* for help – for It
Rolls impotently on as Thou or I.

Edward Fitzgerald *The Rubáiyát of Omar Khayyám*, LII

10 Drink! for you know not whence you came, nor why:
Drink! for you know not why you go, nor where.

Edward Fitzgerald *The Rubáiyát of Omar Khayyám*, LXXIV

11 Tempt not the stars, young man, thou canst not play
With the severity of fate.

John Ford (c. 1586–c. 1640) English dramatist. *The Broken Heart*, I:3

12 Anatomy is destiny.

Sigmund Freud (1856–1939) Austrian psychoanalyst.

13 Never let success hide its emptiness from you, achievement its nothingness, toil its desolation. And so...keep alive the incentive to push on further, that pain in the soul which drives us beyond ourselves... Do not look back. And do not dream about the future, either. It will neither give you back the past, nor satisfy your other daydreams. Your duty, your reward – your destiny – are *here* and *now*.

Dag Hammarskjöld (1905–61) Swedish secretary-general of the United Nations. *Markings*

14 I go the way that Providence dictates with the assurance of a sleepwalker.

Adolf Hitler (1889–1945) German dictator. Referring to his successful re-occupation of the Rhineland, despite advice against the attempt. Speech, Munich, 15 Mar 1936

15 Do not try to find out – we're forbidden to know – what end the gods have in store for me, or for you.

Horace (Quintus Horatius Flaccus; 65–8 BC) Roman poet. *Odes*, I

16 Who can foretell for what high cause
This darling of the Gods was born?

Andrew Marvell (1621–78) English poet. *The Picture of Little T.C. in a Prospect of Flowers*

17 And yet the order of the acts is planned,
The way's end destinate and unconcealed.
Alone. Now is the time of Pharisees.
To live is not like walking through a field.

Boris Pasternak (1890–1960) Russian Jewish poet and novelist. *Hamlet* (trans. Henry Kamen)

18 We may become the makers of our fate when we have ceased to pose as its prophets.

Karl Popper (1902–) Austrian-born British philosopher. *The Observer*, 28 Dec 1975

19 Man never found the deities so kindly
As to assure him that he'd live tomorrow.

François Rabelais (1483–1553) French satirist. *Pantagruel*, Bk. III, Ch. 2

20 Fate sits on these dark battlements, and frowns;
And as the portals open to receive me,
Her voice, in sullen echoes, through the courts,
Tells of a nameless deed.

Ann Radcliffe (1764–1823) British novelist. *The Mysteries of Udolpho*

21 There's a divinity that shapes our ends,
Rough-hew them how we will.

William Shakespeare (1564–1616) English dramatist. *Hamlet*, V:2

22 As flies to wanton boys are we to th' gods –
They kill us for their sport.

William Shakespeare *King Lear*, IV:1

23 The wheel is come full circle.

William Shakespeare *King Lear*, V:3

24 The ancient saying is no heresy:
Hanging and wiving goes by destiny.

William Shakespeare *The Merchant of Venice*, II:9

25 Who can control his fate?

William Shakespeare *Othello*, V:2

26 O! I am Fortune's fool.

William Shakespeare *Romeo and Juliet*, III:1

27 One God, one law, one element,
And one far-off divine event,
To which the whole creation moves.

Alfred, Lord Tennyson (1809–92) British poet. *In Memoriam A.H.H.*, CXXXI

28 I embrace the purpose of God and the doom assigned.

Alfred, Lord Tennyson *Maud*, III

29 We are merely the stars' tennis-balls, struck and bandied
Which way please them.

John Webster (1580–1625) English dramatist. *The Duchess of Malfi*, V:4

30 Every bullet has its billet.

William III (1650–1702) King of England. *Journal* (John Wesley), 6 June 1765

DETERMINATION

See also decision, endurance, inflexibility, persistence, stubbornness

1 He who hesitates is lost.

Proverb

2 Where there's a will there's a way.

Proverb

3 Don't listen to anyone who tells you that you can't do this or that. That's nonsense. Make up your mind, you'll never use crutches or a stick, then have a go at everything. Go to school, join in all the games you can. Go anywhere you want to. But never, never let them persuade you that things are too difficult or impossible.

Douglas Bader (1910–82) British fighter pilot. Speaking to a fourteen-year-old boy who had had a leg amputated after a road accident. Douglas Bader lost both his legs in a flying accident (1931) before becoming a fighter pilot in World War II. *Flying Colours* (Laddie Lucas)

4 There is no such thing as a great talent without great will-power.

Honoré de Balzac (1799–1850) French novelist. *La Muse du département*

5 Let us determine to die here, and we will conquer.
There is Jackson standing like a stone wall. Rally behind the Virginians.

Barnard Elliot Bee (1824–61) US soldier. Said at the First Battle of Bull Run, 1861; hence General Thomas Jackson's nickname, 'Stonewall Jackson'. *Reminiscences of Metropolis* (Poore), II

6 We will not go to Canossa.

Bismarck (1815–98) German statesman. A declaration of his anti-Roman Catholic policy; the Emperor Henry IV had submitted to Pope Gregory VII at Canossa, N. Italy, in 1077. Speech, Reichstag, 14 May 1872

7 The spirit burning but unbent,
May writhe, rebel – the weak alone repent!

Lord Byron (1788–1824) British poet. *The Corsair*, II

8 I purpose to fight it out on this line, if it takes all summer.

Ulysses Simpson Grant (1822–85) US general. Dispatch to Washington, 11 May 1864

9 It will be conquered; I will not capitulate.

Samuel Johnson (1709–84) British lexicographer. Referring to his illness. *Life of Johnson* (J. Boswell), Vol. IV

10 I have not yet begun to fight.

John Paul Jones (1747–92) Scottish-born US naval commander. Retort when informed his ship was sinking. *Life and Letters of J. P. Jones* (De Koven), Vol. I

11 I shall return.

Douglas Macarthur (1880–1964) US general. Message (11 Mar 1942) on leaving for Australia from Corregidor Island (Philippines), which he had been defending against the Japanese

12 What though the field be lost?
All is not lost – the unconquerable will,
And study of revenge, immortal hate,
And courage never to submit or yield:
And what is else not to be overcome?

John Milton (1608–74) English poet. *Paradise Lost*, Bk. I

13 By God, O King, I will neither go nor hang!

Roger Bigod, Earl of Norfolk (1245–1306) Marshal of England. Reply to Edward I's 'By God, Earl, you shall either go or hang!'; Edward had ordered Norfolk and other barons to invade France from Gascony. *Hemingburgh's Chronicle*, Bk. II

14 The Congress will push me to raise taxes and I'll say no, and they'll push, and I'll say no, and they'll push again. And I'll say to them, read my lips, no new taxes.

George Bush (1924–) US politician and president. Speech accepting his nomination as presidential candidate, Republican Party Convention, New Orleans, Aug 1988

15 We must just KBO ('Keep Buggering On').

Winston Churchill (1874–1965) British statesman. Remark, Dec 1941. *Finest Hour* (M. Gilbert)

16 Never let success hide its emptiness from you, achievement its nothingness, toil its desolation. And so…keep alive the incentive to push on further, that pain in the soul which drives us beyond ourselves… Do not look back. And do not dream about the future, either. It will neither give you back the past, nor satisfy your other daydreams. Your duty, your reward – your destiny – are *here* and *now*.

Dag Hammarskjöld (1905–61) Swedish secretary-general of the United Nations. *Markings*

17 Very well, alone.

David Low (1891–1963) British cartoonist. The cartoon showed a British soldier shaking his fist at a hostile sea and a sky full of war planes. Caption to cartoon, *Evening Standard*, 18 June 1940

18 I don't believe I ought to quit because I am not a quitter.

Richard Milhous Nixon (1913–94) US President. TV address, 23 Sept 1952

19 Look for me by moonlight;
Watch for me by moonlight;
I'll come to thee by moonlight, though hell should bar the way!

Alfred Noyes (1880–1958) British poet. *The Highwayman*

20 *Ils ne passeront pas.*
They shall not pass.

Marshal Pétain (1856–1951) French marshal. Attrib; probably derived from General R.-G. Nivelle's Order of the Day, *'Vous ne les laisserez pas passer'* (June 1916). It is also attributed to the Spanish politician Dolores Ibarruri.

21 My resolution's plac'd, and I have nothing
Of woman in me; now from head to foot
I am marble-constant, now the fleeting moon
No planet is of mine.

William Shakespeare (1564–1616) English dramatist. *Antony and Cleopatra*, V:2

22 I will have my bond.

William Shakespeare *The Merchant of Venice*, III:3

23 Even if the doctor does not give you a year, even if he hesitates about a month, make one brave push and see what can be accomplished in a week.

Robert Louis Stevenson (1850–94) Scottish writer. *Virginibus Puerisque*, Ch. 5

24 We are not now that strength which in old days
Moved earth and heaven; that which we are, we are;
One equal temper of heroic hearts,
Made weak by time and fate, but strong in will
To strive, to seek, to find, and not to yield.

Alfred, Lord Tennyson (1809–92) British poet. *Ulysses*

25 I've got a woman's ability to stick to a job and get on with it when everyone else walks off and leaves it.

Margaret Thatcher (1925–) British politician and prime minister. *The Observer*, 'Sayings of the Week', 16 Feb 1975

26 I fight on, I fight to win.

Margaret Thatcher Referring to the election for the leadership of the Conservative Party. *The Times*, 21 Nov 1990

27 I knew what I wanted and determined at an early age that no man would ever tell me what to do. I would make my own rules and down with the double standards.

Mae West (1892–1980) US actress. *Working Woman*, Feb 1979

DEVIL

See also damnation, hell

1 The devil is not so black as he is painted.

Proverb

2 Talk of the devil, and he is bound to appear.
Proverb

3 And he said unto them, I beheld Satan as lightning fall from heaven.
Bible: Luke 10:18

4 And the devil, taking him up into an high mountain, shewed unto him all the kingdoms of the world in a moment of time.
Bible: Luke 4:5

5 And the Lord said unto Satan, Whence comest thou? Then Satan answered the Lord; and said, From going to and fro in the earth, and from walking up and down in it.
Bible: Job 1:7

6 And he asked him, What is thy name? And he answered, saying. My name is Legion: for we are many.
Bible: Mark 5:9

7 And there was war in heaven: Michael and his angels fought against the dragon; and the dragon fought and his angels,
And prevailed not; neither was their place found any more in heaven.
And the great dragon was cast out, that old serpent, called the Devil, and Satan, which deceiveth the whole world: he was cast out into the earth, and his angels were cast out with him.
Bible: Revelations 12:7–9

8 And that no man might buy or sell, save he that had the mark, or the name of the beast, or the number of his name.
Here is wisdom. Let him that hath understanding count the number of the beast: for it is the number of a man; and his number is Six hundred threescore and six.
Bible: Revelations 13:17–18

9 O Thou! Whatever title suit thee –
Auld Hornie, Satan, Nick, or Clootie.
Robert Burns (1759–96) Scottish poet. *Address to the Devil*

10 Wherever God erects a house of prayer,
The Devil always builds a chapel there;
And 'twill be found, upon examination,
The latter has the largest congregation.
Daniel Defoe (1660–1731) British journalist and writer. *The True-Born Englishman*, Pt. I

11 It is so stupid of modern civilization to have given up believing in the devil when he is the only explanation of it.
Ronald Knox (1888–1957) British Roman Catholic priest. *Let Dons Delight*

12 It is no good casting out devils. They belong to us, we must accept them and be at peace with them.
D. H. Lawrence (1885–1930) British novelist. *Phoenix*, 'The Reality of Peace'

13 High on a throne of royal state, which far
Outshone the wealth of Ormus and of Ind,
Or where the gorgeous East with richest hand
Showers on her kings barbaric pearl and gold,
Satan exalted sat, by merit raised
To that bad eminence.
John Milton (1608–74) English poet. *Paradise Lost*, Bk. II

14 The devil can cite Scripture for his purpose.
William Shakespeare (1564–1616) English dramatist. *The Merchant of Venice*, I:3

15 Sometimes
The Devil is a gentleman.
Percy Bysshe Shelley (1792–1822) British poet. *Peter Bell the Third*

DIARIES

1 Let diaries, therefore, be brought in use.
Francis Bacon (1561–1626) English philosopher. *Essays*, 'Of Travel'

2 Only good girls keep diaries. Bad girls don't have the time.
Tallulah Bankhead (1903–68) US actress. Attrib.

3 With the publication of his Private Papers in 1952, he committed suicide 25 years after his death.
Lord Beaverbrook (1879–1964) British newspaper owner and politician. Referring to Earl Haig. *Men and Power*

4 I do not keep a diary. Never have. To write a diary every day is like returning to one's own vomit.
Enoch Powell (1912–) British politician. *Sunday Times*, 6 Nov 1977

5 What is a diary as a rule? A document useful to the person who keeps it, dull to the contemporary who reads it, invaluable to the student, centuries afterwards, who treasures it!
Ellen Terry (1847–1928) British actress. *The Story of My Life*, Ch. 14.

6 I never travel without my diary. One should always have something sensational to read in the train.
Oscar Wilde (1854–1900) Irish-born British dramatist. *The Importance of Being Earnest*, II

DICKENS, CHARLES

(1812–70) British novelist. His career began with contributions to magazines using the pen name Boz, *Pickwick Papers* (1837) bringing him sudden fame. His many subsequent novels, all appearing in monthly instalments and depicting the poverty of the working classes in Victorian England, have remained immensely popular.

Quotations about Dickens

1 We were put to Dickens as children but it never quite took. That unremitting humanity soon had me cheesed off.
Alan Bennett (1934–) British playwright. *The Old Country*, II

2 It does not matter that Dickens' world is not life-like; it is alive.
Lord Cecil (1902–86) British writer and critic. *Early Victorian Novelists*

3 One would have to have a heart of stone to read the death of Little Nell without laughing.
Oscar Wilde (1854–1900) Irish-born British dramatist. Lecturing upon Dickens. *Lives of the Wits* (H. Pearson)

Quotations by Dickens

4 'There are strings', said Mr Tappertit, 'in the human heart that had better not be wibrated.'
Barnaby Rudge, Ch. 22

5 This is a London particular…A fog, miss.
Bleak House, Ch. 3

6 I expect a judgment. Shortly.
Bleak House, Ch. 3

7 'Old girl,' said Mr Bagnet, 'give him my opinion. You know it.'
Bleak House, Ch. 27

8 It is a melancholy truth that even great men have their poor relations.
Bleak House, Ch. 28

9 O let us love our occupations,
Bless the squire and his relations,
Live upon our daily rations,
And always know our proper stations.
The Chimes, '2nd Quarter'

10 'God bless us every one!' said Tiny Tim, the last of all.
A Christmas Carol

11 'I am a lone lorn creetur,' were Mrs Gummidge's words…'and everythink goes contrairy with me.'
David Copperfield, Ch. 3

12 Barkis is willin'.
David Copperfield, Ch. 5

13 Annual income twenty pounds, annual expenditure nineteen nineteen six, result happiness. Annual income twenty pounds, annual expenditure twenty pounds ought and six, result misery.
David Copperfield, Ch. 12

14 I am well aware that I am the 'umblest person going….My mother is likewise a very 'umble person. We live in a numble abode.
Said by Uriah Heep. *David Copperfield*, Ch. 16

15 We are so very 'umble.
David Copperfield, Ch. 17

16 Uriah, with his long hands slowly twining over one another, made a ghastly writhe from the waist upwards.
David Copperfield, Ch. 17

17 Accidents will occur in the best-regulated families.
David Copperfield, Ch. 28

18 I'm Gormed – and I can't say no fairer than that.
David Copperfield, Ch. 63

19 When found, make a note of.
Dombey and Son, Ch. 15

20 There's a young man hid with me, in comparison with which young man I am a Angel. That young man hears the words I speak. That young man has a secret way pecooliar to himself, of getting at a boy, and at his heart, and at his liver.
Said by Magwitch. *Great Expectations*, Ch. 1

21 Now, what I want is Facts…Facts alone are wanted in life.
Hard Times, Bk. I, Ch. 1

22 Whatever was required to be done, the Circumlocution Office was beforehand with all the public departments in the art of perceiving – HOW NOT TO DO IT.
Little Dorrit, Bk. I, Ch. 10

23 In company with several other old ladies of both sexes.
Said by Mr Meagles. *Little Dorrit*, Bk. I, Ch. 17

24 It was not a bosom to repose upon, but it was a capital bosom to hang jewels upon.
Describing Mrs Merdle. *Little Dorrit*, Bk. I, Ch. 21

25 Let us be moral. Let us contemplate existence.
Martin Chuzzlewit, Ch. 10

26 Here's the rule for bargains: 'Do other men, for they would do you.' That's the true business precept.
Martin Chuzzlewit, Ch. 11

27 Buy an annuity cheap, and make your life interesting to yourself and everybody else that watches the speculation.
Martin Chuzzlewit, Ch. 18

28 He'd make a lovely corpse.
Martin Chuzzlewit, Ch. 25

29 'She's the sort of woman now,' said Mould,… 'one would almost feel disposed to bury for nothing: and do it neatly, too!'
Martin Chuzzlewit, Ch. 25

30 He had but one eye, and the popular prejudice runs in favour of two.
Said by Mr Squeers. *Nicholas Nickleby*, Ch. 4

31 When he has learnt that bottinney means a knowledge of plants, he goes and knows 'em. That's our system, Nickleby; what do you think of it?
Said by Mr Squeers. *Nicholas Nickleby*, Ch. 8

32 As she frequently remarked when she made any such mistake, it would be all the same a hundred years hence.
Said by Mrs Squeers. *Nicholas Nickleby*, Ch. 9

33 Every baby born into the world is a finer one than the last.
Nicholas Nickleby, Ch. 36

34 All is gas and gaiters.
Nicholas Nickleby, Ch. 49

35 'Did you ever taste beer?' 'I had a sip of it once,' said the small servant. 'Here's a state of things!' cried Mr Swiveller…. 'She *never* tasted it – it can't be tasted in a sip!'
The Old Curiosity Shop, Ch. 57

36 Oliver Twist has asked for more.
Oliver Twist, Ch. 2

37 Known by the *sobriquet* of 'The artful Dodger.'
Oliver Twist, Ch. 8

38 'If the law supposes that,' said Mr Bumble…, 'the law is a ass – a idiot.'

Oliver Twist, Ch. 51

39 The question about everything was, would it bring a blush to the cheek of a young person?
Pondered by Mr Podsnap. *Our Mutual Friend*, Bk. I, Ch. 11

40 I think...that it is the best club in London.
Mr Tremlow describing the House of Commons. *Our Mutual Friend*, Bk. II, Ch. 3

41 He'd be sharper than a serpent's tooth, if he wasn't as dull as ditch water.
Our Mutual Friend, Bk. III, Ch. 10

42 Kent, sir – everybody knows Kent – apples, cherries, hops and women.
Pickwick Papers, Ch. 2

43 I wants to make your flesh creep.
Pickwick Papers, Ch. 8

44 'It's always best on these occasions to do what the mob do.'
'But suppose there are two mobs?' suggested Mr Snodgrass.
'Shout with the largest,' replied Mr Pickwick.
Pickwick Papers, Ch. 13

45 Take example by your father, my boy, and be very careful o' vidders all your life.
Pickwick Papers, Ch. 13

46 Poverty and oysters always seem to go together.
Pickwick Papers, Ch. 22

47 Wery glad to see you indeed, and hope our acquaintance may be a long 'un, as the gen'l'm'n said to the fi' pun' note.
Pickwick Papers, Ch. 25

48 Poetry's unnat'ral; no man ever talked poetry 'cept a beadle on boxin' day.
Pickwick Papers, Ch. 33

49 It's my opinion, sir, that this meeting is drunk.
Pickwick Papers, Ch. 33

50 I am afeered that werges on the poetical, Sammy.
Said by Sam Weller. *Pickwick Papers*, Ch. 33

51 Never sign a walentine with your own name.
Said by Sam Weller. *Pickwick Papers*, Ch. 33

52 Put it down a we, my lord, put it down a we!
Pickwick Papers, Ch. 34

53 Miss Bolo rose from the table considerably agitated, and went straight home, in a flood of tears and a Sedan chair.
Pickwick Papers, Ch. 35

54 Anythin' for a quiet life, as the man said wen he took the sitivation at the lighthouse.
Pickwick Papers, Ch. 43

55 A smattering of everything, and a knowledge of nothing.
Sketches by Boz, 'Tales', Ch. 3

56 It was the best of times, it was the worst of times, it was the age of wisdom, it was the age of foolishness, it was the epoch of belief, it was the epoch of incredulity, it was the season of Light, it was the season of Darkness, it was the spring of hope, it was the winter of despair, we had everything before us, we had nothing before us, we were all going direct to Heaven, we were all going direct the other way.
The opening words of the book. *A Tale of Two Cities*, Bk. I, Ch. 1

57 It is a far, far, better thing that I do, than I have ever done; it is a far, far, better rest that I go to, than I have ever known.
A Tale of Two Cities, Bk. II, Ch. 15

DICKINSON, EMILY

(1830–86) US poet who has been called 'the New England mystic'. Her works include *Poems by Emily Dickinson* (1890), *The Single Hound: Poems of a Lifetime* (1914), and *Bolts of Melody: New Poems of Emily Dickinson* (1945).

Quotations about Dickinson

1 I saw her but twice, face to face, and brought away the impression of something as unique and remote as Undine or Mignon or Thekla.
Bookman, Oct 1924

2 In a life so retired it was inevitable that the main events should be the death of friends, and Emily Dickinson became a prolific writer of notes of condolence.
Northrop Frye (1912–83) Canadian critic. *Major Writers of America* (ed. Perry Miller)

Quotations by Dickinson

3 Because I could not stop for Death,
He kindly stopped for me;
The carriage held but just ourselves
And Immortality.
The Chariot

4 Parting is all we know of heaven,
And all we need of hell.
My Life Closed Twice Before its Close

5 Pain – has an element of Blank –
It cannot recollect
When it begun – or if there were
A time when it was not –.
Pain

6 Success is counted sweetest
By those who ne'er succeed.
Success is Counted Sweetest

DIETING

1 Unnecessary dieting is because everything from television and fashion ads have made it seem wicked to cast a shadow. This wild, emaciated look appeals to some women, though not to many men, who are seldom seen pinning up a *Vogue* illustration in a machine shop.
Peg Bracken (1918–) US writer and humorist. *The I Hate to Cook Book*

2 As the low-fat diet unfolded, I really felt that God was showing me the way.
Rosemary Conley *The Observer*, 27 June 1993

3 Eating disorders, whether it be anorexia or bulimia, show how individuals can turn the nourishment of the body into a painful attack on themselves and they have at the core a far deeper problem than mere vanity.

Diana, Princess of Wales (1961–) Wife of Prince Charles. *The Times*, 28 Apr 1993

4 A number of small-scale studies have shown that social security benefit levels are insufficient to allow people to eat a healthy diet.

Suzi Leather National Consumer Council. *Your Food: Whose Choice?*

5 Ninety-five per cent of dieters will regain all the weight loss within two or three years...The average woman would not be able to drop two dress-sizes in three weeks without seriously affecting her health.

Alice Mahon (1937–) British politician. *The Independent*, 30 June 1993

6 The first and most important point to remember is that eating should be a pleasure – do not eat purely for health, you won't live much longer, but it will feel like an eternity.

Dr Mark Porter *Radio Times*, 9–15 July 1994

7 We are assaulted by conflicting information about food which appears in the press or on radio and which expose us to passing fads and fancies.

Dilys Wells British nutritionist. *The Good, the Bad and the Fattening*

8 You have a situation where girls of eight want to lose weight and at 12 they can tell you the fat content of an avocado...but they don't know what constitutes a healthy meal.

Mary Evans Young Chairwoman of Dietbreakers *The Observer*, 1 May 1994

DIFFERENCE

See also individuality, opposites, similarity, taste

1 Every man after his fashion.

Proverb

2 Every one to his taste.

Proverb

3 One man's meat is another man's poison.

Proverb

4 There is more than one way to skin a cat.

Proverb

5 There is no accounting for tastes.

Proverb

6 There's nowt so queer as folk.

Proverb

7 All colours will agree in the dark.

Francis Bacon (1561–1626) English philosopher. *Essays*, 'Of Unity in Religion'

8 The only inequalities that matter begin in the mind. It is not income levels but differences in mental equipment that keep people apart, breed feelings of inferiority.

Jacquetta Hawkes (1910–) British archeologist. *New Statesman*, Jan 1957

9 If we cannot now end our differences, at least we can help make the world safe for diversity.

John Fitzgerald Kennedy (1917–63) US statesman. Speech, American University (Washington, DC), 10 June 1963

DIPLOMACY

See also tact

1 Our business is to break with them and yet to lay the breache at their door.

Earl of Arlington (1618–85) Referring to the diplomacy that preceded the third Dutch War (1672–74). *Arlington* (Violet Barbour)

2 We're in the Embassy residence, subject, of course, to some of the discomfiture as a result of a need for, uh, elements of refurbishment and rehabilitation.

Walter Annenberg (1908–) US publisher and diplomat. To Queen Elizabeth II. TV documentary, *Royal Family*

3 It is better for aged diplomats to be bored than for young men to die.

Warren Austin (1877–1962) US politician and diplomat. When asked if he got tired during long debates at the UN. Attrib.

4 There are three groups that no British Prime Minister should provoke: the Vatican, the Treasury and the miners.

Stanley Baldwin (1867–1947) British statesman. A similar remark is often attributed to Harold Macmillan. Attrib.

5 An honest broker.

Bismarck (1815–98) German statesman. His professed role in the diplomacy of 1878, including the Congress of Berlin. Speech, Reichstag, 19 Feb 1878

6 The healthy bones of a single Pomeranian grenadier.

Bismarck A price too high for Germany to pay regarding the Eastern Question. Speech, Reichstag, 5 Dec 1876

7 To jaw-jaw is better than to war-war.

Winston Churchill (1874–1965) British statesman. Speech, Washington, 26 June 1954

8 An appeaser is one who feeds a crocodile – hoping that it will eat him last.

Winston Churchill Attrib.

9 When you have to kill a man it costs nothing to be polite.

Winston Churchill Justifying the fact that the declaration of war against Japan was made in the usual diplomatic language. *The Grand Alliance*

10 Treaties are like roses and young girls – they last while they last.

Charles De Gaulle (1890–1970) French general and statesman. Attrib.

11 America has all that Russia has not. Russia has things America has not. Why will America not reach out a hand to Russia, as I have given my hand?

Isadora Duncan (1878–1927) US dancer. Speaking in support of Russia following the 1917 Revolution. Speech, Symphony Hall, Boston, 1922

12 REPORTER: If Mr Stalin dies, what will be the effect on international affairs?
EDEN: That is a good question for you to ask, not a wise question for me to answer.

Anthony Eden (1897–1977) British statesman. Interview on board the *Queen Elizabeth*, 4 Mar 1953

13 A diplomat is a man who always remembers a woman's birthday but never remembers her age.

Robert Frost (1875–1963) US poet. Attrib.

14 We have stood alone in that which is called isolation – our splendid isolation, as one of our colonial friends was good enough to call it.

George Joachim Goschen (1831–1907) English Conservative politician. Speech, Lewes, 26 Feb 1896

15 I met the great little man, the man who can be silent in several languages.

James Guthrie Harbord (1866–1947) US general. Referring to Colonel House. *Mr Wilson's War* (John Dos Passos), Ch. 3

16 Megaphone diplomacy leads to a dialogue of the deaf.

Geoffrey Howe (1926–) British politician. *The Observer*, 'Sayings of the Week', 29 Sept 1985

17 Official dignity tends to increase in inverse ratio to the importance of the country in which the office is held.

Aldous Huxley (1894–1964) British novelist. *Beyond the Mexique Bay*

18 Our kingdom and whatever anywhere is subject to our rule we place at your disposal and commit to your power, that everything may be arranged at your nod, and that the will of your empire may be carried out in all respects. Let there be between us and our peoples an undivided unity of love and peace and safety of commerce, in such a way that to you, who are pre-eminent in dignity, be given the authority of command, and to us the will to obey shall not be lacking.

Henry II (1133–89) King of England. Letter to the Emperor Frederick Barbarossa, 1157

19 We are not about to send American boys nine or ten thousand miles away from home to do what Asian boys ought to be doing for themselves.

Lyndon B. Johnson (1908–73) US Democratic president. Broadcast address, 21 Oct 1964

20 You let a bully come into your front yard, the next day he'll be on your porch.

Lyndon B. Johnson Referring to Vietnam. *Time*, 15 Apr 1984

21 Let us never negotiate out of fear, but let us never fear to negotiate.

John Fitzgerald Kennedy (1917–63) US statesman. Inaugural address, 20 Jan 1961

22 The great nations have always acted like gangsters, and the small nations like prostitutes.

Stanley Kubrick (1928–) US film director. *The Guardian*, 5 June 1963

23 All diplomacy is a continuation of war by other means.

Chou En Lai (1898–1976) Chinese statesman.

24 *La cordiale entente qui existe entre mon gouvernement et le sien.*
The friendly understanding that exists between my government and hers.

Louis Philippe (1773–1850) King of France. Referring to an informal understanding reached between Britain and France in 1843. The more familiar phrase, 'entente cordiale', was first used in 1844. Speech, 27 Dec 1843

25 The reluctant obedience of distant provinces generally costs more than it is worth.

Lord Macaulay (1800–59) British historian. *Historical Essays Contributed to the 'Edinburgh Review'*, 'Lord Mahon's War of the Succession'

26 Let them especially put their demands in such a way that Great Britain could say that she supported both sides.

Ramsey MacDonald (1866–1937) British statesman and prime minister. Referring to France and Germany. *The Origins of the Second Word War* (A. J. P. Taylor), Ch. 3

27 By intermarriage and by every means in his power he bound the two peoples into a firm union.

Walter Map (c. 1140–c. 1209) Welsh cleric and writer. Referring to Henry I of England, and specifically to his marriage (1100) to Matilda, a descendant of the Anglo-Saxon royal family. *De Nugis Curialium*, Pt. V, Ch. 5

28 Austria will astound the world with the magnitude of her ingratitude.

Prince Schwarzenberg (1800–52) Austrian statesman. On being asked whether Austria was under any obligation to Russia for help received previously. *The Fall of the House of Habsburg* (E. Crankshaw)

29 A diplomat these days is nothing but a head-waiter who's allowed to sit down occasionally.

Peter Ustinov (1921–) British actor. *Romanoff and Juliet*, I

30 Madam, there are fifty thousand men slain this year in Europe, and not one Englishman.

Robert Walpole (1676–1745) British statesman. Referring to his determination not to involve Britain in the War of Polish Succession (1733–35), despite considerable political pressure. Remark to Queen Caroline, 1734

31 No nation is fit to sit in judgement upon any other nation.

Woodrow Wilson (1856–1925) US statesman. Address, Apr 1915

32 An ambassador is an honest man sent to lie abroad for the good of his country.

Henry Wotton (1568–1639) English poet and diplomat. *Life* (Izaak Walton)

DISABILITY

See also blindness

1 If there are any of you at the back who do not hear me, please don't raise your hands because I am also nearsighted.

W. H. Auden (1907–73) British poet. Starting a lecture in a large hall. In *Book of the Month Club News*, Dec 1946

2 I'm a coloured, one-eyed Jew.

Sammy Davis Jnr (1925–90) US singer. When asked what his handicap was during a game of golf. Attrib.

3 I am happy…with who I am and I do not want to be 'fixed'.

Roslyn Rosen President of the National Association of the Deaf. *The Times*, 16 June 1994

4 You are not crippled at all unless your mind is in a splint.

Frank Scully *Bartlett's Unfamiliar Quotations* (Leonard Louis Levinson)

5 There are two kinds of deafness. One is due to wax and is curable; the other is not due to wax and is not curable.

William Wilde (1815–76)

DISAPPOINTMENT

See also disillusion, expectation

1 Unhappiness is best defined as the difference between our talents and our expectations.

Edward de Bono (1933–) British physician and writer. *The Observer*, 'Sayings of the Week', 12 June 1977

2 The best laid schemes o' mice an' men
Gang aft a-gley,
An' lea'e us nought but grief an' pain
For promis'd joy.

Robert Burns (1759–96) Scottish poet. *To a Mouse*

3 Ah, 'all things come to those who wait,'
(I say these words to make me glad),
But something answers soft and sad,
'They come, but often come too late.'

Violet Fane (1843–1905) British poet. 'Tout vient á qui sait attendre'

4 Mountains will heave in childbirth, and a silly little mouse will be born.

Horace (Quintus Horatius Flaccus; 65–8 BC) Roman poet. *Ars Poetica*

5 A mountain in labour shouted so loud that everyone, summoned by the noise, ran up expecting that she would be delivered of a city bigger than Paris; she brought forth a mouse.

Jean de La Fontaine (1621–95) French poet. *Fables*, V, 'La Montagne qui accouche'

6 Levin wanted friendship and got friendliness; he wanted steak and they offered spam.

Bernard Malamud (1914–86) US novelist. *A New Life*, VI

7 Look in my face; my name is Might-have-been.
I am also called No-more, Too-late, Farewell.

Dante Gabriel Rossetti (1828–82) British painter and poet. *The House of Life*, 'A Superscription'

8 Oh, I wish that God had not given me what I prayed for! It was not so good as I thought.

Johanna Spyri (1827–1901) Swiss writer. *Heidi*, Ch. 11

9 He said that he was too old to cry, but it hurt too much to laugh.

Adlai Stevenson (1900–65) US statesman. Said after losing an election, quoting a story told by Abraham Lincoln. Speech, 5 Nov 1952

DISASTER

See also accidents

1 Bad news travels fast.

Proverb

2 Let us hope…that a kind of Providence will put a speedy end to the acts of God under which we have been labouring.

Peter De Vries (1910–93) US novelist. *The Mackerel Plaza*, Ch. 3

3 An Act of God was defined as *something which no reasonable man could have expected.*

A. P. Herbert (1890–1971) British writer and politician. *Uncommon Law*

4 Beautiful Railway Bridge of the Silv'ry Tay!
Alas, I am very sorry to say
That ninety lives have been taken away
On the last Sabbath day of 1879,
Which will be remember'd for a very long time.

William McGonagall (1830–1902) Scottish poet. *The Tay Bridge Disaster*

DISCONTENT

See also envy

1 And sigh that one thing only has been lent
To youth and age in common – discontent.

Matthew Arnold (1822–88) British poet and critic. *Youth's Agitations*

2 The idiot who praises, with enthusiastic tone,
All centuries but this, and every country but his own.

W. S. Gilbert (1836–1911) British dramatist. *The Mikado*, I

3 So have I loitered my life away, reading books, looking at pictures, going to plays, hearing, thinking, writing on what pleased me best. I have wanted only one thing to make me happy, but wanting that have wanted everything.

William Hazlitt (1778–1830) British essayist. *English Literature*, Ch. XVII, 'My First Acquaintance with Poets'

4 How is it, Maecenas, that no one lives contented with his lot, whether he has planned it for himself or fate has flung him into it, but yet he praises those who follow different paths?

Horace (Quintus Horatius Flaccus; 65–8 BC) Roman poet. *Satires*, I

5 Ever let the fancy roam,
Pleasure never is at home.

John Keats (1795–1821) British poet. *Fancy*, I

6 I am sick o' wastin' leather on these gritty pavin'-stones,
An' the blasted English drizzle wakes the fever in my bones;
Tho' I walks with fifty 'ousemaids outer Chelsea to the Strand,
An' they talks a lot o' lovin', but wot do they understand?
Beefy face an' grubby 'and –
Law! Wot do they understand?
I've a neater, sweeter maiden in a cleaner, greener land!

Rudyard Kipling (1865–1936) Indian-born British writer. *The Road to Mandalay*

7 He disdains all things above his reach, and preferreth all countries before his own.

Thomas Overbury (1581–1613) English poet. *Miscellaneous Works*, 'An Affectate Traveller'

8 When in disgrace with fortune and men's eyes
I all alone beweep my outcast state,
And trouble deaf heaven with my bootless cries,
And look upon myself, and curse my fate,
Wishing me like to one more rich in hope
Featur'd like him, like him with friends possess'd,
Desiring this man's art, and that man's scope,
With what I most enjoy contented least.

William Shakespeare (1564–1616) English dramatist. *Sonnet 29*

9 While not exactly disgruntled, he was far from feeling gruntled.

P. G. Wodehouse (1881–1975) British humorous novelist. *The Code of the Woosters*

10 I'd rather be
A Pagan suckled in a creed outworn;
So might I, standing on this pleasant lea,
Have glimpses that would make me less forlorn;
Have sight of Proteus rising from the sea;
Or hear Old Triton blow his wreathed horn.

William Wordsworth (1770–1850) British poet. *Sonnets*, 'The world is too much with us'

DISCOVERY

See also exploration, science, space

1 *Eureka!*
I have found it!

Archimedes (c. 287–212 BC) Greek mathematician. An exclamation of joy supposedly uttered as, stepping into a bath and noticing the water overflowing, he saw the answer to a problem and began the train of thought that led to his principle of buoyancy. Attrib.

2 Look, stranger, at this island now
The leaping light for your delight discovers.

W. H. Auden (1907–73) British poet. *Look, Stranger*

3 Medicinal discovery,
It moves in mighty leaps,
It leapt straight past the common cold
And gave it us for keeps.

Pam Ayres British poet. *Some of Me Poetry*, 'Oh, No, I Got a Cold'

4 They are ill discoverers that think there is no land, when they can see nothing but sea.

Francis Bacon (1561–1626) English philosopher. *The Advancement of Learning*, Bk. II, Ch. 7

5 Upon the whole New Holland, tho' in every respect the most barren country I have seen, is not so bad that between the products of sea and land, a company of people who should have the misfortune of being shipwrecked upon it might support themselves.

Sir Joseph Banks (1744–1820) British scientist. Note, as a participant in Captain Cook's circumnavigation of the world (1768–71), on leaving New South Wales. Journal, Aug 1770

6 At daylight in the morning we discovered a bay, which appeared to be tolerably well sheltered from all winds, into which I resolved to go with the ship.

James Cook (1728–79) British navigator and cartographer. On the discovery of Botany Bay. Journal, 28 Apr 1770

7 Many a man who is brooding over alleged mighty discoveries reminds me of a hen sitting on billiard balls.

J. Chalmers Da Costa (1863–1933) *The Trials and Triumphs of the Surgeon*, Ch. 1

8 We have discovered the secret of life!

Francis Crick (1916–) British scientist. Excitedly bursting into a Cambridge pub with James Watson to celebrate the fact that they had unravelled the structure of DNA. *The Double Helix* (J. D. Watson)

9 None of the great discoveries was made by a 'specialist' or a 'researcher'.

Martin H. Fischer (1879–1962) *Fischerisms* (Howard Fabing and Ray Marr)

10 God could cause us considerable embarrassment by revealing all the secrets of nature to us: we should not know what to do for sheer apathy and boredom.

Goethe (1749–1832) German poet and dramatist. *Memoirs* (Riemer)

11 Then felt I like some watcher of the skies
When a new planet swims into his ken;
Or like stout Cortez when with eagle eyes
He star'd at the Pacific – and all his men
Look'd at each other with a wild surmise –
Silent, upon a peak in Darien.

John Keats (1795–1821) British poet. *On first looking into Chapman's Homer*

12 I do not know what I may appear to the world, but to myself I seem to have been only like a boy playing on the sea-shore, and diverting myself in now and then finding a smoother pebble or a prettier shell than ordinary, whilst the great ocean of truth lay all undiscovered before me.

Isaac Newton (1642–1727) British scientist. *Isaac Newton* (L. T. More)

13 The people – could you patent the sun?

Jonas E. Salk (1914–) US virologist. On being asked who owned the patent on his polio vaccine. *Famous Men of Science* (S. Bolton)

14 We must also keep in mind that discoveries are usually not made by one man alone, but that many brains and many hands are needed before a discovery is made for which one man receives the credit.

Henry E. Sigerist (1891–1957) *A History of Medicine*, Vol. I, Introduction

15 Discovery consists of seeing what everybody has seen and thinking what nobody has thought.

Albert Szent-Györgyi (1893–1986) Hungarian-born US biochemist. *The Scientist Speculates* (I. J. Good)

DISEASE

1 A disease known is half cured.

Proverb

2 'Pray, Mr. Abernethy, what is a cure for gout' was the question of an indolent and luxurious citizen.
'Live upon sixpence a day – and earn it,' was the cogent reply.

John Abernethy (1764–1831) English surgeon. *Medical Portrait Gallery*, Vo. II (Thomas J. Pettigrew)

3 We are led to think of diseases as isolated disturbances in a healthy body, not as the phases of certain periods of bodily development.

Sir Clifford Allbutt (1836–1925) British doctor. *Bulletin of the New York Academy of Medicine*, 4:1000, 1928 (F. H. Garrison)

4 Screw up the vise as tightly as possible – you have rheumatism; give it another turn, and that is gout.

Anonymous

5 Once I am sure a patient has terminal cancer I tell them straight, I say, 'Its time to go visit with the grand-children.' They seem to appreciate it.

Anonymous Said by a doctor from New Mexico. *The Encyclopedia of Alternative Medicine and Self-Help* (ed. Malcolm Hulke)

6 Before this strange disease of modern life,
With its sick hurry, its divided aims.

Matthew Arnold *The Scholar Gipsy*

7 Only those in the last stage of disease could believe that children are true judges of character.

W. H. Auden (1907–73) British poet. *The Orators*, 'Journal of an Airman'

8 Cure the disease and kill the patient.

Francis Bacon (1561–1626) English philosopher. *Essays*, 'Of Friendship'

9 The remedy is worse than the disease.

Francis Bacon *Essays*, 'Of Seditions and troubles'

10 GOUT, n. A physician's name for the rheumatism of a rich patient.

Ambrose Bierce (1842–c. 1914) US writer and journalist. *The Devil's Dictionary*

11 Diseases crucify the soul of man, attenuate our bodies, dry them, wither them, shrivel them up like old apples make them so many anatomies.

Robert Burton (1577–1640) English scholar and churchman. *The Anatomy of Melancholy*, 1

12 Evil comes at leisure like the disease; good comes in a hurry like the doctor.

G. K. Chesterton (1874–1936) British writer. *The Man who was Orthodox*

13 Life is an incurable disease.

Abraham Cowley (1618–67) English poet. *To Dr Scarborough*

14 There is a dread disease which so prepares its victim, as it were, for death…a disease in which death and life are so strangely blended, that death takes a glow and hue of life, and life the gaunt and grisly form of death – a disease which medicine never cured, wealth warded off, or poverty could boast exemption from – which sometimes moves in giant strides, and sometimes at a tardy sluggish pace, but, slow or quick, is ever sure and certain.

Charles Dickens (1812–70) British novelist. *Nicholas Nickleby*, Ch. 49

15 Epidemics have often been more influential than statesman and soldiers in shaping the course of political history, and diseases may also colour the moods of civilizations.

René Dubos (1901–) US microbiologist. *The White Plague*, Ch. 5

16 Disease is an experience of mortal mind. It is fear made manifest on the body.

Mary Baker Eddy (1821–1910) US religious reader and scientist. *Science and Health*, Ch. 14

17 To think that a bottle of wine or a truffled pâté, or even a glass of beer, instead of being absorbed and eliminated by the system in the usual manner, should mine its way through the thighs, knees, calves, ankles, and instep, to explode at last in a fiery volcano in one's great toe, seems a mirth-provoking phenomenon to all but him who is immediately concerned.

George Herman Ellwanger (fl. 1897) *Meditations on Gout*, 'The Malady'

18 Time had robbed her of her personal charms, and that scourge of the human race, the gout, was racking her bones and sinews.

Hannah Farnham Lee (1780–1865) Referring to Catherine de Medici. *The Huguenots in France and America*

19 Many a diabetic has stayed alive by stealing the bread denied him by his doctor.

Martin H. Fischer (1879–1962) *Fischerisms* (Howard Fabing and Ray Marr)

20 Cancer's a Funny Thing:
I wish I had the voice of Homer
To sing of rectal carcinoma,
Which kills a lot more chaps, in fact,
Than were bumped off when Troy
was sacked…

J. B. S. Haldane (1892–1964) British geneticist. Written while mortally ill with cancer. *JBS* (Ronald Clark)

21 If gentlemen love the pleasant titillation of the gout, it is all one to the Town Pump.

Nathaniel Hawthorne (1804–64) US writer. *The Town Pump*

22 Some people are so sensitive they feel snubbed if an epidemic overlooks them.

Frank (Kin) Hubbard (1868–1930) US humorist and journalist. *Abe Martin's Broadcast*

23 Gout is to the arteries what rheumatism is to the heart.

Henri Huchard (1844–1910) *Lancet*, 1:164, 1967 (D. Evan Bedford)

24 We're all going to go crazy, living this epidemic every minute, while the rest of the world goes on out there, all around us, as if nothing is happening, going on with their own lives and not knowing what it's like, what we're going through. We're living through war, but where they're living it's peacetime, and we're all in the same country.

Larry Kramer (1935–) US dramatist and novelist. *The Normal Heart*

25 It is the only disease you don't look forward to being cured of.

Herman J. Mankiewicz (1897–1953) US journalist and screenwriter. Referring to death. *Citizen Kane*

26 While there are several chronic diseases more destructive to life than cancer, none is more feared.

Charles H. Mayo (1865–1939) US physician. *Annals of Surgery*, 83:357, 1926

27 Fever the eternal reproach to the physicians.

John Milton (1608–74) English poet. *Paradise Lost*, Bk. XI

28 I have Bright's disease and he has mine.

S. J. Perelman Attrib.

29 The Muse but serv'd to ease some friend, not Wife,
To help me through this long disease, my life.

Alexander Pope (1688–1744) British poet. *Epistle to Dr. Arbuthnot*

30 Cur'd yesterday of my disease,
I died last night of my physician.

Matthew Prior (1664–1721) British poet. *The Remedy Worse than the Disease*

31 Diseases are the tax on pleasures.

John Ray (1627–1705) English naturalist. *English Proverbs*

32 The diseases which destroy a man are no less natural than the instincts which preserve him.

George Santayana (1863–1952) Spanish-born US philosopher, poet, and critic. *Dialogues in Limbo*, 3

33 Preachers say, Do as I say, not as I do. But if the physician had the same disease upon him that I have, and he should bid me do one thing, and himself do quite another, could I believe him?

John Selden (1584–1654) English historian. *Table Talk*

34 Disease is not of the body but of the place.

Seneca (c. 4 BC–65 AD) Roman writer. *Epistulae ad Lucilium*

35 Not even remedies can master incurable diseases.

Seneca *Epistulae ad Lucilium*

36 The development of industry has created many new sources of danger. Occupational diseases are socially different from other diseases, but not biologically.

Henry E. Sigerist (1891–1957) *Journal of the History of Medicine and Allied Sciences*, 13:214, 1958

37 The man of the present day would far rather believe that disease is connected only with immediate causes for the fundamental tendency in the modern view of life is always to seek what is more convenient.

Rudolf Steiner (1861–1925) Austrian philosopher, founder of anthroposophy. *The Manifestations of Karma*, Lecture III

38 The old saw is that 'if you drink wine you have the gout and if you do not drink wine the gout will have you.'

Thomas Sydenham (1624–89) *Works*, 'A Treatise on Gout and Dropsy'

39 Decay and disease are often beautiful, like the pearly tear of the shellfish and the hectic glow of consumption.

Henry David Thoreau (1817–62) US writer. *Journal*, 11 June 1852

40 The art of medicine consists of amusing the patient while Nature cures the disease.

Voltaire (1694–1788) French writer. Attrib.

41 I would like to remind those responsible for the treatment of tuberculosis that Keats wrote his best poems while dying of this disease. In my opinion he would never have done so under the influence of modern chemotherapy.

Arthur M. Walker (1896–1955) *Walkerisms* (Julius L. Wilson)

DISILLUSION

See also disappointment, innocence of childhood

1 The price one pays for pursuing any profession or calling is an intimate knowledge of its ugly side.

James Baldwin (1924–87) US writer. *Nobody Knows My Name*

2 If you live long enough, you'll see that every victory turns into a defeat.

Simone de Beauvoir (1908–86) French writer. *Tous les hommes sont mortels*

3 The coach has turned into a pumpkin and the mice have all run away.

Ladybird Johnson (1912–) Wife of Lyndon B. Johnson. Said after Lyndon Johnson gave up the presidency. *The Vantage Point* (Lyndon B. Johnson)

4 I have protracted my work till most of those whom I wished to please have sunk into the grave; and success and miscarriage are empty sounds.

Samuel Johnson (1709–84) British lexicographer. *Dictionary of the English Language*

5 One stops being a child when one realizes that telling one's trouble does not make it better.

Cesare Pavese (1908–50) Italian novelist and poet. *The Business of Living: Diaries 1935–50*

6 Thou wretched, rash, intruding fool, farewell!
I took thee for thy better.

William Shakespeare (1564–1616) English dramatist. *Hamlet*, III:4

DISMISSAL

See also departure

1 You have sat too long here for any good you have been doing. Depart, I say, and let us have done with you. In the name of God, *go!*

Leopold Amery (1873–1955) British statesman. Said to Neville Chamberlain using Cromwell's words. Speech, House of Commons, May 1940

2 You have delighted us long enough.

Jane Austen (1775–1817) British novelist. *Pride and Prejudice*, Ch. 18

3 My language fails
Go out and govern new South Wales.

Hilaire Belloc (1870–1953) British writer. *Cautionary Tales*, 'Lord Lundy'

4 It is not fit that you should sit here any longer!...you shall now give place to better men.

Oliver Cromwell (1599–1658) English soldier and statesman. Speech to the Rump Parliament, 22 Jan 1655

5 Take away that fool's bauble, the mace.

Oliver Cromwell Speech dismissing Parliament, 20 Apr 1653

6 Go, and never darken my towels again!

Groucho Marx (Julius Marx; 1895–1977) US comedian. *Duck Soup*

7 There comes a time in every man's life when he must make way for an older man.

Reginald Maudling (1917–77) British politician. Remark made on being replaced in the shadow cabinet by John Davies, his elder by four years. *The Guardian*, 20 Nov 1976

8 We Don't Want To Lose You But We Think You Ought To Go.

Paul Alfred Rubens (1875–1917) British dramatist and songwriter. Song title

9 Stand not upon the order of your going,
But go at once.

William Shakespeare (1564–1616) English dramatist. *Macbeth*, III:4

10 Dropping the pilot.

John Tenniel (1820–1914) British illustrator and cartoonist. Caption of a cartoon. The cartoon refers to Bismarck's resignation portraying him as a ship's pilot walking down the gangway of the ship while Wilhelm II watches from the deck. *Punch*, 29 Mar 1890

11 The son of a bitch isn't going to resign on me, I want him fired.

Harry S. Truman (1884–1972) US statesman. To Omar Bradley, when Truman sacked MacArthur from his command of UN forces in Korea, 1951. Attrib.

DISRAELI, BENJAMIN

(1st Earl of Beaconsfield; 1804–81) British statesman of Italian-Jewish descent, who became Conservative prime minister (1868; 1874–80). He was supported by Queen Victoria, whom he made Empress of India. He also wrote novels including *Coningsby* (1844) and *Sybil* (1845).

Quotations about Disraeli

1 The soul of Dizzy was a chandelier.
Edmund Clerihew Bentley (1875–1956) British writer. *A Ballad of Souls*

2 He was without any rival whatever, the first comic genius who ever installed himself in Downing Street.
Michael Foot (1913–) British Labour politician and journalist. *Debts of Honour*

3 Disraeli lacked two qualities, failing which true eloquence is impossible. He was never quite in earnest, and he was not troubled by dominating conviction.
Henry Lucy (1843–1924) British journalist. *Sixty Years in the Wilderness*

Quotations by Disraeli

4 Youth is a blunder; manhood a struggle; old age a regret.
Coningsby, Bk. III, Ch. 1

5 Almost everything that is great has been done by youth.
Coningsby, Bk. III, Ch. 1

6 His Christianity was muscular.
Endymion, Bk. I, Ch. 14

7 'Sensible men are all of the same religion.' 'And pray what is that?' inquired the prince. 'Sensible men never tell.'
Endymion, Bk. I, Ch. 81

8 The blue ribbon of the turf.
Describing the Derby. *Life of Lord George Bentinck*, Ch. 26

9 When a man fell into his anecdotage it was a sign for him to retire from the world.
Lothair, Ch. 28

10 Every woman should marry – and no man.
Lothair, Ch. 30

11 'My idea of an agreeable person,' said Hugo Bohun, 'is a person who agrees with me.'
Lothair, Ch. 35

12 'Two nations; between whom there is no intercourse and no sympathy; who are as ignorant of each other's habits, thoughts, and feelings, as if they were dwellers in different zones, or inhabitants of different planets; who are formed by a different breeding are fed by a different food, are ordered by different manners, and are not governed by the same laws.'
'You speak of–' said Egremont, hesitatingly.
'THE RICH AND THE POOR.'
Sybil, Bk. II, Ch. 5

13 Little things affect little minds.
Sybil, Bk. III, Ch. 2

14 A majority is always the best repartee.
Tancred, Bk. II, Ch. 14

15 It destroys one's nerves to be amiable every day to the same human being.
The Young Duke

16 There are three kinds of lies: lies, damned lies and statistics.
Autobiography (Mark Twain)

17 I will not go down to posterity talking bad grammar.
Remark made when correcting proofs of his last parliamentary speech, 31 Mar 1881. *Disraeli* (Blake), Ch. 32

18 I know he is, and he adores his maker.
Replying to a remark made in defence of John Bright that he was a self-made man. *The Fine Art of Political Wit* (L. Harris)

19 Thank you for the manuscript; I shall lose no time in reading it.
His customary reply to those who sent him unsolicited manuscripts. *Irreverent Social History* (F. Muir)

20 Though I sit down now, the time will come when you will hear me.
Maiden Speech, House of Commons, 7 Dec 1837

21 The Continent will not suffer England to be the workshop of the world.
Speech, House of Commons, 15 Mar 1838

22 Thus you have a starving population, an absentee aristocracy, and an alien Church, and in addition the weakest executive in the world. That is the Irish Question.
Speech, House of Commons, 16 Feb 1844

23 The right honourable gentleman caught the Whigs bathing, and walked away with their clothes.
Referring to Sir Robert Peel. Speech, House of Commons, 28 Feb 1845

24 A Conservative government is an organized hypocrisy.
Speech, 17 Mar 1845

25 A precedent embalms a principle.
Speech, House of Commons, 22 Feb 1848

26 He has to learn that petulance is not sarcasm, and that insolence is not invective.
Said of Sir C. Wood. Speech, House of Commons, 16 Dec 1852

27 I am myself a gentleman of the Press, and I bear no other scutcheon.
Speech, House of Commons, 18 Feb 1863

28 The question is this: Is man an ape or an angel? I, my lord, am on the side of the angels.
Speech, 25 Nov 1864

29 Assassination has never changed the history of the world.
Speech, House of Commons, 1 May 1865

30 An author who speaks about his own books is almost as bad as a mother who talks about her own children.
Speech, Glasgow, 19 Nov 1873

31 Lord Salisbury and myself have brought you back peace – but a peace I hope with honour.
Speech, House of Commons, 16 July 1878

32 A sophistical rhetorician inebriated with the exuberance of his own verbosity.
Referring to Gladstone. Speech, 27 July 1878

33 Your dexterity seems a happy compound of the smartness of an attorney's clerk and the intrigue of a Greek of the lower empire.
Speaking to Lord Palmerston. Attrib.

34 If a traveller were informed that such a man was leader of the House of Commons, he may well begin to comprehend how the Egyptians worshipped an insect.
Referring to Lord John Russell. Attrib.

35 Pray remember, Mr Dean, no dogma, no Dean.
Attrib.

36 Nobody is forgotten when it is convenient to remember him.
Attrib.

37 Her Majesty is not a subject.
Responding to Gladstone's taunt that Disraeli could make a joke out of any subject, including Queen Victoria. Attrib.

38 When I meet a man whose name I can't remember, I give myself two minutes; then, if it is a hopeless case, I away say, And how is the old complaint?
Attrib.

39 She is an excellent creature, but she never can remember which came first, the Greeks or the Romans.
Referring to his wife. Attrib.

40 When I want to read a novel I write one.
Attrib.

41 I am dead: dead, but in the Elysian fields.
Said on his move to the House of Lords. Attrib.

42 No, it is better not. She will only ask me to take a message to Albert.
On his deathbed, declining an offer of a visit from Queen Victoria. Attrib.

DOCTORS

See also health, illness, medicine, remedies

1 A young doctor makes a humpy graveyard.
Proverb

2 Do not dwell in a city whose governor is a physician.
Proverb

3 God heals, and the doctor takes the fee.
Proverb

4 No man is a good physician who has never been sick.
Proverb

5 Physicians' faults are covered with earth, and rich men's with money.
Proverb

6 The presence of the doctor is the beginning of the cure.
Proverb

7 The superior doctor prevents sickness;
The mediocre doctor attends to impending sickness;
The inferior doctor treats actual sickness.
Proverb

8 While doctors consult, the patient dies.
Proverb

9 I am dying with the help of too many physicians.
Alexander the Great (356–323 BC) King of Macedon. Attrib.

10 These are the duties of a physician: First...to heal his mind and to give help to himself before giving it to anyone else.
Anonymous Epitaph of an Athenian doctor, 2 AD. *Journal of the American Medical Association*, 189:989, 1964

11 In illness the physician is a father; in convalescence a friend; when health is restored, he is a guardian.
Anonymous Brahmanic saying

12 One physician cures you of the colic; two physicians cure you of the medicine.
Anonymous *Journal of the American Medical Association*, 190:765, 1964 (Vincent J. Derbes)

13 Fifty years ago the successful doctor was said to need three things; a top hat to give him Authority, a paunch to give him Dignity, and piles to give him an Anxious Expression.
Anonymous *Lancet*, 1:169, 1951

14 A physician is nothing but a consoler of the mind.
Petronius Arbiter (1st century AD) Roman satirist. *Satyricon*

15 The blunders of a doctor are felt not by himself but by others.
Ar-Rumi (836–896)

16 My dear old friend King George V always told me that he would never have died but for that vile doctor.
Margot Asquith (1865–1945) Wife of Herbert Asquith. Referring to Lord Dawson of Penn.

17 Give me a doctor partridge-plump,
Short in the leg and broad in the rump,
An endomorph with gentle hands
Who'll never make absurd demands
That I abandon all my vices
Nor pull a long face in a crisis,
But with a twinkle in his eye
Will tell me that I have to die.
W. H. Auden (1907–73) British poet. *Nones*, 'Footnotes to Dr. Sheldon'

18 Doctors and undertakers
Fear epidemics of good health.
Gerald Barzan

19 They answered, as they took their fees,
'There is no cure for this disease.'
Hilaire Belloc (1870–1953) British writer. *Cautionary Tales*, 'Henry King'

20 If you think that you have caught a cold, call in a

good doctor. Call in three good doctors and play bridge.

Robert Benchley (1889–1945) *From Bed to Worse*, 'How to Avoid Colds'

21 He would have been better off if they had left him alone – but doctors don't like to leave people alone, especially if their reputations are at stake.

Alan Bennett (1934–) British playwright. Referring to George III. *The Sunday Times*, 24 Nov 1991

22 And he said unto them, Ye will surely say unto me this proverb, Physician, heal thyself: whatsoever we have heard done in Capernaum, do also here in thy country.

Bible: Luke 4:23

23 BODY-SNATCHER, n. A robber of grave-worms. One who supplies the young physicians with that with which the old physicians have supplied the undertaker.

Ambrose Bierce (1842–c. 1914) US writer and journalist. *The Devil's Dictionary*

24 PHYSICIAN, n. One upon whom we set our hopes when ill and our dogs when well.

Ambrose Bierce *The Devil's Dictionary*

25 You medical people will have more lives to answer for in the other world than even we generals.

Napoleon Bonaparte (1769–1821) French Emperor. *Napoleon in Exile* (Barry O'Meara)

26 A skilful leech is better far
Than half a hundred men of war.

Samuel Butler (1612–80) English satirist. *Hudibras*, Pt. I

27 But modern quacks have lost the art,
And reach of life the sacred seat;
They know not how its pulses beat,
Yet take their fee and write their bill,
In barb'rous prose resolved to kill.

Anna Chamber (d. 1777) *Poems, Printed at Strawberry Hill*

28 If the clinician, as observer, wishes to see things as they really are, he must make a *tabula rasa* of his mind and proceed without any preconceived notions whatever.

Jean Martin Charcot (1825–93) French neurologist.

29 Doctors are just the same as lawyers; the only difference is that lawyers merely rob you, whereas doctors rob you and kill you, too.

Anton Chekhov (1860–1904) Russian dramatist. *Ivanov*, I

30 The skilful doctor treats those who are well but the inferior doctor treats those who are ill.

Ch'in Yueh-jen (c. 225 BC)

31 I have noticed a tendency on the part of an occasional elderly and distinguished man to think that the rules of medical ethics were meant for young fellows just starting out, but not for him.

J. Chalmers Da Costa (1863–1933) *The Trials and Triumphs of the Surgeon*, Ch. 1

32 A fashionable surgeon like a pelican can be recognized by the size of his bill.

J. Chalmers Da Costa *The Trials and Triumphs of the Surgeon*, Ch. 1

33 When a doctor does go wrong he is the first of criminals. He has nerve and he has knowledge.

Arthur Conan Doyle (1856–1930) British writer and creator of Sherlock Holmes. *The Speckled Band*

34 'What sort of doctor is he?'
'Oh, well, I don't known much about his ability; but he's got a very good bedside manner!'

George Du Maurier (1834–96) British novelist and cartoonist. Caption to cartoon, *Punch*, 15 Mar 1884

35 He had surrendered all reality, all dread and fear, to the doctor beside him, as people do.

William Faulkner (1897–1962) US novelist. *Light in August*, Ch. 17

36 Medicine is the one place where all the show is stripped of the human drama. You, as doctors, will be in a position to see the human race stark naked – not only physically, but mentally and morally as well.

Martin H. Fischer (1879–1962) *Fischerisms* (Howard Faber and Ray Marr)

37 A doctor must work eighteen hours a day and seven days a week. If you cannot console yourself to this, get out of the profession.

Martin H. Fischer *Fischerisms* (Howard Fabing and Ray Marr)

38 DOCTOR: Always preceded by 'the good.' Among men, in familiar conversation, 'Oh! balls, doctor!' Is a wizard when he enjoys your confidence, a jackass when you're no longer on terms. All are materialists: 'You can't probe for faith with a scalpel.'

Gustave Flaubert (1821–80) French novelist. *Dictionary of Accepted Ideas*

39 We anatomists are like the porters in Paris, who are acquainted with the narrowest and most distant streets, but who know nothing of what takes place in the houses!

Bernard Le Bovier de Fontenelle (1657–1757)

40 There are more old drunkards than old doctors.

Benjamin Franklin (1706–90) US scientist and statesman. Attrib.

41 Quacks are the greatest liars in the world except their patients.

Benjamin Franklin Attrib.

42 Physicians, like beer, are best when they are old.

Thomas Fuller (1608–61) English historian. *The Holy State and the Profane State*

43 That physician will hardly be thought very careful of the health of others who neglects his own.

Galen (fl. 2nd century) Greek physician and scholar. *Of Protecting the Health*, Bk. V

44 The patient's ears remorseless he assails;
Murder with jargon where his medicine fails.

Samuel Garth (1661–1719) English physician and poet. *The Dispensary*

45 See, one physician, like a sculler plies,
The patient lingers and by inches dies,
But two physicians, like a pair of oars
Waft him more swiftly to the Stygian shores.

Samuel Garth Attrib.

46 'Is there no hope?' the sick man said,
The silent doctor shook his head,

And took his leave with signs of sorrow,
Despairing of his fee tomorrow.

John Gay (1685–1732) English poet and dramatist.

47 The doctors are always changing their opinions. They always have some new fad.

David Lloyd George (1863–1945) British liberal statesman. After being told that a well-known surgeon recommended that people sleep on their stomachs. *War Diary*, Ch. 36 (Lord Riddell)

48 It is so hard that one cannot really have confidence in doctors and yet cannot do without them.

Goethe (1749–1832) German poet, dramatist, and scientist.

49 It is a distinct art to talk medicine in the language of the non-medical man.

Edward H. Goodman (b. 1879)

50 The doctor found, when she was dead,
Her last disorder mortal.

Oliver Goldsmith (1728–74) Irish-born British writer. *Elegy on Mrs. Mary Blaize*

51 The crowd of physicians has killed me.

Hadrian (Publius Aelius Hadrianus; 76 AD–138 AD) Roman emperor. *Essays*, Bk. II (Michel de Montaigne)

52 The consultant's first obligation is to the patient, not to his brother physician.

Burton J. Hendrick (1870–1949)

53 A physician who is a lover of wisdom is the equal to a god.

Hippocrates (c. 460–c. 377 BC) Greek physician. *Decorum*, V

54 Foolish the doctor who despises the knowledge acquired by the ancients.

Hippocrates *Entering the World* (M. Odent)

55 I suppose one has a greater sense of intellectual degradation after an interview with a doctor than from any human experience.

Alice James (1848–92) US diarist. *The Diary of Alice James* (ed. Leon Edel), 27 Sept 1890

56 It is incident to physicians, I am afraid, beyond all other men, to mistake subsequence for consequence.

Samuel Johnson (1709–84) British lexicographer. *Life of Johnson* (J. Boswell), Vol. I

57 As long as men are liable to die and are desirous to live, a physician will be made fun of, but he will be well paid.

Jean de La Bruyère (1645–96) French writer and moralist. *Caractères*

58 The doctors allow one to die, the charlatans kill.

Jean de La Bruyère *Caractères*

59 When people's ill, they comes to I,
I physics, bleeds, and sweats 'em;
Sometimes they live, sometimes they die.
What's that to I? I lets 'em.

John Coakley Lettsom (1744–1815) *On Dr. Lettsom, by Himself*

60 A doctor is a man licensed to make grave mistakes.

Leonard Louis Levinson *Bartlett's Unfamiliar Quotations* (Leonard Louis Levinson)

61 But a doctor who has gone into lonely and discouraged homes, where there was fear for the sick, and no one else at hand to administer remedy, and give hope, can really say, 'I amount to something. I'm worth while.'

Carlton K. Matson (1890–1948) *The Cleveland Press*

62 As he approached the place where a meeting of doctors was being held, he saw some elegant limousines and remarked, 'The surgeons have arrived.' Then he saw some cheaper cars and said, 'The physicians are here, too.' A few scattered model-T Fords led him to infer that there were pathologists present. And when he saw a row of overshoes inside, under the hat rack, he is reported to have remarked, 'Ah, I see there are laboratory men here.'

William J. Mayo (1861–1939) US surgeon. *The Way of an Investigator*, Ch. 19 (Walter B. Cannon)

63 English physicians kill you, the French let you die.

William Lamb, Lord Melbourne (1779–1848) British statesman. *Queen Victoria*, Ch. 5 (Elizabeth Longford)

64 No doctor takes pleasure in the health even of his friends.

Michel de Montaigne (1533–92) French essayist. *Essais*, I

65 I used to wonder why people should be so fond of the company of their physician, till I recollected that he is the only person with whom one dares to talk continually of oneself, without interruption, contradiction or censure; I suppose that delightful immunity doubles their fees.

Hannah More (1745–1833) English writer. Letter to Horace Walpole, 27 July 1789

66 One must not count upon all of his patients being willing to steal in order to pay doctor's bills.

Robert Tuttle Morris *Doctors Versus Folks*, Ch. 3

67 The most dangerous physicians are those who can act in perfect mimicry of the born physician.

Friedrich Nietzsche (1844–1900) German philosopher. *Human, All Too Human*, Pt. II

68 We doctors have always been a simple trusting folk. Did we not believe Galen implicitly for 1500 years and Hippocrates for more than 2000?

William Osler (1849–1919) Canadian physician.

69 A physician who treats himself has a fool for a patient.

William Osler *Sir William Osler: Aphorisms*, Ch. I (William B. Bean)

70 One of the first duties of the physician is to educate the masses not to take medicine.

William Osler

71 Physicians who care much for the elderly may find their lives slowly shredded to pieces as their seniors pick at them with minor worries magnified by the rapidly diminishing sands. If the telephone should come into common use, this state of affairs would worsen.

Frank Kittredge Paddock (1841–1901) Attrib.

72 Every physician must be rich in knowledge, and not only of that which is written in books; his patients should be his book, they will never mislead him.

Paracelsus (c. 1493–1541) Swiss philosopher and alchemist. *The Book of Tartaric Diseases*, Ch. 13

73 The doctors were very brave about it.

Dorothy Parker 1893–1967) US writer. Said after she had been seriously ill. *Journal of the American Medical Association*, 194:211, 1965

74 When the physician said to him, 'You have lived to be an old man,' he said, 'That is because I never employed you as my physician.'

Pausanias (fl. 479 BC) Greek traveller. *Moralia* (Plutarch), 'Sayings of Spartans'

75 If your time hasn't come not even a doctor can kill you.

Meyer A. Perlstein (1902–)

76 Life in itself is short enough, but the physicians with their art, know to their amusement, how to make it still shorter.

Petrarch (1304–74) Italian poet. *Invectives*, Preface, Letter to Pope Clement VI

77 After all, a doctor is just to put your mind at rest.

Petronius (fl. 1st century) Roman satirist. *Satyricon*, 42

78 There is not a doctor who desires the health of his friends; not a soldier who desires the peace of his country.

Philemon (c. 361–c. 263 BC) Greek dramatist. *Fabulae Incertae*, Fragment 46

79 A country doctor needs more brains to do his work passably than the fifty greatest industrialists in the world require.

Walter B. Pitkin (1878–1953) *The Twilight of the American Mind*, Ch. 10

80 Who shall decide when doctors disagree?

Alexander Pope (1688–1744) British poet. *Moral Essays*, III

81 Cur'd yesterday of my disease,
I died last night of my physician.

Matthew Prior (1664–1721) British poet. *The Remedy Worse than the Disease*

82 Physicians of all men are most happy; what success soever they have, the world proclaimeth, and what fault they commit, the earth covereth.

Francis Quarles (1592–1644) English poet. *Hieroglyphics of the Life of Man*

83 If you want to get out of medicine the fullest enjoyment, be students all your lives.

David Riesman (1867–1940)

84 The best doctor in the world is the Veterinarian. He can't ask his patients what is the matter – he's got to just know.

Will Rogers (1879–1935) US actor and humorist. *The Autobiography of Will Rogers*, 12

85 First they get *on*, then they get *honour*, then they get *honest*.

Humphrey Rolleston (1862–1944) British physician. Referring to physicians. *Confessions of an Advertising Man* (David Ogilvy)

86 They, on the whole, desire to cure the sick; and, – if they are good doctors, and the choice were fairly put to them, – would rather cure their patient and lose their fee, than kill him, and get it.

John Ruskin (1819–1900) British art critic and writer on sociology and economics. *The Crown of Wild Olive*

87 The doctor occupies a seat in the front row of the stalls of the human drama, and is constantly watching, and even intervening in, the tragedies, comedies and tragi-comedies which form the raw material of the literary art.

W. Russell, Lord Brain (1895–1966) *The Quiet Art: a Doctor's Anthology* (R. Coope), Foreword

88 The common people say, that physicians are the class of people who kill other men in the most polite and courteous manner.

John of Salisbury (c. 1115–80) English churchman, philosopher, and scholar. *Polycraticus*, Bk. II, Ch. 29

89 The physician cannot prescribe by letter the proper time for teating or bathing; he must feel the pulse.

Seneca (c. 4 BC–65 AD) Roman writer. *Epistulae ad Lucilium*, XII

90 Make it compulsory for a doctor using a brass plate to have inscribed on it, in addition to the letters indicating his qualifications, the words 'Remember that I too am mortal'.

George Bernard Shaw (1856–1950) Irish dramatist and critic. *The Doctor's Dilemma*, 'Preface on Doctors'

91 The most tragic thing in the world is a sick doctor.

George Bernard Shaw *The Doctor's Dilemma*, I

92 I had rather follow you to your grave than see you owe your life to any but a regular-bred physician.

Richard Brinsley Sheridan (1751–1816) British dramatist. *St. Patrick's Day*, II:4

93 Our doctor would never really operate unless it was necessary. He was just that way. If he didn't need the money, he wouldn't lay a hand on you.

Herb Shriner

94 A young man, in whose air and countenance appeared all the uncouth gravity and supercilious self-conceit of a physician piping hot from his studies.

Tobias Smollett (1721–71) English novelist and journalist. *The Adventures of Peregrine Pickle*, Ch. 42

95 There are worse occupations in the world than feeling a woman's pulse.

Laurence Sterne (1713–68) Irish-born English writer and churchman.

96 ...the physician...is the flower (such as it is) of our civilization.

Robert Louis Stevenson (1850–94) Scottish writer. *Underwoods*, Dedication

97 The best doctors in the world are Doctor Diet, Doctor Quiet and Doctor Merryman.

Jonathan Swift (1667–1745) Anglo-Irish priest, satirist, and poet.

98 Apollo was held the god of physic and sender of disease. Both were originally the same trade, and still continue.

Jonathan Swift *Thoughts on Various Subjects, Moral and Diverting*

99 An unruly patient makes a harsh physician.

Publius Syrus (1st century BC) Roman dramatist.

100 This is where the strength of the physician lies, be he a quack, a homeopath or an allopath. He supplies the perennial demand for comfort, the craving for sympathy that every human sufferer feels.

Leo Tolstoy (1828–1910) Russian writer. *War and Peace*, Pt. 9, Ch. 16

101 Mr. Anaesthetist, if the patient can keep awake, surely you can.

Wilfred Trotter (1872–1939) Quoted in *Lancet*, 2:1340, 1965

102 He has been a doctor a year now and has had two patients, no, three, I think – yes, it was three; I attended their funerals.

Mark Twain (Samuel L. Clemens; 1835–1910) US writer.

103 The physicians are the natural attorneys of the poor and the social problems should largely be solved by them.

Rudolf Virchow (1821–1902) German pathologist. *Rudolf Virchow*, 'The Doctor' (Erwin H. Ackernecht)

104 Who are the greatest deceivers? The doctors? And the greatest fools? The patients?

Voltaire (François-Marie Arouet; 1694–1778) French writer and philosopher.

105 A physician is one who pours drugs of which he knows little into a body of which he knows less.

Voltaire Attrib.

106 By quack I mean imposter not in opposition to but in common with physicians.

Horace Walpole (1717–97) English writer.

107 Physicians are like kings, – they brook no contradiction.

John Webster (1580–1625) English dramatist. *The Duchess of Malfi*, V:2

108 Doctors are mostly impostors. The older a doctor is and the more venerated he is, the more he must pretend to know everything. Of course, they grow worse with time. Always look for a doctor who is hated by the best doctors. Always seek out a bright young doctor before he comes down with nonsense.

Thornton Wilder (1897–1975) US novelist and dramatist.

109 Doctors are generally dull dogs.

John Wilson (Christopher North; 1785–1854) Scottish poet, essayist, and critic.

DOGS

See also animals

1 A huge dog, tied by a chain, was painted on the wall and over it was written in capital letters 'Beware of the dog.'

Petronius Arbiter (1st century AD) Roman satirist. Latin, *Cave canem*. *Satyricon*: *Cena Trimalchionis*, 29

2 The woman who is really kind to dogs is always one who has failed to inspire sympathy in men.

Max Beerbohm (1872–1956) British writer. *Zuleika Dobson*

3 It's the one species I wouldn't mind seeing vanish from the face of the earth. I wish they were like the White Rhino – six of them left in the Serengeti National Park, and all males.

Alan Bennett (1934–) British playwright. Referring to dogs. *Getting On*, I

4 The great pleasure of a dog is that you may make a fool of yourself with him and not only will he not scold you, he will make a fool of himself too.

Samuel Butler (1835–1902) British writer. *Notebooks*

5 'Tis sweet to hear the watch-dog's honest bark
Bay deep-mouthed welcome as we draw near home;
'Tis sweet to know there is an eye will mark
Our coming, and look brighter when we come.

Lord Byron (1788–1824) British poet. *Don Juan*, I

6 She was always attentive to the feelings of dogs, and very polite if she had to decline their advances.

George Eliot (Mary Ann Evans; 1819–80) British novelist. *Middlemarch*, Ch. 39

7 Anybody who hates children and dogs can't be all bad.

W. C. Fields (1880–1946) US actor. Attrib.

8 Not the least hard thing to bear when they go away from us, these quiet friends, is that they carry away with them so many years of our own lives.

John Galsworthy (1867–1933) British writer. *Memoirs*

9 The dog, to gain some private ends,
Went mad and bit the man.

Oliver Goldsmith (1728–74) Irish-born British writer. *Elegy on the Death of a Mad Dog*

10 The man recovered of the bite,
The dog it was that died.

Oliver Goldsmith *Elegy on the Death of a Mad Dog*

11 Stop running those dogs on your page. I wouldn't have them peeing on my cheapest rug.

William Randolph Hearst (1863–1951) US newspaper owner. Referring to the publication of Thurber's drawings by one of his editors. *The Years with Ross* (James Thurber)

12 Brothers and Sisters, I bid you beware
Of giving your heart to a dog to tear.

Rudyard Kipling (1865–1936) Indian-born British writer. *Power of the Dog*

13 You ain't nothin' but a hound dog,
Cryin' all the time.

Jerry Leiber (1933–) US songwriter. *Hound Dog* (with Mike Stoller)

14 A door is what a dog is perpetually on the wrong side of.

Ogden Nash (1902–71) US poet. *A Dog's Best Friend is his Illiteracy*

15 Regardless of what they say about it, we are going to keep it.

Richard Milhous Nixon (1913–94) US President. Referring to 'Checkers', a dog given to his daughters. He was defending himself against corruption charges. TV address, 23 Sept 1952

16 I am His Highness' dog at Kew;
Pray tell me sir, whose dog are you?

Alexander Pope (1688–1744) British poet. On the collar of a dog given to Frederick, Prince of Wales

17 That indefatigable and unsavoury engine of pollution, the dog.

John Sparrow (1906–92) British lawyer and academic. Letter to *The Times*, 30 Sep 1975

18 I loathe people who keep dogs. They are cowards who haven't got the guts to bite people themselves.

August Strindberg (1849–1912) Swedish dramatist. *A Madman's Diary*

19 Daddy wouldn't buy me a bow-wow, bow-wow.

I've got a little cat
And I'm very fond of that.
Joseph Tabrar (20th century) US songwriter. *Daddy Wouldn't Buy me a Bow-wow*

DONNE, JOHN

(1572–1631) English poet of the metaphysical school. He was ordained at the age of 43 and was appointed Dean of St Pauls (1621). His verse includes *Divine Poems* (1607) and *Epithalamium* (1613).

Quotations about Donne

1 With Donne, whose muse on dromedary trots,
Wreathe iron pokers into true-love knots.
Samuel Taylor Coleridge (1772–1834) British poet. *On Donne's Poetry*

2 Dr Donne's verses are like the peace of God; they pass all understanding.
James I (1566–1625) King of England.

Quotations by Donne

3 And new Philosophy calls all in doubt,
The Element of fire is quite put out;
The Sun is lost, and th' earth, and no man's wit
Can well direct him where to look for it.
An Anatomy of the World, 205

4 Come live with me, and be my love,
And we will some new pleasures prove
Of golden sands, and crystal brooks,
With silken lines, and silver hooks.
The Bait

5 For God's sake hold your tongue and let me love.
The Canonization

6 But I do nothing upon myself, and yet I am mine own Executioner.
Devotions, 12

7 No man is an Island, entire of itself; every man is a piece of the Continent, a part of the main.
Devotions, 17

8 Any man's death diminishes me, because I am involved in Mankind; And therefore never send to know for whom the bell tolls; it tolls for thee.
Devotions, 17

9 Love built on beauty, soon as beauty, dies.
Elegies, 2, 'The Anagram'

10 She, and comparisons are odious.
Elegies, 8, 'The Comparison'

11 Licence my roving hands, and let them go,
Before, behind, between, above, below.
Elegies, 18, 'Love's Progress'

12 O my America! my new-found-land,
My Kingdom, safeliest when with one man man'd.
Elegies, 19, 'Going To Bed'

13 Go, and catch a falling star,
Get with child a mandrake root,
Tell me, where all past years are,
Or who cleft the Devil's foot.
Go and Catch a Falling Star

14 Death be not proud, though some have called thee
Mighty and dreadful, for, thou art not so.
Holy Sonnets, 10

15 It comes equally to us all, and makes us all equal when it comes. The ashes of an Oak in the Chimney, are no epitaph of that Oak, to tell me how high or how large that was; It tells me not what flocks it sheltered while it stood, nor what men it hurt when it fell. The dust of great persons' graves is speechless too, it says nothing, it distinguishes nothing.
Speaking of death. *Sermons*, XV

16 Busy old fool, unruly Sun,
Why dost thou thus,
Through windows and through curtains call on us?
The Sun Rising

17 I am two fools, I know,
For loving, and for saying so
In whining Poetry.
The Triple Fool

DOOMSDAY

1 That at what time ye hear the sound of the cornet, flute, harp, sackbut, psaltery, dulcimer, and all kinds of musick, ye fall down and worship the golden image that Nebuchadnezzar the king hath set up:
And whoso falleth not down and worshippeth shall the same hour be cast into the midst of a burning fiery furnace.
Bible: Daniel 3:5–6

2 Immediately after the tribulation of those days shall the sun be darkened, and the moon shall not give her light, and the stars shall fall from heaven, and the powers of the heavens shall be shaken:
And then shall appear the sign of the Son of man in heaven: and then shall all the tribes of the earth mourn, and they shall see the Son of man coming in the clouds of heaven with power and great glory.
And he shall send his angels with a great sound of a trumpet, and they shall gather together his elect from the four winds, from one end of heaven to the other.
Bible: Matthew 24:29–31

3 'Tis the Last Judgment's fire must cure this place,
Calcine its clods and set my prisoners free.
Robert Browning (1812–89) British poet. *Childe Roland to the Dark Tower Came*, XI

4 Don't wait for the Last Judgement. It takes place every day.
Albert Camus (1913–60) French existentialist writer. *The Fall*

5 When all the world dissolves,
And every creature shall be purified,
All place shall be hell that is not heaven.
Christopher Marlowe (1564–93) English dramatist. *Doctor Faustus*, II:1

DOUBT

See also indecision, scepticism, uncertainty

1 If a man will begin with certainties, he shall end in doubts, but if he will be content to begin with doubts, he shall end in certainties.

Francis Bacon (1561–1626) English philosopher. *The Advancement of Learning*, Bk. I, Ch. 5

2 Oh! let us never, never doubt
What nobody is sure about!

Hilaire Belloc (1870–1953) French-born British poet. *More Beasts for Worse Children*, 'The Microbe'

3 And immediately Jesus stretched forth his hand, and caught him, and said unto him, O thou of little faith, wherefore didst thou doubt?

Bible: Matthew 14:31

4 He who shall teach the child to doubt
The rotting grave shall ne'er get out.

William Blake (1757–1827) British poet. *Auguries of Innocence*

5 All we have gained then by our unbelief
Is a life of doubt diversified by faith,
For one of faith diversified by doubt:
We called the chess-board white, – we call it black.

Robert Browning (1812–89) British poet. *Bishop Blougram's Apology*

6 His doubts are better than most people's certainties.

Lord Hardwicke (1690–1764) English judge. Referring to Dirleton's *Doubts*. *Life of Johnson* (J. Boswell)

7 Negative Capability, that is, when a man is capable of being in uncertainties, mysteries, doubts, without any irritable reaching after fact and reason.

John Keats (1795–1821) British poet. Letter to G. and T. Keats, 21 Dec 1817

8 The trouble with the world is that the stupid are cocksure and the intelligent full of doubt.

Bertrand Russell (1872–1970) British philosopher. *Autobiography*

9 Those obstinate questionings
Of sense and outward things,
Fallings from us, vanishings;
Blank misgivings of a Creature
Moving about in worlds not realised,
High instincts before which our mortal nature
Did tremble like a guilty thing surprised.

William Wordsworth (1770–1850) British poet. *Ode. Intimations of Immortality*, IX

DOYLE, SIR ARTHUR CONAN

(1859–1930) British writer and creator of the detective Sherlock Holmes. Originally a doctor, he ceased to practise in 1890, devoting himself entirely to his writing. He also wrote books on spiritualism.

Quotations about Doyle

1 My contention is that Sherlock Holmes *is* literature on a humble but not ignoble level, whereas the mystery writers most in vogue now are not. The old stories are literature, not because of the conjuring tricks and the puzzles, not because of the lively melodrama, which they have in common with many other detective stories, but by virtue of imagination and style.

Edmund Wilson (1895–1972) US critic and writer. *Classics and Commercials*

2 Conan Doyle, a few words on the subject of. Don't you find as you age in the wood, as we are both doing, that the tragedy of life is that your early heroes lose their glamour?...Now, with Doyle I don't have this feeling. I still revere his work as much as ever. I used to think it swell, and I still think it swell.

P. G. Wodehouse (1881–1975) British humorous novelist. *Performing Flea*

Quotations by Doyle

3 It is an old maxim of mine that when you have excluded the impossible, whatever remains, however improbable, must be the truth.

The Beryl Coronet

4 You know my method. It is founded upon the observance of trifles.

The Boscombe Valley Mystery

5 The husband was a teetotaller, there was no other woman, and the conduct complained of was that he had drifted into the habit of winding up every meal by taking out his false teeth and hurling them at his wife.

A Case of Identity

6 It has long been an axiom of mine that the little things are infinitely the most important.

A Case of Identity

7 Depend upon it, there is nothing so unnatural as the commonplace.

A Case of Identity

8 It is my belief, Watson, founded upon my experience, that the lowest and vilest alleys of London do not present a more dreadful record of sin than does the smiling and beautiful countryside.

Copper Beeches

9 'Excellent!' I cried. 'Elementary,' said he.

Watson talking to Sherlock Holmes; Holmes's reply is often misquoted as 'Elementary, my dear Watson'. *The Crooked Man*

10 'It is my duty to warn you that it will be used against you,' cried the Inspector, with the magnificent fair play of the British criminal law.

The Dancing Men

11 He is the Napoleon of crime.

Referring to Professor Moriarty. *The Final Problem*

12 A man should keep his little brain attic stocked with all the furniture that he is likely to use, and the rest he can put away in the lumber room of his library, where he can get it if he wants it.

Five Orange Pips

13 It is quite a three-pipe problem.

The Red-Headed League

14 An experience of women which extends over many nations and three continents.

The Sign of Four

15 'Is there any other point to which you would

wish to draw my attention?'
'To the curious incident of the dog in the night-time.'
'The dog did nothing in the night-time.'
'That was the curious incident,' remarked Sherlock Holmes.

The Silver Blaze

16 London, that great cesspool into which all the loungers of the Empire are irrestibly drained.

A Study in Scarlet

17 Mediocrity knows nothing higher than itself, but talent instantly recognizes genius.

The Valley of Fear

DRABBLE, MARGARET

(1939–) British novelist and writer. Her novels, which explore the emotional and moral dilemmas of women in contemporary society, include *The Waterfall* (1969), *The Needle's Eye* (1972), *The Middle Ground* (1980), *The Radiant Way* (1987), *A Natural Curiosity* (1989), and *The Gates of Ivory* (1991).

Quotation about Drabble

1 She is becoming the chronicler of contemporary Britain, the novelist people will turn to a hundred years from now to find out how things were, the person who will have done for the late 20th century London what Dickens did for Victorian London, what Balzac did for Paris.

Phyllis Rose *The New York Times Book Review*, Sept 1980

Quotations by Drabble

2 Sex isn't the most important thing in life, she decided, wriggling her body slightly to see if her movement would affect Anthony. It did: he stiffened slightly, but slept on. But if sex isn't the most important thing, what is?

The Ice Age, Part II

3 When nothing is sure, everything is possible.

The Middle Ground

4 Civilized woman can't do the right thing without paying too high a price.

The Middle Ground

5 Poverty, therefore, was comparative. One measured it by a sliding scale. One was always poor, in terms of those who were richer.

The Radiant Way

6 And there isn't any way that one can get rid of the guilt of having a nice body by saying that one can serve society with it, because that would end up with oneself as what? There simply doesn't seem to be any moral place for flesh.

A Summer Bird-Cage, Ch. 10

DREAMS

1 Dreams and predictions ought to serve but for winter talk by the fireside.

Francis Bacon (1561–1626) English philosopher. *Essays*, 'Of Prophecies'

2 It was a dream of perfect bliss,
Too beautiful to last.

Thomas Haynes Bayly (1797–1839) British writer. *It was a Dream*

3 So I awoke, and behold it was a dream.

John Bunyan (1628–88) English writer. *The Pilgrim's Progress*, Pt. I

4 I do not know whether I was then a man dreaming I was a butterfly, or whether I am now a butterfly dreaming I am a man.

Chuang Tse (*or* Zhuangzi; c. 369–286 BC) Chinese philosopher. *Chuang Tse* (H. A. Giles), Ch. 2

5 The people's prayer, the glad diviner's theme,
The young men's vision, and the old men's dream!

John Dryden (1631–1700) British poet and dramatist. *Absalom and Achitophel*, I

6 Last night I dreamt I went to Manderley again.

Daphne Du Maurier (1907–89) British novelist. *Rebecca*, Ch. 1

7 Underneath the arches
We dream our dreams away.

Bud Flanagan (Robert Winthrop; 1896–1968) British comedian. *Underneath the Arches*

8 Abou Ben Adhem (may his tribe increase!)
Awoke one night from a deep dream of peace,
And saw, within the moonlight in his room,
Making it rich, and like a lily in bloom,
An angel writing in a book of gold: – ...

Leigh Hunt (1784–1859) British poet. *Abou Ben Adhem and the Angel*

9 Castles in the air – they're so easy to take refuge in. So easy to build, too.

Henrik Ibsen (1828–1906) Norwegian dramatist. *The Master Builder*, III

10 Alas, all the castles I have, are built with air, thou know'st.

Ben Jonson (1573–1637) English dramatist. *Eastward Ho*, II:2

11 All men dream: but not equally. Those who dream by night in the dusty recesses of their minds wake in the day to find that it was vanity: but the dreamers of the day are dangerous men, for they may act their dream with open eyes, to make it possible.

T. E. Lawrence (1888–1935) British soldier and writer. *Seven Pillars of Wisdom*, Ch. 1

12 From his shelves he picked out a book about dreams and thumbed through...The setting afternoon sun lit up the room. 'An emission during a dream indicates the sexual nature of the whole dream, however obscure and unlikely the contents are. Dreams culminating in emission may reveal the object of the dreamer's desire as well as his inner conflicts. An orgasm can not lie.'

Ian McEwan (1948–) British novelist. *In Between the Sheets*

13 Many's the long night I've dreamed of cheese – toasted, mostly.

Robert Louis Stevenson (1850–94) Scottish writer. *Treasure Island*, Ch. 15

14 Dreams are true while they last, and do we not live in dreams?

Alfred, Lord Tennyson (1809–92) British poet. *The Higher Pantheism*

15 But I, being poor, have only my dreams;
I have spread my dreams under your feet;
Treat softly becuase you treat on my dreams.
W. B. Yeats (1865–1939) Irish poet. *He Wishes for the Cloths of Heaven*

DRINKS

See also alcohol, drunkenness, water

1 The infusion of a China plant sweetened with the pith of an Indian cane.
Joseph Addison (1672–1719) British essayist. *The Spectator*, 69

2 Bowen's Beer Makes You Drunk.
Kingsley Amis (1922–) British novelist, poet, and critic. Suggested advertising slogan. *I Like It Here*

3 Look here, Steward, if this is coffee, I want tea; but if this is tea, then I wish for coffee.
Anonymous Cartoon caption, *Punch*, 1902

4 If I had known there was no Latin word for tea I would have let the vulgar stuff alone.
Hilaire Belloc (1870–1953) French-born British poet. Attrib.

5 Drink no longer water, but use a little wine for thy stomach's sake and thine often infirmities.
Bible: I Timothy 5:23

6 The shortest way out of Manchester is notoriously a bottle of Gordon's gin.
William Bolitho (1890–1930) British writer. Attrib.

7 I the Trinity illustrate,
Drinking watered orange-pulp –
In three sips the Arian frustrate;
While he drains his at one gulp.
Robert Browning (1812–89) British poet. *Soliloquy of the Spanish Cloister*

8 I am willing to taste any drink once.
James Cabell (1879–1958) US novelist and journalist. *Jurgen*, Ch. 1

9 That one day this country of ours, which we love so much, will find dignity and greatness and peace again.
Noël Coward (1899–1973) British dramatist. The toast from *Cavalcade*

10 While the bubbling and loud-hissing urn
Throws up a steamy column, and the cups,
That cheer but not inebriate, wait on each,
So let us welcome peaceful evening in.
William Cowper (1731–1800) British poet. *The Task*

11 If someone asks for a soft drink at a party, we no longer think he is a wimp.
Edwina Currie (1946–) British politician. Speech, Dec 1988

12 Gimme a viskey. Ginger ale on the side. And don't be stingy, baby.
Greta Garbo (1905–90) Swedish-born US film actress. *Anna Christie*

13 Tea for Two, and Two for Tea.
Otto Harback (1873–1963) US dramatist. From the musical *No! No! Nanette.* Song title

14 This wine is too good for toast-drinking, my dear. You don't want to mix emotions up with a wine like that. You lose the taste.
Ernest Hemingway (1898–1961) US novelist. *The Sun also Rises*

15 I would have drunk a lot of Pinot Grigio if I'd lost after leading 5–2 in the third.
Martina Navratilova (1956–) Czech-born US tennis player. *The Times*, 7 May 1994

16 One more drink and I'd be under the host.
Dorothy Parker (1893–1967) US writer. *You Might As Well Live* (J. Keats)

17 Coffee which makes the politician wise,
And see through all things with his half-shut eyes.
Alexander Pope (1688–1744) British poet. *The Rape of the Lock*, III

18 Here thou great Anna! whom three realms obey,
Dost sometimes counsel take – and sometimes Tea.
Alexander Pope *The Rape of the Lock*, III

19 Our trouble is that we drink too much tea. I see in this the slow revenge of the Orient, which has diverted the Yellow River down our throats.
J. B. Priestley (1894–1984) British novelist. *The Observer*, 'Sayings of the Week', 15 May 1949

20 Instant coffee is just old beans that have been cremated.
Jennifer Saunders (1958–) British comedy writer and actress. *Absolutely Fabulous*

21 It's a Naive Domestic Burgundy without Any Breeding, But I Think You'll be Amused by its Presumption.
James Thurber (1894–1961) US humorist. *Men, Women and Dogs*, cartoon caption

22 I think it must be so, for I have been drinking it for sixty-five years and I am not dead yet.
Voltaire (François-Marie Arouet; 1694–1778) French writer. On learning that coffee was considered a slow poison. Attrib.

DROWNING

See also death

1 The western tide crept up along the sand,
And o'er and o'er the sand,
And round and round the sand,
As far as eye could see.
The rolling mist came down and hid the land:
And never home came she.
Charles Kingsley (1819–75) British writer. *The Sands of Dee*

2 O Lord, methought what pain it was to drown,
What dreadful noise of waters in my ears,
What sights of ugly death within my eyes!
William Shakespeare (1564–1616) English dramatist. *Richard III*, I:4

3 Nobody heard him, the dead man,
But still he lay moaning:
I was much further out than you thought
And not waving but drowning.
Stevie Smith (Florence Margaret Smith; 1902–71) British poet. *Not Waving But Drowning*

DRUGS

1 Medicine cures the man who is fated not to die.
Proverb

2 A drug is that substance which, when injected into a rat, will produce a scientific report.

Anonymous

3 Hark! The herald angels sing
Beecham's pills are just the thing.
Peace on earth and mercy mild;
Two for man and one for child.

Anonymous Apparently the result of a Beecham's advertisement in a hymnbook.

4 I'm proving that if you're on drugs then you're in trouble because those drugs aren't working. I'm clean and I'm beating you.

Linford Christie (1960–) British athlete. *The Independent*, 10 June 1994

5 Thou hast the keys of Paradise, oh, just, subtle, and mighty opium!

Thomas De Quincey (1785–1859) British essayist and critic. *Confessions of an English Opium-Eater*, Pt. II

6 Alarmed successively by every fashionable medical terror of the day, she dosed her children with every specific which was publicly advertised or privately recommended. No creatures of their age had taken such quantities of Ching's lozenges, Godbold's elixir, or Dixon's anti-bilious pills. The consequence was, that the dangers, which had at first been imaginary, became real: these little victims of domestic medicine never had a day's health: they looked, and were, more dead than alive.

Maria Edgeworth (1767–1849) British novelist. *Patronage*

7 A man who cannot work without his hypodermic needle is a poor doctor. The amount of narcotic you use is inversely proportional to your skill.

Martin H. Fischer (1879–1962) *Fischerisms* (Howard Fabing and Ray Marr)

8 Half the modern drugs could well be thrown out the window except that the birds might eat them.

Martin H. Fischer *Fischerisms* (Howard Fabing and Ray Marr)

9 A hundred doses of happiness are not enough: send to the drug-store for another bottle – and, when that is finished, for another…There can be no doubt that, if tranquillizers could be bought as easily and cheaply as aspirin they would be consumed, not by the billions, as they are at present, but by the scores and hundreds of billions. And a good, cheap stimulant would be almost as popular.

Aldous Huxley (1894–1963) British writer. *Brave New World Revisited*, Ch. 8

10 What is dangerous about the tranquillizer is that whatever peace of mind they bring is a packaged peace of mind. Where you buy a pill and buy peace with it, you get conditioned to cheap solutions instead of deep ones.

Max Lerner (1902–) Russian-born US teacher, editor, and journalist. *The Unfinished Country*, 'The Assault on the Mind'

11 I will lift up mine eyes unto the pills. Almost everyone takes them, from the humble aspirin to the multi-coloured, king-sized three deckers, which put you to sleep, wake you up, stimulate and soothe you all in one. It is an age of pills.

Malcolm Muggeridge (1903–90) British writer and editor. *The New Statesman*, 3 Aug 1962

12 Two great European narcotics, alcohol and Christianity.

Friedrich Nietzsche (1844–1900) German philosopher. *The Twilight of the Idols*, 'Things the Germans Lack'

13 Imperative drugging – the ordering of medicine in any and every malady – is no longer regarded as the chief function of the doctor.

William Osler *Aequanimitas, with Other Addresses*, 'Medicine in the Nineteenth Century'

14 The treatment with poison medicines comes from the West.

Huang Ti (The Yellow Emperor, 2697 BC–2597 BC) *Nei Ching Su Wen*, Bk. 4

15 I owe my reputation to the fact that I use digitalis in doses the text books say are dangerous and in cases that the text books say are unsuitable.

Karel Frederik Wenckebach (1864–1940) *Lancet*, 2:633, 1937

16 Cocaine is God's way of saying you're making too much money.

Robin Williams (1952–) US actor. *Screen International*, 15 Dec 1990

17 Americans use drugs as if consumption bestowed a 'special license' to be an asshole.

Frank Zappa (1940–93) US rock musician. *The Real Frank Zappa Book*

18 Some rock musicians make a bunch of money and stick it up their noses. I stick mine in my ear.

Frank Zappa *The Real Frank Zappa*

DRUNKENNESS

See also alcohol

1 There are more old drunkards than old doctors.

Proverb

2 His mouth has been used as a latrine by some small animal of the night.

Kingsley Amis (1922–) British novelist. Describing a hangover. *Lucky Jim*

3 Come landlord, fill the flowing bowl,
Until it doth run over…
For tonight we'll merry, merry be,
Tomorrow we'll be sober.

Anonymous *Come, Landlord, Fill the Flowing Bowl*

4 What shall we do with the drunken sailor
Early in the morning?
Hoo-ray and up she rises
Early in the morning.

Anonymous *What shall we do with the Drunken Sailor?*

5 Ha, ha, ha, you and me,
Little brown jug, don't I love thee!

Anonymous *The Little Brown Jug*

6 Lord George-Brown drunk is a better man than the Prime Minister sober.

Anonymous Comparing him with Harold Wilson. *The Times*, 6 Mar 1976

7 One reason I don't drink is that I want to know when I am having a good time.

Nancy Astor (1879–1964) US-born British politician. Attrib.

8 An alcoholic has been lightly defined as a man who drinks more than his own doctor.

Alvan L. Barach (1895–) *Journal of the American Medical Association*, 181:393, 1962

9 Drunkenness, the ruin of reason, the destruction of strength, premature old age, momentary death.

St. Basil the Great (c. 330–c. 379) Bishop of Caesarean Cappadocia. *Homilies*, No. XIV, Ch. 7

10 For when the wine is in, the wit is out.

Thomas Becon (1512–67) English Protestant churchman. *Catechism*, 375

11 Others mocking said, These men are full of new wine.

Bible: Acts 2:13

12 Wine is a mocker, strong drink is raging: and whosoever is deceived thereby is not wise.

Bible: Proverbs 20:1

13 Man, being reasonable, must get drunk;
The best of life is but intoxication.

Lord Byron (1788–1824) British poet. *Don Juan*, II

14 It's my opinion, sir, that this meeting is drunk.

Charles Dickens (1812–70) British novelist. *Pickwick Papers*, Ch. 33

15 I am as sober as a Judge.

Henry Fielding (1707–54) British novelist. *Don Quixote in England*, III:14

16 Drink! for you know not whence you came, nor why:
Drink! for you know not why you go, nor where.

Edward Fitzgerald *The Rubáiyát of Omar Khayyám*, LXXIV

17 Drunkenness is never anything but a substitute for happiness. It amounts to buying the dream of a thing when you haven't money enough to buy the dreamed-of thing materially.

André Gide (1869–1951) French novelist and critic. *Journaux*

18 If merely 'feeling good' could decide, drunkenness would be the supremely valid human experience.

William James (1842–1910) US psychologist and philosopher. *Varieties of Religious Experience*

19 A branch of the sin of drunkenness, which is the root of all sins.

James I (1566–1625) King of England. *A Counterblast to Tobacco*

20 A man who exposes himself when he is intoxicated, has not the art of getting drunk.

Samuel Johnson (1709–84) British lexicographer. *Life of Johnson* (J. Boswell), Vol. III

21 Better sleep with a sober cannibal than a drunken Christian.

Herman Melville (1819–91) US novelist. *Moby Dick*, Ch. 3

22 Drunkenness...spoils health, dismounts the mind, and unmans men.

William Penn (1644–1718) English founder of Pennsylvania. *Fruits of Solitude*, Maxim 72

23 I am as drunk as a lord, but then, I am one, so what does it matter?

Bertrand Russell (1872–1970) British philosopher. *Bertrand Russell, Philosopher of the Century* (Ralph Schoenman)

24 Drunkenness is temporary suicide the happiness that it brings is merely negative, a momentary cessation of unhappiness.

Bertrand Russell *The Conquest of Happiness*

25 No, thank you, I was born intoxicated.

George William Russell (1867–1935) Irish poet and dramatist. Refusing a drink that was offered him. *10,000 Jokes, Toasts, and Stories* (L. Copeland)

26 But I'm not so think as you drunk I am.

John Collings Squire (1884–1958) British journalist. *Ballade of Soporific Absorption*

27 An alcoholic is someone you don't like who drinks as much as you do.

Dylan Thomas (1914–53) Welsh poet. *Dictionary of 20th Century Quotations* (Nigel Rees)

28 Come, Robert, you shall drink twice while I drink once, for I cannot permit the son in his sober senses to witness the intoxication of his father.

Horace Walpole (1717–97) British writer. Explaining why he filled his son's glass twice for every glass he drank himself. Attrib.

DRYDEN, JOHN

(1631–1700) British poet and dramatist. His play *Marriage à la Mode* (1673) and the verse satire *Absalom and Achitophel* (1681) were highly regarded. He was made poet laureate by Charles II in 1668, but having become a Catholic in 1685, he was deprived of the office on the accession of William of Orange.

Quotations about Dryden

1 He never heartily and sincerely praised any human being, or felt any real enthusiasm for any subject he took up.

John Keble (1792–1866) British poet and clergyman. *Lectures on Poetry*

2 Ev'n copious Dryden wanted, or forgot
The last and greatest art – the art to blot.

Alexander Pope (1688–1744) British poet. *Imitations of Horace*

Quotations by Dryden

3 In pious times, e'r Priest-craft did begin,
Before Polygamy was made a Sin.

Absalom and Achitophel, I

4 What e'r he did was done with so much ease,
In him alone, 'twas Natural to please.

Absalom and Achitophel, I

5 Great Wits are sure to Madness near alli'd
And thin Partitions do their Bounds divide.

Absalom and Achitophel, I

6 Bankrupt of Life, yet Prodigal of Ease.

Absalom and Achitophel, I

7 For Politicians neither love nor hate.

Absalom and Achitophel, I

8 But far more numerous was the Herd of such,
Who think too little, and who talk too much.

Absalom and Achitophel, I

9 A man so various, that he seemed to be
Not one, but all Mankind's Epitome.
Stiff in Opinions, always in the wrong;
Was Everything by starts, and Nothing long.
Absalom and Achitophel, I

10 Did wisely from Expensive Sins refrain,
And never broke the Sabbath, but for Gain.
Absalom and Achitophel, I

11 During his Office, Treason was no Crime.
The Sons of Belial had a Glorious Time.
Absalom and Achitophel, I

12 Nor is the Peoples Judgment always true:
The Most may err as grossly as the Few.
Absalom and Achitophel, I

13 Beware the Fury of a Patient Man.
Absalom and Achitophel, I

14 The people's prayer, the glad diviner's theme,
The young men's vision, and the old men's dream!
Absalom and Achitophel, I

15 To die for faction is a common evil,
But to be hanged for nonsense is the Devil.
Absalom and Achitophel, II

16 None but the Brave deserves the Fair.
Alexander's Feast

17 Errors, like Straws, upon the surface flow;
He who would search for Pearls must dive below.
All for Love, Prologue

18 Men are but children of a larger growth;
Our appetites as apt to change as theirs,
And full as craving too, and full as vain.
All for Love, IV

19 So sicken waning moons too near the sun,
And blunt their crescents on the edge of day.
Annus Mirabilis

20 By viewing Nature, Nature's handmaid, art,
Makes mighty things from small beginnings grow.
Annus Mirabilis

21 Here lies my wife; here let her lie!
Now she's at rest, and so am I.
Epitaph Intended for Dryden's Wife

22 He was the man who of all modern, and perhaps ancient poets had the largest and most comprehensive soul.
Referring to Shakespeare. *Essay of Dramatic Poesy*

23 He was naturally learned; he needed not the spectacles of books to read nature; he looked inwards, and found her there.
Referring to Shakespeare. *Essay of Dramatic Poesy*

24 If by the people you understand the multitude, the *hoi polloi*, 'tis no matter what they think; they are sometimes in the right, sometimes in the wrong; their judgement is a mere lottery.
Essay of Dramatic Poesy

25 For present joys are more to flesh and blood
Than a dull prospect of a distant good.
The Hind and the Panther, III

26 All human things are subject to decay,
And, when Fate summons, Monarchs must obey.
MacFlecknoe

27 I am resolved to grow fat and look young till forty, and then slip out of the world with the first wrinkle and the reputation of five-and-twenty.
The Maiden Queen, III

28 I am to be married within these three days; married past redemption.
Marriage à la Mode, I

29 For, Heaven be thanked, we live in such an age,
When no man dies for love, but on the stage.
Mithridates, Epilogue

30 A man is to be cheated into passion, but to be reasoned into truth.
Religio Laici, Preface

31 Happy the Man, and happy he alone,
He who can call today his own:
He who, secure within, can say,
Tomorrow do thy worst, for I have liv'd today.
Translation of Horace, III

DURRELL, LAWRENCE

(1912–90) British novelist and poet. His Alexandria Quartet – *Justine* (1957), *Balthazar* (1958), *Mountolive* (1958), and *Clea* (1960) – established his reputation. Later books include *Tunc* (1968), *Nunquam* (1970), and the Avignon Quintet – *Monsieur* (1974), *Livia* (1978), *Constance* (1982), *Sebastian* (1983), and *Quinx* (1985).

1 No one can go on being a rebel too long without turning into an autocrat.
Balthazar, II

2 No more about sex, it's too boring.
Tunc

3 History is an endless repetition of the wrong way of living.
The Listener, 1978

DUTY

See also obligation

1 From a very early age, I had imbibed the opinion, that it was every man's duty to do all that lay in his power to leave his country as good as he had found it.
William Cobbett (1763–1835) British journalist and writer. *Political Register*, 22 Dec 1832

2 Do your duty and leave the rest to the Gods.
Pierre Corneille (1606–84) French dramatist. *Horace*, II:8

3 She's the sort of woman who lives for others – you can always tell the others by their hunted expression.
C. S. Lewis (1898–1963) British academic and writer. *The Screwtape Letters*

4 If we believe a thing to be bad, and if we have a right to prevent it, it is out duty to try to prevent it and to damn the consequences.
Alfred Milner (1854–1925) British statesman. Speech, Glasgow, 26 Nov 1909

5 England expects every man will do his duty.

Lord Nelson (1758–1805) British admiral. Signal hoisted prior to the Battle of Trafalgar, 1805

6 It is the highest and eternal duty of women – namely, to sacrifice their lives and to seek the good of their husbands.

Adi Parva Hindu text, *Mahabharata*

7 When a stupid man is doing something he is ashamed of, he always declares that it is his duty.

George Bernard Shaw (1856–1950) Irish dramatist and critic. *Caesar and Cleopatra*, III

8 Sunset and evening star,
And one clear call for me!
And may there be no moaning of the bar
When I put out to sea.

Alfred, Lord Tennyson (1809–92) British poet. *Crossing the Bar*

DYLAN, BOB

(Robert Allen Zimmerman; 1941–) US popular singer and songwriter. Originally a member of the 1960s protest movement, producing such albums as *The Times They Are A-Changin'* (1964), in the late 1970s his conversion to Christianity led to such religious albums as *Saved* (1980), *Infidels* (1983), *Oh Mercy* (1989), and *World Gone Wrong* (1994).

1 How many roads must a man walk down
Before you call him a man?

Blowin' in the Wind

2 Yes, 'n' how many years can some people exist
Before they're allowed to be free?
Yes, 'n' how many times can a man turn his head,
Pretending he just doesn't see?
The answer, my friend, is blowin' in the wind.

Blowin' in the Wind

3 But you're gonna have to serve somebody, yes indeed
You're gonna have to serve somebody,
Well, it may be the devil or it may be the Lord
But you're gonna have to serve somebody.

Gotta Serve Somebody

4 I've made shoes for everyone, even you, while I still go barefoot.

I and I

5 Idiot wind, blowing like a circle around my skull,
From the Grand Coulee Dam to the Capitol.
Idiot wind, blowing every time you move your teeth,
You're an idiot, babe.
It's a wonder that you still know how to breathe.

Idiot Wind

6 She takes just like a woman, yes, she does
She makes love just like a woman, yes, she does
And she aches just like a woman
But she breaks just like a little girl.

Just Like a Woman

7 How does it feel
To be without a home
Like a complete unknown
Like a rolling stone?

Like a Rolling Stone

8 She knows there's no success like failure
And that failure's no success at all.

Love Minus Zero No Limit

9 Good intentions can be evil,
Both hands can be full of grease.
You know that sometimes Satan comes as a man of peace.

Man of Peace

10 Hey! Mr Tambourine Man, play a song for me.
I'm not sleepy and there is no place I'm going to.

Mr Tambourine Man

11 You don't need a weather man
To know which way the wind blows

The US revolutionary terrorist group, the Weathermen, took their name from these lines. *Subterranean Homesick Blues*

12 Come mothers and fathers
Throughout the land
And don't criticize
What you can't understand.

The Times They Are A-Changin'

13 I saw thousands who could have overcome the darkness,
For the love of a lousy buck, I've watched them die.

When the Night Comes Falling from the Sky

14 God don't make no promises that He don't keep.
You got some big dreams, baby, but in order to dream you gotta still be asleep.

When You Gonna Wake Up?

16 A Hard Rain's A-Gonna Fall.

Song title

15 Yeah, some of them are about ten minutes long, others five or six.

On being asked, during an interview, if he would say something about his songs

E

ECOLOGY

See also conservation, environment

1 Over increasingly large areas of the United States, spring now comes unheralded by the return of the birds, and the early mornings are strangely silent where once they were filled with the beauty of bird song.

Rachel Carson (1907–64) US biologist. *The Silent Spring*

2 As cruel a weapon as the cave man's club, the chemical barrage has been hurled against the fabric of life.

Rachel Carson *The Silent Spring*

3 Man has been endowed with reason, with the power to create, so that he can add to what he's been given. But up to now he hasn't been a creator, only a destroyer. Forests keep disappearing, rivers dry up, wild life's become extinct, the climate's ruined and the land grows poorer and uglier every day.

Anton Chekhov (1860–1904) Russian dramatist. *Uncle Vanya*, I

4 Both biological and cultural diversity are now severely threatened and working for their preservation is a critical task.

Dr Murray Gell-Man (1929–) US physicist. *The Quark and the Jaguar*

5 It will be said of this generation that it found England a land of beauty and left it a land of beauty spots.

Cyril Joad (1891–1953) British writer and broadcaster. *The Observer*, 'Sayings of Our Times', 31 May 1953

6 We are living beyond our means. As a people we have developed a life-style that is draining the earth of its priceless and irreplaceable resources without regard for the future of our children and people all around the world.

Margaret Mead (1901–78) US anthropologist. *Redbook*, 'The Energy Crisis – Why Our World Will Never Again Be the Same'

7 The Irish Sea is naturally radioactive, the Sellafield discharges are less radioactive than the sea they are discharged into.

Cecil Parkinson (1931–) British politician. Speech, Nov 1987

8 We are wealthy and wasteful but this can't go on. If we don't eat dog biscuits, we could end up eating our dog instead.

Magnus Pyke (1908–92) British scientist, television personality, and writer. *The Observer*, 'Sayings of the Week', 12 Jan 1975

9 Had we gone the way of France and got 60 per cent of our electricity from nuclear power, we should not have environmental problems.

Margaret Thatcher (1925–) British politician and prime minister. Speech, Oct 1988

10 To the average British farmer, organic farming is about as relevant as caviar and a flight on Concorde.

Oliver Walston (1941–) Speech, Jan 1989

ECONOMICS

1 Don't spoil the ship for a ha'porth of tar.

Proverb

2 A budget is a method of worrying before you spend instead of afterwards.

Anonymous

3 John Stuart Mill
By a mighty effort of will
Overcame his natural bonhomie
And wrote 'Principles of Political Economy'.

Edmund Clerihew Bentley (1875–1956) British writer. *Biography for Beginners*

4 Respectable Professors of the Dismal Science.

Thomas Carlyle (1795–1881) Scottish historian and essayist. Referring to economists. *Latter-Day Pamphlets*, 1

5 Provided that the City of London remains as at present, the Clearing-house of the World.

Joseph Chamberlain (1836–1914) British politician. Speech, Guildhall, London, 19 Jan 1904

6 I am not prepared to accept the economics of a housewife.

Jacques Chirac (1932–) French politician. Referring to Margaret Thatcher. Remark, July 1987

7 I have given today's politicians and tomorrow's politicians no choice but to pursue the path of low inflation.

Kenneth Clarke (1940–) British politician. *The Observer*, 'Sayings of the Week', 19 June 1994

8 Annual income twenty pounds, annual expenditure nineteen nineteen six, result happiness. Annual income twenty pounds, annual expenditure twenty pounds ought and six, result misery.

Charles Dickens (1812–70) British novelist. *David Copperfield*, Ch. 12

9 If freedom were not so economically efficient it certainly wouldn't stand a chance.

Milton Friedman (1912–) US economist. Remark, Mar 1987

10 When every blessed thing you hold
Is made of silver, or of gold,
You long for simple pewter.
When you have nothing else to wear
But cloth of gold and satins rare,
For cloth of gold you cease to care –
Up goes the price of shoddy.

W. S. Gilbert (1836–1911) British dramatist. *The Gondoliers*, I

11 Having a little inflation is like being a little pregnant.

Leon Henderson (1895–1986) US economist. Attrib.

12 I will not be a party to debasing the currency.

John Maynard Keynes (1883–1946) British economist. On refusing to pay more than a small tip on having his shoes polished, whilst on a visit to Africa. *John Maynard Keynes* (C. Hession)

13 Economics is a subject that does not greatly respect one's wishes.

Nikita Khrushchev (1894–1971) Soviet statesman. Attrib.

14 Rising unemployment and the recession have been the price that we've had to pay to get inflation down: that is a price well worth paying.

Norman Lamont (1942–) British politician. *The Observer*, 19 May 1991

15 Inflation in the Sixties was a nuisance to be endured, like varicose veins or French foreign policy.

Bernard Levin (1928–) British journalist. *The Pendulum Years*, 'Epilogue'

16 One nanny said, 'Feed a cold'; she was a neo-Keynesian. Another nanny said, 'Starve a cold'; she was a monetarist.

Harold Macmillan (1894–1986) British politician and prime minister. Maiden speech, House of Lords, 1984

17 Population, when unchecked, increases in a geometrical ratio. Subsistence only increases in an arithmetical ratio.

Thomas Robert Malthus (1766–1834) British clergyman and economist. *Essays on the Principle of Population*

18 A nation is not in danger of financial disaster merely because it owes itself money.

Andrew William Mellon (1855–1937) US financier. Attrib.

19 In the days when the nation depended on agriculture for its wealth it made the Lord Chancellor sit on a woolsack to remind him where the wealth came from. I would like to suggest we remove that now and make him sit on a crate of machine tools.

Prince Philip (1921–) The consort of Queen Elizabeth II. Speech, Aug 1986

20 Recession is when a neighbour loses his job; depression is when you lose yours.

Ronald Reagan (1911–) US politician and president. *The Observer*, 'Sayings of the Week', 26 Oct 1980

21 If all economists were laid end to end, they would not reach a conclusion.

George Bernard Shaw (1856–1950) Irish dramatist and critic. Attrib.

22 Give me a one-handed economist! All my economists say, 'on the one hand...on the other'.

Harry S. Truman (1884–1972) US statesman. *Presidential Anecdotes* (P. Boller)

23 From now, the pound is worth 14 per cent or so less in terms of other currencies. It does not mean, of course, that the pound here in Britain, in your pocket or purse or in your bank, has been devalued.

Harold Wilson (1916–) British politician and prime minister. Speech after devaluation of the pound, 20 Nov 1967

24 One man's wage rise is another man's price increase.

Harold Wilson *The Observer*, 'Sayings of the Week', 11 Jan 1970

EDDY, MARY BAKER

(1821–1910) US religious leader who founded the Church of Christ, Scientist, in Boston (1879).

1 The prayer that reforms the sinner and heals the sick is an absolute faith that all things are possible to God – a spiritual understanding of Him, an unselfed love.

Science and Health, with Key to the Scriptures

2 Christian Science explains all cause and effect as mental, not physical.

Science and Health, with Key to the Scriptures

3 Sin brought death, and death will disappear with the disappearance of sin.

Science and Health, with Key to the Scriptures

4 Sickness, sin and death, being inharmonious, do not originate in God, nor belong to His government.

Science and Health, with Key to the Scriptures

5 Disease can carry its ill-effects no farther than mortal mind maps out the way... Disease is an image of thought externalized... We classify disease as error, which nothing but Truth or Mind can heal... Disease is an experience of so-called mortal mind. It is fear made manifest on the body.

Science and Health, with Key to the Scriptures

EDITORS

See also books, journalism, newspapers, publishing

1 Where were you fellows when the paper was blank?

Fred Allen (1894–1956) US comedian. Said to writers who heavily edited one of his scripts. Attrib.

2 Have you heard? The Prime Minister has resigned and Northcliffe has sent for the King.

Anonymous Said by a member of Lord Northcliffe's staff; at the height of his career, Northcliffe owned, among other newspapers, *The Times*, *The Observer*, the *Daily Mail*, the *Daily Mirror*, and the *London Evening News*. *Northcliffe, An Intimate Biography* (Hamilton Fyfe)

3 He made righteousness readable.

James Bone (1872–1962) British journalist. Referring to C. P. Scott, former editor of *The Manchester Guardian*. Attrib.

4 An editor is one who separates the wheat from the chaff and prints the chaff.

Adlai Stevenson (1900–65) US statesman. *The Stevenson Wit*

EDUCATION

See also academics, classics, examinations, indoctrination, learning, punishment

1 Soon learnt, soon forgotten.

Proverb

2 They know enough who know how to learn.

Henry Brooks Adams (1838–1918) US historian. *The Education of Henry Adams*

3 But above all things I strive to train them to be useful to the Holy Church of God and for the glory of your kingdom.

Alcuin (c. 735–804) English theologian. Referring to his school at Tours. Letter to Charlemagne, c. 796

4 ...all the youth now in England of free men, who are rich enough to be able to devote themselves to it, be set to learn as long as they are not fit for any other occupation, until they are able to read English writing well.

Alfred the Great (849–901) King of Wessex *Cura Pastoralis*, Preface

5 I wish I could have a little tape-and-loudspeaker arrangement sewn into the binding of this magazine, to be triggered off by the light reflected from the reader's eyes on to this part of the page, and set to bawl out at several bels: MORE WILL MEAN WORSE.

Kingsley Amis (1922–) British novelist, poet, and critic. Discussing the idea that many students are unable to get university places. *Encounter*, July 1960

6 A maiden at college, named Breeze,
Weighed down by B.A.s and M.D.s
Collapsed from the strain.
Said her doctor, 'It's plain
You are killing yourself by degrees!'

Anonymous

7 What we must look for here is, first, religious and moral principles; secondly, gentlemanly conduct; thirdly, intellectual ability.

Thomas Arnold (1795–1842) British educator. Address to the scholars at Rugby

8 My object will be, if possible to form Christian men, for Christian boys I can scarcely hope to make.

Thomas Arnold Letter on appointment as headmaster of Rugby, 1828

9 I remember when I was young, in the north, they went to the grammar school little children: they came from thence great lubbers: always learning, and little profiting: learning without book everything, understanding within the book little or nothing.

Roger Ascham (1515–68) *The Scholemaster*

10 Universities incline wits to sophistry and affectation.

Francis Bacon (1561–1626) English philosopher. *Valerius Terminus of the Interpretation of Nature*, Ch. 26

11 Studies serve for delight, for ornament, and for ability.

Francis Bacon *Essays*, 'Of Studies'

12 It is Oxford that has made me insufferable.

Max Beerbohm (1872–1956) British writer. *More*, 'Going back to School'

13 The dread of beatings,
Dread of Being Late
And greatest dread of all, the dread of games.

John Betjeman (1906–84) British poet. *Summoned by Bells*

14 Broad of Church and broad of mind,
Broad before and broad behind,
A keen ecclesiologist,
A rather dirty Wykehamist.

John Betjeman *The Wykehamist*

15 The education of the doctor which goes on after he has his degree is, after all, the most important part of his education.

John Shaw Billings (1838–1913) *Boston Medical and Surgical Journal*, 1894

16 Western traditions of education have emphasized knowledge analysis, description and debate. They all have a part to play, but today there is a whole vast aspect of doing that has just been left out. Operacy is what keeps society going.

Edward de Bono (1933–) British physician and writer. *The Times*, 24 Sept 1990

17 Most people...are put off science because maths is the gateway and they can't handle it. What we should be teaching is operational maths because, in general, the maths we need to carry out science is pretty straightforward.

Edward de Bono *The Times*, 24 Sept 1990

18 My students are dismayed when I say to them, 'Half of what you are taught as medical students will in ten years have been shown to be wrong, and the trouble is, none of your teachers knows which half.'

C. Sidney Burwell (1893–1967) *British Medical Journal*, 1956 (G.W. Pickering)

19 Learning is good in and of itself...the mothers of the Jewish ghettoes of the east would pour honey on a book so the children would know that learning is sweet. And the parents who settled hungry Kansas would take their children in from the fields when a teacher came.

George Bush (1924–) US politician and president. Speech accepting his nomination as presidential candidate, Republican Party Convention, New Orleans, Aug 1988

20 The true University of these days is a collection of books.

Thomas Carlyle (1795–1881) Scottish historian and essayist. *Heroes and Hero-Worship*, 'The Hero as Man of Letters'

21 'Reeling and Writhing, of course, to begin with,' the Mock Turtle replied; 'and then the different branches of Arithmetic – Ambition, Distraction, Uglification, and Derision.'

Lewis Carroll (Charles Lutwidge Dodgson; 1832–98) British writer. *Alice's Adventures in Wonderland*, Ch. 9

22 This is to seyn, to syngen and to rede,
As smale children doon in hire childhede.

Geoffrey Chaucer (c. 1342–1400) English poet. *The Canterbury Tales*, 'The Prioress's Tale'

23 His English education at one of the great public schools had preserved his intellect perfectly and permanently at the stage of boyhood.

G. K. Chesterton (1874–1936) British writer. *The Man Who Knew Too Much*

24 Education is simply the soul of a society as it passes from one generation to another.

G. K. Chesterton *The Observer*, 'Sayings of the Week', 6 July 1924

25 Headmasters have powers at their disposal with which Prime Ministers have never yet been invested.

Winston Churchill (1874–1965) British statesman. *My Early Life*, Ch. 2

26 The ape-like virtues without which no one can enjoy a public school.

Cyril Connolly (1903–74) British journalist. *Enemies of Promise*, Ch. 1

27 When he has learnt that bottinney means a knowledge of plants, he goes and knows 'em. That's our system, Nickleby; what do you think of it?

Charles Dickens (1812–70) British novelist. Said by Mr Squeers. *Nicholas Nickleby*, Ch. 8

28 I pay the schoolmaster, but 'tis the schoolboys that educate my son.

Ralph Waldo Emerson (1803–82) US poet and essayist. *Journal*

29 Public schools are the nurseries of all vice and immorality.

Henry Fielding (1707–54) British novelist. *Joseph Andrews*, Bk. III, Ch. 5

30 The great doctors all got their education off dirt pavements and poverty – not marble floors and foundations.

Martin H. Fischer (1879–1962) *Fischerisms* (Howard Fabing and Ray Marr)

31 It is not that the Englishman can't feel – it is that he is afraid to feel. He has been taught at his public school that feeling is bad form. He must not express great joy or sorrow, or even open his mouth too wide when he talks – his pipe might fall out if he did.

E. M. Forster (1879–1970) British novelist. *Abinger Harvest*, 'Notes on the English character'

32 They go forth into it with well-developed bodies, fairly developed minds, and undeveloped hearts.

E. M. Forster Referring to public schoolboys going into the world. *Abinger Harvest*, 'Notes on the English Character'

33 Spoon feeding in the long run teaches us nothing but the shape of the spoon.

E. M. Forster *The Observer*, 'Sayings of the Week', 7 Oct 1951

34 We keep the students within view of their parents; we save them many toils and long foreign journeys; we protect them from robbers. They used to be pillaged while travelling abroad; now, they may study at small cost and short wayfaring, thanks to our liberality.

Frederick II (1194–1250) Holy Roman Emperor. Foundation charter of Naples University

35 A teacher is paid to teach, not to sacrifice rats and hamsters.

Edward A. Gall (1906–) *Journal of Medical Education*, 36:275, 1961

36 To the University of Oxford I acknowledge no obligation; and she will as cheerfully renounce me for a son, as I am willing to disclaim her for a mother. I spent fourteen months at Magdalen College: they proved the fourteen months the most idle and unprofitable of my whole life.

Edward Gibbon (1737–94) British historian. *Autobiography*

37 Let schoolmasters puzzle their brain,
With grammar, and nonsense, and learning,
Good liquor, I stoutly maintain,
Gives genius a better discerning.

Oliver Goldsmith (1728–74) Irish-born British writer. *She Stoops to Conquer*, I

38 Shakespeare is fine for grammar school kids.

Nigel de Gruchy (1943–) British teacher and trade unionist. *The Observer*, 5 July 1992

39 Education made us what we are.

Claude-Adrien Helvétius (1715–71) French philosopher. *Discours* XXX, Ch. 30

40 A good clinical teacher is himself a Medical School.

Oliver Wendell Holmes (1809–94) US writer and physician. *Medical Essays*, 'Scholastic and Bedside Teaching'

41 The bedside is always the true center of medical teaching.

Oliver Wendell Holmes *Medical Essays*, 'Scholastic and Bedside Teaching'

42 The most essential part of a student's instruction is obtained, as I believe, not in the lecture room, but at the beside.

Oliver Wendell Holmes *Medical Essays*, 'Scholastic and Bedside Teaching'

43 And seek for truth in the groves of Academe.

Horace (Quintus Horatius Flaccus; 65–8 BC) Roman poet. *Epistles*, II

44 Those of us who have the duty of training the rising generation of doctors...must not inseminate the virgin minds of the young with the tares of our own fads. It is for this reason that it is easily possible for teaching to be too 'up to date'. It is always well, before handing the cup of knowledge to the young, to wait until the froth has settled.

Robert Hutchison (1871–1960) *British Medical Journal*, 1925

45 You sought the last resort of feeble minds with classical educations. You became a schoolmaster.

Aldous Huxley (1894–1964) British novelist. *Antic Hay*

46 Some experience of popular lecturing had convinced me that the necessity of making things plain to uninstructed people was one of the very best means of clearing up the obscure corners in one's own mind.

T. H. Huxley (1825–95) British biologist. *Man's Place in Nature*, Preface

47 Any attempt to reform the university without attending to the system of which it is an integral part is like trying to do urban renewal in New York City from the twelfth storey up.

Ivan Illich (1926–) Austrian sociologist. *Deschooling Society*, Ch. 3

48 In teaching the medical student the primary requisite is to keep him awake.

Chevalier Jackson (1865–1958) *The Life of Chevalier Jackson*, Ch. 16

49 His mind must be strong indeed, if, rising above juvenile credulity, it can maintain a wise infidelity against the authority of his instructors, and the bewitching delusions of their theories.

Thomas Jefferson (1743–1826) US statesman. Letter to Dr. Caspar Wistar, 21 June 1807

50 It is no matter what you teach them first, any more than what leg you shall put into your breeches first.

Samuel Johnson (1709–84) British lexicographer. *Life of Johnson* (J. Boswell), Vol. I

51 There is now less flogging in our great schools than formerly, but then less is learned there; so that what the boys get at one end they lose at the other.

Samuel Johnson *Life of Johnson* (J. Boswell), Vol. II

52 There mark what ills the scholar's life assail
Toil, envy, want, the patron, and the jail.

Samuel Johnson *Vanity of Human Wishes*

53 I find the three major administrative problems on a campus are sex for the students, athletics for the alumni and parking for the faculty.

Clark Kerr (1911–) US educator. *Time*, 17 Nov 1958

54 Nothing would more effectively further the

development of education than for all flogging pedagogues to learn to educate with the head instead of with the hand.

Ellen Key (Karolina Sofia Key; 1849–1926) Swedish writer. *The Century of the Child*, Ch. 3

55 If every day in the life of a school could be the last day but one, there would be little fault to find with it.

Stephen Leacock (1869–1944) English-born Canadian economist and humorist. *College Days*, 'Memories and Miseries of a Schoolmaster'

56 Four times, under our educational rules, the human pack is shuffled and cut – at eleven-plus, sixteen-plus, eighteen-plus and twenty-plus – and happy is he who comes top of the deck on each occasion, but especially the last. This is called Finals, the very name of which implies that nothing of importance can happen after it. The British postgraduate student is a lonely forlorn soul…for whom nothing has been real since the Big Push.

David Lodge (1935–) British writer. *Changing Places*, Ch. 1

57 Universities are the cathedrals of the modern age. They shouldn't have to justify their existence by utilitarian criteria.

David Lodge *Nice Work*, IV

58 Whenever I look in the glass or see a photograph of myself, I am reminded of Petrarch's simple statement 'Nothing is more hideous than an old schoolmaster'!

G. W. Lyttelton *The Lyttelton Hart-Davis Letters*, 11 Apr 1956

59 If you educate a man you educate a person, but if you educate a woman you educate a family.

Ruby Manikan (20th century) Indian Church leader. *The Observer*, 'Sayings of the Week', 30 Mar 1947

60 …the rustics vie with each other in bringing up their ignoble and degenerate offspring to the liberal arts.

Walter Map (c. 1140–c. 1209) Welsh cleric and writer. Drawing a comparison with the aristocracy, who were 'too poud or too lazy to put their children to learning'. *De Nugis Curialium*, Pt. I, Ch. 10

61 A gentleman need not know Latin, but he should at least have forgotten it.

Brander Matthews (1852–1929) US writer. Attrib.

62 There are two objects of medical education: To heal the sick, and to advance the science.

Charles H. Mayo (1865–1939) *Collected Papers of the Mayo Clinic and Mayo Foundation*, 18:1093, 1926

63 A whale ship was my Yale College and my Harvard.

Herman Melville (1819–91) US novelist. *Moby Dick*, Ch. 24

64 One tongue is sufficient for a woman.

John Milton (1608–74) English poet. On being asked whether he would allow his daughters to learn foreign languages. Attrib.

65 And if education is always to be conceived along the same antiquated lines of a mere transmission of knowledge, there is little to be hoped from it in the bettering of man's future. For what is the use of transmitting knowledge if the individual's total development lags behind?

Maria Montessori (1870–1952) Italian doctor and educationalist. *The Absorbent Mind*

66 We teachers can only help the work going on, as servants wait upon a master.

Maria Montessori *The Absorbent Mind*

67 Discussion in class, which means letting twenty young blockheads and two cocky neurotics discuss something that neither their teacher nor they know.

Vladimir Nabokov (1899–1977) Russian-born US novelist. *Pnin*, Ch. 6

68 Every schoolmaster after the age of 49 is inclined to flatulence, is apt to swallow frequently, and to puff.

Harold Nicolson (1886–1968) British writer. *The Old School*

69 The schoolteacher is certainly underpaid as a childminder, but ludicrously overpaid as an educator.

John Osborne (1929–) British dramatist. *The Observer*, 'Sayings of the Week', 21 July 1985

70 I desire no other epitaph – no hurry about it, I may say – than the statement that I taught medical students in the wards, as I regard this as by far the most useful and important work I have been called upon to do.

William Osler (1849–1919) Canadian physician. *Aequanimitas, with Other Addresses*, 'The Fixed Period'

71 I have learned since to be a better student, and to be ready to say to my fellow students 'I do not know.'

William Osler *Aequanimitas, with Other Addresses*, 'After Twenty-Five Years'

72 School yourself to demureness and patience. Learn to innure yourself to drudgery in science. Learn, compare, collect the facts.

Ivan Pavlov (1849–1936) Russian physiologist. *Bequest to the Academic Youth of Soviet Russia*, 27 Feb 1936

73 He was sent, as usual, to a public school, where a little learning was painfully beaten into him, and from thence to the university, where it was carefully taken out of him.

Thomas Love Peacock (1785–1866) British novelist. *Nightmare Abbey*, Ch. 1

74 'Tis education forms the common mind,
Just as the twig is bent, the tree's inclined.

Alexander Pope (1688–1744) British poet. *Moral Essays*, I

75 Girls and boys grow up more normally together than apart.

Daphne Rae Wife of the headmaster of Westminster School. Remark, May 1988

76 A man who has never gone to school may steal from a freight car, but if he has a university education he may steal the whole railroad.

Franklin D. Roosevelt (1882–1945) US Democratic president. Attrib.

77 But, good gracious, you've got to educate him first.
You can't expect a boy to be vicious till he's been to a good school.

Saki (Hector Hugh Munro; 1870–1916) British writer. *Reginald in Russia*

78 For every person wishing to teach there are thirty not wanting to be taught.

W. C. Sellar (1898–1951) British humorous writer. *And Now All This*

79 No profit grows where is no pleasure ta'en;
In brief, sir, study what you most affect.

William Shakespeare (1564–1616) English dramatist. *The Taming of the Shrew*, I:1

80 A learned man is an idler who kills time by study.

George Bernard Shaw (1856–1950) Irish dramatist and critic. *Man and Superman*

81 There is nothing on earth intended for innocent people so horrible as a school. It is in some respects more cruel than a prison. In a prison, for example, you are not forced to read books written by the warders and the governor.

George Bernard Shaw *Parents and Children*

82 He who can, does. He who cannot, teaches.

George Bernard Shaw *Man and Superman*, 'Maxims for Revolutionists'

83 Educated: in the holidays from Eton.

Osbert Sitwell (1892–1969) British writer. Entry in *Who's Who*

84 Indeed one of the ultimate advantages of an education is simply coming to the end of it.

B. F. Skinner (1904–90) US psychologist. *The Technology of Teaching*

85 Education is what survives when what has been learnt has been forgotten.

B. F. Skinner *New Scientist*, 21 May 1964, 'Education in 1984'

86 I was beaten by almost everyone at Eton, but never by the headmaster.

Nicholas Soames (1948–) British politician. *The Observer*, 'Sayings of the Week', 1 May 1994

87 All my pupils are the crème de la crème.

Muriel Spark (1918–) British novelist. *The Prime of Miss Jean Brodie*

88 To me education is a leading out of what is already there in the pupil's soul. To Miss Mackay it is a putting in of something that is not there, and that is not what I call education, I call it intrusion....

Muriel Spark *The Prime of Miss Jean Brodie*, Ch. 2

89 Education has for its object the formation of character.

Herbert Spencer (1820–1903) British philosopher. *Social Statics*, 2:17

90 Education...has produced a vast population able to read but unable to distinguish what is worth reading.

George Macaulay Trevelyan (1876–1962) British historian. *English Social History*, Ch. 18

91 Soap and education are not as sudden as a massacre, but they are more deadly in the long run.

Mark Twain (Samuel Langhorne Clemens; 1835–1910) US writer. *The Facts concerning the Recent Resignation*

92 People at the top of the tree are those without qualifications to detain them at the bottom.

Peter Ustinov (1921–) British actor. Attrib.

93 I expect you'll be becoming a schoolmaster sir. That's what most of the gentlemen does sir, that gets sent down for indecent behaviour.

Evelyn Waugh (1903–66) British novelist. *Decline and Fall*, Prelude

94 We class schools you see, into four grades: Leading School, First-rate School, Good School, and School.

Evelyn Waugh *Decline and Fall*, Pt. I, Ch. 1

95 We schoolmasters must temper discretion with deceit.

Evelyn Waugh *Decline and Fall*, Pt. I, Ch. 1

96 That's the public-school system all over. They may kick you out, but they never let you down.

Evelyn Waugh *Decline and Fall*, Pt. I, Ch. 3

97 Anyone who has been to an English public school will always feel comparatively at home in prison.

Evelyn Waugh *Decline and Fall*, Pt. III, Ch. 4

98 Assistant masters came and went...Some liked little boys too little and some too much.

Evelyn Waugh *A Little Learning*

99 Medical education is not completed at the medical school: it is only begun.

William H. Welch (1850–1934) *Bulletin of the Harvard Medical School Association*, 3:55, 1892

100 The battle of Waterloo was won on the playing fields of Eton.

Duke of Wellington (1769–1852) British general and statesman. Attrib.

101 A very large part of English middle-class education is devoted to the training of servants...In so far as it is, by definition, the training of upper servants, it includes, of course, the instilling of that kind of confidence which will enable the upper servants to supervise and direct the lower servants.

Raymond Henry Williams (1921–88) British academic and writer. *Culture and Society*, Ch. 3

EFFORT

See also work

1 If a job's worth doing, it's worth doing well.

Proverb

2 Energy is Eternal Delight.

William Blake (1757–1827) British poet. *The Marriage of Heaven and Hell*, 'The Voice of the Devil'

3 I have nothing to offer but blood, toil, tears and sweat.

Winston Churchill (1874–1965) British statesman. On becoming prime minister. Speech, House of Commons, 13 May 1940

4 A world where nothing is had for nothing.

Arthur Hugh Clough (1819–61) British poet. *The Bothie of Tober-na-Vuolich*, Bk. VIII, Ch. 5

5 As is the case in all branches of art, success depends in a very large measure upon individual initiative and exertion, and cannot be achieved except by dint of hard work.

Anna Pavlova (1881–1931) Russian ballet dancer. *Pavlova: A Biography* (ed. A. H. Franks), 'Pages of My Life'

6 And here is the lesson I learned in the army. If you want to do a thing badly, you have to work at it as though you want to do it well.

Peter Ustinov (1921–) British actor. *Dear Me*, Ch. 8

7 Please do not shoot the pianist. He is doing his best.

Oscar Wilde (1854–1900) Irish-born British dramatist. *Impressions of America*, 'Leadville'

EGOTISM

See also arrogance, conceit, pride, selfishness

1 Against whom?

Alfred Adler (1870–1937) Austrian psychiatrist. Said when he heard that an egocentric had fallen in love. *Some of My Best Friends* (J. Bishop), 'Exponent of the Soul'

2 No poet or novelist wishes he were the only one who ever lived, but most of them wish they were the only one alive, and quite a number fondly believe their wish has been granted.

W. H. Auden (1907–73) British poet. *The Dyer's Hand*, 'Writing'

3 EGOTIST, n. A person of low taste, more interested in himself than in me.

Ambrose Bierce (1842–?1914) US writer and journalist. *The Devil's Dictionary*

4 Someone said of a very great egotist: 'He would burn your house down to cook himself a couple of eggs.

Nicolas Chamfort (1741–94) French writer. *Caractères et anecdotes*

5 An author who speaks about his own books is almost as bad as a mother who talks about her own children.

Benjamin Disraeli (1804–81) British statesman. Speech in Glasgow, 19 Nov 1873

6 If the Almighty himself played the violin, the credits would still read 'Rubinstein, God, and Piatigorsky', in that order.

Jascha Heifetz (1901–87) Russian-born US violinist. Whenever Heifetz played in trios with Arthur Rubinstein (piano) and Gregor Piatigorsky (cello), Rubinstein always got top billing. *The Los Angeles Times*, 29 Aug 1982

7 One had rather malign oneself than not speak of oneself at all.

Duc de la Rochefoucauld (1613–80) French writer. *Maximes*, 138

8 As who should say 'I am Sir Oracle,
And when I ope my lips let no dog bark'.

William Shakespeare (1564–1616) English dramatist. *The Merchant of Venice*, I:1

9 A pompous woman of his acquaintance, complaining that the head-waiter of a restaurant had not shown her and her husband immediately to a table, said, 'We had to tell him who we were.' Gerald, interested, enquired, 'And who were you?'

Edith Sitwell (1887–1964) British poet and writer. *Taken Care Of*, Ch. 15

10 No man thinks there is much ado about nothing when the ado is about himself.

Anthony Trollope (1815–82) British novelist. *The Bertrams*, Ch. 27

11 I am the only person in the world I should like to know thoroughly.

Oscar Wilde (1854–1900) Irish-born British dramatist. *Lady Windermere's Fan*, II

EINSTEIN, ALBERT

(1879–1955) German physicist who became a Swiss citizen (1901) and later a US citizen (1940). His theory of relativity revolutionized scientific thought. He was persuaded to write to President Roosevelt to warn him that Germany could possibly make an atomic bomb.

Quotations about Einstein

1 Einstein – the greatest Jew since Jesus. I have no doubt that Einstein's name will still be remembered and revered when Lloyd George, Foch and William Hohenzollern share with Charlie Chaplin that ineluctable oblivion which awaits the uncreative mind.

J. B. S. Haldane (1892–1964) British genetist. *Daedalus or Science and the Future*

2 The genius of Einstein leads to Hiroshima.

Pablo Picasso (1881–1973) Spanish painter. *Life with Picasso* (Françoise Gilot and Carlton Lake)

Quotations by Einstein

3 Science without religion is lame, religion without science is blind.

Science, Philosophy and Religion: a symposium

4 We should take care not to make the intellect our god; it has, of course, powerful muscles, but no personality.

Out of My Later Life, 51

5 If you want to find out anything from the theoretical physicists about the methods they use, I advise you to stick closely to one principle: Don't listen to their words, fix your attention on their deeds.

The World As I See It

6 God does not play dice.

Einstein's objection to the quantum theory, in which physical events can only be known in terms of probabilities. It is sometimes quoted as 'God does not play dice with the Universe'. *Albert Einstein, Creator and Rebel* (B. Hoffman), Ch. 10

7 God is subtle but he is not malicious.

Inscribed over the fireplace in the Mathematical Institute, Princeton. It refers to Einstein's objection to the quantum theory. *Albert Einstein* (Carl Seelig), Ch. 8

8 When you are courting a nice girl an hour seems like a second. When you sit on a red-hot cinder a second seems like an hour. That's relativity.

News Chronicle, 14 Mar 1949

9 If only I had known, I should have become a watchmaker.

Reflecting on his role in the development of the atom bomb. *New Statesman*, 16 Apr 1965

10 Common sense is the collection of prejudices acquired by age eighteen.

Scientific American, Feb 1976

11 A theory can be proved by experiment; but no path leads from experiment to the birth of a theory.

The Sunday Times, 18 July 1976

12 As far as the laws of mathematics refer to reality, they are not certain, and as far as they are certain, they do not refer to reality.

The Tao of Physics (F. Capra), Ch. 2

13 I never think of the future. It comes soon enough.

Interview, 1930

EISENHOWER, DWIGHT D.

(1890–1969) US general and statesman. President (1953–61) during the Cold War and the period of anticommunist witch hunts led by Senator McCarthy. In World War II he became supreme commander and was responsible for the D-day invasion of Europe.

Quotations about Eisenhower

1 Roosevelt proved a man could be president for life; Truman proved anybody could be president; and Eisenhower proved we don't need a president.

Anonymous

2 As an intellectual he bestowed upon the games of golf and bridge all the enthusiasm and perseverance that he withheld from books and ideas.

Emmet John Hughes *The Ordeal of Power*

3 The best clerk I ever fired.

Douglas Macarthur (1880–1964) US general. Attrib

Quotations by Eisenhower

4 The eyes of the world are upon you. The hopes and prayers of liberty-loving people everywhere march with you.

Order to his troops, 6 June 1944 (D-Day)

5 Whatever America hopes to bring to pass in this world must first come to pass in the heart of America.

Inaugural address, 1953

6 There is one thing about being President – nobody can tell you when to sit down.

The Observer, 'Sayings of the Week', 9 Aug 1953

7 You have a row of dominoes set up; you knock over the first one, and what will happen to the last one is that it will go over very quickly.

The so-called 'domino effect'; said during the Battle of Dien Bien Phu, in which the French were defeated by the communist Viet-Minh. Press conference, 7 Apr 1954

8 Your business is to put me out of business.

Addressing a graduating class at a university. *Procession* (J. Gunther)

9 The day will come when the people will make so insistent their demand that there be peace in the world that the Governments will get out of the way and let them have peace.

Attrib.

ELIOT, GEORGE

(Mary Ann Evans; 1819–80) British woman novelist who concealed her identity behind a man's name. Her novels, including *Adam Bede* (1854), *The Mill on the Floss* (1860), *Silas Marner* (1861), and *Middlemarch* (1871–72), were highly acclaimed.

Quotations about George Eliot

1 I found out in the first two pages that it was a woman's writing – she supposed that in making a door, you last of all put in the *panels*!

Referring to *Adam Bede*. **Thomas Carlyle** (1795–1881) Scottish historian and essayist. *George Eliot* (G. H. Haight)

2 I never saw such a woman. There is nothing a bit masculine about her; she is thoroughly feminine and looks and acts as if she were made for nothing but to mother babies. But she has a power of *stating* an argument equal to any man; equal to any man do I say? I have never seen any man, except Herbert Spencer, who could state a case equal to her.

John Fiske (1842–1901) US historian. Letter to his wife, 1873

Quotations by George Eliot

3 A patronizing disposition always has its meaner side.

Adam Bede

4 It's but little good you'll do a-watering the last year's crop.

Adam Bede

5 He was like a cock who thought the sun had risen to hear him crow.

Adam Bede

6 A different taste in jokes is a great strain on the affections.

Daniel Deronda

7 Errors look so very ugly in persons of small means – one feels they are taking quite a liberty in going astray; whereas people of fortune may naturally indulge in a few delinquencies.

Janet's Repentance, Ch. 25

8 I should like to know what is the proper function of women, if it is not to make reasons for husbands to stay at home, and still stronger reasons for bachelors to go out.

The Mill on the Floss, Ch. 6

9 Animals are such agreeable friends – they ask no questions, they pass no criticisms.

Scenes of Clerical Life, 'Mr Gilfil's Love Story', Ch. 7

10 Women who are content with light and easily broken ties do *not* act as I have done. They obtain what they desire and are still invited to dinner.

Referring to her life with George Lewes. *The New Encyclopedia Britannica*

ELIOT, T. S.

(1888–1965) US-born British poet and dramatist. He worked as a bank clerk before publication of his *Prufrock and Other Observations* (1917). *The Waste Land* (1922) established his reputation, which was confirmed by his *Four Quartets* (1935–41). His verse dramas include *Murder in the Cathedral* (1935) and *The Cocktail Party* (1949).

Quotations about T. S. Eliot

1 He likes to look on the bile when it is black.

Aldous Huxley (1894–1964) British novelist and essayist. *Ambrosia and Small Beer* (E. Marsh)

2 He is very yellow and glum. Perfect manners. Dyspeptic, ascetic, eclectic. Inhibitions. Yet obviously a nice man and a great poet.

Harold Nicolson (1886–1968) British writer. *Diary*, 2 May 1932

Quotations by T. S. Eliot

3 Because I do not hope to turn again
Because I do not hope
Because I do not hope to turn.

Ash-Wednesday

4 We can say of Shakespeare, that never has a man turned so little knowledge to such great account.

The Classics and the Man of Letters (lecture)

5 Hell is oneself;
Hell is alone, the other figures in it
Merely projections. There is nothing to escape from
And nothing to escape to. One is always alone.

The Cocktail Party, I:3

6 Time present and time past
Are both perhaps present in time future,
And time future contained in time past.

Four Quartets, 'Burnt Norton'

7 Human kind
Cannot bear very much reality.

Four Quartets, 'Burnt Norton'

8 Here I am, an old man in a dry month,
Being read to by a boy, waiting for rain.

Gerontion

9 We are the hollow men
We are the stuffed men
Leaning together
Headpiece filled with straw. Alas!

The Hollow Men

10 This is the way the world ends
Not with a bang but a whimper.

The Hollow Men

11 Let us go then, you and I,
When the evening is spread out against the sky
Like a patient etherized upon a table.

The Love Song of J. Alfred Prufrock

12 In the room the women come and go
Talking of Michelangelo.

The Love Song of J. Alfred Prufrock

13 I have measured out my life with coffee spoons.

The Love Song of J. Alfred Prufrock

14 I grow old…I grow old…
I shall wear the bottoms of my trousers rolled.

The Love Song of J. Alfred Prufrock

15 Shall I part my hair behind? Do I dare to eat a peach?
I shall wear white flannel trousers, and walk upon the beach.
I have heard the mermaids singing, each to each.

The Love Song of J. Alfred Prufrock

16 Macavity, Macavity, there's no one like Macavity,
There never was a Cat of such deceitfulness and suavity.
He always has an alibi, and one or two to spare:
At whatever time the deed took place – MACAVITY WASN'T THERE!

Old Possum's Book of Practical Cats, 'Macavity: The Mystery Cat'

17 I am aware of the damp souls of the housemaids
Sprouting despondently at area gates.

Morning at the Window

18 The last temptation is the greatest treason:
To do the right deed for the wrong reason.

Murder in the Cathedral, I

19 The winter evening settles down
With smell of steaks in passageways.

Preludes

20 Every street-lamp that I pass
Beats like a fatalistic drum,
And through the spaces of the dark
Midnight shakes the memory
As a madman shakes a dead geranium.

Rhapsody on a Windy Night

21 'Put your shoes at the door, sleep, prepare for life.'
The last twist of the knife.

Rhapsody on a Windy Night

22 Birth, and copulation, and death.
That's all the facts when you come to brass tacks.

Sweeney Agonistes, 'Fragment of an Agon'

23 The host with someone indistinct
Converses at the door apart,
The nightingales are singing near
The Convent of the Sacred Heart.

Sweeney among the Nightingales

24 No poet, no artist of any sort, has his complete meaning alone. His significance, his appreciation is the appreciation of his relation to the dead poets and artists.

Tradition and the Individual Talent

25 Poetry is not a turning loose of emotion, but an escape from emotion; it is not the expression of personality, but an escape from personality.

Tradition and the Individual Talent

26 April is the cruellest month, breeding
Lilacs out of the dead land, mixing
Memory and desire, stirring
Dull roots with spring rain.

The Waste Land, 'The Burial of the Dead'

27 I read, much of the night, and go south in the winter.

The Waste Land, 'The Burial of the Dead'

28 And I will show you something different from either
Your shadow at morning striding behind you,
Or your shadow at evening rising to meet you
I will show you fear in a handful of dust.

The Waste Land, 'The Burial of the Dead'

29 The years between fifty and seventy are the hardest. You are always being asked to do things, and you are not yet decrepit enough to turn them down.

Time, 23 Oct 1950

ELIZABETH I

(1533–1603) Queen of England. The daughter of Henry VIII and Anne Boleyn, she established the Protestant Church in England and had her Catholic cousin, Mary, Queen of Scots, beheaded. The Elizabethan age was one of greatness for England.

Quotations about Elizabeth I

1 The queen did fish for men's souls, and had so sweet a bait that no one could escape her network.
Christopher Hatton. Attrib.

2 ...her face oblong, fair but wrinkled; her eyes small, yet black and pleasant; her nose a little hooked, her lips narrow and her teeth black (a defect the English seem subject to from their too great use of sugar)...She wore false hair and that red.
Paul Hentzner (fl. 1590s) German tutor. *Journey into England*

3 As just and merciful as Nero and as good a Christian as Mahomet.
John Wesley (1703–91) British religious leader. *Journal*, 29 Apr 1768

Quotations by Elizabeth I

4 Though God hath raised me high, yet this I count the glory of my crown: that I have reigned with your loves.
The Golden Speech, 1601

5 Madam I may not call you; mistress I am ashamed to call you; and so I know not what to call you; but howsoever, I thank you.
Writing to the wife of the Archbishop of Canterbury, expressing her disapproval of married clergy. *Brief View of the State of the Church* (Harington)

6 God may pardon you, but I never can.
To the dying Countess of Nottingham. *History of England under the House of Tudor* (Hume), Vol. II, Ch. 7

7 Good-morning, gentlemen both.
When addressing a group of eighteen tailors. *Sayings of Queen Elizabeth* (Chamberlin)

8 I will make you shorter by a head.
To her council leaders, who opposed her course towards Mary Queen of Scots. *Sayings of Queen Elizabeth* (Chamberlin)

9 I am your anointed Queen. I will never be by violence constrained to do anything. I thank God that I am endued with such qualities that if I were turned out of the Realm in my petticoat I were able to live in any place in Christome.
Speech, 5 Nov 1566

10 To me it shall be a full satisfaction both for the memorial of my name, and for the glory also, if when I shall let my last breath, it be engraven upon my marble tomb, 'Here lieth Elizabeth, who reigned a virgin and died a virgin'.
Reply to a petition from the House of Commons, 6 Feb 1559

11 Must! Is *must* a word to be addressed to princes? Little man, little man! thy father, if he had been alive, durst not have used that word.
Said to Robert Cecil, on her death bed. *A Short History of the English People* (J. R. Green), Ch. 7

12 If thy heart fails thee, climb not at all.
Written on a window in reply to Sir Walter RALEIGH's line. *Worthies of England* (Fuller), Vol. I

13 I know I have the body of a weak and feeble woman, but I have the heart and stomach of a King, and of a King of England too.
Speech at Tilbury on the approach of the Spanish Armada, 1588

14 Of myself I must say this, I never was any greedy, scraping grasper, nor a strait fast-holding prince, nor yet a waster; my heart was never set on worldly goods, but only for my subjects' good.
Speech to a deputation from the House of Commons (the Golden Speech), 30 Nov 1601

15 All my possessions for a moment of time.
Last words

EMBARRASSMENT

1 The question about everything was, would it bring a blush to the cheek of a young person?
Charles Dickens (1812–70) British novelist. Pondered by Mr Podsnap. *Our Mutual Friend*, Bk. I, Ch. 11

2 I left the room with silent dignity, but caught my foot in the mat.
George and Weedon Grossmith (1847–1912; 1854–1919) British entertainers and writers. *The Diary of a Nobody*, Ch. 1

EMERSON, RALPH WALDO

(1803–82) US poet and essayist. Ordained in 1829, his book *Nature* (1836) contained his transcendental philosophy. He expressed his optimistic humanism in *Representative Men* (1850) and the *Conduct of Life* (1860).

Quotations about Emerson

1 I could readily see in Emerson a gaping flaw. It was the insinuation that had he lived in those days when the world was made, he might have offered some valuable suggestions.
Herman Melville (1819–91) US novelist. Attrib.

2 Emerson is one who lives instinctively on ambrosia – and leaves everything indigestible on his plate.
Friedrich Nietzsche (1844–1900) German philosopher. Attrib.

Quotations by Emerson

3 A person seldom falls sick, but the bystanders are animated with a faint hope that he will die.
Conduct of Life, 'Considerations by the Way'

4 Art is a jealous mistress.
Conduct of Life, 'Wealth'

5 The louder he talked of his honour, the faster we counted our spoons.
Conduct of Life, 'Worship'

6 The religions we call false were once true.
Essays, 'Character'

7 Nothing great was ever achieved without enthusiasm.
Essays, 'Circles'

8 A Friend may well be reckoned the masterpiece of Nature.

Essays, 'Friendship'

9 There is properly no history; only biography.

Essays, 'History'

10 All mankind love a lover.

Essays, 'Love'

11 The reward of a thing well done is to have done it.

Essays, 'New England Reformers'

12 Every man is wanted, and no man is wanted much.

Essays, 'Nominalist and Realist'

13 In skating over thin ice, our safety is in our speed.

Essays, 'Prudence'

14 Whoso would be a man must be a nonconformist.

Essays, 'Self-Reliance'

15 A foolish consistency is the hobgoblin of little minds, adored by little statesmen and philosophers and divines. With consistency a great soul has simply nothing to do.

Essays, 'Self-reliance'

16 To be great is to be misunderstood.

Essays, 'Self-Reliance'

17 What is a weed? A plant whose virtues have not been discovered.

Fortune of the Republic

18 Talent alone cannot make a writer. There must be a man behind the book.

Goethe

19 I pay the schoolmaster, but 'tis the schoolboys that educate my son.

Journal

20 The book written against fame and learning has the author's name on the title-page.

Journal

21 Old age brings along with its uglinesses the comfort that you will soon be out of it, – which ought to be a substantial relief to such discontented pendulums as we are.

Journal

22 Every hero becomes a bore at last.

Representative Men, 'Uses of Great Men'

23 Hitch your wagon to a star.

Society and Solitude, 'Civilization'

24 We boil at different degrees.

Society and Solitude, 'Eloquence'

25 America is a country of young men.

Society and Solitude, 'Old Age'

26 If a man make a better mouse-trap than his neighbour, though he build his house in the woods, the world will make a beaten path to his door.

Attrib.

EMOTION

See also passion, sentimentality

1 There is a road from the eye to the heart that does not go through the intellect.

G. K. Chesterton (1874–1936) British writer. *The Defendant*

2 'There are strings', said Mr Tappertit, 'in the human heart that had better not be wibrated.'

Charles Dickens (1812–70) British novelist. *Barnaby Rudge*, Ch. 22

3 Grief and disappointment give rise to anger, anger to envy, envy to malice, and malice to grief again, till the whole circle be completed.

David Hume (1711–76) Scottish philosopher. *A Treatise of Human Nature*

4 The intellect is always fooled by the heart.

Duc de la Rochefoucauld (1613–80) French writer. *Maximes*, 102

5 Light breaks where no sun shines;
Where no sea runs, the waters of the heart
Push in their tides.

Dylan Thomas (1914–53) Welsh poet. *Light breaks where no sun shines*

6 Pure and complete sorrow is as impossible as pure and complete joy.

Leo Tolstoy (1828–1910) Russian writer. *War and Peace*, Bk. XV, Ch. 1

ENDING

1 All good things must come to an end.

Proverb

2 All's well that ends well.

Proverb

3 This is the way the world ends
Not with a bang but a whimper.

T. S. Eliot (1888–1965) US-born British poet and dramatist. *The Hollow Men*

4 We'll to the woods no more,
The laurels all are cut.

A. E. Housman (1859–1936) British scholar and poet. *Last Poems*, Introductory

5 The bright day is done,
And we are for the dark.

William Shakespeare (1564-1616) English dramatist. *Antony and Cleopatra*, V:2

6 That but this blow
Might be the be-all and the end-all here –
But here upon this bank and shoal of time –
We'd jump the life to come.

William Shakespeare *Macbeth*, I:7

7 Ring out, wild bells, to the wild sky,
The flying cloud, the frosty light:
The year is dying in the night;
Ring out, wild bells, and let him die.

Alfred, Lord Tennyson (1809–92) British poet. *In Memoriam A.H.H.*, CVI

ENDURANCE

See also comfort, courage, determination, misfortune, suffering

1 Even a worm will turn.
Proverb

2 The last straw breaks the camel's back.
Proverb

3 What can't be cured, must be endured.
Proverb

4 Nothing happens to any man that he is not formed by nature to bear.
Marcus Aurelius (121–180 AD) Roman emperor. *Meditations*, Bk. V, Ch. 18

5 Through the night of doubt and sorrow
Onward goes the pilgrim band,
Singing songs of expectation,
Marching to the Promised Land.
Sabine Baring-Gould (1834–1924) British writer and hymn writer. *Through the Night of Doubt and Sorrow*

6 You put up with the bloody and botched events in the hope of the one occasion when it becomes beautiful.
Peter Brook (1925–) British theatre director. *The Observer*, 'Sayings of the Week', 1 May 1994

7 Virginia's greatest legacy was to show that, even in the midst of personal trials and pain, you can and must keep going. Her lesson was that, no matter how hard life gets, you get up in the morning, say a prayer, put a smile on your face and go out and brave the world to do the best you can.
Hillary Clinton (1947–) US lawyer and First Lady. Referring to her mother-in-law, Virginia Kelley.

8 In the fell clutch of circumstance,
I have not winced nor cried aloud;
Under the bludgeonings of chance
My head is bloody, but unbowed.
William Ernest Henley (1849–1903) British writer. *Echoes*, IV, 'Invictus. In Mem. R.T.H.B.'

9 ...we could never learn to be brave and patient, if there were only joy in the world.
Helen Keller (1880–1968) US writer and lecturer. *Atlantic Monthly* (May 1890)

10 Job endured everything – until his friends came to comfort him, then he grew impatient.
Søren Kierkegaard (1813–55) Danish philosopher. *Journal*

11 Sorrow and silence are strong, and patient endurance is godlike.
Henry Wadsworth Longfellow (1807–82) US poet. *Evangeline*

12 Know how sublime a thing it is
To suffer and be strong.
Henry Wadsworth Longfellow *The Light of Stars*

13 It is not miserable to be blind; it is miserable to be incapable of enduring blindness.
John Milton (1608–74) English poet.

14 The weariest nights, the longest days, sooner or later must perforce come to an end.
Baroness Orczy (1865–1947) British novelist. *The Scarlet Pimpernel*, Ch. 22

15 No pain, no palm; no thorns, no throne; no gall, no glory; no cross, no crown.
William Penn (1644–1718) English preacher. *No Cross, No Crown*

16 The Muse but serv'd to ease some friend, not Wife,
To help me through this long disease, my life.
Alexander Pope (1688–1744) British poet. *Epistle to Dr. Arbuthnot*

17 The pain passes, but the beauty remains.
Pierre Auguste Renoir (1841–1919) French impressionist painter. Explaining why he still painted when his hands were twisted with arthritis. Attrib.

18 Does the road wind up-hill all the way?
Yes, to the very end.
Will the day's journey take the whole long day?
From morn to night, my friend.
Christina Rossetti (1830–74) British poet. *Up-Hill*

19 Had we lived, I should have had a tale to tell of the hardihood, endurance, and courage of my companions which would have stirred the heart of every Englishman. These rough notes and our dead bodies must tell the tale.
Captain Robert Falcon Scott (1868–1912) British explorer. *Message to the Public*

20 I am tied to the stake, and I must stand the course.
William Shakespeare (1564–1616) English dramatist. *King Lear*, III:7

21 The worst is not,
So long as we can say, 'This is the worst.'
William Shakespeare *King Lear*, IV:1

22 Men must endure
Their going hence, even as their coming hither:
Ripeness is all.
William Shakespeare *King Lear*, V:2

23 Still have I borne it with a patient shrug,
For sufferance is the badge of all our tribe.
William Shakespeare *The Merchant of Venice*, I:3

24 For there was never yet philosopher
That could endure the toothache patiently.
William Shakespeare *Much Ado About Nothing*, V:1

25 Let's talk sense to the American people. Let's tell them the truth, that there are no gains without pains.
Adlai Stevenson (1900–65) US statesman. Speech, Chicago, 26 July 1952

26 If you can't stand the heat, get out of the kitchen.
Harry S. Truman (1884–1972) US statesman. Perhaps proverbial in origin, it possibly echoes the expression 'kitchen cabinet'. *Mr Citizen*, Ch. 15

27 O you who have borne even heavier things, God will grant an end to these too.
Virgil (Publius Vergilius Maro; 70–19 BC) Roman poet. *Aeneid*, Bk. I

28 Maybe one day we shall be glad to remember even these hardships.
Virgil *Aeneid*, Bk. I

29 I sing of arms and the man who first from the

shores
of Troy came destined an exile to Italy and the Lavinian beaches, much buffeted he on land and on the deep by force of the gods because of fierce Juno's never-forgetting anger.

Virgil Referring to Aeneas. *Aeneid*, Bk. I

30 Much in sorrow, oft in woe,
Onward, Christians, onward go.

Henry Kirke White (1785–1806) British poet. A hymn, better known in its later form, 'Oft in danger, oft in woe'

ENEMIES

1 Better a thousand enemies outside the house than one inside.

Arabic proverb

2 But I say unto you, That ye resist not evil: but whosoever shall smite thee on thy right cheek, turn to him the other also.
And if any man will sue thee at the law, and take away thy coat, let him have thy cloke also.
And whosoever shall compel thee to go a mile, go with him twain.

Bible: Matthew 5:39–41

3 But I say unto you, Love your enemies, bless them that curse you, do good to them that hate you, and pray for them which despitefully use you, and persecute you;
That ye may be the children of your Father which is in heaven: for he maketh his sun to rise on the evil and on the good, and sendeth rain on the just and on the unjust.
For if ye love them which love you, what reward have ye? do not even the publicans the same?

Bible: Matthew 5:44–46

4 Even a paranoid can have enemies.

Henry Kissinger (1923–) German-born US politician and diplomat. *Time*, 24 Jan 1977

5 They made peace between us; we embraced, and we have been mortal enemies ever since.

Alain-René Lesage (1668–1747) French writer. *Le Diable boiteux*, Ch. 3

6 You must hate a Frenchman as you hate the devil.

Lord Nelson (1758–1805) British admiral. *Life of Nelson* (Southey), Ch. 3

7 I am the enemy you killed, my friend.

Wilfred Owen (1893–1918) British poet. *Strange Meeting*

8 A very great man once said you should love your enemies and that's not a bad piece of advice. We can love them but, by God, that doesn't mean we're not going to fight them.

Norman Schwarzkopf (1934–) US general. Referring to the Gulf War (1991). *The Observer*, 14 July 1991

9 The only good Indians I ever saw were dead.

Philip H. Sheridan (1831–88) US general. *The People's Almanac 2* (D. Wallechinsky)

10 He makes no friend who never made a foe.

Alfred, Lord Tennyson (1809–92) British poet. *Idylls of the King*, 'Lancelot and Elaine'

11 I should be like a lion in a cave of savage Daniels.

Oscar Wilde (1854–1900) Irish-born British dramatist. Explaining why he would not be attending a function at a club whose members were hostile to him. Attrib.

ENGLAND

See also Britain, Cambridge, English, London, Oxford, patriotism

1 The quality of Mersey is not strained.

Anonymous Referring to the polluted condition of the River Mersey. *Sunday Graphic*, 14 Aug 1932

2 A great ship which sailed for many a day in the sea of prosperity is that plenteous realm, the realm of England. The forecastle of this ship is the clergy, prelates, religious, and priests; the hindcastle is the barony, the king with his nobles; the body of the ship is the commons, merchants, craftsmen and labourers.

Anonymous From a sermon preached in the reign of Henry V (1413–22). *Literature and Pulpit in Medieval England* (G. R. Owst)

3 Oh! who can ever be tired of Bath?

Jane Austen (1775–1817) British novelist. *Northanger Abbey*, Ch. 10

4 One has no great hopes from Birmingham. I always say there is something direful in the sound.

Jane Austen *Emma*, Ch. 36

5 When you think about the defence of England you no longer think of the chalk cliffs of Dover. You think of the Rhine. That is where our frontier lies to-day.

Stanley Baldwin (1867–1947) British statesman. Speech, House of Commons, 30 July 1934

6 Come, friendly bombs, and fall on Slough
It isn't fit for humans now.
There isn't grass to graze a cow
Swarm over, Death!
…
Come, friendly bombs, and fall on Slough
To get it ready for the plough.
The cabbages are coming now:
The earth exhales.

John Betjeman (1906–84) British poet. *Slough*

7 And did those feet in ancient time
Walk upon England's mountains green?
And was the holy lamb of God
On England's pleasant pastures seen?
…
I will not cease from mental fight,
Nor shall my sword sleep in my hand,
Till we have built Jerusalem
In England's green and pleasant land.

William Blake (1757–1827) British poet. Better known as the hymn 'Jerusalem', with music by Sir Hubert Parry; not to be confused with Blake's longer poem *Jerusalem*. *Milton*, Preface

8 The smoke of their foul dens
Broodeth on Thy Earth as a black pestilence,
Hiding the kind day's eye. No flower, no grass there groweth,
Only their engines' dung which the fierce furnace throweth.

Wilfred Scawen Blunt (1840–1922) British poet. Describing a northern town. *Satan Absolved: a Victorian Mystery*

9 A population sodden with drink, steeped in vice, eaten up by every social and physical malady, these are the denizens of Darkest England amidst whom my life has been spent.

William Booth (1829–1912) British preacher and founder of the Salvation Army. *In Darkest England, and the Way Out*

10 England is the mother of parliaments.

John Bright (1811–89) British radical politician. Speech, Birmingham, 18 Jan 1865

11 For England's the one land, I know,
Where men with Splendid Hearts may go;
And Cambridgeshire, of all England,
The shire for Men who Understand.

Rupert Brooke (1887–1915) British poet. *The Old Vicarage, Grantchester*

12 A pulse in the eternal mind, no less
Gives somewhere back the thoughts by England given.
Her sights and sounds; dreams happy as her day;
And laughter, learnt of friends; and gentleness,
In hearts at peace, under an English heaven.

Rupert Brooke *The Soldier*

13 Oh, to be in England
Now that April's there.

Robert Browning (1812–89) British poet. *Home Thoughts from Abroad*

14 Without class differences, England would cease to be the living theatre it is.

Anthony Burgess (John Burgess Wilson; 1917–93) British novelist. *The Observer*, 'Sayings of the Week', 26 May 1985

15 In England there are sixty different religions, and only one sauce.

Domenico Caracciolo (1715–89) Governor of Sicily. Attrib.

16 This could have occurred nowhere but in England, where men and sea interpenetrate, so to speak.

Joseph Conrad (Teodor Josef Konrad Korzeniowski; 1857–1924) Polish-born British novelist. *Youth*

17 Very flat, Norfolk.

Noël Coward (1899–1973) British dramatist. *Private Lives*

18 Regions Caesar never knew
Thy posterity shall sway,
Where his eagles never flew,
None invincible as they.

William Cowper (1731–1800) British poet. *Boadicea*

19 There are many things in life more worthwhile than money. One is to be brought up in this our England which is still the envy of less happy lands.

Lord Denning (1899–) British judge. *The Observer*, 'Sayings of the Week', 4 Aug 1968

20 Kent, sir – everybody knows Kent – apples, cherries, hops and women.

Charles Dickens (1812–70) British novelist. *Pickwick Papers*, Ch. 2

21 The Continent will not suffer England to be the workshop of the world.

Benjamin Disraeli (1804–81) British statesman. Speech, House of Commons, 15 Mar 1838

22 England is the paradise of women, the purgatory of men, and the hell of horses.

John Florio (c. 1553–1625) English lexicographer. *Second Fruits*

23 Living in England, provincial England, must be like being married to a stupid but exquisitely beautiful wife.

Margaret Halsey (1910–) US writer. *With Malice Toward Some*

24 All of Stratford, in fact, suggests powdered history – add hot water and stir and you have a delicious, nourishing Shakespeare.

Margaret Halsey *With Malice Toward Some*

25 Dr Johnson's morality was as English an article as a beefsteak.

Nathaniel Hawthorne (1804–64) US novelist and writer. *Our Old Home*, 'Lichfield and Uttoxeter'

26 Those only can care intelligently for the future of England to whom the past is dear.

Dean Inge (1860–1954) British churchman. *Assessments and Anticipations*

27 Pass a law to give every single wingeing bloody Pommie his fare home to England. Back to the smoke and the sun shining ten days a year and shit in the streets. Yer can have it.

Thomas Keneally (1935–) Australian novelist. *The Chant of Jimmy Blacksmith*

28 Winds of the World, give answer! They are whimpering to and fro –
And what should they know of England who only England know?

Rudyard Kipling (1865–1936) Indian-born British writer. *The English Flag*

29 It was one of those places where the spirit of aboriginal England still lingers, the old savage England, whose last blood flows still in a few Englishmen, Welshmen, Cornishmen.

D. H. Lawrence (1885–1930) British novelist. *St Mawr*

30 And suddenly she craved again for the more absolute silence of America. English stillness was so soft, like an inaudible murmur of voices, of presences.

D. H. Lawrence *St Mawr*

31 In an English ship, they say, it is poor grub, poor pay, and easy work; in an American ship, good grub, good pay, and hard work. And this is applicable to the working populations of both countries.

Jack London (1876–1916) US novelist. *The People of the Abyss*, Ch. 20

32 In no country, I believe, are the marriage laws so iniquitous as in England, and the conjugal relation, in consequence, so impaired.

Harriet Martineau (1802–76) British writer. *Society in America*, Vol. III, 'Marriage'

33 In England there is only silence or scandal.

André Maurois (Émile Herzog; 1885–1967) French writer. Attrib.

34 When people say England, they sometimes mean Great Britain, sometimes the United Kingdom, sometimes the British Isles, – but never England.

George Mikes (1912–87) Hungarian-born British writer. *How to be an Alien*

35 It was twenty-one years ago that England and I first set foot on each other. I came for a fortnight; I have stayed ever since.

George Mikes *How to be Inimitable*

36 When you see how in this happy country the lowest and poorest member of society takes an interest in all public affairs; when you see how high and low, rich and poor, are all willing to declare their feelings and convictions; when you see how a carter, a common sailor, a beggar is still a man, nay, even more, an Englishman – then, believe me, you find yourself very differently affected from the experience you feel when staring at our soldiers drilling in Berlin.

Karl Philipp Moritz (1756–93) German Lutheran pastor. Reaction to a by-election at Westminster. Letter to a friend, 1782

37 A family with the wrong members in control – that, perhaps, is as near as one can come to describing England in a phrase.

George Orwell (Eric Blair; 1903–50) British novelist. *The Lion and the Unicorn*, 'The Ruling Class'

38 There can hardly be a town in the South of England where you could throw a brick without hitting the niece of a bishop.

George Orwell *The Road to Wigan Pier*, Ch. 7

39 Damn you, England. You're rotting now, and quite soon you'll disappear.

John Osborne (1929–) British dramatist. Letter in *Tribune*, Aug 1961

40 There'll always be an England
While there's a country lane,
Wherever there's a cottage small
Beside a field of grain.

Clarke Ross Parker (1914–74) British songwriter. *There'll Always Be an England*

41 It is now apparent that this great, this powerful, this formidable Kingdom is considered only as a province of a despicable Electorate.

William Pitt the Elder (1708–78) British statesman. Referring to Hanover, which Pitt accused George II of favouring over England. Speech, House of Commons, 10 Dec 1742

42 The real fact is that I could no longer stand their eternal cold mutton.

Cecil Rhodes (1853–1902) South African statesman. Explaining why he had left his friends in England and come to South Africa. *Cecil Rhodes* (G. le Sueur)

43 My God! this is a wonderful land and a faithless one; for she has exiled, slain, destroyed and ruined so many Kings, so many rulers, so many great men, and she is always diseased and suffering from differences, quarrels and hatred between her people.

Richard II (1365–99) King of England. Attrib. remark, Tower of London, 21 Sept 1399

44 England is the paradise of individuality, eccentricity, heresy, anomalies, hobbies, and humours.

George Santayana (1863–1952) US philosopher. *Soliloquies in England*, 'The British Character'

45 Well, I cannot last ever; but it was always yet the trick of our English nation, if they have a good thing, to make it too common.

William Shakespeare (1564-1616) English dramatist. *Henry IV, Part Two*, I:2

46 This royal throne of kings, this sceptred isle,
This earth of majesty, this seat of Mars,
This other Eden, demi-paradise,
This fortress built by Nature for herself
Against infection and the hand of war,
This happy breed of men, this little world,
This precious stone set in the silver sea,
Which serves it in the office of a wall,
Or as a moat defensive to a house,
Against the envy of less happier lands;
This blessed plot, this earth, this realm, this England,
This nurse, this teeming womb of royal kings,
Fear'd by their breed, and famous by their birth.

William Shakespeare *Richard II*, II:1

47 If I were asked at this moment for a summary opinion of what I have seen in England, I might probably say that its political institutions present a detail of corrupt practices, of profusion, and of personal ambition, under the mask of public spirit very carelessly put on, more disgusting than I should have expected.…On the other hand, I should admit very readily that I have found the great mass of the people richer, happier, and more respectable than any other with which I am acquainted.

L. Simond French traveller and diarist. *Journal of a Tour and Residence in Great Britain during 1810 and 1811 by a French Traveller*

48 And her ways are ways of gentleness, and all her paths are peace.

Cecil Arthur Spring-Rice (1859–1918) British diplomat. *I Vow to Thee, My Country*

49 The English take their pleasures sadly after the fashion of their country.

Duc de Sully (1560–1641) French statesman. *Memoirs*

50 They say that men become attached even to Widnes.

A. J. P. Taylor (1906–) British historian. *The Observer*, 15 Sept 1963

51 Yes. I remember Adlestrop –
The name, because one afternoon
Of heat the express train drew up there
Unwontedly. It was late June.

Edward Thomas (1878–1917) British poet. *Adlestrop*

52 You never find an Englishman among the underdogs – except in England of course.

Evelyn Waugh (1903–66) British novelist. *The Loved One*

ENGLISH

See also British, nationality

1 An Englishman's home is his castle.

Proverb

2 An Englishman's word is his bond.

Proverb

3 That typically English characteristic for which there is no English name – *esprit de corps*.

Frank Ezra Adcock (1886–1968) British classicist. Presidential address

4 The English instinctively admire any man who has no talent and is modest about it.

James Agate (1877–1947) British theatre critic. Attrib.

5 But of all nations in the world the English are perhaps the least a nation of pure philosophers.

Walter Bagehot (1826–77) British economist and journalist. *The English Constitution*, 'The Monarchy'

6 They came from three very powerful nations of the Germans; that is, from the *Saxones*, *Angli*, and *Iutae*.

St Bede (The Venerable Bede; c. 673–735 AD) English churchman and historian. Referring to the Anglo-Saxon invaders of Britain. *Historia Ecclesiastica*, Bk. I

7 I like the English. They have the most rigid code of immorality in the world.

Malcolm Bradbury (1932–) British academic and novelist. *Eating People is Wrong*, Ch. 5

8 The wish to spread those opinions that we hold conducive to our own welfare is so deeply rooted in the English character that few of us can escape its influence.

Samuel Butler (1835–1902) British writer. *Erewhon*, Ch. 20

9 The most dangerous thing in the world is to make a friend of an Englishman, because he'll come sleep in your closet rather than spend 10s on a hotel.

Truman Capote (1924–84) US novelist. *The Observer*, 'Sayings of the Week', 24 Mar 1968

10 Thirty millions, mostly fools.

Thomas Carlyle (1795–1881) Scottish historian and essayist. When asked what the population of England was. Attrib.

11 He's an Anglo-Saxon Messenger – and those are Anglo-Saxon attitudes.

Lewis Carroll (Charles Lutwidge Dodgson; 1832–98) British writer. *Through the Looking-Glass*, Ch. 7

12 All the faces here this evening seem to be bloody Poms.

Charles, Prince of Wales (1948–) Eldest son of Elizabeth II. Remark at Australia Day dinner, 1973

13 Smile at us, pay us, pass us; but do not quite forget.
For we are the people of England, that never have spoken yet.

G. K. Chesterton (1874–1936) British writer. *The Secret People*

14 The wealth of our island may be diminished, but the strength of mind of the people cannot easily pass away...We cannot lose our liberty, because we cannot cease to think.

Humphry Davy (1778–1829) British chemist. Letter to Thomas Poole, 28 Aug 1807

15 O that Ocean did not bound our style
Within these strict and narrow limits so:
But that the melody of our sweet isle
Might now be heard to Tiber, Arne, and Po:
That they might know how far Thames doth outgo
The music of declined Italy.

Michael Drayton (1563–1631) English poet. Referring to the English language. *The Reign of Elizabeth* (J. B. Black), Ch. 8

16 It is said, I believe, that to behold the Englishman at his *best* one should watch him play tip-and-run.

Ronald Firbank (1886–1926) British novelist. *The Flower Beneath the Foot*, Ch. 14

17 *Non Angli sed Angeli*
Not Angles, but angels.

Gregory I (540–604) Pope and saint. Attrib.

18 ...it takes a great deal to produce ennui in an Englishman and if you do, he only takes it as convincing proof that you are well-bred.

Margaret Halsey (1910–) US writer. *With Malice Toward Some*

19 The attitude of the English...toward English history reminds one a good deal of the attitude of a Hollywood director toward love.

Margaret Halsey *With Malice Toward Some*

20 ...the English think of an opinion as something which a decent person, if he has the misfortune to have one, does all he can to hide.

Margaret Halsey *With Malice Toward Some*

21 The English (it must be owned) are rather a foul-mouthed nation.

William Hazlitt (1778–1830) British essayist. *On Criticism*

22 The Englishman never enjoys himself except for a noble purpose.

A. P. Herbert (1890–1971) British writer and politician. *Uncommon Law*

23 When two Englishmen meet, their first talk is of the weather.

Samuel Johnson (1709–84) British lexicographer. *The Idler*

24 The English people on the whole are surely the *nicest* people in the world, and everyone makes everything so easy for everybody else, that there is almost nothing to resist at all.

D. H. Lawrence (1885–1930) British novelist. *Dull London*

25 England is...a country infested with people who love to tell us what to do, but who very rarely seem to know what's going on.

Colin MacInnes (1914–76) British novelist. *England, Half English*, 'Pop Songs and Teenagers'

26 An Englishman, even if he is alone, forms an orderly queue of one.

George Mikes (1912–87) Hungarian-born British writer. *How to be an Alien*

27 Continental people have sex life; the English have hot-water bottles.

George Mikes *How to be an Alien*

28 Many continentals think life is a game, the English think cricket is a game.

George Mikes *How to be an Alien*

29 English women are elegant until they are ten years old, and perfect on grand occasions.

Nancy Mitford (1904–73) British writer. *The Wit of Women* (L. and M. Cowan)

30 The English are busy; they don't have time to be polite.

Baron de Montesquieu (1689–1755) French writer. *Pensées diverses*

31 It has to be admitted that we English have sex on the brain, which is a very unsatisfactory place to have it.

Malcolm Muggeridge (1903–) British writer. *The Observer*, 'Sayings of the Decade', 1964

32 England is a nation of shopkeepers.

Napoleon I (Napoleon Bonaparte; 1769–1821) French emperor. Attrib.

33 To be an Englishman is to belong to the most exclusive club there is.

Ogden Nash (1902–71) US poet. *England Expects*

34 But Lord! to see the absurd nature of Englishmen, that cannot forbear laughing and jeering at everything that looks strange.

Samuel Pepys (1633–1703) English diarist. *Diary*, 27 Nov 1662

35 Remember that you are an Englishman, and have consequently won first prize in the lottery of life.

Cecil Rhodes (1853–1902) South African statesman. *Dear Me* (Peter Ustinov), Ch. 4

36 The English have no respect for their language, and will not teach their children to speak it...It is impossible for an Englishman to open his mouth, without making some other Englishman despise him.

George Bernard Shaw (1856–1950) Irish dramatist and critic. *Pygmalion*, Preface

37 I think for my part one half of the nation is mad – and the other not very sound.

Tobias Smollett (1721–71) British novelist. *The Adventures of Sir Launcelot Greaves*, Ch. 6

38 I cannot but conclude the bulk of your natives to be the most pernicious race of little odious vermin that nature ever suffered to crawl upon the surface of the earth.

Jonathan Swift (1667–1745) Irish-born Anglican priest and writer. *Gulliver's Travels*, 'Voyage to Brobdingnag', Ch. 6

39 The national sport of England is obstacle-racing. People fill their rooms with useless and cumbersome furniture, and spend the rest of their lives in trying to dodge it.

Herbert Beerbohm Tree (1853–1917) British actor and theatre manager. *Beerbohm Tree* (Hesketh Pearson)

40 The English are all right. They're quiet, they're slow, they count things carefully, they hesitate. I'm switching to their track.

Lech Walesa (1943–) Polish statesman. Attrib.

ENTHUSIASM

1 How can I take an interest in my work when I don't like it?

Francis Bacon (1909–92) British painter. *Francis Bacon* (Sir John Rothenstein)

2 It is unfortunate, considering that enthusiasm moves the world, that so few enthusiasts can be trusted to speak the truth.

Arthur Balfour (1848–1930) British statesman. Letter to Mrs Drew, 1918

3 Nothing is so contagious as enthusiasm....It is the genius of sincerity and truth accomplishes no victories without it.

Edward Bulwer-Lytton (1803–73) British novelist and politician. *Dale Carnegie's Scrapbook*

4 Nothing great was ever achieved without enthusiasm.

Ralph Waldo Emerson (1803–82) US poet and essayist. *Essays*, 'Circles'

5 The love of life is necessary to the vigorous prosecution of any undertaking.

Samuel Johnson (1709–84) British lexicographer. *The Rambler*

6 Don't clap too hard – it's a very old building.

John Osborne (1929–) British dramatist. *The Entertainer*

7 Every man loves what he is good at.

Thomas Shadwell (1642–92) English dramatist. *A True Widow*, V:1

8 To business that we love we rise betime,
And go to't with delight.

William Shakespeare (1564–1616) English dramatist. *Antony and Cleopatra*, IV:4

ENVIRONMENT

See also ecology

1 Irritations of the eyes, which are caused by smoke, over-heating, dust, or similar injury, are easy to heal; the patient being advised first of all to avoid the irritating causes... For the disease ceases without the use of any kind of medicine, if only a proper way of living be adopted.

Aetios (c. 535) *Tetrabiblon*, Sermo II

2 The first Care in building of Cities, is to make them airy and well perflated; infectious Distempers must necessarily be propagated amongst Mankind living close together.

John Arbuthnot (1667–1735) Scottish physician and satirist. *An Essay Concerning the Effects of Air on Human Bodies*

3 One cannot assess in terms of cash or exports and imports an imponderable thing like the turn of a lane or an inn or a church tower or a familiar skyline.

John Betjeman (1906–84) British poet. On siting a new London airport at Wing. *The Observer*, 'Sayings of the Week', 20 July 1969

4 They improvidentially piped growing volumes of sewage into the sea, the healing virtues of which were advertised on every railway station.

Robert Cecil (1913–) British writer. Referring to seaside resorts. *Life in Edwardian England*

5 Population growth is the primary source of environmental damage.

Jacques Cousteau (1910–) French underwater explorer. *The Observer*, 'Sayings of the Week', 15 Jan 1989

6 A physician is obligated to consider more than a diseased organ, more even than the whole man – he must view the man in his world.

Harvey Cushing (1869–1939) US surgeon. *Man Adapting*, Ch. 12 (René J. Dubos)

7 It can be said that each civilization has a pattern of disease peculiar to it. The pattern of disease is an expression of the response of man to his total environment (physical, biological, and social); this response is, therefore, determined by anything that affects man himself or his environment.

René J. Dubos (1901–) *Industrial Medicine and Surgery*, 30:369, 1961

8 I am a pasenger on the spaceship, Earth.

Richard Buckminster Fuller (1895–1983) US architect and inventor. *Operating Manual for Spaceship Earth*

9 I say that it touches a man that his blood is sea

water and his tears are salt, that the seed of his loins is scarcely different from the same cells in a seaweed, and that of stuff like his bones are coral made. I say that a physical and biologic law lies down with him, and wakes when a child stirs in the womb, and that the sap in a tree, uprushing in the spring, and the smell of the loam, where the darkness, and the path of the sun in the heaven, these are facts of first importance to his mental conclusions, and that a man who goes in no consciousness of them is a drifter and a dreamer, without a home or any contact with reality.

Donald Culross Peattie (1898–1964) *An Almanac for Moderns*, 'April First'

10 If sunbeams were weapons of war, we would have had solar energy long ago.

George Porter (1920–) British chemist. *The Observer*, 'Sayings of the Week', 26 Aug 1973

11 The emergence of intelligence, I am convinced, tends to unbalance the ecology. In other words, intelligence is the great polluter. It is not until a creature begins to manage its environment that nature is thrown into disorder.

Clifford D. Simak (1904–88) US journalist. *Shakespeare's Planet*

12 It is obvious that the best qualities in man must atrophy in a standing-room-only environment.

Stewart L. Udall (1920–) US politician. *The Quiet Crisis*, 13

ENVY

See also discontent, jealousy

1 Better be envied than pitied.

Proverb

2 The rich man has his motor car,
His country and his town estate.
He smokes a fifty-cent cigar
And jeers at Fate.

F. P. Adams (1881–1960) US journalist. *The Rich Man*

3 Yet though my lamp burns low and dim,
Though I must slave for livelihood –
Think you that I would change with him?
You bet I would!

F. P. Adams *The Rich Man*

4 I am sure the grapes are sour.

Aesop (6th century BC) Reputed Greek writer of fables. *Fables*, 'The Fox and the Grapes'

5 Nearly every man in the city wants a farm until he gets it.

Jacob M. Braude

6 Fools may our scorn, not envy raise,
For envy is a kind of praise.

John Gay (1685–1732) English poet and dramatist. *Fables*

7 A physician ought to be extremely watchful against covetousness, for it is a vice imputed, justly or unjustly, to his Profession.

Thomas Gisborne (1758–1846) *The Duties of Physicians*

8 The man with toothache thinks everyone happy whose teeth are sound.

George Bernard Shaw (1856–1950) Irish dramatist and critic. *Man and Superman*

9 Moral indignation is in most cases 2 per cent moral, 48 per cent indignation and 50 per cent envy.

Vittorio de Sica (1901–74) Italian-born French actor. *The Observer*, 'Sayings of the Decade', 1961

10 Whenever a friend succeeds, a little something in me dies.

Gore Vidal (1925–) US novelist. *The Sunday Times Magazine*, 16 Sept 1973

11 Never having been able to succeed in the world, he took his revenge by speaking ill of it.

Voltaire (François-Marie Arouet; 1694–1778) French writer. *Zadig*, Ch. 4

EPITAPHS

1 She sleeps alone at last.

Robert Benchley (1889–1945) US humorist. Suggested epitaph for an actress. Attrib.

2 Their name, their year, spelt by the unlettered muse,
The place of fame and elegy supply:
On many a holy text around she strews,
That teach the rustic moralist to die.

Thomas Gray (1716–71) British poet. *Elegy Written in a Country Churchyard*

3 In lapidary inscriptions a man is not upon oath.

Samuel Johnson (1709–84) British lexicographer. *Life of Johnson* (J. Boswell), Vol. II

4 Nowhere probably is there more true feeling, and nowhere worse taste, than in a churchyard – both as regards the monuments and the inscriptions. Scarcely a word of true poetry anywhere.

Benjamin Jowett (1817–93) British theologian. *Letters of B. Jowett* (Abbott and Campbell)

Some actual and literary examples

5 Hereabouts died a very gallant gentleman, Captain L. E. G. Oates of the Inniskilling Dragoons. In March 1912, returning from the Pole, he walked willingly to his death in a blizzard, to try and save his comrades, beset by hardships.

E. L. Atkinson (1882–1929) British naval officer. Epitaph on memorial in the Antarctic.

6 I've played everything but the harp.

Lionel Barrymore (1848–1954) US actor. When asked what words he would like engraved on his tombstone. Attrib.

7 When Sir Joshua Reynolds died
All Nature was degraded;
The King dropped a tear in the Queen's ear,
And all his pictures faded.

William Blake (1757–1827) British poet. *On Art and Artists*

8 With death doomed to grapple,
Beneath this cold slab, he
Who lied in the chapel
Now lies in the Abbey.

Lord Byron (1788–1824) British poet. *Epitaph for William Pitt*

9 Here Skugg
Lies snug
As a bug
In a rug.

Benjamin Franklin (1706–90) US scientist and statesman. An epitaph for a squirrel, 'skugg' being a dialect name for the animal. Letter to Georgiana Shipley, 26 Sept 1772

10 The body of
Benjamin Franklin, printer,
(Like the cover of an old book,
Its contents worn out,
And stript of its lettering and gilding)
Lies here, food for worms!
Yet the work itself shall not be lost,
For it will, as he believed, appear once more
In a new
And more beautiful edition,
Corrected and amended
By its Author!

Benjamin Franklin Suggestion for his own epitaph.

11 Here rests his head upon the lap of Earth
A youth to fortune and to fame unknown.
Fair Science frown'd not on his humble birth,
And Melancholy mark'd him for her own.

Thomas Gray (1716–71) British poet. *Elegy Written in a Country Churchyard*

12 He gave to Mis'ry all he had, a tear,
He gain'd from Heav'n ('twas all he wish'd) a friend.

Thomas Gray *Elegy Written in a Country Churchyard*

13 John Brown's body lies a-mouldering in the grave,
His soul is marching on!

Charles Sprague Hall (19th century) US songwriter. The song commemorates the American hero who died in the cause of abolishing slavery. *John Brown's Body*

14 To Oliver Goldsmith, A Poet, Naturalist, and Historian, who left scarcely any style of writing untouched, and touched none that he did not adorn.

Samuel Johnson (1709–84) British lexicographer. Epitaph on Goldsmith. *Life of Johnson* (J. Boswell), Vol. III

15 Over my dead body!

George S. Kaufman (1889–1961) US dramatist. On being asked to suggest his own epitaph. *The Algonquin Wits* (R. Drennan)

16 Here lies one whose name was writ in water.

John Keats (1795–1821) British poet. Suggesting his own epitaph (recalling a line from *Philaster* by Beaumont and Fletcher). *Life of Keats* (Lord Houghton), Ch. 2

17 'There is a report that Piso is dead; it is a great loss; he was an honest man, who deserved to live longer; he was intelligent and agreeable, resolute and courageous, to be depended upon, generous and faithful.' Add: 'provided he is really dead'.

Jean de La Bruyère (1645–96) French satirist. *Les Caractères*

18 Go, stranger, and tell the Lacedaemonians that here we lie, obedient to their commands.

Leonidas (d. 480 BC) King of Sparta. Epitaph over the tomb in which he and his followers were buried after their defeat at Thermopylae.

19 Malcolm Lowry
Late of the Bowery
His prose was flowery
And often glowery
He lived, nightly, and drank, daily,
And died playing the ukulele.

Malcolm Lowry (1909–57) British novelist. *Epitaph*

20 Beneath this slab
John Brown is stowed.
He watched the ads
And not the road.

Ogden Nash (1902–71) US poet. *Lather as You Go*

21 For all the Brothers were valiant, and all the Sisters virtuous.

Margaret, Duchess of Newcastle (1624–74) Second wife of William Cavendish. Epitaph in Westminster Abbey

22 He lies below, correct in cypress wood,
And entertains the most exclusive worms.

Dorothy Parker (1893–1967) US writer. *Epitaph for a Very Rich Man*

23 The poor son-of-a-bitch!

Dorothy Parker Quoting from *The Great Gatsby* on paying her last respects to F. Scott Fitzgerald. *Thalberg: Life and Legend* (B. Thomas)

24 In wit a man; simplicity a child.

Alexander Pope (1688–1744) British poet. *Epitaph on Mr. Gay*

25 At last God caught his eye.

Harry Secombe (1921–) Welsh singer, actor, and comedian. Suggested epitaph for a head waiter. In *Punch*, May 1962

26 Alas, poor Yorick! I knew him, Horatio: a fellow of infinite jest, of most excellent fancy.

William Shakespeare (1564–1616) English dramatist. *Hamlet*, V:1

27 *Si monumentum requiris, circumspice.*
If you seek my monument, look around you.

Sir Christopher Wren (1632–1723) English architect. Inscription in St Paul's Cathedral, London

28 Under bare Ben Bulben's head
In Drumcliff churchyard Yeats is laid…
On limestone quarried near the spot
By his command these words are cut…

W. B. Yeats (1865–1939) Irish poet. *Under Ben Bulben*, VI

Some anonymous examples

29 All you who do my grave pass by
As you are now so once was I,
As I am now so you must be
Prepare in time to follow me.

Epitaph, Dorset churchyard

30 All who come my grave to see
Avoid damp beds and think of me.

Epitaph of Lydia Eason, St Michael's, Stoke

31 Beneath this stone, in hope of Zion,
Doth lie the landlord of the 'Lion'.
His son keeps on the business still,
Resign'd unto the Heavenly will.

Epitaph, Upton-on-Severn churchyard

32 Here lie I and my four daughters,
Killed by drinking Cheltenham waters.
Had we but stick to Epsom salts,
We wouldn't have been in these here vaults.

Cheltenham Waters

33 Here lie I by the chancel door;
They put me here because I was poor.
The further in, the more you pay,
But here lie I as snug as they.

Epitaph, Devon churchyard

34 Here lies a man who was killed by lightning;
He died when his prospects seemed to be

brightening.
He might have cut a flash in this world of trouble,
But the flash cut him, and he lies in the stubble.

Epitaph, Torrington, Devon

35 Here lies a valiant warrior
Who never drew a sword;
Here lies a noble courtier
Who never kept his word;
Here lies the Earl of Leicester
Who governed the estates
Whom the earth could never living love,
And the just heaven now hates.

Attrib. to Ben Jonson in *Collection of Epitaphs* (Tissington), 1857.

36 Here lies father and mother and sister and I,
We all died within the space of one short year;
They all be buried at Wimble, except I,
And I be buried here.

Epitaph, Staffordshire churchyard

37 Here lies Fred,
Who was alive and is dead:
Had it been his father,
I had much rather;
Had it been his brother,
Still better than another;
Had it been his sister,
No one would have missed her;
Had it been the whole generation,
Still better for the nation:
But since 'tis only Fred,
Who was alive and is dead, –
There's no more to be said.

Referring to Frederick, Prince of Wales (d. 1751), eldest son of George II and father of George III. *Memoirs of George II* (Horace Walpole)

38 Here lies my wife,
Here lies she;
Hallelujah!
Hallelujee!

Epitaph, Leeds churchyard

39 Here lies the body of Mary Ann Lowder,
She burst while drinking a seidlitz powder.
Called from the world to her heavenly rest,
She should have waited till it effervesced.

Epitaph

40 Here lies the body of Richard Hind,
Who was neither ingenious, sober, nor kind.

Epitaph

41 Here lies Will Smith – and, what's something rarish,
He was born, bred, and hanged, all in the same parish.

Epitaph

42 Mary Ann has gone to rest,
Safe at last on Abraham's breast,
Which may be nuts for Mary Ann,
But is certainly rough on Abraham.

Epitaph

43 My sledge and anvil lie declined
My bellows too have lost their wind
My fire's extinct, my forge decayed,
And in the Dust my Vice is laid
My coals are spent, my iron's gone
My Nails are Drove, My Work is done.

An epitaph to William Strange, blacksmith, died 6 June 1746 and buried in Nettlebed churchyard.

44 Sacred to the memory of
Captain Anthony Wedgwood
Accidentally shot by his gamekeeper
Whilst out shooting
"Well done thou good and faithful servant".

Epitaph

45 Stranger! Approach this spot with gravity!
John Brown is filling his last cavity.

Epitaph of a dentist

46 This the grave of Mike O'Day
Who died maintaining his right of way.
His right was clear, his will was strong.
But he's just as dead as if he'd been wrong.

Epitaph

47 Warm summer sun shine kindly here:
Warm summer wind blow softly here:
Green sod above lie light, lie light:
Good-night, Dear Heart: good-night, good-night.

Memorial to Clorinda Haywood, St Bartholomew's, Edgbaston

EQUALITY

See also class, feminism, human rights

1 A cat may look at a king.

Proverb

2 All cats are grey in the dark.

Proverb

3 The Prophet Mohamed wanted equality for women. But when Islam went from the desert to the palaces, men put in certain loopholes.

Zeenat Ali Islamic historian. *The Independent*, 16 Sept 1993

4 Anyone who pushes for equality, or criticises the male Anglo-Saxon world, is declared "PC" and thereby discredited and silenced. McCarthyism to counteract imagined totalitarianism. Where have we seen that before?

Jasmin Alibhai-Brown British writer and broadcaster. *The Independent*, 11 Aug 1993

5 Equality may perhaps be a right, but no power on earth can ever turn it into a fact.

Honoré de Balzac (1799–1850) French novelist. *La Duchesse de Langeais*

6 From the point of view of sexual morality the aeroplane is valuable in war in that it destroys men and women in equal numbers.

Ernest William Barnes (1874–1953) British clergyman and mathematician. *Rise of Christianity*

7 What makes equality such a difficult business is that we only want it with our superiors.

Henry Becque (1837–99) French dramatist. *Querelles littéraires*

8 When security and equality are in conflict, it will not do to hesitate a moment. Equality must yield.

Jeremy Bentham (1748–1832) British philosopher. *Principles of Legislation*

9 All service ranks the same with God –
With God, whose puppets, best and worst,
Are we: there is no last or first.

Robert Browning (1812–89) British poet. *Pippa Passes*, Pt. I

10 The terrorist and the policeman both come from the same basket.

Joseph Conrad (Teodor Josef Konrad Korzeniowski; 1857–1924) Polish-born British novelist. *The Secret Agent*, Ch. 4

11 Equality, Child, like freedom, exists only where you are now. Only as an egg in the womb are we all equal.

Oriana Fallaci (1930–) Italian writer. *Letter to a Child Never Born*

12 The majestic egalitarianism of the law, which forbids rich and poor alike to sleep under bridges, to beg in the streets, and to steal bread.

Anatole France (Jacques Anatole François Thibault; 1844–1924) French writer. *The Red Lily*, Ch. 7

13 Men are made by nature unequal. It is vain, therefore, to treat them as if they were equal.

J. A. Froude (1818–94) British historian. *Short Studies on Great Subjects*, 'Party Politics'

14 That all men are equal is a proposition to which, at ordinary times, no sane individual has ever given his assent.

Aldous Huxley (1894–1964) British novelist. *Proper Studies*

15 A just society would be one in which liberty for one person is constrained only by the demands created by equal liberty for another.

Ivan Illich (1926–) Austrian sociologist. *Tools for Conviviality*

16 His foreparents came to America in immigrant ships. My foreparents came to America in slave ships. But whatever the original ships, we are both in the same boat tonight.

Jesse Jackson (1941–) US Black statesman. Speech, July 1988

17 Fair Shares for All, is Labour's Call.

Douglas Jay (1907–) British Labour politician. Slogan, Battersea North by-election, June 1946

18 Your levellers wish to level *down* as far as themselves; but they cannot bear levelling *up* to themselves.

Samuel Johnson (1709–84) British lexicographer. *Life of Johnson* (J. Boswell), Vol. I

19 It is better that some should be unhappy than that none should be happy, which would be the case in a general state of equality.

Samuel Johnson *Life of Johnson* (J. Boswell), Vol. III

20 I have a dream that one day this nation will rise up, live out the true meaning of its creed: we hold these truths to be self-evident, that all men are created equal.

Martin Luther King (1929–68) US Black civil-rights leader. He used the words 'I have a dream' in a number of speeches. Speech, Washington, 27 Aug 1963

21 Every man a king but no man wears a crown.

Huey Long (1893–1935) US demagogue. Quoting William Jennings Bryan. Slogan, 1928

22 Never descend to the ways of those above you.

George Mallaby (1902–78) British diplomat and writer. *From My Level*

23 Every man who comes to England is entitled to the protection of the English law, whatever oppression he may heretofore have suffered, and whatever may be the colour of his skin, whether it is black or whether it is white.

Lord Mansfield (1705–93) British judge and politician. From the judgment in the case of James Somersett, a fugitive negro slave (May 1772); it established the principle that slaves enjoyed the benefits of freedom while in England.

24 The cry of equality pulls everyone down.

Iris Murdoch (1919–) Irish-born British novelist. Remark, Sept 1987

25 This isn't going to be a good country for any of us to live in until it's a good country for all of us to live in.

Richard Milhous Nixon (1913–94) US president. *The Observer*, 'Sayings of the Week', 29 Sep 1968

26 All animals are equal but some animals are more equal than others.

George Orwell (Eric Blair; 1903–50) British novelist. *Animal Farm*, Ch. 10

27 EQUALITY…is the thing. It is the only true and central premise from which constructive ideas can radiate freely and be operated without prejudice.

Mervyn Peake (1911–68) British novelist. *Titus Groan*, 'The Sun goes down'

28 In America everybody is of the opinion that he has no social superiors, since all men are equal, but he does not admit that he has no social inferiors.

Bertrand Russell (1872–1970) British philosopher. *Unpopular Essays*

29 Thersites' body is as good as Ajax'
When neither are alive.

William Shakespeare (1564–1616) English dramatist. *Cymbeline*, IV:2

30 Indeed this counsellor
Is now most still, most secret, and most grave,
Who was in life a foolish prating knave.

William Shakespeare *Hamlet*, III:4

31 I think the King is but a man as I am: the violet smells to him as it doth to me.

William Shakespeare *Henry V*, IV:1

32 What infinite heart's ease
Must kings neglect, that private men enjoy!
And what have kings that privates have not too,
Save ceremony, save general ceremony?

William Shakespeare *Henry V*, IV:1

33 I was born free as Caesar; so were you:
We both have fed as well, and we can both
Endure the winter's cold as well as he:
For once, upon a raw and gusty day,
The troubl'd Tiber chafing with her shores,
Caesar said to me, 'Dar'st thou, Cassius, now,
Leap in with me into this angry flood,
And swim to yonder point?' Upon the word,
Accoutred as I was, I plunged in,
And bade him follow…
But ere we could arrive the point propos'd,
Caesar cried, 'Help me, Cassius, or I sink!'
I, as Aeneas, our great ancestor,
Did from the flames of Troy upon his shoulder
The old Anchises bear, so from the waves of Tiber
Did I the tired Caesar. And this man
Is now become a god.

William Shakespeare *Julius Caesar*, I:2

34 Hath not a Jew eyes? Hath not a Jew hands, organs, dimensions, senses, affections, passions, fed with the same food, hurt with the same weapons, subject to the same diseases, healed by the same means, warmed and cooled by the same winter and summer, as a Christian is? If you prick us, do we not bleed? If you tickle us, do we not laugh? If you poison us, do we not die? And if you wrong us, shall we not revenge?

William Shakespeare *The Merchant of Venice*, III:1

35 Life levels all men: death reveals the eminent.

George Bernard Shaw (1856–1950) Irish dramatist and critic. *Maxims for Revolutionists*

36 *Declaration of Sentiments*:...We hold these truths to be self-evident: that all men and women are created equal.

Elizabeth Stanton (1815–1902) US suffragette. *History of Woman Suffrage*, Vol. I (with Susan B. Anthony and Mathilda Gage)

37 This is a movie, not a lifeboat.

Spencer Tracy (1900–67) US film star. Defending his demand for equal billing with Katherine Hepburn. Attrib.

38 Everybody should have an equal chance – but they shouldn't have a flying start.

Harold Wilson (1916–) British politician and prime minister. *The Observer*, 'Sayings of the Year', 1963

39 Whatever women do, they must do it twice as well as men to be thought half as good. Luckily, this is not difficult.

Charlotte Witton Attrib.

Equality in death

See also death

40 It comes equally to us all, and makes us all equal when it comes. The ashes of an Oak in the Chimney, are no epitaph of that Oak, to tell me how high or how large that was; It tells me not what flocks it sheltered while it stood, nor what men it hurt when it fell. The dust of great persons' graves is speechless too, it says nothing, it distinguishes nothing.

John Donne (1573–1631) English poet. *Sermons*, XV

41 Now at last our child is just like all children.

Charles De Gaulle (1890–1970) French general and statesman. On the death of his daughter Anne, who had Down's Syndrome. *Ten First Ladies of the World* (Pauline Frederick)

42 Pale Death kicks his way equally into the cottages of the poor and the castles of kings.

Horace (Quintus Horatius Flaccus; 65–8 BC) Roman poet. *Odes*, I

43 A heap of dust alone remains of thee;
'Tis all thou art, and all the proud shall be!

Alexander Pope (1688–1744) British poet. *Elegy to the Memory of an Unfortunate Lady*

ESCAPE

1 The view that a peptic ulcer may be the hole in a man's stomach through which he crawls to escape from his wife has fairly wide acceptance.

J. A. D. Anderson (1926–) *A New Look at Social Medicine*

ETERNITY

See also immortality, time

1 Kiss till the cow comes home.

Francis Beaumont (1584–1616) English dramatist. *Scornful Lady*, II:2

2 As it was in the beginning, is now, and ever shall be: world without end.

The Book of Common Prayer *Morning Prayer, Gloria*

3 Thou, silent form, dost tease us out of thought
As doth eternity: Cold Pastoral!

John Keats (1795–1821) British poet. *Ode on a Grecian Urn*

4 Eternity's a terrible thought. I mean, where's it going to end?

Tom Stoppard (1937–) Czech-born British dramatist. *Rosencrantz and Guildenstern Are Dead*, II

ETHNIC CLEANSING

See also racialism

1 The region is undergoing ethnic cleansing.

Anonymous Referring to Bosnia-Hercegovina. Anonymous. Serbian radio, reported in *The Times*, 21 May 1992

2 Defend us, or let us defend ourselves.

Alija Izetbegovic (1925–) Bosnia and Hercegovina politician. Pleading for an end to ethnic cleansing and the siege of Sarajevo. Speech to the UN, 8 Sept 1993

3 The most painful thing for me is seeing the fathers of human rights turning away from what is clearly genocide. By pulling the thread holding Bosnia together, they are pulling apart civilisation in Europe.

Haris Silajdzic Bosnian prime minister. *The Times*, 29 Dec 1993

ETIQUETTE

See also manners

1 Phone for the fish knives Norman,
As Cook is a little unnerved;
You kiddies have crumpled the serviettes
And I must have things daintily served.

John Betjeman (1906–84) British poet. *How to get on in Society*

2 It is necessary to clean the teeth frequently, more especially after meals, but not on any account with a pin, or the point of a penknife, and it must never be done at table.

St Jean Baptiste de la Salle (1651–1719) *The Rules of Christian Manners and Civility*, I

3 He is the only man since my dear husband died, to have the effrontery to kiss me on the lips.

Elizabeth the Queen Mother (1900–) British Royal. Referring to President Carter. Attrib.

4 'It is very pleasant dining with a bachelor,' said Miss Matty, softly, as we settled ourselves in the counting-house. 'I only hope it is not improper; so many pleasant things are!'

Elizabeth Gaskell (1810–65) British novelist. *Cranford*, Ch. 4

5 It's all right, Arthur, the white wine came up with the fish.

Herman J. Mankiewicz (1897–1953) US journalist and screenwriter. After vomiting at the table of a fastidious host. Attrib.

6 At a dinner party one should eat wisely but not too well, and talk well but not too wisely.

W. Somerset Maugham (1874–1965) British novelist. *A Writer's Notebook*

7 We could not lead a pleasant life,
And 'twould be finished soon,
If peas were eaten with the knife,
And gravy with the spoon.
Eat slowly: only men in rags
And gluttons old in sin
Mistake themselves for carpet bags
And tumble victuals in.

Walter Raleigh (1861–1922) British scholar. *Laughter from a Cloud*, 'Stans puer ad mensam'

8 'How did you think I managed at dinner, Clarence?' 'Capitally!' 'I had a knife and two forks left at the end,' she said regretfully.

William Pett Ridge (1860–1930) British novelist. *Love at Paddington Green*, Ch. 6

9 I think she must have been very strictly brought up, she's so desperately anxious to do the wrong thing correctly.

Saki (Hector Hugh Munro; 1870–1916) British writer. *Reginald on Worries*

EUROPE

See also Britain, England, France, Germany, Ireland, Russia, Scotland, Switzerland, Venice, Wales

1 Rome's just a city like anywhere else. A vastly overrated city, I'd say. It trades on belief just as Stratford trades on Shakespeare.

Anthony Burgess (John Burgess Wilson; 1917–93) British novelist. *Mr Enderby*, Pt. II, Ch. 2

2 But the age of chivalry is gone. That of sophisters, economists, and calculators, has succeeded; and the glory of Europe is extinguished for ever.

Edmund Burke (1729–97) British politician. *Reflections on the Revolution in France*

3 The isles of Greece, the isles of Greece!
Where burning Sappho loved and sung,
Where grew the arts of war and peace,
Where Delos rose, and Phoebus sprung!
Eternal summer gilds them yet,
But all, except their sun, is set.

Lord Byron (1788–1824) British poet. *Don Juan*, III

4 The mountains look on Marathon –
And Marathon looks on the sea:
And musing there an hour alone,
I dream'd that Greece might still be free.

Lord Byron *Don Juan*, III

5 While stands the Coliseum, Rome shall stand;
When falls the Coliseum, Rome shall fall;
And when Rome falls – the World.

Lord Byron *Childe Harold's Pilgrimage*, IV

6 We must build a kind of United States of Europe.

Winston Churchill (1874–1965) British statesman. Speech, Zurich, 19 Sept 1946

7 Apart from cheese and tulips, the main product of the country is advocaat, a drink made from lawyers.

Alan Coren (1938–) British humorist and writer. Referring to Holland. *The Sanity Inspector*, 'All You Need to Know about Europe'

8 Europe is not just about material results, it is about spirit. Europe is a state of mind.

Jacques Delors (1925–) French politician and European statesman. *The Independent*, 19 May 1994

9 The construction of Europe is not a boxing match.

Jacques Delors *The Independent*, 19 May 1994

10 The hardest thing is to convince European citizens that even the most powerful nation is no longer able to act alone.

Jacques Delors *The Independent*, 19 May 1994

11 Brussels is a madness. I will fight it from within.

James Goldsmith (1933–) British businessman. *The Times*, 10 June 1994

12 Holland…lies so low they're only saved by being dammed.

Thomas Hood (1799–1845) British poet. *Up the Rhine*

13 It's a tremendous achievement, but it isn't easy to work with British Rail. They're never exactly *against* anything, but they're never in favour of anything either. And they always find ways of putting a spanner in the works.

Jean French senior manager with SNCF. Referring to the Channel tunnel. *The Observer*, 1 May 1994

14 It's not enough to be Hungarian, you must have talent too.

Alexander Korda (Sandor Kellner; 1893–1956) Hungarian-born British film director. *Alexander Korda* (K. Kulik)

15 In Western Europe there are now only small countries – those that know it and those that don't know it yet.

Théo Lefèvre (1914–73) Belgian prime minister. *The Observer*, 'Sayings of the Year', 1963

16 I am inclined to notice the ruin in things, perhaps because I was born in Italy.

Arthur Miller (1915–) US dramatist. *A View from the Bridge*, I

17 Austria is Switzerland speaking pure German and with history added.

J. E. Morpurgo (1918–) British writer and academic. *The Road to Athens*

18 Providence has given to the French the empire of the land, to the English that of the sea, and to the Germans that of the air.

Jean Paul Richter (Johann Paul Friedrich Richter; 1763–1825) German novelist. Quoted by Thomas Carlyle

19 The people of Crete unfortunately make more history than they can consume locally.

Saki (Hector Hugh Munro; 1870–1916) British writer. *The Jesting of Arlington Stringham*

20 We are part of the community of Europe and we must do our duty as such.

Marquess of Salisbury (1830–1903) British statesman. Speech, Caernarvon, 11 Apr 1888

21 We're from Madeira, but perfectly respectable, so far.

George Bernard Shaw (1856–1950) Irish dramatist and critic. *You Never Can Tell*, I

22 Let there be light! said Liberty,

And like sunrise from the sea,
Athens arose!

Percy Bysshe Shelley (1792–1822) British poet. *Hellas*, I

23 Britain does not wish to be ruled by a conglomerate in Europe which include Third World nations such as the Greeks and Irish, nor for that matter the Italians and French, whose standards of political morality are not ours, and never will be.

Alfred Sherman (1919–) British journalist. *The Independent*, 10 Aug 1990

24 Historians will one day look back and think it a curious folly that just as the Soviet Union was forced to recognize reality by dispersing power to its separate states and by limiting the powers of its central government, some people in Europe were trying to create a new artificial state by taking powers away from national states and concentrating them at the centre.

Margaret Thatcher (1925–) British politician and prime minister. Speech, June 1991

25 This going into Europe will not turn out to be the thrilling mutual exchange supposed. It is more like nine middle-aged couples with failing marriages meeting in a darkened bedroom in a Brussels hotel for a Group Grope.

E. P. Thompson (1924–) British historian. On the Europe debate, *Sunday Times*, 27 Apr 1975

26 Every place I look at I work out the cubic feet, and I say it will make a good warehouse or it won't. Can't help myself. One of the best warehouses I ever see was the Vatican in Rome.

Arnold Wesker (1932–) British dramatist. *Chips with Everything*, I:6

27 That Europe's nothin' on earth but a great big auction, that's all it is.

Tennessee Williams (1911–83) US dramatist. *Cat on a Hot Tin Roof*, I

28 A historic document which will allow us to continue our course towards entering Europe without the discrimination which took place in the past. We move forward as equal partners towards our mutual interests.

Boris Yeltsin (1931–) Russian statesman. Signing a partnership and cooperation agreement with the European Union. *The Guardian*, 24 June 1994

EVIL

See also good and evil, sin, vice

1 *Honi soit qui mal y pense.*
Evil be to him who evil thinks.

Anonymous Motto for the Order of the Garter

2 It takes a certain courage and a certain greatness even to be truly base.

Jean Anouilh (1910–87) French dramatist. *Ardele*

3 The fearsome word-and-thought-defying *banality of evil.*

Hannah Arendt (1906–75) German-born US philosopher and historian. *Eichmann in Jerusalem: A Report on the Banality of Evil*

4 Wherefore I praised the dead which are already dead more than the living which are yet alive.
Yea, better is he than both they, which hath not yet been, who hath not seen the evil work that is done under the sun.

Bible: Ecclesiastes 4:2–3

5 But evil men and seducers shall wax worse and worse, deceiving, and being deceived.

Bible: II Timothy 3:13

6 And this is the condemnation, that light is come into the world, and men loved darkness rather than light, because their deeds were evil.

Bible: John 3:19

7 And when the thousand years are expired, Satan shall be loosed out of his prison,
And shall go out to deceive the nations which are in the four quarters of the earth, Gog and Magog, to gather them together to battle: the number of whom is as the sand of the sea.

Bible: Revelations 20:7–8

8 I never saw a brute I hated so;
He must be wicked to deserve such pain.

Robert Browning (1812–89) British poet. *Childe Roland to the Dark Tower Came*, XIV

9 The belief in a supernatural source of evil is not necessary; men alone are quite capable of every wickedness.

Joseph Conrad (Teodor Josef Konrad Korzeniowski; 1857–1924) Polish-born British novelist. *Under Western Eyes*, Part 2

10 There's a young man hid with me, in comparison with which young man I am a Angel. That young man hears the words I speak. That young man has a secret way pecooliar to himself, of getting at a boy, and at his heart, and at his liver.

Charles Dickens (1812–70) British novelist. Said by Magwitch. *Great Expectations*, Ch. 1

11 Something nasty in the woodshed.

Stella Gibbons (1902–89) British poet and novelist. *Cold Comfort Farm*

12 The disease of an evil conscience is beyond the practice of all the physicians of all the countries in the world.

William E. Gladstone (1809–98) British statesman. Speech, Plumstead, 1878

13 But evil is wrought by want of thought,
As well as want of heart!

Thomas Hood (1799–1845) British poet. *The Lady's Dream*

14 He who passively accepts evil is as much involved in it as he who helps to perpetrate it.

Martin Luther King (1929–68) US Black civil-rights leader. *Stride Towards Freedom*

15 Farewell remorse! All good to me is lost;
Evil, be thou my Good.

John Milton (1608–74) English poet. *Paradise Lost*, Bk. IV

16 Take thy beak from out my heart, and take thy form from off my door!
Quoth the Raven, 'Nevermore.'

Edgar Allan Poe (1809–49) US poet and writer. *The Raven*

17 There is scarcely a single man sufficiently aware to know all the evil he does.

Duc de la Rochefoucauld (1613–80) French writer. *Maximes*, 269

18 She is a smart old broad. It is a pity she is so nefarious.

Damon Runyon (1884–1946) US writer. *Runyon à la carte*, 'Broadway Incident'

19 Friends, Romans, countrymen, lend me your ears
I come to bury Caesar, not to praise him.
The evil that men do lives after them;
The good is oft interred with their bones.

William Shakespeare (1564–1616) English dramatist. *Julius Caesar*, III:2

20 Wisdom and goodness to the vile seem vile;
Filths savour but themselves.

William Shakespeare *King Lear*, IV:2

21 Oftentimes, to win us to our harm,
The instruments of darkness tell us truths;
Win us with honest trifles, to betray's
In deepest consequence.

William Shakespeare *Macbeth*, I:3

22 The raven himself is hoarse
That croaks the fatal entrance of Duncan
Under my battlements. Come, you spirits
That tend on mortal thoughts! unsex me here,
And fill me from the crown to the toe top full
Of direst cruelty; make thick my blood,
Stop up the access and passage to remorse,
That no compunctious visitings of nature
Shake my fell purpose, nor keep peace between
The effect and it! Come to my woman's breasts,
And take my milk for gall, you murdering ministers,
Wherever in your sightless substances
You wait on nature's mischief! Come, thick night,
And pall thee in the dunnest smoke of hell,
That my keen knife see not the wound it makes,
Nor heaven peep through the blanket of the dark,
To cry 'Hold, hold!'

William Shakespeare *Macbeth*, I:5

23 And therefore, since I cannot prove a lover,
To entertain these fair well-spoken days,
I am determined to prove a villain,
And hate the idle pleasures of these days.

William Shakespeare *Richard III*, I:1

EVOLUTION

See also survival

1 An ape is ne'er so like an ape
As when he wears a doctor's cape.

Proverb

2 Descended from the apes? My dear, we will hope it is not true. But if it is, let us pray that it may not become generally known.

Anonymous Remark by the wife of a canon of Worcester Cathedral. *Man's Most Dangerous Myth, The Fallacy of Race* (F. Ashley Montagu)

3 A hen is only an egg's way of making another egg.

Samuel Butler (1835–1902) British writer. *Life and Habit*, VIII

4 Some call it Evolution
And others call it God.

William H. Carruth (1859–1924) *Each in His Own Tongue*

5 From an evolutionary point of view, man has stopped moving, if he ever did move.

Pierre Teilhard de Chardin (1881–1955) French Jesuit and palaeontologist. *The Phenomenon of Man*, Postscript

6 I confess freely to you I could never look long upon a Monkey, without very Mortifying Reflections.

William Congreve (1670–1729) English Restoration dramatist. Letter to John Dennis, 10 July 1695

7 Man is developed from an ovule, about the 125th of an inch in diameter, which differs in no respect from the ovules of other animals.

Charles Darwin (1809–82) British life scientist. *The Descent of Man*, Ch. 1

8 We must, however, acknowledge, as it seems to me, that man with all his noble qualities, still bears in his bodily frame the indelible stamp of his lowly origin.

Charles Darwin Closing words. *Descent of Man*, Ch. 21

9 We will now discuss in a little more detail the struggle for existence.

Charles Darwin *Origin of Species*, Ch. 3

10 I have called this principle, by which each slight variation, if useful, is preserved, by the term of Natural Selection.

Charles Darwin *Origin of Species*, Ch. 3

11 The expression often used by Mr Herbert Spencer of the Survival of the Fittest is more accurate, and is sometimes equally convenient.

Charles Darwin *Origin of Species*, Ch. 3

12 A major branch of survival machines, now called plants, started to use sunlight directly themselves…Another branch, now known as animals, 'discovered' how to exploit the chemical labours of the plants, either by eating them, or by eating other animals. Both main branches of survival machines evolved more and more ingenious tricks to increase their efficiency in their various ways of life, and new ways of life were continually being opened up.

Richard Dawkins (1941–) British zoologist. *The Selfish Gene*

13 The question is this: Is man an ape or an angel? I, my lord, am on the side of the angels.

Benjamin Disraeli (1804–81) British statesman. Speech, 25 Nov 1864

14 How like us is that ugly brute, the ape!

Ennius (239 BC–169 BC) Roman poet. *On the Nature of the Gods*, I (Cicero)

15 I am, in point of fact, a particularly haughty and exclusive person, of pre-Adamite ancestral descent. You will understand this when I tell you that I can trace my ancestry back to a protoplasmal primordic atomic globule.

William S. Gilbert (1836–1911) British dramatist and comic writer. *The Mikado*, I

16 Philip is a living example of natural selection. He was as fitted to survive in this modern world as a tapeworm in an intestine.

William Golding (1911–93) British novelist. *Free Fall*, Ch. 2

17 I am quite sure that our views on evolution would be very different had biologists studied genetics and natural selection before and not after most of them were convinced that evolution had occurred.

J. B. S. Haldane (1892–1964) British geneticist.

18 Everything from an egg.

William Harvey (1578–1657) English physician. *De Generatione Animalium*, Frontispiece

19 The probable fact is that we are descended not only from monkeys but from monks.

Elbert G. Hubbard (1856–1915) US writer and editor. *A Thousand and One Epigrams*

20 I asserted – and I repeat – that a man has no reason to be ashamed of having an ape for his grandfather. If there were an ancestor whom I should feel shame in recalling it would rather be a *man* – a man of restless and versatile intellect – who, not content with an equivocal success in his own sphere of activity, plunges into scientific questions with which he has no real acquaintance, only to obscure them by an aimless rhetoric, and distract the attention of his hearers from the real point at issue by eloquent digressions and skilled appeals to religious prejudice.

T. H. Huxley (1825–95) British biologist. Replying to Bishop Samuel WILBERFORCE in the debate on Darwin's theory of evolution at the meeting of the British Association at Oxford. No transcript was taken at the time; the version above is commonly quoted. After hearing Wilberforce's speech, and before rising himself, Huxley is said to have remarked, 'The Lord has delivered him into my hands!' Speech, 30 June 1860

21 Evolution is far more important than living.

Ernst Jünger *The Rebel*, Ch. 3 (Albert Camus)

22 We are very slightly changed
From the semi-apes who ranged
India's prehistoric clay.

Rudyard Kipling (1865–1936) Indian-born British writer. *General Summary*

23 Never neglect the history of a missed menstrual period.

Rutherford Morrison (1853–1939) *The Practitioner*, Oct 1965

24 The tide of evolution carries everything before it, thoughts no less than bodies, and persons no less than nations.

George Santayana (1863–1952) Spanish-born US philosopher, poet, and critic. *Little Essays*, 44

25 We have been God-like in our planned breeding of our domesticated plants and animals, but we have been rabbit-like in our unplanned breeding of ourselves.

Arnold Toynbee (1889–1975) British historian. *National Observer*, 10 June 1963

26 And, in conclusion, I would like to ask the gentleman…whether the ape from which he is descended was on his grandmother's or his grandfather's side of the family.

Samuel Wilberforce (1805–73) British churchman. *See* T. H. HUXLEY. Speech, 30 June 1860

EXAMINATIONS

See also education

1 Examinations are formidable even to the best prepared, for the greatest fool may ask more than the wisest man can answer.

Charles Caleb Colton (?1780–1832) British clergyman and writer. *Lacon*, Vol. II

2 Do not on any account attempt to write on both sides of the paper at once.

W. C. Sellar (1898–1951) British humorous writer. *1066 And All That*, Test Paper 5

3 If silicon had been a gas I should have been a major-general.

James Whistler (1834–1903) US painter. Referring to his failure in a West Point chemistry examination. *English Wits* (L. Russell)

EXAMPLE

1 Practise what you preach.

Proverb

2 Example is the school of mankind, and they will learn at no other.

Edmund Burke (1729–97) British politician. *Letters on a Regicide Peace*, letter 1

3 Do as you would be done by is the surest method that I know of pleasing.

Earl of Chesterfield (1694–1773) English statesman. Letter to his son, 16 Oct 1747

4 What you do not want done to yourself, do not do to others.

Confucius (K'ung Fu-tzu; 551–479 BC) Chinese philosopher. *Analects*

5 Men are not hanged for stealing horses, but that horses may not be stolen.

George Saville (1633–95) English statesman. *Political, Moral and Miscellaneous Thoughts and Reflections*

6 A precedent embalms a principle.

William Scott (1745–1836) British jurist. An opinion given while Advocate-General. Attrib.; also quoted by Benjamin Disraeli (1848)

7 Preachers say, Do as I say, not as I do. But if the physician had the same disease upon him that I have, and he should bid me do one thing, and himself do quite another, could I believe him?

John Selden (1584–1654) English historian. *Table Talk*

8 Do not, as some ungracious pastors do,
Show me the steep and thorny way to heaven,
Whiles, like a puff'd and reckless libertine,
Himself the primrose path of dalliance treads
And recks not his own rede.

William Shakespeare (1564–1616) English dramatist. *Hamlet*, I:3

9 *Dans ce pays-ci, il est bon de tuer de temps en temps un amiral pour encourager les autres.*
In this country it is good to kill an admiral from time to time, to encourage the others.

Voltaire (François-Marie Arouet; 1694–1778) French writer. Referring to England: Admiral Byng was executed for failing to defeat the French at Minorca (1757). *Candide*, Ch. 23

EXCELLENCE

See also superiority

1 Whatever is worth doing at all is worth doing well.

Earl of Chesterfield (1694–1773) English statesman. Letter to his son, 10 Mar 1746

2 The danger chiefly lies in acting well,
No crime's so great as daring to excel.

Charles Churchill (1731–64) British poet. *Epistle to William Hogarth*

3 If you had been mine when you were seven you would have been the crème de la crème.

Muriel Spark (1918–) British novelist. *The Prime of Miss Jean Brodie*, Ch. 2

4 The best is the enemy of the good.

Voltaire (François-Marie Arouet; 1694–1778) French writer. *Dictionnaire philosophique*, 'Art dramatique'

EXCESS

See also moderation

1 Nothing in excess.

Anonymous

2 *L'embarras des richesses.*
A superfluity of good things.

Abbé Lénor Jean d'Allainval (1700–53) French dramatist. Play title

3 What fun it would be to be poor, as long as one was *excessively* poor! Anything in excess is most exhilarating.

Jean Anouilh (1910–87) French dramatist. *Ring Round the Moon*

4 The road of excess leads to the palace of Wisdom.

William Blake (1757–1827) British poet. *The Marriage of Heaven and Hell*, 'Proverbs of Hell'

5 I would remind you that extremism in the defence of liberty is no vice. And let me remind you also that moderation in the pursuit of justice is no virtue!

Barry Goldwater (1909–) US politician. Speech, San Francisco, 17 July 1964

6 ...belching from daily excess he came hiccupping to the war.

William of Malmesbury (c. 1080–c. 1143) English cleric and historian. Referring to Philip I of France. *Gesta Regum*, Bk. II

7 No part of the walls is left undecorated. From everywhere the praise of the Lord is drummed into you.

Nikolaus Pevsner (Bernhard Leon; 1902–83) German-born British art historian. *London, except the Cities of London and Westminster*

8 In baiting a mouse-trap with cheese, always leave room for the mouse.

Saki (Hector Hugh Munro; 1870–1916) British writer. *The Square Egg*

9 'Tis not the drinking that is to be blamed, but the excess.

John Selden (1584–1654) English historian. *Table Talk*

10 Well said; that was laid on with a trowel.

William Shakespeare (1564–1616) English dramatist. *As You Like It*, I:2

11 The lady doth protest too much, methinks.

William Shakespeare *Hamlet*, III:2

12 It out-herods Herod.

William Shakespeare *Hamlet*, III:2

13 Heat not a furnace for your foe so hot
That it do singe yourself. We may outrun
By violent swiftness that which we run at,
And lose by over-running.

William Shakespeare *Henry VIII*, I:1

14 To gild refined gold, to paint the lily,
To throw a perfume on the violet,
To smooth the ice, or add another hue
Unto the rainbow, or with taper-light
To seek the beauteous eye of heaven to garnish,
Is wasteful and ridiculous excess.

William Shakespeare *King John*, IV:2

15 Extreme *busyness*, whether at school or college, kirk or market, is a symptom of deficient vitality.

Robert Louis Stevenson (1850–94) Scottish writer. *Virginibus Puerisque*

16 Battering the gates of heaven with storms of prayer.

Alfred, Lord Tennyson (1809–92) British poet. *St Simeon Stylites*

17 Moderation is a fatal thing, Lady Hunstanton. Nothing succeeds like excess.

Oscar Wilde (1854–1900) Irish-born British dramatist. *A Woman of No Importance*, III

EXECUTION

See also last words, martyrdom, punishment

1 The parliament intended to have hanged him; and he expected no less, but resolved to be hanged with the Bible under one arm and Magna Carta under the other.

John Aubrey (1626–97) English antiquary. David Jenkins (1582–1663), a Welsh judge and royalist, was imprisoned by parliament (1645–60). *Brief Lives*, 'David Jenkins'

2 It's time for me to enjoy another pinch of snuff. Tomorrow my hands will be bound, so as to make it impossible.

Jean Sylvain Bailly (1736–93) French astronomer. Said on the evening before his execution. *Anekdotenschatz* (H. Hoffmeister)

3 And almost all things are by the law purged with blood; and without shedding of blood is no remission.

Bible: Hebrews 9:22

4 And when they were come to the place, which is called Calvary, there they crucified him, and the malefactors, one on the right hand, and the other on the left.

Bible: Luke 23:33

5 'Off with his head!'

Lewis Carroll (Charles Lutwidge Dodgson; 1832–98) British writer. *Alice's Adventures in Wonderland*, Ch. 8

6 I die a Christian, according to the Profession of the Church of England, as I found it left me by my Father.

Charles I (1600–49) King of England. Speech on the scaffold, 30 Jan 1649

7 Thou wilt show my head to the people: it is worth showing.

Georges Jacques Danton (1759–94) French political activist. Said as he mounted the scaffold, 5 Apr 1794. *French Revolution* (Carlyle), Bk. VI, Ch. 2

8 It is a far, far, better thing that I do, than I have ever done; it is a far, far, better rest that I go to, than I have ever known.

Charles Dickens (1812–70) British novelist. Said by Sydney Carton. *A Tale of Two Cities*, Bk. II, Ch. 15

9 To die for faction is a common evil,
But to be hanged for nonsense is the Devil.

John Dryden (1631–1700) British poet and dramatist. *Absalom and Achitophel*, II

10 This year, that is to mean ye 18 day of February, the Duke of Clarence and second brother to the king, then being prisoner in ye Tower, was secretly put to death and drowned in a barrel of malvesye within the said Tower.

Robert Fabyan (d. 1513) English chronicler. This account is apocryphal and reflects popular rumour. *Chronicle*

11 Oh let that day from time be blotted quite,
And let belief of't in next age be waived.
In deepest silence th'act concealed might,
So that the Kingdom's credit might be saved.

But if the Power Divine permitted this,
His Will's the law and ours must acquiesce.

Lord Thomas Fairfax (1612–71) General. Referring to the execution of Charles I. *The Faber Book of English History in Verse* (Kenneth Baker)

12 Son of Saint Louis, ascend to heaven.

Abbé Edgeworth de Firmont (1745–1807) Irish-born confessor to Louis XVI. Said to Louis XVI as he climbed up to the guillotine. Attrib.

13 Let them bestow on every airth a limb;
Then open all my veins, that I may swim
To thee, my Maker! in that crimson lake;
Then place my parboiled head upon a stake –
Scatter my ashes – strew them in the air; –
Lord! since thou know'st where all these atoms are,
I'm hopeful thou'lt recover once my dust,
And confident thou'lt raise me with the just.

James Graham (1612–50) Scottish general. Lines written on the window of his jail the night before his execution.

14 And in that journey was Owen Tudor taken and brought unto Haverfordwest, and he was beheaded at the market place, and his head set upon the highest grice of the market cross, and a mad woman combed his hair and washed away the blood of his face, and she got candles and set about him burning more than a hundred.

William Gregory (d. 1467) Chronicler. Owen Tudor was the grandfather of Henry VII. *Gregory's Chronicle*

15 And have they fixed the where and when?
And shall Trelawny die?
Here's twenty thousand Cornish men
Will know the reason why!

R. S. Hawker (1803–75) British poet. Referring to the imprisonment (1688) of Trelawny, Bishop of Bristol, by James II. *Song of the Western Men*

16 They hang us now in Shrewsbury jail:
The whistles blow forlorn,
And trains all night groan on the rail
To men that die at morn.

A. E. Housman (1859–1936) British scholar and poet. *A Shropshire Lad*, 'Reveillé'

17 O holy simplicity!

John Huss (Jan Hus; c. 1369–1415) Bohemian religious reformer. On noticing a peasant adding a faggot to the pile at his execution. *Apophthegmata* (Zincgreff-Weidner), Pt. III

18 Depend upon it, Sir, when a man knows he is to be hanged in a fortnight, it concentrates his mind wonderfully.

Samuel Johnson (1709–84) British lexicographer. *Life of Johnson* (J. Boswell), Vol. III

19 If we are to abolish the death penalty, I should like to see the first step taken by our friends the murderers.

Alphonse Karr (1808–90) French writer. *Les Guêpes*, Jan 1849

20 For they're hangin' Danny Deever, you can hear the Dead March play,
The Regiment's in 'ollow square – they're hangin' 'im to-day;
They've taken of 'is buttons off an' cut 'is stripes away,
An' they're hangin' Danny Deever in the mornin.

Rudyard Kipling (1865–1936) Indian-born British writer. *Danny Deever*

21 Be of good comfort, Master Ridley, and play the man; we shall this day light such a candle, by God's grace, in England as I trust shall never be put out.

Hugh Latimer (1485–1555) English churchman. Said to Nicholas Ridley as they were about to be burnt at the stake for heresy. *Famous Last Words* (B. Conrad)

22 He nothing common did or mean
Upon that memorable scene,
But with his keener eye
The axe's edge did try.

Andrew Marvell (1621–78) English poet. Referring to the execution of Charles I. *An Horatian Ode upon Cromwell's Return from Ireland*

23 Do not hack me as you did my Lord Russell.

Duke of Monmouth (1649–85) An illegitimate son of Charles II. Said to the headsman before his execution. *History of England* (Macaulay), Vol. I, Ch. 5

24 I pray you, Master Lieutenant, see me safe up, and for coming down let me shift for myself.

Thomas More (1478–1535) English lawyer and scholar. On climbing onto the scaffold prior to his execution. *Life of Sir Thomas More* (William Roper)

25 I cumber you goode Margaret muche, but I woulde be sorye, if it shoulde be any lenger than to morrowe, for it is S. Thomas evin and the vtas of Sainte Peter and therefore to morowe longe I to goe to God, it were a daye very meete and conveniente for me. I neuer liked your maner towarde me better then when you kissed me laste for I loue when doughterly loue and deere charitie hathe no laisor to looke to worldely curtesye. Fare well my deere childe and praye for me, and I shall for you and all your friendes that we maie merily meete in heaven.

Thomas More Last letter to Margaret Roper, his daughter, on the eve of his execution on 6 July 1535

26 Pluck up thy spirits, man, and be not afraid to do thine office; my neck is very short; take heed therefore thou strike not awry, for saving of thine honesty.

Thomas More Said to the headsman. *Life of Sir Thomas More* (Roper)

27 This hath not offended the king.

Thomas More Said as he drew his beard aside before putting his head on the block

28 The sight of it gave me infinite pleasure, as it proved that I was in a civilized society.

Mungo Park (1771–1806) Scottish explorer. Remark on finding a gibbet in an unexplored part of Africa. Attrib.

29 I went out to Charing Cross, to see Major-general Harrison hanged, drawn, and quartered; which was done there, he looking as cheerful as any man could do in that condition.

Samuel Pepys (1633–1703) English diarist. *Diary*, 13 Oct 1660

30 The world itself is but a large prison, out of which some are daily led to execution.

Walter Raleigh (1554–1618) English explorer. Said after his trial for treason, 1603. Attrib.

31 Even such is Time, that takes in trust
Our youth, our joys, our all we have,
And pays us but with age and dust;
Who in the dark and silent grave,
When we have wandered all our ways,
Shuts up the story of our days;
But from this earth, this grave, this dust,
My God shall raise me up, I trust.

Walter Raleigh Written on the night before his execution. Attrib.

32 So the heart be right, it is no matter which way the head lies.

Walter Raleigh On laying his head on the executioner's block. Attrib.

33 Tis a sharp remedy, but a sure one for all ills.

Walter Raleigh Referring to the executioner's axe just before he was beheaded. Attrib.

34 If you give me six lines written by the most honest man, I will find something in them to hang him.

Cardinal Richelieu (1585–1642) French statesman. Exact wording uncertain. Attrib.

35 *'O liberté! O liberté! Que de crimes on commet en ton nom!'*
Oh liberty! Oh liberty! What crimes are committed in thy name!

Madame Roland (1754–93) French revolutionary. Said as she mounted the steps of the guillotine. Attrib.

36 I will burn, but this is a mere incident. We shall continue our discussion in eternity.

Michael Servetus (1511–53) Spanish physician and theologian. Comment to the judges of the Inquisition after being condemned to be burned at the stake as a heretic. *Borges: A Reader* (E. Monegal)

37 FIRST CLOWN: What is he that builds stronger than either the mason, the shipwright, or the carpenter?
SECOND CLOWN: The gallows-maker; for that frame outlives a thousand tenants.

William Shakespeare (1564–1616) English dramatist. *Hamlet*, V:1

38 Then, with that faint fleeting smile playing about his lips, he faced the firing squad; erect and motionless, proud and disdainful, Walter Mitty, the undefeated, inscrutable to the last.

James Thurber (1894–1961) US humorist. *My World and Welcome to It*, 'The Secret Life of Walter Mitty'

EXISTENCE

1 Dear Sir, Your astonishment's odd:
I am always about in the Quad.
And that's why the tree
Will continue to be,
Since observed by Yours faithfully, God.

Anonymous The response to KNOX's limerick

2 Let us be moral. Let us contemplate existence.

Charles Dickens (1812–70) British novelist. *Martin Chuzzlewit*, Ch. 10

3 As far as we can discern, the sole purpose of human existence is to kindle a light in the darkness of mere being.

Carl Gustav Jung (1875–1961) Swiss psychoanalyst. *Memories, Dreams, Reflections*, Ch. 11

4 There once was a man who said 'God
Must think it exceedingly odd
If he find that this tree
Continues to be
When there's no one about in the Quad.'

Ronald Knox (1888–1957) British Roman Catholic priest. For a reply, *see* ANONYMOUS. Attrib.

5 I know perfectly well that I don't want to do anything; to do something is to create existence – and there's quite enough existence as it is.

Jean-Paul Sartre (1905–80) French writer. *Nausea*

6 Never being, but always at the edge of Being.

Stephen Spender (1909–) British poet. *Preludes*

EXPECTATION

See also anticipation, disappointment, hope

1 We joined the Navy to see the world,
And what did we see? We saw the sea.

Irving Berlin (1888–1989) US composer and lyricist. *Follow the Fleet*, 'We Saw the Sea'

2 For there is good news yet to hear and fine things to be seen,
Before we go to Paradise by way of Kensal Green.

G. K. Chesterton (1874–1936) British writer. *The Rolling English Road*

3 As I know more of mankind I expect less of them, and am ready now to call a man *a good man*, upon easier terms than I was formerly.

Samuel Johnson (1709–84) British lexicographer. *Life of Johnson* (J. Boswell), Vol. IV

4 This dumb ox will fill the whole world with his bellowing.

Albertus Magnus (c. 1200–80) German bishop. Referring to his pupil Thomas Aquinas, whose nickname was 'The Dumb Ox'. *Aquinas* (A. Kenny)

5 Dear Mary, We all knew you had it in you.

Dorothy Parker (1893–1967) US writer. Telegram sent to a friend on the successful outcome of her much publicized pregnancy.

6 'Blessed is the man who expects nothing, for he shall never be disappointed' was the ninth beatitude.

Alexander Pope (1688–1744) British poet. Letter to Fortescue, 23 Sept 1725

7 See yon pale stripling! when a boy,
A mother's pride, a father's joy!

Walter Scott (1771–1832) Scottish novelist. *Rokeby*, III

8 Gomer Owen who kissed her once by the pig-sty when she wasn't looking and never kissed her again although she was looking all the time.

Dylan Thomas (1914–53) Welsh poet. *Under Milk Wood*

9 This suspense is terrible. I hope it will last.

Oscar Wilde (1854–1900) Irish-born British dramatist. *The Importance of Being Earnest*, III

EXPEDIENCY

1 Half a loaf is better than no bread.

Proverb

2 And my parents finally realize that I'm kidnapped and they snap into action immediately: they rent out my room.

Woody Allen (Allen Stewart Konigsberg; 1935–) US film actor. *Woody Allen and His Comedy* (E. Lax)

3 I would rather be an opportunist and float than go to the bottom with my principles round my neck.

Stanley Baldwin (1867–1947) British statesman. Attrib.

4 Nobody is forgotten when it is convenient to remember him.

Benjamin Disraeli (1804–81) British statesman. Attrib.

5 You can't learn too soon that the most useful thing about a principle is that it can always be sacrificed to expediency.

W. Somerset Maugham (1874–1965) British novelist. *The Circle*, III

6 Death and taxes and childbirth! There's never any convenient time for any of them!

Margaret Mitchell (1909–49) US novelist. *Gone with the Wind*

7 No man is justified in doing evil on the ground of expediency.

Theodore Roosevelt (1858–1919) US Republican president. *The Strenuous Life*

8 Well, a widow, I see, is a kind of sinecure.

William Wycherley (1640–1716) English dramatist. *The Plain Dealer*, V:3

EXPERIENCE

See also history, past

1 A young physician fattens the churchyard.

Proverb

2 Experience is the best teacher.

Proverb

3 Experience is the mother of wisdom.

Proverb

4 Live and learn.

Proverb

5 Practice makes perfect.

Proverb

6 Experience is a good teacher, but she sends in terrific bills.

Minna Antrim (1861–?) US writer. *Naked Truth and Veiled Allusions*

7 One should try everything once, except incest and folk-dancing.

Arnold Bax (1883–1953) British composer. *Farewell to My Youth*

8 You will think me lamentably crude: my experience of life has been drawn from life itself.

Max Beerbohm (1872–1956) British writer. *Zuleika Dobson*, Ch. 7

9 Experience isn't interesting till it begins to repeat itself – in fact, till it does that, it hardly *is* experience.

Elizabeth Bowen (1899–1973) Irish novelist. *The Death of the Heart*, Pt. I, Ch. 1

10 When all is said and done, no literature can outdo the cynicism of real life; you won't intoxicate with one glass someone who has already drunk up a whole barrel.

Anton Chekhov (1860–1904) Russian dramatist. Letter, 1887

11 If men could learn from history, what lessons it might teach us! But passion and party blind our eyes and the light which experience gives is a lantern on the stern, which shines only on the waves behind us!

Samuel Taylor Coleridge (1772–1834) British poet. *Recollections* (Allsop)

12 An experience of women which extends over many nations and three continents.

Arthur Conan Doyle (1856–1930) British writer. *The Sign of Four*

13 How many roads must a man walk down
Before you call him a man?

Bob Dylan (Robert Allen Zimmerman; 1941–) US popular singer. *Blowin' in the Wind*

14 As for me, I see no such great cause why I should either be fond to live or fear to die. I have had good experience of this world, and I know what it is to be a subject and what to be a sovereign. Good neighbours I have had, and I have met with bad: and in trust I have found treason.

Elizabeth I (1533–1603) Queen of England. Speech to Parliament, 1586

15 What experience and history teach is this – that people and governments never have learned anything from history, or acted on principles deduced from it.

Hegel (1770–1831) German philosopher. *Philosophy of History*, Introduction

16 A moment's insight is sometimes worth a life's experience.

Oliver Wendell Holmes (1809–94) US writer. *The Professor at the Breakfast Table*, Ch. 10

17 Experience is never limited, and it is never complete; it is an immense sensibility, a kind of huge spider-web of the finest silken threads suspended in the chamber of consciousness, and catching every air-borne particle in its tissue.

Henry James (1843–1916) US novelist. *Partial Portraits*, 'The Art of Fiction'

18 Nothing ever becomes real till it is experienced

– even a proverb is no proverb to you till your life has illustrated it.

John Keats (1795–1821) British poet. Letter to George and Georgiana Keats, 19 Mar 1819

19 He was what I often think is a dangerous thing for a statesman to be – a student of history; and like most of those who study history, he learned from the mistakes of the past how to make new ones.

A. J. P. Taylor (1906–90) British historian. Referring to Napoleon III. *The Listener*, 6 June 1963

20 Nourishing a youth sublime
With the fairy tales of science, and the long result of Time.

Alfred, Lord Tennyson (1809–92) British poet. *Locksley Hall*

21 All experience is an arch wherethro'
Gleams that untravelled world, whose margin fades
For ever and for ever when I move.

Alfred, Lord Tennyson *Ulysses*

22 You don't set a fox to watching the chickens just because he has a lot of experience in the hen house.

Harry S. Truman (1884–1972) US statesman. Referring to Vice-President Nixon's nomination for president. Speech, 30 Oct 1960

23 I have learned
To look on nature, not as in the hour
Of thoughtless youth; but hearing often-times
The still, sad music of humanity.

William Wordsworth (1770–1850) British poet. *Lines composed a few miles above Tintern Abbey*

EXPERTS

1 By studying the masters – not their pupils.

Niels Henrik Abel (1809–29) Norwegian mathematician. When asked how he had become a great mathematician so quickly. *Men of Mathematics* (E. T. Bell)

2 An expert is a man who has made all the mistakes, which can be made, in a very narrow field.

Niels Bohr (1885–1962) Danish physicist. Attrib.

3 An expert is someone who knows some of the worst mistakes that can be made in his subject, and how to avoid them.

Werner Heisenberg (1901–76) German physicist. *Physics and Beyond*

4 An accomplished man to his finger-tips.

Horace (Quintus Horatius Flaccus; 65–8 BC) Roman poet. *Satires*, I

5 Specialist – A man who knows more and more about less and less.

William James Mayo (1861–1934) US surgeon. Also attributed to Nicholas Butler

6 The trouble with specialists is that they tend to think in grooves.

Elaine Morgan (1920–) British writer. *The Descent of Woman*, Ch. 1

EXPLANATIONS

1 You will find in politics that you are much exposed to the attribution of false motives. Never complain and never explain.

Stanley Baldwin, 1st Earl of Bewdley (1867–1947) British Conservative prime minister. Quoting Disraeli. Said to Harold Nicolson, 21 July 1943

2 I am one of those unfortunates to whom death is less hideous than explanations.

Wyndham Lewis (1891–1969) British journalist and writer. *Welcome to All This*

3 There is occasions and causes why and wherefore in all things.

William Shakespeare (1564–1616) English dramatist. *Henry V*, V:1

EXPLOITATION

1 Thus the devil played at chess with me, and yielding a pawn, thought to gain a queen of me, taking advantage of my honest endeavours.

Thomas Browne (1605–82) English physician and writer. *Religio Medici*, Pt. I

2 Mortals, whose pleasures are their only care,
First wish to be imposed on, and then are.

William Cowper (1731–1800) British poet. *The Progress of Error*

3 I am confident that the English legal system will not support Mr Justice Parker's decision or uphold what is effectively professional slavery.

George Michael (1963–) British pop singer. Referring to his court action against Sony, who refused to release him from a recording contract he signed in his youth. *The Times*, 22 June 1994

4 A lot of people are going to think, 'My God, I'd like to be ripped off like George Michael's been ripped off.'

Anonymous lawyer Referring to Sony's victory in court enabling them to refuse to release pop singer George Michael from a long-standing recording contract. *The Independent*, 22 June 1994

EXPLORATION

See also discovery

1 The fair breeze blew, the white foam flew,
The furrow followed free;
We were the first that ever burst
Into that silent sea.

Samuel Taylor Coleridge (1772–1834) British poet. *The Rime of the Ancient Mariner*, II

2 Go West, young man, and grow up with the country.

Horace Greeley (1811–72) US politician and journalist. Also attributed to the US writer John Soule (1815–91), *Terre Haute* (Indiana) *Express*, 1851. *Hints toward Reform*

3 Nothing easier. One step beyond the pole, you see, and the north wind becomes a south one.

Robert Edwin Peary (1856–1920) US explorer. Explaining how he knew he had reached the North Pole. Attrib.

4 Had we lived, I should have had a tale to tell of the hardihood, endurance, and courage of my companions which would have stirred the heart of every Englishman. These rough notes and our dead bodies must tell the tale.

Captain Robert Falcon Scott (1868–1912) British explorer. *Message to the Public*

5 Dr Livingstone, I presume?

Henry Morton Stanley (1841–1904) British explorer. On finding David Livingstone at Ujiji on Lake Tanganyika, Nov 1871. *How I found Livingstone*, Ch. 11

EXTRAVAGANCE

See also excess, luxury, money, ostentation, thrift, waste

1 Riches are for spending.

Francis Bacon (1561–1626) English philosopher. *Essays*, 'Of Expense'

2 All progress is based upon a universal innate desire on the part of every organism to live beyond its income.

Samuel Butler (1835–1902) British writer. *Notebooks*

3 He sometimes forgets that he is Caesar, but I always remember that I am Caesar's daughter.

Julia (39 BC–14 AD) Daughter of Augustus. Replying to suggestions that she should live in the simple style of her father, which contrasted with her own extravagance. *Saturnalia* (Macrobius)

4 All decent people live beyond their incomes nowadays, and those who aren't respectable live beyond other people's. A few gifted individuals manage to do both.

Saki (Hector Hugh Munro; 1870–1916) British writer. *The Match-Maker*

5 I suppose that I shall have to die beyond my means.

Oscar Wilde (1854–1900) Irish-born British dramatist. When told that an operation would be expensive. He is also believed to have said 'I am dying beyond my means' on accepting a glass of champagne as he lay on his deathbed. *Life of Wilde* (Sherard)

EYES

See also appearance

1 The eyes are the window of the soul.

Proverb

2 Our sight is the most perfect and most delightful of all our senses. It fills the mind with the largest variety of ideas, converses with its objects at the greatest distance, and continues the longest in action without being tired or satiated with its proper enjoyments.

Joseph Addison (1672–1719) British essayist. *The Spectator*, 411

3 It needs no dictionary of quotations to remind me that the eyes are the windows of the soul.

Max Beerbohm (1872–1956) British writer. *Zuleika Dobson*, Ch. 4

4 The eye of him that hath seen me shall see me no more: thine eyes are upon me, and I am not.

Bible: Job 7:8

5 That youthful sparkle in his eyes is caused by his contact lenses, which he keeps highly polished.

Sheilah Graham Referring to Ronald Reagan. *The Times*, 22 Aug 1981

6 Jeepers Creepers – where'd you get them peepers?

Johnny Mercer (1909–76) US lyricist and composer. *Jeepers Creepers*

7 Who formed the curious texture of the eye,
And cloath'd it with the various tunicles,
And texture exquisite; with chrystal juice
Supply'd it, to transmit the rays of light?

Henry Needler (1685–1760) *A Poem to Prove the Certainty of a God*

8 Out vile jelly!
Where is thy lustre now?

William Shakespeare (1564–1616) English dramatist. Spoken by Cornwall as he puts out Gloucester's remaining eye. *King Lear*, III:7

F

FACTS

See also truth

1 Now, what I want is Facts...Facts alone are wanted in life.

Charles Dickens (1812–70) British novelist. *Hard Times*, Bk. I, Ch. 1

2 Facts are not science – as the dictionary is not literature.

Martin H. Fischer (1879–1962) *Fischerisms* (Howard Faber and Ray Marr)

3 Facts do not cease to exist because they are ignored.

Aldous Huxley (1894–1964) British novelist. *Proper Studies*

4 Facts are ventriloquists' dummies. Sitting on a wise man's knee they may be made to utter words of wisdom; elsewhere they say nothing or talk nonsense.

Aldous Huxley *Time Must Have A Stop*

5 Once a newspaper touches a story, the facts are lost forever, even to the protagonists.

Norman Mailer (1923–) US writer. *The Presidential Papers*

6 Its primary office is the gathering of news. At the peril of its soul it must see that the supply is not tainted. Neither in what it gives, nor in what it does not give, nor in the mode of presentation, must the unclouded face of truth suffer wrong. Comment is free but facts are sacred.

C. P. Scott (1846–1932) British journalist. *Manchester Guardian*, 6 May 1926

7 Facts speak louder than statistics.

Geoffrey Streatfield (1897–1978) British lawyer. *The Observer*, 'Sayings of the Week', 19 Mar 1950

8 The Doctor said that Death was but
A scientific fact.

Oscar Wilde (1854–1900) *The Ballad of Reading Gaol*

FAILURE

See also success

1 A miss is as good as a mile.

Proverb

2 Well, back to the old drawing board.

Peter Arno (1904–68) US cartoonist. Caption to a cartoon of people leaving a crashed plane. *New Yorker*

3 Dear Randolph, utterly unspoiled by failure.

Noël Coward (1899–1973) British dramatist. Referring to Randolph Churchill. Attrib.

4 She knows there's no success like failure
And that failure's no success at all.

Bob Dylan (Robert Allen Zimmerman; 1941–) US popular singer. *Love Minus Zero No Limit*

5 It doesn't hurt to lose my crown, it hurts to lose.

Steffi Graf (1969–) German tennis player. *The Independent*, 22 June 1994

6 Shakespeare's so bloody difficult, and I don't like failure. You can fail on film, but there's nobody actually there in the flesh to watch you failing.

Anthony Hopkins (1937–) Welsh actor. *The Independent*, 12 Feb 1994

7 Here lies Joseph, who failed in everything he undertook.

Joseph II (1741–90) Holy Roman Emperor. Suggesting his own epitaph when reflecting upon the disappointment of his hopes for reform. Attrib.

8 Show me a good and gracious loser and I'll show you a failure.

Knute Rockne (1888–1931) US football coach. Attrib.

9 Like a dull actor now
I have forgot my part and I am out,
Even to a full disgrace.

William Shakespeare (1564–1616) English dramatist. *Coriolanus*, V:3

10 Failure is inevitable. Success is elusive.

Steven Spielberg (1946–) US film director. *OM*, Dec 1984

11 Failure? Do you remember what Queen Victoria once said?
'Failure? – the possibilities do not exist.'

Margaret Thatcher (1925–) British politician and prime minister. Queen Victoria had been speaking about the Boer War. TV news interview, at start of Falklands War, 5 Apr 1982

12 The crime is not to avoid failure. The crime is not to give triumph a chance.

Huw Wheldon (1916–86) British broadcaster and TV executive. Advice given to television producers. Attrib.

FAIRIES

See also supernatural

1 Every time a child says 'I don't believe in fairies' there is a little fairy somewhere that falls down dead.

J. M. Barrie (1860–1937) British novelist and dramatist. *Peter Pan*

2 When the first baby laughed for the first time, the laugh broke into a thousand pieces and they all went skipping about, and that was the beginning of fairies.

J. M. Barrie *Peter Pan*

3 Do you believe in fairies? Say quick that you believe. If you believe, clap your hands!

J. M. Barrie *Peter Pan*

4 There are fairies at the bottom of our garden.

Rose Fyleman (1877–1957) British writer. *Fairies and Chimneys*

5 In a hole in the ground there lived a hobbit.

J. R. R. Tolkien (1892–1973) British writer. *The Hobbit*, Ch. 1

FAITH

See also belief, faithfulness, God, religion, trust

1 Faith will move mountains.

Proverb

2 For we walk by faith, not by sight.

Bible: II Corinthians 5:7

3 Now faith is the substance of things hoped for, the evidence of things not seen.

Bible: Hebrews 11:1

4 These all died in faith, not having received the promises, but having seen them afar off, and were persuaded of them, and embraced them, and confessed that they were strangers and pilgrims on the earth.

Bible: Hebrews 11:13

5 By faith the walls of Jericho fell down, after they were compassed about seven days.

Bible: Hebrews 11:30

6 Even so faith, if it hath not works, is dead, being alone.

Bible: James 2:17

7 The prayer of faith shall save the sick.

Bible: James 5:15

8 And Jesus said unto them, I am the bread of life: he that cometh to me shall never hunger; and he that believeth on me shall never thirst.

Bible: John 6:35

9 And his disciples came to him, and awoke him, saying, Lord, save us: we perish.
And he saith unto them, Why are ye fearful, O ye of little faith? Then he arose, and rebuked the winds and the sea; and there was a great calm.

Bible: Matthew 8:25–26

10 Fight the good fight of faith, lay hold on eternal life, whereunto thou art also called, and hast professed a good profession before many witnesses.

Bible: I Timothy 6:12

11 For I am now ready to be offered, and the time of my departure is at hand.
I have fought a good fight, I have finished my course, I have kept the faith:
Henceforth there is laid up for me a crown of righteousness, which the Lord, the righteous judge, shall give me at that day: and not to me only, but unto all them also that love his appearing.

Bible: II Timothy 4:6–8

12 I feel no need for any other faith than my faith in human beings.

Pearl Buck (1892–1973) US novelist. *I Believe*

13 The prayer that reforms the sinner andheals the sick is an absolute faith that all things are possible to God – a spiritual understanding of Him, an unselfed love.

Mary Baker Eddy (1821–1910) US religious leader. *Science and Health, with Key to the Scriptures*

14 It's only a paper moon,
Sailing over a cardboard sea,
But it wouldn't be make-believe
If you believed in me.

E. Y. Harburg (1898–1981) US lyricist. *The Great Magoo*, 'It's Only a Paper Moon'

15 And I said to the man who stood at the gate of the year: 'Give me a light that I may tread safely into the unknown'. And he replied: 'Go out into the darkness and put your hand into the hand of God. That shall be to you better than light and safer than a known way.'

Minnie Louise Haskins (1875–1957) US writer. Remembered because it was quoted by George VI in his Christmas broadcast, 1939. *The Desert*, Introduction

16 So long as the body is affected through the mind, no audacious device, even of the most manifestly dishonest character, can fail of producing occasional good to those who yield it an implicit or even a partial faith.

Oliver Wendell Holmes (1809–94) US writer and physician. *Medical Essays*, 'Homoeopathy and its Kindred Delusions'

17 If I said that God did not send me, I should condemn myself; truly God did send me.

St Joan of Arc (c. 1412–31) French patriotic leader. Said at her trial

18 My dear child, you must believe in God in spite of what the clergy tell you.

Benjamin Jowett (1817–93) British theologian. *Autobiography* (Asquith), Ch. 8

19 Booth died blind and still by faith he trod,
Eyes still dazzled by the ways of God.

Vachel Lindsay (1879–1931) US poet. *General William Booth Enters Heaven*

20 Be a sinner and sin strongly, but more strongly have faith and rejoice in Christ.

Martin Luther (1483–1546) German Protestant. Letter to Melanchthon

21 Faith may be defined briefly as an illogical belief in the occurrence of the improbable.

H. L. Mencken (1880–1956) US journalist. *Prejudices*, 'Types of Men'

22 It takes a long while for a naturally trustful person to reconcile himself to the idea that after all God will not help him.

H. L. Mencken *Notebooks*, 'Minority Report'

23 Lead, kindly Light, amid the encircling gloom,
Lead thou me on;
The night is dark, and I am far from home,
Lead thou me on.

Cardinal Newman (1801–90) British theologian. *Lead Kindly Light*

24 Nothing in life is more wonderful than faith – the one great moving force which we can neither weigh in the balance nor test in the crucible.

Sir William Osler (1849–1919) Canadian physician. *British Medical Journal*, 1:1470, 1910

25 God and the Doctor we alike adore
But only when in danger, not before;
The danger o'er, both are alike requited,
God is forgotten, and the Doctor slighted.

Robert Owen (1771–1838) British social reformer. Epigram

26 Even such is Time, that takes in trust
Our youth, our joys, our all we have,
And pays us but with age and dust;
Who in the dark and silent grave,
When we have wandered all our ways,
Shuts up the story of our days;
But from this earth, this grave, this dust,
My God shall raise me up, I trust.

Walter Raleigh (1554–1618) English explorer. Written on the night before his execution. Attrib.

27 *Dieu et mon droit.*
God and my right.

Richard I Motto on the royal arms of Great Britain; originally used as a war-cry, Sept 1198

28 A miracle is an event which creates faith. Frauds deceive. An event which creates faith does not deceive; therefore it is not a fraud, but a miracle.

George Bernard Shaw (1856–1950) Irish dramatist and critic. *St Joan*

29 'Tis not the dying for a faith that's so hard, Master Harry – every man of every nation has done that – 'tis the living up to it that is difficult.

William Makepeace Thackeray (1811–63) British novelist. *Henry Esmond*, Ch. 6

30 Life is doubt, and faith without doubt is nothing but death.

Miguel de Unamuno y Jugo (1864–1936) Spanish writer and philosopher. *Poesías*

31 There can be no scientific dispute with respect to faith, for science and faith exclude one another.

Rudolf Virchow (1821–1902) German pathologist. *Disease, Life, and Man*, 'On Man'

32 Faith consists in believing when it is beyond the power of reason to believe. It is not enough that a thing be possible for it to be believed.

Voltaire (François-Marie Arouet; 1694–1778) French writer. *Questions sur l'encyclopédie*

FAITHFULNESS

See also loyalty

1 It is better to be unfaithful than faithful without wanting to be.

Brigitte Bardot (1934–) French film actress. *The Observer*, 'Sayings of the Week', 18 Feb 1968

2 Through perils both of wind and limb,
Through thick and thin she follow'd him.

Samuel Butler (1612–80) English satirist. *Hudibras*, Pt. II

3 I have been faithful to thee, Cynara! in my fashion.

Ernest Dowson (1867–1900) British lyric poet. *Non Sum Qualis Eram Bonae Sub Regno Cynarae*

4 We only part to meet again.
Change, as ye list, ye winds; my heart shall be
The faithful compass that still points to thee.

John Gay (1685–1732) English poet and dramatist. *Sweet William's Farewell*

5 But I'm always true to you, darlin', in my fashion,
Yes, I'm always true to you, darlin', in my way.

Cole Porter (1893–1964) US songwriter. *Kiss Me, Kate*, 'Always True to You in My Fashion'

6 God pardon all oaths that are broke to me!
God keep all vows unbroke are made to thee!

William Shakespeare (1564–1616) English dramatist. *Richard II*, IV:1

7 O heaven! were man
But constant, he were perfect.

William Shakespeare *Two Gentlemen of Verona*, V:4

FAME

See also popularity, posterity, reputation

1 I agree with you that the name of Spiro Agnew is not a household name. I certainly hope that it will become one within the next couple of months.

Spiro T. Agnew (1918–) US Republican politician. TV interview, 8 Aug 1968

2 A celebrity is a person who works hard all his life to become known, then wears dark glasses to avoid being recognized.

Fred Allen (1894–1956) US comedian. *Treadmill to Oblivion*

3 Private faces in public places
Are wise and nicer
Than public faces in private places.

W. H. Auden (1907–73) British poet. *Marginalia*

4 Fame is like a river, that beareth up things light and swollen, and drowns things weighty and solid.

Francis Bacon (1561–1626) English philosopher. *Essays*, 'Of Praise'

5 I should like one of these days to be so well known, so popular, so celebrated, so famous, that it would permit me…to break wind in society, and society would think it a most natural thing.

Honoré de Balzac (1799–1850) French novelist. Attrib.

6 The celebrity is a person who is known for his well-knownness.

Daniel J. Boorstin (1914–) US writer. *The Image*, 'From Hero to Celebrity: The Human Pseudo-event'

7 A best-seller was a book which somehow sold well simply because it was selling well.

Daniel J. Boorstin *The Image*, 'From Shapes to Shadows: Dissolving Forms'

8 I awoke one morning and found myself famous.

Lord Byron (1788–1824) British poet. Remark made after the publication of *Childe Harold's Pilgrimage* (1812). Entry in Memoranda

9 I don't care what you say about me, as long as you say *something* about me, and as long as you spell my name right.

George M. Cohan (1878–1942) US entertainer. *George M. Cohan* (J. McCabe)

10 Being a star has made it possible for me to get insulted in places where the average Negro could never hope to get insulted.

Sammy Davis Jnr (1925–90) US singer. *Yes I Can*

11 If a man make a better mouse-trap than his neighbour, though he build his house in the woods, the world will make a beaten path to his door.

Ralph Waldo Emerson (1803–82) US poet and essayist. Attrib.

12 I was born into big celebrity. It could only diminish.

Carrie Fisher (1956–) US film star. *Vanity Fair*, 1990

13 A big man has no time really to do anything but just sit and be big.

F. Scott Fitzgerald (1896–1940) US novelist. *This Side of Paradise*, Bk. III, Ch. 2

14 Fame is sometimes like unto a kind of mushroom, which Pliny recounts to be the greatest miracle in nature, because growing and having no root.

Thomas Fuller (1608–61) English historian. *The Holy State and the Profane State*

15 I'm into pop because I want to get rich, get famous and get laid.

Bob Geldof (1952–) Irish-born pop singer. Attrib.

16 Fame is a powerful aphrodisiac.

Graham Greene (1904–91) British novelist. *Radio Times*, 10 Sept 1964

17 Every man has a lurking wish to appear considerable in his native place.

Samuel Johnson (1709–84) British lexicographer. Letter to Sir Joshua Reynolds. *Life of Johnson* (J. Boswell), Vol. II

18 People either think I'm famous or they've never heard of me.

Armistead Maupin (1944–) US author. *The Sunday Times*, 4 Feb 1990

19 One of the drawbacks of Fame is that one can never escape from it.

Nellie Melba (Helen Porter Mitchell; 1861–1931) Australian soprano. *Melodies and Memories*

20 Fame is the spur that the clear spirit doth raise
(That last infirmity of noble mind)
To scorn delights, and live laborious days.

John Milton (1608–74) English poet. *Lycidas*

21 I prefer it this way, instead of people leaning out of car windows and shouting obscenities at you.

Kylie Minogue (1968–) Australian pop singer. Referring to her move out of the public eye. *Face*, June 1994

22 'What are you famous *for*?'
'For nothing. I am just famous.'

Iris Murdoch (1919–) Irish-born British novelist. *The Flight from the Enchanter*

23 I'm never going to be famous...I don't do anything. Not one single thing. I used to bite my nails, but I don't even do that any more.

Dorothy Parker (1893–1967) US writer. *The Little Hours*

24 If you have to tell them who you are, you aren't anybody.

Gregory Peck (1916–) US film star. Remarking upon the failure of anyone in a crowded restaurant to recognize him. *Pieces of Eight* (S. Harris)

25 Cannes is where you lie on the beach and stare at the stars – or vice versa.

Rex Reed (1938–) US columnist and actor. Attrib.

26 The more you are talked about, the more you will wish to be talked about. The condemned murderer who is allowed to see the account of his trial in the Press is indignant if he finds a newspaper which has reported it inadequately.... Politicians and literary men are in the same case.

Bertrand Russell (1872–1970) British philosopher. *Human Society in Ethics and Politics*

27 I haven't made any friends since becoming famous.

Seal (1963–) British pop singer. *Vox*, June 1994

28 The names of those who in their lives fought for life,
Who wore at their hearts the fire's centre.

Stephen Spender (1909–) British poet. *I Think Continually of Those*

29 Born of the sun, they travelled a short while towards the sun
And left the vivid air signed with their honour.

Stephen Spender *I Think Continually of Those*

30 Love of fame is the last thing even learned men can bear to be parted from.

Tacitus (c. 55–c. 120 AD) Roman historian. *Histories*, IV, 6

31 He had a genius for backing into the limelight.

Lowell Thomas (1892–1981) US author. Referring to T. E. Lawrence. *Lawrence of Arabia*

32 To famous men all the earth is a sepulchre.

Thucydides (c. 460–c. 400 BC) Greek historian and general. *History of the Peloponnesian War*, Bk. II, Ch. 43

33 The only man who wasn't spoilt by being lionized was Daniel.

Herbert Beerbohm Tree (1853–1917) British actor and theatre manager. *Beerbohm Tree* (Hesketh Pearson)

34 When I pass my name in such large letters I blush, but at the same time instinctively raise my hat.

Herbert Beerbohm Tree *Beerbohm Tree* (Hesketh Pearson)

35 Even the youngest of us will know, in fifty years' time, exactly what we mean by 'a very Noel Coward sort of person'.

Kenneth Tynan (1927–80) British critic. *Curtains*

36 In the future, everyone will be famous for 15 minutes.

Andy Warhol (Andrew Warhola; 1926–87) US pop artist. Attrib.

37 There is only one thing in the world worse than being talked about, and that is not being talked about.

Oscar Wilde (1854–1900) Irish-born British dramatist. *The Picture of Dorian Gray*, Ch. 1

FAMILIARITY

1 Familiarity breeds contempt.

Proverb

2 No man is a hero to his valet.

Anne-Marie Bigot de Cornuel (1605–94) French society hostess. *Lettres de Mlle Aissé*, 13 Aug 1728

3 I like familiarity. In me it does not breed contempt. Only more familiarity.

Gertrude Stein (1874–1946) US writer. *Dale Carnegie's Scrapbook*

4 He began to think the tramp a fine, brotherly, generous fellow. He was also growing accustomed to something – shall I call it an olfactory bar – that had hitherto kept them apart.

H. G. Wells (1866–1946) British writer. *Bealby*, Pt. VI, Ch. 3

FAMILY

See also ancestry, children, marriage

1 Blood is thicker than water.

Proverb

2 Every family has a skeleton in the cupboard.
Proverb

3 Like father, like son.
Proverb

4 The family that prays together stays together.
Proverb

5 There's a black sheep in every flock.
Proverb

6 Sir Walter, being strangely surprised and put out of his countenance at so great a table, gives his son a damned blow over the face. His son, as rude as he was, would not strike his father, but strikes over the face the gentleman that sat next to him and said 'Box about: 'twill come to my father anon'.
John Aubrey (1626–97) English antiquary. *Brief Lives*, 'Sir Walter Raleigh'

7 He that hath wife and children hath given hostages to fortune; for they are impediments to great enterprises, either of virtue or mischief.
Francis Bacon (1561–1626) English philosopher. *See also* LUCAN. *Essays*, 'Of Marriage and Single Life'

8 The joys of parents are secret, and so are their griefs and fears.
Francis Bacon *Essays*, 'Of Parents and Children'

9 Fathers, provoke not your children to anger, lest they be discouraged.
Bible: Colossians 3:21

10 Behold, every one that useth proverbs shall use this proverb against thee, saying, As is the mother, so is her daughter.
Bible: Ezekiel 16:44–45

11 The sort of place everyone should send his mother-in-law for a month, all expenses paid.
Ian Botham (1955–) British cricketer. Referring to Pakistan. BBC Radio 2 interview, Mar 1984

12 Parents are the last people on earth who ought to have children.
Samuel Butler (1835–1902) British writer. *Notebooks*

13 I love all my children, but some of them I don't like.
Lillian Carter (1902–83) The mother of Jimmy Carter, US president (1977–81). In *Woman*, 9 Apr 1977

14 If one is not going to take the necessary precautions to avoid having parents one must undertake to bring them up.
Quentin Crisp (?1910–) Model, publicist, and writer. *The Naked Civil Servant*

15 Fate chooses your relations, you choose your friends.
Jacques Delille (1738–1813) French abbé and poet. *Malheur et pitié*, I

16 There are times when parenthood seems nothing but feeding the mouth that bites you.
Peter De Vries (1910–93) US novelist. *Tunnel of Love*

17 It is a melancholy truth that even great men have their poor relations.
Charles Dickens (1812–70) British novelist. *Bleak House*, Ch. 28

18 I wasn't even aware of the Year of the Family. I couldn't give a toss. These things – the year of the family, the year of the three-legged dog. I think it's all trash.
Roddy Doyle (1958–) Irish novelist and playwright. *The Observer*, 1 May 1994

19 From my experience and observation, if a family is held together in difficult circumstances, nine times out of ten it's the woman who's doing it...You'll find women in their late thirties who look 50, and their husbands of the same age who look 28 or 29 – like the eldest sons. Because, in many ways, they are the eldest sons.
Roddy Doyle *The Observer*, 1 May 1994

20 Come mothers and fathers
Throughout the land
And don't criticize
What you can't understand.
Bob Dylan (Robert Allen Zimmerman; 1941–) US popular singer. *The Times They Are A-Changin'*

21 What a marvellous place to drop one's mother-in-law!
Marshal Foch (1851–1929) French soldier. Remark on being shown the Grand Canyon. Attrib.

22 The mother-child relationship is paradoxical and, in a sense, tragic. It requires the most intense love on the mother's side, yet this very love must help the child grow away from the mother and to become fully independent.
Erich Fromm (1900–80) US psychologist and philosopher.

23 Possessive parents rarely live long enough to see the fruits of their selfishness.
Alan Garner (1934–) British writer. *The Owl Service*

24 My father was frightened of his mother. I was frightened of my father, and I'm damned well going to make sure that my children are frightened of me.
George V (1865–1936) King of the United Kingdom. Attrib.

25 And so do his sisters, and his cousins and his aunts!
His sisters and his cousins,
Whom he reckons up by dozens,
And his aunts!
W. S. Gilbert (1836–1911) British dramatist. *HMS Pinafore*, I

26 LEONTINE. An only son, sir, might expect more indulgence.
CROAKER. An only father, sir, might expect more obedience.
Oliver Goldsmith (1728–74) Irish-born British writer. *The Good-Natured Man*, I

27 I am the family face;
Flesh perishes, I live on.
Thomas Hardy (1840–1928) British novelist. *Heredity*

28 A person may be indebted for a nose or an eye, for a graceful carriage or a voluble discourse, to a great-aunt or uncle, whose existence he has scarcely heard of.
William Hazlitt (1778–1830) British essayist. *On Personal Character*

29 Good families are generally worse than any others.
Anthony Hope (Sir Anthony Hope Hawkins; 1863–1933) British novelist. *The Prisoner of Zenda*, Ch. 1

30 I was the seventh of nine children. When you come from that far down you have to struggle to survive.

Robert Kennedy (1925–68) US politician and younger brother of President John F. Kennedy. *The Kennedy Neurosis* (B. G. Clinch)

31 But there, everything has its drawbacks, as the man said when his mother-in-law died, and they came down upon him for the funeral expenses.

Jerome K. Jerome (1859–1927) British humorist. *Three Men in a Boat*, Ch. 3

32 A poor relation – is the most irrelevant thing in nature.

Charles Lamb (1775–1834) British essayist. *Last Essays of Elia*, 'Poor Relations'

33 They fuck you up, your mum and dad.
They may not mean to, but they do.
They fill you with the faults they had
And add some extra, just for you.

Philip Larkin (1922–85) British poet. *This be the Verse*

34 Far from being the basis of the good society, the family, with its narrow privacy and tawdry secrets, is the source of all our discontents.

Edmund Leach (1910–89) British social anthropologist. In the BBC Reith Lectures for 1967. Lecture reprinted in *The Listener*

35 Kids haven't changed much, but parents seem increasingly unhappy with the child raising phase of their lives.

Penelope Leach (1937–) British writer and child-care specialist. Remark, Oct 1988

36 I have a wife, I have sons: all of them hostages given to fate.

Lucan (Marcus Annaeus Lucanus; 39–65 AD) Roman poet. *See also* BACON. *Works*, VII

37 A group of closely related persons living under one roof; it is a convenience, often a necessity, sometimes a pleasure, sometimes the reverse; but who first exalted it as admirable, an almost religious ideal?

Rose Macaulay (1889–1958) British writer. *The World My Wilderness*, Ch. 20

38 You're a disgrace to our family name of Wagstaff, if such a thing is possible.

Groucho Marx (Julius Marx; 1895–1977) US comedian. *Horse Feathers*

39 Few misfortunes can befall a boy which bring worse consequences than to have a really affectionate mother.

W. Somerset Maugham (1874–1965) British novelist. *A Writer's Notebook*

40 The sink is the great symbol of the bloodiness of family life. All life is bad, but family life is worse.

Julian Mitchell (1935–) British writer. *As Far as You Can Go*, Pt. I, Ch. 1

41 I cumber you goode Margaret muche, but I woulde be sorye, if it shoulde be any lenger than to morrowe, for it is S. Thomas evin and the vtas of Sainte Peter and therefore to morowe longe I to goe to God, it were a daye very meete and conveniente for me. I neuer liked your maner towarde me better then when you kissed me laste for I loue when doughterly loue and deere charitie hathe no laisor to looke to worldely curtesye. Fare well my deere childe and praye for me, and I shall for you and all your friendes that we maie merily meete in heaven.

Thomas More (1478–1535) English lawyer and scholar. Last letter to Margaret Roper, his daughter, on the eve of his execution on 6 July 1535

42 One would be in less danger
From the wiles of a stranger
If one's own kin and kith
Were more fun to be with.

Ogden Nash (1902–71) US poet. *Family Court*

43 Children aren't happy with nothing to ignore,
And that's what parents were created for.

Ogden Nash *The Parents*

44 And Her Mother Came Too.

Ivor Novello (David Ivor Davies; 1893–1951) British actor, composer, and dramatist. Song title

45 There was an old woman who lived in a shoe,
She had so many children she didn't know what to do;
She gave them some broth without any bread;
She whipped them all soundly and put them to bed.

Nursery Rhyme *Gammer Gurton's Garland*

46 The worst misfortune that can happen to an ordinary man is to have an extraordinary father.

Austin O'Malley (1858–1932) US writer.

47 Men are generally more careful of the breed of their horses and dogs than of their children.

William Penn (1644–1718) English preacher. *Some Fruits of Solitude, in Reflections and Maxims relating to the conduct of Humane Life*, Pt. I, No 52

48 Parents are sometimes a bit of a disappointment to their children. They don't fulfil the promise of their early years.

Anthony Powell (1905–) British novelist. *A Buyer's Market*

49 All men are brothers, but, thank God, they aren't all brothers-in-law.

Anthony Powell *A Dance to the Music of Time: At Lady Molly's*, Ch. 4

50 Who has not watched a mother stroke her child's cheek or kiss her child *in a certain way* and felt a nervous shudder at the possessive outrage done to a free solitary human soul?

John Cowper Powys (1872–1963) British novelist. *The Meaning of Culture*

51 For there is no friend like a sister
In calm or stormy weather;
To cheer one on the tedious way,
To fetch one if one goes astray,
To lift one if one totters down,
To strengthen whilst one stands.

Christina Rossetti (1830–74) British poet. *Goblin Market*

52 Two mothers-in-law.

Lord John Russell (1792–1878) British statesman. His answer when asked what he would consider a proper punishment for bigamy. *Anekdotenschatz* (H. Hoffmeister)

53 It is a wise father that knows his own child.

William Shakespeare (1564–1616) English dramatist. *The Merchant of Venice*, II:2

54 There is only one person an English girl hates more than she hates her elder sister; and that is her mother.

George Bernard Shaw (1856–1950) Irish dramatist and critic. *Man and Superman*

55 That dear octopus from whose tentacles we never quite escape, nor in our innermost hearts never quite wish to.

Dodie Smith (1896–90) British dramatist and novelist. *Dear Octopus*

56 I wish either my father or my mother, or indeed both of them, as they were in duty both equally bound to it, had minded what they were about when they begot me.

Laurence Sterne (1713–68) Irish-born British writer. *Tristram Shandy*

57 The greatest destroyer of peace is abortion because if a mother can kill her own child what is left for me to kill you and you to kill me? There is nothing between.

Mother Teresa (Agnes Gonxha Bojaxhui; 1910–) Yugoslavian-born Indian missionary. *Nobel Peace Prize Lecture*

58 If a man's character is to be abused, say what you will, there's nobody like a relation to do the business.

William Makepeace Thackeray (1811–63) British novelist. *Vanity Fair*, Ch. 19

59 All happy families resemble one another, each unhappy family is unhappy in its own way.

Leo Tolstoy (1828–1910) Russian writer. *Anna Karenina*, Pt. I, Ch. 1

60 No man is responsible for his father. That is entirely his mother's affair.

Margaret Turnbull (fl. 1920s–1942) US writer. *Alabaster Lamps*

61 Parents are the bones on which children sharpen their teeth.

Peter Ustinov (1921–) British actor. *Dear Me*

62 'Parents are strange,' said Amy, 'for their age.'

Amanda Vail (Warren Miller; 1921–66) US writer. *Love Me Little*

63 Don't hold your parents up to contempt. After all, you are their son, and it is just possible that you may take after them.

Evelyn Waugh (1903–66) British novelist. *The Tablet*, 9 May 1951

64 The thing that impresses me most about America is the way parents obey their children.

Duke of Windsor (1894–1972) King of the United Kingdom; abdicated 1936. *Look Magazine*, 5 Mar 1957

65 It is no use telling me that there are bad aunts and good aunts. At the core they are all alike. Sooner or later, out pops the cloven hoof.

P. G. Wodehouse (1881–1975) British humorous novelist. *The Code of the Woosters*

66 We could improve world wide mental health if we acknowledged that parents can make you crazy.

Frank Zappa (1940–93) US rock musician. *The Real Frank Zappa Book*

FANATICISM

1 Defined in psychological terms, a fanatic is a man who consciously over-compensates a secret doubt.

Aldous Huxley (1894–1964) British novelist. *Vulgarity in Literature*, Ch. 4

2 Defined in psychological terms, a fanatic is a man who consciously over-compensates a secret doubt.

Aldous Huxley *Vulgarity in Literature*, Ch. 4

3 Fanatics have their dreams, wherewith they weave
A paradise for a sect.

John Keats (1795–1821) British poet. *The Fall of Hyperion*, I

4 You are never dedicated to do something you have complete confidence in. No one is fanatically shouting that the sun is going to rise tomorrow. They *know* it's going to rise tomorrow. When people are fanatically dedicated to political or religious faiths or any other kind of dogmas or goals, it's always because these dogmas or goals are in doubt.

Robert T. Pirsig (1928–) US writer. *Zen and the Art of Motorcycle Maintenance*, Pt. II, Ch. 13

FASCISM

See also Hitler, Nazism

1 *Il Duce ha sempre ragione.*
The Duce is always right.

Anonymous Referring to the Italian dictator, Benito Mussolini (1883–1945). Fascist Slogan

2 I'd love to enter politics. I will one day. I'd adore to be Prime Minister. And yes, I believe very strongly in Fascism.

David Bowie (David Jones; 1947–) British pop singer. *Playboy*, Sept 1976

3 The crafty, cold-blooded, black-hearted Italian.

Winston Churchill (1874–1965) British statesman. Referring to Benito Mussolini. Radio broadcast, 9 Feb 1941

4 With a suitcase full of clothes and underwear in my hand and an indomitable will in my heart, I set out for Vienna...I too hope to become 'something'.

Adolf Hitler (1889–1945) German dictator. *Mein Kampf*

5 It was no secret that this time the revolution would have to be bloody...When we spoke of it, we called it 'The Night of the Long Knives'.

Adolf Hitler Referring to the liquidation of the leadership of the SA, the Sturmabteilung, the Nazi terrorist militia. Speech, Reichstag, 13 July 1934

6 The final solution of the Jewish problem.

Adolf Hitler Referring to the Nazi concentration camps. *The Final Solution* (G. Geitlinger)

7 Before the organization of the Blackshirt movement free speech did not exist in this country.

Oswald Mosley (1896–1980) British politician. Selections from the *New Statesman, This England*, Pt. I

8 I should be pleased, I suppose, that Hitler has carried out a revolution on our lines. But they are Germans. So they will end by ruining our idea.

Benito Mussolini (1883–1945) Italian dictator. *Benito Mussolini* (C. Hibbert), Pt. II, Ch. 1

9 Fascism is a religion; the twentieth century will be known in history as the century of Fascism.

Benito Mussolini On Hitler's seizing power. *Sawdust Caesar* (George Seldes), Ch. 24

10 Fascism is not an article for export.

Benito Mussolini Report in the German press, 1932

11 The keystone of the Fascist doctrine is its conception of the State, of its essence, its functions, and its aims. For Fascism the State is absolute, individuals and groups relative.

Benito Mussolini *Fascism, Doctrine and Institutions*

12 I could have transformed this gray assembly hall into an armed camp of Blackshirts, a bivouac for corpses. I could have nailed up the doors of Parliament.

Benito Mussolini Referring to the Fascist march on Rome, which had resulted in Mussolini becoming prime minister (31 Oct 1922). Speech, Chamber of Deputies, 16 Nov 1922

13 Today in Britain, a fascist has won an election. Can you imagine how we feel? I am a proud and loyal man, madam. We had so much faith in this country. In the war, I thought it is time to help Britain to save democracy and fight fascism. They don't remember what we did, three million of us fought as volunteers remember – in the desert, in Burma. It makes me so sad.

Rajinder Singh British soldier. Referring to the election of a neo-Nazi British National Party councillor. *The Independent*, 22 Nov 1993

14 Every communist has a fascist frown, every fascist a communist smile.

Muriel Spark (1918–) British novelist. *The Girls of Slender Means*, Ch. 4

15 Fascism means war.

John St Loe Strachey (1901–63) British politician. Slogan, 1930s

FASHION

See also clothes

1 Why, Madam, do you know there are upward of thirty yards of bowels squeezed underneath that girdle of your daughter's? Go home and cut it; let Nature have fair play, and you will have no need of my advice.

John Abernethy (1764–1831) English surgeon. Advice to a lady who took her tightly laced daughter to him. *Memoirs of John Abernethy*, Ch. 33 (George Macilwain)

2 No perfumes, but very fine linen, plenty of it, and country washing.

'Beau' Brummell (George Bryan Brummell; 1778–1840) British dandy. *Memoirs* (Harriette Wilson), Ch. 2

3 I do not believe there has ever been a name as important as Pierre Cardin in the general history of couture.

Pierre Cardin (1922–) French fashion designer. *The Sunday Times*, 21 Oct 1990

4 Fashion is architecture: it is a matter of proportions.

Coco Chanel (1883–1971) French dress designer. *Coco Chanel, Her Life, Her Secrets* (Marcel Haedrich)

5 One had as good be out of the world, as out of the fashion.

Colley Cibber (1671–1757) British actor and dramatist. *Love's Last Shift*, II

6 The Englishman's dress is like a traitor's body that hath been hanged, drawn, and quartered, and is set up in various places; his cod-piece is in Denmark, the collar of his doublet and the belly in France; the wing and narrow sleeve in Italy; the short waist hangs over a Dutch butcher's stall in Utrecht; his huge slops speak Spanishly...And thus we that mock every nation for keeping of one fashion, yet steal patches from every one of them to piece out our pride.

Thomas Dekker (c. 1570–1632) English writer. *Seven Deadly Sins of London*

7 I walk down the Strand
With my gloves on my hand,
And I walk down again
With them off.

W. F. Hargreaves (1846–1919) British songwriter. *Burlington Bertie*

8 There are few who would not rather be taken in adultery than in provincialism.

Aldous Huxley (1894–1964) British novelist. *Antic Hay*, Ch. 10

9 A baseball cap is just as valid as a felt hat was 20 years ago.

Stephen Jones (1957–) British milliner. *The Observer*, 'Sayings of the Week', 17 Apr 1994

10 Her frocks are built in Paris but she wears them with a strong English accent.

Saki (Hector Hugh Munro; 1870–1916) British writer. *Reginald on Women*

11 For an idea ever to be fashionable is ominous, since it must afterwards be always old-fashioned.

George Santayana (1863–1952) US philosopher. *Winds of Doctrine*, 'Modernism and Christianity'

12 The only label she wears is 'drip dry'.

Jennifer Saunders (1958–) British comedy writer and actress. *Absolutely Fabulous*

13 Fashions, after all, are only induced epidemics.

George Bernard Shaw (1856–1950) Irish dramatist and critic. *Doctor's Dilemma*, Preface

14 A love of fashion makes the economy go round.

Liz Tilberis (1947–) Editor of *Vogue*. Remark, Aug 1987

FEAR

1 In the Nineteenth Century men lost their fear of God and acquired a fear of microbes.

Anonymous

2 It is a miserable state of mind to have few things to desire and many things to fear.

Francis Bacon (1561–1626) English philosopher. *Essays*, 'Of Empire'

3 There is no fear in love; but perfect love casteth out fear; because fear hath torment. He that feareth is not made perfect in love.

Bible: I John 4:18

4 For God hath not given us the spirit of fear; but of power, and of love, and of a sound mind.

Bible: II Timothy 1:7

5 It takes a brave man to face a brave woman, and man's fear of women's creative energy has never found expression more clear than in the old German clamor, renewed by the Nazis, of 'Kinder, Kuchen und Kirche' for women.

Pearl Buck (1892–1973) US novelist. *To My Daughters with Love*

6 Fear has many eyes and can see things underground.

Miguel de Cervantes (1547–1616) Spanish novelist. *Don Quixote*, Pt. I, Ch. 20

7 Like one, that on a lonesome road
Doth walk in fear and dread,
And having once turned round walks on,
And turns no more his head;
Because he knows, a frightful fiend
Doth close behind him tread.

Samuel Taylor Coleridge (1772–1834) British poet. *The Rime of the Ancient Mainer*, VI

8 Let me assert my firm belief that the only thing we have to fear is fear itself.

Franklin D. Roosevelt (1882–1945) US Democratic president. First Inaugural Address, 4 Mar 1933

9 Fear lent wings to his feet.

Virgil (Publius Vergilius Maro; 70–19 BC) Roman poet. *Aeneid*, Bk. VIII

FEMINISM

See also equality, sexes, woman's role, women

Those in favour

1 Old-fashioned ways which no longer apply to changed conditions are a snare in which the feet of women have always become readily entangled.

Jane Addams (1860–1935) US social worker. In *Newer Ideals of Peace*, 'Utilization of Women in City Government'

2 Burn your bra!

Anonymous Feminist slogan

3 Men their rights and nothing more; women their rights and nothing less.

Susan B. Anthony (1820–1906) US editor. *The Revolution*, Motto

4 …there never will be complete equality until women themselves help to make laws and elect lawmakers.

Susan B. Anthony *The Arena*, 'The Status of Women, Past, Present and Future', May 1897

5 It is probably true to say that the largest scope for change still lies in men's attitude to women, and in women's attitude to themselves.

Vera Brittain (1893–1970) British writer and poet. *Lady into Women*, Ch. 15

6 Feminism is an entire world view or gestalt, not just a laundry list of 'women's issues'.

Charlotte Bunch (1944–) US editor, feminist, educator, and writer. *New Directions for Women*, Sept–Oct 1981

7 From a timid, shy girl I had become a woman of resolute character, who could not longer be frightened by the struggle with troubles.

Anna Dostoevsky (1846–1918) Russian diarist and writer. *Dostoevsky Portrayed by His Wife*

8 The extension of women's rights is the basic principle of all social progress.

Charles Fourier (1772–1837) French social reformer. *Théorie des Quatre Mouvements*

9 Where young boys plan for what they will achieve and attain, young girls plan for whom they will achieve and attain.

Charlotte Perkins Gilman (1860–1935) US writer. *Women and Economics*, Ch. 5

10 A woman needs a man like a fish needs a bicycle.

Graffiti

11 Mother is the dead heart of the family, spending father's earnings on consumer goods to enhance the environment in which he eats, sleeps and watches the television.

Germaine Greer (1939–) Australian-born British writer and feminist. *The Female Eunuch*

12 Women fail to understand how much men hate them.

Germaine Greer *The Female Eunuch*

13 You can now see the Female Eunuch the world over…Wherever you see nail varnish, lipstick, brassieres, and high heels, the Eunuch has set up her camp.

Germaine Greer *The Female Eunuch*

14 I know you do not make the laws but I also know that you are the wives and mothers, the sisters and daughters of those who do.

Angelina Grimké (1805–79) US writer and reformer. *The Anti-Slavery Examiner* (Sep 1836), 'Appeal to the Christian Women of the South'

15 …the emancipation of women is practically the greatest egoistic movement of the nineteenth century, and the most intense affirmation of the right of the self that history has yet seen…

Ellen Key (Karolina Sofia Key; 1849–1926) Swedish writer. *The Century of the Child*, Ch. 2

16 Can anything be more absurd than keeping women in a state of ignorance, and yet so vehemently to insist on their resisting temptation?

Vicesimus Knox (1752–1821) British essayist. *Liberal Education*, Vol. I, 'On the Literary Education of Women'

17 It is ironic that the wife who made Britain great again, and who is the leader of the Western World, has to get her husband to sign her tax form.

Jacqui Lait Referring to the British prime minister, Margaret Thatcher. Speech, Oct 1987

18 Other books have been written by men physicians…One would suppose in reading them that women possess but one class of physical organs, and that these are always diseased. Such teaching is pestiferous, and tends to cause and perpetuate the very evils it professes to remedy.

Mary Ashton Livermore (c. 1820–1905) US writer. *What Shall We Do with Our Daughters?*, Ch. 2

19 I'm furious about the Women's Liberationists. They keep getting up on soapboxes and proclaiming that women are brighter than men. That's true, but it should be kept very quiet or it ruins the whole racket.

Anita Loos (1891–1981) US novelist. *The Observer*, 'Sayings of the Year', 30 Dec 1973

20 …is it to be understood that the principles of the Declaration of Independence bear no relation to half of the human race?

Harriet Martineau (1802–76) British writer. *Society in America*, Vol. III, 'Marriage'

21 The only way a woman can marry now is to agree to become a charwoman, regardless of her education and skills.

Margaret Mead (1901–78) US anthropologist.

22 The most important thing women have to do is to stir up the zeal of women themselves.

John Stuart Mill (1806–73) British philosopher. Letter to Alexander Bain, 14 July 1869

23 ...the rumblings of women's liberation are only one pointer to the fact that you already have a discontented work force. And if conditions continue to lag so far behind the industrial norm and the discomfort increases, you will find...that you will end up with an inferior product.

Elaine Morgan (1920–) British writer. *The Descent of Woman*, Ch. 11

24 In both fiction and non-fiction, women are making their voices heard. My interpretation of women's rights in Islam, like that of countless other Muslim-born feminists, clashes strongly with the conservative, official interpretation.

Taslima Nasreen (1958–) Bangladeshi writer. *The Times*, 18 June 1994

25 No *man*, not even a doctor, ever gives any other definition of what a nurse should be than this – "devoted and obedient." This definition would do just as well for a porter. It might even do for a horse. It would not do for a policeman.

Florence Nightingale (1820–1910) British nurse. *Notes on Nursing*

26 The vote, I thought, means nothing to women. We should be armed.

Edna O'Brien (1936–) Irish novelist. Quoted as epigraph to *Fear of Flying* (Erica Jong), Ch. 16

27 ...if civilisation is to advance at all in the future, it must be through the help of women, women freed of their political shackles, women with full power to work their will in society. It was rapidly becoming clear to my mind that men regarded women as a servant class in the community, and that women were going to remain in the servant class until they lifted themselves out of it.

Emmeline Pankhurst (1858–1928) British suffragette. *My Own Story*

28 Women had always fought for men, and for their children. Now they were ready to fight for their own human rights. Our militant movement was established.

Emmeline Pankhurst *My Own Story*

29 We have taken this action, because as women... we realize that the condition of our sex is so deplorable that it is our duty even to break the law in order to call attention to the reasons why we do so.

Emmeline Pankhurst Speech in court, 21 Oct 1908. *Shoulder to Shoulder* (ed. Midge Mackenzie)

30 Lesbian is a label invented by the man to throw at any woman who dares to be his equal, who dares to challenge his prerogatives...who dares to assert the primacy of her own needs.

Radicalesbians (a political activist group) *The Woman-Identified Woman*

31 So – against odds, the women inch forward, but I'm rather old to be carrying on this fight!

Eleanor Roosevelt (1884–1962) US First Lady, government official, writer, humanitarian, and lecturer. Letter to Joseph P. Lash, 13 Feb 1946

32 The prolonged slavery of women is the darkest page in human history.

Elizabeth Stanton (1815–1902) US suffragette. *History of Woman Suffrage* (with Susan B. Anthony and Mathilda Gage), Vol. I

33 Womanhood is the great fact in her life; wifehood and motherhood are but incidental relations.

Elizabeth Stanton *History of Woman Suffrage* (with Susan B. Anthony and Mathilda Gage), Vol. I

34 *Declaration of Sentiments:*...We hold these truths to be self-evident: that all men and women are created equal...

Elizabeth Stanton *History of Woman Suffrage* (with Susan B. Anthony and Mathilda Gage), Vol. I

35 Men *would* support us (the feminists) we are told, if only we learned how to ask for their support in the right way. It's a subtle and effective way of blaming the victim.

Gloria Steinem (1934–) US writer and feminist. *Outrageous Acts and Everyday Rebellions*

36 People call me a feminist whenever I express sentiments that differentiate me from a doormat or a prostitute.

Rebecca West (Cicely Isabel Fairfield; 1892–1983) British novelist and journalist. Attrib.

37 I think a lot of the women's lib movement came from the war. The women who were growing up then are the mothers of today, and I'm sure they've been affected by the fact that their mothers worked then.

Mary Wolfard British radio journalist. *Don't You Know There's a War On?* (Jonathan Croall)

38 Women have always been the guardians of wisdom and humanity which makes them natural, but usually secret, rulers. The time has come for them to rule openly, but together with and not against men.

Charlotte Wolff (1904–86) German-born British writer. *Bisexuality: A Study*, Ch. 2

39 The *divine right* of husbands, like the divine right of kings, may, it is hoped, in this enlightened age, be contested without danger.

Mary Wollstonecraft (1759–97) British writer. *A Vindication of the Rights of Woman*, Ch. 3

40 I do not wish them to have power over men; but over themselves.

Mary Wollstonecraft Referring to women. *A Vindication of the Rights of Woman*, Ch. 4

41 A king is always a king – and a woman always a woman: his authority and her sex ever stand between them and rational converse.

Mary Wollstonecraft *A Vindication of the Rights of Woman*, Ch. 4

42 Women have served all these centuries as looking-glasses possessing the magic and delicious power of reflecting the figure of man at twice its natural size.

Virginia Woolf (1882–1941) British novelist. *A Room of One's Own*

Those against

43 There is a tide in the affairs of women,
Which, taken at the flood, leads – God knows where.

Lord Byron (1788–1824) British poet. Byron is parodying Brutus's speech from Shakespeare's *Julius Caesar* (IV:3). *Don Juan*, VI

44 Nothing would induce me to vote for giving women the franchise. I am not going to be henpecked into a question of such importance.

Winston Churchill (1874–1965) British statesman. *The Amazing Mr Churchill* (Robert Lewis Taylor)

45 The great question...which I have not been able to answer, despite my thirty years of research into the feminine soul, is 'What does a woman want'?

Sigmund Freud (1856–1939) Austrian psychoanalyst. *Psychiatry in American Life* (Charles Rolo)

46 The First Blast of the Trumpet Against the Monstrous Regiment of Women.

John Knox (c. 1514–72) Scottish religious reformer. Title of Pamphlet, 1558

47 Women's Liberation is just a lot of foolishness. It's the men who are discriminated against. They can't bear children. And no one's likely to do anything about that.

Golda Meir (1898–1978) Russian-born Israeli stateswoman. Attrib.

48 The only good thing about Hammerfall, women's lib was dead milliseconds after Hammerstrike.

Larry Niven (1938–) US science-fiction writer. 'Hammerfall' was a fictional collision in the late 1970s between the Earth and a large comet that destroyed civilization. *Lucifer's Hammer*, Pt. III (with Jerry Pournelle)

49 The rights of women who demand,
Those women are but few:
The greater part had rather staid
Exactly as they do.
Beauty has claims for which she fights
At ease with winning arms;
The women who want women's rights
Want mostly, women's charms.

Punch, 1870

50 Give women the vote, and in five years there will be a crushing tax on bachelors.

George Bernard Shaw (1856–1950) Irish dramatist and critic. *Man and Superman*, Preface

51 The Queen is most anxious to enlist every one who can speak or write to join in checking this mad, wicked folly of 'Woman's Rights', with all its attendant horrors, on which her poor feeble sex is bent, forgetting every sense of womanly feeling and propriety.

Victoria (1819–1901) Queen of the United Kingdom. Letter to Sir Theodore Martin, 29 May 1870

52 The thought could not be avoided that the best home for a feminist was in another person's lab.

James Dewey Watson (1928–) US geneticist. *The Double Helix*, Ch. 2

...and a final word

53 The battle for women's rights has been largely won.

Margaret Thatcher (1925–) British politician and prime minister. *The Guardian*, 1982

54 I do, and I also wash and iron them.

Denis Thatcher (1915–) British businessman married to Margaret Thatcher. Replying to the question 'Who wears the pants in this house?' *The Los Angeles Times*, 21 Apr 1981

55 We are in the midst of a violent backlash against feminism that uses images of female beauty as a political weapon against women's advancement: the beauty myth.

Naomi Wolf US writer. *The Beauty Myth*

56 WOMEN'S RIGHTS NOW!

Followed by
Yes Dear.

Exchange of graffiti

FICTION

See also books, literature, novels, writing

1 Science fiction is no more written for scientists than ghost stories are written for ghosts.

Brian Aldiss (1925–) British science-fiction writer. *Penguin Science Fiction*, Introduction

2 Drunk in charge of a narrative.

Angela Carter (1940–92) British novelist. *Wise Children*

3 Sometimes I don't know whether Zelda and I are real or whether we are characters in one of my novels.

F. Scott Fitzgerald (1896–1940) US novelist. Said of himself and his wife. *A Second Flowering* (Malcolm Cowley)

4 There are many reasons why novelists write, but they all have one thing in common – a need to create an alternative world.

John Fowles (1926–) British novelist. *The Sunday Times Magazine*, 2 Oct 1977

5 Cynics have claimed there are only six basic plots, Frankenstein and My Fair Lady are really the same story.

Leslie Halliwell (1929–89) British film consultant. *Filmgoer's Book of Quotes*, 1973

6 Casting my mind's eye over the whole of fiction, the only absolutely original creation I can think of is Don Quixote.

W. Somerset Maugham (1874–1965) British novelist. *10 Novels and Their Authors*, Ch. 1

7 Contentment and fulfilment don't make for very good fiction.

Joanna Trollope (1943–) British writer. *The Times*, 25 June 1994

FIELDING, HENRY

(1707–54) British novelist and dramatist. He wrote some 25 plays and the novels *Joseph Andrews* (1742), *Jonathan Wild* (1743), and *Tom Jones* (1749).

1 It hath been often said, that it is not death, but dying, which is terrible.

Amelia, Bk. III, Ch. 4

2 These are called the pious frauds of friendship.
Amelia, Bk. III, Ch. 4

3 When widows exclaim loudly against second marriages, I would always lay a wager, that the man, if not the wedding-day, is absolutely fixed on.
Amelia, Bk. VI, Ch. 8

4 One fool at least in every married couple.
Amelia, Bk. IX, Ch. 4

5 I am as sober as a Judge.
Don Quixote in England, III:14

6 Oh! The roast beef of England.
And old England's roast beef.
The Grub Street Opera, III:3

7 Never trust the man who hath reason to suspect that you know he hath injured you.
Jonathan Wild, Bk. III, Ch. 4

8 He in a few minutes ravished this fair creature, or at least would have ravished her, if she had not, by a timely compliance, prevented him.
Jonathan Wild, Bk. III, Ch. 7

9 For clergy are men as well as other folks.
Joseph Andrews, Bk. II, Ch. 6

10 Public schools are the nurseries of all vice and immorality.
Joseph Andrews, Bk. III, Ch. 5

11 What is commonly called love, namely the desire of satisfying a voracious appetite with a certain quantity of delicate white human flesh.
Tom Jones, Bk. VI, Ch. 1

12 His designs were strictly honourable, as the phrase is; that is, to rob a lady of her fortune by way of marriage.
Tom Jones, Bk. XI, Ch. 4

13 Composed that monstrous animal a husband and wife.
Tom Jones, Bk. XV, Ch. 9

14 All Nature wears one universal grin.
Tom Thumb the Great, I:1

FIGHT

1 And did those feet in ancient time
Walk upon England's mountains green?
And was the holy lamb of God
On England's pleasant pastures seen?
...
I will not cease from mental fight,
Nor shall my sword sleep in my hand,
Till we have built Jerusalem
In England's green and pleasant land.
William Blake (1757–1827) British poet. Better known as the hymn 'Jerusalem', with music by Sir Hubert Parry; not to be confused with Blake's longer poem *Jerusalem*. *Milton*, Preface

FIRE

1 All things, oh priests, are on fire...The eye is on fire; forms are on fire; eye-consciousness is on fire; impressions received by the eye are on fire.
Buddha (Gautama Siddhartha; c. 563–c. 483 BC) Indian religious teacher and founder of Buddhism. *The Fire Sermon*

FIRST IMPRESSIONS

1 First impressions are the most lasting.
Proverb

2 First feelings are always the most natural.
Louis XIV (1638–1715) French king. Repeated by Mme de Sévigné.

3 Who ever loved, that loved not at first sight?
Christopher Marlowe (1564–93) English dramatist. *Hero and Leander*, I

4 Mistrust first impulses, they are nearly always good.
Talleyrand (Charles Maurice de Talleyrand-Périgord; 1754–1838) French politician. Sometimes attrib. to Count Montrond. Attrib.

FISHING

See also sport and games

1 Fly fishing may be a very pleasant amusement; but angling or float fishing I can only compare to a stick and a string, with a worm at one end and a fool at the other.
Samuel Johnson (1709–84) British lexicographer. Attrib. in *Instructions to Young Sportsmen* (Hawker)

2 Angling is somewhat like poetry, men are to be born so.
Izaak Walton *The Compleat Angler*, Ch. 1

3 Angling may be said to be so like the mathematics, that it can never be fully learnt.
Izaak Walton *The Compleat Angler*, Epistle to the Reader

4 We may say of angling as Dr Boteler said of strawberries, 'Doubtless God could have made a better berry, but doubtless God never did.'
Izaak Walton *The Compleat Angler*, Ch. 5

5 Let the blessing of St Peter's Master be...upon all that are lovers of virtue; and dare trust in His providence; and be quiet; and go a-Angling.
Izaak Walton *The Compleat Angler*, Ch. 21

FITZGERALD, EDWARD

(1809–83) British poet and translator. His translation of *The Rubáiyát of Omar Khayyám* was a free adaption of the 12th-century Persian original.

1 Taste is the feminine of genius.
Letter to J. R. Lowell, Oct 1877

2 Awake! for Morning in the Bowl of Night
Has flung the Stone that puts the Stars to Flight:
And Lo! the Hunter of the East has caught
The Sultan's Turret in a Noose of Light.
The Rubáiyát of Omar Khayyám (1st edn.), I

3 Come, fill the Cup, and in the Fire of Spring
The Winter Garment of Repentance fling:

The Bird of Time has but a little way
To fly – and Lo! the Bird is on the Wing.

The Rubáiyát of Omar Khayyám (1st edn.), VII

4 The Wine of Life keeps oozing drop by drop,
The Leaves of Life keep falling one by one.

The Rubáiyát of Omar Khayyám (4th edn.), VIII

5 Here with a Loaf of Bread beneath the Bough,
A Flask of Wine, a Book of Verse – and Thou
Beside me singing in the Wilderness –
And Wilderness is Paradise enow.

The Rubáiyát of Omar Khayyám (1st edn.), XI

6 Ah, take the Cash in hand and waive the Rest;
Oh, the brave Music of a *distant* Drum!

The Rubáiyát of Omar Khayyám (1st edn.), XII

7 The Worldly Hope men set their Hearts upon
Turns Ashes – or it prospers; and anon,
Like Snow upon the Desert's dusty face,
Lighting a little Hour or two – is gone.

The Rubáiyát of Omar Khayyám (1st edn.), XIV

8 I sometimes think that never blows so red
The Rose as where some buried Caesar bled;
That every Hyacinth the Garden wears
Dropt in her Lap from some once lovely Head.

The Rubáiyát of Omar Khayyám (1st edn.), XVIII

9 Ah, my Belovéd, fill the Cup that clears
TO-DAY of past Regrets and Future Fears:
To-morrow! – Why, To-morrow I may be
Myself with Yesterday's Sev'n thousand Years.

The Rubáiyát of Omar Khayyám (1st edn.), XX

10 One thing is certain, that Life flies;
One thing is certain, and the Rest is Lies;
The Flower that once has blown for ever dies.

The Rubáiyát of Omar Khayyám (1st edn.), XXVI

11 I came like Water, and like Wind I go.

The Rubáiyát of Omar Khayyám (1st edn.), XXVIII

12 Ah, fill the Cup: – what boots it to repeat
How Time is slipping underneath our Feet:
Unborn TOMORROW, and dead YESTERDAY,
Why fret about them if TODAY be sweet!

The Rubáiyát of Omar Khayyám (1st edn.), XXXVII

13 'Tis all a Chequer-board of Nights and Days
Where Destiny with Men for Pieces plays:
Hither and thither moves, and mates, and slays,
And one by one back in the Closet lays.

The Rubáiyát of Omar Khayyám (1st edn.), XLIX

14 The Moving Finger writes; and, having writ,
Moves on: nor all thy Piety nor Wit
Shall lure it back to cancel half a Line,
Nor all thy Tears wash out a Word of it.

The Rubáiyát of Omar Khayyám (1st edn.), LI

15 And that inverted Bowl we call The Sky,
Whereunder crawling coop't we live and die,
Lift not thy hands to *It* for help – for It
Rolls impotently on as Thou or I.

The Rubáiyát of Omar Khayyám (1st edn.), LII

16 'Who *is* the Potter, pray, and who the Pot?'

The Rubáiyát of Omar Khayyám (1st edn.), LX

17 Strange, is it not? that of the myriads who
Before us pass'd the door of Darkness through,
Not one returns to tell us of the Road,
Which to discover we must travel too.

The Rubáiyát of Omar Khayyám (4th edn.), LXIV

18 Drink! for you know not whence you came, nor why:
Drink! for you know not why you go, nor where.

The Rubáiyát of Omar Khayyám (4th edn.), LXXIV

FITZGERALD, F. SCOTT

(1896–1940) US novelist. His first successful novel was the autobiographical *This Side of Paradise* (1920). This was followed by *The Great Gatsby* (1925) and *Tender is the Night* (1934) before he declined into alcoholism.

Quotations about Fitzgerald

1 Fitzgerald was an alcoholic, a spendthrift and a superstar playboy possessed of a beauty and a glamour that only a Byron could support without artistic ruination.

Anthony Burgess (John Burgess Wilson; 1917–93) British novelist and critic. *The Observer*, 7 Feb 1982

2 The poor son-of-a-bitch!

Dorothy Parker (1893–1967) US writer. Quoting from *The Great Gatsby* on paying her last respects to Fitzgerald. *Thalberg: Life and Legend* (B. Thomas)

Quotations by Fitzgerald

3 In the real dark night of the soul it is always three o'clock in the morning.

See ST JOHN OF THE CROSS. *The Crack-Up*

4 Though the Jazz Age continued, it became less and less an affair of youth. The sequel was like a children's party taken over by the elders.

The Crack-Up

5 FITZGERALD. The rich are different from us.
HEMINGWAY. Yes, they have more money.

The Crack-Up, 'Notebooks, E'

6 I entertained on a cruising trip that was so much fun that I had to sink my yacht to make my guests go home.

The Crack-Up, 'Notebooks, K'

7 One of those men who reach such an acute limited excellence at twenty-one that everything afterward savours of anti-climax.

The Great Gatsby, Ch. 1

8 I was one of the few guests who had actually been invited. People were not invited – they went there.

The Great Gatsby, Ch. 3

9 One girl can be pretty – but a dozen are only a chorus.

The Last Tycoon

10 He differed from the healthy type that was essentially middle-class – he never seemed to perspire.

This Side of Paradise, Bk. I, Ch. 2

11 Beware of the artist who's an intellectual also. The artist who doesn't fit.

This Side of Paradise, Bk. II, Ch. 5

12 'I know myself,' he cried, 'but that is all.'
This Side of Paradise, Bk. II, Ch. 5

13 A big man has no time really to do anything but just sit and be big.
This Side of Paradise, Bk. III, Ch. 2

14 First you take a drink, then the drink takes a drink, then the drink takes you.
Ackroyd (Jules Feiffer), '1964, May 7'

15 Sometimes I don't know whether Zelda and I are real or whether we are characters in one of my novels.
Said of himself and his wife. *A Second Flowering* (Malcolm Cowley)

16 All good writing is *swimming under water* and holding your breath.
Letter to Frances Scott Fitzgerald

FLATTERY

See also compliments, insincerity, praise, servility

1 Imitation is the sincerest form of flattery.
Proverb

2 It is happy for you that you possess the talent of flattering with delicacy. May I ask whether these pleasing attentions proceed from the impulse of the moment, or are the result of previous study?
Jane Austen (1775–1817) British novelist. *Pride and Prejudice*, Ch. 14

3 A rich man's joke is always funny.
Thomas Edward Brown (1830–97) British poet. *The Doctor*

4 Every woman is infallibly to be gained by every sort of flattery, and every man by one sort or other.
Earl of Chesterfield (1694–1773) English statesman. Letter to his son, 16 Mar 1752

5 Madam, before you flatter a man so grossly to his face, you should consider whether or not your flattery is worth his having.
Samuel Johnson (1709–84) British lexicographer. *Diary and Letters* (Mme D'Arblay), Vol. I, Ch. 2

6 Be advised that all flatterers live at the expense of those who listen to them.
Jean de La Fontaine (1621–95) French poet. *Fables*, I, 'Le Corbeau et le Renard'

7 It is always pleasant to be urged to do something on the ground that one can do it well.
George Santayana (1863–1952) US philosopher. *Letters*

8 I will praise any man that will praise me.
William Shakespeare (1564–1616) English dramatist. *Antony and Cleopatra*, II:6

9 He that loves to be flattered is worthy o' the flatterer.
William Shakespeare *Timon of Athens*, I:1

10 Flattery is all right so long as you don't inhale.
Adlai Stevenson (1900–65) US statesman. Attrib.

11 'Tis an old maxim in the schools,
That flattery's the food of fools;
Yet now and then your men of wit
Will condescend to take a bit.
Jonathan Swift (1667–1745) Irish-born Anglican priest and writer. *Cadenus and Vanessa*

FLEMING, SIR ALEXANDER

(1881–1955) British microbiologist. He shared a Nobel prize in 1945 for his discovery of the antibiotic penicillin.

Quotations about Fleming

1 'Pain in the mind' was not the spur that drove him to do research...but rather an urge to do a job better than the next man. Competition was the breath of life to him.
Leonard Colebrook (1883–1967) British medical researcher. *Biographical Memoirs of Fellows of the Royal Society*

2 The catalogue of Fleming's published work leaves little room for doubt that he had to an unusual degree the almost intuitive faculty for original observation coupled with a high degree of technical inventiveness and skill. He had in fact most of the qualities that make a great scientist: an innate curiosity and perceptiveness regarding natural phenomena, insight into the heart of a problem, technical ingenuity, persistence in seeing a job through and that physical and mental toughness that is essential to the top-class investigator.
R. Cruickshank. *Journal of Pathology and Bacteriology*, 1956

Quotations by Fleming

3 I have been trying to point out that in our lives chance may have an astonishing influence and, if I may offer advice to the young laboratory worker, it would be this – never to neglect an extraordinary appearance or happening. It may be – usually is, in fact – a false alarm that leads to nothing, but it may on the other hand be the clue provided by fate to lead you to some important advance.
Lecture at Harvard

4 A good gulp of hot whisky at bedtime – it's not very scientific, but it helps.
When asked about a cure for colds. News summary, 22 Mar 1954

FLOWERS

See also gardens

1 She wore a wreath of roses,
The night that first we met.
Thomas Haynes Bayly (1797–1839) British writer. *She Wore a Wreath of Roses*

2 Just now the lilac is in bloom
All before my little room.
Rupert Brooke (1887–1915) British poet. *The Old Vicarage, Grantchester*

3 Unkempt about those hedges blows
An unofficial English rose.
Rupert Brooke *The Old Vicarage, Grantchester*

4 Tiptoe through the tulips with me.
Al Dubin (20th century) US songwriter. From the musical, *Gold Diggers of Broadway. Tiptoe Through the Tulips*

5 I sometimes think that never blows so red
The Rose as where some buried Caesar bled;

That every Hyacinth the Garden wears
Dropt in her Lap from some once lovely Head.

Edward Fitzgerald (1809–83) British poet. *The Rubáiyát of Omar Khayyám* (1st edn.), XVIII

6 Their smiles,
Wan as primroses gather'd at midnight
By chilly finger'd spring.

John Keats (1795–1821) British poet. *Endymion*, IV

7 Good God, I forgot the violets!

Walter Savage Landor (1775–1864) British poet and writer. Having thrown his cook out of an open window onto the flowerbed below. *Irreverent Social History* (F. Muir)

8 And I will make thee beds of roses
And a thousand fragrant posies.

Christopher Marlowe (1564–93) English dramatist. *The Passionate Shepherd to his Love*

9 Gather the flowers, but spare the buds.

Andrew Marvell (1621–78) English poet. *The Picture of Little T.C. in a Prospect of Flowers*

10 'Tis the last rose of summer
Left blooming alone;
All her lovely companions
Are faded and gone.

Thomas Moore (1779–1852) Irish poet. *Irish Melodies*, 'Tis the Last Rose'

11 Say it with flowers.

Patrick O'Keefe (1872–1934) US advertising agent. Slogan for Society of American Florists

12 They are for prima donnas or corpses – I am neither.

Arturo Toscanini (1867–1957) Italian conductor. Refusing a floral wreath at the end of a performance. *The Elephant that Swallowed a Nightingale* (C. Galtey)

13 But as we went along there were more and yet more and there at last under the boughs of the trees, we saw that there was a long belt of them along the shore, about the breadth of a country turnpike road. I never saw daffodils so beautiful they grew among the mossy stones about and about them, some rested their heads upon these stones as on pillow for weariness and the rest tossed and reeled and danced and seemed as if they verily laughed with the wind that blew upon them over the lake.

Dorothy Wordsworth (1771–1855) British diarist and sister of the poet, William Wordsworth. *The Grasmere Journals*, 15 Apr 1802

14 Thou unassuming common-place
Of Nature.

William Wordsworth (1770–1850) British poet. *To the Daisy*

15 I wandered lonely as a cloud
That floats on high o'er vales and hills,
When all at once I saw a crowd,
A host, of golden daffodils.

William Wordsworth *I Wandered Lonely as a Cloud*

FLYING

See also travel

1 From the point of view of sexual morality the aeroplane is valuable in war in that it destroys men and women in equal numbers.

Ernest William Barnes (1874–1953) British clergyman and mathematician. *Rise of Christianity*

2 Of course I realized there was a measure of danger. Obviously I faced the possibility of not returning when first I considered going. Once faced and settled there really wasn't any good reason to refer to it.

Amelia Earhart (1898–1937) US flyer. Referring to her flight in the 'Friendship'. *20 Hours: 40 Minutes – Our Flight in the Friendship*, Ch. 5

3 Had I been a man I might have explored the Poles or climbed Mount Everest, but as it was my spirit found outlet in the air....

Amy Johnson (1903–41) British flyer. *Myself When Young* (ed. Margot Asquith)

4 I feel about airplanes the way I feel about diets. It seems to me that they are wonderful things for other people to go on.

Jean Kerr (1923–) US dramatist. *The Snake Has All the Lines*, 'Mirror, Mirror, on the Wall'

5 A man with wings large enough and duly attached might learn to overcome the resistance of the air, and conquering it succeed in subjugating it and raise himself upon it.

Leonardo da Vinci (1452–1519) Italian artist. *Flight of Birds*

6 There are only two emotions in a plane: boredom and terror.

Orson Welles (1915–85) US film actor. *The Observer*, 'Sayings of the Week', 12 May 1985

7 Nor law, nor duty bade me fight,
Nor public men, nor cheering crowds,
A lonely impulse of delight
Drove to this tumult in the clouds;
I balanced all, brought all to mind,
The years to come seemed waste of breath,
A waste of breath the years behind
In balance with this life, this death.

W. B. Yeats (1865–1939) Irish poet. *An Irish Airman Foresees his Death*

FOOD

See also etiquette, greed, obesity

1 A meal without flesh is like feeding on grass.

Proverb

2 An apple-pie without some cheese is like a kiss without a squeeze.

Proverb

3 Bread is the staff of life.

Proverb

4 Eat to live and not live to eat.

Proverb

5 The nearer the bone, the sweeter the flesh.

Proverb

6 I always eat peas with honey
I've done it all my life,
They do taste kind of funny,
But it keeps them on the knife.

Anonymous *Peas*

7 There is no such thing as a free lunch.

Anonymous Often attributed to the US economist, Milton Friedman.

8 Carnation milk is the best in the land;
Here I sit with a can in my hand –
No tits to pull, no hay to pitch,
You just punch a hole in the son of a bitch.

Anonymous Referring to a brand of canned milk.

9 'Tis not *her* coldness, father,
That chills my labouring breast;
It's that confounded cucumber
I've eat and can't digest.

R. H. Barham ('Thomas Ingoldsby') (1788–1845) British humorous writer. *The Ingoldsby Legends*, 'The Confession'

10 'Oh, my Friends, be warned by me,
That Breakfast, Dinner, Lunch and Tea
Are all the Human Frame requires...'
With that the Wretched Child expires.

Hilaire Belloc (1870–1953) French-born British poet. *Cautionary Tales*, 'Henry King'

11 The Chief Defect of Henry King
Was chewing little bits of String.

Hilaire Belloc *Cautionary Tales*, 'Henry King'

12 I know what I wanted to ask you;
Is trifle sufficient for sweet?

John Betjeman (1906–84) British poet. *How to get on in Society*

13 And when the children of Israel saw it, they said one to another, It is manna: for they wist not what it was. And Moses said unto them, This is the bread which the Lord hath given you to eat.

Bible: Exodus 16:15

14 There is a lad here, which hath five barley loaves, and two small fishes: but what are they among so many?
And Jesus said, Make the men sit down. Now there was much grass in the place. So the men sat down, in number about five thousand.

Bible: John 6:9–10

15 Your fathers did eat manna in the wilderness, and are dead.
This is the bread which cometh down from heaven, that a man may eat thereof, and not die.
I am the living bread which came down from heaven: if any man eat of this bread, he shall live for ever: and the bread that I will give is my flesh, which I will give for the life of the world.

Bible: John 6:49–51

16 EAT, v.i. To perform successively (and successfully) the functions of mastication, humectation, and deglutition.

Ambrose Bierce (1842–c. 1914) US writer and journalist. *The Devil's Dictionary*

17 I'm a man
More dined against than dining.

Maurice Bowra (1898–1971) British scholar. Echoing King Lear's 'I am a man more sinn'd against than sinning.' (III:2). *Summoned by Bells* (J. Betjeman)

18 A good Kitchen is a good Apothicaries shop.

William Bullein (d. 1576) *The Bulwark Against All Sickness*

19 Some hae meat, and canna eat,
And some wad eat that want it,
But we hae meat and we can eat,
And sae the Lord be thankit.

Robert Burns (1759–96) Scottish poet. *The Selkirk Grace*

20 The Queen of Hearts, she made some tarts,
All on a summer day:
The Knave of Hearts, he stole those tarts,
And took them quite away!

Lewis Carroll (Charles Lutwidge Dodgson; 1832–98) British writer. *Alice's Adventures in Wonderland*, Ch. 11

21 Soup of the evening, beautiful Soup!

Lewis Carroll Said by the Mock Turtle. *Alice's Adventures in Wonderland*, Ch. 10

22 The right diet directs sexual energy into the parts that matter.

Barbara Cartland (1902–) British romantic novelist. Remark, Jan 1981

23 Don't eat too many almonds; they add weight to the breasts.

Colette (1873–1954) French novelist. *Gigi*

24 Do you *know* what breakfast cereal is made of? It's made of all those little curly wooden shavings you find in pencil sharpeners!

Roald Dahl (1916–90) British writer. *Charlie and the Chocolate Factory*, Ch. 27

25 It's a very odd thing –
As odd as can be –
That whatever Miss T eats
Turns into Miss T.

Walter de la Mare (1873–1956) British poet. *Miss T*

26 A good eater must be a good man; for a good eater must have a good digestion, and a good digestion depends upon a good conscience.

Benjamin Disraeli, Lord Beaconsfield (1804–81) British statesman. *The Young Duke*

27 Bouillabaisse is only good because cooked by the French, who, if they cared to try, could produce an excellent and nutritious substitute out of cigar stumps and empty matchboxes.

Norman Douglas (1868–1952) British novelist. *Siren Land*, 'Rain on the Hills'

28 The winter evening settles down
With smell of steaks in passageways.

T. S. Eliot (1888–1965) US-born British poet and dramatist. *Preludes*

29 The way to a man's heart is through his stomach.

Fanny Fern (1811–72) US writer. *Willis Parton*

30 Oh! The roast beef of England.
And old England's roast beef.

Henry Fielding (1707–54) British novelist. *The Grub Street Opera*, III:3

31 First need in the reform of hospital management? That's easy! The death of all dietitians, and the resurrection of a French chef.

Martin H. Fischer (1879–1962) *Fischerisms* (Howard Fabing and Ray Marr)

32 With my little stick of Blackpool rock,
Along the Promenade I stroll.
It may be sticky but I never complain,
It's nice to have a nibble at it now and again.

George Formby (1905–61) British comedian. *With My Little Stick of Blackpool Rock*

33 I eat to live, to serve, and also, if it so happens, to enjoy, but I do not eat for the sake of enjoyment.

Mahatma Gandhi (Mohandas Karamchand Gandhi; 1869–1948) Indian national leader. Attrib.

34 Take your hare when it is cased…

Hannah Glasse (18th century) English writer. Often misquoted as 'First catch your hare'. *The Art of Cookery Made Plain and Easy*, Ch. 1

35 The best number for a dinner party is two – myself and a dam' good head waiter.

Nubar Gulbenkian (1896–1972) Turkish oil magnate. Attrib.

36 Food is so fundamental, more so than sexuality, aggression, or learning, that it is astounding to realize the neglect of food and eating in depth psychology.

James Hillman *Womansize* (Kim Chernin)

37 But one day, one cold winter's day,
He screamed out, 'Take the soup away!'

Heinrich Hoffman (1809–74) German writer. *Struwwelpeter*, 'Augustus'

38 The British hamburger thus symbolised, with savage neatness, the country's failure to provide its ordinary people with food which did anything more for them than sustain life.

Clive James (1939–) Australian-born writer and broadcaster. *Falling Towards England*, Ch.17

39 This was a good dinner enough, to be sure; but it was not a dinner to *ask* a man to.

Samuel Johnson (1709–84) British lexicographer. *Life of Johnson* (J. Boswell), Vol. I

40 It is as bad as bad can be: it is ill-fed, ill-killed, ill-kept, and ill-drest.

Samuel Johnson About the roast mutton at an inn. *Life of Johnson* (J. Boswell), Vol. IV

41 A cucumber should be well sliced, and dressed with pepper and vinegar, and then thrown out, as good for nothing.

Samuel Johnson *Tour to the Hebrides* (J. Boswell)

42 I hate a man who swallows it, affecting not to know what he is eating. I suspect his taste in higher matters.

Charles Lamb (1775–1834) British essayist. Referring to food. *Essays of Elia*, 'Grace before Meat'

43 Any two meals at a boarding-house are together less than two square meals.

Stephen Leacock (1869–1944) British-born Canadian economist and humorist. *Literary Lapses*, 'Boarding-House Geometry'

44 They dined on mince, and slices of quince,
Which they ate with a runcible spoon;
And hand in hand, on the edge of the sand,
They danced by the light of the moon.

Edward Lear (1812–88) British artist and writer. *The Owl and the Pussy-Cat*

45 Food is an important part of a balanced diet.

Fran Lebowitz (1950–) US writer. *Metropolitan Life*, 'Food for Thought and Vice Versa'

46 I told my doctor I get very tired when I go on a diet, so he gave me pep pills. Know what happened? I ate faster.

Joe E. Lewis

47 The Chinese do not draw any distinction between food and medicine.

Lin Yutang (1895–) *The Importance of Living*, Ch. 9, Sect. 7

48 You can't make a soufflé rise twice.

Alice Roosevelt Longworth (1884–1980) US hostess. Referring to Dewey's nomination, in 1948. Attrib.

49 This piece of cod passes all understanding.

Edwin Lutyens (1869–1944) British architect. Comment made in a restaurant. Attrib.

50 Many children are suffering from muesli-belt malnutrition.

Professor Vincent Marks British nutritionist. Remark, June 1986

51 To eat well in England you should have breakfast three times a day.

W. Somerset Maugham (1874–1965) British novelist. Attrib.

52 Kissing don't last: cookery do!

George Meredith (1828–1909) British novelist. *The Ordeal of Richard Feverel*, Ch. 28

53 One should eat to live, not live to eat.

Molière (Jean Baptiste Poquelin; 1622–73) French dramatist. *L'Avare*, III:2

54 Some breakfast food manufacturer hit upon the simple notion of emptying out the leavings of carthorse nosebags, adding a few other things like unconsumed portions of chicken layer's mash, and the sweepings of racing stables, packing the mixture in little bags and selling them in health food shops.

Frank Muir (1920–) British writer and broadcaster. *Upon My Word!*

55 An army marches on its stomach.

Napoleon I (Napoleon Bonaparte; 1769–1821) French emperor. Attrib.

56 Old Mother Hubbard
Went to the cupboard,
To fetch her poor dog a bone;
But when she got there
The cupboard was bare
And so the poor dog had none.

Nursery Rhyme *The Comic Adventures of Old Mother Hubbard and Her Dog*

57 I have often seen the King consume four plates of different soups, a whole pheasant, a partridge, a large plate of salad, two big slices of ham, a dish of mutton in garlic sauce, a plateful of pastries followed by fruit and hard-boiled eggs. The King and Monsieur greatly like hard-boiled eggs.

Duchess of Orleans (1652–1722) Sister-in-law to Louis XIV. Letter, c. 1682

58 I think I could eat one of Bellamy's veal pies.

William Pitt the Younger (1759–1806) British statesman. Last words. Attrib.

59 The vulgar boil, the learned roast an egg.

Alexander Pope (1688–1744) British poet. *Satires and Epistles of Horace Imitated*, Bk. II

60 To the old saying that man built the house but woman made of it a 'home' might be added the modern supplement that woman accepted cooking as a chore but man has made of it a recreation.

Emily Post (1873–1960) US writer. *Etiquette*, Ch. 34

61 Dinner at the Huntercombes' possessed 'only two dramatic features – the wine was a farce and the food a tragedy'.

Anthony Powell (1905–) British novelist. *A Dance to the Music of Time: The Acceptance World*, Ch. 4

62 Great restaurants are, of course, nothing but mouth-brothels. There is no point in going to them if one intends to keep one's belt buckled.

Frederic Raphael (1931–) British author. *The Sunday Times Magazine*, 25 Sep 1977

63 The thought of two thousand people crunching celery at the same time horrified me.

George Bernard Shaw (1856–1950) Irish dramatist and critic. Explaining why he had turned down an invitation to a vegetarian gala dinner. *The Greatest Laughs of All Time* (G. Lieberman)

64 Food is for eating, and good food is to be enjoyed…I think food is, actually, very beautiful in itself.

Delia Smith British cookery writer. *The Times*, 17 Oct 1990

65 Many's the long night I've dreamed of cheese – toasted, mostly.

Robert Louis Stevenson (1850–94) Scottish writer. Said by the castaway Ben Gunn. *Treasure Island*, Ch. 15

66 He was a bold man that first eat an oyster.

Jonathan Swift (1667–1745) Irish-born Anglican priest and writer. *Polite Conversation*, Dialogue 2

67 Kitchen Physic is the best Physic.

Jonathan Swift *Polite Conversation*, Dialogue 2

68 Illness isn't the only thing that spoils the appetite.

Ivan Turgenev (1818–83) Russian novelist and dramatist. *A Month in the Country*, IV

69 Cauliflower is nothing but cabbage with a college education.

Mark Twain (1835–1910) US writer. *Pudd'nhead Wilson's Calendar*

70 The ancient Egyptians used to set large cones of perfumed ointment, which must often have been made with olive oil, upon their heads at dinner parties; as the atmosphere warmed up the cones would gradually melt and deliciously drizzle scented oil down their hair and faces and over their bodies.

Margaret Visser South African writer. *Much Depends on Dinner*

71 Yes, cider and tinned salmon are the staple diet of the agricultural classes.

Evelyn Waugh (1903–66) British novelist. *Scoop*, Bk. I, Ch. 1

72 I saw him even now going the way of all flesh, that is to say towards the kitchen.

John Webster (1580–1625) English dramatist. *Westward Hoe*, II:2

73 You breed babies and you eat chips with everything.

Arnold Wesker (1932–) British dramatist. *Chips with Everything*, I:2

74 MOTHER: It's broccoli, dear.
CHILD: I say it's spinach, and I say the hell with it.

Elwyn Brooks White (1899–1985) US journalist and humorist. Cartoon caption

75 If I had the choice between smoked salmon and tinned salmon, I'd have it tinned. With vinegar.

Harold Wilson (1916–) British politician and prime minister. *The Observer*, 'Sayings of the Week,' 11 Nov 1962

FOOLISHNESS

See also gullibility, ignorance, stupidity, wisdom and foolishness

1 A fool and his money are soon parted.

Proverb

2 A fool at forty is a fool indeed.

Proverb

3 A fool believes everything.

Proverb

4 Better be a fool than a knave.

Proverb

5 Empty vessels make the greatest sound.

Proverb

6 Fools build houses, and wise men buy them.

Proverb

7 Fools live poor to die rich.

Proverb

8 There's no fool like an old fool.

Proverb

9 Give not that which is holy unto the dogs, neither cast ye your pearls before swine, lest they trample them under their feet, and turn again and rend you.

Bible: Matthew 7:6

10 Answer a fool according to his folly, lest he be wise in his own conceit.

Bible: Proverbs 26:5

11 The world is made up for the most part of fools and knaves.

Duke of Buckingham (1628–87) English politician. *To Mr Clifford, on his Humane Reason*

12 He's a muddle-headed fool, with frequent lucid intervals.

Miguel de Cervantes (1547–1616) Spanish novelist. Sancho Panza describing Don Quixote. *Don Quixote*, Pt. II, Ch. 18

13 The wisest fool in Christendom.

Henri IV (1553–1610) King of France. Referring to James I of England. Attrib.

14 Mix a little foolishness with your serious plans: it's lovely to be silly at the right moment.

Horace (Quintus Horatius Flaccus; 65–8 BC) Roman poet. *Odes*, IV

15 Fools are in a terrible, overwhelming majority, all the wide world over.

Henrik Ibsen (1828–1906) Norwegian dramatist. *An Enemy of the People*, IV

16 You cannot fashion a wit out of two half-wits.

Neil Kinnock (1942–) British politician. *The Times*, 1983

17 No creature smarts so little as a fool.

Alexander Pope (1688–1744) British poet. *Epistle to Dr. Arbuthnot*

18 LEAR. Dost thou call me fool, boy?

FOOL. All thy other titles thou hast given away; that thou was born with.

William Shakespeare (1564–1616) English dramatist. *King Lear*, I:4

19 The portrait of a blinking idiot.

William Shakespeare *The Merchant of Venice*, II:9

20 Lord, what fools these mortals be!

William Shakespeare *A Midsummer Night's Dream*, III:2

21 He was a bold man that first eat an oyster.

Jonathan Swift (1667–1745) Irish-born writer. Polite conversation, Dialogue 2

FOOTBALL

See also sport and games

1 Our company only sponsor the arts. I don't think Stenhousemuir could be regarded by any stretch of the imagination as artistic.

Anonymous Reply by a Prudential Insurance public relations officer when fans asked for sponsorship, following a series of advertisements featuring Stenhousemuir.

2 Professional football is no longer a game. It's a war. And it brings out the same primitive instincts that go back thousands of years.

Malcolm Allison British football manager. *The Observer*, 'Sayings of the Week', 14 Mar 1973

3 I do love cricket – it's so very English.

Sarah Bernhardt (Sarah Henriette Rosine Bernard; 1844–1923) French actress. On seeing a game of football. *Nijinsky* (R. Buckle)

4 The great fallacy is that the game is first and last about winning. It's nothing of the kind. The game is about glory. It's about doing things in style, with a flourish, about going out and beating the other lot, not waiting for them to die of boredom.

Danny Blanchflower (1926–93) British football player. *The Glory Game* (Hunter Davies)

5 One of the secrets of football is the simplicity of its laws.

Joseph Blatter FIFA Secretary. *FIFA News*, 1987

6 I'd like to apologise to all the fans who paid good money to watch that. If people are subjected to that kind of garbage every Saturday, the crowds will be down to 200. If that game is the future of British football. I want no part it.

Terry Butcher (1958–) British football manager. Following the defeat of Coventry City by Wimbledon – he managed Coventry City. *Comment in newspaper*, 1991

7 ...wherein is nothing but beastly fury and extreme violence, whereof proceedeth hurt; and consequently rancour and malice do remain with them that be wounded.

Thomas Elyot (?1450–1522) English diplomat. Referring to football. *Boke called the Governour*

8 No one ever taught me and I can't teach anyone. If you can't explain it, how can you take credit for it?

Red Grange (1903–) US football player. Referring to his talent for eluding tackles. Remark

9 The goal stands up, the keeper
Stands up to keep the goal.

A. E. Housman (1859–1936) British scholar and poet. *A Shropshire Lad*, 'Bredon Hill'

10 Winning isn't everything, but wanting to win is.

Vince Lombardi (1913–70) US football coach. Remark

11 The goal was scored a little bit by the hand of God and a little bit by the head of Maradona.

Diego Maradona (1960–) Argentinian soccer player. Referring to a goal he scored against England in the 1986 World Cup quarter-final; although scored illegally with the hand, the referee allowed it to stand. Interview after the game

12 In England, soccer is a grey game played by grey people on grey days.

Rodney Marsh (1944–) British football player. Describing football to an audience on Florida television, 1979.

13 I loathed the game...it was very difficult for me to show courage at it. Football, it seemed to me, is not really played for the pleasure of kicking a ball about, but is a species of fighting.

George Orwell (Eric Blair, 1903–50) British novelist. *Such, Such Were The Joys*

14 The streets were full of footballs.

Samuel Pepys (1633–1703) English diarist. *Diary*, 2 Jan 1665

15 A man who had missed the last home match of 't'United' had to enter social life on tiptoe in Bruddersford.

J. B. Priestley (1894–1984) British novelist and dramatist. *The Good Companions*

16 You play nineteen-twentieths of the game without the ball and that's when you do your thinking. That's when you do your real playing. Any clown can play with the ball when he's got it. It's the good fellows who get into position to receive.

Arthur Rowe (1906–93) British football manager. *The Encyclopedia of Association Football*, 1960

17 Football isn't a matter of life and death – it's much more important than that.

Bill Shankly (1914–81) British football manager. Attrib.

18 Footeball...causeth fighting, brawling, contention, quarrel picking, murder, homicide and great effusion of bloode, as daily experience teacheth.

Philip Stubbes (fl. 1583–91) English Puritan pamphleteer. *Anatomie of Abuses*

19 What they say about footballers being ignorant is rubbish. I spoke to a couple yesterday and they were quite intelligent.

Raquel Welch (Raquel Tejada; 1940–) US film star. After a visit to see Chelsea play in 1973. Attrib.

20 I will not permit thirty men to travel four hundred miles to agitate a bag of wind.

Andrew Dickson White (1832–1918) US educator. Refusing to allow the Cornell American football team to visit Michigan to play a match. *The People's Almanac* (D. Wallechinsky)

FORCE

See also oppression, power politics, violence

1 Do not remove a fly from your friend's forehead with a hatchet.

Anonymous Chinese proverb.

2 Force is not a remedy.

John Bright (1811–89) British radical politician. Speech, Birmingham, 16 Nov 1880

3 The use of force alone is but *temporary*. It may subdue for a moment; but it does not remove the necessity of subduing again: and a nation is not governed, which is perpetually to be conquered.

Edmund Burke (1729–97) British politician. *Speech on Conciliation with America* (House of Commons, 22 Mar 1775)

FOREIGNERS

1 I don't hold with abroad and think that foreigners speak English when our backs are turned.

Quentin Crisp (1910?–) British writer. *The Naked Civil Servant*, Ch. 4

2 Abroad is unutterably bloody and foreigners are fiends.

Nancy Mitford (1904–73) British writer. *The Pursuit of Love*, Ch. 15

3 People are not willing to be governed by those who do not speak their language.

Norman Tebbit (1931–) British politician. *The Observer*, 24 Nov 1991

4 Foreigners fooling about in others' civil wars are a menace. They excite baseless hope of a fair, lasting peace.

Woodrow Wyatt (1918–) British journalist and writer. *News of the World*, June 1993

FORGIVENESS

1 Forgive and forget.

Proverb

2 Even if someone throws a stone at you, respond with food.

Kazakh proverb *The Independent*, 29 Nov 1993

3 Once a woman has forgiven her man, she must not reheat his sins for breakfast.

Marlene Dietrich (Maria Magdalene von Losch; 1904–92) German-born film star. *Marlene Dietrich's ABC*

4 Forgive you? – Oh, of course, dear,
A dozen times a week!
We women were created
Forgiveness but to speak.

Ella Higginson (1862–1940) US poet, writer, and historian. 'Wearing Out Love'

5 She intended to forgive. Not to do so would be un-Christian; but did not intend to do so soon, nor forget how much she had to forgive.

Jessamyn West (c. 1902–) US writer. *The Friendly Perusation*, 'The Buried Leaf'

FORSTER, E. M.

(1879–1970) British novelist. His books include *Where Angels Fear to Tread* (1905), *A Room with a View* (1908), *Howard's End* (1910), and *A Passage to India* (1924).

1 The historian must have...some conception of how men who are not historians behave. Otherwise he will move in a world of the dead.

Abinger Harvest, 'Captain Edward Gibbon'

2 It is not that the Englishman can't feel – it is that he is afraid to feel. He has been taught at his public school that feeling is bad form. He must not express great joy or sorrow, or even open his mouth too wide when he talks – his pipe might fall out if he did.

Abinger Harvest, 'Notes on the English Character'

3 They go forth into it with well-developed bodies, fairly developed minds, and undeveloped hearts.

Referring to public schoolboys going into the world. *Abinger Harvest*, 'Notes on the English Character'

4 Works of art, in my opinion, are the only objects in the material universe to possess internal order, and that is why, though I don't believe that only art matters, I do believe in Art for Art's sake.

Art for Art's Sake

5 Yes – oh dear, yes – the novel tells a story.

Aspects of the Novel, Ch. 2

6 Creative writers are always greater than the causes that they represent.

Gide and George

7 Beethoven's Fifth Symphony is the most sublime noise that has ever penetrated into the ear of man.

Howard's End, Ch. 5

8 Death destroys a man, the idea of Death saves him.

Howard's End, Ch. 27

9 Only connect!

Howard's End, Epigraph

10 The so-called white races are really pinko-gray.

A Passage to India, Ch. 7

11 I hate the idea of causes, and if I had to choose between betraying my country and betraying my friend, I hope I should have the guts to betray my country.

Two Cheers for Democracy, 'What I Believe'

12 Spoon feeding in the long run teaches us nothing but the shape of the spoon.

The Observer, 'Sayings of the Week', 7 Oct 1951

FOWLES, JOHN

(1926–) British novelist. He made his name with such books as *The Collector* (1963), *The Magus* (1966), and *The French Lieutenant's Woman* (1969), all of which have been filmed. Later books include *Mantissa* (1982) and *A Maggot* (1985).

1 The most odious of concealed narcissisms – prayer.

The Aristos

2 In essence the Renaissance was simply the green end of one of civilization's hardest winters.

The French Lieutenant's Woman, Ch. 10

3 We all write poems; it is simply that poets are the ones who write in words.

The French Lieutenant's Woman, Ch. 19

4 There are many reasons why novelists write,

but they all have one thing in common – a need to create an alternative world.

The Sunday Times Magazine, 2 Oct 1977

FRANCE

See also Europe, French Revolution, Paris

1 All Gaul is divided into three parts.

Julius Caesar (100–44 BC) Roman general and statesman. *De Bello Gallico*, Vol. I, Ch. 1

2 France was a long despotism tempered by epigrams.

Thomas Carlyle (1795–1881) Scottish historian and essayist. *History of the French Revolution*, Pt. I, Bk. I, Ch. 1

3 They are short, blue-vested people who carry their own onions when cycling abroad, and have a yard which is 3.37 inches longer than other people's.

Alan Coren (1938–) British humorist and writer. *The Sanity Inspector*, 'All You Need to Know about Europe'

4 Calais should have done more to attract people once the tunnel opens, but the local authority is run by the Communists, and the Communists don't like the English. I can't for the life of me think why!

Cornille French businessman. Referring to the Channel Tunnel. *The Observer*, 1 May 1994

5 There's always something fishy about the French.

Noël Coward (1899–1973) British dramatist. *Conversation Piece*, I:6

6 Bouillabaisse is only good because cooked by the French, who, if they cared to try, could produce an excellent and nutritious substitute out of cigar stumps and empty matchboxes.

Norman Douglas (1868–1952) British novelist. *Siren Land*, 'Rain on the Hills'

7 The French will only be united under the threat of danger. Nobody can simply bring together a country that has 265 kinds of cheese.

Charles De Gaulle (1890–1970) French general and statesman. Speech, 1951

8 To all Frenchmen: France has lost a battle but France has not lost the war.

Charles De Gaulle (1890–1970) French general and statesman. Proclamation, June 1940

9 A revolutionary France would always rather win a war with General Hoche than lose it with Marshal Soubise.

Charles De Gaulle Speech, London, 1 Apr 1942

10 I hate the French because they are all slaves, and wear wooden shoes.

Oliver Goldsmith (1728–74) Irish-born British writer. *Essays*, 'Distresses of a Common Soldier'

11 The best thing I know between France and England is – the sea.

Douglas William Jerrold (1803–57) British dramatist. *Wit and Opinions of Douglas Jerrold*, 'The Anglo-French Alliance'

12 A Frenchman must be always talking, whether he knows anything of the matter or not; an Englishman is content to say nothing, when he has nothing to say.

Samuel Johnson (1709–84) British lexicographer. *Life of Johnson* (J. Boswell), Vol. IV

13 *Allons, enfants, de la patrie,*
Le jour de gloire est arrivé.
Come, children of our native land,
The day of glory has arrived.

Rouget de Lisle (Claude Joseph Rouget de Lisle; 1760–1836) French military engineer and composer. *La Marseillaise* (French national anthem)

14 Yet, who can help loving the land that has taught us
Six hundred and eighty-five ways to dress eggs?

Thomas Moore (1779–1852) Irish poet. *The Fudge Family in Paris*

15 France has more need of me than I have need of France.

Napoleon I (Napoleon Bonaparte; 1769–1821) French emperor. Speech, 31 Dec 1813

16 There's something Vichy about the French.

Ivor Novello (David Ivor Davies; 1893–1951) British actor, composer, and dramatist. *Ambrosia and Small Beer* (Edward Marsh), Ch. 4

17 A mademoiselle from Armenteers,
She hasn't been kissed for forty years,
Hinky, dinky, par-lee-voo.

Edward Rowland (20th century) British songwriter. Armentières was completely destroyed (1918) in World War I. *Mademoiselle from Armentières* (song)

18 They are a loyal, a gallant, a generous, an ingenious, and good-temper'd people as is under heaven – if they have a fault, they are too *serious.*

Laurence Sterne (1713–68) Irish-born British writer. *A Sentimental Journey*, 'The Character. Versailles'

19 I do not dislike the French from the vulgar antipathy between neighbouring nations, but for their insolent and unfounded airs of superiority.

Horace Walpole (1717–97) British writer. Letter to Hannah More, 14 Oct 1787

20 France is a country where the money falls apart in your hands and you can't tear the toilet paper.

Billy Wilder (Samuel Wilder; 1906–) Austrian-born US film director. Attrib.

FRANCE, ANATOLE

(Jacques Anatole François Thibault; 1844–1924) French poet, novelist, and critic. His verse collection *Poèmes Dorés* (1873) was followed by a number of novels, including *La Révolte des Anges* (1914). His *Histoire Contemporaine* comprises a series of books ending with *La Vie en Fleur* (1922).

1 It is only the poor who are forbidden to beg.

Crainquebille

2 To disarm the strong and arm the weak would be to change the social order which it's my job to preserve. Justice is the means by which established injustices are sanctioned.

Crainquebille

3 Man is so made that he can only find relaxation from one kind of labour by taking up another.

The Crime of Sylvestre Bonnard

4 The Arab who builds himself a hut out of the

marble fragments of a temple in Palmyra is more philosophical than all the curators of the museums in London, Munich or Paris.
The Crime of Sylvestre Bonnard

5 The wonder is, not that the field of the stars is so vast, but that man has measured it.
The Garden of Epicurus

6 Christianity has done a great deal for love by making a sin of it.
The Garden of Epicurus

7 A good critic is one who narrates the adventures of his mind among masterpieces.
The Literary Life, Preface

8 It was in the barbarous, gothic times when words had a meaning; in those days, writers expressed thoughts.
The Literary Life, 'M. Charles Morice'

9 The majestic egalitarianism of the law, which forbids rich and poor alike to sleep under bridges, to beg in the streets, and to steal bread.
The Red Lily, Ch. 7

10 It is only the poor who pay cash, and that not from virtue, but because they are refused credit.
A Cynic's Breviary (J. R. Solly)

FRANK, ANNE

(1929–45) German-Jewish girl, who fled with her family from Germany in 1933. While in hiding in a room in Amsterdam she wrote a diary covering the year 1942–43. The family were betrayed and she died in Belsen concentration camp.

Quotations about Frank

1 Her diary endures, full-blooded, unselfpitying, a perpetual reminder that the enormity of the Nazi crime amounted not to the abstraction of 'genocide' but the murder of six million individuals.
Simon Schama (1945–) British historian. *1000 Makers of the 20th Century*

2 Through her diary she remains the most vivid and poignant symbol of Jewish suffering in the 20th century.
Simon Schama (1945–) British historian. *1000 Makers of the 20th century*

Quotations by Frank

3 I soothe my conscience now with the thought that it is better for hard words to be on paper than that Mummy should carry them in her heart.
The Diary of a Young Girl, 2 Jan 1944

4 Mummy herself has told us that she looked upon us more as her friends than her daughters. Now that is all very fine, but still, a friend can't take a mother's place. I need my mother as an example which I can follow, I want to be able to respect her.
The Diary of a Young Girl, 15 Jan 1944

5 We all live with the objective of being happy; our lives are all different and yet the same.
The Diary of a Young Girl, 6 July 1944

6 Laziness may *appear* attractive, but work *gives* satisfaction.
The Diary of a Young Girl, 6 July 1944

7 Parents can only give good advice or put them on the right paths, but the final forming of a person's character lies in their own hands.
The Diary of a Young Girl, 15 July 1944

8 It was a terrible time through which I was living. The war raged about us, and nobody knew whether or not he would be alive the next hour.
Tales from the Secret Annexe, 'Fear', 25 Mar 1944

9 I felt nothing, nothing but fear; I could neither eat nor sleep – fear clawed at my mind and body and shook me.
Tales from the Secret Annexe, 'Fear', 25 Mar 1944

10 I must indeed, try hard to control the talking habit, but I'm afraid that little can be done, as my case is hereditary. My mother, too, is fond of chatting, and has handed this weakness down to me.
Tales from the Secret Annexe, 'A Geometry Lesson', 12 Aug 1943

FRANKLIN, BENJAMIN

(1706–90) US scientist and statesman. His experiments with a kite established the electrical nature of thunderstorms and enabled him to invent lightning conductors. As a diplomat in Paris he negotiated peace with Britain in 1783.

Quotations about Franklin

1 I succeed him; no one can replace him.
Thomas Jefferson (1743–1826) US statesman. Replying to the questions 'Is it you, sir, who replaces Dr Franklin?' Letter, 1791

2 A philosophical Quaker full of mean and thrift maxims.
John Keats (1795–1821) British poet. Letter, 14 Oct 1818

Quotations by Franklin

3 Remember that time is money.
Advice to a Young Tradesman

4 No nation was ever ruined by trade.
Essays, 'Thoughts on Commercial Subjects'

5 A little neglect may breed mischief,...for want of a nail, the shoe was lost; for want of a shoe the horse was lost; and for want of a horse the rider was lost.
Poor Richard's Almanac, Preface

6 Some are weather-wise, some are otherwise.
Poor Richard's Almanac

7 Three may keep a secret, if two of them are dead.
Poor Richard's Almanac

8 At twenty years of age, the will reigns; at thirty, the wit; and at forty, the judgement.
Poor Richard's Almanac

9 Dost thou love life? Then do not squander time, for that's the stuff life is made of.
Poor Richard's Almanac

10 Many a long dispute among divines may be thus abridged: It is so. It is not so. It is so. It is not so.
Poor Richard's Almanac

11 What is the use of a new-born child?
Response when asked the same question of a new invention. *Life and Times of Benjamin Franklin* (J. Parton), Pt. IV

12 Man is a tool-making animal.
Life of Johnson (J. Boswell), 7 Apr 1778

13 A lonesome man on a rainy day who does not know how to read.
On being asked what condition of man he considered the most pitiable. *Wit, Wisdom, and Foibles of the Great* (C. Shriner)

14 Here Skugg
Lies snug
As a bug
In a rug.
An epitaph for a squirrel, 'skug' being a dialect name for the animal. Letter to Georgiana Shipley, 26 Sept 1772

15 We must indeed all hang together, or most assuredly, we shall all hang separately.
Remark on signing the Declaration of Independence, 4 July 1776

16 There never was a good war or a bad peace.
Letter to Josiah Quincy, 11 Sept 1783

17 In this world nothing can be said to be certain but death and taxes.
Letter to Jean-Baptiste Leroy, 13 Nov 1789

18 The body of
Benjamin Franklin, printer,
(Like the cover of an old book,
Its contents worn out,
And stript of its lettering and gilding)
Lies here, food for worms!
Yet the work itself shall not be lost,
For it will, as he believed, appear once more
In a new
And more beautiful edition,
Corrected and amended
By its Author!
Suggestion for his own epitaph.

FRANKNESS

See also honesty, sincerity, truth

1 But of all plagues, good Heaven, thy wrath can send,
Save me, oh, save me, from the candid friend.
George Canning (1770–1827) British statesman. *New Morality*

2 I have two very cogent reasons for not printing any list of subscribers; – one, that I have lost all the names, – the other, that I have spent all the money.
Samuel Johnson (1709–84) British lexicographer. Referring to subscribers to his *Dictionary of the English Language. Life of Johnson* (J. Boswell), Vol. IV

3 I deny the lawfulness of telling a lie to a sick man for fear of alarming him. You have no business with consequences; you are to tell the truth. Besides, you are not sure what effect your telling him that he is in danger may have. It may bring his distemper to a crisis, and that may cure him. Of all lying, I have the greatest abhorrence of this, because I believe it has been frequently practised on myself.
Samuel Johnson *Life of Johnson* (J. Boswell)

4 The great consolation in life is to say what one thinks.
Voltaire (François-Marie Arouet; 1694–1778) French writer. Letter, 1765

5 On an occasion of this kind it becomes more than a moral duty to speak one's mind. It becomes a pleasure.
Oscar Wilde (1854–1900) Irish-born British dramatist. *The Importance of Being Earnest*, II

FREEDOM

See also human rights, imprisonment

1 Wilkes and Liberty.
Anonymous Slogan of the London mob

2 There is a wind of nationalism and freedom blowing round the world, and blowing as strongly in Asia as elsewhere.
Stanley Baldwin, 1st Earl of Bewdley (1867–1947) British Conservative prime minister. Speech, London, 4 Dec 1934

3 I am writing about the conflict between conscience and individual freedom…
Howard Barker (1946–) British playwright. *The Times*, 3 Jan 1990

4 I'll have a fling.
Francis Beaumont (1584–1616) English dramatist. *Rule a Wife and have a Wife*, III:5

5 My policy is to be able to take a ticket at Victoria Station and go anywhere I damn well please.
Ernest Bevin (1881–1951) British trade-union leader and politician. *The Spectator*, 20 Apr 1951

6 And the chief captain answered, With a great sum obtained I this freedom. And Paul said, But I was free born.
Bible: Acts 22:28

7 Conscience, I say, not thine own, but of the other: for why is my liberty judged of another man's conscience?
Bible: I Corinthians 10:29

8 So free we seem, so fettered fast we are!
Robert Browning (1812–89) British poet. *Andrea del Sarto*

9 Liberty, too, must be limited in order to be possessed.
Edmund Burke (1729–97) British politician. Letter to the Sheriffs of Bristol, 1777

10 Hereditary bondsmen! know ye not
Who would be free themselves must strike the blow?
Lord Byron (1788–1824) British poet. *Childe Harold's Pilgrimage*, I

11 England may as well dam up the waters from the Nile with bulrushes as to fetter the step of Freedom, more proud and firm in this youthful land.
Lydia M. Child (1802–80) US abolitionist campaigner. *The Rebels*, Ch. 4

12 But what is Freedom? Rightly understood,
A universal licence to be good.

Hartley Coleridge (1796–1849) British poet. *Liberty*

13 The condition upon which God hath given liberty to man is eternal vigilance.

John Philpot Curran (1750–1817) Irish judge. Speech on the Right of Election of Lord Mayor of Dublin, 10 July 1790

14 Yes, 'n' how many years can some people exist
Before they're allowed to be free?
Yes, 'n' how many times can a man turn his head,
Pretending he just doesn't see?
The answer, my friend, is blowin' in the wind.

Bob Dylan (Robert Allen Zimmerman; 1941–) US popular singer. *Blowin' in the Wind*

15 My people and I have come to an agreement which satisfies us both. They are to say what they please, and I am to do what I please.

Frederick the Great (1712–86) King of Prussia. Attrib.

16 O Freedom, what liberties are taken in thy name!

Daniel George (1890–1967) British writer. *The Perpetual Pessimist*, a parody of Marie Jeanne Philip on Roland's (1754–93; French revolutionary) last words before her execution.

17 This is Liberty-Hall, gentlemen.

Oliver Goldsmith (1728–74) Irish-born British writer. *She Stoops to Conquer*, II

18 *Laissez faire, laissez passer.*
Liberty of action, liberty of movement.

Jean Claude Vincent de Gournay (1712–59) French economist. Speech, Sept 1758

19 Power is so apt to be insolent and Liberty to be saucy, that they are seldom upon good Terms.

Lord Halifax (1633–95) English statesman. *Political, Moral, and Miscellaneous Thoughts and Reflections*

20 What should be said is that Salman has the right to blaspheme, but it is the same citizen's right as anyone at Speakers' Corner.

David Hare (1947–) British playwright. Referring to Salman Rushdie, author of 'The Satanic Verses'. *The Sunday Times*, 11 Feb 1990

21 The love of liberty is the love of others; the love of power is the love of ourselves.

William Hazlitt (1778–1830) British essayist. *The Times*, 1819

22 I know not what course others may take; but as for me, give me liberty or give me death.

Patrick Henry (1736–99) US statesman. Speech, Virginia Convention, 23 Mar 1775

23 I struck the board, and cried, 'No more;
I will abroad.'
What, shall I ever sigh and pine?
My lines and life are free; free as the road,
Loose as the wind, as large as store.

George Herbert (1593–1633) English poet. *The Collar*

24 'Painters and poets alike have always had licence to dare anything.' We know that, and we both claim and allow to others in their turn this indulgence.

Horace (Quintus Horatius Flaccus; 65–8 BC) Roman poet. *Ars Poetica*

25 *Nullius addictus iurare in verba magistri,*
Quo me cumque rapit tempestas, deferor hospes.
Not bound to swear allegiance to any master,
wherever the wind takes me I travel as a visitor.

Horace *Nullius in verba* is the motto of the Royal Society. *Epistles*, I

26 A man should never put on his best trousers when he goes out to battle for freedom and truth.

Henrik Ibsen (1828–1906) Norwegian dramatist. *An Enemy of the People*, V

27 The tree of liberty must be refreshed from time to time with the blood of patriots and tyrants. It is its natural manure.

Thomas Jefferson (1743–1826) US statesman. Letter to W. S. Smith, 13 Nov 1787

28 I have got no further than this: Every man has a right to utter what he thinks truth, and every other man has a right to knock him down for it. Martyrdom is the test.

Samuel Johnson (1709–84) British lexicographer. *Life of Johnson* (J. Boswell), Vol. IV

29 The Liberty of the press is the *Palladium* of all the civil, political and religious rights of an Englishman.

Junius An unidentified writer of letters (1769–72) to the *London Public Advertiser. Letters*, 'Dedication'

30 It's often safer to be in chains than to be free.

Franz Kafka (1883–1924) Czech novelist. *The Trial*, Ch. 8

31 Freedom's just another word for nothing left to lose.

Kris Kristofferson (1936–) US film actor and folk musician. *Me and Bobby McGee*

32 It is true that liberty is precious – so precious that it must be rationed.

Lenin (Vladimir Ilich Ulyanov; 1870–1924) Russian revolutionary leader. Attrib.

33 I intend no modification of my oft-expressed personal wish that all men everywhere could be free.

Abraham Lincoln (1809–65) US statesman. Letter to Horace Greeley, 22 Aug 1862

34 Those who deny freedom to others, deserve it not for themselves.

Abraham Lincoln Speech, 19 May 1856

35 Many politicians of our time are in the habit of laying it down as a self-evident proposition, that no people ought to be free till they are fit to use their freedom. The maxim is worthy of the fool in the old story, who resolved not to go into the water till he had learnt to swim. If men are to wait for liberty till they become wise and good in slavery, they may indeed wait for ever.

Lord Macaulay (1800–59) British historian. *Literary Essays Contributed to the 'Edinburgh Review'*, 'Milton',

36 It would be better that England should be free than that England should be compulsorily sober.

William Connor Magee (1821–91) British clergyman. Speech on the Intoxicating Liquor Bill, House of Lords, 2 May 1872

37 I cannot and will not give any undertaking at a time when I, and you, the people, are not free. Your freedom and mine cannot be separated.

Nelson Mandela (1918–) South African statesman. Message read by his daughter to a rally in Soweto, 10 Feb 1985

38 Letting a hundred flowers blossom and a hundred schools of thought contend is the policy for promoting the progress of the arts and the sciences.

Mao Tse-Tung (1893–1976) Chinese communist leader. *Quotations from Chairman Mao Tse-Tung*, Ch. 32

39 Emancipate yourselves from mental slavery. None but ourselves can free our minds.

Bob Marley (Robert Nesta Marley; 1945–80) Jamaican reggae singer. *Uprising*, 'Redemption Song'

40 The liberty of the individual must be thus far limited; he must not make himself a nuisance to other people.

John Stuart Mill (1806–73) British philosopher. *On Liberty*, Ch. 3

41 ...always with right reason dwells
Twinn'd, and from her hath no dividual being.

John Milton (1608–74) English poet. Referring to liberty. *Paradise Lost*, Bk. XII

42 None can love freedom heartily, but good men; the rest love not freedom, but licence.

John Milton *Tenure of Kings and Magistrates*

43 Liberty is the right to do everything which the laws allow.

Baron de Montesquieu (1689–1755) French writer. *L'Esprit des lois*

44 Before the organization of the Blackshirt movement free speech did not exist in this country.

Oswald Mosley (1896–1980) British politician. Selections from the *New Statesman, This England*, Pt. I

45 My government will protect all liberties but one – the liberty to do away with other liberties.

Gustavo Diaz Ordaz (1911–79) President of Mexico (1964–1970). Inaugural speech

46 Freedom is the right to tell people what they do not want to hear.

George Orwell (Eric Blair; 1903–50) British novelist. *The Road to Wigan Pier*

47 I sometimes think that the price of liberty is not so much eternal vigilance as eternal dirt.

George Orwell *The Road to Wigan Pier*, Ch. 4

48 We must plan for freedom, and not only for security, if for no other reason than that only freedom can make security secure.

Karl Popper (1902–) Austrian-born British philosopher. *The Open Society and Its Enemies*

49 Now: heaven knows, anything goes.

Cole Porter (1893–1964) US songwriter. *Anything Goes*, title song

50 In their rules there was only one clause: Do what you will.

François Rabelais (1483–1553) French satirist. Referring to the fictional Abbey of Thélème. *Gargantua*, Bk. I, Ch. 57

51 *'O liberté! O liberté! Que de crimes on commet en ton nom!'*
Oh liberty! Oh liberty! What crimes are committed in thy name!

Madame Roland (1754–93) French revolutionary. Said as she mounted the steps of the guillotine at her execution. Attrib.

52 Man was born free and everywhere he is in chains.

Jean Jacques Rousseau (1712–78) French philosopher. *Du contrat social*, Ch. 1

53 No human being, however great, or powerful, was ever so free as a fish.

John Ruskin (1819–1900) British art critic and writer. *The Two Paths*, Lecture V

54 Man is condemned to be free.

Jean-Paul Sartre (1905–80) French writer. *Existentialism is a Humanism*

55 You took my freedom away a long time ago and you can't give it back because you haven't got it yourself.

Alexander Solzhenitsyn (1918–) Russian novelist. *The First Circle*, Ch. 17

56 My definition of a free society is a society where it is safe to be unpopular.

Adlai Stevenson (1900–65) US statesman. Speech, Detroit, Oct. 1952

57 It is by the goodness of God that in our country we have those three unspeakably precious things: freedom of speech, freedom of conscience, and the prudence never to practise either of them.

Mark Twain (Samuel Langhorne Clemens; 1835–1910) US writer. *Following the Equator*, heading of Ch. 20

58 Liberty is the hardest test that one can inflict on a people. To know how to be free is not given equally to all men and all nations.

Paul Valéry (1871–1945) French poet and writer. *Reflections on the World Today*, 'On the Subject of Dictatorship'

59 I disapprove of what you say, but I will defend to the death your right to say it.

Voltaire (François-Marie Arouet; 1694–1778) French writer. Attrib.

60 I never approved either the errors of his book, or the trivial truths he so vigorously laid down. I have, however, stoutly taken his side when absurd men have condemned him for these same truths.

Voltaire Referring to Helvetius's *De L'Esprit*, which was publicly burned in 1758; usually misquoted as 'I disapprove of what you say, but I will defend to the death your right to say it'. *Dictionnaire Philosophique Portaif*, 'Homme'

61 Liberty does not consist in mere declarations of the rights of man. It consists in the translation of those declarations into definite action.

Woodrow Wilson (1856–1924) US statesman. Speech, 4 July 1914

62 Me this unchartered freedom tires;
I feel the weight of chance-desires:
My hopes no more must change their name,
I long for a repose that ever is the same.

William Wordsworth (1770–1850) British poet. *Ode to Duty*

63 We must be free or die, who speak the tongue
That Shakespeare spake; the faith and morals hold
Which Milton held.

William Wordsworth *Sonnets*, 'It is not to be thought of'

64 Two voices are there; one is of the sea,
One of the mountains; each a mighty voice:
In both from age to age thou didst rejoice,
They were thy chosen music, Liberty!

William Wordsworth *Sonnets*, 'Two voices are there'

FRENCH REVOLUTION

See also France, revolution

1 The French Revolution is merely the herald of a far greater and much more solemn revolution, which will be the last...The hour has come for founding the Republic of Equals, that great refuge open to every man.

François-Noël Babeuf (1760–97) French revolutionary. *Conjuration des Egaux*

2 Let us take as our emblem green cockades, green the colour of hope!

Camille Desmoulins (1760–94) French Revolutionary leader. *Le Vieux Cordelier*

3 It was the best of times, it was the worst of times, it was the age of wisdom, it was the age of foolishness, it was the epoch of belief, it was the epoch of incredulity, it was the season of Light, it was the season of Darkness, it was the spring of hope, it was the winter of despair, we had everything before us, we had nothing before us, we were all going direct to Heaven, we were all going direct the other way.

Charles Dickens (1812–70) British novelist. The opening words of the book. *A Tale of Two Cities*, Bk. I, Ch. 1

4 How much the greatest event it is that ever happened in the world! and how much the best!

Charles James Fox (1749–1806) British Whig politician. Referring to the fall of the Bastille, 14 July 1789. Letter to Fitzpatrick, 30 July 1789

5 *Rien*
Nothing.

Louis XVI (1754–93) King of France. Diary, 14 July 1789 – the day the Bastille fell

6 No National Assembly ever threatened to be so stormy as that which will decide the fate of the monarchy, and which is gathering in such haste, and with so much distrust on both sides.

Comte de Mirabeau (1749–91) French statesman. Letter, 6 Dec 1788

7 Citizens, we are talking of a republic, and yet Louis lives! We are talking of a republic, and the person of the King still stands between us and liberty.

Robespierre (1758–94) French lawyer and revolutionary. Speech, Convention, 3 Dec 1792

8 Who will dare deny that the Third Estate contains within itself all that is needed to constitute a nation?

Abbé de Sieyès (1748–1836) French churchman. The 'Third Estate' comprised all the French people except the nobility (the First Estate) and the clergy (the Second Estate). *Qu'est-ce que le Tiers État?* (pamphlet, Jan 1789)

9 It is still too early to form a final judgement on the French Revolution.

George Macaulay Trevelyan Speech, National Book League, 30 May 1945

10 There has been reason to fear that the Revolution may, like Saturn, devour each of her children one by one.

Pierre Vergniaud (1753–93) French revolutionary. Said at his trial, Nov 1793. Attrib.

11 Bliss was it in that dawn to be alive,
But to be young was very heaven!

William Wordsworth (1770–1850) British poet. *The Prelude*, XI

12 That which sets
...The budding rose above the rose full blown.

William Wordsworth *The Prelude*, XI

13 Not in Utopia, – subterranean fields, –
Or some secreted island, Heaven knows where!
But in the very world, which is the world
Of all of us, – the place where, in the end,
We find our happiness, or not at all!

William Wordsworth *The Prelude*, XI

FREUD, SIGMUND

(1856–1939) Austrian psychoanalyst. As a physician in Vienna he studied hypnosis but moved on to develop psychoanalysis and the theory that many neuroses were caused by suppressed sexual desires. His works include *The Interpretation of Dreams* (1899) and *Totem and Taboo* (1913).

1 The voice of the intellect is a soft one, but it does not rest till it has gained a hearing.

The Future of an Illusion

2 The psychic development of the individual is a short repetition of the course of development of the race.

Leonardo da Vinci

3 Religion is an illusion and it derives its strength from the fact that it falls in with our instinctual desires.

New Introductory Lectures on Psychoanalysis, 'A Philosophy of Life'

4 Conscience is the internal perception of the rejection of a particular wish operating within us.

Totem and Taboo

5 At bottom God is nothing more than an exalted father.

Totem and Taboo

6 The great question...which I have not been able to answer, despite my thirty years of research into the feminine soul, is 'What does a woman want'?

Psychiatry in American Life (Charles Rolo)

7 What progress we are making. In the Middle Ages they would have burned me. Now they are content with burning my books.

Referring to the public burning of his books in Berlin. Letter to Ernest Jones, 1933

FRIENDS

See also enemies, friendship

1 Books and friends should be few but good.

Proverb

2 Forsake not an old friend; for the new is not comparable to him: a new friend is as new wine; when it is old, thou shalt drink it with pleasure.

Bible: Ecclesiasticus 9:10

3 Cost his enemies a long repentance,
And made him a good friend, but bad acquaintance.

Lord Byron (1788–1824) British poet. *Don Juan*, III

4 Tell me what company thou keepest, and I'll tell thee what thou art.

Miguel de Cervantes (1547–1616) Spanish novelist. *Don Quixote*, Pt. II, Ch. 23

5 Have no friends not equal to yourself.
Confucius (K'ung Fu-tzu; 551–479 BC) Chinese philosopher. *Analects*

6 Fate chooses your relations, you choose your friends.
Jacques Delille (1738–1813) French abbé and poet. *Malheur et pitié*, I

7 *Changez vos amis.*
Change your friends.
Charles De Gaulle (1890–1970) French general and statesman. Replying to the complaint by Jacques Soustelle that he was being attacked by his own friends. Attrib.

8 A Friend may well be reckoned the masterpiece of Nature.
Ralph Waldo Emerson (1803–82) US poet and essayist. *Essays*, 'Friendship'

9 If a man does not make new acquaintance as he advances through life, he will soon find himself left alone. A man, Sir, should keep his friendship in constant repair.
Samuel Johnson (1709–84) British lexicographer. *Life of Johnson* (J. Boswell), Vol. I

10 Friends are God's apology for relations.
Hugh Kingsmill (1889–1949) British writer. *God's Apology* (R. Ingrams)

11 I get by with a little help from my friends.
John Lennon (1940–80) British rock musician. *With a Little Help from My Friends* (with Paul McCartney)

12 He's an oul' butty o' mine – oh, he's a darlin' man, a daarlin' man.
Sean O'Casey (1884–1964) Irish dramatist. *Juno and the Paycock*, I

13 It is more shameful to distrust one's friends than to be deceived by them.
Duc de la Rochefoucauld (1613–80) French writer. *Maximes*, 84

14 A friend should bear his friend's infirmities,
But Brutus makes mine greater than they are.
William Shakespeare (1564–1616) English dramatist. *Julius Caesar*, IV:3

15 If it is abuse – why one is always sure to hear of it from one damned good-natured friend or other!
Richard Brinsley Sheridan (1751–1816) British dramatist. *The Critic*, I

16 I do not believe that friends are necessarily the people you like best, they are merely the people who got there first.
Peter Ustinov (1921–) British actor. *Dear Me*, Ch. 5

17 Associate yourself with men of good quality if you esteem your own reputation; for 'tis better to be alone than in bad company.
George Washington (1732–99) US statesman. *Rules of Civility*

FRIENDSHIP

See also friends, love and friendship

1 A friend in need is a friend indeed.
Proverb

2 A good friend is my nearest relation.
Proverb

3 A hedge between keeps friendship green.
Proverb

4 God defend me from my friends; from my enemies I can defend myself.
Proverb

5 Love is blind; friendship closes its eyes.
Proverb

6 The best of friends must part.
Proverb

7 There is no such thing as a free lunch.
Anonymous Often attributed to Milton Friedman.

8 Two are better than one; because they have a good reward for their labour.
For if they fall, the one will lift up his fellow: but woe to him that is alone when he falleth; for he hath not another to help him up.
Bible: Ecclesiastes 4:9–10

9 Saul and Jonathan were lovely and pleasant in their lives, and in their death they were not divided: they were swifter than eagles, they were stronger than lions.
Bible: II Samuel 1:23–24

10 I've noticed your hostility towards him...I ought to have guessed you were friends.
Malcolm Bradbury (1932–) British academic and novelist. *The History Man*, Ch. 7

11 I don't trust him. We're friends.
Bertolt Brecht (1898–1956) German dramatist. *Mother Courage*, III

12 Should auld acquaintance be forgot,
And never brought to min'?
Robert Burns (1759–96) Scottish poet. *Auld Lang Syne*

13 We'll tak a cup o' kindness yet,
For auld lang syne.
Robert Burns *Auld Lang Syne*

14 Two may talk together under the same roof for many years, yet never really meet; and two others at first speech are old friends.
Mary Catherwood (1847–1901) US writer. *Mackinac and Lake Stories*, 'Marianson'

15 A woman can become a man's friend only in the following stages – first an acquaintance, next a mistress, and only then a friend.
Anton Chekhov (1860–1904) Russian dramatist. *Uncle Vanya*, II

16 There is nothing in the world I wouldn't do for Hope, and there is nothing he wouldn't do for me... We spend our lives doing nothing for each other.
Bing Crosby (Harry Lillis; 1904–77) US singer. Referring to the actor and comedian Bob Hope. *The Observer*, 'Sayings of the Week', 7 May 1950

17 It is not so much our friends' help that helps us as the confident knowledge that they will help us.
Epicurus (341–270 BC) Greek philosopher.

18 These are called the pious frauds of friendship.
Henry Fielding (1707–54) British novelist. *Amelia*, Bk. III, Ch. 4

19 Always, Sir, set a high value on spontaneous kindness. He whose inclination prompts him to cultivate your friendship of his own accord, will love you more than one whom you have been at pains to attach to you.

Samuel Johnson (1709–84) British lexicographer. *Life of Johnson* (J. Boswell), Vol. IV

20 Sir, I look upon every day to be lost, in which I do not make a new acquaintance.

Samuel Johnson *Life of Johnson* (J. Boswell), Vol. IV

21 Greater love than this, he said, no man hath that a man lay down his wife for a friend. Go thou and do likewise. Thus, or words to that effect, saith Zarathustra, sometime regius professor of French letters to the University of Oxtail.

James Joyce (1882–1941) Irish novelist. *Ulysses*

22 Friendship is unnecessary, like philosophy, like art...It has no survival value; rather it is one of those things that give value to survival.

C. S. Lewis (1898–1963) British academic and writer. *The Four Loves, Friendship*

23 That the world will never be quite – what a cliché – the same again
Is what we only learn by the event
When a friend dies out on us and is not there
To share the periphery of a remembered scent.

Louis MacNiece (1907–63) Irish-born British poet. *Tam Cari Capitis*

24 Two buttocks of one bum.

T. Sturge Moore (1870–1944) British poet and illustrator. Referring to the writers Hilaire Belloc and G. K. Chesterton.

25 A true bond of friendship is usually only possible between people of roughly equal status. This equality is demonstrated in many indirect ways, but it is reinforced in face-to-face encounters by a matching of the posture of relaxation or alertness.

Desmond Morris (1928–) British biologist. *Manwatching*, 'Postural Echo'

26 To like and dislike the same things, that is indeed true friendship.

Sallust (Gaius Sallustius Crispus; c. 86–c. 34 BC) Roman historian and politician. *Bellum Catilinae*

27 I might give my life for my friend, but he had better not ask me to do up a parcel.

Logan Pearsall Smith (1865–1946) US writer. *Trivia*

28 Learn to reject friendship, or rather the dream of friendship. To want friendship is a great fault. Friendship ought to be a gratuitous joy, like the joys afforded by art, or life (like aesthetic joys). I must refuse it in order to be worthy to receive it.

Simone Weil (1910–43) French writer, philosopher, and revolutionary. *First and Last Notebooks*, 'The Pre-War Notebook' (ed. Richard Rees)

FROST, ROBERT LEE

(1874–1963) US poet, whose collections *Boy's Will* (1913) and *North of Boston* (1914) brought him considerable acclaim.

1 Most of the change we think we see in life
Is due to truths being in and out of favour.

The Black Cottage

2 No tears in the writer, no tears in the reader.

Collected Poems, Preface

3 Home is the place where, when you have to go there,
They have to take you in.

The Death of the Hired Man

4 Forgive, O Lord, my little jokes on Thee
And I'll forgive Thy great big one on me.

In the Clearing, 'Cluster of Faith'

5 Something there is that doesn't love a wall.

North of Boston, 'Mending Wall'

6 My apple trees will never get across
And eat the cones under his pines, I tell him.
He only says, 'Good fences make good neighbours.'

North of Boston, 'Mending Wall'

7 Two roads diverged in a wood, and I –
I took the one less traveled by,
And that has made all the difference.

The Road Not Taken

8 The woods are lovely, dark, and deep,
But I have promises to keep,
And miles to go before I sleep,
And miles to go before I sleep.

Stopping by Woods on a Snowy Evening

9 Writing free verse is like playing tennis with the net down.

Speech, Milton Academy, 17 May 1935

10 A diplomat is a man who always remembers a woman's birthday but never remembers her age.

Attrib.

11 Poetry is what gets lost in translation. It is also what is lost in interpretation.

Attrib.

FRY, CHRISTOPHER

(1907–) British dramatist. His verse drama *The Lady's Not for Burning* (1948) was very successful. Other plays include *Venus Observed* (1950), *A Sleep of Prisoners* (1951), and *Curtmantle* (1962).

1 Why so shy, my pretty Thomasina?
Thomasin, O Thomasin,
Once you were so promisin'.

The Dark Is Light Enough, II

2 I sometimes think
His critical judgement is so exquisite
It leaves us nothing to admire except his opinion.

The Dark is Light Enough, II

3 Religion
Has made an honest woman of the supernatural,
And we won't have it kicking over the traces again.

The Lady's Not for Burning, II

4 Where in this small-talking world can I find
A longitude with no platitude?

The Lady's Not for Burning, III

5 Try thinking of love, or something.
Amor vincit insomnia.

A Sleep of Prisoners

FUNERALS

See also death

1 Most of the people who will walk after me will be children, so make the beat keep time with short steps.

Hans Christian Andersen (1805–75) Danish writer. Planning the music for his funeral. *Hans Christian Andersen* (R. Godden)

2 This is the last time that I will take part as an amateur.

Daniel-François-Esprit Auber (1782–1871) French composer. Said at a funeral. *Das Buch des Lachens* (W. Scholz)

3 When we attend the funerals of our friends we grieve for them, but when we go to those of other people it is chiefly our own deaths that we mourn for.

Gerald Brenan (Edward Fitzgerald Brenan; 1894–1987) British writer. *Thoughts in a Dry Season*, 'Death'

4 'If you don't go to other men's funerals,' he told Father stiffly, 'they won't go to yours.'

Clarence Shepard Day (1874–1935) US writer. *Life With Father*, 'Father plans'

5 I bet you a hundred bucks he ain't in here.

Charles Bancroft Dillingham (1868–1934) US theatrical manager. Referring to the escapologist Harry Houdini; said at his funeral, while carrying his coffin. Attrib.

6 When I die I want to decompose in a barrel of porter and have it served in all the pubs in Dublin.

J. P. Donleavy (1926–) US novelist. *The Ginger Man*

7 Many funerals discredit a physician.

Ben Jonson (1572–1637) English dramatist.

8 My friends should drink a dozen of Claret on my Tomb.

John Keats (1795–1821) British poet. Letter to Benjamin Bailey, 14 Aug 1819

9 Why should I go? She won't be there.

Arthur Miller (1915–) US dramatist. When asked if he would attend his wife Marilyn Monroe's funeral. Attrib.

10 It proves what they say, give the public what they want to see and they'll come out for it.

Red Skelton (Richard Bernard Skelton; 1913–) US actor and comedian. Said while attending the funeral in 1958 of Hollywood producer Harry Cohn. It has also been attributed to Samuel Goldwyn while attending Louis B. Mayer's funeral in 1957.

11 How Henry would have loved it!

Ellen Terry (1847–1928) British actress. Referring to Sir Henry Irving's funeral. *Yesterdays* (Robert Hitchens)

12 Evan the Death presses hard with black gloves on the coffin of his breast in case his heart jumps out.

Dylan Thomas (1914–53) Welsh poet. *Under Milk Wood*

13 Not a drum was heard, not a funeral note,
As his corse to the rampart we hurried.

Charles Wolfe (1791–1823) Irish poet. *The Burial of Sir John Moore at Corunna*, I

14 We carved not a line, and we raised not a stone –
But we left him alone with his glory.

Charles Wolfe *The Burial of Sir John Moore at Corunna*, VIII

FUTILITY

See also purpose

1 Don't curse the darkness – light a candle.

Chinese Proverb

2 Why buy a cow when milk is so cheap?

Proverb

3 Why keep a dog and bark yourself?

Proverb

4 You can't get blood out of a stone.

Proverb

5 Mock on, mock on, Voltaire, Rousseau;
Mock on, mock on; 'tis all in vain!
You throw the sand against the wind,
And the wind blows it back again.

William Blake (1757–1827) British poet. *Mock on, mock on, Voltaire, Rousseau*

6 A man who has pedalled twenty-five thousand miles on a stationary bicycle has not circled the globe. He has only garnered weariness.

Paul Eldridge *Horns of Glass*

7 It's but little good you'll do a-watering the last year's crop.

George Eliot (Mary Ann Evans; 1819–80) British novelist. *Adam Bede*

8 So we beat on, boats against the current, borne back ceaselessly into the past.

F. Scott Fitzgerald (1896–1940) US novelist. *The Great Gatsby*

9 He is very fond of making things which he does not want, and then giving them to people who have no use for them.

Anthony Hope (Sir Anthony Hope Hawkins; 1863–1933) British novelist. *The Dolly Dialogues*

10 He's a real Nowhere Man,
Sitting in his Nowhere Land,
Making all his nowhere plans for nobody.
Doesn't have a point of view,
Knows not where he's going to,
Isn't he a bit like you and me?

John Lennon (1940–80) British rock musician. *Nowhere Man* (with Paul McCartney)

11 I'm not going to re-arrange the furniture on the deck of the *Titanic*.

Rogers Morton (1914–79) US government official. Refusing attempts to rescue President Ford's re-election campaign, 1976. Attrib.

12 'Tis not necessary to light a candle to the sun.

Algernon Sidney (1622–83) English statesman. *Discourses concerning Government*, Ch. 2

13 People talking without speaking,
People listening without hearing,
People writing songs that voices never shared.

Paul Simon (1942–) US singer. *Sound of Silence*

14 All dressed up, with nowhere to go.

William Allen White (1868–1944) US writer. Referring to the Progressive Party, after Theodore Roosevelt's withdrawal from the 1916 US Presidential election

FUTURE

See also past, present, promises, prophecy, time

1 Tomorrow never comes.
Proverb

2 Years hence, perhaps, may dawn an age,
More fortunate, alas! than we,
Which without hardness will be sage,
And gay without frivolity.
Matthew Arnold (1822–88) British poet and critic. *The Grande Chartreuse*

3 I have a vision of the future, chum.
The workers' flats in fields of soya beans
Tower up like silver pencils.
John Betjeman (1906–84) British poet.

4 Boast not thyself of tomorrow; for thou knowest not what a day may bring forth.
Bible: Proverbs 27:1

5 FUTURE, That period of time in which our affairs prosper, our friends are true and our happiness is assured.
Ambrose Bierce (1842–?1914) US writer and journalist. *The Devil's Dictionary*

6 Not a future. At least not in Europe. America's different, of course, but America's really only a kind of Russia. You've no idea how pleasant it is not to have any future. It's like having a totally efficient contraceptive.
Anthony Burgess (John Burgess Wilson; 1917–93) British novelist. *Honey for the Bears*, Pt. II, Ch. 6

7 I never think of the future. It comes soon enough.
Albert Einstein (1879–1955) German-born US physicist. Interview, 1930

8 This is the way the world ends
Not with a bang but a whimper.
T. S. Eliot (1888–1965) US born British poet and dramatist. *The Hollow Men*

9 The time of our Ford.
Aldous Huxley (1894–1964) British novelist. *Brave New World*, Ch. 3

10 The future will one day be the present and will seem as unimportant as the present does now.
W. Somerset Maugham (1874–1965) British novelist. *The Summing Up*

11 I have seen the future and it works.
Lincoln Steffens (1866–1936) US journalist. Speaking to the US economist and presidential advisor Bernard Baruch, after visiting the Soviet Union, 1919. *Autobiography*, Ch. 18

12 Live Now, Pay Later.
Jack Trevor Story (1917–) British novelist. Title of screenplay

13 The future is made of the same stuff as the present.
Simone Weil (1909–43) French philosopher. *On Science, Necessity, and the Love of God* (ed. Richard Rees), 'Some Thoughts on the Love of God'

14 The Shape of Things to Come.
H. G. Wells (1866–1946) British writer. Book title

G

GALBRAITH, JOHN KENNETH

(1908–) US economist in the Keynesian tradition; he was US ambassador (1961–63) to India and adviser to President Kennedy. His books include *The Affluent Society* (1958), *Economics and the Public Purpose* (1973), and an autobiography, *A Life In Our Times* (1981).

1 Wealth is not without its advantages, and the case to the contrary, although it has often been made, has never proved widely persuasive.
The Affluent Society, Ch. 1

2 Wealth has never been a sufficient source of honour in itself. It must be advertised, and the normal medium is obtrusively expensive goods.
The Affluent Society, Ch. 7

3 Few things are as immutable as the addiction of political groups to the ideas by which they have once won office.
The Affluent Society, Ch. 13

4 In the affluent society no useful distinction can be made between luxuries and necessaries.
The Affluent Society, Ch. 21

5 All races have produced notable economists, with the exception of the Irish who doubtless can protest their devotion to higher arts.
The Age of Uncertainty, Ch. 1

6 Much of the world's work, it has been said, is done by men who do not feel quite well. Marx is a case in point.
The Age of Uncertainty, Ch. 3

7 Money differs from an automobile, a mistress or cancer in being equally important to those who have it and those who do not.
Attrib.

8 The salary of the chief executive of the large corporation is not a market award for achievement. It is frequently in the nature of a warm personal gesture by the individual to himself.
Annals of an Abiding Liberal

GALSWORTHY, JOHN

(1867–1933) British novelist and dramatist. His series of novels, *The Forsyte Saga*, made his name. Plays include *The Silver Box* (1906).

Quotations about Galsworthy

1 Galsworthy had not quite enough of the superb courage of his satire. He faltered, and gave in to the Forsytes. It is a thousand pities. He might have been the surgeon the modern soul needs so badly, to cut away the proud flesh of our Forsytes from the living body of men who are fully alive. Instead, he put down the knife and laid on a soft sentimental poultice, and helped to make the corruption worse.
D. H. Lawrence (1885–1930) British novelist. *Phoenix*

2 He has the gift of becoming, as it were, a statesman of literature.
Robert Lynd (1879–1949) Irish essayist and critic. *John o'London's weekly*, 8 Dec 1928

3 Galsworthy was a bad writer, and some inner trouble, sharpening his sensitiveness, nearly made him into a good one; his discontent healed itself, and he reverted to type.
George Orwell (Eric Blair; 1905–50) British novelist. *New Statesman and Nation*, 12 Mar 1938

Quotations by Galsworthy

4 He was afflicted by the thought that where Beautywas, nothing ever ran quite straight, which, no doubt, was why so many people looked on it as immoral.
In Chancery, Ch. 13

5 Nobody ever tells me anything.
The Man of Property, Pt. I, Ch. 1

6 Oh, your precious 'lame ducks'!
The Man of Property, Pt. II, Ch. 12

GANDHI, INDIRA

(1917–84) Indian stateswoman. The daughter of Jawaharla Nehru, she was prime minister twice (1966–67; 1980–84). She was assassinated by Sikh extremists.

Quotations about Indira Gandhi

1 Her weapon is the snub, a regal, chilling silence. Her silences, as could be testified by ex-President Nixon, whom she disliked, can be disconcerting.
Trevor Fishlock (1941–) British journalist. *The Times*, 'Empress Indira', 22 Mar 1982

2 Mrs Gandhi never gives a performance less than the occasion demands.
The Observer, 'Profile', 21 Mar 1982

Quotations by Indira Gandhi

3 To bear many children is considered not only a religious blessing but also an investment. The greater their number, some Indians reason, the more alms they can beg.
New York Review of Books, 'Indira's Coup' (Oriana Fallaci)

4 There exists no politician in India daring enough to attempt to explain to the masses that cows can be eaten.
New York Review of Books, 'Indira's Coup' (Oriana Fallaci)

5 You cannot shake hands with a clenched fist.
Remark at a press conference, New Delhi, 19 Oct 1971

6 There are moments in history when brooding tragedy and its dark shadows can be lightened by recalling great moments of the past.
Letter to Richard Nixon, 16 Dec 1971

7 I don't mind if my life goes in the service of the

nation. If I die today every drop of my blood will invigorate the nation.

Said the night before she was assassinated by Sikh militants, 30 Oct 1984. *The Sunday Times*, 3 Dec 1989

GANDHI, MAHATMA

(Mohandas Karamchand Gandhi; 1869–1948) Indian national leader who used civil disobedience to achieve political aims. He became leader of the Indian National Congress and was treated as a saint in his own country. He was influential in the achievement of Indian independence, but his advocacy of cooperation between Hindus and Muslims led to his assassination by a Hindu fanatic.

Quotations about Mahatma Gandhi

1 A dear old man with his bald pate and spectacles, beaky nose and birdlike lips and benign but somewhat toothless smile.

Rodney Bennett *Teacher's World*, 7 May 1930

2 It is nauseating to see Mr Gandhi, a seditious Middle Temple lawyer, now posing as a fakir of a type well known in the East, striding half naked up the steps of the Viceregal Palace, while he is still organising and conducting a defiant campaign of civil disobedience, to parley on equal terms with the representative of the King Emperor.

Winston Churchill (1874–1965) British statesman. Speech, 23 Feb 1931

3 Gandhi was very keen on sex. He renounced it when he was 36, so thereafter it was never very far from his thoughts.

Woodrow Wyatt (1918–) British journalist and writer. *The Sunday Times*, 27 Nov 1977

Quotations by Mahatma Gandhi

4 It is better to be violent, if there is violence in our hearts, than to put on the cloak of non-violence to cover impotence.

Non-Violence in Peace and War

5 I think it would be a good idea.

On being asked for his view on Western civilization. Attrib.

6 I eat to live, to serve, and also, if it so happens, to enjoy, but I do not eat for the sake of enjoyment.

Attrib.

GARDENS

See also flowers

1 Mary, Mary, quite contrary,
How does your garden grow?
With silver bells and cockle shells,
And pretty maids all in a row.

Anonymous *Tommy Thumb's Pretty Song Book*

2 God Almighty first planted a garden. And indeed it is the purest of human pleasures.

Francis Bacon (1561–1626) English philosopher. *Essays*, 'Of Gardens'

3 But there went up a mist from the earth, and watered the whole face of the ground.
And the Lord God formed man of the dust of the ground, and breathed into his nostrils the breath of life; and man became a living soul.
And the Lord God planted a garden eastward in Eden; and there he put the man whom he had formed.
And out of the ground made the Lord God to grow every tree that is pleasant to the sight, and good for food; the tree of life also in the midst of the garden, and the tree of knowledge of good and evil.
And a river went out of Eden to water the garden.

Bible: Genesis 2:6–10

4 A garden is a lovesome thing, God wot!

Thomas Edward Brown (1830–97) British poet. *My Garden*

5 To get the best results you must talk to your vegetables.

Charles, Prince of Wales (1948–) Eldest son of Elizabeth II. *The Observer*, 'Sayings of the Week', 28 Sept 1986

6 God the first garden made, and the first city Cain.

Abraham Cowley (1618–67) English poet. *The Garden*

7 The kiss of sun for pardon,
The song of the birds for mirth –
One is nearer God's Heart in a garden
Than anywhere else on earth.

Dorothy Gurney (1858–1932) British poet. *The Lord God Planted a Garden*

8 Oh, Adam was a gardener, and God who made him sees
That half a proper gardener's work is done upon his knees,
So when your work is finished, you can wash your hands and pray
For the Glory of the Garden, that it may not pass away!

Rudyard Kipling (1865–1936) Indian-born British writer. *The Glory of the Garden*

9 A little thin, flowery border, round, neat, not gaudy.

Charles Lamb (1775–1834) British essayist. Letter to Wordsworth, June 1806

10 I have a garden of my own,
But so with roses overgrown,
And lilies, that you would it guess
To be a little wilderness.

Andrew Marvell (1621–78) English poet. *The Nymph Complaining for the Death of her Fawn*

GAY, JOHN

(1685–1732) English poet and dramatist. A member of the Scriblerus Club with Pope and Swift, his *Fables* (1727) were his best-known poems but he is now remembered for his ballad opera *The Beggar's Opera* (1728).

1 A moment of time may make us unhappy for ever.

The Beggar's Opera

2 How, like a moth, the simple maid
Still plays about the flame!

The Beggar's Opera

3 If with me you'd fondly stray,
Over the hills and far away.

The Beggar's Opera

4 Do you think your mother and I should have liv'd comfortably so long together, if ever we had been married?

The Beggar's Opera

5 She who has never loved has never lived.

The Captives

6 In every age and clime we see,
Two of a trade can ne'er agree.

Fables

7 'While there is life, there's hope,' he cried;
'Then why such haste?' so groaned and died.

Fables

8 'Tis a gross error, held in schools,
That Fortune always favours fools.

Fables

9 Fools may our scorn, not envy raise,
For envy is a kind of praise.

Fables

10 Life is a jest; and all things show it.
I thought so once; but now I know it.

My Own Epitaph

11 No sir, tho' I was born and bred in England, I can dare to be poor, which is the only thing now-a-days men are asham'd of.

Polly

12 We only part to meet again.
Change, as ye list, ye winds; my heart shall be
The faithful compass that still points to thee.

Sweet William's Farewell to Black-Eyed Susan

GELDOF, BOB

(1954–) Irish rock musician. Singer with The Boom Town Rats, he played a leading role in the fund raising organisation Band Aid, which was created in 1984 to raise millions of pounds for the starving in Africa. In 1986 he received an honorary knighthood. He now directs a television company.

1 I'm not interested in the bloody system! Why has he no food? Why is he starving to death?

The Observer, 'Sayings of the Week', 27 Oct 1985

2 I'm into pop because I want to get rich, get famous and get laid.

Attrib.

GENERALIZATIONS

See also classification

1 To generalize is to be an idiot.

William Blake (1757–1827) British poet. *Life of Blake* (Gilchrist)

2 All generalizations are dangerous, even this one.

Alexandre Dumas, fils (1824–95) French writer. Attrib.

3 All Stanislavsky ever said was: 'Avoid generalities.'

Anthony Hopkins (1937–) Welsh actor. *Films Illustrated*, Dec 1980

4 The tendency of the casual mind is to pick out or stumble upon a sample which supports or defines its prejudices, and then to make it representative of a whole class.

Walter Lippmann (1889–1974) US editor and writer. *Public Opinion*

5 Any general statement is like a cheque drawn on a bank. Its value depends on what is there to meet it.

Ezra Pound (1885–1972) US poet. *ABC of Reading*, Ch. 2

GENEROSITY

See also charity, gifts, kindness, parasites

1 A bit of fragrance always clings to the hand that gives you roses.

Chinese Proverb

2 Every man according as he purposeth in his heart, so let him give; not grudgingly, or of necessity: for God loveth a cheerful giver.

Bible: II Corinthians 9:7

3 Heal the sick, cleanse the lepers, raise the dead, cast out devils: freely ye have received, freely give.

Bible: Matthew 10:8

4 Experience was to be taken as showing that one might get a five-pound note as one got a light for a cigarette; but one had to check the friendly impulse to ask for it in the same way.

Henry James (1843–1916) US novelist. *The Awkward Age*

5 In the first place, I have only five guineas in my pocket; and in the second, they are very much at your service.

Lord Peterborough (1658–1735) English military and naval commander. Persuading an angry mob that he was not the Duke of Marlborough, notorious for his meanness. *Dictionary of National Biography*

GENIUS

See also talent, talent and genius

1 Genius is an infinite capacity for taking pains.

Proverb

2 Genius (which means transcendent capacity of taking trouble, first of all).

Thomas Carlyle (1795–1881) Scottish historian and essayist. *Frederick the Great*, Vol. IV, Ch. 3

3 I'm going to live forever. Geniuses don't die.

Salvador Dali (1904–89) Spanish painter. Remark, July 1986

4 Great Wits are sure to Madness near alli'd
And thin Partitions do their Bounds divide.

John Dryden (1631–1700) British poet and dramatist. *Absalom and Achitophel*, I

5 Genius is one per cent inspiration and ninety-nine per cent perspiration.

Thomas Edison (1847–1931) US inventor. Attrib.

6 True genius walks along a line, and, perhaps, our greatest pleasure is in seeing it so often near falling, without being ever actually down.

Oliver Goldsmith (1728–74) Irish-born British writer. *The Bee*, 'The Characteristics of Greatness'

7 The true genius is a mind of large general powers, accidentally determined to some particular direction.

Samuel Johnson (1709–84) British lexicographer. *Lives of the English Poets*, 'Cowley'

8 A genius! For thirty-seven years I've practiced fourteen hours a day, and now they call me a genius!

Pablo Sarasate (1844–1908) Spanish violinist and composer. On being hailed as a genius by a critic. Attrib.

9 When a true genius appears in the world, you may know him by this sign, that the dunces are all in confederacy against him.

Jonathan Swift (1667–1745) Irish-born Anglican priest and writer. *Thoughts on Various Subjects*

GERMANY

See also Europe, Hitler, Nazism, World War II

1 Hamelin Town's in Brunswick,
By famous Hanover city;
The river Weser, deep and wide,
Washes its wall on the southern side;
A pleasanter spot you never spied.

Robert Browning (1812–89) British poet. *The Pied Piper of Hamelin*

2 Don't let's be beastly to the Germans.

Noël Coward (1899–1973) British dramatist. Song title

3 *Deutschland, Deutschland über alles.*
Germany, Germany before all else.

Heinrich Hoffmann von Fallersleben (1798–1876) German poet. German national anthem

4 Germany will be either a world power or will not be at all.

Adolf Hitler (1889–1945) German dictator. *Mein Kampf*, Ch. 14

5 How appallingly thorough these Germans always managed to be, how emphatic! In sex no less than in war – in scholarship, in science. Diving deeper than anyone else and coming up muddier.

Aldous Huxley (1894–1964) British novelist.

6 All free men, wherever they may live, are citizens of Berlin. And therefore, as a free man, I take pride in the words *Ich bin ein Berliner.*

John Fitzgerald Kennedy (1917–63) US statesman. Speech, City Hall, West Berlin, 26 June 1963

7 Germany is our fatherland, the united Europe our future.

Helmut Kohl (1930–) German statesman. On the unification of the two Germanies. *The Times*, Oct 1990

8 The German Empire has become a world empire.

Wilhelm II (1859–1941) King of Prussia and Emperor of Germany. Speech, Berlin, 18 Jan 1896

9 America...is the prize amateur nation of the world. Germany is the prize professional nation.

Woodrow Wilson (1856–1925) US statesman. Speech, Aug 1917. *Mr Wilson's War* (John Dos Passos), Pt. III, Ch. 13

10 Germany is our fatherland, the united Europe our future.

Helmut Kohl (1930–) German statesman. On the unification of the two Germanies. *The Times*, Oct 1990

11 This is a day of jubilation, a day of remembrance and gratitude. Our common task now is to establish a new European order.

Hans-Dietrich Genscher (1927–) German politician. Referring to the conclusion of the agreement to reunite East and West Germany. *The Independent*, 10 Sept 1990

12 The highlights and shadows of our history give us cause to reflect in these days, to reflect on that which was done in the name of Germany. That will not repeat itself.

Hans-Dietrich Genscher *The Independent*, 5 Oct 1990

13 It was still a time for open trust, for innocence and illusions.

Christa Wolf (1929–) German writer. Referring to the first few months after the reunification of Germany. *Im Dialog*

14 Silence can sometimes be as bad as lies, for silence can be taken as consent.

Walter Janka Referring to the lack of support he received when he was arrested during Stalinist purges in the 1950s. *Difficulties with the Truth*

15 We must examine our own 'difficulties with the truth' and we shall discover that we too have cause for regret and shame.

Christa Wolf (1929–) German writer. Referring to *Difficulties with the Truth* by Walter Janka *Im Dialog*

GIBBON, EDWARD

(1737–94) British historian whose monumental *The History of the Decline and Fall of the Roman Empire* (1776–88) caused considerable controversy for its treatment of Christianity.

Quotations about Gibbon

1 Gibbon is an ugly, affected, disgusting fellow, and poisons our literary club for me. I class him among infidel wasps and venomous insects.

James Boswell (1740–95) Scottish lawyer and writer. *Diary*, 1779

2 Johnson's style was grand, Gibbon's elegant. Johnson marched to kettle-drums and trumpets. Gibbon moved to flutes and hautboys.

George Colman the Younger (1762–1836) British dramatist. *Ramdom Records*

Quotations by Gibbon

3 To the University of Oxford I acknowledge no obligation; and she will as cheerfully renounce me for a son, as I am willing to disclaim her for a mother. I spent fourteen months at Magdalen College: they proved the fourteen months the most idle and unprofitable of my whole life.

Memoirs

4 Crowds without company, and dissipation without pleasure.

Referring to London. *Memoirs*

5 The romance of *Tom Jones*, that exquisite picture of human manners, will outlive the palace of the Escurial and the imperial eagle of the house of Austria.

Memoirs

6 The various modes of worship, which prevailed in the Roman world, were all considered by the

people as equally true; by the philosopher, as equally false; and by the magistrate, as equally useful. And thus toleration produced not only mutual indulgence, but even religious concord.
Decline and Fall of the Roman Empire, Ch. 2

7 The principles of a free constitution are irrecoverably lost, when the legislative power is nominated by the executive.
Decline and Fall of the Roman Empire, Ch. 3

8 His reign is marked by the rare advantage of furnishing very few materials for history; which is, indeed, little more than the register of the crimes, follies, and misfortunes of mankind.
Referring to the reign of Antoninus Pius. *Decline and Fall of the Roman Empire*, Ch. 3

9 Corruption, the most infallible symptom of constitutional liberty.
Decline and Fall of the Roman Empire, Ch. 21

10 All that is human must retrograde if it does not advance.
Decline and Fall of the Roman Empire, Ch. 71

GIFTS

See also generosity, materialism

1 Every good gift and every perfect gift is from above, and cometh down from the Father of lights, with whom is no variableness, neither shadow of turning.
Bible: James 1:17

2 Heal the sick, cleanse the lepers, raise the dead, cast out devils: freely ye have received, freely give.
Bible: Matthew 10:8

3 'They gave it me,' Humpty Dumpty continued thoughtfully,...'for an un-birthday present.'
Lewis Carroll (Charles Lutwidge Dodgson; 1832–98) British writer. *Through the Looking-Glass*, Ch. 6

4 The manner of giving is worth more than the gift.
Pierre Corneille (1606–84) French dramatist. *Le Menteur*, I:1

5 If one doesn't get birthday presents it can remobilize very painfully the persecutory anxiety which usually follows birth.
Henry Reed (1914–86) British poet and dramatist. *The Primal Scene, as it were*

GILBERT, SIR W. S.

(1836–1911) British dramatist and comic writer. His comic verse published as *Bab Ballads* (1896) preceded his libretti for 14 comic operas written for Arthur Sullivan's music.

1 He led his regiment from behind
He found it less exciting.
The Gondoliers, I

2 Of that there is no manner of doubt –
No probable, possible shadow of doubt –
No possible doubt whatever.
The Gondoliers, I

3 A taste for drink, combined with gout,
Had doubled him up for ever.
The Gondoliers, I

4 All shall equal be.
The Earl, the Marquis, and the Dook,
The Groom, the Butler, and the Cook,
The Aristocrat who banks with Coutts,
The Aristocrat who cleans the boots.
The Gondoliers, I

5 When every blessed thing you hold
Is made of silver, or of gold,
You long for simple pewter.
When you have nothing else to wear
But cloth of gold and satins rare,
For cloth of gold you cease to care –
Up goes the price of shoddy.
The Gondoliers, I

6 Take a pair of sparkling eyes.
The Gondoliers, II

7 I'm called Little Buttercup – dear Little Buttercup,
Though I could never tell why.
HMS Pinafore, I

8 I am the Captain of the *Pinafore*;
And a right good captain too!
HMS Pinafore, I

9 CAPTAIN. I'm never, never sick at sea!
ALL. What never?
CAPTAIN. No, never!
ALL. What, *never*?
CAPTAIN. Hardly ever!
HMS Pinafore, I

10 And so do his sisters, and his cousins and his aunts!
His sisters and his cousins,
Whom he reckons up by dozens,
And his aunts!
HMS Pinafore, I

11 I always voted at my party's call,
And I never thought of thinking for myself at all.
HMS Pinafore, I

12 Stick close to your desks and never go to sea,
And you all may be Rulers of the Queen's Navee!
HMS Pinafore, I

13 When I was a lad I served a term
As office boy to an Attorney's firm.
I cleaned the windows and I swept the floor,
And I polished up the handle of the big front door.
I polished up that handle so carefullee
That now I am the Ruler of the Queen's Navee!
HMS Pinafore, I

14 For he might have been a Roosian,
A French, or Turk, or Proosian,
Or perhaps Ital-ian!
But in spite of all temptations
To belong to other nations,
He remains an Englishman!
HMS Pinafore, II

15 I see no objection to stoutness, in moderation.
Iolanthe, I

16 Bow, bow, ye lower middle classes!
Bow, bow, ye tradesmen, bow, ye masses!
Iolanthe, I

17 When I went to the Bar as a very young man,
(Said I to myself – said I),
I'll work on a new and original plan,
(Said I to myself – said I).
Iolanthe, I

18 The Law is the true embodiment
Of everything that's excellent.
It has no kind of fault or flaw,
And I, my lords, embody the Law.
Iolanthe, I

19 I often think it's comical
How Nature always does contrive
That every boy and every gal
That's born into the world alive
Is either a little Liberal
Or else a little Conservative!
Iolanthe, II

20 The prospect of a lot
Of dull MPs in close proximity,
All thinking for themselves is what
No man can face with equanimity.
Iolanthe, II

21 The House of Peers, throughout the war,
Did nothing in particular,
And did it very well.
Iolanthe, II

22 For you dream you are crossing the Channel, and tossing about in a steamer from Harwich – Which is something between a large bathing machine and a very small second-class carriage.
Iolanthe, II

23 Pooh-Bah (Lord High Everything Else)
The Mikado, Dramatis Personae

24 A wandering minstrel I –
A thing of shreds and patches,
Of ballads, songs and snatches,
And dreamy lullaby!
The Mikado, I

25 I can trace my ancestry back to a protoplasmal primordial atomic globule. Consequently, my family pride is something in-conceivable. I can't help it. I was born sneering.
The Mikado, I

26 As some day it may happen that a victim must be found
I've got a little list – I've got a little list
Of society offenders who might well be underground,
And who never would be missed – who never would be missed!
The Mikado, I

27 The idiot who praises, with enthusiastic tone,
All centuries but this, and every country but his own.
The Mikado, I

28 Three little maids from school are we,
Pert as a school-girl well can be,
Filled to the brim with girlish glee.
The Mikado, I

29 Ah, pray make no mistake,
We are not shy;
We're very wide awake,
The moon and I.
The Mikado, II

30 My object all sublime
I shall achieve in time –
To let the punishment fit the crime –
The punishment fit the crime.
The Mikado, II

31 The billiard sharp whom any one catches,
His doom's extremely hard –
He's made to dwell –
In a dungeon cell
On a spot that's always barred.
And there he plays extravagant matches
In fitless finger-stalls
On a cloth untrue
With a twisted cue
And elliptical billiard balls.
The Mikado, II

32 I have a left shoulder-blade that is a miracle of loveliness. People come miles to see it. My right elbow has a fascination that few can resist.
The Mikado, II

33 Something lingering, with boiling oil in it, I fancy.
The Mikado, II

34 The flowers that bloom in the spring,
Tra la,
Have nothing to do with the case.
I've got to take under my wing,
Tra la,
A most unattractive old thing,
Tra la,
With a caricature of a face.
The Mikado, II

35 On a tree by a river a little tom-tit
Sang 'Willow, titwillow, titwillow!'
The Mikado, II

36 If this young man expresses himself in terms too deep for *me*,
Why, what a very singularly deep young man this deep young man must be!
Patience, I

37 Poor wandering one!
Though thou hast surely strayed,
Take heart of grace,
Thy steps retrace,
Poor wandering one!
The Pirates of Penzance, I

38 I am the very model of a modern Major-General,
I've information vegetable, animal and mineral,
I know the kings of England, and I quote the fights historical,
From Marathon to Waterloo, in order categorical.
The Pirates of Penzance, I

39 About binomial theorems I'm teeming with a lot of news,

With many cheerful facts about the square on the hypoteneuse.

The Pirates of Penzance, I

40 When the foeman bares his steel,
Tarantara! tarantara!
We uncomfortable feel.

The Pirates of Penzance, II

41 When constabulary duty's to be done –
A policeman's lot is not a happy one.

The Pirates of Penzance, II

42 He combines the manners of a Marquis with the morals of a Methodist.

Ruddigore, I

43 Is life a boon?
If so, it must befall
That Death, whene'er he call,
Must call too soon.

The lines are written on Arthur Sullivan's memorial in the Embankment gardens. *The Yeoman of the Guard*, I

44 I have a song to sing O!
Sing me your song, O!

The Yeoman of the Guard, I

45 It's a song of a merryman, moping mum,
Whose soul was sad, and whose glance was glum,
Who sipped no sup, and who craved no crumb,
As he sighed for the love of a ladye.

The Yeoman of the Guard, I

46 She may very well pass for forty-three
In the dusk, with a light behind her!

Trial by Jury

47 Sir, I view the proposal to hold an international exhibition at San Francisco with an equanimity bordering on indifference.

Gilbert, His Life and Strife (Hesketh Pearson)

48 My dear chap! Good isn't the word!

Speaking to an actor after he had given a poor performance. Attrib.

49 Funny without being vulgar.

Referring to Sir Henry Irving's *Hamlet*. Attrib.

GLORY

1 What price Glory?

Maxwell Anderson (1888–1959) US playwright. Play title

2 May God deny you peace but give you glory!

Miguel de Unamuno y Jugo (1864–1936) Spanish writer. Closing words. *The Tragic Sense of Life*

3 *Sic transit gloria mundi.*
Thus the glory of the world passes away.

Thomas à Kempis (Thomas Hemmerken; c. 1380–1471) German monk. *The Imitation of Christ*, I

GOD

See also atheism, creation, faith, prayer, religion

1 Not only is there no God, but try getting a plumber on weekends.

Woody Allen (1935–) US film actor. *Getting Even*, 'My Philosophy'

2 God be in my head,
And in my understanding;
God be in my eyes,
And in my looking;
God be in my mouth,
And in my speaking;
God be in my heart,
And in my thinking;
God be at my end,
And at my departing.

Anonymous *Sarum Missal*

3 Every man thinks God is on his side. The rich and powerful know that he is.

Jean Anouilh (1910–87) French dramatist. *The Lark*

4 It were better to have no opinion of God at all, than such an opinion as is unworthy of him.

Francis Bacon (1561–1626) English philosopher. *Essays*, 'Of Superstition'

5 Then Peter opened his mouth, and said, Of a truth I perceive that God is no respecter of persons.

Bible: Acts 10:34

6 For in him we live, and move, and have our being; as certain also of your own poets have said, For we are also his offspring.

Bible: Acts 17:28

7 Seek him that maketh the seven stars and Orion, and turneth the shadow of death into the morning, and maketh the day dark with night: that calleth for the waters of the sea, and poureth them out upon the face of the earth: The Lord is his name.

Bible: Amos 5:8

8 For the kingdom of God is not in word, but in power.

Bible: I Corinthians 4:20

9 And he changeth the times and the seasons: he removeth kings, and setteth up kings: he giveth wisdom unto the wise, and knowledge to them that know understanding:
He revealeth the deep and secret things: he knoweth what is in the darkness, and the light dwelleth with him.

Bible: Daniel 2:21–22

10 Be strong and of a good courage, fear not, nor be afraid of them: for the Lord thy God, he it is that doth go with thee; he will not fail thee, nor forsake thee.

Bible: Deuteronomy 31:6

11 Let us hear the conclusion of the whole matter: Fear God, and keep his commandments: for this is the whole duty of man.

Bible: Ecclesiastes 12:13

12 I am the Lord thy God, which have brought thee out of the land of Egypt, out of the house of bondage.
Thou shalt have no other gods before me.
Thou shalt not make unto thee any graven image, or any likeness of any thing that is in heaven above, or that is in the earth beneath, or that is in the water under the earth:
Thou shalt not bow down thyself to them, nor serve them: for Lord thy God am a jealous God, visiting the iniquity of the fathers upon the children unto

the third and fourth generation of them that hate me;
And shewing mercy unto thousands of them that love me, and keep my commandments.
Thou shalt not take the name of the Lord thy God in vain; for the Lord will not hold him guiltless that taketh his name in vain.
Remember the sabbath day, to keep it holy.
Six days shalt thou labour, and do all thy work:
But the seventh day is the sabbath of the Lord thy God: in it thou shalt not do any work, thou, nor thy son, nor thy daughter, thy manservant, nor thy maidservant, nor thy cattle, nor thy stranger that is within thy gates:
For in six days the Lord made heaven and earth, the sea, and all that in them is, and rested the seventh day: wherefore the Lord blessed the sabbath day, and hallowed it.
Honour thy father and thy mother: that thy days may be long upon the land which the Lord thy God giveth thee.
Thou shalt not kill.
Thou shalt not commit adultery.
Thou shalt not steal.
Thou shalt not bear false witness against thy neighbour.
Thou shalt not covet thy neighbour's house, thou shalt not covet thy neighbour's wife, nor his manservant, nor his maidservant, nor his ox, nor his ass, nor any thing that is thy neighbour's.

Bible: Exodus 20:2–17

13 And he said, Thou canst not see my face: for there shall no man see me, and live.

Bible: Exodus 33:20

14 And he said, Go forth, and stand upon the mount before the Lord. And, behold, the Lord passed by, and a great and strong wind rent the mountains, and brake in pieces the rocks before the Lord; but the Lord was not in the wind: and after the wind an earthquake; but the Lord was not in the earthquake:
And after the earthquake a fire; but the Lord was not in the fire: and after the fire a still small voice.

Bible: I Kings 19:11–12

15 Man has learned to cope with all questions of importance without recourse to God as a working hypothesis.

Dietrich Bonhoeffer (1906–45) German theologian. *Letters and Papers from Prison*, 8 June 1944

16 A God who let us prove his existence would be an idol.

Dietrich Bonhoeffer *No Rusty Swords*

17 God's gifts put man's best gifts to shame.

Elizabeth Barrett Browning (1806–61) British poet. *Sonnets from the Portuguese*, XXVI

18 Thou shalt have one God only; who
Would be at the expense of two?

Arthur Hugh Clough (1819–61) British poet. *The Latest Decalogue*, 1

19 God moves in a mysterious way
His wonders to perform;
He plants his footsteps in the sea,
And rides upon the storm.

William Cowper (1731–1800) British poet. *Olney Hymns*, 35

20 It is the final proof of God's omnipotence that he need not exist in order to save us.

Peter De Vries (1910–93) US novelist. *The Mackerel Plaza*, Ch. 2

21 What sort of God are we portraying and believing in if we insist on what I will nickname 'the divine laser beam' type of miracle as the heart and basis of the Incarnation and Resurrection?

Bishop of Durham (1925–) British churchman. Speech, July 1986

22 God is subtle but he is not malicious.

Albert Einstein (1879–1955) German-born US physicist. Inscribed over the fireplace in the Mathematical Institute, Princeton. It refers to Einstein's objection to the quantum theory. *Albert Einstein* (Carl Seelig), Ch. 8

23 At bottom God is nothing more than an exalted father.

Sigmund Freud (1856–1939) Austrian psychoanalyst. *Totem and Taboo*

24 O worship the King, all glorious above!
O gratefully sing his power and his love!
Our Shield and Defender – the Ancient of Days,
Pavilioned in splendour, and girded with praise.

Robert Grant (1779–1838) British hymn writer. Hymn

25 Holy, holy, holy, Lord God Almighty!
Early in the morning our song shall rise to thee.

Reginald Heber (1783–1826) British bishop and hymn writer. *Holy, Holy, Holy*

26 The world is charged with the grandeur of God.

Gerard Manley Hopkins (1844–99) British Jesuit and poet. *God's Grandeur*

27 Mine eyes have seen the glory of the coming of the Lord:
He is trampling out the vintage where the grapes of wrath are stored.

Julia Ward Howe (1819–1910) US writer. *Battle Hymn of the American Republic*

28 Operationally, God is beginning to resemble not a ruler but the last fading smile of a cosmic Cheshire cat.

Julian Huxley (1887–1975) British biologist. *Religion without Revelation*

29 The chess-board is the world; the pieces are the phenomena of the universe; the rules of the game are what we call the laws of Nature. The player on the other side is hidden from us. We know that his play is always fair, just, and patient. But also we know, to our cost, that he never overlooks a mistake, or makes the smallest allowance for ignorance.

T. H. Huxley (1825–95) British biologist. *Lay Sermons*, 'A Liberal Education'

30 An honest God is the noblest work of man.

Robert G. Ingersoll (1833–99) US lawyer and agnostic. *Gods*

31 Man proposes but God disposes.

Thomas à Kempis (Thomas Hemmerken; c. 1380–1471) German monk. *The Imitation of Christ*, I

32 A man with God is always in the majority.

John Knox (c. 1514–72) Scottish religious reformer. Inscription, Reformation Monument, Geneva, Switzerland

33 What God does, He does well.

Jean de La Fontaine (1621–95) French poet. *Fables*, IX, 'Le Gland et la Citrouille'

34 I have no need of that hypothesis.

Marquis de Laplace (1749–1827) French mathematician and astronomer. On being asked by Napoleon why he had made no mention of God in his book about the universe, *Mécanique céleste*. *Men of Mathematics* (E. Bell)

35 Though the mills of God grind slowly, yet they grind exceeding small;
Though with patience He stands waiting, with exactness grinds He all.

Friedrich von Logau (1604–55) German poet and writer. *Sinngedichte*, III

36 God is the immemorial refuge of the incompetent, the helpless, the miserable. They find not only sanctuary in His arms, but also a kind of superiority, soothing to their macerated egos; He will set them above their betters.

H. L. Mencken (1880–1956) US journalist. *Notebooks*, 'Minority Report'

37 There's a Friend for little children
Above the bright blue sky,
A Friend who never changes,
Whose love will never die.

Albert Midlane (1825–1909) British hymn writer. Hymn

38 Man has never been the same since God died.
He has taken it very hard.

Edna St Vincent Millay (1892–1950) US poet. *Conversation at Midnight*, 4

39 Let us with a gladsome mind
Praise the Lord, for he is kind,
For his mercies ay endure,
Ever faithful, ever sure.

John Milton (1608–74) English poet. *Psalm*

40 What in me is dark
Illumine, what is low raise and support;
That, to the height of this great argument,
I may assert Eternal Providence,
And justify the ways of God to men.

John Milton *Paradise Lost*, Bk. I

41 God is dead: but considering the state the species Man is in, there will perhaps be caves, for ages yet, in which his shadow will be shown.

Friedrich Nietzsche (1844–1900) German philosopher. *Die Fröhliche Wissenschaft*, Bk. III

42 God is a gentleman. He prefers blondes.

Joe Orton (1933–67) British dramatist. *Loot*, II

43 One on God's side is a majority.

Wendell Phillips (1811–84) US reformer. Speech, Brooklyn, 1 Nov 1859

44 God is really only another artist. He invented the giraffe, the elephant, and the cat. He has no real style, He just goes on trying other things.

Pablo Picasso (1881–1973) Spanish painter. *Life with Picasso* Ch. 1 (Françoise Gilot and Carlton Lake),

45 God can stand being told by Professor Ayer and Marghanita Laski that He doesn't exist.

J. B. Priestley (1894–1984) British novelist. *The Listener*, 1 July 1965, 'The BBC's Duty to Society'

46 Write down that they hope they serve God; and write God first; for God defend but God should go before such villains!

William Shakespeare (1564–1616) English dramatist. *Much Ado About Nothing*, IV:2

47 But already it is time to depart, for me to die, for you to go on living; which of us takes the better course, is concealed from anyone except God.

Socrates (469–399 BC) Athenian philosopher. *Apology* (Plato)

48 In the days of my youth I remembered my God!
And He hath not forgotten my age.

Robert Southey (1774–1843) British poet. *The Old Man's Comforts, and how he Gained them*

49 Yet her conception of God was certainly not orthodox. She felt towards Him as she might have felt towards a glorified sanitary engineer; and in some of her speculations she seems hardly to distinguish between the Deity and the Drains.

Lytton Strachey (1880–1932) British writer. *Eminent Victorians*, 'Florence Nightingale'

50 It is a mistake to assume that God is interested only, or even chiefly, in religion.

William Temple (1881–1944) British churchman. Attrib.

51 O world invisible, we view thee,
O world intangible, we touch theee,
O world unknowable, we know thee.

Francis Thompson (1859–1907) British poet. *The Kingdom of God*

52 If God did not exist, it would be necessary to invent Him.

Voltaire (François-Marie Arouet; 1694–1778) French writer. *Épîtres*, 'À l'auteur du livre des trois Imposteurs'

53 If God made us in His image, we have certainly returned the compliment.

Voltaire *Le Sottisier*

GOETHE, JOHANN WOLFGANG VON

(1749–1832) German poet, dramatist, and scientist. His novel *The Sorrows of Young Werlter* (1774) brought him international fame, which was enhanced by *Faust* (1808), a poetic drama.

1 I do not know myself, and God forbid that I should.

Conversations with Eckermann, 10 Apr 1829

2 Dear friend, theory is all grey,
And the golden tree of life is green.

Faust, Pt. I

3 Two souls dwell, alas! in my breast.

Faust, Pt. I

4 I am the spirit that always denies.

Faust, Pt. I

5 A useless life is an early death.

Iphegenie, I:2

6 Superstition is the poetry of life.

Maximen und Reflexionen

7 Talent develops in quiet places, character in the full current of human life.

Torquato Tasso, I

8 God could cause us considerable

embarrassment by revealing all the secrets of nature to us: we should not know what to do for sheer apathy and boredom.
Memoirs (Riemer)

9 From today and from this place there begins a new epoch in the history of the world.
On witnessing the victory of the French at the Battle of Valmy. *The Story of Civilization* (W. Durant), Vol. II

10 I was not unaware that I had begotten a mortal.
On learning of his son's death. *The Story of Civilization* (W. Durant), Vol. X

11 *Mehr Licht!*
More light!
Attrib. last words. In fact he asked for the second shutter to be opened, to allow more light in.

GOLDING, SIR WILLIAM

(1911–93) British novelist. He made his name with *Lord of the Flies* (1954). Subsequent books include *Free Fall* (1959), *The Spire* (1964), *A Moving Target* (1982), and a trilogy comprising *Rites of Passage* (1980), *Close Quarters* (1987), and *Fire Down Below* (1989). He won a Nobel Prize in 1983.

1 Philip is a living example of natural selection. He was as fitted to survive in this modern world as a tapeworm in an intestine.
Free Fall, Ch. 2

2 Ralph wept for the end of innocence, the darkness of man's heart, and the fall through the air of the true, wise friend called Piggy.
Lord of the Flies, Ch. 12

3 With lack of sleep and too much understanding I grow a little crazy, I think, like all men at sea who live too close to each other and too close thereby to all that is monstrous under the sun and moon.
Rites of Passage

GOLDSMITH, OLIVER

(1730–74) Irish-born British writer, dramatist, and poet. He is remembered for his novel *The Vicar of Wakefield* (1776) and the play *She Stoops to Conquer* (1773) in addition to a considerable amount of verse.

Quotations about Goldsmith

1 No man was more foolish when he had not a pen in his hand, or more wise when he had.
Samuel Johnson (1709–84) British lexicographer. *The Life of Johnson* (J. Boswell)

2 An inspired idiot.
Horace Walpole (1717–97) British writer. Attrib.

Quotations by Goldsmith

3 True genius walks along a line, and, perhaps, our greatest pleasure is in seeing it so often near falling, without being ever actually down.
The Bee, 'The Characteristics of Greatness'

4 As writers become more numerous, it is natural for readers to become more indolent.
The Bee, 'Upon Unfortunate Merit'

5 To a philosopher no circumstance, however trifling, is too minute.
The Citizen of the World

6 Ill fares the land, to hast'ning ills a prey,
Where wealth accumulates, and men decay;
Princes and lords may flourish, or may fade;
A breath can make them, as a breath has made;
But a bold peasantry, their country's pride,
When once destroy'd, can never be supplied.
The Deserted Village

7 In arguing too, the parson own'd his skill,
For e'en though vanquish'd, he could argue still;
While words of learned length, and thund'ring sound
Amazed the gazing rustics rang'd around,
And still they gaz'd, and still the wonder grew,
That one small head could carry all he knew.
The Deserted Village

8 Man wants but little here below,
Nor wants that little long.
Edwin and Angelina, or the Hermit

9 The doctor found, when she was dead,
Her last disorder mortal.
Elegy on Mrs. Mary Blaize

10 The dog, to gain some private ends,
Went mad and bit the man.
Elegy on the Death of a Mad Dog

11 The man recovered of the bite,
The dog it was that died.
Elegy on the Death of a Mad Dog

12 I hate the French because they are all slaves, and wear wooden shoes.
Essays, 'Distresses of a Common Soldier'

13 The true use of speech is not so much to express our wants as to conceal them.
Essays, 'The Use of Language'

14 Friendship is a disinterested commerce between equals; love, an abject intercourse between tyrants and slaves.
The Good-Natured Man, I

15 We must touch his weaknesses with a delicate hand. There are some faults so nearly allied to excellence, that we can scarce weed out the fault without eradicating the virtue.
The Good-Natured Man, I

16 LEONTINE. An only son, sir, might expect more indulgence.
CROAKER. An only father, sir, might expect more obedience.
The Good-Natured Man, I

17 I am told he makes a very handsome corpse, and becomes his coffin prodigiously.
The Good-Natured Man, I

18 Silence is become his mother tongue.
The Good-Natured Man, II

19 I love everything that's old: old friends, old times, old manners, old books, old wine.
She Stoops to Conquer, I

20 In my time, the follies of the town crept slowly among us, but now they travel faster than a stagecoach.
She Stoops to Conquer, I

21 Let schoolmasters puzzle their brain,
With grammar, and nonsense, and learning,
Good liquor, I stoutly maintain,
Gives genius a better discerning.
She Stoops to Conquer, I

22 This is Liberty-Hall, gentlemen.
She Stoops to Conquer, II

23 Where wealth and freedom reign, contentment fails,
And honour sinks where commerce long prevails.
The Traveller

24 Laws grind the poor, and rich men rule the law.
The Traveller

25 A book may be amusing with numerous errors, or it may be very dull without a single absurdity.
The Vicar of Wakefield, Advertisement

26 I...chose my wife, as she did her wedding gown, not for a fine glossy surface, but such qualities as would wear well.
The Vicar of Wakefield, Preface

27 I was ever of opinion, that the honest man who married and brought up a large family, did more service than he who continued single and only talked of population.
The Vicar of Wakefield, Ch. 1

28 Let us draw upon content for the deficiencies of fortune.
The Vicar of Wakefield, Ch. 3

29 When lovely woman stoops to folly,
And finds too late that men betray,
What charm can soothe her melancholy,
What art can wash her guilt away?
The Vicar of Wakefield, Ch. 9

30 Conscience is a coward, and those faults it has not strength enough to prevent it seldom has justice enough to accuse.
The Vicar of Wakefield, Ch. 13

31 There is no arguing with Johnson; for when his pistol misses fire, he knocks you down with the butt end of it.
Life of Johnson (J. Boswell)

32 As I take my shoes from the shoemaker, and my coat from the tailor, so I take my religion from the priest.
Life of Johnson (J. Boswell)

GOLDWYN, SAMUEL

(Samuel Goldfish; 1882–1974) Polish-born US film producer, whose own company merged with others to form Metro-Goldwyn-Mayer (MGM) in 1924 – a company that made many Hollywood successes. He is noted for his so-called 'Goldwynisms', most of which are apocryphal.

1 Let's have some new clichés.
The Observer, 'Sayings of the Week', 24 Oct 1948

2 Why should people go out and pay money to see bad films when they can stay at home and see bad television for nothing?
The Observer, 'Sayings of the Week', 9 Sept 1956

3 Too caustic? To hell with cost; we'll make the picture anyway.
Attrib.

4 We're overpaying him but he's worth it.
Attrib.

5 What we want is a story that starts with an earthquake and works its way up to a climax.
Attrib.

6 I am willing to admit that I may not always be right, but I am never wrong.
Attrib.

7 Chaplin is no business man – all he knows is that he can't take anything less.
Attrib.

8 I don't care if it doesn't make a nickel, I just want every man, woman, and child in America to see it!
Referring to his film *The Best Years of Our Lives*. Attrib.

9 A wide screen just makes a bad film twice as bad.
Attrib.

10 For years I have been known for saying 'Include me out'; but today I am giving it up for ever.
Address, Balliol College, Oxford, 1 Mar 1945

11 In two words: im - possible.
Attrib.

12 Anybody who goes to see a psychiatrist ought to have his head examined.
Attrib.

13 Every director bites the hand that lays the golden egg.
Attrib.

14 I'll give you a definite maybe.
Attrib.

15 A verbal contract isn't worth the paper it's written on.
Attrib.

16 You ought to take the bull between the teeth.
Attrib.

17 We have all passed a lot of water since then.
Attrib.

18 I read part of it all the way through.
Attrib.

19 If Roosevelt were alive he'd turn in his grave.
Attrib.

20 It's more than magnificent – it's mediocre.
Attrib.

21 'Why only twelve?' 'That's the original number.' 'Well, go out and get thousands.'

Referring to the number of disciples whilst filming a scene for *The Last Supper*. Attrib.

22 Yes, I'm going to have a bust made of them.

Replying to an admiring comment about his wife's hands. Attrib.

23 Tell me, how did you love my picture?

Attrib. in *Colombo's Hollywood* (J. R. Colombo)

24 I don't want any yes-men around me. I want everybody to tell me the truth even if it costs them their jobs.

25 The trouble with this business is the dearth of bad pictures.

26 Why should people go out and pay money to see bad films when they can stay at home and see bad television for nothing?

Other examples

Not all Goldwynisms were said by Goldwyn. Here is a selection of remarks that could have been by him, but were, in fact, said by others.

27 The Jews and Arabs should sit down and settle their differences like good Christians.

Warren Austin (1877–1962) US politician and diplomat. Attrib.

28 All my shows are great. Some of them are bad. But they are all great.

Lew Grade (Lewis Winogradsky; 1906–) British film and TV producer. *The Observer*, 'Sayings of the Week', 14 Sept 1975

29 What about it? Do you want to crucify the boy?

Lew Grade Referring to the revelation that an actor portraying Christ on television was living with a woman to whom he was not married. Attrib.

30 Once you're dead, you're made for life.

Jimi Hendrix (1942–70) US rock musician. Attrib.

GOLF

See also sport and games

1 It's not in support of cricket but as an earnest protest against golf.

Max Beerbohm (1872–1956) British writer. Said when giving a shilling towards W. G. Grace's testimonial. *Carr's Dictionary of Extraordinary English Cricketers*

2 I wasn't this nervous playing golf when I was drinking. It's the first tournament I've won on the PGA Tour in a sober manner, so it's a great feeling knowing I can do it sober. I don't think two years ago I could have pulled this off.

John Daly (1966–) US golfer. *The Independent*, 10 May 1994

3 I find it more satisfying to be a bad player at golf. The worse you play, the better you remember the occasional good shot.

Nubar Gulbenkian (1896–1972) Turkish oil magnate. *The Daily Telegraph*, obituary, 12 Jan 1972

4 Golf may be played on Sunday, not being a game within the view of the law, but being a form of moral effort.

Stephen Leacock (1869–1944) British-born Canadian economist and humorist. *Other Fancies*, 'Why I refuse to play Golf'

5 All I've got against it is that it takes you so far from the club house.

Eric Linklater (1889–1974) Scottish novelist. Referring to golf. *Poet's Pub*, Ch. 3

6 Golf is a good walk spoiled.

Mark Twain (Samuel Langhorne Clemens; 1835–1910) US writer. Attrib.

7 Golf is one of the few sports where a white man can dress like a black pimp and not look bad.

Robin Williams (1952–) US actor. *Live*

GOOD

See also good and evil, righteousness, virtue

1 Men have never been good, they are not good, they never will be good.

Karl Barth (1886–1968) Swiss Protestant theologian. *Time*, 12 Apr 1954

2 He who would do good to another must do it in Minute Particulars.
General Good is the plea of the scoundrel, hypocrite, and flatterer.

William Blake (1757–1827) British poet. *Jerusalem*

3 *Summum bonum.*
The greatest good.

Cicero (106–43 BC) Roman orator and statesman. *De Officiis*, I

4 Nice guys finish last.

Leo Durocher (1905–91) US baseball player. Attrib.

5 What is a weed? A plant whose virtues have not been discovered.

Ralph Waldo Emerson (1803–82) US poet and essayist. *Fortune of the Republic*

6 What, after all,
Is a halo? It's only one more thing to keep clean.

Christopher Fry (1907–) British dramatist. *The Lady's Not For Burning*, I

7 Would to God that we might spend a single day really well!

Thomas à Kempis (Thomas Hemmerken; c. 1380–1471) German monk. *The Imitation of Christ*, I

8 Teach us delight in simple things,
And mirth that has no bitter springs;
Forgiveness free of evil done,
And love to all men 'neath the sun!

Rudyard Kipling (1865–1936) Indian-born British writer. *The Children's Song*

9 The greatest pleasure I know, is to do a good action by stealth, and to have it found out by accident.

Charles Lamb (1775–1834) British essayist. *The Athenaeum*, 'Table Talk by the late Elia', 4 Jan 1834

10 Goodness does not more certainly make men happy than happiness makes them good.

Walter Savage Landor (1775–1864) British poet and writer. *Imaginary Conversations*, 'Lord Brooke and Sir Philip Sidney'

11 Dowel, Dobet and Dobest.

William Langland (c. 1330–c. 1400) English poet. Do well, Do better, and Do Best: three concepts central to the search for Truth in *Piers Plowman*, in which they appear as allegorical characters. *The Vision of Piers Plowman*

12 Much benevolence of the passive order may be traced to a disinclination to inflict pain upon oneself.

George Meredith (1828–1909) British novelist. *Vittoria*, Ch. 42

13 Abashed the devil stood,
And felt how awful goodness is.

John Milton (1608–74) English poet. *Paradise Lost*, Bk. IV

14 The good is the beautiful.

Plato (429–347 BC) Greek philosopher. *Lysis*

15 Do good by stealth, and blush to find it fame.

Alexander Pope (1688–1744) British poet. *Epilogue to the Satires*, Dialogue I

16 Sweet are the uses of adversity,
Which like the toad, ugly and venomous,
Wears yet a precious jewel in his head;
And this our life, exempt from public haunt,
Finds tongues in trees, books in the running brooks,
Sermons in stones, and good in everything.

William Shakespeare (1564–1616) English dramatist. *As You Like It*, II:1

17 How far that little candle throws his beams!
So shines a good deed in a naughty world.

William Shakespeare *The Merchant of Venice*, V:1

18 Nothing can harm a good man, either in life or after death.

Socrates (469–399 BC) Athenian philosopher. *Apology* (Plato)

19 – My goodness those diamonds are lovely!
Goodness had nothing whatever to do with it.

Mae West (1892–1980) US actress. Used in 1959 as the title of the first volume of her autobiography. *Diamond Lil*, film 1932

20 You shouldn't say it is not good. You should say you do not like it; and then, you know, you're perfectly safe.

James Whistler (1834–1903) US painter. *Whistler Stories* (D. Seitz)

GOOD AND EVIL

See also evil, good, virtue and vice

1 There is so much good in the worst of us,
And so much bad in the best of us,
That it hardly becomes any of us
To talk about the rest of us.

Anonymous *Good and Bad*

2 Good can imagine Evil; but Evil cannot imagine Good.

W. H. Auden (1907–73) British poet. *A Certain World: A Commonplace Book*

3 Evil comes at leisure like the disease; good comes in a hurry like the doctor.

G. K. Chesterton (1874–1936) British writer. *The Man who was Orthodox*

4 The good die early, and the bad die late.

Daniel Defoe (1660–1731) British journalist and writer. *Character of the late Dr. Annesley*

5 A good man can be stupid and still be good. But a bad man must have brains.

Maxim Gorky (Aleksei Maksimovich Peshkov; 1868–1936) Russian writer. *The Lower Depths*

6 The web of our life is of a mingled yarn, good and ill together.

William Shakespeare (1564–1616) English dramatist. *All's Well that Ends Well*, IV:3

7 Then the liars and swearers are fools, for there are liars and swearers enow to beat the honest men and hang up them.

William Shakespeare *Macbeth*, IV:2

8 O! the more angel she,
And you the blacker devil.

William Shakespeare *Othello*, V:2

9 The good die first,
And they whose hearts are dry as summer dust
Burn to the socket.

William Wordsworth (1770–1850) British poet. *The Excursion*

GORBACHOV, MIKHAIL SERGEEVICH

(1931–) Soviet statesman. He was general secretary of the Soviet Communist party (1985–91) and president (1988–91). He resigned following his failure to prevent the break-up of the Soviet Union into independent states. His *glasnost* (openness) and *perestroika* (progress) policies aimed at radical reform of Soviet society and promoted better relations with the West.

Quotations about Gorbachov

1 This man, comrades, has a nice smile, but he has iron teeth.

Andrei Gromyko, Soviet foreign minister. Speech to Politburo, 1985

2 Gorbachev is a president without a people – just an army, a party and a KGB.

Vitaly Korotich Editor of the radical magazine *Ogonyok*.

3 You bring in your wake destruction, ruin, famine, cold, blood and tears...Amid the applause of the West, Mikhail Sergeievich has forgotten whose President he is.

Sazhi Umalatova Soviet parliament deputy from the North Caucasus. Proposing a motion of no confidence in President Gorbachev, Dec 1990

4 I separate myself from the position and policies of Gorbachev, and I call for his immediate resignation. He has brought the country to dictatorship in the name of presidential rule.

Boris Yeltsin (1931–) Russian president. Television interview, Feb 1991

Quotations by Gorbachov

5 Some comrades apparently find it hard to understand that democracy is just a slogan.

The Observer, 'Sayings of the Week', 1 Feb 1987

6 The essence of perestroika lies in the fact that *it unites socialism with democracy.*

Perestroika

7 And if the Russian word 'perestroika' has easily entered the international lexicon, this is due to more than just interest in what is going on in the Soviet Union. Now the whole world needs restructuring i.e. progressive development, a fundamental change.

Perestroika

8 Our rockets can find Halley's comet and fly to

Venus with amazing accuracy, but side by side with these scientific and technical triumphs is an obvious lack of efficiency in using scientific achievements for economic needs, and many Soviet household appliances are of poor quality.
Perestroika

9 Democracy is the wholesome and pure air without which a socialist public organisation cannot live a full-blooded life.
Report to the 27th Party Congress, 25 Feb 1986

10 No party has a monopoly over what is right.
Speech, Mar 1986

11 The Soviet people want full-blooded and unconditional democracy.
Speech, July 1988

12 Life is making us abandon established stereotypes and outdated views, it is making us discard illusions.
Speech to the United Nations, 7 Dec 1988

13 We must look for ways to improve the international situation and build a new world – and we must do it together.
Speech to the United Nations, 7 Dec 1988

14 Only Socialism would put up with it for so long. Capitalism would have gone bankrupt years ago.
Talking of sub-standard workmanship in the Soviet Union. Television documentary, 23 Mar 1987

GOSSIP

See also secrecy

1 The gossip of two women will destroy two houses.
Arabic proverb

2 A tale never loses in the telling.
Proverb

3 Don't wash your dirty linen in public.
Proverb

4 No names, no pack-drill.
Proverb

5 There's no smoke without fire.
Proverb

6 Throw dirt enough, and some will stick.
Proverb

7 Walls have ears.
Proverb

8 Listeners never hear good of themselves.
Proverb

9 How these curiosities would be quite forgot, did not such idle fellows as I am put them down.
John Aubrey (1626–97) English antiquary. *Brief Lives*, 'Venetia Digby'

10 Men have always detested women's gossip because they suspect the truth: their measurements are being taken and compared.
Erica Jong (1942–) US poet and writer. *Fear of Flying*, Ch. 6

11 Now Nel belonged to the town and all of its ways. She had given herself over to them, and the flick of their tongues would drive her back into her little dry corner where she could cling to her spittle high above the breath of the snake and the fall.
Toni Morrison (Chloe Anthony Morrison; 1931–) US novelist. *Sula*

12 No one gossips about other people's secret virtues.
Bertrand Russell (1872–1970) British philosopher. *On Education*

13 Her first economic drive will be to replace X-ray by hearsay.
Gwyn Thomas (1913–81) British writer. *The Keep*, II

14 I remember that a wise friend of mine did usually say, 'that which is everybody's business is nobody's business'.
Izaak Walton (1593–1683) English writer. *The Compleat Angler*, Ch. 2

GOVERNMENT

See also democracy, Houses of Parliament, monarchy, opposition, politicians, politics

1 I will undoubtedly have to seek what is happily known as gainful employment, which I am glad to say does not describe holding public office.
Dean Acheson (1893–1971) US lawyer and statesman. Remark made on leaving his post as secretary of state, 1952; he subsequently returned to private legal practice

2 The danger is not that a particular class is unfit to govern. Every class is unfit to govern.
Lord Acton (1834–1902) British historian. Letter to Mary Gladstone, 1881

3 The Austrian Government...is a system of despotism tempered by casualness.
Victor Adler (1852–1918) Austrian socialist. Speech, International Socialist Congress, Paris, 17 July 1889

4 Whose Finger do you want on the Trigger When the World Situation Is So Delicate?
Anonymous Headline from the *Daily Mirror* on the day before the General Election, Oct 1951. *Publish and Be Damned* (Hugh Cudlipp), 1953

5 Where some people are very wealthy and others have nothing, the result will be either extreme democracy or absolute oligarchy, or despotism will come from either of those excesses.
Aristotle (384–322 BC) Greek philosopher. *Politics*, Bk. IV

6 One to mislead the public, another to mislead the Cabinet, and the third to mislead itself.
Herbert Henry Asquith (1852–1928) British statesman. Explaining why the War Office kept three sets of figures. *The Price of Glory* (Alastair Horne), Ch. 2

7 My language fails
Go out and govern new South Wales.
Hilaire Belloc (1870–1953) British writer. *Cautionary Tales*, 'Lord Lundy'

8 The object of government in peace and in war is not the glory of rulers or of races, but the happiness of the common man.
Lord Beveridge (1879–1963) British economist. *Social Insurance*

9 Too bad all the people who know how to run the country are busy driving cabs and cutting hair.

George Burns (1896–) US comedian.

10 You had better have one King than five hundred.

Charles II (1630–85) King of England. Remark after dissolving the Oxford Parliament, 28 Mar 1681; he did not summon parliament again

11 A small acquaintance with history shows that all Governments are selfish and the French Governments more selfish than most.

David Eccles (1904–) British politician. *The Observer*, 'Sayings of the Year', 29 Dec 1962

12 The king's council was wont to be chosen of the great princes, and of the greatest lords of the land, both spiritual and temporal.... Wherethrough, when they came together they were so occupied with their own matters that they attended but little, and other whiles nothing, to the king's matters.

John Fortescue (c. 1394–1476) English jurist. *The Governance of England*

13 He was uniformly of an opinion which, though not a popular one, he was ready to aver, that the right of governing was not property but a trust.

Charles James Fox (1749–1806) British Whig politician. Referring to William Pitt's plans for parliamentary reform. *C.J. Fox* (J. L. Hammond)

14 The principles of a free constitution are irrecoverably lost, when the legislative power is nominated by the executive.

Edward Gibbon (1737–94) British historian. *Decline and Fall of the Roman Empire*, Ch. 3

15 A government that is big enough to give you all you want is big enough to take it all away.

Barry Goldwater (1909–) US politician. *Bachman's Book of Freedom Quotations* (M. Ivens and R. Dunstan)

16 We at no time stand so highly in our estate royal as in the time of Parliament, wherein we as head and you as members are conjoined and knit together into one body politic.

Henry VIII (1491–1547) King of England. Speech to a deputation from the House of Commons, 31 Mar 1543

17 They that are discontented under *monarchy*, call it *tyranny*; and they that are displeased with *aristocracy*, call it *oligarchy*: so also, they which find themselves grieved under a *democracy*, call it *anarchy*, which signifies the want of government; and yet I think no man believes, that want of government, is any new kind of government.

Thomas Hobbes (1588–1679) English philosopher. *Leviathan*, Pt. II, Ch. 19

18 I would not give half a guinea to live under one form of government rather than another. It is of no moment to the happiness of an individual.

Samuel Johnson (1709–84) British lexicographer. *Life of Johnson* (J. Boswell), Vol. II

19 We give the impression of being in office but not in power.

Norman Lamont (1942–) British Conservative politician. *The Observer*, 13 June 1993

20 Any cook should be able to run the country.

Lenin (Vladimir Ilich Ulyanov; 1870–1924) Russian revolutionary leader. *The First Circle* (Alexander Solzhenitsyn)

21 What is our task? To make Britain a fit country for heroes to live in.

David Lloyd George (1863–1945) British Liberal statesman. Speech, 24 Nov 1918

22 Government has no other end but the preservation of property.

John Locke (1632–1704) English philosopher. *Second Treatise on Civil Government*

23 The Commons, faithful to their system, remained in a wise and masterly inactivity.

James Mackintosh (1765–1832) Scottish lawyer, philosopher, and historian. *Vindiciae Gallicae*

24 Every country has the government it deserves.

Joseph de Maistre (1753–1821) French monarchist. *Lettres et Opuscules Inédits*, 15 Aug 1811

25 The worst government is the most moral. One composed of cynics is often very tolerant and human. But when fanatics are on top there is no limit to oppression.

H. L. Mencken (1880–1956) US journalist. *Notebooks*, 'Minority Report'

26 One day the don't-knows will get in, and then where will we be?

Spike Milligan (1918–) British comic actor and writer. Attributed remark made about a pre-election poll

27 The rights of parliament should be preserved sacred and inviolable, wherever they are found. This kind of government, once so universal all over Europe, is now almost vanished from amongst the nations thereof. Our king's dominions are the only supporters of this noble Gothic constitution, save only what little remains may be found thereof in Poland.

William Molyneux (1656–98) Irish politician. *The Case of Ireland's being Bound by Acts of Parliament in England stated* (Pamphlet, 1698)

28 Do you not know, my son, with how little wisdom the world is governed?

Axel Oxenstierna (1583–1654) Swedish statesman. Letter to his son, 1648

29 Government, even in its best state, is but a necessary evil; in its worst state, an intolerable one.

Thomas Paine (1737–1809) British writer. *Common Sense*, Ch. 1

30 As to religion, I hold it to be the indispensable duty of government to protect all conscientious professors thereof, and I know of no other business which government hath to do therewith.

Thomas Paine *Common Sense*, Ch. 4

31 Let the people think they govern and they will be governed.

William Penn (1644–1718) English preacher. *Some Fruits of Solitude*, 337

32 We live under a government of men and morning newspapers.

Wendell Phillips (1811–84) US reformer. *Address: The Press*

33 Parliaments are the great lie of our time.

Konstantin Pobedonostsev (1827–1907) Russian jurist and Procurator of the Holy Synod. *Moskovskii Sbornik*

34 Secrecy is the first essential in affairs of the State.

Cardinal Richelieu (1585–1642) French statesman. *Testament Politique*, Maxims

35 I don't make jokes – I just watch the government and report the facts.

Will Rogers (1879–1935) US actor and humorist. *Saturday Review*, 'A Rogers Thesaurus', 25 Aug 1962

36 Hansard is history's ear, already listening.

Herbert Samuel (1870–1963) British Liberal statesman. *The Observer*, 'Sayings of the Week', 18 Dec 1949

37 Parliament is the longest running farce in the West End.

Cyril Smith (1928–) British Liberal politician. *The Times*, 23 Sept 1977

38 It would be desirable if every government, when it comes to power, should have its old speeches burned.

Philip Snowden (1864–1937) British politician. *Biography* (C. E. Bechafer Roberts)

39 Accidentally.

Talleyrand (Charles Maurice de Talleyrand-Périgord; 1754–1838) French politician. Replying, during the reign of Louis Philippe, to the query 'How do you think this government will end?' *The Wheat and the Chaff* (F. Mitterand)

40 People are not willing to be governed by those who do not speak their language.

Norman Tebbit (1931–) British politician. *The Observer*, 24 Nov 1991

41 Governments needs to have both shepherds and butchers.

Voltaire (François-Marie Arouet; 1694–1778) French writer. *Notebooks*

42 Many people consider the things which government does for them to be social progress, but they consider the things government does for others as socialism.

Earl Warren (1891–1971) US lawyer. *Peter's Quotations* (Laurence J. Peter)

43 The people's government, made for the people, made by the people, and answerable to the people.

Daniel Webster (1782–1852) US statesman. Second speech on Foote's resolution, 26 Jan 1830

44 If people behaved in the way nations do they would all be put in straitjackets.

Tennessee Williams (1911–83) US dramatist. BBC interview

45 The foundation of the government of a nation must be built upon the rights of the people, but the administration must be entrusted to experts.

Sun Yat-sen (1867–1925) Chinese revolutionary leader. *The Three Principles of the People*

46 The English nation is the only one on earth which has successfully regulated the power of its kings by resisting them; and which, after repeated efforts, has established that beneficial government under which the Prince, all powerful for good, is restrained from doing ill.

Voltaire (François-Marie Arouet; 1694–1778) French writer. *Lettres philosophiques*

GRAMMAR

See also language, words

1 'Whom are you?' said he, for he had been to night school.

George Ade (1866–1944) US dramatist and humorist. *Bang! Bang!: The Steel Box*

2 When I split an infinitive, god damn it, I split it so it stays split.

Raymond Chandler (1888–1959) US novelist. Letter to his English publisher

3 By being so long in the lowest form I gained an immense advantage over the cleverest boys...I got into my bones the essential structure of the normal British sentence – which is a noble thing.

Winston Churchill (1874–1965) British statesman. *My Early Life*, Ch. 2

4 This is the sort of English up with which I will not put.

Winston Churchill The story is that Churchill wrote the comment in the margin of a report in which a civil servant had used an awkward construction to avoid ending a sentence with a preposition. An alternative version substitutes 'bloody nonsense' for 'English'. *Plain Words* (E. Gowers), Ch. 9

5 I will not go down to posterity talking bad grammar.

Benjamin Disraeli (1804–81) British statesman. Remark made when correcting proofs of his last parliamentary speech, 31 Mar 1881. *Disraeli* (Blake), Ch. 32

6 Grammar, which can govern even kings.

Molière (Jean Baptiste Poquelin; 1622–73) French dramatist. *Les Femmes savantes*, II:6

7 I am the Roman Emperor, and am above grammar.

Sigismund (1368–1437) Holy Roman Emperor. Responding to criticism of his Latin. Attrib.

8 Why care for grammar as long as we are good?

Artemus Ward (Charles Farrar Browne; 1834–67) US humorous writer. *Pyrotechny*

9 Subjunctive to the last, he preferred to ask, 'And that, sir, would be the Hippodrome?'

Alexander Woollcott (1887–1943) US journalist. *While Rome Burns*, 'Our Mrs Parker'

GRANT, ULYSSES S.

(1822–85) US general who became a Republican President (1869–77). As supreme commander of the Federal armies he defeated the Confederates.

Quotations about Grant

1 When Grant once gets possession of a place, he holds on to it as if he had inherited it.

Abraham Lincoln (1809–65) US statesman. Letter, 22 June 1864

2 Grant stood by me when I was crazy and I stood by him when he was drunk.

William Sherman (1820–91) US general and president. *Abraham Lincoln: The War Years* (Carl Sandburg)

Quotations by Grant

3 No terms except unconditional and immediate surrender can be accepted. I propose to move immediately upon your works.

Message to opposing commander, Simon Bolivar Buckner, during siege of Fort Donelson, 16 Feb 1862.

4 I purpose to fight it out on this line, if it takes all summer.

Dispatch to Washington, 11 May 1864

5 Let us have peace.

On accepting the Presidential nomination. Letter, 29 May 1868

6 I know no method to secure the repeal of bad or obnoxious laws so effective as their stringent execution.

Inaugural address, 4 Mar 1869

7 Let no guilty man escape, if it can be avoided… No personal considerations should stand in the way of performing a public duty.

Referring to the Whiskey Ring. Endorsement of a letter, 29 July 1875

GRATITUDE

1 Let me say that the credit belongs to the boys in the back rooms. It isn't the man who sits in the limelight like me who should have the praise. It is not the men who sit in prominent places. It is the men in the back rooms.

Lord Beaverbrook (Maxwell Aitken; 1879–1964) Canadian-born politician and newspaper proprietor. From the song 'The Boys in the Back Room', sung by Marlene Dietrich in the film *Destry Rides Again.*

2 There are minds so impatient of inferiority that their gratitude is a species of revenge, and they return benefits, not because recompense is a pleasure, but because obligation is a pain.

Samuel Johnson (1709–84) British lexicographer. *The Rambler*

3 Thank me no thankings, nor proud me no prouds.

William Shakespeare (1564–1616) English dramatist. *Romeo and Juliet*, III:5

GRAY, THOMAS

(1716–71) British poet. He published several odes but is best known for his *Elegy Written in a Country Churchyard* (1751), written at Stoke Poges in Buckinghamshire.

1 The Curfew tolls the knell of parting day,
The lowing herd winds slowly o'er the lea,
The plowman homeward plods his weary way,
And leaves the world to darkness and to me.

Elegy Written in a Country Churchyard

2 Let not Ambition mock their useful toil,
Their homely joys, and destiny obscure;
Nor Grandeur hear with a disdainful smile,
The short and simple annals of the poor.

Elegy Written in a Country Churchyard

3 The boast of heraldry, the pomp of pow'r,
And all that beauty, all that wealth e'er gave,
Awaits alike th' inevitable hour,
The paths of glory lead but to the grave.

Elegy Written in a Country Churchyard

4 Can storied urn or animated bust
Back to its mansion call the fleeting breath?
Can honour's voice provoke the silent dust,
Or flatt'ry soothe the dull cold ear of death?

Elegy Written in a Country Churchyard

5 Full many a gem of purest ray serene,
The dark unfathom'd caves of ocean bear:
Full many a flower is born to blush unseen,
And waste its sweetness on the desert air.

Elegy Written in a Country Churchyard

6 Some village-Hampden, that with dauntless breast
The little Tyrant of his fields withstood;
Some mute inglorious Milton here may rest,
Some Cromwell guiltless of his country's blood.

Elegy Written in a Country Churchyard

7 Far from the madding crowd's ignoble strife,
Their sober wishes never learn'd to stray;
Along the cool sequester'd vale of life
They kept the noiseless tenor of their way.

Elegy Written in a Country Churchyard

8 Here rests his head upon the lap of Earth
A youth to fortune and to fame unknown.
Fair Science frown'd not on his humble birth,
And Melancholy mark'd him for her own.

Elegy Written in a Country Churchyard

9 Alas, regardless of their doom,
The little victims play!

Ode on a Distant Prospect of Eton College

10 To each his suff'rings, all are men,
Condemn'd alike to groan;
The tender for another's pain,
Th' unfeeling for his own.
Yet ah! why should they know their fate?
Since sorrow never comes too late,
And happiness too swiftly flies.
Thought would destroy their paradise.
No more; where ignorance is bliss,
'Tis folly to be wise.

Ode on a Distant Prospect of Eton College

11 What female heart can gold despise?
What cat's averse to fish?

Ode on the Death of a Favourite Cat

12 A fav'rite has no friend.

Ode on the Death of a Favourite Cat

13 Not all that tempts your wand'ring eyes
And heedless hearts, is lawful prize;
Nor all, that glisters, gold.

Ode on the Death of a Favourite Cat

GREATNESS

1 A truly great man never puts away the simplicity of a child.

Chinese proverb

2 The dullard's envy of brilliant men is always assuaged by the suspicion that they will come to a bad end.

Max Beerbohm (1872–1956) British writer. *Zuleika Dobson*

3 Great men are but life-sized. Most of them, indeed, are rather short.

Max Beerbohm *And Even Now*

4 Great things are done when men and mountains meet;
This is not done by jostling in the street.

William Blake (1757–1827) British poet. *Gnomic Verses*

5 Nothing grows well in the shade of a big tree.

Constantin Brancusi (1876–1957) Romanian sculptor. Refusing Rodin's invitation to work in his studio *Compton's Encyclopedia*

6 No great man lives in vain. The history of the world is but the biography of great men.

Thomas Carlyle (1795–1881) Scottish historian and essayist. *Heroes and Hero-Worship*, 'The Hero as Divinity'

7 To be great is to be misunderstood.

Ralph Waldo Emerson (1803–82) US poet and essayist. *Essays*, 'Self-Reliance'

8 The world's great men have not commonly been great scholars, nor great scholars great men.

Oliver Wendell Holmes (1809–94) US writer. *The Autocrat of the Breakfast Table*, Ch. 6

9 If I am a great man, then a good many of the great men of history are frauds.

Bonar Law (1858–1923) British statesman. Attrib.

10 You are one of the forces of nature.

Jules Michelet (1798–1874) French historian. From a letter received by Dumas *Memoirs*, Vol. VI, Ch. 138 (Alexandre Dumas)

11 To be alone is the fate of all great minds – a fate deplored at times, but still always chosen as the less grievous of two evils.

Arthur Schopenhauer (1788–1860) German philosopher. *Aphorismen zur Lebensweisheit*

12 Some are born great, some achieve greatness, and some have greatness thrust upon 'em.

William Shakespeare (1564–1616) English dramatist. *Twelfth Night*, II:5

13 'My name is Ozymandias, king of kings:
Look on my works, ye Mighty, and despair!'

Percy Bysshe Shelley (1792–1822) British poet. *Ozymandias*

14 Oh, Vanity of vanities!
How wayward the decrees of Fate are;
How very weak the very wise,
How very small the very great are!

William Makepeace Thackeray (1811–63) British novelist. *Vanitas Vanitatum*

15 A great city is that which has the greatest men and women.

Walt Whitman (1819–92) US poet. *Song of the Broad-Axe*, 5

GREED

See also food, materialism, obesity

1 He that eats till he is sick must fast till he is well.

Hebrew proverb

2 Give him an inch and he'll take a yard.

Proverb

3 Kill not the goose that lays the golden egg.

Proverb

4 The eye is bigger than the belly.

Proverb

5 Beware that you do not lose the substance by grasping at the shadow.

Aesop (6th century BC) Reputed Greek writer of fables. *Fables*, 'The Dog and the Shadow'

6 GLUTTON, n. A person who escapes the evils of moderation by committing dyspepsia.

Ambrose Bierce (1842–c. 1914) US writer and journalist. *The Devil's Dictionary*

7 But answer came there none –
And this was scarcely odd because
They'd eaten every one.

Lewis Carroll (Charles Lutwidge Dodgson; 1832–98) British writer. *Through the Looking-Glass*, Ch. 4

8 Gluttony is an emotional escape, a sign something is eating us.

Peter De Vries (1910–93) US novelist. *Comfort me with Apples*, Ch. 7

9 More die in the United States of too much food than of too little.

John Kenneth Galbraith (1908–) US economist. *The Affluent Society*, Ch. 9

10 The mountain sheep are sweeter,
But the valley sheep are fatter;
We therefore deemed it meeter
To carry off the latter.

Thomas Love Peacock (1785–1866) British novelist. *The Misfortunes of Elphin*, Ch. 11, 'The War-Song of Dinas Vawr'

11 These citizens are always willing to bet that what Nicely-Nicely dies of will be over-feeding and never anything small like pneumonia, for Nicely-Nicely is known far and wide as a character who dearly loves to commit eating.

Damon Runyon (1884–1946) US writer. *Take it Easy*, 'Lonely Heart'

12 Wealth is like sea-water; the more we drink, the thirstier we become; and the same is true of fame.

Arthur Schopenhauer (1788–1860) German philosopher. *Parerga and Paralipomena*

13 People will swim through shit if you put a few bob in it.

Peter Sellers (1925–80) British comic actor. *Halliwell's Filmgoer's and Video Viewer's Companion*

14 He hath eaten me out of house and home.

William Shakespeare (1564–1616) English dramatist. *Henry IV, Part Two*, II:1

GREENE, GRAHAM

(1904–91) British novelist. After the success of *The Man Within* (1929), he published *Brighton Rock* (1938), *The Power and the Glory* (1940), *The Heart of the Matter* (1948), *The Human Factor* (1978), *Monsignor Quixote* (1982), *The Captain and the Enemy* (1988), and others. His 'entertainments' (literary thrillers) include *The Third Man* (1950) and *Our Man in Havana* (1958).

1 Those who marry God…can become domesticated too – it's just as humdrum a marriage as all the others.

A Burnt-Out Case, Ch. 1

2 I have often noticed that a bribe…has that effect – it changes a relation. The man who offers a bribe gives away a little of his own importance; the bribe once accepted, he becomes the inferior, like a man who has paid for a woman.

The Comedians, Pt. I, Ch. 4

3 Catholics and Communists have committed great crimes, but at least they have not stood aside, like an established society, and been indifferent. I would rather have blood on my hands than water like Pilate.

The Comedians, Pt. III, Ch. 4

4 He gave the impression that very many cities had rubbed him smooth.

A Gun for Sale, Ch. 4

5 Against the beautiful and the clever and the successful, one can wage a pitiless war, but not against the unattractive.

The Heart of the Matter

6 They had been corrupted by money, and he had been corrupted by sentiment. Sentiment was the more dangerous, because you couldn't name its price. A man open to bribes was to be relied upon below a certain figure, but sentiment might uncoil in the heart at a name, a photograph, even a smell remembered.

The Heart of the Matter

7 That whisky priest, I wish we had never had him in the house.

The Power and the Glory, Pt. I

8 Of course, before we *know* he is a saint, there will have to be miracles.

The Power and the Glory, Pt. IV

9 Perhaps if I wanted to be understood or to understand I would bamboozle myself into belief, but I am a reporter; God exists only for leader-writers.

The Quiet American

10 Fame is a powerful aphrodisiac.

Radio Times, 10 Sept 1964

GREER, GERMAINE

(1939–) Australian-born British writer and feminist. She made her reputation with *The Female Eunuch* (1970). Subsequent books include *Sex and Destiny* (1984).

Quotations about Greer

1 She was once cool but Mr Gravity's been very unkind to that woman.

Jennifer Saunders British comedian. *Absolutely Fabulous*

Quotations by Greer

2 Probably the only place where a man can feel really secure is in a maximum security prison, except for the imminent threat of release.

The Female Eunuch

3 Mother is the dead heart of the family, spending father's earnings on consumer goods to enhance the environment in which he eats, sleeps and watches the television.

The Female Eunuch

4 Love, love, love – all the wretched cant of it, masking egotism, lust, masochism, fantasy under a mythology of sentimental postures, a welter of self-induced miseries and joys, blinding and masking the essential personalities in the frozen gestures of courtship, in the kissing and the dating and the desire, the compliments and the quarrels which vivify its barrenness.

The Female Eunuch

5 When the life of the party wants to express the idea of a pretty woman in mime, he undulates his two hands in the air and leers expressively…The most popular image of the female despite the exigencies of the clothing trade is all boobs and buttocks, a hallucinating sequence of parabolas and bulges.

The Female Eunuch

6 Buttock fetishism is comparatively rare in our culture…Girls are often self-conscious about their behinds, draping themselves in long capes and tunics, but it is more often because they are too abundant in that region than otherwise.

The Female Eunuch

GREETINGS

1 Take me to your leader.

Anonymous Customary line spoken by Martian invaders.

2 *Atque in perpetuum, frater, ave atque vale.*
And for ever, brother, hail and farewell!

Catullus (c 84–c. 54 BC) Roman poet. *Carmina*, CI

3 Dr Livingstone, I presume?

Henry Morton Stanley (1841–1904) British explorer. On finding David Livingstone at Ujiji on Lake Tanganyika, Nov 1871. *How I found Livingstone*, Ch. 11

GUIDANCE

See also leadership

1 Everyman, I will go with thee, and be thy guide.
In thy most need to go by thy side.

Anonymous *Everyman* Pt. 1

2 Wandering in a vast forest at night, I have only a faint light to guide me. A stranger appears and says to me: 'My friend, you should blow out your candle in order to find your way more clearly.' This stranger is a theologian.

Denis Diderot (1713–84) French writer. *Addition aux pensées philosophiques*

3 A little onward lend thy guiding hand
To these dark steps, a little further on.

John Milton (1608–74) English poet. *Samson Agonistes*

GUILT

See also conscience, regret

1 It is quite gratifying to feel guilty if you haven't done anything wrong: how noble! Whereas it is rather hard and certainly depressing to admit guilt and to repent.

Hannah Arendt (1906–75) German-born US philosopher and historian. *Eichmann in Jerusalem*, Ch. 15

2 Alone, alone, about the dreadful wood

Of conscious evil runs a lost mankind,
Dreading to find its Father.

W. H. Auden (1907–73) British poet. *For the Time Being*, 'Chorus'

3 When Pilate saw that he could prevail nothing, but that rather a tumult was made, he took water, and washed his hands before the multitude, saying, I am innocent of the blood of this just person: see ye to it.
Then answered all the people, and said, His blood be on us, and on our children.

Bible: Matthew 27:24–25

4 Dread remorse when you are tempted to err, Miss Eyre: remorse is the poison of life.

Charlotte Brontë (1815–55) British novelist and poet. *Jane Eyre*, Ch. 14

5 Then, my lord, be his blood on your own conscience. You might have saved him if you would. I cannot pardon him because I dare not.

Charles II (1630–85) King of England. Reply to the Earl of Essex, who had protested St Oliver Plunket's innocence of the treason for which he had been sentenced to death. *The Later Stuarts* (Sir George Clark)

6 The many men, so beautiful!
And they all dead did lie:
And a thousand thousand slimy things
Lived on; and so did I.

Samuel Taylor Coleridge (1772–1834) British poet. *The Rime of the Ancient Mariner*, IV

7 St. Thomas, guard for me my kingdom! To you I declare myself guilty of that for which others bear the blame.

Henry II (1133–89) King of England. Said at the outbreak of the Great Rebellion, 1173–74; one of Henry's first actions was to perform a public penance for Thomas Becket's murder. *Chronique de la guerre entre les Anglois et les Ecossais en 1173 et 1174* (Jordan Fantosme)

8 Love bade me welcome; yet my soul drew back,
Guilty of dust and sin.

George Herbert (1593–1633) English poet. *Love*

9 You will put on a dress of guilt
and shoes with broken high ideals.

Roger McGough (1937–) British poet. *Comeclose and Sleepnow*

10 HICKEY: Christ, can you imagine what a guilty skunk she made me feel! If she'd only admitted once she didn't believe any more in her pipe dream that some day I'd behave!

Eugene O'Neill (1888–1953) US dramatist. *The Iceman Cometh*

11 I am alone the villain of the earth,
And feel I am so most.

William Shakespeare (1564–1616) English dramatist. *Antony and Cleopatra*, IV:6

12 I have heard,
That guilty creatures sitting at a play
Have by the very cunning of the scene
Been struck so to the soul that presently
They have proclaim'd their malefactions;
For murder, though it have no tongue, will speak
With most miraculous organ.

William Shakespeare *Hamlet*, II:2

13 The lady doth protest too much, methinks.

William Shakespeare *Hamlet*, III:2

14 O! my offence is rank, it smells to heaven.

William Shakespeare *Hamlet*, III:3

15 Suspicion always haunts the guilty mind;
The thief doth fear each bush an officer.

William Shakespeare *Henry VI, Part Three*, V:6

16 A little water clears us of this deed.

William Shakespeare *Macbeth*, II:2

17 I am in blood
Stepp'd in so far that, should I wade no more,
Returning were as tedious as go o'er.

William Shakespeare *Macbeth*, III:4

18 Out, damned spot! out, I say!

William Shakespeare *Macbeth*, V:1

19 Here's the smell of the blood still. All the perfumes of Arabia will not sweeten this little hand.

William Shakespeare *Macbeth*, V:1

GULLIBILITY

See also foolishness, impressionability

1 There's a sucker born every minute.

Phineas Taylor Barnum (1810–91) US showman. Attrib.

2 When lovely woman stoops to folly,
And finds too late that men betray,
What charm can soothe her melancholy,
What art can wash her guilt away?

Oliver Goldsmith (1728–74) Irish-born British writer. *The Vicar of Wakefield*, Ch. 9

3 Man is a dupable animal. Quacks in medicine, quacks in religion, and quacks in politics know this, and act upon that knowledge.

Robert Southey (1774–1843) British poet. *The Doctor*, Ch. 87

H

HABIT

See also custom

1 Old habits die hard.

Proverb

2 Habit is a great deadener.

Samuel Beckett (1906–89) Irish novelist and dramatist. *Waiting for Godot*, III

3 Curious things, habits. People themselves never knew they had them.

Agatha Christie (1891–1976) British detective-story writer. *Witness for the Prosecution*

4 Men's natures are alike; it is their habits that carry them far apart.

Confucius (K'ung Fu-tzu; 551–479 BC) Chinese philosopher. *Analects*

5 Cultivate only the habits that you are willing should master you.

Elbert Hubbard (1856–1915) US writer. Attrib.

6 They do those little personal things people sometimes do when they think they are alone in railway carriages; things like smelling their own armpits.

Jonathan Miller (1934–) British doctor and television and stage director. *Beyond the Fringe*

HALF MEASURES

1 Two half-truths do not make a truth, and two half-cultures do not make a culture.

Arthur Koestler (1905–83) Hungarian-born British writer . *The Ghost in the Machine*, Preface

2 I'm not really a Jew; just Jew-ish, not the whole hog.

Jonathan Miller (1934–) British doctor and television and stage director. *Beyond the Fringe*

HALIFAX, GEORGE SAVILLE, MARQUIS OF

(1633–95) English statesman. Dismissed from offices he had held by James II, he supported the Glorious Revolution.

1 Men are not hanged for stealing horses, but that horses may not be stolen.

Political, Moral and Miscellaneous Thoughts and Reflections

2 It is a general mistake to think the men we like are good for everything, and those we do not, good for nothing.

Political, Moral and Miscellaneous Thoughts and Reflections

3 It is flattering some men to endure them.

Political, Moral and Miscellaneous Thoughts and Reflections

4 Our virtues and vices couple with one another, and get children that resemble both their parents.

Political, Moral and Miscellaneous Thoughts and Reflections

5 Popularity is a crime from the moment it is sought; it is only a virtue where men have it whether they will or no.

Political, Moral and Miscellaneous Thoughts and Reflections

6 When the People contend for their Liberty, they seldom get anything by their Victory but new masters.

Political, Moral and Miscellaneous Thoughts and Reflections

7 Power is so apt to be insolent and Liberty to be saucy, that they are seldom upon good Terms.

Political, Moral and Miscellaneous Thoughts and Reflections

8 Most men make little use of their speech than to give evidence against their own understanding.

Political, Moral and Miscellaneous Thoughts and Reflections

9 He had said he had known many kicked down stairs, but he never knew any kicked up stairs before.

Original Memoirs (Burnet)

HAMPTON, CHRISTOPHER

(1946–) British writer and dramatist. Plays include *The Philanthropist* (1970), *Savages* (1973), *Treats* (1976), and *Les Liaisons Dangereuses* (1985).

1 You know very well that unless you're a scientist, it's much more important for a theory to be shapely, than for it to be true.

The Philanthropist, Sc. 1

2 You see, I always divide people into two groups. Those who live by what they know to be a lie, and those who live by what they believe, falsely, to be the truth.

The Philanthropist, Sc. 6

3 If I had to give a definition of capitalism I would say: the process whereby American girls turn into American women.

Savages, Sc. 16

4 It's possible to disagree with someone about the ethics of non-violence without wanting to kick his face in.

Treats, Sc. 4

5 Asking a working writer what he thinks about critics is like asking a lamp-post how it feels about dogs.

The Sunday Times Magazine, 16 Oct 1977

HAPPINESS

See also contentment, laughter, pleasure

1 One joy scatters a hundred griefs.

Chinese proverb

2 I wonder why happiness is despised nowadays: dismissively confused with comfort or complacency, judged an enemy of social – even technological – progress.

Julian Barnes (1946–) British novelist. *Metroland*

3 If you haven't been happy very young, you can still be happy later on, but it's much harder. You need more luck.

Simone de Beauvoir (1908–86) French writer. *The Observer*, 'Sayings of the Week', 19 May 1975

4 The greatest happiness of the greatest number is the foundation of morals and legislation.

Jeremy Bentham (1748–1832) British philosopher. *The Commonplace Book*

5 There was a jolly miller once,
Lived on the river Dee;
He worked and sang from morn till night;
No lark more blithe than he.

Isaac Bickerstaffe (c. 1735–c. 1812) Irish dramatist. *Love in a Village*, I

6 When the green woods laugh with
the voice of joy.

William Blake (1757–1827) British poet. *Songs of Innocence*, 'Laughing song'

7 In every adversity of fortune, to have been happy is the most unhappy kind of misfortune.

Boethius (c. 480–524) Roman statesman, philosopher, and scholar. *The Consolation of Philosophy*

8 Happiness is a mystery like religion, and should never be rationalized.

G. K. Chesterton (1874–1936) British writer. *Heretics*, Ch. 7

9 To marvel at nothing is just about the one and only thing, Numicius, that can make a man happy and keep him that way.

Horace (Quintus Horatius Flaccus; 65–8 BC) Roman poet. *Epistles*, I

10 Not the owner of many possessions will you be right to call happy: he more rightly deserves the name of happy who knows how to use the gods' gifts wisely and to put up with rough poverty, and who fears dishonour more than death.

Horace *Odes*, IV

11 That action is best, which procures the greatest happiness for the greatest numbers.

Francis Hutcheson (1694–1746) Scottish philosopher. *Inquiry into the Original of our Ideas of Beauty and Virtue*, Treatise II, 'Concerning Moral Good and Evil'

12 Happiness is like coke - something you get as a by-product in the process of making something else.

Aldous Huxley (1894–1964) British novelist. *Point Counter Point*

13 That all who are happy, are equally happy, is not true. A peasant and a philosopher may be equally *satisfied*, but not equally *happy*. Happiness consists in the multiplicity of agreeable consciousness.

Samuel Johnson (1709–84) British lexicographer. *Life of Johnson* (J. Boswell), Vol. II

14 ...because happiness is not an ideal of reason but of imagination.

Immanuel Kant (1724–1804) German philosopher. *Grundlegung zur Metaphysik der Sitten*, II

15 Ask yourself whether you are happy, and you cease to be so.

John Stuart Mill (1806–73) British philosopher. *Autobiography*, Ch. 5

16 When a small child...I thought that success spelled happiness. I was wrong. Happiness is like a butterfly which appears and delights us for one brief moment, but soon flits away.

Anna Pavlova (1881–1931) Russian ballet dancer. *Pavlova: A Biography* (ed. A. H. Franks), 'Pages of My Life'

17 And we suddenly know, what heaven we're in,
When they begin the beguine.

Cole Porter (1893–1964) US songwriter. *Jubilee*, 'Begin the Beguine'

18 We are never so happy nor so unhappy as we imagine.

Duc de la Rochefoucauld (1613–80) French writer. *Maximes*, 49

19 Happiness is not best achieved by those who seek it directly.

Bertrand Russell (1872–1970) British philosopher. *Mysticism and Logic*

20 Every time I talk to a savant I feel quite sure that happiness is no longer a possibility. Yet when I talk with my gardener, I'm convinced of the opposite.

Bertrand Russell Attrib.

21 To be without some of the things you want is an indispensable part of happiness.

Bertrand Russell Attrib.

22 One is happy as a result of one's own efforts, once one knows the necessary ingredients of happiness – simple tastes, a certain degree of courage, self denial to a point, love of work, and, above all, a clear conscience. Happiness is no vague dream, of that I now feel certain.

George Sand (Aurore Dupin, Baronne Dudevant; 1804–76) French novelist. *Correspondence*, Vol. V

23 There is only one happiness in life, to love and be loved.

George Sand Letter to Lina Calamatta, 31 March 1862

24 Happiness is the only sanction of life; where happiness fails, existence remains a mad and lamentable experiment.

George Santayana (1863–1952) US philosopher. *The Life of Reason*

25 Happiness? That's nothing more than health and a poor memory.

Albert Schweitzer (1875–1965) French Protestant theologian, philosopher, physician and musician. Attrib.

26 A lifetime of happiness: no man alive could bear it: it would be hell on earth.

George Bernard Shaw (1856–1950) Irish dramatist and critic. *Man and Superman*, I

27 Mankind are always happy for having been happy, so that if you make them happy now, you make them happy twenty years hence by the memory of it.

Sydney Smith (1771–1845) British clergyman and essayist. *Elementary Sketches of Moral Philosophy*

28 A man is happy so long as he choose to be happy and nothing can stop him.

Alexander Solzhenitsyn (1918–) Russian novelist. *Cancer Ward*

29 There is no duty we so much underrate as the duty of being happy.

Robert Louis Stevenson (1850–94) Scottish writer. *Virginibus Puerisque*

30 Happiness is an imaginary condition, formerly often attributed by the living to the dead, now usually attributed by adults to children, and by children to adults.

Thomas Szasz (1920–) US psychiatrist. *The Second Sin*

31 If you want to be happy, be.

Leo Tolstoy (1828–1910) Russian writer. *Kosma Prutkov*

32 Happiness is no laughing matter.

Richard Whately (1787–1863) British churchman. *Apohthegms*

33 For the good are always the merry,
Save by an evil chance,
And the merry love the fiddle,
And the merry love to dance

W. B. Yeats (1865–1939) Irish poet. *The Fiddler of Dooney*

34 Happy Days Are Here Again.

Jack Yellen (b. 1892) US lyricist. Used by Roosevelt as a campaign song in 1932. Song title

35 The hell with it. Who never knew the price of happiness will not be happy.

Yevgeny Yevtushenko (1933–) Soviet poet. *Lies*

HARDY, THOMAS

(1840–1928) British novelist and poet. His novels include *The Mayor of Casterbridge* (1886), *Tess of the D'Urbervilles* (1891), and *Jude the Obscure* (1895). His poetry was collected in *Collected Poems* (1930) and he wrote an epic drama *The Dynasts* (1903–08).

Quotations about Hardy

1 Hardy became a sort of village atheist brooding and blaspheming over the village idiot.

G. K. Chesterton (1874–1936) British writer. *The Victorian Age in Literature*

2 The work of Thomas Hardy represents an interesting example of a powerful personality uncurbed by any institutional attachment or by submission to any objective beliefs...He seems to me to have written as nearly for the sake of 'self-expression' as a man well can; and the self which he had to express does not strike me as a particularly wholesome or edifying matter of communication.

T. S. Eliot (1888–1965) US-born British poet and dramatist. *After Strange Gods*

3 What a commonplace genius he has; or a genius for the commonplace, I don't know which. He doesn't rank so terribly high, really. But better than Bernard Shaw, even then.

D. H. Lawrence (1885–1930) British novelist. Letter to Martin Secker, 24 July 1928

4 No one has written worse English than Mr Hardy in some of his novels – cumbrous, stilted, ugly, and inexpressive – yes, but at the same time so strangely expressive of something attractive to us in Mr Hardy himself that we would not change it for the perfection of Sterne at his best. It becomes coloured by its surroundings; it becomes literature.

Virginia Woolf (1882–1941) British novelist. *The Moment*

Quotations by Hardy

5 When the Present has latched its postern behind my tremulous stay,
And the May month flaps its glad green leaves like wings,
Delicate-filmed as new-spun silk, will the neighbours say,
'He was a man who used to notice such things'?

Afterwards

6 A local cult called Christianity.

The Dynasts, I:6

7 My argument is that War makes rattling good history; but Peace is poor reading.

The Dynasts, II:5

8 A lover without indiscretion is no lover at all.

The Hand of Ethelberta, Ch. 20

9 Life's Little Ironies.

Title of book of stories

10 Dialect words – those terrible marks of the beast to the truly genteel.

The Mayor of Casterbridge, Ch. 20

11 Good, but not religious-good.

Under the Greenwood Tree, Ch. 2

12 That man's silence is wonderful to listen to.

Under the Greenwood Tree, Ch. 14

13 This is the weather the cuckoo likes,
And so do I;
When showers betumble the chestnut spikes,
And nestlings fly:
And the little brown nightingale bills his best,
And they sit outside at 'The Travellers' Rest'.

Weathers

14 This is the weather the shepherd shuns,
And so do I.

Weathers

15 If Galileo had said in verse that the world moved, the Inquisition might have let him alone.

The Later Years of Thomas Hardy (F. E. Hardy)

HASTE

See also impetuosity

1 Don't throw the baby out with the bathwater.

Proverb

2 First come, first served.

Proverb

3 Haste makes waste.

Proverb

4 More haste, less speed.

Proverb

5 'Will you walk a little faster?' said a whiting to a snail,
'There's a porpoise close behind us, and he's treading on my tail.'

Lewis Carroll (Charles Lutwidge Dodgson; 1832–98) British writer. *Alice's Adventures in Wonderland*, Ch. 10

6 In skating over thin ice, our safety is in our speed.

Ralph Waldo Emerson (1803–82) US poet and essayist. *Essays*, 'Prudence'

7 Slow and steady wins the race.

Robert Lloyd (1733–64) British poet. *The Hare and the Tortoise*

8 For fools rush in where angels fear to tread.

Alexander Pope (1688–1744) British poet. *An Essay on Criticism*

9 Never before have we had so little time in which to do so much.

Franklin D. Roosevelt (1882–1945) US Democratic president. Radio address, 23 Feb 1942

10 If it were done when 'tis done, then 'twere well
It were done quickly.

William Shakespeare (1564–1616) English dramatist. *Macbeth*, I:7

11 Wisely and slow; they stumble that run fast.

William Shakespeare *Romeo and Juliet*, II:3

12 He sows hurry and reaps indigestion.

Robert Louis Stevenson (1850–94) Scottish writer. *An Apology for Idlers*

13 Hurry! I never hurry. I have no time to hurry.

Igor Stravinsky (1882–1971) Russian-born US composer. Responding to his publisher's request that he hurry his completion of a composition. Attrib.

HATE

See also bitterness, love and hate

1 I do not love thee, Doctor Fell,
The reason why I cannot tell;
But this alone I know full well,
I do not love thee, Doctor Fell.

Thomas Brown (1663–1704) English satirist. Translation of Martial's *Epigrams*

2 Gr-r-r- there go, my heart's abhorrence!
Water your damned flower-pots, do!

Robert Browning (1812–89) British poet. *Soliloquy of the Spanish Cloister*

3 It does not matter much what a man hates, provided he hates something.

Samuel Butler (1835–1902) British writer. *Notebooks*

4 I am free of all prejudice. I hate everyone equally.

W. C. Fields (1880–1946) US actor. Attrib.

5 We can scarcely hate any one that we know.

William Hazlitt (1778–1830) British essayist. *On Criticism*

6 If you hate a person, you hate something in him that is part of yourself. What isn't part of ourselves doesn't disturb us.

Hermann Hesse (1877–1962) German novelist and poet. *Demian*, Ch. 6

7 With a heavy step Sir Matthew left the room and spent the morning designing mausoleums for his enemies.

Eric Linklater (1889–1974) Scottish novelist. *Juan in America*, Prologue

8 Few people can be happy unless they hate some other person, nation or creed.

Bertrand Russell (1872–1970) British philosopher. Attrib.

9 An intellectual hatred is the worst.

W. B. Yeats (1865–1939) Irish poet. *A Prayer for My Daughter*

HAWKING, STEPHEN

(1942–) British physicist. Although a victim of a progressive nervous disease, he is a leading figure in the field of general relativity and the theory of black holes. His publications include *A Brief History of Time* (1987).

Quotation about Hawking

1 Even as he sits helpless in his wheelchair, his mind seems to soar ever more brilliantly across the vastness of space and time to unlock the secrets of the universe.

Time, 1988

Quotations by Hawking

2 I was again fortunate in that I chose theoretical physics, because that is all in the mind. So my disability has not been a serious handicap.

A Brief History of Time, Acknowledgment

3 Why does the universe go to all the bother of existing? Is the unified theory so compelling that it brings about its own existence? Or does it need a creator, and, if so, does he have any other effect on the universe? And who created him?

A Brief History of Time, Ch. 11

4 Then we shall all, philosophers, scientists, and just ordinary people, be able to take part in the discussion of the question of why it is that we and the universe exist. If we find the answer to that, it would be the ultimate triumph of human reason – for then we would know the mind of God.

A Brief History of Time, Ch. 11

5 Not only does God play dice. He does not tell us where they fall.

Commenting on Einstein's remark about quantum theory, 'God does not play dice.' Attrib.

HAZLITT, WILLIAM

(1778–1830) British essayist and journalist. His collections of writings include *Lectures on the English Poets* (1818) and *The Spirit of the Age* (1825).

Quotations about Hazlitt

1 He is your only good damner, and if I am ever damned I should like to be damned by him.

John Keats (1795–1821) British poet. Attrib.

2 He is not a proper person to be admitted into respectable society, being the most perverse and malevolent creature that ill-luck has thrown my way.

William Wordsworth (1770–1850) British poet. Letter to B. R. Haydon, Apr 1817

Quotations by Hazlitt

3 The least pain in our little finger gives us more concern and uneasiness than the destruction of millions of our fellow-beings.
American Literature, 'Dr Channing'

4 If the world were good for nothing else, it is a fine subject for speculation.
Characteristics

5 Man is an intellectual animal, and therefore an everlasting contradiction to himself. His senses centre in himself, his ideas reach to the ends of the universe; so that he is torn in pieces between the two, without a possibility of its ever being otherwise.
Characteristics

6 His sayings are generally like women's letters; all the pith is in the postscript.
Referring to Charles Lamb. *Conversations of Northcote*

7 To great evils we submit; we resent little provocations.
On Great and Little Things

8 He talked on for ever; and you wished him to talk on for ever.
Referring to the poet, Coleridge. *Lectures on the English Poets*, Lecture VIII, 'On the Living Poets'

9 So have I loitered my life away, reading books, looking at pictures, going to plays, hearing, thinking, writing on what pleased me best. I have wanted only one thing to make me happy, but wanting that have wanted everything.
Literary Remains, 'My First Acquaintance with Poets'

10 There is not a more mean, stupid, dastardly, pitiful, selfish, spiteful, envious, ungrateful animal than the public. It is the greatest of cowards, for it is afraid of itself.
On Living to Oneself

11 A person may be indebted for a nose or an eye, for a graceful carriage or a voluble discourse, to a great-aunt or uncle, whose existence he has scarcely heard of.
On Personal Character

12 The dupe of friendship, and the fool of love; have I not reason to hate and to despise myself? Indeed I do; and chiefly for not having hated and despised the world enough.
The Plain Speaker, 'On the Pleasure of Hating'

13 The love of liberty is the love of others; the love of power is the love of ourselves.
Political Essays, 'The Times Newspaper'

14 The art of pleasing consists in being pleased.
The Round Table, 'On Manner'

15 There is nothing good to be had in the country, or, if there is, they will not let you have it.
The Round Table, 'Observation on Mr Wordworth's Poem *The Excursion*'

16 The greatest offence against virtue is to speak ill of it.
Sketches and Essays, 'On Cant and Hypocrisy'

17 There is an unseemly exposure of the mind, as well as of the body.
Sketches and Essays, 'On Disagreeable People'

18 A nickname is the heaviest stone that the devil can throw at a man.
Sketches and Essays, 'Nicknames'

19 We never do anything well till we cease to think about the manner of doing it.
Sketches and Essays, 'On Prejudice'

20 The most fluent talkers or most plausible reasoners are not always the justest thinkers.
Sketches and Essays, 'On Prejudice'

21 He writes as fast as they can read, and he does not write himself down.
The Spirit of the Age, 'Sir Walter Scott'

22 His worst is better than any other person's best.
The Spirit of the Age, 'Sir Walter Scott'

23 Rules and models destroy genius and art.
Sketches and Essays, 'On Taste'

24 Those who make their dress a principal part of themselves, will, in general, become of no more value than their dress.
Table Talk, 'On the Clerical Character'

25 The English (it must be owned) are rather a foul-mouthed nation
Table Talk, 'On Criticism'

26 We can scarcely hate any one that we know.
Table Talk, 'On Criticism'

27 You will hear more good things on the outside of a stagecoach from London to Oxford than if you were to pass a twelvemonth with the undergraduates, or heads of colleges, of that famous university.
Table Talk, 'The Ignorance of the Learned'

28 One of the pleasantest things in the world is going on a journey; but I like to go by myself.
Table Talk, 'On Going a Journey'

29 When I am in the country I wish to vegetate like the country.
Table Talk, 'On Going a Journey'

30 No young man believes he shall ever die.
Uncollected Essays, 'On the Feeling of Immortality in Youth'

31 Spleen can subsist on any kind of food.
On Wit and Humour

32 Well, I've had a happy life.
Last words

HEALTH AND HEALTHY LIVING

See also doctors, illness, medicine, remedies

1 An apple a day keeps the doctor away.
Proverb

2 Health is better than wealth.
Proverb

3 It is a fact that not once in all my life have I gone

out for a walk. I have been taken out for walks; but that is another matter.

Max Beerbohm (1872–1956) British writer. *Going Out of a Walk*

4 I answer 20 000 letters a year and so many couples are having problems because they are not getting the right proteins and vitamins.

Barbara Cartland (1902–) British romantic novelist. *The Observer*, 'Sayings of the Week', 31 Aug 1986

5 The strongest possible piece of advice I would give to any young woman is: Don't screw around, and don't smoke.

Edwina Currie (1946–) British politician. *The Observer*, 'Sayings of the Week', 3 Apr 1988

6 Nutritional research, like a modern star of Bethlehem, brings hope that sickness need not be a part of life.

Adelle Davis (1904–74) US nutritionist and writer. *The New York Times Magazine*, 'The Great Adelle Davis Controversy', 20 May 1973

7 Our body is a magnificently devised, living, breathing mechanism, yet we do almost nothing to insure its optimal development and use...The human organism needs an ample supply of good building material to repair the effects of daily wear and tear.

Indra Devi (1899–) Russian-born US yogini and writer. *Renewing Your Life Through Yoga*, Ch. 2

8 Exercise is bunk. If you are healthy, you don't need it: if you are sick you shouldn't take it.

Henry Ford (1863–1947) US car manufacturer. Attrib.

9 A wise man ought to realize that health is his most valuable possession.

Hippocrates (c. 460 –c. 377 BC) Greek physician. *A Regimen for Health*, 9

10 One swears by wholemeal bread, one by sour milk; vegetarianism is the only road to salvation of some, others insist not only on vegetables alone, but on eating those raw. At one time the only thing that matters is calories; at another time they are crazy about vitamins or about roughage.
The scientific truth may be put quite briefly; eat moderately, having an ordinary mixed diet, and don't worry.

Robert Hutchison (1871–1960) *Newcastle Medical Journal*, Vol. 12, 1932

11 Vegetarianism is harmless enough, though it is apt to fill a man with wind and self righteousness.

Robert Hutchison Attrib.

12 *Orandum est ut sit mens sana in corpore sano.*
Your prayer must be for a sound mind in a sound body.

Juvenal (Decimus Junius Juvenalis; 60–130 AD) Roman satirist. *Satires*, X

13 I don't take pills. I drink herbal tea.

Madonna (Madonna Louise Veronica Ciccone; 1958–) US pop singer and actress.

14 Some breakfast food manufacturer hit upon the simple notion of emptying out the leavings of carthorse nosebags, adding a few other things like unconsumed portions of chicken layer's mash, and the sweepings of racing stables, packing the mixture in little bags and selling them in health food shops.

Frank Muir (1920–) British writer and broadcaster. *Upon My Word!*

15 Early to rise and early to bed makes a male healthy and wealthy and dead.

James Thurber (1894–1961) US humorist. *Fables for Our Time*, 'The Shrike and the Chipmunks'

16 Look to your health: and if you have it, praise God, and value it next to a good conscience; for health is the second blessing that we mortals are capable of; a blessing that money cannot buy.

Izaak Walton (1593–1683) English writer. *The Compleat Angler*, Pt. I, Ch. 21

HEAVEN

See also afterlife

1 And he dreamed, and behold a ladder set up on the earth, and the top of it reached to heaven: and behold the angels of God ascending and descending on it.

Bible: Genesis 28:12

2 And Jacob awaked out of his sleep, and he said, Surely the Lord is in this place; and I knew it not. And he was afraid, and said, How dreadful is this place! this is none other but the house of God, and this is the gate of heaven.

Bible: Genesis 28:16–17

3 In my Father's house are many mansions: if it were not so, I would have told you. I go to prepare a place for you.

Bible: John 14:2

4 Then let him receive the new knowledge and wait us,
Pardoned in heaven, the first by the throne!

Robert Browning (1812–89) British poet. *The Lost Leader*

5 Work and pray, live on hay,
You'll get pie in the sky when you die.

Joe Hill (1879–1915) Swedish-born US songwriter. *The Preacher and the Slave*

6 Even the paradise of fools is not an unpleasant abode while it is inhabitable.

Dean Inge (1860–1954) British churchman. Attrib.

7 Probably no invention came more easily to man than Heaven.

Georg Christoph Lichtenberg (1742–99) German physicist and writer. *Aphorisms*

8 A heav'n on earth.

John Milton (1608–74) English poet. *Paradise Lost*, Bk. IV

9 Glorious things of thee are spoken,
Zion, city of our God.

John Newton (1725–1807) British hymn writer. 'Glorious Things'

10 It may be only glory that we seek here, but I persuade myself that, as long as we remain here, that is right. Another glory awaits us in heaven and he who reaches there will not wish even to think of earthly fame.

Petrarch (Francesco Petrarca; 1304–74) Italian poet. *Secretum*

11 For observe, that to hope for Paradise is to live in Paradise, a very different thing from actually getting there.

Vita Sackville-West (Victoria Sackville-West; 1892–1962) British poet and novelist. *Passenger to Tehran*, Ch. 1

12 I expect no very violent transition.

Catharine Maria Sedgwick (1789–1867) US writer. Comparing heaven with her home-town of Stockbridge, Massachussetts. *Edie* (Jean Stein)

13 If you go to Heaven without being naturally qualified for it you will not enjoy yourself there.

George Bernard Shaw (1856–1950) Irish dramatist and critic. *Man and Superman*

14 Heaven, as conventionally conceived, is a place so inane, so dull, so useless, so miserable, that nobody has ever ventured to describe a whole day in heaven, though plenty of people have described a day at the seaside.

George Bernard Shaw *Misalliance*, Preface

15 Shall shine the traffic of Jacob's ladder
Pitched between Heaven and Charing Cross.

Francis Thompson (1859–1907) British poet. *The Kingdom of God*

16 Grant me paradise in this world; I'm not so sure I'll reach it in the next.

Tintoretto (Jacopo Robusti; 1518–94) Venetian painter. Arguing that he be allowed to paint the *Paradiso* at the doge's palace in Venice, despite his advanced age. Attrib.

17 There is a happy land,
Far, far away,
Where saints in glory stand,
Bright, bright as day.

Andrew Young (1885–1971) Scottish poet. 'There is a Happy Land'

HEINE, HEINRICH

(1797–1856) German poet and writer. His early collection *Buch der Lieder* (1827) preceded his move to Paris (1831), where he remained until his death.

1 Whenever books are burned men also in the end are burned.

Almansor

2 Sleep is good, death is better; but of course, the best thing would be never to have been born at all.

Morphine

3 I just met X in the street, I stopped for a moment to exchange ideas, and now I feel like a complete idiot.

Autant en apportent les mots (Pedrazzini)

4 It is extremely difficult for a Jew to be converted, for how can he bring himself to believe in the divinity of – another Jew?

Attrib.

5 God will pardon me. It is His trade.

Last words. *Journal* (Edmond and Charles Goncourt), 23 Feb 1863

HELL

See also damnation, devil

1 Every wolf's and lion's howl
Raises from Hell a human soul.

William Blake (1757–1827) British poet. *Auguries of Innocence*

2 Abandon hope, all ye who enter here.

Dante (1265–1321) Italian poet. The inscription at the entrance to Hell. *Divine Comedy*, Inferno, III

3 Hell is oneself;
Hell is alone, the other figures in it
Merely projections. There is nothing to escape from
And nothing to escape to. One is always alone.

T. S. Eliot (1888–1965) US-born British poet and dramatist. *The Cocktail Party*, I:3

4 Long is the way
And hard, that out of hell leads up to light.

John Milton (1608–74) English poet. *Paradise Lost*, Bk. II

5 Which way I fly is Hell; myself am Hell;
And, in the lowest deep, a lower deep
Still threat'ning to devour me opens wide,
To which the Hell I suffer seems a Heaven.

John Milton *Paradise Lost*, Bk. IV

6 I fancy that the Hell of Too Many People would occupy a respectable place in the hierarchy of infernal regions.

J. B. Priestley (1894–1984) British novelist. *Self-Selected Essays*, 'Too Many People'

7 Hell is other people.

Jean-Paul Sartre (1905–80) French writer. *Huis clos*

8 Hell is a city much like London –
A populous and smoky city.

Percy Bysshe Shelley (1792–1822) British poet. *Peter Bell the Third*

9 The way down to Hell is easy.

Virgil (Publius Vergilius Maro; 70–19 BC) Roman poet. *Aeneid*, Bk. VI

HELLER, JOSEPH

(1923–) US novelist. He made his name with the war novel *Catch-22* (1961); subsequent books include *Good as Gold* (1979), *God Knows* (1984), and *Picture This* (1988).

1 He was a self-made man who owed his lack of success to nobody.

Catch-22, Ch. 3

2 He had decided to live for ever or die in the attempt.

Catch-22, Ch. 3

3 There was only one catch and that was Catch-22, which specified that a concern for one's own safety in the face of dangers that were real and immediate was the process of a rational mind.

Catch-22, Ch. 5

4 He knew everything about literature except how to enjoy it.

Catch-22, Ch. 8

5 Some men are born mediocre, some men achieve mediocrity, and some men have mediocrity thrust upon them. With Major Major it had been all three.

Catch-22, Ch. 9

6 Hungry Joe collected lists of fatal diseases and arranged them in alphabetical order so that he could put his finger without delay on any one he wanted to worry about.
Catch-22, Ch. 17

7 Prostitution gives her an opportunity to meet people. It provides fresh air and wholesome exercise, and it keeps her out of trouble.
Catch-22, Ch. 33

HELP

See also charity, support

1 Every little helps.
Proverb

2 Many hands make light work.
Proverb

3 One good turn deserves another.
Proverb

4 Scratch my back and I'll scratch yours.
Proverb

5 Too many cooks spoil the broth.
Proverb

6 Two heads are better than one.
Proverb

7 People must help one another; it is nature's law.
Jean de La Fontaine (1621–95) French poet. *Fables*, VIII, 'L'Âne et le Chien'

8 Bind up their wounds – but look the other way.
W. S. Gilbert (1836–1911) British dramatist. *Princess Ida*, III

9 You may help a lame dog over a stile but he is still a lame dog on the other side.
Ernest Newman (1868–1959) British music critic and writer. *Berlioz, Romantic and Classic* (ed. Peter Heyworth)

HEMINGWAY, ERNEST

(1899–1961) US novelist, who lived for much of his life in Paris. His first successful novel was *The Sun Also Rises* (1926); subsequent novels include *A Farewell to Arms* (1929) and *For Whom the Bell Tolls* (1940). He was a keen sportsman and admirer of bullfighting.

Quotations about Hemingway

1 He is the bully on the Left Bank, always ready to twist the milksop's arm.
Cyril Connolly (1903–74) British journalist. *The Observer*, 24 May 1964

2 He has never been known to use a word that might send the reader to the dictionary.
William Faulkner (1897–1962) US novelist. Attrib.

3 He has a capacity for enjoyment so vast that he gives away great chunks to those about him, and never even misses them...He can take you to a bicycle race and make it raise your hair.
Dorothy Parker (1893–1967) US writer. *New Yorker*, 30 Nov 1929

Quotations by Hemingway

4 Bullfighting is the only art in which the artist is in danger of death and in which the degree of brilliance in the performance is left to the fighter's honour.
Death in the Afternoon, Ch. 9

5 But did thee feel the earth move?
For Whom the Bell Tolls, Ch. 13

6 If you are lucky enough to have lived in Paris as a young man, then wherever you go for the rest of your life, it stays with you, for Paris is a moveable feast.
A Moveable Feast, Epigraph

7 A man can be destroyed but not defeated.
The Old Man and the Sea

8 Because I am a bastard.
When asked why he had deserted his wife for another woman.
Americans in Paris (B. Morton)

9 Poor Faulkner. Does he really think big emotions come from big words? He thinks I don't know the ten-dollar words. I know them all right. But there are older and simpler and better words, and those are the ones I use.
In response to Faulkner's jibe (see above). Attrib.

HERBERT, SIR A. P.

(Sir Alan Patrick Herbert; 1890–1971) British writer and politician. His novels include *The Secret Battle* (1919) and *Holy Deadlock* (1934). He also wrote the libretti for a number of musical comedies, of which the most successful was *Bless the Bride* (1947). As an MP, he helped to reform the divorce law and was the prime mover in the act to pay royalties to authors on library books.

1 Other people's babies –
That's my life!
Mother to dozens,
And nobody's wife.
A Book of Ballads, 'Other People's Babies'

2 Let's find out what everyone is doing,
And then stop everyone from doing it.
Let's Stop Somebody

3 The Common Law of England has been laboriously built about a mythical figure – the figure of 'The Reasonable Man'.
Uncommon Law

4 People must not do things for fun. We are not here for fun. There is no reference to fun in any Act of Parliament.
Uncommon Law

5 The critical period in matrimony is breakfast-time.
Uncommon Law

6 The Englishman never enjoys himself except for a noble purpose.
Uncommon Law

7 For any ceremonial purposes the otherwise excellent liquid, water, is unsuitable in colour and other respects.

Uncommon Law

8 An Act of God was defined as *something which no reasonable man could have expected.*

Uncommon Law

HERBERT, GEORGE

(1593–1633) English poet. His religious lyrics were collected in *The Temple* (1633).

1 I struck the board, and cried, 'No more;
I will abroad.'
What, shall I ever sigh and pine?
My lines and life are free; free as the road,
Loose as the wind, as large as store.

The Collar

2 But as I rav'd and grew more fierce and wild
At every word,
Methought I heard one calling, 'Child';
And I replied, 'My Lord.'

The Collar

3 Oh that I were an orange-tree,
That busy plant!
Then I should ever laden be,
And never want
Some fruit for Him that dressed me.

Employment

4 And now in age I bud again,
After so many deaths I live and write;
I once more smell the dew and rain,
And relish versing; O, my only Light,
It cannot be
That I am he
On whom Thy tempests fell all night.

The Flower

5 Death is still working like a mole,
And digs my grave at each remove.

Grace

6 Love bade me welcome; yet my soul drew back,
Guilty of dust and sin.

Love

7 'You must sit down,' says Love, 'and taste My meat,'
So I did sit and eat.

Love

8 He that makes a good war makes a good peace.

Outlandish Proverbs, 420

9 Sweet day, so cool, so calm, so bright,
The bridal of the earth and sky.

Virtue

10 Only a sweet and virtuous soul,
Like season'd timber, never gives;
But though the whole world turn to coal,
Then chiefly lives.

Virtue

HEROISM

See also courage, endurance, patriotism, war

1 Some talk of Alexander, and some of Hercules,
Of Hector and Lysander, and such great names as these;
But of all the world's brave heroes there's none that can compare
With a tow, row, row, row, row, row for the British Grenadier.

Anonymous *The British Grenadiers*

2 Superman, disguised as Clark Kent, mild-mannered reporter for a great metropolitan newspaper, fights a never-ending battle for truth, justice, and the American way.

Anonymous Hence the description 'Mild-mannered Clark Kent'. Introduction to radio series

3 They died to save their country and they only saved the world.

Hilaire Belloc (1870–1953) French-born British poet. *The English Graves*

4 ANDREA. Unhappy the land that has no heroes.
GALILEO. No, unhappy the land that needs heroes.

Bertolt Brecht (1898–1956) German dramatist. *Galileo*, 13

5 In short, he was a perfect cavaliero,
And to his very valet seem'd a hero.

Lord Byron (1788–1824) British poet. *Beppo*

6 Every hero becomes a bore at last.

Ralph Waldo Emerson (1803–82) US poet and essayist. *Representative Men*, 'Uses of Great Men'

7 Show me a hero and I will write you a tragedy.

F. Scott Fitzgerald (1896–1940) US novelist. *The Crack-Up*, 'Notebooks, E'

8 I'm a hero with coward's legs. I'm a hero from the waist up.

Spike Milligan (1918–) British comic actor and author. *Puckoon*

9 Being a hero is about the shortest-lived profession on earth.

Will Rogers (1879–1935) US actor and humorist. *Saturday Review*, 'A Rogers Thesaurus', 25 Aug 1962

10 I think continually of those who were truly great
– The names of those who in their lives fought for life,
Who wore at their hearts the fire's centre.

Stephen Spender (1909–) British poet. *I Think Continually of Those Who Were Truly Great*

HERRICK, ROBERT

(1591–1674) English poet. Ordained in 1623, his religious and secular verse is collected in *Hesperides* (1648).

1 Cherry ripe, ripe, ripe, I cry.
Full and fair ones; come and buy.

See also CAMPION. *Hesperides*, 'Cherry Ripe'

2 A sweet disorder in the dress
Kindles in clothes a wantonness.

Hesperides, 'Delight in Disorder'

3 'Twixt kings and tyrants there's this difference known;
Kings seek their subjects' good: tyrants their own.

Hesperides, 'Kings and Tyrants'

4 Fair daffodils, we weep to see
You haste away so soon:
As yet the early-rising sun

Has not attain'd his noon.
Stay, stay,
Until the hasting day
Has run
But to the even-song;
And, having pray'd together, we
Will go with you along.

We have short time to stay, as you,
We have as short a Spring;
As quick a growth to meet decay,
As you or any thing.

Hesperides, 'To Daffodils'

5 Gather ye rosebuds while ye may,
Old time is still a-flying:
And this same flower that smiles today
Tomorrow will be dying.

Hesperides, 'To the Virgins, to Make Much of Time'

6 Then be not coy, but use your time;
And while ye may, go marry:
For having lost but once your prime,
You may for ever tarry.

Hesperides, 'To the Virgins, to Make Much of Time'

7 Whenas in silks my Julia goes
Then, then (methinks) how sweetly flows
That liquefaction of her clothes.

Hesperides, 'Upon Julia's Clothes'

HILL, GEOFFREY

(1932–) British poet. His publications include *For the Unfallen* (1959), *Mercian Hymns* (1971), and *Collected Poems* (1985).

1 So drummed, so shadowed, your mere trudging voice
Might rave at large while easy truths were told
Bad perjurable stuff, to be forgiven
Because of this lame journey out of mind.
Asmodeus is the prince of demons in Jewish demonology.

For the Unfallen, 'Asmodeus'

2 I love my work and my children. God
Is distant, difficult. Things happen.
Too near the ancient troughs of blood
Innocence is no earthly weapon.

King Log, 'Ovid in the Third Reich'

3 As estimated, you died. Things marched, sufficient, to that end.
Just so much Zyklon and leather, patented terror, so many routine cries.

Zyklon B was the name of the poison gas used in the Nazi extermination camps during World War II. *King Log*, 'September Song'

4 King of the perennial holly-groves, the riven sandstone: overlord of the M5: architect of the historic rampart and ditch, the citadel at Tamworth, the summer hermitage in Holy Cross: guardian of the Welsh Bridge and the Iron Bridge: contractor to the desirable new estates: saltmaster: money-changer: commissioner for oaths: martyrologist: the friend of Charlemagne. 'I liked that,' said Offa, 'sing it again.'

Mercian Hymns, I, 'The Naming of Offa'

5 Fortified in their front parlours, at Yuletide men are the more murderous. Drunk, they defy battle-axes, bellow of whale-bone and dung.

Mercian Hymns, XXVI, 'Offa's Bestiary'

HISTORIANS

See also history

1 A good historian is timeless; although he is a patriot, he will never flatter his country in any respect.

François Fénelon (1651–1715) French writer and prelate. Letter to M. Dacier

2 The historian must have...some conception of how men who are not historians behave. Otherwise he will move in a world of the dead.

E. M. Forster (1879–1970) British novelist. *Abinger Harvest*, 'Captain Edward Gibbon'

3 History repeats itself; historians repeat each other.

Philip Guedalla (1889–1944) British writer. Attrib.

4 Great abilities are not requisite for an Historian... Imagination is not required in any high degree.

Samuel Johnson (1709–84) British lexicographer. *Life of Johnson* (J. Boswell), Vol. I

5 History is too serious to be left to historians.

Iain Macleod (1913–70) British politician. *The Observer*, 'Sayings of the Week', 16 July 1961

6 And even I can remember
A day when the historians left blanks in their writings,
I mean for things they didn't know.

Ezra Pound (1885–1972) US poet. *Cantos*, XIII

7 A historian is a prophet in reverse.

Friedrich von Schlegel (1772–1829) German diplomat, writer, and critic. *Das Athenäum*

8 Historians are like deaf people who go on answering questions that no one has asked them.

Leo Tolstoy (1828–1910) Russian writer. *A Discovery of Australia*, 'Being an Historian' (Manning Clark)

HISTORY

See also experience, historians, past

1 History repeats itself.

Proverb

2 History is the sum total of the things that could have been avoided.

Konrad Adenauer (1876–1967) German statesman.

3 Political history is far too criminal and pathological to be a fit subject of study for the young. Children should acquire their heroes and villains from fiction.

W. H. Auden (1907–73) British poet. *A Certain World*

4 Man is a history-making creature who can neither repeat his past nor leave it behind.

W. H. Auden *The Dyer's Hand*, 'D. H. Lawrence'

5 All things from eternity are of like forms and come round in a circle.

Marcus Aurelius (121–180 AD) Roman emperor. *Meditations*, Bk. II, Ch. 14

6 History does not repeat itself. Historians repeat each other.

Arthur Balfour (1848–1930) British statesman. Attrib.

7 History is the essence of innumerable biographies.

Thomas Carlyle (1795–1881) Scottish historian and essayist. *Critical and Miscellaneous Essays*, 'History'

8 No great man lives in vain. The history of the world is but the biography of great men.

Thomas Carlyle *Heroes and Hero-Worship*, 'The Hero as Divinity'

9 The history of every country begins in the heart of a man or woman.

Willa Cather (1873–1947) US writer and poet. *O Pioneers!*, Pt. II, Ch. 4

10 History is philosophy teaching by examples.

Dionysius of Halicarnassus (40–8 BC) Greek historian. *Ars rhetorica*, XI:2

11 History is an endless repetition of the wrong way of living.

Lawrence Durrell (1912–) British novelist. *The Listener*, 1978

12 There is properly no history; only biography.

Ralph Waldo Emerson (1803–82) US poet and essayist. *Essays*, 'History'

13 History is more or less bunk. It's tradition. We don't want tradition. We want to live in the present and the only history that is worth a tinker's damn is the history we make today.

Henry Ford (1863–1947) US car manufacturer. *Chicago Tribune*, 25 May 1916

14 There are moments in history when brooding tragedy and its dark shadows can be lightened by recalling great moments of the past.

Indira Gandhi (1917–84) Indian stateswoman. Letter to Richard Nixon, 16 Dec 1971

15 History never looks like history when you are living through it. It always looks confusing and messy, and it always feels uncomfortable.

John W. Gardner (1912–) US writer. *No Easy Victories*

16 His reign is marked by the rare advantage of furnishing very few materials for history; which is, indeed, little more than the register of the crimes, follies, and misfortunes of mankind.

Edward Gibbon (1737–94) British historian. Referring to the reign of Antoninus Pius. *Decline and Fall of the Roman Empire*, Ch. 3

17 Each image of Cleopatra...provides clues to the nature of the culture which produced it, in particular to its sexual politics, its racial prejudices, its neuroses and its fantasies.

Lucy Hughes-Hallett (1951–) British writer. *Cleopatra: Histories, Dreams, Distortions*

18 What we know of the past is mostly not worth knowing. What is worth knowing is mostly uncertain. Events in the past may roughly be divided into those which probably never happened and those which do not matter.

Dean Inge (1860–1954) British churchman. *Assessments and Anticipations*, 'Prognostications'

19 It takes a great deal of history to produce a little literature.

Henry James (1843–1916) US novelist. *Life of Nathaniel Hawthorne*, Ch. 1

20 'History', Stephen said, 'is a nightmare from which I am trying to awake'.

James Joyce (1882–1941) Irish novelist. *Ulysses*

21 Hegel says somewhere that all great events and personalities in world history reappear in one fashion or another. He forgot to add: the first time as tragedy, the second as farce.

Karl Marx (1818–83) German philosopher and revolutionary. *The Eighteenth Brumaire of Louis Napoleon*

22 It is impossible to write ancient history because we do not have enough sources, and impossible to write modern history because we have far too many.

Charles Pierre Péguy (1873–1914) French writer. *Clio*

23 There is no history of mankind, there are only many histories of all kinds of aspects of human life. And one of these is the history of political power. This is elevated into the history of the world.

Karl Popper (1902–) Austrian-born British philosopher. *The Open Society and Its Enemies*

24 Progress, far from consisting in change, depends on retentiveness. Those who cannot remember the past are condemned to repeat it.

George Santayana (1863–1952) US philosopher. *The Life of Reason*

25 I have looked upon the face of Agamemnon.

Heinrich Schliemann (1822–90) German archaeologist. On discovering a gold death mask at an excavation in Mycenae. *The Story of Civilization* (W. Durant), Vol. 2

26 History is past politics, and politics present history.

John Robert Seeley (1834–95) British historian. Quoting the historian E. A. Freeman. *The Growth of British Policy*

27 The Cavaliers (Wrong but Wromantic) and the Roundheads (Right but Repulsive).

W. C. Sellar (1898–1951) British humorous writer. *1066 And All That*

28 1066 And All That.

W. C. Sellar Book title

29 The Roman Conquest was, however, a *Good Thing*, since the Britons were only natives at the time.

W. C. Sellar *1066 And All That*

30 Napoleon's armies used to march on their stomachs, shouting: 'Vive l'intérieur!'

W. C. Sellar *1066 And All That*

31 America became top nation and history came to a full stop.

W. C. Sellar *1066 And All That*

32 When in the chronicle of wasted time
I see descriptions of the fairest wights.

William Shakespeare (1564–1616) English dramatist. *Sonnet 106*

33 History gets thicker as it approaches recent times.

A. J. P. Taylor (1906–90) British historian. *English History, 1914–1945*, Bibliography

34 All our ancient history, as one of our wits remarked, is no more than accepted fiction.

Voltaire (François-Marie Arouet; 1694–1778) French writer. *Jeannot et Colin*

35 Indeed, history is nothing more than a tableau of crimes and misfortunes.

Voltaire *L'Ingénu*, Ch. 10

36 Anything but history, for history must be false.

Robert Walpole (1676–1745) British statesman. *Walpoliana*

37 Hindsight is always twenty-twenty.

Billy Wilder (Samuel Wilder; 1906–) Austrian-born US film director. Attrib.

38 The greater part of what passes for diplomatic history is little more than the record of what one clerk said to another clerk.

George Malcolm Young (1882–1959) British historian. *Victorian England: Portrait of an Age*

HITLER, ADOLF

(1889–1945) German dictator, who became president of the Nazi party in 1921 and chancellor of Germany in 1933. His campaign of world conquest led to World War II, defeat and disgrace for Germany, and his own suicide.

Quotations about Hitler

1 The people Hitler never understood, and whose actions continued to exasperate him to the end of his life, were the British.

Allan Bullock (1914–) British academic and historian. *Hitler, A Study in Tyranny*, Ch. 8

2 Hitler showed surprising loyalty to Mussolini, but it never extended to trusting him.

Referring to the Italian dictator, Benito Mussolini (1883–1945). **Alan Bullock** *Hitler, A Study in Tyranny*, Ch. II

3 I have only one purpose, the destruction of Hitler, and my life is much simplified thereby. If Hitler invaded Hell I would make at least a favourable reference to the Devil in the House of Commons.

Winston Churchill (1874–1965) British statesman. *The Grand Alliance*

4 The Italians will laugh at me; every time Hitler occupies a country he sends me a message.

Benito Mussolini (1883–1945) Italian dictator. *Hitler* (Alan Bullock), Ch. 8

5 That garrulous monk.

Benito Mussolini *The Second World War* (W. Churchill)

6 I wouldn't believe Hitler was dead, even if he told me so himself.

Hjalmar Schacht (1877–1970) German banker. Attrib.

7 A racing tipster who only reached Hitler's level of accuracy would not do well for his clients.

A. J. P. Taylor (1906–90) British historian. *The Origins of The Second World War*, Ch. 7

8 Germany was the cause of Hitler just as much as Chicago is responsible for the *Chicago Tribune*.

Alexander Woolcott (1887–1943) US writer and critic. Woollcott died after the broadcast. Radio broadcast, 1943

Quotations by Hitler

9 All those who are not racially pure are mere chaff.

Mein Kampf, Ch. 2

10 Only constant repetition will finally succeed in imprinting an idea on the memory of the crowd.

Mein Kampf, Ch. 6

11 The broad mass of a nation...will more easily fall victim to a big lie than to a small one.

Mein Kampf, Ch. 10

12 Germany will be either a world power or will not be at all.

Mein Kampf, Ch. 14

13 In starting and waging a war it is not right that matters, but victory.

The Rise and Fall of the Third Reich (W. L. Shirer), Ch. 16

14 The essential thing is the formation of the political will of the nation: that is the starting point for political action.

Speech, Düsseldorf, 27 Jan 1932

15 I go the way that Providence dictates with the assurance of a sleepwalker.

Referring to his successful re-occupation of the Rhineland, despite advice against the attempt. Speech, Munich, 15 Mar 1936

16 When Barbarossa commences, the world will hold its breath and make no comment.

Referring to the planned invasion of the USSR, Operation Barbarossa, which began on 22 June 1941. Attrib.

17 Is Paris burning?

Referring to the liberation of Paris, 25 Aug 1944

HOBBES, THOMAS

(1588–1679) English philosopher and political thinker. His *Leviathan* (1651) set out his political philosophy.

1 The condition of man...is a condition of war of everyone against everyone.

Leviathan, Pt. I, Ch. 4

2 True and False are attributes of speech, not of things. And where speech is not, there is neither Truth nor Falsehood.

Leviathan, Pt. I, Ch. 4

3 They that approve a private opinion, call it opinion; but they that mislike it, heresy: and yet heresy signifies no more than private opinion.

Leviathan, Pt. I, Ch. 11

4 No arts; no letters; no society; and which is worst of all, continual fear and danger of violent death; and the life of man, solitary, poor, nasty, brutish, and short.

Leviathan, Pt. I, Ch. 13

5 The only way to erect such a common power, as may be able to defend them from the invasion of foreigners, and the injuries of one another...is, to confer all their power and strength upon one man, or upon one assembly of men, that may reduce all

their wills, by plurality of voices, unto one will… This is the generation of that great Leviathan, or rather (to speak more reverently) of that *Mortal God*, to which we owe under the *Immortal God*, our peace and defence.
Leviathan, Pt. II, Ch. 17

6 They that are discontented under *monarchy*, call it *tyranny*; and they that are displeased with *aristocracy,* call it *oligarchy:* so also, they which find themselves grieved under a *democracy*, call it *anarchy*, which signifies the want of government; and yet I think no man believes, that want of government, is any new kind of government.
Leviathan, Pt. II, Ch. 19

7 The Papacy is not other than the Ghost of the deceased Roman Empire, sitting crowned upon the grave thereof.
Leviathan, Pt. IV, Ch. 47

8 I am about to take my last voyage, a great leap in the dark.
Last words

HOME

See also homesickness, travel

1 East, west, home's best.
Proverb

2 Home is where the heart is.
Proverb

3 A House Is Not a Home.
Polly Adler (1900–62) US madam. Title of memoirs

4 Home is home, though it be never so homely.
John Clarke (fl. 1639) English scholar. *Paroemiologia Anglo-Latina*

5 Home is the place where, when you have to go there,
They have to take you in.
Robert Frost (1875–1963) US poet. *The Death of the Hired Man*

6 What's the good of a home, if you are never in it?
George Grossmith (1847–1912) British singer and comedian. *The Diary of a Nobody*, Ch. 1

7 In fact there was but one thing wrong with the Babbitt house; it was not a home.
Sinclair Lewis (1885–1951) US novelist. *Babbitt*, Ch. 2

8 A man travels the world over in search of what he needs and returns home to find it.
George Moore (1852–1933) Irish writer and art critic. *The Brook Kerith*, Ch. 11

9 Keep the Home Fires Burning.
Ivor Novello (David Ivor Davies; 1893–1951) British actor, composer, and dramatist. Song title (written with Lena Guilbert Ford)

10 Mid pleasures and palaces though we may roam,
Be it ever so humble, there's no place like home;
…
Home, home, sweet, sweet home!
There's no place like home! there's no place like home!
John Howard Payne (1791–1852) US actor and dramatist. *Clari, or the Maid of Milan*

11 Home-keeping youth have ever homely wits.
William Shakespeare (1564–1616) English dramatist. *The Two Gentlemen of Verona*, I:1

12 Seek home for rest,
For home is best.
Thomas Tusser (1524–80) English farmer. *Five Hundred Points of Good Husbandry*, 'Instructions to Housewifery'

13 Look Homeward, Angel!
Thomas Wolfe (1900–38) US novelist. From *Lycidas* by John Milton. Book title

HOMESICKNESS

See also home, nostalgia

1 They say there's bread and work for all,
And the sun shines always there:
But I'll not forget old Ireland,
Were it fifty times as fair.
Helen Selina Blackwood (1807–67) British poet. *Lament of the Irish Emigrant*

2 Weep no more, my lady,
Oh! weep no more today!
We will sing one song for the old Kentucky Home,
For the old Kentucky Home far away.
Stephen Foster (1826–64) US composer of popular songs. *My Old Kentucky Home*

3 'Way down upon de Swanee Ribber,
Far, far away,
Dere's where my heart is turning ebber:
Dere's where de old folks stay.
All up and down de whole creation
Sadly I roam,
Still longing for de old plantation,
And for de old folks at home.
Stephen Foster *Old Folks at Home*

4 Oh give me a home where the buffalo roam,
Where the deer and the antelope play,
Where seldom is heard a discouraging word
And the skies are not cloudy all day.
Brewster Higley (19th century) US songwriter. *Home on the Range*

5 The accent of one's birthplace lingers in the mind and in the heart as it does in one's speech.
Duc de la Rochefoucauld (1613–80) French writer. *Maximes*, 342

6 Breathes there the man, with soul so dead,
Who never to himself hath said,
This is my own, my native land!
Whose heart hath ne'er within him burn'd,
As home his footsteps he hath turn'd
From wandering on a foreign strand!
Walter Scott (1771–1832) Scottish novelist. *The Lay of the Last Minstrel*, VI

7 In home-sickness you must keep moving – it is the only disease that does not require rest.
H. de Vere Stacpoole (1863–1931) Irish-born novelist. *The Bourgeois*

8 Good-bye Piccadilly, Farewell Leicester Square;
It's a long, long way to Tipperary, but my heart's right there!

Harry Williams (1874–1924) British songwriter. Written with Jack Judge (1878–1938). *It's a Long Way to Tipperary*

9 I travelled among unknown men
In lands beyond the sea;
Nor, England! did I know till then
What love I bore to thee.

William Wordsworth (1770–1850) British poet. *I Travelled among Unknown Men*

HOMOSEXUALITY

See also sex

1 Out of the closets and into the streets.

Anonymous Slogan for US Gay Liberation Front

2 Refusal to make herself the object is not always what turns women to homosexuality; most lesbians, on the contrary, seek to cultivate the treasures of their femininity.

Simone de Beauvoir (1908–86) French writer and feminist. *Le Deuxième Sexe*

3 Between women love is contemplative.

Simone de Beauvoir *Le Deuxième Sexe*

4 But the men of Sodom were wicked and sinners before the Lord exceedingly.

Bible: Genesis 13:13

5 If God had meant to have homosexuals he would have created Adam and Bruce.

Anita Bryant US singer. Attrib.

6 We know there have always been gays in the military. The issue is whether they can be in the military without lying about it.

Bill Clinton (1946–) US statesman. *The Independent*, 17 Nov 1992

7 I became one of the stately homos of England.

Quentin Crisp (?1910–) Model, publicist, and writer. *The Naked Civil Servant*

8 The...problem which confronts homosexuals is that they set out to win the love of a 'real' man. If they succeed, they fail. A man who 'goes with' other men is not what they would call a real man.

Quentin Crisp *The Naked Civil Servant*

9 Why didn't you bring him with you? I should be delighted to meet him.

Lady (Maud) 'Emerald' Cunard (1872–1948) US-born society figure in Britain. To Somerset Maugham, who said he was leaving a dinner party early 'to keep his youth'. *Emerald and Nancy* (D. Fielding)

10 I am the Love that dare not speak its name.

Lord Alfred Douglas (1870–1945) British writer and poet. *Two Loves*

11 Gays grow up watching heterosexual movies – *Now Voyager* – and deciding whether they're Bette Davis or Paul Henreid.

Harvey Fierstein (1954–) US actor *Time*, 20 June 1983

12 The sodomite had been a temporary aberration; the homosexual was now a species.

Michel Foucault (1926–84) French philosopher. *A History of Sexuality*

13 It is a perfectly ordinary little case of a man charged with indecency with four or five guardsmen.

Mervyn Griffith-Jones (1909–78) British lawyer. Attrib. in *This England* (Michael Bateman)

14 *The Well of Loneliness*, a novel by Radclyffe Hall, which treats of intimate relationships between women, was withdrawn on the advice of the Home Secretary...the editor of the Sunday Express... declared he 'would sooner give a healthy boy or girl a dose of prussic acid than a copy of it.'

The Daily Telegraph, 20 Dec 1928

15 You're neither unnatural, nor abominable, nor mad; you're as much a part of what people call nature as anyone else; only you're unexplained as yet – you've not got your niche in creation.

Radclyffe Hall (1886–1943) British writer and poet. *The Well of Loneliness*

16 There's nothing wrong with going to bed with somebody of your own sex. People should be very free with sex – they should draw the line at goats.

Elton John (1947–) British rock pianist and singer.

17 I never said I was a dyke even to a dyke because there wasn't a dyke in the land who thought she should be a dyke or even thought she was a dyke so how could we talk about it.

Jill Johnston (1929–) British-born US writer and feminist. *Lesbian Nation: The Feminist Solution*

18 Postumus, are you *really*
Taking a wife?...
isn't it better to sleep with a pretty boy?
Boys don't quarrel all night, or nag you for little presents
While they're on the job, or complain that you don't come
Up to their expectations, or demand more gasping passion.

Juvenal (Decimus Junius Juvenalis; 60–130 AD) Roman satirist. *Satires*, VI

19 The 'homo' is the legitimate child of the 'suffragette'.

Wyndham Lewis (1882–1957) British novelist. *The Art of Being Ruled*, Pt. VIII, Ch. 4

20 Well, he looks like a man.

Abraham Lincoln (1809–65) US statesman. On catching sight of the poet Walt Whitman for the first time. Attrib.

21 Those lesbians and gay men who do have difficulties with their sexuality suffer them because of the prejudice and discrimination they face.

Ian McKellen (1939–) British actor. *The Times*, 5 Dec 1991

22 Constant conditioning in my youth and social pressure in every department of my life all failed to convert me to heterosexuality.

Ian McKellen *The Times*, 5 Dec 1991

23 Terry and I are both from the South and were subjected to the most heterosexual propaganda of all. If propaganda worked we'd be straight.

Armistead Maupin (1944–) US author. *The Sunday Times*, 4 Feb 1990

24 There's nothing I'd like better than to live in a world where my sexuality was utterly irrelevant.

Armistead Maupin *The Sunday Times*, 4 Feb 1990

25 If *Tales of the City* is radical, it's because...the gay characters are on exactly the same footing as the straight characters.

Armistead Maupin *The Sunday Times*, 4 Feb 1990

26 This sort of thing may be tolerated by the French, but we are British – thank God.

Lord Montgomery (1887–1976) British field marshal. Comment on a bill to relax the laws against homosexuals. *Daily Mail*, 27 May 1965

27 Wilde's captors were the police. But his persecutors were to be found on the letters page of the *Daily Telegraph*.

Matthew Parris (1949–) British journalist. *The Times*, 7 Apr 1993

28 I will resist the efforts of some to obtain government endorsement of homosexuality.

Ronald Reagan (1911–) US politician and president. *Communication to the publisher of the Presidential Biblical Scorecard*, 18 Aug 1984

29 People who have a low self-esteem…have a tendency to cling to their own sex because it is less frightening.

Clara Thompson (1893–1958) US physician. *A Study of Interpersonal Relations, New Contributions to Psychiatry*, 'Changing Concepts of Homosexuality in Psychoanalysis' (ed. Patrick Mullahy)

30 If Michelangelo had been straight, the Sistine Chapel would have been wallpapered.

Robin Tyler US comedienne. Speech to gay-rights rally, Washington, 9 Jan 1988

HONESTY

See also frankness, integrity, sincerity, truth

1 An honest man's word is as good as his bond.

Proverb

2 Honesty is the best policy.

Proverb

3 It is impossible that a man who is false to his friends and neighbours should be true to the public.

Bishop Berkeley (1685–1753) Irish churchman and philosopher. *Maxims Concerning Patriotism*

4 To live outside the law, you must be honest.

Bob Dylan (Robert Allen Zimmerman; 1941–) US pop singer. *Absolutely Sweet Marie*

5 You see, I always divide people into two groups. Those who live by what they know to be a lie, and those who live by what they believe, falsely, to be the truth.

Christopher Hampton (1946–) British writer and dramatist. *The Philanthropist*, Sc. 6

6 I keep six honest serving-men
(They taught me all I knew);
Their names are What and Why and When
And How and Where and Who.

Rudyard Kipling (1865–1936) Indian-born British writer. *Just So Stories*

7 Though I be poor, I'm honest.

Thomas Middleton (1580–1627) English dramatist. *The Witch*, III:2

8 To make your children *capable of honesty* is the beginning of education.

John Ruskin (1819–1900) British art critic and writer. *Time and Tide*, Letter VIII

9 To be honest, as this world goes, is to be one man pick'd out of ten thousand.

William Shakespeare (1564–1616) English dramatist. *Hamlet*, II:2

10 I thank God I am as honest as any man living that is an old man and no honester than I.

William Shakespeare *Much Ado About Nothing*, III:5

11 O wretched fool!
That liv'st to make thine honesty a vice.
O monstrous world! Take note, take note, O world!
To be direct and honest is not safe.

William Shakespeare *Othello* III:3

12 Ha, ha! what a fool Honesty is! and Trust his sworn brother, a very simple gentleman!

William Shakespeare *The Winter's Tale*, IV:3

13 Though I am not naturally honest, I am so sometimes by chance.

William Shakespeare *The Winter's Tale*, IV:3

14 Father, I cannot tell a lie. I did it with my little hatchet.

George Washington (1732–99) US statesman. Attrib.

15 Honesty is the best policy; but he who is governed by that maxim is not an honest man.

Richard Whately (1787–1863) British churchman. *Apophthegms*

16 It is a terrible thing for a man to find out suddenly that all his life he has been speaking nothing but the truth.

Oscar Wilde (1854–1900) Irish-born British dramatist. *The Importance of Being Earnest*, III

17 If you do not tell the truth about yourself you cannot tell it about other people.

Virginia Woolf (1882–1941) British novelist. *The Moment and Other Essays*

HONOUR

See also titles

1 And they were offended in him. But Jesus said unto them, A prophet is not without honour, save in his own country, and in his own house.

Bible: Matthew 13:57

2 That chastity of honour, that felt a stain like a wound.

Edmund Burke (1729–97) British politician. *Reflections on the Revolution in France*

3 Remember, men, we're fighting for this woman's honour; which is probably more than she ever did.

Groucho Marx (Julius Marx; 1895–1977) US comedian. *Duck Soup*

4 Honour pricks me on. Yea, but how if honour prick me off when I come on? How then? Can honour set to a leg? No. Or an arm? No. Or take away the grief of a wound? No. Honour hath no skill in surgery, then? No. What is honour? A word. What is in that word? Honour. What is that honour? Air.

William Shakespeare (1564–1616) English dramatist. *Henry IV, Part One*, V:1

5 For Brutus is an honourable man;
So are they all, all honourable men.

William Shakespeare *Julius Caesar*, III:2

6 I once had a sparrow alight upon my shoulder for a moment while I was hoeing in a village garden, and I felt that I was more distinguished by that circumstance than I should have been by any epaulet I could have worn.

Henry David Thoreau (1817–62) US writer. *Walden*, 'Winter Visitors'

7 Brothers all
In honour, as in one community,
Scholars and gentlemen.

William Wordsworth (1770–1850) British poet. *The Prelude*, IX

HOOD, THOMAS

(1799–1845) British poet. His collection *Odes and Addresses* (1825) was followed by several volumes of humorous verse and such political poems as *The Story of the Shirt* (1843).

1 The sedate, sober, silent, serious, sad-coloured sect.

Referring to the Quakers. *Comic Annual*, 'The Doves and the Crows'

2 Ben Battle was a soldier bold,
And used to war's alarms:
But a cannon-ball took off his legs,
So he laid down his arms!

Faithless Nelly Gray

3 For here I leave my second leg,
And the Forty-second Foot!

Faithless Nelly Gray

4 The love that loves a scarlet coat
Should be more uniform.

Faithless Nelly Gray

5 His death, which happen'd in his berth,
At forty-odd befell:
They went and told the sexton, and
The sexton toll'd the bell.

Faithless Sally Brown

6 I remember, I remember,
The house where I was born,
The little window where the sun
Came peeping in at morn;
He never came a wink too soon,
Nor brought too long a day,
But now, I often wish the night
Had borne my breath away!

I Remember

7 I remember, I remember,
The fir trees dark and high;
I used to think their slender tops
Were close against the sky:
It was a childish ignorance,
But now 'tis little joy
To know I'm farther off from heav'n
Than when I was a boy.

I Remember

8 But evil is wrought by want of thought,
As well as want of heart!

The Lady's Dream

9 For that old enemy the gout
Had taken him in toe!

Lieutenant Luff

10 No warmth, no cheerfulness, no healthful ease,
No comfortable feel in any member –
No shade, no shine, no butterflies, no bees,
No fruits, no flowers, no leaves, no birds, –
November!

No!

11 O! men with sisters dear,
O! men with mothers and wives!
It is not linen you're wearing out,
But human creatures' lives!

The Song of the Shirt

12 Oh! God! that bread should be so dear,
And flesh and blood so cheap!

The Song of the Shirt

13 Holland…lies so low they're only saved by being dammed.

Up the Rhine, 'Letter from Martha Penny to Rebecca Page'

14 What is a modern poet's fate?
To write his thoughts upon a slate;
The critic spits on what is done,
Gives it a wipe – and all is gone.

Alfred Lord Tennyson, A Memoir (Hallam Tennyson), Vol. II, Ch. 3

15 There are three things which the public will always clamour for, sooner or later: namely, Novelty, novelty, novelty.

Announcement of *Comic Annual*, 1836

HOPE

See also ambition, desire, expectation, optimism

1 Hope is the physician of each misery.

Irish proverb

2 A drowning man will clutch at a straw.

Proverb

3 Hope for the best.

Proverb

4 It is a long lane that has no turning.

Proverb

5 While there's life there's hope.

Proverb

6 Comin' in on a Wing and a Prayer.

Harold Adamson (1906–) US songwriter. Film and song title

7 Still nursing the unconquerable hope,
Still clutching the inviolable shade.

Matthew Arnold (1822–88) British poet and critic. *The Scholar Gipsy*

8 Charity is the power of defending that which we know to be indefensible. Hope is the power of being cheerful in circumstances which we know to be desperate.

G. K. Chesterton (1874–1936) British writer. *Heretics*, Ch. 12

9 That one day this country of ours, which we love so much, will find dignity and greatness and peace again.

Noël Coward (1899–1973) British dramatist. The toast from *Cavalcade*

10 People will not readily bear pain unless there is hope.

Michael Edwards (1930–) South African businessman. Speech, 2 July 1980

11 He that lives upon hope will die fasting.

Benjamin Franklin (1706–90) US scientist and statesman. *The Way to Wealth*

12 Confidence and hope do be more good than physic.

Galen (fl. 2nd century) Greek physician.

13 While there is life, there's hope,' he cried;
'Then why such haste?' so groaned and died.

John Gay (1685–1732) English poet and dramatist. *Fables*

14 Death is the greatest evil, because it cuts off hope.

William Hazlitt (1778–1830) British essayist and journalist. *Characteristics*, 35

15 Hope is necessary in every condition. The miseries of poverty, sickness, of captivity, would, without this comfort, be insupportable.

Samuel Johnson (1709–84) English lexicographer and writer. *The Rambler*, 67

16 The first qualification for a physician is hopefulness.

James Little (1836–85) US physician.

17 After all, tomorrow is another day.

Margaret Mitchell (1909–49) US novelist. The closing words of the book, *Gone with the Wind*

18 Always give the patient hope, even when death seems at hand.

Ambroise Paré (c. 1517–90) French surgeon.

19 Hope springs eternal in the human breast;
Man never is, but always to be blest.

Alexander Pope (1688–1744) British poet. *An Essay on Man*, I

20 For hope is but the dream of those that wake.

Matthew Prior (1664–1721) British poet. *Solomon*, II

21 The miserable have no other medicine
But only hope.

William Shakespeare (1564–1616) English dramatist. *Measure for Measure*, III:1

22 The doctor says there is no hope, and as he does the killing he ought to know.

Gaspar Zavala y Zamora (d. 1813) *El Triunfo del Amor y de la Amistad*, II:8

HOPE, ANTHONY

(Sir Anthony Hope Hawkins; 1863–1933) British novelist. After the success of *The Prisoner of Zenda* (1894), which was made into a film three times (1922, 1937, and 1952), he wrote many similar romances.

1 Unless one is a genius, it is best to aim at being intelligible.

The Dolly Dialogues

2 He is very fond of making things which he does not want, and then giving them to people who have no use for them.

The Dolly Dialogues

3 Economy is going without something you do want in case you should, some day, want something you probably won't want.

The Dolly Dialogues

4 'You oughtn't to yield to temptation.'
'Well, somebody must, or the thing becomes absurd.'

The Dolly Dialogues

5 Boys will be boys –'
'And even that…wouldn't matter if we could only prevent girls from being girls.'

The Dolly Dialogues

6 '*Bourgeois*,' I observed, 'is an epithet which the riff-raff apply to what is respectable, and the aristocracy to what is decent'.

The Dolly Dialogues

7 I wish you would read a little poetry sometimes. Your ignorance cramps my conversation.

The Dolly Dialogues

8 Good families are generally worse than any others.

The Prisoner of Zenda, Ch. 1

9 His foe was folly and his weapon wit.

Written for the inscription on the memorial to the dramatist W. S. Gilbert, Victoria Embankment, London.

HORACE

(Quintus Horatius Flaccus; 65–8 BC) Roman poet. His *Odes* and *Epistles* portray Roman life in considerable detail.

1 'Painters and poets alike have always had licence to dare anything.' We know that, and we both claim and allow to others in their turn this indulgence.

Ars Poetica

2 I strive to be brief, and I become obscure.

Ars Poetica

3 You will have written exceptionally well if, by skilful arrangement of your words, you have made an ordinary one seem original.

Ars Poetica

4 Many terms which have now dropped out of favour, will be revived, and those that are at present respectable will drop out, if usage so choose, with whom resides the decision and the judgement and the code of speech.

Ars Poetica

5 Scholars dispute, and the case is still before the courts.

Ars Poetica

6 Mountains will heave in childbirth, and a silly little mouse will be born.

Ars Poetica

7 He always hurries to the main event and whisks his audience into the middle of things as though they knew already.
Ars Poetica

8 To the Greeks the Muse gave native wit, to the Greeks the gift of graceful eloquence.
Ars Poetica

9 I'm aggrieved when sometimes even excellent Homer nods.
Ars Poetica

10 Not gods, nor men, nor even booksellers have put up with poets being second-rate.
Ars Poetica

11 Let it be kept till the ninth year, the manuscript put away at home: you may destroy whatever you haven't published; once out, what you've said can't be stopped.
Ars Poetica

12 To save a man's life against his will is the same as killing him.
Ars Poetica

13 *Nullius addictus iurare in verba magistri,*
Quo me cumque rapit tempestas, deferor hospes.
Not bound to swear allegiance to any master, wherever the wind takes me I travel as a visitor.
Nullius in verba is the motto of the Royal Society. *Epistles*, I

14 The happy state of getting the victor's palm without the dust of racing.
Epistles, I

15 If possible honestly, if not, somehow, make money.
Epistles, I

16 Let me remind you what the wary fox said once upon a time to the sick lion: 'Because those footprints scare me, all directed your way, none coming back.'
Epistles, I

17 We are just statistics, born to consume resources.
Epistles, I

18 Believe each day that has dawned is your last. Some hour to which you have not been looking forward will prove lovely. As for me, if you want a good laugh, you will come and find me fat and sleek, in excellent condition, one of Epicurus' herd of pigs.
Epistles, I

19 To marvel at nothing is just about the one and only thing, Numicius, that can make a man happy and keep him that way.
Epistles, I

20 You may drive out nature with a pitchfork, yet she'll be constantly running back.
Epistles, I

21 They change their clime, not their frame of mind, who rush across the sea. We work hard at doing nothing: we look for happiness in boats and carriage rides. What you are looking for is here, is at Ulubrae, if only peace of mind doesn't desert you.
Epistles, I

22 For it is your business, when the wall next door catches fire.
Epistles, I

23 If you believe Cratinus from days of old, Maecenas, (as you must know) no verse can give pleasure for long, nor last, that is written by drinkers of water.
Epistles, I

24 And seek for truth in the groves of Academe.
Epistles, II

25 Hard to train to accept being poor.
Odes, I

26 And if you include me among the lyric poets, I'll hold my head so high it'll strike the stars.
Odes, I

27 Pale Death kicks his way equally into the cottages of the poor and the castles of kings.
Odes, I

28 Life's short span forbids us to enter on far-reaching hopes.
Odes, I

29 Drop the question what tomorrow may bring, and count as profit every day that Fate allows you.
Odes, I

30 Do not try to find out – we're forbidden to know – what end the gods have in store for me, or for you.
Odes, I

31 While we're talking, time will have meanly run on: pick today's fruits, not relying on the future in the slightest.
Odes, I

32 *Carpe diem.*
Seize the day.
Odes, I

33 When things are steep, remember to stay level-headed.
Odes, II

34 *Dulce et decorum est pro patria mori.*
It is a sweet and seemly thing to die for one's country.
Odes, III

35 Force, if unassisted by judgement, collapses through its own mass.
Odes, III

36 Undeservedly you will atone for the sins of your fathers.
Odes, III

37 What do the ravages of time not injure? Our parents' age (worse than our grandparents') has produced us, more worthless still, who will soon give rise to a yet more vicious generation.
Odes, III

38 My life with girls has ended, though till lately I was up to it and soldiered on not ingloriously; now on this wall will hang my weapons and my lyre, discharged from the war.

Odes, III

39 I have executed a memorial longer lasting than bronze.

Odes, III

40 That I make poetry and give pleasure (if I give pleasure) are because of you.

Odes, IV

41 Not to hope for things to last for ever, is what the year teaches and even the hour which snatches a nice day away.

Odes, IV

42 Many brave men lived before Agamemnon's time; but they are all, unmourned and unknown, covered by the long night, because they lack their sacred poet.

Odes, IV

43 Not the owner of many possessions will you be right to call happy: he more rightly deserves the name of happy who knows how to use the gods' gifts wisely and to put up with rough poverty, and who fears dishonour more than death.

Odes, IV

44 Mix a little foolishness with your serious plans: it's lovely to be silly at the right moment.

Odes, IV

45 How is it, Maecenas, that no one lives contented with his lot, whether he has planned it for himself or fate has flung him into it, but yet he praises those who follow different paths?

Satires, I

46 An accomplished man to his finger-tips.

Satires, I

47 Strong enough to answer back to desires, to despise distinctions, and a whole man in himself, polished and well-rounded.

Satires, II

HORSES

See also animals, hunting, sport and games

1 When I appear in public people expect me to neigh, grind my teeth, paw the ground and swish my tail – none of which is easy.

Princess Anne (1950–) The Princess Royal, only daughter of Elizabeth II. *The Observer*, 'Sayings of the Week', 22 May 1977

2 I know two things about the horse,
And one of them is rather coarse.

Anonymous 'The Horse'

3 I sprang to the stirrup, and Joris, and he;
I galloped, Dirck galloped, we galloped all three.

Robert Browning (1812–89) British poet. *How they brought the Good News from Ghent to Aix*

4 As lene was his hors as is a rake.

Geoffrey Chaucer (c. 1342–1400) English poet. *The Canterbury Tales*, Prologue

5 The blue ribbon of the turf.

Benjamin Disraeli (1804–81) British statesman. Describing the Derby. *Life of Lord George Bentinck*, Ch. 26

6 Gwine to run all night!
Gwine to run all day!
I bet my money on the bob-tail nag.
Somebody bet on the bay.

Stephen Foster (1826–64) US composer of popular songs. *Camptown Races*

7 They say princes learn no art truly, but the art of horsemanship. The reason is, the brave beast is no flatterer. He will throw a prince as soon as his groom.

Ben Jonson (1573–1637) English dramatist. *Timber, or Discoveries made upon Men and Matter*

8 It takes a good deal of physical courage to ride a horse. This, however, I have. I get it at about forty cents a flask, and take it as required.

Stephen Leacock (1869–1944) English-born Canadian economist and humorist. *Literary Lapses*, 'Reflections on Riding'

9 To confess that you are totally Ignorant about the Horse, is social suicide: you will be despised by everybody, especially the horse.

W. C. Sellar (1898–1951) British humorous writer. *Horse Nonsense*

10 A horse! a horse ! my kingdom for a horse.

William Shakespeare (1564–1616) English dramatist. *Richard III*, V:4

11 I have endured the Sandhurst riding-school, I have galloped for an impetuous general, I have been steward at regimental races, but none of these feats have altered my opinion that the horse, as a means of locomotion, is obsolete.

E. Œ. Somerville (1858–1949) Irish writer. *Experiences of an Irish R.M.*, 'Great-Uncle McCarthy'

HOSPITALITY

1 A constant guest is never welcome.

Proverb

2 Fish and guests smell in three days.

Proverb

3 The first day a guest, the second day a guest, the third day a calamity.

Indian proverb

4 The guest who outstays his fellow-guests loses his overcoat.

Chinese proverb

5 Fish and guests smell in three days.

Proverb

6 The first day a guest, the second day a guest, the third day a calamity.

Indian proverb

7 The guest who outstays his fellow-guests loses his overcoat.

Chinese proverb

8 I'd rather be a host than a guest. As Beerbohm wonderfully observed, a happy host makes a sad guest.

Harold Acton (1904–) British writer. *The Times*, 18 Apr 1970

9 Let brotherly love continue. Be not forgetful to entertain strangers for thereby some have entertained angels unawares.

Bible: Hebrews 13:1–2

HOSTAGES

See also imprisonment

1 We apologise for having captured you. We recognise now that it was the wrong thing to do, that holding hostages achieves no useful, constructive purpose.

Anonymous Lebanese terrorist, on releasing Terry Waite. *The Times*, 19 Nov 1991

2 Two members of the Order should be sent together among the infidels to treat about the ransom of Christian slaves, and they are hence called Ransomers.

Alban Butler (1710–73) British writer. *The Lives of the Fathers, Martyrs, and Other Principal Saints*

3 The strange paradox of the situation is that on being released, we who have spent so much time on our own still desperately need to be left alone. We need to lick and heal the wounds gradually and unmolested.

Brian Keenan (1950–) Irish hostage. *The Times*, 1990

4 Sometimes it seems that the adulation, affection and warmth in which I am cocooned by friends and family is a kind of hothouse of obligations, both personal and public. I was unprepared for this… This psychological, emotional and social temperature change – from freezing to boiling point – knocks the personality out of balance and makes difficult any meaningful response to the world.

Brian Keenan *The Times*, 1990

5 I am trying to cope with the paradox of being a public figure while desperately wanting to be a man unseen, and at the same time trying to cope with a deeply felt moral and emotional responsibility about the remaining hostages.

Brian Keenan *The Times*, 1990

6 Well hello. It's very nice to be here after five years…I want to go home, to be with my family, to try to make up the time I have lost.

John McCarthy British journalist. Returning home after five years as a hostage in Lebanon. Comment, Aug 1991

7 It's impossible to describe the emotion, the elation. It completely overwhelms you. The main thing is that he is free. Now he has to pick up the threads of his life and start again. He has come out of a black hole into glaring light and he will be overwhelmed by it.

Jill Morrell Friend of John McCarthy, who campaigned for his release. Referring to the release of John McCarthy. *The Times*, 9 Aug 1991

8 An honourable imprisonment…as is due to one who is in treaty for ransom.

Walter Scott (1771–1832) Scottish novelist. *Ivanhoe*

9 They were obliged to ransom not only their prisoners but their dead.

Connop Thirlwall (1797–1875) British historian. *History of Greece*

10 My word, Bunyan, you're a lucky fellow. You've got a window out of which you can look, see the sky, and here I am in a dark room.

Terry Waite (1939–) British church envoy. Contemplating a picture postcard of the author John Bunyan, that had been sent to Waite in captivity. *The Times*, 21 Nov 1991

11 All of us, all hostages, would plead with those who are holding the people of South Lebanon, innocent people being held as hostages, to release them soon; to put an end to this problem; to put an end to terrorism, and to find peaceful, humane and civilised ways of resolving the very complex problems that face the Middle East.

Terry Waite *The Times*, 19 Nov 1991

12 We know that the people of Lebanon have suffered greatly and those from whom I have just come can be assured that we in the church will not rest until all are free and there is justice and peace brought to people who deserve a better deal.

Terry Waite *The Times*, 20 Nov 1991

HOUSES

See also architecture, home, stately homes

1 Houses are built to live in and not to look on; therefore let use be preferred before uniformity, except where both may be had.

Francis Bacon (1561–1626) English philosopher. *Essays*, 'Of Building'

2 A hundred and fifty accurate reproductions of Anne Hathaway's cottage, each complete with central heating and garage.

Osbert Lancaster (1908–86) British cartoonist. *Pillar to Post*, 'Stockbrokers Tudor'

3 A house is a machine for living in.

Le Corbusier (Charles-Édouard Jeanneret; 1887–1965) Swiss-born French architect. *Towards an Architecture*

4 They're all made out of ticky-tacky, and they all look just the same.

Malvina Reynolds (1900–78) US folksinger and songwriter. Song describing a housing scheme built in the hills south of San Francisco. *Little Boxes*

5 It's 'aving 'ouses built by men, I believe, makes all the work and trouble.

H. G. Wells (1866–1946) British writer. *Kipps*, Bk. III, Ch. 1

HOUSES OF PARLIAMENT

See also aristocracy, government, politics

1 This is a rotten argument, but it should be good enough for their lordships on a hot summer afternoon.

Anonymous A note on a ministerial brief read out by mistake in the House of Lords. *The Way the Wind Blows* (Lord Home), 1976

2 The House of Lords is like a glass of champagne that has stood for five days.

Clement Attlee (1883–1967) British statesman and Labour prime minister. Attrib.

3 A severe though not unfriendly critic of our institutions said that 'the cure for admiring the House of Lords was to go and look at it.'

Walter Bagehot (1826–77) British economist and journalist. *The English Constitution*, 'The House of Lords'

4 A lot of hard-faced men who look as if they had done very well out of the war.

Stanley Baldwin (1867–1947) British statesman. Referring to the first House of Commons elected after World War I (1918). *Economic Consequences of the Peace* (J. M. Keynes), Ch. 5

5 The House of Lords is the British Outer Mongolia for retired politicians.

Tony Benn (1925–) British politician. Speech, 11 Feb 1962

6 I have been, though unworthy, a member of this House in six or seven Parliaments, yet never did I see the House in so great confusion. This is more fit for a grammar school than a Court of Parliament.

Robert Cecil, 1st Earl of Salisbury (1563–1612) English statesman. Speech, House of Commons, 24 Nov 1601

7 Well, since I see all the birds are flown, I do expect from you that you shall send them unto me as soon as they return hither.

Charles I (1600–49) King of England. On entering the House of Commons to arrest five MPs. Remark, 4 Jan 1642

8 Better than a play.

Charles II (1630–85) King of England. Referring to House of Lords debate on the Divorce Bill. Attrib.

9 I think...that it is the best club in London.

Charles Dickens (1812–70) British novelist. Mr Tremlow describing the House of Commons. *Our Mutual Friend*, Bk. II, Ch. 3

10 I am dead: dead, but in the Elysian fields.

Benjamin Disraeli (1804–81) British statesman. Said on his move to the House of Lords. Attrib.

11 The House of Lords is a model of how to care for the elderly.

Frank Field (1942–) British politician. *The Observer*, 24 May 1981

12 There are kings enough in England. I am nothing there, I am old and want rest and should only go to be plagued and teased there about that D—d House of Commons.

George II (1683–1760) King of Great Britain and Ireland. George II's reply when urged to leave Hanover and return to England. Letter from the Earl of Holderness to the Duke of Newcastle, 3 Aug 1755

13 The House of Peers, throughout the war,
Did nothing in particular,
And did it very well.

W. S. Gilbert (1836–1911) British dramatist. *Iolanthe*, II

14 I have neither eye to see, nor tongue to speak here, but as the House is pleased to direct me.

William Lenthall (1591–1662) English parliamentarian. Said on 4 Jan 1642 in the House of Commons when asked by Charles I if he had seen five MPs whom the King wished to arrest. It was a succinct restatement of the Speaker's traditional role. *Historical Collections* (Rushworth)

15 Mr Balfour's Poodle.

David Lloyd George (1863–1945) British Liberal statesman. Referring to the House of Lords and its in-built Conservative majority (the Earl of Balfour was a Conservative statesman); said in reply to a claim that it was 'the watchdog of the nation'. Remark, House of Commons, 26 June 1907

16 Every man has a House of Lords in his own head. Fears, prejudices, misconceptions – those are the peers, and they are hereditary.

David Lloyd George Speech, Cambridge, 1927

17 The British, being brought up on team games, enter their House of Commons in the spirit of those who would rather be doing something else. If they cannot be playing golf or tennis, they can at least pretend that politics is a game with very similar rules.

Cyril Northcote Parkinson (1919–93) British historian and writer. *Parkinson's Law*, Ch. 2

18 The House of Lords must be the only institution in the world which is kept efficient by the persistent absenteeism of most of its members.

Herbert Samuel (1870–1963) British Liberal statesman. *News Review*, 5 Feb 1948

19 A life peer is like a mule – no pride of ancestry, no hope of posterity.

Lord Shackleton (1911–) British politician, businessman, and life peer. Attrib.

20 The House of Lords is a perfect eventide home.

Mary Stocks (1891–1975) British politician and writer. *The Observer*, 'Sayings of the Week', 4 Oct 1970

21 The House of Lords, an illusion to which I have never been able to subscribe – responsibility without power, the prerogative of the eunuch throughout the ages.

Tom Stoppard (1937–) Czech-born British dramatist. *Lord Malquist and Mr Moon*, Pt. VI, Ch. 1

22 You must build your House of Parliament upon the river: so...that the populace cannot exact their demands by sitting down round you.

Duke of Wellington (1769–1852) British general and statesman. *Words on Wellington* (Sir William Fraser)

HOUSEWORK

See also woman's role

1 Housekeeping ain't no joke.

Louisa May Alcott (1832–88) US novelist. *Little Women*, Pt. I

2 Our motto: Life is too short to stuff a mushroom.

Shirley Conran (1932–) British designer and journalist. *Superwoman*, Epigraph

3 There was no need to do any housework at all. After the first four years the dirt doesn't get any worse.

Quentin Crisp (c. 1910–) Model, publicist, and writer. *The Naked Civil Servant*

4 Cleaning your house while your kids are still growing
Is like shoveling the walk before it stops snowing.

Phyllis Diller (1917–) US writer and comedienne. *Phyllis Diller's Housekeeping Hints*

5 The whole process of home-making, house-keeping and cooking, which ever has been woman's special province, should be looked on as an art and a profession.

Sarah Joseph Hale (1788–1879) US editor, writer, and poet. Editorial, *Godey's Lady's Book*

6 To housekeep, one had to plan ahead and carry items of motley nature around in the mind and at the same time preside, as mother had, at table, just as if everything, from the liver and bacon, to the succotash, to the French toast and strawberry jam, had not been matters of forethought and speculation.

Fannie Hurst (1889–1968) US writer. *Cosmopolitan*

7 Housework isn't bad in itself – the trouble with it is that it's inhumanely lonely.

Pat Loud (1926–) US writer and television personality. *Pat Loud: a Woman's Story* (with Nora Johnson)

8 I do, and I also wash and iron them.

Denis Thatcher (1915–) British businessman married to the Conservative prime minister Mrs Margaret Thatcher. Replying to the question 'Who wears the pants in this house?' *The Los Angeles Times, 21 Apr 1981*

9 The most dramatic thing is that, even when you look at women who are working full time outside the home – as full time as their men – when it comes to ironing and cleaning, 60 or 70 per cent of that work is still done by the women.

Malcolm Wicks (1947–) British politician. *Move Over Darling*

HOUSMAN, A. E.

(1859–1936) British scholar and poet. His own verse collections include *A Shropshire Lad* (1896) and *Last Poems* (1922).

Quotations about Housman

1 A prim, old-maidish, rather second-rate, rather tired, rather querulous person.

A. C. Benson (1862–1925) British writer. *Dianes*

2 The sad, compassionate, loving, romantic man.

Richard Graves. *A. E. Housman; The Scholar Poet*

Quotations by Housman

3 We'll to the woods no more,
The laurels all are cut.

Last Poems, Introductory

4 The candles burn their sockets,
The blinds let through the day,
The young man feels his pockets
And wonders what's to pay.

Last Poems, 'Eight O'Clock'

5 They say my verse is sad: no wonder;
Its narrow measure spans
Tears of eternity, and sorrow,
Not mine, but man's.

Last Poems, 'Fancy's Knell'

6 Even when poetry has a meaning, as it usually has, it may be inadvisable to draw it out...Perfect understanding will sometimes almost extinguish pleasure.

The Name and Nature of Poetry

7 Loveliest of trees, the cherry now
Is hung with bloom along the bough,
And stands about the woodland ride
Wearing white for Eastertide.

A Shropshire Lad, '1887'

8 They hang us now in Shrewsbury jail:
The whistles blow forlorn,
And trains all night groan on the rail
To men that die at morn.

A Shropshire Lad, 'Reveillé'

9 Look not in my eyes, for fear
They mirror true the sight I see,
And there you find your face too clear
And love it and be lost like me.

A Shropshire Lad, 'March'

10 Here of a Sunday morning
My love and I would lie,
And see the coloured counties,
And hear the larks so high
About us in the sky.

A Shropshire Lad, 'Bredon Hill'

11 Is my team ploughing,
That I was used to drive?

A Shropshire Lad, 'Bredon Hill'

12 The goal stands up, the keeper
Stands up to keep the goal.

A Shropshire Lad, 'Bredon Hill'

13 On Wenlock Edge the wood's in trouble;
His forest fleece the Wrekin heaves;
The wind, it plies the saplings double,
And thick on Severn snow the leaves.

A Shropshire Lad, 'The Welsh Marches'

14 East and west on fields forgotten
Bleach the bones of comrades slain,
Lovely lads and dead and rotten;
None that go return again.

A Shropshire Lad, 'The Welsh Marches'

15 Into my heart an air that kills
From yon far country blows:
What are those blue remembered hills,
What spires, what farms are those?

A Shropshire Lad, 'The Welsh Marches'

16 With rue my heart is laden
For golden friends I had,
For many a rose-lipt maiden
And many a lightfoot lad.

A Shropshire Lad, 'The Welsh Marches'

17 Malt does more than Milton can
To justify God's ways to man.

A Shropshire Lad, 'The Welsh Marches'

HUGHES, TED

(1930–) British poet; poet laureate (1984–), who married the poet Sylvia Plath in 1956. His poetry includes *The Hawk in the Rain* (1957), *Crow* (1970), *River* (1983), and *Flowers and Insects* (1987).

1 Death invented the phone it looks like the altar of death
Do not worship the telephone
It drags its worshippers into actual graves
With a variety of devices, through a variety of disguised voices

Selected Poems 1957–1981, 'Do not Pick up the Telephone'

2 And let her learn through what kind of dust
He has earned his thirst and the right to quench it
And what sweat he has exchanged for his money
And the blood-weight of money. He'll humble her

Selected Poems 1957–1981, 'Her Husband'

3 The war ended, the explosions stopped.
The men surrendered their weapons

And hung around limply.
Peace took them all prisoner.

Selected Poems 1957–1981, 'A Motorbike'

HUGO, VICTOR

(1802–85) French poet, novelist, and dramatist. His novels include *Notre Dame de Paris* (1831), *Le Roi s'amuse* (1832), and *Les Misérables* (1862). Verse collections include *Les Contemplations* (1856); at the age of 80 he wrote the play *Torquemada* (1882). He was regarded as a national hero and the foremost writer of 19th-century France.

Quotations about Hugo

1 In Victor Hugo we have the average sensual man impassioned and grandiloquent; in Zola we have the average sensual man going near the ground.

Matthew Arnold (1822–88) British poet and critic. *Discourses in America*

2 He will be eighty-one in February and walked upright without a stick. His white hair is as thick as his dark eyebrows, and his eyes are as bright and clear as a little child's. After dinner, he drank my health with a little speech of which – though I sat just opposite him – my accursed deafness prevented me hearing a single word.

Algernon Charles Swinburne (1837–1909) British poet. Letter to his mother, 26 Nov 1882

Quotations by Hugo

3 If suffer we must, let's suffer on the heights.

Contemplations, 'Les Malheureux'

4 A stand can be made against invasion by an army; no stand can be made against invasion by an idea.

Histoire d'un Crime, 'La Chute'

5 Symmetry is tedious, and tedium is the very basis of mourning. Despair yawns.

Les Misérables, Vol. II, Bk. IV, Ch. 1

6 The misery of a child is interesting to a mother, the misery of a young man is interesting to a young woman, the misery of an old man is interesting to nobody.

Les Misérables, 'Saint Denis'

7 Popularity? It's glory's small change.

Ruy Blas, III

8 ?

The entire contents of a telegram sent to his publishers asking how *Les Misérables* was selling; the reply was '!' *The Literary Life* (R. Hendrickson)

HUMAN CONDITION

See also human nature, life, mankind

1 A wanderer is man from his birth.
He was born in a ship
On the breast of the river of Time.

Matthew Arnold (1822–88) British poet and critic. *The Future*

2 Thou hast created us for Thyself, and our heart is not quiet until it rests in Thee.

St Augustine of Hippo (354–430) Bishop of Hippo. *Confessions*, Bk. I, Ch. 1

3 Man that is born of a woman is of few days, and full of trouble.

Bible: Job 14:1

4 In real life, of course, it is the hare who wins. Every time. Look around you. And in any case it is my contention that Aesop was writing for the tortoise market...Hares have no time to read. They are too busy winning the game.

Anita Brookner (1928–) British novelist. *Hotel du Lac*

5 We mortals cross the ocean of this world
Each in his average cabin of a life.

Robert Browning (1812–89) British poet. *Bishop Blougram's Apology*

6 The human race, to which so many of my readers belong.

G. K. Chesterton (1874–1936) British writer. *The Napoleon of Notting Hill*, Vol. I, Ch. 1

7 If God were suddenly condemned to live the life which he has inflicted on men, He would kill Himself.

Alexandre Dumas, fils (1824–95) French writer. *Pensées d'album*

8 Every man is wanted, and no man is wanted much.

Ralph Waldo Emerson (1803–82) US poet and essayist. *Essays*, 'Nominalist and Realist'

9 The world is a beautiful place
to be born into
if you don't mind some people dying
all the time
or maybe only starving
some of the time
which isn't half so bad
if it isn't you.

Laurence Ferlinghetti (1919–) US poet. *Pictures of the Gone World*

10 The management of fertility is one of the most important functions of adulthood.

Germaine Greer (1939–) Australian-born British writer and feminist.

11 Oh wearisome condition of humanity!
Born under one law, to another bound.

Fulke Greville (1554–1628) English poet and politician. *Mustapha*, V:6

12 The condition of man...is a condition of war of everyone against everyone.

Thomas Hobbes (1588–1679) English philosopher. *Leviathan*, Pt. I, Ch. 4

13 No arts; no letters; no society; and which is worst of all, continual fear and danger of violent death; and the life of man, solitary, poor, nasty, brutish, and short.

Thomas Hobbes *Leviathan*, Pt. I, Ch. 13

14 Fade far away, dissolve, and quite forget
What thou among the leaves hast never known,
The weariness, the fever, and the fret,
Here, where men sit and hear each other groan.

John Keats (1795–1821) British poet. *Ode to a Nightingale*

15 Man hands on misery to man.

It deepens like a coastal shelf.
Get out as early as you can,
And don't have any kids yourself.

Philip Larkin (1922–85) British poet. *High Windows*, 'This Be the Verse'

16 You come into the world alone, you go out alone. In between it's nice to know a few people, but being alone is a fundamental quality of human life, depressing as that is.

Helen Mirren (1945–) British actress. Remark, Jan 1989

17 Nothing is won forever in human affairs, but everything is always possible.

François Mitterrand (1916–) French politician. *The Observer*, 'Sayings of the Week', 12 June 1994

18 Every man carries the entire form of the human condition.

Michel de Montaigne (1533–92) French essayist and moralist. *Essays*, 'Of repentance'

19 Solomon Grundy,
Born on a Monday,
Christened on Tuesday,
Married on Wednesday,
Took ill on Thursday,
Worse on Friday,
Died on Saturday,
Buried on Sunday.
This is the end
Of Solomon Grundy.

Nursery Rhyme *The Nursery Rhymes of England* (J. O. Halliwell)

20 There, but for a typographical error, is the story of my life.

Dorothy Parker (1893–1967) US writer. At a Hallowe'en party, when someone remarked, 'They're ducking for apples'. *You Might As Well Live* (J. Keats)

21 Created half to rise, and half to fall;
Great lord of all things, yet a prey to all;
Sole judge of truth, in endless error hurl'd;
The glory, jest, and riddle of the world!

Alexander Pope (1688–1744) British poet. *An Essay on Man*, II

22 The universe is so vast and so ageless that the life of one man can only be justified by the measure of his sacrifice.

V. A. Rosewarne (1916–1940) British pilot. Inscribed on the portrait of the 'Young Airman' in the RAF Museum. Letter to his mother, 1940

23 Brief and powerless is Man's life; on him and all his race the slow, sure doom falls pitiless and dark.

Bertrand Russell (1872–1970) British philosopher. *Mysticism and Logic*, 'A Free Man's Worship'

24 Farewell, a long farewell, to all my greatness!
This is the state of man: to-day he puts forth
The tender leaves of hopes: to-morrow blossoms
And bears his blushing honours thick upon him;
The third day comes a frost, a killing frost,
And when he thinks, good easy man, full surely
His greatness is a-ripening, nips his root,
And then he falls, as I do.

William Shakespeare (1564–1616) English dramatist. *Henry VIII*, III:2

25 All the world's a stage,
And all the men and women merely players;
They have their exits and their entrances;
And one man in his time plays many parts,
His acts being seven ages.

William Shakespeare *As You Like It*, II:7

26 When we are born, we cry that we are come
To this great stage of fools.

William Shakespeare *King Lear*, IV:6

27 We have to believe in free-will. We've got no choice.

Isaac Bashevis Singer (1904–91) Polish-born US writer. *The Times*, 21 June 1982

28 But what am I?
An infant crying in the night:
An infant crying for the light:
And with no language but a cry.

Alfred, Lord Tennyson (1809–92) British poet. *In Memoriam A.H.H.*, LIV

29 All men should strive to learn before they die
What they are running from, and to, and why.

James Thurber (1894–1961) American humorist. Attrib.

30 Man has given a false importance to death
Any animal plant or man who dies
adds to Nature's compost heap
becomes the manure without which
nothing could grow nothing could be created
Death is simply part of the process.

Peter Weiss (1916–82) German novelist and dramatist. *Marat/Sade*, I:12

31 For what human ill does not dawn seem to be an alternative?

Thornton Wilder (1897–1975) US novelist and dramatist. *The Bridge of San Luis Rey*

HUMAN NATURE

See also mankind

1 We are usually the best men when in the worst health.

Proverb

2 Human nature is so well disposed towards those who are in interesting situations, that a young person, who either marries or dies, is sure to be kindly spoken of.

Jane Austen (1775–1817) British novelist. *Emma*, Ch. 22

3 A man's nature runs either to herbs, or to weeds; therefore let him seasonably water the one, and destroy the other.

Francis Bacon (1561–1626) English philosopher. *Essays*, 'Of Nature in Men'

4 There is in human nature generally more of the fool than of the wise.

Francis Bacon *Essays*, 'Of Boldness'

5 Nature is often hidden, sometimes overcome, seldom extinguished.

Francis Bacon *Essays*, 'Of Nature in Men'

6 Nature, to be commanded, must be obeyed.

Francis Bacon *Novum Organum*

7 There is no surer way of calling the worst out of anyone than that of taking their worst as being their true selves; no surer way of bringing out the best than by only accepting that as being true of them.

E. F. Benson (1867–1940) British novelist. *Rex*

8 Pleasant people are just as real as horrible people.

John Braine (1922–86) British novelist. Remark, Apr 1983

9 When dealing with people, let us remember we are not dealing with creatures of logic. We are dealing with creatures of emotion, creatures bristling with prejudices and motivated by pride and vanity.

Dale Carnegie (1888–1955) US lecturer and writer. *Dale Carnegie's Scrapbook*

10 I got disappointed in human nature as well and gave it up because I found it too much like my own.

J. P. Donleavy (1926–) US novelist. *Fairy Tales of New York*

11 A man so various, that he seem'd to be
Not one, but all Mankind's Epitome.
Stiff in Opinions, always in the wrong;
Was Everything by starts, and Nothing long.

John Dryden (1631–1700) British poet and dramatist. *Absalom and Achitophel*, I

12 A person seldom falls sick, but the bystanders are animated with a faint hope that he will die.

Ralph Waldo Emerson (1803–82) US poet and essayist. *Conduct of Life*, 'Considerations by the Way'

13 I have always been astonished by the tendency of so many academic psychologists, economists and even anthropologists to treat human beings as entirely rational. My own experience has always been that rationality is only one of many factors governing human behaviour and by no means always the dominant factor.

Murray Gell-Man (1929–) US physicist. *The Quark and the Jaguar*

14 Looks like whatever you try to do, somebody jumps up and hollers and raises cain – then the feller next to him jumps up and hollers how much he likes it.

Woody Guthrie (1912–67) US folk singer. *My Beat: An Intimate Volume of Shop Talk* (Howard Taubman)

15 You may drive out nature with a pitchfork, yet she'll be constantly running back.

Horace (Quintus Horatius Flaccus; 65–8 BC) Roman poet. *Epistles*, I

16 Most human beings have an almost infinite capacity for taking things for granted.

Aldous Huxley (1894–1964) British novelist. *Themes and Variations*

17 We need more understanding of human nature, because the only real danger that exists is man himself...We know nothing of man, far too little. His psyche should be studied because we are the origin of all coming evil.

Carl Gustav Jung (1875–1961) Swiss psychoanalyst. BBC television interview

18 Out of the crooked timber of humanity no straight thing can ever be made.

Immanuel Kant (1724–1804) German philosopher. *Idee zu einer allgemeinen Geschichte in weltbürgerlicher Absicht*

19 Scenery is fine – but human nature is finer.

John Keats (1795–1821) British poet. Letter to Benjamin Bailey, 13 Mar 1818

20 Upon the whole I dislike mankind: whatever people on the other side of the question may advance, they cannot deny that they are always surprised at hearing of a good action and never of a bad one.

John Keats Letter, 1820

21 No absolute is going to make the lion lie down with the lamb unless the lamb is inside.

D. H. Lawrence (1885–1930) British novelist. *The Later D. H. Lawrence*

22 Our humanity rests upon a series of learned behaviors, woven together into patterns that are infinitely fragile and never directly inherited.

Margaret Mead (1901–78) US anthropologist. *Male and Female*, Ch. 9

23 Observe diners arriving at any restaurant and you will see them make a bee-line for the wall-seats. No one ever voluntarily selects a centre table in an open space. Open seating positions are only taken when all the wall-seats are already occupied. This dates back to a primeval feeding practice of avoiding sudden attack during the deep concentration involved in consuming food.

Desmond Morris (1928–) British biologist. *Manwatching*, 'Feeding Behaviour'

24 In the misfortune of our best friends we always find something which is not displeasing to us.

Duc de la Rochefoucauld (1613–80) French writer. *Maximes*, 99

25 'Tis the way of all flesh.

Thomas Shadwell (1642–92) English dramatist. *The Sullen Lovers*, V:2

26 A rarer spirit never
Did steer humanity; but you, gods, will give us
Some faults to make us men.

William Shakespeare (1564–1616) English dramatist. *Antony and Cleopatra*, V:1

27 Get thee to a nunnery: why wouldst thou be a breeder of sinners? I am myself indifferent honest; but yet I could accuse me of such things that it were better my mother had not borne me. I am very proud, revengeful, ambitious; with more offences at my beck than I have thoughts to put them in, imagination to give them shape, or time to act them in. What should such fellows as I do crawling between heaven and earth? We are arrant knaves, all; believe none of us.

William Shakespeare *Hamlet*, III:1

28 How all occasions do inform against me,
And spur my dull revenge! What is a man,
If his chief good and market of his time
Be but to sleep and feed? a beast, no more.
Sure he that made us with such large discourse,
Looking before and after, gave us not
That capability and god-like reason
To fust in us unus'd.

William Shakespeare *Hamlet*, IV:4

29 Virtue! a fig! 'tis in ourselves that we are thus, or thus. Our bodies are our gardens, to the which our wills are gardeners.

William Shakespeare *Othello*, I:3

30 The false division of human nature into 'feminine' and 'masculine' is the root of all other divisions into subject and object, active and passive; the beginning of hierarchy.

Gloria Steinem (1934–) US writer *The Observer Life Magazine*, 15 May 1994

31 It is part of human nature to hate the man you have hurt.

Tacitus (c. 55–c. 120 AD) Roman historian. *Agricola*, 42

32 It is not the ape, nor the tiger in man that I fear, it is the donkey.

William Temple (1881–1944) British churchman. Attrib.

33 ...use thought only to justify their injustices, and speech only to conceal their thoughts.

Voltaire (François-Marie Arouet; 1694–1778) French writer. Referring to men. *Dialogue*, 'Le Chapon et la poularde'

34 The earth does not argue,
Is not pathetic, has no arrangements,
Does not scream, haste, persuade, threaten, promise,
Makes no discriminations, has no conceivable failures,
Closes nothing, refuses nothing, shuts none out.

Walt Whitman (1819–92) US poet. *To the sayers of words*

HUMAN RIGHTS

See also equality, freedom, race

1 All human beings are born free and equal in dignity and rights.

Anonymous *Universal Declaration of Human Rights* (1948), Article 1

2 *Liberté! Égalité! Fraternité!*
Freedom! Equality! Brotherhood!

Anonymous Motto for French Revolutionaries

3 We hold these truths to be self-evident: that all men are created equal; that they are endowed by their Creator with certain unalienable rights; that among these are life, liberty, and the pursuit of happiness.

Thomas Jefferson (1743–1826) US statesman. Declaration of American Independence, 4 July 1776

4 A bill of rights is what the people are entitled to against every government on earth, general or particular and what no just government should refuse to rest on inference.

Thomas Jefferson Letter to James Madison, 20 Dec 1787

5 The poorest he that is in England hath a life to live as the greatest he.

Thomas Rainborowe (d. 1648) English soldier and vice-admiral. *Life of Rainborowe* (Peacock)

6 We look forward to a world founded upon four essential human freedoms. The first is freedom of speech and expression – everywhere in the world. The second is freedom of every person to worship God in his own way – everywhere in the world. The third is freedom from want...everywhere in the world. The fourth is freedom from fear...anywhere in the world.

Franklin D. Roosevelt (1882–1945) US Democratic president. Speech to Congress, 6 Jan 1941

7 Freedom is an indivisible word. If we want to enjoy it, and fight for it, we must be prepared to extend it to everyone, whether they are rich or poor, whether they agree with us or not, no matter what their race or the colour of their skin.

Wendell Lewis Willkie (1892–1944) US lawyer and businessman. *One World*, Ch. 13

8 None ought to be lords or landlords over another, but the earth is free for every son and daughter of mankind to live free upon.

Gerrard Winstanley (c. 1609–c. 1660) English radical. Letter to Lord Fairfax, 1649

HUME, DAVID

(1711–76) Scottish philosopher. His major works were *A Treatise of Human Nature* (1739) and *An Enquiry Concerning Human Understanding* (1748). He also wrote a *History of England* (1754–62).

1 Custom, then, is the great guide of human life.

An Enquiry Concerning Human Understanding

2 If we take in our hand any volume; of divinity or school metaphysics, for instance; let us ask, *Does it contain any abstract reasoning concerning quantity or number?* No. *Does it contain any experimental reasoning, concerning matter of fact and existence?* No. Commit it then to the flames: for it can contain nothing but sophistry and illusion.

An Enquiry Concerning Human Understanding

3 The Christian religion not only was at first attended with miracles, but even at this day cannot be believed by any reasonable person without one. Mere reason is insufficient to convince us of its veracity: and whoever is moved by faith to assent to it, is conscious of a continued miracle in his own person, which subverts all the principles of his understanding, and gives him a determination to believe what is most contrary to custom and experience.

An Enquiry Concerning Human Understanding

4 Beauty in things exists in the mind which contemplates them.

Essays, 'Of Tragedy'

5 We never remark any passion or principle in others, of which, in some degree or other, we may not find a parallel in ourselves.

A Treatise of Human Nature

6 Everyone has observed how much more dogs are animated when they hunt in a pack, than when they pursue their game apart. We might, perhaps, be at a loss to explain this phenomenon, if we had not experience of a similar in ourselves.

A Treatise of Human Nature

7 Grief and disappointment give rise to anger, anger to envy, envy to malice, and malice to grief again, till the whole circle be completed.

A Treatise of Human Nature

8 Philosophers never balance between profit and honesty, because their decisions are general, and neither their passions nor imaginations are interested in the objects.

A Treatise of Human Nature

HUMILITY

See also service, servility

1 Blessed are the meek: for they shall inherit the earth.

Bible: Matthew 5:5

2 Humility is only doubt,
And does the sun and moon blot out.

William Blake (1757–1827) British poet. *The Everlasting Gospel*

3 I do not consider it an insult but rather a compliment to be called an agnostic. I do not pretend to know where many ignorant men are sure.

Clarence Seward Darrow (1857–1938) US lawyer. Remark during the trial (1925) of John Scopes for teaching the theory of evolution in school.

4 It is difficult to be humble. Even if you aim at humility, there is no guarantee that when you have attained the state you will not be proud of the feat.

Bonamy Dobrée (1891–1974) British scholar and writer. *John Wesley*

5 Less than the dust beneath thy chariot wheel,
Less than the weed that grows beside thy door,
Less than the rust that never stained thy sword,
Less than the need thou hast in life of me,
Even less am I.

Laurence Hope (Mrs M. H. Nicolson; 1804–1905) British poet and songwriter. *The Garden of Kama and other Love Lyrics from India*, 'Less than the Dust'

6 The meek do not inherit the earth unless they are prepared to fight for their meekness.

H. J. Laski (1893–1950) British political theorist. Attrib.

7 So I am beginning to wonder if maybe girls wouldn't be happier if we stopped demanding so much respeckt for ourselves and developped a little more respeckt for husbands.

Anita Loos (1888–1981) US writer, dramatist, humorist, and screenwriter. *A Mouse Is Born*, Ch. 19

8 The humble and meek are thirsting for blood.

Joe Orton (1933–67) British dramatist. *Funeral Games*, I

9 Because there's no fourth class.

George Santayana (1863–1952) US philosopher. On being asked why he always travelled third class. *Living Biographies of the Great Philosophers* (H. Thomas)

10 I too had thoughts once of being an intellectual, but I found it too difficult.

Albert Schweitzer (1875–1965) French Protestant theologian, philosopher, physician, and musician. Remark made to an African who refused to perform a menial task on the grounds that he was an intellectual. Attrib.

11 Take physic, pomp;
Expose thyself to feel what wretches feel.

William Shakespeare (1564–1616) English dramatist. *King Lear*, III:4

12 We have the highest authority for believing that the meek shall inherit the Earth; though I have never found any particular corroboration of this aphorism in the records of Somerset House.

F. E. Smith (1872–1930) British lawyer and politician. *Contemporary Personalities*, 'Marquess Curzon'

13 This is not for me. The honour is for the poor.

Mother Teresa (Agnes Gonxha Bojaxhui; 1910–) Yugoslavian-born Indian missionary. Said on receiving the Order of Merit, 24 Nov 1983. *The Sunday Times*, 3 Dec 1989

14 When I survey the wondrous Cross,
On which the Prince of Glory died,
My richest gain I count but loss
And pour contempt on all my pride.

Isaac Watts (1674–1748) English theologian and hymn writer. *When I Survey the Wondrous Cross*

15 Gentle Jesus, meek and mild,
Look upon a little child;
Pity my simplicity,
Suffer me to come to thee.

Charles Wesley (1707–88) British religious leader. *Hymns and Sacred Poems*

HUMOUR

See also laughter, nonsense, puns

On the subject

1 I have a fine sense of the ridiculous, but no sense of humour.

Edward Albee (1928–) US dramatist. *Who's Afraid of Virginia Woolf?*, I

2 Few women care to be laughed at and men not at all, except for large sums of money.

Alan Ayckbourn (1939–) British dramatist. *The Norman Conquests*, Preface

3 The marvellous thing about a joke with a double meaning is that it can only mean one thing.

Ronnie Barker (1929–) British comedian. *Sauce*, 'Daddie's Sauce'

4 The world would not be in such a snarl, had Marx been Groucho instead of Karl.

Irving Berlin (Israel Baline; 1888–1989) US composer. Telegram to the US comedian Groucho Marx on his 71st birthday

5 It's a good deed to forget a poor joke.

Brendan Bracken (1901–58) British newspaper publisher and politician. *The Observer*, 'Sayings of the Week', 17 Oct 1943

6 Comedy is tragedy that happens to other people.

Angela Carter (1940–92) British novelist. *Wise Children*

7 All I need to make a comedy is a park, a policeman and a pretty girl.

Charlie Chaplin (Sir Charles Spencer C.; 1889–1977) British film actor. *My Autobiography*

8 I remain just one thing, and one thing only – and that is a clown.
It places me on a far higher plane than any politician.

Charlie Chaplin *The Observer*, 'Sayings of the Week', 17 June 1960

9 A joke's a very serious thing.

Charles Churchill (1731–64) British poet. *The Ghost*, Bk. IV

10 Men will confess to treason, murder, arson, false teeth, or a wig. How many of them will own up to a lack of humour?

Frank More Colby (1865–1925) US editor. *Essays*, I

11 No mind is thoroughly well organized that is deficient in a sense of humour.

Samuel Taylor Coleridge (1772–1834) British poet. *Table Talk*

12 Total absence of humour renders life impossible.

Colette (1873–1954) French novelist. *Chance Acquaintances*

13 A different taste in jokes is a great strain on the affections.

George Eliot (Mary Ann Evans; 1819–80) British novelist. *Daniel Deronda*

14 Comedy, like sodomy, is an unnatural act.

Marty Feldman (1933–83) British comedian. *The Times*, 9 June 1969

15 As for the Freudian, it is a very low, Central European sort of humour.

Robert Graves (1895–1985) British poet and novelist. *Occupation: Writer*

16 Funny peculiar, or funny ha-ha?

Ian Hay (John Hay Beith; 1876–1952) British novelist and dramatist. *The Housemaster*, III

17 His foe was folly and his weapon wit.

Anthony Hope (Sir Anthony Hope Hawkins; 1863–1933) British novelist. Written for the inscription on the memorial to W. S. Gilbert, Victoria Embankment, London.

18 Every man has, some time in his life, an ambition to be a wag.

Samuel Johnson (1709–84) British lexicographer. *Diary and Letters* (Mme D'Arblay), Vol. III, Ch. 46

19 The essence of any blue material is timing. If you sit on it, it becomes vulgar.

Danny La Rue (Daniel Patrick Carroll; 1928–) British entertainer. Attrib.

20 The coarse joke proclaims that we have here an animal which finds its own animality either objectionable or funny.

C. S. Lewis (1898–1963) British academic and writer. *Miracles*

21 Impropriety is the soul of wit.

W. Somerset Maugham (1874–1965) British novelist. *The Moon and Sixpence*, Ch. 4

22 It is not for nothing that, in the English language alone, to accuse someone of trying to be funny is highly abusive.

Malcolm Muggeridge (1903–90) British writer. *Tread Softly For You Tread on My Jokes*

23 Attic wit.

Pliny the Elder (Gaius Plinius Secundus; 23–79 AD) Roman scholar. *Natural History*, II

24 True wit is nature to advantage dress'd;
What oft was thought, but ne'er so well express'd.

Alexander Pope (1688–1744) British poet. *An Essay on Criticism*

25 Comedy, we may say, is society protecting itself – with a smile.

J. B. Priestley (1894–1984) British novelist. *George Meredith*

26 A comedian can only last till he either takes himself serious or his audience takes him serious.

Will Rogers (1879–1935) US actor and humorist. Newspaper article, 1931

27 Everything is funny, as long as it's happening to somebody else.

Will Rogers *The Illiterate Digest*

28 I am not only witty in myself, but the cause that wit is in other men. I do here walk before thee like a sow that hath overwhelm'd all her litter but one.

William Shakespeare (1564–1616) English dramatist. *Henry IV, Part Two*, I:2

29 A jest's prosperity lies in the ear
Of him that hears it, never in the tongue
Of him that makes it.

William Shakespeare *Love's Labour's Lost*, V:2

30 You just can't have a leisurely farce, and the jokes have to come out of the *plot*, not the people.

Neil Simon (1927–) US dramatist. *The Times*, 4 Aug 1990

31 The truth is that American audiences are still not altogether happy with Woody Allen or me when we stop doing the jokes.

Neil Simon *The Times*, 4 Aug 1990

32 People no longer need the jokes explained; everyone gets irony nowadays.

John Waters (c. 1946–) US film director. *The Times*, 11 June 1994

33 Why have they been telling us women lately that we have no sense of humor – when we are always laughing?...And when we're not laughing, we're smiling.

Naomi Weisstein (1939–) US experimental psychologist, educator, feminist, writer, pianist, and comedienne. *All She Needs*, Introduction (Ellen Levine)

34 It's hard to be funny when you have to be clean.

Mae West (1892–1980) US actress. *The Wit and Wisdom of Mae West* (ed. J. Weintraub)

35 My comedy is like emotional hang-gliding.

Robin Williams (1952–) US actor. *Playboy*, Oct 1982

Some examples

36 There's a wonderful family called Stein,
There's Gert and there's Epp and there's Ein;
Gert's poems are bunk,
Epp's statues are junk,
And no one can understand Ein.

Anonymous

37 Little Willy from his mirror
Licked the mercury right off,
Thinking in his childish error,
It would cure the whooping cough.
At the funeral his mother
Smartly said to Mrs Brown:
''Twas a chilly day for Willie
When the mercury went down'.

Anonymous 'Willie's Epitaph'

38 There was an old man from Darjeeling,
Who boarded a bus bound for Ealing,
He saw on the door:
'Please don't spit on the floor',
So he stood up and spat on the ceiling.

Anonymous

39 I do most of my work sitting down; that's where I shine.

Robert Benchley (1889–1945) US humorist. Attrib.

40 No visit to Dove Cottage, Grasmere, is complete without examining the outhouse where Hazlitt's father, a Unitarian minister of strong liberal views, attempted to put his hand up Dorothy Wordsworth's skirt.

Alan Coren (1938–) British humorist and writer. Dove Cottage, Grasmere was the home of William Wordsworth and his sister Dorothy. *All Except the Bastard*, 'Bohemia'

41 Dear 338171 (May I call you 338?).

Noël Coward (1899–1973) British dramatist. Starting a letter to T. E. Lawrence (Lawrence of Arabia), who had retired from public life to become Aircraftman Shaw, 338171. *Letters to T. E. Lawrence*

42 Miss Bolo rose from the table considerably agitated, and went straight home, in a flood of tears and a Sedan chair.

Charles Dickens (1812–70) British novelist. *Pickwick Papers*, Ch. 35

43 It...was full of dry rot. An unkind visitor said the only reason Menabilly still stood was that the woodworm obligingly held hands.

Daphne Du Maurier (1907–89) British novelist. Interview – referring to her own house in Cornwall upon which Manderley in *Rebecca* was based

44 Wembley, adj. Suffering from a vague *malaise*. 'I feel a bit w. this morning.'

Paul Jennings (1918–89) British humorous writer. *The Jenguin Pennings*, 'Ware, Wye, Watford'

45 The desire of the moth for the star.

James Joyce (1882–1941) Irish novelist. Commenting on the interruption of a music recital when a moth flew into the singer's mouth. *James Joyce* (R. Ellmann)

46 'When I makes tea I makes tea,' as old mother Grogan said. 'And when I makes water I makes water'.

James Joyce *Ulysses*

47 The landlady of a boarding-house is a parallelogram – that is, an oblong angular figure, which cannot be described, but which is equal to anything.

Stephen Leacock (1869–1944) British-born Canadian economist and humorist. *Literary Lapses*, 'Boarding-House Geometry'

48 'Maureen,' they said, 'you are no Joan Bakewell, but you're fairly tart.'

Maureen Lipman (1946–) British actress. BBC radio programme, *The Lipman Test*, June 1994

49 One morning I shot an elephant in my pajamas. How he got into my pajamas I'll never know.

Groucho Marx (Julius Marx; 1895–1977) US comedian. *Animal Crackers*

50 I could dance with you till the cows come home. Better still, I'll dance with the cows and *you* come home.

Groucho Marx *Duck Soup*

51 Go – and never darken my towels again.

Groucho Marx *Duck Soup*

52 I don't have a photograph, but you can have my footprints. They are upstairs in my socks.

Groucho Marx *A Night At the Opera*

53 The strains of Verdi will come back to you tonight, and Mrs Claypool's cheque will come back to you in the morning.

Groucho Marx *A Night at the Opera*

54 Please accept my resignation. I don't want to belong to any club that will accept me as a member.

Groucho Marx Resigning from the Friar's Club in Hollywood. Attrib.

55 Dr Strabismus (Whom God Preserve) of Utrecht is carrying out research work with a view to crossing salmon with mosquitoes. He says it will mean a bite every time for fishermen.

J. B. Morton (1893–1979) British journalist. *By the Way*, 'January Tail-piece'

56 Oh, don't worry about Alan...Alan will always land on somebody's feet.

Dorothy Parker (1893–1967) US writer. Said of her husband on the day their divorce became final. *You Might As Well Live* (J. Keats), Pt. IV, Ch. 1

57 He bit his lip in a manner which immediately awakened my maternal sympathy, and I helped him bite it.

S. J. Perelman (1904–79) US humorous writer. *Crazy Like a Fox*, 'The Love Decoy'

58 I have Bright's disease and he has mine.

S. J. Perelman (Bennet Cerf)

59 A case of the tail dogging the wag.

S. J. Perelman Having escaped with some difficulty from the persistent attentions of some prostitutes in the street. *Another Almanac of Words at Play* (W. Epsy)

60 The cook was a good cook, as cooks go; and as cooks go she went.

Saki (Hector Hugh Munro; 1870–1916) British writer. *Reginald on Besetting Sins*

61 Napoleon's armies used to march on their stomachs, shouting: 'Vive l'intérieur!'

W. C. Sellar (1898–1951) British humorous writer. *1066 And All That*

62 You wait here and I'll bring the etchings down.

James Thurber (1894–1961) US humorist. Cartoon caption

63 Wall is the name – Max Wall. My father was the Great Wall of China. He was a brick.

Max Wall (1908–90) British comedian. Opening line of one of his acts

64 Satire is alive and well and living in the White House.

Robin Williams (1952–) US actor. *Rolling Stone*, 25 Feb 1985

65 He spoke with a certain what-is-it in his voice, and I could see that, if not actually disgruntled, he was far from being gruntled.

P. G. Wodehouse (1881–1975) British humorous novelist. *The Code of the Woosters*

HUNGER

See also desire, food, thirst

1 Hunger is the best sauce.

Proverb

2 Poverty is an anomaly to rich people. It is very difficult to make out why people who want dinner do not ring the bell.

Walter Bagehot (1826–77) British economist and journalist. *Literary Studies*, II

3 When he told men to love their neighbour, their bellies were full. Nowadays things are different.

Bertolt Brecht (1898–1956) German dramatist. *Mother Courage*, II

4 The best sauce in the world is hunger.

Miguel de Cervantes (1547–1616) Spanish novelist. *Don Quixote*, Pt. II, Ch. 5

5 If only it were as easy to banish hunger by rubbing the belly as it is to masturbate.

Diogenes (412–322 BC) Greek philosopher. *Lives and Opinions of Eminent Philosophers* (Diogenes Laertius)

6 They that die by famine die by inches.

Matthew Henry (1662–1714) English nonconformist minister. *Exposition of the Old and New Testaments*

7 The war against hunger is truly mankind's war of liberation.

John Fitzgerald Kennedy (1917–63) US statesman. Speech, World Food Congress, 4 June 1963

8 A hungry stomach has no ears.

Jean de La Fontaine (1621–95) French poet. *Fables*, IX, 'Le Milan et le Rossignol'

9 I came home…hungry as a hunter.

Charles Lamb (1775–1834) British essayist. Letter to Coleridge, Apr 1800

10 Let them eat cake.

Marie-Antoinette (1755–93) Queen of France. On being told that the people had no bread to eat; in fact she was repeating a much older saying. Attrib.

HUNTING

See also sport

1 Happy the hare at morning, for she cannot read
The Hunter's waking thoughts.

W. H. Auden (1907–73) British poet. *The Dog Beneath the Skin* (with Christopher Isherwood)

2 Spirits of well-shot woodcock, partridge, snipe
Flutter and bear him up the Norfolk sky.

John Betjeman (1906–84) British poet. *Death of King George V*

3 Detested sport,
That owes its pleasures to another's pain.

William Cowper (1731–1800) British poet. *The Task*

4 Wild animals never kill for sport. Man is the only one to whom the torture and death of his fellow-creatures is amusing in itself.

J. A. Froude (1818–94) British historian. *Oceana*, Ch. 5

5 D'ye ken John Peel with his coat so gay?
D'ye ken John Peel at the break of the day?
D'ye ken John Peel when he's far far away
With his hounds and his horn in the morning?

'Twas the sound of his horn called me from my bed,
And the cry of his hounds has me oft-times led;
For Peel's view-hollo would waken the dead,
Or a fox from his lair in the morning.

John Woodcock Graves (1795–1886) British poet, huntsman, and songwriter. *John Peel*

6 It is very strange, and very melancholy, that the paucity of human pleasures should persuade us ever to call hunting one of them.

Samuel Johnson (1709–84) British lexicographer. *Johnsonian Miscellanies* (ed. G. B. Hill), Vol. I

7 Most of their discourse was about hunting, in a dialect I understand very little.

Samuel Pepys (1633–1703) English diarist. *Diary*, 22 Nov 1663

8 Hunting people tend to be church-goers on a higher level than ordinary folk. One has a religious experience in the field.

Christopher Seal British churchman. *The Times*, 30 Dec 1993

9 It isn't mere convention. Everyone can see that the people who hunt are the right people and the people who don't are the wrong ones.

George Bernard Shaw (1856–1950) Irish dramatist and critic. *Heartbreak House*

10 But He was never, well,
What I call
A Sportsman;
For forty days
He went out into the desert
– And never shot anything.

Osbert Sitwell (1892–1969) British writer. *Old Fashioned Sportsmen*

11 The English country gentleman galloping after a fox – the unspeakable in full pursuit of the uneatable.

Oscar Wilde (1854–1900) Irish-born British dramatist. *A Woman of No Importance*, I

HURT

See also cruelty, insensitivity, nastiness, suffering

1 Those have most power to hurt us that we love.

Francis Beaumont (1584–1616) English dramatist. *The Maid's Tragedy*, V:6

2 Mrs Montagu has dropt me. Now, Sir, there are people whom one should like very well to drop, but would not wish to be dropped by.

Samuel Johnson (1709–84) British lexicographer. *Life of Johnson* (J. Boswell), Vol. IV

3 It takes your enemy and your friend, working together, to hurt you to the heart; the one to slander you and the other to get the news to you.

Mark Twain (Samuel Langhorne Clemens; 1835–1910) US writer. *Following the Equator*

4 We flatter those we scarcely know,
We please the fleeting guest,
And deal full many a thoughtless blow
To those who love us best.

Ella Wheeler Wilcox (1850–1919) US poet. *Life's Scars*

HUXLEY, ALDOUS

(1894–1963) British novelist and essayist. His novels include *Antic Hay* (1923), *Point Counter Point* (1928), *Brave New World* (1932), and *Eyeless in Gaza* (1936). His non-fiction includes *The Doors of Perception* (1954).

Quotations about Huxley

1 Mr. Huxley is perhaps one of those people who have to perpetrate thirty bad novels before producing a good one.

T. S. Eliot (1888–1965) US-born British poet and dramatist. Attrib.

2 Like a piece of litmus paper he has always been quick to take the colour of his times.
The Observer, Profile, 27 Feb 1949

Quotations by Huxley

3 Thanks to words, we have been able to rise above the brutes; and thanks to words, we have often sunk to the level of the demons.
Adonis and the Alphabet

4 Since Mozart's day composers have learned the art of making music throatily and palpitatingly sexual.
Along the Road, 'Popular music'

5 Christlike in my behaviour,
Like every good believer,
I imitate the Saviour,
And cultivate a beaver.
Antic Hay, Ch. 4

6 He was only the Mild and Melancholy one foolishly disguised as a complete Man.
Antic Hay, Ch. 9

7 There are few who would not rather be taken in adultery than in provincialism.
Antic Hay, Ch. 10

8 Mr Mercaptan went on to preach a brilliant sermon on that melancholy sexual perversion known as continence.
Antic Hay, Ch. 18

9 Lady Capricorn, he understood, was still keeping open bed.
Antic Hay, Ch. 21

10 Official dignity tends to increase in inverse ratio to the importance of the country in which the office is held.
Beyond the Mexique Bay

11 The time of our Ford.
Brave New World, Ch. 3

12 The proper study of mankind is books.
Chrome Yellow

13 We participate in a tragedy; at a comedy we only look.
The Devils of Loudon, Ch. 11

14 Consistency is contrary to nature, contrary to life. The only completely consistent people are the dead.
Do What you Will

15 Thought must be divided against itself before it can come to any knowledge of itself.
Do What You Will

16 People will insist…on treating the *mons Veneris* as though it were Mount Everest.
Eyeless in Gaza, Ch. 30

17 Death…It's the only thing we haven't succeeded in completely vulgarizing.
Eyeless in Gaza, Ch. 31

18 A million million spermatozoa,
All of them alive:
Out of their cataclysm but one poor Noah
Dare hope to survive.
Fifth Philosopher's Song

19 Christianity accepted as given a metaphysical system derived from several already existing and mutually incompatible systems.
Grey Eminence, Ch. 3

20 The quality of moral behaviour varies in inverse ratio to the number of human beings involved.
Grey Eminence, Ch. 10

21 'Bed,' as the Italian proverb succinctly puts it, 'is the poor man's opera.'
Heaven and Hell

22 I can sympathize with people's pains, but not with their pleasures. There is something curiously boring about somebody else's happiness.
Limbo, 'Cynthia'

23 She was a machine-gun riddling her hostess with sympathy.
Mortal Coils, 'The Gioconda Smile'

24 Most of one's life…is one prolonged effort to prevent oneself thinking.
Mortal Coils, 'Green Tunnels'

25 She was one of those indispensables of whom one makes the discovery, when they are gone, that one can get on quite as well without them.
Mortal Coils, 'Nuns at Luncheon'

26 Happiness is like coke – something you get as a by-product in the process of making something else.
Point Counter Point

27 There is no substitute for talent. Industry and all the virtues are of no avail.
Point Counter Point

28 Silence is as full of potential wisdom and wit as the unhewn marble of great sculpture.
Point Counter Point

29 A bad book is as much a labour to write as a good one; it comes as sincerely from the author's soul.
Point Counter Point

30 That all men are equal is a proposition to which, at ordinary times, no sane individual has ever given his assent.
Proper Studies

31 Those who believe that they are exclusively in the right are generally those who achieve something.
Proper Studies

32 Facts do not cease to exist because they are ignored.
Proper Studies

33 Most human beings have an almost infinite capacity for taking things for granted.
Themes and Variations

34 I'm afraid of losing my obscurity. Genuineness only thrives in the dark. Like celery.
Those Barren Leaves, Pt. I, Ch. 1

35 'It's like the question of the authorship of the *Iliad*,' said Mr Cardan. 'The author of that poem is either Homer or, if not Homer, somebody else of the same name.'
Those Barren Leaves, Pt. V, Ch. 4

36 How appallingly thorough these Germans always managed to be, how emphatic! In sex no less than in war – in scholarship, in science. Diving deeper than anyone else and coming up muddier.

37 Knowledge is proportionate to being.... You know in virtue of what you are.
Time Must Have a Stop, Ch. 26

HUXLEY, T. H.

(1825–95) British biologist. A supporter of Darwin's theory of evolution, his books include *Science and Culture* (1881) and *Evolution and Ethics* (1893).

1 The great tragedy of Science – the slaying of a beautiful hypothesis by an ugly fact.
Collected Essays, 'Biogenesis and Abiogenesis'

2 Science is nothing but trained and organized common sense, differing from the latter only as a veteran may differ from a raw recruit: and its methods differ from those of common sense only as far as the guardsman's cut and thrust differ from the manner in which a savage wields his club.
Collected Essays, 'The Method of Zadig'

3 It is the customary fate of new truths to begin as heresies and to end as superstitions.
Science and Culture and Other Essays, 'The Coming of Age of the Origin of Species'

4 One of the unpardonable sins, in the eyes of most people, is for a man to go about unlabelled. The world regards such a person as the police do an unmuzzled dog, not under proper control.
Evolution and Ethics

5 I doubt if the philosopher lives, or ever has lived, who could know himself to be heartily despised by a street boy without some irritation.
Evolution and Ethics

6 The chess-board is the world; the pieces are the phenomena of the universe; the rules of the game are what we call the laws of Nature. The player on the other side is hidden from us. We know that his play is always fair, just, and patient. But also we know, to our cost, that he never overlooks a mistake, or makes the smallest allowance for ignorance.
Lay Sermons, 'A Liberal Education'

7 Some experience of popular lecturing had convinced me that the necessity of making things plain to uninstructed people was one of the very best means of clearing up the obscure corners in one's own mind.
Man's Place in Nature, Preface

8 If a little knowledge is dangerous, where is the man who has so much as to be out of danger?
On Elementary Instruction in Physiology

9 Logical consequences are the scarecrows of fools and the beacons of wise men.
Science and Culture, 'On the Hypothesis that Animals are Automata'

10 I am too much of a sceptic to deny the possibility of anything.
Letter to Herbert Spencer, 22 Mar 1886

11 I asserted – and I repeat – that a man has no reason to be ashamed of having an ape for his grandfather. If there were an ancestor whom I should feel shame in recalling it would rather be a *man* – a man of restless and versatile intellect – who, not content with an equivocal success in his own sphere of activity, plunges into scientific questions with which he has no real acquaintance, only to obscure them by an aimless rhetoric, and distract the attention of his hearers from the real point at issue by eloquent digressions and skilled appeals to religious prejudice.
Replying to Bishop WILBERFORCE in the debate on Darwin's theory of evolution at the meeting of the British Association at Oxford. No transcript was taken at the time; the version above is commonly quoted. After hearing Wilberforce's speech, and before rising himself, Huxley is said to have remarked, 'The Lord has delivered him into my hands!' Speech, 30 June 1860

HYPATIA

(c. 370–415) Egyptian Neoplatonist philosopher and mathematician who became head of the Neoplatonist school of philosophy at Alexandria.

Quotations about Hypatia

1 Donning the philosopher's cloak, and making her way through the midst of the city, she explained publicly the writings of Plato, or Aristotle, or any other philosopher, to all who wished to hear.
Hesychius *Critic*, 1903 (Joseph McCabe)

Quotations by Hypatia

2 Men will fight for a superstition quite as quickly as for a living truth – often more so, since a superstition is so intangible you cannot get at it to refute it, but truth is a point of view, and so is changeable.
Little Journeys to the Homes of Great Teachers (Elbert Hubbard), 'Hypatia'

3 He who influences the thought of his times, influences all the times that follow. He has made his impress on eternity.
Little Journeys to the Homes of Great Teachers (Elbert Hubbard), 'Hypatia'

4 To rule by fettering the mind through fear of punishment in another world, is just as base as to use force.
Little Journeys to the Homes of Great Teachers (Elbert Hubbard), 'Hypatia'

HYPOCHONDRIA

1 He that is uneasy at every little pain is never without some ache.
Proverb

2 People who are always taking care of their health are like misers, who are hoarding a treasure which they have never spirit enough to enjoy.

Laurence Sterne (1713–68) Irish-born British writer. Attrib.

3 The imaginary complaints of indestructible old ladies.

Elwyn Brooks White (1899–1985) US journalist and humorist. *Harper's Magazine*, Nov 1941

HYPOCRISY

See also example, insincerity

1 All are not saints that go to church.

Proverb

2 It is the wisdom of the crocodiles, that shed tears when they would devour.

Francis Bacon (1561–1626) English philosopher. *Essays*, 'Of Wisdom for a Man's Self'

3 But when he saw many of the Pharisees and Sadducees come to his baptism, he said unto them, O generation of vipers, who hath warned you to flee from the wrath to come?

Bible: Matthew 3:7

4 Woe unto you, scribes and Pharisees, hypocrites! for ye are like unto whited sepulchres, which indeed appear beautiful outward, but are within full of dead men's bones, and of all uncleanness.

Bible: Matthew 23:27

5 Prisons are built with stones of Law, brothels with bricks of Religion.

William Blake (1757–1827) British poet. *The Marriage of Heaven and Hell*, 'Proverbs of Hell'

6 God be thanked, the meanest of his creatures
Boasts two soul-sides, one to face the world with,
One to show a woman when he loves her!

Robert Browning (1812–89) British poet. *One Word More*, XVII

7 Man is the only animal that can remain on friendly terms with the victims he intends to eat until he eats them.

Samuel Butler (1835–1902) British writer. *Notebooks*

8 Virtue consisted in avoiding scandal and venereal disease.

Robert Cecil (1913–) British writer. *Life in Edwardian England*

9 The smyler with the knyf under the cloke.

Geoffrey Chaucer (c. 1342–1400) English poet. *The Canterbury Tales*, 'The Knight's Tale'

10 We ought to see far enough into a hypocrite to see even his sincerity.

G. K. Chesterton (1874–1936) British writer. *Heretics*, Ch. 5

11 The book written against fame and learning has the author's name on the title-page.

Ralph Waldo Emerson (1803–82) US poet and essayist. *Journal*

12 Man is the only animal that learns by being hypocritical. He pretends to be polite and then, eventually, he *becomes* polite.

Jean Kerr (1923–) US dramatist. *Finishing Touches*

13 Hypocrisy is the most difficult and nerve-racking vice that any man can pursue; it needs an unceasing vigilance and a rare detachment of spirit. It cannot, like adultery or gluttony, be practised at spare moments; it is a whole-time job.

W. Somerset Maugham (1874–1965) British novelist. *Cakes and Ale*, Ch. 1

14 For neither man nor angel can discern
Hypocrisy, the only evil that walks
Invisible, except to God alone.

John Milton (1608–74) English poet. *Paradise Lost*, Bk. III

15 Ancient sculpture is the true school of modesty. But where the Greeks had modesty, we have cant; where they had poetry, we have cant; where they had patriotism, we have cant; where they had anything that exalts, delights, or adorns humanity, we have nothing but cant, cant, cant.

Thomas Love Peacock (1785–1866) British novelist. *Crotchet Castle*, Ch. 7

16 Hypocrisy is the homage paid by vice to virtue.

Duc de la Rochefoucauld (1613–80) French writer. *Maximes*, 218

17 O villain, villain, smiling, damned villain!
My tables, – meet it is I set it down,
That one may smile, and smile, and be a villain;
At least I'm sure it may be so in Denmark.

William Shakespeare (1564–1616) English dramatist. *Hamlet*, I:5

18 To put an antic disposition on.

William Shakespeare *Hamlet*, I:5

19 I speak of peace, while covert enmity
Under the smile of safety wounds the world.

William Shakespeare *Henry IV, Part Two*, Induction, 9

20 Well, whiles I am a beggar, I will rail
And say there is no sin but to be rich;
And being rich, my virtue then shall be
To say there is no vice but beggary.

William Shakespeare *King John*, II:1

21 Come not, when I am dead,
To drop thy foolish tears upon my grave,
To trample round my fallen head,
And vex the unhappy dust thou wouldst not save.

Alfred, Lord Tennyson (1809–92) British poet. *Come Not, When I Am Dead*

22 I sit on a man's back, choking him and making him carry me, and yet assure myself and others that I am very sorry for him and wish to ease his lot by all possible means – except by getting off his back.

Leo Tolstoy (1828–1910) Russian writer. *What Then Must We Do?*, Ch. 16

23 I hope you have not been leading a double life, pretending to be wicked and being really good all the time. That would be hypocrisy.

Oscar Wilde (1854–1900) Irish-born British dramatist. *The Importance of Being Earnest*, II

24 A Christian is a man who feels
Repentance on a Sunday
For what he did on Saturday
And is going to do on Monday.

Thomas Russell Ybarra (b. 1880) Venezuelan-born US writer. *The Christian*

I

IBSEN, HENRIK

(1828–1906) Norwegian dramatist and poet. His initial successes came with *Brand* (1865) and *Peer Gynt* (1867). Subsequent works, such as *A Doll's House* (1879), *Ghosts* (1881), *An Enemy of the People* (1882), and *Hedda Gabler* (1890) established him as Europe's leading 19th-century playwright.

1 Fools are in a terrible, overwhelming majority, all the wide world over.

An Enemy of the People, IV

2 The majority has the might – more's the pity – but it hasn't right...The minority is always right.

An Enemy of the People, IV

3 The worst enemy of truth and freedom in our society is the compact majority. Yes, the damned, compact, liberal majority.

An Enemy of the People, IV

4 A man should never put on his best trousers when he goes out to battle for freedom and truth.

An Enemy of the People, V

5 Ten o'clock...and back he'll come. I can just see him.
With vine leaves in his hair. Flushed and confident.

Hedda Gabler, II

6 Youth will come here and beat on my door, and force its way in.

The Master Builder, I

7 Castles in the air – they're so easy to take refuge in. So easy to build, too.

The Master Builder, III

8 What's a man's first duty? The answer's brief: To be himself.

Peer Gynt, IV:1

9 Take the life-lie away from the average man and straight away you take away his happiness.

The Wild Duck, V

10 On the contrary!

Ibsen's last words; his nurse had just remarked that he was feeling a little better. *True Remarkable Occurrences* (J. Train)

IDEALISM

1 Of myself I must say this, I never was any greedy, scraping grasper, nor a strait fast-holding prince, nor yet a waster; my heart was never set on wordly goods, but only for my subjects' good.

Elizabeth I Speech to a deputation from the House of Commons (the Golden Speech), 30 Nov 1601

2 You can't be a true idealist without being a true realist.

Jacques Delors (1925–) French politician and European statesman. Speech, European Union Corfu Summit, 21 June 1994

3 If a man hasn't discovered something that he would die for, he isn't fit to live.

Martin Luther King (1929–68) US Black civil-rights leader. Speech, Detroit, 23 June 1963

4 If you can talk with crowds and keep your virtue,
Or walk with Kings – nor lose the common touch,
If neither foes nor loving friends can hurt you,
If all men count with you, but none too much;
If you can fill the unforgiving minute
With sixty seconds' worth of distance run,
Yours is the Earth and everything that's in it,
And – which is more – you'll be a Man my son!

Rudyard Kipling (1865–1936) Indian-born British writer. *If*

5 Ideal mankind would abolish death, multiply itself million upon million, rear up city upon city, save every parasite alive, until the accumulation of mere existence is swollen to a horror.

D. H. Lawrence (1885–1930) British novelist. *St Mawr*

6 An idealist is one who, on noticing that a rose smells better than a cabbage, concludes that it will also make better soup.

H. L. Mencken (1880–1956) US journalist. *Sententiae*

7 Do not despair
For Johnny head-in-air;
He sleeps as sound
As Johnny underground.

John Sleigh Pudney (1909–77) British poet and writer. *For Johnny*

8 A radical is a man with both feet firmly planted in the air.

Franklin D. Roosevelt (1882–1945) US Democratic president. Broadcast, 26 Oct 1939

9 Those who have never dwelt in tents have no idea either of the charm or of the discomfort of a nomadic existence. The charm is purely romantic, and consequently very soon proves to be fallacious.

Vita Sackville-West (Victoria Sackville-West; 1892–1962) British poet and novelist. *Twelve Days*, Ch. 6

10 If a woman like Eva Peron with no ideals can get that far, think how far I can go with all the ideals that I have.

Margaret Thatcher (1925–) British politician. *The Sunday Times*, 1980

11 A liberal dreams of a better world, knowing the dream must ultimately be unattainable. Communism believed it was attainable and felt any means to reach it were justified. That was the corruption.

Mario Vargas Llosa (1936–) Peruvian novelist. *The Observer*, 'Sayings of the Week' 19 June 1994

IDEAS

See also opinions

1 Paradoxes are useful to attract attention to ideas.

Mandell Creighton (1843–1901) British churchman. *Life and Letters*

2 What was once thought can never be unthought.

Friedrich Dürrenmatt (1921–90) Swiss writer. *The Physicists*

3 Man is ready to die for an idea, provided that idea is not quite clear to him.

Paul Eldridge *Horns of Glass*

4 Many ideas grow better when transplanted into another mind than in the one where they sprang up.

Oliver Wendell Holmes Jnr (1841–1935) US jurist.

5 A stand can be made against invasion by an army; no stand can be made against invasion by an idea.

Victor Hugo (1802–85) French writer. *Histoire d'un Crime*, 'La Chute'

6 You cannot endow even the best machine with initiative. The jolliest steam-roller will not plant flowers.

Walter Lippmann (1889–1974) US editor and author. *A Preface to Politics*

7 Society goes on and on and on. It is the same with ideas.

Ramsey MacDonald (1866–1937) British statesman and prime minister. Speech, 1935

8 An idea isn't responsible for the people who believe in it.

Don Marquis (1878–1937) US journalist. *New York Sun*

9 A society made up of individuals who were all capable of original thought would probably be unendurable. The pressure of ideas would simply drive it frantic.

H. L. Mencken (1880–1956) US journalist. *Notebooks*, 'Minority Report'

IDLENESS

See also bed, laziness, leisure, unemployment

1 The devil finds work for idle hands to do.

Proverb

2 The dreadful burden of having nothing to do.

Nicolas Boileau (1636–1711) French writer. *Épitres*, XI

3 Idleness is only the refuge of weak minds.

Earl of Chesterfield (1694–1773) English statesman. Letter to his son, 20 July 1749

4 I don't think necessity is the mother of invention – invention, in my opinion, arises directly from idleness, possibly also from laziness. To save oneself trouble.

Agatha Christie (1891–1976) British detective-story writer. *An Autobiography*

5 What is this life if, full of care,
We have no time to stand and stare?

W. H. Davies (1871–1940) British poet. *Leisure*

6 ...many thousands of idle persons are within this realm which, being no way to be set on work, be either mutinous and seek alteration in the state or at least very burdensome to the common wealth and often fall to pilfering and thieving and other lewdness, whereby all the prisons of the land are daily pestered and stuffed full of them.

Richard Hakluyt (c. 1552–1616) English geographer. *Particular Discourse of Western Planting*

7 It is impossible to enjoy idling thoroughly unless one has plenty of work to do.

Jerome K. Jerome (1859–1927) British humorist. *Idle Thoughts of an Idle Fellow*

8 I like work; it fascinates me. I can sit and look at it for hours. I love to keep it by me; the idea of getting rid of it nearly breaks my heart.

Jerome K. Jerome *Three Men in a Boat*, Ch. 15

9 We would all be idle if we could.

Samuel Johnson (1709–84) British lexicographer. *Life of Johnson* (J. Boswell), Vol. III

10 The affluent society has made everyone dislike work, and come to think of idleness as the happiest life.

Geoffrey Keynes (1887–) British surgeon and literary scholar. *The Observer*, 25 Oct 1981

11 Young people ought not to be idle. It is very bad for them.

Margaret Thatcher (1925–) British politician and prime minister. *The Times*, 1984

12 I am happiest when I am idle. I could live for months without performing any kind of labour, and at the expiration of that time I should feel fresh and vigorous enough to go right on in the same way for numerous more months.

Artemus Ward (Charles Farrar Browne; 1834–67) US humorous writer. *Pyrotechny*

13 For Satan finds some mischief still
For idle hands to do.

Isaac Watts (1674–1748) English theologian and hymn writer. *Divine Songs for Children*, 'Against Idleness and Mischief'

IGNORANCE

See also foolishness, innocence, innocence of childhood, stupidity

1 He that knows little, often repeats it.

Proverb

2 He that knows nothing, doubts nothing.

Proverb

3 What you don't know can't hurt you.

Proverb

4 Happy the hare at morning, for she cannot read
The Hunter's waking thoughts.

W. H. Auden (1907–73) British poet. *The Dog Beneath the Skin* (with Christopher Isherwood)

5 IGNORAMUS, n. A person unacquainted with certain kinds of knowledge familiar to yourself, and having certain other kinds that you know nothing about.

Ambrose Bierce *The Devil's Dictionary*

6 I don't even know what street Canada is on.

Al Capone (1899–1947) US gangster. Attrib.

7 It is the tragedy of the world that no one knows what he doesn't know – and the less a man knows, the more sure he is that he knows everything.

Joyce Cary (1888–1957) British novelist. *Art and Reality*

8 Here's the one who likes all our pretty songs
And he likes to sing along

And he likes to shoot his gun
But he don't know what it means.

Kurt Cobain (1967–94) US rock musician. *Nevermind*

9 She is an excellent creature, but she never can remember which came first, the Greeks or the Romans.

Benjamin Disraeli (1804–81) British statesman. Referring to his wife. Attrib.

10 To each his suff'rings, all are men,
Condemn'd alike to groan;
The tender for another's pain,
Th' unfeeling for his own.
Yet ah! why should they know their fate?
Since sorrow never comes too late,
And happiness too swiftly flies.
Thought would destroy their paradise.
No more; where ignorance is bliss,
'Tis folly to be wise.

Thomas Gray (1716–71) British poet. *Ode on a Distant Prospect of Eton College*

11 Alas, regardless of their doom,
The little victims play!

Thomas Gray *Ode on a Distant Prospect of Eton College*

12 I wish you would read a little poetry sometimes. Your ignorance cramps my conversation.

Anthony Hope (Sir Anthony Hope Hawkins; 1863–1933) British novelist. *The Dolly Dialogues*

13 Ignorance is preferable to error; and he is less remote from the truth who believes nothing, than he who believes what is wrong.

Thomas Jefferson (1743–1826) US statesman. *Notes on the State of Virginia*

14 Ignorance, madam, pure ignorance.

Samuel Johnson (1709–84) British lexicographer. His reply on being questioned, by a lady reader of his *Dictionary*, why he had incorrectly defined 'pastern' as the 'knee' of a horse. *Life of Johnson* (J. Boswell), Vol. I

15 Nothing in the world is more dangerous than sincere ignorance and conscientious stupidity.

Martin Luther King (1929–68) US Black civil-rights leader. *Strength To Love*

16 The ignorant man always adores what he cannot understand.

Cesare Lombroso (1853–1909) Italian criminologist. *The Man of Genius*, Pt. III, Ch. 3

17 I count religion but a childish toy,
And hold there is no sin but ignorance.

Christopher Marlowe (1564–93) English dramatist. *The Jew of Malta*, Prologue

18 His ignorance was an Empire State Building of ignorance. You had to admire it for its size.

Dorothy Parker (1893–1967) US writer. Referring to Harold Ross. Attrib.

19 From ignorance our comfort flows,
The only wretched are the wise.

Matthew Prior (1664–1721) British poet. *To the Hon. Charles Montague*

20 He hath never fed of the dainties that are bred in a book; he hath not eat paper, as it were; he hath not drunk ink; his intellect is not replenished.

William Shakespeare (1564–1616) English dramatist. *Love's Labour's Lost*, IV:2

21 He that is robb'd, not wanting what is stol'n,
Let him not know't, and he's not robb'd at all.

William Shakespeare *Othello*, III:3

22 What you don't know would make a great book.

Sydney Smith (1771–1845) British clergyman and essayist. *Memoir* (Lady Holland)

23 Somebody else's ignorance is bliss.

Jack Vance (1916–) US writer. *Star King*

24 Ignorance is like a delicate exotic fruit; touch it, and the bloom is gone.

Oscar Wilde (1854–1900) Irish-born British dramatist. *The Importance of Being Earnest*, I

ILLEGITIMACY

1 I was born in 1896, and my parents were married in 1919.

J. R. Ackerley (1896–1967) British writer. The opening words of the book. *My Father and Myself* (1968)

2 The American woman, when she is an unmarried mother, simply disappears for a while from her community and then comes back, childless, her secret hidden for life.

Pearl S. Buck (1892–1973) US writer. *Children for Adoption*, Ch. 1

3 The child is different not because he is illegitimate, but because he is fatherless and he is going to miss a father in the same way that any child who loses his father early, through death or separation, misses him.

Lena Jeger British politician, Member of Parliament, civil rights activist, and writer. *Illegitimate Children and Their Parents*, Foreword

4 There are no illegitimate children – only illegitimate parents.

Léon R. Yankwich US lawyer. Quoting columnist O. O. McIntyre. Decision, State District Court, Southern District of California, June 1928

ILLNESS

See also doctors, health, medicine, remedies

1 Feed a cold and starve a fever.

Commonly interpreted as meaning that one should eat with a cold but not with a fever. An alternative explanation is that if one 'feeds' a cold, by not taking care of it, one will end up having to deal with a fever. Proverb

2 Sickness is felt, but health not at all.

Proverb

3 Sickness soaks the purse.

Proverb

4 Sickness tells us what we are.

Proverb

5 If you are too smart to pay the doctor, you had better be too smart to get ill.

African (Transvaal) proverb

6 Coughs and sneezes spread diseases.

Anonymous Wartime health slogan in the UK, c. 1942 *Dictionary of 20th Century Quotations* (Nigel Rees)

7 For want of timely care
Millions have died of medicable wounds.

John Armstrong (1710–79) English physician and poet. *Art of Preserving Health*

8 Nor bring to see me cease to live,
Some doctor full of phrase and fame,
To shake his sapient head, and give
The ill he cannot cure a name.

Matthew Arnold (1822–88) British poet and critic. 'A Wish'

9 Across the wires the electric message came:
'He is no better, he is much the same.'

Alfred Austin (1835–1913) British poet. Generally attrib. to Austin but there is no definite evidence that he wrote it. *On the Illness of the Prince of Wales*

10 Physicians of the utmost fame,
Were called at once; but when they came
They answered, as they took their fees,
'There is no Cure for this Disease.'

Hilaire Belloc (1870–1953) French-born British poet. *Bartlett's Unfamiliar Quotations* (Leonard Louis Levinson)

11 'Ye can call it influenza if ye like,' said Mrs Machin. 'There was no influenza in my young days. We called a cold a cold.'

Arnold Bennett (1867–1931) British novelist. *The Card*, Ch. 8

12 Be not slow to visit the sick: for that shall make thee to be beloved.

Bible: Ecclesiasticus 7:35

13 They that be whole need not a physician, but they that are sick.

Bible: Matthew 9:12

14 INDIGESTION, n. A disease which the patient and his friends frequently mistake for deep religious conviction and concern for the salvation of mankind. As the simple Red Man of the western wild put it, with, it must be confessed, a certain force: 'Plenty well, no pray; big bellyache, heap God.'

Ambrose Bierce (1842–c. 1914) US writer and journalist. *The Devil's Dictionary*

15 A long illness seems to be placed between life and death, in order to make death a comfort both to those who die and to those who remain.

Jean de La Bruyère (1645–96) *Caractères*, Ch. 11

16 I reckon being ill as one of the greatest pleasures of life, provided one is not too ill and is not obliged to work till one is better.

Samuel Butler (1835–1902) British writer. *The Way of All Flesh*, Ch. 80

17 Physicians, when the cause of disease is discovered, consider that the cure is discovered.

Cicero (106 BC–43 BC) Roman orator and statesman. Attrib.

18 I don't have ulcers; I give them.

Harry Cohn (1891–1958) US film producer.

19 My message to the businessmen of this country when they go abroad on business is that there is one thing above all they can take with them to stop them catching Aids, and that is the wife.

Edwina Currie (1946–) British politician. *The Observer*, 'Sayings of the Week', 15 Feb 1987

20 Too late for fruit, too soon for flowers.

Walter De La Mare (1873–1956) British poet. On being asked, as he lay seriously ill, whether he would like some fruit or flowers. Attrib.

21 By focussing their energies on controlling their bodies, they had found a refuge from having to face the more painful issues at the centre of their lives.

Diana, Princess of Wales (1961–) Wife of Prince Charles. On anorexics. *The Times*, 28 Apr 1993

22 To be too conscious is an illness – a real thorough-going illness.

Fyodor Mikhailovich Dostoevsky (1821–81) Russian writer. *Notes from Underground*, 1

23 Disease can carry its ill-effects no farther than mortal mind maps out the way… Disease is an image of thought externalized… We classify disease as error, which nothing but Truth or Mind can heal… Disease is an experience of so-called mortal mind. It is fear made manifest on the body.

Mary Baker Eddy (1821–1910) US religious leader. *Science and Health, with Key to the Scriptures*

24 The multitude of the sick shall not make us deny the existence of health.

Ralph Waldo Emerson (1803–82) US poet and essayist. *The Conduct of Life*, 'Worship'

25 It is dainty to be sick if you have leisure and convenience for it.

Ralph Waldo Emerson *Journals*, Vol. V

26 A weary thing is sickness and its pains!

Euripides (484 BC–406 BC) Greek dramatist. *Hippolytus*, 176

27 Much of the world's work, it has been said, is done by men who do not feel quite well. Marx is a case in point.

John Kenneth Galbraith (1908–) US economist. *The Age of Uncertainty*, Ch. 3

28 Lady Bullock, who had been at death's door for so long now that one might have been pardoned for mistaking her for its knocker.

Leon Garfield (1921–) British writer. *The Prisoners of September*, Ch. 29

29 Every time you sleep with a boy you sleep with all his old girlfriends.

Government-sponsored AIDS advertisement, 1987

30 If you start to think about your physical or moral condition, you usually find that you are sick.

Goethe (1749–1832) German poet and dramatist. *Sprüche in Prosa*, Pt. I, Bk. II

31 Hungry Joe collected lists of fatal diseases and arranged them in alphabetical order so that he could put his finger without delay on any one he wanted to worry about.

Joseph Heller (1923–) US novelist. *Catch-22*, Ch. 17

32 For that old enemy the gout
Had taken him in toe!

Thomas Hood (1799–1845) British poet. *Lieutenant Luff*

33 Indigestion is charged by God with enforcing morality on the stomach.

Victor Hugo (1802–85) French writer. *Les Misérables*, 'Fantine', Bk. III, Ch. 7

34 If my next-door neighbour is to be allowed to let his children go unvaccinated, he might as well be allowed to leave strychnine lozenges about in the way of mine.

T. H. Huxley (1825–95) British biologist. *Method and Results*, 'Administrative Nihilism'

35 In scarcely any house did only one die, but all together, man and wife with their children and household, traversed the same road, the road of death…I leave the parchment for the work to be continued in case in the future any human survivor should remain, or someone of the race of Adam should be able to escape this plague and continue what I have begun.

John of Clyn Irish friar. Recording the effects of the Black Death in Kilkenny. *Annals of Ireland*

36 How few of his friends' houses would a man choose to be at when he is sick.

Samuel Johnson (1709–84) British lexicographer. *Life of Johnson* (J. Boswell), Vol. IV

37 Cough: A convulsion of the lungs, vellicated by some sharp serosity.

Samuel Johnson *Dictionary of the English Language*

38 Illness makes a man a scoundrel.

Samuel Johnson Letter to Fanny Burney, Jan 1788

39 Oh what can ail thee, knight at arms
Alone and palely loitering;
The sedge has wither'd from the lake,
And no birds sing.

John Keats (1795–1821) British poet. *La Belle Dame Sans Merci*

40 How sickness enlarges the dimensions of a man's self to himself.

Charles Lamb (1775–1834) British essayist. *Last Essays of Elia*, 'The Convalescent'

41 To be sick is to enjoy monarchal prerogatives.

Charles Lamb *Last Essays of Elia*, 'The Convalescent'

42 There are things which will not be defined, and Fever is one of them. Besides, when a word had passed into everyday use, it is too late to lay a logical trap for its meaning, and think to apprehend it by a definition.

Peter Mere Latham (1789–1875) US poet and essayist. *General Remarks on the Practice of Medicine*, Ch. 10, Pt. 1

43 I am only half there when I am ill, and so there is only half a man to suffer. To suffer in one's whole self is so great a violation, that it is not to be endured.

D. H. Lawrence (1885–1930) British novelist. Letter to Catherine Carswell, 16 Apr 1916

44 The most important thing in illness is never to lose heart.

V.I. Lenin (Vladimir Ilyich Ulyanov; 1870–1924) Russian Communist leader. *The Secret of Soviet Strength*, Bk. II, Ch. 3, Sect. 2 (Hewlett Johnson)

45 Medicine makes sick patients, for doctors imagine diseases, as mathematics makes hypochondriacs and theology sinners.

Martin Luther (1483–1546) German Protestant reformer.

46 One who is ill has not only the right but also the duty to seek medical aid.

Maimonides (Moses ben Maimon; 1135–1204) Spanish-born Jewish philosopher and physician.

47 Disease makes men more physical, it leaves them nothing but body.

Thomas Mann (1875–1955) German novelist. *The Magic Mountain*, 4

48 Unfortunately, only a small number of patients with peptic ulcer are financially able to make a pet of an ulcer.

William James Mayo (1861–1934) US surgeon. *Journal of the American Medical Association*, 79:19, 1922

49 Illness is in part what the world has done to a victim, but in a larger part it is what the victim has done with his world, and with himself.

Karl Menninger (1893–90) US psychiatrist. *Illness as Metaphor*, Ch. 6 (Susan Sontag)

50 Confirmed dispepsia is the apparatus of illusions.

George Meredith (1828–1909) British novelist. *The Ordeal of Richard Feverel*

51 She didn't fear death itself, welcoming release from her long struggle between mind and body.

Mary Jane Moffat and Charlotte Painter *Womansize* (Kim Chernin)

52 The patient suffered from chronic remunerative appendicitis.

Delbert H. Nickson (1890–1951)

53 The sick are the greatest danger for the healthy; it is not from the strongest that harm comes to the strong, but from the weakest.

Friedrich Nietzsche (1844–1900) German philosopher. *Genealogy of Morals*, Essay 3

54 When meditating over a disease, I never think of finding a remedy for it, but, instead, a means of preventing it.

Louis Pasteur (1822–95) French scientist. Address to the Fraternal Association of Former Students of the École Centrale des Arts et Manufactures, Paris, 15 May 1884

55 Thence I walked to the Tower; but Lord! how empty the streets are and how melancholy, so many poor sick people in the streets full of sores…in Westminster, there is never a physician and but one apothecary left, all being dead.

Samuel Pepys (1633–1703) English diarist. Written during the Great Plague – the last major outbreak of bubonic plague in England, and the worst since the Black Death of 1348. Diary, 16 Sept 1665

56 I've got Bright's disease and he's got mine.

S. J. Perelman (1904–79) US humorous writer. Attrib.

57 Confront disease at its first stage.

Aulus Flaccus Persius (34–62 AD) Roman satirist. *Satires*, III

58 They do certainly give very strange and new-fangled names to diseases.

Plato (c. 427 BC–347 BC) Greek philosopher. *Republic*, III

59 Once Antigonis was told his son, Demetrius, was ill, and went to see him. At the door he met some young beauty. Going in, he sat down by the bed and took his pulse. 'The fever,' said Demetrius, 'has just left me.' 'Oh, yes,' replied the father, 'I met it going out at the door.'

Plutarch (c. 46 AD– c. 120 AD) Greek biographer and essayist. *Bartlett's Unfamiliar Quotations* (Leonard Louis Levinson)

60 Here am I dying of a hundred good symptoms.

Alexander Pope (1688–1744) English poet. Said to George Lyttleton, 15 May 1744

61 He dies every day who lives a lingering life.

Pierrard Poullet (fl. 1590) *La Charité*

62 Every man who feels well is a sick man neglecting himself.

Jules Romains (1885–1972) French writer. *Knock, ou le triomphe de la médecine*

63 The problem of economic loss due to sickness...a very serious matter for many families with and without incomes, and therefore, an unfair burden upon the medical profession.

Franklin D. Roosevelt (1882–1945) US Democratic President. Address on the Problems of Economic and Social Security, 14 Nov 1934

64 When I look back upon the past, I can only dispel the sadness which falls upon me by gazing into that happy future when the infection will be banished.... The conviction that such a time must inevitably sooner or later arrive will cheer my dying hour.

Ignaz Semmelweis (1818–65) Hungarian physician. Semmelweis had discovered that it was the physicians who spread childbirth fever amongst patients, but he was not believed. *Etiology*, Foreword

65 Only do always in health what you have often promised to do when you are sick.

Sigismund (1368–1437) Holy Roman Emperor. His advice on achieving happiness. *Biographiana*, Vol. I

66 Illness is the night-side of life, a more onerous citizenship. Everyone who is born holds dual citizenship, in the kingdom of the well and in the kingdom of the sick. Although we all prefer to use only the good passport, sooner or later each of us is obliged, at least for a spell, to identify ourselves as citizens of that other place.

Susan Sontag (1933–) US novelist and essayist. *Illness as Metaphor*

67 We are so fond of one another because our ailments are the same.

Jonathan Swift (1667–1745) Anglo-Irish priest, poet, and satirist. Letter to Stella, 1 Feb 1711

68 The medicine increases the disease.

Virgil (Publius Vergilius Maro; 70 BC–19 BC) Roman poet. *Aeneid*, Bk. XII

69 Nor do I in any way approve of the modern sympathy with invalids. I consider it morbid. Illness of any kind is hardly a thing to be encouraged in others.

Oscar Wilde (1856–1900) Irish-born British poet and dramatist. *The Importance of Being Earnest*, I

70 Most of the time we think we're sick, it's all in the mind.

Thomas Wolfe (1900–38) US novelist. *Look Homeward, Angel*, Pt. I, Ch. 1

71 Considering how common illness is, how tremendous the spiritual change that it brings, how astonishing, when the lights of health go down, the undiscovered countries that are then disclosed, what wastes and deserts of the soul a slight attack of influenza brings to view, what precipices and lawns sprinkled with bright flowers a little rise of temperature reveals, what ancient and obdurate oaks are uprooted in us by the act of sickness, how we go down into the pit of death and feel the waters of annihilation close above our heads and wake thinking to find ourselves in the presence of the angels and the harpers when we have a tooth out and come to the surface in the dentist's arm-chair and confuse his 'Rinse the mouth – rinse the mouth' with the greeting of the Deity stooping from the floor of Heaven to welcome us – when we think of this, as we are so frequently forced to think of it, it becomes strange indeed that illness has not taken its place with love and battle and jealousy among the prime themes of literature.

Virginia Woolf (1882–1941) British writer. *The Moment and Other Essays*, 'On Being Ill'

IMAGINATION

1 The primary imagination I hold to be the living power and prime agent of all human perception, and as a repetition in the finite mind of the eternal act of creation in the infinite I AM.

Samuel Taylor Coleridge (1772–1834) British poet. *Biographia Literaria*, Ch. 13

2 Art is ruled uniquely by the imagination.

Benedetto Croce (1866–1952) Italian philosopher. *Esthetic*, Ch. 1

3 She has no imagination and that means no compassion.

Michael Foot (1913–) British Labour politician and journalist. Referring to the Conservative politician and prime minister Margaret Thatcher. Attrib.

4 Were it not for imagination, Sir, a man would be as happy in the arms of a chambermaid as of a Duchess.

Samuel Johnson (1709–84) British lexicographer. *Life of Johnson* (J. Boswell), Vol. III

5 I am certain of nothing but the holiness of the heart's affections and the truth of imagination – what the imagination seizes as beauty must be truth – whether it existed before or not.

John Keats (1795–1821) British poet. Letter to Benjamin Bailey, 22 Nov 1817

6 ...that ability to take leave of everything around me, to live in a world of fantasy, to recreate through imagination the make-believe stories that held me spellbound.

Mario Vargas Llosa (1936–) Peruvian novelist. *A Fish in the Water*

7 Imagination and fiction make up more than three quarters of our real life.

Simone Weil (1909–43) French philosopher. *Gravity and Grace*

IMITATION

See also originality

1 A lotta cats copy the Mona Lisa, but people still line up to see the original.

Louis Armstrong (1900–71) US jazz trumpeter. When asked whether he objected to people copying his style. Attrib.

2 Imitation is the sincerest form of flattery.

Charles Caleb Colton (?1780–1832) British clergyman and writer. *Lacon*, Vol. I

3 When people are free to do as they please, they usually imitate each other.

Eric Hoffer (1902–83) US writer. *The Passionate State of Mind*

4 A mere copier of nature can never produce anything great.

Joshua Reynolds (1723–92) British portrait painter. Discourse to Students of the Royal Academy, 14 Dec 1770

5 He who resolves never to ransack any mind but his own, will be soon reduced, from mere barrenness, to the poorest of all imitations; he will be obliged to imitate himself, and to repeat what he has before often repeated.

Joshua Reynolds Discourse to Students of the Royal Academy, 10 Dec 1774

6 Of all my verse, like not a single line;
But like my title, for it is not mine.
That title from a better man I stole;
Ah, how much better, had I stol'n the whole!

Robert Louis Stevenson (1850–94) Scottish writer. *Underwoods*, Foreword

7 You will, Oscar, you will.

James Whistler (1834–1903) US painter. Replying to Oscar Wilde's exclamation 'I wish I had said that!' Attrib.

IMMORTALITY

See also eternity, mortality, posterity

1 I don't want to achieve immortality through my work...I want to achieve it through not dying.

Woody Allen (Allen Stewart Konigsberg; 1935–) US film actor. *Woody Allen and His Comedy* (E. Lax)

2 One cannot live for ever by ignoring the price of coffins.

Ernest Bramah (1868–1942) British writer. *Kai Lung Unrolls His Mat*

3 No young man believes he shall ever die.

William Hazlitt (1778–1830) British essayist. *On the Feeling of Immortality in Youth*

4 He had decided to live for ever or die in the attempt.

Joseph Heller (1923–) US novelist. *Catch-22*, Ch. 3

5 I detest life-insurance agents; they always argue that I shall some day die, which is not so.

Stephen Leacock (1869–1944) English-born Canadian economist and humorist. *Literary Lapses*, 'Insurance. Up to Date'

6 Stuck with placards for 'Deathless', that bitter beer that tastes sweet to its drinkers.

Rainer Maria Rilke (1875–1926) Austrian poet. *Duineser Elegien*, X

7 But thy eternal cummer shall not fade,
Nor lose possession of that fair thou ow'st,
Nor shall death brag thou wander'st in his shade,
When in eternal lines to time thou grow'st;
So long as men can breathe, or eyes can see,
So long lives this, and this gives life to thee.

William Shakespeare (1564–1616) English dramatist. *Sonnets*, 18

8 We feel and know that we are eternal.

Benedict Spinoza (Baruch de Spinoza; 1632–77) Dutch philosopher. *Ethics*

9 A slumber did my spirit seal;
I had no human fears:
She seemed a thing that could not feel
The touch of earthly years.

No motion has she now, no force;
She neither hears nor sees;
Rolled round in earth's diurnal course,
With rocks, and stones, and trees.

William Wordsworth (1770–1850) British poet. *A Slumber did my Spirit seal*

IMPERFECTION

See also mistakes, perfection, weakness

1 Accidents will happen in the best regulated families.

Proverb

2 No man is infallible.

Proverb

3 To err is human.

Proverb

4 Watch and pray, that ye enter not into temptation: the spirit indeed is willing, but the flesh is weak.

Bible: Matthew 26:41

5 He has his talents, his vast and cultivated mind, his vivid imagination, his independence of soul and his high-souled principles of honour. But then – ah, these Buts! Saint Preux never kicked the fireirons, nor made puddings in his tea cup.

Jane Welsh Carlyle (1801–66) The wife of the Scottish historian, Thomas Carlyle. Referring to her husband. Letter to a friend, July 1821

6 When you have faults, do not fear to abandon them.

Confucius (K'ung Fu-tzu; 551–479 BC) Chinese philosopher. *Analects*

7 Even imperfection itself may have its ideal or perfect state.

Thomas De Quincey (1785–1859) British writer. *Murder Considered as one of the Fine Arts*

8 We must touch his weaknesses with a delicate hand. There are some faults so nearly allied to excellence, that we can scarce weed out the fault without eradicating the virtue.

Oliver Goldsmith (1728–74) Irish-born British writer. *The Good-Natured Man*, I

9 I'm aggrieved when sometimes even excellent Homer nods.

Horace (Quintus Horatius Flaccus; 65–8 BC) Roman poet. *Ars Poetica*

10 People often say that, by pointing out to a man the faults of his mistress, you succeed only in strengthening his attachment to her, because he does not believe you; yet how much more so if he does!

Marcel Proust (1871–1922) French novelist. *À La Recherche du temps perdu: Du côté de chez Swann*

11 We only confess our little faults to persuade people that we have no large ones.

Duc de la Rochefoucauld (1613–80) French writer. *Maximes*, 327

12 If we had no faults of our own, we would not take so much pleasure in noticing those of others.

Duc de la Rochefoucauld *Maximes*, 31

13 Oh. I have got lots of human weaknesses, who hasn't?

Margaret Thatcher (1925–) British politician and prime minister. *The Times*, 1983

14 We are none of us infallible – not even the youngest of us.

William Hepworth Thompson (1810–86) British academic. Referring to G. W. Balfour, who was a junior fellow of Trinity College at the time. *Collections and Recollections* (G. W. E. Russell), Ch. 18

IMPERTINENCE

See also frankness, rudeness

1 He has to learn that petulance is not sarcasm, and that insolence is not invective.

Benjamin Disraeli (1804–81) British statesman. Said of Sir C. Wood. Speech, House of Commons, 16 Dec 1852

2 Must! Is *must* a word to be addressed to princes? Little man, little man! thy father, if he had been alive, durst not have used that word.

Elizabeth I (1533–1603) Queen of England. Said to Robert Cecil, on her death bed. *A Short History of the English People* (J. R. Green), Ch. 7

3 The right people are rude. They can afford to be.

W. Somerset Maugham (1874–1965) British novelist. *Our Betters*, II

4 JUDGE WILLIS. You are extremely offensive, young man.
F. E. SMITH. As a matter of fact, we both are, and the only difference between us is that I am trying to be, and you can't help it.

F. E. Smith (1872–1930) British lawyer and politician. *Frederick Elwin, Earl of Birkenhead* (Lord Birkenhead), Vol. I, Ch. 9

IMPETUOSITY

See also haste, spontaneity

1 In me the need to talk is a primary impulse, and I can't help saying right off what comes to my tongue.

Miguel de Cervantes (1547–1616) Spanish novelist. *Don Quixote*, Pt. I, Ch. 30

2 There are some who speak one moment before they think.

Jean de La Bruyère (1645–96) French satirist. *Les Caractères*

3 Celerity is never more admir'd
Than by the negligent.

William Shakespeare (1564–1616) English dramatist. *Antony and Cleopatra*, III:7

4 When a prisoner sees the door of his dungeon open he dashes for it without stopping to think where he shall get his dinner.

George Bernard Shaw (1856–1950) Irish dramatist and critic. *Back to Methuselah*, Preface

5 A youth to whom was given
So much of earth – so much of heaven,
And such impetuous blood.

William Wordsworth (1770–1850) British poet. *Ruth*

IMPORTANCE

See also triviality

1 Are not five sparrows sold for two farthings, and not one of them is forgotten before God?

Bible: Luke 12:6

2 We also demand our own place in the sun.

Bernhard, Prince von Bülow (1849–1929) German statesman. Said at the Reichstag, 6 Dec 1897

3 Not to be sneezed at.

George Colman, the Younger (1762–1836) British dramatist. *Heir-at-Law*, II:1

4 In heaven an angel is nobody in particular.

George Bernard Shaw (1856–1950) Irish dramatist and critic. *Man and Superman*, 'Maxims for Revolutionists'

5 Art and religion first; then philosophy; lastly science. That is the order of the great subjects of life, that's their order of importance.

Muriel Spark (1918–) British novelist. *The Prime of Miss Jean Brodie*, Ch. 2

6 If this is God's world there are no unimportant people.

George Thomas (1909–92) British politician. Remark, in a TV interview

IMPRESSIONABILITY

See also gullibility

1 She had
A heart – how shall I say? – too soon made glad,
Too easily impressed.

Robert Browning (1812–89) British poet. *My Last Duchess*

2 Like a cushion, he always bore the impress of the last man who sat on him.

David Lloyd George (1863–1945) British Liberal statesman. Referring to Lord Derby. Attrib. in *The Listener*, 7 Sep 1978. This remark is also credited to Earl Haig

3 They'll take suggestion as a cat laps milk.

William Shakespeare (1564–1616) English dramatist. *The Tempest*, II:1

4 I am a feather for each wind that blows.

William Shakespeare *The Winter's Tale*, I:3

5 Give me a girl at an impressionable age, and she is mine for life.

Muriel Spark (1918–) British novelist. *The Prime of Miss Jean Brodie*, Ch. 1

IMPRISONMENT

See also freedom, oppression, slavery

1 And say, Thus saith the king, Put this fellow in the prison, and feed him with bread of affliction and with water of affliction, until I come in peace.

Bible: I Kings 22:27

2 A robin redbreast in a cage
Puts all Heaven in a rage.

William Blake (1757–1827) British poet. *Auguries of Innocence*

3 O! dreadful is the check – intense the agony
When the ear begins to hear, and the eye begins to see;
When the pulse begins to throb – the brain to think again –
The soul to feel the flesh, and the flesh to feel the chain.

Emily Brontë (1818–48) British novelist. *The Prisoner*

4 Thirty years' imprisonment is…a declaration of society's intellectual bankruptcy in the field of penology.

Lord Foot (1905–) British politician. *The Observer*, 'Sayings of the Week', 9 Mar 1969

5 Who but my father would keep such a bird in a cage?

Henry, Prince of Wales (1594–1612) First-born son of James I. Referring to Sir Walter Raleigh, who was imprisoned in the Tower of London for treason from 1603. Remark

6 Oh they're taking him to prison for the colour of his hair.

A. E. Housman (1859–1936) British poet. *Collected Poems, Additional Poems*

7 She's only a bird in a gilded cage.

A. J. Lamb (1870–1928) British songwriter. Song title

8 Stone walls do not a prison make,
Nor iron bars a cage.

Richard Lovelace (1618–58) English poet. *To Althea, from Prison*

9 Is not this house as nigh heaven as my own?

Thomas More (1478–1535) English lawyer and scholar. Referring to the Tower of London; More was imprisoned here, and in 1535 executed, for treason arising from his defiance of Henry VIII's religious policies. *Life of Sir Thomas More* (Roper)

10 Come, let's away to prison;
We two alone will sing like birds i' the cage:
When thou dost ask me blessing, I'll kneel down,
And ask of thee forgiveness: and we'll live,
And pray, and sing, and tell old tales, and laugh
At gilded butterflies, and hear poor rogues
Talk of court news; and we'll talk with them too,
Who loses, and who wins; who's in, who's out;
And take upon 's the mystery of things,
As if we were God's spies; and we'll wear out,
In a wall'd prison, packs and sets of great ones
That ebb and flow by the moon.

William Shakespeare (1564–1616) English dramatist. *King Lear*, V:3

11 I have been studying how I may compare
This prison where I live unto the world.

William Shakespeare *Richard II*, V:5

12 Forget the outside world. Life has different laws in here. This is Campland, an invisible country. It's not in the geography books, or the psychology books or the history books. This is the famous country where ninety-nine men weep while one laughs.

Alexander Solzhenitsyn (1918–) Soviet novelist. *The Love-Girl and the Innocent*, I:3

13 We think caged birds sing, when indeed they cry.

John Webster (1580–1625) English dramatist. *The White Devil*, V:4

14 I never saw a man who looked
With such a wistful eye
Upon that little tent of blue
Which prisoners call the sky.

Oscar Wilde (1854–1900) Irish-born British dramatist. *The Ballad of Reading Gaol*, I:3

15 The Governor was strong upon
The Regulations Act:
The Doctor said that Death was but
A scientific fact:
And twice a day the Chaplain called,
And left a little tract.

Oscar Wilde *The Ballad of Reading Gaol*, III:3

16 Something was dead in each of us,
And what was dead was Hope.

Oscar Wilde *The Ballad of Reading Gaol*, III:31

17 I know not whether Laws be right,
Or whether Laws be wrong;
All that we know who lie in gaol
Is that the wall is strong;
And that each day is like a year,
A year whose days are long.

Oscar Wilde *The Ballad of Reading Gaol*, V:1

18 If this is the way Queen Victoria treats her prisoners, she doesn't deserve to have any.

Oscar Wilde Complaining at having to wait in the rain for transport to take him to prison. Attrib.

IMPROVEMENT

See also progress

1 He so improved the city that he justly boasted that he found it brick and left it marble.

Augustus (63 BC–14 AD) Roman emperor. Referring to Rome. *The Lives of the Caesars* (Suetonius), 'Augustus'

2 I've got to admit it's getting better.
It's a little better all the time.

John Lennon (1940–80) British rock musician. *Getting Better* (with Paul McCartney)

3 It is a stupidity second to none, to busy oneself with the correction of the world.

Molière (Jean Baptiste Poquelin; 1622–73) French dramatist. *Le Misanthrope*, I:1

INATTENTION

1 Thank you for the manuscript; I shall lose no time in reading it.

Benjamin Disraeli (1804–81) British statesman. His customary reply to those who sent him unsolicited manuscripts. *Irreverent Social History* (F. Muir)

INCOMPETENCE

1 This island is almost made of coal and surrounded by fish. Only an organizing genius could produce a shortage of coal and fish in Great Britain at the same time.

Aneurin Bevan (1897–1960) British Labour politician. Speech, Blackpool, 18 May 1945

2 The grotesque chaos of a Labour council – a *Labour* council – hiring taxis to scuttle around a city handing out redundancy notices to its own workers.

Neil Kinnock (1942–) British politician. Attacking Militant members in Liverpool. Speech, Labour Party Conference, Bournemouth, 1985

3 He really deserves some sort of decoration…a medal inscribed 'For Vaguery in the Field'.

John Osborne (1929–) British dramatist. *Look Back in Anger*, I

4 Work is accomplished by those employees who have not yet reached their level of incompetence.

Laurence J. Peter (1919–90) Canadian writer. *The Peter Principle*

5 Madame, there you sit with that magnificent instrument between your legs, and all you can do is *scratch* it!

Arturo Toscanini (1867–1957) Italian conductor. Rebuking an incompetent woman cellist. Attrib.

INDECISION

See also uncertainty

1 I will have nothing to do with a man who can blow hot and cold with the same breath.

Aesop (6th century BC) Reputed Greek writer of fables. *Fables*, 'The Man and the Satyr'

2 She didn't say yes,
She didn't say no.

Otto Harbach (1873–1963) US lyricist. *The Cat and the Fiddle*, 'She Didn't Say Yes'

3 Nothing is so exhausting as indecision, and nothing is so futile.

Bertrand Russell (1872–1970) British philosopher. Attrib.

4 But I am pigeon-liver'd, and lack gall
To make oppression bitter, or ere this
I should have fatted all the region kites
With this slave's offal. Bloody, bawdy villain!
Remorseless, treacherous, lecherous, kindless villain!

William Shakespeare (1564–1616) English dramatist. *Hamlet*, II:2

5 I must have a prodigious quantity of mind; it takes me as much as a week, sometimes, to make it up.

Mark Twain (Samuel Langhorne Clemens; 1835–1910) US writer. *The Innocents Abroad*, Ch. 7

INDEPENDENCE

See also self-reliance, society

1 I'm short enough and ugly enough to succeed on my own.

Woody Allen (Allen Stewart Konigsberg; 1935–) US film actor. *Play It Again Sam*

2 I am the cat that walks alone.

Lord Beaverbrook (Maxwell Aitken; 1879–1964) Canadian-born politician and newspaper proprietor. *Beaverbrook* (A. J. P. Taylor)

3 When in the course of human events, it becomes necessary for one people to dissolve the political bonds which have connected them with another, and to assume among the powers of the earth the separate and equal station to which the laws of nature and of Nature's God entitle them, a decent respect to the opinions of mankind requires that they should declare the causes which impel them to the separation.

Thomas Jefferson (1743–1826) US statesman. Declaration of Independence, Preamble bonds

4 I think it much better that…every man paddle his own canoe.

Captain Frederick Marryat (1792–1848) British novelist. *Settlers in Canada*, Ch. 8

INDIFFERENCE

See also insensitivity

1 But what is past my help is past my care.

Francis Beaumont (1584–1616) English dramatist. With John Fletcher. *The Double Marriage*, I:1

2 Nothing is so fatal to religion as indifference, which is, at least, half infidelity.

Edmund Burke (1729–97) British politician. Letter to William Smith, 29 Jan 1795

3 Sir, I view the proposal to hold an international exhibition at San Francisco with an equanimity bordering on indifference.

W. S. Gilbert (1836–1911) British dramatist. *Gilbert, His Life and Strife* (Hesketh Pearson)

4 It's no go the picture palace, it's no go the stadium,
It's no go the country cot with a pot of pink geraniums,
It's no go the Government grants, it's no go the elections,
Sit on your arse for fifty years and hang your hat on a pension.

Louis MacNeice (1907–63) Irish-born British poet. *Bagpipe Music*

5 At length the morn and cold indifference came.

Nicholas Rowe (1674–1718) English dramatist. *The Fair Penitent*, I:1

6 I don't care a twopenny damn what becomes of the ashes of Napoleon Bonaparte.

Duke of Wellington (1769–1852) British general and statesman. Attrib.

7 I hear it was charged against me that I sought to destroy institutions,
But really I am neither for nor against institutions.

Walt Whitman (1819–92) US poet. *I Hear It was Charged against Me*

INDIVIDUALITY

See also difference, opinions, taste

1 Here's tae us wha's like us?
Gey few, and they're a' deid.

Anonymous Scottish toast.

2 Nature made him, and then broke the mould.

Ludovico Ariosto (1474–1533) Italian poet. Referring to Charlemagne's paladin, Roland. *Orlando furioso*

3 It is the common wonder of all men, how among so many million of faces, there should be none alike.

Thomas Browne (1605–82) English physician and writer. *Religio Medici*, Pt. II

4 ...a bore, a bounder and a prig. He was intoxicated with his own youth and loathed any milieu which he couldn't dominate. Certainly he had none of a gentleman's instincts, strutting about Peace Conferences in Arab dress.

Henry Channon (1897–1958) British writer. Referring to T. E. Lawrence, known as Lawrence of Arabia. Diary, 25 May 1935

5 We boil at different degrees.

Ralph Waldo Emerson (1803–82) US poet and essayist. *Society and Solitude*, 'Eloquence'

6 What many men desire! that 'many' may be meant
By the fool multitide, that choose by show,
Not learning more than the fond eye doth teach;
Which pries not to the interior; but, like the martlet,
Builds in the weather on the outward wall,
Even in the force and road of casualty.
I will not choose what many men desire,
Because I will not jump with common spirits
And rank me with the barbarous multitude.

William Shakespeare (1564–1616) English dramatist. *The Merchant of Venice*, II:9

7 Without deviation from the norm 'progress' is not possible.

Frank Zappa (1940–93) US rock musician. *The Real Frank Zappa Book*

INDOCTRINATION

See also education

1 Their teacher had advised them not to read Tolstoy novels, because they were very long and would easily confuse the clear ideas which they had learned from reading critical studies of him.

Alexander Solzhenitsyn (1918–) Soviet novelist. *The First Circle*, Ch. 40

2 This universal, obligatory force-feeding with lies is now the most agonizing aspect of existence in our country – worse than all our material miseries, worse than any lack of civil liberties.

Alexander Solzhenitsyn *Letter to Soviet Leaders*, 6

3 For us, the tasks of education in socialism were closely integrated with those of fighting. Ideas that enter the mind under fire remain there securely and for ever.

Leon Trotsky (Lev Davidovich Bronstein; 1879–1940) Russian revolutionary. *My Life*, Ch. 35

INDULGENCE

1 Love is a boy, by poets styl'd,
Then spare the rod, and spoil the child.

Samuel Butler (1612–80) English satirist. *Hudibras*, Pt. II

2 Every luxury was lavished on you – atheism, breast-feeding, circumcision. I had to make my own way.

Joe Orton (1933–67) British dramatist. *Loot*, I

INDUSTRIAL RELATIONS

See also diplomacy, strikes

1 British management doesn't seem to understand the importance of the human factor.

Charles, Prince of Wales (1948–) Eldest son of Elizabeth II. Speech, Parliamentary and Scientific Committee lunch, 21 Feb 1979

2 Industrial relations are like sexual relations. It's better between two consenting parties.

Vic Feather (1908–76) British trade-union leader. *Guardian Weekly*, 8 Aug 1976

3 I tell you, the only safeguard of order and discipline in the modern world is a standardised worker with interchangeable parts. That would solve the entire problem of management.

Jean Giraudoux (1882–1944) French dramatist. *The Madwoman of Chaillot*

4 It might be said that it is the ideal of the employer to have production without employees and the ideal of the employee is to have income without work.

E. F. Schumacher (1911–77) German-born economist. *The Observer*, 'Sayings of the Week', 4 May 1975

INFERIORITY

See also equality, mediocrity

1 I just met X in the street, I stopped for a moment to exchange ideas, and now I feel like a complete idiot.

Heinrich Heine (1797–1856) German poet and writer. *Autant en apportent les mots* (Pedrazzini)

2 Wherever an inferiority complex exists, there is a good reason for it. There is always something inferior there, although not just where we persuade ourselves that it is.

Carl Gustav Jung (1875–1961) Swiss psychoanalyst. Interview, 1943

3 It is an infallible sign of the second-rate in nature and intellect to make use of everything and everyone.

Ada Beddington Leverson (1862–1933) British writer. *The Limit*

4 There's no such thing as a bad Picasso, but some are less good than others.

Pablo Picasso (1881–1973) Spanish painter. *Come to Judgment* (A. Whitman)

5 Few persons who ever sat for a portrait can have felt anything but inferior while the process is going on.

Anthony Powell (1905–) British novelist. *The Observer*, 9 Jan 1983

6 No one can make you feel inferior without your consent.

Eleanor Roosevelt (1884–1962) US writer and lecturer. *This is My Story*

7 A king of shreds and patches.

William Shakespeare (1564–1616) English dramatist. *Hamlet*, III:4

INFINITY

1 The Desire of Man being Infinite, the possession is Infinite, and himself Infinite.

William Blake (1757–1827) British poet. *There is no Natural Religion*

INFLEXIBILITY

See also determination, stubbornness

1 Whenever you accept our views we shall be in full agreement with you.

Moshe Dayan (1915–81) Israeli general. Said to the US statesman Cyrus Vance during Arab-Israeli negotiations. *The Observer*, 'Sayings of the Week', 14 Aug 1977

2 You cannot shake hands with a clenched fist.

Indira Gandhi (1917–84) Indian stateswoman. Remark at a press conference, New Delhi, 19 Oct 1971

3 U-turn if you want to. The lady's not for turning.

Margaret Thatcher (1925–) British politician and prime minister. Speech, Conservative Conference, 1980

4 Minds like beds always made up,
(more stony than a shore)
unwilling or unable.

William Carlos Williams (1883–1963) US poet. *Patterson*, I, Preface

INFLUENCE

See also inspiration, power

1 Though Rome's gross yoke
Drops off, no more to be endured,
Her teaching is not so obscured
By errors and perversities,
That no truth shines athwart the lies.

Robert Browning (1812–89) British poet. *Christmas Eve*, XI

2 How to Win Friends and Influence People.

Dale Carnegie (1888–1955) US lecturer and writer. Book title

3 In the councils of government, we must guard against the acquisition of unwarranted influence, whether sought or unsought, by the military-industrial complex. The potential for the disastrous rise of misplaced power exists and will persist.

Dwight D. Eisenhower (1890–1969) US president. Farewell address, 17 Jan 1961

4 The proper time to influence the character of a child is about a hundred years before he is born.

Dean Inge (1860–1954) British churchman. *The Observer*, 21 June, 1929

5 We have met too late. You are too old for me to have any effect on you.

James Joyce (1882–1941) Irish novelist. On meeting the Irish poet, W. B. Yeats. *James Joyce* (R. Ellmann)

6 Practical men, who believe themselves to be quite exempt from any intellectual influences, are usually the slaves of some defunct economist. Madmen in authority, who hear voices in the air, are distilling their frenzy from some academic scribbler of a few years back.

John Maynard Keynes (1883–1946) British economist. *The General Theory of Employment, Interest and Money*, Bk. VI, Ch. 24

7 The great man…walks across his century and leaves the marks of his feet all over it, ripping out the dates on his goloshes as he passes.

Stephen Leacock (1869–1944) English-born Canadian economist and humorist. *Literary Lapses*, 'The Life of John Smith'

8 So you're the little woman who wrote the book that made this great war!

Abraham Lincoln (1809–65) US statesman. Said on meeting Harriet Beecher Stowe, the author of *Uncle Tom's Cabin* (1852), which stimulated opposition to slavery before the US Civil War. *Abraham Lincoln: The War Years* (Carl Sandburg), Vol. II, Ch. 39

9 Peace! impudent and shameless Warwick,
peace;
Proud setter up and puller down of kings.

William Shakespeare (1564–1616) English dramatist. *Henry VI, Part Three*, III:3

10 I will shake my little finger – and there will be no more Tito. He will fall.

Joseph Stalin (J. Dzhugashvili; 1879–1953) Soviet statesman. Said to the Soviet statesman Khrushchev. Marshal Tito was the Yugoslav leader (1945–80). Attrib.

11 Athens holds sway over all Greece; I dominate Athens; my wife dominates me; our newborn son dominates her.

Themistocles (c. 528–462 BC) Athenian statesman. Explaining an earlier remark to the effect that his young son ruled all Greece. Attrib.

12 The hand that rocks the cradle
Is the hand that rules the world.

William Ross Wallace (1819–81) US poet and songwriter. *John o'London's Treasure Trove*

13 I took the right sow by the ear.

Robert Walpole Commenting on his perception that, to influence George II, the correct woman to cultivate was Queen Caroline, not any of the King's mistresses – a mistake made by his political opponents. Remark to a friend, c. 1734

14 The man who can dominate a London dinner-table can dominate the world.

Oscar Wilde (1854–1900) Irish-born British dramatist. Attrib. by R. Aldington in his edition of Wilde

INGE, WILLIAM RALPH

(1860–1954) British churchman, who became Dean of St Pauls (1911–34) and wrote a number of books, including *Christian Mysticism* (1899).

1 What we know of the past is mostly not worth knowing. What is worth knowing is mostly uncertain. Events in the past may roughly be divided into those which probably never happened and those which do not matter.

Assessments and Anticipations, 'Prognostications'

2 The enemies of Freedom do not argue; they shout and they shoot.

End of an Age, Ch. 4

3 The effect of boredom on a large scale in history is underestimated. It is a main cause of revolutions, and would soon bring to an end all the static Utopias and the farmyard civilization of the Fabians.

End of an Age, Ch. 6

4 Many people believe that they are attracted by God, or by Nature, when they are only repelled by man.

More Lay Thoughts of a Dean

5 It takes in reality only one to make a quarrel. It is useless for the sheep to pass resolutions in favour

of vegetarianism while the wolf remains of a different opinion.
Outspoken Essays

6 To become a popular religion, it is only necessary for a superstition to enslave a philosophy.
Outspoken Essays

7 Democracy is only an experiment in government, and it has the obvious disadvantage of merely counting votes instead of weighing them.
Possible Recovery?

8 Literature flourishes best when it is half a trade and half an art.
The Victorian Age

9 The proper time to influence the character of a child is about a hundred years before he is born.
The Observer, 21 June, 1929

10 A nation is a society united by a delusion about its ancestry and by a common hatred of its neighbours.
The Perpetual Pessimist (Sagittarius and George)

11 A man may build himself a throne of bayonets, but he cannot sit on it.
Wit and Wisdom of Dean Inge (ed. Marchant)

12 The nations which have put mankind and posterity most in their debt have been small states – Israel, Athens, Florence, Elizabethan England.
Wit and Wisdom of Dean Inge (ed. Marchant)

INGRATITUDE

1 Never look a gift horse in the mouth.
Proverb

2 And having looked to government for bread, on the very first scarcity they will turn and bite the hand that fed them.
Edmund Burke (1729–97) British politician. *Thoughts and Details on Scarcity*

3 Our gratitude to most benefactors is the same as our feeling for dentists who have pulled out teeth. We acknowledge the good they have done and the evil from which they have delivered us, but we remember the pain they occasioned and do not love them very much.
Nicolas Chamfort (1741–94) French writer. *Maximes et pensées*

4 Blow, blow, thou winter wind,
Thou art not so unkind
As man's ingratitude.
William Shakespeare (1564–1616) English dramatist. *As You Like It*, II:7

5 Ingratitude, thou marble-hearted fiend,
More hideous when thou show'st thee in a child
Than the sea-monster!
William Shakespeare *King Lear*, I:4

6 I hate ingratitude more in a man
Than lying, vainness, babbling drunkenness,
Or any taint of vice whose strong corruption
Inhabits our frail blood.
William Shakespeare *Twelfth Night*, III:4

INJUSTICE

1 Give a dog a bad name and hang him.
Proverb

2 If I had been born a man, I would have conquered Europe. As I was born a woman, I exhausted my energy in tirades against fate, and in eccentricities.
Marie Konstantinovna Bashkirtseff (1860–84) Russian artist and diarist. *The Journal of a Young Artist*, 25 June 1884

3 Those who have had no share in the good fortunes of the mighty often have a share in their misfortunes.
Bertolt Brecht (1898–1956) German dramatist. *The Caucasian Chalk Circle*

4 When one has been threatened with a great injustice, one accepts a smaller as a favour.
Jane Welsh Carlyle (1801–66) The wife of the Scottish historian Thomas Carlyle. *Journal*, 21 Nov 1855

5 To disarm the strong and arm the weak would be to change the social order which it's my job to preserve. Justice is the means by which established injustices are sanctioned.
Anatole France (Jacques Anatole François Thibault; 1844–1924) French writer. *Crainquebille*

6 Undeservedly you will atone for the sins of your fathers.
Horace (Quintus Horatius Flaccus; 65–8 BC) Roman poet. *Odes*, III

7 We was robbed!
Joe Jacobs (1896–1940) US boxing manager. Complaining to the audience when the heavyweight title of Max Schmeling, whom he managed, was passed to Jack Sharkey. Attrib.

8 The government burns down whole cities while the people are forbidden to light lamps.
Mao Tse-Tung (1893–1976) Chinese communist leader. Attrib.

9 They invent a legend to put the blame for the existence of humanity on women and, if she wants to stop it, they talk about the wonders of civilizations and the sacred responsibilities of motherhood. They can't have it both ways.
Dorothy Miller Richardson (1873–1957) British writer. *Pilgrimage*, Vol. II, Ch. 24

10 I am a man
More sinn'd against than sinning.
William Shakespeare (1564–1616) English dramatist. *King Lear*, III:2

11 MARIA. Men rail at weakness themselves create,
And boldly stigmatize the female mind,
As though kind nature's just impartial hand
Had form'd its features in a baser mould
Mercy Otis Warren (1728–1814) US poet, historian, and dramatist. *The Ladies of Castile*, I:5

INNOCENCE

See also conscience, ignorance

1 Now I am ashamed of confessing that I have nothing to confess.
Fanny Burney (Frances Burney D'Arblay; 1752–1840) British novelist. *Evelina*, Letter 59

2 She was as immutable as the hills.
But not quite so green.

Rudyard Kipling (1865–1936) Indian-born British writer. *Plain Tales from the Hills*, 'Venus Annodomini'

3 Now my innocence begins to weigh me down.

Jean Racine (1639–99) French dramatist. *Andromaque*, III:1

Innocence of childhood

See also age, children, ignorance

4 'But the Emperor has nothing on at all!' cried a little child.

Hans Christian Andersen (1805–75) Danish writer. *The Emperor's New Clothes*

5 No, it is not only our fate but our business to lose innocence, and once we have lost that, it is futile to attempt a picnic in Eden.

Elizabeth Bowen (1899–1973) Irish novelist. In *Orion III*, 'Out of a Book'

6 Ralph wept for the end of innocence, the darkness of man's heart, and the fall through the air of the true, wise friend called Piggy.

William Golding (1911–93) British novelist. *Lord of the Flies*, Ch. 12

7 I remember, I remember,
The fir trees dark and high;
I used to think their slender tops
Were close against the sky:
It was a childish ignorance,
But now 'tis little joy
To know I'm farther off from heav'n
Than when I was a boy.

Thomas Hood (1799–1845) British poet. *I Remember*

8 Credulity is the man's weakness, but the child's strength.

Charles Lamb (1775–1834) British essayist. *Essays of Elia*, 'Witches and other Night Fears'

9 Childhood is the kingdom where nobody dies. Nobody that matters, that is.

Edna St Vincent Millay (1892–1950) US poet. *Childhood is the Kingdom where Nobody dies*

10 I'd the upbringing a nun would envy and that's the truth. Until I was fifteen I was more familiar with Africa than my own body.

Joe Orton (1933–67) British dramatist. *Entertaining Mr Sloane*, I

11 He hath a person and a smooth dispose
Fram'd to make a woman false.
The Moor is of a free and open nature,
That thinks men honest that but seem to be so.

William Shakespeare (1564–1616) English dramatist. *Othello*, I:3

12 What judgment shall I dread, doing no wrong?

William Shakespeare *The Merchant of Venice*, IV:1

13 Now as I was young and easy under the apple boughs
About the lilting house and happy as the grass was green,
The night above the dingle starry,
Time let me hail and climb
Golden in the heydays of his eyes.

Dylan Thomas (1914–53) Welsh poet. *Fern Hill*

14 And the wild boys innocent as strawberries.

Dylan Thomas *The hunchback in the park*

15 We live in our own world,
A world that is too small
For you to stoop and enter
Even on hands and knees,
The adult subterfuge.

R. S. Thomas *Song at the Year's Turning*, 'Children's Song'

16 There was a time when meadow, grove, and stream,
The earth, and every common sight,
To me did seem
Apparelled in celestial light,
The glory and the freshness of a dream.

William Wordsworth (1770–1850) British poet. *Ode. Intimations of Immortality*, I

INNOVATION

See also conservatism, novelty, originality, progress

1 He that will not apply new remedies must expect new evils: for time is the greatest innovator.

Francis Bacon (1561–1626) English philosopher. *Essays*, 'Of Innovations'

2 I once knew a chap who had a system of just hanging the baby on the clothes line to dry and he was greatly admired by his fellow citizens for having discovered a wonderful innovation on changing a diaper.

Damon Runyon (1884–1946) US writer. *Short Takes*, 'Diaper Dexterity'

INNUENDO

See also meaning

1 There was an old man of Boulogne
Who sang a most topical song.
It wasn't the words
That frightened the birds,
But the horrible double-entendre.

Anonymous

2 I'm one of the ruins that Cromwell knocked about a bit.

Marie Lloyd (1870–1922) British music-hall singer. Song title

3 Where more is meant than meets the ear.

John Milton (1608–74) English poet. *Il Penseroso*

INSENSITIVITY

See also hurt, indifference

1 Miss Buss and Miss Beale
Cupid's darts do not feel.
How different from us,
Miss Beale and Miss Buss.

Anonymous Written about the headmistresses of North London Collegiate School and Cheltenham Ladies' College, respectively

2 Has anyone here been raped and speaks English?

Anonymous Said to have been shouted by a television journalist to a group of Belgian civilians waiting to be evacuated from the Congo in 1960

3 'There's been an accident' they said,
'Your servant's cut in half; he's dead!'
'Indeed!' said Mr Jones, 'and please
Send me the half that's got my keys.'

Harry Graham (1874–1936) British writer. *Ruthless Rhymes for Heartless Homes*, 'Mr. Jones'

4 Just as the meanest and most vicious deeds require spirit and talent, so even the greatest deeds require a certain insensitiveness which on other occasions is called stupidity.

Georg Christoph Lichtenberg (1742–99) German physicist and writer. *Aphorisms*

5 One would have to have a heart of stone to read the death of Little Nell without laughing.

Oscar Wilde (1854–1900) Irish-born British dramatist. Lecturing upon Dickens. *Lives of the Wits* (H. Pearson)

INSIGNIFICANCE

See also triviality

1 There are some people who leave impressions not so lasting as the imprint of an oar upon the water.

Kate Chopin (1851–1904) US writer. *The Awakening*, Ch. 34

2 We are the hollow men
We are the stuffed men
Leaning together
Headpiece filled with straw.

T. S. Eliot (1888–1965) US-born British poet. *The Hollow Men*

3 She was one of those indispensables of whom one makes the discovery, when they are gone, that one can get on quite as well without them.

Aldous Huxley (1894–1964) British novelist. *Mortal Coils*, 'Nuns at Luncheon'

4 We are nothing; less than nothing, and dreams. We are only what might have been, and must wait upon the tedious shores of Lethe millions of ages before we have existence, and a name.

Charles Lamb (1775–1834) British essayist. In Greek mythology, Lethe was a river in the underworld, whose waters were drunk by souls about to be reborn in order to forget their past lives. *Essays of Elia*, 'Dream Children'

5 Apparently if there was a person fiendish enough to set about interfering with your life, the only thing you could do was to concentrate hard on someone they were unlikely ever to have heard of called Martin Amis.

Jeanette Winterson (1959–) British author. *Boating for Beginners*

INSINCERITY

See also hypocrisy

1 Experience teaches you that the man who looks you straight in the eye, particularly if he adds a firm handshake, is hiding something.

Clifton Fadiman (1904–) US writer. *Enter, Conversing*

2 He who praises everybody praises nobody.

Samuel Johnson (1709–84) British lexicographer. *Life of Johnson* (J. Boswell), Vol. III

3 Whatever he may promise me he will break everything to get a regular income from his parliament.

Louis XIV (1638–1715) King of France. Referring to Charles II of England. Letter to Barillon, 1680

4 Went to hear Mrs Turner's daughter...play on the harpsichon; but, Lord! it was enough to make any man sick to hear her; yet was I forced to commend her highly.

Samuel Pepys (1633–1703) English diarist. *Diary*, 1 May 1663

5 Most friendship is feigning, most loving mere folly.

William Shakespeare (1564–1616) English dramatist. *As You Like It*, II:7

6 My nose bleeds for you.

Herbert Beerbohm Tree (1853–1917) British actor and theatre manager. *Beerbohm Tree* (H. Pearson)

INSPIRATION

1 A spur in the head is worth two in the heel.

Proverb

2 That I make poetry and give pleasure (if I give pleasure) are because of you.

Horace (Quintus Horatius Flaccus, 65–8 BC) Roman poet. *Odes*, IV

3 Biting my truant pen, beating myself for spite: 'Fool!' said my Muse to me, 'look in thy heart and write.'

Philip Sidney (1554–86) English poet and courtier. Sonnet, *Astrophel and Stella*

4 I did not write it. God wrote it. I merely did his dictation.

Harriet Beecher Stowe (1811–96) US novelist. Referring to *Uncle Tom's Cabin*. Attrib.

5 The true God, the might God, is the God of ideas.

Alfred de Vigny (1797–1863) French writer. *La Bouteille à la mer*

6 You're best when you're not in charge. The ego locks the muse.

Robin Williams (1952–) US actor. *Premiere*, Jan 1988

INSULTS

See also actors, criticism, politicians, rudeness

1 Sticks and stones may break my bones, but words will never hurt me.

Proverb

2 I don't want you here – now sod off!

Princess Anne (1950–) The Princess Royal, only daughter of Elizabeth II. Remark to the Press, Jan 1987

3 Quite so. But I have not been on a ship for fifteen years and they still call me 'Admiral'.

Italian admiral to whom Eva Peron, the wife of the Argentinian dictator, had complained that she had been called a 'whore' on an Italian visit.

Anonymous

4 TO HELL WITH YOU. OFFENSIVE LETTER FOLLOWS.

Anonymous Telegram to the Conservative statesman Sir Alec Douglas-Home

5 An imitation rough diamond.

Margot Asquith (1865–1945) The second wife of the British statesman Herbert Asquith. *As I Remember*

6 Lloyd George could not see a belt without hitting below it.

Margot Asquith Referring to the Liberal statesman. *The Autiobiography of Margot Asquith*

7 No. The 't' is silent – as in 'Harlow'.

Margot Asquith When the actress Jean Harlow asked whether the 't' was pronounced in 'Margot'.

8 She was a woman of mean understanding, little information, and uncertain temper.

Jane Austen (1775–1817) British novelist. *Pride and Prejudice*, Ch. 1

9 I thought he was a young man of promise; but it appears he was a young man of promises.

Arthur Balfour (1848–1930) British statesman. Said of Winston Churchill on his entry into politics, 1899. *Winston Churchill* (Randolph Churchill), Vol. I

10 Don't bother to thank me. I know what a perfectly ghastly season it's been for you Spanish dancers.

Tallulah Bankhead (1903–68) US actress. Said on dropping fifty dollars into a tambourine held out by a Salvation Army collector. *With Malice Toward All* (D. Hermann)

11 Busy yourselves with *this*, you damned walruses, while the rest of us proceed with the libretto.

John Barrymore (1882–1942) US actor. Throwing a fish to a noisy audience. *Try and Stop Me* (B. Cerf)

12 He's a kind of musical Malcolm Sargent.

Sir Thomas Beecham (1879–1961) British conductor. Comparing the British conductor Sargent to the Austrian conductor Herbert von Karajan. *Beecham Stories* (H. Atkins and A. Newman)

13 I have known many an instance of a man writing a letter and forgetting to sign his name, but this is the only instance I have ever known of a man signing his name and forgetting to write the letter.

Henry Ward Beecher (1813–87) US Congregational minister. Said on receiving a note containing the single word: 'Fool'. *The Best Stories in the World* (T. Masson)

14 Of course we all know that Morris was a wonderful all-round man, but the act of walking round him has always tired me.

Max Beerbohm (1872–1956) British writer. Referring to William Morris, the poet, designer, craftsman, and socialist writer. *Conversations with Max* (S. N. Behrman)

15 I really enjoy only his stage directions; the dialogue is vortical, and, I find, fatiguing. It is like being harangued…He uses the English language like a truncheon.

Max Beerbohm *Conversation with Max* (S. N. Behrens)

16 Come in, you Anglo-Saxon swine
And drink of my Algerian wine.
'Twill turn your eyeballs black and blue,
And damn well good enough for you.

Brendan Behan (1923–64) Irish dramatist. Painted as an advert on the window of a Paris café (the owner of which could not speak English). *My Life with Brendan* (B. Behan)

17 So boring you fall asleep halfway through her name.

Alan Bennett (1934–) British dramatist. Referring to the Greek writer Arianna Stassinopoulos. *The Observer*, 18 Sept 1983

18 Listening to a speech by Chamberlain is like paying a visit to Woolworths; everything in its place and nothing over sixpence.

Aneurin Bevan (1897–1960) Welsh Labour politician. Referring to the Conservative statesman. In *Tribune*

19 He is a man suffering from petrified adolescence.

Aneurin Bevan Referring to the Conservative statesman, Winston Churchill. *Aneurin Bevan* (Vincent Brome), Ch. 11

20 I mock thee not, though I by thee am mockèd;
Thou call'st me madman, but I call thee blockhead.

William Blake (1757–1827) British poet. *To Flaxman*

21 If there is anyone here whom I have not insulted, I beg his pardon.

Johannes Brahms (1833–97) German composer. Said on leaving a gathering of friends. *Brahms* (P. Latham)

22 Listen, dear, you couldn't write fuck on a dusty venetian blind.

Coral Brown (1913–91) Australian-born actress. To a Hollywood writer who had criticized the writer Alan Bennett. Attrib.

23 Who's your fat friend?

'Beau' Brummell (George Bryan Brummell; 1778–1840) British dandy. Referring to George, Prince of Wales. *Reminiscences* (Gronow)

24 If ever he went to school without any boots it was because he was too big for them.

Ivor Bulmer-Thomas (1905–) British writer and politician. Referring to the Labour politician, Harold Wilson. Remark, Conservative Party Conference, 1949

25 A lady of a 'certain age', which means
Certainly aged.

Lord Byron (1788–1824) British poet. *Don Juan*, VI

26 You dirty double-crossing rat!

James Cagney (1899–1986) US actor. Usually misquoted by impressionists as 'You dirty rat'. *Blonde Crazy*

27 That's not writing, that's typing.

Truman Capote (1924–84) US writer. Referring to the writer Jack Kerouac. Attrib.

28 Macaulay is well for a while, but one wouldn't *live* under Niagara.

Thomas Carlyle (1795–1881) Scottish historian and essayist. Referring to the English historian. *Notebook* (R. M. Milnes)

29 Respectable Professors of the Dismal Science.

Thomas Carlyle Referring to economists. *Latter-Day Pamphlets*, 1

30 There goes a woman who knows all the things that can be taught and none of the things that cannot be taught.

Coco Chanel (1883–1971) French dress designer. *Coco Chanel, Her Life, Her Secrets* (Marcel Haedrich)

31 An injury is much sooner forgotten than an insult.

Earl of Chesterfield (1694–1773) English statesman. Letter to his son, 9 Oct 1746

32 If you were my wife, I'd drink it.

Winston Churchill (1874–1965) British statesman. Replying to Lady Astor who had said, 'If you were my husband, I'd put poison in your coffee.' *Nancy Astor and Her Friends* (E. Langhorne)

33 He is like a female llama surprised in her bath.

Winston Churchill Referring to the French general and statesman Charles de Gaulle. Attrib.

34 And you, madam, are ugly. But I shall be sober in the morning.

Winston Churchill Replying to Bessie Braddock MP who told him he was drunk. Attrib.

35 The only time in his life he ever put up a fight was when we asked him for his resignation.

Georges Clemenceau (1841–1929) French statesman. Referring to Marshal Joffre. *Here I Lie* (A.M. Thomson)

36 America is the only nation in history which miraculously has gone directly from barbarism to degeneration without the usual interval of civilization.

Georges Clemenceau Attrib.

37 The Cat, the Rat, and Lovell our dog
Rule all England under a hog.

William Collingbourne (d. 1484) English landowner. The cat was Sir William Catesby; the rat Sir Richard Ratcliffe; the dog Lord Lovell, who had a dog on his crest. The wild boar refers to the emblem of Richard III. *Chronicles* (R. Holinshed), III

38 Pushing forty? She's clinging on to it for dear life.

Ivy Compton-Burnett (1884–1969) British novelist. Attrib.

39 If you weren't the best light comedian in the country, all you'd be fit for would be the selling of cars in Great Portland Street.

Noël Coward (1899–1973) British dramatist. To Rex Harrison. Attrib.

40 How strange, when I saw you acting in *The Glorious Adventure* I laughed all the time.

Noël Coward To Lady Diana Cooper who said she had not laughed once at his comedy *The Young Idea*. *The Noël Coward Diaries*

41 Not even a public figure. A man of no experience. And of the utmost insignificance.

Lord Curzon (1859–1925) British politician. Referring to Stanley Baldwin on his appointment as prime minister. *Curzon: The Last Phase* (Harold Nicolson)

42 I see – she's the original good time that was had by all.

Bette Davis (Ruth Elizabeth Davis; 1908–89) US film star. Referring to a starlet of the time. *The Filmgoer's Book of Quotes* (Leslie Halliwell)

43 Your dexterity seems a happy compound of the smartness of an attorney's clerk and the intrigue of a Greek of the lower empire.

Benjamin Disraeli (1804–81) British statesman. Speaking to his fellow statesman, Lord Palmerston. Attrib.

44 I know he is, and he adores his maker.

Benjamin Disraeli Replying to a remark made in defence of John Bright that he was a self-made man; often also attrib. to Bright referring to Disraeli. *The Fine Art of Political Wit* (L. Harris)

45 He was like a cock who thought the sun had risen to hear him crow.

George Eliot (Mary Ann Evans; 1819–80) British novelist. *Adam Bede*

46 Good-morning, gentlemen both.

Elizabeth I (1533–1603) Queen of England. When addressing a group of eighteen tailors. *Sayings of Queen Elizabeth* (Chamberlin)

47 The nicest old lady I ever met.

William Faulkner (1897–1962) US novelist. Referring to the writer, Henry James. *The Battle and the Books* (E. Stone)

48 He has never been known to use a word that might send the reader to the dictionary.

William Faulkner Referring to Ernest Hemingway. Attrib.

49 A semi-house-trained polecat.

Michael Foot (1913–) British Labour politician and journalist. Referring to the Conservative politician, Norman Tebbitt. Speech, House of Commons

50 He is not only dull in himself, but the cause of dullness in others.

Samuel Foote (1720–77) British actor and dramatist. Parody of a line from Shakespeare's *Henry IV, Part Two*. *Life of Johnson* (J. Boswell)

51 He looks like the guy in a science fiction movie who is the first to see the Creature.

David Frye (1934–) US impressionist and comedian. Referring to Gerald Ford, US president (1974–77). Attrib.

52 Harris, I am not well; pray get me a glass of brandy.

George IV (1762–1830) King of the United Kingdom. On seeing Caroline of Brunswick, whom he was to marry, for the first time. *Diaries* (Earl of Malmesbury)

53 She may very well pass for forty-three
In the dusk, with a light behind her!

W. S. Gilbert (1836–1911) British dramatist. *Trial by Jury*

54 Philip is a living example of natural selection. He was as fitted to survive in this modern world as a tapeworm in an intestine.

William Golding (1911–93) British novelist. *Free Fall*, Ch. 2

55 The reason so many people showed up at his funeral was because they wanted to make sure he was dead.

Samuel Goldwyn (1882–1974) Polish-American film producer. Referring to fellow film producer Louis B. Mayer, often attributed to others. *Hollywood Rajah* (B. Crowther)

56 I met the great little man, the man who can be silent in several languages.

James Guthrie Harbord (1866–1947) US general. Referring to Colonel House. *Mr Wilson's War* (John Dos Passos), Ch. 3

57 If, sir, I possessed the power of conveying unlimited sexual attraction through the potency of my voice, I would not be reduced to accepting a miserable pittance from the BBC for interviewing a faded female in a damp basement.

Gilbert Harding (1907–60) British broadcaster. Said to Mae West's manager, who suggested that he should be more 'sexy' when interviewing her. *Gilbert Harding by His Friends*

58 Like being savaged by a dead sheep.

Denis Healey (1917–) British Labour politician. Referring to the attack launched by the Conservative politician Geoffrey Howe upon his Budget proposals. *The Listener*, 21 Dec 1978

59 She approaches the problems of our country with all the one-dimensional subtlety of a comic strip.

Denis Healey Referring to the prime minister Margaret Thatcher. Speech, House of Commons, 22 May 1979

60 Silly Billy!

Denis Healey Catchphrase invented for him by the impressionist, Mike Yarwood, and then sometimes used by him

61 If the Almighty himself played the violin, the credits would still read 'Rubinstein, God, and Piatigorsky', in that order.

Jascha Heifetz (1901–87) Russian-born US violinist. Whenever Heifetz played in trios with Arthur Rubinstein (piano) and Gregor Piatigorsky (cello), Rubinstein always got top billing. *Los Angeles Times*, 29 Aug 1982

62 You have sent me a Flanders mare.

Henry VIII (1491–1547) King of England. Said on meeting his fourth wife, Anne of Cleves, for the first time. Attrib.

63 Do you call that thing under your hat a head?

Ludwig Holberg (1684–1754) Danish dramatist. Reply to the jibe, 'Do you call that thing on your head a hat?' *Anekdotenschatz* (H. Hoffmeister)

64 I wish you would read a little poetry sometimes. Your ignorance cramps my conversation.

Anthony Hope (Sir Anthony Hope Hawkins; 1863–1933) British novelist. *The Dolly Dialogues*

65 In a disastrous fire in President Reagan's library both books were destroyed. And the real tragedy is that he hadn't finished colouring one.

Jonathan Hunt (1938–) New Zealand politician. *The Observer*, 30 Aug 1981

66 You sought the last resort of feeble minds with classical educations. You became a schoolmaster.

Aldous Huxley (1894–1964) British novelist and essayist. *Antic Hay*

67 The trouble with Senator Long is that he is suffering from halitosis of the intellect. That's presuming Emperor Long has an intellect.

Harold L. Ickes (1874–1952) US Republican politician. *The Politics of Upheaval* (A. M. Schlesinger Jnr), Pt. II, Ch. 14

68 Many people have delusions of grandeur but you're deluded by triviality.

Eugène Ionesco (1912–94) French dramatist. *Exit the King*

69 Sir, you are like a pin, but without either its head or its point.

Douglas William Jerrold (1803–57) British dramatist. Speaking to a small thin man who was boring him. Attrib.

70 Jerry Ford is so dumb that he can't fart and chew gum at the same time.

Lyndon B. Johnson (1908–73) US statesman. Sometimes quoted as '...can't walk and chew gum'. Referring to Gerald Ford, US president (1974–77). *A Ford, Not a Lincoln* (R. Reeves), Ch. 1

71 A very unclubable man.

Samuel Johnson (1709–84) British lexicographer. Referring to the British naval commander, Sir John Hawkins. *Life of Johnson* (J. Boswell), Vol. I

72 I do not care to speak ill of any man behind his back, but I believe the gentleman is an *attorney*.

Samuel Johnson *Life of Johnson* (J. Boswell), Vol. II

73 Sir, your wife, under pretence of keeping a bawdy-house, is a receiver of stolen goods.

Samuel Johnson An example of the customary badinage between travellers on the Thames. *Life of Johnson* (J. Boswell), Vol. IV

74 Sir, there is no settling the point of precedency between a louse and a flea.

Samuel Johnson When Maurice Morgann asked him who he considered to be the better poet – Smart or Derrick. *Life of Johnson* (J. Boswell), Vol. IV

75 No, Sir; there were people who died of dropsies, which they contracted in trying to get drunk.

Samuel Johnson Scornfully criticizing the strength of the wine in Scotland before the Act of Union in response to Boswell's claim that there had been a lot of drunkenness. *Tour to the Hebrides* (J. Boswell)

76 Come, let me know what it is that makes a Scotchman happy!

Samuel Johnson Ordering for himself a glass of whisky. *Tour to the Hebrides* (J. Boswell)

77 Calumnies are answered best with silence.

Ben Jonson (1573–1637) English dramatist. *Volpone*, II:2

78 They travel best in gangs, hanging around like clumps of bananas, thick skinned and yellow.

Neil Kinnock (1942–) British politician. Referring to Tory critics. *The Observer*, 'Sayings of the Week', 22 Feb 1987

79 She only went to Venice because somebody told her she could walk down the middle of the street.

Neil Kinnock Referring to Conservative prime minister, Margaret Thatcher, who attended a meeting in Venice just before the 1987 election. Speech, Leeds, 9 June 1987

80 She looked as though butter wouldn't melt in her mouth – or anywhere else.

Elsa Lanchester (1902–86) British-born US actress. Referring to the actress, Maureen O'Hara. Attrib.

81 Oh, well, you play Bach *your* way. I'll play him *his*.

Wanda Landowska (1877–1959) Hungarian harpsichordist. Remark to fellow musician. Attrib.

82 He looked at me as if I was a side dish he hadn't ordered.

Ring Lardner Jnr (1885–1933) American humorist. Referring to W. H. Taft, US president (1909–13). *The Home Book of Humorous Quotations* (A. K. Adams)

83 Play us a medley of your hit.

Oscar Levant (1906–72) US pianist and actor. Replying to the composer George Gershwin's barb, 'If you had it all over again, would you fall in love with yourself?' Attrib.

84 I'm sure he had a fork in the other.

Ada Beddington Leverson (1862–1933) British writer. Reply when told by Oscar Wilde of a devoted *apache* (Parisian gangster) who used to follow him with a knife in one hand. Attrib.

85 A Catholic layman who has never been averse to giving advice to the Pope, or indeed anybody else who he thought might be in need of it.

Bernard Levin (1928–) British journalist. Referring to the Conservative politician, Norman St John Stevas. *The Pendulum Years*

86 She's the sort of woman who lives for others – you can always tell the others by their hunted expression.

C. S. Lewis (1898–1963) British academic and writer. *The Screwtape Letters*

87 When they circumcised Herbert Samuel they threw away the wrong bit.

David Lloyd George (1863–1945) British Liberal statesman.

Referring to his fellow Liberal politician. Attrib. in *The Listener*, 7 Sept 1978

88 Like a cushion, he always bore the impress of the last man who sat on him.

David Lloyd George Referring to Lord Derby. Attrib. in *The Listener*, 7 Sep 1978. This remark is also credited to Earl Haig

89 The Right Hon. gentleman has sat so long on the fence that the iron has entered his soul.

David Lloyd George Referring to Sir John Simon. Attrib.

90 Dewey looks like the bridegroom on the wedding cake.

Alice Roosevelt Longworth (1884–1980) US hostess. Referring to Thomas E. Dewey. *The New York Times*, 25 Feb 1980

91 He looks as if he had been weaned on a pickle.

Alice Roosevelt Longworth Referring to John Calvin Coolidge, US president (1923–29). *Crowded Hours*

92 The answer is in the plural and they bounce.

Edwin Lutyens (1869–1944) British architect. Attrib.

93 There, but for the Grace of God, goes God.

Herman J. Mankiewicz (1897–1953) US journalist and screenwriter. Said of the actor and director Orson Welles in the making of *Citizen Kane*. Also attributed to others. *The Citizen Kane Book*

94 From the moment I picked up your book until I laid it down, I was convulsed with laughter. Some day I intend reading it.

Groucho Marx (Julius Marx; 1895–1977) US comedian. *The Last Laugh* (S. J. Perelman)

95 Go, and never darken my towels again!

Groucho Marx *Duck Soup*

96 I have forgotten more law than you ever knew, but allow me to say, I have not forgotten much.

John Maynard (1602–90) English judge. Replying to Judge Jeffreys' suggestion that he was so old he had forgotten the law.

97 And I don't feel the attraction of the Kennedys at all...I don't think they are Christians; they may be Catholics but they are not Christians, in my belief anyway.

Mary McCarthy (1912–89) US novelist. *The Observer*, 14 Oct 1979

98 You are the pits.

John McEnroe (1959–) US tennis player. To an umpire at Wimbledon, 1981. *The Sunday Times*, 24 June 1984

99 I think I'm thoroughly in favour of Mrs. Thatcher's visit to the Falklands. I find a bit of hesitation, though, about her coming back.

John Mortimer (1923–) British lawyer and dramatist. *Any Questions?* (BBC radio program)

100 He is not only a bore but he bores for England.

Malcolm Muggeridge (1903–90) British writer. Referring to the Conservative statesman, Sir Anthony Eden. In *Newstatesmanship* (E. Hyams), 'Boring for England'

101 Peel's smile: like the silver plate on a coffin.

Daniel O'Connell (1775–1847) Irish politician. Referring to Sir Robert Peel; the Conservative statesman who founded the Metropolitan Police; quoting J. P. Curran (1750–1817). *Hansard*, 26 Feb 1835

102 Pearls before swine.

Dorothy Parker (1893–1967) US writer. Clare Booth Luce, the dramatist and politician, going through a door with her, said, 'Age before beauty'. *You Might As Well Live* (J. Keats)

103 You know, she speaks eighteen languages. And she can't say 'No' in any of them.

Dorothy Parker Speaking of an acquaintance. Attrib.

104 Where does she find them?

Dorothy Parker In reply to a remark, 'Anyway, she's always very nice to her inferiors'. *Lyttelton Hart-Davis Letters*

105 It is with narrow-souled people as with narrow-necked bottles: the less they have in them, the more noise they make in pouring it out.

Alexander Pope (1688–1744) British poet. *Thoughts on Various Subjects*

106 Dinner at the Huntercombes' possessed 'only two dramatic features – the wine was a farce and the food a tragedy'.

Anthony Powell (1905–) British novelist. *A Dance to the Music of Time: The Acceptance World*, Ch. 4

107 I remember coming across him at the Grand Canyon and finding him peevish, refusing to admire it or even look at it properly. He was jealous of it.

J. B. Priestley (1894–1984) British novelist. Referring to the Irish dramatist, George Bernard Shaw. *Thoughts In the Wilderness*

108 My god, they've shot the wrong person!

James Pryde (1866–1941) British artist. At the unveiling of a statue to Nurse Edith Cavell, who was shot by Germans in World War I for helping Allied prisoners to escape. Attrib.

109 Not a gentleman; dresses too well.

Bertrand Russell (1872–1970) British philosopher. Referring to the Conservative statesman, Sir Anthony Eden. *Six Men* (A. Cooke)

110 He had a smile like a razor-blade.

Anthony Sampson (1926–) British writer and journalist. *The Changing Anatomy of Britain*

111 Thou whoreson zed! thou unnecessary letter!

William Shakespeare (1564–1616) English dramatist. *King Lear*, II:2

112 You are not worth the dust which the rude wind
Blows in your face.

William Shakespeare *King Lear*, IV:2

113 I enjoyed talking to her, but thought *nothing* of her writing. I considered her 'a beautiful little knitter'.

Edith Sitwell (1887–1964) British poet and writer. Referring to Virginia Woolf. Letter to G. Singleton

114 I do not want Miss Mannin's feelings to be hurt by the fact that I have never heard of her...At the moment I am debarred from the pleasure of putting her in her place by the fact that she has not got one.

Edith Sitwell Referring to the novelist Ethel Mannin. *Façades* (J. Pearson)

115 It proves what they say, give the public what they want to see and they'll come out for it.

Red Skelton (Richard Bernard Skelton; 1913–) US actor and comedian. Said while attending the funeral in 1958 of Hollywood producer Harry Cohn. It has also been attributed to Samuel Goldwyn while attending Louis B. Mayer's funeral in 1957.

116 He has occasional flashes of silence, that make his conversation perfectly delightful.

Sydney Smith (1771–1845) British clergyman and essayist. Referring to the historian, Lord Macaulay. *Memoir* (Lady Holland)

117 You silly moo.

Johnny Speight (1920–) British television scriptwriter. *Till Death Do Us Part*

118 Okie use' to mean you was from Oklahoma. Now it means you're scum. Don't mean nothing itself, it's the way they say it.

John Steinbeck (1902–68) US novelist. *The Grapes of Wrath*, Ch. 18

119 I cannot but conclude the bulk of your natives to be the most pernicious race of little odious vermin that nature ever suffered to crawl upon the surface of the earth.

Jonathan Swift (1667–1745) Irish-born Anglican priest and writer. *Gulliver's Travels*, 'Voyage to Brobdingnag', Ch. 6

120 There is a certain class of clergyman whose mendicity is only equalled by their mendacity.

Frederick Temple (1821–1902) British churchman. Remark at a meeting of the Ecclesiastical Commissioners. *Years of Endeavour* (Sir George Leveson Gower)

121 I dunno. Maybe it's that tally-ho lads attitude. You know, there'll always be an England, all that Empire crap they dish out. But I never could cop Poms.

Jeff Thomson Australian cricketer. Remark, Oct 1987

122 It's too late to apologize.

Arturo Toscanini (1867–1957) Italian conductor. Retort to the insult 'Nuts to you!' shouted at him by a player he had just ordered from the stage during rehearsal. *The Humor of Music* (L. Humphrey)

123 He is an old bore; even the grave yawns for him.

Herbert Beerbohm Tree (1853–1917) British actor and theatre manager. Referring to Israel Zangwill. *Beerbohm Tree* (Hesketh Pearson)

124 Forty years ago he was Slightly in Peter Pan, and you might say that he has been wholly in Peter Pan ever since.

Kenneth Tynan (1927–80) British critic. Referring to the actor and dramatist, Noël Coward. *Curtains*

125 A diplomat these days is nothing but a head-waiter who's allowed to sit down occasionally.

Peter Ustinov (1921–) British actor and dramatist. *Romanoff and Juliet*, I

126 A triumph of the embalmer's art.

Gore Vidal (1925–) US novelist. Referring to Ronald Reagan, US president (1981–89) *The Observer*, 26 Apr 1981

127 A typical triumph of modern science to find the only part of Randolph that was not malignant and remove it.

Evelyn Waugh (1903–66) British novelist. Remarking upon the news that the Conservative politician Randolph Churchill had had a noncancerous lung removed. Attrib.

128 Simply a radio personality who outlived his prime.

Evelyn Waugh Referring to the Conservative statesman Winston Churchill. *Evelyn Waugh* (Christopher Sykes)

129 You're a fine woman, Lou. One of the finest women that ever walked the streets.

Mae West (1892–1980). US actress. *She Done Him Wrong*, film 1933

130 Every other inch a gentleman.

Rebecca West (1892–1983) British writer. Attrib.

131 Perhaps not, but then you can't call yourself a great work of nature.

James Whistler (1834–1903) US painter. Responding to a sitter's complaint that his portrait was not a great work of art. *Whistler Stories* (D. Seitz)

132 I do not mind the Liberals, still less do I mind the Country Party, calling me a bastard. In some circumstances I am only doing my job if they do. But I hope you will not publicly call me a bastard, as some bastards in the Caucus have.

Gough Whitlam (1916–) Australian statesman. Speech to the Australian Labor Party, 9 June 1974

133 Dear Frank, we believe you; you have dined in every house in London – *once*.

Oscar Wilde (1854–1900) Irish-born British dramatist. Interrupting Frank Harris's interminable account of the houses he had dined at. Attrib.

134 You have Van Gogh's ear for music.

Billy Wilder (Samuel Wilder; 1906–) Austrian-born US film director. Said to Cliff Osmond. Referring to the fact that Van Gogh had cut off his ear. Attrib.

135 I have always said about Tony that he immatures with age.

Harold Wilson (1916–) British politician and prime minister. Referring to the Labour politician, Anthony Wedgwood Benn. *The Chariot of Israel*

136 She missed the last Lobby briefing, I hear. At the vet's with hard pad, no doubt.

Harold Wilson Referring to a woman journalist he disliked. Attrib.

137 If I had had to choose between him and a cockroach as a companion for a walking-tour, the cockroach would have had it by a short head.

P. G. Wodehouse (1881–1975) British humorous novelist. *My Man Jeeves*, 'The Spot of Art'

138 There is absolutely nothing wrong with Oscar Levant that a miracle cannot fix.

Alexander Woollcott (1887–1943) US writer and critic. *The Vicious Circle* (M. C. Harriman)

139 Then the little man wears a shocking bad hat.

Duke of York and Albany (1763–1827) The second son of George III. Referring to the writer, Horace Walpole. Attrib.

INTEGRITY

See also honesty, morality, principles, righteousness, self, sincerity

1 Be so true to thyself, as thou be not false to others.

Francis Bacon (1561–1626) English philosopher. *Essays*, 'Of Wisdom for a Man's Self'

2 Caesar's wife must be above suspicion.

Julius Caesar (100–44 BC) Roman general and statesman. Said in justification of his divorce from Pompeia, after she was unwittingly involved in a scandal. *Lives*, 'Julius Caesar' (Plutarch)

3 I cannot and will not cut my conscience to fit this year's fashions, even though I long ago came to the conclusion that I was not a political person and could have no comfortable place in any political group.

Lillian Hellman (1905–84) US dramatist. Letter to the US House of Representatives Committee on Un-American Activities, *The Nation*, 31 May 1952

4 Integrity without knowledge is weak and useless, and knowledge without integrity is dangerous and dreadful.

Samuel Johnson (1709–84) British lexicographer. *Rasselas*, Ch. 41

5 It is necessary to the happiness of man that he be mentally faithful to himself. Infidelity does not consist in believing, or in disbelieving, it consists in professing to believe what one does not believe.

Thomas Paine (1737–1809) British writer. *The Age of Reason*, Pt. I

6 Neither a borrower nor a lender be;
For loan oft loses both itself and friend,
And borrowing dulls the edge of husbandry.
This above all: to thine own self be true,
And it must follow, as the night the day,
Thou canst not then be false to any man.

William Shakespeare (1564–1616) English dramatist. *Hamlet*, I:3

7 My strength is as the strength of ten,
Because my heart is pure.

Alfred, Lord Tennyson (1809–92) British poet. *Sir Galahad*

INTELLECT

See also intelligence, mind, thinking

1 Hercule Poirot tapped his forehead. 'These little grey cells, It is 'up to them' – as you say over here.'

Agatha Christie (1890–1976) British detective-story writer. *The Mysterious Affair at Styles*

2 It is generally admitted that with woman the powers of intuition, of rapid perception, and perhaps of imitation, are more strongly marked than in man; but some, at least, of these faculties are characteristic of the lower races, and therefore of a past and lower state of civilisation.

Charles Darwin (1809–82) British life scientist. *The Descent of Man*

3 The chief distinction in the intellectual powers of the two sexes is shewn by man attaining to a higher eminence, in whatever he takes up, than woman can attain – whether requiring deep thought, reason, or imagination, or merely the use of the senses and hands.

Charles Darwin *The Descent of Man*

4 We should take care not to make the intellect our god; it has, of course, powerful muscles, but no personality.

Albert Einstein (1879–1955) German-born US physicist. *Out of My Later Life*, 51

5 The voice of the intellect is a soft one, but it does not rest till it has gained a hearing.

Sigmund Freud (1856–1939) Austrian psychoanalyst. *The Future of an Illusion*

6 Another great Advantage of Deformity is, that it tends to the Improvement of the Mind. A man, that cannot shine in his Person, will have recourse to his Understanding: and attempt to adorn that Part of him, which alone is capable of ornament.

William Hay (1695–1755) *Essay on Deformity*

7 Man is an intellectual animal, and therefore an everlasting contradiction to himself. His senses centre in himself, his ideas reach to the ends of the universe; so that he is torn in pieces between the two, without a possibility of its ever being otherwise.

William Hazlitt (1778–1830) British essayist. *Characteristics*

8 We are thinking beings, and we cannot exclude the intellect from participating in any of our functions.

William James (1842–1910) US psychologist and philosopher. *Varieties of Religious Experience*

9 The highest intellects, like the tops of mountains, are the first to catch and to reflect the dawn.

Lord Macaulay (1800–59) British historian. *Historical Essays Contributed to the 'Edinburgh Review'*, 'Sir James Mackintosh'

10 I had no reason to doubt that brains were suitable for a woman. And as I had my father's kind of mind – which was also his mother's – I learned that the mind is not sex-typed.

Margaret Mead (1901–78) US anthropologist, writer, editor, and museum curator. *Blackberry Winter*

11 The higher the voice the smaller the intellect.

Ernest Newman (1868–1959) British music critic. Attrib.

12 Intellect is invisible to the man who has none.

Arthur Schopenhauer (1788–1860) German philosopher. *Aphorismen zur Lebensweisheit*

INTELLECTUALS

See also academics

1 An intellectual is a man who doesn't know how to park a bike.

Spiro Agnew (1918–) US politician. *See also* WALLACE. Attrib.

2 To the man-in-the-street, who, I'm sorry to say
Is a keen observer of life,
The word Intellectual suggests straight away
A man who's untrue to his wife.

W. H. Auden (1907–73) British poet. *Note on Intellectuals*

3 I've been called many things, but never an intellectual.

Tallulah Bankhead (1903–68) US actress. *Tallulah*, Ch. 15

4 The intellectuals' chief cause of anguish are one another's works.

Jacques Barzun (1907–) US writer. *The House of Intellect*

5 *La trahison des clercs.*
The intellectuals' betrayal.

Julien Benda (1868–1956) French philosopher. Book title

6 Intellectuals are people who believe that ideas are of more importance than values. That is to say, their own ideas and other people's values.

Gerald Brenan (Edward Fitzgerald Brenan; 1894–1987) British writer. *Thoughts in a Dry Season*, 'Life'

7 An intellectual is someone whose mind watches itself.

Albert Camus (1913–60) French existentialist writer. *Notebooks*, 1935–42

8 I muse how men of wit can so hardly use that gift they hold.

Elizabeth I (1533–1603) Queen of England. Speech to a delegation from parliament, 5 Nov 1566

9 There is, however, a pathological condition which occurs so often, in such extreme forms, and in men of such pre-eminent intellectual ability, that it is impossible not to regard it as having a real association with such ability. I refer to gout.

Havelock Ellis (1859–1939) British psychologist. *A Study of British Genius*, Ch. 8

10 Beware of the artist who's an intellectual also. The artist who doesn't fit.

F. Scott Fitzgerald (1896–1940) US novelist. *This Side of Paradise*, Bk. II, Ch. 5

11 You will hear more good things on the outside of a stagecoach from London to Oxford than if you were to pass a twelvemonth with the undergraduates, or heads of colleges, of that famous university.

William Hazlitt (1778–1830) British essayist. *The Ignorance of the Learned*

12 I too had thoughts once of being an intellectual, but I found it too difficult.

Albert Schweitzer (1875–1965) French Protestant theologian, philosopher, and physician. Remark made to an African who refused to perform a menial task on the grounds that he was an intellectual. Attrib.

13 The trouble with me is, I belong to a vanishing race. I'm one of the intellectuals.

Robert E. Sherwood (1896–1955) US writer and dramatist. *The Petrified Forest*

14 Do you think it pleases a man when he looks into a woman's eyes and sees a reflection of the British Museum Reading Room?

Muriel Spark (1918–) British novelist. *The Wit of Women* (L. and M. Cowan)

15 What is a highbrow? It is a man who has found something more interesting than women.

Edgar Wallace (1875–1932) British thriller writer. Interview

16 Pointy-headed intellectuals who can't park their bicycles straight.

George Wallace (1919–) US politician. *See also* AGNEW. Attrib., often repeated

INTELLIGENCE

See also intellect, knowledge, mind, perception, thinking, understanding, wisdom

1 He's very clever, but sometimes his brains go to his head.

Margot Asquith (1865–1945) The second wife of the British statesman, Herbert Asquith. Referring to F. E. Smith. *As I Remember*

2 He has a brilliant mind until he makes it up.

Margot Asquith Referring to the Labour statesman, Sir Stafford Cripps. *The Wit of the Asquiths*

3 The intelligent are to the intelligentsia what a man is to a gent.

Stanley Baldwin (1867–1947) British statesman. Attrib.

4 I never heard tell of any clever man that came of entirely stupid people.

Thomas Carlyle (1795–1881) Scottish historian and essayist. Speech, Edinburgh, 2 Apr 1886

5 One wants to mutter deeply that apart from having two good legs I also have two good degrees and it is just possible that I do know what I'm talking about.

Edwina Currie (1946–) British politician. Remark, Nov 1986

6 Common sense is in medicine the master workman.

Peter Mere Latham (1789–1875) US poet and essayist. *General Remarks on the Practice of Medicine*, Ch. 5

7 NORA. But if God had wanted us to think with our womb, why did He give us a brain?

Clare Boothe Luce (1903–) US politician and writer. *Slam the Door Softly*

8 No one ever went broke underestimating the intelligence of the American people.

H. L. Mencken (1880–1956) US journalist. Attrib.

9 A really intelligent man feels what other men only know.

Baron de Montesquieu (1689–1755) French writer. *Essai sur les causes qui peuvent affecter les esprits et les caractères*

10 The more intelligence one has the more people one finds original. Commonplace people see no difference between men.

Blaise Pascal (1623–62) French philosopher and mathematician. *Pensées*, I

11 The height of cleverness is to be able to conceal it.

Duc de la Rochefoucauld (1613–80) French writer. *Maximes*, 245

12 A short neck denotes a good mind... You see, the messages go quicker to the brain because they've shorter to go.

Muriel Spark (1918–) British novelist. *The Ballad of Peckham Rye*, Ch. 7

13 Intelligence is quickness to apprehend as distinct from ability, which is capacity to act wisely on the thing apprehended.

A. N. Whitehead (1861–1947) British philosopher. *Dialogues*, 135

14 All the unhappy marriages come from the husbands having brains. What good are brains to a man? They only unsettle him.

P. G. Wodehouse (1881–1975) British humorous novelist. *The Adventures of Sally*

INTERRUPTIONS

1 On awaking he...instantly and eagerly wrote down the lines that are here preserved. At this moment he was unfortunately called out by a person on business from Porlock.

Samuel Taylor Coleridge (1772–1834) British poet. *Kubla Khan* (preliminary note)

INTRIGUE

1 Ay, now the plot thickens very much upon us.

Duke of Buckingham (1628–87) English politician. *The Rehearsal*, III:1

2 Everybody was up to something, especially, of course, those who were up to nothing.

Noël Coward (1899–1973) British dramatist. *Future Indefinite*

INTRODUCTIONS

1 'You look a little shy; let me introduce you to that leg of mutton,' said the Red Queen. 'Alice – Mutton; Mutton – Alice.'

Lewis Carroll (Charles Lutwidge Dodgson; 1832–98) British writer. *Through the Looking-Glass*, Ch. 9

INVITATIONS

See also summons

1 Anyone for tennis?

Anonymous

2 Come with me to the Casbah.

Charles Boyer (1899–1978) US film actor. Often quoted, but not actually in the film. *Algiers*

3 'Will you walk into my parlour?' said a spider to a fly:
''Tis the prettiest little parlour that ever you did spy.'

Mary Howitt (1799–1888) British writer. *The Spider and the Fly*

4 If you haven't anything nice to say about anyone, come and sit by me.

Alice Roosevelt Longworth (1884–1980) US hostess. Embroidered on a cushion at her home. *New York Times*, 25 Feb 1980

5 Come into the garden, Maud,
For the black bat, night, has flown,
Come into the garden, Maud,
I am here at the gate alone.

Alfred, Lord Tennyson (1809–92) British poet. *Maud*, I

6 I always did like a man in uniform. And that one fits you grand. Why don't you come up sometime and see me?

Mae West (1892–1980) US actress. Often misquoted as 'Come up and see me some time'. *She Done Him Wrong*, film 1933

IRELAND

See also Britain, Irish

1 I met wid Napper Tandy, and he took me by the hand,
And he said, 'How's poor ould Ireland, and how does she stand?'
She's the most disthressful country that iver yet was seen,
For they're hangin' men an' women there for the wearin' o' the Green.

Anonymous 'The Wearin' o' the Green'

2 In Dublin's fair city, where the girls are so pretty,
I first set my eyes on sweet Molly Malone,
As she wheeled her wheelbarrow, through streets broad and narrow,
Crying, Cockles and mussels! alive, alive, O!

She was a fishmonger, but sure 'twas no wonder,
For so were her father and mother before.

Anonymous '*Cockles and Mussels*'

3 Our day will come.
Tiocfaidh Ar La

Anonymous Slogan of the IRA

4 We are all Home Rulers today.

Anonymous *The Times*, 26 Mar 1919

5 A bit of shooting takes your mind off your troubles – it makes you forget the cost of living.

Brendan Behan (1923–64) Irish playwright. *The Hostage*

6 Ulster will fight; Ulster will be right.

Lord Randolph Churchill (1849–95) British Conservative politician. Letter, 7 May 1886

7 By yesterday morning British troops were patrolling the streets of Belfast. I fear that once Catholics and Protestants get used to our presence they will hate us more than they hate each other.

Richard Crossman (1907–74) British politician. *Diaries*, 17 Aug 1969

8 Thus you have a starving population, an absentee aristocracy, and an alien Church, and in addition the weakest executive in the world. That is the Irish Question.

Benjamin Disraeli (1804–81) British statesman. Speech, House of Commons, 16 Feb 1844

9 I never met anyone in Ireland who understood the Irish question, except one Englishman who had only been there a week.

Keith Fraser (1867–1935) British politician. Speech, House of Commons, May 1919

10 It seems that the historic inability in Britain to comprehend Irish feelings and sensitivities still remains.

Charles Haughey (1925–) Irish statesman. Speech, Feb 1988

11 Worth seeing? yes; but not worth going to see.

Samuel Johnson (1709–84) British lexicographer. Referring to the Giant's Causeway. *Life of Johnson* (J. Boswell), Vol. III

12 Ireland is the old sow that eats her farrow.

James Joyce (1882–1941) Irish novelist. *A Portrait of the Artist as a Young Man*, Ch. 5

13 It is a symbol of Irish art. The cracked looking glass of a servant.

James Joyce *Ulysses*

14 The problem with Ireland is that it's a country full of genius, but with absolutely no talent.

Hugh Leonard (1926–) Irish dramatist. Said during an interview. *The Times*, Aug 1977

15 There is one fundamental point and that is that Northern Ireland's status as part of the UK will not change without the freely expressed consent of the people of Northern Ireland.

John Major (1943–) British statesman. Referring to the Anglo-Irish peace initiative. Speech, House of Commons, 3 Dec 1993

16 We cannot go on spilling blood in the name of the past. There is no excuse, no justification and no future for the use of violence in Northern Ireland.

John Major Referring to the Anglo-Irish peace initiative. Press conference, 15 Dec 1993

17 The harp that once through Tara's halls
The soul of music shed,
Now hangs as mute on Tara's walls
As if that soul were fled. –
So sleeps the pride of former days,
So glory's thrill is o'er;
And hearts, that once beat high for praise,
Now feel that pulse no more.

Thomas Moore (1779–1852) Irish poet. *Irish Melodies*, 'The Harp that Once'

18 It is a city where you can see a sparrow fall to the ground, and God watching it.

Conor Cruise O'Brien (1917–) Irish diplomat and writer. Referring to Dublin. Attrib.

19 You have sold Ulster to buy off the fiendish republican scum. You will learn in a bitter school that all appeasement of these monsters is self-destructive.

Ian Paisley (1926–) Northern Irish politician. Referring to John Major's Anglo-Irish peace initiative. *The Independent*, 16 Dec 1993

20 When a man takes a farm from which another has been evicted, you must show him...by leaving him severely alone, by putting him into a moral Coventry, by isolating him from his kind as if he were a leper of old – you must show him your detestation of the crimes he has committed.

Charles Stewart Parnell (1846–91) Member of Parliament and champion of Irish Home Rule. The first person to be so treated was a Captain Boycott – hence the verb, 'to boycott'. Speech, Ennis, 19 Sept 1880

21 No man has a right to fix the boundary of the march of a nation; no man has a right to say to his country – thus far shalt thou go and no further.

Charles Stewart Parnell Speech at Cork, 21 Jan 1885

22 They must also know, as Edmund Burke once put it, that there is a limit at which forbearance ceases to be a virtue.

Albert Reynolds (1932–) Irish statesman. Referring to both Sinn Fein and the IRA. *The Independent*, 19 May 1994

23 I will drive a coach and six horses through the Act of Settlement.

Stephen Rice (1637–1715) English politician. *State of the Protestants of Ireland* (W. King), Ch. 3

24 The English should give Ireland home rule – and reserve the motion picture rights.

Will Rogers (1879–1935) US actor and humorist. *Autobiography* (published posthumously)

25 Before Irish Home Rule is conceded by the Imperial Parliament, England as the predominant member of the three kingdoms will have to be convinced of its justice and equity.

Lord Rosebery (1847–1929) British statesman. Speech, House of Lords, 11 Mar 1894

26 The moment the very name of Ireland is mentioned, the English seem to bid adieu to common feeling, common prudence, and common sense, and to act with the barbarity of tyrants, and the fatuity of idiots.

Sydney Smith (1771–1845) British clergyman and essayist. *The Letters of Peter Plymley*

27 A disease in the family that is never mentioned.

William Trevor (W. T. Cox; 1928–) Irish writer. Referring to the Troubles in Northern Ireland. *The Observer*, 18 Nov 1990

28 I would have liked to go to Ireland, but my grandmother would not let me. Perhaps she thought I wanted to take the little place.

Wilhelm II (1859–1941) King of Prussia and Emperor of Germany. Queen Victoria was his grandmother. *Carson* (H. Montgomery Hyde), Ch. 9

IRISH

See also British, Ireland

1 Put an Irishman on the spit, and you can always get another Irishman to baste him.

Proverb

2 Other people have a nationality. The Irish and the Jews have a psychosis.

Brendan Behan (1923–64) Irish playwright. *Richard's Cork Leg*, I

3 The English and Americans dislike only *some* Irish – the same Irish that the Irish themselves detest, Irish writers – the ones that *think*.

Brendan Behan *Richard's Cork Leg*, I

4 Not in vain is Ireland pouring itself all over the earth...The Irish, with their glowing hearts and reverent credulity, are needed in this cold age of intellect and skepticism.

Lydia M. Child (1802–80) US abolitionist campaigner. *Letters from New York*, Vol. I, No. 33, 8 Dec 1842

5 All races have produced notable economists, with the exception of the Irish who doubtless can protest their devotion to higher arts.

John Kenneth Galbraith (1908–) US economist. *The Age of Uncertainty*, Ch. 1

6 Irish Americans are about as Irish as Black Americans are African.

Bob Geldof (1952–) Irish rock musician. *The Observer*, 'Sayings of the Week', 22 Jun 1986

7 The Irish are a fair people; – they never speak well of one another.

Samuel Johnson (1709–84) British lexicographer. *Life of Johnson* (J. Boswell), Vol. II

8 The Irish don't know what they want and are prepared to fight to the death to get it.

Sidney Littlewood (1895–1967) President of the Law Society. Speech, 13 Apr 1961

9 [Gladstone] spent his declining years trying to guess the answer to the Irish Question; unfortunately, whenever he was getting warm, the Irish secretly changed the question.

W. C. Sellar (1898–1951) British humorous writer. *1066 And All That*

10 For howbeit the Irish might do very good Service, being a People removed from the Scottish, as well in Affections as Religion; yet it is not safe to train them up more than needs must in the military Way.

Thomas Wentworth (1593–1641) English statesman. Letter to King Charles I, from Ireland, 28 July 1638

IRREVOCABILITY

1 The die is cast.

Julius Caesar (100–44 BC) Roman general and statesman. Said on crossing the Rubicon (49 BC) at the start of his campaign against Pompey. Attrib.

2 The Gods themselves cannot recall their gifts.

Alfred, Lord Tennyson (1809–92) British poet. *Tithonus*

J

JAMES, HENRY

(1843–1916) US novelist, who spent much of his life in Europe (from 1876 in England). *Roderick Hudson* (1875), his first successful novel, was followed by *Washington Square* (1881), *The Bostonians* (1886), *The Turn of the Screw* (1898), *The Ambassadors* (1903), and several others.

Quotations about James

1 Henry James has a mind so fine that no idea could violate it.
T. S. Eliot (1888–1965) US-born British poet and dramatist. Attrib.

2 Henry James was one of the nicest old ladies I ever met.
William Faulkner (1897–1962) US novelist. Attrib.

3 The work of Henry James has always seemed divisible by a simple dynastic arrangement into three reigns. James I, James II, and the Old Pretender.
Philip Guedalla (1889–1944) British writer. *Collected Essays*, 'Men of Letters: Mr. Henry James'

Quotations by James

4 Live all you can; it's a mistake not to. It doesn't so much matter what you do in particular, so long as you have your life. If you haven't had that what *have* you had?
The Ambassadors, Bk. V, Ch. 2

5 Experience was to be taken as showing that one might get a five-pound note as one got a light for a cigarette; but one had to check the friendly impulse to ask for it in the same way.
The Awkward Age

6 It takes a great deal of history to produce a little literature.
Hawthorne, Ch. 1

7 He was imperfect, unfinished, inartistic; he was worse than provincial – he was parochial.
Referring to Thoreau. *Hawthorne*, Ch. 4

8 To kill a human being is, after all, the least injury you can do him.
My Friend Bingham

9 Cats and monkeys, monkeys and cats – all human life is there.
The Madonna of the Future

10 The only obligation to which in advance we may hold a novel, without incurring the accusation of being arbitrary, is that it be interesting.
Partial Portraits, 'The Art of Fiction'

11 Experience is never limited, and it is never complete; it is an immense sensibility, a kind of huge spider-web of the finest silken threads suspended in the chamber of consciousness, and catching every air-borne particle in its tissue.
Partial Portraits, 'The Art of Fiction'

12 What is character but the determination of incident? What is incident but the illustration of character?
Partial Portraits, 'The Art of Fiction'

13 The superiority of one man's opinion over another's is never so great as when the opinion is about a woman.
The Tragic Muse, Ch. 9

14 Nurse, take away the candle and spare my blushes.
On being informed, whilst confined to his bed, that he had been awarded the Order of Merit. *The American Treasury* (C. Fadiman)

15 Summer afternoon – summer afternoon; to me those have always been the two most beautiful words in the English language.
A Backward Glance (Edith Wharton), Ch. 10

16 So it has come at last, the distinguished thing.
Referring to his own death. *A Backward Glance* (Edith Wharton), Ch. 14

JEALOUSY

See also envy

1 For the ear of jealousy heareth all things: and the noise of murmurings is not hid.
Bible: Wisdom 1:10

2 The 'Green-Eyed Monster' causes much woe, but the absence of this ugly serpent argues the presence of a corpse whose name is Eros.
Minna Antrim (b. 1861) US writer. *Naked Truth and Veiled Allusions*

3 Jealousy is no more than feeling alone among smiling enemies.
Elizabeth Bowen (1899–1973) Irish novelist. *The House in Paris*

4 People may go on talking for ever of the jealousies of pretty women; but for real genuine, hard-working envy, there is nothing like an ugly woman with a taste for admiration.
Emily Eden (1797–1869) British-born Indian novelist. *The Semi-Attached Couple, Part One*, Ch. 1

5 The others were only my wives. But you, my dear, will be my widow.
Sacha Guitry (1885–1957) French actor and dramatist. Allaying his fifth wife's jealousy of his previous wives. *Speaker's and Toastmaster's Handbook* (J. Brawle)

6 Though jealousy be produced by love, as ashes are by fire, yet jealousy extinguishes love as ashes smother the flame.
Margaret of Navarre (1492–1549) French poet, writer, and patron of literature. 'Novel XLVIII, the Fifth Day'

7 The secret of my success is that no woman has ever been jealous of me.
Elsa Maxwell (1883–1963) US songwriter, broadcaster, and actress. *The Natives were Friendly* (Noël Barber)

8 O, beware, my lord, of jealousy;

It is the green-ey'd monster which doth mock
The meat it feeds on.

William Shakespeare (1564–1616) English dramatist. *Othello*, III:3

9 O curse of marriage,
That we can call these delicate creatures ours,
And not their appetites! I had rather be a toad,
And live upon the vapour of a dungeon,
Than keep a corner in the thing I love
For others' uses.

William Shakespeare *Othello*, III:3

10 If someone with whom one is having an affair keeps on mentioning some woman whom he knew in the past, however long ago it is since they separated, one is always irritated.

Sei Shonagon (c. 966–c. 1013) Japanese poet and diarist. *The Pillow-Book of Sei Shonagon*

JEFFERSON, THOMAS

(1743–1826) US statesman; the third President (1801–09). He was the chief author of the Declaration of Independence.

Quotations about Jefferson

1 His attachment to those of his friends whom he could make useful to himself was thoroughgoing and exemplary.

John Quincy Adams (1767–1848) Sixth president of the USA. *Diary*, 29 July 1836

2 A gentleman of thirty-two who could calculate an eclipse, survey an estate, tie an artery, plan an edifice, try a cause, break a horse, dance a minuet, and play the violin.

James Parton *Life of Thomas Jefferson*, Ch. 19

Quotations by Jefferson

3 The whole commerce between master and slave is a perpetual exercise of the most boisterous passions, the most unremitting despotism on the one part, and degrading submissions on the other.

Notes on the State of Virginia

4 When in the course of human events, it becomes necessary for one people to dissolve the political bonds which have connected them with another, and to assume among the powers of the earth the separate and equal station to which the laws of nature and of Nature's God entitle them, a decent respect to the opinions of mankind requires that they should declare the causes which impel them to the separation.

Declaration of Independence, Preamble

5 We hold these truths to be sacred and undeniable; that all men are created equal and independent, that from that equal creation they derive rights inherent and inalienable, among which are the preservation of life, and liberty, and the pursuit of happiness.

Declaration of Independence (original draft) pursuit of happiness.

6 We hold these truths to be self-evident: that all men are created equal; that they are endowed by their Creator with certain unalienable rights; that among these are life, liberty, and the pursuit of happiness.

Declaration of Independence, 4 July 1776

7 A little rebellion now and then is a good thing.

Letter to James Madison, 30 Jan 1787

8 The tree of liberty must be refreshed from time to time with the blood of patriots and tyrants. It is its natural manure.

Letter to W. S. Smith, 13 Nov 1787

JEROME, JEROME K.

(1859–1927) British dramatist and humorist. His books include *The Idle Thoughts of an Idle Fellow* (1886), *Three Men in a Boat* (1889), and *The Passing of the Third Floor Buck* (1908).

1 Love is like the measles; we all have to go through with it.

Idle Thoughts of an Idle Fellow

2 Conceit is the finest armour a man can wear.

Idle Thoughts of an Idle Fellow

3 It is easy enough to say that poverty is no crime. No; if it were men wouldn't be ashamed of it. It is a blunder, though, and is punished as such. A poor man is despised the whole world over.

Idle Thoughts of an Idle Fellow

4 If you are foolish enough to be contented, don't show it, but grumble with the rest.

Idle Thoughts of an Idle Fellow

5 It is impossible to enjoy idling thoroughly unless one has plenty of work to do.

Idle Thoughts of an Idle Fellow

6 But there, everything has its drawbacks, as the man said when his mother-in-law died, and they came down upon him for the funeral expenses.

Three Men in a Boat, Ch. 3

7 I like work; it fascinates me. I can sit and look at it for hours. I love to keep it by me; the idea of getting rid of it nearly breaks my heart.

Three Men in a Boat, Ch. 15

JERROLD, DOUGLAS WILLIAM

(1803–57) British dramatist. His plays include *Black-eyed Susan* (1829) and *Time Works Wonders* (1845).

1 Religion's in the heart, not in the knees.

The Devil's Ducat, I.2

2 The best thing I know between France and England is – the sea.

Wit and Opinions of Douglas Jerrold, 'The Anglo-French Alliance'

3 That fellow would vulgarize the day of judgment.

Wit and Opinions of Douglas Jerrold, 'A Comic Author'

4 Talk to him of Jacob's ladder, and he would ask the number of the steps.

Wit and Opinions of Douglas Jerrold, 'A Matter-of-fact Man'

5 Love's like the measles – all the worse when it comes late in life.

Wit and Opinions of Douglas Jerrold, 'Love'

6 The ugliest of trades have their moments of pleasure. Now, if I were a grave-digger, or even a hangman, there are some people I could work for with a great deal of enjoyment.

Wit and Opinions of Douglas Jerrold, 'Ugly Trades'

7 The only athletic sport I ever mastered was backgammon.

Douglas Jerrold (W. Jerrold), Vol. I, Ch. 1

8 Sir, you are like a pin, but without either its head or its point.

Speaking to a small thin man who was boring him. Attrib.

JEWS

See also Nazism, prejudice, race, religion

1 His Majesty's Government views with favour the establishment in Palestine of a national home for the Jewish people...

Arthur Balfour (1848–1930) British statesman. The so-called 'Balfour Declaration'. Letter to Lord Rothschild, 2 Nov 1917

2 Other people have a nationality. The Irish and the Jews have a psychosis.

Brendan Behan (1923–64) Irish playwright. *Richard's Cork Leg*, I

3 The gentleman will please remember that when his half-civilized ancestors were hunting the wild boar in Silesia, mine were princes of the earth.

Judah Philip Benjamin (1811–84) US politician. Replying to a senator of Germanic origin who had made an antisemitic remark. Attrib.

4 Now the Lord had said unto Abram, Get thee out of thy country, and from thy kindred, and from thy father's house, unto a land that I will shew thee:
And I will make of thee a great nation, and I will bless thee, and make thy name great; and thou shalt be a blessing:
And I will bless them that bless thee, and curse him that curseth thee: and in thee shall all families of the earth be blessed.

Bible: Genesis 12:1–3

5 I'm Super-jew!

Lenny Bruce (1923–66) US satirist. Jumping from a window; he got away with a broken leg. *The Observer*, 21 Aug 1966

6 How odd
Of God
To choose
The Jews.

William Norman Ewer (1885–1976) British writer. For a reply see Cecil BROWNE. *How Odd*

7 But not so odd
As those who choose
A Jewish God,
But spurn the Jews.

Cecil Browne In reply to EWER (above)

8 It is extremely difficult for a Jew to be converted, for how can he bring himself to believe in the divinity of – another Jew?

Heinrich Heine (1797–1856) German poet and writer. Attrib.

9 The final solution of the Jewish problem.

Adolf Hitler (1889–1945) German dictator. Referring to the concentration camps. *The Final Solution* (G. Geitlinger).

10 For me this is a vital litmus test: no intellectual society can flourish where a Jew feels even slightly uneasy.

Paul Johnson (1928–) British editor. *The Sunday Times Magazine*, 6 Feb 1977

11 The very best that is in the Jewish blood: a faculty for pure disinterestedness, and warm, physically warm love, that seems to make the corpuscles of the blood glow.

D. H. Lawrence (1885–1930) British novelist. *Kangaroo*, Ch. 6

12 Since my daughter is only half-Jewish, could she go in the water up to her knees?

Groucho Marx (Julius Marx; 1895–1977) US comedian. When excluded from a beach club on racial grounds. *The Observer*, 21 Aug 1977

13 Pessimism is a luxury that a Jew never can allow himself.

Golda Meir (1898–1978) Russian-born Israeli stateswoman. *The Observer*, 'Sayings of the Year', 29 Dec 1974

14 There are not enough prisons and concentration camps in Palestine to hold all the Jews who are ready to defend their lives and property.

Golda Meir Speech, 2 May 1940

15 I'm not really a Jew; just Jew-ish, not the whole hog.

Jonathan Miller (1934–) British doctor and television and stage director. *Beyond the Fringe*

16 And furthermore did you know that behind the discovery of America there was a Jewish financier?

Mordecai Richler (1931–) Canadian novelist. *Cocksure*, Ch. 24

17 Doctor, my doctor, what do you say – let's put the id back in yid!

Philip Roth (1933–) US novelist. *Portnoy's Complaint*

18 A Jewish man with parents alive is a fifteen-year-old boy, and will remain a fifteen-year-old boy till they die.

Philip Roth *Portnoy's Complaint*

19 I believe that the Jews have made a contribution to the human condition out of all proportion to their numbers: I believe them to be an immense people. Not only have they supplied the world with two leaders of the stature of Jesus Christ and Karl Marx, but they have even indulged in the luxury of following neither one nor the other.

Peter Ustinov (1921–) British actor. *Dear Me*, Ch. 19

20 The law of dislike for the unlike will always prevail. And whereas the unlike is normally situated at a safe distance, the Jews bring the unlike into the heart of *every milieu*, and must there defend a frontier line as large as the world.

Israel Zangwill (1864–1926) British writer. *Speeches, Articles and Letters*, 'The Jewish Race'

21 No Jew was ever fool enough to turn Christian unless he was a clever man.

Israel Zangwill *Children of the Ghetto*, Ch. 1

JOHN PAUL II

(Karol Wojtyła; 1920–) Polish pope (1978–); the first non-Italian pope since 1522.

1 It is unbecoming for a cardinal to ski badly.
Replying to the suggestion that it was inappropriate for him, a cardinal, to ski. *John Paul II*

2 We thus denounce the false and dangerous program of the arms race, of the secret rivalry between peoples for military superiority.
The Observer, 'Sayings of the Week', 19 Dec 1976

3 Only before the eyes of God can the human body remain nude and uncovered while fully conserving its splendour and beauty.
The Observer, 'Sayings of the Week', 10 Apr 1994

4 War should belong to the tragic past, to history: it should find no place on humanity's agenda for the future.
Speech, 1982

JOHNSON, LYNDON B.

(1908–73) US statesman. He became Democratic President from 1963 to 1969. His increased involvement in the Vietnam war made him unpopular.

Quotations about L. B. Johnson

1 An extraordinarily gifted president who was the wrong man from the wrong place at the wrong time under the wrong circumstances.
Eric F. Goldman *The Tragedy of Lyndon Johnson*, Ch. 18

2 Lyndon acts like there was never going to be a tomorrow.
Lady Bird Johnson (1912–) Wife of Lyndon B. Johnson. Attrib.

3 Kennedy promised, Johnson delivered.
Arthur Schlesinger Jnr (1917–) US historian, educator, and author. *The Observer*, 20 Nov 1983

Quotations by L. B. Johnson

4 Jerry Ford is so dumb that he can't fart and chew gum at the same time.
Sometimes quoted as '...can't walk and chew gum'. *A Ford, Not a Lincoln* (R. Reeves), Ch. 1

5 If you're in politics and you can't tell when you walk into a room who's for you and who's against you, then you're in the wrong line of work.
The Lyndon Johnson Story (B. Mooney)

6 I am going to build the kind of nation that President Roosevelt hoped for, President Truman worked for and President Kennedy died for.
The Sunday Times, 27 Dec 1964

7 I'd much rather have that fellow inside my tent pissing out, than outside my tent pissing in.
When asked why he retained J. Edgar Hoover at the FBI. *Guardian Weekly*, 18 Dec 1971

JOHNSON, SAMUEL

(1709–84) British lexicographer and writer. His *Dictionary of the English Language* appeared in 1755. The moral fable *Rasselas* (1759) was followed by *The Lives of the English Poets* (1781). His close friend James Boswell wrote his celebrated biography, *Boswell's Life of Johnson* (1791).

Quotations about S. Johnson

1 There is no arguing with Johnson, for when his pistol misses fire, he knocks you down with the butt of it.
Oliver Goldsmith (1728–74) Irish-born British writer. *Life of Johnson* (J. Boswell)

2 That great Cham of Literature, Samuel Johnson.
Tobias Smollett (1721–71) British novelist. Letter to John Wilkes, 16 Mar 1759

3 Johnson made the most brutal speeches to living persons; for though he was good-natured at bottom he was ill-natured at top.
Horace Walpole (1717–97) British writer. *Letters*

Quotations by S. Johnson

4 Every quotation contributes something to the stability or enlargement of the language.
Dictionary of the English Language

5 But these were the dreams of a poet doomed at last to wake a lexicographer.
Dictionary of the English Language

6 I am not yet so lost in lexicography, as to forget that words are the daughters of earth, and that things are the sons of heaven. Language is only the instrument of science, and words are but the signs of ideas: I wish, however, that the instrument might be less apt to decay, and that signs might be permanent, like the things which they denote.
Dictionary of the English Language

7 I have protracted my work till most of those whom I wished to please have sunk into the grave; and success and miscarriage are empty sounds.
Dictionary of the English Language

8 *Dull.* 8. To make dictionaries is dull work.
Dictionary of the English Language

9 *Excise.* A hateful tax levied upon commodities.
Dictionary of the English Language

10 *Lexicographer.* A writer of dictionaries, a harmless drudge.
Dictionary of the English Language

11 *Network.* Anything reticulated or decussated at equal distances, with interstices between the intersections.
Dictionary of the English Language

12 *Oats.* A grain, which in England is generally given to horses, but in Scotland supports the people.
Dictionary of the English Language

13 *Patron.* Commonly a wretch who supports with insolence, and is paid with flattery.
Dictionary of the English Language

14 When the messenger who carried the last sheet to Millar returned, Johnson asked him, 'Well, what did he say?' – 'Sir (answered the messenger), he said, thank God I have done with him.' – 'I am glad (replied Johnson, with a smile) that he thanks God for anything.'
After the final page of his *Dictionary* had been delivered.

15 When two Englishmen meet, their first talk is of the weather.
The Idler

16 Pleasure is very seldom found where it is sought; our brightest blazes of gladness are commonly kindled by unexpected sparks.
The Idler

17 We are inclined to believe those whom we do not know because they have never deceived us.
The Idler

18 A Scotchman must be a very sturdy moralist who does not love Scotland better than truth.
Journey to the Western Islands of Scotland, 'Col'

19 The reciprocal civility of authors is one of the most risible scenes in the farce of life.
Life of Sir Thomas Browne

20 The true genius is a mind of large general powers, accidentally determined to some particular direction.
Lives of the English Poets, 'Cowley'

21 I am disappointed by that stroke of death, which has eclipsed the gaiety of nations and impoverished the public stock of harmless pleasure.
Epitaph on David Garrick. *Lives of the English Poets*, 'Edmund Smith'

22 We are perpetually moralists, but we are geometricians only by chance. Our intercourse with intellectual nature is necessary; our speculations upon matter are voluntary, and at leisure.
Lives of the English Poets, 'Milton'

23 There are minds so impatient of inferiority that their gratitude is a species of revenge, and they return benefits, not because recompense is a pleasure, but because obligation is a pain.
The Rambler

24 I have laboured to refine our language to grammatical purity, and to clear it from colloquial barbarisms, licentious idioms, and irregular combinations.
The Rambler

25 The love of life is necessary to the vigorous prosecution of any undertaking.
The Rambler

26 Almost every man wastes part of his life in attempts to display qualities which he does not possess, and to gain applause which he cannot keep.
The Rambler

27 There is a certain race of men that either imagine it their duty, or make it their amusement, to hinder the reception of every work of learning or genius, who stand as sentinels in the avenues of fame, and value themselves upon giving Ignorance and Envy the first notice of a prey.
The Rambler

28 Human life is everywhere a state in which much is to be endured, and little to be enjoyed.
Rasselas, Ch. 11

29 Marriage has many pains, but celibacy has no pleasures.
Rasselas, Ch. 26

30 Integrity without knowledge is weak and useless, and knowledge without integrity is dangerous and dreadful.
Rasselas, Ch. 41

31 Madam, before you flatter a man so grossly to his face, you should consider whether or not your flattery is worth his having.
Diary and Letters (Mme D'Arblay), Vol. I, Ch. 2

32 Every man has, some time in his life, an ambition to be a wag.
Diary and Letters (Mme D'Arblay), Vol. III, Ch. 46

33 If the man who turnips cries,
Cry not when his father dies,
'Tis a proof that he had rather
Have a turnip than his father.
Johnsonian Miscellanies (ed. G. B. Hill), Vol. I

34 GOLDSMITH. Here's such a stir about a fellow that has written one book, and I have written many.
JOHNSON. Ah, Doctor, there go two-and-forty sixpences you know to one guinea.
Referring to Beattie's *Essay on Truth*. *Johnsonian Miscellanies* (ed. G. B. Hill), Vol. I

35 It is very strange, and very melancholy, that the paucity of human pleasures should persuade us ever to call hunting one of them.
Johnsonian Miscellanies (ed. G. B. Hill), Vol. I

36 Was there ever yet anything written by mere man that was wished longer by its readers, excepting *Don Quixote*, *Robinson Crusoe*, and the *Pilgrim's Progress*?
Johnsonian Miscellanies (ed. G. B. Hill), Vol. I

37 A man is in general better pleased when he has a good dinner upon his table, than when his wife talks Greek.
Johnsonian Miscellanies (ed. G. B. Hill), Vol. II

38 A tavern chair is the throne of human felicity.
Johnsonian Miscellanies (ed. G. B. Hill), Vol. II

39 The only sensual pleasure without vice.
Referring to music. *Johnsonian Miscellanies* (ed. G. B. Hill), Vol. II

40 Difficult do you call it, Sir? I wish it were impossible.
On hearing a famous violinist. *Johnsonian Miscellanies* (ed. G. B. Hill), Vol. II

41 What is written without effort is in general read without pleasure.
Johnsonian Miscellanies (ed. G. B. Hill), Vol. II

42 Love is the wisdom of the fool and the folly of the wise.
Johnsonian Miscellanies (ed. G. B. Hill), Vol. II

43 In my early years I read very hard. It is a sad reflection, but a true one, that I knew almost as much at eighteen as I do now.
Life of Johnson (J. Boswell), Vol. I

44 It is incident to physicians, I am afraid, beyond

all other men, to mistake subsequence for consequence.

Life of Johnson (J. Boswell), Vol. I

45 He was a vicious man, but very kind to me. If you call a dog *Hervey*, I shall love him.

Life of Johnson (J. Boswell), Vol. I

46 I'll come no more behind your scenes, David; for the silk stockings and white bosoms of your actresses excite my amorous propensities.

Said to the actor-manager David Garrick. *Life of Johnson* (J. Boswell), Vol. I

47 A man may write at any time, if he will set himself doggedly to it.

Life of Johnson (J. Boswell), Vol. I

48 Is not a Patron, my Lord, one who looks with unconcern on a man struggling for life in the water, and, when he has reached ground, encumbers him with help? The notice which you have been pleased to take of my labours, had it been early, had been kind; but it has been delayed till I am indifferent, and cannot enjoy it; till I am solitary, and cannot impart it; till I am known, and do not want it.

Letter to Lord Chesterfield, 7 Feb 1755. Lord Chesterfield, the British statesman, was the patron of many writers as well as being a writer noted for his elegance and wit. *Life of Johnson* (J. Boswell), Vol. I

49 A fly, Sir, may sting a stately horse and make him wince; but one is but an insect, and the other is a horse still.

Referring to critics. *Life of Johnson* (J. Boswell), Vol. I

50 This man I thought had been a Lord among wits; but, I find, he is only a wit among Lords.

Referring to Lord Chesterfield. *Life of Johnson* (J. Boswell), Vol. I

51 They teach the morals of a whore, and the manners of a dancing master.

Referring to Lord Chesterfield's *Letters*. *Life of Johnson* (J. Boswell), Vol. I

52 There are two things which I am confident I can do very well: one is an introduction to any literary work, stating what it is to contain, and how it should be executed in the most perfect manner; the other is a conclusion, shewing from various causes why the execution has not been equal to what the author promised to himself and to the public.

Life of Johnson (J. Boswell), Vol. I

53 Ignorance, madam, pure ignorance.

His reply on being questioned, by a lady reader of his *Dictionary*, why he had defined 'pastern' as the 'knee' of a horse. *Life of Johnson* (J. Boswell), Vol. I

54 If a man does not make new acquaintance as he advances through life, he will soon find himself left alone. A man, Sir, should keep his friendship in constant repair.

Life of Johnson (J. Boswell), Vol. I

55 The booksellers are generous liberal-minded men.

Life of Johnson (J. Boswell), Vol. I

56 No man will be a sailor who has contrivance enough to get himself into a jail; for being in a ship is being in a jail, with the chance of being drowned...A man in a jail has more room, better food, and commonly better company.

Life of Johnson (J. Boswell), Vol. I

57 BOSWELL. I do indeed come from Scotland, but I cannot help it...
JOHNSON. That, Sir, I find, is what a very great many of your countrymen cannot help.

Life of Johnson (J. Boswell), Vol. I

58 Yes, Sir, many men, many women, and many children.

When asked by Dr Blair whether any man of their own time could have written the poems of Ossian. *Life of Johnson* (J. Boswell), Vol. I

59 You *may* abuse a tragedy, though you cannot write one. You may scold a carpenter who has made you a bad table, though you cannot make a table. It is not your trade to make tables.

Referring to the qualifications needed to indulge in literary criticism. *Life of Johnson* (J. Boswell), Vol. I

60 He is the richest author that ever grazed the common of literature.

Referring to Dr John Campbell. *Life of Johnson* (J. Boswell), Vol. I

61 Great abilities are not requisite for an Historian... Imagination is not required in any high degree.

Life of Johnson (J. Boswell), Vol. I

62 Norway, too, has noble wild prospects; and Lapland is remarkable for prodigious noble wild prospects. But, Sir, let me tell you, the noblest prospect which a Scotchman ever sees, is the high road that leads him to England!

Life of Johnson (J. Boswell), Vol. I

63 A man ought to read just as inclination leads him; for what he reads as a task will do him little good.

Life of Johnson (J. Boswell), Vol. I

64 But if he does really think that there is no distinction between virtue and vice, why, Sir, when he leaves our houses let us count our spoons.

Life of Johnson (J. Boswell), Vol. I

65 Truth, Sir, is a cow, which will yield such people no more milk, and so they are gone to milk the bull.

Referring to sceptics. *Life of Johnson* (J. Boswell), Vol. I

66 Your levellers wish to level *down* as far as themselves; but they cannot bear levelling *up* to themselves.

Life of Johnson (J. Boswell), Vol. I

67 It is no matter what you teach them first, any more than what leg you shall put into your breeches first.

Referring to the education of children. *Life of Johnson* (J. Boswell), Vol. I

68 It is burning a farthing candle at Dover, to shew light at Calais.

Referring to the impact of Sheridan's works upon the English language. *Life of Johnson* (J. Boswell), Vol. I

69 A woman's preaching is like a dog's walking on his hinder legs. It is not done well; but you are surprised to find it done at all.

Life of Johnson (J. Boswell), Vol. I

70 This was a good dinner enough, to be sure; but it was not a dinner to *ask* a man to.

Life of Johnson (J. Boswell), Vol. I

71 I refute it *thus*.

Replying to Boswell's contention that they were unable to refute Bishop Berkeley's theory of matter, by kicking a large stone with his foot. *Life of Johnson* (J. Boswell), Vol. I

72 A very unclubable man.

Referring to the naval commander, Sir John Hawkins. *Life of Johnson* (J. Boswell), Vol. I

73 That all who are happy, are equally happy, is not true. A peasant and a philosopher may be equally *satisfied*, but not equally *happy*. Happiness consists in the multiplicity of agreeable consciousness.

Life of Johnson (J. Boswell), Vol. II

74 Our tastes greatly alter. The lad does not care for the child's rattle, and the old man does not care for the young man's whore.

Life of Johnson (J. Boswell), Vol. II

75 Shakespeare never had six lines together without a fault. Perhaps you may find seven, but this does not refute my general assertion.

Life of Johnson (J. Boswell), Vol. II

76 Why, Sir, most schemes of political improvement are very laughable things.

Life of Johnson (J. Boswell), Vol. II

77 There is no idolatry in the Mass. They believe God to be there, and they adore him.

Life of Johnson (J. Boswell), Vol. II

78 It matters not how a man dies, but how he lives. The act of dying is not of importance, it lasts so short a time.

Life of Johnson (J. Boswell), Vol. II

79 That fellow seems to me to possess but one idea, and that is a wrong one.

Life of Johnson (J. Boswell), Vol. II

80 I do not care to speak ill of any man behind his back, but I believe the gentleman is an *attorney*.

Life of Johnson (J. Boswell), Vol. II

81 The triumph of hope over experience.

Referring to the hasty remarriage of an acquaintance following the death of his first wife, with whom he had been most unhappy. *Life of Johnson* (J. Boswell), Vol. II

82 Every man has a lurking wish to appear considerable in his native place.

Letter to the portrait painter, Sir Joshua Reynolds. *Life of Johnson* (J. Boswell), Vol. II

83 I would not give half a guinea to live under one form of government rather than another. It is of no moment to the happiness of an individual.

Life of Johnson (J. Boswell), Vol. II

84 Sir, I perceive you are a vile Whig.

Speaking to Sir Adam Fergusson. *Life of Johnson* (J. Boswell), Vol. II

85 A man who is good enough to go to heaven, is good enough to be a clergyman.

Life of Johnson (J. Boswell), Vol. II

86 Much may be made of a Scotchman, if he be *caught* young.

Referring to Lord Mansfield. *Life of Johnson* (J. Boswell), Vol. II

87 ELPHINSTON. What, have you not read it through?...

JOHNSON. No, Sir, do *you* read books *through*?

Life of Johnson (J. Boswell), Vol. II

88 Read over your compositions, and where ever you meet with a passage which you think is particularly fine, strike it out.

Recalling the advice of a college tutor. *Life of Johnson* (J. Boswell), Vol. II

89 The woman's a whore, and there's an end on't.

Referring to Lady Diana Beauclerk. *Life of Johnson* (J. Boswell), Vol. II

90 The Irish are a fair people; – they never speak well of one another.

Life of Johnson (J. Boswell), Vol. II

91 There are few ways in which a man can be more innocently employed than in getting money.

Life of Johnson (J. Boswell), Vol. II

92 He was dull in a new way, and that made many people think him *great*.

Referring to the poet Thomas Gray. *Life of Johnson* (J. Boswell), Vol. II

93 I think the full tide of human existence is at Charing-Cross.

Life of Johnson (J. Boswell), Vol. II

94 A man will turn over half a library to make one book.

Life of Johnson (J. Boswell), Vol. II

95 Patriotism is the last refuge of a scoundrel.

Life of Johnson (J. Boswell), Vol. II

96 Their learning is like bread in a besieged town: every man gets a little, but no man gets a full meal.

Referring to education in Scotland. *Life of Johnson* (J. Boswell), Vol. II

97 Knowledge is of two kinds. We know a subject ourselves, or we know where we can find information upon it.

Life of Johnson (J. Boswell), Vol. II

98 Politics are now nothing more than a means of rising in the world.

Life of Johnson (J. Boswell), Vol. II

99 In lapidary inscriptions a man is not upon oath.

Life of Johnson (J. Boswell), Vol. II

100 There is now less flogging in our great schools than formerly, but then less is learned there; so that what the boys get at one end they lose at the other.

Life of Johnson (J. Boswell), Vol. II

101 When men come to like a sea-life, they are not fit to live on land.

Life of Johnson (J. Boswell), Vol. II

102 There is nothing which has yet been contrived by man, by which so much happiness is produced as by a good tavern or inn.

Life of Johnson (J. Boswell), Vol. II

103 Questioning is not the mode of conversation among gentlemen.

Life of Johnson (J. Boswell), Vol. II

104 Fine clothes are good only as they supply the want of other means of procuring respect.
Life of Johnson (J. Boswell), Vol. II

105 If a madman were to come into this room with a stick in his hand, no doubt we should pity the state of his mind; but our primary consideration would be to take care of ourselves. We should knock him down first, and pity him afterwards.
Life of Johnson (J. Boswell), Vol. III

106 Consider, Sir, how should you like, though conscious of your innocence, to be tried before a jury for a capital crime, once a week.
Life of Johnson (J. Boswell), Vol. III

107 We would all be idle if we could.
Life of Johnson (J. Boswell), Vol. III

108 No man but a blockhead ever wrote, except for money.
Life of Johnson (J. Boswell), Vol. III

109 It is better that some should be unhappy than that none should be happy, which would be the case in a general state of equality.
Life of Johnson (J. Boswell), Vol. III

110 A man who has not been in Italy, is always conscious of an inferiority, from his not having seen what it is expected a man should see. The grand object of travelling is to see the shores of the Mediterranean.
Life of Johnson (J. Boswell), Vol. III

111 Why Sir, it is much easier to say what it is not. We all *know* what light is; but it is not easy to *tell* what it is.
When asked, 'What is poetry'. *Life of Johnson* (J. Boswell), Vol. III

112 Nay, Madam, when you are declaiming, declaim; and when you are calculating, calculate.
Commenting on Mrs Thrales's discourse on the price of children's clothes. *Life of Johnson* (J. Boswell), Vol. III

113 Sir, it is not so much to be lamented that Old England is lost, as that the Scotch have found it.
Life of Johnson (J. Boswell), Vol. III

114 To Oliver Goldsmith, A Poet, Naturalist, and Historian, who left scarcely any style of writing untouched, and touched none that he did not adorn.
Epitaph on Goldsmith. *Life of Johnson* (J. Boswell), Vol. III

115 If I had no duties, and no reference to futurity, I would spend my life in driving briskly in a post-chaise with a pretty woman.
Life of Johnson (J. Boswell), Vol. III

116 Depend upon it, Sir, when a man knows he is to be hanged in a fortnight, it concentrates his mind wonderfully.
Life of Johnson (J. Boswell), Vol. III

117 When a man is tired of London, he is tired of life; for there is in London all that life can afford.
Life of Johnson (J. Boswell), Vol. III

118 He who praises everybody praises nobody.
Life of Johnson (J. Boswell), Vol. III

119 Round numbers are always false.
Life of Johnson (J. Boswell), Vol. III

120 All argument is against it; but all belief is for it.
Of the ghost of a dead person. *Life of Johnson* (J. Boswell), Vol. III

121 Seeing Scotland, Madam, is only seeing a worse England.
Life of Johnson (J. Boswell), Vol. III

122 A country governed by a despot is an inverted cone.
Life of Johnson (J. Boswell), Vol. III

123 I am willing to love all mankind, *except an American.*
Life of Johnson (J. Boswell), Vol. III

124 Sir, the insolence of wealth will creep out.
Life of Johnson (J. Boswell), Vol. III

125 All censure of a man's self is oblique praise. It is in order to shew how much he can spare.
Life of Johnson (J. Boswell), Vol. III

126 Were it not for imagination, Sir, a man would be as happy in the arms of a chambermaid as of a Duchess.
Life of Johnson (J. Boswell), Vol. III

127 There are innumerable questions to which the inquisitive mind can in this state receive no answer: Why do you and I exist? Why was this world created? Since it was to be created, why was it not created sooner?
Life of Johnson (J. Boswell), Vol. III

128 Claret is the liquor for boys; port for men; but he who aspires to be a hero must drink brandy.
Life of Johnson (J. Boswell), Vol. III

129 A man who exposes himself when he is intoxicated, has not the art of getting drunk.
Life of Johnson (J. Boswell), Vol. III

130 Worth seeing? yes; but not worth going to see.
Referring to the Giant's Causeway, a promontory of columnas basalt on the north coast of Northern Ireland, in Antrim. *Life of Johnson* (J. Boswell), Vol. III

131 I have got no further than this: Every man has a right to utter what he thinks truth, and every other man has a right to knock him down for it. Martyrdom is the test.
Life of Johnson (J. Boswell), Vol. IV

132 They are forced plants, raised in a hot-bed; and they are poor plants; they are but cucumbers after all.
Referring to Gray's *Odes*. *Life of Johnson* (J. Boswell), Vol. IV

133 A Frenchman must be always talking, whether he knows anything of the matter or not; an Englishman is content to say nothing, when he has nothing to say.
Life of Johnson (J. Boswell), Vol. IV

134 Sir, your wife, under pretence of keeping a bawdy-house, is a receiver of stolen goods.
An example of the customary badinage between travellers on the Thames. *Life of Johnson* (J. Boswell), Vol. IV

135 Depend upon it that if a man talks of his misfortunes there is something in them that is not disagreeable to him; for where there is nothing but

pure misery there never is any recourse to the mention of it.
Life of Johnson (J. Boswell), Vol. IV

136 Mrs Montagu has dropt me. Now, Sir, there are people whom one should like very well to drop, but would not wish to be dropped by.
Life of Johnson (J. Boswell), Vol. IV

137 Classical quotation is the *parole* of literary men all over the world.
Life of Johnson (J. Boswell), Vol. IV

138 I have two very cogent reasons for not printing any list of subscribers; – one, that I have lost all the names, – the other, that I have spent all the money.
Referring to subscribers to his *Dictionary of the English Language. Life of Johnson* (J. Boswell), Vol. IV

139 Always, Sir, set a high value on spontaneous kindness. He whose inclination prompts him to cultivate your friendship of his own accord, will love you more than one whom you have been at pains to attach to you.
Life of Johnson (J. Boswell), Vol. IV

140 Resolve not to be poor: whatever you have, spend less. Poverty is a great enemy to human happiness; it certainly destroys liberty, and it makes some virtues impracticable and others extremely difficult.
Life of Johnson (J. Boswell), Vol. IV

141 I hate a fellow whom pride, or cowardice, or laziness drives into a corner, and who does nothing when he is there but sit and *growl*; let him come out as I do, and *bark*.
Life of Johnson (J. Boswell), Vol. IV

142 How few of his friends' houses would a man choose to be at when he is sick.
Life of Johnson (J. Boswell), Vol. IV

143 There is a wicked inclination in most people to suppose an old man decayed in his intellects. If a young or middle-aged man, when leaving a company, does not recollect where he laid his hat, it is nothing; but if the same inattention is discovered in an old man, people will shrug up their shoulders, and say, 'His memory is going.'
Life of Johnson (J. Boswell), Vol. IV

144 Sir, there is no settling the point of precedency between a louse and a flea.
When Maurice Morgann asked him who he considered to be the better poet – Smart or Derrick. *Life of Johnson* (J. Boswell), Vol. IV

145 When I observed he was a fine cat, saying, 'why yes, Sir, but I have had cats whom I liked better than this'; and then as if perceiving Hodge to be out of countenance, adding, 'but he is a very fine cat, a very fine cat indeed.'
Life of Johnson (J. Boswell), Vol. IV

146 My dear friend, clear your *mind* of cant... You may *talk* in this manner; it is a mode of talking in Society: but don't *think* foolishly.
Life of Johnson (J. Boswell), Vol. IV

147 As I know more of mankind I expect less of them, and am ready now to call a man *a good man*, upon easier terms than I was formerly.
Life of Johnson (J. Boswell), Vol. IV

148 If a man were to go by chance at the same time with Burke under a shed, to shun a shower, he would say – 'this is an extraordinary man.'
Referring to the Whig statesman, Edmund Burke. *Life of Johnson* (J. Boswell), Vol. IV

149 It is as bad as bad can be: it is ill-fed, ill-killed, ill-kept, and ill-drest.
About the roast mutton at an inn. *Life of Johnson* (J. Boswell), Vol. IV

150 Milton, Madam, was a genius that could cut a Colossus from a rock; but could not carve heads upon cherry-stones.
When Miss Hannah More, the writer, had wondered why Milton could write the epic *Paradise Lost* but only very poor sonnets. *Life of Johnson* (J. Boswell), Vol. IV

151 Sir, I have found you an argument; but I am not obliged to find you an understanding.
Life of Johnson (J. Boswell), Vol. IV

152 No man is a hypocrite in his pleasures.
Life of Johnson (J. Boswell), Vol. IV

153 Dublin, though a place much worse than London, is not so bad as Iceland.
Letter to Mrs Christopher Smart, the wife of the poet. *Life of Johnson* (J. Boswell), Vol. IV

154 Sir, I look upon every day to be lost, in which I do not make a new acquaintance.
Life of Johnson (J. Boswell), Vol. IV

155 It will be conquered; I will not capitulate.
Referring to his illness. *Life of Johnson* (J. Boswell), Vol. IV

156 A cow is a very good animal in the field; but we turn her out of a garden.
Responding to Boswell's objections to the expulsion of six Methodists from Oxford University. *The Personal History of Samuel Johnson* (C. Hibbert)

157 A lawyer has no business with the justice or injustice of the cause which he undertakes, unless his client asks his opinion, and then he is bound to give it honestly. The justice or injustice of the cause is to be decided by the judge.
Tour to the Hebrides (J. Boswell)

158 I have, all my life long, been lying till noon; yet I tell all young men, and tell them with great sincerity, that nobody who does not rise early will ever do any good.
Tour to the Hebrides (J. Boswell)

159 I am always sorry when any language is lost, because languages are the pedigree of nations.
Tour to the Hebrides (J. Boswell)

160 No, Sir; there were people who died of dropsies, which they contracted in trying to get drunk.
Scornfully criticizing the strength of the wine in Scotland before the Act of Union in response to Boswell's claim that there had been a lot of drunkenness. *Tour to the Hebrides* (J. Boswell)

161 A cucumber should be well sliced, and dressed with pepper and vinegar, and then thrown out, as good for nothing.
Tour to the Hebrides (J. Boswell)

162 Come, let me know what it is that makes a Scotchman happy!

Ordering for himself a glass of whisky. *Tour to the Hebrides* (J. Boswell)

163 I am sorry I have not learned to play at cards. It is very useful in life: it generates kindness and consolidates society.

Tour to the Hebrides (J. Boswell)

164 Fly fishing may be a very pleasant amusement; but angling or float fishing I can only compare to a stick and a string, with a worm at one end and a fool at the other.

Attrib. in *Instructions to Young Sportsmen* (Hawker)

JONSON, BEN

(1573–1637) English dramatist and poet. His plays include *Volpone* (1606), *The Alchemist* (1610), and *Bartholomew Fair* (1614); he published two collections of verse.

Quotations about Jonson

1 He invades authors like a monarch and what would be theft in other poets, is only victory in him.

John Dryden (1631–1700) British poet and dramatist. *Essay of Dramatic Poesy*

2 O Rare Ben Jonson.

John Young. Epitaph in Westminster Abbey.

Quotations by Jonson

3 Fortune, that favours fools.

The Alchemist, Prologue

4 Neither do thou lust after that tawney weed tobacco.

Bartholomew Fair, II:6

5 Alas, all the castles I have, are built with air, thou know'st.

Eastward Ho!, II:2

6 Ods me, I marvel what pleasure or felicity they have in taking their roguish tobacco. It is good for nothing but to choke a man, and fill him full of smoke and embers.

Every Man in His Humour, III:5

7 Drink to me only with thine eyes,
And I will pledge with mine;
Or leave a kiss but in the cup,
And I'll not look for wine.
The thirst that from the soul doth rise
Doth ask a drink divine;
But might I of Jove's nectar sup,
I would not change for thine.

I sent thee late a rosy wreath,
Not so much honouring thee,
As giving it a hope that there
It could not wither'd be.

The Forest, IX, 'To Celia'

8 They say princes learn no art truly, but the art of horsemanship. The reason is, the brave beast is no flatterer. He will throw a prince as soon as his groom.

Timber, or Discoveries made upon Men and Matter

9 Talking and eloquence are not the same: to speak, and to speak well, are two things.

Timber, or Discoveries made upon Men and Matter

10 Thou hadst small Latin, and less Greek.

To the Memory of William Shakespeare

11 He was not of an age, but for all time!

To the Memory of William Shakespeare

12 Sweet Swan of Avon!

To the Memory of William Shakespeare

13 She is Venus when she smiles;
But she's Juno when she walks,
And Minerva when she talks.

The Underwood, 'Celebration of Charis, V. His Discourse with Cupid'

14 Good morning to the day: and, next, my gold! –
Open the shrine, that I may see my saint.

Volpone, I:1

15 Calumnies are answered best with silence.

Volpone, II:2

16 Come, my Celia, let us prove,
While we can, the sports of love,
Time will not be ours for ever,
He, at length, our good will sever.

Volpone, III:6

JOURNALISM

See also editors, media, newspapers

1 *Punch* – the official journal of dentists' waiting rooms.

The Times, 7 Oct 1981

2 Have you noticed that life, real honest to goodness life, with murders and catastrophes and fabulous inheritances, happens almost exclusively in newspapers?

Jean Anouilh (1910–87) French dramatist. *The Rehearsal*

3 'Christianity, of course but why journalism?'

Arthur Balfour (1848–1930) British statesman. In reply to Frank Harris's remark, '…all the faults of the age come from Christianity and journalism'. *Autobiography* (Margot Asquith), Ch. 10

4 Go out and speak for the inarticulate and the submerged.

Lord Beaverbrook (1879–1964) British newspaper owner and politician. *Somerset Maugham* (E. Morgan)

5 Because he shakes hands with people's hearts.

Lord Beaverbrook On being asked why the sentimental writer Godfrey Winn was paid so much. *Somerset Maugham* (E. Morgan)

6 If you want to make mischief come and work on my papers.

Lord Beaverbrook Inviting Anthony Howard to join his staff. *Radio Times*, 27 June 1981

7 Who's in charge of the clattering train?

Lord Beaverbrook Attrib.

8 Journalists say a thing that they know isn't true, in the hope that if they keep on saying it long enough it will be true.

Arnold Bennett (1867–1931) British novelist. *The Title*, II

9 No news is good news; no journalists is even better.

Nicolas Bentley (1907–78) British cartoonist and writer. Attrib.

10 I read the newspaper avidly. It is my one form of continuous fiction.

Aneurin Bevan (1897–1960) British Labour politician. *The Observer*, 'Sayings of the Week', 3 Apr 1960

11 There is a bias in television journalism. It is not against any particular party or point of view – it is a bias against *understanding*.

John Birt (1944–) British TV executive. This launched a series of articles written jointly with Peter Jay. *The Times*, 28 Feb 1975

12 Journalism is the only job that requires no degrees, no diplomas and no specialised knowledge of any kind.

Patrick Campbell (1913–80) British humorous writer and editor. *My Life and Easy Times*

13 Journalism largely consists of saying 'Lord Jones is dead' to people who never knew Lord Jones was alive.

G. K. Chesterton (1874–1936) British writer. Attrib.

14 Literature is the art of writing something that will be read twice; journalism what will be grasped at once.

Cyril Connolly (1903–74) British journalist. *Enemies of Promise*, Ch. 3

15 I hesitate to say what the functions of the modern journalist may be; but I imagine that they do not exclude the intelligent anticipation of facts even before they occur.

Lord Curzon (1859–1925) British politician. Speech, House of Commons, 29 Mar 1898

16 I am myself a gentleman of the Press, and I bear no other scutcheon.

Benjamin Disraeli (1804–81) British statesman. Speech, House of Commons, 18 Feb 1863

17 Backward ran sentences until reeled the mind.

Wolcott Gibbs (1902–58) US writer. Parodying the style of *Time* magazine. *More in Sorrow*

18 I'm not allowed to say how many planes joined the raid but I counted them all out and I counted them all back.

Brian Hanrahan (1949–) British journalist. Reporting a British air attack in the opening phase of the Falklands War. BBC broadcast, 1 May 1982

19 Good taste is, of course, an utterly dispensable part of any journalist's equipment.

Michael Hogg *The Daily Telegraph*, 2 Dec 1978

20 Editor: a person employed by a newspaper whose business it is to separate the wheat from the chaff and to see that chaff is printed.

'Kin' Hubbard (1868–1930) US humorist. *A Thousand and One Epigrams*

21 Blood sport is brought to its ultimate refinement in the gossip columns.

Bernard Ingham (1932–) British journalist. *The Observer*, 'Sayings of the Week', 28 Dec 1986

22 ...more attentive to the minute hand of history than to the hour hand.

Desmond Macarthy (1887–1952) British writer and theatre critic. Referring to journalism. *Curtains* (K. Tynan)

23 The gallery in which the reporters sit has become a fourth estate of the realm.

Lord Macaulay (1800–59) British historian. Referring to the press gallery in the House of Commons. *Historical Essays Contributed to the 'Edinburgh Review'*, 'Hallam's "Constitutional History"'

24 Once a newspaper touches a story, the facts are lost forever, even to the protagonists.

Norman Mailer (1923–) US writer. *The Presidential Papers*

25 A good newspaper, I suppose, is a nation talking to itself.

Arthur Miller (1915–) US dramatist. *The Observer*, 'Sayings of the Week', 26 Nov 1961

26 SIXTY HORSES WEDGED IN A CHIMNEY
The story to fit this sensational headline has not turned up yet.

J. B. Morton (1893–1979) British journalist. *The Best of Beachcomber*, 'Mr Justice Cocklecarrot: Home Life'

27 A reporter is a man who has renounced everything in life but the world, the flesh, and the devil.

David Murray (1888–1962) British journalist. *The Observer*, 'Sayings of the Week', 5 July 1931

28 I don't hate the press: I find a lot of it very unpalatable. But if that's the way they want to behave...

Prince Philip (1921–) The consort of Queen Elizabeth II. *Independent on Sunday*, 1992

29 We live under a government of men and morning newspapers.

Wendell Phillips (1811–84) US reformer. *Address: The Press*

30 The *New Yorker* will not be edited for the old lady from Dubuque.

Harold W. Ross (1892–1951) US journalist. Attrib.

31 Its primary office is the gathering of news. At the peril of its soul it must see that the supply is not tainted. Neither in what it gives, nor in what it does not give, nor in the mode of presentation, must the unclouded face of truth suffer wrong. Comment is free but facts are sacred.

C. P. Scott (1846–1932) British journalist. *Manchester Guardian*, 6 May 1926

32 He's someone who flies around from hotel to hotel and thinks the most interesting thing about any story is the fact that he has arrived to cover it.

Tom Stoppard (1937–) Czech-born British dramatist. Referring to foreign correspondents. *Night and Day*, I

33 The only qualities essential for real success in journalism are rat-like cunning, a plausible manner, and a little literary ability.

Nicholas Tomalin (1931–73) British journalist. *The Sunday Times Magazine*, 26 Oct 1969

34 Journalism – an ability to meet the challenge of filling the space.

Rebecca West (Cicely Isabel Fairfield; 1892–1983) British novelist and journalist. *The New York Herald Tribune*, 22 April 1956

35 There is much to be said in favour of modern journalism. By giving us the opinions of the uneducated, it keeps us in touch with the ignorance of the community.

Oscar Wilde (1854–1900) Irish-born British dramatist. *The Critic as Artist*, Pt. 2

36 You cannot hope
to bribe or twist,
thank God! the
British journalist.

But, seeing what
the man will do
unbribed, there's
no occasion to.

Humbert Wolfe (1886–1940) British poet. *The Uncelestial City*, Bk. I, 'Over the Fire'

37 Rock journalism is people who can't write interviewing people who can't talk for people who can't read.

Frank Zappa (1940–93) US rock musician. Attrib.

38 The problem with doing a rock interview in the first place is that the person coming to talk to you a) doesn't know anything about what you do b) doesn't know about music in general and c) has already made up in advance before he comes to you what the answer ought to be to his precious little question.

Frank Zappa *The Real Frank Zappa Book*

JOYCE, JAMES

(1882–1941) Irish novelist and poet. His short stories *The Dubliners* (1914) brought him to public notice, but it was his controversial stream-of-consciousness novel *Ulysses* (1922) that made him famous. *Finnegans Wake* (1939) was his last book.

Quotations about Joyce

1 My God, what a clumsy olla putrida James Joyce is! Nothing but old fags and cabbage-stumps of quotations from the Bible and the rest, stewed in the juice of deliberate, journalistic dirty-mindedness.

D. H. Lawrence (1885–1930) British novelist. Letter to Aldous Huxley, 15 Aug 1928

2 There are passages of *Ulysses* that can be read only in the toilet if one wants to extract the full flavour from them.

Henry Miller (1891–1980) US novelist. *Black Spring*

3 *Ulysses*...I rather wish I had never read it. It gives me an inferiority complex. When I read a book like that and then come back to my own work, I feel like a eunuch who has taken a course in voice production and can pass himself off fairly well as a bass or a baritone, but if you listen closely you can hear the good old squeak just the same as ever.

George Orwell (Eric Blair; 1903–50) British novelist. Letter to Brenda Salkeld, Sept 1934

4 He was not only the greatest literary stylist of his time. He was also the only living representative of the European tradition of the artist who carries on with his creative work unaffected by the storm which breaks around him in the world outside his study.

Stephen Spender (1909–) British poet. *The Listener*, 23 Jan 1941

Quotations by Joyce

5 Three quarks for Muster Mark!

The word quark has since been adopted by physicists for hypothetical elementary particles. *Finnegans Wake*

6 Ireland is the old sow that eats her farrow.

A Portrait of the Artist as a Young Man, Ch. 5

7 'When I makes tea I makes tea,' as old mother Grogan said. 'And when I makes water I makes water'.

Ulysses

8 'History', Stephen said, 'is a nightmare from which I am trying to awake'.

Ulysses

9 Greater love than this, he said, no man hath that a man lay down his wife for a friend. Go thou and do likewise. Thus, or words to that effect, saith Zarathustra, sometime regius professor of French letters to the University of Oxtail.

Ulysses

10 The snotgreen sea. The scrotumtightening sea.

Ulysses

11 It is a symbol of Irish art. The cracked looking glass of a servant.

Ulysses

12 The desire of the moth for the star.

Commenting on the interruption of a music recital when a moth flew into the singer's mouth. *James Joyce* (R. Ellmann)

13 Never mind about my soul, just make sure you get my tie right.

Responding to the painter Patrick Tuohy's assertion that he wished to capture Joyce's soul in his portrait of him. *James Joyce* (R. Ellmann)

14 We have met too late. You are too old for me to have any effect on you.

On meeting the poet, W. B. Yeats, a fellow Irishman. *James Joyce* (R. Ellmann)

JUDGMENT

1 And this is the writing that was written, MENE, MENE, TEKEL, UPHARSIN.
This is the interpretation of the thing: MENE; God hath numbered thy kingdom, and finished it.
TEKEL; Thou art weighed in the balances, and art found wanting.
PERES; Thy kingdom is divided, and given to the Medes and Persians.

Bible: Daniel 5:25–28

2 Judge not, that ye be not judged.

Bible: Matthew 7:1

3 And why beholdest thou the mote that is in thy brother's eye, but considerest not the beam that is in thine own eye?

Bible: Matthew 7:3

4 And I saw a great white throne, and him that sat on it, from whose face the earth and the heaven fled away; and there was found no place for them. And I saw the dead, small and great, stand before God; and the books were opened: and another book was opened, which is the book of life: and the dead were

judged out of those things which were written in the books, according to their works.
And the sea gave up the dead which were in it; and death and hell delivered up the dead which were in them: and they were judged every man according to their works.

Bible: Revelations 20:11–13

5 No man can justly censure or condemn another, because indeed no man truly knows another.

Thomas Browne (1605–82) English physician and writer. *Religio Medici*, Pt. II

6 Your representative owes you, not his industry only, but his judgement; and he betrays instead of serving you if he sacrifices it to your opinion.

Edmund Burke (1729–97) British politician. Speech to the electors of Bristol, 3 Nov 1774

7 You shall judge of a man by his foes as well as by his friends.

Joseph Conrad (Teodor Josef Konrad Korzeniowski; 1857–1924) Polish-born British novelist. *Lord Jim*, Ch. 34

8 Force, if unassisted by judgement, collapses through its own mass.

Horace (Quintus Horatius Flaccus; 65–8 BC) Roman poet. *Odes*, III

9 Everyone complains of his memory, but no one complains of his judgement.

Duc de la Rochefoucauld (1613–80) French writer. *Maximes*, 89

JUNG, CARL GUSTAV

(1875–1961) Swiss psychoanalyst. He collaborated with Freud until 1912, subsequently elaborated his own theory of analysis, described in such books as *The Psychology of the Unconscious* (1916) and *Modern Man in Search of a Soul* (1933).

1 Fortunately, in her kindness and patience, Nature has never put the fatal question as to the meaning of their lives into the mouths of most people. And where no one asks, no one needs to answer.

The Development of Personality

2 The pendulum of the mind oscillates between sense and nonsense, not between right and wrong.

Memories, Dreams, Reflections, Ch. 5

3 A man who has not passed through the inferno of his passions has never overcome them.

Memories, Dreams, Reflections, Ch. 9

4 As far as we can discern, the sole purpose of human existence is to kindle a light in the darkness of mere being.

Memories, Dreams, Reflections, Ch. 11

5 Every form of addiction is bad, no matter whether the narcotic be alcohol or morphine or idealism.

Memories, Dreams, Reflections, Ch. 12

6 Among all my patients in the second half of life...there has not been one whose problem in the last resort was not that of finding a religious outlook on life.

Modern Man in Search of a Soul

7 The least of things with a meaning is worth more in life than the greatest of things without it.

Modern Man in Search of a Soul

8 Sentimentality is a superstructure covering brutality.

Reflections

9 Show me a sane man and I will cure him for you.

The Observer, 19 July 1975

10 Wherever an inferiority complex exists, there is a good reason for it. There is always something inferior there, although not just where we persuade ourselves that it is.

Interview, 1943

11 We need more understanding of human nature, because the only real danger that exists is man himself...We know nothing of man, far too little. His psyche should be studied because we are the origin of all coming evil.

BBC television interview

JUSTICE

See also injustice, judgment, law, lawyers

1 The place of justice is a hallowed place.

Francis Bacon (1561–1626) English philosopher. *Essays*, 'Of Judicature'

2 When I came back to Dublin, I was court-martialled in my absence and sentenced to death in my absence, so I said they could shoot me in my absence.

Brendan Behan (1923–64) Irish playwright. *The Hostage*, I

3 It is better that ten guilty persons escape than one innocent suffer.

William Blackstone (1723–80) British jurist. *Commentaries on the Laws of England*, Bk. IV, Ch. 27

4 The rain it raineth on the just
And also on the unjust fella:
But chiefly on the just, because
The unjust steals the just's umbrella.

Charles Bowen (1835–94) British judge. *Sands of Time* (Walter Sichel)

5 Trial by jury itself, instead of being a security to persons who are accused, will be a delusion, a mockery, and a snare.

Thomas Denman (1779–1854) British judge. Judgment, 4 Sept 1844

6 'It is my duty to warn you that it will be used against you,' cried the Inspector, with the magnificent fair play of the British criminal law.

Arthur Conan Doyle (1856–1930) British writer. *The Dancing Men*

7 Let justice be done, though the world perish.

Ferdinand I (1503–64) Holy Roman Emperor. Attrib.

8 Ah, colonel, all's fair in love and war, you know.

Nathan Bedford Forrest (1821–77) Confederate general. Remark to a captured enemy officer who had been tricked into surrendering. *A Civil War Treasury* (B. Botkin)

9 Let no guilty man escape, if it can be avoided...

No personal considerations should stand in the way of performing a public duty.

Ulysses Simpson Grant (1822–85) US general. Referring to the Whiskey Ring. Indorsement of a letter, 29 July 1875

10 Justice should not only be done, but should manifestly and undoubtedly be seen to be done.

Gordon Hewart (1870–1943) British lawyer and politician. *The Chief* (R. Jackson)

11 I have come to regard the law courts not as a cathedral but rather as a casino.

Richard Ingrams (1937–) British editor. *The Guardian*, 30 July 1977

12 Consider, Sir, how should you like, though conscious of your innocence, to be tried before a jury for a capital crime, once a week.

Samuel Johnson (1709–84) British lexicographer. *Life of Johnson* (J. Boswell), Vol. III

13 A lawyer has no business with the justice or injustice of the cause which he undertakes, unless his client asks his opinion, and then he is bound to give it honestly. The justice or injustice of the cause is to be decided by the judge.

Samuel Johnson *Tour to the Hebrides* (J. Boswell)

14 I am a warrior in the time of women warriors; the longing for justice is the sword I carry, the love of womankind my shield.

Sonia Johnson (c. 1936–) US feminist and writer. *From Housewife to Heretic*

15 Justice is the constant and perpetual wish to render to every one his due.

Justinian I (482–565 AD) Byzantine emperor. *Institutes*, I

16 Justice is such a fine thing that we cannot pay too dearly for it.

Alain-René Lesage (1668–1747) French writer. *Crispin rival de son maître*, IX

17 I'm arm'd with more than complete steel –
The justice of my quarrel.

Christopher Marlowe (1564–93) English dramatist. Play also attributed to others. *Lust's Dominion*, IV:3

18 In England, Justice is open to all, like the Ritz hotel.

James Mathew (1830–1908) British judge. Also attrib. to Lord Darling. *Miscellany-at-Law* (R. E. Megarry)

19 A judge is not supposed to know anything about the facts of life until they have been presented in evidence and explained to him at least three times.

Hubert Lister Parker (1900–72) Lord Chief Justice of England. *The Observer*, 'Sayings of the Week', 12 Mar 1961

20 The hungry judges soon the sentence sign,
And wretches hang that jury-men may dine.

Alexander Pope (1688–1744) British poet. *The Rape of the Lock*, III

21 The love of justice in most men is simply the fear of suffering injustice.

Duc de la Rochefoucauld (1613–80) French writer. *Maximes*, 78

22 A man who is good enough to shed his blood for the country is good enough to be given a square deal afterwards. More than that no man is entitled to, and less than that no man shall have.

Theodore Roosevelt (1858–1919) US Republican president. Speech at the Lincoln Monument, Springfield, Illinois, 4 June 1903

23 Haste still pays haste, and leisure answers leisure;
Like doth quit like, and Measure still for Measure.

William Shakespeare (1564–1616) English dramatist. *Measure for Measure*, V:1

24 This is a British murder inquiry and some degree of justice must be seen to be more or less done.

Tom Stoppard (1937–) Czech-born British dramatist. *Jumpers*, II

25 Under a government which imprisons any unjustly, the true place for a just man is also a prison.

Henry David Thoreau (1817–62) US writer. *Civil Disobedience*

26 The end may justify the means as long as there is something that justifies the end.

Leon Trotsky (Lev Davidovich Bronstein; 1879–1940) Russian revolutionary. *Antonio Gramsci: an introduction to his thought* (A. Pozzolini), Preface

K

KAFKA, FRANZ

(1883–1924) Czech novelist, many of whose books were published posthumously against his wish by Max Brod, his literary executor. His novels include *Metamorphosis* (1912), *The Trial* (1925), and *The Castle* (1926).

1 Don't despair, not even over the fact that you don't despair.
Diary

2 I have the true feeling of myself only when I am unbearably unhappy.
Diary

3 It's often safer to be in chains than to be free.
The Trial, Ch. 8

4 Let me remind you of the old maxim: people under suspicion are better moving than at rest, since at rest they may be sitting in the balance without knowing it, being weighed together with their sins
The Trial, Ch. 8

KANT, IMMANUEL

(1724–1804) German philosopher. His *Critique of Pure Reason* (1781), *Critique of Practical Reason* (1788), and *Critique of Judgment* (1790) summarize his powerful theories.

1 Two things fill the mind with ever new and increasing wonder and awe, the more often and the more seriously reflection concentrates upon them: the starry heaven above me and the moral law within me.
Critique of Practical Reason, Conclusion

2 Finally, there is an imperative which commands a certain conduct immediately...This imperative is Categorical...This imperative may be called that of Morality.
Grundlegung zur Metaphysik der Sitten, II

3 ...because happiness is not an ideal of reason but of imagination.
Grundlegung zur Metaphysik der Sitten, II

4 Out of the crooked timber of humanity no straight thing can ever be made.
Idee zu einer allgemeinen Geschichte in weltbürgerlicher Absicht

KEATS, JOHN

(1795–1821) British poet. Trained as a doctor, he devoted most of his short life to poetry. *Endymion* (1818) was attacked by the critics but he eventually established his reputation with *La Belle Dame Sans Merci* (1820), *Ode to a Nightingale* (1820), and other works. He died in Rome of tuberculosis.

Quotations about Keats

1 What harm he has done in English Poetry. As Browning is a man with a moderate gift passionately desiring movement and fulness, and obtaining but a confused multitudinousness, so Keats with a very high gift, is yet also consumed with this desire: and cannot produce the truly living and moving, as his conscience keeps telling him.
Matthew Arnold (1822–88) British poet and critic. Letter to A. H. Clough, 1848

2 Such writing is a sort of mental masturbation – he is always f–gg–g his *Imagination*. I don't mean he is *indecent*, but viciously soliciting his own ideas into a state, which is neither poetry nor any thing else but a Bedlam vision produced by raw pork and opium.
Lord Byron (1788–1824) British poet. Letter to John Murray, 9 Nov 1820

3 Here is Johnny Keats' piss-a-bed poetry. No more Keats, I entreat; flay him alive; if some of you don't I must skin him myself; there is no bearing the idiotism of the Mankin.
Lord Byron (1788–1824) British poet. Letter to John Murray, 12 Oct 1821

4 In what other English poet (however superior to him in other respects) are you so *certain* of never opening a page without lighting upon the loveliest imagery and the most eloquent expressions? Name one.
Leigh Hunt (1784–1859) British poet. *Imagination and Fancy*

5 I see a schoolboy when I think of him. With face and nose pressed to a sweetshop window.
W. B. Yeats (1865–1939) Irish poet.

Quotations by Keats

6 Bright star, would I were steadfast as thou art.
Bright Star

7 A thing of beauty is a joy for ever:
Its loveliness increases; it will never
Pass into nothingness; but still will keep
A bower quiet for us, and a sleep
Full of sweet dreams, and health, and quiet breathing.
Endymion, I

8 Their smiles,
Wan as primroses gather'd at midnight
By chilly finger'd spring.
Endymion, IV

9 St Agnes' Eve – Ah, bitter chill it was!
The owl, for all his feathers, was a-cold;
The hare limp'd trembling through the frozen grass,
And silent was the flock in woolly fold.
The Eve of Saint Agnes, I

10 The Beadsman, after thousand aves told,
For aye unsought-for slept among his ashes cold.
The Eve of Saint Agnes, I

11 Soft adorings from their loves receive
Upon the honey'd middle of the night.
The Eve of Saint Agnes, VI

12 The music, yearning like a God in pain.

The Eve of Saint Agnes, VII

13 He play'd an ancient ditty, long since mute,
In Provence call'd, 'La belle dame sans mercy'.
The Eve of Saint Agnes, XXXIII

14 And they are gone: aye, ages long ago
These lovers fled away into the storm.
The Eve of Saint Agnes, XLII

15 Fanatics have their dreams, wherewith they weave
A paradise for a sect.
The Fall of Hyperion, I

16 The poet and the dreamer are distinct,
Diverse, sheer opposite, antipodes.
The one pours out a balm upon the world,
The other vexes it.
The Fall of Hyperion, I

17 Ever let the fancy roam,
Pleasure never is at home.
Fancy, I

18 Where's the cheek that doth not fade,
Too much gaz'd at? Where's the maid
Whose lip mature is ever new?
Fancy, I

19 Four seasons fill the measure of the year;
There are four seasons in the mind of man.
Four Seasons

20 O aching time! O moments big as years!
Hyperion, I

21 As when, upon a trancèd summer-night,
Those green-rob'd senators of mighty woods,
Tall oaks, branch-charmèd by the earnest stars,
Dream, and so dream all night without a stir.
Hyperion, I

22 Oh what can ail thee, knight at arms
Alone and palely loitering;
The sedge has wither'd from the lake,
And no birds sing.
La Belle Dame Sans Merci

23 'La belle Dame sans Merci
Hath thee in thrall!'
La Belle Dame Sans Merci

24 Love in a hut, with water and a crust,
Is – Love, forgive us! – cinders, ashes, dust;
Love in a palace is perhaps at last
More grievous torment than a hermit's fast.
Lamia, II

25 Do not all charms fly
At the mere touch of cold philosophy?
Lamia, II

26 Souls of poets dead and gone,
What Elysium have ye known,
Happy field or mossy cavern,
Choicer than the Mermaid Tavern?
Have ye tippled drink more fine
Than mine host's Canary wine?
Lines on the Mermaid Tavern

27 Thou still unravish'd bride of quietness,
Thou foster-child of silence and slow time.
Ode on a Grecian Urn

28 Heard melodies are sweet, but those unheard
Are sweeter; therefore, ye soft pipes, play on.
Ode on a Grecian Urn

29 Thou, silent form, dost tease us out of thought
As doth eternity: Cold Pastoral!
Ode on a Grecian Urn

30 'Beauty is truth, truth beauty,' – that is all
Ye know on earth, and all ye need to know.
Ode on a Grecian Urn

31 For ever warm and still to be enjoy'd,
For ever panting and for ever young;
All breathing human passion far above,
That leaves a heart high-sorrowful and cloy'd,
A burning forehead, and a parching tongue.
Ode on a Grecian Urn

32 No, no, go not to Lethe, neither twist
Wolf's-bane, tight-rooted, for its poisonous wine.
Ode on Melancholy

33 Nor let the beetle, nor the death-moth be
Your mournful Psyche.
Ode on Melancholy

34 Ay, in the very temple of delight
Veil'd Melancholy has her sovran shrine.
Though seen of none save him whose strenuous tongue
Can burst Joy's grape against his palate fine.
Ode on Melancholy

35 My heart aches, and a drowsy numbness pains
My sense.
Ode to a Nightingale

36 O, for a draught of vintage! that hath been
Cool'd a long age in the deep-delved earth.
Ode to a Nightingale

37 O for a beaker full of the warm South,
Full of the true, the blushful Hippocrene,
With beaded bubbles winking at the brim,
And purple-stained mouth.
Ode to a Nightingale

38 Fade far away, dissolve, and quite forget
What thou among the leaves hast never known,
The weariness, the fever, and the fret,
Here, where men sit and hear each other groan.
Ode to a Nightingale

39 Thou wast not born for death, immortal Bird!
No hungry generations tread thee down;
The voice I hear this passing night was heard
In ancient days by emperor and clown:
Perhaps the self-same song that found a path
Through the sad heart of Ruth, when sick for home,
She stood in tears amid the alien corn;
The same that oft-times hath
Charm'd magic casements, opening on the foam
Of perilous seas, in faery lands forlorn.
Ode to a Nightingale

40 Darkling I listen; and, for many a time
I have been half in love with easeful Death,
Call'd him soft names in many a musèd rhyme,
To take into the air my quiet breath;
Now more than ever seems it rich to die,

To cease upon the midnight with no pain,
While thou art pouring forth thy soul abroad
In such an ecstasy!
Ode to a Nightingale

41 Much have I travell'd in the realms of gold,
And many goodly states and kingdoms seen.
On first looking into Chapman's Homer

42 Then felt I like some watcher of the skies
When a new planet swims into his ken;
Or like stout Cortez when with eagle eyes
He star'd at the Pacific – and all his men
Look'd at each other with a wild surmise –
Silent, upon a peak in Darien.
On first looking into Chapman's Homer

43 It keeps eternal whisperings around
Desolate shores, and with its mighty swell
Gluts twice ten thousand Caverns.
On the Sea

44 A drainless shower
Of light is poesy; 'tis the supreme of power;
'Tis might half slumb'ring on its own right arm.
Sleep and Poetry

45 Season of mists and mellow fruitfulness,
Close bosom-friend of the maturing sun;
Conspiring with him how to load and bless
With fruit the vines that round the thatch-eaves run.
To Autumn

46 Where are the songs of Spring? Ay, where are they?
To Autumn

47 O soft embalmer of the still midnight.
To Sleep

48 Turn the key deftly in the oiled wards,
And seal the hushed casket of my soul.
To Sleep

49 Here lies one whose name was writ in water.
Suggesting his own epitaph (recalling a line from *Philaster* by Beaumont and Fletcher). *Life of Keats* (Lord Houghton), Ch. 2

50 A long poem is a test of invention which I take to be the Polar star of poetry, as fancy is the sails, and imagination the rudder.
Letter to Benjamin Bailey, 8 Oct 1817

51 I am certain of nothing but the holiness of the heart's affections and the truth of imagination – what the imagination seizes as beauty must be truth – whether it existed before or not.
Letter to Benjamin Bailey, 22 Nov 1817

52 O for a life of sensations rather than of thoughts!
Letter to Benjamin Bailey, 22 Nov 1817

53 Negative Capability, that is, when a man is capable of being in uncertainties, mysteries, doubts, without any irritable reaching after fact and reason.
Letter to G. and T. Keats, 21 Dec 1817

54 The excellence of every art is its intensity, capable of making all disagreeables evaporate, from their being in close relationship with beauty and truth.
Letter to G. and T. Keats, 21 Dec 1817

55 There is an old saying 'well begun is half done' – 'tis a bad one. I would use instead – Not begun at all until half done.
Letter, 1817

56 We hate poetry that has a palpable design upon us – and if we do not agree, seems to put its hand in its breeches pocket. Poetry should be great and unobtrusive, a thing which enters into one's soul, and does not startle or amaze it with itself, but with its subject.
Letter to J. H. Reynolds, 3 Feb 1818

57 If poetry comes not as naturally as leaves to a tree it had better not come at all.
Letter to John Taylor, 27 Feb 1818

58 Scenery is fine – but human nature is finer.
Letter to Benjamin Bailey, 13 Mar 1818

59 Axioms in philosophy are not axioms until they are proved upon our pulses; we read fine things but never feel them to the full until we have gone the same steps as the author.
Letter to J. H. Reynolds, 3 May 1818

60 I am in that temper that if I were under water I would scarcely kick to come to the top.
Letter to Benjamin Bailey, 25 May 1818

61 I do think better of womankind than to suppose they care whether Mister John Keats five feet high likes them or not.
Letter to Benjamin Bailey, 18 July 1818

62 I think I shall be among the English Poets after my death.
Letter to George and Georgiana Keats, 14 Oct 1818

63 I never can feel certain of any truth but from a clear perception of its beauty.
Letter to George and Georgiana Keats, 16 Dec 1818–4 Jan 1819

64 Nothing ever becomes real till it is experienced – even a proverb is no proverb to you till your life has illustrated it.
Letter to George and Georgiana Keats, 19 Mar 1819

65 My friends should drink a dozen of Claret on my Tomb.
Letter to Benjamin Bailey, 14 Aug 1819

66 Give me books, fruit, French wine and fine weather and a little music out of doors, played by somebody I do not know.
Letter to Fanny Keats, 29 Aug 1819

67 Love is my religion – I could die for that.
Letter to Fanny Brawne, 13 Oct 1819

68 Though a quarrel in the streets is a thing to be hated, the energies displayed in it are fine; the commonest man shows a grace in his quarrel.
Letter

69 I go among the fields and catch a glimpse of a stoat or a fieldmouse peeping out of the withered grass – the creature hath a purpose and its eyes are bright with it. I go amongst the buildings of a city and I see a man hurrying along – to what? the

Creature has a purpose and his eyes are bright with it.

Letter to George and Georgiana Keats, 19 Mar 1819

70 Upon the whole I dislike mankind: whatever people on the other side of the question may advance, they cannot deny that they are always surprised at hearing of a good action and never of a bad one.

Letter, 1820

71 Is there another life? Shall I awake and find all this a dream? There must be, we cannot be created for this sort of suffering.

Letter, 1820

72 I shall soon be laid in the quiet grave – thank God for the quiet grave – O! I can feel the cold earth upon me – the daisies growing over me – O for this quiet – it will be my first.

In a letter to John Taylor by Joseph Severn, 6 Mar 1821

KENNEDY, JOHN FITZGERALD

(1917–63) US statesman; the first Roman Catholic President (1961–63). His liberal New Frontier policies were cut short by his assassination.

Quotations about Kennedy

1 The enviably attractive nephew who sings an Irish ballad for the company and then winsomely disappears before the table-clearing and dishwashing begin.

Lyndon B. Johnson (1908–73) US statesman. *A Political Education* (H. McPherson)

2 Kennedy the politician exuded that musk odour which acts as an aphrodisiac to many women.

Theodore H. White (1906–64) British novelist. *In Search of History*

Quotations by Kennedy

3 It was involuntary. They sank my boat.

Responding to praise of his courage whilst serving in the US navy against the Japanese in World War II. *Nobody Said It Better* (M. Ringo)

4 I can't see that it's wrong to give him a little legal experience before he goes out to practice law.

On being criticized for making his brother Robert attorney general. *Nobody Said It Better* (M. Ringo)

5 I guess this is the week I earn my salary.

Comment made during the Cuban missile crisis. *Nobody Said It Better* (M. Ringo)

6 We must use time as a tool, not as a couch.

The Observer, 'Sayings of the Week', 10 Dec 1961

7 The United States has to move very fast to even stand still.

The Observer, 'Sayings of the Week', 21 July 1963

8 The worse I do, the more popular I get.

Referring to his popularity following the failure of the US invasion of Cuba. *The People's Almanac* (D. Wallechinsky)

KEY, ELLEN

(Karolina Sofia Key; 1849–1926) Swedish writer and feminist. After teaching and lecturing in Sweden, she made a number of lecture tours abroad.

1 ...the emancipation of women is practically the greatest egoistic movement of the nineteenth century, and the most intense affirmation of the right of the self that history has yet seen...

The Century of the Child, Ch. 2

2 At every step the child should be allowed to meet the real experiences of life; the thorns should never be plucked from his roses.

The Century of the Child, Ch. 3

3 Nothing would more effectively further the development of education than for all flogging pedagogues to learn to educate with the head instead of with the hand.

The Century of the Child, Ch. 3

4 Corporal punishment is as humiliating for him who gives it as for him who receives it; it is ineffective besides. Neither shame nor physical pain have any other effect than a hardening one...

The Century of the Child, Ch. 8

5 Love is moral even without legal marriage, but marriage is immoral without love.

The Morality of Woman and Other Essays, 'The Morality of Woman'

6 Formerly, a nation that broke the peace did not trouble to try and prove to the world that it was done solely from higher motives...*Now war has a bad conscience*. Now every nation assures us that it is bleeding for a human cause, the fate of which hangs in the balance of its victory.... No nation dares to admit the guilt of blood before the world.

War, Peace, and the Future, Preface

7 Everything, everything in war is barbaric...But the worst barbarity of war is that it forces men collectively to commit acts against which individually they would revolt with their whole being.

War, Peace, and the Future, Ch. 6

KEYNES, JOHN MAYNARD, BARON

(1883–1946) British economist. His *General Theory of Employment, Interest and Money* (1936), which supports increased public spending as a means of reducing unemployment, still has its advocates.

1 In the long run we are all dead.

Collected Writings, 'A Tract on Monetary Reform'

2 I do not know which makes a man more conservative – to know nothing but the present, or nothing but the past.

The End of Laisser-Faire, I

3 Marxian Socialism must always remain a portent to the historians of Opinion – how a doctrine so illogical and so dull can have exercised so powerful and enduring an influence over the minds of men, and, through them, the events of history.

The End of Laisser-Faire, III

4 This goat-footed bard, this half-human visitor to

our age from the hag-ridden magic and enchanted woods of Celtic antiquity.

Essays and Sketches in Biography, 'Mr Lloyd George'

5 Worldly wisdom teaches that it is better for the reputation to fail conventionally than to succeed unconventionally.

The General Theory of Employment, Interest and Money, Bk. IV, Ch. 12

6 It is better that a man should tyrannize over his bank balance than over his fellow citizens.

The General Theory of Employment, Interest and Money, Bk. VI, Ch. 24

7 Practical men, who believe themselves to be quite exempt from any intellectual influences, are usually the slaves of some defunct economist. Madmen in authority, who hear voices in the air, are distilling their frenzy from some academic scribbler of a few years back.

The General Theory of Employment, Interest and Money, Bk. VI, Ch. 24

8 I will not be a party to debasing the currency.

On refusing to pay more than a small tip on having his shoes polished, whilst on a visit to Africa. *John Maynard Keynes* (C. Hession)

9 Does that mean that because Americans won't listen to sense, you intend to talk nonsense to them?

Said before a monetary conference, 1944 or 1945.

10 No, I don't know his telephone number. But it was up in the high numbers.

Attrib.

11 The avoidance of taxes is the only pursuit that still carries any reward.

Attrib.

KHAYYAM, OMAR

see **Fitzgerald, Edward**

KHRUSHCHEV, NIKITA

(1894–1971) Soviet statesman. Stalin's successor, he became prime minister (1958–64). As a result of his unsuccessful confrontation with Kennedy over the attempted installation of missiles in Cuba he was ousted from office.

1 We had no use for the policy of the Gospels: if someone slaps you, just turn the other cheek. We had shown that anyone who slapped us on our cheek would get his head kicked off.

Khrushchev Remembers, Vol. II

2 When you are skinning your customers, you should leave some skin on to grow so that you can skin them again.

Said to British businessmen. *The Observer*, 'Sayings of the Week', 28 May 1961

3 They talk about who won and who lost. Human reason won. Mankind won.

Referring to the Cuban missiles crisis. *The Observer*, 'Sayings of the Week', 11 Nov 1962

4 If you start throwing hedgehogs under me, I shall throw a couple of porcupines under you.

The Observer, 'Sayings of the Week', 10 Nov 1963

5 Every year humanity takes a step towards Communism. Maybe not you, but at all events your grandson will surely be a Communist.

Said to Sir William Hayter, June 1956

6 We will bury you.

Said at a reception at the Kremlin, 18 Nov 1956

7 Politicians are the same all over. They promise to build a bridge even where there's no river.

Said to journalists while visiting the USA, Oct 1960

8 If you feed people just with revolutionary slogans they will listen today, they will listen tomorrow, they will listen the day after tomorrow, but on the fourth day they will say 'To hell with you!'

Attrib.

KILLING

See also assassination, death, murder, suicide

1 Difficult as it may be to cure, it is always easy to poison and to kill.

Elisha Bartlett (1804–55) *Philosophy of Medical Science*, Pt. II, Ch. 16

2 And Samson said, With the jawbone of an ass, heaps upon heaps, with the jaw of an ass have I slain a thousand men.

Bible: Judges 15:16

3 Euthanasia is a long, smooth-sounding word, and it conceals its danger as long, smooth words do, but the danger is there, nevertheless.

Pearl Buck (1892–1973) US novelist. *The Child Who Never Grew*, Ch. 2

4 Thou shalt not kill; but needst not strive
Officiously to keep alive.

Arthur Hugh Clough (1819–61) British poet. *The Latest Decalogue*, 11

5 Ask any soldier. To kill a man is to merit a woman.

Jean Giraudoux (1882–1944) French writer. *Tiger at the Gates*, I

6 To save a man's life against his will is the same as killing him.

Horace (Quintus Horatius Flaccus; 65–8 BC) Roman poet. *Ars Poetica*

7 To kill a human being is, after all, the least injury you can do him.

Henry James (1843–1916) US novelist. *My Friend Bingham*

8 Killing
Is the ultimate simplification of life.

Hugh MacDiarmid (Christopher Murray Grieve; 1892–1978) Scottish poet. *England's Double Knavery*

9 ...there's no difference between one's killing and making decisions that will send others to kill. It's exactly the same thing, or even worse.

Golda Meir (1898–1978) Russian-born Israeli stateswoman. *L'Europeo* (Oriana Fallaci)

10 Kill a man, and you are a murderer. Kill millions of men, and you are a conqueror. Kill everyone, and you are a god.

Jean Rostand (1894–1977) French biologist and writer. *Pensées d'un biologiste*

11 Yet each man kills the thing he loves,
By each let this be heard,
Some do it with a bitter look,
Some with a flattering word.
The coward does it with a kiss,
The brave man with a sword!

Oscar Wilde (1854–1900) Irish-born British dramatist. *The Ballad of Reading Gaol*, I:7

KINDNESS

See also charity, generosity

1 One kind word can warm three winter months.

Japanese Proverb

2 A word of kindness is better than a fat pie.

Russian proverb

3 Pleasant words are as an honeycomb, sweet to the soul, and health to the bones.

Bible: Proverbs 16:24

4 Recompense injury with justice, and recompense kindness with kindness.

Confucius (K'ung Fu-tzu; 551–479 BC) Chinese philosopher. *Analects*

5 I love thee for a heart that's kind –
Not for the knowledge in thy mind.

W. H. Davies (1871–1940) British poet. *Sweet Stay-at-Home*

6 In the sick room, ten cents' worth of human understanding equals ten dollars' worth of medical science.

Martin H. Fischer (1879–1962) *Fischerisms* (Howard Fabing and Ray Marr)

7 True kindness presupposes the faculty of imagining as one's own the suffering and joy of others.

André Gide (1869–1951) French writer.

8 The natural dignity of our work, its unembarrassed kindness, its insight into life, its hold on science – for these privileges, and for all that they bring with them, up and up, high over the top of the tree, the very heavens open, preaching thankfulness.

Stephen Paget (1855–1926) *Confessio Medici*, Epilogue

9 The purpose of human life is to serve and to show compassion and the will to help others.

Albert Schweitzer (1875–1965) Franco-German medical missionary, theologian, philosopher, and organist. *The Schweitzer Album*

10 People pay the doctor for his trouble; for his kindness they still remain in his debt.

Seneca (c. 4 BC–65 AD) Roman writer and statesman.

11 Yet do I fear thy nature;
It is too full o' th' milk of human kindness
To catch the nearest way.

William Shakespeare (1564–1616) English dramatist. *Macbeth*, I:5

12 This is a way to kill a wife with kindness.

William Shakespeare *The Taming of the Shrew*, IV:1

13 So many gods, so many creeds,
So many paths that wind and wind,
While just the art of being kind
Is all the sad world needs.

Ella Wheeler Wilcox (1850–1919) US poet. *The World's Need*

14 That best portion of a good man's life,
His little, nameless, unremembered acts
Of kindness and of love.

William Wordsworth (1770–1850) British poet. *Lines composed a few miles above Tintern Abbey*

KING, MARTIN LUTHER

(1929–68) US Black clergyman and civil-rights leader. His nonviolent demonstrations led to the Civil Rights Act (1964). He was awarded the Nobel Peace Prize in 1964 and assassinated four years later.

1 A riot is at bottom the language of the unheard.

Where do we go from here?

2 I want to be the white man's brother, not his brother-in-law.

New York Journal-American, 10 Sept 1962

3 If a man hasn't discovered something that he would die for, he isn't fit to live.

Speech, Detroit, 23 June 1963

4 I have a dream that one day this nation will rise up, live out the true meaning of its creed: we hold these truths to be self-evident, that all men are created equal.

He used the words 'I have a dream' in a number of speeches.
Speech, Washington, 27 Aug 1963

KINGSLEY, CHARLES

(1819–75) British writer and clergyman. A chaplain to Queen Victoria, he is remembered for his novels, including *Westward Ho!* (1855) and the children's book *The Water Babies* (1863).

1 Be good, sweet maid, and let who will be clever;
Do lovely things, not dream them, all day long;
And so make Life, Death, and that vast For Ever,
One grand sweet song.

A Farewell. To C. E. G.

2 To be discontented with the divine discontent, and to be ashamed with the noble shame, is the very germ and first upgrowth of all virtue.

Health and Education

3 We have used the Bible as if it was a constable's handbook – an opium-dose for keeping beasts of burden patient while they are being overloaded.

Letters to the Chartists, 2

4 'O Mary, go and call the cattle home,
And call the cattle home,
And call the cattle home,
Across the sands of Dee.'
The western wind was wild and dank with foam,
And all alone went she.

The Sands of Dee

5 The western tide crept up along the sand,

And o'er and o'er the sand,
And round and round the sand,
As far as eye could see.
The rolling mist came down and hid the land:
And never home came she.
The Sands of Dee

6 When all the world is young, lad,
And all the trees are green;
And every goose a swan, lad,
And every lass a queen;
Then hey for boot and horse, lad,
And round the world away:
Young blood must have its course, lad,
And every dog his day.
Songs from The Water Babies, 'Young and Old'

7 For men must work, and women must weep,
And there's little to earn, and many to keep,
Though the harbour bar be moaning.
The Three Fishers

8 He did not know that a keeper is only a poacher turned outside in, and a poacher a keeper turned inside out.
The Water Babies, Ch. 1

9 The loveliest fairy in the world; and her name is Mrs Doasyouwouldbedoneby.
The Water Babies, Ch. 5

10 More ways of killing a cat than choking her with cream.
Westward Ho!, Ch. 20

11 Some say that the age of chivalry is past, that the spirit of romance is dead. The age of chivalry is never past, so long as there is a wrong left unredressed on earth.
Life (Mrs C. Kingsley), Vol. II, Ch. 28

KINNOCK, NEIL

(1942–) British politician; leader of the Labour Party from 1983 to 1992. He succeeded in reuniting the Labour Party, but resigned after his second electoral defeat.

1 It is inconceivable that we could transform this society without a major extension of public ownership.
Marxism Today, 1983

2 Proportional Representation, I think, is fundamentally counter-democratic.
Marxism Today, 1983

3 I want to retire at 50. I want to play cricket in the Summer and geriatric football in the winter, and sing in the choir.
The Times, 28 July 1980

4 You cannot fashion a wit out of two half-wits.
The Times, 1983

5 We cannot remove the evils of capitalism without taking its source of power: ownership.
Tribune, 1975

6 I'm prepared to take advice on leisure from Prince Philip. He's a world expert on leisure. He's been practising for most of his adult life.
Western Mail, 1981

7 Compassion is not a sloppy, sentimental feeling for people who are underprivileged or sick...it is an absolutely practical belief that, regardless of a person's background, ability or ability to pay, he should be provided with the best that society has to offer.
Maiden speech, House of Commons, 1970

8 Like Brighton pier, all right as far as it goes, but inadequate for getting to France.
Speech, House of Commons, 1981

9 Those who prate about Blimpish patriotism in the mode of Margaret Thatcher are also the ones who will take millions off the caring services of this country.
Speech, Labour Party Conference, Brighton, 1983

10 The grotesque chaos of a Labour council – a *Labour* council – hiring taxis to scuttle around a city handing out redundancy notices to its own workers.
Attacking militant members in Liverpool. Speech, Labour Party Conference, Bournemouth, 1985

11 Political renegades always start their career of treachery as 'the best men of all parties' and end up in the Tory knackery.
Speech, Welsh Labour Party Conference, 1985

12 The idea that there is a model Labour voter, a blue-collar council house tenant who belongs to a union and has 2.4 children, a five-year-old car and a holiday in Blackpool, is patronizing and politically immature.
Speech, 1986

13 I would die for my country...but I would not let my country die for me.
Speech on nuclear disarmament, 1987

14 Sanctions are now the only feasible, non-violent way of ending apartheid. The other road to change is covered with blood.
Speech, July 1988

KIPLING, RUDYARD

(1865–1936) Indian-born British writer and poet. His verse collection *Barrack Room Ballads and Other Verses* (1892) included the well-known poems 'If' and 'Gunga Din'. Other works were the *Jungle Books* (1894, 1895), *Kim* (1901) and the children's books *Just So Stories* (1902) and *Puck of Pook's Hill* (1906).

Quotations about Kipling

1 I doubt that the infant monster has any more to give.
Henry James (1843–1916) US novelist. *Letters*, Vol. 3

2 Kipling has done more than any other since Disraeli to show the world that the British race is sound to the core and that rust and dry rot are strangers to it.
Cecil Rhodes (1853–1902) South African statesman. *Rhodes: A Life* (J. G. MacDonald)

3 When the Rudyards cease from Kipling
And the Haggards ride no more.
James Kenneth Stephen (1859–92) British writer. *Lapsus Calami*, 'to R. K.'

Quotations by Kipling

4 Oh, East is East, and West is West, and never the twain shall meet.
The Ballad of East and West

5 And a woman is only a woman, but a good cigar is a smoke.
The Betrothed

6 Teach us delight in simple things,
And mirth that has no bitter springs;
Forgiveness free of evil done,
And love to all men 'neath the sun!
The Children's Song

7 But the Devil whoops, as he whooped of old:
'It's clever, but is it art?'
The Conundrum of the Workshops

8 'For they're hangin' Danny Deever, you can hear the Dead March play,
The Regiment's in 'ollow square – they're hangin' 'im to-day;
They've taken of 'is buttons off an' cut 'is stripes away,
An' they're hangin' Danny Deever in the mornin'.'
Danny Deever

9 Winds of the World, give answer! They are whimpering to and fro –
And what should they know of England who only England know?
The English Flag

10 When the Himalayan peasant meets the he-bear in his pride,
He shouts to scare the monster, who will often turn aside.
But the she-bear thus accosted rends the peasant tooth and nail
For the female of the species is more deadly than the male.
The Female of the Species

11 So 'ere's to you, Fuzzy-Wuzzy, at your 'ome in the Soudan;
You're a pore benighted 'eathen but a first-class fightin' man;
An' 'ere's to you, Fuzzy-Wuzzy, with your 'ayrick 'ead of 'air –
You big black boundin' beggar – for you broke a British square!
Fuzzy-Wuzzy

12 We're poor little lambs who've lost our way,
Baa! Baa! Baa!
We're little black sheep who've gone astray,
Baa-aa-aa!
Gentleman-rankers out on the spree,
Damned from here to Eternity,
God ha' mercy on such as we,
Baa! Yah! Bah!
Gentleman-Rankers

13 Oh, Adam was a gardener, and God who made him sees
That half a proper gardener's work is done upon his knees,
So when your work is finished, you can wash your hands and pray
For the Glory of the Garden, that it may not pass away!
The Glory of the Garden

14 The uniform 'e wore
Was nothin' much before,
An' rather less than 'arf o' that be'ind.
Gunga Din

15 An' for all 'is dirty 'ide
'E was white, clear white, inside
When 'e went to tend the wounded under fire!
Gunga Din

16 Though I've belted you an' flayed you,
By the livin' Gawd that made you,
You're a better man than I am, Gunga Din!
Gunga Din

17 If you can keep your head when all about you
Are losing theirs and blaming it on you,
If you can trust yourself when all men doubt you,
But make allowance for their doubting too;
...
If you can meet with Triumph and Disaster
And treat those two imposters just the same.
If

18 If you can talk with crowds and keep your virtue,
Or walk with Kings – nor lose the common touch,
If neither foes nor loving friends can hurt you,
If all men count with you, but none too much;
If you can fill the unforgiving minute
With sixty seconds' worth of distance run,
Yours is the Earth and everything that's in it,
And – which is more – you'll be a Man my son!
If

19 Asia is not going to be civilized after the methods of the West. There is too much Asia and she is too old.
Life's Handicap, 'The Man Who Was'

20 The Light that Failed.
Novel title

21 The Saxon is not like us Normans. His manners are not so polite.
But he never means anything serious till he talks about justice and right,
When he stands like an ox in the furrow with his sullen set eyes on your own,
And grumbles, 'This isn't fair dealing,' my son, leave the Saxon alone.
Norman and Saxon

22 The silliest woman can manage a clever man; but it needs a very clever woman to manage a fool.
Plain Tales from the Hills, 'Three and – an Extra'

23 If, drunk with sight of power, we loose
Wild tongues that have not Thee in awe,
Such boastings as the Gentiles use,
Or lesser breeds without the Law.
Recessional

24 On the road to Mandalay
Where the flyin'-fishes play.
The Road to Mandalay

25 I am sick o' wastin' leather on these gritty pavin'-stones,
An' the blasted English drizzle wakes the fever in my bones;

Tho' I walks with fifty 'ousemaids outer Chelsea to the Strand,
An' they talks a lot o' lovin', but wot do they understand?
Beefy face an' grubby 'and –
Law! Wot do they understand?
I've a neater, sweeter maiden in a cleaner, greener land!

The Road to Mandalay

26 Ship me somewheres east of Suez, where the best is like the worst,
Where there aren't no Ten Commandments, an' a man can raise a thirst:
For the temple-bells are callin', an' it's there that I would be –
By the old Moulmein Pagoda, looking lazy at the sea.

The Road to Mandalay

27 Being kissed by a man who didn't wax his moustache was – like eating an egg without salt.

Soldiers Three, 'The Gadsbys, Poor Dear Mamma'

28 No one thinks of winter when the grass is green!

A St Helena Lullaby

29 Oh, it's Tommy this, an' Tommy that, an' 'Tommy, go away';
But it's 'Thank you, Mister Atkins,' when the band begins to play.

Tommy

30 It's Tommy this, an' Tommy that, an' 'Chuck him out, the brute!'
But it's 'Saviour of 'is country' when the guns begin to shoot.

Tommy

31 They shut the road through the woods
Seventy years ago.
Weather and rain have undone it again,
And now you would never know
There was once a road through the woods.

The Way Through the Woods

32 Take up the White Man's burden –
And reap his old reward:
The blame of those ye better,
The hate of those ye guard.

The White Man's Burden

33 I've just read that I am dead. Don't forget to delete me from your list of subscribers.

Writing to a magazine that had mistakenly published an announcement of his death. *Anekdotenschatz* (H. Hoffmeister)

34 A Soldier of the Great War Known unto God.

The words he selected to be inscribed on the headstones of the graves of unknown soldiers when he was literary adviser for the Imperial War Graves Commission, 1919. *Silent Cities* (ed. Gavin Stamp)

35 Words are, of course, the most powerful drug used by mankind.

Speech, 14 Feb 1923

36 Power without responsibility – the prerogative of the harlot throughout the ages.

Better known for its subsequent use by BALDWIN. Attrib.

KISSING

1 In the concordance of Nicola Six's kisses there were many subheads and subsections, many genres and phyla – chapter and verse, cross-references, multiple citations.

Martin Amis (1949–) British novelist. *London Fields*, Ch. 11

2 What of soul was left, I wonder, when the kissing had to stop?

Robert Browning (1812–89) British poet. *A Toccata of Galuppi's*

3 I'm fond of kissing. It's part of my job. God sent me down to kiss a lot of people.

Carrie Fisher (1956–) US film star. *Playboy*, July 1983

KNOWLEDGE

See also learning, self-knowledge, wisdom

1 Learning is a treasure which accompanies its owner everywhere.

Chinese proverb

2 Knowledge is the mother of all virtue; all vice proceeds from ignorance.

Proverb

3 *Nam et ipsa scientia potestas est.*
Knowledge itself is power.

Francis Bacon (1561–1626) English philosopher. *Religious Meditations*, 'Of Heresies'

4 I have taken all knowledge to be my province.

Francis Bacon Letter to Lord Burleigh, 1592

5 For all knowledge and wonder (which is the seed of knowledge) is an impression of pleasure in itself.

Francis Bacon *The Advancement of Learning*, Bk. I, Ch. 1

6 Now as touching things offered unto idols, we know that we all have knowledge. Knowledge puffeth up, but charity edifieth.

Bible: I Corinthians 8:1

7 For in much wisdom is much grief: and he that increaseth knowledge increaseth sorrow.

Bible: Ecclesiastes 1:18

8 And the Lord God took the man, and put him into the garden of Eden to dress it and to keep it. And the Lord God commanded the man, saying, Of every tree of the garden thou mayest freely eat: But of the tree of the knowledge of good and evil, thou shalt not eat of it: for in the day that thou eatest thereof thou shalt surely die.

Bible: Genesis 2:15–17

9 An expert is one who knows more and more about less and less.

Nicholas Murray Butler (1862–1947) US educator. Speech, Columbia University

10 Not many people know that.

Michael Caine (1933–) British actor. Attrib., often repeated

11 There goes a woman who knows all the things that can be taught and none of the things that cannot be taught.

Coco Chanel (1883–1971) French dress designer. *Coco Chanel, Her Life, Her Secrets* (Marcel Haedrich)

12 There is no such thing on earth as an uninteresting subject; the only thing that can exist is an uninterested person.

G. K. Chesterton (1874–1936) British writer. *Heretics*, Ch. 3

13 Learning without thought is labour lost; thought without learning is perilous.

Confucius (K'ung Fu-tzu; 551–479 BC) Chinese philosopher. *Analects*

14 Knowledge dwells
In heads replete with thoughts of other men;
Wisdom in minds attentive to their own.

William Cowper (1731–1800) British poet. *The Task*

15 A smattering of everything, and a knowledge of nothing.

Charles Dickens (1812–70) British novelist. *Sketches by Boz*, 'Tales', Ch. 3

16 A man should keep his little brain attic stocked with all the furniture that he is likely to use, and the rest he can put away in the lumber room of his library, where he can get it if he wants it.

Arthur Conan Doyle (1856–1930) British writer. *Five Orange Pips*

17 For lust of knowing what should not be known,
We take the Golden Road to Samarkand.

James Elroy Flecker (1884–1915) British poet. *Hassan*, V:2

18 I now want to know all things under the sun, and the moon, too. For all things are beautiful in themselves, and become more beautiful when known to man. Knowledge is Life with wings.

Kahlil Gibran (1833–1931) Lebanese mystic and poet. *Beloved Prophet* (ed. Virginia Hiln)

19 I am the very model of a modern Major-General,
I've information vegetable, animal and mineral,
I know the kings of England, and I quote the fights historical,
From Marathon to Waterloo, in order categorical.

W. S. Gilbert (1836–1911) British dramatist. *The Pirates of Penzance*, I

20 In arguing too, the parson own'd his skill,
For e'en though vanquish'd, he could argue still;
While words of learned length, and thund'ring sound
Amazed the gazing rustics rang'd around,
And still they gaz'd, and still the wonder grew,
That one small head could carry all he knew.

Oliver Goldsmith (1728–74) Irish-born British writer. *The Deserted Village*

21 The clever men at Oxford
Know all that there is to be knowed.
But they none of them know one half as much
As intelligent Mr Toad.

Kenneth Grahame (1859–1932) Scottish writer. *The Wind in the Willows*, Ch. 10

22 It is the province of knowledge to speak and it is the privilege of wisdom to listen.

Oliver Wendell Holmes (1809–94) US writer. *The Poet at the Breakfast Table*, Ch. 10

23 Knowledge is proportionate to being...You know in virtue of what you are.

Aldous Huxley (1894–1964) British novelist. *Time Must Have a Stop*, Ch. 26

24 If a little knowledge is dangerous, where is the man who has so much as to be out of danger?

T. H. Huxley (1825–95) British biologist. *On Elementary Instruction in Physiology*

25 There was never an age in which useless knowledge was more important than in our own.

Cyril Joad (1891–1953) British writer and broadcaster. *The Observer*, 'Sayings of the Week', 30 Sept 1951

26 All knowledge is of itself of some value. There is nothing so minute or inconsiderable, that I would not rather know it than not.

Samuel Johnson (1709–84) British lexicographer. *Life of Johnson* (J. Boswell)

27 In my early years I read very hard. It is a sad reflection, but a true one, that I knew almost as much at eighteen as I do now.

Samuel Johnson *Life of Johnson* (J. Boswell), Vol. I

28 Knowledge is of two kinds. We know a subject ourselves, or we know where we can find information upon it.

Samuel Johnson *Life of Johnson* (J. Boswell), Vol. II

29 Integrity without knowledge is weak and useless, and knowledge without integrity is dangerous and dreadful.

Samuel Johnson *Rasselas*, Ch. 41

30 The greater our knowledge increases the more our ignorance unfolds.

John Fitzgerald Kennedy (1917–63) US statesman. Speech, Rice University, 12 Sept 1962

31 A study of history shows that civilizations that abandon the quest for knowledge are doomed to disintegration.

Bernard Lovell (1913–) British astronomer and writer. *The Observer*, 'Sayings of the Week', 14 May 1972

32 Knowledge advances by steps, and not by leaps.

Lord Macaulay (1800–59) British historian. *Essays and Biographies*, 'History'. *Edinburgh Review*

33 We have learned the answers, all the answers:
It is the question that we do not know.

Archibald MacLeish (1892–1982) US poet and dramatist. *The Hamlet of A. Macleish*

34 Teach thy tongue to say 'I do not know.'

Maimonides (Moses ben Maimon; 1135–1204) Spanish-born Jewish philosopher and physician.

35 There is no counting the names, that surgeons and anatomists give to the various parts of the human body...I wonder whether mankind could not get along without all those names, which keep increasing every day, and hour, and moment...But people seem to have a great love for names; for to know a great many names seems to look like knowing a good many things.

Herman Melville (1819–91) US novelist. *Redburn*, Ch. 13

36 A little learning is a dangerous thing;
Drink deep, or taste not the Pierian spring:
There shallow draughts intoxicate the brain,
And drinking largely sobers us again.

Alexander Pope (1688–1744) British poet. *An Essay on Criticism*

37 Our knowledge can only be finite, while our ignorance must necessarily be infinite.

Karl Popper (1902–) Austrian-born British philosopher. *Conjectures and Refutations*

38 His had been an intellectual decision founded on his conviction that if a little knowledge was a dangerous thing, a lot was lethal.

Tom Sharpe (1928–) British novelist. *Porterhouse Blue*, Ch. 18

39 These things shall be! A loftier race
Than e'er the world hath known shall rise,
With flame of freedom in their souls,
And light of knowledge in their eyes.

John Addington Symonds (1840–93) British art historian. Hymn

40 Beware you be not swallowed up in books! An ounce of love is worth a pound of knowledge.

John Wesley (1703–91) British religious leader. *Life of Wesley* (R. Southey), Ch. 16

41 'I dunno,' Arthur said. 'I forget what I was taught. I only remember what I've learnt.'

Patrick White (1912–90) British-born Australian novelist. *The Solid Mandala*, Ch. 2

42 I have drunk ale from the Country of the Young
And weep because I know all things now.

W. B. Yeats (1865–1939) Irish poet. *He Thinks of his Past Greatness*

KORAN

(or Qu'ran) Islamic bible. One of the prime sources of Islamic law, the Koran is a compilation of revelations said to have been given to the prophet Mohammed.

1 Praise be to God, the Lord of all creatures; the most merciful, the king of the day of judgment. Thee do we worship, and of thee do we beg assistance. Direct us in the right way, in the way of those to whom thou hast been gracious; not of those against whom thou art incensed, nor of those who go astray.

Opening words of the *Koran*.

2 But the Jews will not be pleased with thee, neither the Christians, until thou follow their religion; say, The Direction of God is the true direction. And verily if thou follow their desires, after the knowledge which hath been given thee, thou shalt find no patron or protector against God. They to whom we have given the book of the Koran, and who read it with its true reading, they believe therein; and whoever believeth not therin, they shall perish.

Ch. II

3 War is enjoined you against the Infidels…They will ask thee concerning the sacred month, whether they may war therein: Answer, To war therein is grievous; but to obstruct the way of God, and infidelity towards him, and to keep men from the holy temple, and to drive out his people from thence, is more grievous in the sight of God, and the temptation to idolatry is more grievous than to kill in the sacred months.

Ch. II

4 The month of Ramadan shall ye fast, in which the Koran was sent down from heaven, a direction unto men, and declarations of direction, and the distinction between good and evil.

Ch. II

5 Ye are forbidden to eat that which dieth of itself, and blood, and swine's flesh, and that on which the name of any besides God hath been invocated; and that which hath been strangled, or killed by a blow, or by a fall, or by the horns of another beast, and that which hath been eaten by a wild beast, except what ye shall kill yourselves; and that which hath been sacrificed unto idols.

Ch. V

6 Marry those who are single among you, and such as are honest of your men-servants and your maid-servants: if they be poor, God will enrich them of his abundance; for God is bounteous and wise.

Ch. XXIV

7 The whore, and the whoremonger, shall ye scourge with a hundred stripes.

Ch. XXIV

8 Suffer the women whom ye divorce to dwell in some part of the houses wherein ye dwell; according to the room and conveniences of the habitations which ye possess; and make them not uneasy, that ye may reduce them to straits.

Ch. LXV

9 Verily the life to come shall be better for thee than this present life: and thy Lord shall give thee a reward wherewith thou shalt be well pleased. Did he not find thee an orphan, and hath he not taken care of thee? And did he not find thee wandering in error, and hath he not guided thee into the truth? And did he not find thee needy, and hath he not enriched thee?

Ch. XCIII

L

LA BRUYERE, JEAN DE

(1645–96) French satirist. He served in the household of Louis II and wrote one book of lasting merit *Les Caractères de Théophraste* (1688).

1 A pious man is one who would be an atheist if the king were.
Les Caractères

2 The majority of men devote the greater part of their lives to making their remaining years unhappy.
Les Caractères

3 There are some who speak one moment before they think.
Les Caractères

4 The pleasure of criticizing robs us of the pleasure of being moved by some very fine things.
Les Caractères

5 Liberality lies less in giving liberally than in the timeliness of the gift.
Les Caractères

6 There are only three events in a man's life; birth, life, and death; he is not conscious of being born, he dies in pain, and he forgets to live.
Les Caractères

7 Women run to extremes; they are either better or worse than men.
Les Caractères

8 One must laugh before one is happy, or one may die without ever laughing at all.
Les Caractères

9 Party loyalty lowers the greatest of men to the petty level of the masses.
Les Caractères

10 There exist some evils so terrible and some misfortunes so horrible that we dare not think of them, whilst their very aspect makes us shudder; but if they happen to fall on us, we find ourselves stronger than we imagined, we grapple with our ill luck, and behave better than we expected we should.
Les Caractères

11 If poverty is the mother of crime, stupidity is its father.
Les Caractères

12 'There is a report that Piso is dead; it is a great loss; he was an honest man, who deserved to live longer; he was intelligent and agreeable, resolute and courageous, to be depended upon, generous and faithful.' Add: 'provided he is really dead'.
Les Caractères

13 If we heard it said of Orientals that they habitually drank a liquor which went to their heads, deprived them of reason and made them vomit, we should say: 'How very barbarous!'
Les Caractères

14 To endeavour to forget anyone is a certain way of thinking of nothing else.
Les Caractères

15 A slave has but one master; an ambitious man has as many masters as there are people who may be useful in bettering his position.
Les Caractères

16 The shortest and best way to make your fortune is to let people see clearly that it is in their interests to promote yours.
Les Caractères

LACLOS, PIERRE CHODERLOS

(1741–1803) French soldier and writer. His scandalous novel *Les Liaisons dangereuses* (1782) reached a wider audience in the 1980s as a stage play and film.

1 How lucky we are that women defend themselves so poorly! We should, otherwise, be no more to them than timid slaves.
Les Liaisons dangereuses, Letter 4

2 Prudence is, it seems to me, the virtue which must be preferred above the rest when one is determining the fate of others; and especially when it is a case of sealing that fate with sacred and indissoluble promises, such as those of marriage.
Les Liaisons dangereuses, Letter 104

3 Have you not as yet observed that pleasure, which is undeniably the sole motive force behind the union of the sexes, is nevertheless not enough to form a bond between them? And that, if it is preceded by desire which impels, it is succeeded by disgust which repels? That is a law of nature which love alone can alter.
Les Liaisons dangereuses, Letter 131

4 Who would not shudder to think of the misery that may be caused by a single dangerous intimacy? And how much suffering could be avoided if it were more often thought of!
Les Liaisons dangereuses, Letter 175

LA FONTAINE, JEAN DE

(1621–95) French poet. His *Fables* (1668–94) was his major work. He repudiated his somewhat bawdy *Contes* (1664) after his religious conversion in 1692.

1 Rather suffer than die is man's motto.
Fables, I, 'La Mort et le Bûcheron'

2 Be advised that all flatterers live at the expense of those who listen to them.
Fables, I, 'Le Corbeau et le Renard'

3 One should oblige everyone to the extent of one's ability. One often needs someone smaller than oneself.
Fables, II, 'Le Lion et le Rat'

4 Patience and passage of time do more than strength and fury.

Fables, II, 'Le Lion et le Rat'

5 This fellow did not see further than his own nose.
Fables, III, 'Le Renard et le Bouc'

6 A mountain in labour shouted so loud that everyone, summoned by the noise, ran up expecting that she would be delivered of a city bigger than Paris; she brought forth a mouse.
Fables, V, 'La Montagne qui accouche'

7 He told me never to sell the bear's skin before one has killed the beast.
Fables, V, 'L'Ours et les deux Compagnons'

8 People must help one another; it is nature's law.
Fables, VIII, 'L'Âne et le Chien'

9 A hungry stomach has no ears.
Fables, IX, 'Le Milan et le Rossignol'

10 What God does, He does well.
Fables, IX, 'Le Gland et la Citrouille'

11 But the shortest works are always the best.
Fables, X, 'Les Lapins'

LAING, R. D.

(1927–89) British psychiatrist. His radical views on schizophrenia were set out in his books *The Divided Self* (1960), *The Politics of Experience* (1967), and *The Politics of the Family* (1971). *Knots* (1970) is a collection of his poetry.

1 The statesmen of the world who boast and threaten that they have Doomsday weapons are far more dangerous, and far more estranged from 'reality', than many of the people on whom the label 'psychotic' is affixed.
The Divided Self, Preface

2 Schizophrenia cannot be understood without understanding despair.
The Divided Self, Ch. 2

3 Few books today are forgivable.
The Politics of Experience, Introduction

4 We are effectively destroying ourselves by violence masquerading as love.
The Politics of Experience, Ch. 13

5 Madness need not be all breakdown. It may also be break-through. It is potential liberation and renewal as well as enslavement and existential death.
The Politics of Experience, Ch. 16

LAMB, CHARLES

(1775–1834) British essayist. He is best remembered for his *Essays of Elia* (1822).

Quotations about Lamb

1 Charles Lamb I sincerely believe to be in some considerable degree insane. A more pitiful, rickety, gasping, staggering, stammering tomfool I do not know.
Thomas Carlyle (1795–1881) Scottish historian and essayist. Attrib.

2 Charles Lamb, a clever fellow certainly, but full of villainous and abortive puns when he miscarries of every minute.
Thomas Moore (1779–1852) Irish poet. *Diary*, 4 Apr 1823

Quotations by Lamb

3 Nothing is to me more distasteful than that entire complacency and satisfaction which beam in the countenances of a new-married couple.
Essays of Elia, 'A Bachelor's Complaint of Married People'

4 We are nothing; less than nothing, and dreams. We are only what might have been, and must wait upon the tedious shores of Lethe millions of ages before we have existence, and a name.
In Greek mythology, Lethe was a river in the underworld, whose waters were drunk by souls about to be reborn in order to forget their past lives. *Essays of Elia*, 'Dream Children'

5 I hate a man who swallows it, affecting not to know what he is eating. I suspect his taste in higher matters.
Referring to food. *Essays of Elia*, 'Grace before Meat'

6 I have been trying all my life to like Scotchmen, and am obliged to desist from the experiment in despair.
Essays of Elia, 'Imperfect Sympathies'

7 Man is a gaming animal. He must always be trying to get the better in something or other.
Essays of Elia, 'Mrs Battle's Opinions on Whist'

8 In everything that relates to science, I am a whole Encyclopaedia behind the rest of the world.
Essays of Elia, 'The Old and the New Schoolmaster'

9 Boys are capital fellows in their own way, among their mates; but they are unwholesome companions for grown people.
Essays of Elia, 'The Old and the New Schoolmaster'

10 The human species, according to the best theory I can form of it, is composed of two distinct races, the men who borrow, and the men who lend.
Essays of Elia, 'The Two Races of Men'

11 Borrowers of books – those mutilators of collections, spoilers of the symmetry of shelves, and creators of odd volumes.
Essays of Elia, 'The Two Races of Men'

12 Credulity is the man's weakness, but the child's strength.
Essays of Elia, 'Witches and other Night Fears'

13 I love to lose myself in other men's minds. When I am not walking, I am reading; I cannot sit and think. Books think for me.
Last Essays of Elia, 'Detached Thoughts on Books and Reading'

14 Newspapers always excite curiosity. No one ever lays one down without a feeling of disappointment.
Last Essays of Elia, 'Detached Thoughts on Books and Reading'

15 A poor relation – is the most irrelevant thing in nature.
Last Essays of Elia, 'Poor Relations'

16 It is a pistol let off at the ear; not a feather to tickle the intellect.

Referring to the nature of a pun. *Last Essays of Elia*, 'Popular Fallacies'

17 How sickness enlarges the dimensions of a man's self to himself.

Last Essays of Elia, 'The Convalescent'

18 The greatest pleasure I know, is to do a good action by stealth, and to have it found out by accident.

The Athenaeum, 'Table Talk by the late Elia', 4 Jan 1834

19 I have had playmates, I have had companions
In my days of childhood, in my joyful schooldays –
All, all are gone, the old familiar faces.

The Old Familiar Faces

20 Riddle of destiny, who can show
What thy short visit meant, or know
What thy errand here below?

On an Infant Dying as soon as Born

21 Damn the age. I'll write for antiquity.

Referring to his lack of payment for the *Essays of Elia*. *English Wits* (L. Russell)

22 DR PARR. How have you acquired your power of smoking at such a rate?
LAMB. I toiled after it, sir, as some men toil after virtue.

Memoirs of Charles Lamb (Talfourd)

23 I came home…hungry as a hunter.

Letter to Coleridge, Apr 1800

24 Separate from the pleasure of your company, I don't much care if I never see another mountain in my life.

Letter to William Wordsworth, 30 Jan 1801

25 A little thin, flowery border, round, neat, not gaudy.

Letter to Wordsworth, June 1806

26 This very night I am going to leave off tobacco! Surely there must be some other world in which this unconquerable purpose shall be realized. The soul hath not her generous aspirings implanted in her in vain.

Letter to Thomas Manning, 26 Dec 1815

LANDOR, WALTER SAVAGE

(1775–1864) British poet and writer. His collections include *Imaginary Conversations of Literary Men and Statesmen* (1824–29), *Hellenics* (1847), and *Dry Sticks, Fagoted* (1858).

1 Stand close around, ye Stygian set,
With Dirce in one boat conveyed!
Or Charon, seeing, may forget
That he is old and she a shade.

In Greek mythology, Dirce, a follower of Dionysius, was killed by her great-nephews Amphion and Zethus because of her mistreatment of their mother Antiope; Charon was the ferryman who transported dead souls across the River Styx to the underworld. *Dirce*

2 Prose on certain occasions can bear a great deal of poetry: on the other hand, poetry sinks and swoons under a moderate weight of prose.

Imaginary Conversations, 'Archdeacon Hare and Walter Landor'

3 Goodness does not more certainly make men happy than happiness makes them good.

Imaginary Conversations, 'Lord Brooke and Sir Philip Sidney'

4 States, like men, have their growth, their manhood, their decrepitude, their decay.

Imaginary Conversations, 'Pollio and Calvus'

5 Clear writers, like clear fountains, do not seem so deep as they are; the turbid look the most profound.

Imaginary Conversations, 'Southey and Porson'

6 Fleas know not whether they are upon the body of a giant or upon one of ordinary size.

Imaginary Conversations, 'Southey and Porson'

7 I strove with none; for none was worth my strife;
Nature I loved, and, next to Nature, Art;
I warmed both hands before the fire of life;
It sinks, and I am ready to depart.

I Strove with None

8 Good God, I forgot the violets!

Having thrown his cook out of an open window onto the flowerbed below. *Irreverent Social History* (F. Muir)

LANGUAGE

See also class, communication, grammar, Goldwynisms, malapropisms, mixed metaphors, opera, pronunciation, speech, spoonerisms, style, words, writing

1 I think as far as which words you use you have a little more freedom in a country where it is not your natural language.

Andre Agassi (1970–) US tennis player. Referring to swearing on court. *The Independent*, 11 May 1994

2 The Greeks Had a Word for It.

Zoë Akins (1886–1958) US dramatist. Play title

3 The sciences were transmitted into the Arabic language from different parts of the world; by it they were embellished and penetrated the hearts of men, while the beauties of the language flowed in their veins and arteries.

Al-Biruni (973–1048) Arabic scholar. *Kitab as-Saidana*

4 Nouns of multitude (e.g., a pair of shoes, a gaggle of geese, a pride of lions)…: a rash of dermatologists, a hive of allergists, a scrub of interns, a chest of phthisiologists, or, a giggle of nurses, a flood of urologists, a pile of proctologists, and eyeful of ophthalmologists; or, a whiff of anesthesiologists, a staff of bacteriologists, a cast of orthopedic rheumatologists, a gargle of laryngologists.

Anonymous *Journal of the American Medical Association*, 190:392, 1964

5 The modern haematologist, instead of describing in English what he can see, prefers to describe in Greek what he can't.

Richard Asher (1912–) *Lancet*, 2:359, 1959

6 Well I ask you? When you take your family on holiday, do you say 'I am taking my gregarious egalitarian sibling group with me'?

Richard Asher *Lancet*, 2:359, 1959

7 A vocabulary that would take the feathers off a hoody crow.

Lillian Beckwith (1916–) US writer. *Lightly Poached*

8 Therefore is the name of it called Babel; because the Lord did there confound the language of all the earth: and from thence did the Lord scatter them abroad upon the face of all the earth.

Bible: Genesis 11:9

9 The cliché is dead poetry. English, being the language of an imaginative race, abounds in clichés, so that English literature is always in danger of being poisoned by its own secretions.

Gerald Brenan (Edward Fitzgerald Brenan; 1894–1987) British writer. *Thoughts in a Dry Season*, 'Literature'

10 'Take some more tea,' the March Hare said to Alice, very earnestly.
'I've had nothing yet,' Alice replied in an offended tone, 'so I can't take more.'
'You mean you can't take *less*,' said the Hatter: 'it's very easy to take *more* than nothing.'

Lewis Carroll (Charles Lutwidge Dodgson; 1832–98) British writer. *Alice's Adventures in Wonderland*, Ch. 7

11 A silly remark can be made in Latin as well as in Spanish.

Miguel de Cervantes (1547–1616) Spanish novelist. *The Dialogue of the Dogs*

12 Well, frankly, the problem as I see it at this moment in time is whether I should just lie down under all this hassle and let them walk all over me, or whether I should just say OK, I get the message, and do myself in.
I mean, let's face it, I'm in a no-win situation, and quite honestly, I'm so stuffed up to here with the whole stupid mess that I can tell you I've just got a good mind to take the easy way out. That's the bottom line. The only problem is, what happens if I find, when I've bumped myself off, there's some kind of...ah, you know, all that mystical stuff about when you die, you might find you're still – know what I mean?

Charles, Prince of Wales (1948–) Eldest son of Elizabeth II. At the presentation of the Thomas Cranmer Schools Prize, 1989, suggesting a possible modern English version of Hamlet's soliloquy. The original version is:
To be, or not to be: that is the question:
Whether 'tis nobler in the mind to suffer
The slings and arrows of outrageous fortune,
Or to take arms against a sea of troubles,
And by opposing end them? To die: to sleep;
No more; and, by a sleep to say we end
The heartache and the thousand natural shocks
That flesh is heir to, 'tis a consummation
Devoutly to be wish'd. To die, to sleep;
To sleep: perchange to dream: aye, there's the rub;
For in that sleep of death what dreams may come
When we have shuffled off this mortal coil,
Must give us pause.

13 I speak Spanish to God, Italian to women, French to men, and German to my horse.

Charles V (1500–58) Holy Roman Emperor. Attrib.

14 And for ther is so greet diversitee
in English and in wryting of our tonge
So preye I God that noon miswryte thee
Ne thee mismetre for defaute of tonge.
And red wherso thou be, or elles songe,
That thou be understonde, I God beseche.

Geoffrey Chaucer (c. 1343–1400) English poet. *Troilus and Criseyde*

15 The one stream of poetry which is continually flowing is slang.

G. K. Chesterton (1874–1936) British writer. *The Defendant*

16 All slang is metaphor, and all metaphor is poetry.

G. K. Chesterton *The Defendant*

17 I don't hold with abroad and think that foreigners speak English when our backs are turned.

Quentin Crisp (c. 1910–) Model, publicist, and writer. *The Naked Civil Servant*

18 Bring on the empty horses!

Michael Curtiz (1888–1962) Hungarian-born US film director. Said during the filming of *The Charge of the Light Brigade.* Curtiz, who was not noted for his command of the English language, meant 'riderless horses'. When people laughed at his order he became very angry, shouting, 'You think I know fuck-nothing, when I know fuck-all!' David Niven used the remark as the title of his second volume of autobiography about his experiences in the film industry. *Bring on the Empty Horses* (David Niven)

19 The liberation of language is rooted in the liberation of ourselves.

Mary Daly (1928–) US educator, writer, and theologian. *The Church and the Second Sex*

20 Imagine the Lord talking French! Aside from a few odd words in Hebrew, I took it completely for granted that God had never spoken anything but the most dignified English.

Clarence Shepard Day (1874–1935) US writer. *Life With Father*, 'Father interferes'

21 Rushing from his laboratory and meeting a curator he embraced him exclaiming, 'I have just made a great discovery. I have separated the sodium ammonium protartrate with two salts of opposite action on the plane of polarization of light. The dextro-salt is in all respects identical with the dextroprotartrate. I am so happy and so overcome by such nervous excitement that I am unable again to place my eye to the polarization instrument.'

Alexander Findlay Referring to the French chemist Louis Pasteur (1822–95). *Chemistry in the Service of Man*

22 You must learn to talk clearly. The jargon of scientific terminology which rolls off your tongues is mental garbage.

Martin H. Fischer (1879–1962) *Fischerisms* (Howard Fabing and Ray Marr)

23 What is the prose for God?

Harley Granville-Barker (1877–1946) British actor and dramatist. *Waste*, I

24 A master of the English language does not need to exaggerate; an illiterate almost always does.

Lord Hailsham (1907–) British Conservative politician. *The Observer* 'Sayings of the Week', 16 March 1975

25 I would never use a long word, even, where a short one would answer the purpose. I know there are professors in this country who 'ligate' arteries. Other surgeons only tie them, and it stops the bleeding just as well.

Oliver Wendell Holmes (1809–94) US writer and physician. *Medical Essays*, 'Scholastic and Bedside Teaching'

26 I have laboured to refine our language to grammatical purity, and to clear it from colloquial barbarisms, licentious idioms, and irregular combinations.

Samuel Johnson (1709–84) British lexicographer. *The Rambler*

27 I am always sorry when any language is lost, because languages are the pedigree of nations.

Samuel Johnson *Tour to the Hebrides* (J. Boswell)

28 I am not yet so lost in lexicography, as to forget that words are the daughters of earth, and that things are the sons of heaven. Language is only the instrument of science, and words are but the signs of ideas: I wish, however, that the instrument might be less apt to decay, and that signs might be permanent, like the things which they denote.

Samuel Johnson *Dictionary of the English Language*

29 The baby doesn't understand English and the Devil knows Latin.

Ronald Knox (1888–1957) British Roman Catholic priest. Said when asked to conduct a baptism service in English. *Ronald Knox* (Evelyn Waugh), Pt. I, Ch. 5

30 There are things which will not be defined, and Fever is one of them. Besides, when a word had passed into everyday use, it is too late to lay a logical trap for its meaning, and think to apprehend it by a definition.

Peter Mere Latham (1789–1875) US poet and essayist. *General Remarks on the Practice of Medicine*, Ch. 10, Pt. 1

31 The contraction of his obicular, the lateral obtusion of his sense centres, his night fears, his stomach trouble, the polyencephalitic condition of his youth, and above all the heredity of his old father and young mother, combined to make him an hysterico-epileptic type, traceable in the paranoic psychoses evident in all he wrote.

Cesare Lombroso (1853–1909) Italian criminologist. Referring to Émile Zola. *Paris Was Yesterday* (Janet Flanner)

32 A man of true science…uses but few hard words, and those only when none other will answer his purpose; whereas the smatterer in science… thinks, that by mouthing hard words, he proves that he understands hard things.

Herman Melville (1819–91) US novelist. *White Jacket*, Ch. 63

33 If the English language had been properly organized…then there would be a word which meant both 'he' and 'she', and I could write, 'If John or Mary comes heesh will want to play tennis,' which would save a lot of trouble.

A. A. Milne (1882–1956) British writer. *The Christopher Robin Birthday Book*

34 Most of their discourse was about hunting, in a dialect I understand very little.

Samuel Pepys (1633–1703) English diarist. *Diary*, 22 Nov 1663

35 I include 'pidgin-English'…even though I am referred to in that splendid language as 'Fella belong Mrs Queen'.

Prince Philip (1921–) The consort of Queen Elizabeth II. Speech, English-Speaking Union Conference, Ottawa, 29 Oct 1958

36 Life is too short to learn German.

Richard Porson (1759–1808) British classicist. *Gryll Grange* (T. L. Peacock), Ch. 3

37 Sign language is the equal of speech, lending itself equally to the rigorous and the poetic, to philosophical analysis or to making love.

Oliver Sacks (1933–) British neurologist. *The Times*, 16 June 1994

38 The language of the men of medicine is a fearful concoction of sesquipedalian words, numbered by thousands.

Frederick Saunders (1807–1902)

39 Honi soie qui mal y pense ('Honey, your silk stocking's hanging down').

W. C. Sellar (1898–1951) British humorous writer. *1066 And All That*

40 The language I have learn'd these forty years,
My native English, now I must forego;
And now my tongue's use is to me no more
Than an unstringed viol or a harp.

William Shakespeare (1564–1616) English dramatist. *Richard II*, I:3

41 O! know, sweet love, I always write of you,
And you and love are still my argument;
So all my best is dressing old words new,
Spending again what is already spent.

William Shakespeare *Sonnets*, 76

42 You taught me language; and my profit on't
Is, I know how to curse: the red plague rid you
For learning me your language!

William Shakespeare *The Tempest*, I:2

43 England and America are two countries separated by the same language.

George Bernard Shaw (1856–1950) Irish dramatist and critic. Attrib.

44 So now they have made our English tongue a gallimaufry or hodgepodge of all other speeches.

Edmund Spenser (1552–99) English poet.

The Shepherd's Calender, 'Letter to Gabriel Harvey'

45 Language grows out of life, out of its needs and experiences…*Language* and *knowledge* are indissolubly connected; they are interdependent. Good work in language presupposes and depends on a real knowledge of things.

Annie Sullivan (1866–1936) US teacher of the handicapped. Speech, American Association to Promote the Teaching of Speech to the Deaf, July 1894

46 A foreign swear-word is practically inoffensive except to the person who has learnt it early in life and knows its social limits.

Paul Theroux (1941–) US-born writer. *Saint Jack*, Ch. 12

47 Political correctness is a really inane concept. It automatically gives the impression that left-wing ideas are about toeing some line, it makes people think that being left-wing means being a Stalinist. I find the idea of PC petty. Plus it makes the racists look like the rebels.

Mark Thomas British comedian. Comment, Feb 1993

48 The most attractive sentences are not perhaps the wisest, but the surest and soundest.

Henry David Thoreau (1817–62) US writer. *Journal*, 1842

49 I am not like a lady at the court of Versailles, who said: 'What a dreadful pity that the bother at the tower of Babel should have got language all mixed up, but for that, everyone would always have spoken French.

Voltaire (François-Marie Arouet; 1694–1778) French writer. Letter to Catherine the Great, Empress of Russia, 26 May 1767

50 We should constantly use the most common,

little, easy words (so they are pure and proper) which our language affords.

John Wesley (1703–91) British religious leader. Advice for preaching to 'plain people'. Attrib.

51 But they underestimate the cumulative effect of always hearing Stone-Age man, postman, chairman; of the different reactions you have to 'landlord' and 'landlady' or 'a bit of a bitch' and 'a bit of a dog'.

Katherine Whitehorn (1926–) British journalist. *The Observer*, 18 Aug 1991

52 We dissect nature along lines laid down by our native language... Language is not simply a reporting device for experience but a defining framework for it.

Benjamin Lee Whorf (1897–1941) US linguist. *New Directions in the Study of Language* (ed. Hoyer), 'Thinking in Primitive Communities'

LARKIN, PHILIP

(1922–85) British poet. Collections include *The Whitsun Weddings* (1964) and *High Windows* (1974). He also edited *The Oxford Book of Twentieth Century Verse* (1973) and wrote two novels.

1 Clearly money has something to do with life
– In fact, they've a lot in common, if you enquire:
You can't put off being young until you retire.

Money

2 Perhaps being old is having lighted rooms
Inside your head, and people in them, acting.
People you know, yet can't quite name.

The Old Fools

3 Get stewed:
Books are a load of crap.

A Study of Reading Habits

4 They fuck you up, your mum and dad.
They may not mean to, but they do.
They fill you with the faults they had
And add some extra, just for you.

This be the Verse

5 Far too many relied on the classic formula of a beginning, a muddle, and an end.

Referring to modern novels. *New Fiction*, 15 (January 1978)

LAST WORDS

Not always the actual last words said, but including remarks made when dying. Many are apocryphal, hence the fact that some people have more than one set of attributed 'last words'.
See also death, execution

1 A lot of people, on the verge of death, utter famous last words or stiffen into attitudes, as if the final stiffening in three days' time were not enough; they will have ceased to exist three days' hence, yet they still want to arouse admiration and adopt a pose and tell a lie with their last gasp.

Henri de Montherlant (1896–1972) French novelist. *Explicit Mysterium*

Some examples

2 I inhabit a weak, frail, decayed tenement; battered by the winds and broken in on by the storms, and, from all I can learn, the landlord does not intend to repair.

John Quincy Adams (1767–1848) Sixth president of the USA. Said during his last illness. Attrib.

3 See in what peace a Christian can die.

Joseph Addison (1672–1719) British essayist.

4 *Ave Caesar, morituri te salutant.*
Hail Caesar; those who are about to die salute you.

Anonymous Greeting to the Roman Emperor by gladiators

5 Jakie, is it my birthday or am I dying?

Viscountess Nancy Astor (1879–1964) American-born British politician. To her son on her death bed. He replied: 'A bit of both, Mum.'

6 How were the receipts today in Madison Square Garden?

Phineas Taylor Barnum (1810–91) US showman.

7 I am ready to die for my Lord, that in my blood the Church may obtain liberty and peace.

Thomas Becket (c. 1118–79) English churchman. One version of his last words. *Vita S. Thomae, Cantuariensis Archiepiscopi et Martyris* (Edward Grim)

8 Thank you, sister. May you be the mother of a bishop!

Brendan Behan (1923–64) Irish playwright. Said to a nun nursing him on his deathbed. Attrib.

9 When Jesus therefore had received the vinegar, he said, It is finished: and he bowed his head, and gave up the ghost.

Bible: John 19:30

10 And when Jesus had cried with a loud voice, he said, Father, into thy hands I commend my spirit: and having said thus, he gave up the ghost.

Bible: Luke 23:46

11 Jesus, when he had cried again with a loud voice, yielded up the ghost.
And, behold, the veil of the temple was rent in twain from the top to the bottom; and the earth did quake, and the rocks rent;
And the graves were opened; and many bodies of the saints which slept arose.

Bible: Matthew 27:50–52

12 *Et tu, Brute?*
You too, Brutus?

Julius Caesar (100–44 BC) Roman general and statesman.

13 All right, then, I'll say it: Dante makes me sick.

Lope Félix de Vega Carpio (1562–1635) Spanish dramatist and poet. On being informed he was about to die. Attrib.

14 I realize that patriotism is not enough. I must have no hatred or bitterness towards anyone.

Edith Cavell (1865–1915) British nurse. Before her execution by the Germans in 1915.

15 A Subject and a Sovereign are clean different things.

Charles I (1600–49) King of England. Speech on the scaffold, 30 Jan 1649

16 Let not poor Nelly starve.

Charles II (1630–85) King of England. Referring to his mistress Nell Gwynne. Said on his death bed

17 He had been, he said, a most unconscionable time dying; but he hoped that they would excuse it.

Charles II *History of England* (Macaulay), Vol. I, Ch. 4

18 Give Dayrolles a chair.

Earl of Chesterfield (1694–1773) English statesman. Said on his deathbed when visited by his godson, Solomon Dayrolles. Last words

19 Take a step forward, lads. It will be easier that way.

Erskine Childers (1870–1922) British-born author and Irish patriot. Last words before being executed by firing squad, 24 Nov 1922. *The Riddle of Erskine Childers* (A. Boyle)

20 I'm so bored with it all.

Winston Churchill (1874–1965) British statesman. Said to be his last words. *Clementine* (M. Soames)

21 Goodnight, my darlings. I'll see you tomorrow.

Noël Coward (1899–1973) British dramatist. *The Life of Noël Coward* (C. Lesley)

22 It much grieves me that I should be noted a traitor when I always had your laws on my breast, and that I should be a sacramentary. God he knoweth the truth, and that I am of the one and the other guiltless.

Thomas Cromwell (c. 1485–1540) English statesman. On being condemned to death for treason and heresy. Letter to Henry VIII, 30 June 1540

23 Nurse, it was I who discovered that leeches have red blood.

Baron Georges Cuvier (1769–1832) French zoologist. On his deathbed when the nurse came to apply leeches. *The Oxford Book of Death* (D. Enright)

24 Too late for fruit, too soon for flowers.

Walter De La Mare (1873–1956) British poet. On being asked, as he lay seriously ill, whether he would like some fruit or flowers. Attrib.

25 No, it is better not. She will only ask me to take a message to Albert.

Benjamin Disraeli (1804–81) British statesman. On his deathbed, declining an offer of a visit from Queen Victoria.

26 Shakespeare, I come!

Theodore Dreiser (1871–1945) US novelist. His intended last words. *The Constant Circle* (S. Mayfield)

27 Goodbye, my friends, I go on to glory.

Isadora Duncan (1878–1927) US dancer. She was strangled when her long scarf became entangled in the wheel of a sports car. Attrib.

28 My work is done. Why wait?

George Eastman (1854–1932) US inventor and industrialist. His suicide note

29 All my possessions for a moment of time.

Elizabeth I (1533–1603) Queen of England.

30 Must! Is *must* a word to be addressed to princes? Little man, little man! thy father, if he had been alive, durst not have used that word.

Elizabeth I Said to Robert Cecil, on her death bed. *A Short History of the English People* (J. R. Green), Ch. 7

31 Death is my neighbour now.

Edith Evans (1888–1976) British actress. Said a week before her death. BBC radio interview, 14 Oct 1976

32 I have no pain, dear mother, now;
But oh! I am so dry:
Just moisten poor Jim's lips once more;
And, mother, do not cry!

Edward Farmer (1809–76) British writer. A typical sentimental verse of the time. *The Collier's Dying Child*

33 Now I'll have *eine kleine Pause.*

Kathleen Ferrier (1912–53) British contralto. Said shortly before her death. *Am I Too Loud?* (Gerald Moore)

34 I have spent a lot of time searching through the Bible for loopholes.

W. C. Fields (1880–1946) US comedian. Said during his last illness. Attrib.

35 It is high time for me to depart, for at my age I now begin to see things as they really are.

Bernard de Fontenelle (1657–1757) French philosopher. Remark on his deathbed. *Anekdotenschatz* (H. Hoffmeister)

36 I feel nothing, apart from a certain difficulty in continuing to exist.

Bernard de Fontenelle Remark on his deathbed. *Famous Last Words* (B. Conrad)

37 I die happy.

Charles James Fox (1749–1806) British Whig politician. *Life and Times of C. J. Fox* (Russell), Vol. III

38 Why fear death? It is the most beautiful adventure in life.

Charles Frohman (1860–1915) US theatre producer. Said before going down with the liner *Lusitania*, alluding to 'To die will be an awfully big adventure' from Barrie's *Peter Pan*, which Frohman had produced. *J. M. Barrie and the Lost Boys* (A. Birkin)

39 We are all going to Heaven, and Vandyke is of the company.

Thomas Gainsborough (1727–88) British painter. Referring to the Flemish painter Anthony Vandyke (1599–1641) who was court painter to Charles I of England (1632–41). *Thomas Gainsborough* (Boulton), Ch. 9

40 I don't mind if my life goes in the service of the nation. If I die today every drop of my blood will invigorate the nation.

Indira Gandhi (1917–84) Indian stateswoman. Said the night before she was assassinated by Sikh militants, 30 Oct 1984. *The Sunday Times*, 3 Dec 1989

41 Bugger Bognor.

George V (1865–1936) King of the United Kingdom. His alleged last words, when his doctor promised him he would soon be well enough to visit Bognor Regis.

42 How is the Empire?

George V Last words. *The Times*, 21 Jan 1936

43 We are as near to heaven by sea as by land.

Humphrey Gilbert (c. 1539–83) English navigator. Remark made shortly before he went down with his ship *Squirrel*. *A Book of Anecdotes* (D. George)

44 *Mehr Licht!*
More light!

Goethe (1749–1832) German poet and dramatist. Attrib. last words. In fact he asked for the second shutter to be opened, to allow more light in.

45 It is. But not as hard as farce.

Edmund Gwenn (1875–1959) British actor. On his deathbed, in reply to the comment 'It must be very hard'. *Time*, 30 Jan 1984

46 Well, I've had a happy life.

William Hazlitt (1778–1830) British essayist.

47 You might make that a double.

Neville Heath (1917–46) British murderer. Comment made when offered a drink before his execution. Attrib.

48 Only one man ever understood me...And he didn't understand me.

Hegel (1770–1831) German philosopher. Said on his deathbed. *Famous Last Words* (B. Conrad)

49 God will pardon me. It is His trade.

Heinrich Heine (1797–1856) German poet and writer. *Journal* (Edmond and Charles Goncourt), 23 Feb 1863

50 Turn up the lights, I don't want to go home in the dark.

O. Henry (William Sidney Porter; 1862–1910) US short-story writer. Quoting a popular song of the time. *O. Henry* (C. A. Smith), Ch. 9

51 I am about to take my last voyage, a great leap in the dark.

Thomas Hobbes (1588–1679) English philosopher.

52 If heaven had granted me five more years, I could have become a real painter.

Hokusai (1760–1849) Japanese painter. Said on his deathbed. *Famous Last Words* (B. Conrad)

53 On the contrary!

Henrik Ibsen (1828–1906) Norwegian dramatist. His nurse had just remarked that he was feeling a little better. *True Remarkable Occurrences* (J. Train)

54 So it has come at last, the distinguished thing.

Henry James (1843–1916) US novelist. *A Backward Glance* (Edith Wharton), Ch. 14

55 Above ground I shall be food for kites; below I shall be food for mole-crickets and ants. Why rob one to feed the other?

Juang-zu (4th century BC) Chinese Taoist philosopher. When asked on his deathbed what his wishes were regarding the disposal of his body. *Famous Last Words* (B. Conrad)

56 Don't give up the ship.

James Lawrence (1781–1813) US naval officer. As he lay dying in his ship, the US frigate *Chesapeake*, during the battle with the British frigate *Shannon*.

57 It's all been rather lovely.

John Le Mesurier (1912–83) British actor. *The Times*, 15 Nov 1983

58 Why are you weeping? Did you imagine that I was immortal?

Louis XIV (1638–1715) French king. Noticing as he lay on his deathbed that his attendants were crying. *Louis XIV* (V. Cronin)

59 *Tête d'Armée.*
Chief of the Army.

Napoleon I (Napoleon Bonaparte; 1769–1821) French emperor. Last words. Attrib.

60 I do not have to forgive my enemies, I have had them all shot.

Ramón Maria Narváez (1800–68) Spanish general and political leader. Said on his deathbed, when asked by a priest if he forgave his enemies. *Famous Last Words* (B. Conrad)

61 Kiss me, Hardy.

Lord Nelson (1758–1805) British admiral. Spoken to Sir Thomas Hardy, captain of the *Victory*, during the Battle of Trafalgar, 1805.

62 Too kind, too kind.

Florence Nightingale (1820–1910) British nurse. When given the Order of Merit on her deathbed. *Life of Florence Nightingale*, Vol. II, Pt. 7, Ch. 9 (E. Cook)

63 I am just going outside and may be some time.

Captain Lawrence Oates (1880–1912) British soldier and explorer. Before leaving the tent and vanishing into the blizzard on the ill-fated Antarctic expedition (1910–12). Oates was afraid that his lameness would slow down the others. *Journal* (R. F. Scott), 17 Mar 1912

64 Die, my dear Doctor, that's the last thing I shall do!

Lord Palmerston (1784–1865) British statesman.

65 I am curious to see what happens in the next world to one who dies unshriven.

Pietro Perugino (1446–1523) Italian painter. Giving his reasons for refusing to see a priest as he lay dying. Attrib.

66 Oh, my country! How I leave my country!

William Pitt the Younger (1759–1806) British statesman.

67 I think I could eat one of Bellamy's veal pies.

William Pitt the Younger

68 I have not told half of what I saw.

Marco Polo (c. 1254–1324) Venetian traveller. *The Story of Civilization* (W. Durant), Vol. I

69 Here am I, dying of a hundred good symptoms.

Alexander Pope (1688–1744) British poet. *Anecdotes by and about Alexander Pope* (Joseph Spence)

70 I owe much; I have nothing; the rest I leave to the poor.

François Rabelais (1483–1553) French satirist.

71 Ring down the curtain, the farce is over.

François Rabelais

72 I am going in search of a great perhaps.

François Rabelais

73 My dear hands. Farewell, my poor hands.

Sergei Rachmaninov (1873–1943) Russian composer. On being informed that he was dying from cancer. *The Great Pianists* (H. Schonberg)

74 I have a long journey to take, and must bid the company farewell.

Walter Raleigh (1554–1618) English explorer. *Sir Walter Raleigh* (Edward Thompson), Ch. 26

75 So little done, so much to do.

Cecil Rhodes (1853–1902) South African statesman.

76 You can keep the things of bronze and stone and give me one man to remember me just once a year.

Damon Runyon (1884–1946) US writer.

77 Dear World, I am leaving you because I am bored. I am leaving you with your worries. Good luck.

George Sanders (1906–72) British film actor. Suicide note

78 Everybody has got to die, but I have always believed an exception would be made in my case. Now what?

William Saroyan (1908–81) US dramatist. *Time*, 16 Jan 1984

79 At last I am going to be well!

Paul Scarron (1610–60) French poet. As he lay dying. Attrib.

80 Nonsense, they couldn't hit an elephant at this distance

John Sedgwick (1813–64) US general. In response to a suggestion that he should not show himself over the parapet during the Battle of the Wilderness. Attrib.

81 His nose was as sharp as a pen, and 'a babbl'd of green fields.

William Shakespeare (1564–1616) English dramatist. Referring to Falstaff on his deathbed. *Henry V*, II:3

82 Thank heavens the sun has gone in and I don't have to go out and enjoy it.

Logan Pearsall Smith (1865–1946) US writer.

83 Crito, we owe a cock to Aesculapius; please pay it and don't let it pass.

Socrates (469–399 BC) Athenian philosopher. Before his execution by drinking hemlock. *Phaedo* (Plato), 118

84 Beautifully done.

Stanley Spencer (1891–1959) British artist. Said to the nurse who had injected him, just before he died. *Stanley Spencer, a Biography* (Maurice Collis), Ch. 19

85 What *is* the answer?...In that case, what is the question?

Gertrude Stein (1874–1946) US writer.

86 If this is dying, I don't think much of it.

Lytton Strachey (1880–1932) British writer. *Lytton Strachey* (Michael Holroyd), Pt. V, Ch. 17

87 Ah, a German and a genius! a prodigy, admit him!

Jonathan Swift (1667–1745) Irish-born Anglican priest and writer. Learning of the arrival of the composer Handel (1685–1759).

88 I did not know that we had ever quarrelled.

Henry David Thoreau (1817–62) US writer. On being urged to make his peace with God. Attrib.

89 God bless ... God damn.

James Thurber (1894–1961) US humorist.

90 Even in the valley of the shadow of death, two and two do not make six.

Leo Tolstoy (1828–1910) Russian writer. Refusing to reconcile himself with the Russian Orthodox Church as he lay dying.

91 I have had no real gratification or enjoyment of any sort more than my neighbor on the next block who is worth only half a million.

William Henry Vanderbilt (1821–85) US railway chief. *Famous Last Words* (B. Conrad)

92 Dear me, I believe I am becoming a god. An emperor ought at least to die on his feet.

Vespasian (9–79 AD) Roman emperor. *Lives of the Caesars* (Suetonius)

93 Either that wallpaper goes, or I do.

Oscar Wilde (1854–1900) Irish-born British dramatist. As he lay dying in a drab Paris bedroom. *Time*, 16 Jan 1984

94 I expect I shall have to die beyond my means.

Oscar Wilde On accepting a glass of champagne on his deathbed.

95 I haven't got time to be tired.

Wilhelm I (1797–1888) King of Prussia and Emperor of Germany. Said during his last illness

96 Now God be praised, I will die in peace.

James Wolfe (1727–59) British general. After being mortally wounded at the Battle of Quebec, 1759. *Historical Journal of Campaigns, 1757–60* (J. Knox), Vol. II

97 Germany was the cause of Hitler just as much as Chicago is responsible for the *Chicago Tribune*.

Alexander Woollcott (1887–1943) US writer and critic. Woollcott died after the broadcast. Radio broadcast, 1943

LAUGHTER

See also happiness, humour

1 Laugh and grow fat.

Proverb

2 Laugh before breakfast, you'll cry before supper.

Proverb

3 Laughter is the best medicine.

Proverb

4 A good laugh and a long sleep are the best cures in the doctor's book.

Irish proverb

5 I make myself laugh at everything, so that I do not weep.

Beaumarchais (1732–99) French dramatist. *Le Barbier de Séville*, I:2

6 I said of laughter, It is mad: and of mirth, What doeth it?

Bible: Ecclesiastes 2:2

7 The most wasted of all days is that on which one has not laughed.

Nicolas Chamfort (1741–94) French writer. *Maximes et pensées*

8 But laughter is weakness, corruption, the foolishness of our flesh.

Umberto Eco (1932–) Italian semiologist and writer. *The Name of the Rose*

9 One must laugh before one is happy, or one may die without ever laughing at all.

Jean de La Bruyère (1645–96) French satirist. *Les Caractères*

10 Laughter is pleasant, but the exertion is too much for me.

Thomas Love Peacock (1785–1866) British novelist. Said by the Hon. Mr Listless. *Nightmare Abbey*, Ch. 5

11 Born with the gift of laughter and a sense that the world was mad.

Rafael Sabatini (1875–1950) Italian-born novelist. *Scaramouche*

12 I live in a constant endeavour to fence against the infirmities of ill health, and other evils of life, by mirth.

Laurence Sterne (1713–68) Irish-born English writer and churchman. *Tristram Shandy*, Dedication

13 Laugh, and the world laughs with you;
Weep, and you weep alone,
For the sad old earth must borrow its mirth,
But has trouble enough of its own.

Ella Wheeler Wilcox (1850–1919) US poet. *Solitude*

LAW

See also crime, justice, lawyers

1 A judge knows nothing unless it has been explained to him three times.
Proverb

2 Every dog is allowed one bite.
Proverb

3 Every one is innocent until he is proved guilty.
Proverb

4 Possession is nine points of the law.
Proverb

5 The law does not concern itself about trifles.
Proverb

6 Human law is law only by virtue of its accordance with right reason, and by this means it is clear that it flows from Eternal law. In so far as it deviates from right reason it is called an Unjust law; and in such a case, it is no law at all, but rather an assertion of violence.
St Thomas Aquinas (1225–74) Italian theologian. *Summa Theologiae*

7 One of the Seven was wont to say: 'That laws were like cobwebs; where the small flies were caught, and the great brake through.'
Francis Bacon (1561–1626) English philosopher. *See also* SHENSTONE; SOLON; SWIFT. *Apothegms*

8 Every law is an evil, for every law is an infraction of liberty.
Jeremy Bentham (1748–1832) British philosopher. *An Introduction to the Principles of Morals and Legislation*

9 The good of the people is the chief law.
Cicero (106–43 BC) Roman orator and statesman. *De Legibus*, III

10 The law of the realm cannot be changed but by Parliament.
Edward Coke (1552–1634) English lawyer and politician. Dictum, in the case *Articuli Cleri*, 1605

11 The Law of England is a very strange one; it cannot compel anyone to tell the truth...But what the Law can do is to give you seven years for not telling the truth.
Lord Darling (1849–1936) British judge. *Lord Darling* (D. Walker-Smith), Ch. 27

12 'If the law supposes that,' said Mr Bumble..., 'the law is a ass – a idiot.'
Charles Dickens (1812–70) British novelist. *Oliver Twist*, Ch. 51

13 We must face the fact that the United Nations is not yet the international equivalent of our own legal system and the rule of law.
Anthony Eden (1897–1977) British statesman and prime minister. Speech, House of Commons, 1 Nov 1956

14 Although we have some laws which are unfair to women, some women can live their whole lives and not know the law as it affects them.
Taujan Faisal Jordanian politician. *The Times*, 15 June 1994

15 The majestic egalitarianism of the law, which forbids rich and poor alike to sleep under bridges, to beg in the streets, and to steal bread.
Anatole France (Jacques Anatole François Thibault; 1844–1924) French writer. *The Red Lily*, Ch. 7

16 Public opinion is always in advance of the law.
John Galsworthy (1867–1933) British writer. *Windows*

17 When I went to the Bar as a very young man,
(Said I to myself – said I),
I'll work on a new and original plan,
(Said I to myself – said I).
W. S. Gilbert (1836–1911) British dramatist. *Iolanthe*, I

18 The Law is the true embodiment
Of everything that's excellent.
It has no kind of fault or flaw,
And I, my lords, embody the Law.
W. S. Gilbert *Iolanthe*, I

19 There's no better way of exercising the imagination than the study of law. No poet ever interpreted nature as freely as a lawyer interprets truth.
Jean Giraudoux (1882–1944) French dramatist. *Tiger at the Gates*, I

20 Laws grind the poor, and rich men rule the law.
Oliver Goldsmith (1728–74) Irish-born British writer. *The Traveller*

21 I know no method to secure the repeal of bad or obnoxious laws so effective as their stringent execution.
Ulysses Simpson Grant (1822–85) US general. Inaugural address, 4 Mar 1869

22 The Common Law of England has been laboriously built about a mythical figure – the figure of 'The Reasonable Man'.
A. P. Herbert (1890–1971) British writer and politician. *Uncommon Law*

23 In *this* country, my Lords,...the individual subject...'has nothing to do with the laws but to obey them.'
Bishop Samuel Horsley (1733–1806) British bishop. House of Lords, 13 Nov 1795

24 Oh, Mr. President, do not let so great an achievement suffer from any taint of legality.
Philander Chase Knox (1853–1921) US lawyer and politician. Responding to Theodore Roosevelt's request for legal justification of his acquisition of the Panama Canal Zone. *Violent Neighbours* (T. Buckley)

25 In university they don't tell you that the greater part of the law is learning to tolerate fools.
Doris Lessing (1919–) British novelist. *Martha Quest*, Pt. III, Ch. 2

26 No brilliance is needed in the law. Nothing but common sense, and relatively clean finger nails.
John Mortimer (1923–) British lawyer and dramatist. *A Voyage Round My Father*, I

27 Laws were made to be broken.
Christopher North (John Wilson; 1785–1854) Scottish writer. *Noctes Ambrosianae*, 24 May 1830

28 Let us consider the reason of the case. For nothing is law that is not reason.
John Powell (1645–1713) English judge. Coggs v. Bernard, 2 Lord Raymond, 911

29 Any institution which does not suppose the people good, and the magistrate corruptible is evil.
Robespierre (1758–94) French lawyer and revolutionary. *Déclaration des droits de l'homme*, 24 Apr 1793

30 Every law is a contract between the king and the people and therefore to be kept.

John Selden (1584–1654) English historian. *Table Talk*

31 Ignorance of the law excuses no man; not that all men know the law, but because 'tis an excuse every man will plead, and no man can tell how to confute him.

John Selden *Table Talk*

32 We must not make a scarecrow of the law,
Setting it up to fear the birds of prey,
And let it keep one shape, till custom make it
Their perch and not their terror.

William Shakespeare (1564–1616) English dramatist. *Measure for Measure*, II:1

33 Let him look to his bond.

William Shakespeare *The Merchant of Venice*, III:1

34 Wrest once the law to your authority:
To do a great right, do a little wrong.

William Shakespeare *The Merchant of Venice*, IV:1

35 Still you keep o' th' windy side of the law.

William Shakespeare *Twelfth Night*, III:4

36 Laws are generally found to be nets of such a texture, as the little creep through, the great break through, and the middle-sized are alone entangled in.

William Shenstone *See also* BACON; SOLON; SWIFT. *Essays on Men, Manners, and Things*, 'On Politics'

37 Laws are like spider's webs: if some poor weak creature come up against them, it is caught; but a bigger one can break through and get away.

Solon (6th century BC) Athenian statesman. *See also* BACON; SHENSTONE; SWIFT. *Lives of the Eminent Philosophers* (Diogenes Laertius), I

38 Laws are like cobwebs, which may catch small flies, but let wasps and hornets break through.

Jonathan Swift (1667–1745) Irish-born Anglican priest and writer. *See also* BACON; SHENSTONE; SOLON. *A Critical Essay upon the Faculties of the Mind*

39 Everybody talks of the constitution, but all sides forget that the constitution is extremely well, and would do very well, if they would but let it alone.

Horace Walpole (1717–97) British writer. Letter to Sir Horace Mann, 1770

40 It is only those with the deepest pockets who can risk going to law.

Lord Woolf (1933–) British lawyer. *The Times*, 23 June 1994

LAWRENCE, D. H.

(1885–1930) British novelist. The son of a coalminer, he earned his reputation with the autobiographical *Sons and Lovers* (1913). Subsequent novels include *Women in Love* (1921), *Kangaroo* (1923), and *Lady Chatterley's Lover* (1928).

Quotations about D. H. Lawrence

1 Interesting, but a type I could not get on with. Obsessed with self. Dead eyes and a red beard, long narrow face. A strange bird.

John Galsworthy (1867–1933) British novelist. *Life and Letters* (edited by H. V. Marriot)

2 For Lawrence, existence was one long convalescence, it was as though he were newly reborn from a mortal illness every day of his life.

Aldous Huxley (1894–1964) British novelist. *The Olive Tree*

Quotations by D. H. Lawrence

3 You must always be a-waggle with LOVE.

Bibbles

4 The English people on the whole are surely the *nicest* people in the world, and everyone makes everything so easy for everybody else, that there is almost nothing to resist at all.

Dull London

5 To the Puritan all things are impure, as somebody says.

Etruscan Places, 'Cerveteri'

6 The Romans and Greeks found everything human. Everything had a face, and a human voice. Men spoke, and their fountains piped an answer.

Fantasia of the Unconscious, Ch. 4

7 The refined punishments of the spiritual mode are usually much more indecent and dangerous than a good smack.

Fantasia of the Unconscious, Ch. 4

8 Morality which is based on ideas, or on an ideal, is an unmitigated evil.

Fantasia of the Unconscious, Ch. 7

9 When Eve ate this particular apple, she became aware of her own womanhood, mentally. And mentally she began to experiment with it. She has been experimenting ever since. So has man. To the rage and horror of both of them.

Fantasia of the Unconscious, Ch. 7

10 O pity the dead that are dead, but cannot make
the journey, still they moan and beat
against the silvery adamant walls of life's exclusive city.

The Houseless Dead

11 How beastly the bourgeois is
especially the male of the species.

How beastly the bourgeois is

12 You may be the most liberal Liberal Englishman, and yet you cannot fail to see the categorical difference between the responsible and the irresponsible classes.

Kangaroo, Ch. 1

13 And all lying mysteriously within the Australian underdark, that peculiar, lost weary aloofness of Australia. There was the vast town of Sydney. And it didn't seem to be real, it seemed to be sprinkled on the surface of a darkness into which it never penetrated.

Kangaroo, Ch. 1

14 The very best that is in the Jewish blood: a faculty for pure disinterestedness, and warm, physically warm love, that seems to make the corpuscles of the blood glow.

Kangaroo, Ch. 6

15 We have all lost the war. All Europe.

The Ladybird, 'The Ladybird'

16 The young Cambridge group, the group that stood for 'freedom' and flannel trousers and flannel shirts open at the neck, and a well-bred sort of emotional anarchy, and a whispering, murmuring sort of voice, and an ultra-sensitive sort of manner.
Lady Chatterley's Lover, Ch. 1

17 It's all this cold-hearted fucking that is death and idiocy.
Lady Chatterley's Lover, Ch. 14

18 But tha mun dress thysen, an' go back to thy stately homes of England, how beautiful they stand. Time's up! Time's up for Sir John, an' for little Lady Jane! Put thy shimmy on, Lady Chatterley!
Lady Chatterley's Lover, Ch. 15

19 Water is H_2O, hydrogen two parts, oxygen one, but there is also a third thing, that makes it water and nobody knows what that is.
Pansies, 'The Third Thing'

20 It always seemed to me that men wore their beards, like they wear their neckties, for show. I shall always remember Lewis for saying his beard was part of him.
St Mawr

21 The modern pantheist not only sees the god in everything, he takes photographs of it.
St Mawr

22 It was one of those places where the spirit of aboriginal England still lingers, the old savage England, whose last blood flows still in a few Englishmen, Welshmen, Cornishmen.
St Mawr

23 Ideal mankind would abolish death, multiply itself million upon million, rear up city upon city, save every parasite alive, until the accumulation of mere existence is swollen to a horror.
St Mawr

24 And suddenly she craved again for the more absolute silence of America. English stillness was so soft, like an inaudible murmur of voices, of presences.
St Mawr

25 You may have my husband, but not my horse. My husband won't need emasculating, and my horse I won't have you meddle with. I'll preserve one last male thing in the museum of this world, if I can.
St Mawr

26 There's nothing so artificial as sinning nowadays. I suppose it once was real.
St Mawr

27 One realizes with horror, that the race of men is almost extinct in Europe. Only Christ-like heroes and woman-worshipping Don Juans, and rabid equality-mongrels.
Sea and Sardinia, Ch. 3

28 A snake came to my water-trough
On a hot, hot day, and I in pyjamas for the heat,
To drink there.
Snake

29 And so, I missed my chance with one of the lords
Of life.
And I have something to expiate;
A pettiness.
Snake

30 When I read Shakespeare I am struck with wonder
That such trivial people should muse and thunder
In such lovely language.
When I Read Shakespeare

31 Be a good animal, true to your animal instincts.
The White Peacock, Pt. II, Ch. 2

32 No absolute is going to make the lion lie down with the lamb unless the lamb is inside.
The Later D. H. Lawrence

33 Away with all ideals. Let each individual act spontaneously from the for ever incalculable prompting of the creative wellhead within him. There is no universal law.
Phoenix, Preface to 'All Things are Possible' by Leo Shostov

34 Russia will certainly inherit the future. What we already call the greatness of Russia is only her pre-natal struggling.
Phoenix, Preface to 'All Things are Possible' by Leo Shostov

35 Pornography is the attempt to insult sex, to do dirt on it.
Phoenix, 'Pornography and Obscenity'

36 It is no good casting out devils. They belong to us, we must accept them and be at peace with them.
Phoenix, 'The Reality of Peace'

37 Neither can you expect a revolution, because there is no new baby in the womb of our society. Russia is a collapse, not a revolution.
Phoenix, 'The Good Man'

38 I am a man, and alive...For this reason I am a novelist. And being a novelist, I consider myself superior to the saint, the scientist, the philosopher, and the poet, who are all great masters of different bits of man alive, but never get the whole hog.
Phoenix, 'Why the Novel Matters'

39 We know these new English Catholics. They are the last words in Protest. They are Protestants protesting against Protestantism.
Phoenix, 'Review of Eric Gill, *Art Nonsense*'

40 To every man who struggles with his own soul in mystery, a book that is a book flowers once, and seeds, and is gone.
Phoenix, 'A Bibliography of D.H.L.'

41 I like to write when I feel spiteful: it's like having a good sneeze.
Letter to Lady Cynthia Asquith, Nov 1913

42 They are great parables, the novels, but false art. They are only parables. All the people are *fallen angels* – even the dirtiest scrubs. This I cannot stomach. People are not fallen angels, they are merely people.
Referring to the novels of Dostoevsky. Letter to J. Middleton Murry and Katherine Mansfield, 17 Feb 1916

43 I am only half there when I am ill, and so there

is only half a man to suffer. To suffer in one's whole self is so great a violation, that it is not to be endured.

Letter to Catherine Carswell, 16 Apr 1916

44 The dead don't die. They look on and help.

Letter to J. Middleton Murry, 2 Feb 1923

45 I'm not sure if a mental relation with a woman doesn't make it impossible to love her. To know the *mind* of a woman is to end in hating her. Love means the pre-cognitive flow…it is the honest state before the apple.

Letter to Dr Trigant Burrow, 3 Aug 1927

LAWRENCE, T. E.

(1888–1935) British soldier and writer, known as Lawrence of Arabia. He became famous after leading a successful Arab revolt against the Turks (1917–18). He wrote *The Seven Pillars of Wisdom* (1926) and *The Mint* (1955).

Quotations about T. E. Lawrence

1 Arabian Lawrence, who, whatever his claims as a man, was surely a sonorous fake as a writer.

Kingsley Amis (1922–) British novelist. *What Became of Jane Austen?*

2 He's always backing into the limelight.

Gerald Hugh Tyrwhitt-Wilson Berners (1883–1950) British writer and composer. Attrib.

3 …a bore and a bounder and a prig. He was intoxicated with his own youth, and loathed any milieu which he couldn't dominate. Certainly he had none of a gentleman's instincts, strutting about Peace Conferences in Arab dress.

Henry Channon (1897–1958) US-born British politician. *Diary*, 25 May 1935

4 There are those who have tried to dismiss his story with a flourish of the Union Jack, a psycho-analytical catchword, or a sneer. It should move our deepest admiration and pity. Like Shelley and like Baudelaire it may be said of him that he suffered, in his own person, the neurotic ills of an entire generation.

Christopher Isherwood (1904–86) British novelist. *Exhumations*

5 He was retiring and yet craved to be seen, he was sincerely shy and naively exhibitionist. He had to rise above others and then humble himself, and in his self-inflicted humiliation demonstrate his superiority.

Lewis B. Namier (1888–1960) Polish educator and historian. *T. E. Lawrence by His Friends* (A. W. Lawrence)

Quotations by T. E. Lawrence

6 Many men would take the death-sentence without a whimper to escape the life-sentence which fate carries in her other hand.

The Mint, Pt. I, Ch. 4

7 I loved you, so I drew these tides of men into my hands and wrote my will across the sky in stars
To earn you Freedom, the seven pillared worthy house, that your eyes might be shining for me
When we came.

Seven Pillars of Wisdom, Epigraph

8 All men dream: but not equally. Those who dream by night in the dusty recesses of their minds wake in the day to find that it was vanity: but the dreamers of the day are dangerous men, for they may act their dream with open eyes, to make it possible.

Seven Pillars of Wisdom, Ch. 1

9 I fancy, for myself, that they are rather out of touch with reality; by reality I mean shops like Selfridges, and motor buses, and the *Daily Express*.

Referring to expatriate authors living in Paris, such as James Joyce. Letter to W. Hurley, 1 Apr 1929

10 I'm re-reading it with a slow deliberate carelessness.

Letter to Edward Marsh, 18 Apr 1929

LAWYERS

See also law

1 He that is his own lawyer has a fool for a client.

Proverb

2 A lawyer never goes to law himself.

Proverb

3 A lawyer's opinion is worth nothing unless paid for.

Proverb

4 Lawyers are the only persons in whom ignorance of the law is not punished.

Jeremy Bentham (1748–1832) British philosopher. Attrib.

5 Woe unto you, lawyers! for ye have taken away the key of knowledge: ye entered not in yourselves, and them that were entering in ye hindered.

Bible: Luke 11:52

6 A client is fain to hire a lawyer to keep from the injury of other lawyers – as Christians that travel in Turkey are forced to hire Janissaries, to protect them from the insolencies of other Turks.

Samuel Butler (1835–1902) British writer. *Prose Observations*

7 Hence it comes about that there is scarcely a man learned in the laws to be found in the realm who is not noble or sprung of noble lineage.

Sir John Fortescue (c. 1394–c. 1476) Chief justice of the King's Bench. *The Governance of England*

8 I do not care to speak ill of any man behind his back, but I believe the gentleman is an *attorney*.

Samuel Johnson (1709–84) British lexicographer. *Life of Johnson* (J. Boswell), Vol. II

9 A lawyer with his briefcase can steal more than a thousand men with guns.

Mario Puzo (1920–) US novelist. *The Godfather*

10 CADE. There shall be in England seven halfpenny loaves sold for a penny; the three-hooped pot shall have ten hoops; and I will make it felony to drink small beer. All the realm shall be in common, and in Cheapside shall my palfrey go to grass. And when I am king, – as king I will be, –…there shall be no money; all shall eat and drink on my score; and I will apparel them all in one livery, that they

may agree like brothers, and worship me their lord.
DICK. The first thing we do, let's kill all the lawyers.

William Shakespeare (1564–1616) English dramatist. *Henry VI, Part Two, IV:2*

11 It is a very salutary check for a judge to realise that if he does say something silly it is liable to get into the papers.

Mr Justice Templeman (1920–) British judge. *The Observer*, 20 Aug 1978

LAZINESS

See also bed, idleness

1 You can tell a British workman by his hands. They are always in his pockets.

Anonymous *Quote Unquote* (radio programme), 26 June 1980

2 We grow old more through indolence, than through age.

Christina of Sweden (1626–89) Swedish queen. *Maxims (1660–1680)*

3 I make no secret of the fact that I would rather lie on a sofa than sweep beneath it. But you have to be efficient if you're going to be lazy.

Shirley Conran (1932–) British designer and journalist. *Superwoman*, 'The Reason Why'

4 I get my exercise acting as a pallbearer to my friends who exercise.

Chauncey Depew (1834–1928) US politician.

5 The only exercise I get is when I take the studs out of one shirt and put them in another.

Ring Lardner Jnr (1885–1933) US humorist. *Bartlett's Unfamiliar Quotations* (Leonard Louis Levinson)

6 Happy is the man with a wife to tell him what to do and a secretary to do it.

Lord Mancroft (1917–87) British businessman and writer. *The Observer*, 'Sayings of the Week', 18 Dec 1966

7 Alas! The hours we waste in work
And similar inconsequence,
Friends, I beg you do not shirk
Your daily task of indolence.

Don Marquis (1878–1937) US journalist. *The Almost Perfect State*

8 For one person who dreams of making fifty thousand pounds, a hundred people dream of being left fifty thousand pounds.

A. A. Milne (1882–1956) British writer. *If I May*, 'The Future'

9 Henry has always led what could be called a sedentary life, if only he'd ever got as far as actually sitting up.

Henry Reed (1914–) British poet and dramatist. *Not a Drum was Heard: The War Memoirs of General Gland*

10 It is better to have loafed and lost than never to have loafed at all.

James Thurber (1894–1961) US humorist. *Fables for Our Time*, 'The Courtship of Arthur and Al'

11 'Tis the voice of the sluggard, I heard him complain:
'You have waked me too soon, I must slumber again.'

Isaac Watts (1674–1748) English theologian and hymn writer. *The Sluggard*

LEACOCK, STEPHEN

(1869–1944) British-born Canadian economist and humorist. His *Literary Lapses* (1910) and *Nonsense Novels* (1911) were two of some 30 humorous books.

1 If every day in the life of a school could be the last day but one, there would be little fault to find with it.

College Days, 'Memories and Miseries of a Schoolmaster'

2 The classics are only primitive literature. They belong in the same class as primitive machinery and primitive music and primitive medicine.

Homer and Humbug

3 I detest life-insurance agents; they always argue that I shall some day die, which is not so.

Literary Lapses, 'Insurance. Up to Date'

4 Get your room full of good air, then shut up the windows and keep it. It will keep for years. Anyway, don't keep using your lungs all the time. Let them rest.

Literary Lapses, 'How to Live to be 200'

5 Astronomy teaches the correct use of the sun and the planets.

Literary Lapses, 'A Manual of Education'

6 The landlady of a boarding-house is a parallelogram – that is, an oblong angular figure, which cannot be described, but which is equal to anything.

Literary Lapses, 'Boarding-House Geometry'

7 Any two meals at a boarding-house are together less than two square meals.

Literary Lapses, 'Boarding-House Geometry'

8 It takes a good deal of physical courage to ride a horse. This, however, I have. I get it at about forty cents a flask, and take it as required.

Literary Lapses, 'Reflections on Riding'

9 The great man...walks across his century and leaves the marks of his feet all over it, ripping out the dates on his goloshes as he passes.

Literary Lapses, 'The Life of John Smith'

10 Lord Ronald said nothing; he flung himself from the room, flung himself upon his horse and rode madly off in all directions.

Nonsense Novels, 'Gertrude the Governess'

11 Golf may be played on Sunday, not being a game within the view of the law, but being a form of moral effort.

Over the Footlights, 'Why I refuse to play Golf'

12 A 'Grand Old Man'. That means on our continent any one with snow white hair who has kept out of jail till eighty.

The Score and Ten

13 The general idea, of course, in any first-class laundry is to see that no shirt or collar ever comes back twice.

Winnowed Wisdom, Ch. 6

LEADERSHIP

See also guidance

1 I know that the right kind of political leader for the Labour Party is a desiccated calculating machine.

Aneurin Bevan (1897–1960) Welsh Labour politician. Usually regarded as a gibe at the leader of the Labour Party, Hugh Gaitskell. Speech during Labour Party Conference, 29 Sept 1954

2 The trouble in modern democracy is that men do not approach to leadership until they have lost the desire to lead anyone.

Lord Beveridge (1879–1963) British economist. *The Observer*, 'Sayings of the Week', 15 Apr 1934

3 And he shall rule them with a rod of iron; as the vessels of a potter shall they be broken to shivers: even as I received of my Father.

Bible: Revelations 2:27

4 I believe in benevolent dictatorship provided I am the dictator.

Richard Branson (1950–) British entrepreneur. Remark, Nov 1984

5 Captains of industry.

Thomas Carlyle (1795–1881) Scottish historian and essayist. *Past and Present*, Bk. IV, Ch. 4

6 As the Prime Minister put it to me...he saw his role as being that of Moses.

Peter Jay (1937–) British economist and broadcaster. Referring to a conversation with James Callaghan. *Guardian Weekly*, 18 Sept 1977

7 Let me pass, I have to follow them, I am their leader.

Alexandre Auguste Ledru-Rollin (1807–74) French lawyer and politician. Trying to force his way through a mob during the Revolution of 1848, of which he was one of the chief instigators. A similar remark is attributed to the British Conservative Statesman, Bonar Law. *The Fine Art of Political Wit* (L. Harris)

8 Lions led by donkeys.

Erich Ludendorff (1865–1937) German general. Referring to British troops in World War I. Attrib.

9 Only one man in a thousand is a leader of men – the other 999 follow women.

Groucho Marx (Julius Marx; 1895–1977) US comedian. *News Review*

10 A leader who doesn't hesitate before he sends his nation into battle is not fit to be a leader.

Golda Meir (1898–1978) Russian-born Israeli stateswoman. *As Good as Golda* (ed. Israel and Mary Shenker)

11 No general in the midst of battle has a great discussion about what he is going to do if defeated.

David Owen (1938–) British politician. *The Observer*, 'Sayings of the Week', 6 June 1987

12 Out great captain's captain.

William Shakespeare (1564–1616) English dramatist. *Othello*, II:1

13 We were not born to sue, but to command.

William Shakespeare *Richard II*, I:1

14 A constant effort to keep his party together, without sacrificing either principle or the essentials of basic strategy, is the very stuff of political leadership. Macmillan was canonised for it.

Harold Wilson (1916–) British politician and prime minister. Referring to the Conservative prime minister Harold Macmillan (1894–1986). *Final Term: The Labour Government 1974–76*

LEAR, EDWARD

(1812–88) British artist and writer. His *Book of Nonsense* (1846) was the forerunner of several others, such as *Laughable Lyrics* (1876).

1 There was an Old Man with a beard,
Who said, 'It is just as I feared! –
Two Owls and a Hen,
Four Larks and a Wren,
Have all built their nests in my beard!'

Book of Nonsense

2 On the Coast of Coromandel
Where the early pumpkins blow,
In the middle of the woods
Lived the Yonghy-Bonghy-Bò.

The Courtship of the Yonghy-Bonghy-Bò

3 The Dong! – the Dong!
The wandering Dong through the forest goes!
The Dong! – the Dong!
The Dong with a luminous Nose!

The Dong with a Luminous Nose

4 They went to sea in a sieve, they did
In a sieve they went to sea.

The Jumblies

5 Far and few, far and few,
Are the lands where the Jumblies live;
Their heads are green, and their hands are blue,
And they went to sea in a sieve.

The Jumblies

6 Serve up in a clean dish, and throw the whole out of the window as fast as possible.

To make an Amblongus Pie

7 He has many friends, laymen and clerical.
Old Foss is the name of his cat:
His body is perfectly spherical,
He weareth a runcible hat.

Nonsense Songs, Preface

8 The Owl and the Pussy-Cat went to sea
In a beautiful pea-green boat,
They took some honey, and plenty of money,
Wrapped up in a five-pound note.

The Owl and the Pussy-Cat

9 They dined on mince, and slices of quince,
Which they ate with a runcible spoon;
And hand in hand, on the edge of the sand,
They danced by the light of the moon.

The Owl and the Pussy-Cat

LEARNING

See also education, knowledge

1 I learned just by going around. I know all about Kleenex factories, and all sorts of things.

Princess Anne (1950–) The Princess Royal, only daughter of Elizabeth II. Attrib.

2 What we have to learn to do, we learn by doing.

Aristotle (384–322 BC) Greek philosopher. *Nicomachean Ethics*, Bk. II

3 Miss not the discourse of the elders: for they also learned of their fathers, and of them thou shalt learn understanding, and to give answer as need requireth.

Bible: Ecclesiasticus 8:9

4 Read, mark, learn and inwardly digest.

The Book of Common Prayer *Collect, 2nd Sunday in Advent*

5 An art can only be learned in the workshop of those who are winning their bread by it.

Samuel Butler (1835–1902) British writer. *Erewhon*, Ch. 20

6 LIBOV ANDREEVNA. Are you still a student?
TROFIMOV. I expect I shall be a student to the end of my days.

Anton Chekhov (1860–1904) Russian dramatist. *The Cherry Orchard*, I

7 I am always ready to learn although I do not always like being taught.

Winston Churchill (1874–1965) British statesman. *The Observer*, 9 Nov 1952

8 In the traditional method the child must say something that he has merely learned. There is all the difference in the world between having something to say, and having to say something.

John Dewey (1859–1952) US philosopher and educator. *Dewey On Education*

9 Remember that even the learned ignorance of a nomenclature is something to have mastered, and may furnish pegs to hang facts upon which would otherwise have strewed the floor of memory in loose disorder.

Oliver Wendell Holmes (1809–94) US writer and physician. *Medical Essays*, 'The Young Practitioner'

10 It is the true nature of mankind to learn from mistakes, not from example.

Fred Hoyle (1915–) British astronomer. *Into Deepest Space*

11 Thus men of more enlighten'd genius and more intrepid spirit must compose themselves to the risque of public censure, and the contempt of their jealous contemporaries, in order to lead ignorant and prejudic'd minds into more happy and successful methods.

John Jones (1729–91) Introductory lecture to his course in surgery

12 ...that is what learning is. You suddenly understand something you've understood all your life, but in a new way.

Doris Lessing (1919–) British novelist. *The Four-Gated City*

13 You will have to learn many tedious things,... which you will forget the moment you have passed your final examination, but in anatomy it is better to have learned and lost than never to have learned at all.

W. Somerset Maugham (1874–1965) British writer and doctor. Given as advice to first-year medical students. *Of Human Bondage*, Ch. 54

14 The safest thing for a patient is to be in the hands of a man engaged in teaching medicine. In order to be a teacher of medicine the doctor must always be a student.

Charles H. Mayo (1865–1939) US physician. *Proceedings of the Staff Meetings of the Mayo Clinic*, 2:233, 1927

15 He intended, he said, to devote the rest of his life to learning the remaining twenty-two letters of the alphabet.

George Orwell (Eric Blair; 1903–50) British novelist. *Animal Farm*, Ch. 9

16 For where is any author in the world
Teaches such beauty as a woman's eye?
Learning is but an adjunct to oneself.

William Shakespeare (1564–1616) English dramatist. *Love's Labour's Lost*, IV:3

17 Not with blinded eyesight poring over miserable books.

Alfred, Lord Tennyson (1809–92) British poet. *Locksley Hall*

18 One impulse from a vernal wood
May teach you more of man,
Of moral evil and of good,
Than all the sages can.

William Wordsworth (1770–1850) British poet. *The Tables Turned*

19 Some for renown, on scraps of learning dote,
And think they grow immortal as they quote.

Edward Young (1683–1765) British poet. *Love of Fame*, I

LE CORBUSIER

(Charles-Édouard Jeanneret; 1887–1965) Swiss-born French architect. He progressed from cubist-style houses to more innovative ideas, such as the *unité d'habitation* at Marseilles. The city of Chandigarh in India was his most ambitious town-planning project.

1 A house is a machine for living in.

Towards a New Architecture

2 'A great epoch has begun. There exists a new spirit.'

Towards a New Architecture

3 If you want to see bad taste, go into the houses of the rich.

Attrib.

LEE, LAURIE

(1914–) British novelist and poet. His most famous publication is the novel *Cider with Rosie* (1959), about his rural childhood; other works include *As I Walked Out One Midsummer Morning* (1969) and *I Can't Stay Long* (1976).

1 As the drought continued, prayer was abandoned and more devilish steps adopted. Finally soldiers with rifles marched to the tops of the hills and began shooting at passing clouds.

Cider With Rosie, 'First Names'

2 Being so recently born, birth had no meaning; it was the other extreme that enthralled me. Death was absorbing, and I saw much of it; it was my childhood's continuous fare.

Cider With Rosie, 'Public Death, Private Murder'

3 The old couple were shocked and terrified, and lay clutching each other's hands. 'The Workhouse' – always a word of shame, grey shadow falling on the close of life, most feared by the old (even when called The Infirmary); abhorred more than debt, or prison, or beggary, or even the stain of madness.

Cider with Rosie, 'Public Death, Private Murder'

4 Myself, my family, my generation, were born in

a world of silence; a world of hard work and necessary patience...Man and horse were all the power we had – abetted by levers and pulleys. But the horse was king, and almost everything grew around him...This was what we were born to, and all we knew at first. Then, to the scream of the horse, the change began. The brass-lamped motor-car came coughing up the road.

Cider With Rosie, 'Last Days'

LEISURE

See also idleness, merrymaking, pleasure, rest

1 The wisdom of a learned man cometh by opportunity of leisure: and he that hath little business shall become wise.
How can he get wisdom that holdeth the plough, and that glorieth in the goad, that driveth oxen, and is occupied in their labours, and whose talk is of bullocks?

Bible: Ecclesiasticus 38:24–25

2 We are closer to the ants than to the butterflies. Very few people can endure much leisure.

Gerald Brenan (Edward Fitzgerald Brenan; 1894–1987) British writer. *Thoughts in a Dry Season*

3 Hey! Mr Tambourine Man, play a song for me.
I'm not sleepy and there is no place I'm going to.

Bob Dylan (Robert Allen Zimmerman; 1941–) US popular singer. *Mr Tambourine Man*

4 I am interested in leisure in the way that a poor man is interested in money. I can't get enough of it.

Prince Philip (1921–) The consort of Queen Elizabeth II. Attrib.

5 If all the year were playing holidays, To sport would be as tedious as to work.

William Shakespeare (1564–1616) English dramatist. *Henry IV, Part One*, I:2

6 Days off.

Spencer Tracy (1900–67) US film star. Explaining what he looked for in a script. Attrib.

LENIN, VLADIMIR ILICH

(Vladimir Ilich Ulyanov; 1870–1924) Russian revolutionary leader, who led the Bolsheviks to victory, establishing the Soviet of People's Commissars and the Third International. He died after a series of strokes resulting from an assassination attempt.

1 If it were necessary to give the briefest possible definition of imperialism we should have to say that imperialism is the monopoly stage of capitalism.

Imperialism, the Highest Stage of Capitalism, Ch. 7

2 One step forward, two steps back...It happens in the lives of individuals, and it happens in the history of nations and in the development of parties.

One Step Forward, Two Steps Back

3 Under capitalism we have a state in the proper sense of the word, that is, a special machine for the suppression of one class by another.

The State and Revolution, Ch. 5

4 While the state exists there can be no freedom. When there is freedom there will be no state.

The State and Revolution, Ch. 5

5 Under socialism *all* will govern in turn and will soon become accustomed to no one governing.

The State and Revolution, Ch. 6

6 A Social-Democrat must never forget that the proletariat will inevitably have to wage a class struggle for Socialism even against the most democratic and republican bourgeoisie and petty bourgeoisie.

The State and Revolution, Ch. 10

7 Any cook should be able to run the country.

The First Circle (Alexander Solzhenitsyn)

8 When a liberal is abused, he says: Thank God they didn't beat me. When he is beaten, he thanks God they didn't kill him. When he is killed, he will thank God that his immortal soul has been delivered from its mortal clay.

Lenin heard this characterization at a meeting, and repeated it with approval. *The Government's Falsification of the Duma and the Tasks of the Social-Democrats*, 'Proletary', Dec 1906

9 Communism is Soviet power plus the electrification of the whole country.

Political slogan of 1920, promoting the programme of electrification

10 A good man fallen among Fabians.

Referring to George Bernard Shaw. Attrib.

11 It is true that liberty is precious – so precious that it must be rationed.

Attrib.

LENNON, JOHN

(1940–80) British rock musician and member of the Beatles. His most distinctive solo recording was *Imagine* (1971). He was assassinated in 1980.

1 Life is what happens to you while you're busy making other plans.

Beautiful Boy

2 For I don't care too much for money,
For money can't buy me love.

Can't Buy Me Love (with Paul McCartney)

3 Waits at the window, wearing the face that she keeps in a jar by the door
Who is it for? All the lonely people, where do they all come from?
All the lonely people, where do they all belong?

Eleanor Rigby (with Paul McCartney)

4 If there's anything that you want,
If there's anything I can do,
Just call on me,
And I'll send it along with love from me to you.

From Me to You (with Paul McCartney)

5 I've got to admit it's getting better.
It's a little better all the time.

Getting Better (with Paul McCartney)

6 It's been a hard day's night.

A Hard Day's Night (with Paul McCartney)

7 Picture yourself in a boat on a river with tangerine trees and marmalade skies.
Somebody calls you, you answer quite slowly a girl with kaleidoscope eyes.
Lucy in the Sky with Diamonds (with Paul McCartney)

8 He's a real Nowhere Man,
Sitting in his Nowhere Land,
Making all his nowhere plans for nobody.
Doesn't have a point of view,
Knows not where he's going to,
Isn't he a bit like you and me?
Nowhere Man (with Paul McCartney)

9 Sergeant Pepper's Lonely Hearts Club Band.
Song title (with Paul McCartney)

10 She loves you, yeh, yeh, yeh,
And with a love like that you know you should be glad.
She Loves You (with Paul McCartney)

11 She's leaving home after living alone for so many years.
She's Leaving Home (with Paul McCartney)

12 I get by with a little help from my friends.
With a Little Help from My Friends (with Paul McCartney)

13 We're more popular than Jesus Christ now. I don't know which will go first. Rock and roll or Christianity.
The Beatles Illustrated Lyrics

LEONARDO DA VINCI

1452–1519) Italian artist, engineer, and scientist. His best-known paintings are the *Last Supper* and the *Mona Lisa*. His *Notebooks* (1508–18) cover a wide range of subjects.

Quotations about Leonardo da Vinci

1 He was the most relentlessly curious man in history. Everything he saw made him ask how and why. Why does one find sea-shells in the mountains? How do they build locks in Flanders? How does a bird fly? What accounts for cracks in walls? What is the origin of winds and clouds? Find out; write it down; if you can see it, draw it.
Sir Kenneth Clark (1903–83) British art historian and writer. *Civilization*

2 Of all these questions the one he asks most insistently is about man. How does he walk. How does the heart pump blood. What happens when he yawns and sneezes? How does a child live in the womb. Why does he die of old age? Leonardo discovered a centenarian in a hospital in Florence and waited gleefully for his demise so that he could examine his veins.
Sir Kenneth Clark (1903–83) British art historian and writer. *Civilization*

3 He bores me. He ought to have stuck to his flying machines.
Pierre Auguste Renoir (1841–1919) French impressionist painter.

4 Leonardo undertook for Francesco Zanobi del Giocondo the portrait of his wife Mona Lisa. She was very beautiful and while he was drawing her portrait he engaged people to play and sing, and jesters to keep her merry, and remove that melancholy which painting usually gives to portraits. This figure of Leonardo's has such a pleasant smile that it seems rather divine than human, and was considered marvellous, an exact copy of Nature.
Giorgio Vasari (1511–74) Italian art historian. *Lives of Painters, Architects and Sculptors*

Quotations by Leonardo da Vinci

5 A man with wings large enough and duly attached might learn to overcome the resistance of the air, and conquering it succeed in subjugating it and raise himself upon it.
Flight of Birds

6 While I thought that I was learning how to live, I have been learning how to die.
Notebooks

7 Those who are enamoured of practice without science are like a pilot who goes into a ship without rudder or compass and never has any certainty where he is going.
Practice should always be based upon a sound knowledge of theory.
Notebooks

LESSING, DORIS

(1919–) British novelist, brought up in Rhodesia. Her works include the five-novel sequence *Children of Violence* (1952–69), *The Golden Notebook* (1962), *Memoirs of a Survivor* (1974), *The Good Terrorist* (1985), *The Fifth Child* (1988), and *London Observed* (1992).

1 ...that is what learning is. You suddenly understand something you've understood all your life, but in a new way.
The Four-Gated City

2 When old settlers say 'One has to understand the country', what they mean is, 'You have to get used to our ideas about the native.' They are saying, in effect, 'Learn our ideas, or otherwise get out; we don't want you.'
Referring specifically to South Africa. *The Grass is Singing*, Ch. 1

3 When a white man in Africa by accident looks into the eyes of a native and sees the human being (which it is his chief preoccupation to avoid), his sense of guilt, which he denies, fumes up in resentment and he brings down the whip.
The Grass is Singing, Ch. 8

4 If people dug up the remains of this civilization a thousand years hence, and found Epstein's statues and that man Ellis, they would think we were just savages.
Martha Quest, Pt. I, Ch. 1

5 In university they don't tell you that the greater part of the law is learning to tolerate fools.
Martha Quest, Pt. III, Ch. 2

6 If a fish is the movement of water embodied, given shape, then cat is a diagram and pattern of subtle air.
Particularly Cats, Ch. 2

LETTER-WRITING

See also communication

1 …a habit the pleasure of which increases with practise, but becomes more urksome with neglect.

Abigail Adams (1744–1818) US feminist. Letter to her daughter, 8 May 1808

2 Someone, somewhere, wants a letter from you.

Anonymous British Post Office slogan

3 When he wrote a letter, he would put that which was most material in the postscript, as if it had been a by-matter.

Francis Bacon (1561–1626) English philosopher. *Essays*, 'Of Cunning'

4 His sayings are generally like women's letters; all the pith is in the postscript.

William Hazlitt (1778–1830) British essayist. Referring to Charles Lamb *Conversations of Northcote*

LEWIS, C. S.

(1898–1963) British academic and writer. An Oxford professor, his books on Christianity include *The Problem of Pain* (1940) and *The Screwtape Letters* (1942). He also wrote children's books and science fiction.

1 Friendship is unnecessary, like philosophy, like art…It has no survival value; rather it is one of those things that give value to survival.

The Four Loves, Friendship

2 The coarse joke proclaims that we have here an animal which finds its own animality either objectionable or funny.

Miracles

3 There is wishful thinking in Hell as well as on earth.

The Screwtape Letters, Preface

4 There must be several young women who would render the Christian life intensely difficult to him if only you could persuade him to marry one of them.

The Screwtape Letters

5 The Future is something which everyone reaches at the rate of sixty minutes an hour, whatever he does, whoever he is.

The Screwtape Letters

6 She's the sort of woman who lives for others – you can always tell the others by their hunted expression.

The Screwtape Letters

LEWIS, WYNDHAM

(1882–1957) British novelist and painter. He helped to found the Vorticist movement in 1913; his novels include *The Apes of God* (1930) and the trilogy *The Human Age* (1928–55).

1 The soul started at the knee-cap and ended at the navel.

The Apes of God, Pt. XII

2 'Dying for an idea,' again, sounds well enough, but why not let the idea die instead of you?

The Art of Being Ruled, Pt. I, Ch. 1

3 I believe that (in one form or another) castration may be the solution. And the feminization of the white European and American is already far advanced, coming in the wake of the war.

The Art of Being Ruled, Pt. II, Ch. 2

4 The 'homo' is the legitimate child of the 'suffragette'.

The Art of Being Ruled, Pt. VIII, Ch. 4

5 You persisted for a certain number of years like a stammer. You were a *stammer*, if you like, of Space-Time.

The Human Age, 'The Childermass'

6 The revolutionary simpleton is everywhere.

Time and Western Man, Bk. I, Ch. 6

LEXICOGRAPHY

1 To finish is both a relief and a release from an extraordinarily pleasant prison.

Robert Burchfield (1923–) New Zealand editor. On completing the supplements to the Oxford English Dictionary *The Observer*, 'Sayings of the Week', 11 Sept 1986

2 Like Webster's Dictionary
We're Morocco bound.

Johnny Burke (1908–64) US songwriter. Song, 'Road to Morocco' from the film *The Road to Morocco*

3 The responsibility of a dictionary is to record a language, not set its style.

Philip Babcock Gove (1902–72) US dictionary editor. Letter to *Life Magazine*, 17 Nov 1961

4 But these were the dreams of a poet doomed at last to wake a lexicographer.

Samuel Johnson (1709–84) British lexicographer. *Dictionary of the English Language*

5 *Dull.* 8. To make dictionaries is dull work.

Samuel Johnson *Dictionary of the English Language*

6 *Lexicographer.* A writer of dictionaries, a harmless drudge.

Samuel Johnson *Dictionary of the English Language*

7 I've been in *Who's Who*, and I know what's what, but this is the first time I ever made the dictionary.

Mae West (1892–1980) US actress. On having a life-jacket named after her. Attrib.

LIBERALISM

1 You Liberals think that goats are just sheep from broken homes.

Malcolm Bradbury (1932–) British academic and novelist. *After Dinner Game* (with Christopher Bigsby)

2 When a liberal is abused, he says: Thank God they didn't beat me. When he is beaten, he thanks God they didn't kill him. When he is killed, he will thank God that his immortal soul has been delivered from its mortal clay.

Lenin (Vladimir Ilich Ulyanov; 1870–1924) Russian revolutionary leader. Lenin heard this characterization at a meeting, and repeated it with approval. *The Government's Falsification of the Duma and the Tasks of the Social-Democrats,* 'Proletary', Dec 1906.

3 A pleasant old buffer, nephew to a lord,
Who believed that the bank was mightier than the sword,
And that an umbrella might pacify barbarians abroad:
Just like an old liberal
Between the wars.

William Plomer (1903–73) South African poet and novelist. *Father and Son: 1939*

LIBERTY

1 It is not our frowning battlements...or the strength of our gallant and disciplined army. These are not our reliance against a resumption of tyranny in our fair land....Our defence is in the preservation of the spirit which prizes liberty as the heritage of all men, in all lands, everywhere.

Abraham Lincoln (1809–65) US statesman. Speech, 11 Sept 1858

2 Liberty means responsibility. That is why most men dread it.

George Bernard Shaw (1856–1950) Irish dramatist and critic.

LIFE

See also afterlife, human condition, life and death, mortality, purpose, time, world-weariness

1 Life begins at forty.

Proverb

2 Life is just a bowl of cherries.

Proverb

3 Life is sweet.

Proverb

4 Life, the Universe and Everything.

Douglas Adams (1952–) British writer. Book title

5 Is it so small a thing
To have enjoy'd the sun,
To have lived light in the spring,
To have loved, to have thought, to have done?

Matthew Arnold (1822–88) British poet and critic. *Empedocles on Etna*

6 Before this strange disease of modern life,
With its sick hurry, its divided aims.

Matthew Arnold *The Scholar Gipsy*

7 Who saw life steadily, and saw it whole:
The mellow glory of the Attic stage.

Matthew Arnold *Sonnets to a Friend*

8 Remember that no man loses any other life than this which he now lives, nor lives any other than this which he now loses.

Marcus Aurelius (121–180 AD) Roman emperor. *Meditations,* Bk. II, Ch. 14

9 The universe is transformation; our life is what our thoughts make it.

Marcus Aurelius *Meditations,* Bk. IV, Ch. 3

10 You don't get to choose how you're going to die. Or when. You can only decide how you're going to live. Now.

Joan Baez (1941–) US folksinger and civil rights activist. *Daybreak*

11 The present life of men on earth, O king, as compared with the whole length of time which is unknowable to us, seems to me to be like this: as if, when you are sitting at dinner with your chiefs and ministers in wintertime,...one of the sparrows from outside flew very quickly through the hall; as if it came in one door and soon went out through another. In that actual time it is indoors it is not touched by the winter's storm; but yet the tiny period of calm is over in a moment, and having come out of the winter it soon returns to the winter and slips out of your sight. Man's life appears to be more or less like this; and of what may follow it, or what preceded it, we are absolutely ignorant.

St Bede (The Venerable Bede; c. 673–735 AD) English churchman and historian. *Ecclesiastical History of the English People,* Bk. II, Ch. 13

12 Life is rather like a tin of sardines – we're all of us looking for the key.

Alan Bennett (1934–) British playwright. *Beyond the Fringe*

13 Your whole life is on the other side of the glass. And there is nobody watching.

Alan Bennett *The Old Country,* I

14 A man of sixty has spent twenty years in bed and over three years eating.

Arnold Bennett (1867–1931) British novelist. *Bartlett's Unfamiliar Quotations* (Leonard Louis Levinson)

15 One should not exaggerate the importance of trifles. Life, for instance, is much too short to be taken seriously.

Nicolas Bentley (1907–78) British cartoonist and writer. Attrib.

16 Life is a partial, continuous, progressive, multiform and conditionally interactive self-realization of the potentialities of atomic electron states.

John Desmond Bernal (1901–71) *The Origin of Life*

17 For everything that lives is holy, life delights in life.

William Blake (1757–1827) British poet. *America*

18 At last awake
From life, that insane dream we take
For waking now.

Robert Browning (1812–89) British poet. *Easter-Day,* XIV

19 How good is man's life, the mere living! how fit to employ
All the heart and the soul and the senses for ever in joy!

Robert Browning *Saul,* IX

20 Life is one long process of getting tired.

Samuel Butler (1835–1902) British writer. *Notebooks*

21 Life is the art of drawing sufficient conclusions from insufficient premises.

Samuel Butler *Notebooks*

22 To live is like love, all reason is against it, and all healthy instinct for it.

Samuel Butler *Notebooks*

23 Is life worth living? This is a question for an embryo, not for a man.

Samuel Butler *Notebooks*

24 Life is a dusty corridor, I say,
Shut at both ends.

Roy Campbell (1901–57) South African poet. *The Flaming Terrapin*

25 It's as large as life, and twice as natural!

Lewis Carroll (Charles Lutwidge Dodgson; 1832–98) British writer *Through the Looking-Glass*, Ch. 7

26 Living is a sickness from which sleep provides relief every sixteen hours. It's a pallative. The remedy is death.

Nicolas Chamfort (1741–94) French writer and wit.

27 Life is a tragedy when seen in close-up, but a comedy in long-shot.

Charlie Chaplin (Sir Charles Spencer C.; 1889–1977) British film actor. *The Guardian*, Obituary, 28 Dec 1977

28 For there is good news yet to hear and fine things to be seen,
Before we go to Paradise by way of Kensal Green.

G. K. Chesterton (1874–1936) British writer. *The Rolling English Road*

29 Life is a maze in which we take the wrong turning before we have learnt to walk.

Cyril Connolly (1903–74) British journalist. *The Unquiet Grave*

30 Magnificently unprepared
For the long littleness of life.

Frances Cornford (1886–1960) British poet. *Rupert Brooke*

31 Life is an incurable disease.

Abraham Cowley (1618–67) English poet. *To Dr Scarborough*

32 Life was a funny thing that happened to me on the way to the grave.

Quentin Crisp (c. 1910–) British model, publicist, and writer. *The Naked Civil Servant*, Ch. 18

33 What a fine comedy this world would be if one did not play a part in it!

Denis Diderot (1713–84) French writer. *Letters to Sophie Volland*

34 People do not live nowadays – they get about ten percent out of life.

Isadora Duncan (1878–1927) US dancer. *This Quarter Autumn*, 'Memoirs'

35 'Put your shoes at the door, sleep, prepare for life.'
The last twist of the knife.

T. S. Eliot (1888–1965) US-born British poet and dramatist. *Rhapsody on a Windy Night*

36 I have measured out my life with coffee spoons.

T. S. Eliot *The Love Song of J. Alfred Prufrock*

37 Yet we have gone on living,
Living and partly living.

T. S. Eliot *Murder in the Cathedral, Part One*

38 Pain and death are a part of life. To reject them is to reject life itself.

Havelock Ellis (1859–1939) British psychologist. *On Life and Sex: Essays of Love and Virtue*, 2

39 One thing is certain, that Life flies;
One thing is certain, and the Rest is Lies;
The Flower that once has blown for ever dies.

Edward Fitzgerald (1809–83) British poet. *The Rubáiyát of Omar Khayyám* (1st edn.), XXVI

40 Personal relations are the important thing for ever and ever, and not this outer life of telegrams and anger.

E. M. Forster (1879–1970) British novelist. *Howards End*

41 Between
Our birth and death we may touch understanding
As a moth brushes a window with its wing.

Christopher Fry (1907–) British dramatist. *The Boy with a Cart*

42 Life is a jest; and all things show it.
I thought so once; but now I know it.

John Gay (1685–1732) English poet and dramatist. *My Own Epitaph*

43 I must consider more closely this cycle of good and bad days which I find coursing within myself. Passion, attachment, the urge to action, inventiveness, performance, order all alternate and keep their orbit; cheerfulness, vigor, energy, flexibility and fatigue, serenity as well as desire. Nothing disturbs the cycle for I lead a simple life, but I must still find the time and order in which I rotate.

Goethe (1749–1832) German poet and dramatist. *The Encyclopedia of Alternative Medicine and Self-Help* (ed. Malcolm Hulke)

44 Life is a sexually transmitted disease.

Graffiti

45 Life's Little Ironies.

Thomas Hardy (1840–1928) British novelist. Title of book of stories

46 Life is made up of sobs, sniffles and smiles, with sniffles predominating.

O. Henry (William Sydney Porter; 1862–1910) US short-story writer. *The Gifts of the Magi*

47 Men to whom life had appeared as a reversible coat – seamy on both sides.

O. Henry *The Hiding of Black Bill*

48 Life is a fatal complaint, and an eminently contagious one.

Oliver Wendell Holmes (1809–94) US writer and physician. *The Poet at the Breakfast Table*, XII

49 I'm more and more convinced that life is a dream. What has happened to me is surely a dream.

Anthony Hopkins (1937–) Welsh actor. *The Independent*, 12 Feb 1994

50 Life is just one damned thing after another.

Elbert Hubbard (1856–1915) US writer. *A Thousand and One Epigrams*

51 Life isn't all beer and skittles.

Thomas Hughes (1822–96) British novelist. *Tom Brown's Schooldays*, Pt. I, Ch. 2

52 Live all you can; it's a mistake not to. It doesn't so much matter what you do in particular, so long as you have your life. If you haven't had that what *have* you had?

Henry James (1843–1916) US novelist. *The Ambassadors*, Bk. V, Ch. 2

53 The art of life is the art of avoiding pain.

Thomas Jefferson (1743–1826) US statesman. Letter to Maria Cosway, 12 Oct 1786

54 Pain is life – the sharper, the more evidence of life.

Charles Lamb (1775–1834) English essayist. Letter to Bernard Barton, 9 Jan 1824

55 Life is something to do when you can't get to sleep.

Fran Lebowitz (1950–) US writer. *The Observer*, 21 Jan 1979

56 Life is like a sewer. What you get out of it depends on what you put into it.

Tom Lehrer (1928–) US university teacher and songwriter. *We Will all Go together When We Go*

57 Life is what happens to you while you're busy making other plans.

John Lennon (1940–80) British rock musician. *Beautiful Boy*

58 Our ingress into the world
Was naked and bare;
Our progress through the world
Is trouble and care.

Henry Wadsworth Longfellow (1807–82) US poet. *Tales of A Wayside Inn*, 'The Student's Tale'

59 And thou wilt give thyself relief, if thou doest every act of thy life as if it were the last.

Marcus Aurelius (121–180 AD) Roman emperor. *Meditations*, Bk. II, Ch. 5

60 The living are just the dead on holiday.

Maurice Maeterlinck (1862–1949) Belgian poet and playwright. Attrib.

61 All interest in disease and death is only another expression of interest in life.

Thomas Mann (1875–1955) German novelist. *The Magic Mountain*, 6

62 Life to me is like boarding-house wallpaper. It takes a long time to get used to it, but when you finally do, you never notice that it's there. And then you hear the decorators are arriving.

Derek Marlowe (1938–) British writer. *A Dandy in Aspic*

63 Life is not living, but living in health.

Martial (c. 40 AD–c. 104 AD) Roman poet. *Epigrams*, VI

64 It is not true that life is one damn thing after another – it's one damn thing over and over.

Edna St. Vincent Millay (1892–1950) US poet. *Letters of Edna St. Vincent Millay*

65 The aim of life is to live, and to live means to be aware, joyously, drunkenly, serenely, divinely aware.

Henry Miller (1891–1980) US novelist. *The Wisdom of the Heart*, 'Creative Death'

66 I've looked at life from both sides now
From win and lose and still somehow
It's life's illusions I recall
I really don't know life at all.

Joni Mitchell (1943–) U.S. singer and songwriter. *Both Sides Now*

67 There are three ingredients in the good life: learning, earning and yearning.

Christopher Darlington Morley (1890–1957) US writer. *Parnassus on Wheels*, Ch. 10

68 Life is a foreign language: all men mispronounce it.

Christopher Darlington Morley *Thunder on the Left*, Ch. 14

69 Life itself is a mystery which defies solution.

John Mortimer (1923–) British lawyer and dramatist. *The Sunday Times*, 1 Apr 1990

70 Life is just one damned thing after another.

Frank Ward O'Malley (1875–1932) US writer. Attrib.

71 Our lives are merely strange dark interludes in the electric display of God the Father.

Eugene O'Neill (1888–1953) US dramatist. *Strange Interlude*

72 Life is for each man a solitary cell whose walls are mirrors.

Eugene O'Neill (1888–1953) US dramatist. *Lazarus Laughed*

73 Life is perhaps best regarded as a bad dream between two awakenings.

Eugene O'Neill *Marco Millions*

74 Most people get a fair amount of fun out of their lives, but on balance life is suffering and only the very young or the very foolish imagine otherwise.

George Orwell (Eric Blair; 1903–50) British novelist. *Shooting an Elephant*

75 Life Begins at Forty.

William B. Pitkin (1878–1953) US professor in journalism. Book title

76 The vanity of human life is like a river, constantly passing away, and yet constantly coming on.

Alexander Pope (1688–1744) British poet. *Thoughts on Various Subjects*

77 A Dance to the Music of Time.

Anthony Powell (1905–) British novelist. From the name of a painting by Nicolas Poussin. Book title

78 Life has got to be lived – that's all there is to it. At 70, I would say the advantage is that you take life more calmly. You know that 'this, too, shall pass!'

Eleanor Roosevelt (1884–1962) US First Lady, government official, writer, humanitarian, and lecturer. *The New York Times*, 8 Oct 1954

79 Life is not a spectacle or a feast; it is a predicament.

George Santayana (1863–1952) US philosopher. *The Perpetual Pessimist* (Sagittarius and George)

80 There is no cure for birth and death save to enjoy the interval.

George Santayana *Soliloquies in England*, 24, 'War Shrines'

81 It is only in the microscope that our life looks so big. It is an indivisible point, drawn out and magnified by the powerful lenses of Time and Space.

Arthur Schopenhauer (1788–1860) German philosopher. *Parerga and Paralipomena*, 'The Vanity of Existence'

82 And so, from hour to hour, we ripe and ripe,
And then, from hour to hour, we rot and rot;
And thereby hangs a tale.

William Shakespeare (1564–1616) English dramatist. *As You Like It*, II:7

83 O, how full of briers is this working-day world!

William Shakespeare *As You Like It*, I:3

84 ...the time of life is short;
To spend that shortness basely were too long.

William Shakespeare *Henry IV, Part 1*, V:2

85 Life is as tedious as a twice-told tale
Vexing the dull ear of a drowsy man.

William Shakespeare *King John*, III:4

86 Tomorrow, and tomorrow, and tomorrow,
Creeps in this petty pace from day to day
To the last syllable of recorded time,
And all our yesterdays have lighted fools
The way to dusty death. Out, out, brief candle!
Life's but a walking shadow, a poor player,
That struts and frets his hour upon the stage,
And then is heard no more; it is a tale
Told by an idiot, full of sound and fury,
Signifying nothing.

William Shakespeare *Macbeth*, V:5

87 I hold the world but as the world, Gratiano;
A stage where every man must play a part,
And mine a sad one.

William Shakespeare *The Merchant of Venice*, I:1

88 Lift not the painted veil which those who live
Call life.

Percy Bysshe Shelley (1792–1822) British poet. *Lift not the Painted Veil*

89 Living well and beautifully and justly are all one thing.

Socrates (469 BC–399 BC) Greek philosopher. *Crito* (Plato)

90 Life is a gamble, at terrible odds – if it was a bet, you wouldn't take it.

Tom Stoppard (1937–) Czech-born British dramatist. *Rosencrantz and Guildenstern Are Dead*, III

91 As our life is very short, so it is very miserable, and
therefore it is well it is short.

Jeremy Taylor (1613–67) English Anglican theologian. *The Rule and Exercise of Holy Dying*, Ch. 1

92 To preserve a man alive in the midst of so many chances and hostilities, is as great a miracle as to create him.

Jeremy Taylor *The Rule and Exercise of Holy Dying*

93 A life that moves to gracious ends
Thro' troops of unrecording friends,
A deedful life, a silent voice.

Alfred, Lord Tennyson (1809–92) British poet. *To –, after reading a Life and Letters*

94 Oh, isn't life a terrible thing, thank God?

Dylan Thomas (1914–53) Welsh poet. *Under Milk Wood*

95 For life is but a dream whose shapes return,
Some frequently, some seldom, some by night
And some by day.

James Thomson (1834–82) British poet. *The City of Dreadful Night*, I

96 The world is a comedy to those who think, a tragedy to those who feel.

Horace Walpole (1717–97) British writer. Letter to Sir Horace Mann, 1769

97 I spent the afternoon musing on Life. If you come to think of it, what a queer thing Life is! So unlike anything else, don't you know, if you see what I mean.

P. G. Wodehouse (1881–1975) British humorous novelist. *My Man Jeeves*, 'Rallying Round Old George'

98 When I think of all the books I have read, and of the wise words I have heard spoken, and of the anxiety I have given to parents and grandparents, and of the hopes that I have had, all life weighed in the scales of my own life seems to me preparation for something that never happens.

W. B. Yeats (1865–1939) Irish poet. *Autobiography*

99 We begin to live when we have conceived life as a tragedy.

W. B. Yeats *Autobiography*

100 Never to have lived is best, ancient writers say;
Never to have drawn the breath of life,
never to have looked into the eye of day
The second best's a gay goodnight and quickly turn away.

W. B. Yeats *Oedipus at Colonus*

LIFE AND DEATH

See also death, life

1 The first breath is the beginning of death.

Proverb

2 Dying is as natural as living.

Proverb

3 The thing to remember is that each time of life has its appropriate rewards, whereas when you're dead it's hard to find the light switch. The chief problem about death, incidentally, is the fear that there may be no afterlife – a depressing thought, particularly for those who have bothered to shave. Also, there is the fear that there is an afterlife but no one will know where it's being held. On the plus side, death is one of the few things that can be done as easily lying down.

Woody Allen (Allen Stewart Konigsberg; 1935–) US film actor and director. *Without Feathers*, 'The Early Essays'

4 In my happier days I used to remark on the aptitude of the saying, 'When in life we are in the midst of death'. I have since learnt that it's more apt to say, 'When in death we are in the midst of life'.

Anonymous Said by a survivor from Belsen. *The Oxford Book of Death* (D.J. Enright)

5 Every moment dies a man,
Every moment one and one sixteenth is born.

Charles Babbage (1792–1871) British mathematician. A parody of TENNYSON's *Vision of Sin*. Letter to Tennyson

6 It is as natural to die as to be born; and to a little infant, perhaps, the one is as painful as the other.

Francis Bacon (1561–1626) English philosopher, lawyer, and politician. *Essays*, 'Of Death'

7 Life, the permission to know death.

Djuna Barnes (1892–1982) US writer. *Nightwood*

8 I imagine, sometimes, that if a film could be made of one's life, every other frame would be death. It goes so fast we're not aware of it. Destruction and resurrection in alternate beats of being, but speed makes it seem continuous. But you see, kid, with ordinary consciousness you can't even begin to know what's happening.

Saul Bellow (1915–) Canadian-born US novelist. *The Dean's December*

9 ...Human life is mainly a process of filling in time until the arrival of death, or Santa Claus, with very little choice, if any, of what kind of business one is going to transact during the long wait.

Eric Berne *Games People Play*, Ch. 18

10 I call heaven and earth to record this day against you, that I have set before you life and death, blessing and cursing: therefore choose life, that both thou and thy seed may live.

Bible: Deuteronomy 30:19

11 But Jesus said unto him, Follow me; and let the dead bury their dead.

Bible: Matthew 8:22

12 Life itself is but the shadow of death, and souls but the shadows of the living. All things fall under this name. The sun itself is but the dark *simulacrum*, and light but the shadow of God.

Thomas Browne (1605–82) English physician and writer. *The Garden of Cyrus*

13 This world nis but a thurghfare ful of wo,
And we ben pilgrimes, passinge to and fro;
Deeth is an ende of every worldly sore.

Geoffrey Chaucer (c. 1342–1400) English poet. *The Canterbury Tales*, 'The Knight's Tale'

14 Birth, and copulation, and death.
That's all the facts when you come to brass tacks.

T. S. Eliot (1888–1965) US-born British poet and dramatist. *Sweeney Agonistes*, 'Fragment of an Agon'

15 I came like Water, and like Wind I go.

Edward Fitzgerald (1809–83) British poet. *The Rubáiyát of Omar Khayyám* (1st edn.), XXVIII

16 The memory of birth and the expectation of death always lurk within the human being, making him separate from his fellows and consequently capable of intercourse with them.

E. M. Forster (1879–1970) British writer. 'What I Believe'

17 A man is not completely born until he be dead.

Benjamin Franklin (1706–90) US scientist and statesman. *Letters to Miss Hubbard*

18 When he can keep life no longer in, he makes a fair and easie passage for it to go out.

Thomas Fuller (1608–61) English historian. *The Holy State*, Ch. 17

19 The most rational cure after all for the inordinate fear of death is to set a just value on life.

William Hazlitt (1778–1830) British essayist and journalist. *Table Talk*, 'On the Fear of Death'

20 I believe that the struggle against death, the unconditional and self-willed determination to live, is the motive power behind the lives and activities of all outstanding men.

Hermann Hesse (1877–1962) German novelist and poet. *Steppenwolf*, 'Treatise on the Steppenwolf'

21 There are only three events in a man's life; birth, life, and death; he is not conscious of being born, he dies in pain, and he forgets to live.

Jean de La Bruyère (1645–96) French satirist. *Les Caractères*

22 I strove with none; for none was worth my strife;
Nature I loved, and, next to Nature, Art;
I warmed both hands before the fire of life;
It sinks, and I am ready to depart.

Walter Savage Landor (1775–1864) British poet and writer. *I Strove with None*

23 Many men would take the death-sentence without a whimper to escape the life-sentence which fate carries in her other hand.

T. E. Lawrence (1888–1935) British soldier and writer. *The Mint*, Pt. I, Ch. 4

24 If you wish to live, you must first attend your own funeral.

Katherine Mansfield (1888–1923) New-Zealand-born British writer. *Katherine Mansfield* (Antony Alpers)

25 Life is a great surprise. I do not see why death should not be an even greater one.

Vladimir Nabokov (1899–1977) Russian-born US novelist. *Pale Fire*, 'Commentary'

26 Who was it that said the living are the dead on holiday?

Terry Nation *Dr Who*, BBC TV, 1980

27 When a man lies dying, he does not die from the disease alone. He dies from his whole life.

Charles Péguy (1873–1914) *Basic Verities*, 'The Search for Truth'

28 There is no cure for birth and death save to enjoy the interval.

George Santayana (1863–1952) US philosopher. *Soliloquies in England*, 'War Shrines'

29 Fare thee well, great heart!
Ill-weav'd ambition, how much art thou shrunk!
When that this body did contain a spirit,
A kingdom for it was too small a bound;
But now two paces of the vilest earth
Is room enough: this earth, that bears thee dead,
Bears not alive so stout a gentleman.

William Shakespeare (1564–1616) English dramatist. *Henry IV, Part 1*, V:4

30 He hath awakened from the dream of life –
'Tis we, who lost in stormy visions, keep
With phantoms an unprofitable strife,
And in mad trance, strike with our spirit's knife
Invulnerable nothings.

Percy Bysshe Shelley (1792–1822) British poet. *Adonais*, XXXIX

31 If we are aware of what indicates life, which everyone may be supposed to know, though perhaps no one can say that he truly and clearly understands what constitutes it, we at once arrive at the discrimination of death. It is the cessation of the phenomena with which we are so especially familiar – the phenomena of life.

J. G. Smith *Principles of Forensic Medicine*

32 Every moment dies a man,
Every moment one is born.

Alfred, Lord Tennyson (1809–92) British poet. For a parody, *see* BABBAGE. *The Vision of Sin*

33 Because there is no difference.

Thales (c. 624–547 BC) Greek philosopher and astronomer. His reply when asked why he chose to carry on living after saying there was no difference between life and death. *The Story of Civilization* (W. Durant), Vol. 2

34 All say, 'How hard it is that we have to die' – a strange complaint to come from the mouths of people who have had to live.

Mark Twain (Samuel L. Clemens; 1835–1910) US writer. *Pudd'nhead Wilson*

35 Science says: 'We must live,' and seeks the means of prolonging, increasing, facilitating and amplifying life, of making it tolerable and acceptable; wisdom says: 'We must die,' and seeks how to make us die well.

Miguel de Unamuno y Jugo (1864–1936) Spanish writer and philosopher. *Essays and Soliloquies*, 'Arbitrary Reflections'

LIMERICKS

A small selection

1 There's a wonderful family called Stein,
There's Gert and there's Epp and there's Ein;
Gert's poems are bunk,
Epp's statues are junk,
And no one can understand Ein.

Anonymous

2 There was a faith-healer of Deal,
Who said, 'Although pain isn't real,
If I sit on a pin
And it punctures my skin,
I dislike what I fancy I feel.'

Anonymous

3 There was an old man from Darjeeling,
Who boarded a bus bound for Ealing,
He saw on the door:
'Please don't spit on the floor,'
So he stood up and spat on the ceiling.

Anonymous

4 There was an old man of Boulogne
Who sang a most topical song.
It wasn't the words
That frightened the birds,
But the horrible double-entendre.

Anonymous

5 There was a young lady of Riga,
Who went for a ride on a tiger;
They returned from the ride
With the lady inside,
And a smile on the face of the tiger.

Anonymous

6 There was a young man of Japan
Whose limericks never would scan;
When they said it was so,
He replied, 'Yes, I know,
But I always try to get as many words into the last line as ever I possibly can.'

Anonymous

7 There was a young lady named Bright,
Whose speed was far faster than light;
She set out one day
In a relative way,
And returned home the previous night.

Arthur Henry Reginald Buller (1874–1944) British botanist. *Limerick*

8 There once was a man who said 'God
Must think it exceedingly odd
If he find that this tree
Continues to be
When there's no one about in the Quad.'

Ronald Knox (1888–1957) British Roman Catholic priest. For a reply, see below. Atrrib.

9 Dear Sir, Your astonishment's odd:
I am always about in the Quad.
And that's why the tree
Will continue to be,
Since observed by Yours faithfully, God.

Anonymous A reply to KNOX.

10 There was an Old Man with a beard,
Who said, 'It is just as I feared! –
Two Owls and a Hen,
Four Larks and a Wren,
Have all built their nests in my beard!'

Edward Lear (1812–88) British artist and writer. *Book of Nonsense*

11 A wonderful bird is the pelican,
His bill will hold more than his belican.
He can take in his beak,
Enough food for a week,
But I'm damned if I know how the helican.

Dixon Lanier Merritt (1879–1954) *The Pelican*

LINCOLN, ABRAHAM

(1809–65) US statesman and Republican president (1861–65). He achieved freedom for slaves and the prohibition of slavery. He was assassinated a few days after the surrender of the South in the Civil War.

Quotations about Lincoln

1 Mr. Lincoln is like a waiter in a large eating house where all the bells are ringing at once; he cannot serve them all at once and so some grumblers are to be expected.

John Bright (1811–89) British radical politician. Cincinnati Gazette, 1864

2 My heart burned within me with indignation and grief; we could think of nothing else. All night long we had but little sleep, waking up perpetually to the sense of a great shock and grief. Everyone is feeling the same. I never knew such a universal feeling.

Elizabeth Gaskell (1810–65) British novelist. Letter to C. E. Norton, 28 Apr 1865

3 Lincoln had faith in time, and time has justified his faith.

Benjamin Harrison (1833–92) US president. Lincoln Day Address, 1898

4 Mr Lincoln's soul seems made of leather, and incapable of any grand or noble emotion...He lowers, he never elevates you.

New York Post, 1863

Quotations by Lincoln

5 So you're the little woman who wrote the book that made this great war!

Said on meeting Harriet Beecher Stowe, the author of *Uncle Tom's Cabin* (1852), which stimulated opposition to slavery before the US Civil War. *Abraham Lincoln: The War Years* (Carl Sandburg), Vol. II, Ch. 39

6 The Lord prefers common-looking people. That is why he makes so many of them.

Our President (James Morgan), Ch. 6

7 Die when I may, I want it said of me by those who know me best, that I have always plucked a thistle and planted a flower where I thought a flower would grow.

Presidential Anecdotes (P. Boller)

8 I intend no modification of my oft-expressed personal wish that all men everywhere could be free.

Letter to Horace Greeley, 22 Aug 1862

9 If you don't want to use the army, I should like to borrow it for a while. Yours respectfully, A. Lincoln.

Letter to General George B. McClellan, whose lack of activity during the US Civil War irritated Lincoln.

10 No man is good enough to govern another man without that other's consent.

Speech, 1854

11 The ballot is stronger than the bullet.

Speech, 19 May 1856

12 Those who deny freedom to others, deserve it not for themselves.

Speech, 19 May 1856

13 It is not our frowning battlements...or the strength of our gallant and disciplined army. These are not our reliance against a resumption of tyranny in our fair land...Our defense is in the preservation of the spirit which prizes liberty as the heritage of all men, in all lands, everywhere.

Speech, 11 Sept 1858

14 What is conservatism? Is it not adherence to the old and tried, against the new and untried?

Speech, 27 Feb 1860

15 This country, with its institutions, belongs to the people who inhabit it. Whenever they shall grow weary of the existing government, they can exercise their constitutional right of amending it, or their revolutionary right to dismember or overthrow it.

First Inaugural Address, 4 Mar 1861

16 An old Dutch farmer, who remarked to a companion once that it was not best to swap horses in mid-stream.

Speech, 9 June 1864

17 Fourscore and seven years ago our fathers brought forth upon this continent a new nation, conceived in liberty, and dedicated to the proposition that all men are created equal. In a larger sense we cannot dedicate, we cannot consecrate, we cannot hallow this ground. The brave men, living and dead, who struggled here, have consecrated it far above our power to add or detract. The world will little note, nor long remember, what we say here, but it can never forget what they did here. It is for us, the living, rather to be dedicated here to the unfinished work which they who fought here have thus far so nobly advanced. It is rather for us to be here dedicated to the great task remaining before us...that we here highly resolve that the dead shall not have died in vain, that this nation, under God, shall have a new birth of freedom; and that government of the people, by the people, and for the people, shall not perish from the earth.

Report of Lincoln's address at the dedication (19 Nov 1863) of the national cemetery on the site of the Battle of Gettysburg.

18 You can fool some of the people all the time and all the people some of the time; but you can't fool all the people all the time.

Attrib.

19 People who like this sort of thing will find this is the sort of thing they like.

A comment on a book. Attrib.

20 I can't spare this man; he fights.

Resisting demands for the dismissal of Ulysses Grant. Attrib.

21 Well, he looks like a man.

On catching sight of Walt Whitman for the first time. Attrib.

22 I don't know who my grandfather was; I am much more concerned to know what his grandson will be.

Taking part in a discussion on ancestry. Attrib.

LITERACY

See also reading, writing

1 The ratio of literacy to illiteracy is constant, but nowadays the illiterates can read and write.

Alberto Moravia (Alberto Pincherle; 1907–90) Italian novelist. *The Observer*, 14 Oct 1979

2 To be a well-favoured man is the gift of fortune; but to write and read comes by nature.

William Shakespeare (1564–1616) English dramatist. *Much Ado About Nothing*, III:3

LITERATURE

See also arts, books, criticism, fiction, novels, plays, poetry, poetry and prose, poets, prose, reading, theatre, writers, writing

1 Literature is the art of writing something that will be read twice; journalism what will be grasped at once.

Cyril Connolly (1903–74) British journalist. *Enemies of Promise*, Ch. 3

2 A work that aspires, however humbly, to the condition of art should carry its justification in every line.

Joseph Conrad (Teodor Josef Konrad Korzeniowski; 1857–1924) Polish-born British novelist. *The Nigger of the Narcissus*, Preface

3 The reading of all good books is like a conversation with the finest men of past centuries.

René Descartes (1596–1650) French philosopher. *Le Discours de la méthode*

4 Only two classes of books are of universal appeal. The very best and the very worst.

Ford Maddox Ford (1873–1939) British novelist, critic, and poet. *Joseph Conrad*

5 I'm able to bolt down a cheap thriller but I couldn't read Troilus and Cressida or Coriolanus with any great pleasure.

John Gielgud (1904–) British actor. *The Observer*, 'Sayings of the Week', 17 Apr 1994

6 God forbid people should read our books to find the juicy passages.

Graham Greene (1904–91) British novelist. *The Observer*, 'Sayings of the Week', 14 Oct 1979

7 He knew everything about literature except how to enjoy it.

Joseph Heller (1923–) US novelist. *Catch-22*, Ch. 8

8 The proper study of mankind is books.

Aldous Huxley (1894–1964) British novelist. *Chrome Yellow*

9 That was the chief difference between literature and life. In books, the proportion of exceptional to commonplace people is high; in reality, very low.

Aldous Huxley *Eyeless in Gaza*

10 Literature flourishes best when it is half a trade and half an art.

Dean Inge (1860–1954) British churchman. *The Victorian Age*

11 It takes a great deal of history to produce a little literature.

Henry James (1843–1916) US novelist. *Life of Nathaniel Hawthorne*, Ch. 1

12 Was there ever yet anything written by mere man that was wished longer by its readers, excepting *Don Quixote*, *Robinson Crusoe*, and the *Pilgrim's Progress*?

Samuel Johnson (1709–84) British lexicographer. *Johnsonian Miscellanies* (ed. G. B. Hill), Vol. I

13 *Sturm und Drang.*
Storm and stress.

Friedrich Maximilian von Klinger (1752–1831) German dramatist and novelist. Used to designate a late 18th-century literary movement in Germany. Play title

14 Compared with this revolution the Renaissance is a mere ripple on the surface of literature.

C. S. Lewis (1898–1963) British academic and writer. Referring to the appearance of the concept of courtly love in the 12th century. *The Allegory of Love*

15 Our American professors like their literature clear and cold and pure and very dead.

Sinclair Lewis (1885–1951) US novelist. Speech, on receiving the Nobel Prize, 1930

16 Literature is mostly about having sex and not much about having children; life is the other way round.

David Lodge (1935–) British author. *The British Museum is Falling Down*, Ch. 4

17 Suddenly I realized this literary stuff doesn't just come out of a hat. It has a mechanism which you can take apart like a watch.

David Lodge *The Times Educational Supplement*, 18 May 1990

18 You understand *Epipsychidion* best when you are in love; *Don Juan* when anger is subsiding into indifference. Why not Strindberg when you have a temperature?

Desmond MacCarthy (1877–1952) British writer and theatre critic. *Theatre*, 'Miss Julie and the Pariah'

19 The idea of going to a writers' congress in Moscow is rather like attending a human rights conference in Nazi Germany.

David Markstein Member of the Writers' Guild of Great Britain.

20 Great works of literature, perhaps the greatest – the Oresteia, Hamlet, even the Bible – have been stories of mystery and crime.

John Mortimer (1923–) British lawyer and dramatist. *The Sunday Times*, 1 Apr 1990

21 Literature and butterflies are the two sweetest passions known to man.

Vladimir Nabokov (1899–1977) Russian-born US novelist. *Radio Times*, Oct 1962

22 Literature is news that STAYS news.

Ezra Pound (1885–1972) US poet. *ABC of Reading*, Ch. 2

23 Great Literature is simply language charged with meaning to the utmost possible degree.

Ezra Pound *How to Read*

24 His most rational response to my attempts at drawing him out about literature and art was 'I adore italics, don't you?'

Siegfried Sassoon (1886–1967) British poet. Referring to Ronald Fairbanks. *Siegfried's Journey*

25 Romanticism is the art of presenting people with the literary works which are capable of affording them the greatest possible pleasure, in the present state of their customs and beliefs. Classicism, on the other hand, presents them with the literature that gave the greatest possible pleasure to their great-grandfathers.

Stendhal (Henri Beyle; 1783–1842) French novelist. *Racine et Shakespeare*, Ch. 3

26 Something that everybody wants to have read and nobody wants to read.

Mark Twain (Samuel Langhorne Clemens; 1835–1910) US writer. Definition of a classic of literature. Speech at Nineteenth Century Club, New York, 20 Nov 1900

27 '*Language*, man!' roared Parsons; 'why, it's LITERATURE!'

H. G. Wells (1866–1946) British writer. *The History of Mr Polly*, Pt. I, Ch. 3

28 Literature is the orchestration of platitudes.

Thornton Wilder (1897–1975) US novelist and dramatist. *Time* magazine

LLOYD GEORGE, DAVID

(David Lloyd George, Earl of Dwyfor; 1863–1945) British Liberal statesman. As prime minister (1916–22), he replaced Asquith as leader of a coalition government during World War I and for four years after it.

Quotations about Lloyd George

1 He couldn't see a belt without hitting below it.

Margot Asquith (1865–1945) The second wife of Herbert Asquith. *Autobiography*

2 He spent his whole life in plastering together the true and the false and therefrom extracting the plausible.

Stanley Baldwin (1867–1947) British statesman. *The Fine Art of Political Wit* (Leon Harris)

3 He did not care in which direction the car was travelling, so long as he remained in the driver's seat.

Lord Beaverbrook (1879–1964) Canadian-born British newspaper proprietor. *New Statesman*, 14 June 1963

4 My one ardent desire is that after the war he

should be publicly castrated in front of Nurse Cavell's statue.

Lytton Strachey (1880–1932) British writer. *The Times*, 15 Jan 1972

Quotations by Lloyd George

5 He saw foreign policy through the wrong end of a municipal drainpipe.

Referring to the Conservative statesman Neville Chamberlain. *The Fine Art of Political Wit* (Harris), Ch. 6

6 Poor Bonar can't bear being called a liar. Now I don't mind.

Referring to Bonar Law, prime minister 1922–23. *Stanley Baldwin* (G. M. Young)

7 You cannot feed the hungry on statistics.

Advocating Tariff Reform. Speech, 1904

8 Mr Balfour's Poodle.

Referring to the House of Lords and its in-built Conservative majority; said in reply to a claim that it was 'the watchdog of the nation'. Remark, House of Commons, 26 June 1907

9 There are no credentials. They do not even need a medical certificate. They need not be sound either in body or mind. They only require a certificate of birth – just to prove that they are first of the litter. You would not choose a spaniel on these principles.

Referring to the law of primogeniture. Budget Speech, 1909

10 A fully equipped Duke costs as much to keep up as two Dreadnoughts, and Dukes are just as great a terror, and they last longer.

Speech, Newcastle, 9 Oct 1909

11 What is our task? To make Britain a fit country for heroes to live in.

Speech, Wolverhampton, 24 Nov 1918

12 Every man has a House of Lords in his own head. Fears, prejudices, misconceptions – those are the peers, and they are hereditary.

Speech, Cambridge, 1927

13 If we are going in without the help of Russia we are walking into a trap.

Speech, House of Commons, 3 Apr 1939

14 The Right Hon. gentleman has sat so long on the fence that the iron has entered his soul.

Referring to Sir John Simon. Attrib.

15 When they circumcised Herbert Samuel they threw away the wrong bit.

Referring to the British Liberal politician Herbert Samuel (1870–1963). Attrib. in *The Listener*, 7 Sept 1978

16 Like a cushion, he always bore the impress of the last man who sat on him.

Referring to the British Conservative statesman Lord Derby. Attrib. in *The Listener*, 7 Sept 1978. This remark is also credited to Earl Haig

17 Well, I find that a change of nuisances is as good as a vacation.

On being asked how he maintained his cheerfulness when beset by numerous political obstacles. Attrib.

18 This war, like the next war, is a war to end war.

Referring to the popular opinion that World War I would be the last major war.

19 The world is becoming like a lunatic asylum run by lunatics.

The Observer, 8 Jan 1933

20 A politician is a person with whose politics you did not agree. When you did agree with him he was a statesman.

Speech, Central Hall, Westminster, 2 July 1935

LODGE, DAVID JOHN

(1935–) British author and critic whose novels include *The British Museum is Falling Down* (1965), *Changing Places* (1975), *Small World* (1984), *Nice Work* (1988), and *Paradise News* (1991).

1 Literature is mostly about having sex and not much about having children; life is the other way round.

The British Museum is Falling Down, Ch. 4

2 Rummidge...had lately suffered the mortifying fate of most English universities of its type (civic redbrick): having competed strenuously for fifty years with two universities chiefly valued for being old, it was, at the moment of drawing level, rudely overtaken in popularity and prestige by a batch of universities chiefly valued for being new.

Changing Places, Ch. 1

3 Four times, under our educational rules, the human pack is shuffled and cut – at eleven-plus, sixteen-plus, eighteen-plus and twenty-plus – and happy is he who comes top of the deck on each occasion, but especially the last. This is called Finals, the very name of which implies that nothing of importance can happen after it. The British postgraduate student is a lonely forlorn soul...for whom nothing has been real since the Big Push.

Changing Places, Ch. 1

4 The British, he thought, must be gluttons for satire: even the weather forecast seemed to be some kind of spoof, predicting every possible combination of weather for the next twenty-four hours without actually committing itself to anything specific.

Changing Places, Ch. 2

5 Walt Whitman who laid end to end words never seen in each other's company before outside of a dictionary.

Changing Places, Ch. 5

6 It was difficult to decide whether the system that produced the kettle was a miracle of human ingenuity and co-operation or a colossal waste of resources, human and natural. Would we all be better off boiling our water in a pot hung over an open fire? Or was it the facility to do things at the touch of a button that freed men, and more particularly women, from servile labour and made it possible for them to become literary critics?

Nice Work, V

LOGIC

See also philosophy

1 LOGIC, n. The art of thinking and reasoning in

strict accordance with the limitations and incapacities of the human understanding.

Ambrose Bierce (1842–?1914) US writer and journalist. *The Devil's Dictionary*

2 'Contrariwise,' continued Tweedledee, 'if it was so, it might be; and if it were so, it would be: but as it isn't, it ain't. That's logic.'

Lewis Carroll (Charles Lutwidge Dodgson; 1832–98) British writer. *Through the Looking-Glass*, Ch. 4.

3 A Clerk ther was of Oxenford also,
That un-to logik hadde longe y-go.

Geoffrey Chaucer (c. 1342–1400) English poet. *The Canterbury Tales*, Prologue

4 You can only find truth with logic if you have already found truth without it.

G. K. Chesterton (1874–1936) British writer. *The Man who was Orthodox*

5 Orr was crazy and could be grounded. All he had to do was ask; and as soon as he did, he would no longer be crazy and would have to fly more missions...Yossarian was moved very deeply by the absolute simplicity of this clause of Catch-22 and let out a respectful whistle.

Joseph Heller (1923–) US novelist. *Catch-22*

6 Logical consequences are the scarecrows of fools and the beacons of wise men.

T. H. Huxley (1825–95) British biologist. *Science and Culture*, 'On the Hypothesis that Animals are Automata'

7 The world is everything that is the case.

Ludwig Wittgenstein (1889–1951) Austrian philosopher. *Tractatus Logico-Philosophicus*, Ch. 1

8 Logic must take care of itself.

Ludwig Wittgenstein *Tractatus Logico-Philosophicus*, Ch. 5

LONDON

See also England

1 The streets of London are paved with gold.

Proverb

2 Oranges and lemons,
Say the bells of St Clement's.
You owe me five farthings,
Say the bells of St Martin's.
When will you pay me?
Say the bells of Old Bailey.
When I grow rich,
Say the bells of Shoreditch.
When will that be?
Say the bells of Stepney.
I'm sure I don't know,
Says the great bell at Bow.
Here comes a candle to light you to bed,
Here comes a chopper to chop off your head.

Tommy Thumb's Pretty Song Book

3 Nobody is healthy in London, nobody can be.

Jane Austen (1775–1817) British novelist. *Emma*, Ch. 12

4 London is a splendid place to live in for those who can get out of it.

Lord Balfour of Burleigh (1884–1967) British financier. Attrib.

5 What a place to plunder!

Gebhard Blücher (1742–1819) Prussian general. Referring to London. Attrib.

6 Where's Troy, and where's the Maypole in the Strand?
Pease, cabbages and turnips once grew where
Now stands New Bond Street and a newer Square;
Such piles of buildings now rise up and down,
London itself seems going out of Town.
Our Fathers crossed from Fulham in a Wherry,
Their sons enjoy a Bridge at Putney Ferry.

James Bramston (c. 1694–1744) British poet. *The Whig Supremacy* (Basil Williams), Ch. 15

7 Let's all go down the Strand.

Harry Castling (19th century) British songwriter. Song title

8 But what is to be the fate of the great wen of all?

William Cobbett (1763–1835) British journalist and writer. A wen is a sebaceous cyst. *Rural Rides*

9 I don't know what London's coming to – the higher the buildings the lower the morals.

Noël Coward (1899–1973) British dramatist. *Law and Order*

10 London, that great cesspool into which all the loungers of the Empire are irresistibly drained.

Arthur Conan Doyle (1856–1930) British writer. *A Study in Scarlet*

11 Strong be thy wallis that about thee standis;
Wise be the people that within thee dwellis;
Fresh be thy ryver with his lusty strandis;
Blithe by thy chirches, wele swonyng be thy bellis;
Riche by they merchauntis in substaunce that excellis;
Fair be their wives, right lovesom, white and small;
Clere by thy virgyns, lusty under kellis:
London, thou art the flour of Cities all.

William Dunbar (1460–1530) *The Earlier Tudors* (J. D. Mackie)

12 This fatal night about ten, began that deplorable fire near Fish Street in London...all the sky were of a fiery aspect, like the top of a burning Oven, and the light seen above 40 miles round about for many nights.

John Evelyn (1620–1706) English diarist. The Fire of London (2–5 Sept 1666) began in a bakehouse in Pudding Lane and spread to two thirds of the city. Diary, 23 Sept 1666

13 It is not the walls that make the city, but the people who live within them. The walls of London may be battered, but the spirit of the Londoner stands resolute and undismayed.

George VI (1895–1952) King of the United Kingdom. Radio broadcast to the Empire, 23 Sept 1940

14 Crowds without company, and dissipation without pleasure.

Edward Gibbon (1737–94) British historian. *Autobiography*

15 The tourists who come to our island take in the Monarchy along with feeding the pigeons in Trafalgar Square.

William Hamilton (1917–) Scottish MP. *My Queen and I*, Ch. 9

16 ...the illustrious place, built by the skill of the ancient Romans, called throughout the world the great city of London.

Bishop Helmstan of Winchester *Cartularium Saxonicum*

17 I think the full tide of human existence is at Charing-Cross.

Samuel Johnson (1709–84) British lexicographer. *Life of Johnson* (J. Boswell), Vol. II

18 When a man is tired of London, he is tired of life; for there is in London all that life can afford.

Samuel Johnson *Life of Johnson* (J. Boswell), Vol. III

19 Here out of the window it was a most pleasant sight to see the City from one end to the other with a glory about it, so high was the light of the bonfires, and so thick round the City, and the bells rang everywhere.

Samuel Pepys (1633–1703) English diarist. Describing the celebrations in London at the end of the Commonwealth. Diary, 21 Feb 1660

20 I would sell London, if I could find a suitable purchaser.

Richard I (1157–1199) King of England. Comment while raising money for the third Crusade. *Historia Rerum Anglicarum* (William of Newburgh), Bk. IV, Ch. 5

21 London, that great sea, whose ebb and flow
At once is deaf and loud, and on the shore
Vomits its wrecks, and still howls on for more.

Percy Bysshe Shelley (1792–1822) British poet. *Letter to Maria Gisborne*, I

22 Hell is a city much like London –
A populous and smoky city.

Percy Bysshe Shelley *Peter Bell the Third*

23 Crossing Piccadilly Circus.

Joseph Thomson (1858–95) Scottish explorer. His reply when asked by J. M. Barrie what was the most hazardous part of his expedition to Africa. *J. M. Barrie* (D. Dunbar)

24 Earth has not anything to show more fair:
Dull would he be of soul who could pass by
A sight so touching in its majesty:
The City now doth, like a garment, wear
The beauty of the morning; silent, bare,
Ships, towers, domes, theatres, and temples lie
Open unto the fields, and to the sky;
All bright and glittering in the smokeless air.

William Wordsworth (1770–1850) British poet. *Sonnets*, 'Composed upon Westminster Bridge'

LONELINESS

See also solitude

1 Oh! why does the wind blow upon me so wild? –
It is because I'm nobody's child?

Phila Henrietta Case (fl. 1864) British poet. *Nobody's Child*

2 But who can count the beatings of the lonely heart?

Susan Edmonstone Ferrier (1782–1854) Scottish novelist. *The Inheritance*, Ch. 1.

3 A fav'rite has no friend.

Thomas Gray (1716–71) British poet. *Ode on the Death of a Favourite Cat*

4 Pray that your loneliness may spur you into finding something to live for, great enough to die for.

Dag Hammarskjöld (1905–61) Swedish diplomat. *Diaries*, 1951

5 So lonely am I
My body is a floating weed
Severed at the roots
Were there water to entice me,
I would follow it, I think.

Ono no Komachi (834–880) Japanese poet. *Kokinshu, Anthology of Japanese Literature* (ed. Donald Keene)

6 Waits at the window, wearing the face that she keeps in a jar by the door
Who is it for? All the lonely people, where do they all come from?
All the lonely people, where do they all belong?

John Lennon (1940–80) British rock musician. *Eleanor Rigby* (with Paul McCartney)

7 None But the Lonely Heart.

Richard Llewellyn British writer. Adapted from the English title of Tchaikovsky's song 'None But the Weary Heart' (original words by Goethe). Book title

8 My heart is a lonely hunter that hunts on a lonely hill.

Fiona Macleod (William Sharp; 1856–1905) Scottish poet and writer. *The Lonely Hunter*

9 I grow lean
in loneliness,
like a water lily
gnawed by a beetle.

Kaccipettu Nannakaiyar (3rd century) Indian poet. *Interior Landscape: Love Poems from a Tamil Anthology* (ed. A. K. Tamanaujan)

10 At the moment of childbirth, every woman has the same aura of isolation, as though she were abandoned, alone.

Boris Pasternak (1890–1950) Russian writer. *Doctor Zhivago*, Ch. 9, Sect. 3

11 To be alone is the fate of all great minds – a fate deplored at times, but still always chosen as the less grievous of two evils.

Arthur Schopenhauer (1788–1860) German philosopher. *Aphorismen zur Lebensweisheit*

12 Don't think you can frighten me by telling me I am alone. France is alone; and God is alone; and what is my loneliness before the loneliness of my country and my God.

George Bernard Shaw (1856–1950) Irish dramatist and critic. *St. Joan*

13 When my bed is empty,
Makes me feel awful mean and blue.
My springs are getting rusty,
Living single like I do.

Bessie Smith (1894–1937) US blues singer. *Empty Bed Blues*

14 Loneliness and the feeling of being unwanted is the most terrible poverty.

Mother Teresa (Agnes Gonxha Bojaxhui; 1910–) Yugoslavian-born Indian missionary. *Time*, 'Saints Among Us', 29 Dec 1975

15 The hunchback in the park
A solitary mister
Propped between trees and water.

Dylan Thomas (1914–53) Welsh poet. *The Hunchback in the Park*

16 She dwelt among the untrodden ways
Beside the springs of Dove,
A maid whom there were none to praise
And very few to love...

William Wordsworth (1770–1850) British poet. *She Dwelt Among the Untrodden Ways*

17 The wind blows out of the gates of the day,
The wind blows over the lonely of heart,
And the lonely of heart is withered away.

W. B. Yeats (1865–1939) Irish poet. *The Land of Heart's Desire*

LONGEVITY

See also age, life, old age

1 He that would live for aye, must eat sage in May.

Latin proverb

2 Get up at five, have lunch at nine,
Supper at five, retire at nine.
And you will live to ninety-nine.

Anonymous *Works*, Bk. IV, Ch. 64 (François Rabelais)

3 Ageing seems to be the only available way to live a long time.

Daniel-François-Esprit Auber (1782–1871) French composer. *Dictionnaire Encyclopédique* (E. Guérard)

4 LONGEVITY, n. Uncommon extension of the fear of death.

Ambrose Bierce (1842–c. 1914) US writer and journalist. *The Devil's Dictionary*

5 People always wonder how I have achieved such a ripe age, and I can only say I never felt the urge to partake of the grape, the grain, or the weed, but I do eat everything.

Mrs Mary Borah Said at the age of 100. *Bartlett's Unfamiliar Quotations* (Leonard Louis Levinson)

6 Despair of all recovery spoils longevity,
And makes men's miseries of alarming brevity.

Lord Byron (1788–1824) British poet. *Don Juan*, II

7 Longevity is the revenge of talent upon genius.

Cyril Connolly (1903–74) British journalist. *The Sunday Times*, 19 June 1966

8 There is no short-cut to longevity. To win it is the work of a lifetime, and the promotion of it is a branch of preventive medicine.

Sir James Crichton-Browne (1840–1938) *The Prevention of Senility*

9 Have a chronic disease and take care of it.

Oliver Wendell Holmes (1809–94) US writer and physician. His formula for longevity.

10 Life protracted is protracted woe.

Samuel Johnson (1709–84) English lexicographer and writer. *The Vanity of Human Wishes*

11 Get your room full of good air, then shut up the windows and keep it. It will keep for years. Anyway, don't keep using your lungs all the time. Let them rest.

Stephen Leacock (1869–1944) English-born Canadian economist and humorist. *Literary Lapses*, 'How to Live to be 200'

12 The brain is the organ of longevity.

George Alban Sacher (1917–) *Perspectives in Experimental Gerontology*

13 Do not try to live forever. You will not succeed.

George Bernard Shaw (1856–1950) Irish dramatist and critic. *The Doctor's Dilemma*, 'Preface on Doctors'

14 I smoke almost constantly, sometimes in the middle of the night. And I drink anything I can get my hands on.

Joe Smart On his 100th birthday. *Bartlett's Unfamiliar Quotations* (Leonard Louis Levinson)

15 If you live long enough, the venerability factor creeps in; you get accused of things you never did and praised for virtues you never had.

I. F. Stone (1907–89) US writer and publisher. *Peter's Quotations* (Laurence J. Peter)

16 They live ill who expect to live always.

Publilius Syrus (1st century BC) Roman dramatist. *Moral Sayings*, 457

17 Keep breathing.

Sophie Tucker (1884–1966) Russian-born US singer and vaudeville star. Her reply, at the age of 80, when asked the secret of her longevity. Attrib.

LONGFELLOW, HENRY WADSWORTH

(1807–82) US poet. A professor of modern languages, he travelled widely in Europe. His narrative poems, including *Evangeline* (1847) and *The Song of Hiawatha* (1855), achieved great popularity.

Quotations about Longfellow

1 Longfellow is to poetry what the barrel-organ is to music.

Van Wyck Brooks *The Flowering of New England*

2 The gentleman was a sweet, beautiful soul, but I have entirely forgotten his name.

Ralph Waldo Emerson (1803–82) US poet and essayist. Attending Longfellow's funeral. Attrib.

Quotations by Longfellow

3 I shot an arrow into the air,
It fell to earth, I knew not where.

The Arrow and the Song

4 I stood on the bridge at midnight,
As the clocks were striking the hour.

The Bridge

5 If you would hit the mark, you must aim a little above it;
Every arrow that flies feels the attraction of earth.

Elegiac Verse

6 Sorrow and silence are strong, and patient endurance is godlike.

Evangeline

7 The shades of night were falling fast,
As through an Alpine village passed
A youth, who bore, 'mid snow and ice,
A banner with the strange device,
Excelsior!

Opening of a poem best known as a Victorian drawing-room ballad, and the butt of many music hall jokes. Excelsior means 'higher' (Latin). *Excelsior*

8 Know how sublime a thing it is
To suffer and be strong.

The Light of Stars

9 You would attain to the divine perfection,
And yet not turn your back upon the world.

Michael Angelo

10 Art is long, and Time is fleeting,
And our hearts, though stout and brave,
Still, like muffled drums, are beating
Funeral marches to the grave.

See also HIPPOCRATES. *A Psalm of Life*

11 There is a Reaper whose name is Death,
And, with his sickle keen,
He reaps the bearded grain at a breath,
And the flowers that grow between.

The Reaper and the Flowers

12 'Wouldst thou' – so the helmsman answered –
'Learn the secret of the sea?
Only those who brave its dangers
Comprehend its mystery!'

The Secret of the Sea

13 By the shore of Gitche Gumee,
By the shining Big-Sea-Water.

The Song of Hiawatha, III

14 Onaway! Awake, beloved!

Opening of the song sung by Chibiabos at Hiawatha's wedding feast; best known in the setting by Coleridge-Taylor. *The Song of Hiawatha*, XI, 'Hiawatha's Wedding-feast'

15 Our ingress into the world
Was naked and bare;
Our progress through the world
Is trouble and care.

Tales of A Wayside Inn, 'The Student's Tale'

16 Ships that pass in the night, and speak each other in passing;
Only a signal shown and a distant voice in the darkness;
So on the ocean of life we pass and speak one another,
Only a look and a voice; then darkness again and a silence.

Tales of a Wayside Inn, 'The Theologian's Tale. Elizabeth'

17 Under a spreading chestnut tree
The village smithy stands;
The smith, a mighty man is he,
With large and sinewy hands;
And the muscles of his brawny arms
Are strong as iron bands.

The Village Blacksmith

18 Looks the whole world in the face,
For he owes not any man.

The Village Blacksmith

19 It was the schooner Hesperus,
That sailed the wintry sea;
And the skipper had taken his little daughter,
To bear him company.

The Wreck of the Hesperus

LOSS

See also defeat, mourning

1 'Tis better to have loved and lost than never to have lost at all.

Samuel Butler (1835–1902) British writer. *The Way of All Flesh*, Ch. 77

2 What's lost upon the roundabouts we pulls up on the swings!

Patrick Reginald Chalmers (1872–1942) British banker and novelist. *Green Days and Blue Days: Roundabouts and Swings*

3 And much more am I sorrier for my good knights' loss than for the loss of my fair queen; for queens I might have enough, but such a fellowship of good knights shall never be together in no company.

Thomas Malory (1400–71) English writer. *Morte d'Arthur*, Bk. XX, Ch. 9

4 There is a ghost
That eats handkerchiefs;
It keeps you company
On all your travels.

Christian Morgenstern (1871–1914) German poet. *Der Gingganz*, 'Gespenst'

5 Where have all the flowers gone?
Young girls picked them every one.

Pete Seeger (1919–) US folksinger and songwriter. *Where Have All the Flowers Gone?*

6 Hast thou no care of me? shall I abide
In this dull world, which in thy absence is
No better than a sty? O! see my women,
The crown o' the earth doth melt. My lord!

William Shakespeare (1564–1616) English dramatist. *Antony and Cleopatra*, IV:13

7 My daughter! O my ducats! O my daughter!
Fled with a Christian! O my Christian ducats!
Justice! the law! my ducats, and my daughter!

William Shakespeare *The Merchant of Venice*, II:8

8 I've lost the only playboy of the western world.

John Millington Synge (1871–1909) Anglo-Irish dramatist. The closing words. *The Playboy of the Western World*, III

9 I've lost one of my children this week.

Joseph Turner (1775–1851) British painter. His customary remark following the sale of one of his paintings. *Sketches of Great Painters* (E. Chubb)

10 To lose one parent, Mr Worthing, may be regarded as a misfortune; to lose both looks like carelessness.

Oscar Wilde (1854–1900) Irish-born British dramatist. *The Importance of Being Earnest*, I

LOUIS XIV

(1638–1715) French king. He believed in the divine right of kings, held a lavish court at Versailles, and was a generous patron of the arts.

1 How could God do this to me after all I have done for him?

On receiving news of the French army's defeat at the Battle of Blenheim. *Saint-Simon at Versailles* (L. Norton)

2 Has God then forgotten what I have done for him?

Reportedly said after Marlborough's pyrrhic victory over the French at the Battle of Malplaquet, 11 Sept 1709.

3 First feelings are always the most natural.

First impressions at the Battle of Malplaquet, 11 Sept 1709
Recorded by Mme de Sévigné

4 *L'État c'est moi.*
I am the State.

Attrib.

5 The Pyrenees have ceased to exist.

On the accession of his grandson to the Spanish throne (1700); attributed by Voltaire.

6 Ah, if I were not king, I should lose my temper.

Attrib.

7 Why are you weeping? Did you imagine that I was immortal?

Noticing as he lay on his deathbed that his attendants were crying. *Louis XIV* (V. Cronin)

LOVE

See also admiration, love and death, love and friendship, love and hate, love and marriage, lust, passion, sex

1 All is fair in love and war.

Proverb

2 All the world loves a lover.

Proverb

3 Love laughs at locksmiths.

Proverb

4 Love makes the world go round.

Proverb

5 Love me, love my dog.

Proverb

6 Love will find a way.

Proverb

7 Lucky at cards, unlucky in love.

Proverb

8 No love like the first love.

Proverb

9 Salt water and absence wash away love.

Proverb

10 The way to a man's heart is through his stomach.

Proverb

11 True love never grows old.

Proverb

12 When poverty comes in at the door, love flies out of the window.

Proverb

13 In Scarlet town, where I was born,
There was a fair maid dwellin',
Made every youth cry *Well-a-way!*
Her name was Barbara Allen.

All in the merry month of May,
When green buds they were swellin',
Young Jemmy Grove on his death-bed lay,
For love of Barbara Allen.

So slowly, slowly rase she up,
And slowly she came nigh him,
And when she drew the curtain by –
'Young man, I think you're dyin'!'.

Anonymous *Barbara Allen's Cruelty*

14 Greensleeves was all my joy,
Greensleeves was my delight,
Greensleeves was my heart of gold,
And who but Lady Greensleeves.

Anonymous *Greensleeves*

15 There were twa sisters sat in a bour;
Binnorie, O Binnorie!
There came a knight to be their wooer,
By the bonnie milldams o' Binnorie.

Anonymous *Binnorie*

16 Oh, love is real enough, you will find it some day, but it has one arch-enemy – and that is life.

Jean Anouilh (1910–87) French dramatist. *Ardèle*

17 Love is, above all, the gift of oneself.

Jean Anouilh *Ardèle*

18 Tell me about yourself – your struggles, your dreams, your telephone number.

Peter Arno (1904–68) US cartoonist. Caption to a cartoon of a man talking to a woman

19 *Falling in love*, we said; *I fell for him*. We were falling women. We believed in it, this downward motion: so lovely, like flying, and yet at the same time so dire, so extreme, so unlikely.

Margaret Atwood (1939–) Canadian novelist. *The Handmaid's Tale*

20 When it comes, will it come without warning
Just as I'm picking my nose?
Will it knock on my door in the morning,
Or tread in the bus on my toes?
Will it come like a change in the weather?
Will its greeting be courteous or rough?
Will it alter my life altogether?
O tell me the truth about love.

W. H. Auden (1907–73) British poet. *Twelve Songs*, XII

21 We must love one another or die.

W. H. Auden *September 1, 1939*

22 Nuptial love maketh mankind; friendly love perfecteth it; but wanton love corrupteth and embaseth it.

Francis Bacon (1561–1626) English philosopher. *Essays*, 'Of Love'

23 Love is just a system for getting someone to call you darling after sex.

Julian Barnes (1946–) British novelist. *Talking It Over*, Ch. 16

24 Those have most power to hurt us that we love.

Francis Beaumont (1584–1616) English dramatist. *The Maid's Tragedy*, V:6

25 Women who love the same man have a kind of bitter freemasonry.

Max Beerbohm (1872–1956) British writer. *Zuleika Dobson*, Ch. 4

26 Love ceases to be a pleasure, when it ceases to be a secret.

Aphra Behn (1640–89) English novelist and dramatist. *The Lover's Watch*, 'Four o'clock'

27 And the king loved Esther above all the women, and she obtained grace and favour in his sight more than all the virgins; so that he set the royal crown upon her head, and made her queen instead of Vashti.

Bible: Esther 2:17

28 Beloved, let us love one another: for love is of

God; and every one that loveth is born of God, and knoweth God.
He that loveth not knoweth not God; for God is love.

Bible: I John 4:7–8

29 There is no fear in love; but perfect love casteth out fear: because fear hath torment. He that feareth is not made perfect in love.

Bible: I John 4:18

30 If a man say, I love God, and hateth his brother, he is a liar: for he that loveth not his brother whom he hath seen, how can he love God whom he hath not seen?

Bible: I John 4:20

31 Greater love hath no man than this, that a man lay down his life for his friends.

Bible: John 15:13

32 Jesus said unto him, Thou shalt love the Lord thy God with all thy heart, and with all thy soul, and with all thy mind.
This is the first and great commandment.
And the second is like unto it, Thou shalt love thy neighbour as thyself.
On these two commandments hang all the law and the prophets.

Bible: Matthew 22:37–40

33 He brought me to the banqueting house, and his banner over me was love.
Stay me with flagons, comfort me with apples: for I am sick of love.
His left hand is under my head, and his right hand doth embrace me.

Bible: Song of Solomon 2:4–6

34 The voice of my beloved! behold, he cometh leaping upon the mountains, skipping upon the hills.

Bible: Song of Solomon 2:8

35 My beloved is mine, and I am his: he feedeth among the lilies.
Until the day break, and the shadows flee away, turn, my beloved, and be thou like a roe or a young hart upon the mountains of Bether.

Bible: Song of Solomon 2:16–17

36 Love seeketh not itself to please,
Nor for itself hath any care,
But for another gives its ease,
And builds a Heaven in Hell's despair.

William Blake (1757–1827) British poet. *Songs of Experience*, 'The Clod and the Pebble'

37 Love seeketh only Self to please,
To bind another to its delight,
Joys in another's loss of ease,
And builds a Hell in Heaven's despite.

William Blake *Songs of Experience*, 'The Clod and the Pebble'

38 Although love dwells in gorgeous palaces, and sumptuous apartments, more willingly than in miserable and desolate cottages, it cannot be denied but that he sometimes causes his power to be felt in the gloomy recesses of forests, among the most bleak and rugged mountains, and in the dreary caves of a desert...

Giovanni Boccaccio (1313–75) Italian writer and poet. *Decameron*, 'Third Day'

39 Love is also like a coconut which is good while it is fresh, but you have to spit it out when the juice is gone, what's left tastes bitter.

Bertolt Brecht (1898–1956) German dramatist. *Baal*

40 My love for Linton is like the foliage in the woods: time will change it, I'm well aware, as winter changes the trees. My love for Heathcliff resembles the eternal rocks beneath: a source of little visible delight, but necessary. Nelly, I *am* Heathcliff!

Emily Brontë (1818–48) British novelist and poet. *Wuthering Heights*, Ch. 9

41 I love thee with a love I seemed to lose
With my lost saints – I love thee with the breath,
Smiles, tears, of all my life! – and, if God choose,
I shall but love thee better after death.

Elizabeth Barrett Browning (1806–61) British poet. *Sonnets from the Portuguese*, XLIII

42 Such ever was love's way; to rise, it stoops.

Robert Browning (1812–89) British poet. *A Death in the Desert*

43 Green grow the rashes O,
Green grow the rashes O,
The sweetest hours that e'er I spend,
Are spent amang the lasses O!

Robert Burns (1759–96) Scottish poet. *Green Grow the Rashes*

44 My love is like a red red rose
That's newly sprung in June:
My love is like the melodie
That's sweetly play'd in tune.

Robert Burns *A Red, Red Rose*

45 Gin a body meet a body
Coming through the rye;
Gin a body kiss a body,
Need a body cry?

Robert Burns *Coming through the Rye*

46 Absence is to love what wind is to fire; it extinguishes the small, it inflames the great.

Bussy-Rabutin (Roger de Rabutin, Comte de Bussy; 1618–93) French soldier and writer. *Histoire amoureuse des Gaules*

47 Man's love is of man's life a thing apart,
'Tis woman's whole existence.

Lord Byron (1788–1824) British poet. *Don Juan*, I

48 Though the night was made for loving,
And the day returns too soon,
Yet we'll go no more a roving
By the light of the moon.

Lord Byron *So, we'll go no more a roving*

49 God is Love – I dare say. But what a mischievous devil Love is!

Samuel Butler (1835–1902) British writer. *Notebooks*

50 Of all the girls that are so smart
There's none like pretty Sally;
She is the darling of my heart
And she lives in our alley.

Henry Carey (c. 1690–1743) English poet and musician. *Sally in our Alley*

51 I have fallen in love with all sorts of girls and I fully intend to go on doing so.

Charles, Prince of Wales (1948–) Eldest son of Elizabeth II. *The Observer*, 21 Dec 1975

52 Yes...whatever that may mean.

Charles, Prince of Wales On his engagement, when asked whether he was in love. TV news interview, Feb 1981

53 There ain't a lady livin' in the land
As I'd swop for my dear old Dutch!

Albert Chevalier (1861–1923) British music-hall artist. *My Old Dutch*

54 Many a man has fallen in love with a girl in a light so dim he would not have chosen a suit by it.

Maurice Chevalier (1888–1972) French singer and actor. Attrib.

55 To the men and women who own men and women
those of us meant to be lovers
we will not pardon you
for wasting our bodies and time

Leonard Cohen (1934–) Canadian poet. *The Energy of Slaves*

56 Love and a cottage! Eh, Fanny! Ah, give me indifference and a coach and six!

George Colman, the Elder (1732–94) British dramatist. *The Clandestine Marriage*, I:2

57 See how love and murder will out.

William Congreve (1670–1729) British Restoration dramatist. *The Double Dealer*, IV:6

58 Say what you will, 'tis better to be left than never to have been loved.

William Congreve *The Way of the World*, II:1

59 Lord, what is a lover that it can give? Why one makes lovers as fast as one pleases, and they live as long as one pleases, and they die as soon as one pleases: and then if one pleases one makes more.

William Congreve *The Way of the World*, II:4

60 Mad about the boy.

Noël Coward (1899–1973) British dramatist. Song title

61 Love is a sickness full of woes,
All remedies refusing;
A plant that with most cutting grows,
Most barren with best using.
Why so?
More we enjoy it, more it dies;
If not enjoyed, it sighing cries,
Hey ho.

Samuel Daniel (c. 1562–1619) English poet and dramatist. *Hymen's Triumph*, I

62 It has been said that love robs those who have it of their wit, and gives it to those who have none.

Denis Diderot (1713–84) French writer. *Paradoxe sur le comédien*

63 Come live with me, and be my love,
And we will some new pleasures prove
Of golden sands, and crystal brooks,
With silken lines, and silver hooks.

John Donne (1573–1631) English poet. *The Bait*

64 Love built on beauty, soon as beauty, dies.

John Donne *Elegies*, 2, 'The Anagram'

65 I am two fools, I know,
For loving, and for saying so
In whining Poetry.

John Donne *The Triple Fool*

66 It seems to me that he has never loved, that he has only imagined that he has loved, that there has been no real love on his part. I even think that he is incapable of love; he is too much occupied with other thoughts and ideas to become strongly attached to anyone earthly.

Anna Dostoevsky (1846–1918) Russian diarist and writer. *Dostoevsky Portrayed by His Wife*

67 And I was desolate and sick of an old passion.

Ernest Dowson (1867–1900) British lyric poet. *Non Sum Qualis Eram Bonae Sub Regno Cynarae*

68 You may not be an angel
'Cause angels are so few,
But until the day that one comes along
I'll string along with you.

Al Dubin (20th century) US songwriter. *Twenty Million Sweethearts*

69 All mankind love a lover.

Ralph Waldo Emerson (1803–82) US poet and essayist. *Essays*, 'Love'

70 Don't you think I was made for you? I feel like you had me ordered – and I was delivered to you – to be worn – I want you to wear me, like a watch-charm or a button hole bouquet – to the world.

Zelda Fitzgerald (1900–48) US writer. Letter to F. Scott Fitzgerald, 1919

71 ...I don't want to live – I want to love first, and live incidentally...

Zelda Fitzgerald Letter to F. Scott Fitzgerald, 1919

72 *Plaisir d'amour ne dure qu'un moment,*
Chagrin d'amour dure toute la vie.
Love's pleasure lasts but a moment; love's sorrow lasts all through life.

Jean-Pierre Claris de Florian (1755–94) French writer of fables. *Celestine*

73 I'm leaning on a lamp-post at the corner of the street,
In case a certain little lady walks by.

George Formby (1905–61) British comedian. *Leaning on a Lamp-post*

74 Try thinking of love, or something.
Amor vincit insomnia.

Christopher Fry (1907–) British dramatist. *A Sleep of Prisoners*

75 If with me you'd fondly stray,
Over the hills and far away.

John Gay (1685–1732) English poet and dramatist. *The Beggar's Opera*

76 She who has never loved has never lived.

John Gay *Captives*

77 Everyone has experienced that truth: that love, like a running brook, is disregarded, taken for granted; but when the brook freezes over, then people begin to remember how it was when it ran, and they want it to run again.

Kahlil Gibran (1833–1931) Lebanese mystic and poet. *Beloved Prophet* (ed. Virginia Hilu)

78 Love one another, but make not a bond of love:
Let it rather be a moving sea between the shores of your souls.
Fill each other's cup but drink not from one cup.
Give one another of your bread but eat not from the same loaf...
And stand together yet not too near together:
For the pillars of the temple stand apart,

And the oak tree and the cypress grow not in each other's shadow.

Kahlil Gibran *The Prophet*

79 It's a song of a merryman, moping mum,
Whose soul was sad, and whose glance was glum,
Who sipped no sup, and who craved no crumb,
As he sighed for the love of a ladye.

W. S. Gilbert (1836–1911) British dramatist. *The Yeoman of the Guard*, I

80 In love as in sport, the amateur status must be strictly maintained.

Robert Graves (1895–1985) British poet and novelist. *Occupation: Writer*

81 Love, love, love – all the wretched cant of it, masking egotism, lust, masochism, fantasy under a mythology of sentimental postures, a welter of self-induced miseries and joys, blinding and masking the essential personalities in the frozen gestures of courtship, in the kissing and the dating and the desire, the compliments and the quarrels which vivify its barrenness.

Germaine Greer (1939–) Australian-born British writer and feminist. *The Female Eunuch*

82 If you were the only girl in the world,
And I were the only boy.

George Grossmith the Younger (1874–1935) British singer, actor, and songwriter. *The Bing Boys*, 'If you were the Only Girl' (with Fred Thompson; 1884–1949)

83 Hello, Young Lovers, Wherever You Are.

Oscar Hammerstein (1895–1960) US lyricist. From the musical *The King and I* Song title

84 A lover without indiscretion is no lover at all.

Thomas Hardy (1840–1928) British novelist. *The Hand of Ethelberta*, Ch. 20

85 'You must sit down,' says Love, 'and taste My meat,'
So I did sit and eat.

George Herbert (1593–1633) English poet. *Love*

86 My love she's but a lassie yet.

James Hogg (1770–1835) Scottish poet and writer. Song title

87 Pale hands I loved beside the Shalimar,
Where are you now? Who lies beneath your spell?

Laurence Hope (Mrs M. H. Nicolson; 1804–1905) British poet and songwriter. *The Garden of Kama and other Love Lyrics from India*, 'Pale Hands I Loved'

88 Look not in my eyes, for fear
They mirror true the sight I see,
And there you find your face too clear
And love it and be lost like me.

A. E. Housman (1859–1936) British scholar and poet. *A Shropshire Lad*, 'March'

89 I know nothing about platonic love except that it is not to be found in the works of Plato.

Edgar Jepson (1863–1938) British novelist. *EGO 5* (James Agate)

90 Love is like the measles; we all have to go through with it.

Jerome K. Jerome (1859–1927) British humorist. *Idle Thoughts of an Idle Fellow*

91 Love's like the measles – all the worse when it comes late in life.

Douglas William Jerrold (1803–57) British dramatist. *Wit and Opinions of Douglas Jerrold*, 'A Philanthropist'

92 Love is the wisdom of the fool and the folly of the wise.

Samuel Johnson (1709–84) British lexicographer. *Johnsonian Miscellanies* (ed. G. B. Hill), Vol. II

93 Drink to me only with thine eyes,
And I will pledge with mine;
Or leave a kiss but in the cup,
And I'll not look for wine.
The thirst that from the soul doth rise
Doth ask a drink divine;
But might I of Jove's nectar sup,
I would not change for thine.

I sent thee late a rosy wreath,
Not so much honouring thee,
As giving it a hope that there
It could not wither'd be.

Ben Jonson (1573–1637) English dramatist. *The Forest, IX*, 'To Celia'

94 Come, my Celia, let us prove,
While we can, the sports of love,
Time will not be ours for ever,
He, at length, our good will sever.

Ben Jonson *Volpone*, III:6

95 Love me, love my umbrella.

James Joyce (1882–1941) Irish novelist. Attrib.

96 Love in a hut, with water and a crust,
Is – Love, forgive us! – cinders, ashes, dust;
Love in a palace is perhaps at last
More grievous torment than a hermit's fast.

John Keats (1795–1821) British poet. *Lamia*, II

97 Soft adorings from their loves receive
Upon the honey'd middle of the night.

John Keats *The Eve of Saint Agnes*, VI

98 It is said there is no happiness, and no love to be compared to that which is felt for the first time. Most persons erroneously think so; but love like other arts requires experience, and terror and ignorance, on its first approach, prevent our feeling it as strongly as at a later period.

Caroline Lamb (1785–1828) British novelist. *Glenarvon*, Vol. I, Ch. 11

99 What will survive of us is love.

Philip Larkin (1922–85) British poet. *The Whitsun Weddings*, 'An Arundel Tomb'

100 I love a lassie.

Harry Lauder (Hugh MacLennon; 1870–1950) Scottish music-hall artist. Song title

101 You must always be a-waggle with LOVE.

D. H. Lawrence (1885–1930) British novelist. *Bibbles*

102 I'm not sure if a mental relation with a woman doesn't make it impossible to love her. To know the *mind* of a woman is to end in hating her. Love means the pre-cognitive flow…it is the honest state before the apple.

D. H. Lawrence Letter to Dr Trigant Burrow, 3 Aug 1927

103 I loved you, so I drew these tides of men into my hands and wrote my will across the sky in stars to earn you freedom, the seven pillared worthy house, that your eyes might be shining for me when we came.

T. E. Lawrence (1888–1935) British soldier and writer. *The Seven Pillars of Wisdom*, Epigraph 'To S.A.'

104 All You Need Is Love.

John Lennon (1940–80) British rock musician. Song title (with Paul McCartney)

105 If there's anything that you want,
If there's anything I can do,
Just call on me,
And I'll send it along with love from me to you.

John Lennon *From Me to You* (with Paul McCartney)

106 She loves you, yeh, yeh, yeh,
And with a love like that you know you should be glad.

John Lennon *She Loves You* (with Paul McCartney)

107 Finally found a fellow
He says 'Murder!' – he says!
Every time we kiss he says 'Murder!' – he says!
Is that the language of love?

Frank Loesser (1910–69) US songwriter. *Happy Go Lucky*

108 Two souls with but a single thought,
Two hearts that beat as one.

Maria Lovell (1803–77) British actress and dramatist. *Ingomar the Barbarian*, II (transl. of Friedrich Halm)

109 Time was away and somewhere else,
There were two glasses and two chairs
And two people with one pulse.

Louis MacNeice (1907–63) Irish-born British poet. *Meeting Point*

110 Come live with me, and be my love;
And we will all the pleasures prove
That hills and valleys, dales and fields,
Woods or steepy mountain yields.

Christopher Marlowe (1564–93) English dramatist. *The Passionate Shepherd to his Love*

111 Let us roll all our strength and all
Our sweetness up into one ball,
And tear our pleasures with rough strife
Thorough the iron gates of life:
Thus, though we cannot make our sun
Stand still, yet we will make him run.

Andrew Marvell (1621–78) English poet. *To His Coy Mistress*

112 Send two dozen roses to Room 424 and put 'Emily, I love you' on the back of the bill.

Groucho Marx (Julius Marx; 1895–1977) US comedian. *A Night in Casablanca*

113 Because women can do nothing except love, they've given it a ridiculous importance.

W. Somerset Maugham (1874–1965) British novelist. *The Moon and Sixpence*, Ch. 41

114 If the heart bleeds love, bare it,
If the martyr's crown fits, wear it.

Roger McGough (1937–) British poet. *Russian Bear*

115 I loved Kirk so much, I would have skied down Mount Everest in the nude with a carnation up my nose.

Joyce McKinney (1950–) US former beauty queen. Ms McKinney was accused of kidnapping an ex-lover who had rejected her. Evidence in court, 1977

116 Love is based on a view of women that is impossible to those who have had any experience with them.

H. L. Mencken (1880–1956) US journalist.

117 My heart shall be thy garden.

Alice Meynell (1847–1922) British poet. *The Garden*

118 Falling out of love is very enlightening. For a short while you see the world with new eyes.

Iris Murdoch (1919–) Irish-born British novelist. *The Observer*, 'Sayings of the Week', 4 Feb 1968

119 When a man is in love he endures more than at other times; he submits to everything.

Friedrich Wilhelm Nietzsche (1844–1900) German philosopher. *The Antichrist*

120 I do not love thee! – no! I do not love thee!
And yet when thou art absent I am sad.

Caroline Elizabeth Sarah Norton (1808–77) British poet. *I do Not Love Thee*

121 K-K-Katy, beautiful Katy,
You're the only g-g-g-girl that I adore,
When the m-m-m-moon shines over the cow-shed,
I'll be waiting at the k-k-k-kitchen door.

Geoffrey O'Hara (1882–1967) Canadian-born US songwriter. *K-K-Katy* (song)

122 By the time you swear you're his,
Shivering and sighing,
And he vows his passion is
Infinite, undying –
Lady, make a note of this:
One of you is lying.

Dorothy Parker (1893–1967) US writer. *Unfortunate Coincidence*

123 Every love is the love before
In a duller dress.

Dorothy Parker *Death and Taxes*

124 Love is like quicksilver in the hand. Leave the fingers open and it stays. Clutch it, and it darts away.

Dorothy Parker Attrib.

125 Love's perfect blossom only blows
Where noble manners veil defect.
Angels may be familiar; those
Who err each other must respect.

Coventry Patmore (1823–96) British poet. *The Angel in the House*, Bk. I, Prelude 2

126 Ye gods! annihilate but space and time.
And make two lovers happy.

Alexander Pope (1688–1744) British poet. *The Art of Sinking in Poetry*, 11

127 I've Got You Under My Skin.

Cole Porter (1893–1964) US songwriter. *Born to Dance*, song title

128 Night and day, you are the one,
Only you beneath the moon and under the sun.

Cole Porter *The Gay Divorcee*, 'Night and Day'

129 Let's Do It; Let's Fall in Love.

Cole Porter *Paris*, song title

130 I have sometimes regretted living so close to Marie...because I may be very fond of her, but I am not quite so fond of her company.

Marcel Proust (1871–1922) French novelist. *À la Recherche du temps perdu: Sodome et Gomorrhe*

131 There can be no peace of mind in love, since the advantage one has secured is never anything but a fresh starting-point for further desires.

Marcel Proust *À la Recherche du temps perdu: À l'ombre des jeunes filles en fleurs*

132 I loved you when you were inconstant. What should I have done if you had been faithful?

Jean Racine (1639–99) French dramatist. *Andromaque*, IV:5

133 If all the world and love were young,
And truth in every shepherd's tongue,
These pretty pleasures might me move
To live with thee, and be thy love.

Walter Raleigh (1554–1618) English explorer. *Answer to Marlow*

134 There are very few people who are not ashamed of having been in love when they no longer love each other.

Duc de la Rochefoucauld (1613–80) French writer. *Maximes*, 71

135 It takes a woman twenty years to make a man of her son, and another woman twenty minutes to make a fool of him.

Helen Rowland (1876–1950) US writer. *Reflections of a Bachelor Girl*

136 Of all forms of caution, caution in love is perhaps the most fatal to true happiness.

Bertrand Russell (1872–1970) British philosopher. *Autobiography*

137 To fear love is to fear life, and those who fear life are already three parts dead.

Bertrand Russell *Marriage and Morals*

138 Every little girl knows about love. It is only her capacity to suffer because of it that increases.

Françoise Sagan (1935–) French writer. *Daily Express*

139 Liszt said to me today that God alone deserves to be loved. It may be true, but when one has loved a man it is very different to love God.

George Sand (Aurore Dupin, Baronne Dudevant; 1804–76) French novelist. *Intimate Journal*

140 True love's the gift which God has given
To man alone beneath the heaven.

Walter Scott (1771–1832) Scottish novelist. *The Lay of the Last Minstrel*, V

141 When we love animals and children too much we love them at the expense of men.

Jean-Paul Sartre (1905–80) French writer. *The Words*

142 The triple pillar of the world transform'd
Into a strumpet's fool.

William Shakespeare (1564–1616) English dramatist. *Antony and Cleopatra*, I:1

143 There's beggary in the love that can be reckon'd.

William Shakespeare *Antony and Cleopatra*, I:1

144 If thou rememb'rest not the slightest folly
That ever love did make thee run into,
Thou hast not lov'd.

William Shakespeare *As You Like It*, II:4

145 But love is blind, and lovers cannot see
The pretty follies that themselves commit.

William Shakespeare *The Merchant of Venice*, II:6

146 For aught that I could ever read,
Could ever hear by tale or history,
The course of true love never did run smooth.

William Shakespeare *A Midsummer Night's Dream*, I:1

147 Love looks not with the eyes, but with the mind;
And therefore is wing'd Cupid painted blind.

William Shakespeare *A Midsummer Night's Dream*, I:1

148 The lunatic, the lover, and the poet,
Are of imagination all compact.

William Shakespeare *A Midsummer Night's Dream*, V:1

149 A woman's face, with Nature's own hand painted,
Hast thou, the Master Mistress of my passion.

William Shakespeare *Sonnet 20*

150 Let me not to the marriage of true minds
Admit impediments. Love is not love
Which alters when it alteration finds,
Or bends with the remover to remove.
O, no! it is an ever-fixed mark,
That looks on tempests and is never shaken.

William Shakespeare *Sonnet 116*

151 Love alters not with his brief hours and weeks,
But bears it out even to the edge of doom.
If this be error, and upon me prov'd,
I never writ, nor no man ever lov'd.

William Shakespeare *Sonnet 116*

152 To be wise and love
Exceeds man's might.

William Shakespeare *Troilus and Cressida*, III:2

153 She never told her love,
But let concealment, like a worm i' th' bud,
Feed on her damask cheek. She pin'd in thought;
And with a green and yellow melancholy
She sat like Patience on a monument,
Smiling at grief.

William Shakespeare *Twelfth Night*, II:4

154 Love sought is good, but given unsought is better.

William Shakespeare *Twelfth Night*, III:1

155 Then must you speak
Of one that lov'd not wisely, but too well;
Of one not easily jealous, but, being wrought,
Perplexed in the extreme; of one whose hand,
Like the base Indian, threw a pearl away
Richer than all his tribe.

William Shakespeare *Othello*, V:2

156 Nowadays we don't think much of a man's love for an animal; we laugh at people who are attached to cats. But if we stop loving animals, aren't we bound to stop loving humans too?

Alexander Solzhenitsyn (1918–) Russian novelist. *Cancer Ward*, Pt. I, Ch. 20

157 And all for love, and nothing for reward.

Edmund Spenser (1552–99) English poet. *The Faerie Queene*

158 Love is above the laws, above the opinion of

men; it is the truth, the flame, the pure element, the primary idea of the moral world.

Germaine de Staël (1766–1817) French novelist, literary critic, and feminist. *Zulma, and Other Tales*

159 A woman despises a man for loving her, unless she returns his love.

Elizabeth Drew Stoddard (1823–1902) US novelist and poet. *Two Men*, Ch. 32

160 I know she likes me,
Because she says so.

Eugene Stratton (1861–1918) British music-hall singer. *The Lily of Laguna*

161 I hold it true, whate'er befall;
I feel it, when I sorrow most;
'Tis better to have loved and lost
Than never to have loved at all.

Alfred, Lord Tennyson (1809–92) British poet. *In Memoriam A.H.H.*, XXVII

162 Such a one do I remember, whom to look at was to love.

Alfred, Lord Tennyson *Locksley Hall*

163 The rose was awake all night for your sake,
Knowing your promise to me;
The lilies and roses were all awake,
They sighed for the dawn and thee.

Alfred, Lord Tennyson *Maud*, I

164 O tell her, brief is life but love is long.

Alfred, Lord Tennyson *The Princess*, IV

165 God gives us love. Something to love
He lends us; but, when love is grown
To ripeness that on which it throve
Falls off, and love is left alone.

Alfred, Lord Tennyson *To J.S.*

166 'Tis strange what a man may do, and a woman yet think him an angel.

William Makepeace Thackeray (1811–63) British novelist. *Henry Esmond*, Ch. 7

167 All, everything that I understand, I understand only because I love.

Leo Tolstoy (1828–1910) Russian writer. *War and Peace*, Bk. VII, Ch. 16

168 One can't live on love alone; and I am so stupid that I can do nothing but think of him.

Sophie Tolstoy (1844–1919) Russian writer. *A Diary of Tolstoy's Wife, 1860–1891*

169 Those who have courage to love should have courage to suffer.

Anthony Trollope (1815–82) British novelist. *The Bertrams*, Ch. 27

170 I doubt whether any girl would be satisfied with her lover's mind if she knew the whole of it.

Anthony Trollope *The Small House at Allington*, Ch. 4

171 Walking My Baby Back Home.

Roy Turk (20th century) US songwriter. Song title

172 Love conquers all things: let us too give in to Love.

Virgil (Publius Vergilius Maro; 70–19 BC) Roman poet. *Eclogue*, Bk. X

173 The boy I love is up in the gallery,
The boy I love is looking down at me.

George Ware (19th century) British songwriter. *The Boy in the Gallery*

174 It is like a cigar. If it goes out, you can light it again but it never tastes quite the same.

Lord Wavell (1883–1950) British field marshall. Attrib.

175 Beware you be not swallowed up in books! An ounce of love is worth a pound of knowledge.

John Wesley (1703–91) British religious leader. *Life of Wesley* (R. Southey), Ch. 16

176 I have found it impossible to carry the heavy burden of responsibility and to discharge my duties as King as I would wish to do without the help and support of the woman I love.

Duke of Windsor (1894–1972) King of the United Kingdom; abdicated 1936. Radio broadcast, 11 Dec 1936

177 'Ah, love, love' he said. 'Is there anything like it? Were you ever in love, Beach?'
'Yes, sir, on one occasion, when I was a young under-footman. But it blew over.'

P. G. Wodehouse (1881–1975) British humorous novelist. *Pigs Have Wings*

178 There is a comfort in the strength of love;
'Twill make a thing endurable, which else
Would overset the brain, or break the heart.

William Wordsworth (1770–1850) British poet. *Michael*, 448

179 Love fled
And paced upon the mountains overhead
And hid his face amid a crowd of stars.

W. B. Yeats (1865–1939) Irish poet. *When you are Old*

180 But Love has pitched his mansion in
The place of excrement.

W. B. Yeats *Crazy Jane Talks with the Bishop*

181 A pity beyond all telling
Is hid in the heart of love.

W. B. Yeats *The Pity of Love*

LOVE AND DEATH

See also death, love

1 And for bonnie Annie Laurie
I'll lay me doun and dee.

William Douglas (1672–1748) Scottish poet. *Annie Laurie*

2 For, Heaven be thanked, we live is such an age,
When no man dies for love, but on the stage.

John Dryden (1631–1700) British poet and dramatist. *Mithridates*, Epilogue

3 Love is my religion – I could die for that.

John Keats (1795–1821) British poet. Letter to Fanny Brawne, 13 Oct 1819

4 How alike are the groans of love to those of the dying.

Malcolm Lowry (1909–57) British novelist. *Under the Volcano*, Ch. 12

5 It is very rarely that a man loves
And when he does it is nearly always fatal.

Hugh MacDiarmid (Christopher Murray Grieve; 1892–1978) Scottish poet. *The International Brigade*

6 Men have died from time to time, and worms have eaten them, but not for love.

William Shakespeare (1564–1616) English dramatist. *As You Like It*, IV:1

7 She shall be buried by her Antony:
No grave upon the earth shall clip in it
A pair so famous.

William Shakespeare *Antony and Cleopatra*, V:2

8 I kiss'd thee ere I kill'd thee, no way but this,
Killing myself to die upon a kiss.

William Shakespeare *Othello*, V:2

9 Romeo, come forth; come forth, thou fearful man:
Affliction is enamour'd of thy parts,
And thou are wedded to calamity.

William Shakespeare *Romeo and Juliet*, III:3

10 'Tis said that some have died for love.

William Wordsworth (1770–1850) British poet. *'Tis Said that some have Died*

LOVE AND FRIENDSHIP

See also friendship, love

1 Love is blind; friendship closes its eyes.

Proverb

2 A woman can become a man's friend only in the following stages – first an acquaintance, next a mistress, and only then a friend.

Anton Chekhov (1860–1904) Russian dramatist. *Uncle Vanya*, II

3 No human relation gives one possession in another – every two souls are absolutely different. In friendship or in love, the two side by side raise hands together to find what one cannot reach alone.

Kahlil Gibran (1833–1931) Lebanese mystic and poet. *Beloved Prophet* (Virginia Hilu)

4 Friendship is a disinterested commerce between equals; love, an abject intercourse between tyrants and slaves.

Oliver Goldsmith (1728–74) Irish-born British writer. *The Good-Natured Man*, I

5 Most friendship is feigning, most loving mere folly.

William Shakespeare (1564–1616) English dramatist. *As You Like It*, II:7

6 Friendship is constant in all other things
Save in the office and affairs of love.

William Shakespeare *Much Ado About Nothing*, II:1

LOVE AND HATE

See also hate, love

1 Now hatred is by far the longest pleasure;
Men love in haste, but they detest at leisure.

Lord Byron (1788–1824) British poet. *Don Juan*, XIII

2 *Odi et amo.*
I hate and love.

Catullus (c. 84–c. 54 BC) Roman poet. *Carmina*, LXXXV

3 Heaven has no rage like love to hatred turned,
Nor hell a fury like a woman scorned.

William Congreve (1670–1729) British Restoration dramatist. *The Mourning Bride*, III

4 Oh, I have loved him too much to feel no hate for him.

Jean Racine (1639–99) French dramatist. *Andromaque*, II:1

5 If one judges love by its visible effects, it looks more like hatred than like friendship.

Duc de la Rochefoucauld (1613–80) French writer. *Maximes*, 72

6 My only love sprung from my only hate!
Too early seen unknown, and known too late!

William Shakespeare (1564–1616) English dramatist. *Romeo and Juliet*, I:5

LOVE AND MARRIAGE

See also love, marriage

1 Next to being married, a girl likes to be crossed in love a little now and then.

Jane Austen (1775–1817) British novelist. *Pride and Prejudice*, Ch. 24

2 Love and marriage, love and marriage,
Go together like a horse and carriage.

Sammy Cahn (Samuel Cohen; 1913–) US songwriter. *Our Town*, 'Love and Marriage'

3 ALMA. I rather suspect her of being in love with him.
MARTIN. Her own husband? Monstrous! What a selfish woman!

Jennie Jerome Churchill (1854–1921) US-born British hostess and writer. *His Borrowed Plumes*

4 Love is moral even without legal marriage, but marriage is immoral without love.

Ellen Key (Karolina Sofia Key; 1849–1926) Swedish writer. *The Morality of Woman and Other Essays*, 'The Morality of Woman'

5 Many a man in love with a dimple makes the mistake of marrying the whole girl.

Stephen Leacock (1869–1944) British-born Canadian economist and humorist. *Literary Lapses*

6 Any one must see at a glance that if men and women marry those whom they do not love, they must love those whom they do not marry.

Harriet Martineau (1802–76) British writer. *Society in America*, Vol. III, 'Marriage'

7 Can't you read? The score demands *con amore*, and what are you doing? You are playing it like married men!

Arturo Toscanini (1867–1957) Italian conductor. Criticizing the playing of an Austrian orchestra during rehearsal. Attrib.

8 The amount of women in London who flirt with their own husbands is perfectly scandalous. It looks so bad. It is simply washing one's clean linen in public.

Oscar Wilde (1854–1900) Irish-born British dramatist. *The Importance of Being Earnest*, I

LOYALTY

See also betrayal, faithfulness, patriotism, support

1 Dog does not eat dog.

Proverb

2 There is honour among thieves.
Proverb

3 You cannot run with the hare and hunt with the hounds.
Proverb

4 Here's a health unto his Majesty...
Confusion to his enemies,...
And he that will not drink his health,
I wish him neither wit nor wealth,
Nor yet a rope to hang himself.

Anonymous *Here's a Health unto his Majesty*

5 And Ruth said, Intreat me not to leave thee, or to return from following after thee: for whither thou goest, I will go; and where thou lodgest, I will lodge: thy people shall be my people, and thy God my God:
Where thou diest, will I die, and there will I be buried: the Lord do so to me, and more also, if ought but death part thee and me.

Bible: Ruth 1:16–17

6 The State, in choosing men to serve it, takes no notice of their opinions. If they be willing faithfully to serve it, that satisfies.

Oliver Cromwell (1599–1658) English soldier and statesman. Said before the Battle of Marston Moor, 2 July 1644

7 We are all the President's men.

Henry Kissinger (1923–) German-born US politician and diplomat. Said regarding the invasion of Cambodia, 1970. *The Sunday Times Magazine*, 4 May 1975

8 A man who will steal *for* me will steal *from* me.

Theodore Roosevelt (1858–1919) US Republican president. Firing a cowboy who had applied Roosevelt's brand to a steer belonging to a neighbouring ranch. *Roosevelt in the Bad Lands* (Herman Hagedorn)

9 Those he commands move only in command,
Nothing in love; now does he feel his title
Hang loose about him, like a giant's robe
Upon a dwarfish thief.

William Shakespeare (1564–1616) English dramatist. *Macbeth*, V:2

10 Myn hert ys set and all myn hole entent,
To serve this flour in my most humble wyse
As faythfully as can be thought or ment,
Wythout feynyng or slouthe in my servyse;
For wytt the wele, yt ys a paradyse
To se this floure when yt begyn to sprede,
Wyth colours fressh ennewyd, white and rede.

Duke of Suffolk (1396–1450) English nobleman. Poem dedicated to Margaret of Anjou, Queen of England. *Secular Lyrics of XIVth and XVth Centuries* (ed. R. H. Robbins)

11 He was my crowned King, and if the Parliamentary authority of England set the Crown upon a stock, I will fight for that stock: And as I fought then for him, I will fight for you, when you are established by the said authority.

Earl of Surrey Reply when asked by Henry VII why he had fought for Richard III at the Battle of Bosworth (22 Aug 1485). *Remains Concerning Britain* (W. Camden)

12 If this man is not faithful to his God, how can he be faithful to me, a mere man?

Theodoric (c. 445–526) King of the Ostrogoths. Explaining why he had had a trusted minister, who had said he would adopt his master's religion, beheaded. *Dictionnaire Encyclopédique* (E. Guérard)

13 When I forget my sovereign, may God forget me!

Lord Thurlow (1731–1806) British lawyer. Speech, House of Lords, 15 Dec 1778

14 Had I but served God as diligently as I have served the king, he would not have given me over in my gray hairs.

Cardinal Wolsey (1475–1530) English churchman. Remark to Sir William Kingston. *Negotiations of Thomas Wolsey* (Cavendish)

LUCK

See also chance, superstition

1 A bad penny always turns up.
Proverb

2 A cat has nine lives.
Proverb

3 Finders keepers, losers weepers.
Proverb

4 It is better to be born lucky than rich.
Proverb

5 The devil looks after his own.
Proverb

6 Today we were unlucky. But remember, we have only to be lucky once. You will have to be lucky always.

Anonymous Telephone call from the IRA following their unsuccessful attempt to blow up Margaret Thatcher and other ministers at the Grand Hotel, Brighton, in 1984

7 There, but for the grace of God, goes John Bradford.

John Bradford (c. 1510–55) English Protestant martyr. Said on seeing some criminals being led to execution. Attrib.

8 This is the temple of Providence where disciples still hourly mark its ways and note the system of its mysteries. Here is the one God whose worshippers prove their faith by their works and in their destruction still trust in Him.

F. H. Bradley (1846–1924) British philosopher. Referring to Monte Carlo. *Aphorisms*

9 Fortune, that favours fools.

Ben Jonson (1573–1637) English dramatist. *The Alchemist*, Prologue

10 I am a great believer in luck, and I find the harder I work the more I have of it.

Stephen Leacock (1869–1944) British-born Canadian economist and humorist. *Literary Lapses*

11 The Eskimo had his own explanation. Said he: 'The devil is asleep or having trouble with his wife, or we should never have come back so easily.'

Robert Edwin Peary (1856–1920) US explorer. *The North Pole*

12 We need greater virtues to sustain good fortune than bad.

Duc de la Rochefoucauld (1613–80) French writer. *Maximes*, 25

13 'My aunt was suddenly prevented from going a voyage
in a ship what went down – would you call that a case

of Providential interference?'
'Can't tell: didn't know your aunt.'

Frederick Temple (1821–1902) British churchman. *Memoirs of Archbishop Temple* (Sandford), Vol. II

LUST

See also animalism, desire, love, sex

1 For all that is in the world, the lust of the flesh, and the lust of the eyes, and the pride of life, is not of the Father, but is of the world.

Bible: I John 2:16

2 For the bewitching of naughtiness doth obscure things that are honest; and the wandering of concupiscence doth undermine the simple mind. He, being made perfect in a short time, fulfilled a long time.

Bible: Wisdom 4:12–13

3 Licence my roving hands, and let them go,
Before, behind, between, above, below.

John Donne (1573–1631) English poet. *Elegies*, 18, 'Love's Progress'

4 What is commonly called love, namely the desire of satisfying a voracious appetite with a certain quantity of delicate white human flesh.

Henry Fielding (1707–54) British novelist. *Tom Jones*, Bk. VI, Ch. 1

5 ...kept a hearth-girl in his house who kindled his fire but extinguished his virtue.

Gerald of Wales (c. 1146–c. 1220) Welsh topographer, archdeacon, and writer. Referring to the parish priest. *Gemma Ecclesiastica*

6 I'll come no more behind your scenes, David; for the silk stockings and white bosoms of your actresses excite my amorous propensities.

Samuel Johnson (1709–84) British lexicographer. Said to the actor-manager David Garrick. *Life of Johnson* (J. Boswell), Vol. I

7 Oh, to be seventy again!

Oliver Wendell Holmes Jnr (1841–1935) US jurist. Said in his eighty-seventh year, while watching a pretty girl. *The American Treasury* (C. Fadiman)

8 Stand close around, ye Stygian set,
With Dirce in one boat conveyed!
Or Charon, seeing, may forget
That he is old and she a shade.

Walter Savage Landor (1775–1864) British poet and writer. In Greek mythology, Dirce, a follower of Dionysius, was killed by her great-nephews Amphion and Zethus because of her mistreatment of their mother Antiope; Charon was the ferryman who transported dead souls across the River Styx to the underworld. *Dirce*

9 Lolita, light of my life, fire of my loins. My sin, my Soul.

Vladimir Nabokov (1899–1977) Russian-born US novelist. *Lolita*

10 Th' expense of spirit in a waste of shame
Is lust in action; and till action, lust
Is perjur'd, murd'rous, bloody, full of blame,
Savage, extreme, rude, cruel, not to trust;
Enjoy'd no sooner but despised straight.

William Shakespeare (1564–1616) English dramatist. *Sonnet 129*

11 All witchcraft comes from carnal lust which in women is insatiable.

Jacob Sprenger and Hendrich Kramer German Dominican monks. The indispensable handbook for the Inquisition. *Malleus Maleficarum*

12 Nonconformity and lust stalking hand in hand through the country, wasting and ravaging.

Evelyn Waugh (1903–66) British novelist. *Decline and Fall*, Pt. I, Ch. 5

13 Outside every thin girl there is a fat man trying to get in.

Katharine Whitehorn (1928–) British journalist. Attrib.

LUXURY

See also extravagance, wealth

1 It's grand, and ye canna expect to be baith grand and comfortable.

J. M. Barrie (1860–1937) British novelist and dramatist. *The Little Minister*, Ch. 10

2 The saddest thing I can imagine is to get used to luxury.

Charlie Chaplin (Sir Charles Spencer C.; 1889–1977) British film actor. *My Autobiography*

3 In the affluent society no useful distinction can be made between luxuries and necessaries.

John Kenneth Galbraith (1908–) US economist. *The Affluent Society*, Ch. 21

4 Give us the luxuries of life, and we will dispense with its necessities.

John Lothrop Motley (1814–77) US historian and diplomat. Also quoted by Frank Lloyd Wright. *The Autocrat of the Breakfast Table* (O. W. Holmes), Ch. 6

5 How many things I can do without!

Socrates (469–399 BC) Athenian philosopher. Examining the range of goods on sale at a market. *Lives of the Eminent Philosophers* (Diogenes Laertius), II

6 Beulah, peel me a grape.

Mae West (1892–1980) US actress. *I'm No Angel*, film 1933

LYING

See also deception, honesty, truth

1 A liar is worse than a thief.

Proverb

2 The boy cried 'Wolf, wolf!' and the villagers came out to help him.

Aesop (6th century BC) Reputed Greek writer of fables. *Fables*, 'The Shepherd's Boy'

3 It contains a misleading impression, not a lie. I was being economical with the truth.

Robert Armstrong (1913–) British civil servant. Giving evidence on behalf of the British Government in an Australian court case, Nov 1986. Armstrong was, in fact, quoting Edmund Burke (1729–97).

4 She tells enough white lies to ice a wedding cake.

Margot Asquith (1865–1945) The second wife of Herbert Asquith. Referring to Lady Desborough. *As I Remember*

5 Matilda told such Dreadful Lies
It made one Gasp and Stretch one's Eyes.
For every time she shouted 'Fire'
They only answered 'Little Liar'. And therefore
when her Aunt returned
Matilda, and the House, were Burned.

Hilaire Belloc (1870–1953) French-born British poet. *Cautionary Tales*

6 The moment a man talks to his fellows he begins to lie.

Hilaire Belloc *The Silence of the Sea*

7 Woe unto them that call evil good, and good evil; that put darkness for light, and light for darkness; that put bitter for sweet, and sweet for bitter!

Bible: Isaiah 5:20

8 Nobody speaks the truth when there's something they must have.

Elizabeth Bowen (1899–1973) Irish novelist. *The House in Paris*, Ch. 5

9 A lie can be half-way round the world before the truth has got its boots on.

James Callaghan (1912–) British politician and prime minister. Speech, 1 Nov 1976

10 It cannot in the opinion of His Majesty's Government be classified as slavery in the extreme acceptance of the word without some risk of terminological inexactitude.

Winston Churchill (1874–1965) British statesman. Speech, House of Commons, 22 Feb 1906

11 Whoever would lie usefully should lie seldom.

Lord Hervey (1696–1743) English writer and pamphleteer. *Memoirs of the Reign of George II*, Vol. I

12 The broad mass of a nation…will more easily fall victim to a big lie than to a small one.

Adolf Hitler (1889–1945) German dictator. *Mein Kampf*, Ch. 10

13 She's too crafty a woman to invent a new lie when an old one will serve.

W. Somerset Maugham (1874–1965) British novelist. *The Constant Wife*, II

14 It is hard to believe that a man is telling the truth when you know that you would lie if you were in his place.

H. L. Mencken (1880–1956) US journalist. *Prejudices*

15 Unless a man feels he has a good enough memory, he should never venture to lie.

Michel de Montaigne (1533–92) French essayist. Also quoted in *Le Menteur*, IV:5 by Pierre Corneille (1606–84). *Essais*, I

16 He led a double life. Did that make him a liar? He did not feel a liar. He was a man of two truths.

Iris Murdoch (1919–) Irish-born British novelist. *The Sacred and Profane Love Machine*

17 He who does not need to lie is proud of not being a liar.

Friedrich Wilhelm Nietzsche (1844–1900) German philosopher. *Nachgelassene Fragmente*

18 By the time you say you're his,
Shivering and sighing
And he vows his passion is
Infinite, undying –
Lady, make a note of this
One of you is lying.

Dorothy Parker (1893–1967) US writer. *Not So Deep as a Well*

19 It has made more liars out of the American people than Golf.

Will Rogers (1879–1935) US actor and humorist. Referring to income tax. *Saturday Review*, 'A Rogers Thesaurus', 25 Aug 1962

20 I have never but once succeeded in making him tell a lie and that was by a subterfuge. 'Moore,' I said, 'Do you *always* tell the truth?' 'No', he replied. I believe this to be the only lie he ever told.

Bertrand Russell (1872–1970) British philosopher. Referring to the British philosopher George Edward Moore. *Autobiography*

21 O what a tangled web we weave,
When first we practise to deceive!

Sir Walter Scott (1771–1832) Scottish novelist. *Marmion*, VI:17

22 For my part, if a lie may do thee grace,
I'll gild it with the happiest terms I have.

William Shakespeare (1564–1616) English dramatist. *Henry IV, Part One*, V:4

23 Lord, Lord! how subject we old men are to this vice of lying.

William Shakespeare *Henry IV, Part Two*, III:2

24 In our country the lie has become not just a moral category but a pillar of the State.

Alexander Solzhenitsyn (1918–) Russian novelist. *The Observer*, 'Sayings of the Year', 29 Dec 1974

25 A lie is an abomination unto the Lord and a very present help in trouble.

Adlai Stevenson (1900–65) US statesman. Speech, Jan 1951

26 That a lie which is all a lie may be met and fought with outright,
But a lie which is part a truth is a harder matter to fight.

Alfred, Lord Tennyson (1809–92) British poet. *The Grandmother*

27 There was things which he stretched, but mainly he told the truth.

Mark Twain (Samuel Langhorne Clemens; 1835–1910) US writer. *The Adventures of Huckleberry Finn*, Ch. 1

M

MACAULAY, THOMAS BABINGTON

(1800–59) British historian and writer. An MP for many years, he is remembered for his five-volume *History of England* (1849–61).

1 The English Bible, a book which, if everything else in our language should perish, would alone suffice to show the whole extent of its beauty and power.

Essays and Biographies, 'John Dryden'. *Edinburgh Review*

2 His imagination resembled the wings of an ostrich. It enabled him to run, though not to soar.

Essays and Biographies, 'John Dryden'. *Edinburgh Review*

3 Knowledge advances by steps, and not by leaps.

Essays and Biographies, 'History'. *Edinburgh Review*

4 The gallery in which the reporters sit has become a fourth estate of the realm.

Referring to the press gallery in the House of Commons. *Essays Contributed to the 'Edinburgh Review'*, 'Hallam's "Constitutional History"'

5 The reluctant obedience of distant provinces generally costs more than it is worth.

Essays Contributed to the 'Edinburgh Review', 'Lord Mahon's War of the Succession'

6 The dust and silence of the upper shelf.

Essays Contributed to the 'Edinburgh Review', 'Milton'

7 As civilization advances, poetry almost necessarily declines.

Essays Contributed to the 'Edinburgh Review', 'Milton'

8 Perhaps no person can be a poet, or can even enjoy poetry, without a certain unsoundness of mind.

Essays Contributed to the 'Edinburgh Review', 'Milton'

9 Many politicians of our time are in the habit of laying it down as a self-evident proposition, that no people ought to be free till they are fit to use their freedom. The maxim is worthy of the fool in the old story, who resolved not to go into the water till he had learnt to swim. If men are to wait for liberty till they become wise and good in slavery, they may indeed wait for ever.

Essays Contributed to the 'Edinburgh Review', 'Milton'

10 We know no spectacle so ridiculous as the British public in one of its periodical fits of morality.

Essays Contributed to the 'Edinburgh Review', 'Moore's 'Life of Lord Byron"

11 His writing bears the same relation to poetry which a Turkey carpet bears to a picture. There are colours in the Turkey carpet out of which a picture might be made. There are words in Mr Montgomery's writing which, when disposed in certain orders and combinations, have made, and will make again, good poetry. But, as they now stand, they seem to be put together on principle in such a manner as to give no image of anything 'in the heavens above, or in the earth beneath, or in the waters under the earth'.

Essays Contributed to the 'Edinburgh Review', 'Mr. Robert Montgomery's Poems'

12 The highest intellects, like the tops of mountains, are the first to catch and to reflect the dawn.

Contributed to the 'Edinburgh Review', 'Sir James Mackintosh'

13 He...felt towards those whom he had deserted that peculiar malignity which has, in all ages, been characteristic of apostates.

History of England, Vol. I, Ch. 1

14 The Puritan hated bear-baiting, not because it gave pain to the bear, but because it gave pleasure to the spectators.

History of England, Vol. I, Ch. 2

15 There were gentlemen and there were seamen in the navy of Charles the Second. But the seamen were not gentlemen; and the gentlemen were not seamen.

History of England, Vol. I, Ch. 3

16 In every age the vilest specimens of human nature are to be found among demagogues.

History of England, Vol. I, Ch. 5

17 Then out spake brave Horatius,
The Captain of the Gate:
'To every man upon this earth
Death cometh soon or late.
And how can man die better
Than facing fearful odds,
For the ashes of his fathers,
And the temples of his Gods?'

Lays of Ancient Rome, 'Horatius', 27

18 Thank you, madam, the agony is abated.

Replying, aged four, to a lady who asked if he had hurt himself having had hot coffee spilt over his legs.

Life and Letters of Macaulay (Trevelyan), Ch. 1

19 Ye diners-out from whom we guard our spoons.

Letter to Hannah Macaulay, 29 June 1831

20 I shall not be satisfied unless I produce something that shall for a few days supersede the last fashionable novel on the tables of young ladies.

Letter to Macvey Napier, 5 Nov 1841

21 A broken head in Cold Bath Fields produces a greater sensation among us than three pitched battles in India.

Speech, 10 July 1833

MACMILLAN, HAROLD

(Earl of Stockton; 1894–1986) British statesman and publisher; Conservative prime minister (1957–63). His last year in office was notorious for the Profumo scandal.

Quotations about Macmillan

1 By far the most radical man I've known in politics wasn't on the labour side at all – Harold Macmillan. If it hadn't been for the war he'd have joined the Labour party. If that had happened Macmillan would have been Labour Prime Minister, and not me.

Clement Attlee (1883–1967) British statesman and Labour prime minister. *The Abuse of Power* (James Margach)

2 One can never escape the suspicion, with Mr Macmillan, that all his life was a preparation for elder statesmanship.

Frank Johnson. *The Times*, 30 Mar 1981

3 Harold Macmillan was the first person to recognise that in the modern world of media exposure a Prime Minister has to be something of a showman, equally at home in the theatre spotlight or the sawdust of the circus ring.

James Margach. *The Abuse of Power*

4 What a pity it is that now we have the most intelligent Prime Minister of the century, he has to conceal his intelligence from the public for fear they will suspect it.

Harold Nicolson (1886–1968) British diplomat and literary critic. Diary, 9 Feb 1957

Quotations by Macmillan

5 Most of our people have never had it so good.

Speech, Bedford Football Ground, 20 July 1957

6 I thought the best thing to do was to settle up these little local difficulties, and then turn to the wider vision of the Commonwealth.

Referring to resignation of ministers. Remark, London Airport, 7 Jan 1958

7 When you're abroad you're a statesman: when you're at home you're just a politician.

Speech, 1958

8 The wind of change is blowing through the continent. Whether we like it or not, this growth of national consciousness is a political fact.

Referring to South Africa.

Speech, South African Parliament, 3 Feb 1960

9 One nanny said, 'Feed a cold'; she was a neo-Keynesian. Another nanny said, 'Starve a cold'; she was a monetarist.

Maiden speech, House of Lords, 1984

10 Selling the family silver.

Referring to privatization of profitable nationalized industries. Speech, House of Lords, 1986

11 There are three groups that no prime minister should provoke: the Treasury, the Vatican, and the National Union of Mineworkers.

First used by Stanley BALDWIN. Attrib.

12 Power? It's like a dead sea fruit; when you achieve it, there's nothing there.

Attrib.

MACNEICE, LOUIS

(1907–63) Irish-born British poet. His verse publications include *Blind Fireworks* (1929), *Autumn Journal* (1939), and *The Burning Perch* (1963). He also wrote radio plays and worked for the BBC.

1 For the last blossom is the first blossom
And the first blossom is the best blossom
And when from Eden we take our way
The morning after is the first day.

Apple Blossom

2 It's no go the picture palace, it's no go the stadium,
It's no go the country cot with a pot of pink geraniums,
It's no go the Government grants, it's no go the elections,
Sit on your arse for fifty years and hang your hat on a pension.

Bagpipe Music

3 He looked at us coldly
And his eyes were dead and his hands on the oar
Were black with obols and varicose veins
Marbled his hands and he said to us coldly:
If you want to die you will have to pay for it.

Charon

4 Time was away and somewhere else,
There were two glasses and two chairs
And two people with one pulse.

Meeting Point

5 Down the road someone is practising scales,
The notes like little fishes vanish with a wink of tails,
Man's heart expands to tinker with his car
For this is Sunday morning, Fate's great bazaar.

Sunday Morning

6 That the world will never be quite – what a cliché – the same again
Is what we only learn by the event
When a friend dies out on us and is not there
To share the periphery of a remembered scent

Tam Cari Capitis

MADNESS

See also psychiatry, psychology

1 Whom God wishes to destroy, he first makes mad.

Proverb

2 Lucid intervals and happy pauses.

Francis Bacon (1561–1626) English philosopher. *The History of the Reign of King Henry VII*

3 I cultivate my hysteria with joy and terror. Now I am always dizzy, and today, January 23, 1862, I experienced a singular premonition, I felt pass over me a breath of wind from the wings of madness.

Charles Baudelaire (1821–67) French poet. *Journaux intimes*, 'Fusées', XVI

4 We all are born mad. Some remain so.

Samuel Beckett (1906–89) Irish novelist and dramatist. *Waiting for Godot*, II

5 There's a streak of madness in the family. I've a horrible fear it's genetic. One of the reasons I've never been in analysis is I've always been afraid of what I might find out.

David Bowie (David Jones; 1947–) British pop singer. *Photoplay*, Sept 1983

6 A knight errant who turns mad for a reason deserves neither merit nor thanks. The thing is to do it without cause.

Miguel de Cervantes (1547–1616) Spanish novelist. *Don Quixote*, Pt. I, Ch. 25

7 The madman is not the man who has lost his reason. The madman is the man who has lost everything except his reason.

G. K. Chesterton (1874–1936) British writer. *Orthodoxy*, Ch. 1

8 Much Madness is divinest Sense –
To a discerning Eye –
Much Sense – the starkest Madness –

Emily Dickinson (1830–86) US poet. *Poems*, 'Much Madness is Divinest Sense'

9 There is less harm to be suffered in being mad among madmen than in being sane all by oneself.

Denis Diderot (1713–84) French writer and editor. *Supplement to Bougainville's 'Voyage'*

10 There is a pleasure sure
In being mad which none but madmen know.

John Dryden (1631–1700) English poet and dramatist. *The Spanish Friar*, 2

11 Where does one go from a world of insanity? Somewhere on the other side of despair.

T. S. Eliot (1888–1965) US-born British poet and dramatist. *The Family Reunion*, II:2

12 Sanity is very rare: every man almost, and every woman, has a dash of madness.

Ralph Waldo Emerson (1803–82) US poet and essayist. *Journals*

13 Those whom God wishes to destroy, he first makes mad.

Euripides (c. 480–406 BC) Greek dramatist. *Fragment*

14 It is his reasonable conversation which mostly frightens us in a madman.

Anatole France (Jacques Anatole François Thibault; 1844–1924) French writer.

15 Madness is part of all of us, all the time, and it comes and goes, waxes and wanes.

Otto Friedrich

16 What is madness
To those who only observe, is often wisdom
To those to whom it happens.

Christopher Fry (1907–) British dramatist. *A Phoenix Too Frequent*

17 I saw the best minds of my generation destroyed by madness, starving hysterical naked.

Allen Ginsberg (1926–) US poet. *Howl*

18 The world is so full of simpletons and madmen, that one need not seek them in a madhouse.

Johann Wolfgang von Goethe (1749–1832) German poet, dramatist, and scientist. *Conversations with Goethe*, 17 Mar 1830 (Johann Peter Eckermann)

19 With lack of sleep and too much understanding I grow a little crazy, I think, like all men at sea who live too close to each other and too close thereby to all that is monstrous under the sun and moon.

William Golding (1911–93) British novelist. *Rites of Passage*, '&'

20 Insanity is a kind of innocence.

Graham Greene (1904–91) British novelist. *The Quiet American*, Ch. 3, Pt. 2

21 Ordinarily he is insane, but he has lucid moments when he is only stupid.

Heinrich Heine (1797–1856) German poet and writer. Comment about Savoye, appointed ambassador to Frankfurt by Lamartine, 1848

22 Insanity is often the logic of an accurate mind overtaxed.

Oliver Wendell Holmes (1809–94) US writer and physician.

23 Show me a sane man and I will cure him for you.

Carl Gustav Jung (1875–1961) Swiss psychoanalyst. *The Observer*, 19 July 1975

24 Every one is more or less mad on one point.

Rudyard Kipling (1865–1936) Indian-born British writer. *Plain Tales from the Hills*, 'On the Strength of a Likeness'

25 Madness need not be all breakdown. It may also be break-through. It is potential liberation and renewal as well as enslavement and existential death.

R. D. Laing (1927–89) British psychiatrist. *The Politics of Experience*, Ch. 16

26 The world is becoming like a lunatic asylum run by lunatics.

David Lloyd George (1863–1945) British Liberal statesman. *The Observer*, 'Sayings of Our Times', 31 May 1953

27 Insanity is hereditary – you can get it from your children.

Sam Levinson

28 The great proof of madness is the disproportion of one's designs to one's means.

Napoleon I (Napoleon Bonaparte; 1769–1821) French emperor. *Maxims*

29 Insanity in individuals is something rare – but in groups, parties, nations, and epochs it is the rule.

Friedrich Nietzsche (1844–1900) German philosopher. *Beyond Good and Evil*, Ch. 4

30 Men are so necessarily mad, that not to be mad would amount to another form of madness.

Blaise Pascal (1623–62) French philosopher and mathematician. *Pensées*, 414

31 His father's sister had bats in the belfry and was put away.

Eden Phillpotts (1862–1960) British novelist and dramatist. *Peacock House*, 'My First Murder'

32 A body seriously out of equilibrium, either with itself or with its environment, perishes outright. Not so a mind. Madness and suffering can set themselves no limit.

George Santayana (1863–1952) US philosopher. *The Life of Reason: Reason in Common Sense*, 2

33 Sanity is madness put to good uses; waking life is a dream controlled.

George Santayana (1863–1952) US philosopher and poet.

34 Our occasional madness is less wonderful than our occasional sanity.

George Santayana *Interpretations of Poetry and Religion*

35 I am but mad north-north-west. When the wind is southerly I know a hawk from a handsaw.

William Shakespeare (1564–1616) English dramatist. *Hamlet*, II:2

36 Though this be madness, yet there is method in't.

William Shakespeare *Hamlet*, II:2

37 Madness in great ones must not unwatch'd go.

William Shakespeare *Hamlet*, III:1

38 O, let me not be mad, not mad, sweet heaven!
Keep me in temper; I would not be mad!

William Shakespeare *King Lear*, I:5

39 MACBETH. Canst thou not minister to a mind diseas'd,
Pluck from the memory a rooted sorrow,
Raze out the written troubles of the brain,
And with some sweet oblivious antidote
Cleanse the stuff'd bosom of that perilous stuff
Which weighs upon the heart?
DOCTOR. Therein the patient
Must minister to himself.
MACBETH. Throw physic to the dogs,
I'll none of it!

William Shakespeare *Macbeth*, V:3

40 We want a few mad people now. See where the sane ones have landed us!

George Bernard Shaw (1856–1950) Irish dramatist and critic. *Saint Joan*

41 The madman thinks the rest of the world crazy.

Publilius Syrus (1st century BC) Roman dramatist. *Moral Sayings*, 386

42 Whom Fortune wishes to destroy she first makes mad.

Publilius Syrus *Moral Sayings*, 911

43 If you talk to God, you are praying; if God talks to you, you have schizophrenia. If the dead talk to you, you are a spiritualist; if God talks to you, you are a schizophrenic.

Thomas Szasz (1920–) US psychiatrist. *The Second Sin*

44 When we remember that we are all mad, the mysteries disappear and life stands explained.

Mark Twain (Samuel Longhorne Clemens; 1835–1910) US writer.

45 The way it is now, the asylums can hold the sane people, but if we tried to shut up the insane we should run out of building materials.

Mark Twain *Bartlett's Unfamiliar Quotations* (Leonard Louis Levinson)

46 Men will always be mad and those who think they can cure them are the maddest of all.

Voltaire (François-Marie Arouet; 1694–1778) French writer. Letter, 1762

47 What is madness? To have erroneous perceptions and to reason correctly from them.

Voltaire *Philosophical Dictionary*, 'Madness'

48 I shudder and I sigh to think
That even Cicero
And many-minded Homer were
Mad as the mist and snow.

W. B. Yeats (1865–1939) Irish poet. *Mad as the Mist and Snow*

MAJOR, JOHN

(1943–) British politician. He became prime minister in 1990 following the resignation of Margaret Thatcher. He entered parliament in 1979 and served as minister for social security (1986–87), chief secretary to the Treasury (1987–89), foreign secretary (July–Oct 1989), and chancellor of the exchequer (1989–90).

Quotations about Major

1 All Tories are monsters. John Major is charming. Therefore John Major isn't a Tory.

Ken Livingstone (1945–) British Labour politician. Referring to his experience of Major as chairman of Lambeth housing committee.

2 The only man who has ever run away from the circus to become an accountant.

Anonymous Referring to John Major's background – his father had once been a trapeze artist.

3 He is another one of us.

Margaret Thatcher (1925–) British politician and prime minister. After Major's success in the leadership election.

4 I don't accept that all of a sudden Major is his own man.

Margaret Thatcher On his re-election as prime minister in 1992.

Quotations by Major

5 If it's not hurting, it's not working.

Defending high interest rates when chancellor. Speech, Oct 1990

6 Well, who would have thought it?

At his first cabinet meeting as prime minister. Remark, 1990

7 I've got it, I like it, and with your help I'm going to keep it.

Speech, Conservative party conference, 1991

8 I'm feeling lucky.

Referring to the imminent British general election. *The Times*, 9 Apr 1992

9 You can think of ex-Ministers who are going around causing all sorts of trouble. We don't want another three more of the bastards out there.

Remark made after a television interview, when he thought that recording had stopped. *The Times*, 26 July 1993

10 I could name eight people. Half of those eight people are barmy. How many apples short of a picnic?

Referring to backbenchers who opposed him on Europe. Press conference, Tokyo, 20 Sept 1993

11 It is time to get back to basics: to self-discipline and respect for the law, to consideration for others, to accepting responsibility for yourself and your family, and not shuffling it off on the state.

Speech, Conservative party conference, Blackpool, 8 Oct 1993

MAJORITY

See also democracy, minority, public

1 The one pervading evil of democracy is the tyranny of the majority.

Lord Acton (1834–1902) British historian. *The History of Freedom*

2 When great changes occur in history, when great principles are involved, as a rule the majority are wrong.

Eugene V. Debs (1855–1926) US socialist, pacifist, and labor unionist. Speech, 12 Aug 1918

3 'It's always best on these occasions to do what the mob do.'
'But suppose there are two mobs?' suggested Mr Snodgrass.
'Shout with the largest,' replied Mr Pickwick.

Charles Dickens (1812–70) British novelist. *Pickwick Papers*, Ch. 13

4 A majority is always the best repartee.

Benjamin Disraeli (1804–81) British statesman. *Tancred*, Bk. II, Ch. 14

5 The majority has the might – more's the pity – but it hasn't right...The minority is always right.

Henrik Ibsen (1828–1906) Norwegian dramatist. *An Enemy of the People*, IV

6 The worst enemy of truth and freedom in our society is the compact majority. Yes, the damned, compact, liberal majority.

Henrik Ibsen *An Enemy of the People*, IV

7 It is time for the great silent majority of Americans to stand up and be counted.

Richard Milhous Nixon (1913–94) US president. Election speech, Oct 1970

MALAPROPISMS

Remarks of a type associated with Mrs Malaprop in Sheridan's play *The Rivals*.

1 Our watch, sir, have indeed comprehended two aspicious persons.

William Shakespeare (1564–1616) English dramatist. *Much Ado About Nothing*, III:5

2 Comparisons are odorous.

William Shakespeare *Much Ado About Nothing*, III:5

3 A progeny of learning.

Richard Brinsley Sheridan (1751–1816) British dramatist. *The Rivals*, I

4 Illiterate him, I say, quite from your memory.

Richard Brinsley Sheridan *The Rivals*, II

5 It gives me the hydrostatics to such a degree.

Richard Brinsley Sheridan *The Rivals*, III

6 As headstrong as an allegory on the banks of the Nile.

Richard Brinsley Sheridan *The Rivals*, III

7 He is the very pine-apple of politeness!

Richard Brinsley Sheridan *The Rivals*, III

8 If I reprehend any thing in this world, it is the use of my oracular tongue, and a nice derangement of epitaphs!

Richard Brinsley Sheridan *The Rivals*, III

MALORY, SIR THOMAS

(?1400–71) English writer. Probably a Warwickshire knight and MP, he is remembered as the author of *Morte d'Arthur*, an account of the legendary court of King Arthur, based on French sources.

1 Whoso pulleth out this sword of this stone and anvil is
rightwise King born of all England.

Morte d'Arthur, Bk. I, Ch. 4

2 For, as I suppose, no man in this world hath lived better than I have done, to achieve that I have done.

Morte d'Arthur, Bk. XVII, Ch. 16

3 For love that time was not as love is nowadays.

Morte d'Arthur, Bk. XX, Ch. 3

4 And much more am I sorrier for my good knights' loss than for the loss of my fair queen; for queens I might have enough, but such a fellowship of good knights shall never be together in no company.

Morte d'Arthur, Bk. XX, Ch. 9

5 Then Sir Launcelot saw her visage, but he wept not greatly, but sighed!

Morte d'Arthur, Bk. XXI, Ch. 11

MANDELA, NELSON

(1918–) Black South African lawyer and statesman. An active member of the African National Congress, he was charged with treason, acquitted in 1961, retried in 1963–64, and sentenced to life imprisonment. He was released in 1990 after an international campaign and travelled widely as deputy president of the ANC. He became president of South Africa in 1994.

Quotations about Mandela

1 Mr Mandela has walked a long road and now stands at the top of the hill. A traveller would sit down and admire the view. But a man of destiny knows that beyond this hill lies another and another.

F. W. de Klerk (1936–) South African statesman. Speech, 2 May 1994

Quotations by Mandela

2 I have fought against white domination, and I have fought against black domination. I have cherished the ideal of a democratic and free society in which all persons will live together in harmony and with equal opportunities. It is an ideal which I hope to live for and achieve. But, if needs be, it is an ideal for which I am prepared to die.

Speech from the dock, 20 Apr 1964 The closing words of his defence statement.

3 The soil of our country is destined to be the scene of the fiercest fight and the sharpest struggles to rid our continent of the last vestiges of white minority rule.

The Observer, 'Sayings of the Eighties', 15 June 1980

4 I cannot and will not give any undertaking at a time when I, and you, the people, are not free. Your freedom and mine cannot be separated.

Message read by his daughter to a rally in Soweto, 10 Feb 1985

5 Only free men can negotiate; prisoners cannot enter into contracts.

Statement from prison, 10 Feb 1985 Replying to an offer to release him if he renounced violence.

6 It indicates the deadly weight of the terrible tradition of a dialogue between master and servant which we have to overcome.

Referring to the first meeting between the government and the

ANC. *The Independent*, 5 May 1990 @Quote:7 We stand for majority rule, we don't stand for black majority rule.
Speech, 24 Apr 1994

8 Years of imprisonment could not stamp out our determination to be free. Years of intimidation and violence could not stop us. And we will not be stopped now.
Press conference, 26 Apr 1994

9 My fellow South Africans, today we are entering a new era for our country and its people. Today we celebrate not the victory of a party, but a victory for all the people of South Africa.
Speech, Cape Town, 9 May 1994 Following his election to the presidency.

10 Let there be work, bread, water and salt for all.
The Observer, 'Sayings of the Week', 15 May 1994

MANKIND

See also evolution, human condition, human nature, men, misanthropy, philanthropy, public, society, women

1 Pray consider what a figure a man would make in the republic of letters.
Joseph Addison (1672–1719) British essayist. *Ancient Medals*

2 I am a human being: Do not fold, spindle or mutilate.
Anonymous Hippy slogan

3 Either a beast or a god.
Aristotle (384–322 BC) Greek philosopher. *Politics*, Bk. I

4 Man, when perfected, is the best of animals, but, when separated from law and justice, he is the worst of all.
Aristotle *Politics*, Bk. I

5 Whatever this is that I am, it is a little flesh and breath, and the ruling part.
Marcus Aurelius (121–180 AD) Roman emperor. *Meditations*, Bk. II, Ch. 2

6 Is a man a salvage at heart, skinned o'er with fragile Manners? Or is salvagery but a faint taint in the natural man's gentility, which erupts now and again like pimples on an angel's arse?
John Barth (1930–) US novelist and academic. *The Sot-Weed Factor*, 3

7 Drinking when we are not thirsty and making love all year round, madam; that is all there is to distinguish us from other animals.
Beaumarchais (1732–99) French dramatist. *Le Mariage de Figaro*, II:21

8 And God said, Let us make man in our image, after our likeness: and let them have dominion over the fish of the sea, and over the fowl of the air, and over the cattle, and over all the earth, and over every creeping thing that creepeth upon the earth. So God created man in his own image, in the image of God created he him; male and female created he them.
And God blessed them, and God said unto them, Be fruitful, and multiply, and replenish the earth, and subdue it: and have dominion over the fish of the sea, and over the fowl of the air, and over every living thing that moveth upon the earth.
Bible: Genesis 1:26–28

9 MAN, n. An animal so lost in rapturous contemplation of what he thinks he is as to overlook what he indubitably ought to be.
Ambrose Bierce (1842–c. 1914) US writer and journalist. *The Devil's Dictionary*

10 For Mercy has a human heart,
Pity a human face,
And Love, the human form divine,
And Peace, the human dress.
William Blake (1757–1827) British poet. *Songs of Innocence*, 'The Divine Image'

11 What is man, when you come to think upon him, but a minutely set, ingenious machine for turning, with infinite artfulness, the red wine of Shiraz into urine?
Karen Blixen (Isak Dinesen; 1885–1962) Danish writer. *Seven Gothic Tales*, 'The Dreamers'

12 Every animal leaves traces of what it was; man alone leaves traces of what he created.
Jacob Bronowski (1908–74) British scientist and writer. *The Ascent of Man*, Ch. 1

13 Man is a noble animal, splendid in ashes, and pompous in the grave.
Thomas Browne (1605–82) English physician and writer. *Urn Burial*, Ch. 5

14 There is surely a piece of divinity in us, something that was before the elements, and owes no homage unto the sun.
Thomas Browne *Religio Medici*

15 A single sentence will suffice for modern man: he fornicated and read the papers.
Albert Camus (1913–60) French existentialist writer. *The Fall*

16 The true science and the true study of man is man.
Pierre Charron (1541–1603) French theologian and philosopher. *Traité de la sagesse*, Bk. I, Ch. 1

17 Man is an exception, whatever else he is. If he is not the image of God, then he is a disease of the dust.
G. K. Chesterton (1874–1936) British writer. *All Things Considered*, 'Wine When It Is Red'

18 Carlyle said that men were mostly fools. Christianity, with a surer and more reverend realism, says that they are all fools.
G. K. Chesterton *Heretics*, Ch. 12

19 Individually, men may present a more or less rational appearance, eating, sleeping and scheming. But humanity as a whole is changeful, mystical, fickle and delightful. Men are men, but Man is a woman.
G. K. Chesterton *The Napoleon of Notting Hill*

20 Mankind is not a tribe of animals to which we owe compassion. Mankind is a club to which we owe our subscription.
G. K. Chesterton *Daily News*, 10 Apr 1906

21 The evolution of the human race will not be accomplished in the ten thousand years of tame animals, but in the million years of wild animals, because man is and will always be a wild animal.
Charles Darwin (1887–1962) British life scientist. *The Next Ten Million Years*, Ch. 4

22 A wonderful fact to reflect upon, that every human creature is constituted to be that profound secret and mystery to every other.

Charles Dickens (1812–70) British novelist. *A Tale of Two Cities*, 1

23 What is man, when you come to think upon him, but a minutely set, ingenious machine for turning, with infinite artfulness, the red wine of Shiraz into urine.

Isak Dinesen (1885–1962) Danish writer. *Seven Gothic Tales, The Dreamers*

24 Any man's death diminishes me, because I am involved in Mankind; And therefore never send to know for whom the bell tolls; it tolls for thee.

John Donne (1573–1631) English poet. *Devotions*, 17

25 It's a burden to us even to be human beings – men with our own real body and blood; we are ashamed of it, we think it a disgrace and try to contrive to be some sort of impossible generalized man.

Fyodor Mikhailovich Dostoevsky (1821–81) Russian writer. *Notes from Underground*, 2

26 Man is physically as well as metaphysically a thing of shreds and patches, borrowed unequally from good and bad ancestors, and a misfit from the start.

Ralph Waldo Emerson (1803–82) US poet and essayist. *The Conduct of Life*, 'Beauty'

27 Every man has a wild beast within him.

Frederick the Great (1712–86) Prussian king. *Letter to Voltaire*, 1759

28 Man is Nature's sole mistake.

W. S. Gilbert (1836–1911) British dramatist. *Princess Ida*, I

29 Human beings are like timid punctuation marks sprinkled among the incomprehensible sentences of life.

Jean Giraudoux (1882–1944) French dramatist and writer. *Siegfried*, 2

30 On earth there is nothing great but man; in man there is nothing great but mind.

William Hamilton (1788–1856) Scottish philosopher. *Lectures on Metaphysics*

31 The human race will be the cancer of the planet.

Julian Huxley (1887–1975) British biologist.

32 Man as we know him is a poor creature; but he is halfway between an ape and a god and he is travelling in the right direction.

W. R. Inge (1860–1954) British clergyman. *Outspoken Essays: Second Series*, 'Confessio Fidei'

33 There are only two classes of mankind in the world – doctors and patients.

Rudyard Kipling (1865–1936) Indian-born British writer and poet. *A Doctor's Work*, address to medical students at London's Middlesex Hospital, 1 Oct 1908

34 The majority of men devote the greater part of their lives to making their remaining years unhappy.

Jean de La Bruyère (1645–96) French satirist. *Les Caractères*

35 The anthropologist respects history, but he does not accord it a special value. He conceives it as a study complementary to his own: one of them unfurls the range of human societies in time, the other in space.

Claude Lévi-Strauss (1908–) French anthropologist. *The Savage Mind*

36 Man appears to be the missing link between anthropoid apes and human beings.

Konrad Lorenz (1903–89) Austrian zoologist and pioneer of ethology. *The New York Times Magazine*, 11 Apr 1965 (John Pfeiffer)

37 I'll give you my opinion of the human race... Their heart's in the right place, but their head is a thoroughly inefficient organ.

W. Somerset Maugham (1874–1965) British novelist. *The Summing Up*

38 Man is a beautiful machine that works very badly. He is like a watch of which the most that can be said is that its cosmetic effect is good.

H. L. Mencken (1880–1956) US journalist and editor. *Minority Report*, 20

39 A human being, he wrote, is a whispering in the steam pipes on a cold night; dust sifted through a locked window; one or the other half of an unsolved equation; a pun made by God; an ingenious assembly of portable plumbing.

Christopher Morley (1890–1957) US writer and journalist. *Human Being*, Ch. 11

40 A human being is an ingenious assembly of portable plumbing.

Robert Morley (1908–92) British actor. *Human Being*

41 Clearly, then, the city is not a concrete jungle, it is a human zoo.

Desmond Morris (1928–) British biologist and writer. *The Human Zoo*, Introduction

42 There are one hundred and ninety-three living species of monkeys and apes. One hundred and ninety-two of them are covered with hair. The exception is a naked ape self-named *Homo sapiens*.

Desmond Morris *The Naked Ape*, Introduction

43 He is proud that he has the biggest brain of all the primates, but attempts to conceal the fact that he also has the biggest penis.

Desmond Morris *The Naked Ape*, Introduction

44 Man's the bad child of the universe.

James Oppenheim *Laughter*

45 Man, as he is, is not a genuine article. He is an imitation of something, and a very bad imitation.

P. D. Ouspensky (1878–1947) Russian-born occultist. *The Psychology of Man's Possible Evolution*, Ch. 2

46 The proper study of Mankind is Man.

Alexander Pope (1688–1744) English poet. *An Essay on Man*, Epistle II

47 The human face is indeed, like the face of the God of some Oriental theogony, a whole cluster of faces, crowded together but on different surfaces so that one does not see them all at once.

Marcel Proust (1871–1922) French novelist. *À La Recherche du temps perdu: À l'ombre des jeunes filles en fleurs*

48 Man is Heaven's masterpiece.

Francis Quarles (1592–1644) English writer. *Emblems*, Bk. II

49 I wish I loved the Human Race;

I wish I loved its silly face;
I wish I liked the way it walks;
I wish I liked the way it talks;
And when I'm introduced to one
I wish I thought *What Jolly Fun!*

Walter Raleigh (1861–1922) British scholar. *Laughter from a Cloud*, 'Wishes of an Elderly Man'

50 Everything is good when it leaves the Creator's hands; everything degenerates in the hands of man.

Jean Jacques Rousseau (1712–78) French philosopher. Attrib.

51 Man is not a solitary animal, and so long as social life survives, self-realization cannot be the supreme principle of ethics.

Bertrand Russell (1872–1970) British philosopher. *History of Western Philosophy*, 'Romanticism'

52 The mass of mankind is divided into two classes, the Sancho Panzas who have a sense for reality, but no ideals, and the Don Quixotes with a sense for ideals, but mad.

George Santayana (1863–1952) Spanish-born US philosopher, poet, and critic. *Interpretations of Poetry and Religion*, Preface

53 Doctors, priests, magistrates, and officers know men as thoroughly as if they had made them.

Jean-Paul Sartre (1905–80) French philosopher, dramatist, and novelist. *Nausea*, 'Shrove Tuesday'

54 I love mankind – it's people I can't stand.

Charles M. Schultz (1922–) US cartoonist. *Go Fly a Kite, Charlie Brown*

55 After all, for mankind as a whole there are no exports. We did not start developing by obtaining foreign exchange from Mars or the moon. Mankind is a closed society.

E. F. Schumacher (1911–77) German-born economist. *Small is Beautiful, A Study of Economics as if People Mattered*, Ch. 14

56 What a piece of work is a man! How noble in reason! how infinite in faculties! in form and moving, how express and admirable! in action, how like an angel! in apprehension, how like a god! the beauty of the world! the paragon of animals! And yet, to me, what is this quintessence of dust? Man delights not me – no, nor woman neither.

William Shakespeare (1564–1616) English dramatist. *Hamlet*, II:2

57 But man, proud man
Dress'd in a little brief authority,
Most ignorant of what he's most assur'd,
His glassy essence, like an angry ape,
Plays such fantastic tricks before high heaven
As makes the angels weep.

William Shakespeare *Measure for Measure*, II:2

58 How beauteous mankind is! O brave new world
That has such people in't!

William Shakespeare *The Tempest*, V:1

59 You fools of fortune, trencher-friends, time's flies.

William Shakespeare *Timon of Athens*, III:6

60 Physically there is nothing to distinguish human society from the farm-yard except that children are more troublesome and costly than chickens and women are not so completely enslaved as farm stock.

George Bernard Shaw (1856–1950) Irish dramatist and critic. *Getting Married*, Preface

61 Man, unlike any other thing organic or inorganic in the universe, grows beyond his work, walks up the stairs of his concepts, emerges ahead of his accomplishments.

John Steinbeck (1902–68) US novelist. *The Grapes of Wrath*, Ch. 14

62 Glory to Man in the highest! for Man is the master of things.

Algernon Charles Swinburne (1837–1909) British poet. *Hymn of Man*

63 The fish in the water is silent, the animal on the earth is noisy, the bird in the air is singing.
But Man has in him the silence of the sea, the noise of the earth and the music of the air.

Rabindranath Tagore (1861–1941) Indian poet and philosopher. *Stray Birds*, 43

64 I am a man, I count nothing human foreign to me.

Terence (Publius Terentius Afer; c. 190–159 BC) Roman poet. *Heauton Timorumenos*

65 …he willed that the hearts of Men should seek beyond the world and should find no rest therein; but they should have a virtue to shape their life, amid the powers and chances of the world.

J. R. R. Tolkien (1892–1973) British writer. 'He' is Ilúvatar, the Creator. *The Silmarillion*, Ch. 1

66 The highest wisdom has but one science – the science of the whole – the science explaining the whole creation and man's place in it.

Leo Tolstoy (1828–1910) Russian writer. *War and Peace*, Bk.V, Ch. 2

67 Man is a museum of diseases, a home of impurities; he comes today and is gone tomorrow; he begins as dirt and departs as stench.

Mark Twain (Samuel L. Clemens; 1835–1910) US writer.

68 The noblest work of God? Man. Who found it out? Man.

Mark Twain *Autobiography*

69 We should expect the best and the worst from mankind, as from the weather.

Marquis de Luc de Clapiers Vauvenargues (1715–47) French moralist. *Reflections and Maxims*, 102

70 One thousand years more. That's all *Homo sapiens* has before him.

H. G. Wells (1866–1946) British writer. *Diary* (Harold Nicolson)

71 If anything is sacred the human body is sacred.

Walt Whitman (1819–92) US poet. *I Sing the Body Electric*, 8

72 But there comes a moment in everybody's life when he must decide whether he'll live among human beings or not – a fool among fools or a fool alone.

Thornton Wilder (1897–1975) US novelist and dramatist. *The Matchmaker*, IV

73 We're all of us guinea pigs in the laboratory of God. Humanity is just a work in progress.

Tennessee Williams (1911–83) US dramatist. *Camino Real*, 12

74 If this belief from heaven be sent,
If such be Nature's holy plan,
Have I not reason to lament
What man has made of man?

William Wordsworth (1770–1850) British poet. *Lines written in Early Spring*

MANNERS

See also courtesy, etiquette

1 Leave off first for manners' sake: and be not unsatiable, lest thou offend.
Bible: Ecclesiasticus 31:17

2 'Speak when you're spoken to!' the Red Queen sharply interrupted her.
Lewis Carroll (Charles Lutwidge Dodgson; 1832–98) British writer. *Through the Looking-Glass*, Ch. 9

3 Don't tell your friends about your indigestion: 'How are you!' is a greeting, not a question.
Arthur Guiterman *A Poet's Proverbs*, 'Of Tact'

4 To Americans English manners are far more frightening than none at all.
Randall Jarrell (1914–65) US author. *Pictures from an Institution*, Pt. I, Ch. 5

5 On the Continent people have good food; in England people have good table manners.
George Mikes (1912–87) Hungarian-born British writer. *How to be an Alien*

6 Good breeding consists in concealing how much we think of ourselves and how little we think of other persons.
Mark Twain (Samuel Langhorne Clemens; 1835–1910) US writer. *Notebooks*

7 Politeness is organised indifference.
Paul Valéry (1871–1945) French poet and writer. *Tel Quel*

8 Manners are especially the need of the plain. The pretty can get away with anything.
Evelyn Waugh (1903–66) British novelist. *The Observer*, 'Sayings of the Year,' 1962

9 Manners maketh man.
William of Wykeham (1324–1404) English churchman. Motto of Winchester College and New College, Oxford

MAO TSE-TUNG

(1893–1976) Chinese communist leader. As chairman of the Communist Party, in 1949 he proclaimed the People's Republic of China and in 1966–68 launched the Cultural Revolution. He developed the form of communism known as Maoism.

Quotations about Mao Tse-Tung

1 No Chinese thinker in the period since Confucius has attained the degree of acceptance and authority which Mao has acquired.
C. P. Fitzgerald *Mao Tse-Tung and China*

2 He dominated the room as I have never seen any person do except Charles de Gaulle.
Henry Kissinger (1923–) German-born US politician and diplomat. *Memoirs*

Quotations by Mao Tse-Tung

3 'War is the continuation of politics'. In this sense war is politics and war itself is a political action.
See also CHOU EN-LAI; CLAUSEWITZ. *Quotations from Chairman Mao Tse-Tung*, Ch. 5

4 We are advocates of the abolition of war, we do not want war; but war can only be abolished through war, and in order to get rid of the gun it is necessary to take up the gun.
Quotations from Chairman Mao Tse-Tung, Ch. 5

5 All reactionaries are paper tigers.
Quotations from Chairman Mao Tse-Tung, Ch. 6

6 Letting a hundred flowers blossom and a hundred schools of thought contend is the policy for promoting the progress of the arts and the sciences.
Speech, Peking, 27 Feb 1957

7 Every Communist must grasp the truth, 'Political power grows out of the barrel of a gun.'
Speech, 6 Nov 1938

8 To read too many books is harmful.
The New Yorker, 7 Mar 1977

9 The atom bomb is a paper tiger which the United States reactionaries use to scare people.
Interview, Aug 1946

10 The government burns down whole cities while the people are forbidden to light lamps.
Attrib.

MARCUS AURELIUS ANTONINUS

(121–180 AD) Roman emperor (161–180). He is remembered for his *Meditations*, 12 books of Stoic aphorisms.

1 Whatever this is that I am, it is a little flesh and breath, and the ruling part.
Meditations, Bk. II, Ch. 2

2 And thou wilt give thyself relief, if thou doest every act of thy life as if it were the last.
Meditations, Bk. II, Ch. 5

3 Remember that no man loses any other life than this which he now lives, nor lives any other than this which he now loses.
Meditations, Bk. II, Ch. 14

4 All things from eternity are of like forms and come round in a circle.
Meditations, Bk. II, Ch. 14

5 The universe is transformation; our life is what our thoughts make it.
Meditations, Bk. IV, Ch. 3

6 Everything that happens happens as it should, and if you observe carefully, you will find this to be so.
Meditations, Bk. IV, Ch. 10

7 Everything is only for a day, both that which remembers and that which is remembered.
Meditations, Bk. IV, Ch. 35

8 Time is like a river made up of the events which happen, and its current is strong; no sooner does anything appear than it is swept away, and another comes in its place, and will be swept away too.

Meditations, Bk. IV, Ch. 43

9 Nothing happens to any man that he is not formed by nature to bear.

Meditations, Bk. V, Ch. 18

10 Live with the gods. And he does so who constantly shows them that his soul is satisfied with what is assigned to him.

Meditations, Bk. V, Ch. 27

11 Remember that to change your mind and follow him who sets you right is to be none the less free than you were before.

Meditations, Bk. VIII, Ch. 16

12 Whatever may happen to you was prepared for you from all eternity; and the implication of causes was from eternity spinning the thread of your being.

Meditations, Bk. X, Ch. 5

MARLOWE, CHRISTOPHER

(1564–93) English dramatist and poet. His plays include *Tamburlaine the Great* (1587), *The Jew of Malta* (1590), *Doctor Faustus* (c. 1592), and *Edward II* (1592). He was killed in a fight in a Deptford tavern.

1 When all the world dissolves,
And every creature shall be purified,
All place shall be hell that is not heaven.

Doctor Faustus, II:1

2 Was this the face that launch'd a thousand ships
And burnt the topless towers of Ilium?
Sweet Helen, make me immortal with a kiss.

Doctor Faustus, V:1

3 Oh, thou art fairer than the evening air
Clad in the beauty of a thousand stars.

Doctor Faustus, V:1

4 Now hast thou but one bare hour to live,
And then thou must be damn'd perpetually!
Stand still, you ever-moving spheres of heaven,
That time may cease, and midnight never come.

Doctor Faustus, V:2

5 Ugly hell, gape not! come not, Lucifer!
I'll burn my books!

Doctor Faustus, V:2

6 Cut is the branch that might have grown full straight,
And burned is Apollo's laurel-bough,
That sometime grew within this learned man.

Doctor Faustus, Epilogue

7 My men, like satyrs grazing on the lawns,
Shall with their goat-feet dance an antic hay.

Edward II, I:1

8 Who ever loved, that loved not at first sight?

Hero and Leander, I

9 I count religion but a childish toy,
And hold there is no sin but ignorance.

The Jew of Malta, Prologue

10 And, as their wealth increaseth, so enclose
Infinite riches in a little room.

The Jew of Malta, I:1

11 FRIAR BARNARDINE. Thou hast committed –
BARABAS. Fornication: but that was in another country;
And beside the wench is dead.

The Jew of Malta, IV:1

12 I'm arm'd with more than complete steel –
The justice of my quarrel.

Play also attributed to others. *Lust's Dominion*, IV:3

13 Come live with me, and be my love;
And we will all the pleasures prove
That valleys, groves, hills and fields,
Woods or steepy mountain yields.

The Passionate Shepherd to his Love

14 And I will make thee beds of roses
And a thousand fragrant posies.

The Passionate Shepherd to his Love

MARRIAGE

See also adultery, family, love and marriage, unfaithfulness

1 Better be an old man's darling than a young man's slave.

Proverb

2 Marriages are made in heaven.

Proverb

3 Marry in haste, and repent at leisure.

Proverb

4 Marry in Lent, and you'll live to repent.

Proverb

5 Marry in May, rue for aye.

Proverb

6 The first wife is matrimony, the second company, the third heresy.

Proverb

7 I had vaguely supposed that marriage in a registry office, while lacking both sanctity and style, was at least a swift, straightforward business. If not, then what was the use of it, even to the heathen? A few inquiries, however, showed it to be no such thing.

Richard Adams (1920–) British novelist. *The Girl in a Swing*, Ch. 13

8 EGGHEAD WEDS HOURGLASS.

Anonymous On marriage of playwright Arthur Miller to Marilyn Monroe. *Variety*, headline 1956

9 To marry a man out of pity is folly; and, if you think you are going to influence the kind of fellow who has 'never had a chance, poor devil,' you are profoundly mistaken. One can only influence the strong characters in life, not the weak; and it is the height of vanity to suppose that you can make an honest man of anyone.

Margot Asquith (1865–1945) The second wife of Herbert Asquith. *The Autobiography of Margot Asquith*, Ch. 6

10 I married beneath me – all women do.

Nancy Astor (1879–1964) American-born British politician. *Dictionary of National Biography*

11 It is a truth universally acknowledged, that a

single man in possession of a good fortune must be in want of a wife.

Jane Austen (1775–1817) British novelist. The opening words of the book. *Pride and Prejudice*, Ch. 1

12 Happiness in marriage is entirely a matter of chance.

Jane Austen *Pride and Prejudice*, Ch. 6

13 Mrs Hall of Sherbourne was brought to bed yesterday of a dead child, some weeks before she expected, owing to a fright. I suppose she happened unawares to look at her husband.

Jane Austen Letter, 27 Oct 1798

14 Wives are young men's mistresses, companions for middle age, and old men's nurses.

Francis Bacon (1561–1626) English philosopher. *Essays*, 'Of Marriage and Single Life'

15 He was reputed one of the wise men, that made answer to the question, when a man should marry? A young man not yet, an elder man not at all.

Francis Bacon *Essays*, 'Of Marriage and Single Life'

16 I rather think of having a career of my own.

Arthur Balfour (1848–1930) British statesman. When asked whether he was going to marry Margot Tennant. *Autobiography* (Margot Asquith), Ch. 9

17 It is easier to be a lover than a husband, for the same reason that it is more difficult to show a ready wit all day long than to produce an occasional *bon mot*.

Honoré de Balzac (1799–1850) French novelist. Attrib.

18 The majority of husbands remind me of an orangutang trying to play the violin.

Honoré de Balzac *La Physiologie du mariage*

19 No man should marry until he has studied anatomy and dissected at least one woman.

Honoré de Balzac *La Physiologie du mariage*

20 My father argued sair – my mother didna speak,
But she looked in my face till my heart was like to break;
They gied him my hand but my heart was in the sea;
And so auld Robin Gray, he was gudeman to me.

Lady Ann Barnard (1750–1825) British poet. *Auld Robin Gray*

21 Maybe today's successful marriage is when a man is in love with his wife and only one other woman.

Matt Basile US private detective. *The Observer*, 'Sayings of the Week', 31 Aug 1975

22 I don't like your Christian name. I'd like to change it.

Thomas Beecham ((1879–1961) British conductor. To his future wife. She replied, 'You can't, but you can change my surname.' Attrib.

23 I think weddings is sadder than funerals, because they remind you of your own wedding. You can't be reminded of your own funeral because it hasn't happened. But weddings always make me cry.

Brendan Behan (1923–64) Irish playwright. *Richard's Cork Leg*, I

24 Being a husband is a whole-time job. That is why so many husbands fail. They cannot give their entire attention to it.

Arnold Bennett (1867–1931) British novelist. *The Title*, I

25 Husbands, love your wives, and be not bitter against them.

Bible: Colossians 3:19

26 Let the husband render unto the wife due benevolence: and likewise also the wife unto the husband.

Bible: I Corinthians 7:3

27 But if they cannot contain, let them marry: for it is better to marry than to burn.

Bible: I Corinthians 7:9

28 But he that is married careth for the things that are of the world, how he may please his wife.

Bible: I Corinthians 7:33

29 And the Lord God said, It is not good that the man should be alone; I will make him an help meet for him.

Bible: Genesis 2:18

30 Wherefore they are no more twain, but one flesh. What therefore God hath joined together, let not man put asunder.

Bible: Matthew 19:6

31 Even as Sara obeyed Abraham, calling him lord: whose daughters ye are, as long as ye do well, and are not afraid with any amazement.
Likewise, ye husbands, dwell with them according to knowledge, giving honour unto the wife, as unto the weaker vessel, and as being heirs together of the grace of life; that your prayers be not hindered.

Bible: I Peter 3:6–7

32 MARRIAGE, n. The state or condition of a community consisting of a master, a mistress and two slaves, making in all two.

Ambrose Bierce (1842–c. 1914) US writer and journalist. *The Devil's Dictionary*

33 To have and to hold from this day forward, for better for worse, for richer for poorer, in sickness and in health, to love and to cherish, till death us do part.

The Book of Common Prayer *Solemnization of Matrimony*

34 Splendid couple – slept with both of them.

Maurice Bowra (1898–1971) British academic. Referring to a well-known literary couple. Attrib.

35 'We stay together, but we distrust one another.'
'Ah, yes...but isn't that a definition of marriage?'

Malcolm Bradbury (1932–) British academic and novelist. *The History Man*, Ch. 3

36 Most married couples in the end arrive at tolerable arrangements for living – arrangements that may strike others as odd, but which suit them very well.

John Braine (1922–86) British author. Remark, June 1970

37 In a happy marriage it is the wife who provides the climate, the husband the landscape.

Gerald Brenan (1894–1987) British writer. *Thoughts in a Dry Season*

38 Ah, gentle dames! It gars me greet
To think how mony counsels sweet,

How mony lengthen'd sage advices,
The husband frae the wife despises!

Robert Burns (1759–96) Scottish poet. *Tam o' Shanter*

39 It was very good of God to let Carlyle and Mrs Carlyle marry one another and so make only two people miserable instead of four, besides being very amusing.

Samuel Butler (1835–1902) British novelist. Letter to Miss Savage, 21 Nov 1884

40 Marriage is distinctly and repeatedly excluded from heaven. Is this because it is thought likely to mar the general felicity?

Samuel Butler *Notebooks*

41 Wedlock – the deep, deep peace of the double bed after the hurly-burly of the chaise-longue.

Mrs Patrick Campbell (Beatrice Stella Tanner; 1865–1940) British actress. *Jennie* (Ralph G. Martin), Vol. II

42 They call it 'serial monogamy'.

Angela Carter (1940–92) British novelist. *Wise Children*

43 I never doubted I couldn't enter into any marriage that denied me my career. But equally I never doubted that my husband was of very great importance to me. OK, perhaps I could employ someone to iron his shirts, but I wanted to spoil him. He was my man. I'm just saying my femininity is big enough to embrace everything. That's to me the richness of life. I want my man at the other side of it. I don't like aridities.

Barbara Castle (1910–) British politician. *The Guardian*, June 1993.

44 The one advantage about marrying a princess – or someone from a royal family – is that they do know what happens.

Charles, Prince of Wales (1948–) Eldest son of Elizabeth II. Attrib.

45 She was a worthy womman al hir lyve,
Housbondes at chirche-dore she hadde fyve,
Withouten other companye in youthe.

Geoffrey Chaucer (c. 1342–1400) English poet. Referring to the wife of Bath. *The Canterbury Tales*, Prologue

46 An archaeologist is the best husband any woman can have: the older she gets, the more interested he is in her.

Agatha Christie (1891–1976) British detective-story writer. Attrib.

47 He loved me, and 'twas right that he should, for I had come to him as a girl-bride; we two had made such wise provision in all our love that our two hearts were moved in all things, whether of joy or of sorrow, by a common wish, more united in love than the hearts of brother and sister.

Christine de Pisan (c. 1363–c. 1430) Italian poet. *Women of Medieval France* (Pierce Butler)

48 Marriage without love means love without marriage.

Kenneth Clark (1903–83) British art historian. *Civilization*

49 The most happy marriage I can picture or imagine to myself would be the union of a deaf man to a blind woman.

Samuel Taylor Coleridge (1772–1834) British poet. *Recollections* (Allsop)

50 Yang – positive cosmic force, the heavens, man.
Yin – negative cosmic force, earth, woman.

Confucian text. *Tung Chung Shu*

51 SHARPER: Thus grief still treads upon the heels of pleasure:
Marry'd in haste, we may repent at leisure.
SETTER: Some by experience find those words misplac'd:
At leisure marry'd, they repent in haste.

William Congreve (1670–1729) British Restoration dramatist. *The Old Bachelor*, V:8

52 Courtship to marriage, as a very witty prologue to a very dull Play.

William Congreve *The Old Bachelor*, V:10

53 I hope you do not think me prone to any iteration of nuptials.

William Congreve *The Way of the World*, IV:12

54 Marriage is a wonderful invention; but then again so is a bicycle repair kit.

Billy Connolly (1942–) British comedian. *The Authorized Version*

55 Dear Mrs A., hooray hooray,
At last you are deflowered
On this as every other day
I love you. Noël Coward.

Noël Coward (1899–1973) British dramatist. Telegram to Gertrude Lawrence on her marriage to Richard S. Aldrich

56 Says John, It is my wedding-day,
And all the world would stare,
If wife should dine at Edmonton,
And I should dine at Ware.

William Cowper (1731–1800) British poet. *John Gilpin*

57 To-morrow is our wedding-day,
And we will then repair
Unto the Bell at Edmonton,
All in a chaise and pair.

William Cowper *John Gilpin*

58 Daisy, Daisy, give me your answer, do!
I'm half crazy, all for the love of you!
It won't be a stylish marriage,
I can't afford a carriage,
But you'll look sweet upon the seat
Of a bicycle made for two!

Harry Dacre (19th century) British songwriter. *Daisy Bell*

59 If a man stays away from his wife for seven years, the law presumes the separation to have killed him; yet according to our daily experience, it might well prolong his life.

Lord Darling (1849–1936) British judge. *Scintillae Juris*

60 This man, she reasons, as she looks at her husband, is a poor fish. But he is the nearest I can get to the big one that got away.

Nigel Dennis (1912–89) British writer. *Cards of Identity*

61 The value of marriage is not that adults produce children but that children produce adults.

Peter de Vries (1906–93) US writer. *Tunnel of Love*, Ch. 8

62 'Old girl,' said Mr Bagnet, 'give him my opinion. You know it.'

Charles Dickens (1812–70) British novelist. *Bleak House*, Ch. 27

63 Every woman should marry – and no man.

Benjamin Disraeli (1804–81) British statesman. *Lothair*, Ch. 30

64 It destroys one's nerves to be amiable every day to the same human being.

Benjamin Disraeli *The Young Duke*

65 Now one of the great reasons why so many husbands and wives make shipwreck of their lives together is because a man is always seeking for happiness, while a woman is on a perpetual still hunt for trouble.

Dorothy Dix (Elizabeth Meriwether Gilmer; 1861–1951) US journalist and writer. *Dorothy Dix, Her Book*, Ch. 1

66 The husband was a teetotaller, there was no other woman, and the conduct complained of was that he had drifted into the habit of winding up every meal by taking out his false teeth and hurling them at his wife.

Arthur Conan Doyle (1856–1930) British writer. *A Case of Identity*

67 Here lies my wife; here let her lie!
Now she's at rest, and so am I.

John Dryden (1631–1700) British poet and dramatist. *Epitaph Intended for Dryden's Wife*

68 I am to be married within these three days; married past redemption.

John Dryden *Marriage à la Mode*, I

69 So that ends my first experience with matrimony, which I always thought a highly overrated performance.

Isadora Duncan (1878–1927) US dancer. *The New York Times*, 1923

70 Being an old maid is like death by drowning, a really delightful sensation after you cease to struggle.

Edna Ferber (1887–1968) US writer. *Wit's End* (R. E. Drennan), 'Completing the Circle'

71 When widows exclaim loudly against second marriages, I would always lay a wager, that the man, if not the wedding-day, is absolutely fixed on.

Henry Fielding *Amelia*, Bk. VI, Ch. 8

72 One fool at least in every married couple.

Henry Fielding *Amelia*, Bk. IX, Ch. 4

73 His designs were strictly honourable, as the phrase is; that is, to rob a lady of her fortune by way of marriage.

Henry Fielding (1707–54) British novelist. *Tom Jones*, Bk. XI, Ch. 4

74 Composed that monstrous animal a husband and wife.

Henry Fielding *Tom Jones*, Bk. XV, Ch. 9

75 Most marriages don't add two people together. They subtract one from the other.

Ian Fleming (1908–64) British journalist and author. *Diamonds are Forever*

76 All men are rapists and that's all they are. They rape us with their eyes, their laws and their codes.

Marilyn French (1929–) US novelist. *The Women's Room*

77 Husbands are like fires. They go out when unattended.

Zsa Zsa Gabor (1919–) Hungarian-born US film star. *Newsweek*, 28 Mar 1960

78 A man in love is incomplete until he has married. Then he's finished.

Zsa Zsa Gabor *Newsweek*, 28 Mar 1960

79 Do you think your mother and I should have liv'd comfortably so long together, if ever we had been married?

John Gay (1685–1732) English poet and dramatist. *The Beggar's Opera*

80 No, I shall have mistresses.

George II (1683–1760) King of Great Britain and Ireland. Reply to Queen Caroline's suggestion, as she lay on her deathbed, that he should marry again after her death. *Memoirs of George the Second* (Hervey), Vol. II

81 When you marry your mistress, you create a job vacancy.

James Goldsmith (1933–) British businessman. Attrib.

82 I was ever of opinion, that the honest man who married and brought up a large family, did more service than he who continued single and only talked of population.

Oliver Goldsmith (1728–74) Irish-born British writer. *The Vicar of Wakefield*, Ch. 1

83 I...chose my wife, as she did her wedding gown, not for a fine glossy surface, but such qualities as would wear well.

Oliver Goldsmith *The Vicar of Wakefield*, Preface

84 The trouble with my wife is that she is a whore in the kitchen and a cook in bed.

Geoffrey Gorer (1905–85) British writer and anthropologist. *Exploring the English Character*

85 When a woman gets married it is like jumping into a hole in the ice in the middle of winter; you do it once and you remember it the rest of your days.

Maxim Gorky (Aleksei Maksimovich Peshkov; 1868–1936) Russian writer. *The Lower Depths*

86 The concept of two people living together for 25 years without having a cross word suggests a lack of spirit only to be admired in sheep.

A. P. Herbert (1890–1971) British writer and politician. *News Chronicle*, 1940

87 The critical period in matrimony is breakfast-time.

A. P. Herbert *Uncommon Law*

88 Then be not coy, but use your time;
And while ye may, go marry:
For having lost but once your prime,
You may for ever tarry.

Robert Herrick (1591–1674) English poet. *Hesperides*, 'To the Virgins, to Make Much of Time'

89 If a man avoids
Marriage and all the troubles women bring
And never takes a wife, at last he comes
To a miserable old age, and does not have
Anyone to care for the old man.

Hesiod (8th century BC) Greek epic poet. *Theogony*, 602–7

90 Marriage has many pains, but celibacy has no pleasures.

Samuel Johnson (1709–84) British lexicographer. *Rasselas*, Ch. 26

91 The triumph of hope over experience.

Samuel Johnson Referring to the hasty remarriage of an

acquaintance following the death of his first wife, with whom he had been most unhappy. *Life of Johnson* (J. Boswell), Vol. II

92 Always see a fellow's weak point in his wife.

James Joyce (1882–1941) Irish novelist. *Ulysses*

93 It has been discovered experimentally that you can draw laughter from an audience anywhere in the world, of any class or race, simply by walking on to a stage and uttering the words 'I am a married man'.

Ted Kavanagh (1892–1958) British radio scriptwriter. *News Review*, 10 July 1947

94 Marriage in modern times is regarded as a partnership of equals and no longer one in which the wife must be the subservient chattel of the husband.

Lord Keith of Kinkel (1922–) British judge. Giving judgment in the House of Lords that rape can occur within marriage. *The Independent*, 24 Oct 1991

95 Marry those who are single among you, and such as are honest of your men-servants and your maid-servants: if they be poor, God will enrich them of his abundance; for God is bounteous and wise.

Koran Ch. XXIV

96 Suffer the women whom ye divorce to dwell in some part of the houses wherein ye dwell; according to the room and conveniences of the habitations which ye possess; and make them not uneasy, that ye may reduce them to straits.

Koran Ch. LXV

97 Nothing is to me more distasteful than that entire complacency and satisfaction which beam in the countenances of a new-married couple.

Charles Lamb (1775–1834) British essayist. *Essays of Elia*, 'A Bachelor's Complaint of Married People'

98 Same old slippers,
Same old rice,
Same old glimpse of
Paradise.

William James Lampton (1859–1917) British writer. *June Weddings*

99 He married a woman to stop her getting away
Now she's there all day.

Philip Larkin (1922–85) British poet. *Self's The Man*

100 There was I, waiting at the church,
Waiting at the church, waiting at the church,
When I found he'd left me in the lurch,
Lor', how it did upset me!...
Can't get away to marry you today –
My wife won't let me.

Fred W. Leigh (19th century) British songwriter. *Waiting at the Church*

101 I'm getting married in the morning!
Ding dong! the bells are gonna chime.
Pull out the stopper!
Let's have a whopper!
But get me to the church on time!

Alan Jay Lerner (1918–86) US songwriter. *My Fair Lady*, II:3

102 A bachelor lives like a king and dies like a beggar.

L. S. Lowry (1887–1976) British painter. Attrib.

103 Being married six times shows a degree of optimism over wisdom, but I am incorrigibly optimistic.

Norman Mailer (1923–) US writer. *The Observer*, 'Sayings of the Week', 17 Jan 1988

104 I am in truth very thankful for not having married at all.

Harriet Martineau (1802–76) British writer. *Harriet Martineau's Autobiography*, Vol. I

105 ...the early marriages of silly children... where...every woman is married before she well knows how serious a matter human life is.

Harriet Martineau *Society in America*, Vol. III, 'Marriage'

106 In no country, I believe, are the marriage laws so iniquitous as in England, and the conjugal relation, in consequence, so impaired.

Harriet Martineau *Society in America*, Vol. III, 'Marriage'

107 When married people don't get on they can separate, but if they're not married it's impossible. It's a tie that only death can sever.

W. Somerset Maugham (1874–1965) British novelist. *The Circle*, III

108 No man is genuinely happy, married, who has to drink worse gin than he used to drink when he was single.

H. L. Mencken (1880–1956) US journalist and editor. *Prejudices*, 'Reflections on Monogamy'

109 Marriage is like a cage; one sees the birds outside desperate to get in, and those inside equally desperate to get out.

Michel de Montaigne (1533–92) French essayist. *Essais*, III

110 Why did He not marry? Could the answer be that Jesus was not by nature the marrying sort?

Hugh Montefiore (1920–) British Anglican clergyman. Speech, Oxford, 26 July 1967

111 It has been said that a bride's attitude towards her betrothed can be summed up in three words: Aisle. Altar. Hymn.

Frank Muir (1920–) British writer and broadcaster. *Upon My Word!* (Frank Muir and Dennis Norden), 'A Jug of Wine'

112 One doesn't have to get anywhere in a marriage. It's not a public conveyance.

Iris Murdoch (1919–) Irish-born British novelist. *A Severed Head*

113 Writing is like getting married. One should never commit oneself until one is amazed at one's luck.

Iris Murdoch *The Black Prince*, 'Bradley Pearson's Foreword'

114 Marriage is an insult and women shouldn't touch it.

Jenni Murray (1950–) British broadcaster. *The Independent*, 20 June 1992

115 Why have hamburger out when you've got steak at home? That doesn't mean it's always tender.

Paul Newman (1925–) US film actor. Remark, Mar 1984

116 It is now known...that men enter local politics solely as a result of being unhappily married.

Cyril Northcote Parkinson (1919–93) British historian and writer. *Parkinson's Law*, Ch. 10

117 Marriage may often be a stormy lake, but celibacy is almost always a muddy horse-pond.
Thomas Love Peacock (1785–1866) British novelist. *Melincourt*

118 Sir, I have quarrelled with my wife; and a man who has quarrelled with his wife is absolved from all duty to his country.
Thomas Love Peacock *Nightmare Abbey*, Ch. 11

119 Strange to say what delight we married people have to see these poor fools decoyed into our condition.
Samuel Pepys (1633–1703) English diarist. *Diary*, 25 Dec 1665

120 When a man opens the car door for his wife, it's either a new car or a new wife.
Prince Philip (1921–) The consort of Queen Elizabeth II. Remark, Mar 1988

121 I don't think a prostitute is more moral than a wife, but they are doing the same thing.
Prince Philip Remark, Dec 1988

122 A loving wife will do anything for her husband except stop criticising and trying to improve him.
J. B. Priestley (1894–1984) British novelist. *Rain on Godshill*

123 When you're bored with yourself, marry and be bored with someone else.
David Pryce-Jones (1936–) British author and critic. *Owls and Satyrs*

124 It doesn't much signify whom one marries, for one is sure to find next morning that it was someone else.
Samuel Rogers (1763–1855) British poet. *Table Talk* (ed. Alexander Dyce)

125 A married couple are well suited when both partners usually feel the need for a quarrel at the same time.
Jean Rostand (1894–1977) French biologist and writer. *Le Mariage*

126 Never feel remorse for what you have thought about your wife; she has thought much worse things about you.
Jean Rostand *Le Mariage*

127 When you see what some girls marry, you realize how they must hate to work for a living.
Helen Rowland (1876–1950) US writer. *Reflections of a Bachelor Girl*

128 Marriage is for women the commonest mode of livelihood, and the total amount of undesired sex endured by women is probably greater in marriage than in prostitution.
Bertrand Russell (1872–1970) British philosopher. *Marriage and Morals*

129 The Western custom of one wife and hardly any mistresses.
Saki (Hector Hugh Munro; 1870–1916) British writer. *Reginald in Russia*

130 It takes two to make a marriage a success and only one a failure.
Herbert Samuel (1870–1963) British Liberal statesman. *A Book of Quotations*

131 Marriage is nothing but a civil contract.
John Selden (1584–1654) English historian. *Table Talk*

132 For a light wife doth make a heavy husband.
William Shakespeare (1564–1616) English dramatist. *The Merchant of Venice*, V:1

133 The world must be peopled. When I said I would die a bachelor, I did not think I should live till I were married.
William Shakespeare *Much Ado About Nothing*, II:3

134 Kiss me Kate, we will be married o' Sunday.
William Shakespeare *The Taming of the Shrew*, II:1

135 Such duty as the subject owes the prince,
Even such a woman oweth to her husband.
William Shakespeare *The Taming of the Shrew*, V:2

136 MIRANDA. I am your wife, if you will marry me;
If not, I'll die your maid: to be your fellow
You may deny me; but I'll be your servant
Whether you will or no.
FERDINAND. My mistress, dearest;
And thus I humble ever.
MIRANDA. My husband then?
FERDINAND. Ay, with a heart as willing
As bondage e'er of freedom; here's my hand.
MIRANDA. And mine, with my heart in't.
William Shakespeare *The Tempest*, III:1

137 Many a good hanging prevents a bad marriage.
William Shakespeare *Twelfth Night*, I:5

138 My mother married a very good man...and she is not at all keen on my doing the same.
George Bernard Shaw (1856–1950) Irish dramatist and critic. *Heartbreak House*

139 Marriage is popular because it combines the maximum of temptation with the maximum of opportunity.
George Bernard Shaw *Man and Superman*

140 It is a woman's business to get married as soon as possible, and a man's to keep unmarried as long as he can.
George Bernard Shaw *Man and Superman*, II

141 Have you not heard
When a man marries, dies, or turns Hindoo,
His best friends hear no more of him?
Percy Bysshe Shelley (1792–1822) British poet. Referring to the novelist Thomas Love Peacock, who worked for the East India Company and had recently married. *Letter to Maria Gisborne*, I

142 Be assured on the faith of a monkey that your frog lives in hope.
Jean de Simier The 'monkey' was Elizabeth I's pet name for Simier, who tried unsuccessfully to arrange a marriage between Elizabeth and his master, the Duke of Anjou (the 'frog').

143 Married women are kept women, and they are beginning to find it out.
Logan Pearsall Smith (1865–1946) US writer. *Afterthoughts*, 'Other people'

144 My definition of marriage:....it resembles a pair of shears, so joined that they cannot be separated; often moving in opposite directions, yet always punishing anyone who comes between them.
Sydney Smith (1771–1845) British clergyman and essayist. *Memoir* (Lady Holland)

145 A little in drink, but at all times yr faithful husband.

Richard Steele (1672–1729) Dublin-born British essayist. Letter to his wife, 27 Sep 1708

146 Even if we take matrimony at its lowest, even if we regard it as no more than a sort of friendship recognized by the police.

Robert Louis Stevenson (1850–94) Scottish writer. *Virginibus Puerisque*

147 Marriage is a step so grave and decisive that it attracts light-headed, variable men by its very awfulness.

Robert Louis Stevenson *Virginibus Puerisque*

148 Marriage is like life in this – that it is a field of battle, and not a bed of roses.

Robert Louis Stevenson *Virginibus Puerisque*

149 In marriage, a man becomes slack and selfish and undergoes a fatty degeneration of his moral being.

Robert Louis Stevenson *Virginibus Puerisque*

150 Lastly (and this is, perhaps, the golden rule), no woman should marry a teetotaller, or a man who does not smoke.

Robert Louis Stevenson *Virginibus Puerisque*

151 Bachelor's fare; bread and cheese, and kisses.

Jonathan Swift (1667–1745) Irish-born Anglican priest and writer. *Polite Conversation*, Dialogue 1

152 What they do in heaven we are ignorant of; what they do *not* we are told expressly, that they neither marry, nor are given in marriage.

Jonathan Swift *Thoughts on Various Subjects*

153 He that loves not his wife and children, feeds a lioness at home and broods a nest of sorrows.

Jeremy Taylor (1613–67) English Anglican theologian. *Sermons*, 'Married Love'

154 Or when the moon was overhead,
Came two young lovers lately wed;
'I am half sick of shadows,' said
The Lady of Shalott.

Alfred, Lord Tennyson (1809–92) British poet. *The Lady of Shalott*, Pt. II

155 Remember, it is as easy to marry a rich woman as a poor woman.

William Makepeace Thackeray (1811–63) British novelist. *Pendennis*, Ch. 28

156 This I set down as a positive truth. A woman with fair opportunities and without a positive hump, may marry whom she likes.

William Makepeace Thackeray *Vanity Fair*, Ch. 4

157 Men marry, indeed, so as to get a manager for the house, to solace wariness, to banish solitude; but a faithful slave is a far better manager, more submissive to the master, more observant of his ways, than a wife who thinks she proves herself mistress if she acts in opposition to her husband, that is, if she does what pleases her not what she is commanded.

Theophrastus (c. 372–287 BC) Greek philosopher. *On Marriage*

158 Every night of her married life she has been late for school.

Dylan Thomas (1914–53) Welsh poet. *Under Milk Wood*

159 It should be a very happy marriage – they are both so much in love with ***him***.

Irene Thomas (1920–) British writer. Attrib.

160 Divorce? Never. But murder often!

Sybil Thorndike (1882–1976) British actress. Replying to a query as to whether she had ever considered divorce during her long marriage to Sir Lewis Casson. Attrib.

161 A man should not insult his wife publicly, at parties. He should insult her in the privacy of the home.

James Thurber (1894–1961) US humorist. *Thurber Country*

162 Nearly all marriages, even happy ones, are mistakes: in the sense that almost certainly (in a more perfect world, or even with a little more care in this very imperfect one) both partners might have found more suitable mates. But the real soul-mate is the one you are actually married to.

J. R. R. Tolkien (1892–1973) British writer. Letter to Michael Tolkien, 6–8 Mar 1941

163 Marriage is the only adventure open to the cowardly.

Voltaire (François-Marie Arouet; 1694–1778) French writer. *Thoughts of a Philosopher*

164 Marriage is a great institition, but I'm not ready for an institution, yet.

Mae West (1892–1980) US actress.

165 I think women are basically quite lazy. Marriage is still a woman's best investment, because she can con some man into supporting her for the rest of his life.

Alan Whicker (1925–) British television broadcaster and writer. *The Observer*, 'Sayings of the Week', 10 Sept 1972

166 And what would happen to my illusion that I am a force for order in the home if I wasn't married to the only man north of the Tiber who is even untidier than I am?

Katherine Whitehorn (1926–) British journalist. *Sunday Best*, 'Husband-Swapping'

167 In married life three is company and two is none.

Oscar Wilde (1854–1900) Irish-born British dramatist. *The Importance of Being Earnest*, I

168 Twenty years of romance makes a woman look like a ruin; but twenty years of marriage make her something like a public building.

Oscar Wilde *A Woman of No Importance*, I

169 The best part of married life is the fights. The rest is merely so-so.

Thornton Wilder (1897–1975) US novelist and dramatist. *The Matchmaker*, II

170 I married the Duke for better or worse but not for lunch.

Duchess of Windsor (Wallis Warfield Simpson; 1896–1986) The wife of the Duke of Windsor (formerly Edward VIII). *The Windsor Story* (J. Bryan III and J. V. Murphy)

171 Of course, I do have a slight advantage over the rest of you. It helps in a pinch to be able to remind your bride that you gave up a throne for her.

Duke of Windsor (1894–1972) King of the United Kingdom; abdicated 1936. Discussing the maintenance of happy marital relations. Attrib.

172 Marriage isn't a process of prolonging the life of love, but of mummifying the corpse.

P. G. Wodehouse (1881–1975) British humorous novelist. *Bring on the Girls* (with Guy Bolton)

173 Judges, as a class, display, in the matter of arranging alimony, that reckless generosity that is found only in men who are giving away somebody else's cash.

P. G. Wodehouse *Louder and Funnier*

174 I can honestly say that I always look on Pauline as one of the nicest girls I was ever engaged to.

P. G. Wodehouse *Thank You Jeeves*, Ch. 6

175 Wondering why one's friends chose to marry the people they did is unprofitable, but recurrent. One could so often have done so much better for them.

John Wyndham (1903–69) British science-fiction writer. *The Kraken Wakes*

MARTINEAU, HARRIET

(1802–76) British writer. She wrote novels and books on history, religion, and economics.

1 I am in truth very thankful for not having married at all.

Harriet Martineau's Autobiography, Vol. I

2 If there is any country on earth where the course of true love may be expected to run smooth, it is America.

Society in America, Vol. III, 'Marriage'

3 …the early marriages of silly children… where…every woman is married before she well knows how serious a matter human life is.

Society in America, Vol. III, 'Marriage'

4 In no country, I believe, are the marriage laws so iniquitous as in England, and the conjugal relation, in consequence, so impaired.

Society in America, Vol. III, 'Marriage'

5 Any one must see at a glance that if men and women marry those whom they do not love, they must love those whom they do not marry.

Society in America, Vol. III, 'Marriage'

6 …is it to be understood that the principles of the Declaration of Independence bear no relation to half of the human race?

Society in America, Vol. III, 'Marriage'

MARTYRDOM

See also execution

1 The king has been very good to me. He promoted me from a simple maid to be a marchioness. Then he raised me to be a queen. Now he will raise me to be a martyr.

Anne Boleyn (1507–36) Second wife of Henry VIII. *Notable Women in History* (W. Abbot)

2 To die for a religion is easier than to live it absolutely.

Jorge Luis Borges (1899–1986) Argentinian writer. *Labyrinthes*

3 'Dying for an idea,' again, sounds well enough, but why not let the idea die instead of you?

Wyndham Lewis (1882–1957) British novelist. *The Art of Being Ruled*, Pt. I, Ch. 1

4 I look on martyrs as mistakes
But still they burned for it at stakes.

John Masefield (1878–1967) British poet. *The Everlasting Mercy*

5 I will burn, but this is a mere incident. We shall continue our discussion in eternity.

Michael Servetus (1511–53) Spanish physician and theologian. Comment to the judges of the Inquisition after being condemned to be burned at the stake as a heretic. *Borges: A Reader* (E. Monegal)

6 It is a heretic that makes the fire,
Not she which burns in 't.

William Shakespeare (1564–1616) English dramatist. *The Winter's Tale*, II:3

7 And they blest him in their pain, that they were not left to Spain,
To the thumbscrew and the stake, for the glory of the Lord.

Alfred, Lord Tennyson (1809–92) British poet. *The Revenge*, III

8 A thing is not necessarily true because a man dies for it.

Oscar Wilde (1854–1900) Irish-born British dramatist. *Oscariana*

MARVELL, ANDREW

(1621–78) English poet. MP for Hull for nearly 20 years, he published many pamphlets attacking corruption in the government. His poetry, much of which was published posthumously, includes 'To His Coy Mistress' and 'The Garden'.

1 How vainly men themselves amaze
To win the palm, the oak, or bays.

The Garden

2 Annihilating all that's made
To a green thought in a green shade.

The Garden

3 So restless Cromwell could not cease
In the inglorious arts of peace.

An Horatian Ode upon Cromwell's Return from Ireland

4 He nothing common did or mean
Upon that memorable scene,
But with his keener eye
The axe's edge did try.

Referring to the execution of Charles I. *An Horatian Ode upon Cromwell's Return from Ireland*

5 Ye living lamps, by whose dear light
The nightingale does sit so late,
And studying all the summer night,
Her matchless songs does meditate.

The Mower to the Glow-worms

6 I have a garden of my own,
But so with roses overgrown,
And lilies, that you would it guess
To be a little wilderness.

The Nymph Complaining for the Death of her Fawn

7 Who can foretell for what high cause
This darling of the Gods was born?
The Picture of Little T.C. in a Prospect of Flowers

8 Gather the flowers, but spare the buds.
The Picture of Little T.C. in a Prospect of Flowers

9 Had we but world enough, and time,
This coyness, lady, were no crime.
To His Coy Mistress

10 But at my back I always hear
Time's winged chariot hurrying near;
And yonder all before us lie
Deserts of vast eternity.
To His Coy Mistress

11 Let us roll all our strength and all
Our sweetness up into one ball,
And tear our pleasures with rough strife
Thorough the iron gates of life:
Thus, though we cannot make our sun
Stand still, yet we will make him run.
To His Coy Mistress

12 The grave's a fine and private place,
But none, I think, do there embrace.
To His Coy Mistress

MARX, GROUCHO

(Julius Marx; 1895–1977) US comedian and film actor; the member of the Marx brothers team who specialized in wisecracks. Their films included *Monkey Business* (1931), *Horse Feathers* (1932), *A Night at the Opera* (1935), and *A Night in Casablanca* (1945).

1 You're the most beautiful woman I've ever seen, which doesn't say much for you.
Animal Crackers

2 One morning I shot an elephant in my pajamas. How he got into my pajamas I'll never know.
Animal Crackers

3 What's a thousand dollars? Mere chicken feed. A poultry matter.
The Cocoanuts

4 Your eyes shine like the pants of my blue serge suit.
The Cocoanuts

5 Either he's dead or my watch has stopped.
A Day at the Races

6 A child of five would understand this. Send somebody to fetch a child of five.
Duck Soup

7 My husband is dead.
– I'll bet he's just using that as an excuse.
I was with him to the end.
– No wonder he passed away.
I held him in my arms and kissed him.
– So it was murder!
Duck Soup

8 Go, and never darken my towels again!
Duck Soup

9 Remember, men, we're fighting for this woman's honour; which is probably more than she ever did.
Duck Soup

10 There's a man outside with a big black moustache.
– Tell him I've got one.
Horse Feathers

11 You're a disgrace to our family name of Wagstaff, if such a thing is possible.
Horse Feathers

12 You've got the brain of a four-year-old boy, and I bet he was glad to get rid of it.
Horse Feathers

13 Look at me: I worked my way up from nothing to a state of extreme poverty.
Monkey Business

14 I want to register a complaint. Do you know who sneaked into my room at three o'clock this morning?...
– Who?...
Nobody, and that's my complaint.
Monkey Business

15 Do you suppose I could buy back my introduction to you?
Monkey Business

16 Sir, you have the advantage of me.
– Not yet I haven't, but wait till I get you outside.
Monkey Business

17 Do they allow tipping on the boat?
– Yes, sir.
Have you got two fives?
– Oh, yes, sir.
Then you won't need the ten cents I was going to give you.
A Night at the Opera

18 The strains of Verdi will come back to you tonight, and Mrs Claypool's cheque will come back to you in the morning.
A Night at the Opera

19 Send two dozen roses to Room 424 and put 'Emily, I love you' on the back of the bill.
A Night in Casablanca

20 I never forget a face, but I'll make an exception in your case.
The Guardian, 18 June 1965

21 I was so long writing my review that I never got around to reading the book.
Attrib.

22 Time wounds all heels.
Attrib.

23 Please accept my resignation. I don't want to belong to any club that will accept me as a member.
Resigning from the Friar's Club in Hollywood; *see also* BENCHLEY.
Attrib.

24 No, Groucho is not my real name. I'm breaking it in for a friend.
Attrib.

25 Whoever named it necking was a poor judge of anatomy.
Attrib.

26 A man is only as old as the woman he feels.
Attrib.

MARX, KARL

(1818–83) German philosopher and revolutionary. *The Communist Manifesto* (1848), *A Contribution to the Critique of Political Economy* (1859), and *Das Kapital* (1867) are some of his books on the theory of communism. He became leader of the First International and lived abroad (in London from 1849) for much of his life.

1 The history of all hitherto existing society is the history of class struggles.
The Communist Manifesto, 1

2 The workers have nothing to lose but their chains. They have a world to gain. Workers of the world, unite.
The Communist Manifesto, 4

3 From each according to his abilities, to each according to his needs.
Criticism of the Gotha Programme

4 Religion...is the opium of the people.
Criticism of the Hegelian Philosophy of Right, Introduction

5 Capitalist production begets, with the inexorability of a law of nature, its own negation.
Das Kapital, Ch. 15

6 Hegel says somewhere that all great events and personalities in world history reappear in one fashion or another. He forgot to add: the first time as tragedy, the second as farce.
The Eighteenth Brumaire of Louis Napoleon

7 The dictatorship of the proletariat.
Attrib.

MARXISM

See also Communism, socialism

1 The Marxist analysis has got nothing to do with what happened in Stalin's Russia; it's like blaming Jesus Christ for the Inquisition in Spain.
Tony Benn (1925–) British politician. *The Observer*, 27 Apr 1980

2 I was a man who was lucky enough to have discovered a political theory, a man who was caught up in the whirlpool of Cuba's political crisis long before becoming a fully fledged Communist... discovering Marxism...was like finding a map in the forest.
Fidel Castro (1926–) Cuban statesman. Speech, Chile, 18 Nov 1971

3 Karl Marx wasn't a Marxist all the time. He got drunk in the Tottenham Court Road.
Michael Foot (1913–) British Labour politician and journalist. *Behind The Image* (Susan Barnes)

4 Much of the world's work, it has been said, is done by men who do not feel quite well. Marx is a case in point.
John Kenneth Galbraith (1908–) US economist. *The Age of Uncertainty*, Ch. 3

5 He is the apostle of class-hatred, the founder of a Satanic anti-religion, which resembles some religions in its cruelty, fanaticism and irrationality.
Dean Inge (1860–1954) British churchman. Referring to Karl Marx. *Assessments and Anticipations*

6 Marxian Socialism must always remain a portent to the historians of Opinion – how a doctrine so illogical and so dull can have exercised so powerful and enduring an influence over the minds of men, and, through them, the events of history.
John Maynard Keynes (1883–1946) British economist. *The End of Laissez-Faire*, III

7 A Social-Democrat must never forget that the proletariat will inevitably have to wage a class struggle for Socialism even against the most democratic and republican bourgeoisie and petty bourgeoisie.
Lenin (Vladimir Ilich Ulyanov; 1870–1924) Russian revolutionary leader. *The State and Revolution*, Ch. 10

8 Marxism is like a classical building that followed the Renaissance; beautiful in its way, but incapable of growth.
Harold Macmillan (1894–1986) British politician and prime minister. Speech to the Primrose League, 29 Apr 1981

9 The history of all hitherto existing society is the history of class struggles.
Karl Marx (1818–83) German philosopher and revolutionary. *The Communist Manifesto*, 1

10 The workers have nothing to lose but their chains. They have a world to gain. Workers of the world, unite.
Karl Marx *The Communist Manifesto*, 4

11 From each according to his abilities, to each according to his needs.
Karl Marx *Criticism of the Gotha Programme*

12 Capitalist production begets, with the inexorability of a law of nature, its own negation.
Karl Marx *Das Kapital*, Ch. 15

13 All I know is that I am not a Marxist.
Karl Marx Attrib.

14 The dictatorship of the proletariat.
Karl Marx Attrib.

15 Property is theft.
Pierre Joseph Proudhon (1809–65) French socialist. *See also* SHAW. *Qu'est-ce que la Propriété?*, Ch. 1

16 And what a prize we have to fight for: no less than the chance to banish from our land the dark divisive clouds of Marxist socialism.
Margaret Thatcher (1925–) British politician and prime minister. Speech, Scottish Conservative Conference, 1983

MASCULINITY

See also men

1 It makes me feel masculine to tell you that I do

not answer questions like this without being paid for answering them.

Lillian Hellman (1905–84) US dramatist. When asked by *Harper's* magazine when she felt most masculine; this question had already been asked of several famous men. *Reader's Digest*, July 1977

2 You may have my husband, but not my horse. My husband won't need emasculating, and my horse I won't have you meddle with. I'll preserve one last male thing in the museum of this world, if I can.

D. H. Lawrence (1885–1930) British novelist. *St Mawr*

MASEFIELD, JOHN

(1878–1967) British poet. His poetry includes *Salt-Water Ballads* (1902) and *Reynard the Fox* (1919). He also wrote several novels of which *Sard Harker* (1924) is the best known. He was poet laureate from 1930 to 1967.

1 He was one of those born neither to obey nor to command, but to be evil to the commander and the obeyer alike. Perhaps there was nothing in life that he had much wanted to do, except to shoot rabbits and hit his father on the jaw, and both these things he had done.

The Bird of Dawning

2 Quinquireme of Nineveh from distant Ophir
Rowing home to haven in sunny Palestine,
With a cargo of ivory,
And apes and peacocks,
Sandalwood, cedarwood, and sweet white wine.

Cargoes

3 Dirty British coaster with a salt-caked smoke stack,
Butting through the Channel in the mad March days,
With a cargo of Tyne coal,
Road-rail, pig-lead,
Firewood, iron-ware, and cheap tin trays.

Cargoes

4 The stars grew bright in the winter sky,
The wind came keen with a tang of frost,
The brook was troubled for new things lost,
The copse was happy for old things found,
The fox came home and he went to ground.

Reynard the Fox

5 I must down to the seas again, to the lonely sea and the sky,
And all I ask is a tall ship and a star to steer her by,
And the wheel's kick and the wind's song and the white sail's shaking,
And a grey mist on the sea's face and a grey dawn breaking.

Often quoted using 'sea' rather than 'seas'. *Sea Fever*

MATERIALISM

See also greed, money, wealth

1 Benefits make a man a slave.

Arabic proverb

2 Thinking to get at once all the gold that the goose could give, he killed it, and opened it only to find – nothing.

Aesop (6th century BC) Reputed Greek writer of fables. *Fables*, 'The Goose with the Golden Eggs'

3 You don't want no pie in the sky when you die,
You want something here on the ground while you're still around.

Muhammad Ali (Cassius Clay; 1942–) US heavyweight boxer. Attrib.

4 Jesus said unto him, If thou wilt be perfect, go and sell that thou hast, and give to the poor, and thou shalt have treasure in heaven: and come and follow me.
But when the young man heard that saying, he went away sorrowful: for he had great possessions.

Bible: Matthew 19:21–22

5 They say unto him, Caesar's. Then saith he unto them, Render therefore unto Caesar the things which are Caesar's; and unto God the things that are God's.

Bible: Matthew 22:21

6 The gentleman's name that met him was Mr Worldly Wiseman.

John Bunyan (1628–88) English writer. *The Pilgrim's Progress*, Pt. I

7 Maidens, like moths, are ever caught by glare,
And Mammon wins his way where Seraphs might despair.

Lord Byron (1788–1824) British poet. *Childe Harold's Pilgrimage*, I

8 For gold in phisik is a cordial,
Therfore he lovede gold in special.

Geoffrey Chaucer (c. 1342–1400) English poet. Referring to the doctor. *The Canterbury Tales*, Prologue

9 To be clever enough to get all that money, one must be stupid enough to want it.

G. K. Chesterton (1874–1936) British writer. *The Innocence of Father Brown*

10 I never hated a man enough to give him diamonds back.

Zsa Zsa Gabor (1919–) Hungarian-born US film star. *The Observer*, 'Sayings of the Week', 28 Aug 1957

11 Increase of material comforts, it may be generally laid down, does not in any way whatsoever conduce to moral growth.

Mahatma Gandhi (Mohandas Karamchand Gandhi; 1869–1948) Indian national leader. Obituary, *News Chronicle*

12 What female heart can gold despise?
What cat's averse to fish?

Thomas Gray (1716–71) British poet. *Ode on the Death of a Favourite Cat*

13 Man must choose whether to be rich in things or in the freedom to use them.

Ivan Illich (1926–) Austrian sociologist. *Deschooling Society*, Ch. 4

14 In a consumer society there are inevitably two kinds of slaves: the prisoners of addiction and the prisoners of envy.

Ivan Illich *Tools for Conviviality*

15 The almighty dollar, that great object of

universal devotion throughout our land, seems to have no genuine devotees in these peculiar villages.
Washington Irving (1783–1859) US writer. *Wolfert's Roost*, 'The Creole Village'

16 Good morning to the day: and, next, my gold! – Open the shrine, that I may see my saint.
Ben Jonson (1573–1637) English dramatist. *Volpone*, I:1

17 The spread of personal ownership is in harmony with the deepest instincts of the British people. Few changes have done more to create one nation.
Nigel Lawson (1932–) British politician. Speech, Jan 1988

18 Kissing your hand may make you feel very very good but a diamond and safire bracelet lasts forever.
Anita Loos (1891–1981) US novelist. *Gentlemen Prefer Blondes*, Ch. 4

19 When an American heiress wants to buy a man, she at once crosses the Atlantic. The only really materialistic people I have ever met have been Europeans.
Mary McCarthy (1912–89) US novelist. *On the Contrary* 1962

20 Years ago a person, he was unhappy, didn't know what to do with himself – he'd go to church, start a revolution – *something*. Today you're unhappy? Can't figure it out? What is the salvation? Go shopping.
Arthur Miller (1915–) US dramatist. *The Price*, I

21 Why is it no one ever sent me yet
One perfect limousine, do you suppose?
Ah no, it's always just my luck to get
One perfect rose.
Dorothy Parker (1893–1967) US writer. *One Perfect Rose*

22 Diamonds Are A Girl's Best Friend.
Leo Robin (1899–1984) US songwriter. *Gentlemen Prefer Blondes*, song title

23 Bell, book, and candle, shall not drive me back,
When gold and silver becks me to come on.
William Shakespeare (1564–1616) English dramatist. *King John*, III:3

24 The want of a thing is perplexing enough, but the possession of it is intolerable.
John Vanbrugh (1664–1726) English architect and dramatist. *The Confederacy*, I:2

25 Conspicuous consumption of valuable goods is a means of reputability to the gentleman of leisure.
Thorstein Bunde Veblen (1857–1929) US social scientist. *The Theory of the Leisure Class*

26 What do you not drive human hearts into, cursed
craving for gold!
Virgil (Publius Vergilius Maro; 70–19 BC) Roman poet. *Aeneid*, Bk. III

27 There's something about a crowd like that that brings a lump to my wallet.
Eli Wallach (1915–) US actor. Remarking upon the long line of people at the box office before one of his performances. Attrib.

28 A gold rush is what happens when a line of chorus girls spot a man with a bank roll.
Mae West (1892–1980) US actress. *Klondike Annie*, film 1936

MATHEMATICS

See also numbers

1 All science requires mathematics
Roger Bacon (c. 1214–c. 1292) English monk, scholar, and scientist. *Opus Maius*, Pt. IV

2 What is algebra exactly; is it those three-cornered things?
J. M. Barrie (1860–1937) British novelist and dramatist. *Quality Street*, II

3 I never could make out what those damned dots meant.
Lord Randolph Churchill (1849–95) British Conservative politician. Referring to decimal points. *Lord Randolph Churchill* (W. S. Churchill)

4 As far as the laws of mathematics refer to reality, they are not certain, and as far as they are certain, they do not refer to reality.
Albert Einstein (1879–1955) German-born US physicist. *The Tao of Physics* (F. Capra), Ch. 2

5 When we reach the sphere of mathematics we are among processes which seem to some the most inhuman of all human activities and the most remote from poetry. Yet it is here that the artist has fullest scope for his imagination.
Havelock Ellis (1859–1939) British sexologist. *The Dance of Life*, 1923

6 The mathematician has reached the highest rung on the ladder of human thought.
Havelock Ellis *The Dance of Life*, 1923

7 There is no 'royal road' to geometry.
Euclid (c. 300 BC) Greek mathematician. Said to Ptolemy I when asked if there were an easier way to solve theorems. *Comment on Euclid* (Proclus)

8 *Quod erat demonstrandum.*
Which was to be proved.
Euclid Hence, of course, Q.E.D. *Elements*, I:5

9 About binomial theorems I'm teeming with a lot of news,
With many cheerful facts about the square on the hypoteneuse.
W. S. Gilbert (1836–1911) British dramatist. *The Pirates of Penzance*, I

10 One has to be able to count, if only so that at fifty one doesn't marry a girl of twenty.
Maxim Gorky (Aleksei Maksimovich Peshkov; 1868–1936) Russian writer. *The Zykovs*

11 Once I had learnt my twelve times table (at the age of three) it was downhill all the way.
Fred Hoyle (1915–) British astronomer.

12 MORIARTY. How are you at Mathematics?
HARRY SECOMBE. I speak it like a native.
Spike Milligan (1918–) British comic actor and author. *The Goon Show*

13 The only way I can distinguish proper from improper fractions
Is by their actions.
Ogden Nash (1902–71) US poet. *Ask Daddy, He Won't Know*

14 One geometry cannot be more true than another; it can only be more convenient. Geometry is not true, it is advantageous.

Robert T. Pirsig (1928–) US writer. *Zen and the Art of Motorcycle Maintenance*, Pt. III, Ch. 22

15 Let no one ignorant of mathematics enter here.

Plato (429–347 BC) Greek philosopher. Inscription written over the entrance to the Academy. *Biographical Encyclopedia* (I. Asimov)

16 The true spirit of delight, the exaltation, the sense of being more than Man, which is the touchstone of the highest excellence is to be found in mathematics as surely as in poetry.

Bertrand Russell (1872–1970) British philosopher. *Mysticism and Logic*

17 Mathematics, rightly viewed, possesses not only truth by supreme beauty – a beauty cold and austere like that of sculpture.

Bertrand Russell *Mysticism and Logic*

18 Mathematics may be defined as the subject in which we never know what we are talking about, nor whether what we are saying is true.

Bertrand Russell *Mysticism and Logic*, Ch. 4

19 Pure mathematics consists entirely of assertions to the effect that, if such and such a proposition is true of *anything*, then such and such another proposition is true of that thing. It is essential not to discuss whether the first proposition is really true, and not to mention what the anything is, of which it is supposed to be true.

Bertrand Russell *Mysticism and Logic*, Ch. 5

20 Mathematics possesses not only truth, but supreme beauty – a beauty cold and austere, like that of sculpture.

Bertrand Russell *The Study of Mathematics*

21 I like mathematics because it is *not* human and has nothing particular to do with this planet or with the whole accidental universe – because, like Spinoza's God, it won't love us in return.

Bertrand Russell Letter to Lady Ottoline Morrell, Mar 1912

22 It is with medicine as with mathematics: we should occupy our minds only with what we continue to know; what we once knew is of little consequence.

Charles Augustin Sainte-Beuve (1804–69) French critic.

23 I knew a mathematician who said 'I do not know as much as God. But I know as much as God knew at my age'.

Milton Shulman (1925–) Canadian writer, journalist, and critic. *Stop The Week*, BBC Radio 4

24 Numbers constitute the only universal language.

Nathaniel West (Nathan Weinstein; 1903–40) US novelist. *Miss Lonelyhearts*

25 Mathematics is thought moving in the sphere of complete abstraction from any particular instance of what it is talking about.

A. N. Whitehead (1861–1947) British philosopher. *Science and the Modern World*

MAUGHAM, W. SOMERSET

(1874–1965) British novelist and doctor. After practising medicine, he became a full-time writer with the success of *Liza of Lambeth* (1896). *Of Human Bondage* (1915), *The Moon and Sixpence* (1919), and *The Razor's Edge* (1944) were among his most successful books.

1 You know, of course, that the Tasmanians, who never committed adultery, are now extinct.

The Bread-Winner

2 Hypocrisy is the most difficult and nerve-racking vice that any man can pursue; it needs an unceasing vigilance and a rare detachment of spirit. It cannot, like adultery or gluttony, be practised at spare moments; it is a whole-time job.

Cakes and Ale, Ch. 1

3 From the earliest times the old have rubbed it into the young that they are wiser than they, and before the young had discovered what nonsense this was they were old too, and it profited them to carry on the imposture.

Cakes and Ale, Ch. 11

4 You can't learn too soon that the most useful thing about a principle is that it can always be sacrificed to expediency.

The Circle, III

5 A woman will always sacrifice herself if you give her the opportunity. It is her favourite form of self-indulgence.

The Circle, III

6 When married people don't get on they can separate, but if they're not married it's impossible. It's a tie that only death can sever.

The Circle, III

7 She's too crafty a woman to invent a new lie when an old one will serve.

The Constant Wife, II

8 The mystic sees the ineffable, and the psychopathologist the unspeakable.

The Moon and Sixpence, Ch. 1

9 Impropriety is the soul of wit.

The Moon and Sixpence, Ch. 4

10 Because women can do nothing except love, they've given it a ridiculous importance.

The Moon and Sixpence, Ch. 41

11 Like all weak men he laid an exaggerated stress on not changing one's mind.

Of Human Bondage, Ch. 39

12 People ask you for criticism, but they only want praise.

Of Human Bondage, Ch. 50

13 Money is like a sixth sense without which you cannot make a complete use of the other five.

Of Human Bondage, Ch. 51

14 The degree of a nation's civilization is marked by its disregard for the necessities of existence.

Our Betters, I

15 The right people are rude. They can afford to be.

Our Betters, II

16 It was such a lovely day I thought it was a pity to get up.
Our Betters, II

17 For to write good prose is an affair of good manners. It is, unlike verse, a civil art...Poetry is baroque.
The Summing Up

18 I would sooner read a time-table or a catalogue than nothing at all. They are much more entertaining than half the novels that are written.
The Summing Up

19 Life is too short to do anything for oneself that one can pay others to do for one.
The Summing Up

20 There is an impression abroad that everyone has it in him to write one book; but if by this is implied a good book the impression is false.
The Summing Up

21 I'll give you my opinion of the human race... Their heart's in the right place, but their head is a thoroughly inefficient organ.
The Summing Up

22 Casting my mind's eye over the whole of fiction, the only absolutely original creation I can think of is Don Quixote.
10 Novels and Their Authors, Ch. 1

23 Music-hall songs provide the dull with wit, just as proverbs provide them with wisdom.
A Writer's Notebook

24 I recognize that I am made up of several persons and that the person that at the moment has the upper hand will inevitably give place to another. But which is the real one? All of them or none?
A Writer's Notebook

25 Sentimentality is only sentiment that rubs you up the wrong way.
A Writer's Notebook

26 Dying is a very dull, dreary affair. And my advice to you is to have nothing whatever to do with it.
Escape from the Shadows (Robin Maugham)

27 I am sick of this way of life. The weariness and sadness of old age make it intolerable. I have walked with death in hand, and death's own hand is warmer than my own. I don't wish to live any longer.
Said on his ninetieth birthday. *Familiar Medical Quotations* (M. B. Strauss)

28 I've always been interested in people, but I've never liked them.
The Observer, 'Sayings of the Week', 28 Aug 1949

29 The trouble with our younger authors is that they are all in the sixties.
The Observer, 'Sayings of the Week', 14 Oct 1951

MCCARTHY, MARY

(1912–89) US novelist. Her books include *Groves of Academe* (1952), *On the Contrary* (1961), *The Group* (1963), and *Cannibals and Missionaries* (1979).

1 If someone tells you he is going to make 'a realistic decision', you immediately understand that he has resolved to do something bad.
On the Contrary

2 There are no new truths, but only truths that have not been recognized by those who have perceived them without noticing.
On the Contrary

3 When an American heiress wants to buy a man, she at once crosses the Atlantic. The only really materialistic people I have ever met have been Europeans.
On the Contrary

4 The immense popularity of American movies abroad demonstrates that Europe is the unfinished negative of which America is the proof.
On the Contrary

5 An interviwer asked me what book I thought best represented the modern American woman. All I could think of to answer was: *Madame Bovary*.
On the Contrary

6 And I don't feel the attraction of the Kennedys at all...I don't think they are Christians; they may be Catholics but they are not Christians, in my belief anyway.
The Observer, 14 Oct 1979

MCCARTNEY, PAUL

(1943–) British rock musician and composer. Formerly a member of the Beatles, he wrote many songs with John Lennon. He later formed the band Wings and released such hit albums as *Band on the Run* (1973) before launching a new solo career. *See* JOHN LENNON.

1 The issues are the same. We wanted peace on earth, love, and understanding between everyone around the world. We have learned that change comes slowly.
The Observer, 'Sayings of the Week', 7 June 1987

2 The reason I couldn't do the music is that I don't *really* like words by Shakespeare.
Declining to write music for a production of *As You Like It*. Letter to Kenneth Tynan, 1968

MEANING

See also purpose, words

1 'Then you should say what you mean,' the March Hare went on. 'I do,' Alice hastily replied; 'at least – at least I mean what I say – that's the same thing, you know.'
'Not the same thing a bit!' said the Hatter. 'Why, you might just as well say that 'I see what I eat' is the same thing as 'I eat what I see!''
Lewis Carroll (Charles Lutwidge Dodgson; 1832–98) British writer. *Alice's Adventures in Wonderland*, Ch. 7

2 Take care of the sense, and the sounds will take care of themselves.
Lewis Carroll *Alice's Adventures in Wonderland*, Ch. 9

3 'When *I* use a word,' Humpty Dumpty said in

rather a scornful tone, 'it means just what I choose it to mean – neither more nor less.'

Lewis Carroll *Through the Looking-Glass*, Ch. 6

4 Where in this small-talking world can I find
A longitude with no platitude?

Christopher Fry (1907–) British dramatist. *The Lady's Not for Burning*, III

5 The least of things with a meaning is worth more in life than the greatest of things without it.

Carl Gustav Jung (1875–1961) Swiss psychoanalyst. *Modern Man in Search of a Soul*

MEDIA

See also journalism, newspapers, television

1 I want to be punished for what I did, not what a tabloid distorted it into.

Anonymous Prisoner serving life imprisonment for murder. Letter, 1993

2 What do we want? Radio 4! Where do we want it? Long wave! And what do we say? Please!

Anonymous Chanted by protesters who opposed the BBC's plans to broadcast Radio 4 on FM only. *The Guardian*, 5 Apr 1993

3 What the proprietorship of these papers is aiming at is power, and power without responsibility – the prerogative of the harlot through the ages.

Stanley Baldwin (1867–1947) Attacking the press barons Lords Rothermere and Beaverbrook. It was first used by KIPLING. *See also* DEVONSHIRE (10th Duke). Speech, election rally, 18 Mar 1931

4 If I rescued a child from drowning, the Press would no doubt headline the story 'Benn grabs child'.

Tony Benn (1925–) British politician. *The Observer*, 'Sayings of the Week', 2 Mar 1975

5 When a dog bites a man that is not news, but when a man bites a dog that is news.

John B. Bogart (1845–1920) US journalist. Sometimes attributed to Charles Dana and Amos Cummings. Attrib.

6 I try to find Radio 4 but I can't with all those bloody music channels.

Jack Charlton (1935–) British footballer and football manager. *The Guardian*, June 1994

7 Good God, that's done it. He's lost us the tarts' vote.

Duke of Devonshire (1895–1950) Conservative politician. Referring to Stanley Baldwin's attack on newspaper proprietors; recalled by Harold Macmillan. Attrib.

8 The only thing I don't like about the press is I can give as many answers as you want, and be totally honest, but finally it's you who shapes the final product...often what comes out isn't what I meant at all.

Roddy Doyle (1958–) Irish novelist and playwright. *The Observer*, 1 May 1994

9 TV...is our latest medium – we call it a medium because nothing's well done.

Ace Goodman (1899–) US writer. Letter to Groucho Marx, 1954 *The Groucho Letters*

10 The Liberty of the press is the *Palladium* of all the civil, political and religious rights of an Englishman.

Junius An unidentified writer of letters (1769–72) to the *London Public Advertiser*. *Letters*, 'Dedication'

11 A medium, so called because it is neither rare nor well done.

Ernie Kovacs (1919–62) US entertainer. Referring to television. Attrib.

12 Newspapers always excite curiosity. No one ever lays one down without a feeling of disappointment.

Charles Lamb (1775–1834) British essayist. *Last Essays of Elia*, 'Detached Thoughts on Books and Reading'

13 On the whole I would not say that our Press is obscene. I would say that it trembles on the brink of obscenity.

Lord Longford (1905–) British politician and social reformer. *The Observer*, 'Sayings of the Year', 1963

14 MILNE. No matter how imperfect things are, if you've got a free press everything is correctable, and without it everything is conceivable.
RUTH. I'm with you on the free press. It's the newspapers I can't stand.

Tom Stoppard (1937–) Czech-born British dramatist. *Night and Day*, I

15 Freedom of the press in Britain is freedom to print such of the proprietor's prejudices as the advertisers don't object to.

Hannen Swaffer (1879–1962) British journalist. Attrib.

16 Facing the press is more difficult than bathing a leper.

Mother Teresa (Agnes Gonxha Bojaxhiu; 1910–) Yugoslavian-born Indian missionary. *Eileen Egan, Such a Vision of the Street*

MEDICINE

See also doctors, health, illness, nurses, remedies

1 Nature, time and patience are the three great physicians.

Bulgarian proverb

2 Medicine can only cure curable diseases, and then not always.

Chinese proverb

3 Dermatology is the best speciality. The patient never dies – and never gets well.

Anonymous

4 If every man would mend a man, then all the world would be mended.

Anonymous

5 If I were summing up the qualities of a good teacher of medicine, I would enumerate human sympathy, moral and intellectual integrity, enthusiasm, and ability to talk, in addition, of course, to knowledge of his subject.

Anonymous

6 The deficiencies which I think good to note...I will enumerate...The first is the discontinuance of the ancient and serious diligence of Hippocrates, which used to set down a narrative of the special cases of his patients, and how they proceeded, and how they were judged by recovery or death.

Francis Bacon (1561–1626) English philosopher, lawyer, and politician. *The Advancement of Learning*, Bk. II

7 The poets did well to conjoin Music and Medicine in Apollo: because the office of medicine is but to tune this curious harp of man's body and to reduce it to harmony.

Francis Bacon *The Advancement of Learning*, Bk. II

8 Medicine is a science which hath been, as we have said, more professed than laboured, and yet more laboured than advanced; the labour having been, in my judgment, rather in a circle than in progression.

Francis Bacon *Advancement of Learning*, Bk. II

9 The prime goal is to alleviate suffering, and not to prolong life. And if your treatment does not alleviate suffering, but only prolongs life, that treatment should be stopped.

Christiaan Barnard (1922–) South African surgeon.

10 With certain limited exceptions, the laws of physical science are positive and absolute, both in their aggregate, and in their elements – in their sum, and in their details; but the ascertainable laws of the science of life are approximative only, and not absolute.

Elisha Bartlett (1804–55) *Philosophy of Medical Science*, Pt. II, Ch. 2

11 Of all the lessons which a young man entering upon the profession of medicine needs to learn, this is perhaps the first – that he should resist the fascination of doctrines and hypotheses till he has won the privilege of such studies by honest labor and faithful pursuit of real and useful knowledge.

William Beaumont (1785–1853) US physician. *Notebook*

12 Medicine is like a woman who changes with the fashions.

August Bier (1861–1949) Aphorism

13 GRAVE, n. A place in which the dead are laid to await the coming of the medical student.

Ambrose Bierce (1842–c. 1914) US writer and journalist. *The Devil's Dictionary*

14 HOMEOPATHY, n. A school of medicine midway between Allopathy and Christian Science. To the last both the others are distinctly inferior, for Christian Science will cure imaginary diseases, and they can not.

Ambrose Bierce *The Devil's Dictionary*

15 Every hospital should have a plaque in the physicians' and students' entrances: 'There are some patients whom we cannot help, there are none whom we cannot harm.'

Arthur L. Bloomfield (1888–1962) Personal communication after iatrogenic tragedy, c. 1930–36

16 Medicine…the only profession that labours incessantly to destroy the reason for its own existence.

Sir James Bryce (1838–1922) British liberal politician, historian, and ambassador to America. Address, 23 Mar 1914

17 Among the arts, medicine, on account of its eminent utility, must always hold the highest place.

Henry Thomas Buckle (1821–62) *Miscellaneous and Posthumous Works*, Vol. II

18 Vaccination is the medical sacrament corresponding to baptism.

Samuel Butler (1835–1902) British writer.

19 Medical men all over the world having merely entered into a tacit agreement to call all sorts of maladies people are liable to, in cold weather, by one name; so that one sort of treatment may serve for all, and their practice thereby be greatly simplified.

Jane Welsh Carlyle (1801–66) The wife of Thomas Carlyle. Letter to John Welsh, 4 Mar 1837

20 Quackery gives birth to nothing; gives death to all things.

Thomas Carlyle (1795–1881) Scottish essayist and historian. *Heroes and Hero-Worship*

21 The Art of Medicine is in need really of reasoning,…for this is a conjectural art. However, in many cases not only does conjecture fail, but experience as well.

Celsus (25 BC–50 AD) Roman encyclopedist. *De re medicina*

22 It is obvious that we cannot instruct women as we do men in the science of medicine; we cannot carry them into the dissecting room.

Walter Channing Remarks on the Employment of Females as Practitioners in Midwifery, by a Physician

23 The whole imposing edifice of modern medicine is like the celebrated tower of Pisa – slightly off balance.

Charles, Prince of Wales (1948–) Eldest son of Elizabeth II.

24 Nature heals, under the auspices of the medical profession.

Haven Emerson (1874–1957) Lecture

25 To a physician, each man, each woman, is an amplification of one organ.

Ralph Waldo Emerson (1803–82) US poet and essayist. *Bartlett's Unfamiliar Quotations* (Leonard Louis Levinson)

26 Homeopathy is insignificant as an act of healing, but of great value as criticism on the hygeia or medical practice of the time.

Ralph Waldo Emerson *Essays* (Second Series), 'Nominalist and Realist'

27 In the hands of the discoverer, medicine becomes a heroic art…wherever life is dear he is a demigod.

Ralph Waldo Emerson *Uncollected Lectures*, 'Resources'

28 Anatomy is to physiology as geography to history; it describes the theatre of events.

Jean Fernel (1497–1558) *On the Natural Part of Medicine*, Ch. 1

29 Patience is the best medicine.

John Florio (1553–1625) English lexicographer and translator. *First Frutes*

30 Study sickness while you are well.

Thomas Fuller (1654–1734) English physician and writer. *Gnomologia*

31 Medicine absorbs the physician's whole being because it is concerned with the entire human organism.

Johann Wolfgang von Goethe (1749–1832) German poet, dramatist and scientist.

32 A well chosen anthology is a complete dispensary of medicine for the more common mental disorders, and may be used as much for prevention as cure.

Robert Graves (1895–1985) British poet and novelist. *On English Poetry*, Ch. 29

33 Comedy is medicine.

Trevor Griffiths (1935–) *Comedians*, I

34 The foundation of the study of Medicine, as of all scientific inquiry, lies in the belief that every natural phenomenon, trifling as it may seem, has a fixed and invariable meaning.

Sir William Withey Gull (1816–90) *Published Writings*, 'Study of Medicine'

35 Medicine is as old as the human race, as old as the necessity for the removal of disease.

Heinrich Haeser (1811–84) *Lehrbuch der Geschichte der Medizin*, Erste Periode

36 Solving the mysteries of heaven has not given birth to as many abortive findings as has the quest into the mysteries of the human body. When you think of yourselves as scientists, I want you always to remember everything you learn from me will probably be regarded tomorrow as the naive confusions of a pack of medical aborigines. Despite all our toil and progress, the art of medicine still falls somewhere between trout casting and spook writing.

Ben Hecht (1894–1964) *Miracle of the Fifteen Murderers*

37 I swear by Apollo the physician, by Asclepius, by Health, by Panacea and by all the gods and goddesses, making them my witnesses, that I will carry out, according to my ability and judgment, this oath and this indenture. To hold my teacher in this art equal to my own parents; to make him partner in my livelihood; when he is in need of money to share mine with him; to consider his family as my own brothers and to teach them this art, if they want to learn it, without fee or indenture; to impart precept, oral instruction, and all other instruction to my own sons, the sons of my teacher, and to indentured pupils who have taken the physician's oath, but to nobody else. I will use treatment to help the sick according to my ability and judgment, but never with a view to injury and wrong-doing. Neither will I administer a poison to anybody when asked to do so, nor will I suggest such a course. Similarly, I will not give a woman a pessary to cause abortion. But I will keep pure and holy both in my life and my art. I will not use the knife, not even, verily, on sufferers from stone but I will give place to such as are craftsmen therein. Into whatsoever houses I enter, I will enter to help the sick, and I will abstain from all intentional wrong-doing and harm, especially from abusing the bodies of man or woman, bond or free. And whatsoever I shall see or hear in the course of my profession, as well as outside my profession in my intercourse with men, if it be what should not be published abroad, I will never divulge holding such things to be holy secret. Now if I carry out this oath, and break it not, may I gain for ever reputation among all men for my life and for my art; but if I transgress it and forswear myself, may the opposite befall me.

Hippocrates (c. 460 BC–c. 357 BC) Greek physician. *The Hippocratic Oath*

38 Life is short, the Art long, opportunity fleeting, experience treacherous, judgment difficult. The physician must be ready, not only to do his duty himself, but also to secure the co-operation of the patient, of the attendants and of externals.

Hippocrates *Aphorisms*, I, 1

39 The art has three factors, the disease, the patient, and physician. The physician is the servant of the art. The patient must co-operate with the physician in combating the disease.

Hippocrates *Epidemics*, I

40 A miracle drug is any drug that will do what the label says it will do.

Eric Hodgins (1899–1971) US writer and editor. *Episode*

41 Homeopathy…a mingled mass of perverse ingenuity, of tinsel erudition, of imbecile credulity, and of artful misrepresentation, too often mingled in practice…with heartless and shameless imposition.

Oliver Wendell Holmes (1809–94) US writer and physician. *Medical Essays*, 'Homeopathy and Its Kindred Delusions'

42 It is so hard to get anything out of the dead hand of medical tradition!

Oliver Wendell Holmes *Medical Essays*, 'Currents and Counter-Currents in Medical Science'

43 The truth is, that medicine, professedly founded on observation, is as sensitive to outside influences, political, religious, philosophical, imaginative, as is the barometer to the changes of atmospheric density.

Oliver Wendell Holmes *Medical Essays*, 'Currents and Counter-Currents in Medical Science'

44 *Nature*, in medical language, as opposed to Art, means trust in the reactions of the living system against ordinary normal impressions.
Art, in the same language, as opposed to Nature, means an intentional resort to extraordinary abnormal impressions for the relief of disease.

Oliver Wendell Holmes *Medical Essays*, 'Currents and Counter-Currents in Medical Science'

45 The lancet was the magician's wand of the dark ages of medicine.

Oliver Wendell Holmes *Medical Essays*, 'Some of My Early Teachers'

46 It is unnecessary – perhaps dangerous – in medicine to be too clever.

Sir Robert Hutchison (1871–1960) *Lancet*, 2:61, 1938

47 The only sure foundations of medicine are, an intimate knowledge of the human body, and observation on the effects of medicinal substances on that.

Thomas Jefferson (1743–1826) US statesman. Letter to Dr. Caspar Wistar, 21 June 1807

48 Fasting is a medicine.

St John Chrysostom (c. 345–407) Bishop of Constantinopole and Doctor of the Church. *Homilies on the Statutes*, III

49 One of the most difficult things to contend with in a hospital is the assumption on the part of the staff that because you have lost your gall bladder you have also lost your mind.

Jean Kerr (1923–) US dramatist. *Please Don't Eat the Daisies*

50 No costs have increased more rapidly in the last decade than the cost of medical care. And no group of Americans has felt the impact of these sky-rocketing costs more than our older citizens.

John F. Kennedy (1917–63) US statesman. Address on the 25th Anniversary of the Social Security Act, 14 Aug 1960

51 The ultimate indignity is to be given a bedpan by a stranger who calls you by your first name.

Maggie Kuhn (1905–) US writer and social activist. *The Observer*, 20 Aug 1978

52 Medicine is a strange mixture of speculation and action. We have to cultivate a science and to exercise an art. The calls of science are upon our leisure and our choice; the calls of practice are of daily emergence and necessity.

Peter Mere Latham (1789–1875) US poet and essayist. *Diseases of the Heart*

53 The practice of physic is jostled by quacks on the one side, and by science on the other.

Peter Mere Latham *Collected Works*, Vol. I, 'In Memoriam' (Sir Thomas Watson)

54 In the old-fashioned days when a man got sick he went to the family doctor and said he was sick. The doctor gave him a bottle of medicine. He took it home and drank it and got well.
On the bottle was written, 'Three times a day in water.' The man drank it three times a day the first day, twice the second day, and once the third day. On the fourth day he forgot it. But that didn't matter. He was well by that time....
Such medicine was, of course, hopelessly unscientific, hopelessly limited. Death could beat it round every corner. But it was human, gracious, kindly.

Stephen Leacock (1869–1944) British-born Canadian economist and humorist. *The Leacock Roundabout*, 'The Doctor and the Contraption'

55 When you buy a pill and buy peace with it you get conditioned to cheap solutions instead of deep ones.

Max Lerner (1902–) US author and journalist. *The Unfinished Country*

56 Medicine is not a lucrative profession. It is a divine one.

John Coakley Lettsom (1744–1815) Letter to a friend, 6 Sept 1791

57 Medicine makes people ill, mathematics makes them sad and theology makes them sinful.

Martin Luther (1483–1546) German Protestant reformer.

58 Medical practice is not knitting and weaving and the labor of the hands, but it must be inspired with soul and be filled with understanding and equipped with the gift of keen observation; these together with accurate scientific knowledge are the indispensable requisites for proficient medical practice.

Maimonides (Moses ben Maimon; 1135–1204) Spanish-born Jewish philosopher and physician. *Bulletin of the Institute of the History of Medicine*, 3:555, 1935

59 Medicine is a conjectural art.

Jean Nicolas Corvisart des Marets (1755–1821)

60 Medicine heals doubts as well as diseases.

Karl Marx (1796–1877) German philosopher, economist, and revolutionary. *Bulletin of the New York Academy of Medicine* (F. H. Garrison)

61 The prevention of disease today is one of the most important factors in the line of human endeavor.

Charles H. Mayo (1865–1939) US surgeon. *Collected Papers of the Mayo Clinic and Mayo Foundation*, 5:17, 1913

62 The aim of medicine is to prevent disease and prolong life, the ideal of medicine is to eliminate the need of a physician.

William J. Mayo (1861–1939) US physician. *National Education Association: Proceedings and Addresses*, 66:163, 1928

63 Medicine may be defined as the art or the science of keeping a patient quiet with frivolous reasons for his illness and amusing him with remedies good or bad until nature kills him or cures him.

Gilles Ménage (1613–92) *Ménagiana*, Pt. III

64 The aim of medicine is surely not to make men virtuous; it is to safeguard and rescue them from the consequences of their vices.

H. L. Mencken (1880–1956) US journalist and editor. *Prejudices*, 'Types of Men: the Physician'

65 Medicine is for the patient. Medicine is the people. It is not for the profits.

George Merck (1894–1957)

66 I wasn't driven into medicine by a social conscience but by rampant curiosity.

Jonathan Miller (1936–) British writer and doctor.

67 GERONTE. It was very clearly explained, but there was just one thing which surprised me that you got them the wrong way about, that the heart should be on the left side, and the liver on the right.
SGANARELLE. Yes, it used to be so but we have changed all that. Everything's quite different in medicine nowadays.

Molière (Jean-Baptiste Poquelin; 1622–73) French dramatist. *Le Médecin malgré lui*, II:4

68 The art of medicine is my discovery. I am called Help-Bringer throughout the world, and all the potency of herbs is known to me.

Ovid (Publius Ovidius Naso; 43 BC–17 AD) Roman poet. Spoken by Apollo. *Metamorphoses*

69 The art of medicine is generally a question of time.

Ovid *Remedia Amoris*

70 Medicine sometimes snatches away health, sometimes gives it.

Ovid *Tristia*

71 A hospital should also have a recovery room adjoining the cashier's office.

Francis O'Walsh *Bartlett's Unfamiliar Quotations* (Leonard Louis Levinson)

72 Medicine is not only a science; it is also an art. It does not consist of compounding pills and plasters; it deals with the very processes of life, which must be understood before they may be guided.

Paracelsus (c. 1493–1541) Swiss physician and alchemist. *Die grosse Wundarznei*

73 The art of healing comes from nature not from the physician. Therefore the physician must start from nature, with an open mind.

Paracelsus *Seven Defenses*, Ch. 4

74 Experiment alone crowns the efforts of medicine, experiment limited only by the natural range of the powers of the human mind. Observation discloses in the animal organism numerous phenomena existing side by side, and interconnected now profoundly, now indirectly, or accidentally. Confronted with a multitude of different assumptions the mind must *guess* the real nature of this connection.

Ivan Pavlov (1849–1936) Russian physiologist. *Experimental Psychology and Other Essays*, Pt. X

75 This basis of medicine is sympathy and the desire to help others, and whatever is done with this end must be called medicine.

Frank Payne (1840–1910) *English Medicine in the Anglo-Saxon Times*

76 Medicine is not yet liberated from the medieval idea that disease is the result of sin and must be expiated by mortification of the flesh.

Sir George W. Pickering (1904–) *Resident Physician*, II (No. 9): 71, 1965

77 Medicine is an art, and attends to the nature and constitution of the patient, and has principles of action and reason in each case.

Plato (427 BC–347 BC) Greek philosopher. *Gorgias*

78 And this is what the physician has to do, and in this the art of medicine consists: for medicine may be regarded generally as the knowledge of the loves and desires of the body, and how to satisfy them or not; and the best physician is he who is able to separate fair love from foul, or to convert one into the other; and he who knows how to eradicate and how to implant love, whichever is required, and can reconcile the most hostile elements in the constitution and make them loving friends, is a skilful practitioner.

Plato *Symposium*

79 The first staggering fact about medical education is that after two and a half years of being taught on the assumption that everyone is the same, the student has to find out for himself that everyone is different, which is really what his experience has taught him since infancy. And the second staggering fact about medical education is that after being taught for two and half years not to trust any evidence except that based on the measurements of physical science, the student has to find out for himself that all important decisions are in reality made, almost at unconscious level, by that most perfect and complex of computers the human brain, about which he has as yet learnt almost nothing, and will probably go on learning nothing to the end of his course – this computer which can take in and analyse an incredible number of data in an extremely short time. And the data are mostly not of the hard crude type with which that simple fellow the scientist has to deal, but are of a much more subtle, human, and interesting character, each tinted in its own colours of personality and emotion. All this the student has to discover for himself which his teachers strangely pretend to believe that the secrets of medicine are revealed only to those whose biochemical background is beyond reproach.

Sir Robert Platt (1900–) *British Medical Journal*, 2:551, 1965

80 Medicine, to produce health, has to examine disease.

Plutarch (c. 46–c. 120) Greek biographer and essayist. *Lives*, 'Demetrius', I

81 Medicine for the dead is too late.

Quintilian (Marcus Fabius Quintilianus; c. 35 AD–c. 96 AD) Roman rhetorician and teacher.

82 Truth in medicine is an unattainable goal, and the art as described in books is far beneath the knowledge of an experienced and thoughtful physician.

Rhazes (Ar-Razi; c. 865–c. 928) Persian physician and philosopher. *History of Medicine* (Max Neuburger)

83 In treating a patient, let your first thought be to strengthen his natural vitality.

Rhazes

84 The first cry of pain through the primitive jungle was the first call for a physician…Medicine is a natural art, conceived in sympathy and born of necessity; from instinctive procedures developed the specialized science that is practised today.

Victor Robinson (1886–1947) *The Story of Medicine*

85 Medicine is a noble profession but a damn bad business.

Humphrey Rolleston (1862–1944) British physician. Attrib.

86 Medicine is an occupation for slaves.

Benjamin Rush (c. 1745–1813) *Autobiography*

87 It is with medicine as with mathematics: we should occupy our minds only with what we continue to know; what we once knew is of little consequence.

Charles Augustin Sainte-Beuve (1804–69) French critic.

88 After twenty years one is no longer quoted in the medical literature. Every twenty years one sees a republication of the same ideas.

Béla Schick (1877–1967) Austrian pediatrician. *Aphorisms and Facetiae of Béla Schick*, 'Early Years' (I.J. Wolf)

89 Not even medicine can master incurable diseases.

Seneca (c. 4 BC–65 AD) Roman author. *Epistulae ad Lucilium*, XCIV

90 By medicine life may be prolonged, yet death
Will seize the doctor too.

William Shakespeare (1564–1616) English dramatist and poet. *Cymbeline*, V:5

91 Optimistic lies have such immense therapeutic value that a doctor who cannot tell them convincingly has mistaken his profession.

George Bernard Shaw (1856–1950) Irish dramatist and critic. *Misalliance*, Preface

92 Medical science is as yet very imperfectly differentiated from common curemongering witchcraft.

George Bernard Shaw *The Doctor's Dilemma*, 'Preface on Doctors'

93 …the department of witchcraft called medical science.

George Bernard Shaw *The Philanderer*

94 The very popular hunting for 'Fathers' of every branch of medicine and every treatment is, therefore, rather foolish; it is unfair not only to the mothers and ancestors but also to the obstetricians and midwives.

Henry E. Sigerist (1891–1957) *A History of Medicine*, Vol. I, Introduction

95 *Prevention* of disease must become the goal of every physician.

Henry E. Sigerist *Medicine and Human Welfare*, Ch. 3

96 I've already had medical attention – a dog licked me when I was on the ground.

Neil Simon (1927–) US playwright. *Only When I Laugh* (screenplay)

97 There are worse occupations in this world than feeling a woman's pulse.

Laurence Sterne (1713–68) British novelist. *A Sentimental Journey*, 'The Pulse'

98 Medicine can never abdicate the obligation to care for the patient and to teach patient care.

Maurice B. Strauss (1904–74) *Medicine*, 43:19, 1964

99 If they are not interested in the care of the patient, in the phenomena of disease in the sick, they should not be in the clinical department of medicine, since they cannot teach students clinical medicine.

Maurice B. Strauss *Medicine*, 43:619, 1964

100 Formerly, when religion was strong and science weak, men mistook magic for medicine, now, when science is strong and religion weak, men mistake medicine for magic.

Thomas Szasz (1920–) US psychiatrist. *The Second Sin*

101 The history of medicine is a story of amazing foolishness and amazing intelligence.

Jerome Tarshis

102 Human beings, yes, but not surgeons.

Rudolph Virchow (1821–1902) German pathologist. Answering a query as to whether human beings could survive appendectomy, which had recently become a widespread practice. *Anekdotenschatz* (H. Hoffmeister)

103 He preferred to know the power of herbs and their value for curing purposes, and, heedless of glory, to exercise that quiet art.

Virgil (Publius Vergilius Maro; 70 BC–19 BC) Roman poet. *Aeneid*

104 The art of medicine consists of amusing the patient while Nature cures the disease.

Voltaire (François-Marie Arouet; 1694–1788) French writer. Attrib.

105 Medical education is not completed at the medical school: it is only begun.

William H. Welch (1850–1934) *Bulletin of the Harvard Medical School Association*, 3:55, 1892

MEDIOCRITY

See also inferiority

1 The most insidious influence on the young is not violence, drugs, tobacco, drink or sexual perversion, but our pursuit of the trivial and our tolerance of the third rate.

Eric Anderson (1936–) British teacher; headmaster of Eton. *The Observer*, 'Sayings of the Week', 12 June 1994

2 Only mediocrity can be trusted to be always at its best.

Max Beerbohm (1872–1956) British writer. *Conversations with Max* (S.N. Behrman)

3 The world is made of people who never quite get into the first team and who just miss the prizes at the flower show.

Jacob Bronowski (1908–74) British scientist and writer. *The Face of Violence*, Ch. 6

4 Mediocrity knows nothing higher than itself, but talent instantly recognizes genius.

Arthur Conan Doyle (1856–1930) British writer. *The Valley of Fear*

5 Only the mediocre are always at their best.

Jean Giraudoux (1882–1944) French dramatist. Attrib.

6 Some men are born mediocre, some men achieve mediocrity, and some men have mediocrity thrust upon them. With Major Major it had been all three.

Joseph Heller (1923–) US novelist. *Catch-22*, Ch. 9

7 Women want mediocre men, and men are working to be as mediocre as possible.

Margaret Mead (1901–78) US anthropologist. *Quote Magazine*, 15 May 1958

8 With first-rate sherry flowing into second-rate whores,
And third-rate conversation without one single pause:
Just like a couple
Between the wars.

William Plomer (1903–73) South African poet and novelist. *Father and Son: 1939*

9 It isn't evil that is ruining the earth, but mediocrity. The crime is not that Nero played while Rome burned, but that he played badly.

Ned Rorem (1923–) US composer and writer. *The Final Diary*

10 Much of a muchness.

John Vanbrugh (1664–1726) English architect and dramatist. *The Provok'd Husband*, I:1

MEIR, GOLDA

(1898–1978) Russian-born Israeli stateswoman, who was brought up in the USA. A founder of the Israeli Workers' Party, she became minister of Labour (1949–56) and foreign minister (1956–66), before becoming prime minister (1969–74).

1 A leader who doesn't hesitate before he sends his nation into battle is not fit to be a leader.

As Good as Golda (ed. Israel and Mary Shenker)

2 I can honestly say that I was never affected by the question of the success of an undertaking. If I felt it was the right thing to do, I was for it regardless of the possible outcome.

Golda Meir: Woman with a Cause (Marie Syrkin)

3 ...there's no difference between one's killing and making decisions that will send others to kill. It's exactly the same thing, or even worse.

L'Europeo (Oriana Fallaci)

4 Pessimism is a luxury that a Jew never can allow himself.

The Observer, 'Sayings of the Year', 29 Dec 1974

5 Being seventy is not a sin.

Reader's Digest (July 1971), 'The Indestructible Golda Meir'

6 We intend to remain alive. Our neighbors want

to see us dead. This is not a question that leaves much room for compromise.

Reader's Digest (July 1971), 'The Indestructible Golda Meir'

7 There are not enough prisons and concentration camps in Palestine to hold all the Jews who are ready to defend their lives and property.

Speech, 2 May 1940

MELANCHOLY

See also despair, sorrow

1 Nothing's so dainty sweet as lovely melancholy.

Francis Beaumont (1584–1616) English dramatist. *The Nice Valour*, III:3

2 All my joys to this are folly,
Naught so sweet as Melancholy.

Robert Burton (1577–1640) English scholar and explorer. *Anatomy of Melancholy*, Abstract

3 If there is a hell upon earth, it is to be found in a melancholy man's heart.

Robert Burton *Anatomy of Melancholy*, Pt. I

4 Twentieth-Century Blues.

Noël Coward (1899–1973) British dramatist. Song title

5 I am aware of the damp souls of the housemaids
Sprouting despondently at area gates.

T. S. Eliot (1888–1965) US-born British poet and dramatist. *Morning at the Window*

6 I am in that temper that if I were under water I would scarcely kick to come to the top.

John Keats (1795–1821) British poet. Letter to Benjamin Bailey, 21 May 1818

7 Ay, in the very temple of delight
Veil'd Melancholy has her sovran shrine.
Though seen of none save him whose strenuous tongue
Can burst Joy's grape against his palate fine.

John Keats *Ode on Melancholy*

8 My heart aches, and a drowsy numbness pains
My sense.

John Keats *Ode to a Nightingale*

9 Wrapt in a pleasing fit of melancholy.

John Milton (1608-74) English poet. *Comus*

10 Where glowing embers through the room
Teach light to counterfeit a gloom,
Far from all resort of mirth,
Save the cricket on the hearth.

John Milton *Il Penseroso*

11 I was told I am a true cosmopolitan. I am unhappy everywhere.

Stephen Vizinczey (1933–) Hungarian-born British writer. *The Guardian*, 7 Mar 1968

MELBA, DAME NELLIE

(Helen Porter Mitchell; 1861–1931) Australian soprano.

1 The first rule in opera is the first rule in life: see to everything yourself.

Melodies and Memories

2 Music is not written in red, white and blue. It is written in the heart's blood of the composer.

Melodies and Memories

3 One of the drawbacks of Fame is that one can never escape from it.

Melodies and Memories

4 So you're going to Australia! Well, I made twenty thousand pounds on my tour there, but of course *that* will never be done again. Still, it's a wonderful country, and you'll have a good time. What are you going to sing? All I can say is – sing 'em muck! It's all they can understand!

Speaking to Clara Butt. *Clara Butt: Her Life Story* (W. H. Ponder)

MELBOURNE, WILLIAM LAMB, VISCOUNT

(1779–1848) British statesman. Whig prime minister (1934; 1835–41). His marriage to Lady Caroline Ponsonby (1805) ended in divorce after her affair with Lord Byron.

Quotations about Melbourne

1 He is nothing more than a sensible, honest man who means to do his duty to the Sovereign and his country, instead of the ignorant man he pretends to be.

Sydney Smith (1771–1845) British clergyman and essayist. Attrib.

2 He is the person who makes us feel safe and comfortable.

Victoria (1819–1901) Queen of the United Kingdom. *Journal*, 4 July 1838

Quotations by Melbourne

3 Now, is it to lower the price of corn, or isn't it? It is not much matter which we say, but mind, we must all say *the same.*

Said at a cabinet meeting. *The English Constitution* (Bagehot), Ch. 1

4 What I want is men who will support me when I am in the wrong.

Replying to someone who said he would support Melbourne as long as he was in the right. *Lord M.* (Lord David Cecil)

5 For God's sake, ma'am, let's have no more of that. If you get the English people into the way of making kings, you'll get them into the way of *un*making them.

Advising Queen Victoria against granting Prince Albert the title of King Consort. *Lord M.* (Lord David Cecil)

6 I like the Garter; there is no damned merit in it.

Lord Melbourne (H. Dunckley), 'On the Order of the Garter'

7 I wish I was as cocksure of anything as Tom Macaulay is of everything.

Preface to Lord Melbourne's Papers (Earl Cowper)

8 Nobody ever did anything very foolish except from some strong principle.

The Young Melbourne (Lord David Cecil)

9 Damn it all, another Bishop dead, – I verily believe they die to vex me.

Attrib.

10 While I cannot be regarded as a pillar, I must be regarded as a buttress of the church, because I support it from the outside.
Attrib.

11 Things have come to a pretty pass when religion is allowed to invade the sphere of private life.
On hearing an evangelical sermon.
Attrib.

MEMORIALS

See also epitaphs, memory, obituaries, reputation

1 When I am dead, and laid in grave,
And all my bones are rotten,
By this may I remembered be
When I should be forgotten.
Anonymous On a girl's sampler, 1736

2 You must not miss Whitehall. At one end you will find a statue of one of our kings who was beheaded; at the other the monument to the man who did it. This is just an example of our attempts to be fair to everybody.
Edward Appleton (1892–1965) British physicist. Referring to Charles I and Cromwell. Speech, Stockholm, 1 Jan 1948

3 All your better deeds
Shall be in water writ, but this in marble.
Francis Beaumont (1584–1616) English dramatist. *The Nice Valour*, V:3

4 Such as did bear rule in their kingdoms, men renowned for their power, giving counsel by their understanding, and declaring prophecies:
Leaders of the people by their counsels, and by their knowledge of learning meet for the people, wise and eloquent in their instructions:
Such as found out musical tunes and recited verses in writing:
Rich men furnished with ability living peaceably in their habitations:
All these were honoured in their generations, and were the glory of their times.
There be of them, that have left a name behind them, that their praises might be reported.
And some there be, which have no memorial; who are perished, as though they had never been; and are become as though they had never been born; and their children after them.
Bible: Ecclesiasticus 44:3–9

5 Their bodies are buried in peace; but their name liveth for evermore.
Bible: Ecclesiasticus 44:14

6 They shall grow not old, as we that are left grow old:
Age shall not weary them, nor the years condemn.
At the going down of the sun and in the morning
We will remember them.
Laurence Binyon (1869–1943) British poet. *Poems For the Fallen*

7 John Brown's body lies a-mouldering in the grave,
His soul is marching on!
Charles Sprague Hall (19th century) US songwriter. The song commemorates the American hero who died in the cause of abolishing slavery. *John Brown's Body*

8 I have executed a memorial longer lasting than bronze.
Horace (Quintus Horatius Flaccus; 65–8 BC) Roman poet. *Odes*, III

9 In a larger sense we cannot dedicate, we cannot consecrate, we cannot hallow this ground. The brave men, living and dead, who struggled here, have consecrated it far above our power to add or detract. The world will little note, nor long remember, what we say here, but it can never forget what they did here. It is for us, the living, rather to be dedicated here to the unfinished work which they who fought here have thus far so nobly advanced. It is rather for us to be here dedicated to the great task remaining before us...that we here highly resolve that the dead shall not have died in vain, that this nation, under God, shall have a new birth of freedom; and that government of the people, by the people, and for the people, shall not perish from the earth.
Abraham Lincoln (1809–65) US statesman. Report of Lincoln's address at the dedication (19 Nov 1863) of the national cemetery on the site of the Battle of Gettysburg.

10 The monument sticks like a fishbone
in the city's throat.
Robert Lowell (1917–77) US poet. *For the Union Dead*

11 In Flanders fields the poppies blow
Between the crosses, row on row,
That mark our place.
John McCrae (1872–1918) Canadian poet and doctor. *In Flanders Fields*, 'Ypres Salient', 3 May 1915

12 The shrill demented choirs of wailing shells
And buglers calling for them from sad shires.
Wilfred Owen (1893–1918) British poet. *Anthem for Doomed Youth*

13 I was told that the Chinese said they would bury me by the Western Lake and build a shrine to my memory. I have some slight regret that this did not happen, as I might have become a god, which would have been very *chic* for an atheist.
Bertrand Russell (1872–1970) British philosopher. *The Autobiography of Bertrand Russell*, Vol. II, Ch. 3

14 Who will remember, passing through this gate
The unheroic dead who fed the guns?
Who shall absolve the foulness of their fate –
Those doomed, conscripted, unvictorious ones?
Siegfried Sassoon (1886–1967) British poet. *On Passing the New Menin Gate*

15 Remembrance is the secret of reconciliation.
Rudolf Scharping German politician *The Observer*, 'Sayings of the Week', 17 Apr 1994

16 Men's evil manners live in brass: their virtues
We write in water.
William Shakespeare (1564–1616) English dramatist. *Henry VIII*, IV:2

17 I met a traveller from an antique land
Who said: Two vast and trunkless legs of stone
Stand in the desert.
Percy Bysshe Shelley (1792–1822) British poet. Referring to the legs of a broken statue of the Pharaoh Rameses II (1301–1234 BC; Greek name, Ozymandias). *Ozymandias*

18 Move Queen Anne? Most certainly not! Why it might some day be suggested that *my* statue should be moved, which I should much dislike.

Victoria (1819–1901) Queen of the United Kingdom. Said at the time of her Diamond Jubilee (1897), when it was suggested that the statue of Queen Anne should be moved from outside St. Paul's. *Men, Women and Things* (Duke of Portland), Ch. 5

MEMORY

See also memorials, nostalgia, past

1 Memories are hunting horns whose sound dies on the wind.

Guillaume Apollinaire (Wilhelm de Kostrowitzky; 1880–1918) Italian-born French poet. *Cors de Chasse*

2 I have more memories than if I were a thousand years old.

Charles Baudelaire (1821–67) French poet. *Spleen*

3 Time whereof the memory of man runneth not to the contrary.

William Blackstone (1723–80) British jurist. *Commentaries on the Laws of England*, Bk. I, Ch. 18

4 Like the empty words of a dream
Remembered on waking.

Robert Bridges (1844–1930) British poet. *I Love All Beauteous Things*

5 Memory is the thing you forget with.

Alexander Chase *Perspectives*

6 Am in Birmingham. Where ought I to be?

G. K. Chesterton (1874–1936) British writer. Telegram to his wife during a lecture tour. *Portrait of Barrie* (C. Asquith)

7 When I meet a man whose name I can't remember, I give myself two minutes; then, if it is a hopeless case, I always say, And how is the old complaint?

Benjamin Disraeli (1804–81) British statesman. Attrib.

8 I have forgot much, Cynara! gone with the wind,
Flung roses, roses riotously with the throng.

Ernest Dowson (1867–1900) British lyric poet. *Non Sum Qualis Eram Bonae Sub Regno Cynarae*

9 Oh! don't you remember sweet Alice, Ben Bolt,
Sweet Alice, whose hair was so brown,
Who wept with delight when you gave her a smile,
And trembled with fear at your frown?

Thomas Dunn English (1819–1902) US lawyer and writer. *Ben Bolt*

10 To endeavour to forget anyone is a certain way of thinking of nothing else.

Jean de La Bruyère (1645–96) French satirist. *Les Caractères*

11 Oh, yes I remember it well.

Alan Jay Lerner (1918–86) US lyricist and playwright. *Gigi*, 'I Remember It Well'

12 I never forget a face, but I'll make an exception in your case.

Groucho Marx (Julius Marx; 1895–1977) US comedian. *The Guardian*, 18 June 1965

13 The sigh of midnight trains in empty stations…
The smile of Garbo and the scent of roses
These foolish things
Remind me of you.

Eric Maschwitz (1901–69) British songwriter. Song

14 What a strange thing is memory, and hope; one looks backward, the other forward. The one is of today, the other is the Tomorrow. Memory is history recorded in our brain, memory is a painter, it paints pictures of the past and of the day.

Grandma Moses (Anna Mary Robertson Moses; 1860–1961) US primitive painter. *Grandma Moses, My Life's History* (ed. Aotto Kallir), Ch. 1

15 The taste was that of the little crumb of madeleine which on Sunday mornings at Combray…, when I used to say good-day to her in her bedroom, my aunt Léonie used to give me, dipping it first in her own cup of real or of lime-flower tea.

Marcel Proust (1871–1922) French novelist. *À La Recherche du temps perdu: Du côté de chez Swann*

16 Thanks For the Memory.

Leo Robin (1899–1984) US songwriter. *Big Broadcast*, song title

17 Everyone complains of his memory, but no one complains of his judgement.

Duc de la Rochefoucauld (1613–80) French writer. *Maximes*, 89

18 Remember me when I am gone away,
Gone far away into the silent land.

Christina Rossetti (1830–74) British poet. *Remember*

19 Better by far you should forget and smile
Than that you should remember and be sad.

Christina Rossetti *Remember*

20 To expect a man to retain everything that he has ever read is like expecting him to carry about in his body everything that he has ever eaten.

Arthur Schopenhauer (1788–1860) German philosopher. *Parerga and Paralipomena*

21 Old men forget; yet all shall be forgot,
But he'll remember, with advantages,
What feats he did that day.

William Shakespeare (1564–1616) English dramatist. *Henry V*, IV:3

22 Music, when soft voices die,
Rose leaves, when the rose is dead,
Are heaped for the beloved's bed;
And so thy thoughts, when thou art gone,
Love itself shall slumber on.

Percy Bysshe Shelley (1792–1822) British poet. *To –*

23 There are three things I always forget. Names, faces and—the third I can't remember.

Italo Svevo (Ettore Schmitz; 1861–1928) Italian writer. Attrib.

24 Till life forget and death remember,
Till thou remember and I forget.

Algernon Charles Swinburne (1837–1909) British poet. *Itylus*

25 As a perfume doth remain
In the folds where it hath lain,
So the thought of you, remaining
Deeply folded in my brain,
Will not leave me: all things leave me:
You remain.

Arthur Symons (1865–1945) British poet. *Memory*

26 Yes, I remember Adlestrop –
The name, because one afternoon
Of heat the express train drew up there
Unwontedly. It was late June.

Edward Thomas (1878–1917) British poet. *Adlestrop*

27 I suppose that the high-water mark of my youth

in Columbus, Ohio, was the night the bed fell on my father.

James Thurber (1894–1961) US humorist. *My Life and Hard Times*, Ch. 1

28 The nice thing about having memories is that you can choose.

William Trevor (1928–) British writer. *Matilda's England*

29 Memories are like mulligatawny soup in a cheap restaurant. It is best not to stir them.

P. G. Wodehouse (1881–1975) British humorous novelist. *Bring on the Girls* (with Guy Bolton)

MEN

See also mankind, marriage, masculinity, sexes, women

1 One cannot be always laughing at a man without now and then stumbling on something witty.

Jane Austen (1775–1817) British novelist. *Pride and Prejudice*, Ch. 40

2 A man's a man for a' that.

Robert Burns (1759–96) Scottish poet. *For a' that and a' that*

3 It is men who face the biggest problems in the future, adjusting to their new and complicated role.

Anna Ford British newscaster. Remark, Jan 1981

4 All men are rapists and that's all they are. They rape us with their eyes, their laws and their codes.

Marilyn French (1929–) US novelist. *The Women's Room*

5 A man…is *so* in the way in the house!

Elizabeth Gaskell (1810–65) British novelist. *Cranford*, Ch. 1

6 Probably the only place where a man can feel really secure is in a maximum security prison, except for the imminent threat of release.

Germaine Greer (1939–) Australian-born British writer and feminist. *The Female Eunuch*

7 And let her learn through what kind of dust
He has earned his thirst and the right to quench it
And what sweat he has exchanged for his money
And the blood-weight of money. He'll humble her

Ted Hughes (1930–) British poet. *Selected Poems 1957–1981*, 'Her Husband'

8 Christ called as his Apostles only men. He did this in a totally free and sovereign way.

John Paul II (Karol Wojtyla; 1920–) Polish Pope. *The Observer*, 'Sayings of the Week', 25 Sept 1988

9 How beastly the bourgeois is
especially the male of the species.

D. H. Lawrence (1885–1930) British novelist. *How beastly the bourgeois is*

10 One realizes with horror, that the race of men is almost extinct in Europe. Only Christ-like heroes and woman-worshipping Don Juans, and rabid equality-mongrels.

D. H. Lawrence *Sea and Sardinia*, Ch. 3

11 Why can't a woman be more like a man?
Men are so honest, so thoroughly square;
Eternally noble, historically fair.

Alan Jay Lerner (1918–86) US songwriter. *My Fair Lady*, II:4

12 He was formed for the ruin of our sex.

Tobias Smollett (1721–71) British novelist. *Roderick Random*, Ch. 22

13 It is an ancient contention of my wife that I, in common with all other men, in any dispute between a female relative and a tradesman, side with the tradesman, partly from fear, partly from masculine clannishness, and most of all from a desire to stand well with the tradesman.

E. Œ. Somerville (1858–1949) Irish writer. *Experiences of an Irish R.M.*, 'The Pug-nosed Fox'

14 Sometimes I think if there was a third sex men wouldn't get so much as a glance from me.

Amanda Vail (Warren Miller; 1921–66) US writer. *Love Me Little*, Ch. 6

15 A man in the house is worth two in the street.

Mae West (1892–1980) US actress. *Belle of the Nineties*, film 1934

MENCKEN, H. L.

(1880–1956) US journalist and editor. His collected essays were published in *Prejudices* (6 vols; 1919–27).

1 Puritanism – The haunting fear that someone, somewhere, may be happy.

Chrestomathy 1949

2 Conscience is the inner voice that warns us somebody may be looking.

A Little Book in C Major 1916

3 We must respect the other fellow's religion, but only in the sense and to the extent that we respect his theory that his wife is beautiful and his children smart.

Notebooks, 'Minority Report'

4 It is now quite lawful for a Catholic woman to avoid pregnancy by a resort to mathematics, though she is still forbidden to resort to physics and chemistry.

Notebooks, 'Minority Report'

5 War will never cease until babies begin to come into the world with larger cerebrums and smaller adrenal glands.

Notebooks, 'Minority Report'

6 One of the things that makes a Negro unpleasant to white folk is the fact that he suffers from their injustice. He is thus a standing rebuke to them.

Notebooks, 'Minority Report'

7 The chief contribution of Protestantism to human thought is its massive proof that God is a bore.

Notebooks, 'Minority Report'

8 The worst government is the most moral. One composed of cynics is often very tolerant and human. But when fanatics are on top there is no limit to oppression.

Notebooks, 'Minority Report'

9 God is the immemorial refuge of the incompetent, the helpless, the miserable. They find not only sanctuary in His arms, but also a kind of superiority, soothing to their macerated egos; He will set them above their betters.

Notebooks, 'Minority Report'

10 It takes a long while for a naturally trustful person to reconcile himself to the idea that after all God will not help him.
Notebooks, 'Minority Report'

11 A society made up of individuals who were all capable of original thought would probably be unendurable. The pressure of ideas would simply drive it frantic.
Notebooks, 'Minority Report'

12 Poetry is a comforting piece of fiction set to more or less lascivious music.
Prejudices, 'The Poet and his Art'

13 No man is genuinely happy, married, who has to drink worse gin than he used to drink when he was single.
Prejudices, 'Reflections on Monogamy'

14 Faith may be defined briefly as an illogical belief in the occurrence of the improbable.
Prejudices, 'Types of Men'

15 He is the only man who is for ever apologizing for his occupation.
Referring to businessmen. *Prejudices*, 'Types of Men'

16 An idealist is one who, on noticing that a rose smells better than a cabbage, concludes that it will also make better soup.
Sententiae

17 Opera in English, is, in the main, just about as sensible as baseball in Italian.
The Frank Muir Book (Frank Muir)

18 I've made it a rule never to drink by daylight and never to refuse a drink after dark.
New York Post, 18 Sept 1945

MERCY

1 And he said, He that shewed mercy on him.
Then said Jesus unto him, Go, and do thou likewise.
Bible: Luke 10:37

2 The quality of mercy is not strain'd;
It droppeth as the gentle rain from heaven
Upon the place beneath. It is twice blest;
It blesseth him that gives and him that takes.
William Shakespeare (1564–1616) English dramatist. *The Merchant of Venice*, IV:1

3 God tempers the wind, said Maria, to the shorn lamb.
Laurence Sterne (1713–68) British novelist. *A Sentimental Journey*, 'Maria'

4 And her face so sweet and pleading, yet with sorrow pale and worn,
Touched his heart with sudden pity – lit his eye with misty light;
'Go, your lover lives!' said Cromwell; 'Curfew shall not ring tonight!'
Rose Hartwick Thorpe (1850–1939) US poet and novelist. *Curfew Shall Not Ring Tonight*

MERIT

1 A good dog deserves a good bone.
Proverb

2 I don't deserve this, but I have arthritis, and I don't deserve that either.
Jack Benny (Benjamin Kubelsky; 1894–1974) US actor. Said when accepting an award. Attrib.

3 But many that are first shall be last; and the last shall be first.
Bible: Matthew 19:30

4 GOLDSMITH: Here's such a stir about a fellow that has written one book, and I have written many.
JOHNSON: Ah, Doctor, there go two-and-forty sixpences you know to one guinea.
Samuel Johnson (1709–84) British lexicographer. Referring to Beattie's *Essay on Truth*. *Johnsonian Miscellanies* (ed. G. B. Hill), Vol. I

5 I guess this is the week I earn my salary.
John Fitzgerald Kennedy (1917–63) US statesman. Comment made during the Cuban missile crisis. *Nobody Said It Better* (M. Ringo)

6 Use every man after his desert, and who shall scape whipping?
William Shakespeare (1564–1616) English dramatist. *Hamlet*, II:2

7 I wasn't lucky. I deserved it.
Margaret Thatcher (1925–) British politician and prime minister. Said after receiving school prize, aged nine. Attrib.

8 The Rise of the Meritocracy.
Michael Young (1915–) British political writer. Book title

MERRYMAKING

See also parties, pleasure

1 Come lasses and lads, get leave of your dads,
And away to the Maypole hie,
For every he has got him a she,
And the fiddler's standing by.
Anonymous *Come Lasses and Lads*

2 There was a sound of revelry by night,
And Belgium's capital had gather'd then
Her Beauty and her Chivalry, and bright
The lamps shone o'er fair women and brave men.
Lord Byron (1788–1824) British poet. *Childe Harold's Pilgrimage*, III

3 We have heard the chimes at midnight.
William Shakespeare (1564–1616) English dramatist. *Henry IV, Part Two*, III:2

4 Dost thou think, because thou art virtuous, there shall be no more cakes and ale?
William Shakespeare *Twelfth Night*, II:3

5 You must wake and call me early, call me early, mother dear;
To-morrow 'ill be the happiest time of all the glad New-year;
Of all the glad New-year, mother, the maddest merriest day;
For I'm to be Queen o' the May, mother, I'm to be Queen o' the May.
Alfred, Lord Tennyson (1809–92) British poet. *The May Queen*

6 I love such mirth as does not make friends ashamed to look upon one another next morning.

Izaak Walton (1593–1683) English writer. *The Compleat Angler*, Ch. 5

METAPHYSICS

See also philosophy

1 A blind man in a dark room – looking for a black hat – which isn't there.

Lord Bowen (1835–94) British judge. Characterization of a metaphysician. Attrib.

2 Metaphysics is the finding of bad reasons for what we believe upon instinct; but to find these reasons is no less an instinct.

F. H. Bradley (1846–1924) British philosopher. *Appearance and Reality*, Preface

3 We used to think that if we knew one, we knew two, because one and one are two. We are finding that we must learn a great deal more about 'and'.

Arthur Eddington (1882–1944) British astronomer. *The Harvest of a Quiet Eye* (A. L. Mackay)

4 In other words, apart from the known and the unknown, what else is there?

Harold Pinter (1930–) British dramatist. *The Homecoming*, II

5 Whither is fled the visionary gleam?
Where is it now, the glory and the dream?

Our birth is but a sleep and a forgetting:
The Soul that rises with us, our life's Star,
Hath had elsewhere its setting,
And cometh from afar;
Not in entire forgetfulness,
And not in utter nakedness,
But trailing clouds of glory do we come
From God, who is our home:
Heaven lies about us in our infancy!
Shades of the prison-house begin to close
Upon the growing boy.

William Wordsworth (1770–1850) British poet. *Ode. Intimations of Immortality*, IV

6 Hence in a season of calm weather
Though inland far we be,
Our souls have sight of that immortal sea
Which brought us hither…

William Wordsworth *Ode. Intimations of Immortality*, IX

MILLER, ARTHUR

(1915–) US dramatist. His plays include *Death of a Salesman* (1947), *The Crucible* (1953), *After the Fall* (1964), based on the life of his late wife, Marilyn Monroe, *The Price* (1968), and *The Last Yankee* (1990).

1 There are many who stay away from church these days because you hardly ever mention God any more.

The Crucible, I

2 He's liked, but he's not well liked.

Death of a Salesman, I

3 Years ago a person, he was unhappy, didn't know what to do with himself – he'd go to church, start a revolution – *something*. Today you're unhappy? Can't figure it out? What is the salvation? Go shopping.

The Price, I

4 I am inclined to notice the ruin in things, perhaps because I was born in Italy.

A View from the Bridge, I

5 A good newspaper, I suppose, is a nation talking to itself.

The Observer, 'Sayings of the Week', 26 Nov 1961

6 Why should I go? She won't be there.

When asked if he would attend Marilyn Monroe's funeral. Attrib.

MILLIGAN, SPIKE

(1918–) British comic actor and author, best known as co-author of and performer in the BBC radio series *The Goon Show*.

1 I shook hands with a friendly Arab…I still have my right hand to prove it.

A Dustbin of Milligan, 'Letters to Harry Secombe'

2 I have for instance among my purchases… several original Mona Lisas and all painted (according to the Signature) by the great artist Kodak.

A Dustbin of Milligan, 'Letters to Harry Secombe'

3 – 'Do you come here often?'
'Only in the mating season.'

The Goon Show

4 I don't like this game.

The Goon Show

5 I'm walking backwards till Christmas.

The Goon Show

6 MORIARTY. How are you at Mathematics?
HARRY SECOMBE. I speak it like a native.

The Goon Show

7 You silly twisted boy.

The Goon Show

8 Contraceptives should be used on every conceivable occasion.

The Last Goon Show of All

9 Policemen are numbered in case they get lost.

The Last Goon Show of All

10 Money can't buy friends, but you can get a better class of enemy.

Puckoon, Ch. 6

11 One day the don't-knows will get in, and then where will we be?

Attributed remark made about a pre-election poll

MILNE, A. A.

(1882–1956) British writer, best known for his books for and about his son Christopher Robin, including *When We Were Very Young* (1924), *Winnie-the-Pooh* (1926), and *Now We Are Six* (1927).

1 I am old enough to be – in fact am – your mother.

Belinda

2 If the English language had been properly organized…then there would be a word which meant both 'he' and 'she', and I could write, 'If John or Mary comes heesh will want to play tennis,' which would save a lot of trouble.

The Christopher Robin Birthday Book

3 For one person who dreams of making fifty thousand pounds, a hundred people dream of being left fifty thousand pounds.

If I May, 'The Future'

4 They're changing guard at Buckingham Palace –
Christopher Robin went down with Alice.
Alice is marrying one of the guard.
'A soldier's life is terrible hard,'
Says Alice.

When We Were Very Young, 'Buckingham Palace'

5 And some of the bigger bears try to pretend
That they came round the corner to look for a friend;
And they'll try to pretend that nobody cares
Whether you walk on the lines or the squares.

When We Were Very Young, 'Lines and Squares'

6 I am a Bear of Very Little Brain, and long words Bother me.

Winnie-the-Pooh, Ch. 4

7 Time for a little something.

Winnie-the-Pooh, Ch. 6

MILTON, JOHN

(1608–74) English poet. His poems include *L'Allegro* and *Il Penseroso* (1632) and the great epics *Paradise Lost* (1667) and *Paradise Regained* (1671).

Quotations about Milton

1 Our Language sunk under him, and was unequal to that greatness of soul which furnished him with such glorious conceptions.

Joseph Addison (1672–1719) British essayist. *The Spectator*

2 Milton the prince of poets – so we say
A little heavy but no less divine
An independent being in his day –
Learn'd, pious, temperate in love and wine.

Lord Byron (1788–1824) British poet. *Don Juan*

3 The whole of Milton's poem, *Paradise Lost*, is such barbarous trash, so outrageously offensive to reason and to common sense that one is naturally led to wonder how it can have been tolerated by a people amongst whom astronomy, navigation and chemistry are understood.

William Cobbett (1763–1835) British journalist and writer. *A Year's Residence in The United States*

4 As a poet, Milton seems to me the greatest of eccentrics. His work illustrates no general principles of good writing; the only principles of writing that it illustrates are such as are valid only for Milton himself to observe.

T. S. Eliot (1888–1965) US-born British poet and dramatist. *Essays: Milton*

5 Milton, Madam, was a genius that could cut a Colossus from a rock; but could not carve heads upon cherry-stones.

Samuel Johnson (1709–84) British lexicographer. *Life of Johnson* (James Boswell)

Quotations by Milton

6 Who kills a man kills a reasonable creature, God's image; but he who destroys a good book, kills reason itself, kills the image of God, as it were in the eye.

Areopagitica

7 A good book is the precious life-blood of a master spirit, embalmed and treasured up on purpose to a life beyond life.

Areopagitica

8 Let her and Falsehood grapple; who ever knew Truth put to the worse, in a free and open encounter?

Areopagitica

9 Blest pair of Sirens, pledges of Heaven's joy,
Sphere-born harmonious sisters, Voice and Verse.

At a Solemn Music

10 Wrapt in a pleasing fit of melancholy.

Comus

11 Hence, vain deluding Joys,
The brood of Folly without father bred!

Il Penseroso

12 And looks commercing with the skies,
Thy rapt soul sitting in thine eyes.

Il Penseroso

13 Sweet bird, that shunn'st the noise of folly,
Most musical, most melancholy!

Referring to the nightingale. *Il Penseroso*

14 Where glowing embers through the room
Teach light to counterfeit a gloom,
Far from all resort of mirth,
Save the cricket on the hearth.

Il Penseroso

15 Where more is meant than meets the ear.

Il Penseroso

16 Come, and trip it as ye go
On the light fantastic toe.

L'Allegro

17 To hear the lark begin his flight,
And singing startle the dull night,
From his watch-tower in the skies,
Till the dappled dawn doth rise.

L'Allegro

18 Then to the spicy nut-brown ale.

L'Allegro

19 Or sweetest Shakespeare, Fancy's child,
Warble his native wood-notes wild.

L'Allegro

20 The melting voice through mazes running;
Untwisting all the chains that tie
The hidden soul of harmony.

L'Allegro

21 Yet once more, O ye laurels, and once more,
Ye myrtles brown, with ivy never sere,
I come to pluck your berries harsh and crude,
And with forced fingers rude
Shatter your leaves before the mellowing year.
Lycidas

22 Under the opening eye-lids of the morn.
Lycidas

23 As killing as the canker to the rose.
Lycidas

24 To sport with Amaryllis in the shade,
Or with the tangles of Neaera's hair.
Lycidas

25 Fame is the spur that the clear spirit doth raise
(That last infirmity of noble mind)
To scorn delights, and live laborious days.
Lycidas

26 The hungry sheep look up, and are not fed,
But, swoln with wind and the rank mist they draw,
Rot inwardly, and foul contagion spread.
Lycidas

27 At last he rose, and twitched his mantle blue:
To-morrow to fresh woods, and pastures new.
Lycidas

28 Rhyme being no necessary adjunct or true ornament of poem or good verse, in longer works especially, but the invention of a barbarous age, to set off wretched matter and lame metre.
Paradise Lost, The Verse. Preface to 1668 ed.

29 The troublesome and modern bondage of Rhyming.
Paradise Lost, The Verse. Preface to 1668 ed.

30 Of Man's first disobedience, and the fruit
Of that forbidden tree, whose mortal taste
Brought death into the World, and all our woe…
Paradise Lost, Bk. I

31 What in me is dark
Illumine, what is low raise and support;
That, to the height of this great argument,
I may assert Eternal Providence,
And justify the ways of God to men.
Paradise Lost, Bk. I

32 What though the field be lost?
All is not lost – the unconquerable will,
And study of revenge, immortal hate,
And courage never to submit or yield:
And what is else not to be overcome?
Paradise Lost, Bk. I

33 A mind not to be changed by place or time.
The mind is its own place, and in itself
Can make a Heaven of Hell, a Hell of Heaven.
Paradise Lost, Bk. I

34 To reign is worth ambition, though in Hell:
Better to reign in Hell than serve in Heaven.
Paradise Lost, Bk. I

35 Care
Sat on his faded cheek.
Paradise Lost, Bk. I

36 Tears such as angels weep, burst forth.
Paradise Lost, Bk. I

37 Who overcomes
By force, hath overcome but half his foe.
Paradise Lost, Bk. I

38 From morn
To noon he fell, from noon to dewy eve,
A summer's day, and with the setting sun
Dropped from the zenith, like a falling star.
Paradise Lost, Bk. I

39 High on a throne of royal state, which far
Outshone the wealth of Ormus and of Ind,
Or where the gorgeous East with richest hand
Showers on her kings barbaric pearl and gold,
Satan exalted sat, by merit raised
To that bad eminence.
Paradise Lost, Bk. II

40 Long is the way
And hard, that out of hell leads up to light.
Paradise Lost, Bk. II

41 Vain wisdom all, and false philosophy.
Paradise Lost, Bk. II

42 For neither man nor angel can discern
Hypocrisy, the only evil that walks
Invisible, except to God alone.
Paradise Lost, Bk. III

43 Which way I fly is Hell; myself am Hell;
And, in the lowest deep, a lower deep
Still threat'ning to devour me opens wide,
To which the Hell I suffer seems a Heaven.
Paradise Lost, Bk. IV

44 Farewell remorse! All good to me is lost;
Evil, be thou my Good.
Paradise Lost, Bk. IV

45 A heav'n on earth.
Paradise Lost, Bk. IV

46 Now came still Evening on, and Twilight grey
Had in her sober livery all things clad.
Paradise Lost, Bk. IV

47 Abashed the devil stood,
And felt how awful goodness is.
Paradise Lost, Bk. IV

48 Midnight brought on the dusky hour
Friendliest to sleep and silence.
Paradise Lost, Bk. V

49 In solitude
What happiness? who can enjoy alone,
Or, all enjoying, what contentment find?
Paradise Lost, Bk. VIII

50 Accuse not Nature, she hath done her part;
Do thou but thine.
Paradise Lost, Bk. VIII

51 Revenge, at first though sweet,
Bitter ere long back on itself recoils.
Paradise Lost, Bk. IX

52 The world was all before them, where to choose
Their place of rest, and Providence their guide:

They, hand in hand, with wandering steps and slow,
Through Eden took their solitary way.
Paradise Lost, Bk. XII

53 Most men admire
Virtue, who follow not her lore.
Paradise Regained, Bk. I

54 Beauty stands
In the admiration only of weak minds
Led captive.
Paradise Regained, Bk. II

55 Let us with a gladsome mind
Praise the Lord, for he is kind,
For his mercies ay endure,
Ever faithful, ever sure.
Psalm

56 A little onward lend thy guiding hand
To these dark steps, a little further on.
Samson Agonistes

57 Ask for this great deliverer now, and find him
Eyeless in Gaza at the mill with slaves.
Samson Agonistes

58 O dark, dark, dark, amid the blaze of noon,
Irrecoverably dark, total eclipse,
Without all hope of day!
Samson Agonistes

59 How soon hath Time, the subtle thief of youth,
Stolen on his wing my three-and-twentieth year!
Sonnet: 'On Being Arrived at the Age of Twenty-three'

60 When I consider how my light is spent
Ere half my days in this dark world and wide,
And that one talent which is death to hide
Lodged with me useless.
Sonnet: 'On his Blindness'

61 God doth not need
Either man's work or his own gifts. Who best
Bear his mild yoke, they serve him best: his state
Is kingly; thousands at his bidding speed,
And post o'er land and ocean without rest;
They also serve who only stand and wait.
Sonnet: 'On his Blindness'

62 New Presbyter is but old Priest writ large.
Sonnet: 'On the New Forcers of Conscience under the Long Parliament'

63 Peace hath her victories
No less renowned than war.
Sonnet: 'To the Lord General Cromwell, May 1652'

64 None can love freedom heartily, but good men; the rest love not freedom, but licence.
Tenure of Kings and Magistrates

65 One tongue is sufficient for a woman.
On being asked whether he would allow his daughters to learn foreign languages. Attrib.

MIND

See also intellect, intelligence, thinking

1 BRAIN, n. An apparatus with which we think that we think.
Ambrose Bierce (1842–c. 1914) US writer and journalist. *The Devil's Dictionary*

2 A great many open minds should be closed for repairs.
Toledo Blade

3 The brain is not an organ to be relied upon. It is developing monstrously. It is swelling like a goitre.
Aleksandr Blok (1880–1921) Russian poet.

4 As long as our brain is a mystery, the universe, the reflection of the structure of the brain, will also be a mystery.
Santiago Ramón y Cajal (1852–1934) Spanish scientist. *Charlas de Café*

5 We know the human brain is a device to keep the ears from grating on one another.
Peter de Vries (1910–93) US novelist. *Comfort me with Apples*, Ch. 1

6 Minds like bodies, will often fall into a pimpled, ill-conditioned state from mere excess of comfort.
Charles Dickens (1812–70) British novelist. *Barnaby Rudge*, Ch. 7

7 The mind is an iceberg it floats with only 17 of its bulk above water.
Sigmund Freud (1856–1939) Austrian psychoanalyst. *Bartlett's Unfamiliar Quotations* (Leonard Louis Levinson)

8 The conscious mind may be compared to a fountain playing in the sun and falling back into the great subterranean pool of subconscious from which it rises.
Sigmund Freud *Bartlett's Unfamiliar Quotations* (Leonard Louis Levinson)

9 My life and work has been aimed at one goal only: to infer or guess how the mental apparatus is constructed and what forces interplay and counteract in it.
Sigmund Freud *Life and Work of Sigmund Freud* (E. Jones)

10 The remarkable thing about the human mind is its range of limitations.
Celia Green *The Decline and Fall of Science*, 'Aphorisms'

11 We have rudiments of reverence for the human body, but we consider as nothing the rape of the human mind.
Eric Hoffer (1902–83) US writer. *Bartlett's Unfamiliar Quotations* (Leonard Louis Levinson)

12 Little minds are interested in the extraordinary; great minds in the commonplace.
Elbert Hubbard (1856–1915) US writer and editor. *Roycroft Dictionary and Book of Epigrams*

13 What we think and feel and are is to a great extent determined by the state of our ductless glands and our viscera.
Aldous Huxley (1894–1964) British writer. *Music at Night*, 'Meditation on El Greco'

14 The natural course of the human mind is certainly from credulity to scepticism.
Thomas Jefferson (1743–1826) US statesman. Letter to Dr. Caspar Wistar, 21 June 1807

15 Bodily decay is gloomy in prospect, but of all human contemplations the most abhorrent is body without mind.

Thomas Jefferson Letter to John Adams, 1 Aug 1816

16 The pendulum of the mind oscillates between sense and nonsense, not between right and wrong.

Carl Gustav Jung (1875–1961) Swiss psychoanalyst. *Memories, Dreams, Reflections*, Ch. 5

17 You should pray for a healthy mind in a healthy body.

Juvenal (c. 60–130 AD) Roman satirist. *Satires*, X

18 The highest function of *mind* is its function of messenger.

D. H. Lawrence (1885–1930) British writer. *Kangaroo*, Ch. 16

19 And the mind must sweat a poison
...that, discharged not thence
Gangrenes the vital sense
And makes disorder true.
It is certain we shall attain
No life till we stamp on all
Life the tetragonal
Pure symmetry of the brain.

C. Day Lewis (1904–72) British poet. *Collected Poems 1929–1933*

20 The mind like a sick body can be healed and changed by medicine.

Lucretius (c. 96 BC–55 BC) Roman philosopher and poet. *On the Nature of Things*, III

21 A mind not to be changed by place or time.
The mind is its own place, and in itself
Can make a Heaven of Hell, a Hell of Heaven.

John Milton (1608–74) English poet. *Paradise Lost*, Bk. I

22 The mind has great influence over the body, and maladies often have their origin there.

Molière (Jean Baptiste Poquelin; 1622–73) French dramatist. *Love's the Best Doctor*, III

23 It is good to rub and polish our brain against that of others.

Michel de Montaigne (1533–92) French essayist and moralist. *Essays*, Bk. I

24 A sick mind cannot endure any harshness.

Ovid (Publius Ovidius Naso; 43 BC–17 AD) Roman poet. *Epistulae ex Ponto*, Bk. I

25 That's the classical mind at work, runs fine inside but looks dingy on the surface.

Robert T. Pirsig (1928–) US writer. *Zen and the Art of Motorcycle Maintenance*, Pt. III, Ch. 25

26 Mind is ever the ruler of the universe.

Plato (429 BC–347 BC) Greek philosopher. *Philebus*

27 Happiness is beneficial for the body, but it is grief that develops the powers of the mind.

Marcel Proust (1871–1922) French novelist. *À La Recherche du temps perdu: Le Temps retrouvé*, Ch. 3

28 Our minds are lazier than our bodies.

Duc François de la Rochefoucauld (1613–80) French writer. *Bartlett's Unfamiliar Quotations* (Leonard Louis Levinson)

29 The dogma of the Ghost in the Machine.

Gilbert Ryle (1900–76) British philosopher. *The Concept of Mind*, Ch. 1

30 If it is for mind that we are seaching the brain, then we are supposing the brain to be much more than a telephone-exchange. We are supposing it a telephone-exchange along with the subscribers as well.

Charles Scott Sherrington (1857–1952) British physiologist. *Man on his Nature*

31 Once we are destined to live out our lives in the prison of our mind, our one duty is to furnish it well.

Peter Ustinov (1921–) British actor, director, and writer. *Dear Me*, Ch. 20

32 Mind over matter.

Virgil (Publius Vergilius Maro; 70 BC–19 BC) Roman poet. *Aeneid*, Bk. VI

33 When people will not weed their own minds, they are apt to be overrun with nettles.

Horace Walpole (1717–97) British writer. Letter to Lady Ailesbury, 10 July 1779

34 The mind can also be an erogenous zone.

Raquel Welch (Raquel Tejada; 1940–) US film star. *Colombo's Hollywood* (J. R. Colombo)

35 At 83 Shaw's mind was perhaps not quite as good as it used to be, but it was still better than anyone else's.

Alexander Woollcott (1887–1943) US journalist. Referring to George Bernard Shaw. *While Rome Burns*

36 Strongest minds
Are often those of whom the noisy world
Hears least.

William Wordsworth (1770–1850) British poet. *The Excursion*

MINORITY

See also majority

1 What's a cult? It just means not enough people to make a minority.

Robert Altman (1922–) US film director. *The Observer*, 1981

2 The majority has the might – more's the pity – but it hasn't right...The minority is always right.

Henrik Ibsen (1828–1906) Norwegian dramatist. *An Enemy of the People*, IV

3 Minorities...are almost always in the right.

Sydney Smith (1771–1845) British clergyman and essayist. *The Smith of Smiths* (H. Pearson), Ch. 9

MISANTHROPY

See also mankind

1 What though the spicy breezes
Blow soft o'er Ceylon's isle;
Though every prospect pleases,
And only man is vile...

Reginald Heber (1783–1826) British bishop and hymn writer. *From Greenland's Icy Mountains*

2 I've always been interested in people, but I've never liked them.

W. Somerset Maugham (1874–1965) British novelist. *The Observer*, 'Sayings of the Week', 28 Aug 1949

3 A young, earnest American brought up the subject of nuclear warfare which, he said might well destroy the entire human race. 'I can't wait' P. G. Wodehouse murmured.

Malcolm Muggeridge (1903–90) British writer. *Tread Softly for You Tread On My Jokes*

4 I love mankind – it's people I can't stand.

Charles M. Schultz (1922–) US cartoonist. *Go Fly a Kite, Charlie Brown*

5 Other people are quite dreadful. The only possible society is oneself.

Oscar Wilde (1854–1900) Irish-born British dramatist. *An Ideal Husband*, III

MISFORTUNE

See also accidents, curses, sorrow, suffering

1 It is easy to bear the misfortunes of others.

Proverb

2 It never rains but it pours.

Proverb

3 Drink wine, and have the gout; drink no wine, and have the gout too.

Proverb

4 Prosperity doth best discover vice; but adversity doth best discover virtue.

Francis Bacon (1561–1626) English philosopher. *Essays*, 'Of Adversity'

5 Calamities are of two kinds. Misfortune to ourselves and good fortune to others.

Ambrose Bierce (1842–c. 1914) US writer and journalist. *The Devil's Dictionary*

6 There remaineth a rest for the people of God:
And I have had troubles enough, for one.

Robert Browning (1812–89) British poet. *Old Pictures in Florence*, XVII

7 Tragedie is to seyn a certeyn storie,
As olde bokes maken us memorie,
Of him that stood in greet prosperitee
And is y-fallen out of heigh degree
Into miserie, and endeth wrecchedly.

Geoffrey Chaucer (c. 1342–1400) English poet. *The Canterbury Tales*, 'The Monk's Prologue'

8 For of fortunes sharp adversitee
The worst kinde of infortune is this,
A man to have ben in prosperitee,
And it remembren, what is passed is.

Geoffrey Chaucer *Troilus and Criseyde*, 3

9 A chapter of accidents.

Earl of Chesterfield (1694–1773) English statesman. Letter to his son, 16 Feb 1753

10 The Dodo never had a chance. He seems to have been invented for the sole purpose of becoming extinct and that was all he was good for.

Will Cuppy (1884–1949) US humorist. *How to Become Extinct*

11 'I am a lone lorn creetur,' were Mrs Gummidge's words…'and everythink goes contrairy with me.'

Charles Dickens (1812–70) British novelist. *David Copperfield*, Ch. 3

12 Life is mostly froth and bubble;
Two things stand like stone,
Kindness in another's trouble,
Courage in your own.

Adam Lindsay Gordon (1833–70) Australian poet. *Ye Wearie Wayfarer*, Fytte 8

13 Depend upon it that if a man talks of his misfortunes there is something in them that is not disagreeable to him; for where there is nothing but pure misery there never is any recourse to the mention of it.

Samuel Johnson (1709–84) British lexicographer. *Life of Johnson* (J. Boswell), Vol. IV

14 There exist some evils so terrible and some misfortunes so horrible that we dare not think of them, whilst their very aspect makes us shudder; but if they happen to fall on us, we find ourselves stronger than we imagined, we grapple with our ill luck, and behave better than we expected we should.

Jean de La Bruyère (1645–96) French satirist. *Les Caractères*

15 I never knew any man in my life who could not bear another's misfortunes perfectly like a Christian.

Alexander Pope (1688–1744) British poet. *Thoughts on Various Subjects*

16 We are all strong enough to bear the misfortunes of others.

Duc de la Rochefoucauld (1613–80) French writer. *Maximes*, 19

17 In the misfortune of our best friends, we always find something which is not displeasing to us.

Duc de la Rochefoucauld *Maximes*, 99

18 When sorrows come, they come not single spies,
But in battalions!

William Shakespeare (1564–1616) English dramatist. *Hamlet*, IV:5

19 This is the excellent foppery of the world, that, when we are sick in fortune, often the surfeits of our own behaviour, we make guilty of our disasters the sun, the moon, and stars.

William Shakespeare *King Lear*, I:2

20 Misery acquaints a man with strange bedfellows.

William Shakespeare *The Tempest*, II:2

MISOGYNY

See also women

1 I'd be equally as willing
For a dentist to be drilling
Than to ever let a woman in my life.

Alan Jay Lerner (1918–86) US songwriter. *My Fair Lady*, I:2

2 How can I possibly dislike a sex to which Your Majesty belongs?

Cecil Rhodes (1853–1902) South African statesman. Replying to Queen Victoria's suggestion that he disliked women. *Rhodes* (Lockhart)

3 Would you have me speak after my custom, as being a professed tyrant to their sex?

William Shakespeare (1564–1616) English dramatist. *Much Ado About Nothing*, I:1

MISQUOTATIONS

1 Misquotations are the only quotations that are never misquoted.

Hesketh Pearson (1887–1964) British biographer. *Common Misquotations*

2 A widely-read man never quotes accurately… Misquotation is the pride and privilege of the learned.

Hesketh Pearson *Common Misquotations*

Some examples

3 Had I been present at the Creation, I would have given some useful hints for the better ordering of the universe.

Alfonso the Wise (c. 1221–84) King of Castile and Léon. Referring to the complicated Ptolemaic model of the universe. Often quoted as, 'Had I been consulted I would have recommended something simpler'. Attrib.

4 We have ways of making men talk.

Anonymous Film catchphrase, often repeated as 'We have ways of making you talk'. *Lives of a Bengal Lancer*

5 That's one small step for man, one giant leap for mankind.

Neil Armstrong (1930–) US astronaut. Said on stepping onto the moon. Often quoted as, 'small step for a man…' (which is probably what he intended). Remark, 21 July 1969

6 I have seldom spoken with greater regret, for my lips are not yet unsealed. Were these troubles over I would make a case, and I guarantee that not a man would go into the Lobby against us.

Stanley Baldwin (1867–1947) British statesman. Referring to the Abyssinian crisis; usually misquoted as 'My lips are sealed'. Speech, House of Commons, 10 Dec 1935

7 And behold joy and gladness, slaying oxen, and killing sheep, eating flesh, and drinking wine: let us eat and drink; for tomorrow we shall die.

Bible: Isaiah 22:13 A similar sentiment is expressed in Corinthians 15:32–33. Often misquoted as 'let us eat, drink, and be merry'.

8 So when they continued asking him, he lifted up himself, and said unto them, He that is without sin among you, let him first cast a stone at her.

Bible: John 8:7 Often misquoted as 'cast the first stone'.

9 Then said Jesus unto him, Put up again thy sword into his place: for all they that take the sword shall perish with the sword.

Bible: Matthew 26:52 Often msiquoted as 'They that live by the sword shall die by the sword'.

10 Pride goeth before destruction, and an haughty spirit before a fall.

Bible: Proverbs 16:18 Often misquoted as 'Pride goeth before a fall'.

11 Play it, Sam. Play 'As Time Goes By.'

Humphrey Bogart (1899–1957) US film star. Often misquoted as 'Play it again, Sam'. *Casablanca*

12 You dirty double-crossing rat!

James Cagney (1899–1986) US actor. Usually misquoted by impressionists as 'You dirty rat'. *Blonde Crazy*

13 I have nothing to offer but blood, toil, tears and sweat.

Winston Churchill (1874–1965) British statesman. On becoming prime minister. Often misquoted as 'blood, sweat and tears'. Speech, House of Commons, 13 May 1940

14 War is the continuation of politics by other means.

Karl von Clausewitz (1780–1831) Prussian general. The usual misquotation of 'War is nothing but a continuation of politics with the admixture of other means'. *Vom Kriege*

15 'Excellent!' I cried. 'Elementary,' said he.

Arthur Conan Doyle (1856–1930) British writer. Watson talking to Sherlock Holmes; Holmes's reply is often misquoted as 'Elementary, my dear Watson'. *The Crooked Man*

16 I got there fustest with the mostest.

Nathan Bedford Forrest (1821–77) Confederate general. Popular misquotation of his explanation of his success in capturing Murfreesboro; his actual words were, 'I just took the short cut and got there first with the most men'. *A Civil War Treasury* (B. Botkin)

17 I never said, 'I want to be alone.' I only said, 'I want to be *left* alone.' There is all the difference.

Greta Garbo (1905–90) Swedish-born US film star. *Garbo* (John Bainbridge)

18 Take your hare when it is cased…

Hannah Glasse (18th century) English writer. Often misquoted as, 'First catch your hare' and wrongly attributed to Mrs Beaton. *The Art of Cookery Made Plain and Easy*, Ch. 1

19 Once I built a rail-road,
Now it's done.
Brother, can you spare a dime?

E. Y. Harburg (1898–1981) US lyricist. Often quoted as 'Buddy can you spare a dime'. *New Americana*, 'Brother Can You Spare a Dime'.

20 I am happy now that Charles calls on my bedchamber less frequently than of old. As it is, I now endure but two calls a week and when I hear his steps outside my door I lie down on my bed, close my eyes, open my legs and think of England.

Lady Alice Hillingdon (1857–1940) Wife of 2nd Baron Hillingdon. Often mistakenly attributed to Queen Victoria. *Journal* (1912)

21 Jerry Ford is so dumb that he can't fart and chew gum at the same time.

Lyndon B. Johnson (1908–73) US statesman. Sometimes quoted as '…can't walk and chew gum'. *A Ford, Not a Lincoln* (R. Reeves), Ch. 1

22 Alas, poor Yorick! I knew him,
Horatio: a fellow of infinite jest, of most excellent fancy.

William Shakespeare (1564–1616) English dramatist. Often misquoted as 'I knew him well'. *Hamlet*, V:1

23 I always did like a man in uniform. And that one fits you grand. Why don't you come up sometime and see me?

Mae West (1892–1980) US actress. Often misquoted as 'Come up and see me some time'. *She Done Him Wrong*, film 1933

MISTAKES

See also imperfection

1 Two wrongs do not make a right.

Proverb

2 It is worse than immoral, it's a mistake.

Dean Acheson (1893–1971) US lawyer and statesman. Describing the Vietnam war. *See also* BOULAY DE LA MEURTHE.

Quoted by Alistair Cooke in his radio programme *Letter from America*

3 The weak have one weapon: the errors of those who think they are strong.

Georges Bidault (1899–1983) French statesman. *The Observer*, 1962

4 It is worse than a crime, it is a blunder.

Antoine Boulay de la Meurthe (1761–1840) French politician. *See also* ACHESON. Referring to the summary execution of the Duc d'Enghien by Napoleon, 1804. Attrib.

5 I guess that'll hold the little bastards.

Don Carney (1897–1954) US broadcaster. Carney was ending a children's radio show and thought that he was off the air. Attrib.

6 The medical errors of one century constitute the popular faith of the next.

Alonzo Clark (1807–87)

7 I beseech you, in the bowels of Christ, think it possible you may be mistaken.

Oliver Cromwell (1599–1658) English soldier and statesman. Letter to the General Assembly of the Church of Scotland, 3 Aug 1650

8 Better send them a Papal Bull.

Lord Curzon (1859–1925) British politician. Written in the margin of a Foreign Office document. The phrase 'the monks of Mount Athos were violating their vows' had been misprinted as '...violating their cows'. *Life of Lord Curzon* (Ronaldshay), Vol. III, Ch. 15

9 What we call experience is often a dreadful list of ghastly mistakes.

J. Chalmers Da Costa (1863–1933) *The Trials and Triumphs of the Surgeon*, Ch. 1

10 Yes, once – many, many years ago. I thought I had made a wrong decision. Of course, it turned out that I had been right all along. But I was wrong to have *thought* that I was wrong.

John Foster Dulles (1888–1959) US politician. On being asked whether he had ever been wrong. *Facing the Music* (H. Temianka)

11 Pardon me, madam, but *I* am my brother.

Karl Gustav Jacob Jacobi (1804–51) German mathematician. On being mistaken by a lady for his brother. *Men of Mathematics* (M. H. Jacobi)

12 Erratum. In my article on the Price of Milk, 'Horses' should have read 'Cows' throughout.

J. B. Morton (1893–1979) British journalist. *The Best of Beachcomber*

13 The man who makes no mistakes does not usually make anything.

Edward John Phelps (1822–1900) US lawyer and diplomat. Speech, Mansion House, London, 24 Jan 1899

14 Dentopedology is the science of opening your mouth and putting your foot in it. I've been practising it for years.

Prince Philip (1921–) The consort of Queen Elizabeth II. Attrib.

15 A man should never be ashamed to own he has been in the wrong, which is but saying, in other words, that he is wiser to-day than he was yesterday.

Alexander Pope (1688–1744) British poet. *Thoughts on Various Subjects*

16 To err is human, to forgive, divine.

Alexander Pope *An Essay on Criticism*

17 The follies which a man regrets the most in his life, are those which he didn't commit when he had the opportunity.

Helen Rowland (1876–1950) US writer. *Guide To Men*

18 What time is the next swan?

Leo Slezak (1873–1946) Czechoslovakian-born tenor. When the mechanical swan left the stage without him during a performance of *Lohengrin*. *What Time Is the Next Swan?* (Walter Slezak)

19 We often discover what *will* do, by finding out what will not do; and probably he who never made a mistake never made a discovery.

Samuel Smiles (1812–1904) British writer. *Self-Help*, Ch. 11

20 Human blunders usually do more to shape history than human wickedness.

A. J. P. Taylor (1906–90) British historian. *The Origins of the Second World War*, Ch. 10

21 Well, if I called the wrong number, why did you answer the phone?

James Thurber (1894–1961) US humorist. Cartoon caption

22 If we had more time for discussion we should probably have made a great many more mistakes.

Leon Trotsky (Lev Davidovich Bronstein; 1879–1940) Russian revolutionary. *My Life*

23 The physician can bury his mistakes, but the architect can only advise his client to plant vines.

Frank Lloyd Wright (1869–1959) US architect. *The New York Times Magazine*, 4 Oct 1953

MISTRUST

See also suspicion, trust

1 After shaking hands with a Greek, count your fingers.

Proverb

2 While I see many hoof-marks going in, I see none coming out.

Aesop (6th century BC) Reputed Greek writer of fables. *Fables*, 'The Lion, the Fox, and the Beasts'

3 The lion and the calf shall lie down together but the calf won't get much sleep.

Woody Allen (Allen Stewart Konigsberg; 1935–) US film actor. *Without Feathers*, 'The Scrolls'

4 The louder he talked of his honour, the faster we counted our spoons.

Ralph Waldo Emerson (1803–82) US poet and essayist. *Conduct of Life*, 'Worship'

5 Let me remind you what the wary fox said once upon a time to the sick lion: 'Because those footprints scare me, all directed your way, none coming back.'

Horace (Quintus Horatius Flaccus; 65–8 BC) Roman poet. *Epistles*, I back

6 But if he does really think that there is no distinction between virtue and vice, why, Sir, when he leaves our houses let us count our spoons.

Samuel Johnson (1709–84) British lexicographer. *Life of Johnson* (J. Boswell), Vol. I

7 *Quis custodiet ipsos*

custodes?
Who is to guard the guards themselves?

Juvenal (Decimus Junius Juvenalis; 60–130 AD) Roman satirist. *Satires*, VI

8 Ye diners-out from whom we guard our spoons.

Lord Macaulay (1800–59) British historian. Letter to Hannah Macaulay, 29 June 1831

9 Everyone likes a kidder, but no one lends him money.

Arthur Miller (1915–) US dramatist. *Death of a Salesman*

10 Let me have men about me that are fat;
Sleek-headed men, and such as sleep o' nights.
Yon Cassius has a lean and hungry look;
He thinks too much. Such men are dangerous.

William Shakespeare (1564–1616) English dramatist. *Julius Caesar*, I:2

11 An ally has to be watched just like an enemy.

Leon Trotsky (Lev Davidovich Bronstein; 1879–1940) Russian revolutionary. *Expansion and Coexistence* (A. Ulam)

12 *Equo ne credite, Teucri.*
Quidquid id est timeo Danaos et dona ferentis.
Do not trust the horse, Trojans. Whatever it is, I fear the Greeks even when they bring gifts.

Virgil (Publius Vergilius Maro; 70–19 BC) Roman poet. *Aeneid*, Bk. II

MITCHELL, MARGARET

(1909–49) US novelist, whose single success was *Gone with the Wind* (1936, filmed 1939).

1 Until you've lost your reputation, you never realize what a burden it was or what freedom really is.

Gone with the Wind

2 Fighting is like champagne. It goes to the heads of cowards as quickly as of heroes. Any fool can be brave on a battle field when it's be brave or else be killed.

Gone with the Wind

3 Death and taxes and childbirth! There's never any convenient time for any of them!

Gone with the Wind

4 After all, tomorrow is another day.

The closing words of the book. *Gone with the Wind*

5 Frankly, my dear, I don't give a damn.

Gone with the Wind (screen version)

6 Gone With the Wind.

From the poem *Non Sum Qualis Eram* (Ernest Dowson): 'I have forgotten much, Cynara! Gone with the wind…'. Book title

MIXED METAPHORS

See also Goldwynisms

1 If you open that Pandora's Box you never know what Trojan 'orses will jump out.

Ernest Bevin (1881–1951) British trade-union leader and politician. Referring to the Council of Europe. *Ernest Bevin and the Foreign Office* (Sir Roderick Barclay)

2 Every director bites the hand that lays the golden egg.

Samuel Goldwyn (Samuel Goldfish; 1882–1974) Polish-born US film producer. Attrib.

3 You ought to take the bull between the teeth.

Samuel Goldwyn Attrib.

4 Mr Speaker, I smell a rat; I see him forming in the air and darkening the sky; but I'll nip him in the bud.

Boyle Roche (1743–1807) British politician. Attrib.

MODERATION

See also excess

1 Moderation in all things.

Proverb

2 You can have too much of a good thing.

Proverb

3 Eat and drink measurely, and defy the mediciners.

Proverb

4 Temperance is the best physic.

Proverb

5 I have changed my ministers, but I have not changed my measures; I am still for moderation and will govern by it.

Anne (1665–1714) Queen of Great Britain To members of the new Tory ministry, Jan 1711

6 By God, Mr Chairman, at this moment I stand astonished at my own moderation!

Clive of India (1725–74) British soldier and governor of Bengal. Reply during Parliamentary Inquiry, 1773

7 Eat not to dullness; drink not to elevation.

Benjamin Franklin (1706–90) US scientist and statesman. *Autobiography*, Ch. 5

8 Moderation is a virtue only in those who are thought to have an alternative.

Henry Kissinger (1923–) German-born US politician and diplomat. *The Observer*, 24 Jan 1982

9 What have I gained by health? intolerable dullness. What by early hours and moderate meals? – a total blank.

Charles Lamb (1775–1834) British essayist. Letter to William Wordsworth, 22 Jan 1830

10 Temperance is the love of health, or the inability to overindulge.

Duc de La Rochefoucauld (1613–80) French writer. *Maxims*, No. 583

11 Not too much zeal.

Talleyrand (Charles Maurice de Talleyrand-Périgord; 1754–1838) French politician. Attrib.

12 Moderation is a fatal thing, Lady Hunstanton. Nothing succeeds like excess.

Oscar Wilde (1854–1900) Irish-born British dramatist. *A Woman of No Importance*, III

MODESTY

1 His modesty amounts to deformity.

Margot Asquith (1865–1945) The second wife of Herbert Asquith. Referring to her husband. *As I Remember*

2 Nurse, take away the candle and spare my blushes.

Henry James (1843–1916) US novelist. On being informed, whilst confined to his bed, that he had been awarded the Order of Merit. *The American Treasury* (C. Fadiman)

3 It was involuntary. They sank my boat.

John Fitzgerald Kennedy (1917–63) US statesman. Responding to praise of his courage whilst serving in the US navy against the Japanese in World War II. *Nobody Said It Better* (M. Ringo)

4 Age will bring all things, and everyone knows, Madame, that twenty is no age to be a prude.

Molière (Jean Baptiste Poquelin; 1622–73) French dramatist. *Le Misanthrope*, III:4

5 In some remote regions of Islam it is said, a woman caught unveiled by a stranger will raise her skirt to cover her face.

Raymond Mortimer (1895–1980) British literary critic and writer. *Colette*

6 If you want people to think well of you, do not speak well of yourself.

Blaise Pascal (1623–62) French philosopher and mathematician. *Pensées*, I

7 Be modest! It is the kind of pride least likely to offend.

Jules Renard (1894–1910) French writer. *Journal*

8 ...the nuns who never take a bath without wearing a bathrobe all the time. When asked why, since no man can see them, they reply 'Oh, but you forget the good God.'

Bertrand Russell (1872–1970) British philosopher. *The Basic Writings*, Pt. II, Ch. 7

9 I have often wished I had time to cultivate modesty...But I am too busy thinking about myself.

Edith Sitwell (1887–1964) British poet and writer. *The Observer*, 'Sayings of the Week', 30 Apr 1950

10 Put off your shame with your clothes when you go in to your husband, and put it on again when you come out.

Theano (fl. 420s BC) Greek priestess. *Lives, Teachings, and Sayings of Famous Philosophers; Pythagoras*, Bk VIII (Diogenes Laertius)

MOLIERE

(Jean Baptiste Poquelin; 1622–73) French dramatist. In his plays, such as *Tartuffe* (1664), *Le Bourgeois Gentilhomme* (1670), and *Le Malade imaginaire* (1673), he satirized contemporary society.

1 He who lives without tobacco is not worthy to live.

Don Juan, I:1

2 One should eat to live, not live to eat.

L'Avare, III:1

3 Good heavens! I have been talking prose for over forty years without realizing it.

Le Bourgeois Gentilhomme, II:4

4 One dies only once, and it's for such a long time!

Le Dépit amoureux, V:3

5 He must have killed a lot of men to have made so much money.

Le Malade imaginaire, I:5

6 It is a stupidity second to none, to busy oneself with the correction of the world.

Le Misanthrope, I:1

7 One should examine oneself for a very long time before thinking of condemning others.

Le Misanthrope, III:4

8 Age will bring all things, and everyone knows, Madame, that twenty is no age to be a prude.

Le Misanthrope, III:4

9 Grammar, which can govern even kings.

Les Femmes savantes, II:6

10 It is public scandal that constitutes offence, and to sin in secret is not to sin at all.

Tartuffe, IV:5

MONARCHY

See also royalty

1 *Rex illiteratus, asinus coronatus.*
An unlettered king is a crowned ass.

Anonymous

2 The best reason why Monarchy is a strong government is that it is an intelligible government. The mass of mankind understand it, and they hardly anywhere in the world understand any other.

Walter Bagehot (1826–77) British economist and journalist. *The English Constitution*, 'The Monarchy'

3 The Sovereign has, under a constitutional monarchy such as ours, three rights – the right to be consulted, the right to encourage, the right to warn.

Walter Bagehot *The English Constitution*, 'The Monarchy'

4 God grant him peace and happiness but never understanding of what he has lost.

Stanley Baldwin (1867–1947) British statesman. Referring to Edward VIII's abdication.

5 The king never dies.

William Blackstone (1723–80) British jurist. *Commentaries on the Laws of England*, Bk. I, Ch. 7

6 That the king can do no wrong, is a necessary and fundamental principle of the English constitution.

William Blackstone *Commentaries on the Laws of England*, Bk. III, Ch. 17

7 If everything became entirely based on politics, I think this country would lose a great deal.

Charles, Prince of Wales (1948–) Eldest son of Elizabeth II. His views on the abolition of the monarchy. ITV programme *Charles: The Private Man, the Public Role*, 29 June 1994

8 I would rather hew wood than be a king under the conditions of the King of England.

Charles X (1757–1836) King of France. *Encyclopaedia Britannica*

9 There is no middle course between the throne and the scaffold.

Charles X Said to Talleyrand, who is said to have replied 'You are forgetting the postchaise'. Attrib.

10 Magna Charta is such a fellow, that he will have no sovereign.

Edward Coke (1552–1634) English lawyer and politician. Speaking on the Lords Amendment to the Petition of Right, 17 May 1628. *Hist. Coll.* (Rushworth), I

11 The influence of the Crown has increased, is increasing, and ought to be diminished.

John Dunning (1731–83) British lawyer and politician. Motion passed by the House of Commons, 1780

12 There will soon be only five kings left – the Kings of England, Diamonds, Hearts, Spades and Clubs.

Farouk I (1920–65) The last king of Egypt. Remark made to Lord Boyd-Orr

13 Kings govern by means of popular assemblies only when they cannot do without them.

Charles James Fox (1749–1806) British Whig politician. Attrib.

14 I did not usurp the crown, but was duly elected.

Henry IV (1367–1413) King of England. Reply when accused by Richard Frisby, a Franciscan on trial for plotting (1402) to overthrow him. *Eulogium Historiarum*

15 I will govern according to the common weal, but not according to the common will.

James I (1566–1625) King of England. *History of the English People* (J. R. Green)

16 A constitutional king must learn to stoop.

Leopold II (1835–1909) King of the Belgians. Instructing Prince Albert, the heir apparent, to pick up some papers that had fallen onto the floor. *The Mistress* (Betty Kelen)

17 *L'État c'est moi.*
I am the State.

Louis XIV (1638–1715) French king. Attrib.

18 There is something behind the throne greater than the King himself.

William Pitt the Elder (1708–78) British statesman. Speech, House of Lords, 2 Mar 1770

19 The right divine of kings to govern wrong.

Alexander Pope (1688–1744) British poet. *The Dunciad*, IV

20 A king is a thing men have made for their own sakes, for quietness' sake. Just as if in a family one man is appointed to buy the meat.

John Selden (1584–1654) English historian. *Table Talk*

21 There's such divinity doth hedge a king
That treason can but peep to what it would.

William Shakespeare (1564–1616) English dramatist. *Hamlet*, IV:5

22 Uneasy lies the head that wears a crown.

William Shakespeare *Henry IV, Part Two*, III:1

23 Every subject's duty is the King's; but every subject's soul is his own.

William Shakespeare *Henry V*, IV:1

24 Not all the water in the rough rude sea
Can wash the balm from an anointed king;
The breath of worldly men cannot depose
The deputy elected by the Lord.

William Shakespeare *Richard II*, III:2

25 The king reigns, and the people govern themselves.

Louis Adolphe Thiers (1797–1877) French statesman and historian. In an unsigned article attributed to Thiers. *Le National*, 20 Jan 1830

26 As guardian of His Majesty's conscience.

Lord Thurlow (1731–1806) British lawyer. Speech, House of Lords, 1779

27 The monarchy is a labour-intensive industry.

Harold Wilson (1916–) British politician and prime minister. *The Observer*, 13 Feb 1977

28 The king reigns, but does not govern.

Jan Zamoyski (1541–1605) Grand chancellor of Poland. Speech, Polish Parliament, 1605

MONEY

See also bribery, economics, extravagance, greed, materialism, thrift, wealth

1 Easy come, easy go.

Proverb

2 Out of debt, out of danger.

Proverb

3 Take care of the pence, and the pounds will take care of themselves.

Proverb

4 I can't afford to waste my time making money.

Jean Louis Rodolphe Agassiz (1807–73) Swiss naturalist. When asked to give a lecture for a fee. Attrib.

5 It does seem to be true that the more you get the more you spend. It is rather like being on a golden treadmill.

Charles Allsop (1940–) Commodities broker. Remark, Dec 1988

6 Business, you know, may bring money, but friendship hardly ever does.

Jane Austen (1775–1817) British novelist. *Emma*, Ch. 34

7 Money is like muck, not good except it be spread.

Francis Bacon (1561–1626) English philosopher. *See also* MURCHISON. *Essays*, 'Of Seditions and Troubles'

8 Money, it turned out, was exactly like sex, you thought of nothing else if you didn't have it and thought of other things if you did.

James Baldwin (1924–87) US writer. *Nobody Knows My Name*

9 I'm tired of Love: I'm still more tired of Rhyme.
But Money gives me pleasure all the Time.

Hilaire Belloc (1870–1953) French-born British poet. *Fatigue*

10 A feast is made for laughter, and wine maketh merry: but money answereth all things.

Bible: Ecclesiastes 10:19

11 For the love of money is the root of all evil: which while some coveted after, they have erred from the faith, and pierced themselves through with many sorrows.

Bible: I Timothy 6:10

12 If it's a good script, I'll do it. And if it's a bad script, and they pay me enough, I'll do it.

George Burns (1896–) US comedian. Remark, Nov 1988

13 Straighteners, managers and cashiers of the Musical Banks.

Samuel Butler (1835–1902) British writer. *Erewhon*, Ch. 9

14 It has been said that the love of money is the root of all evil. The want of money is so quite as truly.

Samuel Butler *Erewhon*, Ch. 20

15 What makes all doctrines plain and clear?
About two hundred pounds a year.

Samuel Butler *Hudibras*, Pt. III

16 It is a kind of spiritual snobbery that makes people think that they can be happy without money.

Albert Camus (1913–60) French existentialist writer. *Notebooks, 1935–1942*

17 Where large sums of money are concerned, it is advisable to trust nobody.

Agatha Christie (1891–1976) British detective-story writer. *Endless Night*, Bk. II, Ch. 15

18 How pleasant it is to have money.

Arthur Hugh Clough (1819–61) British poet. *Dipsychus*, Bk. I

19 But then one is always excited by descriptions of money changing hands. It's much more fundamental than sex.

Nigel Dennis (1912–89) British writer. *Cards of Identity*

20 Buy an annuity cheap, and make your life interesting to yourself and everybody else that watches the speculation.

Charles Dickens (1812–70) British novelist. *Martin Chuzzlewit*, Ch. 18

21 Making money is pretty pointless and it needs constant attention.

Adam Faith (1940–) British pop singer. *The Observer*, 'Sayings of the Week', 8 May 1994

22 Ah, take the Cash in hand and waive the Rest;
Oh, the brave Music of a *distant* Drum!

Edward Fitzgerald (1809–83) British poet. *The Rubáiyát of Omar Khayyám* (1st edn.), XII

23 It is only the poor who pay cash, and that not from virtue, but because they are refused credit.

Anatole France (Jacques Anatole François Thibault; 1844–1924) French writer. *A Cynic's Breviary* (J. R. Solly)

24 Money differs from an automobile, a mistress or cancer in being equally important to those who have it and those who do not.

John Kenneth Galbraith (1908–) US economist. Attrib.

25 You can call an ecu a pound in Britain. A single currency does not need a single name, but it does need a single value.

Michael Heseltine (1933–) British politician. *The Times*, 19 Nov 1990

26 If possible honestly, if not, somehow, make money.

Horace (Quintus Horatius Flaccus; 65–8 BC) Roman poet. *Epistles*, I

27 We all know how the size of sums of money appears to vary in a remarkable way according as they are being paid in or paid out.

Julian Huxley (1887–1975) British biologist. *Essays of a Biologist*, 5

28 There are few ways in which a man can be more innocently employed than in getting money.

Samuel Johnson (1709–84) British lexicographer. *Life of Johnson* (J. Boswell), Vol. II

29 You don't seem to realize that a poor person who is unhappy is in a better position than a rich person who is unhappy. Because the poor person has hope. He thinks money would help.

Jean Kerr (1923–) US dramatist. *Poor Richard*

30 Clearly money has something to do with life
– In fact, they've a lot in common, if you enquire:
You can't put off being young until you retire.

Philip Larkin (1922–85) British poet. *Money*

31 For I don't care too much for money,
For money can't buy me love.

John Lennon (1940–80) British rock musician. *Can't Buy Me Love* (with Paul McCartney)

32 The working classes are never embarrassed by money – only the absence of it.

Ken Livingstone (1945–) British Labour politician. Speech, Sept 1987

33 What's a thousand dollars? Mere chicken feed. A poultry matter.

Groucho Marx (Julius Marx; 1895–1977) US comedian. *The Cocoanuts*

34 Do they allow tipping on the boat?
– Yes, sir.
Have you got two fives?
– Oh, yes, sir.
Then you won't need the ten cents I was going to give you.

Groucho Marx *A Night at the Opera*

35 Money is like a sixth sense without which you cannot make a complete use of the other five.

W. Somerset Maugham (1874–1965) British novelist. *Of Human Bondage*, Ch. 51

36 Money can't buy friends, but you can get a better class of enemy.

Spike Milligan (1918–) British comic actor and author. *Puckoon*, Ch. 6

37 Money is like manure. If you spread it around it does a lot of good. But if you pile it up in one place it stinks like hell.

Clint Murchison Jnr (1895–1969) US industrialist. Following BACON. *Time Magazine*, 16 June 1961

38 Some people's money is merited
And other people's is inherited.

Ogden Nash (1902–71) US poet. *The Terrible People*

39 Check enclosed.

Dorothy Parker (1893–1967) US writer. Giving her version of the two most beautiful words in the English language. Attrib.

40 Money is good for bribing yourself through the inconveniences of life.

Gottfried Reinhardt (1911–) Austrian film producer. *Picture*, 'Looks Like We're Still in Business' (Lillian Ross)

41 My boy...always try to rub up against money, for if you rub up against money long enough, some of it may rub off on you.

Damon Runyon (1884–1946) US writer. *Furthermore*, 'A Very Honourable Guy'

42 He that wants money, means, and content, is without three good friends.

William Shakespeare (1564–1616) English dramatist. *As You Like It*, III:2

43 I can get no remedy against this consumption of the purse; borrowing only lingers and lingers it out, but the disease is incurable.

William Shakespeare *Henry IV, Part Two*, I:2

44 Put money in thy purse.

William Shakespeare *Othello*, I:3

45 Lack of money is the root of all evil.

George Bernard Shaw (1856–1950) Irish dramatist and critic. *Man and Superman*, 'Maxims for Revolutionists.'

46 The trouble, Mr Goldwyn is that you are only interested in art and I am only interested in money.

George Bernard Shaw Turning down Goldwyn's offer to buy the screen rights of his plays. *The Movie Moguls* (Philip French), Ch. 4

47 Nothing links man to man like the frequent passage from hand to hand of cash.

Walter Richard Sickert (1860–1942) British impressionist painter. *A Certain World* (W. H. Auden)

48 There are few sorrows, however poignant, in which a good income is of no avail.

Logan Pearsall Smith (1865–1946) US writer. *Afterthoughts*

49 Pieces of eight!

Robert Louis Stevenson (1850–94) Scottish writer. *Treasure Island*, Ch. 10

50 I think I could be a good woman if I had five thousand a year.

William Makepeace Thackeray (1811–63) British novelist. *Vanity Fair*, Ch. 36

51 No one would have remembered the Good Samaritan if he'd only had good intentions. He had money as well.

Margaret Thatcher (1925–) British politician and prime minister. Television interview, 1980

52 The easiest way for your children to learn about money is for you not to have any.

Katherine Whitehorn (1926–) British journalist. *How to Survive Children*

53 You can be young without money but you can't be old without it.

Tennessee Williams (1911–83) US dramatist. *Cat on a Hot Tin Roof*, I

54 All these financiers, all the little gnomes of Zürich and the other financial centres, about whom we keep on hearing.

Harold Wilson (1916–) British politician and prime minister. Speech, House of Commons, 12 Nov 1956

MONTAIGNE, MICHEL DE

(1533–92) French essayist. His *Essais* (1580 and 1588) started a new literary genre, in which he expressed his philosophy of humanism.

1 The greatest thing in the world is to know how to be self-sufficient.

Essais, I

2 A man must keep a little back shop where he can be himself without reserve. In solitude alone can he know true freedom.

Essais, I

3 Unless a man feels he has a good enough memory, he should never venture to lie.

Essais, I

4 The daughter-in-law of Pythagoras said that a woman who goes to bed with a man ought to lay aside her modesty with her skirt, and put it on again with her petticoat.

Essais, I

5 When I play with my cat, who knows whether she is not amusing herself with me more than I with her?

Essais, II

6 Man is quite insane. He wouldn't know how to create a maggot and he creates Gods by the dozen.

Essais, II

7 Marriage is like a cage; one sees the birds outside desperate to get in, and those inside equally desperate to get out.

Essais, III

8 Many a man has been a wonder to the world, whose wife and valet have seen nothing in him that was even remarkable. Few men have been admired by their servants.

Essais, III

9 The world is but a school of inquiry.

Essais, III

10 Poverty of goods is easily cured; poverty of soul, impossible.

Essais, III

11 A man who fears suffering is already suffering from what he fears.

Essais, III

MONTESQUIEU, BARON DE

(1689–1755) French writer and historian. He is remembered for his influential *Considérations sur les causes de la grandeur et de la décadence des romains* (1734) and *Esprit des lois* (1748).

1 An empire founded by war has to maintain itself by war.

Considérations sur les causes de la grandeur et de la décadence des romains, Ch. 8

2 A really intelligent man feels what other men only know.

Essai sur les causes qui peuvent affecter les esprits et les caractères

3 Liberty is the right to do everything which the laws allow.

L'Esprit des lois

4 There is a very good saying that if triangles invented a god, they would make him three-sided.

Lettres persanes

5 No kingdom has ever had as many civil wars as the kingdom of Christ.

Lettres persanes

6 Great lords have their pleasures, but the people have fun.

Pensées diverses

7 The English are busy; they don't have time to be polite.

Pensées diverses

8 I suffer from the disease of writing books and being ashamed of them when they are finished.

Pensées diverses

MONTHS

See also seasons

1 March comes in like a lion and goes out like a lamb.

Proverb

2 Ne'er cast a clout till May be out.

Proverb

3 The cuckoo comes in April, and stays the month of May; sings a song at midsummer, and then goes away.

Proverb

4 Thirty days hath September,
April, June, and November;
All the rest have thirty-one,
Excepting February alone,
And that has twenty-eight days clear
And twenty-nine in each leap year.

Anonymous *See also* GRAFTON. Stevins Manuscript, c. 1555

5 There are twelve months in all the year,
As I hear many men say,
But the merriest month in all the year
Is the merry month of May.

Anonymous *Robin Hood and the Widow's Three Sons*

6 And after April, when May follows,
And the whitethroat builds, and all the swallows!

Robert Browning (1812–89) British poet. *Home Thoughts from Abroad*

7 Whan that Aprille with his shoures sote
The droghte of Marche hath perced to the rote.

Geoffrey Chaucer (c. 1342–1400) English poet. *The Canterbury Tales*, Prologue

8 April is the cruellest month, breeding
Lilacs out of the dead land, mixing
Memory and desire, stirring
Dull roots with spring rain.

T. S. Eliot (1888–1965) US-born British poet and dramatist. *The Waste Land*, 'The Burial of the Dead'

9 Thirty days hath November,
April, June and September,
February hath twenty-eight alone,
And all the rest have thirty-one.

Richard Grafton (d. c. 1572) English chronicler and printer. *Abridgement of the Chronicles of England*, Introduction

10 No warmth, no cheerfulness, no healthful ease,
No comfortable feel in any member –
No shade, no shine, no butterflies, no bees,
No fruits, no flowers, no leaves, no birds, –
November!

Thomas Hood (1799–1845) British poet. *No!*

11 February, fill the dyke
With what thou dost like.

Thomas Tusser (1524–80) English farmer. *Five Hundred Points of Good Husbandry*, 'February's Husbandry'

12 Sweet April showers
Do spring May flowers.

Thomas Tusser *Five Hundred Points of Good Husbandry*, 'April's Husbandry'

MOON

See also astronomy, space, universe

1 I saw the new moon late yestreen
Wi' the auld moon in her arm;
And if we gang to sea master;
I fear we'll come to harm.

Anonymous The 'new moon in the old moon's arms' is generally regarded as a sign of bad weather. Sir Patrick Spens

2 The moving Moon went up the sky,
And no where did abide:
Softly she was going up,
And a star or two beside.

Samuel Taylor Coleridge (1772–1834) British poet. *The Rime of the Ancient Mariner*, IV

3 who knows if the moon's
a balloon, coming out of a keen city
in the sky – filled with pretty people?

e. e. cummings (1894–1962) US poet. Used for the title and epigraph of David Niven's first volume of autobiography, *The Moon's a Balloon*, about his experiences in the film industry.

4 So sicken waning moons too near the sun,
And blunt their crescents on the edge of day.

John Dryden (1631–1700) British poet and dramatist. *Annus Mirabilis*

5 For years politicians have promised the moon,
I'm the first one to be able to deliver it.

Richard Milhous Nixon (1913–94) US president. Radio message to astronauts on the moon, 20 Jul 1969

6 Oh! shine on, shine on, harvest moon
Up in the sky.
I ain't had no lovin'
Since April, January, June or July.

Jack Norworth (1879–1959) US vaudeville comedian and songwriter. *Shine On, Harvest Moon* (song)

MOORE, THOMAS

(1779–1852) Irish poet. His most popular works are the collection *Irish Melodies* (1807–34) and the oriental romance *Lalla Rookh* (1817).

1 Yet, who can help loving the land that has taught us
Six hundred and eighty-five ways to dress eggs?

The Fudge Family in Paris

2 The harp that once through Tara's halls
The soul of music shed,
Now hangs as mute on Tara's walls
As if that soul were fled. –
So sleeps the pride of former days,
So glory's thrill is o'er;
And hearts, that once beat high for praise,
Now feel that pulse no more.

Irish Melodies, 'The Harp that Once'

3 The Minstrel Boy to the war is gone,
In the ranks of death you'll find him;
His father's sword he has girded on,
And his wild harp slung behind him.

Irish Melodies, 'The Minstrel Boy'

4 She is far from the land where her young hero sleeps,
And lovers are round her, sighing:
But coldly she turns from their gaze, and weeps,
For her heart in his grave is lying.

Irish Melodies, 'She is Far'

5 'Tis the last rose of summer
Left blooming alone;
All her lovely companions
Are faded and gone.

Irish Melodies, ''Tis the Last Rose'

6 I never nurs'd a dear gazelle,
To glad me with its soft black eye
But when it came to know me well,
And love me, it was sure to die!

See also PAYN. *Lalla Rookh*

7 Oft in the stilly night,
Ere Slumber's chain has bound me,
Fond Memory brings the light
Of other days around me;
The smiles, the tears,
Of boyhood's years,
The words of love then spoken;
The eyes that shone,
Now dimmed and gone,
The cheerful hearts now broken!

National Airs, 'Oft in the Stilly Night'

MORALITY

See also integrity, principles, righteousness

1 In his own way each man must struggle, lest the moral law become a far-off abstraction utterly separated from his active life.

Jane Addams (1860–1935) US social worker. *Twenty Years at Hull House*

2 No morality can be founded on authority, even if the authority were divine.

A. J. Ayer (1910–89) British philosopher. *Essay on Humanism*

3 Morality's not practical. Morality's a gesture. A complicated gesture learnt from books.

Robert Bolt (1924–) British playwright. *A Man for All Seasons*

4 The propriety of some persons seems to consist in having improper thoughts about their neighbours.

F. H. Bradley (1846–1924) British philosopher. *Aphorisms*

5 And there isn't any way that one can get rid of the guilt of having a nice body by saying that one can serve society with it, because that would end up with oneself as what? There simply doesn't seem to be any moral place for flesh.

Margaret Drabble (1939–) British novelist. *A Summer Bird-Cage*, Ch. 10

6 What is moral is what you feel good after, and what is immoral is what you feel bad after.

Ernest Hemingway (1899–1961) US novelist. *Death in the Afternoon*

7 The quality of moral behaviour varies in inverse ratio to the number of human beings involved.

Aldous Huxley (1894–1964) British novelist. *Grey Eminence*, Ch. 10

8 Finally, there is an imperative which commands a certain conduct immediately...This imperative is Categorical...This imperative may be called that of Morality.

Immanuel Kant (1724–1804) German philosopher. *Grundlegung zur Metaphysik der Sitten*, II

9 Morality which is based on ideas, or on an ideal, is an unmitigated evil.

D. H. Lawrence (1885–1930) British novelist. *Fantasia of the Unconscious*, Ch. 7

10 We know no spectacle so ridiculous as the British public in one of its periodical fits of morality.

Lord Macaulay (1800–59) British historian. *Literary Essays Contributed to the 'Edinburgh Review'*, 'Moore's 'Life of Lord Byron''

11 It is a public scandal that gives offence, and it is no sin to sin in secret.

Molière (Jean Baptiste Poquelin; 1622–73) French dramatist. *Tartuffe*, IV:5

12 Morality in Europe today is herd-morality.

Friedrich Nietzsche (1844–1900) German philosopher. *Jenseits von Gut und Böse*

13 Morality, like language, is an invented structure for conserving and communicating order. And morality is learned, like language, by mimicking and remembering.

Jane Rule (1931–) US-born Canadian writer. *Lesbian Images*, 'Myth and Morality, Sources of Law and Prejudice'

14 We have, in fact, two kinds of morality side by side; one which we preach but do not practise, and another which we practise but seldom preach.

Bertrand Russell (1872–1970) British philosopher. *Sceptical Essays*

15 All universal moral principles are idle fancies.

Marquis de Sade (1740–1814) French novelist. *The 120 Days of Sodom*

16 Without doubt the greatest injury...was done by basing morals on myth, for sooner or later myth is recognized for what it is, and disappears. Then morality loses the foundation on which it has been built.

Herbert Samuel (1870–1963) British Liberal statesman. Romanes Lecture, 1947

17 Morality consists in suspecting other people of not being legally married.

George Bernard Shaw (1856–1950) Irish dramatist and critic. *The Doctor's Dilemma*

18 He never does a proper thing without giving an improper reason for it.

George Bernard Shaw *Major Barbara*, III

19 The so-called new morality is too often the old immorality condoned.

Lord Shawcross (1902–) British Labour politician and lawyer. *The Observer*, 17 Nov 1963

20 'Twas Peter's drift
To be a kind of moral eunuch.

Percy Bysshe Shelley (1792–1822) British poet. *Peter Bell the Third*

21 Moral indignation is in most cases 2 percent moral, 48 percent indignation and 50 percent envy.
Vittorio De Sica (1901–74) Italian film director. *The Observer*, 1961

22 If your morals make you dreary, depend upon it, they are wrong.
Robert Louis Stevenson (1850–94) Scottish writer. *Across the Plains*

23 Victorian values...were the values when our country became great.
Margaret Thatcher (1925–) British politician and prime minister. Television interview, 1982

24 Morals are an acquirement – like music, like a foreign language, like piety, poker, paralysis – no man is born with them.
Mark Twain (Samuel Langhorne Clemens; 1835–1910) US writer. *Seventieth Birthday*

MORRIS, DESMOND

(1928–) British biologist and writer. His books, including *The Naked Ape* (1967), *Manwatching* (1977), *Bodywatching* (1985), and *The World of Animals* (1993), draw parallels between human and animal behaviour.

1 Clearly, then, the city is not a concrete jungle, it is a human zoo.
The Human Zoo, Introduction

2 Observe diners arriving at any restaurant and you will see them make a bee-line for the wall-seats. No one ever voluntarily selects a centre table in an open space. Open seating positions are only taken when all the wall-seats are already occupied. This dates back to a primeval feeding practice of avoiding sudden attack during the deep concentration involved in consuming food.
Manwatching, 'Feeding Behaviour'

3 There are one hundred and ninety-three living species of monkeys and apes. One hundred and ninety-two of them are covered with hair. The exception is a naked ape self-named *Homo sapiens.*
The Naked Ape, Introduction

4 He is proud that he has the biggest brain of all the primates, but attempts to conceal the fact that he also has the biggest penis.
The Naked Ape, Introduction

MORRIS, WILLIAM

(1834–96) British designer, artist, and poet. Associated with the Pre-Raphaelite Brotherhood, he designed stained glass, carpets, wallpaper, and furniture and founded the Kelmscott Press in 1890; his ideas influenced both the Arts and Crafts movement and the development of British socialism.

1 It is not this or that tangible steel or brass machine which we want to get rid of, but the great intangible machine of commercial tyrrany which oppresses the lives of us all.
Arts and Crafts Movement

2 Nothing should be made by man's labour which is not worth making or which must be made by labour degrading to the makers.
Arts and Crafts Movement

3 I don't want art for a few, any more than education for a few, or freedom for a few.
Arts and Crafts Movement

4 Art will make our streets as beautiful as the woods, as elevating as the mountain-side: it will be a pleasure and a rest, and not a weight upon the spirits to come from the open country into a town. Every man's house will be fair and decent, soothing to his mind and helpful to his work.
Arts and Crafts Movement

MORTALITY

See also death, equality in death, human condition, immortality, life, life and death, time, transience

1 All men are mortal.
Proverb

2 Mortality, behold and fear!
What a change of flesh is here!
Francis Beaumont (1584–1616) English dramatist. *On the Tombs in Westminster Abbey*

3 That lyf so short, the craft so long to lerne,
Th' assay so hard, so sharp the conquerynge.
Geoffrey Chaucer (c. 1342–1400) English poet. *See also* HIPPOCRATES. *The Parliament of Fowls*

4 What argufies pride and ambition?
Soon or late death will take us in tow:
Each bullet has got its commission,
And when our time's come we must go.
Charles Dibdin (1745–1814) British actor and dramatist. *Each Bullet has its Commission*

5 All humane things are subject to decay,
And, when Fate summons, Monarchs must obey.
John Dryden (1631–1700) British poet and dramatist. *Mac Flecknoe*

6 The Wine of Life keeps oozing drop by drop,
The Leaves of Life keep falling one by one.
Edward Fitzgerald (1809–83) British poet. *The Rubáiyát of Omar Khayyám* (4th edn.), VIII

7 Is life a boon?
If so, it must befall
That Death, whene'er he call,
Must call too soon.
W. S. Gilbert (1836–1911) British dramatist. The lines are written on Arthur Sullivan's memorial in the Embankment gardens. *The Yeoman of the Guard*, I

8 I was not unaware that I had begotten a mortal.
Goethe (1749–1832) German poet and dramatist. On learning of his son's death. *The Story of Civilization* (W. Durant), Vol. X

9 Man wants but little here below,
Nor wants that little long.
Oliver Goldsmith (1728–74) Irish-born British writer. *Edwin and Angelina, or the Hermit*

10 The boast of heraldry, the pomp of pow'r,
And all that beauty, all that wealth e'er gave,
Awaits alike th' inevitable hour,
The paths of glory lead but to the grave.
Thomas Gray (1716–71) British poet. *Elegy Written in a Country Churchyard*

11 I expect to pass through this world but once; any good thing therefore that I can do, or any kindness that I can show to any fellow-creature, let me do it now; let me not defer or neglect it, for I shall not pass this way again.

Stephen Grellet (1773–1855) French-born US missionary. Attrib. *Treasure Trove* (John o'London)

12 The life so short, the craft so long to learn.

Hippocrates (c. 460–c. 377 BC) Greek physician. Describing medicine. It is often quoted in Latin as *Ars longa, vita brevis,* and interpreted as 'Art lasts, life is short'. *See also* CHAUCER. *Aphorisms*, I

13 Life's short span forbids us to enter on far-reaching hopes.

Horace (Quintus Horatius Flaccus; 65–8 BC) Roman poet. *Odes*, I

14 Art is long, and Time is fleeting,
And our hearts, though stout and brave,
Still, like muffled drums, are beating
Funeral marches to the grave.

Henry Wadsworth Longfellow (1807–82) US poet. *See also* HIPPOCRATES. *A Psalm of Life*

15 *Inque brevi spatio mutantur saecla animantum*
Et quasi cursores vitai lampada tradunt.
The generations of living things pass in a short time, and like runners hand on the torch of life.

Lucretius (Titus Lucretius Carus; c. 99–55 BC) Roman philosopher. *On the Nature of the Universe*, II

16 Fear no more the heat o' th' sun
Nor the furious winter's rages;
Thou thy worldly task hast done,
Home art gone, and ta'en thy wages.
Golden lads and girls all must,
As chimney-sweepers, come to dust.

William Shakespeare (1564–1616) English dramatist. *Cymbeline*, IV:2

17 Our revels now are ended. These our actors,
As I foretold you, were all spirits, and
Are melted into air, into thin air;
And, like the baseless fabric of this vision,
The cloud-capp'd towers, the gorgeous palaces,
The solemn temples, the great globe itself,
Yea, all which it inherit, shall dissolve,
And, like this insubstantial pageant faded,
Leave not a rack behind. We are such stuff
As dreams are made on; and our little life
Is rounded with a sleep.

William Shakespeare *The Tempest*, IV:1

18 Old and young, we are all on our last cruise.

Robert Louis Stevenson (1850–94) Scottish writer. *Virginibus Puerisque*

19 The woods decay, the woods decay and fall,
The vapours weep their burthen to the ground,
Man comes and tills the field and lies beneath,
And after many a summer dies the swan.

Alfred, Lord Tennyson (1809–92) British poet. *Tithonus*

20 A power is passing from the earth
To breathless Nature's dark abyss;
But when the great and good depart,
What is it more than this –

That Man who is from God sent forth,
Doth yet again to God return? –
Such ebb and flow must ever be,
Then wherefore should we mourn?

William Wordsworth (1770–1850) British poet. Referring to Charles James Fox, the hero of the liberal Whigs, who died in 1806. *Lines on the Expected Dissolution of Mr. Fox*

21 The clouds that gather round the setting sun
Do take a sober colouring from an eye
That hath kept watch o'er man's mortality.

William Wordsworth *Ode. Intimations of Immortality*, XI

22 I am moved to pity, when I think of the brevity of human life, seeing that of all this host of men not one will still be alive in a hundred years' time.

Xerxes (d. 465 BC) King of Persia. On surveying his army.

23 That is no country for old men. The young
In one another's arms, birds in the trees
– Those dying generations – at their song,
The salmon-falls, the mackerel-crowded seas,
Fish, flesh, or fowl, commend all summer long
Whatever is begotten, born, and dies.

W. B. Yeats (1865–1939) Irish poet. *Sailing to Byzantium*, I

24 Man wants but little, nor that little long.

Edward Young (1683–1765) British poet. *Night Thoughts*

MOTHERHOOD

See also babies, birth, children, pregnancy

1 The best thing that could happen to motherhood already has. Fewer women are going into it.

Victoria Billings (1945–) US journalist and writer. *Womansbook*, 'Meeting Your Personal Needs'

2 Women, who are, beyond all doubt, the mothers of all mischief, also nurse that babe to sleep when he is too noisy.

R. D. Blackmore (1825–1900) British writer. *Lorna Doone*

3 Womanliness means only motherhood;
All love begins and ends there.

Robert Browning (1812–89) British poet. *The Inn Album*

4 Motherhood meant I have written four fewer books, but I know more about life.

A. S. Byatt (1936–) British novelist. *The Sunday Times*, 21 Oct 1990

5 An author who speaks about his own books is almost as bad as a mother who talks about her own children.

Benjamin Disraeli (1804–81) British statesman. Speech in Glasgow, 19 Nov 1873

6 Claudia...remembered that when she'd had her first baby she had realised with astonishment that the perfect couple consisted of a mother and child and not, as she had always supposed, a man and woman.

Alice Thomas Ellis (1932–) British writer. *The Other Side of the Fire*

7 Mother is the dead heart of the family; spending father's earnings on consumer goods to enhance the environment in which he eats, sleeps and watches the television.

Germaine Greer (1939–) Australian-born British writer and feminist. *The Female Eunuch*

8 Now, as always, the most automated appliance in a household is the mother.

Beverly Jones (1927–) US writer and feminist. *The Florida Paper on Women's Liberation*

9 Who has not watched a mother stroke her child's cheek or kiss her child *in a certain way* and felt a nervous shudder at the possessive outrage done to a free solitary human soul?

John Cowper Powys (1872–1963) British writer. *The Meaning of Culture*

10 Maternity is on the face of it an unsocial experience. The selfishness that a woman has learned to stifle or to dissemble where she alone is concerned, blooms freely and unashamed on behalf of her offspring.

Emily James Putnam (1865–1944) US educator, writer, and college administrator. First dean of Barnard College, New York. *The Lady*, Introduction

11 No matter how old a mother is she watches her middle-aged children for signs of improvement.

Florida Scott-Maxwell (b. 1883) US-born British writer, psychologist, playwright, suffragette, and actress. *The Measure of My Days*

12 Though motherhood is the most important of all the professions – requiring more knowledge than any other department in human affairs – there was no attention given to preparation for this office.

Elizabeth Cady Stanton (1815–1902) US suffragette and abolitionist. *Eighty Years and More*

13 A mother! What are we worth really? They all grow up whether you look after them or not.

Christina Stead (c. 1900–) Australian writer. *The Man Who Loved Children*, Ch. 10

MOTIVE

See also purpose

1 Never ascribe to an opponent motives meaner than your own.

J. M. Barrie (1860–1937) British novelist and dramatist. Speech, St Andrews, 3 May 1922

2 The last temptation is the greatest treason:
To do the right deed for the wrong reason.

T. S. Eliot (1888–1965) US-born British poet and dramatist. *Murder in the Cathedral*, I

3 Because it is there.

George Mallory (1886–1924) British mountaineer. Answer to the question 'Why do you want to climb Mt. Everest?' *George Mallory* (D. Robertson)

4 Nobody ever did anything very foolish except from some strong principle.

Lord Melbourne (1779–1848) British statesman. *The Young Melbourne* (Lord David Cecil)

5 The heart has its reasons which reason does not know.

Blaise Pascal (1623–62) French philosopher and mathematician. *Pensées*, IV

6 Men are rewarded and punished not for what they do, but rather for how their acts are defined. This is why men are more interested in better justifying themselves than in better behaving themselves.

Thomas Szasz (1920–) US psychiatrist. *The Second Sin*

MOUNTAINS

1 Mountains interposed
Make enemies of nations, who had else,
Like kindred drops, been mingled into one.

William Cowper (1731–1800) British poet. *The Task*

2 Separate from the pleasure of your company, I don't much care if I never see another mountain in my life.

Charles Lamb (1775–1834) British essayist. Letter to William Wordsworth, 30 Jan 1801

3 Mountains are the beginning and the end of all natural scenery.

John Ruskin (1819–1900) British art critic and writer. *Modern Painters*, Vol. IV

4 They say that if the Swiss had designed these mountains they'd be rather flatter.

Paul Theroux (1941–) US-born writer. Referring to the Alps. *The Great Railway Bazaar*, Ch. 28

MOUNTBATTEN, LORD

(Earl Mountbatten of Burma; 1900–79) British admiral and diplomat. After active service in World War II, he was appointed the last Viceroy of India in 1947 and was governor general (1947–48). He was killed in Ireland by an IRA bomb.

Quotations about Mountbatten

1 When he finally retired as Chief of Defence Staff in 1965 there was a sigh of relief among the professionals. One can see why and understand, but his departure was the eclipse of a genius – maddening, unveracious, and arrogant, but a genius nevertheless.

Lord Blake. *The Times*, 14 Mar 1985

2 Not everyone liked him. He was too successful, too rich, too vain, and not quite clever enough to compensate for his faults, but surely no one would deny that he was a hero.

David Holloway (1924–) Literary editor. *The Daily Telegraph*, 20 Aug 1980

3 I am sure that Dickie has done marvellously. But it is curious that we should regard as a hero the man who liquidated the Empire which other heroes such as Clive, Warren Hastings, and Napier won for us. Very odd indeed.

Harold Nicolson (1886–1968) British writer. Diary, 3 June 1947

Quotations by Mountbatten

4 You can divide my life into two. During the first part of my life I was an ordinary conventional naval officer, trying not to be different in the sense of being royal, trying not to show myself off as being rich and ostentatious – like always using a small car to drive to the dockyard instead of my Rolls Royce.

Mountbatten, Hero of Our Time, Ch. 9 (Richard Hough)

5 Do you really think the IRA would think me a worthwhile target?

Mountbatten, Hero of Our Time, Ch. 11 (Richard Hough)

6 As a military man who has given half a century of active service, I say in all sincerity that the nuclear arms race has no military purpose. Wars cannot be fought with nuclear weapons; their existence only adds to our perils because of the illusions which they have generated.

Speech, Strasbourg, 11 May 1979

7 Actually I vote Labour, but my butler's a Tory.

Said to a Tory canvasser during the 1945 election

MOURNING

See also death, loss, regret, sorrow

1 We met…Dr Hall in such very deep mourning that either his mother, his wife, or himself must be dead.

Jane Austen (1775–1817) British novelist. Letter to Cassandra Austen, 17 May 1799

2 I am distressed for thee, my brother Jonathan: very pleasant hast thou been unto me: thy love to me was wonderful, passing the love of women.
How are the mighty fallen, and the weapons of war perished!

Bible: II Samuel 1:26–27

3 With proud thanksgiving, a mother for her children,
England mourns for her dead across the sea.

Laurence Binyon (1869–1943) British poet. In response to the slaughter of World War I. *Poems For the Fallen*

4 MEDVEDENKO. Why do you wear black all the time?
MASHA. I'm in mourning for my life, I'm unhappy.

Anton Chekhov (1860–1904) Russian dramatist. *The Seagull*, I

5 There's a one-eyed yellow idol to the north of Khatmandu,
There's a little marble cross below the town;
There's a broken-hearted woman tends the grave of Mad Carew
And the Yellow God forever gazes down.

J. Milton Hayes (1884–1940) British writer. *The Green Eye of the Yellow God*

6 What we call mourning for our dead is perhaps not so much grief at not being able to call them back as it is grief at not being able to want to do so.

Thomas Mann (1875–1955) German novelist. *The Magic Mountain*

7 In a cavern, in a canyon,
Excavating for a mine
Dwelt a miner, Forty-niner,
And his daughter, Clementine.
Oh, my darling, Oh, my darling, Oh, my darling Clementine!
Thou art lost and gone for ever, dreadful sorry, Clementine.

Percy Montrose (19th century) US songwriter. *Clementine*

8 She is far from the land where her young hero sleeps,
And lovers are round her, sighing:
But coldly she turns from their gaze, and weeps,
For her heart in his grave is lying.

Thomas Moore (1779–1852) Irish poet. *Irish Melodies*, 'She is Far'

9 O, wither'd is the garland of the war,
The soldier's pole is fall'n! Young boys and girls
Are level now with men. The odds is gone,
And there is nothing left remarkable
Beneath the visiting moon.

William Shakespeare (1564–1616) English dramatist. *Antony and Cleopatra*, IV:13

10 But I have that within which passes show –
these but the trappings and the suits of woe.

William Shakespeare *Hamlet*, I:2

11 Alas, poor Yorick! I knew him, Horatio: a fellow of infinite jest, of most excellent fancy.

William Shakespeare *Hamlet*, V:1

12 If thou didst ever hold me in thy heart,
Absent thee from felicity awhile,
And in this harsh world draw thy breath in pain,
To tell my story.

William Shakespeare *Hamlet*, V:2

13 And my poor fool is hang'd! No, no, no life!
Why should a dog, a horse, a rat have life,
And thou no breath at all? Thou'lt come no more,
Never, never, never, never.

William Shakespeare *King Lear*, V:3

14 I weep for Adonais – he is dead!
O, weep for Adonais! though our tears
Thaw not the frost which binds so dear a head!

Percy Bysshe Shelley (1792–1822) British poet. Prompted by the death of Keats. *Adonais*, I

15 A lady asked me why, on most occasions, I wore black. 'Are you in mourning?'
'Yes.'
'For whom are you in mourning?'
'For the world.'

Edith Sitwell (1887–1964) British poet and writer. *Taken Care Of*, Ch. 1

16 Home they brought her warrior dead.
She nor swoon'd, nor utter'd cry:
All her maidens, watching said,
'She must weep or she will die.'

Alfred, Lord Tennyson (1809–92) British poet. *The Princess*, VI

MUGGERIDGE, MALCOLM

(1903–90) British writer and editor. The editor of *Punch* (1953–57), he wrote a number of books including *The Thirties* (1940), *Affairs of the Heart* (1949), and *Jesus Rediscovered* (1969), as well as an autobiography and diaries.

1 An orgy looks particularly alluring seen through the mists of righteous indignation.

The Most of Malcolm Muggeridge, 'Dolce Vita in a Cold Climate'

2 The orgasm has replaced the Cross as the focus of longing and the image of fulfilment.

The Most of Malcolm Muggeridge, 'Down with Sex'

3 Macmillan seemed, in his very person, to embody the national decay he supposed himself to be confuting. He exuded a flavour of moth-balls.

Tread Softly For You Tread on My Jokes, 'England, whose England'

4 A ready means of being cherished by the English is to adopt the simple expedient of living a long time. I have little doubt that if, say, Oscar Wilde had lived into his nineties, instead of dying in his forties, he would have been considered a benign, distinguished figure suitable to preside at a school prize-giving or to instruct and exhort scoutmasters at their jamborees. He might even have been knighted.

Tread Softly for you Tread on my Jokes

5 Its avowed purpose is to excite sexual desire, which, I should have thought, it unnecessary in the case of the young, inconvenient in the case of the middle aged, and unseemly in the old.

Tread Softly For You Tread On My Jokes

6 He is not only a bore but he bores for England.

Referring to the Conservative statesman Sir Anthony Eden. In *Newstatesmanship* (E. Hyams), 'Boring for England'

MURDER

See also assassination, crime, killing

1 Lizzie Borden took an axe
And gave her mother forty whacks;
When she saw what she had done
She gave her father forty-one!

Anonymous On 4 Aug 1892 in Fall River, Massachusetts, Lizzie Borden was acquitted of the murder of her stepmother and her father.

2 And the Lord said unto Cain, Where is Abel thy brother? And he said, I know not: Am I my brother's keeper?
And he said, What hast thou done? the voice of thy brother's blood crieth unto me from the ground.

Bible: Genesis 4:9–10

3 I've been accused of every death except the casualty list of the World War.

Al Capone (1899–1947) Italian-born US gangster. *The Bootleggers* (Kenneth Allsop), Ch. 11

4 Mordre wol out, that see we day by day.

Geoffrey Chaucer (c. 1342–1400) English poet. *The Canterbury Tales*, 'The Nun's Priest's Tale'

5 See how love and murder will out.

William Congreve (1670–1729) British Restoration dramatist. *The Double Dealer*, IV:6

6 Murder considered as one of the Fine Arts.

Thomas De Quincey (1785–1859) British writer. Essay title

7 I made a remark a long time ago. I said I was very pleased that television was now showing murder stories, because it's bringing murder back into its rightful setting – in the home.

Alfred Hitchcock (1889–1980) British film director. *The Observer*, 'Sayings of the Week', 17 Aug 1969

8 It takes two to make a murder. There are born victims, born to have their throats cut.

Aldous Huxley (1894–1964) British novelist. *Point Counter Point*

9 Murder, like talent, seems occasionally to run in families.

G. H. Lewes (1817–78) British philosopher and writer. *The Physiology of Common Life*, Ch. 12

10 Murder most foul, as in the best it is;
But this most foul, strange, and unnatural.

William Shakespeare 1564–1616) English dramatist. *Hamlet*, I:5

11 Put out the light, and then put out the light.
If I quench thee, thou flaming minister,
I can again thy former light restore,
Should I repent me; but once put out thy light,
Thou cunning'st pattern of excelling nature,
I know not where is that Promethean heat
That can thy light relume.

William Shakespeare *Othello*, V:2

12 I met Murder on the way –
He had a mask like Castlereagh.

Percy Bysshe Shelley (1792–1822) British poet. Viscount Castlereagh (1769–1822) was British foreign secretary (1812–22); he was highly unpopular and became identified with such controversial events as the Peterloo massacre of 1819. *The Mask of Anarchy*, 5

13 Other sins only speak; murder shrieks out.

John Webster (1580–1625) English dramatist. *The Duchess of Malfi*, IV:2

14 The person by far the most likely to kill you is yourself.

Jock Young British criminologist. *The Observer*, 'Sayings of the Week', 8 May 1994

MURDOCH, DAME IRIS

(1919–) Irish-born British novelist and philosophy teacher. Her novels include *The Bell* (1958), *A Severed Head* (1961), *The Sea, The Sea* (1978), *The Good Apprentice* (1985), and *The Message to the Planet* (1989).

1 All art deals with the absurd and aims at the simple. Good art speaks truth, indeed *is* truth, perhaps the only truth.

The Black Prince, 'Bradley Pearson's Foreword'

2 Writing is like getting married. One should never commit oneself until one is amazed at one's luck.

The Black Prince, 'Bradley Pearson's Foreword'

3 'What are you famous *for*?'
'For nothing. I am just famous.'

The Flight from the Enchanter

4 He led a double life. Did that make him a liar? He did not feel a liar. He was a man of two truths.

The Sacred and Profane Love Machine

5 Only lies and evil come from letting people off.

A Severed Head

MUSEUMS

1 The Arab who builds himself a hut out of the marble fragments of a temple in Palmyra is more philosophical than all the curators of the museums in London, Munich or Paris.

Anatole France (Jacques Anatole François Thibault; 1844–1924) French writer. *The Crime of Sylvestre Bonnard*

2 If there was a little room somewhere in the British Museum that contained only about twenty exhibits and good lighting, easy chairs, and a notice imploring you to smoke, I believe I should become a museum man.

J. B. Priestley (1894–1984) British novelist. *Self-Selected Essays*, 'In the British Museum'

3 There is in the British Museum an enormous mind. Consider that Plato is there cheek by jowl with Aristotle; and Shakespeare with Marlowe. This great mind is hoarded beyond the power of any single mind to possess it.

Virginia Woolf (1882–1941) British novelist. *Jacob's Room*, Ch. 9

MUSIC

See also criticism, musicians, opera, singing

1 Music helps not the toothache.
Proverb

2 Nothing is capable of being well set to music that is not nonsense.
Joseph Addison (1672–1719) British essayist. *The Spectator,* 18

3 The music teacher came twice each week to bridge the awful gap between Dorothy and Chopin.
George Ade (1866–1944) US dramatist and humorist. Attrib.

4 A musicologist is a man who can read music but can't hear it.
Thomas Beecham (1879–1961) British conductor. *Beecham Remembered* (H. Procter-Gregg)

5 There are two golden rules for an orchestra: start together and finish together. The public doesn't give a damn what goes on in between.
Thomas Beecham *Beecham Stories* (H. Atkins and A. Newman)

6 The English may not like music – but they absolutely love the noise it makes.
Thomas Beecham *The Wit of Music* (L. Ayre)

7 Brass bands are all very well in their place – outdoors and several miles away.
Thomas Beecham Attrib.

8 The sound of the harpsichord resembles that of a bird-cage played with toasting-forks.
Thomas Beecham Attrib.

9 When I composed that, I was conscious of being inspired by God Almighty. Do you think I can consider your puny little fiddle when He speaks to me?
Ludwig van Beethoven (1770–1827) German composer. Said when a violinist complained that a passage was unplayable. *Music All Around Me* (A. Hopkins)

10 I shall hear in heaven.
Last words. Attrib.

11 FIDDLE, n. An instrument to tickle human ears by function of a horse's tail on the entrails of a cat.
Ambrose Bierce (1842–c. 1914) US writer and journalist. *The Devil's Dictionary*

12 Down South where I come from you don't go around hitting too many white keys.
Eubie Blake (1883–1983) US pianist and ragtime composer. When asked why his compositions contained so many sharps and flats. Attrib.

13 Piping down the valleys wild,
Piping songs of pleasant glee,
On a cloud I saw a child.
William Blake (1757–1827) British poet. *Songs of Innocence,* Introduction

14 'Pipe a song about a Lamb!'
So I piped with merry cheer.
William Blake *Songs of Innocence,* Introduction

15 No one really understood music unless he was a scientist, her father had declared, and not just a scientist, either, oh, no, only the real ones, the theoreticians, whose language was mathematics.
Pearl Buck (1892–1973) US novelist. *The Goddess Abides,* Pt. I

16 The heart of the melody can never be put down on paper.
Pablo Casals (1876–1973) Spanish cellist. *Conversations*

17 Music has charms to soothe a savage breast.
William Congreve (1670–1729) British Restoration dramatist. *The Mourning Bride,* I

18 Strange how potent cheap music is.
Noël Coward (1899–1973) British dramatist. *Private Lives*

19 Music is the arithmetic of sounds as optics is the geometry of light.
Claude Debussy (1862–1918) French composer. Attrib.

20 The century of aeroplanes deserves its own music. As there are no precedents I must create anew.
Claude Debussy Attrib.

21 If you're not able to do the music of our day well, you're certainly not able to do the music of the past. I'm not interested in people who do Brahms without knowing Schoenberg. You cannot read Dostoyevsky without knowing Proust.
Christopher von Dohnányi (1929–) German musician. Interview, *The Independent,* 29 Apr 1994

22 When I was 25, Bartok needed me, a young man who would get up on the podium, play his music and be whistled at for it.
Antal Dorati (1906–88) American conductor and composer. Remark, Apr 1986

23 A song belongs to no man, said Joey The Lips.
The Lord holds copyright on all songs.
Me arse, said Outspan.
Roddy Doyle (1958–) Irish novelist and playwright. *The Commitments*

24 Music was invented to confirm human loneliness.
Lawrence Durrell (1912–90) British novelist. *Clea*

25 There is music in the air, music all round us: the world is full of it, and you simply take as much as you require.
Sir Edward Elgar (1857–1934) British composer. Basil Maine, *Elgar, his Life and Works*

26 Beethoven's Fifth Symphony is the most sublime noise that has ever penetrated into the ear of man.
E. M. Forster (1879–1970) British novelist. *Howards End,* Ch. 5

27 This poor teacher was trying to keep control of this class of rowdy 13-year-olds, and after a while she just gave up and started playing the piano to us. She stopped and said 'Does anybody know what key that is in? Without thinking I said: 'C sharp minor.' And she looked at me and said: 'See me afterwards.'
Jane Glover (1949–) British conductor. On how she discovered she had perfect pitch. *The Independent on Sunday,* 5 June 1994

28 The hills are alive with the sound of music
With the songs they have sung
For a thousand years.
Oscar Hammerstein (1895–1960) US lyricist. *The Sound of Music,* title song

29 I do not see any reason why the devil should have all the good tunes.

Rowland Hill (1744–1833) British clergyman. Attrib.

30 Never compose anything unless the not composing of it becomes a positive nuisance to you.

Gustav Holst (1874–1934) British composer. Letter to W. G. Whittaker

31 Since Mozart's day composers have learned the art of making music throatily and palpitatingly sexual.

Aldous Huxley (1894–1964) British novelist. *Along the Road*, 'Popular music'

32 The only sensual pleasure without vice.

Samuel Johnson (1709–84) British lexicographer. Referring to music. *Johnsonian Miscellanies* (ed. G. B. Hill), Vol. II

33 Heard melodies are sweet, but those unheard
Are sweeter; therefore, ye soft pipes, play on.

John Keats (1795–1821) British poet. *Ode on a Grecian Urn*

34 Oh well, you play Bach *your* way. I'll play him *his*.

Wanda Landowska (1877–1959) US harpsichordist. To fellow musician. Attrib.

35 A woman may be elected Prime Minister. She may administer justice in the High Courts, and the sacraments in the Church, but she cannot be trusted with a symphony orchestra for a couple of hours.

Norman Lebrecht *The Maestro Myth*

36 But I can't listen to music too often. It affects your nerves, makes you want to say stupid, nice things, and stroke the heads of people who could create such beauty while living in this vile hell.

Lenin (Vladimir Ilich Ulyanov; 1870–1924) Russian revolutionary leader. *Lenin and the Russian Revolution* (Christopher Hill)

37 There's sure no passion in the human soul,
But finds its food in music.

George Lillo (1693–1739) English dramatist. *Fatal Curiosity*, I:2

38 Music, Maestro, Please.

Herb Magidson (20th century) US songwriter. Song title

39 Every day people come forward with new songs. Music goes on forever.

Bob Marley (Robert Nesta Marley; 1945–80) Jamaican reggae singer. Attrib.

40 Music is not written in red, white and blue. It is written in the heart's blood of the composer.

Nellie Melba (Helen Porter Mitchell; 1861–1931) Australian soprano. *Melodies and Memories*

41 Music creates order out of chaos; for rhythm imposes unanimity upon the divergent, melody imposes continuity upon the disjointed, and harmony imposes compatibility upon the incongruous.

Yehudi Menuhin (1916–) US-born British violinist. *The Sunday Times*, 10 Oct 1976

42 The melting voice through mazes running;
Untwisting all the chains that tie
The hidden soul of harmony.

John Milton (1608–74) English poet. *L'Allegro*

43 I sometimes wonder which would be nicer – an opera without an interval, or an interval without an opera.

Ernest Newman (1868–1959) British music critic and writer. *Berlioz, Romantic and Classic* (ed. Peter Heyworth)

44 The song that we hear with our ears is only the song that is sung in our hearts.

Ouida (Marie Louise de la Ramée; 1839–1908) British novelist. *Wisdom, Wit and Pathos*, 'Ariadne'

45 What a terrible revenge by the culture of the Negroes on that of the whites.

Ignacy Paderewski (1860–1941) Polish pianist, composer, and statesman. Referring to jazz. Attrib.

46 Music is your own experience, your thoughts, your wisdom. If you don't live it, it won't come out of your horn.

Charlie Parker (1920–55) US black jazz musician. *Hear Me Talkin' to Ya* (Nat Shapiro and Nat Hentoff)

47 Music and women I cannot but give way to, whatever my business is.

Samuel Pepys (1633–1703) English diarist. *Diary*, 9 Mar 1666

48 The basic difference between classical music and jazz is that in the former the music is always greater than its performance – whereas the way jazz is performed is always more important than what is being played.

André Previn (1929–) German-born conductor. *An Encyclopedia of Quotations about Music* (Nat Shapiro)

49 Seated one day at the organ,
I was weary and ill at ease,
And my fingers wandered idly
Over the noisy keys.
...
But I struck one chord of music,
Like the sound of a great Amen.

Adelaide Anne Procter (1825–64) British poet. Better known in the setting by Sir Arthur Sullivan. *Legends and Lyrics*, 'A Lost Chord'

50 I have already heard it. I had better not go: I will start to get accustomed to it and finally like it.

Nikolai Rimsky-Korsakov (1844–1908) Russian composer. Referring to music by Debussy. *Conversations with Stravinsky* (Robert Craft and Igor Stravinsky)

51 Give me a laundry-list and I'll set it to music.

Gioacchino Rossini (1792–1868) Italian operatic composer. Attrib.

52 To be played with both hands in the pocket.

Erik Satie (1866–1925) French composer. Direction on one of his piano pieces. *The Unimportance of Being Oscar* (O. Levant)

53 The sonatas of Mozart are unique; they are too easy for children, and too difficult for artists.

Artur Schnabel (1882–1951) Austrian concert pianist. *An Encyclopedia of Quotations about Music* (Nat Shapiro)

54 This is not Beethoven lying here.

Franz Peter Schubert (1797–1828) Austrian-born composer. His last words

55 I am never merry when I hear sweet music.

William Shakespeare (1564–1616) English dramatist. *The Merchant of Venice*, V:1

56 The man that hath no music in himself,
Nor is not mov'd with concord of sweet sounds,
Is fit for treasons, stratagems, and spoils.

William Shakespeare *The Merchant of Venice*, V:1

57 If music be the food of love, play on,

Give me excess of it, that, surfeiting,
The appetite may sicken and so die.

William Shakespeare *Twelfth Night*, I:1

58 I wish the Government would put a tax on pianos for the incompetent.

Edith Sitwell (1887–1964) British poet and writer. *Letters, 1916–1964*

59 Jazz will endure just as long as people hear it through their feet instead of their brains.

John Philip Sousa (1854–1932) US composer, conductor, and writer. Attrib.

60 I don't write modern music. I only write good music.

Igor Stravinsky (1882–1971) Russian-born US composer. To journalists on his first visit to America, 1925

61 My music is best understood by children and animals.

Igor Stravinsky *The Observer*, 'Sayings of the Week', 8 Oct 1961

62 Music that gentlier on the spirit lies,
Than tir'd eyelids upon tir'd eyes.

Alfred, Lord Tennyson (1809–92) British poet. *The Lotos-Eaters*, 'Choric Song'

63 Oh I'm a martyr to music.

Dylan Thomas (1914–53) Welsh poet. *Under Milk Wood*

64 The cello is not one of my favourite instruments. It has such a lugubrious sound, like someone reading a will.

Irene Thomas (1920–) British writer. Attrib.

65 God tells me how he wants this music played – and you get in his way.

Arturo Toscanini (1867–1957) Italian conductor. *Etude* (Howard Tubman)

66 You know, sometimes I don't even like music.

Sir William Walton (1902–83) British composer. Remark, Mar 1982

67 When I play on my fiddle in Dooney,
Folk dance like a wave of the sea.

W. B. Yeats (1865–1939) Irish poet. *The Fiddler of Dooney*

MUSICIANS

See also critics, singers

General quotes

1 Musicians don't retire; they stop when there's no more music in them.

Louis Armstrong (1900–71) US jazz trumpeter. *The Observer*, 'Sayings of the Week', 21 Apr 1968

2 Off with you! You're a happy fellow, for you'll give happiness and joy to many other people. There is nothing better or greater than that!

Ludwig van Beethoven (1770–1827) German composer. Said to Franz Liszt when Liszt, aged 11, had visited Beethoven and played for him. *Beethoven: Letters, Journals and Conversations* (M. Hamburger)

3 The public doesn't want a new music: the main thing it demands of a composer is that he be dead.

Arthur Honegger (1892–1955) French composer. Attrib.

4 Of all musicians, flautists are most obviously the ones who know something we don't know.

Paul Jennings (1918–89) British humorous writer. *The Jenguin Pennings*, 'Flautists Flaunt Afflatus'

5 The conductor has the advantage of not seeing the audience.

André Kostalenetz (1903–80) Russian-born conductor. Attrib.

6 You see, our fingers are circumcised, which gives it a very good dexterity, you know, particularly in the pinky.

Itzhak Perlman (1945–) Israeli violinist. Responding to an observation that many great violinists are Jewish. *Close Encounters* (M. Wallace)

7 Sometimes, I think, not so much am I a pianist, but a vampire. All my life I have lived off the blood of Chopin.

Arthur Rubinstein (1887–1982) Polish-born US pianist. Attrib.

8 The notes I handle no better than many pianists. But the pauses between the notes – ah, that is where the art resides.

Artur Schnabel (1882–1951) Austrian concert pianist. *Chicago Daily News*, 11 June 1958

9 A good composer does not imitate; he steals.

Igor Stravinsky (1882–1971) Russian-born composer. *Twentieth Century Music* (Peter Yates)

Specific quotes

10 A master is dead. Today we sing no more.

Johannes Brahms (1833–97) German composer. Stopping a choral rehearsal on hearing of the death of Wagner *Brahms* (P. Latham).

11 Bach is like an astronomer who, with the aid of ciphers, finds the most wonderful stars.

Frédéric Chopin (1810–49) Polish composer and pianist. *Letter to Delphine Potocka*

12 Wagner is the Puccini of music.

J. B. Morton (1893–1979) British journalist. Attrib.

13 My dear hands. Farewell, my poor hands.

Sergei Rachmaninov (1873–1943) Russian composer. On being informed that he was dying from cancer. *The Great Pianists* (H. Schonberg)

14 When a piece gets difficult make faces.

Artur Schnabel (1882–1951) Austrian concert pianist. Advice given to the pianist Vladimir Horowitz. *The Unimportance of Being Oscar* (O. Levant)

15 Music owes as much to Bach as religion to its founder.

Robert Schumann (1810–56) German composer. Attrib.

16 Brahms is just like Tennyson, an extraordinary musician with the brains of a third-rate village policeman.

George Bernard Shaw (1856–1950) Irish dramatist and critic. Letter to Packenham Beatty, 4 Apr 1893

17 Unlike many contemporaries, he never writes paper music; everything has first been vividly heard by an inner ear of amazing acuteness. This faculty explains the speed at which he composes. The processes of trial and error take place mostly in the head.

Desmond Shaw-Taylor (1907–) British music critic. Referring to Benjamin Britten. *Sunday Times*, 17 Nov 1963

18 Walton wrote *Belshazzar's Feast* in that barn out

there. He made such a frightful din on the piano we had to banish him from the house.

Sacheverell Sitwell (1897–) British writer. *The Times, Profile,* 16 Nov 1982

19 He was the only pianist I have ever seen who did not grimace. That is a great deal.

Igor Stravinsky (1882–1971) Russian-born US composer. Referring to Rachmaninov. *Conversations with Igor Stravinsky* (Igor Stravinsky and Robert Craft)

20 Rachmaninov's immortalizing totality was his scowl. He was a six-and-a-half-foot-tall scowl.

Igor Stravinsky *Conversations with Igor Stravinsky* (Igor Stravinsky and Robert Craft)

21 Ah, a German and a genius! a prodigy, admit him!

Jonathan Swift (1667–1745) Irish-born Anglican priest and writer. Learning of the arrival in England of the German composer Handel: Swift's last words. Attrib.

MUSSOLINI, BENITO

(1883–1945) Italian dictator, responsible for the organization and spread of fascism in Italy. In World War II he formed the Axis with Germany (1940); after the Allied invasion of Italy, he was deposed (1943) and murdered.

1 I should be pleased, I suppose, that Hitler has carried out a revolution on our lines. But they are Germans. So they will end by ruining our idea.

Benito Mussolini (C. Hibbert), Pt. II, Ch. 1

2 The Italians will laugh at me; every time Hitler occupies a country he sends me a message.

Hitler (Alan Bullock), Ch. 8

3 We cannot change our policy now. After all, we are not political whores.

Hitler (Alan Bullock), Ch. 8

4 Fascism is a religion; the twentieth century will be known in history as the century of Fascism.

On Hitler's seizing power. *Sawdust Caesar* (George Seldes), Ch. 24

5 Fascism is not an article for export.

Report in the German press, 1932

MYTHS

1 Science must begin with myths, and with the criticism of myths.

Karl Popper (1902–) Austrian-born British philosopher. *British Philosophy in the Mid-Century* (ed. C. A. Mace)

2 A myth is, of course, not a fairy story. It is the presentation of facts belonging to one category in the idioms appropriate to another. To explode a myth is accordingly not to deny the facts but to re-allocate them.

Gilbert Ryle (1900–76) British philosopher. *The Concept of Mind*, Introduction

N

NABOKOV, VLADIMIR

(1899–1977) Russian-born US novelist. He was educated at Cambridge but emigrated to the USA in 1945. Of his many novels *Lolita* (1955) is the best known.

1 Lolita, light of my life, fire of my loins. My sin, my Soul.
Lolita

2 Life is a great surprise. I do not see why death should not be an even greater one.
Pale Fire, 'Commentary'

3 Like so many ageing college people, Pnin had long ceased to notice the existence of students on the campus.
Pnin, Ch. 3

4 Discussion in class, which means letting twenty young blockheads and two cocky neurotics discuss something that neither their teacher nor they know.
Pnin, Ch. 6

5 Poor Knight! he really had two periods, the first – a dull man writing broken English, the second – a broken man writing dull English.
The Real Life of Sebastian Knight, Ch. 1

6 Spring and summer did happen in Cambridge almost every year.
The Real Life of Sebastian Knight, Ch. 5

7 A novelist is, like all mortals, more fully at home on the surface of the present than in the ooze of the past.
Strong Opinions, Ch. 20

8 Literature and butterflies are the two sweetest passions known to man.
Radio Times, Oct 1962

NAKEDNESS

1 My Love in her attire doth show her wit,
It doth so well become her:
For every season she hath dressings fit,
For winter, spring, and summer.
No beauty she doth miss,
When all her robes are on;
But beauty's self she is,
When all her robes are gone.
Anonymous Madrigal

2 Lives there the man that can figure a naked Duke of Windlestraw addressing a naked House of Lords?
Thomas Carlyle (1795–1881) Scottish historian and essayist. *Sartor Resartus*, Bk. I, Ch. 9

3 a pretty girl who naked is
is worth a million statues.
e. e. cummings (1894–1962) US poet. *Collected Poems*, 133

4 No woman so naked as one you can see to be naked underneath her clothes.
Michael Frayn (1933–) British journalist and writer. *Constructions*

5 How idiotic civilization is! Why be given a body if you have to keep it shut up in a case like a rare, rare fiddle?
Katherine Mansfield (1888–1923) New-Zealand-born British writer. *Bliss and Other Stories*, 'Bliss'

6 JOURNALIST. Didn't you have anything on?
M. M. I had the radio on.
Marilyn Monroe (Norma-Jean Baker; 1926–62) US film star. Attrib.

NAMES

1 Ball...how very singular.
Thomas Beecham (1879–1961) British conductor. To a man called Ball. *Sir Thomas Beecham* (N. Cardus)

2 Known by the *sobriquet* of 'The artful Dodger.'
Charles Dickens (1812–70) British novelist. *Oliver Twist*, Ch. 8

3 I'm called Little Buttercup – dear Little Buttercup,
Though I could never tell why.
W. S. Gilbert (1836–1911) British dramatist. *HMS Pinafore*, I

4 A nickname is the heaviest stone that the devil can throw at a man.
William Hazlitt (1778–1830) British essayist. *Nicknames*

5 No, Groucho is not my real name. I'm breaking it in for a friend.
Groucho Marx (Julius Marx; 1895–1977) US comedian. Attrib.

6 O Romeo, Romeo! wherefore art thou Romeo?
William Shakespeare (1564–1616) English dramatist. *Romeo and Juliet*, II:2

7 What's in a name? That which we call a rose
By any other name would smell as sweet.
William Shakespeare *Romeo and Juliet*, II:2

8 'It's giving girls names like that', said Buggins, 'that nine times out of ten makes 'em go wrong. It unsettles 'em. If ever I was to have a girl, if ever I was to have a dozen girls, I'd call 'em all Jane.'
H. G. Wells (1866–1946) British writer. Referring to the name Euphemia. *Kipps*, Bk. I, Ch. 4

NAPOLEON I

(Napoleon Bonaparte; 1769–1821) French emperor. Having extended his power into most of Europe, the disastrous invasion of Russia (1812) marked a turning point; after his defeat at Waterloo (1815) he was exiled to St Helena, where he died.

Quotations about Napoleon

1 That infernal creature who is the curse of all the human race becomes every day more and more abominable.
Alexander I (1777–1825) Tsar of Russia. Letter to his sister Catherine, 5 Jan 1812

2 Napoleon is a dangerous man in a free country.

He seems to me to have the makings of a tyrant, and I believe that were he to be king he would be fully capable of playing such a part, and his name would become an object of detestation to posterity and every right-minded patriot.

Lucien Bonaparte (1775–1840) Younger brother of Napoleon. Letter to his brother Joseph, 1790

3 Napoleon – mighty somnambulist of a vanished dream.

Victor Hugo (1802–85) French writer. *Les Misérables*

4 Bonaparte's whole life, civil, political and military, was a fraud. There was not a transaction, great or small, in which lying and fraud were not introduced.

Duke of Wellington (1769–1852) British general and statesman. Letter, 29 Dec 1835

Quotations by Napoleon

5 I still love you, but in politics there is no heart, only head.

Referring to his divorce, for reasons of state, from the Empress Josephine (1809). *Bonaparte* (C. Barnett)

6 Maybe it would have been better if neither of us had been born.

Said while looking at the tomb of the philosopher Jean-Jacques Rousseau, whose theories had influenced the French Revolution. *The Story of Civilization* (W. Durant), Vol. II

7 There rises the sun of Austerlitz.

Said at the Battle of Borodino (7 Sept 1812), near Moscow; the Battle of Austerlitz (2 Dec 1805) was Napoleon's great victory over the Russians and Austrians.

8 It's the most beautiful battlefield I've ever seen.

Referring to carnage on the field of Borodino, near Moscow, after the battle (7 Sept 1812). Attrib.

9 It is only a step from the sublime to the ridiculous.

Remark following the retreat from Moscow, 1812. Attrib.

10 France has more need of me than I have need of France.

Speech, 31 Dec 1813

11 The bullet that is to kill me has not yet been moulded.

In reply to his brother Joseph, King of Spain, who had asked whether he had ever been hit by a cannonball. Attrib.

12 Oh well, no matter what happens, there's always death.

Attrib.

13 England is a nation of shopkeepers.

Attrib.

14 An army marches on its stomach.

Attrib.

15 *Tête d'Armée.*
Chief of the Army.

Last words. Attrib.

NASH, OGDEN

(1902–71) US poet. He wrote many books of satirical verse, including *I'm a Stranger Here Myself* (1938) and *Collected Verse* (1961).

1 The cow is of the bovine ilk;
One end is moo, the other, milk.

The Cow

2 A door is what a dog is perpetually on the wrong side of.

A Dog's Best Friend Is His Illiteracy

3 To be an Englishman is to belong to the most exclusive club there is.

England Expects

4 Women would rather be right than reasonable.

Frailty, Thy Name Is a Misnomer

5 Home is heaven and orgies are vile
But you need an orgy, once in a while.

Home, 99.44 100% Sweet Home

6 Beneath this slab
John Brown is stowed.
He watched the ads
And not the road.

Lather as You Go

7 Do you think my mind is maturing late,
Or simply rotted early?

Lines on Facing Forty

8 Children aren't happy with nothing to ignore,
And that's what parents were created for.

The Parents

9 I prefer to forget both pairs of glasses and pass my declining years saluting strange women and grandfather clocks.

Peekaboo, I Almost See You

10 I think that I shall never see
A billboard lovely as a tree.
Perhaps unless the billboards fall,
I'll never see a tree at all.

Song of the Open Road

NASTINESS

See also cruelty, hurt

1 But are they all horrid, are you sure they are all horrid?

Jane Austen (1775–1817) British novelist. *Northanger Abbey*, Ch. 6

2 I do not want people to be very agreeable, as it saves me the trouble of liking them a great deal.

Jane Austen Letter, 24 Dec 1798

3 There is an unseemly exposure of the mind, as well as of the body.

William Hazlitt (1778–1830) British essayist. *On Disagreeable People*

4 Because I am a bastard.

Ernest Hemingway (1899–1961) US novelist. When asked why he had deserted his wife for another woman. *Americans in Paris* (B. Morton)

5 He was one of those born neither to obey nor to command, but to be evil to the commander and the obeyer alike. Perhaps there was nothing in life that he had much wanted to do, except to shoot rabbits and hit his father on the jaw, and both these things he had done.

John Masefield (1878–1967) British poet. *The Bird of Dawning*

6 One of the worst things about life is not how nasty the nasty people are. You know that already. It is how nasty the nice people can be.

Anthony Powell (1905–) British novelist. *A Dance to the Music of Time: The Kindly Ones*, Ch. 4

7 I can't see that she could have found anything nastier to say if she'd thought it out with both hands for a fortnight.

Dorothy L. Sayers (1893–1957) British writer. *Busman's Holiday*, 'Prothalamion'

8 'I grant you that he's not two-faced,' I said. 'But what's the use of that when the one face he has got is so peculiarly unpleasant?'

C. P. Snow (1905–80) British novelist. *The Affair*, Ch. 4

9 Malice is like a game of poker or tennis; you don't play it with anyone who is manifestly inferior to you.

Hilde Spiel (1911–90) Austrian writer. *The Darkened Room*

NATIONALITY

See also Americans, British

1 The French are wiser than they seem, and the Spaniards seem wiser than they are.

Francis Bacon (1561–1626) English philosopher. *Essays*, 'Of Seeming Wise'

2 He was born an Englishman and remained one for years.

Brendan Behan (1923–64) Irish playwright. *The Hostage*, I

3 PAT. He was an Anglo-Irishman.
MEG. In the blessed name of God, what's that?
PAT. A Protestant with a horse.

Brendan Behan *The Hostage*, I

4 One of themselves, even a prophet of their own, said, The Cretians are alway liars, evil beasts, slow bellies.

Bible: Titus 1:12

5 England is a paradise for women, and hell for horses: Italy a paradise for horses, hell for women.

Robert Burton (1577–1640) English scholar and explorer. *Anatomy of Melancholy*, Pt. III

6 The Almighty in His infinite wisdom did not see fit to create Frenchmen in the image of Englishmen.

Winston Churchill (1874–1965) British statesman. Speech, House of Commons, 10 Dec 1942

7 For he might have been a Roosian,
A French, or Turk, or Proosian,
Or perhaps Ital-ian!
But in spite of all temptations
To belong to other nations,
He remains an Englishman!

W. S. Gilbert (1836–1911) British dramatist. *HMS Pinafore*, II

8 The Saxon is not like us Normans. His manners are not so polite.
But he never means anything serious till he talks about justice and right,
When he stands like an ox in the furrow with his sullen set eyes on your own,
And grumbles, 'This isn't fair dealing,' my son, leave the Saxon alone.

Rudyard Kipling (1865–1936) Indian-born British writer. *Norman and Saxon*

9 Great artists have no country.

Alfred de Musset (1810–57) French dramatist and poet. *Lorenzaccio*, I:5

10 I am not an Athenian or a Greek, but a citizen of the world.

Socrates (469–399 BC) Athenian philosopher. *Of Banishment* (Plutarch)

11 Men of England! You wish to kill me because I am a Frenchman. Am I not punished enough in not being born an Englishman?

Voltaire (François-Marie Arouet; 1694–1778) French writer. Addressing an angry London mob who desired to hang him because he was a Frenchman. Attrib.

12 We are all American at puberty; we die French.

Evelyn Waugh (1903–66) British novelist. *Diaries*, 'Irregular Notes', 18 July 1961

NATIONS

See also places

1 The day of small nations has long passed away. The day of Empires has come.

Joseph Chamberlain (1836–1914) British politician. Speech, Birmingham, 12 May 1904

2 What kind of people do they think we are?

Winston Churchill (1874–1965) British statesman. Referring to the Japanese. Speech to US Congress, 26 Dec 1941

3 Swiss peacekeepers would be the personification of an active neutrality.

Flavio Cotti (1939–) Swiss politician. *The Observer*, 'Sayings of the Week', 22 May 1994

4 The nations which have put mankind and posterity most in their debt have been small states – Israel, Athens, Florence, Elizabethan England.

Dean Inge (1860–1954) British churchman. *Wit and Wisdom of Dean Inge* (ed. Marchant)

5 This agglomeration which was called and which still calls itself the Holy Roman Empire was neither holy, nor Roman, nor an empire.

Voltaire (François-Marie Arouet; 1694–1778) French writer. *Essai sur les moeurs et l'esprit des nations*, LXX

NATURE

See also animals, birds, countryside, ecology, flowers, human nature, science

1 All things are artificial, for nature is the art of God.

Thomas Browne (1605–82) English physician and writer. *Religio Medici*, Pt. I

2 Ye banks and braes o' bonnie Doon,
How can ye bloom sae fresh and fair?
How can ye chant, ye little birds,
And I sae weary fu' o' care?

Robert Burns (1759–96) Scottish poet. *Ye Banks and Braes*

3 There is a pleasure in the pathless woods,
There is a rapture on the lonely shore,

There is society, where none intrudes,
By the deep Sea, and music in its roar:
I love not Man the less, but Nature more.

Lord Byron (1788–1824) British poet. *Childe Harold's Pilgrimage*, IV

4 Nature admits no lie.

Thomas Carlyle (1795–1881) Scottish historian and essayist. *Latter-Day Pamphlets*, 5

5 Is ditchwater dull? Naturalists with microscopes have told me that it teems with quiet fun.

G. K. Chesterton (1874–1936) British writer. *The Spice of Life*

6 Nature is but a name for an effect
Whose cause is God.

William Cowper (1731–1800) British poet. *The Task*

7 Nature can do more than physicians.

Oliver Cromwell (1599–1658) English soldier and statesman.

8 All my life through, the new sights of Nature made me rejoice like a child.

Marie Curie (1867–1934) Polish chemist. *Pierre Curie*

9 By viewing Nature, Nature's handmaid, art,
Makes mighty things from small beginnings grow.

John Dryden (1631–1700) British poet and dramatist. *Annus Mirabilis*

10 Whatever Nature has in store for mankind, unpleasant as it may be, men must accept, for ignorance is never better than knowledge.

Enrico Fermi (1901–54) *Atoms in the Family* (Laura Fermi)

11 All Nature wears one universal grin.

Henry Fielding (1707–54) British novelist. *Tom Thumb the Great*, I:1

12 Here's good advice for practice: go into partnership with nature; she does more than half the work and asks none of the fee.

Martin H. Fischer (1879–1962) *Fischerisms* (Howard Fabing and Ray Marr)

13 The spectacular advances made in therapeutics by industry during recent years tend to make us forget the medicinal value of plants. Their usefulness is far from negligible; their active principles are manifold and well-balanced.

Paul Fruictier *Grandmother's Secrets* (Jean Palaiseul)

14 The irregular side of nature, the discontinuous and erratic side – these have been puzzles to science, or worse, monstrosities.

James Gleick US science writer. *Chaos* (1987)

15 Natural science does not simply describe and explain nature, it is part of the interplay between nature and ourselves.

Werner Heisenberg (1901–76) German physicist. *Physics and Philosophy*

16 We must turn to nature itself, to the observations of the body in health and disease to learn the truth.

Hippocrates (c. 460 BC–c. 377 BC) Greek physician.

17 Man's chief goal in life is still to become and stay human, and defend his achievements against the encroachment of nature.

Eric Hoffer (1902–83) US writer and philosopher. *The Temper of Our Time*, 'The Return of Nature'

18 Nature is a benevolent old hypocrite; she cheats the sick and the dying with illusions better than any anodynes.

Oliver Wendell Holmes (1809–94) US writer and physician. *Medical Essays*, 'The Young Practitioner'

19 The axis of the earth sticks out visibly through the center of each and every town or city.

Oliver Wendell Holmes *The Autocrat of the Breakfast Table*, Ch. 6

20 Though you drive away Nature with a pitchfork she always returns.

Horace (Quintus Horatius Flaccus; 65 BC–8 BC) Roman poet. *Epistles*, I

21 Nature is as wasteful of promising young men as she is of fish spawn.

Richard Hughes (1900–79) British novelist and playwright. *The Fox in the Attic*

22 The whole of nature is a conjugation of the verb to eat, in the active and the passive.

Dean Inge (1860–1954) British churchman. *Outspoken Essays*

23 In nature there are neither rewards nor punishments – there are consequences.

Robert G. Ingersoll (1833–99) US lawyer and agnostic. *Lectures & Essays*, 'Some Reasons Why'

24 Anything green that grew out of the mould
Was an excellent herb to our fathers of old.

Rudyard Kipling (1865–1936) Indian-born British writer. *Grandmother's Secrets* (Jean Palaiseul)

25 Gentlemen know that fresh air should be kept in its proper place – out of doors – and that, God having given us indoors and out-of-doors, we should not attempt to do away with this distinction.

Rose Macaulay (1889–1958) British writer. *Crewe Train*, Pt. I, Ch. 5

26 Nature is very consonant and conformable with herself.

Isaac Newton (1642–1727) British scientist. *Opticks*, Bk. III

27 It is far from easy to determine whether she has proved a kind parent to man or a merciless step-mother.

Pliny the Elder (Gaius Plinius Secundus; 23–79 AD) Roman scholar. *Natural History*, VII

28 Nature abhors a vacuum.

François Rabelais (1483–1553) French satirist. Attrib.

29 O mickle is the powerful grace that lies in herbs, plants, stones and their true qualities.

William Shakespeare (1564–1616) English dramatist and poet. *Romeo and Juliet*, II

30 Are God and Nature then at strife
That Nature lends such evil dreams?
So careful of the type she seems,
So careless of the single life.

Alfred, Lord Tennyson (1809–92) British poet. *In Memoriam A.H.H.*

31 Nature has always had more power than education.

Voltaire (François Marie Arouet; 1694–1778) French writer and philosopher. *Vie de Molière*

32 Nature is usually wrong.

James Whistler (1834–1903) US painter. *The Gentle Art of Making Enemies*

33 After you have exhausted what there is in business, politics, conviviality, and so on – have found that none of these finally satisfy, or permanently wear – what remains? Nature remains.

Walt Whitman (1819–92) US poet. *Specimen Days*, 'New Themes Entered Upon'

34 A vacuum is a hell of a lot better than some of the stuff that nature replaces it with.

Tennessee Williams (1911–83) US dramatist. *Cat On A Hot Tin Roof*

35 Nature never did betray
The heart that loved her.

William Wordsworth (1770–1850) British poet. *Lines Composed a Few Miles above Tintern Abbey*

36 Earth fills her lap with pleasures of her own:
Yearnings she hath in her own natural kind.

William Wordsworth *Ode. Intimations of Immortality*, VI

37 Another race hath been, and other palms are won.
Thanks to the human heart by which we live,
Thanks to its tenderness, its joys and fears,
To me the meanest flower that blows can give
Thoughts that do often lie too deep for tears.

William Wordsworth *Ode. Intimations of Immortality*, IX

38 Come forth into the light of things,
Let Nature be your Teacher.

William Wordsworth *The Tables Turned*

39 O chestnut tree, great rooted blossomer,
Are you the leaf, the blossom or the bole?
O body swayed to music; O brightening glance,
How can we know the dancer from the dance?

W. B. Yeats (1865–1939) Irish poet. *Among School Children*

NAVY

See also boats, officers, sea, war

1 We joined the Navy, to see the world
And what did we see? We saw the sea.

Irving Berlin (Israel Baline; 1888–1989) US composer. Song

2 The Royal Navy of England has ever been its greatest defence and ornament; it is its ancient and natural strength, the floating bulwark of the island.

Willian Blackstone (1723–80) British jurist. *Commentaries on the Laws of England*, Bk. I, Ch. 13

3 Ye Mariners of England
That guard our native seas,
Whose flag has braved, a thousand years,
The battle and the breeze –
Your glorious standard launch again
To match another foe!
And sweep through the deep,
While the stormy winds do blow, –
While the battle rages loud and long,
And the stormy winds do blow.

Thomas Campbell (1777–1844) British poet. *Ye Mariners of England*

4 It is upon the navy under the Providence of God that the safety, honour, and welfare of this realm do chiefly attend.

Charles II (1630–1685) King of England. Articles of War

5 Don't talk to me about naval tradition. It's nothing but rum, sodomy, and the lash.

Winston Churchill (1874–1965) British statesman. *Former Naval Person* (Sir Peter Gretton), Ch. 1

6 The British navy always travels first class.

Lord Fisher (1841–1920) British admiral. *The Second World War*, Vol. 1 (W. Churchill)

7 I do not say the French cannot come, I only say they cannot come by sea.

John Jervis, Earl St Vincent (1735–1823) British admiral. Remark to the Cabinet, 1803

8 There were gentlemen and there were seamen in the navy of Charles the Second. But the seamen were not gentlemen; and the gentlemen were not seamen.

Lord Macaulay (1800–59) British historian. *History of England*, Vol. I, Ch. 3

9 England's chief defence depends upon the navy being always ready to defend the realm against invasion.

Philip II (1527–98) King of Spain. Philip, as husband of Mary I, was King-Consort of England (1554–58). Submission to the Privy Council

10 Most men were in fear that the French would invade, but I was always of another opinion, for I always said that, whilst we had a fleet in being, they would not dare to make an attempt.

Earl of Torrington English admiral. Justifying his refusal to give battle to a numerically superior French fleet; when subsequently ordered to do so, he was defeated off Beachy Head (10 July 1690). *The Later Stuarts* (Sir George Clark)

11 The Fleet's lit up. It is like fairyland; the ships are covered with fairy lights.

Thomas Woodroofe (1899–1978) British radio broadcaster. Said during commentary at the Coronation Review of the Royal Navy, May 1937

NAZISM

See also fascism, Germany, Hitler, Jews, World War II

1 *Ein Reich, Ein Volk, Ein Führer.*
One Realm, One People, One Leader.

Anonymous Slogan of the Nazi Party; first used at Nuremberg, Sept 1934

2 I herewith commission you to carry out all preparations with regard to…a *total solution* of the Jewish question, in those territories of Europe which are under German influence.

Hermann Goering (1893–1946) German leader. *The Rise and Fall of the Third Reich* (William Shirer)

3 Our movement took a grip on cowardly Marxism and from it extracted the meaning of socialism. It also took from the cowardly middle-class parties their nationalism. Throwing both into the cauldron of our way of life there emerged, as clear as a crystal, the synthesis – German National Socialism.

Hermann Goering Speech, Berlin, 9 Apr 1933

4 *Kraft durch Freude.*
Strength through joy.

Robert Ley (1890–1945) German Nazi. German Labour Front slogan

5 The former allies had blundered in the past by offering Germany too little, and offering even that too late, until finally Nazi Germany had become a menace to all mankind.

Allan Nevins (1890–1971) US historian. *Current History*, May 1935

6 In Germany, the Nazis came for the Communists and I didn't speak up because I was not a Communist. Then they came for the Jews and I didn't speak up because I was not a Jew. Then they came for the trade unionists and I didn't speak up because I was not a trade unionist. Then they came for the Catholics and I was a Protestant so I didn't speak up. Then they came for me…By that time there was no one to speak up for anyone.

Martin Niemöller (1892–1984) German pastor. *Concise Dictionary of Religious Quotations* (W. Neil)

NECESSITY

1 Beggars can't be choosers.

Proverb

2 Necessity is the mother of invention.

Proverb

3 Needs must when the devil drives.

Proverb

4 Necessity is the plea for every infringement of human freedom. It is the argument of tyrants; it is the creed of slaves.

William Pitt the Younger (1759–1806) British statesman. Speech, House of Commons, 18 Nov 1783

5 O, reason not the need! Our basest beggars
Are in the poorest thing superfluous.
Allow not nature more than nature needs,
Man's life is cheap as beast's.

William Shakespeare (1564–1616) English dramatist. *King Lear*, II:4

6 Teach thy necessity to reason thus:
There is no virtue like necessity.

William Shakespeare *Richard II*, I:3

7 Necessity knows no law.

Publilius Syrus (1st century BC) Roman dramatist. Attrib.

8 I find no hint throughout the universe
Of good or ill, of blessing or of curse;
I find alone Necessity Supreme.

James Thomson (1834–82) British poet. *The City of Dreadful Night*, XIV

NEGLECT

1 A little neglect may breed mischief,…for want of a nail, the shoe was lost; for want of a shoe the horse was lost; and for want of a horse the rider was lost.

Benjamin Franklin (1706–90) US scientist and statesman. *Poor Richard's Almanack*

2 The general idea, of course, in any first-class laundry is to see that no shirt or collar ever comes back twice.

Stephen Leacock (1869–1944) British-born Canadian economist and humorist. *Winnowed Wisdom*, Ch. 6

3 The dust and silence of the upper shelf.

Lord Macaulay (1800–59) British historian. *Literary Essays Contributed to the 'Edinburgh Review'*, 'Milton'

4 What time he can spare from the adornment of his person he devotes to the neglect of his duties.

William Hepworth Thompson (1810–86) British academic. Referring to the Cambridge Professor of Greek, Sir Richard Jebb. *With Dearest Love to All* (M. R. Bobbit), Ch. 7

NEIGHBOURS

1 Love your neighbour, yet pull not down your hedge.

Proverb

2 Thou shalt love thy neighbour as thy self.

Bible: Matthew 22:39

3 My apple trees will never get across
And eat the cones under his pines, I tell him.
He only says, 'Good fences make good neighbours.'

Robert Frost (1875–1963) US poet. *North of Boston*, 'Mending Wall'

4 For it is your business, when the wall next door catches fire.

Horace (Quintus Horatius Flaccus; 65–8 BC) Roman poet. *Epistles*, I

NELSON, HORATIO

(1758–1805) British admiral. Hero of many naval battles, he defeated the French at Trafalgar (1805) but was killed during the battle. His affair with Lady Hamilton caused a considerable scandal.

1 The Nelson touch.

Diary, 9 Oct 1805

2 You must hate a Frenchman as you hate the devil.

Life of Nelson (Southey), Ch. 3

3 I have only one eye: I have a right to be blind sometimes: I really do not see the signal.

Remark, Battle of Copenhagen, 2 Apr 1801; Nelson ignored Admiral Parker's order to disengage by placing his telescope to his blind eye; an hour later, he was victorious. *Life of Nelson* Ch. 7 (Robert Southey)

4 England expects every man will do his duty.

Signal hoisted prior to the Battle of Trafalgar, 1805.

5 In case signals can neither be seen nor perfectly understood, no captain can do very wrong if he places his ship alongside that of an enemy.

Memorandum before Trafalgar, 9 Oct 1805

6 Kiss me, Hardy.

Last words, spoken to Sir Thomas Hardy, captain of the *Victory*, during the Battle of Trafalgar, 1805.

NEPOTISM

1 I am against government by crony.

Harold L. Ickes (1874–1952) US Republican politician. Comment on his resignation as Secretary of the Interior (1946) after a dispute with President Truman

2 I can't see that it's wrong to give him a little legal experience before he goes out to practice law.

John Fitzgerald Kennedy (1917–63) US statesman. On being criticized for making his brother Robert attorney general. *Nobody Said It Better* (M. Ringo)

NEUROSIS

See also psychiatry, psychology

1 The psychotic person knows that two and two make five and is perfectly happy about it; the neurotic person knows that two and two make four, but is terribly worried about it.

Anonymous

2 A mistake which is commonly made about neurotics is to suppose that they are interesting. It is not interesting to be always unhappy, engrossed with oneself, malignant and ungrateful, and never quite in touch with reality.

Cyril Connolly (1903–74) British journalist and writer. *The Unquiet Grave*, Pt. II

3 A man should not strive to eliminate his complexes, but to get into accord with them: they are legitimately what directs his conduct in the world.

Sigmund Freud (1856–1939) Austrian psychoanalyst.

4 There are those who have tried to dismiss his story with a flourish of the Union Jack, a psycho-analytical catchword or a sneer; it should move our deepest admiration and pity. Like Shelley and like Baudelaire, it may be said of him that he suffered, in his own person, the neurotic ills of an entire generation.

Christopher Isherwood (1904–86) British novelist. Referring to T. E. Lawrence. *Exhumations*

5 Neurosis is always a substitute for legitimate suffering.

C. G. Jung (1875–1961) Swiss psychologist.

6 This is, I think, very much the Age of Anxiety, the age of the neurosis, because along with so much that weighs on our minds there is perhaps even more that grates on our nerves.

Louis Kronenberger (1904–) US writer, critic, and editor. *Company Manners*, 'The Spirit of the Age'

7 Modern neurosis began with the discoveries of Copernicus. Science made man feel small by showing him that the earth was not the center of the universe.

Mary McCarthy (1912–89) US novelist. *On the Contrary*, 'Tyranny of the Orgasm'

8 Neurotic means he is not as sensible as I am, and psychotic means he's even worse than my brother-in-law.

Karl Menninger (1893–1990) US psychiatrist.

9 Freud is all nonsense; the secret of neurosis is to be found in the family battle of wills to see who can refuse longest to help with the dishes. The sink is the great symbol of the bloodiness of family life. All life is bad, but family life is worse.

Julian Mitchell (1935–) British writer and dramatist. *As Far as You Can Go*, I, Ch. 1

10 Neurosis has an absolute genius for malingering. There is no illness which it cannot counterfeit perfectly...If it is capable of deceiving the doctor, how should it fail to deceive the patient?

Marcel Proust (1871–1922) French novelist. *À la Recherche du temps perdu: Le Côté de Guermantes*

11 The 'sensibility' claimed by neurotics is matched by their egotism; they cannot abide the flaunting by others of the sufferings to which they pay an ever increasing attention in themselves.

Marcel Proust *À la Recherche du temps perdu: Le Côté de Guermantes*

12 Everything great in the world is done by neurotics; they alone founded our religions and created our masterpieces.

Marcel Proust *The Perpetual Pessimist* (Sagittarius and George)

13 Work and love – these are the basics. Without them there is neurosis.

Theodor Reik

14 Neurosis is the way of avoiding non-being by avoiding being.

Paul Tillich (1886–1965) German-born US theologian. *The Courage to Be*

NEWBOLT, SIR HENRY

(1862–1938) British poet. An authority on the British navy, many of his poems are about the sea and his *Songs of the Sea* (1904) and *Songs of the Fleet* (1910) were set to music by Stanford.

1 He clapped the glass to his sightless eye,
And 'I'm damned if I see it', he said.

Referring to Lord Nelson at the Battle of Copenhagen (1801). *Admirals All*

2 'Take my drum to England, hang et by the shore,
Strike et when your powder's runnin' low;
If the Dons sight Devon, I'll quit the port o' Heaven,
An' drum them up the Channel as we drummed them long ago.'

Drake's Drum

3 Drake he's in his hammock till the great Armadas come.
(Capten, art tha sleepin' there below?)
Slung atween the round shot, listenin' for the drum,
An dreamin' arl the time o' Plymouth Hoe.

Drake's Drum

4 Now the sunset breezes shiver,
And she's fading down the river,
But in England's song for ever
She's the Fighting Téméraire.

The Fighting Téméraire

5 But cared greatly to serve God and the King,
And keep the Nelson touch.

See NELSON. *Minora Sidera*

6 There's a breathless hush in the Close tonight –
Ten to make and the match to win –
A bumping pitch and a blinding light,
An hour to play and the last man in.

Vitaï Lampada

7 The sand of the desert is sodden red, –
Red with the wreck of a square that broke; –
The gatling's jammed and the colonel dead,
And the regiment blind with the dust and smoke.
The river of death has brimmed its banks
And England's far and honour a name.

But the voice of a schoolboy rallies the ranks:
'Play up! play up! and play the game!'
Vitaï Lampada

NEWSPAPERS

See also journalism, media

1 Top people take *The Times.*
Anonymous Advertisement

2 *The Times* has made many ministries.
Walter Bagehot (1826–77) British economist and journalist. *The English Constitution*, 'The Cabinet'

3 Deleted by French censor.
James Gordon Bennett (1841–1918) US newspaper owner and editor. Used to fill empty spaces in his papers during World War I when news was lacking. *Americans in Paris* (B. Morton)

4 Price of Herald three cents daily. Five cents Sunday. Bennett.
James Gordon Bennett Telegram to William Randolph Hearst, when he heard that Hearst was trying to buy his paper. *The Life and Death of the Press Barons* (P. Brandon)

5 Reading someone else's newspaper is like sleeping with someone else's wife. Nothing seems to be precisely in the right place, and when you find what you are looking for, it is not clear then how to respond to it.
Malcolm Bradbury (1932–) British academic and novelist. *Stepping Westward*, Bk. I, Ch. 1

6 *The Times* is speechless and takes three columns to express its speechlessness.
Winston Churchill (1874–1965) British statesman. Referring to Irish Home Rule. Speech, Dundee, 14 May 1908

7 I believe it has been said that one copy of *The Times* contains more useful information than the whole of the historical works of Thucydides.
Richard Cobden (1804–65) British politician. Speech, Manchester, 27 Dec 1850

8 Small earthquake in Chile. Not many dead.
Claud Cockburn Put forward as an example of a dull newspaper headline. *I Claud*

9 Nothing is news until it has appeared in *The Times.*
Ralph Deakin (1888–1952) Foreign News Editor of *The Times.* Attrib.

10 And when it's gay priests, even the tabloids suddenly find they have a religious affairs correspondent.
David Hare (1947–) British playwright. *The Sunday Times*, 11 Feb 1990

11 All the news that's fit to print.
Adolph Simon Ochs (1858–1935) US newspaper publisher. The motto of *The New York Times*

12 Never believe in mirrors or newspapers.
John Osborne (1929–) British dramatist. *The Hotel in Amsterdam*

13 Well, there are only two posh papers on a Sunday – the one you're reading and this one.
John Osborne *Look Back in Anger*, I

14 Written by office boys for office boys.
Marquess of Salisbury (1830–1903) British statesman. Reaction to the launch of the *Daily Mail*, 1896. *Northcliffe, an Intimate Biography* (Hamilton Fyfe), Ch. 4

15 They have been just as spiteful to me in the American press as the Soviet press was.
Alexander Solzhenitsyn (1918–) Russian novelist. *The Observer*, 'Sayings of the Week', 1 May 1994

16 The *Pall Mall Gazette* is written by gentlemen for gentlemen.
William Makepeace Thackeray (1811–63) British novelist. *Pendennis*, Ch. 32

17 '*The Beast* stands for strong mutually antagonistic governments everywhere', he said. 'Self-sufficiency at home, self-assertion abroad.'
Evelyn Waugh (1903–66) British novelist. *Scoop*, Bk. I, Ch. 1

18 News is what a chap who doesn't care much about anything wants to read. And it's only news until he's read it. After that it's dead.
Evelyn Waugh *Scoop*, Bk. I, Ch. 5

19 They were not so much published as carried screaming into the street.
H. G. Wells (1866–1946) British writer. *War In the Air*

NEWTON, SIR ISAAC

(1642–1727) British scientist, one of the greatest of all time, who discovered gravitation, recognized that white light is a mixture of coloured lights, invented calculus, and laid the foundations of dynamics with his laws of motion. His principal publications were the *Principia Mathematica* (1686–87) and *Optiks* (1704).

Quotations about Newton

1 He lived the life of a solitary, and like all men who are occupied with profound meditation, he acted strangely. Sometimes, in getting out of bed, an idea would come to him, and he would sit on the edge of the bed, half dressed, for hours at a time.
Louis Figuier (1819–94) French writer. *Vies des savants* (translated by B.H. Clark)

2 Sir Isaac Newton, though so deep in algebra and fluxions, could not readily make up a common account; and whilst he was Master of the Mint, used to get someone to make up the accounts for him.
Alexander Pope (1688–1744) British poet. *Observations, Anecdotes and characters* (Rev. Joseph Spence)

3 He was a highly neurotic young don at Trinity College, Cambridge, who became the most revolutionary mathematician in Europe at the age of 24.
Michael Ratcliffe *The Times*, 26 Mar 1981

Quotations by Newton

4 Nature is very consonant and conformable with herself.
Opticks, Bk. III

5 I do not know what I may appear to the world, but to myself I seem to have been only like a boy playing on the sea-shore, and diverting myself in now and then finding a smoother pebble or a prettier shell than ordinary, whilst the great ocean of truth lay all undiscovered before me.
Isaac Newton (L. T. More)

6 O Diamond! Diamond! thou little knowest the mischief done!

Said to a dog that set fire to some papers, representing several years' work, by knocking over a candle. *Wensley-Dale…a Poem* (Thomas Maude)

7 If I have seen further it is by standing on the shoulders of giants.

Letter to Robert Hooke, 5 Feb 1676. The quotation was in fact used by many others before Newton.

NIETZSCHE, FRIEDRICH

(1844–1900) German philosopher. His rejection of all religion and his glorification of the superman in *Thus Spake Zarathustra* (1883–92) influenced Nazi philosophy in Germany.

Quotations about Nietzsche

1 Nietzsche…was a confirmed Life Force worshipper. It was he who raked up the Superman, who is as old as Prometheus.

George Bernard Shaw (1856–1950) Irish dramatist and critic. *Man and Superman*, III

Quotations by Nietzsche

2 When a man is in love he endures more than at other times; he submits to everything.

The Antichrist

3 God created woman. And boredom did indeed cease from that moment – but many other things ceased as well! Woman was God's *second* mistake.

The Antichrist

4 I call Christianity the one great curse, the one enormous and innermost perversion, the one great instinct of revenge, for which no means are too venomous, too underhand, too underground and too petty – I call it the one immortal blemish of mankind.

The Antichrist

5 God is dead: but considering the state the species Man is in, there will perhaps be caves, for ages yet, in which his shadow will be shown.

Die Fröhliche Wissenschaft, Bk. III

6 Believe me! The secret of reaping the greatest fruitfulness and the greatest enjoyment from life is to *live dangerously*!

Die Fröhliche Wissenschaft, Bk. IV

7 As an artist, a man has no home in Europe save in Paris.

Ecce Homo

8 My time has not yet come either; some are born posthumously.

Ecce Homo

9 My doctrine is: Live that thou mayest desire to live again – that is thy duty – for in any case thou wilt live again!

Eternal Recurrence

10 Do you really believe that the sciences would ever have originated and grown if the way had not been prepared by magicians, alchemists, astrologers and witches whose promises and pretensions first had to create a thirst, a hunger, a taste for *hidden* and *forbidden* powers? Indeed, infinitely more had to be *promised* than could ever be fulfilled in order that anything at all might be fulfilled in the realms of knowledge.

The Gay Science

11 The thought of suicide is a great source of comfort: with it a calm passage is to be made across many a bad night.

Jenseits von Gut und Böse

12 Morality in Europe today is herd-morality.

Jenseits von Gut und Böse

13 Is not life a hundred times too short for us to bore ourselves?

Jenseits von Gut und Böse

14 In the philosopher there is nothing whatever impersonal; and, above all, his morality bears decided and decisive testimony to *who he is* – that is to say, to the order of rank in which the innermost drives of his nature stand in relation to one another.

Jenseits von Gut und Böse

15 Insects sting, not from malice, but because they want to live. It is the same with critics – they desire our blood, not our pain.

Miscellaneous Maxims and Reflections

16 He who does not need to lie is proud of not being a liar.

Nachgelassene Fragmente

17 I teach you the Superman. Man is something that is to be surpassed.

Thus Spake Zarathustra

18 To show pity is felt as a sign of contempt because one has clearly ceased to be an object of *fear* as soon as one is pitied.

The Wanderer and His Shadow

NIGHTINGALE, FLORENCE

(1820–1910) British nurse famous for her work in army hospitals during the Crimean War (1854–56), when she became known as the 'Lady with the Lamp'. Following the war she brought about radical reforms in army medical practice and was a noted hospital reformer and founder of the modern nursing profession. She was the first woman to be awarded the Order of Merit (1907).

Quotations about Nightingale

1 Miss Nightingale did inspire awe, not because one felt afraid of her *per se*, but because the very essence of *Truth* seemed to emanate from her, and because of her perfect fearlessness in telling it.

William Richmond *The Richmond Papers*

2 What a comfort it was to see her pass. She would speak to one, and nod and smile to as many more; but she could not do it to all you know. We lay there by the hundreds; but we could kiss her shadow as it fell and lay our heads on the pillow again content.

A patient in the Crimean War. *Florence Nightingale* (Cecil Woodham-Smith)

Quotations by Nightingale

3 It may seem a strange principle to enunciate as the very first requirement in a Hospital that it should do the sick no harm.

Notes on Hospitals, Preface

4 No *man*, not even a doctor, ever gives any other definition of what a nurse should be than this – 'devoted and obedient.' This definition would do just as well for a porter. It might even do for a horse. It would not do for a policeman.

Notes on Nursing

5 The first possibility of rural cleanliness lies in *water supply*.

Letter to Medical Officer of Health, Nov 1891

6 Too kind, too kind.

When given the Order of Merit on her death bed. *Life of Florence Nightingale*, Vol. II, Pt. 7, Ch. 9 (E. Cook)

NIXON, RICHARD MILHOUS

(1913–94) US president. A republican, he became president in 1969 and was responsible for ending the US commitment in Vietnam (1973). He was forced to resign after the Watergate scandal (1974), but was pardoned by his successor, President Ford.

Quotations about Nixon

1 President Nixon's motto was, if two wrongs don't make a right, try three.

Norman Cousins *Daily Telegraph*, 17 July 1969

2 Nixon is the kind of politician who would cut down a redwood tree and then mount the stump to make a speech for conservation.

Adlai Stevenson (1900–65) US statesman. Attrib.

Quotations by Nixon

3 There can be no whitewash at the White House.

Referring to the Watergate scandal. *The Observer*, 'Sayings of the Week', 30 Apr 1973

4 I let down my friends, I let down my country. I let down our system of government.

The Observer, 'Sayings of the Week', 8 May 1977

5 You won't have Nixon to kick around any more, gentlemen. This is my last Press Conference.

Press conference for governorship of California, 2 Nov 1962

6 Let us begin by committing ourselves to the truth, to see it like it is and to tell it like it is, to find the truth, to speak the truth and live with the truth. That's what we'll do.

Nomination acceptance speech, Miami, 8 Aug 1968

7 It is time for the great silent majority of Americans to stand up and be counted.

Election speech, Oct 1970

8 This is the greatest week in the history of the world since the creation.

Said when men first landed on the moon. Attrib., 24 July 1969

9 I don't give a shit what happens. I want you all to stonewall it, let them plead the Fifth Amendment, cover-up or anything else, if it'll save it, save the plan.

Referring to the Watergate cover-up. In conversation, 22 Mar 1973 (tape transcript)

10 I am not a crook.

Attrib., 17 Nov 1973

11 When the President does it, that means it is not illegal.

Television interview, May 1977

12 I have as my ideal the life of Jesus.

Nixon, a Life (Jonathan Aitken)

NOBILITY

See also aristocracy, honour

1 There is surely a piece of divinity in us, something that was before the elements, and owes no homage unto the sun.

Thomas Browne (1605–82) English physician and writer. *Religio Medici*, Pt. II

2 Real nobility is based on scorn, courage, and profound indifference.

Albert Camus (1913–60) French existentialist writer. *Notebooks*

3 *Noblesse oblige.*
Nobility has its own obligations.

Duc de Lévis (1764–1830) French writer and soldier. *Maximes et Réflexions*

4 The high sentiments always win in the end, the leaders who offer blood, toil, tears and sweat always get more out of their followers than those who offer safety and a good time. When it comes to the pinch, human beings are heroic.

George Orwell (Eric Blair; 1903–50) British novelist. *The Art of Donald McGill*

5 Thou hast a grim appearance, and thy face
Bears a command in't; though thy tackle's torn,
Thou show'st a noble vessel. What's thy name?

William Shakespeare (1564–1616) English dramatist. *Coriolanus*, IV:5

6 This was the noblest Roman of them all.
All the conspirators save only he
Did that they did in envy of great Caesar.

William Shakespeare *Julius Caesar*, V:5

7 His life was gentle, and the elements
So mixed in him that Nature might stand up
And say to all the world, 'This was a man!'

William Shakespeare *Julius Caesar*, V:5

8 There is
One great society alone on earth:
The noble living and the noble dead.

William Wordsworth (1770–1850) British poet. *The Prelude*, XI

9 Thy soul was like a star, and dwelt apart.

William Wordsworth *Sonnets*, 'Milton! thou shouldst'

NONCOMMITMENT

1 We know what happens to people who stay in the middle of the road. They get run over.

Aneurin Bevan (1897–1960) British Labour politician. *The Observer*, 'Sayings of the Week', 9 Dec 1953

2 Let them eat the lie and swallow it with their

bread. Whether the two were lovers or no, they'll have accounted to God for it by now. I have my own fish to fry.

Miguel de Cervantes (1547–1616) Spanish novelist. *Don Quixote*, Pt. I, Ch. 25

3 The Right Hon. gentleman has sat so long on the fence that the iron has entered his soul.

David Lloyd George (1863–1945) British Liberal statesman. Referring to Sir John Simon. Attrib.

NONSENSE

See also humour

1 If all the world were paper,
And all the sea were ink,
And all the trees were bread and cheese,
What should we do for drink?

Anonymous *If All the World were Paper*

2 If ever there was a case of clearer evidence than this of persons acting in concert together, this case is that case.

William Arabin (1773–1841) British judge. *Arabinesque at Law* (Sir R. Megarry)

3 The fleas that tease in the high Pyrenees.

Hilaire Belloc (1870–1953) French-born British poet. *Tarantella*

4 What happens to the hole when the cheese is gone?

Bertolt Brecht (1898–1956) German dramatist. *Mother Courage*, VI

5 Twinkle, twinkle, little bat!
How I wonder what you're at!
Up above the world you fly!
Like a teatray in the sky.

Lewis Carroll (Charles Lutwidge Dodgson; 1832–98) British writer. *Alice's Adventures in Wonderland*, Ch. 7

6 For the Snark *was* a Boojum, you see.

Lewis Carroll *The Hunting of the Snark*

7 'Twas brillig, and the slithy toves
Did gyre and gimble in the wabe;
All mimsy were the borogoves,
And the mome raths outgrabe.

Lewis Carroll *Through the Looking-Glass*, Ch. 1

8 Now, *here*, you see, it takes all the running *you* can do, to keep in the same place. If you want to get somewhere else, you must run at least twice as fast as that!

Lewis Carroll *Through the Looking-Glass*, Ch. 2

9 'The time has come,' the Walrus said,
'To talk of many things:
Of shoes – and ships – and sealing-wax –
Of cabbages – and kings –
And why the sea is boiling hot –
And whether pigs have wings.'

Lewis Carroll *Through the Looking-Glass*, Ch. 4

10 Colourless green ideas sleep furiously.

Noam Chomsky (1928–) US academic linguist. Used by Chomsky to demonstrate that an utterance can be grammatical without having meaning. *Syntactic Structures*

11 Go, and catch a falling star,
Get with child a mandrake root,
Tell me, where all past years are,
Or who cleft the Devil's foot.

John Donne (1573–1631) English poet. *Go and Catch a Falling Star*

12 Gertrude Stein is the mama of dada.

Clifton Fadiman (1904–) US writer. Referring to the US writer Gertrude Stein (1874–1946) who lived in Paris from 1903 and was involved in Dada, the nihilistic artistic movement. Attrib.

13 So she went into the garden to cut a cabbage-leaf; to make an apple-pie; and at the same time a great she-bear, coming up the street, pops its head into the shop. 'What! no soap?' So he died, and she very imprudently married the barber; and there were present the Picninnies, and the Joblillies, and the Garyalies, and the grand Panjandrum himself, with the little round button at top, and they all fell to playing the game of catch as catch can, till the gun powder ran out at the heels of their boots.

Samuel Foote (1720–77) British actor and dramatist. Nonsense composed to test the actor Charles Macklin's claim that he could memorize anything.

14 This particularly rapid, unintelligible patter
Isn't generally heard, and if it is it doesn't matter.

W. S. Gilbert (1836–1911) British dramatist. *Ruddigore*, II

15 If the man who turnips cries,
Cry not when his father dies,
'Tis a proof that he had rather
Have a turnip than his father.

Samuel Johnson (1709–84) British lexicographer. *Johnsonian Miscellanies* (ed. G. B. Hill), Vol. I

16 Three quarks for Muster Mark!

James Joyce (1882–1941) Irish novelist. The word quark has since been adopted by physicists for hypothetical elementary particles. *Finnegans Wake*

17 Lord Ronald said nothing; he flung himself from the room, flung himself upon his horse and rode madly off in all directions.

Stephen Leacock (1869–1944) English-born Canadian economist and humorist. *Nonsense Novels*, 'Gertrude the Governess'

18 On the Coast of Coromandel
Where the early pumpkins blow,
In the middle of the woods
Lived the Yonghy-Bonghy-Bò.

Edward Lear (1812–88) British artist and writer. *Nonsense Songs*, 'The Courtship of the Yonghy-Bonghy-Bò'

19 The Dong! – the Dong!
The wandering Dong through the forest goes!
The Dong! – the Dong!
The Dong with a luminous Nose!

Edward Lear *Nonsense Songs*, 'The Dong with a Luminous Nose'

20 The Pobble who has no toes
Had once as many as we;
When they said, 'Some day you may lose them all';
He replied, 'Fish fiddle de-dee!'

Edward Lear *Nonsense Songs*, 'The Pobble who has no Toes'

21 Far and few, far and few,
Are the lands where the Jumblies live;
Their heads are green, and their hands are blue,
And they went to sea in a sieve.

Edward Lear *The Jumblies*

22 He has many friends, laymen and clerical.

Old Foss is the name of his cat:
His body is perfectly spherical,
He weareth a runcible hat.

Edward Lear *Nonsense Songs*, Preface

23 The Owl and the Pussy-Cat went to sea
In a beautiful pea-green boat,
They took some honey, and plenty of money,
Wrapped up in a five-pound note.

Edward Lear *The Owl and the Pussy-Cat*

24 Serve up in a clean dish, and throw the whole out of the window as fast as possible.

Edward Lear *To make an Amblongus Pie*

25 As I was going up the stair
I met a man who wasn't there.
He wasn't there again to-day.
I wish, I wish he'd stay away.

Hughes Mearns (1875–1965) US writer. *The Psychoed*

26 I'm walking backwards till Christmas.

Spike Milligan (1918–) British comic actor and author. *The Goon Show*

NORMALITY

1 She always says she dislikes the abnormal, it is so obvious. She says the normal is so much more simply complicated and interesting.

Gertrude Stein (1874–1946) US writer. *The Autobiography of Alice B. Toklas*

2 My suit is pale yellow. My nationality is French, and my normality has been often subject to question.

Tennessee Williams (1911–83) US dramatist. *Camino Real*, Block 4

NOSTALGIA

See also homesickness, memory, past, regret

1 Were we closer to the ground as children, or is the grass emptier now?

Alan Bennett (1934–) British playwright. *Forty Years On*

2 Play it, Sam. Play 'As Time Goes By.'

Humphrey Bogart (1899–1957) US film star. Often misquoted as 'Play it again, Sam'. *Casablanca*

3 Stands the Church clock at ten to three?
And is there honey still for tea?

Rupert Brooke (1887–1915) British poet. *The Old Vicarage, Grantchester*

4 John Anderson my jo, John,
When we were first acquent,
Your locks were like the raven,
Your bonnie brow was brent.

Robert Burns (1759–96) Scottish poet. *John Anderson My Jo*

5 The 'good old times' – all times when old are good –
Are gone.

Lord Byron (1788–1824) British poet. *The Age of Bronze*, I

6 Nothing recalls the past so potently as a smell.

Winston Churchill (1874–1965) British statesman. *My Early Life*

7 What peaceful hours I once enjoyed!
How sweet their memory still!
But they have left an aching void
The world can never fill.

William Cowper (1731–1800) British poet. *Olney Hymns*, 1

8 I'm sitting on the stile, Mary,
Where we sat, side by side.

Countess of Dufferin (1807–67) British poet. *Lament of the Irish Emigrant*

9 Despair abroad can always nurse pleasant thoughts of home.

Christopher Fry (1907–) British dramatist. *A Phoenix Too Frequent*

10 I remember, I remember,
The house where I was born,
The little window where the sun
Came peeping in at morn;
He never came a wink too soon,
Nor brought too long a day,
But now, I often wish the night
Had borne my breath away!

Thomas Hood (1799–1845) British poet. *I Remember*

11 Into my heart an air that kills
From yon far country blows:
What are those blue remembered hills,
What spires, what farms are those?

A. E. Housman (1859–1936) British scholar and poet. *A Shropshire Lad*, 'The Welsh Marches'

12 With rue my heart is laden
For golden friends I had,
For many a rose-lipt maiden
And many a lightfoot lad.

A. E. Housman *A Shropshire Lad*, 'The Welsh Marches'

13 I have had playmates, I have had companions
In my days of childhood, in my joyful schooldays –
All, all are gone, the old familiar faces.

Charles Lamb (1775–1834) British essayist. *The Old Familiar Faces*

14 …the glamour
Of childish days is upon me, my manhood is cast
Down in the flood of remembrance, I weep like a child for the past.

D. H. Lawrence (1885–1930) British novelist. *Piano*

15 Yesterday, all my troubles seemed so far away.

John Lennon (1940–80) British rock musician. *Yesterday* (with Paul McCartney)

16 For love that time was not as love is nowadays.

Thomas Malory (1400–71) English writer. *Morte d'Arthur*, Bk. XX, Ch. 3

17 Oft in the stilly night,
Ere Slumber's chain has bound me,
Fond Memory brings the light
Of other days around me;
The smiles, the tears,
Of boyhood's years,
The words of love then spoken;
The eyes that shone,
Now dimmed and gone,
The cheerful hearts now broken!

Thomas Moore (1779–1852) Irish poet. *National Airs*, 'Oft in the Stilly Night'

18 Fings Ain't Wot They Used T'Be.

Frank Norman (1931–80) British dramatist and broadcaster. Title of musical

19 Before the war, and especially before the Boer War, it was summer all the year round.

George Orwell (Eric Blair; 1903–50) British novelist. *Coming Up for Air*, Pt. II, Ch. 1

20 They spend their time mostly looking forward to the past.

John Osborne (1929–) British dramatist. *Look Back in Anger*, II:1

21 The earth's about five thousand million years old. Who can afford to live in the past?

Harold Pinter (1930–) British dramatist. *The Homecoming*

22 Come to me in the silence of the night;
Come in the speaking silence of a dream;
Come with soft rounded cheeks and eyes as bright
As sunlight on a stream;
Come back in tears,
O memory, hope, love of finished years.

Christina Rossetti (1830–74) British poet. *Echo*

23 We have seen better days.

William Shakespeare (1564–1616) English dramatist. *Timon of Athens*, IV:2

24 And the stately ships go on
To their haven under the hill;
But O for the touch of a vanish'd hand,
And the sound of a voice that is still!

Alfred, Lord Tennyson (1809–92) British poet. *Break, Break, Break*

25 For now I see the true old times are dead,
When every morning brought a noble chance,
And every chance brought out a noble knight.

Alfred, Lord Tennyson *Idylls of the King*, 'The Passing of Arthur'

26 Dear as remembered kisses after death,
And sweet as those by hopeless fancy feign'd
On lips that are for others: deep as love,
Deep as first love, and wild with all regret;
O Death in Life, the days that are no more.

Alfred, Lord Tennyson *The Princess*, IV

27 *Mais où sont les neiges d'antan?*
But where are the snows of yesteryear?

François Villon (1431–85) French poet. *Ballade des dames du temps jadis*

28 Where are the boys of the Old Brigade?

Frederic Edward Weatherly (1848–1929) British lawyer and songwriter. *The Old Brigade*

29 Sweet childish days, that were as long
As twenty days are now.

William Wordsworth (1770–1850) British poet. *To a Butterfly, I've Watched You Now*

NOTHING

1 Nothing can be created out of nothing.

Lucretius (Titus Lucretius Carus; c. 99–55 BC) Roman philosopher. *On the Nature of the Universe*, I

2 Nothing, like something, happens anywhere.

Philip Larkin (1922–85) British poet. *I Remember, I Remember*

3 Nothing will come of nothing. Speak again.

William Shakespeare (1564–1616) English dramatist. *King Lear*, I:1

NOVELS

See also books, criticism, fiction, literature, writers, writing

1 My scrofulous French novel
On grey paper with blunt type!

Robert Browning (1812–89) British poet. *Soliloquy of the Spanish Cloister*

2 A good novel tells us the truth about its hero; but a bad novel tells us the truth about its author.

G. K. Chesterton (1874–1936) British writer. *Heretics*, Ch. 15

3 When I want to read a novel I write one.

Benjamin Disraeli (1804–81) British statesman. Attrib.

4 Yes – oh dear, yes – the novel tells a story.

E. M. Forster (1879–1970) British novelist. *Aspects of the Novel*, Ch. 2

5 The romance of *Tom Jones*, that exquisite picture of human manners, will outlive the palace of the Escurial and the imperial eagle of the house of Austria.

Edward Gibbon (1737–94) British historian. *Autobiography*

6 Historians tell the story of the past, novelists the story of the present.

Edmond de Goncourt (1822–96) French novelist. *Journal*

7 The only obligation to which in advance we may hold a novel, without incurring the accusation of being arbitrary, is that it be interesting.

Henry James (1843–1916) US novelist. *Partial Portraits*, 'The Art of Fiction'

8 It's an odd thing, but now one knows it's profoundly moral and packed with deep spiritual significance a lot of the old charm seems to have gone.

Osbert Lancaster (1908–86) British cartoonist. Referring to *Lady Chatterley's Lover*, after the obscenity trial. Caption to cartoon in the *Daily Express*

9 Far too many relied on the classic formula of a beginning, a muddle, and an end.

Philip Larkin (1922–85) British poet. Referring to modern novels. *New Fiction*, 15 (January 1978)

10 I am a man, and alive...For this reason I am a novelist. And being a novelist, I consider myself superior to the saint, the scientist, the philosopher, and the poet, who are all great masters of different bits of man alive, but never get the whole hog.

D. H. Lawrence (1885–1930) British novelist. *Phoenix*, 'Why the Novel Matters'

11 I would sooner read a time-table or a catalogue than nothing at all. They are much more entertaining than half the novels that are written.

W. Somerset Maugham (1874–1965) British novelist. *The Summing Up*

12 An interviewer asked me what book I thought best represented the modern American woman. All I could think of to answer was: *Madame Bovary.*

Mary McCarthy (1912–89) US novelist. *On the Contrary*

13 People think that because a novel's invented, it isn't true. Exactly the reverse is the case. Biography and memoirs can never be wholly true, since they cannot include every conceivable circumstance of what happened. The novel can do that.

Anthony Powell (1905–) British novelist. *A Dance to the Music of Time: Hearing Secret Harmonies*, Ch. 3

14 The detective novel is the art-for-art's-sake of yawning Philistinism.

V. S. Pritchett (1900–) British short-story writer. *Books in General*, 'The Roots of Detection'

15 It is the sexless novel that should be distinguished: the sex novel is now normal.

George Bernard Shaw (1856–1950) Irish dramatist and critic. *Table-Talk of G.B.S.*

16 A novel is a mirror walking along a main road.

Stendhal (Henri Beyle; 1783–1842) French novelist. *Le Rouge et le noir*, Ch. 49

17 A novel is a static thing that one moves through; a play is a dynamic thing that moves past one.

Kenneth Tynan (1927–80) British theatre critic. *Curtains*

18 The novel being dead, there is no point to writing made-up stories. Look at the French who will not and the Americans who cannot.

Gore Vidal (1925–) US novelist. *Myra Breckinridge*, Ch. 2

NOVELTY

See also conservatism, innovation, progress

1 All the rivers run into the sea; yet the sea is not full; unto the place from whence the rivers come, thither they return again.
All things are full of labour; man cannot utter it: the eye is not satisfied with seeing, nor the ear filled with hearing.
The thing that hath been, it is that which shall be; and that which is done is that which shall be done: and there is no new thing under the sun.

Bible: Ecclesiastes 1:7–9

2 Most of the change we think we see in life
Is due to truths being in and out of favour.

Robert Frost (1875–1963) US poet. *The Black Cottage*

3 There are three things which the public will always clamour for, sooner or later: namely, Novelty, novelty, novelty.

Thomas Hood (1799–1845) British poet. Announcement of *Comic Annual*, 1836

4 It is the customary fate of new truths to begin as heresies and to end as superstitions.

T. H. Huxley (1825–95) British biologist. *The Coming of Age of the Origin of Species*

5 New opinions are always suspected, and usually opposed, without any other reason but because they are not already common.

John Locke (1632–1704) English philosopher. *An Essay Concerning Human Understanding*, dedicatory epistle

6 Rummidge…had lately suffered the mortifying fate of most English universities of its type (civic redbrick): having competed strenuously for fifty years with two universities chiefly valued for being old, it was, at the moment of drawing level, rudely overtaken in popularity and prestige by a batch of universities chiefly valued for being new.

David Lodge (1935–) British author. *Changing Places*, Ch. 1

7 There are no new truths, but only truths that have not been recognized by those who have perceived them without noticing.

Mary McCarthy (1912–89) US novelist. *On the Contrary*

8 There is always something new out of Africa.

Pliny the Elder (Gaius Plinius Secundus; 23–79 AD) Roman scholar. *Natural History*, VIII

9 All great truths begin as blasphemies.

George Bernard Shaw (1856–1950) Irish dramatist and critic. *Annajanska*

10 If we do not find anything pleasant, at least we shall find something new.

Voltaire (François-Marie Arouet; 1694–1778) French writer. *Candide*, Ch. 17

NUCLEAR WEAPONS

See also weapons

1 Ban the bomb.

Anonymous Slogan of nuclear disarmament campaigners

2 Better red than dead.

Anonymous Slogan of the British nuclear disarmament movement

3 Now we are all sons of bitches.

Kenneth Bainbridge (1904–) US physicist. After the first atomic test. *The Decision to Drop the Bomb*

4 If you carry this resolution and follow out all its implications and do not run away from it you will send a Foreign Minister, whoever he may be, naked into the conference chamber.

Aneurin Bevan (1897–1960) British Labour politician. Opposing a motion advocating unilateral nuclear disarmament. Speech, Labour Party Conference, 3 Oct 1957

5 The way to win an atomic war is to make certain it never starts.

Omar Nelson Bradley (1893–1981) US general. *The Observer*, 'Sayings of the Week', 20 Apr 1952

6 The Bomb brought peace but man alone can keep that peace.

Winston Churchill (1874–1965) British statesman. Speech, House of Commons, 16 Aug 1945

7 If only I had known, I should have become a watchmaker.

Albert Einstein (1879–1955) German-born US physicist. Reflecting on his role in the development of the atom bomb. *New Statesman*, 16 Apr 1965

8 Surely the right course is to test the Russians, not the bombs.

Hugh Gaitskell (1906–63) British Labour politician. *The Observer*, 'Sayings of the Week', 23 June 1957

9 We thus denounce the false and dangerous programme of the arms race, of the secret rivalry between peoples for military superiority.

John Paul II (Karol Wojtyla; 1920–) Polish pope (1978–). *The Observer*, 'Sayings of the Week', 19 Dec 1976

10 Preparing for suicide is not a very intelligent means of defence.

Bruce Kent (1929–) British campaigner for nuclear disarmament. *The Observer*, 'Sayings of the Week', 10 Aug 1986

11 Hitherto man had to live with the idea of death

as an individual; from now onward mankind will have to live with the idea of its death as a species.

Arthur Koestler (1905–83) Hungarian-born British writer. Referring to the development of the atomic bomb. *Peter's Quotations* (Laurence J. Peter)

12 The statesmen of the world who boast and threaten that they have Doomsday weapons are far more dangerous, and far more estranged from 'reality', than many of the people on whom the label 'psychotic' is affixed.

R. D. Laing (1927–89) British psychiatrist. *The Divided Self*, Preface

13 At first it was a giant column that soon took the shape of a supramundane mushroom.

William L. Laurence (1888–1977) US journalist. Referring to the explosion of the first atomic bomb, over Hiroshima, 6 Aug 1945. *The New York Times*, 26 Sept 1945

14 The atom bomb is a paper tiger which the United States reactionaries use to scare people.

Mao Tse-Tung (1893–1976) Chinese communist leader. Interview, Aug 1946

15 As a military man who has given half a century of active service, I say in all sincerity that the nuclear arms race has no military purpose. Wars cannot be fought with nuclear weapons; their existence only adds to our perils because of the illusions which they have generated.

Louis Mountbatten of Burma (1900–79) British admiral and colonial administrator. Speech, Strasbourg, 11 May 1979

16 We knew the world would not be the same.

J. Robert Oppenheimer (1904–67) US physicist. After the first atomic test *The Decision to Drop the Bomb*

17 I am become death, the destroyer of worlds.

J. Robert Oppenheimer Quoting Vishnu from the *Gita*, at the first atomic test in New Mexico, 16 July 1945. Attrib.

18 It was on this issue, the nuclear defence of Britain, on which I left the Labour Party, and on this issue I am prepared to stake my entire political career.

David Owen (1938–) British politician. *The Observer*, 'Sayings of the Week', 9 Nov 1986

19 To adopt nuclear disarmament would be akin to behaving like a virgin in a brothel.

David Penhaligon (1944–86) British politician. *The Guardian*, 1980

20 Building up arms is not a substitute for diplomacy.

Samuel Pisar (1929–) Polish-born US writer and lawyer. *Of Blood and Hope*

21 You may reasonably expect a man to walk a tightrope safely for ten minutes; it would be unreasonable to do so without accident for two hundred years.

Bertrand Russell (1872–1970) British philosopher. On the subject of nuclear war. *The Tightrope Men* (D. Bagley)

22 Man has wrested from nature the power to make the world a desert or to make the deserts bloom. There is no evil in the atom, only in men's souls.

Adlai Stevenson (1900–65) US statesman. Speech, Hartford, Connecticut, 18 Sept 1952

23 For Hon. Members opposite the deterrent is a phallic symbol. It convinces them that they are men.

George Wigg (1900–76) British politician. *The Observer*, 'Sayings of the Week', 8 Mar 1964

24 It's summit time again...They're talking of partial nuclear disarmament. This is also like talking about partial circumcision. It's a strange thing. You either go all the way or you fucking forget it.

Robin Williams (1952–) US actor. *Live*

25 A bigger bang for a buck.

Charles E. Wilson (1890–1961) US Republican politician. On the hydrogen bomb test at Bikini, 1954. *Political Dictionary* (W. Safire)

NUMBERS

A selection of nursery rhymes is given here. The wording used is the one most commonly used today; not necessarily the form in the original publication.

See also mathematics, statistics

1 I'll sing you twelve O.
Green grow the rushes O.
What is your twelve O?
Twelve for the twelve apostles,
Eleven for the eleven who went to heaven,
Ten for the ten commandments,
Nine for the nine bright shiners,
Eight for the eight bold rangers,
Seven for the seven stars in the sky,
Six for the six proud walkers,
Five for the symbol at your door,
Four for the Gospel makers,
Three for the rivals,
Two, two, the lily-white boys,
Clothed all in green O,
One is one and all alone
And ever more shall be so.

Anonymous *The Dilly Song*

2 Round numbers are always false.

Samuel Johnson (1709–84) British lexicographer. *Life of Johnson* (J. Boswell), Vol. III

3 No, I don't know his telephone number. But it was up in the high numbers.

John Maynard Keynes (1883–1946) British economist. Attrib.

4 One, two, Buckle my shoe;
Three, four, Knock at the door.

Nursery Rhyme *Songs for the Nursery*

5 No, it is a very interesting number, it is the smallest number expressible as a sum of two cubes in two different ways.

Srinivasa Ramanujan (1887–1920) Indian mathematician. The mathematician G. H. Hardy had referred to the number '1729' as 'dull'. *Collected Papers of Srinivasa Ramanujan*

6 Oh, quite easy! The Septuagint minus the Apostles.

Arthur Woollgar Verrall (1851–1912) British classicist. Reply to a person who thought the number 58 difficult to remember

NURSERY RHYMES

A selection of nursery rhymes is given here. The wording used is the one most commnly used today; not necessarily the form in the original publication.

1 A frog he would a-wooing go,
Heigh ho! says Rowley,
A frog he would a-wooing go,
Whether his mother would let him or no.
With a rowley, powley, gammon and spinach,
Heigh ho! says Anthony Rowley.
Melismata (Thomas Ravenscroft)

2 All the birds of the air
Fell a-sighing and a-sobbing,
When they heard the bell toll
For poor Cock Robin.
Tommy Thumb's Pretty Song Book

3 As I was going to St Ives,
I met a man with seven wives.
Each wife had seven sacks
Each sack had seven cats,
Each cat had seven kits,
How many were going to St Ives?
Mother Goose's Quarto

4 Baa, baa, black sheep,
Have you any wool?
Yes, sir, yes, sir,
Three bags full;
One for the master,
And one for the dame,
And one for the little boy
Who lives down the lane.
Tommy Thumb's Pretty Song Book

5 Bobby Shafto's gone to sea,
Silver buckles on his knee;
He'll come back and marry me,
Bonny Bobby Shafto!
Songs for the Nursery

6 Boys and girls come out to play,
The moon doth shine as bright as day.
Useful Transactions in Philosophy (William King)

7 Come, let's to bed
Says Sleepy-head;
Tarry a while, says Slow;
Put on the pan;
Says Greedy Nan,
Let's sup before we go.
Gammer Gurton's Garland (R. Christopher)

8 Curly locks, Curly locks,
Wilt thou be mine?
Thou shalt not wash dishes
Nor yet feed the swine,
But sit on a cushion
And sew a fine seam,
And feed upon strawberries,
Sugar and cream.
Infant Institutes

9 Ding dong, bell,
Pussy's in the well.
Who put her in?
Little Johnny Green.
Who pulled her out?
Little Tommy Stout.
Mother Goose's Melody

10 Doctor Foster went to Gloucester
In a shower of rain:
He stepped in a puddle,
Right up to his middle,
And never went there again.
The Nursery Rhymes of England (J. O. Halliwell)

11 Eena, meena, mina, mo,
Catch a nigger by his toe;
If he hollers, let him go,
Eena, meena, mina, mo.
Games and Songs of American Children (Newell)

12 Georgie Porgie, pudding and pie,
Kissed the girls and made them cry;
When the boys came out to play,
Georgie Porgie ran away.
The Nursery Rhymes of England (J. O. Halliwell)

13 Goosey, goosey gander,
Whither shall I wander?
Upstairs and downstairs
And in my lady's chamber.
Gammer Gurton' Garland

14 Hey diddle diddle,
The cat and the fiddle,
The cow jumped over the moon;
The little dog laughed
To see such sport,
And the dish ran away with the spoon.
Mother Goose's Melody

15 Hickory, dickory, dock,
The mouse ran up the clock.
The clock struck one,
The mouse ran down,
Hickory, dickory, dock.
Tommy Thumb's Pretty Song Book

16 Hot cross buns!
Hot cross buns!
One a penny, two a penny,
Hot cross buns!
Christmas Box

17 How many miles to Babylon?
Three score miles and ten.
Can I get there by candle-light?
Yes, and back again.
If your heels are nimble and light,
You may get there by candle-light.
Songs for the Nursery

18 Humpty Dumpty sat on a wall,
Humpty Dumpty had a great fall.
All the king's horses,
And all the king's men,
Couldn't put Humpty together again.
Gammer Gurton's Garland

19 Hush-a-bye, baby, on the tree top,
When the wind blows the cradle will rock;
When the bough breaks the cradle will fall,
Down will come baby, cradle, and all.
Mother Goose's Melody

20 I had a little nut tree,
Nothing would it bear
But a silver nutmeg
And a golden pear;
The King of Spain's daughter
Came to visit me,
And all for the sake
Of my little nut tree.
Newest Christmas Box

21 I had a little pony,

His name was Dapple Grey;
I lent him to a lady
To ride a mile away.
She whipped him, she lashed him,
She rode him through the mire;
I would not lend my pony now,
For all the lady's hire.
Poetical Alphabet

22 I love sixpence, jolly little sixpence,
I love sixpence better than my life;
I spent a penny of it, I lent a penny of it,
And I took fourpence home to my wife.
Gammer Gurton's Garland

23 I'm the king of the castle,
Get down you dirty rascal.
Brand's Popular Antiquities

24 I see the moon,
And the moon sees me;
God bless the moon,
And God bless me.
Gammer Gurton's Garland

25 Jack and Jill went up the hill
To fetch a pail of water;
Jack fell down and broke his crown,
And Jill came tumbling after.
Mother Goose's Melody

26 Jack Sprat could eat no fat,
His wife could eat no lean,
And so between them both you see,
They licked the platter clean.
Paroemiologia Anglo-Latina (John Clark)

27 Ladybird, ladybird,
Fly away home,
Your house is on fire
And your children all gone.
Tommy Thumb's Pretty Song Book

28 Little Bo-peep has lost her sheep,
And can't tell where to find them;
Leave them alone, and they'll come home,
Bringing their tails behind them.
Gammer Gurton's Garland

29 Little Boy Blue,
Come blow your horn,
The sheep's in the meadow,
The cow's in the corn.
Famous Tommy Thumb's Little Story Book

30 Little Jack Horner
Sat in the corner,
Eating a Christmas pie;
He put in his thumb,
And pulled out a plum,
And said, What a good boy am I!
Namby Pamby (Henry Carey)

31 Little Miss Muffet
Sat on a tuffet,
Eating her curds and whey;
There came a big spider,
Who sat down beside her
And frightened Miss Muffet away.
Songs for the Nursery

32 Little Tommy Tucker,
Sings for his supper:
What shall we give him?
White bread and butter
How shall he cut it
Without a knife?
How will he be married
Without a wife?
Tommy Thumb's Pretty Song Book

33 London Bridge is broken down,
My fair lady.
Namby Pamby (Henry Carey)

34 Mary, Mary, quite contrary,
How does your garden grow?
With silver bells and cockle shells,
And pretty maids all in a row.
Tommy Thumb's Pretty Song Book

35 Monday's child is fair of face,
Tuesday's child is full of grace,
Wednesday's child is full of woe,
Thursday's child has far to go,
Friday's child is loving and giving,
Saturday's child works hard for his living,
And the child that is born on the Sabbath day
Is bonny and blithe, and good and gay.
Traditions of Devonshire (A. E. Bray)

36 My mother said that I never should
Play with the gypsies in the wood;
If I did, she would say,
Naughty girl to disobey.
Come Hither (Walter de la Mare)

37 Oh! the grand old Duke of York
He had ten thousand men;
He marched them up to the top of the hill,
And he marched them down again.
And when they were up they were up,
And when they were down they were down,
And when they were only half way up,
They were neither up nor down.
Traditional

38 Old King Cole
Was a merry old soul,
And a merry old soul was he;
He called for his pipe,
And he called for his bowl,
And he called for his fiddlers three.
Useful Transactions in Philosophy (William King)

39 Old Mother Hubbard
Went to the cupboard,
To fetch her poor dog a bone;
But when she got there
The cupboard was bare
And so the poor dog had none.
The Comic Adventures of Old Mother Hubbard and Her Dog

40 One, two, Buckle my shoe;
Three, four, Knock at the door.
Songs for the Nursery

41 Oranges and lemons,
Say the bell of St Clement's.
You owe me five farthings,
Say the bells of St Martin's.
When will you pay me?
Say the bells of Old Bailey.
When I grow rich,
Say the bells of Shoreditch.
When will that be?

Say the bells of Stepney.
I'm sure I don't know,
Says the great bell at Bow.
Here comes a candle to light you to bed,
Here comes a chopper to chop off your head.
Tommy Thumb's Pretty Song Book

42 Pat-a-cake, pat-a-cake, baker's man,
Bake me a cake as fast as you can;
Pat it and prick it, and mark it with B,
Put it in the oven for baby and me.
The Campaigners (Tom D'Urfey)

43 Peter Piper picked a peck of pickled pepper;
A peck of pickled pepper Peter Piper picked;
If Peter Piper picked a peck of pickled pepper,
Where's the peck of pickled pepper Peter Piper picked?
Peter Piper's Practical Principles of Plain and Perfect Pronunciation

44 Polly put the kettle on,
Polly put the kettle on,
Polly put the kettle on,
We'll all have tea.
Sukey take it off again,
Sukey take it off again,
Sukey take it off again,
They've all gone away.
Traditional

45 Pussy cat, pussy cat, where have you been?
I've been to London to look at the queen.
Pussy cat, pussy cat, what did you there?
I frightened a little mouse under her chair.
Songs for the Nursery

46 Ride a cock-horse to Banbury Cross,
To see a fine lady upon a white horse;
Rings on her fingers and bells on her toes,
And she shall have music wherever she goes.
Gammer Gurton's Garland

47 Ring-a-ring o'roses,
A pocket full of posies,
A-tishoo! A-tishoo!
We all fall down.
Mother Goose (Kate Greenway)

48 Round and round the garden
Like a teddy bear;
One step, two step,
Tickle you under there!
Traditional

49 Rub-a-dub-dub,
Three men in a tub,
And who do you think they be?
The butcher, the baker,
The candlestick-maker,
And they all sailed out to sea.
Christmas Box

50 See-saw, Margery Daw,
Jacky shall have a new master;
He shall have but a penny a day,
Because he can't work any faster.
Mother Goose's Melody

51 Simple Simon met a pieman,
Going to the fair;
Says Simple Simon to the pieman,
Let me taste your ware.
Says the pieman to Simple Simon,
Show me first your penny;
Says Simple Simon to the pieman,
Indeed I have not any.
Simple Simon (Chapbook Advertisement)

52 Sing a song of sixpence,
A pocket full of rye;
Four and twenty blackbirds,
Baked in a pie.
When the pie was opened,
The birds began to sing;
Was not that a dainty dish,
To set before the king?
The king was in his counting-house,
Counting out his money;
The queen was in the parlour,
Eating bread and honey.
The maid was in the garden,
Hanging out the clothes,
When down came a blackbird,
And pecked off her nose.
Tommy Thumb's Pretty Song Book

53 Solomon Grundy,
Born on a Monday,
Christened on Tuesday,
Married on Wednesday,
Took ill on Thursday,
Worse on Friday,
Died on Saturday,
Buried on Sunday.
This is the end
Of Solomon Grundy.
The Nursery Rhymes of England (J. O. Halliwell)

54 The lion and the unicorn
Were fighting for the crown;
The lion beat the unicorn
All round about the town.
Useful Transactions in Philosophy (William King)

55 The Queen of Hearts
She made some tarts,
All on a summer's day;
The Knave of Hearts
He stole the tarts,
And took them clean away.
The European Magazine

56 There was a crooked man, and he walked a crooked mile,
He found a crooked sixpence against a crooked stile:
He bought a crooked cat, which caught a crooked mouse,
And they all lived together in a little crooked house.
The Nursery Rhymes of England (J. O. Halliwell)

57 There was an old woman
Lived under a hill,
And if she's not gone
She lives there still.
Academy of Complements

58 There was an old woman who lived in a shoe,
She had so many children she didn't know what to do;
She gave them some broth without any bread;
She whipped them all soundly and put them to bed.
Gammer Gurton's Garland

59 The twelfth day of Christmas,
My true love sent to me
Twelve lords a-leaping,
Eleven ladies dancing,
Ten pipers piping,
Nine drummers drumming,
Eight maids a-milking,
Seven swans a-swimming,
Six geese a-laying,
Five gold rings,
Four colly birds,
Three French hens,
Two turtle doves, and
A partridge in a pear tree.

Mirth without Mischief

60 Thirty days hath September,
April, June, and November;
All the rest have thirty-one,
Excepting February alone
And that has twenty-eight days clear
And twenty-nine in each leap year.

Abridgement of the Chronicles of England (Richard Grafton)

61 This is the farmer sowing his corn,
That kept the cock that crowed in the morn,
That waked the priest all shaven and shorn,
That married the man all tattered and torn,
That kissed the maiden all forlorn,
That milked the cow with the crumpled horn,
That tossed the dog,
That worried the cat,
That killed the rat,
That ate the corn,
That lay in the house that Jack built.

Nurse Truelove's New-Year-Gift

62 This little piggy went to market,
This little piggy stayed at home,
This little piggy had roast beef,
This little piggy had none,
And this little piggy cried, Wee-wee-wee-wee-wee,
I can't find my way home.

The Famous Tommy Thumb's Little Story Book

63 Three blind mice, see how they run!
They all run after the farmer's wife,
Who cut off their tails with a carving knife,
Did you ever see such a thing in your life,
As three blind mice?

Deuteromelia (Thomas Ravenscroft)

64 Tinker,
Tailor,
Soldier,
Sailor,
Rich man,
Poor man,
Beggarman,
Thief.

Popular Rhymes and Nursery Tales (J. O. Halliwell)

65 Tom, he was a piper's son,
He learnt to play when he was young,
And all the tune that he could play
Was 'Over the hills and far away'.

Tom, The Piper's Son

66 Tom, Tom, the piper's son,
Stole a pig and away he run;
The pig was eat
And Tom was beat,
And Tom went howling down the street.

Tom, The Piper's Son

67 Two little dicky birds, Sitting on a wall;
One named Peter, The other named Paul,
Fly away, Peter! Fly away, Paul!
Come back, Peter! Come back, Paul!

Mother Goose's Melody

68 Wee Willie Winkie runs through the town
Upstairs and downstairs and in his nightgown,
Rapping at the window, crying through the lock,
Are the children all in bed? It's past eight o'clock.

In *Whistle-Binkie* (W. Miller)

69 What are little boys made of?
Frogs and snails
And puppy-dogs' tails,
That's what little boys are made of.
What are little girls made of?
Sugar and spice
And all that's nice,
That's what little girls are made of.

Nursery Rhymes (J. O. Halliwell)

70 What is your fortune, my pretty maid?
My face is my fortune, sir, she said.
Then I can't marry you, my pretty maid.
Nobody asked you, sir, she said.

Archaeologia Cornu-Britannica (William Pryce)

71 Where are you going to, my pretty maid?
I'm going a-milking, sir, she said.

Archaeologia Cornu-Britannica (William Pryce)

72 Who killed Cock Robin?
I, said the Sparrow,
With my bow and arrow,
I killed Cock Robin.
Who saw him die?
I, said the Fly,
With my little eye,
I saw him die.

Tommy Thumb's Pretty Song Book

73 Yankee Doodle came to town,
Riding on a pony;
He stuck a feather in his cap
And called it macaroni.

Gammer Gurton's Garland

O

OBEDIENCE

1 Children, obey your parents in the Lord: for this is right.

Bible: Ephesians 6:1

2 'She still seems to me in her own way a person born to command,' said Luce...
'I wonder if anyone is born to obey,' said Isabel.
'That may be why people command rather badly, that
they have no suitable material to work on.'

Ivy Compton-Burnett (1892–1969) British novelist. *Parents and Children*, Ch. 3

3 It is much safer to obey than to rule.

Thomas à Kempis (Thomas Hemmerken; c. 1380–1471) German monk. *The Imitation of Christ*, I

4 'Forward the Light Brigade!'
Was there a man dismay'd?
Not tho' the soldier knew
Some one had blunder'd:
Their's not to make reply,
Their's not to reason why,
Their's but to do and die:
Into the valley of Death
Rode the six hundred.

Alfred, Lord Tennyson (1809–92) British poet. *The Charge of the Light Brigade*

OBESITY

See also food, greed

1 Outside every fat man there is an even fatter man trying to close in.

Kingsley Amis (1922–) British novelist. *See also* CONNOLLY, ORWELL. *One Fat Englishman*, Ch. 3

2 A fat paunch never bred a subtle mind.

Anonymous

3 Who's your fat friend?

'Beau' Brummel (George Bryan Brummell; 1778–1840) British dandy. Referring to George, Prince of Wales. *Reminiscences* (Gronow)

4 Just the other day in the Underground I enjoyed the pleasure of offering my seat to three ladies.

G. K. Chesterton (1874–1936) British writer. Suggesting that fatness has its consolations. *Das Buch des Lachens* (W. Scholz)

5 I want to reassure you I am not this size, really – dear me no, I'm being amplified by the mike.

G. K. Chesterton At a lecture in Pittsburgh. *The Outline of Sanity: A Life of G. K. Chesterton* (S. D. Dale)

6 Imprisoned in every fat man a thin one is wildly signalling to be let out.

Cyril Connolly (1903–74) British journalist. *See also* AMIS, ORWELL. *The Unquiet Grave*

7 Obesity is a mental state, a disease brought on by boredom and disappointment.

Cyril Connolly *The Unquiet Grave*

8 The one way to get thin is to re-establish a purpose in life.

Cyril Connolly *The Unquiet Grave*

9 O fat white woman whom nobody loves,
Why do you walk through the fields in gloves...
Missing so much and so much?

F. M. Cornford (1886–1960) British poet. *To a Fat Lady Seen from a Train*

10 That dark day when a man decides he must wear his belt under instead of over his cascading paunch.

Peter De Vries (1910–93) US novelist. *Consenting Adults*, 1980

11 I see no objection to stoutness, in moderation.

W. S. Gilbert (1836–1911) British dramatist. *Iolanthe*, I

12 I'm fat, but I'm thin inside. Has it ever struck you that there's a thin man inside every fat man, just as they say there's a statue inside every block of stone?

George Orwell (Eric Blair; 1903–50) British novelist. *See also* AMIS, CONNOLLY. *Coming Up For Air*, Pt. I, Ch. 3

13 My advice if you insist on slimming: Eat as much as you like – just don't swallow it.

Harry Secombe (1921–) Welsh singer, actor, and comedian. *Daily Herald*, 5 Oct 1962

14 Falstaff sweats to death
And lards the lean earth as he walks along.

William Shakespeare (1564–1616) English dramatist. *Henry IV, Part One*, II:2

15 I have more flesh than another man, and therefore more frailty.

William Shakespeare *Henry IV, Part One*, III:3

16 Enclosing every thin man, there's a fat man demanding elbow-room.

Evelyn Waugh (1903–66) British novelist. *Officers and Gentlemen*, Interlude

17 Outside every thin girl there is a fat man trying to get in.

Katharine Whitehorn (1928–) British journalist. Attrib.

18 She fitted into my biggest armchair as if it had been built round her by someone who knew they were wearing armchairs tight about the hips that season.

P. G. Wodehouse (1881–1975) British humorous novelist. *My Man Jeeves*, 'Jeeves and the Unbidden Guest'

19 The Right Hon. was a tubby little chap who looked as if he had been poured into his clothes and had forgotten to say 'When!'

P. G. Wodehouse *Very Good Jeeves!*, 'Jeeves and the Impending Doom'

OBITUARIES

See also death, epitaphs, memorials

1 He caused castles to be built
Which were a sore burden to the poor,
A hard man was the king
And took from his subjects many marks

In gold and many more hundreds of pounds in silver.
These sums he took by weight from his people,
Most unjustly and for little need.
He was sunk in greed
And utterly given up to avarice.
He set apart a vast deer preserve and imposed laws concerning it.
Whoever slew a hart or a hind
Was to be blinded.
He forbade the killing of boars
Even as the killing of harts.
For he loved the stags as dearly
As though he had been their father.
Hares, also, he decreed should go unmolested.
The rich complained and the poor lamented,
But he was too relentless to care though all might hate him,
And they were compelled, if they wanted
To keep their lives and their lands
And their goods and the favour of the king,
To submit themselves wholly to his will.
Alas! that any man should bear himself so proudly
And deem himself exalted above all other men!
May Almighty God shew mercy to his soul
And pardon him his sins.

Anonymous Written on the death of William the Conqueror. The Peterborough Chronicle (part of *The Anglo-Saxon Chronicle*)

2 I have never killed a man, but I have read many obituaries with a lot of pleasure.

Clarence Darrow (1857–1938) US lawyer. *Medley*

3 With the newspaper strike on I wouldn't consider it.

Bette Davis (Ruth Elizabeth Davis; 1908–89) US film star. When told that a rumour was spreading that she had died. *Book of Lists* (I. Wallace)

4 He will be looked upon by posterity as a brave bad man.

Edward Hyde, Earl of Clarendon (1609–74) English statesman and historian. Referring to Oliver Cromwell. *History of the Great Rebellion*

5 I've just read that I am dead. Don't forget to delete me from your list of subscribers.

Rudyard Kipling (1865–1936) Indian-born British writer. Writing to a magazine that had mistakenly published an announcement of his death. *Anekdotenschatz* (H. Hoffmeister)

6 John Le Mesurier wishes it to be known that he conked out on November 15th. He sadly misses family and friends.

John Le Mesurier (1912–83) British actor. His death announcement. *The Times*, 15 Nov 1983

7 You should have known that it was not easy for me to die. But, tell me, were my obituaries good?

Makarios (Mikhail Christodoulou Mouskos; 1913–77) Cypriot archbishop, patriarch, and statesman.

8 At social gatherings he was liable to engage in heated and noisy arguments which could ruin a dinner party, and made him the dread of hostesses on both sides of the Atlantic. The tendency was exacerbated by an always generous, and occasionally excessive alcoholic intake.

Malcolm Muggeridge (1903–90) British writer. Referring to Randolph Churchill. *The Times*, 7 June 1968

9 ...that great lover of peace, a man of giant stature who moulded, as few other men have done, the destinies of his age.

Jawaharlal Nehru (1889–1964) First Indian prime minister. Referring to Stalin. Obituary tribute, Indian Parliament, 9 Mar 1953

10 In these days a man is nobody unless his biography is kept so far posted up that it may be ready for the national breakfast-table on the morning after his demise.

Anthony Trollope (1815–82) British novelist. *Doctor Thorne*, Ch. 25

11 Reports of my death are greatly exaggerated.

Mark Twain (Samuel Langhorne Clemens; 1835–1910) US writer. On learning that his obituary had been published. Cable to the Associated Press

OBJECTIVITY

See also perspective, subjectivity

1 *Sir Roger* told them, with the air of a man who would not give his judgment rashly, that 'much might be said on both sides'.

Joseph Addison (1672–1719) British essayist. Sir Roger de Coverley was a fictional archetype of the old-fashioned and eccentric country squire. *The Spectator*, 122

2 Thus I live in the world rather as a Spectator of mankind, than as one of the species, by which means I have made myself a speculative statesman, soldier, merchant, and artisan, without ever meddling with any practical part of life.

Joseph Addison *The Spectator*, 1

3 Only reason can convince us of those three fundamental truths without a recognition of which there can be no effective liberty: that what we believe is not necessarily true; that what we like is not necessarily good; and that all questions are open.

Clive Bell (1881–1964) British art critic. *Civilization*, Ch. 5

4 I am a camera with its shutter open, quite passive, recording, not thinking.

Christopher Isherwood (1904–86) British novelist. *Goodbye to Berlin*

5 The man who sees both sides of a question is a man who sees absolutely nothing at all.

Oscar Wilde (1854–1900) Irish-born British dramatist. *The Critic as Artist*, Pt. 2

OBLIGATION

See also duty

1 The debt which cancels all others.

Charles Caleb Colton (?1780–1832) British clergyman and writer. *Lacon*, Vol. II

2 We are so much bounden to the See of Rome that we cannot do too much honour to it...for we received from that See our Crown Imperial.

Henry VIII (1491–1547) King of England. Remark to Thomas More

3 It is the nature of men to be bound by the benefits they confer as much as by those they receive.

Machiavelli (1469–1527) Italian statesman. *The Prince*

OBLIVION

1 Many brave men lived before Agamemnon's time; but they are all, unmourned and unknown, covered by the long night, because they lack their sacred poet.

Horace (Quintus Horatius Flaccus; 65–8 BC) Roman poet. *Odes*, IV

2 No, no, go not to Lethe, neither twist
Wolf's-bane, tight-rooted, for its poisonous wine.

John Keats (1795–1821) British poet. *Ode on Melancholy*

3 Annihilating all that's made
To a green thought in a green shade.

Andrew Marvell (1621–78) English poet. *The Garden*

O'BRIEN, EDNA

(1936–) Irish novelist. Her books include *The Country Girls* (1966), *The Lonely Girl* (1962), *Night* (1972), *Returning* (1982), and *Lantern Slides* (1990). She has also written plays and film scripts.

1 I did not sleep. I never do when I am over-happy, over-unhappy, or in bed with a strange man.

The Love Object

2 Do you know what I hate about myself, I have never done a brave thing, I have never risked death.

A Scandalous Woman, 'Over'

3 To Crystal, hair was the most important thing on earth. She would never get married because you couldn't wear curlers in bed.

Winter's Tales, 8, 'Come into the Drawing Room, Doris'

4 The vote, I thought, means nothing to women. We should be armed.

Quoted as epigraph to *Fear of Flying* (Erica Jong), Ch. 16

OBSESSIONS

1 I have three phobias which, could I mute them, would make my life as slick as a sonnet, but as dull as ditch water: I hate to go to bed, I hate to get up, and I hate to be alone.

Tallulah Bankhead (1903–68) US actress. *Tallulah*, Ch. 1

2 *Papyromania* – compulsive accumulation of papers...
Papyrophobia – abnormal desire for 'a clean desk'.

Laurence J. Peter (1919–90) Canadian writer. *The Peter Principle*, Glossary

OBSTRUCTION

1 I'll put a spoke among your wheels.

Francis Beaumont (1584–1616) English dramatist. *The Mad Lover*, III:6

2 If any of you know cause, or just impediment.

The Book of Common Prayer *Solemnization of Matrimony*

3 There was only one catch and that was Catch-22, which specified that a concern for one's own safety in the face of dangers that were real and immediate was the process of a rational mind.

Joseph Heller (1923–) US novelist. *Catch-22*, Ch. 5

OCCUPATIONS

See also doctors, lawyers, police

1 A priest sees people at their best, a lawyer at their worst, but a doctor sees them as they really are.

Proverb

2 Every man to his trade.

Proverb

3 Jack of all trades, master of none.

Proverb

4 Old soldiers never die, they simply fade away.

Proverb

5 Once a parson always a parson.

Proverb

6 Sailors have a port in every storm.

Proverb

7 Medicine would be the ideal profession if it did not involve giving pain.

Samuel Hopkins Adams (1871–1958) US politician. *The Health Master*, Ch. 3

8 After quitting radio I was able to live on the money I saved on aspirins.

Fred Allen (1894–1956) US comedian.

9 Doctors bury their mistakes. Lawyers hang them. But journalists put theirs on the front page.

Anonymous

10 CLINICIAN. learns less and less about more and more until he knows nothing about everything. RESEARCHER. learns more and more about less and less until he knows everything about nothing.

Anonymous

11 The work of a Prime Minister is the loneliest job in the world.

Stanley Baldwin (1867–1947) British statesman. Speech, 9 Jan 1927

12 The ugliest of trades have their moments of pleasure. Now, if I were a grave-digger, or even a hangman, there are some people I could work for with a great deal of enjoyment.

Douglas William Jerrold (1803–57) British dramatist. *Wit and Opinions of Douglas Jerrold*, 'Ugly Trades'

13 He did not know that a keeper is only a poacher turned outside in, and a poacher a keeper turned inside out.

Charles Kingsley (1819–75) British writer. *The Water Babies*, Ch. 1

14 When I caught a glimpse of Rita
Filling in a ticket in her little white book
In a cap she looked much older
And the bag across her shoulder
Made her look a little like a military man
Lovely Rita Meter Maid.

John Lennon (1940–80) British rock musician. *Lovely Rita* (with Paul McCartney)

15 What do you want to be a sailor for? There are greater storms in politics than you'll ever find at sea. Piracy, broadsides, blood on the deck – you'll find them all in politics.

David Lloyd George (1863–1945) British Liberal statesman. Remark to Julian Amery. *The Observer*, 2 Jan 1966

16 Under the spreading chestnut tree
The village smithy stands;
The smith, a mighty man is he,
With large and sinewy hands;
And the muscles of his brawny arms
Are strong as iron bands.

Henry Wadsworth Longfellow (1807–82) US poet. *The Village Blacksmith*

17 The trained nurse has given nursing the human, or shall we say, the divine touch, and made the hospital desirable for patients with serious ailments regardless of their home advantages.

Charles H. Mayo (1865–1939) US physician. *Collected Papers of the Mayo Clinic and Mayo Foundation*

18 I have nothing against undertakers personally. It's just that I wouldn't want one to bury my sister.

Jessica Mitford (1917–) British writer. Attrib. in *Saturday Review*, 1 Feb 1964

19 If I didn't start painting, I would have raised chickens.

Grandma Moses (Anna Mary Robertson Moses; 1860–1961) US primitive painter. *Grandma Moses, My Life's History* (ed. Aotto Kallir), Ch. 3

20 No *man*, not even a doctor, ever gives any other definition of what a nurse should be than this – 'devoted and obedient'. This definition would do just as well for a porter. It might even do for a horse. It would not do for a policeman.

Florence Nightingale (1820–1910) British nurse. *Notes on Nursing*

21 Tinker,
Tailor,
Soldier,
Sailor,
Rich man,
Poor man,
Beggarman,
Thief.

Nursery Rhyme *Popular Rhymes and Nursery Tales* (J. O. Halliwell)

22 The trained nurse has become one of the great blessings of humanity, taking a place beside the physician and the priest, and not inferior to either in her mission.

William Osler (1849–1919) Canadian physician. *Aequanimitas, with Other Addresses*, 'Nurse and Patient'

23 A doctor who doesn't say too many foolish things is a patient half-cured, just as a critic is a poet who has stopped writing verse and a policeman a burglar who has retired from practice.

Marcel Proust (1871–1922) French novelist. *À la recherche du temps perdu: Le Côté de Guermantes*

24 Everybody hates house-agents because they have everybody at a disadvantage. All other callings have a certain amount of give and take; the house-agent simply takes.

H. G. Wells (1866–1946) British writer. *Kipps*, Bk. III, Ch. 1

25 The best careers advice to give to the young is 'Find out what you like doing best and get someone to pay you for doing it.'

Katherine Whitehorn (1926–) British journalist. *The Observer*, 1975

OFFICERS

See also army, navy, soldiers, war

1 Any officer who shall behave in a scandalous manner, unbecoming the character of an officer and a gentleman shall...be cashiered.

Anonymous The words 'conduct unbecoming the character of an officer' are a direct quotation from the Naval Discipline Act (10 Aug 1860), Article 24. *Articles of War* (1872), *Disgraceful Conduct*, 79

2 If Kitchener was not a great man, he was, at least, a great poster.

Margot Asquith (1865–1945) The second wife of Herbert Asquith. *Kitchener: Portrait of an Imperialist* (Sir Philip Magnus), Ch. 14

3 In defeat unbeatable; in victory unbearable.

Winston Churchill (1874–1965) British statesman. Referring to Viscount Montgomery. *Ambrosia and Small Beer* (E. Marsh), Ch. 5

4 Jellicoe was the only man on either side who could lose the war in an afternoon.

Winston Churchill Referring to Earl Jellicoe (1859–1935), the British admiral who commanded the Grand Fleet at the Battle of Jutland (1916). *The Observer*, 'Sayings of the Week', 13 Feb 1927

5 War is too important to be left to the generals.

Georges Clemenceau (1841–1929) French statesman. A similar remark is attributed to another French statesman, Talleyrand (1754–1838). Attrib.

6 When I was a lad I served a term
As office boy to an Attorney's firm.
I cleaned the windows and I swept the floor,
And I polished up the handle of the big front door.
I polished up that handle so carefullee
That now I am the Ruler of the Queen's Navee!

W. S. Gilbert (1836–1911) British dramatist. *HMS Pinafore*, I

7 Stick close to your desks and never go to sea,
And you all may be Rulers of the Queen's Navee!

W. S. Gilbert *HMS Pinafore*, I

8 LUDENDORFF: The English soldiers fight like lions.
HOFFMANN: True. But don't we know that they are lions led by donkeys.

Max Hoffmann (1869–1927) German general. Referring to the performance of the British army in World War I. *The Donkeys* (A. Clark)

9 I can't spare this man; he fights.

Abraham Lincoln (1809–65) US statesman. Resisting demands for the dismissal of Ulysses Grant, commander in chief of the Union forces during the American Civil War. Attrib.

10 The Nelson touch.

Lord Nelson (1758–1805) British admiral. Diary, 9 Oct 1805

11 Nelson, born in a fortunate hour for himself and for his country, was always in his element and always on his element.

George Macaulay Trevelyan (1876–1962) British historian. *History of England*, Bk. V, Ch. 5

12 I didn't fire him because he was a dumb son of a bitch, although he was, but that's not against the law for generals. If it was, half to three-quarters of them would be in gaol.

Harry S. Truman (1884–1972) US statesman. Referring to General MacArthur. *Plain Speaking* (Merle Miller)

13 I don't know what effect these men will have on the enemy, but, by God, they frighten me.
Duke of Wellington (1769–1852) British general and statesman. Referring to his generals. Attrib.

14 It is not the business of generals to shoot one another.
Duke of Wellington Refusing an artillery officer permission to fire upon Napoleon himself during the Battle of Waterloo, 1815. Attrib.

15 Not upon a man from the colonel to the private in a regiment – both inclusive. We may pick up a marshal or two perhaps; but not worth a damn.
Duke of Wellington Said during the Waterloo campaign, when asked whether he anticipated any desertions from Napoleon's army. *Creevey Papers*, Ch. X

16 I used to say of him that his presence on the field made the difference of forty thousand men.
Duke of Wellington Referring to Napoleon. *Notes of Conversations with the Duke of Wellington* (Stanhope), 2 Nov 1831

OLD AGE

See also age, longevity

1 All would live long, but none would be old.
Proverb

2 Grey hairs are death's blossoms.
Proverb

3 Man fools himself. He prays for a long life, and he fears an old age.
Chinese proverb

4 Forty is the old age of youth; fifty is the youth of old age.
French proverb

5 Old men are twice children.
Greek proverb

6 Dying while young is a boon in old age.
Yiddish proverb

7 You can't teach an old dog new tricks.
Proverb

8 Nobody hears old people complain because people think that's all old people do. And that's because old people are gnarled and sagged and twisted into the shape of a complaint.
Edward Albee (1928–) US dramatist. *The American Dream*

9 As men draw near the common goal
Can anything be sadder
Than he who, master of his soul,
Is servant to his bladder?
Anonymous *The Speculum*, Melbourne, 1938

10 Everyone faces at all times two fateful possibilities: one is to grow older, the other not.
Anonymous

11 The principal objection to old age is that there's no future in it.
Anonymous

12 You are getting old when the gleam in your eyes is from the sun hitting your bifocals.
Anonymous

13 It's a sign of age if you feel like the day after the night before and you haven't been anywhere.
Anonymous

14 When you are forty, half of you belongs to the past...And when you are seventy, nearly all of you.
Jean Anouilh (1910–87) French dramatist.

15 When men desire old age, what else do they desire but prolonged infirmity?
St Augustine (354–430) Bishop of Hippo in North Africa. *Of the Catechizing of the Unlearned*, XVI

16 I will never be an old man. To me, old age is always fifteen years older than I am.
Bernard Baruch (1870–1965) US financier and presidential adviser. *The Observer* 'Sayings of the Week', 21 Aug 1955

17 An old man looks permanent, as if he had been born an old man.
H. E. Bates (1905–74) British novelist. *Death In Spring*

18 ...no one ever speaks of 'a beautiful old woman'.
Simone de Beauvoir (1908–86) French writer. *The Coming of Age*

19 Tidy the old into tall flats. Desolation at fourteen storeys becomes a view.
Alan Bennett (1934–) British dramatist. *Forty Years On*

20 Tranquillity comes with years, and that horrid thing which Freud calls sex is expunged.
E. F. Benson (1867–1940) British novelist. *Mapp and Lucia*

21 Now all the world she knew is dead
In this small room she lives her days.
The wash-hand stand and single bed
Screened from the public gaze.
John Betjeman (1906–84) British poet. *A Few Late Chrysanthemums*, 'House of Rest'

22 Better is a poor and a wise child than an old and foolish king, who will no more be admonished.
Bible: Ecclesiastes 4:13

23 With the ancient is wisdom; and in length of days understanding.
Bible: Job 12:12

24 To be old is to be part of a huge and ordinary multitude...the reason why old age was venerated in the past was because it was extraordinary.
Ronald Blythe (1922–) British writer. *The View in Winter*

25 Old age takes away from us what we have inherited and gives us what we have earned.
Gerald Brenan (Edward Fitzgerald Brenan; 1894–1987) British writer. *Thoughts in a Dry Season*, 'Life'

26 I smoke 10 to 15 cigars a day, at my age I have to hold on to something.
George Burns (1896–) US comedian. Attrib.

27 As a white candle
In a holy place,
So is the beauty
Of an aged face.
Joseph Campbell (1879–1944) Irish poet. *The Old Woman*

28 'You are old, Father William,' the young man said,
'And your hair has become very white;

And yet you incessantly stand on your head –
Do you think at your age, it is right?'

Lewis Carroll (Charles Lutwidge Dodgson; 1832–98) British writer. *See also* SOUTHEY. *Alice's Adventures in Wonderland*, Ch. 5

29 I'll keep going till my face falls off.

Barbara Cartland (1902–) British romantic novelist. *The Observer*, 'Sayings of the Week', 17 Aug 1975

30 Old age is the out-patients' department of purgatory.

Lord Cecil (1869–1956) British politician. *The Cecils of Hatfield House* (David Cecil)

31 I prefer old age to the alternative.

Maurice Chevalier (1888–1972) French singer and actor. Attrib.

32 Old-age, a second child, by Nature curs'd
With more and greater evils than the first,
Weak, sickly, full of pains; in ev'ry breath
Railing at life, and yet afraid of death.

Charles Churchill (1731–64) British poet. *Gotham*, I

33 I am ready to meet my Maker. Whether my Maker is ready for the ordeal of meeting me is another matter.

Winston Churchill (1874–1965) British statesman. On his 75th birthday. Speech, 30 Nov 1949

34 Dead birds don't fall out of their nests.

Winston Churchill When someone told him that his trouser fly-buttons were undone. Attrib.

35 It is not by muscle, speed, or physical dexterity that great things are achieved, but by reflection, force of character, and judgement; in these qualities old age is usually not only not poorer, but is even richer.

Cicero (106–43 BC) Roman orator and statesman. *On Old Age*, VI

36 Oh to be seventy again.

Georges Clemenceau (1841–1929) French statesman. Remark on his eightieth birthday, noticing a pretty girl in the Champs Elysées. *Ego 3* (James Agate)

37 So, perhaps, I may escape otherwise than by death the last humiliation of an aged scholar, when his juniors conspire to print a volume of essays and offer it to him as a sign that they now consider him senile.

Robin George Collingwood (1889–1943) British philosopher and archaeologist. *Autobiography*

38 A man is as old as he's feeling,
A woman as old as she looks.

Mortimer Collins (1827–76) British writer. *The Unknown Quantity*

39 Let's go out and buy playing-cards, good wine, bridge-scorers, knitting needles – all the paraphernalia to fill a gaping void, all that's required to disguise that monster, an old woman.

Colette (1873–1954) French writer. *Cheri*

40 Body and mind, like man and wife, do not always agree to die together.

Charles C. Colton (c. 1780–1832) British churchman and writer. *Lacon*, Vol. I, Ch. 324

41 Old age is a shipwreck.

Charles De Gaulle (1890–1970) French general and president. *The Life of Arthur Ransome* (H. Brogan)

42 When a man fell into his anecdotage it was a sign for him to retire from the world.

Benjamin Disraeli (1804–81) British statesman. *Lothair*, Ch. 28

43 In 1716 he had a paralytic stroke which was followed by senile decay. The story is famous of the broken man, hobbling to gaze at Kneller's portrait which showed him in the full splendour of manhood and murmuring, 'That was once a man'.

T. Charles Edwards and Brian Richardson Referring to John Churchill, First Duke of Marlborough. *They Saw it Happen*

44 I grow old…I grow old…
I shall wear the bottoms of my trousers rolled.

T. S. Eliot (1888–1965) US-born British poet and dramatist. *The Love Song of J. Alfred Prufrock*

45 Shall I part my hair behind? Do I dare to eat a peach?
I shall wear white flannel trousers, and walk upon the beach.
I have heard the mermaids singing, each to each.

T. S. Eliot *The Love Song of J. Alfred Prufrock*

46 Old age brings along with its uglinesses the comfort that you will soon be out of it, – which ought to be a substantial relief to such discontented pendulums as we are.

Ralph Waldo Emerson (1803–82) US poet and essayist. *Journal*

47 All diseases run into one, old age.

Ralph Waldo Emerson *Journals*

48 He cannot bear old men's jokes. That is not new. But now he begins to think of them himself.

Max Frisch (1911–91) Swiss dramatist and novelist. *Sketchbook 1966–71*

49 No skill or art is needed to grow old; the trick is to endure it.

Johann Wolfgang von Goethe (1749–1832) German poet, dramatist and scientist.

50 The first sign of his approaching end was when my old aunts, while undressing him, removed a toe with one of his socks.

Graham Greene (1904–91) British novelist. *Travels With My Aunt*

51 Time goes by: reputation increases, ability declines.

Dag Hammarskjöld (1905–61) Swedish diplomat. *Diaries*, 1964

52 A woman would rather visit her own grave than the place where she had been young and beautiful after she is aged and ugly.

Corra May Harris (1869–1935) US writer. *Eve's Second Husband*, Ch. 14

53 And now in age I bud again,
After so many deaths I live and write;
I once more smell the dew and rain,
And relish versing; O, my only Light,
It cannot be
That I am he
On whom Thy tempests fell all night.

George Herbert (1593–1633) English poet. *The Flower*

54 Some people reach the age of 60 before others.

Lord Hood (1910–) British civil servant. *The Observer*, 'Sayings of the Week', 23 Feb 1969

55 The misery of a child is interesting to a mother,

the misery of a young man is interesting to a young woman, the misery of an old man is interesting to nobody.

Victor Hugo (1802–85) French poet, novelist, and dramatist. *Les Misérables*, 'Saint Denis'

56 The ageing man of the middle twentieth century lives, not in the public world of atomic physics and conflicting ideologies, of welfare states and supersonic speed, but in his strictly private universe of physical weakness and mental decay.

Aldous Huxley (1894–1964) British writer. *Themes and Variations*, 'Variations on a Philosopher'

57 It is so comic to hear oneself called old, even at ninety I suppose!

Alice James (1848–92) US diarist. Letter to William James, 14 June 1889. *The Diary of Alice James* (ed. Leon Edel)

58 There is a wicked inclination in most people to suppose an old man decayed in his intellects. If a young or middle-aged man, when leaving a company, does not recollect where he laid his hat, it is nothing; but if the same inattention is discovered in an old man, people will shrug up their shoulders, and say, 'His memory is going.'

Samuel Johnson (1709–84) British lexicographer. *Life of Johnson* (J. Boswell), Vol. IV

59 When the first few wrinkles appear,
When her skin goes dry and slack, when her teeth begin
To blacken, when her eyes turn lustreless, then: 'Pack
Your bags!' his steward will tell her. 'Be off with you!'

Juvenal (Decimus Junius Juvenalis; 60–130 AD) Roman satirist. *Satires*, VI

60 A medical revolution has extended the life of our elder citizens without providing the dignity and security those later years deserve.

John F. Kennedy (1917–63) US statesman. Acceptance speech, Democratic National Convention, Los Angeles, 15 July 1960

61 Prolonged and costly illness in later years robs too many of our elder citizens of pride, purpose and savings.

John F. Kennedy *Message to Congress on the Nation's Health Needs*, 27 Feb 1962

62 Alas! the colours of the flowers
Have faded in the long continued rain;
My beauty ageing, too, as in this world
I gazed, engrossed, on things that were but vain.

Ono no Komachi (834–880) Japanese poet. *'The Colours of Flowers'*

63 Perhaps being old is having lighted rooms
Inside your head, and people in them, acting.
People you know, yet can't quite name.

Philip Larkin (1922–85) British poet. *The Old Fools*

64 A 'Grand Old Man'. That means on our continent any one with snow white hair who has kept out of jail till eighty.

Stephen Leacock (1869–1944) British-born Canadian economist and humorist. *The Score and Ten*

65 Old age is woman's hell.

Ninon de Lenclos (1620–1705) French courtesan. Attrib.

66 Only stay quiet while my mind remembers
The beauty of fire from the beauty of embers.

John Masefield (1878–1967) British poet. *On Growing Old*

67 From the earliest times the old have rubbed it into the young that they are wiser than they, and before the young had discovered what nonsense this was they were old too, and it profited them to carry on the imposture.

W. Somerset Maugham (1874–1965) British novelist. *Cakes and Ale*, Ch. 9

68 When you have loved as she has loved you grow old beautifully.

W. Somerset Maugham *The Circle*

69 What makes old age hard to bear is not the failing of one's faculties, mental and physical, but the burden of one's memories.

W. Somerset Maugham *Points of View*, Ch. 1

70 Growing old is a bad habit which a busy man has no time to form.

André Maurois (Émile Herzog; 1885–1967) French writer. *The Ageing American*

71 Being seventy is not a sin.

Golda Meir (1898–1978) Russian-born Israeli stateswoman. *Reader's Digest* (July 1971), 'The Indestructible Golda Meir'

72 Old age puts more wrinkles in our minds than on our faces.

Michel de Montaigne (1533–92) French essayist. *Essays*, Bk. III, Ch. 2, 'Of Repentance'

73 Old age is an island surrounded by death.

Juan Montalvo

74 A ready means of being cherished by the English is to adopt the simple expedient of living a long time. I have little doubt that if, say, Oscar Wilde had lived into his nineties, instead of dying in his forties, he would have been considered a benign, distinguished figure suitable to preside at a school prize-giving or to instruct and exhort scoutmasters at their jamborees. He might even have been knighted.

Malcolm Muggeridge (1903–90) British writer. *Tread Softly for you Tread on my Jokes*

75 I prefer to forget both pairs of glasses and pass my declining years saluting strange women and grandfather clocks.

Ogden Nash (1902–71) US poet. *Peekaboo, I Almost See You*

76 Senescence begins
And middle age ends,
The day your descendants,
Outnumber your friends.

Ogden Nash

77 Age only matters when one is ageing. Now that I have arrived at a great age, I might just as well be twenty.

Pablo Picasso (1881–1973) Spanish painter. *The Observer, Shouts and Murmurs*, 'Picasso in Private' (John Richardson)

78 See how the world its veterans rewards!
A youth of frolics, an old age of cards.

Alexander Pope (1688–1744) British poet. *Moral Essays*, II

79 Growing old is like being increasingly penalized for a crime you haven't committed.

Anthony Powell (1905–) British novelist. *A Dance to the Music of Time: Temporary Kings*, Ch. 1

80 As you get older you become more boring and better behaved.

Simon Raven (1927–) British writer. *The Observer* 'Sayings Of the Week', 22 Aug 1976

81 Darling, I am growing old,
Silver threads among the gold.

Eben Rexford (1848–1916) British songwriter. *Silver Threads Among the Gold*

82 Age seldom arrives smoothly or quickly. It's more often a succession of jerks.

Jean Rhys (1894–1979) Dominican-born British novelist. *The Observer*, 'Sayings of the Week', 25 May 1975

83 If you want to be a dear old lady at seventy, you should start early, say about seventeen.

Maude Royden (1876–1956)

84 Gentle ladies, you will remember till old age what we did together in our brilliant youth!

Sappho (fl. c. 610–635 BC) Greek poet. *Distinguished Women Writers* (Virginia Moore)

85 As I grow older and older,
And totter towards the tomb,
I find that I care less and less
Who goes to bed with whom.

Dorothy L. Sayers (1893–1957) British writer. *That's Why I Never Read Modern Novels*

86 Old age is a disease which we cannot cure.

Seneca (c. 4 BC–65 AD) Roman author and statesman. *Epistulae ad Lucilium*, CVIII

87 Last scene of all,
That ends this strange eventful history,
Is second childishness and mere oblivion;
Sans teeth, sans eyes, sans taste, sans every thing.

William Shakespeare (1564–1616) English dramatist. *As You Like It*, II:7

88 For mine own part, I could be well content
To entertain the lag-end of my life
With quiet hours.

William Shakespeare *Henry IV, Part One*, V:1

89 I know thee not, old man: fall to thy prayers;
How ill white hairs become a fool and jester!
I have long dream'd of such a kind of man,
So surfeit-swell'd, so old, and so profane.

William Shakespeare *Henry IV, Part Two*, V:5

90 I am a very foolish, fond old man,
Fourscore and upward, not an hour more or less;
And, to deal plainly,
I fear I am not in my perfect mind.

William Shakespeare *King Lear*, IV:7

91 I have liv'd long enough.
My way of life
Is fall'n into the sear, the yellow leaf;
And that which should accompany old age,
As honour, love, obedience, troops of friends,
I must not look to have.

William Shakespeare *Macbeth*, V:3

92 Doth not the appetite alter? A man loves the meat in his youth that he cannot endure in his age.

William Shakespeare *Much Ado About Nothing*, II:3

93 You and I are past our dancing days.

William Shakespeare *Romeo and Juliet*, I:5

94 That time of year thou mayst in me behold
When yellow leaves, or none, or few, do hang
Upon those boughs which shake against the cold,
Bare ruin'd choirs, where late the sweet birds sang.

William Shakespeare *Sonnet 73*

95 Old men are dangerous; it doesn't matter to them what is going to happen to the world.

George Bernard Shaw (1856–1950) Irish dramatist and critic. *Heartbreak House*

96 The denunciation of the young is a necessary part of the hygiene of older people, and greatly assists the circulation of their blood.

Logan Pearsall Smith (1865–1946) US writer. *All Trivia*, 'Last Words'

97 You are old, Father William, the young man cried,
The few locks which are left you are grey;
You are hale, Father William, a hearty old man,
Now tell me the reason, I pray.

Robert Southey (1774–1843) British poet. *See also* CARROLL. *The Old Man's Comforts, and How He Gained Them*

98 Being over seventy is like being engaged in a war. All our friends are going or gone and we survive amongst the dead and the dying as on a battlefield.

Muriel Spark (1918–) British novelist. *Memento Mori*, Ch. 4

99 There are so few who can grow old with a good grace.

Richard Steele (1672–1729) Dublin-born British essayist. *The Spectator*, 263

100 A man is as old as his arteries.

Thomas Sydenham (1624–89) *Bulletin of the New York Academy of Medicine*, 4:993, 1928 (F. H. Garrison)

101 The greatest problem about old age is the fear that it may go on too long.

A. J. P. Taylor (1906–90) British historian. *Observer* 'Sayings of the Week', 1 Nov 1981

102 Sleeping as quiet as death, side by wrinkled side, toothless, salt and brown, like two old kippers in a box.

Dylan Thomas (1914–53) Welsh poet. *Under Milk Wood*

103 Old age is the most unexpected of all the things that happen to a man.

Leon Trotsky (Lev Davidovich Bronstein; 1879–1940) Russian revolutionary. *Diary in Exile*, 8 May 1935

104 Man can have only a certain number of teeth, hair and ideas; there comes a time when he necessarily loses his teeth, hair and ideas.

Voltaire (François-Marie Arouet; 1694–1778) French writer and philosopher. *Philosophical Dictionary*

105 There is nothing funny or commendable about old age. It is a miserable affliction which brings a sort of imbecility to those who suffer from it and distresses everyone else.

Auberon Waugh (1939–) British novelist. *The Diaries of Auberon Waugh 1976–1985*, 'July 21, 1982'

106 The gods bestowed on Max the gift of perpetual old age.

Oscar Wilde (1854–1900) Irish-born British dramatist. Referring to Max Beerbohm. Attrib.

107 It is a terrible thing for an old woman to outlive her dogs.

Tennessee Williams (1911–83) US dramatist. *Camino Real*

108 He was either a man of about a hundred and fifty who was rather young for his years or a man of about a hundred and ten who had been aged by trouble.

P. G. Wodehouse (1881–1975) British humorous novelist. *Wodehouse at Work to the End* (Richard Usborne), Ch. 6

109 The wiser mind
Mourns less for what age takes away
Than what it leaves behind.

William Wordsworth (1770–1850) British poet. *The Fountain*

110 Provoke
The years to bring the inevitable yoke.

William Wordsworth *Ode. Intimations of Immortality*, VIII

111 I pray – for fashion's word is out
And prayer comes round again –
That I may seem, though I die old,
A foolish passionate man.

W. B. Yeats (1865–1939) Irish poet. *A Prayer for Old Age*

112 An aged man is but a paltry thing
A tattered coat upon a stick, unless
Soul clap its hands and sing.

W. B. Yeats *Sailing to Byzantium*

113 When you are old and gray and full of sleep,
And nodding by the fire, take down this book,
And slowly read, and dream of the soft look
Your eyes had once, and of their shadows deep...

W. B. Yeats *When you are Old*

ONE-UPMANSHIP

See also snobbery, superiority

1 Keeping up with the Joneses was a full-time job with my mother and father. It was not until many years later when I lived alone that I realized how much cheaper it was to drag the Joneses down to my level.

Quentin Crisp (c. 1910–) Model, publicist, and writer. *The Naked Civil Servant*

2 There is no doubt that basic weekendmanship should contain some reference to Important Person Play.

Stephen Potter (1900–69) British writer. *Lifemanship*, Ch. 2

3 *How to be one up* – how to make the other man feel that something has gone wrong, however slightly.

Stephen Potter *Lifemanship*, Introduction

OPERA

See also music, singing

1 Opera is like a husband with a foreign title: expensive to support, hard to understand, and therefore a supreme social challenge.

Cleveland Amory NBC TV, 6 Apr 1960

2 I do not mind what language an opera is sung in so long as it is a language I don't understand.

Edward Appleton (1892–1965) British physicist. *The Observer*, 'Sayings of the Week,' 28 Aug 1955

3 No good opera plot can be sensible, for people do not sing when they are feeling sensible.

W. H. Auden (1907–73) British poet. *Time*, 29 Dec 1961

4 The opera isn't over till the fat lady sings.

Dan Cook US journalist. *Washington Post*, 13 June 1978

5 People are wrong when they say the opera isn't what it used to be. It is what it used to be. That's what's wrong with it.

Noël Coward (1899–1973) British dramatist. *Design for Living*

6 Opera is when a guy gets stabbed in the back and instead of bleeding he sings.

Ed Gardener *Duffy's Tavern* (American radio show)

7 Opera in English, is, in the main, just about as sensible as baseball in Italian.

H. L. Mencken (1880–1956) US journalist. *The Frank Muir Book* (Frank Muir)

8 I sometimes wonder which would be nicer – an opera without an interval, or an interval without an opera.

Ernest Newman (1868–1959) British music critic. *Berlioz, Romantic and Classic* (ed. Peter Heyworth)

9 His vocal cords were kissed by God.

Harold Schoenberg (1915–) US music critic. Referring to Luciano Pavarotti. *The Times*, 30 June 1981

10 Our mistake, you see, was to write interminable large operas, which had to fill an entire evening... And now along comes someone with a one- or two-act opera without all that pompous nonsense...that was a happy reform.

Giuseppe Verdi (1813–1901) Italian composer. Referring to Mascagni.

11 Tenors are noble, pure and heroic and get the soprano. But baritones are born villains in opera. Always the heavy and never the hero.

Leonard Warren (1911–60) US baritone singer. *The New York World Telegram*, 13 Feb 1957

12 Like German opera, too long and too loud.

Evelyn Waugh (1903–66) British novelist. Giving his opinions of warfare after the Battle of Crete, 1941. Attrib.

13 An unalterable and unquestioned law of the musical world required that the German text of French operas sung by Swedish artists should be translated into Italian for the clearer understanding of English speaking audiences.

Edith Wharton (1862–1937) US novelist. *The Age of Innocence*, Bk. I, Ch. 1

OPINIONS

See also ideas

1 We must say that the same opinions have arisen among men in cycles, not once, twice, nor a few times, but infinitely often.

Aristotle (384–322 BC) Greek philosopher. *Meteorologica*

2 A man's opinion on tramcars matters; his opinion on Botticelli matters; his opinion on all things does not matter.

G. K. Chesterton (1874–1936) British writer. *Heretics*

3 Science is the father of knowledge, but opinion breeds ignorance.
Hippocrates (c. 460 BC–c. 377 BC) Greek physician. *The Canon Law*, IV

4 They that approve a private opinion, call it opinion; but they that mislike it, heresy: and yet heresy signifies no more than private opinion.
Thomas Hobbes (1588–1679) English philosopher. *Leviathan*, Pt. I, Ch. 11

5 The superiority of one man's opinion over another's is never so great as when the opinion is about a woman.
Henry James (1843–1916) US novelist. *The Tragic Muse*, Ch. 9

6 'Tis with our judgments as our watches, none
Go just alike, yet each believes his own.
Alexander Pope (1688–1744) British poet. *An Essay on Criticism*

7 The average man's opinions are much less foolish than they would be if he thought for himself.
Bertrand Russell (1872–1970) British philosopher. *Autobiography*

8 The fact that an opinion has been widely held is no evidence whatever that it is not utterly absurd.
Bertrand Russell Attrib.

9 It is folly of too many to mistake the echo of a London coffee-house for the voice of the kingdom.
Jonathan Swift (1667–1745) Irish-born Anglican priest and writer. *The Conduct of the Allies*

10 So many men, so many opinions.
Terence (Publius Terentius Afer; c. 190–159 BC) Roman poet. *Phormio*

11 I agree with no man's opinion. I have some of my own.
Ivan Turgenev (1818–83) Russian novelist. *Fathers and Sons*, Ch. 13

12 It is just when opinions universally prevail and we have added lip service to their authority that we become sometimes most keenly conscious that we do not believe a word that we are saying.
Virginia Woolf (1882–1941) British novelist. *The Common Reader*

OPPORTUNITY

See also chance, present

1 All's grist that comes to the mill.
Proverb

2 Every dog has his day.
Proverb

3 Hoist your sail when the wind is fair.
Proverb

4 Make hay while the sun shines.
Proverb

5 Nothing ventured, nothing gained.
Proverb

6 Opportunity seldom knocks twice.
Proverb

7 Strike while the iron is hot.
Proverb

8 Whenever you fall, pick up something.
Oswald Theodore Avery (1877–1955) Canadian bacteriologist. Attrib.

9 A wise man will make more opportunities than he finds.
Francis Bacon (1561–1626) English philosopher. *Essays*, 'Of Ceremonies and Respects'

10 Cast thy bread upon the waters: for thou shalt find it after many days.
Bible: Ecclesiastes 11:1

11 Let him now speak, or else hereafter for ever hold his peace.
The Book of Common Prayer *Solemnization of Matrimony*

12 Healing is a matter of time, but it is sometimes also a matter of opportunity.
Hippocrates (c. 460 BC–c. 377 BC) Greek physician. *Precepts*, I

13 Carpe diem, quam minimum credula postero.
Seize today, and put as little trust as you can in the morrow.
Horace (Quintus Horatius Flaccus; 65–8 BC) Roman poet. *Odes*, I

14 Opportunities are usually disguised as hard work, so most people don't recognise them.
Ann Landers (1918–) US journalist. Attrib.

15 One can present people with opportunities. One cannot make them equal to them.
Rosamond Lehmann (1901–90) British novelist. *The Ballad and the Source*

16 There is no security in this life. There is only opportunity.
Douglas MacArthur (1880–1964) US general. *MacArthur, His Rendezvous with History* (Courtney Whitney)

17 Equality of opportunity means equal opportunity to be unequal.
Iain Macleod (1913–70) British politician. *Way Of Life* (John Boyd Carpenter)

18 Grab a chance and you won't be sorry for a might have been.
Arthur Ransome (1884–1967) British novelist. *We Didn't Mean to Go to Sea*

19 There is a tide in the affairs of men
Which, taken at the flood, leads on to fortune;
Omitted, all the voyage of their life
Is bound in shallows and in miseries.
On such a full sea are we now afloat,
And we must take the current when it serves,
Or lose our ventures.
William Shakespeare (1564–1616) English dramatist. *Julius Caesar*, IV:3

20 Why, then the world's mine oyster,
Which I with sword will open.
William Shakespeare *The Merry Wives of Windsor*, II:2

21 A man who never missed an occasion to let slip an opportunity.
George Bernard Shaw (1856–1950) Irish dramatist and critic. Referring to Lord Rosebery. Attrib.

22 I missed the chance of a lifetime, too. Fifty lovelies in the rude and I'd left my Bunsen burner home.

Dylan Thomas (1914–53) Welsh poet. *Portrait of the Artist as a Young Dog*, 'One Warm Saturday'

23 Never miss a chance to have sex or appear on television.

Gore Vidal (1925–) US novelist. Attrib.

OPPOSITES

See also conflict, difference

1 It takes all sorts to make a world.

Proverb

2 Fish die belly-upward and rise to the surface; it is their way of falling.

André Gide (1869–1951) French novelist. *Journals*

3 The poet and the dreamer are distinct,
Diverse, sheer opposite, antipodes.
The one pours out a balm upon the world,
The other vexes it.

John Keats (1795–1821) British poet. *The Fall of Hyperion*, I

4 Oh, East is East, and West is West, and never the twain shall meet.

Rudyard Kipling (1865–1936) Indian-born British writer. *The Ballad of East and West*

5 War is Peace, Freedom is Slavery, Ignorance is Strength.

George Orwell (Eric Blair; 1903–50) British novelist. *Nineteen Eighty-Four*

6 Doublethink means the power of holding two contradictory beliefs in one's mind simultaneously, and accepting both of them.

George Orwell *Nineteen Eighty-Four*

7 The sublime and the ridiculous are often so nearly related that it is difficult to class them separately. One step above the sublime makes the ridiculous; and one step above the ridiculous makes the sublime again.

Thomas Paine (1737–1809) British writer. *The Age of Reason*, Pt. 2

OPPOSITION

See also government, politics

1 It has been said that England invented the phrase, 'Her Majesty's Opposition'.

Walter Bagehot (1826–77) British economist and journalist. *See* HOBHOUSE. *The English Constitution*, 'The Monarchy'

2 The duty of an opposition is to oppose.

Lord Randolph Churchill (1849–95) British Conservative politician. *Lord Randolph Churchill* (W. S. Churchill)

3 When I invented the phrase 'His Majesty's Opposition' he paid me a compliment on the fortunate hit.

John Cam Hobhouse (1786–1869) British politician. Speaking about the British statesman, Earl Canning (1812–62). *Recollections of a Long Life*, II, Ch. 12

4 One fifth of the people are against everything all the time.

Robert Kennedy (1925–68) US politician. *The Observer*, 'Sayings of the Week', 10 May 1964

5 ...I have spent many years of my life in opposition and I rather like the role.

Eleanor Roosevelt (1884–1962) US writer and lecturer. Letter to Bernard Baruch, 18 Nov 1952

6 The tragedy of the Police State is that it always regards all opposition as a crime, and there are no degrees.

Lord Vansittart (1881–1957) British politician. Speech, House of Lords, June 1947

OPPRESSION

See also imprisonment, indoctrination, power politics, slavery, tyranny

1 When Israel was in Egypt land,
Let my people go,
Oppressed so hard they could not stand,
Let my people go.
Go down, Moses,
Way-down in Egypt land,
Tell old Pharaoh
To let my people go.

Anonymous Negro spiritual

2 To the capitalist governors Timor's petroleum smells better than Timorese blood and tears.

Distant Voices (John Pilger; 1994)

3 Christ in this country would quite likely have been arrested under the Suppression of Communism Act.

Joost de Blank (1908–68) Dutch-born British churchman. Referring to South Africa. *The Observer*, 'Sayings of the Week', 27 Oct 1963

4 The enemies of Freedom do not argue; they shout and they shoot.

Dean Inge (1860–1954) British churchman. *The End of an Age*, Ch. 4

5 All the government gives us is charity at election time...Afterwards, death returns to our homes.

Marcos Mexican rebel leader. *The Independent*, 12 Jan 1994

6 If you want a picture of the future, imagine a boot stamping on a human face – for ever.

George Orwell (Eric Blair; 1903–50) British novelist. *Nineteen Eighty-Four*

7 In the first days of the revolt you must kill: to shoot down a European is to kill two birds with one stone, to destroy an oppressor and the man he oppresses at the same time: there remain a dead man, and a free man.

Jean-Paul Sartre (1905–80) French writer. *The Wretched of the Earth* (F. Fanon), Preface

8 Where today are the Pequot? Where are the Narraganset, the Mohican, the Pocanet, and other powerful tribes of our people? They have vanished before the avarice and oppression of the white man, as snow before the summer sun.

Tecumseh Shawnee leader. Speech, July 1811

OPTIMISM

See also hope

1 After a storm comes a calm.

Proverb

2 Every cloud has a silver lining.
Proverb

3 It's an ill wind that blows nobody any good.
Proverb

4 It will all come right in the wash.
Proverb

5 Look on the bright side.
Proverb

6 No news is good news.
Proverb

7 Nothing so bad but it might have been worse.
Proverb

8 The darkest hour is just before the dawn.
Proverb

9 Tomorrow is another day.
Proverb

10 When one door shuts, another opens.
Proverb

11 While there's life there's hope.
Proverb

12 Are we downhearted? No!
Anonymous A favourite expression of the British soldiers during World War I. Attrib.

13 What's the use of worrying?
It never was worth while,
So, pack up your troubles in your old kit-bag,
And smile, smile, smile.
George Asaf (George H. Powell; 1880–1951) US songwriter. *Pack up Your Troubles in Your Old Kit-bag*

14 Let other pens dwell on guilt and misery.
Jane Austen (1775–1817) British novelist. *Mansfield Park*, Ch. 48

15 A Scout smiles and whistles under all circumstances.
Robert Baden-Powell (1857–1941) British soldier and founder of the Boy Scouts. *Scouting for Boys*

16 FUTURE, n. That period of time in which our affairs prosper, our friends are true and our happiness is assured.
Ambrose Bierce (1842–?1914) US writer and journalist. *The Devil's Dictionary*

17 My sun sets to rise again.
Robert Browning (1812–89) British poet. *At the 'Mermaid'*

18 No, at noonday in the bustle of man's worktime
Greet the unseen with a cheer!
Robert Browning *Epilogue to Asolando*

19 The pessimist is the man who believes things couldn't possibly be worse, to which the optimist replies 'Oh yes they could.'
Vladimir Bukovsky (1942–) Russian writer and scientist. *The Guardian Weekly*, 10 July 1977

20 Don't you know each cloud contains
Pennies from Heaven?
Johnny Burke (1908–64) US songwriter. *Pennies from Heaven*

21 The optimist proclaims we live in the best of all possible worlds; and the pessimist fears this is true.
James Cabell (1879–1958) US novelist and journalist. *The Silver Stallion*

22 But you have no silver linings without a cloud.
Angela Carter (1940–92) British novelist. *Wise Children*

23 We are not downhearted. The trouble is, we cannot understand what is happening to our neighbours.
Joseph Chamberlain (1836–1914) British politician. Speech, 1906

24 Like the Mississippi, it just keeps rolling along. Let it roll. Let it roll on full flood, inexorable, irresistible, benignant, to broader lands and better days.
Winston Churchill (1874–1965) British statesman. Referring to cooperation with the US. Speech, House of Commons, 20 Aug 1940

25 The place where optimism most flourishes is the lunatic asylum.
Havelock Ellis (1859–1939) British sexologist. *The Dance of Life*

26 Optimism is the content of small men in high places.
F. Scott Fitzgerald (1896–1940) US novelist. *The Crack-Up*

27 Let us draw upon content for the deficiencies of fortune.
Oliver Goldsmith (1728–74) Irish-born British dramatist. *The Vicar of Wakefield*, Ch. 3

28 The corn is as high as an elephant's eye.
Oscar Hammerstein II (1895–1960) US lyricist. *Oklahoma!*, 'Oh, What a Beautiful Mornin''

29 Optimism: A kind of heart stimulant – the digitalis of failure.
Elbert G. Hubbard (1856–1915) *The Roycroft Dictionary*

30 Cheer up, the worst is yet to come.
Philander Chase Johnson (1866–1939) US journalist. *Shooting Stars*

31 Two men look out through the same bars:
One sees the mud, and one the stars.
Frederick Langbridge (1849–1923) British religious writer. *A Cluster of Quiet Thoughts*

32 An optimist is a guy that never had much experience.
Don Marquis (1878–1937) US journalist. *archy and mehitabel*

33 The Power of Positive Thinking.
Norman Vincent Peale (1899–93) US clergyman and writer. Book title

34 The worst is not
So long as we can say 'This is the worst'.
William Shakespeare (1564–1616) English dramatist. *King Lear*, IV:1

35 Now is the winter of our discontent
Made glorious summer by this sun of York.
William Shakespeare *Richard III*, I:1

36 Life may change, but it may fly not;
Hope may vanish, but can die not;
Truth be veiled, but still it burneth;
Love repulsed, – but it returneth!
Percy Bysshe Shelley (1792–1822) British poet. *Hellas*, I

37 The latest definition of an optimist is one who fills up his crossword puzzle in ink.

Clement King Shorter (1857–1926) British journalist and critic. *The Observer*, 'Sayings of the Week', 22 Feb 1925

38 I am an optimist, unrepentant and militant. After all, in order not to be a fool an optimist must know how sad a place the world can be. It is only the pessimist who finds this out anew every day.

Peter Ustinov (1921–) British actor. *Dear Me*, Ch. 9

39 All is for the best in the best of possible worlds.

Voltaire (François-Marie Arouet; 1694–1778) French writer. *Candide*, Ch. 30

40 We are all in the gutter, but some of us are looking at the stars.

Oscar Wilde (1854–1900) Irish-born British dramatist. *Lady Windermere's Fan*, III

41 I'm an optimist, but I'm an optimist who carries a raincoat.

Harold Wilson (1916–) British politician and prime minister. Attrib.

42 Nor greetings where no kindness is, nor all
The dreary intercourse of daily life,
Shall e'er prevail against us, or disturb
Our cheerful faith, that all which we behold
Is full of blessings.

William Wordsworth (1770–1850) British poet. *Lines Composed a Few Miles above Tintern Abbey*

ORDER

1 I am an orderly man. I say this with no sense of false modesty, or of conceit....Being orderly, as a matter of fact, can be excessively tiresome and it often irritates me greatly, but I cannot pull away.

Dirk Bogarde (1921–) British actor and writer. *An Orderly Man*, Ch.1

2 'Where shall I begin, please your Majesty?' he asked.
'Begin at the beginning' the King said, gravely, 'and go on till you come to the end: then stop.'

Lewis Carroll (Charles Lutwidge Dodgson; 1832–98) British writer. *Alice's Adventures in Wonderland*, Ch. 11

3 Order is heaven's first law.

Alexander Pope (1688–1744) British poet. *An Essay on Man*, IV

4 How sour sweet music is
When time is broke and no proportion kept!
So is it in the music of men's lives.

William Shakespeare (1564–1616) English dramatist. *Richard II*, V:5

5 O, when degree is shak'd,
Which is the ladder of all high designs,
The enterprise is sick!

William Shakespeare *Troilus and Cressida*, I:3

6 A place for everything, and everything in its place.

Samuel Smiles (1812–1904) British writer. *Thrift*, Ch. 5

ORIGINALITY

See also imitation, innovation

1 Anything that is worth doing has been done frequently. Things hitherto undone should be given, I suspect, a wide berth.

Max Beerbohm (1872–1956) British writer. *Mainly on the Air*

2 An original writer is not one who imitates nobody, but one whom nobody can imitate.

Vicomte de Chateaubriand (1768–1848) French diplomat and writer. *Génie du Christianisme*

3 A thought is often original, though you have uttered it a hundred times.

Oliver Wendell Holmes (1809–94) US writer. *The Autocrat of the Breakfast Table*, Ch. 1

4 All good things which exist are the fruits of originality.

John Stuart Mill (1806–73) British philosopher. *On Liberty*, Ch. 3

5 Nothing has yet been said that's not been said before.

Terence (Publius Terentius Afer; c. 190–159 BC) Roman poet. *Eunuchus*, Prologue

6 Another unsettling element in modern art is that common symptom of immaturity, the dread of doing what has been done before.

Edith Wharton (1862–1937) US novelist. *The Writing of Fiction*, Ch. 1

ORTHODOXY

See also conformity

1 The difference between Orthodoxy or My-doxy and Heterodoxy or Thy-doxy.

Thomas Carlyle (1795–1881) Scottish historian and essayist. A similar remark is attributed to the British churchman William Warburton (1698–1779). *History of the French Revolution*, Pt. II, Bk. IV, Ch. 2

2 The word 'orthodoxy' not only no longer means being right; it practically means being wrong.

G. K. Chesterton (1874–1936) British writer. *Heretics*, Ch. 1

3 Worldly wisdom teaches that it is better for the reputation to fail conventionally than to succeed unconventionally.

John Maynard Keynes (1883–1946) British economist. *The General Theory of Employment, Interest and Money*, Bk. IV, Ch. 12

ORTON, JOE

(1933–67) British dramatist. His black comedies include *Entertaining Mr Sloane* (1964), *Loot* (1965), and *What the Butler Saw* (1969). He was battered to death by his homosexual lover.

1 I'd the upbringing a nun would envy and that's the truth. Until I was fifteen I was more familiar with Africa than my own body.

Entertaining Mr Sloane, I

2 It's all any reasonable child can expect if the dad is present at the conception.

Entertaining Mr Sloane, III

3 The humble and meek are thirsting for blood.

Funeral Games, I

4 Every luxury was lavished on you – atheism, breast-feeding, circumcision. I had to make my own way.

Loot, I

5 Reading isn't an occupation we encourage among police officers. We try to keep the paper work down to a minimum.

Loot, II

6 God is a gentleman. He prefers blondes.

Loot, II

7 You were born with your legs apart. They'll send you to the grave in a Y-shaped coffin.

What the Butler Saw, I

ORWELL, GEORGE

(Eric Blair; 1903–50) British novelist. His books include *The Road to Wigan Pier* (1937), *Animal Farm* (1945), and *Nineteen Eighty-Four* (1949).

Quotations about Orwell

1 He could not blow his nose without moralising on the state of the handkerchief industry.

Cyril Connolly (1903–74) British journalist. *The Evening Colonnade*

2 He was a kind of saint, and in that character, more likely in politics to chastise his own side than the enemy.

V. S. Pritchett (1900–) British short-story writer. *New Statesman*, 1950

Quotations by Orwell

3 Man is the only creature that consumes without producing.

An allegory of the Marxist analysis of capitalism, with man representing the capitalist. *Animal Farm*, Ch. 1

4 Four legs good, two legs bad.

Animal Farm, Ch. 3

5 War is war. The only good human being is a dead one.

Animal Farm, Ch. 4

6 He intended, he said, to devote the rest of his life to learning the remaining twenty-two letters of the alphabet.

Animal Farm, Ch. 9

7 All animals are equal but some animals are more equal than others.

Animal Farm, Ch. 10

8 The high sentiments always win in the end, the leaders who offer blood, toil, tears and sweat always get more out of their followers than those who offer safety and a good time. When it comes to the pinch, human beings are heroic.

The Art of Donald McGill

9 I'm fat, but I'm thin inside. Has it ever struck you that there's a thin man inside every fat man, just as they say there's a statue inside every block of stone?

Coming Up For Air, Pt. I, Ch. 3

10 Before the war, and especially before the Boer War, it was summer all the year round.

Coming Up for Air, Pt. II, Ch. 1

11 Prolonged, indiscriminate reviewing of books involves constantly *inventing* reactions towards books about which one has no spontaneous feelings whatever.

Confessions of a Book Reviewer

12 He was an embittered atheist (the sort of atheist who does not so much disbelieve in God as personally dislike Him).

Down and Out in Paris and London, Ch. 30

13 Probably the Battle of Waterloo *was* won on the playing-fields of Eton, but the opening battles of all subsequent wars have been lost there.

The Lion and the Unicorn, 'England, Your England'

14 A family with the wrong members in control – that, perhaps, is as near as one can come to describing England in a phrase.

The Lion and the Unicorn, 'The Ruling Class'

15 Who controls the past controls the future. Who controls the present controls the past.

Nineteen Eighty-Four

16 If you want a picture of the future, imagine a boot stamping on a human face – for ever.

Nineteen Eighty-Four

17 Big Brother is watching you.

Nineteen Eighty-Four

18 War is Peace, Freedom is Slavery, Ignorance is Strength.

Nineteen Eighty-Four

19 Doublethink means the power of holding two contradictory beliefs in one's mind simultaneously, and accepting both of them.

Nineteen Eighty-Four

20 The quickest way of ending a war is to lose it.

Polemic, 'Second thoughts on James Burnham'

21 In our time, political speech and writing are largely the defence of the indefensible.

Politics and the English Language

22 The books one reads in childhood, and perhaps most of all the bad and good bad books, create in one's mind a sort of false map of the world, a series of fabulous countries into which one can retreat at odd moments throughout the rest of life, and which in some cases can even survive a visit to the real countries which they are supposed to represent.

Riding Down from Bangor

23 It is brought home to you...that it is only because miners sweat their guts out that superior persons can remain superior.

The Road to Wigan Pier, Ch. 2

24 I sometimes think that the price of liberty is not so much eternal vigilance as eternal dirt.

The Road to Wigan Pier, Ch. 4

25 We may find in the long run that tinned food is a deadlier weapon than the machine-gun.

The Road to Wigan Pier, Ch. 6

26 There can hardly be a town in the South of England where you could throw a brick without hitting the niece of a bishop.

The Road to Wigan Pier, Ch. 7

27 As with the Christian religion, the worst advertisement for Socialism is its adherents.
The Road to Wigan Pier, Ch. 11

28 To the ordinary working man, the sort you would meet in any pub on Saturday night, Socialism does not mean much more than better wages and shorter hours and nobody bossing you about.
The Road to Wigan Pier, Ch. 11

29 The higher-water mark, so to speak, of Socialist literature is W. H. Auden, a sort of gutless Kipling.
The Road to Wigan Pier, Ch. 11

30 We have nothing to lose but our aitches.
Referring to the middle classes. *The Road to Wigan Pier*, Ch. 13

31 Most people get a fair amount of fun out of their lives, but on balance life is suffering and only the very young or the very foolish imagine otherwise.
Shooting an Elephant

32 Serious sport has nothing to do with fair play. It is bound up with hatred, jealousy, boastfulness, disregard of all rules and sadistic pleasure in witnessing violence; in other words it is war minus the shooting.
Shooting an Elephant

33 To a surprising extent the war-lords in shining armour, the apostles of the martial virtues, tend not to die fighting when the time comes. History is full of ignominious getaways by the great and famous.
Who Are the War Criminals?

34 He is pretty certain to come back into favour. One of the surest signs of his genius is that women dislike his books.
Referring to Joseph Conrad. *New English Weekly*, 23 July 1936

35 Each generation imagines itself to be more intelligent than the one that went before it, and wiser than the one that comes after it.
Book Review

36 At 50, everyone has the face he deserves.
Last words in his manuscript notebook, 17 Apr 1949.

OSBORNE, JOHN

(1929–) British dramatist. He made his reputation as one of the Angry Young Men with *Look Back in Anger* (1956). His subsequent plays include *The Entertainer* (1957), *Luther* (1960), *Inadmissible Evidence* (1964), *West of Suez* (1971), and *A Better Class of Person* (1981).

1 Don't clap too hard – it's a very old building.
The Entertainer

2 Well, there are only two posh papers on a Sunday – the one you're reading and this one.
Look Back in Anger, I

3 He really deserves some sort of decoration…a medal inscribed 'For Vaguery in the Field'.
Look Back in Anger, I

4 I don't think one 'comes down' from Jimmy's university. According to him, it's not even red brick, but white tile.
Look Back in Anger, II:1

5 They spend their time mostly looking forward to the past.
Look Back in Anger, II:1

6 Poor old Daddy – just one of those sturdy old plants left over from the Edwardian Wilderness, that can't understand why the sun isn't shining any more.
Look Back in Anger, II:2

7 She's like the old line about justice – not only must be done but must be seen to be done.
Time Present, I

8 I never deliberately set out to shock, but when people don't walk out of my plays I think there is something wrong.
The Observer, 'Sayings of the Week', 19 Jan 1975

OSTENTATION

See also affectation

1 That's it, baby, if you've got it, flaunt it.
Mel Brooks (Melvyn Kaminsky; 1926–) US film director. *The Producers*

2 The possession of a book becomes a substitute for reading it.
Anthony Burgess (John Burgess Wilson; 1917–) British novelist. *The New York Times Book Review*

3 Wealth has never been a sufficient source of honour in itself. It must be advertised, and the normal medium is obtrusively expensive goods.
John Kenneth Galbraith (1908–) US economist. *The Affluent Society*, Ch. 7

4 When I meet those remarkable people whose company is coveted, I often wish they would show off a little more.
Desmond MacCarthy (1877–1952) British writer and theatre critic. *Theatre*, 'Good Talk'

5 She's like the old line about justice – not only must be done but must be seen to be done.
John Osborne (1929–) British dramatist. *Time Present*, I

6 With the great part of rich people, the chief employment of riches consists in the parade of riches.
Adam Smith (1723–90) Scottish economist. *The Wealth of Nations*

OVID

(Publius Ovidius Naso; 43 BC–17 AD) Roman poet. He is remembered for his love poems, including the *Amores* and *Heroides*, and his *Metamorphoses*, a collection of mythical and historical tales.

Quotations about Ovid

1 Ovid had nothing in common with the older Roman poets; their dignity, virility and piety were entirely lacking in him. But he possessed an exquisite sensitiveness to beauty, and abounding imaginative power, which they lacked.
Concise Universal Biography (J.A. Hammerton)

2 The true cause of Ovid's sudden exile is not known; some attribute it to a shameful amour with

Livia, wife of Augustus; others support that it arose from the knowledge which Ovid had of the unpardonable incest of the emperor with his daughter Julia; these reasons are indeed merely conjectural; the cause was of a private and secret nature of which Ovid himself was afraid to speak.

John Lemprière (1765–1824) British scholar. *Classical Dictionary*

Quotations by Ovid

3 Whether a pretty woman grants or withholds her favours, she always likes to be asked for them.

Ars Amatoria

4 Dripping water hollows out a stone, a ring is worn away by use.

See also LATIMER, LUCRETIUS. *Epistulae Ex Ponto*, Bk. IV

5 Now there are fields where Troy once was.

Heroides, Bk. I

6 *Tu quoque.*
You also.

Tristia

7 All things can corrupt perverted minds.

Tristia, Bk. II

OWEN, WILFRED

(1893–1918) British poet. Written during World War I, his poetry expresses the horror of war and includes 'Strange Meeting' and 'Anthem for Doomed Youth'. He was killed in action.

1 The pallor of girls' brows shall be their pall;
Their flowers the tenderness of patient minds,
And each slow dusk a drawing-down of blinds.

Anthem for Doomed Youth

2 And in the happy no-time of his sleeping
Death took him by the heart.

Asleep

3 The old Lie: *Dulce et decorum est*
Pro patria mori.

The Latin quotation means 'it is sweet and fitting to die for one's country', and it comes from Horace, *Odes*, III. *Dulce et decorum est*

4 Was it for this the clay grew tall?
–O what made fatuous sunbeams toil
To break earth's sleep at all?

Futility

5 Red lips are not so red
As the stained stones kissed by the English dead.

Greater Love

6 Above all I am not concerned with Poetry. My subject is War, and the pity of War. The Poetry is in the pity.

Poems, Preface

7 I am the enemy you killed, my friend.
I knew you in this dark: for so you frowned
Yesterday through me as you jabbed and killed.
I parried; but my hands were loath and cold.
Let us sleep now...

Strange Meeting

OXFORD

See also Cambridge, education, England

1 Home of lost causes, and forsaken beliefs, and unpopular names, and impossible loyalties!

Matthew Arnold (1822–88) British poet and critic. *Essays in Criticism*, First Series, Preface

2 That sweet City with her dreaming spires
She needs not June for beauty's heightening.

Matthew Arnold *Thyrsis*

3 Oxford is on the whole more attractive than Cambridge to the ordinary visitor; and the traveller is therefore recommended to visit Cambridge first, or to omit it altogether if he cannot visit both.

Karl Baedeker (1801–59) German publisher. *Baedeker's Great Britain*, 'From London to Oxford'

4 ...a young man with so superior a voice that he might have been to Oxford twice.

Vernon Bartlett (1894–) British journalist and writer. *And Now, Tomorrow*

5 It is Oxford that has made me insufferable.

Max Beerbohm (1872–1956) British writer. *More*, 'Going back to School'

6 The King to Oxford sent a troop of horse,
For Tories own no argument but force:
With equal skill to Cambridge books he sent,
For Whigs admit no force but argument.

William Browne (1692–1774) English physician. A reply to TRAPP. *Literary Anecdotes* (Nichols), Vol. III

7 It is a secret in the Oxford sense: you may tell it to only one person at a time.

Oliver Franks (1905–92) British philosopher and administrator. *The Sunday Telegraph*, 30 Jan 1977

8 To the University of Oxford I acknowledge no obligation; and she will as cheerfully renounce me for a son, as I am willing to disclaim her for a mother. I spent fourteen months at Magdalen College: they proved the fourteen months the most idle and unprofitable of my whole life.

Edward Gibbon (1737–94) British historian. *Autobiography*

9 Oxford had not taught me, nor had any other place or person, the value of liberty as an essential condition of excellence in human things.

William Ewart Gladstone (1809–98) British statesman. Gladstone graduated from Oxford in 1831.

10 The clever men at Oxford
Know all that there is to be knowed.
But they none of them know one half as much
As intelligent Mr Toad.

Kenneth Grahame (1859–1932) Scottish writer. *The Wind in the Willows*, Ch. 10

11 I often think how much easier the world would have been to manage if Herr Hitler and Signor Mussolini had been at Oxford.

Viscount Halifax (1881–1959) British politician. Speech, York, 4 Nov 1937

12 Cambridge sees Oxford as the Latin quarter of Cowley.

Marjorie Knight Letter to *The Daily Telegraph*, 15 Aug 1979

13 Very nice sort of place, Oxford, I should think, for people that like that sort of place.

George Bernard Shaw (1856–1950) Irish dramatist and critic. *Man and Superman*, II

14 The King, observing with judicious eyes
The state of both his universities,
To Oxford sent a troop of horse, and why?
That learned body wanted loyalty;
To Cambridge books, as very well discerning
How much that loyal body wanted learning.

Joseph Trapp (1679–1747) English churchman and academic. Written after George I donated the Bishop of Ely's library to Cambridge; for the reply see BROWNE. *Literary Anecdotes* (Nichols), Vol. III

15 Oxford is, and always has been, full of cliques, full of factions, and full of a particular non-social snobbiness.

Mary Warnock (1924–) British philosopher and educationalist. *The Observer*, 2 Nov 1980

16 We think of Cambridge as a little town and Oxford as a hive of industry, but they aren't that different.

Katherine Whitehorn (1926–) British journalist. *The Observer*, 14 Jan 1979

P

PAINTING

See also art, artists

1 One picture is worth ten thousand words.
Frederick R. Barnard Ascribed to Chinese origin. *Printer's Ink*, 8 Dec 1921

2 Buy old masters. They fetch a better price than old mistresses.
Lord Beaverbrook (1879–1964) British newspaper owner and politician. Attrib.

3 PAINTING, n. The art of protecting flat surfaces from the weather and exposing them to the critic.
Ambrose Bierce (1842–c. 1914) US writer and journalist. *The Devil's Dictionary*

4 Good painters imitate nature, bad ones spew it up.
Miguel de Cervantes (1547–1616) Spanish novelist. *El Licenciado Vidriera*

5 The day is coming when a single carrot, freshly observed, will set off a revolution.
Paul Cézanne (1839–1906) French postimpressionist painter. Attrib.

6 It's either easy or impossible.
Salvador Dali (1904–89) Spanish painter. Reply when asked if he found it hard to paint a picture. Attrib.

7 I do not paint a portrait to look like the subject, rather does the person grow to look like his portrait.
Salvador Dali Spanish painter. Attrib.

8 Never mind about my soul, just make sure you get my tie right.
James Joyce (1882–1941) Irish novelist. Responding to the painter Patrick Tuohy's assertion that he wished to capture Joyce's soul in his portrait of him. *James Joyce* (R. Ellmann)

9 If people only knew as much about painting as I do, they would never buy my pictures.
Edwin Landseer (1802–73) British painter and sculptor. Said to W. P. Frith. *Landseer the Victorian Paragon* (Campbell Lennie), Ch. 12

10 I mix them with my brains, sir.
John Opie (1761–1807) British painter. When asked what he mixed his colours with. *Self-Help* (Samuel Smiles), Ch. 4

11 A picture has been said to be something between a thing and a thought.
Samuel Palmer (1805–81) British landscape painter. *Life of Blake* (Arthur Symons)

12 If I like it, I say it's mine. If I don't I say it's a fake.
Pablo Picasso (1881–1973) Spanish painter. When asked how he knew which paintings were his. *The Sunday Times*, 10 Oct 1965

13 I paint objects as I think them, not as I see them.
Pablo Picasso Attrib.

14 Painting is a blind man's profession. He paints not what he sees, but what he feels, what he tells himself about what he has seen.
Pablo Picasso *Journals* (Jean Cocteau), 'Childhood'

15 It's better like that, if you want to kill a picture all you have to do is to hang it beautifully on a nail and soon you will see nothing of it but the frame. When it's out of place you see it better.
Pablo Picasso Explaining why a Renoir in his apartment was hung crooked. *Picasso: His Life and Work* (Ronald Penrose)

16 It is bad enough to be condemned to drag around this image in which nature has imprisoned me. Why should I consent to the perpetuation of the image of this image?
Plotinus (205–270 AD) Egyptian-born Greek philosopher. Refusing to have his portrait painted. Attrib.

17 I just keep painting till I feel like pinching. Then I know it's right.
Pierre Auguste Renoir (1841–1919) French impressionist painter. Explaining how he achieved such lifelike flesh tones in his nudes. Attrib.

18 Every time I paint a portrait I lose a friend.
John Singer Sargent (1856–1925) US portrait painter. Attrib.

19 Portraits of famous bards and preachers, all fur and wool from the squint to the kneecaps.
Dylan Thomas (1914–53) Welsh poet. *Under Milk Wood*

20 My business is to paint not what I know, but what I see.
Joseph Turner (1775–1851) British painter. Responding to a criticism of the fact that he had painted no portholes on the ships in a view of Plymouth. *Proust: The Early Years* (G. Painter)

PANKHURST, DAME CHRISTABEL

(1880–1958) British suffragette. The daughter of Emmeline Pankhurst, she was arrested for assaulting the policeman who removed her from an election meeting.

Quotations about Christabel Pankhurst

1 She knows everything and can see through everything.
Mrs Flora Drummond (1869–1949) British suffragette. *Suffragette*, 12 Dec 1913

2 I heard Christabel Pankhurst the other day. She was very able, very clever, and very unpleasant. Her idea of progress is that females should meet together in masses and orate. But I agreed with most of her remarks, and her tone did not unconvert me.
E. M. Forster (1879–1970) British novelist. *Letters*, Vol. I

Quotations by Christabel Pankhurst

3 Never lose your temper with the Press or the public is a major rule of political life.
Unshackled

4 We are not ashamed of what we have done, because, when you have a great cause to fight for, the moment of greatest humiliation is the moment when the spirit is proudest.
Speech, Albert Hall, London, 19 Mar 1908

5 We are here to claim our rights as women, not only to be free, but to fight for freedom. It is our privilege, as well as our pride and our joy, to take some part in this militant movement, which, as we believe, means the regeneration of all humanity.

Speech, 23 Mar 1911

6 What we suffragettes aspire to be when we are enfranchised is ambassadors of freedom to women in other parts of the world, who are not so free as we are.

Speech, Carnegie Hall, New York, 25 Oct 1915

PANKHURST, EMMELINE

(1858–1928) British suffragette. She founded, in Manchester, the Women's Social and Political Union (1903). She was frequently imprisoned for destroying property, but during World War I abandoned her campaign and encouraged women to do industrial war work.

Quotations about Emmeline Pankhurst

1 What an extraordinary mixture of idealism and lunacy. Hasn't she the sense to see that the very worst method of campaigning for the franchise is to try and intimidate or blackmail a man into giving her what he would gladly give her otherwise.

David Lloyd George (1863–1945) British Liberal statesman. *Lloyd George* (Richard Lloyd George)

2 She was as she instinctively knew, cast for a great role. She had a temperament akin to genius. She could have been a queen on the Stage or in the Salon.

Emmeline Pethwick-Lawrence (1867–1954) British suffragette. *My Part in a Changing World*

Quotations by Emmeline Pankhurst

3 …if civilisation is to advance at all in the future, it must be through the help of women, women freed of their political shackles, women with full power to work their will in society. It was rapidly becoming clear to my mind that men regarded women as a servant class in the community, and that women were going to remain in the servant class until they lifted themselves out of it.

My Own Story

4 Women had always fought for men, and for their children. Now they were ready to fight for their own human rights. Our militant movement was established.

My Own Story

5 I have no sense of guilt. I look upon myself as a prisoner of war. I am under no moral obligation to conform to, or in any way accept, the sentence imposed upon me.

Speech in court, Apr 1913. *The Fighting Pankhursts* (David Mitchell)

6 We have taken this action, because as women… we realize that the condition of our sex is so deplorable that it is our duty even to break the law in order to call attention to the reasons why we do so.

Speech in court, 21 Oct 1908. *Shoulder to Shoulder* (ed. Midge Mackenzie)

PARASITES

1 Many a man who thinks to found a home discovers that he has merely opened a tavern for his friends.

Norman Douglas (1868–1952) British novelist. *South Wind*, Ch. 24

2 A free-loader is a confirmed guest. He is the man who is always willing to come to dinner.

Damon Runyon (1884–1946) US writer. *Short Takes*, 'Free-Loading Ethics'

3 So, naturalist observe, a flea
Hath smaller fleas that on him prey,
And these have smaller fleas to bite 'em.
And so proceed *ad infinitum*.

Jonathan Swift (1667–1745) Irish-born Anglican priest and writer. *On Poetry*

4 But was there ever dog that praised his fleas?

W. B. Yeats (1865–1939) Irish poet. *To a Poet, who would have me Praise certain Bad Poets, Imitators of His and Mine*

PARIS

See also France

1 The last time I saw Paris, her heart was warm and gay,
I heard the laughter of her heart in every street café.

Oscar Hammerstein II (1895–1960) US lyricist. *Lady Be Good*, 'The Last Time I Saw Paris'

2 If you are lucky enough to have lived in Paris as a young man, then wherever you go for the rest of your life, it stays with you, for Paris is a moveable feast.

Ernest Hemingway (1899–1961) US novelist. *A Moveable Feast*, Epigraph

3 Paris is worth a mass.

Henri IV (1553–1610) King of France. Said on entering Paris (March 1594), having secured its submission to his authority by becoming a Roman Catholic. Attrib.

4 Is Paris burning?

Adolf Hitler (1889–1945) German dictator. Referring to the liberation of Paris, 1944

5 As an artist, a man has no home in Europe save in Paris.

Friedrich Wilhelm Nietzsche (1844–1900) German philosopher. *Ecce Homo*

6 I love Paris in the springtime.

Cole Porter (1893–1964) US songwriter. *Can-Can*, 'I Love Paris'

7 Paris Loves Lovers.

Cole Porter *Silk Stockings*

PARKER, DOROTHY

(1893–1967) US writer and wit. Her New York circle in the 1920s included Ogden Nash and James Thurber. She is best known for her short stories, sketches, and poems; her books include *Not So Deep As a Well* (1936).

Quotations about Parker

1 She has put into what she has written a voice, a state of mind, an era, a few moments of human experience that nobody else has conveyed.
Edmund Wilson (1895–1972) US critic and writer. Attrib.

2 She is a combination of Little Nell and Lady Macbeth.
Alexander Woollcott (1887–1943) US journalist. *While Rome Burns*

Quotations by Parker

3 Razors pain you
Rivers are damp;
Acids stain you;
And drugs cause cramp.
Guns aren't lawful;
Nooses give;
Gas smells awful;
You might as well live.
Enough Rope, 'Resumé'

4 He lies below, correct in cypress wood,
And entertains the most exclusive worms.
Epitaph for a Very Rich Man

5 All I say is, nobody has any business to go around looking like a horse and behaving as if it were all right. You don't catch horses going around looking like people, do you?
Horsie

6 How do people go to sleep? I'm afraid I've lost the knack. I might try busting myself smartly over the temple with the nightlight. I might repeat to myself, slowly and soothingly, a list of quotations beautiful from minds profound; if I can remember any of the damn things.
The Little Hours

7 I'm never going to be famous...I don't do anything. Not one single thing. I used to bite my nails, but I don't even do that any more.
The Little Hours

8 And I'll stay off Verlaine too; he was always chasing Rimbauds.
The Little Hours

9 Why is it no one ever sent me yet
One perfect limousine, do you suppose?
Ah no, it's always just my luck to get
One perfect rose.
One Perfect Rose

10 Sorrow is tranquillity remembered in emotion.
Sentiment

11 It costs me never a stab nor squirm
To tread by chance upon a worm.
"Aha, my little dear," I say,
"Your clan will pay me back one day."
Sunset Gun, 'Thought for a Sunshiny Morning'

12 By the time you say you're his,
Shivering and sighing,
And he vows his passion is
Infinite, undying –
Lady, make a note of this:
One of you is lying.
Unfortunate Coincidence

13 That should assure us of at least forty-five minutes of undisturbed privacy.
Pressing a button marked NURSE during a stay in hospital. *The Algonquin Wits* (R. Drennan)

14 The poor son-of-a-bitch!
Quoting from *The Great Gatsby* on paying her last respects to F. Scott Fitzgerald. *Thalberg: Life and Legend* (B. Thomas)

15 If all the young ladies who attended the Yale promenade dance were laid end to end, no one would be the least surprised.
While Rome Burns (Alexander Woollcott)

16 Brevity is the soul of lingerie.
While Rome Burns (Alexander Woollcott)

17 This is not a novel to be tossed aside lightly. It should be thrown with great force.
Book review. *Wit's End* (R. E. Dremman)

18 A list of authors who have made themselves most beloved and therefore, most comfortable financially, shows that it is our national joy to mistake for the first-rate, the fecund rate.
Wit's End (R. E. Drennan)

19 You can't teach an old dogma new tricks.
Wit's End (R. E. Drennan)

20 I was fired from there, finally, for a lot of things, among them my insistence that the Immaculate Conception was spontaneous combustion.
Writers at Work, First Series (Malcolm Cowley)

21 This is on me.
Suggesting words for tombstone. *You Might As Well Live* (J. Keats), Pt. I, Ch. 5

22 It serves me right for putting all my eggs in one bastard.
Said on going into hospital to get an abortion. *You Might as Well Live* (J. Keats), Pt. II, Ch. 3

23 Oh, don't worry about Alan...Alan will always land on somebody's feet.
Said of her husband on the day their divorce became final. *You Might As Well Live* (J. Keats), Pt. IV, Ch. 1

24 How do they know?
Reaction to news of the death of Calvin Coolidge, US President 1923–29; also attributed to H. L. Mencken. *You Might As Well Live* (J. Keats)

25 Dear Mary, We all knew you had it in you.
Telegram sent to a friend on the successful outcome of her much-publicized pregnancy

26 You can lead a whore to culture but you can't make her think.
Speech to American Horticultural Society

27 You know, she speaks eighteen languages. And she can't say 'No' in any of them.
Speaking of an acquaintance. Attrib.

28 Men seldom make passes
At girls who wear glasses.
Attrib.

29 Check enclosed.
Giving her version of the two most beautiful words in the English language. Attrib.

Referring to a performance by Katharine Hepburn on Broadway. Attrib.

31 Excuse my dust.

Her own epitaph

PARKINSON, CYRIL NORTHCOTE

(1909–93) British historian and writer. He is best known for his book *Parkinson's Law* (1958), a study of business administration.

1 Work expands so as to fill the time available for its completion.

Parkinson's Law, Ch. 1

2 The rise in the total of those employed is governed by Parkinson's Law and would be much the same whether the volume of work were to increase, diminish or even disappear.

Parkinson's Law, Ch. 1

3 The British, being brought up on team games, enter their House of Commons in the spirit of those who would rather be doing something else. If they cannot be playing golf or tennis, they can at least pretend that politics is a game with very similar rules.

Parkinson's Law, Ch. 2

4 It is now known…that men enter local politics solely as a result of being unhappily married.

Parkinson's Law, Ch. 10

PAROCHIALISM

See also self-interest, selfishness

1 This fellow did not see further than his own nose.

Jean de La Fontaine (1621–95) French poet. *Fables*, III, 'Le Renard et le Bouc'

2 A broken head in Cold Bath Fields produces a greater sensation among us than three pitched battles in India.

Lord Macaulay (1800–59) British historian. Speech, 10 July 1833

3 'That is well said,' replied Candide, 'but we must cultivate our garden.'

Voltaire (François-Marie Arouet; 1694–1778) French writer. *Candide*, Ch. 30

PARTIES

See also society

1 I'll tell you what game we'll play. We're done with Humiliate the Host…and we don't want to play Hump the Hostess…We'll play a round of Get the Guests.

Edward Albee (1928–) US playwright. *Who's Afraid of Virginia Woolf?*

2 The sooner every party breaks up the better.

Jane Austen (1775–1817) British novelist. *Emma*, Ch. 25

3 And bring hither the fatted calf, and kill it; and let us eat, and be merry:
For this my son was dead, and is alive again; he was lost, and is found. And they began to be merry.

Bible: Luke 15:23–24

4 ELYOT. Delightful parties Lady Bundle always gives, doesn't she?
AMANDA. Entrancing. Such a dear old lady.
ELYOT. And so gay. Did you notice her at supper blowing all those shrimps through her ear trumpet.

Noël Coward (1899–1973) British dramatist. *Private Lives*

5 I entertained on a cruising trip that was so much fun that I had to sink my yacht to make my guests go home.

F. Scott Fitzgerald (1896–1940) US novelist. *The Crack-Up*, 'Notebooks, K'

6 I was one of the few guests who had actually been invited. People were not invited – they went there.

F. Scott Fitzgerald *The Great Gatsby*, Ch. 3

7 HE. Have you heard it's in the stars
Next July we collide with Mars?
SHE. Well, did you evah! What a swell party this is.

Cole Porter (1893–1964) US songwriter. *High Society* 'Well, Did You Evah!'

8 Certainly, there is nothing else here to enjoy.

George Bernard Shaw (1856–1950) Irish dramatist and critic. Said at a party when his hostess asked him whether he was enjoying himself. *Pass the Port* (Oxfam)

9 'So like one's first parties' said Miss Runcible 'being sick with other people singing.'

Evelyn Waugh (1903–66) British novelist. *Vile Bodies*

10 She had heard someone say something about an Independent Labour Party, and was furious that she had not been asked.

Evelyn Waugh *Vile Bodies*

11 The Life and Soul, the man who will never go home while there is one man, woman or glass of anything not yet drunk.

Katherine Whitehorn (1926–) British journalist. *Sunday Best*, 'Husband-Swapping'

12 He would give them his every imitation from 'Eton and Oxford' to the flushing of the lavatory cistern, and so, perhaps, carry the evening through.

Angus Wilson (1913–91) British novelist. *A Bit Off the Map*

13 This party is a moral crusade, or it is nothing.

Harold Wilson (1916–) British politician and prime minister. Speech, 1962

PARTING

See also departure, greetings, separation

1 Adieu, adieu, kind friends, adieu, adieu, adieu,
I can no longer stay with you, stay with you.
I'll hang my harp on a weeping willow-tree.
And may the world go well with thee.

Anonymous *There is a Tavern in the Town*

2 There is a tavern in the town,
And there my dear love sits him down,
And drinks his wine 'mid laughter free,
And never, never thinks of me.

Fare thee well, for I must leave thee,
Do not let this parting grieve thee,
And remember that the best of friends must part.

Anonymous *There is a Tavern in the Town*

3 Farewell and adieu to you,
Fair Spanish Ladies
Farewell and adieu to you, Ladies of Spain.

Anonymous *Spanish Ladies*

4 Forty years on, when afar and asunder
Parted are those who are singing to-day.

E. E. Bowen (1836–1901) British writer. *Forty Years On* (the Harrow school song)

5 Parting is all we know of heaven,
And all we need of hell.

Emily Dickinson (1830–86) US poet. *My Life Closed Twice Before its Close*

6 Since there's no help, come let us kiss and part –
Nay, I have done, you get no more of me;
And I am glad, yea glad with all my heart
That thus so cleanly I myself can free.

Michael Drayton (1563–1631) English poet. *Sonnets*, 61

7 But tha mun dress thysen, an' go back to thy stately homes of England, how beautiful they stand. Time's up! Time's up for Sir John, an' for little Lady Jane! Put thy shimmy on, Lady Chatterley!

D. H. Lawrence (1885–1930) British novelist. *Lady Chatterley's Lover*, Ch. 15

8 It was not like your great and gracious ways!
Do you, that have nought other to lament,
Never, my Love, repent
Of how, that July afternoon,
You went,
With sudden, unintelligible phrase, – And frightened eye,
Upon your journey of so many days,
Without a single kiss or a good-bye?

Coventry Patmore (1823–96) British poet. *The Unknown Eros*, Bk. I, 'Departure'

9 It is seldom indeed that one parts on good terms, because if one were on good terms one would not part.

Marcel Proust (1871–1922) French novelist. *À La Recherche du temps perdu: La Prisonnière*

10 Good night, good night! Parting is such sweet sorrow
That I shall say good night till it be morrow.

William Shakespeare (1564–1616) English dramatist. *Romeo and Juliet*, II:2

11 Farewell! thou art too dear for my possessing,
And like enough thou know'st thy estimate:
The charter of thy worth gives thee releasing;
My bonds in thee are all determinate.

William Shakespeare *Sonnet 87*

12 Good-by-ee! – good-bye-ee!
Wipe the tear, baby dear, from your eye-ee.
Tho' it's hard to part, I know,
I'll be tickled to death to go.
Don't cry-ee! – don't sigh-ee!
There's a silver lining in the sky-ee! –
Bonsoir, old thing! cheerio! chin-chin!
Nahpoo! Toodle-oo! Good-bye-ee!

R. P. Weston (20th century) British songwriter. *Good-bye-ee!* (with Bert Lee)

PASCAL, BLAISE

(1623–62) French philosopher and mathematician. At the age of 18 he invented the first calculating machine. His works include *Lettres provinciales* (1656), a defence of Jansenist doctrine, and *Pensées sur la religion* (1669).

1 I have made this letter longer than usual, only because I have not had the time to make it shorter.

Lettres provinciales, XVI

2 Not to care for philosophy is to be a true philosopher.

Pensées, I

3 The more intelligence one has the more people one finds original. Commonplace people see no difference between men.

Pensées, I

4 If you want people to think well of you, do not speak well of yourself.

Pensées, I

5 I cannot forgive Descartes; in all his philosophy he did his best to dispense with God. But he could not avoid making Him set the world in motion with a flip of His thumb; after that he had no more use for God.

Pensées, II

6 Had Cleopatra's nose been shorter, the whole face of the world would have changed.

Pensées, II

7 The heart has its reasons which reason knows nothing of.

Pensées, IV

PASSION

See also emotion, love

1 Asthma is a disease that has practically the same symptoms as passion except that with asthma it lasts longer.

Anonymous

2 The man who is master of his passions is Reason's slave.

Cyril Connolly (1903–74) British journalist. *Turnstile One* (ed. V. S. Pritchett)

3 Nothing kills passion faster than an exploding harpoon in the guts.

Ben Elton British comedian. *Stark*

4 A man who has not passed through the inferno of his passions has never overcome them.

Carl Gustav Jung (1875–1961) Swiss psychoanalyst. *Memories, Dreams, Reflections*, Ch. 9

5 For ever warm and still to be enjoy'd,
For ever panting and for ever young;
All breathing human passion far above,
That leaves a heart high-sorrowful and cloy'd,
A burning forehead, and a parching tongue.

John Keats (1795–1821) British poet. *Ode on a Grecian Urn*

6 It is with our passions as it is with fire and water, they are good servants, but bad masters.

Roger L'Estrange (1616–1704) English journalist and writer. *Aesop's Fables*, 38

7 And hence one master-passion in the breast,
Like Aaron's serpent,
swallows up the rest.

Alexander Pope (1688–1744) British poet. *An Essay on Man*, II

8 The ruling passion, be it what it will
The ruling passion conquers reason still.

Alexander Pope *Moral Essays*, III

9 Passion, you see, can be destroyed by a doctor.
It cannot be created.

Peter Shaffer (1926–) British dramatist. *Equus*, II:35

10 Give me that man
That is not passion's slave, and I will wear him
In my heart's core, ay, in my heart of heart,
As I do thee.

William Shakespeare (1564–1616) English dramatist. *Hamlet*, III:2

11 So I triumphed ere my passion, sweeping thro' me, left me dry,
Left me with the palsied heart, and left me with the jaundiced eye.

Alfred, Lord Tennyson (1809–92) British poet. *Locksley Hall*

12 Strange fits of passion have I known:
And I will dare to tell,
But in the lover's ear alone,
What once to me befell.

William Wordsworth (1770–1850) British poet. *Strange Fits of Passion*

PAST

See also experience, future, history, memory, nostalgia, present, regret, time

1 Even God cannot change the past.

Agathon (c. 446–401 BC) Athenian poet and playwright. *Nicomachean Ethics* (Aristotle), VI

2 There is always something rather absurd about the past.

Max Beerbohm (1872–1956) British writer. *1880*

3 A king lived long ago,
In the morning of the world,
When earth was nigher heaven than now.

Robert Browning (1812–89) British poet. *Pippa Passes*, Pt. I

4 There was a house we all had in common and it was called the past.

Angela Carter (1940–92) British novelist. *Wise Children*

5 Study the past, if you would divine the future.

Confucius (K'ung Fu-tzu; 551–479 BC) Chinese philosopher. *Analects*

6 The past is a foreign country: they do things differently there.

L. P. Hartley (1895–1972) British novelist. *The Go-Between*

7 Why doesn't the past decently bury itself, instead of sitting and waiting to be admitted by the present?

D. H. Lawrence (1885–1930) British novelist. *St. Mawr*

8 Yesterday, all my troubles seemed so far away.

John Lennon (1940–80) British rock musician. *Yesterday* (with Paul McCartney)

9 Those who cannot remember the past are condemned to repeat it.

George Santayana (1863–1952) US philosopher. *The Life of Reason*, Vol. I, Ch. 12

10 Look back, and smile at perils past.

Walter Scott (1771–1832) Scottish novelist. *The Bridal of Triermain*, Introduction

11 The past is the only dead thing that smells sweet.

Edward Thomas (1878–1917) British poet. *Early One Morning*

12 Keep off your thoughts from things that are past and done;
For thinking of the past wakes regret and pain.

Arthur Waley (1889–1966) British poet and translator. Translation from the Chinese of Po-Chü-I. *Resignation*

13 The past, at least, is secure.

Daniel Webster (1782–1852) US statesman. Speech, US Senate, 26 Jan 1830

14 Each has his past shut in him like the leaves of a book known to him by heart and his friends can only read the title.

Virginia Woolf (1882–1941) British novelist. *Jacob's Room*

PATIENCE

See also endurance, persistence

1 A watched pot never boils.

Proverb

2 Everything comes to him who waits.

Proverb

3 First things first.

Proverb

4 Patience is a virtue.

Proverb

5 Rome was not built in a day.

Proverb

6 We must learn to walk before we can run.

Proverb

7 Wait and see.

Herbert Henry Asquith (1852–1928) British statesman. In various speeches, 1910

8 PATIENCE, n. A minor form of despair, disguised as a virtue.

Ambrose Bierce (1842–c. 1914) US writer and journalist. *The Devil's Dictionary*

9 The bud may have a bitter taste,
But sweet will be the flower.

William Cowper (1731–1800) British poet. *Olney Hymns*, 35

10 Beware the Fury of a Patient Man.

John Dryden (1631–1700) British poet and dramatist. *Absalom and Achitophel*, I

11 And now before us stands the last problem that must be solved and will be solved. It is the last territorial claim which I have to make in Europe, but it is the claim from which I will not recede and which, God willing, I will make good...With regard to the problem of the Sudeten Germans, my patience is now at an end.

Adolf Hitler (1889–1945) German dictator. Speech, Berlin, 26 Sept 1938

12 Patience and passage of time do more than strength and fury.

Jean de La Fontaine (1621–95) French poet. *Fables*, II, 'Le Lion et le Rat'

13 Very well, I can wait.

Arnold Schoenberg (1874–1951) German composer. Replying to a complaint that his violin concerto would need a musician with six fingers. Attrib.

14 Though patience be a tired mare, yet she will plod.

William Shakespeare (1564–1616) English dramatist. *Henry V*, II:1

15 It is very strange...that the years teach us patience; that the shorter our time, the greater our capacity for waiting.

Elizabeth Taylor (1912–75) British writer. *A Wreath of Roses*, Ch. 10

PATIENTS

1 Every invalid is a physician.

Irish proverb

2 Keep a watch also on the faults of the patients, which often make them lie about the taking of things prescribed.

Hippocrates (c. 460–c. 377 BC) Greek physician. *Decorum*, 14

3 The sick man is a parasite of society. In certain cases it is indecent to go on living. To continue to vegetate in a state of cowardly dependence upon doctors and special treatments, once the meaning of life, the right to life has been lost, ought to be regarded with the greatest contempt by society.

Friedrich Nietzsche (1844–1900) German philosopher. *The Twilight of the Idols*, 'Skirmishes in a War with the Age'

PATRIOTISM

See also homesickness, loyalty, war

1 What pity is it
That we can die but once to serve our country!

Joseph Addison (1672–1719) British essayist. *Cato*, IV:4

2 Speak for England.

Leopold Amery (1873–1955) British statesman. Shouted to Arthur Greenwood, Labour Party spokesman, before he began to speak in a House of Commons debate immediately preceding the declaration of war, 2 Sept 1939

3 I know my own heart to be entirely English.

Queen Anne (1665–1714) Queen of England (1702–14). Drawing a contrast with her predecessor, the Dutch William III. Speech on opening parliament, 1702

4 That this house will in no circumstances fight for its King and country.

Anonymous Motion passed at the Oxford Union, 9 Feb 1933

5 The *Daily Mirror* does not believe that patriotism had to be proved in blood. Especially someone else's blood.

Anonymous Referring to the Falklands War. *Daily Mirror*, Apr 1982

6 Patriotism is seen not only as the last refuge of the scoundrel but as the first bolt-hole of the hypocrite.

Melvyn Bragg (1939–) British author and television presenter. *Speak for England*, Introduction

7 The religion of Hell is patriotism and the government is an enlightened democracy.

James Branch Cabell (1879–1958) US writer. *Jurgen*

8 'My country, right or wrong' is a thing that no patriot would think of saying, except in a desperate case. It is like saying 'My mother, drunk or sober.'

G. K. Chesterton (1874–1936) British writer. *The Defendant*

9 Be England what she will,
With all her faults, she is my country still.

Charles Churchill (1731–64) British poet. *The Farewell*

10 England, with all thy faults, I love thee still,
My country.

William Cowper (1731–1800) British poet. *The Task*

11 The tocsin you hear today is not an alarm but an alert: it sounds the charge against our enemies. To conquer them we must dare, and dare again, and dare for ever; and thus will France be saved

Georges Jacques Danton (1759–94) French political activist. Speech, Paris, 2 Sept 1792

12 Our country! In her intercourse with foreign nations, may she always be in the right; but our country, right or wrong.

Stephen Decatur (1779–1820) US naval officer. Speech, Norfolk, Virginia, Apr 1816

13 Nationalism is an infantile disease. It is the measles of mankind.

Albert Einstein (1879–1955) German-born US physicist. *Einstein: A Study in Simplicity* (Edwin Muller)

14 I have never understood why one's affections must be confined, as once with women, to a single country.

John Kenneth Galbraith (1908–) US economist. *A Life in our Times*

15 Anyone who wants to carry on the war against the outsiders, come with me. I can't offer you either honours or wages; I offer you hunger, thirst, forced marches, battles and death. Anyone who loves his country, follow me.

Giuseppe Garibaldi (1807–82) Italian general and political leader. *Garibaldi* (Guerzoni)

16 That kind of patriotism which consists in hating all other nations.

Elizabeth Gaskell (1810–65) British novelist. *Sylvia's Lovers*, Ch. 1

17 Born and educated in this country I glory in the name of Briton.

George III (1738–1820) King of Great Britain and Ireland. Speech on opening parliament, 18 Nov 1760

18 I only regret that I have but one life to lose for my country.

Nathan Hale (1755–76) US revolutionary hero. Speech before his execution, 22 Sept 1776

19 Unlike so many who find success, she remained a 'dinkum hard-swearing Aussie' to the end.

Arnold Haskell (1903–80) English writer on ballet. Referring to the Australian soprano Dame Nellie Melba. *Waltzing Matilda*

20 *Dulce et decorum est pro patria mori.*
It is a sweet and seemly thing to die for one's country.

Horace (Quintus Horatius Flaccus; 65–8 BC) Roman poet. Odes, III

21 We don't want to fight, but, by jingo if we do,
We've got the ships, we've got the men, we've got the money too.
We've fought the Bear before, and while Britons shall be true,
The Russians shall not have Constantinople.

George William Hunt (c. 1829–1904) British writer. *We Don't Want to Fight*

22 One of the great attractions of patriotism – it fulfils our worst wishes. In the person of our nation we are able, vicariously, to bully and to cheat. Bully and cheat, what's more, with a feeling that we are profoundly virtuous.

Aldous Huxley (1894–1964) British novelist. *Eyeless in Gaza*

23 I have often heretofore ventured my life in defence of this nation; and I shall go as far as any man in preserving it in all its just rights and liberties.

James II (1633–1701) Address to the Privy Council on becoming King (1685).

24 Patriotism is the last refuge of a scoundrel.

Samuel Johnson (1709–84) British lexicographer. *Life of Johnson* (J. Boswell), Vol. II

25 And so, my fellow Americans: ask not what your country can do for you – ask what you can do for your country. My fellow citizens of the world: ask not what America will do for you, but what together we can do for the freedom of man.

John Fitzgerald Kennedy (1917–63) US statesman. Inaugural address, 20 Jan 1961

26 Those who prate about Blimpish patriotism in the mode of Margaret Thatcher are also the ones who will take millions off the caring services of this country.

Neil Kinnock (1942–) British politician. Speech, Labour Party Conference, Brighton, 1983

27 I would die for my country...but I would not let my country die for me.

Neil Kinnock Speech on nuclear disarmament, 1987

28 My principle is: France before everything.

Napoleon I (Napoleon Bonaparte; 1769–1821) French emperor. Letter to Eugène de Beauharnais, 23 Aug 1810

29 Patriotism is often an arbitrary veneration of real estate above principles.

G. J. Nathan (1882–1958) US drama critic. *Testament of a Critic*

30 'Take my drum to England, hang et by the shore,
Strike et when your powder's runnin' low;
If the Dons sight Devon, I'll quit the port o' Heaven,
An' drum them up the Channel as we drummed them long ago.'

Henry John Newbolt (1862–1938) British poet. *Drake's Drum*

31 But cared greatly to serve God and the King,
And keep the Nelson touch.

Henry John Newbolt *Minora Sidera*

32 The old Lie: *Dulce et decorum est*
Pro patria mori.

Wilfred Owen (1893–1918) British poet. *See also* HORACE. *Dulce et decorum est*

33 If I were an American, as I am an Englishman, while a foreign troop was landed in my country, I never would lay down my arms, – never – never – never!

William Pitt the Elder (1708–78) British statesman. Speech, House of Lords, 18 Nov 1777

34 There is no room in this country for hyphenated Americanism.

Theodore Roosevelt (1858–1919) US Republican president. Speech, New York, 12 Oct 1915

35 There can be no fifty-fifty Americanism in this country. There is room here for only one hundred per cent Americanism.

Theodore Roosevelt Speech, Saratoga, 19 July 1918

36 Patriots always talk of dying for their country and never of killing for their country.

Bertrand Russell (1872–1970) British philosopher. *The Autobiography of Bertrand Russell*

37 We few, we happy few, we band of brothers;
For he to-day that sheds his blood with me
Shall be my brother; be he ne'er so vile
This day shall gentle his condition:
And gentlemen in England, now a-bed
Shall think themselves accurs'd they were not here,
And hold their manhoods cheap whiles any speaks
That fought with us upon Saint Crispin's day.

William Shakespeare (1564–1616) English dramatist. *Henry V*, IV:3

38 Not that I lov'd Caesar less, but that I lov'd Rome more.

William Shakespeare *Julius Caesar*, III:2

39 You'll never have a quiet world till you knock the patriotism out of the human race.

George Bernard Shaw (1856–1950) Irish dramatist and critic. *O'Flaherty V.C.*

40 True patriotism is of no party.

Tobias Smollett (1721–71) British novelist. *The Adventures of Sir Launcelote Greaves*

41 I vow to thee, my country – all earthly things above –
Entire and whole and perfect, the service of my love.

Cecil Arthur Spring-Rice (1859–1918) British diplomat. *I Vow to Thee, My Country*

42 Patriotism to the Soviet State is a revolutionary duty, whereas patriotism to a bourgeois State is treachery.

Leon Trotsky (Lev Davidovich Bronstein; 1879–1940) Russian revolutionary. *Disputed Barricade* (Fitzroy Maclean)

43 I was born an American; I will live an American; I shall die an American.

Daniel Webster (1782–1852) US statesman. Speech, US Senate, 17 July 1850

44 'Shoot, if you must, this old gray head,

But spare your country's flag,' she said.

A shade of sadness, a blush of shame,
Over the face of the leader came.

John Greenleaf Whittier (1807–92) US poet. *Barbara Frietchie*

45 There is one certain means by which I can be sure never to see my country's ruin; I will die in the last ditch.

William III (1650–1702) King of England. *History of England* (Hume)

PATRONAGE

See also promotion

1 *Patron.* Commonly a wretch who supports with insolence, and is paid with flattery.

Samuel Johnson (1709–84) British lexicographer. *Dictionary of the English Language*

2 Is not a Patron, my Lord, one who looks with unconcern on a man struggling for life in the water, and, when he has reached ground, encumbers him with help? The notice which you have been pleased to take of my labours, had it been early, had been kind; but it has been delayed till I am indifferent, and cannot enjoy it; till I am solitary, and cannot impart it; till I am known, and do not want it.

Samuel Johnson Letter to Lord Chesterfield, 7 Feb 1755. *Life of Johnson* (J. Boswell), Vol. I

PEACE

See also war and peace

1 'Here you are – don't lose it again.'

Anonymous Caption to cartoon showing a wounded soldier handing over 'victory and peace in Europe'. *Daily Mirror*, 8 May 1945

2 The wolf also shall dwell with the lamb, and the leopard shall lie down with the kid; and the calf and the young lion and the fatling together: and a little child shall lead them.
And the cow and the bear shall feed; their young ones shall lie down together: and the lion shall eat straw like the ox.
And the sucking child shall play on the hole of the asp, and the weaned child shall put his hand on the cockatrice' den.
They shall not hurt nor destroy in all my holy mountain: for the earth shall be full of the knowledge of the Lord, as the waters cover the sea.

Bible: Isaiah 11:6–9

3 There is no peace, saith the Lord, unto the wicked.

Bible: Isaiah 48:22

4 Peace I leave with you, my peace I give unto you: not as the world giveth, give I unto you. Let not your heart be troubled, neither let it be afraid.

Bible: John 14:27

5 PEACE, n. In international affairs, a period of cheating between two periods of fighting.

Ambrose Bierce (1842–c. 1914) US writer and journalist. *The Devil's Dictionary*

6 Give peace in our time, O Lord.

The Book of Common Prayer *Morning Prayer*, Versicles

7 Don't tell me peace has broken out.

Bertolt Brecht (1898–1956) German dramatist. *Mother Courage*, VIII

8 I believe it is peace for our time...peace with honour.

Neville Chamberlain (1869–1940) British statesman. Broadcast after Munich Agreement, 1 Oct 1938

9 Anythin' for a quiet life, as the man said wen he took the sitivation at the lighthouse.

Charles Dickens (1812–70) British novelist. *Pickwick Papers*, Ch. 43

10 Lord Salisbury and myself have brought you back peace – but a peace I hope with honour.

Benjamin Disraeli (1804–81) British statesman. Speech, House of Commons, 16 July 1878

11 Let us have peace.

Ulysses Simpson Grant (1822–85) US general. On accepting nomination. Letter, 29 May 1868

12 Arms alone are not enough to keep the peace – it must be kept by men.

John Fitzgerald Kennedy (1917–63) US statesman. *The Observer*, 'Sayings of the Decade', 1962

13 And who will bring white peace
That he may sleep upon his hill again?

Vachel Lindsay (1879–1931) US poet. *Abraham Lincoln Walks at Midnight*

14 Peace is indivisible.

Maxim Litvinov (1876–1951) Russian statesman. Speech to the League of Nations, 1 July 1936

15 I would make great sacrifices to preserve peace....But if a situation were to be forced upon us, in which peace could only be preserved by the surrender of the great and beneficent position Britain has won by centuries of heroism and achievement...I say emphatically that peace at that price would be a humiliation intolerable for a great country like ours to endure.

David Lloyd George (1863–1945) British Liberal statesman. *British Documents* (Gooch and Temperley), Vol. VII

16 The issues are the same. We wanted peace on earth, love, and understanding between everyone around the world. We have learned that change comes slowly.

Paul McCartney (1943–) British rock musician. *The Observer*, 'Sayings of the Week', 7 June 1987

17 Roll up that map: it will not be wanted these ten years.

William Pitt the Younger (1759–1806) British statesman. On learning that Napoleon had won the Battle of Austerlitz. Attrib.

18 Nation shall speak peace unto nation.

Montague John Rendall (1862–1950) British schoolmaster. Motto of BBC, 1927

19 When peace has been broken anywhere, the peace of all countries everywhere is in danger.

Franklin D. Roosevelt (1882–1945) US Democratic president. Radio broadcast, 3 Sept 1939

20 Here, where the world is quiet;
Here, where all trouble seems
Dead winds' and spent waves' riot
In doubtful dreams of dreams.

Algernon Charles Swinburne (1837–1909) British poet. *The Garden of Proserpine*

21 We are the true peace movement.
Margaret Thatcher (1925–) British politician and prime minister. *The Times*, 1983

22 And I shall have some peace there, for peace comes dropping slow,
Dropping from the veils of the morning to where the cricket sings.
W. B. Yeats (1865–1939) Irish poet. *The Lake Isle of Innisfree*

PEACOCK, THOMAS LOVE

(1785–1866) British novelist. His satirical novels include *Nightmare Abbey* (1818) and *Gryll Grange* (1860).

1 Respectable means rich, and decent means poor. I should die if I heard my family called decent.
Crotchet Castle, Ch. 3

2 Ancient sculpture is the true school of modesty. But where the Greeks had modesty, we have cant; where they had poetry, we have cant; where they had patriotism, we have cant; where they had anything that exalts, delights, or adorns humanity, we have nothing but cant, cant, cant.
Crotchet Castle, Ch. 7

3 A book that furnishes no quotations is, *me judice*, no book – it is a plaything.
Crotchet Castle, Ch. 9

4 Nothing can be more obvious than that all animals were created solely and exclusively for the use of man.
Headlong Hall, Ch. 2

5 Marriage may often be a stormy lake, but celibacy is almost always a muddy horse-pond.
Melincourt

6 There are two reasons for drinking; one is, when you are thirsty, to cure it; the other, when you are not thirsty, to prevent it...Prevention is better than cure.
Melincourt

7 The mountain sheep are sweeter,
But the valley sheep are fatter;
We therefore deemed it meeter
To carry off the latter.
The Misfortunes of Elphin, Ch. 11, 'The War-Song of Dinas Vawr'

8 He was sent, as usual, to a public school, where a little learning was painfully beaten into him, and from thence to the university, where it was carefully taken out of him.
Nightmare Abbey, Ch. 1

9 Laughter is pleasant, but the exertion is too much for me.
Said by the Hon. Mr Listless. *Nightmare Abbey*, Ch. 5

10 Sir, I have quarrelled with my wife; and a man who has quarrelled with his wife is absolved from all duty to his country.
Nightmare Abbey, Ch. 11

PEPYS, SAMUEL

(1633–1703) English diarist. His *Diary* (1660–1669) includes detailed descriptions of the Plague and the Fire of London.

Quotations about Pepys

1 A vain, silly, transparent coxcomb without either solid talents or a solid nature.
J.G. Lockhart (1794–1854) Scottish biographer and critic.

2 Matter-of-fact, like the screech of a sash window being thrown open, begins one of the greatest texts in our history and our literature.
Richard Ollard *Pepys*

3 Obliged to give up writing today – read Pepys instead.
Walter Scott (1771–1832) Scottish novelist. Journal, 5 Jan 1826

4 He had a kind of idealism in pleasure; like the princess in the fairy story, he was conscious of a rose-leaf out of place.
Robert Louis Stevenson (1850–94) Scottish writer. *Samuel Pepys*

Quotations by Pepys

5 And so to bed.
Diary, 20 Apr 1660

6 I went out to Charing Cross, to see Major-general Harrison hanged, drawn, and quartered; which was done there, he looking as cheerful as any man could do in that condition.
Diary, 13 Oct 1660

7 But Lord! to see the absurd nature of Englishmen, that cannot forbear laughing and jeering at everything that looks strange.
Diary, 27 Nov 1662

8 My wife, who, poor wretch, is troubled with her lonely life.
Diary, 19 Dec 1662

9 Went to hear Mrs Turner's daughter...play on the harpsichon; but, Lord! it was enough to make any man sick to hear her; yet was I forced to commend her highly.
Diary, 1 May 1663

10 Most of their discourse was about hunting, in a dialect I understand very little.
Diary, 22 Nov 1663

11 Pretty witty Nell.
Referring to Charles II's mistress Nell Gwynne. *Diary*, 3 Apr 1665

12 Thence I walked to the Tower; but Lord! how empty the streets are and how melancholy, so many poor sick people in the streets full of sores...in Westminster, there is never a physician and but one apothecary left, all being dead.
Written during the Great Plague – the last major outbreak of bubonic plague in England, and the worse since the Black Death of 1348. Diary, 16 Sept 1665

13 Strange to say what delight we married people have to see these poor fools decoyed into our condition.
Diary, 25 Dec 1665

14 Music and women I cannot but give way to, whatever my business is.
Diary, 9 Mar 1666

15 To church; and with my mourning, very handsome, and new periwig, make a great show.
Diary, 31 Mar 1667

16 My wife hath something in her gizzard, that only waits an opportunity of being provoked to bring up.
Diary, 17 June 1668

17 And so I betake myself to that course, which is almost as much as to see myself go into my grave – for which, and all the discomforts that will accompany my being blind, the good God prepare me!
The closing words of Pepys's *Diary*; he lived another 34 years and did not go blind. *Diary*, 31 May 1669

PERCEPTION

1 If the doors of perception were cleansed everything would appear to man as it is, infinite.
William Blake (1757–1827) British poet. *The Marriage of Heaven and Hell*, 'A Memorable Fancy'

2 Man's Desires are limited by his Perceptions; none can desire what he has not perceived.
William Blake *There is no Natural Religion*

3 'What,' it will be questioned, 'when the sun rises, do you not see a round disc of fire somewhat like a guinea?' 'O no, no, I see an innumerable company of the heavenly host crying, 'Holy, Holy, Holy is the Lord God Almighty!''
William Blake *Descriptive Catalogue*, 'The Vision of Judgment'

4 I saw it, but I did not realize it.
Elizabeth Peabody (1804–94) US educationalist. Giving a Transcendentalist explanation for her accidentally walking into a tree. *The Peabody Sisters of Salem* (L. Tharp)

PERFECTION

See also imperfection

1 The pursuit of perfection, then, is the pursuit of sweetness and light...He who works for sweetness and light united, works to make reason and the will of God prevail.
Matthew Arnold (1822–88) British poet and critic. *Culture and Anarchy*, Ch. 1

2 Be ye therefore perfect, even as your Father which is in heaven is perfect.
Bible: Matthew 5:48

3 The year's at the spring,
And day's at the morn;
Morning's at seven;
The hill-side's dew-pearled;
The lark's on the wing;
The snail's on the thorn;
God's in His heaven –
All's right with the world.
Robert Browning (1812–89) British poet. *Pippa Passes*, Pt. I

4 What's come to perfection perishes.
Things learned on earth, we shall practise in heaven.
Works done least rapidly, Art most cherishes.
Robert Browning *Old Pictures in Florence*, XVII

5 You would attain to the divine perfection,
And yet not turn your back upon the world.
Henry Wadsworth Longfellow (1807–82) US poet. *Michael Angelo*

6 Perfection has one grave defect; it is apt to be dull.
W. Somerset Maugham (1874–1965) British novelist. *The Summing Up*

7 The essence of being human is that one does not seek perfection.
George Orwell (1903–50) British novelist. *Shooting an Elephant*, 'Reflections on Gandhi'

8 Whoever thinks a faultless piece to see,
Thinks what ne'er was, nor is, nor e'er shall be.
Alexander Pope (1688–1744) British poet. *An Essay on Criticism*

9 Oysters are more beautiful than any religion... There's nothing in Christianity or Buddhism that quite matches the sympathetic unselfishness of an oyster.
Saki (Hector Hugh Munro; 1870–1916) British writer. *The Match-Maker*

10 Everything's Coming Up Roses.
Stephen Sondheim (1930–) US composer and lyricist. Song title

11 Finality is death. Perfection is finality. Nothing is perfect. There are lumps in it.
James Stephens (1882–1950) Irish novelist. *The Crock of Gold*

PERSISTENCE

See also determination, endurance, patience

1 If the mountain will not come to Mahomet, Mahomet must go to the mountain.
Proverb

2 Never say die.
Proverb

3 Slow but sure wins the race.
Proverb

4 And ye shall be hated of all men for my name's sake: but he that endureth to the end shall be saved.
Bible: Matthew 10:22

5 If at first you don't succeed,
Try, try again.
William Edward Hickson (1803–70) British educationalist. *Try and Try Again*

6 A man may write at any time, if he will set himself doggedly to it.
Samuel Johnson (1709–84) British lexicographer. *Life of Johnson* (J. Boswell), Vol. I

7 The drop of rain maketh a hole in the stone, not by violence, but by oft falling.
Hugh Latimer (1485–1555) English churchman. *See also* LUCRETIUS; OVID. Sermon preached before Edward VI

8 Keep Right on to the End of the Road.

Harry Lauder (Hugh MacLennon; 1870–1950) Scottish music-hall artist. Song title

9 You persisted for a certain number of years like a stammer. You were a *stammer*, if you like, of Space-Time.

Wyndham Lewis (1882–1957) British novelist. *The Human Age*, 'The Childermass'

10 Constant dripping hollows out a stone.

Lucretius (Titus Lucretius Carus; c. 99–55 BC) Roman philosopher. *On the Nature of the Universe*, I. *See also* LATIMER; OVID

11 Dripping water hollows out a stone, a ring is worn away by use.

Ovid (Publius Ovidius Naso; 43 BC–17 AD) Roman poet. *See also* LATIMER; LUCRETIUS. *Epistulae Ex Ponto*, Bk. IV

12 I am a kind of burr; I shall stick.

William Shakespeare (1564–1616) English dramatist. *Measure for Measure*, IV:3

PERSPECTIVE

See also objectivity

1 'Tis distance lends enchantment to the view,
And robes the mountain in its azure hue.

Thomas Campbell (1777–1844) British poet. *Pleasures of Hope*, I

2 One sees great things from the valley; only small things from the peak.

G. K. Chesterton (1874–1936) British writer. *The Hammer of God*

3 Fleas know not whether they are upon the body of a giant or upon one of ordinary size.

Walter Savage Landor (1775–1864) British poet and writer. *Imaginary Conversations*, 'Southey and Porson'

4 Everything must be taken seriously, nothing tragically.

Louis Adolphe Thiers (1797–1877) French statesman and historian. Speech, French National Assembly, 24 May 1873

PERSUASION

1 They will conquer, but they will not convince.

Miguel de Unamuno y Jugo (1864–1936) Spanish writer. Referring to the Franco rebels. Attrib.

2 There is a holy, mistaken zeal in politics, as well as religion. By persuading others we convince ourselves.

Junius An unidentified writer of letters (1769–72) to the *London Public Advertiser*. Letter, 19 Dec 1769

3 For a priest to turn a man when he lies a-dying, is just like one that has a long time solicited a woman, and cannot obtain his end; at length makes her drunk, and so lies with her.

John Selden (1584–1654) English historian. *Table Talk*

4 The President spends most of his time kissing people on the cheek in order to get them to do what they ought to do without getting kissed.

Harry S. Truman (1884–1972) US statesman. *The Observer*, 'Sayings of the Week', 6 Feb 1949

PERVERSITY

See also petulance, stubbornness

1 If it's heaven for climate, it's hell for company.

J. M. Barrie (1860–1937) British novelist and dramatist. *The Little Minister*, Ch. 3

2 Never the time and the place
And the loved one all together!

Robert Browning (1812–89) British poet. *Never the Time and the Place*

3 For 'tis a truth well known to most,
That whatsoever thing is lost –
We seek it, ere it come to light,
In every cranny but the right.

William Cowper (1731–1800) British poet. *The Retired Cat*

4 Let's find out what everyone is doing,
And then stop everyone from doing it.

A. P. Herbert (1890–1971) British writer and politician. *Let's Stop Somebody*

5 I had never had a piece of toast
Particularly long and wide,
But fell upon the sanded floor,
And always on the buttered side.

James Payn (1830–98) British writer and editor. *Chambers's Journal*, 2 Feb 1884

6 Adam was but human – this explains it all. He did not want the apple for the apple's sake, he wanted it only because it was forbidden.

Mark Twain (Samuel Langhorne Clemens; 1835–1910) US writer. *Pudd'nhead Wilson's Calendar*, Ch. 2

PESSIMISM

1 Pessimism, when you get used to it, is just as agreeable as optimism.

Arnold Bennett (1867–1931) British novelist. *Things that have Interested Me*, 'The Slump in Pessimism'

2 Scratch a pessimist, and you find often a defender of privilege.

Lord Beveridge (1879–1963) British economist. *The Observer*, 'Sayings of the Week', 17 Dec 1943

3 The optimist proclaims we live in the best of all possible worlds; and the pessimist fears this is true.

James Cabell (1879–1958) US novelist and journalist. *The Silver Stallion*

4 He who despairs over an event is a coward, but he who holds hopes for the human condition is a fool.

Albert Camus (1913–60) French existentialist writer. *The Rebel*

5 A Hard Rain's A-Gonna Fall.

Bob Dylan (Robert Allen Zimmerman; 1941–) US popular singer. Song title

6 Sleep is good, death is better; but of course, the best thing would be never to have been born at all.

Heinrich Heine (1797–1856) German poet and writer. *Morphine*

7 Nothing to do but work,
Nothing to eat but food,
Nothing to wear but clothes,
To keep one from going nude.

Benjamin Franklin King (1857–94) US humorist. *The Pessimist*

8 If we see light at the end of the tunnel it is the light of an oncoming train.

Robert Lowell (1917–77) US poet. *Day by Day*

9 How many pessimists end up by desiring the things they fear, in order to prove that they are right.

Robert Mallet (1915–) French writer. *Apostilles*

10 A pessimist is a man who looks both ways before crossing a one-way street.

Laurence J. Peter (1919–90) Canadian writer. *Peter's Quotations*

11 It is not, nor it cannot come to good.

William Shakespeare (1564–1616) English dramatist. *Hamlet*, I:2

PETULANCE

See also perversity, stubbornness

1 She refused to begin the 'Beguine'
Tho' they besought her to
And with language profane and obscene
She curs'd the man who taught her to
She curs'd Cole Porter too!

Noël Coward (1899–1973) British dramatist. *Sigh No More*, 'Nina'

2 He has to learn that petulance is not sarcasm, and that insolence is not invective.

Benjamin Disraeli (1804–81) British statesman. Said of Sir C. Wood. Speech, House of Commons, 16 Dec 1852

3 I am the emperor, and I want dumplings.

Ferdinand I (1793–1875) Emperor of Austria. *The Fall of the House of Habsburg* (E. Crankshaw)

4 I hate a fellow whom pride, or cowardice, or laziness drives into a corner, and who does nothing when he is there but sit and *growl*; let him come out as I do, and *bark*.

Samuel Johnson (1709–84) British lexicographer. *Life of Johnson* (J. Boswell), Vol. IV

PHILISTINISM

See also arts, books, culture

1 For this class we have a designation which now has become pretty well known, and which we may as well still keep for them, the designation of Philistines.

Matthew Arnold (1822–88) British poet and critic. Referring to the middle class. *Culture and Anarchy*, Ch. 3

2 The great apostle of the Philistines, Lord Macaulay.

Matthew Arnold *Joubert*

3 The finest collection of frames I ever saw.

Humphry Davy (1778–1829) British chemist. When asked what he thought of the Paris art galleries. Attrib.

4 When I hear anyone talk of Culture, I reach for my revolver.

Hermann Goering (1893–1946) German leader. Attrib. to Goering but probably said by Hanns Johst

5 I've never been in there…but there are only three things to see, and I've seen colour reproductions of all of them.

Harold W. Ross (1892–1951) US journalist. Referring to the Louvre. *A Farewell to Arms* (Ernest Hemingway)

6 All my wife has ever taken from the Mediterranean – from that whole vast intuitive culture – are four bottles of Chianti to make into lamps, and two china condiment donkeys labelled Sally and Peppy.

Peter Shaffer (1926–) British dramatist. *Equus*, I:18

7 Particularly against books the Home Secretary is. If we can't stamp out literature in the country, we can at least stop it being brought in from outside.

Evelyn Waugh (1903–66) British novelist. *Vile Bodies*, Ch. 2

8 Listen! There never was an artistic period. There never was an Art-loving nation.

James Whistler (1834–1903) US painter. Attrib.

PHILOSOPHERS

See also philosophy

1 All are lunatics, but he who can analyze his delusion is called a philosopher.

Ambrose Bierce (1842–c. 1914) US writer and journalist. *Epigrams*

2 There is nothing so absurd but some philosopher has said it.

Cicero (106–43 BC) Roman orator and statesman. *De Divinatione*, II

3 To a philosopher no circumstance, however trifling, is too minute.

Oliver Goldsmith (1728–74) Irish-born British writer. *The Citizen of the World*

4 Philosophers never balance between profit and honesty, because their decisions are general, and neither their passions nor imaginations are interested in the objects.

David Hume (1711–76) Scottish philosopher. *A Treatise of Human Nature*

5 I doubt if the philosopher lives, or ever has lived, who could know himself to be heartily despised by a street boy without some irritation.

T. H. Huxley (1825–95) British biologist. *Evolution and Ethics*

6 The philosophers have only interpreted the world in various ways; the point is to change it.

Karl Marx (1818–1883) German philosopher and revolutionary. *Theses on Feuerbach*

7 In the philosopher there is nothing whatever impersonal; and, above all, his morality bears decided and decisive testimony to *who he is* – that is to say, to the order of rank in which the innermost drives of his nature stand in relation to one another.

Friedrich Nietzsche (1844–1900) German philosopher. *Jenseits von Gut und Böse*

8 Not to care for philosophy is to be a true philosopher.

Blaise Pascal (1623–62) French philosopher and mathematician. *Pensées*, I

9 Nowadays there are no serious philosophers who are not looking forward to the pension to which their involvement with the subject entitles them.

Anthony Quinton (1925–) British philosopher. *Thoughts and Thinkers*

10 Three passions, simple but overwhelmingly strong, have governed my life: the longing for love, the search for knowledge, and unbearable pity for the suffering of mankind.

Bertrand Russell (1872–1970) British philosopher. *The Autobiography of Bertrand Russell*, Prologue

11 Philosophers are as jealous as women. Each wants a monopoly of praise.

George Santayana (1863–1952) US philosopher. *Dialogues In Limbo*

12 For there was never yet philosopher
That could endure the toothache patiently.

William Shakespeare (1564–1616) English dramatist. *Much Ado About Nothing*, V:1

13 The philosopher is Nature's pilot. And there you have our difference; to be in hell is to drift; to be in heaven is to steer.

George Bernard Shaw (1856–1950) Irish dramatist and critic. *Man and Superman*

14 There are now-a-days professors of philosophy but not philosophers.

Henry David Thoreau (1817–62) US writer. *Walden*, 'Economy'

15 A philosopher of imposing stature doesn't think in a vacuum. Even his most abstract ideas are, to some extent, conditioned by what is or what is not known in the time when he lives.

A. N. Whitehead (1861–1947) British philosopher. *Dialogues*

PHILOSOPHY

See also logic, metaphysics, philosophers, thinking

1 The principles of logic and metaphysics are true simply because we never allow them to be anything else.

A. J. Ayer (1910–89) British philosopher. *Language, Truth and Logic*

2 The formula 'Two and two make five' is not without its attractions.

Fedor Mikhailovich Dostoevsky (1821–81) Russian novelist. *Notes from the Underground*

3 If we take in our hand any volume; of divinity or school metaphysics, for instance; let us ask, *Does it contain any abstract reasoning concerning quantity or number?* No. *Does it contain any experimental reasoning, concerning matter of fact and existence?* No. Commit it then to the flames: for it can contain nothing but sophistry and illusion.

David Hume (1711–76) Scottish philosopher. *An Enquiry Concerning Human Understanding*

4 We are perpetually moralists, but we are geometricians only by chance. Our intercourse with intellectual nature is necessary; our speculations upon matter are voluntary, and at leisure.

Samuel Johnson (1709–84) British lexicographer. *Lives of the English Poets*, 'Milton'

5 I refute it *thus*.

Samuel Johnson Replying to Boswell's contention that they were unable to refute Bishop Berkeley's theory of matter, by kicking a large stone with his foot. *Life of Johnson* (J. Boswell), Vol. I

6 There are innumerable questions to which the inquisitive mind can in this state receive no answer: Why do you and I exist? Why was this world created? Since it was to be created, why was it not created sooner?

Samuel Johnson *Life of Johnson* (J. Boswell), Vol. III

7 Do not all charms fly
At the mere touch of cold philosophy?

John Keats (1795–1821) British poet. *Lamia*, II

8 Axioms in philosophy are not axioms until they are proved upon our pulses; we read fine things but never feel them to the full until we have gone the same steps as the author.

John Keats Letter to J. H. Reynolds, 3 May 1818

9 The Power of Positive Thinking.

Norman Vincent Peale (1899–93) US clergyman and writer. Book title

10 Zen and the Art of Motorcycle Maintenance.

Robert M. Pirsig (1929–) US writer. Book title

11 There will be no end to the troubles of states, or indeed, my dear Glaucon, of humanity itself, till philosophers become kings in this world, or till those we now call kings and rulers really and truly become philosophers.

Plato (429–347 BC) Greek philosopher. *Republic*, Bk. 5

12 We thought philosophy ought to be patient and unravel people's mental blocks. Trouble with doing that is, once you've unravelled them, their heads fall off.

Frederic Raphael (1931–) British author. *The Glittering Prizes: A Double Life*, III:2

13 Matter...a convenient formula for describing what happens where it isn't.

Bertrand Russell (1872–1970) British philosopher. *An Outline of Philosophy*

14 To teach how to live without certainty and yet without being paralysed by hesitation is perhaps the chief thing that philosophy, in our age, can do for those who study it.

Bertrand Russell *The History of Western Philosophy*

15 The point of philosophy is to start with something so simple as to seem not worth stating, and to end with something so paradoxical that no one will believe it.

Bertrand Russell *Logic and Knowledge*

16 Science is what you know, philosophy is what you don't know.

Bertrand Russell

17 Philosophy is the replacement of category-habits by category-disciplines.

Gilbert Ryle (1900–76) British philosopher. *The Concept of Mind*, Introduction

18 It is a great advantage for a system of philosophy to be substantially true.

George Santayana (1863–1952) US philosopher. *The Unknowable*

19 Because he is the highest vertebrate he can do what no other vertebrate can do: when, out of whatever desire and knowledge may be his, he makes a choice, he can say 'I will.'... And knowing how and why he says 'I will', he comes to his own as a philosopher.

Homer W. Smith (1895–1962) *From Fish to Philosopher*, Ch. 13

20 Philosophy is the product of wonder.

A. N. Whitehead (1861–1947) British philosopher. *Nature and Life*, Ch. 1

21 The safest general characterization of the European philosophical tradition is that it consists of a series of footnotes to Plato.

A. N. Whitehead *Process and Reality*

22 The history of Western philosophy is, after all, no more than a series of footnotes to Plato's philosophy.

A. N. Whitehead (1861–1947) British philosopher. Attrib.

23 My advice to you is not to inquire why or whither, but just enjoy your ice-cream while it's on your plate, – that's my philosophy.

Thornton Wilder (1897–1975) US novelist and dramatist. *The Skin of Our Teeth*, I

24 Philosophy, as we use the word, is a fight against the fascination which forms of expression exert upon us.

Ludwig Wittgenstein (1889–1951) Austrian philosopher. *The Blue Book*

25 Philosophy is not a theory but an activity.

Ludwig Wittgenstein *Tractatus Logico-Philosophicus*, Ch. 4

PHOTOGRAPHY

1 Photography can never grow up if it imitates some other medium. It has to walk alone; it has to be itself.

Berenice Abbott (1898–1991) US photographer. *Infinity*, 'It Has to Walk Alone'

2 Most things in life are moments of pleasure and a lifetime of embarrassment; photography is a moment of embarrassment and a lifetime of pleasure.

Tony Benn (1925–) British politician. *The Sunday Times*, 31 Dec 1989

3 In a portrait, I'm looking for the silence in somebody.

Henri Cartier-Bresson (1908–) French photographer. *The Observer*, 'Sayings of the Week', 15 May 1994

4 The camera cannot lie. But it can be an accessory to untruth.

Harold Evans (1928–) British journalist. *Pictures on a Page*

5 As far as I knew, he had never taken a photograph before, and the summit of Everest was hardly the place to show him how.

Edmund Hillary (1919–) New Zealand mountaineer. Referring to the Napalese mountaineer Tenzing Norgay, his companion on the conquest of Mt Everest (1953). *High Adventure*

6 The modern pantheist not only sees the god in everything, he takes photographs of it.

D. H. Lawrence (1885–1930) British novelist. *St Mawr*

7 I have for instance among my purchases... several original Mona Lisas and all painted (according to the Signature) by the great artist Kodak.

Spike Milligan (1918–) British comic actor and author. *A Dustbin of Milligan*, 'Letters to Harry Secombe'

8 A photograph is not only an image (as a painting is an image), an interpretation of the real; it is also a trace, something directly stencilled off the real, like a footprint or a death mask.

Susan Sontag (1933–) US novelist and essayist. *On Photography*

PICASSO, PABLO

(1881–1973) Spanish painter, sculptor, and stage designer. An exceptionally versatile artist, his work was influenced by cubism, surrealism, African sculpture, and classicism.

Quotations about Picasso

1 A Catalan wizard who fools with shapes.

Bernhard Berenson (1865–1959) US art critic and writer. *Berenson: A Biography* (Sylvia Sprigge)

2 His sickness has created atrocities that are repellent. Every one of his paintings deforms man, his body and his face.

V. Kemenov Soviet art critic.

3 Nothing unites the English like war. Nothing divides them like Picasso.

Hugh Mills (1913–71) British screenwriter. *Prudence and The Pill*

4 If my husband would ever meet a woman on the street who looked like the women in his paintings he would fall over in a dead faint.

Mme Picasso

Quotations by Picasso

5 There's no such thing as a bad Picasso, but some are less good than others.

Come to Judgment (A. Whitman)

6 Painting is a blind man's profession. He paints not what he sees, but what he feels, what he tells himself about what he has seen.

Journals (Jean Cocteau), 'Childhood'

7 God is really only another artist. He invented the giraffe, the elephant, and the cat. He has no real style, He just goes on trying other things.

Life with Picasso (Françoise Gilot and Carlton Lake), Ch. 1

8 I hate that aesthetic game of the eye and the mind, played by these connoisseurs, these mandarins who 'appreciate' beauty. What *is* beauty, anyway? There's no such thing. I never 'appreciate', any more than I 'like'. I love or I hate.

Life with Picasso (Françoise Gilot and Carlton Lake), Ch. 2

9 Age only matters when one is ageing. Now that I have arrived at a great age, I might just as well be twenty.

The Observer, Shouts and Murmurs, 'Picasso in Private' (John Richardson)

10 When I was their age, I could draw like Raphael, but it took me a lifetime to learn to draw like them.

Visiting an exhibition of drawings by children. *Picasso: His Life and Work* (Ronald Penrose)

11 The earth doesn't have a cleaning woman to dust it off.
Interview, 20 Oct 1943

12 My joining the Communist Party is the logical outcome of my whole life and of the whole body of my work.
New Masses

13 It's better like that, if you want to kill a picture all you have to do is to hang it beautifully on a nail and soon you will see nothing of it but the frame. When it's out of place you see it better.
Explaining why a Renoir in his apartment was hung crookedly. *Picasso: His Life and Work* (Ronald Penrose)

PINTER, HAROLD

(1930–) British dramatist. His well-known plays include *The Birthday Party* (1958), *The Caretaker* (1960), *Family Voices* (1981), and *Party Time* (1992). He has also written film scripts and directed plays.

1 If only I could get down to Sidcup! I've been waiting for the weather to break. He's got my papers, this man I left them with, it's got it all down there, I could prove everything.
The Caretaker, I

2 Them bastards at the monastery let me down again.
the Caretaker, I

3 In other words, apart from the known and the unknown, what else is there?
The Homecoming, II

4 The earth's about five thousand million years old. Who can afford to live in the past?
The Homecoming

5 The weasel under the cocktail cabinet.
Reply when asked what his plays were about. *Anger and After* (J. Russell Taylor)

6 I'm not a theorist. I'm not an authoritative or reliable commentator on the dramatic scene, the social scene, any scene. I write plays, when I can manage it, and that's all.
Speech to the National Student Drama Festival, Bristol, 1962

7 There are two silences. One where no word is spoken. The other where perhaps a torrent of language is being employed.
Speech addressed to the National Student Drama Festival, Bristol, 1962

PITT THE ELDER

(William Pitt, 1st Earl of Chatham; 1708–78) British statesman. An outstanding orator, he entered parliament in 1735, becoming paymaster general (1746–55) and secretary of state in 1756. He was in charge of foreign affairs during the Seven Years' War. Pitt resigned in 1761, returning to form a new ministry (1766–68) as Earl of Chatham.

1 The poorest man may in his cottage bid defiance to all the forces of the Crown. It may be frail – its roof may shake – the wind may blow through it – the storm may enter – the rain may enter – but the King of England cannot enter! – all his force dares not cross the threshold of the ruined tenement!
Statesmen in the Time of George III (Lord Brougham), Vol. I

2 The atrocious crime of being a young man…I shall neither attempt to palliate nor deny.
Speech, House of Commons, 2 Mar 1741

3 Unlimited power is apt to corrupt the minds of those who possess it.
See also Lord ACTON. Speech, House of Lords, 9 Jan 1770

4 Where laws end, tyranny begins.
Speech, House of Lords, referring to the Wilkes case, 9 Jan 1770

5 There is something behind the throne greater than the King himself.
Speech, House of Lords, 2 Mar 1770

6 If I were an American, as I am an Englishman, while a foreign troop was landed in my country, I never would lay down my arms, – never – never – never!
Speech, House of Lords, 18 Nov 1777

PITT THE YOUNGER

(William Pitt, 2nd Earl of Chatham; 1759–1806) British statesman, Britain's youngest prime minister at the age of 24 (1783–1801). He resigned following George III's refusal to accept Catholic emancipation, but returned to office (1804–06) for a second administration.

1 Necessity is the plea for every infringement of human freedom. It is the argument of tyrants; it is the creed of slaves.
Speech, House of Commons, 18 Nov 1783

2 Roll up that map: it will not be wanted these ten years.
On learning that Napoleon had won the Battle of Austerlitz. Attrib.

3 I think I could eat one of Bellamy's veal pies.
Last words. Attrib.

4 Oh, my country! How I leave my country!
Last words. Attrib.

PLACES

See also Britain, Europe

1 All roads lead to Rome.
Proverb

2 See Naples and die.
Proverb

3 This is beautiful downtown Burbank.
Anonymous Catchphrase in the US TV comedy series, *Rowan and Martin's Laugh-In.*

4 I went to New Zealand but it was closed.
Anonymous

5 The shortest way out of Manchester is notoriously a bottle of Gordon's gin.
William Bolitho (1890–1930) British writer. Attrib.

6 The sort of place everyone should send his mother-in-law for a month, all expenses paid.

Ian Botham (1955–) British cricketer. Referring to Pakistan. BBC Radio 2 interview, Mar 1984

7 For Cambridge people rarely smile,
Being urban, squat, and packed with guile.

Rupert Brooke (1887–1915) British) poet. *The Old Vicarage, Grantchester*

8 I don't even know what street Canada is on.

Al Capone (1899–1947) US gangster. Attrib.

9 Hollywood is a world with all the personality of a paper cup.

Raymond Chandler (1888–1959) US novelist. Attrib.

10 India is a geographical term. It is no more a united nation than the Equator.

Winston Churchill (1874–1965) British statesman. Speech, Royal Albert Hall, 18 Mar 1931

11 There are few virtues which the Poles do not possess and there are few errors they have ever avoided.

Winston Churchill Speech, House of Commons, 1945

12 Oh what a pity were the greatest and most virtuous of kings, of that real virtue which makes the greatest of princes, to be measured by the yardstick of Versailles!

Jean-Baptiste Colbert (1619–83) French statesman. Letter to Louis XIV, 28 Sept 1665

13 I believe that the earthly Paradise lies here, which no one can enter except by God's leave. I believe that this land which your Highnesses have commanded me to discover is very great, and that there are many other lands in the south of which there have never been reports.

Christopher Columbus (1451–1506) Italian navigator. From the narrative of his third voyage, on which he discovered South America

14 Latins are tenderly enthusiastic. In Brazil they throw flowers at you. In Argentina they throw themselves.

Marlene Dietrich (Maria Magdalene von Losch; 1904–92) German-born film star. *Newsweek*, 24 Aug 1959

15 I find it hard to say, because when I was there it seemed to be shut.

Clement Freud (1924–) British Liberal politician and broadcaster. On being asked for his opinion of New Zealand. Similar remarks have been attributed to others. BBC radio, 12 Apr 1978

16 Some word that teems with hidden meaning – like Basingstoke.

W. S. Gilbert (1836–1911) British dramatist. *Ruddigore*, II

17 From Greenland's icy mountains,
From India's coral strand,
Where Afric's sunny fountains
Roll down their golden sand.

Reginald Heber (1783–1826) British bishop and hymn writer. *From Greenland's Icy Mountains*

18 Dublin, though a place much worse than London, is not so bad as Iceland.

Samuel Johnson (1709–84) British lexicographer. Letter to Mrs Christopher Smart. *Life of Johnson* (J. Boswell), Vol. IV

19 Liverpool is the pool of life.

Carl Jung (1875–1961) Swiss psychologist. Attrib.

20 Asia is not going to be civilized after the methods of the West. There is too much Asia and she is too old.

Rudyard Kipling (1865–1936) Indian-born British writer. *Life's Handicap*, 'The Man Who Was'

21 On the road to Mandalay
Where the flyin'-fishes play.

Rudyard Kipling *The Road to Mandalay*

22 And all lying mysteriously within the Australian underdark, that peculiar, lost weary aloofness of Australia. There was the vast town of Sydney. And it didn't seem to be real, it seemed to be sprinkled on the surface of a darkness into which it never penetrated.

D. H. Lawrence (1885–1930) British novelist. *Kangaroo*, Ch. 1

23 Don't let it be forgot
That once there was a spot
For one brief shining moment that was known
As Camelot.

Alan Jay Lerner (1918–86) US lyricist and playwright. *Camelot*

24 So you're going to Australia! Well, I made twenty thousand pounds on my tour there, but of course *that* will never be done again. Still, it's a wonderful country, and you'll have a good time. What are you going to sing? All I can say is – sing 'em muck! It's all they can understand!

Nellie Melba (Helen Porter Mitchell; 1861–1931) Australian soprano. Speaking to Clara Butt. *Clara Butt: Her Life Story* (W. H. Ponder)

25 I shook hands with a friendly Arab…I still have my right hand to prove it.

Spike Milligan (1918–) British comic actor and author. *A Dustbin of Milligan*, 'Letters to Harry Secombe'

26 That bastard of the Versailles treaty.

Vyacheslav Mikhailovich Molotov (1890–1986) Soviet statesman. Referring to Poland.

27 Jerusalem the golden,
With milk and honey blest,
Beneath thy contemplation
Sink heart and voice oppressed.

John Mason Neale (1818–66) British churchman. *Jerusalem the Golden*

28 The Great White Way.

Albert Bigelow Paine (1861–1937) US writer. Later used as a name for Broadway. Book title

29 Once a jolly swagman camped by a billy-bong,
Under the shade of a coolibah tree,
And he sang as he sat and waited for his billy-boil,
'You'll come a-waltzing, Matilda, with me.'

Andrew Barton Paterson (1864–1941) Australian journalist and poet. *Waltzing Matilda*

30 The whole city is arrayed in squares just like a chess-board, and disposed in a manner so perfect and masterly that it is impossible to give a description that should do it justice.

Marco Polo (c. 1254–1324) Venetian traveller. Referring to Kublai Khan's capital, Cambaluc (later Peking). *The Book of Marco Polo*

31 Even the Hooligan was probably invented in China centuries before we thought of him.

Saki (Hector Hugh Munro; 1870–1916) British writer. *Reginald on House-Parties*

32 Great God! this is an awful place.

Captain Robert Falcon Scott (1868–1912) British explorer. Referring to the South Pole. *Journal*, 17 Jan 1912

33 Cusins is a very nice fellow, certainly: nobody would ever guess that he was born in Australia.

George Bernard Shaw (1856–1950) Irish dramatist and critic. *Major Barbara*, I

34 The Japanese have perfected good manners and made them indistinguishable from rudeness.

Paul Theroux (1941–) US-born writer. *The Great Railway Bazaar*, Ch. 2

35 I'm Charley's aunt from Brazil, where the nuts come from.

Brandon Thomas (1856–1914) British actor and dramatist. *Charley's Aunt*, I

36 Oh, Calcutta!

Kenneth Tynan From the French expression, *'Oh quel cul t'as'* ('what a lovely arse you've got'). Play title

PLATH, SYLVIA

(1932–63) US poet and novelist. She married Ted Hughes in 1956; her only novel, *The Bell Jar*, was published less than a month after she committed suicide. Other works include *Ariel* (1965), *Crossing the Water* (1971), *Winter Trees* (1971), and *Collected Poems* (1981).

1 They all wanted to adopt me in some way and, for the price of their care and influence, have me resemble them.

The Bell Jar

2 Stars open among the liles.
Are you not blinded by such expressionless sirens?
This is the silence of astounded souls.

Crossing the Water

3 Dying
is an art, like everything else.
I do it exceptionally well.

Lady Lazarus

4 The fountains are dry and the roses over.
Incense of death. Your day approaches.
The pears fatten like litle buddhas.
A blue mist is dragging the lake.

The Manor Garden

5 The hills step off into whiteness.
People or stars
Regard me sadly I disappoint them.

Sheep in Fog

6 The surgeon is quiet, he does not speak.
He has seen too much death, his hands are full of it.

Winter Trees, 'The Courage of Shutting-Up'

7 I am no shadow
Though there is a shadow starting from my feet. I am a wife.
The city waits and aches. The little grasses
Crack through stone, and they are green with life.

Winter Trees, 'The Three Women'

PLATO

(429–347 BC) Greek philosopher. A disciple of Socrates and teacher of Aristotle, he founded the first university (the Academy) in Athens. His works include the *Phaedo* (on immortality), *Symposium* (on love), and *Republic* (on government).

1 The good is the beautiful.

Lysis

2 Our object in the construction of the state is the greatest happiness of the whole, and not that of any one class.

Republic, Bk. 4

3 I wonder if we could contrive...some magnificent myth that would in itself carry conviction to our whole community.

Republic, Bk. 5

4 There will be no end to the troubles of states, or indeed, my dear Glaucon, of humanity itself, till philosophers become kings in this world, or till those we now call kings and rulers really and truly become philosophers.

Republic, Bk. 5

5 Democracy passes into despotism.

Republic, Bk. 8

6 Let no one ignorant of mathematics enter here.

Inscription written over the entrance to the Academy. *Biographical Encyclopedia* (I. Asimov)

PLAYS

See also acting, actors, criticism, literature, Shakespeare, theatre, writers, writing

1 Now a whole is that which has a beginning, a middle, and an end.

Aristotle (384–322 BC) Greek philosopher. Referring specifically to the dramatic form of tragedy. *Poetics*, Ch. 7

2 One of Edward's Mistresses was Jane Shore, who has had a play written about her, but it is a tragedy and therefore not worth reading.

Jane Austen (1775–1817) British novelist. *The History of England*

3 In the theatre the audience want to be surprised – but by things that they expect.

Tristan Bernard (1866–1947) French dramatist. *Contes, Repliques et Bon Mots*

4 Prologues precede the piece – in mournful verse;
As undertakers – walk before the hearse.

David Garrick (1717–79) British actor and manager. *Apprentice*, Prologue

5 I'd say award winning plays are written only for the critics.

Lew Grade (Lewis Winogradsky; 1906–) British film and TV producer. *The Observer*, 'Sayings of the Week', 18 Oct 1970

6 Oh, for an hour of Herod!

Anthony Hope (1863–1933) British novelist. Said at the children's play *Peter Pan* (J. M. Barrie). *J. M. Barrie and the Lost Boys* (A. Birkin)

7 He always hurries to the main event and whisks his audience into the middle of things as though they knew already.

Horace (Quintus Horatius Flaccus; 65–8 BC) Roman poet. *Ars Poetica*

8 The weasel under the cocktail cabinet.

Harold Pinter (1930–) British playwright. Reply when asked what his plays were about. *Anger and After* (J. Russell Taylor)

9 I think you would have been very glad if I had written it.

Alexis Piron (1689–1773) French poet and dramatist. Discussing Voltaire's *Sémiramis* with him after its poor reception on the first night. *Cyclopaedia of Anecdotes* (K. Arvine)

10 Depending upon shock tactics is easy, whereas writing a good play is difficult. Pubic hair is no substitute for wit.

J. B. Priestley (1894–1984) British novelist. *Outcries and Asides*

11 My soul; sit thou a patient looker-on;
Judge not the play before the play is done:
Her plot hath many changes, every day
Speaks a new scene; the last act crowns the play.

Francis Quarles (1592–1644) English poet. *Epigram, Respice Finem*

12 Rehearsing a play is making the word flesh. Publishing a play is reversing the process.

Peter Shaffer (1926–) British dramatist. *Equus*, Note

13 If it be true that good wine needs no bush, 'tis true that a good play needs no epilogue.

William Shakespeare (1564–1616) English dramatist. *As You Like It*, Epilogue

14 The play's the thing
Wherein I'll catch the conscience of the King.

William Shakespeare *Hamlet*, II:2

15 A novel is a static thing that one moves through; a play is a dynamic thing that moves past one.

Kenneth Tynan (1927–80) British theatre critic. *Curtains*

16 A good many inconveniences attend play-going in any large city, but the greatest of them is usually the play itself.

Kenneth Tynan *New York Herald Tribune*

17 The play was a great success, but the audience was a disaster.

Oscar Wilde (1854–1900) Irish-born British dramatist. Referring to a play that had recently failed. Attrib.

PLEASURE

See also debauchery, happiness, leisure, merrymaking

1 No pleasure without pain.

Proverb

2 And if the following day, he chance to find
A new repast, or an untasted spring,
Blesses his stars, and thinks it luxury.

Joseph Addison (1672–1719) British essayist. *Cato*, I:4

3 One half of the world cannot understand the pleasures of the other.

Jane Austen (1775–1817) British novelist. *Emma*, Ch. 9

4 Then I commended mirth, because a man hath no better thing under the sun, than to eat, and to drink, and to be merry: for that shall abide with him of his labour the days of his life, which God giveth him under the sun.

Bible: Ecclesiastes 8:15

5 He who bends to himself a Joy
Doth the wingèd life destroy;
But he who kisses the Joy as it flies
Lives in Eternity's sunrise.

William Blake (1757–1827) British poet. *Gnomic Verses*

6 He said once to myself that he was no atheist but he could not think God would make a man miserable only for taking a little pleasure out of the way.

Gilbert Burnet (1643–1715) English bishop and historian. Referring to Charles II. *History of My Own Times*

7 I love the gay Eastertide, which brings forth leaves and flowers; and I love the joyous song of the birds, re-echoing through the copse. But I also love to see, amidst the meadows, tents and pavilions spread; it gives me great joy to see, drawn up on the field, knights and horses in battle array.

Bertrand le Born French troubadour.

8 Pleasure after all is a safer guide than either right or duty.

Samuel Butler (1835–1902) British writer. *The Way of All Flesh*, Ch. 19

9 Though sages may pour out their wisdom's treasure,
There is no sterner moralist than Pleasure.

Lord Byron (1788–1824) British poet. *Don Juan*, III

10 In Xanadu did Kubla Khan
A stately pleasure-dome decree:
Where Alph, the sacred river, ran
Through caverns measureless to man
Down to a sunless sea.

Samuel Taylor Coleridge (1772–1834) British poet. *Kubla Khan*

11 It was a miracle of rare device,
A sunny pleasure-dome with caves of ice!

Samuel Taylor Coleridge *Kubla Khan*

12 Nothing can permanently please, which does not contain in itself the reason why it is so, and not otherwise.

Samuel Taylor Coleridge *Biographia Literaria*, Ch. 14

13 For present joys are more to flesh and blood
Than a dull prospect of a distant good.

John Dryden (1631–1700) British poet and dramatist. *The Hind and the Panther*, III

14 The art of pleasing consists in being pleased.

William Hazlitt (1778–1830) British essayist. *On Manner*

15 People must not do things for fun. We are not here for fun. There is no reference to fun in any Act of Parliament.

A. P. Herbert (1890–1971) British writer and politician. *Uncommon Law*

16 Pleasure is very seldom found where it is sought; our brightest blazes of gladness are commonly kindled by unexpected sparks.

Samuel Johnson (1709–84) British lexicographer. *The Idler*

17 If I had no duties, and no reference to futurity, I would spend my life in driving briskly in a post-chaise with a pretty woman.

Samuel Johnson *Life of Johnson* (J. Boswell), Vol. III

18 No man is a hypocrite in his pleasures.

Samuel Johnson *Life of Johnson* (J. Boswell), Vol. IV

19 Give me books, fruit, French wine and fine weather and a little music out of doors, played by somebody I do not know.

John Keats (1795–1821) British poet. Letter to Fanny Keats, 29 Aug 1819

20 Life would be tolerable, were it not for its amusements.

George Cornewall Lewis (1806–63) British statesman and writer. *The Perpetual Pessimist* (Sagittarius and George)

21 A Little of What You Fancy Does You Good.

Marie Lloyd (1870–1922) British music-hall singer. Song title

22 Who loves not wine, woman and song,
Remains a fool his whole life long.

Martin Luther (1483–1546) German Protestant. Attrib.

23 My candle burns at both ends;
It will not last the night;
But ah, my foes, and oh my friends –
It gives a lovely light!

Edna St Vincent Millay (1892–1950) US poet. *A Few Figs from Thistles*, 'First Fig'

24 To sport with Amaryllis in the shade,
Or with the tangles of Neaera's hair.

John Milton (1608–74) English poet. *Lycidas*

25 Hence, vain deluding Joys,
The brood of Folly without father bred!

John Milton *Il Penseroso*

26 Great lords have their pleasures, but the people have fun.

Baron de Montesquieu (1689–1755) French writer. *Pensées diverses*

27 It was great fun,
But it was just one of those things.

Cole Porter (1891–1964) US composer and lyricist. *Jubilee*, 'Just One of Those Things'

28 It's delightful, it's delicious, it's de-lovely.

Cole Porter *Red, Hot and Blue*, 'It's De-Lovely'

29 I wish thee as much pleasure in the reading, as I had in the writing.

Francis Quarles (1592–1644) English poet. *Emblems*, 'To the Reader'

30 A life of pleasure requires an aristocratic setting to make it interesting.

George Santayana (1863–1952) US philosopher. *Life of Reason*, 'Reason in Society'

31 Pleasures are all alike simply considered in themselves…He that takes pleasure to hear sermons enjoys himself as much as he that hears plays.

John Selden (1584–1654) English historian. *Table Talk*

32 Pleasure is nothing else but the intermission of pain.

John Selden *Table Talk*

33 A Good Time Was Had by All.

Stevie Smith (Florence Margaret Smith; 1902–71) British poet. Book title

34 This is the best moment of my life, since my Granny caught her tit in the mangle.

Daley Thompson (Francis Morgan T.; 1958–) British decathlete. On winning the decathlon at the Olympics. *The Guardian*, 1984

35 Everyone is dragged on by their favourite pleasure.

Virgil (Publius Vergilius Maro; 70–19 BC) Roman poet. *Eclogue*, Bk. II

36 All the things I really like to do are either immoral, illegal, or fattening.

Alexander Woollcott (1887–1943) US journalist. Attrib.

37 Pleasures newly found are sweet
When they lie about our feet.

William Wordsworth (1770–1850) British poet. *To the Small Celandine*

PLINY THE ELDER

(Gaius Plinius Secundus; 23–79 AD) Roman scholar. His *Natural History* was a major source of knowledge until the 17th century. He died while closely observing an eruption of Vesuvius.

1 Attic wit.

Natural History, II

2 Amid the miseries of our life on earth, suicide is God's best gift to man.

Natural History, II

3 It is far from easy to determine whether she has proved a kind parent to man or a merciless step-mother.

Referring to Nature. *Natural History*, VII

4 There is always something new out of Africa.

Natural History, VIII

5 *In vino veritas.*
Truth comes out in wine.

Natural History, XIV

POETRY

See also criticism, inspiration, literature, poetry and prose, poets

1 For this reason poetry is something more philosophical and more worthy of serious attention than history.

Aristotle (384–322 BC) Greek philosopher. *Poetics*, Ch. 9

2 A criticism of life under the conditions fixed for such a criticism by the laws of poetic truth and poetic beauty.

Matthew Arnold (1822–88) British poet and critic. *Essays in Criticism*, Second Series, 'The Study of Poetry'

3 I think it will be found that the grand style arises in poetry, when a noble nature, poetically gifted, treats with simplicity or with severity a serious subject.

Matthew Arnold Closing words. *On Translating Homer*

4 The difference between genuine poetry and the poetry of Dryden, Pope, and all their school, is briefly this: their poetry is conceived and composed in their wits, genuine poetry is conceived and composed in the soul.

Matthew Arnold *Thomas Gray*

5 Now Ireland has her madness and her weather

still,
For poetry makes nothing happen.

W. H. Auden (1907–73) British poet. *In Memory of W. B. Yeats*, II

6 Poetry makes nothing happen, it survives
In the valley of its saying.

W. H. Auden *In Memory of W. B. Yeats*

7 A verbal art like poetry is reflective. It stops to think. Music is immediate, it goes on to become.

W. H. Auden Attrib.

8 It is not possible for a poet to be a professional. Poetry is essentially an amateur activity.

Lord Barrington (1908–) British barrister and peer. Speech, House of Lords, 23 Nov 1978

9 It is a pretty poem, Mr Pope, but you must not call it Homer.

Richard Bentley (1662–1742) English scholar. Referring to Alexander Pope's *Iliad. Samuel Johnson, Life of Pope*

10 Too many people in the modern world view poetry as a luxury, not a necessity like petrol. But to me it's the oil of life.

John Betjeman (1906–84) British poet. *The Observer*, 'Sayings of the Year', 1974

11 Poetry is as much a part of the universe as mathematics and physics. It is not a cleverer device or recreation, unless the Eternal is clever.

Edmund Blunden (1896–1974) British poet. Speech on his election as Professor of Poetry at Oxford University, 1966

12 Masefield's sonnets? Ah yes. Very nice. Pure Shakespeare. Masefield's 'Reynard the Fox'? Very nice, too. Pure Chaucer. Masefield's 'Everlasting Mercy'? H'm. Yes. Pure Masefield.

Robert Bridges (1844–1930) British poet. *Twenty-Five* (Beverley Nichols)

13 Nothing so difficult as a beginning
In poesy, unless perhaps the end.

Lord Byron (1788–1824) British poet. *Don Juan*, IV

14 I have nothing to say, I am saying it, and that is poetry.

John Cage (1912–92) US composer. *The Sunday Times* (quoted by Cyril Connolly), 10 Sept 1972

15 Or like a poet woo the moon,
Riding an armchair for my steed,
And with a flashing pen harpoon
Terrific metaphors of speed.

Roy Campbell (1901–57) South African poet. *The Festivals of Flight*

16 For the godly poet must be chaste himself, but there is no need for his verses to be so.

Catullus (c. 84–c. 54 BC) Roman poet. *Carmina*, XVI

17 You don't make a poem with thoughts; you must make it with words.

Jean Cocteau (1889–1963) French poet and artist. *The Sunday Times*, 20 Oct 1963

18 That willing suspension of disbelief for the moment, which constitutes poetic faith.

Samuel Taylor Coleridge (1772–1834) British poet. *Biographia Literaria*, Ch. 14

19 Poetry's unnat'ral; no man ever talked poetry 'cept a beadle on boxin' day.

Charles Dickens (1812–70) British novelist. *Pickwick Papers*, Ch. 33

20 I am afeered that werges on the poetical, Sammy.

Charles Dickens Said by Sam Weller. *Pickwick Papers*, Ch. 33

21 Poetry is not a turning loose of emotion, but an escape from emotion; it is not the expression of personality, but an escape from personality.

T. S. Eliot (1888–1965) US-born British poet and dramatist. *Tradition and the Individual Talent*

22 All one's inventions are true, you can be sure of that. Poetry is as exact a science as geometry.

Gustave Flaubert (1821–80) French novelist. Letter to Louise Colet, 14 Aug 1853

23 We all write poems; it is simply that poets are the ones who write in words.

John Fowles (1926–) British novelist. *The French Lieutenant's Woman*, Ch. 19

24 Writing free verse is like playing tennis with the net down.

Robert Frost (1875–1963) US poet. Speech, Milton Academy, 17 May 1935

25 Poetry is the language in which man explores his own amazement.

Christopher Fry (1907–) British dramatist. *Time*, 3 Apr 1950

26 Rightly thought of there is poetry in peaches... even when they are canned.

Harley Granville-Barker (1877–1946) British actor and dramatist. *The Madras House*, I

27 If Galileo had said in verse that the world moved, the Inquisition might have let him alone.

Thomas Hardy (1840–1928) British novelist. *The Later Years of Thomas Hardy* (F. E. Hardy)

28 It's hard to say why writing verse
Should terminate in drink or worse.

A. P. Herbert (1890–1971) British writer and politician. *Punch*, 'Lines for a Worldly Person'

29 Even when poetry has a meaning, as it usually has, it may be inadvisable to draw it out...Perfect understanding will sometimes almost extinguish pleasure.

A. E. Housman (1859–1936) British scholar and poet. Lecture, *The Name and Nature of Poetry*, Cambridge, 9 May 1933

30 If a line of poetry strays into my memory, my skin bristles so that the razor ceases to act.

A. E. Housman Lecture, *The Name and Nature of Poetry*, Cambridge, 9 May 1933

31 'Why Sir, it is much easier to say what it is not. We all *know* what light is; but it is not easy to *tell* what it is.'

Samuel Johnson (1709–84) British lexicographer. When asked, 'What is poetry?' *Life of Johnson* (J. Boswell), Vol. III

32 A drainless shower
Of light is poesy; 'tis the supreme of power;
'Tis might half slumb'ring on its own right arm.

John Keats (1795–1821) British poet. *Sleep and Poetry*

33 A long poem is a test of invention which I take to be the Polar star of poetry, as fancy is the sails, and imagination the rudder.

John Keats Letter to Benjamin Bailey, 8 Oct 1817

34 We hate poetry that has a palpable design upon us – and if we do not agree, seems to put its hand in its breeches pocket. Poetry should be great and unobtrusive, a thing which enters into one's soul, and does not startle or amaze it with itself, but with its subject.

John Keats Letter to J. H. Reynolds, 3 Feb 1818

35 If poetry comes not as naturally as leaves to a tree it had better not come at all.

John Keats Letter to John Taylor, 27 Feb 1818

36 When power narrows the areas of man's concern, poetry reminds him of the richness and diversity of his existence.

John Fitzgerald Kennedy (1917–63) US statesman. Address at Dedication of the Robert Frost Library, 26 Oct 1963

37 Deprivation is for me what daffodils were for Wordsworth.

Philip Larkin (1922–85) British poet. Interview in *The Observer*

38 Perhaps no person can be a poet, or can even enjoy poetry, without a certain unsoundness of mind.

Lord Macaulay (1800–59) British historian. *Literary Essays Contributed to the 'Edinburgh Review'*, 'Milton'

39 Poem me no poems.

Rose Macaulay (1889–1958) British writer. *Poetry Review*, Autumn 1963

40 Poetry is a comforting piece of fiction set to more or less lascivious music.

H. L. Mencken (1880–1956) US journalist. *Prejudices*, 'The Poet and his Art'

41 Verse libre; a device for making poetry easier to read and harder to write.

H. L. Mencken *A Book of Burlesques*

42 Blest pair of Sirens, pledges of Heaven's joy,
Sphere-born harmonious sisters, Voice and Verse.

John Milton (1608–74) English poet. *At a Solemn Music*

43 Rhyme being no necessary adjunct or true ornament of poem or good verse, in longer works especially, but the invention of a barbarous age, to set off wretched matter and lame metre.

John Milton *Paradise Lost*, The Verse. Preface to 1668 ed.

44 The troublesome and modern bondage of Rhyming.

John Milton *Paradise Lost*, The Verse. Preface to 1668 ed.

45 ...poetry, 'The Cinderella of the Arts.'

Harriet Monroe (1860–1936) US poet and editor. *Famous American Women* (Hope Stoddard), 'Harriet Monroe'

46 Above all I am not concerned with Poetry. My subject is War, and the pity of War. The Poetry is in the pity.

Wilfred Owen (1893–1918) British poet. *Poems*, Preface

47 Poetry is the monster hiding in a child's dark room, it is the scar on a beautiful person's face. It is the last blade of grass being picked from the city park.

Brian Patten (1946–) British poet. *Prose Poem Towards a Definition of Itself*

48 Curst be the verse, how well so'er it flow,
That tends to make one worthy man my foe.

Alexander Pope (1688–1744) British poet. *Epistle to Dr. Arbuthnot*

49 For three years, out of key with his time,
He strove to resuscitate the dead art
Of poetry to maintain 'the sublime'
In the old sense. Wrong from the start.

Ezra Pound (1885–1972) US poet. *Pour l'élection de son sépulcre*

50 It is a perfectly possible means of overcoming chaos.

I. A. Richards (1893–1979) British critic. *Science and Poetry*

51 A sonnet is a moment's monument, –
Memorial from the Soul's eternity
To one dead deathless hour.

Dante Gabriel Rossetti (1828–82) British painter and poet. *The House of Life*, Introduction

52 What is poetry? The suggestion, by the imagination, of noble grounds for the noble emotions.

John Ruskin (1819–1900) British art critic and writer. *Modern Painters*, Vol. III

53 The truest poetry is the most feigning.

William Shakespeare (1564–1616) English dramatist. *As You Like It*, III:3

54 The poet's eye, in a fine frenzy rolling,
Doth glance from heaven to earth, from earth to heaven;
And as imagination bodies forth
The forms of things unknown, the poet's pen
Turns them to shapes, and gives to airy nothing
A local habitation and a name.

William Shakespeare *A Midsummer Night's Dream*, V:1

55 The lunatic, the lover, and the poet,
Are of imagination all compact.

William Shakespeare *A Midsummer Night's Dream*, V:1

56 Not marble, nor the gilded monuments
Of princes, shall outlive this powerful rhyme.

William Shakespeare *Sonnet 55*

57 Poetry is the record of the best and happiest moments of the happiest and best minds.

Percy Bysshe Shelley (1792–1822) British poet. *A Defence of Poetry*

58 My poems are hymns of praise to the glory of life.

Edith Sitwell (1887–1964) British poet and writer. *Collected Poems*, 'Some Notes on My Poetry'

59 One of the purposes of poetry is to show the dimensions of man that are, as Sir Arthur Eddington said 'midway in scale between the atom and the star.'

Edith Sitwell *Rhyme and Reason*

60 Poetry ennobles the heart and the eyes and unveils the meaning of things upon which the heart and the eyes dwell.

Edith Sitwell *Rhyme and Reason*

61 It is as unseeing to ask what is the *use* of poetry as it would be to ask what is the use of religion.

Edith Sitwell *The Outcasts*, Preface

62 A man does not write poems about what he knows, but about what he does not know.

Robin Skelton (1925–) British academic. *Teach Yourself Poetry*

63 Poetry is the supreme fiction, madame.
Wallace Stevens (1879–1955) US poet. *A High-Toned Old Christian Woman*

64 These poems, with all their crudities, doubts, and confusions, are written for the love of Man and in praise of God, and I'd be a damn' fool if they weren't.
Dylan Thomas (1914–53) Welsh poet. *Collected Poems*, Note

65 What was it Chaucer
Said once about the long toil
That goes like blood to the poem's making?
Leave it to nature and the verse sprawls,
Limp as bindweed, if it break at all
Life's iron crust.
R. S. Thomas (1913–) Welsh poet. *Poetry for Supper*

66 A poem is never finished, only abandoned.
Paul Valéry (1871–1945) French poet and writer. *A Certain World* (W. H. Auden)

67 Having verse set to music is like looking at a painting through a stained glass window.
Paul Valéry Attrib.

68 There are no poetic ideas; only poetic utterances.
Evelyn Waugh (1903–66) British novelist. *Books On Trial*

69 Hence no force however great can stretch a cord however fine into an horizontal line which is accurately straight: there will always be a bending downwards.
William Whewell (1794–1866) British philosopher and mathematician. An example of unintentional versification. *Elementary Treatise on Mechanics* (1819 edition), Ch. 4

70 No one will ever get at my verses who insists upon viewing them as a literary performance.
Walt Whitman (1819–92) US poet. *A Backward Glance O'er Travel'd Roads*

71 I would rather have written those lines than take Quebec.
James Wolfe (1727–59) British general. Referring to Gray's Elegy, on the eve of the Battle of Quebec, 1759. Attrib.

72 Poetry is the spontaneous overflow of powerful feelings: it takes its origin from emotion recollected in tranquillity.
William Wordsworth (1770–1850) British poet. *Lyrics Ballads*, Preface

73 Out of the quarrel with others we make rhetoric; out of the quarrel with ourselves we make poetry.
W. B. Yeats (1865–1939) Irish poet. *Essay*

74 Too true, too sincere. The Muse prefers the liars, the gay and warty lads.
W. B. Yeats Referring to the poetry of James Reed. *The Long Week End* (Robert Graves and Alan Hodge)

POETRY AND PROSE

See also poetry, prose

1 Poetry is not the proper antithesis to prose, but to science. Poetry is opposed to science, and prose to metre.
Samuel Taylor Coleridge (1772–1834) British poet. *Lectures and Notes of 1818*, I

2 I wish our clever young poets would remember my homely definitions of prose and poetry; that is, prose = words in their best order; – poetry = the best words in the best order.
Samuel Taylor Coleridge *Table Talk*

3 Prose on certain occasions can bear a great deal of poetry: on the other hand, poetry sinks and swoons under a moderate weight of prose.
Walter Savage Landor (1775–1864) British poet and writer. *Imaginary Conversations*, 'Archdeacon Hare and Walter Landor'

4 For to write good prose is an affair of good manners. It is, unlike verse, a civil art...Poetry is baroque.
W. Somerset Maugham (1874–1965) British novelist. *The Summing Up*

5 Poetry is to prose as dancing is to walking.
John Wain (1925–94) British novelist and poet. Talk, BBC radio, 13 Jan 1976

6 The poet gives us his essence, but prose takes the mould of the body and mind entire.
Virginia Woolf (1882–1941) British novelist. *The Captain's Death Bed*, 'Reading'

7 There neither is, nor can be, any *essential* difference between the language of prose and metrical composition.
William Wordsworth (1770–1850) British poet. *Lyrical Ballads*, Preface

8 O'CONNOR. How are you?
W.B.Y. Not very well, I can only write prose today.
W. B. Yeats (1865–1939) Irish poet. Attrib.

POETS

See also Chaucer, criticism, Milton, poetry, Shakespeare, writers

General quotations

1 Poets and painters are outside the class system, or rather they constitute a special class of their own, like the circus people and the gipsies.
Gerald Brenan (Edward Fitzgerald Brenan; 1894–1987) British writer. *Thoughts in a Dry Season*, 'Writing'

2 The Fleshly School of Poetry.
Robert Williams Buchanan (1841–1901) British poet and writer. Referring to Swinburne, William Morris, D. G. Rossetti, etc. Title of article in the *Contemporary Review*, Oct 1871

3 A poet without love were a physical and metaphysical impossibility.
Thomas Carlyle (1795–1881) Scottish historian and essayist. *Critical and Miscellaneous Essays*, 'Burns'

4 A true poet does not bother to be poetical. Nor does a nursery gardener scent his roses.
Jean Cocteau (1889–1963) French poet and artist. *Professional Secrets*

5 Immature poets imitate; mature poets steal.
T. S. Eliot (1888–1965) US-born British poet and dramatist. *Philip Massinger*

6 To be a poet is a condition rather than a profession.
Robert Graves (1895–1985) British poet and novelist. *Horizon*

7 Shelley and Keats were the last English poets

who were at all up to date in their chemical knowledge.

J. B. S. Haldane (1892–1964) British geneticist. *Daedalus or Science and the Future*

8 Not gods, nor men, nor even booksellers have put up with poets' being second-rate.

Horace (Quintus Horatius Flaccus; 65–8 BC) Roman poet. *Ars Poetica*

9 Sir, there is no settling the point of precedency between a louse and a flea.

Samuel Johnson (1709–84) British lexicographer. When Maurice Morgann asked him who he considered to be the better poet – Smart or Derrick. *Life of Johnson* (J. Boswell), Vol. IV

10 For ne'er
Was flattery lost on poet's ear:
A simple race! they waste their toil
For the vain tribute of a smile.

Walter Scott (1771–1832) Scottish novelist. *The Lay of the Last Minstrel*, IV

11 There have been many most excellent poets that have never versified, and now swarm many versifiers that need never answer to the name of poets.

Philip Sidney (1554–86) English poet and courtier. *The Defence of Poesy*

12 I hate the whole race...There is no believing a word they say – your professional poets, I mean – there never existed a more worthless set than Byron and his friends for example.

Duke of Wellington (1769–1852) British general and statesman. Lady Salisbury's diary, 26 Oct 1833

Specific quotations

13 Reader! I am to let thee know,
Donne's Body only, lyes below:
For, could the grave his Soul comprize,
Earth would be richer than the skies.

Anonymous Epitaph, written on the wall above Donne's grave the day after his burial

14 It always seems to me that the right sphere for Shelley's genius was the sphere of music, not of poetry.

Matthew Arnold (1822–88) British poet and critic. *Maurice de Guérin*, Footnote

15 When Byron's eyes were shut in death,
We bow'd our head and held our breath.
He taught us little: but our soul
Had *felt* him like the thunder's roll.

Matthew Arnold *Memorial Verses*

16 He spoke, and loos'd our heart in tears.
He laid us as we lay at birth
On the cool flowery lap of earth.

Matthew Arnold Referring to Wordsworth. *Memorial Verses*

17 Time may restore us in his course
Goethe's sage mind and Byron's force:
But where will Europe's latter hour
Again find Wordsworth's healing power?

Matthew Arnold *Memorial Verses*

18 Earth, receive an honoured guest:
William Yeats is laid to rest.
Let the Irish vessel lie
Emptied of its poetry.

W. H. Auden (1907–73) British poet. *In Memory of W. B. Yeats*, III

19 So long as Byron tried to write Poetry with a capital P, to express deep emotions and profound thoughts, his work deserved that epithet he most dreaded, *una seccatura*...His attempts to write satirical heroic couplets were less unsuccessful, but aside from the impossibility of equaling Dryden and Pope in their medium, Byron was really a comedian, not a satirist.

W. H. Auden *The Dyer's Hand*

20 He was the one English love poet who was not afraid to acknowledge that he was composed of body, soul, and mind; and who faithfully recorded all the pitched battles, alarms, treaties, sieges, and fanfares of that extraordinary triangular warfare.

Rupert Brooke (1887–1915) British poet. Referring to John Donne. *John Donne*

21 The great Metaquizzical poet.

Lord Byron (1788–1824) British poet. Said of Wordsworth. Letter to John Murray, 19 Jan 1821

22 Here is Johnny Keats piss-a-bed poetry. No more Keats, I entreat.

Lord Byron Letter to the publisher John Murray, 12 Oct 1821

23 If they had said the sun and the moon was gone out of the heavens it could not have struck me with the idea of a more awful and dreary blank in the creation than the words: Byron is dead.

Jane Welsh Carlyle (1801–66) The wife of Thomas Carlyle. Letter to Thomas Carlyle, 1824

24 A weak, diffusive, weltering, ineffectual man.

Thomas Carlyle (1795–1881) Scottish historian and essayist. Referring to Coleridge. Attrib.

25 How great a possibility; how small a realized result.

Thomas Carlyle Referring to Coleridge. Letter to Ralph Waldo Emerson, 12 Aug 1834

26 A gifted Byron rises in his wrath; and feeling too surely that he for his part is not 'happy', declares the same in very violent language, as a piece of news that may be interesting. It evidently has surprised him much. One dislikes to see a man and poet reduced to proclaim on the streets such tidings.

Thomas Carlyle *Past and Present*

27 He could not think up to the height of his own towering style.

G. K. Chesterton (1874–1936) British writer. Speaking of Tennyson. *The Victorian Age in Literature*, Ch. 3

28 With Donne, whose muse on dromedary trots,
Wreathe iron pokers into true-love knots.

Samuel Taylor Coleridge (1772–1834) British poet. *On Donne's Poetry*

29 The misfortune is, that he has begun to write verses without very well understanding what metre is.

Samuel Taylor Coleridge Referring to Tennyson. *Table Talk*

30 The world is rid of Lord Byron, but the deadly slime of his touch still remains.

John Constable (1776–1837) British landscape painter. Letter to John Fisher, three weeks after Byron's death

31 Few writers have shown a more extraordinary compass of powers than Donne; for he combined what no other man has ever done – the last sublimation of subtlety with the most impassioned majesty.

Thomas De Quincey (1785–1859) British writer. Referring to John Donne. *Blackwood's Magazine*, Dec 1828

32 This illustrious man, the largest and most spacious intellect, the subtlest and the most comprehensive, in my judgement, that has yet existed amongst men.

Thomas De Quincey Referring to Coleridge. *Recollections of the Lake Poets*

33 He seems to me the most *vulgar-minded* genius that ever produced a great effect in literature.

George Eliot (Mary Ann Evans; 1819–80) British novelist. Referring to Byron. Letter, 21 Sept 1869

34 Blake...knew what interested him, and he therefore presents only the essential, only, in fact, what can be presented, and need not be explained...He approached everything with a mind unclouded by current opinions. There was nothing of the superior person about him. This makes him terrifying.

T. S. Eliot (1888–1965) US-born British poet and dramatist. *The Sacred Wood*

35 Blake is damned good to steal from!

Henry Fuseli (1741–1825) Swiss artist. *Life of Blake* (Alexander Gilchrist)

36 *Hugo – hélas!*

André Gide (1869–1951) French novelist. Replying to an inquiry as to whom he considered the finest poet of the 19th century. *André Gide–Paul Valéry Correspondence 1890–1942*

37 He has no sense of the ludicrous, and, as to God, a worm crawling in a privy is as worthy an object as any other, all being to him indifferent. So to Blake the Chimney Sweeper etc. He is ruined by vain struggles to get rid of what presses on his brain – he attempts impossibles.

William Hazlitt (1778–1830) British essayist. Referring to Blake. *Diary* (Henry Crabb Robinson)

38 He talked on for ever; and you wished him to talk on for ever.

William Hazlitt Referring to Coleridge. *Lectures on the English Poets*, Lecture VIII, 'On the Living Poets'

39 His thoughts did not seem to come with labour and effort; but as if borne on the gusts of genius, and as if the wings of his imagination lifted him from off his feet.

William Hazlitt Referring to Coleridge. *Lectures on the English Poets*, Lecture VIII, 'On the Living Poets'

40 He had a fire in his eye, a fever in his blood, a maggot in his brain, a hectic flutter in his speech, which mark out the philosophic fanatic.

William Hazlitt Referring to Shelley. *Table Talk*

41 The most original poet now living, and the one whose writings could the least be spared; for they have no substitutes elsewhere.

William Hazlitt Referring to Wordsworth. *The Spirit of the Age*

42 Dr Donne's verses are like the peace of God; they pass all understanding.

James I (1566–1625) King of England. Attrib.

43 He was dull in a new way, and that made many people think him *great*.

Samuel Johnson (1709–84) British lexicographer. Referring to Thomas Gray. *Life of Johnson* (J. Boswell), Vol. II

44 Milton, Madam, was a genius that could cut a Colossus from a rock; but could not carve heads upon cherry-stones.

Samuel Johnson When Miss Hannah More had wondered why Milton could write the epic *Paradise Lost* but only very poor sonnets. *Life of Johnson* (J. Boswell), Vol. IV

45 For Shelley's nature is utterly womanish. Not merely his weak points, but his strong ones, are those of a woman. Tender and pitiful as a woman; and yet, when angry, shrieking, railing, hysterical as a woman...The nature of a woman looks out of that wild, beautiful, girlish face – the nature: but not the spirit.

Charles Kingsley (1819–75) British writer. *Thoughts on Shelley and Byron*

46 Mad, bad, and dangerous to know.

Lady Caroline Lamb (1785–1828) The wife of William Lamb. Said of Byron in her journal. *Journal*

47 Separate from the pleasure of your company, I don't much care if I never see another mountain in my life.

Charles Lamb (1775–1834) British essayist. Letter to Wordsworth, 30 Jan 1801

48 His face when he repeats his verses hath its ancient glory, an Archangel a little damaged.

Charles Lamb Referring to Coleridge. Letter, 26 Apr 1816

49 Keats, at a time when the phrase had not yet been invented, practised the theory of art for art's sake. He is the type, not of the poet, but of the artist. He was not a great personality, his work comes to us as a greater thing than his personality. When we read his verse, we think of the verse, not of John Keats.

F. R. Leavis (1895–1978) British literary critic. *Revaluation*

50 Walt Whitman who laid end to end words never seen in each other's company before outside of a dictionary.

David Lodge (1935–) British author. *Changing Places*, Ch. 5

51 Your works will be read after Shakespeare and Milton are fogotten – and not till then.

Richard Porson (1759–1808) British classicist. Giving his opinion of the poems of Robert Southey. *Quotable Anecdotes* (L. Meissen)

52 Mr Wordsworth, a stupid man, with a decided gift for portraying nature in vignettes, never yet ruined anyone's morals, unless, perhaps, he has driven some susceptible persons to crime in a very fury of boredom.

Ezra Pound (1885–1972) US poet. *Future*, Nov 1917

53 I weep for Adonais – he is dead!
O, weep for Adonais! though our tears
Thaw not the frost which binds so dear a head!
And thou, sad Hour, selected from all years
To mourn our loss, rouse thy obscure compeers,
And teach them thine own sorrow, say: 'With me
Died Adonais; till the Future dares
Forget the Past, his fate and fame shall be
An echo and a light unto eternity!'

Percy Bysshe Shelley (1792–1822) British poet. Written on the death of Keats. *Adonais*

54 People sometimes divide others into those you laugh at and those you laugh with. The young Auden was someone you could laugh-at-with.

Stephen Spender (1909–) British poet. Address, W. H. Auden's memorial service, Oxford 27 Oct 1973

55 Blake, in the hierarchy of the inspired, stands very high indeed. If one could strike an average among poets, it would probably be true to say that, as far as inspiration is concerned, Blake is to the average poet, as the average poet is to the man in the street. All poetry, to be poetry at all, must have the power of making one, now and then, involuntarily ejaculate: 'What made him think of that?' With Blake, one is asking the question all the time.

Lytton Strachey (1880–1932) British writer. *Books and Characters*

56 Blake is the only poet who sees all temporal things under a form of eternity...Where other poets use reality as a spring-board into space, he uses it as a foothold on his return from flight.

Arthur Symons (1865–1945) British poet. *William Blake*

57 Wordsworth was a tea-time bore, the great Frost of literature, the verbose, the humourless, the platitudinary reporter of Nature in her dullest moods. Open him at any page: and there lies the English language not, as George Moore said of Pater, in a glass coffin, but in a large, sultry, and unhygienic box.

Dylan Thomas (1914–53) Welsh poet. Letter to Pamela Hansford Johnson, 1933

58 The Poet of Immortal Youth.

Henry Van Dyke *Keats*

59 He found in stones the sermons he had already hidden there.

Oscar Wilde (1854–1900) Irish-born British dramatist. Referring to Wordsworth. *The Decay of Lying*

60 There is no doubt that this poor man was mad, but there is something in the madness of this man which interests me more than the sanity of Lord Byron and Walter Scott.

William Wordsworth (1770–1850) British poet. Talking of Blake. *Reminiscences* (Henry Crabb Robinson)

61 I see a schoolboy when I think of him
With face and nose pressed to a sweetshop window.

W. B. Yeats (1865–1939) Irish poet. Referring to Keats. Attrib.

62 That William Blake
Who beat upon the wall
Till Truth obeyed his call.

W. B. Yeats *An Acre of Grass*

POLICE

1 I have never seen a situation so dismal that a policeman couldn't make it worse.

Brendan Behan (1923–64) Irish playwright. Attrib.

2 When constabulary duty's to be done –
A policeman's lot is not a happy one.

W. S. Gilbert (1836–1911) British dramatist. *The Pirates of Penzance*, II

3 The police are the only 24-hour social service in the country.

Commander Alex Marnoch Remark, Feb 1983

4 Policemen are numbered in case they get lost.

Spike Milligan (1918–) British comic actor and author. *The Last Goon Show of All*

5 A thing of duty is a boy for ever.

Flann O'Brien (Brian O'Nolan; 1911–66) Irish novelist and journalist. About policemen always seeming to be young-looking. *The Listener*, 24 Feb 1977

6 Reading isn't an occupation we encourage among police officers. We try to keep the paper work down to a minimum.

Joe Orton (1933–67) British dramatist. *Loot*, II

7 My father didn't create you to arrest me.

Lord Peel (1829–1912) British politician. Protesting against his arrest by the police, recently established by his father. Attrib.

8 One always has the air of someone who is lying when one speaks to a policeman.

Charles-Louis Philippe (1874–1909) French novelist. *Les Chroniques du canard sauvage*

POLITICIANS

See also Churchill, compliments, government, Hitler, Houses of Parliament, insults, politics

General quotes

1 He therefore was at strenuous pains
To atrophy his puny brains
And registered success in this
Beyond the dreams of avarice
Till when he had at last become
Blind, paralytic, deaf and dumb
Insensible and cretinous
He was admitted ONE OF US.

Hilaire Belloc *The Statesman*

2 Politics and the fate of mankind are shaped by men without ideas and without greatness. Men who have greatness within them don't go in for politics.

Albert Camus (1913–60) French existentialist writer. *Notebooks*, 1935–42

3 a politician is an arse upon which everyone has sat except a man.

e. e. cummings (1894–1962) US poet. *A Politician*

4 When I was a boy I was told that anybody could become President of the United States. I am beginning to believe it.

Clarence Seward Darrow (1857–1938) US lawyer. Attrib.

5 Since a politician never believes what he says, he is surprised when others believe him.

Charles De Gaulle (1890–1970) French general and statesman. Attrib.

6 In order to become the master, the politician poses as the servant.

Charles De Gaulle Attrib.

7 I have come to the conclusion that politics are too serious a matter to be left to the politicians.

Charles De Gaulle Attrib.

8 For Politicians neither love nor hate.

John Dryden (1631–1700) British poet and dramatist. *Absalom and Achitophel*, I

9 There is just one rule for politicians all over the world. Don't say in Power what you say in Opposition: if you do you only have to carry out what the other fellows have found impossible.

John Galsworthy (1867–1933) British novelist. *Maid in Waiting*

10 I always voted at my party's call,
And I never thought of thinking for myself at all.

W. S. Gilbert (1836–1911) British dramatist. *HMS Pinafore*, I

11 The prospect of a lot
Of dull MPs in close proximity,
All thinking for themselves is what
No man can face with equanimity.

W. S. Gilbert *Iolanthe*, I

12 'Do you pray for the senators, Dr Hale?' 'No, I look at the senators and I pray for the country.'

Edward Everett Hale (1822–1909) US author and clergyman. *New England Indian Summer* (Van Wyck Brooks)

13 Politicians are the same everywhere. They promise to build bridges even where there are no rivers.

Nikita Khrushchev (1894–1971) Soviet statesman. Attrib., Oct 1960

14 Political renegades always start their career of treachery as 'the best men of all parties' and end up in the Tory knackery.

Neil Kinnock (1942–) British politician. Speech, Welsh Labour Party Conference, 1985

15 A politician is a person with whose politics you don't agree; if you agree with him he is a statesman.

David Lloyd George (1863–1945) British Liberal statesman. Attrib.

16 When you're abroad you're a statesman: when you're at home you're just a politician.

Harold Macmillan (1894–1986) British politician and prime minister. Speech, 1958

17 It is very unfair to expect a politician to live in private up to the statements he makes in public.

W. Somerset Maugham (1874–1965) British novelist. *The Circle*

18 A statesman is a politician who places himself at the service of the nation. A politician is a statesman who places the nation at his service.

Georges Pompidou (1911–74) French statesman. *The Observer*, 'Sayings of the Year', 30 Dec 1973

19 All political lives, unless they are cut off in midstream at a happy juncture, end in failure.

Enoch Powell (1912–) British politician. *The Sunday Times*, 6 Nov 1977

20 Above any other position of eminence, that of Prime Minister is filled by fluke.

Enoch Powell *The Observer*, 'Sayings of the Week' 8 Mar 1987

21 A number of anxious dwarfs trying to grill a whale.

J. B. Priestley (1894–1984) British novelist. *Outcries and Asides*

22 I don't want Labour MPs sitting on the green benches at Westminster fighting for a four-day week for themselves and a seven-day week for miners.

Arthur Scargill (1941–) British trades union leader. *The Independent*, 29 Sept 1993

23 Get thee glass eyes,
And, like a scurvy politician, seem
To see the things thou dost not.

William Shakespeare (1564–1616) English dramatist. *King Lear*, IV:6

24 He knows nothing; and he thinks he knows everything. That points clearly to a political career.

George Bernard Shaw (1856–1950) Irish dramatist and critic. *Major Barbara*, III

25 Most Conservatives believe that a creche is something that happens between two Range Rovers in Tunbridge Wells.

Caroline Shorten SLD spokesperson *The Independent*, 22 Sept 1993

26 All politicians have vanity. Some wear it more gently than others.

David Steel (1938–) British politician. *The Observer*, 'Sayings of the Week', 14 July 1985

27 A politician is a statesman who approaches every question with an open mouth.

Adlai Stevenson Also attrib. to Arthur Goldberg. *The Fine Art of Political Wit* (L. Harris)

28 Whoever could make two ears of corn or two blades of grass to grow upon a spot of ground where only one grew before would deserve better of mankind and do more essential service to his country than the whole race of politicians put together.

Jonathan Swift (1667–1745) Irish-born Anglican priest and writer. *Gulliver's Travels*, 'Voyage to Brobdingnag', Ch. 7

29 A politician is a man who understands government, and it takes a politician to run a government. A statesman is a politician who's been dead ten or fifteen years.

Harry S. Truman (1884–1972) US statesman. *New York World Telegram and Sun*, 12 Apr 1958

30 Politicians can forgive almost anything in the way of abuse; they can forgive subversion, revolution, being contradicted, exposed as liars, even ridiculed, but they can never forgive being ignored.

Auberon Waugh (1939–) British novelist and critic. *The Observer*, 11 Oct 1981

31 It is a pity, as my husband says, that more politicians are not bastards by birth instead of vocation.

Katherine Whitehorn (1926–) British journalist. *The Observer*, 1964

Specific quotations

32 No wonder Harold is back in form – every Labour politician feels more at home attacking his own party's politics.

Anonymous Referring to Harold Wilson. Cartoon caption, *Punch*, 31 Jan 1973

33 The G.O.M., when his life ebbs out,
Will ride in a fiery chariot,
And sit in state
On a red-hot plate
Between Pilate and Judas Iscariot.

Anonymous Gladstone, known as the Grand Old Man, was blamed for the death of General Gordon at Khartoum. *See also* Lord NORTHCOTE. *The Faber Book of English History in Verse* (Kenneth Baker)

34 The Iron Lady of British politics is seeking to revive the cold war.

Anonymous Commenting on a speech by Margaret Thatcher. *Red Star*, 23 Jan 1976

35 Margaret Thatcher is David Owen in drag.

Anonymous *The Rhodesia Herald*, 8 Aug 1979

36 Would you buy a used car from this man?

Anonymous Referring to Richard Nixon.

37 Lord George-Brown drunk is a better man than the Prime Minister sober.

Anonymous Comparing him with Harold Wilson. *The Times*, 6 Mar 1976

38 It is fitting that we should have buried the Unknown Prime Minister by the side of the Unknown Soldier.

Herbert Henry Asquith (1852–1928) British statesman. Said at Bonar Law's funeral, 5 Nov 1923. Attrib.

39 He always has his arm round your waist and his eye on the clock.

Margot Asquith (1865–1945) The second wife of Herbert Asquith. *As I Remember*

40 He could not see a belt without hitting below it.

Margot Asquith Referring to Lloyd George. *Autobiography*, Introduction

41 You'll never get on in politics, my dear, with *that* hair.

Viscountess Nancy Astor (1879–1964) American-born British politician. Attrib.

42 You have no right whatever to speak on behalf of the Government. Foreign Affairs are in the capable hands of Ernest Bevin. His task is quite sufficiently difficult without the embarrassment of irresponsible statements of the kind which you are making…a period of silence on your part would be welcome.

Clement Attlee (1883–1967) British Labour prime minister. Letter to Harold Laski, Chairman of the Labour Party, 20 Aug 1945. *British Political Facts 1900–75*

43 He believes, with all his heart and soul and strength, that there *is* such a thing as truth; he has the soul of a martyr with the intellect of an advocate.

Walter Bagehot (1826–77) British economist and journalist. Referring to Gladstone. *Historical Essays*, 'Mr Gladstone'

44 No man has come so near our definition of a constitutional statesman – the powers of a first-rate man and the creed of a second-rate man.

Walter Bagehot *Historical Essays*, 'The Character of Sir Robert Peel'

45 He did not care in which direction the car was travelling, so long as he remained in the driver's seat.

Max(well) Aitken Beaverbrook, 1st Baron (1879–1964) Canadian-born British newspaper proprietor. Referring to Lloyd George. *New Statesman*, 14 June 1963

46 Of all the politicians I ever saw
The least significant was Bonar Law.
Unless it was MacDonald, by the way:
Or Baldwin – it's impossible to say.

Hilaire Belloc (1870–1953) French-born British poet. *The Faber Book of English History in Verse* (Kenneth Baker)

47 If I rescued a child from drowning, the Press would no doubt headline the story 'Benn grabs child'.

Tony Benn (1925–) British politician. *The Observer*, 'Sayings of the Week', 2 Mar 1975

48 I am on the right wing of the middle of the road and with a strong radical bias.

Tony Benn Attrib.

49 Mr Lloyd George spoke for a hundred and seventeen minutes, in which period he was detected only once in the use of an argument.

Arnold Bennett (1867–1931) British writer. *Things That Have Interested Me*, 'After the March Offensive'

50 A dessicated calculating machine.

Aneurin Bevan (1897–1960) British Labour politician. Referring to Hugh Gaitskell. *Hugh Gaitskell* (W. T. Rodgers)

51 There is no reason to attack the monkey when the organ-grinder is present.

Aneurin Bevan The 'monkey' was Selwyn Lloyd; the 'organ-grinder' was Harold Macmillan. Speech, House of Commons

52 Not while I'm alive, he ain't.

Ernest Bevin (1881–1951) British Labour politician. When told that Aneurin Bevan was 'his own worst enemy'. Also attributed to others. *Aneurin Bevan* (M. Foot)

53 She is trying to wear the trousers of Winston Churchill.

Leonid Brezhnev (1906–82) Soviet statesman. Referring to Margaret Thatcher. Speech, 1979

54 Most British statesmen have either drunk too much or womanized too much. I never fell into the second category.

Lord George Brown (1914–85) British Labour politician. *The Observer*, 11 Nov 1974

55 He was not merely a chip off the old block, but the old block itself.

Edmund Burke (1729–97) British politician. Referring to William Pitt the Younger's first speech in the House of Commons, 26 Feb 1781. Attrib.

56 Mr Macmillan is the best prime minister we have.

R. A. Butler (1902–82) British Conservative politician. Often quoted in the form above. In fact, Butler simply answered 'Yes' to the question 'Would you say that this is the best prime minister we have?' Interview, London Airport, Dec 1955

57 I think the Prime Minister has to be a butcher, and know the joints. That is perhaps where I have not been quite competent enough in knowing the ways that you cut up a carcass.

R. A. Butler Television interview, June 1966

58 Pitt is to Addington
As London is to Paddington.

George Canning (1770–1827) British statesman. Comparing two British prime ministers, William Pitt the Younger and Henry Addington. *The Oracle*

59 The seagreen Incorruptible.

Thomas Carlyle (1795–1881) Scottish historian and essayist. Referring to the French revolutionary Robespierre. *History of the French Revolution*, Pt. II, Bk. IV, Ch. 4

60 She is clearly the best man among them.

Barbara Castle (1910–) British politician. Referring to Margaret Thatcher. *The Castle Diaries*

61 An old man in a hurry.

Lord Randolph Churchill (1849–95) British Conservative politician. Referring to Gladstone. Speech, June 1886

62 For the purposes of recreation he has selected the felling of trees, and we may usefully remark that his amusements, like his politics, are essentially destructive…The forest laments in order that Mr Gladstone may perspire.

Randolph Churchill Speech, Blackpool, 24 Jan 1884

63 Their worst misfortune was his birth; their next worst – his death.

Winston Churchill (1874–1965) British statesman. Referring to Lenin. *The World Crisis*

64 He is like a female llama surprised in her bath.

Winston Churchill Referring to Charles de Gaulle. Attrib.

65 The Happy Warrior of Squandermania.

Winston Churchill Referring to Lloyd George. Attrib.

66 I remember, when I was a child, being taken to the celebrated Barnum's circus, which contained an exhibition of freaks and monstrosities, but the exhibit…which I most desired to see was the one described as 'The Boneless Wonder'. My parents judged that that spectacle would be too revolting and demoralising for my youthful eyes, and I have waited 50 years to see the boneless wonder sitting on the Treasury Bench.

Winston Churchill Referring to Ramsey MacDonald. Speech, House of Commons, 28 Jan 1931

67 I have never seen a human being who more perfectly represented the modern conception of a robot.

Winston Churchill Referring to the Soviet statesman Molotov. *The Second World War*

68 In Franklin Roosevelt there died the greatest American friend we have ever known and the greatest champion of freedom who has ever brought help and comfort from the New World to the Old.

Winston Churchill *The Second World War*

69 The good Lord has only ten.

Georges Clemenceau (1841–1929) French politician. On President Wilson's Fourteen Points (1918). Attrib.

70 She put back the chance of another woman becoming PM by 50 years – by going over the top, becoming a dictator, having illusions of infallibility, which of course brought her downfall.

Ann Clwyd (1937–) British journalist and politician. Referring to Margaret Thatcher. *The Independent*, 28 Apr 1992

71 In the eighteenth century he would have become Prime Minister before he was thirty; as it was he appeared honourably ineligible for the struggle of life.

Cyril Connolly (1903–74) British writer. Referring to the British prime minister Sir Alec Douglas-Home at Eton. *Enemies of Promise*

72 I do not choose to run for President in 1928.

Calvin Coolidge (1872–1933) US president. Announcement in 1927

73 President Nixon's motto was, if two wrongs don't make a right, try three.

Norman Cousins (1915–90) US editor and author. *The Daily Telegraph*, 17 July 1979

74 Dear Randolph, utterly unspoiled by failure.

Noël Coward (1899–1973) British dramatist. Referring to Randolph Churchill. Attrib.

75 In private conversation he tries on speeches like a man trying on ties in his bedroom to see how he would look in them.

Lionel Curtis (1872–1955) British writer. Referring to Winston Churchill. Letter to Nancy Astor, 1912

76 Not even a public figure. A man of no experience. And of the utmost insignificance.

Lord Curzon (1859–1925) British politician. Referring to Stanley Baldwin on his appointment as Prime Minister. *Curzon: The Last Phase* (Harold Nicolson)

77 I myself have become a Gaullist only little by little.

Charles De Gaulle (1890–1970) French general and statesman. *The Observer*, 'Sayings of the Year', 29 Dec 1963

78 …a great master of gibes and flouts and jeers.

Benjamin Disraeli (1804–81) British statesman. Referring to Lord Salisbury. Speech, House of Commons, 5 Aug 1874

79 Gladstone, like Richelieu, can't write. Nothing can be more unmusical, more involved or more uncouth than all his scribblement.

Benjamin Disraeli Letter, 3 Oct 1877

80 If a traveller were informed that such a man was leader of the House of Commons, he may well begin to comprehend how the Egyptians worshipped an insect.

Benjamin Disraeli Referring to Lord John Russell. Attrib.

81 There are two problems in my life. The political ones are insoluble and the economic ones are incomprehensible.

Alec Douglas-Home (1903–) British statesman. Speech, Jan 1964

82 He is used to dealing with estate workers. I cannot see how anyone can say he is out of touch.

Lady Caroline Douglas-Home (1937–) Daughter of Alec Douglas-Home. Referring to her father's suitability to his new role as prime minister. *Daily Herald*, 21 Oct 1963 (Jon Akass)

83 He was the only man I knew who could make a curse sound like a caress.

Michael Foot (1913–) British politician *Aneurin Bevan 1897–1945*

84 This cardinal is the person who rules both the king and the entire kingdom.

Sebastian Giustiniani Venetian ambassador to England. Referring to Cardinal Wolsey. *Wolsey* (A. F. Pollard)

85 Nothing pleased him more than to be styled the arbitrator of the affairs of Christendom.

Sebastian Giustiniani Referring to Cardinal Wolsey. *Letters and Papers of Henry VIII*, Vol. III

86 Count not his broken pledges as a crime
He MEANT them, HOW he meant them – at the time.

Kensal Green Referring to Lloyd George. *The Faber Book of English History in Verse* (Kenneth Baker)

87 A sad day this for Alexander
And many another dead commander.
Jealousy's rife in heroes' hall –
Winston Churchill has bluffed them all.

Kensal Green *The Faber Book of English History in Verse* (Kenneth Baker)

88 His fame endures; we shall not quite forget
The name of Baldwin till we're out of debt.

Kensal Green *The Faber Book of English History in Verse* (Kenneth Baker)

89 This man has a nice smile, but he has got iron teeth.

Andrei Gromyko (1909–89) Soviet politician. In proposing Mikhail Gorbachev for the post of Soviet Communist Party leader. Speech, 1985

90 For the past few months she has been charging about like some bargain-basement Boadicea.

Denis Healey (1917–) British Labour politician. Referring to Margaret Thatcher. *The Observer*, 'Sayings of the Week', 7 Nov 1982

91 I am the Gromyko of the Labour party.

Denis Healey Alluding to Andrei Gromyko (1909–89), Soviet statesman who was foreign minister from 1957 to 1985. Attrib.

92 He would rather follow public opinion than lead it.

Harry Hopkins (1890–1946) US politician. Referring to Roosevelt. Attrib.

93 If a man were to go by chance at the same time with Burke under a shed, to shun a shower, he would say – 'this is an extraordinary man.'

Samuel Johnson (1709–84) British lexicographer. Referring to Edmund Burke. *Life of Johnson* (J. Boswell), Vol. IV

94 Do you realize the responsibility I carry? I'm the only person standing between Nixon and the White House.

John Fitzgerald Kennedy (1917–63) US statesman. Said to Arthur Schlesinger, 13 Oct 1960; Richard Nixon was the Republican candidate in the 1960 US Presidential election. *A Thousand Days* (Arthur M. Schlesinger, Jnr)

95 This goat-footed bard, this half-human visitor to our age from the hag-ridden magic and enchanted woods of Celtic antiquity.

John Maynard Keynes (1883–1946) British economist. Referring to Lloyd George. *Essays and Sketches in Biography*

96 An ego fat on arrogance and drunk on ambition.

Neil Kinnock (1942–) British politician. Describing David Owen.

97 There is another thing that connects Bill Clinton, Boris Yeltsin and François Mitterand; we all like to eat, I perhaps most of all.

Helmut Kohl (1930–) German statesman. *The Observer*, 'Sayings of the Week', 12 June 1994

98 We have heard of people being thrown to the wolves, but never before have we heard of a man being thrown to the wolves with a bargain on the part of the wolves that they would not eat him.

Bonar Law (1858–1923) British statesman. Referring to the fact that the then war minister, Col Seely, had offered his resignation. Speech, House of Common, Mar 1914

99 Look at that man's eyes. You will hear more of him later.

Bonar Law Referring to Mussolini. Attrib.

100 Poor Bonar can't bear being called a liar. Now I don't mind.

David Lloyd George (1863–1945) British Liberal statesman. Referring to Bonar Law, prime minister 1922–23. *Stanley Baldwin* (G. M. Young)

101 He saw foreign policy through the wrong end of a municipal drainpipe.

David Lloyd George Referring to Neville Chamberlain. *The Fine Art of Political Wit* (Harris), Ch. 6

102 A savage old Nabob, with an immense fortune, a tawny complexion, a bad liver and a worse heart.

Lord Macaulay (1800–59) British historian. Referring to Clive of India (1725–74). *Historical Essays*, 'Lord Clive'

103 I am MacWonder one moment and MacBlunder the next.

Harold Macmillan (1894–1986) British politician and prime minister. *The Daily Telegraph*, 15 Nov 1973

104 He displayed unswerving loyalty to his party and a deep concern with the welfare of his country…I will miss him not only as a formidable opponent but also as a man whom I liked and respected.

John Major (1943–) British Conservative politician. Referring to British Labour politician John Smith (1938–94). *The Independent*, 13 May 1994

105 So restless Cromwell could not cease
In the inglorious arts of peace.

Andrew Marvell (1621–78) English poet. *An Horatian Ode upon Cromwell's Return from Ireland*

106 Sit down, man. You're a bloody tragedy.

James Maxton (1885–1946) Scottish Labour leader. Said to Ramsay MacDonald when he made his last speech in Parliament. Attrib.

107 The rogue elephant among British prime ministers.

Dr Kenneth Morgan (1934–) British historian. Referring to Lloyd George. *Life of David Lloyd George*

108 I am not and never have been, a man of the right. My position was on the left and is now in the centre of politics.

Oswald Mosley (1896–1980) British politician. *The Times*, 26 Apr 1968

109 Argue as you please, you are nowhere, that grand old man, the Prime Minister, insists on the other thing.

Lord Northcote (1818–87) British statesman. Referring to Gladstone; the phrase, and its acronym GOM, became his nickname – temporarily reversed to MOG ('Murderer of Gordon') in 1885, after the death of General Gordon at Khartoum. *See also* ANONYMOUS (33). Speech, Liverpool, 12 Apr 1882

110 …reminds me of nothing so much as a recently dead fish before it has had time to stiffen.

George Orwell (Eric Blair; 1903–50) British novelist. Referring to Clement Attlee. Diary, 19 May 1942

111 How could they tell?

Dorothy Parker (1893–1967) US writer. Reaction to news of the death of Calvin Coolidge, US President 1923–29; also attributed to H. L. Mencken. *You Might As Well Live* (J. Keats)

112 Coolidge is a better example of evolution than either Bryan or Darrow, for he knows when not to talk, which is the biggest asset the monkey possesses over the human.

Will Rogers (1879–1935) US actor and humorist. *Saturday Review*, 'A Rogers Thesaurus', 25 Aug 1962

113 Stalin hates the guts of all your top people. He thinks he likes me better, and I hope he will continue to do so.

Franklin D. Roosevelt (1882–1945) US Democratic president. *The Hinge of Fate* (Winston S. Churchill), Ch. 11

114 ...a man who, with all his great qualities, was unable to decide a general principle of action, or to ensure that when decided on it should be carried out by his subordinates.

Marquess of Salisbury (1830–1903) British statesman. Referring to Benjamin Disraeli. *Chapters of Autobiography* (A. J. Balfour)

115 The Right Honourable gentleman is indebted to his memory for his jests, and to his imagination for his facts.

Richard Brinsley Sheridan (1751–1816) British dramatist. Replying to a speech in the House of Commons. Attrib.

116 I will not accept if nominated, and will not serve if elected.

General William Sherman (1820–91) US general. Replying to a request that he accept the Republican presidential nomination. Attrib.

117 He was the Messiah of the new age, and his crucifixion was yet to come.

George Edward Slocombe (1894–1963) British journalist. Referring to Woodrow Wilson and his visit to the Versailles conference. *Mirror to Geneva*

118 Nixon is the kind of politician who would cut down a redwood tree, then mount the stump for a conservation speech.

Adlai Stevenson (1900–65) US statesman. Attrib.

119 With favour and fortune fastidiously blest,
He's loud in his laugh and he's coarse in his jest;
...
Though I name not the wretch you know who I mean –
'Tis the cur dog of Britain and spaniel of Spain.

Jonathan Swift Referring to Sir Robert Walpole. *Two Character Studies*

120 A master of improvised speech and improvised policies.

A. J. P. Taylor (1906–90) British historian. Referring to Lloyd George. *English History 1914–1945*

121 I hope Mrs Thatcher will go until the turn of the century looking like Queen Victoria.

Norman Tebbitt (1931–) British Conservative politician. *The Observer*, 'Sayings of the Week', 17 May 1987

122 If a woman like Eva Peron with no ideals can get that far, think how far I can go with all the ideals that I have.

Margaret Thatcher (1925–) British politician and prime minister. *The Sunday Times*, 1980

123 Ladies and gentlemen, I stand before you tonight in my green chiffon evening gown, my face softly made up, my fair hair gently waved...the Iron Lady of the Western World. Me? A cold war warrior? Well, yes – if that is how they wish to interpret my defence of values, and freedoms fundamental to our way of life.

Margaret Thatcher Referring to the nickname 'The Iron Lady' used by the Soviet paper. *Red Star*. Speech, Dorking, 31 Jan 1976

124 I like old Joe Stalin. He's a good fellow but he's a prisoner of the Politburo. He would make certain agreements but they won't let him keep them.

Harry S. Truman (1884–1972) US statesman. *News Review*, 24 June 1948

125 Introducing Super-Mac.

Vicky (Victor Weisz; 1913–66) German-born British cartoonist. Cartoon caption depicting Harold Macmillan as Superman. *Evening Standard*, 6 Nov 1958

126 The danger to the country, to Europe, to her vast Empire, which is involved in having all these great interests entrusted to the shaking hand of an old, wild, and incomprehensible man of 82½, is very great!

Victoria (1819–1901) Queen of the United Kingdom. Reaction to Gladstone's fourth and last appointment as prime minister, 1892. Letter to Lord Lansdowne, 12 Aug 1892

127 He speaks to Me as if I was a public meeting.

Victoria Referring to Gladstone. *Collections and Recollections* (G. W. E. Russell), Ch. 14

POLITICS

See also Communism, democracy, diplomacy, government, Houses of Parliament, monarchy, opposition, politicians, power politics, socialism

1 When the political columnists say 'Every thinking man' they mean themselves and when the candidates appeal to 'Every intelligent voter' they mean everybody who is going to vote for them.

Franklin P. Adams (1881–1960) US journalist and humorist. *Nods And Becks*

2 Politics, as a practice, whatever its professions, has always been the systematic organisation of hatreds.

Henry Brooks Adams (1838–1918) US historian. *The Education of Henry Adams*

3 Practical politics consists in ignoring facts.

Henry Brooks Adams (1838–1918) US historian. *The Education of Henry Adams*

4 Don't tell my mother I'm in politics – she thinks I play the piano in a whorehouse.

Anonymous US saying.

5 He warns the heads of parties against believing their own lies.

John Arbuthnot (1667–1735) Scottish writer and physician. *The Art of Political Lying*

6 Man is by nature a political animal.

Aristotle (384–322 BC) Greek philosopher. *Politics*, Bk. I

7 Anybody who thinks that the Liberal Democrats are a racist party are staring the facts in the face.

Paddy Ashdown (Jeremy John Durham Ashdown; 1941–) British politician. ITV TV programme *Lunchtime News*, Sept 1993

8 We believe in a League system in which the whole world should be ranged against an aggressor.

Clement Attlee (1883–1967) British statesman and Labour prime minister. Speech, House of Commons, 11 Mar 1935

9 I am a Tory Anarchist, I should like everyone to go about doing just as he pleased – short of altering any of the things to which I have grown accustomed.

Max Beerbohm (1872–1956) British writer. Attrib.

10 We are not just here to manage capitalism but to change society and to define its finer values.

Tony Benn Speech, Labour Party Conference, 1 Oct 1975

11 The connection between humbug and politics is too long established to be challenged.

Ronald Bell British politician. Speech, 5 Dec 1979

12 The accursed power which stands on Privilege
(And goes with Women, and Champagne, and Bridge)
Broke – and Democracy resumed her reign:
(Which goes with Bridge, and Women and Champagne).

Hilaire Belloc (1870–1953) French-born British poet. *Epigrams*, 'On a Great Election'

13 Every Briton is at heart a Tory – especially every British Liberal.

Arnold Bennett (1867–1931) British novelist. *Journal*

14 Politics is a blood sport.

Aneurin Bevan (1897–1960) British Labour politician. *My Life with Nye* (Jennie Lee)

15 No attempt at ethical or social seduction can eradicate from my heart a deep burning hatred for the Tory Party...So far as I am concerned they are lower than vermin.

Aneurin Bevan Speech, Manchester, 4 July 1949

16 We know what happens to people who stay in the middle of the road. They get run over.

Aneurin Bevan *The Observer*, 9 Dec 1953

17 I know that the right kind of political leader for the Labour Party is a desiccated calculating machine.

Aneurin Bevan Usually regarded as a gibe at Hugh Gaitskell. Speech during Labour Party Conference, 29 Sept 1954

18 And you call that statesmanship. I call it an emotional spasm.

Aneurin Bevan Speech, Labour Party Conference, 3 Oct 1957

19 Politics is not an exact science.

Bismarck (1815–98) German statesman. Speech, Prussian Chamber, 18 Dec 1863

20 Politics is not a science...but an art.

Bismarck Speech, Reichstag, 15 Mar 1884

21 Faction is to party what the superlative is to the positive: party is a political evil and faction is the worst of all parties.

Bolingbroke, Henry St John, Viscount (1678–1751) British politician and writer. *The Patriot King*

22 Politics are usually the executive expression of human immaturity.

Vera Brittain (1893–1970) British writer and feminist. *The Rebel Passion*

23 Politics is the art of the possible.

R. A. Butler (1902–82) British Conservative politician. Often attrib. to Butler but used earlier by others, including Bismarck. *The Art of the Possible*, Epigraph

24 The healthy stomach is nothing if not conservative. Few radicals have good digestions.

Samuel Butler (1835–1902) British writer. *Notebooks*

25 I am not made for politics because I am incapable of wishing for, or accepting the death of my adversary.

Albert Camus (1913–60) French existentialist writer. *The Rebel*

26 Detente is like the race in 'Alice in Wonderland' where everyone had to have a prize.

Lord Carrington (1919–) British politician. Speech, Mar 1980

27 What a genius the Labour Party has for cutting itself in half and letting the two parts writhe in public.

Cassandra (William Neil Cannon; 1910–67) Irish journalist. *The Daily Mirror*

28 Labour is not fit to govern.

Winston Churchill (1874–1965) British statesman. Election speech, 1920

29 Would a special relationship between the United States and the British Commonwealth be inconsistent with our over-riding loyalty to the World Organization?

Winston Churchill Speech, 5 Mar 1946

30 Do not criticize your government when out of the country. Never cease to do so when at home.

Winston Churchill Attrib.

31 The disastrous element in the Labour party is its intellectuals.

George Norman Clark (1890–1979) British historian. *A Man of the Thirties* (A. L. Rowse)

32 My home policy? I wage war. My foreign policy? I wage war. Always, everywhere, I wage war.

Georges Clemenceau Speech to the Chamber of Deputies, 8 Mar 1918

33 We now are, as we always have been, decidedly and conscientiously attached to what is called the Tory, and which might with more propriety be called the Conservative, party.

John Wilson Croker (1780–1857) British Tory politician. The first use of the term 'Conservative Party'. In *Quarterly Review*, Jan 1830

34 The right honourable gentleman caught the Whigs bathing, and walked away with their clothes.

Benjamin Disraeli (1804–81) British statesman. Referring to Sir Robert Peel. Speech, House of Commons, 28 Feb 1845

35 A Conservative government is an organized hypocrisy.

Benjamin Disraeli . Speech, 17 Mar 1845

36 During the last few weeks I have felt that the Suez Canal was flowing through my drawing room.

Clarissa Eden (1920–85) Wife of Anthony Eden. Said during the Suez crisis of 1956. Attrib.

37 All terrorists, at the invitation of the Government, end up with drinks at the Dorchester.

Hugh Gaitskell (1906–63) British Labour politician. Letter to *The Guardian*, 23 Aug 1977 (Dora Gaitskell)

38 There are some of us...who will fight, fight, fight, and fight again to save the party we love.

Hugh Gaitskell After his policy for a nuclear deterrent had been defeated. Speech, Labour Party conference, Scarborough, 3 Oct 1960

39 There are times in politics when you must be on the right side and lose.

John Kenneth Galbraith (1908–) US economist. *The Observer*, 'Sayings of the Week', 11 Feb 1968

40 Few things are as immutable as the addiction of political groups to the ideas by which they have once won office.

John Kenneth Galbraith *The Affluent Society*, Ch. 13

41 It isn't worth a pitcher of warm spit.

John Nance Garner (1868–1937) US Democratic vice-president. Referring to the Vice-Presidency; sometimes 'piss' is substituted for 'spit'. Attrib.

42 Today 23 years ago dear Grandmama died. I wonder what she would have thought of a Labour Government.

George V (1865–1936) King of the United Kingdom. On the formation of the first Labour Government. His grandmother was Queen Victoria. Diary, 22 Jan 1924

43 It does no harm to throw the occasional man overboard, but it does not do much good if you are steering full speed ahead for the rocks.

Ian Gilmour (1926–) British Conservative politician. Said after being sacked as Deputy Foreign Secretary. *Time*, Sept 1981

44 I often think it's comical
How Nature always does contrive
That every boy and every gal
That's born into the world alive
Is either a little Liberal
Or else a little Conservative!

W. S. Gilbert (1836–1911) British dramatist. *Iolanthe*, II

45 Christchurch was the place where the difference between the Tories and the Alfred Chicken Party was that members of the Alfred Chicken Party ran around with their heads still on.

Philip Goldenberg (1946–) British politician. Referring to a by-election that the Conservatives unexpectedly lost. *The Independent*, 21 Sept 1993

46 If the British public falls for this, I say it will be stark, staring bonkers.

Lord Hailsham (1907–) British Conservative politician. Referring to Labour policy in the 1964 general-election campaign. Press conference, Conservative Central Office, 12 Oct 1964

47 A great party is not to be brought down because of a scandal by a woman of easy virtue and a proved liar.

Lord Hailsham Referring to the Profumo affair, in BBC interview, 13 June 1963. *The Pendulum Years*, Ch. 3 (Bernard Levin)

48 Their Europeanism is nothing but imperialism with an inferiority complex.

Denis Healey (1917–) British Labour politician. Referring to the policies of the Conservative party. *The Observer*, 'Sayings of the Week', 7 Oct 1962

49 I don't think that modesty is the oustanding characteristic of contemporary politics, do you?

Edward Heath (1916–) British politician and prime minister. Remark, Dec 1988

50 Never judge a country by its politics. After all, we English are quite honest by nature, aren't we?

Alfred Hitchcock (1889–1980) British film director. *The Lady Vanishes*

51 The essential thing is the formation of the political will of the nation: that is the starting point for political action.

Adolf Hitler (1889–1945) German dictator. Speech, Düsseldorf, 27 Jan 1932

52 You can't adopt politics as a profession and remain honest.

Louis McHenry Howe (1871–1936) US diplomat. Speech, Columbia University, 17 Jan 1933

53 The Politics of Joy.

Hubert H. Humphrey (1911–78) US Democratic vice-president. Campaign slogan, 1964

54 For in the case of nutrition and health, just as in the case of education, the gentleman in Whitehall really does know better what is good for people than the people know themselves.

Douglas Jay (1907–) British Labour politician. *The Socialist Case*

55 Fair Shares for All, is Labour's Call.

Douglas Jay Slogan, Battersea North by-election, June 1946

56 A little rebellion, now and then, is a good thing, and as necessary in the political world as storms in the physical.

Thomas Jefferson (1743–1826) US statesman.

57 If you're in politics and you can't tell when you walk into a room who's for you and who's against you, then you're in the wrong line of work.

Lyndon B. Johnson (1908–73) US statesman. *The Lyndon Johnson Story* (B. Mooney)

58 Sir, I perceive you are a vile Whig.

Samuel Johnson (1709–84) British lexicographer. Speaking to Sir Adam Fergusson. *Life of Johnson* (J. Boswell), Vol. II

59 Why, Sir, most schemes of political improvement are very laughable things.

Samuel Johnson *Life of Johnson* (J. Boswell), Vol. II

60 Politics are now nothing more than a means of rising in the world.

Samuel Johnson *Life of Johnson* (J. Boswell), Vol. II

61 Mothers all want their sons to grow up to become president, but they don't want them to become politicians in the process.

John Fitzgerald Kennedy (1917–63) US statesman. Attrib.

62 What is objectionable, what is dangerous about extremists is not that they are extreme but that they are intolerant.

Robert Kennedy (1925–68) US politician. *The Pursuit of Justice*

63 The idea that there is a model Labour voter, a blue-collar council house tenant who belongs to a union and has 2.4 children, a five-year-old car and a holiday in Blackpool, is patronizing and politically immature.

Neil Kinnock (1942–) British politician. Speech, 1986

64 Proportional Representation, I think, is fundamentally counter-democratic.

Neil Kinnock *Marxism Today*, 1983

65 Party loyalty lowers the greatest of men to the petty level of the masses.

Jean de La Bruyère (1645–96) French satirist. *Les Caractères*

66 States, like men, have their growth, their manhood, their decrepitude, their decay.

Walter Savage Landor (1775–1864) British poet and writer. *Imaginary Conversations*, 'Pollio and Calvus'

67 If it were necessary to give the briefest possible definition of imperialism we should have to say that imperialism is the monopoly stage of capitalism.

Lenin (Vladimir Ilich Ulyanov; 1870–1924) Russian

revolutionary leader. *Imperialism, the Highest Stage of Capitalism*, Ch. 7

68 In every age the vilest specimens of human nature are to be found among demagogues.

Lord Macaulay (1800–59) British historian. *History of England*, Vol. I, Ch. 5

69 Forever poised between a cliché and an indiscretion.

Harold Macmillan (1894–1986) British politician and prime minister. Referring to a Foreign Secretary's life. *Newsweek*, 30 Apr 1956

70 I thought the best thing to do was to settle up these little local difficulties, and then turn to the wider vision of the Commonwealth.

Harold Macmillan (1894–1986) British politician and prime minister. Referring to resignation of ministers. Attrib., London Airport, 7 Jan 1958

71 There are three groups that no prime minister should provoke: the Treasury, the Vatican, and the National Union of Mineworkers.

Harold Macmillan First used by Stanley Baldwin. Attrib.

72 First of all the Georgian silver goes, and then that nice furniture that used to be in the saloon. Then the Canalettos go.

Harold Macmillan Referring to privatization of profitable nationalized industries. Often misquoted as 'selling the family silver'. Speech, House of Lords, 1985

73 In politics, as in grammar, one should be able to tell the substantives from the adjectives. Hitler was a substantive; Mussolini only an adjective. Hitler was a nuisance. Mussolini was bloody. Together a bloody nuisance.

Salvador de Madariaga y Rogo (1886–1978) Spanish diplomat and writer. Attrib.

74 Every intellectual attitude is latently political.

Thomas Mann (1875–1955) German novelist. *The Observer*, 11 Aug 1974

75 All reactionaries are paper tigers.

Mao Tse-Tung (1893–1976) Chinese communist leader. *Quotations from Chairman Mao Tse-Tung*, Ch. 6

76 McCarthyism is Americanism with its sleeves rolled.

Joseph R. McCarthy (1908–57) US senator. Speech, 1952

77 The expression 'positive neutrality' is a contradiction in terms. There can be no more positive neutrality than there can be a vegetarian tiger.

V. K. Krishna Menon (1896–1974) Indian barrister and writer. *The New York Times*, 18 Oct 1960

78 Any party which takes credit for the rain must not be surprised if its opponents blame it for the drought.

Dwight W. Morrow (1873–1931) US politician. Speech, Oct 1930

79 We cannot change our policy now. After all, we are not political whores.

Benito Mussolini (1883–1945) Italian dictator. *Hitler* (Alan Bullock), Ch. 8

80 I still love you, but in politics there is no heart, only head.

Napoleon I (Napoleon Bonaparte; 1769–1821) French emperor. Referring to his divorce, for reasons of state, from the Empress Josephine (1809). *Bonaparte* (C. Barnett)

81 In our time, political speech and writing are largely the defence of the indefensible.

George Orwell (Eric Blair; 1903–50) British novelist. *Politics and the English Language*

82 As these two, the kingdom and the priesthood, are brought together by divine mystery, so are their two heads, by the force of mutual loves; the King may be found in the Roman pontiff, and the Roman pontiff be found in the King.

St Peter Damian (1007–72) Bishop of Ostia. Written just after the enthronement of Pope Alexander II (1061). *Disceptatio synodalis*

83 All political lives, unless they are cut off in midstream at a happy juncture, end in failure, because that is the nature of politics and of human affairs.

Enoch Powell (1912–) British politician. *Joseph Chamberlain*

84 I used to say that politics was the second lowest profession and I have come to know that it bears a great similarity to the first.

Ronald Reagan (1911–) US politician and president. *The Observer*, 13 May 1979

85 Remember this, Griffin. The revolution eats its own. Capitalism re-creates itself.

Mordecai Richler (1931–) Canadian novelist. *Cocksure*, Ch. 22

86 The more you read about politics, you got to admit that each party is worse than the other.

Will Rogers (1879–1935) US actor and humorist. *Saturday Review*, 'A Rogers Thesaurus', 25 Aug 1962

87 England elects a Labour Government. When a man goes in for politics over here, he has no time to labour, and any man that labours has no time to fool with politics. Over there politics is an obligation; over here it's a business.

Will Rogers *Autobiography*, Ch. 14

88 I am reminded of four definitions. A radical is a man with both feet firmly planted – in the air; a conservative is a man with two perfectly good legs who, however, has never learned to walk; a reactionary is a somnambulist walking backwards; a liberal is a man who uses his legs and his hands at the behest of his head.

Franklin D. Roosevelt (1882–1945) US Democratic president. Radio broadcast, 26 Oct 1939

89 You have to clean your plate.

Lord Rosebery (1847–1929) British statesman. Said to the Liberal Party. Speech, Chesterfield, 16 Dec 1901

90 Revolutionary spirits of my father's generation waited for Lefty. Existentialist heroes of my youth waited for Godot. Neither showed up.

Theodore Roszak (1933–) US writer and editor. Referring to the play by Samuel Beckett *Waiting for Godot* (1952). *Unfinished Animal*

91 An Englishman has to have a Party, just as he has to have trousers.

Bertrand Russell (1872–1970) British philosopher. Letter to Maurice Amos MP, 16 June 1936

92 The collection of prejudices which is called political philosophy is useful provided that it is not called philosophy.

Bertrand Russell (1872–1970) British philosopher. *The Observer*, 'Sayings of the Year', 1962

93 History is past politics, and politics present history.

John Robert Seeley (1834–95) British historian. Quoting the historian E. A. Freeman. *The Growth of British Policy*

94 If ever there's any emergence of a fourth party in this country, the task of the Liberal party is to strangle it at birth.

Cyril Smith (1928–) British Liberal politician. *The Guardian*, 1981

95 If Her Majesty stood for Parliament – if the Tory Party had any sense and made Her its leader instead of that grammar school twit Heath – us Tories, mate, would win every election we went in for.

Johnny Speight (1920–) British television scriptwriter. *Till Death Do Us Part*

96 The Republican form of Government is the highest form of government; but because of this it requires the highest type of human nature – a type nowhere at present existing.

Herbert Spencer (1820–1903) British philosopher. *Essays*, 'The Americans'

97 The tasks of the party are...to be cautious and not allow our country to be drawn into conflicts by warmongers who are accustomed to have others pull the chestnuts out of the fire for them.

Joseph Stalin (J. Dzhugashvili; 1879–1953) Soviet statesman. Speech, 8th Congress of the Communist Party, 6 Jan 1941

98 Disdain is the wrong word, but perhaps affection is too strong a word.

David Steel (1938–) British politician. Referring to his attitude to the Liberal party of which he was the leader (1976–88). *The Observer*, 'Sayings of the Week', 22 Sept 1985

99 Go back to your constituencies and prepare for government!

David Steel Speech to party conference, 1985

100 I sense that the British electorate is now itching to break out once and for all from the discredited straight-jacket of the past.

David Steel *The Times*, 2 June 1987

101 An independent is a guy who wants to take the politics out of politics.

Adlai Stevenson (1900–65) US statesman. *The Art Of Politics*.

102 Politics is perhaps the only profession for which no preparation is thought necessary.

Robert Louis Stevenson (1850–94) Scottish writer. *Familiar Studies of Men and Books*, 'Yoshida-Torajiro'

103 Socialists treat their servants with respect and then wonder why they vote Conservative.

Tom Stoppard (1937–) Czech-born British dramatist. *Lord Malquist and Mr Moon*, Pt. V, Ch. 1

104 Revolts, republics, revolutions, most
No graver than a schoolboy's barring out.

Alfred, Lord Tennyson (1809–92) British poet. *The Princess*, Conclusion

105 Any woman who understands the problems of running a home will be nearer to understanding the problems of running a country.

Margaret Thatcher (1925–) British politician and prime minister. *The Observer*, 8 May 1979

106 I can trust my husband not to fall asleep on a public platform and he usually claps in the right places.

Margaret Thatcher *The Observer*, 20 Aug 1978

107 Britain is no longer in the politics of the pendulum, but of the ratchet.

Margaret Thatcher Speech, Institute of Public Relations, 1977

108 In politics, if you want anything said, ask a man; if you want anything done, ask a woman.

Margaret Thatcher (1925–) British politician and prime minister. *The Changing Anatomy of Britain* (Anthony Sampson)

109 Looking around the House, one realizes that we are all minorities now.

Jeremy Thorpe (1929–) British Liberal politician. After a General Election which resulted in no clear majority for any party. Speech, House of Commons, 6 Mar 1974

110 Politics is the art of preventing people from taking part in affairs which properly concern them.

Paul Valéry (1871–1945) French poet and writer. *Tel quel*

111 Real politics, not the kind one reads and writes about...has little to do with ideas, values and imagination...and everything to do with manoeuvres, intrigues, plots, paranoias, betrayals, a great deal of calculation, no little cynicism and every kind of con game.

Mario Vargas Llosa (1936–) Peruvian novelist. *A Fish in the Water*

112 Any American who is prepared to run for President should automatically, by definition, be disqualified from ever doing so.

Gore Vidal (1925–) US novelist. Attrib.

113 Politics come from man. Mercy, compassion and justice come from God.

Terry Waite (1939–) British churchman. *The Observer*, 'Sayings of the Week', 13 Jan 1985

114 The hungry hare has no frontiers and doesn't follow ideologies. The hungry hare goes where it finds the food. And the other hares don't block its passage with the tanks.

Lech Walesa (1943–) Polish trade unionist. Interview, 1981

115 A writer of crook stories ought never to stop seeking new material.

Edgar Wallace (1875–1932) British thriller writer. Said when a candidate for Parliament. *The Long Weekend* (Alan Hodge)

116 He stood twice for Parliament, but so diffidently that his candidature passed almost unnoticed.

Evelyn Waugh (1903–66) British novelist. *Decline and Fall*, Pt. III, Ch. 1

117 Pappenhacker says that every time you are polite to a proletarian you are helping to bolster up the capitalist system.

Evelyn Waugh *Scoop*, Bk. I, Ch. 5

118 The Labour Party is going about the country stirring up apathy.

William Whitelaw (1918–) British Conservative politician. Attrib.

119 In vain will such a minister, or the foul dregs of his power, the tools of despotism and corruption, preach up 'the spirit of concord...' They have sent the spirit of discord through the land and I will prophesy it will never be distingushed but by the extinction of their power.

John Wilkes (1725–97) British politician. Part of a libellous article on George III's speech (which was drafted by George Grenville, the 'minister') at the opening of parliament. This article led to a celebrated legal battle, and launched his career as a champion of the common man against overbearing government. *North Briton*, 45 (23 Apr 1763)

120 The Labour party is like a stage-coach. If you rattle along at great speed everybody inside is too exhilarated or too seasick to cause any trouble. But if you stop everybody gets out and argues about where to go next.

Harold Wilson (1916–) British politician and prime minister. *Harold Wilson, The Authentic Portrait* (Leslie Smith)

121 Hence the practised performances of latter-day politicians in the game of musical daggers: never be left holding the dagger when the music stops.

Harold Wilson *The Governance of Britain*, Ch. 2

122 A week is a long time in politics.

Harold Wilson First said in 1965 or 1966, and repeated on several occasions. Attrib.

123 Every dog is allowed one bite, but a different view is taken of a dog that goes on biting all the time. He may not get his licence returned when it falls due.

Harold Wilson (1916–) Referring to opposition within his own party. Speech, 2 Mar 1967

124 Politics is the entertainment branch of Industry.

Frank Zappa (1940–93) US rock musician.

125 For socialists, going to bed with the Liberals is like having oral sex with a shark.

Larry Zolf (1934–) Canadian TV journalist and writer.

POPE, ALEXANDER

(1688–1744) British poet. His witty and satirical poems include the mock-heroic *The Rape of the Lock* (1712), the mock epic *The Dunciad* (1728), and the philosophical *An Essay on Man* (1733).

Quotations about Pope

1 The wicked asp of Twickenham.

Lady Mary Wortley Montague (1689–1762) English writer. Attrib.

2 In Pope I cannot read a line,
But with a sigh I wish it mine;
When he can in one couplet fix
More sense than I can do in six:
It gives me such a jealous fit,
I cry, 'Pox take him and his wit!'

Jonathan Swift (1667–1745) Irish-born Anglican priest and writer. *On the Death of Dr. Swift*

Quotations by Pope

3 Ye gods! annihilate but space and time.
And make two lovers happy.

The Art of Sinking in Poetry, 11

4 The right divine of kings to govern wrong.

The Dunciad, IV

5 When man's whole frame is obvious to a flea.

The Dunciad, IV

6 I mount! I fly!
O grave! where is thy victory?
O death! where is thy sting?

The Dying Christian to his Soul

7 A heap of dust alone remains of thee;
'Tis all thou art, and all the proud shall be!

Elegy to the Memory of an Unfortunate Lady

8 Line after line my gushing eyes o'erflow,
led through a sad variety of woe.

Eloisa to Abelard

9 You beat your pate, and fancy wit will come;
Knock as you please, there's nobody at home.

Epigram

10 Do good by stealth, and blush to find it fame.

Epilogue to the Satires, Dialogue I

11 Ask you what provocation I have had?
The strong antipathy of good to bad.

Epilogue to the Satires, Dialogue II

12 Yes; I am proud, I must be proud to see
Men not afraid of God, afraid of me.

Epilogue to the Satires, Dialogue II

13 The Muse but serv'd to ease some friend, not Wife,
To help me through this long disease, my life.

Epistle to Dr. Arbuthnot

14 Damn with faint praise, assent with civil leer,
And, without sneering, teach the rest to sneer.

Epistle to Dr. Arbuthnot

15 Curst be the verse, how well so'er it flow,
That tends to make one worthy man my foe.

Epistle to Dr. Arbuthnot

16 Wit that can creep, and pride that licks the dust.

Epistle to Dr. Arbuthnot

17 No creature smarts so little as a fool.

Epistle to Dr. Arbuthnot

18 In wit a man; simplicity a child.

Epitaph on Mr. Gay

19 Nature, and Nature's laws lay hid in night:
God said, *Let Newton be!* and all was light.

For a reply, *see* SQUIRE. *Epitaphs*, 'Intended for Sir Isaac Newton'

20 'Tis hard to say, if greater want of skill
Appear in writing or in judging ill.

An Essay on Criticism

21 'Tis with our judgments as our watches, none
Go just alike, yet each believes his own.

An Essay on Criticism

22 Of all the causes which conspire to blind
Man's erring judgment, and misguide the mind,
What the weak head with strongest bias rules,
Is Pride, the never-failing vice of fools.

An Essay on Criticism

23 A little learning is a dangerous thing;
Drink deep, or taste not the Pierian spring:

There shallow draughts intoxicate the brain,
And drinking largely sobers us again.
An Essay on Criticism

24 Whoever thinks a faultless piece to see,
Thinks what ne'er was, nor is, nor e'er shall be.
An Essay on Criticism

25 True wit is nature to advantage dress'd;
What oft was thought, but ne'er so well express'd.
An Essay on Criticism

26 True ease in writing comes from art, not chance,
As those move easiest who have learn'd to dance.
'Tis not enough no harshness gives offence,
The sound must seem an echo to the sense.
An Essay on Criticism

27 Fondly we think we honour merit then,
When we but praise ourselves in other men.
An Essay on Criticism

28 To err is human, to forgive, divine.
An Essay on Criticism

29 For fools rush in where angels fear to tread.
An Essay on Criticism

30 Words are like leaves; and where they most abound,
Much fruit of sense beneath is rarely found.
An Essay on Criticism

31 Nor in the critic let the man be lost.
An Essay on Criticism

32 Hope springs eternal in the human breast;
Man never is, but always to be blest.
An Essay on Man, I

33 Created half to rise, and half to fall;
Great lord of all things, yet a prey to all;
Sole judge of truth, in endless error hurl'd;
The glory, jest, and riddle of the world!
An Essay on Man, II

34 Know then thyself, presume not God to scan,
The proper study of Mankind is Man.
An Essay on Man, II

35 And hence one master-passion in the breast,
Like Aaron's serpent, swallows up the rest.
An Essay on Man, II

36 That true self-love and social are the same;
That virtue only makes our bliss below;
And all our knowledge is, ourselves to know.
An Essay on Man, IV

37 Order is heaven's first law.
An Essay on Man, IV

38 Not to admire, is all the art I know
To make men happy, and to keep them so.
Imitations of Horace, 'To Mr. Murray'

39 To observations which ourselves we make.
We grow more partial for th' observer's sake.
Moral Essays, I

40 'Tis education forms the common mind,
Just as the twig is bent, the tree's inclined.
Moral Essays, I

41 Most women have no characters at all.
Moral Essays, II

42 Men, some to business, some to pleasure take;
But every woman is at heart a rake.
Moral Essays, II

43 Woman's at best a contradiction still.
Moral Essays, II

44 See how the world its veterans rewards!
A youth of frolics, an old age of cards.
Moral Essays, II

45 The ruling passion, be it what it will
The ruling passion conquers reason still.
Moral Essays, III

46 Who shall decide when doctors disagree?
Moral Essays, III

47 Where'er you walk, cool gales shall fan the glade,
Trees, where you sit, shall crowd into a shade:
Where'er you tread, the blushing flow'rs shall rise,
And all things flourish where you turn your eyes.
Pastorals, 'Summer'

48 What dire offence from am'rous causes springs,
What mighty contests rise from trivial things.
The Rape of the Lock, I

49 Here thou great Anna! whom three realms obey,
Dost sometimes counsel take – and sometimes Tea.
The Rape of the Lock, III

50 Not louder shrieks to pitying heav'n are cast,
When husbands, or when lap-dogs breathe their last.
The Rape of the Lock, III

51 The hungry judges soon the sentence sign,
And wretches hang that jury-men may dine.
The Rape of the Lock, III

52 Coffee which makes the politician wise,
And see through all things with his half-shut eyes.
The Rape of the Lock, III

53 The vulgar boil, the learned roast an egg.
Satires and Epistles of Horace Imitated, Bk. II

54 A man should never be ashamed to own he has been in the wrong, which is but saying, in other words, that he is wiser to-day than he was yesterday.
Thoughts on Various Subjects

55 It is with narrow-souled people as with narrow-necked bottles: the less they have in them, the more noise they make in pouring it out.
Thoughts on Various Subjects

56 When men grow virtuous in their old age, they only make a sacrifice to God of the devil's leavings.
Thoughts on Various Subjects

57 I never knew any man in my life who could not bear another's misfortunes perfectly like a Christian.
Thoughts on Various Subjects

58 The vanity of human life is like a river, constantly passing away, and yet constantly coming on.

Thoughts on Various Subjects

59 Here am I, dying of a hundred good symptoms.

To George, Lord Lyttelton, 15 May 1744.

Anecdotes by and about Alexander Pope (Joseph Spence)

60 'Blessed is the man who expects nothing, for he shall never be disappointed' was the ninth beatitude.

Letter to Fortescue, 23 Sept 1725

61 How often are we to die before we go quite off this stage? In every friend we lose a part of ourselves, and the best part.

Letter to Jonathan Swift, 5 Dec 1732

62 I am His Highness' dog at Kew;
Pray tell me sir, whose dog are you?

On the collar of a dog given to Frederick, Prince of Wales

POPULARITY

See also fame

1 Do not let that trouble Your Excellency; perhaps the greetings are intended for me.

Ludwig van Beethoven (1770–1827) German composer. Said when walking with the poet Goethe, when Goethe complained about greetings from passers-by. *Thayer's Life of Beethoven* (E. Forbes)

2 Everybody hates me because I'm so universally liked.

Peter De Vries (1910–93) US novelist. *The Vale of Laughter*, Pt. I

3 Popularity is a crime from the moment it is sought; it is only a virtue where men have it whether they will or no.

Lord Halifax (1633–95) English statesman. *Political, Moral and Miscellaneous Thoughts and Reflections*

4 Popularity? It's glory's small change.

Victor Hugo (1802–85) French writer. *Ruy Blas*, III

5 The worse I do, the more popular I get.

John Fitzgerald Kennedy (1917–63) US statesman. Referring to his popularity following the failure of the US invasion of Cuba. *The People's Almanac* (D. Wallechinsky)

6 We're more popular than Jesus Christ now. I don't know which will go first. Rock and roll or Christianity.

John Lennon (1940–80) British rock musician. *The Beatles Illustrated Lyrics*

7 He's liked, but he's not well liked.

Arthur Miller (1915–) US dramatist. *Death of a Salesman*, I

8 I don't resent his popularity or anything else. Good Lord, I co-starred with Errol Flynn once.

Ronald Reagan (1911–) US politician and president. Remark, Dec 1987

9 He hasn't an enemy in the world, and none of his friends like him.

Oscar Wilde (1854–1900) Irish-born British dramatist. Said of G. B. Shaw. *Sixteen Self Sketches* (Shaw), Ch. 17

POPULAR MUSIC

1 Rock'n'roll is part of a pest to undermine the morals of the youth of our nation. It...brings people of both races together.

Anonymous Statement by the North Alabama Citizens' Council in the 1950s

2 It was three o'clock in the morning in New York. It was pouring with rain, and it came to me... 'And now the end is near and so I face the final curtain'...And I said wow that's it, that's for Sinatra...and then I cried.

Paul Anka (1941–) Canadian songwriter. On completing the English lyrics to the Claude Francois original called *Comme D'Habitude*.

3 Give me that rock'n'roll music,
Any old way you choose it,
It's got to be rock'n'roll music,
If you want to dance with me.

The Beatles British pop group. *Rock'n'roll music*

4 Listen kid, take my advice, never hate a song that has sold half a million copies.

Irving Berlin (Israel Baline; 1888–1989) Russian-born US composer. Giving advice to the composer Cole Porter. Attrib.

5 Roll Over Beethoven.

Chuck Berry (1931–) US rock-and-roll musician. Song title.

6 Hail, hail rock'n'roll.
Deliver me from the days of old.

Chuck Berry *Hail, hail, rock'n'roll*

7 The greatest composers since Beethoven.

Richard Buckle (1916–) British writer. Referring to John Lennon and Paul McCartney. Attrib.

8 Do they merit vitriol, even a drop of it? Yes, because they corrupt the young, persuading them that the mature world, which produced Beethoven and Schweitzer, sets an even higher value on the transient anodynes of youth than does youth itself...They are the Hollow Men. They are electronic lice.

Anthony Burgess (1917–) British novelist. Referring to disc jockeys. *Punch*, 20 Sept 1967

9 Canned music is like audible wallpaper.

Alistair Cooke (1908–) British broadcaster. Attrib.

10 Strange how potent cheap music is.

Noël Coward (1899–1973) British dramatist. *Private Lives*

11 I think popular music in this country is one of the few things in the twentieth century that have made giant strides in reverse.

Bing Crosby (Harry Lillis Crosby; 1904–77) US singer. Interview in *This Week*

12 That's jazz, Brother. That's what jazz does. It makes the man selfish. He doesn't give a fuck about his brothers. That's what jazz is doing to Dean, said Joey The Lips.

Roddy Doyle (1958–) Irish novelist and playwright. *The Commitments*

13 Soul is the rhythm o' sex. It's the rhythm o' the factory too. The workin' man's rhythm. Sex an' factory. Not the factory I'm in, said Natalie. There isn't much rhythm guttin' fish.

Roddy Doyle *The Commitments*

14 Yea, some of them are about ten minutes long, others five or six.

Bob Dylan (Robert Allen Zimmerman; 1941–) US songwriter. On being asked in an interview, to say something about his songs. Attrib.

15 Rock Around the Clock.

Bill Haley and The Comets US rock-and-roll band. Song title

16 Everybody is sleeping with everybody else in this business, but the artist is the only one that's getting screwed.

Billy Joel (1949–) US pop singer. *The Independent*, 24 June 1994

17 We're more popular than Jesus Christ now. I don't know which will go first, Rock and Roll or Christianity.

John Lennon (1940–80) British rock musician. *The Beatles Illustrated Lyrics*

18 George Harrison is a sweet sort of hapless character who doesn't have a mean bone in his body.

Madonna (Madonna Louise Veronica Ciccone; 1958–) US pop singer and film star. *Rolling Stone*, 5 June 1986

19 I could eat alphabet soup and *shit* better lyrics.

Johnny Mercer (1909–76) US lyricist and composer. Speaking about a British musical. Attrib.

20 What a terrible revenge by the culture of the Negroes on that of the Whites.

Ignacy Paderewski (1860–1941) Polish pianist. Referring to jazz. Attrib.

21 Every popular song has at least one line or sentence that is perfectly clear – the line that fits the music.

Ezra Pound (1885–1972) US poet and critic. Attrib.

22 It's only rock and roll
But I like it.

The Rolling Stones British rock band. *It's Only Rock and Roll*

23 Rock and roll is phony and false, and it's sung, written and played for the most part by cretinous goons.

Frank Sinatra (1915–) US singer and actor. Remark, 1957

24 Jazz will endure just as long as people hear it through their feet instead of their brains.

John Philip Sousa (1854–1932) US composer, conductor, and writer. Attrib.

25 How dare they describe this thing I've worked at in my voicebox as shouting? I always feel my voice is like black velvet on sandpaper.

Rod Stewart (1945–) British singer. Attrib.

26 No change in musical style...will survive unless it is accompanied by a change in clothing style.

Frank Zappa (1940–93) US rock musician. *The Real Frank Zappa Book*

PORNOGRAPHY

See also censorship, prudery, sex

1 This is the kind of show that gives pornography a bad name.

Clive Barnes (1927–) British-born theatre and ballet critic. Reviewing *Oh, Calcutta!* Attrib.

2 I don't think pornography is very harmful, but it is terribly, terribly boring.

Noël Coward (1899–1973) British dramatist. *The Observer*, 'Sayings of the Week', 24 Sept 1972

3 Women do not believe that men believe what pornography says about women. But they do. From the worst to the best of them, they do.

Andrea Dworkin (1946–) US writer and journalist. *Pornography: Men Possessing Women*

4 Pornography is the attempt to insult sex, to do dirt on it.

D. H. Lawrence (1885–1930) British novelist. *Phoenix*, 'Pornography and Obscenity'

5 It is heartless and it is mindless and it is a lie.

John McGahern (1934–) British writer. *The Pornographer*

6 Its avowed purpose is to excite sexual desire, which, I should have thought, is unnecessary in the case of the young, inconvenient in the case of the middle aged, and unseemly in the old.

Malcolm Muggeridge (1903–90) British writer. *Tread Softly For You Tread On My Jokes*, 1966

7 *Lady Chatterley's Lover* is a book that all Christians might read with profit.

John Robinson (1919–83) Bishop of Woolwich. Said in the court case against Penguin Books. Attrib.

8 Don't be daft. You don't get any pornography on there, not on the telly. Get filth, that's all. The only place you get pornography is in yer Sunday papers.

Johnny Speight (1920–) British television scriptwriter. *Till Death Do Us Part*

PORTER, COLE

(1893–1964) American songwriter and composer, noted for his witty lyrics. He wrote scores for such musicals as *Kiss Me Kate* (1953), *High Society* (1956), and *Can-Can* (1959).

1 Now: heaven knows, anything goes.

Anything Goes, title song

2 I've Got You Under My Skin.

Born to Dance, song title

3 I love Paris in the springtime.

Can-Can, 'I Love Paris'

4 Night and day, you are the one,
Only you beneath the moon and under the sun.

The Gay Divorcee, 'Night and Day'

5 Miss Otis regrets she's unable to lunch today.

Hi Diddle Diddle, Miss Otis Regrets

6 HE. Have you heard it's in the stars
Next July we collide with Mars?
SHE. Well, did you evah! What a swell party this is.

High Society, 'Well, Did You Evah!'

7 And we suddenly know, what heaven we're in,
When they begin the beguine.

Jubilee, 'Begin the Beguine'

8 But I'm always true to you, darlin', in my fashion,
Yes, I'm always true to you, darlin', in my way.

Kiss Me, Kate, 'Always True to You in My Fashion'

9 Let's Do It; Let's Fall in Love.
Paris, song title

10 Who Wants to Be a Millionaire? I don't.
Who Wants to be a Millionaire?, title song

POSSIBILITY

1 The grand Perhaps!
Robert Browning (1812–89) British poet. *Bishop Blougram's Apology*

2 However, one cannot put a quart in a pint cup.
Charlotte Perkins Gilman (1860–1935) US writer. *The Living of Charlotte Perkins Gilman*

3 Your If is the only peace-maker; much virtue in If.
William Shakespeare (1564–1616) English dramatist. *As You Like It*, V:4

POSTERITY

See also death, fame, future, immortality, reputation

1 Think of your forefathers! Think of your posterity!
John Quincy Adams (1767–1848) Sixth president of America. Speech, Plymouth, Massachusetts, 22 Dec 1802

2 We are always doing something for posterity, but I would fain see posterity do something for us.
Joseph Addison (1672–1719) British essayist. *The Spectator*, 583

3 Let us honour if we can
The vertical man
Though we value none
But the horizontal one.
W. H. Auden (1907–73) British poet. *Epigraph for Poems*

4 Posterity is as likely to be wrong as anybody else.
Heywood Brown *Sitting on the World*

5 When a man is in doubt about this or that in his writing, it will often guide him if he asks himself how it will tell a hundred years hence.
Samuel Butler (1835–1902) British writer. *Notebooks*

6 I think I shall be among the English Poets after my death.
John Keats (1795–1821) British poet. Letter to George and Georgiana Keats, 14 Oct 1818

7 A writer's ambition should be to trade a hundred contemporary readers for ten readers in ten years' time and for one reader in a hundred years' time.
Arthur Koestler (1905–83) Hungarian-born British writer. *New York Times Book Review*, 1 Apr 1951

8 Damn the age. I'll write for antiquity.
Charles Lamb (1775–1834) British essayist. Referring to his lack of payment for the *Essays of Elia*. *English Wits* (L. Russell)

9 Now I'm dead in the grave with my lips moving
And every schoolboy repeating my words by heart.
Osip Mandelstam (1891–1938) Russian poet. *Poems*, No. 306

10 My time has not yet come either; some are born posthumously.
Friedrich Nietzsche (1844–1900) German philosopher. *Ecce Homo*

POTTER, STEPHEN

(1900–70) British writer and critic. He is best known for his humorous studies on how to outwit an opponent, including *Gamesmanship* (1947), *Lifemanship* (1950), and *One-Upmanship* (1952).

1 Gamesmanship or The Art of Winning Games Without Actually Cheating.
Book title

2 *How to be one up* – how to make the other man feel that something has gone wrong, however slightly.
Lifemanship, Introduction

3 It is an important general rule always to refer to your friend's country establishment as a 'cottage'.
Lifemanship, Ch. 2

4 There is no doubt that basic weekendmanship should contain some reference to Important Person Play.
Lifemanship, Ch. 2

5 Donsmanship…'the art of criticizing without actually listening'.
Lifemanship, Ch. 6

6 It is WRONG to do what everyone else does – namely, to hold the wine list just out of sight, look for the second cheapest claret on the list, and say, 'Number 22, please'.
One-Upmanship, Ch. 14

7 A good general rule is to state that the bouquet is better than the taste, and vice versa.
One-Upmanship, Ch. 14

POUND, EZRA

(1885–1972) US poet and critic. His poetry includes *Hugh Selwyn Mauberly* (1920) and *The Pisan Cantos* (1925–69). His support for Mussolini led to his confinement in a US mental hospital (1946–58).

Quotations about Pound

1 To me Pound remains the exquisite showman minus the show.
Ben Hecht *Pounding Ezra*

2 I confess I am seldom interested in what he is saying, but only in the way he says it.
T. S. Eliot (1888–1965) US-born British poet and dramatist. *The Dial*, 'Isolated superiority'

Quotations by Pound

3 Music begins to atrophy when it departs too far from the dance;…poetry begins to atrophy when it gets too far from music.
ABC of Reading, 'Warning'

4 One of the pleasures of middle age is to *find out* that one WAS right, and that one was much righter than one knew at say 17 or 23.
ABC of Reading, Ch. 1

5 Literature is news that STAYS news.
ABC of Reading, Ch. 1

6 Any general statement is like a cheque drawn on a bank. Its value depends on what is there to meet it.
ABC of Reading, Ch. 1

7 Winter is icummen in,
Lhude sing Goddamm,
Raineth drop and staineth slop
And how the wind doth ramm!
Sing: Goddamm.
Ancient Music

8 And even I can remember
A day when the historians left blanks in their writings,
I mean for things they didn't know.
Cantos, XIII

9 Bah! I have sung women in three cities,
But it is all the same;
And I will sing of the sun.
Cino

10 The difference between a gun and a tree is a difference of tempo. The tree explodes every spring.
Criterion, July 1937

11 Great Literature is simply language charged with meaning to the utmost possible degree.
How to Read

12 For three years, out of key with his time,
He strove to resuscitate the dead art
Of poetry to maintain 'the sublime'
In the old sense. Wrong from the start.
Pour L'Élection de son sépulcre

POVERTY

See also hunger, poverty and wealth

1 From clogs to clogs in three generations.
Proverb

2 Poverty is not a crime.
Proverb

3 Hunger is the best sauce.
Proverb

4 To some extent, if you've seen one city slum you've seen them all.
Spiro Agnew (1918–) US politician. Election speech, Detroit, 18 Oct 1968

5 When you have learnt all that Oxford can teach you, go and discover why, with so much wealth in Britain, there continues to be so much poverty and how poverty can be cured.
Edward Caird (1835–1908) British philosopher and theologian. Said to Lord Beveridge

6 To be poor and independent is very nearly an impossibility.
William Cobbett (1763–1835) British journalist and writer. *Advice to Young Men*

7 He found it inconvenient to be poor.
William Cowper (1731–1800) British poet. *Charity*

8 Poverty and oysters always seem to go together.
Charles Dickens (1812–70) British novelist. *Pickwick Papers*, Ch. 22

9 Poverty, therefore, was comparative. One measured it by a sliding scale. One was always poor, in terms of those who were richer.
Margaret Drabble (1939–) British novelist. *The Radiant Way*

10 There's no scandal like rags, nor any crime so shameful as poverty.
George Farquhar (1678–1707) Irish dramatist. *The Beaux' Strategem*, I:1

11 The very poor are unthinkable and only to be approached by the statistician and the poet.
E. M. Forster (1879–1970) British novelist. *Howards End*

12 It is only the poor who are forbidden to beg.
Anatole France (Jacques Anatole François Thibault; 1844–1924) French writer. *Crainquebille*

13 For every talent that poverty has stimulated, it has blighted a hundred.
John W. Gardner (1912–) US writer. *Excellence*

14 No sir, tho' I was born and bred in England, I can dare to be poor, which is the only thing now-a-days men are asham'd of.
John Gay (1685–1732) English poet and dramatist. *Polly*

15 Is it possible that my people live in such awful conditions?...I tell you, Mr Wheatley, that if I had to live in conditions like that I would be a revolutionary myself.
George V (1865–1936) King of the United Kingdom. On being told Mr Wheatley's life story. *The Tragedy of Ramsay MacDonald* (L. MacNeill Weir), Ch. 16

16 Let not Ambition mock their useful toil,
Their homely joys, and destiny obscure;
Nor Grandeur hear with a disdainful smile,
The short and simple annals of the poor.
Thomas Gray (1716–71) British poet. *Elegy Written in a Country Churchyard*

17 People who are much too sensitive to demand of cripples that they run races ask of the poor that they get up and act just like everyone else in society.
Michael Harrington (1928–89) US socialist and writer. *The Other America*

18 I want there to be no peasant in my kingdom so poor that he is unable to have a chicken in his pot every Sunday.
Henri IV (1553–1610) King of France. *Hist. de Henry le Grand* (Hardouin de Péréfixe)

19 Seven cities warr'd for Homer, being dead,
Who, living, had no roof to shroud his head.
Thomas Heywood (c. 1574–1641) English dramatist. *The Hierarchy of the Blessed Angels*

20 Oh! God! that bread should be so dear,
And flesh and blood so cheap!
Thomas Hood (1799–1845) British poet. *The Song of the Shirt*

21 Hard to train to accept being poor.
Horace (Quintus Horatius Flaccus; 65–8 BC) Roman poet. *Odes*, I

22 It is easy enough to say that poverty is no crime. No; if it were men wouldn't be ashamed of it. It is a blunder, though, and is punished as such. A poor man is despised the whole world over.

Jerome K. Jerome (1859–1927) British humorist. *Idle Thoughts of an Idle Fellow*

23 This Administration here and now declares unconditional war on poverty in America.

Lyndon B. Johnson (1908–73) US statesman. State of the Union message, 8 Jan 1964

24 Resolve not to be poor: whatever you have, spend less. Poverty is a great enemy to human happiness; it certainly destroys liberty, and it makes some virtues impracticable and others extremely difficult.

Samuel Johnson (1709–84) British lexicographer. *Life of Johnson* (J. Boswell), Vol. IV

25 The misfortunes of poverty carry with them nothing harder to bear than that it exposes men to ridicule.

Juvenal (Decimus Junius Juvenalis; 60–130 AD) Roman satirist. *Satires*, III

26 It's not easy for people to rise out of obscurity when they have to face straitened circumstances at home.

Juvenal *Satires*, III

27 We're really all of us bottomly broke.
I haven't had time to work in weeks.

Jack Kerouac (1922–69) US novelist. *On the Road*, Pt. I

28 The trouble with being poor is that it takes up all your time.

William de Kooning Attrib.

29 Few, save the poor, feel for the poor.

Letitia Landon (1802–38) British poet and novelist. *The Poor*

30 'The Workhouse' – always a word of shame, grey shadow falling on the close of life, most feared by the old (even when called The Infirmary); abhorred more than debt, or prison, or beggary, or even the stain of madness.

Laurie Lee (1914–) British novelist and poet. *Cider with Rosie*

31 I (Who Have Nothing).

Jerry Leiber (1933–) US songwriter. Credited to 'Donida; Leiber, Stoller, Mogol'. Song title

32 Look at me: I worked my way up from nothing to a state of extreme poverty.

Groucho Marx (Julius Marx; 1895–1977) US comedian. *Monkey Business*

33 The forgotten man at the bottom of the economic pyramid.

Franklin D. Roosevelt (1882–1945) US Democratic president. Speech on radio, 7 Apr 1932

34 The poor don't know that their function in life is to exercise our generosity.

Jean-Paul Sartre (1905–80) French writer. *Words*

35 The heart of the matter, as I see it, is the stark fact that world poverty is primarily a problem of two million villages, and thus a problem of two thousand million villagers.

E. F. Schumacher (1911–77) German-born economist. *Small is Beautiful, A Study of Economics as if People Mattered*, Ch. 13

36 CUSINS. Do you call poverty a crime?
UNDERSHAFT. The worst of all crimes. All the other crimes are virtues beside it.

George Bernard Shaw (1856–1950) Irish dramatist and critic. *Major Barbara*, IV

37 Disease creates poverty and poverty disease. The vicious circle is closed.

Henry E. Sigerist (1891–1957) *Medicine and Human Welfare*, Ch. 1

38 Moving through the silent crowd
Who stand behind dull cigarettes,
These men who idle in the road,
I have the sense of falling light.

They lounge at corners of the street
And greet friends with a shrug of the shoulder
And turn their empty pockets out,
The cynical gestures of the poor.

Stephen Spender (1909–) British poet. *Unemployed*

39 ...the poor are our brothers and sisters.... people in the world who need love, who need care, who have to be wanted.

Mother Teresa (Agnes Gonxha Bojaxhui; 1910–) Yugoslavian-born Indian missionary. *Time*, 'Saints Among Us', 29 Dec 1975

40 I have achieved poverty with distinction, but never poverty with dignity; the best I can manage is dignity with poverty.

Dylan Thomas (1914–53) Welsh poet. Letter to Henry Treece

41 It is very good, sometimes, to have nothing. I want society, not me, to have places to sit in and beds to lie in; and who wants a hatstand of his very own?

Dylan Thomas *Dylan Thomas: Poet of His People* (Andrew Sinclair)

42 There were times my pants were so thin I could sit on a dime and tell if it was heads or tails.

Spencer Tracy (1900–67) US film star. *Spencer Tracy* (L. Swindell)

43 As for the virtuous poor, one can pity them, of course, but one cannot possibly admire them.

Oscar Wilde (1854–1900) Irish-born British dramatist. *The Soul of Man under Socialism*

44 But I, being poor, have only my dreams;
I have spread my dreams under your feet;
Tread softly because you tread on my dreams.

W. B. Yeats (1865–1939) Irish poet. *He Wishes for the Cloths of Heaven*

POVERTY AND WEALTH

See also money, poverty, wealth

1 If the rich could hire other people to die for them, the poor could make a wonderful living.

Yiddish proverb

2 She was poor but she was honest
Victim of a rich man's game.
First he loved her, then he left her,
And she lost her maiden name.

See her on the bridge at midnight,
Saying 'Farewell, blighted love.'
Then a scream, a splash and goodness,
What is she a-doin' of?

It's the same the whole world over,
It's the poor wot gets the blame,
It's the rich wot gets the gravy.
Ain't it all a bleedin' shame?

Anonymous *She was Poor but she was Honest*

3 There was a certain rich man, which was clothed in purple and fine linen, and fared sumptuously every day:
And there was a certain beggar named Lazarus, which was laid at his gate, full of sores,
And desiring to be fed with the crumbs which fell from the rich man's table: moreover the dogs came and licked his sores.
And it came to pass, that the beggar died, and was carried by the angels into Abraham's bosom: the rich man also died, and was buried;
And in hell he lift up his eyes, being in torments, and seeth Abraham afar off, and Lazarus in his bosom.

Bible: Luke 16:19–23

4 There are only two families in the world, my old grandmother used to say, The *Haves* and the *Have-Nots*.

Miguel de Cervantes (1547–1616) Spanish novelist. *Don Quixote*, Pt. II, Ch. 20

5 'Two nations; between whom there is no intercourse and no sympathy; who are as ignorant of each other's habits, thoughts, and feelings, as if they were dwellers in different zones, or inhabitants of different planets; who are formed by a different breeding, are fed by a different food, are ordered by different manners, and are not governed by the same laws.'
'You speak of –' said Egremont, hesitatingly
'THE RICH AND THE POOR.'

Benjamin Disraeli (1804–81) British statesman. *Sybil*, Bk. II, Ch. 5

6 Errors look so very ugly in persons of small means – one feels they are taking quite a liberty in going astray; whereas people of fortune may naturally indulge in a few delinquencies.

George Eliot (Mary Ann Evans; 1819–80) British novelist. *Janet's Repentance*, Ch. 25

7 Whereas it has long been known and declared that the poor have no right to the property of the rich, I wish it also to be known and declared that the rich have no right to the property of the poor.

John Ruskin (1819–1900) British art critic and writer. *Unto this Last*, Essay III

8 When the rich wage war it is the poor who die.

Jean-Paul Sartre (1905–80) French writer. *The Devil and the Good Lord*

9 As long as men are men, a poor society cannot be too poor to find a right order of life, nor a rich society too rich to have need to seek it.

R. H. Tawney (1880–1962) British economist and historian. *The Acquisitive Society*

POWELL, ANTHONY

(1905–) British novelist. His satirical *A Dance to the Music of Time* comprises twelve volumes published between 1951 and 1975; later novels include *The Fisher King* (1986).

1 He fell in love with himself at first sight and it is a passion to which he has always remained faithful. Self-love seems so often unrequited.

A Dance to the Music of Time: The Acceptance World, Ch. 1

2 Dinner at the Huntercombes' possessed 'only two dramatic features – the wine was a farce and the food a tragedy'.

A Dance to the Music of Time: The Acceptance World, Ch. 4

3 All men are brothers, but, thank God, they aren't all brothers-in-law.

A Dance to the Music of Time: At Lady Molly's, Ch. 4

4 It must be generations since anyone but highbrows lived in this cottage...I imagine most of the agricultural labourers round here commute from London.

A Dance to the Music of Time: The Kindly Ones, Ch. 2

5 One of the worst things about life is not how nasty the nasty people are. You know that already. It is how nasty the nice people can be.

A Dance to the Music of Time: The Kindly Ones, Ch. 4

6 Growing old is like being increasingly penalized for a crime you haven't committed.

A Dance to the Music of Time: Temporary Kings, Ch. 1

7 People think that because a novel's invented, it isn't true. Exactly the reverse is the case. Biography and memoirs can never be wholly true, since they cannot include every conceivable circumstance of what happened. The novel can do that.

A Dance to the Music of Time: Hearing Secret Harmonies, Ch. 3

POWER

See also influence, leadership, responsibility

1 Divide and rule.

Proverb

2 He who pays the piper calls the tune.

Proverb

3 Power tends to corrupt, and absolute power corrupts absolutely. Great men are almost always bad men...There is no worse heresy than that the office sanctifies the holder of it.

Lord Acton (1834–1902) British historian. Often misquoted as 'Power corrupts...' Letter to Bishop Mandell Creighton, 5 Apr 1887

4 A friend in power is a friend lost.

Henry Brooks Adams (1838–1918) US historian. *The Education of Henry Adams*

5 Nothing destroyeth authority so much as the unequal and untimely interchange of power pressed too far, and relaxed too much.

Francis Bacon (1561–1626) English philosopher. *Essays*, 'Of Empire'

6 He did not care in which direction the car was travelling, so long as he remained in the driver's seat.

Lord Beaverbrook (1879–1964) British newspaper owner and politician. Referring to Lloyd George. *New Statesman*, 14 June 1963

7 The strongest poison ever known
Came from Caesar's laurel crown.

William Blake (1757–1827) British poet. *Auguries of Innocence*

8 The greater the power, the more dangerous the abuse.

Edmund Burke (1729–97) British politician. Speech, House of Commons, 7 Feb 1771

9 If you think you have someone eating out of your hand, it's a good idea to count your fingers.

Martin Buxbaume Attrib.

10 Obtain power, then, by all means; power is the law of man; make it yours.

Maria Edgeworth (1767–1849) Irish novelist and essayist. *An Essay on the Noble Science of Self-Justification*

11 There is one thing about being President – nobody can tell you when to sit down.

Dwight D. Eisenhower (1890–1969) US general and statesman. *The Observer*, 'Sayings of the Week', 9 Aug 1953

12 Men of power have not time to read; yet men who do not read are unfit for power.

Michael Foot (1913–) British Labour politician and journalist. *Debts Of Honour*

13 Power is so apt to be insolent and Liberty to be saucy, that they are seldom upon good Terms.

Lord Halifax (1633–95) English statesman. *Political, Moral, and Miscellaneous Thoughts and Reflections*

14 The Communist Party, the KGB, and the army – the three ugly sisters – are the instruments of control in the Soviet Union.

Douglas Hurd (1930–) British politician. Referring to an abortive coup in the Soviet Union (Aug 1991). *The Observer*, 25 Aug 1991

15 It was a symptom of Britain's post-war condition that anyone given power before his hair turned white was called a whizz-kid.

Clive James (1939–) Australian-born writer and broadcaster. *Falling Towards England*, Ch. 18

16 Power is the ultimate aphrodisiac.

Henry Kissinger (1923–) German-born US politician and diplomat. *The Guardian*, 28 Nov 1976

17 Power? It's like a dead sea fruit; when you achieve it, there's nothing there.

Harold Macmillan (1894–1986) British politician and prime minister. Attrib.

18 To reign is worth ambition, though in Hell:
Better to reign in Hell than serve in Heaven.

John Milton (1608–74) English poet. *Paradise Lost*, Bk. I

19 It could never be a correct justification that, because the whites oppressed us yesterday when they had power, that the blacks must oppress them today because they have power.

Robert Mugabe (1925–) Zimbabwe politician and president. Speech, Mar 1980

20 Who controls the past controls the future. Who controls the present controls the past.

George Orwell (Eric Blair; 1903–50) British novelist. *Nineteen Eighty-Four*

21 Unlimited power is apt to corrupt the minds of those who possess it.

William Pitt the Elder (1708–78) British statesman. *See also* Lord ACTON. Speech, House of Lords, 9 Jan 1770

22 The megalomaniac differs from the narcissist by the fact that he wishes to be powerful rather than charming, and seeks to be feared rather than loved. To this type belong many lunatics and most of the great men of history.

Bertrand Russell (1872–1970) British philosopher. *The Conquest of Happiness*

23 We are the masters at the moment – and not only for the moment, but for a very long time to come.

Lord Shawcross (1902–) British Labour politician and lawyer. Sometimes quoted as, 'We are the masters now!' House of Commons, 2 Apr 1946

24 The official world, the corridors of power, the dilemmas of conscience and egotism – she disliked them all.

C. P. Snow (1905–80) British novelist. *Homecomings*, Ch. 22

25 You only have power over people so long as you don't take *everything* away from them. But when you've robbed a man of everything he's no longer in your power – he's free again.

Alexander Solzhenitsyn (1918–) Russian novelist. *The First Circle*, Ch. 17

26 The only emperor is the emperor of ice-cream.

Wallace Stevens (1879–1955) US poet. *The Emperor of Ice-Cream*

27 Power corrupts, but lack of power corrupts absolutely.

Adlai Stevenson (1900–65) US statesman. *The Observer*, Jan 1963

28 He aspired to power instead of influence, and as a result forfeited both.

A. J. P. Taylor (1906–90) British historian. Referring to Lord Northcliffe. *English History, 1914–1945*, Ch. 1

29 One Ring to rule them all, One Ring to find them,
One Ring to bring them all and in the darkness bind them.

J. R. R. Tolkien (1892–1973) British writer. *The Lord of the Rings*, Pt. I: *The Fellowship of the Ring*, Ch. 2

30 The balance of power.

Robert Walpole (1676–1745) British statesman. Speech, House of Commons

31 The good old rule
Sufficeth them, the simple plan,
That they should take, who have the power,
And they should keep who can.

William Wordsworth (1770–1850) British poet. *Rob Roy's Grave*

32 The wrong sort of people are always in power because they would not be in power if they were not the wrong sort of people.

Jon Wynne-Tyson (1924–) British humorous writer. *Times Literary Supplement*

POWER POLITICS

See also force, oppression, violence, weapons

1 Whatever happens, we have got
The Maxim Gun, and they have not.

Hilaire Belloc (1870–1953) French-born British poet. Referring to African natives. *The Modern Traveller*

2 The great questions of our day cannot be solved

by speeches and majority votes...but by iron and blood.

Bismarck (1815–98) German statesman. Usually misquoted as 'blood and iron' – a form Bismarck himself used in 1886. Speech, Prussian Chamber, 30 Sept 1862

3 Guns will make us powerful; butter will only make us fat.

Hermann Goering (1893–1946) German leader. Radio broadcast, 1936

4 A man may build himself a throne of bayonets, but he cannot sit on it.

Dean Inge (1860–1954) British churchman. *Wit and Wisdom of Dean Inge* (ed. Marchant)

5 Every Communist must grasp the truth, 'Political power grows out of the barrel of a gun.'

Mao Tse-Tung (1893–1976) Chinese communist leader. *Selected Works*, Vol II, 'Problems of War and Strategy', 6 Nov 1938

6 There is a homely adage which runs 'Speak softly and carry a big stick, you will go far'.

Theodore Roosevelt (1858–1919) US Republican president. Speech, Minnesota State Fair, 2 Sept 1901

7 God is always on the side of the big battalions.

Vicomte de Turenne (1611–75) French marshal. Attrib.

8 God is on the side not of the heavy battalions, but of the best shots.

Voltaire (François-Marie Arouet; 1694–1778) French writer. *Notebooks*

PRACTICALITY

1 I have no dress except the one I wear every day. If you are going to be kind enough to give me one, please let it be practical and dark so that I can put it on afterwards to go to the laboratory.

Marie Curie (1867–1934) Polish chemist. Referring to a wedding dress. Letter to a friend

2 What would you do with it? It is full of leprosy.

Father Damien (Joseph de Veuster; 1840–89) Belgian Roman Catholic missionary. When asked on his deathbed whether he would leave another priest his mantle, like Elijah. *Memoirs of an Aesthete* (H. Acton)

3 The Arab who builds himself a hut out of the marble fragments of a temple in Palmyra is more philosophical than all the curators of the museums in London, Munich or Paris.

Anatole France (Jacques Anatole François Thibault; 1844–1924) French writer. *The Crime of Sylvestre Bonnard*

4 Talk to him of Jacob's ladder, and he would ask the number of the steps.

Douglas William Jerrold (1803–57) British dramatist. *Wit and Opinions of Douglas Jerrold*, 'A Matter-of-fact Man'

5 Don't carry away that arm till I have taken off my ring.

Lord Raglan (1788–1855) British field marshal. Request immediately after his arm had been amputated following the Battle of Waterloo. *Dictionary of National Biography*

6 Very well, then I shall not take off my boots.

Duke of Wellington (1769–1852) British general and statesman. Responding to the news, as he was going to bed, that the ship in which he was travelling seemed about to sink. Attrib.

PRAISE

See also admiration, boasts, compliments, flattery

1 Self-praise is no recommendation.

Proverb

2 If I were not Alexander, I would be Diogenes.

Alexander the Great (356–323 BC) King of Macedon. Plutarch, *Life of Alexander*, Bk. XIV

3 Just as it is always said of slander that something always sticks when people boldly slander, so it might be said of self-praise (if it is not entirely shameful and ridiculous) that if we praise ourselves fearlessly, something will always stick.

Francis Bacon (1561–1626) English philosopher. *The Advancement of Learning*

4 Let us now praise famous men, and our fathers that begat us.

Bible: Ecclesiasticus 44:1

5 Watch how a man takes praise and there you have the measure of him.

Thomas Burke (1886–1945) British writer. *T. P.'s Weekly*, 8 June 1928

6 The advantage of doing one's praising for oneself is that one can lay it on so thick and exactly in the right places.

Samuel Butler (1835–1902) British writer. *The Way of All Flesh*, Ch. 34

7 Fondly we think we honour merit then,
When we but praise ourselves in other men.

Alexander Pope (1688–1744) British poet. *An Essay on Criticism*

8 To refuse praise reveals a desire to be praised twice over.

Duc de la Rochefoucauld (1613–80) French writer. *Maximes*, 149

PRAYER

See also Christianity, faith, God, religion

1 Hail Mary, full of grace, the Lord is with thee:
Blessed art thou among women, and blessed is the fruit of thy womb, Jesus.

Anonymous *Ave Maria*, 11th century

2 From ghoulies and ghosties and long-leggety beasties
And things that go bump in the night,
Good Lord, deliver us!

Anonymous Cornish

3 O Lord! thou knowest how busy I must be this day: if I forget thee, do not thou forget me.

Lord Astley (1579–1652) English Royalist general. Prayer before taking part in the Battle of Edgehill. *Memoires* (Sir Philip Warwick)

4 *Da mihi castitatem et continentiam, sed noli modo.*
Give me chastity and continence, but not yet.

St Augustine of Hippo (354–430) Bishop of Hippo. *Confessions*

5 O God, send me some good actors – cheap.

Lilian Baylis (1874–1937) British theatre owner and producer. *The Guardian*, 1 Mar 1976

6 But when ye pray, use not vain repetitions, as the heathen do: for they think that they shall be heard for their much speaking.
Be not ye therefore like unto them: for your Father knoweth what things ye have need of, before ye ask him.
After this manner therefore pray ye: Our Father which art in heaven, Hallowed be thy name.
Thy kingdom come. Thy will be done in earth, as it is in heaven.
Give us this day our daily bread.
And forgive us our debts, as we forgive our debtors.
And lead us not into temptation, but deliver us from evil: For thine is the kingdom, and the power, and the glory, for ever. Amen.

Bible: Matthew 6:7–13

7 PRAY, V. To ask that the rules of the universe be annulled on behalf of a single petitioner, confessedly unworthy.

Ambrose Bierce (1842–c. 1914) US writer and journalist. *The Devil's Dictionary*

8 To Mercy, Pity, Peace, and Love
All pray in their distress.

William Blake (1757–1827) British poet. *Songs of Innocence*, 'The Divine Image'

9 When two or three are gathered together in thy Name thou wilt grant their requests.

The Book of Common Prayer *Morning Prayer, Prayer of St Chrysostom*

10 A leap over the hedge is better than good men's prayers.

Miguel de Cervantes (1547–1616) Spanish novelist. *Don Quixote*, Pt. I, Ch. 21

11 He prayeth well, who loveth well
Both man and bird and beast.

Samuel Taylor Coleridge (1772–1834) British poet. *The Rime of the Ancient Mariner*, VII

12 He prayeth best, who loveth best
All things both great and small;
For the dear God who loveth us,
He made and loveth all.

Samuel Taylor Coleridge *The Rime of the Ancient Mariner*, VII

13 'Does God always answer prayer?' the cardinal was asked. 'Yes' he said. 'And sometimes the answer is – 'No'.'

Alistair Cooke (1908–) British writer and broadcaster. *Letter from America* (BBC radio)

14 Prayer makes the Christian's armour bright;
And Satan trembles when he sees
The weakest saint upon his knees.

William Cowper (1731–1800) British poet. *Olney Hymns*, 29

15 The idea that He would take his attention away from the universe in order to give me a bicycle with three speeds is just so unlikely I can't go along with it.

Quentin Crisp (c. 1910–) Model, publicist, and writer. *The Sunday Times*, 18 Dec 1977

16 Some day when you have time, look into the business of prayer, amulets, baths and poultices, and discover for yourself how much valuable therapy the profession has cast on the dump.

Martin H. Fischer (1879–1962) *Fisherisms* (Howard Fabing and Ray Marr)

17 Forgive, O Lord, my little jokes on Thee
And I'll forgive Thy great big one on me.

Robert Frost (1875–1963) US poet. *In the clearing*, 'Cluster of Faith'

18 Your cravings as a human animal do not become a prayer just because it is God whom you must ask to attend to them.

Dag Hammarskjöld (1905–61) Swedish diplomat. *Markings*

19 Religion's in the heart, not in the knees.

Douglas William Jerrold (1803–57) British dramatist. *The Devil's Ducat*, I.2

20 The Beadsman, after thousand aves told,
For aye unsought-for slept among his ashes cold.

John Keats (1795–1821) British poet. *The Eve of Saint Agnes*, I

21 If thou may not continually gather thyself together, do it some time at least once a day, morning or evening.

Thomas à Kempis (1380–1471) German monk and writer. *The Imitation of Christ*, 1

22 Better to enjoy and suffer than sit around with folded arms. You know the only true prayer? Please God, lead me into temptation.

Jennie Lee (1904–88) British politician and writer. *My Life with Nye*

23 Arise, O Lord, plead Thine own cause; remember how the foolish man reproacheth Thee daily; the foxes are wasting Thy vineyard, which Thou hast given to Thy Vicar Peter, the boar out of the wood doth waste it, and the wild beast of the field doth devour it.

Leo X (Giovanni de' Medici; 1475–1521) Pope (1513–21). Papal Bull, *Exsurge, Domine*, Preface

24 Nowhere can man find a quieter or more untroubled retreat than in his own soul.

Marcus Aurelius (Marcus Aurelius Antoninus; 121–180) Roman emperor and Stoic philosopher. *Meditations*, 4

25 Our dourest parsons, who followed the nonconformist fashion of long extemporary prayers, always seemed to me to be bent on bullying God. After a few 'beseech thees' as a mere politeness, they adopted a sterner tone and told Him what they expected from Him and more than hinted He must attend to His work.

J. B. Priestley (1894–1984) British novelist. *Outcries and Asides*

26 I am just going to pray for you at St Paul's, but with no very lively hope of success.

Sydney Smith (1771–1845) British clergyman and essayist. On meeting an acquaintance. *The Smith of Smiths* (H. Pearson), Ch. 13

27 If thou shouldst never see my face again,
Pray for my soul. More things are wrought by prayer
Than this world dreams of.

Alfred, Lord Tennyson (1809–92) British poet. *Idylls of the King*, 'The Passing of Arthur'

28 Whatever a man prays for, he prays for a miracle. Every prayer reduces itself to this: 'Great God grant that twice two be not four.'

Ivan Turgenev (1818–83) Russian novelist. *Prayer*

PRECOCITY

See also children, youth

1 When you were quite a little boy somebody ought to have said 'hush' just once.

Mrs Patrick Campbell (1865–1940) British actress. Letter to George Bernard Shaw, 1 Nov 1912

2 One of those men who reach such an acute limited excellence at twenty-one that everything afterward savours of anti-climax.

F. Scott Fitzgerald (1896–1940) US novelist. *The Great Gatsby,* Ch. 1

3 Thank you, madam, the agony is abated.

Lord Macaulay (1800–59) British historian. Replying, aged four, to a lady who asked if he had hurt himself. *Life and Letters of Macaulay* (Trevelyan), Ch. 1

4 He is pretty certain to come back into favour. One of the surest signs of his genius is that women dislike his books.

George Orwell (Eric Blair; 1903–50) British novelist. Referring to Conrad. *New English Weekly,* 23 July 1936

5 So wise so young, they say, do never live long.

William Shakespeare (1564–1616) English dramatist. *Richard III,* III:1

PREGNANCY

See also babies, birth, motherhood

1 The baby bounced gently off the wall of her uterus. She opened her dressing gown and put her hands back on her belly. It moved again like a dolphin going through the water; that was the way she imagined it. Are yeh normal? she said.

Roddy Doyle (1958–) Irish novelist and playwright. *The Snapper*

2 Hormonal changes are perfectly normal. Part an' parcel of the pregnancy, if yeh follows me. But sometimes there are side effects. Snottiness or depression or actin' a bit queer.

Roddy Doyle *The Snapper*

3 It seems an insult to nature and to the Creator to imagine that pregnancy was ever intended to be a sickness...False states of society, false modes of dress, false habits of life, etc., all contribute to bring suffering at this time.

Mrs E. B. Duffey *What Women Should Know*

4 It is the woman who is ultimately held responsible for pregnancy. While not being allowed to have control over her body, she is nevertheless held responsible for its products.

Carol Glassman (c. 1942–) US civil rights activist. *Sisterhood Is Powerful* (ed. Robin Morgan)

5 Thy ruddy face shall turn lean, and grown green as grass. Thine eyes shall be dusky, and underneath grow pale; and by the giddiness of thy brain, thy head shall ache sorely. Within thy belly, the uterus shall swell and strut out like a water bag; thy bowels shall have pains and there shall be stitches in thy flank, and pain rife in thy loins, heaviness in every limb.

Hali Meidenhad

6 In men nine out of ten abdominal tumours are malignant; in women nine out of ten abdominal swellings are the pregnant uterus.

Rutherford Morison (1853–1939) British doctor. *The Practitioner,* Oct 1965

7 Dear Mary, We all knew you had it in you.

Dorothy Parker (1893–1967) US writer. Telegram sent to a friend on the successful outcome of her much-publicized pregnancy

8 Pregnancy is not a disease, and the pregnant woman should not consider herself a patient, but she should be more careful than ever to lead a really physiological life.

Mary Scharlieb (1845–1930) British gynaecological surgeon. *A Woman's Words to Women on the Care of their Health in England and in India*

9 Pregnancy is associated with an increase in blood volume that would help the endurance competitor.

Craig Sharp British physiologist. *The Times,* 17 Apr 1993

PREJUDICE

See also equality, feminism, Jews, objectivity, racism, religion, subjectivity

1 I am a Catholic. As far as possible I go to Mass every day. As far as possible I kneel down and tell these beads every day. If you reject me on account of my religion, I shall thank God that he has spared me the indignity of being your representative.

Hilaire Belloc (1870–1953) French-born British poet. Said in his first election campaign. Speech, Salford, 1906

2 Mother is far too clever to understand anything she does not like.

Arnold Bennett (1867–1931) British novelist. *The Title*

3 Don't half-quote me to reinforce your own prejudices.

Brian Clark (1932–) British playwright. *Kipling*

4 Common sense is the collection of prejudices acquired by age eighteen.

Albert Einstein (1879–1955) German-born US physicist. *Scientific American,* Feb 1976

5 I am free of all prejudice. I hate everyone equally.

W. C. Fields (1880–1946) US actor. Attrib.

6 I've lived my entire life with heterosexual hatred. All my life, I've been the queer down the hall.

Harvey Fierstein (1954–) US actor. *Playboy,* Aug 1988

7 My corns ache, I get gouty, and my prejudices swell like varicose veins.

James Gibbons Huneker (1860–1921) *Old Fogy,* Ch. 1

8 Since my daughter is only half-Jewish, could she go in the water up to her knees?

Groucho Marx (Julius Marx; 1895–1977) US comedian. When excluded from a beach club on racial grounds. *The Observer,* 21 Aug 1977

9 Vegetarians have wicked, shifty eyes, and laugh in a cold and calculating manner. They pinch little children, steal stamps, drink water, favour beards... wheeze, squeak, drawl and maunder.

J. B. Morton (1893–1979) British journalist. *By the Way,* '4 June'

10 Why bastard? wherefore base?
When my dimensions are as well compact,
My mind as generous, and my shape as true,
As honest madam's issue? Why brand they us
With base? with baseness? bastardy? base, base?
Who in the lusty stealth of nature take
More composition and fierce quality
Than doth, within a dull, stale, tired bed,
Go to creating a whole tribe of fops,
Got 'tween asleep and wake?

William Shakespeare (1564–1616) English dramatist. *King Lear*, I:2

11 I will buy with you, sell with you, talk with you, walk with you, and so following; but I will not eat with you, drink with you, nor pray with you. What news on the Rialto?

William Shakespeare *The Merchant of Venice*, I:3

12 How like a fawning publican he looks!
I hate him for he is a Christian;

William Shakespeare *The Merchant of Venice*, I:3

13 Mislike me not for my complexion,
The shadow'd livery of the burnish'd sun,
To whom I am neighbour and near bred.

William Shakespeare *The Merchant of Venice*, II:1

14 I'll refer me to all things of sense,
Whether a maid so tender, fair, and happy,
So opposite to marriage that she shunn'd
The wealthy curled darlings of our nation,
Would ever have, to incur a general mock,
Run from her guardage to the sooty bosom
Of such a thing as thou.

William Shakespeare *Othello*, I:2

15 …I *too well* know its truth, from experience, that whenever any poor Gipsies are encamped anywhere and crimes and robberies &c. occur, it is invariably laid to their account, which is shocking; and if they are always looked upon as vagabonds, how *can* they become good people?

Victoria (1819–1901) Queen of the United Kingdom. Journal, 29 Dec 1836

16 I do not intend to prejudge the past.

William Whitelaw (1918–) British politician. Said on arriving in Ulster as Minister for Northern Ireland. *The Times*, 3 Dec 1973

17 No Jewish blood runs among my blood,
but I am as bitterly and hardly hated
by every anti-semite
as if I were a Jew. By this
I am a Russian.

Yevgeny Yevtushenko (1933–) Soviet poet. *Babi Yar*

PRESENT

See also future, opportunity, past, time

1 No time like the present.

Proverb

2 The past was nothing to her; offered no lesson which she was willing to heed. The future was a mystery which she never attempted to penetrate. The present alone was significant…

Kate Chopin (1851–1904) US writer. *The Awakening*, Ch. 15

3 I have learned to live each day as it comes, and not to borrow trouble by dreading tomorrow. It is the dark menace of the future that makes cowards of us.

Dorothy Dix (Elizabeth Meriwether Gilmer; 1861–1951) US journalist and writer. *Dorothy Dix, Her Book*, Introduction

4 Happy the Man, and happy he alone,
He who can call today his own:
He who, secure within, can say,
Tomorrow do thy worst, for I have liv'd today.

John Dryden (1631–1700) British poet and dramatist. *Translation of Horace*, III

5 Ah, my Belovéd, fill the Cup that clears
TO-DAY of past Regrets and Future Fears:
To-morrow! – Why, To-morrow I may be
Myself with Yesterday's Sev'n thousand Years.

Edward Fitzgerald (1809–83) British poet. *The Rubáiyát of Omar Khayyám* (1st edn.), XX

6 Gather ye rosebuds while ye may,
Old time is still a-flying:
And this same flower that smiles today
Tomorrow will be dying.

Robert Herrick (1591–1674) English poet. *Hesperides*, 'To the Virgins, to Make Much of Time'

7 *Carpe diem.*
Seize the day.

Horace (Quintus Horatius Flaccus; 65–8 BC) Roman poet. *Odes*, I

8 Drop the question what tomorrow may bring, and count as profit every day that Fate allows you.

Horace *Odes*, I

9 While we're talking, time will have meanly run on: pick today's fruits, not relying on the future in the slightest.

Horace *Odes*, I

10 Believe each day that has dawned is your last. Some hour to which you have not been looking forward will prove lovely. As for me, if you want a good laugh, you will come and find me fat and sleek, in excellent condition, one of Epicurus' herd of pigs.

Horace *Epistles*, I

11 We live in stirring times – tea-stirring times.

Christopher Isherwood (1904–86) British novelist. *Mr Norris Changes Trains*

12 Redeem thy mis-spent time that's past;
Live this day, as if 'twere thy last.

Thomas Ken (1637–1711) English bishop. *A Morning Hymn*

13 What is love? 'Tis not hereafter;
Present mirth hath present laughter;
What's to come is still unsure.
In delay there lies no plenty,
Then come kiss me, sweet and twenty;
Youth's a stuff will not endure.

William Shakespeare (1564–1616) English dramatist. *Twelfth Night*, II:3

PRIDE

See also arrogance, conceit, egotism, self-respect

1 Pride goeth before destruction, and an haughty spirit before a fall.

Bible: Proverbs 16:18

2 He that is down needs fear no fall;
He that is low, no pride.

John Bunyan (1628–88) English writer. *The Pilgrim's Progress*, 'Shepherd Boy's Song'

3 TREVES. In my experience, pride is a word often on women's lips – but they display little sign of it where love affairs are concerned.

Agatha Christie (1891–1975) British writer. *Toward's Zero*

4 I know of no case where a man added to his dignity by standing on it.

Winston Churchill (1874–1965) British politician. Attrib.

5 When the Lord sent me forth into the world, He forbade me to put off my hat to any high or low.

George Fox (1624–91) English religious leader. *Journal*

6 And if you include me among the lyric poets, I'll hold my head so high it'll strike the stars.

Horace (Quintus Horatius Flaccus; 65–8 BC) Roman poet. *Odes*, I

7 We are not ashamed of what we have done, because, when you have a great cause to fight for, the moment of greatest humiliation is the moment when the spirit is proudest.

Christabel Pankhurst (1880–1958) British suffragette. Speech, Albert Hall, London, 19 Mar 1908

8 Yes; I am proud, I must be proud to see
Men not afraid of God, afraid of me.

Alexander Pope (1688–1744) British poet. *Epilogue to the Satires*, Dialogue II

9 Of all the causes which conspire to blind
Man's erring judgment, and misguide the mind,
What the weak head with strongest bias rules,
Is Pride, the never-failing vice of fools.

Alexander Pope *An Essay on Criticism*

10 There is false modesty, but there is no false pride.

Jules Renard (1894–1910) French writer. *Journal*

11 If women be proud (or addicted to pride) it is ten to one to be laid, that it is the men that make them so; for like inchaunters, they do never leave or cease to bewitch & charme poore women with their flatteries.

Mary Tattlewell (fl. 1640) English writer. 'Epistle to the Reader: Long Megge of Westminster, hearing the abuse, offeres to women to riseth out of her grave and thus speaketh'

12 I am proud to have a son who died doing the job he loved for the country he loved.

Harry Taylor Father of soldier killed in Falklands war. Remark, May 1982

13 The French want no-one to be their *superior*. The English want *inferiors*. The Frenchman constantly raises his eyes above him with anxiety. The Englishman lowers his beneath him with satisfaction. On either side it is pride, but understood in a different way.

Alexis de Tocqueville (1805–59) French writer, historian, and politician. *Voyage en Angleterre et en Irlande de 1835*, 18 May

14 We cannot bring ourselves to believe it possible that a foreigner should in any respect be wiser than ourselves. If any such point out to us our follies, we at once claim those follies as the special evidences of our wisdom.

Anthony Trollope (1815–82) British novelist. *Orley Farm*, Ch. 18

PRIESTLEY, J. B.

(1894–1984) British novelist and dramatist, who also published books of criticism and memoirs. His many successful works include *The Good Companions* (1929) and *Dangerous Corner* (1932). He was a popular radio broadcaster during World War II.

1 Comedy, we may say, is society protecting itself – with a smile.

George Meredith

2 They will review a book by a writer much older than themselves as if it were an over-ambitious essay by a second-year student...It is the little dons I complain about, like so many corgis trotting up, hoping to nip your ankles.

Outcries and Asides

3 A number of anxious dwarfs trying to grill a whale.

Referring to politicians. *Outcries and Asides*

4 The greater part of critics are parasites, who, if nothing had been written, would find nothing to write.

Outcries and Asides

5 If there was a little room somewhere in the British Museum that contained only about twenty exhibits and good lighting, easy chairs, and a notice imploring you to smoke, I believe I should become a museum man.

Self-Selected Essays, 'In the British Museum'

6 Our trouble is that we drink too much tea. I see in this the slow revenge of the Orient, which has diverted the Yellow River down our throats.

The Observer, 'Sayings of the Week', 15 May 1949

7 It is hard to tell where MCC ends and the Church of England begins.

New Statesman, 20 July 1962, 'Topside Schools'

8 God can stand being told by Professor Ayer and Marghanita Laski that He doesn't exist.

The Listener, 1 July 1965, 'The BBC's Duty to Society'

9 A novelist who writes nothing for 10 years finds his reputation rising. Because I keep on producing books they say there must be something wrong with this fellow.

The Observer, 'Sayings of the Week', 21 Sept 1969

10 Our great-grandchildren, when they learn how we began this war by snatching glory out of defeat...may also learn how the little holiday steamers made an excursion to hell and came back glorious.

Referring to the British Expeditionary Force's evacuation from Dunkirk. Broadcast, 5 June 1940

PRINCIPLES

See also integrity, morality

1 It is easier to fight for one's principles than to live up to them.

Alfred Adler (1870–1937) Austrian psychiatrist. *Alfred Adler* (P. Bottome)

2 Ethics and Science need to shake hands.

Richard Clarke Cabot (1868–1939) *The Meaning of Right and Wrong*, Introduction

3 If one sticks too rigidly to one's principles one would hardly see anybody.

Agatha Christie (1891–1976) British detective-story writer. *Towards Zero*, I

4 Whenever two good people argue over principles, they are both right.

Marie Ebner von Eschenbach (1830–1916) Austrian writer. *Aphorism*

5 Well, sir, you never can tell. That's a principle in life with me, sir, if you'll excuse my having such a thing, sir.

George Bernard Shaw (1856–1950) Irish dramatist and critic. *You Never Can Tell*, II

6 It is often easier to fight for principles than to live up to them.

Adlai Stevenson (1900–65) US statesman. Speech, New York, 27 Aug 1952

PRIVACY

1 Private faces in public places
Are wiser and nicer
Than public faces in private places.

W. H. Auden (1907–73) British-born poet. *Marginalia*

2 The house of every one is to him as his castle and fortress.

Edward Coke (1552–1634) English lawyer and politician. *Semayne's Case*

3 I never said, 'I want to be alone.' I only said, 'I want to be *left* alone.' There is all the difference.

Greta Garbo (1905–90) Swedish-born US film star. *Garbo* (John Bainbridge)

4 The story of my life is about back entrances and side doors and secret elevators and other ways of getting in and out of places so that people won't bother you.

Greta Garbo Attrib.

5 The poorest man may in his cottage bid defiance to all the forces of the Crown. It may be frail – its roof may shake – the wind may blow through it – the storm may enter – the rain may enter – but the King of England cannot enter! – all his force dares not cross the threshold of the ruined tenement!

William Pitt the Elder (1708–78) British statesman. *Statesmen in the Time of George III* (Lord Brougham), Vol. I

6 This is a free country, madam. We have a right to share your privacy in a public place.

Peter Ustinov (1921–) British actor. *Romanoff and Juliet*, I

PROCRASTINATION

1 Never put off till tomorrow what you can do today.

Proverb

2 Put off the evil hour as long as you can.

Proverb

3 The road to hell is paved with good intentions.

Proverb

4 Give me chastity and continence, but not yet.

St Augustine of Hippo (354–430) Bishop of Hippo. *Confessions*, Bk. VIII, Ch. 7

5 Procrastination is the thief of time.

Edward Young (1683–1765) British poet. *Night Thoughts*

PROGRESS

See also change, conservatism, improvement, innovation, novelty, technology

1 We've made great medical progress in the last generation. What used to be merely an itch is now an allergy.

Anonymous

2 Surely every medicine is an innovation, and he that will not apply new remedies, must expect new evils.

Sir Francis Bacon (1561–1626) English philosopher, lawyer, and politician. *Essays*, 'Of Innovations'

3 The Coming of Post-Industrial Society.

Daniel Bell (1919–) US sociologist. Book title

4 The people who live in the past must yield to the people who live in the future. Otherwise the world would begin to turn the other way round.

Arnold Bennett (1867–1931) British novelist. *Milestones*

5 We have stopped believing in progress. What progress that is!

Jorge Luis Borges (1899–1986) Argentinian writer. *Ibarra, Borges et Borges*

6 Progress is
The law of life, man is not man as yet.

Robert Browning (1812–89) British poet. *Paracelsus*, 5

7 All progress is based upon a universal innate desire on the part of every organism to live beyond its income.

Samuel Butler (1835–1902) British writer. *Notebooks*

8 Disease is very old, and nothing about it has changed. It is we who change, as we learn to recognize what was formerly imperceptible.

Jean Martin Charcot (1825–93) *De L'Expectation en médecine*

9 As enunciated today, 'progress' is simply a comparative of which we have not settled the superlative.

G. K. Chesterton (1874–1936) British writer. *Heretics*, Ch. 2

10 New roads: new ruts.

G. K. Chesterton Attrib.

11 A man of destiny knows that beyond this hill lies another and another. The journey is never complete.

F. W. de Klerk (1936–) South African statesman. Referring to Nelson Mandela. *The Observer*, 'Sayings of the Week', 8 May 1994

12 What we call progress is the exchange of one nuisance for another nuisance.

Havelock Ellis (1859–1939) British sexologist. Attrib.

13 All that is human must retrograde if it does not advance.

Edward Gibbon (1737–94) British historian. *Decline and Fall of the Roman Empire*, Ch. 71

14 You cannot fight against the future. Time is on our side.

William Ewart Gladstone (1809–98) British statesman. Advocating parliamentary reform. Speech, 1866

15 And if the Russian word 'perestroika' has easily entered the international lexicon, this is due to more than just interest in what is going on in the Soviet Union. Now the whole world needs restructuring i.e. progressive development, a fundamental change.

Mikhail Gorbachov (1931–) Soviet statesman. *Perestroika*

16 In your time we have the opportunity to move not only toward the rich society and the powerful society but upward to the Great Society.

Lyndon B. Johnson (1908–73) US Democratic president. Speech, University of Michigan, May 1964

17 Human salvation lies in the hands of the creatively maladjusted.

Martin Luther King (1929–68) US Black civil-rights leader. *Strength to Love*

18 One step forward, two steps back...It happens in the lives of individuals, and it happens in the history of nations and in the development of parties.

Lenin (Vladimir Ilich Ulyanov; 1870–1924) Russian revolutionary leader. *One Step Forward, Two Steps Back*

19 If I have seen further it is by standing on the shoulders of giants.

Isaac Newton (1642–1727) British scientist. Letter to Robert Hooke, 5 Feb 1675

20 You can't say civilization don't advance, however, for in every war they kill you a new way.

Will Rogers (1879–1935) US actor and humorist. *Autobiography*, Ch. 12

21 Organic life, we are told, has developed gradually from the protozoon to the philosopher, and this development, we are assured, is indubitably an advance. Unfortunately it is the philosopher, not the protozoon, who gives us this assurance.

Bertrand Russell (1872–1970) British philosopher. *Mysticism and Logic*, Ch. 6

22 Man's 'progress' is but a gradual discovery that his questions have no meaning.

Antoine de Saint-Exupéry (1900–44) French novelist and aviator. *The Wisdom of the Sands*

23 Progress, far from consisting in change, depends on retentiveness. Those who cannot remember the past are condemned to repeat it.

George Santayana (1863–1952) US philosopher. *The Life of Reason*

24 To slacken the tempo...would mean falling behind. And those who fall behind get beaten.... We are fifty or a hundred years behind the advanced countries. We must make good this distance in ten years. Either we do it, or they crush us.

Joseph Stalin (J. Dzhugashvili; 1879–1953) Soviet statesman.

25 In England we have come to rely upon a comfortable time lag of fifty years or a century intervening between the perception that something ought to be done and a serious attempt to do it.

H. G. Wells (1866–1946) British writer. *The Work, Wealth and Happiness of Mankind*

PROMISCUITY

See also sex

1 Every time you sleep with a boy you sleep with all his old girlfriends.

Government advert warning about AIDS, 1987

2 I see – she's the original good time that was had by all.

Bette Davis (Ruth Elizabeth Davis; 1908–89) US film star. Referring to a starlet of the time. *The Filmgoer's Book of Quotes* (Leslie Halliwell)

3 My message to the businessmen of this country when they go abroad on business is that there is one thing above all they can take with them to stop them catching AIDS, and that is the wife.

Edwina Currie (1946–) British politician. *The Observer*, 15 Feb 1987

4 The strongest possible piece of advice I would give to any young woman is: Don't screw around, and don't smoke.

Edwina Currie *The Observer*, 3 Apr 1988

5 Lady Capricorn, he understood, was still keeping open bed.

Aldous Huxley (1894–1964) British novelist. *Antic Hay*, Ch. 21

6 The woman's a whore, and there's an end on't.

Samuel Johnson (1709–84) British lexicographer. Referring to Lady Diana Beauclerk. *Life of Johnson* (J. Boswell), Vol. II

7 The whore, and the whoremonger, shall ye scourge with a hundred stripes.

Koran Ch. XXIV

8 You mustn't think I advocate perpetual sex. Far from it. Nothing nauseates me more than promiscuous sex in and out of season.

D. H. Lawrence (1885–1930) British novelist. Letter to Lady Ottoline Morrell, 20 Dec 1928

9 You were born with your legs apart. They'll send you to the grave in a Y-shaped coffin.

Joe Orton (1933–67) British dramatist. *What the Butler Saw*, I

10 You know, she speaks eighteen languages. And she can't say 'No' in any of them.

Dorothy Parker (1893–1967) US writer. Speaking of an acquaintance. Attrib.

11 Your idea of fidelity is not having more than one man in the bed at the same time...You're a whore, baby, that's all, just a whore, and I don't take whores in taxis.

Frederick Raphael (1931–) British writer. *Darling* (film)

12 I have made love to ten thousand women.

Georges Simenon (1903–89) Belgian novelist. Interview with *Die Tat*, 1977

13 I'm glad you like my Catherine. I like her too. She ruled thirty million people and had three thousand lovers. I do the best I can in two hours.

Mae West (1892–1980) US actress. After her performance in *Catherine the Great.* Speech from the stage

PROMISES

1 On my honour I promise that I will do my best...to do my duty to God and the King...to help other people at all times...to obey the Scout Law.

Robert Baden-Powell (1857–1941) British soldier and founder of the Boy Scouts. The Scout's oath. *Scouting for Boys*

2 Better is it that thou shouldest not vow, than that thou shouldest vow and not pay.

Bible: Ecclesiastes 5:5

3 I do set my bow in the cloud, and it shall be for a token of a covenant between me and the earth.

Bible: Genesis 9:13

4 The rule is, jam tomorrow and jam yesterday – but never jam today.

Lewis Carroll (Charles Lutwidge Dodgson; 1832–98) British writer. *Through the Looking-Glass*, Ch. 5

5 If you feed people just with revolutionary slogans they will listen today, they will listen tomorrow, they will listen the day after tomorrow, but on the fourth day they will say 'To hell with you!'

Nikita Khrushchev (1894–1971) Soviet statesman. Attrib.

6 A promise made is a debt unpaid.

Robert William Service (1874–1958) Canadian poet. *The Cremation of Sam McGee*

7 Jam today, and men aren't at their most exciting: Jam tomorrow, and one often sees them at their noblest.

C. P. Snow (1905–80) British novelist. *The Two Cultures and the Scientific Revolution*, 4

8 Promises and pie-crust are made to be broken.

Jonathan Swift (1667–1745) Irish-born Anglican priest and writer. *Polite Conversation*, Dialogue 1

PROMOTION

See also patronage

1 Tired of knocking at Preferment's door.

Matthew Arnold (1822–88) British poet and critic. *The Scholar Gipsy*

2 He had said he had known many kicked down stairs, but he never knew any kicked up stairs before.

Lord Halifax (1633–95) English statesman. *Original Memoirs* (Burnet)

3 Every time I make an appointment, I make one ungrateful person and a hundred with a grievance.

Louis XIV (1638–1715) French king. *Siècle de Louis XIV* (Voltaire), Ch. 26

4 The Thane of Cawdor lives; why do you dress me
In borrow'd robes?

William Shakespeare (1564–1616) English dramatist. *Macbeth*, I:3

PROMPTNESS

1 Liberality lies less in giving liberally than in the timeliness of the gift.

Jean de La Bruyère (1645–96) French satirist. *Les Caractères*

2 Punctuality is the politeness of kings.

Louis XVIII (1755–1824) French king. Attrib.

3 Better never than late.

George Bernard Shaw (1856–1950) Irish dramatist and critic. Responding to an offer by a producer to present one of Shaw's plays, having earlier rejected it. *The Unimportance of Being Oscar* (Oscar Levant)

4 He gives twice who gives promptly.

Publilius Syrus (1st century BC) Roman dramatist. Attrib.

5 Punctuality is the virtue of the bored.

Evelyn Waugh (1903–66) British novelist. *Diaries*, 'Irregular Notes', 26 Mar 1962

PRONUNCIATION

See also class, language, speech, spelling

1 The 't' is silent as in Harlow.

Margot Asquith (1865–1945) The 2nd wife of Herbert Asquith. Referring to her name being mispronounced by Jean Harlow.

2 Everybody has a right to pronounce foreign names as he chooses.

Winston Churchill (1874–1965) British statesman. *The Observer*, 'Sayings of the Week', 5 Aug 1951

3 To correct an Englishman's pronunciation is to imply that he is not quite a gentleman.

George Bernard Shaw (1856–1950) Irish dramatist and critic. When chairman of the BBC's committee on standard pronunciation

4 Oh my God! Remember you're in Egypt. The *skay* is only seen in Kensington.

Herbert Beerbohm Tree (1853–1917) British actor and theatre manager. To a leading lady. *Beerbohm Tree* (Hesketh Pearson)

5 They spell it Vinci and pronounce it Vinchy; foreigners always spell better than they pronounce.

Mark Twain (Samuel Langhorne Clemens; 1835–1910) US writer. *The Innocents Abroad*, Ch. 19

PROOF

1 One swallow does not make a summer.

Proverb

2 What is now proved was once only imagined.

William Blake (1757–1827) British poet. *The Marriage of Heaven and Hell*, 'Proverbs of Hell'

3 If a man could pass through Paradise in a dream, and have a flower presented to him as a pledge that his soul had really been there, and if he found that flower in his hand when he awoke – Aye, and what then?

Samuel Taylor Coleridge (1772–1834) British poet. *Anima Poetae*

4 Of course, before we *know* he is a saint, there will have to be miracles.

Graham Greene (1904–) British novelist. *The Power and the Glory*, Pt. IV

5 If only I could get down to Sidcup! I've been waiting for the weather to break. He's got my papers, this man I left them with, it's got it all down there, I could prove everything.

Harold Pinter (1930–) British dramatist. *The Caretaker*, I

6 Some circumstantial evidence is very strong, as when you find a trout in the milk.

Henry David Thoreau (1817–62) US writer. *Journal*, 1850

PROPAGANDA

1 Propaganda is that branch of the art of lying which consists in nearly deceiving your friends without quite deceiving your enemies.

F. M. Cornford (1886–1960) British poet. *New Statesman*, 15 Sept 1978

2 The greater the lie, the greater the chance that it will be believed.

Adolf Hitler (1889–1945) German dictator. *Mein Kampf*

3 I wonder if we could contrive...some magnificent myth that would in itself carry conviction to our whole community.

Plato (429–347 BC) Greek philosopher. *Republic*, Bk. 5

PROPHECY

See also beginning, future

1 'I saw the new moon late yestreen
Wi' the auld moon in her arm;
And if we gang to sea master,
I fear we'll come to harm.'

Anonymous *Sir Patrick Spens*

2 And there arose not a prophet since in Israel like unto Moses, whom the Lord knew face to face.

Bible: Deuteronomy 34:10

3 I am signing my death warrant.

Michael Collins (1890–1922) Irish nationalist. Said on signing the agreement with Great Britain, 1921, that established the Irish Free State. He was assassinated in an ambush some months later. *Peace by Ordeal* (Longford), Pt. 6, Ch. 1

4 I will sit down now, but the time will come when you will hear me.

Benjamin Disraeli (1804–81) British statesman. Maiden Speech, House of Commons, 7 Dec 1837

5 The lamps are going out over all Europe; we shall not see them lit again in our lifetime.

Lord Grey (1862–1933) British statesman. Remark made on 3 Aug 1914, the eve of World War I.

6 You ain't heard nothin' yet, folks.

Al Jolson (Asa Yoelson; 1886–1950) US actor and singer. In the film *The Jazz Singer*, July 1927.

7 For not wanting to consent to the divorce, which then afterwards will be recognized as unworthy, the King of the islands will be forced to flee, and one put in his place who has no sign of kingship.

Nostradamus (1503–66) French astrologer. Thought to refer to the abdication of Edward VIII. *The Prophecies of Nostradamus*, Century X, 22

8 At night they will think they have seen the sun, when they see the half pig man: Noise, screams, battles seen fought in the skies. The brute beasts will be heard to speak.

Nostradamus Thought to prophecy a 20th-century air-battle. *The Prophecies of Nostradamus*, Century I, 64

9 The blood of the just will be demanded of London burnt by fire in three times twenty plus six. The ancient lady will fall from her high position, and many of the same denomination will be killed.

Nostradamus Believed to refer to the Great Fire of London, 1666. The 'ancient lady' is interpreted as the Cathedral of St. Paul's, which was destroyed in the fire. *The Prophecies of Nostradamus*, Century II, 51

10 *Après nous le déluge.*
After us the deluge.

Madame de Pompadour (1721–64) The mistress of Louis XV of France. After the Battle of Rossbach, 1757

11 As I look ahead, I am filled with foreboding. Like the Roman, I seem to see 'the River Tiber foaming with much blood'.

Enoch Powell (1912–) British politician. Talking about immigration. *See* VIRGIL. Speech in Birmingham, 20 Apr 1968

12 Beware the ides of March.

William Shakespeare (1564–1616) English dramatist. *Julius Caesar*, I:2

13 Mr Turnbull had predicted evil consequences... and was now doing the best in his power to bring about the verification of his own prophecies.

Anthony Trollope (1815–82) British novelist. *Phineas Finn*, Ch. 25

14 I see wars, horrible wars, and the Tiber foaming with
much blood.

Virgil (Publius Vergilius Maro; 70–19 BC) Roman poet. Part of the Sibyl's prophecy to Aeneas, foretelling his difficulties in winning a home in Italy. *Aeneid*, Bk. VI

15 When the Paris Exhibition closes, electric light will close with it and no more will be heard of it.

Erasmus Wilson

PROSE

See also books, criticism, fiction, literature, novels, poetry and prose, writing

1 Yet no one hears his own remarks as prose.

W. H. Auden (1907–73) British poet. *At a Party*

2 I could also have stepped into a style much higher than this in which I have here discoursed, and could have adorned all things more than here I have seemed to do, but I dare not. God did not play in convincing of me, the devil did not play in tempting of me neither did I play when I sunk into a bottomless pit, when the pangs of hell caught hold upon me; wherefore I may not play in my relating of them, but be plain and simple, and lay down the thing as it was.

John Bunyan (1628–88) Referring to literary style. *Grace Abounding to the Chief of Sinners*, Preface

3 Men will forgive a man anything except bad prose.

Winston Churchill (1874–1965) British statesman. Election speech, Manchester, 1906

4 ...the pulpit was the cradle of English prose.

A. G. Little (1863–1945) British historian. *English Historical Review*, xlix (1934)

5 It has been said that good prose should resemble the conversation of a well-bred man.

W. Somerset Maugham (1874–1965) British novelist and doctor. *The Summing Up*

6 Good heavens! I have been talking prose for over forty years without realizing it.

Molière (Jean Baptiste Poquelin; 1622–73) French dramatist. *Le Bourgeois Gentilhomme*, II:4

PROTESTANTISM

See also Catholicism, Christianity, religion

1 The three great elements of modern civilization, Gunpowder, Printing, and the Protestant Religion.

Thomas Carlyle (1795–1881) Scottish historian and essayist. *Critical and Miscellaneous Essays*, 'The State of German Literature'

2 A single friar who goes counter to all Christianity for a thousand years must be wrong.

Charles V (1500–58) Holy Roman Emperor. Referring to Martin Luther. Remark, Diet of Worms, 19 Apr 1521

3 I shall never be a heretic, I may err in dispute; but I do not wish to decide anything finally; on the other hand, I am not bound by the opinions of men.

Martin Luther (1483–1546) German Protestant. Letter to the chaplain to the Elector of Saxony, 28 Aug 1518

4 If I had heard that as many devils would set on me in Worms as there are tiles on the roofs, I should none the less have ridden there.

Martin Luther Referring to the Diet of Worms. *Luthers Sämmtliche Schriften*

5 Anyone who can be proved to be a seditious person is an outlaw before God and the emperor; and whoever is the first to put him to death does right and well.

Martin Luther Referring to the 'Peasants' War', an uprising (1524–25) of peasants in Germany partly inspired by Luther's teachings. *Against the Robbing and Murdering Hordes of Peasants* (Broadsheet, May 1525)

6 The chief contribution of Protestantism to human thought is its massive proof that God is a bore.

H. L. Mencken (1880–1956) US journalist. *Notebooks*, 'Minority Report'

7 'You're a Christian?' 'Church of England,' said Mr Polly. 'Mm,' said the employer, a little checked. 'For good all round business work, I should have preferred a Baptist.'

H. G. Wells (1866–1946) British writer. *The History of Mr Polly*, Pt. III, Ch. 1

8 Take heed of thinking. *The farther you go from the church of Rome, the nearer you are to God.*

Henry Wotton (1568–1639) English poet and diplomat. *Reliquiae Wottonianae* (Izaak Walton)

PROUST, MARCEL

(1871–1922) French novelist. His masterpiece was a series of partly autobiographical novels, *À la recherche du temps perdu* (1913–27), which give a detailed portrait of the life of his time.

Quotations about Proust

1 Reading Proust is like bathing in someone else's dirty water.

Alexander Woollcott Attrib.

Quotations by Proust

2 The taste was that of the little crumb of madeleine which on Sunday mornings at Combray…, when I used to say good-day to her in her bedroom, my aunt Léonie used to give me, dipping it first in her own cup of tea or tisane.

À La Recherche du temps perdu: Du côté de chez Swann

3 People often say that, by pointing out to a man the faults of his mistress, you succeed only in strengthening his attachment to her, because he does not believe you; yet how much more so if he does!

À La Recherche du temps perdu: Du côté de chez Swann

4 The human face is indeed, like the face of the God of some Oriental theogony, a whole cluster of faces, crowded together but on different surfaces so that one does not see them all at once.

À La Recherche du temps perdu: À l'ombre des jeunes filles en fleurs

5 There can be no peace of mind in love, since the advantage one has secured is never anything but a fresh starting-point for further desires.

À La Recherche du temps perdu: À l'ombre des jeunes filles en fleurs

6 As soon as one is unhappy one becomes moral.

À La Recherche du temps perdu: À l'ombre des jeunes filles en fleurs

7 A PUSHING LADY. What are your views on love?
MME LEROI. Love? I make it constantly but I never talk about it.

À La Recherche du temps perdu: Le Côté de Guermantes

8 It has been said that the highest praise of God consists in the denial of Him by the atheist, who finds creation so perfect that he can dispense with a creator.

À La Recherche du temps perdu: Le Côté de Guermantes

9 A doctor who doesn't say too many foolish things is a patient half-cured, just as a critic is a poet who has stopped writing verse and a policeman a burglar who has retired from practice.

À La Recherche du temps perdu: Le Côté de Guermantes

10 Neurosis has an absolute genius for malingering. There is no illness which it cannot counterfeit perfectly…If it is capable of deceiving the doctor, how should it fail to deceive the patient?

À La Recherche du temps perdu: Le Côté de Guermantes

11 As soon as he ceased to be mad he became merely stupid. There are maladies we must not seek to cure because they alone protect us from others that are more serious.

À La Recherche du temps perdu: Le Côté de Guermantes

12 His hatred of snobs was a derivative of his snobbishness, but made the simpletons (in other words, everyone) believe that he was immune from snobbishness.

À La Recherche du temps perdu: Le Côté de Guermantes

13 There is nothing like desire for preventing the thing one says from bearing any resemblance to what one has in mind.
À La Recherche du temps perdu: Le Côté de Guermantes

14 Good-bye, I've barely said a word to you, it is always like that at parties, we never see the people, we never say the things we should like to say, but it is the same everywhere in this life. Let us hope that when we are dead things will be better arranged.
À La Recherche du temps perdu: Sodome et Gomorrhe

15 I have sometimes regretted living so close to Marie...because I may be very fond of her, but I am not quite so fond of her company.
À La Recherche du temps perdu: Sodome et Gomorrhe

16 I have a horror of sunsets, they're so romantic, so operatic.
À La Recherche du temps perdu: Sodome et Gomorrhe

17 It is seldom indeed that one parts on good terms, because if one were on good terms one would not part.
À La Recherche du temps perdu: La Prisonnière

18 One of those telegrams of which M. de Guermantes had wittily fixed the formula: 'Cannot come, lie follows'.
À La Recherche du temps perdu: Le Temps retrouvé

19 Happiness is beneficial for the body, but it is grief that develops the powers of the mind.
À La Recherche du temps perdu: Le Temps retrouvé

20 Everything great in the world is done by neurotics; they alone founded our religions and created our masterpieces.
The Perpetual Pessimist (Sagittarius and George)

PROVERBS

A selection of the commonest proverbs and other sayings is given here. The proverbs are arranged in alphabetical order.

1 A bad penny always turns up.

2 A bad workman always blames his tools.

3 A bird in the hand is worth two in the bush.

4 Absence makes the heart grow fonder.

5 A cask of wine works more miracles than a church full of saints.
Italian proverb.

6 A cat has nine lives.

7 A cat may look at a king.

8 Accidents will happen in the best regulated families.

9 A chain is no stronger than its weakest link.

10 A constant guest is never welcome.

11 Actions speak louder than words.

12 Adam's ale is the best brew.

13 A dimple in the chin, a devil within.

14 A drowning man will clutch at a straw.

15 A fool and his money are soon parted.

16 A fool at forty is a fool indeed.

17 A fool believes everything.

18 A friend in need is a friend indeed.

19 After a storm comes a calm.

20 After shaking hands with a Greek, count your fingers.

21 A good dog deserves a good bone.

22 A good drink makes the old young.

23 A good face is a letter of recommendation.

24 A good friend is my nearest relation.

25 A good scare is worth more than good advice.

26 A hedge between keeps friendship green.

27 A judge knows nothing unless it has been explained to him three times.

28 A lawyer never goes to law himself.

29 A lawyer's opinion is worth nothing unless paid for.

30 A liar is worse than a thief.

31 All are not saints that go to church.

32 All cats are grey in the dark.

33 All good things must come to an end.

34 All is fair in love and war.

35 All men are mortal.

36 All roads lead to Rome.

37 All's grist that comes to the mill.

38 All's well that ends well.

39 All that glitters is not gold.

40 All the world loves a lover.

41 All work and no play makes Jack a dull boy.

42 Although there exist many thousand subjects for elegant conversation, there are persons who cannot meet a cripple without talking about feet.
Chinese proverb.

43 A man can die but once.

44 A man is as old as he feels, and a woman as old as she looks.

45 A man of straw is worth a woman of gold.

46 A meal without flesh is like feeding on grass.
Indian proverb.

47 A miss is as good as a mile.

48 An apple a day keeps the doctor away.

49 An apple-pie without some cheese is like a kiss without a squeeze.

50 An atheist is one point beyond the devil.

51 An Englishman's home is his castle.

52 An Englishman's word is his bond.

53 An honest man's word is as good as his bond.

54 An hour in the morning is worth two in the evening.

55 A nod is as good as a wink to a blind horse.

56 Any port in a storm.

57 Any publicity is good publicity.

58 A penny saved is a penny earned.

59 A piece of churchyard fits everybody.

60 Appearances are deceptive.

61 A priest sees people at their best, a lawyer at their worst, but a doctor sees them as they really are.

62 A rainbow in the morning is the shepherd's warning; a rainbow at night is the shepherd's delight.

63 Ask a silly question and you'll get a silly answer.

64 Ask no questions and hear no lies.

65 A spur in the head is worth two in the heel.

66 As soon as man is born he begins to die.

67 A still tongue makes a wise head.

68 A stitch in time saves nine.

69 A tale never loses in the telling.

70 A trouble shared is a trouble halved.

71 A truly great man never puts away the simplicity of a child.
Chinese proverb.

72 Attack is the best form of defence.

73 A watched pot never boils.

74 A woman's place is in the home.

75 A woman's work is never done.

76 A young physician fattens the churchyard.

77 Bad news travels fast.

78 Barking dogs seldom bite.

79 Beauty is in the eye of the beholder.

80 Beauty is only skin-deep.

81 Beauty is potent but money is omnipotent.

82 Beggars can't be choosers.

83 Believe nothing of what you hear, and only half of what you see.

84 Benefits make a man a slave.
Arabic proverb.

85 Better a lie that heals than a truth that wounds.

86 Better an egg today than a hen tomorrow.

87 Better a thousand enemies outside the house than one inside.
Arabic proverb.

88 Better be a fool than a knave.

89 Better be an old man's darling than a young man's slave.

90 Better be envied than pitied.

91 Better be safe than sorry.

92 Better late than never.

93 Birds of a feather flock together.

94 Blood is thicker than water.

95 Books and friends should be few but good.

96 Borrowed garments never fit well.

97 Bread is the staff of life.

98 Caesar's wife must be above suspicion.

99 Charity begins at home.

100 Christmas comes but once a year.

101 Civility costs nothing.

102 Cold hands, warm heart.

103 Constant dripping wears away the stone.

104 Curiosity killed the cat.

105 Cut your coat according to your cloth.

106 Dead men tell no tales.

107 Death defies the doctor.

108 Death is the great leveller.

109 Desperate cuts must have desperate cures.

110 Divide and rule.

111 Do as I say, not as I do.

112 Do as you would be done by.

113 Dog does not eat dog.

114 Doing is better than saying.

115 Don't count your chickens before they are hatched.

116 Don't cross the bridge till you get to it.

117 Don't cut off your nose to spite your face.

118 Don't meet troubles half-way.

119 Don't put all your eggs in one basket.

120 Don't spoil the ship for a ha'porth of tar.

121 Don't teach your grandmother to suck eggs.

122 Don't throw the baby out with the bathwater.

123 Don't wash your dirty linen in public.

124 Early to bed and early to rise, makes a man healthy, wealthy and wise.

125 Easier said than done.

126 East, west, home's best.

127 Easy come, easy go.

128 Eat to live and not live to eat.

129 Empty vessels make the greatest sound.

130 Even a worm will turn.

131 Every book must be chewed to get out its juice.
Chinese proverb.

132 Every cloud has a silver lining.

133 Every dog has his day.

134 Every dog is allowed one bite.

135 Every family has a skeleton in the cupboard.

136 Every little helps.

137 Every man after his fashion.

138 Every man for himself, and the devil take the hindmost.

139 Every man is his own worst enemy.

140 Every man to his trade.

141 Every one is innocent until he is proved guilty.

142 Every one to his taste.

143 Every picture tells a story.

144 Everything comes to him who waits.

145 Experience is the best teacher.

146 Experience is the mother of wisdom.

147 Faith will move mountains.

148 Familiarity breeds contempt.

149 Fear of death is worse than death itself.

150 Fight fire with fire.

151 Finders keepers, losers seekers.

152 Fine feathers make fine birds.

153 Fine words butter no parsnips.

154 Fingers were made before forks, and hands before knives.

155 First come, first served.

156 First impressions are the most lasting.

157 First things first.

158 Fish and guests smell in three days.

159 Fools build houses, and wise men buy them.

160 Fools live poor to die rich.

161 Footprints on the sands of time are not made by sitting down.

162 Forbidden fruit is sweet.

163 Forewarned is forearmed.

164 Forgive and forget.

165 Fortune favours fools.

166 For want of a nail the shoe was lost; for want of a shoe the horse was lost; for want of a horse the rider was lost.

167 From clogs to clogs is only three generations.

168 From small beginnings come great things.

169 From the sublime to the ridiculous is only a step.

170 Garbage in, garbage out.

171 Genius is an infinite capacity for taking pains.

172 Give a dog a bad name and hang him.

173 Give a thief enough rope and he'll hang himself.

174 Give him an inch and he'll take a yard.

175 Give me a child for the first seven years, and you may do what you like with him afterwards.

176 God defend me from my friends; from my enemies I can defend myself.

177 God helps them that help themselves.

178 God is always on the side of the big battalions.

179 Good fences make good neighbours.

180 Go to bed with the lamb, and rise with the lark.

181 Great minds think alike.

182 Great oaks from little acorns grow.

183 Grey hairs are death's blossoms.

184 Half a loaf is better than no bread.

185 Handsome is as handsome does.

186 Haste makes waste.

187 Health is better than wealth.

188 He helps little that helps not himself.

189 He that fights and runs away, may live to fight another day.

190 He that has no children brings them up well.

191 He that has no wife, beats her oft.

192 He that is his own lawyer has a fool for a client.

193 He that knows little, often repeats it.

194 He that knows nothing, doubts nothing.

195 He that lives long suffers much.

196 He travels fastest who travels alone.

197 He was a bold man that first ate an oyster.

198 He who drinks a little too much drinks much too much.

199 He who hesitates is lost.

200 He who lives by the sword dies by the sword.

201 He who pays the piper calls the tune.

202 He who rides a tiger is afraid to dismount.

203 He who sups with the devil should have a long spoon.

204 History repeats itself.

205 Hoist your sail when the wind is fair.

206 Home is home, though it be never so homely.

207 Home is where the heart is.

208 Honesty is the best policy.

209 Hope for the best.

210 Hunger is the best sauce.

211 If a job's worth doing, it's worth doing well.

212 If anything can go wrong, it will.

213 If at first you don't succeed, try, try, try again.

214 If ifs and ans were pots and pans, there'd be no trade for tinkers.

215 If the mountain will not come to Mahomet, Mahomet must go to the mountain.

216 If wishes were horses, beggars would ride.

217 If you can't be good, be careful.

218 If you don't like the heat, get out of the kitchen.

219 If you play with fire you get burnt.

220 If you trust before you try, you may repent before you die.

221 If you want a thing well done, do it yourself.

222 Imitation is the sincerest form of flattery.

223 In for a penny, in for a pound.

224 In the country of the blind, the one-eyed man is king.

225 It is a long lane that has no turning.

226 It is better to be born lucky than rich.

227 It is easy to bear the misfortunes of others.

228 It is easy to be wise after the event.

229 It is no use crying over spilt milk.

230 It never rains but it pours.

231 It's an ill wind that blows nobody any good.

232 It's a small world.

233 It's too late to shut the stable door after the horse has bolted.

234 It takes all sorts to make a world.

235 It takes two to make a quarrel.

236 It takes two to tango.

237 It will all come right in the wash.

238 It will be all the same in a hundred years.

239 Jack of all trades, master of none.

240 Keep something for a rainy day.

241 Keep your mouth shut and your eyes open.

242 Keep your weather-eye open.

243 Kill not the goose that lays the golden egg.

244 Knowledge is power.

245 Knowledge is the mother of all virtue; all vice proceeds from ignorance.

246 Know thyself.

247 Laugh and grow fat.

248 Laugh before breakfast, you'll cry before supper.

249 Laughter is the best medicine.

250 Learning is a treasure which accompanies its owner everywhere.
Chinese proverb.

251 Least said soonest mended.

252 Leave well alone.

253 Lend only that which you can afford to lose.

254 Let bygones be bygones.

255 Let sleeping dogs lie.

256 Let the cobbler stick to his last.

257 Life begins at forty.

258 Life is just a bowl of cherries.

259 Life is not all beer and skittles.

260 Life is sweet.

261 Like breeds like.

262 Like father, like son.

263 Listeners never hear good of themselves.

264 Live and learn.

265 Long absent, soon forgotten.

266 Look after number one.

267 Look before you leap.

268 Look on the bright side.

269 Love conquers all.

270 Love is blind.

271 Love laughs at locksmiths.

272 Love makes the world go round.

273 Love me, love my dog.

274 Love will find a way.

275 Love your neighbour, yet pull not down your hedge.

276 Lucky at cards, unlucky in love.

277 Mackerel sky and mares' tails make lofty ships carry low sails.

278 Make hay while the sun shines.

279 Manners maketh man.

280 Man proposes, God disposes.

281 Many a mickle makes a muckle.

282 Many a true word is spoken in jest.

283 Many hands make light work.

284 Many irons in the fire, some must cool.

285 March comes in like a lion and goes out like a lamb.

286 March winds and April showers bring forth May flowers.

287 Marriages are made in heaven.

288 Marry in haste, and repent at leisure.

289 Marry in Lent, and you'll live to repent.

290 Marry in May, rue for aye.

291 Meet on the stairs and you won't meet in heaven.

292 Mind your own business.

293 Moderation in all things.

294 Monday's child is fair of face, Tuesday's child is full of grace; Wednesday's child is full of woe, Thursday's child has far to go; Friday's child is loving and giving, Saturday's child works hard for its living; and the child that's born on the Sabbath day, is fair and wise and good and gay.

295 More haste, less speed.

296 Music helps not the toothache.

297 Music is the food of love.

298 Necessity is the mother of invention.

299 Needs must when the devil drives.

300 Ne'er cast a clout till May be out.

301 Never do things by halves.

302 Never judge from appearances.

303 Never look a gift horse in the mouth.

304 Never put off till tomorrow what you can do today.

305 Never say die.

306 Never speak ill of the dead.

307 Never too late to learn.

308 Ninety per cent of inspiration is perspiration.

309 No bees, no honey; no work, no money.

310 No love like the first love.

311 No man is a hero to his valet.

312 No man is infallible.

313 No names, no pack-drill.

314 No news is good news.

315 No pleasure without pain.

316 Nothing is certain but death and taxes.

317 Nothing so bad but it might have been worse.

318 Nothing succeeds like success.

319 Nothing ventured, nothing gained.

320 No time like the present.

321 Old habits die hard.

322 Old sins cast long shadows.

323 Old soldiers never die, they simply fade away.

324 Once a parson always a parson.

325 One for sorrow, two for mirth; three for a wedding, four for a birth; five for silver, six for gold; seven for a secret, not to be told; eight for heaven, nine for hell; and ten for the devil's own sel.
Referring to magpies or crows; there are numerous variants.

326 One good turn deserves another.

327 One hour's sleep before midnight, is worth two after.

328 One joy scatters a hundred griefs.
Chinese proverb.

329 One man's meat is another man's poison.

330 One swallow does not make a summer.

331 Opportunity seldom knocks twice.

332 Out of debt, out of danger.

333 Out of sight, out of mind.

334 Patience is a virtue.

335 Penny wise, pound foolish.

336 Pigs might fly, if they had wings.

337 Possession is nine points of the law.

338 Poverty is not a crime.

339 Practice makes perfect.

340 Practise what you preach.

341 Prevention is better than cure.

342 Promises are like pie-crust, made to be broken.

343 Punctuality is the politeness of princes.

344 Put an Irishman on the spit, and you can always get another Irishman to baste him.

345 Put off the evil hour as long as you can.

346 Rain before seven: fine before eleven.

347 Rain, rain, go away, come again another day.

348 Red sky at night, shepherd's delight; red sky in the morning, shepherd's warning.

349 Revenge is a dish that tastes better cold.

350 Revenge is sweet.

351 Rome was not built in a day.

352 Sailors have a port in every storm.

353 Salt water and absence wash away love.

354 Save your breath to cool your porridge.

355 Saying is one thing, and doing another.

356 Scratch my back and I'll scratch yours.

357 See a pin and pick it up, all the day you'll have good luck; see a pin and let it lie, you'll want a pin before you die.

358 Seeing is believing.

359 See Naples and die.

360 Self-praise is no recommendation.

361 Send a fool to the market and a fool he will return again.

362 Silence is golden.

363 Slow but sure wins the race.

364 Small is beautiful.

365 Soon learnt, soon forgotten.

366 Spare the rod and spoil the child.

367 Speak when you are spoken to.

368 Speech is silver, silence is golden.

369 Sticks and stones may break my bones, but words will never hurt me.

370 Still waters run deep.

371 Strike while the iron is hot.

372 St. Swithin's Day, if thou dost rain, for forty days it will remain; St. Swithin's Day, if thou be fair, for forty days 'twill rain no more.

373 Take a hair of the dog that bit you.

374 Take care of the pence, and the pounds will take care of themselves.

375 Take things as they come.

376 Talk of the devil, and he is bound to appear.

377 Tell the truth and shame the devil.

378 The best of friends must part.

379 The best things come in small parcels.

380 The best things in life are free.

381 The better the day, the better the deed.

382 The cuckoo comes in April, and stays the month of May; sings a song at midsummer, and then goes away.

383 The darkest hour is just before the dawn.

384 The devil finds work for idle hands to do.

385 The devil is not so black as he is painted.

386 The devil looks after his own.

387 The early bird catches the worm.

388 The end justifies the means.

389 The exception proves the rule.

390 The eye is bigger than the belly.

391 The eyes are the window of the soul.

392 The family that prays together stays together.

393 The first day a guest, the second day a guest, the third day a calamity.
Indian proverb.

394 The first step is the hardest.

395 The first wife is matrimony, the second company, the third heresy.

396 The good die young.

397 The guest who outstays his fellow-guests loses his overcoat.
Chinese proverb.

398 The hand that rocks the cradle rules the world.

399 The last straw breaks the camel's back.

400 The law does not concern itself about trifles.

401 The more the merrier; the fewer the better fare.

402 The nearer the bone, the sweeter the flesh.

403 The north wind does blow, and we shall have snow.

404 The old man has his death before his eyes; the young man behind his back.

405 There are more old drunkards than old doctors.

406 There are only twenty-four hours in the day.

407 There is a time and place for everything.

408 There is honour among thieves.

409 There is more than one way to skin a cat.

410 There is no accounting for tastes.

411 There is safety in numbers.

412 There's a black sheep in every flock.

413 There's always room at the top.

414 There's many a good tune played on an old fiddle.

415 There's many a slip 'twixt the cup and the lip.

416 There's no fool like an old fool.

417 There's no place like home.

418 There's no smoke without fire.

419 There's nowt so queer as folk.

420 There's one law for the rich, and another for the poor.

421 There's only one pretty child in the world, and every mother has it.

422 There will be sleeping enough in the grave.

423 The road to hell is paved with good intentions.

424 The shoemaker's son always goes barefoot.

425 The streets of London are paved with gold.

426 The style is the man.

427 The way to a man's heart is through his stomach.

428 The weakest goes to the wall.

429 Things are not always what they seem.

430 Third time lucky.

431 Throw dirt enough, and some will stick.

432 Throw out a sprat to catch a mackerel.

433 Time and tide wait for no man.

434 Time is a great healer.

435 Time will tell.

436 To deceive oneself is very easy.

437 To err is human.

438 Tomorrow is another day.

439 Tomorrow never comes.

440 Too many cooks spoil the broth.

441 Travel broadens the mind.

442 True love never grows old.

443 Truth fears no trial.

444 Truth is stranger than fiction.

445 Truth will out.

446 Two heads are better than one.

447 Two wrongs do not make a right.

448 Union is strength.

449 United we stand, divided we fall.

450 Vice is often clothed in virtue's habit.

451 Walls have ears.

452 Waste not, want not.

453 We must learn to walk before we can run.

454 What can't be cured, must be endured.

455 What must be, must be.

456 What's done cannot be undone.

457 What you don't know can't hurt you.

458 What you lose on the swings you gain on the roundabouts.

459 When one door shuts, another opens.

460 When poverty comes in at the door, love flies out of the window.

461 When the cat's away, the mice will play.

462 When the wine is in, the wit is out.

463 Where there's a will there's a way.

464 While there's life there's hope.

465 Whom the gods love dies young.

466 Who spits against the wind, it falls in his face.

467 Why buy a cow when milk is so cheap?

468 Why keep a dog and bark yourself?

469 You can have too much of a good thing.

470 You can lead a horse to the water, but you can't make him drink.

471 You cannot run with the hare and hunt with the hounds.

472 You can't get a quart into a pint pot.

473 You can't get blood out of a stone.

474 You can't make an omelette without breaking eggs.

475 You can't make bricks without straw.

476 You can't please everyone.

477 You can't take it with you when you go.

478 You can't teach an old dog new tricks.

479 You can't tell a book by its cover.

PROVOCATION

1 My wife hath something in her gizzard, that only waits an opportunity of being provoked to bring up.

Samuel Pepys (1633–1703) English diarist. *Diary*, 17 June 1668

2 Ask you what provocation I have had?
The strong antipathy of good to bad.

Alexander Pope (1688–1744) British poet. *Epilogue to the Satires*, Dialogue II

PRUDENCE

See also caution, wisdom

1 A bird in the hand is worth two in the bush.

Proverb

2 Forewarned is forearmed.

Proverb

3 For want of a nail the shoe was lost; for want of a shoe the horse was lost; for want of a horse the rider was lost.

Proverb

4 Prevention is better than cure.

Proverb

5 One does not insult the river god while crossing the river.

Anonymous Chinese proverb.

6 It is always good
When a man has two irons in the fire.

Francis Beaumont (1584–1616) English dramatist. *The Faithful Friends*, I:2

7 Put your trust in God, my boys, and keep your powder dry.

Valentine Blacker (1778–1823) British soldier. *Oliver Cromwell's Advice*

8 I'd much rather have that fellow inside my tent pissing out, than outside my tent pissing in.

Lyndon B. Johnson (1908–73) US statesman. When asked why he retained J. Edgar Hoover at the FBI. *Guardian Weekly*, 18 Dec 1971

9 One should oblige everyone to the extent of one's ability. One often needs someone smaller than oneself.

Jean de La Fontaine (1621–95) French poet. *Fables*, II, 'Le Lion et le Rat'

10 Any girl who was a lady would not even think of having such a good time that she did not remember to hang on to her jewelry.

Anita Loos (1891–1981) US novelist. *Gentlemen Prefer Blondes*, Ch. 4

11 Be nice to people on your way up because you'll meet 'em on your way down.

Wilson Mizner (1876–1933) US writer and wit. Also attributed to Jimmy Durante. *A Dictionary of Catch Phrases* (Eric Partridge)

PRUDERY

See also censorship, pornography, puritanism

1 Would you allow your wife or your servant to read this book?

Mervyn Griffith-Jones (1909–78) British lawyer. As counsel for the prosecution in the *Lady Chatterley's Lover* trial

2 We have long passed the Victorian Era when asterisks were followed after a certain interval by a baby.

W. Somerset Maugham (1874–1965) British novelist. *The Constant Wife*

3 Age will bring all things, and everyone knows, Madame, that twenty is no age to be a prude.

Molière (Jean Baptiste Poquelin; 1622–73) French dramatist. *Le Misanthrope*, III:4

4 An orgy looks particularly alluring seen through the mists of righteous indignation.

Malcolm Muggeridge (1903–90) British writer. *The Most of Malcolm Muggeridge*, 'Dolce Vita in a Cold Climate'

5 Obscenity is what happens to shock some elderly and ignorant magistrate.

Bertrand Russell (1872–1970) British philosopher. *Look*

PSALMS

The version of the Psalms included here is the more familiar Coverdale version taken from The Book of Common Prayer, rather than that from the Authorized Version of the Bible.

1 Blessed is the man that hath not walked in the counsel of the ungodly, nor stood in the way of sinners, and hath not sat in the seat of the scornful.
But his delight is in the law of the Lord; and in his law will he exercise himself day and night.
And he shall be like a tree planted by the water-side, that will bring forth his fruit in due season.
His leaf also shall not wither; and look, whatsoever he doeth shall prosper.

1:1–4

2 All mine enemies shall be confounded, and sore vexed: they shall be turned back, and put to shame suddenly.

6:10

3 Out of the mouth of very babes and sucklings hast thou ordained strength, because of thine enemies, that thou mightest still the enemy, and the avenger.
For I will consider thy heavens, even the works of thy fingers, the moon and the stars, which thou hast ordained.
What is man, that thou art mindful of him? and the son of man, that thou visitest him?
Thou madest him lower than the angels, to crown him with glory and worship.

8:2–5

4 In the Lord put I my trust: how say ye then to my soul, that she should flee as a bird unto the hill?
For lo, the ungodly bend their bow, and make ready their arrows within the quiver that they may privily shoot at them which are true of heart.

11:1–2

5 Upon the ungodly he shall rain snares, fire and brimstone, storm and tempest: this shall be their portion to drink.

11:7

6 Keep me as the apple of an eye; hide me under the shadow of thy wings.

17:8

7 Thou also shalt light my candle: the Lord my God shall make my darkness to be light.
For in thee I shall discomfit an host of men; and with the help of my God I shall leap over the wall.

18:28–29

8 In them hath he set a tabernacle for the sun, which cometh forth as a bridegroom out of his chamber, and rejoiceth as a giant to run his course.

19:5

9 The fear of the Lord is clean, and endureth for ever: the judgments of the Lord are true, and righteous altogether.
More to be desired are they than gold, yea, than much fine gold: sweeter also than honey, and the honey-comb.

19:9–10

10 Let the words of my mouth, and the meditation

of my heart, be alway acceptable in thy sight,
O Lord, my strength, and my redeemer.
19:14–15

11 The Lord is my shepherd; therefore can I lack nothing.
He shall feed me in a green pasture: and lead me forth beside the waters of comfort.
He shall convert my soul: and bring me forth in the paths of righteousness, for his Name's sake.
Yea, though I walk through the valley of the shadow of death, I will fear no evil: for thou art with me; thy rod and thy staff comfort me.
Thou shalt prepare a table before me against them that trouble me: thou hast anointed my head with oil, and my cup shall be full.
But thy loving-kindness and mercy shall follow me all the days of my life: and I will dwell in the house of the Lord for ever.
23:1–6

12 The Lord is my shepherd; I shall not want.
He maketh me to lie down in green pastures: he leadeth me beside the still waters.
Authorised Version 23:1–2

13 Thou preparest a table before me in the presence of mine enemies: thou anointest my head with oil; my cup runneth over.
Surely goodness and mercy shall follow me all the days of my life: and I will dwell in the house of the Lord for ever.
Authorised Version 23:5–6

14 Lift up your heads, O ye gates, and be ye lift up, ye everlasting doors; and the King of glory shall come in.
Who is the King of glory? it is the Lord strong and mighty, even the Lord mighty in battle.
24:7–8

15 The Lord is my light, and my salvation; whom then shall I fear? the Lord is the strength of my life; of whom then shall I be afraid?
27:1

16 The voice of the Lord breaketh the cedar-trees; yea, the Lord breaketh the cedars of Libanus.
29:5

17 For his wrath endureth but the twinkling of an eye, and in his pleasure is life: heaviness may endure for a night, but joy cometh in the morning.
And in my prosperity I said, I shall never be removed; thou, Lord, of thy goodness hast made my hill so strong.
30:5–6

18 In thee, O Lord, have I put my trust: let me never be put to confusion; deliver me in thy righteousness.
31:1

19 Into thy hands I commend my spirit: for thou hast redeemed me, O Lord, thou God of truth.
31:6

20 I am clean forgotten, as a dead man out of mind: I am become like a broken vessel.
31:14

21 He loveth righteousness and judgment: the earth is full of the goodness of the Lord.
33:5

22 I will alway give thanks unto the Lord: his praise shall ever be in my mouth.
34:1

23 When thou with rebukes dost chasten man for sin, thou makest his beauty to consume away, like as it were a moth fretting a garment: every man therefore is but vanity.
39:12

24 As for me, I am poor and needy; but the Lord careth for me.
Thou art my helper and redeemer; make no long tarrying, O my God.
40:20–21

25 Yea, even mine own familiar friend, whom I trusted, who did also eat of my bread, hath laid great wait for me.
41:9

26 Like as the hart desireth the water-brooks, so longeth my soul after thee, O God.
My soul is athirst for God, yea, even for the living God: when shall I come to appear before the presence of God?
42:1–2

27 God is in the midst of her, therefore shall she not be removed God shall help her, and that right early.
The heathen make much ado, and the kingdoms are moved: but God hath shewed his voice, and the earth shall melt away.
46:5–6

28 He maketh wars to cease in all the world; he breaketh the bow, and knappeth the spear in sunder, and burneth the chariots in the fire.
Be still then, and know that I am God: I will be exalted among the heathen, and I will be exalted in the earth.
The Lord of hosts is with us; the God of Jacob is our refuge.
46:9–11

29 Man being in honour hath no understanding: but is compared unto the beasts that perish.
49:20

30 Wash me throughly from my wickedness, and cleanse me from my sin.
For I acknowledge my faults: and my sin is ever before me.
51:2–3

31 Behold, I was shapen in wickedness: and in sin hath my mother conceived me.
But lo, thou requirest truth in the inward parts: and shalt make me to understand wisdom secretly.
Thou shalt purge me with hyssop, and I shall be clean: thou shalt wash me, and I shall be whiter than snow.
Thou shalt make me hear of joy and gladness: that the bones which thou hast broken may rejoice.
Turn thy face from my sins: and put out all my misdeeds.
Make me a clean heart, O God: and renew a right spirit within me.
51:5–10

32 For thou desirest no sacrifice, else would I give it thee: but thou delightest not in burnt-offerings.

The sacrifice of God is a troubled spirit: a broken and contrite heart, O God, shalt thou not despise.
51:16–17

33 And I said, O that I had wings like a dove: for then would I flee away, and be at rest.
55:6

34 We took sweet counsel together, and walked in the house of God as friends.
55:15

35 For thou hast delivered my soul from death, and my feet from falling, that I may walk before God in the light of the living.
56:13

36 God shall send forth his mercy and truth: my soul is among lions.
And I lie even among the children of men, that are set on fire: whose teeth are spears and arrows, and their tongue a sharp sword.
57:4–5

37 O set me up upon the rock that is higher than I: for thou hast been my hope, and a strong tower for me against the enemy.
I will dwell in thy tabernacle for ever; and my trust shall be under the covering of thy wings.
61:3–4

38 Then shall the earth bring forth her increase; and God, even our own God, shall give us his blessing.
67:6

39 Let them be wiped out of the book of the living, and not be written among the righteous.
69:29

40 Let them for their reward be soon brought to shame, that cry over me, There, there.
70:3

41 They that dwell in the wilderness shall kneel before him; his enemies shall lick the dust.
72:9

42 So man did eat angels' food: for he sent them meat enough.
78:26

43 So the Lord awaked as one out of sleep, and like a giant refreshed with wine.
78:66

44 O how amiable are thy dwellings, thou Lord of hosts!
My soul hath a desire and longing to enter into the courts of the Lord: my heart and my flesh rejoice in the living God.
Yea, the sparrow hath found her an house, and the swallow a nest where she may lay her young, even thy altars, O Lord of hosts, my King and my God.
84:1–3

45 For one day in thy courts is better than a thousand.
I had rather be a door-keeper in the house of my God, than to dwell in the tents of ungodliness.
84:10–11

46 Mercy and truth are met together; righteousness and peace have kissed each other.
Truth shall flourish out of the earth; and righteousness hath looked down from heaven.
85:10–11

47 Her foundations are upon the holy hills; the Lord loveth the gates of Sion more than all the dwellings of Jacob.
Very excellent things are spoken of thee, thou city of God.
87:1–2

48 Lord, thou hast been our refuge from one generation to another.
Before the mountains were brought forth, or ever the earth and the world were made, thou art God from everlasting, and world without end.
90:1–2

49 For a thousand years in thy sight are but as yesterday, seeing that is past as a watch in the night.
As soon as thou scatterest them they are even as a sleep; and fade away suddenly like the grass.
In the morning it is green, and groweth up; but in the evening it is cut down, dried up, and withered.
90:4–6

50 For when thou art angry all our days are gone: we bring our years to an end, as it were a tale that is told.
The days of our age are threescore years and ten; and though men be so strong that they come to fourscore years, yet is their strength then but labour and sorrow; so soon passeth it away, and we are gone.
90:9–10

51 For he shall deliver thee from the snare of the hunter, and from the noisome pestilence.
He shall defend thee under his wings, and thou shalt be safe under his feathers: his faithfulness and truth shall be thy shield and buckler.
Thou shalt not be afraid for any terror by night; nor for the arrow that flieth by day;
For the pestilence that walketh in darkness; nor for the sickness that destroyeth in the noon-day.
A thousand shall fall beside thee, and ten thousand at thy right hand; but it shall not come nigh thee.
91:3–7

52 The righteous shall flourish like a palm-tree: and shall spread abroad like a cedar in Libanus.
92:11

53 He that planted the ear, shall he not hear? or he that made the eye, shall he not see?
94:9

54 O come, let us sing unto the Lord: let us heartily rejoice in the strength of our salvation.
Let us come before his presence with thanksgiving, and shew ourselves glad in him with psalms.
For the Lord is a great God, and a great King above all gods.
In his hand are all the corners of the earth: and the strength of the hills is his also.
The sea is his, and he made it: and his hands prepared the dry land.
95:1–5

55 Venite, exultemus
Vulgate 95:1

56 For he is the Lord our God; and we are the people of his pasture, and the sheep of his hand.
To-day if ye will hear his voice, harden not your hearts; as in the provocation, and as in the day of temptation in the wilderness.
95:7–8

57 Whoso hath also a proud look and high stomach, I will not suffer him.
101:7

58 The days of man are but as grass: for he flourisheth as a flower of the field.
For as soon as the wind goeth over it, it is gone; and the place thereof shall know it no more.
103:15–16

59 O give thanks unto the Lord, for he is gracious: and his mercy endureth for ever.
106:1

60 They that go down to the sea in ships, and occupy their business in great waters;
These men see the works of the Lord, and his wonders in the deep.
For at his word the stormy wind ariseth, which lifteth up the waves thereof.
They are carried up to the heaven, and down again to the deep: their soul melteth away because of the trouble.
They reel to and fro, and stagger like a drunken man, and are at their wit's end.
107:23–27

61 The Lord said unto my Lord, Sit thou on my right hand, until I make thine enemies thy footstool.
110:1

62 The fear of the Lord is the beginning of wisdom; a good understanding have all they that do thereafter; the praise of it endureth for ever.
111:10

63 The sea saw that, and fled: Jordan was driven back.
The mountains skipped like rams, and the little hills like young sheep.
114:3–4

64 Their idols are silver and gold, even the work of men's hands.
They have mouths, and speak not; eyes have they, and see not.
They have ears, and hear not; noses have they, and smell not.
They have hands, and handle not; feet have they, and walk not; neither speak they through their throat.
115:4–7

65 The snares of death compassed me round about; and the pains of hell gat hold upon me.
116:3

66 And why? thou hast delivered my soul from death, mine eyes from tears, and my feet from falling.
I will walk before the Lord in the land of the living.
I believed, and therefore will I speak; but I was sore troubled: I said in my haste, All men are liars.
116:8–10

67 I will lift up mine eyes unto the hills, from whence cometh my help.
121:1

68 The Lord himself is thy keeper: the Lord is thy defence upon thy right hand;
So that the sun shall not burn thee by day, neither the moon by night.
The Lord shall preserve thee from all evil: yea, it is even he that shall keep thy soul.
The Lord shall preserve thy going out, and thy coming in, from this time forth for evermore.
121:5–8

69 Turn our captivity, O Lord, as the rivers in the south.
They that sow in tears shall reap in joy.
He that now goeth on his way weeping, and beareth forth good seed, shall doubtless come again with joy, and bring his sheaves with him.
126:5–7

70 By the waters of Babylon we sat down and wept, when we remembered thee, O Sion.
As for our harps, we hanged them up upon the trees that are therein.
For they that led us away captive required of us then a song, and melody, in our heaviness: Sing us one of the songs of Sion.
How shall we sing the Lord's song in a strange land?
If I forget thee, O Jerusalem, let my right hand forget her cunning.
If I do not remember thee, let my tongue cleave to the roof of my mouth; yea, if I prefer not Jerusalem in my mirth.
137:1–6

71 Such knowledge is too wonderful and excellent for me: I cannot attain unto it.
139:5

72 Man is like a thing of nought: his time passeth away like a shadow.
144:4

73 O put not your trust in princes, nor in any child of man; for there is no help in them.
For when the breath of man goeth forth he shall turn again to his earth; and then all his thoughts perish.
146:2–3

74 The Lord looseth men out of prison: the Lord giveth sight to the blind.
The Lord helpeth them that are fallen: the Lord careth for the righteous.
The Lord careth for the strangers: he defendeth the fatherless and widow; as for the way of the ungodly, he turneth it upside down.
146:7–9

75 The Lord doth build up Jerusalem, and gather together the out-casts of Israel.
He healeth those that are broken in heart, and giveth medicine to heal their sickness.
He telleth the number of the stars, and calleth them all by their names.
147:2–4

76 Let the saints be joyful with glory: let them rejoice in their beds.

Let the praises of God be in their mouth, and a two-edged sword in their hands.
149:5–6

77 Praise him in the cymbals and dances: praise him upon the strings and pipe.
Praise him upon the well-tuned cymbals: praise him upon the loud cymbals.
150:4–5

PSYCHIATRY

See also madness, neurosis, psychology

1 The new definition of psychiatry is the care of the id by the odd.
Anonymous

2 The psychiatrist is the obstetrician of the mind.
Anonymous

3 Just because you're paranoid doesn't mean you're not being followed.
Anonymous

4 I have myself spent nine years in a lunatic asylum and have never suffered from the obsession of wanting to kill myself; but I know that each conversation with a psychiatrist in the morning, made me want to hang myself because I knew I could not strangle him.
Antonin Artaud (1896–1948) French theatre producer, actor, and theorist.

5 To us he is no more a person
Now but a climate of opinion.
W. H. Auden (1907–73) British poet. *In Memory of Sigmund Freud*

6 Of course, Behaviourism 'works'. So does torture. Give me a no-nonsense, down-to-earth behaviourist, a few drugs, and simple electrical appliances, and in six months I will have him reciting the Athanasian creed in public.
W. H. Auden *A Certain World*, 'Behaviourism'

7 Psychiatrist: A man who asks you a lot of expensive questions your wife asks you for nothing.
Sam Bardell (1915–)

8 No man is a hero to his wife's psychiatrist.
Dr. Eric Berne *Bartlett's Unfamiliar Quotations* (Leonard Louis Levinson)

9 Psychiatry's chief contribution to philosophy is the discovery that the toilet is the seat of the soul.
Alexander Chase (1926–) US journalist. *Perspectives*

10 I can think of no better step to signalize the inauguration of the National Health service than that a person who so obviously needs psychiatric attention should be among the first of its patients.
Winston Churchill (1874–1965) British statesman. Referring to Aneurin Bevan who introduced the National Health Service (1948). Speech, July 1948

11 A mental stain can neither be blotted out by the passage of time nor washed away by any waters.
Cicero (106 BC–43 BC) Roman orator and statesman. *De Legibus*, Bk. II

12 In a disordered mind, as in a disordered body, soundness of health is impossible.
Cicero *Tusculanarum Disputationum*, Bk. III

13 The trouble with Freud is that he never played the Glasgow Empire Saturday night.
Ken Dodd (1931–) British comedian. TV interview, 1965

14 The psychic development of the individual is a short repetition of the course of development of the race.
Sigmund Freud (1856–1939) Austrian psychoanalyst. *Leonardo da Vinci*

15 Sometimes a cigar is just a cigar.
Sigmund Freud When asked by one of his students whether there was any symbolism in the large cigars that Freud smoked. Attrib.

16 Anybody who goes to see a psychiatrist ought to have his head examined.
Samuel Goldwyn (Samuel Goldfish; 1882–1974) Polish-born US film producer. Attrib.

17 Freud is the father of psychoanalysis. It has no mother.
Germaine Greer (1939–) Australian-born British writer and feminist. *The Female Eunuch*

18 If a patient is poor he is committed to a public hospital as 'psychotic'; if he can afford the luxury of a private sanitarium, he is put there with the diagnosis of 'neurasthenia'; if he is wealthy enough to be isolated in his own home under constant watch of nurses and physicians he is simply an indisposed 'eccentric'.
Pierre Marie Félix Janet (1859–1947) French psychologist and neurologist. *La Force et la faiblesse psychologiques*

19 The relation between psychiatrists and other kinds of lunatics is more or less the relation of a convex folly to a concave one.
Karl Kraus *Bartlett's Unfamiliar Quotations* (Leonard Louis Levinson)

20 Schizophrenic behaviour is a special strategy that a person invents in order to live in an unlivable situation.
R. D. Laing (1927–89) British psychiatrist. *The Politics of Experience*

21 Schizophrenia cannot be understood without understanding despair.
R. D. Laing *The Divided Self*, Ch. 2

22 The mystic sees the ineffable, and the psychopathologist the unspeakable.
W. Somerset Maugham (1874–1965) British novelist. *The Moon and Sixpence*, Ch. 1

23 If the nineteenth century was the age of the editorial chair, ours is the century of the psychiatrist's couch.
Marshall McLuhan (1911–81) Canadian sociologist. *Understanding Media*, Introduction

24 They have a financial interest in being wrong; the more children they can disturb, the larger their adult clientele.
Geoffrey Robinson *Hedingham Harvest*

25 The care of the human mind is the most noble branch of medicine.
Aloysius Sieffert (fl. 1858) *Medical and Surgical Practitioner's Memorandum*

26 One should only see a psychiatrist out of boredom.

Muriel Spark (1918–) British novelist.

27 A psychiatrist is a man who goes to the Folies-Bergère and looks at the audience.

Mervyn Stockwood (1913–) British churchman. *The Observer*, 'Sayings of the Week', 15 Oct 1961

28 Psychiatrists classify a person as neurotic if he suffers from his problems in living, and a psychotic if he makes others suffer.

Thomas Szasz (1920–) US psychiatrist. *The Second Sin*

29 In the past, men created witches: now they create mental patients.

Thomas Szasz

30 We must remember that every 'mental' symptom is a veiled cry of anguish. Against what? Against oppression, or what the patient experiences as oppression. The oppressed speak a million tongues...

Thomas Szasz

31 A neurotic is the man who builds a castle in the air. A psychotic is the man who lives in it. And a psychiatrist is the man who collects the rent.

Lord Robert Webb-Johnstone (b. 1879) *Collected Papers*

32 The ideas of Freud were popularized by people who only imperfectly understood them, who were incapable of the great effort required to grasp them in their relationship to larger truths, and who therefore assigned to them a prominence out of all proportion to their true importance.

Alfred North Whitehead (1861–1947) British philosopher and mathematician. *Dialogues*, Dialogue XXVIII (June 3, 1943)

33 He was meddling too much in my private life.

Tennessee Williams (1911–83) US dramatist. Explaining why he had given up visiting his psychoanalyst. Attrib.

34 He is always called a nerve specialist because it sounds better, but everyone knows he's a sort of janitor in a looney bin.

P. G. Wodehouse (1881–1975) British humorous novelist. *The Inimitable Jeeves*

PSYCHOLOGY

See also mind, psychiatry

1 An animal psychologist is a man who pulls habits out of rats.

Anonymous

2 Behavioural psychology is the science of pulling habits out of rats.

Douglas Busch *Peter's Quotations* (Laurence J. Peter)

3 It seems a pity that psychology should have destroyed all our knowledge of human nature.

G. K. Chesterton (1874–1936) British essayist, novelist, and poet. *The Observer*, 9 Dec 1934

4 Every day, in every way, I am getting better and better.

Emile Coué (1857–1926) French psychologist and pharmacist. Formula for a cure by auto-suggestion used at his clinic in Nancy. *My Method*, Ch. 3

5 Popular psychology is a mass of cant, of slush and of superstition worthy of the most flourishing days of the medicine man.

John Dewey (1859–1952) US philosopher. *The Public and Its Problems*, Ch. 5

6 Psychology has a long past, but only a short history.

Hermann Ebbinghaus (1850–1909) German psychologist. *Summary of Psychology*

7 A woman who is very anxious to get children always read *storks* instead of *stocks*.

Sigmund Freud (1856–1939) Austrian psychoanalyst. *Psychopathology of Everyday Life*

8 What progress we are making. In the Middle Ages they would have burned me. Now they are content with burning my books.

Sigmund Freud Referring to the public burning of his books in Berlin. Letter to Ernest Jones, 1933

9 The separation of psychology from the premises of biology is purely artificial, because the human psyche lives in indissoluble union with the body.

C. G. Jung (1875–1961) Swiss psychoanalyst. *Factors Determining Human Behaviour*, 'Psychological Factors Determining Human Behaviour'

10 It is indeed high time for the clergyman and the psychotherapist to join forces.

Carl Jung *Modern Man in Search of a Soul*, Ch. 11

11 Psychology is as unnecessary as directions for using poison.

Karl Kraus (1874–1936)

12 Psychology which explains everything
explains nothing,
and we are still in doubt.

Marianne Moore (1887–1972) US poet. *Collected Poems*, 'Marriage'

13 Idleness is the parent of all psychology.

Friedrich Nietzsche (1844–1900) German philosopher. *Twilight of the Idols*, 'Maxims and Missiles'

14 I never saw a person's id
I hope I never see one.
But I can tell you if I did
I'd clamp an ego as a lid
Upon the id to keep it hid,
Which is, I gather, what God did
When he first saw a free one.

Helen Harris Perlman (1905–) *National Association of Social Workers News*, 9:2, 1964

15 I don't think the profession of historian fits a man for psychological analysis. In our work we have to deal only with simple feelings to which we give generic names such as Ambition and Interest.

Jean-Paul Sartre (1905–80) French writer. *Nausea*

16 I maintain that today many an inventor, many a diplomat, many a financier is a sounder philosopher than all those who practise the dull craft of experimental psychology.

Oswald Spengler (1880–1936) German philosopher. *Decline of the West*

17 A large part of the popularity and persuasiveness of psychology comes from its being a sublimated spiritualism: a secular, ostensibly scientific way of affirming the primacy of 'spirit' over matter.

Susan Sontag (1933–) US novelist and essayist. *Illness as Metaphor*, Ch. 7

18 There is no psychology; there is only biography and autobiography.

Thomas Szasz (1920–) US psychiatrist. *The Second Sin*, 'Psychology'

19 Man, by the very fact of being man, by possessing consciousness, is, in comparison with the ass or the crab, a diseased animal. Consciousness is a disease.

Miguel de Unamuno y Jugo (1864–1937) Spanish writer and philosopher. *The Tragic Sense of Life*, 1

20 The object of psychology is to give us a totally different idea of the things we know best.

Paul Valéry (1871–1945) French writer. *Tel quel*

PUBLIC

See also class, majority

1 *Vox populi, vox dei.*
The voice of the people is the voice of God.

Alcuin (c. 735–804) English theologian. Letter to Charlemagne

2 But that vast portion, lastly, of the working-class which, raw and half-developed, has long lain half-hidden amidst its poverty and squalor, and is now issuing from its hiding-place to assert an Englishman's heaven-born privilege of doing as he likes, and is beginning to perplex us by marching where it likes, meeting where it likes, bawling what it likes, breaking what it likes – to this vast residuum we may with great propriety give the name of Populace.

Matthew Arnold (1822–88) British poet and critic. *Culture and Anarchy*, Ch. 3

3 Our researchers into Public Opinion are content
That he held the proper opinions for the time of year;
When there was peace, he was for peace; when there was war, he went.

W. H. Auden (1907–73) British poet. *The Unknown Citizen*

4 You cannot make a man by standing a sheep on its hind legs. But by standing a flock of sheep in that position you can make a crowd of men.

Max Beerbohm (1872–1956) British writer. *Zuleika Dobson*, Ch. 9

5 The great Unwashed.

Henry Peter Brougham (1778–1868) Scottish lawyer and politician. Attrib.

6 The people are the masters.

Edmund Burke (1729–97) British politician. *Speech on the Economical Reform* (House of Commons, 11 Feb 1780)

7 The public buys its opinions as it buys its meat, or takes in its milk, on the principle that it is cheaper to do this than to keep a cow. So it is, but the milk is more likely to be watered.

Samuel Butler (1835–1902) British writer. *Notebooks*

8 The Public is an old woman. Let her maunder and mumble.

Thomas Carlyle (1795–1881) Scottish historian and essayist. *Journal*, 1835

9 The public are usually more sensible than politicians or the press.

Kenneth Clarke (1940–) British Conservative politician. Speech at the Mansion House, 15 June 1994

10 The people would be just as noisy if they were going to see me hanged.

Oliver Cromwell (1599–1658) English soldier and statesman. Referring to a cheering crowd.

11 If by the people you understand the multitude, the *hoi polloi*, 'tis no matter what they think; they are sometimes in the right, sometimes in the wrong; their judgement is a mere lottery.

John Dryden (1631–1700) British poet and dramatist. *Essay of Dramatic Poesy*

12 Nor is the Peoples Judgment always true:
The Most may err as grossly as the Few.

John Dryden *Absalom and Achitophel*, I

13 Ill fares the land, to hast'ning ills a prey,
Where wealth accumulates, and men decay;
Princes and lords may flourish, or may fade;
A breath can make them, as a breath has made;
But a bold peasantry, their country's pride,
When once destroy'd, can never be supplied.

Oliver Goldsmith (1728–74) Irish-born British writer. *The Deserted Village*

14 There is not a more mean, stupid, dastardly, pitiful, selfish, spiteful, envious, ungrateful animal than the public. It is the greatest of cowards, for it is afraid of itself.

William Hazlitt (1778–1830) British essayist. *On Living to Oneself*

15 Only constant repetition will finally succeed in imprinting an idea on the memory of the crowd.

Adolf Hitler (1889–1945) German dictator. *Mein Kampf*, Ch. 6

16 The people long eagerly for just two things – bread and circuses.

Juvenal (Decimus Junius Juvenalis; 60–130 AD) Roman satirist. *Satires*, X

17 They are only ten.

Lord Northcliffe (1865–1922) Irish-born British newspaper proprietor. Rumoured to have been a notice to remind his staff of his opinion of the mental age of the general public. Attrib.

18 The multitude is always in the wrong.

Earl of Roscommon (1633–85) Irish-born English poet. *Essay on Translated Verse*

19 Once the people begin to reason, all is lost.

Voltaire (François-Marie Arouet; 1694–1778) French writer. Letter to Damilaville, 1 Apr 1766

20 The century on which we are entering – the century which will come out of this war – can be and must be the century of the common man.

Henry Wallace (1888–1965) US economist and politician. Speech, 'The Price of Free World Victory', 8 May 1942

21 Our supreme governors, the mob.

Horace Walpole (1717–97) British writer. Letter to Sir Horace Mann, 7 Sept 1743

22 I have no concern for the common man except that he should not be so common.

Angus Wilson (1913–91) British novelist. *No Laughing Matter*

PUBLIC HOUSES

See also alcohol, drunkenness

1 A tavern chair is the throne of human felicity.

Samuel Johnson (1709–84) British lexicographer. *Johnsonian Miscellanies* (ed. G. B. Hill), Vol. II

2 There is nothing which has yet been contrived by man, by which so much happiness is produced as by a good tavern or inn.

Samuel Johnson *Life of Johnson* (J. Boswell), Vol. II

3 Souls of poets dead and gone,
What Elysium have ye known,
Happy field or mossy cavern,
Choicer than the Mermaid Tavern?
Have ye tippled drink more fine
Than mine host's Canary wine?

John Keats (1795–1821) British poet. *Lines on the Mermaid Tavern*

4 The hands of the clock have stayed still at half past eleven for fifty years. It is always opening time in the Sailors Arms.

Dylan Thomas (1914–53) Welsh poet. *Under Milk Wood*

5 Come, Come, Come and have a drink with me
Down at the old 'Bull and Bush'.

Harry Tilzer (Albert von Tilzer; 1878–1956) British songwriter. *The Old Bull and Bush*

PUBLISHING

See also books, editors

1 Publication is the male equivalent of childbirth.

Richard Acland (1906–) British politician and writer. *The Observer*, 'Sayings of the Week', 19 May 1974

2 If I had been someone not very clever, I would have done an easier job like publishing. That's the easiest job I can think of.

A. J. Ayer (1910–89) British philosopher. Remark, Sept 1984

3 I'll publish, right or wrong:
Fools are my theme, let satire be my song.

Lord Byron (1788–1824) British poet. *English Bards and Scotch Reviewers*

4 Now Barabbas was a publisher.

Thomas Campbell (1777–1844) British poet. Attrib.

5 Gentlemen, you must not mistake me. I admit that he is the sworn foe of our nation, and, if you will, of the whole human race. But, gentlemen, we must be just to our enemy. We must not forget that he once shot a bookseller.

Thomas Campbell Excusing himself in proposing a toast to Napoleon at a literary dinner. *The Life and Letters of Lord Macaulay* (G. O. Trevelyan)

6 As repressed sadists are supposed to become policemen or butchers so those with irrational fear of life become publishers.

Cyril Connolly (1903–74) British journalist. *Enemies of Promise*, Ch. 3

7 Let it be kept till the ninth year, the manuscript put away at home: you may destroy whatever you haven't published; once out, what you've said can't be stopped.

Horace (Quintus Horatius Flaccus; 65–8 BC) Roman poet. *Ars Poetica*

8 My own motto is publish and be sued.

Richard Ingrams (1937–) British editor. Referring to his editorship of *Private Eye*. *See* Duke of WELLINGTON. BBC radio broadcast, 4 May 1977

9 The booksellers are generous liberal-minded men.

Samuel Johnson (1709–84) British lexicographer. *Life of Johnson* (J. Boswell), Vol. I

10 Curse the blasted, jelly-boned swines, the slimy, the belly-wriggling invertebrates, the miserable sodding rutters, the flaming sods, the snivelling, dribbling, dithering, palsied, pulse-less lot that make up England today. They've got white of egg in their veins and their spunk is that watery it's a marvel they can breed.

D. H. Lawrence (1885–1930) British novelist. Letter to Edward Garnet, 3 July 1912, on Heinemann's rejection of *Sons and Lovers*

11 Publish and be damned!

Duke of Wellington (1769–1852) British general and statesman. On being offered the chance to avoid mention in the memoirs of Harriette Wilson by giving her money. Attrib.

12 Being published by the O.U.P. is rather like being married to a duchess; the honour is almost greater than the pleasure.

G. M. Young Letter to Rupert Hart-Davis, 20 Nov 1956

PUNISHMENT

See also education, execution, imprisonment, retribution

1 Spare the rod and spoil the child.

Proverb

2 Wherefore putting away lying, speak every man truth with his neighbour: for we are members one of another.
Be ye angry, and sin not: let not the sun go down upon your wrath:
Neither give place to the devil.
Let him that stole steal no more: but rather let him labour, working with his hands the thing which is good, that he may have to give to him that needeth.

Bible: Ephesians 4:25–28

3 When thou tillest the ground, it shall not henceforth yield unto thee her strength; a fugitive and a vagabond shalt thou be in the earth.
And Cain said unto the Lord, My punishment is greater than I can bear.

Bible: Genesis 4:12–13

4 And surely your blood of your lives will I require; at the hand of every beast will I require it, and at the hand of man; at the hand of every man's brother will I require the life of man.
Whoso sheddeth man's blood, by man shall his blood be shed: for in the image of God made he man.

Bible: Genesis 9:5–6

5 Then the Lord rained upon Sodom and upon Gomorrah brimstone and fire from the Lord out of heaven.

Bible: Genesis 19:24

6 There is no peace, saith the Lord, unto the wicked.

Bible: Isaiah 48:22

7 He that spareth his rod hateth his son: but he that loveth him chasteneth him betimes.

Bible: Proverbs 13:24

8 Love is a boy, by poets styl'd,
Then spare the rod, and spoil the child.

Samuel Butler (1612–80) English satirist. *Hudibras*, Pt. II

9 Never under the most despotic of infidel governments did I behold such squalid wretchedness as I have seen since my return in the very heart of a Christian country.

Lord Byron (1788–1824) British poet. Speaking against the death penalty for machine wrecking. Speech, House of Lords, 27 Feb 1812

10 The use of the birch is not to be deplored. All the best men in the country have been beaten, archbishops, bishops and even deans. Without sensible correction they could not be the men they are today.

Very Rev. Michael S. Carey (1913–) British churchman. Attrib.

11 Quoth he, 'The man hath penance done,
And penance more will do.'

Samuel Taylor Coleridge (1772–1834) British poet. *The Rime of the Ancient Mariner*, V

12 Punishment is not for revenge, but to lessen crime and reform the criminal.

Elizabeth Fry (1780–1845) British prison reformer. *Biography of Distinguished Women* (Sarah Josepha Hale)

13 As some day it may happen that a victim must be found
I've got a little list – I've got a little list
Of society offenders who might well be underground,
And who never would be missed – who never would be missed!

W. S. Gilbert (1836–1911) British dramatist. *The Mikado*, I

14 My object all sublime
I shall achieve in time –
To let the punishment fit the crime –
The punishment fit the crime.

W. S. Gilbert *The Mikado*, II

15 The billiard sharp whom any one catches,
His doom's extremely hard –
He's made to dwell –
In a dungeon cell
On a spot that's always barred.
And there he plays extravagant matches
In fitless finger-stalls
On a cloth untrue
With a twisted cue
And elliptical billiard balls.

W. S. Gilbert *The Mikado*, II

16 Something lingering, with boiling oil in it, I fancy.

W. S. Gilbert *The Mikado*, II

17 The door flew open, in he ran,
The great, long, red-legged scissor-man.

Heinrich Hoffman (1809–74) German writer. *Struwwelpeter*, 'The Little Suck-a-Thumb'

18 The only thing I really mind about going to prison is the thought of Lord Longford coming to visit me.

Richard Ingrams (1937–) British editor. Attrib.

19 Corporal punishment is as humiliating for him who gives it as for him who receives it; it is ineffective besides. Neither shame nor physical pain have any other effect than a hardening one...

Ellen Key (Karolina Sofia Key; 1849–1926) Swedish writer. *The Century of the Child*, Ch. 8

20 The refined punishments of the spiritual mode are usually much more indecent and dangerous than a good smack.

D. H. Lawrence (1885–1930) British novelist. *Fantasia of the Unconscious*, Ch. 4

21 Men are not hanged for stealing horses, but that horses may not be stolen.

George Saville (1633–95) English statesman. *Political, Moral and Miscellaneous Thoughts and Reflections*

22 And where the offence is let the great axe fall.

William Shakespeare (1564–1616) English dramatist. *Hamlet*, IV:5

23 Condemn the fault and not the actor of it?

William Shakespeare *Measure for Measure*, II:2

24 Nay, take my life and all; pardon not that:
You take my house when you do take the prop
That doth sustain my house; you take my life
When you do take the means whereby I live.

William Shakespeare *The Merchant of Venice*, IV:1

25 Eating the bitter bread of banishment.

William Shakespeare *Richard II*, III:1

26 Every child should have an occasional pat on the back, as long as it is applied low enough, and hard enough.

J. Fulton Sheen (1895–1979) US Roman Catholic archbishop. *On Children* (Frank Muir)

27 Whipping and abuse are like laudanum: You have to double the dose as the sensibilities decline.

Harriet Beecher Stowe (1811–96) US novelist. *Uncle Tom's Cabin*, Ch. 20

28 People should not be sent to prison if there are other acceptable ways of dealing with them.

Lord Taylor of Gosforth (1930–) British lawyer; Lord Chief Justice of England. *The Times*, 27 June 1994

29 He must have known me had he seen me as he was wont to see me, for he was in the habit of flogging me constantly. Perhaps he did not recognize me by my face.

Anthony Trollope (1815–82) British novelist. *Autobiography*, Ch. 1

30 I'm all for bringing back the birch, but only between consenting adults.

Gore Vidal (1925–) US novelist. Said when asked by David Frost in a TV interview for his views about corporal punishment.

31 We spared the rod and wound up with the beat generation.

L. J. Wolf *Bartlett's Unfamiliar Quotations* (Leonard Louis Levinson)

32 You cannot cane someone and expect it to be painless. You might as well give him a book to read.

George Yeo Singaporean politician. *The Observer*, 'Sayings of the Week', 1 May 1994

PUNS

See also humour

1 When I am dead, I hope it may be said:
'His sins were scarlet, but his books were read.'

Hilaire Belloc (1870–1953) French-born British poet. *Epigrams*, 'On His Books'

2 VISITOR. Ah, Bottomley, sewing?
BOTTOMLEY. No, reaping.

Horatio William Bottomley (1860–1933) British newspaper editor. When found sewing mail bags. *Horatio Bottomley* (Julian Symons)

3 Like Webster's Dictionary
We're Morocco bound.

Johnny Burke (1908–64) US songwriter. Song, 'Road to Morocco' from the film *The Road to Morocco*

4 A man who could make so vile a pun would not scruple to pick a pocket.

John Dennis (1657–1734) British critic and dramatist. *The Gentleman's Magazine*, 1781

5 'In our case,' says the Frenchman, addressing the Englishman, 'we have 'goût' for the taste; in your case, you have 'gout' for the result!'

George Herman Ellwanger (fl. 1897) *Meditations on Gout*, 'The Theory'

6 Any stigma will do to beat a dogma.

Philip Guedalla (1889–1944) British writer. Attrib.

7 His death, which happen'd in his berth,
At forty-odd befell:
They went and told the sexton, and
The sexton toll'd the bell.

Thomas Hood (1799–1845) British poet. *Faithless Sally Brown*

8 For that old enemy the gout
Had taken him in toe!

Thomas Hood *Lieutenant Luff*

9 The love that loves a scarlet coat
Should be more uniform.

Thomas Hood *Faithless Nelly Gray*

10 Ben Battle was a soldier bold,
And used to war's alarms:
But a cannon-ball took off his legs,
So he laid down his arms!

Thomas Hood *Faithless Nelly Gray*

11 For here I leave my second leg,
And the Forty-second Foot!

Thomas Hood *Faithless Nelly Gray*

12 It is a pistol let off at the ear; not a feather to tickle the intellect.

Charles Lamb (1775–1834) British essayist. Referring to the nature of a pun. *Last Essays of Elia*, 'Popular Fallacies'

13 Thou canst not serve both cod and salmon.

Ada Beddington Leverson (1862–1933) British writer. Reply when offered a choice of fish at dinner. *The Times*, 7 Nov 1970

14 You know it's hard to hear what a bearded man is saying. He can't speak above a whisker.

Herman J. Mankiewicz (1897–1953) US journalist and screenwriter. *Wit's End* (R. E. Drennan)

15 What's a thousand dollars? Mere chicken feed. A poultry matter.

Groucho Marx (Julius Marx; 1895–1977) US comedian. *The Cocoanuts*

16 Contraceptives should be used on all conceivable occasions.

Spike Milligan (1918–) British comedian and humorous writer.

17 It has been said that a bride's attitude towards her betrothed can be summed up in three words: Aisle. Altar. Hymn.

Frank Muir (1920–) British writer and broadcaster. *Upon My Word!* (Frank Muir and Dennis Norden), 'A Jug of Wine'

18 A thing of duty is a boy for ever.

Flann O'Brien (Brian O'Nolan; 1911–66) Irish novelist and journalist. About policemen always seeming to be young-looking. *The Listener*, 24 Feb 1977

19 You can lead a whore to culture but you can't make her think.

Dorothy Parker (1893–1967) US writer. Speech to American Horticultural Society

20 You can't teach an old dogma new tricks.

Dorothy Parker *Wit's End* (R. E. Drennan)

21 I tried to resist his overtures, but he plied me with symphonies, quartettes, chamber music and cantatas.

S. J. Perelman (1904–79) US humorous writer. *Crazy Like a Fox*, 'The Love Decoy'

22 Mother always told me my day was coming, but I never realized that I'd end up being the shortest knight of the year.

Gordon Richards (1904–86) British champion jockey. Referring to his diminutive size, on learning of his knighthood. Attrib.

23 Private Means is dead,
God rest his soul,
Officers and fellow-rankers said.

Stevie Smith (Florence Margaret Smith; 1902–71) British poet. *Private Means is Dead*

24 That's right. 'Taint yours, and 'taint mine.

Mark Twain (Samuel Langhorne Clemens; 1835–1910) US writer. Agreeing with a friend's comment that the money of a particular rich industrialist was 'tainted'. Attrib.

25 To me Adler will always be Jung.

Max Wall (1908–90) British comedian. Telegram to the US harmonica-player Larry Adler on his 60th birthday

PURITANISM

See also prudery

1 A puritan's a person who pours righteous indignation into the wrong things.

G. K. Chesterton (1874–1936) British writer. Attrib.

2 To the Puritan all things are impure, as somebody says.

D. H. Lawrence (1885–1930) British novelist. *Etruscan Places*, 'Cerveteri'

3 The Puritan hated bear-baiting, not because it gave pain to the bear, but because it gave pleasure to the spectators.

Lord Macaulay (1800–59) British historian. *History of England*, Vol. I, Ch. 2

4 Persecution produced its natural effect on them. It found them a sect; it made them a faction.

Lord Macaulay Referring to the early Puritans. *History of England*

5 Puritanism – The haunting fear that someone, somewhere, may be happy.

H. L. Mencken (1880–1956) US journalist. *A Book of Burlesques*

PURITY

1 Caesar's wife must be above suspicion.

Proverb

2 I'm as pure as the driven slush.

Tallulah Bankhead (1903–68) US actress. *The Observer*, 'Sayings of the Week', 24 Feb 1957

3 A simple maiden in her flower
Is worth a hundred coats-of-arms.

Alfred, Lord Tennyson (1809–92) British poet. *Lady Clara Vere de Vere*, II

4 It is one of the superstitions of the human mind to have imagined that virginity could be a virtue.

Voltaire (François-Marie Arouet; 1694–1778) French writer. *Notebooks*

5 Age cannot wither her, nor custom stale her infinite virginity.

Daniel Webster (1782–1852) US statesman. Paraphrasing a line from Shakespeare's *Antony and Cleopatra*. on hearing of Andrew Jackson's steadfast maintenance that his friend Peggy Eaton did not deserve her scandalous reputation *Presidential Anecdotes* (P. Boller)

6 I used to be Snow White…but I drifted.

Mae West (1892–1980) US actress. *The Wit and Wisdom of Mae West* (ed. J. Weintraub)

PURPOSE

See also futility, motive

1 Everything's got a moral, if only you can find it.

Lewis Carroll (Charles Lutwidge Dodgson; 1832–98) British writer. *Alice's Adventures in Wonderland*, Ch. 9

2 What is the use of a new-born child?

Benjamin Franklin (1706–90) US scientist and statesman. Response when asked the same question of a new invention. *Life and Times of Benjamin Franklin* (J. Parton), Pt. IV

3 A useless life is an early death.

Goethe (1749–1832) German poet and dramatist. *Iphegenie*, I:2

4 A mission to explain.

Peter Jay (1937–) British journalist and broadcaster. Explaining his philosophy for a new breakfast-television company. Said on many occasions

5 Fortunately, in her kindness and patience, Nature has never put the fatal question as to the meaning of their lives into the mouths of most people. And where no one asks, no one needs to answer.

Carl Gustav Jung (1875–1961) Swiss psychoanalyst. *The Development of Personality*

6 I go among the fields and catch a glimpse of a stoat or a fieldmouse peeping out of the withered grass – the creature hath a purpose and its eyes are bright with it. I go amongst the buildings of a city and I see a man hurrying along – to what? the Creature has a purpose and his eyes are bright with it.

John Keats (1795–1821) British poet. Letter, 1819

7 Riddle of destiny, who can show
What thy short visit meant, or know
What thy errand here below?

Charles Lamb (1775–1834) British essayist. *On an Infant Dying as soon as Born*

8 The purpose of population is not ultimately peopling earth. It is to fill heaven.

Graham Leonard (1921–) British churchman (Bishop of London). Said during a debate on the Church and the Bomb. Speech, General Synod of the Church of England, 10 Feb 1983

9 If people want a sense of purpose they should get it from their archbishop. They should certainly not get it from their politicians.

Harold Macmillan (1894–1986) British politician and prime minister. *The Life of Politics* (H. Fairlie)

10 Yes there is a meaning; at least for me, there is one thing that matters – to set a chime of words tinkling in the minds of a few fastidious people.

Logan Pearsall Smith (1865–1946) US writer. Attrib.

11 It should not merely be useful and ornamental; it should preach a high moral lesson.

Lytton Strachey (1880–1932) British writer. Referring to Prince Albert's plans for the Great Exhibition. *Queen Victoria*, Ch. 4

Q

QUAYLE, DAN

(James Danforth Quayle; 1947–) US Republican politician; vice-president (1989–93). During his vice presidency, Quayle became noted for making unfortunate remarks in public, and a large number of stories were circulated about things he had said. Many of these so-called 'Quaylisms' are not genuine.

Quotations about Quayle

1 A heart flutters, a nation shudders.

Referring to the fact that Quayle would succeed to the presidency if George Bush were to die. *Chicago Tribune*, Editorial

2 Anyone who knows Dan Quayle knows that he would rather play golf than have sex any day.

Marilyn Quayle. Defending her husband against suggestions that he might be involved in a sex scandal.

3 I served with Jack Kennedy. I knew Jack Kennedy. Jack Kennedy was a friend of mine. Senator, you're no Jack Kennedy.

Lloyd Bentsen US politician. Televised presidential debate, 1988, replying to Quayle's claim that he had as much experience in the Congress as Kennedy did when he became president.

Quotations by Quayle

4 What a waste it is to lose one's mind or not to have a mind is very wasteful.

Address to United Negro College Fund, May 1989. In 1972 the Fund used an advertising slogan, 'A mind is a terrible thing to waste.'

5 Space is almost infinite. As a matter of fact we think it is infinite.

The Sunday Times, 31 Dec 1989

6 My friends, we can and we will never, never, never surrender to what is right.

Address to Republican meeting

7 A stirring victory for the forces of aggression against lawlessness.

Comment on the Gulf War. Attrib.

8 I had no problem communicating with Latin American heads of state – though now I do wish I had paid more attention to Latin when I was in school.

Attrib. There is no evidence that Quayle ever said this

QUOTATIONS

See also misquotation

1 It is a good thing for an uneducated man to read books of quotations.

Winston Churchill (1874–1965) British statesman. *My Early Life*, Ch. 9

2 We prefer to believe that the absence of inverted commas guarantees the originality of a thought, whereas it may be merely that the utterer has forgotten its source.

Clifton Fadiman (1904–) US writer. *Any Number Can Play*

3 When a thing has been said and said well, have no scruple. Take it and copy it.

Anatole France (Jacques Anatole François Thibault; 1844–1924) French writer. *The Routledge Dictionary of Quotations* (Robert Andrews)

4 Classical quotation is the *parole* of literary men all over the world.

Samuel Johnson (1709–84) British lexicographer. *Life of Johnson* (J. Boswell), Vol. IV

5 Every quotation contributes something to the stability or enlargement of the language.

Samuel Johnson *Dictionary of the English Language*

6 I wish they wouldn't start their programme with fictitious quotes from me.

John Major (1943–) British Conservative politician. Referring to the BBC TV programme *Have I Got News for You*. Attrib.

7 To be amused at what you read – that is the great spring of happy quotation.

C. E. Montague (1867–1928) British editor and writer. *A Writer's Notes on his Trade*

8 If with the literate I am
Impelled to try an epigram
I never seek to take the credit
We all assume that Oscar said it.

Dorothy Parker (1893–1967) US writer. *Oscar Wilde*

9 I might repeat to myself...a list of quotations from minds profound – if I can remember any of the damn things.

Dorothy Parker *The Little Hours*

10 A book that furnishes no quotations is, *me judice*, no book – it is a plaything.

Thomas Love Peacock (1785–1866) British novelist. *Crotchet Castle*, Ch. 9

11 It is gentlemanly to get one's quotations very slightly wrong. In that way one unprigs oneself and allows the company to correct one.

Lord Ribblesdale (1854–1925) British aristocrat. *The Light of Common Day* (Lady D. Cooper)

12 To say that anything was a quotation was an excellent method, in Eleanor's eyes, for withdrawing it from discussion.

Saki (Hector Hugh Munro; 1870–1916) British writer. *The Jesting of Arlington Stringham*

13 The devil can cite Scripture for his purpose.

William Shakespeare (1564–1616) English dramatist. *The Merchant of Venice*, I:3

14 It's better to be quotable than to be honest.

Tom Stoppard (1937–) Czech-born British dramatist. *The Guardian*

15 In the dying world I come from quotation is a national vice. It used to be the classics, now it's lyric verse.

Evelyn Waugh (1903–66) British novelist. *The Loved One*

16 The nicest thing about quotes is that they give us a nodding acquaintance with the originator which is often socially impressive.

Kenneth Williams (1926–88) British comic actor. *Acid Drops*

R

RABBITS

See also animals

1 The rabbit has a charming face;
Its private life is a disgrace.

Anonymous *The Rabbit*

2 I shall tell you a tale of four little rabbits whose names were Flopsy, Mopsy, Cottontail and Peter.

Beatrix Potter (1866–1943) British children's writer. *The Tale of Peter Rabbit*

RABELAIS, FRANCOIS

(1483–1553) French humanist and satirist. He is best known for his *Pantagruel* (1532) and *Gargantua* (1534), which are renowned for their bawdiness.

Quotations about Rabelais

1 Rabelais is the wondrous mask of ancient comedy...henceforth a human living face, remaining enormous and coming among us to laugh at us and with us.

Victor Hugo (1802–85) French writer. Attrib.

Quotations by Rabelais

2 I drink for the thirst to come.

Gargantua, Bk. I, Ch. 5

3 Appetite comes with eating.

Gargantua, Bk. I, Ch. 5

4 Nature abhors a vacuum.

Gargantua, Bk. I, Ch. 5

5 In their rules there was only one clause: Do what you will.

Referring to the fictional Abbey of Thélème. *Gargantua*, Bk. I, Ch. 57

6 Man never found the deities so kindly
As to assure him that he'd live tomorrow.

Pantagruel, Bk. III, Ch. 2

7 Not everyone is a debtor who wishes to be; not everyone who wishes makes creditors.

Pantagruel, Bk. III, Ch. 3

8 I owe much; I have nothing; the rest I leave to the poor.

Last words. Attrib.

9 Ring down the curtain, the farce is over.

Last words. Attrib.

10 I am going in search of a great perhaps.

Last words. Attrib.

RACISM

See also equality, freedom, human rights, Jews, oppression, prejudice, slavery

1 There was a young woman called Starkie,
Who had an affair with a darky.
The result of her sins
Was quadruplets, not twins –
One black, and one white, and two khaki.

Anonymous

2 It is a great shock at the age of five or six to find that in a world of Gary Coopers you are the Indian.

James Baldwin (1924–87) US writer. Gary Cooper, the US film actor, was best known for his roles as cowboy heroes in Westerns. Speech, Cambridge Union, 17 Feb 1965

3 The future is...black.

James Baldwin *The Observer*, 'Sayings of the Week', 25 Aug 1963

4 Down South where I come from you don't go around hitting too many white keys.

Eubie Blake (1883–1983) US pianist and ragtime composer. When asked why his compositions contained so many sharps and flats. Attrib.

5 My mother bore me in the southern wild.
And I am black, but O! my soul is white;
White as an angel is the English child,
But I am black, as if bereav'd of light.

William Blake (1757–1827) British poet. *Songs of Innocence*, 'The Little Black Boy'

6 People think we do not understand our black and coloured countrymen. But there is a special relationship between us.

Elize Botha Wife of South African President, P. W. Botha. Remark, May 1987

7 Black people are doing what they have been told and bettering themselves, but it is not getting them anywhere.

Donna Covey British trade union official. *The Independent*, 7 Sept 1993

8 To like an individual because he's black is just as insulting as to dislike him because he isn't white.

e. e. cummings (1894–1962) US poet. Attrib.

9 I suffer from an incurable disease – colour blindness.

Joost de Blank (1908–68) Dutch-born British churchman. Attrib.

10 I'm a coloured, one-eyed Jew.

Sammy Davis Jnr (1925–90) US singer. When asked what his handicap was during a game of golf. Attrib.

11 The so-called white races are really pinko-gray.

E. M. Forster (1879–1970) British novelist. *A Passage to India*, Ch. 7

12 When the white man came we had the land and they had the Bibles; now they have the land and we have the Bibles.

Dan George (1899–1982) Canadian Indian chief. Attrib.

13 All those who are not racially pure are mere chaff.

Adolf Hitler (1889–1945) German dictator. *Mein Kampf*, Ch. 2

14 I want to be the white man's brother, not his brother-in-law.

Martin Luther King (1929–68) US Black civil-rights leader. *New York Journal-American*, 10 Sept 1962

15 Take up the White Man's burden –
And reap his old reward:
The blame of those ye better,
The hate of those ye guard.

Rudyard Kipling (1865–1936) Indian-born British writer. *The White Man's Burden*

16 So 'ere's to you, Fuzzy-Wuzzy, at your 'ome in the Soudan;
You're a pore benighted 'eathen but a first-class fightin' man;
An' 'ere's to you, Fuzzy-Wuzzy, with your 'ayrick 'ead of 'air –
You big black boundin' beggar – for you broke a British square!

Rudyard Kipling *Fuzzy-Wuzzy*

17 When old settlers say 'One has to understand the country', what they mean is, 'You have to get used to our ideas about the native.' They are saying, in effect, 'Learn our ideas, or otherwise get out; we don't want you.'

Doris Lessing (1919–) British novelist. Referring specifically to South Africa. *The Grass is Singing*, Ch. 1

18 When a white man in Africa by accident looks into the eyes of a native and sees the human being (which it is his chief preoccupation to avoid), his sense of guilt, which he denies, fumes up in resentment and he brings down the whip.

Doris Lessing *The Grass is Singing*, Ch. 8

19 A coloured man can tell, in five seconds dead, whether a white man likes him or not. If the white man *says* he does, he is instantly – and usually quite rightly – mistrusted.

Colin MacInnes (1914–76) British novelist. *England, Half English*, 'A Short Guide for Jumbles'

20 It's just like when you've got some coffee that's too black, which means it's too strong. What do you do? You integrate it with cream, you make it weak... It used to wake you up, now it puts you to sleep.

Malcolm X (1925–65) US Black leader. Referring to Black Power and the Civil Rights movement. *Malcolm X Speaks*, Ch. 14

21 The soil of our country is destined to be the scene of the fiercest fight and the sharpest struggles to rid our continent of the last vestiges of white minority rule.

Nelson Mandela (1918–) South African lawyer and politician. Speech, from prison, June 1980

22 I have cherished the ideal of a democratic and free society in which all persons live together in harmony and with equal opportunites...if needs be, it is an ideal for which I am prepared to die.

Nelson Mandela Speech, 11 Feb 1990, after his release from prison. Mandela was reiterating his words at his trial in 1964

23 One of the things that makes a Negro unpleasant to white folk is the fact that he suffers from their injustice. He is thus a standing rebuke to them.

H. L. Mencken (1880–1956) US journalist. *Notebooks*, 'Minority Report'

24 He's really awfully fond of coloured people. Well, he says himself, he wouldn't have white servants.

Dorothy Parker (1893–1967) US writer. *Arrangements in Black and White*

25 If you stay much longer you will go back with slitty eyes.

Prince Philip (1921–) The consort of Queen Elizabeth II. Said to English students on a visit to China. Remark, Oct 1986

26 As I look ahead, I am filled with foreboding. Like the Roman, I seem to see 'the River Tiber foaming with much blood'.

Enoch Powell (1912–) British politician. Talking about immigration. Speech in Birmingham, 20 Apr 1968

27 He liked to patronise coloured people and treated them as equals because he was quite sure they were not.

Bertrand Russell (1872–1970) British philosopher. *The Autobiography of Bertrand Russell*

28 I don't believe in black majority rule ever in Rhodesia...not in a thousand years.

Ian Smith (1919–) Rhodesian (Zimbabwe) politician. Speech, Mar 1976

29 We don't want apartheid liberalized. We want it dismantled. You can't improve something that is intrinsically evil.

Bishop Desmond Tutu (1931–) South African clergyman. *The Observer*, 'Sayings of the Week', 10 Mar 1985

30 It seems that the British Government sees black people as expendable.

Bishop Desmond Tutu Speech, June 1986

31 There are two kinds of blood, the blood that flows in the veins and the blood that flows out of them.

Julian Tuwim (1894–1954) Polish writer and poet. *We, the Polish Jews*

RALEIGH, SIR WALTER

(1554–1618) English explorer and writer. A favourite of Elizabeth I, he introduced the potato and tobacco plant from America into England. Under James I he was imprisoned for treason and eventually executed.

1 If all the world and love were young,
And truth in every shepherd's tongue,
These pretty pleasures might me move
To live with thee, and be thy love.

Answer to Marlow

2 Fain would I climb, yet fear I to fall.

Written on a window pane. For the reply *see* ELIZABETH I. Attrib.

3 Even such is Time, that takes in trust
Our youth, our joys, and all we have,
And pays us but with age and dust;
Who in the dark and silent grave,
When we have wandered all our ways,
Shuts up the story of our days;
And from which earth, and grave, and dust,
The Lord shall raise me up, I trust.

Written on the night before his execution. Attrib.

4 The world itself is but a large prison, out of which some are daily led to execution.

Said after his trial for treason, 1603. Attrib.

5 'Tis a sharp remedy, but a sure one for all ills.

Referring to the executioner's axe just before he was beheaded. Attrib.

6 So the heart be right, it is no matter which way the head lies.

On being asked which way he preferred to lay his head on the executioner's block. Attrib.

7 I have a long journey to take, and must bid the company farewell.

Last words. *Sir Walter Raleigh* (Edward Thompson), Ch. 26

RAPE

1 It is little wonder that rape is one of the least-reported crimes. Perhaps it is the only crime in which the victim becomes the accused and, in reality, it is she who must prove her good reputation, her mental soundness, and her impeccable propriety.

Freda Adler (1934–) US educator. *Sisters in Crime*, Ch. 9

2 There's no money in rape warrants.

Martin Amis (1949–) British novelist. *Money*

3 However rape is a perfectly natural function. It means that a man so desires a woman that he takes her by force. Since a man is much stronger than a woman it does not necessarily involve much violence, and in many cases the woman duly submits.

Professor J. M. V. Browner *Vive la Différence*

4 Words such as 'beast', 'monster' and 'sex fiend' are commonly used to describe the rapist. Yet we rarely see the simple word 'man', which the rapist invariably is.

Cambridge Rape Crisis Centre *Out of Focus*

5 Rape is a form of mass terrorism...The fear of rape keeps women off the streets at night. Keeps women at home. Keeps women passive and modest for fear that they be thought provocative.

Susan Griffin (1943–) US poet, writer, and educator. *Women: a Feminist Perspective* (ed. Jo Freeman)

6 We take the view that the time has now arrived when the law should declare that a rapist remains a rapist and is subject to the criminal law, irrespective of his relationship with his victim.

Lord Lane (1918–) British judge and Lord Chief Justice. Dismissing the appeal of a man who argued, on the 1736 principle of Chief Justice Hale, that he could not be guilty of raping his wife. *The Times*, 15 Mar 1991

7 What they love to yield
They would often rather have stolen. Rough seduction
Delights them, the boldness of near rape
Is a compliment.

Ovid (Publius Ovidius Naso; 43 BC–17 AD) Roman poet. *The Art of Love*

8 Women are entitled to dress attractively, even provocatively if you like, be friendly with casual acquaintances and still say no at the end of the evening without being brutally assaulted...This sort of brutal violence, particularly to women, has got to be dealt with severely. You broke her jaw just because she wasn't prepared to go to bed with you.

Richard Rougier (1932–) British judge. Sentencing an attacker at the Old Bailey. *The Daily Telegraph*, 4 Mar 1988

9 Women who say no do not always mean no. It is not just a question of saying no, it is a question of how she says it, how she shows and makes it clear. If she doesn't want it she only has to keep her legs shut and she would not get it without force and there would be marks of force being used.

David Wild (1927–) British judge. Cambridge, 1982

RAPHAEL, FREDERIC

(1931–) British author of novels, short stories, and screenplays. His books include *A Wild Surmise* (1961), *The Glittering Prizes* (1976), and *After the War* (1988); he wrote the screenplays for *Darling* (1965), *Far From the Madding Crowd* (1967), *Rogue Male* (1976), and other films.

1 This is the city of perspiring dreams.

Referring to Cambridge – Oxford is known as the city of dreaming spires. *The Glittering Prizes: An Early Life*, III

2 We thought philosophy ought to be patient and unravel people's mental blocks. Trouble with doing that is, once you've unravelled them, their heads fall off.

The Glittering Prizes: A Double Life, III:2

3 I come from suburbia, Dan, personally, I don't ever want to go back. It's the one place in the world that's further away than anywhere else.

The Glittering Prizes: A Sex Life, I:3

4 Great restaurants are, of course, nothing but mouth-brothels. There is no point in going to them if one intends to keep one's belt buckled.

The Sunday Times Magazine, 25 Sept 1977

READING

See also books, criticism, fiction, literacy, literature, novels, writing

1 Reading maketh a full man; conference a ready man; and writing an exact man.

Francis Bacon (1561–1626) English philosopher. *Essays*, 'Of Studies'

2 He has only half learned the art of reading who has not added to it the even more refined accomplishments of skipping and skimming.

Arthur Balfour (1848–1930) British statesman. *Mr. Balfour* (E. T. Raymond)

3 I read, much of the night, and go south in the winter.

T. S. Eliot (1888–1965) US-born British poet and dramatist. *The Waste Land*, 'The Burial of the Dead'

4 A lonesome man on a rainy day who does not know how to read.

Benjamin Franklin (1706–90) US scientist and statesman. On being asked what condition of man he considered the most pitiable. *Wit, Wisdom, and Foibles of the Great* (C. Shriner)

5 As writers become more numerous, it is natural for readers to become more indolent.

Oliver Goldsmith (1728–74) Irish-born British writer. *The Bee*, 'Upon Unfortunate Merit'

6 Reading is sometimes an ingenious device for avoiding thought.

Arthur Helps (1813–75) British historian. *Friends in Council*

7 ELPHINSTON. What, have you not read it

through?...
JOHNSON. No, Sir, do *you* read books *through*?
Samuel Johnson (1709–84) British lexicographer. *Life of Johnson* (J. Boswell), Vol. II

8 A man ought to read just as inclination leads him; for what he reads as a task will do him little good.
Samuel Johnson *Life of Johnson* (J. Boswell), Vol. I

9 I love to lose myself in other men's minds. When I am not walking, I am reading; I cannot sit and think. Books think for me.
Charles Lamb (1775–1834) British essayist. *Last Essays of Elia*, 'Detached Thoughts on Books and Reading'

10 I'm re-reading it with a slow deliberate carelessness.
T. E. Lawrence (1888–1935) British soldier and writer. Letter to Edward Marsh, 18 Apr 1929

11 To read too many books is harmful.
Mao Tse-Tung (1893–1976) Chinese communist leader. *The New Yorker*, 7 Mar 1977

12 I have only read one book in my life and that is *White Fang*. It's so frightfully good I've never bothered to read another.
Nancy Mitford (1904–73) British writer. *The Pursuit Of Love*

13 There are two motives for reading a book: one, that you enjoy it, the other that you can boast about it.
Bertrand Russell (1872–1970) British philosopher. *The Conquest of Happiness*

14 People say that life is the thing, but I prefer reading.
Logan Pearsall Smith (1865–1946) US writer. *Afterthoughts*, 'Myself'

15 Reading is to the mind what exercise is to the body.
Richard Steele (1672–1729) Dublin-born British essayist. *The Tatler*, 147

16 Education...has produced a vast population able to read but unable to distinguish what is worth reading.
George Macaulay Trevelyan (1876–1962) British historian. *English Social History*, Ch. 18

17 I have led a life of business so long that I have lost my taste for reading, and now – what shall I do?
Horace Walpole (1717–97) British writer. *Thraliana* (K. Balderston)

18 Lady Peabury was in the morning room reading a novel; early training gave a guilty spice to this recreation, for she had been brought up to believe that to read a novel before luncheon was one of the gravest sins it was possible for a gentlewoman to commit.
Evelyn Waugh (1903–66) British novelist. *Work Suspended*, 'An Englishman's Home'

19 As in the sexual experience, there are never more than two persons present in the act of reading – the writer who is the impregnator, and the reader who is the respondent.
Elwyn Brooks White (1899–1985) US journalist and humorist. *The Second Tree from the Corner*

REAGAN, RONALD

(1911–) US Republican president (1981–89). He entered politics as governor of California (1966–74) after a career as a film actor.

Quotations about Reagan

1 That youthful sparkle in his eyes is caused by his contact lenses, which he keeps highly polished.
Sheilah Graham *The Times*, 22 Aug 1981

2 Reagan is the most popular figure in the history of the US. No candidate we put up would have been able to beat Reagan this year.
Thomas P. O'Neill (1912–) US Democratic politician. Remark, 1984

3 As the age of television progresses the Reagans will be the rule, not the exception. To be perfect for television is all a President has to be these days.
Gore Vidal (1925–) US novelist. Attrib.

4 A triumph of the embalmer's art.
Gore Vidal Attrib.

5 Here is a man in a presidential debate who referred to army uniforms as costumes.
Robin Williams (1952–) US actor. *Live*

6 Ask him the time, and he'll tell you how the watch was made.
Jane Wyman (1914–) US film actress and the first wife of Reagan. Attrib.

Quotations by Reagan

7 Please assure me that you are all Republicans!
Addressing the surgeons on being wheeled into the operating theatre for an emergency operation after an assassination attempt. *Presidential Anecdotes* (P. Boller)

8 No one can kill Americans and brag about it. No one.
The Observer, 'Sayings of the Week', 27 Apr 1986

9 You know, by the time you reach my age, you've made plenty of mistakes if you've lived your life properly.
The Observer, 'Sayings of the Week', 8 Mar 1987

10 I used to say that politics was the second lowest profession and I have come to know that it bears a great similarity to the first.
The Observer, 13 May 1979

11 Honey, I forgot to duck.
Said to his wife, Nancy, after an assassination attempt by John Hinckley III, 30 Mar 1981. *The Sunday Times*, 3 Dec 1989

12 They say hard work never hurt anybody, but I figure why take the chance.
Attrib.

13 Government is not the solution to the problem – government is the problem.
Attrib.

14 Government is a referee; it shouldn't try to be a player in the game.
Attrib.

REALISM

1 Mr Lely, I desire you would use all your skill to paint my picture truly like me, and not flatter me at all; but remark all these roughnesses, pimples, warts, and everything as you see me, otherwise I will never pay a farthing for it.

Oliver Cromwell (1599–1658) English soldier and statesman. The origin of the expression 'warts and all'. *Anecdotes of Painting* (Horace Walpole), Ch. 12

2 If at first you don't succeed, try, try again. Then quit. No use being a damn fool about it.

W. C. Fields (1880–1946) US actor.

3 We must rediscover the distinction between hope and expectation.

Ivan Illich (1926–) Austrian sociologist. *Deschooling Society*, Ch. 7

4 The glass is falling hour by hour, the glass will fall for ever,
But if you break the bloody glass, you won't hold up the weather.

Louis MacNeice (1907–63) Irish-born British poet. *Bagpipe Music*

5 Better by far
For Johnny-the-bright-star,
To keep your head
And see his children fed.

John Sleigh Pudney (1909–77) British poet and writer. *For Johnny*

REALITY

1 For I see now that I am asleep that I dream when I am awake.

Pedro Calderón de la Barca (1600–81) Spanish dramatist. *La Vida es Sueño*, II

2 Human kind
Cannot bear very much reality.

T. S. Eliot (1888–1965) US-born British poet and dramatist. *Four Quartets*, 'Burnt Norton'

3 There may always be another reality
To make fiction of the truth we think we've arrived at.

Christopher Fry (1907–) British dramatist. *A Yard of Sun*, II

4 Dear friend, theory is all grey,
And the golden tree of life is green.

Goethe (1749–1832) German poet and dramatist. *Faust*, Pt. I

5 I fancy, for myself, that they are rather out of touch with reality; by reality I mean shops like Selfridges, and motor buses, and the *Daily Express*.

T. E. Lawrence (1888–1935) British soldier and writer. Referring to expatriate writers living in Paris, such as James Joyce. Letter to W. Hurley, 1 Apr 1929

6 We live in a fantasy world, a world of illusion. The great task in life is to find reality.

Iris Murdoch (1919–) Irish-born British novelist. *The Times*, 15 Apr 1983

7 Things are entirely what they appear to be and *behind them*...there is nothing.

Jean-Paul Sartre (1905–80) French writer. *Nausea*

8 If this were play'd upon a stage now, I could condemn it as an improbable fiction.

William Shakespeare (1564–1616) English dramatist. *Twelfth Night*, III:4

9 And even the most solid of things and the most real, the best-loved and the well-known, are only hand-shadows on the wall. Empty space and points of light.

Jeanette Winterson (1959–) British author. *Sexing the Cherry*

REASON

See also motive

1 Some who had received a liberal education at the Colleges of Unreason, and taken the highest degrees in hypothetics, which are their principal study.

Samuel Butler (1835–1902) British writer. *Erewhon*, Ch. 9

2 Reason is itself a matter of faith. It is an act of faith to assert that our thoughts have any relation to reality at all.

G. K. Chesterton (1874–1936) British writer. *Orthodoxy*, Ch. 3

3 Fools give you reasons, wise men never try.

Oscar Hammerstein II (1895–1960) US lyricist. *South Pacific*, 'Some Enchanted Evening'

4 Reason has moons, but moons not hers
Lie mirror'd on her sea,
Confounding her astronomers,
But, O! delighting me.

Ralph Hodgson (1871–1962) British poet. *Reason Has Moons*

5 Come now, let us reason together.

Lyndon B. Johnson (1908–73) US Democratic president. Attrib., often used

6 My dear friend, clear your *mind* of cant... You may *talk* in this manner; it is a mode of talking in Society: but don't *think* foolishly.

Samuel Johnson (1709–84) British lexicographer. *Life of Johnson* (J. Boswell), Vol. IV

7 A man who does not lose his reason over certain things has none to lose.

Gotthold Ephraim Lessing (1729–81) German dramatist. *Emilia Galotti*, IV:7

8 There is occasions and causes why and wherefore in all things.

William Shakespeare (1564–1616) English dramatist. *Henry V*, V:1

REBELLION

See also revolution

1 In this king's time there was nothing but disturbance and wickedness and robbery, for forthwith the powerful men who were traitors rose against him.

Anonymous Referring to the reign of Stephen, 1135–54. *Anglo-Saxon Chronicle*

2 The defiance of established authority, religious and secular, social and political, as a world-wide phenomenon may well one day be accounted the outstanding event of the last decade.

Hannah Arendt (1906–75) German-born US philosopher and historian. *Crises of the Republic*, 'Civil Disobedience'

3 Son of man, thou dwellest in the midst of a rebellious house, which have eyes to see, and see not; they have ears to hear, and hear not: for they are a rebellious house.

Bible: Ezekiel 12:2

4 What is a rebel? A man who says no.

Albert Camus (1913–60) French existentialist writer. *The Rebel*

5 No one can go on being a rebel too long without turning into an autocrat.

Lawrence Durrell (1912–90) British novelist. *Balthazar*, II

6 The whole of the Welsh nation in these parts are concerned in this rebellion.

John Fairfield Receiver of Brecon. Referring to the rebellion led by Owen Glendower against Henry IV's rule in Wales (1400–15). Letter to Henry IV

7 When the People contend for their Liberty, they seldom get anything by their Victory but new masters.

Lord Halifax (1633–95) English statesman. *Political, Moral, and Miscellaneous Thoughts and Reflections*

8 This is a standard of rebellion.

James II (1633–1701) King of England. Referring to a petition from seven bishops against his Declaration of Indulgence (1687; reissued 7 May 1688); the bishops were prosecuted for sedititious libel, but acquitted. Remark, ?2 June 1688

9 A little rebellion now and then is a good thing.

Thomas Jefferson (1743–1826) US statesman. Letter to James Madison, 30 Jan 1787

10 A riot is at bottom the language of the unheard.

Martin Luther King (1929–68) US Black civil-rights leader. *Chaos or Community*, Ch. 4

11 In my opinion it is better that all of these peasants should be killed rather than that the sovereigns and magistrates should be destroyed, because the peasants take up the sword without God's authorization.

Martin Luther (1483–1546) German Protestant. Letter to Nicholas von Ansdorf, 30 May 1525

12 Angry Young Man.

Leslie Paul (1905–85) British writer. Book title

13 You noble Diggers all, stand up now,
The waste land to maintain, seeing Cavaliers by name
Your digging do disdain and persons all defame.

Gerrard Winstanley (c. 1609–c. 1660) Leader of the Diggers. The Diggers were a radical group that believed in land reform and practiced a primitive agrarian communism. Important in 1649, they were dispersed by the Commonwealth government in 1650. *The Diggers' Song*

14 Seeing the common people of England by joint consent of person and purse have cast out Charles our Norman oppressor, we have by this victory recovered ourselves from under his Norman yoke.

Gerrard Winstanley Referring to the trial and execution of Charles I after his defeat in the Civil War. Remark to Lord Fairfax, 8 Dec 1649

REED, HENRY

(1914–86) British poet and dramatist. His collected poems appeared in *A Map of Verona* (1946) and *The Lessons of the War* (1970). He wrote many plays for radio.

1 And the various holds and rolls and throws and breakfalls
Somehow or other I always seemed to put
In the wrong place. And as for war, my wars
Were global from the start.

Lessons of the War, 'Unarmed Combat'

2 Today we have naming of parts. Yesterday,
We had daily cleaning. And tomorrow morning
We shall have what to do after firing. But today,
Today we have naming of parts.

Lessons of the War, 'Naming of Parts'

3 They call it easing the Spring: it is perfectly easy
If you have any strength in your thumb: like the bolt,
And the breech, and the cocking-piece, and the point of balance,
Which in our case we have not got.

Lessons of the War, 'Naming of Parts'

4 A barn is not called a barn, to put it more plainly,
Or a field in the distance, where sheep may be safely grazing.
You must never be over-sure. You must say, when reporting:
At five o'clock in the central sector is a dozen
Of what appear to be animals; whatever you do,
Don't call the bleeders *sheep*.

Lessons of the War, 'Judging Distances'

5 In a civil war, a general must know – and I'm afraid it's a thing rather of instinct than of practice – he must know exactly when to move over to the other side.

Not a Drum was Heard: The War Memoirs of General Gland

6 If one doesn't get birthday presents it can remobilize very painfully the persecutory anxiety which usually follows birth.

The Primal Scene, as it were

7 I have known her pass the whole evening without mentioning a single book, or *in fact anything unpleasant* at all.

A Very Great Man Indeed

REGRET

See also apologies, memory, mourning, nostalgia, past, sorrow

1 It is no use crying over spilt milk.

Proverb

2 It's too late to shut the stable door after the horse has bolted.

Proverb

3 What's done cannot be undone.

Proverb

4 Then said I, Woe is me. For I am undone; because I am a man of unclean lips, and I dwell in the midst of a people of unclean lips: for mine eyes have seen the King, the Lord of Hosts. Then flew one of the seraphims unto me, having a live coal in his hand, which he had taken with the tongs from off the altar: and he laid it upon my mouth, and said, Lo, this hath touched thy lips; and thine iniquity is taken away, and thy sin purged.

Bible: Isaiah 6:5–7

5 I say unto you, that likewise joy shall be in heaven over one sinner that repenteth, more than over ninety and nine just persons, which need no repentance.

Bible: Luke 15:7

6 One doesn't recognize in one's life the really important moments – not until it's too late.

Agatha Christie (1891–1976) British detective-story writer. *Endless Night*, Bk. II, Ch. 14

7 This hand hath offended.

Thomas Cranmer (1489–1556) English churchman. *Memorials of Cranmer* (Strype)

8 All I have, I would have given gladly not to be standing here today.

Lyndon B. Johnson (1908–73) US Democratic president. Following the assassination of President Kennedy. Speech to Congress, 27 Nov 1963

9 Were it not better to forget
Than but remember and regret?

Letitia Landon (1802–38) British poet and novelist. *Despondency*

10 We might have been – These are but common words,
And yet they make the sum of life's bewailing.

Letitia Landon *Three Extracts from the Diary of a Week*

11 And so, I missed my chance with one of the lords
Of life.
And I have something to expiate;
A pettiness.

D. H. Lawrence (1885–1930) British novelist. *Snake*

12 Make it a rule of life never to regret and never to look back. Regret is an appalling waste of energy; you can't build on it; it's only good for wallowing in.

Katherine Mansfield (1888–1923) New Zealand-born British writer. Attrib.

13 Maybe it would have been better if neither of us had been born.

Napoleon I (Napoleon Bonaparte; 1769–1821) French emperor. Said while looking at the tomb of the philosopher Jean-Jacques Rousseau, whose theories had influenced the French Revolution. *The Story of Civilization* (W. Durant), Vol. II

14 It serves me right for putting all my eggs in one bastard.

Dorothy Parker (1893–1967) US writer and wit. On going into hospital for an abortion. *You Might As Well Live*, II, Ch. 3 (J. Keats)

15 Good-bye, I've barely said a word to you, it is always like that at parties, we never see the people, we never say the things we should like to say, but it is the same everywhere in this life. Let us hope that when we are dead things will be better arranged.

Marcel Proust (1871–1922) French novelist. *À La Recherche du temps perdu: Sodome et Gomorrhe*

16 Had I been brighter, the ladies been gentler, the Scotch been weaker, had the gods been kinder, had the dice been hotter, this could have been a one-sentence story: Once upon a time I lived happily ever after.

Mickey Rooney (1920–) US actor. Attrib.

17 The follies which a man regrets most in his life are those which he didn't commit when he had the opportunity.

Helen Rowland (1876–1950) US writer. *Reflections of a Bachelor Girl*

18 But with the morning cool repentance came.

Walter Scott (1771–1832) Scottish novelist. *Rob Roy*, Ch. 12

19 Had I but serv'd my God with half the zeal
I serv'd my King, he would not in mine age
Have left me naked to mine enemies.

William Shakespeare (1564–1616) English dramatist. *Henry VIII*, III:2

20 O, pardon me, thou bleeding piece of earth,
That I am meek and gentle with these butchers!
Thou art the ruins of the noblest man
That ever lived in the tide of times.

William Shakespeare *Julius Caesar*, III:1

21 To mourn a mischief that is past and gone
Is the next way to draw new mischief on.

William Shakespeare *Othello*, I:3

22 Things sweet to taste prove in digestion sour.

William Shakespeare *Richard II*, I:3

23 What's gone and what's past help
Should be past grief.

William Shakespeare *The Winter's Tale*, III:2

24 When to the sessions of sweet silent thought
I summon up remembrance of things past,
I sigh the lack of many a thing I sought,
And with old woes new wail my dear time's waste.

William Shakespeare *Sonnet 30*

25 O! call back yesterday, bid time return.

William Shakespeare *Richard II*, III:2

26 The bitterest tears shed over graves are for words left unsaid and deeds left undone.

Harriet Beecher Stowe (1811–96) US novelist. *Little Foxes*, Ch. 3.

27 I never wonder to see men wicked, but I often wonder to see them not ashamed.

Jonathan Swift (1667–1745) Irish-born Anglican priest and writer. *Thoughts on Various Subjects*

28 Though nothing can bring back the hour
Of splendour in the grass, of glory in the flower;
We will grieve not, rather find
Strength in what remains behind...

William Wordsworth (1770–1850) British poet. *Ode. Intimations of Immortality*, IX

29 Men are we, and must grieve when even the shade
Of that which once was great is passed away.

William Wordsworth *Sonnets*, 'Once did she hold'

RELIGION

See also atheism, belief, Bible, Catholicism, Christianity, Christmas, Church, damnation, devil, doomsday, faith, God, heaven, hell, Jews, martyrdom, prayer, Protestantism, Sunday

1 Karin needed nothing from God. He just had

the power to kill her that's all; to destroy her flesh and blood, the tools without which she could not work.

Richard Adams (1920–) British novelist. *The Girl in a Swing*, Ch. 28

2 Nearer, my God, to thee,
Nearer to thee!

Sarah F. Adams (1805–48) British poet and hymn writer. *Nearer My God to Thee*

3 ...of middle stature, neither tall nor short. His complexion was rosy white; his eyes black; his hair, thick, brilliant, and beautiful, fell to his shoulders. His profuse beard fell to his breast...There was such sweetness in his visage that no one, once in his presence, could leave him. If I hungered, a single look at the Prophet's face dispelled the hunger. Before him all forgot their griefs and pains.

Ali (c. 600–661) Son-in-law of Mohammed and fourth caliph. Describing Mohammed (570–632). *Chronique* (Abu Jafar Mohammed al-Tabari), Pt. III, Ch. 46

4 He was of the faith chiefly in the sense that the church he currently did not attend was Catholic.

Kingsley Amis (1922–) British novelist. *One Fat Englishman*

5 As long as you said you were some sort of a Christian and you were married, for the first time that is, they were still leaving you pretty much alone. They were concentrating first on the others.

Margaret Atwood (1939–) Canadian novelist. *The Handmaid's Tale*

6 There is no salvation outside the church.

St Augustine of Hippo (354–430) Bishop of Hippo. *De Bapt.*, IV

7 The Jews and Arabs should sit down and settle their differences like good Christians.

Warren Austin (1877–1962) US politician and diplomat. Attrib.

8 One cathedral is worth a hundred theologians capable of proving the existence of God by logic.

Julian Barnes (1946–) British novelist. *Staring at the Sun*

9 I'm a Communist by day and a Catholic as soon as it gets dark.

Brendan Behan (1923–64) Irish playwright. Attrib.

10 Ye shall circumcise the flesh of your foreskin; and it shall be a token of the covenant betwixt me and you.

Bible: Genesis 17:11

11 Blessed are the pure in heart: for they shall see God.
Blessed are the peacemakers: for they shall be called the children of God.
Blessed are they which are persecuted for righteousness' sake: for theirs is the kingdom of heaven.

Bible: Matthew 5:8–10

12 If the concept of God has any validity or use, it can only be to make us larger, freer, and more loving. If God cannot do this, then it is time we got rid of Him.

James Baldwin (1924–87) US writer. *The Fire next Time*

13 INDIGESTION, n. A disease which the patient and his friends frequently mistake for deep religious conviction and concern for the salvation of mankind. As the simple Red Man of the western wild put it, with, it must be confessed, a certain force: 'Plenty well, no pray; big bellyache, heap God.'

Ambrose Bierce (1842–?1914) US writer and journalist. *The Devil's Dictionary*

14 SAINT, n. a dead sinner revised and edited.

Ambrose Bierce *The Devil's Dictionary*

15 As for the British churchman, he goes to church as he goes to the bathroom, with the minimum of fuss and no explanation if he can help it.

Ronald Blythe (1922–) British writer. *The Age of Illusion*

16 If I really believed that the Church of England came out of the loins of Henry VIII I could be as free as I liked about making changes, but I do not believe that.

Canon Peter Boulton British clergyman. Remark, Mar 1987

17 Every day people are straying away from the church and going back to God. Really.

Lenny Bruce (1925–66) US comedian. *The Essential Lenny Bruce* (ed. J. Cohen), 'Religions Inc.'

18 This Ariyan Eightfold Path, that is to say: Right view, right aim, right speech, right action, right living, right effort, right mindfulness, right contemplation.

Buddha (Gautama Siddhartha; c. 563–c. 483 BC) Indian religious teacher. *Some Sayings of the Buddha* (F. L. Woodward)

19 Man is by his constitution a religious animal.

Edmund Burke (1729–97) British politician. *Reflections on the Revolution in France*

20 One religion is as true as another.

Robert Burton (1577–1640) English scholar and explorer. *Anatomy of Melancholy*, Pt. III

21 To be at all is to be religious more or less.

Samuel Butler (1835–1902) British writer. *Notebooks*

22 He no play-a da game. He no make-a da rules!

Earl Butz (1909–) US politician. Referring to the Pope's strictures against contraception. Remark, 1974

23 It is a mockery to allow women to baptise. Even the Virgin Mary was not allowed this.

John Calvin (1509–64) French Protestant reformer. *Institution de la religion Chrestienne*

24 The idea that only a male can represent Christ at the altar is a most serious heresy.

Dr George Carey (1935–) British churchman and Archbishop of Canterbury (1991–). *Reader's Digest*, Apr 1991

25 Not a religion for gentlemen.

Charles II (1630–85) King of England. Referring to Presbyterianism. *History of My Own Time* (Burnet), Vol. I, Bk. II, Ch. 2

26 Religion is by no means a proper subject of conversation in a mixed company.

Earl of Chesterfield (1694–1773) English statesman. Letter to his godson

27 When your ladyship's faith has removed them, I will go thither with all my heart.

Earl of Chesterfield Said to his sister, Lady Gertrude Hotham, when she suggested he go to a Methodist seminary in Wales to recuperate, recommending the views of the mountains. Attrib.

28 Talk about the pews and steeples

And the cash that goes therewith!
But the souls of Christian peoples...
Chuck it, Smith!

G. K. Chesterton (1874–1936) British writer. *Antichrist, or the Reunion of Christendom*

29 Men will wrangle for religion; write for it; fight for it; anything but – live for it.

Charles Caleb Colton (?1780–1832) British clergyman and writer. *Lacon*, Vol. I

30 Pray remember, Mr Dean, no dogma, no Dean.

Benjamin Disraeli (1804–81) British statesman. Attrib.

31 'Sensible men are all of the same religion.' 'And pray what is that?' inquired the prince. 'Sensible men never tell.'

Benjamin Disraeli *Endymion*, Bk. I, Ch. 81

32 I neglect God and his angels for the noise of a fly, for the rattling of a coach, for the whining of a door.

John Donne (1573–1631) English poet. *Sermons*, 80

33 When you go to church where two men stand behind the Communion table, and ten men serve Communion, and another man stands at the lectern and reads the scripture, and another man stands up and preaches, and three more men stand in the aisles handing out bulletins, you hear a fairly loud statement about the nature of the Church.

Harold Dowler British churchman. *Ms*, Mar 1982

34 In pious times, e'r Priest-craft did begin,
Before Polygamy was made a Sin.

John Dryden (1631–1700) British poet and dramatist. *Absalom and Achitophel*, I

35 It would be better to see the royal turban of the Turks in the midst of the city than the Latin mitre.

Michael Ducas (?1400–?70) Byzantine historian. Referring to Emperor Constantine XI's reunification of the Orthodox and Roman Churches (1452), in an attempt to save the Byzantine Empire from the Turks. Attrib.

36 Christian Science explains all cause and effect as mental, not physical.

Mary Baker Eddy (1821–1910) US religious leader. *Science and Health, with Key to the Scriptures*

37 Sickness, sin and death, being inharmonious, do not originate in God, nor belong to His government.

Mary Baker Eddy *Science and Health, with Key to the Scriptures*

38 Science without religion is lame, religion without science is blind.

Albert Einstein (1879–1955) German-born US physicist. *Out of My Later Years*

39 The whole religious complexion of the modern world is due to the absence from Jerusalem of a lunatic asylum.

Havelock Ellis (1859–1939) British sexologist. *Impressions and Comments*

40 The religions we call false were once true.

Ralph Waldo Emerson (1803–82) US poet and essayist. *Essays*, 'Character'

41 Religion is an illusion and it derives its strength from the fact that it falls in with our instinctual desires.

Sigmund Freud (1856–1939) Austrian psychoanalyst. *New Introductory Lectures on Psychoanalysis*, 'A Philosophy of Life'

42 Religion
Has made an honest woman of the supernatural,
And we won't have it kicking over the traces again.

Christopher Fry (1907–) British dramatist. *The Lady's Not for Burning*, II

43 There exists no politician in India daring enough to attempt to explain to the masses that cows can be eaten.

Indira Gandhi (1917–84) Indian stateswoman. *The New York Review of Books*, 'Indira's Coup' (Oriana Fallaci)

44 God has no religion.

Mahatma Gandhi (Mohandas Karamchand 'Mahatma' Gandhi; 1869–1948) Indian national leader. Attrib.

45 The various modes of worship, which prevailed in the Roman world, were all considered by the people as equally true; by the philosopher, as equally false; and by the magistrate, as equally useful. And thus toleration produced not only mutual indulgence, but even religious concord.

Edward Gibbon (1737–94) British historian. *Decline and Fall of the Roman Empire*, Ch. 2

46 As I take my shoes from the shoemaker, and my coat from the tailor, so I take my religion from the priest.

Oliver Goldsmith (1728–74) Irish-born British writer. *Life of Johnson* (J. Boswell)

47 Decide for Christ.

Billy Graham (1918–) US evangelist. Slogan

48 Those who marry God...can become domesticated too – it's just as humdrum a marriage as all the others.

Graham Greene (1904–91) British novelist. *A Burnt-Out Case*, Ch. 1

49 They illuminate our whole country with the bright light of their preaching and teaching.

Robert Grosseteste (c. 1175–1253) Bishop of Lincoln. Referring to the Franciscans. Letter to Pope Gregory IX, 1238

50 Pray, good people, be civil. I am the Protestant whore.

Nell Gwyn (1650–87) English actress and mistress of Charles II. On being surrounded in her coach by an angry mob in Oxford at the time of the Popish Plot. *Nell Gwyn* (Bevan), Ch. 13

51 I could always not deal with my problems by referring to God, my comfort...Religion was my protection against pain.

David Hare (1947–) British playwright. *The Sunday Times*, 11 Feb 1990

52 But as I rav'd and grew more fierce and wild
At every word,
Methought I heard one calling, 'Child';
And I replied, 'My Lord.'

George Herbert (1593–1633) English poet. *The Collar*

53 The sedate, sober, silent, serious, sad-coloured sect.

Thomas Hood (1799–1845) British poet. Referring to the Quakers. *The Doves and the Crows*

54 A lot of people have a very confused idea of what Christianity is. I hope I've stimulated people's interest in the intellectual side of it. There's so much bad religion around...Christianity is good because in 2000 years so much crap's been worked out.

Susan Howatch (1940–) British writer. *The Observer*, 8 May 1994

55 To become a popular religion, it is only necessary for a superstition to enslave a philosophy.

Dean Inge (1860–1954) British churchman. *Outspoken Essays*

56 Many people believe that they are attracted by God, or by Nature, when they are only repelled by man.

Dean Inge *More Lay Thoughts of a Dean*

57 Many people think they have religion when they are troubled with dyspepsia.

Robert G. Ingersoll (1833–99) US lawyer and agnostic. *Liberty of Man, Woman and Child*, Section 3

58 There are as many miracles as there are articles of the *Summa*.

John XXII (Jacques d'Euse; c. 1249–1334) Pope. Referring to the *Summa Theologiae* of Thomas Aquinas, who was in the process of being canonized. Attrib.

59 Among all my patients in the second half of life...there has not been one whose problem in the last resort was not that of finding a religious outlook on life.

Carl Gustav Jung (1875–1961) Swiss psychoanalyst. *Modern Man in Search of a Soul*

60 The author of the Satanic Verses book, which is against Islam, the Prophet and the Koran, and all those involved in its publication who were aware of its content, are sentenced to death. I ask all Moslems to execute them wherever they find them.

Ayatollah Ruholla Khomeini (1900-89) Iranian Shiite Muslim leader. The fatwa against Salman Rushdie. Speech, 14 Feb 1989

61 The month of Ramadan shall ye fast, in which the Koran was sent down from heaven, a direction unto men, and declarations of direction, and the distinction between good and evil.

Koran Ch. II

62 But I suppose even God was born
too late to trust the old religion –
all those setting out
that never left the ground,
beginning in wisdom, dying in doubt.

Robert Lowell (1917–77) US poet. *Tenth Muse*

63 Here stand I. I can do no other. God help me. Amen.

Martin Luther (1483–1546) German Protestant. Speech at the Diet of Worms, 18 Apr 1521

64 Abide with me; fast falls the eventide;
The darkness deepens; Lord, with me abide;
When other helpers fail, and comforts flee,
Help of the helpless, O, abide with me.

Henry Francis Lyte (1793–1847) British hymn writer. *Abide with Me*

65 Religion...is the opium of the people.

Karl Marx (1818–83) German philosopher and revolutionary. *Criticism of the Hegelian Philosophy of Right*, Introduction

66 Things have come to a pretty pass when religion is allowed to invade the sphere of private life.

Lord Melbourne (1779–1848) British statesman. Attrib.

67 There are many who stay away from church these days because you hardly ever mention God any more.

Arthur Miller (1915–) US dramatist. *The Crucible*, I

68 New Presbyter is but old Priest writ large.

John Milton (1608–74) English poet. *Sonnet*: 'On the New Forcers of Conscience under the Long Parliament'

69 Man is quite insane. He wouldn't know how to create a maggot and he creates Gods by the dozen.

Michel de Montaigne (1533–92) French essayist. *Essais*, II

70 There is a very good saying that if triangles invented a god, they would make him three-sided.

Baron de Montesquieu (1689–1755) French writer. *Lettres persanes*

71 I hold the Koran, the Vedas, the Bible, and all such religious texts determining the lives of their followers, as out of place and out of time...We have to move beyond these ancient texts if we want progress.

Taslima Nasreen (1958–) Bangladeshi novelist. She has had two fatwas pronounced against her.

72 Our religion doesn't give women any human dignity. Women are considered slaves...I write against the religion because if women want to live like human beings, they will have to live outside the religion and Islamic law.

Taslima Nasreen *The Times*, 22 June 1994

73 The Christian resolution to find the world ugly and bad has made the world ugly and bad.

Friedrich Nietzsche (1844–1900) German philosopher. *Die Fröhliche Wissenschaft*

74 There's no reason to bring religion into it. I think we ought to have as great a regard for religion as we can, so as to keep it out of as many things as possible.

Sean O'Casey (1884–1964) Irish dramatist. *The Plough and the Stars*, I

75 Religion has always been the wound, not the bandage.

Dennis Potter (1935–94) British dramatist. *The Observer*, 'Sayings of the Week', 10 Apr 1994

76 If women in the priesthood has come as a result of women's liberation, then I think it is satanic.

William Pwaisiho Malaitan churchman. *The Daily Telegraph*, Aug 1988

77 The brotherhood of man under the fatherhood of God.

Nelson Rockefeller (1908–79) US Republican politician and vice-president. Attrib.

78 We must reject a privatization of religion which results in its reduction to being simply a matter of personal salvation.

Robert Runcie (1921–) British churchman; Archbishop of Canterbury (1980–91). *The Observer*, 'Sayings of the Week', 17 Apr 1988

79 Unlike Christianity, which preached a peace that it never achieved, Islam unashamedly came with a sword.

Steven Runciman (1903–) British academic and diplomat. *A History of the Crusades*, 'The First Crusade'

80 I call upon the intellectual community in this

country and abroad to stand up for freedom of the imagination, an issue much larger than my book or indeed my life.

Salman Rushdie (1947–) Indian-born British novelist. Press statement, 14 Feb 1989

81 Religious law is like the grammar of a language. Any language is governed by such rules; otherwise it ceases to be a language. But within them, you can say many different sentences and write many different books. Historically speaking, Jews throughout the world and throughout the centuries, though bound by the same rules, have written many different books. So we have the resources today to write a book that women will read and say: 'This is my story'.

Jonathan Sacks (1948–) British Chief Rabbi. *The Independent*, 30 June 1994

82 I have been into many of the ancient cathedrals – grand, wonderful, mysterious. But I always leave them with a feeling of indignation because of the generations of human beings who have struggled in poverty to build these altars to the unknown god.

Elizabeth Stanton (1815–1902) US suffragette. *Diary*

83 Whenever a man talks loudly against religion, – always suspect that it is not his reason, but his passions which have got the better of his creed.

Laurence Sterne (1713–68) Irish-born British writer. *Tristram Shandy*

84 I believe in the Church, One Holy, Catholic and Apostolic, and I regret that it nowhere exists.

William Temple (1881–1944) British churchman. Attrib.

85 Alas, O Lord, to what a state dost Thou bring those who love Thee!

St Teresa of Ávila (1515–82) Spanish mystic. *The Interior Castle*, VI

86 And do you know that you are an Eve? God's sentence hangs over all your sex and His punishment weighs down upon you. You are the devil's gateway; it was you who first violated the forbidden tree and broke God's law…You should always go in mourning and rags.

Tertullian (Quintus Septimus Florens Tertullianus; c. 160–225 AD) Roman theologian. *De cultu feminarum* (On Female Dress)

87 It is spring, moonless night in the small town, starless and bible-black.

Dylan Thomas (1914–53) Welsh poet. *Under Milk Wood*

88 I fled Him, down the nights and down the days;
I fled Him, down the arches of the years;
I fled Him, down the labyrinthine ways
Of my own mind; and in the mist of tears
I hid from Him, and under running laughter.

Francis Thompson (1859–1907) British poet. *The Hound of Heaven*

89 Rock of ages, cleft for me,
Let me hide myself in Thee.

Augustus Montague Toplady (1740–78) British hymn writer. *Rock of Ages*

90 Beware when you take on the Church of God. Others have tried and have bitten the dust.

Bishop Desmond Tutu (1931–) South African clergyman. Speech, Apr 1987

91 In general the churches, visited by me too often on weekdays… bore for me the same relation to God that billboards did to Coca-Cola: they promoted thirst without quenching it.

John Updike (1932–) US novelist. *A Month of Sundays*, Ch. 2

92 Organized religion is making Christianity political rather than making politics Christian.

Laurens Van der Post (1906–) South African novelist. *The Observer*, 'Sayings of the Week', 9 Nov 1986

93 Jesus loves me – this I know,
For the Bible tells me so.

Susan Warner (1819–85) US novelist. *The Love of Jesus*

94 Lord, I ascribe it to Thy grace,
And not to chance, as others do,
That I was born of Christian race,
And not a Heathen, or a Jew.

Isaac Watts (1674–1748) English theologian and hymn writer. *Divine Songs for Children*, 'Praise for the Gospel'

95 Our God, our help in ages past,
Our hope for years to come,
Our shelter from the stormy blast,
And our eternal home.

Isaac Watts *Our God, Our Help in Ages Past*

96 I have noticed again and again since I have been in the Church that lay interest in ecclesiastical matters is often a prelude to insanity.

Evelyn Waugh (1903–66) British novelist. *Decline and Fall*, Pt. I, Ch. 8

97 There is a species of person called a 'Modern Churchman' who draws the full salary of a beneficed clergyman and need not commit himself to any religious belief.

Evelyn Waugh *Decline and Fall*, Pt. II, Ch. 4

98 Mrs. Ape, as was her invariable rule, took round the hat and collected nearly two pounds. 'Salvation doesn't do them the same good if they think it's free' was her favourite axiom.

Evelyn Waugh *Vile Bodies*

99 Religion is love; in no case is it logic.

Beatrice Webb (1858–1943) British economist and writer. *My Apprenticeship*, Ch. 2

100 I look upon all the world as my parish.

John Wesley (1703–91) British religious leader. *Journal*, 11 June 1739

101 Why do born-again people so often make you wish they'd never been born the first time?

Katherine Whitehorn (1926–) British journalist. *The Observer*, 20 May 1979

102 So many gods, so many creeds,
So many paths that wind and wind,
While just the art of being kind
Is all the sad world needs.

Ella Wheeler Wilcox (1850–1919) US poet. *The World's Need*

103 The question of the rights of women to hold secular office is a quite separate matter and should not in any way be connected to or paralleled with the question of women's ordination.

Cardinal Willebrands (1909–) Dutch ecclesiastic. Remark, June 1986

104 The itch of disputing will prove the scab of churches.

Henry Wotton (1568–1639) English poet and diplomat. *A Panegyric to King Charles*

105 The Ethiopians say that their gods are snub-nosed and black, the Thracians that theirs have light blue eyes and red hair.

Xenophanes (c. 560–c. 478 BC) Greek poet and philosopher. *Fragment 15*

106 No Jew was ever fool enough to turn Christian unless he was a clever man.

Israel Zangwill (1864–1926) British writer. *Children of the Ghetto*, Ch. 1

107 The only difference between a religion and a cult is the amount of real estate they own.

Frank Zappa (1940–93) US rock musician. *Interview*

REMEDIES

See also doctors, illness, medicine

1 He's the best physician that knows the worthlessness of the most medicines.

Proverb

2 Many medicines, few cures.

Proverb

3 Visitors' footfalls are like medicine; they heal the sick.

Bantu proverb

4 A single untried popular remedy often throws the scientific doctor into hysterics.

Chinese proverb

5 Three remedies of the physicians of Myddfai: water, honey, and labour.

Welsh proverb

6 Modern therapy, particularly of malignancy, makes good use of the Borgia effect – two poisons are more efficacious than one.

Anonymous

7 Why should a man die who has sage in his garden?

Anonymous *Regimen Sanitatis, Salernitanum*

8 You give medicine to a sick man; the sick man hands you gold in return. You cure his disease, he cures yours.

Anonymous

9 Cure the disease and kill the patient.

Francis Bacon (1561–1626) English philosopher. *Essays*, 'Of Friendship'

10 The remedy is worse than the disease.

Francis Bacon *Essays*, 'Of Seditions and Troubles'

11 Then Peter said, Silver and gold have I none; but such as I have give I thee: In the name of Jesus Christ of Nazareth rise up and walk.

Bible: Acts 3:6

12 The Lord hath created medicines out of the earth; and he that is wise will not abhor them.

Bible: Ecclesiasticus 38:4

13 And besought him that they might only touch the hem of his garment: and as many as touched were made perfectly whole.

Bible: Matthew 14:36

14 My father invented a cure for which there was no disease and unfortunately my mother caught it and died of it.

Victor Borge (1909–) Danish-born US composer, actor, and musical comedian. *In Concert*

15 We all labour against our own cure, for death is the cure of all diseases.

Thomas Browne (1605–82) English physician and writer.

16 *Diseases* of their own Accord,
But *Cures* come difficult and hard.

Samuel Butler (1612–80) English poet and satirist. *Satyr upon the Weakness and Misery of Man*

17 Medical men all over the world...merely entered into a tacit agreement to call all sorts of maladies people are liable to, in cold weather, by one name; so that one sort of treatment may serve for all, and their practice be thereby greatly simplified.

Jane Welsh Carlyle (1801–66) The wife of Thomas Carlyle. Letter to John Welsh, 4 Mar 1837

18 A reckoning up of the cause often solves the malady.

Celsus (25 BC–50 AD) Roman scholar. *De Medicina*, Prooemium

19 Well, now, there's a remedy for everything except death.

Miguel de Cervantes (1547–1616) Spanish novelist. *Don Quixote*, Pt. II, Ch. 10

20 When a lot of remedies are suggested for a disease, that means it can't be cured.

Anton Chekhov (1860–1904) Russian dramatist. *The Cherry Orchard*, II

21 Men worry over the great number of diseases; doctors worry over the small number of remedies.

Pien Ch'iao (c. 225 BC)

22 When ill, indeed,
E'en dismissing the doctor don't *always* succeed.

George Colman, the Younger (1762–1836) British dramatist. *Lodgings for Single Gentlemen*

23 If you are too fond of new remedies, first you will not cure your patients; secondly, you will have no patients to cure.

Astley Paston Cooper (1768–1841)

24 What destroys one man preserves another.

Pierre Corneille (1606–84) French dramatist. *Cinna*, II:1

25 Every day, in every way, I am getting better and better.

Émile Coué (1857–1920) French doctor. Formula for a cure by autosuggestion

26 You see – he's got a perfectly new idea. He never sees his patients. He's not interested in individuals, he prefers to treat a crowd. And he's organized these mass cures... And he cures thirty thousand people every Thursday.

Ruth Draper *Doctors and Diets*

27 Then comes the question, how do drugs, hygiene and animal magnetism heal? It may be affirmed that they do not heal, but only relieve suffering temporarily, exchanging one disease for another.

Mary Baker Eddy (1821–1910) US religious leader. *Science and Health, with Key to the Scriptures*

28 The poisons are our principal medicines, which kill the disease and save the life.

Ralph Waldo Emerson (1803–82) US poet and essayist. *The Conduct of Life*, Ch. 7

29 His *Majestie* began first to Touch for the Evil according to costome; Thus, his Majestie sitting under his State in the *Banqueting* house: The *Chirurgeons* cause the sick to be brought or led up to the throne, who kneeling, the King strokes their faces or cheekes with both his hands at once: at which instant a *Chaplaine* in his formalities, says, *He put his hands upon them, & he healed them.*

John Evelyn (1620–1706) English diarist. *Diary*, 6 July 1660

30 Life as we find it is too hard for us; it entails too much pain, too many disappointments, impossible tasks. We cannot do without palliative remedies.

Sigmund Freud (1856–1939) Austrian psychoanalyst. *Civilization and Its Discontents*

31 Like cures like.

Samuel Hahnemann (1755–1843) Motto for homeopathy

32 Extreme remedies are most appropriate for extreme diseases.

Hippocrates (c. 460–c. 377 BC) Greek physician. *Aphorisms*, I

33 To do nothing is also a good remedy.

Hippocrates

34 By opposites opposites are cured.

Hippocrates *Deflatibus*, Vol. I

35 Like cures like.

Hippocrates Attrib.

36 One of the most successful physicians I have ever known, has assured me, that he used more bread pills, drops of colored water, and powders of hickory ashes, than of all other medicines put together. It was certainly a pious fraud.

Thomas Jefferson (1743–1826) US statesman. Letter to Dr. Caspar Wistar, 21 June 1807

37 The patient, treated on the fashionable theory, sometimes gets well in spite of the medicine. The medicine therefore restored him, and the young doctor receives new courage to proceed in his bold experiments on the lives of his fellow creatures.

Thomas Jefferson Letter to Dr. Caspar Wistar, 21 June 1807

38 Poisons and medicine are oftentimes the same substance given with different intents.

Peter Mere Latham (1789–1875) US poet and essayist. *General Remarks on the Practice of Medicine*, Ch. 7

39 Remedies, indeed, are our great analysers of disease.

Peter Mere Latham *General Remarks on the Practice of Medicine*, Ch. 7

40 You know that medicines when well used restore health to the sick: they will be well used when the doctor together with his understanding of their nature shall understand also what man is, what life is, and what constitution and health are. Know these well and you will know their opposites; and when this is the case you will know well how to devise a remedy.

Leonardo da Vinci (1452–1519) Italian artist, sculptor, architect, and engineer. *Codice Atlantico*, 270

41 Is getting well ever an art
Or art a way to get well.

Robert Lowell (1917–77) US poet. *Unwanted*

42 Most men die of their remedies, and not of their illnesses.

Molière (1622–73) French dramatist. *Le Malade imaginaire*, III:3

43 We are more sensible of one little touch of a surgeon's lancet than of twenty wounds with a sword in the heat of fight.

Michel de Montaigne (1533–92) French essayist and moralist.

44 Medicines are only fit for old people.

Napoleon I (Napoleon Bonaparte; 1769–1821) French Emperor. *Napoleon in Exile* (Barry O'Meara)

45 The best of healers is good cheer.

Pindar (c. 522–443 BC) *Nemean Ode*, IV

46 As soon as he ceased to be mad he became merely stupid. There are maladies we must not seek to cure because they alone protect us from others that are more serious.

Marcel Proust (1871–1922) French novelist. *À La Recherche du temps perdu: Le Côté de Guermantes*

47 Happiness is salutary for the body but sorrow develops the powers of the spirit.

Marcel Proust *À La Recherche du temps perdu: Le temps retrouvé*

48 The number of unexplained cures has dropped enormously in the last few years and...will continue to drop.

Theodore Mangipan French physician. Referring to Lourdes, where he worked for 18 years. *The Independent*, 12 May 1994

49 Nothing hinders a cure so much as frequent change of medicine.

Seneca (c. 4 BC–65 AD) Roman writer. *Epistulae ad Lucilium*

50 It is medicine not scenery, for which a sick man must go searching.

Seneca *Epistulae ad Lucilium*

51 It is part of the cure to wish to be cured.

Seneca *Hippolytus*, 249

52 Our remedies oft in ourselves do lie,
Which we ascribe to heaven.

William Shakespeare (1564–1616) English dramatist and poet. *All's Well That Ends Well*, I:1

53 They all thought she was dead; but my father he kept ladling gin down her throat till she came to so sudden that she bit the bowl off the spoon.

George Bernard Shaw (1856–1950) Irish dramatist and critic. *Pygmalion*, III

54 Nicotinic acid cures pellagra, but a beefsteak prevents it.

Henry E. Sigerist (1891–1957) *Atlantic Monthly*, June 1939

55 I watched what method Nature might take, with intention of subduing the symptom by treading in her footsteps.

Thomas Sydenham (1624–89) *Medical Observations*, 5, Ch. 2

56 Our body is a machine for living. It is organized for that, it is its nature. Let life go on in it unhindered and let it defend itself, it will do more than if you paralyse it by encumbering it with remedies.

Leo Tolstoy (1828–1910) Russian writer. *War and Peace*, Bk. X, Ch. 29

57 Wonderful is the skill of a physician; for a rich man he prescribeth various admixtures and compounds, by which the patient is rought to health in many days at an expense of fifty pounds; while for a poor man for the same disease he giveth a more common name, and prescribeth a dose of oil, which worketh a cure in a single night charging fourpence therefor.

James Townley (1714–78)

58 We do not know the mode of action of almost all remedies. Why therefore fear to confess our ignorance? In truth, it seems that the words 'I do not know' stick in every physician's throat.

Armand Trousseau (1801–67) *Bulletin de l'académie impériale de médecine*, 25:733, 1860

59 Dr. Snow gave that blessed Chloroform & the effect was soothing, quieting & delightful beyond measure.

Victoria (1819–1901) Queen of England. Describing her labour. *Journal*

60 Sparrowhawks, Ma'am.

Duke of Wellington (1769–1852) British general and statesman. Advice when asked by Queen Victoria how to remove sparrows from the Crystal Palace. Attrib.

61 There is only one cure for grey hair. It was invented by a Frenchman. It is called the guillotine.

P. G. Wodehouse (1881–1975) British humorous novelist. *The Old Reliable*

62 Some reckoned he killed himself with purgations.

Charles Wriothesley *Chronicle*, Vol. I

RENUNCIATION

See also dismissal

1 Renounce the devil and all his works.

The Book of Common Prayer *Publick Baptism of Infants*

2 I would rather be a brilliant memory than a curiosity.

Emma Eames (1865–1952) US opera singer. Referring to her retirement at the age of 47. *The Elephant that Swallowed a Nightingale* (C. Galtey)

3 You won't have Nixon to kick around any more, gentlemen. This is my last Press Conference.

Richard Milhous Nixon (1913–94) US president. Press conference, after losing the election for the governorship of California, 2 Nov 1962

4 I'll break my staff,
Bury it certain fathoms in the earth,
And deeper than did ever plummet sound
I'll drown my book.

William Shakespeare (1564–1616) English dramatist. *The Tempest*, V:1

5 It is very simple. The artists retired. The British remained.

James Whistler (1834–1903) US painter. Explaining his resignation as president of the Royal Society of British Artists. *Whistler Stories* (D. Seitz)

REPARTEE

1 It hasn't taken Winston long to get used to American ways. He hadn't been an American citizen for three minutes before attacking an ex-secretary of state!

Dean Acheson (1893–1971) US lawyer and statesman. At a ceremony in 1963 to make Churchill an honorary American citizen, Churchill obliquely attacked Acheson's reference to Britain losing an empire. *Randolph Churchill* (K. Halle)

2 Stand a little less between me and the sun.

Diogenes (412–322 BC) Greek philosopher. When Alexander the Great asked if there was anything he wanted. *Life of Alexander* (Plutarch)

3 Oh! he is mad, is he? Then I wish he would bite some other of my generals.

George II (1683–1760) King of Great Britain and Ireland. Replying to advisors who told him that General James Wolfe was mad. Attrib.

4 JUDGE WILLIS. What do you suppose I am on the Bench for, Mr Smith?
SMITH. It is not for me to attempt to fathom the inscrutable workings of Providence.

F. E. Smith (1872–1930) British lawyer and politician. *Frederick Elwin, Earl of Birkenhead* (Lord Birkenhead), Vol. I, Ch. 9

5 LORD SANDWICH. You will die either on the gallows, or of the pox.
WILKES. That must depend on whether I embrace your lordship's principles or your mistress.

John Wilkes (1725–97) British politician. Sometimes attrib. to Samuel Foote. *Portrait of a Patriot* (Charles Chenevix-Trench), Ch. 3

REPRESENTATION

1 In Scotland there is no shadow even of representation. There is neither a representation of property for the counties, nor of population for the towns.

Charles James Fox (1749–1806) British politician. *Parliamentary History of England* (W. Cobbett), Vol. XXXIII

2 Taxation without representation is tyranny.

James Otis (1725–83) US political activist. As 'No taxation without representation' this became the principal slogan of the American Revolution. Attrib.

3 No annihilation without representation.

Arnold Toynbee (1889–1975) British historian. Urging the need for a greater British influence in the UN 1947

REPUBLIC

See also democracy, State

1 Our object in the construction of the state is the greatest happiness of the whole, and not that of any one class.

Plato (429–347 BC) Greek philosopher. *Republic*, Bk. 4

2 As there was no form of government common to the peoples thus segregated, nor tie of language, history, habit, or belief, they were called a Republic.

Evelyn Waugh (1903–66) British novelist. *Scoop*, Bk. II, Ch. 1

REPUTATION

See also fame, posterity

1 For my name and memory, I leave it to men's charitable speeches, and to foreign nations, and the next ages.

Francis Bacon (1561–1626) English philosopher. Will, 19 Dec 1625

2 I hold it as certain, that no man was ever written out of reputation but by himself.

Richard Bentley (1662–1742) English academic. *The Works of Alexander Pope* (W. Warburton), Vol. IV

3 Dead flies cause the ointment of the apothecary to send forth a stinking savour: so doth a little folly him that is in reputation for wisdom and honour.

Bible: Ecclesiastes 10:1

4 The Doctor fared even better. The fame of his new case spread far and wide. People seemed to think that if he could cure an elephant he could cure anything.

Henry Cuyler Bunner (1855–96) *Short Sixes*, 'The Infidelity of Zenobia'

5 Reputation is a bubble which bursts when a man tries to blow it up for himself.

Emma Carleton Attrib.

6 Die when I may, I want it said of me by those who know me best, that I have always plucked a thistle and planted a flower where I thought a flower would grow.

Abraham Lincoln (1809–65) US statesman. *Presidential Anecdotes* (P. Boller)

7 Until you've lost your reputation, you never realize what a burden it was or what freedom really is.

Margaret Mitchell (1909–49) US novelist. *Gone with the Wind*

8 This famous store needs no name on the door.

H. Gordon Selfridge (1856–1947) US businessman. Slogan

9 Reputation, reputation, reputation! O, I have lost my reputation! I have lost the immortal part of myself, and what remains is bestial.

William Shakespeare (1564–1616) English dramatist. *Othello*, II:3

10 Good name in man and woman, dear my lord,
Is the immediate jewel of their souls:
Who steals my purse steals trash; 'tis something, nothing;
'Twas mine, 'tis his, and has been slave to thousands;
But he that filches from me my good name
Robs me of that which not enriches him
And makes me poor indeed.

William Shakespeare *Othello*, III:3

11 The purest treasure mortal times afford
Is spotless reputation; that away,
Men are but gilded loam or painted clay.

William Shakespeare *Richard II*, I:1

12 The king's name is a tower of strength.

William Shakespeare *Richard III*, V:3

13 Even the fact that doctors themselves die of the very diseases they profess to cure passes unnoticed. We do not shoot out our lips and shake our heads, saying, 'They save others: themselves they cannot save': their reputation stands, like an African king's palace, on a foundation of dead bodies.

George Bernard Shaw (1856–1950) Irish dramatist and critic. *The Doctor's Dilemma*, 'Preface on Doctors'

14 My reputation grew with every failure.

George Bernard Shaw Referring to his unsuccessful early novels. *Bernard Shaw* (Hesketh Pearson)

15 I'm called away by particular business. But I leave my character behind me.

Richard Brinsley Sheridan (1751–1816) British dramatist. *The School for Scandal*, II

16 Everything.

Mae West (1892–1980) US actress. When asked what she wanted to be remembered for. Attrib.

RESEARCH

1 We vivisect the nightingale
To probe the secret of his note.

T. B. Aldrich (1836–1907) US writer and editor.

2 O speculator concerning this machine of ours let it not distress you that you impart knowledge of it through another's death, but rejoice that our Creator has ordained the intellect to such excellence of perception.

Leonardo da Vinci (1452–1519) Italian artist. *Quaderni d'Anatomia*, Vol. II

3 Research! A mere excuse for idleness; it has never achieved, and will never achieve any results of the slightest value.

Benjamin Jowett (1817–93) British theologian. *Unforgotten Years* (Logan Pearsall Smith)

4 The aim of research is the discovery of the equations which subsist between the elements of phenomena.

Ernst Mach (1838–1916) Austrian physicist and philosopher. *Popular Scientific Lectures*

5 Always verify your references.

Martin Joseph Routh (1755–1854) British scholar. Attrib.

6 We haven't the money, so we've got to think.

Ernest Rutherford (1871–1937) British physicist. Attrib.

7 The outcome of any serious research can only be to make two questions grow where only one grew before.

Thorstein Bunde Veblen (1857–1929) US social scientist. *The Place of Science in Modern Civilization*

RESPECT

See also courtesy, self-respect

1 Let them hate, so long as they fear.

Lucius Accius (170–c. 85 BC) Roman tragic dramatist. *Atreus*, 'Seneca'

2 One does not arrest Voltaire.

Charles De Gaulle (1890–1970) French general and statesman. Explaining why he had not arrested the philosopher Jean-Paul Sartre for urging French soldiers in Algeria to desert. Attrib.

3 I hate victims who respect their executioners.

Jean-Paul Sartre (1905–80) French writer and philosopher. *Altona*

4 We owe respect to the living; to the dead we owe only truth.

Voltaire (François-Marie Arouet; 1694–1778) French writer. *Oeuvres*, 'Première lettre sur Oedipe'

5 His indolence was qualified with enough basic bad temper to ensure the respect of those about him.

Evelyn Waugh (1903–66) British novelist. *Put Out More Flags*

6 The old-fashioned respect for the young is fast dying out.

Oscar Wilde (1854–1900) Irish-born British dramatist. *The Importance of Being Earnest*, I

RESPECTABILITY

1 Since when was genius found respectable?

Elizabeth Barrett Browning (1806–61) British poet. *Aurora Leigh*, Bk. VI

2 Let them cant about decorum
Who have characters to lose.

Robert Burns (1759–96) Scottish poet. *The Jolly Beggars*

3 Respectable means rich, and decent means poor. I should die if I heard my family called decent.

Thomas Love Peacock (1785–1866) British novelist. *Crotchet Castle*, Ch. 3

4 So live that you wouldn't be ashamed to sell the family parrot to the town gossip.

Will Rogers (1879–1935) US actor and humorist. Attrib.

RESPONSIBILITY

See also accusation

1 A bad workman always blames his tools.

Proverb

2 What the proprietorship of these papers is aiming at is power, and power without responsibility – the prerogative of the harlot through the ages.

Stanley Baldwin (1867–1947) British statesman. Attacking the press barons Lords Rothermere and Beaverbrook. It was first used by KIPLING. *See also* DUKE OF DEVONSHIRE; STOPPARD. Speech, election rally, 18 Mar 1931

3 Each man the architect of his own fate.

Appius Caecus (4th–3rd century BC) Roman statesman. *De Civitate* (Sallust), Bk. I

4 Everyone threw the blame on me. I have noticed that they nearly always do. I suppose it is because they think I shall be able to bear it best.

Winston Churchill (1874–1965) British statesman. *My Early Life*, Ch. 17

5 Perhaps it is better to be irresponsible and right than to be responsible and wrong.

Winston Churchill Party Political Broadcast, London, 26 Aug 1950

6 Good God, that's done it. He's lost us the tarts' vote.

Duke of Devonshire (1895–1950) Conservative politician. Referring to Stanley BALDWIN's attack on newspaper proprietors; recalled by Harold Macmillan. Attrib.

7 What a man does defiles him, not what is done by others.

William Golding (1911–93) British novelist. *Rites of Passage*, 'Next Day'

8 It matters not how strait the gate,
How charged with punishments the scroll,
I am the master of my fate:
I am the captain of my soul.

William Ernest Henley (1849–1903) British writer. *Echoes*, IV, 'Invictus. In Mem. R.T.H.B.'

9 It often happens that I wake at night and begin to think about a serious problem and decide I must tell the Pope about it. Then I wake up completely and remember I am the Pope.

John XXIII (1881–1963) Italian-born pope. Attrib.

10 Power without responsibility – the prerogative of the harlot throughout the ages.

Rudyard Kipling (1865–1936) Indian-born British writer. Better known for its subsequent use by BALDWIN. Attrib.

11 Accuse not Nature, she hath done her part;
Do thou but thine.

John Milton (1608–74) English poet. *Paradise Lost*, Bk. VIII

12 *We can believe what we choose.* We are answerable for what we choose to believe.

Cardinal Newman (1801–90) British theologian. Letter to Mrs Froude, 27 June 1848

13 You become responsible, forever, for what you have tamed. You are responsible for your rose.

Antoine de Saint-Exupéry (1900–44) French novelist and aviator. *The Little Prince*, Ch. 21

14 What infinite heart's ease
Must kings neglect, that private men enjoy!
And what have kings that privates have not too,
Save ceremony, save general ceremony?

William Shakespeare (1564–1616) English dramatist. *Henry V*, IV:1

15 'Tis not the balm, the sceptre and the ball,
The sword, the mace, the crown imperial,
The intertissued robe of gold and pearl,
The farced title running 'fore the king,
The throne he sits on, nor the tide of pomp
That beats upon the high shore of this world,
No, not all these, thrice-gorgeous ceremony,
Can sleep so soundly as the wretched slave,
Who with a body fill'd and vacant mind
Gets him to rest, cramm'd with distressful bread;
Never sees horrid night, the child of hell,
But, like a lackey, from the rise to set
Sweats in the eye of Phoebus, and all night
Sleeps in Elysium.

William Shakespeare *Henry V*, IV:1

16 O God! methinks it were a happy life,
To be no better than a homely swain;
To sit upon a hill, as I do now,
To carve out dials, quaintly, point by point,
Thereby to see the minutes how they run,
How many make the hour full complete;
How many hours bring about the day;
How many days will finish up the year;
How many years a mortal man may live.

William Shakespeare *Henry VI, Part Three*, II:5

17 The salvation of mankind lies only in making everything the concern of all.

Alexander Solzhenitsyn (1918–) Russian novelist. Nobel Lecture, 1970

18 The House of Lords, an illusion to which I have never been able to subscribe – responsibility without power, the prerogative of the eunuch throughout the ages.

Tom Stoppard (1937–) Czech-born British dramatist. *See also* BALDWIN. *Lord Malquist and Mr Moon*, Pt. VI, Ch. 1

19 For man is man and master of his fate.

Alfred, Lord Tennyson (1809–92) British poet. *Idylls of the King*, 'The Marriage of Geraint'

20 The buck stops here.

Harry S. Truman (1884–1972) US statesman. Sign kept on his desk during his term as president. *Presidential Anecdotes* (P. Boller)

21 I don't know whether you fellows ever had a load of hay fall on you, but when they told me yesterday what had happened, I felt like the moon, the stars, and all the planets had fallen on me.

Harry S. Truman On succeeding Roosevelt as president. Attrib.

22 Every man who takes office in Washington either grows or swells, and when I give a man office I watch him carefully to see whether he is growing or swelling.

Woodrow Wilson (1856–1925) US statesman. Speech, 15 May 1916

23 In dreams begins responsibility.

W. B. Yeats (1865–1939) Irish poet. *Old Play, Epigraph, Responsibilities*

REST

See also bed, idleness, leisure, sleep

1 Will there be beds for me and all who seek?
Yea, beds for all who come.

Christina Rossetti (1830–74) British poet. *Up-Hill*

2 Unarm, Eros; the long day's task is done,
And we must sleep.

William Shakespeare (1564–1616) English dramatist. *Antony and Cleopatra*, IV:12

3 I enjoy convalescence. It is the part that makes the illness worth while.

George Bernard Shaw (1856–1950) Irish dramatist and critic. *Back to Methuselah*, Pt. II

4 It is well to lie fallow for a while.

Martin Farquhar Tupper (1810–89) British writer. *Proverbial Philosophy*, 'Of Recreation'

RESULTS

1 Desperate cuts must have desperate cures.

Proverb

2 The little bit (two inches wide) of ivory on which I work with so fine a brush as produces little effect after much labour.

Jane Austen (1775–1817) British novelist. Letter, 16 Dec 1816

3 Ye shall know them by their fruits. Do men gather grapes of thorns, or figs of thistles?
Even so every good tree bringeth forth good fruit; but a corrupt tree bringeth forth evil fruit.
A good tree cannot bring forth evil fruit, neither can a corrupt tree bring forth good fruit.
Every tree that bringeth not forth good fruit is hewn down, and cast into the fire.
Wherefore by their fruits ye shall know them.

Bible: Matthew 7:16–20

4 Our love of what is beautiful does not lead to extravagance; our love of the things of the mind does not make us soft.

Pericles (c. 495–429 BC) Greek statesman. Part of the funeral oration, 430 BC, for the dead of the first year of the Peloponnesian War. Attrib. in *Histories* Bk. II, Ch. 40 (Thucydides)

5 What dire offence from am'rous causes springs,
What mighty contests rise from trivial things.

Alexander Pope (1688–1744) British poet. *The Rape of the Lock*, I

RETRIBUTION

See also punishment, revenge

1 Give a thief enough rope and he'll hang himself.

Proverb

2 *Nemo me impune lacessit.*
No one provokes me with impunity.

Anonymous Motto of the Crown of Scotland

3 And if any mischief follow, then thou shalt give life for life,
Eye for eye, tooth for tooth, hand for hand, foot for foot,
Burning for burning, wound for wound, stripe for stripe.

Bible: Exodus 21:23–25

4 Be not deceived: God is not mocked: for whatsoever a man soweth, that shall he also reap.
For he that soweth to his flesh shall of the flesh reap corruption; but he that soweth to the Spirit shall of the Spirit reap life everlasting.
And let us not be weary in well doing: for in due season we shall reap, if we faint not.

Bible: Galatians 6:7–9

5 For they have sown the wind, and they shall reap the whirlwind: it hath no stalk: the bud shall yield no meal: if so be it yield, the strangers shall swallow it up.

Bible: Hosea 8:7

6 For I say unto you, That except your righteousness shall exceed the righteousness of the scribes and Pharisees, ye shall in no case enter into the kingdom of heaven.

Bible: Matthew 5:20

7 And if thy right eye offend thee, pluck it out, and cast it from thee: for it is profitable for thee that one of thy members should perish, and not that thy whole body should be cast into hell.

Bible: Matthew 5:29

8 For thou shalt heap coals of fire upon his head, and the Lord shall reward thee.

Bible: Proverbs 25:22

9 But men never violate the laws of God without suffering the consequences, sooner or later.

Lydia M. Child (1802–80) US abolitionist campaigner. *The Freedmen's Book*, 'Toussaint L'Ouverture'

10 The Germans, if this Government is returned, are going to pay every penny; they are going to be squeezed, as a lemon is squeezed – until the pips squeak. My only doubt is not whether we can squeeze hard enough, but whether there is enough juice.

Eric Campbell Geddes (1875–1937) British politician. Speech, Cambridge, 10 Dec 1918

RETURN

1 Winston's back.

Anonymous Signal to all ships of the Royal Navy from the Admiralty when Churchill was reappointed First Sea Lord, 3 Sept 1939.

2 Poor wandering one!
Though thou hast surely strayed,
Take heart of grace,
Thy steps retrace,
Poor wandering one!

W. S. Gilbert (1836–1911) British dramatist. *The Pirates of Penzance*, I

3 Ten o'clock…and back he'll come. I can just see him.
With vine leaves in his hair. Flushed and confident.

Henrik Ibsen (1828–1906) Norwegian dramatist. *Hedda Gabler*, II

4 Better lo'ed ye canna be,
Will ye no come back again?

Carolina Nairne (1766–1845) Scottish songwriter. Referring to Bonnie Prince Charlie. *Bonnie Charlie's now awa!*

REVENGE

See also retribution

1 Don't cut off your nose to spite your face.

Proverb

2 Revenge is a dish that tastes better cold.

Proverb

3 Revenge is sweet.

Proverb

4 And the Lord said unto him, Therefore whosoever slayeth Cain, vengeance shall be taken on him sevenfold. And the Lord set a mark upon Cain, lest any finding him should kill him.
And Cain went out from the presence of the Lord, and dwelt in the land of Nod, on the east of Eden.

Bible: Genesis 4:15–16

5 But I say unto you, That ye resist not evil; but whosoever shall smite thee on thy right cheek, turn to him the other also.

Bible: Matthew 5:39 *See also* HOLMES; KHRUSCHEV.

6 Revenge is a kind of wild justice; which the more man's nature runs to, the more ought law to weed it out.

Francis Bacon (1561–1626) English philosopher. *Essays*, 'Of Revenge'

7 A man that studieth revenge keeps his own wounds green.

Francis Bacon *Essays*, 'Of Revenge'

8 Perish the Universe, provided I have my revenge.

Cyrano de Bergerac (1619–55) French writer. *La Mort d'Agrippine*, IV

9 I make war on the living, not on the dead.

Charles V (1500–58) Holy Roman Emperor. After the death of the leader of the Protestant Reformation, Martin Luther, when it was suggested that he hang the corpse on a gallows. Attrib.

10 Rome shall perish – write that word
In the blood that she has spilt.

William Cowper (1731–1800) British poet. *Boadicea*

11 Wisdom has taught us to be calm and meek,
To take one blow, and turn the other cheek;
It is not written what a man shall do
If the rude caitiff smite the other too!

Oliver Wendell Holmes (1809–94) US writer. *Non-Resistance*

12 No one delights more in vengeance than a woman.

Juvenal (Decimus Junius Juvenalis; 60–130 AD) Roman satirist. *Satires*, XIII

13 Don't get mad, get even.

Joseph P. Kennedy (1888–1969) US politician; father of President Kennedy. *Conversations with Kennedy* (B. Bradlee)

14 We had no use for the policy of the Gospels: if someone slaps you, just turn the other cheek. We had shown that anyone who slapped us on our cheek would get his head kicked off.

Nikita Khrushchev (1894–1971) Soviet statesman. *Khrushchev Remembers*, Vol. II

15 Revenge, at first though sweet,
Bitter ere long back on itself recoils.

John Milton (1608–74) English poet. *Paradise Lost*, Bk. IX

16 Revenge his foul and most unnatural murder.

William Shakespeare (1564–1616) English dramatist. *Hamlet*, I:5

17 Set you down this;
And say besides, that in Aleppo once,
Where a malignant and a turban'd Turk
Beat a Venetian and traduc'd the state,
I took by the throat the circumcised dog,
And smote him thus.

William Shakespeare *Othello*, V:2

18 I do begin to have bloody thoughts.

William Shakespeare *The Tempest*, IV:1

19 I'll be revenged on the whole pack of you.

William Shakespeare *Twelfth Night*, V:1

20 No more tears now; I will think upon revenge.

Mary Stuart (1542–87) Queen of Scots. Remark on hearing of the murder (9 Mar 1566) of her secretary, David Riccio, by her husband, Lord Darnley

21 Those who offend us are generally punished for the offence they give; but we so frequently miss the satisfaction of knowing that we are avenged!

Anthony Trollope (1815–82) British novelist. *The Small House at Allington*, Ch. 50

REVOLUTION

See also French Revolution, rebellion, Russian Revolution

1 Inferiors revolt in order that they may be equal and equals that they may be superior. Such is the state of mind which creates revolutions.

Aristotle (384–322 BC) Greek philosopher. *Politics*, Bk. V

2 One of the strangest catastrophes that is in any history. A great king, with strong armies and mighty fleets, a great treasure and powerful allies, fell all at once, and his whole strength, like a spider's web, was...irrecoverably broken at a touch.

Gilbert Burnet (1643–1715) English bishop and historian. Referring to the Glorious Revolution, 1688. *History of My Own Times*

3 All modern revolutions have ended in a reinforcement of the power of the State.

Albert Camus (1913–60) French existentialist writer. *The Rebel*

4 A revolution is not a bed of roses. A revolution is a struggle to the death between the future and the past.

Fidel Castro (1926–) Cuban statesman. Speech, Havana, Jan 1961 (2nd anniversary of the Cuban Revolution)

5 The uprising of the masses implies a fabulous increase of vital possibilities; quite the contrary of what we hear so often about the decadence of Europe.

José Ortega y Gasset (1883–1955) Spanish philosopher. *The Revolt of the Masses*, Ch. 2

6 Revolution is not the uprising against pre-existing order, but the setting-up of a new order contradictory to the traditional one.

José Ortega y Gasset *The Revolt of the Masses*, Ch. 6

7 I believe in the armed struggle as the only solution for those people who fight to free themselves, and I am consistent with my beliefs. Many will call me an adventurer – and that I am, only one of a different sort: one of those who risks his skin to prove his platitudes.

Che Guevara (Ernesto G.; 1928–67) Argentine-born revolutionary. On leaving Cuba to join guerrillas in the Bolivian jungle. Last letter to his parents, 1965

8 What is wrong with a revolution is that it is natural. It is as natural as natural selection, as devastating as natural selection, and as horrible.

William Golding (1911–93) British novelist. *The Observer*, 'Sayings of the Year', 1974

9 'Liberty Mr Gumboil?' he said, 'you don't suppose any serious minded person imagines a revolution is going to bring liberty do you?'

Aldous Huxley (1894–1964) British novelist. *Antic Hay*

10 Revolution is delightful in the preliminary stages. So long as it's a question of getting rid of the people at the top.

Aldous Huxley *Eyeless in Gaza*

11 We are dancing on a volcano.

Comte de Salvandy (1795–1856) French nobleman. A remark made before the July Revolution in 1830.

12 To attempt to export revolution is nonsense.

Joseph Stalin (J. Dzhugashvili; 1879–1953) Soviet statesman. Remark, 1 Mar 1936, to Roy Howard (US newspaper owner)

13 Insurrection is an art, and like all arts it has its laws.

Leon Trotsky (Lev Davidovich Bronstein; 1879–1940) Russian revolutionary. *History of the Russian Revolution*, Pt. III, Ch. 6

14 Revolutions are always verbose.

Leon Trotsky *History of the Russian Revolution*, Pt. II, Ch. 12

15 The fundamental premise of a revolution is that the existing social structure has become incapable of solving the urgent problems of development of the nation.

Leon Trotsky *History of the Russian Revolution*, Pt. III, Ch. 6

16 Revolution by its very nature is sometimes compelled to take in more territory than it is capable of holding. Retreats are possible – when there is territory to retreat from.

Leon Trotsky *Diary in Exile*, 15 Feb 1935

17 The word 'revolution' is a word for which you kill, for which you die, for which you send the labouring masses to their death, but which does not possess any content.

Simone Weil (1909–43) French philosopher. *Oppression and Liberty*, 'Reflections Concerning the Causes of Liberty and Social Oppression'

18 We invented the Revolution
but we don't know how to run it.

Peter Weiss (1916–82) German novelist and dramatist. *Marat/Sade*, 15

19 Where the populace rise at once against the never-ending audacity of elected persons.

Walt Whitman (1819–92) US poet. *Song of the Broad Axe*, 5

RHODES, CECIL JOHN

(1853–1902) South African financier and statesman. Prime minister of Cape Colony (1890–96), he helped to found Rhodesia, which was named in his honour.

1 The real fact is that I could no longer stand their eternal cold mutton.

Explaining why he had left his friends in England and come to South Africa. *Cecil Rhodes* (G. le Sueur)

2 Remember that you are an Englishman, and have consequently won first prize in the lottery of life.

Dear Me (Peter Ustinov), Ch. 4

3 How can I possibly dislike a sex to which Your Majesty belongs?

Replying to Queen Victoria's suggestion that he disliked women. *Rhodes* (Lockhart)

4 So little done, so much to do.

Last words

RHYS, JEAN

(c. 1890–1979) Dominican-born British novelist. Her books include *Voyage in the Dark* (1934), *Good Morning, Midnight* (1939), and *The Wide Sargasso Sea* (1966).

1 Next week, or next month, or next year I'll kill myself. But I might as well last out my month's rent, which has been paid up, and my credit for breakfast in the morning.

Good Morning, Midnight, Pt. II

2 I often want to cry. That is the only advantage women have over men – at least they can cry.

Good Morning, Midnight, Pt. II

3 The feeling of Sunday is the same everywhere, heavy, melancholy, standing still. Like when they say, 'As it was in the beginning, is now, and ever shall be, world without end.'
Voyage in the Dark, Ch. 4

RIDICULE

See also contempt, satire

1 For what do we live, but to make sport for our neighbours, and laugh at them in our turn?
Jane Austen (1775–1817) British novelist. *Pride and Prejudice*, Ch. 57

2 Few women care to be laughed at and men not at all, except for large sums of money.
Alan Ayckbourn (1939–) British dramatist. *The Norman Conquests*, Preface

3 It often happens, that he who endeavours to ridicule other people, especially in things of a serious nature, becomes himself a jest, and frequently to his great cost.
Giovanni Boccaccio (1313–75) Italian writer and poet. *Decameron*, 'Second Day'

4 Ridicule often checks what is absurd, and fully as often smothers that which is noble.
Walter Scott (1771–1832) Scottish novelist. *Quentin Durward*

RIGHT

1 This the grave of Mike O'Day
Who died maintaining his right of way.
His right was clear, his will was strong.
But he's just as dead as if he'd been wrong.
Anonymous Epitaph

2 A child becomes an adult when he realizes that he has a right not only to be right but also to be wrong.
Thomas Szasz (1920–) US psychiatrist. *The Second Sin*

3 While I'd rather be right than president, at any time I'm ready to be both.
Norman M. Thomas (1884–1968) US politician. Referring to his lack of success in presidential campaigns. The expression 'I'd rather be right than president' is also attributed to the US politician Henry Clay (1777–1852). *Come to Judgment* (A. Whitman)

4 Right is more precious than peace.
Woodrow Wilson (1856–1925) US statesman. *Radio Times*, 10 Sept 1964

RIGHTEOUSNESS

See also good, integrity, morality, virtue

1 The eternal *not ourselves* that makes for righteousness.
Matthew Arnold (1822–88) British poet and critic. *Literature and Dogma*, Ch. 8

2 Righteous people terrify me…Virtue is its own punishment.
Aneurin Bevan (1897–1960) British Labour politician. *Aneurin Bevan 1897–1945* (Michael Foot)

3 Neither do men light a candle, and put it under a bushel, but on a candlestick; and it giveth light unto all that are in the house.
Let your light so shine before men, that they may see your good works, and glorify your Father which is in heaven.
Bible: Matthew 5:15–16

4 And I saw heaven opened, and behold a white horse; and he that sat upon him was called Faithful and True, and in righteousness he doth judge and make war.
Bible: Revelations 19:11

5 Ye must leave righteous ways behind, not to speak of unrighteous ways.
Buddha (Gautama Siddhartha; c. 563–c. 483 BC) Indian religious teacher. *Some Sayings of the Buddha* (F. L. Woodward)

6 The man of life upright,
Whose guiltless heart is free
From all dishonest deeds
Or thought of vanity.
Thomas Campion (1567–1620) English poet. *The Man of Life Upright*

7 Good thoughts his only friends,
His wealth a well-spent age,
The earth his sober inn
And quiet pilgrimage.
Thomas Campion *The Man of Life Upright*

8 Perhaps it is better to be irresponsible and right than to be responsible and wrong.
Winston Churchill (1874–1965) British statesman. Party Political Broadcast, London, 26 Aug 1950

9 Looks the whole world in the face,
For he owes not any man.
Henry Wadsworth Longfellow (1807–82) US poet. *The Village Blacksmith*

10 Live among men as if God beheld you; speak to God as if men were listening.
Seneca (c. 4 BC–65 AD) Roman author. *Epistles*

RILKE, RAINER MARIA

(1875–1926) Austrian poet. His collections include *Das Stunden Buch* (1905), *Duineser Elegien* (1923), and *Die Sonette an Orpheus* (1923).

1 Spring has returned. The earth is like a child that knows poems.
Die Sonette an Orpheus, I, 21

2 The machine threatens all achievement.
Die Sonette an Orpheus, II, 10

3 The hero is strangely akin to those who die young.
Duineser Elegien, VI

4 Stuck with placards for 'Deathless', that bitter beer that tastes sweet to its drinkers.
Duineser Elegien, X

5 I never read anything concerning my work. I feel that criticism is a letter to the public which the author, since it is not directed to him, does not have to open and read.
Letters

RIVERS

1 I have seen the Mississippi. That is muddy water. I have seen the St Lawrence. That is crystal water. But the Thames is liquid history.

John Burns (1858–1943) British Labour politician. Attrib.

2 Ol' man river, dat ol' man river,
He must know sumpin', but don't say nothin',
He just keeps rollin', he keeps on rollin' along.

Oscar Hammerstein (1895–1960) US lyricist. From the musical *Show Boat*. 'Ol' Man River'

3 What is there to make so much of in the Thames? I am quite tired of it. Flow, flow, flow, always the same.

Duke of Queensberry (1724–1810) British peer. *Century of Anecdote* (J. Timbs)

4 *Die Wacht am Rhein.*
The Watch on the Rhine.

Max Schneckenburger (1819–49) German poet. Song title

5 Sweet Thames! run softly, till I end my Song.

Edmund Spenser (1552–99) English poet. *Prothalamion*, 18

6 I come from haunts of coot and hern,
I make a sudden sally
And sparkle out among the fern,
To bicker down a valley.

Alfred, Lord Tennyson (1809–92) British poet. *The Brook*

ROCHEFOUCAULD, FRANCOIS, DUC DE LA

(1613–80) French writer. His literary circle included Mme de Sévigné and the Comtesse de La Fayette. He is best known for his *Maximes*, published in five editions between 1665 and 1678.

1 Self-love is the greatest of all flatterers.

Maximes, 2

2 We are all strong enough to bear the misfortunes of others.

Maximes, 19

3 We need greater virtues to sustain good fortune than bad.

Maximes, 25

4 If we had no faults of our own, we would not take so much pleasure in noticing those of others.

Maximes, 31

5 Self-interest speaks all sorts of tongues, and plays all sorts of roles, even that of disinterestedness.

Maximes, 39

6 We are never so happy nor so unhappy as we imagine.

Maximes, 49

7 To succeed in the world, we do everything we can to appear successful.

Maximes, 50

8 There are very few people who are not ashamed of having been in love when they no longer love each other.

Maximes, 71

9 If one judges love by its visible effects, it looks more like hatred than like friendship.

Maximes, 72

10 The love of justice in most men is simply the fear of suffering injustice.

Maximes, 78

11 Silence is the best tactic for him who distrusts himself.

Maximes, 79

12 It is more shameful to distrust one's friends than to be deceived by them.

Maximes, 84

13 Everyone complains of his memory, but no one complains of his judgement.

Maximes, 89

14 In the misfortune of our best friends, we always find something which is not displeasing to us.

Maximes, 99

15 The intellect is always fooled by the heart.

Maximes, 102

16 One gives nothing so freely as advice.

Maximes, 110

17 One had rather malign oneself than not speak of oneself at all.

Maximes, 138

18 To refuse praise reveals a desire to be praised twice over.

Maximes, 149

19 Hypocrisy is the homage paid by vice to virtue.

Maximes, 218

20 The height of cleverness is to be able to conceal it.

Maximes, 245

21 There is scarcely a single man sufficiently aware to know all the evil he does.

Maximes, 269

22 We only confess our little faults to persuade people that we have no large ones.

Maximes, 327

23 The accent of one's birthplace lingers in the mind and in the heart as it does in one's speech.

Maximes, 342

24 We seldom attribute common sense except to those who agree with us.

Maximes, 347

25 Nothing prevents us from being natural so much as the desire to appear so.

Maximes, 431

26 Quarrels would not last so long if the fault were on only one side.

Maximes, 496

27 Most usually our virtues are only vices in disguise.

Maximes, added to the 4th edition

ROGERS, WILL

(1879–1935) US actor and humorist. He starred in many films and contributed daily articles to *The New York Times* (from 1926). He also wrote several books.

1 You can't say civilization don't advance, however, for in every war they kill you a new way.
Autobiography, Ch. 12

2 England elects a Labour Government. When a man goes in for politics over here, he has no time to labour, and any man that labours has no time to fool with politics. Over there politics is an obligation; over here it's a business.
Autobiography, Ch. 14

3 Communism is like prohibition, it's a good idea but it won't work.
Autobiography, Nov 1927

4 Everything is funny, as long as it's happening to somebody else.
The Illiterate Digest

5 Being a hero is about the shortest-lived profession on earth.
Saturday Review, 'A Rogers Thesaurus', 25 Aug 1962

6 Coolidge is a better example of evolution than either Bryan or Darrow, for he knows when not to talk, which is the biggest asset the monkey possesses over the human.
Referring to three US politicians. *Saturday Review*, 'A Rogers Thesaurus', 25 Aug 1962

7 I don't make jokes – I just watch the government and report the facts.
Saturday Review, 'A Rogers Thesaurus', 25 Aug 1962

8 It has made more liars out of the American people than Golf.
Referring to income tax. *Saturday Review*, 'A Rogers Thesaurus', 25 Aug 1962

9 The more you read and observe about this politics thing, you got to admit that each party is worse than the other.
Saturday Review, 'A Rogers Thesaurus', 25 Aug 1962

10 A comedian can only last till he either takes himself serious or his audience takes him serious.
Newspaper article, 1931

11 See what will happen to you if you don't stop biting your fingernails.
Message written on a postcard of the Venus de Milo that he sent to his young niece.

12 So live that you wouldn't be ashamed to sell the family parrot to the town gossip.
Attrib.

ROOSEVELT, FRANKLIN D.

(1882–1945) US Democratic president. Although partially paralysed by polio (from 1921), he was re-elected three times and became an effective war leader.

Quotations about F. D. Roosevelt

1 A chameleon on plaid.
Herbert Hoover (1874–1964) US statesman. Attrib.

2 The man who started more creations since Genesis – and finished none.
Hugh Johnson. Attrib.

Quotations by F. D. Roosevelt

3 I murdered my grandmother this morning.
His habitual greeting to any guest at the White House he suspected of paying no attention to what he said. *Ear on Washington* (D. McClellan)

4 It is fun to be in the same decade with you.
After Churchill had congratulated him on his 60th birthday. *The Hinge of Fate* (Winston S. Churchill), Ch. 4

5 Stalin hates the guts of all your top people. He thinks he likes me better, and I hope he will continue to do so.
The Hinge of Fate (Winston S. Churchill), Ch. 11

6 Defeat of Germany means the defeat of Japan, probably without firing a shot or losing a life.
The Hinge of Fate (Winston S. Churchill), Ch. 25

7 The best immediate defence of the United States is the success of Great Britain defending itself.
At press conference, 17 Dec 1940. *Their Finest Hour* (Winston S. Churchill), Ch. 28

8 The forgotten man at the bottom of the economic pyramid.
Speech on radio, 7 Apr 1932

9 I pledge you, I pledge myself, to a new deal for the American people.
Speech accepting nomination for presidency, Chicago, 2 July 1932

10 Let me assert my firm belief that the only thing we have to fear is fear itself.
First Inaugural Address, 4 Mar 1933

11 In the field of world policy; I would dedicate this nation to the policy of the good neighbor.
First Inaugural Address, 4 Mar 1933

12 A radical is a man with both feet firmly planted in air.
Broadcast, 26 Oct 1939

13 We must be the great arsenal of democracy.
Broadcast address to Forum on Current Problems, 29 Dec 1940

14 We look forward to a world founded upon four essential human freedoms. The first is freedom of speech and expression – everywhere in the world. The second is freedom of every person to worship God in his own way – everywhere in the world. The third is freedom from want...everywhere in the world. The fourth is freedom from fear...anywhere in the world.
Speech to Congress, 6 Jan 1941

15 Never before have we had so little time in which to do so much.
Radio address, 23 Feb 1942

16 We all know that books burn – yet we have the greater knowledge that books cannot be killed by fire. People die, but books never die. No man and no force can abolish memory...In this war, we know, books are weapons.
Message to American Booksellers Association, 6 May 1942

17 More than an end of this war, an end to the beginnings of all wars.

Speech broadcast on the day after his death (13 Apr 1945)

ROOSEVELT, THEODORE

(1858–1919) US Republican president. His presidency (1901–09) is remembered for his Square Deal programme for social reform and the construction of the Panama Canal.

Quotations about Theodore Roosevelt

1 I always enjoy his society, he is so hearty, so straightforward, outspoken and, for the moment, so absolutely sincere.

Mark Twain (Samuel Langhorne Clemens; 1835–1910) US writer. *Autobiography*

2 Father always wanted to be the bride at every wedding and the corpse at every funeral.

Nicholas Roosevelt *A Front Row Seat*

Quotations by Theodore Roosevelt

3 No man is justified in doing evil on the ground of expediency.

The Strenuous Life

4 Kings and such like are just as funny as politicians.

Mr Wilson's War (John Dos Passos), Ch. 1

5 A man who will steal *for* me will steal *from* me.

Firing a cowboy who had applied Roosevelt's brand to a steer belonging to a neighbouring ranch. *Roosevelt in the Bad Lands* (Herman Hagedorn)

6 I wish to preach, not the doctrine of ignoble ease, but the doctrine of the strenuous life.

Speech, Chicago, 10 Apr 1899

7 There is a homely adage which runs 'Speak softly and carry a big stick, you will go far'.

Speech, Minnesota State Fair, 2 Sept 1901

8 A man who is good enough to shed his blood for the country is good enough to be given a square deal afterwards. More than that no man is entitled to, and less than that no man shall have.

Speech at the Lincoln Monument, Springfield, Illinois, 4 June 1903

9 There is no room in this country for hyphenated Americanism.

Speech, New York, 12 Oct 1915

10 There can be no fifty-fifty Americanism in this country. There is room here for only one hundred per cent Americanism.

Speech, Saratoga, 19 July 1918

ROSSETTI, CHRISTINA

(1830–94) British poet and supporter of the Pre-Raphaelite Brotherhood founded by her brother, Dante Gabriel Rossetti. Her collections include *Goblin Market* (1862), *The Prince's Progress* (1866), and *New Poems* (1896). Twice refusing offers of marriage, she lived a solitary, sickly, and religious life.

1 Come to me in the silence of the night;
Come in the speaking silence of a dream;
Come with soft rounded cheeks and eyes as bright
As sunlight on a stream;
Come back in tears,
O memory, hope, love of finished years.

Echo

2 For there is no friend like a sister
In calm or stormy weather;
To cheer one on the tedious way,
To fetch one if one goes astray,
To lift one if one totters down,
To strengthen whilst one stands.

Goblin Market

3 In the bleak mid-winter
Frosty wind made moan,
Earth stood hard as iron,
Water like a stone;
Snow had fallen, snow on snow,
Snow on snow,
In the bleak mid-winter,
Long ago.

Mid-Winter

4 Remember me when I am gone away,
Gone far away into the silent land.

Remember

5 Better by far you should forget and smile
Than that you should remember and be sad.

Remember

6 Does the road wind up-hill all the way?
Yes, to the very end.
Will the day's journey take the whole long day?
From morn to night, my friend.

Up-Hill

7 Will there be beds for me and all who seek?
Yea, beds for all who come.

Up-Hill

8 When I am dead, my dearest,
Sing no sad songs for me;
Plant thou no roses at my head,
Nor shady cypress tree:
Be the green grass above me
With showers and dewdrops wet;
And if thou wilt, remember,
And if thou wilt, forget.

When I am Dead

9 Who has seen the wind?
Neither you nor I:
But when the trees bow down their heads,
The wind is passing by.

Who Has Seen the Wind?

ROSSETTI, DANTE GABRIEL

(1828–82) British painter and poet. With Millais and Holman Hunt he founded the Pre-Raphaelite Brotherhood. His poetic works include *Poems* (1870) and *Ballads and Sonnets* (1881).

1 The blessèd damozel leaned out
From the gold bar of Heaven;
Her eyes were deeper than the depth
Of waters stilled at even;
She had three lilies in her hand,
And the stars in her hair were seven.

The Blessèd Damozel

2 A sonnet is a moment's monument, –
Memorial from the Soul's eternity
To one dead deathless hour.

The House of Life, Introduction

3 Look in my face; my name is Might-have-been.
I am also called No-more, Too-late, Farewell.

The House of Life, 'A Superscription'

4 I have been here before.
But when or how I cannot tell:
I know the grass beyond the door,
The sweet keen smell,
The sighing sound, the lights around the shore.

Sudden Light

5 The Stealthy School of Criticism.

Letter to the *Athenaeum*, 1871.

ROUSSEAU, JEAN JACQUES

(1712–78) French philosopher and writer. His most influential work was *Du Contrat social* (1762). Other works include *La Nouvelle Héloise* (1760) and *Émile* (1762).

1 Man was born free and everywhere he is in chains.

Du Contrat social, Ch. 1

2 He who pretends to look on death without fear lies. All men are afraid of dying, this is the great law of sentient beings, without which the entire human species would soon be destroyed.

Julie, ou la nouvelle Héloise

3 Everything is good when it leaves the Creator's hands; everything degenerates in the hands of man.

Attrib.

ROYALTY

See also monarchy

1 Be the Emperor, be Peter the Great, John the Terrible, the Emperor Paul – crush them all under you – Now don't you laugh, naughty one – but I long to see you so with those men who try to govern *you* and it must be the contrary.

Alexandra (1872–1918) Empress-Consort of Russia. Letter (in English) to Nicholas II, 27 Dec 1916

2 The personality conveyed by the utterances which are put into her mouth is that of a priggish schoolgirl, captain of the hockey team, a prefect, and a recent candidate for confirmation. It is not thus that she will be able to come into her own as an independent and distinctive character.

Lord Altrincham (John Grigg; 1924–) British writer. Referring to Queen Elizabeth II. *National and English Review*, Aug 1958

3 Your experience will be a lesson to all of us men to be careful not to marry ladies in very high positions.

Idi Amin (1925–) Ugandan soldier and president. Message to Lord Snowdon, on the break-up of his marriage to Princess Margaret. *International Gossip* (A. Barrow)

4 Bloody hell, Ma'am, what's he doing here?

Elizabeth Andrews Royal chambermaid. Discovering an intruder sitting on Queen Elizabeth II's bed. *Daily Mail*, July 1982

5 There is no romance between us. He is here solely to exercise the horses.

Anne (1950–) The Princess Royal, only daughter of Elizabeth II. Shortly before her engagement to Captain Phillips. Attrib.

6 One was presented with a small, hairy individual and, out of general curiosity, one climbed on.

Anne Referring to her first horse ride. *Princess Anne and Mark Phillips Talking Horses with Genevieve Murphy*

7 It's a very boring time. I am not particularly maternal – it's an occupational hazard of being a wife.

Anne TV interview, talking about pregnancy. *Daily Express*, 14 Apr 1981

8 Why don't you naff off!

Anne To reporters. *Daily Mirror*, 17 Apr 1982

9 The King over the Water.

Anonymous Jacobite toast

10 How different, how very different from the home life of our own dear Queen!

Anonymous Remark about the character of Cleopatra as performed by Sarah Bernhardt. It refers to Queen Victoria.

11 Here lies Fred,
Who was alive and is dead:
Had it been his father,
I had much rather;
Had it been his brother,
Still better than another;
Had it been his sister,
No one would have missed her;
Had it been the whole generation,
Still better for the nation:
But since 'tis only Fred,
Who was alive and is dead, –
There's no more to be said.

Anonymous Referring to Frederick, Prince of Wales, eldest son of George II and father of George III. *Memoirs of George II* (Horace Walpole)

12 ...his lieges who from their hearts entirely thank God who has given them such a lord and governor, who has delivered them from servitude to other lands and from the charges sustained by them in times past.

Anonymous A tribute by the Commons to Edward III. *Rotuli Parliamentorum*, Vol. II

13 It was not, as our enemies say, our intention to kill the king and his sons, but to make him the duke of Lancaster, which is what he ought to be.

Anonymous Referring to Henry IV; said by one of the Franciscans condemned for plotting (1402) to overthrow him. *Eulogium Historiarum*

14 In Hide Park he rides like a hog in armour,
In Whitehall he creeps like a country farmer,
Old England may boast of a godly reformer;
A dainty fine king indeed.

Anonymous Referring to William III, known as William of Orange because of his Dutch descent. *The Faber Book of English History in Verse* (Kenneth Baker)

15 Good People come buy
The Fruit that I cry,
That now is in Season, tho' Winter is nigh;

'Twill do you all good
And sweeten your Blood,
I'm sure it will please when you've once understood
'tis an *Orange*.

Anonymous Referring to William III, known as William of Orange because of his Dutch descent. *The Faber Book of English History in Verse* (Kenneth Baker)

16 Lost or strayed out of this house, a man who left a wife and six children on the parish; whoever will give any tidings of him to the churchwardens of St. James's Parish, so he may be got again, shall receive four shillings and sixpence. N.B. This reward will not be increased, nobody judging him to deserve a Crown.

Anonymous Referring to George II, whose frequent absences in Hanover made him unpopular. Notice posted on the gate of St. James's Palace

17 My Lord Archbishop, what a scold you are
And when a man is down, how bold you are,
Of Christian charity how scant you are
You auld Lang Swine, how full of cant you are!

Anonymous Archbishop Lang was one of the chief opponents of Edward VIII's marriage to Mrs Wallis Simpson. *The Faber Book of English History in Verse* (Kenneth Baker)

18 Hark the herald angels sing
Mrs Simpson's pinched our king.

Anonymous Referring to the abdication of Edward VIII.

19 We shall not pretend that there is nothing in his long career which those who respect and admire him would wish otherwise.

Anonymous On the accession of King Edward VII, referring to his wild lifestyle as Prince of Wales. *The Times*, Jan 1901

20 The King told me he would never have died if it had not been for that fool Dawson of Penn.

Margot Asquith (1865–1945) The second wife of Herbert Asquith. Referring to Lord Dawson of Penn. *George V* (K. Rose)

21 George, be a King.

Augusta of Saxe-Gotha, Princess of Wales (1719–72) Mother of King George III. Attrib.

22 The house is well, but it is you, Your Majesty, who have made me too great for my house.

Francis Bacon (1561–1626) English philosopher. Reply when Elizabeth I remarked on the smallness of his house. *After-dinner Stories and Anecdotes* (L. Meissen)

23 Throughout the greater part of his life George III was a kind of 'consecrated obstruction'.

Walter Bagehot (1826–1877) British economist and journalist. *The English Constitution*, 'The Monarchy'

24 Our cock won't fight.

Lord Beaverbrook (Maxwell Aitken; 1879–1964) Canadian-born politician and newspaper proprietor. To Winston Churchill referring to Edward VIII during the abdication crisis. *Edward VIII* (F. Donaldson)

25 So whether it is that the King, misled
By flattering talk to giving his consent,
And truly ignorant of their designs
Unknowingly approves such wrongs as these
Whose only end can be destruction, and
The ruin of his land; or whether he,
With malice in his heart, and ill-intent,
Commits these shameful crimes by raising up
His royal state and power far beyond
The reach of all his country's laws, so that
His whim is satisfied by the abuse
Of royal privilege and strength; if thus
Or otherwise this land of ours is brought
To total rack and ruin, and at last
The kingdom is left destitute, it is
The duty of the great and noble men
To rescue it, to purge the land of all
Corruption and all false authority.

Roger de Berksted Referring to the civil war between Henry III and his barons. *The Song of Lewes*

26 The benefit of the King's Coronation depends under God upon…the faith, prayer and self-dedication of the King himself…We hope that he is aware of this need. Some of us wish that he gave more positive signs of such awareness.

Alfred Blunt (1879–1957) British bishop. Referring to Edward VIII shortly before the abdication crisis. Address to diocesan conference, 1 Dec 1936

27 Speed, bonny boat, like a bird on the wing;
'Onward', the sailors cry;
Carry the lad that's born to be king
Over the sea to Skye.

H. E. Boulton (1859–1935) Scottish songwriter. Referring to Bonnie Prince Charlie. *Skye Boat Song*

28 It is neither fitting nor safe that all the keys should hang from the belt of one woman.

Thomas Brinton (c. 1320–89) Bishop of Rochester. Criticizing the influence of Alice Perrers over the ageing Edward III. Sermon, Westminister Abbey, 18 May 1376

29 Such grace had kings when the world begun!

Robert Browning (1812–89) British poet. *Pippa Passes*, Pt. I

30 Kings are naturally lovers of low company.

Edmund Burke (1729–97) British politician. *Speech on the Economical Reform* (House of Commons, 11 Feb 1780)

31 The Duke of Buckingham gave me once a short but severe character of the two brothers. It was the more severe, because it was true: the King (he said) could see things if he would, and the Duke would see things if he could.

Gilbert Burnet (1643–1715) English bishop and historian. Referring to Charles II and James II. *History of My Own Times*

32 …was apt to suffer things to run on till there was a great heap of papers laid before him, so then he signed them a little too precipitately.

Gilbert Burnet Referring to William III; his authorization of the Glencoe Massacre (1692) may have been one consequence of this habit. *History of My Own Times*

33 A better farmer ne'er brushed dew from lawn,
A worse king never left a realm undone!

Lord Byron (1788–1824) British poet. Referring to George III. *The Vision of Judgment*, VIII

34 …by putting her hand to her head, when the King of Scots was named to succeed her, they all knew he was the man she desired should reign after her.

Sir Robert Carey (c. 1560–1639) English courtier. Referring to the death of Elizabeth I and the succession of James VI of Scotland, who became James I of England and Ireland. *Memoirs*

35 I shall be an autocrat: that's my trade. And the good Lord will forgive me: that's his.

Catherine the Great (1729–96) Empress of Russia (1762–96). Attrib.

36 The sovereign is absolute; for, in a state whose expanse is so vast, there can be no other appropriate authority except that which is concentrated in him.

Catherine the Great *Nakaz*

37 Conquering kings their titles take.

John Chandler (1806–76) British clergyman and writer. Poem title

38 Brother, I am too old to go again to my travels.

Charles II (1630–85) King of England. Referring to his exile, 1651–60. *History of Great Britain (Hume)*, Vol. II, Ch. 7

39 Retirement, for a monarch, is not a good idea.

Charles, Prince of Wales (1948–) Eldest son of Elizabeth II. Speech, 1974

40 The monarchy is the oldest profession in the world.

Charles, Prince of Wales Attrib.

41 The one advantage about marrying a princess – or someone from a royal family – is that they do know what happens.

Charles, Prince of Wales Attrib.

42 Yes, until it became clear that the marriage had irretrievably broken down.

Charles, Prince of Wales On being asked if he had been faithful to his wife. ITV programme *Charles: The Private Man, The Public Role*

43 One could forgive the fiend for becoming a torrent, but to become an earthquake was really too much.

Charles-Joseph, Prince de Ligne (1735–1814) Austrian diplomat. Referring to Napoleon I. Attrib.

44 His views and affections were singly confined to the narrow compass of the Electorate; England was too big for him.

Earl of Chesterfield (1694–1773) English statesman. Referring to George I. *Letters*

45 I still get teased mercilessly about the royal family. 'What d'you want to go hanging around with the Queen for?'...I could hardly refuse when Andrew and the Duchess asked me to dinner. I couldn't very well say: 'I can't come to dinner with you, I'm working class.'...Actually you're not invited, you're ordered.

Billy Connolly (1942–) Scottish comedian. *The Times*, 15 Dec 1990

46 My lord, if this be so, why did we take up arms at first? This is against fighting ever hereafter.

Oliver Cromwell (1599–1658) English soldier and statesman. Reply to the Earl of MANCHESTER. Remark

47 Most excellent Royall Majesty, of our *Elizabeth* (sitting at the *Helm* of this Imperial Monarchy: or rather, at the Helm of the Imperiall Ship).

John Dee (1527–1608) English mathematician and astrologer. *General and Rare Memorials pertaining to the Perfect Arte of Navigation*

48 Her Majesty is not a subject.

Benjamin Disraeli (1804–81) British statesman. Responding to Gladstone's taunt that Disraeli could make a joke out of any subject, including Queen Victoria. Attrib.

49 The courtiers who surrounded him have forgotten nothing and learnt nothing.

Charles-François Dumouriez (1739–1823) French general. Referring to Louis XVIII. This remark is also attributed to the French statesman Talleyrand. Attrib.

50 Royalty must think the whole country always smells of fresh paint.

Elizabeth Dunn *The Sunday Times*

51 There's this myth that the Royal Family is worth £6 billion. It's madness...where is it all, that's what I'd like to know.

Prince Edward (1964–) Youngest son of Elizabeth II. *The Sun*, 1993

52 ...the king of France, hardened in his malice, would assent to no peace or treaty, but called together his strong host to take into his hand the duchy of Aquitaine, declaring against all truth that it was forfeit to him.

Edward III (1312–77) King of England. Proclamation on the outbreak of the Hundred Years War. *Foedera* (ed. T. Rymer), Vol. IV

53 I know I have the body of a weak and feeble woman, but I have the heart and stomach of a King, and of a King of England too.

Elizabeth I (1533–1603) Queen of England. Speech at Tilbury on the approach of the Spanish Armada

54 Though God hath raised me high, yet this I count the glory of my crown: that I have reigned with your loves.

Elizabeth I *The Golden Speech*, 1601

55 I will make you shorter by a head.

Elizabeth I *Sayings of Queen Elizabeth* (Chamberlin)

56 The queen of Scots is this day leichter of a fair son, and I am but a barren stock.

Elizabeth I *Memoirs of Sir James Melville* (1549–93)

57 The daughter of debate, that eke discord doth sow.

Elizabeth I Referring to Mary Queen of Scots. *Sayings of Queen Elizabeth* (Chamberlin)

58 I will that a king succeed me, and who but my kinsman the king of Scots.

Elizabeth I Said shortly before she died, when pressed concerning the succession. She referred to James VI of Scotland, who became James I of England and Ireland. *The Reign of Elizabeth* (J. D. Black), Ch. 13

59 I should like to be a horse.

Elizabeth II (1926–) Queen of the United Kingdom. When asked about her ambitions when a child. Attrib.

60 I think that everyone will concede that – today of all days – I should begin by saying, 'My husband and I'.

Elizabeth II On her silver-wedding. The phrase, 'My husband and I,' is mistakenly associated with her through the humorous idea that this is the way in which she begins all her speeches. Speech, Guildhall, 1972

61 1992 is not a year I shall look back on with undiluted pleasure. In the words of one of my more sympathetic correspondents, it has turned out to be an 'annus horribilis'.

Elizabeth II Alluding to *Annus Mirabilis*, a poem by John Dryden.

62 In the midst stood Prince Henry, who showed already something of royalty in his demeanour, in which there was a certain dignity combined with singular courtesy.

Erasmus (1466–1536) Dutch humanist, scholar, and writer. Remark on first meeting the future Henry VIII

63 ...to long for and desire the landing of that Prince, whom they looked on as their deliverer from Popish tyranny, praying incessantly for an Easterly wind...

John Evelyn (1620–1706) English diarist. Referring to William of Orange who was invited to come from The Netherlands, as the Protestant husband of James II's daughter Mary and grandson of Charles I, to invade England to secure a Protestant succession. William III and Mary II ruled jointly from 1689. Diary, 6 Oct 1688

64 She came into Whitehall laughing and jolly, as to a wedding, so as to seem quite transported.

John Evelyn Referring to Mary II's arrival in London. Diary, 21 Feb 1689

65 Your peoples die of hunger. Agriculture is almost stationary, industry languishes everywhere, all commerce is destroyed...You relate everything to yourself as though you were God on earth.

François Fénelon (1651–1715) French writer and prelate. Letter to Louis XIV

66 A crown is merely a hat that lets the rain in.

Frederick the Great (1712–86) King of Prussia. Remark

67 The King of England changes his ministers as often as he changes his shirts.

Frederick the Great Referring to George III. Attrib.

68 After I am dead the boy will ruin himself in twelve months.

George V (1865–1936) King of the United Kingdom. Referring to the Prince of Wales, later Edward VIII; said to the politician Stanley Baldwin. Attrib.

69 We're not a family; we're a firm.

George VI (1895–1952) King of the United Kingdom. *Our Future King* (Peter Lane)

70 ...her face oblong, fair but wrinkled; her eyes small, yet black and pleasant; her nose a little hooked, her lips narrow and her teeth black (a defect the English seem subject to from their too great use of sugar)...She wore false hair and that red.

Paul Hentzner (fl. 1590s) German tutor. Referring to Elizabeth I. *Journey into England*

71 After all the stormy, tempestuous, and blustering windy weather of Queen Mary was overblown, the darksome clouds of discomfort dispersed, the palpable fogs and mist of the most intolerable misery consumed, and the dashing showers of persecution overpast: it pleased God to send England calm and quiet season, a clear and lovely sunshine, a quitsest from former broils of a turbulent estate, and a world of blessings by good Queen Elizabeth.

Raphael Holinshed (d. 1580) English chronicler. *Chronicles*

72 This delightful, blissful, wise, pleasurable, honourable, virtuous, true and immortal Prince was a violator of his word, a libertine over head and ears in debt and disgrace, and despiser of domestic ties, the companion of gamblers and demireps, a man who has just closed half a century without one single claim on the gratitude of his country or the respect of posterity.

Leigh Hunt (1784–1859) British poet. Referring to the Prince Regent. Hunt was imprisoned for two years for this libellous attack. *The Examiner*, 22 Mar 1812

73 A more virtuous man, I believe, does not exist, nor one who is more enthusiastically devoted to better the condition of mankind.

Thomas Jefferson (1743–1826) US statesman. Referring to Tsar Alexander I. Letter to William Duane, 20 July 1807

74 For, he said, albeit unworthy, he was a king's son and one of the greatest lords in the kingdom after the king: and what had been so evilly spoken of him could rightly be called plain treason...And if any man were so bold as to charge him with treason or other disloyalty or with anything prejudicial to the realm, he was ready to defend himself with his body as though he were the poorest bachelor in the land.

John of Gaunt (1340–99) Duke of Lancaster. Report of a speech to Richard II's first parliament. *Rotuli Parliamentorum*, Vol. III

75 George the First knew nothing, and desired to know nothing; did nothing, and desired to do nothing; and the only good thing that is told of him is, that he wished to restore the crown to its hereditary successor.

Samuel Johnson (1709–84) British lexicographer. *Life of Johnson* (J. Boswell)

76 I'm prepared to take advice on leisure from Prince Philip. He's a world expert on leisure. He's been practising for most of his adult life.

Neil Kinnock (1942–) British politician. *Western Mail*, 1981

77 Walk wide o' the Widow at Windsor,
For 'alf o' Creation she owns:
We have bought 'er the same with sword an' the flame,
An' we've salted it down with our bones.

Rudyard Kipling (1865–1936) Indian-born British writer. Referring to Queen Victoria. *The Widow at Windsor*

78 I don't mind your being killed, but I object to your being taken prisoner.

Lord Kitchener (1850–1916) British field marshal. Said to the Prince of Wales (later Edward VIII) when he asked to go to the Front. *Journal* (Viscount Esher), 18 Dec 1914

79 He contents the people where he goes best that ever did Prince, for many a poor man that hath suffered wrong many days has been relieved and helped by him.

Thomas Langton (c. 1440–1501) Bishop of St David's. Referring to Richard III. Remark

80 When it comes to culture, you'll find more on a month-old carton of yoghurt than between the ears of the Princess of Wales.

Richard Littlejohn *The Sun*, 1993

81 Ah, if I were not king, I should lose my temper.

Louis XIV (1638–1715) French king. Attrib.

82 Junker Henry means to be God and do as he pleases.

Martin Luther (1483–1546) German Protestant. Referring to Henry VIII's religious policy. *The Earlier Tudors* (J. D. Mackie)

83 ...this haughty, vigilant, resolute, sagacious blue-stocking, half Mithridates and half Trissotin, bearing up against a world in arms.

Lord Macaulay (1800–59) British historian. Referring to Frederick the Great. *Historical Essays*, 'Frederick the Great'

84 If we beat the King ninety and nine times yet he is King still, and so will his posterity be after him; but if the King beat us once we shall all be hanged, and our posterity made slaves.

Earl of Manchester (1602–71) English peer and soldier. For reply *see* CROMWELL. Remark

85 Well, Mr Baldwin! *this* is a pretty kettle of fish!

Queen Mary (1867–1953) Consort of George V. Referring to the abdication of Edward VIII. *Life of Queen Mary* (James Pope-Hennessy)

86 For God's sake, ma'am, let's have no more of that. If you get the English people into the way of making kings, you'll get them into the way of *un*making them.

Lord Melbourne (1779–1848) British statesman. Advising Queen Victoria against granting Prince Albert the title of King Consort. *Lord M.* (Lord David Cecil)

87 Of hearte couragious, politique in counsaile in adversitie nothynge abashed, in peace juste and mercifull, in warre sharpe and fyerce, in the fielde bolde and hardye and natheless no farther than wysedome woulde adventurouse. Whose warres whoso will consyder, hee shall no lesse commende hys wysedome where he voyded than hys mannehode where he vanquished. He was of visage louelye, of body myghtie, strong and cleane made.

Thomas More (1478–1535) English lawyer and scholar. Referring to Edward IV. *The Historie of Kyng Rychardе the Thirde*

88 The King has a way of making every man feel that he is enjoying his special favour, just as the London wives pray before the image of Our Lady by the Tower till each of them believes it is smiling upon her.

Thomas More Referring to Henry VIII. Letter to Bishop John Fisher, 1518

89 You can divide my life into two. During the first part of my life I was an ordinary conventional naval officer, trying not to be different in the sense of being royal trying not to show myself off as being rich and ostentatious – like always using a small car to drive to the dockyard instead of my Rolls Royce.

Louis Mountbatten of Burma (1900–79) British admiral and colonial administrator. *Mountbatten, Hero of Our Time*, Ch. 9 (Richard Hough)

90 Oh, my Erasmus, if you could see how all the world here is rejoicing in the possession of so great a prince, how his life is all their desire, you could not contain your tears for joy. The heavens laugh, the earth exults, all things are full of milk, of honey and of nectar! Avarice is expelled the country. Liberality scatters wealth with bounteous hand. Our king does not desire gold or gems or precious metals, but virtue, glory, immortality...The other day he wished he was more learned. I said, that is not what we expect of your Grace, but that you will foster and encourage learned men. Yea, surely, said he, for indeed without them we should scarcely exist at all.

Lord Mountjoy Referring to Henry VIII. Letter to Erasmus, 27 May 1509

91 Frumpish and banal.

Malcolm Muggeridge (1903–90) British writer. Referring to Queen Elizabeth II. Magazine article, Oct 1957

92 I shall maintain the principle of autocracy just as firmly and unflinchingly as it was upheld by my own ever to be remembered dead father.

Nicholas II (1868–1918) Tsar of Russia. Declaration to representatives of Tver, 17 Jan 1896

93 Our dear King James is good and honest, but the most incompetent man I have ever seen in my life. A child of seven years would not make such silly mistakes as he does.

Duchess of Orleans (1652–1722) Sister-in-law to Louis XIV. Referring to James II, who was in exile in France. Letter to the Electress Sophia, 6 June 1692

94 He will go from resort to resort getting more tanned and more tired.

Westbrook Pegler (1894–1969) US journalist. On the abdication of Edward VIII. *Six Men* (Alistair Cooke), Pt. II

95 I'm self-employed.

Prince Philip (1921–) The consort of Queen Elizabeth II. Answering a query as to what nature of work he did. Attrib.

96 I know of no one in the realm who would not more fitly to come to me than I to him.

Richard, Duke of York (1411–60) Father of Edward IV. Reply when asked, in parliament, whether he wished to go and see the king; York formally claimed the throne six days later. Remark, 10 Oct 1460

97 Not least among the qualities in a great King is a capacity to permit his ministers to serve him.

Cardinal Richelieu (1585–1642) French statesman. *Testament politique*, Maxims

98 To know how to dissimulate is the knowledge of kings.

Cardinal Richelieu. *Testament politique*, Maxims

99 A merry monarch, scandalous and poor.

Earl of Rochester (1647–80) English poet. Referring to Charles II. *A Satire on King Charles II*

100 Kings and such like are just as funny as politicians.

Theodore Roosevelt (1858–1919) US Republican president. *Mr Wilson's War* (John Dos Passos), Ch. 1

101 Royalty puts a human face on the operations of government.

Robert Runcie (1921–) British churchman; Archbishop of Canterbury (1980–91). Sermon for the 80th birthday of Elizabeth the Queen Mother

102 The sun does not set in my dominions.

Friedrich von Schiller (1759–1805) German dramatist. Said by Philip II. *Don Carlos*, I:6

103 Kings are earth's gods; in vice their law's their will.

William Shakespeare (1564–1616) English dramatist. *Pericles*, I:1

104 For God's sake let us sit upon the ground
And tell sad stories of the death of kings:
How some have been depos'd, some slain in war,
Some haunted by the ghosts they have depos'd,
Some poison'd by their wives, some sleeping kill'd,
All murder'd – for within the hollow crown
That rounds the mortal temples of a king
Keeps Death his court.

William Shakespeare *Richard II*, III:2

105 Ay, every inch a king.

William Shakespeare *King Lear*, IV:6

106 I would not be a queen
For all the world.

William Shakespeare *Henry VIII*, II:3

107 Albert was merely a young foreigner, who suffered from having no vices, and whose only claim to distinction was that he had happened to marry the Queen of England.

Lytton Strachey (1880–1932) British writer. *Queen Victoria*, Ch. 5

108 The king is incompetent to govern in person. Throughout his reign he has been controlled and governed by others who have given him evil counsel.

John de Stratford (d. 1348) Archbishop of Canterbury. Referring to Edward II. *Historiae Anglicanae Scriptores* (Twysden)

109 Authority forgets a dying king.

Alfred, Lord Tennyson (1809–92) British poet. *Idylls of the King*, 'The Passing of Arthur'

110 In this year King Edward of England made Lord Edward, his son and heir, Prince of Wales and Earl of Chester. When the Welsh heard this, they were overjoyed, thinking him their lawful master, as he was born in their lands.

Thomas of Walsingham (d. 1419) English monk and chronicler. Edward of Caernarfon, later Edward II, began the tradition that male heirs to the English throne were invested with these titles. *Historia Anglicana*

111 I'd punch him in the snoot.

William Hale 'Big Bill' Thompson (1867–1944) US politician and Mayor of Chicago. His reaction if ever King George V were to come to Chicago. Attrib.

112 He used towardes every men of highe and low degree more than mete famylyarytie which trade of life he never changed.

Polydore Vergil (c. 1470–c. 1555) Italian historian. Referring to Edward IV. *Anglica Historia*

113 We are not amused!

Victoria (1819–1901) Queen of the United Kingdom. Attrib.

114 I sat between the King and Queen. We left supper soon. My health was drunk. I then danced one more quadrille with Lord Paget.…I was *very* much amused.

Victoria Journal, 16 June 1833

115 It has none, your Highness. Its history dates from today.

James Whistler (1834–1903) US painter. Replying to a query from the Prince of Wales about the history of the Society of British Artists, which he was visiting for the first time. *Whistler Stories* (D. Seitz)

116 The Tsar is not treacherous but he is weak. Weakness is not treachery, but it fulfils all its functions.

Wilhelm II (1859–1941) King of Prussia and Emperor of Germany. Referring to Nicholas II. Comment written on a despatch from the German ambassador to Russia, 16 Mar 1907

117 Now what do I do with *this*?

Duke of Windsor (1894–1972) King of the United Kingdom; abdicated 1936. On being handed the bill after a lengthy stay in a luxury hotel. Attrib.

118 He is a prince of royal courage and hath a princely heart; and rather than he will miss or want part of his appetite, he will hazard the loss of one-half of his kingdom.

Cardinal Wolsey (1475–1530) English churchman. Referring to Henry VIII. Remark, Nov 1530

119 I go to therapy, and I'm very proud of that.

The Duchess of York (1959–) *The Times*, 26 Aug 1993

RULES

1 The exception proves the rule.

Proverb

2 Rules and models destroy genius and art.

William Hazlitt (1778–1830) British essayist. *On Taste*

3 The golden rule is that there are no golden rules.

George Bernard Shaw (1856–1950) Irish dramatist and critic. *Man and Superman*, 'Maxims for Revolutionists'

RUNYON, DAMON

(1884–1946) US writer and journalist. His works include *Rhymes of the Firing Line* (1912), the collection of short stories *Guys and Dolls* (1932), and the play *A Slight Case of Murder* (1935).

1 All she has to do is to walk around and about Georgie White's stage with only a few light bandages on, and everybody considers her very beautiful, especially from the neck down.

Furthermore, 'A Very Honourable Guy'

2 My boy…always try to rub up against money, for if you rub up against money long enough, some of it may rub off on you.

Furthermore, 'A Very Honourable Guy'

3 More than Somewhat.

Title of a collection of stories

4 And you cannot tell by the way a party looks or how he lives in this town, if he has any scratch, because many a party who is around in automobiles, and wearing good clothes, and chucking quite a swell is nothing but a phonus bolonus and does not have any real scratch whatever.

More than Somewhat, 'The Snatching of Bookie Bob'

5 She is a smart old broad. It is a pity she is so nefarious.

Runyon à la carte, 'Broadway Incident'

6 At such an hour the sinners are still in bed resting up from their sinning of the night before, so they will be in good shape for more sinning a little later on.

Runyon à la carte, 'The Idyll of Miss Sarah Brown'

7 I once knew a chap who had a system of just hanging the baby on the clothes line to dry and he was greatly admired by his fellow citizens for having discovered a wonderful innovation on changing a diaper.

Short Takes, 'Diaper Dexterity'

8 A free-loader is a confirmed guest. He is the man who is always willing to come to dinner.

Short Takes, 'Free-Loading Ethics'

9 He is without strict doubt a Hoorah Henry, and he is generally figured as nothing but a lob as far as doing anything useful in this world is concerned.
Short Takes, 'Tight Shoes'

10 These citizens are always willing to bet that what Nicely-Nicely dies of will be over-feeding and never anything small like pneumonia, for Nicely-Nicely is known far and wide as a character who dearly loves to commit eating.
Take it Easy, 'Lonely Heart'

RUSKIN, JOHN

(1819–1900) British art critic and writer on sociology and economics. His books include *Modern Painters* (1843–60), *The Seven Lamps of Architecture* (1849), and *Munera Pulveris* (1862).

Quotations about Ruskin

1 A certain girlish petulance of style that distinguishes Ruskin was not altogether a defect. It served to irritate and fix attention where a more evenly judicial writer might have remained unread.
W. R. Sickert (1860–1942) British impressionist painter. *New Age*, 'The Spirit of the Hive'

2 I doubt that art needed Ruskin any more than a moving train needs one of its passengers to shove it.
Tom Stoppard (1937–) Czech-born British dramatist. *The Times Literary Supplement*, 3 June 1977

Quotations by Ruskin

3 No person who is not a great sculptor or painter can be an architect. If he is not a sculptor or painter, he can only be a *builder*.
Lectures on Architecture and Painting

4 Life without industry is guilt, and industry without art is brutality.
Lectures on Art, 'The Relation of Art to Morals', 23 Feb 1870

5 What is poetry? The suggestion, by the imagination, of noble grounds for the noble emotions.
Modern Painters, Vol. III

6 Mountains are the beginning and the end of all natural scenery.
Modern Painters, Vol. IV

7 If a book is worth reading, it is worth buying.
Sesame and Lilies, 'Of Kings' Treasuries'

8 All books are divisible into two classes, the books of the hour, and the books of all time.
Sesame and Lilies, 'Of Kings' Treasuries'

9 How long most people would look at the best book before they would give the price of a large turbot for it!
Sesame and Lilies, 'Of Kings' Treasuries'

10 When we build let us think that we build for ever.
The Seven Lamps of Architecture, 'The Lamp of Memory'

11 Remember that the most beautiful things in the world are the most useless, peacocks and lilies for instance.
Stones of Venice, Vol. I, Ch. 2

12 To make your children *capable of honesty* is the beginning of education.
Time and Tide, Letter VIII

13 Fine art is that in which the hand, the head, and the heart of man go together.
The Two Paths, Lecture II

14 Nobody cares much at heart about Titian, only there is a strange undercurrent of everlasting murmur about his name, which means the deep consent of all great men that he is greater than they.
The Two Paths, Lecture II

15 No human being, however great, or powerful was ever so free as a fish.
The Two Paths, Lecture V

16 Whereas it has long been known and declared that the poor have no right to the property of the rich, I wish it also to be known and declared that the rich have no right to the property of the poor.
Unto this Last, Essay III

17 I have seen, and heard, much of Cockney impudence before now; but never expected to hear a coxcomb ask two hundred guineas for flinging a pot of paint in the public's face.
On Whistler's painting 'Nocturne in Black and Gold'. Letter, 18 June 1877

18 What have we to say to India?
Referring to the completion of the British-Indian cable. Attrib.

RUSSELL, BERTRAND

(1872–1970) British philosopher. His many books include *Principia Mathematica* (with A. N. Whitehead; 1910) and *Our Knowledge of the External World* (1914). He was an ardent pacifist and campaigner for nuclear disarmament.

Quotations about Russell

1 In trying to recall his face I am able to see it only in profile – the sharp, narrow silhouette of an aggressive jester.
Arthur Koestler (1905–83) Hungarian-born British writer. *Stranger on the Square*

2 The beauty of Bertrand Russell's beautiful mathematical mind is absolute, like the third movement of Beethoven's A Minor Quartet.
Ethel Mannin *Confessions and Impressions*

Quotations by Russell

3 I have a certain hesitation in starting my biography too soon for fear of something important having not yet happened. Suppose I should end my days as President of Mexico; the biography would seem incomplete if it did not mention this fact.
Letter to Stanley Unwin, Nov 1930

4 Three passions, simple but overwhelmingly strong, have governed my life: the longing for love, the search for knowledge, and unbearable pity for the suffering of mankind.

The Autobiography of Bertrand Russell, Prologue

5 I was told that the Chinese said they would bury me by the Western Lake and build a shrine to my memory. I have some slight regret that this did not happen, as I might have become a god, which would have been very *chic* for an atheist.

The Autobiography of Bertrand Russell, Vol. II, Ch. 3

6 One of the symptoms of approaching nervous breakdown is the belief that one's work is terribly important. If I were a medical man, I should prescribe a holiday to any patient who considered his work important.

The Autobiography of Bertrand Russell, Vol. II, Ch. 5

7 ...the nuns who never take a bath without wearing a bathrobe all the time. When asked why, since no man can see them, they reply 'Oh, but you forget the good God.'

The Basic Writings, Pt. II, Ch. 7

8 The megalomaniac differs from the narcissist by the fact that he wishes to be powerful rather than charming, and seeks to be feared rather than loved. To this type belong many lunatics and most of the great men of history.

The Conquest of Happiness

9 There are two motives for reading a book: one, that you enjoy it, the other that you can boast about it.

The Conquest of Happiness

10 Of all forms of caution, caution in love is perhaps the most fatal to true happiness.

The Conquest of Happiness

11 Man is not a solitary animal, and so long as social life survives, self-realization cannot be the supreme principle of ethics.

History of Western Philosophy, 'Romanticism'

12 The more you are talked about, the more you will wish to be talked about. The condemned murderer who is allowed to see the account of his trial in the Press is indignant if he finds a newspaper which has reported it inadequately... Politicians and literary men are in the same case.

Human Society in Ethics and Politics

13 Mathematics may be defined as the subject in which we never know what we are talking about, nor whether what we are saying is true.

Mysticism and Logic, Ch. 4

14 Pure mathematics consists entirely of assertions to the effect that, if such and such a proposition is true of *anything*, then such and such another proposition is true of that thing. It is essential not to discuss whether the first proposition is really true, and not to mention what the anything is, of which it is supposed to be true.

Mysticism and Logic, Ch. 5

15 Organic life, we are told, has developed gradually from the protozoon to the philosopher, and this development, we are assured, is indubitably an advance. Unfortunately it is the philosopher, not the protozoon, who gives us this assurance.

Mysticism and Logic, Ch. 6

16 Brief and powerless is Man's life; on him and all his race the slow, sure doom falls pitiless and dark.

Mysticism and Logic, 'A Free Man's Worship'

17 No one gossips about other people's secret virtues.

On Education

18 Matter...a convenient formula for describing what happens where it isn't.

An Outline of Philosophy

19 Mathematics rightly viewed, possesses not only truth, but supreme beauty – a beauty cold and austere, like that of sculpture.

Philosophical Essays

20 It is undesirable to believe a proposition when there is no ground whatever for supposing it true.

Sceptical Essays

21 We have, in fact, two kinds of morality side by side; one which we preach but do not practise, and another which we practise but seldom preach.

Sceptical Essays

22 In America everybody is of the opinion that he has no social superiors, since all men are equal, but he does not admit that he has no social inferiors.

Unpopular Essays

23 People don't seem to realize that it takes time and effort and preparation to think. Statesmen are far too busy making speeches to think.

Kenneth Harris Talking To: 'Bertrand Russell' (Kenneth Harris)

24 There's a Bible on that shelf there. But I keep it next to Voltaire – poison and antidote.

Kenneth Harris Talking To: 'Bertrand Russell' (Kenneth Harris)

25 Obscenity is what happens to shock some elderly and ignorant magistrate.

Look

26 The collection of prejudices which is called political philosophy is useful provided that it is not called philosophy.

The Observer, 'Sayings of the Year', 1962

27 Not a gentleman; dresses too well.

Referring to Anthony Eden, the British Conservative prime minister. *Six Men* (A. Cooke)

28 Many people would sooner die than think. In fact they do.

Thinking About Thinking (A. Flew)

29 You may reasonably expect a man to walk a tightrope safely for ten minutes; it would be unreasonable to do so without accident for two hundred years.

On the subject of nuclear war between the US and the Soviets. *The Tightrope Men* (D. Bagley)

30 Few people can be happy unless they hate some other person, nation or creed.

Attrib.

31 Patriots always talk of dying for their country, and never of killing for their country.

Attrib.

32 Of course not. After all, I may be wrong.

On being asked whether he would be prepared to die for his beliefs. Attrib.

33 Every time I talk to a savant I feel quite sure that happiness is no longer a possibility. Yet when I talk with my gardener, I'm convinced of the opposite.

Attrib.

RUSSIA

See also Cold War, oppression, Russian Revolution

1 Reforms mean you can have a big car if you're in the mafia. Reforms mean hard-currency shops for a handful of people who have it. I'm a factory worker. I'll never have a big car or dollars, so reform for me will be when the milk isn't sour, that's all.

Anonymous Remark by a Russian woman while queuing for food. *The Times*, 25 Nov 1992

2 We all know the Iron Curtain has been demolished, but in its place an economic and social curtain might come down.

Jozsef Antall (1932–) Hungarian statesman *The Independent*, 29 Oct 1992

3 I cannot forecast to you the action of Russia. It is a riddle wrapped in a mystery inside an enigma.

Winston Churchill (1874–1965) British statesman. Broadcast talk, 1 Oct 1939

4 The Democrats only come here when they want votes. They brought sweets to bribe us.
The Communists used to bring vodka. It was more successful.

Galina Denisova Russian shopkeeper speaking to her neighbour. *The Times*, 11 Aug 1993

5 There is a discussion in my country about a new name for the USSR...Philip Morris is sending us billions of cigarettes. So some people suggest our new name should be Marlboro Country.

Gennadi Gerasimov (1930–) Russian journalist. *The Sunday Times*, 21 Oct 1990

6 The Soviet people want full-blooded and unconditional democracy.

Mikhail Gorbachov (1931–) Soviet statesman. Speech, July 1988

7 We have no borders, no customs, no visas, no army, no currency, no language other than Russian. We are not leaving Russia and have no plans to do so.

Anatoly Grebenkin Council chairman of the new Urals Republic. *The Independent*, 14 July 1993

8 The Communist Party, the KGB, and the army – the three ugly sisters – are the instruments of control in the Soviet Union.

Douglas Hurd (1930–) British politician. Referring to an abortive coup in the Soviet Union (Aug 1991). *The Observer*, 25 Aug 1991

9 It is one thing if a small poodle tries to walk through these gates but quite another matter when an elephant like Russia tries to do the same thing.

Andrei Kozyrev (1951–) Russian politician. Referring to the Nato Partnership for Peace agreement. *The Observer*, 'Sayings of the Week', 26 June 1994

10 Russia will certainly inherit the future. What we already call the greatness of Russia is only her pre-natal struggling.

D. H. Lawrence (1885–1930) British novelist. *Phoenix*, Preface

11 Neither can you expect a revolution, because there is no new baby in the womb of our society. Russia is a collapse, not a revolution.

D. H. Lawrence *Phoenix*, 'The Good Man'

12 Scratch the Russian and you will find the Tartar.

Joseph de Maistre (1753–1821) French monarchist. Attributed also to Napoleon and Prince de Ligne

13 Absolutism tempered by assassination.

Ernst Friedrich Herbert Münster (1766–1839) Hanoverian statesman. Referring to the Russian Constitution. Letter

14 This is a historic moment. Russia has entered the family of civilized nations.

Gavrill Popov (1936–) Russian economist and politician. Remark on his election as the first elected mayor of Moscow. *The Observer*, 16 June 1991

15 Comrade democrats, you have scattered. The reformers have gone to ground. Dictatorship is coming. I state it with complete responsibility. No one knows what kind of dictatorship this will be.

Eduard Shevardnadze (1928–) Georgian president. Resignation speech delivered to the USSR Congress of People's Deputies, Dec 1990.

16 Gaiety is the most outstanding feature of the Soviet Union.

Joseph Stalin (J. Dzhugashvili; 1879–1953) Soviet statesman. Attrib.

17 It was the supreme expression of the mediocrity of the apparatus that Stalin himself rose to his position.

Leon Trotsky (Lev Davidovich Bronstein; 1879–1940) Russian revolutionary. *My Life*, Ch. 40

18 From being a patriotic myth, the Russian people have become an awful reality.

Leon Trotsky *History of the Russian Revolution*, Pt. III, Ch. 7

19 We are still too dependent upon dachas, cars, special government telephone lines and armoured doors – the perquisites of power.

Boris Nikolayevich Yeltsin (1931–) Russian politician. *The View from the Kremlin*

20 It is a historic document which will allow us to continue our course towards entering Europe without the discrimination which took place in the past. We move forward as equal partners towards our mutual interest.

Boris Nikolayevich Yeltsin Referring to a partnership agreement between the European Union and Russia. *The Guardian*, 24 June 1994

21 People in our country don't like it when foreigners take too active a hand in our affairs.

Boris Nikolayevich Yeltsin *The View from the Kremlin*

22 How can I explain the process of privatising our bread shop to you, when I understand very little about it myself?...I don't even know whom to bribe any more, or how much. After all, your man could be there one day and gone the next.

Olga Zaiko Manager of a bread shop in Moscow. *The Guardian*, 25 June, 1994

23 This is a ridiculous country. It can't do anything properly, not even carry out a coup.

Igor Zakharov Russian journalist. Referring to an abortive coup in the Soviet Union (Aug 1991). *The Observer*, 25 Aug 1991

24 America has brought us McDonald's and horror movies. The West is trying to tell us how to live.

Vladimir Zhirinovsky (1946–) Russian politician. *The Sunday Times*, 3 Apr 1994

RUSSIAN REVOLUTION

See also revolution, Russia

1 Peace, Bread and Land.

Anonymous Slogan of workers in Petrograd (St Petersburg) during the February Revolution

2 All Power to the Soviets!

Anonymous Slogan of workers in Petrograd (St Petersburg) during the October Revolution

3 The Germans turned upon Russia the most grisly of all weapons. They transported Lenin in a sealed truck like a plague bacillus from Switzerland to Russia.

Winston Churchill (1874–1965) British statesman. *The World Crisis*

4 Of all tyrannies in history the Bolshevik tyranny is the worst, the most destructive, the most degrading

Winston Churchill Speech, London, 11 Apr 1919

5 Dear comrades, soldiers, sailors and workers! I am happy to greet in you the victorious Russian Revolution!

V.I. Lenin (Vladimir Ilich Ulyanov; 1870–1924) Russian revolutionary leader. Speech, Finland Station (Petrograd), 16 Apr 1917

6 The substitution of the proletarian for the bourgeois state is impossible without a violent revolution.

V.I. Lenin *State and Revolution*, Ch. 1

7 Ten Days that Shook the World.

John Reed (1887–1920) American journalist. Referring to the Bolshevik Revolution in Russia (Nov 1917). Book title

8 Our hand will not tremble.

Joseph Stalin (J. Dzhugashvili; 1879–1953) Soviet statesman. Reply to a telegraph from Lenin at the start of the Red Terror (1918) urging him to be merciless against the Bolsheviks' enemies

9 The 23rd of February was International Woman's Day…It had not occurred to anyone that it might become the first day of the revolution.

Leon Trotsky (Lev Davidovich Bronstein; 1879–1940) Russian revolutionary. *History of the Russian Revolution*, Pt. I, Ch. 7

10 The revolution does not choose its paths: it made its first steps towards victory under the belly of a Cossack's horse.

Leon Trotsky *History of the Russian Revolution*, Pt. I, Ch. 7

RUTHLESSNESS

1 Would that the Roman people had but one neck!

Caligula (Gaius Caesar; 12–41 AD) Roman Emperor. *Life of Caligula* (Suetonius), Ch. 30

2 What millions died – that Caesar might be great!

Thomas Campbell (1777–1844) British poet. *Pleasures of Hope*, II

3 Exterminate all brutes.

Joseph Conrad (Teodor Josef Konrad Korzeniowski; 1857–1924) Polish-born British novelist. *Heart of Darkness*

4 I do not have to forgive my enemies, I have had them all shot.

Ramón Maria Narváez (1800–68) Spanish general and political leader. Said on his deathbed, when asked by a priest if he forgave his enemies. *Famous Last Words* (B. Conrad)

5 3RD FISHERMAN. Master, I marvel how the fishes live in the sea.
1ST FISHERMAN. Why, as men do a-land – the great ones eat up the little ones.

William Shakespeare (1564–1616) English dramatist. *Pericles*, II:1

6 The world continues to offer glittering prizes to those who have stout hearts and sharp swords.

F. E. Smith (1872–1930) British lawyer and politician. Speech, Glasgow University, 7 Nov 1923

7 It is not enough to succeed. Others must fail.

Gore Vidal (1925–) US novelist. *Antipanegyric for Tom Driberg* (G. Irvine)

S

SACKVILLE-WEST, VITA

(Victoria Sackville-West; 1892–1962) British poet and novelist. She established her reputation as a poet with *The Land* (1926); her novels include *The Edwardians* (1930), *All Passion Spent* (1931), and *Grand Canyon* (1942).

1 Among the many problems which beset the novelist, not the least weighty is the choice of the moment at which to begin his novel.
The Edwardians, Ch. 1

2 The country habit has me by the heart,
For he's bewitched for ever who has seen,
Not with his eyes but with his vision, Spring
Flow down the woods and stipple leaves with sun.
The Land, 'Winter'

3 Travel is the most private of pleasures. There is no greater bore than the travel bore. We do not in the least want to hear what he has seen in Hong-Kong.
Passenger to Tehran, Ch. 1

4 For observe, that to hope for Paradise is to live in Paradise, a very different thing from actually getting there.
Passenger to Tehran, Ch. 1

5 Those who have never dwelt in tents have no idea either of the charm or of the discomfort of a nomadic existence. The charm is purely romantic, and consequently very soon proves to be fallacious.
Twelve Days, Ch. 6

SAKI

(Hector Hugh Munro; 1870–1916) British writer. He is best known for his collections of humorous short stories, including *Reginald* (1904), *The Chronicles of Clovis* (1911), and *Beasts and Super-Beasts* (1914).

1 By insisting on having your bottle pointing to the north when the cork is being drawn, and calling the waiter Max, you may induce an impression on your guests which hours of laboured boasting might be powerless to achieve. For this purpose, however, the guests must be chosen as carefully as the wine.
The Chaplet

2 Addresses are given to us to conceal our whereabouts.
Cross Currents

3 'I believe I take precedence,' he said coldly; 'you are merely the club Bore: I am the club Liar.'
A Defensive Diamond

4 Waldo is one of those people who would be enormously improved by death.
Referring to Ralph Waldo Emerson. *The Feast of Nemesis*

5 Children with Hyacinth's temperament don't know better as they grow older; they merely know more.
Hyacinth

6 The people of Crete unfortunately make more history than they can consume locally.
The Jesting of Arlington Stringham

7 To say that anything was a quotation was an excellent method, in Eleanor's eyes, for withdrawing it from discussion.
The Jesting of Arlington Stringham

8 He's simply got the instinct for being unhappy highly developed.
The Match-Maker

9 All decent people live beyond their incomes nowadays, and those who aren't respectable live beyond other people's. A few gifted individuals manage to do both.
The Match-Maker

10 Oysters are more beautiful than any religion... There's nothing in Christianity or Buddhism that quite matches the sympathetic unselfishness of an oyster.
The Match-Maker

11 His socks compelled one's attention without losing one's respect.
Ministers of Grace

12 The young have aspirations that never come to pass, the old have reminiscences of what never happened.
Reginald at the Carlton

13 There may have been disillusionments in the lives of the medieval saints, but they would scarcely have been better pleased if they could have foreseen that their names would be associated nowadays chiefly with racehorses and the cheaper clarets.
Reginald at the Carlton

14 The Western custom of one wife and hardly any mistresses.
Reginald in Russia

15 But, good gracious, you've got to educate him first.
You can't expect a boy to be vicious till he's been to a good school.
Reginald in Russia

16 The cook was a good cook, as cooks go; and as cooks go she went.
Reginald on Besetting Sins

17 People may say what they like about the decay of Christianity; the religious system that produced green Chartreuse can never really die.
Reginald on Christmas Presents

18 Even the Hooligan was probably invented in China centuries before we thought of him.
Reginald on House-Parties

19 Every reformation must have its victims. You can't expect the fatted calf to share the enthusiasm of the angels over the prodigal's return.
Reginald on the Academy

20 I think she must have been very strictly brought up, she's so desperately anxious to do the wrong thing correctly.

Reginald on Worries

21 I always say beauty is only sin deep.

Reginald's Choir Treat

22 In baiting a mouse-trap with cheese, always leave room for the mouse.

The Square Egg

23 Sherard Blaw, the dramatist who had discovered himself, and who had given so ungrudgingly of his discovery to the world.

Referring to George Bernard Shaw. *The Unbearable Bassington*, Ch. 13

SALINGER, J. D.

(1919–) US novelist who achieved success with *The Catcher in the Rye* (1951); later books include *Franny and Zooey* (1961), *Seymour, An Introduction* (1963), and *Raise High the Roof Beam, Carpenters* (1963).

Quotations about Salinger

1 Salinger was the perfect *New Yorker* writer, whose promise and celebrity delivered less and less.

Leo Brandy US Professor of English *Harvard Guide to Contemporary American Writing* (Daniel Hoffman) 'Realists, Naturalists, and Novelists of Manners'

2 That quality of sensitive innocence which Holden Caulfield retained beneath his rebellious mannerisms has developed into a note of religious mysticism.

Ian Ousby British critic.*50 American Novels* 1979

Quotations by Salinger

3 If you really want to hear about it, the first thing you'll probably want to know is where I was born and what my lousy childhood was like, and how my parents were occupied and all before they had me, and all that David Copperfield kind of crap.

The opening words of the book. *The Catcher in the Rye*

4 Sex is something I really don't understand too hot. You never know *where* the hell you are. I keep making up these sex rules for myself, and then I break them right away.

The Catcher in the Rye, Ch. 9

5 They didn't act like people and they didn't act like actors. It's hard to explain. They acted more like they knew they were celebrities and all. I mean they were good, but they were *too* good.

The Catcher in the Rye, Ch. 17

6 What really knocks me out is a book that, when you're all done reading it, you wish the author that wrote it was a terrific friend of yours and you could call him up on the phone whenever you felt like it.

The Catcher in the Rye

7 I'm trying to hold on to some old, useful feelings of obscurity. If I had to do it over again, I'm pretty sure I'd use a pseudonym during publication years. It's a great pity that noms de plume have gone out of fashion.

Declining to appear in one of Tynan's television programmes. Letter to Kenneth Tynan, 1959

SANTAYANA, GEORGE

(1863–1952) US philosopher and poet. His books include *Realms of Being* (1927–40), *Background of my Life* (1945), several volumes of poetry, and a novel.

Quotations about Santayana

1 He stood on the flat road to heaven and buttered slides to hell for all the rest.

Oliver Wendell Holmes (1809–94) US writer. Letter, 5 Dec 1913

Quotations by Santayana

2 The working of great institutions is mainly the result of a vast mass of routine, petty malice, self interest, carelessness, and sheer mistake. Only a residual fraction is thought.

The Crime of Galileo

3 The young man who has not wept is a savage, and the old man who will not laugh is a fool.

Dialogues in Limbo, Ch. 3

4 The Bible is literature, not dogma.

Introduction to the Ethics of Spinoza

5 Happiness is the only sanction of life; where happiness fails, existence remains a mad and lamentable experiment.

The Life of Reason

6 Progress, far from consisting in change, depends on retentiveness. Those who cannot remember the past are condemned to repeat it.

The Life of Reason

7 Because there's no fourth class.

On being asked why he always travelled third class. *Living Biographies of the Great Philosophers* (H. Thomas)

8 Life is not a spectacle or a feast; it is a predicament.

The Perpetual Pessimist (Sagittarius and George)

9 England is the paradise of individuality, eccentricity, heresy, anomalies, hobbies, and humours.

Soliloquies in England, 'The British Character'

10 Trust the man who hesitates in his speech and is quick and steady in action, but beware of long arguments and long beards.

Soliloquies in England, 'The British Character'

11 There is no cure for birth and death save to enjoy the interval.

Soliloquies in England, 'War Shrines'

12 It is a great advantage for a system of philosophy to be substantially true.

The Unknowable

13 For an idea ever to be fashionable is ominous, since it must afterwards be always old-fashioned.

Winds of Doctrine, 'Modernism and Christianity'

14 If all the arts aspire to the condition of music, all the sciences aspire to the condition of mathematics.

The Observer, 'Sayings of the Week', 4 Mar 1928

SARCASM

1 Sarcasm I now see to be, in general, the language of the devil.

Thomas Carlyle (1795–1881) Scottish historian and essayist. *Sartor Resartus*, Bk. II, Ch. 4

2 If you don't want to use the army, I should like to borrow it for a while. Yours respectfully, A. Lincoln.

Abraham Lincoln (1809–65) US statesman. Letter to General George B. McClellan, whose lack of activity during the US Civil War irritated Lincoln.

SARTRE, JEAN-PAUL

(1905–80) French philosopher, dramatist, and novelist. The principal exponent of existentialism, he wrote a number of books on this subject, including *Being and Nothingness* (1943). His novels include the trilogy *The Roads to Freedom* (1945–49), and *The Respectable Prostitute* (1946) is the best known of his plays.

Quotations about Sartre

1 His adult life resembled his childhood in the sense that he lorded it over admiring women.

James Fenton (1949–) British writer and editor. *The Times*, 22 Nov 1984

2 He is a philosopher remarkable for the force, one might almost say the animal vigour, of his thought; a novelist of great fecundity and a sumptuous flow of words, mixed a little too carefully with vulgar expressions and low-class slang; a playwright able to sustain themes apparently void of dramatic interest; and a political journalist with a word to say on all contemporary problems.

The Observer, 7 Mar 1947

3 The ineptitude of M. Sartre's political performance has tempted some British critics to dismiss him as a phoney, particularly as he rarely hesitates to adapt the facts to fit the cause for which he currently cares.

The Observer, 4 Dec 1960

Quotations by Sartre

4 I hate victims who respect their executioners.

Altona

5 An American is either a Jew, or an anti-Semite, unless he is both at the same time.

Altona

6 Man is condemned to be free.

Existentialism is a Humanism

7 Three o'clock is always too late or too early for anything you want to do.

Nausea

8 Things are entirely what they appear to be and *behind them*...there is nothing.

Nausea

9 My thought is *me*: that is why I can't stop. I exist by what I think...and I can't prevent myself from thinking.

Nausea

10 I know perfectly well that I don't want to do anything; to do something is to create existence – and there's quite enough existence as it is.

Nausea

11 I don't think the profession of historian fits a man for psychological analysis. In our work we have to deal only with simple feelings to which we give generic names such as Ambition and Interest.

Nausea

12 I think they do that to pass the time, nothing more. But time is too large, it refuses to let itself be filled up.

Nausea

13 You get the impression that their normal condition is silence and that speech is a slight fever which attacks them now and then.

Nausea

14 The poor don't know that their function in life is to exercise our generosity.

Words

15 A kiss without a moustache, they said then, is like an egg without salt; I will add to it: and it is like Good without Evil.

Words

16 She believed in nothing; only her scepticism kept her from being an atheist.

Words

17 There is no such thing as psychological. Let us say that one can improve the biography of the person.

The Divided Self (R. D. Laing), Ch. 8

18 In the first days of the revolt you must kill: to shoot down a European is to kill two birds with one stone, to destroy an oppressor and the man he oppresses at the same time: there remain a dead man, and a free man.

The Wretched of the Earth (F. Fanon), Preface

SASSOON, SIEGFRIED

(1886–1967) British poet and writer. After serving in World War I he published several collections of anti-war verse, including *The Old Huntsman* (1917) and *Counter Attack* (1918). His autobiographical prose work, *Memoirs of George Sherston*, included the well-known *Memoirs of a Fox-Hunting Man* (1928).

1 If I were fierce and bald and short of breath,
I'd live with scarlet Majors at the Base,
And speed glum heroes up the line to death.

Base Details

2 And when the war is done and youth stone dead
I'd toddle safely home and die – in bed.

Base Details

3 Soldiers are citizens of death's grey land,
Drawing no dividend from time's tomorrows.

Dreamers

4 'Good morning; good morning!' the general said
When we met him last week on our way to the line.
Now the soldiers he smiled at are most of 'em dead,
And we're cursing his staff for incompetent swine.

The General

5 Man, it seemed, had been created to jab the life out of Germans.

Memoirs of an Infantry Officer, Pt. I, Ch. 1

6 Deep in water I splashed my way
Up the trench to our bogged front line
Rain had fallen the whole damned night.
O Jesus, send me a wound today,
And I'll believe in Your bread and wine,
And get my bloody old sins washed white!

Stand-to: Good Friday Morning

7 I am making this statement as a wilful defiance of military authority because I believe that the War is being deliberately prolonged by those who have the power to end it.

Memoirs of an Infantry Officer, Pt. X, Ch. 3

8 Safe with his wound, a citizen of life,
He hobbled blithely through the garden gate,
And thought: 'Thank God they had to amputate!'

The One-Legged Man

SATIRE

See also ridicule, sarcasm

1 It's hard not to write satire.

Juvenal (Decimus Junius Juvenalis; 60–130 AD) Roman satirist. *Satires*, I

2 Satire should, like a polished razor keen,
Wound with a touch that's scarcely felt or seen.

Lady Mary Wortley Montagu (1689–1762) English writer.

To the Imitator of the First Satire of Horace, Bk. II

3 Satire is a sort of glass, wherein beholders do generally discover everybody's face but their own.

Jonathan Swift (1667–1745) Irish-born Anglican priest and writer. *The Battle of the Books*, 'Preface'

SATISFACTION

See also contentment

1 Youth will be served, every dog has his day, and mine has been a fine one.

George Henry Borrow (1803–81) British writer. *Lavengro*, Ch. 92

2 I wasna fou, but just had plenty.

Robert Burns (1759–96) Scottish poet. *Death and Doctor Hornbrook*

3 The reward of a thing well done is to have done it.

Ralph Waldo Emerson (1803–82) US poet and essayist. *Essays*, 'New England Reformers'

4 I can't get no satisfaction.

Mick Jagger (1943–) British rock musician and songwriter. 'Satisfaction' (With Keith Richard)

5 Open your eyes and look within. Are you satisfied with the life you're living?

Bob Marley (Robert Nesta Marley; 1945–80) Jamaican reggae singer. *Exodus*

SAYINGS

See also quotations

1 A platitude is simply a truth repeated till people get tired of hearing it.

Stanley Baldwin (1867–1947) British statesman. Attrib.

2 The hunter for aphorisms on human nature has to fish in muddy water, and he is even condemned to find much of his own mind.

F. H. Bradley (1846–1924) British philosopher. *Aphorisms*

3 The great writers of aphorisms read as if they had all known each other well.

Elias Canetti (1905–) Bulgarian-born novelist. *The Human Province*

4 A proverb is much matter decorated into few words.

Thomas Fuller (1608–61) English historian. *The History of the Worthies of England*, Ch. 2

5 A new maxim is often a brilliant error.

Chrétien Guillaume de Lamoignonde Malesherbes (1721–94) French statesman. *Pensées et maximes*

6 A proverb is one man's wit and all men's wisdom.

Lord John Russell (1792–1878) British statesman. Attrib.

7 A truism is on that account none the less true.

Herbert Samuel (1870–1963) British Liberal statesman. *A Book of Quotations*

SCEPTICISM

See also doubt, proof

1 We don't believe in rheumatism and true love until after the first attack.

Marie Ebner von Eschenbach (1830–1916) Austrian writer. *Aphorism*

2 I am too much of a sceptic to deny the possibility of anything.

T. H. Huxley (1825–95) British biologist. Letter to Herbert Spencer, 22 Mar 1886

3 Truth, Sir, is a cow, which will yield such people no more milk, and so they are gone to milk the bull.

Samuel Johnson (1709–84) British lexicographer. Referring to sceptics. *Life of Johnson* (J. Boswell), Vol. I

4 It is undesirable to believe a proposition when there is no ground whatever for supposing it true.

Bertrand Russell (1872–1970) British philosopher. *Sceptical Essays*

5 She believed in nothing; only her scepticism kept her from being an atheist.

Jean-Paul Sartre (1905–80) French writer. *Words*

6 The temerity to believe in nothing.

Ivan Turgenev (1818–83) Russian novelist. *Fathers and Sons*, Ch. 14

SCHOPENHAUER, ARTHUR

(1788–1860) German philosopher. His books include *Die Welt als Wille und Vorstellung* (1819) and *Die Beiden Grundprobleme der Ethik* (1841).

1 To be alone is the fate of all great minds – a fate deplored at times, but still always chosen as the less grievous of two evils.
Aphorismen zur Lebensweisheit

2 Intellect is invisible to the man who has none.
Aphorismen zur Lebensweisheit

3 Every parting gives a foretaste of death; every coming together again a foretaste of the resurrection.
Gedanken über vielerlei Gegenstände, XXVI

4 The fundamental fault of the female character is that it has no sense of justice.
Gedanken über vielerlei Gegenstände, XXVII

5 The thing-in-itself, the will-to-live, exists whole and undivided in every being, even in the tiniest; it is present as completely as in all that ever were, are, and will be, taken together.
Parerga and Paralipomena

6 To expect a man to retain everything that he has ever read is like expecting him to carry about in his body everything that he has ever eaten.
Parerga and Paralipomena

7 After your death you will be what you were before your birth.
Parerga and Paralipomena

8 Wealth is like sea-water; the more we drink, the thirstier we become; and the same is true of fame.
Parerga and Paralipomena

SCIENCE

See also discovery, mathematics, Nature, progress, research, scientists, technology

1 On 13 September 1765 people in fields near Luce, in France, saw a stone-mass drop from the sky after a violent thunderclap. The great physicist Lavoisier, who knew better than any peasant that this was impossible, reported to the Academy of Science that the witnesses were mistaken or lying. The Academy would not accept the reality of meteorites until 1803.
Anonymous *Fortean Times*

2 *Eureka!*
I have found it!
Archimedes (c. 287–212 BC) Greek mathematician. An exclamation of joy supposedly uttered as, stepping into a bath and noticing the water overflowing, he saw the answer to a problem and began the train of thought that led to his principle of buoyancy. Attrib.

3 There are no such things as incurable, there are only things for which man has not found a cure.
Bernard Baruch (1870–1965) US financier and statesman. Quoting his father Simon Baruch, the pioneer surgeon, in a speech to the President's Committee on Employment of the Physically Handicapped, 30 Apr 1954

4 Science seldom renders men amiable; women, never.
Edmone-Pierre Chanvot de Beauchêne (1748–1824) *Maximes, réflexions et pensées diverses*

5 The Microbe is so very small
You cannot make him out at all,
But many sanguine people hope
To see him through a microscope.
His jointed tongue that lies beneath
A hundred curious rows of teeth;
His seven tufted tails with lots
Of lovely pink and purple spots,
On each of which a pattern stands,
Composed of forty separate bands;
His eyebrows of a tender green;
But Scientists, who ought to know,
Assure us that they must be so…
Oh! let us never, never doubt
What nobody is sure about!
Hilaire Belloc (1870–1953) French-born British poet, essayist and historian. *Cautionary Verses*, 'The Microbe'

6 There are more microbes *per person* than the entire population of the world. Imagine that. Per person. This means that if the time scale is diminished in proportion to that of space it would be quite possible for the whole story of Greece and Rome to be played out between farts.
Alan Bennett (1934–) British dramatist and actor. *The Old Country*, II

7 Medical scientists are nice people, but you should not let them treat you.
August Bier (1861–1949) Attrib.

8 O Timothy, keep that which is committed to thy trust, avoiding profane and vain babblings, and oppositions of science falsely so called.
Bible: I Timothy 6:20

9 A first-rate laboratory is one in which mediocre scientists can produce outstanding work.
Patrick Maynard Stuart Blackett (1897–1974) Attrib.

10 It is my intent to beget a good understanding between the chymists and the mechanical philosophers who have hitherto been too little acquainted with one another's learning.
Robert Boyle (1627–91) British scientist. *The Sceptical Chymist*

11 Private practice and marriage – those twin extinguishers of science.
Paul Broca (1824–80) Letter, 10 Apr 1851

12 That is the essence of science: ask an impertinent question, and you are on the way to the pertinent answer.
Jacob Bronowski (1908–74) British scientist and writer. *The Ascent of Man*, Ch. 4

13 Physics becomes in those years the greatest collective work of science – no, more than that, the great collective work of art of the twentieth century.
Jacob Bronowski Referring to the period around the turn of the century marked by the elucidation of atomic structure and the development of the quantum theory. *The Ascent of Man*, Ch. 10

14 Science has nothing to be ashamed of, even in the ruins of Nagasaki.
Jacob Bronowski *Science and Human Values*

15 No one should approach the temple of science with the soul of a money changer.
Thomas Browne (1605–82) English physician and writer.

16 There was a young lady named Bright,
Whose speed was far faster than light;
She set out one day

In a relative way,
And returned home the previous night.

Arthur Henry Reginald Buller (1874–1944) British botanist. *Limerick*

17 X-RAYS: Their moral is this – that a right way of looking at things will see through almost anything.

Samuel Butler (1835–1902) British writer. *Note-Books*, Vol. V

18 That is how the atom is split. But what does it mean? To us who think in terms of practical use it means – Nothing!

Ritchie Calder (1898–1976) US engineer and sculptor. *The Daily Herald*, 27 June 1932

19 It is, of course, a bit of a drawback that science was invented after I left school.

Lord Carrington (1919–) British statesman. *The Observer*, 23 Jan 1983

20 When a distinguished but elderly scientist states that something is possible, he is almost certainly right. When he states that something is impossible, he is very probably wrong.

Arthur C. Clarke (1917–) British science-fiction writer. *Profiles of the Future*

21 We have discovered the secret of life!

Francis Crick (1916–) British biophysicist. Excitedly bursting into a Cambridge pub with James Watson to celebrate the fact that they had unravelled the structure of DNA. *The Double Helix* (J. D. Watson)

22 I also suspect that many workers in this field and related fields have been strongly motivated by the desire, rarely actually expressed, to refute vitalism.

Francis H. C. Crick Referring to molecular biology. *British Medical Bulletin*, 21:183, 1965

23 After all, science is essentially international, and it is only through lack of the historical sense that national qualities have been attributed to it.

Marie Curie (1867–1934) Polish chemist. *Memorandum*, 'Intellectual Co-operation'

24 One never notices what has been done; one can only see what remains to be done…

Marie Curie Letter to her brother, 18 Mar 1894

25 But in science the credit goes to the man who convinces the world, not to the man to whom the idea first occurs.

Francis Darwin (1848–1925) British scientist. *Eugenics Review*, 6:1, 1914

26 Every great advance in science has issued from a new audacity of imagination.

John Dewey (1859–1952) US philosopher and educator. *The Quest for Certainty*, Ch. 11

27 Putting on the spectacles of science in expectation of finding the answer to everything looked at signifies inner blindness.

J. Frank Dobie (1888–1964) *The Voice of Coyote*, Introduction

28 And new Philosophy calls all in doubt,
The Element of fire is quite put out;
The Sun is lost, and th' earth, and no man's wit
Can well direct him where to look for it.

John Donne (1573–1631) English poet. *An Anatomy of the World*, 205

29 The content of physics is the concern of physicists, its effect the concern of all men.

Friedrich Dürrenmatt (1921–90) Swiss writer. *The Physicists*

30 Electrical force is defined as something which causes motion of electrical charge; an electrical charge is something which exerts electric force.

Arthur Eddington (1882–1944) British astronomer. *The Nature of the Physical World*

31 Man is slightly nearer to the atom than the stars. From his central position he can survey the grandest works of Nature with the astronomer, or the minutest works with the physicist.

Arthur Eddington *Stars and Atoms*

32 When you are courting a nice girl an hour seems like a second. When you sit on a red-hot cinder a second seems like an hour. That's relativity.

Albert Einstein (1879–1955) German-born US physicist. *News Chronicle*, 14 Mar 1949

33 The whole of science is nothing more than a refinement of everyday thinking.

Albert Einstein *Out of My Later Years*

34 Science without religion is lame, religion without science is blind.

Albert Einstein *Out of My Later Years*

35 God does not play dice.

Albert Einstein Einstein's objection to the quantum theory, in which physical events can only be known in terms of probabilities. It is sometimes quoted as 'God does not play dice with the Universe'. *Albert Einstein, Creator and Rebel* (B. Hoffman), Ch. 10

36 I believe my theory of relativity to be true. But it will only be proved for certain in 1981, when I am dead.

Albert Einstein *Einstein: A Study in Simplicity*

37 God is subtle but he is not malicious.

Albert Einstein Inscribed over the fireplace in the Mathematical Institute, Princeton. It refers to Einstein's objection to the quantum theory. *Albert Einstein* (Carl Seelig), Ch. 8

38 Everything should be made as simple as possible, but not simpler.

Albert Einstein Attrib.

39 Physicists like to think that all you have to do is say, these are the conditions, now what happens next?

Richard Phillips Feynman (1918–88) US theoretical physicist. *Chaos* (James Gleick)

40 All the world is a laboratory to the inquiring mind.

Martin H. Fischer (1879–1962) *Fischerisms* (Howard Fabing and Ray Marr)

41 A vacuum can only exist, I imagine, by the things which enclose it.

Zelda Fitzgerald (1900–48) US writer. Journal, 1932

42 Simple systems give rise to complex behavior. Complex systems give rise to simple behavior. And most important, the laws of complexity hold universally, caring not at all for the details of a system's constituent atoms.

James Gleick US science writer.

43 To some physicists chaos is a science of process rather than state, of becoming rather than being.

James Gleick *Chaos*

44 Thus I saw that most men only care for science so far as they get a living by it, and that they worship even error when it affords them a subsistence.

Goethe (1749–1832) German poet, dramatist, and scientist. *Conversations with Goethe* (Johann Peter Eckermann)

45 Science is not to be regarded merely as a storehouse of facts to be used for material purposes, but as one of the great human endeavours to be ranked with arts and religion as the guide and expression of man's fearless quest for truth.

Richard Arman Gregory (1864–1952) *The Harvest of a Quiet Eye* (Alan L. Mackay)

46 Shelley and Keats were the last English poets who were at all up to date in their chemical knowledge.

J. B. S. Haldane (1892–1964) British geneticist. *Daedalus or Science and the Future*

47 MASTER: They split the atom by firing particles at it, at 5,500 miles a second.
BOY: Good heavens. And they only split it?

Will Hay (1888–1949) British comedian. *The Fourth Form at St Michael's*

48 Oh, powerful bacillus,
With wonder how you fill us,
Every day!
While medical detectives,
With powerful objectives,
Watch your play.

William T. Helmuth (1833–1902) *Ode to the Bacillus*

49 Science has 'explained' nothing; the more we know the more fantastic the world becomes and the profounder the surrounding darkness.

Aldous Huxley (1894–1964) British novelist. *Views Of Holland*

50 Along with many scientists he considered the discovery of psychedelics one of the three major scientific break-throughs of the twentieth century, the other two being the splitting of the atom and the manipulation of genetic structures.

Laura Huxley Referring to Aldous Huxley. *This Timeless Moment*

51 Science is nothing but trained and organized common sense, differing from the latter only as a veteran may differ from a raw recruit: and its methods differ from those of common sense only as far as the guardsman's cut and thrust differ from the manner in which a savage wields his club.

T. H. Huxley (1825–95) British biologist. *Collected Essays*, 'The Method of Zadig'

52 The great tragedy of Science – the slaying of a beautiful hypothesis by an ugly fact.

T. H. Huxley *Collected Essays*, 'Biogenesis and Abiogenesis'

53 Science...commits suicide when it adopts a creed.

T. H. Huxley *Darwiniana*, 'The Darwin Memorial'

54 Reason, Observation, and Experience – the Holy Trinity of Science.

Robert G. Ingersoll (1833–99) US lawyer and agnostic. *The Gods*

55 Many persons nowadays seem to think that any conclusion must be very scientific if the arguments in favor of it are derived from twitching of frogs' legs – especially if the frogs are decapitated – and that – on the other hand – any doctrine chiefly vouched for by the feelings of human beings – with heads on their shoulders – must be benighted and superstitious.

William James (1842–1910) US psychologist and philosopher. *Pragmatism*

56 Life exists in the universe only because the carbon atom possesses certain exceptional properties.

James Jeans (1877–1946) British scientist. *The Mysterious Universe*, Ch. 1

57 Science should leave off making pronouncements: the river of knowledge has too often turned back on itself.

James Jeans *The Mysterious Universe*, Ch. 5

58 Three quarks for Muster Mark!

James Joyce (1882–1941) Irish novelist. The word quark has since been adopted by physicists for hypothetical elementary particles. *Finnegans Wake*

59 Let both sides seek to invoke the wonders of science instead of its terrors. Together let us explore the stars, conquer the deserts, eradicate disease, tap the ocean depths, and encourage the arts and commerce.

John F. Kennedy (1917–63) US statesman. Inaugural Address, 20 Jan 1961

60 We have genuflected before the god of science only to find that it has given us the atomic bomb, producing fears and anxieties that science can never mitigate.

Martin Luther King (1929–68) US Black civil-rights leader. *Strength through Love*, Ch. 13

61 In everything that relates to science, I am a whole Encyclopaedia behind the rest of the world.

Charles Lamb (1775–1834) British essayist. *Essays of Elia*, 'The Old and the New Schoolmaster'

62 Water is H_2O, hydrogen two parts, oxygen one, but there is also a third thing, that makes it water and nobody knows what that is.

D. H. Lawrence (1885–1930) British novelist. *Pansies*, 'The Third Thing'

63 It is a good morning exercise for a research scientist to discard a pet hypothesis every day before breakfast.

Konrad Lorenz (1903–89) Austrian zoologist and pioneer of ethology. *On Aggression*, Ch. 2

64 Science conducts us, step by step, through the whole range of creation, until we arrive, at length, at God.

Marguerite of Valois (1553–1615) *Memoirs (1594–1600)*, Letter XII

65 Scientific discovery is a private event, and the delight that accompanies it, or the despair of finding it illusory does not travel.

Peter Medawar (1915–87) British immunologist. *Hypothesis and Imagination*

66 *Laboratorium est oratorium.* The place where we do our scientific work is a place of prayer.

Joseph Needham (1900–) British biochemist. *The Harvest of a Quiet Eye* (A. L. Mackay)

67 In my view this should not be an ethical debate,

but a debate about trade…If you allow the Americans to gain patents that cover vast stretches of the entire human genome, the economic consequences could be disastrous.

Peter Neville Goodfellow (1951–) British biotechnologist. *The Independent*, 27 Apr 1994

68 I do not know what I may appear to the world, but to myself I seem to have been only like a boy playing on the sea-shore, and diverting myself in now and then finding a smoother pebble or a prettier shell than ordinary, whilst the great ocean of truth lay all undiscovered before me.

Isaac Newton (1642–1727) British scientist. *Isaac Newton* (L. T. More)

69 O Diamond! Diamond! thou little knowest the mischief done!

Isaac Newton Said to a dog that set fire to some papers, representing several years' work, by knocking over a candle. *Wensley-Dale…a Poem* (Thomas Maude)

70 Do you really believe that the sciences would ever have originated and grown if the way had not been prepared by magicians, alchemists, astrologers and witches whose promises and pretensions first had to create a thirst, a hunger, a taste for *hidden* and *forbidden* powers? Indeed, infinitely more had to be *promised* than could ever be fulfilled in order that anything at all might be fulfilled in the realms of knowledge.

Friedrich Wilhelm Nietzsche (1844–1900) German philosopher. *The Gay Science*

71 There are no such things as applied sciences, only applications of science.

Louis Pasteur (1822–95) French scientist. Address, 11 Sept 1872

72 Traditional scientific method has always been at the very *best*, 20-20 hindsight. It's good for seeing where you've been.

Robert T. Pirsig (1928–) US writer. *Zen and the Art of Motorcycle Maintenance*, Pt. III, Ch. 24

73 We have no right to assume that any physical laws exist, or if they have existed up to now, that they will continue to exist in a similar manner in the future.

Max Planck (1858–1947) German physicist. *The Universe in the Light of Modern Physics*

74 Science must begin with myths, and with the criticism of myths.

Karl Popper (1902–) Austrian-born British philosopher. *British Philosophy in the Mid-Century* (ed. C. A. Mace)

75 Science may be described as the art of systematic over-simplification.

Karl Popper Remark, Aug 1982

76 Should we force science down the throats of those that have no taste for it? Is it our duty to drag them kicking and screaming into the twenty-first century? I am afraid that it is.

George Porter (1920–) British chemist. Speech, Sept 1986

77 A device which enables us to see how the bones in the back room are doing.

Don Quinn *Bartlett's Unfamiliar Quotations* (Leonard Louis Levinson)

78 Science without conscience is the death of the soul.

François Rabelais (1483–1553) French satirist.

79 The simplest schoolboy is now familiar with truths for which Archimedes would have sacrified his life.

Ernest Renan (1823–92) French philosopher and theologian. *Souvenirs d'enfance et de jeunesse*

80 When we have found how the nucleus of atoms are built-up we shall have found the greatest secret of all – except life. We shall have found the basis of everything – of the earth we walk on, of the air we breathe, of the sunshine, of our physical body itself, of everything in the world, however great or however small – except life.

Ernest Rutherford (1871–1937) British physicist. *Passing Show 24*

81 The people – could you patent the sun?

Jonas E. Salk (1914–) US virologist. On being asked who owned the patent on his polio vaccine. *Famous Men of Science* (S. Bolton)

82 If all the arts aspire to the condition of music, all the sciences aspire to the condition of mathematics.

George Santayana (1863–1952) US philosopher. *The Observer*, 'Sayings of the Week', 4 Mar 1928

83 People must understand that science is inherently neither a potential for good nor for evil. It is a potential to be harnessed by man to do his bidding.

Glenn T. Seaborg (1912–) US physicist. Associated Press interview with Alton Blakeslee, 29 Sept 1964

84 Science is always wrong. It never solves a problem without creating ten more.

George Bernard Shaw (1856–1950) Irish dramatist and critic.

85 Science is the great antidote to the poison of enthusiasm and superstition.

Adam Smith (1723–90) Scottish economist. *The Wealth of Nations*, Bk. V, Ch. 1

86 Art and religion first; then philosophy; lastly science. That is the order of the great subjects of life, that's their order of importance.

Muriel Spark (1918–) British novelist. *The Prime of Miss Jean Brodie*, Ch. 2

87 Science is organized knowledge.

Herbert Spencer (1820–1903) British philosopher. *Education*, Ch. 2

88 Fifty-five crystal spheres geared to God's crankshaft is my idea of a satisfying universe. I can't think of anything more trivial than quarks, quasars, big bangs and black holes.

Tom Stoppard (1937–) Czech-born British dramatist. *The Observer*, 'Sayings of the Week', 22 May 1994

89 Discovery consists of seeing what everybody has seen and thinking what nobody has thought.

Albert Szent-Györgyi (1893–92) Hungarian-born US biochemist. *The Scientist Speculates* (I. J. Good)

90 Mystics always hope that science will some day overtake them.

Booth Tarkington (1869–1946) US novelist. *Looking Forward to the Great Adventure*

91 Her own mother lived the latter years of her life in the horrible suspicion that electricity was dripping invisibly all over the house.

James Thurber (1894–1961) US humorist. *My Life and Hard Times*, Ch. 2

92 Modern Physics is an instrument of Jewry for the destruction of Nordic science...True physics is the creation of the German spirit.

Rudolphe Tomaschek (20th century) German scientist. *The Rise and Fall of the Third Reich* (W. L. Shirer), Ch. 8

93 Science robs men of wisdom and usually converts them into phantom beings loaded up with facts.

Miguel de Unamuno y Jugo (1864–36) Spanish writer. *Essays and Soliloquies*

94 Whenever science makes a discovery, the devil grabs it while the angels are debating the best way to use it.

Alan Valentine

95 The term Science should not be given to anything but the aggregate of the recipes that are always successful. All the rest is literature.

Paul Valéry (1871–1945) French poet and writer. *Moralités*

96 As long as vitalism and spiritualism are open questions so long will the gateway of science be open to mysticism.

Rudolf Virchow (1821–1902) German pathologist. *Bulletin of the New York Academy of Medicine*, 4:994, 1928

97 Classical physics has been superseded by quantum theory: quantum theory is verified by experiments. Experiments must be described in terms of classical physics.

C. F. von Weizsäcker (1912–) German physicist and philosopher. Attrib.

98 If silicon had been a gas I should have been a major-general.

James Whistler (1834–1903) US painter. Referring to his failure in a West Point chemistry examination. *English Wits* (L. Russell)

99 A science which hesitates to forget its founders is lost.

A. N. Whitehead (1861–1947) British philosopher. Attrib.

100 The airplane stays up because it doesn't have the time to fall.

Orville Wright (1871–1948) US aviator. Explaining the principles of powered flight. Attrib.

SCIENCE FICTION

1 Far out in the uncharted backwaters of the unfashionable end of the Western Spiral arm of the Galaxy lies a small unregarded yellow sun. Orbiting this at a distance of roughly ninety-two million miles is an utterly insignificant little blue green planet whose ape-descended life forms are so amazingly primitive that they still think digital watches are a pretty neat idea.

Douglas Adams (1952–) British writer. *The Hitch Hiker's Guide to the Galaxy*, Introduction

2 Science fiction is the search for a definition of mankind and his status in the universe which will stand in our advanced but confused state of knowledge (science), and is characteristically cast in the Gothic or post-Gothic mode.

Brian Aldiss (1925–) British science-fiction writer. *Trillion Year Spree*, Ch. 1

3 *Star Maker* is really the one great grey holy book of science fiction...

Brian Aldiss Referring to Olaf Stapledon's novel *Star Maker*. *Trillion Year Spree*, Ch. 8

SCIENTISTS

See also science

General quotations

1 When I find myself in the company of scientists, I feel like a shabby curate who has strayed by mistake into a drawing-room full of dukes.

W. H. Auden (1907–73) British poet. *The Dyer's Hand*

2 The true men of action in our time, those who transform the world, are not the politicians and statesmen, but the scientists. Unfortunately, poetry cannot celebrate them, because their deeds are concerned with things, not persons and are, therefore, speechless.

W. H. Auden *The Dyer's Hand*

3 If you want to find out anything from the theoretical physicists about the methods they use, I advise you to stick closely to one principle: Don't listen to their words fix your attention on their deeds.

Albert Einstein (1879–1955) German-born US physicist. *The World As I See It*

4 Scientists are treated like gods handing down new commandments. People tend to assume that religion has been disproved by science. But the scientist may tell us how the world works, not why it works, not how we should live our lives, not how we face death or make moral decisions.

Susan Howatch (1940–) British writer. *The Observer*, 8 May 1994

5 The physicists have known sin; and this is a knowledge which they cannot lose.

J. Robert Oppenheimer (1904–67) US physicist. Lecture, Massachusetts Institute of Technology, 25 Nov 1947

6 He doubted the existence of the Deity but accepted Carnot's cycle, and he had read Shakespeare and found him weak in chemistry.

H. G. Wells (1866–1946) British writer. *Short Stories*, 'The Lord of the Dynamos'

Specific quotations

7 Sir Humphry Davy
Abominated gravy.
He lived in the odium
Of having discovered Sodium.

Edmund Clerihew Bentley (1875–1956) British writer. *Biography for Beginners*

8 Edison, whose inventions did as much as any to add to our material convenience, wasn't what we would call a scientist at all, but a supreme 'do-it-yourself' man – the successor to Benjamin Franklin.

Kenneth Clark (1903–83) British art historian. *Civilization*

9 I believe the souls of five hundred Sir Isaac Newtons would go to the making up of a Shakespeare or a Milton.

Samuel Taylor Coleridge (1772–1834) British poet. Letter to Thomas Poole, 23 Mar 1801

10 I went to the Society where were divers experiments in Mr Boyle's Pneumatic Engine. We put in a snake but could not kill it by exhausting the air, only making it extremely sick, but a chick died of convulsions in a short space.

John Evelyn (1620–1706) English diarist. *Diary*, 22 Apr 1661

11 Einstein – the greatest Jew since Jesus. I have no doubt that Einstein's name will still be remembered and revered when Lloyd George, Foch and William Hohenzollern share with Charlie Chaplin that uneluctable oblivion which awaits the uncreative mind.

J. B. S. Haldane (1892–1964) British geneticist. *Daedalus or Science and the Future*

12 Bacon discovered the art of making reading-glasses...and various other mathematical and astronomical instruments....That the ingredients of gunpowder and the art of making it were known to him is now undeniable; but the *humane philosopher* dreading the consequences of communicating the discovery to the world, transposed the letters of the Latin words which signify charcoal, which made the whole obscure.

Robert Henry *History of England*

13 Had he not been an untidy man and apt to leave his cultures exposed on the laboratory table the spore of hyssop mould, the *penicillin notatum*, might never have floated in from Praed Street and settled on his dish of staphylococci.

André Maurois (Émile Herzog; 1885–1967) French writer. *Life of Alexander Fleming*

14 Nature, and Nature's laws lay hid in night:
God said, Let *Newton be!* and all was light.

Alexander Pope (1688–1744) British poet. For a reply, *see* John Collings SQUIRE. *Epitaphs*, 'Intended for Sir Isaac Newton'

15 It did not last: the Devil howling 'Ho!
Let Einstein be!' restored the status quo.

John Collings Squire (1884–1958) British journalist. Answer to POPE's Epitaph for Newton. *Epigrams*, 'The Dilemma'

16 He snatched the lightning shaft from heaven, and the sceptre from tyrants.

Anne-Robert-Jacques Turgot (1727–81) French economist. An inscription for a bust of Benjamin Franklin, alluding both to Franklin's invention of the lightning conductor and to his role in the American Revolution. *Vie de Turgot* (A. N. de Condorcet)

17 Already for thirty-five years he had not stopped talking and almost nothing of fundamental value had emerged.

James Dewey Watson (1928–) US geneticist. Referring to the British biophysicist Francis Crick with whom he discovered the structure of DNA (1953). *The Double Helix*, Ch. 8

SCOTLAND

See also Britain, Scots

1 O ye'll tak' the high road, and I'll tak' the low road,
And I'll be in Scotland afore ye,
But me and my true love will never meet again,
On the bonnie, bonnie banks o' Loch Lomon'.

Anonymous *The Bonnie Banks o' Loch Lomon'*

2 My heart's in the Highlands, my heart is not here;
My heart's in the Highlands a-chasing the deer;
Chasing the wild deer, and following the roe,
My heart's in the Highlands, wherever I go.

Robert Burns (1759–96) Scottish poet. *My Heart's in the Highlands*

3 *Oats.* A grain, which in England is generally given to horses, but in Scotland supports the people.

Samuel Johnson (1709–84) British lexicographer. *Dictionary of the English Language*

4 Norway, too, has noble wild prospects; and Lapland is remarkable for prodigious noble wild prospects. But, Sir, let me tell you, the noblest prospect which a Scotchman ever sees, is the high road that leads him to England!

Samuel Johnson *Life of Johnson* (J. Boswell), Vol. I

5 Seeing Scotland, Madam, is only seeing a worse England.

Samuel Johnson *Life of Johnson* (J. Boswell), Vol. III

6 Roamin' in the gloamin',
By the bonny banks of Clyde.

Harry Lauder (Hugh MacLennon; 1870–1950) Scottish music-hall artist. Song

7 O Caledonia! stern and wild,
Meet nurse for a poetic child!
Land of brown heath and shaggy wood,
Land of the mountain and the flood,
Land of my sires! what mortal hand
Can e'er untie the filial band
That knits me to thy rugged strand!

Walter Scott (1771–1832) Scottish novelist. *The Lay of the Last Minstrel*, VI

8 That knuckle-end of England – that land of Calvin, oat-cakes, and sulphur.

Sydney Smith (1771–1845) British clergyman and essayist. *Memoir* (Lady Holland)

SCOTS

See also British, Scotland

1 You've forgotten the grandest moral attribute of a Scotsman, Maggie, that he'll do nothing which might damage his career.

J. M. Barrie (1860–1937) British novelist and dramatist. *What Every Woman Knows*, II

2 There are few more impressive sights in the world than a Scotsman on the make.

J. M. Barrie *What Every Woman Knows*, II

3 A Scotchman must be a very sturdy moralist who does not love Scotland better than truth.

Samuel Johnson (1709–84) British lexicographer. *Journey to the Western Islands of Scotland*, 'Col'

4 BOSWELL. I do indeed come from Scotland, but I cannot help it...
JOHNSON. That, Sir, I find, is what a very great many of your countrymen cannot help.

Samuel Johnson *Life of Johnson* (J. Boswell), Vol. I

5 Much may be made of a Scotchman, if he be *caught* young.

Samuel Johnson Referring to Lord Mansfield. *Life of Johnson* (J. Boswell), Vol. II

6 Their learning is like bread in a besieged town: every man gets a little, but no man gets a full meal.
Samuel Johnson Referring to education in Scotland. *Life of Johnson* (J. Boswell), Vol. II

7 I have been trying all my life to like Scotchmen, and am obliged to desist from the experiment in despair.
Charles Lamb (1775–1834) British essayist. *Essays of Elia*, 'Imperfect Sympathies'

8 In all my travels I never met with any one Scotchman but what was a man of sense. I believe everybody of that country that has any, leaves it as fast as they can.
Francis Lockier (1667–1740) English writer. *Anecdotes* (Joseph Spence)

9 Join a Highland regiment, me boy. The kilt is an unrivalled garment for fornication and diarrhoea.
John Masters (1914–83) British writer. *Bugles and a Tiger*

10 It's ill taking the breeks aff a wild Highlandman.
Walter Scott (1771–1832) Scottish novelist. *The Fair Maid of Perth*, Ch. 5

11 It is never difficult to distinguish between a Scotsman with a grievance and a ray of sunshine.
P. G. Wodehouse (1881–1975) British humorous novelist. *Wodehouse at Work to the End* (Richard Usborne), Ch. 8

SCOTT, PAUL

(1920–78) British novelist. He is best remembered for the Raj Quartet, consisting of *Jewel in the Crown* (1966), *The Day of the Scorpion* (1968), *The Towers of Silence* (1971), and *A Division of the Spoils* (1975).

1 Our Eastern Empire, I mean. It was, you know, what *made* the English middle class. It taught us the hitherto upper-class secrets of government and civil administration. Now we must largely be content again with commerce and science.
The Bender

2 I have been in the houses of very rich people who are rich because they have talents or vital statistics and in such places you have but definitely to wet your finger and hold it up and you may then go like without hesitation following the wind blowing from looward and presently drop anchor. But in the houses of people who have both money and class it is like of no use to wet your finger and hold it up because someone will simply stick upon it a canapé filled with *pâté de foie*.
The Bender

3 There were people in Mayapore who said I only kept up with Lady Manners for snob reasons, *Indian* snob reasons, like calling an English person by his Christian name.
The Jewel in the Crown

SCOTT, SIR WALTER

(1771–1832) Scottish novelist. Originally a lawyer, he turned to writing for a living after the success of his narrative poem, *The Lay of the Last Minstrel* (1805). *Waverley* (1814) was the first of many successful historical novels, including *Rob Roy* (1817), *The Heart of Midlothian* (1818), *The Bride of Lammermoor* (1818), *Ivanhoe* (1819), and *The Talisman* (1825).

Quotations about Scott

1 It can be said of him, when he departed he took a Man's life with him. No sounder piece of British manhood was put together in that eighteenth century of time.
Thomas Carlyle (1795–1881) Scottish historian and essayist. *Essays*, 'Lockhart's Life of Scott'

2 Sir Walter Scott, when all is said and done, is an inspired butler.
William Hazlitt (1778–1830) British essayist. *Mrs Siddons*

Quotations by Scott

3 Look back, and smile at perils past.
The Bridal of Triermain, Introduction

4 It's ill taking the breeks aff a wild Highlandman.
The Fair Maid of Perth, Ch. 5

5 The Big Bow-Wow strain I can do myself like any now going; but the exquisite touch, which renders ordinary commonplace things and characters interesting, from the truth of the description and the sentiment, is denied to me.
In praise of Jane Austen. *Journal*, 14 Mar 1826

6 For ne'er
Was flattery lost on poet's ear:
A simple race! they waste their toil
For the vain tribute of a smile.
The Lay of the Last Minstrel, IV

7 True love's the gift which God has given
To man alone beneath the heaven.
The Lay of the Last Minstrel, V

8 Breathes there the man, with soul so dead,
Who never to himself hath said,
This is my own, my native land!
Whose heart hath ne'er within him burn'd,
As home his footsteps he hath turn'd
From wandering on a foreign strand!
The Lay of the Last Minstrel, VI

9 O Caledonia! stern and wild,
Meet nurse for a poetic child!
Land of brown heath and shaggy wood,
Land of the mountain and the flood,
Land of my sires! what mortal hand
Can e'er untie the filial band
That knits me to thy rugged strand!
The Lay of the Last Minstrel, VI

10 His morning walk was beneath the elms in the churchyard; 'for death,' he said, 'had been his next-door neighbour for so many years, that he had no apology for dropping the acquaintance.'
The Legend of Montrose, Introduction

11 There is a Southern proverb, – fine words butter no parsnips.
The Legend of Montrose, Ch. 3

12 To that dark inn, the grave!
The Lord of the Isles, VI

13 But search the land of living men,
Where wilt thou find their like agen?
Marmion, I

14 O, young Lochinvar is come out of the west,
Through all the wide Border his steed was the best.
Marmion, V

15 So faithful in love, and so dauntless in war,
There never was knight like the young Lochinvar.
Marmion, V

16 The stubborn spear-men still made good
Their dark impenetrable wood,
Each stepping where his comrade stood,
The instant that he fell.
Marmion, VI

17 Ridicule often checks what is absurd, and fully as often smothers that which is noble.
Quentin Durward

18 But with the morning cool repentance came.
Rob Roy, Ch. 12

19 See yon pale stripling! when a boy,
A mother's pride, a father's joy!
Rokeby, III

20 O, Brignal banks are wild and fair,
And Gretna woods are green,
And you may gather garlands there
Would grace a summer queen.
Rokeby, III

21 My heart's in the Highlands, my heart is not here,
My heart's in the Highlands a-chasing the deer.
Waverley, Ch. 28

22 No, this right hand shall work it all off.
Refusing offers of help following his bankruptcy in 1826. *Century of Anecdote* (J. Timbs)

23 All health is better than wealth.
Familiar Letters, Letter to C. Carpenter, 4 Aug 1812

SEA

See also boats, Navy, seaside

1 The sea is calm to-night,
The tide is full, the moon lies fair
Upon the Straits.
Matthew Arnold (1822–88) British poet and critic. *Dover Beach*

2 For all at last return to the sea – to Oceanus, the ocean river, like the ever-flowing stream of time, the beginning and the end.
Rachel Carson (1907–64) US biologist. The closing words of the book. *The Sea Around Us*

3 The voice of the sea speaks to the soul. The touch of the sea is sensuous, enfolding the body in its soft, close embrace.
Kate Chopin (1851–1904) US writer. *The Awakening*, Ch. 6

4 The ice was here, the ice was there,
The ice was all around:
It cracked and growled, and roared and howled,
Like noises in a swound!
Samuel Taylor Coleridge (1772–1834) British poet. *The Rime of the Ancient Mariner*, I

5 We are as near to heaven by sea as by land.
Humphrey Gilbert (c. 1539–83) English navigator. Remark made shortly before he went down with his ship *Squirrel*. *A Book of Anecdotes* (D. George)

6 When men come to like a sea-life, they are not fit to live on land.
Samuel Johnson (1709–84) British lexicographer. *Life of Johnson* (J. Boswell), Vol. II

7 The snotgreen sea. The scrotumtightening sea.
James Joyce (1882–1941) Irish novelist. *Ulysses*

8 It keeps eternal whisperings around
Desolate shores, and with its mighty swell
Gluts twice ten thousand Caverns.
John Keats (1795–1821) British poet. *On the Sea*

9 'Wouldst thou' – so the helmsman answered–
'Learn the secret of the sea?
Only those who brave its dangers
Comprehend its mystery!'
Henry Wadsworth Longfellow (1807–82) US poet. *The Secret of the Sea*

10 I must down to the seas again, to the lonely sea and the sky,
And all I ask is a tall ship and a star to steer her by,
And the wheel's kick and the wind's song and the white sail's shaking,
And a grey mist on the sea's face and a grey dawn breaking.
John Masefield (1878–1967) British poet. Often quoted using 'sea' rather than 'seas', and 'I must go down' rather than 'I must down'. *Sea Fever*

11 Rocked in the cradle of the deep.
Emma Millard (1787–1870) British songwriter. Song

12 ...the sea, trembling with a long line of radiance, and showing in the clear distance the sails of vessels stealing in every direction along its surface.
Ann Radcliffe (1764–1823) British novelist. *The Italian*

13 A life on the ocean wave,
A home on the rolling deep.
Epes Sargent (1813–80) US writer and dramatist. *A Life on the Ocean Wave*

14 O hear us when we cry to Thee
For those in peril on the sea.
William Whiting (1825–78) British hymn writer. *Eternal Father Strong to Save*

15 The sea! the sea!
Xenophon (430–354 BC) Greek historian. *Anabasis*, IV:7

16 That dolphin-torn, that gong-tormented sea.
W. B. Yeats (1865–1939) Irish poet. *Byzantium*

SEASIDE

See also sea

1 The King bathes, and with great success; a machine follows the Royal one into the sea, filled with fiddlers, who play *God Save the King* as his Majesty takes his plunge.
Fanny Burney (Frances Burney D'Arblay; 1752–1840) British novelist. Referring to George III at Weymouth. Diary, 8 July 1789

2 The Walrus and the Carpenter
Were walking close at hand;
They wept like anything to see

Such quantities of sand:
'If this were only cleared away,'
They said, 'it *would* be grand!'

Lewis Carroll (Charles Lutwidge Dodgson; 1832–98) British writer. *Through the Looking-Glass*, Ch. 4

3 It is the drawback of all sea-side places that half the landscape is unavailable for purposes of human locomotion, being covered by useless water.

Norman Douglas (1868–1952) British novelist. *Alone*, 'Mentone'

4 I do Like to be Beside the Seaside.

John A. Glover-Kind (19th century) US songwriter. Song title

SEASONS

See also months

1 Sumer is icumen in,
Lhude sing cuccu!
Groweth sed, and bloweth med,
And springth the wude nu.

Anonymous *Cuckoo Song*

2 Many human beings say that they enjoy the winter, but what they really enjoy is feeling proof against it.

Richard Adams (1920–) British novelist. *Watership Down*, Ch. 50

3 All the live murmur of a summer's day.

Matthew Arnold (1882–88) British poet and critic. *The Scholar Gipsy*

4 It is time for the destruction of error.
The chairs are being brought in from the garden.
The summer talk stopped on that savage coast
Before the storms.

W. H. Auden (1907–73) British poet. *It is time*

5 My beloved spake, and said unto me, Rise up, my love, my fair one, and come away. For, lo, the winter is past, the rain is over and gone;
The flowers appear on the earth; the time of the singing of birds is come, and the voice of the turtle is heard in our land.

Bible: Song of Solomon 2:10–12

6 Now Spring, sweet laxative of Georgian strains,
Quickens the ink in literary veins,
The Stately Homes of England ope their doors
To piping Nancy-boys and Crashing Bores.

Roy Campbell (1901–57) South African poet. *The Georgiad*

7 Summer has set in with its usual severity.

Samuel Taylor Coleridge (1772–1834) British poet. Quoted in Lamb's letter to V. Novello, 9 May 1826

8 Summer afternoon – summer afternoon; to me those have always been the two most beautiful words in the English language.

Henry James (1843–1916) US novelist. *A Backward Glance* (Edith Wharton), Ch. 10

9 St Agnes Eve – Ah, bitter chill it was!
The owl, for all his feathers, was a-cold;
The hare limp'd trembling through the frozen grass,
And silent was the flock in woolly fold.

John Keats (1795–1821) British poet. *The Eve of Saint Agnes*, I

10 Four seasons fill the measure of the year;
There are four seasons in the mind of men.

John Keats *Four Seasons*

11 Where are the songs of Spring? Ay, where are they?

John Keats *To Autumn*

12 Season of mists and mellow fruitfulness,
Close bosom-friend of the maturing sun;
Conspiring with him how to load and bless
With fruit the vines that round the thatch-eaves run.

John Keats *To Autumn*

13 No one thinks of winter when the grass is green!

Rudyard Kipling (1865–1936) Indian-born British writer. *A St Helena Lullaby*

14 In a somer season, when soft was the sonne.

William Langland (c. 1330–c. 1400) English poet. *The Vision of Piers Plowman*, Prologue

15 Russia has two generals in whom she can confide – Generals Janvier and Février.

Nicholas I (1796–1855) Tsar of Russia. Referring to the Russian winter. Nicholas himself succumbed to a February cold in 1855 – the subject of the famous *Punch* Cartoon, 'General Février turned traitor', 10 Mar 1855. Attrib.

16 Winter is icummen in,
Lhude sing Goddamm,
Raineth drop and staineth slop
And how the wind doth ramm!
Sing: Goddamm.

Ezra Pound (1885–1972) US poet. *Ancient Music*

17 Spring has returned. The earth is like a child that knows poems.

Rainer Maria Rilke (1875–1926) Austrian poet. *Die Sonette an Orpheus*, I, 21

18 In the bleak mid-winter
Frosty wind made moan,
Earth stood hard as iron,
Water like a stone;
Snow had fallen, snow on snow,
Snow on snow,
In the bleak mid-winter,
Long ago.

Christina Rossetti (1830–74) British poet. *Mid-Winter*

19 The country habit has me by the heart,
For he's bewitched for ever who has seen,
Not with his eyes but with his vision, Spring
Flow down the woods and stipple leaves with sun.

Vita Sackville-West (Victoria Sackville-West; 1892–1962) British poet and novelist. *The Land*, 'Winter'

20 When icicles hang by the wall,
And Dick the shepherd blows his nail,
And Tom bears logs into the hall,
And milk comes frozen home in pail,
When blood is nipp'd, and ways be foul,
Then nightly sings the staring owl:
'Tu-who;
Tu-whit, Tu-who' – A merry note.
While greasy Joan doth keel the pot.

William Shakespeare (1564–1616) English dramatist. *Love's Labour's Lost*, V:2

21 If Winter comes, can Spring be far behind?

Percy Bysshe Shelley (1792–1822) British poet. *Ode to the West Wind*

22 When the hounds of spring are on winter's traces,
The mother of months in meadow or plain
Fills the shadows and windy places
With lisp of leaves and ripple of rain…

Algernon Charles Swinburne (1837–1909) British poet. *Atlanta in Calydon*

23 The moans of doves in immemorial elms,
And murmuring of innumerable bees.

Alfred, Lord Tennyson (1809–92) British poet. *The Princess*, VII

24 In the Spring a young man's fancy lightly turns to thoughts of love.

Alfred, Lord Tennyson *Locksley Hall*

25 It is a winter's tale
That the snow blind twilight ferries over the lakes
And floating fields from the farm in the cup of the vales.

Dylan Thomas (1914–53) Welsh poet. *A Winter's Tale*

26 Spring is come home with her world-wandering feet.
And all the things are made young with young desires.

Francis Thompson (1859–1907) British poet. *The Night of Forebeing*, 'Ode to Easter'

27 The comic almanacs give us dreadful pictures of January and February; but, in truth, the months which should be made to look gloomy in England are March and April. Let no man boast himself that he has got through the perils of winter till at least the seventh of May.

Anthony Trollope (1815–82) British novelist. *Doctor Thorne*, Ch. 47

28 Like an army defeated
The snow hath retreated.

William Wordsworth (1770–1850) British poet. *Written in March*

SECRECY

See also gossip

1 Only the nose knows
Where the nose goes
When the door close.

Muhammad Ali (Cassius Clay; 1942–) US boxer. When asked whether a boxer should have sex before a big fight. Remark, reported by Al Silverman

2 I have seldom spoken with greater regret, for my lips are not yet unsealed. Were these troubles over I would make a case, and I guarantee that not a man would go into the Lobby against us.

Stanley Baldwin (1867–1947) British statesman. Referring to the Abyssinian crisis; usually misquoted as 'My lips are sealed'. Speech, House of Commons, 10 Dec 1935

3 Curse not the king, no not in thy thought; and curse not the rich in thy bedchamber: for a bird of the air shall carry the voice, and that which hath wings shall tell the matter.

Bible: Ecclesiastes 10:20

4 If thou hast heard a word, let it die with thee; and be bold, it will not burst thee.

Bible: Ecclesiasticus 19:10

5 Stolen waters are sweet, and bread eaten in secret is pleasant.

Bible: Proverbs 9:17

6 Mum's the word.

George Colman, the Younger (1762–1836) British dramatist. *The Battle of Hexham*, II:1

7 O fie miss, you must not kiss and tell.

William Congreve (1670–1729) British Restoration dramatist. *Love for Love*, II:10

8 I know that's a secret, for it's whispered every where.

William Congreve *Love for Love*, III:3

9 Three may keep a secret, if two of them are dead.

Benjamin Franklin (1706–90) US scientist and statesman. *Poor Richard's Almanack*

10 It is a secret in the Oxford sense: you may tell it to only one person at a time.

Oliver Franks (1905–) British philosopher and administrator. *The Sunday Telegraph*, 30 Jan 1977

11 Nobody tells me anything.

John Galsworthy (1867–1933) British writer. *The Man of Property*

SELDEN, JOHN

(1584–1654) English historian, jurist, antiquary, and statesman. He wrote many erudite works but is best remembered for *Table Talk* (1689), a posthumously published collection of his sayings.

1 A king is a thing men have made for their own sakes, for quietness' sake. Just as if in a family one man is appointed to buy the meat.

Table Talk

2 Every law is a contract between the king and the people and therefore to be kept.

Table Talk

3 Ignorance of the law excuses no man; not that all men know the law, but because 'tis an excuse every man will plead, and no man can tell how to confute him.

Table Talk

4 Pleasure is nothing else but the intermission of pain.

Table Talk

5 Preachers say, Do as I say, not as I do. But if the physician had the same disease upon him that I have, and he should bid me do one thing, and himself do quite another, could I believe him?

Table Talk

6 For a priest to turn a man when he lies a-dying, is just like one that has a long time solicited a woman, and cannot obtain his end; at length makes her drunk, and so lies with her.

Table Talk

7 Pleasures are all alike simply considered in

themselves...He that takes pleasure to hear sermons enjoys himself as much as he that hears plays.
Table Talk

8 'Tis not the drinking that is to be blamed, but the excess.
Table Talk

9 Marriage is nothing but a civil contract.
Table Talk

SELF

See also self-confidence, etc.

1 Every man is his own worst enemy.
Proverb

2 God helps them that help themselves.
Proverb

3 He helps little that helps not himself.
Proverb

4 He travels fastest who travels alone.
Proverb

5 And now the end is near
And so I face the final curtain,
My friend, I'll say it clear,
I'll state my case of which I'm certain.
I've lived a life that's full, I've traveled each and evr'y high-way
And more, much more than this, I did it my way.
Paul Anka (1941–) US singer and songwriter. Based on the French composition, 'Comme d'habitude'. *My Way*

6 He is, after all, the reflection of the tenderness I bear for myself. It is always ourselves we love.
Beryl Bainbridge (1934–) British novelist. *A Weekend with Claud, 'Maggie'*

7 Lord, deliver me from myself.
Thomas Browne (1605–82) English physician and writer. *Religio Medici*, Pt. II

8 I have always disliked myself at any given moment; the total of such moments is my life.
Cyril Connolly (1903–74) British journalist. *Enemies of Promise*, Ch. 18

9 But I do nothing upon myself, and yet I am mine own Executioner.
John Donne (1573–1631) English poet. *Devotions*, 12

10 What we must decide is perhaps how we are valuable, rather than how valuable we are.
F. Scott Fitzgerald (1896–1940) US novelist. *The Crack-Up*

11 We never remark any passion or principle in others, of which, in some degree or other, we may not find a parallel in ourselves.
David Hume (1711–76) Scottish philosopher. *A Treatise of Human Nature*

12 Whenever I look inside myself I am afraid.
Cyril Joad (1891–1953) British writer and broadcaster. *The Observer*, 'Sayings of the Week', 8 Nov 1942

13 All censure of a man's self is oblique praise. It is in order to shew how much he can spare.
Samuel Johnson (1709–84) British lexicographer. *Life of Johnson* (J. Boswell), Vol. III

14 One should examine oneself for a very long time before thinking of condemning others.
Molière (Jean Baptiste Poquelin; 1622–73) French dramatist. *Le Misanthrope*, III:4

15 Self-love seems so often unrequited.
Anthony Powell (1905–) British novelist. *The Acceptance World*

16 Why, man, he doth bestride the narrow world
Like a Colossus; and we petty men
Walk under his huge legs, and peep about
To find ourselves dishonourable graves.
Men at some time are masters of their fates:
The fault, dear Brutus, is not in our stars,
But in ourselves that we are underlings.
William Shakespeare (1564–1616) English dramatist. *Julius Caesar*, I:2

17 Do not love your neighbour as yourself. If you are on good terms with yourself it is an impertinence; if on bad, an injury.
George Bernard Shaw (1856–1950) Irish dramatist and critic. *Man and Superman*, 'Maxims for Revolutionists'

18 Self-sacrifice enables us to sacrifice
Other people without blushing.
George Bernard Shaw *Man and Superman*

19 The unexamined life is not worth living.
Socrates (469–399 BC) Athenian philosopher. *Apology* (Plato)

20 I am greater than the stars for I know that they are up there and they do not know that I am down here.
William Temple (1881–1944) British churchman. Attrib.

21 I am always with myself, and it is I who am my tormentor.
Leo Tolstoy (1828–1910) Russian writer. *Memoirs of a Madman*

22 Meanwhile you will write an essay on 'self-indulgence'. There will be a prize of half a crown for the longest essay, irrespective of any possible merit.
Evelyn Waugh (1903–66) British novelist. *Decline and Fall*, Pt. I, Ch. 5

23 I can't quite explain it, but I don't believe one can ever be unhappy for long provided one does just exactly what one wants to and when one wants to.
Evelyn Waugh *Decline and Fall*, Pt. I, Ch. 5

24 I celebrate myself, and sing myself,
And what I assume you shall assume.
Walt Whitman (1819–92) US poet. *Song of Myself*, 1

25 Behold, I do not give lectures or a little charity,
When I give I give myself.
Walt Whitman *Song of Myself*, 40

26 I have said that the soul is not more than the body,
And I have said that the body is not more than the soul,
And nothing, but God, is greater to one than one's self is.
Walt Whitman *Song of Myself*, 48

27 Do I contradict myself?

Very well then I contradict myself,
(I am large, I contain multitudes).

Walt Whitman *Song of Myself*, 51

28 Self-determination is not a mere phrase. It is an imperative principle which statesmen will henceforth ignore at their peril.

Woodrow Wilson (1856–1925) US statesman. Speech to Congress, 11 Feb 1918

SELF-CONFIDENCE

See also shyness

1 I know I'm not clever but I'm always right.

J. M. Barrie (1860–1937) British playwright. *Peter Pan*

2 I think I'm getting a little confidence now.

John Gielgud (1904–) British actor. *The Sunday Times*, Dec 1975

3 Those who believe that they are exclusively in the right are generally those who achieve something.

Aldous Huxley (1894–1964) British novelist. *Proper Studies*

4 I can honestly say that I was never affected by the question of the success of an undertaking. If I felt it was the right thing to do, I was for it regardless of the possible outcome.

Golda Meir (1898–1978) Russian-born Israeli stateswoman. *Golda Meir: Woman with a Cause* (Marie Syrkin)

5 I wish I was as cocksure of anything as Tom Macaulay is of everything.

Lord Melbourne (1779–1848) British statesman. *Preface to Lord Melbourne's Papers* (Earl Cowper)

6 Bring me no more reports; let them fly all:
Till Birnam wood remove to Dunsinane
I cannot taint with fear.

William Shakespeare (1564–1616) English dramatist. *Macbeth*, V:3

7 Hang out our banners on the outward walls;
The cry is still, 'They come'; our castle's strength
Will laugh a siege to scorn.

William Shakespeare *Macbeth*, V:5

8 'Tis an ill cook that cannot lick his own fingers.

William Shakespeare *Romeo and Juliet*, IV:2

9 'Are you not,' a Rugby master had asked him in discussing one of his essays, 'a little out of your depth here?' 'Perhaps, Sir,' was the confident reply, 'but I can swim.'

William Temple (1881–1944) British churchman. *William Temple* (F. A. Iremonger)

10 Why not be oneself? That is the whole secret of a successful appearance. If one is a grey-hound why try to look like a Pekinese?

Edith Sitwell (1887–1965) British poet and writer. *Why I Look As I Do*

11 I am certain that we will win the election with a good majority. Not that I am ever over-confident.

Margaret Thatcher (1925–) British politician and prime minister. *Evening Standard*, 1987

12 If I ever felt inclined to be timid as I was going into a room full of people, I would say to myself, 'You're the cleverest member of one of the cleverest families in the cleverest class of the cleverest nation in the world, why should you be frightened?'

Beatrice Webb (1858–1943) British economist and writer. *Portraits from Memory* (Bertrand Russell), 'Sidney and Beatrice Webb'

13 Speak up for yourself, or you'll end up a rug.

Mae West (1892–1980) US actress. Attrib.

SELF-CONTROL

1 He that is slow to anger is better than the mighty; and he that ruleth his spirit than he that taketh a city.

Bible: Proverbs 16:32

2 No one who cannot limit himself has ever been able to write.

Nicolas Boileau (1636–1711) French writer. *L'Art poétique*, I

3 The highest possible stage in moral culture is when we recognize that we ought to control our thoughts.

Charles Darwin (1809–82) British life scientist. *Descent of Man*, Ch. 4

4 When things are steep, remember to stay level-headed.

Horace (Quintus Horatius Flaccus; 65–8 BC) Roman poet. *Odes*, II

5 If you can keep your head when all about you
Are losing theirs and blaming it on you.

Rudyard Kipling (1865–1936) Indian-born British writer. *If*

6 He that would govern others, first should be
The master of himself.

Philip Massinger (1583–1640) English dramatist. *The Bondman*, I

7 Never lose your temper with the Press or the public is a major rule of political life.

Christabel Pankhurst (1880–1958) British suffragette. *Unshackled*

SELF-DENIAL

See also abstinence, selflessness

1 Self-denial is not a virtue; it is only the effect of prudence on rascality.

George Bernard Shaw (1856–1950) Irish dramatist and critic. *Man and Superman*, 'Maxims for Revolutionists'

2 Thy need is yet greater than mine.

Philip Sidney (1554–86) English poet and courtier. Giving his own water bottle to a humble wounded soldier after he had himself been wounded. Attrib.

SELF-INTEREST

See also parochialism, selfishness

1 Every man for himself, and the devil take the hindmost.

Proverb

2 The land self-interest groans from shore to shore,
For fear that plenty should attain the poor.

Lord Byron (1788–1824) British poet. *The Age of Bronze*, XIV

3 Anyone informed that the universe is expanding and contracting in pulsations of eighty billion years has a right to ask, 'What's in it for me?'

Peter De Vries (1910–93) US novelist. *The Glory of the Hummingbird*, Ch. 1

4 The least pain in our little finger gives us more concern and uneasiness than the destruction of millions of our fellow-beings.

William Hazlitt (1778–1830) British essayist. *American Literature*, 'Dr Channing'

5 It is difficult to love mankind unless one has a reasonable private income and when one has a reasonable private income one has better things to do than loving mankind.

Hugh Kingsmill (1889–1949) British writer. *God's Apology* (R. Ingrams)

6 Self-interest speaks all sorts of tongues, and plays all sorts of roles, even that of disinterestedness.

Duc de la Rochefoucauld (1613–80) French writer. *Maximes*, 39

SELFISHNESS

See also egotism, self-interest

1 I have been a selfish being all my life, in practice, though not in principle.

Jane Austen (1775–1817) British novelist. *Pride and Prejudice*, Ch. 58

2 And this the burthen of his song,
For ever us'd to be,
I care for nobody, not I,
If no one cares for me.

Isaac Bickerstaffe (c. 1735–c. 1812) Irish dramatist. *Love in a Village*, I

3 It's 'Damn you, Jack – I'm all right!' with you chaps.

David Bone (1874–1959) British sea captain and writer. *The Brassbounder*, Ch. 3

4 The proud, the cold untroubled heart of stone,
That never mused on sorrow but its own.

Thomas Campbell (1777–1844) British poet. *Pleasures of Hope*, I

SELF-KNOWLEDGE

1 Resolve to be thyself: and know, that he
Who finds himself, loses his misery.

Matthew Arnold (1822–88) British poet and critic. *Self-Dependence*

2 We confess our bad qualities to others out of fear of appearing naive or ridiculous by not being aware of them.

Gerald Brenan (Edward Fitzgerald Brenan; 1894–1987) British writer. *Thoughts in a Dry Season*

3 'I know myself,' he cried, 'but that is all.'

F. Scott Fitzgerald (1896–1940) US novelist. *This Side of Paradise*, Bk. II, Ch. 5

4 I do not know myself, and God forbid that I should.

Goethe (1749–1832) German poet and dramatist. *Conversations with Eckermann*, 10 Apr 1829

5 Know then thyself, presume not God to scan,
The proper study of Mankind is Man.

Alexander Pope (1688–1744) British poet. *An Essay on Man*, II

6 That true self-love and social are the same;
That virtue only makes our bliss below;
And all our knowledge is, ourselves to know.

Alexander Pope *An Essay on Man*, IV

SELFLESSNESS

See also charity, self-denial

1 Of gold she would not wear so much as a seal-ring, choosing to store her money in the stomachs of the poor rather than to keep it at her own disposal.

St Jerome (c. 347–c. 420) Italian monk and scholar. *Letter CXXVII*

2 The way to get things done is not to mind who gets the credit of doing them.

Benjamin Jowett (1817–93) British theologian. Attrib.

3 To give and not to count the cost;
To fight and not to heed the wounds;
To toil and not to seek for rest;
To labour and not ask for any reward
Save that of knowing that we do Thy will.

St Ignatius Loyola (1491–1556) Spanish priest. *Prayer for Generosity*

4 'I haven't got time to be sick!' he said. 'People need me.' For he was a country doctor, and he did not know what it was to spare himself.

Don Marquis (1878–1937) US journalist and writer. *Country Doctor*

5 There is nothing in Christianity or Buddhism that quite matches the sympathetic unselfishness of an oyster.

Saki (Hector Hugh Munro; 1870–1916) British writer. *Chronicles of Clovis*

6 O good old man! how well in thee appears
The constant service of the antique world,
When service sweat for duty, not for meed!
Thou art not for the fashion of these times,
Where none will sweat but for promotion,
And having that, do choke their service up
Even with the having.

William Shakespeare (1564–1616) English dramatist. *As You Like It*, II:3

SELF-MADE MEN

1 I know he is, and he adores his maker.

Benjamin Disraeli (1804–81) British statesman. Replying to a remark made in defence of John Bright that he was a self-made man. *The Fine Art of Political Wit* (L. Harris)

2 He was a self-made man who owed his lack of success to nobody.

Joseph Heller (1923–) US novelist. *Catch-22*, Ch. 3

3 A self-made man is one who believes in luck and sends his son to Oxford.

Christina Stead (1902–83) Australian novelist. *House of All Nations*, 'Credo'

SELF-PRESERVATION

See also survival

1 Look after number one.
Proverb

2 I want to get out with my greatness intact.
Muhammad Ali (Cassius Clay; 1942–) US heavyweight boxer. Announcing his retirement. *The Observer*, 4 July 1974

3 He that fights and runs away
May live to fight another day.
Anonymous *Musarum Deliciae*

4 This animal is very bad; when attacked it defends itself.
Anonymous *La Ménagerie* (P. K. Théodore), 1828

5 In good King Charles's golden days,
When loyalty no harm meant,
A zealous High Churchman was I,
And so I got preferment.

And this is law, that I'll maintain,
Unto my dying day, Sir,
That whatsoever King shall reign,
I'll be the Vicar of Bray, Sir.
Anonymous *The Vicar of Bray*

6 Kill the other guy before he kills you.
Jack Dempsey (1895–1983) US heavyweight boxer. *The Times*, 2 June 1983

7 There was only one catch and that was Catch-22, which specified that a concern for one's own safety in the face of dangers that were real and immediate was the process of a rational mind.
Joseph Heller (1923–) US novelist. *Catch-22*, Ch. 5

8 If a madman were to come into this room with a stick in his hand, no doubt we should pity the state of his mind; but our primary consideration would be to take care of ourselves. We should knock him down first, and pity him afterwards.
Samuel Johnson (1709–84) British lexicographer. *Life of Johnson* (J. Boswell), Vol. III

9 We intend to remain alive. Our neighbors want to see us dead. This is not a question that leaves much room for compromise.
Golda Meir (1898–1978) Russian-born Israeli stateswoman. *Reader's Digest* (July 1971), 'The Indestructible Golda Meir'

10 England has saved herself by her exertions, and will, as I trust, save Europe by her example.
William Pitt the Younger (1759–1806) British statesman. Speech, Guildhall, 1805

11 The better part of valour is discretion; in the which better part I have saved my life.
William Shakespeare (1564–1616) English dramatist. *Henry IV, Part One*, V:4

12 *J'ai vécu.*
I survived.
Abbé de Sieyès (1748–1836) French churchman. Replying to an enquiry concerning what he had done during the Terror. *Dictionnaire Encyclopédique* (E. Guérard)

13 Greater love hath no man than this, that he lay down his friends for his life.
Jeremy Thorpe (1929–) British politician. After Macmillan's 1962 Cabinet reshuffle. *The Pendulum Years* (Bernard Levin), Ch. 12

14 He was gifted with the sly, sharp instinct for self-preservation that passes for wisdom among the rich.
Evelyn Waugh (1903–66) British novelist. *Scoop*

15 Scheherazade is the classical example of a woman saving her head by using it.
Esme Wynne-Tyson (1898–) British writer. Attrib.

SELF-RELIANCE

See also independence

1 If you want a thing well done, do it yourself.
Proverb

2 The gods help them that help themselves.
Aesop (6th century BC) Reputed Greek writer of fables. *Fables*, 'Hercules and the Waggoner'

3 Be Prepared…the meaning of the motto is that a scout must prepare himself by previous thinking out and practising how to act on any accident or emergency so that he is never taken by surprise; he knows exactly what to do when anything unexpected happens.
Robert Baden-Powell (1857–1941) British soldier and founder of the Boy Scouts. Motto of the Scout movement. *Scouting for Boys*

4 I am the cat that walks alone.
Lord Beaverbrook (Maxwell Aitken; 1879–1964) Canadian-born politician and newspaper proprietor. *Beaverbrook* (A. J. P. Taylor)

5 They do most by Books, who could do much without them, and he that chiefly owes himself unto himself, is the substantial Man.
Thomas Browne (1605–82) English physician and writer. *Christian Morals*, Pt. II

6 Let the boy win his spurs.
Edward III (1312–77) King of England. Replying to a suggestion that he should send reinforcements to his son, the Black Prince, during the Battle of Crécy, 1346. Attrib.

7 I am your anointed Queen. I will never be by violence constrained to do anything. I thank God that I am endued with such qualities that if I were turned out of the Realm in my petticoat I were able to live in any place in Christome.
Elizabeth I (1533–1603) Queen of England. *Sayings of Queen Elizabeth* (Chamberlin)

8 Very well, alone.
David Low (1891–1963) British cartoonist. The cartoon showed a British soldier shaking his fist at a hostile sea and a sky full of war planes. Caption to cartoon, *Evening Standard*, 18 June 1940

9 The first rule in opera is the first rule in life: see to everything yourself.
Nellie Melba (Helen Porter Mitchell; 1861–1931) Australian soprano. *Melodies and Memories*

10 The greatest thing in the world is to know how to be self-sufficient.
Michel de Montaigne (1533–92) French essayist. *Essais*, I

11 I think it is about time we pulled our fingers out…The rest of the world most certainly does not owe us a living.

Prince Philip (1921–) The consort of Queen Elizabeth II. Speech, London, 17 Oct 1961

12 Our remedies oft in ourselves do lie,
Which we ascribe to heaven.

William Shakespeare (1564–1616) English dramatist. *All's Well that Ends Well*, I:1

13 I'll never
Be such a gosling to obey instinct, but stand
As if a man were author of himself
And knew no other kin.

William Shakespeare *Coriolanus*, V:3

14 Cassius from bondage will deliver Cassius.

William Shakespeare *Julius Caesar*, I:3

SELF-RESPECT

See also pride, respect

1 I will rather risk my Crown than do what I think personally disgraceful, and whilst I have no wish but for the good and prosperity of my country, it is impossible that the nation shall not stand by me; if they will not, they shall have another King.

George III (1738–1820) King of Great Britain and Ireland. Letter to Lord North, 17 Mar 1778

2 It is better to die on your feet than to live on your knees.

Dolores Ibarruri (1895–1989) Spanish politician. Speech, Paris, 1936

3 Self-respect – the secure feeling that no one, as yet, is suspicious.

H. L. Mencken (1880–1956) US journalist. *A Mencken Chrestomathy*

4 Whatever talents I possess may suddenly diminish or suddenly increase. I can with ease become an ordinary fool. I may be one now. But it doesn't do to upset one's own vanity.

Dylan Thomas (1914–53) Welsh poet. *Notebooks*

5 As for conceit, what man will do any good who is not conceited? Nobody holds a good opinion of a man who has a low opinion of himself.

Anthony Trollope (1815–82) British novelist. *Orley Farm*, Ch. 22

6 And, above all things, never think that you're not good enough yourself. A man should never think that. My belief is that in life people will take you very much at your own reckoning.

Anthony Trollope *The Small House at Allington*, Ch. 32

7 When people do not respect us we are sharply offended; yet deep down in his heart no man much respects himself.

Mark Twain (Samuel Langhorne Clemens; 1835–1910) US writer. *Notebooks*

SELLAR, WALTER CARRUTHERS

(1898–1951) British humorous writer who collaborated with Robert Julius Yeatman (1897–1968).

1 For every person wishing to teach there are approximately thirty who don't want to learn – much.

And Now All This, 'Introduction'

2 To confess that you are totally Ignorant about the Horse, is social suicide: you will be despised by everybody, especially the horse.

Horse Nonsense

3 1066 And All That.

Book title

4 The Roman Conquest was, however, a *Good Thing*, since the Britons were only natives at the time.

1066 And All That

5 The Cavaliers (Wrong but Wromantic) and the Roundheads (Right but Repulsive).

1066 And All That

6 Napoleon's armies used to march on their stomachs, shouting: 'Vive l'intérieur!'

1066 And All That

7 America became top nation and history came to a full stop.

1066 And All That

8 Do not on any account attempt to write on both sides of the paper at once.

1066 And All That, Test Paper 5

SENSATION

1 O for a life of sensations rather than of thoughts!

John Keats (1795–1821) British poet. Letter to Benjamin Bailey, 22 Nov 1817

2 'The story is like the wind', the Bushman prisoner said. 'It comes from a far off place, and we feel it.'

Laurens Van der Post (1906–) South African novelist. *A Story Like the Wind*

SENTIMENTALITY

See also emotion

1 They had been corrupted by money, and he had been corrupted by sentiment. Sentiment was the more dangerous, because you couldn't name its price. A man open to bribes was to be relied upon below a certain figure, but sentiment might uncoil in the heart at a name, a photograph, even a smell remembered.

Graham Greene (1904–91) British novelist. *The Heart of the Matter*

2 Sentimentality is a superstructure covering brutality.

Carl Gustav Jung (1875–1961) Swiss psychoanalyst. *Reflections*

3 One may not regard the world as a sort of metaphysical brothel for emotions.

Arthur Koestler (1905–83) Hungarian-born British writer. *Darkness at Noon*, 'The Second Hearing'

4 Sentimentality is only sentiment that rubs you up the wrong way.

W. Somerset Maugham (1874–1965) British novelist. *A Writer's Notebook*

5 She likes stories that make her cry – I think we

all do, it's so nice to feel sad when you've nothing particular to be sad about.

Annie Sullivan (1866–1936) US teacher of the handicapped. Referring to Helen Keller. Letter, 12 Dec 1887

SEPARATION

See also absence, parting

1 My Bonnie lies over the ocean,
My Bonnie lies over the sea,
My Bonnie lies over the ocean,
Oh, bring back my Bonnie to me.

Anonymous *My Bonnie*

2 If I should meet thee
After long years,
How should I greet thee? –
With silence and tears.

Lord Byron (1788–1824) British poet. *When we two parted*

3 Absence from whom we love is worse than death.

William Cowper (1731–1800) British poet. *'Hope, like the Short-lived Ray'*

4 As it will be the right of all, so it will be the duty of some, definitely to prepare for a separation, amicably if they can, violently if they must.

Josiah Quincy (1772–1864) US statesman. *Abridgement of Debates of Congress*, Vol. IV, 14 Jan 1811

5 Every parting gives a foretaste of death; every coming together again a foretaste of the resurrection.

Arthur Schopenhauer (1788–1860) German philosopher. *Gedanken über vielerlei Gegenstände*, XXVI

6 I do desire we may be better strangers.

William Shakespeare (1564–1616) English dramatist. *As You Like It*, III:2

SERIOUSNESS

1 Angels can fly because they take themselves lightly.

G. K. Chesterton (1874–1936) British writer. *Orthodoxy*, Ch. 7

2 Though this may be play to you, 'tis death to us.

Roger L'Estrange (1616–1704) English journalist and writer. *Aesop's Fables*, 398

3 You must not think me necessarily foolish because I am facetious, nor will I consider you necessarily wise because you are grave.

Sydney Smith (1771–1845) British clergyman and essayist. Letter to Bishop Blomfield

4 He rose by gravity; I sank by levity.

Sydney Smith Comparing his career with that of his brother, Robert Percy Smith. Attrib.

SERMONS

See also brevity, speeches, verbosity

1 The British churchgoer prefers a severe preacher because he thinks a few home truths will do his neighbours no harm.

George Bernard Shaw (1856–1950) Irish dramatist and critic. Attrib.

2 They are written as if sin were to be taken out of man like Eve out of Adam – by putting him to sleep.

Sydney Smith (1771–1845) British clergyman and essayist. Referring to boring sermons. *Anecdotes of the Clergy* (J. Larwood)

3 I never quite forgave Mahaffy for getting himself suspended from preaching in the College Chapel. Ever since his sermons were discontinued, I suffer from insomnia in church.

George Tyrrell (1861–1909) Irish Catholic theologian. *As I Was Going Down Sackville Street* (Oliver St John Gogarty), Ch. 25

4 Yes, about ten minutes.

Duke of Wellington (1769–1852) British general and statesman. Responding to a vicar's query as to whether there was anything he would like his forthcoming sermon to be about. Attrib.

SERVICE

See also help

1 His lord said unto him, Well done, thou good and faithful servant: thou hast been faithful over a few things, I will make thee ruler over many things: enter thou into the joy of thy lord.

Bible: Matthew 25:21

2 He was caught
Red-handed with the silver and his Grace
Being short of staff at the time asked him to stay
And clean it.

Christopher Fry (1907–) British dramatist. *Venus Observed*

3 Oh that I were an orange-tree,
That busy plant!
Then I should ever laden be,
And never want
Some fruit for Him that dressed me.

George Herbert (1593–1633) English poet. *Employment*

4 All English shop assistants are Miltonists. All Miltonists firmly believe that 'they serve who only stand and wait.'

George Mikes (1912–87) Hungarian-born British writer. *How to be Inimitable*

5 God doth not need
Either man's work or his own gifts. Who best
Bear his mild yoke, they serve him best: his state
Is kingly; thousands at his bidding speed,
And post o'er land and ocean without rest;
They also serve who only stand and wait.

John Milton (1608–74) English poet. *Sonnet*: 'On his Blindness'

6 Small service is true service, while it lasts.

William Wordsworth (1770–1850) British poet. *To a Child, Written in her Album*

SERVILITY

See also flattery, humility

1 Fine words and an insinuating appearance are seldom associated with true virtue.

Confucius (K'ung Fu-tzu; 551–479 BC) Chinese philosopher. *Analects*

2 I am well aware that I am the 'umblest person going…My mother is likewise a very 'umble person. We live in a numble abode.

Charles Dickens (1812–70) British novelist. Said by Uriah Heep. *David Copperfield*, Ch. 16

3 Uriah, with his long hands slowly twining over one another, made a ghastly writhe from the waist upwards.

Charles Dickens *David Copperfield*, Ch. 17

4 A pious man is one who would be an atheist if the king were.

Jean de La Bruyère (1645–96) French satirist. *Les Caractères*

5 Wit that can creep, and pride that licks the dust.

Alexander Pope (1688–1744) British poet. *Epistle to Dr. Arbuthnot*

6 You know that nobody is strongminded around a President…it is always: 'yes sir', 'no sir' (the 'no sir' comes when he asks whether you're dissatisfied).

George Edward Reedy (1917–) US government official. *The White House* (ed. R. Gordon Hoxie)

7 Whenever he met a great man he grovelled before him, and my-lorded him as only a free-born Briton can do.

William Makepeace Thackeray (1811–63) British novelist. *Vanity Fair*, Ch. 13

SEX

See also abstinence, adultery, animalism, contraception, debauchery, illegitimacy, lust, pornography, promiscuity, prudery, purity, sexes

1 There are many females who never feel any sexual excitement whatever. The best mothers, wives, and managers of households, know little or nothing of sexual indulgences. Love of home, children, and domestic duties are the only passions they feel.

W. Acton *The Functions and Disorders of the Reproductive Organs*

2 Is sex dirty? Only if it's done right.

Woody Allen (Allen Stewart Konigsberg; 1935–) US film actor. *All You've Ever Wanted to Know About Sex*

3 It was the most fun I ever had without laughing.

Woody Allen *Annie Hall*

4 Don't knock it, it's sex with someone you love.

Woody Allen Referring to masturbation. *Annie Hall*

5 WOMAN. You are the greatest lover I have ever known.
ALLEN. Well, I practice a lot when I'm on my own.

Woody Allen *Love and Death*

6 My brain: it's my second favorite organ.

Woody Allen *Sleeper*

7 Sex between a man and a woman can be wonderful – provided you get between the right man and the right woman.

Woody Allen Attrib.

8 Virginity is rather a state of mind.

Maxwell Anderson (1888–1959) *Elizabeth the Queen*, II:3

9 She sighed, she cried, she damned near died:
she said 'What shall I do?'
So I took her into bed and covered up her head
Just to save her from the foggy, foggy dew.

Anonymous *Weaver's Song*

10 You are the first American to make sex funny.

Anonymous Said to Anita Loos by a friend on reading her *Gentlemen Prefer Blondes* (1928).

11 The Seven Year Itch.

George Axelrod (1922–) US screenwriter. Play and film title

12 It is called in our schools 'beastliness', and this is about the best name for it…should it become a habit it quickly destroys both health and spirits; he becomes feeble in body and mind, and often ends in a lunatic asylum.

Robert Baden-Powell (1857–1941) British soldier and founder of the Boy Scouts. Referring to masturbation. *Scouting for Boys*

13 The great and terrible step was taken. What else could you expect from a girl so expectant? 'Sex,' said Frank Harris, 'is the gateway to life.' So I went through the gateway in an upper room in the Cafe Royal.

Enid Bagnold (1889–1981) British playwright. *Enid Bagnold's Autobiography*

14 Money, it turned out, was exactly like sex, you thought of nothing else if you didn't have it and thought of other things if you did.

James Baldwin (1924–87) US writer. *Nobody Knows My Name*

15 I'll come and make love to you at five o'clock. If I'm late start without me.

Tallulah Bankhead (1903–68) US actress. *Somerset Maugham* (E. Morgan)

16 Sexuality is the lyricism of the masses.

Charles Baudelaire (1821–67) French poet. *Journaux intimes*, 93

17 My beloved put in his hand by the hole of the door, and my bowels were moved for him.

Bible: Song of Solomon 5:4

18 If God had meant us to have group sex, I guess he'd have given us all more organs.

Malcolm Bradbury (1932–) British academic and novelist. *Who Do You Think You Are?*, 'A Very Hospitable Person'

19 Sex and the Single Girl.

Helen Gurley Brown (1922–) US journalist. Book title

20 He said it was artificial respiration but now I find I'm to have his child.

Anthony Burgess (John Burgess Wilson; 1917–93) British novelist. *Inside Mr. Enderby*

21 It doesn't matter what you do in the bedroom as long as you don't do it in the street and frighten the horses.

Mrs Patrick Campbell (Beatrice Stella Tanner; 1865–1940) British actress. *The Duchess of Jermyn Street* (Daphne Fielding), Ch. 2

22 The Summer hath his joys,
And Winter his delights.
Though Love and all his pleasures are but toys,
They shorten tedious nights.

Thomas Campion (1567–1620) English poet. *Now Winter Nights Enlarge*

23 I'll wager you that in 10 years it will be fashionable again to be a virgin.

Barbara Cartland (1902–) British romantic novelist. *The Observer*, 'Sayings of the Week', 20 June 1976

24 I answer 20 000 letters a year and so many couples are having problems because they are not getting the right proteins and vitamins.

Barbara Cartland *The Observer*, 'Sayings of the Week', 31 Aug 1986

25 I said 10 years ago that in 10 years time it would be smart to be a virgin. Now everyone is back to virgins again.

Barbara Cartland *The Observer*, 'Sayings of the Week', 12 July 1987

26 She gave me a smile I could feel in my hip pocket.

Raymond Chandler (1888–1959) US novelist. *Farewell, My Lovely*, Ch. 18

27 The pleasure is momentary, the position ridiculous and the expense damnable.

Earl of Chesterfield (1694–1773) English statesman. *Nature*, 1970, 227, 772

28 Dead birds don't fall out of their nests.

Winston Churchill (1874–1965) British statesman. When someone told him that his trouser fly-buttons were undone. Attrib.

29 When she raises her eyelids it's as if she were taking off all her clothes.

Colette (1873–1954) French novelist. *Claudine and Annie*

30 The doggie in front has suddenly gone blind, and the other one has very kindly offered to push him all the way to St Dunstan's.

Noël Coward (1899–1973) British dramatist. To a small child, who asked what two dogs were doing together in the street. St Dunstan's is a British institution for the blind. *Two Hands Clapping* (K. Tynan)

31 Ignorance of the necessity for sexual intercourse to the health and virtue of both man and woman, is the most fundamental error in medical and moral philosophy.

George Drysdale *The Elements of Social Science*

32 You notice that the tabetic has the power of holding water for an indefinite period. He also is impotent – in fact two excellent properties to possess for a quiet day on the river.

Dr. Dunlop (fl. early 20th century) Lecture at Charing Cross Hospital, London

33 No more about sex, it's too boring. Everyone's got one. Nastiness is a real stimulant though – but poor honest sex, like dying, should be a private matter.

Laurence Durrell (1912–90) British novelist and poet. *Prospero's Cell*, Ch. 1

34 You think intercourse is a private act; it's not, it's a social act. Men are sexually predatory in life; and women are sexually manipulative. When two individuals come together and leave their gender outside the bedroom door, then they make love. If they take it inside with them, they do something else, because society is in the room with them.

Andrea Dworkin US feminist. *Intercourse*

35 We're all wankers underneath...if we were honest about ourselves we'd know we're all wankers under the table...I'm a wanker, I have known the pleasures of the palm...why can't we be honest? Once we acknowledge everyone's a wanker it'll be easy – suddenly all authority figures disappear.

Ben Elton British comedian. BBC TV programme, *The Man from Auntie*, 1990

36 He in a few minutes ravished this fair creature, or at least would have ravished her, if she had not, by a timely compliance, prevented him.

Henry Fielding (1707–54) British novelist. *Jonathan Wild*, Bk. III, Ch. 7

37 Older women are best because they always think they may be doing it for the last time.

Ian Fleming (1908–64) British journalist and author. *Life of Ian Fleming* (John Pearson)

38 In an uncorrupted woman the sexual impulse does not manifest itself at all, but only love; and this love is the natural impulse of a woman to satisfy a man.

Johann Fichte (1762–1814) German philosopher. *The Science of Rights*

39 Well, what does it do this nine-inch penis? Where does it go?...Do I have a clitoris halfway up my stomach?

Carrie Fisher (1956–) US film star. *Life*, 1 May 1994

40 The members of our secret service have apparently spent so much time looking under the beds for Communists, they haven't had time to look in the bed.

Michael Foot (1913–) British Labour politician and journalist. Referring to the Profumo affair. Attrib.

41 The sole criterion of frigidity is the absence of the vaginal orgasm.

Sigmund Freud (1856–1939) Austrian psychoanalyst. *Three Essays on the Theory of Sexuality*

42 Personally I know nothing about sex because I've always been married.

Zsa Zsa Gabor (1919–) Hungarian-born US film star. *The Observer*, 'Sayings of the Week', 16 Aug 1987

43 Ah, the sex thing. I'm glad that part of my life is over.

Greta Garbo (1905–90) Swedish-born US film star. Attrib.

44 As women have known since the dawn of our times, the primary site for stimulation to orgasm centers upon the clitoris. The revolution unleashed by the Kinsey report of 1953 has, by now, made this information available to men who, for whatever reason, had not figured it out for themselves by the more obvious routes of experience and sensitivity.

Stephen Jay Gould (1941–) US geologist and writer. *Bully for Brontosaurus*

45 Despite a lifetime of service to the cause of sexual liberation I have never caught a venereal disease, which makes me feel rather like an arctic explorer who has never had frostbite.

Germaine Greer (1939–) Australian-born British writer and feminist. *The Observer*, 'Sayings of the Week', 4 Mar 1973

46 For all the pseudo-sophistication of twentieth-century sex theory, it is still assumed that a man should make love as if his principal intention was to people the wilderness.

Germaine Greer Attrib.

47 No sex is better than bad sex.

Germaine Greer Attrib.

48 Masturbation is the thinking man's television.

Christopher Hampton (1946–) British playwright. *The Philanthropist*

49 Prostitution gives her an opportunity to meet people. It provides fresh air and wholesome exercise, and it keeps her out of trouble.

Joseph Heller (1923–) US novelist. *Catch-22*, Ch. 33

50 But did thee feel the earth move?

Ernest Hemingway (1899–1961) US novelist. *For Whom the Bell Tolls*, Ch. 13

51 I am happy now that Charles calls on my bedchamber less frequently than of old. As it is, I now endure but two calls a week and when I hear his steps outside my door I lie down on my bed, close my eyes, open my legs and think of England.

Lady Alice Hillingdon (1857–1940) Wife of 2nd Baron Hillingdon. Often mistakenly attributed to Queen Victoria. *Journal* (1912)

52 My life with girls has ended, though till lately I was up to it and soldiered on not ingloriously; now on this wall will hang my weapons and my lyre, discharged from the war.

Horace (Quintus Horatius Flaccus; 65–8 BC) Roman poet. *Odes*, III

53 People will insist…on treating the *mons Veneris* as though it were Mount Everest.

Aldous Huxley (1894–1964) British novelist. *Eyeless in Gaza*, Ch. 30

54 A million million spermatozoa,
All of them alive:
Out of their cataclysm but one poor Noah
Dare hope to survive.

Aldous Huxley *Fifth Philosopher's Song*

55 'Bed,' as the Italian proverb succinctly puts it, 'is the poor man's opera.'

Aldous Huxley *Heaven and Hell*

56 The zipless fuck is the purest thing there is. And it is rarer than the unicorn. And I have never had one.

Erica Jong (1942–) US novelist. *Fear of Flying*

57 My response…was…to evolve my fantasy of the Zipless Fuck…Zipless because when you come together zippers fell away like petals.

Erica Jong *Fear of Flying*

58 The discussion of the sexual problem is, of course, only the somewhat crude beginning of a far deeper question, namely, that of the psychic of human relationship between the sexes. Before this later question the sexual problem pales into significance.

C. G. Jung (1875–1961) Swiss psychologist. *Bartlett's Unfamiliar Quotations* (Leonard Louis Levinson)

59 To be solemn about the organs of generation is only possible to someone who, like Lawrence, has deified the will and denied the spirit.

Hugh Kingsmill Referring to D. H. Lawrence. *Tread Softly for You Tread on My Jokes* (Malcolm Muggeridge)

60 The vagina walls are quite insensitive in the great majority of females…There is no evidence that the vagina is ever the sole source of arousal, or even the primary source of erotic arousal in any female.

Alfred Charles Kinsey (1894–1956) US zoologist and director of the Institute for Sex Research. *Sexual Behaviour in the Human Female*

61 Have you not as yet observed that pleasure, which is undeniably the sole motive force behind the union of the sexes, is nevertheless not enough to form a bond between them? And that, if it is preceded by desire which impels, it is succeeded by disgust which repels? That is a law of nature which love alone can alter.

Pierre Choderlos de Laclos (1741–1803) French novelist. *Les Liaisons dangereuses*, Letter 131

62 Who would not be curious to see the lineaments of a man who, having himself been twice married wished that mankind were propagated like trees.

Charles Lamb (1775–1834) British essayist. Referring to Thomas Browne. *New Monthly Magazine*, Jan 1826

63 Sexual intercourse began
In nineteen sixty-three
(Which was rather late for me) –
Between the end of the *Chatterley* ban
And the Beatles' first LP.

Philip Larkin (1922–85) British poet. *High Windows*, 'Annus Mirabilis'

64 When Eve ate this particular apple, she became aware of her own womanhood, mentally. And mentally she began to experiment with it. She has been experimenting ever since. So has man. To the rage and horror of both of them.

D. H. Lawrence (1885–1930) British novelist. *Fantasia of the Unconscious*, Ch. 7

65 It's all this cold-hearted fucking that is death and idiocy.

D. H. Lawrence (1885–1930) British novelist and poet. *Lady Chatterley's Lover*, Ch. 14 (1928)

66 John Thomas says good-night to Lady Jane, a little droopingly, but with a hopeful heart.

D. H. Lawrence The closing words of the book. *Lady Chatterley's Lover*

67 You mustn't think I advocate perpetual sex. Far from it. Nothing nauseates me more than promiscuous sex in and out of season.

D. H. Lawrence Referring to *Lady Chatterley's Lover*. Letter to Lady Ottoline Morrell, 22 Dec 1928

68 Making love is the sovereign remedy for anguish.

Frédérick Leboyer (1918–) French obstetrician. *Birth without Violence*

69 The trouble with Ian is that he gets off with women because he can't get on with them.

Rosamond Lehmann (1901–90) British writer. Referring to Ian Fleming. *The Life of Ian Fleming* (J. Pearson)

70 He was into animal husbandry – until they caught him at it.

Tom Lehrer (1928–) US songwriter and entertainer. *An Evening Wasted with Tom Lehrer*

71 You know the worst thing about oral sex? The view.

Maureen Lipman (1946–) British actress. Remark, 1990.

72 There was sex of course, but although both of them were extremely interested in sex, and enjoyed nothing better than discussing it, neither of them, if the truth be told, was quite so interested in actually having it, or at any rate in having it very frequently.

David Lodge (1935–) British author. *Nice Work*, I

73 No sex without responsibility.

Lord Longford (1905–) British politician and social reformer. *The Observer*, 'Sayings of the Week', 3 May 1954

74 The reproduction of mankind is a great marvel and mystery. Had God consulted me in the matter, I should have advised him to continue the generation of the species by fashioning them of clay.

Martin Luther (1483–1546) German Protestant reformer.

75 Nuns are sexy.

Madonna (Madonna Louise Veronica Ciccone; 1958–) US pop singer and film star. *Time*, 27 May 1985

76 Pussy rules the world.

Madonna BBC TV programme *Omnibus*, 1 Dec 1990

77 The Duke returned from the wars today and did pleasure me in his top-boots.

Sarah, Duchess of Marlborough (1660–1744) Wife of John Churchill, 1st Duke of Marlborough. Attributed to her in various forms; a more ambitious version goes '...pleasure me three times in his top-boots'.

78 FRIAR BARNARDINE. Thou hast committed –
BARABAS. Fornication: but that was in another country;
And beside the wench is dead.

Christopher Marlowe (1564–93) English dramatist. *The Jew of Malta*, IV:1

79 Whoever named it necking was a poor judge of anatomy.

Groucho Marx (Julius Marx; 1895–1977) US comedian. Attrib.

80 If sex is such a natural phenomenon, how come there are so many books on how to?

Bette Midler (1944–) US actress and comedienne.

81 Continental people have sex life; the English have hot-water bottles.

George Mikes (1912–) Hungarian-born British writer and humorist. *How to be an Alien*

82 Sex is one of the nine reasons for reincarnation...The other eight are unimportant.

Henry Miller (1891–1980) US novelist. *Big Sur and the Oranges of Hieronymus Bosch*

83 There was a little girl
Who had a little curl
Right in the middle of her forehead,
When she was good she was very very good
And when she was bad she was very very popular.

Max Miller (Harold Sargent; 1895–1963) British music-hall comedian. *The Max Miller Blue Book*

84 When she saw the sign 'Members Only' she thought of him.

Spike Milligan (1918–) British comic actor and author. *Puckoon*

85 The daughter-in-law of Pythagoras said that a woman who goes to bed with a man ought to lay aside her modesty with her skirt, and put it on again with her petticoat.

Michel de Montaigne (1533–92) French essayist. *Essais*, I

86 Two minutes with Venus, two years with mercury.

J. Earle Moore (1892–1957) US physician. Alluding to the former use of mercury compounds in the treatment of syphilis. Aphorism

87 Why do they put the Gideon Bibles only in the bedrooms where it's usually too late?

Christopher Darlington Morley (1890–1957) US writer. *Quotations for Speakers and Writers*

88 The orgasm has replaced the Cross as the focus of longing and the image of fulfilment.

Malcolm Muggeridge (1903–90) British writer. *The Most of Malcolm Muggeridge*, 'Down with Sex'

89 It has to be admitted that we English have sex on the brain, which is a very unsatisfactory place to have it.

Malcolm Muggeridge *The Observer*, 'Sayings of the Decade', 1964

90 It's all any reasonable child can expect if the dad is present at the conception.

Joe Orton (1933–67) British dramatist. *Entertaining Mr Sloane*, III

91 If all the young ladies who attended the Yale promenade dance were laid end to end, no one would be the least surprised.

Dorothy Parker (1893–1967) US writer. *While Rome Burns* (Alexander Woollcott)

92 Tell him I've been too fucking busy – or vice versa.

Dorothy Parker When asked why she had not delivered her copy on time. *You Might As Well Live* (J. Keats)

93 There, but for a typographical error, is the story of my life.

Dorothy Parker At a Hallowe'en party, when someone remarked, 'They're ducking for apples'. *You Might As Well Live* (J. Keats)

94 I know it does make people happy but to me it is just like having a cup of tea.

Cynthia Payne (1934–) London housewife. After her acquittal on a charge of controlling prostitutes in a famous 'sex-for-luncheon-vouchers' case, 8 Nov 1987

95 Love is not the dying moan of a distant violin – it's the triumphant twang of a bedspring.

S. J. Perelman (1904–79) US humorous writer. *Quotations for Speakers and Writers* (A. Andrews)

96 I tend to believe that cricket is the greatest thing that God ever created on earth...certainly greater than sex, although sex isn't too bad either.

Harold Pinter (1930–) British playwright. *The Observer*, 5 Oct 1980

97 On a sofa upholstered in panther skin
Mona did researches in original sin.

William Plomer (1903–73) South African poet and novelist. *Mews Flat Mona*

98 A PUSHING LADY. What are your views on love?
MME LEROI. Love? I make it constantly but I never talk about it.

Marcel Proust (1871–1922) French novelist. *À La Recherche du temps perdu: Le Côté de Guermantes*

99 One orgasm in the bush is worth two in the hand.

Robert Reisner *Graffiti*, 'Masturbation'

100 Everything You Always Wanted to Know About Sex But Were Afraid to Ask.

David Reuben (1933–) US doctor and author. Book title

101 The Christian view of sex is that it is, indeed, a form of holy communion.

John Robinson (1919–83) Bishop of Woolwich. Giving evidence in the prosecution of Penguin Books for publishing *Lady Chatterly's Lover.*

102 Love is two minutes fifty-two seconds of squishing noises. It shows your mind isn't clicking right.

Johnny Rotten (1957–) British punk musician. In the *Daily Mirror* in 1983 Rotten said that owing to a new-found technique, the time was now about five minutes. Attrib.

103 Love as a relation between men and women was ruined by the desire to make sure of the legitimacy of the children.

Bertrand Russell (1872–1970) British philosopher. *Marriage and Morals*

104 Civilized people cannot fully satisfy their sexual instinct without love.

Bertrand Russell *Marriage and Morals*, 'The Place of Love in Human Life'

105 His excessive emphasis on sex was due to the fact that in sex alone he was compelled to admit that he was not the only human being in the universe. It was so painful that he conceived of sex relations as a perpetual fight in which each is attempting to destroy the other.

Bertrand Russell Referring to D.H. Lawrence. *Autobiography*

106 Sex is something I really don't understand too hot. You never know *where* the hell you are. I keep making up these sex rules for myself, and then I break them right away.

J. D. Salinger (1919–) US novelist. *The Catcher in the Rye*, Ch. 9

107 Is it not strange that desire should so many years outlive performance?

William Shakespeare (1564–1616) English dramatist. *Henry IV, Part Two*, II:4

108 Even now, now, very now, an old black ram
Is tupping your white ewe.

William Shakespeare *Othello*, I:1

109 Your daughter and the Moor are now making the beast with two backs.

William Shakespeare *Othello*, I:1

110 Lechery, lechery! Still wars and lechery! Nothing else holds fashion.

William Shakespeare *Troilus and Cressida*, V:2

111 A determining point in the history of gynecology is to be found in the fact that sex plays a more important part in the life of woman than in that of man, and that she is more burdened by her sex.

Henry E. Sigerist (1891–1957) *American Journal of Obstetrics and Gynecology* 42:714, 1941

112 Someone asked Sophocles, 'How do you feel now about sex? Are you still able to have a woman?' He replied, 'Hush, man; most gladly indeed am I rid of it all, as though I had escaped from a mad and savage master.'

Sophocles (c. 496–406 BC) Greek dramatist. *Republic* (Plato), Bk. I

113 'Sex,' she says, 'is a subject like any other subject. Every bit as interesting as agriculture.'

Muriel Spark (1918–) British writer and poet. *The Hothouse by the East River*, Ch. 4

114 What women want is not to be treated with respect and care. They want to be treated like shit. They seem to like it.

John Steed British rapist and murderer. Referring to the rape and murder he committed on the M4, 1986.

115 For me, there was always this part of the brain reliably devoted to sex. Now there is this whole part of your brain which is freed up.

Gloria Steinem (1934–) US writer and feminist. *The Observer Life Magazine*, 15 May 1994

116 Masturbation: the primary sexual activity of mankind. In the nineteenth century it was a disease; in the twentieth, it's a cure.

Thomas Szasz (1920–) US psychiatrist. *The Second Sin*

117 Traditionally, sex has been a very private, secretive activity. Herein perhaps lies its powerful force for uniting people in a strong bond. As we make sex less secretive, we may rob it of its power to hold men and women together.

Thomas Szasz (1920–) US psychiatrist. *The Second Sin*

118 Chasing the naughty couples down the grassgreen gooseberried double bed of the wood.

Dylan Thomas (1914–53) Welsh poet. *Under Milk Wood*

119 Old Nat Burge sat…He was…watching the moon come up lazily out of the old cemetery in which nine of his daughters were lying, and only two of them were dead.

James Thurber (1894–1961) US humorist. *Let Your Mind Alone*, 'Bateman Comes Home'

120 Surely you don't mean by unartificial insemination!

James Thurber On being accosted at a party by a drunk woman who claimed she would like to have a baby by him. Attrib.

121 Is Sex Necessary?

James Thurber and E. B. White (1894–1961 and 1899–) US writers, humorists, and cartoonists. Title of a book

122 Familiarity breeds contempt – and children.

Mark Twain (Samuel Langhorne Clemens; 1835–1910) US writer. *Notebooks*

123 Sex is the biggest nothing of all time.

Andy Warhol (Andrew Warhola; 1926–87) US pop artist. *Halliwell's Filmgoer's and Video Viewer's Companion*

124 All this fuss about sleeping together. For physical pleasure I'd sooner go to my dentist any day.

Evelyn Waugh (1903–66) British novelist. *Vile Bodies*, Ch. 6

125 The mind can also be an erogenous zone.

Raquel Welch (1940–) US film star. *Colombo's Hollywood* (J.R. Colombo)

126 When women go wrong, men go right after them.

Mae West (1892–1980) US actress. *The Wit and Wisdom of Mae West* (ed. J. Weintraub)

127 It's not the men in my life that count; it's the life in my men.

Mae West Attrib.

128 When I'm good I'm very good, but when I'm bad I'm better.

Mae West Attrib.

129 I shall not say why and how I became, at the age of fifteen, the mistress of the Earl of Craven.

Harriette Wilson (1789–1846) British writer and courtesan. *Memoirs*, Opening

130 Sex is the tabasco sauce which an adolescent national palate sprinkles on every course in the menu.

Mary Day Winn (1888–1965) US writer. *Adam's Rib*

131 Freud found sex an outcast in the outhouse and left it in the living room an honored guest.

W. Beran Wolfe Referring to Sigmund Freud. *The Great Quotations* (George Seldes)

132 A mistress should be like a little country retreat near the town, not to dwell in constantly, but only for a night and away.

William Wycherley (1640–1716) English dramatist. *The Country Wife*, I:1

133 The artificial categories 'heterosexual' and 'homosexual' have been laid on us by a sexist society.

Allen Young US gay activist. *Out of the Closets: Voices of Gay Liberation*

SEXES

See also feminism, marriage, men, sex, woman's role, women

1 Between man and woman there is little difference, but *vive la différence*.

French proverb

2 Physically, a man is a man for a much longer time than a woman is a woman.

Honoré de Balzac (1799–1850) French writer. *The Physiology of Marriage*

3 As men
Do walk a mile, women should talk an hour,
After supper. 'Tis their exercise.

Francis Beaumont (1584–1616) English dramatist. *Philaster*, II:4

4 And the man said, The woman whom thou gavest to be with me, she gave me of the tree, and I did eat.
And the Lord God said unto the woman, What is this that thou hast done? And the woman said, The serpent beguiled me, and I did eat.
And the Lord God said unto the serpent, Because thou hast done this, thou art cursed above all cattle, and above every beast of the field; upon thy belly shalt thou go, and dust shalt thou eat all the days of thy life:
And I will put enmity between thee and the woman, and between thy seed and her seed; it shall bruise thy head, and thou shalt bruise his heel.
Unto the woman he said, I will greatly multiply thy sorrow and thy conception; in sorrow thou shalt bring forth children; and thy desire shall be to thy husband, and he shall rule over thee.
And unto Adam he said, Because thou hast hearkened unto the voice of thy wife, and has eaten of the tree, of which I commanded thee, saying, Thou shalt not eat of it: cursed is the ground for thy sake; in sorrow shalt thou eat of it all the days of thy life.

Bible: Genesis 3:12–17

5 Mr. Darwin…has failed to hold definitely before his mind the principle that the difference of sex, whatever it may consist in, must itself be subject to natural selection and to evolution.

Antoinette Brown Blackwell (1825–1921) US feminist writer. *The Sexes Throughout Nature*

6 Man's love is of man's life a thing apart,
'Tis woman's whole existence.

Lord Byron (1788–1824) British poet. *Don Juan*, I

7 There is more difference within the sexes than between them.

Ivy Compton-Burnett (1892–1969) British novelist. *Mother and Son*

8 In the sex-war thoughtlessness is the weapon of the male, vindictiveness of the female.

Cyril Connolly (1903–74) British journalist. *The Unquiet Grave*

9 The average man is more interested in a woman who is interested in him than he is in a woman – any woman – with beautiful legs.

Marlene Dietrich (Maria Magdalene von Losch; 1904–92) German-born film star. News item, 13 Dec 1954

10 Most women set out to try to change a man, and when they have changed him they do not like him.

Marlene Dietrich Attrib.

11 The reason that husbands and wives do not understand each other is because they belong to different sexes.

Dorothy Dix (Elizabeth Meriwether Gilmer; 1861–1951) US journalist and writer. News item

12 I don't think men and women were meant to live together. They are totally different animals.

Diana Dors (1931–84) British actress. Remark, May 1988

13 Where young boys plan for what they will achieve and attain, young girls plan for whom they will achieve and attain.

Charlotte Perkins Gilman (1860–1935) US writer. *Women and Economics*, Ch. 5

14 Man has his will, – but woman has her way.

Oliver Wendell Holmes (1809–94) US writer. *The Autocrat of the Breakfast Table*, Prologue

15 Boys will be boys – '
'And even that…wouldn't matter if we could only prevent girls from being girls.'

Anthony Hope (Anthony Hope Hawkins; 1863–1933) British novelist. *The Dolly Dialogues*

16 If Nature had arranged that husbands and wives should have children alternatively, there would never be more than *three* in a family.

Laurence Housman (1865–1959)

17 Christ called as his Apostles only men. He did this in a totally free and sovereign way.

John Paul II (Karol Wotjyla; 1920–) Polish pope. Speech, Sept 1988

18 For men must work, and women must weep,

And there's little to earn, and many to keep,
Though the harbour bar be moaning.

Charles Kingsley (1819–75) British writer. *The Three Fishers*

19 The silliest woman can manage a clever man; but it needs a very clever woman to manage a fool.

Rudyard Kipling (1865–1936) Indian-born British writer. *Plain Tales from the Hills*, 'Three and – an Extra'

20 Men have broad and large chests, and small narrow hips, and more understanding than women, who have but small and narrow breasts, and broad hips, to the end they should remain at home, sit still, keep house, and bear and bring up children.

Martin Luther (1483–1546) German Protestant reformer. *Table-Talk*, 'Of Marriage and Celibacy'

21 The only really happy people are married women and single men.

H. L. Mencken (1880–1956) US journalist. Attrib.

22 Perhaps at fourteen every boy should be in love with some ideal woman to put on a pedestal and worship. As he grows up, of course, he will put her on a pedestal the better to view her legs.

Barry Norman (1933–) British cinema critic and broadcaster. *The Listener*

23 The seldom female in a world of males!

Ruth Pitter (1897–92) British poet. *The Kitten's Eclogue*, IV

24 Women have smaller brains than men.

Hojatolislam Rafsanjani Iranian politician. Remark, July 1986

25 I often want to cry. That is the only advantage women have over men – at least they can cry.

Jean Rhys (1894–1979) Dominican-born British novelist. *Good Morning, Midnight*, Pt. II

26 Woman's virtue is man's greatest invention.

Cornelia Otis Skinner (1901–79) US stage actress. Attrib.

27 A man may sympathize with a woman in childbed, though it is impossible that he should conceive himself as suffering her pains in his own proper person and character.

Adam Smith (1723–90) Scottish economist. *The Theory of Moral Sentiments*, Pt. VII

28 Man is a creature who lives not upon bread alone, but principally by catchwords; and the little rift between the sexes is astonishingly widened by simply teaching one set of catchwords to the girls and another to the boys.

Robert Louis Stevenson (1850–94) Scottish writer. *Virginibus Puerisque*

29 Man is the hunter; woman is his game:
The sleek and shining creatures of the chase,
We hunt them for the beauty of their skins.

Alfred, Lord Tennyson (1809–92) British poet. *The Princess*, V

30 Man for the field and woman for the hearth:
Man for the sword and for the needle she:
Man with the head and woman with the heart:
Man to command and woman to obey;
All else confusion.

Alfred, Lord Tennyson *The Princess*, V

31 There are some meannesses which are too mean even for man – woman, lovely woman alone, can venture to commit them.

William Makepeace Thackeray (1811–63) British novelist. *A Shabby-Genteel Story*, Ch. 3

32 The War between Men and Women.

James Thurber (1894–1961) US humorist. Title of a series of cartoons

33 When a man confronts catastrophe on the road, he looks in his purse – but a woman looks in her mirror.

Margaret Turnbull (fl. 1920s–1942) US writer. *The Left Lady*

34 Instead of this absurd division into sexes they ought to class people as static and dynamic.

Evelyn Waugh (1903–66) British novelist. *Decline and Fall*, Pt. III, Ch. 7

35 All women become like their mothers. That is their tragedy. No man does. That's his.

Oscar Wilde (1854–1900) Irish-born British dramatist. *The Importance of Being Earnest*, I

36 Women represent the triumph of matter over mind, just as men represent the triumph of mind over morals.

Oscar Wilde *The Picture of Dorian Gray*, Ch. 4

37 Can the fact that Our Lord chose men as his Twelve Apostles be lightly dismissed?

Bishop of Winchester (1926–) British churchman. Remark, July 1988

38 Why are women...so much more interesting to men than men are to women?

Virginia Woolf (1882–1941) British novelist. *A Room of One's Own*

SHAKESPEARE, WILLIAM

(1564–1616) English dramatist and poet, universally acknowledged to be the greatest English writer of historical plays, comedies, and tragedies. His sonnets have love and friendship as their themes.

Quotations about Shakespeare

1 Others abide our question, Thou art free,
We ask and ask: Thou smilest and art still,
Out-topping knowledge.

Matthew Arnold (1822–88) British poet and critic. *Shakespeare*

2 When he killed a calf he would do it in a high style, and make a speech.

John Aubrey (1626–1697) English antiquary. *Brief Lives*, 'William Shakespeare'

3 Shakespeare was something of an Establishment creep...a man who could be trusted to have a safe pair of hands when it came to politics dramatised on the stage.

Howard Brenton (1942–) British dramatist. *The Guardian*, 'Soundbites', 3 June 1993

4 Our myriad-minded Shakespeare.

Samuel Taylor Coleridge (1772–1834) British poet. *Biographia Literaria*, Ch. 15

5 I have tried lately to read Shakespeare, and found it so intolerably dull that it nauseated me.

Charles Darwin (1809–82) British life scientist. *Autobiography*

6 He was the man who of all modern, and perhaps ancient poets had the largest and most comprehensive soul.

John Dryden (1631–1700) British poet and dramatist. *Essay of Dramatic Poesy*

7 He was naturally learned; he needed not the spectacles of books to read nature; he looked inwards, and found her there.

John Dryden *Essay of Dramatic Poesy*

8 We can say of Shakespeare, that never has a man turned so little knowledge to such great account.

T. S. Eliot (1888–1965) US-born British poet and dramatist. *The Classics and the Man of Letters* (lecture)

9 The remarkable thing about Shakespeare is that he is really very good – in spite of all the people who say he is very good.

Robert Graves (1895–1985) British poet and novelist. *The Observer*, 'Sayings of the Week', 6 Dec 1964

10 Shakespeare never had six lines together without a fault. Perhaps you may find seven, but this does not refute my general assertion.

Samuel Johnson (1709–84) British lexicographer. *Life of Johnson* (J. Boswell), Vol. II

11 He was not of an age, but for all time!

Ben Jonson (1573–1637) English dramatist. *To the Memory of William Shakespeare*

12 Sweet Swan of Avon!

Ben Jonson *To the Memory of William Shakespeare*

13 When I read Shakespeare I am struck with wonder
That such trivial people should muse and thunder
In such lovely language.

D. H. Lawrence (1885–1930) British novelist. *When I Read Shakespeare*

14 Or sweetest Shakespeare, Fancy's child,
Warble his native wood-notes wild.

John Milton (1608–74) English poet. *L'Allegro*

15 Shakespeare – The nearest thing in incarnation to the eye of God.

Laurence Olivier (1907–89) British actor. *Kenneth Harris Talking To*, 'Sir Laurence Olivier'

16 A man can be forgiven a lot if he can quote Shakespeare in an economic crisis.

Prince Philip (1921–) The consort of Queen Elizabeth II. Attrib.

17 Brush Up Your Shakespeare.

Cole Porter (1891–1964) US composer and lyricist. *Kiss Me Kate*

18 With the single exception of Homer, there is no eminent writer, not even Sir Walter Scott, whom I can despise so entirely as I despise Shakespeare when I measure my mind against his...It would positively be a relief to me to dig him up and throw stones at him.

George Bernard Shaw (1856–1950) Irish dramatist and critic. *Dramatic Opinions and Essays*, Vol. 2

19 Wonderful women! Have you ever thought how much we all, and women especially, owe to Shakespeare for his vindication of women in these fearless, high-spirited, resolute and intelligent heroines?

Ellen Terry (1847–1928) British actress. *Four Lectures on Shakespeare*, 'The Triumphant Women'

20 One of the greatest geniuses that ever existed, Shakespeare, undoubtedly wanted taste.

Horace Walpole (1717–97) British writer. Letter to Wren, 9 Aug 1764

Quotations by Shakespeare

The quotations by William Shakespeare are arranged in alphabetical order of his plays. These are followed by the poems and sonnets.

All's Well that Ends Well

21 HELENA. Our remedies oft in ourselves do lie,
Which we ascribe to heaven.

I:1

22 PAROLLES. A young man married is a man that's marred.

II:3

23 FIRST LORD. The web of our life is of a mingled yarn, good and ill together.

IV:3

24 KING. Th' inaudible and noiseless foot of Time.

V:3

Antony and Cleopatra

25 PHILO. The triple pillar of the world transform'd
Into a strumpet's fool.

I:1

26 ANTONY. There's beggary in the love that can be reckon'd.

I:1

27 CHARMIAN. In time we hate that which we often fear.

I:3

28 CLEOPATRA. Where's my serpent of old Nile?

I:5 Quoting Antony's name for her

29 CLEOPATRA. My salad days,
When I was green in judgment, cold in blood,
To say as I said then!

I:5

30 ENOBARBUS. The barge she sat in, like a burnish'd throne,
Burn'd on the water. The poop was beaten gold;
Purple the sails, and so perfumed that
The winds were love-sick with them; the oars were silver,
Which to the tune of flutes kept stroke and made
The water which they beat to follow faster,
As amorous of their strokes. For her own person,
It beggar'd all description.

II:2

31 ENOBARBUS. Age cannot wither her, nor custom stale
Her infinite variety. Other women cloy
The appetites they feed, but she makes hungry
Where most she satisfies.

II:2

32 ENOBARBUS. I will praise any man that will praise me.

II:6

33 CLEOPATRA. Celerity is never more admir'd
Than by the negligent.

III:7

34 ANTONY. To business that we love we rise betime,
And go to't with delight.
IV:4

35 ANTONY. Unarm, Eros; the long day's task is done,
And we must sleep.
IV:14

36 ANTONY. I am dying, Egypt, dying; only
I here importune death awhile, until
Of many thousand kisses the poor last
I lay upon thy lips.
IV:15

37 CLEOPATRA. The crown o' the earth doth melt. My lord!
O, wither'd is the garland of the war,
The soldier's pole is fall'n! Young boys and girls
Are level now with men. The odds is gone,
And there is nothing left remarkable
Beneath the visiting moon.
IV:15

38 IRAS. The bright day is done,
And we are for the dark.
V:2

39 CLEOPATRA. Dost thou not see my baby at my breast
That sucks the nurse asleep?
Holding the asp to her breast. V:2

40 CAESAR. She shall be buried by her Antony!
No grave upon the earth shall clip in it
A pair so famous.
V:2

As You Like It

41 CELIA. Well said; that was laid on with a trowel.
I:2

42 ROSALIND. O, how full of briers is this working-day world!
I:3

43 DUKE SENIOR. And this our life, exempt from public haunt,
Finds tongues in trees, books in the running brooks,
Sermons in stones and good in everything.
II:1

44 TOUCHSTONE. I had rather bear with you than bear you.
II:4

45 SILVIUS. If thou remembr'rest not the slightest folly
That ever love did make thee run into,
Thou hast not lov'd.
II:4

46 AMIENS. Under the greenwood tree
Who loves to lie with me,
And turn his merry note
Unto the sweet bird's throat,
Come hither, come hither, come hither.
Here shall he see
No enemy
But winter and rough weather.
II:5

47 JACQUES. And so, from hour to hour, we ripe and ripe,
And then, from hour to hour, we rot and rot;
And thereby hangs a tale.
II:7

48 JACQUES. All the world's a stage,
And all the men and women merely players;
They have their exits and their entrances;
And one man in his time plays many parts,
His acts being seven ages.
II:7

49 JACQUES. Last scene of all,
That ends this strange eventful history,
Is second childishness and mere oblivion;
Sans teeth, sans eyes, sans taste, sans every thing.
II:7

50 AMIENS. Blow, blow, thou winter wind,
Thou art not so unkind
As man's ingratitude.
II:7

51 AMIENS. Most friendship is feigning, most loving mere folly.
II:7

52 CORIN. He that wants money, means, and content, is without three good friends.
III:2

53 ROSALIND. Do you not know I am a woman? When I think, I must speak.
III:2

54 ORLANDO. I do desire we may be better strangers.
III:2

55 TOUCHSTONE. The truest poetry is the most feigning.
III:3

56 ROSALIND. Men have died from time to time, and worms have eaten them, but not for love.
IV:1

57 TOUCHSTONE. Your 'If' is the only peace-maker; much virtue in 'If'.
V:4

58 ROSALIND. If it be true that 'good wine needs no bush', 'tis true that a good play needs no epilogue.
Epilogue

Coriolanus

59 CORIOLANUS. Custom calls me to't.
What custom wills, in all things should we do't,
The dust on antique time would lie unswept,
And mountainous error be too highly heap'd
For truth to o'erpeer.
II:3

60 CORIOLANUS. Like a dull actor now
I have forgot my part and I am out,
Even to a full disgrace.
V:3

Cymbeline

61 BELARIUS. O, this life
Is nobler than attending for a check,
Richer than doing nothing for a bribe,
Prouder than rustling in unpaid-for silk.
III:3

62 IMOGEN. Society is no comfort
To one not sociable.
IV:2

63 GUIDERIUS. Fear no more the heat o' th' sun
Nor the furious winter's rages;
Thou thy worldly task hast done,
Home art gone, and ta'en thy wages.
Golden lads and girls all must,
As chimney-sweepers, come to dust.
IV:2

64 POSTHUMUS. Every good servant does not all commands.
V:1

Hamlet

65 FRANCISCO. For this relief much thanks. 'Tis bitter cold,
And I am sick at heart.
I:1

66 HAMLET. A little more than kin, and less than kind.
I:2

67 HAMLET. But I have that within which passes show –
these but the trappings and the suits of woe.
I:2

68 HAMLET. O! that this too too solid flesh would melt,
Thaw, and resolve itself into a dew.
Or that the Everlasting had not fix'd
His canon 'gainst self-slaughter! O God! O God!
How weary, stale, flat, and unprofitable,
Seem to me all the uses of this world!
I:2

69 HAMLET. Frailty, thy name is woman!
I:2

70 HAMLET. It is not, nor it cannot come to good.
I:2

71 HAMLET. 'A was a man, take him for all in all,
I shall not look upon his like again.
I:2

72 HAMLET. Foul deeds will rise,
Though all the earth o'erwhelm them, to men's eyes.
I:2

73 OPHELIA. Do not, as some ungracious pastors do,
Show me the steep and thorny way to heaven,
Whiles, like a puff'd and reckless libertine,
Himself the primrose path of dalliance treads
And recks not his own rede.
I:3

74 POLONIUS. Costly thy habit as thy purse can buy,
But not express'd in fancy; rich, not gaudy;
For the apparel oft proclaims the man.
I:3

75 POLONIUS. Neither a borrower nor a lender be;
For loan oft loses both itself and friend,
And borrowing dulls the edge of husbandry.
This above all: to thine own self be true,
And it must follow, as the night the day,
Thou canst not then be false to any man.
I:3

76 HAMLET. But to my mind, though I am native here
And to the manner born, it is a custom
More honour'd in the breach than the observance.
I:4

77 MARCELLUS. Something is rotten in the state of Denmark.
I:4

78 GHOST. Murder most foul, as in the best it is;
But this most foul, strange, and unnatural.
I:5

79 HAMLET. There are more things in heaven and earth, Horatio,
Than are dreamt of in your philosophy.
I:5

80 HAMLET. The time is out of joint; O cursed spite,
That ever I was born to set it right!
I:5

81 POLONIUS. Brevity is the soul of wit.
II:2

82 HAMLET. To be honest, as this world goes, is to be one man pick'd out of ten thousand.
II:2

83 POLONIUS. Though this be madness, yet there is method in't.
II:2

84 HAMLET. There is nothing either good or bad, but thinking makes it so.
II:2

85 HAMLET. What a piece of work is a man! How noble in reason! how infinite in faculties! in form and moving, how express and admirable! in action, how like an angel! in apprehension, how like a god! the beauty of the world! the paragon of animals! And yet, to me, what is this quintessence of dust? Man delights not me – no, nor woman neither.
II:2

86 HAMLET. I am but mad north-north-west; when the
wind is southerly, I know a hawk from a handsaw.
II:2

87 HAMLET. The play, I remember, pleas'd not the million; 'twas caviare to the general.
II:2

88 HAMLET. Use every man after his desert, and who should 'scape whipping?
II:2

89 HAMLET. The play's the thing
Wherein I'll catch the conscience of the King.
II:2

90 HAMLET. To be, or not to be – that is the question;
Whether 'tis nobler in the mind to suffer
The slings and arrows of outrageous fortune,
Or to take arms against a sea of troubles,
And by opposing end them? To die, to sleep –
No more; and by a sleep to say we end
The heart-ache and the thousand natural shocks
That flesh is heir to, 'tis a consummation
Devoutly to be wish'd. To die, to sleep;
To sleep, perchance to dream. Ay, there's the rub;
For in that sleep of death what dreams may come,
When we have shuffled off this mortal coil,
Must give us pause.
III:1

91 HAMLET. The dread of something after death –
The undiscover'd country, from whose bourn
No traveller returns.
III:1

92 HAMLET. Thus conscience does make cowards of us all;
And thus the native hue of resolution
Is sicklied o'er with the pale cast of thought.
III:1

93 HAMLET. Get thee to a nunnery: why wouldst thou be a breeder of sinners?
III:1

94 KING. Madness in great ones must not unwatch'd go.
III:1

95 HAMLET. It out-herods Herod.
III:2

96 HAMLET. Suit the action to the word, the word to the action; with this special observance, that you o'erstep not the modesty of nature.
III:2

97 QUEEN. The lady doth protest too much, methinks.
III:2

98 POLONIUS. Very like a whale.
III:2

99 HAMLET. A king of shreds and patches.
III:4

100 HAMLET. How all occasions do inform against me,
And spur my dull revenge! What is a man,
If his chief good and market of his time
Be but to sleep and feed? a beast, no more.
IV:4

101 HAMLET. Some craven scruple
Of thinking too precisely on th' event.
IV:4

102 KING. When sorrows come, they come not single spies,
But in battalions!
IV:5

103 KING. There's such divinity doth hedge a king
That treason can but peep to what it would.
IV:5

104 OPHELIA. There's rosemary, that's for remembrance; pray, love, remember: and there is pansies, that's for thoughts.
IV:5

105 LAERTES. Too much of water hast thou, poor Ophelia,
And therefore I forbid my tears.
IV:7

106 HAMLET. Alas, poor Yorick! I knew him, Horatio: a fellow of infinite jest, of most excellent fancy.
V:1

107 HAMLET. There's a divinity that shapes our ends,
Rough-hew them how we will.
V:2

108 HAMLET. If thou didst ever hold me in thy heart,
Absent thee from felicity awhile,
And in this harsh world draw thy breath in pain,
To tell my story.
V:2

109 HAMLET. The rest is silence.
V:2

Henry IV, Part One

110 PRINCE HENRY: If all the year were playing holidays, To sport would be as tedious as to work.
I:2

111 PRINCE HENRY. Falstaff sweats to death
And lards the lean earth as he walks along.
II:2

112 HOTSPUR. Out of this nettle, danger, we pluck this flower, safety.
II:3

113 FALSTAFF. I have more flesh than another man, and therefore more frailty.
III:3

114 FALSTAFF. Honour pricks me on. Yea, but how if honour prick me off when I come on? How then? Can honour set to a leg? No. Or an arm? No. Or take away the grief of a wound? No. Honour hath no skill in surgery, then? No. What is honour? A word. What is in that word? Honour. What is that honour? Air.
V:1

115 HOTSPUR. But thoughts, the slaves of life, and life, time's fool,
And time, that takes survey of all the world,
Must have a stop.
V:4

116 FALSTAFF. The better part of valour is discretion; in the which better part I have saved my life.
V:4

Henry IV, Part Two

117 FALSTAFF. I am not only witty in myself, but the

cause that wit is in other men. I do here walk before thee like a sow that hath overwhelm'd all her litter but one.
I:2

118 FALSTAFF. Well, I cannot last ever; but it was always yet the trick of our English nation, if they have a good thing, to make it too common.
I:2

119 FALSTAFF. I can get no remedy against this consumption of the purse; borrowing only lingers and lingers it out, but the disease is incurable.
I:2

120 HOSTESS. He hath eaten me out of house and home.
II:1

121 POINS. Is it not strange that desire should so many years outlive performance?
II:4

122 KING HENRY IV. Uneasy lies the head that wears a crown.
III:1

123 FALSTAFF. We have heard the chimes at midnight.
III:2

124 FEEBLE. I care not; a man can die but once; we owe God a death.
III:2

125 FALSTAFF. Care I for the limb, the thews, the stature, bulk, and big assemblance of a man! Give me the spirit.
III:2

Henry V

126 NYM. I dare not fight; but I will wink and hold out mine iron.
II:1

127 NYM. Though patience be a tired mare, yet she will plod.
II:1

128 HOSTESS. His nose was as sharp as a pen, and 'a babbl'd of green fields.
Referring to Falstaff on his deathbed. II:3

129 KING HENRY V Once more unto the breach, dear friends, once more;
Or close the wall up with our English dead.
III:1

130 KING HENRY V. But when the blast of war blows in our ears,
Then imitate the action of the tiger;
Stiffen the sinews, summon up the blood,
Disguise fair nature with hard-favoured rage;
Then lend the eye a terrible aspect.
III:1

131 KING HENRY V. On, on you noblest English.
Whose blood is fet from fathers of war-proof!
III:1

132 KING HENRY V. The game's afoot:
Follow your spirit; and, upon this charge
Cry 'God for Harry! England and Saint George!'
III:1

133 BOY. Men of few words are the best men.
III:2

134 KING HENRY V. I think the King is but a man as I am: the violet smells to him as it doth to me.
IV:1

135 KING HENRY V. Every subject's duty is the King's; but every subject's soul is his own.
IV:1

136 KING HENRY V. Old men forget; yet all shall be forgot,
But he'll remember, with advantages,
What feats he did that day.
IV:3

137 KING HENRY V. And gentlemen in England, now a-bed
Shall think themselves accurs'd they were not here,
And hold their manhoods cheap whiles any speaks
That fought with us upon Saint Crispin's day.
IV:3

138 FLUELLEN. There is occasions and causes why and wherefore in all things.
V:1

Henry VIII

139 NORFOLK. Heat not a furnace for your foe so hot
That it do singe yourself. We may outrun
By violent swiftness that which we run at,
And lose by over-running.
I:1

140 ANNE BULLEN. I would not be a queen
For all the world.
II:3

141 WOLSEY. Farewell, a long farewell, to all my greatness!
This is the state of man: to-day he puts forth
The tender leaves of hopes: to-morrow blossoms
And bears his blushing honours thick upon him;
The third day comes a frost, a killing frost,
And when he thinks, good easy man, full surely
His greatness is a-ripening, nips his root,
And then he falls, as I do.
III:2

142 WOLSEY. Had I but serv'd my God with half the zeal
I serv'd my King, he would not in mine age
Have left me naked to mine enemies.
III:2

143 GRIFFITH. Men's evil manners live in brass: their virtues
We write in water.
IV:2

Julius Caesar

144 SOOTHSAYER. Beware the ides of March.
I:2

145 CASSIUS. Why, man, he doth bestride the narrow world

Like a Colossus; and we petty men
Walk under his huge legs, and peep about
To find ourselves dishonourable graves.
Men at some time are masters of their fates:
The fault, dear Brutus, is not in our stars,
But in ourselves, that we are
underlings.
I:2

146 CAESAR. Let me have men about me that are fat;
Sleek-headed men, and such as sleep o' nights.
Yond Cassius has a lean and hungry look;
He thinks too much. Such men are dangerous.
I:2

147 CASCA. For mine own part, it was Greek to me.
I:2

148 CAESAR. Cowards die many times before their deaths:
The valiant never taste of death but once.
II:2

149 CAESAR. *Et tu, Brute?*
III:1

150 CASSIUS. Why, he that cuts off twenty years of life
Cuts off so many years of fearing death.
III:1

151 ANTONY. O mighty Caesar! dost thou lie so low?
Are all thy conquests, glories, triumphs, spoils,
Shrunk to this little measure?
III:1

152 ANTONY. O, pardon me, thou bleeding piece of earth,
That I am meek and gentle with these butchers!
Thou art the ruins of the noblest man
That ever lived in the tide of times.
III:1

153 ANTONY. Cry 'Havoc!' and let slip the dogs of war.
III:1

154 BRUTUS. Not that I lov'd Caesar less, but that I lov'd Rome more.
III:2

155 ANTONY. Friends, Romans, countrymen, lend me your ears
I come to bury Caesar, not to praise him.
The evil that men do lives after them;
The good is oft interred with their bones.
III:2

156 ANTONY. For Brutus is an honourable man;
So are they all, all honourable men.
III:2

157 ANTONY. Ambition should be made of sterner stuff.
III:2

158 ANTONY. If you have tears, prepare to shed them now.
III:2

159 ANTONY. For I have neither wit, nor words, nor worth,
Action, nor utterance, nor the power of speech,
To stir men's blood; I only speak right on.
III:2

160 CASSIUS. A friend should bear his friend's infirmities,
But Brutus makes mine greater than they are.
IV:3

161 BRUTUS. There is a tide in the affairs of men
Which, taken at the flood, leads on to fortune;
Omitted, all the voyage of their life
Is bound in shallows and in miseries.
On such a full sea are we now afloat,
And we must take the current when it serves,
Or lose our ventures.
IV:3

162 ANTONY. This was the noblest Roman of them all.
All the conspirators save only he
Did that they did in envy of great Caesar.
V:5

163 ANTONY. His life was gentle; and the elements
So mix'd in him that Nature might stand up
And say to all the world 'This was a man!'
Referring to Brutus. V:5

King John

164 PHILIP THE BASTARD. Well, whiles I am a beggar, I will rail
And say there is no sin but to be rich;
And being rich, my virtue then shall be
To say there is no vice but beggary.
II:1

165 PHILIP THE BASTARD. Bell, book, and candle, shall not drive me back,
When gold and silver becks me to come on.
III:3

166 LEWIS. Life is as tedious as a twice-told tale
Vexing the dull ear of a drowsy man.
III:4

167 SALISBURY. To gild refined gold, to paint the lily,
To throw a perfume on the violet,
To smooth the ice, or add another hue
Unto the rainbow, or with taper-light
To seek the beauteous eye of heaven to garnish,
Is wasteful and ridiculous excess.
IV:2

168 KING JOHN. How oft the sight of means to do ill deeds
Makes ill deeds done!
IV:2

169 KING JOHN. I beg cold comfort.
V:7

King Lear

170 LEAR. Nothing will come of nothing. Speak again.
I:1

171 EDMUND. This is the excellent foppery of the world, that, when we are sick in fortune, often the

surfeit of our own behaviour, we make guilty of our disasters the sun, the moon, and stars.
I:2

172 LEAR. Ingratitude, thou marble-hearted fiend,
More hideous when thou show'st thee in a child
Than the sea-monster!
I:4

173 LEAR. How sharper than a serpent's tooth it is
To have a thankless child!
I:4

174 LEAR. O, let me not be mad, not mad, sweet heaven!
Keep me in temper; I would not be mad!
I:5

175 KENT. Thou whoreson zed! thou unnecessary letter!
II:2

176 LEAR. Down, thou climbing sorrow,
Thy element's below.
II:4

177 LEAR. O, reason not the need! Our basest beggars
Are in the poorest thing superfluous.
Allow not nature more than nature needs,
Man's life is cheap as beast's.
II:4

178 LEAR. Blow, winds, and crack your cheeks; rage, blow.
You cataracts and hurricanoes, spout
Till you have drench'd our steeples, drown'd the cocks.
III:2

179 LEAR. Rumble thy bellyful. Spit, fire; spout rain.
Nor rain, wind, thunder, fire, are my daughters
I tax not you, you elements, with unkindness.
III:2

180 LEAR. I am a man
More sinn'd against than sinning.
III:2

181 LEAR. O! that way madness lies; let me shun that.
III:4

182 LEAR. Poor naked wretches, wheresoe'er you are,
That bide the pelting of this pitiless storm,
How shall your houseless heads and unfed sides,
Your loop'd and window'd raggedness, defend you
From seasons such as these?
III:4

183 LEAR. Take physic, pomp;
Expose thyself to feel what wretches feel.
III:4

184 CORNWALL. Out vile jelly!
Where is thy lustre now?
Spoken by Cornwall as he puts out Gloucester's remaining eye.
III:7

185 GLOUCESTER. I have no way, and therefore want no eyes;
I stumbled when I saw.
IV:1

186 EDGAR. The worst is not
So long as we can say 'This is the worst'.
IV:1

187 GLOUCESTER. As flies to wanton boys are we to th' gods –
They kill us for their sport.
IV:1

188 LEAR. Ay, every inch a king.
IV:6

189 LEAR. The wren goes to't, and the small gilded fly
Does lecher in my sight.
IV:6

190 LEAR. Through tatter'd clothes small vices do appear;
Robes and furr'd gowns hide all.
IV:6

191 LEAR. Get thee glass eyes,
And, like a scurvy politician, seem
To see the things thou dost not.
IV:6

192 LEAR. When we are born, we cry that we are come
To this great stage of fools.
IV:6

193 LEAR. Thou art a soul in bliss; but I am bound
Upon a wheel of fire, that mine own tears
Do scald like molten lead.
IV:7

194 EDGAR. Men must endure
Their going hence, even as their coming hither:
Ripeness is all.
V:2

195 EDGAR. The gods are just, and of our pleasant vices
Make instruments to plague us.
V:3

196 LEAR. And my poor fool is hang'd! No, no, no life!
Why should a dog, a horse, a rat have life,
And thou no breath at all? Thou'lt come no more,
Never, never, never, never.
V:3

Love's Labour's Lost

197 BIRON. At Christmas I no more desire a rose
Than wish a snow in May's newfangled mirth;
But like of each thing that in season grows.
I:1

198 NATHANIEL. He hath never fed of the dainties that are bred in a book; he hath not eat paper, as it were; he hath not drunk ink; his intellect is not replenished.
IV:2

199 BIRON. For where is any author in the world

Teaches such beauty as a woman's eye?
Learning is but an adjunct to oneself.
IV:3

200 ROSALINE. A jest's prosperity lies in the ear
Of him that hears it, never in the tongue
Of him that makes it.
V:2

201 WINTER. When icicles hang by the wall,
And Dick the shepherd blows his nail,
And Tom bears logs into the hall,
And milk comes frozen home in pail,
When blood is nipp'd, and ways be foul,
Then nightly sings the staring owl:
'Tu-who;
Tu-whit, Tu-who' – A merry note,
While greasy Joan doth keel the pot.
V:2

Macbeth

202 FIRST WITCH. When shall we three meet again
In thunder, lightning, or in rain?
I:1

203 MACBETH. So foul and fair a day I have not seen.
I:3

204 MACBETH. This supernatural soliciting
Cannot be ill; cannot be good.
I:3

205 MACBETH. Come what come may,
Time and the hour runs through the roughest day.
I:3

206 MALCOLM. Nothing in his life
Became him like the leaving it: he died
As one that had been studied in his death
To throw away the dearest thing he ow'd
As 'twere a careless trifle.
I:4

207 LADY MACBETH. Yet do I fear thy nature;
It is too full o' th' milk of human kindness
To catch the nearest way.
I:5

208 LADY MACBETH. The raven himself is hoarse
That croaks the fatal entrance of Duncan
Under my battlements.
I:5

209 MACBETH. If it were done when 'tis done, then 'twere well
It were done quickly.
I:7

210 MACBETH. That but this blow
Might be the be-all and the end-all here –
But here upon this bank and shoal of time –
We'd jump the life to come.
I:7

211 MACBETH. I have no spur
To prick the sides of my intent, but only
Vaulting ambition, which o'er-leaps itself,
And falls on th' other.
I:7

212 MACBETH. False face must hide what the false heart doth know.
I:7

213 MACBETH. Is this a dagger which I see before me,
The handle toward my hand? Come, let me clutch thee:
I have thee not, and yet I see thee still.
II:1

214 MACBETH. Methought I heard a voice cry, 'Sleep no more!'
Macbeth doth murder sleep,' the innocent sleep,
Sleep that knits up the ravell'd sleave of care,
The death of each day's life, sore labour's bath,
Balm of hurt minds, great nature's second course,
Chief nourisher in life's feast.
II:2

215 PORTER. It provokes the desire, but it takes away the performance. Therefore much drink may be said to be an equivocator with lechery.
II:3

216 LADY MACBETH. Nought's had, all's spent,
Where our desire is got without content.
'Tis safer to be that which we destroy,
Than by destruction dwell in doubtful joy.
III:2

217 LADY MACBETH. Stand not upon the order of your going,
But go at once.
III:4

218 MACBETH. I had else been perfect,
Whole as the marble, founded as the rock,
As broad and general as the casing air,
But now I am cabin'd, cribb'd, confin'd, bound in
To saucy doubts and fears.
III:4

219 MACBETH. I am in blood
Stepp'd in so far that, should I wade no more,
Returning were as tedious as go o'er.
III:4

220 SECOND WITCH. Eye of newt, and toe of frog,
Wool of bat, and tongue of dog,
Adder's fork, and blind-worm's sting,
Lizard's leg, and howlet's wing,
For a charm of powerful trouble,
Like a hell-broth boil and bubble.
IV:1

221 SECOND APPARITION. Be bloody bold, and resolute, laugh to scorn
The power of man, for none of woman born
Shall harm Macbeth.
IV:1

222 LADY MACBETH. Out, damned spot! out, I say!
V:1

223 LADY MACBETH. Yet who would have thought the old man to have had so much blood in him?
V:1

224 LADY MACBETH. Here's the smell of the blood still. All the perfumes of Arabia will not sweeten this little hand.
V:1

225 MACBETH. I have liv'd long enough.
My way of life
Is fall'n into the sear, the yellow leaf;
And that which should accompany old age,
As honour, love, obedience, troops of friends,
I must not look to have.
V:3

226 MACBETH. I have supp'd full with horrors.
V:5

227 MACBETH. Tomorrow, and tomorrow, and tomorrow,
Creeps in this petty pace from day to day
To the last syllable of recorded time,
And all our yesterdays have lighted fools
The way to dusty death. Out, out, brief candle!
Life's but a walking shadow, a poor player,
That struts and frets his hour upon the stage,
And then is heard no more; it is a tale
Told by an idiot, full of sound and fury,
Signifying nothing.
V:5

228 MACBETH. I gin to be aweary of the sun,
And wish th' estate o' th' world were now undone.
V:5

229 MACBETH. I bear a charmed life, which must not yield
To one of woman born.
MACDUFF. Despair thy charm;
And let the angel whom thou still hast serv'd
Tell thee Macduff was from his mother's womb
Untimely ripp'd.
V:8

Measure for Measure

230 ISABELLA. But man, proud man
Dress'd in a little brief authority,
Most ignorant of what he's most assur'd,
His glassy essence, like an angry ape,
Plays such fantastic tricks before high heaven
As makes the angels weep.
II:2

231 ISABELLA. That in the captain's but a choleric word
Which in the soldier is flat blasphemy.
II:2

232 CLAUDIO. The miserable have no other medicine
But only hope.
III:1

233 DUKE VINCENTIO. Thou hast nor youth nor age;
But, as it were, an after-dinner's sleep,
Dreaming on both.
III:1

234 CLAUDIO. Ay, but to die, and go we know not where;
To lie in cold obstruction, and to rot;
This sensible warm motion to become
A kneaded clod; and the delighted spirit
To bathe in fiery floods or to reside
In thrilling region of thick-ribbed ice.
III:1

235 LUCIO. I am a kind of burr; I shall stick.
IV:3

236 DUKE VINCENTIO. Haste still pays haste, and leisure answers leisure;
Like doth quit like, and Measure still for Measure.
V:1

237 MARIANA. They say best men are moulded out of faults
And, for the most, become much more the better
For being a little bad.
V:1

The Merchant of Venice

238 GRATIANO. As who should say 'I am Sir Oracle,
And when I ope my lips let no dog bark'.
I:1

239 PORTIA. If to do were as easy as to know what were good to do, chapels had been churches, and poor men's cottages princes' palaces.
I:2

240 SHYLOCK. How like a fawning publican he looks!
I hate him for he is a Christian.
But more for that in low simplicity
He lends out money gratis, and brings down
The rate of usance here with us in Venice.
I:3

241 ANTONIO. The devil can cite Scripture for his purpose.
I:3

242 SHYLOCK. You call me misbeliever, cut-throat dog,
And spit upon my Jewish gaberdine,
And all for use of that which is mine own.
I:3

243 LAUNCELOT. It is a wise father that knows his own child.
II:2

244 JESSICA. But love is blind, and lovers cannot see
The pretty follies that themselves commit.
II:6

245 SHYLOCK. My daughter! O my ducats! O my daughter!
Fled with a Christian! O my Christian ducats!
Justice! the law! my ducats, and my daughter!
II:8

246 NERISSA. The ancient saying is no heresy:
Hanging and wiving goes by destiny.
II:9

247 SHYLOCK. Hath not a Jew eyes? Hath not a Jew hands, organs, dimensions, senses, affections, passions, fed with the same food, hurt with the same weapons, subject to the same diseases, healed by the same means, warmed and cooled by the same winter and summer, as a Christian is? If you prick us, do we not bleed? If you tickle us, do we not laugh? If you poison us, do we not die? And if you wrong us, shall we not revenge?
III:1

248 PORTIA. The quality of mercy is not strain'd;
It droppeth as the gentle rain from heaven
Upon the place beneath. It is twice blest;
It blesseth him that gives and him that takes.
IV:1

249 SHYLOCK. A Daniel come to judgment! yea, a Daniel!
IV:1

250 LORENZO. The moon shines bright: in such a night as this,
...in such a night
Troilus methinks mounted the Troyan walls,
And sigh'd his soul toward the Grecian tents,
Where Cressid lay that night.
V:1

251 LORENZO. How sweet the moonlight sleeps upon this bank!
Here will we sit, and let the sounds of music
Creep in our ears; soft stillness and the night
Become the touches of sweet harmony.
V:1

252 JESSICA. I am never merry when I hear sweet music.
V:1

253 LORENZO. The man that hath no music in himself,
Nor is not mov'd with concord of sweet sounds,
Is fit for treasons, stratagems, and spoils.
V:1

254 PORTIA. How far that little candle throws his beams!
So shines a good deed in a naughty world.
V:1

255 PORTIA. For a light wife doth make a heavy husband.
V:1

The Merry Wives of Windsor

256 PISTOL. Why, then the world's mine oyster,
Which I with sword will open.
II:2

257 ANNE. O, what a world of vile ill-favour'd faults
Looks handsome in three hundred pounds a year!
III:4

258 FALSTAFF. They say there is divinity in odd numbers, either in nativity, chance, or death.
V:1

A Midsummer Night's Dream

259 LYSANDER. For aught that I could ever read,
Could ever hear by tale or history,
The course of true love never did run smooth.
I:1

260 HELENA. Love looks not with the eyes, but with the mind;
And therefore is wing'd Cupid painted blind.
I:1

261 SNUG. I am slow of study.
I:2

262 OBERON. Ill met by moonlight, proud Titania.
II:1

263 BOTTOM. A lion among ladies is a most dreadful thing; for there is not a more fearful wild-fowl than your lion living.
III:1

264 PUCK. Lord, what fools these mortals be!
III:2

265 THESEUS. The lunatic, the lover, and the poet,
Are of imagination all compact.
V:1

266 THESEUS. The poet's eye, in a fine frenzy rolling,
Doth glance from heaven to earth, from earth to heaven;
And as imagination bodies forth
The forms of things unknown, the poet's pen
Turns them to shapes, and gives to airy nothing
A local habitation and a name.
V:1

267 PUCK. If we shadows have offended,
Think but this, and all is mended, That you have but slumber'd here While these visions did appear.
V:2

Much Ado About Nothing

268 BENEDICK. Would you have me speak after my custom, as being a professed tyrant to their sex?
I:1

269 CLAUDIO. Friendship is constant in all other things
Save in the office and affairs of love.
II:1

270 CLAUDIO. Silence is the perfectest herald of joy:
I were but little happy if I could say how much.

II:1

271 BENEDICK. Doth not the appetite alter? A man loves the meat in his youth that he cannot endure in his age.
II:3

272 DOGBERRY. To be a well-favoured man is the gift of fortune; but to write and read comes by nature.
III:3

273 VERGES. I thank God I am as honest as any man living that is an old man and no honester than I.
III:5

274 DOGBERRY. Comparisons are odorous.
III:5

275 DOGBERRY. Our watch, sir, have indeed comprehended two aspicious persons.
III:5

276 DOGBERRY. Write down that they hope they serve God; and write God first; for God defend but God should go before such villains!
IV:2

277 LEONATO. For there was never yet philosopher
That could endure the toothache patiently.
V:1

Othello

278 DUKE OF VENICE. To mourn a mischief that is

past and gone
Is the next way to draw new mischief on.
I:3

279 IAGO. Put money in thy purse.
I:3

280 IAGO. There are many events in the womb of time which will be delivered.
I:3

281 IAGO. For I am nothing if not critical.
II:1

282 IAGO. To suckle fools and chronicle small beer.
II:1

283 CASSIO. Reputation, reputation, reputation! O, I have lost my reputation! I have lost the immortal part of myself, and what remains is bestial.
II:3

284 IAGO. Good name in man and woman, dear my lord,
Is the immediate jewel of their souls:
Who steals my purse steals trash; 'tis something, nothing;
'Twas mine, 'tis his, and has been slave to thousands;
But he that filches from me my good name
Robs me of that which not enriches him
And makes me poor indeed.
III:3

285 IAGO. O, beware, my lord, of jealousy;
It is the green-ey'd monster which doth mock
The meat it feeds on.
III:3

286 OTHELLO. O curse of marriage,
That we can call these delicate creatures ours,
And not their appetites! I had rather be a toad,
And live upon the vapour of a dungeon,
Than keep a corner in the thing I love
For others' uses.
III:3

287 OTHELLO. He that is robb'd, not wanting what is stol'n,
Let him not know't, and he's not robb'd at all.
III:3

288 OTHELLO. Farewell the neighing steed and the shrill trump,
The spirit-stirring drum, th'ear piercing fife,
The royal banner, and all quality,
Pride, pomp, and circumstance, of glorious war!
III:3

289 OTHELLO. Put out the light, and then put out the light.
If I quench thee, thou flaming minister,
I can again thy former light restore,
Should I repent me; but once put out thy light,
Thou cunning'st pattern of excelling nature,
I know not where is that Promethean heat
That can thy light relume.
V:2

290 LODOVICO. Then must you speak
Of one that lov'd not wisely, but too well;
Of one not easily jealous, but, being wrought,
Perplexed in the extreme; of one whose hand,
Like the base Indian, threw a pearl away
Richer than all his tribe.
V:2

Pericles

291 PERICLES. Kings are earth's gods; in vice their law's their will.
I:1

292 3RD FISHERMAN. Master, I marvel how the fishes live in the sea.
1ST FISHERMAN. Why, as men do a-land – the great ones eat up the little ones.
II:1

293 PERICLES. O you gods!
Why do you make us love your goodly gifts
And snatch them straight away?
III:1

Richard II

294 MOWBRAY. The purest treasure mortal times afford
Is spotless reputation; that away,
Men are but gilded loam or painted clay.
I:1

295 GAUNT. Things sweet to taste prove in digestion sour.
I:3

296 GAUNT. Teach thy necessity to reason thus:
There is no virtue like necessity.
I:3

297 GAUNT. This royal throne of kings, this sceptred isle,
This earth of majesty, this seat of Mars,
This other Eden, demi-paradise,
This fortress built by Nature for herself
Against infection and the hand of war,
This happy breed of men, this little world,
This precious stone set in the silver sea,
Which serves it in the office of a wall,
Or as a moat defensive to a house,
Against the envy of less happier lands;
This blessed plot, this earth, this realm, this England,
This nurse, this teeming womb of royal kings,
Fear'd by their breed, and famous by their birth.
II:1

298 KING RICHARD. Not all the water in the rough rude sea
Can wash the balm from an anointed king;
The breath of worldly men cannot depose
The deputy elected by the Lord.
III:2

299 KING RICHARD. The worst is death, and death will have his day.
III:2

300 KING RICHARD. For God's sake let us sit upon the ground
And tell sad stories of the death of kings:
How some have been depos'd, some slain in war,
Some haunted by the ghosts they have depos'd,
Some poison'd by their wives, some sleeping kill'd,
All murder'd – for within the hollow crown

That rounds the mortal temples of a king
Keeps Death his court.
III:2

301 KING RICHARD. How sour sweet music is
When time is broke and no proportion kept!
So is it in the music of men's lives.
V:5

Richard III

302 GLOUCESTER. Now is the winter of our discontent
Made glorious summer by this sun of York.
I:1

303 CLARENCE. Lord, Lord, methought what pain it was to drown,
What dreadful noise of waters in mine ears,
What ugly sights of death within mine eyes!
I:4

304 THIRD CITIZEN. Woe to the land that's govern'd by a child!
II:3

305 KING RICHARD. A horse! a horse ! my kingdom for a horse.
V:4

Romeo and Juliet

306 PROLOGUE. From forth the fatal loins of these two foes
A pair of star-cross'd lovers take their life.
Prologue

307 MERCUTIO. O! then, I see, Queen Mab hath been with you.
She is the fairies' midwife…
And in this state she gallops night by night
Through lovers' brains, and then they dream of love.
I:4

308 ROMEO. O! she doth teach the torches to burn bright
It seems she hangs upon the cheek of night
Like a rich jewel in an Ethiop's ear;
Beauty too rich for use, for earth too dear.
I:5

309 JULIET. My only love sprung from my only hate!
Too early seen unknown, and known too late!
I:5

310 ROMEO. He jests at scars, that never felt a wound.
But, soft! what light through yonder window breaks?
It is the east, and Juliet is the sun.
II:2

311 JULIET. O Romeo, Romeo! wherefore art thou Romeo?
II:2

312 ROMEO. What's in a name? That which we call a rose
By any other name would smell as sweet.
II:2

313 JULIET. O, swear not by the moon, th' inconstant moon,
That monthly changes in her circled orb,
Lest that thy love prove likewise variable.
II:2

314 ROMEO. Good night, good night! Parting is such sweet sorrow
That I shall say good night till it be morrow.
II:2

315 FRIAR LAURENCE. Wisely and slow; they stumble that run fast.
II:3

316 FRIAR LAURENCE. Therefore love moderately: long love doth so;
Too swift arrives as tardy as too slow.
II:6

317 MERCUTIO. A plague o' both your houses!
They have made worms' meat of me.
III:1

318 CAPULET. Thank me no thankings, nor proud me no prouds.
III:5

319 SECOND SERVANT. 'Tis an ill cook that cannot lick his own fingers.
IV:2

The Taming of the Shrew

320 TRANIO. No profit grows where is no pleasure ta'en;
In brief, sir, study what you most affect.
I:1

321 PETRUCHIO. This is a way to kill a wife with kindness.
IV:1

322 PETRUCHIO. Our purses shall be proud, our garments poor;
For 'tis the mind that makes the body rich;
And as the sun breaks through the darkest clouds,
So honour peereth in the meanest habit.
IV:3

The Tempest

323 ARIEL. Full fathom five thy father lies;
Of his bones are coral made;
Those are pearls that were his eyes;
Nothing of him that doth fade
But doth suffer a sea-change
Into something rich and strange.
I:2

324 TRINCULO. When they will not give a doit to relieve a lame beggar, they will lay out ten to see a dead Indian.
II:2

325 TRINCULO. Misery acquaints a man with strange bedfellows.
II:2

326 STEPHANO. He that dies pays all debts.
III:2

327 PROSPERO. Our revels now are ended. These our actors,

As I foretold you, were all spirits, and
Are melted into air, into thin air;
And, like the baseless fabric of this vision,
The cloud-capp'd towers, the gorgeous palaces,
The solemn temples, the great globe itself,
Yea, all which it inherit, shall dissolve,
And, like this insubstantial pageant faded,
Leave not a rack behind. We are such stuff
As dreams are made on; and our little life
Is rounded with a sleep.
IV:1

328 PROSPERO. I'll break my staff,
Bury it certain fathoms in the earth,
And deeper than did ever plummet sound
I'll drown my book.
V:1

329 MIRANDA. How beauteous mankind is! O brave new world
That has such people in't!
V:1

Troilus and Cressida

330 CRESSIDA. That she belov'd knows nought that knows not this:
Men prize the thing ungain'd more than it is.
I:2

331 ULYSSES. O, when degree is shak'd,
Which is the ladder of all high designs,
The enterprise is sick!
I:3

332 CRESSIDA. To be wise and love
Exceeds man's might.
III:2

333 ULYSSES. Time hath, my lord, a wallet at his back,
Wherein he puts alms for oblivion,
A great-siz'd monster of ingratitudes.
III:3

334 HECTOR.The end crowns all,
And that old common arbitrator, Time,
Will one day end it.
IV:5

335 THERSITES. Lechery, lechery! Still wars and lechery! Nothing else holds fashion.
V:2

Twelfth Night

336 ORSINO. If music be the food of love, play on,
Give me excess of it, that, surfeiting,
The appetite may sicken and so die.
I:1

337 SIR TOBY BELCH. Is it a world to hide virtues in?
I:3

338 CLOWN. Many a good hanging prevents a bad marriage.
I:5

339 SIR TOBY BELCH. Not to be abed after midnight is to be up betimes.
II:3

340 CLOWN. What is love? 'Tis not hereafter;
Present mirth hath present laughter;
What's to come is still unsure.
In delay there lies no plenty,
Then come kiss me, sweet and twenty;
Youth's a stuff will not endure.
II:3

341 SIR TOBY BELCH. Dost thou think, because thou art virtuous, there shall be no more cakes and ale?
II:3

342 VIOLA. She never told her love,
But let concealment, like a worm i' th' bud,
Feed on her damask cheek. She pin'd in thought;
And with a green and yellow melancholy
She sat like Patience on a monument,
Smiling at grief.
II:4

343 MALVOLIO. Some men are born great, some achieve greatness, and some have greatness thrust upon 'em.
II:5

344 OLIVIA. Love sought is good, but given unsought is better.
III:1

345 FABIAN. If this were play'd upon a stage now, I could condemn it as an improbable fiction.
III:4

346 FABIAN. Still you keep o' th' windy side of the law.
III:4

347 VIOLA. I hate ingratitude more in a man
Than lying, vainness, babbling drunkenness,
Or any taint of vice whose strong corruption
Inhabits our frail blood.
III:4

The Two Gentlemen of Verona

348 VALENTINE. Home-keeping youth have ever homely wits.
I:1

349 LUCETTA. I have no other but a woman's reason:
I think him so, because I think him so.
I:2

350 Who is Silvia? What is she,
That all our swains commend her?
Holy, fair, and wise is she.
Song performed by Thurio's musicians beneath Silvia's window.
IV:2

The Winter's Tale

351 PAULINA. What's gone and what's past help
Should be past grief.
III:2

352 SHEPHERD. I would there were no age between ten and three and twenty, or that youth would sleep out the rest; for there is nothing in the between but getting wenches with child, wronging the ancientry, stealing, fighting.
III:3

353 *Exit, pursued by a bear.*
Stage direction. III:3

354 AUTOLYCUS. A snapper-up of unconsidered trifles.
IV:2

355 AUTOLYCUS. Though I am not naturally honest, I am so sometimes by chance.
IV:4

356 CLOWN. Though authority be a stubborn bear, yet he is oft led by the nose with gold.
IV:4

Poems and Sonnets

357 Crabbed age and youth cannot live together:
Youth is full of pleasure, age is full of care;
Youth like summer morn, age like winter weather;
Youth like summer brave, age like winter bare.
The Passionate Pilgrim, XII

358 Beauty itself doth of itself persuade
The eyes of men without an orator.
The Rape of Lucrece, I

359 From fairest creatures we desire increase,
That thereby beauty's rose might never die.
Sonnet 1

360 Shall I compare thee to a summer's day?
Thou art more lovely and more temperate.
Rough winds do shake the darling buds of May,
And summer's lease hath all too short a date.
Sonnet 18

361 A woman's face, with Nature's own hand painted,
Hast thou, the Master Mistress of my passion.
Sonnet 20

362 When in disgrace with fortune and men's eyes
I all alone beweep my outcast state,
And trouble deaf heaven with my bootless cries,
And look upon myself, and curse my fate,
Wishing me like to one more rich in hope
Featur'd like him, like him with friends possess'd,
Desiring this man's art, and that man's scope,
With what I most enjoy contented least.
Sonnet 29

363 When to the sessions of sweet silent thought
I summon up remembrance of things past,
I sigh the lack of many a thing I sought,
And with old woes new wail my dear time's waste.
Sonnet 30

364 Not marble, nor the gilded monuments
Of princes, shall outlive this powerful rhyme.
Sonnet 55

365 Like as the waves make towards the pebbled shore,
So do our minutes hasten to their end.
Sonnet 60

366 That time of year thou mayst in me behold
When yellow leaves, or none, or few, do hang
Upon those boughs which shake against the cold,
Bare ruin'd choirs, where late the sweet birds sang.
Sonnet 73

367 Farewell! thou art too dear for my possessing,
And like enough thou know'st thy estimate:
The charter of thy worth gives thee releasing;
My bonds in thee are all determinate.
Sonnet 87

368 For sweetest things turn sourest by their deeds:
Lilies that fester smell far worse than weeds.
Sonnet 94

369 When in the chronicle of wasted time
I see descriptions of the fairest wights.
Sonnet 106

370 Let me not to the marriage of true minds
Admit impediments. Love is not love
Which alters when it alteration finds,
Or bends with the remover to remove.
O, no! it is an ever-fixed mark,
That looks on tempests and is never shaken.
Sonnet 116

371 Love alters not with his brief hours and weeks,
But bears it out even to the edge of doom.
If this be error, and upon me prov'd,
I never writ, nor no man ever lov'd.
Sonnet 116

372 Th' expense of spirit in a waste of shame
Is lust in action; and till action, lust
Is perjur'd, murd'rous, bloody, full of blame,
Savage, extreme, rude, cruel, not to trust;
Enjoy'd no sooner but despised straight.
Sonnet 129

373 My mistress' eyes are nothing like the sun;
Coral is far more red than her lips' red.
Sonnet 130

374 And yet, by heaven, I think my love as rare
As any she belied with false compare.
Sonnet 130

375 Two loves I have, of comfort and despair,
Which like two spirits do suggest me still;
The better angel is a man right fair,
The worser spirit a woman colour'd ill.
Sonnet 144

SHAW, GEORGE BERNARD

(1856–1950) Irish dramatist and critic. His plays, with their long prefaces, established him as the leading British playwright of his time. Included among his prose works are *The Intelligent Woman's Guide to Socialism and Capitalism* (1928) and *The Black Girl in Search of God* (1932).

Quotations about Shaw

1 Shaw's works make me admire the magnificent tolerance and broadmindedness of the English.
James Joyce (1882–1941) Irish novelist. *The Wild Geese* (Gerald Griffin)

2 He writes like a Pakistani who has learned English when he was twelve years old in order to become a chartered accountant.
John Osborne (1929–) British dramatist. Attrib.

Quotations by Shaw

3 Whether you think Jesus was God or not, you

must admit that he was a first-rate political economist.
Androcles and the Lion, Preface, 'Jesus as Economist'

4 All great truths begin as blasphemies.
Annajanska

5 You are a very poor soldier: a chocolate cream soldier!
Arms and the Man, I

6 Silence is the most perfect expression of scorn.
Back to Methuselah

7 When a stupid man is doing something he is ashamed of, he always declares that it is his duty.
Caesar and Cleopatra, III

8 A man of great common sense and good taste, – meaning thereby a man without originality or moral courage.
Referring to Julius Caesar. *Caesar and Cleopatra*, Notes

9 The British soldier can stand up to anything except the British War Office.
The Devil's Disciple, III

10 I never expect a soldier to think.
The Devil's Disciple, III

11 With the single exception of Homer, there is no eminent writer, not even Sir Walter Scott, whom I can despise so entirely as I despise Shakespeare when I measure my mind against his…It would positively be a relief to me to dig him up and throw stones at him.
Dramatic Opinions and Essays, Vol. 2

12 Physically there is nothing to distinguish human society from the farm-yard except that children are more troublesome and costly than chickens and women are not so completely enslaved as farm stock.
Getting Married, Preface

13 My way of joking is to tell the truth. It's the funniest joke in the world.
John Bull's Other Island, II

14 Cusins is a very nice fellow, certainly: nobody would ever guess that he was born in Australia.
Major Barbara, I

15 Nobody can say a word against Greek: it stamps a man at once as an educated gentleman.
Major Barbara, I

16 Alcohol is a very necessary article…It enables Parliament to do things at eleven at night that no sane person would do at eleven in the morning.
Major Barbara, II

17 He never does a proper thing without giving an improper reason for it.
Major Barbara, III

18 He knows nothing; and he thinks he knows everything. That points clearly to a political career.
Major Barbara, III

19 CUSINS. Do you call poverty a crime?
UNDERSHAFT. The worst of all crimes. All the other crimes are virtues beside it.
Major Barbara, IV

20 Give women the vote, and in five years there will be a crushing tax on bachelors.
Man and Superman, Preface

21 A lifetime of happiness: no man alive could bear it: it would be hell on earth.
Man and Superman, I

22 Very nice sort of place, Oxford, I should think, for people that like that sort of place.
Man and Superman, II

23 It is a woman's business to get married as soon as possible, and a man's to keep unmarried as long as he can.
Man and Superman, II

24 There are two tragedies in life. One is to lose your heart's desire. The other is to gain it.
Man and Superman, IV

25 In heaven an angel is nobody in particular.
Man and Superman, 'Maxims for Revolutionists'

26 Beware of the man who does not return your blow: he neither forgives you nor allows you to forgive yourself.
Man and Superman, 'Maxims for Revolutionists'

27 Do not love your neighbour as yourself. If you are on good terms with yourself it is an impertinence; if on bad, an injury.
Man and Superman, 'Maxims for Revolutionists'

28 Titles distinguish the mediocre, embarrass the superior, and are disgraced by the inferior.
Man and Superman, 'Maxims for Revolutionists'

29 Self-denial is not a virtue; it is only the effect of prudence on rascality.
Man and Superman, 'Maxims for Revolutionists'

30 If you strike a child, take care that you strike it in anger, even at the risk of maiming it for life. A blow in cold blood neither can nor should be forgiven.
Man and Superman, 'Maxims for Revolutionists'

31 The golden rule is that there are no golden rules.
Man and Superman, 'Maxims for Revolutionists'

32 He who can, does. He who cannot, teaches.
Man and Superman, 'Maxims for Revolutionists'

33 Optimistic lies have such immense therapeutic value that a doctor who cannot tell them convincingly has mistaken his profession.
Misalliance, Preface

34 Heaven, as conventionally conceived, is a place so inane, so dull, so useless, so miserable, that nobody has ever ventured to describe a whole day in heaven, though plenty of people have described a day at the seaside.
Misalliance, Preface

35 The secret of being miserable is to have leisure to bother about whether you are happy or not.
Misalliance, Preface

36 The English have no respect for their language, and will not teach their children to speak it…It is

impossible for an Englishman to open his mouth, without making some other Englishman despise him.
Pygmalion, Preface

37 They all thought she was dead; but my father he kept ladling gin down her throat till she came to so sudden that she bit the bowl off the spoon.
Pygmalion, III

38 Gin was mother's milk to her.
Pygmalion, III

39 Assassination is the extreme form of censorship.
The Shewing-Up of Blanco Posnet, 'Limits to Toleration'

40 It is the sexless novel that should be distinguished: the sex novel is now normal.
Table-Talk of G.B.S.

41 It does not follow...that the right to criticize Shakespeare involves the power of writing better plays. And in fact...I do not profess to write better plays.
Three Plays for Puritans, Preface

42 We're from Madeira, but perfectly respectable, so far.
You Never Can Tell, I

43 Well, sir, you never can tell. That's a principle in life with me, sir, if you'll excuse my having such a thing, sir.
You Never Can Tell, II

44 I've been offered titles, but I think they get one into disreputable company.
Gossip (A. Barrow)

45 The thought of two thousand people crunching celery at the same time horrified me.
Explaining why he had turned down an invitation to a vegetarian gala dinner. *The Greatest Laughs of All Time* (G. Lieberman)

46 It's a funny thing about that bust. As time goes on it seems to get younger and younger.
Referring to a portrait bust sculpted for him by Rodin. *More Things I Wish I'd Said* (K. Edwards)

47 The trouble, Mr Goldwyn is that you are only interested in art and I am only interested in money.
Turning down Goldwyn's offer to buy the screen rights of his plays. *The Movie Moguls* (Philip French), Ch. 4

48 I quite agree with you, sir, but what can two do against so many?
Responding to a solitary hiss heard amongst the applause at the first performance of *Arms and the Man* in 1894. *Oxford Book of Literary Anecdotes*

49 Certainly, there is nothing else here to enjoy.
Said at a party when his hostess asked him whether he was enjoying himself. *Pass the Port* (Oxfam)

50 Far too good to waste on children.
Reflecting upon youth. *10,000 Jokes, Toasts, and Stories* (L. Copeland)

51 Better never than late.
Responding to an offer by a producer to present one of Shaw's plays, having earlier rejected it. *The Unimportance of Being Oscar* (Oscar Levant)

52 LORD NORTHCLIFFE. The trouble with you, Shaw, is that you look as if there were famine in the land.
G.B.S. The trouble with you, Northcliffe, is that you look as if you were the cause of it.
Attrib.

53 If all economists were laid end to end, they would not reach a conclusion.
Attrib.

SHELLEY, PERCY BYSSHE

(1792–1822) British poet. Most of his poetry was written in Italy, including *Prometheus Unbound* (1818–19), *Adonais* (1821), and much lyrical poetry.

Quotations about Shelley

1 In his poetry as well as in his life Shelley was indeed 'a beautiful and ineffectual angel', beating in the void his luminous wings in vain.
Matthew Arnold (1822–88) British poet and critic. *Literature and Drama*, 'Shelley'

2 Poor Shelley always was, and is, a kind of ghastly object; colourless, pallid, tuneless, without health or warmth or vigour.
Thomas Carlyle (1795–1881) Scottish historian and essayist. *Reminiscences*

Quotations by Shelley

3 I weep for Adonais – he is dead!
O, weep for Adonais! though our tears
Thaw not the frost which binds so dear a head!
Prompted by the death of Keats. *Adonais*, I

4 He hath awakened from the dream of life –
'Tis we, who lost in stormy visions, keep
With phantoms an unprofitable strife,
And in mad trance, strike with our spirit's knife
Invulnerable nothings.
Adonais, XXXIX

5 I wield the flail of the lashing hail,
And whiten the green plains under,
And then again I dissolve it in rain,
And laugh as I pass in thunder.
The Cloud

6 I am the daughter of Earth and Water,
And the nursling of the Sky;
I pass through the pores of the ocean and shores;
I change, but I cannot die,
For after the rain when with never a stain
The pavilion of Heaven is bare,
And the winds and sunbeams with their convex gleams
Build up the blue dome of air,
I silently laugh at my own cenotaph,
And out of the caverns of rain,
Like a child from the womb, like a ghost from the tomb,
I arise and unbuild it again.
The Cloud

7 Poetry is the record of the best and happiest moments of the happiest and best minds.
A Defence of Poetry

8 Life may change, but it may fly not;
Hope may vanish, but can die not;

Truth be veiled, but still it burneth;
Love repulsed, – but it returneth!

Hellas, I

9 Let there be light! said Liberty,
And like sunrise from the sea,
Athens arose!

Hellas, I

10 London, that great sea, whose ebb and flow
At once is deaf and loud, and on the shore
Vomits its wrecks, and still howls on for more.

Letter to Maria Gisborne, I

11 Have you not heard
When a man marries, dies, or turns Hindoo,
His best friends hear no more of him?

Referring to the novelist Thomas Love Peacock, who worked for the East India Company and had recently married. *Letter to Maria Gisborne*, I

12 Lift not the painted veil which those who live
Call life.

Lift not the Painted Veil

13 I met Murder on the way –
He had a mask like Castlereagh.

Viscount Castlereagh (1769–1822) was British foreign secretary (1812–22); he was highly unpopular and became identified with such controversial events as the Peterloo massacre of 1819. *The Mask of Anarchy*, 5

14 O Wild West Wind, thou breath of Autumn's being,
Thou, from whose unseen presence the leaves dead
Are driven, like ghosts from an enchanter fleeing,
Yellow, and black, and pale, and hectic red,
Pestilence-stricken multitudes.

Ode to the West Wind

15 If Winter comes, can Spring be far behind?

Ode to the West Wind

16 I met a traveller from an antique land
Who said: Two vast and trunkless legs of stone
Stand in the desert.

Referring to the legs of a broken statue of the Pharaoh Rameses II (1301–1234 BC; Greek name, Ozymandias). *Ozymandias*

17 'My name is Ozymandias, king of kings:
Look on my works, ye Mighty, and despair!'

Ozymandias

18 Sometimes
The Devil is a gentleman.

Peter Bell the Third

19 Teas,
Where small talk dies in agonies.

Peter Bell the Third

20 'Twas Peter's drift
To be a kind of moral eunuch.

Peter Bell the Third

21 Hell is a city much like London –
A populous and smoky city.

Peter Bell the Third

22 Death is the veil which those who live call life:
They sleep, and it is lifted.

Prometheus Unbound, III

23 It is a modest creed, and yet
Pleasant if one considers it,
To own that death itself must be,
Like all the rest, a mockery.

The Sensitive Plant, III

24 Hail to thee, blithe Spirit!
Bird thou never wert,
That from Heaven, or near it,
Pourest thy full heart
In profuse strains of unpremeditated art.

To a Skylark

25 Music, when soft voices die,
Vibrates in the memory –
Odours, when sweet violets sicken,
Live within the sense they quicken.
Rose leaves, when the rose is dead,
Are heaped for the beloved's bed;
And so thy thoughts, when thou art gone,
Love itself shall slumber on.

To –

26 For she was beautiful – her beauty made
The bright world dim, and everything beside
Seemed like the fleeting image of a shade.

The Witch of Atlas, XII

SHERIDAN, RICHARD BRINSLEY

(1751–1816) British dramatist. His best-known comedies are *The Rivals* (1775) and *The School for Scandal* (1777). He was manager of the Drury Lane Theatre and a Whig MP (1780–1812).

Quotations about Sheridan

1 Good at a fight, but better at a play
God-like in giving, but the devil to pay.

Lord Byron (1788–1824) British poet. *On a Cast of Sheridan's Hand*

2 He could not make enemies. If anyone came to request the payment of a loan from him he borrowed more. A cordial shake of his hand was a receipt in full for all demands.

William Hazlitt (1778–1830) British essayist. *New Monthly Magazine*, Jan 1824

Quotations by Sheridan

3 If it is abuse – why one is always sure to hear of it from one damned good-natured friend or other!

The Critic, I

4 A progeny of learning.

The Rivals, I

5 Illiterate him, I say, quite from your memory.

The Rivals, II

6 It gives me the hydrostatics to such a degree.

The Rivals, III

7 As headstrong as an allegory on the banks of the Nile.

The Rivals, III

8 He is the very pine-apple of politeness!

The Rivals, III

9 If I reprehend any thing in this world, it is the

use of my oracular tongue, and a nice derangement of epitaphs!
The Rivals, III

10 You had no taste when you married me.
The School for Scandal, I

11 I'm called away by particular business. But I leave my character behind me.
The School for Scandal, II

12 Well, then, my stomach must just digest in its waistcoat.
On being warned that his drinking would destroy the coat of his stomach. *The Fine Art of Political Wit* (L. Harris)

13 What His Royal Highness most particularly prides himself upon, is the excellent harvest.
Lampooning George IV's habit of taking credit for everything good in England. *The Fine Art of Political Wit* (L. Harris)

14 My dear fellow, be reasonable; the sum you ask me for is a very considerable one, whereas I only ask you for twenty-five pounds.
On being refused a further loan of £25 from a friend to whom he already owed £500. *Literary and Scientific Anecdotes* (W. Keddie)

15 Whatsoever might be the extent of the private calamity, I hope it will not interfere with the public business of the country.
On learning, whilst in the House of Commons, that his Drury Lane Theatre was on fire. *Memoirs of Life of the R. Hon. Richard Brinsley Sheridan* (T. Moore)

16 A man may surely be allowed to take a glass of wine by his own fireside.
As he sat in a coffeehouse watching his Drury Lane Theatre burn down. *Memoirs of the Life of the Rt. Hon. Richard Brinsley Sheridan* (T. Moore)

17 Thank God, that's settled.
Handing one of his creditors an IOU. *Wit, Wisdom, and Foibles of the Great* (C. Shriner)

18 Won't you come into the garden? I would like my roses to see you.
Said to a young lady. Attrib. in *The Perfect Hostess*

19 It is not my interest to pay the principal, nor my principle to pay the interest.
To his tailor when he requested the payment of a debt, or of the interest on it at least. Attrib.

20 The Right Honourable gentleman is indebted to his memory for his jests, and to his imagination for his facts.
Replying to a speech in the House of Commons. Attrib.

21 Mr. Speaker, I said the honorable member was a liar it is true and I am sorry for it. The honourable member may place the punctuation where he pleases.
On being asked to apologize for calling a fellow MP a liar. Attrib.

SHYNESS

See also self-confidence

1 I'm really a timid person – I was beaten up by Quakers.
Woody Allen (Allen Stewart Konigsberg; 1935–) US film actor. *Sleeper*

2 A timid question will always receive a confident answer.
Lord Darling (1849–1936) British judge. *Scintillae Juris*

3 Why so shy, my pretty Thomasina?
Thomasin, O Thomasin,
Once you were so promisin'.
Christopher Fry (1907–) British dramatist. *The Dark Is Light Enough*, II

4 I was a total loner, not by self-design. I just didn't know what the hell to say to people. I was so shy. I used to stammer and lisp and dribble at the mouth.
Anthony Hopkins (1937–) Welsh actor. *Films Illustrated*, Dec 1980

5 Shyness is just egotism out of its depth.
Penelope Keith British actress. Remark, July 1988

6 Had we but world enough, and time,
This coyness, lady, were no crime.
Andrew Marvell (1621–78) English poet. *To His Coy Mistress*

7 Shyness is *common*...Self-consciousness it was always called when I was young, and that is what it is. To imagine that it shows a sense of modesty is absurd. *Modesty*. Why, I have never known a *truly* modest person to be the least bit shy.
Elizabeth Taylor (1912–75) British writer. *The Bush*, 'You'll Enjoy It When You Get There'

SIGNATURES

1 Never sign a walentine with your own name.
Charles Dickens (1812–70) British novelist. Said by Sam Weller. *Pickwick Papers*, Ch. 33

2 There, I guess King George will be able to read that.
John Hancock (1737–93) US revolutionary. Referring to his signature, written in a bold hand, on the US Declaration of Independence. *The American Treasury* (C. Fadiman)

3 The hand that signed the treaty bred a fever,
And famine grew, and locusts came;
Great is the hand that holds dominion over
Man by a scribbled name.
Dylan Thomas (1914–53) Welsh poet. *The Hand that Signed the Paper*

SILENCE

See also speech

1 A still tongue makes a wise head.
Proverb

2 Speech is silver, silence is golden.
Proverb

3 No voice; but oh! the silence sank
Like music on my heart.
Samuel Taylor Coleridge (1772–1834) British poet. *The Rime of the Ancient Mariner*, VI

4 When you have nothing to say, say nothing.
Charles Caleb Colton (?1780–1832) British clergyman and writer. *Lacon*, Vol. I

5 For God's sake hold your tongue and let me love.

John Donne (1573–1631) English poet. *The Canonization*

6 Silence is become his mother tongue.

Oliver Goldsmith (1728–74) Irish-born British writer. *The Good-Natured Man*, II

7 That man's silence is wonderful to listen to.

Thomas Hardy (1840–1928) British novelist. *Under the Greenwood Tree*, Ch. 14

8 Silence is as full of potential wisdom and wit as the unhewn marble of great sculpture.

Aldous Huxley (1894–1964) British novelist. *Point Counter Point*

9 Thou still unravish'd bride of quietness,
Thou foster-child of silence and slow time.

John Keats (1795–1821) British poet. *Ode on a Grecian Urn*

10 Silence is the best tactic for him who distrusts himself.

Duc de la Rochefoucauld (1613–80) French writer. *Maximes*, 79

11 You get the impression that their normal condition is silence and that speech is a slight fever which attacks them now and then.

Jean-Paul Sartre (1905–80) French writer. *Nausea*

12 Silence is the perfectest herald of joy: I were but little happy if I could say how much.

William Shakespeare (1564–1616) English dramatist. *Much Ado About Nothing*, II:1

13 Silence is the most perfect expression of scorn.

George Bernard Shaw (1856–1950) Irish dramatist and critic. *Back to Methuselah*

14 My personal hobbies are reading, listening to music, and silence.

Edith Sitwell (1887–1964) British poet and writer. Attrib.

15 The cruellest lies are often told in silence.

Robert Louis Stevenson (1850–94) Scottish writer. *Virginibus Puerisque*

16 God is the friend of silence. Trees, flowers, grass grow in silence. See the stars, moon and sun, how they move in silence.

Mother Teresa (Agnes Gonxha Bojaxhui; 1910–) Yugoslavian-born Indian missionary. *For the Brotherhood of Man*

17 Whereof one cannot speak, thereon one must remain silent.

Ludwig Wittgenstein (1889–1951) Austrian philosopher. *Tractatus Logico-Philosophicus*, Ch. 7

SIMILARITY

See also analogy, difference

1 Birds of a feather flock together.

Proverb

2 Great minds think alike.

Proverb

3 Like breeds like.

Proverb

4 Never mind, dear, we're all made the same, though some more than others.

Noël Coward (1899–1973) British dramatist. *The Café de la Paix*

5 I never knows the children. It's just six of one and half-a-dozen of the other.

Captain Frederick Marryat (1792–1848) British novelist. *The Pirate*, Ch. 4

SIMPLICITY

1 'Excellent!' I cried. 'Elementary,' said he.

Arthur Conan Doyle (1856–1930) British writer. Watson talking to Sherlock Holmes; Holmes's reply is often misquoted as 'Elementary, my dear Watson'. *The Crooked Man*

2 The ability to simplify means to eliminate the unnecessary so that the necessary may speak.

Hans Hofmann (1880–1966) German-born US painter. *Search for the Real*

3 O holy simplicity!

John Huss (Jan Hus; c. 1369–1415) Bohemian religious reformer. On noticing a peasant adding a faggot to the pile at his execution. *Apophthegmata* (Zincgreff-Weidner), Pt. III

4 The trivial round, the common task,
Would furnish all we ought to ask;
Room to deny ourselves; a road
To bring us, daily, nearer God.

John Keble (1792–1866) British poet and clergyman. *The Christian Year*, 'Morning'

5 A child of five would understand this.
Send somebody to fetch a child of five.

Groucho Marx (Julius Marx; 1895–1977) US comedian. *Duck Soup*

6 Entities should not be multiplied unnecessarily. No more things should be presumed to exist than are absolutely necessary.

William of Okham (c. 1280–1349) English philosopher. 'Okham's Razor'. Despite its attribution to William of Okham, it was in fact a repetition of an ancient philosophical maxim.

7 Anybody can shock a baby, or a television audience. But it's too easy, and the effect is disproportionate to the effort.

Richard G. Stern (1928–) US writer. *Golk*, Ch. 4

8 Our life is frittered away by detail...Simplify, simplify.

Henry David Thoreau (1817–62) US writer. *Walden*, 'Where I lived, and What I Lived For'

SIN

See also evil, vice

1 Old sins cast long shadows.

Proverb

2 All sin tends to be addictive, and the terminal point of addiction is what is called damnation.

W. H. Auden (1907–73) British poet. *A Certain World*

3 Wherefore putting away lying, speak every man truth with his neighbour: for we are members one of another.
Be ye angry, and sin not: let not the sun go down upon your wrath:
Neither give place to the devil.
Let him that stole steal no more: but rather let him labour, working with his hands the thing which is good, that he may have to give to him that needeth.

Bible: Ephesians 4:25–28

4 So when they continued asking him, he lifted up himself, and said unto them, He that is without sin among you, let him first cast a stone at her.

Bible: John 8:7

5 If we say that we have no sin, we deceive ourselves, and the truth is not in us.
If we confess our sins, he is faithful and just to forgive us our sins, and to cleanse us from all unrighteousness.

Bible: I John 1:8–9

6 Wherefore I say unto thee, Her sins, which are many, are forgiven; for she loved much: but to whom little is forgiven, the same loveth little.

Bible: Luke 7:47

7 But if ye will not do so, behold, ye have sinned against the Lord: and be sure your sin will find you out.

Bible: Numbers 32:23

8 We have erred, and strayed from thy ways like lost sheep.

The Book of Common Prayer *Morning Prayer, General Confession*

9 We have left undone those things which we ought to have done; and we have done those things we ought not to have done.

The Book of Common Prayer *Morning Prayer, General Confession*

10 I am not in the business of allotting sins.

George Carey (1935–) British churchman; Archbishop of Canterbury. *The Observer*, 'Sayings of the Week', 22 May 1994

11 A private sin is not so prejudicial in the world as a public indecency.

Miguel de Cervantes (1547–1616) Spanish novelist. *Don Quixote*, Pt. II, Ch. 22

12 He said he was against it.

Calvin Coolidge (1872–1933) US president. Reply when asked what a clergyman had said regarding sin in his sermon. Attrib.

13 It is my belief, Watson, founded upon my experience, that the lowest and vilest alleys of London do not present a more dreadful record of sin than does the smiling and beautiful countryside.

Arthur Conan Doyle (1856–1930) British writer. *Copper Beeches*

14 Did wisely from Expensive Sins refrain,
And never broke the Sabbath, but for Gain.

John Dryden (1631–1700) British poet and dramatist. *Absalom and Achitophel*, I

15 Sin brought death, and death will disappear with the disappearance of sin.

Mary Baker Eddy (1821–1910) US religious leader. *Science and Health, with Key to the Scriptures*

16 Fashions in sin change.

Lillian Hellman (1906–) US playwright and writer. *Watch on the Rhine*

17 Don't tell my mother I'm living in sin,
Don't let the old folks know:
Don't tell my twin that I breakfast on gin,
He'd never survive the blow.

A. P. Herbert (1890–1971) British writer. *Don't Tell My Mother*

18 There's nothing so artificial as sinning nowadays. I suppose it once was real.

D. H. Lawrence (1885–1930) British novelist. *St Mawr*

19 Sin...has been made out not only ugly but passé. People are no longer sinful, they are only immature or under privileged or frightened or, more particularly, sick.

Phyllis McGinley (1905–78) US poet and humorist. *The Province of the Heart*, 'In Defense of Sin'

20 Of Man's first disobedience, and the fruit
Of that forbidden tree, whose mortal taste
Brought death into the World, and all our woe...

John Milton (1608–74) English poet. *Paradise Lost*, Bk. I

21 The only people who should really sin
Are the people who can sin with a grin.

Ogden Nash (1902–71) US poet. *I'm a Stranger Here Myself*

22 She holds that it were better for sun and moon to drop from heaven, for the earth to fail, and for all the many millions who are upon it to die of starvation in extremest agony, as far as temporal affliction goes, than that one soul, I will not say, should be lost, but should commit one single venial sin, should tell one wilful untruth,...or steal one poor farthing without excuse.

Cardinal Newman (1801–90) British theologian. Referring to the Roman Catholic Church. *Lectures on Anglican Difficulties*, VIII

23 At such an hour the sinners are still in bed resting up from their sinning of the night before, so they will be in good shape for more sinning a little later on.

Damon Runyon (1884–1946) US writer. *Runyon à la carte*, 'The Idyll of Miss Sarah Brown'

24 I delight in sinning and hate to compose a mask for gossip.

Sulpicia (fl. 63 BC–AD 14) Roman poet. *A Book of Women Poets* (ed. Aliki and Willis Barnstone)

25 Were't not for gold and women, there would be no damnation.

Cyril Tourneur (1575–1626) English dramatist. *The Revenger's Tragedy*, II:1

SINCERITY

See also frankness, honesty, integrity

1 Best be yourself, imperial, plain and true!

Robert Browning (1812–89) British poet. *Bishop Blougram's Apology*

2 What comes from the heart, goes to the heart.

Samuel Taylor Coleridge (1772–1834) British poet. *Table Talk*

3 Some of the worst men in the world are sincere and the more sincere they are the worse they are.

Lord Hailsham (1907–) British Conservative politician. *The Observer*, 'Sayings of the Week', 7 Jan 1968

4 I'm afraid of losing my obscurity. Genuineness only thrives in the dark. Like celery.

Aldous Huxley (1894–1964) British novelist. *Those Barren Leaves*, Pt. I, Ch. 1

5 What's a man's first duty? The answer's brief:
To be himself.

Henrik Ibsen (1828–1906) Norwegian dramatist. *Peer Gynt*, IV:1

6 A little sincerity is a dangerous thing, and a great deal of it is absolutely fatal.

Oscar Wilde (1854–1900) Irish-born British dramatist. *The Critic as Artist*, Pt. 2

SINGERS

See also musicians, singing

1 Swans sing before they die – 'twere no bad thing,
Did certain persons die before they sing.

Samuel Taylor Coleridge (1772–1834) British poet. *Epigram on a Volunteer Singer*

2 A wandering minstrel I –
A thing of shreds and patches,
Of ballads, songs and snatches,
And dreamy lullaby!

W. S. Gilbert (1836–1911) British dramatist. *The Mikado*, I

3 The Last of the Red-Hot Mamas.

Sophie Tucker (Sophia Abuza; 1884–1966) Russian-born US singer. Description of herself. *Dictionary of Biographical Quotation* (J. Wintle and R. Kenin)

SINGING

See also music, opera, singers

1 You know whatta you do when you shit?
Singing, it's the same thing, only up!

Enrico Caruso (1873–1921) Italian tenor. *Whose Little Boy Are You?* (H. Brown)

2 I have a song to sing O!
Sing me your song, O!

W. S. Gilbert (1836–1911) British dramatist. *The Yeoman of the Guard*, I

3 Just a little more reverence, please, and not so much astonishment.

Malcolm Sargent (1895–1967) British conductor. Rehearsing the female chorus in 'For Unto Us a Child is Born' from Handel's *Messiah*. *2500 Anecdotes* (E. Fuller)

SITWELL, DAME EDITH

(1887–1964) British poet and writer, sister of Osbert Sitwell. *Façade* (1923) was set to music by William Walton; her other collections include *Gold Coast Customs* (1929).

Quotations about Sitwell

1 Then Edith Sitwell appeared, her nose longer than an ant-eater's, and read some of her absurd stuff.

Lytton Strachey (1880–1932) British writer. Letter to Dora Carrington, 28 June 1921

2 So you've been reviewing Edith Sitwell's latest piece of virgin dung, have you? Isn't she a poisonous thing of a woman, lying, concealing, flipping, plagiarising, misquoting, and being as clever a crooked literary publicist as ever.

Dylan Thomas (1914–53) Welsh poet. Letter to Glyn Jones, 1934

Quotations by Sitwell

3 My poems are hymns of praise to the glory of life.

Collected Poems, 'Some Notes on My Poetry'

4 Who dreamed that Christ has died in vain?
He walks again on the Seas of Blood,
He comes in the terrible Rain.

The Shadow of Cain

5 When
Sir
Beelzebub called for his syllabub in the hotel in Hell
Where Proserpine first fell,
Blue as the gendarmerie were the waves of the sea,
(Rocking and shocking the bar-maid).

6 A lady asked me why, on most occasions, I wore black. 'Are you in mourning?'
'Yes.'
'For whom are you in mourning?'
'For the world.'

Taken Care Of, Ch. 1

7 A pompous woman of his acquaintance, complaining that the head-waiter of a restaurant had not shown her and her husband immediately to a table, said, 'We had to tell him who we were.' Gerald, interested, enquired, 'And who were you?'

Taken Care Of, Ch. 15

8 I have often wished I had time to cultivate modesty...But I am too busy thinking about myself.

The Observer, 'Sayings of the Week', 30 Apr 1950

9 I enjoyed talking to her, but thought *nothing* of her writing. I considered her 'a beautiful little knitter'.

Referring to Virginia Woolf. Letter to G. Singleton

SLAVERY

See also oppression

1 From the beginning all were created equal by nature, slavery was introduced through the injust oppression of worthless men, against the will of God; for, if God had wanted to create slaves, he would surely have decided at the beginning of the world who was to be slave and who master.

John Ball Sermon, Blackheath, 1381

2 The future is the only kind of property that the masters willingly concede to slaves.

Albert Camus (1913–60) French existentialist writer. *The Rebel*

3 There they are cutting each other's throats, because one half of them prefer hiring their servants for life, and the other by the hour.

Thomas Carlyle (1795–1881) Scottish historian and essayist. Referring to the American Civil War. Attrib.

4 Slaves cannot breathe in England; if their lungs
Receive our air, that moment they are free;
They touch our country, and their shackles fall.

William Cowper (1731–1800) British poet. A situation resulting from a judicial decision in 1772. *The Task*

5 The compact which exists between the North and the South is a covenant with death and an agreement with hell.

William Lloyd Garrison (1805–79) US abolitionist. Resolution, Massachusetts Anti-Slavery Society, 27 Jan 1843

6 The whole commerce between master and slave is a perpetual exercise of the most boisterous passions, the most unremitting despotism on the one part, and degrading submissions on the other.

Thomas Jefferson (1743–1826) US statesman. *Notes on the State of Virginia*

7 No man should be a serf, nor do homage or any manner of service to any lord, but should give fourpence rent for an acre of land, and that no one should work for any man but as his own will, and on terms of a regular covenant.

Wat Tyler (d. 1381) English rebel. *Anonimalle Chronicle*

SLEEP

See also bed, dreams

1 One hour's sleep before midnight, is worth two after.

Proverb

2 Sleep is better than medicine.

Proverb

3 The beginning of health is sleep.

Irish proverb

4 Now I lay me down to sleep,
I pray the Lord my soul to keep.
If I should die before I wake,
I pray the Lord my soul to take.

Anonymous *New England Primer*, 1781

5 The amount of sleep required by the average person is just five minutes more.

Anonymous

6 Lay your sleeping head, my love,
Human on my faithless arm.

W. H. Auden (1907–73) British poet. *Lullaby*

7 Rock-a-bye baby on the tree top,
When the wind blows the cradle will rock,
When the bough bends the cradle will fall,
Down comes the baby, cradle and all.

Charles Dupee Blake (1846–1903) British writer of nursery rhymes. Attrib.

8 Laugh and the world laughs with you; snore and you sleep alone.

Anthony Burgess (John Burgess Wilson; 1917–93) British novelist. *Inside Mr. Enderby*

9 Oh sleep! it is a gentle thing,
Beloved from pole to pole!

Samuel Taylor Coleridge (1772–1834) British poet. *The Rime of the Ancient Mariner*, V

10 Golden slumbers kiss your eyes,
Smiles awake you when you rise.

Thomas Dekker (c. 1572–1632) English dramatist. *Patient Grissil*, IV:2

11 Sleep is that golden chaine that ties health and our bodies together.

Thomas Dekker *The Guls Horn-Booke*, Ch. 2

12 Health is the first muse, and sleep is the condition to produce it.

Ralph Waldo Emerson (1803–82) US poet and essayist. *Uncollected Lectures*, 'Resources'

13 It appears that every man's insomnia is as different from his neighbor's as are their daytime hopes and aspirations.

F. Scott Fitzgerald (1896–1940) US novelist. *The Crack-up*, 'Sleeping and Waking'

14 Try thinking of love, or something.
Amor vincit insomnia.

Christopher Fry (1907–) British dramatist. *A Sleep of Prisoners*

15 Sleep is when all the unsorted stuff comes flying out as from a dustbin upset in a high wind.

William Golding (1911–93) British novelist. *Pincher Martin*

16 Sleep is gross, a form of abandonment, and it is impossible for anyone to awake and observe its sordid consequences save with a faint sense of recent dissipation, of minute personal disquiet and remorse.

Patrick Hamilton *Slaves of Solitude*

17 Sleep and watchfulness, both of them, when immoderate, constitute disease.

Hippocrates (c. 460 BC–c. 377 BC) Greek physician. *Aphorisms*, II

18 He's a wicked man that comes after children when they won't go to bed and throws handfuls of sand in their eyes.

Ernst Hoffmann (1776–1822) German composer. *The Sandman*

19 Three natural anaesthetics...sleep, fainting, death.

Oliver Wendell Holmes (1809–94) US writer and physician. *Medical Essays*, 'The Medical Profession in Massachusetts'

20 Insomnia never comes to a man who has to get up exactly at six o'clock. Insomnia troubles only those who can sleep any time.

Elbert G. Hubbard (1856–1915) *The Philistine*, 'In Re Muldoon'

21 Now deep in my bed I turn
And the world turns on the other side.

Elizabeth Jennings (1926–) British poet *In the Night*

22 The amount of sleep required by the average person is about five minutes more.

Max Kauffmann Attrib.

23 O soft embalmer of the still midnight.

John Keats (1795–1821) British poet. *To Sleep*

24 Turn the key deftly in the oiled wards,
And seal the hushed casket of my soul.

John Keats *To Sleep*

25 How do people go to sleep? I'm afraid I've lost the knack. I might try busting myself smartly over the temple with the nightlight. I might repeat to myself, slowly and soothingly, a list of quotations beautiful from minds profound; if I can remember any of the damn things.

Dorothy Parker (1893–1967) US writer. *The Little Hours*

26 Slepe is the nouryshment and food of a sucking child.

Thomas Phaer (c. 1510–60) *The Boke of Chyldren*

27 Those no-sooner-have-I-touched-the-pillow people are past my comprehension. There is something bovine about them.

J. B. Priestley (1894–1984) British novelist. *All About Ourselves*

28 Our foster nurse of nature is repose.

William Shakespeare (1564–1616) English dramatist and poet. *King Lear*, IV

29 Sleep that knits up the ravell'd sleave of care,
The death of each day's life, sore labour's bath,
Balm of hurt minds, great nature's second course,
Chief nourisher in life's feast.

William Shakespeare *Macbeth*, II:2

30 Sleep's the only medicine that gives ease.

Sophocles (c. 496–406 BC) Greek dramatist. *Philoctetes*, 766

31 Of all the soft, delicious functions of nature this is the chiefest; what a happiness it is to man, when the anxieties and passions of the day are over.

Laurence Sterne (1713–68) Irish-born English novelist.

32 Sleep, Death's twin-brother, knows not Death,
Nor can I dream of thee as dead.

Alfred, Lord Tennyson (1809–92) British poet. *In Memoriam A.H.H.*, LXVIII

33 I have come to the borders of sleep,
The unfathomable deep
Forest where all must lose
Their way.

Edward Thomas (1878–1917) British poet. *Lights Out*

34 There ain't no way to find out why a snorer can't hear himself snore.

Mark Twain (Samuel Langhorne Clemens; 1835–1910) US writer. *Tom Sawyer Abroad*, Ch. 10

35 It was the time when first sleep begins for weary
mortals and by the gift of the gods creeps over them
most welcomely.

Virgil (Publius Vergilius Maro; 70–19 BC) Roman poet. *Aeneid*, Bk. II

36 That sweet, deep sleep, so close to tranquil death.

Virgil *Aeneid*, VI

37 I haven't been to sleep for over a year. That's why I go to bed early. One needs more rest if one doesn't sleep.

Evelyn Waugh (1903–66) British novelist. *Decline and Fall*, Pt. II, Ch. 3

38 I believe the greatest asset a head of state can have is the ability to get a good night's sleep.

Harold Wilson (1916–) British politician and prime minister. *The World Tonight*, BBC Radio, 16 Apr 1975

39 Dear God! the very houses seem asleep;
And all that mighty heart is lying still!

William Wordsworth (1770–1850) British poet. *Sonnets*, 'Composed upon Westminster Bridge'

SMALLNESS

See also triviality

1 The best things come in small parcels.

Proverb

2 The Microbe is so very small
You cannot make him out at all.

Hilaire Belloc (1870–1953) French-born British poet. *More Beasts for Worse Children*, 'The Microbe'

3 One cubic foot less of space and it would have constituted adultery.

Robert Benchley (1889–1945) US humorist. Describing an office shared with Dorothy Parker. Attrib.

4 Small is beautiful.

E. F. Schumacher (1911–77) German-born economist. Title of book

SMITH, ADAM

(1723–90) Scottish economist. He lectured on logic and moral philosophy (1752–63) and wrote *An Enquiry into the Nature and Causes of the Wealth of Nations* (1776).

1 People of the same trade seldom meet together but the conversation ends in a conspiracy against the public, or in some contrivance to raise prices.

The Wealth of Nations

2 With the great part of rich people, the chief employment of riches consists in the parade of riches.

The Wealth of Nations

3 There is no art which one government sooner learns of another than that of draining money from the pockets of the people.

The Wealth of Nations

4 Science is the great antidote to the poison of enthusiasm and supersition.

The Wealth of Nations

SMITH, LOGAN PEARSALL

(1865–1946) US writer. He spent most of his life in England and is best known for his collections *Trivia* (1902) and *Afterthoughts* (1931) as well as his books on language, such as *The English Language* (1912).

1 A best-seller is the gilded tomb of a mediocre talent.

Afterthoughts, 'Art and Letters'

2 It is the wretchedness of being rich that you have to live with rich people.

Afterthoughts, 'In the World'

3 People say that life is the thing, but I prefer reading.

Afterthoughts, 'Myself

4 Married women are kept women, and they are beginning to find it out.

Afterthoughts, 'Other people'

5 I might give my life for my friend, but he had better not ask me to do up a parcel.

Trivia

6 I am one of the unpraised, unrewarded millions without whom Statistics would be a bankrupt science. It is we who are born, who marry, who die, in constant ratios.

Trivia

7 I cannot forgive my friends for dying: I do not find these vanishing acts of theirs at all amusing.

Trivia

8 Thank heavens the sun has gone in and I don't have to go out and enjoy it.

Attrib.

9 Yes there is a meaning; at least for me, there is one thing that matters – to set a chime of words tinkling in the minds of a few fastidious people.

Contemplating whether life has any meaning, shortly before his death. *New Statesman*, 9 Mar 1946

SMITH, SYDNEY

(1771–1845) British clergyman, essayist, and wit. He helped to found the *Edinburgh Review* (1802), and published many of his sermons, essays, speeches, and letters.

1 Mankind are always happy for having been happy, so that if you make them happy now, you make them happy twenty years hence by the memory of it.

Elementary Sketches of Moral Philosophy

2 The moment the very name of Ireland is mentioned, the English seem to bid adieu to common feeling, common prudence, and common sense, and to act with the barbarity of tyrants, and the fatuity of idiots.

The Letters of Peter Plymley

3 They are written as if sin were to be taken out of man like Eve out of Adam – by putting him to sleep.

Referring to boring sermons. *Anecdotes of the Clergy* (J. Larwood)

4 Heat, madam! It was so dreadful that I found there was nothing for it but to take off my flesh and sit in my bones.

Discussing the hot weather with a lady acquaintance. *Lives of the Wits* (H. Pearson)

5 You never expected justice from a company, did you? They have neither a soul to lose nor a body to kick.

Memoir (Lady Holland)

6 What you don't know would make a great book.

Memoir (Lady Holland)

7 That knuckle-end of England – that land of Calvin, oat-cakes, and sulphur.

Referring to Scotland. *Memoir* (Lady Holland)

8 How can a bishop marry? How can he flirt? The most he can say is, 'I will see you in the vestry after service'.

Memoir (Lady Holland)

9 You find people ready enough to do the Samaritan, without the oil and twopence.

Memoir (Lady Holland)

10 My definition of marriage:...it resembles a pair of shears, so joined that they cannot be separated; often moving in opposite directions, yet always punishing anyone who comes between them.

Memoir (Lady Holland)

11 He has occasional flashes of silence, that make his conversation perfectly delightful.

Referring to the historian Lord Macaulay. *Memoir* (Lady Holland)

12 No furniture so charming as books.

Memoir (Lady Holland)

13 Minorities...are almost always in the right.

The Smith of Smiths (H. Pearson), Ch. 9

14 I am just going to pray for you at St Paul's, but with no very lively hope of success.

On meeting an acquaintance. *The Smith of Smiths* (H. Pearson), Ch. 13

15 I look upon Switzerland as an inferior sort of Scotland.

Letter to Lord Holland, 1815

16 He who drinks a tumbler of London water has literally in his stomach more animated beings than there are men, women and children on the face of the globe.

Letter

17 You must not think me necessarily foolish because I am facetious, nor will I consider you necessarily wise because you are grave.

Letter to Bishop Blomfield

18 He rose by gravity; I sank by levity.

Comparing his career with that of his brother, Robert Percy Smith. Attrib.

SMOKING

See also abstinence

1 It is better to be without a wife for a bit than without tobacco for an hour.

Proverb

2 Tobacco hic,
Will make a man well if he be sick.

Proverb

3 Caution: Cigarette Smoking May Be Hazardous to Your Health.

Anonymous Statement required on cigarette packages and cartons by the 89th US Congress, 1st Session

4 The Elizabethan age might be better named the beginning of the smoking era.

J. M. Barrie (1860–1937) British novelist and dramatist. *My Lady Nicotine*

5 Certainly not – if you don't object if I'm sick.

Thomas Beecham (1879–1961) British conductor. When asked whether he minded if someone smoked in a non-smoking compartment. Attrib.

6 Tobacco, divine, rare, superexcellent tobacco, which goes far beyond all their panaceas, potable gold, and philosopher's stones, a sovereign remedy to all diseases.

Robert Burton (1577–1640) English scholar and explorer. *Anatomy of Melancholy*

7 Jones – (who, I'm glad to say,
Asked leave of Mrs J. –)
Daily absorbs a clay
After his labours.

C. S. Calverley (1831–84) British poet. *Ode to Tobacco*

8 I must point out that my rule of life prescribed as an absolutely sacred rite smoking cigars and also the drinking of alcohol before, after, and if need be during all meals and in the intervals between them.

Winston Churchill (1874–1965) British statesman. Said during a lunch with the Arab leader Ibn Saud, when he heard that the king's religion forbade smoking and alcohol. *The Second World War*

9 Smokers, male and female, inject and excuse idleness in their lives every time they light a cigarette.

Colette (1873–1954) French novelist. *Earthly Paradise*, 'Freedom'

10 It is quite a three-pipe problem.

Arthur Conan Doyle (1856–1930) British writer. *The Red-Headed League*

11 I have seen many a man turn his gold into smoke, but you are the first who has turned smoke into gold.

Elizabeth I (1533–1603) Queen of England. Speaking to Sir Walter Raleigh who brought the tobacco plant to England from America

12 What smells so? Has somebody been burning a Rag, or is there a Dead Mule in the Back yard? No, the Man is Smoking a Five-Cent Cigar.

Eugene Field (1850–95) US poet and journalist. *The Tribune Primer*, 'The Five-Cent Cigar'

13 Tobacco surely was designed
To poison, and destroy mankind.

Philip Freneau (1752–1832) US poet. *Poems*, 'Tobacco'

14 What a blessing this smoking is! perhaps the greatest that we owe to the discovery of America.

Arthur Helps (1813–75) British historian. *Friends in Council*

15 Tobacco is a dirty weed. I like it.
It satisfies no normal need. I like it.
It makes you thin, it makes you lean,
It takes the hair right off your bean.
It's the worst darn stuff I've ever seen.
I like it.

Graham Lee Hemminger (1896–1949) *Penn State Froth*, Nov 1915

16 A custom loathsome to the eye, hateful to the nose, harmful to the brain, dangerous to the lungs, and in the black, stinking fume thereof, nearest resembling the horrible Stygian smoke of the pit that is bottomless.

James I (1566–1625) King of England. *A Counterblast to Tobacco*

17 Smoking...is a shocking thing, blowing smoke out of our mouths into other people's mouths, eyes and noses, and having the same thing done to us.

Samuel Johnson (1709–84) British lexicographer. *Tour to the Hebrides* (James Boswell)

18 Neither do thou lust after that tawney weed tobacco.

Ben Jonson (1573–1637) English dramatist. *Bartholomew Fair*, II:6

19 Ods me, I marvel what pleasure or felicity they have in taking their roguish tobacco. It is good for nothing but to choke a man, and fill him full of smoke and embers.

Ben Jonson *Every Man in His Humour*, III:5

20 The tobacco business is a conspiracy against womanhood and manhood. It owes its origin to that scoundrel Sir Walter Raleigh, who was likewise the founder of American slavery.

Dr. John Harvey Kellogg *Tobacco*

21 A woman is only a woman, but a good cigar is a smoke.

Rudyard Kipling (1865–1936) Indian-born British writer and poet. *The Betrothed*

22 It is now proved beyond doubt that smoking is one of the leading causes of statistics.

Fletcher Knebel *Reader's Digest*, Dec 1961

23 This very night I am going to leave off tobacco! Surely there must be some other world in which this unconquerable purpose shall be realized. The soul hath not her generous aspirings implanted in her in vain.

Charles Lamb (1775–1834) British essayist. Letter to Thomas Manning, 26 Dec 1815

24 Dr Parr...asked him, how he had acquired his power of smoking at such a rate? Lamb replied, 'I toiled after it, sir, as some men toil after virtue.'

Charles Lamb *Memoirs of Charles Lamb* (Talfourd)

25 No matter what Aristotle and all philosophy may say, there's nothing like tobacco. 'Tis the passion of decent folk; he who lives without tobacco isn't worthy of living.

Molière (Jean Baptiste Poquelin; 1622–73) French dramatist. *Don Juan, ou le festin de Pierre*, I:1

26 The very act of smoking a cigarette is, for many, a major source of Displacement Activities...They are stress-smokers, not drug-smokers, and in that capacity at least, smoking can play a valuable role in a society full of minute-by-minute tensions and pressures. It is so much more than a question of inhaling smoke.

Desmond Morris (1928–) British biologist. *Manwatching*, 'Displacement Activities'

27 This vice brings in one hundred million francs in taxes every year. I will certainly forbid it at once – as soon as you can name a virtue that brings in as much revenue.

Napoleon III (1808–73) French emperor. Reply when asked to ban smoking. *Anekdotenschatz* (H. Hoffmeister)

28 Cigarettes are killers that travel in packs.

Mary S. Ott *Bartlett's Unfamiliar Quotations* (Leonard Louis Levinson)

29 My doctor has always told me to smoke. He even explains himself: 'Smoke, my friend. Otherwise someone else will smoke in your place.'

Erik Satie (1866–1925) French composer. *Mémoires d'un amnésique*

30 I have every sympathy with the American who was so horrified by what he had read of the effects of smoking that he gave up reading.

Henry G. Strauss *Quotations for Speakers and Writers* (A. Andrews)

31 I asked a coughing friend of mine why he doesn't stop smoking. 'In this town it wouldn't do any good,' he explained. 'I happen to be a chain breather.'

Robert Sylvester (1907–75) US writer. *Bartlett's Unfamiliar Quotations* (Leonard Louis Levinson)

32 We shall not refuse tobacco the credit of being

sometimes medical, when used temperately, though an acknowledged poison.

Jesse Torrey (1787–1834) *The Moral Instructor*, Pt. IV

33 When I was young, I kissed my first woman, and smoked my first cigarette on the same day. Believe me, never since have I wasted any more time on tobacco.

Arturo Toscanini (1867–1957) Italian conductor. Attrib.

34 There are people who strictly deprive themselves of each and every eatable, drinkable and smokable which has in any way acquired a shady reputation. They pay this price for health. And health is all they get for it.

Mark Twain (Samuel Langhorne Clemens; 1835–1910) US writer.

35 To cease smoking is the easiest thing I ever did. I ought to know because I've done it a thousand times.

Mark Twain (Samuel L. Clemens; 1835–1910) US writer.

36 Tobacco drieth the brain, dimmeth the sight, vitiateth the smell, hurteth the stomach, destroyeth the concoction, disturbeth the humors and spirits, corrupteth the breath, induceth a trembling of the limbs, exsiccateth the windpipe, lungs, and liver, annoyeth the milt, scorcheth the heart, and causeth the blood to be adjusted.

Tobias Venner (1577–1660) *Via Recta ad Vitam Longam*

37 A cigarette is the perfect type of a perfect pleasure. It is exquisite, and it leaves one unsatisfied. What more can one want?

Oscar Wilde (1854–1900) Irish-born British dramatist. *The Picture of Dorian Gray*, Ch. 6

SMOLLETT, TOBIAS

(1721–71) British novelist and journalist. His novels include *Roderick Random* (1748) and *Peregrine Pickle* (1751). He also wrote a *Complete History of England* (1757–58).

1 I think for my part one half of the nation is mad – and the other not very sound.

Referring to the English. *The Adventures of Sir Launcelot Greaves*, Ch. 6

2 True patriotism is of no party.

The Adventures of Sir Launcelot Greaves

3 Hark ye, Clinker, you are a most notorious offender. You stand convicted of sickness, hunger, wretchedness, and want.

Humphrey Clinker, Letter to Sir Watkin Phillips, 24 May

4 Some folk are wise, and some are otherwise.

Roderick Random, Ch. 6

5 He was formed for the ruin of our sex.

Roderick Random, Ch. 22

6 That great Cham of literature, Samuel Johnson.

Letter to John Wilkes, 16 Mar 1759

SNOBBERY

See also aristocracy, class, one-upmanship

1 We would not mind so much if it was called Reginald Jones Close.

Anonymous A Midsomer Norton resident objecting to the renaming of her street as Reg Jones Close. *The Observer*, 'Sayings of the Week', 19 June 1994

2 In our way we were both snobs, and no snob welcomes another who has risen with him.

Cecil Beaton (1904–80) British photographer. Referring to the writer Evelyn Waugh. Attrib.

3 And this is good old Boston,
The home of the bean and the cod,
Where the Lowells talk only to Cabots,
And the Cabots talk only to God.

John Collins Bossidy (1860–1928) US writer. Toast at Holy Cross Alumni dinner, 1910

4 Of course they have, or I wouldn't be sitting here talking to someone like you.

Barbara Cartland (1902–) British romantic novelist. When asked in a radio interview whether she thought that British class barriers had broken down. *Class* (J. Cooper)

5 I've danced with a man, who's danced with a girl, who's danced with the Prince of Wales.

Herbert Farjeon (1887–1945) British writer. *Picnic*

6 His hatred of snobs was a derivative of his snobbishness, but made the simpletons (in other words, everyone) believe that he was immune from snobbishness.

Marcel Proust (1871–1922) French novelist. *À La Recherche du temps perdu: Le Côté de Guermantes*

7 Skullion had little use for contraceptives at the best of times. Unnatural, he called them, and placed them in the lower social category of things along with elastic-sided boots and made-up bow ties. Not the sort of attire for a gentleman.

Tom Sharpe (1928–) British novelist. *Porterhouse Blue*, Ch. 9

8 I mustn't go on singling out names. One must not be a name-dropper, as Her Majesty remarked to me yesterday.

Norman St John Stevas (1929–) British politician. Speech, Museum of the Year luncheon, 20 June 1979

9 He who meanly admires mean things is a Snob.

William Makepeace Thackeray (1811–63) British novelist. *The Book of Snobs*, Ch. 2

10 It is impossible, in our condition of society, not to be sometimes a Snob.

William Makepeace Thackeray *The Book of Snobs*, Ch. 3

11 She was – but I assure you that she was a very bad cook.

Louis Adolphe Thiers (1797–1877) French statesman and historian. Defending his social status after someone had remarked that his mother had been a cook. Attrib.

12 My dear – the people we should have been seen dead with.

Rebecca West (Cicely Isabel Fairfield; 1892–1983) British novelist and journalist. Cable sent to Noël Coward after learning they had both been on a Nazi death list. *Times Literary Supplement*, 1 Oct 1982

13 CECILY: When I see a spade I call it a spade.
GWENDOLEN: I am glad to say I have never seen a spade. It is obvious that our social spheres have been widely different.

Oscar Wilde (1854–1900) Irish-born British dramatist. *The Importance of Being Earnest*, II

14 Never speak disrespectfully of Society, Algernon. Only people who can't get into it do that.

Oscar Wilde *The Importance of Being Earnest*, III

15 I don't owe a penny to a single soul – not counting tradesmen, of course.

P. G. Wodehouse (1881–1975) British humorous novelist. *My Man Jeeves*, 'Jeeves and the Hard-Boiled Egg'

SOCIALISM

See also Communism, Marxism

1 Why is it always the intelligent people who are socialists?

Alan Bennett (1934–) British playwright. *Forty Years On*

2 A divorced woman on the throne of the House of Windsor would be a pretty big feather in the cap of that bunch of rootless intellectuals, alien Jews and international pederasts who call themselves the Labour Party.

Alan Bennett (1934–) British playwright and actor. Parodying Bulldog Drummond. *Forty Years On*

3 The language of priorities is the religion of Socialism.

Aneurin Bevan (1897–1960) British Labour politician. *Aneurin Bevan* (Vincent Brome), Ch. 1

4 Socialism in the context of modern society (means) the conquest of the commanding heights of the economy.

Aneurin Bevan Speech, Labour Party Conference, Nov 1959

5 ...when internal and external forces that are hostile to socialism try to turn the development of some socialist country towards the restoration of a capitalist regime, when socialism in that country and the socialist community as a whole is threatened...

Leonid Brezhnev (1906–82) Soviet statesman. The 'Brezhnev doctrine', used to justify Russia's intervention in Czechoslovakia, stated the circumstances when Russia had a right to intervene.

6 The people's flag is deepest red;
It shrouded oft our martyred dead,
And ere their limbs grew stiff and cold,
Their heart's blood dyed its every fold.
Then raise the scarlet standard high!
Within its shade we'll live or die.
Tho' cowards flinch and traitors sneer,
We'll keep the red flag flying here.

James Connell (1852–1929) British socialist. Traditionally sung at the close of annual conferences of the British Labour Party. *The Red Flag*, in *Songs that made History* (H. E. Piggot), Ch. 6

7 Socialism with a human face must function again for a new generation. We have lived in the darkness for long enough.

Alexander Dubček (1921–92) Czech statesman. Speech, Wenceslas Square, Prague, 24 Nov 1989

8 There is nothing in Socialism that a little age or a little money will not cure.

Will Durant (1885–1982) US teacher, philosopher, and historian. Attrib.

9 Socialism can only arrive by bicycle.

José Antonio Viera Gallo (1943–) Chilean politician. *Energy and Equity* (Ivan Illich)

10 Only socialism would put up with it for so long. Capitalism would have gone bankrupt years ago.

Mikhail Gorbachov (1931–) Soviet statesman. Talking of sub-standard workmanship in the Soviet Union. TV documentary, 23 March 1987

11 Well, what are you socialists going to do about me?

George V (1865–1936) King of the United Kingdom. To Ramsay MacDonald at his first meeting as prime minister. Attrib.

12 The essence of perestroika lies in the fact that *it unites socialism with democracy* and revives the feminist concept of socialist construction both in theory and in practice.

Mikhail Gorbachov *Perestroika*

13 We are all Socialists now.

William Harcourt (1827–1904) British statesman. Attrib.

14 Compassion is not a sloppy, sentimental feeling for people who are underprivileged or sick...it is an absolutely practical belief that, regardless of a person's background, ability or ability to pay, he should be provided with the best that society has to offer.

Neil Kinnock (1942–) British politician. Maiden speech, House of Commons, 1970

15 It is inconceivable that we could transform this society without a major extension of public ownership.

Neil Kinnock *Marxism Today*, 1983

16 We shall now proceed to construct the socialist order.

V. I. Lenin (Vladimir Ilich Ulyanov; 1870–1924) Russian revolutionary leader. First words to the Congress of Soviets after the capture of the Winter Palace, 26 Oct 1917

17 Under socialism *all* will govern in turn and will soon become accustomed to no one governing.

V. I. Lenin *The State and Revolution*, Ch. 6

18 In so far as socialism means anything, it must be about the wider distribution of smoked salmon and caviar.

Richard Marsh (1928–) British businessman. Remark, Oct 1976

19 As with the Christian religion, the worst advertisement for Socialism is its adherents.

George Orwell (Eric Blair; 1903–50) British novelist. *The Road to Wigan Pier*, Ch. 11

20 To the ordinary working man, the sort you would meet in any pub on Saturday night, Socialism does not mean much more than better wages and shorter hours and nobody bossing you about.

George Orwell *The Road to Wigan Pier*, Ch. 11

21 The higher-water mark, so to speak, of Socialist literature is W. H. Auden, a sort of gutless Kipling.

George Orwell *The Road to Wigan Pier*, Ch. 11

22 I am a socialist – and I only wish the Labour Party was.

Donald Soper (1903–) British Methodist Minister and writer. *Any Questions* (radio programme), 11 May 1979

23 In place of the conception of the Power-State we are led to that of the Welfare-State.

Archbishop William Temple (1881–1944) British churchman. *Citizen and Churchman*, Ch. 11

24 State socialism is totally alien to the British character.

Margaret Thatcher (1925–) British politician and prime minister. *The Times*, 1983

25 We are redefining and we are restating our socialism in terms of the scientific revolution…the Britain that is going to be forged in the white heat of this revolution will be no place for restrictive practices or out-dated methods on either side of industry.

Harold Wilson (1916–) British politician and prime minister. Speech, Labour Party Conference, 1 Oct 1963

26 …if there was one word I would use to identify modern socialism, it was 'Science'.

Harold Wilson (1916–) British politician and prime minister. Speech, 17 June 1967

SOCIETY

See also mankind

1 A characteristic of Thatcherism is a reversion to the idea of nature, irreparable in its forces. Poverty and sickness are seen as part of an order.

Howard Barker (1946–) British playwright. *The Times*, 3 Jan 1990

2 I am a sociable worker.

Brendan Behan (1923–64) Irish playwright. *The Hostage*, II

3 Man was formed for society.

William Blackstone (1723–80) British jurist. *Commentaries on the Laws of England*, Introduction

4 There are those who collect the refuse of the public streets, but in order to be received into the band it is necessary to have been born one of the Hereditary Confederacy of Superfluity Removers and Abandoned Oddment Gatherers.

Ernest Bramah (1869–1942) British writer. *Kai Lung Unrolls His Mat*

5 Society, being codified by man, decrees that woman is inferior: she can do away with this inferiority only by destroying the male's superiority.

Simone de Beauvoir (1908–86) French writer and feminist. *Le Deuxième Sexe* (The Second Sex)

6 I do not think British industry has made any recognition whatsoever of the social revolution of the 1980s and 1990s. Two out of every three families are dual-career families, but industry has not designed itself in any way to help women – or, indeed, men who have working wives – to cope with the new family circumstance.

Cary Cooper (1940–) British psychologist. *Move Over Darling* (Kathy Barnby and Loretta Loach)

7 I don't think the state can simply be removed from the economy…My ideal is a society full of responsible men and women who show solidarity to those who can't keep up.

Jacques Delors (1925–) French politician and European statesman. *The Independent*, 22 June 1994

8 No man is an Island, entire of itself; every man is a piece of the Continent, a part of the main.

John Donne (1573–1631) English poet. *Devotions*, 17

9 The term 'primitive' is clearly a highly subjective one.

Ben Elton British comedian. *Stark*

10 Problem children tend to grow up into problem adults and problem adults tend to produce more problem children.

David Farrington (1944–) British criminal psychologist. *The Times*, 19 May 1994

11 They hated everybody, and abused everybody, and would sit together in White's bay window, or the pit boxes at the Opera, weaving tremendous crammers. They swore a good deal, never laughed, looked hazy after dinner, and had most of them been patronized at one time or other by Brummel and the Prince Regent.

Rees Howell Gronow (1795–1865) British MP and social observer. Referring to Regency 'dandies'. *Reminiscences*, Vol. I

12 It is intuitively obvious that a society which looks after the interests of a few, at the expense of the welfare of the majority, is likely to incur real economic costs in terms of policing, security and damage resulting from civil unrest.

Tim Jackson and Nic Marks *Measuring Sustainable Economic Welfare – a Pilot Index: 1950–1990*

13 The permissive society has been allowed to become a dirty phrase. A better phrase is the civilized society.

Roy Jenkins (1920–) British Liberal Democrat politician (formerly a Labour Home Secretary). Speech, Abingdon, 19 July 1969

14 The great society is a place where men are more concerned with the quality of their goods than the quantity of their goods.

Lyndon B. Johnson (1908–73) US statesman. Speech, 22 May 1964

15 If a free society cannot help the many who are poor, it cannot save the few who are rich.

John Fitzgerald Kennedy (1917–63) US statesman. Speech, 20 Jan 1961

16 People who need people are the luckiest people in the world.

Bob Merrill (Robert Merrill; 1890–1977) US lyricist and composer. *People Who Need People*

17 Our civilization…has not yet fully recovered from the shock of its birth – the transition from the tribal or 'closed society', with its submission to magical forces, to the 'open society' which sets free the critical powers of man.

Karl Popper (1902–) Austrian-born British philosopher. *The Open Society and Its Enemies*

18 Man is not a solitary animal, and so long as social life survives, self-realization cannot be the supreme principle of ethics.

Bertrand Russell (1872–1970) British philosopher. *History of Western Philosophy*, 'Romanticism'

19 Society is no comfort
To one not sociable.

William Shakespeare (1564–1616) English dramatist. *Cymbeline*, IV:2

20 The liberty the citizen enjoys is to be measured not by the governmental machinery he lives under, whether representative or other, but by the paucity of restraints it imposes on him.

Herbert Spencer (1820–1903) British philospher. *Man versus the State*

21 Man is a social animal.

Benedict Spinoza (Baruch de Spinoza; 1632–77) Dutch philosopher. *Ethics*

22 Women are the real architects of society.

Harriet Beecher Stowe (1811–96) US writer and social critic. *Atlantic Monthly*, 'Dress, or Who Makes the Fashions'

23 What men call social virtues, good fellowship, is commonly but the virtue of pigs in a litter, which lie close together to keep each other warm. It brings men together in crowds and mobs in bar-rooms and elsewhere, but it does not deserve the name of virtue.

Henry David Thoreau (1817–62) US writer. *Journal*, 1852

SOCRATES

(469–399 BC) Athenian philosopher. Although he wrote nothing himself, much is known of his philosophy from the writings of his pupils, especially Plato. Charged with corrupting youth and atheism, he was condemned to death.

Quotations about Socrates

1 Socrates was the first to call philosophy down from the heavens and to place it in cities, and even to introduce it into homes and compel it to enquire about life and standards and good and ill.

Cicero (106–43 BC) Roman orator and statesman. *Tusculanae Disputationes*

2 He was so orderly in his way of life that on several occasions when pestilence broke out in Athens he was the only man who escaped infection.

Diogenes Laertius (fl. 3rd century AD) Greek author. *Lives of Eminent Philosophers*

3 Socrates is a doer of evil, who corrupts the youth; and who does not believe in the gods of the state, but has other new divinities of his own. Such is the charge.

Plato (429–347 BC) Greek Philosopher. *Dialogue*

Quotations by Socrates

4 Nothing can harm a good man, either in life or after death.

Apology (Plato)

5 The unexamined life is not worth living.

Apology (Plato)

6 But already it is time to depart, for me to die, for you to go on living; which of us takes the better course, is concealed from anyone except God.

Apology (Plato)

7 How many things I can do without!

Examining the range of goods on sale at a market. *Lives of the Eminent Philosophers* (Diogenes Laertius), II

8 I am not an Athenian or a Greek, but a citizen of the world.

Of Banishment (Plutarch)

9 Crito, we owe a cock to Aesculapius; please pay it and don't let it pass.

Last words before his execution by drinking hemlock. *Phaedo* (Plato), 118

SOLDIERS

See also army, officers, war

1 Some talk of Alexander, and some of Hercules,
Of Hector and Lysander, and such great names as these;
But of all the world's brave heroes there's none that can compare
With a tow, row, row, row, row, row for the British Grenadier.

Anonymous *The British Grenadiers*

2 The mounted knight is irresistable; he would bore his way through the walls of Babylon.

Anna Comnena Describing the French knights of the First Crusade, who passed through Constantinople in 1097. *The Alexiad*

3 It's Tommy this, an' Tommy that, an' 'Chuck him out, the brute!'
But it's 'Saviour of 'is country' when the guns begin to shoot.

Rudyard Kipling (1865–1936) Indian-born British writer. *Tommy*

4 Oh, it's Tommy this, an' Tommy that, an' 'Tommy, go away';
But it's 'Thank you, Mister Atkins,' when the band begins to play.

Rudyard Kipling *Tommy*

5 Lions led by donkeys.

Erich Ludendorff (1865–1937) German general. Referring to British troops in World War I. Attrib.

6 They're changing guard at Buckingham Palace
Christopher Robin went down with Alice.
Alice is marrying one of the guard.
'A soldier's life is terrible hard,'
Says Alice.

A. A. Milne (1882–1956) British writer. *When We Were Very Young*, 'Buckingham Palace'

7 Then was seen with what a strength and majesty the British soldier fights.

Sir William Napier (1785–1860) British general and historian. *History of the War in the Peninsula* Bk. XII, Ch. 6

8 Every French soldier carries in his cartridge-pouch the baton of a marshal of France.

Napoleon I (1769–1821) French emperor. *La Vie militaire sous l'empire* (E. Blaze)

9 It must have been a little trying to the colonel who came up to him and asked him if he was fond of horses to be told 'No but I adore giraffes.'

John Beverley Nichols (1898–1983) British writer. Referring to the writer Osbert Sitwell. *Twenty Five*

10 Volunteers usually fall into two groups. There are the genuinely courageous who are itching to get at the throat of the enemy, and the restless who will volunteer for anything in order to escape from the boredom of what they are presently doing.

David Niven (1909–83) British film actor. *The Moon's a Balloon*, Ch. 12

11 The soldier's body becomes a stock of accessories that are not his property.

Antoine de Saint-Exupéry (1900–44) French novelist and aviator. *Flight To Arras*

12 Soldiers are citizens of death's grey land,
Drawing no dividend from time's tomorrows.

Siegfried Sassoon (1886–1967) British poet. *Dreamers*

13 A soldier is better accommodated than with a wife.

William Shakespeare (1564–1616) English dramatist. *Henry IV, Part 2*, III:2

14 You are a very poor soldier: a chocolate cream soldier!

George Bernard Shaw (1856–1950) Irish dramatist and critic. *Arms and the Man*, I

15 I never expect a soldier to think.

George Bernard Shaw *The Devil's Disciple*, III

16 They're overpaid, overfed, oversexed and over here.

Tommy Trinder (1909–89) British entertainer. Referring to the G.I.s in Britain during World War II. Attrib.

17 He (the recruiting officer) asked me 'Why tanks?' I replied that I preferred to go into battle sitting down.

Peter Ustinov (1921–) British actor. *Dear Me*

18 It all depends upon that article there.

Duke of Wellington (1769–1852) British general and statesman. Indicating a passing infantryman when asked if he would be able to defeat Napoleon. *The Age of Elegance* (A. Bryant)

SOLITUDE

See also loneliness

1 Whosoever is delighted in solitude is either a wild beast or a god.

Francis Bacon (1561–1626) English philosopher. *Essays*, 'Of Friendship'

2 Alone, alone, all, all alone,
Alone on a wide wide sea!
And never a saint took pity on
My soul in agony.

Samuel Taylor Coleridge (1772–1834) British poet. *The Rime of the Ancient Mariner*, IV

3 Oh for a lodge in some vast wilderness,
Some boundless contiguity of shade,
Where rumour of oppression and deceit,
Of unsuccessful or successful war,
Might never reach me more!

William Cowper (1731–1800) British poet. *The Task*

4 Society, friendship, and love,
Divinely bestowed upon man,
Oh, had I the wings of a dove,
How soon would I taste you again!

William Cowper *Verses supposed to be written by Alexander Selkirk*

5 I am monarch of all I survey,
My right there is none to dispute;
From the centre all round to the sea
I am lord of the fowl and the brute.
Oh, solitude! where are the charms
That sages have seen in thy face?
Better dwell in the midst of alarms,
Than reign in this horrible place.

William Cowper *Verses supposed to be written by Alexander Selkirk*

6 As *sickness* is the greatest misery so the greatest misery of sickness is *solitude*. *Solitude* is a torment which is not threatened in *hell* itselfe.

John Donne (1573–1631) English poet. *Awakenings* (Oliver W. Sacks)

7 I want to be alone.

Greta Garbo (1905–90) Swedish-born US film star. Words spoken by Garbo in the film *Grand Hotel*, and associated with her for the rest of her career.

8 Far from the madding crowd's ignoble strife,
Their sober wishes never learn'd to stray;
Along the cool sequester'd vale of life
They kept the noiseless tenor of their way.

Thomas Gray (1716–71) British poet. *Elegy Written in a Country Churchyard*

9 One of the pleasantest things in the world is going on a journey; but I like to go by myself.

William Hazlitt (1778–1830) British essayist. *On Going a Journey*

10 It is a fine thing to be out on the hills alone. A man can hardly be a beast or a fool alone on a great mountain.

Francis Kilvert (1840–79) British diarist and clergyman. *Diary*, 29 May 1871

11 In solitude
What happiness? who can enjoy alone,
Or, all enjoying, what contentment find?

John Milton (1608–74) English poet. *Paradise Lost*, Bk. VIII

12 I want to be a movement
But there's no one on my side.

Adrian Mitchell (1932–) British writer and dramatist. *Loose Leaf Poem*

13 A man must keep a little back shop where he can be himself without reserve. In solitude alone can he know true freedom.

Michel de Montaigne (1533–92) French essayist. *Essais*, I

14 Solitude is the playfield of Satan.

Vladimir Nabokov (1899–1977) Russian-born US novelist. *Pale Fire*

15 I never found the companion that was so companionable as solitude.

Henry David Thoreau (1817–62) US writer. *Walden*, 'Solitude'

16 Alas, Lord, I am powerful but alone. Let me sleep the sleep of the earth.

Alfred de Vigny (1797–1863) French writer. *Moise*

17 For oft, when on my couch I lie
In vacant or in pensive mood,
They flash upon that inward eye
Which is the bliss of solitude.

William Wordsworth (1770–1850) British poet. *I Wandered Lonely as a Cloud*

18 Behold her, single in the field,
Yon solitary Highland lass!

William Wordsworth *The Solitary Reaper*

19 I will arise and go now, and go to Innisfree,
And a small cabin build there, of clay and wattles made;
Nine bean rows will I have there, a hive for the honey bee,
And live alone in the bee-loud glade.

W. B. Yeats (1865–1939) Irish poet. *The Lake Isle of Innisfree*

SOLZHENITSYN, ALEXANDER

(1918–) Russian novelist. Imprisoned for political dissent, he left the Soviet Union in 1974 to live in America. His books include *One Day in the Life of Ivan Denisovich* (1962), *Cancer Ward* (1968), *Gulag Archipelago* (1974–78), and *October 1916* (1985). In 1991 the Soviet authorities dropped all charges against him and he returned to Russia in 1994.

Quotations about Solzhenitsyn

1 What is there about the *Gulag Archipelago* that made it a kind of last straw and that drove the politburo to arbitrary arrest and expulsion of its author?

Robert Conquest (1917–) British literary editor.

2 Solzhenitsyn's novel is one of the steps in the completion of the literature of the Twenties and Thirties.

F.D. Reeve (1928–) US editor and translator.

3 Solzhenitsyn's analysis of the butcher-like amorality of contemporary men absorbed in the niceties of trimming a carcass whose former life they thought they did not need and therefore undervalued is couched in a superbly artful fiction. Like Tolstoy, he is a man of great talent and of stupendous moral dignity.

F.D. Reeve (1928–) US editor and translator.

Quotations by Solzhenitsyn

4 The whole of his life had prepared Podduyev for living, not for dying.

Cancer Ward, Pt. I, Ch. 8

5 Nowadays we don't think much of a man's love for an animal; we laugh at people who are attached to cats. But if we stop loving animals, aren't we bound to stop loving humans too?

Cancer Ward, Pt. I, Ch. 20

6 When truth is discovered by someone else, it loses something of its attractiveness.

Candle in the Wind, 3

7 You took my freedom away a long time ago and you can't give it back because you haven't got it yourself.

The First Circle, Ch. 17

8 You only have power over people so long as you don't take *everything* away from them. But when you've robbed a man of everything he's no longer in your power – he's free again.

The First Circle, Ch. 17

9 Their teacher had advised them not to read Tolstoy novels, because they were very long and would easily confuse the clear ideas which they had learned from reading critical studies of him.

The First Circle, Ch. 40

10 No regime has ever loved great writers, only minor ones.

The First Circle, Ch. 57

11 This universal, obligatory force-feeding with lies is now the most agonizing aspect of existence in our country – worse than all our material miseries, worse than any lack of civil liberties.

Letter to Soviet Leaders, 6

12 Forget the outside world. Life has different laws in here. This is Campland, an invisible country. It's not in the geography books, or the psychology books or the history books. This is the famous country where ninety-nine men weep while one laughs.

The Love-Girl and the Innocent, I:3

13 For us in Russia communism is a dead dog, while, for many people in the West, it is still a living lion.

The Listener, 15 Feb 1979

14 In our country the lie has become not just a moral category but a pillar of the State.

The Observer, 'Sayings of the Year', 29 Dec 1974

15 The salvation of mankind lies only in making everything the concern of all.

Nobel Lecture, 1970

16 They have been just as spiteful to me in the American press as the Soviet press was before.

In a 'Farewell to the US' interview. *The Times*, 26 Apr 1994

SORROW

See also despair, melancholy, mourning, regret

1 A wound heals but the scar remains.

Proverb

2 My eye cried and woke me.
The night was pain.

Al-Khansa (575–646) Arabic poet. 'The Night'

3 Every tear from every eye
Becomes a babe in Eternity.

William Blake (1757–1827) British poet. *Auguries of Innocence*

4 Do you hear the children weeping, O my brothers,
Ere the sorrow comes with years?

Elizabeth Barrett Browning (1806–61) British poet. *The Cry of the Children*

5 Follow thy fair sun, unhappy shadow.

Thomas Campion (1567–1620) English poet. *Follow Thy Fair Sun*

6 Does anybody wonder so many women die. Grief and constant anxiety kill nearly as many women as men die on the battlefield.

Mary Chesnut (1823–86) US diarist. *Diary from Dixie*, 9 June 1862

7 One often calms one's grief by recounting it.

Pierre Corneille (1606–84) French dramatist. *Polyeucte*, I:3

8 Tears were to me what glass beads are to African traders.

Quentin Crisp (c. 1910–) Model, publicist, and writer. *The Naked Civil Servant*

9 There is no greater sorrow than to recall a time of happiness when in misery.

Dante (1265–1321) Italian poet. *Divine Comedy, Inferno*, V

10 *Adieu tristesse*
Bonjour tristesse
Tu es inscrite dans les lignes du plafond.

Farewell sadness
Good day sadness
You are written in the lines of the ceiling.

Paul Éluard (Eugène Grindel; 1895–1952) French surrealist poet. *La Vie immédiate*

11 A moment of time may make us unhappy for ever.

John Gay (1685–1732) English poet and dramatist. *The Beggar's Opera*

12 Sadness is almost never anything but a form of fatigue.

André Gide (1869–1951) French novelist. *Journals*, 1922

13 They say my verse is sad: no wonder;
Its narrow measure spans
Tears of eternity, and sorrow,
Not mine, but man's.

A. E. Housman (1859–1936) British scholar and poet. *Last Poems*, 'Fancy's Knell'

14 I envy aire because it dare
Still breathe, and he not so;
Hate earthe, that doth entomb his youth,
And who can blame my woe?

Anne Dacre Howard (1557–1630) English poet. 'Elegy on the Death of Her Husband'

15 A woman's heart always has a burned mark.

Louise Labé (c. 1524–66) French poet, linguist, feminist, and soldier. *Oeuvres*, Sonnet II

16 Then Sir Launcelot saw her visage, but he wept not greatly, but sighed!

Thomas Malory (1400–71) English writer. *Morte d'Arthur*, Bk. XXI, Ch. 11

17 Tears such as angels weep, burst forth.

John Milton (1608–74) English poet. *Paradise Lost*, Bk. I

18 Have you any idea
How long a night can last, spent
Lying alone and sobbing?!

Mother of Michitsuna (fl. 954–974) Japanese diarist. *One Hundred Poems from the Japanese*

19 Art thou weary, art thou languid,
Art thou sore distressed?

John Mason Neale (1818–66) British churchman. *Art thou Weary?*

20 Sorrow is tranquillity remembered in emotion.

Dorothy Parker (1893–1967) US writer. *Sentiment*

21 Line after line my gushing eyes o'erflow,
Led through a sad variety of woe.

Alexander Pope (1688–1744) British poet. *Eloisa to Abelard*

22 Not louder shrieks to pitying heav'n are cast,
When husbands, or when lap-dogs breathe their last.

Alexander Pope *The Rape of the Lock*, III

23 As soon as one is unhappy one becomes moral.

Marcel Proust (1871–1922) French novelist. *À La Recherche du temps perdu: À l'ombre des jeunes filles en fleurs*

24 Happiness is beneficial for the body, but it is grief that develops the powers of the mind.

Marcel Proust *À La Recherche du temps perdu: Le Temps retrouvé*

25 It is such a secret place, the land of tears.

Antoine de Saint-Exupéry (1900–44) French novelist and aviator. *The Little Prince*, Ch. 7

26 He's simply got the instinct for being unhappy highly developed.

Saki (Hector Hugh Munro; 1870–1916) British writer. *The Match-Maker*

27 If you have tears, prepare to shed them now.

William Shakespeare (1564–1616) English dramatist. *Julius Caesar*, III:2

28 Down, thou climbing sorrow,
Thy element's below.

William Shakespeare *King Lear*, II:4

29 When sorrows come, they come not single spies,
But in battalions.

William Shakespeare (1564–1616) English dramatist. *Hamlet*, IV:5

30 This sorrow's heavenly,
It strikes where it doth love.

William Shakespeare *Othello*, V:2

31 The secret of being miserable is to have leisure to bother about whether you are happy or not.

George Bernard Shaw (1856–1950) Irish dramatist and critic. *Misalliance*, Preface

32 'Tis held that sorrow makes us wise.

Alfred, Lord Tennyson (1809–92) British poet. *In Memoriam A.H.H.*, CXIII

33 My regret
Becomes an April violet,
And buds and blossoms like the rest.

Alfred, Lord Tennyson *In Memoriam A.H.H.*, CXV

34 Tears, idle tears, I know not what they mean,
Tears from the depth of some divine despair.

Alfred, Lord Tennyson *The Princess*, IV

35 Indescribable, O queen, is the grief you bid me to renew.

Virgil (Publius Vergilius Maro; 70–19 BC) Roman poet. The opening words of Aeneas' account to Dido of the fall of Troy. *Aeneid*, Bk. II

SOUL

1 The eyes are the window of the soul.

Proverb

2 We cannot kindle when we will
The fire which in the heart resides,
The spirit bloweth and is still,
In mystery our soul abides.

Matthew Arnold (1822–88) British poet and critic. *Morality*

3 And see all sights from pole to pole,
And glance, and nod, and bustle by;
And never once possess our soul
Before we die.

Matthew Arnold *A Southern Night*

4 Man has no Body distinct from his Soul; for that called Body is a portion of Soul discerned by the five Senses, the chief inlets of Soul in this age.

William Blake (1757–1827) British poet. *The Marriage of Heaven and Hell*, 'The Voice of the Devil'

5 Leave the flesh to the fate it was fit for! the spirit be thine!

Robert Browning (1812–89) British poet. *Saul*, XIII

6 They had escaped pollution on earth, only to discover that they had carried with them another pollution, a pollution that they could not escape. The pollution in their own souls.

Ben Elton British comedian. *Stark*

7 In the real dark night of the soul it is always three o'clock in the morning.

F. Scott Fitzgerald (1896–1940) US novelist. *See* ST JOHN OF THE CROSS. *The Crack-Up*

8 That night, that year
Of now done darkness I wretch lay wrestling with
(my God!) my God.

Gerard Manley Hopkins (1844–99) British Jesuit and poet. *Carrion Comfort*

9 The dark night of the soul.

St John of the Cross (Juan de Yepes y Alvarez; 1542–91) Spanish churchman and poet. *See also* F. SCOTT FITZGERALD. English translation of *Noche obscura del alma*, the title of a poem.

10 Nor let the beetle, nor the death-moth be
Your mournful Psyche.

John Keats (1795–1821) British poet. *Ode on Melancholy*

11 And looks commercing with the skies,
Thy rapt soul sitting in thine eyes.

John Milton (1608–74) English poet. *Il Penseroso*

12 I am positive I have a soul; nor can all the books with which materialists have pestered the world ever convince me of the contrary.

Laurence Sterne (1713–68) Irish-born British writer. *A Sentimental Journey*, 'Maria, Moulines'

13 Fair seed-time had my soul, and I grew up
Fostered alike by beauty and by fear.

William Wordsworth (1770–1850) British poet. *The Prelude*, I

SOUTH AFRICA

1 South Africa will not allow the double standards and hypocrisy of the Western world, even in the application of legal principles, to stand in the way of our responsibility to protect our country.

P. W. Botha (1916–) South African politician and president. Speech, May 1986

2 You won't force South Africans to commit national suicide.

P. W. Botha Speech, Aug 1986

3 My feelings are that for the first time we are participating in an election that will have legitimacy. Now we can go to the polling booth without a bad conscience.

P. W. Botha *The Independent*, 28 Apr 1994

4 South Africa, renowned both far and wide
For politics and little else beside.

Roy Campbell (1901–57) South African poet. *The Wayzgoose*

5 Today we have closed the book on apartheid.

F. W. de Klerk (1936–) South African president. Remark after a referendum of white South Africans had endorsed his government's reform programme. *The Independent*, 19 Mar 1992

6 I've a bad case of the Buthelezi Blues, or is it post-Natal depression?

Graffiti

7 On your feet and let them know
This is why we love her!
For she is South Africa –
Is Our Own South Africa –
Africa all over!

Rudyard Kipling (1865–96) Indian-born British writer. *South Africa*

8 The task at hand will not be easy, but you have mandated us to change South Africa from a land in which the majority lived with little hope, to one in which they can live and work with dignity, with a sense of self-esteem and confidence in the future.

Nelson Mandela (1918–) South African president. Speech at his inauguration, 10 May 1994

9 For many years I was ashamed of being South African. Now I allow myself to feel nostalgic.

Anthony Sher (1949–) South African actor. *The Sunday Times*, 8 July 1990

10 It is an incredible feeling, like falling in love.

Archbishop Desmond Tutu (1931–) South African clergyman. Referring to voting in the first multiracial elections in South Africa. *The Independent*, 27 Apr 1994

11 The paradox in South Africa is that after all these years of white racism, oppression and injustice there is hardly any anti-white feeling.

Archbishop Desmond Tutu *Black Sash: The Beginning Of A Bridge in South Africa*, Foreword

SOUTHEY, ROBERT

(1774–1843) British poet and writer. A friend of Wordsworth, his epics include *Thalaba* (1801) and *Madoc* (1805); shorter poems include *The Battle of Blenheim* and *The Inchcape Rock*. He also wrote a *Life of Nelson* (1813) and became poet laureate in 1813.

1 'And everybody praised the Duke,
Who this great fight did win.'
'But what good came of it at last?'
Quoth little Peterkin.
'Why that I cannot tell,' said he,
'But 'twas a famous victory.'

The Battle of Blenheim

2 Curses are like young chickens, they always come home to roost.

The Curse of Kehama, Motto

3 Live as long as you may, the first twenty years are the longest half of your life.

The Doctor, Ch. 130

4 You are old, Father William, the young man cried,
The few locks which are left you are grey;
You are hale, Father William, a hearty old man,
Now tell me the reason, I pray.

See also Lewis CARROLL. *The Old Man's Comforts, and how he Gained them*

5 In the days of my youth I remembered my God!
And He hath not forgotten my age.

The Old Man's Comforts, and how he Gained them

SPACE

See also astronomy, discovery, exploration, moon, science, stars, sun, technology, universe

1 Space...is big. Really big. You just won't believe how vastly hugely mindbogglingly big it is. I mean you may think it's a long way down the road to the chemist, but that's just peanuts to space.
Douglas Adams (1952–) British writer. *The Hitch Hiker's Guide to the Galaxy*, Ch. 8

2 That's one small step for man, one giant leap for mankind.
Neil Armstrong (1930–) US astronaut. Said on stepping onto the moon. In his autobiography Armstrong claimed that he had said, 'small step for a man...', but that the radio transmission had distorted his words. Remark, 21 July 1969

3 Outer space is no place for a person of breeding.
Violet Bonham Carter (1887–1969) British politician. *The New Yorker*

4 I am a passenger on the spaceship, Earth.
Richard Buckminster Fuller (1895–1983) US architect and inventor. *Operating Manual for Spaceship Earth*

5 The Earth is just too small and fragile a basket for the human race to keep all its eggs in.
Robert Heinlein (1907–88) US science-fiction writer. Speech

6 Space isn't remote at all. It's only an hour's drive away if your car could go straight upwards.
Fred Hoyle (1915–) British astronomer. *The Observer*, 9 Sept 1979

7 This is the greatest week in the history of the world since the creation.
Richard Milhous Nixon (1913–94) US president. Said when men first landed on the moon. Attrib., 24 July 1969

8 Space is almost infinite. As a matter of fact we think it *is* infinite.
Dan Quayle (James Danforth Q.; 1946–) US statesman. *The Sunday Times*, 31 Dec 1989

9 Space is out of this world.
Helen Sharman (1963–) First Briton in space. Remark, May 1991

10 The astronauts!...Rotarians in outer space.
Gore Vidal (1925–) US novelist. *Two Sisters*

SPARK, MURIEL

(1918–) British novelist, born in Edinburgh. Her popular novels include *The Prime of Miss Jean Brodie* (1961), *The Abbess of Crewe* (1974), *Territorial Rights* (1979), *The Only Problem* (1984), and *A Far Cry From Kensington* (1988).

Quotation about Spark

1 Her prose is like a bird darting from place to place, palpitating with nervous energy; but a bird with a bright beady eye and a sharp beak as well.
Francis Hope *The Observer*, 28 Apr 1963

Quotations by Spark

2 A short neck denotes a good mind...You see, the messages go quicker to the brain because they've shorter to go.
The Ballad of Peckham Rye, Ch. 7

3 Parents learn a lot from their children about coping with life.
The Comforters, Ch. 6

4 Every communist has a fascist frown, every fascist a communist smile.
The Girls of Slender Means, Ch. 4

5 Selwyn Macgregor, the nicest boy who ever committed the sin of whisky.
The Go-Away Bird, 'A Sad Tale's Best for Winter'

6 Being over seventy is like being engaged in a war. All our friends are going or gone and we survive amongst the dead and the dying as on a battlefield.
Memento Mori, Ch. 4

7 Give me a girl at an impressionable age, and she is mine for life.
The Prime of Miss Jean Brodie, Ch. 1

8 One's prime is elusive. You little girls, when you grow up, must be on the alert to recognize your prime at whatever time of your life it may occur. You must then live it to the full.
The Prime of Miss Jean Brodie, Ch. 1

9 If you had been mine when you were seven you would have been the crème de la crème.
The Prime of Miss Jean Brodie, Ch. 2

10 Art and religion first; then philosophy; lastly science. That is the order of the great subjects of life, that's their order of importance.
The Prime of Miss Jean Brodie, Ch. 2

11 To me education is a leading out of what is already there in the pupil's soul. To Miss Mackay it is a putting in of something that is not there, and that is not what I call education, I call it intrusion.
The Prime of Miss Jean Brodie, Ch. 2

12 But I did not remove my glasses, for I had not asked for her company in the first place, and there is a limit to what one can listen to with the naked eye.
Voices at Play, 'The Dark Glasses'

13 Do you think it pleases a man when he looks into a woman's eyes and sees a reflection of the British Museum Reading Room?
The Wit of Women (L. and M. Cowan)

SPECULATION

1 While to deny the existence of an unseen kingdom is bad, to pretend that we know more about it than its bare existence is no better.
Samuel Butler (1835–1902) British writer. *Erewhon*, Ch. 15

2 If the world were good for nothing else, it is a fine subject for speculation.
William Hazlitt (1778–1830) British essayist. *Characteristics*

3 I think the primary notion back of most gambling is the excitement of it. While gamblers naturally want to win, the majority of them derive pleasure even if they lose. The desire to win, rather than the excitement involved, seems to me the compelling force behind speculation.

Joseph Kennedy (1888–1969) US businessman. *The Kennedys*, Ch. 2 (Peter Collier and David Horowitz)

SPEECH

See also silence, speeches, verbosity, words

1 Save your breath to cool your porridge.

Proverb

2 Speak when you are spoken to.

Proverb

3 This god-forsaken city, with a climate so evil that no self-respecting singer would ever set foot in it! It is a catarrhal place that has been the cause through the centuries of the nasal Liverpool accent.

Thomas Beecham (1879–1961) British conductor. *Beecham Stories* (Harold Atkins and Archie Newman)

4 Let your speech be alway with grace, seasoned with salt, that ye may know how ye ought to answer every man.

Bible: Colossians 4:6

5 Let thy speech be short, comprehending much in few words; be as one that knoweth and yet holdeth his tongue.

Bible: Ecclesiasticus 32:8

6 Even so the tongue is a little member, and boasteth great things. Behold, how great a matter a little fire kindleth!

Bible: James 3:5

7 But the tongue can no man tame; it is an unruly evil, full of deadly poison.

Bible: James 3:8

8 To know how to say what others only know how to think is what makes men poets or sages; and to dare to say what others only dare to think makes men martyrs or reformers – or both.

Elizabeth Charles (1828–96) British writer. *Chronicle of the Schönberg-Cotta Family*

9 No, Sir, because I have time to think before I speak, and don't ask impertinent questions.

Erasmus Darwin (1731–1802) British physician, biologist, and poet. Reply when asked whether he found his stammer inconvenient. *Reminiscences of My Father's Everyday Life* (Sir Francis Darwin)

10 The metaphor is probably the most fertile power possessed by man.

José Ortega y Gasset (1883–1955) Spanish philosopher. *The Dehumanization of Art*

11 The true use of speech is not so much to express our wants as to conceal them.

Oliver Goldsmith (1728–74) Irish-born British writer. *Essays*, 'The Use of Language'

12 Most men make little use of their speech than to give evidence against their own understanding.

Lord Halifax (1633–95) English statesman. *Political, Moral, and Miscellaneous Thoughts and Reflections*

13 Talking and eloquence are not the same: to speak, and to speak well, are two things.

Ben Jonson (1573–1637) English dramatist. *Timber, or Discoveries made upon Men and Matter*

14 Speech is civilisation itself. The word, even the most contradictory word, preserves contact – it is silence which isolates.

Thomas Mann (1875–1955) German novelist. *The Magic Mountain*

15 The thoughtless are rarely wordless.

Howard W. Newton Attrib.

16 The most precious things in speech are pauses.

Ralph Richardson (1902–83) British actor. Attrib.

17 But words once spoke can never be recall'd.

Earl of Roscommon (1633–85) Irish-born English poet. *Art of Poetry*

18 Words may be false and full of art,
Sighs are the natural language of the heart.

Thomas Shadwell (1642–92) English dramatist. *Psyche*, III

19 I don't want to talk grammar, I want to talk like a lady.

George Bernard Shaw (1856–1950) Irish dramatist and critic. *Pygmalion*

20 Speech was given to man to disguise his thoughts.

Talleyrand (Charles Maurice de Talleyrand-Périgord; 1754–1838) French politician. Attrib.

SPEECHES

See also brevity, sermons, verbosity

1 Frankly a pain in the neck.

Lord Altrincham (John Grigg; 1924–) British writer. Referring to Queen Elizabeth II's public speaking. *National and English Review*, Aug 1958

2 Mr Lloyd George spoke for a hundred and seventeen minutes, in which period he was detected only once in the use of an argument.

Arnold Bennett (1867–1931) British writer. *Things That Have Interested Me*, 'After the March Offensive'

3 Listening to a speech by Chamberlain is like paying a visit to Woolworths; everything in its place and nothing over sixpence.

Aneurin Bevan (1897–1960) Welsh Labour politician. *Tribune*

4 I take the view, and always have done, that if you cannot say what you have to say in twenty minutes, you should go away and write a book about it.

Lord Brabazon of Tara (1910–74) British businessman and Conservative politician. Attrib.

5 An after-dinner speech should be like a lady's dress – long enough to cover the subject and short enough to be interesting.

R. A. Butler (1902–82) British Conservative politician. Remark made at an Anglo-Jewish dinner

6 He is one of those orators of whom it was well said, 'Before they get up they do not know what they are going to say; when they are speaking, they do not know what they are saying; and when they sit down, they do not know what they have said'.

Winston Churchill (1874–1965) British statesman. Referring to Lord Charles Beresford. Speech, House of Commons, 20 Dec 1912

7 Haven't you learned yet that I put something more than whisky into my speeches.

Winston Churchill To his son Randolph. Attrib.

8 Call that a maiden speech? I call it a brazen hussy of a speech.

Winston Churchill To A. P. Herbert. *Immortal Jester* (L. Frewin)

9 I dreamt that I was making a speech in the House. I woke up, and by Jove I was!

Duke of Devonshire (1833–1908) Conservative politician. *Thought and Adventures* (W. S. Churchill)

10 Did y'ever think, Ken, that making a speech on economics is a lot like pissing down your leg? It seems hot to you, but it never does to anyone else.

Lyndon B. Johnson (1908–73) US Democratic president. *A Life in Our Times*

11 For I have neither wit, nor words, nor worth,
Action, nor utterance, nor the power of speech,
To stir men's blood; I only speak right on.

William Shakespeare (1564–1616) English dramatist. *Julius Caesar*, III:2

12 Don't quote Latin; say what you have to say, and then sit down.

Duke of Wellington (1769–1852) British general and statesman. Advice to a new Member of Parliament. Attrib.

13 If you want me to talk for ten minutes I'll come next week. If you want me to talk for an hour I'll come tonight.

Woodrow Wilson (1856–1925) US statesman. Answering an invitation to make a speech. Attrib.

SPELLING

See also language, pronunciation, words, writing

1 Put it down a we, my lord, put it down a we!

Charles Dickens (1812–70) British novelist. *Pickwick Papers*, Ch. 34

2 They spell it Vinci and pronounce it Vinchy; foreigners always spell better than they pronounce.

Mark Twain (Samuel Langhorne Clemens; 1835–1910) US writer. *The Innocents Abroad*, Ch. 19

SPENDER, SIR STEPHEN

(1909–) British poet, who became famous as one of the left-wing poets of the 1930s. His *Collected Poems* was published in 1985, other publications include *The Temple* (1988)and *Dolphins* (1994).

1 Marston, dropping it in the grate,broke his pipe.
Nothing hung on this act, it was no symbol
Ludicrous for calamity, but merely ludicrous.

Marston

2 Pylons, those pillars
Bare like nude giant girls that have no secret.

The Pylons

3 And she was never one to miss
plausible happiness
Of a new experience.

Song

4 Moving thought the silent crowd
Who stand behind dull cigarettes,
These men who idle in the road,
I have the sense of falling light.
They lounge at corners of the street
And greet friends with a shrug of the shoulder
And turn their empty pockets out,
The cynical gestures of the poor.

Unemployed

5 Who live under the shadow of a war,
What can I do that matters?

Who live under the Shadow

6 People sometimes divide others into those you laugh at and those you laugh with. The young Auden was someone you could laugh-at-with.

Address, W. H. Auden's memorial service, Oxford, 27 Oct 1973

SPONTANEITY

See also impetuosity

1 Spontaneity is only a term for man's ignorance of the gods.

Samuel Butler (1835–1902) British writer. *Erewhon*, Ch. 25

2 *L'acte gratuite.*
The unmotivated action.

André Gide (1869–1951) French novelist. *Les Caves du Vatican*

3 Away with all ideals. Let each individual act spontaneously from the for ever incalculable prompting of the creative wellhead within him. There is no universal law.

D. H. Lawrence (1885–1930) British novelist. *Phoenix*, Preface to 'All Things are Possible' by Leo Shostov

4 Nothing prevents us from being natural so much as the desire to appear so.

Duc de la Rochefoucauld (1613–80) French writer. *Maximes*, 431

SPOONER, WILLIAM ARCHIBALD

(1844–1930) British clergyman and academic, remembered for his 'spoonerisms', phrases in which the first letters of words are transposed.

1 You will find as you grow older that the weight of rages will press harder and harder on the employer.

Spooner (Sir W. Hayter), Ch. 6

2 I remember your name perfectly, but I just can't think of your face.

Attrib.

3 Kinquering Congs their titles take.

A scrambled announcement of the hymn in New College Chapel, (probably apocryphal)

4 Let us drink to the queer old Dean.

Attrib.

5 Sir, you have tasted two whole worms; you have hissed all my mystery lectures and have been caught fighting a liar in the quad; you will leave Oxford by the town drain.

Attrib.

6 Poor soul – very sad; her late husband, you know, a very sad death – eaten by missionaries – poor soul.

Spooner (Sir W. Hayter)

SPORT AND GAMES

See also cricket, fishing, football, golf, horses, hunting

1 Float like a butterfly
Sting like a bee.

Muhammad Ali (Cassius Clay; 1942–) US boxer. Describing his boxing style. Remark

2 Anyone for tennis?

Anonymous

3 I don't think sportsmen can use 'sports and politics don't mix' as an excuse. I didn't want to represent 50 million English people touring a country where the regime was abhorrent.

Stuart Barnes English rugby player. Referring to his refusal to tour South Africa in 1984. *The Independent*, 11 May 1994

4 The game isn't over till it's over.

Yogi Berra (1925–) US baseball player. Attrib.

5 I'm a bit like an old, battered Escort. You might find one panel that's original. I've had about ten operations – back, shoulder, wrist, knee, cheek.

Ian Botham (1955–) British cricketer. On his retirement. *The Times*, 30 Dec 1993

6 Follow up! Follow up! Follow up! Follow up! Follow up!
Till the field ring again and again,
With the tramp of the twenty-two men,
Follow up!

E. E. Bowen (1836–1901) British writer. *Forty Years On* (the Harrow school song)

7 Life's too short for chess.

Henry James Byron (1834–84) British dramatist and actor. *Our Boys*, I

8 It's altogether quieter, more reflective, less controversial and more physical.

Sebastian Coe (1956–) British politician and athlete. Remark on pursuing a career in politics, 1989

9 This government says it intends to drive hooliganism out of sport – yet it appoints a hooligan to oversee it.

Richard Course Executive Director of the League Against Cruel Sports. Referring to Minister of Sport, Dick Tracey. Speech, 1986

10 I've got a career that depends a lot on being tall and blonde, and if I ended up growing a beard I don't think it would do me much good.

Sharon Davis British swimmer and model. Explaining why she doesn't take drugs. Remark, 1989

11 Sport is cut and dried. You always know when you succeed…You are not an actor; you don't wonder 'did my performance go down all right?' You've lost.

Steve Davis (1957–) British snooker player.

12 I just forgot to duck.

Jack Dempsey (1895–1983) US boxer. Said after losing the world heavyweight title, 23 Sept 1926

13 I think women as a group are better team members than men. We communicate better and are more compatible. We're also more perfectionist and take instruction better.

Sue Dorrington Captain of the England women's rugby team. *The Times*, 3 May 1994

14 There is plenty of time to win this game, and to thrash the Spaniards too.

Francis Drake (1540–96) British navigator and admiral. Referring to the sighting of the Armada during a game of bowls, 20 July 1588. Attrib.

15 Any boxer who says he loves boxing is either a liar or a fool. I'm not looking for glory…I'm looking for money. I'm looking for readies.

Chris Eubank British boxer. *The Times*, 30 Dec 1993

16 Swearing at the polo club? It's a load of bollocks.

Major Ronald Ferguson Polo club secretary and father of the Duchess of York. Denying that Prince Charles had used bad language in a chukkah. Remark, 1987

17 Exercise is bunk. If you are healthy, you don't need it: if you are sick, you shouldn't take it.

Henry Ford (1863–1947) US car manufacturer. Attrib.

18 Bullfighting is the only art in which the artist is in danger of death and in which the degree of brilliance in the performance is left to the fighter's honour.

Ernest Hemingway (1899–1961) US novelist. *Death in the Afternoon*, Ch. 9

19 When in doubt, win the trick.

Edmond Hoyle (1672–1769) English writer on card games. *Hoyle's Games*, 'Whist, Twenty-four Short Rules for Learners'

20 The only athletic sport I ever mastered was backgammon.

Douglas William Jerrold (1803–57) British dramatist. *Douglas Jerrold* (W. Jerrold), Vol. I, Ch. 1

21 It is unbecoming for a cardinal to ski badly.

John Paul II (Karol Wojtyla; 1920–) Polish pope (1978–). Replying to the suggestion that it was inappropriate for him, a cardinal, to ski. *John Paul II*

22 I am sorry I have not learned to play at cards. It is very useful in life: it generates kindness and consolidates society.

Samuel Johnson (1709–84) British lexicographer. *Tour to the Hebrides* (J. Boswell)

23 I've always wanted to equalize things for us… Women can be great athletes. And I think we'll find in the next decade that women athletes will finally get the attention they deserve.

Billie Jean King (c. 1943–) US professional tennis player. Interview, Sept 1973

24 Man is a gaming animal. He must always be trying to get the better in something or other.

Charles Lamb (1775–1834) British essayist. *Essays of Elia*, 'Mrs Battle's Opinions on Whist'

25 O, he flies through the air with the greatest of ease,
This daring young man on the flying trapeze.

George Leybourne (?–1884) British songwriter. *The Man on the Flying Trapeze*

26 It is a major tragedy of the struggle against doping that the atmosphere has been poisoned in this way.

Professor Arne Ljungqvist Head of medical commission of the International Amateur Athletic Federation. *The Times*, 15 Sept 1993

27 The gladiators and champions through the ages confirm quite clearly that aggressive competition is part of the human make-up. For the sport of professional boxing to be banned would be the most terrible error.

Barry McGuigan (Finbar Patrick McGuigan; 1961–) British and Irish boxer. *The Observer*, 1 May 1994

28 Mountaineering, sailing, riding and, as yesterday's fatal crash in San Marino showed, motor racing have seen more tragic loss of life than the square ring.

Barry McGuigan *The Observer*, 1 May 1994

29 Ayrton and I shared some of the most exciting races ever staged. When a truly great driver and a great champion loses his life, there is a very big void left behind.

Nigel Mansell (1954–) British motor racing driver. Referring to the Brazilian racing driver Ayrton Senna (1960–94). *The Independent*, 3 May 1994

30 I didn't take drugs and above all I did not let down those who love me.

Diego Maradona (1960–) Argentinian footballer. Having been expelled from the 1994 World Cup for taking drugs. *The Independent*, 1 July 1994

31 I don't like this game.

Spike Milligan (1918–) British comic actor and author. *The Goon Show*

32 I'm playing as well as I ever have in my career. It's just hard to get out of bed in the morning.

Martina Navratilova (1956–) Czech-born US tennis player. *The Guardian*, 30 June 1993

33 Serious sport has nothing to do with fair play. It is bound up with hatred, jealousy, boastfulness, disregard of all rules and sadistic pleasure in witnessing violence; in other words it is war minus the shooting.

George Orwell (Eric Blair; 1903–50) British novelist. *The Sporting Spirit*

34 There is no way sport is so important that it can be allowed to damage the rest of your life.

Steve Ovett (1955–) British athlete. At the Olympic Games, Los Angeles, 1984

35 Gamesmanship or The Art of Winning Games Without Actually Cheating.

Stephen Potter (1900–69) British writer. Book title

36 For when the One Great Scorer comes
To write against your name,
He marks – not that you won or lost –
But how you played the game.

Grantland Rice (1880–1954) US sportswriter. *Alumnus Football*

37 Show me a good and gracious loser and I'll show you a failure.

Knute Rockne (1888–1931) US football coach. Attrib.

38 I've been training for about 2 weeks...For once, I've had a normal life.

Pete Sampras (1971–) US tennis player. *The Independent*, 10 May 1994

39 To survive in grand prix racing, you need to be afraid. Fear is an important feeling. It helps you to race longer and live longer.

Ayrton Senna (1960–94) Brazilian motor racing driver. *The Times*, 3 May 1994

40 The cars are very fast and difficult to drive. It's going to be a season with lots of accidents and I'll risk saying we'll be lucky if something really serious doesn't happen.

Ayrton Senna Referring to his fears for the 1994 season. *The Times*, 3 May 1994

41 It was remarked to me by the late Mr Charles Roupell...that to play billiards well was a sign of an ill-spent youth.

Herbert Spencer (1820–1903) British philosopher. *Life and Letters of Spencer* (Duncan), Ch. 20

42 Like you, during a long and tempestuous history, we came under the yoke of our Anglo-Saxon brothers. You, wisely, had more sense than us, in that you devoured as many as you could.

Alun Thomas Welsh Rugby Union president. Welcoming the Fijian tourists in 1985. Attrib.

43 I wanted a play that would paint the full face of sensuality, rebellion and revivalism. In South Wales these three phenomena have played second fiddle only to the Rugby Union which is a distillation of all three.

Gwyn Thomas (1913–81) British writer. *Jackie the Jumper* (Introduction), 'Plays and Players' 19 Jan 1963

44 There's no secret. You just press the accelerator to the floor and steer left.

Bill Vukovich (1918–55) US motor-racing driver. Explaining his success in the Indianapolis 500. Attrib.

STALIN, JOSEPH

(J. Dzhugashvili; 1879–1953) Soviet statesman. A Bolshevik under Lenin, he became supreme dictator in 1929. In the 1930s he eliminated his rivals in various purges, but led the Soviet Union to victory in World War II. After the war his autocratic rule was intensified and he built up an empire of Eastern European Communist countries.

1 The Pope! How many divisions has *he* got?

When urged by Pierre Laval to tolerate Catholicism in the USSR to appease the Pope, 13 May 1935. *The Second World War* (W. S. Churchill), Vol. I, Ch. 8

2 The state is an instrument in the hands of the ruling class for suppressing the resistance of its class enemies.

Foundations of Leninism

3 The tasks of the party are...to be cautious and not allow our country to be drawn into conflicts by warmongers who are accustomed to have others pull the chestnuts out of the fire for them.

Speech, 8th Congress of the Communist Party, 6 Jan 1941

4 The party is the rallying-point for the best elements of the working class.

Attrib.

5 Gaiety is the most outstanding feature of the Soviet Union.

Attrib.

6 A single death is a tragedy; a million is a statistic.

Attrib.

STARING

1 It is better to be looked over than overlooked.

Mae West (1892–1980) US actress. *The Wit and Wisdom of Mae West* (ed. J. Weintraub)

2 Don't go on looking at me like that, because you'll wear your eyes out.

Émile Zola (1840–1902) French novelist. *La Bête humaine*, Ch. 5

STARS

See also astronomy, moon, space, sun, universe

1 ...things called Stars appeared, which robbed men of their souls and left them unreasoning brutes, so that they destroyed the civilization they themselves had built up.

Isaac Asimov (1920–92) US science-fiction writer. On the fictional world of Lagash night comes once every 2049 years. *Nightfall*

2 And God made two great lights: the greater light to rule the day, and the lesser light to rule the night: he made the stars also.

Bible: Genesis 1:16

3 I stood upon that silent hill
And stared into the sky until
My eyes were blind with stars and still
I stared into the sky.

Ralph Hodgson (1871–1962) British poet. *The Song of Honour*

4 Look at the stars! look, look up at the skies!
O look at all the fire-folk sitting in the air!
The bright boroughs, the circle-citadels there!

Gerard Manley Hopkins (1844–99) British Jesuit and poet. *The Starlight Night*

5 Bright star, would I were steadfast as thou art.

John Keats (1795–1821) British poet. *Bright Star*

6 Twinkle, twinkle, little star,
How I wonder what you are!
Up above the world so high,
Like a diamond in the sky!

Jane Taylor (1783–1824) British writer. *Rhymes for the Nursery* (with Ann Taylor), 'The Star'

7 For still I looked on that same star,
That fitful, fiery Lucifer,
Watching with mind as quiet as moss
Its light nailed to a burning cross.

Andrew Young (1885–1971) Scottish poet. *The Evening Star*

8 Stars lay like yellow pollen
That from a flower has fallen;
And single stars I saw
Crossing themselves in awe;
Some stars in sudden fear
Fell like a falling tear.

Andrew John Young *The Stars*

STATE

See also democracy, government, republic

1 The only way to erect such a common power, as may be able to defend them from the invasion of foreigners, and the injuries of one another...is, to confer all their power and strength upon one man, or upon one assembly of men, that may reduce all their wills, by plurality of voices, unto one will... This is the generation of that great Leviathan, or rather (to speak more reverently) of that *Mortal God*, to which we owe under the *Immortal God*, our peace and defence.

Thomas Hobbes (1588–1679) English philosopher. *Leviathan*, Pt. II, Ch. 17

2 So long as the state exists there is no freedom. When there is freedom there will be no state.

V. I. Lenin (Vladimir Ilich Ulyanov; 1870–1924) Russian revolutionary leader. *The State and Revolution*, Ch. 5

3 In a free society the state does not administer the affairs of men. It administers justice among men who conduct their own affairs.

Walter Lippman (1889–1974) US editor and writer. *An Enquiry into the Principles of a Good Society*

4 The worth of a State in the long run is the worth of the individuals composing it.

John Stuart Mill (1806–73) British philosopher. *On Liberty*, Ch. 5

5 The state is an instrument in the hands of the ruling class for suppressing the resistance of its class enemies.

Joseph Stalin (J. Dzhugashvili; 1879–1953) Soviet statesman. *Foundations of Leninism*

STATELY HOMES

See also architecture, aristocracy, houses

1 One way a peer can make a bit of extra money is by letting the public into his house. Another way is by letting the public into his head. Either way, the dottier the contents the better.

Anonymous Referring to the Earl of Avon's column in *The Evening News*. *The Sunday Times*, 15 Jan 1967

2 An extraordinary aspect of running a stately home is that much of its success depends, not on how many Van Dycks you have, but how many loos. No amount of beautiful objects can compensate a visitor who is kept queuing in the cold.

Duchess of Bedford *Nicole Nobody*

3 Now Spring, sweet laxative of Georgian strains,
Quickens the ink in literary veins,
The Stately Homes of England ope their doors
To piping Nancy-boys and Crashing Bores.

Roy Campbell (1901–57) South African poet. *The Georgiad*

4 The Stately Homes of England
How beautiful they stand,
To prove the upper classes
Have still the upper hand.

Noël Coward (1899–1973) British dramatist. *Operette*, 'The Stately Homes of England'

5 And though the Van Dycks have to go
And we pawn the Bechstein grand,
We'll stand by the Stately Homes of England.

Noël Coward *Operette*, 'The Stately Homes of England'

6 The stately homes of England,
How beautiful they stand!
Amidst their tall ancestral trees,
O'er all the pleasant land.

Felicia Dorothea Hemans (1793–1835) British poet. *The Homes of England*

7 Those comfortably padded lunatic asylums which are known, euphemistically, as the stately homes of England.

Virginia Woolf (1882–1941) British novelist. *The Common Reader*, 'Lady Dorothy Nevill'

STATISTICS

1 Medical statistics are like a bikini. What they reveal is interesting but what they conceal is vital.

Anonymous

2 A witty statesman said, you might prove anything by figures.

Thomas Carlyle (1795–1881) Scottish historian and essayist. *Critical and Miscellaneous Essays*, 'Chartism'

3 There are three kinds of lies: lies, damned lies and statistics.

Benjamin Disraeli (1804–81) British statesman. *Autobiography* (Mark Twain)

4 We are just statistics, born to consume resources.

Horace (Quintus Horatius Flaccus; 65–8 BC) Roman poet. *Epistles*, I

5 He uses statistics as a drunken man uses lamp-posts – for support rather than illumination.

Andrew Lang (1844–1912) Scottish writer and poet. *Treasury of Humorous Quotations*

6 You cannot feed the hungry on statistics.

David Lloyd George (1863–1945) British Liberal statesman. Advocating Tariff Reform. Speech, 1904

7 Statistics will prove anything, even the truth.

Noël Moynihan (1916–) British doctor and writer. Attrib.

8 To understand God's thoughts we must study statistics, for these are the measure of his purpose.

Florence Nightingale (1820–1910) British nurse. *Life...of Francis Galton* (K. Pearson), Vol. II, Ch. 13

9 I am one of the unpraised, unrewarded millions without whom Statistics would be a bankrupt science. It is we who are born, who marry, who die, in constant ratios.

Logan Pearsall Smith (1865–1946) US writer. *Trivia*

10 A single death is a tragedy; a million is a statistic.

Joseph Stalin (J. Dzhugashvili; 1879–1953) Soviet statesman. Attrib.

11 There are two kinds of statistics, the kind you look up and the kind you make up.

Rex Todhunter Stout (1886–1975) US writer. *Death of a Doxy*, Ch. 9

12 Facts speak louder than statistics.

Geoffrey Streatfield (1897–1978) British lawyer. *The Observer*, 'Sayings of the Week', 19 Mar 1950

STEIN, GERTRUDE

(1874–1946) US writer, who lived in Paris from 1903. Her books include *Tender Buttons* (1914) and *The Autobiography of Alice B. Toklas* (1933).

Quotations about Stein

1 Reading Gertrude Stein at length is not unlike making one's way through an interminable and badly printed game book.

Richard Bridgeman *Gertrude Stein in Pieces*

2 Miss Stein was a past master in making nothing happen very slowly

Clifton Fadiman (1904–) US writer and broadcaster. *The Selected Writings of Clifton Fadiman*, 'Puzzlements'

Quotations by Stein

3 She always says she dislikes the abnormal, it is so obvious. She says the normal is so much more simply complicated and interesting.

The Autobiography of Alice B. Toklas

4 In the United States there is more space where nobody is than where anybody is. That is what makes America what it is.

The Geographical History of America

5 Rose is a rose is a rose is a rose.

Sacred Emily

6 Besides Shakespeare and me, who do you think there is?

Speaking to a friend she considered knew little about literature. *Charmed Circle* (J. Mellow)

7 The Jews have produced only three originative geniuses: Christ, Spinoza, and myself.

Charmed Circle (J. Mellow)

8 That's what you are. That's what you all are. All of you young people who served in the war. You are all a lost generation.

A Moveable Feast (E. Hemingway)

STEINBECK, JOHN

(1902–68) US novelist. Many of his novels are set in the mid-west of America during the Depression; they include *Of Mice and Men* (1937), *The Grapes of Wrath* (1939), and *East of Eden* (1952).

1 The American Standard translation *orders* men to triumph over sin, and you can call sin ignorance. The King James translation makes a promise in 'Thou shalt', meaning that men will surely triumph over sin. But the Hebrew word, the word *timshel* – 'Thou mayest' – that gives a choice. It might be the most important word in the world. That says the way is open. That throws it right back on a man. For if 'Thou mayest' – it is also true that 'Thou mayest not'.

Referring to Genesis 4:7. *East of Eden*, Ch. 24

2 Man, unlike any other thing organic or inorganic in the universe, grows beyond his work, walks up the stairs of his concepts, emerges ahead of his accomplishments.

The Grapes of Wrath, Ch. 14

3 Okie use' to mean you was from Oklahoma. Now it means you're a dirty son-of-a-bitch. Okie means you're scum. Don't mean nothing itself, it's the way they say it.

The Grapes of Wrath, Ch. 18

STERNE, LAURENCE

(1713–68) Irish-born British writer and clergyman. *Tristram Shandy* (1759) established his reputation and was followed by *A Sentimental Journey* (1768). He also published books of sermons.

1 He gave a deep sigh – I saw the iron enter into his soul!

A Sentimental Journey, 'The Captive. Paris'

2 They are a loyal, a gallant, a generous, an ingenious, and good-temper'd people as is under heaven – if they have a fault, they are too *serious*.

Referring to the French. *A Sentimental Journey*, 'The Character. Versailles'

3 I am positive I have a soul; nor can all the books with which materialists have pestered the world ever convince me of the contrary.

A Sentimental Journey, 'Maria, Moulines'

4 I wish either my father or my mother, or indeed both of them, as they were in duty both equally bound to it, had minded what they were about when they begot me.

Tristram Shandy

5 So long as a man rides his hobby-horse peaceably and quietly along the king's highway, and neither compels you or me to get up behind him, – pray, Sir, what have either you or I to do with it?

Tristram Shandy

6 'Tis known by the name of perseverance in a good cause, – and of obstinacy in a bad one.

Tristram Shandy

7 Writing, when properly managed, (as you may be sure I think mine is) is but a different name for conversation.

Tristram Shandy

8 Whenever a man talks loudly against religion, – always suspect that it is not his reason, but his passions which have got the better of his creed.

Tristram Shandy

9 A man should know something of his own country, too, before he goes abroad.

Tristram Shandy

10 An ounce of a man's own wit is worth a ton of other people's.

Tristram Shandy

STEVENSON, ADLAI

(1900–65) US statesman. Governor of Illinois (1949–53), he twice stood unsuccessfully for the presidency (1952; 1956) as Democratic candidate.

1 An editor is one who separates the wheat from the chaff and prints the chaff.

The Stevenson Wit

2 A politician is a statesman who approaches every question with an open mouth.

Also attrib. to Arthur Goldberg. *The Fine Art of Political Wit* (L. Harris)

3 Power corrupts, but lack of power corrupts absolutely.

The Observer, Jan 1963

4 Let's talk sense to the American people. Let's tell them the truth, that there are no gains without pains.

Speech, Chicago, 26 July 1952

5 There is no evil in the atom; only in men's souls.

Speech, Hartford, Connecticut, 18 Sept 1952

6 My definition of a free society is a society where it is safe to be unpopular.

Speech, Detroit, 7 Oct 1952

7 He said that he was too old to cry, but it hurt too much to laugh.

Said after losing an election, quoting a story told by Abraham Lincoln. Speech, 5 Nov 1952

8 She would rather light a candle than curse the darkness, and her glow has warmed the world.

Referring to the writer Eleanor Roosevelt who was a delegate to the United Nations (1945–52). Address, United Nations General Assembly, 9 Nov 1962

STEVENSON, ROBERT LOUIS

(1850–94) Scottish writer. His books include *Treasure Island* (1883), *Kidnapped* (1886), and *The Strange Case of Dr Jekyll and Mr Hyde* (1886).

Quotations about Stevenson

1 Stevenson seemed to pick the right word up on the point of his pen, like a man playing spillikins.

G. K. Chesterton (1874–1936) British writer. *The Victorian Age in Literature*

2 I think of Mr Stevenson as a consumptive youth weaving garlands of sad flowers with pale, weak hands.

George Moore (1852–1933) Irish writer and art critic. *Confessions of a Young Man*

Quotations by Stevenson

3 If your morals make you dreary, depend upon it, they are wrong.

Across the Plains

4 Politics is perhaps the only profession for which no preparation is thought necessary.

Familiar Studies of Men and Books, 'Yoshida-Torajiro'

5 Vanity dies hard; in some obstinate cases it outlives the man.

Prince Otto

6 Wealth I seek not; hope nor love,
Nor a friend to know me;
All I seek, the heaven above
And the road below me.

Songs of Travel, 'The Vagabond'

7 For my part, I travel not to go anywhere, but to go. I travel for travel's sake. The great affair is to move.

Travels with a Donkey, 'Cheylard and Luc'

8 Fifteen men on the dead man's chest
Yo-ho-ho, and a bottle of rum!
Drink and the devil had done for the rest –
Yo-ho-ho, and a bottle of rum!

Treasure Island, Ch. 1

9 Pieces of eight!
Treasure Island, Ch. 10

10 Many's the long night I've dreamed of cheese – toasted, mostly.
Treasure Island, Ch. 15

11 Of all my verse, like not a single line;
But like my title, for it is not mine.
That title from a better man I stole;
Ah, how much better, had I stol'n the whole!
Underwoods, Foreword

12 Under the wide and starry sky
Dig the grave and let me lie.
Glad did I live and gladly die,
– And I laid me down with a will.
This is the verse you grave for me:
'Here he lies where he longed to be;
Home is the sailor, home from sea,
And the hunter home from the hill.'
Underwoods, Bk. I, 'Requiem'

13 Even if we take matrimony at its lowest, even if we regard it as no more than a sort of friendship recognized by the police.
Virginibus Puerisque

14 Man is a creature who lives not upon bread alone, but principally by catchwords; and the little rift between the sexes is astonishingly widened by simply teaching one set of catchwords to the girls and another to the boys.
Virginibus Puerisque

15 The cruellest lies are often told in silence.
Virginibus Puerisque

16 When the torrent sweeps a man against a boulder, you must expect him to scream, and you need not be surprised if the scream is sometimes a theory.
Virginibus Puerisque

17 Old and young, we are all on our last cruise.
Virginibus Puerisque

18 Books are good enough in their own way, but they are a mighty bloodless substitute for life.
Virginibus Puerisque

19 Extreme *busyness*, whether at school or college, kirk or market, is a symptom of deficient vitality.
Virginibus Puerisque

20 There is no duty we so much underrate as the duty of being happy.
Virginibus Puerisque

21 Give me the young man who has brains enough to make a fool of himself!
Virginibus Puerisque

22 Lastly (and this is, perhaps, the golden rule), no woman should marry a teetotaller, or a man who does not smoke.
Virginibus Puerisque

23 Marriage is a step so grave and decisive that it attracts light-headed, variable men by its very awfulness.
Virginibus Puerisque

24 In marriage, a man becomes slack and selfish and undergoes a fatty degeneration of his moral being.
Virginibus Puerisque

25 Marriage is like life in this – that it is a field of battle, and not a bed of roses.
Virginibus Puerisque

26 To travel hopefully is a better thing than to arrive, and the true success is to labour.
Virginibus Puerisque

27 It's deadly commonplace, but, after all, the commonplaces are the great poetic truths.
Weir of Hermiston, Ch. 6

STOPES, MARIE

(1880–1958) British campaigner for birth control. She opened the first birth control clinic in Holloway in 1921; her books include *Married Love* (1918), *Wise Parenthood* (1918) and *Contraception: Its Theory, History and Practice* (1923).

Quotations about Stopes

1 A fascinating combination of scientist and would-be poet, of mystic and crank, of propagandist and neurotic, Marie Stopes splendidly embraced the challenge of society and set up her first birth-control clinic in London in 1921, but she completely failed to write a poem of any consequence.
Keith Briant *Marie Stopes*

2 Her frontal attacks on old taboos, her quasi-prophetic tone, her flowery fervour, aroused strong opposition from those who disagreed with her for religious reasons or felt that she had overstepped the bounds of good taste.
The Daily Telegraph, Obituary, 3 Oct 1958

3 Dr Marie Stopes made contraceptive devices respectable in a somewhat gushing book, *Married Love*. For this she deserves to be remembered among the great benefactors of the age.
A.J.P. Taylor (1906–90) British historian. *English History 1914–45*

Quotations by Stopes

4 An impersonal and scientific knowledge of the structure of our bodies is the surest safeguard against prurient curiosity and lascivious gloating.
Married Love, Ch. 5

5 ...each coming together of man and wife, even if they have been mated for many years, should be a fresh adventure; each winning should necessitate a fresh wooing.
Married Love, Ch. 10

6 We are not much in sympathy with the typical hustling American business man, but we have often felt compunction for him, seeing him nervous and harassed, sleeplessly, anxiously hunting dollars and all but overshadowed by his overdressed, extravagant and idle wife, who sometimes insists that her spiritual development necessitates that she shall have no children...Yet such wives imagine that they are upholding women's emancipation.

The Fighting Pankhursts (David Mitchell)

STOPPARD, TOM

(1937–) Czech-born British dramatist. He achieved notice with his play *Rosencrantz and Guildenstern Are Dead* (1967), subsequently building on this success with *Jumpers* (1972), *Travesties* (1975), *Night and Day* (1978), *The Real Thing* (1983), and *Hapgood* (1988).

1 Skill without imagination is craftsmanship and gives us many useful objects such as wickerwork picnic baskets. Imagination without skill gives us modern art.

Artist Descending a Staircase

2 This is a British murder inquiry and some degree of justice must be seen to be more or less done.

Jumpers, II

3 Socialists treat their servants with respect and then wonder why they vote Conservative.

Lord Malquist and Mr Moon, Pt. V, Ch. 1

4 The House of Lords, an illusion to which I have never been able to subscribe – responsibility without power, the prerogative of the eunuch throughout the ages.

See Lord ACTON. *Lord Malquist and Mr Moon*, Pt. VI, Ch. 1

5 He's someone who flies around from hotel to hotel and thinks the most interesting thing about any story is the fact that he has arrived to cover it.

Referring to foreign correspondents. *Night and Day*, I

6 The media. It sounds like a convention of spiritualists.

Night and Day, I

7 MILNE. No matter how imperfect things are, if you've got a free press everything is correctable, and without it everything is conceivable.
RUTH. I'm with you on the free press. It's the newspapers I can't stand.

Night and Day, I

8 Eternity's a terrible thought. I mean, where's it going to end?

Rosencrantz and Guildenstern Are Dead, II

9 The bad end unhappily, the good unluckily. That is what tragedy means.

Rosencrantz and Guildenstern Are Dead, II

10 Life is a gamble, at terrible odds – if it was a bet, you wouldn't take it.

Rosencrantz and Guildenstern Are Dead, III

11 What is an artist? For every thousand people there's nine hundred doing the work, ninety doing well, nine doing good, and one lucky bastard who's the artist.

Travesties, I

12 It's better to be quotable than to be honest.

The Guardian

13 I doubt that art needed Ruskin any more than a moving train needs one of its passengers to shove it.

Referring to the art critic John Ruskin. *Times Literary Supplement*, 3 June 1977

STOWE, HARRIET BEECHER

(1811–96) US novelist. She achieved fame with *Uncle Tom's Cabin* (1852), which greatly helped the antislavery lobby. Her other books include *The Minister's Wooing* (1859) and *Oldtown Folks* (1864). Her article accusing Lord Byron of incest with his sister caused great controversy.

1 The bitterest tears shed over graves are for words left unsaid and deeds left undone.

Little Foxes, Ch. 3

2 'Do you know who made you?' 'Nobody, as I knows on,' said the child, with a short laugh... 'I 'spect I grow'd.'

Uncle Tom's Cabin, Ch. 20

3 Whipping and abuse are like laudanum: You have to double the dose as the sensibilities decline.

Uncle Tom's Cabin, Ch. 20

4 I did not write it. God wrote it. I merely did his dictation.

Referring to *Uncle Tom's Cabin*. Attrib.

STRAVINSKY, IGOR

(1882–1971) Russian-born US composer. His early ballet scores, commissioned by Diaghilev, include *The Firebird* (1910), *Petrushka* (1911), and *The Rite of Spring* (1913). His later work includes a piano concerto (1924), the oratorio *Oedipus Rex* (1927) and the opera *The Rake's Progress* (1951).

1 Rachmaninov's immortalizing totality was his scowl. He was a six-and-a-half-foot-tall scowl.

Conversations with Igor Stravinsky (Igor Stravinsky and Robert Craft)

2 He was the only pianist I have ever seen who did not grimace. That is a great deal.

Referring to Rachmaninov. *Conversations with Igor Stravinsky* (Igor Stravinsky and Robert Craft)

3 I had another dream the other day about music critics. They were small and rodent-like with padlocked ears, as if they had stepped out of a painting by Goya.

The Evening Standard, 29 Oct 1969

4 My music is best understood by children and animals.

The Observer, 'Sayings of the Week', 8 Oct 1961

5 A good composer does not imitate; he steals.

Twentieth Century Music (Peter Yates)

6 I don't write modern music. I only write good music.

To journalists on his first visit to America, 1925.

7 Hurry! I never hurry. I have no time to hurry.

Responding to his publisher's request that he hurry his completion of a composition. Attrib.

STRIKES

See also industrial relations

1 The rights and interests of the laboring man will be protected and cared for, not by the labor agitators, but by the Christian men to whom God in His infinite wisdom has given control of the property interests of the country.

George Baer (1842–1914) US railroad magnate. Written during the Pennsylvania miners' strike. Letter to the press, Oct 1902

2 Constitutional Government is being attacked... The general strike is a challenge to Parliament, and is the road to anarchy and ruin.

Stanley Baldwin (1867–1947) British politician and prime minister. *The British Gazette*, 6 May 1926

3 Not a penny off the pay; not a minute on the day.

A. J. Cook (1885–1931) British trade-union leader. Slogan used in the miners' strike, 1926

4 There is no right to strike against the public safety by anybody, anywhere, any time.

Calvin Coolidge (1872–1933) US president. Referring to the Boston police strike. Remark, 14 Sept 1919

5 It is difficult to go on strike if there is no work in the first place.

Lord George-Brown (1914–85) British statesman. *The Observer*, 24 Feb 1980

6 The trouble with employers is that they only like ballots so long as you lose them.

Jimmy Knapp (1940–) General Secretary of the National Union of Railwaymen. Referring to British Rail's decision to go to court following a ballot solidly in favour of strike action. *The Guardian*, 1989

7 Another fact of life that will not have escaped you is that, in this country, the twenty-four-hour strike is like the twenty-four-hour flu. You have to reckon on it lasting at least five days.

Frank Muir (1920–) British writer and broadcaster. *You Can't Have Your Kayak and Heat It* (Frank Muir and Dennis Norden), 'Great Expectations'

8 Have you noticed, the last four strikes we've had, it's pissed down? It wouldn't be a bad idea to check the weather reports before they pull us out next time.

Johnny Speight (1920–) British television scriptwriter. *Till Death Do Us Part*

STUBBORNNESS

See also determination, inflexibility, petulance

1 You can lead a horse to the water, but you can't make him drink.

Proverb

2 None so blind as those who won't see.

Proverb

3 Obstinate people can be divided into the opinionated, the ignorant, and the boorish.

Aristotle (384–322 BC) Greek philosopher. *Nicomachean Ethics*, Bk. VII

4 'Tis known by the name of perseverance in a good cause, – and of obstinacy in a bad one.

Laurence Sterne (1713–68) Irish-born British writer. *Tristram Shandy*

STUPIDITY

See also foolishness, ignorance

1 His mind is open; yes, it is so open that nothing is retained; ideas simply pass through him.

F. H. Bradley (1846–1924) British philosopher. Attrib.

2 He'd be sharper than a serpent's tooth, if he wasn't as dull as ditch water.

Charles Dickens (1812–70) British novelist. *Our Mutual Friend*, Bk. III, Ch. 10

3 He is not only dull in himself, but the cause of dullness in others.

Samuel Foote (1720–77) British actor and dramatist. Parody of a line from Shakespeare's *Henry IV, Part Two*. *Life of Johnson* (J. Boswell)

4 The trouble with Senator Long is that he is suffering from halitosis of the intellect. That's presuming Emperor Long has an intellect.

Harold L. Ickes (1874–1952) US Republican politician. *The Politics of Upheaval* (A. M. Schlesinger Jnr), Pt. II, Ch. 14

5 Jerry Ford is so dumb that he can't fart and chew gum at the same time.

Lyndon B. Johnson (1908–73) US statesman. Sometimes quoted as '...can't walk and chew gum'. *A Ford, Not a Lincoln* (R. Reeves), Ch. 1

6 That fellow seems to me to possess but one idea, and that is a wrong one.

Samuel Johnson (1709–84) British lexicographer. *Life of Johnson* (J. Boswell), Vol. II

7 I've been married six months. She looks like a million dollars, but she only knows a hundred and twenty words and she's only got two ideas in her head. The other one's hats.

Eric Linklater (1889–1974) Scottish novelist. *Juan in America*, Pt. II, Ch. 5

8 You've got the brain of a four-year-old boy, and I bet he was glad to get rid of it.

Groucho Marx (Julius Marx; 1895–1977) US comedian. *Horse Feathers*

9 Music-hall songs provide the dull with wit, just as proverbs provide them with wisdom.

W. Somerset Maugham (1874–1965) British novelist. *A Writer's Notebook*

10 Stupidity does not consist in being without ideas. Such stupidity would be the sweet, blissful stupidity of animals, molluscs and the gods. Human Stupidity consists in having lots of ideas, but stupid ones.

Henry de Montherlant (1896–1972) French novelist. *Notebooks*

11 She has a Rolls body and a Balham mind.

J. B. Morton (1893–1979) British journalist. *The Best of Beachcomber*, 'A Foul Innuendo'

12 I've examined your son's head, Mr Glum, and there's nothing there.

Frank Muir (1920–) British writer and broadcaster. *Take It from Here* (Frank Muir and Dennis Norden), 1957

13 You beat your pate, and fancy wit will come; Knock as you please, there's nobody at home.

Alexander Pope (1688–1744) British poet. *Epigram*

14 Against stupidity the gods themselves struggle in vain.

Friedrich von Schiller (1759–1805) German dramatist. *Die Jungfrau von Orleans*, III:6

15 There is no sin except stupidity.

Oscar Wilde (1854–1900) Irish-born British dramatist. *The Critic as Artist*, Pt. 2

STYLE

1 Style is the man himself.

Comte de Buffon (1707–88) French naturalist. *Discours sur le style*

2 Style, like sheer silk, too often hides eczema.

Albert Camus (1913–60) French existentialist writer. *The Fall*

3 There goes a woman who knows all the things that can be taught and none of the things that cannot be taught.

Coco Chanel (1883–1971) French dress designer. *Coco Chanel, Her Life, Her Secrets* (Marcel Haedrich)

4 An author arrives at a good style when his language performs what is required of it without shyness.

Cyril Connolly (1903–74) British journalist. *Enemies of Promise*, Ch. 3

5 Glamour is what makes a man ask for your telephone number. But it also is what makes a woman ask for the name of your dressmaker.

Lilly Daché (1904–) French-born US fashion designer and writer. *Woman's Home Companion*, July 1955

6 He has never been known to use a word that might send the reader to the dictionary.

William Faulkner (1897–1962) US novelist. Referring to Ernest HEMINGWAY. Attrib.

7 Poor Faulkner. Does he really think big emotions come from big words? He thinks I don't know the ten-dollar words. I know them all right. But there are older and simpler and better words, and those are the ones I use.

Ernest Hemingway (1899–1961) US novelist. In response to a jibe by William FAULKNER. Attrib.

8 English women are elegant until they are ten years old, and perfect on grand occasions.

Nancy Mitford (1904–73) British writer. *The Wit of Women* (L. and M. Cowan)

9 I wanted one more chance and I'm there. This is what I dreamed about. This is what I wanted – to go out in style. Win or lose, I'll be going out in style. I'm going to enjoy the moment.

Martina Navratilova (1956–) Czech-born US tennis player. Referring to Wimbledon. She was defeated in the finals. *The Independent*, 1 July 1994

10 All styles are good except the tiresome sort.

Voltaire (François-Marie Arouet; 1694–1778) French writer. *L'Enfant prodigue*, Preface

11 In matters of grave importance, style, not sincerity, is the vital thing.

Oscar Wilde (1854–1900) Irish-born British dramatist. *The Importance of Being Earnest*, III

SUBJECTIVITY

See also objectivity, prejudice

1 She was one of the people who say, 'I don't know anything about music really, but I know what I like'.

Max Beerbohm (1872–1956) British writer. *Zuleika Dobson*, Ch. 16

2 An apology for the Devil – it must be remembered that we have only heard one side of the case. God has written all the books.

Samuel Butler (1835–1902) British writer. *Notebooks*

3 It is a general mistake to think the men we like are good for everything, and those we do not, good for nothing.

Lord Halifax (1633–95) English statesman. *Political, Moral and Miscellaneous Thoughts and Reflections*

4 He who knows only his own side of the case knows little of that.

John Stuart Mill (1806–73) British philosopher. *On Liberty*, Ch. 2

5 All the world is queer save thee and me, and even thou art a little queer.

Robert Owen (1771–1858) British social reformer. Referring to William Allen, his partner in business. Attrib., 1828

6 To observations which ourselves we make
We grow more partial for th' observer's sake.

Alexander Pope (1688–1744) British poet. *Moral Essays*, I

7 Partisanship is our great curse. We too readily assume that everything has two sides and that it is our duty to be on one or the other.

James Harvey Robinson (1863–1936) US historian and educator. *The Mind in the Making*

SUBURBIA

1 I come from suburbia, Dan, personally, I don't ever want to go back. It's the one place in the world that's further away than anywhere else.

Frederic Raphael (1931–) British author. *The Glittering Prizes: A Sex Life*, I:3

2 She was more than ever proud of the position of the bungalow, so almost in the country.

Angus Wilson (1913–) British novelist. *A Bit Off the Map*, 'A Flat Country Christmas'

SUCCESS

See also achievement, failure, victory

1 Nothing succeeds like success.

Proverb

2 Nothing is harder on your laurels than resting on them.

Anonymous

3 'Tis not in mortals to command success,
But we'll do more, Sempronius; we'll deserve it.

Joseph Addison (1672–1719) British essayist. *Cato*, I:2

4 The penalty of success is to be bored by people who used to snub you.

Nancy Astor (1879–1964) US-born British politician. *Sunday Express*, 12 Jan 1956

5 One's religion is whatever he is most interested in, and yours is Success.

J. M. Barrie (1860–1937) British novelist and dramatist. *The Twelve-Pound Look*

6 A woman who is loved always has success.

Vicki Baum (1888–1960) Austrian-born US writer, playwright, and scenarist. *Grand Hotel*

7 Ask, and it shall be given you; seek, and ye shall find; knock, and it shall be opened unto you:
For every one that asketh receiveth; and he that seeketh findeth; and to him that knocketh it shall be opened.

Bible: Matthew 7:7–8

8 All I think about is winning that bleedin' title.

Frank Bruno (1961–) British boxer. Remark, Jan 1989

9 The only infallible criterion of wisdom to vulgar minds – success.

Edmund Burke (1729–97) British politician. *Letter to a Member of the National Assembly*

10 Success is counted sweetest
By those who ne'er succeed.

Emily Dickinson (1830–86) US poet. *Success is Counted Sweetest*

11 Success is relative. It is what we can make of the mess we have made of things.

T. S. Eliot (1888–1965) US-born British poet and dramatist. *The Family Reunion*

12 There are two reasons why I am successful in show business and I am standing on both of them.

Betty Grable (1916–73) US actress. Attrib.

13 The moral flabbiness born of the bitch-goddess Success.

William James (1842–1910) US psychologist and philosopher. Letter to H. G. Wells, 11 Sept 1906

14 Victory has a thousand fathers but defeat is an orphan.

John Fitzgerald Kennedy (1917–63) US statesman. Attrib.

15 The shortest and best way to make your fortune is to let people see clearly that it is in their interests to promote yours.

Jean de La Bruyère (1645–96) French satirist. *Les Caractères*

16 Powerful men often succeed through the help of their wives. Powerful women only succeed in spite of their husbands.

Linda Lee-Potter British journalist. *Daily Mail*, 16 May 1984

17 Sweet Smell of Success.

Ernest Lehman (1920–) US screenwriter. Novel and film title

18 You write a hit the same way you write a flop.

Alan Jay Lerner (1918–86) US lyricist and playwright. Attrib.

19 We in this industry know that behind every successful screenwriter stands a woman. And behind her stands his wife.

Groucho Marx (Julius Marx; 1895–1977) US comedian. Attrib.

20 The secret of my success is that no woman has ever been jealous of me.

Elsa Maxwell (1883–1963) US songwriter, broadcaster, and actress. *The Natives were Friendly* (Noël Barber)

21 Nothing fails like success; nothing is so defeated as yesterday's triumphant Cause.

Phyllis McGinley (1905–78) US poet and humorist. *The Province of the Heart*, 'How to Get Along with Men'

22 I don't think success is harmful, as so many people say. Rather, I believe it indispensable to talent, if for nothing else than to increase the talent.

Jeanne Moreau (1929–) French actress. *The Egotists* (Oriana Fallaci)

23 As is the case in all branches of art, success depends in a very large measure upon individual initiative and exertion, and cannot be achieved except by dint of hard work.

Anna Pavlova (1881–1931) Russian ballet dancer. *Pavlova: A Biography* (ed. A. H. Franks), 'Pages of My Life'

24 No pain, no palm; no thorns, no throne;
no gall, no glory; no cross, no crown.

William Penn (1644–1718) English founder of Pennsylvania. *No Cross, No Crown*

25 To succeed in the world, we do everything we can to appear successful.

Duc de la Rochefoucauld (1613–80) French writer. *Maximes*, 50

26 The idea has gained currency that women have often been handicapped not only by a fear of failure – not unknown to men either – but by a fear of success as well.

Sonya Rudikoff US writer. *Commentary*, 'Women and Success', Oct 1974

27 The only place where success comes before work is a dictionary.

Vidal Sassoon (1928–) British hair stylist. Quoting one of his teachers in a BBC radio broadcast

28 The only way to succeed is to make people hate you. That way, they remember you.

Joseph von Sternberg (1894–1969) US film director. *Autobiography* (*Fun in a Chinese Laundry*)

29 There are no gains without pains.

Adlai Stevenson (1900–65) US statesman. Speech, Chicago, 26 July 1952

30 It is not enough to succeed. Others must fail.

Gore Vidal (1925–) US novelist. *Antipanegyric for Tom Driberg* (G. Irvine)

31 Success? Ah yes, the first three-piece suit, first lawsuit…

Robin Williams (1952–) US actor. *Playboy*, 1979

SUFFERING

1 He that lives long suffers much.

Proverb

2 Oh, torture. Torture. My pubic hairs went grey.

Steven Spielberg (1946–) US film director. Referring to the filming of ET. *Rolling Stone*, 24 Oct 1985

3 If drama shows people dealing nobly with their misery, it disenfranchises those watching who cannot cope like that.

Juliet Stevenson (1956–) British actress. *The Observer*, 'Sayings of the Week', 22 May 1994

SUICIDE

See also death

1 I was suicidal, and would have killed myself, but I was in analysis with a strict Freudian, and if you kill yourself they make you pay for the lessons you miss.

Woody Allen (Allen Stewart Konigsberg; 1935–) US film actor and director. *Halliwell's Filmgoers' and Video Viewers' Companion*

2 To run away from trouble is a form of cowardice and, while it is true that the suicide braves death, he does it not for some noble object but to escape some ill.

Aristotle (384 BC–322 BC) Greek philosopher and scientist. *Nicomachean Ethics*, 3

3 If I had the use of my body I would throw it out of the window.

Samuel Beckett (1906–89) Irish novelist and dramatist. *Malone Dies*

4 If you must commit suicide…always contrive to do it as decorously as possible; the decencies, whether of life or of death, should never be lost sight of.

George Borrow (1803–81) British writer. *Lavengro*, Ch. 23

5 There is but one truly serious philosophical problem, and that is suicide. Judging whether life is, or is not worth living amounts to answering the fundamental question of philosophy.

Albert Camus (1913–60) French existentialist writer. *The Myth of Sisyphus*

6 As soon as one does not kill oneself, one must keep silent about life.

Albert Camus *Notebooks 1935–1942*, 1

7 To attempt suicide is a criminal offense. Any man who, of his own will, tries to escape the treadmill to which the rest of us feel chained incites our envy, and therefore our fury. We do not suffer him to go unpunished.

Alexander Chase (1926–) US journalist. *Perspectives*

8 The strangest whim has seized me…After all I think I will not hang myself today.

G. K. Chesterton (1874–1936) British writer. *A Ballade of Suicide*

9 Not only is suicide a sin, it is the sin. It is the ultimate and absolute evil, the refusal to take the oath of loyalty to life. The man who kills a man, kills a man. The man who kills himself kills all men; as far as he is concerned he wipes out the world.

G. K. Chesterton *Orthodoxy*

10 The worst crime is faking it.

Kurt Cobain (1967–94) US rock musician. *The Observer*, 'Sayings of the Week', 17 Apr 1994

11 Suicide is the worst form of murder, because it leaves no opportunity for repentance.

John Churton Collins (1848–1908) *Life and Memoirs of John Churton Collins* (L. C. Collins), Appendix VII

12 There are many who dare not kill themselves for fear of what the neighbours might say.

Cyril Connolly (1903–74) British journalist. *The Unquiet Grave*

13 Self-destruction is the effect of cowardice in the highest extreme.

Daniel Defoe (c. 1659–1731) English journalist and writer. *An Essay Upon Projects*, 'Of Projectors'

14 My work is done. Why wait?

George Eastman (1854–1932) US inventor and industrialist. His suicide note

15 The prevalence of suicide is a test of height in civilization; it means that the population is winding up its nervous and intellectual system to the utmost point of tension and that sometimes it snaps.

Havelock Ellis (1859–1939) British psychologist.

16 Suicide is not a remedy.

James A. Garfield (1831–81) US statesman. Inaugural address, 4 Mar 1881

17 However great a man's fear of life…suicide remains the courageous act, the clear-headed act of a mathematician. The suicide has judged by the laws of chance – so many odds against one, that to live will be more miserable than to die. His sense of mathematics is greater than his sense of survival.

Graham Greene (1904–91) British novelist. *The Comedians*, I

18 Hatred and the feeling of solidarity pay a high psychological dividend. The statistics of suicide show that, for noncombatants at least, life is more interesting in war than in peace.

Dean Inge (1860–1954) British writer and churchman. *The End of an Age*, Ch. 3

19 I take it that no man is educated who has never dallied with the thought of suicide.

William James (1842–1910) US psychologist and philosopher.

20 Nature puts upon no man an unbearable burden; if her limits be exceeded, man responds by suicide. I have always respected suicide as a regulator of nature.

Emil Ludwig (1881–1948) *I Believe* (Clifton Fadiman)

21 The thought of suicide is a great source of comfort: with it a calm passage is to be made across many a bad night.

Friedrich Wilhelm Nietzsche (1844–1900) German philosopher. *Jenseits von Gut und Böse*

22 You fellows, in your business, you have a way of handling problems like this. Somebody leaves a pistol in the drawer. I don't have a pistol.

Richard Milhous Nixon (1913–94) US President. To General Alexander Haig. *Final Days* (R. Woodward and C. Bernstein)

23 When you go to drown yourself always take off your clothes, they may fit your wife's next husband.

Gregory Nunn

24 Razors pain you
Rivers are damp;
Acids stain you;
And drugs cause cramp.
Guns aren't lawful;
Nooses give;
Gas smells awful;
You might as well live.

Dorothy Parker (1893–1967) US writer. *Enough Rope*, 'Resumé'

25 No one ever lacks a good reason for suicide.

Cesare Pavese (1908–50) Italian writer. *The Savage God* (A. Alvarez)

26 Amid the miseries of our life on earth, suicide is God's best gift to man.

Pliny the Elder (23–79 AD) Roman scholar. *Natural History*, II

27 When you're between any sort of devil and the

deep blue sea, the deep blue sea sometimes looks very inviting.

Terence Rattigan (1911–77) British dramatist. *The Deep Blue Sea*

28 How many people have wanted to kill themselves, and have been content with tearing up their photograph!

Jules Renard (1864–1910) French writer. *Journal*

29 Next week, or next month, or next year I'll kill myself. But I might as well last out my month's rent, which has been paid up, and my credit for breakfast in the morning.

Jean Rhys (1894–1979) Dominican-born British novelist. *Good Morning, Midnight*, Pt. II

30 It is against the law to commit suicide in this man's town…although what the law can do to a guy who commits suicide I am never able to figure out.

Damon Runyon (1884–1946) US writer. *Guys and Dolls*

31 The miserable change now at my end
Lament nor sorrow at; but please your thoughts
In feeding them with those my former fortunes
Wherein I liv'd the greatest prince o' the world,
The noblest; and do now not basely die,
Not cowardly put off my helmet to
My countryman; a Roman by a Roman
Valiantly vanquished.

William Shakespeare (1564–1616) English dramatist. *Antony and Cleopatra*, IV:13

32 Dost thou not see my baby at my breast
That sucks the nurse asleep?

William Shakespeare Holding the asp to her breast. *Antony and Cleopatra*, V:2

33 My desolation does begin to make
A better life. 'Tis paltry to be Caesar;
Not being Fortune, he's but Fortune's knave,
A minister of her will; and it is great
To do that thing that ends all other deeds,
Which shackles accidents, and bolts up change,
Which sleeps, and never palates more the dug,
The beggar's nurse and Caesar's.

William Shakespeare *Antony and Cleopatra*, V:2

34 She hath pursu'd conclusions infinite
Of easy ways to die.

William Shakespeare *Antony and Cleopatra*, V:2

35 To be, or not to be – that is the question;
Whether 'tis nobler in the mind to suffer
The slings and arrows of outrageous fortune,
Or to take arms against a sea of troubles,
And by opposing end them? To die, to sleep –
No more; and by a sleep to say we end
The heart-ache and the thousand natural shocks
That flesh is heir to, 'tis a consummation
Devoutly to be wish'd. To die, to sleep;
To sleep, perchance to dream. Ay, there's the rub;
For in that sleep of death what dreams may come,
When we have shuffled off this mortal coil,
Must give us pause.

William Shakespeare *Hamlet*, III:1

36 A still small voice spake unto me,
'Thou art so full of misery,
Were it not better not to be?'

Alfred, Lord Tennyson (1809–92) British poet. *The Two Voices*

37 I am the only man in the world who cannot commit suicide.

Rev. Chad Varah (1911–) Founder of the Samaritans. Attrib.

38 Not that suicide always comes from madness. There are said to be occasions when a wise man takes that course: but, generally speaking, it is not in an access of reasonableness that people kill themselves.

Voltaire (François-Marie Arouet; 1694–1778) French writer and philosopher. Letter to James Marriott, 1767

39 There is no refuge from confession but suicide; and suicide is confession.

Daniel Webster (1782–1852) US statesman. *The Murder of Captain Joseph White: Argument on the Trial of John Francis Knapp*

40 Never murder a man who is committing suicide.

Woodrow Wilson (1856–1925) US statesman. *Mr Wilson's War* (John Dos Passos), Pt. II, Ch. 10

SUITABILITY

1 In seed time learn, in harvest teach, in winter enjoy.

William Blake (1757–1827) British poet. *The Marriage of Heaven and Hell*, 'Proverbs of Hell'

2 A cow is a very good animal in the field; but we turn her out of a garden.

Samuel Johnson (1709–84) British lexicographer. Responding to Boswell's objections to the expulsion of six Methodists from Oxford University. *The Personal History of Samuel Johnson* (C. Hibbert)

3 Today I dressed to meet my father's eyes; yesterday it was for my husband's.

Julia (39 BC–14 AD) Daughter of Augustus. On being complimented by her father, the emperor Augustus, on her choice of a more modest dress than the one she had worn the previous day. *Saturnalia* (Macrobius)

4 At Christmas I no more desire a rose
Than wish a snow in May's newfangled shows.

William Shakespeare (1564–1616) English dramatist. *Love's Labour's Lost*, I:1

SUMMONS

See also invitations

1 Go, for they call you, Shepherd, from the hill.

Matthew Arnold (1822–88) British poet and critic. *The Scholar Gipsy*

2 Whistle and she'll come to you.

Francis Beaumont (1584–1616) English dramatist. *Wit Without Money*, IV:4

3 Mr Watson, come here; I want you.

Alexander Graham Bell (1847–1922) Scottish scientist. The first telephone conversation, 10 Mar 1876, in Boston. Attrib.

4 Dauntless the slug-horn to my lips I set,
And blew. *Childe Roland to the Dark Tower came.*

Robert Browning (1812–89) British poet. *Childe Roland to the Dark Tower Came*, XXXIV

SUN

See also weather

1 The night has a thousand eyes,
And the day but one;
Yet the light of the bright world dies
With the dying sun.

Francis William Bourdillon (1852–1921) British writer. *Light*

2 The Sun came up upon the left,
Out of the sea came he!
And he shone bright, and on the right
Went down into the sea.

Samuel Taylor Coleridge (1772–1834) British poet. *The Rime of the Ancient Mariner*, I

3 Busy old fool, unruly Sun,
Why dost thou thus,
Through windows and through curtains call on us?

John Donne (1573–1631) English poet. *The Sun Rising*

4 Mother, give me the sun.

Henrik Ibsen (1828–1906) Norwegian dramatist. *Ghosts*, III

5 I have a horror of sunsets, they're so romantic, so operatic.

Marcel Proust (1871–1922) French novelist. *À La Recherche du temps perdu: Sodome et Gomorrhe*

6 Thank heavens, the sun has gone in, and I don't have to go out and enjoy it.

Logan Pearsall Smith (1865–1946) US writer. *Afterthoughts*

7 Hath Britain all the sun that shines?

William Shakespeare (1564–1616) English dramatist. *Cymbeline*, III:4

8 …twentieth-century woman appears to regard sunlight as a kind of cosmetic effulgence with a light aphrodisiac content – which makes it a funny thing that none of her female ancestors are recorded as seeing it the same way. Men, of course, just go on sweating in it from century to century.

John Wyndham (1903–69) British science-fiction writer. *The Kraken Wakes*

SUNDAY

1 And on the seventh day God ended his work which he had made; and he rested on the seventh day from all his work which he had made.

Bible: Genesis 2:2

2 And he said unto them, The sabbath was made for man, and not man for the sabbath: Therefore the Son of man is Lord also of the sabbath.

Bible: Mark 2:27–28

3 Of all the days that's in the week
I dearly love but one day –
And that's the day that comes betwixt
A Saturday and Monday.

Henry Carey (c. 1690–1743) English poet and musician. *Sally in our Alley*

4 The better day, the worse deed.

Matthew Henry (1662–1714) English nonconformist minister. *Exposition of the Old and New Testaments*

5 The feeling of Sunday is the same everywhere, heavy, melancholy, standing still. Like when they say, 'As it was in the beginning, is now, and ever shall be, world without end.'

Jean Rhys (1894–1979) Dominican-born British novelist. *Voyage in the Dark*, Ch. 4

SUPERIORITY

See also equality, excellence, one-upmanship, snobbery

1 My name is George Nathaniel Curzon,
I am a most superior person.
My face is pink, my hair is sleek,
I dine at Blenheim once a week.

Anonymous *The Masque of Balliol*

2 Spare your ships, and do not risk a battle; for these people are as much superior to your people in seamanship, as men to women.

Artemisia (fl. 480 BC) Carian queen of Halicarnassus and military leader. The people she was referring to were the Greeks. *The Persian Wars*, Bk. VIII (Herodotus)

3 The slave begins by demanding justice and ends by wanting to wear a crown. He must dominate in his turn.

Albert Camus (1913–60) French existentialist writer. *The Rebel*

4 The superior man is satisfied and composed; the mean man is always full of distress.

Confucius (K'ung Fu-tzu; 551–479 BC) Chinese philosopher. *Analects*

5 The superior man is distressed by his want of ability.

Confucius *Analects*

6 When you meet someone better than yourself, turn your thoughts to becoming his equal. When you meet someone not as good as you are, look within and examine your own self.

Confucius *Analects*

7 And lo! Ben Adhem's name led all the rest.

Leigh Hunt (1784–1859) British poet. *Abou Ben Adhem and the Angel*

8 Though I've belted you an' flayed you,
By the livin' Gawd that made you,
You're a better man than I am, Gunga Din!

Rudyard Kipling (1865–1936) Indian-born British writer. *Gunga Din*

9 Sir, you have the advantage of me.
– Not yet I haven't, but wait till I get you outside.

Groucho Marx (Julius Marx; 1895–1977) US comedian. *Monkey Business*

10 What men value in this world is not rights but privileges.

H. L. Mencken (1880–1956) US journalist. *Minority Report*

11 Considering the company I keep in this place, that is hardly surprising.

Robert Menzies (1894–1978) Australian prime minister. When accused of having a superiority complex in parliament. *Time*, 29 May 1978

12 Above the vulgar flight of common souls.

Arthur Murphy (1727–1805) Irish dramatist, writer, and actor. *Zenobia*, V

13 I teach you the Superman. Man is something that is to be surpassed.

Friedrich Wilhelm Nietzsche (1844–1900) German philosopher. *Thus Spake Zarathustra*

14 It is brought home to you…that it is only because miners sweat their guts out that superior persons can remain superior.

George Orwell (Eric Blair; 1903–50) British novelist. *The Road to Wigan Pier*, Ch. 2

15 My parents just didn't have that sense of innate superiority that the successful parents had.

Michael Palin (1943–) British actor and writer. *The Times*, 24 Feb 1990

16 'I believe I take precedence,' he said coldly; 'you are merely the club Bore: I am the club Liar.'

Saki (Hector Hugh Munro; 1870–1916) British writer. *A Defensive Diamond*

17 In the Country of the Blind the One-eyed Man is King.

H. G. Wells (1866–1946) British writer. *The Country of the Blind*

SUPERNATURAL

See also fairies

1 From ghoulies and ghosties and long-leggety beasties
And things that go bump in the night,
Good Lord, deliver us!

Anonymous Cornish prayer

2 Open Sesame!

The Arabian Nights (c. 1500) A collection of tales from the East. *The History of Ali Baba*

3 Thou shalt not suffer a witch to live.

Bible: Exodus 22:18

4 For my part, I have ever believed, and do now know, that there are witches.

Thomas Browne (1605–82) English physician and writer. *Religio Medici*, Pt. I

5 This time it vanished quite slowly, beginning with the end of the tail, and ending with the grin, which remained some time after the rest of it had gone.

Lewis Carroll (Charles Lutwidge Dodgson; 1832–98) British writer. Describing the Cheshire Cat. *Alice's Adventures in Wonderland*, Ch. 6

6 A savage place! as holy and enchanted
As e'er beneath a waning moon was haunted
By woman wailing for her demon-lover!

Samuel Taylor Coleridge (1772–1834) British poet. *Kubla Khan*

7 The girl is lost; she is burnt flesh.

Umberto Eco (1932–) Italian semiologist and writer. Referring to a suspected witch. *The Name of the Rose*

8 Religion
Has made an honest woman of the supernatural,
And we won't have it kicking over the traces again.

Christopher Fry (1907–) British dramatist. *The Lady's Not for Burning*, II

9 All argument is against it; but all belief is for it.

Samuel Johnson (1709–84) British lexicographer. Of the ghost of a dead person. *Life of Johnson* (J. Boswell), Vol. III

10 'La belle Dame sans Merci
Hath thee in thrall!'

John Keats (1795–1821) British poet. *La Belle Dame Sans Merci*

11 That old black magic has me in its spell.

Johnny Mercer (1909–76) US lyricist and composer. *That Old Black Magic*

12 Once upon a midnight dreary, while I pondered, weak and weary,
Over many a quaint and curious volume of forgotten lore,
While I nodded, nearly napping, suddenly there came a tapping,
As of some one gently rapping, rapping at my chamber door.

Edgar Allan Poe (1809–49) US poet and writer. *The Raven*

13 There are more things in heaven and earth, Horatio,
Than are dreamt of in your philosophy.

William Shakespeare (1564–1616) English dramatist. *Hamlet*, I:5

14 This supernatural soliciting
Cannot be ill; cannot be good.

William Shakespeare *Macbeth*, I:3

15 His face was a strong – a very strong – aquiline, with high bridge of the thin nose and peculiarly arched nostrils...The mouth...was fixed and rather cruel-looking, with peculiarly sharp white teeth; these protruded over the lips, whose remarkable ruddiness showed astonishing vitality in a man of his years.

Bram Stoker (1847–1912) Irish novelist. Referring to Count Dracula. *Dracula*, Ch. 2

16 His eyes flamed red with devilish passion; the great nostrils of the white aquiline nose opened wide and quivered at the edges; and the white sharp teeth, behind the full lips of the blood-dripping mouth, champed together like those of a wild beast.

Bram Stoker *Dracula*, Ch. 21

SUPERSTITION

See also luck

1 A dimple in the chin, a devil within.

Proverb

2 Meet on the stairs and you won't meet in heaven.

Proverb

3 One for sorrow, two for mirth; three for a wedding, four for a birth; five for silver, six for gold; seven for a secret, not to be told; eight for heaven, nine for hell; and ten for the devil's own sel.

Referring to magpies or crows; there are numerous variants.
Proverb

4 See a pin and pick it up, all the day you'll have good luck; see a pin and let it lie, you'll want a pin before you die.

Proverb

5 Third time lucky.

Proverb

6 (For all the Athenians and strangers which were there spent their time in nothing else, but either to tell, or to hear some new thing.)
Then Paul stood in the midst of Mars' hill, and said, Ye men of Athens, I perceive that in all things ye are too superstitious.
For as I passed by, and beheld your devotions, I found an altar with this inscription, TO THE UNKNOWN GOD. Whom therefore ye ignorantly

worship, him declare I unto you.
God that made the world and all things therein, seeing that he is Lord of heaven and earth, dwelleth not in temples made with hands.

Bible: Acts 17:21–24

7 Of course I don't believe in it. But I understand that it brings you luck whether you believe in it or not.

Niels Bohr (1885–1962) Danish physicist. When asked why he had a horseshoe on his wall. Attrib.

8 Superstition is the religion of feeble minds.

Edmund Burke (1729–97) British politician. *Reflections on the Revolution in France*

9 Superstition is the poetry of life.

Goethe (1749–1832) German poet and dramatist. *Sprüche in Prosa*, III

10 And some of the bigger bears try to pretend
That they came round the corner to look for a friend;
And they'll try to pretend that nobody cares
Whether you walk on the lines or the squares.

A. A. Milne (1882–1956) British writer. *When We Were Very Young*, 'Lines and Squares'

11 They say there is divinity in odd numbers, either in nativity, chance, or death.

William Shakespeare (1564–1616) English dramatist. *The Merry Wives of Windsor*, V:1

12 Superstition sets the whole world in flames; philosophy quenches them.

Voltaire (François-Marie Arouet; 1694–1778) French writer. *Dictionnaire philosophique*, 'Superstition'

SUPPORT

See also loyalty

1 He found him in a desert land, and in the waste howling wilderness; he led him about, he instructed him, he kept him as the apple of his eye.

Bible: Deuteronomy 32:10

2 The finest plans have always been spoiled by the littleness of those that should carry them out. Even emperors can't do it all by themselves.

Bertolt Brecht (1898–1956) German dramatist. *Mother Courage*, VI

3 Either back us or sack us.

James Callaghan (1912–) British politician and prime minister. Speech, Labour Party Conference, Brighton, 5 Oct 1977

4 Give me your arm, old Toad;
Help me down Cemetery Road.

Philip Larkin (1922–85) British poet. *The Whitsun Weddings*, 'Toads Revisited'

5 What I want is men who will support me when I am in the wrong.

Lord Melbourne (1779–1848) British statesman. Replying to someone who said he would support Melbourne as long as he was in the right. *Lord M.* (Lord David Cecil)

6 While I cannot be regarded as a pillar, I must be regarded as a buttress of the church, because I support it from the outside.

Lord Melbourne Attrib.

7 And so, tonight – to you, the great silent majority of my fellow Americans – I ask for your support.

Richard Milhous Nixon (1913–94) US President. On a plan for peace in Vietnam. Broadcast address, 3 Nov 1969

8 Ladies and gentleman, it takes more than one to make a ballet.

Ninette de Valois (Edris Stannus; 1898–) British ballet dancer and choreographer. *The New Yorker*

SURVIVAL

See also evolution, self-preservation

1 I haven't asked you to make me young again. All I want is to go on getting older.

Konrad Adenauer (1876–1967) German statesman. Replying to his doctor. Attrib.

2 It isn't important to come out on top; what matters is to come out alive.

Bertolt Brecht (1898–1956) German dramatist. *Jungle of Cities*

3 People are inexterminable – like flies and bed-bugs. There will always be some that survive in cracks and crevices – that's us.

Robert Frost (1875–1963) US poet. *The Observer*, 29 Mar 1959

4 Ideal mankind would abolish death, multiply itself million upon million, rear up city upon city save every parasite alive, until the accumulation of mere existence is swollen to a horror.

D. H. Lawrence (1885–1930) British novelist. *St. Mawr*

5 The perpetual struggle for room and food.

Thomas Robert Malthus (1766–1834) British clergyman and economist. *Essays on the Principle of Population*

6 Species do not evolve toward perfection, but quite the contrary. The weak, in fact, always prevail over the strong, not only because they are in the majority, but also because they are the more crafty.

Friedrich Nietzsche (1844–1900) German philosopher. *The Twilight of the Idols*

7 When you get to the end of your rope, tie a knot and hang on.

Franklin D. Roosevelt (1882–1945) US Democratic president. Attrib.

8 The thing-in-itself, the will-to-live, exists whole and undivided in every being, even in the tiniest; it is present as completely as in all that ever were, are, and will be, taken together.

Arthur Schopenhauer (1788–1860) German philosopher. *Parerga and Paralipomena*

9 This is the Law of the Yukon, that only the strong shall thrive;
That surely the weak shall perish, and only the Fit survive.

Robert William Service (1874–1958) Canadian poet. *The Law of the Yukon*

10 Survival of the fittest.

Herbert Spencer (1820–1903) British philosopher. *Principles of Biology*, Pt. III, Ch. 12

11 One can survive everything nowadays, except death.

Oscar Wilde (1854–1900) Irish-born British dramatist. *A Woman of No Importance*, I

SUSPICION

See also mistrust

1 Suspicions amongst thoughts are like bats amongst birds, they ever fly by twilight.

Francis Bacon (1561–1626) English philosopher. *Essays*, 'Of Suspicion'

2 He had the sort of convoluted mind that could attribute evil and devious motives to a bee-keeper offering him a pot of honey as a gift.

Hugh Cudlipp Referring to H. G. Bartholomew, editor of *The Daily Mirror*. *Walking on the Water*

3 I found a long gray hair on Kevin's jacket last night – If it's another woman's I'll kill him. If it's mine I'll kill myself.

Neil Simon (1927–) US playwright. *It Hurts Only When I Laugh*

4 By heaven, he echoes me,
As if there were some monster in his thought
Too hideous to be shown.

William Shakespeare (1564–1616) English dramatist. *Othello*, III:3

SWIFT, JONATHAN

(1667–1745) Irish-born Anglican priest who became a poet and satirist in London. He is remembered for his *Journal to Stella* (1710–13) and *A Tale of A Tub* (1704), but best of all for *Gulliver's Travels* (1726), written after his return to Dublin as dean of St Patrick's.

Quotations about Swift

1 He delivered Ireland from plunder and oppression; and showed that wit, confederated with truth, had such force as authority was unable to resist.

Samuel Johnson (1709–84) British lexicographer. Attrib.

2 A monster gibbering, shrieking and gnashing imprecations against mankind.

William Makepeace Thackeray (1811–63) British novelist. Attrib.

Quotations by Swift

3 Satire is a sort of glass, wherein beholders do generally discover everybody's face but their own.

The Battle of the Books, 'Preface'

4 'Tis an old maxim in the schools,
That flattery's the food of fools;
Yet now and then your men of wit
Will condescend to take a bit.

Cadenus and Vanessa

5 It is folly of too many to mistake the echo of a London coffee-house for the voice of the kingdom.

The Conduct of the Allies

6 I have heard of a man who had a mind to sell his house, and therefore carried a piece of brick in his pocket, which he shewed as a pattern to encourage purchasers.

The Drapier's Letters, 2 (4 Aug 1724)

7 I cannot but conclude the bulk of your natives to be the most pernicious race of little odious vermin that nature ever suffered to crawl upon the surface of the earth.

Referring to the English. *Gulliver's Travels*, 'Voyage to Brobdingnag', Ch. 6

8 Whoever could make two ears of corn or two blades of grass to grow upon a spot of ground where only one grew before would deserve better of mankind and do more essential service to his country than the whole race of politicians put together.

Gulliver's Travels, 'Voyage to Brobdingnag', Ch. 7

9 So, naturalist observe, a flea
Hath smaller fleas that on him prey,
And these have smaller fleas to bite 'em.
And so proceed *ad infinitum*.

On Poetry

10 Promises and pie-crust are made to be broken.

Polite Conversation, Dialogue 1

11 Bachelor's fare; bread and cheese, and kisses.

Polite Conversation, Dialogue 1

12 He was a bold man that first eat an oyster.

Polite Conversation, Dialogue 2

13 I never saw, heard, nor read, that the clergy were beloved in any nation where Christianity was the religion of the country. Nothing can render them popular, but some degree of persecution.

Thoughts on Religion

14 When a true genius appears in the world, you may know him by this sign, that the dunces are all in confederacy against him.

Thoughts on Various Subjects

15 What they do in heaven we are ignorant of; what they do *not* we are told expressly, that they neither marry, nor are given in marriage.

Thoughts on Various Subjects

16 I never wonder to see men wicked, but I often wonder to see them not ashamed.

Thoughts on Various Subjects

17 Most sorts of diversion in men, children, and other animals, are an imitation of fighting.

Thoughts on Various Subjects

18 Laws are like cobwebs, which may catch small flies, but let wasps and hornets break through.

Similar remarks have been made by others; *see* SHENSTONE; SOLON. *A Critical Essay upon the Faculties of the Mind*

19 For God's sake, madam, don't say that in England for if you do, they will surely tax it.

Responding to Lady Carteret's admiration for the quality of the air in Ireland. *Lives of the Wits* (H. Pearson)

20 I shall be like that tree; I shall die from the top.

Predicting his own mental decline on seeing a tree with a withered crown. *Lives of the Wits* (H. Pearson)

21 If Heaven had looked upon riches to be a valuable thing, it would not have given them to such a scoundrel.

Letter to Miss Vanhomrigh, 12–13 Aug 1720

22 Ah, a German and a genius! a prodigy, admit him!

Learning of the arrival in England of the German composer Handel: Swift's last words. Attrib.

SWITZERLAND

See also Europe

1 Since both its national products, snow and chocolate, melt, the cuckoo clock was invented solely in order to give tourists something solid to remember it by.

Alan Coren (1938–) British humorist and writer. *The Sanity Inspector*, 'And Though They Do Their Best'

2 The Swiss who are not a people so much as a neat clean quite solvent business.

William Faulkner (1897–1962) US novelist. *Intruder in the Dust*, Ch. 7

3 I look upon Switzerland as an inferior sort of Scotland.

Sydney Smith (1771–1845) British clergyman and essayist. Letter to Lord Holland, 1815

4 They say that if the Swiss had designed these mountains they'd be rather flatter.

Paul Theroux (1941–) US-born writer. Referring to the Alps. *The Great Railway Bazaar*, Ch. 28

5 In Italy for thirty years under the Borgias they had warfare, terror, murder, bloodshed – they produced Michelangelo, Leonardo da Vinci and the Renaissance. In Switzerland they had brotherly love, five hundred years of democracy and peace, and what did they produce…? The cuckoo clock.

Orson Welles (1915–85) US film actor. *The Third Man*

SYMPATHY

See also comfort

1 Sympathy – for all these people, for being foreigners – lay over the gathering like a woolly blanket; and no one was enjoying it at all.

Malcolm Bradbury (1932–) British academic and novelist. *Eating People is Wrong*, Ch. 2

2 To be sympathetic without discrimination is so very debilitating.

Ronald Firbank (1886–1926) British novelist. *Vainglory*

3 This is for all ill-treated fellows
Unborn and unbegot,
For them to read when they're in trouble
And I am not.

A. E. Housman (1859–1936) British poet. Epigraph, *More Poems*

4 She was a machine-gun riddling her hostess with sympathy.

Aldous Huxley (1894–1964) British novelist. *Mortal Coils*, 'The Gioconda Smile'

5 I can sympathize with people's pains, but not with their pleasures. There is something curiously boring about somebody else's happiness.

Aldous Huxley *Limbo*, 'Cynthia'

6 To show pity is felt as a sign of contempt because one has clearly ceased to be an object of *fear* as soon as one is pitied.

Friedrich Wilhelm Nietzsche (1844–1900) German philosopher. *The Wanderer and His Shadow*

7 I can sympathize with everything, except suffering.

Oscar Wilde (1854–1900) Irish-born British dramatist. *The Picture of Dorian Gray*, Ch. 3

SZASZ, THOMAS

(1920–) US psychiatrist and writer. His writings include *Pain and Pleasure* (1957) and *The Second Sin* (1974).

1 Men are rewarded and punished not for what they do, but rather for how their acts are defined. This is why men are more interested in better justifying themselves than in better behaving themselves.

The Second Sin

2 Traditionally, sex has been a very private, secretive activity. Herein perhaps lies its powerful force for uniting people in a strong bond. As we make sex less secretive, we may rob it of its power to hold men and women together.

The Second Sin

3 Formerly, when religion was strong and science weak, men mistook magic for medicine, now, when science is strong and religion weak, men mistake medicine for magic.

The Second Sin

4 A child becomes an adult when he realizes that he has a right not only to be right but also to be wrong.

The Second Sin

5 Happiness is an imaginary condition, formerly often attributed by the living to the dead, now usually attributed by adults to children, and by children to adults.

The Second Sin

6 The stupid neither forgive nor forget; the naive forgive and forget; the wise forgive but do not forget.

The Second Sin

7 Psychiatrists classify a person as neurotic if he suffers from his problems in living, and a psychotic if he makes others suffer.

The Second Sin

8 If you talk to God, you are praying; if God talks to you, you have schizophrenia. If the dead talk to you, you are a spiritualist; if God talks to you, you are a schizophrenic.

The Second Sin

9 Masturbation: the primary sexual activity of mankind. In the nineteenth century it was a disease; in the twentieth, it's a cure.

The Second Sin

T

TACITUS, CORNELIUS

(c. 55–c. 120 AD) Roman historian. He became governor of Asia (112–13 AD). His major works were the *Histories* and the *Annals*, surveying Roman history in the periods 69–96 AD and 14–68 AD, respectively.

1 They make a wilderness and call it peace.
Agricola, 30

2 It is part of human nature to hate the man you have hurt.
Agricola, 42

3 Love of fame is the last thing even learned men can bear to be parted from.
Histories, IV, 6

TACT

See also diplomacy

1 Leave well alone.
Proverb

2 Let sleeping dogs lie.
Proverb

3 Social tact is making your company feel at home, even though you wish they were.
Anonymous

4 One shouldn't talk of halters in the hanged man's house.
Miguel de Cervantes (1547–1616) Spanish novelist. *Don Quixote*, Pt. I, Ch. 25

5 Tact consists in knowing how far we may go too far.
Jean Cocteau (1889–1963) French poet and artist. In *Treasury of Humorous Quotations*

6 My advice was delicately poised between the cliché and the indiscretion.
Robert Runcie (1921–) British churchman; Archbishop of Canterbury (1980–91). Comment to the press concerning his advice to the Prince of Wales and Lady Diana Spencer on their approaching wedding, 13 July 1981

TALENT

See also genius, talent and genius

1 The English instinctively admire any man who has no talent and is modest about it.
James Agate (1877–1947) British theatre critic. Attrib.

2 Whom the gods wish to destroy they first call promising.
Cyril Connolly (1903–74) British journalist. *Enemies of Promise*, Ch. 3

3 I believe that since my life began
The most I've had is just
A talent to amuse.
Noël Coward (1899–1973) British dramatist. *Bitter Sweet*, 'If Love Were All'

4 Talent develops in quiet places, character in the full current of human life.
Goethe (1749–1832) German poet and dramatist. *Torquato Tasso*, I

5 Middle age snuffs out more talent than even wars or sudden deaths do.
Richard Hughes (1900–79) British writer. *The Fox in the Attic*

6 There is no substitute for talent. Industry and all the virtues are of no avail.
Aldous Huxley (1894–1964) British novelist. *Point Counter Point*

7 I think it's the most extraordinary collection of talent, of human knowledge, that has ever been gathered together at the White House – with the possible exception of when Thomas Jefferson dined alone.
John Fitzgerald Kennedy (1917–63) US statesman. Said at a dinner for Nobel Prizewinners, 29 Apr 1962.

8 It's not enough to be Hungarian, you must have talent too.
Alexander Korda (Sandor Kellner; 1893–1956) Hungarian-born British film director. *Alexander Korda* (K. Kulik)

9 Let our children grow tall, and some taller than others if they have it in them to do so.
Margaret Thatcher (1925–) British politician and prime minister. Speech, US tour, 1975

10 Talent is hereditary; it may be the common possession of a whole family (e.g., the Bach family); genius is not transmitted; it is never diffused, but is strictly individual.
Otto Weininger (1880–1903) *Sex and Character*, Pt. II, Ch. 4

TALENT AND GENIUS

See also genius, talent

1 It takes people a long time to learn the difference between talent and genius, especially ambitious young men and women.
Louisa May Alcott (1832–88) US novelist. *Little Women*, Pt. II

2 Mediocrity knows nothing higher than itself, but talent instantly recognizes genius.
Arthur Conan Doyle (1856–1930) British writer. *The Valley of Fear*

3 Genius does what it must, and Talent does what it can.
Owen Meredith (Robert Bulwer-Lytton, 1st Earl of Lytton; 1831–91) British statesman and poet. *Last Words of a Sensitive Second-rate Poet*

TALLEYRAND

(Charles Maurice de Talleyrand-Périgord; 1754–1838) French politician. During the French Revolution he attempted to reform the Church, but was excommunicated by the pope. He was foreign minister (1797–1807) and ambassador to Britain (1830–34).

1 I found there a country with thirty-two religions and only one sauce.

Referring to America. *Autant en apportent les mots* (Pedrazzini)

2 Accidentally.

Replying, during the reign of Louis Philippe, to the query 'How do you think this government will end?' *The Wheat and the Chaff* (F. Mitterrand)

3 This is the beginning of the end.

Referring to Napoleon's defeat at Borodino, 1812. Attrib.

4 Speech was given to man to disguise his thoughts.

Attrib.

5 Above all gentlemen, not too much zeal.

Attrib.

6 War is much too serious a thing to be left to military men.

Attrib.

7 Mistrust first impulses; they are nearly always good.

Sometimes attrib. to Count Montrond. Attrib.

8 Well, you might try getting crucified and rising again on the third day.

Giving his opinion upon what action might impress the French peasantry. Attrib.

TASTE

See also difference, individuality

1 Between friends differences in taste or opinions are irritating in direct proportion to their triviality.

W. H. Auden (1907–73) British poet. *The Dyer's Hand*

2 Good taste is better than bad taste, but bad taste is better than no taste.

Arnold Bennett (1867–1931) British novelist. *The Observer*, 'Sayings of the Week', 24 Aug 1930

3 Taste is the feminine of genius.

Edward Fitzgerald (1809–83) British poet. Letter to J. R. Lowell, Oct 1877

4 Our tastes greatly alter. The lad does not care for the child's rattle, and the old man does not care for the young man's whore.

Samuel Johnson (1709–84) British lexicographer. *Life of Johnson* (J. Boswell), Vol. II

5 What is food to one man is bitter poison to others.

Lucretius (Titus Lucretius Carus; c. 99–55 BC) Roman philosopher. *On the Nature of the Universe*, IV

6 The kind of people who always go on about whether a thing is in good taste invariably have very bad taste.

Joe Orton (1933–67) British dramatist. Attrib.

7 The play, I remember, pleas'd not the million; 'twas caviare to the general.

William Shakespeare (1564–1616) English dramatist. *Hamlet*, II:2

8 Do not do unto others as you would they should do unto you. Their tastes may not be the same.

George Bernard Shaw (1856–1950) Irish dramatist and critic. *Man and Superman*, 'Maxims for Revolutionists'

9 You had no taste when you married me.

Richard Brinsley Sheridan (1751–1816) British dramatist. *The School for Scandal*, I

TAXATION

1 Neither will it be, that a people overlaid with taxes should ever become valiant and martial.

John Aubrey (1626–97) English antiquary. *Essays*, 'Of the True Greatness of Kingdoms'

2 The hardest thing in the world to understand is income tax.

Albert Einstein (1879–1955) German-born US physicist. Attrib.

3 The greatest harm that cometh of a king's poverty is, that he shall by necessity be forced to find exquisite means of getting goods, as to put in default some of his subjects that be innocent, and upon the rich men more than the poor, because they may the better pay.

John Fortescue (c. 1394–1476) English jurist. *The Governance of England*

4 In this world nothing is certain but death and taxes.

Benjamin Franklin (1706–90) US scientist and statesman. Letter to Jean-Baptiste Leroy, 13 Nov 1789

5 *Excise.* A hateful tax levied upon commodities.

Samuel Johnson (1709–84) British lexicographer. *Dictionary of the English Language*

6 Sir, I now pay you this exorbitant charge, but I must ask you to explain to her Majesty that she must not in future look upon me as a source of income.

Charles Kemble (1775–1854) British actor. On being obliged to hand over his income tax to the tax collector. *Humour in the Theatre* (J. Aye)

7 The avoidance of taxes is the only pursuit that still carries any reward.

John Maynard Keynes (1883–1946) British economist. Attrib.

8 The Chancellor of the Exchequer is a man whose duties make him more or less of a taxing machine. He is intrusted with a certain amount of misery which it is his duty to distribute as fairly as he can.

Robert Lowe (1811–92) British lawyer and politician. Speech, House of Commons, 11 Apr 1870

9 It is ironic that the wife who made Britain great again, and who is the leader of the Western World, has to get her husband to sign her tax form.

Jacqui Lait Referring to Margaret Thatcher. Speech, Oct 1987

10 The taxpayer is someone who works for the federal government but doesn't have to take a civil service examination.

Ronald Reagan (1911–) US politician and president. Attrib.

11 There is no art which one government sooner learns of another than that of draining money from the pockets of the people.

Adam Smith (1723–90) Scottish economist. *The Wealth of Nations*

12 I am humbly following in your footsteps and having a row with the Government over the iniquity of the Marriage Tax in the form of supertax…our incomes being added together we are liable for supertax which we are refusing to pay on the grounds of morality as I consider in a Christian country it is an immoral and outrageous act to tax me because I am living in Holy matrimony instead of as my husband's mistress.

Marie Stopes (1880–1958) British birth-control campaigner. Letter to George Bernard Shaw, 29 June 1925

13 For God's sake, madam, don't say that in England for if you do, they will surely tax it.

Jonathan Swift (1667–1745) Irish-born Anglican priest and writer. Responding to Lady Carteret's admiration for the quality of the air in Ireland. *Lives of the Wits* (H. Pearson)

TAYLOR, A. J. P.

(1906–90) British historian. His best-known book is *The Origins of the Second World War* (1961).

1 History gets thicker as it approaches recent times.

English History, 1914–1945, Bibliography

2 He aspired to power instead of influence, and as a result forfeited both.

Referring to the British newspaper proprietor, Lord Northcliffe. *English History, 1914–1945*, Ch. 1

3 Communism continued to haunt Europe as a spectre – a name men gave to their own fears and blunders. But the crusade against Communism was even more imaginary than the spectre of Communism.

The Origins of the Second World War, Ch. 2

4 Lenin was the first to discover that capitalism 'inevitably' caused war; and he discovered this only when the First World War was already being fought. Of course he was right. Since every great state was capitalist in 1914, capitalism obviously 'caused' the First World War; but just as obviously it had 'caused' the previous generation of Peace.

The Origins of the Second World War, Ch. 6

5 A racing tipster who only reached Hitler's level of accuracy would not do well for his clients.

The Origins of the Second World War, Ch. 7

6 Psychoanalysts believe that the only 'normal' people are those who cause no trouble either to themselves or anyone else.

The Trouble Makers

7 He was what I often think is a dangerous thing for a statesman to be – a student of history; and like most of those who study history, he learned from the mistakes of the past how to make new ones.

Referring to Napoleon III. *The Listener*, 6 June 1963

8 They say that men become attached even to Widnes.

The Observer, 15 Sept 1963

TECHNOLOGY

See also progress, science

1 At sixty miles an hour the loudest noise in this new Rolls-Royce comes from the electric clock.

Anonymous Advertising slogan for Rolls-Royce

2 Give me a firm place to stand, and I will move the earth.

Archimedes (c. 287–212 BC) Greek mathematician. *On the Lever*

3 Man is a tool-using animal.

Thomas Carlyle (1795–1881) Scottish historian and essayist. *Sartor Resartus*, Bk. I, Ch. 5

4 Machines from the Maxim gun to the computer, are for the most part means by which a minority can keep free men in subjection.

Kenneth Clark (1903–83) British art historian. *Civilisation*

5 Any sufficiently advanced technology is indistinguishable from magic.

Arthur C. Clarke (1917–) British science-fiction writer. *The Lost Worlds of 2001*

6 Man is a tool-making animal.

Benjamin Franklin (1706–90) US scientist and statesman. *Life of Johnson* (J. Boswell), 7 Apr 1778

7 Our rockets can find Halley's comet and fly to Venus with amazing accuracy, but side by side with these scientific and technical triumphs is an obvious lack of efficiency in using scientific achievements for economic needs, and many Soviet household appliances are of poor quality.

Mikhail Gorbachov (1931–) Soviet statesman. *Perestroika*

8 One machine can do the work of fifty ordinary men. No machine can do the work of one extraordinary man.

Elbert Hubbard (1856–1915) US writer. *Roycroft Dictionary and Book of Epigrams*

9 That plastic Buddha jars out a Karate screech

Before the soft words with their spores
The cosmetic breath of the gravestone

Death invented the phone it looks like the altar of death

Ted Hughes (1930–) British poet. *Selected Poems 1957–1981*, 'Do not Pick up the Telephone'

10 Have strong suspicions that Crippen London cellar murderer and accomplice are amongst saloon passengers moustache taken off growing beard accomplice dressed as boy voice manner and build undoubtedly a girl both travelling as Mr and Master Robinson

Captain Kendall This was the first time a wireless telegraphy message from a ship at sea led to the arrest of criminals. Telegram to Scotland Yard, 22 July 1910

11 It was difficult to decide whether the system that produced the kettle was a miracle of human ingenuity and co-operation or a colossal waste of resources, human and natural. Would we all be better off boiling our water in a pot hung over an open fire? Or was it the facility to do such things at the touch of a button that freed men, and more particularly women, from servile labour and made it possible for them to become literary critics?

David Lodge (1935–) British writer. *Nice Work*, V

12 The new electronic interdependence recreates the world in the image of a global village.

Marshall McLuhan (1911–81) Canadian sociologist. *The Gutenberg Galaxy*

13 For tribal man space was the uncontrollable mystery. For technological man it is time that occupies the same role.

Marshall McLuhan *The Mechanical Bride*, 'Magic that Changes Mood'

14 The machine threatens all achievement.

Rainer Maria Rilke (1875–1926) Austrian poet. *Die Sonette an Orpheus*, II, 10

15 The technology of medicine has outrun its sociology.

Henry E. Sigerist (1891–1957) *Medicine and Human Welfare*, Ch. 3

16 Pylons, those pillars
Bare like nude giant girls that have no secret.

Stephen Spender (1909–) British poet. *The Pylons*

17 No man…who has wrestled with a self-adjusting card table can ever quite be the man he once was.

James Thurber (1894–1961) US humorist. *Let Your Mind Alone*, 'Sex ex Machina'

18 Sir, I have tested your machine. It adds new terror to life and makes death a long-felt want.

Herbert Beerbohm Tree (1853–1917) British actor and theatre manager. Referring to a gramophone. *Beerbohm Tree* (H. Pearson)

19 I see no reason to suppose that these machines will ever force themselves into general use.

Duke of Wellington (1769–1852) British general and statesman. Referring to steam locomotives. *Geoffrey Madan's Notebooks* (J. Gere)

TEETH

1 Removing the teeth will cure something, including the foolish belief that removing the teeth will cure everything.

Anonymous

2 For years I have let dentists ride roughshod over my teeth: I have been sawed, hacked, chopped, whittled, bewitched, bewildered, tattooed, and signed on again; but this is cuspid's last stand.

S. J. Perelman (1904–79) US humorous writer. *Crazy Like a Fox*, 'Nothing but the Tooth'

3 I'll dispose of my teeth as I see fit, and after they've gone, I'll get along. I started off living on gruel, and by God, I can always go back to it again.

S. J. Perelman *Crazy Like a Fox*, 'Nothing but the Tooth'

4 Certain people are born with natural false teeth.

Robert Robinson (1927–) British writer and broadcaster. BBC radio programme, *Stop the Week*, 1977

5 Adam and Eve had many advantages, but the principal one was that they escaped teething.

Mark Twain (Samuel Langhorne Clemens; 1835–1910) US writer. *The Tragedy of Pudd'nhead Wilson*, Ch. 4

6 To lose a lover or even a husband or two during the course of one's life can be vexing. But to lose one's teeth is a catastrophe.

Hugh Wheeler (1912–87) British-born US writer. *A Little Night Music*

TELEGRAMS

1 To hell with you. Offensive letter follows.

Anonymous Telegram to Sir Alec Douglas-Home

2 Winston's back.

Anonymous Signal to all ships of the Royal Navy from the Admiralty when Churchill was reappointed First Sea Lord, 3 Sept 1939

3 Streets full of water. Please advise.

Robert Benchley (1889–1945) US humorist. Telegram sent to his editor on arriving in Venice. Attrib.

4 Price of Herald three cents daily.

James Gordon Bennett (1841–1918) US editor. Telegram to William Randolph Hearst, when he heard that Hearst was trying to buy his paper. *The Life and Death of the Press Barons* (P. Brandon)

5 Nothing to be fixed except your performance.

Noël Coward (1899–1973) British dramatist. Replying to a telegram from the actress Gertrude Lawrence – 'Nothing wrong that can't be fixed' – referring to her part in Coward's play. *Private Lives. Noël Coward and his Friends*

6 Dear Mrs A., hooray hooray,
At last you are deflowered
On this as every other day
I love you. Noël Coward.

Noël Coward Telegram to Gertrude Lawrence on her marriage to Richard S. Aldrich

7 'Old Cary Grant fine. How you?'

Cary Grant (Archibald Leach; 1904–86) British-born US film star. Replying to a telegram sent to his agent inquiring: 'How old Cary Grant?' *The Filmgoer's Book of Quotes* (Leslie Halliwell)

8 ?

Victor Hugo (1802–85) French writer. The entire contents of a telegram sent to his publishers asking how *Les Misérables* was selling the reply was '!'. *The Literary Life* (R. Hendrickson)

9 Have strong suspicions that Crippen London cellar murderer and accomplice are amongst saloon passengers moustache taken off growing beard accomplice dressed as boy voice manner and build undoubtedly a girl both travelling as Mr and Master Robinson

Captain Kendall This was the first time a wireless telegraphy message from a ship at sea led to the arrest of criminals. Telegram to Scotland Yard, 22 July 1910

10 We have finished the job, what shall we do with the tools?

Haile Selassie (1892–1975) Emperor of Ethiopia. Telegram sent to Winston Churchill, mimicking his 'Give us the tools, and we will finish the job'. *Ambrosia and Small Beer*, Ch. 4 (Edward Marsh)

11 Reports of my death are greatly exaggerated.

Mark Twain (Samuel Langhorne Clemens; 1835–1910) US writer. On learning that his obituary had been published in the *New York Journal*. Cable to the Associated Press

12 Nurse unupblown.

Evelyn Waugh (1903–66) British novelist. Cable sent after he had failed, while a journalist serving in Ethiopia, to substantiate a rumour that an English nurse had been blown up in an Italian air raid. *Our Marvelous Native Tongue* (R. Claiborne)

13 No, no, Oscar, you forget. When you and I are together we never talk about anything except me.

James Whistler (1834–1903) US painter. Cable replying to Oscar Wilde's message: 'When you and I are together we never talk about anything except ourselves.' *The Gentle Art of Making Enemies*

TELEVISION

See also media, journalism

1 That's the sixty-four thousand dollar question.
Anonymous Title of US TV quizzes

2 There is a bias in television journalism. It is not against any particular party or point of view – it is a bias against *understanding*.
John Birt (1944–) British TV executive. This launched a series of articles written jointly with Peter Jay. *The Times*, 28 Feb 1975

3 Some television programs are so much chewing gum for the eyes.
John Mason Brown (1900–69) US critic. Interview, 28 July 1955

4 Television is for appearing on, not looking at.
Noël Coward (1899–1973) British dramatist. Attrib.

5 Why should people go out and pay to see bad films when they can stay at home and see bad television for nothing?
Samuel Goldwyn (Samuel Goldfish; 1882–1974) Polish-born US film producer. *The Observer*, 9 Sept 1956

6 TV...is our latest medium – we call it a medium because nothing's well done.
Ace Goodman (1899–) US writer. Letter to Groucho Marx, 1954. *The Groucho Letters*

7 Television – the drug of the nation
Breeding ignorance and feeding radiation.
The Disposable Heroes of Hiphoprisy US rap band. 'Television, the Drug of the Nation'

8 A medium, so called because it is neither rare nor well done.
Ernie Kovacs (1919–62) US entertainer. Referring to television. Attrib.

9 Television won't matter in your lifetime or mine.
Rex Lambert *The Listener*

10 I have had my aerials removed – it's the moral equivalent of a prostate operation.
Malcolm Muggeridge (1903–90) British writer. *Radio Times*, Apr 1981

TEMPTATION

1 Forbidden fruit is sweet.
Proverb

2 If you can't be good, be careful.
Proverb

3 I am not over-fond of resisting temptation.
William Beckford (1759–1844) British writer. *Vathek*

4 Blessed is the man that endureth temptation: for when he is tried, he shall receive the crown of life, which the Lord hath promised to them that love him.
Bible: James 1:12

5 All the deceits of the world, the flesh, and the devil.
The Book of Common Prayer *Morning Prayer, Prayer of St Chrysostom*

6 Not all that tempts your wand'ring eyes
And heedless hearts, is lawful prize;
Nor all, that glisters, gold.
Thomas Gray (1716–71) British poet. *Ode on the Death of a Favourite Cat*

7 'You oughtn't to yield to temptation.'
'Well, somebody must, or the thing becomes absurd.'
Anthony Hope (Sir Anthony Hope Hawkins; 1863–1933) British novelist. *The Dolly Dialogues*

8 ...with peaches and women, it's only the side next the sun that's tempting.
Ouida (Marie Louise de la Ramée; 1839–1908) British novelist. *Strathmore*

9 I never resist temptation because I have found that things that are bad for me never tempt me.
George Bernard Shaw (1856–1950) Irish dramatist and critic. *The Apple Cart*

10 I can resist everything except temptation.
Oscar Wilde (1854–1900) Irish-born British dramatist. *Lady Windermere's Fan*, I

11 The only way to get rid of a temptation is to yield to it.
Oscar Wilde Repeating a similar sentiment expressed by Clementina Stirling Graham (1782–1877). *The Picture of Dorian Gray*, Ch. 2

TENNYSON, ALFRED, LORD

(Baron Tennyson; 1809–92) British poet. He established his reputation with *Morte d'Arthur* (1842). Of his many other works, *In Memoriam* (1850), *The Charge of the Light Brigade* (1854), *Maud* (1855), and *The Idylls of the King* (1859) are outstanding. He became poet laureate in 1850.

Quotations about Tennyson

1 ... there was little about melancholia that he didn't know; there was little else that he did.
W. H. Auden (19079–73) British poet. *Selected Poems of Tennyson*, Introduction

2 Let school-miss Alfred vent her chaste delight
On 'darling little rooms so warm and bright.'
Edward Bulwer-Lytton (1803–73) British novelist and politician. Attrib.

3 Alfred is always carrying a bit of chaos round with him, and turning it into cosmos.
Thomas Carlyle (1795–1881) Scottish historian and essayist.

4 Tennyson was not Tennysonian.
Henry James (1843–1916) US novelist. *The Middle Years*

Quotations by Tennyson

5 And the stately ships go on
To their haven under the hill;
But O for the touch of a vanish'd hand,
And the sound of a voice that is still!
Break, Break, Break

6 For men may come and men may go
But I go on for ever.
The Brook

7 I come from haunts of coot and hern,
I make a sudden sally

And sparkle out among the fern,
To bicker down a valley.
The Brook

8 Half a league, half a league,
Half a league onward,
All in the valley of Death
Rode the six hundred.
The Charge of the Light Brigade

9 'Forward the Light Brigade!'
Was there a man dismay'd?
Not tho' the soldier knew
Some one had blunder'd:
Their's not to make reply,
Their's not to reason why,
Their's but to do and die:
Into the valley of Death
Rode the six hundred.
The Charge of the Light Brigade

10 Into the jaws of Death,
Into the mouth of Hell.
The Charge of the Light Brigade

11 Come not, when I am dead,
To drop thy foolish tears upon my grave,
To trample round my fallen head,
And vex the unhappy dust thou wouldst not save.
Come Not, When I Am Dead

12 Sunset and evening star,
And one clear call for me!
And may there be no moaning of the bar
When I put out to sea.
Crossing the Bar

13 God made the woman for the man,
And for the good and increase of the world.
Edwin Morris

14 Half light, half shade,
She stood, a sight to make an old man young.
The Gardener's Daughter

15 That a lie which is all a lie may be met and fought with outright,
But a lie which is part a truth is a harder matter to fight.
The Grandmother

16 Dreams are true while they last, and do we not live in dreams?
The Higher Pantheism

17 His honour rooted in dishonour stood,
And faith unfaithful kept him falsely true.
Idylls of the King, 'Lancelot and Elaine'

18 He makes no friend who never made a foe.
Idylls of the King, 'Lancelot and Elaine'

19 For man is man and master of his fate.
Idylls of the King, 'The Marriage of Geraint'

20 An arm
Rose up from out the bosom of the lake,
Clothed in white samite, mystic, wonderful.
Idylls of the King, 'The Passing of Arthur'

21 Authority forgets a dying king.
Idylls of the King, 'The Passing of Arthur'

22 For now I see the true old times are dead,
When every morning brought a noble chance,
And every chance brought out a noble knight.
Idylls of the King, 'The Passing of Arthur'

23 And slowly answer'd Arthur from the barge:
'The old order changeth, yielding place to new,
And God fulfils himself in many ways.'
Idylls of the King, 'The Passing of Arthur'

24 If thou shouldst never see my face again,
Pray for my soul. More things are wrought by prayer
Than this world dreams of.
Idylls of the King, 'The Passing of Arthur'

25 I am going a long way
With these thou seest – if indeed I go
(For all my mind is clouded with a doubt) –
To the island-valley of Avilion;
Where falls not hail, or rain, or any snow,
Nor ever wind blows loudly; but it lies
Deep-meadow'd, happy, fair with orchard lawns
And bowery hollows crown'd with summer sea,
Where I will heal me of my grievous wound.
Idylls of the King, 'The Passing of Arthur'

26 Our little systems have their day;
They have their day and cease to be.
In Memoriam A.H.H., Prologue

27 For words, like Nature, half reveal
And half conceal the Soul within.
In Memoriam A.H.H., V

28 I hold it true, whate'er befall;
I feel it, when I sorrow most;
'Tis better to have loved and lost
Than never to have loved at all.
In Memoriam A.H.H., XXVII

29 And so the Word had breath, and wrought
With human hands the creed of creeds
In loveliness of perfect deeds,
More strong than all poetic thought.
In Memoriam A.H.H., XXXVI

30 But what am I?
An infant crying in the night:
An infant crying for the light:
And with no language but a cry.
In Memoriam A.H.H., LIV

31 Are God and Nature then at strife
That Nature lends such evil dreams?
So careful of the type she seems,
So careless of the single life.
In Memoriam A.H.H., LV

32 Sleep, Death's twin-brother, knows not Death,
Nor can I dream of thee as dead.
In Memoriam A.H.H., LXVIII

33 I dreamed there would be Spring no more,
That Nature's ancient power was lost.
In Memoriam A.H.H., LXIX

34 So many worlds, so much to do,
So little done, such things to be.
In Memoriam A.H.H., LXXIII

35 Ring out, wild bells, to the wild sky,
The flying cloud, the frosty light:

The year is dying in the night;
Ring out, wild bells, and let him die.
In Memoriam A.H.H., CVI

36 'Tis held that sorrow makes us wise.
In Memoriam A.H.H., CXIII

37 My regret
Becomes an April violet,
And buds and blossoms like the rest.
In Memoriam A.H.H., CXV

38 One God, one law, one element,
And one far-off divine event,
To which the whole creation moves.
In Memoriam A.H.H., CXXXI

39 A simple maiden in her flower
Is worth a hundred coats-of-arms.
Lady Clara Vere de Vere, II

40 Kind hearts are more than coronets,
And simple faith than Norman blood.
Lady Clara Vere de Vere, VI

41 On either side the river lie
Long fields of barley and of rye,
That clothe the wold and meet the sky;
And thro' the field the road runs by
To many-tower'd Camelot.
The Lady of Shalott, Pt. I

42 Willows whiten, aspens quiver,
Little breezes dusk and shiver.
The Lady of Shalott, Pt. I

43 Or when the moon was overhead,
Came two young lovers lately wed;
'I am half sick of shadows,' said
The Lady of Shalott.
The Lady of Shalott, Pt. II

44 She has heard a whisper say,
A curse is on her if she stay
To look down to Camelot.
The Lady of Shalott, Pt. II

45 A bow-shot from her bower-eaves,
He rode between the barley-sheaves,
The sun came dazzling thro' the leaves
And flamed upon the brazen graves
Of bold Sir Lancelot.
The Lady of Shalott, Pt. III

46 'The curse is come upon me,' cried
The Lady of Shalott.
The Lady of Shalott, Pt. III

47 But Lancelot mused a little space;
He said, 'She has a lovely face;
God in his mercy lend her grace,
The Lady of Shalott.'
The Lady of Shalott, Pt. IV

48 Ah God! the petty fools of rhyme
That shriek and sweat in pigmy wars.
Literary Squabbles

49 Nourishing a youth sublime
With the fairy tales of science, and the long result of Time.
Locksley Hall

50 In the Spring a young man's fancy lightly turns to thoughts of love.
Locksley Hall

51 Such a one do I remember, whom to look at was to love.
Locksley Hall

52 So I triumphed ere my passion, sweeping thro' me, left me dry,
Left me with the palsied heart, and left me with the jaundiced eye.
Locksley Hall

53 Not with blinded eyesight poring over miserable books.
Locksley Hall

54 Time driveth onward fast,
And in a little while our lips are dumb.
Let us alone. What is it that will last?
All things are taken from us, and become
Portions and parcels of the dreadful Past.
The Lotos-Eaters, 'Choric Song'

55 Music that gentlier on the spirit lies,
Than tir'd eyelids upon tir'd eyes.
The Lotos-Eaters, 'Choric Song'

56 Come into the garden, Maud,
For the black bat, night, has flown,
Come into the garden, Maud,
I am here at the gate alone.
Maud, I

57 The rose was awake all night for your sake,
Knowing your promise to me;
The lilies and roses were all awake,
They sighed for the dawn and thee.
Maud, I

58 I embrace the purpose of God and the doom assigned.
Maud, III

59 But the churchmen fain would kill their church,
As the churches have kill'd their Christ.
Maud, V

60 You must wake and call me early, call me early, mother dear;
To-morrow 'ill be the happiest time of all the glad New-year;
Of all the glad New-year, mother, the maddest merriest day;
For I'm to be Queen o' the May, mother, I'm to be Queen o' the May.
The May Queen

61 The splendour falls on castle walls
And snowy summits old in story.
The Princess, III

62 Tears, idle tears, I know not what they mean,
Tears from the depth of some divine despair.
The Princess, IV

63 Dear as remembered kisses after death,
And sweet as those by hopeless fancy feign'd
On lips that are for others: deep as love,
Deep as first love, and wild with all regret;
O Death in Life, the days that are no more.
The Princess, IV

64 O tell her, brief is life but love is long.
The Princess, IV

65 Man is the hunter; woman is his game:
The sleek and shining creatures of the chase,
We hunt them for the beauty of their skins.
The Princess, V

66 Man for the field and woman for the hearth:
Man for the sword and for the needle she:
Man with the head and woman with the heart:
Man to command and woman to obey;
All else confusion.
The Princess, V

67 Home they brought her warrior dead.
She nor swoon'd, nor utter'd cry:
All her maidens, watching said,
'She must weep or she will die.'
The Princess, VI

68 The moans of doves in immemorial elms,
And murmuring of innumerable bees.
The Princess, VII

69 Revolts, republics, revolutions, most
No graver than a schoolboy's barring out.
The Princess, Conclusion

70 And they blest him in their pain, that they were not left to Spain,
To the thumbscrew and the stake, for the glory of the Lord.
The Revenge, III

71 A day less or more
At sea or ashore,
We die – does it matter when?
The Revenge, XI

72 My strength is as the strength of ten,
Because my heart is pure.
Sir Galahad

73 How sweet are looks that ladies bend
On whom their favours fall!
Sir Galahad

74 Battering the gates of heaven with storms of prayer.
St Simeon Stylites

75 The woods decay, the woods decay and fall,
The vapours weep their burthen to the ground,
Man comes and tills the field and lies beneath,
And after many a summer dies the swan.
Tithonus

76 The Gods themselves cannot recall their gifts.
Tithonus

77 A life that moves to gracious ends
Thro' troops of unrecording friends,
A deedful life, a silent voice.
To –, after reading a Life and Letters

78 God gives us love. Something to love
He lends us; but, when love is grown
To ripeness that on which it throve
Falls off, and love is left alone.
To J.S.

79 A still small voice spake unto me,
'Thou art so full of misery,
Were it not better not to be?'
The Two Voices

80 All experience is an arch wherethro'
Gleams that untravelled world, whose margin fades
For ever and for ever when I move.
Ulysses

81 We are not now that strength which in old days
Moved earth and heaven; that which we are, we are;
One equal temper of heroic hearts,
Made weak by time and fate, but strong in will
To strive, to seek, to find, and not to yield.
Ulysses

82 Every moment dies a man,
Every moment one is born.
The Vision of Sin

TERENCE

(Publius Terentius Afer; c. 190–159 BC) Roman poet.

1 Nothing has yet been said that's not been said before.
Eunuchus, Prologue

2 I am a man, I count nothing human foreign to me.
Heauton Timorumenos

3 Fortune favours the brave.
Phormio

4 So many men, so many opinions.
Phormio

TERESA, MOTHER

(Agnes Gonxha Bojaxhui; 1910–) Yugoslavian-born nun of Albanian parents. She founded the Order of the Missionaries of Charity in Calcutta, her nuns helping lepers, cripples, and the poor and aged throughout the world.

Quotations about Mother Teresa

1 She is among the last of the great missionary superstars.
Arun Chacko *The Times*, 14 Aug 1983

2 Without her faith Mother Teresa would be remarkable only for her ordinariness, and she rejoices in this fact for it is evidence of the power for which she and many others with her are but channels.
Kathryn Spink *For the Brotherhood of Man Under the Fatherhood of God*, 1981

Quotations by Mother Teresa

3 ...the poor are our brothers and sisters...people in the world who need love, who need care, who have to be wanted.
Time, 'Saints Among Us', 29 Dec 1975

4 Loneliness and the feeling of being unwanted is the most terrible poverty.
Time, 'Saints Among Us', 29 Dec 1975

5 To keep a lamp burning we have to keep putting oil in it.

Time, 'Saints Among Us', 29 Dec 1975

6 I would not give a baby from one of my homes for adoption to a couple who use contraception. People who use contraceptives do not understand love.

Radio broadcast, while on a visit to London

7 This is not for me. The honour is for the poor.

Said on receiving the Order of Merit, 24 Nov 1983. *The Sunday Times*, 3 Dec 1989

TERRY, DAME ELLEN

(1847–1928) British actress. She performed with Sir Henry Irving at the Lyceum Theatre and later managed the Imperial Theatre.

1 Wonderful women! Have you ever thought how much we all, and women especially, owe to Shakespeare for his vindication of women in these fearless, high-spirited, resolute and intelligent heroines?

Four Lectures on Shakespeare, 'The Triumphant Women'

2 Imagination! imagination! I put it first years ago, when I was asked what qualities I thought necessary for success upon the stage.

The Story of My Life, Ch. 2

3 What is a diary as a rule? A document useful to the person who keeps it, dull to the contemporary who reads it, invaluable to the student, centuries afterwards, who treasures it!

The Story of My Life, Ch. 14

4 How Henry would have loved it!

Referring to Sir Henry Irving's funeral. *Yesterdays* (Robert Hitchens)

TERTULLIAN

(c. 160–225 AD) Carthaginian father of the church. He was converted to Christianity (190 AD) but withdrew from the church in 207 to form a Montanist group. His many works include *Apologeticus* and *De Baptismo*.

1 The blood of the martyrs is the seed of the Church.

Traditional misquotation: more accurately, 'Our numbers increase as often as you cut us down: the blood of Christians is the seed.' *Apologeticus*, L

2 See how these Christians love one another.

Apologeticus, XXXIX

3 I believe because it is impossible.

The usual misquotation of 'It is certain because it is impossible.' *De Carne Christi*, V

THACKERAY, WILLIAM MAKEPEACE

(1811–63) British novelist. He became a full-time writer after the success of *Vanity Fair* (1847). Later novels include *Pendennis* (1848), *The History of Henry Esmond* (1852), and *The Newcomes* (1853).

1 He who meanly admires mean things is a Snob.

The Book of Snobs, Ch. 2

2 It is impossible, in our condition of society, not to be sometimes a Snob.

The Book of Snobs, Ch. 3

3 'Tis not the dying for a faith that's so hard, Master Harry – every man of every nation has done that – 'tis the living up to it that is difficult.

The History of Henry Esmond, Ch. 6

4 'Tis strange what a man may do, and a woman yet think him an angel.

The History of Henry Esmond, Ch. 7

5 Remember, it is as easy to marry a rich woman as a poor woman.

Pendennis, Ch. 28

6 The *Pall Mall Gazette* is written by gentlemen for gentlemen.

Pendennis, Ch. 32

7 There are some meannesses which are too mean even for man – woman, lovely woman alone, can venture to commit them.

A Shabby-Genteel Story, Ch. 3

8 Oh, Vanity of vanities!
How wayward the decrees of Fate are;
How very weak the very wise,
How very small the very great are!

Vanitas Vanitatum

9 This I set down as a positive truth. A woman with fair opportunities and without a positive hump, may marry whom she likes.

Vanity Fair, Ch. 4

10 Whenever he met a great man he grovelled before him, and my-lorded him as only a free-born Briton can do.

Vanity Fair, Ch. 13

11 If a man's character is to be abused, say what you will, there's nobody like a relation to do the business.

Vanity Fair, Ch. 19

12 I think I could be a good woman if I had five thousand a year.

Vanity Fair, Ch. 36

THATCHER, MARGARET

(1925–) British politician, prime minister 1979–90. Trained as a chemist and a barrister, she became a Conservative MP in 1959 and minister of education and science (1970–74).

Quotations about Thatcher

1 Paddy Ashdown is the first trained killer to be a party leader...Mrs Thatcher being self-taught.

Gilbert Archer, President of Edinburgh Chamber of Commerce. Remark, 1992

2 I am not prepared to accept the economics of a housewife.

Jacques Chirac (1932–) French politician. Remark, July 1987

3 She put back the chance of another woman

becoming PM by 50 years – by going over the top, becoming a dictator, having illusions of infallibility, which of course brought her downfall.

Ann Clwyd (1937–) British journalist and politician. *The Independent*, 28 Apr 1992

4 Mrs Thatcher is a woman of common views but uncommon abilities.

Julian Critchley (1930–) British Conservative politician. *The Times*, 'Profile: Margaret Thatcher'

5 Attila the Hen.

Clement Freud (1924–) British Liberal politician and broadcaster. BBC Radio programme, *The News Quiz*

6 She approaches the problems of our country with all the one-dimensional subtlety of a comic-strip.

Denis Healey (1917–) British Labour politician. Speech, House of Commons, 22 May 1979

7 It is rather like sending your opening batsman to the crease, only for them to find that their bats have been broken before the game by the team captain.

Geoffrey Howe (1926–) British Conservative politician. Referring, on his resignation from the government, to his differences with Margaret Thatcher over European policy; Thatcher had previously likened her position as prime minister to the captaincy of a cricket team. Speech, House of Commons, Nov 1990

8 She sounded like the *Book of Revelation* read out over a railway address system by a headmistress of a certain age wearing calico knickers.

Clive James (1939–) Writer and broadcaster, born in Australia. Attrib.

9 She only went to Venice because somebody told her she could walk down the middle of the street.

Neil Kinnock (1942–) British Labour politician.

10 When you see the way she was done down, you are bound to think that the people who organized the coup must have had a conscience bypass.

Neil Kinnock Referring to the removal of Margaret Thatcher as leader of the Conservative Party. Attrib.

11 A towering Prime Minister who left her country in a far better position than she found it.

John Major (1943–) British statesman. Following her resignation in 1990

12 I wish the old cow would resign.

Richard Needham (1942–) Northern Ireland Minister. Nov 1990

13 Margaret Thatcher's great strength seems to be the better people know her, the better they like her. But, of course, she has one great disadvantage – she is a daughter of the people and looks trim, as the daughters of the people desire to be. Shirley Williams has such an advantage over her because she's a member of the upper-middle class and can achieve that kitchen-sink-revolutionary look that one cannot get unless one has been to a really good school.

Rebecca West (Cicely Isabel Fairfield; 1892–1993) British novelist and journalist. Said in an interview with Jilly Cooper. *The Sunday Times*, 25 July 1976

Quotations by Thatcher

14 I wasn't lucky. I deserved it.

Said after receiving school prize, aged nine. Attrib.

15 I'm not hard – I'm frightfully soft. But I will not be hounded.

Daily Mail, 1972

16 Let our children grow tall, and some taller than others if they have it in them to do so.

Speech, US tour, 1975

17 Britain is no longer in the politics of the pendulum, but of the ratchet.

Speech, Institute of Public Relations, 1977

18 I love argument, I love debate. I don't expect anyone just to sit there and agree with me, that's not their job.

The Times, 1980

19 If a woman like Eva Péron with no ideals can get that far, think how far I can go with all the ideals that I have.

Referring to the wife of the Argentinian statesman, Juan Péron. She was famous for her charity work. *The Sunday Times*, 1980

20 To those waiting with bated breath for that favourite media catchphrase, the U-turn, I have only one thing to say.
You turn if you want to. The lady's not for turning.

Speech, Conservative Party Conference, 1980

21 There is no easy popularity in that but I believe people accept there is no alternative.

The oft-used phrase 'There is no alternative' led to the acronymic nickname 'TINA'. Speech, Conservative Women's Conference, 21 May 1980

22 No one would have remembered the Good Samaritan if he'd only had good intentions. He had money as well.

Television interview, 6 Jan 1986

23 The battle for women's rights has been largely won.

The Guardian, 1982

24 Pennies do not come from heaven. They have to be earned here on earth.

The Sunday Telegraph, 1982

25 Victorian values...were the values when our country became great.

Television interview, 1982

26 Oh. I have got lots of human weaknesses, who hasn't?

The Times, 1983

27 State socialism is totally alien to the British character.

The Times, 1983

28 I am painted as the greatest little dictator, which is ridiculous – you always take some consultations.

The Times, 1983

29 We are the true peace movement.

The Times, 1983

30 And what a prize we have to fight for: no less than the chance to banish from our land the dark divisive clouds of Marxist socialism.

Speech, Scottish Conservative Conference, 1983

31 Young people ought not to be idle. It is very bad for them.

The Times, 1984

32 I love being at the centre of things.

Reader's Digest, 1984

33 This was the day I was meant not to see.

On her feelings the Sunday after she had escaped death in the IRA bomb explosion at the Grand Hotel, Brighton. TV interview, Oct 1984

34 I think, historically, the term 'Thatcherism' will be seen as a compliment.

Remark, Oct 1985

35 I am certain that we will win the election with a good majority. Not that I am ever over-confident.

Evening Standard, 1987

36 There is no such thing as Society. There are individual men and women, and there are families.

Woman's Own, 31 Oct 1987

37 I think I have become a bit of an institution – you know, the sort of thing people expect to see around the place.

Remark, July 1987

38 I don't mind how much my ministers talk – as long as they do what I say.

The Times, 1987

39 Had I faltered, we would have neither the success nor international reputation we have. Yet when a woman is strong, she is strident. If a man is strong, he's a good guy.

The Times, 19 Nov 1990

40 Having consulted widely among colleagues I have concluded that the unity of the party and the prospects of victory in a general election would be better served if I stood down to enable cabinet colleagues to enter the ballot for leadership.

The Times, 23 Nov 1990

41 It's a funny old world.

Remark, Nov 1990, after informing the Cabinet of her decision to withdraw from the Conservative Party leadership election

42 I think Essex Man will vote for a Conservative government.

Referring to the imminent British general election. *The Independent*, 2 Apr 1992

THEATRE

See also acting, actors, audiences, criticism, literature, plays, Shakespeare

1 The reason why Absurdist plays take place in No Man's Land with only two characters is primarily financial.

Arthur Adamov (1908–70) Russian-born French dramatist. Said at the Edinburgh International Drama Conference, 13 Sept 1963

2 It's one of the tragic ironies of the theatre that only one man in it can count on steady work – the night watchman.

Tallulah Bankhead (1903–68) US actress. *Tallulah*, Ch. 1

3 The complexities of poetry are destroyed by the media. In the theatre, spoken language can be defended and expanded.

Howard Barker (1946–) British playwright. *The Times*, 3 Jan 1990

4 Drama is the back-stairs of the intellect. Philosophers and historians go in by the front door, but playwrights and novelists sneak up the back stairs with their more disreputable luggage.

Alan Bennett (1934–) British playwright. *The Sunday Times*, 24 Nov 1991

5 Tragedy is if I cut my finger. Comedy is if I walk into an open sewer and die.

Mel Brooks (Melvyn Kaminsky; 1926–) US film director. *New Yorker*, 30 Oct 1978

6 All tragedies are finish'd by a death,
All comedies are ended by a marriage.

Lord Byron (1788–1824) British poet. *Don Juan*, III

7 You know, I go to the theatre to be entertained...I don't want to see plays about rape, sodomy and drug addiction...I can get all that at home.

Peter Cook (1937–) British writer and entertainer. *The Observer*, caption to cartoon, 8 July 1962

8 Don't put your daughter on the stage, Mrs Worthington.

Noël Coward (1899–1973) British dramatist. Song title

9 Farce is the essential theatre. Farce refined becomes high comedy: farce brutalized becomes tragedy.

Gordon Craig (1872–1966) British actor. *The Story of my Days*

10 We participate in a tragedy; at a comedy we only look.

Aldous Huxley (1894–1964) British novelist. *The Devils of Loudon*, Ch. 11

11 Drama never changed anybody's mind about anything.

David Mamet (1947–) US playwright. *The Times*, 15 Sept 1993

12 I never deliberately set out to shock, but when people don't walk out of my plays I think there is something wrong.

John Osborne (1929–) British dramatist. *The Observer*, 'Sayings of the Week', 19 Jan 1975

13 I depict men as they ought to be, but Euripides portrays them as they are.

Sophocles (c. 496–406 BC) Greek dramatist. *Poetics* (Aristotle)

14 The bad end unhappily, the good unluckily. That is what tragedy means.

Tom Stoppard (1937–) Czech-born British dramatist. *Rosencrantz and Guildenstern Are Dead*, II

15 I would just like to mention Robert Houdin who in the eighteenth century invented the vanishing bird-cage trick and the theater matinée – may he rot and perish. Good afternoon.

Orson Welles (1915–85) US film actor. Addressing the audience at the end of a matinée performance. *Great Theatrical Disasters* (G. Brandreth)

THEFT

See also crime

1 The fault is great in man or woman

Who steals a goose from off a common;
But what can plead that man's excuse
Who steals a common from a goose?

Anonymous *The Tickler Magazine*, 1 Feb 1821

2 They will steal the very teeth out of your mouth as you walk through the streets. I know it from experience.

William Arabin (1773–1841) British judge. Referring to the people of Uxbridge. *Arabinesque at Law* (Sir R. Megarry)

3 Prisoner, God has given you good abilities, instead of which you go about the country stealing ducks.

William Arabin *Arabinesque at Law* (Sir R. Megarry)

4 I am laughing to think what risks you take to try to find money in a desk by night where the legal owner can never find any by day.

Honoré de Balzac (1799–1850) French novelist. Said on waking to find a burglar in the room. Attrib.

5 Stolen sweets are best.

Colley Cibber (1671–1757) British actor and dramatist. *The Rival Fools*, I

6 Travel light and you can sing in the robber's face.

Juvenal (Decimus Junius Juvenalis; 60–130 AD) Roman satirist. *Satires*, X

7 Stolen sweets are always sweeter,
Stolen kisses much completer,
Stolen looks are nice in chapels,
Stolen, stolen, be your apples.

Hunt Leigh (1784–1859) British poet. *Song of Fairies Robbing an Orchard*

THEORY

See also ideas

1 Medical theories are most of the time even more peculiar than the facts themselves.

August Bier (1861–1949) Aphorism

2 A thing may look specious in theory, and yet be ruinous in practice; a thing may look evil in theory, and yet be in practice excellent.

Edmund Burke (1729–97) British politician. Impeachment of Warren Hastings, 19 Feb 1788

3 A theory can be proved by experiment; but no path leads from experiment to the birth of a theory.

Albert Einstein (1879–1955) German-born US physicist. *The Sunday Times*, 18 July 1976

4 Don't confuse *hypothesis* and *theory*. The former is a possible explanation; the latter, the correct one. The establishment of theory is the very purpose of science.

Martin H. Fischer (1879–1962) *Fischerisms* (Howard Fabing and Ray Marr)

5 For hundreds of pages the closely-reasoned arguments unroll, axioms and theorems interlock. And what remains with us in the end? A general sense that the world can be expressed in closely-reasoned arguments, in interlocking axioms and theorems.

Michael Frayn (1933–) British journalist and writer. *Constructions*

6 Factual evidence can never 'prove' a hypothesis; it can only fail to disprove it, which is what we generally mean when we say, somewhat inexactly, that the hypothesis is 'confirmed' by experience.

Milton Friedman (1912–) US economist. *Essays in Positive Economics*

7 Dear friend, theory is all grey,
And the golden tree of life is green.

Goethe (1749–1832) German poet and dramatist. *Faust*, Pt. I

8 You know very well that unless you're a scientist, it's much more important for a theory to be shapely, than for it to be true.

Christopher Hampton (1946–) British writer and dramatist. *The Philanthropist*, 1

9 A first rate theory predicts; a second rate theory forbids, and a third rate theory explains after the event.

A. I. Kitaigorodskii *Harvest of a Quiet Eye*

10 Those who are enamoured of practice without science are like a pilot who goes into a ship without rudder or compass and never has any certainty where he is going.
Practice should always be based upon a sound knowledge of theory.

Leonardo da Vinci (1452–1519) Italian artist, sculptor, architect, and engineer. *The Notebooks of Leonardo da Vinci* (Edward MacCurdy)

11 It is a good morning exercise for a research scientist to discard a pet hypothesis every day before breakfast. It keeps him young.

Konrad Lorenz (1903–89) Austrian zoologist. *On Aggression*, Ch. 2

12 Theory, glamorous mother of the drudge experiment.

Harlan Mayer, Jr. *Physics for the Inquiring Mind*

13 Physicians are inclined to engage in hasty generalizations. Possessing a natural or acquired distinction, endowed with a quick intelligence, an elegant and facile conversation...the more eminent they are...the less leisure they have for investigative work...Eager for knowledge...they are apt to accept too readily attractive but inadequately proven theories.

Louis Pasteur (1822–95) French scientist. *Études sur la bière*, Ch. 3

14 In making theories always keep a window open so that you can throw one out if necessary.

Béla Schick (1877–1967) Austrian pediatrician. *Aphorisms and Facetiae of Béla Schick* (I. J. Wolf)

15 When the torrent sweeps a man against a boulder, you must expect him to scream, and you need not be surprised if the scream is sometimes a theory.

Robert Louis Stevenson (1850–94) Scottish writer. *Virginibus Puerisque*

THINKING

See also intellect, intelligence, mind, philosophy

1 I have always found that the man whose second thoughts are good is worth watching.

J. M. Barrie (1860–1937) British novelist and dramatist. *What Every Woman Knows*, III

2 He can't think without his hat.

Samuel Beckett (1906–89) Irish novelist and dramatist. *Waiting for Godot*

3 Mirrors should think longer before they reflect.

Jean Cocteau (1889–1963) French poet and artist. *The Sunday Times*, 20 Oct 1963

4 *Cogito, ergo sum.*
I think, therefore I am.

René Descartes (1596–1650) French philosopher. *Le Discours de la méthode*

5 There was a pause – just long enough for an angel to pass, flying slowly.

Ronald Firbank (1886–1926) British novelist. *Vainglory*, Ch. 6

6 It would not be at all a bad thing if the elite of the medical world would be a little less clever, and would adopt a more primitive method of thinking, and reason more as children do.

George Groddeck (1866–1934) *The Book of the It*, Letter XII

7 The most fluent talkers or most plausible reasoners are not always the justest thinkers.

William Hazlitt (1778–1830) British essayist. *On Prejudice*

8 Most of one's life…is one prolonged effort to prevent oneself thinking.

Aldous Huxley (1894–1964) British novelist. *Mortal Coils*, 'Green Tunnels'

9 Meditation is not a means to an end. It is both the means and the end.

Jiddu Krishnamurti (1895–1985) Indian Hindu philosopher. *The Penguin Krishnamurti Reader*

10 The brain has muscles for thinking as the legs have muscles for walking.

Julien Offroy de la Mettrie (1709–51) *L'Homme machine*

11 His thoughts, few that they were, lay silent in the privacy of his head.

Spike Milligan (1918–) British comedian. *Puckoon*, Ch. 1

12 You can't think rationally on an empty stomach, and a whole lot of people can't do it on a full one either.

Lord Reith (1889–1971) British administrator and first director general of the BBC. Attrib.

13 One of the worst diseases to which the human creature is liable is its disease of thinking.

John Ruskin (1819–1900) British art critic and social reformer. *The Political Economy of Art*, 'A Joy For Ever'

14 People don't seem to realize that it takes time and effort and preparation to think. Statesmen are far too busy making speeches to think.

Bertrand Russell (1872–1970) British philosopher. *Kenneth Harris Talking To:* 'Bertrand Russell' (Kenneth Harris)

15 Many people would sooner die than think. In fact they do.

Bertrand Russell *Thinking About Thinking* (A. Flew)

16 My thought is *me*: that is why I can't stop. I exist by what I think…and I can't prevent myself from thinking.

Jean-Paul Sartre (1905–80) French writer. *Nausea*

17 There is nothing either good or bad, but thinking makes it so.

William Shakespeare (1564–1616) English dramatist. *Hamlet*, II:2

18 Thinking is to me the greatest fatigue in the world.

John Vanbrugh (1664–1726) English architect and dramatist. *The Relapse*, II:1

19 Great thoughts come from the heart.

Marquis de Vauvenargues (1715–47) French soldier and writer. *Réflexions et maximes*

20 Thinking is the most unhealthy thing in the world, and people die of it just as they die of any other disease.

Oscar Wilde (1854–1900) Irish-born British writer and wit. *The Decay of Lying*

21 In order to draw a limit to thinking, we should have to be able to think both sides of this limit.

Ludwig Wittgenstein (1889–1951) Austrian philosopher. *Tractatus Logico-Philosophicus*, Preface

THIRST

See also alcohol, desire, drinks, hunger

1 There are two reasons for drinking; one is, when you are thirsty, to cure it; the other, when you are not thirsty, to prevent it…Prevention is better than cure.

Thomas Love Peacock (1785–1866) British novelist. *Melincourt*

2 I drink for the thirst to come.

François Rabelais (1483–1553) French satirist. *Gargantua*, Bk. I, Ch. 5

3 As pants the hart for cooling streams
When heated in the chase.

Nahum Tate (1652–1715) Irish-born English poet. *New Version of the Psalms*, 'As Pants the Hart'

THOMAS, DYLAN

(1914–53) Welsh poet. His collections include *18 Poems* (1934) and *Deaths and Entrances* (1946). His radio play *Under Milk Wood* (1954) is also well known. His early death resulted from alcoholism.

Quotations about Thomas

1 The first time I saw Dylan Thomas I felt as if Rubens had suddenly taken it into his head to paint a youthful Silenus.

Edith Sitwell (1887–1964) British poet and writer. *Taken Care of: An Autobiography*

2 He was a detestable man. Men pressed money on him, and women their bodies. Dylan took both with equal contempt. His great pleasure was to humiliate people.

A. J. P. Taylor (1906–90) British historian. *Autobiography*

Quotations by Thomas

3 Though they go mad they shall be sane,
Though they sink through the sea they shall rise again.
Though lovers be lost love shall not;
And death shall have no dominion.

And death shall have no dominion

4 I, born of flesh and ghost, was neither
A ghost nor man, but mortal ghost.
And I was struck down by death's feather.
Before I knocked

5 These poems, with all their crudities, doubts, and confusions, are written for the love of Man and in praise of God, and I'd be a damn' fool if they weren't.
Collected Poems, Note

6 When *I* take up assassination, I shall start with the surgeons in this city and work *up* to the gutter.
The Doctor and the Devils, 88

7 Do not go gentle into that good night,
Old age should burn and rave at close of day;
Rage, rage, against the dying of the light.
Do not go gentle into that good night

8 Now as I was young and easy under the apple boughs
About the lilting house and happy as the grass was green.
Fern Hill

9 Time held me green and dying
Though I sang in my chains like the sea.
Fern Hill

10 The force that through the green fuse drives the flower
Drives my green age.
The force that through the green fuse drives the flower

11 The hand that signed the treaty bred a fever,
And famine grew, and locusts came;
Great is the hand that holds dominion over
Man by a scribbled name.
The hand that signed the paper

12 The hunchback in the park
A solitary mister
Propped between trees and water.
The hunchback in the park

13 And the wild boys innocent as strawberries.
The hunchback in the park

14 Light breaks where no sun shines;
Where no sea runs, the waters of the heart
Push in their tides.
Light breaks where no sun shines

15 I missed the chance of a lifetime, too. Fifty lovelies in the rude and I'd left my Bunsen burner home.
Portrait of the Artist as a Young Dog, 'One Warm Saturday'

16 After the first death, there is no other.
A Refusal to Mourn the Death, by Fire, of a Child in London

17 This bread I break was once the oat,
This wine upon a foreign tree
Plunged in its fruit;
Man in the day or wind at night
Laid the crops low, broke the grape's joy.
This bread I break

18 It is spring, moonless night in the small town, starless and bible black.
Under Milk Wood

19 MR PRITCHARD. I must dust the blinds and then I must raise them.
MRS OGMORE-PRITCHARD. And before you let the sun in, mind it wipes its shoes.
Under Milk Wood

20 Gomer Owen who kissed her once by the pigsty when she wasn't looking and never kissed her again although she was looking all the time.
Under Milk Wood

21 Sleeping as quiet as death, side by wrinkled side, toothless, salt and brown, like two old kippers in a box.
Under Milk Wood

22 The hands of the clock have stayed still at half past eleven for fifty years. It is always opening time in the Sailors Arms.
Under Milk Wood

23 Chasing the naughty couples down the grassgreen gooseberried double bed of the wood.
Under Milk Wood

24 Every night of her married life she has been late for school.
Under Milk Wood

25 Oh, isn't life a terrible thing, thank God?
Under Milk Wood

26 Oh I'm a martyr to music.
Under Milk Wood

27 ...his nicotine eggyellow weeping walrus Victorian moustache worn thick and long in memory of Doctor Crippen.
Under Milk Wood

28 Portraits of famous bards and preachers, all fur and wool from the squint to the kneecaps.
Under Milk Wood

29 It is a winter's tale
That the snow blind twilight ferries over the lakes
And floating fields from the farm in the cup of the vales.
A Winter's Tale

30 The land of my fathers. My fathers can have it.
Referring to Wales. *Dylan Thomas* (John Ackerman)

31 Somebody's boring me, I think it's me.
Remark made after he had been talking continuously for some time. *Four Absentees* (Rayner Heppenstall)

32 Too many of the artists of Wales spend too much time about the position of the artist of Wales. There is only one position for an artist anywhere: and that is, upright.
New Statesman, 18 Dec 1964

THOMAS, GWYN

(1913–81) British writer and dramatist. His novels include *The Dark Philosophers* (1946), *Now Lead Us Home* (1952), and *The Sky of Our Lives* (1972). His best-known plays are *The Keep* (1961) and *Jackie the Jumper* (1962).

1 I wanted a play that would paint the full face of sensuality, rebellion and revivalism. In South Wales these three phenomena have played second fiddle only to the Rugby Union which is a distillation of all three.

Jackie the Jumper (Introduction), 'Plays and Players' 19 Jan 1963

2 My life's been a meeting, Dad, one long meeting. Even on the few committees I don't yet belong to, the agenda winks at me when I pass.

The Keep, I

3 A bit like God in his last years, the Alderman.

The Keep, I

4 Her first economic drive will be to replace X-ray by hearsay.

The Keep, II

5 There are still parts of Wales where the only concession to gaiety is a striped shroud.

Punch, 18 June 1958

THOREAU, HENRY DAVID

(1817–62) US writer. He is best known for *Walden* (1854), an account of his year spent as a recluse in the Walden woods in Massachusetts. He also wrote poetry and many essays, including one on *Civil Disobedience*.

Quotations about Thoreau

1 Whatever question there may be of his talent, there can be none I think of his genius. It was a slim and crooked one, but it was eminently personal.

Henry James (1843–1916) US novelist. *Hawthorne*

2 I love Henry, but I cannot like him; and as for taking his arm, I should as soon think of taking the arm of an elm tree.

Remark by an unknown friend

Quotations by Thoreau

3 Under a government which imprisons any unjustly, the true place for a just man is also a prison.

Civil Disobedience

4 The most attractive sentences are not perhaps the wisest, but the surest and soundest.

Journal, 1842

5 Whatever sentence will bear to be read twice, we may be sure was thought twice.

Journal, 1842

6 Some circumstantial evidence is very strong, as when you find a trout in the milk.

Journal, 1850

7 What men call social virtues, good fellowship, is commonly but the virtue of pigs in a litter, which lie close together to keep each other warm. It brings men together in crowds and mobs in bar-rooms and elsewhere, but it does not deserve the name of virtue.

Journal, 1852

8 As if you could kill time without injuring eternity.

Walden, 'Economy'

9 The mass of men lead lives of quiet desperation.

Walden, 'Economy'

10 I have lived some thirty years on this planet, and I have yet to hear the first syllable of valuable or even earnest advice from my seniors.

Walden, 'Economy'

11 There are now-a-days professors of philosophy but not philosophers.

Walden, 'Economy'

12 As for doing good, that is one of the professions which are full.

Walden, 'Economy'

13 Beware of all enterprises that require new clothes.

Walden, 'Economy'

14 I never found the companion that was so companionable as solitude.

Walden, 'Solitude'

15 The three-o'-clock in the morning courage, which Bonaparte thought was the rarest.

Walden, 'Sounds'

16 Our life is frittered away by detail…Simplify, simplify.

Walden, 'Where I Lived, and What I Lived For'

17 Time is but the stream I go a-fishing in.

Walden, 'Where I Lived, and What I Lived For'

18 I once had a sparrow alight upon my shoulder for a moment while I was hoeing in a village garden, and I felt that I was more distinguished by that circumstance than I should have been by any epaulet I could have worn.

Walden, 'Winter Animals'

19 It takes two to speak the truth – one to speak, and another to hear.

A Week on the Concord and Merrimack Rivers

20 Not that the story need be long, but it will take a long while to make it short.

Letter, 16 Nov 1867

21 One world at a time.

On being asked his opinion of the hereafter. Attrib.

22 I did not know that we had ever quarrelled.

On being urged to make his peace with God. Attrib.

23 Yes – around Concord.

On being asked whether he had travelled much. Concord, in Massachusetts, is the town where he was born, grew up, and lived most of his life. Attrib.

THREATS

1 Today we were unlucky. But remember, we have only to be lucky once. You will have to be lucky always.

Anonymous Telephone call from the IRA following their unsuccessful attempt to blow up Margaret Thatcher and other ministers at the Grand Hotel, Brighton, in 1984

2 Violet Elizabeth dried her tears. She saw that they were useless and she did not believe in wasting her effects. 'All right,' she said calmly, 'I'll thcream then. I'll thcream, an' thcream, an' thcream till I'm thick.'

Richmal Crompton (Richmal Crompton Lamburn; 1890–1969) British writer. Violet Elizabeth Bott, a character in the *William* books, had both a lisp and an exceptional ability to get her own way. *Just William*

3 If you start throwing hedgehogs under me, I shall throw two porcupines under you.

Nikita Khrushchev (1894–1971) Soviet statesman. *The Observer*, 'Sayings of the Week', 10 Nov 1963

4 I'll make him an offer he can't refuse.

Mario Puzo (1920–) US novelist. *The Godfather*

5 After I die, I shall return to earth as a gatekeeper of a bordello and I won't let any of you – not a one of you – enter!

Arturo Toscanini (1867–1957) Italian conductor. Rebuking an incompetent orchestra. *The Maestro: The Life of Arturo Toscanini* (Howard Taubman)

THRIFT

See also extravagance, money

1 A penny saved is a penny earned.

Proverb

2 Keep something for a rainy day.

Proverb

3 Penny wise, pound foolish.

Proverb

4 Many a mickle makes a muckle.

Proverb

5 I knew once a very covetous, sordid fellow, who used to say, 'Take care of the pence, for the pounds will take care of themselves.'

Earl of Chesterfield (1694–1773) English statesman. Possibly referring to William Lowndes. Letter to his son, 6 Nov 1747

6 …we owe something to extravagance, for thrift and adventure seldom go hand in hand.

Jennie Jerome Churchill (1854–1921) US-born British hostess and writer. *Pearson's*, 'Extravagance'

7 Thrift has nearly killed her on several occasions, through the agency of old sausages, slow-punctured tyres, rusty blades.

Margaret Drabble (1939–) British novelist. *The Radiant Way*

8 Everybody is always in favour of general economy and particular expenditure.

Anthony Eden (1897–1977) British statesman. *The Observer*, 'Sayings of the Week', 17 June 1956

9 Economy is going without something you do want in case you should, some day, want something you probably won't want.

Anthony Hope (Sir Anthony Hope Hawkins; 1863–1933) British novelist. *The Dolly Dialogues*

10 What! Can't a fellow even enjoy a biscuit any more?

Duke of Portland (1857–1943) British peer. On being informed that as one of several measures to reduce his own expenses he would have to dispense with one of his two Italian pastry cooks. *Their Noble Lordships* (S. Winchester)

11 A hole is the accident of a day, while a darn is premeditated poverty.

Edward Shuter (1728–76) British actor. Explaining why he did not mend the holes in his stocking. *Dictionary of National Biography*

12 I belong to a generation that don't spend until we have the money in hand.

Margaret Thatcher (1925–) British politician and prime minister. *The Observer*, 'Sayings of the Week', 13 Feb 1977

13 Beware of all enterprises that require new clothes.

Henry David Thoreau (1817–62) US writer. *Walden*, 'Economy'

THURBER, JAMES

(1894–1961) US writer, humorist, and cartoonist. A contributor to *The New Yorker*, he published a number of collected writings, including *The Thurber Carnival* (1945).

Quotations about Thurber

1 A tall, thin, spectacled man with the face of a harassed rat.

Russell Maloney *Saturday Review*, 'Tilley the Toiler'

Quotations by Thurber

2 'Joe,' I said, 'was perhaps the first great nonstop literary drinker of the American nineteenth century. He made the indulgences of Coleridge and De Quincey seem like a bit of mischief in the kitchen with the cooking sherry.'

Alarms and Diversions, 'The Moribundant Life…'

3 I was seized by the stern hand of Compulsion, that dark, unseasonable Urge that impels women to clean house in the middle of the night.

Alarms and Diversions, 'There's a Time for Flags'

4 It is better to have loafed and lost than never to have loafed at all.

Fables for Our Time, 'The Courtship of Arthur and Al'

5 You can fool too many of the people too much of the time.

Fables for Our Time, 'The Owl Who Was God'

6 Early to rise and early to bed makes a male healthy and wealthy and dead.

Fables for Our Time, 'The Shrike and the Chipmunks'

7 Old Nat Burge sat…He was…watching the moon come up lazily out of the old cemetery in which nine of his daughters were lying, and only two of them were dead.

Let Your Mind Alone, 'Bateman Comes Home'

8 No man…who has wrestled with a self-adjusting card table can ever quite be the man he once was.

Let Your Mind Alone, 'Sex ex Machina'

9 I suppose that the high-water mark of my youth in Columbus, Ohio, was the night the bed fell on my father.

My Life and Hard Times, Ch. 1

10 Her own mother lived the latter years of her life in the horrible suspicion that electricity was dripping invisibly all over the house.

My Life and Hard Times, Ch. 2

11 Then, with that faint fleeting smile playing about

his lips, he faced the firing squad; erect and motionless, proud and disdainful, Walter Mitty, the undefeated, inscrutable to the last.
My World and Welcome to It, 'The Secret Life of Walter Mitty'

12 A man should not insult his wife publicly, at parties. He should insult her in the privacy of the home.
Thurber Country

13 The difference between our decadence and the Russians' is that while theirs is brutal, ours is apathetic.
The Observer, 'Sayings of the Week', 5 Feb 1961

14 The War between Men and Women.
Title of a series of cartoons. *The New Yorker*, 20 Jan–28 Apr 1934

15 Well, if I called the wrong number, why did you answer the phone?
Cartoon caption. *The New Yorker*, 5 June 1937

16 You wait here and I'll bring the etchings down.
Cartoon caption

17 I said the hounds of spring are on winter's traces – but let it pass, let it pass!
Cartoon caption

18 Why do you have to be a nonconformist like everybody else?
Attrib. Actually a cartoon caption by Stan Hunt in *The New Yorker*

19 Surely you don't mean by unartificial insemination!
On being accosted at a party by a drunk woman who claimed she would like to have a baby by him. Attrib.

20 It had only one fault. It was kind of lousy.
Remark made about a play. Attrib.

21 God bless…God damn.
His last words. Attrib.

TIME

See also eternity, future, life, past, present, transience

1 An hour in the morning is worth two in the evening.
Proverb

2 There are only twenty-four hours in the day.
Proverb

3 There is a time and place for everything.
Proverb

4 Time and tide wait for no man.
Proverb

5 Time is a great healer.
Proverb

6 Time will tell.
Proverb

7 Time cures the sick man, not the ointment.
Proverb

8 Except Time all other things are created. Time is the creator; and Time has no limit, neither top nor bottom.
The Persian Rivayat

9 To choose time is to save time.
Francis Bacon (1561–1626) English philosopher. *Essays*, 'Of Dispatch'

10 We should count time by heart-throbs.
Philip James Bailey (1816–1902) British poet. *Festus*

11 VLADIMIR. That passed the time.
ESTRAGON. It would have passed in any case.
VLADIMIR. Yes, but not so rapidly.
Samuel Beckett (1906–89) Irish novelist and dramatist. *Waiting for Godot*, I

12 I believe the twenty-four hour day has come to stay.
Max Beerbohm (1872–1956) British writer. *A Christmas Garland*, 'Perkins and Mankind'

13 Time is a great teacher, but unfortunately it kills all its pupils.
Hector Berlioz (1803–69) French composer. *Almanach des lettres françaises*

14 To every thing there is a season, and a time to every purpose under the heaven:
A time to be born, and a time to die; a time to plant, and a time to pluck up that which is planted;
A time to kill, and a time to heal; a time to break down, and a time to build up;
A time to weep, and a time to laugh; a time to mourn, and a time to dance;
A time to cast away stones, and a time to gather stones together; a time to embrace, and a time to refrain from embracing;
A time to get, and a time to lose; a time to keep, and a time to cast away;
A time to rend, and a time to sew; a time to keep silence, and a time to speak;
A time to love, and a time to hate; a time of war, and a time of peace.
Bible: Ecclesiastes 3:1–8

15 Men talk of killing time, while time quietly kills them.
Dion Boucicault (Dionysius Lardner Boursiquot; 1820–90) Irish-born US actor and dramatist. *London Assurance*, II:1

16 Time, like a loan from the bank, is something you're only given when you possess so much that you don't need it.
John Braine (1922–86) British novelist. *Room at the Top*, Ch. 15

17 I recommend you to take care of the minutes: for hours will take care of themselves.
Earl of Chesterfield (1694–1773) English statesman. Letter to his son, 6 Nov 1747

18 Time is a physician that heals every grief.
Diphilius (4th century BC)

19 Time is the great physician.
Benjamin Disraeli (1804–81) British statesman. *Henrietta Temple*, Bk. VI, Ch. 9

20 Time present and time past
Are both perhaps present in time future
And time future contained in time past.
T. S. Eliot (1888–1965) US-born British poet and dramatist. *Four Quartets*

21 Come, fill the Cup, and in the Fire of Spring
The Winter Garment of Repentance fling:
The Bird of Time has but a little way
To fly – and Lo! the Bird is on the Wing.

Edward Fitzgerald (1809–83) British poet. *The Rubáiyát of Omar Khayyám*

22 Ah, fill the Cup: – what boots it to repeat
How Time is slipping underneath our Feet:
Unborn TOMORROW, and dead YESTERDAY,
Why fret about them if TODAY be sweet!

Edward Fitzgerald *The Rubáiyát of Omar Khayyám*

23 Dost thou love life? Then do not squander time, for that's the stuff life is made of.

Benjamin Franklin (1706–90) US scientist and statesman. *Poor Richard's Almanack*

24 In order to be utterly happy the only thing necessary is to refrain from comparing this moment with other moments in the past, which I often did not fully enjoy because I was comparing them with other moments of the future.

André Gide (1869–1951) French novelist. *Journals*

25 Counting the beats,
Counting the slow heart beats,
The bleeding to death of time in slow heart beats,
Wakeful they lie.

Robert Graves (1895–1985) British writer. *Counting the Beats*

26 You must remember this;
A kiss is just a kiss,
A sigh is just a sigh –
The fundamental things apply
As time goes by.

Herman Hupfeld (20th century) US songwriter. From the film *Casablanca. As Time Goes By*

27 The now, the here, through which all future plunges to the past.

James Joyce (1882–1941) Irish novelist. *Ulysses*

28 O aching time! O moments big as years!

John Keats (1795–1821) British poet. *Hyperion*, I

29 We must use time as a tool, not as a couch.

John Fitzgerald Kennedy (1917–63) US statesman. *The Observer*, 'Sayings of the Week', 10 Dec 1961

30 They shut the road through the woods
Seventy years ago.
Weather and rain have undone it again,
And now you would never know
There was once a road through the woods.

Rudyard Kipling (1865–1936) Indian-born British writer. *The Way Through the Woods*

31 God seems to have left the receiver off the hook, and time is running out.

Arthur Koestler (1905–1983) Hungarian-born British writer. *The Ghost in the Machine*, Ch. 18

32 The Future is something which everyone reaches at the rate of sixty minutes an hour, whatever he does, whoever he is.

C. S. Lewis (1898–1963) British academic and writer. *The Screwtape Letters*

33 Yes, time heals all things,
So I needn't cling to this fear,
It's merely that Spring
Will be a little late this year.

Frank Loesser (1910–69) US songwriter. *Christmas Holiday*, 'Spring Will Be a Little Late This Year'

34 I stood on the bridge at midnight,
As the clocks were striking the hour.

Henry Wadsworth Longfellow (1807–82) US poet. *The Bridge*

35 The man is killing time – there's nothing else.

Robert Lowell (1917–77) US poet. *The Drinker*

36 Time wounds all heels.

Groucho Marx (Julius Marx; 1895–1977) US comedian. Attrib.

37 'Twenty-three and a quarter minutes past', Uncle Matthew was saying furiously, 'in precisely six and three-quarter minutes the damned fella will be late.'

Nancy Mitford (1904–73) British writer. *Love in a Cold Climate*

38 A physician can sometimes parry the scythe of death, but has no power over the sand in the hourglass.

Hester Lynch Piozzi (Mrs. Henry Thrale; 1741–1821) British writer. Letter to Fanny Burney, 22 Nov 1781

39 It is only time that weighs upon our hands.
It is only time, and that is not material.

Sylvia Plath (1932–63) British poet. *Winter Trees*, 'The Three Women'

40 Distances are only the relation of space to time and vary with that relation.

Marcel Proust (1871–1922) French novelist. *A La Recherche du temps perdu, Sodome et Gomorrhe*

41 If you want to know the time,
Ask a Policeman.

E. W. Rogers (1864–1913) *Ask a P'liceman*

42 They do that to pass the time, nothing more. But Time is too large, it refuses to let itself be filled up.

Jean-Paul Sartre (1905–80) French writer. *Nausea*

43 The physician's best remedy is *Tincture of Time!*

Béla Schick (1877–1967) Austrian pediatrician. *Aphorisms and Facetiae of Béla Schick* (I. J. Wolf)

44 Time heals what reason cannot.

Seneca (c. 4 BC–65 AD) Roman writer and statesman. *Agamemnon*, 130

45 Ah! the clock is always slow;
It is later than you think.

Robert William Service (1874–1958) Canadian poet. *It is Later than You Think*

46 Th' inaudible and noiseless foot of Time.

William Shakespeare (1564–1616) English dramatist and poet. *All's Well that Ends Well*, V:3

47 Come what come may,
Time and the hour runs through the roughest day.

William Shakespeare *Macbeth*, I:3

48 Time's glory is to calm contending kings,
To unmask falsehood, and bring truth to light.

William Shakespeare *The Rape of Lucrece*, Dedication

49 I wasted time, and now doth time waste me.

William Shakespeare *Richard II*, V:5

50 Like as the waves make towards the pebbled

shore,
So do our minutes hasten to their end.

William Shakespeare *Sonnet 60*

51 Time's thievish progress to eternity.

William Shakespeare *Sonnet 77*

52 Time hath, my lord, a wallet at his back,
Wherein he puts alms for oblivion,
A great-siz'd monster of ingratitudes.

William Shakespeare *Troilus and Cressida*, III:3

53 Beauty, wit,
High birth, vigour of bone, desert in service,
Love, friendship, charity, are subjects all
To envious and calumniating time.
One touch of nature makes the whole world kin,
That all with one consent praise new-born gawds,
Though they are made and moulded of things past,
And give to dust that is a little gilt
More laud than gilt o'er-dusted.

William Shakespeare *Troilus and Cressida*, III:3

54 The end crowns all,
And that old common arbitrator, Time,
Will one day end it.

William Shakespeare *Troilus and Cressida*, IV:5

55 Thus the whirligig of time brings in his revenges.

William Shakespeare *Twelfth Night*, V:1

56 In reality, *killing time*
Is only the name for another of the multifarious ways
By which Time kills us.

Osbert Sitwell (1892–1969) British writer. *Milordo Inglese*

57 Time driveth onward fast,
And in a little while our lips are dumb.
Let us alone. What is it that will last?
All things are taken from us, and become
Portions and parcels of the dreadful Past.

Alfred, Lord Tennyson (1809–92) British poet. *The Lotos-Eaters*, 'Choric Song'

58 Time held me green and dying
Though I sang in my chains like the sea.

Dylan Thomas (1914–53) Welsh poet. *Fern Hill*

59 Time is but the stream I go a-fishing in.

Henry David Thoreau (1817–62) US writer. *Walden*, 'Where I Lived, and What I Lived For'

60 As if you could kill time without injuring eternity.

Henry David Thoreau *Walden*, 'Economy'

61 But meanwhile it is flying, irretrievable time is flying.

Virgil (Publius Vergilius Maro; 70 BC–19 BC) Roman poet. *Georgics*, Bk. III

62 Times carries all things, even our wits, away.

Virgil *Eclogues*, Bk. IX

63 The Hopi, an Indian tribe, have a language as sophisticated as ours, but no tenses for past, present and future. The division does not exist. What does this say about time?

Jeanette Winterson (1959–) British author. *Sexing the Cherry*

64 Time drops in decay,
Like a candle burnt out.

W. B. Yeats (1865–1939) Irish poet. *The Moods*

65 The bell strikes one. We take no note of time
But from its loss.

Edward Young (1683–1765) British poet. *Night Thoughts*

66 Time flies, death urges, knells call, heaven invites,
Hell threatens.

Edward Young *Night Thoughts*

TITLES

See also aristocracy, courtesy, honour, nobility

1 As far as the 14th Earl is concerned, I suppose Mr Wilson, when you come to think of it, is the 14th Mr Wilson.

Alec Douglas-Home (1903–) British statesman. On renouncing his peerage (as 14th Earl of Home) to become prime minister. Replying to the leader of the opposition, Harold Wilson. *See* WILSON. TV interview, 21 Oct 1963

2 Madam I may not call you; mistress I am ashamed to call you; and so I know not what to call you; but howsoever, I thank you.

Elizabeth I (1533–1603) Queen of England. Writing to the wife of the Archbishop of Canterbury, expressing her disapproval of married clergy. *Brief View of the State of the Church* (Harington)

3 Tyndall, I must remain plain Michael Faraday to the last; and let me now tell you, that if I accepted the honour which the Royal Society desires to confer upon me, I would not answer for the integrity of my intellect for a single year.

Michael Faraday (1791–1867) British scientist. Said when Faraday was offered the Presidency of the Royal Society. *Faraday as a Discoverer* (J. Tyndall), 'Illustrations of Character'

4 Pooh-Bah (Lord High Everything Else).

W. S. Gilbert (1836–1911) British dramatist. *The Mikado, Dramatis Personae*

5 I like the Garter; there is no damned merit in it.

Lord Melbourne (1779–1848) British statesman. *Lord Melbourne* (H. Dunckley), 'On the Order of the Garter'

6 When I want a peerage, I shall buy one like an honest man.

Lord Northcliffe (1865–1922) Irish-born British newspaper proprietor. Attrib.

7 Call me madame.

Frances Perkins (1882–1965) US social worker and politician. Deciding the term of address she would prefer when made the first woman to hold a cabinet office in America. *Familiar Quotations* (J. Bartlett)

8 A person seeking a quiet life is greatly helped by not having a title.

Captain Mark Phillips (1948–) Ex-husband of Princess Anne. Attrib.

9 Mother always told me my day was coming, but I never realized that I'd end up being the shortest knight of the year.

Gordon Richards (1904–86) British champion jockey. Referring to his diminutive size, on learning of his knighthood. Attrib.

10 Members rise from CMG (known sometimes in Whitehall as 'Call me God') to the KCMG ('Kindly Call me God') to…The GCMG ('God Calls me God').

Anthony Sampson (1926–) British writer and journalist. *Anatomy of Britain*, Ch. 18

11 Titles distinguish the mediocre, embarrass the superior, and are disgraced by the inferior.

George Bernard Shaw (1856–1950) Irish dramatist and critic. *Man and Superman*, 'Maxims for Revolutionists'

12 I've been offered titles, but I think they get one into disreputable company.

George Bernard Shaw *Gossip* (A. Barrow)

13 After half a century of democratic advance, the whole process has ground to a halt with a 14th Earl.

Harold Wilson (1916–) British politician and prime minister. Referring to Alec Douglas-Home. For the reply, *see* DOUGLAS-HOME. Speech, Manchester, 19 Oct 1963

TOLERANCE

1 There is, however, a limit at which forbearance ceases to be a virtue.

Edmund Burke (1729–97) British politician. *Observations on a Publication, 'The Present State of the Nation'*

2 No party has a monopoly over what is right.

Mikhail Gorbachov (1931–) Soviet statesman. Speech, Mar 1986

3 It is flattering some men to endure them.

Lord Halifax (1633–95) English statesman. *Political, Moral and Miscellaneous Thoughts and Reflections*

4 If you cannot mould yourself as you would wish, how can you expect other people to be entirely to your liking?

Thomas à Kempis (Thomas Hemmerken; c. 1380–1471) German monk. *The Imitation of Christ*, I

5 We must respect the other fellow's religion, but only in the sense and to the extent that we respect his theory that his wife is beautiful and his children smart.

H. L. Mencken (1880–1956) US journalist. *Notebooks*, 'Minority Report'

6 Steven's mind was so tolerant that he could have attended a lynching every day without becoming critical.

Thorne Smith (1892–1934) US humorist. *The Jovial Ghosts*, Ch. 11

7 So long as a man rides his hobby-horse peaceably and quietly along the king's highway, and neither compels you or me to get up behind him, – pray, Sir, what have either you or I to do with it?

Laurence Sterne (1713–68) Irish-born British writer. *Tristram Shandy*

8 It is because we put up with bad things that hotel-keepers continue to give them to us.

Anthony Trollope (1815–82) British novelist. *Orley Farm*, Ch. 18

TOLKIEN, J. R. R.

(1892–1973) British writer. While professor of English literature at Oxford he wrote *The Lord of the Rings* (1954–55). Related works include *The Hobbit* (1937) and *The Silmarillion* (1977).

Quotations about Tolkien

1 Though Tolkien lived in the twentieth century he can scarcely be called a modern writer. His roots were buried deep in early literature, and the major names in twentieth-century writing meant little or nothing to him.

Humphrey Carpenter *The Inklings*

2 He is a smooth, pale, fluent little chap – can't read Spenser because of the forms – thinks all literature is written for the amusement of *men* between thirty and forty...His pet abomination is the idea of 'liberal studies'. Technical hobbies are more in his line. No harm in him; only needs a smack or so.

C.S. Lewis (1898–1963) British academic and writer. Diary, May 1926

3 All who love that kind of children's book that can be read and re-read by adults should take note that a new star has appeared in this constellation. To the trained eye some of the characters will seem almost mythopoeic.

C.S. Lewis (1898–1963) British academic and writer. *The Times*, 7 Oct 1937

Quotations by Tolkien

4 In a hole in the ground there lived a hobbit.

The Hobbit, Ch. 1

5 One Ring to rule them all, One Ring to find them,
One Ring to bring them all and in the darkness bind them.

The Lord of the Rings, Pt. I: *The Fellowship of the Ring*, Ch. 2

6 Where iss it, where iss it: my Precious, my Precious? It's ours, it is, and we wants it.

The Lord of the Rings, Pt. II: *The Two Towers*, Ch. 1

7 ...he willed that the hearts of Men should seek beyond the world and should find no rest therein; but they should have a virtue to shape their life, amid the powers and chances of the world, beyond the Music of the Ainur, which is a fate to all things else.

'He' is Ilúvatar, the Creator. *The Silmarillion*, Ch. 1

8 Nearly all marriages, even happy ones, are mistakes: in the sense that almost certainly (in a more perfect world, or even with a little more care in this very imperfect one) both partners might be found more suitable mates. But the real soul-mate is the one you are actually married to.

Letter to Michael Tolkien, 6–8 Mar 1941

TOLSTOY, LEO, COUNT

(1828–1910) Russian writer. His fame rests on his two epic novels *War and Peace* (1865–69) and *Anna Karenina* (1875–77). In 1876 he was converted to a form of Christian mysticism, about which he wrote copiously.

Quotations about Tolstoy

1 Tolstoy towered above his age as Dante and Michelangelo and Beethoven had done. His novels are marvels of sustained imagination, but his life was full of inconsistencies. He wanted to be one with the peasants, yet he continued to live like an aristocrat. He preached universal love, yet he quarrelled so painfully with his poor demented wife that at the age of 82 he ran away from her.

Sir Kenneth Clark (1938–69) British art historian and writer. *Civilisation*

2 I like Leo Tolstoy enormously, but in my opinion he won't write much of anything else. (I could be wrong.)

Fedor Mikhailovich Dostoevsky (1821–81) Russian novelist.

3 It has been said that a careful reading of *Anna Karenina*, if it teaches you nothing else, will teach you how to make strawberry jam.

Julian Mitchell (1935–) British writer. *Radio Times*, 30 Oct 1976

4 Tolstoy, like myself, wasn't taken in by superstititions like science and medicine.

George Bernard Shaw (1856–1950) Irish dramatist and critic.

Quotations by Tolstoy

5 All happy families resemble one another, each unhappy family is unhappy in its own way.

Anna Karenina, Pt. I, Ch. 1

6 If you want to be happy, be.

Kosma Prutkov

7 I am always with myself, and it is I who am my tormentor.

Memoirs of a Madman

8 The highest wisdom has but one science – the science of the whole – the science explaining the whole creation and man's place in it.

War and Peace, Bk. V, Ch. 2

9 The chief attraction of military service has consisted and will consist in this compulsory and irreproachable idleness.

War and Peace, Bk. VII, Ch. 1

10 All, everything that I understand, I understand only because I love.

War and Peace, Bk. VII, Ch. 16

11 Our body is a machine for living. It is organized for that, it is its nature. Let life go on in it unhindered and let it defend itself, it will do more than if you paralyse it by encumbering it with remedies.

War and Peace, Bk. X, Ch. 29

12 Pure and complete sorrow is as impossible as pure and complete joy.

War and Peace, Bk. XV, Ch. 1

13 Art is not a handicraft, it is the transmission of feeling the artist has experienced.

What is Art?, Ch. 19

14 I sit on a man's back, choking him and making him carry me, and yet assure myself and others that I am very sorry for him and wish to ease his lot by all possible means – except by getting off his back.

What Then Must We Do?, Ch. 16

15 Historians are like deaf people who go on answering questions that no one has asked them.

A Discovery of Australia, 'Being an Historian' (Manning Clark)

16 Even in the valley of the shadow of death, two and two do not make six.

Refusing to reconcile himself with the Russian Orthodox Church as he lay dying. Attrib.

TOLSTOY, SOPHIE

(1844–1919) Russian writer. The wife of Leo Tolstoy, she kept a revealing diary of her life with him.

1 One can't live on love alone; and I am so stupid that I can do nothing but think of him.

A Diary of Tolstoy's Wife, 1860–1891

2 I am a source of satisfaction to him, a nurse, a piece of furniture, a *woman* – nothing more.

A Diary of Tolstoy's Wife, 1860–1891

3 He would like to destroy his old diaries and to appear before his children and the public only in his patriarchal robes. His vanity is immense!

A Diary of Tolstoy's Wife, 1860–1891

TOSCANINI, ARTURO

(1867–1957) Italian conductor. Originally a cellist, he became famous as a conductor of opera at La Scala, Milan, and at the Metropolitan Opera in New York. He was conductor of the NBC Symphony Orchestra (1937–57).

1 They are for prima donnas or corpses – I am neither.

Refusing a floral wreath at the end of a performance. *The Elephant that Swallowed a Nightingale* (C. Galtey)

2 It's too late to apologize.

Retort to the insult 'Nuts to you!' shouted at him by a player he had just ordered from the stage during rehearsal. *The Humor of Music* (L. Humphrey)

3 After I die, I shall return to earth as a gatekeeper of a bordello and I won't let any of you – not a one of you – enter!

Rebuking an incompetent orchestra. *The Maestro: The Life of Arturo Toscanini* (Howard Taubman)

4 Can't you read? The score demands *con amore*, and what are you doing? You are playing it like married men!

Criticizing the playing of an Austrian orchestra during rehearsal. Attrib.

5 Madame, there you sit with that magnificent instrument between your legs, and all you can do is *scratch* it!

Rebuking an incompetent woman cellist. Attrib.

TRANSIENCE

See also life, mortality, time

1 So passes the glory of the world.

Anonymous Referring to the large number of ruined castles in England, Normandy, and Anjou, which had been demolished after the rebellion (1173–74) against Henry II. *Histoire de Guillaume le Maréchal*

2 Everything is only for a day, both that which remembers and that which is remembered.

Marcus Aurelius (121–180 AD) Roman emperor. *Meditations*, Bk. IV, Ch. 35

3 Time is like a river made up of the events which happen, and its current is strong; no sooner does anything appear than it is swept away, and another comes in its place, and will be swept away too.

Marcus Aurelius *Meditations*, Bk. IV, Ch. 43

4 Faith, Sir, we are here to-day, and gone tomorrow.

Aphra Behn (1640–89) English novelist and dramatist. *The Lucky Chance*, IV

5 Vanity of vanities, saith the Preacher, vanity of vanities; all is vanity.
What profit hath a man of all his labour which he taketh under the sun?
One generation passeth away, and another generation cometh: but the earth abideth for ever.

Bible: Ecclesiastes 1:2–4

6 And I gave my heart to seek and search out by wisdom concerning all things that are done under heaven: this sore travail hath God given to the sons of man to be exercised therewith.
I have seen all the works that are done under the sun; and, behold, all is vanity and vexation of spirit.

Bible: Ecclesiastes 1:13–14

7 Whatsoever thy hand findeth to do, do it with thy might; for there is no work, nor device, nor knowledge, nor wisdom, in the grave, whither thou goest.

Bible: Ecclesiastes 9:10

8 And behold joy and gladness, slaying oxen, and killing sheep, eating flesh, and drinking wine: let us eat and drink; for tomorrow we shall die.

Bible: Isaiah A similar sentiment is expressed in Corinthians 15:32–33. 22:13

9 Heaven and earth shall pass away, but my words shall not pass away.

Bible: Matthew 24:35

10 Suddenly, as rare things will, it vanished.

Robert Browning (1812–89) British poet. *One Word More*, IV

11 Now the peak of summer's past, the sky is overcast
And the love we swore would last for an age seems deceit.

C. Day Lewis (1904–72) British poet. *Hornpipe*

12 They are not long, the days of wine and roses.

Ernest Dowson (1867–1900) British lyric poet. *Vitae Summa Brevis Spem Nos Vetat Incohare Longam*

13 A little rule, a little sway,
A sunbeam in a winter's day,
Is all the proud and mighty have
Between the cradle and the grave.

John Dyer (1700–58) British poet. *Grongar Hill*

14 The Worldly Hope men set their Hearts upon
Turns Ashes – or it prospers; and anon,
Like Snow upon the Desert's dusty face,
Lighting a little Hour or two – is gone.

Edward Fitzgerald (1809–83) British poet. *The Rubáiyát of Omar Khayyám*, XIV

15 Fair daffodils, we weep to see
You haste away so soon:
As yet the early-rising sun
Has not attain'd his noon.
Stay, stay,
Until the hasting day
Has run
But to the even-song;
And, having pray'd together, we
Will go with you along.

We have short time to stay, as you,
We have as short a Spring;
As quick a growth to meet decay,
As you or any thing.

Robert Herrick (1591–1674) English poet. *Hesperides*, 'To Daffodils'

16 Not to hope for things to last for ever, is what the year teaches and even the hour which snatches a nice day away.

Horace (Quintus Horatius Flaccus; 65–8 BC) Roman poet. *Odes*, IV

17 Ships that pass in the night, and speak each other in passing;
Only a signal shown and a distant voice in the darkness;
So on the ocean of life we pass and speak one another,
Only a look and a voice; then darkness again and a silence.

Henry Wadsworth Longfellow (1807–82) US poet. *Tales of a Wayside Inn*, 'The Theologian's Tale. Elizabeth'

18 But she was of the world where the fairest things have the worst fate. Like a rose, she has lived as long as roses live, the space of one morning.

François de Malherbe (1555–1628) French poet. *Consolation à M. du Périer*

19 Gone With the Wind.

Margaret Mitchell (1909–49) US novelist. From the poem *Non Sum Qualis Eram* (Ernest Dowson): 'I have forgot much, Cynara! Gone with the wind…' Book title

20 O ruin'd piece of nature! This great world
Should so wear out to nought.

William Shakespeare (1564–1616) English dramatist. *King Lear*, IV:4

21 The painful warrior famoused for fight,
After a thousand victories once foil'd,
Is from the book of honour razed quite,
And all the rest forgot for which he toil'd.

William Shakespeare *Sonnet 25*

22 What's past, and what's to come is strew'd with husks
And formless ruin of oblivion.

William Shakespeare *Troilus and Cressida*, IV:5

23 Our little systems have their day;
They have their day and cease to be.

Alfred, Lord Tennyson (1809–92) British poet. *In Memoriam A.H.H.*, Prologue

24 Will anyone, a hundred years from now, consent to live in the houses the Victorians built, travel by their roads or railways, value the furnishings they made to live among or esteem, except for curious or historial reasons, their prevalent art and the clipped and limited literature that satisfied their souls?

H. G. Wells (1866–1946) British writer. *The New Machiavelli*

TRANSLATION

1 The original is unfaithful to the translation.

Jorge Luis Borges (1899–1986) Argentinian writer. Referring to Henley's translation of Beckford's *Vathek. Sobre el 'Vathek' de William Beckford*

2 Translations (like wives) are seldom faithful if they are in the least attractive.

Roy Campbell (1901–57) South African poet. *Poetry Review*

3 Poetry is what gets lost in translation.

Robert Frost (1875–1963) US poet. Attrib.

4 An idea does not pass from one language to another without change.

Miguel de Unamuno y Jugo (1864–1936) Spanish writer. *The Tragic Sense of Life*

5 Humour is the first of the gifts to perish in a foreign tongue.

Virginia Woolf (1882–1941) British novelist. *The Common Reader*

TRAVEL

See also boats, flying

1 Travel broadens the mind.

Proverb

2 The time to enjoy a European tour is about three weeks after you unpack.

George Ade (1866–1944) US dramatist and humorist. *Forty Modern Fables*

3 Is your journey really necessary?

Anonymous British wartime slogan

4 If It's Tuesday, This Must be Belgium.

Anonymous Title of film about US tourists in Europe

5 This is the Night Mail crossing the Border
Bringing the cheque and the postal order.

W. H. Auden (1907–73) British poet. Commentary for Post Office documentary film. *Night Mail*

6 Travel, in the younger sort, is a part of education; in the elder, a part of experience.

Francis Bacon (1561–1626) English philosopher. *Essays*, 'Of Travel'

7 Second to the right, and straight on till morning.

J. M. Barrie (1860–1937) British dramatist. *Peter Pan*

8 I have recently been all round the world and have formed a very poor opinion of it.

Thomas Beecham (1879–1961) British conductor. Speech at the Savoy. *The News Review*, 22 Aug 1946

9 Rumbling under blackened girders, Midland, bound for Cricklewood,
Puffed its sulphur to the sunset where the Land of Laundries stood.
Rumble under, thunder over, train and tram alternate go.

John Betjeman (1906–84) British poet. *Parliament Hill Fields*

10 My experience of ships is that on them one makes an interesting discovery about the world. One finds one can do without it completely.

Malcolm Bradbury (1932–) British novelist. *Stepping Westward*, Bk. I, Ch. 2

11 May not and ought not the children of these fathers rightly say: 'Our fathers were Englishmen which came over this great ocean, and were ready to perish in this wilderness.'

William Bradford (1590–1657) Pilgrim Father. Referring to the Pilgrim Fathers, after their arrival at Cape Cod. *Of Plymouth Plantation*, Ch. 10

12 Before the Roman came to Rye or out to Severn strode,
The rolling English drunkard made the rolling English road.

G. K. Chesterton (1874–1936) British writer. *The Rolling English Road*

13 The only way to be sure of catching a train is to miss the one before it.

G. K. Chesterton *Vacances à tous prix*, 'Le Supplice de l'heure' (P. Daninos)

14 Travelling is almost like talking with men of other centuries.

René Descartes (1596–1650) French philosopher. *Le Discours de la méthode*

15 How does it feel
To be without a home
Like a complete unknown
Like a rolling stone?

Bob Dylan (Robert Allen Zimmerman; 1941–) US popular singer. *Like a Rolling Stone*

16 I read, much of the night, and go south in the winter.

T. S. Eliot (1888–1965) US-born British poet and dramatist. *The Waste Land*, 'The Burial of the Dead'

17 The woods are lovely, dark, and deep,
But I have promises to keep,
And miles to go before I sleep,
And miles to go before I sleep.

Robert Frost (1875–1963) US poet. *Stopping by Woods on a Snowy Evening*

18 He gave the impression that very many cities had rubbed him smooth.

Graham Greene (1904–91) British novelist. *A Gun for Sale*, Ch. 4

19 Follow the Yellow Brick Road.

E. Y. Harburg (1898–1981) US lyricist. *The Wizard of Oz*, Song title

20 Motorists (as they used to be called) were utterly irresponsible in their dealings with each other and with the pedestrian public; for their benefit homicide was legalised. The basic principles of Equality were flouted, while the opposing principle of Envy was disastrously encouraged.

L. P. Hartley (1895–1972) British novelist. *Facial Justice*, Ch. 5

21 One of the pleasantest things in the world is going on a journey; but I like to go by myself.

William Hazlitt (1778–1830) British essayist. *On Going a Journey*

22 They change their clime, not their frame of mind, who rush across the sea. We work hard at doing nothing: we look for happiness in boats and carriage rides. What you are looking for is here, is at Ulubrae, if only peace of mind doesn't desert you.

Horace (Quintus Horatius Flaccus; 65–8 BC) Roman poet. *Epistles*, I

23 A man who has not been in Italy, is always conscious of an inferiority, from his not having seen what it is expected a man should see. The grand object of travelling is to see the shores of the Mediterranean.

Samuel Johnson (1709–84) British lexicographer. *Life of Johnson* (J. Boswell), Vol. III

24 Much have I travell'd in the realms of gold,
And many goodly states and kingdoms seen.

John Keats (1795–1821) British poet. *On First Looking into Chapman's Homer*

25 Mr Stephenson having taken me on the bench of the engine with him, we started at about ten miles an hour. You cannot imagine how strange it seemed to be journeying on thus, without any visible cause of progressing other than that magical machine, with its flying white breath, and rhythmical unwearying pace.

Fanny Kemble (1809–93) British actress and writer. *Record of a Girlhood*

26 Of all noxious animals, too, the most noxious is a tourist. And of all tourists the most vulgar, ill-bred, offensive and loathsome is the British tourist.

Francis Kilvert (1840–79) British diarist and clergyman. *Diary*, 5 Apr 1870

27 Like Brighton pier, all right as far as it goes, but inadequate for getting to France.

Neil Kinnock (1942–) British politician. Speech, House of Commons, 1981

28 Give me your arm, old Toad;
Help me down Cemetery Road.

Philip Larkin (1922–85) British poet. *The Whitsun Weddings*, 'Toads Revisited'

29 Oh, mister porter, what shall I do?
I wanted to go to Birmingham, but they've carried me on to Crewe.

Marie Lloyd (1870–1922) British music-hall singer. *Oh, Mister Porter*

30 Americans are people who prefer the Continent to their own country but refuse to learn its languages.

E. V. Lucas (1868–1938) British publisher and writer. *Wanderings and Diversions*

31 The great and recurrent question about abroad is, is it worth getting there?

Rose Macaulay (1889–1958) British writer. Attrib.

32 Whenever I prepare for a journey I prepare as though for death. Should I never return, all is in order. This is what life has taught me.

Katherine Mansfield (1888–1923) New-Zealand-born British writer. *The Journal of Katherine Mansfield*, 1922

33 The car has become the carapace, the protective and aggressive shell, of urban and suburban man.

Marshall McLuhan (1911–81) Canadian sociologist. *Understanding Media*, Ch. 22

34 SEAGOON. I want you to accompany me on the safari.

BLOODNOCK. Gad sir, I'm sorry, I've never played one.

Spike Milligan (1918–) British comic actor and writer. *The Goon Show*

35 *Rush hour:* that hour when traffic is almost at a standstill.

J. B. Morton (1893–1979) British journalist. *Morton's Folly*

36 It is the overtakers who keep the undertakers busy.

William Ewart Pitts (b. 1900) British chief constable. *The Observer*, 'Sayings of the Week', 22 Dec 1963

37 A trip to the moon on gossamer wings.

Cole Porter (1891–1964) US composer and lyricist. *Jubilee*, 'Just One of Those Things'

38 In the middle ages people were tourists because of their religion, whereas now they are tourists because tourism is their religion.

Robert Runcie (1921–) British churchman; Archbishop of Canterbury (1980–91). *The Observer*, 'Sayings of the Week', 11 Dec 1988

39 Travel is the most private of pleasures. There is no greater bore than the travel bore. We do not in the least want to hear what he has seen in Hong-Kong.

Vita Sackville-West (Victoria Sackville-West; 1892–1962) British poet and novelist. *Passenger to Tehran*, Ch. 1

40 A man should know something of his own country, too, before he goes abroad.

Laurence Sterne (1713–68) Irish-born British writer. *Tristram Shandy*

41 Wealth I ask not; hope nor love,
Nor a friend to know me;
All I seek, the heaven above
And the road below me.

Robert Louis Stevenson (1850–94) Scottish writer. *Songs of Travel*, 'The Vagabond'

42 For my part, I travel not to go anywhere, but to go. I travel for travel's sake. The great affair is to move.

Robert Louis Stevenson *Travels with a Donkey*, 'Cheylard and Luc'

43 Travel is glamorous only in retrospect.

Paul Theroux (1941–) US-born writer. *The Observer*, 'Sayings of the Week', 7 Oct 1979

44 Ever since childhood, when I lived within earshot of the Boston and Maine, I have seldom heard a train go by and not wished I was on it.

Paul Theroux *The Great Railway Bazaar*

45 Yes – around Concord.

Henry David Thoreau (1817–62) US writer. On being asked whether he had travelled much. Concord, in Massachusetts, is the town where he was born, grew up, and lived most of his life. Attrib.

46 He travelled in order to come home.

William Trevor (1928–) British writer. *Matilda's England*

47 If you ever plan to motor west,
Travel my way, take the highway, that's the best,
Get your kicks on Route 66.

Bobby Troup (1919–) US songwriter. *Route 66*

48 Commuter – one who spends his life
In riding to and from his wife;

A man who shaves and takes a train,
And then rides back to shave again.

Elwyn Brooks White (1899–1985) US journalist and humorist. *The Commuter*

49 The Victorians had not been anxious to go away for the weekend. The Edwardians, on the contrary, were nomadic.

T. H. White (1906–64) British novelist. *Farewell Victoria*, Ch. 4

TREASON

See also betrayal

1 Please to remember the Fifth of November,
Gunpowder Treason and Plot.
We know no reason why gunpowder treason
Should ever be forgot.

Anonymous Traditional

2 ...in general sorrow that so monstrous a wickedness should be found harboured within the breast of any of their religion.

Charles Cornwallis (c. 1580–1629) British ambassador in Madrid. Describing Spanish reaction to the Gunpowder Plot. Letter to Lord Salisbury, Nov 1605

3 During his Office, Treason was no Crime.
The Sons of Belial had a Glorious Time.

John Dryden (1631–1700) British poet and dramatist. *Absalom and Achitophel*, I

4 A desperate disease requires a dangerous remedy.

Guy Fawkes (1570–1606) English conspirator. In justification of the Gunpowder Plot; said when questioned by the King and council immediately after his arrest (5 Nov 1605). *Dictionary of National Biography*

5 ...to blow the Scots back again into Scotland.

Guy Fawkes One of his professed objectives for the Gunpowder Plot, referring to the Scottish-born King James I; said when questioned by the King and council immediately after his arrest, 5 Nov 1605. *Dictionary of National Biography*

6 Treason doth never prosper: what's the reason?
For if it prosper, none dare call it treason.

John Harington (1561–1612) English writer. *Epigrams*, 'Of Treason'

7 He maintained his denial. He was offered immunity from prosecution. He sat in silence for a while. He got up, looked out of the window, poured himself a drink and after a few minutes confessed. Later he co-operated, and he continued to co-operate. That is how the immunity was given and how Blunt responded.

Michael Havers (1923–) British lawyer and Conservative politician. Referring to the immunity from prosecution offered to the spy, Sir Anthony Blunt, in 1964. Speech, House of Commons, 21 Nov 1979

8 Germany calling, Germany calling.

'Lord Haw-Haw' (William Joyce; 1906–46) US-born propagandist for German Nazis. Radio broadcasts to Britain, during World War II

9 Caesar had his Brutus – Charles the First, his Cromwell – and George the Third – ('Treason,' cried the Speaker)...*may profit by their example*. If *this* be treason, make the most of it.

Patrick Henry (1736–99) US statesman. Speech, Virginia Convention, May 1765

10 On the 5th of November we began our Parliament, to which the King should have come in person, but refrained, through a practice but that morning discovered. The plot was to have blown up the King.

Edward Hoby (1560–1617) English politician. Letter to Sir Thomas Edmondes, 19 Nov 1605

11 Any service rendered to the temporal king to the prejudice of the eternal king is, without doubt, an act of treachery.

Stephen Langton (c. 1150–1228) Archbishop of Canterbury. Letter to the barons of England, 1207

12 Gives not the hawthorn bush a sweeter shade
To shepherds, looking on their silly sheep,
Than doth a rich embroider'd canopy
To kings that fear their subjects' treachery?

William Shakespeare (1564–1616) English dramatist. *Henry VI, Part Three*, II:5

13 O villains, vipers, damn'd without redemption!
Dogs, easily won to fawn on any man!
Snakes, in my heart-blood warm'd, that sting my heart!
Three Judases, each one thrice worse than Judas!
Would they make peace? terrible hell make war
Upon their spotted souls for this offence!

William Shakespeare *Richard II*, III:2

14 Mine eyes are full of tears, I cannot see:
And yet salt water blinds them not so much
But they can see a sort of traitors here.
Nay, if I turn my eyes upon myself,
I find myself a traitor with the rest.

William Shakespeare *Richard II*, IV:1

15 Talk'st thou to me of 'ifs'? Thou art a traitor:
Off with his head!

William Shakespeare *Richard III*, III:4

TREE, SIR HERBERT BEERBOHM

(1852–1917) British actor and theatre manager. He managed both the Haymarket Theatre and Her Majesty's Theatre and founded RADA.

1 I was born old and get younger every day. At present I am sixty years young.

Beerbohm Tree (Hesketh Pearson)

2 My poor fellow, why not carry a watch?

Remark made to a man carrying a grandfather clock. *Beerbohm Tree* (Hesketh Pearson)

3 He is an old bore; even the grave yawns for him.

Referring to Israel Zangwill. *Beerbohm Tree* (Hesketh Pearson)

4 The only man who wasn't spoilt by being lionized was Daniel.

Beerbohm Tree (Hesketh Pearson)

5 A whipper-snapper of criticism who quoted dead languages to hide his ignorance of life.

Refering to A. B. Walleley. *Beerbohm Tree* (Hesketh Pearson)

6 The national sport of England is obstacle-racing. People fill their rooms with useless and cumbersome furniture, and spend the rest of their lives in trying to dodge it.

Beerbohm Tree (Hesketh Pearson)

7 Oh my God! Remember you're in Egypt. The *skay* is only seen in Kensington.

To a leading lady. *Beerbohm Tree* (Hesketh Pearson)

8 When I pass my name in such large letters I blush, but at the same time instinctively raise my hat.

Beerbohm Tree (Hesketh Pearson)

9 Take that black box away. I can't act in front of it.

Objecting to the presence of the camera while performing in a silent film. *Hollywood: The Pioneers* (K. Brownlow)

10 Ladies, just a little more virginity, if you don't mind.

Directing a group of sophisticated actresses. *Smart Aleck* (H. Teichmann)

TREES

See also countryside, Nature

1 And the Lord God took the man, and put him into the garden of Eden to dress it and to keep it. And the Lord God commanded the man, saying, Of every tree of the garden thou mayest freely eat: But of the tree of the knowledge of good and evil, thou shalt not eat of it: for in the day that thou eatest thereof thou shalt surely die.

Bible: Genesis 2:15–17

2 O leave this barren spot to me!
Spare, woodman, spare the beechen tree.

Thomas Campbell (1777–1844) British poet. *The Beech-Tree's Petition*

3 The poplars are felled, farewell to the shade,
And the whispering sound of the cool colonnade!

William Cowper (1731–1800) British poet. *The Poplar Field*

4 On Wenlock Edge the wood's in trouble;
His forest fleece the Wrekin heaves;
The gale, it plies the saplings double,
And thick on Severn snow the leaves.

A. E. Housman (1859–1936) British scholar and poet. *A Shropshire Lad*, 'The Welsh Marches'

5 Loveliest of trees, the cherry now
Is hung with bloom along the bough,
And stands about the woodland ride
Wearing white for Eastertide.

A. E. Housman *A Shropshire Lad*, '1887'

6 I'm replacing some of the timber used up by my books. Books are just trees with squiggles on them.

Hammond Innes (1913–) British novelist. Interview in *Radio Times*, 18 Aug 1984

7 As when, upon a trancèd summer-night,
Those green-rob'd senators of mighty woods,
Tall oaks, branch-charmed by the earnest stars,
Dream, and so dream all night without a stir.

John Keats (1795–1821) British poet. *Hyperion*, I

8 I think that I shall never see
A poem lovely as a tree.

Alfred Joyce Kilmer (1886–1918) US poet. *Trees*

9 Poems are made by fools like me,
But only God can make a tree.

Alfred Joyce Kilmer *Trees*

10 Yet once more, O ye laurels, and once more,
Ye myrtles brown, with ivy never sere,
I come to pluck your berries harsh and crude,
And with forced fingers rude
Shatter your leaves before the mellowing year.

John Milton (1608–74) English poet. *Lycidas*

11 Woodman, spare that tree!
Touch not a single bough!
In youth it sheltered me,
And I'll protect it now.

George Pope Morris (1802–64) US journalist. *Woodman, Spare That Tree*

12 I think that I shall never see
A billboard lovely as a tree.
Perhaps unless the billboards fall,
I'll never see a tree at all.

Ogden Nash (1902–71) US poet. *Song of the Open Road*

13 The difference between a gun and a tree is a difference of tempo. The tree explodes every spring.

Ezra Pound (1885–1972) US poet. *Criterion*, July 1937

TRIVIALITY

See also insignificance

1 Nothing matters very much, and very few things matter at all.

Arthur Balfour (1848–1930) British statesman. Attrib.

2 A Storm in a Teacup.

W. B. Bernard (1807–75) British dramatist. Play title

3 It beareth the name of Vanity Fair, because the town where 'tis kept is lighter than vanity.

John Bunyan (1628–88) English writer. *The Pilgrim's Progress*, Pt. I

4 As she frequently remarked when she made any such mistake, it would be all the same a hundred years hence.

Charles Dickens (1812–70) British novelist. Said by Mrs Squeers. *Martin Chuzzlewit*, Ch. 9

5 Little things affect little minds.

Benjamin Disraeli (1804–81) British statesman. *Sybil*, Bk. III, Ch. 2

6 You know my method. It is founded upon the observance of trifles.

Arthur Conan Doyle (1856–1930) British writer. *The Boscombe Valley Mystery*

7 It has long been an axiom of mine that the little things are infinitely the most important.

Arthur Conan Doyle *A Case of Identity*

8 Depend upon it, there is nothing so unnatural as the commonplace.

Arthur Conan Doyle *A Case of Identity*

9 'Is there any point to which you would wish to draw my attention?'
'To the curious incident of the dog in the night-time.'
'The dog did nothing in the night-time.'
'That was the curious incident,' remarked Sherlock Holmes.

Arthur Conan Doyle *The Silver Blaze*

10 To great evils we submit; we resent little provocations.

William Hazlitt (1778–1830) British essayist. *On Great and Little Things*

11 Little minds are interested in the extraordinary; great minds in the commonplace.

Elbert Hubbard (1856–1915) US writer. *Roycroft Dictionary and Book of Epigrams*

12 What should I do? I think the best thing is to order a new stamp to be made with my face on it.

Charles (1887–1922) Emperor of Austria. On hearing of his accession to emperor. *Anekdotenschatz* (H. Hoffmeister)

13 To suckle fools and chronicle small beer.

William Shakespeare (1564–1616) English dramatist. *Othello*, II:1

14 It's deadly commonplace, but, after all, the commonplaces are the great poetic truths.

Robert Louis Stevenson (1850–94) Scottish writer. *Weir of Hermiston*, Ch. 6

15 Ah God! the petty fools of rhyme
That shriek and sweat in pigmy wars.

Alfred, Lord Tennyson (1809–92) British poet. *Literary Squabbles*

TROLLOPE, ANTHONY

(1815–82) British novelist. He established his reputation with the Barsetshire series of novels, including *The Warden* (1855) and *Barchester Towers* (1857). Later books include *Phineas Finn* (1869).

Quotations about Trollope

1 He has a gross and repulsive face but appears *bon enfant* when you talk to him. But he is the dullest Briton of them all.

Henry James (1843–1916) US novelist. Letter to his family, 1 Nov 1875

Quotations by Trollope

2 He must have known me had he seen me as he was wont to see me, for he was in the habit of flogging me constantly. Perhaps he did not recognize me by my face.

Autobiography, Ch. 1

3 Three hours a day will produce as much as a man ought to write.

Autobiography, Ch. 15

4 No man thinks there is much ado about nothing when the ado is about himself.

The Bertrams, Ch. 27

5 Those who have courage to love should have courage to suffer.

The Bertrams, Ch. 27

6 In these days a man is nobody unless his biography is kept so far posted up that it may be ready for the national breakfast-table on the morning after his demise.

Doctor Thorne, Ch. 25

7 The comic almanacs give us dreadful pictures of January and February; but, in truth, the months which should be made to look gloomy in England are March and April. Let no man boast himself that he has got through the perils of winter till at least the seventh of May.

Doctor Thorne, Ch. 47

8 It's dogged as does it. It ain't thinking about it.

Last Chronicle of Barset, Ch. 61

9 With many women I doubt whether there be any more effectual way of touching their hearts than ill-using them and then confessing it. If you wish to get the sweetest fragrance from the herb at your feet, tread on it and bruise it.

Miss Mackenzie, Ch. 10

10 We cannot bring ourselves to believe it possible that a foreigner should in any respect be wiser than ourselves. If any such point out to us our follies, we at once claim those follies as the special evidences of our wisdom.

Orley Farm, Ch. 18

11 It is because we put up with bad things that hotel-keepers continue to give them to us.

Orley Farm, Ch. 18

12 As for conceit, what man will do any good who is not conceited? Nobody holds a good opinion of a man who has a low opinion of himself.

Orley Farm, Ch. 22

13 Mr Turnbull had predicted evil consequences... and was now doing the best in his power to bring about the verification of his own prophecies.

Phineas Finn, Ch. 25

14 I doubt whether any girl would be satisfied with her lover's mind if she knew the whole of it.

The Small House at Allington, Ch. 4

15 And, above all things, never think that you're not good enough yourself. A man should never think that. My belief is that in life people will take you very much at your own reckoning.

The Small House at Allington, Ch. 32

16 Those who offend us are generally punished for the offence they give; but we so frequently miss the satisfaction of knowing that we are avenged!

The Small House at Allington, Ch. 50

TROTSKY, LEON

(Lev Davidovich Bronstein; 1879–1940) Russian revolutionary. Originally a Menshevik, he returned from exile to become a Bolshevik and played a major role in the October (1917) Revolution. After Lenin's death he was exiled by Stalin and murdered in Mexico (possibly by a Soviet agent).

1 Revolution by its very nature is sometimes compelled to take in more territory than it is capable of holding. Retreats are possible – when there is territory to retreat from.

Diary in Exile, 15 Feb 1935

2 Old age is the most unexpected of all the things that happen to a man.

Diary in Exile, 8 May 1935

3 The 23rd of February was International

Woman's Day…It had not occurred to anyone that it might become the first day of the revolution.
History of the Russian Revolution, Pt. I, Ch. 7

4 The revolution does not choose its paths: it made its first steps towards victory under the belly of a Cossack's horse.
History of the Russian Revolution, Pt. I, Ch. 7

5 Revolutions are always verbose.
History of the Russian Revolution, Pt. II, Ch. 12

6 Insurrection is an art, and like all arts it has its laws.
History of the Russian Revolution, Pt. III, Ch. 6

7 The fundamental premise of a revolution is that the existing social structure has become incapable of solving the urgent problems of development of the nation.
History of the Russian Revolution, Pt. III, Ch. 6

8 From being a patriotic myth, the Russian people have become an awful reality.
History of the Russian Revolution, Pt. III, Ch. 7

9 For us, the tasks of education in socialism were closely integrated with those of fighting. Ideas that enter the mind under fire remain there securely and for ever.
My Life, Ch. 35

10 It was the supreme expression of the mediocrity of the apparatus that Stalin himself rose to his position.
My Life, Ch. 40

11 Lenin's method leads to this: the party organization at first substitutes itself for the party as a whole. Then the central committee substitutes itself for the party organization, and finally a single dictator substitutes himself for the central committee.
The Communist Parties of Western Europe (N. McInnes), Ch. 3

12 Patriotism to the Soviet State is a revolutionary duty, whereas patriotism to a bourgeois State is treachery.
Disputed Barricade (Fitzroy Maclean)

13 An ally has to be watched just like an enemy.
Expansion and Coexistence (A. Ulam)

TRUMAN, HARRY S.

(1884–1972) US statesman. He became president (1945–53) after the death of Roosevelt and ordered the dropping of the atom bombs on Hiroshima and Nagasaki. His administration also established NATO.

Quotations about Truman

1 The captain with the mighty heart.
Dean Acheson (1893–1971) US lawyer and statesman. *Present at the Creation.*

2 Truman is short, square, simple, and looks one straight in the face.
Harold Nicolson (1886–1968) British writer. *Diaries*, 8 Aug 1945

Quotations by Truman

3 If you can't stand the heat, get out of the kitchen.
Perhaps proverbial in origin, possibly echoes the expression 'kitchen cabinet'. *Mr Citizen*, Ch. 15

4 If we see that Germany is winning the war we ought to help Russia, and if Russia is winning we ought to help Germany, and in that way let them kill as many as possible.
The New York Times, 24 July 1941, when Russia was invaded by Germany

5 A politician is a man who understands government, and it takes a politician to run a government. A statesman is a politician who's been dead ten or fifteen years.
New York World Telegram and Sun, 12 Apr 1958

6 The President spends most of his time kissing people on the cheek in order to get them to do what they ought to do without getting kissed.
The Observer, 'Sayings of the Week', 6 Feb 1949

7 It's a recession when your neighbour loses his job; it's a depression when you lose yours.
The Observer, 'Sayings of the Week', 13 Apr 1958

8 I didn't fire him because he was a dumb son of a bitch, although he was, but that's not against the law for generals. If it was, half to three-quarters of them would be in gaol.
Referring to General MacArthur. *Plain Speaking* (Merle Miller)

9 Give me a one-handed economist! All my economists say, 'on the one hand…on the other'.
Presidential Anecdotes (P. Boller)

10 The buck stops here.
Sign kept on his desk during his term as president. *Presidential Anecdotes* (P. Boller)

11 You don't set a fox to watching the chickens just because he has a lot of experience in the hen house.
Referring to Vice-President Nixon's nomination for president. Speech, 30 Oct 1960

TRUST

See also faith, mistrust

1 Trust ye not in a friend, put ye not confidence in a guide: keep the doors of thy mouth from her that lieth in thy bosom.
Bible: Micah 7:5

2 Never trust the man who hath reason to suspect that you know he hath injured you.
Henry Fielding (1707–54) British novelist. *Jonathan Wild*, Bk. III, Ch. 4

3 Some patients, though conscious that their condition is perilous, recover their health simply through their contentment with the goodness of the physician.
Hippocrates (c. 460–c. 377 BC) Greek physician. *Precepts*, VI

4 We are inclined to believe those whom we do not know because they have never deceived us.
Samuel Johnson (1709–84) British lexicographer. *The Idler*

5 Never trust a husband too far, nor a bachelor too near.

Helen Rowland (1876–1950) US writer. *The Rubaiyat of a Bachelor*

6 Would you buy a second-hand car from this man?

Mort Sahl (1926–) US political comedian. Referring to President Nixon. Attrib.

TRUTH

See also facts, frankness, honesty, lying, sincerity

1 Better a lie that heals than a truth that wounds.

Proverb

2 Many a true word is spoken in jest.

Proverb

3 Tell the truth and shame the devil.

Proverb

4 Truth fears no trial.

Proverb

5 Truth is stranger than fiction.

Proverb

6 Truth will out.

Proverb

7 The truth that makes men free is for the most part the truth which men prefer not to hear.

Herbert Sebastian Agar (1897–1980) US writer. *A Time for Greatness*

8 Plato is dear to me, but dearer still is truth.

Aristotle (384–322 BC) Greek philosopher. Attrib.

9 Truth sits upon the lips of dying men.

Matthew Arnold (1822–88) British poet and critic. *Sohrab and Rustum*

10 What is truth? said jesting Pilate, and would not stay for an answer.

Francis Bacon (1561–1626) English philosopher. *Essays*, 'Of Truth'

11 And ye shall know the truth, and the truth shall make you free.

Bible: John 8:32

12 Pilate saith unto him, What is truth? And when he had said this, he went out again unto the Jews, and saith unto them, I find in him no fault at all.

Bible: John 18:38

13 A truth that's told with bad intent
Beats all the lies you can invent.

William Blake (1757–1827) British poet. *Auguries of Innocence*

14 To treat your facts with imagination is one thing, to imagine your facts is another.

John Burroughs (1837–1921) US naturalist. *The Heart of Burroughs Journals*

15 Some men love truth so much that they seem to be in continual fear lest she should catch a cold on overexposure.

Samuel Butler (1835–1902) British writer. *Notebooks*

16 Agree to a short armistice with truth.

Lord Byron (1788–1824) British poet. *Don Juan*, III

17 'Tis strange – but true; for truth is always strange;
Stranger than fiction: if it could be told,
How much would novels gain by the exchange!

Lord Byron *Don Juan*, XIV

18 You can only find truth with logic if you have already found truth without it.

G. K. Chesterton (1874–1936) British writer. *The Man who was Orthodox*

19 Much truth is spoken, that more may be concealed.

Lord Darling (1849–1936) British judge. *Scintillae Juris*

20 Perjury is often bold and open. It is truth that is shamefaced – as, indeed, in many cases is no more than decent.

Lord Darling *Scintillae Juris*

21 I tore myself away from the safe comfort of certainties through my love for truth; and truth rewarded me.

Simone de Beauvoir (1908–86) French writer and feminist. *All Said and Done*

22 It is an old maxim of mine that when you have excluded the impossible, whatever remains, however improbable, must be the truth.

Arthur Conan Doyle (1856–1930) British writer. *The Beryl Coronet*

23 Errors, like Straws, upon the surface flow;
He who would search for Pearls must dive below.

John Dryden (1631–1700) British poet and dramatist. *All for Love*, Prologue

24 A man is to be cheated into passion, but to be reasoned into truth.

John Dryden *Religio Laici*, Preface

25 I do not want to use the word 'true'. There are only opinions, some of which are preferable to others. One cannot say: 'Ah. If it is just a matter of preference to hell with it'...One can die for an opinion which is only preferable.

Umberto Eco (1932–) Italian semiologist and writer. *Index on Censorship*, Vol. 23, May/June 1994

26 Ethical axioms are found and tested not very differently from the axioms of science. Truth is what stands the test of experience.

Albert Einstein (1879–1955) German-born US physicist. *Out of My Later Years*

27 If nobody is telling the truth then the lies they are telling are no longer lies but the norm is the truth.

Stephen Fry (1957–) British actor and writer. *The Liar*

28 Truth, like a torch, the more it's shook it shines.

William Hamilton (1788–1856) Scottish philosopher. *Discussions on Philosophy*, title page

29 True and False are attributes of speech, not of things. And where speech is not, there is neither Truth nor Falsehood.

Thomas Hobbes (1588–1679) English philosopher. *Leviathan*, Pt. I, Ch. 4

30 It's easy to make a man confess the lies he tells

to himself; it's far harder to make him confess the truth.

Geoffrey Household (1900–88) British writer. *Rogue Male*

31 I am certain of nothing but the holiness of the heart's affections and the truth of imagination – what the imagination seizes as beauty must be truth – whether it existed before or not.

John Keats (1795–1821) British poet. Letter to Benjamin Bailey, 22 Nov 1817

32 I never can feel certain of any truth but from a clear perception of its beauty.

John Keats Letter to George and Georgiana Keats, 16 Dec 1818–4 Jan 1819

33 'Beauty is truth, truth beauty,' – that is all
Ye know on earth, and all ye need to know.

John Keats *Ode on a Grecian Urn*

34 It is one thing to show a man that he is in an error, and another to put him in possession of truth.

John Locke (1632–1704) English philosopher. *An Essay Concerning Human Understanding*, Bk. IV, Ch. 7

35 It is hard to believe that a man is telling the truth when you know that you would lie if you were in his place.

Henry Louis Mencken (1880–1956) US journalist.

36 No one wants the truth if it is inconvenient.

Arthur Miller (1915–) US dramatist. *The Observer*, 'Sayings of the Week', 8 Jan 1989

37 Let her and Falsehood grapple; who ever knew Truth put to the worse, in a free and open encounter?

John Milton (1608–74) English poet. *Areopagitica*

38 There can be no whitewash at the White House.

Richard Milhous Nixon (1913–94) US president. Referring to the Watergate scandal. *The Observer*, 'Sayings of the Week', 30 Dec 1973

39 Let us begin by committing ourselves to the truth, to see it like it is and to tell it like it is, to find the truth, to speak the truth and live with the truth. That's what we'll do.

Richard Milhous Nixon Nomination acceptance speech, Miami, 8 Aug 1968

40 Truth has no special time of its own. Its hour is now – always.

Albert Schweitzer (1875–1965) French Protestant theologian, philosopher, physician, and musician. *Out of My Life and Thought*

41 Truth telling is not compatible with the defence of the realm.

George Bernard Shaw (1856–1950) Irish dramatist and critic. *Heartbreak House*

42 My way of joking is to tell the truth. It's the funniest joke in the world.

George Bernard Shaw *John Bull's Other Island*, II

43 When truth is discovered by someone else, it loses something of its attractiveness.

Alexander Solzhenitsyn (1918–) Russian novelist. *Candle in the Wind*, 3

44 It takes two to speak the truth – one to speak, and another to hear.

Henry David Thoreau (1817–62) US writer. *A Week on the Concord and Merrimack Rivers*

45 The only truths which are universal are those gross enough to be thought so.

Paul Valéry (1871–1945) French poet and writer. *Mauvaises Pensées et autres*

46 But not even Marx is more precious to us than the truth.

Simone Weil (1909–43) French philosopher. *Oppression and Liberty*, 'Revolution Proletarienne'

47 There are no whole truths; all truths are half-truths. It is trying to treat them as whole truths that plays the devil.

A. N. Whitehead (1861–1947) British philosopher. *Dialogues*, 16

48 I believe that in the end the truth will conquer.

John Wycliffe (1329–84) English religious reformer. Said to John of Gaunt, Duke of Lancaster, 1381. *Short History of the English People* (J. R. Green)

49 Truth is on the march; nothing can stop it now.

Émile Zola (1840–1902) French novelist. Referring to the Dreyfus scandal. Attrib.

TURGENEV, IVAN

(1818–83) Russian novelist. A critic of the Russian system in *Sportsman's Sketches* (1852), he was briefly imprisoned. The novels *Fathers and Sons* (1862) and *The Torrents of Spring* (1872) established his reputation, but he is best known for the play *A Month in the Country* (1870).

1 I agree with no man's opinion. I have some of my own.

Fathers and Sons, Ch. 13

2 The temerity to believe in nothing.

Fathers and Sons, Ch. 14

3 Go and try to disprove death. Death will disprove you, and that's all!

Fathers and Sons, Ch. 27

4 Whatever a man prays for, he prays for a miracle. Every prayer reduces itself to this: 'Great God grant that twice two be not four.'

Poems in Prose, 'Prayer'

TWAIN, MARK

(Samuel Langhorne Clemens; 1835–1910) US writer. A steamboat pilot, he wrote a novel, *The Adventures of Huckleberry Finn* (1884), which established his reputation as a writer.

Quotations about Twain

1 The average American loves his family. If he has any love left over for some other person, he generally selects Mark Twain.

Thomas Edison (1847–1931) US inventor. Attrib.

2 Mark Twain and I are in the same position. We have to put things in such a way as to make people, who would otherwise hang us, believe that we are joking.

George Bernard Shaw (1856–1950) Irish dramatist and critic. Attrib.

Quotations by Twain

3 There was things which he stretched, but mainly he told the truth.

The Adventures of Huckleberry Finn, Ch. 1

4 There are three kinds of lies: lies, damned lies, and statistics.

Autobiography

5 Soap and education are not as sudden as a massacre, but they are more deadly in the long run.

A Curious Dream, 'The Facts concerning the Recent Resignation'

6 It takes your enemy and your friend, working together, to hurt you to the heart; the one to slander you and the other to get the news to you.

Following the Equator, Ch. 45

7 It is by the goodness of God that in our country we have those three unspeakably precious things: freedom of speech, freedom of conscience, and the prudence never to practise either of them.

Following the Equator, heading of Ch. 20

8 Man is the only animal that blushes. Or needs to.

Following the Equator, heading of Ch. 27

9 I must have a prodigious quantity of mind; it takes me as much as a week, sometimes, to make it up.

The Innocents Abroad, Ch. 7

10 They spell it Vinci and pronounce it Vinchy; foreigners always spell better than they pronounce.

The Innocents Abroad, Ch. 19

11 The radical invents the views. When he has worn them out, the conservative adopts them.

Notebooks

12 Familiarity breeds contempt – and children.

Notebooks

13 When people do not respect us we are sharply offended; yet deep down in his heart no man much respects himself.

Notebooks

14 Good breeding consists in concealing how much we think of ourselves and how little we think of other persons.

Notebooks

15 Adam was but human – this explains it all. He did not want the apple for the apple's sake, he wanted it only because it was forbidden.

Pudd'nhead Wilson, Ch. 2

16 There ain't no way to find out why a snorer can't hear himself snore.

Tom Sawyer Abroad, Ch. 10

17 Something that everybody wants to have read and nobody wants to read.

Definition of a classic of literature. Speech at Nineteenth Century Club, New York, 20 Nov 1900

18 Reports of my death are greatly exaggerated.

On learning that his obituary had been published in the *New York Journal*. Cable to the Associated Press

19 That's right. 'Taint yours, and 'taint mine.

Agreeing with a friend's comment that the money of a particular rich industrialist was 'tainted'. Attrib.

20 Scarce, sir. Mighty scarce.

Responding to the question 'In a world without women what would men become?' Attrib.

21 To cease smoking is the easiest thing I ever did. I ought to know because I've done it a thousand times.

Referring to giving up smoking. Attrib.

TYNAN, KENNETH

(1927–80) British theatre critic and producer. He became literary manager of the National Theatre. His books inlcude *He That Plays the King* (1950) and *Curtains* (1961).

1 A novel is a static thing that one moves through; a play is a dynamic thing that moves past one.

Curtains

2 William Congreve is the only sophisticated playwright England has produced; and like Shaw, Sheridan, and Wilde, his nearest rivals, he was brought up in Ireland.

Curtains, 'The Way of the World'

3 A good drama critic is one who perceives what is happening in the theatre of his time. A great drama critic also perceives what is not happening.

Tynan Right and Left, Foreword

4 A good many inconveniences attend play-going in any large city, but the greatest of them is usually the play itself.

New York Herald Tribune

5 A critic is a man who knows the way but can't drive the car.

The New York Times Magazine, 9 Jan 1966

6 What, when drunk, one sees in other women, one sees in Garbo sober.

The Sunday Times, 25 Aug 1963

TYRANNY

See also authoritarianism, oppression

1 Churchill on top of the wave has in him the stuff of which tyrants are made.

Lord Beaverbrook (1879–1964) Canadian-born British newspaper proprietor. *Politicians and the War*

2 He is an ordinary human being after all!...now he will put himself above everyone else and become a tyrant.

Ludwig van Beethoven (1770–1827) German composer. Referring to Napoleon, on hearing that he had declared himself emperor. Remark to Ferdinand Ries, a pupil

3 To tell the truth, Napoleon is a dangerous man in a free country. He seems to me to have the makings of a tyrant.

Lucien Bonaparte (1775–1840) Brother of Napoleon I. Letter to Joseph Bonaparte, 1790

4 Nature has left this tincture in the blood,
That all men would be tyrants if they could.

Daniel Defoe (1660–1731) British journalist and writer. *The Kentish Petition*, Addenda

5 'Twixt kings and tyrants there's this difference known;
Kings seek their subjects' good: tyrants their own.

Robert Herrick (1591–1674) English poet. *Hesperides*, 'Kings and Tyrants'

6 So long as men worship the Caesars and Napoleons, Caesars and Napoleons will arise to make them miserable.

Aldous Huxley (1894–1964) British novelist. *Ends and Means*

7 A country governed by a despot is an inverted cone.

Samuel Johnson (1709–84) British lexicographer. *Life of Johnson* (J. Boswell), Vol. III

8 It is better that a man should tyrannize over his bank balance than over his fellow citizens.

John Maynard Keynes (1883–1946) British economist. *The General Theory of Employment, Interest and Money*, Bk. VI, Ch. 24

9 ...whenever kingship approaches tyranny it is near its end, for by this it becomes ripe for division, change of dynasty, or total destruction, especially in a temperate climate...where men are habitually, morally and naturally free.

Nicholas of Oresme (c. 1320–82) Chaplain to Charles V of France. *De Moneta*

10 Where laws end, tyranny begins.

William Pitt the Elder (1708–78) British statesman. Referring to John Wilkes, an 18th century journalist and radical politician, regarded as a champion of liberty. Speech, House of Lords, 9 Jan 1770

11 The only tyrannies from which men, women and children are suffering in real life are the tyrannies of minorities.

Theodore Roosevelt (1858–1919) US Republican president. Speech, 22 Mar 1912

12 The laity found him more than a king, the clergy more than a pope, and both an intolerable tyrant.

William of Newburgh (1136–c. 1198) English monk and historian. Referring to William Longchamp, Justiciar and Chancellor of England during Richard I's absence on Crusade. *Historia Rerum Anglicarum*, Bk. IV, Ch. 14

U

UNAMUNO, MIGUEL DE

(1864–1936) Spanish writer and philosopher. His major philosophical work is *The Tragic Sense of Life* (1913).

1 All right, my lord creator, Don Miguel, you too will die and return to the nothing whence you came. God will cease to dream you!
Mist

2 Man, by the very fact of being man, by possessing consciousness, is, in comparison with the ass or the crab, a disease animal. Consciousness is a disease.
The Tragic Sense of Life, 1

3 May God deny you peace but give you glory!
Closing words. *The Tragic Sense of Life*

4 They will conquer, but they will not convince.
Referring to the Franco rebels. Attrib.

UNCERTAINTY

See also doubt, indecision

1 If ifs and ans were pots and pans, there'd be no trade for tinkers.
Proverb

2 I have known uncertainty: a state unknown to the Greeks.
Jorge Luis Borges (1899–1986) Argentinian writer. *Ficciones*, 'The Babylonian Lottery'

3 Without measureless and perpetual uncertainty the drama of human life would be destroyed.
Winston Churchill (1874–1965) British statesman. *The Gathering Storm*

4 Of course not. After all, I may be wrong.
Bertrand Russell (1872–1970) British philosopher. On being asked whether he would be prepared to die for his beliefs. Attrib.

UNDERSTANDING

See also intelligence, wisdom

1 And come hither, and I shall light a candle of understanding in thine heart, which shall not be put out, till the things be performed which thou shalt begin to write.
Bible: II Esdras 14:25

2 It is good to know what a man is, and also what the world takes him for. But you do not understand him until you have learnt how he understands himself.
F. H. Bradley (1846–1924) British philosopher. *Aphorisms*

3 The people may be made to follow a course of action, but they may not be made to understand it.
Confucius (K'ung Fu-tzu; 551–479 BC) Chinese philosopher. *Analects*

4 Only one man ever understood me…And he didn't understand me.
Hegel (1770–1831) German philosopher. Said on his deathbed. *Famous Last Words* (B. Conrad)

5 Even when poetry has a meaning, as it usually has, it may be inadvisable to draw it out…Perfect understanding will sometimes almost extinguish pleasure.
A. E. Housman (1859–1936) British scholar and poet. *The Name and Nature of Poetry*

6 Thought must be divided against itself before it can come to any knowledge of itself.
Aldous Huxley (1894–1964) British novelist. *Do What You Will*

7 She did her work with the thoroughness of a mind that reveres details and never quite understands them.
Sinclair Lewis (1885–1951) US novelist. *Babbitt*, Ch. 18

8 I used to tell my husband that, if he could make *me* understand something, it would be clear to all the other people in the country.
Eleanor Roosevelt (1884–1962) US writer and lecturer, wife of President Franklin Delano Roosevelt. Newspaper column, 'My Day', 12 Feb 1947

9 I have striven not to laugh at human actions, not to weep at them, nor to hate them, but to understand them.
Benedict Spinoza (Baruch de Spinoza; 1632–77) Dutch philosopher. *Tractatus Theologico-Politicus*, Ch. 1

10 All, everything that I understand, I understand only because I love.
Leo Tolstoy (1828–1910) Russian writer. *War and Peace*, Bk. VII, Ch. 16

UNEMPLOYMENT

See also idleness, work

1 We must do more than attack the scourge of unemployment. We should also get rid of dead-end, low-paid work with no prospects.
Tony Blair (1953–) British Labour politician. *The Independent*, 14 June 1994

2 Giz a job, I could do that.
Alan Bleasdale (1946–) British playwright. Said by his character Yosser Hughes. *Boys From the Blackstuff*

3 When a great many people are unable to find work, unemployment results.
Calvin Coolidge (1872–1933) US president. *City Editor*

4 Rising unemployment and the recession have been the price that we've had to pay to get inflation down: that is a price well worth paying.
Norman Lamont (1931–) British politician. *The Observer*, 24 Nov 1991

5 My father did not wait around…he got on his bike and went out looking for work.
Norman Tebbitt (1931–) British Conservative politician. Speech, Conservative Party conference, 1981

6 It's a recession when your neighbour loses his job; it's a depression when you lose your own.
Harry S. Truman (1884–1972) US statesman. *The Observer*, 'Sayings of the Week', 6 Apr 1958

7 Something must be done.

Duke of Windsor (1894–1972) King of the United Kingdom; abdicated 1936. Said while visiting areas of high unemployment in South Wales during the 1930s. Attrib.

UNFAITHFULNESS

See also adultery

1 Early one morning, just as the sun was rising,
I heard a maiden singing in the valley below:
'Oh, don't deceive me; Oh, never leave me!
How could you use a poor maiden so?'

Anonymous *Early One Morning*

2 Swore to be true to each other, true as the stars above;
He was her man, but he done her wrong.

Anonymous *Frankie and Johnny*

3 Reading someone else's newspaper is like sleeping with someone else's wife. Nothing seems to be precisely in the right place, and when you find what you are looking for, it is not clear then how to respond to it.

Malcolm Bradbury (1932–) British academic and novelist. *Stepping Westward*, Bk I, Ch. 1

4 ...today I was driving a little more slowly because of the rain, but that was the only difference between yesterday and today.
My wife had been unfaithful to me but there was still the same number of traffic lights to obey...

John Braine (1922–86) British novelist. *Life at the Top*, Ch. 16

5 Translations (like wives) are seldom faithful if they are in the least attractive.

Roy Campbell (1901–57) South African poet. *Poetry Review*

6 But I kissed her little sister,
And forgot my Clementine.

Percy Montrose (19th century) US songwriter. *Clementine*

7 O, swear not by the moon, th' inconstant moon,
That monthly changes in her circled orb,
Lest that thy love prove likewise variable.

William Shakespeare (1564–1616) English dramatist. *Romeo and Juliet*, II:2

8 His honour rooted in dishonour stood,
And faith unfaithful kept him falsely true.

Alfred, Lord Tennyson (1809–92) British poet. *Idylls of the King*, 'Lancelot and Elaine'

9 No man worth having is true to his wife, or can be true to his wife, or ever was, or ever will be so.

John Vanbrugh (1664–1726) English architect and dramatist. *The Relapse*, III:2

10 Why should marriage bring only tears?
All I wanted was a man
With a single heart,
And we would stay together
As our hair turned white,
Not somebody always after wriggling fish
With his big bamboo rod.

Chuo Wên-chün (?179–117 BC) Chinese poet. *Orchid Boat, Women Poets of China* (Kenneth Rexroth and Ling Chung)

UNITY

1 A chain is no stronger than its weakest link.

Proverb

2 Union is strength.

Proverb

3 United we stand, divided we fall.

Proverb

4 That typically English characteristic for which there is no English name – *esprit de corps*.

Frank Ezra Adcock (1886–1968) British classicist. Presidential address

5 And if one prevail against him, two shall withstand him; and a threefold cord is not quickly broken.

Bible: Ecclesiastes 4:12

6 And the whole earth was of one language, and of one speech.

Bible: Genesis 11:1

7 When bad men combine, the good must associate; else they will fall one by one, an unpitied sacrifice in a contemptible struggle.

Edmund Burke (1729–97) British politician. *Thoughts on the Cause of the Present Discontents*

8 All for one, and one for all.

Alexandre Dumas, père (1802–70) French novelist and dramatist. *The Three Musketeers*

9 We must indeed all hang together, or most assuredly, we shall all hang separately.

Benjamin Franklin (1706–90) US scientist and statesman. Remark on signing the Declaration of Independence, 4 July 1776

10 No human relation gives one possession in another – every two souls are absolutely different. In friendship or in love, the two side by side raise hands together to find what one cannot reach alone.

Kahil Gibran (1833–1931) Lebanese mystic and poet. *Beloved Prophet* (ed. Virginia Hilu)

11 Everyone has observed how much more dogs are animated when they hunt in a pack, than when they pursue their game apart. We might, perhaps, be at a loss to explain this phenomenon, if we had not experience of a similar in ourselves.

David Hume (1711–76) Scottish philosopher. *A Treatise of Human Nature*

12 Now, is it to lower the price of corn, or isn't it? It is not much matter which we say, but mind, we must all say *the same*.

Lord Melbourne (1779–1848) British statesman. Said at a cabinet meeting. *The English Constitution* (Bagehot), Ch. 1

UNIVERSE

See also astronomy, moon, space, stars, sun, world

1 Had I been present at the Creation, I would have given some useful hints for the better ordering of the universe.

Alfonso the Wise (c. 1221–84) King of Castile and Léon. Referring to the complicated Ptolemaic model of the universe. Often quoted as, 'Had I been consulted I would have recommended something simpler'. Attrib.

2 The visible universe was an illusion or, more precisely, a sophism. Mirrors and fatherhood are abominable because they multiply it and extend it.

Jorge Luis Borges (1899–1986) Argentinian writer. *Ficciones*, 'Tlön, Uqbar, Orbis Tertius'

3 In this unbelievable universe in which we live there are no absolutes. Even parallel lines, reaching into infinity, meet somewhere yonder.

Pearl Buck (1892–1973) US novelist. *A Bridge for Passing*

4 I don't pretend to understand the Universe – it's a great deal bigger than I am...People ought to be modester.

Thomas Carlyle (1795–1881) Scottish historian and essayist. Attrib.

5 MARGARET FULLER. I accept the universe.
CARLYLE. Gad! she'd better!

Thomas Carlyle Attrib.

6 The cosmos is about the smallest hole that a man can hide his head in.

G. K. Chesterton (1874–1936) British writer. *Orthodoxy*, Ch. 1

7 There is no reason to assume that the universe has the slightest interest in intelligence – or even in life. Both may be random accidental by-products of its operations like the beautiful patterns on a butterfly's wings. The insect would fly just as well without them.

Arthur C. Clarke (1917–) British science-fiction writer. *The Lost Worlds of 2001*

8 I am very interested in the Universe – I am specializing in the universe and all that surrounds it.

Peter Cook (1937–) British writer and entertainer. *Beyond the Fringe*

9 Listen; there's a hell of a good universe next door: let's go.

e. e. cummings (1894–1962) US poet. *Pity this Busy Monster, Mankind*

10 Anyone informed that the universe is expanding and contracting in pulsations of eighty billion years has a right to ask, 'What's in it for me?'

Peter De Vries (1910–) US novelist. *The Glory of the Hummingbird*, Ch. 1

11 My own suspicion is that the universe is not only queerer than we suppose, but queerer than we *can* suppose.

J. B. S. Haldane (1892–1964) British geneticist. *Possible Worlds*, 'On Being the Right Size'

12 The universe is not hostile, nor yet is it friendly. It is simply indifferent.

John Haynes Holmes (1879–1964) US clergyman. *A Sensible Man's View of Religion*

13 The universe begins to look more like a great thought than like a great machine.

James Jeans (1877–1946) British scientist. *The Mysterious Universe*

14 In my youth I regarded the universe as an open book, printed in the language of physical equations, whereas now it appears to me as a text written in invisible ink, of which in our rare moments of grace we are able to decipher a small fragment.

Arthur Koestler (1905–83) Hungarian-born British writer. *Bricks to Babel*, Epilogue

15 Out of all possible universes, the only one which can exist, in the sense that it can be known, is simply the one which satisfies the narrow conditions necessary for the development of intelligent life.

Bernard Lovell (1913–) British astronomer and writer. *In the Centre of Immensities*

16 My theology, briefly, is that the universe was dictated but not signed.

Christopher Morley (1890–1957) US writer. Attrib.

17 The universe ought to be presumed too vast to have any character.

C. S. Peirce (1839–1914) US physicist. *Collected Papers*, VI

UPDIKE, JOHN

(1932–) US novelist and writer. His novels include *Rabbit, Run* (1960), *Couples* (1968), *Marry Me* (1976), *Rabbit is Rich* (1981), and *The Witches of Eastwick* (1984).

1 A healthy male adult bore consumes each year one and a half times his own weight in other people's patience.

Assorted Prose, 'Confessions of a Wild Bore'

2 In general the churches, visited by me too often on weekdays... bore for me the same relation to God that billboards did to Coca-Cola: they promoted thirst without quenching it.

A Month of Sundays, Ch. 2

3 Americans have been conditioned to respect newness, whatever it costs them.

A Month of Sundays, Ch. 18

4 He is a man of brick. As if he was born as a baby literally of clay and decades of exposure have baked him to the colour and hardness of brick.

Rabbit, Run

USTINOV, SIR PETER

(1921–) British actor, director, and dramatist. His plays include *The Love of Four Colonels* (1951), *Romanoff and Juliet* (1956), and *Beethoven's Tenth* (1983). He is also a well-known impersonator and raconteur.

1 Thanks to the movies, gunfire has always sounded unreal to me, even when being fired at.

Dear Me, Ch. 7

2 And here is the lesson I learned in the army. If you want to do a thing badly, you have to work at it as though you want to do it well.

Dear Me, Ch. 8

3 I am an optimist, unrepentant and militant. After all, in order not to be a fool an optimist must know how sad a place the world can be. It is only the pessimist who finds this out anew every day.

Dear Me, Ch. 9

4 There are no old men any more. *Playboy* and *Penthouse* have between them made an ideal of eternal adolescence, sunburnt and saunaed, with the grey dorianed out of it.

Dear Me, Ch. 18

5 I believe that the Jews have made a contribution to the human condition out of all proportion to their

numbers: I believe them to be an immense people. Not only have they supplied the world with two leaders of the stature of Jesus Christ and Karl Marx, but they have even indulged in the luxury of following neither one nor the other.
Dear Me, Ch. 19

6 This is a free country, madam. We have a right to share your privacy in a public place.
Romanoff and Juliet, I

7 As for being a General, well, at the age of four with paper hats and wooden swords we're all Generals. Only some of us never grow out of it.
Romanoff and Juliet, I

8 A diplomat these days is nothing but a head-waiter who's allowed to sit down occasionally.
Romanoff and Juliet, I

9 If Botticelli were alive today he'd be working for *Vogue*.
The Observer, 'Sayings of the Week', 21 Oct 1962

10 People at the top of the tree are those without qualifications to detain them at the bottom.
Attrib.

V

VENICE

See also Europe

1 Streets full of water. Please advise.

Robert Benchley (1889–1945) US humorist. Telegram sent to his editor on arriving in Venice. Attrib.

2 Venice is like eating an entire box of chocolate liqueurs at one go.

Truman Capote (1924–84) US novelist. *The Observer*, 'Sayings of the Week', 26 Nov 1961

3 Venice, the eldest Child of Liberty.
She was a maiden City, bright and free.

William Wordsworth (1770–1850) British poet. Venice, a republic since the Middle Ages, was conquered by Napoleon in 1797 and absorbed into his Kingdom of Italy in 1805. *Sonnets*, 'Once did she hold'

4 Once did she hold the gorgeous east in fee;
And was the safeguard of the west.

William Wordsworth *Sonnets*, 'Once did she hold'

5 When she took unto herself a mate,
She must espouse the everlasting sea.

William Wordsworth *Sonnets*, 'Once did she hold'

VERBOSITY

See also brevity, sermons, speech, speeches, writing

1 There was a young man of Japan
Whose limericks never would scan;
When they said it was so,
He replied, 'Yes, I know,
But I always try to get as many words into the last line as ever I possibly can.'

Anonymous

2 As far as I can see, you have used every cliché except 'God is love' and 'Please adjust your dress before leaving'.

Winston Churchill (1874–1965) British statesman. Complaining about a memorandum from the Conservative statesman Anthony Eden. *The Mirror: A Political History* (M. Edelman)

3 A sophistical rhetorician inebriated with the exuberance of his own verbosity.

Benjamin Disraeli (1804–81) British statesman. Referring to the Liberal statesman Gladstone. Speech, 27 July 1878

4 But far more numerous was the Herd of such,
Who think too little, and who talk too much.

John Dryden (1631–1700) British poet and dramatist. *Absalom and Achitophel*, I

5 Nothing is more despicable than a professional talker who uses his words as a quack uses his remedies.

François Fénelon (1651–1715) French writer and prelate. Letter to M. Dacier

6 I have made this letter longer than usual, only because I have not had the time to make it shorter.

Blaise Pascal (1623–62) French philosopher and mathematician. *Lettres provinciales*, XVI

7 Words are like leaves; and where they most abound,
Much fruit of sense beneath is rarely found.

Alexander Pope (1688–1744) British poet. *An Essay on Criticism*

VICE

See also crime, evil, sin, virtue and vice

1 When vice prevails, and impious men bear sway,
The post of honour is a private station.

Joseph Addison (1672–1719) British essayist. *Cato*, IV:1

2 We make ourselves a ladder out of our vices if we trample the vices themselves underfoot.

St Augustine of Hippo (354–430) Bishop of Hippo. *Sermons*, Bk. III, 'De Ascensione'

3 And when Jehu was come to Jezreel, Jezebel heard of it; and she painted her face, and tired her head, and looked out at a window.

Bible: II Kings 9:30

4 Often the fear of one evil leads us into a worse.

Nicolas Boileau (1636–1711) French writer. *L'Art poétique*, I

5 The wickedness of the world is so great you have to run your legs off to avoid having them stolen from under you.

Bertolt Brecht (1898–1956) German dramatist. *The Threepenny Opera*, I:3

6 Vice itself lost half its evil, by losing all its grossness.

Edmund Burke (1729–97) British politician. *Reflections on the Revolution in France*

7 Half the vices which the world condemns most loudly have seeds of good in them and require moderate use rather than total abstinence.

Samuel Butler (1835–1902) British writer. *The Way of All Flesh*

8 Vice is its own reward.

Quentin Crisp (c. 1910–) Model, publicist, and writer. *The Naked Civil Servant*

9 In my time, the follies of the town crept slowly among us, but now they travel faster than a stagecoach.

Oliver Goldsmith (1728–74) Irish-born British writer. *She Stoops to Conquer*, I

10 It is the restrictions placed on vice by our social code which makes its pursuit so peculiarly agreeable.

Kenneth Grahame (1859–1932) Scottish writer. *Pagan Papers*

11 We have become, Nina, the sort of people our parents warned us about.

Augustus John (1878–1961) British artist. To Nina Hamnet. Attrib.

12 She was too fond of her most filthy bargain.

William Shakespeare (1564–1616) English dramatist. *Othello*, V:2

13 Vice is waste of life. Poverty, obedience and celibacy are the canonical vices.

George Bernard Shaw (1856–1950) Irish dramatist and critic. *Man and Superman*

14 Wrongdoing can only be avoided if those who are not wronged feel the same indignation at it as those who are.

Solon (6th century BC) Athenian statesman. *Greek Wit* (F. Paley)

15 Whenever I'm caught between two evils, I take the one I've never tried.

Mae West (1892–1980) US actress. Attrib.

16 Never support two weaknesses at the same time. It's your combination sinners – your lecherous liars and your miserly drunkards – who dishonour the vices and bring them into bad repute.

Thornton Wilder (1897–1975) US novelist and dramatist. *The Matchmaker*, III

VICTORIA

(1819–1901) Queen of the United Kingdom (1837–1901). She succeeded her uncle William IV and married her cousin Prince Albert of Saxe-Coburg-Gotha. Disraeli, her close ally after Albert's death in 1861, made her Empress of India.

Quotations about Victoria

1 Victoria has greatly improved, and has become very reasonable and good-natured.

Prince Albert (1819–61) The consort of Queen Victoria. Letter to his brother Ernst, 1843

2 Queen Victoria in her eighties was more known, more revered, and a more important part of the life of the country than she had ever been. Retirement, for a monarch, is not a good idea.

Charles, Prince of Wales (1948–) Eldest son of Elizabeth II

3 She's more of a man than I expected.

Henry James (1843–1916) US novelist. *Diary* (E.M. Forster)

4 Nowadays a parlourmaid as ignorant as Queen Victoria was when she came to the throne would be classed as mentally defective.

George Bernard Shaw (1856–1950) Irish dramatist and critic.

Quotations by Victoria

5 I sat between the King and Queen. We left supper soon. My health was drunk. I then danced one more quadrille with Lord Paget...I was *very* much amused.

Journal, 16 June 1833

6 ...I *too well* know its truth, from experience, that whenever any poor Gipsies are encamped anywhere and crimes and robberies &c. occur, it is invariably laid to their account, which is shocking; and if they are always looked upon as vagabonds, how *can* they become good people?

Journal, 29 Dec 1836

7 The Queen is most anxious to enlist every one who can speak or write to join in checking this mad, wicked folly of 'Woman's Rights', with all its attendant horrors, on which her poor feeble sex is bent, forgetting every sense of womanly feeling and propriety.

Letter to Sir Theodore Martin, 29 May 1870

8 The danger to the country, to Europe, to her vast Empire, which is involved in having all these great interests entrusted to the shaking hand of an old, wild, and incomprehensible man of 82½, is very great!

Reaction to Gladstone's fourth and last appointment as prime minister, 1892. Letter to Lord Lansdowne, 12 Aug 1892

9 He speaks to Me as If I was a public meeting.

Referring to the Liberal statesman Gladstone. *Collections and Recollections* (G. W. E. Russell), Ch. 14

10 A strange, horrible business, but I suppose good enough for Shakespeare's day.

Giving her opinion of *King Lear*. *Living Biographies of Famous Rulers* (H. Thomas)

11 Move Queen Anne? Most certainly not! Why it might some day be suggested that *my* statue should be moved, which I should much dislike.

Said at the time of her Diamond Jubilee (1897), when it was suggested that the statue of Queen Anne should be moved from outside St. Paul's. *Men, Women and Things* (Duke of Portland), Ch. 5

12 We are not amused!

Attrib.

VICTORY

See also war

1 *Veni, vidi, vici.*
I came, I saw, I conquered.

Julius Caesar (100–44 BC) Roman general and statesman. *The Twelve Caesars* (Suetonius)

2 I came, I saw, God conquered.

Charles V (1500–58) Holy Roman Emperor. Echoing Caesar's '*veni, vidi, vici*'. *See also* JOHN III SOBIESKI. Remark after the Battle of Mühlberg, 23 Apr 1547

3 Victory at all costs, victory in spite of all terror, victory however long and hard the road may be; for without victory there is no survival.

Winston Churchill (1874–1965) British statesman. Speech, House of Commons, 13 May 1940

4 This is *your* victory.

Winston Churchill Speech, London, 8 May 1945

5 As always, victory finds a hundred fathers, but defeat is an orphan.

Count Galeazzo Ciano (1903–44) Italian foreign minister. Diary entry, 9 Sept 1942

6 We triumph without glory when we conquer without danger.

Pierre Corneille (1606–84) French dramatist. *Le Cid*, II:2

7 The most important thing in the Olympic Games is not winning but taking part...The essential thing in life is not conquering but fighting well.

Pierre de Coubertin (1863–1937) French educator and sportsman. Speech, Banquet for Officials of the Olympic Games, London, 24 July 1908

8 A game which a sharper once played with a dupe, entitled 'Heads I win, tails you lose.'

John Wilson Croker (1780–1857) British Tory politician. *Croker Papers*

9 The happy state of getting the victor's palm without the dust of racing.

Horace (Quintus Horatius Flaccus; 65–8 BC) Roman poet. *Epistles*, I

10 We've got no place in this outfit for good losers. We want tough hombres who will go in there and *win*!

Jonas Ingram US admiral. Remark, 1926

11 I came; I saw; God conquered.

John III Sobieski (1624–96) King of Poland. Announcing his victory over the Turks at Vienna to the pope (echoing Caesar's '*veni, vidi, vici*'). *See also* CHARLES V. Attrib.

12 They talk about who won and who lost. Human reason won. Mankind won.

Nikita Khrushchev (1894–1971) Soviet statesman. Referring to the Cuban missiles crisis. *The Observer*, 'Sayings of the Week', 11 Nov 1962

13 Winning isn't everything, but wanting to win is.

Vince Lombardi (1913–70) US football coach.

14 I have not time to say more, but to beg you will give my duty to the Queen, and let her know her army has had a glorious victory. Monsieur Tallard and two other generals are in my coach, and I am following the rest...

Duke of Marlborough (1650–1722) British military commander. Referring to the Battle of Blenheim, 13 Aug 1704. Note to his wife, written on a tavern bill

15 How vainly men themselves amaze
To win the palm, the oak, or bays.

Andrew Marvell (1621–78) English poet. *The Garden*

16 Who overcomes
By force, hath overcome but half his foe.

John Milton (1608–74) English poet. *Paradise Lost*, Bk. I

17 See, the conquering hero comes!
Sound the trumpets, beat the drums!

Thomas Morell (1703–84) British classicist. The libretto for Handel's oratorio. *Joshua*, Pt. III

18 We have met the enemy, and they are ours.

Oliver Hazard Perry (1785–1819) US naval officer. Message sent reporting his victory in a naval battle on Lake Erie. *Familiar Quotations* (J. Bartlett)

19 Now indeed with God's help the final stone has been laid in the foundation of St Petersburg.

Peter the Great (1672–1725) Tsar of Russia. Referring to his victory over Charles XII of Sweden at the Battle of Poltava (28 June 1709). Letter to Admiral Apraksin, 27 June 1709

20 Such another victory and we are ruined.

Pyrrhus (319–272 BC) King of Epirus. Commenting upon the costliness of his victory at the Battle of Asculum (279 BC). *Life of Pyrrhus* (Plutarch)

21 For when the One Great Scorer comes
To write against your name,
He marks – not that you won or lost –
But how you played the game.

Grantland Rice (1880–1954) US sportswriter. *Alumnus Football*

22 Thus we have defeated the king of France at Gisors but it is not we who have done it, but God and our right through us.

Richard I (1157–99) King of England. Letter to the Bishop of Durham, 1198

23 The earth is still bursting with the dead bodies of the victors.

George Bernard Shaw (1856–1950) Irish dramatist and critic. *Heartbreak House*, Preface

24 'And everybody praised the Duke,
Who this great fight did win.'
'But what good came of it at last?'
Quoth little Peterkin.
'Why that I cannot tell,' said he,
'But 'twas a famous victory.'

Robert Southey (1774–1843) British poet. *The Battle of Blenheim*

25 Since it is neither right nor natural for Frenchmen to be subject to Englishmen, but rather for Englishmen to be subject to Frenchmen, the outcome of the event mocked his vile expectation.

Suger, Abbot of St Denis (1081–1152) French monk and diplomat. Referring to William II of England's campaigns in Normandy. *Life of Louis VI*

26 Just rejoice at that news and congratulate our forces and the Marines. Goodnight. Rejoice!

Margaret Thatcher (1925–) British politician and prime minister. On the recapture of South Georgia, to newsmen outside 10 Downing Street. TV news coverage, 25 Apr 1982

27 It was easier to conquer it than to know what to do with it.

Horace Walpole (1717–97) British writer. Referring to the East. Letter to Sir Horace Mann, 27 Mar 1772

28 The next greatest misfortune to losing a battle is to gain such a victory as this.

Duke of Wellington (1769–1852) British general and statesman. *Recollections* (S. Rogers)

29 I always say that, next to a battle lost, the greatest misery is a battle gained.

Duke of Wellington *Diary* (Frances, Lady Shelley)

30 By the splendour of God I have taken possession of my realm; the earth of England is in my two hands.

William the Conqueror (1027–87) King of England. Said after falling over when coming ashore at Pevensey with his army of invasion. Attrib.

VIDAL, GORE

(1925–) US novelist. His books include *Myra Breckinridge* (1968), *Burr* (1974), *Lincoln* (1984), and *Live from Golgotha* (1992).

Quotation about Vidal

1 Novelist, essayist, dramatist, epigramist, television polemicist, contraversialist, pensexualist, socialist and socialite: if there is a key to Gore Vidal's public character it has something to do with his towering immodesty, the enjoyable superbity of his self love.

Martin Amis (1949–) British novelist. *The Moronic Inferno*

Quotations by Vidal

2 The novel being dead, there is no point to writing made-up stories. Look at the French who will not and the Americans who cannot.

Myra Breckinridge, Ch. 2

3 American writers want to be not good but great; and so are neither.
Two Sisters

4 The astronauts!...Rotarians in outer space.
Two Sisters

5 Never have children, only grandchildren.
Two Sisters

6 It is not enough to succeed. Others must fail.
Antipanegyric for Tom Driberg (G. Irvine)

7 Whenever a friend succeeds, a little something in me dies.
The Sunday Times Magazine, 16 Sept 1973

8 I'm all for bringing back the birch, but only between consenting adults.
Said when asked by David Frost in a TV interview for his views about corporal punishment.

VIOLENCE

See also cruelty, force

1 You know I hate fighting. If I knew how to make a living some other way, I would.
Muhammad Ali (Cassius Clay; 1942–) US boxer. *The Observer*, 'Sayings of the Week', 21 Nov 1971

2 I would be quite happy for men to hit women if there was a law saying that women could carry guns. Because then, if a man hit you, you could shoot him.
Jo Brand (1958–) British comic. *Q*, June 1994

3 A bit of shooting takes your mind off your troubles – it makes you forget the cost of living.
Brendan Behan (1923–64) Irish dramatist. *The Hostage*

4 Violence is the repartee of the illiterate.
Alan Brien (1925–) British journalist. *Punch*, 7 Feb 1973

5 So soon as the man overtook me, he was but a word and a blow.
John Bunyan (1628–88) English writer. *The Pilgrim's Progress*, Pt. I

6 Two lovely black eyes,
Oh, what a surprise!
Only for telling a man he was wrong.
Two lovely black eyes!
Charles Coborn (1852–1945) US songwriter. *Two Lovely Black Eyes*

7 It is better to be violent, if there is violence in our hearts, than to put on the cloak of non-violence to cover impotence.
Mahatma Gandhi (Mohandas Karamchand Gandhi; 1869–1948) Indian national leader. *Non-Violence in Peace and War*

8 Let the Turks now carry away their abuses in the only possible manner, namely by carrying off themselves. Their Zaptiehs and their Mudirs, their Bimbashis and their Yuzbachis, their Kaimakans and their Pashas, one and all, bag and baggage, shall, I hope, clear out from the province they have desolated and profaned.
William Ewart Gladstone (1809–98) British statesman. Reaction to the massacres of Bulgarians committed by Turkish Bashi-Bazouks (irregular troops). *The Bulgarian Horrors and the Question of the East* (pamphlet, 6 Sept 1876)

9 Brute force, the law of violence, rules to a great extent in the poor man's domicile; and woman is little more than his drudge.
Sarah Moore Grimké (1792–1873) US abolitionist and women's rights pioneer. Letter from Brookline, Sept 1837

10 It's possible to disagree with someone about the ethics of non-violence without wanting to kick his face in.
Christopher Hampton (1946–) British writer and dramatist. *Treats*, Sc. 4

11 In Japan, we live life with no guns. We hope that you too can live life without guns.
Masaichi Hattori His 16-year-old son was shot dead by a trigger-happy householder, while on a student cultural exchange. *The Independent*, 19 Nov 1993

12 We are effectively destroying ourselves by violence masquerading as love.
R. D. Laing (1927–89) British psychiatrist. *The Politics of Experience*, Ch. 13

13 If someone puts his hand on you, send him to the cemetery.
Malcolm X (1925–65) US Black leader. *Malcolm X Speaks*

14 Remove your pants before resorting to violence.
Yoko Ono (1933–) Japanese-born US rock musician and composer. Attrib.

15 Today violence is the rhetoric of the period.
José Ortega y Gasset (1883–1955) Spanish philosopher. *The Revolt of the Masses*

16 Women are entitled to dress attractively, even provocatively if you like, be friendly with casual acquaintances and still say no at the end of the evening without being brutally assaulted...This sort of brutal violence, particularly to women, has got to be dealt with severely. You broke her jaw just because she wasn't prepared to go to bed with you.
Richard Rougier (1932–) British judge. Sentencing an attacker at the Old Bailey. *Daily Telegraph*, 4 May 1988

17 Every puny whipster gets my sword.
William Shakespeare (1564–1616) English dramatist. *Othello*, V:2

18 If you strike a child, take care that you strike it in anger, even at the risk of maiming it for life. A blow in cold blood neither can nor should be forgiven.
George Bernard Shaw (1856–1950) Irish dramatist and critic. *Man and Superman*, 'Maxims for Revolutionists'

19 The only difference is that the stress and the violence is worse at home, because it happens younger, it happens at the hands of someone you love and there is no recognition that this is the enemy.
Gloria Steinem (1934–) US writer and feminist. Referring to similarities between the trauma suffered by men who have fought in wars and women and girls who have been victims of domestic violence. *The Observer Life Magazine*, 15 May 1994

20 Blows are fitter for beasts than for rational creatures.
Hannah Wooley (1623–c. 1675) English pioneer educator and governess. *The Gentlewoman's Companion*

VIRGIL

(Publius Vergilius Maro; 70–19 BC) Roman poet. His *Eclogues* (42–37 BC) were followed by the *Georgics* (36–29 BC), works that expressed his pastoral and agricultural interests. His national epic in 12 books, the *Aeneid*, led to his veneration by subsequent generations.

Quotations about Virgil

1 A crawling and disgusting parasite, a base scoundrel, and pander to unnatural passions.
William Cobbett (1763–1835) British journalist and writer.

2 Thou are my master and my author, thou art he from whom alone I took the style whose beauty has done me honour.
Dante (1265–1321) Italian poet. *Divine Comedy*, 'Inferno', I

3 Virgil's great judgement appears in putting things together, and in his picking gold out of the dunghills of old Roman writers.
Alexander Pope (1688–1744) British poet. *Observations, Anecdotes and Characters* (Rev. Joseph Spence)

Quotations by Virgil

4 Anger supplies the arms.
Aeneid, Bk. I

5 I sing of arms and the man who first from the shores
of Troy came destined an exile to Italy and the Lavinian beaches, much buffeted he on land and on the deep by force of the gods because of fierce Juno's never-forgetting anger.
Referring to Aeneas. *Aeneid*, Bk. I

6 O you who have borne even heavier things, God will grant an end to these too.
Aeneid, Bk. I

7 Maybe one day we shall be glad to remember even these hardships.
Aeneid, Bk. I

8 A grief too much to be told, O queen, you bid me renew.
The opening words of Aeneas' account to Dido of the fall of Troy. *Aeneid*, Bk. II

9 *Equo ne credite, Teucri.*
Quidquid id est timeo Danaos et dona ferentis.
Do not trust the horse, Trojans. Whatever it is, I fear the Greeks even when they bring gifts.
Aeneid, Bk. II

10 It was the time when first sleep begins for weary
mortals and by the gift of the gods creeps over them
most welcomely.
Aeneid, Bk. II

11 What do you not drive human hearts into, cursed
craving for gold!
Aeneid, Bk. III

12 Woman is always fickle and changing.
Aeneid, Bk. IV

13 The way down to Hell is easy.
Aeneid, Bk. VI

14 I see wars, horrible wars, and the Tiber foaming with
much blood.
Part of the Sibyl's prophecy to Aeneas, foretelling his difficulties in winning a home in Italy. *Aeneid*, Bk. VI

15 Fear lent wings to his feet.
Aeneid, Bk. VIII

16 Everyone is dragged on by their favourite pleasure.
Eclogue, Bk. II

17 There's a snake hidden in the grass.
Eclogue, Bk. III

18 Love conquers all things: let us too give in to Love.
Eclogue, Bk. X

19 But meanwhile it is flying, irretrievable time is flying.
Georgics, Bk. III

VIRGINITY

1 The error of Jovian consisted in holding virginity not to be preferable to marriage. This error is refuted above all by the example of Christ Who both chose a virgin for His mother and remained Himself a virgin.
St Thomas Aquinas (1225–74) Italian theologian. *Summa Theologica*

2 Although it is true that the hymen is often relaxed in virgins, or broken and diminished by accidents independent of all coition, such accidents are very rare, and the absence of the hymen is assuredly a good ground of strong suspicion.
T. Bell British doctor. *Kalogynomia*, 1821

3 I'll wager you that in 10 years it will be fashionable again to be a virgin.
Barbara Cartland (1902–) British romantic novelist. *The Observer*, 'Sayings of the Week', 20 June 1976

4 I said 10 years ago that in 10 years time it would be smart to be a virgin. Now everyone is back to virgins again.
Barbara Cartland *The Observer*, 'Sayings of the Week', 12 July 1987

5 The men you meet aren't naive enough to expect virgins but they certainly don't want to hear about the 'ghosts' of your past life. Yet I can't imagine a man sticking around much after two or three months if you hadn't slept together.
Sacha Cowlam (1963–) *Out of the Doll's House* (Angela Holdsworth)

6 The endeavour to protect virginity or otherwise to control female sexuality is a feature of most societies ancient and modern, though the diverse efforts to achieve this particular end change form, depending on patterns of kinship, economic and power relationships.
Michel Foucault (1926–84) French philosopher. *The Archaeology of Knowledge*

7 Are there still virgins? One is tempted to answer no. There are only girls who have not yet crossed the line, because they want to preserve their market value...Call them virgins if you wish, these travellers in transit.

Françoise Giroud (1916–) Swiss-born French politician, journalist, editor, and French Minister of Women. *Coronet*, Nov 1960

8 Nothing is more horrible than the terror, the sufferings, and the revulsion of a poor girl, ignorant of the facts of life, who finds herself raped by a brute. As far as possible we bring them up as saints, and then we hand them over as if they were fillies.

George Sand (Aurore Dupin, Baronne Dudevant; 1804–76) French novelist. Letter to Hippolyte Chatiron, 1843

9 It is one of the superstitions of the human mind to have imagined that virginity could be a virtue.

Voltaire (François-Marie Arouet; 1694–1778) French writer. *Notebooks*

10 I used to be Snow White...but I drifted.

Mae West (1892–1980) US actress. *The Wit and Wisdom of Mae West* (ed. J. Weintraub)

VIRTUE

See also good, morality, purity, righteousness, virtue and vice

1 A fair woman without virtue is like palled wine.

Proverb

2 Unhappy as the event must be for Lydia, we may draw from it this useful lesson: that loss of virtue in a female is irretrievable; that one false step involves her in endless ruin; that her reputation is no less brittle than it is beautiful; and that she cannot be too much guarded in her behaviour towards the undeserving of the other sex.

Jane Austen (1775–1817) British novelist. *Pride and Prejudice*, Ch. 47

3 Virtue is like a rich stone, best plain set.

Francis Bacon (1561–1626) English philosopher. *Essays*, 'Of Beauty'

4 As in nature things move violently to their place and calmly in their place, so virtue in ambition is violent, in authority settled and calm.

Francis Bacon *Essays*, 'Of Great Place'

5 A good name is better than precious ointment; and the day of death than the day of one's birth.
It is better to go to the house of mourning, than to go to the house of feasting: for that is the end of all men; and the living will lay it to his heart.

Bible: Ecclesiastes 7:1–2

6 Enter ye in at the strait gate: for wide is the gate, and broad is the way, that leadeth to destruction, and many there be which go in thereat:
Because strait is the gate, and narrow is the way, which leadeth unto life, and few there be that find it.

Bible: Matthew 7:13–14

7 Then shall the King say unto them on his right hand, Come, ye blessed of my Father, inherit the kingdom prepared for you from the foundation of the world:
For I was an hungred, and ye gave me meat: I was thirsty, and ye gave me drink: I was a stranger, and ye took me in:
Naked, and ye clothed me: I was sick, and ye visited me: I was in prison, and ye came unto me.

Bible: Matthew 25:34–36

8 Finally, brethren, whatsoever things are true, whatsoever things are honest, whatsoever things are just, whatsoever things are pure, whatsoever things are lovely, whatsoever things are of good report; if there be any virtue; and if there be any praise, think on these things.

Bible: Philippians 4:8

9 But the path of the just is as the shining light, that shineth more and more unto the perfect day.

Bible: Proverbs 4:18

10 Whenever there are tremendous virtues it's a sure sign something's wrong.

Bertolt Brecht (1898–1956) German dramatist. *Mother Courage*

11 Virtue consisted in avoiding scandal and venereal disease.

Robert Cecil (1913–) British writer. *Life in Edwardian England*

12 My virtue's still far too small, I don't trot it out and about yet.

Colette (1873–1954) French novelist. *Claudine at School*

13 To be able to practise five things everywhere under heaven constitutes perfect virtue...gravity, generosity of soul, sincerity, earnestness, and kindness.

Confucius (K'ung Fu-tzu; 551–479 BC) Chinese philosopher. *Analects*

14 How next to impossible is the exercise of virtue! It requires a constant watchfulness, constant guard.

William Golding (1911–93) British novelist. *Rites of Passage*, 'Colley's Letter'

15 Good, but not religious-good.

Thomas Hardy (1840–1928) British novelist. *Under the Greenwood Tree*, Ch. 2

16 The greatest offence against virtue is to speak ill of it.

William Hazlitt (1778–1830) British essayist. *On Cant and Hypocrisy*

17 Only a sweet and virtuous soul,
Like season'd timber, never gives;
But though the whole world turn to coal,
Then chiefly lives.

George Herbert (1593–1633) English poet. *Virtue*

18 Be good, sweet maid, and let who will be clever;
Do lovely things, not dream them, all day long;
And so make Life, and Death, and that For Ever,
One grand sweet song.

Charles Kingsley (1819–75) British writer. *A Farewell. To C. E. G.*

19 To be discontented with the divine discontent, and to be ashamed with the noble shame, is the very germ and first upgrowth of all virtue.

Charles Kingsley *Health and Education*

20 Most men admire
Virtue, who follow not her lore.

John Milton (1608–74) English poet. *Paradise Regained*, Bk. I

21 When men grow virtuous in their old age, they only make a sacrifice to God of the devil's leavings.

Alexander Pope (1688–1744) British poet. *Thoughts on Various Subjects*

22 Most good women are hidden treasures who are only safe because nobody looks for them.

Dorothy Parker (1893–1967) US writer. *The New York Times*, Obituary, 8 June 1967

23 Woman's virtue is man's greatest invention.

Cornelia Otis Skinner (1901–79) US stage actress. Attrib.

VIRTUE AND VICE

See also good and evil, vice, virtue

1 Oh the gladness of her gladness when she's glad,
And the sadness of her sadness when she's sad,
But the gladness of her gladness
And the sadness of her sadness
Are as nothing, Charles,
To the badness of her badness when she's bad.

J. M. Barrie (1860–1937) British novelist and dramatist. *Rosalind*

2 Good girls go to heaven, bad girls go everywhere.

Helen Gurley Brown (1922–) US journalist. *Cosmopolitan*

3 It is the function of vice to keep virtue within reasonable bounds.

Samuel Butler (1835–1902) British writer. *Notebooks*

4 Our virtues and vices couple with one another, and get children that resemble both their parents.

Lord Halifax (1633–95) English statesman. *Political, Moral and Miscellaneous Thoughts and Reflections*

5 There was a little girl
Who had a little curl
Right in the middle of her forehead;
When she was good
She was very very good,
But when she was bad she was horrid.

Henry Wadsworth Longfellow (1807–82) US poet. *There was a Little Girl*

6 Most usually our virtues are only vices in disguise.

Duc de la Rochefoucauld (1613–80) French writer. *Maximes*, added to the 4th edition

7 Vice and virtues are products like sulphuric acid and sugar.

Hippolyte Adolphe Taine (1828–93) French writer and philosopher. *Histoire de la littérature anglaise*, Introduction

VOLTAIRE

(François-Marie Arouet; 1694–1778) French writer and philosopher. A fearless campaigner against injustice, he was imprisoned in the Bastille, exiled to England, Germany, and Switzerland, and later became a hero of French culture. His works include *Lettres philosophiques* (1734), the fable *Candide* (1759), and the *Dictionnaire philosophique* (1764).

Quotations about Voltaire

1 He does not inflame his mind with grand hopes of the immortality of the soul. He says it may be, but he knows nothing of it. And his mind is in perfect tranquillity.

James Boswell (1740–95) Scottish lawyer and writer. *Boswell on the Grand Tour* (F.A. Pottle)

2 When he talked our language he was animated with the soul of a Briton. He had bold fights. He had humour. He had an extravagance.

James Boswell (1740–95) Scottish lawyer and writer. *Boswell on the Grand Tour* (ed. by F. A. Pottle)

3 I have done but very little but read Voltaire since I saw you. He is an exquisite fellow. One thing in him is peculiarly striking – his clear knowledge of the limits of human understanding.

Dr J. Currie (1756–1805) Scottish physician and writer. Letter to Thomas Creevey, 17 Dec 1798

4 I was born much too soon, but I do not regret it; I have seen Voltaire.

Frederick the Great (1712–86) King of Prussia. Attrib.

5 Here lies the child spoiled by the world which he spoiled.

Baronne de Montolieu. Epitaph on Voltaire

Quotations by Voltaire

6 If we do not find anything pleasant, at least we shall find something new.

Candide, Ch. 17

7 *Dans ce pays-ci, il est bon de tuer de temps en temps un amiral pour encourager les autres.*
In this country it is good to kill an admiral from time to time, to encourage the others.

Referring to England: Admiral Byng was executed for failing to defeat the French at Minorca (1757). *Candide*, Ch. 23

8 All is for the best in the best of all possible worlds.

Candide, Ch. 1

9 'That is well said,' replied Candide, 'but we must cultivate our garden.'

Candide, Ch. 30

10 Work banishes those three great evils, boredom, vice, and poverty.

Candide, Ch. 30

11 The best is the enemy of the good.

Contes, 'La Begueule'

12 ...use thought only to justify their injustices, and speech only to conceal their thoughts.

Referring to men. *Dialogue*, 'Le Chapon et la poularde'

13 Superstition sets the whole world in flames; philosophy quenches them.

Dictionnaire philosophique, 'Superstition'

14 If God did not exist, it would be necessary to invent Him.

Épîtres, 'À l'auteur du livre des trois' Imposteurs'

15 The secret of the arts is to correct nature.

Épîtres, 'À M. de Verrière'

16 This agglomeration which was called and which still calls itself the Holy Roman Empire was neither holy, nor Roman, nor an empire.

Essai sur les moeurs et l'esprit des nations, LXX

17 All our ancient history, as one of our wits remarked, is no more than accepted fiction.
Jeannot et Colin

18 All styles are good except the tiresome sort.
L'Enfant prodigue, Preface

19 If God made us in His image, we have certainly returned the compliment.
Le Sottisier

20 Indeed, history is nothing more than a tableau of crimes and misfortunes.
L'Ingénu, Ch. 10

21 It is one of the superstitions of the human mind to have imagined that virginity could be a virtue.
Notebooks

22 Governments need to have both shepherds and butchers.
Notebooks

23 God is on the side not of the heavy battalions, but of the best shots.
Notebooks

24 We owe respect to the living; to the dead we owe only truth.
Oeuvres, 'Première lettre sur Oedipe'

25 Faith consists in believing when it is beyond the power of reason to believe. It is not enough that a thing be possible for it to be believed.
Questions sur l'encyclopédie

26 Marriage is the only adventure open to the cowardly.
Thoughts of a Philosopher

27 Never having been able to succeed in the world, he took his revenge by speaking ill of it.
Zadig, Ch. 4

28 There are two things for which animals are to be envied: they know nothing of future evils, or of what people say about them.
Letter, 1739

29 Men will always be mad and those who think they can cure them are the maddest of all.
Letter, 1762

30 The great consolation in life is to say what one thinks.
Letter, 1765

31 Once the people begin to reason, all is lost.
Letter to Damilaville, 1 Apr 1766

32 I am not like a lady at the court of Versailles, who said: 'What a dreadful pity that the bother at the tower of Babel should have got language all mixed up, but for that, everyone would always have spoken French.'
French was the dominant language in the educated circles of 18th-century Europe. Letter to Catherine the Great, Empress of Russia, 26 May 1767

33 The man who leaves money to charity in his will is only giving away what no longer belongs to him.
Letter, 1769

34 Men of England! You wish to kill me because I am a Frenchman. Am I not punished enough in not being born an Englishman?
Addressing an angry London mob who desired to hang him because he was a Frenchman. Attrib.

35 I think it must be so, for I have been drinking it for sixty-five years and I am not dead yet.
On learning that coffee was considered a slow poison. Attrib.

36 He was a great patriot, a humanitarian, a loyal friend – provided, of course, that he really is dead.
Giving a funeral oration. Attrib.

37 I do not think this poem will reach its destination.
Reviewing Rousseau's poem 'Ode to Posterity'. Attrib.

38 Once: a philosopher; twice: a pervert!
Turning down an invitation to an orgy, having attended one the previous night for the first time. Attrib.

39 I disapprove of what you say, but I will defend to the death your right to say it.
Attrib.

VULGARITY

See also humour

1 You gotta have a swine to show you where the truffles are.
Edward Albee (1928–) US dramatist. *Who's Afraid of Virginia Woolf?*, I

2 The aristocratic pleasure of displeasing is not the only delight that bad taste can yield. One can love a certain kind of vulgarity for its own sake.
Aldous Huxley (1894–1964) British novelist. *Vulgarity in Literature*, Ch. 4

3 That fellow would vulgarize the day of judgment.
Douglas William Jerrold (1803–57) British dramatist. *Wit and Opinions of Douglas Jerrold*, 'A Comic Author'

4 It is disgusting to pick your teeth. What is vulgar is to use a gold toothpick.
Louis Kronenberger (1904–80) US writer and literary critic. *The Cat and the Horse*

5 With our James vulgarity begins at home, and should be allowed to stay there.
Oscar Wilde (1854–1900) Irish-born British dramatist.
Referring to the artist James Whistler. Letter to the *World*

6 I can't stand a naked light bulb, any more than I can a rude remark or a vulgar action.
Tennessee Williams (1911–83) US dramatist. *A Streetcar Named Desire*, II:3

W

WALES

See also Britain, Welsh

1 The thing I value about Wales and Welsh background is that it has always been a genuinely more classless society than many people present England as being.

Geoffrey Howe (1926–) British politician. *The Observer*, 'Sayings of the Week', 9 Nov 1986

2 The land of my fathers. My fathers can have it.

Dylan Thomas (1914–53) Welsh poet. Referring to Wales. *Dylan Thomas* (John Ackerman)

3 Too many of the artists of Wales spend too much time about the position of the artist of Wales. There is only one position for an artist anywhere: and that is, upright.

Dylan Thomas *New Statesman*, 18 Dec 1964

4 Make me content
With some sweetness
From Wales
Whose nightingales
Have no wings.

Edward Thomas (1878–1917) British poet. *Words*

5 We can trace almost all the disasters of English history to the influence of Wales.

Evelyn Waugh (1903–66) British novelist. *Decline and Fall*, Pt. I, Ch. 8

WAŁESA, LECH

(1943–) Polish politician and trade unionist. He became leader of Solidarity on its formation in 1980 and was awarded the Nobel Peace Prize in 1983; in 1989 he helped form Poland's first noncommunist government since World War II.

1 I've never worked for prizes...I'm as ready to receive prizes as I am to be thrown into prison, not that I'm ungrateful for this honor; it's just that neither the one nor the other could ever divert me from the course I've set myself.

Wałesa's response when awarded the Nobel Peace Prize, 1983. *A Path of Hope*, 'Private Citizen'

2 SOLIDARITY was born at that precise moment when the shipyard strike evolved from a local success in the shipyard, to a strike in support of other factories and business enterprises, large and small, in need of our protection: moral reasons impelled us toward solidarity with our neighbors and our co-workers in every line of endeavor.

A Path of Hope, 'The Strike and the August Agreements'

3 The hungry hare has no frontiers and doesn't follow ideologies. The hungry hare goes where it finds the food. And the other hares don't block its passage with the tanks.

Interview, 1981

WALKER, ALICE

(1944–) US writer whose novels and poetry have won many awards. Her works include *The Color Purple* (1983), *Her Blue Body Everything We Know* (1991), and *Possessing the Secret of Joy* (1992).

1 If it is true that it is what we run from that chases us, then *The Color Purple*...is the book that ran me down while I sat with my back to it in a field.

Preface to the Tenth Anniversary Edition of *The Color Purple*

2 Any God I ever felt in church I brought in with me.

The Color Purple

3 I think it pisses God off if you walk by the color purple in a field somewhere and don't notice it.

The Color Purple

4 People think pleasing God is all God care about. But any fool living in the world can see it always trying to please us back.

The Color Purple

5 He never had a kind word to say to me. Just say You gonna do what your mammy wouldn't. First he put his thing up gainst my hip and sort of wiggle it around. Then he grab hold my titties. Then he push his thing inside my pussy. When that hurt, I cry. He start to choke me, saying You better shut up and git used to it.

The Color Purple

6 This Book is Dedicated with Tenderness and Respect To the Blameless Vulva.

Dedication, *Possessing the Secret of Joy*

7 There are those who believe Black people possess the secret of joy and that it is this that will sustain them through any spiritual or moral or physical devastation.

Possessing the Secret of Joy

8 When someone informs you your wife is to be assassinated publicly, it is a very bitter thing.

Possessing the Secret of Joy

9 I will concentrate on the beauty of one blue hill in the distance, and for me, that moment will be eternity.

Possessing the Secret of Joy

10 It now took a quarter of an hour for her to pee. Her menstrual periods lasted ten days. She was incapacitated by cramps...lasting nearly half the month. There were premenstrual cramps: cramps caused by the near impossibility of flow passing through so tiny an aperture as M'Lissa had left after fastening together the raw sides of Tashi's vagina with a couple of thorns and inserting a straw so that in healing, the traumatized flesh might not grow together, shutting the opening completely: cramps caused by the residual flow that could not find its way out, was not reabsorbed into her body and had nowhere to go. There was the odour too, of soured blood, which no amount of scrubbing ever washed off.

Possessing the Secret of Joy

11 Womanist is to feminist as purple is to lavender.

Preface, *In Search of our Mother's Gardens*

12 My major advice to young black artists would be that they shut themselves up somewhere away from all debates about who they are and what color they are and just turn out paintings and poems and stories and novels.

In Search of our Mother's Gardens, II, 2

WALPOLE, HORACE

(4th Earl of Orford; 1717–97) British writer and fourth son of the statesman Robert Walpole. He is remembered for his gothic novel *The Castle of Otranto* (1765) and his gothic-revival villa at Twickenham, Strawberry Hill.

1 I am, sir for the last time in my life, Your Humble Servant Horace Walpole.

Ending a letter written to an uncle with whom he had recently quarrelled. *Horace Walpole* (R. Ketton-Cremes)

2 I have led a life of business so long that I have lost my taste for reading, and now – what shall I do?

Thraliana (K. Balderston)

3 Our supreme governors, the mob.

Letter to Horace Mann, 7 Sept 1743

4 One of the greatest geniuses that ever existed, Shakespeare, undoubtedly wanted taste.

Letter to Christopher Wren, 9 Aug 1764

5 It is charming to totter into vogue.

Letter to G. A. Selwyn, 2 Dec 1765

6 This world is a comedy to those that think, a tragedy to those that feel.

Letter to Anne, Countess of Upper Ossory, 16 Aug 1776

7 By the waters of Babylon we sit down and weep, when we think of thee, O America!

On the eve of the American Revolution. Letter to Mason, 12 June 1775

8 When people will not weed their own minds, they are apt to be overrun with nettles.

Letter to Lady Ailesbury, 10 July 1779

9 I do not dislike the French from the vulgar antipathy between neighbouring nations, but for their insolent and unfounded airs of superiority.

Letter to Hannah More, 14 Oct 1787

10 Come, Robert, you shall drink twice while I drink once, for I cannot permit the son in his sober senses to witness the intoxication of his father.

Explaining why he filled his son's glass twice for every glass he drank himself. Attrib.

WALPOLE, SIR ROBERT

(1st Earl of Orford; 1676–1745) British statesman. A Whig MP, he became secretary for war (1708–10) and chancellor of the exchequer (1715). He then became Britain's first prime minister (1721–42), maintaining his power by skilful management of parliament.

1 Anything but history, for history must be false.

Walpoliana

2 They now *ring* the bells, but they will soon *wring* their hands.

Said when war declared in 1739 with Spain, against Walpole's wishes. *Memoirs of Sir Robert Walpole* (W. Coxe)

3 All those men have their price.

Memoirs of Sir Robert Walpole (W. Coxe)

4 My Lord Bath, you and I are now two as insignificant men as any in England.

Said to William Pulteney, Earl of Bath, when they were promoted to the peerage (1742). *Political & Literary Anecdotes* (W. King)

5 The balance of power.

Speech, House of Commons

WALTON, IZAAK

(1593–1683) English writer, remembered for his treatise on fishing, *The Compleat Angler* (1653).

1 Angling may be said to be so like the mathematics, that it can never be fully learnt.

The Compleat Angler, Epistle to the Reader

2 Angling is somewhat like poetry, men are to be born so.

The Compleat Angler, Ch. 1

3 I remember that a wise friend of mine did usually say, 'that which is everybody's business is nobody's business'.

The Compleat Angler, Ch. 2

4 We may say of angling as Dr Boteler said of strawberries, 'Doubtless God could have made a better berry, but doubtless God never did.'

The Compleat Angler, Ch. 5

5 I love such mirth as does not make friends ashamed to look upon one another next morning.

The Compleat Angler, Ch. 5

6 Let the blessing of St Peter's Master be…upon all that are lovers of virtue; and dare trust in His providence; and be quiet; and go a-Angling.

The Compleat Angler, Ch. 21

7 Of this blest man, let his just praise be given,
Heaven was in him, before he was in heaven.

Referring to Dr Richard Sibbes. Written in a copy of *Returning Backslider* by Richard Sibbes

WAR

See also army, Cold War, defeat, navy, nuclear weapons, officers, patriotism, soldiers, victory, war and peace, weapons, World War II

1 We have suffered the inevitable consequences of a combination of unpreparedness and feeble counsel.

Julian Amery (1919–) British Conservative politician. Referring to Argentina's seizure of the Falkland Islands. Speech, House of Commons, 3 Apr 1982

2 *Flavit deus et dissipati sunt.*
God blew and they were scattered.

Anonymous Inscription on the medallion minted to commemorate the defeat of the Spanish Armada.

3 They did not, in all their sailing round about England, so much as sink or take one ship, bark, pinnace, or cockboat of ours, or even burn so much as one sheepcote in this land.

Anonymous Referring to the Spanish Armada. *The Reign of Elizabeth* (J. D. Black), Ch. 10

4 Oh! the grand old Duke of York
He had ten thousand men;
He marched them up to the top of the hill,
And he marched them down again.
And when they were up they were up,
And when they were down they were down,
And when they were only half way up,
They were neither up nor down.

Anonymous Referring to Frederick Augustus, son of George III and Duke of York, who commanded two unsuccessful campaigns against the French (1793 and 1799). Traditional

5 Your country needs YOU.

Anonymous British recruiting poster featuring Lord Kitchener

6 Oh, my dear fellow, the noise…and the people!

Anonymous A soldier describing battle conditions.

7 Here on 11 November 1918 succumbed the criminal pride of the German Reich, vanquished by the free peoples which it tried to enslave.

Anonymous In the forest of Compiègne, France, where the Armistice was signed at the end of World War I.

8 It became necessary to destroy the town of Ben Tre to save it.

Anonymous Said by a US Major in Vietnam. *The Observer*, 'Sayings of the Week', 11 Feb 1968

9 Hell no, we won't go!

Anonymous US anti-war chant during the time of the Vietnam war

10 Give them the cold steel, boys!

Lewis Addison Arminstead (1817–63) US general. Exhortation given to his troops during the US Civil War. Attrib.

11 And we are here as on a darkling plain
Swept with confused alarms of struggle and flight,
Where ignorant armies clash by night.

Matthew Arnold (1822–88) British poet and critic. *Dover Beach*

12 We shall never sheathe the sword which we have not lightly drawn until Belgium receives in full measure all and more than all that she has sacrificed, until France is adequately secured against the menace of aggression, until the rights of the smaller nationalities of Europe are placed upon an unassailable foundation, and until the military domination of Prussia is wholly and finally destroyed.

Herbert Henry Asquith (1852–1928) British statesman. Speech, Guildhall, 9 Nov 1914

13 To save your world you asked this man to die:
Would this man, could he see you now, ask why?

W. H. Auden (1907–73) British poet. *Epitaph for an Unknown Soldier*

14 Well, if you knows of a better 'ole, go to it.

Bruce Bairnsfather (1888–1959) British cartoonist. *Fragments from France*

15 The only defence is in offence, which means that you have to kill more women and children more quickly than the enemy if you want to save yourselves.

Stanley Baldwin (1867–1947) British statesman. Speech, Nov 1932

16 I think it is well also for the man in the street to realise that there is no power on earth that can protect him from being bombed. Whatever people may tell him, the bomber will always get through, and it is very easy to understand that, if you realise the area of space.

Stanley Baldwin Speech, House of Commons, 10 Nov 1932

17 From the point of view of sexual morality the aeroplane is valuable in war in that it destroys men and women in equal numbers.

Ernest William Barnes (1874–1953) British clergyman and mathematician. *Rise of Christianity*

18 It takes twenty years or more of peace to make a man, it takes only twenty seconds of war to destroy him.

Baudouin I (1930–93) King of Belgium. Addressing US Congress, 12 May 1959

19 I have never understood this liking for war. It panders to instincts already catered for within the scope of any respectable domestic establishment.

Alan Bennett (1934–) British dramatist. *Forty Years On*, I

20 And ye shall hear of wars and rumours of wars: see that ye be not troubled: for all these things must come to pass, but the end is not yet.
For nation shall rise against nation, and kingdom against kingdom: and there shall be famines, and pestilences, and earthquakes, in divers places.
All these are the beginning of sorrows.

Bible: Matthew 24:6–8

21 Then said Jesus unto him, Put up again thy sword into his place: for all they that take the sword shall perish with the sword.

Bible: Matthew 26:52

22 If there is ever another war in Europe, it will come out of some damned silly thing in the Balkans.

Bismarck (1815–98) German statesman. Remark to Ballen, shortly before Bismarck's death.

23 The Falklands thing was a fight between two bald men over a comb.

Jorge Luis Borges (1899–1986) Argentinian novelist. Referring to the war with the UK over the Falklands (1982). *Time*, 14 Feb 1983

24 *C'est magnifique, mais ce n'est pas la guerre.*
It is magnificent, but it is not war.

Pierre Bosquet (1810–61) French marshal. Referring to the Charge of the Light Brigade at the Battle of Balaclava, 25 Oct 1854. Attrib.

25 The wrong war, at the wrong place, at the wrong time, and with the wrong enemy.

Omar Nelson Bradley (1893–1981) US general. Said in evidence to a Senate inquiry, May 1951, over a proposal by MacArthur that the Korean War should be extended into China.

26 What they could do with round here is a good war.

Bertolt Brecht (1898–1956) German dramatist. *Mother Courage*, I

27 A war of which we could say it left nothing to be desired will probably never exist.

Bertolt Brecht *Mother Courage*, VI

28 War is like love, it always finds a way.

Bertolt Brecht *Mother Courage*, VI

29 The Angel of Death has been abroad throughout the land: you may almost hear the beating of his wings.

John Bright (1811–89) British radical politician. Referring to the Crimean War. Speech, House of Commons, 23 Feb 1855

30 If I should die, think only this of me:
That there's some corner of a foreign field
That is forever England.

Rupert Brooke (1887–1915) British poet. *The Soldier*

31 Now, God be thanked who has matched us with His hour,
And caught our youth, and wakened us from sleeping.

Rupert Brooke *Peace*

32 War knows no power. Safe shall be my going,
Secretly armed against all death's endeavour;
Safe though all safety's lost; safe where men fall;
And if these poor limbs die, safest of all.

Rupert Brooke *Safety*

33 Scots, wha hae wi' Wallace bled,
Scots, wham Bruce has aften led,
Welcome tae your gory bed,
Or tae victorie.

Robert Burns (1759–96) Scottish poet. *Scots, Wha Hae*

34 I will draw a line in the sand.

George Bush (1924–) US president. Referring to the defence of Saudi Arabia by US forces following the Iraqi invasion of Kuwait (1990). Speech, 1990

35 Our goal is not the conquest of Iraq. It is the liberation of Kuwait.

George Bush Referring to the Gulf War (1991). *The Times*, 16 Jan 1991

36 War is never cheap or easy.

George Bush Referring to the Gulf War (1991). *The Observer*, 20 Jan 1991

37 The war wasn't fought about democracy in Kuwait.

George Bush Referring to the Gulf War (1991). *The Observer*, 14 July 1991

38 When civil fury first grew high,
And men fell out they knew not why.

Samuel Butler (1612–80) English satirist. *Hudibras*, Pt. I

39 War, war is still the cry, 'War even to the knife!'

Lord Byron (1788–1824) British poet. *Childe Harold's Pilgrimage*, I

40 When was a war not a war? When it was carried on by methods of barbarism.

Henry Campbell-Bannerman (1836–1908) British statesman. Referring to the Boer War. Speech, National Reform Union Dinner, 14 June 1901

41 Tweedledum and Tweedledee
Agreed to have a battle;
For Tweedledum said Tweedledee
Had spoiled his nice new rattle.

Lewis Carroll (Charles Lutwidge Dodgson; 1832–98) British writer. *Through the Looking-Glass*, Ch. 4

42 Carthage must be destroyed.

Cato the Elder (Marcius Porcius C.; 234–149 BC) Roman statesman. *Life of Cato* (Plutarch)

43 In war, whichever side may call itself the victor, there are no winners, but all are losers.

Neville Chamberlain (1869–1940) British statesman. Speech, Kettering, 3 July 1938

44 Wars, conflict, it's all business. One murder makes a villain. Millions a hero. Numbers sanctify.

Charlie Chaplin (Sir Charles Spencer C.; 1889–1977) British film actor. *Monsieur Verdoux*

45 The redress of the grievances of the vanquished should precede the disarmament of the victors.

Winston Churchill (1874–1965) British statesman. *The Gathering Storm*, Ch. 3

46 I said that the world must be made safe for at least fifty years. If it was only for fifteen to twenty years then we should have betrayed our soldiers.

Winston Churchill *Closing the Ring*, Ch. 20

47 No one can guarantee success in war, but only deserve it.

Winston Churchill *Their Finest Hour*

48 All great civilizations, in their early stages, are based on success in war.

Kenneth Clark (1903–83) British art historian. *Civilization*

49 War is the continuation of politics by other means.

Karl von Clausewitz (1780–1831) Prussian general. The usual misquotation of 'War is nothing but a continuation of politics with the admixture of other means'. *Vom Kriege*

50 My home policy? I wage war. My foreign policy? I wage war. Always, everywhere, I wage war…And I shall continue to wage war until the last quarter of an hour.

Georges Clemenceau (1841–1929) French statesman. Speech, Chamber of Deputies, 8 Mar 1918

51 Now, gentlemen, let us do something today which the world may talk of hereafter.

Lord Collingwood (1750–1810) British admiral. Said before the Battle of Trafalgar, 21 Oct 1805. *Correspondence and Memoir of Lord Collingwood* (G. L. Newnham; ed. Collingwood)

52 Our troops are all moving from this place at present. Lord Wellington was at the ball tonight as composed as ever.

Thomas Creevey (1768–1838) British politician and diarist. Written at Brussels. *Journal*, 16 June 1815

53 *C'est une drôle de guerre.*
It is a phoney war.

Edouard Daladier (1884–1970) French prime minister. Speech, Chamber of Deputies, 22 Dec 1939

54 Come on, you sons of bitches! Do you want to live for ever?

Dan Daly (20th century) Sergeant in the US Marines. Remark during Allied resistance at Belleau Wood, June 1918. *See also* FREDERICK THE GREAT. Attrib.

55 If we lose this war, I'll start another in my wife's name.

Moshe Dayan (1915–81) Israeli general. Attrib.

56 France has lost a battle, but France has not lost the war!

Charles de Gaulle (1890–1970) French general and statesman. Proclamation, 18 June 1940

57 There is plenty of time to win this game, and to thrash the Spaniards too.

Francis Drake (1540–96) British navigator and admiral.

Referring to the sighting of the Armada during a game of bowls, 20 July 1588. Attrib.

58 The advantage of time and place in all practical actions is half a victory; which being lost is irrecoverable.

Francis Drake Letter to Elizabeth I, 1588

59 I have singed the Spanish king's beard.

Francis Drake Referring to the raid on Cadiz harbour, 1587. Attrib.

60 We are not at war with Egypt. We are in an armed conflict.

Anthony Eden (1897–1977) British statesman. Speech, House of Commons, 4 Nov 1956

61 There is nothing that war has ever achieved that we could not better achieve without it.

Havelock Ellis (1859–1939) British sexologist. *The Philosophy of Conflict*

62 My centre is giving way, my right is in retreat; situation excellent. I shall attack.

Marshal Foch (1851–1929) French soldier. Message sent during the second Battle of the Marne, 1918. *Biography of Foch* (Aston), Ch. 13

63 Praise the Lord and pass the ammunition!

Howell Maurice Forgy (1908–83) US naval lieutenant. Remark made during the Japanese attack on Pearl Harbor, 7 Dec 1941. Attrib. in *The Los Angeles Times*

64 I got there fustest with the mostest.

Nathan Bedford Forrest (1821–77) Confederate general. Popular misquotation of his explanation of his success in capturing Murfreesboro; his actual words were, 'I just took the short cut and got there first with the most men'. *A Civil War Treasury* (B. Botkin)

65 He kept us out of war!

Martin H. Glynn (1891–1924) Governor of New York State. Referring to President Wilson. Speech, Democratic Convention, St Louis, 15 June 1916

66 The English do not treat very kindly the men who conduct their wars for them.

Joseph Goebbels (1897–1945) German politician. *Diaries*

67 We can now look forward with something like confidence to the time when war between civilized nations will be considered as antiquated as a duel.

George Peabody Gooch (1873–1968) British historian and Liberal MP. *History of Our Time*

68 When the days of rejoicing are over,
When the flags are stowed safely away,
They will dream of another wild 'War to End Wars'
And another wild Armistice day.

But the boys who were killed in the trenches,
Who fought with no rage and no rant,
We left them stretched out on their pallets of mud
Low down with the worm and the ant.

Robert Graves (1895–1985) British poet and novelist. *Armistice Day, 1918*

69 Rascals, would you live for ever?

Frederick the Great (1712–86) King of Prussia. Addressed to reluctant soldiers at the Battle of Kolin, 18 June 1757. *See also* DALY.

70 Madam, I am the civilization they are fighting to defend.

Heathcote William Garrod (1878–1960) British classical scholar. Replying to criticism that he was not fighting to defend civilization, during World War I. *Oxford Now and Then* (D. Balsdon)

71 I have many times asked myself whether there can be more potent advocates of peace upon earth through the years to come than this massed multitude of silent witnesses to the desolation of war.

George V (1865–1936) King of the United Kingdom. Referring to the massed World War I graves in Flanders, 1922. *Silent Cities* (ed. Gavin Stamp)

72 You've got to forget about this civilian. Whenever you drop bombs, you're going to hit civilians.

Barry Goldwater (1909–) US politician. Speech, New York, 23 Jan 1967

73 No terms except unconditional and immediate surrender can be accepted. I propose to move immediately upon your works.

Ulysses Simpson Grant (1822–85) US general. Message to opposing commander, Simon Bolivar Buckner, during Siege of Fort Donelson, 16 Feb 1862.

74 Every position must be held to the last man: there must be no retirement. With our backs to the wall, and believing in the justice of our cause, each one of us must fight on to the end.

Douglas Haig (1861–1928) British general. Order to the British Army, 12 Apr 1918

75 I'm not allowed to say how many planes joined the raid but I counted them all out and I counted them all back.

Brian Hanrahan (1949–) British journalist. Reporting a British air attack in the opening phase of the Falklands War. BBC broadcast, 1 May 1982

76 Gentlemen of the French Guard, fire first!

Lord Charles Hay (d. 1760) British soldier. Said at the Battle of Fontenoy, 1745. Attrib.

77 I'd like to see the government get out of war altogether and leave the whole feud to private industry.

Joseph Heller (1923–) US novelist. *Catch 22*

78 In starting and waging a war it is not right that matters, but victory.

Adolf Hitler (1889–1945) German dictator. *The Rise and Fall of the Third Reich* (W. L. Shirer), Ch. 16

79 War? War is an organized bore.

Oliver Wendell Holmes Jnr (1841–1935) US jurist. *Yankee from Olympus* (C. Bowen)

80 Older men declare war. But it is youth that must fight and die.

Herbert Clark Hoover (1874–1964) US statesman. Speech, Republican National Convention, Chicago, 27 June 1944

81 East and west on fields forgotten
Bleach the bones of comrades slain,
Lovely lads and dead and rotten;
None that go return again.

A. E. Housman (1859–1936) British scholar and poet. *A Shropshire Lad*, 'The Welsh Marches'

82 They will drown in their own blood.

Saddam Hussein (1937–) Iraqi dictator. Referring to the coalition forces assembing in Saudi Arabia to expel the Iraqis from Kuwait. Speech, 1990

83 The mother of battles will be our battle of victory and martyrdom.

Saddam Hussein Referring to the imminent Gulf War. Speech, 1991

84 Elevate them guns a little lower.

Andrew Jackson (1767–1845) US statesman. Order given whilst watching the effect of the US artillery upon the British lines at the Battle of New Orleans. Attrib.

85 I had always to remember that I could have lost the war in an afternoon.

Lord Jellicoe (1859–1935) British admiral. Referring to the Battle of Jutland, 1916

86 We are about to engage in a battle on which the fate of our country depends and it is important to remind all ranks that the moment has passed for looking to the rear; all our efforts must be directed to attacking and driving back the enemy. Troops that can advance no farther must, at any price, hold on to the ground they have conquered and die on the spot rather than give way. Under the circumstances which face us, no act of weakness can be tolerated.

Joseph Jacques Césaire Joffre (1852–1931) French soldier. *The Memoirs of Marshall Joffre*

87 War should belong to the tragic past, to history: it should find no place on humanity's agenda for the future.

John Paul II (Karol Wojtyla; 1920–) Polish pope (1978–). Speech, 1982

88 The first casualty when war comes is truth.

Hiram Warren Johnson (1866–1945) US politician. Speech, U.S. Senate, 1917

89 Some men are killed in a war and some men are wounded, and some men never leave the country... Life is unfair.

John Fitzgerald Kennedy (1917–63) US statesman. *Robert Kennedy and His Times* (A. M. Schlesinger)

90 Formerly, a nation that broke the peace did not trouble to try and prove to the world that it was done solely from higher motives...*Now war has a bad conscience*. Now every nation assures us that it is bleeding for a human cause, the fate of which hangs in the balance of its victory...No nation dares to admit the guilt of blood before the world.

Ellen Key (Karolina Sofia Key; 1849–1926) Swedish writer. *War, Peace, and the Future*, Preface

91 Everything, everything in war is barbaric...But the worst barbarity of war is that it forces men collectively to commit acts against which individually they would revolt with their whole being.

Ellen Key *War, Peace, and the Future*, Ch. 6

92 Our scientific power has outrun our spiritual power. We have guided missiles and misguided men.

Martin Luther King (1929–68) US Black civil-rights leader. *Strength to Love*

93 The conventional army loses if it does not win. The guerrilla wins if he does not lose.

Henry Kissinger (1923–) German-born US politician and diplomat. *Foreign Affairs*, XIII (Jan 1969), 'The Vietnam Negotiations'

94 The most persistent sound which reverberates through men's history is the beating of war drums.

Arthur Koestler (1905–83) Hungarian-born British writer. *Janus: A Summing Up*, Prologue

95 Where do all the women who have watched so carefully over the lives of their beloved ones get the heroism to send them to face the canon?

Käthe Kollwitz (1867–1945) German painter, sculptor, and graphic artist. Diary entry, 27 Aug 1914

96 Napoleon is a torrent which as yet we are unable to stem. Moscow will be the sponge that will suck him dry.

Mikhail Kutuzov (1745–1813) Russian marshal. Address to the commanders of the Russian army, 13 Sept 1812

97 If, therefore, war should ever come between these two countries, which Heaven forbid! it will not, I think, be due to irresistible natural laws, it will be due to the want of human wisdom.

Bonar Law (1858–1923) British statesman. Referring to the UK and Germany. Speech, House of Commons, 27 Nov 1911

98 We have all lost the war. All Europe.

D. H. Lawrence (1885–1930) British novelist. *The Ladybird*, 'The Ladybird'

99 It is well that war is so terrible; else we would grow too fond of it.

Robert E. Lee (1807–70) US general. Speaking to another general during the Battle of Fredericksburg. *The American Treasury* (C. Fadiman)

100 My solution to the problem would be to tell them...they've got to draw in their horns or we're going to bomb them into the Stone Age.

Curtis E. LeMay (1906–90) US general and air-force chief. On the North Vietnamese. *Mission with LeMay*

101 This war, like the next war, is a war to end war.

David Lloyd George (1863–1945) British Liberal statesman. Referring to the popular opinion that World War I would be the last major war.

102 In war there is no substitute for victory.

Douglas MacArthur (1880–1964) US general. Speech, US Congress, 19 Apr 1951

103 'War is the continuation of politics'. In this sense war is politics and war itself is a political action.

Mao Tse-Tung (1893–1976) Chinese communist leader. *See also* CLAUSEWITZ. *Quotations from Chairman Mao Tse-Tung*, Ch. 5

104 We are advocates of the abolition of war, we do not want war; but war can only be abolished through war, and in order to get rid of the gun it is necessary to take up the gun.

Mao Tse-Tung *Quotations from Chairman Mao Tse-Tung*, Ch. 5

105 Television brought the brutality of war into the comfort of the living room. Vietnam was lost in the living rooms of America – not on the battlefields of Vietnam.

Marshall McLuhan (1911–81) Canadian sociologist. *Montreal Gazette*, 16 May 1975

106 War will never cease until babies begin to come into the world with larger cerebrums and smaller adrenal glands.

H. L. Mencken (1880–1956) US journalist. *Notebooks*, 'Minority Report'

107 War is the national industry of Prussia.

Comte de Mirabeau (1749–91) French statesman. Attrib.

108 Fighting is like champagne. It goes to the heads of cowards as quickly as of heroes. Any fool can be brave on a battle field when it's be brave or else be killed.

Margaret Mitchell (1909–49) US novelist. *Gone with the Wind*

109 *La quinta columna.*
The Fifth Column.

Emilio Mola (1887–1937) Spanish Nationalist General. Reply when asked (Oct 1937) which of four Nationalist armies would capture Madrid; Mola was referring to Nationalist elements within the city.

110 War hath no fury like a non-combatant.

C. E. Montague (1867–1928) British editor and writer. *Disenchantment*, Ch. 15

111 An empire founded by war has to maintain itself by war.

Baron de Montesquieu (1689–1755) French writer. *Considérations sur les causes de la grandeur et de la décadence des romains*, Ch. 8

112 The U.S. has broken the second rule of war. That is, don't go fighting with your land army on the mainland of Asia. Rule One is don't march on Moscow. I developed these two rules myself.

Lord Montgomery (1887–1976) British field marshal. Referring to the Vietnam War. *Montgomery of Alamein* (Chalfont)

113 The Minstrel Boy to the war has gone,
In the ranks of death you'll find him;
His father's sword he has girded on,
And his wild harp slung behind him.

Thomas Moore (1779–1852) Irish poet. *Irish Melodies*, 'The Minstrel Boy'

114 War alone brings up to their highest tension all human energies and imposes the stamp of nobility upon the peoples who have the courage to make it.

Benito Mussolini (1883–1945) Italian dictator. *Encyclopedia Italiane*

115 It's the most beautiful battlefield I've ever seen.

Napoleon I (Napoleon Bonaparte; 1769–1821) French emperor. Referring to carnage on the field of Borodino, near Moscow, after the battle (7 Sept 1812). Attrib.

116 There rises the sun of Austerlitz.

Napoleon I Said at the Battle of Borodino (7 Sept 1812), near Moscow; the Battle of Austerlitz (2 Dec 1805) was Napoleon's great victory over the Russians and Austrians.

117 I don't care for war, there's far too much luck in it for my liking.

Napoleon III (1808–73) French emperor. Said after the narrow but bloody French victory at Solferino (24 June 1859). *The Fall of the House of Habsburg* (E. Crankshaw)

118 In case signals can neither be seen nor perfectly understood, no captain can do very wrong if he places his ship alongside that of an enemy.

Lord Nelson (1758–1805) British admiral. Memorandum before Trafalgar, 9 Oct 1805

119 The sand of the desert is sodden red, –
Red with the wreck of a square that broke; –
The gatling's jammed and the colonel dead,
And the regiment blind with the dust and smoke.
The river of death has brimmed its banks
And England's far and honour a name.
But the voice of a schoolboy rallies the ranks:
'Play up! play up! and play the game!'

Henry John Newbolt (1862–1938) British poet. *Vitaï Lampada*

120 Drake he's in his hammock till the great Armadas come.
(Capten, art tha sleepin' there below?)
Slung atween the round shot, listenin' for the drum,
An dreamin' arl the time o' Plymouth Hoe.

Henry John Newbolt *Drake's Drum*

121 War is war. The only good human being is a dead one.

George Orwell (Eric Blair; 1903–50) British novelist. *Animal Farm*, Ch. 4

122 Probably the Battle of Waterloo *was* won on the playing-fields of Eton, but the opening battles of all subsequent wars have been lost there.

George Orwell *The Lion and the Unicorn*, 'England, Your England'

123 The quickest way of ending a war is to lose it.

George Orwell *Second Thoughts on James Burnham*

124 The pallor of girls' brows shall be their pall;
Their flowers the tenderness of patient minds,
And each slow dusk a drawing-down of blinds.

Wilfred Owen (1893–1918) British poet. *Anthem for Doomed Youth*

125 Red lips are not so red
As the stained stones kissed by the English dead.

Wilfred Owen *Greater Love*

126 I could not give my name to aid the slaughter in this war, fought on both sides for grossly material ends, which did not justify the sacrifice of a single mother's son. Clearly I must continue to oppose it, and expose it, to all whom I could reach with voice or pen.

Sylvia Pankhurst (1882–1960) British suffragette. *The Home Front*, Ch. 25

127 Stand your ground. Don't fire unless fired upon, but if they mean to have a war, let it begin here!

John Parker (1729–75) US general. Command given at the start of the Battle of Lexington. *Familiar Quotations* (J. Bartlett)

128 This is how war is begun: such is my advice. First destroy the land, deal after with the foe.

Philip, Count of Flanders Advice to William, King of Scotland. *Chronique de la guerre entre les Anglois et les Ecossois en 1173 et 1174* (Jordan Fantosme)

129 Don't cheer, boys; the poor devils are dying.

John Woodward Philip (1840–1900) US naval officer. Restraining his victorious crew during the naval battle off Santiago in the Spanish-American War. Attrib.

130 If sunbeams were weapons of war, we would have had solar energy long ago.

George Porter (1920–) British chemist. *The Observer*, 'Sayings of the Week', 26 Aug 1973

131 Don't fire until you see the whites of their eyes.

William Prescott (1726–95) US revolutionary soldier. Command given at the Battle of Bunker Hill

132 War is, after all, the universal perversion. We are all tainted: if we cannot experience our perversion at first hand we spend our time reading war stories, the pornography of war; or seeing war films, the blue films of war; or titillating our senses with the imagination of great deeds, the masturbation of war.

John Rae (1931–) British schoolmaster and writer. *The Custard Boys*, Ch. 6

133 As a woman I can't go to war, and I refuse to send anyone else.

Jeannette Rankin (1880–1973) US suffragette, pacifist, and politician. *Jeannette Rankin: First Lady in Congress*, Prologue

134 In a civil war, a general must know – and I'm afraid it's a thing rather of instinct than of practice – he must know exactly when to move over to the other side.

Henry Reed (1914–86) British poet and dramatist. *Not a Drum was Heard: The War Memoirs of General Gland*

135 And the various holds and rolls and throws and breakfalls
Somehow or other I always seemed to put
In the wrong place. And as for war, my wars
Were global from the start.

Henry Reed *A Map of Verona*, 'Lessons of the War', III

136 All Quiet on the Western Front.

Erich Maria Remarque (1898–1970) German novelist. Title of novel

137 All wars are planned by old men
In council rooms apart.

Grantland Rice (1880–1954) US sportswriter. *Two Sides of War*

138 (Fire – without hatred.)

Antonio Rivera (d. 1936) Spanish Nationalist hero. Giving the order to open fire at the Siege of the Alcázar. *The Siege of the Alcázar* (C. Eby)

139 More than an end to war, we want an end to the beginnings of all wars.

Franklin D. Roosevelt (1882–1945) US Democratic president. Speech broadcast on the day after his death (13 Apr 1945)

140 I discovered to my amazement that average men and women were delighted at the prospect of war. I had fondly imagined what most pacifists contended, that wars were forced upon a reluctant population by despotic and Machiavellian governments.

Bertrand Russell (1872–1970) British philosopher. *The Autobiography of Bertrand Russell*

141 They dashed on towards that *thin red line tipped with steel.*

William Howard Russell (1820–1907) British journalist. Description of the Russian charge against the British at the Battle of Balaclava, 1854. *The British Expedition to the Crimea*

142 War is not an adventure. It is a disease. It is like typhus.

Antoine de Saint-Exupéry (1900–44) French novelist and aviator. *Flight to Arras*

143 Sometime they'll give a war and nobody will come.

Carl Sandburg (1878–1967) US author and poet. *The People, Yes*

144 Man, it seemed, had been created to jab the life out of Germans.

Siegfried Sassoon (1886–1967) British poet. *Memoirs of an Infantry Officer*, Pt. I, Ch. 1

145 Safe with his wound, a citizen of life,
He hobbled blithely through the garden gate,
And thought: 'Thank God they had to amputate!'

Siegfried Sassoon *The One-Legged Man*

146 If I were fierce and bald and short of breath,
I'd live with scarlet Majors at the Base,
And speed glum heroes up the line to death.

Siegfried Sassoon *Base Details*

147 And when the war is done and youth stone dead
I'd toddle safely home and die – in bed.

Siegfried Sassoon *Base Details*

148 'Good morning; good morning!' the general said
When we met him last week on our way to the line.
Now the soldiers he smiled at are most of 'em dead,
And we're cursing his staff for incompetent swine.

Siegfried Sassoon *The General*

149 I am making this statement as a wilful defiance of military authority because I believe that the War is being deliberately prolonged by those who have the power to end it.

Siegfried Sassoon *Memoirs of an Infantry Officer*, Pt. X, Ch. 3

150 All wars are popular for the first thirty days.

Arthur Schlesinger Jnr (1917–) US historian, educator, and author. Attrib.

151 When you march into France, let the last man on the right brush the Channel with his sleeve.

Alfred Graf von Schlieffen (1833–1913) German general. Referring to the Schlieffen plan. *August 1914* (Barbara Tuchman), Ch. 2

152 Wars come because not enough people are sufficiently afraid.

Hugh Schonfield (1901–) British writer and editor. *The News Review*, 26 Feb 1948

153 We're going around, over, through, on top, underneath.

Norman Schwarzkopf (1934–) US general. Describing his tactics for attacking the Iraqi army. Press conference, 24 Feb 1991

154 The Cavaliers (wrong but Wromantic) and the Roundheads (Right but Repulsive).

W. C. Sellar (1898–1951) British humorous writer. *1066 And All That*

155 We have always borne part of the weight of war, and the major part…Men have made boomerangs, bows, swords, or guns with which to destroy one another; we have made the men who destroyed and were destroyed!…*We pay the first cost on all human life.*

Olive Schreiner (1855–1920) South African writer, feminist, and social critic. *Woman and Labor*, Ch. 4

156 Everyone is always talking about our defense effort in terms of defending women and children, but no one ever asks the women and children what they think.

Patricia Schroeder (1940–) US politician, lawyer, and educator. *American Political Women*

157 When we, the Workers, all demand: 'What are we fighting for?…
Then, then we'll end that stupid crime, that devil's madness – War.

Robert William Service (1874–1958) Canadian poet. *Michael*

158 Cry 'Havoc!' and let slip the dogs of war.

William Shakespeare (1564–1616) English dramatist. *Julius Caesar*, III:1

159 Farewell the neighing steed and the shrill trump,
The spirit-stirring drum, th'ear piercing fife,
The royal banner, and all quality,
Pride, pomp, and circumstance, of glorious war!

William Shakespeare *Othello*, III:3

160 The British soldier can stand up to anything except the British War Office.

George Bernard Shaw (1856–1950) Irish dramatist and critic. *The Devil's Disciple*, II

161 Nothing is ever done in this world until men are prepared to kill each other if it is not done.

George Bernard Shaw

162 I am tired and sick of war. Its glory is all moonshine…War is hell.

General William Sherman (1820–91) US general. Attrib. in address, Michigan Military Academy, 19 June 1879

163 Who live under the shadow of a war,
What can I do that matters?

Stephen Spender (1909–) British poet. *Who live under the Shadow*

164 To win in Vietnam, we will have to exterminate a nation.

Dr Benjamin Spock (1903–) US paediatrician and psychiatrist. *Dr Spock on Vietnam*, Ch.7

165 Yonder are the Hessians. They were bought for seven pounds and tenpence a man. Are you worth more? Prove it. Tonight the American flag floats from yonder hill or Molly Stark sleeps a widow!

John Stark (1728–1822) US general. Urging on his troops at the Battle of Bennington in 1777. *The American Treasury* (C. Fadiman)

166 That's what you are. That's what you all are. All of you young people who served in the war. You are a lost generation.

Gertrude Stein (1874–1946) US writer. *A Moveable Feast* (E. Hemingway)

167 War is capitalism with the gloves off.

Tom Stoppard (1937–) Czech-born British dramatist. *Travesties*

168 Most sorts of diversion in men, children, and other animals, are an imitation of fighting.

Jonathan Swift (1667–1745) Irish-born Anglican priest and writer. *Thoughts on Various Subjects*

169 The guerrilla fights the war of the flea, and his military enemy suffers the dog's disadvantages: too much to defend; too small, ubiquitous, and agile an enemy to come to grips with.

Robert Taber (20th century) US writer. *The War of the Flea*, Ch. 2

170 They make a wilderness and call it peace.

Tacitus (c. 55–c. 120 AD) Roman historian. *Agricola*, 30

171 Now all roads lead to France
And heavy is the tread
Of the living; but the dead
Returning lightly dance.

Edward Thomas (1878–1917) British poet. *Roads*

172 Dead battles, like dead generals, hold the military mind in their dead grip.

Barbara W. Tuchman (1912–89) US editor and writer. *August 1914*, Ch. 2

173 They now *ring* the bells, but they will soon *wring* their hands.

Robert Walpole (1676–1745) British statesman. Said when war was declared in 1739 with Spain, against Walpole's wishes. *Memoirs of Sir Robert Walpole* (W. Coxe)

174 I heard the bullets whistle, and believe me, there is something charming in the sound.

George Washington (1732–99) US statesman. Referring to a recent skirmish in the French and Indian War. *Presidential Anecdotes* (P. Boller)

175 When the war broke out she took down the signed photograph of the Kaiser and, with some solemnity, hung it in the menservants' lavatory; it was her one combative action.

Evelyn Waugh (1903–66) British novelist. *Vile Bodies*, Ch. 3

176 Like German opera, too long and too loud.

Evelyn Waugh Giving his opinions of warfare after the Battle of Crete, 1941. Attrib.

177 It has been a damned serious business – Blücher and I have lost 30,000 men. It has been a damned nice thing – the nearest run thing you ever saw in your life…By God! I don't think it would have done if I had not been there.

Duke of Wellington (1769–1852) British general and statesman. Referring to the Battle of Waterloo, 18 June 1815. *Creevey Papers*, Ch. X

178 Yes, and they went down very well too.

Duke of Wellington Replying to the observation that the French cavalry had come up very well during the Battle of Waterloo. *The Age of Elegance* (A. Bryant)

179 A battle of giants.

Duke of Wellington Referring to the Battle of Waterloo; said to Samuel Rogers. Attrib.

180 Up, Guards, and at 'em.

Duke of Wellington Order given at the Battle of Waterloo. Attrib.

181 The military don't start wars. The politicians start wars.

William Westmorland (1914–) US army officer. Attrib.

182 As long as war is regarded as wicked, it will always have its fascination. When it is looked upon as vulgar, it will cease to be popular.

Oscar Wilde (1854–1900) Irish-born British dramatist. *The Critic as Artist*, Pt. 2

183 You will be home before the leaves have fallen from the trees.

Wilhelm II (1859–1941) King of Prussia and Emperor of Germany. Said to troops leaving for the Front, Aug 1914. *August 1914* (Barbara Tuchman), Ch. 9

184 It is my Royal and Imperial Command that you…exterminate first the treacherous English, and…walk over General French's contemptible little Army.

Wilhelm II Referring to the British Expeditionary Force; veterans of this force became known as 'Old Contemptibles'. *The Times*, 1 Oct 1914

185 We draw the sword with a clear conscience and with clean hands.

Wilhelm II Speech, Berlin, 4 Aug 1914

186 There is such a thing as a man being too proud to fight.

Woodrow Wilson (1856–1925) US statesman. Address to foreign-born citizens, 10 May 1915

187 The war we have just been through, though it was shot through with terror, is not to be compared with the war we would have to face next time.

Woodrow Wilson *Mr Wilson's War* (John Dos Passos), Pt. V, Ch. 22

188 Once lead this people into war and they'll forget there ever was such a thing as tolerance.

Woodrow Wilson *Mr Wilson's War* (John Dos Passos), Pt. III, Ch. 2

189 It takes only one gramme of explosive to kill a man, so why waste five tons?

Solly Zuckerman (1904–93) South African-born British anatomist. *From Apes to War Lords*

WAR AND PEACE

See also peace, war

1 Since wars begin in the minds of men, it is in the minds of men that the defences of peace must be constructed.

Anonymous Constitution of UNESCO

2 The Israelis are now what we call the 'enemy-friends.

Anonymous adviser to the Palestinian leader Yasser Arafat. *The Independent*, 5 July 1994

3 And he shall judge among the nations, and shall rebuke many people: and they shall beat their swords into plowshares, and their spears into pruning-hooks: nation shall not lift up sword against nation, neither shall they learn war any more.

Bible: Isaiah 2:4

4 In war, resolution; in defeat, defiance; in victory, magnanimity; in peace, goodwill.

Winston Churchill (1874–1965) British statesman. Epigram used by Sir Edward Marsh after World War II; used as 'a moral of the work' in Churchill's book. *The Second World War*

5 Those who can win a war well can rarely make a good peace and those who could make a good peace would never have won the war.

Winston Churchill *My Early Life*, Ch. 26

6 My pacifism is not based on any intellectual theory but on a deep antipathy to every form of cruelty and hatred.

Albert Einstein (1879–1955) German-born US physicist. Said on the outbreak of World War I. Attrib.

7 There never was a good war or a bad peace.

Benjamin Franklin (1706–90) US scientist and statesman. Letter to Josiah Quincy, 11 Sept 1783

8 My argument is that War makes rattling good history; but Peace is poor reading.

Thomas Hardy (1840–1928) British novelist. *The Dynasts*, II:5

9 He that makes a good war makes a good peace.

George Herbert (1593–1633) English poet. *Outlandish Proverbs*, 420

10 The war ended, the explosions stopped.
The men surrendered their weapons
And hung around limply.
Peace took them all prisoner.

Ted Hughes (1930–) British poet. *Selected Poems 1957–1981*, 'A Motorbike'

11 The statistics of suicide show that, for non-combatants at least, life is more interesting in war than in peace.

Dean Inge (1860–1954) British churchman. *The End of an Age*

12 Peace hath her victories
No less renowned than war.

John Milton (1608–74) English poet. *Sonnet*: 'To the Lord General Cromwell, May 1652'

13 Peace is not only better than war, but infinitely more arduous.

George Bernard Shaw (1856–1950) Irish dramatist and critic. *Heartbreak House* (Preface)

14 Let him who desires peace, prepare for war.

Vegetius (Flavius Vegetius Renatus; 4th century AD) Roman writer. *Epitoma Rei Militaris*, 3, 'Prologue'

15 When you're at war you think about a better life; when you're at peace you think about a more comfortable one.

Thornton Wilder (1897–1975) US novelist and dramatist. *The Skin of Our Teeth*, III

WASHINGTON, GEORGE

(1732–99) US statesman and first president of the USA (1789–97). Commander in chief of the American forces in the American Revolution, he presided over the Constitutional Convention (1787) and was elected president of the new republic.

Quotations about Washington

1 First in war, first in peace, first in the hearts of his countrymen.

Henry Lee Addressing the House of Representatives, Dec 1799

2 The crude commercialism of America, its materializing spirit are entirely due to the country having adopted for its natural hero a man who could not tell a lie.

Oscar Wilde (1854–1900) Irish-born British dramatist. *The Decay of Lying*

Quotations by Washington

3 Associate yourself with men of good quality if you esteem your own reputation; for 'tis better to be alone than in bad company.

Rules of Civility

4 I heard the bullets whistle, and believe me, there is something charming in the sound.

Referring to a recent skirmish in the French and Indian War. *Presidential Anecdotes* (P. Boller)

5 Father, I cannot tell a lie. I did it with my little hatchet.

Attrib.

WASTE

See also extravagance

1 Waste not, want not.

Proverb

2 Full many a gem of purest ray serene,
The dark unfathom'd caves of ocean bear:
Full many a flower is born to blush unseen,
And waste its sweetness on the desert air.

Thomas Gray (1716–71) British poet. *Elegy Written in a Country Churchyard*

3 The world is too much with us; late and soon,
Getting and spending, we lay waste our powers:
Little we see in Nature that is ours.

William Wordsworth (1770–1850) British poet. *Sonnets*, 'The world is too much with us'

WATER

See also drinks

1 Well, the principle seems the same. The water still keeps falling over.

Winston Churchill (1874–1965) British statesman. When asked whether the Niagara Falls looked the same as when he first saw them. *Closing the Ring*, Ch. 5

2 Water, water, every where,
And all the boards did shrink;
Water, water, every where,
Nor any drop to drink.

Samuel Taylor Coleridge (1772–1834) British poet. *The Rime of the Ancient Mariner*, II

3 Instead of drinking Coca Colas, turn on the tap and drink what the good Lord gave us.

Edwina Currie (1946–) British politician. Speech, Nov 1988

4 Fish fuck in it.

W. C. Fields (1880–1946) US actor. His reason for not drinking water. Attrib.

5 For any ceremonial purposes the otherwise excellent liquid, water, is unsuitable in colour and other respects.

A. P. Herbert (1890–1971) British writer and politician. *Uncommon Law*

6 If you believe Cratinus from days of old, Maecenas, (as you must know) no verse can give pleasure for long, nor last, that is written by drinkers of water.

Horace (Quintus Horatius Flaccus; 65–8 BC) Roman poet. *Epistles*, I

7 The biggest waste of water in the country by far. You spend half a pint and flush two gallons.

Prince Philip (1921–) The consort of Queen Elizabeth II. Speech, 1965

8 Human beings were invented by water as a device for transporting itself from one place to another.

Tom Robbins (1936–) US novelist. *Another Roadside Attraction*

9 He who drinks a tumbler of London water has literally in his stomach more animated beings than there are men, women and children on the face of the globe.

Sydney Smith (1771–1845) British clergyman and essayist. Letter

WATTS, ISAAC

(1674–1748) English theologian and hymn writer. His 600 hymns include 'O God, our help in ages past' and 'There is a land of pure delight'.

1 For Satan finds some mischief still
For idle hands to do.

Divine Songs for Children, 'Against Idleness and Mischief'

2 How doth the little busy bee
Improve each shining hour,
And gather honey all the day
From every opening flower!

Divine Songs for Children, 'Against Idleness and Mischief'

3 Let dogs delight to bark and bite,
For God hath made them so;
Let bears and lions growl and fight,
For 'tis their nature too.

Divine Songs for Children, 'Against Quarrelling'

4 Lord, I ascribe it to Thy grace,
And not to chance, as others do,
That I was born of Christian race,
And not a Heathen, or a Jew.

Divine Songs for Children, 'Praise for the Gospel'

5 There's no repentance in the grave.

Divine Songs for Children, 'Solemn Thoughts of God and Death'

6 Our God, our help in ages past,
Our hope for years to come,
Our shelter from the stormy blast,
And our eternal home.

Our God, Our Help in Ages Past

7 'Tis the voice of the sluggard, I heard him complain:
'You have waked me too soon, I must slumber again.'

Divine Songs for Children, 'The Sluggard'

8 When I survey the wondrous Cross,
On which the Prince of Glory died,
My richest gain I count but loss
And pour contempt on all my pride.

Crucifixion to the World, by the Cross of Christ.

WAUGH, EVELYN

(1903–66) British novelist. He established his reputation with *Decline and Fall* (1928) and *Vile Bodies* (1930). Later books, after his conversion to Catholicism, include *Brideshead Revisited* (1945) and the war trilogy *Sword of Honour* (1952–61).

Quotations about Waugh

1 I expect you know my friend Evelyn Waugh, who, like you, your Holiness, is a Roman Catholic.

Randolph Churchill (1911–68) British political journalist. Remark made during an audience with the Pope

2 Mr. Waugh, I always feel, is an antique in search of a period, a snob in search of a class, perhaps even a mystic in search of a beatific vision.

Malcolm Muggeridge (1903–90) British writer. *The Most of Malcolm Muggeridge*

Quotations by Waugh

3 Venice is the *one* town in Italy where *no one* ever *has* gone to church.

Brideshead Revisited, Bk. I, Ch. 1

4 'It is typical of Oxford', I said, 'to start the new year in autumn.'

Brideshead Revisited, Bk. I, Ch. 5

5 O God, if there is a God, forgive him his sins, if there is such a thing as sin.
Brideshead Revisited, Bk. III, Ch. 5

6 I expect you'll be becoming a schoolmaster sir. That's what most of the gentlemen does sir, that gets sent down for indecent behaviour.
Decline and Fall, Prelude

7 The sound of the English county families baying for broken glass.
Decline and Fall, Prelude

8 We class schools you see, into four grades: Leading School, First-rate School, Good School, and School.
Decline and Fall, Pt. I, Ch. 1

9 We schoolmasters must temper discretion with deceit.
Decline and Fall, Pt. I, Ch. 1

10 Very hard for a man with a wig to keep order.
Decline and Fall, Pt. I, Ch. 3

11 That's the public-school system all over. They may kick you out, but they never let you down.
Decline and Fall, Pt. I, Ch. 3

12 Meanwhile you will write an essay on 'self-indulgence'. There will be a prize of half a crown for the longest essay, irrespective of any possible merit.
Decline and Fall, Pt. I, Ch. 5

13 I can't quite explain it, but I don't believe one can ever be unhappy for long provided one does just exactly what one wants to and when one wants to.
Decline and Fall, Pt. I, Ch. 5

14 Nonconformity and lust stalking hand in hand through the country, wasting and ravaging.
Decline and Fall, Pt. I, Ch. 5

15 For generations the British bourgeoisie have spoken of themselves as gentlemen, and by that they have meant, among other things, a self-respecting scorn of irregular perquisites. It is the quality that distinguishes the gentleman from both the artist and the aristocrat.
Decline and Fall, Pt. I, Ch. 6

16 There aren't many left like him nowadays, what with education and whisky the price it is.
Decline and Fall, Pt. I, Ch. 7

17 'The Welsh,' said the Doctor, 'are the only nation in the world that has produced no graphic or plastic art, no architecture, no drama. They just sing,' he said with disgust, 'sing and blow down wind instruments of plated silver.'
Decline and Fall, Pt. I, Ch. 8

18 We can trace almost all the disasters of English history to the influence of Wales.
Decline and Fall, Pt. I, Ch. 8

19 I have noticed again and again since I have been in the Church that lay interest in ecclesiastical matters is often a prelude to insanity.
Decline and Fall, Pt. I, Ch. 8

20 I have often observed in women of her type a tendency to regard all athletics as inferior forms of fox-hunting.
Decline and Fall, Pt. I, Ch. 10

21 I haven't been to sleep for over a year. That's why I go to bed early. One needs more rest if one doesn't sleep.
Decline and Fall, Pt. II, Ch. 3

22 There is a species of person called a 'Modern Churchman' who draws the full salary of a beneficed clergyman and need not commit himself to any religious belief.
Decline and Fall, Pt. II, Ch. 4

23 I came to the conclusion many years ago that almost all crime is due to the repressed desire for aesthetic expression.
Decline and Fall, Pt. III, Ch. 1

24 He stood twice for Parliament, but so diffidently that his candidature passed almost unnoticed.
Decline and Fall, Pt. III, Ch. 1

25 Anyone who has been to an English public school will always feel comparatively at home in prison.
Decline and Fall, Pt. III, Ch. 4

26 He was greatly pained at how little he was pained by the events of the afternoon.
Decline and Fall, Pt. III, Ch. 4

27 Instead of this absurd division into sexes they ought to class people as static and dynamic.
Decline and Fall, Pt. III, Ch. 7

28 We are all American at puberty; we die French.
Diaries, 'Irregular Notes', 18 July 1961

29 Punctuality is the virtue of the bored.
Diaries, 'Irregular Notes', 26 Mar 1962

30 Assistant masters came and went…Some liked little boys too little and some too much.
A Little Learning

31 You never find an Englishman among the underdogs – except in England of course.
The Loved One

32 In the dying world I come from quotation is a national vice. It used to be the classics, now it's lyric verse.
The Loved One

33 Enclosing every thin man, there's a fat man demanding elbow-room.
Similar sentiments have been expressed by others. *See* AMIS; CONNOLLY; ORWELL. *Officers and Gentlemen*, Interlude

34 Feather-footed through the plashy fen passes the questing vole.
Scoop, Bk. I, Ch. 1

35 '*The Beast* stands for strong mutually antagonistic governments everywhere', he said. 'Self-sufficiency at home, self-assertion abroad.'
Scoop, Bk. I, Ch. 1

36 Yes, cider and tinned salmon are the staple diet of the agricultural classes.

Scoop, Bk. I, Ch. 1

37 Pappenhacker says that every time you are polite to a proletarian you are helping to bolster up the capitalist system.

Scoop, Bk. I, Ch. 5

38 News is what a chap who doesn't care much about anything wants to read. And it's only news until he's read it. After that it's dead.

Scoop, Bk. I, Ch. 5

39 'I will not stand for being called a woman in my own house,' she said.

Scoop, Bk. II, Ch. 1

40 As there was no form of government common to the peoples thus segregated, nor tie of language, history, habit, or belief, they were called a Republic.

Scoop, Bk. II, Ch. 1

41 The better sort of Ishmaelites have been Christian for many centuries and will not publicly eat human flesh uncooked in Lent, without special and costly dispensation from their bishop.

Scoop, Bk. II, Ch. 1

42 Other nations use 'force'; we Britons alone use 'Might'.

Scoop, Bk. II, Ch. 5

43 Up to a point, Lord Copper.

A euphemism for 'No'. *Scoop*, passim

44 Particularly against books the Home Secretary is. If we can't stamp out literature in the country, we can at least stop it being brought in from outside.

Vile Bodies, Ch. 2

45 When the war broke out she took down the signed photograph of the Kaiser and, with some solemnity, hung it in the menservants' lavatory; it was her one combative action.

Vile Bodies, Ch. 3

46 She had heard someone say something about an Independent Labour Party, and was furious that she had not been asked.

Vile Bodies, Ch. 4

47 All this fuss about sleeping together. For physical pleasure I'd sooner go to my dentist any day.

Vile Bodies, Ch. 6

48 Lady Peabury was in the morning room reading a novel; early training gave a guilty spice to this recreation, for she had been brought up to believe that to read a novel before luncheon was one of the gravest sins it was possible for a gentlewoman to commit.

Work Suspended, 'An Englishman's Home'

49 I wouldn't give up writing about God at this stage, if I was you. It would be like P. G. Wodehouse dropping Jeeves half-way through the Wooster series.

Said to Grahame Greene, who proposed to write a political novel. *Evelyn Waugh* (Christopher Sykes)

50 Simply a radio personality who outlived his prime.

Referring to Winston Churchill. *Evelyn Waugh* (Christopher Sykes)

51 Manners are especially the need of the plain. The pretty can get away with anything.

The Observer, 'Sayings of the Year,' 15 Apr 1962

52 No writer before the middle of the 19th century wrote about the working classes other than as grotesque or as pastoral decoration. Then when they were given the vote certain writers started to suck up to them.

Interview. *Paris Review*, 1963

53 Nurse unupblown.

Cable sent after he had failed, while a journalist serving in Ethiopia, to substantiate a rumour that an English nurse had been blown up in an Italian air raid. *Our Marvellous Native Tongue* (R. Claiborne)

54 A typical triumph of modern science to find the only part of Randolph that was not malignant and remove it.

Remarking upon the news that Randolph Churchill had had a noncancerous lung removed. Attrib.

55 Like German opera, too long and too loud.

Giving his opinions of warfare after the Battle of Crete, 1941. Attrib.

56 I put the words down and push them a bit.

Obituary, *The New York Times*, 11 Apr 1966

WEAKNESS

See also imperfection, yielding

1 The weakest goes to the wall.

Proverb

2 Oh, your precious 'lame ducks'!

John Galsworthy (1867–1933) British novelist. *The Man of Property*, Pt. II, Ch. 12

3 A sheep in sheep's clothing.

Edmund Gosse (1849–1928) British writer and critic. Referring to T. Sturge Moore. Sometimes attributed to Winston Churchill, referring to Clement Attlee. *Under the Bridge* (Ferris Greenslet), Ch. 12

4 My brother John is not the man to conquer a country if there is anyone to offer even the feeblest resistance.

Richard I (1157–99) King of England. *From Domesday Book to Magna Carta* (A. L. Poole)

5 Frailty, thy name is woman!

William Shakespeare (1564–1616) English dramatist. *Hamlet*, I:2

6 Thou knowest in the state of innocency Adam fell; and what should poor Jack Falstaff do in the days of villany. Thou seest I have more flesh than another man, and therefore more frailty.

William Shakespeare *Henry IV, Part One*, III:3

WEALTH

See also capitalism, extravagance, materialism, money, ostentation, poverty and wealth

1 The best things in life are free.

Proverb

2 You can't take it with you when you go.
Proverb

3 A good wife and health are a man's best wealth.
Proverb

4 It does seem to be true that the more you get the more you spend. It is rather like being on a golden treadmill.
Charles Allsop (1940–) Commodities broker. Remark, Dec 1988

5 A rich man is one who isn't afraid to ask the salesman to show him something cheaper.
Anonymous *Ladies Home Journal*, Jan 1946

6 Rich men's houses are seldom beautiful, rarely comfortable, and never original. It is a constant source of surprise to people of moderate means to observe how little a big fortune contributes to Beauty.
Margot Asquith (1865–1945) The second wife of the British statesman Herbert Asquith. *The Autobiography of Margot Asquith*, Ch. 17

7 A man who has a million dollars is as well off as if he were rich.
John Jacob Astor (1763–1848) US millionaire. Attrib.

8 Being a king that loved wealth and treasure, he could not endure to have trade sick.
Francis Bacon (1561–1626) English philosopher. Referring to Henry VII. *The Life of Henry VII*

9 For the Lord thy God bringeth thee into a good land, a land of brooks of water, of fountains and depths that spring out of valleys and hills;
A land of wheat, and barley, and vines, and fig trees, and pomegranates; a land of oil olive, and honey;
A land wherein thou shalt eat bread without scarceness, thou shalt not lack any thing in it; a land whose stones are iron, and out of whose hills thou mayest dig brass.
When thou hast eaten and art full, then thou shalt bless the Lord thy God for the good land which he hath given thee.
Bible: Deuteronomy 8:7–10

10 So the Lord blessed the latter end of Job more than his beginning: for he had fourteen thousand sheep, and six thousand camels, and a thousand yoke of oxen, and a thousand she asses.
Bible: Job 42:12

11 For what shall it profit a man, if he shall gain the whole world, and lose his own soul? Or what shall a man give in exchange for his soul?
Bible: Mark 8:36–37

12 Lay not up for yourselves treasures upon earth, where moth and rust doth corrupt, and where thieves break through and steal:
But lay up for yourselves treasures in heaven, where neither moth nor rust doth corrupt, and where thieves do not break through nor steal:
For where your treasure is, there will your heart be also.
Bible: Matthew 6:19–21

13 Then said Jesus unto his disciples, Verily I say unto you, That a rich man shall hardly enter into the kingdom of heaven.
And again I say unto you, It is easier for a camel to go through the eye of a needle, than for a rich man to enter into the kingdom of God.
Bible: Matthew 19:23–24

14 For we brought nothing into this world, and it is certain we carry nothing out.
Bible: I Timothy 6:7

15 Maidens, like moths, are ever caught by glare,
And Mammon wins his way where Seraphs might despair.
Lord Byron (1788–1824) British poet. *Childe Harold's Pilgrimage*, I

16 Nothing melts a Woman's Heart like gold.
Susannah Centlivre (c. 1667–1723) English poet, playwright, and actress. *The Basset-Table*, IV

17 The rich are the scum of the earth in every country.
G. K. Chesterton (1874–1936) British writer. *The Flying Inn*

18 People don't resent having nothing nearly as much as too little.
Ivy Compton-Burnett (1892–1969) British novelist. *A Family and a Fortune*

19 Poor Little Rich Girl.
Noël Coward (1899–1973) British dramatist. *Song title*

20 Riches have wings, and grandeur is a dream.
William Cowper (1731–1800) British poet. *The Task*

21 FITZGERALD. The rich are different from us.
HEMINGWAY. Yes, they have more money.
F. Scott Fitzgerald (1896–1940) US novelist. *The Crack-Up*, 'Notebooks, E'

22 Wealth is not without its advantages, and the case to the contrary, although it has often been made, has never proved widely persuasive.
John Kenneth Galbraith (1908–) US economist. *The Affluent Society*, Ch. 1

23 The meek shall inherit the earth but not the mineral rights.
J. Paul Getty (1892–1976) US oil magnate. Attrib.

24 If you can actually count your money you are not really a rich man.
J. Paul Getty *Gossip* (A. Barrow)

25 As I walk along the Bois Bou-long,
With an independent air,
You can hear the girls declare,
'He must be a millionaire',
You can hear them sigh and wish to die,
You can see them wink the other eye
At the man who broke the Bank at Monte Carlo.
Fred Gilbert (1850–1903) British songwriter. The Bois de Boulogne was a fashionable recreational area on the outskirts of Paris. *The Man who Broke the Bank at Monte Carlo* (song)

26 I think people still want to marry rich. Girls especially…It's simple. Don't date poor boys. Go where the rich are…You don't have to be rich to go where they go.
Sheilah Graham (c. 1908–) British-born US writer. *The Los Angeles Times*, 13 Oct 1974

27 The rich hate signing cheques. Hence the success of credit cards.
Graham Greene (1904–91) British novelist. *Dr. Fischer of Geneva*

28 Sir, the insolence of wealth will creep out.

Samuel Johnson (1709–84) British lexicographer. *Life of Johnson* (J. Boswell), Vol. III

29 Wealth covers sin – the poor
Are naked as a pin.

Kassia (fl. c. 840) Byzantine poet. *Women Poets of the World* (eds Joanna Bankier and Deirdre Lashgari)

30 If Enterprise is afoot, Wealth accumulates whatever may be happening to Thrift; and if Enterprise is asleep, Wealth decays, whatever Thrift may be doing.

John Maynard Keynes (1883–1946) British economist. *Treatise on Money*

31 I don't know how much money I've got…I did ask the accountant how much it came to. I wrote it down on a bit of paper. But I've lost the bit of paper.

John Lennon (1940–80) British rock musician. *The Beatles* (Hunter Davies)

32 Those in the cheaper seats clap. The rest of you rattle your jewellery.

John Lennon Remark, Royal Variety Performance, 15 Nov 1963

33 Your lord the King of England, who lacks nothing, has men, horses, gold, silk, jewels, fruits, game and everything else. We in France have nothing but bread and wine and gaiety.

Louis VII (c. 1120–80) King of France. By 'France' Louis meant the comparatively small area around Paris that he ruled directly. Remark to the Welsh ecclesiastic and writer, Walter Map; cited in *Richard the Lionheart* (J. Gillingham), Ch. 4

34 So our Lord God commonly gives riches to those gross asses to whom he vouchsafes nothing else.

Martin Luther (1483–1546) German Protestant. *Colloquia* (J. Aurifaber), Ch. XX

35 Most of our people have never had it so good.

Harold Macmillan (1894–1986) British politician and prime minister. Speech, Bedford Football Ground, 20 July 1957

36 They gave me star treatment because I was making a lot of money. But I was just as good when I was poor.

Bob Marley (Robert Nesta Marley; 1945–80) Jamaican reggae singer. *The Radio Times*, 18 Sept 1981

37 And, as their wealth increaseth, so inclose
Infinite riches in a little room.

Christopher Marlowe (1564–93) English dramatist. *The Jew of Malta*, I:1

38 He must have killed a lot of men to have made so much money.

Molière (Jean Baptiste Poquelin; 1622–73) French dramatist. *Le Malade imaginaire*, I:5

39 I am rich beyond the dreams of avarice.

Edward Moore (1712–57) British dramatist. *The Gamester*, II

40 God shows his contempt for wealth by the kind of person he selects to receive it.

Austin O'Malley (1858–1932) US writer.

41 Gout is not relieved by a fine shoe nor a hangnail by a costly ring nor migraine by a tiara.

Plutarch (46 AD–120 AD) Greek biographer and essayist. *Moralia*, 'Contentment'

42 Who Wants to Be a Millionaire? I don't.

Cole Porter (1893–1964) US songwriter. *Who Wants to be a Millionaire?*, title song

43 I am a millionaire. That is my religion.

George Bernard Shaw (1856–1950) Irish dramatist and critic. *Major Barbara*

44 With the great part of rich people, the chief employment of riches consists in the parade of riches.

Adam Smith (1723–90) Scottish economist. *The Wealth of Nations*

45 It is the wretchedness of being rich that you have to live with rich people.

Logan Pearsall Smith (1865–1946) US writer. *Afterthoughts*, 'In the World'

46 I don't feel guilty as long as the Queen and Prince Charles are swimming about. I've just got more money than I need. I give it away, it's as simple as that.

Robert Smith (1959–) British pop singer. Attrib.

47 If Heaven had looked upon riches to be a valuable thing, it would not have given them to such a scoundrel.

Jonathan Swift (1667–1745) Irish-born Anglican priest and writer. Letter to Miss Vanhomrigh, 12–13 Aug 1720

48 I have had no real gratification or enjoyment of any sort more than my neighbor on the next block who is worth only half a million.

William Henry Vanderbilt (1821–85) US railway chief. *Famous Last Words* (B. Conrad)

49 One can never be too thin or too rich.

Duchess of Windsor (Wallis Warfield Simpson; 1896–1986) The wife of the Duke of Windsor (formerly Edward VIII). Attrib.

50 Just what God would have done if he had the money.

Alexander Woollcott (1887–1943) US journalist. On being shown round Moss Hart's elegant country house and grounds. Attrib.

WEAPONS

See also nuclear weapons, power politics, war

1 I put before the whole House my own view with appalling frankness…supposing I had gone to the country and said…that we must rearm, does anybody think that this pacific democracy would have rallied to that cry at that moment? I cannot think of anything that would have made the loss of the election from my point of view more certain.

Stanley Baldwin (1867–1947) British Conservative prime minister. Speech, House of Commons, 12 Nov 1936

2 If you carry this resolution and follow out all its implications and do not run away from it, you will send a Foreign Secretary, whoever he may be, naked into the conference chamber.

Aneurin Bevan (1897–1960) British Labour politician. Referring to unilateral disarmament. Speech, Labour Party Conference, 2 Oct 1957

3 In Place of Fear.

Aneurin Bevan Title of book about disarmament

4 It was very successful, but it fell on the wrong planet.

Wernher von Braun (1912–77) German rocket engineer.

Referring to the first V2 rocket to hit London during World War II. Attrib.

5 We may find in the long run that tinned food is a deadlier weapon than the machine-gun.

George Orwell (Eric Blair; 1903–50) British novelist. *The Road to Wigan Pier*, Ch. 6

6 Arms control so easily becomes an incantation rather than policy.

Richard Perle US politician. Remark, Mar 1987

7 Today we have naming of parts. Yesterday,
We had daily cleaning. And tomorrow morning
We shall have what to do after firing. But today,
Today we have naming of parts.

Henry Reed (1914–86) British poet and dramatist. *Naming of Parts*

8 They call it easing the Spring: it is perfectly easy
If you have any strength in your thumb: like the bolt,
And the breech, and the cocking-piece, and the point of balance,
Which in our case we have not got.

Henry Reed *Naming of Parts*

9 Though loaded firearms were strictly forbidden at St Trinian's to all but Sixth-Formers...one or two of them carried automatics acquired in the holidays, generally the gift of some indulgent relative.

Ronald Searle (1920–) British cartoonist. *The Terror of St Trinian's*, Ch. 3

10 But bombs *are* unbelievable until they actually fall.

Patrick White (1912–90) British-born Australian novelist. *Riders in the Chariot*, I:4

WEATHER

See also sun

1 Mackerel sky and mares' tails make lofty ships carry low sails.

Proverb

2 Rain before seven: fine before eleven.

Proverb

3 Rain, rain, go away, come again another day.

Proverb

4 Red sky at night, shepherd's delight; red sky in the morning, shepherd's warning.

Proverb

5 St. Swithin's Day, if thou dost rain, for forty days it will remain; St. Swithin's Day, if thou be fair, for forty days 'twill rain no more.

Proverb

6 The north wind does blow, and we shall have snow.

Proverb

7 What dreadful hot weather we have! It keeps me in a continual state of inelegance.

Jane Austen (1775–1817) British novelist. Letter, 18 Sept 1796

8 I like the weather, when it is not rainy,
That is, I like two months of every year.

Lord Byron (1788–1824) British poet. *Beppo*

9 This is a London particular...A fog, miss.

Charles Dickens (1812–70) British novelist. *Bleak House*, Ch. 3

10 It ain't a fit night out for man or beast.

W. C. Fields (1880–1946) US actor. *The Fatal Glass of Beer*

11 I'm singing in the rain, just singing in the rain;
What a wonderful feeling, I'm happy again.

Arthur Freed (1894–1973) US film producer and songwriter. From the musical, *Hollywood Revue of 1929. Singing in the Rain*

12 This is the weather the cuckoo likes,
And so do I;
When showers betumble the chestnut spikes,
And nestlings fly:
And the little brown nightingale bills his best,
And they sit outside at 'The Travellers' Rest'.

Thomas Hardy (1840–1928) British novelist. *Weathers*

13 This is the weather the shepherd shuns,
And so do I.

Thomas Hardy *Weathers*

14 When two Englishmen meet, their first talk is of the weather.

Samuel Johnson (1709–84) British lexicographer. *The Idler*

15 A snake came to my water-trough
On a hot, hot day, and I in pyjamas for the heat,
To drink there.

D. H. Lawrence (1885–1930) British novelist. *Snake*

16 The British, he thought, must be gluttons for satire: even the weather forecast seemed to be some kind of spoof, predicting every possible combination of weather for the next twenty-four hours without actually committing itself to anything specific.

David Lodge (1935–) British author. *Changing Places*, Ch. 2

17 Who has seen the wind?
Neither you nor I:
But when the trees bow down their heads,
The wind is passing by.

Christina Rossetti (1830–74) British poet. *Who Has Seen the Wind?*

18 The fog comes on little cat feet

Carl Sandburg (1878–1967) US poet. *Fog*

19 Blow, winds, and crack your cheeks; rage, blow.
You cataracts and hurricanoes, spout
Till you have drench'd our steeples, drown'd the cocks.

William Shakespeare (1564–1616) English dramatist. *King Lear*, III:2

20 Rumble thy bellyful. Spit, fire; spout rain.
Nor rain, wind, thunder, fire, are my daughters
I tax not you, you elements, with unkindness.

William Shakespeare *King Lear*, III:2

21 Poor naked wretches, wheresoe'er you are,
That bide the pelting of this pitiless storm,
How shall your houseless heads and unfed sides,
Your loop'd and window'd raggedness, defend you
From seasons such as these?

William Shakespeare *King Lear*, III:4

22 So foul and fair a day I have not seen.

William Shakespeare *Macbeth*, I:3

23 I am the daughter of Earth and Water,
And the nursling of the Sky;
I pass through the pores of the ocean and shores;
I change, but I cannot die,
For after the rain when with never a stain
The pavilion of Heaven is bare,
And the winds and sunbeams with their convex gleams
Build up the blue dome of air,
I silently laugh at my own cenotaph,
And out of the caverns of rain,
Like a child from the womb, like a ghost from the tomb,
I arise and unbuild it again.

Percy Bysshe Shelley (1792–1822) British poet. *The Cloud*

24 I wield the flail of the lashing hail,
And whiten the green plains under,
And then again I dissolve it in rain,
And laugh as I pass in thunder.

Percy Bysshe Shelley *The Cloud*

25 O Wild West Wind, thou breath of Autumn's being,
Thou, from whose unseen presence the leaves dead
Are driven, like ghosts from an enchanter fleeing,
Yellow, and black, and pale, and hectic red,
Pestilence-stricken multitudes.

Percy Bysshe Shelley *Ode to the West Wind*

26 Heat, madam! It was so dreadful that I found there was nothing for it but to take off my flesh and sit in my bones.

Sydney Smith (1771–1845) British clergyman and essayist. Discussing the hot weather with a lady acquaintance. *Lives of the Wits* (H. Pearson)

27 Willows whiten, aspens quiver,
Little breezes dusk and shiver.

Alfred, Lord Tennyson (1809–92) British poet. *The Lady of Shalott*, Pt. I

28 It was the wrong kind of snow.

Terry Worrall British railway manager. Explaining why British Rail's anti-snow measures had not worked. *The Observer*, 17 Feb 1991

WEBSTER, DANIEL

(1782–1852) US statesman. A senator and renowned orator, he became secretary of state (1841–43; 1850–52) and an unsuccessful presidential candidate.

Quotations about Webster

1 Daniel Webster struck me much like a steam engine in trousers.

Sydney Smith (1771–1845) British clergyman and essayist. *A Memoir of the Reverend Sydney Smith* (Lady Holland)

2 God is the only president of the day, and Webster is his orator.

Henry David Thoreau (1817–62) US writer. Attrib.

Quotations by Webster

3 Age cannot wither her, nor custom stale her infinite virginity.

Paraphrasing a line from Shakespeare's *Antony and Cleopatra* on hearing of Andrew Jackson's steadfast maintenance that his friend Peggy Eaton did not deserve her scandalous reputation. *Presidential Anecdotes* (P. Boller)

4 The people's government, made for the people, made by the people, and answerable to the people.

Second speech on Foote's resolution, 26 Jan 1830

5 The past, at least, is secure.

Speech, US Senate, 26 Jan 1830

6 I was born an American; I will live an American; I shall die an American.

Speech, US Senate on 'The Compromise Bill', 17 July 1850

7 There is always room at the top.

When advised not to become a lawyer because the profession was overcrowded. Attrib.

WEBSTER, JOHN

(1580–1625) English dramatist. His plays include *The White Devil* (1612) and *The Duchess of Malfi* (1613). He also collaborated with other dramatists, including Thomas Dekker.

1 Other sins only speak; murder shrieks out.

The Duchess of Malfi, IV:2

2 Physicians are like kings, – they brook no contradiction.

The Duchess of Malfi, V:2

3 We are merely the stars' tennis-balls, struck and bandied
Which way please them.

The Duchess of Malfi, V:4

4 I saw him even now going the way of all flesh, that is to say towards the kitchen.

Westward Ho!, II:2

5 We think caged birds sing, when indeed they cry.

The White Devil, V:4

WEIL, SIMONE

(1909–43) French philosopher and religious mystic. An active socialist in the 1930s, she became a Roman Catholic in 1938. Her books include *Waiting for God* (1951) and *The Need for Roots* (1952).

1 Culture is an instrument wielded by professors to manufacture professors, who when their turn comes will manufacture professors.

The Need for Roots

2 The word 'revolution' is a word for which you kill, for which you die, for which you send the labouring masses to their death, but which does not possess any content.

Oppression and Liberty, 'Reflections Concerning the Causes of Liberty and Social Oppression'

3 But not even Marx is more precious to us than the truth.

Oppression and Liberty, 'Revolution Proletarienne'

4 The future is made of the same stuff as the present.

On Science, Necessity, and the Love of God (ed. Richard Rees), 'Some Thoughts on the Love of God'

WELLINGTON, DUKE OF

(Arthur Wellesley, Duke of Wellington; 1769–1852) British general and statesman. He defeated the French in the Peninsular War and Napoleon at Waterloo. Known as the 'Iron Duke', he became Tory prime minister (1828–30). Under Peel he served as foreign secretary (1834–35).

Quotations about Wellington

1 He accepted peace as if he had been defeated.
Napoleon I (Napoleon Bonaparte; 1769–1821) French emperor. Attrib.

2 The Duke of Wellington has exhausted nature and exhausted glory. His career was one unclouded longest day.
The Times, Obituary, 16 Sept 1852

Quotations by Wellington

3 It all depends upon that article there.
Indicating a passing infantryman when asked if he would be able to defeat Napoleon. *The Age of Elegance* (A. Bryant)

4 Yes, and they went down very well too.
Replying to the observation that the French cavalry had come up very well during the Battle of Waterloo (18 June 1815). *The Age of Elegance* (A. Bryant)

5 In my situation as Chancellor of the University of Oxford, I have been much exposed to authors.
Collections and Recollections (G. W. E. Russell)

6 Not upon a man from the colonel to the private in a regiment – both inclusive. We may pick up a marshal or two perhaps; but not worth a damn.
Said during the Waterloo campaign, when asked whether he anticipated any desertions from Napoleon's army. *Creevey Papers*, Ch. X

7 It has been a damned serious business – Blücher and I have lost 30,000 men. It has been a damned nice thing – the nearest run thing you ever saw in your life...By God! I don't think it would have done if I had not been there.
Referring to the Battle of Waterloo. *Creevey Papers*, Ch. X

8 I always say that, next to a battle lost, the greatest misery is a battle gained.
Diary (Frances, Lady Shelley)

9 I see no reason to suppose that these machines will ever force themselves into general use.
Referring to steam locomotives. *Geoffrey Madan's Notebooks* (J. Gere)

10 I hate the whole race...There is no believing a word they say – your professional poets, I mean – there never existed a more worthless set than Byron and his friends for example.
Lady Salisbury's diary, 26 Oct 1833

11 I used to say of him that his presence on the field made the difference of forty thousand men.
Referring to Napoleon. *Notes of Conversations with the Duke of Wellington* (Stanhope), 2 Nov 1831

12 The next greatest misfortune to losing a battle is to gain such a victory as this.
Recollections (S. Rogers)

13 The greatest tragedy in the world, Madam, except a defeat.
In reply to the remark, 'What a glorious thing must be a victory'. *Recollections* (S. Rogers).

14 You must build your House of Parliament upon the river: so...that the populace cannot exact their demands by sitting down round you.
Words on Wellington (Sir William Fraser)

15 I don't know what effect these men will have on the enemy, but, by God, they frighten me.
Referring to his generals. Attrib.

16 I have got an infamous army, very weak and ill-equipped, and a very inexperienced staff.
Written at the beginning of the Waterloo campaign. Letter to Lord Stewart, 8 May 1815

17 It is not the business of generals to shoot one another.
Refusing an artillery officer permission to fire upon Napoleon himself during the Battle of Waterloo, 1815. Attrib.

18 Up, Guards, and at 'em.
Order given at the Battle of Waterloo. Attrib.

19 The battle of Waterloo was won on the playing fields of Eton.
Attrib.

20 Yes, about ten minutes.
Responding to a vicar's query as to whether there was anything he would like his forthcoming sermon to be about. Attrib.

21 Very well, then I shall not take off my boots.
Responding to the news, as he was going to bed, that the ship in which he was travelling seemed about to sink. Attrib.

22 Ours is composed of the scum of the earth.
Of the British army. Remark, 4 Nov 1831

23 Publish and be damned!
On being offered the chance to avoid mention in the memoirs of Harriette Wilson by giving her money. Attrib.

24 I don't care a twopenny damn what becomes of the ashes of Napoleon Bonaparte.
Attrib.

25 Don't quote Latin; say what you have to say, and then sit down.
Advice to a new Member of Parliament. Attrib.

26 A battle of giants.
Referring to the Battle of Waterloo; said to Samuel Rogers. Attrib.

27 Sparrowhawks, Ma'am.
Advice when asked by Queen Victoria how to remove sparrows from the Crystal Palace. Attrib.

WELLS, H. G.

(1866–1946) British writer. After studying science, he won a literary reputation with *The Time Machine* (1895) and *Kipps* (1905). His other books included *An Outline of History* (1920) and *The Shape of Things to Come* (1933).

Quotations about Wells

1 Whatever Wells writes is not only alive, but kicking.
Henry James (1843–1916) US novelist. Attrib.

2 I doubt whether in the whole course of our history, any one individual has explored as many avenues, turned over so many stones, ventured along so many culs-de-sac. Science, history, politics, all were within his compass.

Malcolm Muggeridge (1903–) British writer. *The Observer*, 11 Sept 1966

Quotations by Wells

3 The cat is the offspring of a cat and the dog of a dog, but butlers and lady's maids do not reproduce their kind. They have other duties.

Bealby, Pt. I, Ch. 1

4 He was quite sure that he had been wronged. Not to be wronged is to forgo the first privilege of goodness.

Bealby, Pt. IV, Ch. 1

5 Miss Madeleine Philips was making it very manifest to Captain Douglas that she herself was a career; that a lover with any other career in view need not – as the advertisements say – apply.

Bealby, Pt. V, Ch. 5

6 He began to think the tramp a fine, brotherly, generous fellow. He was also growing accustomed to something – shall I call it an olfactory bar – that had hitherto kept them apart.

Bealby, Pt. VI, Ch. 3

7 The army ages men sooner than the law and philosophy; it exposes them more freely to germs, which undermine and destroy, and it shelters them more completely from thought, which stimulates and preserves.

Bealby, Pt. VIII, Ch. 1

8 He had one peculiar weakness; he had faced death in many forms but he had never faced a dentist. The thought of dentists gave him just the same sick horror as the thought of Socialism.

Bealby, Pt. VIII, Ch. 1

9 In the Country of the Blind the One-eyed Man is King.

The Country of the Blind

10 '*Language*, man!' roared Parsons; 'why, it's LITERATURE!'

The History of Mr Polly, Pt. I, Ch. 3

11 'You're a Christian?' 'Church of England,' said Mr Polly. 'Mm,' said the employer, a little checked. 'For good all round business work, I should have preferred a Baptist.'

The History of Mr Polly, Pt. III, Ch. 1

12 Arson, after all, is an artificial crime...A large number of houses deserve to be burnt.

The History of Mr Polly, Pt. X, Ch. 1

13 'It's giving girls names like that', said Buggins, 'that nine times out of ten makes 'em go wrong. It unsettles 'em. If ever I was to have a girl, if ever I was to have a dozen girls, I'd call 'em all Jane.'

Referring to the name Euphemia.
Kipps, Bk. I, Ch. 4

14 It's 'aving 'ouses built by men, I believe, makes all the work and trouble.

Kipps, Bk. III, Ch. 1

15 Everybody hates house-agents because they have everybody at a disadvantage. All other callings have a certain amount of give and take; the house-agent simply takes.

Kipps, Bk. III, Ch. 1

16 We were taught as the chief subjects of instruction Latin and Greek. We were taught very badly because the men who taught us did not habitually use either of these languages.

The New Machiavelli, Bk. I., Ch. 3

17 Cynicism is humour in ill-health.

Short Stories, 'The Last Trump'

18 He doubted the existence of the Deity but accepted Carnot's cycle, and he had read Shakespeare and found him weak in chemistry.

Short Stories, 'The Lord of the Dynamos'

19 Bricklayers kick their wives to death, and dukes betray theirs; but it is among the small clerks and shopkeepers nowadays that it comes most often to the cutting of throats.

Short Stories, 'The Purple Pileus'

20 The War that will End War.

Book title

21 If Max gets to Heaven he won't last long. He will be chucked out for trying to pull off a merger between Heaven and Hell...after having secured a controlling interest in key subsidiary companies in both places, of course.

Referring to the newspaper proprietor and politician, Lord Beaverbrook. *Beaverbrook* (A. J. P. Taylor)

22 One thousand years more. That's all *Homo sapiens* has before him.

Diary (Harold Nicolson)

WELSH

See also British, Wales

1 Eddy was a tremendously tolerant person, but he wouldn't put up with the Welsh. He always said, surely there's enough English to go round.

John Mortimer (1923–) British lawyer and dramatist. *Two Stars for Comfort*, I:2

2 There are still parts of Wales where the only concession to gaiety is a striped shroud.

Gwyn Thomas (1913–81) British writer. *Punch*, 18 June 1958

3 ...an impotent people,
Sick with inbreeding,
Worrying the carcase of an old song.

R. S. Thomas (1913–) Welsh poet.
Welsh Landscape

4 'The Welsh,' said the Doctor, 'are the only nation in the world that has produced no graphic or plastic art, no architecture, no drama. They just sing,' he said with disgust, 'sing and blow down wind instruments of plated silver.'

Evelyn Waugh (1903–66) British novelist. *Decline and Fall*, Pt. I, Ch. 8

WEST, MAE

(1892–1980) US actress, sex symbol, and comedienne. She made her reputation in the theatre with *Diamond Lil* (1928). Her films included *She Done Him Wrong* (1933) and *I'm No Angel* (1933).

Quotations about Mae West

1 In a non-permissive age, she made remarkable inroads against the taboos of her day, and did so without even lowering her neckline.

Leslie Halliwell (1929–) British journalist and author. *The Filmgoer's Book of Quotes*

2 She stole everything but the cameras.

George Raft (1895–1980) US actor. Attrib.

Quotations by Mae West

3 A man in the house is worth two in the street.

Belle of the Nineties, film 1934

4 My goodness those diamonds are lovely! Goodness had nothing to do with it.

Used in 1959 as the title of the first volume of her autobiography. *Diamond Lil*, film 1932

5 I have a lot of respect for that dame. There's one lady barber that made good.

Referring to Delilah. *Going to Town*, film 1934

6 Beulah, peel me a grape.

I'm No Angel, film 1933

7 A gold rush is what happens when a line of chorus girls spot a man with a bank roll.

Klondike Annie, film 1936

8 I always did like a man in uniform. And that one fits you grand. Why don't you come up sometime and see me?

Often misquoted as 'Come up and see me some time'. *She Done Him Wrong*, film 1933

9 You're a fine woman, Lou. One of the finest women that ever walked the streets.

She Done Him Wrong, film 1933

10 You can say what you like about long dresses, but they cover a multitude of shins.

Peel Me a Grape (J. Weintraub)

11 It's hard to be funny when you have to be clean.

The Wit and Wisdom of Mae West (ed. J. Weintraub)

12 It is better to be looked over than overlooked.

The Wit and Wisdom of Mae West (ed. J. Weintraub)

13 I used to be Snow White…but I drifted.

The Wit and Wisdom of Mae West (ed. J. Weintraub)

14 When women go wrong, men go right after them.

The Wit and Wisdom of Mae West (ed. J. Weintraub)

15 I'm glad you like my Catherine. I like her too. She ruled thirty million people and had three thousand lovers. I do the best I can in two hours.

After her performance in *Catherine the Great.* Speech from the stage.

16 Everything.

When asked what she wanted to be remembered for. Attrib.

17 When I'm good I'm very good, but when I'm bad I'm better.

Attrib.

18 Whenever I'm caught between two evils, I take the one I've never tried.

Attrib.

19 I've been in *Who's Who,* and I know what's what, but this is the first time I ever made the dictionary.

On having a life-jacket named after her. Attrib.

WEST, DAME REBECCA

(Cicely Isabel Fairfield; 1892–1983) British novelist and journalist. Novels include *The Thinking Reed* (1936) and *The Birds Fall Down* (1966). Other books, such as *The Meaning of Treason* (1949) and *A Train of Powder*, are essays in political journalism.

Quotations about Rebecca West

1 She regarded me as a piece of fiction – like one of her novels – that she could edit and improve.

Anthony West (1914–) British writer (Rebecca West's son) *Heritage*

Quotations by Rebecca West

2 But there are other things than dissipation that thicken the features. Tears, for example.

Black Lamb and Grey Falcon, 'Serbia'

3 …any authentic work of art must start an argument between the artist and his audience.

The Court and the Castle, Pt. I, Ch. 1

4 The point is that nobody likes having salt rubbed into their wounds, even if it is the salt of the earth.

The Salt of the Earth, Ch. 2

5 God forbid that any book should be banned. The practice is as indefensible as infanticide.

The Strange Necessity, 'The Tosh Horse'

6 There is no such thing as conversation. It is an illusion. There are intersecting monologues, that is all.

There Is No Conversation, Ch. 1

7 Margaret Thatcher's great strength seems to be the better people know her, the better they like her. But, of course, she has one great disadvantage – she is a daughter of the people and looks trim, as the daughters of the people desire to be. Shirley Williams has such an advantage over her because she's a member of the upper-middle class and can achieve that kitchen-sink-revolutionary look that one cannot get unless one has been to a really good school.

Said in an interview with Jilly Cooper. *The Sunday Times*, 25 July 1976

8 My dear – the people we should have been seen dead with.

Cable sent to Noël Coward after learning they had both been on a Nazi death list. *Times Literary Supplement*, 1 Oct 1982

9 Just how difficult it is to write biography can be reckoned by anybody who sits down and considers

just how many people know the real truth about his or her love affairs.
Vogue

WHISTLER, JAMES ABBOTT MCNEILL

(1834–1903) US painter. Living mostly in Europe, he established his reputation with *The Artist's Mother* and *Nocturne in Blue and Gold*. He was also the author of *The Gentle Art of Making Enemies* (1890).

Quotations about Whistler

1 I have seen, and heard, much of cockney impudence before now, but never expected to hear a coxcomb ask two hundred guineas for flinging a pot of paint in the public's face.
John Ruskin (1819–1900) British art critic and writer. *Fors Clavigera*, 2 July 1877

2 That he is indeed one of the very greatest master of painting, is my opinion. And I may add that in this opinion Mr. Whistler himself entirely concurs.
Oscar Wilde (1854–1900) Irish-born British dramatist. *Pall Mall Gazette*, 21 Feb 1885

Quotations by Whistler

3 I am not arguing with you – I am telling you.
The Gentle Art of Making Enemies

4 Nature is usually wrong.
Mr Whistler's 'Ten O'Clock'

5 No, no, Oscar, you forget. When you and I are together we never talk about anything except me.
Cable replying to Oscar Wilde's message: 'When you and I are together we never talk about anything except ourselves'. *The Gentle Art of Making Enemies*

6 If silicon had been a gas I should have been a major-general.
Referring to his failure in a West Point chemistry examination. *English Wits* (L. Russell)

7 No, I ask it for the knowledge of a lifetime.
Replying to the taunt, during the Ruskin trial, that he was asking a fee of 200 guineas for two days' painting. *Lives of the Wits* (H. Pearson)

8 Isn't it? I know in my case I would grow intolerably conceited.
Replying to the pointed observation that it was as well that we do not not see ourselves as others see us. *The Man Whistler* (H. Pearson)

9 A LADY. I only know of two painters in the world: yourself and Velasquez.
WHISTLER. Why drag in Velasquez?
Whistler Stories (D. Seitz)

10 You shouldn't say it is not good. You should say you do not like it; and then, you know, you're perfectly safe.
Whistler Stories (D. Seitz)

11 A LADY. This landscape reminds me of your work.
WHISTLER. Yes madam, Nature is creeping up.
Whistler Stories (D. Seitz)

12 Perhaps not, but then you can't call yourself a great work of nature.
Responding to a sitter's complaint that his portrait was not a great work of art. *Whistler Stories* (D. Seitz)

13 I cannot tell you that, madam. Heaven has granted me no offspring.
Replying to a lady who had inquired whether he thought genius hereditary. *Whistler Stories* (D. Seitz)

14 It has none, your Highness. Its history dates from today.
Replying to a query from the Prince of Wales about the history of the Society of British Artists, which he was visiting for the first time. *Whistler Stories* (D. Seitz)

15 It is very simple. The artists retired. The British remained.
Explaining his resignation as president of the Royal Society of British Artists. *Whistler Stories* (D. Seitz)

16 Well, not bad, but there are decidedly too many of them, and they are not very well arranged. I would have done it differently.
His reply when asked if he agreed that the stars were especially beautiful one night. Attrib.

17 You will, Oscar, you will.
Replying to Oscar Wilde's exclamation 'I wish I had said that!' Attrib.

18 The explanation is quite simple. I wished to be near my mother.
Explaining to a snobbish lady why he had been born in such an unfashionable place as Lowell, Massachusetts. Attrib.

19 Listen! There never was an artistic period. There never was an Art-loving nation.
Mr Whistler's 'Ten O'Clock'

WHISTLING

See also fear

1 You know you don't have to act with me, Steve. You don't have to say anything, and you don't have to do anything. Not a thing. Oh, maybe just whistle. You know how to whistle, don't you, Steve? You just put your lips together and blow.
Lauren Bacall (1924–) US film actress. *To Have and Have Not*

2 The schoolboy, with his satchel in his hand, Whistling aloud to bear his courage up.
Robert Blair (1699–1746) Scottish poet. *The Grave*

3 I Whistle a Happy Tune.
Oscar Hammerstein (1895–1960) US lyricist. From the musical *The King and I*. Song title

WHITE, PATRICK

(1912–90) British-born Australian novelist. His novels include *The Tree of Man* (1955), *Voss* (1957), *The Solid Mandala* (1966), and *Memoirs of Many in One* (1986).

1 But bombs *are* unbelievable until they actually fall.
Riders in the Chariot, I:4

2 'I dunno,' Arthur said. 'I forget what I was taught. I only remember what I've learnt.'
The Solid Mandala, Ch. 2

3 All my novels are an accumulation of detail. I'm a bit of a bower-bird.

Southerly, 139

4 Well, good luck to you, kid! I'm going to write the Great Australian Novel.

The Vivisector, 112

WHITEHEAD, A. N.

(1861–1947) British philosopher and mathematician. With Bertrand Russell he wrote *Principia Mathematica* (1910–13). Other books include *The Principles of Natural Knowledge* (1919) and *The Concept of Nature* (1920).

1 Where are no whole truths; all truths are half-truths. It is trying to treat them as whole truths that plays the devil.

Dialogues, 16

2 Intelligence is quickness to apprehend as distinct from ability, which is capacity to act wisely on the thing apprehended.

Dialogues, 135 15 Dec 1939

3 Art is the imposing of a pattern on experience, and our aesthetic enjoyment is recognition of the pattern.

Dialogues, 228 10 June 1943

4 Philosophy is the product of wonder.

Nature and Life, Ch. 1

5 A science which hesitates to forget its founders is lost.

Attrib.

6 The history of Western philosophy is, after all, no more than a series of footnotes to Plato's philosophy.

Attrib.

WHITEHORN, KATHERINE

(1926–) British journalist and writer. She has written a column in *The Observer* since 1960. Her books include *Only on Sundays* (1966), *How to Survive Children* (1975), and *View from a Column* (1981).

1 Hats divide generally into three classes: offensive hats, defensive hats, and shrapnel.

Shouts and Murmurs, 'Hats'

2 And what would happen to my illusion that I am a force for order in the home if I wasn't married to the only man north of the Tiber who is even untidier than I am?

Sunday Best, 'Husband-Swapping'

3 The Life and Soul, the man who will never go home while there is one man, woman or glass of anything not yet drunk.

Sunday Best, 'Husband-Swapping'

4 It is a pity, as my husband says, that more politicians are not bastards by birth instead of vocation.

The Observer, 1964

5 Have you ever taken anything out of the clothes basket because it had become, relatively, the cleaner thing?

The Observer, 'On Shirts', 1964

6 The best careers advice to give to the young is 'Find out what you like doing best and get someone to pay you for doing it.'

The Observer, 1975

7 A good listener is not someone who has nothing to say. A good listener is a good talker with a sore throat.

Attrib.

WHITMAN, WALT

(1819–92) US poet. His first verse collection, *Leaves of Grass* (1855), was poorly received at first, although it went through nine editions in his lifetime. Other books include *Democratic Vistas* (1871), *November Boughs* (1888), and *Goodbye, My Fancy* (1891).

Quotations about Whitman

1 Walt Whitman who laid end to end words never seen in each other's company before outside of a dictionary.

David Lodge (1935–) British writer. *Changing Places*, Ch. 5

2 He is a writer of something occasionally like English, and a man of something occasionally like genius.

Algernon Charles Swinburne (1837–1909) British poet. *Whitmania*

Quotations by Whitman

3 No one will ever get at my verses who insists upon viewing them as a literary performance.

A Backward Glance O'er Travel'd Roads

4 I hear it was charged against me that I sought to destroy institutions,
But really I am neither for nor against institutions.

I Hear It was Charged against Me

5 If anything is sacred the human body is sacred.

I Sing the Body Electric, 8

6 I celebrate myself, and sing myself,
And what I assume you shall assume.

Song of Myself, 1

7 I think I could turn and live with animals, they're so placid and self-contained,
I stand and look at them long and long.

Song of Myself, 32

8 Behold, I do not give lectures or a little charity,
When I give I give myself.

Song of Myself, 40

9 I have said that the soul is not more than the body,
And I have said that the body is not more than the soul,
And nothing, but God, is greater to one than one's self is.

Song of Myself, 48

10 Do I contradict myself?

Very well then I contradict myself,
(I am large, I contain multitudes).
Song of Myself, 51

11 Where the populace rise at once against the never-ending audacity of elected persons.
Song of the Broad Axe, 5

12 A great city is that which has the greatest men and women.
Song of the Broad-Axe, 5

13 After you have exhausted what there is in business, politics, conviviality, and so on – have found that none of these finally satisfy, or permanently wear – what remains? Nature remains.
Specimen Days, 'New Themes Entered Upon'

14 The earth does not argue,
Is not pathetic, has no arrangements,
Does not scream, haste, persuade, threaten, promise,
Makes no discriminations, has no conceivable failures,
Closes nothing, refuses nothing, shuts none out.
A Song of the Rolling Earth

WILDE, OSCAR FINGAL O'FLAHERTIE WILLS

(1854–1900) Irish-born British poet and dramatist. His comedies *Lady Windermere's Fan* (1892), *An Ideal Husband* (1895), and *The Importance of Being Earnest* (1895) made him a leading figure in London society. However he was ruined by a trial (1895) arising from his homosexual relationships, especially with Lord Alfred Douglas. During his imprisonment he wrote *De Profundis* (1905) and the *The Ballad of Reading Gaol* (1898).

Quotations about Wilde

1 From the beginning Wilde performed his life and continued to do so even after fate had taken the plot out of his hands.
W. H. Auden (1907–73) British poet. *Forwards and Afterwards*

2 If with the literate I am
Impelled to try an epigram
I never seek to take the credit
We all assume that Oscar said it.
Dorothy Parker (1893–1967) US writer. Attrib.

3 He was over-dressed, pompous, snobbish, sentimental and vain. But he had an undeniable *flair* for the possibilities of commercial theatre.
Evelyn Waugh (1903–66) British novelist. *Harper's Bazaar*, Nov 1930

Quotations by Wilde

4 I never saw a man who looked
With such a wistful eye
Upon that little tent of blue
Which prisoners call the sky.
The Ballad of Reading Gaol, I:3

5 Yet each man kills the thing he loves,
By each let this be heard,
Some do it with a bitter look,
Some with a flattering word.
The coward does it with a kiss,
The brave man with a sword!
The Ballad of Reading Gaol, I:7

6 The Governor was strong upon
The Regulations Act:
The Doctor said that Death was but
A scientific fact:
And twice a day the Chaplain called,
And left a little tract.
The Ballad of Reading Gaol, III:3

7 Something was dead in each of us,
And what was dead was Hope.
The Ballad of Reading Gaol, III:31

8 For he who lives more lives than one
More deaths than one must die.
The Ballad of Reading Gaol, III:37

9 I know not whether Laws be right,
Or whether Laws be wrong;
All that we know who lie in gaol
Is that the wall is strong;
And that each day is like a year,
A year whose days are long.
The Ballad of Reading Gaol, V:1

10 As long as war is regarded as wicked, it will always have its fascination. When it is looked upon as vulgar, it will cease to be popular.
The Critic as Artist, Pt. 2

11 The man who sees both sides of a question is a man who sees absolutely nothing at all.
The Critic as Artist, Pt. 2

12 A little sincerity is a dangerous thing, and a great deal of it is absolutely fatal.
The Critic as Artist, Pt. 2

13 Ah! don't say you agree with me. When people agree with me I always feel that I must be wrong.
The Critic as Artist, Pt. 2

14 There is no sin except stupidity.
The Critic as Artist, Pt. 2

15 There is much to be said in favour of modern journalism. By giving us the opinions of the uneducated, it keeps us in touch with the ignorance of the community.
The Critic as Artist, Pt. 2

16 Art never expresses anything but itself.
The Decay of Lying

17 To love oneself is the beginning of a lifelong romance.
An Ideal Husband, III

18 Other people are quite dreadful. The only possible society is oneself.
An Ideal Husband, III

19 Really, if the lower orders don't set us a good example, what on earth is the use of them?
The Importance of Being Earnest, I

20 I have invented an invaluable permanent invalid called Bunbury, in order that I may be able to go down into the country whenever I choose.
The Importance of Being Earnest, I

21 All women become like their mothers. That is their tragedy. No man does. That's his.
The Importance of Being Earnest, I

22 The amount of women in London who flirt with their own husbands is perfectly scandalous. It looks so bad. It is simply washing one's clean linen in public.
The Importance of Being Earnest, I

23 The old-fashioned respect for the young is fast dying out.
The Importance of Being Earnest, I

24 In married life three is company and two none.
The Importance of Being Earnest, I

25 Ignorance is like a delicate exotic fruit; touch it, and the bloom is gone.
The Importance of Being Earnest, I

26 To lose one parent, Mr Worthing, may be regarded as a misfortune; to lose both looks like carelessness.
The Importance of Being Earnest, I

27 I hope you have not been leading a double life, pretending to be wicked and being really good all the time. That would be hypocrisy.
The Importance of Being Earnest, II

28 On an occasion of this kind it becomes more than a moral duty to speak one's mind. It becomes a pleasure.
The Importance of Being Earnest, II

29 CECILY. When I see a spade I call it a spade. GWENDOLEN. I am glad to say I have never seen a spade. It is obvious that our social spheres have been widely different.
The Importance of Being Earnest, II

30 I never travel without my diary. One should always have something sensational to read in the train.
The Importance of Being Earnest, II

31 In matters of grave importance, style, not sincerity, is the vital thing.
The Importance of Being Earnest, III

32 Three addresses always inspire confidence, even in tradesmen.
The Importance of Being Earnest, III

33 Never speak disrespectfully of Society, Algernon. Only people who can't get into it do that.
The Importance of Being Earnest, III

34 No woman should ever be quite accurate about her age. It looks so calculating.
The Importance of Being Earnest, III

35 This suspense is terrible. I hope it will last.
The Importance of Being Earnest, III

36 It is a terrible thing for a man to find out suddenly that all his life he has been speaking nothing but the truth.
The Importance of Being Earnest, III

37 Please do not shoot the pianist. He is doing his best.
Impressions of America, 'Leadville'

38 I can resist everything except temptation.
Lady Windermere's Fan, I

39 It is absurd to divide people into good and bad. People are either charming or tedious.
Lady Windermere's Fan, I

40 I am the only person in the world I should like to know thoroughly.
Lady Windermere's Fan, II

41 We are all in the gutter, but some of us are looking at the stars.
Lady Windermere's Fan, III

42 There is nothing in the whole world so unbecoming to a woman as a Nonconformist conscience.
Lady Windermere's Fan, III

43 A man who knows the price of everything and the value of nothing.
A cynic. *Lady Windermere's Fan*, III

44 There is no such thing as a moral or an immoral book. Books are well written, or badly written.
The Picture of Dorian Gray, Preface

45 All Art is quite useless.
The Picture of Dorian Gray, Preface

46 There is only one thing in the world worse than being talked about, and that is not being talked about.
The Picture of Dorian Gray, Ch. 1

47 The only way to get rid of a temptation is to yield to it.
The Picture of Dorian Gray, Ch. 2

48 It is only shallow people who do not judge by appearances.
The Picture of Dorian Gray, Ch. 2

49 I can sympathize with everything, except suffering.
The Picture of Dorian Gray, Ch. 3

50 Women represent the triumph of matter over mind, just as men represent the triumph of mind over morals.
The Picture of Dorian Gray, Ch. 4

51 A cigarette is the perfect type of a perfect pleasure. It is exquisite, and it leaves one unsatisfied. What more can one want?
The Picture of Dorian Gray, Ch. 6

52 Anybody can be good in the country.
The Picture of Dorian Gray, Ch. 19

53 As for the virtuous poor, one can pity them, of course, but one cannot possibly admire them.
The Soul of Man under Socialism

54 Democracy means simply the bludgeoning of the people by the people for the people.
See LINCOLN. *The Soul of Man under Socialism*

55 Art is the most intense mode of individualism that the world has known.
The Soul of Man Under Socialism

56 Twenty years of romance makes a woman look like a ruin; but twenty years of marriage make her something like a public building.
A Woman of No Importance, I

57 MRS ALLONBY. They say, Lady Hunstanton, that when good Americans die they go to Paris.
LADY HUNSTANTON. Indeed? And when bad Americans die, where do they go to?
LORD ILLINGWORTH. Oh, they go to America.
See APPLETON, Thomas Gold. *A Woman of No Importance*, I

58 The English country gentleman galloping after a fox – the unspeakable in full pursuit of the uneatable.
A Woman of No Importance, I

59 One should never trust a woman who tells one her real age. A woman who would tell one that, would tell one anything.
A Woman of No Importance, I

60 LORD ILLINGWORTH. The Book of Life begins with a man and a woman in a garden.
MRS ALLONBY. It ends with Revelations.
A Woman of No Importance, I

61 Moderation is a fatal thing, Lady Hunstanton. Nothing succeeds like excess.
A Woman of No Importance, III

62 Ah, every day dear Herbert becomes *de plus en plus Oscarié*. It is a wonderful case of nature imitating art.
Referring to Beerbohm Tree's unconscious adoption of some of the mannerisms of a character he was playing in one of Wilde's plays. *Great Theatrical Disasters* (G. Brandreth)

63 I suppose that I shall have to die beyond my means.
When told that an operation would be expensive. He is also believed to have said 'I am dying beyond my means' on accepting a glass of champagne as he lay on his deathbed. *Life of Wilde* (Sherard)

64 One would have to have a heart of stone to read the death of Little Nell without laughing.
Lecturing upon Dickens. *Lives of the Wits* (H. Pearson)

65 A thing is not necessarily true because a man dies for it.
Sebastian Melmoth

66 He hasn't an enemy in the world, and none of his friends like him.
Said of G. B. Shaw. *Sixteen Self Sketches* (Shaw), Ch. 17

67 With our James vulgarity begins at home, and should be allowed to stay there.
Referring to the artist James Whistler. Letter to the *World*

68 The man who can dominate a London dinner-table can dominate the world.
Attrib. by R. Aldington in his edition of Wilde

69 The gods bestowed on Max the gift of perpetual old age.
Referring to Max Beerbohm. Attrib.

70 The play was a great success, but the audience was a disaster.
Referring to a play that had recently failed. Attrib.

71 Who am I to tamper with a masterpiece?
Refusing to make alterations to one of his own plays. Attrib.

72 It requires one to assume such indecent postures.
Explaining why he did not play cricket. Attrib.

73 If this is the way Queen Victoria treats her prisoners, she doesn't deserve to have any.
Complaining at having to wait in the rain for transport to take him to prison. Attrib.

74 Grief has turned her fair.
Referring to the fact that a recently bereaved lady friend had dyed her hair blonde. Attrib.

75 Work is the curse of the drinking classes.
Attrib.

76 Nothing, except my genius.
Replying to a US customs official on being asked if he had anything to declare. Attrib.

77 I should be like a lion in a cave of savage Daniels.
Explaining why he would not be attending a function at a club whose members were hostile to him. Attrib.

78 Dear Frank, we believe you; you have dined in every house in London – *once*.
Interrupting Frank Harris's interminable account of the houses he had dined at. Attrib.

79 Either that wall paper goes, or I do.
Last words, as he lay dying in a drab Paris bedroom. *Time*, 16 Jan 1984

WILDER, THORNTON

(1897–1975) US novelist and dramatist. His works include the novel *The Bridge of San Luis Rey* (1927) and the plays *Our Town* (1938) and *The Skin of Our Teeth* (1942).

1 A living is made, Mr Kemper, by selling something that everybody needs at least once a year. Yes, sir! And a million is made by producing something that everybody needs every day. You artists produce something that nobody needs at any time.
The Matchmaker, II

2 The best part of married life is the fights. The rest is merely so-so.
The Matchmaker, II

3 Never support two weaknesses at the same time. It's your combination sinners – your lecherous liars and your miserly drunkards – who dishonour the vices and bring them into bad repute.
The Matchmaker, III

4 But there comes a moment in everybody's life when he must decide whether he'll live among human beings or not – a fool among fools or a fool alone.
The Matchmaker, IV

5 My advice to you is not to inquire why or whither, but just enjoy your ice-cream while it's on your plate, – that's my philosophy.
The Skin of Our Teeth, I

6 When you're at war you think about a better life;

when you're at peace you think about a more comfortable one.

The Skin of Our Teeth, III

7 Literature is the orchestration of platitudes.

Time, 12 Jan 1953

WILHELM II

(1859–1941) King of Prussia and Emperor of Germany (1888–1918). After Germany's defeat in World War I (in which he was known as 'Kaiser Bill') he was forced to abdicate.

1 You will be home before the leaves have fallen from the trees.

Said to troops leaving for the Front, Aug 1914. *August 1914* (Barbara Tuchman), Ch. 9

2 I would have liked to go to Ireland, but my grandmother would not let me. Perhaps she thought I wanted to take the little place.

Queen Victoria was his grandmother. *Carson* (H. Montgomery Hyde), Ch. 9

3 The Admiral of the Atlantic salutes the Admiral of the Pacific.

Telegram sent to Tsar Nicholas II during a naval exercise. *The Shadow of the Winter Palace* (E. Crankshaw)

4 It is my Royal and Imperial Command that you…exterminate first the treacherous English, and…walk over General French's contemptible little Army.

Referring to the British Expeditionary Force; veterans of this force are known as 'Old Contemptibles'. *The Times*, 1 Oct 1914

5 The machine is running away with *him* as it ran away with *me*.

Referring to Hitler. Remark to Sir Robert Bruce-Lockhart and Sir John Wheeler-Bennett, 27 Aug 1939

WILLIAMS, TENNESSEE

(1911–83) US dramatist. He established his reputation with *The Glass Menagerie* (1945). Subsequent successes include *A Streetcar Named Desire* (1947) and *Cat on a Hot Tin Roof* (1955).

1 My suit is pale yellow. My nationality is French, and my normality has been often subject to question.

Camino Real, Block 4

2 You can be young without money but you can't be old without it.

Cat on a Hot Tin Roof, I

3 That Europe's nothin' on earth but a great big auction, that's all it is.

Cat on a Hot Tin Roof, I

4 A vacuum is a hell of a lot better than some of the stuff that nature replaces it with.

Cat on a Hot Tin Roof

5 I can't stand a naked light bulb, any more than I can a rude remark or a vulgar action.

A Streetcar Named Desire, II:3

6 I have always depended on the kindness of strangers.

A Streetcar Named Desire, II:3

7 If people behaved in the way nations do they would all be put in straitjackets.

BBC interview

8 He was meddling too much in my private life.

Explaining why he had given up visiting his psychoanalyst. Attrib.

WILSON, HAROLD

(Baron Wilson of Rievaulx; 1916–   ) British Labour statesman. He became prime minister (1964–70; 1974–76), after succeeding Gaitskell as leader of the Labour Party in 1963.

1 Hence the practised performances of latter-day politicians in the game of musical daggers: never be left holding the dagger when the music stops.

The Governance of Britain, Ch. 2

2 If I had the choice between smoked salmon and tinned salmon, I'd have it tinned. With vinegar.

The Observer, 'Sayings of the Week,' 11 Nov 1962

3 Everybody should have an equal chance – but they shouldn't have a flying start.

The Observer, 'Sayings of the Year', 1963

4 One man's wage rise is another man's price increase.

The Observer, 'Sayings of the Week', 11 Jan 1970

5 The monarchy is a labour-intensive industry.

The Observer, 'Sayings of the Week', 13 Feb 1977

6 All these financiers, all the little gnomes of Zürich and the other financial centres, about whom we keep on hearing.

Speech, House of Commons, 12 Nov 1956

7 There is something utterly nauseating about a system of society which pays a harlot 25 times as much as it pays its Prime Minister, 250 times as much as it pays its Members of Parliament, and 500 times as much as it pays some of its ministers of religion.

Referring to the case of Christine Keeler, the woman at the centre of the Profumo scandal. Speech, House of Commons, June 1963

8 We are redefining and we are restating our socialism in terms of the scientific revolution…the Britain that is going to be forged in the white heat of this revolution will be no place for restrictive practices or out-dated methods on either side of industry.

Speech, Labour Party Conference, 1 Oct 1963

9 After half a century of democratic advance, the whole process has ground to a halt with a 14th Earl.

Referring to Sir Alec Douglas-Home. Speech, Manchester, 19 Oct 1963

10 From now, the pound is worth 14 per cent or so less in terms of other currencies. It does not mean, of course, that the pound here in Britain, in your pocket or purse or in your bank, has been devalued.

Speech after devaluation of the pound, 20 Nov 1967

11 A week is a long time in politics.

First said in 1965 or 1966, and repeated on several occasions. Attrib.

12 I believe the greatest asset a head of state can have is the ability to get a good night's sleep.
The World Tonight, BBC Radio, 16 Apr 1975

WILSON, WOODROW

(1856–1924) US statesman. He became Democratic president in 1913 and declared war on Germany in 1917. He negotiated the peace treaty in 1918, making the League of Nations a part of the treaty. For this measure he received no support in the Senate.

Quotations about Wilson

1 The spacious philanthropy which he exhaled upon Europe stopped quite sharply at the coasts of his own country.
Winston Churchill (1874–1965) British statesman. *World Crisis*

2 Like Odysseus, he looked wiser when seated.
John Maynard Keynes (1883–1946) British economist. *The Worldly Philosophers* (R. Heilbron)

Quotations by Wilson

3 Never murder a man who is committing suicide.
Mr Wilson's War (John Dos Passos), Pt. II, Ch. 10

4 Once lead this people into war and they'll forget there ever was such a thing as tolerance.
Mr Wilson's War (John Dos Passos), Pt. III, Ch. 2

5 America…is the prize amateur nation of the world. Germany is the prize professional nation.
Speech, Aug 1917. *Mr Wilson's War* (John Dos Passos), Pt. III, Ch. 13

6 The war we have just been through, though it was shot through with terror, is not to be compared with the war we would have to face next time.
Mr Wilson's War (John Dos Passos), Pt. V, Ch. 22

7 Business underlies everything in our national life, including our spiritual life. Witness the fact that in the Lord's Prayer the first petition is for daily bread. No one can worship God or love his neighbour on an empty stomach.
Speech, New York, 1912

8 No nation is fit to sit in judgement upon any other nation.
Address, New York, Apr 1915

9 There is such a thing as a man being too proud to fight.
Address to foreign-born citizens, 10 May 1915

10 Right is more precious than peace.
Address to Congress, 2 Apr 1917

11 The world must be made safe for democracy.
Address to Congress, asking for a declaration of war, 2 Apr 1917

12 Sometimes people call me an idealist. Well, that is the way I know I am an American. America is the only idealistic nation in the world.
Speech, Sioux Falls, 8 Sept 1919

WISDOM

See also intelligence, knowledge, prudence, wisdom and foolishness

1 It is easy to be wise after the event.
Proverb

2 For in much wisdom is much grief: and he that increaseth knowledge increaseth sorrow.
Bible: Ecclesiastes 1:18

3 The words of wise men are heard in quiet more than the cry of him that ruleth among fools.
Bible: Ecclesiastes 9:17

4 The wisdom of a learned man cometh by opportunity of leisure: and he that hath little business shall become wise.
How can he get wisdom that holdeth the plough, and that glorieth in the goad, that driveth oxen, and is occupied in their labours, and whose talk is of bullocks?
Bible: Ecclesiasticus 38:24–25

5 With the ancient is wisdom; and in length of days understanding.
Bible: Job 12:12

6 No mention shall be made of coral, or of pearls: for the price of wisdom is above rubies.
Bible: Job 28:18

7 A wise man will hear, and will increase learning; and a man of understanding shall attain unto wise counsels:
To understand a proverb, and the interpretation; the words of the wise, and their dark sayings.
The fear of the Lord is the beginning of knowledge: but fools despise wisdom and instruction.
Bible: Proverbs 1:5–7

8 Wisdom is the principal thing; therefore get wisdom: and with all thy getting get understanding.
Bible: Proverbs 4:7

9 Wisdom hath builded her house, she hath hewn out her seven pillars.
Bible: Proverbs 9:1

10 Wisdom reacheth from one end to another mightily: and sweetly doth she order all things.
Bible: Wisdom 8:1

11 For wisdom is more moving than any motion: she passeth and go through all things by reason of her pureness.
For she is the breath of the power of God, and a pure influence flowing from the glory of the Almighty: therefore can no defiled thing fall into her.
Bible: Wisdom 7:24–25

12 Does the Eagle know what is in the pit
Or wilt thou go ask the Mole?
Can Wisdom be put in a silver rod,
Or love in a golden bowl?
William Blake (1757–1827) British poet. *The Book of Thel*, 'Thel's Motto'

13 I care not whether a man is Good or Evil; all that I care
Is whether he is a Wise Man or a Fool. Go! put off

Holiness,
And put on Intellect.

William Blake *Jerusalem*

14 Be wiser than other people if you can, but do not tell them so.

Earl of Chesterfield (1694–1773) English statesman. Letter to his son, 19 Nov 1745

15 A sadder and a wiser man,
He rose the morrow morn.

Samuel Taylor Coleridge (1772–1834) British poet. *The Rime of the Ancient Mariner*, VII

16 If one is too lazy to think, too vain to do a thing badly, too cowardly to admit it, one will never attain wisdom.

Cyril Connolly (1903–74) British journalist. *The Unquiet Grave*

17 Knowledge dwells
In heads replete with thoughts of other men;
Wisdom in minds attentive to their own.

William Cowper (1731–1800) British poet. *The Task*

18 Some are weather-wise, some are otherwise.

Benjamin Franklin (1706–90) US scientist and statesman. *Poor Richard's Almanack*

19 Self-reflection is the school of wisdom.

Baltasar Gracián (1601–58) Spanish writer and Jesuit. *The Art of Worldly Wisdom*, 69

20 Knowledge can be communicated but not wisdom.

Hermann Hesse (1877–1962) German novelist and poet. *Siddhartha*

21 It is the province of knowledge to speak and it is the privilege of wisdom to listen.

Oliver Wendell Holmes (1809–94) US writer. *The Poet at the Breakfast Table*, Ch. 10

22 Vain wisdom all, and false philosophy.

John Milton (1608–74) English poet. *Paradise Lost*, Bk. II

23 There is more wisdom in your body than in your deepest philosophy.

Friedrich Nietzsche (1844–1900) German philosopher. *Human, All Too Human*, Pt. II

24 The young man who has not wept is a savage, and the old man who will not laugh is a fool.

George Santayana (1863–1952) US philosopher. *Dialogues in Limbo*, Ch. 3

25 Thou speakest wiser than thou art ware of.

William Shakespeare (1564–1616) English dramatist. *As You Like It*, II:4

26 I never knew so young a body with so old a head.

William Shakespeare *The Merchant of Venice*, IV:1

27 This fellow's wise enough to play the fool,
And to do that well craves a kind of wit.

William Shakespeare *Twelfth Night*, III:1

28 Possibly no wiser, My Lord, but far better informed.

F. E. Smith (1872–1930) British lawyer and politician. To judge who complained that he had listened to Smith's argument but was still none the wiser. *Life of F. E. Smith* (Birkenhead)

29 Some folk are wise, and some are otherwise.

Tobias Smollett (1721–71) British novelist. *Roderick Random*, Ch. 6

30 An ounce of a man's own wit is worth a ton of other people's.

Laurence Sterne (1713–68) Irish-born British writer. *Tristram Shandy*

31 Sciences may be learned by rote, but Wisdom not.

Laurence Sterne *Tristram Shandy*

32 Oh, Vanity of vanities!
How wayward the decrees of Fate are;
How very weak the very wise,
How very small the very great are!

William Makepeace Thackeray (1811–63) British novelist. *Vanitas Vanitatum*

33 It is never wise to try to appear to be more clever than you are. It is sometimes wise to appear slightly less so.

William Whitelaw (1918–) British politician. *The Observer*, 'Sayings of the Year', 1975

WISDOM AND FOOLISHNESS

1 A wise man makes his own decisions, an ignorant man follows the public opinion.

Chinese Proverb

2 Then I saw that wisdom excelleth folly, as far as light excelleth darkness.
The wise man's eyes are in his head; but the fool walketh in darkness: and I myself perceived also that one event happeneth to them all.

Bible: Ecclesiastes 2:13–14

3 But God hath chosen the foolish things of the world to confound the wise; and God hath chosen the weak things of the world to confound the things which are mighty.

Bible: I Corinthians 1:27

4 For ye suffer fools gladly, seeing ye yourselves are wise.

Bible: II Corinthians 11:19

5 A fool sees not the same tree that a wise man sees.

William Blake (1757–1827) British poet. *The Marriage of Heaven and Hell*, 'Proverbs of Hell'

6 Many have been the wise speeches of fools, though not so many as the foolish speeches of wise men.

Thomas Fuller (1608–61) English historian. *The Holy State and the Profane State*

7 Give me the young man who has brains enough to make a fool of himself!

Robert Louis Stevenson (1850–94) Scottish writer. *Virginibus Puerisque*

WODEHOUSE, SIR P. G.

(1881–1975) British humorous novelist. His books feature the 1920s upper-class bachelor Bertie Wooster and his immaculate manservant Jeeves. He lived abroad, becoming a US citizen in 1955.

Quotations about Wodehouse

1 P. G. Wodehouse, whose works I place a little below Shakespeare's and any distance you like above anybody else's.
James Agate (1877–1947) British theatre critic. *P. G. Wodehouse* (David A. Jensen)

2 English Literature's performing flea.
Sean O'Casey (1884–1964) Irish dramatist. Attrib.

Quotations by Wodehouse

3 All the unhappy marriages come from the husbands having brains. What good are brains to a man? They only unsettle him.
The Adventures of Sally

4 It is no use telling me that there are bad aunts and good aunts. At the core they are all alike. Sooner or later, out pops the cloven hoof.
The Code of the Woosters

5 He spoke with a certain what-is-it in his voice, and I could see that, if not actually disgruntled, he was far from being gruntled.
The Code of the Woosters

6 Big chap with a small moustache and the sort of eye that can open an oyster at sixty paces.
The Code of the Woosters

7 Jeeves coughed one soft, low, gentle cough like a sheep with a blade of grass stuck in its throat.
The Inimitable Jeeves, Ch. 13

8 It was my Uncle George who discovered that alcohol was a food well in advance of medical thought.
The Inimitable Jeeves, Ch. 16

9 It is a good rule in life never to apologize. The right sort of people do not want apologies, and the wrong sort take a mean advantage of them.
The Man Upstairs

10 New York is a small place when it comes to the part of it that wakes up just as the rest is going to bed.
My Man Jeeves, 'The Aunt and the Sluggard'

11 His ideas of first-aid stopped short at squirting soda-water.
My Man Jeeves, 'Doing Clarence a Bit of Good'

12 I don't owe a penny to a single soul – not counting tradesmen, of course.
My Man Jeeves, 'Jeeves and the Hard-Boiled Egg'

13 She fitted into my biggest armchair as if it had been built round her by someone who knew they were wearing armchairs tight about the hips that season.
My Man Jeeves, 'Jeeves and the Unbidden Guest'

14 I spent the afternoon musing on Life. If you come to think of it, what a queer thing Life is! So unlike anything else, don't you know, if you see what I mean.
My Man Jeeves, 'Rallying Round Old George'

15 If I had had to choose between him and a cockroach as a companion for a walking-tour, the cockroach would have had it by a short head.
My Man Jeeves, 'The Spot of Art'

16 There is only one cure for grey hair. It was invented by a Frenchman. It is called the guillotine.
The Old Reliable

17 I can honestly say that I always look on Pauline as one of the nicest girls I was ever engaged to.
Thank You Jeeves, Ch. 6

18 The Right Hon. was a tubby little chap who looked as if he had been poured into his clothes and had forgotten to say 'When!'
Very Good Jeeves!, 'Jeeves and the Impending Doom'

19 The stationmaster's whiskers are of a Victorian bushiness and give the impression of having been grown under glass.
Wodehouse at Work to the End (Richard Usborne), Ch. 2

20 Like so many substantial Americans, he had married young and kept on marrying, springing from blonde to blonde like the chamois of the Alps leaping from crag to crag.
Wodehouse at Work to the End (Richard Usborne), Ch. 2

21 Unlike the male codfish which, suddenly finding itself the parent of three million five hundred thousand little codfish, cheerfully resolves to love them all, the British aristocracy is apt to look with a somewhat jaundiced eye on its younger sons.
Wodehouse at Work to the End (Richard Usborne), Ch. 5

22 He was either a man of about a hundred and fifty who was rather young for his years or a man of about a hundred and ten who had been aged by trouble.
Wodehouse at Work to the End (Richard Usborne), Ch. 6

23 It is never difficult to distinguish between a Scotsman with a grievance and a ray of sunshine.
Wodehouse at Work to the End (Richard Usborne), Ch. 8

WOLLSTONECRAFT, MARY

(1759–97) British writer and feminist. She is remembered for *A Vindication of the Rights of Women* (1792). The wife of William Goodwin, the social philosopher, she died giving birth to her daughter Mary, who married the poet Shelley.

Quotations about Wollstonecraft

1 In all probability had she been married well in early life, she had then been a happy woman and universally respected.
Monthly Visitor, Feb 1798

2 Among the writers whose extravagant doctrines have not only been published in this country, but circulated with uncommon avidity, loaded with extravagant praise and insinuated into every recess, the name of Mary Wollstonecraft has obtained a lamentable distinction.
Jane West *Letters to a Young Man*

Quotations by Wollstonecraft

3 The *divine right* of husbands, like the divine

right of kings, may, it is hoped, in this enlightened age, be contested without danger.

A Vindication of the Rights of Woman, Ch. 3

4 I do not wish them to have power over men; but over themselves.

Referring to women. *A Vindication of the Rights of Woman*, Ch. 4

5 I know what you are thinking of, but I have nothing to communicate on the subject of religion.

Last words, spoken to her husband.

WOMAN'S ROLE

See also feminism, housework, marriage, women, sexes

1 God could not be everywhere and therefore he made mothers.

Jewish proverb

2 Whoever rightly considers the order of things may plainly see the whole race of woman-kind is by nature, custom, and the laws, made subject to man, to be governed according to his discretion: therefore it is the duty of every one of us that desires to have ease, comfort, and repose, with those men to whom we belong, to be humble, patient, and obedient, as well as chaste…

Giovanni Boccaccio (1313–75) Italian writer and poet. *Decameron*, 'Ninth Day'

3 We are unimportant. We are here to serve, to heal the wounds and give love.

Marike de Klerk The wife of F. W. de Klerk, South African president. Referring to the role of women. *The Observer*, 12 May 1991

4 What they say of us is that we have a peaceful time
Living at home, while they do the fighting in war.
How wrong they are! I would very much rather stand
Three times in the front of battle than bear one child.

Euripides (484 BC–406 BC) Greek tragic dramatist. *Medea*, 248

5 Females get hired along procreative lines. After 40, we're kind of cooked.

Carrie Fisher (1956–) US film star. *Time*, 18 Feb 1991

6 Mother is the dead heart of the family, spending father's earnings on consumer goods to enhance the environment in which he eats, sleeps and watches the television.

Germaine Greer (1939–) Australian-born British writer and feminist. *The Female Eunuch*

7 She-who-must-be-obeyed.

Henry Rider Haggard (1856–1925) British novelist. *She*

8 These are rare attainments for a damsel, but pray tell me, can she spin?

James I (1566–1625) King of England. On being introduced to a young girl proficient in Latin, Greek, and Hebrew. Attrib.

9 A man is in general better pleased when he has a good dinner upon his table, than when his wife talks Greek.

Samuel Johnson (1709–84) British lexicographer. *Johnsonian Miscellanies* (ed. G. B. Hill), Vol. II

10 To promote a Woman to bear rule, superiority, dominion or empire, above any Realm, Nation, or City, is repugnant to Nature; contumely to God, a thing most contrarious to his revealed will and approved ordinance, and finally it is the subversion of good Order, of all equity and justice.

John Knox (c. 1514–72) Scottish religious reformer. Opening words. *First Blast of the Trumpet against the Monstrous Regiment of Women*

11 We had a certain image of the Jewish woman as a mother. And now we have a generation of Jewish women with huge educational attainments. We had to learn that there is a huge tension between the roles these women are alotted in the outside world and the roles that have been open to them in, for example, synagogue management.

Jonathan Sacks (1948–) British Chief Rabbi. *The Independent*, 30 June 1994

12 Women exist in the main solely for the propagation of the species.

Arthur Schopenhauer (1788–1860) German philosopher.

13 Vain man is apt to think we were merely intended for the world's propagation and to keep its humane inhabitants sweet and clean; but, by their leaves, had we the same literature he would find our brains as fruitful as our bodies.

Hanna Woolley *Gentlewoman's Companion*, 1675

WOMEN

See also feminism, men, sexes, woman's role

1 A man of straw is worth a woman of gold.

Proverb

2 A woman's place is in the home.

Proverb

3 A woman's work is never done.

Proverb

4 The hand that rocks the cradle rules the world.

Proverb

5 Six men give a doctor less to do than one woman.

Proverb

6 An ailing woman lives forever.

Spanish proverb

7 Old-fashioned ways which no longer apply to changed conditions are a snare in which the feet of women have always become readily entangled.

Jane Addams (1860–1935) US social worker. In *Newer Ideals of Peace*, 'Utilization of Women in City Government'

8 The woman that deliberates is lost.

Joseph Addison (1672–1719) British essayist. *Cato*, IV:1

9 A woman seldom asks advice until she has bought her wedding clothes.

Joseph Addison *The Spectator*, 475

10 …girls are so queer you never know what they mean. They say No when they mean Yes, and drive a man out of his wits for the fun of it…

Louisa May Alcott (1832–88) US novelist. *Little Women*, Pt. II

11 Votes for Women.

Anonymous Slogan

12 It is almost a pity that a woman has a womb.
Anonymous *Woman and Nature* (Susan Griffin)

13 The sort of woman who, if accidentally locked in alone in the National Gallery, would start rearranging the pictures.
Anonymous

14 A woman, especially if she have the misfortune of knowing anything, should conceal it as well as she can.
Jane Austen *Northanger Abbey*, Ch. 14

15 A lady's imagination is very rapid; it jumps from admiration to love, from love to matrimony in a moment.
Jane Austen *Pride and Prejudice*, Ch. 6

16 Next to being married, a girl likes to be crossed in love a little now and then.
Jane Austen *Pride and Prejudice*, Ch. 24

17 Women – one half the human race at least – care fifty times more for a marriage than a ministry.
Walter Bagehot (1826–77) British economist and journalist. *The English Constitution*, 'The Monarchy'

18 Every man who is high up likes to feel that he has done it himself; and the wife smiles, and lets it go at that. It's our only joke. Every woman knows that.
J. M. Barrie (1860–1937) British playwright. *Peter Pan*

19 One is not born a woman, one becomes one.
Simone de Beauvoir (1908–86) French writer. *Le Deuxième Sexe* (trans. The Second Sex)

20 It is in great part the anxiety of being a woman that devastates the feminine body.
Simone de Beauvoir *Womansize* (Kim Chernin)

21 You will find that the woman who is really kind to dogs is always one who has failed to inspire sympathy in men.
Max Beerbohm (1872–1956) British writer. *Zuleika Dobson*, Ch. 6

22 They have perfect eyelashes, they have unscratched legs without varicose veins, they have shoes with soles as thin as pancakes; they have hands white and smooth as peeled potatoes and when you smell their smell, it fills you with a God-forsaken longing.
John Berger (1926–) British author and art critic. *Lilac and Flag*

23 And the Lord God caused a deep sleep to fall upon Adam, and he slept: and he took one of his ribs, and closed up the flesh instead thereof;
And the rib, which the Lord God had taken from man, made he a woman, and brought her unto the man.
And Adam said, This is now bone of my bones, and flesh of my flesh: she shall be called Woman, because she was taken out of Man.
Therefore shall a man leave his father and his mother, and shall cleave unto his wife: and they shall be one flesh.
And they were both naked, the man and his wife, and were not ashamed.
Bible: Genesis 2:21–25

24 For the lips of a strange woman drop as an honeycomb, and her mouth is smoother than oil:
But her end is bitter as wormwood, sharp as a two-edged sword.
Bible: Proverbs 5:3–4

25 Who can find a virtuous woman? for her price is far above rubies
The heart of her husband doth safely trust in her, so that he shall have no need of spoil.
She will do him good and not evil all the days of her life.
Bible: Proverbs 31:10–12

26 Women do not have the right to have a child.
Virginia Bottomley (Virginia Hilda Brunette Maxwell Bottomley; 1948–) British Conservative politician. *The Times*, 28 Dec 1993

27 Intimacies between women often go backwards, beginning in revelations and ending in small talk without loss of esteem.
Elizabeth Bowen (1899–1973) Irish novelist. *The Death of the Heart*

28 The Blessed One said, 'Amrapali, the mind of a woman is easily disturbed and misled. She yields to her desires and surrenders to jealousy more easily than a man. Therefore it is more difficult for a woman to follow the Noble Path.'
The Teachings of Buddha

29 Why need the other women know so much?
Robert Browning (1812–89) British poet. *Any Wife to any Husband*

30 The souls of women are so small,
That some believe they've none at all.
Samuel Butler (1612–80) English satirist. *Miscellaneous Thoughts*

31 Brigands demand your money or your life; women require both.
Samuel Butler Attrib.

32 I thought it would appear
That there had been a lady in the case.
Lord Byron (1788–1824) British poet. *Don Juan*, V

33 Do you know why God withheld the sense of humour from women?
That we may love you instead of laughing at you.
Mrs Patrick Campbell (1865–1940) British actress. To a man. *The Life of Mrs Pat* (M. Peters)

34 Women are much more like each other than men: they have, in truth, but two passions, vanity and love; these are their universal characteristics.
Earl of Chesterfield (1694–1773) English statesman. Letter to his son, 19 Dec 1749

35 There is no fury like an ex-wife searching for a new lover.
Cyril Connolly (1903–74) British journalist. *The Unquiet Grave*

36 Certain women should be struck regularly, like gongs.
Noël Coward (1899–1973) British dramatist. *Private Lives*

37 Mother love, particularly in America, is a highly respected and much publicised emotion and when exacerbated by gin and bourbon it can become extremely formidable.
Noël Coward *Future Indefinite*

38 What is woman? – only one of Nature's agreeable blunders.

Hannah Cowley (1743–1809) British poet and dramatist. *Who's the Dupe?*, II

39 Here's to the lot of them, murderer, thief,
Forger and lunatic too, Sir –
Infants, and those who get parish relief,
And women, it's perfectly true, Sir –
Please to take note, they are in the same boat:
They have not a chance of recording the vote.

H. Crawford Referring to the women's suffrage movement. *In the Same Boat*

40 It is an unfortunate fact that where two ladies get in the same kitchen it is often a recipe for disaster.

Graham Davis British chairman of an industrial tribunal. *The Observer*, 'Sayings of the Week', 22 May 1994

41 There are some women who should barely be spoken to; they should only be caressed.

Edgar Degas (1834–1917) French artist. *Degas by himself* (ed. R. Kendall)

42 Women never have young minds. They are born three thousand years old.

Shelagh Delaney (1939–) British dramatist. *A Taste of Honey*, I:1

43 'She's the sort of woman now,' said Mould,... 'one would almost feel disposed to bury for nothing: and do it neatly, too!'

Charles Dickens (1812–70) British novelist. *Martin Chuzzlewit*, Ch. 25

44 Women are most fascinating between the ages of thirty-five and forty, after they have won a few races and know how to pace themselves. Since few women ever pass forty, maximum fascination can continue indefinitely.

Christian Dior (1905–57) French couturier. *Colliers Magazine*, 10 June 1955

45 Girls bored me–they still do. I love Mickey Mouse more than any woman I've ever known.

Walt Disney (1901–66) US film-maker. *You Must Remember This* (W. Wagner)

46 It is only the women whose eyes have been washed clear with tears who get the broad vision that makes them little sisters to all the world.

Dorothy Dix (Elizabeth Meriwether Gilmer; 1861–1951) US journalist and writer. *Dorothy Dix, Her Book*, Introduction

47 There are only three things to be done with a woman. You can love her, you can suffer for her, or you can turn her into literature.

Lawrence Durrell (1912–90) British novelist. *Justine*

48 All Berkshire women are very silly. I don't know why women in Berkshire are more silly than anywhere else.

Claude Duveen (1903–) British judge. Said in Reading County Court, July 1972.

49 She takes just like a woman, yes, she does
She makes love just like a woman, yes, she does
And she aches just like a woman
But she breaks just like a little girl.

Bob Dylan (Robert Allen Zimmerman; 1941–) US popular singer. *Just Like a Woman*

50 I'm not denyin' the women are foolish: God Almighty made 'em to match the men.

George Eliot (Mary Ann Evans; 1819–80) British novelist. *Adam Bede*, Ch. 53

51 I should like to know what is the proper function of women, if it is not to make reasons for husbands to stay at home, and still stronger reasons for bachelors to go out.

George Eliot *The Mill on the Floss*, Ch. 6

52 The happiest women, like the happiest nations, have no history.

George Eliot *The Mill on the Floss*, Ch. 6

53 In the room the women come and go
Talking of Michelangelo.

T. S. Eliot (1888–1965) US-born British poet and dramatist. *The Love Song of J. Alfred Prufrock*

54 When a woman behaves like a man, why doesn't she behave like a nice man?

Edith Evans (1888–1976) British actress. *The Observer*, 'Sayings of the Week', 30 Sept 1956

55 She is abstract femininity...the prototype of a galactic New Woman.

Federico Fellini (1920–93) Italian film director. Referring to the US actress Kim Basinger.

56 A woman should be an illusion.

Ian Fleming (1908–64) British writer. *Life of Ian Fleming* (John Pearson)

57 The great question...which I have not been able to answer, despite my thirty years of research into the feminine soul, is 'What does a woman want'?

Sigmund Freud (1856–1939) Austrian psychoanalyst. *Psychiatry in American Life* (Charles Rolo)

58 Women are equal because they are not different any more.

Erich Fromm (1910–80) US writer. *The Art of Loving*

59 How, like a moth, the simple maid
Still plays about the flame!

John Gay (1685–1732) English poet and dramatist. *The Beggar's Opera*

60 You have to admit that most women who have done something with their lives have been disliked by almost everyone.

Françoise Gilot Artist and mistress of Picasso. Remark, Oct 1987

61 Fighting is essentially a masculine idea; a woman's weapon is her tongue.

Hermione Gingold (1897–1987) British actress. Attrib.

62 I know you do not make the laws but I also know that you are the wives and mothers, the sisters and daughters of those who do...

Angelina Grimké (1805–79) US writer and reformer. *The Anti-Slavery Examiner* (Sep 1836), 'Appeal to the Christian Women of the South'

63 My mother said it was simple to keep a man, you must be a maid in the living room, a cook in the kitchen and a whore in the bedroom. I said I'd hire the other two and take care of the bedroom bit.

Jerry Hall US model and actress. Remark, Oct 1985

64 There Is Nothin' Like a Dame.

Oscar Hammerstein II (1895–1960) US lyricist. *South Pacific*, Song title

65 If men knew how women pass their time when they are alone, they'd never marry.

O. Henry (William Sidney Porter; 1862–1910) US short-story writer. *The Four Million Memoirs of a Yellow Dog*

66 O! men with sisters dear,
O! men with mothers and wives!
It is not linen you're wearing out,
But human creatures' lives!

Thomas Hood (1799–1845) British poet. *The Song of the Shirt*

67 Oh, she's a splendid girl.
Wonderfully pneumatic.

Aldous Huxley (1894–1963) British writer. *Brave New World*, Ch. 3

68 Why should human females become sterile in the forties, while female crocodiles continue to lay eggs into their third century?

Aldous Huxley *After Many a Summer*, I, Ch. 5

69 A woman's preaching is like a dog's walking on his hinder legs. It is not done well; but you are surprised to find it done at all.

Samuel Johnson (1709–84) British lexicographer. *Life of Johnson* (J. Boswell), Vol. I

70 No one delights more in vengeance than a woman.

Juvenal (Decimus Junius Juvenalis; 60–130 AD) Roman satirist. *Satires*, XIII

71 When the Himalayan peasant meets the he-bear in his pride,
He shouts to scare the monster, who will often turn aside.
But the she-bear thus accosted rends the peasant tooth and nail
For the female of the species is more deadly than the male.

Rudyard Kipling (1865–1936) Indian-born British writer. *The Female of the Species*

72 And a woman is only a woman, but a good cigar is a smoke.

Rudyard Kipling *The Betrothed*

73 The First Blast of the Trumpet Against the Monstrous Regiment of Women.

John Knox (c. 1514–72) Scottish religious reformer. Title of Pamphlet, 1558

74 Women run to extremes; they are either better or worse than men.

Jean de La Bruyère (1645–96) French satirist. *Les Caractères*

75 How lucky we are that women defend themselves so poorly! We should, otherwise, be no more to them than timid slaves.

Pierre Choderlos de Laclos (1741–1803) French novelist. *Les Liaisons dangereuses*, Letter 4

76 Nobody can have the soul of me. My mother has had it, and nobody can have it again. Nobody can come into my very self again, and breathe me like an atmosphere.

D. H. Lawrence (1885–1930) British novelist. *Letters*

77 Thank heaven for little girls,
For little girls get bigger every day.

Alan Jay Lerner (1918–86) US lyricist and playwright. *Gigi*, 'Thank Heaven for Little Girls'

78 The female breast has been called 'the badge of feminity'. In order for the breast to be aesthetically pleasing, it should be a relatively firm, full breast which stands out from the chest wall and states with certainty, 'I am feminine'.

John Ransom Lewis Jnr M.D. *Atlas of Aesthetic Plastic Surgery*

79 I see some rats have got in; let them squeal, it doesn't matter.

David Lloyd George (1863–1945) British Liberal statesman. Said when suffragettes interrupted a meeting. *The Faber Book of English History in Verse* (Kenneth Baker)

80 So this gentleman said a girl with brains ought to do something else with them besides think.

Anita Loos (1891–1981) US novelist. *Gentlemen Prefer Blondes*, Ch. 1

81 Women do not find it difficult nowadays to behave like men; but they often find it extremely difficult to behave like gentlemen.

Compton Mackenzie (1883–1972) British writer. *On Moral Courage*

82 If you educate a man you educate a person, but if you educate a woman you educate a family.

Ruby Manikan (20th century) Indian Church leader. *The Observer*, 'Sayings of the Week', 30 Mar 1947

83 A woman should open everything to a man except her mouth.

Derek Marlowe *A Dandy in Aspic*

84 The Professor of Gynaecology began his course of lectures as follows: Gentlemen, woman is an animal that micturates once a day, defecates once a week, menstruates once a month, parturates once a year and copulates whenever she has the opportunity.

W. Somerset Maugham (1874–1965) British novelist. *A Writer's Notebook*

85 American women expect to find in their husbands a perfection that English women only hope to find in their butlers.

W. Somerset Maugham *A Writer's Notebook*

86 A woman will always sacrifice herself if you give her the opportunity. It is her favourite form of self-indulgence.

W. Somerset Maugham *The Circle*, III

87 Because women can do nothing except love, they've given it a ridiculous importance.

W. Somerset Maugham *The Moon and Sixpence*, Ch. 41

88 Thousands of American women know far more about the subconscious than they do about sewing.

H. L. Mencken (1880–1956) US journalist. *Prejudices*

89 When women kiss, it always reminds me of prize-fighters shaking hands.

H. L. Mencken Attrib.

90 I expect that Woman will be the last thing civilized by Man.

George Meredith (1828–1909) British novelist. *The Ordeal of Richard Feverel*, Ch. 1

91 One tongue is sufficient for a woman.

John Milton (1608–74) English poet. On being asked whether he would allow his daughters to learn foreign languages. Attrib.

92 I shrug my shoulders in despair at women who moan at the lack of opportunities and then take two weeks off as a result of falling out with their boyfriends.

Sophie Mirman British business woman. On receiving the *Business Woman of the Year Award.*

93 The moral world of the sick-bed explains in a measure some of the things that are strange in daily life, and the man who does not know sick women does not know women.

S. Weir Mitchell (1829–1914) *Doctor and Patient*, Introduction

94 Women would rather be right than reasonable.

Ogden Nash (1902–71) US poet. *Frailty, Thy Name Is a Misnomer*

95 God created woman. And boredom did indeed cease from that moment – but many other things ceased as well! Woman was God's *second* mistake.

Friedrich Wilhelm Nietzsche (1844–1900) German philosopher. *The Antichrist*

96 When I think of women, it is their hair which first comes to my mind. The very idea of womanhood is a storm of hair....

Friedrich Nietzsche *My Sister and I*

97 When a woman becomes a scholar there is usually something wrong with her sexual organs.

Friedrich Wilhelm Nietzsche *Bartlett's Unfamiliar Quotations* (Leonard Louis Levinson)

98 There are already so many women in the world! Why then...was I born a woman, to be scorned by men in words and deeds?

Isotta Nogarola (1418–1466) Italian scholar and author. Letter to Guarino Veronese

99 If women didn't exist, all the money in the world would have no meaning.

Aristotle Onassis (1906–75) Greek businessman. Attrib.

100 The surgical cycle in woman: Appendix removed, right kidney hooked up, gall-bladder taken out, gastro-enterostomy, clean sweep of uterus and adnexa.

William Osler (1849–1919) Canadian physician. *Sir William Osler: Aphorisms* (William B. Bean)

101 Whether a pretty woman grants or withholds her favours, she always likes to be asked for them.

Ovid (Publius Ovidius Naso; 43 BC–17 AD) Roman poet. *Ars Amatoria*

102 So greatly did she care for freedom that she died for it. So dearly did she love women that she offered her life as their ransom. That is the verdict given at the great Inquest of the Nation on the death of Emily Wilding Davison.

Christabel Pankhurst (1880–1958) British suffragette. Emily Davison threw herself under the King's horse in protest at the imprisoning of suffragettes. *The Suffragette*, 13 June 1913

103 Most good women are hidden treasures who are only safe because nobody looks for them.

Dorothy Parker (1893–1967) US writer. Obituary, *The New York Times*, 8 June 1967

104 My wife, who, poor wretch, is troubled with her lonely life.

Samuel Pepys (1633–1703) English diarist. *Diary*, 19 Dec 1662

105 I don't think a prostitute is more moral than a wife, but they are doing the same thing.

Prince Philip (1921–) The consort of Queen Elizabeth II. Remark, Dec 1988

106 There are two kinds of women – goddesses and doormats.

Pablo Picasso (1881–1973) Spanish painter. Attrib.

107 Most women have no characters at all.

Alexander Pope (1688–1744) British poet. *Moral Essays*, II

108 Men, some to business, some to pleasure take;
But every woman is at heart a rake.

Alexander Pope *Moral Essays*, II

109 Woman's at best a contradiction still.

Alexander Pope *Moral Essays*, II

110 Bah! I have sung women in three cities,
But it is all the same;
And I will sing of the sun.

Ezra Pound (1885–1972) US poet. *Cino*

111 In a matriarchy men should be encouraged to take it easy, for most women prefer live husbands to blocks of shares and seats on the board.

J. B. Priestley (1894–1984) British novelist. *Thoughts in the Wilderness*

112 ...it being natural and comely to women to nourish their hair, which even God and nature have given them for a covering, a token of subjection, and a natural badge to distinguish them from men.

William Prynne (1600–69) English Puritan. *Histriomastix*

113 She really is a woman just like my mum.

Cliff Richard (1940–) British pop singer. Remark, Aug 1988

114 The doctors said at the time that she couldn't live more than a fortnight, and she's been trying ever since to see if she could. Women are so opinionated.

Saki (Hector Hugh Munro; 1870–1916) British writer. *Reginald on Women*

115 The fundamental fault of the female character is that it has no sense of justice.

Arthur Schopenhauer (1788–1860) German philosopher. *Gedanken über vielerlei Gegenstände*, XXVII

116 Women exist in the main solely for the propagation of the species.

Arthur Schopenhauer Attrib.

117 I know that a woman is a dish for the gods, if the devil dress her not.

William Shakespeare (1564–1616) English dramatist. *Antony and Cleopatra*, V:2

118 Do you not know I am a woman? When I think, I must speak.

William Shakespeare *As You Like It*, III:2

119 Frailty, thy name is woman!

William Shakespeare *Hamlet*, I:2

120 She's beautiful and therefore to be woo'd;
She is a woman therefore to be won.

William Shakespeare *Henry VI, Part One*, V:3

121 O tiger's heart wrapp'd in a woman's hide!

William Shakespeare *Henry VI, Part Three*, I:4

122 Would it not grieve a woman to be over-mastered with a piece of valiant dust? to make an account of her life to a clod of wayward marl?

William Shakespeare *Much Ado About Nothing*, II:1

123 I have no other but a woman's reason:
I think him so, because I think him so.

William Shakespeare *The Two Gentlemen of Verona*, I:2

124 This Englishwoman is so refined
She has no bosom and no behind.

Stevie Smith (Florence Margaret Smith; 1902–71) British poet. *This Englishwoman*

125 Womanhood is the great fact in her life; wifehood and motherhood are but incidental relations.

Elizabeth Stanton (1815–1902) US suffragette. *History of Woman Suffrage* (with Susan B. Anthony and Mathilda Gage), Vol. I

126 A ship is sooner rigged than a gentlewoman made ready.

Philip Stubbs *The Anatomie of Abuses*

127 The really original woman is the one who first imitates a man.

Italo Svevo (Ettore Schmitz; 1861–1928) Italian writer. *A Life*, Ch. 8

128 God made the woman for the man,
And for the good and increase of the world.

Alfred, Lord Tennyson (1809–92) British poet. *Edwin Morris*

129 How sweet are looks that ladies bend
On whom their favours fall!

Alfred, Lord Tennyson *Sir Galahad*

130 I've got a woman's ability to stick to a job and get on with it when everyone else walks off and leaves it.

Margaret Thatcher (1925–) British politician and prime minister. *The Observer*, 'Sayings of the Week', 16 Feb 1975

131 It is a great glory in a woman to show no more weakness than is natural to her sex, and not be talked of, either for good or evil by men.

Thucydides (c. 460–c. 400 BC) Greek historian and general. *History of the Peloponnesian War*, Bk. II, Ch. 45

132 I was seized by the stern hand of Compulsion, that dark, unseasonable Urge that impels women to clean house in the middle of the night.

James Thurber (1894–1961) US humorist. *Alarms and Diversions*, 'There's a Time for Flags'

133 I am a source of satisfaction to him, a nurse, a piece of furniture, a *woman* – nothing more.

Sophie Tolstoy (1844–1919) Russian writer. *A Diary of Tolstoy's Wife, 1860–1891*

134 With many women I doubt whether there be any more effectual way of touching their hearts than ill-using them and then confessing it. If you wish to get the sweetest fragrance from the herb at your feet, tread on it and bruise it.

Anthony Trollope (1815–82) British novelist. *Miss Mackenzie*, Ch. 10

135 Scarce, sir. Mighty scarce.

Mark Twain (Samuel Langhorne Clemens; 1835–1910) US writer. Responding to the question 'In a world without women what would men become?' Attrib.

136 Woman is unrivaled as a wet nurse.

Mark Twain Attrib.

137 As if a woman of education bought things because she wanted 'em.

John Vanbrugh (1664–1726) English architect and dramatist. *The Confederacy*, II:1

138 Once a woman has given you her heart you can never get rid of the rest of her.

John Vanbrugh *The Relapse*, II:1

139 Woman is always fickle and changing.

Virgil (Publius Vergilius Maro; 70–19 BC) Roman poet. *Aeneid*, Bk. IV

140 I have often observed in women of her type a tendency to regard all athletics as inferior forms of fox-hunting.

Evelyn Waugh (1903–66) British novelist. *Decline and Fall*, Pt. I, Ch. 10

141 'I will not stand for being called a woman in my own house,' she said.

Evelyn Waugh *Scoop*, Bk. I, Ch. 5

142 There is nothing in the whole world so unbecoming to a woman as a Nonconformist conscience.

Oscar Wilde (1854–1900) Irish-born British dramatist. *Lady Windermere's Fan*, III

143 The question of the rights of women to hold secular office is a quite separate matter and should not in any way be connected to or paralleled with the question of women's ordination.

Cardinal Willebrands (1909–) Dutch ecclesiastic. Remark, June 1986

144 I would venture to guess that Anon, who wrote so many poems without signing them, was often a woman.

Virginia Woolf (1882–1941) British novelist. *A Room of One's Own*

145 Women have served all these centuries as looking-glasses possessing the magic and delicious power of reflecting the figure of man at twice its natural size.

Virginia Woolf *A Room of One's Own*

WONDER

See also admiration, curiosity

1 For all knowledge and wonder (which is the seed of knowledge) is an impression of pleasure in itself.

Francis Bacon (1561–1626) English philosopher. *The Advancement of Learning*, Bk. I, Ch. 1

2 To see a World in a grain of sand,
And a Heaven in a wild flower,
Hold Infinity in the palm of your hand,
And Eternity in an hour.

William Blake (1757–1827) British poet. *Auguries of Innocence*

3 Two things fill the mind with ever new and increasing wonder and awe, the more often and the more seriously reflection concentrates upon them: the starry heaven above me and the moral law within me.

Immanuel Kant (1724–1804) German philosopher. *Critique of Practical Reason*, Conclusion

4 ...now in Ireland, now in England, now in Normandy, he must fly rather than travel by horse or ship.

Louis VII (c. 1120–80) King of France. Referring to Henry II of England. *Imagines Historiarum* (Ralph de Diceto)

5 Philosophy is the product of wonder.

A. N. Whitehead (1861–1947) British philosopher. *Nature and Life*, Ch. 1

WOOLF, VIRGINIA

(1882–1941) British novelist and writer, a member of the Bloomsbury Group, with her husband Leonard Woolf, the writer and publisher. She suffered from clinical depression and eventually drowned herself. Her novels include *Mrs Dalloway* (1925), *To the Lighthouse* (1927), *Orlando* (1928), and *The Waves* (1931).

Quotations about Woolf

1 Virginia Woolf is dead, a grey, highly-strung woman of dignity and charm, but she was unstable and often had periods of madness. She led the Bloomsbury movement, did much to make England so Left – yet she always remained a lady, and was never violent. She could not stand human contacts, and people fatigued her.

Sir Henry Channon (1897–1958) British politician and writer. Diary, 5 Apr 1941

2 I do not believe that she wrote one word of fiction which does not put out boundaries a little way; one book which does not break new ground and form part of the total experiment.

Susan Hill (1942–) British novelist and playwright. *The Daily Telegraph* 5 May 1974

3 I enjoyed talking to her, but thought *nothing* of her writing. I considered her 'a beautiful little knitter'.

Edith Sitwell (1887–1964) British poet and writer. Letter to G. Singleton

Quotations by Woolf

4 The poet gives us his essence, but prose takes the mould of the body and mind entire.

The Captain's Death Bed, 'Reading'

5 *Middlemarch*, the magnificent book which with all its imperfections is one of the few English novels for grown up people.

The Common Reader, 'George Eliot'

6 Trivial personalities decomposing in the eternity of print.

The Common Reader, 'The Modern Essay'

7 Those comfortably padded lunatic asylums which are known, euphemistically, as the stately homes of England.

The Common Reader, 'Lady Dorothy Nevill'

8 Fraser...left his children unbaptized – his wife did it secretly in the washing basin.

Jacob's Room, Ch. 9

9 There is in the British Museum an enormous mind. Consider that Plato is there cheek by jowl with Aristotle; and Shakespeare with Marlowe. This great mind is hoarded beyond the power of any single mind to possess it.

Jacob's Room, Ch. 9

10 If you do not tell the truth about yourself you cannot tell it about other people.

The Moment and Other Essays

11 The older one grows the more one likes indecency.

Monday or Tuesday

12 Women have served all these centuries as looking-glasses possessing the magic and delicious power of reflecting the figure of man at twice its natural size.

A Room of One's Own

13 Why are women...so much more interesting to men than men are to women?

A Room of One's Own

14 When one reads of a witch being ducked, of a woman possessed by devils, of a wise woman selling herbs, or even of a very remarkable man who had a mother, then I think we are on the track of a lost novelist, a suppressed poet, of some mute and inglorious Jane Austen, some Emily Brontë who dashed her brains out on the moor or moped and mowed about the high-ways crazed with the torture her gift had put her to. Indeed I would venture that Anon, who wrote so many poems without signing them, was a woman.

A Room of One's Own

15 Literature is strewn with the wreckage of men who have minded beyond reason the opinions of others.

A Room of One's Own

16 If we didn't live venturously, plucking the wild goat by the beard; and trembling over precipices, we should never be depressed, I've no doubt; but already should be faded, fatalistic and aged.

A Writer's Diary, 26 May 1924

17 Dearest I feel certain that I am going mad again: I feel we cant go through another of those terrible times. And I shant recover this time. I begin to hear voices, and cant concentrate. So I am doing what seems the best thing to do...If anybody could have saved me it would have been you. Everything has gone from me but the certainty of your goodness. I cant go on spoiling your life any longer.
I dont think two people could have been happier than we have been.

Suicide note to her husband, c. 18 Mar 1941

WORDS

See also language, speech, verbosity

1 In the beginning was the Word, and the Word was with God, and the Word was God.

Bible: John 1:1

2 Actions speak louder than words.

Proverb

3 He said true things, but called them by wrong names.

Robert Browning (1812–89) British poet. *Bishop Blougram's Apology*

4 Oaths are but words, and words but wind.

Samuel Butler (1612–80) English satirist. *Hudibras*, Pt. II

5 Be not the slave of Words.

Thomas Carlyle (1795–1881) Scottish historian and essayist. *Sartor Resartus*, Bk. I, Ch. 8

6 We must have a better word than 'prefabricated'. Why not 'ready-made'?

Winston Churchill (1874–1965) British statesman. *Closing the Ring*, Appendix C

7 Words as is well known, are great foes of reality.

Joseph Conrad (Teodor Josef Konrad Korzeniowski; 1857–1924) Polish-born British novelist. *Under Western Eyes*

8 Until we learn the use of living words we shall continue to be waxworks inhabited by gramophones.

Walter De La Mare (1873–1956) British poet. *The Observer*, 'Sayings of the Week', 12 May 1929

9 When a diplomat says yes, he means perhaps. When he says perhaps he means no. When he says no, he is not a diplomat. When a lady says no, she means perhaps. When she says perhaps, she means yes. But when she says yes, she is no lady.

Lord Denning (1899–) British lawyer. Speech, 14 Oct 1982

10 Ad-i-ad-o-cho-kin-e-sis
Is a term that will bolster my thesis
That 'tis idle to seek
Such precision in Greek
When confusion it only increases.

Horace B. and Ava C. English (1892–1961; fl. 20th century) *A Comprehensive Dictionary of Psychological and Psychoanalytical Terms*

11 When there is no explanation, they give it a name, which immediately explains everything.

Martin H. Fischer (1879–1962) *Fischerisms* (Howard Fabing and Ray Marr)

12 Whenever ideas fail, men invent words.

Martin H. Fischer *Fischerisms* (Howard Fabing and Ray Marr)

13 You can stroke people with words.

F. Scott Fitzgerald (1896–1940) US novelist. *The Crack-up*

14 It was in the barbarous, gothic times when words had a meaning; in those days, writers expressed thoughts.

Anatole France (Jacques Anatole François Thibault; 1844–1924) French writer. *The Literary Life*, 'M. Charles Morice'

15 A spade is never so merely a spade as the word Spade would imply.

Christopher Fry (1907–) British dramatist. *Venus Observed*, II

16 Some seventy years ago a promising young neurologist made a discovery that necessitated the addition of a new word to the English vocabulary. He insisted that this should be ***knee-jerk***, and ***knee-jerk*** it has remained, in spite of the efforts of ***patellar reflex*** to dislodge it. He was my father; so perhaps I have inherited a prejudice in favour of home-made words.

Ernest Gowers (1880–1966) *Plain Words*, Ch. 5

17 The Spanish doctor who treated Yeats in Majorca reported to his Irish colleague. 'We have here an antique cardio-sclerotic of advanced years.' Gogarty tried to slur over the death sentence. 'Read it slowly and distinctly,' Yeats ordered. He inclined his head. He followed the cadence with his finger. As the sound died away he exclaimed, 'Do you know, I would rather be called 'Cardio-Sclerotic' than Lord of Lower Egypt.'

T. R. Henn *The Lonely Tower*

18 Many terms which have now dropped out of favour, will be revived, and those that are at present respectable will drop out, if usage so choose, with whom resides the decision and the judgement and the code of speech.

Horace (Quintus Horatius Flaccus; 65–8 BC) Roman poet. *Ars Poetica*

19 Thanks to words, we have been able to rise above the brutes; and thanks to words, we have often sunk to the level of the demons.

Aldous Huxley (1894–1964) British novelist. *Adonis and the Alphabet of the demons*

20 *Net.* Anything reticulated or decussated at equal distances, with interstices between the intersections.

Samuel Johnson (1709–84) British lexicographer. *Dictionary of the English Language*

21 He mobilized the English language and sent it into battle.

John Fitzgerald Kennedy (1917–63) US statesman. At a ceremony to confer honorary US citizenship on Winston Churchill. Speech, 9 Apr 1963

22 Words are, of course, the most powerful drug used by mankind.

Rudyard Kipling (1865–1936) Indian-born British writer. Speech, 14 Feb 1923

23 Words are men's daughters, but God's sons are things.

Samuel Madden (1686–1765) Irish writer. *Boulter's Monument*

24 I am a Bear of Very Little Brain, and long words Bother me.

A. A. Milne (1882–1956) British writer. *Winnie-the-Pooh*, Ch. 4

25 It is an important general rule always to refer to your friend's country establishment as a 'cottage'.

Stephen Potter (1900–69) British writer. *Lifemanship*, Ch. 2

26 My father still reads the dictionary every day. He says your life depends on your power to master words.

Arthur Scargill (1941–) British trades union leader. *The Sunday Times*, 10 Jan 1982

27 There is a Southern proverb, – fine words butter no parsnips.

Walter Scott (1771–1832) Scottish novelist. *The Legend of Montrose*, Ch. 3

28 POLONIUS. What do you read, my lord?
HAMLET. Words, words, words.

William Shakespeare (1564–1616) English dramatist. *Hamlet*, II:2

29 Let me be cruel, not unnatural;
I will speak daggers to her, but use none.

William Shakespeare *Hamlet*, III:2

30 My words fly up, my thoughts remain below:
Words without thoughts never to heaven go.

William Shakespeare *Hamlet*, III:3

31 But words are words; I never yet did hear
That the bruis'd heart was pierced through the ear.

William Shakespeare *Othello*, I:3

32 Man does not live by words alone, despite the fact that sometimes he has to eat them.

Adlai Stevenson (1900–65) US statesman. Attrib.

33 She shrank from words, thinking of the scars they leave, which she would be left to tend when he had gone. If he spoke the truth, she could not bear it; if he tried to muffle it with tenderness, she would look upon it as pity.

Elizabeth Taylor (1912–75) British writer. *The Blush*, 'The Letter Writers'

34 For words, like Nature, half reveal
And half conceal the Soul within.

Alfred, Lord Tennyson (1809–92) British poet. *In Memoriam A.H.H.*, V

35 One forgets words as one forgets names. One's vocabulary needs constant fertilisation or it will die.

Evelyn Waugh (1903–66) British novelist. *Diaries*

36 No, my dear, it is *I* who am surprised; you are merely astonished.

Noah Webster (1758–1843) US lexicographer. Responding to his wife's comment that she had been surprised to find him embracing their maid. Attrib.

WORDSWORTH, WILLIAM

(1770–1850) British poet. His reputation was based on his *Lyrical Ballads* (1798), written with Samuel Taylor Coleridge. After settling in the Lake District with his wife and sister he produced *The Prelude*, a verse autobiography published posthumously, and much other verse.

Quotations about Wordsworth

1 Time may restore us in his course Goethe's sage mind and Byron's force:
But where will Europe's latter hour
Again find Wordsworth's healing power?

Matthew Arnold (1822–88) British poet and critic. *Memorial Verses*

2 Two voices are there: one is of the deep…
And one is of an old half-witted sheep…
And, Wordsworth, both are thine.

James Kenneth Stephen (1859–92) British writer. *Lapsus Calami*, 'Sonnet'

3 Wordsworth went to the Lakes, but he never was a lake poet. He found in stones the sermons he had already put there.

Oscar Wilde (1854–1900) Irish-born British dramatist. *The Decay of Lying*

Quotations by Wordsworth

4 Strongest minds
Are often those of whom the noisy world
Hears least.

The Excursion

5 The good die first,
And they whose hearts are dry as summer dust
Burn to the socket.

The Excursion

6 The wiser mind
Mourns less for what age takes away
Than what it leaves behind.

The Fountain

7 I travelled among unknown men
In lands beyond the sea;
Nor, England! did I know till then
What love I bore to thee.

I Travelled among Unknown Men

8 I wandered lonely as a cloud
That floats on high o'er vales and hills,
When all at once I saw a crowd,
A host, of golden daffodils.

I Wandered Lonely as a Cloud

9 For oft, when on my couch I lie
In vacant or in pensive mood,
They flash upon that inward eye
Which is the bliss of solitude.

I Wandered Lonely as a Cloud

10 That best portion of a good man's life,
His little, nameless, unremembered acts
Of kindness and of love.

Lines composed a few miles above Tintern Abbey

11 That blessed mood,
In which the burthen of the mystery,
In which the heavy and the weary weight
Of all this unintelligible world,
Is lightened.

Lines composed a few miles above Tintern Abbey

12 We are laid asleep
In body, and become a living soul:
While with an eye made quiet by the power
Of harmony, and the deep power of joy,
We see into the life of things.

Lines composed a few miles above Tintern Abbey

13 I have learned
To look on nature, not as in the hour
Of thoughtless youth; but hearing often-times
The still, sad music of humanity.

Lines composed a few miles above Tintern Abbey

14 Nature never did betray
The heart that loved her.

Lines composed a few miles above Tintern Abbey

15 Nor greetings where no kindness is, nor all
The dreary intercourse of daily life,
Shall e'er prevail against us, or disturb
Our cheerful faith, that all which we behold
Is full of blessings.

Lines composed a few miles above Tintern Abbey

16 A power is passing from the earth
To breathless Nature's dark abyss;
But when the great and good depart,
What is it more than this –

That Man who is from God sent forth,
Doth yet again to God return? –
Such ebb and flow must ever be,
Then wherefore should we mourn?

Referring to Charles James Fox, the hero of the liberal Whigs, who died in 1806. *Lines on the Expected Dissolution of Mr. Fox*

17 If this belief from heaven be sent,
If such be Nature's holy plan,
Have I not reason to lament
What man has made of man?
Lines written in Early Spring

18 The sweetest thing that ever grew
Beside a human door!
Lucy Gray

19 There neither is, nor can be, any *essential* difference between the language of prose and metrical composition.
Lyrical Ballads, Preface

20 Poetry is the spontaneous overflow of powerful feelings: it takes its origin from emotion recollected in tranquillity.
Lyrics Ballads, Preface

21 Every great and original writer, in proportion as he is great and original, must himself create the taste by which he is to be relished.
Lyrical Ballads, Preface

22 There is a comfort in the strength of love;
'Twill make a thing endurable, which else
Would overset the brain, or break the heart.
Michael, 448

23 Why art thou silent! Is thy love a plant
Of such weak fibre that the treacherous air
Of absence withers what was once so fair?
Miscellaneous Sonnets, III

24 My heart leaps up when I behold
A rainbow in the sky:
So was it when my life began;
So is it now I am a man;
So be it when I shall grow old,
Or let me die!
The Child is Father of the Man;
And I could wish my days to be
Bound each to each by natural piety.
My Heart Leaps Up

25 There was a time when meadow, grove, and stream,
The earth, and every common sight,
To me did seem
Apparelled in celestial light,
The glory and the freshness of a dream.
Ode. Intimations of Immortality, I

26 Whither is fled the visionary gleam?
Where is it now, the glory and the dream?

Our birth is but a sleep and a forgetting:
The Soul that rises with us, our life's Star,
Hath had elsewhere its setting,
And cometh from afar;
Not in entire forgetfulness,
And not in utter nakedness,
But trailing clouds of glory do we come
From God, who is our home:
Heaven lies about us in our infancy!
Shades of the prison-house begin to close
Upon the growing boy.
Ode. Intimations of Immortality, IV

27 Earth fills her lap with pleasures of her own:
Yearnings she hath in her own natural kind.
Ode. Intimations of Immortality, VI

28 Provoke
The years to bring the inevitable yoke.
Ode. Intimations of Immortality, VIII

29 Hence in a season of calm weather
Though inland far we be,
Our souls have sight of that immortal sea
Which brought us hither…
Ode. Intimations of Immortality, IX

30 Those obstinate questionings
Of sense and outward things,
Fallings from us, vanishings;
Blank misgivings of a Creature
Moving about in worlds not realised,
High instincts before which our mortal nature
Did tremble like a guilty thing surprised.
Ode. Intimations of Immortality, IX

31 Though nothing can bring back the hour
Of splendour in the grass, of glory in the flower;
We will grieve not, rather find
Strength in what remains behind…
Ode. Intimations of Immortality, X

32 Another race hath been, and other palms are won.
Thanks to the human heart by which we live,
Thanks to its tenderness, its joys and fears,
To me the meanest flower that blows can give
Thoughts that do often lie too deep for tears.
Ode. Intimations of Immortality, XI

33 The clouds that gather round the setting sun
Do take a sober colouring from an eye
That hath kept watch o'er man's mortality.
Ode. Intimations of Immortality, XI

34 Me this unchartered freedom tires;
I feel the weight of chance-desires:
My hopes no more must change their name,
I long for a repose that ever is the same.
Ode to Duty

35 O Nightingale, thou surely art
A creature of a 'fiery heart'.
O Nightingale

36 Fair seed-time had my soul, and I grew up
Fostered alike by beauty and by fear.
The Prelude, I

37 When the deed was done
I heard among the solitary hills
Low breathings coming after me, and sounds
Of undistinguishable motion, steps
Almost as silent as the turf they trod.
The Prelude, I

38 The grim shape
Towered up between me and the stars, and still,
For so it seemed, with purpose of its own
And measured motion like a living thing,
Strode after me.
The Prelude, I

39 I was taught to feel, perhaps too much,
The self-sufficing power of Solitude.
The Prelude, II

40 We were brothers all
In honour, as in one community,
Scholars and gentlemen.

The Prelude, IX

41 Bliss was it in that dawn to be alive,
But to be young was very heaven!

Referring to the French Revolution. *The Prelude*, XI

42 That which sets
... The budding rose above the rose full blown.

Referring to the French Revolution. *The Prelude*, XI

43 Not in Utopia, – subterranean fields, –
Or some secreted island, Heaven knows where!
But in the very world, which is the world
Of all of us, – the place where, in the end,
We find our happiness, or not at all!

Referring to the French Revolution. *The Prelude*, XI

44 There is
One great society alone on earth:
The noble living and the noble dead.

The Prelude, XI

45 The pious bird with the scarlet breast,
Our little English robin.

The Redbreast chasing the Butterfly

46 Still glides the Stream, and shall for ever glide;
The Form remains, the Function never dies.

The River Duddon, 'After-Thought'

47 The good old rule
Sufficeth them, the simple plan,
That they should take, who have the power,
And they should keep who can.

Rob Roy's Grave

48 A youth to whom was given
So much of earth – so much of heaven,
And such impetuous blood.

Ruth

49 She dwelt among the untrodden ways
Beside the springs of Dove,
A maid whom there were none to praise
And very few to love...

She Dwelt Among the Untrodden Ways

50 A slumber did my spirit seal;
I had no human fears:
She seemed a thing that could not feel
The touch of earthly years.

No motion has she now, no force;
She neither hears nor sees;
Rolled round in earth's diurnal course,
With rocks, and stones, and trees.

A Slumber did my Spirit seal

51 Behold her, single in the field,
Yon solitary Highland lass!

The Solitary Reaper

52 Another year! – another deadly blow!
Another mighty empire overthrown!
And we are left, or shall be left, alone.

Napoleon defeated Prussia at the Battles of Jena and Anerstädt, 14 Oct 1806. *Sonnets*, 'Another year!'

53 Earth has not anything to show more fair:
Dull would he be of soul who could pass by
A sight so touching in its majesty:
The City now doth, like a garment, wear
The beauty of the morning; silent, bare,
Ships, towers, domes, theatres, and temples lie
Open unto the fields, and to the sky;
All bright and glittering in the smokeless air.

Sonnets, 'Composed upon Westminster Bridge'

54 Dear God! the very houses seem asleep;
And all that mighty heart is lying still!

Sonnets, 'Composed upon Westminster Bridge'

55 We must be free or die, who speak the tongue
That Shakspeare spake; the faith and morals hold
Which Milton held.

Sonnets, 'It is not to be thought of'

56 Milton! thou shouldst be living at this hour:
England hath need of thee; she is a fen
Of stagnant waters: altar, sword, and pen,
Fireside, the heroic wealth of hall and bower,
Have forfeited their ancient English dower
Of inward happiness.

Sonnets, 'Milton! thou shouldst'

57 Thy soul was like a star, and dwelt apart.

Sonnets, 'Milton! thou shouldst'

58 Plain living and high thinking are no more.

Sonnets, 'O friend! I know not'

59 Once did she hold the gorgeous east in fee;
And was the safeguard of the west.

Sonnets, 'Once did she hold'

60 Venice, the eldest Child of Liberty.
She was a maiden City, bright and free.

Venice, a republic since the Middle Ages, was conquered by Napoleon in 1797 and absorbed into his Kingdom of Italy in 1805. *Sonnets*, 'Once did she hold'

61 When she took unto herself a mate,
She must espouse the everlasting sea.

Sonnets, 'Once did she hold'

62 Men are we, and must grieve when even the shade
Of that which once was great is passed away.

Sonnets, 'Once did she hold'

63 Thou hast great allies;
Thy friends are exultations, agonies,
And love, and man's unconquerable mind.

Sonnets, 'Toussaint, the most unhappy man'

64 Two voices are there; one is of the sea,
One of the mountains; each a mighty voice:
In both from age to age thou didst rejoice,
They were thy chosen music, Liberty!

Sonnets, 'Two voices are there'

65 The world is too much with us; late and soon,
Getting and spending, we lay waste our powers:
Little we see in Nature that is ours.

Sonnets, 'The world is too much with us'

66 I'd rather be
A Pagan suckled in a creed outworn;
So might I, standing on this pleasant lea,
Have glimses that would make me less forlorn;
Have sight of Proteus rising from the sea;
Or hear Old Triton blow his wreathed horn.

Sonnets, 'The world is too much with us'

67 Strange fits of passion have I known:
And I will dare to tell,

But in the lover's ear alone,
What once to me befell.
Strange Fits of Passion

68 Come forth into the light of things,
Let Nature be your Teacher.
The Tables Turned

69 One impulse from a vernal wood
May teach you more of man,
Of moral evil and of good,
Than all the sages can.
The Tables Turned

70 Three years she grew in sun and shower,
Then Nature said, 'A lovelier flower
On earth was never sown;
This child I to myself will take;
She shall be mine, and I will make
A Lady of my own.'
Three Years she Grew

71 'Tis said that some have died for love.
'Tis Said that some have Died

72 Sweet childish days, that were as long
As twenty days are now.
To a Butterfly, I've Watched you now

73 Small service is true service, while it lasts.
To a Child, Written in her Album

74 Ethereal minstrel! pilgrim of the sky!
Dost thou despise the earth where cares abound?
To a Skylark

75 Thrice welcome, darling of the spring!
Even yet thou art to me
No bird, but an invisible thing,
A voice, a mystery.
To the Cuckoo

76 Thou unassuming common-place
Of Nature.
To the Daisy

77 Pleasures newly found are sweet
When they lie about our feet.
To the Small Celandine

78 Like an army defeated
The snow hath retreated.
Written in March

WORK

See also effort, unemployment

1 All work and no play makes Jack a dull boy.
Proverb

2 No bees, no honey; no work, no money.
Proverb

3 In work the greatest satisfaction lies – the satisfaction of stretching yourself, using your abilities and making them expand, and knowing that you have accomplished something that could have been done only by you using your unique apparatus. This is really the centre of life, and those who never orientate themselves in this direction are missing more than they ever know.
Kenneth Allsop (1920–73) British writer and broadcaster. *Letters to His Daughter*

4 Whatsoever thy hand findeth to do, do it with thy might; for there is no work, nor device, nor knowledge, nor wisdom, in the grave, whither thou goest.
Bible: Ecclesiastes 9:10

5 For even when we were with you, this we commanded you, that if any would not work, neither should he eat.
Bible: II Thessalonians 3:10

6 There is dignity in work only when it is work freely accepted.
Albert Camus (1913–60) French existentialist writer. *Notebooks, 1935–42*

7 Work is the grand cure of all the maladies and miseries that ever beset mankind.
Thomas Carlyle (1795–1881) Scottish historian and essayist. Speech, Edinburgh, 2 Apr 1886

8 Work is much more fun than fun.
Noël Coward (1899–1973) British dramatist. *The Observer*, 'Sayings of the Week', 21 June 1963

9 By working faithfully eight hours a day you may eventually get to be a boss and work twelve hours a day.
Robert Frost (1875–1963) US poet. Attrib.

10 The brain is a wonderful organ. It starts working the moment you get up in the morning, and does not stop until you get into the office.
Robert Frost Attrib.

11 Employment is nature's physician, and is essential to human happiness.
Galen (fl. 2nd century) Greek physician and scholar.

12 One of the best ways of avoiding necessary and even urgent tasks is to seem to be busily employed on things that are already done.
John Kenneth Galbraith (1908–) US economist. *The Affluent Society*, Ch. 1

13 When work is a pleasure, life is a joy! When work is a duty, life is slavery.
Maxim Gorky (Aleksei Maksimovich Peshkov; 1868–1936) Russian writer. *The Lower Depths*

14 Idleness begets ennui, ennui the hypochondriac, and that a diseased body. No laborious person was ever yet hysterical.
Thomas Jefferson (1743–1826) US statesman. Letter to Martha Jefferson, 28 Mar 1787

15 That one must do some work seriously and must be independent and not merely amuse oneself in life – this our mother has told us always, but never that science was the only career worth following.
Iréne Joliot-Curie (1897–1956) French scientist. Recalling the advice of her mother, Marie Curie. *A Long Way from Missouri* (Mary Margaret McBride), Ch. 10

16 Horny-handed sons of toil.
Denis Kearney (1847–1907) US Labor leader. Speech, San Francisco, c. 1878

17 Why should I let the toad *work*
Squat on my life?

Can't I use my wit as a pitchfork
And drive the brute off?

Philip Larkin (1922–85) British poet. *The Less Deceived*, 'Toads'

18 There must be love
Without love you will be merely skilful.

Frédérick Leboyer (1918–) French obstetrician. *Entering the World* (M. Odent)

19 It's been a hard day's night.

John Lennon (1940–80) British rock musician. *A Hard Day's Night* (with Paul McCartney)

20 ...she had always found occupation to be one of the best medicines for an afflicted mind...

Eliza Leslie (1787–1858) *Pencil Sketches; or, Outlines of Character and Manners*, 'Constance Allerton; or the Mourning Suits'

21 Life is too short to do anything for oneself that one can pay others to do for one.

W. Somerset Maugham (1874–1965) British novelist. *The Summing Up*

22 Few men of action have been able to make a graceful exit at the appropriate time.

Malcolm Muggeridge (1903–90) British writer. *Chronicles Of Wasted Time*

23 The rise in the total of those employed is governed by Parkinson's Law and would be much the same whether the volume of work were to increase, diminish or even disappear.

Cyril Northcote Parkinson (1919–) British historian and writer. *Parkinson's Law*, Ch. 1

24 Work expands so as to fill the time available for its completion.

Cyril Northcote Parkinson *Parkinson's Law*, Ch. 1

25 In a hierarchy every employee tends to rise to his level of incompetence.

Laurence J. Peter (1919–) Canadian writer. *Peter Principle*, Ch. 1

26 Work is accomplished by those employees who have not yet reached their level of incompetence.

Laurence J. Peter *Peter principle*, Ch. 1

27 Work is necessary for man. Man invented the alarm clock.

Pablo Picasso (1881–1973) Spanish painter. Attrib.

28 The harder you work, the luckier you get.

Gary Player (1935–) South African golfer. Attrib.

29 They say hard work never hurt anybody, but I figure why take the chance.

Ronald Reagan (1911–) US politician and president. Attrib.

30 If you have great talents, industry will improve them: if you have but moderate abilities, industry will supply their deficiency.

Joshua Reynolds (1723–92) British portrait painter. Discourse to Students of the Royal Academy, 11 Dec 1769

31 I wish to preach, not the doctrine of ignoble ease, but the doctrine of the strenuous life.

Theodore Roosevelt (1858–1919) US Republican president. Speech, Chicago, 10 Apr 1899

32 Temperance and labour are the two real physicians of man: labour sharpens his appetite and temperance prevents his abusing it.

Jean Jacques Rousseau (1712–78) French philosopher. *Émile*, Bk. I

33 One of the symptoms of approaching nervous breakdown is the belief that one's work is terribly important. If I were a medical man, I should prescribe a holiday to any patient who considered his work important.

Bertrand Russell (1872–1970) British philosopher. *The Autobiography of Bertrand Russell*, Vol. II, Ch. 5

34 The only place where success comes before work is a dictionary.

Vidal Sassoon (1928–) British hair stylist. Quoting one of his teachers in a BBC radio broadcast

35 Pennies do not come from heaven. They have to be earned here on earth.

Margaret Thatcher (1925–) British politician and prime minister. *The Sunday Telegraph*, 1982

36 I should have worked just long enough to discover that I didn't like it.

Paul Theroux (1941–) US-born writer. *The Observer Magazine*, 1 Apr 1979

37 Work banishes those three great evils, boredom, vice, and poverty.

Voltaire (François-Marie Arouet; 1694–1778) French writer. *Candide*, Ch. 30

38 How doth the little busy bee
Improve each shining hour,
And gather honey all the day
From every opening flower!

Isaac Watts (1674–1748) English theologian and hymn writer. *Divine Songs for Children*, 'Against Idleness and Mischief'

39 Work is the curse of the drinking classes.

Oscar Wilde (1854–1900) Irish-born British dramatist. Attrib.

40 I haven't got time to be tired.

Wilhelm I (1797–1888) King of Prussia and Emperor of Germany. Said during his last illness

WORLD

See also confusion

1 For the world, I count it not an inn, but an hospital, and a place, not to live, but to die in.

Thomas Browne (1605–82) English physician and writer. *Religio Medici*, Pt. II

2 As I walked through the wilderness of this world.

John Bunyan (1628–88) English writer. *The Pilgrim's Progress*, Pt. I

3 The world degenerates and grows worse every day...The calamities inflicted on Adam...were light in comparison with those inflicted on us.

Martin Luther (1483–1546) German Protestant. Commentary on the Book of Genesis

4 Sell a country! Why not sell the air, the great sea, as well as the earth? Did not the Great Spirit make them all for the use of his children?

Tecumseh (c.1718–1813) Shawnee leader. Protesting to Governor W. H. Harrison over the breach of the Treaty of Greenville, 1810.

WORLD WAR I

1 Belgium put the kibosh on the Kaiser,
Europe took a stick and made him sore;
And if Turkey makes a stand
She'll get ghurka'd and japanned,
And it won't be Hoch the Kaiser any more.

Anonymous Song of World War I

2 Six million young men lie in premature graves, and four old men sit in Paris partitioning the earth.

Anonymous *New York Nation*, 1919

3 Just for the word 'neutrality', a word which in wartime has so often been disregarded – just for a scrap of paper, Great Britain is going to make war on a kindred nation who desires nothing better than to be friends with her.

Theobald von Bethmann-Hollweg (1856–1921) German statesman. Letter to Sir Edward Goschen, 4 Aug 1914

4 The battlefield is fearful. One is overcome by a peculiar sour, heavy and penetrating smell of corpses...The legs of an Englishman, still encased in puttees, stick out of a trench, the corpse being built into the parapet; a soldier hangs his rifle on them.

Rudolph Binding *A Fatalist At War*

5 The effects of the successful gas attack were horrible. I am not pleased with the idea of poisoning men. Of course the entire world will rage about it first and then imitate us. All the dead lie on their backs with clenched fists; the whole field is yellow.

Rudolph Binding *A Fatalist At War*

6 What did you do in the Great War, Daddy?

British Recruiting Poster

7 I shall fight before Paris, I shall fight in Paris, I shall fight behind Paris.

Georges Clemenceau (1841–1929) French statesman. Speech, June 1918

8 We'll be over, we're coming over,
And we won't come back till it's over, over there.

George M. Cohan (1878–1942) US comedian. American song of World War I

9 My centre is giving way, my right is in retreat; situation excellent. I shall attack.

Marshal Foch (1851–1929) French soldier. Message sent during the second battle of the Marne, 1918. *Biography of Foch* (Aston), Ch. 13

10 This is not peace: it is an armistice for twenty years.

Marshal Foch Attrib.

11 Please God – let there be victory, before the Americans arrive.

Douglas Haig Diary, 1917

12 Every position must be held to the last man: there must be no retirement. With our backs to the wall, and believing in the justice of our cause, each one of us must fight on to the end.

Douglas Haig (1861–1928) British general. Order to the British Army, 12 Apr 1918

13 If any question why we died,
Tell them because our fathers lied.

Rudyard Kipling (1865–1936) Indian-born British writer. *Epitaphs of War*

14 I cannot get any sense of an enemy – only of a disaster.

D. H. Lawrence (1885–1930) British novelist. Letter to Edward Marsh, Oct 1914

15 This war, like the next war, is a war to end war.

David Lloyd George (1863–1945) British Liberal statesman.

16 We travelled miles of trenches to reach the point we occupy. Some of the places we passed were liquid mud up to our knees. The town we passed through was an absolute ruin, not a house that is not blown to bits. I never saw the like of it, not a soul anywhere. I can't describe the look it has. It made me shiver – wooden crosses on the roadside and in places in the town marking the heroes' death – what devastation – a day of judgement more like. Man builds and then builds machines to destroy, well he seems to have made a better job of destroying this town.

Peter McGregor (1871–1916) Private soldier. Letter to his wife, 21 June 1916

17 I feel my own life all the more precious and more dear in the presence of this deflowering of Europe. While it is true that the guns will effect a little useful weeding, I am furious with chagrin to think that the Minds, which were to have excelled the civilization of two thousand years, are being annihilated – and bodies, the product of aeons of Natural Selection, melted down to pay for political statues.

Wilfred Owen (1893–1918) British poet. Letter, 28 Aug 1914

18 What passing-bells for these who die as cattle?
Only the monstrous anger of the guns,
Only the stuttering rifles' rapid rattle
Can patter out their hasty orisons.

Wilfred Owen *Anthem for Doomed Youth*

19 Man, it seemed, had been created to jab the life out of Germans.

Siegfried Sassoon (1886–1967) British poet. *Memoirs of an Infantry Officer*, Pt. I, Ch. 1

20 ...The lecturer's voice still battered on my brain. 'The bullet and the bayonet are brother and sister.' 'If you don't kill him, he'll kill you.' 'Stick him between the eyes, in the throat, in the chest.' 'Don't waste good steel. Six inches are enough. What's the use of a foot of steel sticking out at the back of a man's neck? Three inches will do for him; when he coughs, go and look for another.'

Siegfried Sassoon *Memoirs of an Infantry Officer*

21 On St Paul's steps I watched a recruiting meeting for some time. There was a tremendous crowd round and a soldier who looked like a Colonial was letting out for all he was worth. He had a number of men in uniform with him and every little while stopped and pointed his finger at some man in the crowd and shouted 'Why haven't you joined?' Of course everyone looked at the victim who felt called upon to make an excuse if he could, and one of the assistants pushed through the crowd to tackle the one singled out.

Robert Saunders Headmaster. Letter to his son, 31 May 1915

22 When you march into France, let the last man on the right brush the Channel with his sleeve.

Alfred Graf von Schlieffen (1833–1913) German general. Referring to the Schlieffen plan. *August 1914* (Barbara Tuchman), Ch. 2

23 We drove the Boche across the Rhine,
The Kaiser from his throne.
Oh, Lafayette, we've paid our debt,
For Christ's sake, send us home.

US Army song

24 You will be home before the leaves have fallen from the trees.

Wilhelm II (1859–1941) King of Prussia and Emperor of Germany. Said to troops leaving for the Front, Aug 1914. *August 1914* (Barbara Tuchman), Ch. 9

25 It is my Royal and Imperial Command that you...exterminate first the treacherous English, and...walk over General French's contemptible little Army.

Wilhelm II Referring to the British Expeditionary Force; veterans of this force became known as 'Old Contemptibles'. *The Times*, 1 Oct 1914

26 There is such a thing as a man being too proud to fight.

Woodrow Wilson (1856–1925) US statesman. Address to foreign-born citizens, 10 May 1915

27 My message today was a message of death for our young men. How strange it seems to applaud that.

Woodrow Wilson Remark after his speech to Congress asking for a declaration of war, Apr 1917

28 There is a price which is too great to pay for peace, and that price can be put into one word. One cannot pay the price of self-respect.

Woodrow Wilson Speech, Des Moines, Iowa, 1 Feb 1916

WORLD WAR II

See also Churchill, Germany, Hitler, Nazism, war

1 World War II began last week at 5.20 a.m. (Polish time) Friday, September 1, when a German bombing plane dropped a projectile on Puck, fishing village and air base in the armpit of the Hel Peninsula.

Anonymous *Time*, 11 Sept 1939

2 Hitler
Has only got one ball!
Goering
Has two, but very small!
Himmler
Has something similar,
But poor old Goebbels
Has no balls at all!

Anonymous World War II song (to the tune of 'Colonel Bogey')

3 Any gum, chum?

Anonymous Children's cry in Britain to US GIs.

4 You wear no uniforms and your weapons differ from ours – but they are not less deadly. The fact that you wear no uniforms is your strength. The Nazi official and the German soldier don't know you. But they fear you...The night is your friend. The 'V' is your sign.

Colonel Britton (Douglas Ritchie; 1905–67) British propagandist. Broadcast to the resistance movement in occupied Europe. Radio broadcast, 1941

5 How horrible, fantastic, incredible, it is that we should be digging trenches and trying on gas-masks here because of a quarrel in a far-away country between people of whom we know nothing.

Neville Chamberlain (1869–1940) British statesman. Referring to Germany's annexation of the Sudetenland. Radio broadcast, 27 Sept 1938

6 This morning I had another talk with the German Chancellor, Herr Hitler, and here is the paper which bears his name upon it as well as mine...'We regard the agreement signed last night – and the Anglo-German Naval Agreement – as symbolic of the desire of our two peoples never to go to war with one another again.'

Neville Chamberlain On returning from signing the Munich agreement. Speech, Heston airport, 30 Sept 1938

7 This morning the British Ambassador in Berlin handed the German Government a final note stating that, unless we heard from them by eleven o'clock that they were prepared at once to withdraw their troops from Poland, a state of war would exist between us. I have to tell you that no such undertaking has been received, and that consequently this country is at war with Germany.

Neville Chamberlain Radio broadcast from Downing Street, London, 3 Sept 1939

8 Hitler has missed the bus.

Neville Chamberlain Speech, House of Commons, 4 Apr 1940

9 We have sustained a defeat without a war.

Winston Churchill (1874–1965) Speech, House of Commons, 5 Oct 1938

10 If we can stand up to Hitler, all Europe may be free and the life of the world may move forward into broad, sunlit uplands.

Winston Churchill Speech, House of Commons, 18 June 1940

11 We shall not flag or fail. We shall fight in France, we shall fight on the seas and oceans, we shall fight with growing confidence and growing strength in the air, we shall defend our island, whatever the cost may be, we shall fight on the beaches, we shall fight on the landing grounds, we shall fight in the fields and in the streets, we shall fight in the hills; we shall never surrender.

Winston Churchill Speech, House of Commons, 4 June 1940

12 Let us therefore brace ourselves to our duties, and so bear ourselves that, if the British Empire and its Commonwealth last for a thousand years, men will still say: 'This was their finest hour'.

Winston Churchill Referring to the forthcoming Battle of Britain. Speech, House of Commons, 18 June 1940

13 The battle of Britain is about to begin.

Winston Churchill Speech, House of Commons, 18 June 1940

14 Never in the field of human conflict was so much owed by so many to so few.

Winston Churchill Referring to the Battle of Britain pilots. Speech, House of Commons, 20 Aug 1940

15 We are waiting for the long-promised invasion. So are the fishes.

Winston Churchill Radio broadcast to the French people, 21 Oct 1940

16 Give us the tools, and we will finish the job.

Winston Churchill Referring to Lend-lease, which was being legislated in America. Radio broadcast, 9 Feb 1941

17 This whipped jackal ... is frisking up by the side of the German tiger.

Winston Churchill Referring to the Italian dictator, Mussolini. Speech, House of Commons, Apr 1941

18 You do your worst, and we will do our best.

Winston Churchill Addressed to Hitler. Speech, 14 July 1941

19 Do not let us speak of darker days; let us rather speak of sterner days. These are not dark days: these are great days – the greatest days our country has ever lived.

Winston Churchill Address, Harrow School, 29 Oct 1941

20 When I warned them that Britain would fight on alone whatever they did, their Generals told their Prime Minister and his divided Cabinet: 'In three weeks England will have her neck wrung like a chicken.'
Some chicken! Some neck!

Winston Churchill Referring to the French Government; *see* WEYGAND. Speech, Canadian Parliament, 30 Dec 1941

21 This is not the end. It is not even the beginning of the end. But it is, perhaps, the end of the beginning.

Winston Churchill Referring to the Battle of Egypt. Speech, Mansion House, 10 Nov 1942

22 This is *your* victory.

Winston Churchill Speech, London, 8 May 1945

23 Wars are not won by evacuations.

Winston Churchill Referring to the British Expeditionary Force's evacuation from Dunkirk. *Their Finest Hour*

24 Before Alamein we never had a victory. After Alamein we never had a defeat.

Winston Churchill *The Hinge of Fate*, Ch. 33

25 Peace with Germany and Japan on our terms will not bring much rest...As I observed last time, when the war of the giants is over the wars of the pygmies will begin.

Winston Churchill *Triumph and Tragedy*, Ch. 25

26 I, General de Gaulle, now in London, call on all French officers and men who are at present on British soil, or who may be in the future...to get in touch with me. Whatever happens the flame of French resistance must not and shall not be extinguished.

Charles De Gaulle (1890–1970) French general and statesman. Broadcast, 18 June 1940

27 Now we can look the East End in the face.

Elizabeth the Queen Mother (1900–) The widow of King George VI. Surveying the damage caused to Buckingham Palace by a bomb during the Blitz in World War II. Attrib.

28 This was the Angel of History! We felt its wings flutter through the room. Was that not the fortune we awaited so anxiously?

Joseph Goebbels (1897–1945) German politician. Referring to Roosevelt's death. *Diary*

29 They entered the war to prevent us from going into the East, not to have the East come to the Atlantic.

Hermann Goering (1893–1946) German leader. Referring to the war aims of the British in World War II. *Nuremberg Diary* (G. M. Gilbert)

30 The little ships, the unforgotten Homeric catalogue of *Mary Jane* and *Peggy IV*, of *Folkestone Belle*, *Boy Billy*, and *Ethel Maud*, of *Lady Haig* and *Skylark*...the little ships of England brought the Army home.

Philip Guedalla (1889–1944) British writer. Referring to the evacuation of Dunkirk. *Mr. Churchill*

31 Our ships have been salvaged and are retiring at high speed toward the Japanese fleet.

W. C. Halsey (1882–1959) US admiral. Following Japanese claims that most of the American Third Fleet had been sunk or were retiring. Radio message, Oct 1944

32 Germany calling, Germany calling.

'Lord Haw-Haw' (William Joyce; 1906–46) US-born propagandist for German Nazis. Radio broadcasts to Britain, during World War II

33 The war situation has developed not necessarily to Japan's advantage.

Hirohito (1901–89) Japanese head of state. Announcing Japan's surrender, 15 Aug 1945

34 When Barbarossa ommences, the world will hold its breath and ma e no comment.

Adolf Hitler (1889–1945) German dictator. Referring to the planned invasion of the USSR, Operation Barbarossa, which began on 22 June 1941. Attrib.

35 Before us stands the last problem that must be solved and will be solved. It is the last territorial claim which I have to make in Europe, but it is the claim from which I will not recede.

Adolf Hitler (1889–1945) German dictator. Referring to the Sudetenland (Czechoslovakia). Speech, Berlin, 26 Sept 1938

36 Well, he seemed such a nice old gentleman, I thought I would give him my autograph as a souvenir.

Adolf Hitler Referring to Neville Chamberlain and the Munich agreement. Attrib.

37 If we are going in without the help of Russia we are walking into a trap.

David Lloyd George (1863–1945) British Liberal statesman. Speech, House of Commons, 3 Apr 1939

38 And here we are – just as before – safe in our skins;
Glory to God for Munich.
And stocks go up and wrecks
Are salved and politicians' reputations
Go up like Jack-on-the-Beanstalk; only the Czechs
Go down and without fighting.

Louis Macneice (1907–63) Irish-born British poet. *Autumn Journal*

39 This Berlin–Rome connection is not so much a diaphragm as an axis, around which can revolve all those states of Europe with a will towards collaboration and peace.

Benito Mussolini (1883–1945) Italian dictator. Speech, Milan, 1 Nov 1936

40 Dear Ike, Today I spat in the Seine.

General George Patton (1885–1945) US general. Message sent to Eisenhower reporting his crossing of the Seine in World War II. *The American Treasury* (C. Fadiman)

41 To make a union with Great Britain would be fusion with a corpse.

Marshal Pétain (1856–1951) French marshal. On hearing Churchill's suggestion for an Anglo-French union, 1940. *Their Finest Hour* (Winston S. Churchill), Ch. 10

42 Our great-grandchildren, when they learn how we began this war by snatching glory out of defeat...may also learn how the little holiday steamers made an excursion to hell and came back glorious.

J. B. Priestley (1894–1984) British novelist. Referring to the British Expeditionary Force's evacuation from Dunkirk. Broadcast, 5 June 1940

43 The best immediate defence of the United States is the success of Great Britain defending itself.

Franklin D. Roosevelt (1882–1945) US Democratic president. At press conference, 17 Dec 1940. *Their Finest Hour* (Winston S. Churchill), Ch. 28

44 A date that shall live in infamy.

Franklin D. Roosevelt Referring to 7 Dec 1941, when Japan attacked Pearl Harbor. Message to Congress, 8 Dec 1941

45 Defeat of Germany means the defeat of Japan, probably without firing a shot or losing a life.

Franklin D. Roosevelt *The Hinge of Fate* (Winston S. Churchill), Ch. 25

46 We have finished the job, what shall we do with the tools?

Haile Selassie (1892–1975) Emperor of Ethiopia. Telegram sent to Winston Churchill, mimicking his 'Give us the tools, and we will finish the job'. *Ambrosia and Small Beer*, Ch. 4 (Edward Marsh)

47 This war is not as in the past; whoever occupies a territory also imposes on it his own social system. Everyone imposes his own system as far as his army has power to do so. It cannot be otherwise.

Joseph Stalin (J. Dzhugashvili; 1879–1953) Soviet statesman. *Conversations with Stalin* (Milovan Djilas)

48 If we see that Germany is winning the war we ought to help Russia, and if Russia is winning we ought to help Germany, and in that way let them kill as many as possible.

Harry S. Truman (1884–1972) US statesman. *The New York Times*, 24 July 1941, when Russia was invaded by Germany.

49 In three weeks England will have her neck wrung like a chicken.

Maxime Weygand (1867–1965) French general. Said at the fall of France; *see* CHURCHILL. *Their Finest Hour* (Winston S. Churchill)

50 I fear we have only awakened a sleeping giant, and his reaction will be terrible.

Isoroku Yamamoto (1884–1943) Japanese admiral. Said after the Japanese attack on Pearl Harbor, 1941.

WORLD-WEARINESS

1 Bankrupt of Life, yet Prodigal of Ease.

John Dryden (1631–1700) British poet and dramatist. *Absalom and Achitophel*, I

2 Spare all I have, and take my life.

George Farquhar (1678–1707) Irish dramatist. *The Beaux' Strategem*, V:2

3 Death is a delightful hiding-place for weary men.

Herodotus (c. 484–c. 424 BC) Greek historian. *Histories*, VII, 46

4 I am sick of this way of life. The weariness and sadness of old age make it intolerable. I have walked with death in hand, and death's own hand is warmer than my own. I don't wish to live any longer.

W. Somerset Maugham (1874–1965) British novelist. Said on his ninetieth birthday. *Familiar Medical Quotations* (M. B. Strauss)

5 Stop the World, I Want to Get Off.

Anthony Newley (1931–) British actor, composer, singer, and comedian. With Leslie Bricusse. Title of musical

6 How weary, stale, flat, and unprofitable,
Seem to me all the uses of this world!

William Shakespeare (1564–1616) English dramatist. *Hamlet*, I:2

7 I have supp'd full with horrors.

William Shakespeare *Macbeth*, V:5

8 I gin to be aweary of the sun,
And wish th' estate o' th' world were now undone.

William Shakespeare *Macbeth*, V:5

9 Death is not the greatest of ills; it is worse to want to die, and not be able to.

Sophocles (c. 496–406 BC) Greek dramatist. *Electra*, 1007

WORRY

See also misfortune

1 A trouble shared is a trouble halved.

Proverb

2 Don't meet troubles half-way.

Proverb

3 It will be all the same in a hundred years.

Proverb

4 Take things as they come.

Proverb

5 Every little yielding to anxiety is a step away from the natural heart of man.

Japanese proverb

6 Begone, dull care! I prithee begone from me!
Begone, dull care, you and I shall never agree.

Anonymous *Begone Dull Care*

7 'Life's too short for worrying.'
'Yes, that's what worries me.'

Anonymous

8 Behold the fowls of the air: for they sow not, neither do they reap, nor gather into barns; yet your heavenly Father feedeth them. Are ye not much better than they?
Which of you by taking thought can add one cubit unto his stature?
And why take ye thought for raiment? Consider the lilies of the field, how they grow; they toil not, neither do they spin:
And yet I say unto you, That even Solomon in all his glory was not arrayed like one of these.
Wherefore, if God so clothe the grass of the field, which today is, and tomorrow is cast into the oven, shall he not much more clothe you, O ye of little faith?
Therefore take no thought, saying, What shall we eat? or, What shall we drink? or, Wherewithal shall we be clothed?

Bible: Matthew 6:26–31

9 But seek ye first the kingdom of God, and his righteousness; and all these things shall be added unto you.
Take therefore no thought for the morrow: for the morrow shall take thought for the things of itself. Sufficient unto the day is the evil thereof.

Bible: Matthew 6:33–34

10 Just when we are safest, there's a sunset-touch,
A fancy from a flower-bell, some one's death,
A chorus-ending from Euripides, –
And that's enough for fifty hopes and fears
As old and new at once as Nature's self,
To rap and knock and enter in our soul.

Robert Browning (1812–89) British poet. *Bishop Blougram's Apology*

11 Before the cherry orchard was sold everybody was worried and upset, but as soon as it was all settled finally and once for all, everybody calmed down, and felt quite cheerful.

Anton Chekhov (1860–1904) Russian dramatist. *The Cherry Orchard*, IV

12 When I look back on all these worries I remember the story of the old man who said on his deathbed that he had had a lot of trouble in his life, most of which had never happened.

Winston Churchill (1874–1965) British statesman. *Their Finest Hour*

13 But Jesus, when you don't have any money, the problem is food. When you have money, it's sex. When you have both, it's health, you worry about getting ruptured or something. If everything is simply jake then you're frightened of death.

J. P. Donleavy (1926–) US writer.

14 Worry affects circulation, the heart and the glands, the whole nervous sytem, and profoundly affects the heart. I have never known a man who died from overwork, but many who died from doubt.

Charles H. Mayo (1865–1939) US physician. *Bartlett's Unfamiliar Quotations* (Leonard Louis Levinson)

15 Care
Sat on his faded cheek.

John Milton (1608–74) English poet. *Paradise Lost*, Bk. I

16 Worrying is the most natural and spontaneous of all human functions. It is time to acknowledge this, perhaps even to learn to do it better.

Lewis Thomas (1913–90) US pathologist. *More Notes of a Biology Watcher*, 'The Medusa and the Snail'

WRITERS

See also Chaucer, criticism, Dickens, Milton, poets, Shakespeare, writing

General quotations

1 A reader seldom peruses a book with pleasure until he knows whether the writer of it be a black man or a fair man, of a mild or choleric disposition, married or a bachelor.

Joseph Addison (1672–1719) British essayist. *The Spectator*, 1

2 Writers, like teeth, are divided into incisors and grinders.

Walter Bagehot (1826–77) British economist and journalist. *Estimates of some Englishmen and Scotchmen*, 'The First Edinburgh Reviewers

3 The idea that it is necessary to go to a university in order to become a successful writer, or even a man or woman of letters (which is by no means the same thing), is one of those phantasies that surround authorship.

Vera Brittain (1893–1970) British writer and feminist. *On Being an Author*, Ch. 2

4 I'm not very good at ordinary socialising. I prefer to be thinking or reading.

A. S. Byatt (1936–) British novelist. *The Sunday Times*, 21 Oct 1990

5 Literary men are…a perpetual priesthood.

Thomas Carlyle (1795–1881) Scottish historian and essayist. *Critical and Miscellaneous Essays*, 'The State of German Literature'

6 I believe the souls of five hundred Sir Isaac Newtons would go to the making up of a Shakespeare or a Milton.

Samuel Taylor Coleridge (1772–1834) British poet. Letter to Thomas Poole, 23 Mar 1801

7 The faults of great authors are generally excellences carried to an excess.

Samuel Taylor Coleridge *Miscellanies*, 149

8 A great writer creates a world of his own and his readers are proud to live in it. A lesser writer may entice them in for a moment, but soon he will watch them filing out.

Cyril Connolly (1903–74) British journalist. *Enemies of Promise*, Ch. 1

9 The only way for writers to meet is to share a quick pee over a common lamp-post.

Cyril Connolly *The Unquiet Grave*

10 Talent alone cannot make a writer. There must be a man behind the book.

Ralph Waldo Emerson (1803–82) US poet and essayist. *Goethe*

11 Alas! a woman that attempts the pen,
Such an intruder on the rights of men,
Such a presumptuous creature, is esteemed,
The fault can by no virtue be redeemed.

Anne Finch (1661–c. 1722) English poet. *Miscellany Poems, Written by a Lady*

12 Creative writers are always greater than the causes that they represent.

E. M. Forster (1879–1970) British novelist. *Gide and George*

13 The reciprocal civility of authors is one of the most risible scenes in the farce of life.

Samuel Johnson (1709–84) British lexicographer. *Life of Sir Thomas Browne*

14 Authors are easy to get on with – if you're fond of children.

Michael Joseph (1897–1958) British publisher. *The Observer*, 1949

15 One man is as good as another until he has written a book.

Benjamin Jowett (1817–93) British theologian. *Letters of B. Jowett* (Abbott and Campbell)

16 There is a vanity and a paranoia about writers – which makes excellent dramatic material – but which also makes me question the nature of writing.

David Lodge (1935–) British author. *The Times Educational Supplement*, 18 May 1990

17 Our principal writers have nearly all been fortunate in escaping regular education.

Hugh MacDiarmid (Christopher Murray Grieve; 1892–1978) Scottish poet. *The Observer*, 'Sayings of the Week', 29 Mar 1953

18 The trouble with our younger authors is that they are all in the sixties.

W. Somerset Maugham (1874–1965) British novelist. *The Observer*, 'Sayings of the Week', 14 Oct 1951

19 A novelist is, like all mortals, more fully at home on the surface of the present than in the ooze of the past.

Vladimir Nabokov (1899–1977) Russian-born US novelist. *Strong Opinions*, Ch. 20

20 I think that if a third of all the novelists and maybe two-thirds of all the poets now writing dropped dead suddenly, the loss to literature would not be great.

Charles Osborne (1927–) Author, critic, and Director of Arts Council. Remark, Nov 1985

21 A list of authors who have made themselves most beloved and therefore, most comfortable financially, shows that it is our national joy to mistake for the first-rate, the fecund rate.

Dorothy Parker (1893–1967) US writer. *Wit's End* (R. E. Drennan)

22 A novelist who writes nothing for 10 years finds his reputation rising. Because I keep on producing books they say there must be something wrong with this fellow.

J. B. Priestley (1894–1984) British novelist. *The Observer*, 'Sayings of the Week', 21 Sept 1969

23 Everybody writes a book too many.

Mordecai Richler (1931–) Canadian novelist. *The Observer*, 'Sayings of the Week', 9 Jan 1985

24 Among the many problems which beset the novelist, not the least weighty is the choice of the moment at which to begin his novel.

Vita Sackville-West (Victoria Sackville-West; 1892–1962) British poet and novelist. *The Edwardians*, Ch. 1

25 When I was a little boy they called me a liar but now that I am a grown up they call me a writer.

Isaac Bashevis Singer (1904–91) US novelist and short-story writer. Remark, July 1983

26 No regime has ever loved great writers, only minor ones.

Alexander Solzhenitsyn (1918–) Russian novelist. *The First Circle*, Ch. 57

27 It is a sad feature of modern life that only women for the most part have time to write novels, and they seldom have much to write about.

Auberon Waugh (1939–) British novelist and critic. Remark, June 1981

28 In my situation as Chancellor of the University of Oxford, I have been much exposed to authors.

Duke of Wellington (1769–1852) British general and statesman. *Collections and Recollections* (G. W. E. Russell)

29 I think it's good for a writer to think he's dying; he works harder.

Tennessee Williams (1911–83) US dramatist. *The Observer*, 'Sayings of the Week', 31 Oct 1976

30 There's nothing worse than the writer who learns to do something and then goes on doing it because it's comfortable and safe. It is a gift of wings, and you learn to trust yourself, that you will not fall – or if you do, that you will just swoop up again.

Jeanette Winterson (1959–) British author. *The Guardian*, 18 June 1994

31 Literature is strewn with the wreckage of men who have minded beyond reason the opinions of others.

Virginia Woolf (1882–1941) British novelist. *A Room of One's Own*

32 It's not a writer's business to hold opinions.

W. B. Yeats (1865–1939) Irish poet. Speaking to playwright, Denis Johnston. *The Guardian*, 5 May 1977

Specific quotations

33 More can be learnt from Miss Austen about the nature of the novel than from almost any other writer.

Walter Allen (1911–) British author and literary journalist. *The English Novel*

34 From the beginning Wilde performed his life and continued to do so even after fate had taken the plot out of his hands.

W. H. Auden (1907–73) British poet. *Forewords and Afterwords*

35 Shaw's judgements are often scatterbrained, but at least he has brains to scatter.

Max Beerbohm (1872–1956) British writer. *Conversation With Max* (S. N. Behrens)

36 I have been told by hospital authorites that more copies of my works are left behind by departing patients than those of any other author.

Robert Benchley (1889–1945) US humorist. *Chips off the Old Benchley*, 'Why Does Nobody Collect Me?'

37 He sipped at a weak hock and seltzer,
As he gazed at the London skies
Through the Nottingham lace of the curtains
Or was it his bees-winged eyes?

John Betjeman (1906–84) British poet. *The Arrest of Oscar Wilde at the Cadogan Hotel*

38 That sovereign of insufferables.

Ambrose Bierce (1842–?1914) US writer and journalist. Referring to Oscar Wilde. *Wasp* (San Francisco), 1882

39 Miller is not really a writer but a non-stop talker to whom someone has given a typewriter.

Gerald Brenan (Edward Fitzgerald Brenan; 1894–1987) British writer. Referring to Henry Miller. *Thoughts in a Dry Season*, 'Literature'

40 I had not seen *Pride and Prejudice* till I read that sentence of yours, and then I got the book. And what did I find? An accurate daguerreotyped portrait of a commonplace face; a carefully fenced, highly cultivated garden, with neat borders and delicate flowers; but no glance of a bright, vivid physiognomy, no open country, no fresh air, no blue hill, no bonny beck. I should hardly like to live with her ladies and gentlemen, in their elegant but confined houses.

Charlotte Brontë (1816–55) British novelist. Referring to Jane Austen. Letter to G. H. Lewes, 12 Jan 1848

41 A budding young anthologist sought to include a Shaw piece in a new collection. 'I hope you understand', he wrote to Shaw, 'that I cannot afford to pay your usual fee as I am a very young man.' Shaw replied 'I'll wait for you to grow up.'

Bennett Cerf (1898–1971) US publisher, editor and writer. *Shake Well Before Using*

42 G.B.S. looked aged and feeble and was dressed in very dark tweeds and a black overcoat. His white whiskers and pink face looked like an enamelled portrait, and had that pink lifeless quality of the very old.

Henry Channon (1897–1958) Politician and writer. Referring to George Bernard Shaw. Diary, 26 Feb 1944

43 Mr Shaw is (I suspect) the only man on earth who has never written any poetry.

G. K. Chesterton (1874–1936) British writer. *Orthodoxy*, Ch. 3

44 His gaze was constantly fixed on himself; yet not on himself, but on his reflection in the looking-glass...Introspection of the genuine kind he never achieved...Wilde grew into a Pierrot who liked to play the prophet.

Harold Child *Times Literary Supplement*, 18 June 1908

45 ...Old dread-death and dread-evil Johnson, that teacher of moping and melancholy...If the writings of this time-serving, mean, dastardly old pensioner had got a firm hold of the minds of the people at large, the people would have been bereft of their very souls.

William Cobbett (1763–1835) British journalist and writer.

46 Shaw relished every opportunity to have himself painted, sketched, photographed or carved, because each likeness provided him with a new extension of himself.

Peter Conrad *The Observer*, Multitude of Shaws, 7 Oct 1979

47 Wilde's voice was of the brown velvet order – mellifluous – rounded – in a sense giving it a plummy quality – rather on the adenotic side – but practically pure cello – and very pleasing.

Franklin Dyall *Life of Oscar Wilde* (Hesketh Pearson)

48 A dangerous person to disagree with.

T. S. Eliot (1888–1965) US-born British poet and dramatist. Referring to Samuel Johnson. *The Metaphysical Poets*

49 I am at a loss to understand why people hold Miss Austen's novels at so high a rate, which seem to me vulgar in tone, sterile in artistic invention, imprisoned in the wretched conventions of English society, without genius, wit, or knowledge of the world. Never was life so pinched and narrow. The one problem in the mind of the writer in both the stories I have read...is marriageableness.

Ralph Waldo Emerson (1803–82) US poet and essayist. *Journal*, 1861

50 This pictorial account of the day-to-day life of an English gamekeeper is full of considerable interest to outdoor minded readers, as it contains many passages on pheasant-raising, the apprehending of poachers, ways to control vermin, and other chores and duties of the professional gamekeeper. Unfortunately, one is obliged to wade through many pages of extraneous material in order to discover and savour those sidelights on the management of a midland shooting estate, and in this reviewer's opinion the book cannot take the place of J. R. Miller's *Practical Gamekeeping*.

Review of *Lady Chatterley's Lover. Field and Stream*

51 Lawrence himself is, as far as I know, the only prophetic novelist writing today – all the rest are fantasists or preachers: the only living novelist in whom the song predominates, who has the rapt bardic quality, and whom it is idle to criticize... Nothing is more disconcerting than to sit down, so to speak, before your prophet, and then suddenly to receive his boot in the pit of your stomach.

E. M. Forster (1879–1970) British novelist. *Aspects of the Novel*

52 Scott misunderstood it when he congratulated her for painting on a square of ivory. She is a miniaturist, but never two-dimensional. All her characters are round, or capable of rotundity.

E. M. Forster Referring to Jane Austen. *Aspects of the Novel*

53 It's not good enough to spend time and ink in describing the penultimate sensations and physical movements of people getting into a state of rut... The body's never worthwhile, and the sooner Lawrence recognizes that, the better – the men we swear by – Tolstoy, Turgenev, Chekov, Maupassant, Flaubert, France – knew that great truth, they only use the body, and that sparingly, to reveal the soul.

John Galsworthy (1867–1933) British novelist. Letter to Edward Garnett, 13 Apr 1914

54 Lunched with Pinker to meet D. H. Lawrence, that provincial genius. Interesting, but a type I could not get on with. Obsessed with self. Dead eyes, and a red beard, long pale narrow face. A strange bird.

John Galsworthy *Life and Letters of John Galsworthy* (H. V. Marrot)

55 There is no arguing with Johnson; for when his pistol misses fire, he knocks you down with the butt end of it.

Oliver Goldsmith (1728–74) Irish-born British writer. *Life of Johnson* (J. Boswell)

56 ...But Mr Hardy's women are moulded of the same flesh as his men; they are liable to flutterings and tremblings; they are not always constant even when they are 'quite nice'; and some of them are actually 'of a coming-on disposition'.

Edmund Gosse (1849–1928) British writer and critic. *Speaker*, 13 Sept 1890

57 Oscar Wilde did not dive very deeply below the surface of human nature, but found, to a certain extent rightly, that there is more on the surface of life than is seen by the eyes of most people.

J. T. Grein *Sunday Special*, 9 Dec 1900

58 The work of Henry James has always seemed divisible by a simple dynastic arrangement into three reigns: James I, James II, and the Old Pretender.

Philip Guedalla (1889–1944) British writer. *Collected Essays*, 'Men of Letters: Mr. Henry James'

59 His worst is better than any other person's best.

William Hazlitt (1778–1830) British essayist. Referring to Walter Scott. *English Literature*, Ch. XIV, 'Sir Walter Scott'

60 He writes as fast as they can read, and he does not write himself down.

William Hazlitt Referring to Walter Scott. *English Literature*, CH. XIV, 'Sir Walter Scott'

61 Dr Johnson's sayings would not appear so extraordinary, were it not for his *bow-wow way*.

Henry Herbert (1734–94) British general. *Life of Johnson* (J. Boswell)

62 He identified genius with immunity from the cravings and turpitudes which make us human. Hence his regime of sexual continence which so confused and dismayed the women he persisted in loving, and hence too his abstinent diet of grated vegetables.

Michael Holroyd (1935–) British writer. Referring to George Bernard Shaw. *The Genius of Shaw*

63 To be with Lawrence was a kind of adventure, a voyage of discovery into newness and otherness… For Lawrence, existence was one continuous convalescence; it was as though he were newly re-born from a mortal illness every day of his life.

Aldous Huxley (1894–1964) British novelist. *The Letters of D. H. Lawrence*, Introduction

64 He was imperfect unfinished, inartistic; he was worse than provincial – he was parochial.

Henry James (1843–1916) US novelist. Referring to Henry Thoreau. *Life of Nathaniel Hawthorne*, Ch. 4

65 He is the richest author that ever grazed the common of literature.

Samuel Johnson (1709–84) British lexicographer. Referring to Dr John Campbell. *Life of Johnson* (J. Boswell), Vol. I

66 What a commonplace genius he has, or a genius for the commonplace, I don't know which. He doesn't rank so terribly high, really. But better than Bernard Shaw, even then.

D. H. Lawrence (1885–1930) British novelist. Referring to Thomas Hardy. Letter to Martin Secker, 24 July 1928

67 Charlotte Brontë, one cannot but feel after comparing her early work with modern bestsellers, was only unlike them in being fortunate in her circumstances, which gave her a cultured background, and in the age in which she lived, which did not get between her and her spontaneities.

Q. D. Leavis (1906–81) British writer. *Fiction and the Reading Public*

68 A good man fallen among Fabians.

Lenin (Vladimir Ilich Ulyanov; 1870–1924) Russian revolutionary leader. Referring to George Bernard Shaw. Attrib.

69 The last gentleman in Europe.

Ada Beddington Leverson (1862–1933) British writer. Said of Oscar Wilde. *Letters to the Sphinx* (Wilde), 'Reminiscences', 2

70 I ask you, is anything in life or literature, past or present, in earth, heaven or hell, anything more devastatingly tedious than D.H.L.'s interest in the human genitalia.

G. W. Lyttelton Referring to D. H. Lawrence. *The Lyttelton Hart-Davis Letters*, 29 Mar 1956

71 In the foreground is that strange figure which is as familiar to us as the figures of those among whom we have been brought up, the gigantic body, the huge massy face, seamed with the scars of disease, the brown coat, the black worsted stockings, the grey wig with the scorched foretop, the dirty hands, the nails bitten and pared to the quick.

Lord Macaulay (1800–59) British historian. Describing Samuel Johnson. *Essays:* 'Boswell's Life of Johnson'

72 Nothing very much happens in her books, and yet, when you come to the bottom of a page, you eagerly turn it to learn what will happen next. Nothing very much does and again you eagerly turn the page. The novelist who has the power to achieve this has the most precious gift a novelist can possess.

W. Somerset Maugham (1874–1965) British novelist. Referring to Jane Austen. *Ten Novels and Their Authors*

73 I have discovered that our great favourite, Miss Austen, is my countrywoman…with whom mamma before her marriage was acquainted. Mamma says that she was then the prettiest, silliest, most affected, husband-hunting butterfly she ever remembers.

Mary Russell Mitford (1787–1855) British writer. Referring to Jane Austen. Letter to Sir William Elford, 3 Apr 1815

74 English literature's performing flea.

Sean O'Casey (1884–1964) Irish dramatist. Referring to P. G. Wodehouse. Attrib.

75 He is pretty certain to come back into favour. One of the surest signs of his genius is that women dislike his books.

George Orwell (Eric Blair; 1903–50) British novelist. Referring to Joseph Conrad. *New English Weekly*, 23 July 1936

76 The foaming denouncers of the bourgeoisie, and the more-water-in-your-beer reformers of whom Shaw is the prototype.

George Orwell *The Road to Wigan Pier*

77 If with the literate I am
Impelled to try an epigram
I never seek to take the credit
We all assume that Oscar said it.

Dorothy Parker (1893–1967) US writer. Referring to Oscar Wilde. Attrib.

78 The poor son-of-a-bitch!

Dorothy Parker Quoting from *The Great Gatsby* on paying her last respects to F. Scott Fitzgerald. *Thalberg: Life and Legend* (B. Thomas)

79 Now that the old lion is dead, every ass thinks he may kick at him.

Samuel Parr (1747–1825) British writer and scholar. Referring to Samuel Johnson. *Life of Johnson* (J. Boswell)

80 Even when conversing he could not keep still: jumping up and down, crossing and uncrossing his legs, shoving his hands in his pockets and pulling them out, sitting straight up or lying right back in his chair, bending forward, stretching backward, never remaining in one position for two minutes together.

Hesketh Pearson (1887–1964) British biographer. *Bernard Shaw*

81 Undeterred…,Mr Lawrence has penned another novel, *Women in Love*, which justly merits the fate of its predecessor. I do not claim to be a literary critic, but I know dirt when I smell it and here it is in heaps – festering, putrid heaps which smell to high Heaven.

W. Charles Pilley Critic. Review of *Women in Love. John Bull*, 17 Sept 1921

82 Detestable person but needs watching. I think he learned the proper treatment of modern subjects before I did.

Ezra Pound (1885–1972) US poet. Referring to D. H. Lawrence. Letter to Harriet Monroe, Mar 1913

83 Waldo is one of those people who would be enormously improved by death.

Saki (Hector Hugh Munro; 1870–1916) British writer. Referring to Ralph Waldo Emerson. *The Feast of Nemesis*

84 Sherard Blaw, the dramatist who had discovered himself, and who had given so ungrudgingly of his discovery to the world.

Saki Referring to George Bernard Shaw. *The Unbearable Bassington*, Ch. 13

85 The Big Bow-Wow strain I can do myself like any now going; but the exquisite touch, which renders ordinary commonplace things and characters interesting, from the truth of the description and the sentiment, is denied to me.

Walter Scott (1771–1832) Scottish novelist. In praise of Jane Austen. *Journal*, 14 Mar 1826

86 That young lady has a talent for describing the involvements and feelings and characters of ordinary life which is to me the most wonderful thing I ever met with.

Walter Scott Referring to Jane Austen. *Journals*, 14 Mar 1826

87 I enjoyed talking to her, but thought *nothing* of her writing. I considered her 'a beautiful little knitter'.

Edith Sitwell (1887–1964) British poet and writer. Referring to Virginia Woolf. Letter to G. Singleton

88 That great Cham of literature, Samuel Johnson.

Tobias Smollett (1721–71) British novelist. Letter to John Wilkes, 16 Mar 1759

89 I wish you had not sent me Jane Eyre. It interested me so much that I have lost (or won if you like) a whole day in reading it at the busiest period, with the printers I know waiting for copy. Who the author can be I can't guess – if a woman she knows her language better than most ladies do, or has had a 'classical' education. It is a fine book though – the man & woman capital – the style very generous and upright so to speak. I thought it was Kinglake for some time.

W. M. Thackeray (1811–63) British novelist. Referring to Charlotte Brontë. Letter to W. S. Williams, 23 Oct 1847

90 The poor little woman of genius! the fiery little eager brave tremulous homely-faced creature!...But you see she is a little bit of a creature without a penny worth of good looks, thirty years old I should think, buried in the country, and eating up her own heart there.

W. M. Thackeray Referring to Charlotte Brontë. Letter to Lucy Baxter, 11 Mar 1853

91 George Too Shaw To Be Good.

Dylan Thomas (1914–53) Welsh poet. Letter to Pamela Hansford Johnson, Oct 1933

92 William Congreve is the only sophisticated playwright England has produced; and like Shaw, Sheridan, and Wilde, his nearest rivals, he was brought up in Ireland.

Kenneth Tynan (1927–80) British theatre critic. *Curtains*, 'The Way of the World'

93 Jane Austen's books, too, are absent from this library. Just that one omission alone would make a fairly good library out of a library that hadn't a book in it.

Mark Twain (Samuel Langhorne Clemens; 1835–1910) US writer. *Following the Equator*, Pt. II

94 I wouldn't give up writing about God at this stage, if I was you. It would be like P. G. Wodehouse dropping Jeeves half-way through the Wooster series.

Evelyn Waugh (1903–66) British novelist. Said to Graham Greene, who proposed to write a political novel. *Evelyn Waugh* (Christopher Sykes)

95 He was over-dressed, pompous, snobbish, sentimental and vain. But he had an indeniable *flair* for the possibilities of commercial theatre.

Evelyn Waugh Referring to Oscar Wilde. *Harper's Bazaar*, Nov 1930

96 Mr Bernard Shaw has no enemies but is intensely disliked by all his friends.

Oscar Wilde (1854–1900) Irish-born British dramatist. *Autobiographies* (W. B. Yeats)

97 Of all the great Victorian writers, he was probably the most antagonistic to the Victorian age itself.

Edmund Wilson (1895–1972) US critic and writer. Referring to Charles Dickens. *The Wound and the Bow*, 'The Two Scrooges'

98 No one has written worse English than Mr Hardy in some of his novels – cumbrous, stilted, ugly, and inexpressive – yes, but at the same time so strangely expressive of something attractive to us in Mr Hardy himself that we would not change it for the perfection of Sterne at his best. It becomes coloured by its surroundings; it becomes literature.

Virginia Woolf (1882–1941) British novelist. *The Moment*

99 I agree about Shaw – he is haunted by the mystery he flouts. He is an atheist who trembles in the haunted corridor.

W. B. Yeats (1865–1939) Irish poet. Letter to George Russell, 1 July 1921

WRITING

See also books, criticism, fiction, inspiration, letter-writing, literacy, literature, novels, plays, poetry, poetry and prose, prose, reading, style, writers

1 Every book must be chewed to get out its juice.

Chinese proverb

2 The style is the man.

Proverb

3 Most people enjoy the sight of their own handwriting as they enjoy the smell of their own farts.

W. H. Auden (1907–73) British poet. *The Dyer's Hand*, 'Writing'

4 My characters often advance both an idea and its opposite. They seduce each other by their articulateness.

Howard Barker (1946–) British playwright. *The Times*, 3 Jan 1990

5 It is all very well to be able to write books, but can you waggle your ears?

J. M. Barrie (1860–1937) British playwright. Speaking to H. G. Wells. *Barrie: The Story of A Genius* (J. A. Hamerton)

6 Sapper, Buchan, Dornford Yates, practitioners in that school of Snobbery with Violence that runs like a thread of good-class tweed through twentieth-century literature.

Alan Bennett (1934–) British playwright and actor. Obituary in *The Times* for Colin Watson, 21 Jan 1983

7 Beneath the rule of men entirely great,
The pen is mightier than the sword.

Edward Bulwer-Lytton (1803–73) British novelist and politician. *Richelieu*, II:2

8 From this it is clear how much more cruel the pen is than the sword.

Robert Burton (1577–1640) English scholar and explorer. *Anatomy of Melancholy*, Pt. I

9 That's not writing, that's typing.

Truman Capote (1924–84) US writer. Referring to the writer Jack Kerouac. Attrib.

10 When in doubt have a man come through a door with a gun in his hand.

Raymond Chandler (1888–1959) US novelist. *The Simple Art of Murder*

11 NINA. Your play's hard to act, there are no living people in it.
TREPLEV. Living people! We should show life neither as it is nor as it ought to be, but as we see it in our dreams.

Anton Chekhov (1860–1904) Russian dramatist. *The Seagull*, I

12 Better to write for yourself and have no public, than write for the public and have no self.

Cyril Connolly (1903–74) British journalist. *Turnstile One* (ed. V. S. Pritchett)

13 Neither am I.

Peter Cook (1937–) British writer and entertainer. On being told that the person sitting next to him at a dinner party was 'writing a book'. Attrib.

14 All good writing is *swimming under water* and holding your breath.

F. Scott Fitzgerald (1896–1940) US novelist. Letter to Frances Scott Fitzgerald

15 No tears in the writer, no tears in the reader.

Robert Frost (1875–1963) US poet. *Collected Poems*, Preface

16 Another damned, thick, square book! Always scribble, scribble, scribble! Eh! Mr Gibbon?

William, Duke of Gloucester (1743–1805) The brother of George III. Addressing Edward Gibbon, author of the six-volume *The History of the Decline and Fall of the Roman Empire. Literary Memorials* (Best)

17 You must write for children in the same way as you do for adults, only better.

Maxim Gorky (Aleksei Maksimovich Peshkov; 1868–1936) Russian writer. Attrib.

18 I cannot write as well as some people; my talent is in coming up with good stories about lawyers. That is what I am good at.

John Grisham (1955–) US writer. *The Independent on Sunday*, 5 June 1994

19 I wasn't born until I started to write.

David Hare (1947–) British dramatist. *The Sunday Times*, 11 Feb 1990

20 You will have written exceptionally well if, by skilful arrangement of your words, you have made an ordinary one seem original.

Horace (Quintus Horatius Flaccus; 65–8 BC) Roman poet. *Ars Poetica*

21 A bad book is as much a labour to write as a good one; it comes as sincerely from the author's soul.

Aldous Huxley (1894–1964) British novelist. *Point Counter Point*

22 A man will turn over half a library to make one book.

Samuel Johnson (1709–84) British lexicographer. *Life of Johnson* (J. Boswell), Vol. II

23 What is written without effort is in general read without pleasure.

Samuel Johnson *Johnsonian Miscellanies* (ed. G. B. Hill), Vol. II

24 Read over your compositions, and where ever you meet with a passage which you think is particularly fine, strike it out.

Samuel Johnson Recalling the advice of a college tutor. *Life of Johnson* (J. Boswell), Vol. II

25 No man but a blockhead ever wrote, except for money.

Samuel Johnson *Life of Johnson* (J. Boswell), Vol. III

26 Many suffer from the incurable disease of writing, and it becomes chronic in their sick minds.

Juvenal (Decimus Junius Juvenalis; 60–130 AD) Roman satirist. *Satires*, VII

27 I happen to belive that *The Dark Stuff* contains some of the greatest, most truly heroic stories of my time and generation…and no one else has written them quite like me.

Nick Kent Rock journalist. Referring to a collection of his own work. *The Independent on Sunday*, 5 June 1994

28 Clear writers, like clear fountains, do not seem so deep as they are; the turbid look the most profound.

Walter Savage Landor (1775–1864) British poet and writer. *Imaginary Conversations*, 'Southey and Porson'

29 I like to write when I feel spiteful: it's like having a good sneeze.

D. H. Lawrence (1885–1930) British novelist. Letter to Lady Cynthia Asquith, Nov 1913

30 Nothing but old fags and cabbage-stumps of quotations from the Bible and the rest, stewed in the juice of deliberate, journalistic dirty-mindedness.

D. H. Lawrence Referring to James Joyce. Letter to Aldous Huxley, 15 Aug 1928

31 When once the itch of literature comes over a man, nothing can cure it but the scratching of a pen.

Samuel Lover (1797–1868) Irish novelist. *Handy Andy*, Ch. 36

32 I shall not be satisfied unless I produce something that shall for a few days supersede the last fashionable novel on the tables of young ladies.

Lord Macaulay (1800–59) British historian. Letter to Macvey Napier, 5 Nov 1841

33 There is an impression abroad that everyone has it in him to write one book; but if by this is implied a good book the impression is false.

W. Somerset Maugham (1874–1965) British novelist. *The Summing Up*

34 When you steal from one author, it's plagiarism; if you steal from many, it's research.

Wilson Mizner (1876–1933) US writer and wit. Attrib.

35 I suffer from the disease of writing books and being ashamed of them when they are finished.

Baron de Montesquieu (1689–1755) French writer. *Pensées diverses*

36 Writing is like getting married. One should never commit oneself until one is amazed at one's luck.

Iris Murdoch (1919–) Irish-born British novelist. *The Black Prince*, 'Bradley Pearson's Foreword'

37 Poor Knight! he really had two periods, the first – a dull man writing broken English, the second – a broken man writing dull English.

Vladimir Nabokov (1899–1977) Russian-born US novelist. *The Real Life of Sebastian Knight*, Ch. 1

38 One always writes comedy at the moment of deepest hysteria.

V. S. Naipaul (1932–) West Indian-born British novelist. *The Observer*, 'Sayings of the Week', 1 May 1994

39 True ease in writing comes from art, not chance,
As those move easiest who have learn'd to dance.
'Tis not enough no harshness gives offence,
The sound must seem an echo to the sense.

Alexander Pope (1688–1744) British poet. *An Essay on Criticism*

40 What is the future of my kind of writing?… Perhaps in retirement…a quieter, narrower kind of life can be worked out and adopted. Bounded by English literature and the Anglican Church and small pleasures like sewing and choosing dress material for this uncertain summer.

Barbara Pym (1928–80) British novelist. Diary, 6 Mar 1972

41 Make 'em laugh; make 'em cry; make 'em wait.

Charles Reade (1814–84) British novelist and dramatist. Advice to an aspiring writer. Attrib.

42 The profession of letters is, after all, the only one in which one can make no money without being ridiculous.

Jules Renard (1894–1910) French writer. *Journal*

43 My scribbling pays me zero francs per line – not including the white spaces.

Marquis de Rochefort (1830–1913) French journalist. Referring to his salary as a writer. *Autant en apportent les mots* (Pedrazzini)

44 I have a certain hesitation in starting my biography too soon for fear of something important having not yet happened. Suppose I should end my days as President of Mexico; the biography would seem incomplete if it did not mention this fact.

Bertrand Russell (1872–1970) British philosopher. Letter to Stanley Unwin, Nov 1930

45 No, this right hand shall work it all off.

Walter Scott (1771–1832) Scottish novelist. Refusing offers of help following his bankruptcy in 1826. *Century of Anecdote* (J. Timbs)

46 Writing, when properly managed, (as you may be sure I think mine is) is but a different name for conversation.

Laurence Sterne (1713–68) Irish-born British writer. *Tristram Shandy*

47 Whatever sentence will bear to be read twice, we may be sure was thought twice.

Henry David Thoreau (1817–62) US writer. *Journal*, 1842

48 Not that the story need be long, but it will take a long while to make it short.

Henry David Thoreau Letter, 16 Nov 1867

49 Three hours a day will produce as much as a man ought to write.

Anthony Trollope (1815–82) British novelist. *Autobiography*, Ch. 15

50 I put the words down and push them a bit.

Evelyn Waugh (1903–66) British novelist. Obituary, *The New York Times*, 11 Apr 1966

51 The fact that – these books – two novels, a book of travel, a biography, a work of contemporary history – never got beyond the first ten thousand words was testimony to the resilience of his character.

Evelyn Waugh *Put Out More Flags*

52 All my novels are an accumulation of detail. I'm a bit of a bower-bird.

Patrick White (1912–90) British-born Australian novelist. *Southerly*, 139

53 Praise and blame are much the same for the writer. One is better for your vanity, but neither gets you much further with your work.

Jeanette Winterson (1959–) British author. *The Guardian*, 18 June 1994

54 Every great and original writer, in proportion as he is great and original, must himself create the taste by which he is to be relished.

William Wordsworth (1770–1850) British poet. *Lyrical Ballads*, Preface

YZ

YEATS, W. B.

(1865–1939) Irish poet and dramatist. His verse collections include *The Tower* (1928) and *The Winding Stair* (1929). With Lady Gregory, he founded the Abbey Theatre in Dublin, for which he wrote many plays.

Quotations about Yeats

1 Willie Yeats stood for enchantment.

G. K. Chesterton (1874–1936) British writer. Attrib.

2 Yeats is not a man of this world; and when you hurl an enormous, smashing chunk of it at him, he dodges it, small blame to him.

George Bernard Shaw (1856–1950) Irish dramatist and critic. Letter to Sean O'Casey

Quotations by Yeats

3 That William Blake
Who beat upon the wall
Till Truth obeyed his call.

An Acre of Grass

4 O chestnut tree, great rooted blossomer,
Are you the leaf, the blossom or the bole?
O body swayed to music; O brightening glance,
How can we know the dancer from the dance?

Among School Children

5 When I think of all the books I have read, and of the wise words I have heard spoken, and of the anxiety I have given to parents and grandparents, and of the hopes that I have had, all life weighed in the scales of my own life seems to me preparation for something that never happens.

Autobiography

6 Now that my ladder's gone
I must lie down where all the ladders start,
In the foul rag-and-bone shop of the heart.

The Circus Animals' Desertion

7 Though leaves are many, the root is one;
Through all the lying days of my youth
I swayed my leaves and flowers in the sun;
Now I may wither into the truth.

The Coming of Wisdom with Time

8 But Love has pitched his mansion in
The place of excrement.

Crazy Jane Talks with the Bishop 1932

9 Wine comes in at the mouth
And love comes in at the eye;
That's all we shall know for truth
Before we grow old and die.

A Drinking Song

10 All changed, changed utterly:
A terrible beauty is born

Easter 1916

11 Out of the quarrel with others we make rhetoric; out of the quarrel with ourselves we make poetry.

Essay

12 When I play on my fiddle in Dooney,
Folk dance like a wave of the sea.

The Fiddler of Dooney

13 For the good are always the merry,
Save by an evil chance,
And the merry love the fiddle,
And the merry love to dance

The Fiddler of Dooney

14 One that is ever kind said yesterday:
'Your well-belovèd's hair has threads of grey,
And little shadows come about her eyes.'

The Folly of Being Comforted

15 I have drunk ale from the Country of the Young
And weep because I know all things now.

He Thinks of his Past Greatness

16 Nor law, nor duty bade me fight,
Nor public men, nor cheering crowds,
A lonely impulse of delight
Drove to this tumult in the clouds;
I balanced all, brought all to mind,
The years to come seemed waste of breath,
A waste of breath the years behind
In balance with this life, this death.

An Irish Airman Foresees his Death

17 I will arise and go now, and go to Innisfree,
And a small cabin build there, of clay and wattles made;
Nine bean rows will I have there, a hive for the honey bee,
And live alone in the bee-loud glade.

The Lake Isle of Innisfree

18 And I shall have some peace there, for peace comes dropping slow,
Dropping from the veils of the morning to where the cricket sings.

The Lake Isle of Innisfree

19 The wind blows out of the gates of the day,
The wind blows over the lonely of heart,
And the lonely of heart is withered away.

The Land of Heart's Desire

20 I shudder and I sigh to think
That even Cicero
And many-minded Homer were
Mad as the mist and snow.

Mad as the Mist and Snow

21 Time drops in decay,
Like a candle burnt out.

The Moods

22 Never to have lived is best, ancient writers say;
Never to have drawn the breath of life,
never to have looked into the eye of day
The second best's a gay goodnight and quickly turn away.

Oedipus at Colonus 1928

23 In dreams begins responsibility.

Old Play, Epigraph, Responsibilities

24 Where, where but here have Pride and Truth,

That long to give themselves for wage,
To shake their wicked sides at youth
Restraining reckless middle age?

On hearing that the Students of our New University have joined the Agitation against Immoral Literature

25 A pity beyond all telling
Is hid in the heart of love.

The Pity of Love 1893

26 An intellectual hatred is the worst.

A Prayer for My Daughter

27 That is no country for old men. The young
In one another's arms, birds in the trees
– Those dying generations – at their song,
The salmon-falls, the mackerel-crowded seas,
Fish, flesh, or fowl, commend all summer long
Whatever is begotten, born, and dies.

Sailing to Byzantium, I

28 Things fall apart; the centre cannot hold;
Mere anarchy is loosed upon the world,
The blood-dimmed tide is loosed, and everywhere
The ceremony of innocence is drowned;
The best lack all conviction, while the worst
Are full of passionate intensity.

The Second Coming

29 A woman of so shining loveliness
That men threshed corn at midnight by a tress,
A little stolen tress.

The Secret Rose

30 And pluck till time and times are done
The silver apples of the moon
The golden apples of the sun.

Song of Wandering Aengus

31 But where's the wild dog that has praised his fleas?

To a Poet, who would have me Praise certain Bad Poets, Imitators of His and Mine

32 Under bare Ben Bulben's head
In Drumcliff churchyard Yeats is laid...
On limestone quarried near the spot
By his command these words are cut:
Cast a cold eye
On life, on death.
Horseman, pass by!

Under Ben Bulben, VI

33 When you are old and gray and full of sleep,
And nodding by the fire, take down this book,
And slowly read, and dream of the soft look
Your eyes had once, and of their shadows deep...

When you are Old

34 Love fled
And paced upon the mountains overhead
And hid his face amid a crowd of stars.

When you are Old

35 But I, being poor, have only my dreams;
I have spread my dreams under your feet;
Tread softly because you tread on my dreams.

He Wishes for the Cloths of Heaven

36 It's not a writer's business to hold opinions.

Speaking to playwright, Denis Johnston. *The Guardian*, 5 May 1977

37 He is all blood, dirt and sucked sugar stick.

Referring to the poet Wilfred Owen. *Letters on Poetry to Dorothy Wellesley*, Letter, 21 Dec 1936

38 O'CONNOR. How are you?
W.B.Y. Not very well, I can only write prose today.

Attrib.

YIELDING

See also determination, weakness

1 The concessions of the weak are the concessions of fear.

Edmund Burke (1729–97) British politician. *Speech on Conciliation with America* (House of Commons, 22 Mar 1775)

2 He that complies against his will,
Is of his own opinion still.

Samuel Butler (1612–80) English satirist. *Hudibras*, Pt. III

YOUNG, EDWARD

(1683–1765) British poet. His verse collection *Night Thoughts* (1742–45) gave rise to the 'graveyard poets'. His plays include *Busiris* (1719), *Revenge* (1721), and *The Brothers* (1726).

1 Some for renown, on scraps of learning dote,
And think they grow immortal as they quote.

Love of Fame, I

2 Be wise with speed,
A fool at forty is a fool indeed.

Love of Fame, II

3 All men think all men mortal, but themselves.

Night Thoughts

4 By night an atheist half believes a God.

Night Thoughts

5 Procrastination is the thief of time.

Night Thoughts

6 The bell strikes one. We take no note of time
But from its loss.

Night Thoughts

7 Time flies, death urges, knells call, heaven invites,
Hell threatens.

Night Thoughts

8 To know the world, not love her is thy point,
She gives but little, nor that little long.

Night Thoughts

YOUTH

See also age, children

1 The younger members of our society are not different from what they have always been...At the time of the world when there were only two young people, Cain and Abel, one of them was a delinquent.

Lord Aberdare (1919–) *The Observer*, 'Sayings of the Week', 25 Feb 1968

2 A stage between infancy and adultery.

Anonymous

3 Better is a poor and a wise child than an old and foolish king, who will no more be admonished.

Bible: Ecclesiastes 4:13

4 It is good for a man that he bear the yoke in his youth.

Bible: Lamentations 3:27

5 Youth is something very new: twenty years ago no one mentioned it.

Coco Chanel (1883–1971) French dress designer. *Coco Chanel, Her Life, Her Secrets* (Marcel Haedrich)

6 This day I am thirty years old. Let me now bid a cheerful adieu to my youth. My young days are now surely over, and why should I regret them? Were I never to grow old I might be always here, and might never bid farewell to sin and sorrow.

Janet Colquhoun (1781–1846) Diary, 17 Apr 1811

7 I remember my youth and the feeling that will never come back any more – the feeling that I could last for ever, outlast the sea, the earth, and all men; the deceitful feeling that lures us on to perils, to love, to vain effort – to death…

Joseph Conrad (Teodor Josef Konrad Korzeniowski; 1857–1924) Polish-born British novelist. *Youth*

8 The young always have the same problem – how to rebel and conform at the same time. They have now solved this by defying their parents and copying one another.

Quentin Crisp (c. 1910–) Model, publicist, and writer. *The Naked Civil Servant*

9 Almost everything that is great has been done by youth.

Benjamin Disraeli (1804–81) British statesman. *Coningsby*, Bk. III, Ch. 1

10 'And youth is cruel, and has no remorse
And smiles at situations which it cannot see.'
I smile of course,
And go on drinking tea.

T. S. Eliot (1888–1965) US-born British poet and dramatist. *Portrait of a Lady*

11 I never dared be radical when young, for fear it would make me conservative when old.

Robert Frost (1875–1963) US poet. *Precaution*

12 *Les enfants terribles.*
The embarrassing young.

Paul Gavarni (1801–66) French illustrator. Title of a series of prints

13 No young man believes he shall ever die.

William Hazlitt (1778–1830) British essayist. *The Monthly Magazine*, Mar 1827

14 It is the malady of our age that the young are so busy teaching us that they have no time left to learn.

Eric Hoffer (1902–83) US writer.

15 A majority of young people seem to develop mental arteriosclerosis forty years before they get the physical kind.

Aldous Huxley (1894–1964) British writer. Interview. *Writers at Work: Second Series*

16 Youth will come here and beat on my door, and force its way in.

Henrik Ibsen (1828–1906) Norwegian dramatist. *The Master Builder*, I

17 Young men make great mistakes in life; for one thing, they idealize love too much.

Benjamin Jowett (1817–93) British theologian. *Letters of B. Jowett* (Abbott and Campbell)

18 When all the world is young, lad,
And all the trees are green;
And every goose a swan, lad,
And every lass a queen;
Then hey for boot and horse, lad,
And round the world away:
Young blood must have its course, lad,
And every dog his day.

Charles Kingsley (1819–75) British writer. *Songs from The Water Babies*, 'Young and Old'

19 Youth is a malady of which one becomes cured a little every day.

Benito Mussolini (1883–1945) Italian dictator. Said on his 50th birthday.

20 One starts to get young at the age of sixty and then it is too late.

Pablo Picasso (1881–1973) Spanish painter. *The Sunday Times*, 20 Oct 1963

21 The atrocious crime of being a young man…I shall neither attempt to palliate nor deny.

William Pitt the Elder (1708–78) British statesman. Speech, House of Commons, 27 Jan 1741

22 He whom the gods love dies young, while he has his strength and senses and wits.

Plautus (c. 254 BC–184 BC) Roman dramatist. *Bacchides*, IV:8

23 One of the pleasures of middle age is to *find out* that one WAS right, and that one was much righter than one knew at say 17 or 23.

Ezra Pound (1885–1972) US poet. *ABC of Reading*, Ch. 1

24 I will not make age an issue of this campaign. I am not going to exploit for political purposes my opponent's youth and inexperience.

Ronald Reagan (1911–) US president. TV debate, 22 Oct 1984

25 Youth is in itself so amiable, that were the soul as perfect as the body, we could not forbear adoring it.

Marie de Sévigné (1626–96) French letter-writer. Letter to her daughter

26 My salad days,
When I was green in judgment, cold in blood,
To say as I said then!

William Shakespeare (1564–1616) English dramatist. *Antony and Cleopatra*, I:5

27 Crabbed age and youth cannot live together:
Youth is full of pleasure, age is full of care;
Youth like summer morn, age like winter weather;
Youth like summer brave, age like winter bare.

William Shakespeare *The Passionate Pilgrim*, XII

28 I would there were no age between ten and three and twenty, or that youth would sleep out the rest; for there is nothing in the between but getting wenches with child, wronging the ancientry, stealing, fighting.

William Shakespeare *The Winter's Tale*, III:3

29 Far too good to waste on children.

George Bernard Shaw (1856–1950) Irish dramatist and critic. *10,000 Jokes, Toasts, and Stories* (L. Copeland)

30 Live as long as you may, the first twenty years are the longest half of your life.

Robert Southey (1774–1843) British poet. *The Doctor*, Ch. 130

31 Proficiency at billiards is proof of a misspent youth.

Herbert Spencer (1820–1903) British philosopher. Attrib.

32 I looked younger than 26. I looked 17, and I had acne, and that doesn't help instil confidence in seasoned film crews.

Steven Spielberg (1946–) US film director. *New Yorker*, 1994

33 No wise man ever wished to be younger.

Jonathan Swift (1667–1745) Anglo-Irish priest, satirist, and poet. *Thoughts on Various Subjects, Moral and Diverting*

34 Young people ought not to be idle. It is very bad for them.

Margaret Thatcher (1925–) British politician and prime minister. *The Times*, 1984

35 'Smart Juniors,' said Polly to himself, 'full of Smart Juniosity. The Shoveacious Cult.'

H. G. Wells (1866–1946) British writer. *The History of Mr Polly*, Pt. III, Ch. 1

ZOLA, EMILE

(1840–1902) French novelist. His first successful novel, *Thérèse Raquin* (1867), was followed by the 20-novel series *Les Rougon-Macquart* (1871–93). *Nana* (1880) and *Germinal* (1885) were later successes. His open letter *J'accuse* (1898), supporting Dreyfus, led to his exile in England followed by a hero's return after Dreyfus was cleared.

1 Don't go on looking at me like that, because you'll wear your eyes out.

La Bête humaine, Ch. 5

2 *J'accuse.*
I accuse.

Title of an open letter to the French President, denouncing the French army's conduct in the Dreyfus affair. *L'Aurore*, 13 Jan 1898

3 Truth is on the march; nothing can stop it now.

Referring to the Dreyfus scandal. Attrib.

4 Do you need a damn God and his paradise to make you happy? Can't you make your own happiness on earth all by yourselves?

Germinal, Pt. III, Ch. 3

5 She defended herself, not on account of any sense of rebellion, but only with the passive resignation of all girls who come under the male thumb at an early age.

Germinal, Pt. IV, Ch. 3

6 It dawned on him that indignation was rather old fashioned.

Nana, Ch. 3

7 Venus was decomposing.

Nana, Ch. 14

8 A passion for her body, an ecstatic admiration of her satin skin and the supple lines of her figure, kept her serious, attentive and absorbed in her love of herself.

Nana, Ch. 7

KEYWORD INDEX

A

Aaron A.'s rod BIBLE, 108
abandon A. hope, all ye who enter DANTE ALIGHIERI, 2; HELL, 2
abashed A. the devil…felt how awful goodness is MILTON, J, 47
A. the devil stood GOOD, 13
abated the agony is a. MACAULAY, T, 18; PRECOCITY, 3
Abbey Who lied in the chapel /Now lies in the A. BYRON, 39
abdominal nine out of ten a. swellings PREGNANCY, 6
Abdul A. the Bulbul Amir ANONYMOUS, 98; COURAGE, 2
abed Not to be a. after midnight BED, 11; SHAKESPEARE, 339
aberration sodomite had been a temporary a. HOMOSEXUALITY, 12
abhorrence my heart's a. BROWNING, R, 52; HATE, 2
abide A. with me; fast falls the eventide RELIGION, 64
abideth now a. faith, hope, charity BIBLE, 38; CHARITY, 7
abilities From each according to his a. MARX, K, 3; MARXISM, 11
Great a. are not requisite for an Historian HISTORIANS, 4; JOHNSON, S, 61
ability a.…is capacity to act wisely INTELLIGENCE, 13; WHITEHEAD, A, 2
A young Scotsman of your a. BARRIE, J, 9; BRITISH, 2
distressed by his want of a. CONFUCIUS, 13; SUPERIORITY, 5
One should oblige everyone to…one's a. LA FONTAINE, J, 3; PRUDENCE, 9
to every man according to his several a. BIBLE, 417
woman's a. to stick to a job DETERMINATION, 25
abnormal she dislikes the a. NORMALITY, 1; STEIN, G, 3
abolish Don't be snobbish, we seek to a. CLASS, 25
to a. the death penalty EXECUTION, 19
abolished The state is not 'a.', it withers away COMMUNISM, 5
war can only be a. through war CHINA, 18; MAO TSE-TUNG, 4
abortion I will not give a woman a pessary to cause a. MEDICINE, 37
The greatest destroyer of peace is a. FAMILY, 57
abortions A. will not let you forget ABORTION, 3
Abou Ben Adhem A. (may his tribe increase!) DREAMS, 8
Abraham A.'s bosom BIBLE, 333; POVERTY AND WEALTH, 3
abroad A. is unutterably bloody FOREIGNERS, 2
an honest man sent to lie a. for…his country DIPLOMACY, 32
I don't hold with a. LANGUAGE, 17
know something of his own country…before he goes a. STERNE, L, 9; TRAVEL, 40
recurrent question about a. is TRAVEL, 31
Absalom A. hanged in an oak BIBLE, 484
O A., my son BIBLE, 485
absence A. from whom we love COWPER, W, 8; SEPARATION, 3
A. is to love ABSENCE, 6; LOVE, 46
A. makes the heart grow fonder ABSENCE, 4
shall I abide /In this dull world, which in thy a. is /No better than a sty LOSS, 6
they could shoot me in my a. BEHAN, B, 3; JUSTICE, 2
total a. of humour COLETTE, S, 1; HUMOUR, 12
treacherous air /Of a. ABSENCE, 10; WORDSWORTH, W, 23
absent Long a. ABSENCE, 1; PROVERBS, 265
when thou art a. I am sad LOVE, 120
absolute For Fascism the State is a. FASCISM, 11
he is the A. – she is the Other BEAUVOIR, S, 5
the more a. silence of America ENGLAND, 30; LAWRENCE, D, 24
The sovereign is a. ROYALTY, 36
absolutes unbelievable universe…there are no a. BUCK, P, 1
Absolutism A. tempered by assassination RUSSIA, 13
absolved a. from all duty to his country MARRIAGE, 118; PEACOCK, T, 10
absorbing Death was a. LEE, L, 2
abstinence a. from spirituous liquors ABSTINENCE, 7
The few bad poems…created during a. ABSTINENCE, 8
vices…require moderate use rather than total a. VICE, 7
abstract *a. reasoning concerning quantity or number* PHILOSOPHY, 3
She is a. femininity WOMEN, 55
absurd All art deals with the a. ART, 25; MURDOCH, I, 1
His work presents the feeling of the *A.* CAMUS, A, 1
I have…taken his side when a. men have condemned him FREEDOM, 60
something rather a. about the past BEERBOHM, M, 3; PAST, 2
There is nothing so a. PHILOSOPHERS, 2
Absurdism The Humphrey Bogart of A. CAMUS, A, 3
Absurdist why A. plays take place in No Man's Land THEATRE, 1
abundant a. shower of curates BRONTE, C, 7
abuse If it is a. FRIENDS, 15; SHERIDAN, R, 3
the more dangerous the a. BURKE, E, 25; POWER, 8
Whipping and a. are like laudanum CRUELTY, 6; PUNISHMENT, 27; STOWE, H, 3
You *may* a. a tragedy CRITICISM, 26; JOHNSON, S, 59
abusive to accuse someone of trying to be funny is highly a. HUMOUR, 22
Academe And seek for truth in the groves of A. EDUCATION, 43; HORACE, 24
Academy last words which I should pronounce in this A. ARTISTS, 21
The A. would not accept the reality of meteorites until 1803 SCIENCE, 1
accelerator You just press the a. to the floor and steer left SPORT AND GAMES, 44
accent a. of one's birthplace lingers HOMESICKNESS, 5; ROCHEFOUCAULD, 23
accept I will not a. if nominated POLITICIANS, 116
acceptable let the words of my mouth…be alway a. in thy sight PSALMS, 10
the a. face of capitalism CAPITALISM, 8
acceptance the degree of a. and authority which Mao has acquired MAO TSE-TUNG, 1
accessible artist…a. is self-destructive ARTISTS, 1
accessory The camera…an a. to untruth PHOTOGRAPHY, 4
accident A. n. An inevitable occurrence ACCIDENTS, 1
a. with a contraceptive ADAMS, D, 11
A hole is the a. THRIFT, 11
good action…found out by a. GOOD, 9; LAMB, C, 18
'There's been an a.' they said INSENSITIVITY, 3
accidental A. and fortuitous concurrence of atoms CHANCE, 5
accidentally A. GOVERNMENT, 39; TALLEYRAND, 2
A. shot by his gamekeeper ANONYMOUS, 70
accidents A. will happen IMPERFECTION, 1; PROVERBS, 8
A. will occur CONTRACEPTION, 5; DICKENS, C, 17
chapter of a. CHESTERFIELD, P, 18; MISFORTUNE, 9
season with lots of a. SPORT AND GAMES, 40
accommodated better a. than with a wife SOLDIERS, 13
accomplished An a. man to his finger-tips EXPERTS, 4; HORACE, 46
accord My cousin Francis and I are in perfect a. AGREEMENT, 1
according judged every man a. to their works JUDGMENT, 4
accountant run away from the circus to become an a. MAJOR, J, 2
accuracy A racing tipster…Hitler's level of a. HITLER, A, 7
accurate No woman should ever be quite a. about her age AGE, 99; WILDE, O, 34
accurs'd think themselves a. they were not here SHAKESPEARE, 137
accuse A. not Nature, she hath done her part MILTON, J, 50; RESPONSIBILITY, 11
I a. ACCUSATION, 4; ZOLA, 2
accused Never make a defence…before you be a. ACCUSATION, 3
accustomed become a. to no one governing LENIN, V, 5; SOCIALISM, 17
I will start to get a. to it MUSIC, 50
ace someone else was about to play the a. CRITICISM, 19
aches My heart a. KEATS, J, 35; MELANCHOLY, 8
achieve no man…hath lived…to a. that I have done ACHIEVEMENT, 12; MALORY, T, 2
those who a. something HUXLEY, A, 31; SELF-CONFIDENCE, 3
To a. great things ACHIEVEMENT, 14
achieved Nothing great was ever a. EMERSON, R, 7; ENTHUSIASM, 4
achievement do not let so great an a. suffer from…legality LAW, 24

It's a tremendous a., but it isn't easy to work with British Rail EUROPE, 13
aching an a. void COWPER, W, 14; NOSTALGIA, 7
acquaintance a good friend, but bad a. FRIENDS, 3
auld a. be forgot BURNS, R, 4; FRIENDSHIP, 12
first an a. LOVE AND FRIENDSHIP, 2
hope our a. may be a long 'un DICKENS, C, 47
act A. of God...*something which no reasonable man could have expected* HERBERT, A, 8
art of acting is not to a. ACTING, 14
Can't a.. Can't sing ACTORS, 11
Can't a., can't sing, slightly bald ACTING, 3
I cannot a. ACTING, 24
last a. crowns the play PLAYS, 11
More of an a. than an actress BANKHEAD, T, 1
no reference to fun in any A. of Parliament HERBERT, A, 4; PLEASURE, 15
The A. of God designation ACCIDENTS, 2
the second a. and the child's throat CHILDREN, 26; CRITICISM, 16
they didn't a. like actors ACTORS, 10
They didn't a. like people SALINGER, J, 5
to conceal the fact that the players cannot a. ACTING, 1
acting A. is the expression of a neurotic impulse ACTING, 5
A. is...the lowest of the arts ACTING, 17
The art of a. consists ACTING, 18
The danger chiefly lies in a. well EXCELLENCE, 2
action *A. will furnish belief* BELIEF, 6
Chi Wen Tzu always thought three times before taking a. CONFUCIUS, 2
Liberty of a. FREEDOM, 18
lust in a. LUST, 10; SHAKESPEARE, 372
man...unable to decide a general principle of a. POLITICIANS, 114
No a. is in itself good or bad ACTION, 10
Suit the a. to the word ACTION, 11; SHAKESPEARE, 96
The true men of a....are...the scientists AUDEN, W, 7
The unmotivated a. SPONTANEITY, 2
thought three times before taking a. CAUTION, 10
true men of a....the scientists SCIENTISTS, 2
actions A. speak louder PROVERBS, 11; WORDS, 2
active foreigners take too a. a hand in our affairs RUSSIA, 21
actor a. is something less than a man ACTORS, 5
a.....qualifications, including no money ACTORS, 9
An a.'s a guy who ACTORS, 4
Condemn the fault and not the a. of it PUNISHMENT, 23
easier to get an a. to be a cowboy ACTING, 12
hard for an a. to open his gob ACTORS, 3
Like a dull a. now FAILURE, 9; SHAKESPEARE, 60
actors A. should be treated like cattle ACTORS, 8
Never meddle with play-a. CERVANTES, M, 18
send me some good a. – cheap PRAYER, 5
actress More of an act than an a. BANKHEAD, T, 1
She was always a star...intermittently a good a. BANKHEAD, T, 2
acts And yet the order of the a. is planned DESTINY, 17
He who desires but a. not ACTION, 7; BLAKE, W, 26
Adam A.'s ale ALCOHOL, 2; PROVERBS, 12
A. was but human PERVERSITY, 6; TWAIN, M, 15
grant that the old A. in this Child BOOK OF COMMON PRAYER, 21
Oh, A. was a gardener GARDENS, 8; KIPLING, R, 13
When A. delved CLASS, 5
adamant the silvery a. walls of life's exclusive city DEATH, 97; LAWRENCE, D, 10
addiction a. of political groups to ideas GALBRAITH, J, 3; POLITICS, 40
Every form of a. is bad JUNG, C, 5
prisoners of a. and...prisoners of envy MATERIALISM, 14
the terminal point of a. is...damnation AUDEN, W, 5; SIN, 2
Addison give his days and nights to the volumes of A. ADDISON, J, 1
address Old age is...crossed off names in an a. book AGE, 19
addresses A....conceal our whereabouts SAKI, 2
Three a. always inspire confidence WILDE, O, 32
adieu a., kind friends, a. ANONYMOUS, 1; PARTING, 1
A.! my native shore BYRON, 9; DEPARTURE, 4
adjectives tell the substantives from the a. POLITICS, 73
Adler A. will always be Jung PUNS, 25
Adlestrop I remember A. ENGLAND, 51; MEMORY, 26
administration a. must be entrusted to experts GOVERNMENT, 45
admiral good to kill an a. EXAMPLE, 9; VOLTAIRE, 7
I have not been on a ship...they still call me 'A.' INSULTS, 3
salutes the A. of the Pacific ARROGANCE, 10
The A. of the Atlantic salutes the A. of the Pacific WILHELM II, 3
admiration Beauty stands /In the a....of weak minds BEAUTY, 33; MILTON, J, 54
admire a greater fool to a. him ADMIRATION, 3
Not to a. ADMIRATION, 12; POPE, A, 38
one cannot possibly a. them POVERTY, 43; WILDE, O, 53
The English instinctively a. ENGLISH, 4; TALENT, 1
admired Few men have been a. by their servants ADMIRATION, 10; MONTAIGNE, M, 8
admiring the cure for a. the House of Lords BAGEHOT, W, 2; HOUSES OF PARLIAMENT, 3
admit refuse to a. that I am more than fifty-two AGE, 8
ado much a. about nothing when the a. is about himself EGOTISM, 10; TROLLOPE, A, 4
the heathen make much a. PSALMS, 27
adolescence Acting engenders...qualities that are best left way behind in a. ACTING, 11
a man suffering from petrified a. BEVAN, A, 3; INSULTS, 19
infancy, childhood, a. and obsolescence AGE, 58
maturity is only a short break in a. AGE, 40
Adonais I weep for A. MOURNING, 14; SHELLEY, P, 3
I weep for A. – he is dead POETS, 53
adopt all wanted to a. me in some way PLATH, S, 1
adores he a. his maker DISRAELI, B, 18
The ignorant man always a. IGNORANCE, 16
adorned as a bride a. for her husband BIBLE, 473
adornment What time he can spare from the a. of his person NEGLECT, 4
adrenal larger cerebrums and smaller a. glands MENCKEN, H, 5; WAR, 106
ads He watched the a. /And not the road NASH, O, 6
adult A child becomes an a. when RIGHT, 2; SZASZ, T, 4
His a. life resembled his childhood SARTRE, J, 1
The a. subterfuge INNOCENCE, 15
the larger their a. clientele PSYCHIATRY, 24
What is an a. AGE, 14; BEAUVOIR, S, 1
adultery and gods a. ADULTERY, 1; BYRON, 19
between infancy and a. YOUTH, 2
commit a. at one end ADULTERY, 3
I've committed a. in my heart ADULTERY, 2
rather be taken in a. than in provincialism FASHION, 8; HUXLEY, A, 7
the Tasmanians, who never committed a. ADULTERY, 5; MAUGHAM, W, 1
thou shalt not commit a. BIBLE, 115; GOD, 12
would have constituted a. SMALLNESS, 3
adulthood a....now eat dessert without eating her vegetables CHILDREN, 3
adults Problem children tend to grow up into problem a. SOCIETY, 10
The value of marriage is...that children produce a. MARRIAGE, 61
advance Every great a. in science SCIENCE, 26
if civilisation is to a....it must be through...women PANKHURST, E, 3
advanced years behind the a. countries PROGRESS, 24
advantage a. of time and place...is half a victory WAR, 58
him who desires his own a. not harm another BUDDHA, 2
not necessarily to Japan's a. DEFEAT, 8; WORLD WAR II, 33
The a. of doing one's praising BUTLER, S, 26; PRAISE, 6
you have the a. of me MARX, G, 16; SUPERIORITY, 9
advantages Wealth is not without its a. GALBRAITH, J, 1; WEALTH, 22
adventure coming together of man and wife...should be a fresh a. STOPES, M, 5
extravagance...thrift and a. THRIFT, 6
Marriage is the only a. open to the cowardly MARRIAGE, 163; VOLTAIRE, 26
To die will be an awfully big a. BARRIE, J, 5; DEATH, 31
adventures A good critic...narrates the a. of his mind CRITICS, 5; FRANCE, A, 7
adversity a. doth best discover virtue BACON, F, 8; MISFORTUNE, 4
advertised dosed her children with every specific which was publicly a. DRUGS, 6
Wealth...must be a. GALBRAITH, J, 2; OSTENTATION, 3
advertisement the worst a. for Socialism is its adherents CHRISTIANITY, 50; ORWELL, G, 27
advertisers as the a. don't object to MEDIA, 15

advice A. is seldom welcome CHESTERFIELD, P, 12
a....poised between the cliché TACT, 6
nothing so freely as a. ROCHEFOUCAULD, 16
Parents can only give good a. FRANK, A, 7
to hear...valuable or even earnest a. from my seniors THOREAU, H, 10
woman seldom asks a. ADDISON, J, 16; WOMEN, 9
you will have no need of my a. FASHION, 1
advocaat a., a drink made from lawyers ALCOHOL, 28; EUROPE, 7
advocate the soul of a martyr with the intellect of an a. BAGEHOT, W, 10; POLITICIANS, 43
aeroplane a. is valuable...destroys men and women EQUALITY, 6; FLYING, 1; WAR, 17
aeroplanes century of a. deserves its own music MUSIC, 20
Aesculapius we owe a cock to A. LAST WORDS, 83; SOCRATES, 9
Aesop prettily devised of A. BACON, F, 58; CONCEIT, 3
aesthetic the degree of my a. emotion CRITICISM, 7; CRITICS, 1
afar a. and asunder PARTING, 4
affair The great a. is to move STEVENSON, R, 7; TRAVEL, 42
affairs tide in the a. of men OPPORTUNITY, 19; SHAKESPEARE, 161
affectation Universities incline wits to sophistry and a. BACON, F, 65; EDUCATION, 10
affection a. is too strong a word POLITICS, 98
affections A different taste in jokes is a...strain on the a. ELIOT, G, 6; HUMOUR, 13
affliction feed him with bread of a. IMPRISONMENT, 1
affluent The a., educated, liberated women of the First World APPEARANCE, 77
the a. society GALBRAITH, J, 4; LUXURY, 3
The a. society...made everyone dislike work IDLENESS, 10
afford purest treasure mortal times a. REPUTATION, 11; SHAKESPEARE, 294
afraid be not a. to do thine office EXECUTION, 26
Englishman...is a. to feel EDUCATION, 31; FORSTER, E, 2
Men not a. of God, a. of me POPE, A, 12; PRIDE, 8
they are not a. to die for democracy CHINA, 3
thou shalt not be a. for any terror by night PSALMS, 51
Whenever I look inside myself I am a. SELF, 12
Afric Where A.'s sunny fountains PLACES, 17
Africa more familiar with A. than my own body INNOCENCE, 10; ORTON, J, 1
something new out of A. NOVELTY, 8; PLINY THE ELDER, 4
When a white man in A. RACISM, 18
after-dinner a. speech should be like a lady's dress CLOTHES, 7
an a.'s sleep AGE, 80; SHAKESPEARE, 233
afterlife that the a. will be any less exasperating AFTERLIFE, 3; COWARD, N, 3
after-lives Lazarus was not /Questioned about a. DEATH, 86
afternoon could lose the war in an a. CHURCHILL, W, 35; OFFICERS, 4
I could have lost the war in an a. WAR, 85
Summer a. – summer a. JAMES, H, 15
against A. whom EGOTISM, 1
He said he was a. it SIN, 12
If...you can't tell...who's for you and who's a. you JOHNSON, L, 5
neither for nor a. institutions INDIFFERENCE, 7; WHITMAN, W, 4
This is a. fighting ever hereafter ROYALTY, 46
who's for you and who's a. you POLITICS, 57
Agamemnon I have looked upon the face of A. HISTORY, 25
Many brave men...before A.'s time OBLIVION, 1
age A child blown up by a. AGE, 14; BEAUVOIR, S, 1
A. cannot wither her SHAKESPEARE, 31
a. of chivalry is gone BURKE, E, 9; EUROPE, 2
A. only matters when one is ageing OLD AGE, 77; PICASSO, P, 9
A. seldom arrives smoothly or quickly OLD AGE, 82
A. shall not weary them MEMORIALS, 6
A. will bring all things MOLIERE, 8; PRUDERY, 3
A. will not be defied AGE, 10; BACON, F, 42
an a. in which useless knowledge KNOWLEDGE, 25
And now in a. I bud again HERBERT, G, 4; OLD AGE, 53
an old a. of cards OLD AGE, 78; POPE, A, 44
a sign of a. if you feel like the day after the night before OLD AGE, 13
A tart temper never mellows with a. CHARACTER, 12
at my a. I have to hold on to something OLD AGE, 26
At twenty years of a. AGE, 43; FRANKLIN, B, 8
Cool'd a long a. in the deep-delved earth ALCOHOL, 46; KEATS, J, 36
Crabbed a. and youth AGE, 82; YOUTH, 27
Damn the a.. I'll write for antiquity LAMB, C, 21; POSTERITY, 8
do not necessarily improve with a. AGE, 50
Do you think at your a., it is right CARROLL, L, 6; OLD AGE, 28
Drives my green a. THOMAS, D, 10
gift of perpetual old a. OLD AGE, 106; WILDE, O, 69
He hath not forgotten my a. GOD, 48; SOUTHEY, R, 5
He prays for a long life, and he fears an old a. OLD AGE, 3
how I have achieved such a ripe a. LONGEVITY, 5
I prefer old a. to the alternative OLD AGE, 31
I summon a. /To grant youth's heritage AGE, 21; BROWNING, R, 49
It is...at my a. I now begin to see things as they really are LAST WORDS, 35
lady of a certain a. AGE, 24; BYRON, 32; INSULTS, 25
Lo, Hudled up, together Lye /Gray A., Grene youth, White Infancy ANONYMOUS, 53
Man arrives as a novice at each a. of his life AGE, 26
no a. between ten and three and twenty SHAKESPEARE, 352; YOUTH, 28
nothing in thy youth, how canst thou find any thing in thine a. AGE, 15; BIBLE, 87
not of an a., but for all time JONSON, B, 11
No woman should ever be quite accurate about her a. AGE, 99; WILDE, O, 34
Old-a., a second child OLD AGE, 32
Old a....gives us what we have earned OLD AGE, 25
old a. is...older than I am OLD AGE, 16
Old a. is the most unexpected OLD AGE, 103
Old a. is the most unexpected of all...things TROTSKY, L, 2
Old a. is the out-patients' department OLD AGE, 30
old a....the fear that it may go on too long OLD AGE, 101
Our parents' a....has produced us AGE, 53; HORACE, 37
Socialism...a. or a little money will not cure SOCIALISM, 8
Some people reach the a. of 60 OLD AGE, 54
The a. of chivalry is never past KINGSLEY, C, 11
Thou has nor youth nor a. AGE, 80; SHAKESPEARE, 233
treat...her a. with ambiguity AGE, 76
what a. takes away OLD AGE, 109; WORDSWORTH, W, 6
When men grow virtuous in their old a. POPE, A, 56; VIRTUE, 21
when Mozart was my a. AGE, 56
who tells one her real a. AGE, 100; WILDE, O, 59
Years hence, perhaps, may dawn an a. ARNOLD, M, 20; FUTURE, 2
aged a. diplomats...bored than for young men to die DIPLOMACY, 3
a man of about a hundred and ten who had been a. OLD AGE, 108; WODEHOUSE, P, 22
An a. man is but a paltry thing OLD AGE, 112
the beauty /Of an a. face OLD AGE, 27
ageing A....the only...way to live a long time LONGEVITY, 3
Age only matters when one is a. OLD AGE, 77; PICASSO, P, 9
Like so many a. college people ACADEMICS, 6; NABOKOV, V, 3
The a. man of the middle twentieth century OLD AGE, 56
agenda the a. winks at me THOMAS, G, 2
agent prime a. of all human perception COLERIDGE, S, 5; IMAGINATION, 1
ages His acts being seven a. HUMAN CONDITION, 25; SHAKESPEARE, 48
Our God, our help in a. past RELIGION, 95; WATTS, I, 6
Rock of a., cleft for me RELIGION, 89
the a. of other women AGE, 32
aggregate the a. of the recipes SCIENCE, 95
aggression the forces of a. against lawlessness QUAYLE, D, 7
aggressive a. competition is part of the human make-up SPORT AND GAMES, 27
aggressor whole world should be ranged against an a. POLITICS, 8
Agnes St A. Eve – Ah, bitter chill it was SEASONS, 9
agnostic rather a compliment to be called an a. HUMILITY, 3
agonies Thy friends are exultations, a., /And love WORDSWORTH, W, 63
agony a lonely spasm of helpless a. DEATH, 85
agree colours will a. in the dark BACON, F, 57; DIFFERENCE, 7
don't say you a. with me WILDE, O, 13
If two men on the same job a. BUSINESS, 40
those who a. with us ROCHEFOUCAULD, 24
Two of a trade can ne'er a. GAY, J, 6
agreeable I do not want people to be very a. AUSTEN, J, 30; NASTINESS, 2
My idea of an a. person DISRAELI, B, 11
agreement My people and I have come to an a. FREEDOM, 15

Whenever you accept our views we shall be in full a. INFLEXIBILITY, 1
agrees a person who a. with me DISRAELI, B, 11
agricultural the a. labourers…commute from London COUNTRYSIDE, 9; POWELL, A, 4
agriculture Sex…Every bit as interesting as a. SEX, 113
when the nation depended on a. for its wealth ECONOMICS, 19
aid One who is ill has…the duty to seek medical a. ILLNESS, 46
Aids stop them catching A.…the wife AIDS, 3; PROMISCUITY, 3
ail what can a. thee, knight at arms ILLNESS, 39; KEATS, J, 22
ailments our a. are the same ILLNESS, 67
ain't bet you a hundred bucks he a. in here FUNERALS, 5
air cat is a diagram and pattern of subtle a. CATS, 11; LESSING, D, 6
Get your room full of good a. LEACOCK, S, 4; LONGEVITY, 11
music in the a. MUSIC, 25
my spirit found outlet in the a. FLYING, 3
the castles I have, are built with a. DREAMS, 10; JONSON, B, 5
to the Germans that of the a. EUROPE, 18
waste its sweetness on the desert a. GRAY, T, 5; WASTE, 2
airplane The a. stays up because it doesn't have the time to fall SCIENCE, 100
airplanes a.…are wonderful things for other people to FLYING, 4
I feel about a. the way I feel about diets FLYING, 4
airth Let them bestow on every a. a limb EXECUTION, 13
aisle A.. Altar. Hymn MARRIAGE, 111; PUNS, 17
aitches We have nothing to lose but our a. CLASS, 33; ORWELL, G, 30
Alamein Before A. we never had a victory CHURCHILL, W, 15; WORLD WAR II, 24
alarm The tocsin you hear today is not an a. but an alert PATRIOTISM, 11
alarms confused a. of struggle and flight ARNOLD, M, 11; WAR, 11
albatross I shot the a. COLERIDGE, S, 27
Albert A. was merely a young foreigner ROYALTY, 107
ask me to take a message to A. DISRAELI, B, 42
that A. married beneath him COWARD, N, 24; CRITICISM, 15
alcohol A.…enables Parliament to do things at eleven ALCOHOL, 73; SHAW, G, 16
A. is like love ALCOHOL, 25
discovered that a. was a food ALCOHOL, 88; WODEHOUSE, P, 8
The sway of a. over mankind ALCOHOL, 41
alcoholic a. liquors have been used by the…best races ALCOHOL, 65
An a.…drinks as much as you do ALCOHOL, 80
An a. has been lightly defined DRUNKENNESS, 8
An a. is someone you don't like DRUNKENNESS, 27
Fitzgerald was an a. FITZGERALD, F, 1
ale a. from the Country of the Young KNOWLEDGE, 42; YEATS, W, 15
no more cakes and a. MERRYMAKING, 4; SHAKESPEARE, 341
the spicy nut-brown a. ALCOHOL, 58; MILTON, J, 18
ale-house jangled in every a. and tavern BIBLE, 531
alert The tocsin you hear today is not an alarm but an a. PATRIOTISM, 11
Alexander If I were not A. PRAISE, 2
Some talk of A., and some of Hercules ANONYMOUS, 73; HEROISM, 1; SOLDIERS, 1
Alfred school-miss A. vent her chaste delight TENNYSON, 2
Alfred Chicken Party Christchurch…the difference between the Tories and the A. POLITICS, 45
algebra Sir Isaac Newton…deep in a. and fluxions NEWTON, I, 2
What is a. exactly BARRIE, J, 6; MATHEMATICS, 2
Algerian And drink of my A. wine BEHAN, B, 9; INSULTS, 16
Alice A. – Mutton; Mutton – A. CARROLL, L, 37; INTRODUCTIONS, 1
Oh! don't you remember sweet A., Ben Bolt MEMORY, 9
alien amid the a. corn KEATS, J, 39
State socialism is totally a. SOCIALISM, 24; THATCHER, M, 27
alike so many million of faces…none a. APPEARANCE, 13; INDIVIDUALITY, 3
alimony Judges…in the matter of arranging a. MARRIAGE, 173
alive Bliss was it in that dawn to be a. FRENCH REVOLUTION, 11; WORDSWORTH, W, 41
he is no longer a. DEATH, 33
he shall save his soul a. BIBLE, 127
if I am a. DEATH, 69
needst not strive /…to keep a. KILLING, 4
nobody knew whether…he would be a. the next hour FRANK, A, 8
not one will still be a. in a hundred years' time MORTALITY, 22
Not while I'm a., he ain't POLITICIANS, 52
Thersites' body is as good as Ajax' /When neither are a. EQUALITY, 29
this earth, that bears thee dead, /Bears not a. so stout a gentleman LIFE AND DEATH, 29
We intend to remain a. MEIR, G, 6; SELF-PRESERVATION, 9
Whatever Wells writes is not only a. WELLS, H, 1
what matters is to come out a. SURVIVAL, 2
all A. for one, and one for a. UNITY, 8
A. good things ENDING, 1; PROVERBS, 33
a. our yesterdays LIFE, 86; SHAKESPEARE, 227
A.'s well ENDING, 2; PROVERBS, 38
a man, take him for a. in a. ADMIRATION, 17; ADMIRATION, 17; COMPLIMENTS, 30; COMPLIMENTS, 30
are you sure they are a. horrid AUSTEN, J, 14; NASTINESS, 1
'A was a man, take him for a. in a. SHAKESPEARE, 71
Christ is a., and in a. BIBLE, 20; CHRISTIANITY, 8
Damn you, Jack – I'm a. right SELFISHNESS, 3
Let there be work…for a. MANDELA, N, 10
Ripeness is a. ENDURANCE, 22; SHAKESPEARE, 194
'Tis a. thou art EQUALITY, 43; POPE, A, 7
allegiance Not bound to swear a. to any master FREEDOM, 25; HORACE, 13
allegory headstrong as an a. MALAPROPISMS, 6; SHERIDAN, R, 7
Allen Woody A. or me when we stop doing the jokes HUMOUR, 31
allergists a hive of a. LANGUAGE, 4
allergy What used to be merely an itch is now an a. PROGRESS, 1
alley she lives in our a. LOVE, 50
allies former a. had blundered NAZISM, 5
Thou hast great a. WORDSWORTH, W, 63
allowed I should never be a. out in private APOLOGIES, 2
all-round a wonderful a. man BEERBOHM, M, 20; INSULTS, 14
ally An a. has to be watched MISTRUST, 11; TROTSKY, L, 13
Almighty If the A. himself played the violin EGOTISM, 6; INSULTS, 61
almonds Don't eat too many a. COLETTE, S, 5; FOOD, 23
alms a. for oblivion SHAKESPEARE, 333; TIME, 52
alone A., a., all, all a. COLERIDGE, S, 31; SOLITUDE, 2
A. and palely loitering ILLNESS, 39; KEATS, J, 22
And we are left, or shall be left, a. DEFEAT, 18; WORDSWORTH, W, 52
better to be a. than in bad company FRIENDS, 17; WASHINGTON, G, 3
doctors don't like to leave people a. DOCTORS, 21
even the most powerful nation is no longer able to act a. EUROPE, 10
Hell is a. ELIOT, T, 5
I am here at the gate a. INVITATIONS, 5; TENNYSON, 56
I am the cat that walks a. BEAVERBROOK, M, 1; SELF-RELIANCE, 4
I hate to be a. BANKHEAD, T, 4; OBSESSIONS, 1
I want to be a. MISQUOTATIONS, 17; PRIVACY, 3
Lying a. and sobbing SORROW, 18
No poet…has…meaning a. ELIOT, T, 24
powerful but a. SOLITUDE, 16
She sleeps a. at last EPITAPHS, 1
strange paradox…need to be left a. HOSTAGES, 3
To be a. is the fate of all great minds GREATNESS, 11; SCHOPENHAUER, A, 1
Very well, a. DETERMINATION, 17; SELF-RELIANCE, 8
We perish'd, each a. COWPER, W, 6; DEATH, 52
We two a. will sing like birds i' the cage IMPRISONMENT, 10
woe to him that is a. when he falleth BIBLE, 69; FRIENDSHIP, 8
You come into the world a. HUMAN CONDITION, 16
Alph Where A., the sacred river, ran COLERIDGE, S, 14; PLEASURE, 10
Alpha A. and Omega BIBLE, 459
alphabet could eat a. soup POPULAR MUSIC, 19
the remaining twenty-two letters of the a. LEARNING, 15; ORWELL, G, 6
also You a. OVID, 6
altar Aisle. A.. Hymn MARRIAGE, 111; PUNS, 17
altars struggled in poverty to build these a. RELIGION, 82
alternative a need to create an a. world FICTION, 4; FOWLES, J, 4
I prefer old age to the a. OLD AGE, 31
there is no a. THATCHER, M, 21
alway lo, I am with you a. BIBLE, 433

always Minorities...are almost a. in the right MINORITY, 3; SMITH, S, 13
am I a. not what I a. APPEARANCES, 32
I A. THAT I A. BIBLE, 107
in the infinite I A. COLERIDGE, S, 5; IMAGINATION, 1
I think therefore I a. THINKING, 4
Amaryllis sport with A. in the shade MILTON, J, 24; PLEASURE, 24
amateur a. is an artist who supports himself with outside jobs ARTISTS, 6
America...is the prize a. nation AMERICA, 45; GERMANY, 9; WILSON, W, 5
In love...the a. status LOVE, 80
the last time that I will take part as an a. FUNERALS, 2
amateurs a disease that afflicts a. CHESTERTON, G, 25
nation of a. BRITISH, 13
amaze How vainly men themselves a. MARVELL, A, 1; VICTORY, 15
amazing Pretty a. ADMIRATION, 5
ambiguity treat...her age with a. AGE, 76
ambition A., Distraction, Uglification, and Derision CARROLL, L, 15; EDUCATION, 21
A. is the grand enemy of all peace AMBITION, 19
A. should be made of sterner stuff AMBITION, 22; SHAKESPEARE, 157
A writer's a. should be POSTERITY, 7
Cromwell was a man in whom a. had...suspended,... religion CROMWELL, O, 1
Every man has...an a. to be a wag HUMOUR, 18; JOHNSON, S, 32
Let not A. mock GRAY, T, 2; POVERTY, 16
Vaulting a., which o'er-leaps itself AMBITION, 23; SHAKESPEARE, 211
What argufies pride and a. MORTALITY, 4
ambitious an a. man has as many masters AMBITION, 13; LA BRUYERE, J, 15
Amblongus A. Pie LEAR, E, 6; NONSENSE, 24
ambrosia Emerson is one who lives...on a. EMERSON, R, 2
ambulance Knocked down a doctor? With an a. ACCIDENTS, 9
Amen sound of a great A. MUSIC, 49
America A....based on the dreams of spinsters AMERICA, 35
A. became top nation HISTORY, 31; SELLAR, W, 7
A.!.../God shed His grace on thee AMERICA, 4
A. has brought us McDonald's and horror movies RUSSIA, 24
A....has gone directly from barbarism to degeneration AMERICA, 9; INSULTS, 36
A. is a country of young men AMERICA, 15; EMERSON, R, 25
A. is a large, friendly dog AMERICA, 39
A. is just ourselves AMERICA, 1; ARNOLD, M, 4
A. is...the great Melting-Pot AMERICA, 47
A. is the only idealistic nation AMERICA, 44; WILSON, W, 12
A....is the prize amateur nation AMERICA, 45; GERMANY, 9; WILSON, W, 5
A.'s freedom BUSH, G, 3
A.'s really only a kind of Russia BURGESS, A, 2; FUTURE, 6
ask not what A. will do for you PATRIOTISM, 25
behind the discovery of A. JEWS, 16
declares unconditional war on poverty in A. POVERTY, 23
first come to pass in the heart of A. AMERICA, 14; EISENHOWER, D, 5
His foreparents came to A. EQUALITY, 16
my A.! my new-found-land DONNE, J, 12
The business of A. is business AMERICA, 12; BUSINESS, 7
The crude commercialism of A. WASHINGTON, G, 2
the greatest that we owe to the discovery of A. SMOKING, 14
the more absolute silence of A. ENGLAND, 30; LAWRENCE, D, 24
The national dish of A. AMERICA, 33
Vietnam was lost in the living rooms of A. WAR, 105
what makes A. what it is AMERICA, 36; STEIN, G, 4
when we think of thee, O A. AMERICA, 40; WALPOLE, H, 7
Why will A. not reach out...to Russia DIPLOMACY, 11
woman governs A. AMERICA, 29
American A. heiress wants to buy a man MATERIALISM, 19; MCCARTHY, M, 3
A. system of rugged individualism AMERICA, 21
an A. citizen...attacking an ex-secretary of state CHURCHILL, W, 1
An A. is either a Jew, or an anti-Semite SARTRE, J, 5
as spiteful to me in the A. press as the Soviet press NEWSPAPERS, 15
capitalism...the process whereby A. girls turn into A women CAPITALISM, 6; HAMPTON, C, 3
I am willing to love all mankind, *except an A.* JOHNSON, S, 123
If I were an A., as I am an Englishman PATRIOTISM, 33; PITT THE ELDER, 6
intelligence of the A. people INTELLIGENCE, 8
It hasn't taken Winston long to get used to A. ways ACHESON, D, 3; REPARTEE, 1
I was born an A. PATRIOTISM, 43; WEBSTER, D, 6
Let's talk sense to the A. people ENDURANCE, 25; STEVENSON, A, 4
the feminization of the white European and A. is already far advanced LEWIS, W, 3
the greatest A. friend we have ever known CHURCHILL, W, 25; POLITICIANS, 68
truth, justice, and the A. way HEROISM, 2
We are all A. at puberty NATIONALITY, 12; WAUGH, E, 28
We are not about to send A. boys nine or ten thousand miles DIPLOMACY, 19
Americanism hyphenated A. PATRIOTISM, 34; ROOSEVELT, T, 9
McCarthyism is A. POLITICS, 76
There can be no fifty-fifty A. PATRIOTISM, 35; ROOSEVELT, T, 10
Americans A. are people who prefer the Continent TRAVEL, 30
A. have been conditioned to respect newness UPDIKE, J, 3
because A. won't listen to sense KEYNES, J, 9
Good A., when they die, go to Paris AMERICANS, 1
No one can kill A. and brag REAGAN, R, 8
the great silent majority of my fellow A. – I ask for your support SUPPORT, 7
the matter with A. CHESTERTON, G, 44
when good A. die they go to Paris WILDE, O, 57
amiable how a. are thy dwellings PSALMS, 44
It destroys one's nerves to be a. every day DISRAELI, B, 15; MARRIAGE, 64
amis *Changez vos a.* DE GAULLE, C, 9; FRIENDS, 7
Amis concentrate hard on someone...called Martin A. INSIGNIFICANCE, 5
ammunition Praise the Lord and pass the a. WAR, 63
amo *Odi et a.* LOVE AND HATE, 2
Amor *A. vincit insomnia* FRY, C, 5; LOVE, 74
A. vincit insomnia SLEEP, 14
amorality the butcher-like a. of...men SOLZHENITSYN, A, 3
amorous the silk stockings and white bosoms...excite my a. propensities LUST, 6
the silk stockings and white bosoms of your actresses excite my a. propensities JOHNSON, S, 46
amplified I'm being a. by the mike CHESTERTON, G, 47; OBESITY, 5
amputate 'Thank God they had to a.!' SASSOON, S, 8; WAR, 145
am'rous dire offence from a. causes springs POPE, A, 48; RESULTS, 5
amuse A talent to a. TALENT, 3
amused how to be a. rather than shocked AGE, 22; BUCK, P, 4
I was *very* much a. ROYALTY, 114; VICTORIA, 5
one has to be very old before one learns how to be a. AGE, 22; BUCK, P, 4
We are not a. ROYALTY, 113; VICTORIA, 12
You'll be A. by its Presumption DRINKS, 21
amusement all literature is written for the a. of *men* TOLKIEN, J, 2
amusing Any a. deaths DEATH, 41
anaesthetics Three natural a. SLEEP, 19
analogy Though a. is often misleading ANALOGY, 1; BUTLER, S, 17
analysed Everything has been discussed and a. BOOKS, 2
analysis historian fits a man for psychological a. PSYCHOLOGY, 15
in a. with a strict Freudian SUICIDE, 1
the profession of historian fits a man for psychological a. SARTRE, J, 11
Anarchist I am a Tory A. POLITICS, 9
anarchy a well-bred sort of emotional a. CLASSIFICATION, 2; LAWRENCE, D, 16
grieved under a *democracy*, call it *a.* GOVERNMENT, 17; HOBBES, T, 6
Anathema A. Maranatha BIBLE, 43
anatomists There is no counting the names, that surgeons and a. give KNOWLEDGE, 35
We a. are like the porters DOCTORS, 39
anatomy A. is destiny DESTINY, 12
A. is to physiology MEDICINE, 28
he has studied a. and dissected at least one woman MARRIAGE, 19
in a. it is better to have learned and lost LEARNING, 13

My a. is only part of an infinitely complex organisation CARTER, A, 6
ancestor I am my own a. ANCESTRY, 1
ancestors a. on either side of the Battle of Hastings ANCESTRY, 4
when his half-civilized a. were hunting the wild boar JEWS, 3
ancestry I can trace my a. back to a…globule ANCESTRY, 2; GILBERT, W, 25
nation is a society united by a delusion about its a. INGE, W, 10
ancient an a. Mariner COLERIDGE, S, 24
beyond these a. texts if we want progress RELIGION, 71
with the a. is wisdom BIBLE, 228; OLD AGE, 23; WISDOM, 5
anecdotage man fell into his a. DISRAELI, B, 9; OLD AGE, 42
anesthesiologists whiff of a. LANGUAGE, 4
angel An a. writing in a book of gold DREAMS, 8
A. of Death has been abroad WAR, 29
A. of the Lord came down CHRISTMAS, 22
a. to pass, flying slowly THINKING, 5
in action, how like an a. MANKIND, 56; SHAKESPEARE, 85
in comparison with which…I am a A. DICKENS, C, 20; EVIL, 10
In heaven an a. is nobody in particular IMPORTANCE, 4; SHAW, G, 25
Is man an ape or an a. DISRAELI, B, 28; EVOLUTION, 13
Look Homeward, A. HOME, 13
This was the A. of History WORLD WAR II, 28
woman yet think him an a. LOVE, 166; THACKERAY, W, 4
You may not be an a. LOVE, 68
angels A. can fly CHESTERTON, G, 36; SERIOUSNESS, 1
fools rush in where a. fear to tread HASTE, 8; POPE, A, 29
gave you manna…a.' bread BIBLE, 97
have entertained a. unawares BIBLE, 189
I…am on the side of the a. DISRAELI, B, 28; EVOLUTION, 13
Its visits, /Like those of a. DEATH, 39
Not Angles, but a. ENGLISH, 17
One more devils'-triumph and sorrow for a. BROWNING, R, 32; DAMNATION, 1
People are not fallen a. CRITICISM, 33; LAWRENCE, D, 42
Tears such as a. weep MILTON, J, 36; SORROW, 17
the tongues of men and of a. BIBLE, 38; CHARITY, 7
thou madest him lower than the a. PSALMS, 3
angels' food man did eat a. PSALMS, 42
anger A. supplies the arms VIRGIL, 4
fierce /Juno's never-forgetting a. VIRGIL, 5
Grief and disappointment give rise to a. EMOTION, 3; HUME, D, 7
he that is slow to a. is better than the mighty BIBLE, 452; SELF-CONTROL, 1
Juno's never-forgetting a. ENDURANCE, 29
Angles Not A., but angels ENGLISH, 17
Angli the *Saxones*, *A.*, and *Iutae* ENGLISH, 6
angling A. is somewhat like poetry FISHING, 2; WALTON, I, 2
A. may be said to be…like the mathematics FISHING, 3; WALTON, I, 1
lovers of virtue…and go a-A. FISHING, 5; WALTON, I, 6
We may say of a. as Dr Boteler said of strawberries FISHING, 4; WALTON, I, 4
Anglo-Catholic Becoming an A. must…be a sad business CATHOLICISM, 15
Anglo-Saxon Come in, you A. swine BEHAN, B, 9; INSULTS, 16
those are A. attitudes CARROLL, L, 33; ENGLISH, 11
angry A. Young Man REBELLION, 12
cannot be a. at God BEAUVOIR, S, 8
not one of those 'a. feminists' ANGER, 7
The man who gets a.…in the right way…is commended ARISTOTLE, 2
anguish drinking deep of that divinest a. BRONTE, E, 6
every 'mental' symptom is a veiled cry of a. PSYCHIATRY, 30
Making love is the sovereign remedy for a. SEX, 68
angular an oblong a. figure HUMOUR, 47; LEACOCK, S, 6
animal 'Are you a. – or vegetable – or mineral?' CARROLL, L, 35
He was into a. husbandry SEX, 70
information vegetable, a. and mineral GILBERT, W, 38; KNOWLEDGE, 19
Man is a gaming a. LAMB, C, 7; SPORT AND GAMES, 24
man is and will always be a wild a. MANKIND, 21
Man is an intellectual a. HAZLITT, W, 5; INTELLECT, 7
Man is a noble a. BROWNE, T, 12; MANKIND, 13
man is…a religious a. BURKE, E, 11; RELIGION, 19
Man is a social a. SOCIETY, 21
Man is by nature a political a. ARISTOTLE, 6; POLITICS, 6
Man is the only a.…on friendly terms with the victims…he eats BUTLER, S, 20; HYPOCRISY, 7
MAN, n. An a. so lost in rapturous contemplation MANKIND, 9
This a. is very bad ANONYMOUS, 100; SELF-PRESERVATION, 4
true to your a. instincts ANIMALISM, 3; LAWRENCE, D, 31
Whenever you observe an a. closely ANIMALS, 10
animality its own a. either objectionable or funny HUMOUR, 20; LEWIS, C, 2
animals All a. are equal EQUALITY, 26; ORWELL, G, 7
all a. were created…for the use of man ANIMALS, 20; PEACOCK, T, 4
all there is to distinguish us from other a. MANKIND, 7
A. are such agreeable friends ANIMALS, 13; ELIOT, G, 9
a.…know nothing…of what people say about them ANIMALS, 24; VOLTAIRE, 28
But if we stop loving a. LOVE, 156; SOLZHENITSYN, A, 5
differs in no respect from the ovules of other a. EVOLUTION, 7
give my wisdom and experience to a. CONSERVATION, 1
I could…live with a. ANIMALS, 27; WHITMAN, W, 7
love a. and children too much LOVE, 141
Man, when perfected, is the best of a. MANKIND, 4
My music…understood by children and a. MUSIC, 61; STRAVINSKY, I, 4
Never work with a. or children ACTING, 2
paragon of a. MANKIND, 56; SHAKESPEARE, 85
some a. are more equal than others EQUALITY, 26; ORWELL, G, 7
The a. went in one by one ANONYMOUS, 78
There are two things for which a. are…envied ANIMALS, 24; VOLTAIRE, 28
Wild a. never kill for sport HUNTING, 4
animated a. with the soul of a Briton VOLTAIRE, 2
Anna great A.! whom three realms obey DRINKS, 18; POPE, A, 49
annals short and simple a. of the poor GRAY, T, 2; POVERTY, 16
Anne Move Queen A.? Most certainly not MEMORIALS, 18
Annie for bonnie A. Laurie LOVE AND DEATH, 1
annihilating A. all that's made MARVELL, A, 2; OBLIVION, 3
annihilation No a. REPRESENTATION, 3
anno A. domini…the most fatal complaint DEATH, 80
announced be a. as…'Doreen' BLEASDALE, A, 2
annual A. income twenty pounds DICKENS, C, 13; ECONOMICS, 8
annuity Buy an a. cheap DICKENS, C, 27; MONEY, 20
annus it has turned out to be an 'a. horribilis' ROYALTY, 61
anomaly Poverty is an a. to rich people BAGEHOT, W, 11; HUNGER, 2
Anon I would…guess that A.…was often a woman WOMEN, 144
another A. year! – a. deadly blow DEFEAT, 18; WORDSWORTH, W, 52
He who would do good to a. BLAKE, W, 16; GOOD, 2
I would have given you a. CHIVALRY, 6
Life is just one damned thing after a. LIFE, 50
may always be a. reality REALITY, 3
No man can…condemn a. BROWNE, T, 7
answer a. a fool according to his folly BIBLE, 456; FOOLISHNESS, 10
a. ought to be to his precious little question JOURNALISM, 38
a. to Life ADAMS, D, 7
A timid question will…receive a confident a. SHYNESS, 2
But a. came there none CARROLL, L, 29; GREED, 7
give a. as need requireth BIBLE, 82; LEARNING, 3
I do not a. questions like this without being paid MASCULINITY, 1
more than the wisest man can a. EXAMINATIONS, 1
The a.…is blowin' in the wind DYLAN, B, 2; FREEDOM, 14
the inquisitive mind can…receive no a. JOHNSON, S, 127; PHILOSOPHY, 6
What *is* the a. LAST WORDS, 85
where no one asks, no one needs to a. JUNG, C, 1; PURPOSE, 5
would not stay for an a. BACON, F, 56; TRUTH, 10
answers I can give as many a. as you want, and be totally honest MEDIA, 8
antagonistic the most a. to the Victorian age WRITERS, 97
antan *les neiges d'a.* NOSTALGIA, 27
anthology a. is like all the plums and orange peel BOOKS, 36
A well chosen a. is a complete dispensary of medicine MEDICINE, 32
antic dance an a. hay MARLOWE, C, 7
anticipation the intelligent a. of facts JOURNALISM, 15
anti-clerical it makes me understand a. things BELLOC, H, 20; CLERGY, 1

a. to what is decent CLASS, 20
displeased with *a.*, call it *oligarchy* GOVERNMENT, 17; HOBBES, T, 6
If human beings could be propagated…a. would be… sound ARISTOCRACY, 13
riff-raff apply to what is respectable…a. to what is decent HOPE, A, 6
Unlike the male codfish…the British a. is ARISTOCRACY, 22; WODEHOUSE, P, 21
aristocrat the gentleman from both the artist and the a. CLASS, 51; WAUGH, E, 15
aristocratic To be a. in Art ART, 24
to distinguish…the a. class from the Philistines ARNOLD, M, 8; CLASS, 4
arithmetic different branches of A. CARROLL, L, 15; EDUCATION, 21
Music is the a. of sounds MUSIC, 19
ark an a. of bulrushes BIBLE, 103
into the a., two and two BIBLE, 158
arm An a. /Rose up from…the lake TENNYSON, 20
disarm the strong and a. the weak INJUSTICE, 5
Don't carry away that a. till I have…my ring PRACTICALITY, 5
Human on my faithless a. AUDEN, W, 20; SLEEP, 6
soon think of taking the a. of an elm tree THOREAU, H, 2
Armageddon a place called…A. BIBLE, 467
armchair She fitted into my biggest a. OBESITY, 18; WODEHOUSE, P, 13
arm'd a. with more than complete steel JUSTICE, 17; MARLOWE, C, 12
armed We should be a. FEMINISM, 26; O'BRIEN, E, 4
Armenteers A mademoiselle from A. FRANCE, 17
armies ignorant a. clash by night ARNOLD, M, 11; WAR, 11
not a.…but flocks of sheep CERVANTES, M, 5; DELUSION, 3
armistice an a. for twenty years WORLD WAR I, 10
a short a. with truth BYRON, 25; TRUTH, 16
dream of…another wild A. day WAR, 68
armour a. of light BOOK OF COMMON PRAYER, 4
Conceit is the finest a. CONCEIT, 12; JEROME, J, 2
Prayer makes the Christian's a. bright COWPER, W, 15; PRAYER, 14
arms Anger supplies the a. VIRGIL, 4
A. control so easily becomes an incantation WEAPONS, 6
Building up a. is not a substitute for diplomacy NUCLEAR WEAPONS, 20
For the theatre one needs long a. ACTING, 6
I never would lay down my a. PATRIOTISM, 33; PITT THE ELDER, 6
I sing of a. and the man ENDURANCE, 29; VIRGIL, 5
opening time in the Sailors A. PUBLIC HOUSES, 4; THOMAS, D, 22
So he laid down his a. HOOD, T, 2; PUNS, 10
army An a. is a nation within a nation ARMY, 5
An a. marches on its stomach FOOD, 55; NAPOLEON I, 14
Chief of the A. LAST WORDS, 59; NAPOLEON I, 15
contemptible little A. WAR, 184; WILHELM II, 4
her a. has had a glorious victory VICTORY, 14
If you don't want to use the a., I should like to borrow it LINCOLN, A, 9; SARCASM, 2
little ships of England brought the A. home BOATS, 8; WORLD WAR II, 30
no longer have an a. DEFEAT, 5
referred to a. uniforms as costumes REAGAN, R, 5
terrible as an a. with banners BIBLE, 496
The a. ages men sooner than the law ARMY, 8; WELLS, H, 7
The conventional a. loses if it does not win WAR, 93
Arnold A. is a dandy Isaiah ARNOLD, M, 2
around We're going a. WAR, 153
arrest arbitrary a. and expulsion SOLZHENITSYN, A, 1
My father didn't create you to a. me POLICE, 7
One does not a. Voltaire DE GAULLE, C, 10; RESPECT, 2
arrested Christ…would quite likely have been a. OPPRESSION, 3
arrive To travel hopefully is…better…than to a. ANTICIPATION, 7; STEVENSON, R, 26
arrogance ego fat on a. POLITICIANS, 96
the a. you have when you are 20 AGE, 31
arrow Every a.…feels the attraction of earth AMBITION, 15; LONGFELLOW, H, 5
I, said the Sparrow, /With my bow and a. NURSERY RHYMES, 72
I shot an a. into the air CHANCE, 4; LONGFELLOW, H, 3
the a. that flieth by day PSALMS, 51
arrows whose teeth are spears and a. PSALMS, 36
arse a politician is an a. CUMMINGS, 6; POLITICIANS, 3
Sit on your a. for fifty years INDIFFERENCE, 4; MACNEICE, L, 2
arsenal a. of democracy DEMOCRACY, 21; ROOSEVELT, F, 13
arson A., after all, is an artificial crime WELLS, H, 12
art A burglar who respects his a. CRIME, 5
All a. deals with the absurd ART, 25; MURDOCH, I, 1
All A. is quite useless ART, 40; WILDE, O, 45
An a. can only be learned BUTLER, S, 5; LEARNING, 5
an artist in the here and now of both life and a. CARTER, A, 1
any authentic work of a. must start an argument WEST, R, 3
A. and religion first; then philosophy SPARK, M, 10
A.…can go on mattering ART, 5
a. constantly aspires towards…music ART, 26
A. for a.'s sake ART, 8
A. for A.'s sake ART, 11; FORSTER, E, 4
A. has to move you ART, 14; DESIGN, 1
A. is a jealous mistress ART, 10; EMERSON, R, 4
A. is long, and Time is fleeting LONGFELLOW, H, 10; MORTALITY, 14
A. is not a mirror…but a hammer ART, 22
A. is not a pastime ART, 7
A. is not a special sauce ART, 18
a. is not a weapon ART, 15
A. is ruled…imagination IMAGINATION, 2
A. is the imposing of a pattern ART, 38; WHITEHEAD, A, 3
A. is the most intense mode ART, 41; WILDE, O, 55
A. is…the transmission of feeling ART, 35; TOLSTOY, L, 13
a. is to give life a shape ANOUILH, J, 5; ART, 2
A. never expresses anything ART, 39; WILDE, O, 16
a. of acting is not to act ACTING, 14
a. of pleasing consists HAZLITT, W, 14; PLEASURE, 14
aspires…to the condition of a. CONRAD, J, 5; LITERATURE, 2
Bullfighting is the only a. HEMINGWAY, E, 4; SPORT AND GAMES, 18
Desiring this man's a. DISCONTENT, 8; SHAKESPEARE, 362
Dying /is an a. DEATH, 121; PLATH, S, 3
excellence of every a. is its intensity KEATS, J, 54
Fine a. is that in which the hand ART, 31; RUSKIN, J, 13
great parables…but false a. CRITICISM, 33; LAWRENCE, D, 42
half a trade and half an a. INGE, W, 8; LITERATURE, 10
home-making…should be looked on as an a. HOUSEWORK, 5
I don't want a. for a few MORRIS, W, 3
I doubt that a. needed Ruskin RUSKIN, J, 2; STOPPARD, T, 13
industry without a. is brutality ART, 30; RUSKIN, J, 4
Insurrection is an a. REVOLUTION, 13; TROTSKY, L, 6
It's clever but is it a. ART, 16; KIPLING, R, 7
learnt the a. of upstaging ACTING, 15
Medicine is a natural a. MEDICINE, 84
Mr Goldwyn…you are only interested in a. ART, 32; MONEY, 46; SHAW, G, 47
nature is the a. of God BROWNE, T, 3; NATURE, 1
Nature's handmaid, a. DRYDEN, J, 20; NATURE, 9
Politics is not a science…but an a. POLITICS, 20
princes learn no a. truly, but…horsemanship HORSES, 7
Rules and models destroy genius and a. HAZLITT, W, 23; RULES, 2
sombre enemy of good a. BABIES, 2; CONNOLLY, C, 10
the a. of the possible POLITICS, 23
The last and greatest a. – the a. to blot DRYDEN, J, 2
They say princes learn no a. truly, but…horsemanship JONSON, B, 8
To be aristocratic in A. ART, 24
True ease in writing comes from a. POPE, A, 26; WRITING, 39
wonderful case of nature imitating a. ACTORS, 31; WILDE, O, 62
work of a. must start an argument ART, 37
art-attacks Everything is dying of a. ARTS, 2
arteries A man is as old as his a. OLD AGE, 100
arteriosclerosis young people seem to develop mental a. YOUTH, 15
artery the a. ceases to beat DEATH, 76
artful The a. Dodger DICKENS, C, 37; NAMES, 2
article It all depends upon that a. there SOLDIERS, 18; WELLINGTON, 3
articulateness seduce each other by their a. WRITING, 4
artificial All things are a. BROWNE, T, 3; NATURE, 1
nothing so a. as sinning nowadays LAWRENCE, D, 26; SIN, 18
artist amateur is an a. who supports himself with outside jobs ARTISTS, 6
an a. in the here and now of both life and art CARTER, A, 1
a. is someone who produces things that people don't need ARTISTS, 9
As an a., a man has no home NIETZSCHE, F, 7; PARIS, 5
Beware of the a. who's an intellectual FITZGERALD, F, 11
God is really only another a. GOD, 44; PICASSO, P, 7

No a. is ahead of his time ART, 12
only one position for an a. anywhere THOMAS, D, 32; WALES, 3
Remember I'm an a. ARTISTS, 3
the a. is forgotten ARTISTS, 18
the gentleman from both the a. and the aristocrat CLASS, 51
the quality that distinguishes the gentleman from both the a. and the aristocrat WAUGH, E, 15
What is an a. ARTISTS, 7
What is an a. STOPPARD, T, 11
artistic a. temperament…afflicts amateurs CHESTERTON, G, 25
There never was an a. period PHILISTINISM, 8; WHISTLER, J, 19
artists architects were a. ARTISTS, 13
A. are not engineers of the soul ART, 15
Great a. have no country NATIONALITY, 9
My major advice to young black a. WALKER, A, 12
The a. retired. The British remained WHISTLER, J, 15
You a. produce something that nobody needs ARTISTS, 10
art-loving an A. nation PHILISTINISM, 8; WHISTLER, J, 19
arts If all the a. aspire to the condition of music SANTAYANA, G, 14; SCIENCE, 82
Murder…one of the Fine A. MURDER, 6
Our company only sponsor the a. FOOTBALL, 1
rustics…bringing up their…offspring to the liberal a. EDUCATION, 60
secret of the a. is to correct nature VOLTAIRE, 15
ascertainable the a. laws of the science of life are approximative MEDICINE, 10
ashamed few people who are not a. of having been in love ROCHEFOUCAULD, 8
I am a. of confessing INNOCENCE, 1
not a. of having been in love LOVE, 134
to see them not a. REGRET, 27; SWIFT, J, 16
We are not a. of what we have done PANKHURST, C, 4; PRIDE, 7
ashes a. of Napoleon INDIFFERENCE, 6; WELLINGTON, 24
Asia There is too much A. KIPLING, R, 19; PLACES, 20
ask a., and it shall be given BIBLE, 375; SUCCESS, 7
A. a silly question PROVERBS, 63
A. no questions CURIOSITY, 1; PROVERBS, 64
those things which we a. faithfully BOOK OF COMMON PRAYER, 7
To labour and not a. for any reward SELFLESSNESS, 3
Who could a. for anything more CONTENTMENT, 4
asks where no one a., no one needs to answer JUNG, C, 1; PURPOSE, 5
asleep The devil is a. LUCK, 11
to dream you gotta still be a. DYLAN, B, 14
you fall a. halfway through her name INSULTS, 17
asp wicked a. of Twickenham POPE, A, 1
aspect Meet in her a. BEAUTY, 16; BYRON, 40
aspens Willows whiten, a. quiver TENNYSON, 42; WEATHER, 27
aspicious two a. persons MALAPROPISMS, 1; SHAKESPEARE, 275
aspirations The young have a. AGE, 77; SAKI, 12
aspires art constantly a. towards…music ART, 26
a.…to the condition of art CONRAD, J, 5; LITERATURE, 2
aspirin if tranquillizers could be bought as easily and cheaply as a. DRUGS, 9
aspirings The soul hath not her generous a. LAMB, C, 26; SMOKING, 23
aspirins I was able to live on the money I saved on a. OCCUPATIONS, 8
ass An unlettered king is a crowned a. MONARCHY, 1
a strong a. BIBLE, 181
every a. thinks he may kick at him WRITERS, 79
the law is a a. DICKENS, C, 38; LAW, 12
the Lord opened the mouth of the a. BIBLE, 438
with the jawbone of an a. KILLING, 2
assassination Absolutism tempered by a. RUSSIA, 13
A. has never changed ASSASSINATION, 3; DISRAELI, B, 29
A.…the extreme form of censorship ASSASSINATION, 7; SHAW, G, 39
assemblance Care I for the…a. of a man APPEARANCES, 26; SHAKESPEARE, 125
assemblies Kings govern by…a. only when MONARCHY, 13
assembly an ingenious a. of portable plumbing MANKIND, 39
assertions Pure mathematics consists entirely of a. MATHEMATICS, 19; RUSSELL, B, 14
asset the greatest a. a head of state can have SLEEP, 38; WILSON, H, 12
asshole Americans use drugs as…license' to be an a. DRUGS, 17
assigned purpose of God and the doom a. DESTINY, 28; TENNYSON, 58
associate good must a. BURKE, E, 20; UNITY, 7
I…like to a. with…priests BELLOC, H, 20; CLERGY, 1
assure a. him that he'd live tomorrow DESTINY, 19; RABELAIS, F, 6
asthma A. is a disease that has practically the same symptoms as passion PASSION, 1
astonished a. at my own moderation MODERATION, 6
you are merely a. WORDS, 36
astonishment a little more reverence…and not so much a. SINGING, 3
Dear Sir, Your a.'s odd ANONYMOUS, 15; EXISTENCE, 1
astound Austria will a. the world DIPLOMACY, 28
astronauts The a.!…Rotarians in outer space SPACE, 10; VIDAL, G, 4
astronomer Bach is like an a. MUSICIANS, 11
astronomy A. teaches the correct use ASTRONOMY, 4; LEACOCK, S, 5
asunder afar and a. PARTING, 4
let no man put a. BOOK OF COMMON PRAYER, 29
let not man put a. MARRIAGE, 30
asylum I have myself spent nine years in a lunatic a. PSYCHIATRY, 4
the absence from Jerusalem of a lunatic a. RELIGION, 39
world is…like a lunatic a. LLOYD GEORGE, D, 19; MADNESS, 26
asylums lunatic a.…the stately homes STATELY HOMES, 7; WOOLF, V, 7
the a. can hold the sane people MADNESS, 45
ate I a. faster FOOD, 46
atheism Every luxury…a., breast-feeding INDULGENCE, 2; ORTON, J, 4
miracle to convince a. ATHEISM, 2; BACON, F, 9
atheist an a. half believes a God ATHEISM, 13; YOUNG, E, 4
An a.…has no invisible means of support ATHEISM, 6
an a. if the king were SERVILITY, 4
An a. is one point ATHEISM, 1; PROVERBS, 50
an a. who trembles in the haunted corridor WRITERS, 99
A pious man…would be an a. if the king were LA BRUYERE, J, 1
Hardy became a sort of village a. HARDY, T, 1
He was an embittered a. ATHEISM, 10; ORWELL, G, 12
he was no a. PLEASURE, 6
I am an a.…thank God ATHEISM, 4
scepticism kept her from being an a. SARTRE, J, 16; SCEPTICISM, 5
very *chic* for an a. MEMORIALS, 13; RUSSELL, B, 5
Athens A. arose EUROPE, 22; SHELLEY, P, 9
A. holds sway over all Greece INFLUENCE, 11
men of A.…ye are too superstitious SUPERSTITION, 6
athirst my soul is a. for God PSALMS, 26
athletes Women can be great a. SPORT AND GAMES, 23
athletic The only a. sport I ever mastered JERROLD, D, 7; SPORT AND GAMES, 20
athletics a. as inferior forms of fox-hunting WAUGH, E, 20; WOMEN, 140
Atlantic The Admiral of the A. ARROGANCE, 10; WILHELM II, 3
the dread of hostesses on both sides of the A. OBITUARIES, 8
to have the East come to the A. WORLD WAR II, 29
atmosphere a. has been poisoned SPORT AND GAMES, 26
A to B She ran…emotions from A. PARKER, D, 30
atom carbon a. possesses certain exceptional properties SCIENCE, 56
how the a. is split SCIENCE, 18
nearer to the a. than the stars SCIENCE, 31
The a. bomb is a paper tiger MAO TSE-TUNG, 9; NUCLEAR WEAPONS, 14
There is no evil in the a. NUCLEAR WEAPONS, 22; STEVENSON, A, 5
They split the a. by firing particles at SCIENCE, 47
atomic The way to win an a. war NUCLEAR WEAPONS, 5
atoms fortuitous concurrence of a. CHANCE, 5
atone a. for the sins of your fathers HORACE, 36; INJUSTICE, 6
atrocities His sickness has created a. that are repellent PICASSO, P, 2
atrophy Music begins to a. POUND, E, 3
attached men become a. even to Widnes ENGLAND, 50; TAYLOR, A, 8
attachment His a. to…his friends…was thoroughgoing and exemplary JEFFERSON, T, 1
attack A. is the best form CONFLICT, 1; PROVERBS, 72
love until after the first a. SCEPTICISM, 1
more than a. the scourge of unemployment UNEMPLOYMENT, 1
situation excellent. I shall a. WAR, 62

attacks Her frontal a. on old taboos STOPES, M, 2
attainments rare a.…but…can she spin WOMAN'S ROLE, 8
attention a. to the inside…contempt for the outside BOOKS, 16; CHESTERFIELD, P, 14
take his a. away from the universe PRAYER, 15
attentive always a. to the feelings of dogs DOGS, 6
attic A. wit HUMOUR, 23; PLINY THE ELDER, 1
brain a. stocked with all the furniture that he is likely to use DOYLE, A, 12; KNOWLEDGE, 16
glory of the A. stage ARNOLD, M, 42; LIFE, 7
Attila A. the Hen THATCHER, M, 5
attitude his a. of a king in exile DE GAULLE, C, 1
the largest scope for change still lies in men's a. to women BRITTAIN, V, 2
attitudes Anglo-Saxon a. CARROLL, L, 33; ENGLISH, 11
attorney the gentleman is an *a.* INSULTS, 72; JOHNSON, S, 80
attraction Every arrow…feels the a. of earth AMBITION, 15; LONGFELLOW, H, 5
The chief a. of military service ARMY, 4; TOLSTOY, L, 9
attractive if they are in the least a. CAMPBELL, R, 4; TRANSLATION, 2
seldom faithful if they are in the least a. UNFAITHFULNESS, 5
The most a. sentences are not perhaps the wisest LANGUAGE, 48; THOREAU, H, 4
audacity a. of elected persons REVOLUTION, 19; WHITMAN, W, 11
Auden A. was someone you could laugh-at-with POETS, 54; SPENDER, S, 6
high watermark…of Socialist literature is W. H. A. AUDEN, W, 2
to write like Tennyson…rather than Eliot or A. BETJEMAN, J, 2
We have one poet of genius in A. AUDEN, W, 1
W. H. A., a sort of gutless Kipling ORWELL, G, 29; SOCIALISM, 21
audience a. was a disaster WILDE, O, 70
I know two kinds of a. AUDIENCES, 6
the a. want to be surprised…by things that they expect PLAYS, 3
the a. was a disaster PLAYS, 17
think of the a. when I'm directing AUDIENCES, 8
whether the a. thinks you are crying ACTING, 4
auld a. acquaintance be forgot BURNS, R, 4; FRIENDSHIP, 12
for a. lang syne BURNS, R, 5; FRIENDSHIP, 13
aunt Charley's a. from Brazil PLACES, 35
aunts bad a. and good a. FAMILY, 65; WODEHOUSE, P, 4
Aussie a dinkum hard-swearing A. PATRIOTISM, 19
Austen Jane A. SCOTT, W, 5; WRITERS, 85
Jane A.'s books, too, are absent from this library AUSTEN, J, 3
Miss A.'s novels…sterile in artistic invention WRITERS, 49
Miss A.…the prettiest, silliest, most affected, husband-hunting /butterfly WRITERS, 73
More can be learnt from Miss A. AUSTEN, J, 1; WRITERS, 33
Austerlitz There rises the sun of A. NAPOLEON I, 7; WAR, 116
Australia guess…he was born in A. PLACES, 33; SHAW, G, 14
So you're going to A. MELBA, N, 4; PLACES, 24
Australian I'm going to write the Great A. Novel AMBITION, 28; WHITE, P, 4
Austria A. is Switzerland…with history added EUROPE, 17
A. will astound the world DIPLOMACY, 28
author An a. who speaks about his own books DISRAELI, B, 30; EGOTISM, 5
bad novel tells us…about its a. CHESTERTON, G, 24; NOVELS, 2
He is the richest a. that ever grazed JOHNSON, S, 60
Thou are my master and my a. VIRGIL, 2
authoress a.…whose books have set all London talking BRONTE, C, 2
authority a top hat to give him A. DOCTORS, 13
a. be a stubborn bear BRIBERY, 5; SHAKESPEARE, 356
A. forgets a dying king ROYALTY, 109; TENNYSON, 21
it can maintain a wise infidelity against the a. of his instructors EDUCATION, 49
man /Dress'd in a little brief a. MANKIND, 57; SHAKESPEARE, 230
No morality can be founded on a. MORALITY, 2
Nothing destroyeth a. so much BACON, F, 22; POWER, 5
place him in a. CHARACTER, 2
purge the land of…false a. ROYALTY, 25
The defiance of established a. REBELLION, 2
the degree of acceptance and a. which Mao has acquired MAO TSE-TUNG, 1
the highest a. for believing that the meek shall inherit the Earth HUMILITY, 12
authors A. are easy to get on with WRITERS, 14
much exposed to a. WELLINGTON, 5; WRITERS, 28
The faults of great a. COLERIDGE, S, 20
their a. could not endure being wrong CAMUS, A, 7; CRIME, 2
The reciprocal civility of a. JOHNSON, S, 19
The trouble with our younger a. is MAUGHAM, W, 29
autobiography a. is an obituary BIOGRAPHY, 2
autocracy maintain the principle of a. ROYALTY, 92
autocrat be an a.: that's my trade ROYALTY, 35
autograph give him my a. as a souvenir WORLD WAR II, 36
automobile Money differs from an a. GALBRAITH, J, 7; MONEY, 24
avarice rich beyond the dreams of a. WEALTH, 39
vanished before the a. and oppression of the white man OPPRESSION, 8
avenged the satisfaction of knowing that we are a. REVENGE, 21; TROLLOPE, A, 16
average a. American loves his family TWAIN, M, 1
no great compliment to say that a man is above the a. COMPLIMENTS, 19
Take the life-lie away from the a. man DELUSION, 4; IBSEN, H, 9
aves Beadsman, after thousand a. told KEATS, J, 10; PRAYER, 20
Avilion To the island-valley of A. AFTERLIFE, 11; TENNYSON, 25
avocado fat content of an a. DIETING, 8
avoidance The a. of taxes…still carries…reward KEYNES, J, 11; TAXATION, 7
avoiding Reading…ingenious device for a. thought READING, 6
Avon Sweet Swan of A. JONSON, B, 12; SHAKESPEARE, 12
a-waggle You must always be a. LAWRENCE, D, 3; LOVE, 101
awake At last a. BROWNING, R, 24; LIFE, 18
A.! for Morning in the Bowl of Night DAY, 5; FITZGERALD, E, 2
I dream when I am a. REALITY, 1
Onaway! A., beloved LONGFELLOW, H, 14
The lilies and roses were all a. LOVE, 163; TENNYSON, 57
We're very wide a., /The moon and I APPEARANCES, 19; GILBERT, W, 29
aware wasn't even a. of the Year of the Family FAMILY, 18
away Over the hills and far a. GAY, J, 3; LOVE, 75
Take the soup a. FOOD, 37
the big one that got a. MARRIAGE, 60
aweary I gin to be a. of the sun SHAKESPEARE, 228; WORLD-WEARINESS, 8
awful Abashed the devil…felt how a. goodness is MILTON, J, 47
And felt how a. goodness is GOOD, 13
a. things that rabbits ANONYMOUS, 84
awfulness by its very a. MARRIAGE, 147; STEVENSON, R, 23
awoke I a. one morning BYRON, 45; FAME, 8
axe his keener eye /The a.'s edge did try EXECUTION, 22; MARVELL, A, 4
let the great a. fall PUNISHMENT, 22
Lizzie Borden took an a. ANONYMOUS, 52; MURDER, 1
axioms A. in philosophy are not a. KEATS, J, 59; PHILOSOPHY, 8
the world can be expressed in…arguments…a. and theorems THEORY, 5
axis a. of the earth sticks out visibly through…every town or city NATURE, 19
This Berlin–Rome connection is…an a. WORLD WAR II, 39
aye A., and what then COLERIDGE, S, 4; PROOF, 3

B

baa B., b., black sheep NURSERY RHYMES, 4
God ha' mercy on such as we, /B.! Yah! Bah DEBAUCHERY, 8; KIPLING, R, 12
Babbitt one thing wrong with the B. house HOME, 7
babbl'd 'a b. of green fields DEATH, 144; LAST WORDS, 81
babblings vain b. SCIENCE, 8
Babel B.; because the Lord did there confound the language BIBLE, 164; LANGUAGE, 8
the tower of B. should have got language all mixed up LANGUAGE, 49; VOLTAIRE, 32
babes out of the mouth of…b. and sucklings PSALMS, 3
babies bit the b. in the cradles ANIMALS, 7; BROWNING, R, 42
If men had to have b. BIRTH, 9
Other people's b. BABIES, 6; HERBERT, A, 1
putting milk into b. BABIES, 1; CHURCHILL, W, 62
War will never cease until b. MENCKEN, H, 5; WAR, 106
wretched b. don't come until BABIES, 4

You breed b. and you eat chips FOOD, 73
baby Anybody can shock a b. SIMPLICITY, 7
Don't throw the b. out HASTE, 1; PROVERBS, 122
Every b. born into the world BABIES, 3; DICKENS, C, 33
Hanging head downwards between cliffs of bone, was the b. BIRTH, 2
hanging the b. on the clothes line to dry INNOVATION, 2; RUNYON, D, 7
Hush-a-bye, b., on the tree top NURSERY RHYMES, 19
my b. at my breast SHAKESPEARE, 39; SUICIDE, 32
no new b. in the womb of our society LAWRENCE, D, 37; RUSSIA, 11
Rock-a-bye b. on the tree top SLEEP, 7
The b. bounced gently off the wall of her uterus PREGNANCY, 1
Walking My B. Back Home LOVE, 171
Babylon B. the great BIBLE, 469
By the waters of B. AMERICA, 40; PSALMS, 70
How many miles to B. NURSERY RHYMES, 17
Bach B. is like an astronomer MUSICIANS, 11
J. S. B. BEECHAM, T, 6; CRITICISM, 4
Music owes as much to B. MUSICIANS, 15
you play B. *your* way INSULTS, 81; MUSIC, 34
bachelor A b.…dies like a beggar MARRIAGE, 102
B.'s fare MARRIAGE, 151; SWIFT, J, 11
die a b. MARRIAGE, 133
Never trust…a b. too near TRUST, 5
Now I am a b., I live by myself ANONYMOUS, 63
bachelors crushing tax on b. FEMINISM, 50
reasons for b. to go out ELIOT, G, 8; WOMEN, 51
bacillus Oh, powerful b. SCIENCE, 48
back any of you at the b. who do not hear me AUDEN, W, 28; DISABILITY, 1
But at my b. I always hear AGE, 61; MARVELL, A, 10
Either b. us or sack us SUPPORT, 3
I sit on a man's b. HYPOCRISY, 22; TOLSTOY, L, 14
the book that ran me down while I sat with my b. to it WALKER, A, 1
the credit belongs to the boys in the b. rooms GRATITUDE, 1
turn your b. upon the world LONGFELLOW, H, 9; PERFECTION, 5
Will ye no come b. again RETURN, 4
Winston's b. RETURN, 1
backing b. into the limelight LAWRENCE, T, 2
backlash violent b. against feminism FEMINISM, 55
backs With our b. to the wall WAR, 74; WORLD WAR I, 12
back-stairs Drama is the b. of the intellect THEATRE, 4
backward In a country economically b., the proletariat can take power earlier CAPITALISM, 19
Bacon B. discovered the art of making reading-glasses SCIENTISTS, 12
When their lordships asked B. BRIBERY, 1
bacteriologists staff of b. LANGUAGE, 4
bad a b. man must have brains GOOD AND EVIL, 5
a b. novel tells us the truth about its author CHESTERTON, G, 24; NOVELS, 2
A b. penny LUCK, 1; PROVERBS, 1
a brave b. man CROMWELL, O, 2; OBITUARIES, 4
a good friend, but b. acquaintance BYRON, 23
A truth that's told with b. intent BLAKE, W, 6; TRUTH, 13
b. book is as much a labour to write as a good one HUXLEY, A, 29
B. girls don't have the time BANKHEAD, T, 13; DIARIES, 2
b. taste is better than no taste BENNETT, A, 9; TASTE, 2
Defend the b. against the worse DECLINE, 4
Galsworthy was a b. writer GALSWORTHY, J, 3
Housework isn't b. in itself HOUSEWORK, 7
It is as b. as b. can be FOOD, 40; JOHNSON, S, 149
Mad, b., and dangerous to know BYRON, 3
never was a b. peace FRANKLIN, B, 16; WAR AND PEACE, 7
nothing either good or b. SHAKESPEARE, 84; THINKING, 17
Nothing so b. but it might have been worse OPTIMISM, 7; PROVERBS, 317
put up with b. things TOLERANCE, 8; TROLLOPE, A, 11
resolved to do something b. DECISION, 4; MCCARTHY, M, 1
she was a very b. cook SNOBBERY, 11
so much b. in the best of us ANONYMOUS, 88; GOOD AND EVIL, 1
strong antipathy of good to b. POPE, A, 11; PROVOCATION, 2
the b. die late DEFOE, D, 1; GOOD AND EVIL, 4
the name of…obstinacy in a b. one STERNE, L, 6; STUBBORNNESS, 4
There's no such thing as a b. Picasso INFERIORITY, 4; PICASSO, P, 5
they are…surprised at hearing of a good action and never of a b. one KEATS, J, 70
two legs b. ORWELL, G, 4
When b. men combine BURKE, E, 20; UNITY, 7
when I'm b. I'm better SEX, 128; WEST, M, 17
when she was b. she was horrid VIRTUE AND VICE, 5
badge Red B. of Courage COURAGE, 8
badly If you want to do a thing b. EFFORT, 6; USTINOV, P, 2
badness the b. of her b. VIRTUE AND VICE, 1
bag b. and baggage VIOLENCE, 8
Bailey When will you pay me? /Say the bells of Old B. LONDON, 2; NURSERY RHYMES, 41
baker The butcher, the b., /The candlestick-maker NURSERY RHYMES, 49
Bakewell no Joan B., but you're fairly tart HUMOUR, 48
balance The b. of power POWER, 30; WALPOLE, R, 5
balanced Food is an important part of a b. diet FOOD, 45
balances thou art weighed in the b., and art found wanting BIBLE, 52; JUDGMENT, 1
bald being b. – one can hear snowflakes APPEARANCE, 22
Can't act, can't sing, slightly b. ACTING, 3
Falklands…a fight between two b. men over a comb WAR, 23
baldness a light form of premature b. AGE, 41
There is more felicity on the far side of b. AGE, 85; APPEARANCE, 66
There's one thing about b. APPEARANCE, 30
Baldwin not quite forget…B. till we're out of debt POLITICIANS, 88
Balfour Mr B.'s Poodle HOUSES OF PARLIAMENT, 15; LLOYD GEORGE, D, 8
Balham She has a Rolls body and a B. mind STUPIDITY, 11
Balkans some damned silly thing in the B. WAR, 22
ball Any clown can play with the b. FOOTBALL, 16
B.…how very singular BEECHAM, T, 3; NAMES, 1
Hitler /Has only got one b. WORLD WAR II, 2
ballet it takes more than one to make a b. SUPPORT, 8
balloon the moon's /a b. CUMMINGS, 1; MOON, 3
ballot The b. is stronger than the bullet DEMOCRACY, 14; LINCOLN, A, 11
ballots employers…only like b. so long as you lose them STRIKES, 6
balm wash the b. from an anointed king MONARCHY, 24; SHAKESPEARE, 298
banal Frumpish and b. ROYALTY, 91
banality The fearsome…*b. of evil* EVIL, 3
bananas b. or oranges, the Americans would not go AMERICANS, 2
hanging around like clumps of b. INSULTS, 78
Banbury Ride a cock-horse to B. Cross NURSERY RHYMES, 46
bandage Religion…the wound, not the b. RELIGION, 75
bandages to walk around…with only a few light b. on BEAUTY, 37; RUNYON, D, 1
bands Brass b. are all very well in their place BEECHAM, T, 9; MUSIC, 7
ladies who pursue Culture in b. CULTURE, 4
banes Here lie Willie Michie's b. BURNS, R, 9
bang bigger b. for a buck NUCLEAR WEAPONS, 25
Not with a b. but a whimper ELIOT, T, 10; ENDING, 3; FUTURE, 8
banish to b.…the dark divisive clouds of Marxist socialism MARXISM, 16; THATCHER, M, 30
banishment bitter bread of b. PUNISHMENT, 25
bank b. and shoal of time ENDING, 6; SHAKESPEARE, 210
better that a man should tyrannize over his b. balance KEYNES, J, 6; TYRANNY, 8
I cried all the way to the b. CRITICISM, 36
the b. was mightier than the sword LIBERALISM, 3
the man who broke the B. at Monte Carlo WEALTH, 25
bankrupt B. of Life DRYDEN, J, 6; WORLD-WEARINESS, 1
banks cashiers of the Musical B. BUTLER, S, 2; MONEY, 13
Ye b. and braes BURNS, R, 24; NATURE, 2
banned any book should be b. BOOKS, 52; CENSORSHIP, 13; WEST, R, 5
banner A b. with the strange device, /Excelsior AMBITION, 14; LONGFELLOW, H, 7
banners terrible as an army with b. BIBLE, 496
banqueting beggar by b. upon borrowing BORROWING, 2
baptise mockery to allow women to b. RELIGION, 23
Baptist For good all round business work, I should have preferred a B. PROTESTANTISM, 7; WELLS, H, 11
bar an olfactory b. WELLS, H, 6

Into the B. ALCOHOL, 86
no moaning of the b. DUTY, 8; TENNYSON, 12
though hell should b. the way DETERMINATION, 19
When I went to the B. as a very young man GILBERT, W, 17; LAW, 17
Barabbas B. was a publisher PUBLISHING, 4
now B. was a robber BIBLE, 266
Barbara Her name was B. Allen LOVE, 13
There was a fair maid dwellin', /.../Her name was B. Allen ANONYMOUS, 49
Barbarians society distributes itself into B., Philistines, and Populace AMERICA, 1; ARNOLD, M, 4
barbarity the...b. of war...forces men...to commit acts KEY, E, 7; WAR, 91
the English seem...to act with the b. of tyrants IRELAND, 26; SMITH, S, 2
barbarous *Paradise Lost*, is such b. trash MILTON, J, 3
the invention of a b. age MILTON, J, 28; POETRY, 43
bard This goat-footed b. KEYNES, J, 4; POLITICIANS, 95
bards Portraits of famous b. and preachers PAINTING, 19; THOMAS, D, 28
bare Our ingress.../Was naked and b. LIFE, 58; LONGFELLOW, H, 15
Pylons, those pillars /B. SPENDER, S, 2; TECHNOLOGY, 16
barefoot I still go b. DYLAN, B, 4
bargains rule for b. BUSINESS, 8; DICKENS, C, 26
barge The b. she sat in, like a burnish'd throne ADMIRATION, 15; COMPLIMENTS, 28
baritones b. are born villains in opera OPERA, 11
bark to hear the watch-dog's honest b. BYRON, 18; DOGS, 5
barking B. dogs ACTION, 1; PROVERBS, 78
b. mad about crime CRIME, 9
Barkis B. is willin' DICKENS, C, 12
Barnum the celebrated B.'s circus CHURCHILL, W, 44; POLITICIANS, 66
barrage chemical b. has been hurled against the fabric of life CARSON, R, 3; ECOLOGY, 2
barrel drowned in a b. of malvesye EXECUTION, 10
out of the b. of a gun CHINA, 20; MAO TSE-TUNG, 7; POWER POLITICS, 5
you won't intoxicate with one glass someone who has... drunk...a...b. CHEKHOV, A, 13; EXPERIENCE, 10
barren I am but a b. stock ROYALTY, 56
most b. country I have seen DISCOVERY, 5
barrenness quarrels which vivify its b. GREER, G, 4; LOVE, 81
barricade At some disputed b. DEATH, 136
barring a schoolboy's b. out POLITICS, 104; TENNYSON, 69
bar-rooms It brings men together in crowds and mobs in b. SOCIETY, 23; THOREAU, H, 7
bars Nor iron b. a cage IMPRISONMENT, 8
barter All government...is founded on compromise and b. BURKE, E, 14; COMPROMISE, 4
base doing good to b. fellows CERVANTES, M, 9; CHARITY, 13
It takes a certain courage...to be truly b. EVIL, 2
scorning the b. degrees /...he did ascend AMBITION, 21
Why brand they us /With b. PREJUDICE, 10
baseball as sensible as b. in Italian MENCKEN, H, 17; OPERA, 7
b. cap is just as valid as a felt hat FASHION, 9
based All progress is b. BUTLER, S, 11; EXTRAVAGANCE, 2; PROGRESS, 7
basement interviewing a faded female in a damp b. INSULTS, 57
basics time to get back to b. MAJOR, J, 11
basing b. morals on myth MORALITY, 16
Basingstoke teems with hidden meaning – like B. PLACES, 16
basket Have you ever taken anything out of the clothes b. CLEANNESS, 4
bastard all my eggs in one b. ABORTION, 11; REGRET, 14
Because I am a b. HEMINGWAY, E, 8; NASTINESS, 4
I hope you will not publicly call me a b. INSULTS, 132
one lucky b. who's the artist STOPPARD, T, 11
we knocked the b. off ACHIEVEMENT, 9
bastards b. at the monastery PINTER, H, 2
It is a pity...that more politicians are not b. POLITICIANS, 31; WHITEHORN, K, 4
that'll hold the little b. CHILDREN, 22; MISTAKES, 5
three more of the b. out there MAJOR, J, 9
bat black b., night, has flown INVITATIONS, 5; TENNYSON, 56
They came to see me b. not to see you bowl CRICKET, 3
Twinkle, twinkle, little b. CARROLL, L, 10; NONSENSE, 5
bath a female llama surprised in her b. INSULTS, 33; POLITICIANS, 64
B....once a week to avoid being a public menace BURGESS, A, 4; CLEANNESS, 2
the nuns who never take a b. MODESTY, 8; RUSSELL, B, 7
Bath Oh! who can ever be tired of B. AUSTEN, J, 15; ENGLAND, 3
bathe B. early every day and sickness will avoid you CLEANNESS, 1
bathes The King b. SEASIDE, 1
bathing b. in someone else's dirty water PROUST, M, 1
caught the Whigs b. DISRAELI, B, 23; POLITICS, 34
something between a large b. machine BOATS, 6; GILBERT, W, 22
bathroom he goes to church as he goes to the b. CLERGY, 3; RELIGION, 15
horse in the b. ADAMS, D, 1
bats b. in the belfry MADNESS, 31
their b. have been broken...by the team captain THATCHER, M, 7
battalions God is always on the side of the big b. POWER POLITICS, 7
God is on the side not of the heavy b. POWER POLITICS, 8; VOLTAIRE, 23
battered bit like an old, b. Escort SPORT AND GAMES, 5
battering B. the gates of heaven EXCESS, 16; TENNYSON, 74
battle A b. of giants WAR, 179; WELLINGTON, 26
b. to the strong BIBLE, 74
France has lost a b. FRANCE, 8; WAR, 56
greatest misery is a b. gained VICTORY, 29; WELLINGTON, 8
next greatest misfortune to losing a b. VICTORY, 28; WELLINGTON, 12
preferred to go into b. sitting down SOLDIERS, 17
The b. for women's rights FEMINISM, 53; THATCHER, M, 23
The b. of Britain CHURCHILL, W, 52; WORLD WAR II, 13
the B. of Waterloo ORWELL, G, 13
battlefield b. is fearful WORLD WAR I, 4
the most beautiful b. NAPOLEON I, 8; WAR, 115
we survive amongst the dead and the dying as on a b. OLD AGE, 98; SPARK, M, 6
battlements Fate sits on these dark b. DESTINY, 20
battles Dead b., like dead generals WAR, 172
mother of b. WAR, 83
bauble that fool's b., the mace DISMISSAL, 5
What shall we do with this b. CROMWELL, O, 6
bay we discovered a b. DISCOVERY, 6
baying b. for broken glass ARISTOCRACY, 21; WAUGH, E, 7
bayonet bullet and the b. are brother and sister WORLD WAR I, 20
bayonets A man may build...a throne of b. INGE, W, 11; POWER POLITICS, 4
bays To win the palm, the oak, or b. MARVELL, A, 1; VICTORY, 15
bazaar Sunday morning, Fate's great b. MACNEICE, L, 5
be If you want to b. happy, b. HAPPINESS, 31; TOLSTOY, L, 6
To b., or not to b. LANGUAGE, 12; SHAKESPEARE, 90
What must b., must b. DESTINY, 1; PROVERBS, 455
beaches we shall fight on the b. CHURCHILL, W, 50; WORLD WAR II, 11
beacons Logical consequences are the scarecrows of fools and the b. of wise men HUXLEY, T, 9; LOGIC, 6
beadle a b. on boxin' day DICKENS, C, 48; POETRY, 19
beads what glass b. are to African traders SORROW, 8
Beadsman The B., after thousand aves told KEATS, J, 10; PRAYER, 20
beak Take thy b. from out my heart EVIL, 16
beaker a b. full of the warm South ALCOHOL, 47; KEATS, J, 37
Beale Miss Buss and Miss B. /Cupid's darts do not feel ANONYMOUS, 56; INSENSITIVITY, 1
be-all b. and the end-all here ENDING, 6; SHAKESPEARE, 210
bean The home of the b. and the cod SNOBBERY, 3
beans Instant coffee is just old b. DRINKS, 20
bear a B. of Very Little Brain MILNE, A, 6; WORDS, 24
any man...who could not b. another's misfortunes...like a Christian MISFORTUNE, 15; POPE, A, 57
authority be a stubborn b. BRIBERY, 5; SHAKESPEARE, 356
Exit, pursued by a b. ANIMALS, 23; SHAKESPEARE, 353
Human kind cannot b. ELIOT, T, 7; REALITY, 2
I had rather b. with you than b. you SHAKESPEARE, 44
never...sell the b.'s skin ANTICIPATION, 6; LA FONTAINE, J, 7
Round and round the garden /Like a teddy b. NURSERY RHYMES, 48
they think I shall be able to b. it best CHURCHILL, W, 21; RESPONSIBILITY, 4

bear-baiting Puritan hated b. MACAULAY, T, 14; PURITANISM, 3
beard b. the lion in his den COURAGE, 26
Dead eyes and a red b. LAWRENCE, D, 1
singed the Spanish king's b. WAR, 59
There was an Old Man with a b. APPEARANCE, 37; LEAR, E, 1
bearded hard to hear what a b. man is saying PUNS, 14
He reaps the b. grain at a breath DEATH, 101; LONGFELLOW, H, 11
beards beware of long arguments and long b. BREVITY, 7; SANTAYANA, G, 10
men wore their b., like they wear their neckties APPEARANCE, 36; LAWRENCE, D, 20
bears And dancing dogs and b. ANIMALS, 15
And some of the bigger b. try to pretend MILNE, A, 5; SUPERSTITION, 10
b. and lions growl and fight ANIMALS, 25; WATTS, I, 3
beast b. of the earth BIBLE, 141; CREATION, 5
Dialect words – those terrible marks of the b. CLASS, 19; HARDY, T, 10
Either a b. or a god ARISTOTLE, 7; MANKIND, 3
Every man has a wild b. within him MANKIND, 27
for man or b. WEATHER, 10
hardly be a b. or a fool alone on a great mountain SOLITUDE, 10
Man's life is cheap as b.'s NECESSITY, 5; SHAKESPEARE, 177
The B. stands for strong mutually antagonistic governments NEWSPAPERS, 17; WAUGH, E, 35
the b. with two backs SEX, 109
the mark…of the b. BIBLE, 466; DEVIL, 8
beastie Wee, sleekit, cow'rin', tim'rous b. ANIMALS, 9; BURNS, R, 21
beastliness It is called in our schools 'b.' SEX, 12
beastly Don't let's be b. to the Germans COWARD, N, 7; GERMANY, 2
nothing but b. fury and extreme violence FOOTBALL, 7
beasts Blows are fitter for b. VIOLENCE, 20
man…compared unto the b. that perish PSALMS, 29
beat make the b. keep time with short steps FUNERALS, 1
Two hearts that b. as one LOVE, 108
wound up with the b. generation PUNISHMENT, 31
beaten All the best men…have been b. PUNISHMENT, 10
I was b. by almost everyone at Eton, but never by the headmaster. EDUCATION, 86
I was b. up by Quakers ALLEN, W, 5; SHYNESS, 1
public school, where…learning was painfully b. into him EDUCATION, 73; PEACOCK, T, 8
beautiful Against the b.…one can wage a pitiless war BEAUTY, 24; GREENE, G, 5
b. downtown Burbank PLACES, 3
b.…for someone who could not read AMERICA, 8; CHESTERTON, G, 50
food is, actually, very b. FOOD, 64
Give me my golf clubs…and a b. partner DESIRE, 1
Incredibly,…adorably b. BEAUTY, 13; COMPLIMENTS, 5
light, shade, and perspective…make it b. BEAUTY, 18
many men, so b. COLERIDGE, S, 32; GUILT, 6
most b. in Britain…in private hands BRITAIN, 14
most b. things…are the most useless BEAUTY, 38; RUSKIN, J, 11
Our love of what is b. does not lead to extravagance RESULTS, 4
Rich men's houses are seldom b. WEALTH, 6
Small is B. CONSERVATION, 11
summer afternoon…two most b. words SEASONS, 8
The good is the b. GOOD, 14; PLATO, 1
the most b. battlefield NAPOLEON I, 8; WAR, 115
the most b. woman I've ever seen BEAUTY, 32; MARX, G, 1
the name of which was B. ARCHITECTURE, 2; BUNYAN, J, 4
when a woman isn't b. BEAUTY, 17; CHEKHOV, A, 12
beautifully B. done LAST WORDS, 84
Living well and b. and justly LIFE, 89
beauty A thing of b. is a joy for ever BEAUTY, 28; KEATS, J, 7
B. and the lust for learning BEAUTY, 9; BEERBOHM, M, 15
b. being the best of all we know BEAUTY, 11
B. in distress BEAUTY, 15; BURKE, E, 7
B. in things exists in the mind which contemplates them BEAUTY, 26; HUME, D, 4
B. is altogether in the eye of the beholder BEAUTY, 27; PROVERBS, 79
b. is only sin deep BEAUTY, 39; SAKI, 21
B. is only skin-deep BEAUTY, 3; PROVERBS, 80
B. is potent BEAUTY, 4; PROVERBS, 81
B. is truth, truth b. KEATS, J, 30; TRUTH, 33
B. itself doth of itself persuade /The eyes of men BEAUTY, 41; SHAKESPEARE, 358
B. sat with me all the summer day BEAUTY, 12
B. stands /In the admiration…of weak minds BEAUTY, 33; MILTON, J, 54
B. too rich for use SHAKESPEARE, 308
better to be first with an ugly woman than the hundredth with a b. BEAUTY, 14; BUCK, P, 6
But b.'s self she is, /When all her robes are gone ANONYMOUS, 58; NAKEDNESS, 1
Charm is a delusion and b. fleeting CHARM, 1
Clad in the b. of a thousand stars MARLOWE, C, 3
concubine for her b. BEAUTY, 1
Exuberance is B. BEAUTY, 10; BLAKE, W, 29
feeling for b. BEAUTY, 21
Fostered alike by b. and by fear SOUL, 13; WORDSWORTH, W, 36
Health is b. BEAUTY, 44
heavily and cruelly images of female b. BEAUTY, 47
her b. made /The bright world dim BEAUTY, 43; COMPLIMENTS, 33; SHELLEY, P, 26
imagination seizes as b. must be truth IMAGINATION, 5
Love built on b. BEAUTY, 20; DONNE, J, 9
love permanence more than…b. BRITISH, 4
Mathematics possesses…b. MATHEMATICS, 20; RUSSELL, B, 21
perceive real b. in a person…older BEAUTY, 7
She walks in b. BEAUTY, 16; BYRON, 40
Teaches such b. as a woman's eye LEARNING, 16; SHAKESPEARE, 199
the b. /Of an aged face OLD AGE, 27
the laws of poetic truth and poetic b. ARNOLD, M, 15; POETRY, 2
The pain passes, but the b. remains ART, 28; ENDURANCE, 17
There is no excellent b. BACON, F, 12; BEAUTY, 8
this generation…found England a land of b. ECOLOGY, 5
'Tisn't b.…just IT ATHEISM, 14
What *is* b., anyway? There's no such thing BEAUTY, 34; PICASSO, P, 8
where B.was, nothing ever ran quite straight GALSWORTHY, J, 4
beaver And cultivate a b. HUXLEY, A, 5
because B. it is there MOTIVE, 3
Becket Thomas B. ASSASSINATION, 5
become How ill white hairs b. a fool and jester OLD AGE, 89
What's b. of Waring ABSENCE, 5; BROWNING, R, 58
becoming I believe I am b. a god LAST WORDS, 92
Sunburn is very b. APPEARANCE, 20; COWARD, N, 10
bed A man of sixty has spent twenty years in b. LIFE, 14
and die – in b. SASSOON, S, 2; WAR, 147
And so to b. BED, 10; PEPYS, S, 5
B.…is the poor man's opera HUXLEY, A, 21; SEX, 55
Each within our narrow b. DEATH, 47
Go to b. with the lamb BED, 2; PROVERBS, 180
Here comes a candle to light you to b. LONDON, 2; NURSERY RHYMES, 41
in b. with a strange man O'BRIEN, E, 1
It's just hard to get out of b. in the morning SPORT AND GAMES, 32
Lady Capricorn…was…keeping open b. HUXLEY, A, 9; PROMISCUITY, 5
nicer to stay in b. BED, 7
Now deep in my b. I turn SLEEP, 21
So I took her into b. and covered up her head ANONYMOUS, 63; SEX, 9
The b. be blest BLESSING, 1
the night the b. fell on my father MEMORY, 27; THURBER, J, 9
Wedlock – the…deep peace of the double b. after the… chaise-longue MARRIAGE, 41
We should have stood in b. DEFEAT, 9
Who goes to b. with whom OLD AGE, 85
woman who goes to b. with a man MONTAIGNE, M, 4; SEX, 85
you have to get up early if you want to get out of b. BED, 8
bedfellows Misery acquaints…strange b. MISFORTUNE, 20; SHAKESPEARE, 325
bedroom meeting in a darkened b. in a Brussels hotel EUROPE, 25
beds Minds like b. always made up INFLEXIBILITY, 4
Will there be b. for me and all who seek REST, 1; ROSSETTI, C, 7
bedspring the triumphant twang of a b. SEX, 95
bee How doth the little busy b. WATTS, I, 2; WORK, 38
Sting like a b. SPORT AND GAMES, 1
Beecham B.'s pills are just the thing DRUGS, 3
beechen spare the b. tree TREES, 2
beef The roast b. of England FIELDING, H, 6; FOOD, 30

beefsteak a b. prevents it REMEDIES, 54
Dr Johnson's morality was as English…as a b. ENGLAND, 25
beer Bowen's B. Makes You Drunk DRINKS, 2
chronicle small b. SHAKESPEARE, 282; TRIVIALITY, 13
Did you ever taste b. ALCOHOL, 30; DICKENS, C, 35
Life isn't all b. and skittles LIFE, 51
that bitter b. that tastes sweet IMMORTALITY, 6; RILKE, R, 4
Beerbohm Max B. OLD AGE, 106; WILDE, O, 69
bees murmuring of innumerable b. SEASONS, 23; TENNYSON, 68
No b., no honey PROVERBS, 309; WORK, 2
No shade, no shine, no butterflies, no b. HOOD, T, 10; MONTHS, 10
bees-winged Or was it his b. eyes WRITERS, 37
Beethoven B.'s Fifth Symphony is the most sublime noise FORSTER, E, 7; MUSIC, 26
greatest composers since B. POPULAR MUSIC, 7
not B. lying here MUSIC, 54
Roll Over B. POPULAR MUSIC, 5
beetle gnawed by a b. LONELINESS, 9
before I have been here b. ROSSETTI, D, 4
beg only the poor…are forbidden to b. FRANCE, A, 1; POVERTY, 12
beggar A bachelor…dies like a b. MARRIAGE, 102
b. by banqueting upon borrowing BORROWING, 2
how a carter, a common sailor, a b. is still…an Englishman ENGLAND, 36
beggar'd b. all description ADMIRATION, 15; SHAKESPEARE, 30
beggars B. can't be choosers NECESSITY, 1; PROVERBS, 82
beggary b. in the love that can be reckon'd LOVE, 143; SHAKESPEARE, 26
no vice but b. HYPOCRISY, 20; SHAKESPEARE, 164
begin Are you sitting comfortably? Then I'll b. BEGINNING, 15
B. at the beginning CARROLL, L, 20; ORDER, 2
beginning a b., a muddle, and an end LARKIN, P, 5; NOVELS, 9
As it was in the b. BOOK OF COMMON PRAYER, 16; ETERNITY, 2
a whole is that which has a b., a middle, and an end ARISTOTLE, 4; PLAYS, 1
b. and the ending BIBLE, 459
b. of fairies BARRIE, J, 3; FAIRIES, 2
b. of time according to our Chronologie CREATION, 15
end of the b. CHURCHILL, W, 59; WORLD WAR II, 21
every man at the b. doth set forth good wine ALCOHOL, 17; BIBLE, 242
I like a film to have a b., a middle and an end CINEMA, 12
In my b. is my end BEGINNING, 9
in the b. God BIBLE, 137; CREATION, 2
in the b. was the word BIBLE, 238; WORDS, 1
Nothing so difficult as a b. BYRON, 28; POETRY, 13
the b. of the end DEFEAT, 16; TALLEYRAND, 3
beginnings end to the b. of all wars ROOSEVELT, F, 17; WAR, 139
mighty things from small b. DRYDEN, J, 20; NATURE, 9
begins exception of the equator, everything b. somewhere BEGINNING, 10
Life B. at Forty LIFE, 75
my family b. with me ANCESTRY, 3
begot what they were about when they b. me FAMILY, 56; STERNE, L, 4
begotten Whatever is b., born, and dies MORTALITY, 23; YEATS, W, 27
beguine She refused to begin the 'B.' COWARD, N, 19; PETULANCE, 1
When they begin the b. HAPPINESS, 17; PORTER, C, 7
begun There is an old saying 'well b. is half done' BEGINNING, 13; KEATS, J, 55
behaving men are more interested in…justifying themselves than in…b. MOTIVE, 6; SZASZ, T, 1
behaviour rationality…factors governing human b. HUMAN NATURE, 13
The quality of moral b. varies HUXLEY, A, 20; MORALITY, 7
behaviourism Of course, B. 'works' PSYCHIATRY, 6
beheaded Owen Tudor…was b. at the market place EXECUTION, 14
behind another Yank half a step b. CLINTON, B, 5
In the dusk, with a light b. her AGE, 47; GILBERT, W, 46; INSULTS, 53
led his regiment from b. COWARDICE, 4; GILBERT, W, 1
part my hair b. ELIOT, T, 15; OLD AGE, 45
behold all which we b. /Is full of blessings OPTIMISM, 42; WORDSWORTH, W, 15
B. her, single in the field SOLITUDE, 18; WORDSWORTH, W, 51
b. it was a dream BUNYAN, J, 8; DREAMS, 3
b. the man BIBLE, 267
beholder Beauty is…in the eye of the b. BEAUTY, 27
beige It's b.! My color ARCHITECTURE, 20
being always at the edge of B. EXISTENCE, 6
in him we live, and move, and have our b. BIBLE, 13; GOD, 6
Knowledge is proportionate to b. HUXLEY, A, 37; KNOWLEDGE, 23
To kill a human b. JAMES, H, 8; KILLING, 7
beings We tolerate shapes in human b. APPEARANCE, 32
Belfast British troops were patrolling the streets of B. IRELAND, 7
belfry bats in the b. MADNESS, 31
belief *Action will furnish b.* BELIEF, 6
Bible demands suspension of b. BIBLE, 529
believe a verb meaning 'to b. falsely' BELIEF, 13
b. in the life to come AFTERLIFE, 1; BECKETT, S, 1
B. it or not BELIEF, 10
B. nothing of what you hear BELIEF, 1; PROVERBS, 83
be ready to b. that what seems to us white is black CHURCH, 8
don't b. in…true love until after the first attack SCEPTICISM, 1
Do you b. in fairies FAIRIES, 3
except I…thrust my hand into his side, I will not b. BIBLE, 277
I b. because it is impossible BELIEF, 11; TERTULLIAN, 3
I b. I am becoming a god LAST WORDS, 92
I b. in the Church RELIGION, 84
I b. very strongly in Fascism FASCISM, 2
I don't b. in fairies BARRIE, J, 4; FAIRIES, 1
If you b., clap your hands FAIRIES, 3
inclined to b. those whom we do not know JOHNSON, S, 17; TRUST, 4
Infidelity…consists in professing to b. INTEGRITY, 5
it brings you luck whether you b.…or not SUPERSTITION, 7
They didn't b. me BEAUTY, 35
undesirable to b. a proposition RUSSELL, B, 20; SCEPTICISM, 4
We are arrant knaves, all; b. none of us HUMAN NATURE, 27
We can b. what we choose RESPONSIBILITY, 12
what we b. is not necessarily true OBJECTIVITY, 3
when you cease to b. you may cease to behave BELIEF, 9
you must b. in God FAITH, 18
believes He b.…that there *is* such a thing as truth BAGEHOT, W, 10; POLITICIANS, 43
politician never b. what he says DE GAULLE, C, 11; POLITICIANS, 5
bell B., book, and candle MATERIALISM, 23; SHAKESPEARE, 165
for whom the b. tolls DEATH, 59; DONNE, J, 8; MANKIND, 24
I'll b. the cat COURAGE, 12
The b. strikes one TIME, 65; YOUNG, E, 6
The sexton toll'd the b. HOOD, T, 5; PUNS, 7
Unto the B. at Edmonton COWPER, W, 10; MARRIAGE, 57
Bellamy I could eat one of B.'s veal pies LAST WORDS, 67; PITT THE YOUNGER, 3
belle La b. Dame sans Merci KEATS, J, 13, 23; SUPERNATURAL, 10
bellies their b. were full BRECHT, B, 4; HUNGER, 3
bells Ring out, wild b., and let him die ENDING, 7; TENNYSON, 35
Rings on her fingers and b. on her toes NURSERY RHYMES, 46
The b. of hell go ting-a-ling-a-ling ANONYMOUS, 65; DEATH, 21
'Twould ring the b. of Heaven ANIMALS, 15
With silver b. and cockle shells GARDENS, 1; NURSERY RHYMES, 34
belly Every man with a b. full of the classics CLASSICS, 7
the b. for meats BIBLE, 27
to banish hunger by rubbing the b. HUNGER, 5
upon thy b. shalt thou go BIBLE, 151; SEXES, 4
victory under the b. of a Cossack's horse RUSSIAN REVOLUTION, 10; TROTSKY, L, 4
bellyful Rumble thy b. SHAKESPEARE, 179; WEATHER, 20
beloved I am my b.'s, and his desire is toward me BIBLE, 499
I am my b.'s, and my b. is mine BIBLE, 495
Onaway! Awake, b. LONGFELLOW, H, 14
the voice of my b. BIBLE, 488; LOVE, 34
this is my b. Son BIBLE, 355; CHRISTIANITY, 24
below Capten, art tha sleepin' there b. NEWBOLT, H, 3; WAR, 120
Down and away b. ARNOLD, M, 16; DEPARTURE, 1
What thy errand here b. LAMB, C, 20; PURPOSE, 7
belt could not see a b. without hitting below it LLOYD GEORGE, D, 1; POLITICIANS, 40
Ben Under bare B. Bulben's head YEATS, W, 32
And lo! B. Adhem's name led all the rest SUPERIORITY, 7
B. Battle was a soldier bold HOOD, T, 2; PUNS, 10
bench What do you suppose I am on the B. for REPARTEE, 4
benefactors gratitude to most b. INGRATITUDE, 3
benefits B. make a man a slave MATERIALISM, 1; PROVERBS, 84

It is the nature of men to be bound by the b. they confer OBLIGATION, 3
benevolence husband render unto the wife due b. BIBLE, 29; MARRIAGE, 26
bereav'd I am black, as if b. of light BLAKE, W, 48; RACISM, 5
Berlin when staring at our soldiers drilling in B. ENGLAND, 36
Berliner *Ich bin ein B.* GERMANY, 6
Bernhardt Sarah B.'s funeral ACTORS, 15
berries I come to pluck your b. MILTON, J, 21; TREES, 10
berth His death, which happen'd in his b. HOOD, T, 5; PUNS, 7
Things hitherto undone should be given…a wide b. BEERBOHM, M, 7; ORIGINALITY, 1
Bertie I'm Burlington B. BED, 5
beside not in the lecture room, but at the b. EDUCATION, 42
best all that's b. of dark and bright BEAUTY, 16; BYRON, 40
as in the b. it is MURDER, 10; SHAKESPEARE, 78
beauty being the b. of all we know BEAUTY, 11
b. men are moulded out of faults SHAKESPEARE, 237
b. of life is but intoxication BYRON, 21; DRUNKENNESS, 13
b. that is known and thought in the world ARNOLD, M, 14; CRITICISM, 2
b. words in the b. order COLERIDGE, S, 41; POETRY AND PROSE, 2
Carnation milk is the b. in the land FOOD, 8
Culture, the acquainting ourselves with the b. ARNOLD, M, 22; CULTURE, 1
For home is b. HOME, 12
His worst is better than any other person's b. COMPLIMENTS, 12; HAZLITT, W, 22
It was the b. of times DICKENS, C, 56; FRENCH REVOLUTION, 3
I will do my b. PROMISES, 1
look at the b. book…price of a turbot… BOOKS, 42; RUSKIN, J, 9
Men of few words are the b. BREVITY, 9; SHAKESPEARE, 133
Stolen sweets are b. THEFT, 5
The b. is the enemy of the good EXCELLENCE, 4; VOLTAIRE, 11
The b. lack all conviction YEATS, W, 28
the b. of all possible worlds VOLTAIRE, 8
The b. of friends FRIENDSHIP, 6; PROVERBS, 378
The b. things in life PROVERBS, 380; WEALTH, 1
the b. which has been thought and said in the world ARNOLD, M, 3
the shortest works are always the b. BREVITY, 5; LA FONTAINE, J, 11
we will do our b. CHURCHILL, W, 56; WORLD WAR II, 18
bestial what remains is b. REPUTATION, 9; SHAKESPEARE, 283
bestow Let them b. on every airth a limb EXECUTION, 13
bestride he doth b. the narrow world /Like a Colossus SELF, 16; SHAKESPEARE, 145
best-seller A b.…because it was selling well BOOKS, 15; FAME, 7
A b. is the gilded tomb of a mediocre talent BOOKS, 45; SMITH, L, 1
bet I b. my money on the bob-tail nag HORSES, 6
Bethlehem O come ye to B. CHRISTMAS, 19
O little town of B. CHRISTMAS, 12
betimes to be up b. BED, 11; SHAKESPEARE, 339
betray All a man can b. is his conscience CONSCIENCE, 2
Nature never did b. NATURE, 35; WORDSWORTH, W, 14
betrayal intellectuals' b. INTELLECTUALS, 5
betrayed woe unto that man by whom the Son of man is b. BETRAYAL, 1; BIBLE, 423
betraying if I had to choose between b. my country and b. my friend BETRAYAL, 7; FORSTER, E, 11
betrothed a bride's attitude towards her b. MARRIAGE, 111; PUNS, 17
better a far, far, b. thing DICKENS, C, 57; EXECUTION, 8
always…trying to get the b. LAMB, C, 7; SPORT AND GAMES, 24
b. is he…who hath not seen the evil work under the sun BIBLE, 68; EVIL, 4
b. strangers SEPARATION, 6; SHAKESPEARE, 54
B. than a play CHARLES II, 5; HOUSES OF PARLIAMENT, 8
b. to have loved and lost LOVE, 161; TENNYSON, 28
b. to have no opinion of God BACON, F, 52; GOD, 4
b. to marry than to burn BIBLE, 30; MARRIAGE, 27
for b. for worse BOOK OF COMMON PRAYER, 27; MARRIAGE, 33
He is no b. ILLNESS, 9
I am getting b. and b. PSYCHOLOGY, 4; REMEDIES, 25
if you knows of a b. 'ole WAR, 14
I've got to admit it's getting b. IMPROVEMENT, 2; LENNON, J, 5
nae b. than he should be BURNS, R, 8
no b. than you should be BEAUMONT, F, 1
something b. than our brains to depend upon ARISTOCRACY, 8; CHESTERFIELD, P, 20

the old is b. AGE, 17; ALCOHOL, 18; BIBLE, 321
We have seen b. days NOSTALGIA, 23
when I'm bad I'm b. SEX, 128; WEST, M, 17
When you meet someone b.…turn your thoughts to becoming his equal CONFUCIUS, 1; SUPERIORITY, 6
You're a b. man than I am, Gunga Din KIPLING, R, 16; SUPERIORITY, 8
bettering Black people are…b. themselves RACISM, 7
Beulah B., peel me a grape LUXURY, 6; WEST, M, 6
bewailing the sum of life's b. REGRET, 10
beware all should cry, B. CAUTION, 9; COLERIDGE, S, 17
B. of the artist who's an intellectual FITZGERALD, F, 11; INTELLECTUALS, 10
B. of the dog DOGS, 1
B. of the man who does not return your blow SHAW, G, 26
bewildered Bewitched, Bothered and B. CONFUSION, 7
I was b. once CONFUSION, 3
bewitching the b. of naughtiness BIBLE, 519; LUST, 2
beyond All decent people live b. their incomes nowadays EXTRAVAGANCE, 4; SAKI, 9
We are living b. our means CONSERVATION, 7
bias a b. against *understanding* JOURNALISM, 11; TELEVISION, 2
Bible B.…straightforward language…work of lesser influence BIBLE, 530
have used the B. as if it was a constable's handbook BIBLE, 532; KINGSLEY, C, 3
quotations from the B. and the rest JOYCE, J, 1
searching through the B. for loopholes BIBLE, 528; LAST WORDS, 34
starless and b. black THOMAS, D, 18
that book is the B. ARNOLD, M, 31; BIBLE, 523
The B. is literature BIBLE, 536; SANTAYANA, G, 4
the B. tells me so RELIGION, 93
The English B. BIBLE, 533; MACAULAY, T, 1
There's a B. on that shelf there BIBLE, 535; RUSSELL, B, 24
Bibles they have the land and we have the B. RACISM, 12
bicycle a b. made for two MARRIAGE, 58
like a fish needs a b. FEMINISM, 10
Socialism can only arrive by b. SOCIALISM, 9
big A b. man has no time FAME, 13; FITZGERALD, F, 13
A government…b. enough to give you all you want GOVERNMENT, 15
B. Brother is watching you AUTHORITARIANISM, 6; ORWELL, G, 17
b. emotions come from b. words HEMINGWAY, E, 9; STYLE, 7
he was too b. for them CONCEIT, 5; INSULTS, 24
the b. one that got away MARRIAGE, 60
The b. print giveth and the fine print taketh away BUSINESS, 29
bigger it's a great deal b. CARLYLE, T, 33; UNIVERSE, 4
bike he got on his b. UNEMPLOYMENT, 5
bile He likes…the b. when it is black ELIOT, T, 1
bill put 'Emily, I love you' on the back of the b. LOVE, 112; MARX, G, 19
billboard A b. lovely as a tree NASH, O, 10; TREES, 12
billboards the churches…bore for me the same relation to God that b. did to Coca-Cola RELIGION, 91; UPDIKE, J, 2
billiard The b. sharp whom any one catches GILBERT, W, 31; PUNISHMENT, 15
billiards Proficiency at b.…misspent youth YOUTH, 31
to play b. well SPORT AND GAMES, 41
Billy Silly B. INSULTS, 60
billy-bong Once a jolly swagman camped by a b. PLACES, 29
biographies History is the essence of…b. CARLYLE, T, 6; HISTORY, 7
biography a man is nobody unless his b. OBITUARIES, 10; TROLLOPE, A, 6
hesitation in starting my b. too soon RUSSELL, B, 3; WRITING, 44
history…the b. of great men CARLYLE, T, 11; GREATNESS, 6; HISTORY, 8
how difficult it is to write b. WEST, R, 9
no history; only b. EMERSON, R, 9; HISTORY, 12
biology The separation of psychology from the premises of b. PSYCHOLOGY, 9
birch I'm all for bringing back the b. PUNISHMENT, 30; VIDAL, G, 8
bird A b. in the hand PROVERBS, 3; PRUDENCE, 1
a b. of the air shall carry the voice SECRECY, 3
Her prose is like a b. SPARK, M, 1
keep such a b. in a cage IMPRISONMENT, 5
Lo! the B. is on the Wing FITZGERALD, E, 3; TIME, 21
my soul…should flee as a b. PSALMS, 4
She's only a b. in a gilded cage IMPRISONMENT, 7

The B. of Time FITZGERALD, E, 3; TIME, 21
bird-cage a b. played with toasting-forks BEECHAM, T, 7; MUSIC, 8
Robert Houdin who…invented the vanishing b. THEATRE, 15
birds All the b. of the air NURSERY RHYMES, 2
b.…caught in the snare CHANCE, 2
B. of a feather PROVERBS, 93; SIMILARITY, 1
Dead b. don't fall out of their nests OLD AGE, 34; SEX, 28
I see all the b. are flown HOUSES OF PARLIAMENT, 7
no b. sing ILLNESS, 39; KEATS, J, 22
No fruits, no flowers, no leaves, no b. HOOD, T, 10; MONTHS, 10
spring now comes unheralded by the return of the b. CARSON, R, 4; ECOLOGY, 1
that make fine b. AESOP, 5; CLOTHES, 2
Two little dicky b., /Sitting on a wall NURSERY RHYMES, 67
where late the sweet b. sang OLD AGE, 94; SHAKESPEARE, 366
Birmingham Am in B. CHESTERTON, G, 48; MEMORY, 6
One has no great hopes from B. AUSTEN, J, 10; ENGLAND, 4
birth B., and copulation, and death ELIOT, T, 22; LIFE AND DEATH, 14
b. had no meaning LEE, L, 2
B. may be a matter of a moment BIRTH, 11
From b. to age eighteen, a girl needs good parents AGE, 95
Man's main task in life is to give *b.* to himself BIRTH, 10
no credentials…not even…a certificate of b. ARISTOCRACY, 14; LLOYD GEORGE, D, 9
no cure for b. and death LIFE, 80; SANTAYANA, G, 11
Our b. is but a sleep BIRTH, 17
The history of man for the nine months preceding his b. BIRTH, 8
The memory of b. LIFE AND DEATH, 16
what you were before your b. AFTERLIFE, 9; SCHOPENHAUER, A, 7
birthday A diplomat…always remembers a woman's b. AGE, 44; DIPLOMACY, 13; FROST, R, 10
If one doesn't get b. presents GIFTS, 5; REED, H, 6
is it my b. or am I dying LAST WORDS, 5
birthplace accent of one's b. lingers HOMESICKNESS, 5; ROCHEFOUCAULD, 23
biscuit Can't a fellow even enjoy a b. THRIFT, 10
bishop a b.…must be blameless BIBLE, 507; CLERGY, 2
another B. dead CLERGY, 10; MELBOURNE, 9
blonde to make a b. kick a hole APPEARANCE, 17; COMPLIMENTS, 9
How can a b. marry CLERGY, 11; SMITH, S, 8
Make him a b., and you will silence him CHESTERFIELD, P, 21; CLERGY, 4
May you be the mother of a b. BEHAN, B, 11; LAST WORDS, 8
No B., no King CHURCH, 6
the symbol of a b. is a crook CLERGY, 5
bisier he semed b. than he was APPEARANCES, 11; CHAUCER, G, 10
bit He b. his lip in a manner HUMOUR, 57
The dog…/Went mad and b. the man DOGS, 9; GOLDSMITH, O, 10
bitch The son of a b. isn't going to resign on me DISMISSAL, 11
bitches burn the bloody b. CLERGY, 18
Now we are all sons of b. NUCLEAR WEAPONS, 3
bite b. the hand that fed them BURKE, E, 19; INGRATITUDE, 2
Every dog is allowed one b. POLITICS, 123
would b. some other of my generals REPARTEE, 3
bites when a man b. a dog that is news MEDIA, 5
biting if you don't stop b. your fingernails ARTISTS, 22; ROGERS, W, 11
bivouac an armed camp of Blackshirts, a b. for corpses FASCISM, 12
black A lady asked me why… I wore b. MOURNING, 15; SITWELL, E, 6
an old b. ram /Is tupping your white ewe SEX, 108
Any colour, so long as it's b. CHOICE, 1
B. people are…bettering themselves RACISM, 7
B. people possess the secret of joy WALKER, A, 7
British Government sees b. people as expendable RACISM, 30
coffee that's too b.…You integrate it with cream RACISM, 20
I am b., as if bereav'd of light BLAKE, W, 48; RACISM, 5
I don't believe in b. majority rule RACISM, 28
looking for a b. hat METAPHYSICS, 1
My major advice to young b. artists WALKER, A, 12
One b., and one white, and two khaki ANONYMOUS, 95; RACISM, 1
People think we do not understand our b.…countrymen RACISM, 6
Take that b. box away CINEMA, 27; TREE, H, 9
That old b. magic SUPERNATURAL, 11
The Ethiopians say that their gods are…b. RELIGION, 105
The future is…b. BALDWIN, J, 4; RACISM, 3
There's a b. sheep FAMILY, 5; PROVERBS, 412
To like an individual because he's b. RACISM, 8
Two lovely b. eyes VIOLENCE, 6
Who art as b. as hell, as dark as night APPEARANCE, 63
blackbird When down came a b. NURSERY RHYMES, 52
blackbirds Four and twenty b., /Baked in a pie NURSERY RHYMES, 52
blacker you the b. devil GOOD AND EVIL, 8
Blackpool With my little stick of B. rock FOOD, 32
Blackshirt Before the organization of the B. movement FASCISM, 7; FREEDOM, 44
Blackshirts an armed camp of B., a bivouac for corpses FASCISM, 12
bladder master of his soul, /Is servant to his b. OLD AGE, 9
Blake B. is damned good to steal from POETS, 35
B. is to the average poet…man in the street POETS, 55
B.…presents only the essential POETS, 34
That William B. /Who beat upon the wall POETS, 62
blame Everyone threw the b. on me CHURCHILL, W, 21; RESPONSIBILITY, 4
Praise and b. are much the same WRITING, 53
put the b. for the existence of humanity INJUSTICE, 9
blaming subtle and effective way of b. the victim FEMINISM, 35
blank Where were you fellows when the paper was b. EDITORS, 1
blanket not a b. woven from one thread AMERICA, 23
blankets rough male kiss of b. BED, 4; BROOKE, R, 1
blanks historians left b. in their writings HISTORIANS, 6; POUND, E, 8
blaspheme the right to b. FREEDOM, 20
blasphemies All great truths begin as b. NOVELTY, 9; SHAW, G, 4
blasphemy Your b.…can't be forgiven CENSORSHIP, 7
blast b. of war SHAKESPEARE, 130
bleak In the b. mid-winter SEASONS, 18
bleed If you prick us, do we not b. EQUALITY, 34; SHAKESPEARE, 247
bleeds My nose b. for you INSINCERITY, 6
blemish Christianity…the one immortal b. of mankind CHRISTIANITY, 49; NIETZSCHE, F, 4
lamb…without b. BIBLE, 109
Blenheim I dine at B. once a week ANONYMOUS, 59; SUPERIORITY, 1
bless B. relaxes BLAKE, W, 28
God b. us, every one BLESSING, 8; DICKENS, C, 10
blessed all generations shall call me b. BIBLE, 309
B. are the meek HUMILITY, 1
b. are the poor in spirit BIBLE, 360
b. are they that have not seen, and yet have believed BIBLE, 278
b. is he that cometh in the name of the Lord BIBLE, 407
b. is the man that endureth temptation BIBLE, 216; TEMPTATION, 4
B. is the man who expects nothing EXPECTATION, 6; POPE, A, 60
I b. them unaware BLESSING, 7
blessing a b. that money cannot buy HEALTH AND HEALTHY LIVING, 16
a b.…very well disguised DEFEAT, 1
b. of God Almighty BOOK OF COMMON PRAYER, 11
Let the b.…be…upon all that are lovers of virtue FISHING, 5; WALTON, I, 6
blessings all which we behold /Is full of b. OPTIMISM, 42; WORDSWORTH, W, 15
a world of b. by good Queen Elizabeth ROYALTY, 71
The trained nurse has become one of the great b. of humanity OCCUPATIONS, 22
blest for this gift I feel b. BLESSING, 6
It is twice b. MERCY, 2; SHAKESPEARE, 248
The bed be b. BLESSING, 1
they b. him in their pain MARTYRDOM, 7; TENNYSON, 70
this b. man, let his just praise be given COMPLIMENTS, 37; WALTON, I, 7
blind A b. man in a dark room METAPHYSICS, 1
Acting in English…I'm like a b. man ACTING, 10
all the discomforts that will accompany my being b. BLINDNESS, 13
b. as those who won't see STUBBORNNESS, 2

b. in their own cause BLINDNESS, 2
Booth died b. FAITH, 19
Country of the B. SUPERIORITY, 17; WELLS, H, 9
discomforts that will accompany my being b. PEPYS, S, 17
It is not miserable to be b. ENDURANCE, 13
I was eyes to the b. BIBLE, 235
Lord giveth sight to the b. PSALMS, 74
love is b. LOVE, 145; SHAKESPEARE, 244
Painting is a b. man's profession PAINTING, 14; PICASSO, P, 6
The doggie in front has suddenly gone b. SEX, 30
union of a deaf man to a b. woman COLERIDGE, S, 22; MARRIAGE, 49
whereas I was b., now I see BIBLE, 255
wing'd Cupid painted b. LOVE, 147; SHAKESPEARE, 260
blinded with b. eyesight BOOKS, 49; LEARNING, 17; TENNYSON, 53
blindness it is miserable to be incapable of enduring b. ENDURANCE, 13
My b. is my sight BLINDNESS, 5
the…world was stumbling…in social b. BLINDNESS, 6
blinking The portrait of a b. idiot FOOLISHNESS, 19
bliss B. was it in that dawn to be alive FRENCH REVOLUTION, 11; WORDSWORTH, W, 41
where ignorance is b., /'Tis folly to be wise GRAY, T, 10; IGNORANCE, 10
blithe Hail to thee, b. Spirit SHELLEY, P, 24
No lark more b. than he HAPPINESS, 5
blitz A b. of a boy is Timothy Winters APPEARANCE, 16
block a chip off the old b. BURKE, E, 27; POLITICIANS, 55
there's a statue inside every b. of stone OBESITY, 12; ORWELL, G, 9
blockbuster everyone in Hollywood is looking for the b. COMMERCIALISM, 5
blockhead No man but a b. ever wrote JOHNSON, S, 108; WRITING, 25
blocks philosophy ought to…unravel people's mental b. PHILOSOPHY, 12
blonde A b. to make a bishop kick a hole APPEARANCE, 17; COMPLIMENTS, 9
a career that depends a lot on being tall and b. SPORT AND GAMES, 10
springing from b. to b. like the chamois of the Alps WODEHOUSE, P, 20
think I'm a dumb b.…then they're dumber APPEARANCE, 54
blondes Gentlemen always seem to remember b. APPEARANCE, 42
blood be his b. on your own conscience GUILT, 5
b. and iron POWER POLITICS, 2
B. is thicker FAMILY, 1; PROVERBS, 94
B. sport is brought to its ultimate refinement JOURNALISM, 21
b., toil, tears and sweat CHURCHILL, W, 48; EFFORT, 3
cannot go on spilling b. IRELAND, 16
critics…desire our b., not our pain CRITICS, 13; NIETZSCHE, F, 15
day burns through their b. CAMPBELL, R, 5
drown in their own b. WAR, 82
He is all b., dirt and sucked sugar stick CRITICISM, 69; YEATS, W, 37
his b. be on us BIBLE, 430; GUILT, 3
How does the heart pump b. LEONARDO DA VINCI, 2
humble and meek are thirsting for b. HUMILITY, 8; ORTON, J, 3
I am in b. /Stepp'd in so far GUILT, 17; SHAKESPEARE, 219
If I die today every drop of my b. LAST WORDS, 40
I have lived off the b. of Chopin MUSICIANS, 7
increase in b. volume that would help the endurance competitor PREGNANCY, 9
it touches a man that his b. is sea water ENVIRONMENT, 9
leeches have red b. LAST WORDS, 23
men with our own real body and b. MANKIND, 25
my b. of the new testament BIBLE, 424; CHRISTIANITY, 29
rather have b. on my hands COMMITMENT, 6; GREENE, G, 3
Seas of B. CHRISTIANITY, 56; SITWELL, E, 4
shed his b. for the country JUSTICE, 22; ROOSEVELT, T, 8
The b. of the martyrs is the seed of the Church CHRISTIANITY, 61; TERTULLIAN, 1
the b. that she has spilt COWPER, W, 5; REVENGE, 10
the old savage England, whose last b. flows still ENGLAND, 29; LAWRENCE, D, 22
There are two kinds of b. RACISM, 31
the River Tiber foaming with much b. PROPHECY, 11; RACISM, 26
thought the old man…had so much b. in him SHAKESPEARE, 223
thy brother's b. crieth unto me MURDER, 2
white in the b. of the Lamb BIBLE, 463
Who so sheddeth man's b. BIBLE, 160
without shedding of b. is no remission BIBLE, 186; EXECUTION, 3
You can't get b. FUTILITY, 4; PROVERBS, 473
your b. of your lives will I require CRIME, 1; PUNISHMENT, 4
bloodcurdling good, old-fashioned, b. revenge AYCKBOURN, A, 3
bloodiness The sink is the great symbol of the b. of family life FAMILY, 40; NEUROSIS, 9
bloody Abroad is unutterably b. FOREIGNERS, 2
All the faces…seem to be b. Poms CHARLES, PRINCE, 1; ENGLISH, 12
Be b. bold, and resolute SHAKESPEARE, 221
My head is b., but unbowed ENDURANCE, 8
to have b. thoughts REVENGE, 18
You put up with the b. and botched events ENDURANCE, 6
bloom It's a sort of b. on a woman BARRIE, J, 8; CHARM, 3
lilac is in b. BROOKE, R, 3; FLOWERS, 2
blossom Love's perfect b. LOVE, 125
blot The last and greatest art – the art to b. DRYDEN, J, 2
blow A b. in cold blood SHAW, G, 30; VIOLENCE, 18
Another year! – another deadly b. DEFEAT, 18; WORDSWORTH, W, 52
Beware of the man who does not return your b. SHAW, G, 26
B., b., thou winter wind INGRATITUDE, 4; SHAKESPEARE, 50
b. his nose…state of the handkerchief industry ORWELL, G, 1
b. the Scots back again into Scotland TREASON, 5
B.…till you burst BROWNING, R, 44; CONTEMPT, 2
B., winds, and crack your cheeks SHAKESPEARE, 178; WEATHER, 19
but a word and a b. BUNYAN, J, 6; VIOLENCE, 5
themselves must strike the b. BYRON, 12; FREEDOM, 10
this b. /Might be the be-all and the end-all here ENDING, 6; SHAKESPEARE, 210
You know how to whistle…just put your lips together and b. WHISTLING, 1
blows B. are fitter for beasts VIOLENCE, 20
bludgeoning the b. of the people DEMOCRACY, 28; WILDE, O, 54
blue Little Boy B., /Come blow your horn NURSERY RHYMES, 29
that little tent of b. IMPRISONMENT, 14; WILDE, O, 4
The b. ribbon of the turf HORSES, 5
The essence of any b. material HUMOUR, 19
What are those b. remembered hills HOUSMAN, A, 15; NOSTALGIA, 11
Blues Twentieth-Century B. COWARD, N, 20; MELANCHOLY, 4
blue-vested short, b. people FRANCE, 3
bluffed Winston Churchill has b. them all POLITICIANS, 87
blunder poverty…is a b. JEROME, J, 3; POVERTY, 22
worse than a crime, it is a b. MISTAKES, 4
Youth is a b. AGE, 33; DISRAELI, B, 4
blunders b. usually do more to shape history than…wickedness MISTAKES, 20
The b. of a doctor DOCTORS, 15
blush a b. to the cheek of a young person DICKENS, C, 39; EMBARRASSMENT, 1
b. to find it fame GOOD, 15; POPE, A, 10
flower is born to b. unseen GRAY, T, 5; WASTE, 2
blushes Man is the only animal that b. TWAIN, M, 8
take away the candle and spare my b. JAMES, H, 14; MODESTY, 2
Boadicea some bargain-basement B. POLITICIANS, 90
boar the b. out of the wood doth waste it PRAYER, 23
when his half-civilized ancestors were hunting the wild b. JEWS, 3
boarding-house Any two meals at a b. FOOD, 43; LEACOCK, S, 7
boat a beautiful pea-green b. LEAR, E, 8; NONSENSE, 23
Do they allow tipping on the b. MARX, G, 17; MONEY, 34
in the same b.…not a chance of recording the vote WOMEN, 39
It was involuntary. They sank my b. KENNEDY, J, 3; MODESTY, 3
On a slow b. to China BOATS, 11
boating Jolly b. weather BOATS, 4
boats b. against the current FUTILITY, 8
messing about in b. BOATS, 7
we look for happiness in b. and carriage rides HORACE, 21; TRAVEL, 22
Bobby B. Shafto's gone to sea NURSERY RHYMES, 5
bob-tail I bet my money on the b. nag HORSES, 6
Boche drove the B. across the Rhine WORLD WAR I, 23

unprintable b. that is readable BOOKS, 35
What is the use of a b. BOOKS, 13; CARROLL, L, 4
What you don't know would make a great b. IGNORANCE, 22; SMITH, S, 6
When a b. is boring, they yawn openly BOOKS, 44
without mentioning a single b. BOOKS, 37; REED, H, 7
Would you allow your wife…to read this b. PRUDERY, 1
You can't tell a b. APPEARANCES, 7; PROVERBS, 479
books against b. the Home Secretary is PHILISTINISM, 7; WAUGH, E, 44
All b. are divisible into two classes BOOKS, 41; RUSKIN, J, 8
An author who speaks about his own b. DISRAELI, B, 30; EGOTISM, 5
authoress…whose b. have set all London talking BRONTE, C, 2
be not swallowed up in b. KNOWLEDGE, 40; LOVE, 175
between a man of sense and his b. BOOKS, 16; CHESTERFIELD, P, 14
B. and friends BOOKS, 1; FRIENDS, 1; PROVERBS, 95
B. are a load of crap BOOKS, 26; LARKIN, P, 3
B. are…a mighty bloodless substitute for life BOOKS, 47; STEVENSON, R, 18
B. are made…like pyramids BOOKS, 20
B. are well written, or badly written BOOKS, 53; WILDE, O, 44
b. by which the printers have lost BOOKS, 22
B. cannot always please BOOKS, 17
b. cannot be killed by fire BOOKS, 39; ROOSEVELT, F, 16
B., I don't know what you see in them BOOKS, 51
B. must follow sciences BACON, F, 63; BOOKS, 5
B.…propose to *instruct* or to *amuse* BOOKS, 18
B. think for me LAMB, C, 13; READING, 9
b.…written by people who don't understand them BOOKS, 29
Borrowers of b. BOOKS, 25; LAMB, C, 11
but b. never die BOOKS, 39; ROOSEVELT, F, 16
come not, Lucifer! /I'll burn my b. DAMNATION, 4; MARLOWE, C, 5
Few b. today are forgivable BOOKS, 24; LAING, R, 3
Give me b., fruit, French wine and fine weather KEATS, J, 66; PLEASURE, 19
God has written all the b. BUTLER, S, 13; SUBJECTIVITY, 2
His b. were read BELLOC, H, 14; BOOKS, 7; PUNS, 1
If my b. had been any worse CINEMA, 5
I keep my b. at the British Museum BOOKS, 10; BUTLER, S, 8
Morality's a gesture.…learnt from b. MORALITY, 3
Motherhood meant I have written four fewer b. MOTHERHOOD, 4
No furniture so charming as b. BOOKS, 46; SMITH, S, 12
of making many b. there is no end BIBLE, 78; BOOKS, 9
poring over miserable b. LEARNING, 17; TENNYSON, 53
Prolonged…reviewing of b. involves constantly *inventing* reactions CRITICISM, 46; ORWELL, G, 11
proper study of mankind is b. HUXLEY, A, 12; LITERATURE, 8
read our b. to find the juicy LITERATURE, 6
replacing some of the timber used up by my b. TREES, 6
Some b. are to be tasted BACON, F, 50; BOOKS, 4
Some b. are undeservedly forgotten AUDEN, W, 10; BOOKS, 3
the b. of the hour BOOKS, 41; RUSKIN, J, 8
The b. one reads in childhood…create in one's mind a…false map BOOKS, 34; ORWELL, G, 22
the disease of writing b. MONTESQUIEU, 8; WRITING, 35
The reading of all good b. LITERATURE, 3
To read too many b. MAO TSE-TUNG, 8; READING, 11
true University…collection of b. CARLYLE, T, 12
two classes of b. are of universal appeal LITERATURE, 4
We all know that b. burn BOOKS, 39; ROOSEVELT, F, 16
Whenever b. are burned CENSORSHIP, 4; HEINE, H, 1
When I think of all the b. I have read LIFE, 98; YEATS, W, 5
women dislike his b. ORWELL, G, 34; WRITERS, 75
bookseller he once shot a b. PUBLISHING, 5
booksellers b. are generous liberal-minded men JOHNSON, S, 55; PUBLISHING, 9
nor even b. have put up with poets being second-rate HORACE, 10; POETS, 8
boon Is life a b. GILBERT, W, 43; MORTALITY, 7
boorish the opinionated, the ignorant, and the b. ARISTOTLE, 3; STUBBORNNESS, 3
boot imagine a b. stamping on a human face OPPRESSION, 6; ORWELL, G, 16
Booth B. died blind FAITH, 19
boots before the truth has got its b. on LYING, 9
If ever he went to school without any b. CONCEIT, 5; INSULTS, 24
look at his b. CLASS, 45
Very well, then I shall not take off my b. PRACTICALITY, 6; WELLINGTON, 21
Bo-peep Little B. has lost her sheep NURSERY RHYMES, 28
bordello After I die, I shall return to earth as a gatekeeper of a b. THREATS, 5; TOSCANINI, A, 3
border the Night Mail crossing the B. TRAVEL, 5
Through all the wide B. CHIVALRY, 11; SCOTT, W, 14
borders We have no b.…no language other than Russian RUSSIA, 7
bore a b., a bounder and a prig INDIVIDUALITY, 4; LAWRENCE, T, 3
A b. is a man who BORES, 5
A healthy male adult b. BORES, 8; UPDIKE, J, 1
B., n. A person who talks BIERCE, A, 3; BORES, 1
Every hero becomes a b. EMERSON, R, 22; HEROISM, 6
He is an old b. BORES, 7; INSULTS, 123; TREE, H, 3
He is…decrepit and forgetful…a b. BELLOC, H, 2
Is not life…too short…to b. ourselves BOREDOM, 9; NIETZSCHE, F, 13
no greater b. than the travel b. SACKVILLE-WEST, V, 3; TRAVEL, 39
proof that God is a b. MENCKEN, H, 7; PROTESTANTISM, 6
War is an organized b. WAR, 79
you are…the club B.: I am the club Liar SAKI, 3; SUPERIORITY, 16
bored aged diplomats to be b. DIPLOMACY, 3
Bores and *B.* BORES, 2; BYRON, 34
Dear World, I am leaving you because I am b. LAST WORDS, 77
I wanted to be b. to death BOREDOM, 3
other people less b. for 100 minutes CINEMA, 19
Punctuality is the virtue of the b. PROMPTNESS, 5; WAUGH, E, 29
so b. with it all BOREDOM, 2; LAST WORDS, 20
We were as nearly b. as enthusiasm would permit CRITICISM, 23
When you're b. with yourself BOREDOM, 10; MARRIAGE, 123
boredom sheer apathy and b. DISCOVERY, 10; GOETHE, J, 8
The effect of b. on a large scale BOREDOM, 7; INGE, W, 3
three great evils, b., vice, and poverty VOLTAIRE, 10; WORK, 37
bores he b. for England INSULTS, 100; MUGGERIDGE, M, 6
the *B.* and *Bored* BORES, 2; BYRON, 34
Borgia makes good use of the B. effect REMEDIES, 6
boring curiously b. about…happiness HUXLEY, A, 22; SYMPATHY, 5
Somebody's b. me, I think it's me BORES, 6; THOMAS, D, 31
you ought to be ashamed of…being b. BOREDOM, 5
born A man is not completely b. LIFE AND DEATH, 17
a silly little mouse will be b. DISAPPOINTMENT, 4; HORACE, 6
As soon as man is b. DEATH, 4; PROVERBS, 66
a time to be b., and a time to die BIBLE, 67; TIME, 14
best…never to have been b. at all HEINE, H, 2; PESSIMISM, 6
better if neither of us had been b. NAPOLEON I, 6; REGRET, 13
b. again, not of corruptible seed BIBLE, 440; DEATH, 36
b. to obey OBEDIENCE, 2
B. under one law HUMAN CONDITION, 11
b. until I started to write WRITING, 19
Every moment one is b. LIFE AND DEATH, 32; TENNYSON, 82
except a man be b. again BIBLE, 243; CHRISTIANITY, 16
Fascism…future refusing to be b. BEVAN, A, 11
he is not conscious of being b. LA BRUYERE, J, 6; LIFE AND DEATH, 21
He was b. an Englishman BEHAN, B, 1; NATIONALITY, 2
It is as natural to die as to be b. LIFE AND DEATH, 6
I was b. at the age of twelve CINEMA, 9
I was b. in 1896 ILLEGITIMACY, 1
I was b. into big celebrity FAME, 12
I was b. old AGE, 93; TREE, H, 1
I was free b. BIBLE, 15; FREEDOM, 6
joy that a man is b. into the world BIBLE, 263; BIRTH, 3
let the day perish wherein I was b. BIBLE, 225
Man that is b. of a woman…short time to live BOOK OF COMMON PRAYER, 2
Man was b. free FREEDOM, 52; ROUSSEAU, J, 1
natural to die as to be b. BACON, F, 19; BIRTH, 1; DEATH, 30
none of woman b. /Shall harm Macbeth SHAKESPEARE, 221
No, thank you, I was b. intoxicated DRUNKENNESS, 25
One is not b. a woman BEAUVOIR, S, 3; WOMEN, 19
one of woman b. BIRTH, 15; SHAKESPEARE, 229
powerless to be b. ARNOLD, M, 19
Some are b. great GREATNESS, 12; SHAKESPEARE, 343
Some men are b. mediocre HELLER, J, 5; MEDIOCRITY, 6
sucker b. every minute GULLIBILITY, 1
that thou was b. with FOOLISHNESS, 18

that which is b. of the flesh is flesh BIBLE, 244
The house where I was b. HOOD, T, 6; NOSTALGIA, 10
to have been b. BIRTH, 6
to the manner b. CUSTOM, 4; SHAKESPEARE, 76
We are all b. mad BECKETT, S, 5; MADNESS, 4
Whatever is begotten, b., and dies MORTALITY, 23; YEATS, W, 27
born-again b. people...make you wish RELIGION, 101
boroughs The bright b., the circle-citadels there STARS, 4
borrow If you don't want to use the army, I should like to b. it LINCOLN, A, 9; SARCASM, 2
the men who b., and the men who lend LAMB, C, 10
borrow'd why do you dress me /In b. robes PROMOTION, 4
borrowed B. garments BORROWING, 1; PROVERBS, 96
Britain has lived...on b. time BRITAIN, 5
borrower Neither a b. nor a lender be INTEGRITY, 6; SHAKESPEARE, 75
borrowers B. of books BOOKS, 25; LAMB, C, 11
borrowing be not made a beggar by banqueting upon b. BIBLE, 86
b. dulls the edge of husbandry INTEGRITY, 6; SHAKESPEARE, 75
bosom Abraham's b. BIBLE, 333; POVERTY AND WEALTH, 3
a capital b. to hang jewels upon APPEARANCE, 24
not a b. to repose upon APPEARANCE, 24; DICKENS, C, 24
bosoms the silk stockings and white b. of your actresses JOHNSON, S, 46
boss working...eight hours a day...get to be a b. WORK, 9
Boston this is good old B. SNOBBERY, 3
botch sundial, and I make a b. BELLOC, H, 7
botched You put up with the bloody and b. events ENDURANCE, 6
both Dreaming on b. AGE, 80; SHAKESPEARE, 233
said on b. sides ADDISON, J, 13; OBJECTIVITY, 1
bother long words B. me MILNE, A, 6; WORDS, 24
bothered Bewitched, B. and Bewildered CONFUSION, 7
Botticelli If B. were alive today ARTISTS, 24; USTINOV, P, 9
bottinney b. means a knowledge of plants DICKENS, C, 31; EDUCATION, 27
bottle Yo-ho-ho, and a b. of rum ALCOHOL, 78; STEVENSON, R, 8
bottles It is with...people as with...b. CHARACTER, 17; INSULTS, 105; POPE, A, 55
the English have hot-water b. ENGLISH, 27; SEX, 81
bottom b. of the economic pyramid POVERTY, 33; ROOSEVELT, F, 8
Jesus picked up twelve men from the b. ranks CHRISTIANITY, 4
the best reasons...for remaining at the b. AMBITION, 7
bough Loaf of Bread beneath the B. CONTENTMENT, 3; FITZGERALD, E, 5
boughs young and easy under the apple b. THOMAS, D, 8
bought b. things because she wanted 'em WOMEN, 137
bouillabaisse B. is only good because cooked by the French FOOD, 27; FRANCE, 6
boulder When the torrent sweeps a man against a b. STEVENSON, R, 16; THEORY, 15
Boulogne There was an old man of B. ANONYMOUS, 92; INNUENDO, 1
bound grandmother's feet had been b. CHINA, 11
Tomorrow my hands will be b. EXECUTION, 2
boundary right to fix the b. of...a nation IRELAND, 21
bounder a bore and a b. and a prig LAWRENCE, T, 3
Bountiful Lady B. CHARITY, 16
bouquet the b. is better than the taste ALCOHOL, 64; POTTER, S, 7
bourgeois *B.*...is an epithet CLASS, 20; HOPE, A, 6
Gentleness was considered 'b.' CHINA, 13
How beastly the b. is LAWRENCE, D, 11; MEN, 9
bourgeoisie The British B. CLASS, 47
the British b. have spoken of themselves as gentlemen CLASS, 51; WAUGH, E, 15
bourn from whose b. /No traveller returns AFTERLIFE, 10; SHAKESPEARE, 91
bovine The cow is of the b. ilk ANIMALS, 19; NASH, O, 1
bow at the name of Jesus every knee should b. BIBLE, 443; CHRISTIANITY, 30
B., b., ye lower middle classes CLASS, 17; GILBERT, W, 16
I'm sure I don't know, /Says the great bell at B. NURSERY RHYMES, 41
I, said the Sparrow, /With my b. and arrow NURSERY RHYMES, 72
Says the great bell at B. LONDON, 2
bowels in the b. of Christ CROMWELL, O, 5; MISTAKES, 7
my b. were moved for him BIBLE, 494; SEX, 17
thirty yards of b. FASHION, 1
bower-bird I'm a bit of a b. WHITE, P, 3; WRITING, 52
bowl inverted B. we call The Sky DESTINY, 9; FITZGERALD, E, 15
love in a golden b. BLAKE, W, 11; WISDOM, 12
They came to see me bat not to see you b. CRICKET, 3
bow-wow Daddy wouldn't buy me a b. DOGS, 19
box B. about: 'twill come to my father anon FAMILY, 6
Take that black b. away CINEMA, 27; TREE, H, 9
boxing loves b. is either a liar or a fool SPORT AND GAMES, 15
boxing match Europe is not a b. EUROPE, 9
boy And said, What a good b. am I NURSERY RHYMES, 30
a secret way...of getting at a b. DICKENS, C, 20; EVIL, 10
A thing of duty is a b. for ever POLICE, 5; PUNS, 18
every b. and every gal /That's born into the world alive GILBERT, W, 19; POLITICS, 44
If...I were the only b. LOVE, 82
I'm farther off from heav'n /Than when...a b. INNOCENCE, 7
Let the b. win his spurs SELF-RELIANCE, 6
Love is a b. BUTLER, S, 4; INDULGENCE, 1
Mad about the b. COWARD, N, 11; LOVE, 60
rarely...one can see in a little b. the promise of a man CHILDREN, 27
Shades of the prison-house begin to close /Upon the growing b. METAPHYSICS, 5; WORDSWORTH, W, 26
The b. I love is up in the gallery LOVE, 173
The b. stood on the burning deck COURAGE, 18
the b. will ruin himself ROYALTY, 68
the little b. /Who lives down the lane NURSERY RHYMES, 4
To know I'm farther off from heav'n /Than when...a b. HOOD, T, 7
When I was a little b. they called me a liar WRITERS, 25
boyhood The smiles, the tears, /Of b.'s years MOORE, T, 7; NOSTALGIA, 17
boys As flies to wanton b. DESTINY, 22; SHAKESPEARE, 187
B. and girls come out to play NURSERY RHYMES, 6
B. are capital fellows in their own way CHILDREN, 44; LAMB, C, 9
B. do not grow up gradually CHILDREN, 25; CONNOLLY, C, 13
B. will be boys HOPE, A, 5; SEXES, 15
Claret is the liquor for b. ALCOHOL, 42; JOHNSON, S, 128
Girls and b. grow up more normally together EDUCATION, 75
the credit belongs to the b. in the back rooms GRATITUDE, 1
Where are the b. of the Old Brigade NOSTALGIA, 28
Where...b. plan for what...young girls plan for whom SEXES, 13
Written by office b. for office b. NEWSPAPERS, 14
young b. plan for what...achieve FEMINISM, 9
bra Burn your b. FEMINISM, 2
bracelet diamond and safire b. lasts forever MATERIALISM, 18
braces Damn b. BLAKE, W, 28
I had b. on my teeth and got high marks APPEARANCE, 43
braes Ye banks and b. BURNS, R, 24; NATURE, 2
Brahms B....an extraordinary musician MUSICIANS, 16
people who do B. without knowing Schoenberg MUSIC, 21
brain a Bear of Very Little B. MILNE, A, 6; WORDS, 24
b. attic stocked with all the furniture that he is likely to use DOYLE, A, 12; KNOWLEDGE, 16
B., n. An apparatus with which we think BIERCE, A, 4; MIND, 1
b. the size of a planet ADAMS, D, 5
If it is for mind that we are seaching the b. MIND, 30
It is good to rub and polish our b. MIND, 23
Let schoolmasters puzzle their b. EDUCATION, 37; GOLDSMITH, O, 21
My b.: it's my second favorite organ SEX, 6
our b. is a mystery MIND, 4
part of the b. reliably devoted to sex SEX, 115
Pure symmetry of the b. MIND, 19
that most perfect and complex of computers the human b. MEDICINE, 79
the biggest b. of all the primates MANKIND, 43; MORRIS, D, 4
The b. has muscles for thinking THINKING, 10
The b. is a wonderful organ WORK, 10
The b. is not an organ to be relied upon MIND, 3
The b. is the organ of longevity LONGEVITY, 12
the human b. is a device to keep the ears from grating MIND, 5
the universe, the reflection of the structure of the b. MIND, 4
Tobacco drieth the b. SMOKING, 36
we are supposing the b....more than a telephone-exchange MIND, 30
with no deep researches vex the b. CLARITY, 1
You've got the b. of a four-year-old boy MARX, G, 12; STUPIDITY, 8

brains a girl with b. ought to do something else WOMEN, 80
b. enough to make a fool of himself STEVENSON, R, 21; WISDOM AND FOOLISHNESS, 7
b. were suitable for a woman INTELLECT, 10
gallops night by night /Through lovers' b. SHAKESPEARE, 307
I mix them with my b. PAINTING, 10
many b. and many hands are needed DISCOVERY, 14
our b. as fruitful as our bodies WOMAN'S ROLE, 13
something better than our b. to depend upon ARISTOCRACY, 8; CHESTERFIELD, P, 20
sometimes his b. go to his head INTELLIGENCE, 1
What good are b. to a man INTELLIGENCE, 14; WODEHOUSE, P, 3
branch Cut is the b. that might have grown DEATH, 104; MARLOWE, C, 6
brandy I am not well; pray get me…b. INSULTS, 52
brass B. bands are all very well in their place BEECHAM, T, 9; MUSIC, 7
Make it compulsory for a doctor using a b. plate DOCTORS, 90
Men's evil manners live in b. MEMORIALS, 16; SHAKESPEARE, 143
sounding b. BIBLE, 38; CHARITY, 7
brat than it is to turn one b. into a decent human being CHILDREN, 43
brave Any fool can be b. on a battle field MITCHELL, M, 2; WAR, 108
b. new world…such people in't MANKIND, 58; SHAKESPEARE, 329
Fortune favours the b. COURAGE, 35; TERENCE, 3
land of the free, and the home of the b. AMERICA, 25
looked upon by posterity as a b., bad man CROMWELL, O, 2
Many b. men…before Agamemnon's time HORACE, 42; OBLIVION, 1
never done a b. thing O'BRIEN, E, 2
the B. deserves the Fair COURAGE, 13; DRYDEN, J, 16
we could never learn to be b.…if there were only joy COURAGE, 21; ENDURANCE, 9
Brazil B., where the nuts come from PLACES, 35
breach a custom more honour'd in the b. CUSTOM, 4; SHAKESPEARE, 76
Once more unto the b. COURAGE, 27; SHAKESPEARE, 129
breache lay the b. at their door DIPLOMACY, 1
bread b. and cheese, and kisses MARRIAGE, 151; SWIFT, J, 11
b. and circuses PUBLIC, 16
b. eaten in secret is pleasant BIBLE, 449; SECRECY, 5
b. enough and to spare BIBLE, 331
B. is the staff of life FOOD, 3; PROVERBS, 97
cast thy b. upon the waters BIBLE, 77; OPPORTUNITY, 10
gave you manna…angels' b. BIBLE, 97
I am the b. of life BIBLE, 250; FAITH, 8
if his son ask b., will he give him a stone BIBLE, 376; CHARITY, 10
Jesus took b., and blessed it BIBLE, 424; CHRISTIANITY, 29
Loaf of B. beneath the Bough CONTENTMENT, 3; FITZGERALD, E, 5
man shall not live by b. alone BIBLE, 356
One swears by wholemeal b. HEALTH AND HEALTHY LIVING, 10
Peace, B. and Land RUSSIAN REVOLUTION, 1
that b. should be so dear HOOD, T, 12; POVERTY, 20
Their learning is like b. in a besieged town JOHNSON, S, 96; SCOTS, 6
the living b. FOOD, 15
This b. I break was once the oat AGRICULTURE, 5; THOMAS, D, 17
breakdown One of the symptoms of approaching nervous b. WORK, 33
breakfast b.. I told Jeeves to drink it himself ALCOHOL, 87
breakfast-table ready for the national b. OBITUARIES, 10; TROLLOPE, A, 6
breakfast-time critical period in matrimony is b. HERBERT, A, 5; MARRIAGE, 87
break-throughs discovery of psychedelics one of the three major scientific b. SCIENCE, 50
breast charms to soothe a savage b. CONGREVE, W, 8; MUSIC, 17
my baby at my b. SHAKESPEARE, 39; SUICIDE, 32
The female b. has been called 'the badge of feminity' WOMEN, 78
breast-feeding Every luxury…atheism, b. INDULGENCE, 2; ORTON, J, 4
breasts there are no b. in space CINEMA, 8
they add weight to the b. COLETTE, S, 5; FOOD, 23
women, who have but small and narrow b. SEXES, 20
breath blow hot and cold with the same b. AESOP, 7; INDECISION, 1
Can storied urn…/Back to its mansion call the fleeting b. DEATH, 74; GRAY, T, 4
Competition was the b. of life to him FLEMING, A, 1
He reaps the bearded grain at a b. DEATH, 101; LONGFELLOW, H, 11
in this harsh world draw thy b. in pain MOURNING, 12; SHAKESPEARE, 108
The first b. is the beginning of death LIFE AND DEATH, 1
The years to come seemed waste of b. FLYING, 7; YEATS, W, 16
wish the night /Had borne my b. away HOOD, T, 6; NOSTALGIA, 10
world will hold its b. HITLER, A, 16; WORLD WAR II, 34
breathed God…b. into his nostrils BIBLE, 144; GARDENS, 3
breather I happen to be a chain b. SMOKING, 31
breathing Keep b. LONGEVITY, 17
breathings heard among the solitary hills /Low b. WORDSWORTH, W, 37
breed happy b. of men ENGLAND, 46; SHAKESPEARE, 297
more careful of the b. of their horses and dogs than of their children FAMILY, 47
breeder b. of sinners SHAKESPEARE, 93
breeding formed by a different b. DISRAELI, B, 12; POVERTY AND WEALTH, 5
God-like in our…b. of…plants and animals EVOLUTION, 25
Good b. consists in concealing how…we think of ourselves MANNERS, 6; TWAIN, M, 14
breeks taking the b. aff a wild Highlandman SCOTS, 10; SCOTT, W, 4
breeze The fair b. blew COLERIDGE, S, 28; EXPLORATION, 1
breezes spicy b. /Blow soft o'er Ceylon's isle MISANTHROPY, 1
brethren the least of these my b. BIBLE, 422
brevity B. is the soul of lingerie CLOTHES, 18; PARKER, D, 16
B. is the soul of wit BREVITY, 8; SHAKESPEARE, 81
brewery O take me to a b. ALCOHOL, 11; ANONYMOUS, 43
The b. is the best drugstore ALCOHOL, 9
bribe doing nothing for a b. CONTENTMENT, 9; SHAKESPEARE, 61
The man who offers a b. BRIBERY, 4; GREENE, G, 2
You cannot hope to b. or twist JOURNALISM, 36
bribes How many b. he had taken BRIBERY, 1
bribing Money is good for b. yourself MONEY, 40
brick carried a…b. in his pocket BUSINESS, 32; SWIFT, J, 6
he found it b. IMPROVEMENT, 1
He is a man of b. CHARACTER, 24; UPDIKE, J, 4
the Yellow B. Road TRAVEL, 19
bricklayers B. kick their wives to death CLASS, 53; WELLS, H, 19
bricks You can't make b. PROVERBS, 475
bride a b.'s attitude towards her betrothed MARRIAGE, 111; PUNS, 17
as a b. adorned for her husband BIBLE, 473
It helps…to remind your b. that you gave up a throne for her MARRIAGE, 171
the b. at every wedding ROOSEVELT, T, 2
unravish'd b. of quietness KEATS, J, 27; SILENCE, 9
bridegroom behold, the b. cometh BIBLE, 416
like the b. on the wedding cake APPEARANCE, 41; INSULTS, 90
the sun…cometh forth as a b. PSALMS, 8
bridge Beautiful Railway B. of the Silv'ry Tay DISASTER, 4
he bestowed upon the games of golf and b. EISENHOWER, D, 2
I am not going to speak to the man on the b. DEPARTURE, 3
I stood on the b. at midnight LONGFELLOW, H, 4; TIME, 34
Like a b. over troubled water COMFORT, 6
London B. is broken down NURSERY RHYMES, 33
over the B. of Sighs into eternity DEATH, 96
They promise to build a b. even where there's no river KHRUSHCHEV, N, 7
brief I strive to be b., and I become obscure BREVITY, 3; HORACE, 2
Out, out, b. candle LIFE, 86; SHAKESPEARE, 227
briefcase A lawyer with his b. can steal more LAWYERS, 9
briers how full of b. SHAKESPEARE, 42
O, how full of b. is this working-day world LIFE, 83
brigade Forward the Light B. OBEDIENCE, 4
Where are the boys of the Old B. NOSTALGIA, 28
brigands B. demand your money BUTLER, S, 29; WOMEN, 31
bright her beauty made /The b. world dim COMPLIMENTS, 33; SHELLEY, P, 26
Look on the b. side OPTIMISM, 5; PROVERBS, 268
she doth teach the torches to burn b. SHAKESPEARE, 308
the creature hath a purpose and its eyes are b. with it KEATS, J, 69; PURPOSE, 6
Tiger! burning b. ANIMALS, 6; BLAKE, W, 39

Bright I've got B.'s disease and he's got mine ILLNESS, 56
young lady named B. LIMERICKS, 7; SCIENCE, 16
brightening He died when his prospects seemed to be b. ANONYMOUS, 27
brighter Had I been b. REGRET, 16
brightness To pass away ere life hath lost its b. DEATH, 77
Brighton Like B. pier…inadequate for getting to France KINNOCK, N, 8; TRAVEL, 27
bright-star Johnny-the-b. REALISM, 5
brilliance No b. is needed in the law LAW, 26
brilliant a b. mind until he makes it up INTELLIGENCE, 2
a far less b. pen than mine BEERBOHM, M, 4; CONCEIT, 4
b. men…will come to a bad end BEERBOHM, M, 11; GREATNESS, 2
brillig Twas b., and the slithy toves CARROLL, L, 23; NONSENSE, 7
brimstone b. and fire BIBLE, 167; PUNISHMENT, 5
bring thou knowest not what a day may b. forth BIBLE, 457; FUTURE, 4
Why didn't you b. him with you HOMOSEXUALITY, 9
brink scared to go to the b. COURAGE, 14; COWARDICE, 2
Britain a time when B. had a savage culture CIVILIZATION, 2
battle of B. is about to begin CHURCHILL, W, 52; WORLD WAR II, 13
B. does not wish to be ruled by a conglomerate in Europe EUROPE, 23
B.…Fabian Society writ large BRITAIN, 8
B. fit country for heroes to live in GOVERNMENT, 21; LLOYD GEORGE, D, 11
B. is no longer in the politics of the pendulum POLITICS, 107; THATCHER, M, 17
B. is not…easily rocked by revolution BRITAIN, 8
Today in B., a fascist has won an election FASCISM, 13
to help B. to become a Third Programme BRITAIN, 16
When B. first, at heaven's command BRITAIN, 15
Britannia Rule, B., rule the waves BRITAIN, 15
British B. loathe the middle-aged AGE, 92
but we are B. – thank God HOMOSEXUALITY, 26
Hitler never understood…the B. HITLER, A, 1
I would rather be B. than just BRITISH, 12
Kipling has done more…to show…that the B. race is sound to the core KIPLING, R, 2
less known by the B. than these selfsame B. Islands BRITISH, 3
socialism…alien to the B. character SOCIALISM, 24; THATCHER, M, 27
The artists retired. The B. remained WHISTLER, J, 15
The B., being brought up on team games HOUSES OF PARLIAMENT, 17; PARKINSON, C, 3
The B. love permanence BRITISH, 4
The B. won't fight BRITISH, 9
the magnificent fair play of the B. criminal law DOYLE, A, 10; JUSTICE, 6
the most vulgar…is the B. tourist BRITISH, 10; TRAVEL, 26
when a B. Prime Minister sneezed BRITAIN, 13
you broke a B. square RACISM, 16
British Empire liquidation of the B. CHURCHILL, W, 60
British Museum a little room somewhere in the B. that MUSEUMS, 2; PRIESTLEY, J, 5
a reflection of the B. Reading Room INTELLECTUALS, 14; SPARK, M, 13
I keep my books at the B. BOOKS, 10; BUTLER, S, 8
There is in the B. an enormous mind MUSEUMS, 3; WOOLF, V, 9
British Rail It's a tremendous achievement, but it isn't easy to work with B. EUROPE, 13
Briton animated with the soul of a B. VOLTAIRE, 2
as only a free-born B. can do SERVILITY, 7; THACKERAY, W, 10
dullest B. of them all TROLLOPE, A, 1
I glory in the name of B. PATRIOTISM, 17
Britons B. never will be slaves BRITAIN, 15
B. were only natives HISTORY, 29; SELLAR, W, 4
broad B. of Church and b. of mind EDUCATION, 14
b., sunlit uplands WORLD WAR II, 10
She is a smart old b. EVIL, 18; RUNYON, D, 5
She's the B. and I'm the High ACADEMICS, 8
broadmindedness magnificent tolerance and b. of the English SHAW, G, 1
broken A b. head in Cold Bath Fields MACAULAY, T, 21; PAROCHIALISM, 2
baying for b. glass ARISTOCRACY, 21; WAUGH, E, 7
healeth those that are b. in heart PSALMS, 75
He liked the sound of b. glass ARISTOCRACY, 4; BELLOC, H, 18
I am become like a b. vessel PSALMS, 20
Laws were made to be b. LAW, 27
marriage had irretrievably b. down ROYALTY, 42
peace has b. out BRECHT, B, 10; PEACE, 7
the bones which thou hast b. PSALMS, 31
broker An honest b. DIPLOMACY, 5
bronchitis nobody goes to the theatre unless he…has b. AUDIENCES, 1
Brontë Charlotte B.…was/ only unlike them in being fortunate in her circumstances WRITERS, 67
bronze executed a memorial longer lasting than b. HORACE, 39; MEMORIALS, 8
broody b. hen sitting on a china egg BUREAUCRACY, 5
brook b. no contradiction DOCTORS, 107; WEBSTER, J, 2
brothel a sort of metaphysical b. for emotions SENTIMENTALITY, 3
brothels b. with bricks of Religion BLAKE, W, 20; HYPOCRISY, 5
brother Big B. is watching you AUTHORITARIANISM, 6
I want to be the white man's b. KING, M, 2; RACISM, 14
love God, and hateth his b. BIBLE, 284; LOVE, 30
my b. Jonathan BIBLE, 483
Pardon me…*I* am my b. MISTAKES, 11
the mote that is in thy b.'s eye JUDGMENT, 3
the same is my b. BIBLE, 390
brotherhood b. of man under the fatherhood of God RELIGION, 77
Freedom! Equality! B. ANONYMOUS, 50; HUMAN RIGHTS, 2
brother-in-law not his b. KING, M, 2; RACISM, 14
psychotic means he's even worse than my b. NEUROSIS, 8
brotherly let b. love continue BIBLE, 189
tramp a fine, b., generous fellow FAMILIARITY, 4
brothers All men are b. FAMILY, 49; POWELL, A, 3
B. all /In honour HONOUR, 7; WORDSWORTH, W, 40
happy few, we band of b. PATRIOTISM, 37
I grew up with a lot of b. and sisters AMBITION, 17
the poor are our b. and sisters POVERTY, 39; TERESA, 3
am I my b. keeper BIBLE, 154; MURDER, 2
brought b. nothing into this world BIBLE, 510; WEALTH, 14
never b. to min' BURNS, R, 4; FRIENDSHIP, 12
Brown John B.'s body MEMORIALS, 7
bruise it shall b. thy head SEXES, 4
sweetest fragrance from the herb…tread on it and b. it TROLLOPE, A, 9; WOMEN, 134
bruised it is often a comfort to…be b. in a new place CHANGE, 15
Brummel patronized…by B. and the Prince Regent SOCIETY, 11
Brunswick Hamelin Town's in B. BROWNING, R, 41; GERMANY, 1
brush B. Up Your Shakespeare SHAKESPEARE, 17
Brussels B. is a madness EUROPE, 11
meeting in a darkened bedroom in a B. hotel EUROPE, 25
brutality industry without art is b. ART, 30; RUSKIN, J, 4
Sentimentality is a superstructure covering b. JUNG, C, 8; SENTIMENTALITY, 2
brute B. force…rules VIOLENCE, 9
I never saw a b. I hated so BROWNING, R, 17; EVIL, 8
brutes Exterminate all b. CONRAD, J, 1; RUTHLESSNESS, 3
Thanks to words, we have been able to rise above the b. HUXLEY, A, 3; WORDS, 19
Brutus B. is an honourable man HONOUR, 5; SHAKESPEARE, 156
Caesar had his B. – Charles the First, his Cromwell TREASON, 9
The fault, dear B., is not in our stars SHAKESPEARE, 145
bubble Life is mostly froth and b. MISFORTUNE, 12
Like a hell-broth boil and b. SHAKESPEARE, 220
bubbles With beaded b. winking at the brim ALCOHOL, 47; KEATS, J, 37
buck The b. stops here RESPONSIBILITY, 20; TRUMAN, H, 10
Buckingham changing guard at B. Palace MILNE, A, 4; SOLDIERS, 6
buckle One, two, /B. my shoe NUMBERS, 4; NURSERY RHYMES, 40
buckler his faithfulness and truth shall be thy shield and b. PSALMS, 51
bucks bet you a hundred b. he ain't in here FUNERALS, 5
bud And now in age I b. again HERBERT, G, 4; OLD AGE, 53
Buddha plastic B. jars out a Karate screech TECHNOLOGY, 9
Buddhism nothing in Christianity or B. that quite matches SAKI, 10
budding That which sets…The b. rose above the rose full blown FRENCH REVOLUTION, 12; WORDSWORTH, W, 42
budget b. is a method of worrying ECONOMICS, 2
buds Gather the flowers, but spare the b. FLOWERS, 9; MARVELL, A, 8
the darling b. of May COMPLIMENTS, 31; SHAKESPEARE, 360
buffalo give me a home where the b. roam HOMESICKNESS, 4

bugger B. Bognor LAST WORDS, 41
build let us think that we b. for ever ARCHITECTURE, 14; RUSKIN, J, 10
The *end* is to b. well ARCHITECTURE, 21
They promise to b. a bridge even where there's no river KHRUSHCHEV, N, 7
builder he can only be a *b.* ARCHITECTURE, 13; RUSKIN, J, 3
building twenty years of marriage make her…like a public b. MARRIAGE, 168; WILDE, O, 56
Well b. hath three Conditions ARCHITECTURE; 21
buildings b.…condemned now in advance ARCHITECTURE, 16
I go amongst the b. of a city KEATS, J, 69; PURPOSE, 6
jostling scrum of office b. ARCHITECTURE, 5
Luftwaffe…knocked down our b. ARCHITECTURE, 3; CHARLES, PRINCE, 4
piles of b. now rise up and down LONDON, 6
built till we have b. Jerusalem BLAKE, W, 33; ENGLAND, 7; FIGHT, 1
Bulben Under bare Ben B.'s head YEATS, W, 32
bull Better send them a Papal B. MISTAKES, 8
Down at the old 'B. and Bush' PUBLIC HOUSES, 5
take the b. between the teeth GOLDWYN, S, 16; MIXED METAPHORS, 3
When you take the b. by the horns CHANCE, 6
bullet ballot is stronger than the b. DEMOCRACY, 14; LINCOLN, A, 11
b. and the bayonet are brother and sister WORLD WAR I, 20
Each b. has got its commission MORTALITY, 4
Every b. has its billet DESTINY, 30
The b. that is to kill me ARROGANCE, 6; NAPOLEON I, 11
bullets I heard the b. whistle WAR, 174; WASHINGTON, G, 4
bullfighting B. is the only art HEMINGWAY, E, 4; SPORT AND GAMES, 18
bully He is the b.…ready to twist the milksop's arm HEMINGWAY, E, 1
let a b. come into your front yard DIPLOMACY, 20
bulrushes an ark of b. BIBLE, 103
dam…the Nile with b. FREEDOM, 11
bump And things that go b. in the night PRAYER, 2; SUPERNATURAL, 1
don't b. into the furniture ACTING, 7
bums art and literature are left to a lot of shabby b. AMERICA, 27; ART, 19
Bunbury an invaluable permanent invalid called B. DECEPTION, 11; WILDE, O, 20
bungalow proud of the position of the b.,…in the country SUBURBIA, 2
bunk Exercise is b. HEALTH AND HEALTHY LIVING, 8
History is more or less b. HISTORY, 13
buns Hot cross b.! /…/One a penny, two a penny NURSERY RHYMES, 16
Bunsen and I'd left my B. burner home OPPORTUNITY, 22; THOMAS, D, 15
Bunyan My word, B., you're a lucky fellow HOSTAGES, 10
Burbank beautiful downtown B. PLACES, 3
burden Take up the White Man's b. KIPLING, R, 32; RACISM, 15
The dreadful b. IDLENESS, 2
burglar A b. who respects his art CRIME, 5
Burgundy a Naive Domestic B. ALCOHOL, 82
buried They all be b. at Wimble ANONYMOUS, 29
Burlington I'm B. Bertie BED, 5
burn better to marry than to b. BIBLE, 30; MARRIAGE, 27
b. the bloody bitches CLERGY, 18
come not, Lucifer! /I'll b. my books DAMNATION, 4; MARLOWE, C, 5
He would b. your house down EGOTISM, 4
I will b., but…continue our discussion in eternity EXECUTION, 36; MARTYRDOM, 5
sun shall not b. thee by day PSALMS, 68
burned A woman's heart always has a b. mark SORROW, 15
every government…should have its old speeches b. GOVERNMENT, 38
Whenever books are b. CENSORSHIP, 4; HEINE, H, 1
burning The boy stood on the b. deck COURAGE, 18
The spirit b. but unbent BYRON, 17; DETERMINATION, 7
they think we're b. witches CHESTERTON, G, 29
To keep a lamp b. CHARITY, 26; TERESA, 5
burnings B. of people ART, 29
burnish'd Furnish'd and b. by Aldershot sun ADMIRATION, 1; BETJEMAN, J, 12
burns day b. through their blood CAMPBELL, R, 5
burnt lamb for a b. BIBLE, 169
she is b. flesh SUPERNATURAL, 7
burnt-offerings but thou delightest not in b. PSALMS, 32
burr kind of b.; I shall stick PERSISTENCE, 12; SHAKESPEARE, 235
burst Blow your pipe there till you b. BROWNING, R, 44; CONTEMPT, 2
burthen the b. of the mystery…/Is lightened CONFUSION, 11; WORDSWORTH, W, 11
bury I come to b. Caesar, not to praise him EVIL, 19; SHAKESPEARE, 155
let the dead b. their dead BIBLE, 382; LIFE AND DEATH, 11
the sort of woman now…one would almost feel disposed to b. for nothing DICKENS, C, 29; WOMEN, 43
We will b. you KHRUSHCHEV, N, 6
bus Hitler has missed the b. CHAMBERLAIN, N, 7; WORLD WAR II, 8
bush the b. burned with fire BIBLE, 105
business A b. that makes nothing but money BUSINESS, 11
All b. sagacity reduces itself…to…sabotage BUSINESS, 34
a successful b. BUSINESS, 9
a woman's b. to get married MARRIAGE, 140; SHAW, G, 23
B. as usual BRITISH, 6; CHURCHILL, W, 42
B.…may bring money…friendship hardly ever does AUSTEN, J, 9; MONEY, 6
b. of allotting sins SIN, 10
B. underlies everything in our national life BUSINESS, 39; WILSON, W, 7
Chaplin is no b. man GOLDWYN, S, 7
dinner lubricates b. BUSINESS, 25
don't advise any one to take it up as a b. proposition ARTISTS, 5
everybody's b. is nobody's b. GOSSIP, 14; WALTON, I, 3
For good all round b. work, I should have preferred a Baptist PROTESTANTISM, 7; WELLS, H, 11
friendship founded on b. BUSINESS, 24
If everybody minded their own b. CARROLL, L, 7; CURIOSITY, 4
I have led a life of b. so long that I have lost my taste for reading READING, 17; WALPOLE, H, 2
it is…our b. to lose innocence INNOCENCE, 5
limit to what one can learn about normal b. transactions DEATH, 132
That's the true b. precept BUSINESS, 8; DICKENS, C, 26
The b. of America is b. AMERICA, 12; BUSINESS, 7
the future Englishmen must take b. as seriously as their grandfathers had done BUSINESS, 20
The Swiss…are not a people so much as a…b. SWITZERLAND, 2
To b. that we love we rise betime ENTHUSIASM, 8; SHAKESPEARE, 34
Whatsoever…the private calamity, I hope it will not interfere with the public b. of the country SHERIDAN, R, 15
Your b. is to put me out of b. EISENHOWER, D, 8
businessmen My message to the b. of this country ILLNESS, 19
Buss Miss B. and Miss Beale /Cupid's darts do not feel ANONYMOUS, 56; INSENSITIVITY, 1
bust I'm going to have a b. made of them GOLDWYN, S, 22
It's a funny thing about that b. AGE, 84; SHAW, G, 46
Buster B. Jones in white spats CATS, 3
bustle the b. of man's worktime BROWNING, R, 6; OPTIMISM, 18
busy How doth the little b. bee WATTS, I, 2; WORK, 38
It is a stupidity…to b. oneself with the correction of the world IMPROVEMENT, 3; MOLIERE, 6
The English are b. ENGLISH, 30; MONTESQUIEU, 7
thou knowest how b. I must be this day PRAYER, 3
too fucking b. – or vice versa SEX, 92
busyness Extreme *b.* EXCESS, 15; STEVENSON, R, 19
butcher The b., the baker, /The candlestick-maker NURSERY RHYMES, 49
the Prime Minister has to be a b. POLITICIANS, 57
butchers Governments needs to have both shepherds and b. GOVERNMENT, 41; VOLTAIRE, 22
Buthelezi bad case of the B. Blues SOUTH AFRICA, 6
butler I vote Labour, but my b.'s a Tory CLASS, 32; MOUNTBATTEN OF BURMA, L, 7
Sir Walter Scott…is an inspired b. SCOTT, W, 2
butlers b. and lady's maids do not reproduce their kind WELLS, H, 3
butter b. in a lordly dish BIBLE, 293
b. will only make us fat POWER POLITICS, 3
b. wouldn't melt in her mouth ACTORS, 24; INSULTS, 80
fine words b. no parsnips SCOTT, W, 11; WORDS, 27
Buttercup I'm called Little B. GILBERT, W, 7; NAMES, 3
buttered a piece of toast…fell…always/ on the b. side PERVERSITY, 5

butterflies Literature and b. are the two sweetest passions LITERATURE, 21; NABOKOV, V, 8
No shade, no shine, no b., no bees HOOD, T, 10; MONTHS, 10
butterfly a man dreaming I was a b. DREAMS, 4
Float like a b. SPORT AND GAMES, 1
Happiness is like a b. HAPPINESS, 16
Miss Austen,...the prettiest, silliest, most affected, husband-hunting /b. WRITERS, 73
buttock B. fetishism is comparatively rare GREER, G, 6
buttocks Two b. of one bum FRIENDSHIP, 24
button facility to do such things at the touch of a b. TECHNOLOGY, 11
buttress a b. of the church MELBOURNE, 10; SUPPORT, 6
buy American heiress wants to b. a man MATERIALISM, 19; MCCARTHY, M, 3
I could b. back my introduction MARX, G, 15
I will b. with you PREJUDICE, 11
would never b. my pictures PAINTING, 9
bygones Let b. be b. PROVERBS, 254
Byron A gifted B. rises in his wrath POETS, 26
a more worthless set than B. POETS, 12; WELLINGTON, 10
B. is dead POETS, 23
B. tried to write Poetry with a capital P POETS, 19
B. was really a comedian, not a satirist POETS, 19
Goethe's sage mind and B.'s force WORDSWORTH, W, 1
the words: B. is dead CARLYLE, J, 3
The world is rid of Lord B. POETS, 30
When B.'s eyes were shut in death ARNOLD, M, 26; POETS, 15

C

cabbage Cauliflower is nothing but c. FOOD, 69
cabbages c. and kings CARROLL, L, 28; NONSENSE, 9
The c. are coming now BETJEMAN, J, 11; ENGLAND, 6
cabbage-stumps Nothing but old fags and c. CRITICISM, 34; WRITING, 30
cabin'd c., cribb'd, confin'd, bound in SHAKESPEARE, 218
cabs busy driving c. and cutting hair GOVERNMENT, 9
Caesar *Ave C., morituri te salutant* ANONYMOUS, 9; LAST WORDS, 4
C.! dost thou lie so low DEATH, 146; SHAKESPEARE, 151
C. had his Brutus – Charles the First, his Cromwell TREASON, 9
C.'s laurel crown BLAKE, W, 4; POWER, 7
C.'s wife PROVERBS, 98; PURITY, 1
hast thou appealed unto C. BIBLE, 17
I always remember that I am C.'s daughter EXTRAVAGANCE, 3
I come to bury C. EVIL, 19; SHAKESPEARE, 155
Not that I lov'd C. less PATRIOTISM, 38; SHAKESPEARE, 154
Regions C. never knew COWPER, W, 3; ENGLAND, 18
render...unto C. the things which are C.'s BIBLE, 410; MATERIALISM, 5
Rose...where some buried C. bled FITZGERALD, E, 8; FLOWERS, 5
that C. might be great RUTHLESSNESS, 2
Caesars So long as men worship the C. and Napoleons TYRANNY, 6
cage keep such a bird in a c. IMPRISONMENT, 5
Marriage is like a c. MARRIAGE, 109; MONTAIGNE, M, 7
Nor iron bars a c. IMPRISONMENT, 8
robin redbreast in a c. BLAKE, W, 10; IMPRISONMENT, 2
She's only a bird in a gilded c. IMPRISONMENT, 7
caged We think c. birds sing, when indeed they cry IMPRISONMENT, 13; WEBSTER, J, 5
Cain the Lord set a mark upon C. BIBLE, 155; REVENGE, 4
caitiff If the rude c. smite the other too REVENGE, 11
cake Bake me a c. as fast as you can NURSERY RHYMES, 42
enough white lies to ice a wedding c. LYING, 4
Let them eat c. HUNGER, 10
like the bridegroom on the wedding c. APPEARANCE, 41; INSULTS, 90
my face looks like a wedding c. left out in the rain APPEARANCE, 7
cakes no more c. and ale MERRYMAKING, 4; SHAKESPEARE, 341
Calais 'C.' lying in my heart DEFEAT, 11
C....attract people once the tunnel opens FRANCE, 4
calamities C. are of two kinds MISFORTUNE, 5
the c. of life CLASS, 12; DEFOE, D, 3
calamity the third day a c. HOSPITALITY, 3; HOSPITALITY, 6
thou are wedded to c. LOVE AND DEATH, 9
Whatsoever...the private c., I hope it will not interfere with the public business of the country SHERIDAN, R, 15
calculating A dessicated c. machine BEVAN, A, 4
Calcutta Oh, C. PLACES, 36
Caledonia C.! stern and wild SCOTLAND, 7; SCOTT, W, 9
calf a molten c. BIBLE, 120
but the c. won't get much sleep ALLEN, W, 8; MISTRUST, 3
killed a c. he would do it in a high style SHAKESPEARE, 2
the fatted c. BIBLE, 332; PARTIES, 3
call one clear c. for me DUTY, 8; TENNYSON, 12
called c. a cold a cold BENNETT, A, 3; ILLNESS, 11
calling Germany c. TREASON, 8; WORLD WAR II, 32
calm sea is c. to-night ARNOLD, M, 10; SEA, 1
Wisdom has taught us to be c. and meek REVENGE, 11
calories the only thing that matters is c. HEALTH AND HEALTHY LIVING, 10
calumnies C. are answered best INSULTS, 77; JONSON, B, 15
Calvary the place, which is called C. BIBLE, 338; EXECUTION, 4
Calvin land of C., oat-cakes, and sulphur SCOTLAND, 8; SMITH, S, 7
Calvinist That maniacal C. and coddled poet COWPER, W, 2
Cambridge C. as a little town and Oxford OXFORD, 16
C. people rarely smile CAMBRIDGE, 2; PLACES, 7
Oxford is on the whole more attractive than C. CAMBRIDGE, 1; OXFORD, 3
Spring and summer did happen in C. CAMBRIDGE, 4; NABOKOV, V, 6
The young C. group CLASSIFICATION, 2; LAWRENCE, D, 16
To C. books CAMBRIDGE, 6; OXFORD, 14
With equal skill to C. books he sent CAMBRIDGE, 3; OXFORD, 6
came I c., I saw, God conquered VICTORY, 2, 11
I c., I saw, I conquered CAESAR, J, 4; VICTORY, 1
I c. like Water FITZGERALD, E, 11; LIFE AND DEATH, 15
camel easier for a c. to go through the eye of a needle BIBLE, 405; WEALTH, 13
Camelot many-tower'd C. TENNYSON, 41
there was a spot...known /As C. PLACES, 23
To look down to C. CURSES, 5; TENNYSON, 44
camels the c. and the sand CINEMA, 26
camera I am a c. OBJECTIVITY, 4
The c. cannot lie. But... PHOTOGRAPHY, 4
cameras She stole everything but the c. WEST, M, 2
camp an armed c. of Blackshirts, a bivouac for corpses FASCISM, 12
campaign as well as he ran his c. CLINTON, B, 3
Campbells The C. are comin' ANONYMOUS, 79
Campland This is C., an invisible country IMPRISONMENT, 12; SOLZHENITSYN, A, 12
campus three major administrative problems on a c. EDUCATION, 53
can Talent does what it c. TALENT AND GENIUS, 3
Canada what street C. is on IGNORANCE, 6; PLACES, 8
cancel to c. half a Line DESTINY, 8; FITZGERALD, E, 14
cancels debt which c. all others OBLIGATION, 1
cancer c....close to the Presidency CORRUPTION, 2
C.'s a Funny Thing DISEASE, 20
chronic diseases more destructive to life than c. DISEASE, 26
candid save me, from the c. friend FRANKNESS, 1
candidates C. should not attempt more than six BIBLE, 524
candle a c. of understanding BIBLE, 100; UNDERSTANDING, 1
Bell, book, and c. SHAKESPEARE, 165
blow out your c....to find your way ATHEISM, 5; GUIDANCE, 2
It is burning a farthing c. at Dover CRITICISM, 25; JOHNSON, S, 68
light a c., and put it under a bushel BIBLE, 361; RIGHTEOUSNESS, 3
light a c. to the sun FUTILITY, 12
Like a c. burnt out TIME, 64; YEATS, W, 21
little c. throws his beams GOOD, 17; SHAKESPEARE, 254
My c. burns at both ends PLEASURE, 23
Out, out, brief c. LIFE, 86; SHAKESPEARE, 227
She would rather light a c. than curse the darkness STEVENSON, A, 8
take away the c. and spare my blushes JAMES, H, 14; MODESTY, 2
thou...shalt light my c. PSALMS, 7
we shall this day light such a c. EXECUTION, 21
candle-light Can I get there by c. NURSERY RHYMES, 17
candles She would rather light c. than curse the darkness COMPLIMENTS, 35
The c. burn their sockets HOUSMAN, A, 4

candlestick The butcher, the baker, /The c.-maker NURSERY RHYMES, 49
cane c. someone and expect it to be painless PUNISHMENT, 32
canem *Cave c.* DOGS, 1
canker killing as the c. to the rose CORRUPTION, 8; MILTON, J, 23
canned C. music is like audible wallpaper POPULAR MUSIC, 9
Cannes C.…lie on the beach FAME, 25
cannibal Better sleep with a sober c. than a drunken Christian DRUNKENNESS, 21
cannon-ball c. took off his legs HOOD, T, 2; PUNS, 10
cannot I c. pardon him because I dare not GUILT, 5
canoe every man paddle his own c. INDEPENDENCE, 4
Canossa We will not go to C. DETERMINATION, 6
cant auld Lang Swine, how full of c. you are ROYALTY, 17
clear your *mind* of c. JOHNSON, S, 146; REASON, 6
love – all the wretched c. of it GREER, G, 4; LOVE, 81
Popular psychology is a mass of c. PSYCHOLOGY, 5
where the Greeks had modesty, we have c. HYPOCRISY, 15; PEACOCK, T, 2
capability Negative C. DOUBT, 7; KEATS, J, 53
capable c. of being well set to music ADDISON, J, 11; MUSIC, 2
capital Boys are c. fellows in their own way CHILDREN, 44; LAMB, C, 9
capitalism C. is the exploitation of man by man CAPITALISM, 1
C. re-creates POLITICS, 85
c.…: the process whereby American girls turn into American women CAPITALISM, 6; HAMPTON, C, 3
I am going to fight c. CAPITALISM, 15
imperialism is the monopoly stage of c. LENIN, V, 1; POLITICS, 67
Lenin was the first to discover that c. 'inevitably' caused war CAPITALISM, 18; TAYLOR, A, 4
militarism…is one of the chief bulwarks of c. CAPITALISM, 9
not just here to manage c. POLITICS, 10
the acceptable face of c. CAPITALISM, 8
unacceptable face of c. CAPITALISM, 7
We cannot remove the evils of c. CAPITALISM, 10; KINNOCK, N, 5
capitalist C. production begets…its own negation MARX, K, 5
Not every problem someone has with his girlfriend is…due to…c.…production CAPITALISM, 12
capitulate It will be conquered; I will not c. DETERMINATION, 9
Capricorn Lady C.,…was…keeping open bed HUXLEY, A, 9; PROMISCUITY, 5
caps We touch our c. ANTHONY, S, 2
captain C. of the *Pinafore* CONCEIT, 9; GILBERT, W, 8
captain's c. LEADERSHIP, 12
I am the c. of my soul RESPONSIBILITY, 8
their bats have been broken…by the team c. THATCHER, M, 7
captains C. of industry CARLYLE, T, 22; LEADERSHIP, 5
capten C., art tha sleepin' there below NEWBOLT, H, 3; WAR, 120
captive Beauty stands…Led c. BEAUTY, 33; MILTON, J, 54
car always using a small c. to drive to the dockyard instead of my Rolls Royce MOUNTBATTEN OF BURMA, L, 4; ROYALTY, 89
heart expands to tinker with his c. MACNEICE, L, 5
in which direction the c. was travelling LLOYD GEORGE, D, 3
I thought I told you to wait in the c. BANKHEAD, T, 12
The c. has become the carapace TRAVEL, 33
Would you buy a used c. from this man POLITICIANS, 36
carapace The car has become the c. TRAVEL, 33
carbon c. atom possesses certain exceptional properties SCIENCE, 56
carbuncle Like a c. on the face of an old and valued friend ARCHITECTURE, 4; CHARLES, PRINCE, 3
card wrestled with a self-adjusting c. table TECHNOLOGY, 17; THURBER, J, 8
Cardin a name as important as Pierre C. FASHION, 3
cardinal This c. is the person who rules POLITICIANS, 84
unbecoming for a c. to ski badly JOHN PAUL II, 1; SPORT AND GAMES, 21
cardio-sclerotic We have here an antique c. WORDS, 17
cards an old age of c. OLD AGE, 78; POPE, A, 44
I have not learned to play at c. JOHNSON, S, 163; SPORT AND GAMES, 22
care age is full of c. AGE, 82; SHAKESPEARE, 357; YOUTH, 27
always taking c. of their health HYPOCHONDRIA, 2
Begone, dull c. ANONYMOUS, 10; WORRY, 6
can c. intelligently for the future of England ENGLAND, 26
C. /Sat on his faded cheek MILTON, J, 35; WORRY, 15
For want of timely c. ILLNESS, 7
I c. for nobody SELFISHNESS, 2
I don't c. for war WAR, 117
Our progress…/Is trouble and c. LIFE, 58; LONGFELLOW, H, 15
pleasures are their only c. COWPER, W, 20
Sleep that knits up the ravell'd sleave of c. SHAKESPEARE, 214; SLEEP, 29
so vain…c. for the opinion of those we don't c. for CONCEIT, 8
take c. of the minutes CHESTERFIELD, P, 11; TIME, 17
Take c. of the pence CHESTERFIELD, P, 10; THRIFT, 5
The first C. in building of Cities ENVIRONMENT, 2
what is past my help is past my c. BEAUMONT, F, 2; INDIFFERENCE, 1
career a c. that depends a lot on being tall and blonde SPORT AND GAMES, 10
a lover with any other c. in view COMMITMENT, 10; WELLS, H, 5
having a c. of my own BALFOUR, A, 1; MARRIAGE, 16
lost my virginity as a c. move AMBITION, 18
marriage that denied me my c. MARRIAGE, 43
Miss Madeleine Philips…was a c. COMMITMENT, 10; WELLS, H, 5
nothing in his long c. which those…would wish otherwise ROYALTY, 19
nothing which might damage his c. BARRIE, J, 10; SCOTS, 1
science was the only c. worth following WORK, 15
sign a piece of paper at the beginning of your c. BUSINESS, 22
careers The best c. advice to give to the young OCCUPATIONS, 25; WHITEHORN, K, 6
careful be very c. o' vidders CAUTION, 11; DICKENS, C, 45
careless first fine c. rapture BROWNING, R, 27
carelessness To lose one parent…a misfortune; to lose both looks like c. LOSS, 10; WILDE, O, 26
with a slow deliberate c. LAWRENCE, T, 10; READING, 10
cares Nobody c. much at heart about Titian ARTISTS, 23
the earth where c. abound WORDSWORTH, W, 74
careth he that is married c.…how he may please his wife BIBLE, 31; MARRIAGE, 28
cargo With a c. of ivory BOATS, 13; MASEFIELD, J, 2
With a c. of Tyne coal BOATS, 14; MASEFIELD, J, 3
caring take millions off the c. services KINNOCK, N, 9; PATRIOTISM, 26
Carnation C. milk is the best in the land FOOD, 8
carpe *C. diem* HORACE, 32; PRESENT, 7
carpenter Walrus and the C. CARROLL, L, 27; SEASIDE, 2
carpet a Turkey c. bears to a picture CRITICISM, 38; MACAULAY, T, 11
only men in rags…/Mistake themselves for c. bags ETIQUETTE, 7
carriage Go together like a horse and c. LOVE AND MARRIAGE, 2
very small second-class c. BOATS, 6; GILBERT, W, 22
we look for happiness in boats and c. rides HORACE, 21; TRAVEL, 22
carriages when they think they are alone in railway c. HABIT, 6
carry certain we can c. nothing out BIBLE, 510; WEALTH, 14
cars the selling of c. in Great Portland Street INSULTS, 39
carter how a c., a common sailor, a beggar is still…an Englishman ENGLAND, 36
Carthage C. must be destroyed WAR, 42
Cary Grant Old C. fine TELEGRAMS, 7
Casbah Come with me to the C. INVITATIONS, 2
case If ever there was a c. of clearer evidence NONSENSE, 2
in our c. we have not got REED, H, 3; WEAPONS, 8
the c. is still before the courts HORACE, 5
the reason of the c. LAW, 28
there had been a lady in the c. BYRON, 29; WOMEN, 32
The world is everything that is the c. LOGIC, 7
casements Charm'd magic c. KEATS, J, 39
cases a narrative of the special c. of his patients MEDICINE, 6
cash Nothing links man to man like…c. MONEY, 47
One cannot assess in terms of c.…a church tower ENVIRONMENT, 3
only the poor who pay c. FRANCE, A, 10; MONEY, 23
take the C. in hand FITZGERALD, E, 6; MONEY, 22
cashiers c. of the Musical Banks BUTLER, S, 2; MONEY, 13
casino I have come to regard…courts…as a c. JUSTICE, 11
cask A c. of wine ALCOHOL, 1; PROVERBS, 5
casket seal the hushed c. of my soul KEATS, J, 48; SLEEP, 24
Cassius C. has a lean and hungry look MISTRUST, 10; SHAKESPEARE, 146
cassock C., band, and hymn-book too CLERGY, 15
cassowary If I were a c. CLERGY, 15

cast c. thy bread upon the waters BIBLE, 77; OPPORTUNITY, 10
he that is without sin…let him first c. a stone BIBLE, 251; SIN, 4
pale c. of thought CONSCIENCE, 7; COWARDICE, 8; SHAKESPEARE, 92
set my life upon a c. CHANCE, 7
she was…c. for a great role PANKHURST, E, 2
The die is c. CAESAR, J, 3; IRREVOCABILITY, 1
caste measure the social c. of a person CLASS, 3
casteth perfect love c. out fear BIBLE, 283; LOVE, 29
casting It is no good c. out devils DEVIL, 12; LAWRENCE, D, 36
castle A c. called Doubting C. BUNYAN, J, 7; DESPAIR, 4
A neurotic is the man who builds a c. in the air PSYCHIATRY, 31
The house of every one is to him as his c. PRIVACY, 2
Castlereagh Murder…had a mask like C. MURDER, 12; SHELLEY, P, 13
castles C. in the air DREAMS, 9; IBSEN, H, 7
Pale Death kicks his way…into…the c. of kings EQUALITY, 42; HORACE, 27
the c. I have, are built with air DREAMS, 10; JONSON, B, 5
castrated after the war he should be publicly c. LLOYD GEORGE, D, 4
casualty except the c. list of the World War MURDER, 3
The first c. when war comes WAR, 88
cat A c. has nine lives LUCK, 2; PROVERBS, 6
A c. may look EQUALITY, 1; PROVERBS, 7
a C. of such deceitfulness CATS, 4; ELIOT, T, 16
c. is a diagram and pattern of subtle air CATS, 11; LESSING, D, 6
God…a cosmic Cheshire c. GOD, 28
Had Tiberius been a c. ARNOLD, M, 33; CATS, 1
He bought a crooked c., which caught a crooked mouse NURSERY RHYMES, 56
he is a very fine c. CATS, 9; JOHNSON, S, 145
Hey diddle diddle, /The c. and the fiddle NURSERY RHYMES, 14
I am the c. that walks alone BEAVERBROOK, M, 1; INDEPENDENCE, 2; SELF-RELIANCE, 4
I'll bell the c. COURAGE, 12
More ways of killing a c. CHOICE, 3; KINGSLEY, C, 10
That tossed the dog, /That worried the c. NURSERY RHYMES, 61
The C., the Rat, and Lovell our dog INSULTS, 37
What c.'s averse to fish GRAY, T, 11; MATERIALISM, 12
When I play with my c. CATS, 12; MONTAIGNE, M, 5
When the c.'s away ABSENCE, 3; PROVERBS, 461
cataclysm Out of their c. but one poor Noah /Dare hope to survive HUXLEY, A, 18; SEX, 54
catastrophe to lose one's teeth is a c. TEETH, 6
When a man confronts c.…a woman looks in her mirror SEXES, 33
Catch-22 moved very deeply by…this clause of C. LOGIC, 5
only one catch and that was C. OBSTRUCTION, 3
catch Go, and c. a falling star DONNE, J, 13; NONSENSE, 11
catches it is your business, when the wall next door c. fire HORACE, 22
catchwords Man is a creature who lives…by c. SEXES, 28; STEVENSON, R, 14
categorical This imperative is C. KANT, I, 2; MORALITY, 8
cathedral c. is worth a hundred theologians RELIGION, 8
cathedrals the ancient c. – grand, wonderful, mysterious RELIGION, 82
Catherine I'm glad you like my C. PROMISCUITY, 13; WEST, M, 15
Catholic A C. layman who has never been averse INSULTS, 85
Evelyn Waugh…is a Roman C. WAUGH, E, 1
he clings to the Roman C. Church BELLOC, H, 1
I am a C.….I go to Mass every day BELLOC, H, 21; PREJUDICE, 1
I have a C. soul, but a Lutheran stomach CATHOLICISM, 4
I'm still a C. CATHOLICISM, 16
One cannot…be a C. and grown-up CATHOLICISM, 12
quite lawful for a C. woman to avoid pregnancy by…mathematics CONTRACEPTION, 10; MENCKEN, H, 4
who, like you, your Holiness, is a Roman C. CATHOLICISM, 3
Catholics C. and Communists have committed great crimes COMMITMENT, 6; GREENE, G, 3
they may be C. but they are not Christians INSULTS, 97; MCCARTHY, M, 6
We know these new English C. LAWRENCE, D, 39
cats All c. are grey EQUALITY, 2; PROVERBS, 32
A lotta c. copy the Mona Lisa IMITATION, 1
what c. most appreciate…is…entertainment value CATS, 8
cattle Actors should be treated like c. ACTORS, 8
O Mary, go and call the c. home AGRICULTURE, 4; KINGSLEY, C, 4

these who die as c. WORLD WAR I, 18
thou art cursed above all c. BIBLE, 151
cauliflower C. is nothing but cabbage FOOD, 69
cause A c. is like champagne and high heels BELIEF, 3
A reckoning up of the c. often solves the malady REMEDIES, 18
Arise, O Lord, plead Thine own c. PRAYER, 23
for what high c. /This darling of the Gods DESTINY, 16; MARVELL, A, 7
the name of perseverance in a good c. STERNE, L, 6; STUBBORNNESS, 4
causes Home of lost c. ARNOLD, M, 13; OXFORD, 1
they should declare the c. which impel them to…separation INDEPENDENCE, 3; JEFFERSON, T, 4
caustic Too c.? To hell with cost GOLDWYN, S, 3
caution c. in love LOVE, 136
cautious he was c. of his own words CROMWELL, O, 3
cavaliero a perfect c. BYRON, 6; HEROISM, 5
Cavaliers C. (Wrong but Wromantic) HISTORY, 27; SELLAR, W, 5
cave *C. canem* DOGS, 1
I should be like a lion in a c. of savage Daniels ENEMIES, 11; WILDE, O, 77
caverns Gluts twice ten thousand C. KEATS, J, 43; SEA, 8
Through c. measureless to man COLERIDGE, S, 14; PLEASURE, 10
caves be c.…in which his shadow will be shown GOD, 41; NIETZSCHE, F, 5
sunny pleasure-dome with c. of ice COLERIDGE, S, 15; PLEASURE, 11
caviare c. to the general SHAKESPEARE, 87; TASTE, 7
cavity John Brown is filling his last c. ANONYMOUS, 74
cease have their day and c. to be TENNYSON, 26; TRANSIENCE, 23
he maketh wars to c. in all the world PSALMS, 28
I will not c. from mental fight BLAKE, W, 33; ENGLAND, 7; FIGHT, 1
restless Cromwell could not c. MARVELL, A, 3; POLITICIANS, 105
ceases forbearance c. to be a virtue BURKE, E, 5; TOLERANCE, 1
cedar spread abroad like a c. in Libanus PSALMS, 52
cedars the c. of Libanus PSALMS, 16
celebrate I c. myself SELF, 24; WHITMAN, W, 6
poetry cannot c. them AUDEN, W, 7
celebrity A c.…works hard…to become known FAME, 2
I was born into big c. FAME, 12
owes his c. merely to his antiquity CHAUCER, G, 1
The c.…known for his well-knownness FAME, 6
celerity C. is never more admir'd IMPETUOSITY, 3; SHAKESPEARE, 33
celery Genuineness…Like c. HUXLEY, A, 34; SINCERITY, 4
two thousand people crunching c. at the same time FOOD, 63; SHAW, G, 45
Celia Come, my C., let us prove JONSON, B, 16; LOVE, 94
celibacy c. is…a muddy horse-pond MARRIAGE, 117; PEACOCK, T, 5
cello The c. is not one of my favourite instruments MUSIC, 64
cells These little grey c. CHRISTIE, A, 3; INTELLECT, 1
celluloid The most expensive habit in the world is c. not heroin CINEMA, 24
cemetery Help me down C. Road SUPPORT, 4; TRAVEL, 28
old c. in which nine of his daughters THURBER, J, 7
send him to the c. VIOLENCE, 13
censor Deleted by French c. NEWSPAPERS, 3
censorship Assassination…the extreme form of c. ASSASSINATION, 7; SHAW, G, 39
C.…depraving and corrupting CENSORSHIP, 12
censure All c. of a man's self JOHNSON, S, 125; SELF, 13
No man can justly c. or condemn JUDGMENT, 5
centre I love being at the c. of things COMMITMENT, 9; THATCHER, M, 32
My c. is giving way WORLD WAR I, 9
the c. cannot hold YEATS, W, 28
century The c. on which we are entering…must be the c. of the common man PUBLIC, 20
The great man…walks across his c. INFLUENCE, 7; LEACOCK, S, 9
the twentieth c. will be…the c. of Fascism FASCISM, 9; MUSSOLINI, B, 4
cereal Do you *know* what breakfast c. is made of FOOD, 24
cerebrums larger c. and smaller adrenal glands MENCKEN, H, 5; WAR, 106
certain I am c. that we will win the election with a good majority SELF-CONFIDENCE, 11; THATCHER, M, 35
nothing can be said to be c. but death and taxes FRANKLIN, B, 17
Nothing is c. but death DEATH, 12; PROVERBS, 316; TAXATION, 4

One thing is c. FITZGERALD, E, 10; LIFE, 39
certainties begin with c. BACON, F, 2; CERTAINTY, 1; DOUBT, 1
His doubts are better than…c. DOUBT, 6
the safe comfort of c. TRUTH, 21
certainty The mind longs for c. CERTAINTY, 2
cesspit people swirling about in a human c. AIDS, 1
cesspool London, that great c. DOYLE, A, 16; LONDON, 10
Ceylon spicy breezes /Blow soft o'er C.'s isle MISANTHROPY, 1
chaff An editor…separates the wheat from the c. EDITORS, 4; STEVENSON, A, 1
not racially pure are mere c. RACISM, 13
chain A c. is no stronger PROVERBS, 9; UNITY, 1
the flesh to feel the c. BRONTE, E, 5; IMPRISONMENT, 3
chains c. that tie /The hidden soul of harmony MILTON, J, 20; MUSIC, 42
It's often safer to be in c. FREEDOM, 30; KAFKA, F, 3
Man…everywhere he is in c. FREEDOM, 52; ROUSSEAU, J, 1
nothing to lose but their c. MARX, K, 2; MARXISM, 10
chair Give Dayrolles a c. CHESTERFIELD, P, 23; LAST WORDS, 18
the nineteenth century was the age of the editorial c. PSYCHIATRY, 23
chairs The c. are being brought in from the garden AUDEN, W, 18
chaise All in a c. and pair COWPER, W, 10; MARRIAGE, 57
chaise-longue Wedlock – the…deep peace of the double bed after the…c. MARRIAGE, 41
chalices In old time we had treen c. and golden priests CLERGY, 8
Cham That great C. JOHNSON, S, 2
chamber rapping at my c. door SUPERNATURAL, 12
Upstairs and downstairs /And in my lady's c. NURSERY RHYMES, 13
Chamberlain a speech by C. is like…Woolworths INSULTS, 18; SPEECHES, 3
chambermaid a man would be as happy in the arms of a c. JOHNSON, S, 126
chameleon A c. on plaid ROOSEVELT, F, 1
chamois springing from blonde to blonde like the c. of the Alps WODEHOUSE, P, 20
champagne Fighting is like c. MITCHELL, M, 2; WAR, 108
I get no kick from c. COMPLIMENTS, 23
like a glass of c. that has stood HOUSES OF PARLIAMENT, 2
water flowed like c. ABSTINENCE, 4
champion great driver and a great c. loses his life SPORT AND GAMES, 29
chance every c. brought out a noble knight NOSTALGIA, 25; TENNYSON, 22
Grab a c. OPPORTUNITY, 18
in our lives c. may have an astonishing influence FLEMING, A, 3
time and c. happeneth to them all BIBLE, 74; CHANCE, 2
Chancellor C. of the Exchequer TAXATION, 8
chandelier The soul of Dizzy was a c. DISRAELI, B, 1
change c.…due to truths being in and out of favor CHANGE, 10
c. in musical style…c. in clothing style POPULAR MUSIC, 26
C. is not made without inconvenience CHANGE, 14
c. is the very essence of life CHANGE, 9
I c., but I cannot die SHELLEY, P, 6; WEATHER, 23
If you leave a thing alone you leave it to a torrent of c. CHESTERTON, G, 35; CONSERVATISM, 2
Most of the c. we think we see FROST, R, 1; NOVELTY, 2
Most women set out to try to c. a man CHANGE, 5; SEXES, 10
often we support c., and then are swept away CHANGE, 11
Plus ça c. CONSTANCY, 3
Popularity?…glory's small c. POPULARITY, 4
the largest scope for c. BRITTAIN, V, 2; FEMINISM, 5
The miserable c. now at my end /Lament nor sorrow at SUICIDE, 31
The more things c. CONSTANCY, 3
There is a certain relief in c. CHANGE, 15
The wind of c. CHANGE, 18; MACMILLAN, H, 8
changed All c., c. utterly BEAUTY, 49; YEATS, W, 10
changeth The old order c. CHANGE, 25; TENNYSON, 23
changez *C. vos amis* DE GAULLE, C, 9; FRIENDS, 7
changing c. scenes of life CHANGE, 24
Woman is always fickle and c. VIRGIL, 12; WOMEN, 139
Channel dream you are crossing the C. BOATS, 6; GILBERT, W, 22
let the last man…brush the C. with his sleeve WAR, 151
chaos a perfectly possible means of overcoming c. POETRY, 50
carrying a bit of c. round with him TENNYSON, 3
c. is a science of process SCIENCE, 43
The grotesque c. of a Labour council – a *Labour* council KINNOCK, N, 10
chapel Devil always builds a c. there DEFOE, D, 5; DEVIL, 10
Who lied in the c. /Now lies in the Abbey BYRON, 39
chapels c. had been churches ACTION, 13; SHAKESPEARE, 239
Chaplain twice a day the C. called IMPRISONMENT, 15; WILDE, O, 6
Chaplin C. is no business man ACTORS, 20; GOLDWYN, S, 7
chaps Biography is about C. BIOGRAPHY, 1
chapter c. of accidents CHESTERFIELD, P, 18; MISFORTUNE, 9
character Education…formation of c. EDUCATION, 89
George Harrison is a sweet sort of hapless c. POPULAR MUSIC, 18
I had become a woman of…c. CHARACTER, 6
I leave my c. behind REPUTATION, 15; SHERIDAN, R, 11
proper time to influence the c. of a child INGE, W, 9
to influence the c. of a child INFLUENCE, 4
What is c. but the determination of incident JAMES, H, 12
characteristic c. of Thatcherism SOCIETY, 1
typically English c. ENGLISH, 3; UNITY, 4
characters c. in one of my novels FICTION, 3; FITZGERALD, F, 15
her c. are round, or capable of rotundity WRITERS, 52
involvements and feelings and c. of ordinary life WRITERS, 86
Most women have no c. POPE, A, 41; WOMEN, 107
some of the c. will seem almost mythopoeic TOLKIEN, J, 3
charge Electrical force…causes motion of electrical c. SCIENCE, 30
charged it was c. against me INDIFFERENCE, 7; WHITMAN, W, 4
Charing Cross between Heaven and C. HEAVEN, 15
I went out to C., to see Major-general Harrison hanged EXECUTION, 29; PEPYS, S, 6
the full tide of human existence is at C. JOHNSON, S, 93; LONDON, 17
chariot a c.…of fire BIBLE, 301
Swing low sweet c. ANONYMOUS, 76; DEATH, 22
the dust beneath thy c. wheel HUMILITY, 5
Time's winged c. AGE, 61; MARVELL, A, 10
charity C. begins at home BROWNE, T, 8; PROVERBS, 99
C. is the power of defending that which we know to be indefensible CHESTERTON, G, 22; HOPE, 8
c. never faileth BIBLE, 38; CHARITY, 7
c. offers to the poor the gains in medical skill CHARITY, 18
c. suffereth long, and is kind BIBLE, 38; CHARITY, 7
government gives us is c. at election time OPPRESSION, 5
In c. there is no excess BACON, F, 27; CHARITY, 4
knowledge puffeth up, but c. edifieth BIBLE, 32; CHARITY, 8; KNOWLEDGE, 6
lectures or a little c. SELF, 25; WHITMAN, W, 8
now abideth faith, hope, c. BIBLE, 38; CHARITY, 7
the greatest of these is c. BIBLE, 38; CHARITY, 7
The house which is not opened for c. CHARITY, 25
The living need c. CHARITY, 3
The man who leaves money to c. in his will VOLTAIRE, 33
without c. are nothing worth BOOK OF COMMON PRAYER, 8; CHARITY, 11
Charles Caesar had his Brutus – C. the First, his Cromwell TREASON, 9
cast out C. our Norman oppressor REBELLION, 14
There were gentlemen and…seamen in the navy of C. the Second NAVY, 8
Charley I'm C.'s aunt from Brazil PLACES, 35
Charlie C. is my darling ADMIRATION, 11; COMPLIMENTS, 20
charm Conversation has a kind of c. CONVERSATION, 8
The c. is purely romantic IDEALISM, 9
the c.…of a nomadic existence SACKVILLE-WEST, V, 5
charming c. people have something to conceal CONNOLLY, C, 11
I heard the bullets whistle…c. in the sound WAR, 174; WASHINGTON, G, 4
It is c. to totter into vogue AGE, 97; WALPOLE, H, 5
People are either c. or tedious WILDE, O, 39
charms Whose c. all other maids surpass ADMIRATION, 9; COMPLIMENTS, 16
Charon C., seeing, may forget LANDOR, W, 1; LUST, 8
Chartreuse religious system that produced green C. ALCOHOL, 66; CHRISTIANITY, 53
charwoman agree to become a c. FEMINISM, 21
chasing always c. Rimbauds PARKER, D, 8

chaste godly poet must be c. himself POETRY, 16
My English text is c. CENSORSHIP, 3
school-miss Alfred vent her c. delight TENNYSON, 2
chastise in politics to c. his own side than the enemy ORWELL, G, 2
chastity Give me c. and continence PRAYER, 4; PROCRASTINATION, 4
Chatterley Put thy shimmy on, Lady C. LAWRENCE, D, 18; PARTING, 7
cheap flesh and blood so c. HOOD, T, 12; POVERTY, 20
Pile it high, sell it c. BUSINESS, 6; CAPITALISM, 3
send me some good actors – c. PRAYER, 5
War is never c. BUSH, G, 14; WAR, 36
cheating PEACE, n.... a period of c. BIERCE, A, 10
check C. enclosed PARKER, D, 29
dreadful is the c. BRONTE, E, 5
cheek Care /Sat on his faded c. MILTON, J, 35; WORRY, 15
the c. that doth not fade APPEARANCE, 35; KEATS, J, 18
turn the other c. REVENGE, 11
whosoever shall smite thee on thy right c. BIBLE, 364; ENEMIES, 2
cheeks Blow, winds, and crack your c. SHAKESPEARE, 178; WEATHER, 19
cheer cups, /That c. but not inebriate COWPER, W, 25; DRINKS, 10
Don't c., boys; the poor devils are dying WAR, 129
cheerful God loveth a c. giver BIBLE, 45
cheerfulness No warmth, no c., no healthful ease HOOD, T, 10; MONTHS, 10
cheese 265 kinds of c. DE GAULLE, C, 8; FRANCE, 7
bread and c., and kisses MARRIAGE, 151; SWIFT, J, 11
c. – toasted, mostly DREAMS, 13; FOOD, 65; STEVENSON, R, 10
when the c. is gone BRECHT, B, 8; NONSENSE, 4
cheesed unremitting humanity soon had me c. off DICKENS, C, 1
chef the resurrection of a French c. FOOD, 31
Cheltenham Here lie I.../Killed by drinking C. waters ANONYMOUS, 25
chemical c. barrage...against the fabric of life CARSON, R, 3; ECOLOGY, 2
Shelley and Keats were...up to date in...c. knowledge POETS, 7; SCIENCE, 46
chemistry he had read Shakespeare and found him weak in c. WELLS, H, 18
cheque Any general statement is like a c. GENERALIZATIONS, 5; POUND, E, 6
Mrs Claypool's c. will come back to you HUMOUR, 53; MARX, G, 18
chequer-board a C. of Nights and Days DESTINY, 7; FITZGERALD, E, 13
cheques The rich hate signing c. WEALTH, 27
cherish to love and to c. MARRIAGE, 33
cherry Before the c. orchard was sold CHEKHOV, A, 6; WORRY, 11
C. ripe, ripe, ripe HERRICK, R, 1
Loveliest of trees, the c. HOUSMAN, A, 7; TREES, 5
Till 'C. ripe' themselves do cry ADMIRATION, 4; CAMPION, T, 2; COMPLIMENTS, 7
chess Life's too short for c. SPORT AND GAMES, 7
the devil played at c. with me BROWNE, T, 4; EXPLOITATION, 1
chess-board c. is the world; the pieces...the phenomena of the universe GOD, 29; HUXLEY, T, 6
chest Fifteen men on the dead man's c. ALCOHOL, 78; STEVENSON, R, 8
chestnut O c. tree NATURE, 39; YEATS, W, 4
spreading c. tree LONGFELLOW, H, 17; OCCUPATIONS, 16
chestnuts warmongers who...have others pull the c. out of the fire POLITICS, 97; STALIN, J, 3
chests Men have broad and large c. SEXES, 20
chew he can't fart and c. gum at the same time INSULTS, 70; JOHNSON, L, 4; STUPIDITY, 5
chewing c. little bits of String BELLOC, H, 9; FOOD, 11
television programs are so much c. gum TELEVISION, 3
chic very *c.* for an atheist MEMORIALS, 13
chicken a c. in his pot every Sunday POVERTY, 18
England will have her neck wrung like a c. WORLD WAR II, 49
Some c. CHURCHILL, W, 58; WORLD WAR II, 20
chickens children are more troublesome and costly than c. MANKIND, 60; SHAW, G, 12
count their c. ere they're hatched ANTICIPATION, 5; BUTLER, S, 3
Don't count your c. AESOP, 8; ANTICIPATION, 4
If I didn't start painting, I would have raised c. OCCUPATIONS, 19
You don't set a fox to watching the c. EXPERIENCE, 22; TRUMAN, H, 11
chief C. Defect of Henry King BELLOC, H, 9; FOOD, 11
C. of the Army LAST WORDS, 59; NAPOLEON I, 15
child A c. becomes an adult when RIGHT, 2; SZASZ, T, 4
A c. deserves the maximum respect CHILDREN, 40
A c.'s a plaything for an hour CHILDREN, 45
A c.... would have no more idea of death than a cat or a plant DEATH, 179
all any reasonable c. can expect ORTON, J, 2; SEX, 90
better...a poor and a wise c. than an old and foolish king YOUTH, 3
C.! do not throw this book about BELLOC, H, 3
c. of five would understand this MARX, G, 6; SIMPLICITY, 5
Every c. should have an occasional pat on the back PUNISHMENT, 26
flourish in a c. of six BELLOC, H, 8
getting wenches with c. SHAKESPEARE, 352; YOUTH, 28
give her the living c. BIBLE, 298
Give me a c. for the first seven years PROVERBS, 175
grant that the old Adam in this C. BOOK OF COMMON PRAYER, 21
He who shall teach the c. to doubt BLAKE, W, 8; DOUBT, 4
I don't care if it doesn't make a nickel, I just want every man, woman, and c. in America to see it GOLDWYN, S, 8
If the c. is father of the man CARTER, A, 11
If you strike a c. SHAW, G, 30; VIOLENCE, 18
institute for the study of c. guidance CHILDREN, 43
I would...stand /Three times in the front of battle than bear one c. WOMAN'S ROLE, 4
nobody's c. LONELINESS, 1
Now at last our c. is just like all children DE GAULLE, C, 6; EQUALITY, 41
One stops being a c. when...telling one's trouble does not make it better DISILLUSION, 5
receive one such little c. in my name BIBLE, 400; CHILDREN, 18
right to have a c. WOMEN, 26
simplicity a c. POPE, A, 18
spoil the c. INDULGENCE, 1; PUNISHMENT, 8
sweetest Shakespeare, Fancy's c. MILTON, J, 19
The business of being a c. CHILDREN, 36
The C. is Father of the Man AGE, 102; WORDSWORTH, W, 24
The mother-c. relationship is paradoxical FAMILY, 22
There are only two things a c. will share willingly CHILDREN, 57
To have a thankless c.! SHAKESPEARE, 173
to influence the character of a c. INFLUENCE, 4
unless the play is stopped, the c. cannot...go on AUDIENCES, 3
unto us a c. is born BIBLE, 201; CHRISTMAS, 7
What is the use of a new-born c. FRANKLIN, B, 11; PURPOSE, 2
when I was a c., I spake as a c. BIBLE, 38; CHARITY, 7
wise father that knows his own c. FAMILY, 53; SHAKESPEARE, 243
Woe to the land that's govern'd by a c. SHAKESPEARE, 304
childbearing Common morality now treats c. as an aberration CHILDREN, 32
childbed A man may sympathize with a woman in c. SEXES, 27
childbirth At the moment of c., every woman has the same aura of isolation LONELINESS, 10
Death and taxes and c. EXPEDIENCY, 6
Mountains will heave in c. DISAPPOINTMENT, 4; HORACE, 6
the male equivalent of c. PUBLISHING, 1
Childe C. Roland to the Dark Tower BROWNING, R, 18; SUMMONS, 4
childhood C. is the kingdom where nobody dies INNOCENCE, 9
His adult life resembled his c. SARTRE, J, 1
his egotism was all but second c. CARROLL, L, 2
infancy, c., adolescence and obsolescence AGE, 58
Prejudice is planted in c. BAINBRIDGE, B, 7
The books one reads in c.... create in one's mind a...false map BOOKS, 34; ORWELL, G, 22
childish I put away c. things BIBLE, 38; CHARITY, 7
Sweet c. days NOSTALGIA, 29; WORDSWORTH, W, 72
childishness second c. OLD AGE, 87; SHAKESPEARE, 49
children a Friend for little c. /Above the bright blue sky GOD, 37
Anybody who hates c. and dogs CHILDREN, 28; DOGS, 7

Are the c. all in bed? It's past eight o'clock NURSERY RHYMES, 68
as c. fear to go in the dark BACON, F, 18; DEATH, 29
a wicked man that comes after c. SLEEP, 18
A woman...anxious to get c. PSYCHOLOGY, 7
c. are more troublesome and costly than chickens MANKIND, 60; SHAW, G, 12
C. aren't happy with nothing to ignore FAMILY, 43; NASH, O, 8
c. are true judges of character AUDEN, W, 23; CHILDREN, 5
C. have never been very good at listening CHILDREN, 7
C....have no use for psychology BOOKS, 44
c., obey your parents BIBLE, 95; OBEDIENCE, 1
C. should acquire...heroes and villains from fiction AUDEN, W, 4; HISTORY, 3
C. sweeten labours BACON, F, 39; CHILDREN, 6
C. with Hyacinth's temperament...merely know more CHARACTER, 18; SAKI, 5
Come dear c. ARNOLD, M, 16; DEPARTURE, 1
desire not a multitude of unprofitable c. BIBLE, 85; CHILDREN, 14
Do you hear the c. weeping BROWNING, E, 3; SORROW, 4
English are growing demented about c. CHILDREN, 61
except ye...become as little c. BIBLE, 399; CHILDREN, 17
Familiarity breeds...c. SEX, 122; TWAIN, M, 12
Far too good to waste on c. SHAW, G, 50; YOUTH, 29
Having no c. had been a kind of choice CHILDREN, 13
He that has no c. PROVERBS, 190
He that loves not his wife and c. MARRIAGE, 153
his wife is beautiful and his c. smart MENCKEN, H, 3; TOLERANCE, 5
I love all my c. FAMILY, 13
in sorrow thou shalt bring forth c. SEXES, 4
I've lost one of my c. this week LOSS, 9
Let our c. grow tall TALENT, 9; THATCHER, M, 16
like a c.'s party taken over by the elders AGE, 42; FITZGERALD, F, 4
love animals and c. too much LOVE, 141
make your c. *capable of honesty* is the beginning of education HONESTY, 8; RUSKIN, J, 12
Many c. are suffering from muesli-belt malnutrition FOOD, 50
Men are but c. of a larger growth AGE, 35; DRYDEN, J, 18
more careful of the breed of their horses and dogs than of their c. FAMILY, 47
Most of the people...will be c. FUNERALS, 1
My music...understood by c. and animals MUSIC, 61; STRAVINSKY, I, 4
Never have c. CHILDREN, 60; VIDAL, G, 5
Never work with animals or c. ACTING, 2
no illegitimate c. ILLEGITIMACY, 4
no one ever asks the women and c. what they think WAR, 156
Now at last our child is just like all c. DE GAULLE, C, 6; EQUALITY, 41
Old men are twice c. OLD AGE, 5
Parents learn a lot from their c. CHILDREN, 56; SPARK, M, 3
Problem c. tend to grow up into problem adults SOCIETY, 10
provoke not your c. BIBLE, 22; FAMILY, 9
She had so many c. she didn't know what to do FAMILY, 45; NURSERY RHYMES, 58
that husbands and wives should have c. alternatively SEXES, 16
the c. I might have had CHILDREN, 49; CONTRACEPTION, 8
the early marriages of silly c. MARRIAGE, 105; MARTINEAU, H, 3
the more c. they can disturb PSYCHIATRY, 24
the Revolution may...devour each of her c. FRENCH REVOLUTION, 10
The value of marriage is...that c. produce adults MARRIAGE, 61
to avoid having c. CONTRACEPTION, 17
To bear many c. is considered...an investment CHILDREN, 29; GANDHI, I, 3
to seyn, to syngen and to rede, /As smale c. doon EDUCATION, 22
We have no c., except me BEHAN, B, 10; CHILDREN, 8
Were we closer to the ground as c. NOSTALGIA, 1
We want far better reasons for having c. CONTRACEPTION, 14
when they started life as c. CHILDREN, 4
write for c....as you do for adults WRITING, 17
You can do anything with c. if you only play with them CHILDREN, 20
you can get it from your c. MADNESS, 27

Chile Small earthquake in C. NEWSPAPERS, 8
chill St Agnes' Eve – Ah, bitter c. it was KEATS, J, 9
chime to set a c. of words tinkling in...a few fastidious people PURPOSE, 10; SMITH, L, 9
chimes c. at midnight MERRYMAKING, 3; SHAKESPEARE, 123
chimney sixty horses wedged in a c. JOURNALISM, 26
chimney-sweepers As c., come to dust MORTALITY, 16; SHAKESPEARE, 63
china broody hen sitting on a c. egg BUREAUCRACY, 5
China Even the Hooligan was probably invented in C. PLACES, 31; SAKI, 18
On a slow boat to C. BOATS, 11
The infusion of a C. plant ADDISON, J, 12; DRINKS, 1
Chinese Nothing...can destroy the C. people BUCK, P, 3; CHINA, 1
chip c. off the old block POLITICIANS, 55
c. of the old block BURKE, E, 27
chips You breed babies and you eat c. FOOD, 73
chirche-dore Housbondes at c. CHAUCER, G, 12; MARRIAGE, 45
chivalry age of c. is gone BURKE, E, 9; EUROPE, 2
Cervantes laughed c. out of fashion CERVANTES, M, 2
The age of c. is never past CHIVALRY, 7
truant been to c. CHIVALRY, 13
Chi Wen Tzu C. always thought three times before taking action CONFUCIUS, 2
Chloë In the spring...your lovely C. APPEARANCE, 59
chloroform that blessed C. & the effect was soothing REMEDIES, 59
chocolate a c. cream soldier SHAW, G, 5; SOLDIERS, 14
both its national products, snow and c., melt SWITZERLAND, 1
Venice is like eating...c. liqueurs VENICE, 2
choice Having no children had been a kind of c. CHILDREN, 13
Hebrew word...*timshel*...gives a c. CHOICE, 5
he makes a c. PHILOSOPHY, 19
'Thou mayest' – that gives a c. STEINBECK, J, 1
choir Sweet singing in the c. ANONYMOUS, 81; CHRISTMAS, 5
choirs Bare ruin'd c. OLD AGE, 94; SHAKESPEARE, 366
choose c. people who offer us money CORRUPTION, 6
I will not c. what many men desire INDIVIDUALITY, 6
We can believe what we c. RESPONSIBILITY, 12
Chopin I have lived off the blood of C. MUSICIANS, 7
to bridge the awful gap between Dorothy and C. MUSIC, 3
chord c. of music MUSIC, 49
chorus a dozen are only a c. BEAUTY, 22; FITZGERALD, F, 9
chose *plus c'est la même c.* CONSTANCY, 3
chosen a c. vessel BIBLE, 8
but few are c. BIBLE, 409
Christ C. called as his Apostles only men MEN, 8
C. is all, and in all BIBLE, 20; CHRISTIANITY, 8
C....would quite likely have been arrested OPPRESSION, 3
churches have kill'd their C. CLERGY, 14; TENNYSON, 59
Decide for C. RELIGION, 47
I beseech you, in the bowels of C. CROMWELL, O, 5; MISTAKES, 7
only a male can represent C. CLERGY, 16; RELIGION, 24
The Jews have produced...C., Spinoza, and myself CONCEIT, 16; STEIN, G, 7
We're more popular than Jesus C. LENNON, J, 13; POPULARITY, 6
Who dreamed that C. has died in vain CHRISTIANITY, 56; SITWELL, E, 4
Christchurch C. was the place where the difference between the Tories and the Alfred Chicken Party POLITICS, 45
Christendom Of the two lights of C. DEFEAT, 14
wisest fool in C. FOOLISHNESS, 13
Christian A C....feels /Repentance on a Sunday CHRISTIANITY, 64; HYPOCRISY, 24
any man...who could not bear another's misfortunes...like a C. MISFORTUNE, 15; POPE, A, 57
Better sleep with a sober cannibal than a drunken C. DRUNKENNESS, 21
centres of strong C. presence...kind of Walt Disney Theme Park COMMERCIALISM, 2
C. and you were married, for the first time RELIGION, 5
C. glories in the death of a pagan CHRISTIANITY, 5
C. resolution to find the world ugly RELIGION, 73
good a C. as Mahomet ELIZABETH I, 3
How very hard.../To be a C. BROWNING, R, 23; CHRISTIANITY, 31
I die a C. EXECUTION, 6
Indian snob reasons, like calling an English person by his C. name SCOTT, P, 3
in what peace a C. can die ADDISON, J, 19; LAST WORDS, 3

civil Foreigners fooling about in others' c. wars are a menace FOREIGNERS, 4
In a c. war, a general must know REED, H, 5; WAR, 134
The British c. service BUREAUCRACY, 9
civilian forget about this c. WAR, 72
civilians drop bombs…hit c. WAR, 72
civilisation Disinterested intellectual curiosity…life blood of…c. CURIOSITY, 9
if c. is to advance FEMINISM, 27
if c. is to advance…it must be through…women PANKHURST, E, 3
civilised we delude ourselves if we think that humanity is becoming ever more c. CHARLES, PRINCE, 5
civility C. costs nothing COURTESY, 1
The reciprocal c. of authors JOHNSON, S, 19
The reciprocal c. of authors WRITERS, 13
civilization As c. advances, poetry…declines CIVILIZATION, 9; MACAULAY, T, 7
C. is a method of living CIVILIZATION, 1
C. is…equal respect for all men CIVILIZATION, 1
decline in c. CIVILIZATION, 11
each c. has a pattern of disease ENVIRONMENT, 7
How idiotic c. is NAKEDNESS, 5
If people dug up the remains of this c. ARTISTS, 19
It is so stupid of modern c. DEVIL, 11
little in c. to appeal to a Yeti CIVILIZATION, 7
Madam, I am the c. they are fighting to defend WAR, 70
Our c. is founded on the shambles DEATH, 85
The degree of a nation's c. CIVILIZATION, 10; MAUGHAM, W, 14
the physician…is the flower…of our c. DOCTORS, 96
the Renaissance was…the green end of one of c.'s hardest winters CIVILIZATION, 5; FOWLES, J, 2
without the usual interval of c. AMERICA, 9; INSULTS, 36
You can't say c. don't advance PROGRESS, 20; ROGERS, W, 1
civilizations All great c./, in their early stages, are based on success in war WAR, 48
civilized it proved that I was in a c. society EXECUTION, 28
the family of c. nations RUSSIA, 14
Woman will be the last thing c. by Man WOMEN, 90
clap Don't c. too hard ENTHUSIASM, 6; OSBORNE, J, 1
If you believe, c. your hands FAIRIES, 3
clapped c. the glass to his sightless eye BLINDNESS, 12; NEWBOLT, H, 1
claret C. is the liquor for boys ALCOHOL, 42; JOHNSON, S, 128
drink a dozen of C. on my Tomb ALCOHOL, 45; FUNERALS, 8; KEATS, J, 65
look for the second cheapest c.…and say, 'Number 22 ALCOHOL, 63; POTTER, S, 6
said of c. ALCOHOL, 15
class a special machine for the suppression of one c. by another CAPITALISM, 11; LENIN, V, 3
Because there's no fourth c. HUMILITY, 9; SANTAYANA, G, 7
British navy always travels first c. NAVY, 6
Discussion in c., which means EDUCATION, 67; NABOKOV, V, 4
Every c. is unfit to govern GOVERNMENT, 2
for one c. to appreciate the wrongs of another CLASS, 48
For this c. we have…the designation of Philistines ARNOLD, M, 7; PHILISTINISM, 1
Like many of the upper c. ARISTOCRACY, 4; BELLOC, H, 18
Mr. Waugh…is…a snob in search of a c. WAUGH, E, 2
Poets and painters are outside the c. system ARTISTS, 2
Poets and painters…constitute a special c. POETS, 1
The constitution…first and second c. citizens CLASS, 57
The history of all…society is the history of c. struggles CLASS, 26; MARX, K, 1; MARXISM, 9
The one c. you do *not* belong to CLASS, 29
the proletariat will…wage a c. struggle for Socialism CLASS, 22; LENIN, V, 6; MARXISM, 7
The state is an instrument…of the ruling c. STATE, 5
Without c. differences…living theatre BURGESS, A, 7; ENGLAND, 14
young Englishman of our upper c. ARISTOCRACY, 2; ARNOLD, M, 6
classes back the masses against the c. CLASS, 18
Hats divide generally into three c. CLOTHES, 28; WHITEHORN, K, 1
I'm not interested in c. CLASS, 24
responsible and the irresponsible c. CLASS, 21; LAWRENCE, D, 12
the lower c. had such white skins CLASS, 11
classical C. quotation is the *parole* of literary men JOHNSON, S, 137; QUOTATIONS, 4
That's the c. mind at work MIND, 25
The basic difference between c. music and jazz MUSIC, 48
Classicism C.…the literature that gave…pleasure to their great-grandfathers LITERATURE, 25
classics Every man with a belly full of the c. CLASSICS, 7
The c. are only primitive literature CLASSICS, 6; LEACOCK, S, 2
clattering in charge of the c. train JOURNALISM, 7
clay absorbs a c. /After his labours SMOKING, 7
clean Bath…once a day to be passably c. BURGESS, A, 4; CLEANNESS, 2
c. your plate POLITICS, 89
hard to be funny when you have to be c. HUMOUR, 34; WEST, M, 11
We draw the sword…with c. hands WAR, 185
cleaning woman earth doesn't have a c. PICASSO, P, 11
clear His right was c., his will was strong ANONYMOUS, 102; RIGHT, 1
if he could make *me* understand…it would be c. to all UNDERSTANDING, 8
clearing-house the C. of the World ECONOMICS, 5
clears water c. us of this deed GUILT, 16
cleft Rock of ages, c. for me RELIGION, 89
Clementine Dwelt a miner, Forty-niner, /And his daughter, C. MOURNING, 7
clenched You cannot shake hands with a c. fist GANDHI, I, 5; INFLEXIBILITY, 2
Cleopatra Had C.'s nose been shorter APPEARANCE, 55; PASCAL, B, 6
image of C.…provides clues to the nature of the culture HISTORY, 17
clergy c. are men CLERGY, 6; FIELDING, H, 9
I never saw…the c. were beloved in any nation CLERGY, 12; SWIFT, J, 13
clergyman c. whose mendicity is only equalled by their mendacity CLERGY, 13; INSULTS, 120
good enough to be a c. CLERGY, 9; JOHNSON, S, 85
time for the c. and the psychotherapist to join forces PSYCHOLOGY, 10
clerk C. ther was of Oxenford also CHAUCER, G, 7; LOGIC, 3
diplomatic history is…what one c. said to another c. HISTORY, 38
The best c. I ever fired EISENHOWER, D, 3
the smartness of an attorney's c. DISRAELI, B, 33; INSULTS, 43
clever Be good, sweet maid, and let who will be c. VIRTUE, 18
Charles Lamb, a c. fellow certainly LAMB, C, 2
c. man…came of…stupid people CARLYLE, T, 32; INTELLIGENCE, 4
it needs a very c. woman to manage a fool KIPLING, R, 22
It's c., but is it art ART, 16
never wise to try to appear…more c. WISDOM, 33
not c. but I'm always right SELF-CONFIDENCE, 1
not quite c. enough to compensate for his faults MOUNTBATTEN OF BURMA, L, 2
no use trying to be *c.* ACADEMICS, 5
The silliest woman can manage a c. man KIPLING, R, 22
To be c. enough to get…money, one must be stupid CHESTERTON, G, 26; MATERIALISM, 9
cleverest You're the c. member of…the c. nation in the world SELF-CONFIDENCE, 12
cleverness height of c. is…to conceal it INTELLIGENCE, 11; ROCHEFOUCAULD, 20
cliché poised between a c. and an indiscretion POLITICS, 69
The c. is dead poetry LANGUAGE, 9
you have used every c. VERBOSITY, 2
clichés Let's have some new c. GOLDWYN, S, 1
cliffs the chalk c. of Dover BALDWIN, S, 6
climate common where the c.'s sultry ADULTERY, 1; BYRON, 19
If it's heaven for c. BARRIE, J, 1; PERVERSITY, 1
climax a story that starts with an earthquake and…a c. GOLDWYN, S, 5
climb Fain would I c., yet fear I to fall AMBITION, 20; RALEIGH, W, 2
clime change their c., not their frame of mind, who rush across the sea HORACE, 21; TRAVEL, 22
cling c. to their own sex because it is less frightening HOMOSEXUALITY, 29
clinician c.. learns less and less about more and more OCCUPATIONS, 10
If the c., as observer, wishes to see things as they really are DOCTORS, 28
Clinton Bill C., Boris Yeltsin and François Mitterand; we all like to eat POLITICIANS, 97

clitoris Do I have a c. halfway up my stomach SEX, 39
stimulation to orgasm centers upon the c. SEX, 44
Clive What I like about C. DEATH, 33
cloak Donning the philosopher's c. HYPATIA, 1
clock c. in the steeple strikes one ALCOHOL, 90
his arm round your waist and his eye on the c. POLITICIANS, 39
loudest noise…electric c. TECHNOLOGY, 1
Rock Around the C. POPULAR MUSIC, 15
Stands the Church c. at ten to three BROOKE, R, 5; NOSTALGIA, 3
The c. struck one, /The mouse ran down NURSERY RHYMES, 15
clocks hands of c. in railway stations CHILDREN, 25; CONNOLLY, C, 13
pass my declining years saluting…grandfather c. OLD AGE, 75
the c. were striking the hour LONGFELLOW, H, 4; TIME, 34
clod a c. of wayward marl WOMEN, 122
clogs From c. to c. POVERTY, 1; PROVERBS, 167
cloke knyf under the c. CHAUCER, G, 13; HYPOCRISY, 9
Clootie Satan, Nick, or C. BURNS, R, 3; DEVIL, 9
close a breathless hush in the C. tonight NEWBOLT, H, 6
regretted living so c. to Marie LOVE, 130; PROUST, M, 15
closed I went to New Zealand but it was c. PLACES, 4
Mankind is a c. society MANKIND, 55
the transition from the…'c. society'…to the 'open society' SOCIETY, 17
closer c. to the ground as children CHILDREN, 12
closet sleep in your c. rather than ENGLISH, 9
closets Out of the c. HOMOSEXUALITY, 1
close-up Life is a tragedy…in c. CHAPLIN, C, 9; LIFE, 27
closing c. time in the gardens of the West CAPITALISM, 4
clothe feed and c. 1.2 billion Chinese CHINA, 16
clothes After that you just take the girl's c. off ALCOHOL, 25
as if she were taking off all her c. COLETTE, S, 2; SEX, 29
bought her wedding c. ADDISON, J, 16; WOMEN, 9
C. do matter BAINBRIDGE, B, 2
c. have stretch marks CLOTHES, 23
enterprises that require new c. THOREAU, H, 13; THRIFT, 13
Fine c. are good CLOTHES, 14; JOHNSON, S, 104
hanging the baby on the c. line to dry INNOVATION, 2
Have you ever taken anything out of the c. basket CLEANNESS, 4
if it be our c. alone which fit us for society CLOTHES, 9
Nothing to wear but c. PESSIMISM, 7
No woman so naked as…underneath her c. NAKEDNESS, 4
walked away with their c. DISRAELI, B, 23; POLITICS, 34
wrapped him in swaddling c. BIBLE, 313; CHRISTMAS, 8
clothing change in musical style…change in c. style POPULAR MUSIC, 26
cloud a c. received him out of their sight BIBLE, 1
a pillar of a c. BIBLE, 111
Every c. has a silver lining OPTIMISM, 2; PROVERBS, 132
fiend hid in a c. BIRTH, 5; BLAKE, W, 38
I wandered lonely as a c. FLOWERS, 15; WORDSWORTH, W, 8
no silver linings without a c. OPTIMISM, 22
clouds But trailing c. of glory METAPHYSICS, 5; WORDSWORTH, W, 26
c. that gather round the setting sun MORTALITY, 21; WORDSWORTH, W, 33
clout Ne'er cast a c. MONTHS, 2; PROVERBS, 300
clown Any c. can play with the ball FOOTBALL, 16
I remain…a c. CHAPLIN, C, 8
I remain just one thing…and that is a c. HUMOUR, 8
club I don't want to belong to any c. HUMOUR, 54; MARX, G, 23
Mankind is a c. CHESTERTON, G, 42; MANKIND, 20
takes you so far from the c. house GOLF, 5
the best c. in London DICKENS, C, 40; HOUSES OF PARLIAMENT, 9
the most exclusive c. there is ENGLISH, 33; NASH, O, 3
cluster The human face is…a whole c. of faces MANKIND, 47; PROUST, M, 4
Clyde the bonny banks of C. SCOTLAND, 6
CMG Members rise from C. TITLES, 10
coach c. and six horses through the Act of Settlement IRELAND, 23
indifference and a c. and six LOVE, 56
coal best sun…made of Newcastle c. BUSINESS, 35
having a live c. in his hand REGRET, 4
though the whole world turn to c. HERBERT, G, 10; VIRTUE, 17
coalitions period of c.…is now over ASHDOWN, P, 1
coals heap c. of fire upon his head BIBLE, 454; RETRIBUTION, 8
coaster Dirty British c. BOATS, 14; MASEFIELD, J, 3
coat a c. of many colours BIBLE, 174
cobbler Let the c. stick CLASS, 2; PROVERBS, 256
cobwebs Laws are like c. LAW, 38; SWIFT, J, 18
laws were like c. BACON, F, 5; LAW, 7
Coca-Cola the churches…bore for me the same relation to God that billboards did to C. RELIGION, 91; UPDIKE, J, 2
Coca Colas Instead of drinking C. WATER, 3
cocaine C. is God's way of saying DRUGS, 16
C. isn't habit-forming ADDICTION, 1; BANKHEAD, T, 7
cock before the c. crow, thou shalt deny me BETRAYAL, 2; BIBLE, 425
He was like a c. ARROGANCE, 3; ELIOT, G, 5; INSULTS, 45
Our c. won't fight BEAVERBROOK, M, 5; ROYALTY, 24
That kept the c. that crowed in the morn NURSERY RHYMES, 61
waiting for the c. to crow BETRAYAL, 8
we owe a c. to Aesculapius LAST WORDS, 83; SOCRATES, 9
cockles Crying, C. and mussels! alive, alive, O ANONYMOUS, 472
cockroach c. world of compromise COMPROMISE, 5
to choose between him and a c. as a companion INSULTS, 137; WODEHOUSE, P, 15
cockroaches The huge laughing c. APPEARANCE, 44
cocksure as c. of anything MELBOURNE, 7; SELF-CONFIDENCE, 5
cocktail Mona Lisa c.…can't get the silly grin ALCOHOL, 12
weasel under the c. cabinet PINTER, H, 5; PLAYS, 8
cod piece of c. passes all understanding FOOD, 49
serve both c. and salmon PUNS, 13
the c.'s wallop is always fresh made COMMUNISM, 11
The home of the bean and the c. SNOBBERY, 3
codfish Unlike the male c.…the British aristocracy is ARISTOCRACY, 22; WODEHOUSE, P, 21
coffee c. that's too black…You integrate it with cream RACISM, 20
C. which makes the politician wise DRINKS, 17; POPE, A, 52
if this is c., I want tea DRINKS, 3
Instant c. is just old beans DRINKS, 20
measured out my life with c. spoons ELIOT, T, 13; LIFE, 36
coffee-house It is folly…to mistake the echo of a…c. for the…kingdom OPINIONS, 9; SWIFT, J, 5
coffin the silver plate on a c. INSULTS, 101
coffins ignoring the price of c. IMMORTALITY, 2
cogito *C., ergo sum* THINKING, 4
cognitive I have created a lot of c. dissonance CONFUSION, 5
coherence the church, it does provide a c. CHURCH, 13
coil shuffled off this mortal c. SHAKESPEARE, 90; SUICIDE, 35
coke Happiness is like c. HAPPINESS, 12; HUXLEY, A, 26
Colbert I can pay some of my debt with this gift – C. BETRAYAL, 10
cold blow hot and c. with the same breath AESOP, 7; INDECISION, 1
C. hands, warm heart PROVERBS, 102
C. Pastoral ETERNITY, 3; KEATS, J, 29
Feed a c. ILLNESS, 1
I beg c. comfort COMFORT, 5; SHAKESPEARE, 169
If you think that you have caught a c., call in a good doctor DOCTORS, 20
It leapt straight past the common c. DISCOVERY, 3
she should catch a c. on overexposure BUTLER, S, 18; TRUTH, 15
The Irish…are needed in this c. age IRISH, 4
we are…in the midst of a c. war COLD WAR, 1
We called a c. a c. BENNETT, A, 3; ILLNESS, 11
Whiskey is the most popular of…remedies that won't cure a c. ALCOHOL, 84
coldly c. she turns from their gaze, and weeps MOORE, T, 4; MOURNING, 8
Cole Old King C. /Was a merry old soul NURSERY RHYMES, 38
colic One physician cures you of the c. DOCTORS, 12
Coliseum While stands the C., Rome shall stand BYRON, 15; EUROPE, 5
collapse Russia is a c., not a revolution LAWRENCE, D, 37; RUSSIA, 11
collapses Force…c. through its own mass HORACE, 35
collar no shirt or c. ever comes back twice LEACOCK, S, 13; NEGLECT, 2
collections those mutilators of c. BOOKS, 25; LAMB, C, 11
collective the greatest c. work of science BRONOWSKI, J, 3; SCIENCE, 13
college I am Master of this c. ACADEMICS, 2
Like so many ageing c. people ACADEMICS, 6; NABOKOV, V, 3
colleges a liberal education at the C. of Unreason REASON, 1
colonel The gatling's jammed and the c. dead NEWBOLT, H, 7; WAR, 119

colonnade whispering sound of the cool c. COWPER, W, 19; TREES, 3
Colossus a genius that could cut a C. MILTON, J, 5
he doth bestride the narrow world /Like a C. SHAKESPEARE, 145
colour an incurable disease – c. blindness RACISM, 9
Any c., so long as it's black CHOICE, 1
Like a piece of litmus paper…take the c. of his times HUXLEY, A, 2
water, is unsuitable in c. HERBERT, A, 7; WATER, 5
coloured I'm a c., one-eyed Jew DISABILITY, 2; RACISM, 10
colourless C. green ideas NONSENSE, 10
colours a coat of many c. BIBLE, 174
All c. will agree in the dark BACON, F, 57; DIFFERENCE, 7
clashed his c. together like cymbals ARTISTS, 11
column The Fifth C. WAR, 109
coma shuffle off in a c. DEATH, 84
comb Falklands…a fight between two bald men over a c. WAR, 23
combine When bad men c. BURKE, E, 20; UNITY, 7
combustion the Immaculate Conception was spontaneous c. CATHOLICISM, 13
come 'Cannot c., lie follows' PROUST, M, 18
C. what come may SHAKESPEARE, 205; TIME, 47
I c. as a thief BIBLE, 467
I do not say the French cannot c. NAVY, 7
mine hour is not yet c. BIBLE, 241
Mr Watson, c. here; I want you SUMMONS, 3
O c. all ye faithful CHRISTMAS, 19
Our day will c. IRELAND, 3
Shape of Things to C. FUTURE, 14
Thou'lt c. no more MOURNING, 13; SHAKESPEARE, 196
Whistle and she'll c. to you BEAUMONT, F, 13; SUMMONS, 2
Why don't you c. up sometime WEST, M, 8
Will ye no c. back again RETURN, 4
comedian A c. can only last HUMOUR, 26; ROGERS, W, 10
comedies c. are ended by a marriage BYRON, 22; THEATRE, 6
comedy All I need to make a c. CHAPLIN, C, 5; HUMOUR, 7
at a c. we only look HUXLEY, A, 13; THEATRE, 10
c. at the moment of deepest hysteria WRITING, 38
C. is if I walk into an open sewer and die THEATRE, 5
C. is medicine MEDICINE, 33
C. is tragedy HUMOUR, 6
C., like sodomy, is an unnatural act HUMOUR, 14
C., we may say, is society HUMOUR, 25; PRIESTLEY, J, 1
Farce refined becomes high c. THEATRE, 9
Life is…a c. in long-shot CHAPLIN, C, 9; LIFE, 27
Rabelais is the wondrous mask of ancient c. RABELAIS, F, 1
What a fine c. this world would be LIFE, 33
world is a c. to those who think LIFE, 96; WALPOLE, H, 6
comes Everything c. to him who waits PATIENCE, 2; PROVERBS, 144
cometh he c. with clouds BIBLE, 459
comfort carrion c., Despair, not feast on thee DESPAIR, 5
c. me with apples BIBLE, 487; LOVE, 33
From ignorance our c. flows IGNORANCE, 19
happiness is…confused with c. or complacency HAPPINESS, 2
He supplies the perennial demand for c. DOCTORS, 100
I beg cold c. COMFORT, 5; SHAKESPEARE, 169
the waters of c. PSALMS, 11
thought of suicide is a great…c. NIETZSCHE, F, 11; SUICIDE, 21
thy rod and thy staff c. me PSALMS, 11
Two loves I have, of c. and despair CONFLICT, 7; SHAKESPEARE, 375
until his friends came to c. him ENDURANCE, 10
What a c. it was to see her pass NIGHTINGALE, F, 2
Wilt thou love her, c. her BOOK OF COMMON PRAYER, 26
comfortable not believe that our place is at the c. mid-point ASHDOWN, P, 3
something more c. CLOTHES, 10
to be baith grand and c. BARRIE, J, 2; LUXURY, 1
comfortably Are you sitting c.? Then I'll begin BEGINNING, 15
comforted he refused to be c. BIBLE, 176
comforters miserable c. are ye all BIBLE, 231
comforts Increase of material c.…moral growth MATERIALISM, 11
comic It is so c. to hear oneself called old OLD AGE, 57
comic strip the one-dimensional subtlety of a c. INSULTS, 59
one-dimensional subtlety of a c. THATCHER, M, 6
coming C. through the rye BURNS, R, 6; LOVE, 45
he…c. after me is preferred before me BIBLE, 239; CHRISTIANITY, 14
command but to c. LEADERSHIP, 13
mortals to c. success ADDISON, J, 4; SUCCESS, 3
one of those born neither to obey nor to c. MASEFIELD, J, 1; NASTINESS, 5
people c. rather badly OBEDIENCE, 2
commandments fear God, and keep his c. BIBLE, 79; GOD, 11
gods handing down new c. SCIENTISTS, 4
Where there aren't no Ten C. DESIRE, 9; KIPLING, R, 26
commands good servant does not all c. SHAKESPEARE, 64
commas absence of inverted c. guarantees…originality QUOTATIONS, 2
commend forced to c. her highly INSINCERITY, 4; PEPYS, S, 9
into thy hands I c. my spirit BIBLE, 340; LAST WORDS, 10; PSALMS, 19
commended The man who gets angry…in the right way…is c. ARISTOTLE, 2
commendeth obliquely c. himself BROWNE, T, 1; CRITICISM, 12
comment C. is free but facts are sacred FACTS, 6; JOURNALISM, 31
commentators rather give me c. plain CLARITY, 1
commerce difficult business of c. BUSINESS, 5
Friendship is a disinterested c. between equals GOLDSMITH, O, 14; LOVE AND FRIENDSHIP, 4
honour sinks where c. long prevails BUSINESS, 17; GOLDSMITH, O, 23
commercialism The crude c. of America WASHINGTON, G, 2
commercing looks c. with the skies MILTON, J, 12; SOUL, 11
commission Each bullet has got its c. MORTALITY, 4
commit woman alone, can…c. them SEXES, 31; THACKERAY, W, 7
committed fight in your own cause…c. to winning COMMITMENT, 7
committee A c. is a cul-de-sac BUREAUCRACY, 3
A c. is an animal DEMOCRACY, 3
A c. should consist of three men DEMOCRACY, 26
The number one book…was written by a c. BIBLE, 534
commodity *C., Firmness,* and *Delight* ARCHITECTURE, 21
common All the realm shall be in c. LAWYERS, 10
C. Law of England LAW, 22
good thing, to make it too c. ENGLAND, 45; SHAKESPEARE, 118
He nothing c. did or mean EXECUTION, 22; MARVELL, A, 4
house we all had in c. PAST, 4
lose the c. touch IDEALISM, 4; KIPLING, R, 18
that old c. arbitrator, Time SHAKESPEARE, 334
the happiness of the c. man GOVERNMENT, 8
The trivial round, the c. task SIMPLICITY, 4
'Tis education forms the c. mind EDUCATION, 74; POPE, A, 40
woman of c. views but uncommon abilities THATCHER, M, 4
common-looking The Lord prefers c. people APPEARANCE, 39; LINCOLN, A, 6
common man I have no concern for the c. PUBLIC, 22
commonplace nothing so unnatural as the c. DOYLE, A, 7; TRIVIALITY, 8
renders…c. things and characters interesting SCOTT, W, 5
What a c. genius he has HARDY, T, 3
unassuming c. /Of Nature FLOWERS, 14; WORDSWORTH, W, 76
commonplaces c. are the great poetic truths STEVENSON, R, 27; TRIVIALITY, 14
Commons The C., faithful to their system GOVERNMENT, 23
common sense C. is the collection of prejudices EINSTEIN, A, 10
Science is nothing but trained and organized c. HUXLEY, T, 2
seldom attribute c. ROCHEFOUCAULD, 24
Commonwealth C. of Nations BRITISH EMPIRE, 6
turn to the wider vision of the C. MACMILLAN, H, 6; POLITICS, 70
communications evil c. corrupt good manners BIBLE, 40
communism arrested under the Suppression of C. Act OPPRESSION, 3
C. continued to haunt Europe as a spectre COMMUNISM, 18; TAYLOR, A, 3
C. is in fact the completion of Socialism COMMUNISM, 12
C. is like prohibition COMMUNISM, 13; ROGERS, W, 3
C. is Soviet power plus the electrification COMMUNISM, 8; LENIN, V, 9
For us in Russia c. is a dead dog COMMUNISM, 15; SOLZHENITSYN, A, 13
Russian c. is the illegitimate child COMMUNISM, 2
communist Every c. has a fascist frown COMMUNISM, 16; FASCISM, 14; SPARK, M, 4
I'm a C. by day RELIGION, 9
joining the C. Party is the logical outcome PICASSO, P, 12
your grandson will…be a C. COMMUNISM, 6; KHRUSHCHEV, N, 5

communists Catholics and C. have committed great crimes COMMITMENT, 6; GREENE, G, 3
C. used to bring vodka RUSSIA, 4
In Germany, the Nazis came for the C. NAZISM, 6
looking under the beds for C. SEX, 40
community journalism....keeps us in touch with the ignorance of the c. JOURNALISM, 35; WILDE, O, 15
MARRIAGE...a c....making in all two MARRIAGE, 32
the c. of Europe EUROPE, 20
commute the agricultural labourers...c. from London COUNTRYSIDE, 9; POWELL, A, 4
commuter C....riding to and from his wife TRAVEL, 48
compact the damned, c., liberal majority IBSEN, H, 3; MAJORITY, 6
companion to choose between him and a cockroach as a c. INSULTS, 137; WODEHOUSE, P, 15
companionable so c. as solitude SOLITUDE, 15; THOREAU, H, 14
companions Boys...are unwholesome c. for grown people CHILDREN, 44; LAMB, C, 9
c. for middle age BACON, F, 34; MARRIAGE, 14
company better to be alone than in bad c. FRIENDS, 17; WASHINGTON, G, 3
c....have neither a soul to lose nor a body to kick BUSINESS, 31; SMITH, S, 5
c. of their own sex BROOKNER, A, 5
Considering the c....hardly surprising SUPERIORITY, 11
Crowds without c. GIBBON, E, 4; LONDON, 14
find myself in the c. of scientists SCIENTISTS, 1
I've been offered titles...get one into disreputable c. SHAW, G, 44
Our c. only sponsor the arts FOOTBALL, 1
pleasure of your c. LAMB, C, 24; MOUNTAINS, 2
Take the tone of the c. CHESTERFIELD, P, 8; CONFORMITY, 3
Tell me what c. thou keepest CERVANTES, M, 22; FRIENDS, 4
You never expected justice from a c. BUSINESS, 31; SMITH, S, 5
comparative progress is simply a c. CHESTERTON, G, 19; PROGRESS, 9
compare any she belied with false c. ANALOGY, 5; SHAKESPEARE, 374
c. thee to a summer's day COMPLIMENTS, 31; SHAKESPEARE, 360
Learn, c., collect the facts EDUCATION, 72
compared The war we have just been through,...is not to be c. WAR, 187; WILSON, W, 6
comparisons c. are odious ANALOGY, 2
C. are odorous MALAPROPISMS, 2
compass my heart shall be /The faithful c. FAITHFULNESS, 4; GAY, J, 12
compassed snares of death c. me round PSALMS, 65
compassion But a certain Samaritan...had c. on him BIBLE, 325; CHARITY, 9
C. is not a sloppy, sentimental feeling for people who are underprivileged KINNOCK, N, 7
no imagination...no c. IMAGINATION, 3
The purpose of human life is to serve and to show c. KINDNESS, 9
competition C. was the breath of life to him FLEMING, A, 1
happiest conversation where there is no c. CONVERSATION, 5
competitor increse in blood volume that would help the endurance c. PREGNANCY, 9
complacency c. and satisfaction...in...a new-married couple LAMB, C, 3; MARRIAGE, 97
happiness is...confused with comfort or c. HAPPINESS, 2
complain Never c. and never explain EXPLANATIONS, 1
one hardly knows to whom to c. COMPLAINTS, 2
complains no one c. of his judgement JUDGMENT, 9
complaint Anno domini...the most fatal c. DEATH, 80
how is the old c. DISRAELI, B, 38; MEMORY, 7
I want to register a c. COMPLAINTS, 5; MARX, G, 14
Life is a fatal c. LIFE, 48
complete disguised as a C. Man HUXLEY, A, 6
now I feel like a c. idiot HEINE, H, 3; INFERIORITY, 1
complex Simple systems give rise to c. behavior SCIENCE, 42
Wherever an inferiority c. exists, there is...reason INFERIORITY, 2; JUNG, C, 10
complexes A man should not strive to eliminate his c. NEUROSIS, 3
complexion Mislike me not for my c. PREJUDICE, 13
complexities c. of poetry are destroyed by the media THEATRE, 3
compliance by a timely c. FIELDING, H, 8; SEX, 36
compliment returned the c. GOD, 53; VOLTAIRE, 19
compose Never c....unless...not composing...becomes a positive nuisance MUSIC, 30
composed When I c. that, I was...inspired by God MUSIC, 9
composer A good c. does not imitate MUSICIANS, 9
A good c....steals STRAVINSKY, I, 5
composers greatest c. since Beethoven POPULAR MUSIC, 7
composition difference between...prose and metrical c. POETRY AND PROSE, 7
comprehended c. two aspicious persons MALAPROPISMS, 1; SHAKESPEARE, 275
comprehensive largest and most c. soul SHAKESPEARE, 6
compromise All government...is founded on c. and barter BURKE, E, 14; COMPROMISE, 4
C. used to mean that half a loaf CHESTERTON, G, 41; COMPROMISE, 6
not a question that leaves much room for c. MEIR, G, 6; SELF-PRESERVATION, 9
compulsion seized by the stern hand of C. THURBER, J, 3
compulsive Brando is always c. viewing ACTORS, 22
compulsory c. and irreproachable idleness ARMY, 4; TOLSTOY, L, 9
computers so many c....use them in the search for love CRITICISM, 64
comrade stepping where his c. stood COURAGE, 25; SCOTT, W, 16
comrades Bleach the bones of c. slain WAR, 81
Dear c., soldiers, sailors and workers RUSSIAN REVOLUTION, 5
East and west on fields forgotten /Bleach the bones of c. slain HOUSMAN, A, 14
con no little cynicism and every kind of c. game POLITICS, 111
conceal Addresses...c. our whereabouts SAKI, 2
height of cleverness is...to c. it INTELLIGENCE, 11; ROCHEFOUCAULD, 20
speech only to c. their thoughts HUMAN NATURE, 33; VOLTAIRE, 12
concealed Much truth is spoken...more...c. TRUTH, 19
concealing Good breeding consists in c. how...we think of ourselves MANNERS, 6; TWAIN, M, 14
concealment c., like a worm i' th' bud LOVE, 153; SHAKESPEARE, 342
conceit C. is the finest armour CONCEIT, 12; JEROME, J, 2
conceited I would grow intolerably c. CONCEIT, 21; WHISTLER, J, 8
what man will do any good who is not c. SELF-RESPECT, 5; TROLLOPE, A, 12
concentrate c. hard on someone...called Martin Amis INSIGNIFICANCE, 5
concept If the c. of God has BALDWIN, J, 1; RELIGION, 12
Political correctness is a really inane c. LANGUAGE, 47
conception if the dad is present at the c. ORTON, J, 2; SEX, 90
the Immaculate C. was spontaneous combustion CATHOLICISM, 13
concepts walks up the stairs of his c. MANKIND, 61; STEINBECK, J, 2
concerned great society...men are more c. with the quality of their goods SOCIETY, 14
concessions The c. of the weak are the c. of fear BURKE, E, 13; YIELDING, 1
conclusions Life is the art of drawing...c. BUTLER, S, 10; LIFE, 21
concord toleration produced...religious c. GIBBON, E, 6; RELIGION, 45
Concord Yes – around C. THOREAU, H, 23; TRAVEL, 45
concordance c. of Nicola Six's kisses KISSING, 1
concrete your life being set in c....a feeling of being constantly observed CHARLES, PRINCE, 7
concubine c. for her beauty BEAUTY, 1
concurrence fortuitous c. of atoms CHANCE, 5
condemn No man can justly censure or c. JUDGMENT, 5
No man can justly censure or c. another BROWNE, T, 7
condemned If God were suddenly c. to live the life HUMAN CONDITION, 7
I have...taken his side when absurd men have c. him FREEDOM, 60
Man is c. to be free FREEDOM, 54; SARTRE, J, 6
condemning One should examine oneself...before...c. others MOLIERE, 7; SELF, 14
condition fools decoyed into our c. MARRIAGE, 119
hopes for the human c. CAMUS, A, 16; PESSIMISM, 4
The c. of man...is a c. of war HOBBES, T, 1; HUMAN CONDITION, 12

the c. of our sex is so deplorable that it is our duty…to break the law PANKHURST, E, 6
the Jews have made a contribution to the human c. JEWS, 19
To be a poet is a c. POETS, 6
wearisome c. of humanity HUMAN CONDITION, 11
what delight we married people have to see…fools decoyed into our c. PEPYS, S, 13
conditioned Americans have been c. to respect newness UPDIKE, J, 3
conditions my people live in such awful c. POVERTY, 15
these are the c., now what happens SCIENCE, 39
condolence prolific writer of notes of c. DICKINSON, E, 2
condoms c. are not only necessary but mandatory AIDS, 8
spent £167 million on c. CONTRACEPTION, 6
conducive anything c. to our national stability CHINA, 10
conduct C.…to the prejudice of good order and military discipline ANONYMOUS, 14; ARMY, 2
conductor c. has the advantage MUSICIANS, 5
dare look back lest…the c. DEPARTURE, 9
conference naked into the c. chamber BEVAN, A, 10; WEAPONS, 2
confess It's easy to make a man c.…lies TRUTH, 30
Men will c. HUMOUR, 10
only c. our little faults IMPERFECTION, 11; ROCHEFOUCAULD, 22
We c. our bad qualities…out of fear SELF-KNOWLEDGE, 2
confessed poured himself a drink and…c. TREASON, 7
confessing I am ashamed of c. INNOCENCE, 1
women…ill-using them and then c. it TROLLOPE, A, 9; WOMEN, 134
confession There is no refuge from c. but suicide SUICIDE, 39
confidence c. in seasoned film crews YOUTH, 32
getting a little c. SELF-CONFIDENCE, 2
never dedicated to do something you have complete c. in FANATICISM, 4
one cannot really have c. in doctors DOCTORS, 48
Three addresses always inspire c. WILDE, O, 32
confident There are two things which I am c. I can do very well CRITICISM, 24; JOHNSON, S, 52
confin'd cabin'd, cribb'd, c., bound in SHAKESPEARE, 218
confined I should hardly like to live…in their elegant but c. houses WRITERS, 40
conflict the c. between conscience and individual freedom FREEDOM, 3
We are in an armed c. WAR, 60
conform how to rebel and c. at the same time YOUTH, 8
conformable Nature is very consonant and c. NATURE, 26; NEWTON, I, 4
confound the weak things of the world to c. the…mighty WISDOM AND FOOLISHNESS, 3
confounded mine enemies shall be c. PSALMS, 2
confused Anyone who isn't c. here doesn't really understand CONFUSION, 1
c. idea of what Christianity is RELIGION, 54
confusion let me never be put to c. PSALMS, 18
conglomerate Britain does not wish to be ruled by a c. in Europe EUROPE, 23
congratulate rejoice at that news and c. our forces VICTORY, 26
Congreve C. is the only sophisticated playwright TYNAN, K, 2; WRITERS, 92
congs Kinquering C. their titles take SPOONER, W, 3
conked John Le Mesurier…c. out on November 15th OBITUARIES, 6
connect Only c. COMMUNICATION, 1; FORSTER, E, 9
conquer easier to c. it VICTORY, 27
in the end the truth will c. TRUTH, 48
not the man to c. a country WEAKNESS, 4
They will c., but…not convince PERSUASION, 1; UNAMUNO, M, 4
We'll fight and we'll c. COURAGE, 17
when we c. without danger VICTORY, 6
conquered I came, I saw, God c. VICTORY, 2, 11
I came, I saw, I c. CAESAR, J, 4; VICTORY, 1
It will be c.; I will not capitulate DETERMINATION, 9
conquering C. kings ROYALTY, 37
not c. but fighting well VICTORY, 7
See, the c. hero comes VICTORY, 17
conquest goal is not the c. of Iraq BUSH, G, 13
Socialism…the c. of the…economy SOCIALISM, 4
The Roman C. was, however, a *Good Thing* HISTORY, 29; SELLAR, W, 4
conscience a good digestion depends upon a good c. FOOD, 26
a Nonconformist c. WILDE, O, 42; WOMEN, 142
As guardian of His Majesty's c. MONARCHY, 26
A still and quiet c. CONSCIENCE, 8
c. does make cowards of us all CONSCIENCE, 7; COWARDICE, 8; SHAKESPEARE, 92
c. hath a thousand several tongues CONSCIENCE, 11
C. is a coward CONSCIENCE, 4; GOLDSMITH, O, 30
C. is but a word that cowards use CONSCIENCE, 12
C. is…rejection of a particular wish FREUD, S, 4
C. is the inner voice CONSCIENCE, 6; MENCKEN, H, 2
C. is the internal perception of the rejection of a particular wish CONSCIENCE, 3
dilemmas of c. and egotism POWER, 24
freedom of speech, freedom of c., and the prudence never to practise…them FREEDOM, 57
I cannot…cut my c. to fit this year's fashions INTEGRITY, 3
I'll catch the c. of the King PLAYS, 14; SHAKESPEARE, 89
I wasn't driven into medicine by a social c. MEDICINE, 66
Now war has a bad c. KEY, E, 6; WAR, 90
Now we can go to the polling booth without a bad c. SOUTH AFRICA, 3
O coward c. CONSCIENCE, 10
people who organized the coup must have had a c. bypass THATCHER, M, 10
Science without c. SCIENCE, 78
the conflict between c. and individual freedom FREEDOM, 3
We draw the sword with a clear c. WAR, 185
why is my liberty judged of another man's c. BIBLE, 36; CONSCIENCE, 1; FREEDOM, 7
conscious To be too c. is an illness ILLNESS, 22
consciousness C. is a disease PSYCHOLOGY, 19
man, by possessing c., is…a diseased animal UNAMUNO, M, 2
consent freely expressed c. of the people of Northern Ireland IRELAND, 15
No one can make you feel inferior without your c. INFERIORITY, 6
silence can be taken as c. GERMANY, 14
consequence It is incident to physicians…to mistake subsequence for c. JOHNSON, S, 44
physicians…mistake subsequence for c. DOCTORS, 56
consequences men never violate the laws of God without suffering the c. RETRIBUTION, 9
out duty…and to damn the c. DUTY, 4
conservatism c.…adherence to the old and tried CONSERVATISM, 6; LINCOLN, A, 14
c. is based upon the idea CHESTERTON, G, 35; CONSERVATISM, 2
conservative most c. man…is the British Trade Unionist CONSERVATISM, 1
C. government is an organized hypocrisy DISRAELI, B, 24
The radical invents the views.…the c. adopts them CONSERVATISM, 8
which makes a man more c. CONSERVATISM, 5; KEYNES, J, 2
Conservative Or else a little C. GILBERT, W, 19; POLITICS, 44
the C. Party at prayer CHURCH, 11
to what is called the Tory…called the C., party POLITICS, 33
consider c. your ways BIBLE, 184
When I c. how my light is spent BLINDNESS, 9; MILTON, J, 60
considerable to appear c. in his native place FAME, 17; JOHNSON, S, 82
considered hast thou c. my servant Job BIBLE, 222
consistency C. is contrary to nature HUXLEY, A, 14
consoler A physician is…a c. of the mind DOCTORS, 14
consonant Nature is very c. and conformable NATURE, 26; NEWTON, I, 4
conspiracy not a Party, it is a c. BEVAN, A, 1; COMMUNISM, 3
People of the same trade…conversation ends in a c. BUSINESS, 30
conspirators All the c. NOBILITY, 6; SHAKESPEARE, 162
constabulary When c. duty's to be done GILBERT, W, 41; POLICE, 2
constant A c. guest HOSPITALITY, 1; PROVERBS, 10
C. dripping PROVERBS, 103
Friendship is c. in all other things SHAKESPEARE, 269
constitution c. is extremely well LAW, 39
The c.…first and second class citizens CLASS, 57
The principles of a free c. GIBBON, E, 7; GOVERNMENT, 14
constitutional A c. king must learn to stoop MONARCHY, 16
c. right DEMOCRACY, 15; LINCOLN, A, 15
definition of a c. statesman BAGEHOT, W, 9

constitutionally woman's right to abortion was c. protected ABORTION, 7
construction Our object in the c. of the state PLATO, 2; REPUBLIC, 1
consultant c.'s first obligation is to the patient DOCTORS, 52
consultations dictator...always take some c. AUTHORITARIANISM, 7; THATCHER, M, 28
consulted the right to be c....to encourage...to warn BAGEHOT, W, 7; MONARCHY, 3
consume I have often seen the King c. FOOD, 57
more history than they can c. EUROPE, 19; SAKI, 6
statistics, born to c. resources HORACE, 17; STATISTICS, 4
consumed is yet also c. with this desire KEATS, J, 1
consumer In a c. society there are...two kinds of slaves MATERIALISM, 14
consumes Man...c. without producing CAPITALISM, 14; ORWELL, G, 3
consummation a c. /Devoutly to be wish'd SHAKESPEARE, 90; SUICIDE, 35
consummatum c. est BIBLE, 272
consumption Conspicuous c....is a means of reputability MATERIALISM, 25
this c. of the purse MONEY, 43; SHAKESPEARE, 119
consumptive c. youth weaving garlands of sad flowers STEVENSON, R, 2
contemplate passers-by who can c. it...are those...with a white stick and a dog ARCHITECTURE, 8
contemplates Beauty in things exists in the mind which c. them BEAUTY, 26; HUME, D, 4
contemplation right mindfulness, right c. BUDDHA, 4; RELIGION, 18
contemplative Between women love is c. BEAUVOIR, S, 4; HOMOSEXUALITY, 3
contemporary to trade a hundred c. readers for POSTERITY, 7
contempt attention to the inside...c. for the outside BOOKS, 16; CHESTERFIELD, P, 14
she was only an Object of C. AUSTEN, J, 12; CONTEMPT, 1
To show pity is felt as a sign of c. NIETZSCHE, F, 18; SYMPATHY, 6
contemptible c. little Army WAR, 184; WILHELM II, 4
content desire is got without c. CONTENTMENT, 10; SHAKESPEARE, 216
glad of other men's good, c. with my harm CONTENTMENT, 8
Let us draw upon c. for the deficiencies of fortune GOLDSMITH, O, 28; OPTIMISM, 27
contented How is it...that no one lives c. with his lot DISCONTENT, 4; HORACE, 45
If you are foolish enough to be c., don't show it COMPLAINTS, 3; JEROME, J, 4
With what I most enjoy c. least DISCONTENT, 8; SHAKESPEARE, 362
contentment C. and fulfilment don't make for very good fiction FICTION, 7
Where wealth and freedom reign, c. fails BUSINESS, 17; GOLDSMITH, O, 23
contests mighty c. rise from trivial things POPE, A, 48; RESULTS, 5
continence Give me chastity and c. PROCRASTINATION, 4
that melancholy sexual perversion known as c. ABSTINENCE, 6; HUXLEY, A, 8
Continent On the C. people have good food MANNERS, 5
Continental C. people have sex life ENGLISH, 27; SEX, 81
continual c. state of inelegance AUSTEN, J, 28; WEATHER, 7
continuation All diplomacy is a c. of war CHINA, 2; DIPLOMACY, 23
War is the c. of politics WAR, 49
contraception a terrific story about oral c. ALLEN, W, 11; CONTRACEPTION, 2
leave c. on the long finger CONTRACEPTION, 9
we demand free access to c. ABORTION, 1
contraceptive accident with a c. ADAMS, D, 11
Dr Marie Stopes made c. devices respectable STOPES, M, 3
It's like having a totally efficient c. BURGESS, A, 2; FUTURE, 6
The best c. is a glass of cold water CONTRACEPTION, 3
contraceptives C. should be used MILLIGAN, S, 8
People who use c. do not understand love TERESA, 6
Skullion had little use for c. CONTRACEPTION, 15; SNOBBERY, 7
contract A verbal c. isn't worth the paper GOLDWYN, S, 15
Every law is a c. LAW, 30; SELDEN, J, 2
Marriage is...but a civil c. MARRIAGE, 131; SELDEN, J, 9
contradict Do I c. myself SELF, 27; WHITMAN, W, 10
contradiction brook no c. DOCTORS, 107; WEBSTER, J, 2
Man is...an everlasting c. to himself HAZLITT, W, 5; INTELLECT, 7
Woman's at best a c. POPE, A, 43; WOMEN, 109
contradictory Doublethink means the power of holding two c. beliefs ORWELL, G, 19
Our world is highly c. AUDIENCES, 2
contrairy everythink goes c. with me DICKENS, C, 11
contraries Without C. is no progression BLAKE, W, 18; CONFLICT, 4
contrariwise 'C.,' continued Tweedledee CARROLL, L, 26
contrary Mary, Mary, quite c. GARDENS, 1; NURSERY RHYMES, 34
On the c. IBSEN, H, 10; LAST WORDS, 53
control c. his fate DESTINY, 25
I must...try hard to c. the talking habit, but...my case is hereditary FRANK, A, 10
protect virginity or otherwise to c. female sexuality VIRGINITY, 6
we ought to c. our thoughts DARWIN, C, 6; SELF-CONTROL, 3
controversial It's altogether...less c. and more physical SPORT AND GAMES, 8
convalescence For Lawrence, existence was one long c. LAWRENCE, D, 2
I enjoy c. REST, 3
in c. a friend DOCTORS, 11
convenient modern view of life is always to seek what is more c. DISEASE, 37
Nobody is forgotten when it is c. to remember him DISRAELI, B, 36; EXPEDIENCY, 4
Convent C. of the Sacred Heart ELIOT, T, 23
convention a c. which says you must not make species extinct CONSERVATION, 9
conventional The c. army loses if it does not win WAR, 93
conventionally to fail c. KEYNES, J, 5; ORTHODOXY, 3
conversation a c. with the finest men LITERATURE, 3
And third-rate c. MEDIOCRITY, 8
a proper subject of c. CHESTERFIELD, P, 19; RELIGION, 26
C....elicits secrets from us CONVERSATION, 8
C. has a kind of charm CONVERSATION, 8
c. must be an exchange of thought CONVERSATION, 7
happiest c. where there is no competition CONVERSATION, 5
make his c. perfectly delightful INSULTS, 116; SMITH, S, 11
Questioning is not the mode of c. CONVERSATION, 4; JOHNSON, S, 103
There is no such thing as c. CONVERSATION, 10; WEST, R, 6
Writing...is but a different name for c. STERNE, L, 7; WRITING, 46
Your ignorance cramps my c. HOPE, A, 7; INSULTS, 64
conversationalist the c. who adds 'in other words' CONVERSATION, 6
conversing Even when c. he could not keep still WRITERS, 80
converted difficult for a Jew to be c. HEINE, H, 4; JEWS, 8
conviction The best lack all c. YEATS, W, 28
convince They will conquer, but...not c. PERSUASION, 1; UNAMUNO, M, 4
cook a good c., as cooks go HUMOUR, 60; SAKI, 16
Any c. should be able to GOVERNMENT, 20; LENIN, V, 7
C. is a little unnerved BETJEMAN, J, 6; ETIQUETTE, 1
ill c. that cannot lick his own fingers SELF-CONFIDENCE, 8; SHAKESPEARE, 319
she was a very bad c. SNOBBERY, 11
cookery c. do FOOD, 52
cooking woman accepted c....but man...made of it a recreation FOOD, 60
cooks Too many c. HELP, 5; PROVERBS, 440
cool She was once c. but Mr Gravity's been very unkind GREER, G, 1
Coolidge C. is a better example of evolution POLITICIANS, 112
Cooper shock to see Gary C. killing off the Indians BALDWIN, J, 7
copier c. of nature can never produce anything great IMITATION, 4
copies more c. of my works are left behind WRITERS, 36
copulation Birth, and c., and death ELIOT, T, 22; LIFE AND DEATH, 14
copy A lotta cats c. the Mona Lisa IMITATION, 1
copying by defying their parents and c. one another YOUTH, 8
copyright The Lord holds c. on all songs MUSIC, 23
coral C. is far more red ANALOGY, 4; SHAKESPEARE, 373
Of his bones are c. made DEATH, 154; SHAKESPEARE, 323
cord a threefold c. is not quickly broken BIBLE, 70; UNITY, 5
cordial gold in phisik is a c. CHAUCER, G, 11; MATERIALISM, 8

cordiale *La c. entente* DIPLOMACY, 24
corn amid the alien c. KEATS, J, 39
make two ears of c.…grow…where only one grew before POLITICIANS, 28; SWIFT, J, 8
That ate the c. NURSERY RHYMES, 61
The c. is as high OPTIMISM, 28
the meadows rich with c. AMERICA, 41
corner a c. in the thing I love JEALOUSY, 9; SHAKESPEARE, 286
her little dry c. GOSSIP, 11
some c. of a foreign field BROOKE, R, 7; WAR, 30
Cornish twenty thousand C. men EXECUTION, 15
Coromandel On the Coast of C. LEAR, E, 2; NONSENSE, 18
coronets Kind hearts are more than c. ARISTOCRACY, 18; TENNYSON, 40
corps English characteristic…*esprit de c.* ENGLISH, 3
corpse He'd make a lovely c. DEATH, 54; DICKENS, C, 28
he makes a very handsome c. DEATH, 72; GOLDSMITH, O, 17
the c. at every funeral ROOSEVELT, T, 2
the sort of greeting a c. would give to an undertaker BALDWIN, S, 5
corpses an armed camp of Blackshirts, a bivouac for c. FASCISM, 12
They are for prima donnas or c.… FLOWERS, 12; TOSCANINI, A, 1
corpuscles make the c. of the blood glow JEWS, 11; LAWRENCE, D, 14
correct Astronomy teaches the c. use ASTRONOMY, 4; LEACOCK, S, 5
correction It is a stupidity…to busy oneself with the c. of the world IMPROVEMENT, 3; MOLIERE, 6
correctly anxious to do the wrong thing c. ETIQUETTE, 9; SAKI, 20
corridor Life is a dusty c. LIFE, 24
corridors c. of power POWER, 24
corroboration c.…in the records of Somerset House HUMILITY, 12
corrupt Among a people generally c. BURKE, E, 22; CORRUPTION, 1
appointment by the c. few DEMOCRACY, 23
power is apt to c. PITT THE ELDER , 3; POWER, 21
Power tends to c. POWER, 3
corrupted one whom fame has not c. CURIE, M, 2
They had been c. by money GREENE, G, 6; SENTIMENTALITY, 1
corruptible born again, not of c. seed BIBLE, 440; DEATH, 36
corruption C., the most infallible symptom of constitutional liberty CORRUPTION, 4; GIBBON, E, 9
I have said to c., thou art my father BIBLE, 232
purge the land of all /C. ROYALTY, 25
strong c. /Inhabits our frail blood INGRATITUDE, 6
the foul dregs of his power, the tools of despotism and c. POLITICS, 119
corruptly O! that estates, degrees, and offices /Were not deriv'd c. CORRUPTION, 14
corrupts lack of power c. absolutely POWER, 27; STEVENSON, A, 3
Socrates is a doer of evil, who c. the youth SOCRATES, 3
corse As his c. to the rampart FUNERALS, 13
cosmetic sunlight as a kind of c. effulgence SUN, 8
cosmetics In the factory we make c. COSMETICS, 5
cosmopolitan I was told I am a true c. MELANCHOLY, 11
cosmos c. is about the smallest hole CHESTERTON, G, 32; UNIVERSE, 6
cost To give and not to count the c. SELFLESSNESS, 3
Too caustic? To hell with c. GOLDWYN, S, 3
Why so large c.…upon thy fading mansion spend APPEARANCE, 62
costumes referred to army uniforms as c. REAGAN, R, 5
cottage Love and a c. LOVE, 56
poorest man may in his c. bid defiance to…the Crown PITT THE ELDER , 1; PRIVACY, 5
to refer to your friend's country establishment as a 'c.' POTTER, S, 3; WORDS, 25
cottages Pale Death kicks his way equally into the c. of the poor EQUALITY, 42
couch the century of the psychiatrist's c. PSYCHIATRY, 23
time as a tool not as a c. KENNEDY, J, 6; TIME, 29
when on my c. I lie SOLITUDE, 17; WORDSWORTH, W, 9
cough C.: A convulsion of the lungs ILLNESS, 37
Jeeves coughed one soft, low, gentle c. ANALOGY, 6; WODEHOUSE, P, 7
coughing keeping people from c. ACTING, 18
coughs C. and sneezes spread diseases ILLNESS, 6
council The grotesque chaos of a Labour c. – a *Labour* c. KINNOCK, N, 10
counsel consequences of…unpreparedness and feeble c. WAR, 1
C. of her country's gods BRITAIN, 7; COWPER, W, 4
sometimes c. take – and sometimes Tea DRINKS, 18; POPE, A, 49
the c. of the ungodly PSALMS, 1
we took sweet c. together PSALMS, 34
count Don't c. your chickens AESOP, 8; ANTICIPATION, 4
If you can…c. your money you are not…rich man WEALTH, 24
I won the c. DEMOCRACY, 24
Let me c. the ways BROWNING, E, 5
One has to be able to c. MATHEMATICS, 10
To give and not to c. the cost SELFLESSNESS, 3
counted I c. them all out and I c. them all back JOURNALISM, 18; WAR, 75
countenance the Lord lift up his c. upon thee BIBLE, 436; BLESSING, 4
counter-democratic Proportional Representation,…is fundamentally c. KINNOCK, N, 2
counterpoint Too much c.; what is worse, Protestant c. BEECHAM, T, 6; CRITICISM, 4
counties see the coloured c. COUNTRYSIDE, 7; HOUSMAN, A, 10
countries preferreth all c. before his own DISCONTENT, 7
country absolved from all duty to his c. MARRIAGE, 118; PEACOCK, T, 10
a c. diversion CONGREVE, W, 15; COUNTRYSIDE, 1
A c. governed by a despot JOHNSON, S, 122; TYRANNY, 7
a c. of young men AMERICA, 15; EMERSON, R, 25
affections must be confined…to a single c. PATRIOTISM, 14
A man should know something of his own c. STERNE, L, 9; TRAVEL, 40
an honest man sent to lie abroad for…his c. DIPLOMACY, 32
Anybody can be good in the c. COUNTRYSIDE, 13; WILDE, O, 52
Anyone who loves his c., follow me PATRIOTISM, 15
became entirely based on politics, I think this c. would lose MONARCHY, 7
Counsel of her c.'s gods BRITAIN, 7; COWPER, W, 4
c. from whose bourn no traveller returns AFTERLIFE, 10; SHAKESPEARE, 91
died to save their c. CHESTERTON, G, 14
every time Hitler occupies a c. HITLER, A, 4
God made the c. COUNTRYSIDE, 2; COWPER, W, 22
go down into the c. DECEPTION, 11; WILDE, O, 20
good news from a far c. BIBLE, 455
Great artists have no c. NATIONALITY, 9
heartbeat of the c. BUSH, G, 8
How I leave my c. LAST WORDS, 66; PITT THE YOUNGER, 4
I have but one life to lose for my c. PATRIOTISM, 18
I love thee still, My c. COWPER, W, 23; PATRIOTISM, 10
In the c. of the blind PROVERBS, 224
I vow to thee, my c. PATRIOTISM, 41
I would die for my c. PATRIOTISM, 27
loathe the c. CONGREVE, W, 15; COUNTRYSIDE, 1
My c., right or wrong CHESTERTON, G, 8; PATRIOTISM, 8
nothing good…in the c. COUNTRYSIDE, 5; HAZLITT, W, 15
Our c. is the world AMERICA, 16
our c., right or wrong PATRIOTISM, 12
Patriots…talk of dying for their c. RUSSELL, B, 31
proud of the position of the bungalow,…in the c. SUBURBIA, 2
Sell a c. WORLD, 4
she is my c. still PATRIOTISM, 9
soil of our c. is destined to be the /scene of the fiercest fight MANDELA, N, 3
supposing I had gone to the c. and said…rearm WEAPONS, 1
That is no c. for old men MORTALITY, 23; YEATS, W, 27
The history of every c. begins in the heart HISTORY, 9
The idiot who praises…every c. but his own DISCONTENT, 2; GILBERT, W, 27
The past is a foreign c. PAST, 6
The soil of our c. RACISM, 21
The undiscover'd c. AFTERLIFE, 10; SHAKESPEARE, 91
This c.…belongs to the people who inhabit it DEMOCRACY, 15; LINCOLN, A, 15
This isn't going to be a good c. EQUALITY, 25
to leave his c. as good as he had found it DUTY, 1
understanding the problems of running a c. POLITICS, 105
we can die but once to serve our c. ADDISON, J, 8; PATRIOTISM, 1
what was good for our c. BUSINESS, 38
When I am in the c. I wish to vegetate COUNTRYSIDE, 6; HAZLITT, W, 29
Your c. needs YOU WAR, 5

countrymen first in the hearts of his c. WASHINGTON, G, 1
countryside a more dreadful record of sin than…c. DOYLE, A, 8; SIN, 13
c. is one of the most heavily man-made habitats CONSERVATION, 10
county The sound of the English c. families ARISTOCRACY, 21; WAUGH, E, 7
coup people who organized the c. must have had a conscience bypass THATCHER, M, 10
couple A married c. are well suited MARRIAGE, 125
Splendid c. – slept with both MARRIAGE, 34
the perfect c.…a mother and child MOTHERHOOD, 6
couples so many c.…not getting the right proteins SEX, 24
courage be strong and of a good c. BIBLE, 58
be strong and of a good c. GOD, 10
C. is the price…for granting peace COURAGE, 15
c. to love…courage to suffer LOVE, 169; TROLLOPE, A, 5
good deal of physical c. to ride a horse ALCOHOL, 52; HORSES, 8; LEACOCK, S, 8
not quite enough of the superb c. of his satire GALSWORTHY, J, 1
prince of royal c. ROYALTY, 118
screw your c. to the sticking-place AMBITION, 24
tale…of…c. of my companions ENDURANCE, 19; EXPLORATION, 4
The Red Badge of C. COURAGE, 8
three o'clock in the morning c. COURAGE, 36; THOREAU, H, 15
Whistling aloud to bear his c. up WHISTLING, 2
couragious Of hearte c., politique in counsaile ROYALTY, 87
course c. of true love never did run smooth LOVE, 146; SHAKESPEARE, 259
courteous If a man be…c. to strangers BACON, F, 28; COURTESY, 2
courtesy C. is not dead BRITISH, 8; COURTESY, 4
courtier Here lies a noble c. /Who never kept his word ANONYMOUS, 28
courtiers c.…forgotten nothing and learnt nothing ROYALTY, 49
courting When you are c. a nice girl EINSTEIN, A, 8; SCIENCE, 32
courts I have come to regard…c.…as a casino JUSTICE, 11
my soul hath a desire and longing to enter into the c. of the Lord PSALMS, 44
the case is still before the c. HORACE, 5
courtship C. to marriage CONGREVE, W, 11; MARRIAGE, 52
covenant a c. between me and the earth BIBLE, 161; PROMISES, 3
a c. with death SLAVERY, 5
Coventry putting him into a moral C. IRELAND, 20
cover I…will c. thee with my hand BIBLE, 122
Never judge a c. by its book BOOKS, 28
covet thou shalt not c. BIBLE, 115
covetousness A physician ought to be extremely watchful against c. ENVY, 7
cow A c. is a very good animal in the field JOHNSON, S, 156; SUITABILITY, 2
I wish the old c. would resign THATCHER, M, 12
That milked the c. with the crumpled horn NURSERY RHYMES, 61
The c. is of the bovine ilk ANIMALS, 19; NASH, O, 1
The c. jumped over the moon NURSERY RHYMES, 14
The c.'s in the corn NURSERY RHYMES, 29
till the c. comes home BEAUMONT, F, 12; ETERNITY, 1
Truth, Sir, is a c. JOHNSON, S, 65; SCEPTICISM, 3
Why buy a c. FUTILITY, 2; PROVERBS, 467
coward better…widow of a hero than the wife of a c. COURAGE, 19
Conscience is a c. CONSCIENCE, 4; GOLDSMITH, O, 30
No c. soul is mine BRONTE, E, 3; COURAGE, 4
None but a c.…has never known fear COWARDICE, 3
The c. does it with a kiss KILLING, 11; WILDE, O, 5
Coward a very Noel C. sort of person FAME, 35
Cowardice guilty of Noël C. COWARDICE, 1
cowardly Marriage is the only adventure open to the c. MARRIAGE, 163; VOLTAIRE, 26
took a grip on c. Marxism NAZISM, 3
cowards C. die many times COWARDICE, 11; SHAKESPEARE, 148
the future…makes c. of us PRESENT, 3
Thus conscience does make c. of us all SHAKESPEARE, 92
cowboy easier to get an actor to be a c. ACTING, 12
cowering c. on the very island BRITISH, 1
cows daring…to explain…that c. can be eaten GANDHI, I, 4; RELIGION, 43
'Horses' should have read 'C.' MISTAKES, 12
coxcomb A vain…c. without…solid talents PEPYS, S, 1
to hear a c. ask two hundred guineas CRITICISM, 56; RUSKIN, J, 17
coyness This c., lady, were no crime MARVELL, A, 9; SHYNESS, 6
cracked The c. looking glass of a servant IRELAND, 13
cradle Between the c. and the grave TRANSIENCE, 13
Rocked in the c. of the deep SEA, 11
The hand that rocks the c. INFLUENCE, 12
cradles bit the babies in the c. ANIMALS, 7; BROWNING, R, 42
craft the c. so long to lerne CHAUCER, G, 19; MORTALITY, 3
The life so short, the c. so long to learn MORTALITY, 12
craftsmanship Skill without imagination is c. ART, 34; STOPPARD, T, 1
crafty too c. a woman to invent a new lie LYING, 13; MAUGHAM, W, 7
cramps incapacitated by c.…sides of Tashi's vagina with a couple of thorns WALKER, A, 10
crankshaft Fifty-five crystal spheres geared to God's c. SCIENCE, 88
cranny We seek…In every c. but the right PERVERSITY, 3
crap Books are a load of c. BOOKS, 26; LARKIN, P, 3
Craven why and how I became…mistress of the Earl of C. SEX, 129
crazy a little c.…like all men at sea GOLDING, W, 3
going to go c., living this epidemic every minute DISEASE, 24
grow a little c.…like all men at sea MADNESS, 19
I was c. and…he was drunk GRANT, U, 2
cream coffee that's too black…You integrate it with c. RACISM, 20
create c. a world CINEMA, 2
My father didn't c. you to arrest me POLICE, 7
rail at weakness themselves c. INJUSTICE, 11
created God c.…the earth BIBLE, 137;
man alone leaves traces of what he c. BRONOWSKI, J, 1; MANKIND, 12
Man…had been c. to jab the life out of Germans SASSOON, S, 5; WAR, 144
that all men and women are c. equal FEMINISM, 34
Thou hast c. us for Thyself HUMAN CONDITION, 2
we cannot be c. for this sort of suffering AFTERLIFE, 7; KEATS, J, 71
creates he c. Gods by the dozen MONTAIGNE, M, 6; RELIGION, 69
creation an ugly *woman* is a blot on the fair face of c. BRONTE, C, 4
greatest week…since the c. NIXON, R, 8; SPACE, 7
Had I been present at the C. UNIVERSE, 1
Science conducts us…through the whole range of c. SCIENCE, 64
The art of c. /is older CREATION, 17
you've not got your niche in c. HOMOSEXUALITY, 15
creations The man who started more c. since Genesis ROOSEVELT, F, 2
creative man's fear of women's c. energy FEAR, 5
creativity mistake…to put…c. first DESIGN, 9
creator All right, my lord c., Don Miguel DEATH, 91; UNAMUNO, M, 1
c. had a purpose in equipping us with a neck COURAGE, 22
Man…hasn't been a c., only a destroyer CHEKHOV, A, 10; ECOLOGY, 3
virtue in the c. is not the same as virtue in the creature CREATION, 13
creature every c. of God is good BIBLE, 508
No c. smarts…as a fool FOOLISHNESS, 17; POPE, A, 17
the c. hath a purpose and its eyes are bright with it KEATS, J, 69; PURPOSE, 6
Who kills a man kills a reasonable c. BOOKS, 32; MILTON, J, 6
creatures call these delicate c. ours JEALOUSY, 9; SHAKESPEARE, 286
From fairest c. we desire increase BEAUTY, 42; SHAKESPEARE, 359
creche c.…happens between two Range Rovers POLITICIANS, 25
credentials no c.…not even…a certificate of birth ARISTOCRACY, 14; LLOYD GEORGE, D, 9
credit If you can't explain it, how can you take c. FOOTBALL, 8
the c. belongs to the boys in the back rooms GRATITUDE, 1
The way to get things done is not to mind who gets the c. SELFLESSNESS, 2
creditors my oldest c. would hardly know me APPEARANCE, 26
not everyone who wishes makes c. RABELAIS, F, 7

credits c. would still read 'Rubinstein, God, and Piatigorsky' EGOTISM, 6; INSULTS, 61
credulity C. is...the child's strength INNOCENCE, 8; LAMB, C, 12
natural course of the human mind is...from c. to scepticism MIND, 14
creed got the better of his c. RELIGION, 83; STERNE, L, 8
Science...commits suicide when it adopts a c. SCIENCE, 53
the c. of a second-rate man POLITICIANS, 44
the powers of a first-rate man and the c. of a second-rate man BAGEHOT, W, 9
wrought /...the c. of creeds CHRISTIANITY, 60; TENNYSON, 29
creeds So many gods, so many c. KINDNESS, 13; RELIGION, 102
Vain are the thousand c. BELIEF, 4; BRONTE, E, 4
creep I wants to make your flesh c. DICKENS, C, 43
Shakespeare was something of an Establishment c. SHAKESPEARE, 3
Wit that can c. POPE, A, 16; SERVILITY, 5
creepers Jeepers C. EYES, 6
creetur lone lorn c. DICKENS, C, 11; MISFORTUNE, 11
crème c. de la c. EDUCATION, 87; SPARK, M, 9
Crete The people of C....make more history EUROPE, 19; SAKI, 6
Cretians the C. are alway liars BIBLE, 515; NATIONALITY, 4
cricket c. as organised loafing CRICKET, 11
c. is the greatest thing that God ever created CRICKET, 9
English think c. is a game ENGLISH, 28
I do love c. – it's so very English CRICKET, 2; FOOTBALL, 3
If the French noblesse had been capable of playing c. with their peasants ARISTOCRACY, 19; CRICKET, 12
It's not in support of c. BEERBOHM, M, 19; CRICKET, 1; GOLF, 1
the c. on the hearth MELANCHOLY, 10; MILTON, J, 14
where the c. sings PEACE, 22; YEATS, W, 18
Cricklewood Midland, bound for C. BETJEMAN, J, 9; TRAVEL, 9
cried I c. all the way to the bank CRITICISM, 36
crieth thy brother's blood c. unto me MURDER, 2
crime all c. is due to the repressed desire for aesthetic expression CRIME, 10; WAUGH, E, 23
Arson, after all, is an artificial c. WELLS, H, 12
Count not his broken pledges as a c. POLITICIANS, 86
C., like virtue, has its degrees CRIME, 7
Do you call poverty a c. POVERTY, 36; SHAW, G, 19
If poverty is the mother of c., stupidity is its father CRIME, 6; LA BRUYERE, J, 11
man's greatest c. BIRTH, 6
no...c. so shameful as poverty POVERTY, 10
stories of mystery and c. LITERATURE, 20
The atrocious c. of being a young man PITT THE ELDER , 2; YOUTH, 21
the Napoleon of c. CRIME, 4; DOYLE, A, 11
The punishment fit the c. GILBERT, W, 30; PUNISHMENT, 14
This coyness, lady, were no c. MARVELL, A, 9; SHYNESS, 6
Treason was no C. DRYDEN, J, 11; TREASON, 3
worse than a c., it is a blunder MISTAKES, 4
worst c. is faking it SUICIDE, 10
crimes Catholics and Communists have committed great c. COMMITMENT, 6; GREENE, G, 3
history...a tableau of c. and misfortunes VOLTAIRE, 20
how many c. committed CAMUS, A, 7; CRIME, 2
Oh liberty!...What c. are committed in thy name EXECUTION, 35; FREEDOM, 51
Crippen strong suspicions that C. London cellar murderer TECHNOLOGY, 10; TELEGRAMS, 9
crippled You are not c. at all DISABILITY, 4
crisis It may bring his distemper to a c. FRANKNESS, 3
Nor pull a long face in a c. DOCTORS, 17
crisp Deep and c. and even CHRISTMAS, 16
critic A c. is a man who CRITICS, 22; TYNAN, K, 5
A good c....narrates the adventures of his mind CRITICS, 5; FRANCE, A, 7
A good drama c. is CRITICS, 23
c. spits on what is done CRITICS, 8; HOOD, T, 14
Nor in the c. let the man be lost CRITICS, 14; POPE, A, 31
the function of the c. CRITICISM, 7; CRITICS, 1
critical c. judgement is so exquisite CRITICS, 6; FRY, C, 2
nothing if not c. CRITICISM, 57; SHAKESPEARE, 281
criticism A great deal of contemporary c. CHESTERTON, G, 4
As far as c. is concerned CRITICISM, 63
c. is a letter to the public RILKE, R, 5
my own definition of c. ARNOLD, M, 14; CRITICISM, 2
People ask you for c. CRITICISM, 42; MAUGHAM, W, 12
The Stealthy School of C. CRITICISM, 54; ROSSETTI, D, 5
criticize Do not c. your government when out of the country POLITICS, 30
don't c. /What you can't understand CHANGE, 7; DYLAN, B, 12; FAMILY, 20
criticizing The pleasure of c. CRITICISM, 32; LA BRUYERE, J, 4
critics Asking a working writer...about c. CRITICS, 7; HAMPTON, C, 5
award winning plays are written only for the c. PLAYS, 5
c. all are ready made BYRON, 38; CRITICS, 2
C. are more malicious about poetry CRITICS, 9
c....desire our blood, not our pain NIETZSCHE, F, 15
music c.....small and rodent-like with padlocked ears CRITICS, 20
The greater part of c. are parasites PRIESTLEY, J, 4
crocodile An appeaser is one who feeds a c. CHURCHILL, W, 69; DIPLOMACY, 8
crocodiles wisdom of the c. BACON, F, 60; HYPOCRISY, 2
Cromwell Caesar had his Brutus – Charles the First, his C. TREASON, 9
C. was a man in whom ambition had...suspended,...religion CROMWELL, O, 1
restless C. could not cease MARVELL, A, 3; POLITICIANS, 105
ruins that C. knocked about a bit INNUENDO, 2
Some C. guiltless GRAY, T, 6
crony government by c. NEPOTISM, 1
crook A writer of c. stories POLITICS, 115
I am not a c. NIXON, R, 10
the symbol of a bishop is a c. CLERGY, 5
crooked the c. timber of humanity HUMAN NATURE, 18; KANT, I, 4
There was a c. man, and he walked a c. mile NURSERY RHYMES, 56
crop watering the last year's c. ELIOT, G, 4; FUTILITY, 7
crops Man.../Laid the c. low AGRICULTURE, 5; THOMAS, D, 17
cross Don't c. the bridge ANTICIPATION, 2; PROVERBS, 116
Hot c. buns! NURSERY RHYMES, 16
no c., no crown ENDURANCE, 15
sign of the c....an indulgence for all the sins CHRISTIANITY, 6
The orgasm has replaced the C. MUGGERIDGE, M, 2; SEX, 88
When I survey the wondrous C. HUMILITY, 14; WATTS, I, 8
cross-bow With my c. /I shot COLERIDGE, S, 27
crossed a girl likes to be c. in love a little now and then AUSTEN, J, 24; WOMEN, 16
crosses wooden c. on the roadside WORLD WAR I, 16
crossword an optimist...fills up his c. puzzle in ink OPTIMISM, 37
crow before the cock c., thou shalt deny me BETRAYAL, 2; BIBLE, 425
sun had risen to hear him c. ARROGANCE, 3; ELIOT, G, 5; INSULTS, 45
waiting for the cock to c. BETRAYAL, 8
crowd a c. like that...brings a lump to my wallet MATERIALISM, 27
And hid his face amid a c. of stars LOVE, 179; YEATS, W, 34
Far from the madding c. GRAY, T, 7; SOLITUDE, 8
crowds C. without company GIBBON, E, 4; LONDON, 14
If you can talk with c. and keep your virtue IDEALISM, 4; KIPLING, R, 18
It brings men together in c. and mobs in bar-rooms SOCIETY, 23; THOREAU, H, 7
crown c. o' the earth doth melt SHAKESPEARE, 37
no cross, no c. ENDURANCE, 15
poorest man... bid defiance to...the C. PRIVACY, 5; PITT THE ELDER, 1
risk my C. than do what I think personally disgraceful SELF-RESPECT, 1
the c. of life BIBLE, 216; TEMPTATION, 4
The influence of the C. has increased MONARCHY, 11
Uneasy lies the head that wears a c. MONARCHY, 22; SHAKESPEARE, 122
we received from that See our C. OBLIGATION, 2
within the hollow c. ROYALTY, 104; SHAKESPEARE, 300
crowned An unlettered king is a c. ass MONARCHY, 1
He was my c. King LOYALTY, 11
crucible America is God's C. AMERICA, 47
crucified preach Christ c. BIBLE, 24
Where the dear Lord was c. CHRISTIANITY, 1
you might try getting c. CHRISTIANITY, 58; TALLEYRAND, 8
crucify Diseases c. the soul of man DISEASE, 11
Do you want to c. the boy CHRISTIANITY, 39; GOLDWYN, S, 29
cruel A c. story runs on wheels CRUELTY, 4
As c. a weapon...the chemical barrage CONSERVATION, 2

be c. only to be kind CRUELTY, 5
C., but composed and bland ARNOLD, M, 33; CATS, 1
cruellest April is the c. month ELIOT, T, 26; MONTHS, 8
cruelly heavily and c. images of female beauty BEAUTY, 47
cruelty Fear is the parent of c. CRUELTY, 2
unsex me here, /And fill me...full /Of direst c. EVIL, 22
cruise we are all on our last c. MORTALITY, 18; STEVENSON, R, 17
crumbs c. which fell from the rich man's table BIBLE, 333; POVERTY AND WEALTH, 3
crusade This party is a moral c. PARTIES, 13
cry I often want to c. RHYS, J, 2; SEXES, 25
let them...be soon brought to shame, that c. over me, there, there PSALMS, 40
make 'em c. WRITING, 41
mother, do not c. LAST WORDS, 32
She likes stories that make her c. SENTIMENTALITY, 5
the c. of him that ruleth among fools BIBLE, 75; WISDOM, 3
the only advantage women have over men –...they can c. RHYS, J, 2; SEXES, 25
the stones would immediately c. out BIBLE, 337
We think caged birds sing, when indeed they c. IMPRISONMENT, 13; WEBSTER, J, 5
when we c. to Thee SEA, 14
crying An infant c. in the night HUMAN CONDITION, 28; TENNYSON, 30
It is no use c. PROVERBS, 229; REGRET, 1
crystal as clear as a c., the synthesis – German National Socialism NAZISM, 3
cubic One c. foot less SMALLNESS, 3
cuckold make her husband a c. to make him a monarch AMBITION, 25
cuckoo the c. clock was invented...to give tourists something solid SWITZERLAND, 1
The c. comes in April MONTHS, 3; PROVERBS, 382
This is the weather the c. likes HARDY, T, 13; WEATHER, 12
cucumber A c. should be well sliced FOOD, 41; JOHNSON, S, 161
cucumbers they are but c. after all CRITICISM, 31; JOHNSON, S, 132
cul-de-sac A committee is a c. BUREAUCRACY, 3
cult difference between a religion and a c. RELIGION, 107
local c. called Christianity CHRISTIANITY, 42; HARDY, T, 6
What's a c. MINORITY, 1
cultivate c. our garden PAROCHIALISM, 3; VOLTAIRE, 9
cultivated I do not want to die...until I have...c. the seed ACHIEVEMENT, 11
culture C. being a pursuit of our total perfection ARNOLD, M, 3
C. is an instrument wielded by professors WEIL, S, 1
C. is the passion for sweetness and light ARNOLD, M, 232
C., the acquainting ourselves with the best ARNOLD, M, 22
c., you'll find more on a month-old carton of yoghurt ROYALTY, 80
image of Cleopatra...provides clues to the nature of the c. HISTORY, 17
ladies who pursue C. in bands CULTURE, 4
terrible revenge by the c. of the Negroes POPULAR MUSIC, 20
two half-cultures do not make a c. HALF MEASURES, 1
When I hear anyone talk of C. PHILISTINISM, 4
You can lead a whore to c. PARKER, D, 26; PUNS, 19
cultures apt to leave his c. exposed on the laboratory table SCIENTISTS, 13
cumulative they underestimate the c. effect LANGUAGE, 51
cunning rat-like c., a plausible manner JOURNALISM, 33
cup Ah, fill the C. FITZGERALD, E, 12; TIME, 22
Come, fill the C., and in the Fire of Spring FITZGERALD, E, 3; TIME, 21
Hollywood...the personality of a paper c. CINEMA, 6; PLACES, 9
my c. runneth over PSALMS, 13
my c. shall be full PSALMS, 11
tak a c. o' kindness yet BURNS, R, 5; FRIENDSHIP, 13
the c. of the vales THOMAS, D, 29
cupboard But when she got there /The c. was bare FOOD, 56; NURSERY RHYMES, 39
Cupid wing'd C. painted blind LOVE, 147; SHAKESPEARE, 260
cups c., That cheer but not inebriate COWPER, W, 25; DRINKS, 10
cur the c. dog of Britain and spaniel of Spain POLITICIANS, 119
curable One is due to wax and is c. DISABILITY, 5
curates abundant shower of c. BRONTE, C, 7
curators The Arab who builds...a hut out of...a temple...is more philosophical than...c. of the museums FRANCE, A, 4; MUSEUMS, 1
cur'd C....of my disease DOCTORS, 81
curds Eating her c. and whey NURSERY RHYMES, 31
cure a c. for which there was no disease REMEDIES, 14
consider that the c. is discovered ILLNESS, 17
C. the disease BACON, F, 25; REMEDIES, 9
death is the c. of all diseases DEATH, 42
Difficult as it may be to c. KILLING, 1
first you will not c. your patients REMEDIES, 23
It is part of the c. to wish to be cured REMEDIES, 51
no c. for birth and death LIFE AND DEATH, 28; SANTAYANA, G, 11
Nothing hinders a c. so much as frequent change of medicine REMEDIES, 49
People seemed to think that if he could c. an elephant he could c. anything REPUTATION, 4
Show me a sane man and I will c. him for you JUNG, C, 9; MADNESS, 23
the c. for admiring the House of Lords BAGEHOT, W, 2; HOUSES OF PARLIAMENT, 3
The most rational c....for the...fear of death LIFE AND DEATH, 19
The presence of the doctor is the beginning of the c. DOCTORS, 6
There are maladies we must not seek to c. REMEDIES, 47
there are only things for which man has not found a c. SCIENCE, 3
'There is no c. for this disease.' DOCTORS, 19
We all labour against our own c. DEATH, 42; REMEDIES, 15
Work is the grand c. CARLYLE, T, 31; WORK, 7
cured By opposites opposites are c. REMEDIES, 34
Groan so in perpetuity, than be c. DEATH, 140
Poverty of goods is easily c. MONTAIGNE, M, 10
the only disease you don't look forward to being c. of DEATH, 103
What can't be c. ENDURANCE, 3; PROVERBS, 454
cures A good laugh and a long sleep are the best c. in the doctor's book LAUGHTER, 4
But *C.* come difficult and hard REMEDIES, 16
he's organized these mass c. REMEDIES, 26
Many medicines, few c. REMEDIES, 2
Nicotinic acid c. pellagra REMEDIES, 54
number of unexplained c. has dropped REMEDIES, 48
curfew 'C. shall not ring tonight!' MERCY, 4
The C. tolls the knell of parting day DAY, 6; GRAY, T, 1
curiosities How these c. would be quite forgot GOSSIP, 9
curiosity C. killed the cat CURIOSITY, 2; PROVERBS, 104
C. will conquer fear CURIOSITY, 8
Disinterested intellectual c....life blood of...civilisation CURIOSITY, 9
I would rather be a brilliant memory than a c. RENUNCIATION, 2
curious Be not c. in unnecessary matters BIBLE, 81; CURIOSITY, 3
I am c. to see what happens...to one who dies unshriven LAST WORDS, 65
'That was the c. incident,' remarked...Holmes DOYLE, A, 15; TRIVIALITY, 9
curiouser C. and c. CARROLL, L, 5; CONFUSION, 4
curl There was a little girl /Who had a little c. SEX, 83
curly C. locks, C. locks, /Wilt thou be mine NURSERY RHYMES, 8
currency I will not be a party to debasing the c. ECONOMICS, 12; KEYNES, J, 8
curse A c. is on her if she stay CURSES, 5; TENNYSON, 44
Christianity the one great c. CHRISTIANITY, 49; NIETZSCHE, F, 4
c. God, and die BIBLE, 224; CURSES, 1
c. not the king, no not in thy thought SECRECY, 3
Don't c. the darkness FUTILITY, 1
make a c. sound like a caress POLITICIANS, 83
She would rather light a candle than c. the darkness STEVENSON, A, 8
The c. is come upon me CURSES, 4; TENNYSON, 46
the c. of all the human race NAPOLEON I, 1
the c. of the present British Prime Minister CHAMBERLAIN, N, 1
Work is the c. of the drinking classes WILDE, O, 75; WORK, 39
cursed thou art c. above all cattle BIBLE, 151; SEXES, 4
curses C....always come home to roost CURSES, 3; SOUTHEY, R, 2
curst C. be the verse POETRY, 48; POPE, A, 15
curtain An iron c. CHURCHILL, W, 64; COLD WAR, 2

d. sayings WISDOM, 7
Genuineness only thrives in the d. HUXLEY, A, 34; SINCERITY, 4
great leap in the d. HOBBES, T, 8; LAST WORDS, 51
never to refuse a drink after d. ALCOHOL, 56; MENCKEN, H, 18
O d., d., d., amid the blaze of noon BLINDNESS, 8; MILTON, J, 58
slow, sure doom falls pitiless and d. HUMAN CONDITION, 23; RUSSELL, B, 16
The d. night of the soul SOUL, 9
they grope in the d. BIBLE, 229
Turn up the lights, I don't want to go home in the d. LAST WORDS, 50
we are for the d. ENDING, 5; SHAKESPEARE, 38
What in me is d. /Illumine GOD, 40; MILTON, J, 31
darken never d. my towels again INSULTS, 95; MARX, G, 8
darker people who sit out in the sun to become d. APPEARANCE, 33
darkest The d. hour OPTIMISM, 8; PROVERBS, 383
darkling as on a d. plain ARNOLD, M, 11; WAR, 11
D. I listen DEATH, 92; KEATS, J, 40
darkly through a glass, d. BIBLE, 38; CHARITY, 7
darkness Before us pass'd the door of D. DEATH, 64; FITZGERALD, E, 17
cast away the works of d. BOOK OF COMMON PRAYER, 4
d. was upon the face of the deep BIBLE, 137; CREATION, 2
fool walketh in d. BIBLE, 66
God shall make my d. to be light PSALMS, 7
instruments of d. tell us truths EVIL, 21
Lighten our d. BOOK OF COMMON PRAYER, 9
men loved d.…because their deeds were evil BIBLE, 246; EVIL, 6
outer d. BIBLE, 381
She would rather light a candle than curse the d. COMPLIMENTS, 35; STEVENSON, A, 8
The d. falls at Thy behest DAY, 4
the people that walked in d. BIBLE, 200
the pestilence that walketh in d. PSALMS, 51
we wrestle…against the rulers of the d. BIBLE, 96
darlin' he's a d. man FRIENDS, 12
darling Charlie is my d. ADMIRATION, 11; COMPLIMENTS, 20
d. of the Gods was born DESTINY, 16; MARVELL, A, 7
Thrice welcome, d. of the spring WORDSWORTH, W, 75
darlings Goodnight, my d. LAST WORDS, 21
darn a d. is…poverty THRIFT, 11
Darwin D. was to the nineteenth DARWIN, C, 3
dashes prisoner sees the door of his dungeon open he d. IMPETUOSITY, 4
date A d. that shall live in infamy WORLD WAR II, 44
dates Its history d. from today ROYALTY, 115; WHISTLER, J, 14
daughter as is the mother, so is her d. BIBLE, 125; FAMILY, 10
d. of Earth and Water SHELLEY, P, 6; WEATHER, 23
Don't put your d. on the stage COWARD, N, 8; THEATRE, 8
Dwelt a miner, Forty-niner, /And his d., Clementine MOURNING, 7
I always remember that I am Caesar's d. EXTRAVAGANCE, 3
My d.! O my ducats LOSS, 7; SHAKESPEARE, 245
skipper had taken his little d. BOATS, 12; LONGFELLOW, H, 19
the earth is free for every son and d. of mankind HUMAN RIGHTS, 8
daughters old cemetery in which nine of his d. were lying SEX, 119; THURBER, J, 7
Words are men's d. WORDS, 23
dauntless faithful in love…d. in war CHIVALRY, 12; SCOTT, W, 15
David D. Copperfield kind of crap BEGINNING, 16; SALINGER, J, 3
D. his ten thousands BIBLE, 481
Once in royal D.'s city CHRISTMAS, 2
Davy Sir Humphry D. SCIENTISTS, 7
dawn a grey d. breaking MASEFIELD, J, 5; SEA, 10
Bliss was it in that d. to be alive FRENCH REVOLUTION, 11; WORDSWORTH, W, 41
the dappled d. doth rise MILTON, J, 17
They sighed for the d. and thee LOVE, 163; TENNYSON, 57
dawned each day that has d. is your last HORACE, 18; PRESENT, 10
day compare thee to a summer's d. COMPLIMENTS, 31; SHAKESPEARE, 360
count as profit every d. that Fate allows you HORACE, 29; PRESENT, 8
death will have his d. DEATH, 152; SHAKESPEARE, 299
each d. is like a year IMPRISONMENT, 17; WILDE, O, 9
each d. that has dawned is your last HORACE, 18; PRESENT, 10
Every d., in every way, I am getting better and better PSYCHOLOGY, 4
every dog has his d. SATISFACTION, 1
from this d. forward BOOK OF COMMON PRAYER, 27; MARRIAGE, 33
God called the light D. BIBLE, 137; CREATION, 2
Good morning to the d.: and, next, my gold JONSON, B, 14; MATERIALISM, 16
If every d. in the life of a school EDUCATION, 55; LEACOCK, S, 1
I look upon every d. to be lost FRIENDSHIP, 20; JOHNSON, S, 154
in the d. of judgement BOOK OF COMMON PRAYER, 13; DEATH, 40
It takes place every d. CAMUS, A, 9; DOOMSDAY, 4
It was such a lovely d. BED, 9; MAUGHAM, W, 16
let the d. perish wherein I was born BIBLE, 225
live murmur of a summer's d. ARNOLD, M, 35
Live this d., as…thy last PRESENT, 12
long d.'s task is done REST, 2; SHAKESPEARE, 35
Night and d. LOVE, 128; PORTER, C, 4
Now the d. is over DAY, 1
one d. in thy courts is better than a thousand PSALMS, 45
Our d. will come IRELAND, 3
Our little systems have their d. TENNYSON, 26; TRANSIENCE, 23
Seize the d. HORACE, 32; PRESENT, 7
So foul and fair a d. SHAKESPEARE, 203; WEATHER, 22
spend a single d. really well GOOD, 7
Stay, stay, /Until the hasting d. /Has run HERRICK, R, 4; TRANSIENCE, 15
Sweet d., so cool, so calm DAY, 8; HERBERT, G, 9
That fellow would vulgarize the d. of judgment JERROLD, D, 3; VULGARITY, 3
the arrow that flieth by d. PSALMS, 51
The better the d. PROVERBS, 381
The bright d. is done ENDING, 5; SHAKESPEARE, 38
The d. begins to droop DAY, 2
the d. I was meant not to see ASSASSINATION, 8; THATCHER, M, 33
the d. returns too soon BYRON, 42; LOVE, 48
the twenty-four hour d. BEERBOHM, M, 6; TIME, 12
thou knowest not what a d. may bring forth BIBLE, 457; FUTURE, 4
when the d. of Pentecost was fully come BIBLE, 2
Without all hope of d. BLINDNESS, 8; MILTON, J, 58
daylight a rule never to drink by d. ALCOHOL, 56; MENCKEN, H, 18
Dayrolles Give D. a chair CHESTERFIELD, P, 23; LAST WORDS, 18
days D. and moments quickly flying DEATH, 47
D. off LEISURE, 6
d. of man are but as grass PSALMS, 58
d. of wine and roses TRANSIENCE, 12
Do not let us speak of darker d. CHURCHILL, W, 57; WORLD WAR II, 19
Shuts up the story of our d. FAITH, 26; RALEIGH, W, 3
Sweet childish d. NOSTALGIA, 29; WORDSWORTH, W, 72
Ten D. that Shook the World RUSSIAN REVOLUTION, 7
the d. of our age are threescore years and ten PSALMS, 50
Thirty d. hath November MONTHS, 9
dead Add: 'provided he is really d.' ADMIRATION, 8; LA BRUYERE, J, 12
all the world she knew is d. OLD AGE, 21
And what was d. was Hope IMPRISONMENT, 16; WILDE, O, 7
A statesman is a politician who's been d. POLITICIANS, 29; TRUMAN, H, 5
Better red than d. NUCLEAR WEAPONS, 2
Bloomin' Well D. DEATH, 133
But he's just as d. as if he'd been wrong ANONYMOUS, 102; RIGHT, 1
Come not, when I am d. HYPOCRISY, 21; TENNYSON, 11
D.! and…never called me mother DEATH, 182
d., but in the Elysian fields DISRAELI, B, 41; HOUSES OF PARLIAMENT, 10
D. men tell no tales DEATH, 5; PROVERBS, 106
Either he's d. or my watch has stopped DEATH, 106; MARX, G, 5
England mourns for her d. across the sea MOURNING, 3
Fifteen men on the d. man's chest ALCOHOL, 78; STEVENSON, R, 8
forgotten, as a d. man out of mind PSALMS, 20
for those who like it better d. CRITICISM, 40
God is d. GOD, 41; NIETZSCHE, F, 5
great deal to be said for being d. DEATH, 33
Here lies Fred, /Who was alive and is d. ANONYMOUS, 30; ROYALTY, 11
He was a great patriot…provided…that he really is d. ADMIRATION, 19; VOLTAIRE, 36
if I am d. he would like to see me DEATH, 69
If the d. talk to you, you are a spiritualist MADNESS, 43; SZASZ, T, 8

I have been drinking it for sixty-five years and I am not d. DRINKS, 22; VOLTAIRE, 35
It does not then concern either the living or the d. DEATH, 61
I've just read that I am d. KIPLING, R, 33; OBITUARIES, 5
I wouldn't believe Hitler was d. HITLER, A, 6
let the d. bury their d. BIBLE, 382; LIFE AND DEATH, 11
more to say when I am d. DEATH, 128
most of 'em d. SASSOON, S, 4; WAR, 148
Mother is the d. heart of the family GREER, G, 3; WOMAN'S ROLE, 6
move in a world of the d. FORSTER, E, 1; HISTORIANS, 2
My husband is d. DEATH, 107; MARX, G, 7
Nobody heard him, the d. man DROWNING, 3
Now he is d. ARNOLD, M, 30; DEATH, 26
Now I'm d. in the grave with my lips moving POSTERITY, 9
Once you're d., you're made for life DEATH, 78; GOLDWYN, S, 30
O pity the d. that are d. DEATH, 97; LAWRENCE, D, 10
ransom not only their prisoners but their d. HOSTAGES, 9
she was d.; but my father he kept ladling gin REMEDIES, 53; SHAW, G, 37
The d. don't die DEATH, 98; LAWRENCE, D, 44
The d.…look on and help DEATH, 98; LAWRENCE, D, 44
the d. shall be raised incorruptible BIBLE, 42; DEATH, 35
the d. shall hear the voice of the Son of God BIBLE, 248
the living are the d. on holiday LIFE AND DEATH, 26
The noble living and the noble d. NOBILITY, 8; WORDSWORTH, W, 44
The novel being d. NOVELS, 18; VIDAL, G, 2
The only completely consistent people are the d. CONSTANCY, 2; HUXLEY, A, 14
The only good Indians I ever saw were d. ENEMIES, 9
The past is the only d. thing PAST, 11
the people we should have been seen d. with SNOBBERY, 12; WEST, R, 8
this earth, that bears thee d., /Bears not alive so stout a gentleman LIFE AND DEATH, 29
To one d. deathless hour POETRY, 51; ROSSETTI, D, 2
to resuscitate the d. art /Of poetry POETRY, 49; POUND, E, 12
to the d. we owe only truth RESPECT, 4; VOLTAIRE, 24
wanted to make sure he was d. INSULTS, 55
we are all d. DEATH, 95; KEYNES, J, 1
we survive amongst the d. and the dying as on a battlefield OLD AGE, 98; SPARK, M, 6
When I am d., and laid in grave ANONYMOUS, 106; MEMORIALS, 1
When I am d., my dearest DEATH, 129; ROSSETTI, C, 8
when you're d. it's hard to find the light switch LIFE AND DEATH, 3
who quoted d. languages CRITICS, 21; TREE, H, 5
year d. for tax reasons ADAMS, D, 12

deadener Habit is a great d. BECKETT, S, 6; HABIT, 2

deadly Soap and education…are more d. EDUCATION, 91; TWAIN, M, 5
the female of the species is more d. than the male KIPLING, R, 10; WOMEN, 71

deaf Historians are like d. people HISTORIANS, 8; TOLSTOY, L, 15
union of a d. man to a blind woman COLERIDGE, S, 22; MARRIAGE, 49

deafness There are two kinds of d. DISABILITY, 5

deal a new d. for the American people AMERICA, 34; ROOSEVELT, F, 9
Shed his blood…given a square d. JUSTICE, 22

dean no dogma, no D. DISRAELI, B, 35; RELIGION, 30
the queer old D. SPOONER, W, 4

dear D. 338171 COWARD, N, 23; HUMOUR, 41
that bread should be so d. HOOD, T, 12; POVERTY, 20

dearer d. still is truth ARISTOTLE, 10; TRUTH, 8
met with anything that was d. to anyone than his own self BUDDHA, 2

death A bridegroom in my d. DEATH, 138
A child…would have no more idea of d. than a cat or a plant DEATH, 179
a covenant with d. SLAVERY, 5
After all, what *is* d. DEATH, 156
After d. the doctor DEATH, 1
After the first d., there is no other DEATH, 172; THOMAS, D, 16
After your d. you will be AFTERLIFE, 9; SCHOPENHAUER, A, 7
All interest in disease and d. LIFE, 61
A long illness seems to be placed between life and d. ILLNESS, 15
and d. remember MEMORY, 24
Angel of D. has been abroad WAR, 29
an intelligent man at the point of d. DEATH, 20
Any man's d. diminishes me DEATH, 59; DONNE, J, 8
A physician can sometimes parry the scythe of d. TIME, 38
a Reaper whose name is D. DEATH, 101; LONGFELLOW, H, 11
a remedy for everything except d. CERVANTES, M, 17; REMEDIES, 19
artist is in danger of d. HEMINGWAY, E, 4; SPORT AND GAMES, 18
A single d. is a tragedy STALIN, J, 6; STATISTICS, 10
a tie that only d. can sever MARRIAGE, 107; MAUGHAM, W, 6
A useless life is an early d. GOETHE, J, 5; PURPOSE, 3
author of the Satanic Verses book…sentenced to d. RELIGION, 60
Because I could not stop for D. DEATH, 55
Birth, and copulation, and d. ELIOT, T, 22; LIFE AND DEATH, 14
Christianity has made of d. a terror CHRISTIANITY, 51; DEATH, 115
could not stop for D. DICKINSON, E, 3
D.…a friend that alone can bring the peace DEATH, 50
d. after life does greatly please DEATH, 164
D. and taxes and childbirth EXPEDIENCY, 6; MITCHELL, M, 3
D. be not proud DEATH, 58; DONNE, J, 14
d.…can be done as easily lying down LIFE AND DEATH, 3
D. cometh soon or late COURAGE, 23; MACAULAY, T, 17
D. defies the doctor DEATH, 6; PROVERBS, 107
D. destroys a man DEATH, 67; FORSTER, E, 8
D. has got something to be said for it DEATH, 19
D. is a delightful hiding-place WORLD-WEARINESS, 3
D. is an acquired trait DEATH, 17
D. is a punishment to some DEATH, 137
D. is better than disease DEATH, 100
D. is my neighbour now DEATH, 62; LAST WORDS, 31
D. is nothing AFTERLIFE, 6; DEATH, 81
D. is not the greatest of ills WORLD-WEARINESS, 9
D. is simply part of the process HUMAN CONDITION, 30
D. is still working like a mole DEATH, 79; HERBERT, G, 5
d. is the cure of all diseases DEATH, 42; REMEDIES, 15
D. is the greatest evil HOPE, 14
D. is the greatest kick of all DEATH, 126
D. is the great leveller DEATH, 7; PROVERBS, 108
D. is the poor man's best physician DEATH, 8
D. is the price paid by life DEATH, 176
D. is the privilege of human nature DEATH, 131
D. is the veil DEATH, 157; SHELLEY, P, 22
d. itself must be…a mockery DEATH, 158; SHELLEY, P, 23
D. must…become the discreet…exit DEATH, 25
D. must be distinguished from dying DEATH, 161
d. of Little Nell without laughing WILDE, O, 64
d. reveals the eminent EQUALITY, 35
D. Shall Have No Dominion DEATH, 174; THOMAS, D, 3
d.'s own hand is warmer than my own MAUGHAM, W, 27; WORLD-WEARINESS, 4
d.…the least of all evils BACON, F, 6; DEATH, 27
d., the most terrifying of ills DEATH, 61
D. took him by the heart DEATH, 116; OWEN, W, 2
D. was absorbing LEE, L, 2
D. was but /A scientific fact IMPRISONMENT, 15; WILDE, O, 6
D.…we haven't succeeded in…vulgarizing DEATH, 83; HUXLEY, A, 17
D. will disprove you DEATH, 177; TURGENEV, I, 3
d. will have his day SHAKESPEARE, 299
dread disease which so prepares its victim…for d. DISEASE, 14
dread of something after d. AFTERLIFE, 10; SHAKESPEARE, 91
easy d. only to the just DEATH, 18
enormously improved by d. SAKI, 4; WRITERS, 83
faith without doubt is nothing but d. FAITH, 30
Football isn't a matter of life and d. FOOTBALL, 17
give me liberty or give me d. FREEDOM, 22
Go and try to disprove d. DEATH, 177; TURGENEV, I, 3
Graveyards…people associate them with d. DEATH, 32
Growth is a greater mystery than d. AGE, 60
half in love with easeful D. DEATH, 92; KEATS, J, 40
He has seen too much d. PLATH, S, 6
He who pretends to look on d. without fear lies DEATH, 130; ROUSSEAU, J, 2
His d., which happen'd in his berth HOOD, T, 5; PUNS, 7
Human life is…filling in time until…d. LIFE AND DEATH, 9
I am able to follow my own d. step by step DEATH, 89
I am become d., the destroyer of worlds NUCLEAR WEAPONS, 17
I am disappointed by that stroke of d. JOHNSON, S, 21
I am not so much afraid of d. DEATH, 43
I am signing my d. warrant PROPHECY, 3

Ideal mankind would abolish d. LAWRENCE, D, 23; SURVIVAL, 4
I do really think that d. will be marvellous DEATH, 160
If everything is simply jake then you're frightened of d. WORRY, 13
Ignore d. up to the last moment DEATH, 84
I here importune d. awhile SHAKESPEARE, 36
I know I shall love d. as well DEATH, 168
Incense of d. PLATH, S, 4
in their d. they were not divided BIBLE, 482; FRIENDSHIP, 9
In the midst of life we are in d. BOOK OF COMMON PRAYER, 3
Into the jaws of D. COURAGE, 34; TENNYSON, 10
Into the valley of D. OBEDIENCE, 4; TENNYSON, 9
I prepare for a journey...as though for d. TRAVEL, 32
I shall but love thee better after d. BROWNING, E, 6; LOVE, 41
it is not d., but dying, which is terrible DEATH, 63; FIELDING, H, 1
it may be so the moment after d. AFTERLIFE, 4
I've been accused of every d. MURDER, 3
I wanted to be bored to d. BOREDOM, 3
I will defend to the d. your right to say it FREEDOM, 60
Life itself is but the shadow of d. LIFE AND DEATH, 12
Life, the permission to know d. LIFE AND DEATH, 7
man and wife...traversed...the road of d. ILLNESS, 35
man fears...only the stroke of d. BACON, F, 7; DEATH, 28
Man has given a false importance to d. HUMAN CONDITION, 30
Many men on the point of an edifying d. DEATH, 119
Many men would take the d.-sentence LAWRENCE, T, 6; LIFE AND DEATH, 23
Men fear d. BACON, F, 18; DEATH, 29
message of d. for our young men WORLD WAR I, 27
My name is d. DEATH, 163
never risked d. O'BRIEN, E, 2
no cure for birth and d. SANTAYANA, G, 11
no drinking after d. ALCOHOL, 33
nothing can be said to be certain but d. and taxes FRANKLIN, B, 17
O d., where is thy sting BIBLE, 42; DEATH, 35
O d.! where is thy sting DEATH, 123; POPE, A, 6
O D., where is thy sting-a-ling-a-ling ANONYMOUS, 65; DEATH, 21
Old age is an island surrounded by d. OLD AGE, 73
One can survive everything nowadays, except d. SURVIVAL, 11
one of those unfortunates to whom d. is EXPLANATIONS, 2
one that had been studied in his d. DEATH, 147; SHAKESPEARE, 206
one ultimate and effectual preventive...is d. DEATH, 53
Pain and d. are a part of life LIFE, 38
Pale D. kicks his way...into...the castles of kings EQUALITY, 42; HORACE, 27
passed from d. unto life BIBLE, 248
Railing at life, and yet afraid of d. OLD AGE, 32
Reports of my d. are greatly exaggerated TELEGRAMS, 11; TWAIN, M, 18
sad stories of the d. of kings ROYALTY, 105; SHAKESPEARE, 300
sentenced to d. in my absence BEHAN, B, 3; JUSTICE, 2
She didn't fear d. itself ILLNESS, 51
Sickness, sin and d....do not originate in God EDDY, M, 4; RELIGION, 37
Sin brought d. DEATH, 60; EDDY, M, 3; SIN, 15
Sleeping as quiet as d. OLD AGE, 102; THOMAS, D, 21
Sleep is good, d. is better HEINE, H, 2; PESSIMISM, 6
Sleep...knows not D. SLEEP, 32; TENNYSON, 32
snares of d. compassed me round PSALMS, 65
Soldiers are citizens of d.'s grey land SASSOON, S, 3; SOLDIERS, 12
so natural, so necessary, and so universal as d. DEATH, 167
Swarm over, D. BETJEMAN, J, 11; ENGLAND, 6
That sweet, deep sleep, so close to tranquil d. SLEEP, 36
that...turneth the shadow of d. into the morning BIBLE, 18; GOD, 7
the discrimination of d. LIFE AND DEATH, 31
The Doctor said that D. was but /A scientific fact FACTS, 8
the expectation of d. LIFE AND DEATH, 16
The first breath is the beginning of d. LIFE AND DEATH, 1
the idea of d. as an individual NUCLEAR WEAPONS, 11
the land of the shadow of d. BIBLE, 200
the last enemy...is d. AUTHORITARIANISM, 2
The most rational cure...for the...fear of d. LIFE AND DEATH, 19
There is...no d. DEATH, 102
The remedy is d. LIFE, 26
there's always d. DEATH, 114; NAPOLEON I, 12
The sense of d. is most in apprehension DEATH, 148
The stroke of d. is as a lover's pinch DEATH, 139
the struggle against d. LIFE AND DEATH, 20
the sure physician, d. DEATH, 140
the valley of the shadow of d. PSALMS, 11
this is d., and the sole d. BROWNING, R, 21; DEATH, 45
this may be play to you, 'tis d. to us SERIOUSNESS, 2
thought of d. came DEATH, 117
Thou wast not born for d. KEATS, J, 39
till d. us do part BOOK OF COMMON PRAYER, 27; MARRIAGE, 33
Time flies, d. urges TIME, 66; YOUNG, E, 7
to abolish the d. penalty EXECUTION, 19
to make d. a comfort ILLNESS, 15
tragedies are finished by a d. BYRON, 22; THEATRE, 6
valiant never taste of d. but once COWARDICE, 11; SHAKESPEARE, 148
way to dusty d. LIFE, 86; SHAKESPEARE, 227
we all contain failure and d. within us AGE, 60
we owe God a d. DEATH, 143; SHAKESPEARE, 124
what a man still plans...shows the...injustice in his d. DEATH, 46
When Byron's eyes were shut in d. ARNOLD, M, 26; BYRON, 1
'When in d. we are in the midst of life' LIFE AND DEATH, 4
'When in life we are in the midst of d.' LIFE AND DEATH, 4
who fears dishonour more than d. HAPPINESS, 10; HORACE, 43
Why fear d. DEATH, 70; LAST WORDS, 38
worse than d. COWPER, W, 8; SEPARATION, 3
you impart knowledge of it through another's d. RESEARCH, 2
deaths Any amusing d. DEATH, 41
it is chiefly our own d. that we mourn for FUNERALS, 3
debasing I will not be a party to d. the currency ECONOMICS, 12; KEYNES, J, 8
debate daughter of d. ROYALTY, 57
I love argument, I love d. THATCHER, M, 18
debauchee D., n. One who has...pursued pleasure BIERCE, A, 5; DEBAUCHERY, 3
debt A promise made is a d. unpaid PROMISES, 6
d. which cancels all others OBLIGATION, 1
I can pay some of my d. with this gift – Colbert BETRAYAL, 10
not quite forget...Baldwin till we're out of d. POLITICIANS, 88
Out of d. MONEY, 2; PROVERBS, 332
paid its d. to her too generously BRONTE, E, 1
The nations which have put mankind...most in their d. INGE, W, 12; NATIONS, 4
debtor Not everyone is a d. RABELAIS, F, 7
debts He that dies pays all d. DEATH, 155; SHAKESPEARE, 326
decade fun to be in the same d. AGE, 74; ROOSEVELT, F, 4
decadence The difference between our d. and the Russians' DECLINE, 13; THURBER, J, 13
decades D. have a delusive edge CLASSIFICATION, 3
decay as short a Spring; /As quick a growth to meet d. HERRICK, R, 4; TRANSIENCE, 15
Bodily d. is gloomy in prospect MIND, 15
D. and disease are often beautiful DISEASE, 39
Macmillan seemed...to embody the national d. DECLINE, 6; MUGGERIDGE, M, 3
private universe of physical weakness and mental d. OLD AGE, 56
Time drops in d. TIME, 64; YEATS, W, 21
woods d. and fall MORTALITY, 19; TENNYSON, 75
deceit love we swore...seems d. TRANSIENCE, 11
philosophy and vain d. BIBLE, 19; CHRISTIANITY, 7
temper discretion with d. EDUCATION, 95; WAUGH, E, 9
Where rumour of oppression and d. COWPER, W, 27; SOLITUDE, 3
deceitfulness a Cat of such d. CATS, 4; ELIOT, T, 16
deceive if we say that we have no sin, we d. BIBLE, 281; SIN, 5
Oh, don't d. me; Oh, never leave me ANONYMOUS, 16
To d. oneself DECEPTION, 1; PROVERBS, 436
When first we practise to d. LYING, 21
deceived take heed...that your heart be not d. BIBLE, 55; CHRISTIANITY, 9
The world is still d. with ornament APPEARANCES, 35
deceivers Men were d. ever DECEPTION, 8
deceiving without quite d. your enemies PROPAGANDA, 1
decent aristocracy to what is d. CLASS, 20
d. means poor PEACOCK, T, 1; RESPECTABILITY, 3
Every man's house will be fair and d. MORRIS, W, 4
most d. nation on the face of the earth AMERICA, 5
the only d. thing...is to die at once BEQUESTS, 1; BUTLER, S, 28

decision he is going to make 'a realistic d.' DECISION, 4; MCCARTHY, M, 1
if usage so choose, with whom resides the d. HORACE, 4; WORDS, 18
decisive Marriage is a step so grave and d. MARRIAGE, 147; STEVENSON, R, 23
deck I am not going to spit on the d. DEPARTURE, 3
declaim Nay, Madam, when you are declaiming, d. COMPLAINTS, 4; JOHNSON, S, 112
declaration the principles of the D. of Independence FEMINISM, 20; MARTINEAU, H,6
declare they should d. the causes which impel them to…separation INDEPENDENCE, 3; JEFFERSON, T, 4
declining pass my d. years saluting…grandfather clocks NASH, O, 9; OLD AGE, 75
decompose d. in a barrel of porter FUNERALS, 6
decomposing d. in the eternity of print CRITICISM, 67; WOOLF, V, 6
decorated proverb…much matter d. SAYINGS, 4
decorum *Dulce et d. est* HORACE, 34; PATRIOTISM, 20
Let them cant about d. BURNS, R, 13; RESPECTABILITY, 2
decrepit He is…d. and forgetful…a bore BELLOC, H, 2
you are not yet d. enough AGE, 37; ELIOT, T, 29
decussated Anything reticulated or d. at equal distances JOHNSON, S, 11; WORDS, 20
dedicated never d. to do something FANATICISM, 4
You must all grow up to be d. women COMMITMENT, 8
Dee Across the sands of D. AGRICULTURE, 4; KINGSLEY, C, 4
deed a good d. to forget a poor joke HUMOUR, 5
good d. in a naughty world GOOD, 17; SHAKESPEARE, 254
right d. for the wrong reason ELIOT, T, 18; MOTIVE, 2
The better day, the worse d. SUNDAY, 4
deeds better d. shall be in water writ BEAUMONT, F, 8; MEMORIALS, 3
Don't listen to their words, fix your attention on their d. EINSTEIN, A, 5
Foul d. will rise SHAKESPEARE, 72
means to do ill d. SHAKESPEARE, 168
The bitterest tears…are for d.…undone REGRET, 26
deep beauty is only sin d. BEAUTY, 39; SAKI, 21
D. and crisp and even CHRISTMAS, 16
Rocked in the cradle of the d. SEA, 11
what a very singularly d. young man ARROGANCE, 4; GILBERT, W, 36
deeper d. than did ever plummet sound RENUNCIATION, 4; SHAKESPEARE, 328
whelm'd in d. gulphs COWPER, W, 6; DEATH, 52
deeth D. is an ende of every worldly sore CHAUCER, G, 14; LIFE AND DEATH, 13
defeat a d. without a war CHURCHILL, W, 46; WORLD WAR II, 9
d. is an orphan DEFEAT, 2; SUCCESS, 14; VICTORY, 5
D. of Germany means ROOSEVELT, F, 6; WORLD WAR II, 45
every victory turns into a d. BEAUVOIR, S, 6; DISILLUSION, 2
In d. unbeatable CHURCHILL, W, 32; OFFICERS, 3
The greatest tragedy…except a d. WELLINGTON, 13
we are not interested in the possibilities of d. DEFEAT, 17
defeated Like an army d. /The snow hath retreated WORDSWORTH, W, 78
man can be destroyed…not d. DEFEAT, 6; HEMINGWAY, E, 7
defect Chief D. of Henry King BELLOC, H, 9; FOOD, 11
defence England's chief d. depends upon the navy NAVY, 9
Never make a d. or apology ACCUSATION, 3
Preparing for suicide…means of d. NUCLEAR WEAPONS, 10
The best immediate d. of the United States ROOSEVELT, F, 7; WORLD WAR II, 43
the d. of England BALDWIN, S, 6
The only d. is in offence BALDWIN, S, 4; WAR, 15
Truth telling is not compatible with the d. of the realm TRUTH, 41
When you think about the d. of England ENGLAND, 5
defend D., O Lord, this thy Child BOOK OF COMMON PRAYER, 20
D. us ETHNIC CLEANSING, 2
I will d. to the death your right to say it VOLTAIRE, 39; FREEDOM, 59
Defender of Faith my title as D. CHARLES, PRINCE, 6
defiance in defeat, d. CHURCHILL, W, 26; WAR AND PEACE, 4
poorest man may in his cottage bid d. to…the Crown PITT THE ELDER , 1; PRIVACY, 5
The d. of established authority REBELLION, 2
deficiencies The d. which I think good to note MEDICINE, 6
defied Age will not be d. AGE, 10; BACON, F, 42
defiles What a man does d. him RESPONSIBILITY, 7
defined There are things which will not be d. ILLNESS, 42; LANGUAGE, 30
defining Language is…a d. framework LANGUAGE, 52
definite a d. maybe GOLDWYN, S, 14
definition Science fiction is the search for a d. of mankind SCIENCE FICTION, 2
deflowered At last you are d. COWARD, N, 25; MARRIAGE, 55
deflowering more dear in the presence of this d. of Europe WORLD WAR I, 17
deformity Another great Advantage of D. INTELLECT, 6
His modesty amounts to d. MODESTY, 1
defying by d. their parents and copying one another YOUTH, 8
degenerates everything d. in the hands of man MANKIND, 50; ROUSSEAU, J, 3
world d. and grows worse every day WORLD, 3
degeneration fatty d. of his moral being MARRIAGE, 149; STEVENSON, R, 24
degradation intellectual d. after an interview with a doctor DOCTORS, 55
degree d. of delight BURKE, E, 6
when d. is shak'd ORDER, 5; SHAKESPEARE, 331
degrees Crime, like virtue, has its d. CRIME, 7
We boil at different d. EMERSON, R, 24; INDIVIDUALITY, 5
deid Gey few, and they're a' d. ANONYMOUS, 36; INDIVIDUALITY, 1
deities the d. so kindly DESTINY, 19; RABELAIS, F, 6
deity doubted the existence of the D. SCIENTISTS, 6
to distinguish between the D. and the Drains GOD, 49
deleted D. by French censor NEWSPAPERS, 3
deliberate with a slow d. carelessness LAWRENCE, T, 10; READING, 10
deliberates woman that d. is lost ADDISON, J, 6; WOMEN, 8
deliberation D. is the work of many men ACTION, 9; DE GAULLE, C, 4
delicacy the talent of flattering with d. AUSTEN, J, 22; FLATTERY, 2
delicious delightful, it's d., it's de-lovely PLEASURE, 28
delight a degree of d. BURKE, E, 6
Commodity, Firmness, and *D.* ARCHITECTURE, 21
Energy is Eternal D. BLAKE, W, 32; EFFORT, 2
go to't with d. ENTHUSIASM, 8; SHAKESPEARE, 34
his d. is in the law of the Lord PSALMS, 1
Studies serve for d. BACON, F, 49; EDUCATION, 11
Teach us d. in simple things GOOD, 8; KIPLING, R, 6
The leaping light for your d. discovers AUDEN, W, 19; DISCOVERY, 2
very temple of d. KEATS, J, 34; MELANCHOLY, 7
wept with d. when you gave her a smile MEMORY, 9
delighted Whosoever is d. in solitude BACON, F, 24; SOLITUDE, 1
You have d. us long enough AUSTEN, J, 23; DISMISSAL, 2
delightful d., it's delicious, it's de-lovely PLEASURE, 28
make his conversation perfectly d. INSULTS, 116; SMITH, S, 11
What a d. thing this perspective is ART, 36
delights Man d. not me MANKIND, 56; SHAKESPEARE, 85
deliver d. me from myself BROWNE, T, 9; SELF, 7
delivered thou hast d. my soul from death PSALMS, 35
deliverer their d. from Popish tyranny ROYALTY, 63
de-lovely delightful, it's delicious, it's d. PLEASURE, 28
delude we d. ourselves CHARLES, PRINCE, 5
deluge After us the d. PROPHECY, 10
Après nous le d. PROPHECY, 10
delusion Charm is a d. and beauty fleeting CHARM, 1
he who can analyze his d. is called a philosopher PHILOSOPHERS, 1
nation is a society united by a d. about its ancestry INGE, W, 10
delusions Many people have d. of grandeur DELUSION, 5; INSULTS, 68
delusive Decades have a d. edge CLASSIFICATION, 3
delved When Adam d. CLASS, 5
demagogues the vilest specimens of human nature are…found among d. MACAULAY, T, 16; POLITICS, 68
demands the populace cannot exact their d. HOUSES OF PARLIAMENT, 22; WELLINGTON, 14
demented shrill d. choirs of wailing shells MEMORIALS, 12
demigod wherever life is dear he is a d. MEDICINE, 27
democracy arsenal of d. DEMOCRACY, 21; ROOSEVELT, F, 13
D. can't work DEMOCRACY, 9
D.…government by the uneducated CHESTERTON, G, 45; DEMOCRACY, 5
d. in Kuwait WAR, 37
d. is just a slogan GORBACHOV, M, 5

D. is only an experiment in government DEMOCRACY, 10; INGE, W, 7
D. is the wholesome and pure air DEMOCRACY, 7; GORBACHOV, M, 9
D. means government by discussion DEMOCRACY, 1
D. passes into despotism DEMOCRACY, 19; PLATO, 5
d....recognises the subjecting of the minority DEMOCRACY, 12
D. resumed her reign BELLOC, H, 13; POLITICS, 12
D. substitutes election by the incompetent many DEMOCRACY, 23
extreme d. or absolute oligarchy, or despotism will come ARISTOTLE, 8; GOVERNMENT, 5
grieved under a *d.*, call it *anarchy* GOVERNMENT, 17
In Switzerland they had...five hundred years of d. and peace SWITZERLAND, 5
Man's capacity for evil makes d. necessary DEMOCRACY, 18
not the voting that's d. DEMOCRACY, 25
they are not afraid to die for d. CHINA, 3
war wasn't fought about d. BUSH, G, 15
world...made safe for d. DEMOCRACY, 29; WILSON, W, 11
you often need less, not more, d. DEMOCRACY, 17
democratic the ideal of a d. and free society RACISM, 22
thoroughly d. and patronise everybody CLASS, 41; DEMOCRACY, 22
democrats Comrade d., you have scattered RUSSIA, 15
D. only come here when they want votes RUSSIA, 4
demon woman wailing for her d.-lover COLERIDGE, S, 16; SUPERNATURAL, 6
demons we have often sunk to the level of the d. HUXLEY, A, 3
demonstrations d. from Chengdu to Tiananmen Square CHINA, 5
den a d. of thieves BIBLE, 408; CHRISTIANITY, 28
denial the highest praise of God consists in the d. of Him ATHEISM, 11; PROUST, M, 8
denies spirit that always d. GOETHE, J, 4
Denmark rotten in the state of D. CORRUPTION, 12; SHAKESPEARE, 77
denounce We thus d....the arms race JOHN PAUL II, 2; NUCLEAR WEAPONS, 9
dentist fuss about sleeping together...sooner go to my d. SEX, 124; WAUGH, E, 47
dentists I have let d. ride roughshod over my teeth TEETH, 2
The thought of d. gave him just the same sick horror WELLS, H, 8
Dentopedology D. is the science of opening your mouth MISTAKES, 14
deny before the cock crow, thou shalt d. me thrice BETRAYAL, 2; BIBLE, 425
let him d. himself BIBLE, 398; CHRISTIANITY, 27
Those who d. freedom FREEDOM, 34; LINCOLN, A, 12
depart D....and let us have done with you DISMISSAL, 1
lettest thou thy servant d. in peace BIBLE, 317; DEATH, 37
when the great and good d. MORTALITY, 20; WORDSWORTH, W, 16
departure the time of my d. is at hand BIBLE, 514; FAITH, 11
dependent too d. upon dachas RUSSIA, 19
depends It all d. upon that article there SOLDIERS, 18; WELLINGTON, 3
depraved No one...suddenly became d. DEBAUCHERY, 7
depression Recession...a neighbour loses...d....you lose ECONOMICS, 20
deprivation D. is for me what daffodils were POETRY, 37
depth out of your d. SELF-CONFIDENCE, 9
derangement a nice d. of epitaphs MALAPROPISMS, 8; SHERIDAN, R, 9
derision Ambition, Distraction, Uglification, and D. CARROLL, L, 15; EDUCATION, 21
dermatologists a rash of d. LANGUAGE, 4
dermatology D. is the best speciality MEDICINE, 3
descend Never d. to the ways of those above you EQUALITY, 22
descendants The day your d., /Outnumber your friends OLD AGE, 76
descended D. from the apes...hope it is not true EVOLUTION, 2
we are d. not only from monkeys but from monks EVOLUTION, 19
descent of pre-Adamite ancestral d. EVOLUTION, 15
description beggar'd all d. ADMIRATION, 15; SHAKESPEARE, 30
descriptions d. of the fairest wights HISTORY, 32; SHAKESPEARE, 369
desert The d., the abode of enforced sterility CARTER, A, 3
The sand of the d. is sodden red NEWBOLT, H, 7; WAR, 119
Use every man after his d. MERIT, 6; SHAKESPEARE, 88
deserts D. of vast eternity AGE, 61; MARVELL, A, 10
deserve I have arthritis, and I don't d. that either MERIT, 2
deserved I wasn't lucky. I d. it MERIT, 7; THATCHER, M, 14
deserves At 50, everyone has the face he d. AGE, 66; ORWELL, G, 36
the government it d. GOVERNMENT, 24
designing I am d. St Paul's ARCHITECTURE, 1
desire antidote to d. CONGREVE, W, 17; DESIRE, 6
a universal innate d. BUTLER, S, 11; PROGRESS, 7
d. is got without content CONTENTMENT, 10; SHAKESPEARE, 216
D. is the very essence of man DESIRE, 16
d. should so many years outlive performance SEX, 107; SHAKESPEARE, 121
d. to be praised twice over PRAISE, 8; ROCHEFOUCAULD, 18
few things to d. FEAR, 2
I am my beloved's, and his d. is toward me BIBLE, 499
is yet also consumed with this d. KEATS, J, 1
It provokes the d. ALCOHOL, 69; SHAKESPEARE, 215
my soul hath a d. PSALMS, 44
nothing like d. for preventing the thing one says DESIRE, 12; PROUST, M, 13
not really d. the things they failed to obtain AMBITION, 16
object of the dreamer's d. DREAMS, 12
The D. of Man being Infinite BLAKE, W, 50; INFINITY, 1
Those who restrain D. BLAKE, W, 30; DESIRE, 2
to have few things to d. BACON, F, 21
to lose your heart's d. DESIRE, 15; SHAW, G, 24
desired more to be d....than gold PSALMS, 9
war which...left nothing to be d. BRECHT, B, 7; WAR, 27
desires He who d. but acts not ACTION, 7; BLAKE, W, 26
him who d. his own advantage not harm another BUDDHA, 2
Man's D. are limited by his Perceptions BLAKE, W, 49; DESIRE, 4
Strong enough to answer back to d. CHARACTER, 11; HORACE, 47
than nurse unacted d. BLAKE, W, 21; DESIRE, 3
desireth like as the hart d. the water-brooks PSALMS, 26
desiring pessimists end up by d. the things they fear PESSIMISM, 9
desist to d. from the experiment in despair LAMB, C, 6; SCOTS, 7
desk what risks you take...to find money in a d. BALZAC, H, 4; THEFT, 4
desks Stick...to your d. and never go to sea GILBERT, W, 12; OFFICERS, 7
desolate d. and sick of an old passion LOVE, 67
desolated from the province they have d. and profaned VIOLENCE, 8
desolation My d. does begin to make /A better life SUICIDE, 33
despair carrion comfort, D., not feast on thee DESPAIR, 5
D. is better treated with hope not dope DESPAIR, 1
Don't d., not even over...d. DESPAIR, 6; KAFKA, F, 1
Look on my works, ye Mighty, and d. SHELLEY, P, 17
PATIENCE, n. A minor form of d. BIERCE, A, 9; PATIENCE, 8
some divine d. SORROW, 34; TENNYSON, 62
Somewhere on the other side of d. MADNESS, 11
to desist from the experiment in d. LAMB, C, 6; SCOTS, 7
without understanding d. LAING, R, 2; PSYCHIATRY, 21
despairs He who d. over an event is a coward CAMUS, A, 16; PESSIMISM, 4
desperate D. cuts PROVERBS, 109; RESULTS, 1
desperation lives of quiet d. DESPAIR, 9; THOREAU, H, 9
despicable this formidable Kingdom is...a province of a d. Electorate ENGLAND, 41
despise I d. Shakespeare SHAW, G, 11
some other Englishman d. him CLASS, 44; SHAW, G, 36
despised A poor man is d. the whole world over JEROME, J, 3; POVERTY, 22
who could know himself...d. by a street boy HUXLEY, T, 5; PHILOSOPHERS, 5
despises A woman d. a man for loving her LOVE, 159
Despond name of the slough was D. BUNYAN, J, 2; DESPAIR, 3
despot A country governed by a d. JOHNSON, S, 122; TYRANNY, 7
despotism Democracy passes into d. DEMOCRACY, 19; PLATO, 5
d. tempered by casualness GOVERNMENT, 3
extreme democracy or absolute oligarchy, or d. will come ARISTOTLE, 8; GOVERNMENT, 5

France was a long d. CARLYLE, T, 14; FRANCE, 2
the foul dregs of his power, the tools of d. and corruption POLITICS, 119
dessicated A d. calculating machine POLITICIANS, 50
destination I do not think this poem will reach its d. CRITICISM, 62; VOLTAIRE, 37
The d. of all journeys CARTER, A, 5
destinies in determining the future d. of mankind BRITISH EMPIRE, 1
destiny Anatomy is d. DESTINY, 12
I were walking with d. CHURCHILL, W, 12; DESTINY, 5
man of d. MANDELA, N, 1; PROGRESS, 11
Riddle of d. LAMB, C, 20; PURPOSE, 7
destroy Doth the wingèd life d. BLAKE, W, 15; PLEASURE, 5
He would like to d. his old diaries CONCEIT, 20; TOLSTOY, S, 3
Man…builds machines to d. WORLD WAR I, 16
necessary to d. the town…to save it WAR, 8
sought to d. institutions INDIFFERENCE, 7; WHITMAN, W, 4
they shall not hurt nor d. in all my holy mountain BIBLE, 203; PEACE, 2
Whom God wishes to d. MADNESS, 1, 13
Whom the gods wish to d. CONNOLLY, C, 9; TALENT, 2
destroy'd a bold peasantry…/When once d. GOLDSMITH, O, 6; PUBLIC, 13
destroyed man can be d.…not defeated DEFEAT, 6; HEMINGWAY, E, 7
destroyer greatest d. of peace is abortion ABORTION, 13
I am become death, the d. of worlds NUCLEAR WEAPONS, 17
Man…hasn't been a creator, only a d. CHEKHOV, A, 10; ECOLOGY, 3
destroying simplifying something by d. nearly everything CHESTERTON, G, 5; CIVILIZATION, 4
destroys an unwanted pregnancy d. two lives ABORTION, 10
he who d. a good book, kills reason BOOKS, 32; MILTON, J, 6
What d. one man preserves another REMEDIES, 24
destruction broad is the way, that leadeth to d. BIBLE, 377; VIRTUE, 6
D. and resurrection in alternate beats LIFE AND DEATH, 8
It is time for the d. of error AUDEN, W, 18
one purpose…d. of Hitler CHURCHILL, W, 13
Pride goeth before d. MISQUOTATIONS, 10
the d. of Hitler HITLER, A, 3
detail life is frittered away by d. SIMPLICITY, 8; THOREAU, H, 16
details with the thoroughness of a mind that reveres d. UNDERSTANDING, 7
detective The d. novel is NOVELS, 14
detente D. is like the race POLITICS, 26
determination character but the d. of incident CHARACTER, 13
deterrent the d. is a phallic symbol NUCLEAR WEAPONS, 23
detest they d. at leisure BYRON, 33; LOVE AND HATE, 1
detestable D. person but needs watching WRITERS, 82
He was a d. man THOMAS, D, 2
detested D. sport COWPER, W, 31; HUNTING, 3
Deuteronomy Old D.'s lived a long time CATS, 7
Deutschland *D., D. über alles* GERMANY, 3
deviation d. from the norm 'progress' INDIVIDUALITY, 7
device A banner with the strange d., /Excelsior AMBITION, 14; LONGFELLOW, H, 7
devil Abashed the d.…felt how awful goodness is GOOD, 13; MILTON, J, 47
between any sort of d. and the deep blue sea SUICIDE, 27
cleft the D.'s foot DONNE, J, 13; NONSENSE, 11
D. always builds a chapel there DEFOE, D, 5; DEVIL, 10
d. can cite Scripture DEVIL, 14; SHAKESPEARE, 241
d.'s walking parody CHESTERTON, G, 12
given up believing in the d. DEVIL, 11
I do not see…why the d. should have all the good tunes MUSIC, 29
Mirrors are the windows of the d. APPEARANCES, 18
nickname is the heaviest stone that the d. can throw HAZLITT, W, 18; NAMES, 4
Renounce the d. BOOK OF COMMON PRAYER, 22
resist the d., and he will flee BIBLE, 218
sacrifice…of the d.'s leavings POPE, A, 56; VIRTUE, 21
Sarcasm…the language of the d. CARLYLE, T, 26; SARCASM, 1
the d. did not play in tempting of me PROSE, 2
The d. finds work IDLENESS, 1; PROVERBS, 384
The D. is a gentleman DEVIL, 15; SHELLEY, P, 18
The d. is not so black DEVIL, 1; PROVERBS, 385
the D. knows Latin LANGUAGE, 29
The d. looks after his own LUCK, 5; PROVERBS, 386
the d. played at chess with me BROWNE, T, 4; EXPLOITATION, 1
the world, the flesh, and the d. JOURNALISM, 27; TEMPTATION, 5
devilish eyes flamed red with d. passion SUPERNATURAL, 16
devils It is no good casting out d. DEVIL, 12; LAWRENCE, D, 36
many d. would set on me in Worms PROTESTANTISM, 4
One more d.'-triumph and sorrow for angels BROWNING, R, 32; DAMNATION, 1
d. walking parody ANIMALS, 11
devotion The almighty dollar…object of universal d. MATERIALISM, 15
devour he shall d. the prey BIBLE, 182
shed tears when they would d. BACON, F, 60; HYPOCRISY, 2
the Revolution may…d. each of her children FRENCH REVOLUTION, 10
devoured you d. as many as you could SPORT AND GAMES, 42
dew his body was wet with the d. of heaven BIBLE, 50
Just to save her from the foggy, foggy d. ANONYMOUS, 63; SEX, 9
dexterity Your d. seems a happy compound DISRAELI, B, 33; INSULTS, 43
diabetic Many a d. has stayed alive DISEASE, 19
diagram cat is a d. and pattern of subtle air CATS, 11; LESSING, D, 6
dialect a d. I understand very little HUNTING, 7; PEPYS, S, 10
D. words – those terrible marks of the beast CLASS, 19; HARDY, T, 10
diamond An imitation rough d. INSULTS, 5
D.! D. ACCIDENTS, 8; NEWTON, I, 6; SCIENCE, 69
more of rough than polished d. BRITISH, 5; CHESTERFIELD, P, 13
Diamonds D. Are MATERIALISM, 22
My goodness those d. are lovely GOOD, 19; WEST, M, 4
to give him d. back MATERIALISM, 10
diaries He would like to destroy his old d. CONCEIT, 20; TOLSTOY, S, 3
Let d., therefore BACON, F, 55; DIARIES, 1
Only good girls keep d. BANKHEAD, T, 13; DIARIES, 2
diary Her d. endures, full-blooded FRANK, A, 1
I never travel without my d. DIARIES, 6; WILDE, O, 30
To write a d.…returning to one's own vomit DIARIES, 4
What is a d. as a rule DIARIES, 5; TERRY, D, 3
dice God play d. HAWKING, S, 5
Dickens D.…never quite took BENNETT, A, 5
does not matter that D.' world is not life-like DICKENS, C, 2
dictated universe was d. but not signed UNIVERSE, 16
dictation I merely did his d. STOWE, H, 4; INSPIRATION, 4
dictator and finally a single d. substitutes himself COMMUNISM, 19; TROTSKY, L, 11
I am painted as the greatest little d. AUTHORITARIANISM, 7; THATCHER, M, 28
I believe in benevolent dictatorship provided I am the d. LEADERSHIP, 4
dictators D. ride to and fro upon tigers AUTHORITARIANISM, 4; CHURCHILL, W, 31
dictatorship The d. of the proletariat MARX, K, 7; MARXISM, 14
dictionaries To make d. is dull work JOHNSON, S, 8; LEXICOGRAPHY, 5
dictionary send the reader to the d. STYLE, 6; HEMINGWAY, E, 2
The responsibility of a d. LEXICOGRAPHY, 3
this is the first time I ever made the d. LEXICOGRAPHY, 7; WEST, M, 19
words never seen…before outside of a d. LODGE, D, 5; POETS, 50
diddle Hey d. d., /The cat and the fiddle NURSERY RHYMES, 14
die A man can d. DEATH, 2; PROVERBS, 43
argue that I shall some day d. DEATH, 99
As long as men are liable to d. DOCTORS, 57
better to d. on your feet than to live on your knees SELF-RESPECT, 2
Body and mind…do not always agree to d. together OLD AGE, 40
but to do and d. OBEDIENCE, 4; TENNYSON, 9
curse God, and d. BIBLE, 224; CURSES, 1
d. on the spot rather than give way WAR, 86
d. on your feet than to live on your knees COURAGE, 20
D.…the last thing I shall do LAST WORDS, 64
D. when I may LINCOLN, A, 7; REPUTATION, 6
easy ways to d. SUICIDE, 34
either do, or d. ACTION, 6; BEAUMONT, F, 4
Everybody has got to d.…. Now what LAST WORDS, 78
expedient that one man should d. for the people BIBLE, 264
for me to d., for you to go on living GOD, 47; SOCRATES, 6
have to d. beyond my means LAST WORDS, 94
'How hard it is that we have to d.' LIFE AND DEATH, 34

How often are we to d. DEATH, 125; POPE, A, 61
I am ready to d. for my Lord LAST WORDS, 7
I d. a Christian EXECUTION, 6
I d. because I do not d. DEATH, 87
I d. happy LAST WORDS, 37
I do not want to d.…until I have…cultivated the seed ACHIEVEMENT, 11
If a man hasn't discovered something that he would d. for IDEALISM, 3; KING, M, 3
If I d. today every drop of my blood LAST WORDS, 40
If I should d. BROOKE, R, 7; WAR, 30
I have been learning how to d. DEATH, 178; LEONARDO DA VINCI, 6
in what peace a Christian can d. ADDISON, J, 19; LAST WORDS, 3
I shall be like that tree; I shall d. from the top DECLINE, 11; SWIFT, J, 20
It is as natural to d. BACON, F, 19; LIFE AND DEATH, 6
it is worse to want to d. WORLD-WEARINESS, 9
it is youth that must fight and d. WAR, 80
it was not easy for me to d. OBITUARIES, 7
I will d. in peace LAST WORDS, 96
I will d. in the last ditch PATRIOTISM, 45
I would d. for my country… KINNOCK, N, 13; PATRIOTISM, 27
let me d. drinking in an inn ALCOHOL, 54
Let us determine to d. here DETERMINATION, 5
Let us do or d. ACTION, 8; BURNS, R, 18
let us eat and drink; for tomorrow we d. BIBLE, 40
live for ever or d. in the attempt HELLER, J, 2; IMMORTALITY, 4
man can d. but once DEATH, 143; SHAKESPEARE, 124
Many people would sooner d. than think RUSSELL, B, 28; THINKING, 15
me…who is going to d. DEATH, 102
More d. in the United States GREED, 9
Never say d. PERSISTENCE, 2; PROVERBS, 305
No young man believes he shall ever d. HAZLITT, W, 30; IMMORTALITY, 3
one may d. without ever laughing LA BRUYERE, J, 8; LAUGHTER, 9
people d. from pregnancy CONTRACEPTION, 13
pie in the sky when you d. AFTERLIFE, 5; HEAVEN, 5; MATERIALISM, 3
place…to d. in BROWNE, T, 10; WORLD, 1
Rather suffer than d. LA FONTAINE, J, 1
Ring out, wild bells, and let him d. ENDING, 7; TENNYSON, 35
save your world you asked this man to d. AUDEN, W, 13; WAR, 13
so afraid I will d. in the middle of shooting AGE, 46
sometimes they d. DOCTORS, 59
The dead don't d. DEATH, 98; LAWRENCE, D, 44
The d. is cast CAESAR, J, 3; IRREVOCABILITY, 1
The human race is the only one that knows it must d. DEATH, 179
the only decent thing…is to d. at once BEQUESTS, 1; BUTLER, S, 28
those who are about to d. salute you ANONYMOUS, 9; LAST WORDS, 4
to d., and go we know not where DEATH, 150; SHAKESPEARE, 234
To d. will be an awfully big adventure BARRIE, J, 5; DEATH, 31
to d. you will have to pay MACNEICE, L, 3
to live will be more miserable than to d. SUICIDE, 17
trains all night groan on the rail /To men that d. at morn EXECUTION, 16; HOUSMAN, A, 8
we can d. but once to serve our country ADDISON, J, 8; PATRIOTISM, 1
We d. – does it matter when DEATH, 170; TENNYSON, 71
we must live as though…never going to d. ACHIEVEMENT, 14
We must love one another or d. LOVE, 21
we shall d. as usual DEATH, 65
when good Americans d. they go to Paris WILDE, O, 57
Will tell me that I have to d. DOCTORS, 17
wisdom says: 'We must d.,' LIFE AND DEATH, 35

died A piece of each of us d. at that moment ASSASSINATION, 6
As estimated, you d. HILL, G, 3
d. to save their country CHESTERTON, G, 14
dog it was that d. DOGS, 10; GOLDSMITH, O, 11
I d.…of my physician DOCTORS, 81
Men have d. from time to time LOVE AND DEATH, 6; SHAKESPEARE, 56
never been the same since God d. GOD, 38
there were people who d. of dropsies ALCOHOL, 43; JOHNSON, S, 160
'Tis said that some have d. for love LOVE AND DEATH, 10; WORDSWORTH, W, 71

diem *Carpe d.* HORACE, 32; PRESENT, 7

dies A bachelor…d. like a beggar MARRIAGE, 102
a young person, who…marries or d. AUSTEN, J, 7; HUMAN NATURE, 2
because a man d. for it MARTYRDOM, 8; WILDE, O, 65
Childhood is the kingdom where nobody d. INNOCENCE, 9
Every moment d. a man LIFE AND DEATH, 5
He d. every day who lives a lingering life ILLNESS, 61
He d. from his whole life LIFE AND DEATH, 27
he d. in pain LA BRUYERE, J, 6; LIFE AND DEATH, 21
He that d. pays all debts DEATH, 155; SHAKESPEARE, 326
It matters not how a man d. DEATH, 88; JOHNSON, S, 78
king never d. BLACKSTONE, W, 2; MONARCHY, 5
One d. only once DEATH, 112; MOLIERE, 4
Whatever is begotten, born, and d. MORTALITY, 23; YEATS, W, 27
When a friend d. out on us MACNEICE, L, 6

diet As the low-fat d. unfolded DIETING, 2
Doctor D., /Doctor Quiet and Doctor Merryman DOCTORS, 97
Food is an important part of a balanced d. FOOD, 45
I told my doctor I get very tired…on a d. FOOD, 46
The right d. directs sexual energy into the parts that matter FOOD, 22

dieters d. will regain all the weight loss DIETING, 5

dietitians The death of all d. FOOD, 31

diets I feel about airplanes the way I feel about d. FLYING, 4

Dieu *D. et mon droit* FAITH, 27

difference Because there is no d. LIFE AND DEATH, 33
Between man and woman there is little d. SEXES, 1
d. between…prose and metrical composition POETRY AND PROSE, 7; WORDSWORTH, W, 19
made the d. of forty thousand men OFFICERS, 16; WELLINGTON, 11
more d. within the sexes than between them SEXES, 7
the d. of sex, if there is any ANTHONY, S, 5

differences If we cannot now end our d. DIFFERENCE, 9
The Jews and Arabs should…settle their d. GOLDWYN, S, 27; RELIGION, 7

different child is d.…because he is fatherless ILLEGITIMACY, 3
populism that rejects anything d. DEMOCRACY, 6
rich are d. FITZGERALD, F, 5; WEALTH, 21

differently I would have done it d. ARROGANCE, 9; WHISTLER, J, 16

differeth one star d. from another…in glory ASTRONOMY, 1; BIBLE, 41

difficult Christian ideal…found d. CHRISTIANITY, 34
D. do you call it, Sir CRITICISM, 30; JOHNSON, S, 40
It is d. to be humble HUMILITY, 4
Naming of Cats is a d. matter CATS, 6
never let them persuade you that things are too d. DETERMINATION, 3
When a piece gets d. MUSICIANS, 14

difficulties settle up these little local d. MACMILLAN, H, 6; POLITICS, 70

difficulty d. for every solution BUREAUCRACY, 6
I feel…a certain d. in continuing to exist LAST WORDS, 36

digest It's that confounded cucumber /I've eat and can't d. FOOD, 9
mark, learn and inwardly d. LEARNING, 4
my stomach must just d. in its waistcoat ALCOHOL, 75; SHERIDAN, R, 12

digestion Things sweet to taste prove in d. sour REGRET, 22; SHAKESPEARE, 295

digestions Few radicals have good d. BUTLER, S, 16; POLITICS, 24

diggers You noble D. all REBELLION, 13

digital still think d. watches are a pretty neat idea SCIENCE FICTION, 1

digitalis I use d. in doses the text books say are dangerous DRUGS, 15

dignity a paunch to give him D. DOCTORS, 13
d. and greatness and peace again DRINKS, 9; HOPE, 9
free and equal in d. and rights ANONYMOUS, 3; HUMAN RIGHTS, 1
man added to his d. by standing on it PRIDE, 4
man is capable of a certain degree of d. CAMUS, A, 2
Official d.…in inverse ratio to…importance DIPLOMACY, 17; HUXLEY, A, 10

dilemmas d. of conscience and egotism POWER, 24

diligently Had I…served God as d. as I have served the king LOYALTY, 14

dim My eyes are d. BLINDNESS, 3

my lamp burns low and d. ENVY, 3
dime Brother, can you spare a d. MISQUOTATIONS, 19
dimensions sickness enlarges the d. of a man's self ILLNESS, 40; LAMB, C, 17
diminished ought to be d. MONARCHY, 11
dimmed The eyes that shone, /Now d. and gone MOORE, T, 7; NOSTALGIA, 17
dimple A d. in the chin, a devil within PROVERBS, 13; SUPERSTITION, 1
din made such a frightful d. on the piano MUSICIANS, 18
dine wretches hang that jury-men may d. JUSTICE, 20; POPE, A, 51
dined More d. against than dining FOOD, 17
when Thomas Jefferson d. alone TALENT, 7
you have d. in every house in London – *once* INSULTS, 133; WILDE, O, 78
diners Observe d. arriving at any restaurant HUMAN NATURE, 23; MORRIS, D, 2
diners-out d. from whom we guard our spoons MACAULAY, T, 19; MISTRUST, 8
ding D. dong, bell, /Pussy's in the well NURSERY RHYMES, 9
dinkum a 'd. hard-swearing Aussie' PATRIOTISM, 19
dinky Hinky, d., par-lee-voo FRANCE, 17
dinner A d. lubricates business BUSINESS, 25
A man is...better pleased when he has a good d. upon his table JOHNSON, S, 37; WOMAN'S ROLE, 9
Breakfast, D., Lunch and Tea BELLOC, H, 10; FOOD, 10
people...would ask him to d. BELIEF, 5; CARLYLE, T, 28; CHRISTIANITY, 33
still invited to d. ELIOT, G, 10
This was a good d. enough FOOD, 39; JOHNSON, S, 70
dinner-table dominate a London d. INFLUENCE, 14; WILDE, O, 68
diplomacy All d. is a continuation of war CHINA, 2; DIPLOMACY, 23
Building up arms is not a substitute for d. NUCLEAR WEAPONS, 20
diplomat A d....always remembers a woman's birthday FROST, R, 10
d. these days is nothing but a head-waiter INSULTS, 125; USTINOV, P, 8
diplomatic d. history is...what one clerk said to another clerk HISTORY, 38
diplomats aged d. to be bored DIPLOMACY, 3
Dirce With D. in one boat conveyed LANDOR, W, 1; LUST, 8
direct can't d. a Laughton picture ACTORS, 21
directing think of the audience when I'm d. AUDIENCES, 8
direction in which d. the car was travelling LLOYD GEORGE, D, 3
Protestants...have any sense of d. CATHOLICISM, 16
directions rode madly off in all d. LEACOCK, S, 10; NONSENSE, 17
director Every d. bites the hand GOLDWYN, S, 13; MIXED METAPHORS, 2
Theatre d.: a person ACTING, 1
want to be a d. CINEMA, 22
dirt After the first four years the d. doesn't get any worse HOUSEWORK, 3
he begins as d. and departs as stench MANKIND, 67
I know d. when I smell it and here it is WRITERS, 81
Throw d. enough GOSSIP, 6; PROVERBS, 431
dirty A rather d. Wykehamist EDUCATION, 14
bathing in someone else's d. water PROUST, M, 1
Is sex d. ALLEN, W, 1; SEX, 2
The permissive society has...become a d. phrase SOCIETY, 13
You d. double-crossing rat INSULTS, 26
disability d. has not been a serious handicap HAWKING, S, 2
disadvantage d. of merely counting votes DEMOCRACY, 10; INGE, W, 7
disagree Who shall decide when doctors d. DOCTORS, 80; POPE, A, 46
disappointed I am d. by that stroke of death JOHNSON, S, 21
disappointment Grief and d. give rise to anger EMOTION, 3; HUME, D, 7
disapprove I d. of what you say FREEDOM, 60; VOLTAIRE, 39
disarm d. the strong and arm the weak INJUSTICE, 5
disarmament partial nuclear d....partial circumcision NUCLEAR WEAPONS, 24
precede the d. of the victors CHURCHILL, W, 11; WAR, 45
disaster audience was a d. WILDE, O, 70
meet with Triumph and D. KIPLING, R, 17
the audience was a d. PLAYS, 17
disasters the middle station had the fewest d. CLASS, 12; DEFOE, D, 3
trace...the d. of English history to...Wales WALES, 5; WAUGH, E, 18
disbelief willing suspension of d. COLERIDGE, S, 8; POETRY, 18
disciple a d....of the fiend, called the Pucelle ACCUSATION, 1
disciples d....mark its ways and note...its mysteries LUCK, 8
discomfiture We're in the Embassy residence, subject...to some...d. DIPLOMACY, 2
discomforts all the d. that will accompany my being blind BLINDNESS, 13; PEPYS, S, 17
discommendeth He who d. others BROWNE, T, 1; CRITICISM, 12
discontent lent /To youth and age...d. ARNOLD, M, 46; DISCONTENT, 1
To be discontented with the divine d. KINGSLEY, C, 2; VIRTUE, 19
winter of our d. OPTIMISM, 35; SHAKESPEARE, 302
discontents the family...source of all our d. FAMILY, 34
discourse their d. was about hunting HUNTING, 7; PEPYS, S, 10
discovered We have d. the secret of life DISCOVERY, 8; SCIENCE, 21
discoverers They are ill d. that think there is no land BACON, F, 3; DISCOVERY, 4
discoveries d. are usually not made by one man alone DISCOVERY, 14
Many a man who is brooding over alleged mighty d. DISCOVERY, 7
None of the great d. DISCOVERY, 9
discovery behind the d. of America JEWS, 16
D. consists of seeing what everybody has seen DISCOVERY, 15; SCIENCE, 89
he who never made a mistake never made a d. MISTAKES, 19
Scientific d. is a private event SCIENCE, 65
Whenever science makes a d. SCIENCE, 94
discretion better part of valour is d. SELF-PRESERVATION, 11; SHAKESPEARE, 116
temper d. with deceit EDUCATION, 95; WAUGH, E, 9
the years of d. AGE, 20; BOOK OF COMMON PRAYER, 19
discrimination sympathetic without d. SYMPATHY, 2
discussed Everything has been d. and analysed BOOKS, 2
discussion D. in class, which means EDUCATION, 67; NABOKOV, V, 4
more time for d....more mistakes MISTAKES, 22
disdains He d. all things above his reach DISCONTENT, 7
disease a cure for which there was no d. REMEDIES, 14
All interest in d. and death LIFE, 61
amusing the patient while Nature cures the d. MEDICINE, 104
an incurable d. – colour blindness RACISM, 9
a poor man for the same d. he giveth a more common name REMEDIES, 57
Confront d. at its first stage ILLNESS, 57
Consciousness is a d. PSYCHOLOGY, 19; UNAMUNO, M, 2
Cur'd...of my d. DOCTORS, 81
Cure the d. BACON, F, 25; REMEDIES, 9
Decay and d. are often beautiful DISEASE, 39
desperate d. requires a dangerous remedy TREASON, 4
Despite a lifetime of service...venereal d. SEX, 45
D. can carry its ill-effects no farther than mortal mind ILLNESS, 23
D. creates poverty POVERTY, 37
d. in the family IRELAND, 27
D. is an image of thought externalized EDDY, M, 5; ILLNESS, 23
D. is...of the place DISEASE, 34
d. is the result of sin MEDICINE, 76
D. is very old PROGRESS, 8
d. known is half cured DISEASE, 1
D. makes men more physical ILLNESS, 47
dread d. which so prepares its victim...for death DISEASE, 14
each civilization has a pattern of d. ENVIRONMENT, 7
Evil comes...like the d.; good...like the doctor CHESTERTON, G, 27; GOOD AND EVIL, 3
Have a chronic d. and take care of it LONGEVITY, 9
he does not die from the d. alone LIFE AND DEATH, 27
he is a d. of the dust MANKIND, 17
if the physician had the same d. upon him that I have EXAMPLE, 7; SELDEN, J, 5
I've got Bright's d. and he's got mine ILLNESS, 56
let us...eradicate d. SCIENCE, 59
Life is an incurable d. DISEASE, 13; LIFE, 31
Life is a sexually transmitted d. LIFE, 44
Medicine, to produce health, has to examine d. MEDICINE, 80
Old age is a d. OLD AGE, 86
only d. you don't look forward to being cured of DISEASE, 25
Only those in the last stage of d. AUDEN, W, 23; CHILDREN, 5
Remedies...are our great analysers of d. REMEDIES, 39

how much more d. are animated when they hunt in a pack HUME, D, 6; UNITY, 11
I loathe people who keep d. DOGS, 18
let slip the d. of war SHAKESPEARE, 153; WAR, 158
like asking a lamp-post…about d. CRITICS, 7; HAMPTON, C, 5
Mad d. and Englishmen COWARD, N, 12
more careful of the breed of their horses and d. FAMILY, 47
Rats…fought the d. ANIMALS, 7; BROWNING, R, 42
Stop…those d.…peeing on my cheapest rug DOGS, 11
woman who is…kind to d. DOGS, 2; WOMEN, 21
doing Anything that is worth d. BEERBOHM, M, 7; ORIGINALITY, 1
D. is better than saying ACTION, 2; PROVERBS, 114
Find out what you like d. best OCCUPATIONS, 25; WHITEHORN, K, 6
let us not be weary in well d. RETRIBUTION, 4
we learn by d. ARISTOTLE, 1; LEARNING, 2
Whatever is worth d. CHESTERFIELD, P, 6; EXCELLENCE, 1
doings All our d. without charity BOOK OF COMMON PRAYER, 8; CHARITY, 11
do-it-yourself Edison…a supreme 'd.' man SCIENTISTS, 8
doleful Knight of the D. Countenance CERVANTES, M, 6
dollar The almighty d.…object of universal devotion MATERIALISM, 15
dollars What's a thousand d. MARX, G, 3; MONEY, 33; PUNS, 15
dolphin Irish d., swift and single ANIMALS, 22
dolphins man…more intelligent than d. ADAMS, D, 6
dominate d. the world INFLUENCE, 14; WILDE, O, 68
dominated He d. the room MAO TSE-TUNG, 2
dominion Death Shall Have No D. DEATH, 174
death shall have no d. THOMAS, D, 3
dominions His Majesty's d. BRITISH EMPIRE, 5
The sun does not set in my d. ROYALTY, 102
dominoes a row of d. set up; you knock over the first EISENHOWER, D, 7
dona *timeo Danaos et d. ferentis* MISTRUST, 12; VIRGIL, 9
done bright day is d. ENDING, 5; SHAKESPEARE, 38
Do as you would be d. by CHESTERFIELD, P, 9; EXAMPLE, 3
d. those things we ought not BOOK OF COMMON PRAYER, 15; SIN, 9
If it were d. when 'tis d. HASTE, 10; SHAKESPEARE, 209
Justice should…be seen to be d. JUSTICE, 10
Let justice be d. JUSTICE, 7
long day's task is d. REST, 2; SHAKESPEARE, 35
Oh, he's d. for AGE, 45
One never notices what has been d. CURIE, M, 7; SCIENCE, 24
so little d. ACTION, 14; TENNYSON, 34
the dread of doing what has been d. before ORIGINALITY, 6
The way to get things d. is not to mind who gets the credit SELFLESSNESS, 2
thy worldly task hast d. MORTALITY, 16; SHAKESPEARE, 63
What's d. cannot be undone PROVERBS, 456; REGRET, 3
What you do not want d. to yourself CONFUCIUS, 14; EXAMPLE, 4
Dong The D. with a luminous Nose LEAR, E, 3; NONSENSE, 19
Don Juan *D.* when anger is subsiding into indifference LITERATURE, 18
Don Juans Christ-like heroes and woman-worshipping D. LAWRENCE, D, 27; MEN, 10
donkeys lions led by d. LEADERSHIP, 8
Don Miguel All right, my lord creator, D. DEATH, 91; UNAMUNO, M, 1
Donne D.'s Body only, lyes below POETS, 13
D.…sublimation of subtlety with…impassioned majesty POETS, 31
D.'s verses…pass all understanding POETS, 42
With D., whose muse on dromedary trots DONNE, J, 1
Don Quixote the only absolutely original creation…is D. FICTION, 6; MAUGHAM, W, 22
dons d., whose arguments…populated the ether ACADEMICS, 9
If the D. sight Devon NEWBOLT, H, 2; PATRIOTISM, 30
It is the little d. I complain about CRITICS, 15; PRIESTLEY, J, 2
Donsmanship D.…the art of criticizing POTTER, S, 5
don't-knows One day the d. will get in GOVERNMENT, 26; MILLIGAN, S, 11
Doodle Yankee D. came to town AMERICA, 3; NURSERY RHYMES, 73
doom bears it out even to the edge of d. LOVE, 151; SHAKESPEARE, 371
purpose of God and the d. assigned DESTINY, 28; TENNYSON, 58
regardless of their d. GRAY, T, 9; IGNORANCE, 11
slow, sure d. falls pitiless and dark HUMAN CONDITION, 23; RUSSELL, B, 16
door A d. is what a dog is…on the wrong side of DOGS, 14; NASH, O, 2
sweetest thing that ever grew /Beside a human d. ADMIRATION, 20; WORDSWORTH, W, 18
the judge standeth before the d. BIBLE, 219
When one d. shuts OPTIMISM, 10; PROVERBS, 459
world will make a beaten path to his d. EMERSON, R, 26; FAME, 11
Youth will come…beat on my d. IBSEN, H, 6; YOUTH, 16
door-keeper I had rather be a d. in the house of my God PSALMS, 45
doormat differentiate me from a d. FEMINISM, 36
doors be ye lift up, ye everlasting d. PSALMS, 14
story of my life is about back entrances and side d. PRIVACY, 4
the d. of perception were cleansed BLAKE, W, 19; PERCEPTION, 1
dope Despair is better treated with hope, not d. DESPAIR, 1
doping struggle against d. SPORT AND GAMES, 26
Dorchester All terrorists…end up with drinks at the D. POLITICS, 37
Doreen be announced as…'D.' BLEASDALE, A, 2
dosed d. her children DRUGS, 6
dots those damned d. MATHEMATICS, 3
double down the grassgreen gooseberried d. bed SEX, 118; THOMAS, D, 23
down with the d. standards DETERMINATION, 27
make that a d. LAST WORDS, 47
double-crossing You dirty d. rat MISQUOTATIONS, 12
double-entendre But the horrible d. ANONYMOUS, 92; INNUENDO, 1
doublethink D. means…holding two contradictory beliefs OPPOSITES, 6; ORWELL, G, 19
doubt a life of d. diversified by faith BROWNING, R, 12; DOUBT, 5
all my mind is clouded with a d. AFTERLIFE, 11; TENNYSON, 25
faith without d. is nothing but death FAITH, 30
Humility is only d. BLAKE, W, 13; HUMILITY, 2
new Philosophy calls all in d. DONNE, J, 3; SCIENCE, 28
No…shadow of d. CERTAINTY, 3; GILBERT, W, 2
O thou of little faith, wherefore didst thou d. BIBLE, 395; DOUBT, 3
Through the night of d. and sorrow ENDURANCE, 5
trust yourself when all men d. you KIPLING, R, 17
When a man is in d. about…his writing BUTLER, S, 12; POSTERITY, 5
When in d., win the trick SPORT AND GAMES, 19
Doubting castle called D. Castle BUNYAN, J, 7; DESPAIR, 4
doubts end in d. BACON, F, 2; DOUBT, 1
His d. are better than…certainties DOUBT, 6
Medicine heals d. as well as diseases MEDICINE, 60
douche the rattling of a thousand d. bags CHILDREN, 49; CONTRACEPTION, 8
dove and the d. came in to him BIBLE, 159
No visit to D. Cottage, Grasmere, is complete HUMOUR, 40
the Spirit of God descending like a d. BIBLE, 355; CHRISTIANITY, 24
the wings of a d. COWPER, W, 33; SOLITUDE, 4
wings like a d. PSALMS, 33
Dover It is burning a farthing candle at D. CRITICISM, 25; JOHNSON, S, 68
the chalk cliffs of D. BALDWIN, S, 6
doves The moans of d. in immemorial elms TENNYSON, 68
Dowel D., Dobet and Dobest GOOD, 11
dower forfeited their ancient English d. DECLINE, 16; WORDSWORTH, W, 56
down for coming d. let me shift for myself EXECUTION, 24
He that is d. BUNYAN, J, 10; PRIDE, 2
I brought myself d. DEFEAT, 12
I started at the top and worked my way d. DECLINE, 14
put it d. a we DICKENS, C, 52; SPELLING, 1
Yes, and they went d. very well too WAR, 178; WELLINGTON, 4
downcast causes many people to feel a little d. DEATH, 109
downfall illusions of infallibility, which of course brought her d. POLITICIANS, 70
downhearted Are we d.? No ANONYMOUS, 7; OPTIMISM, 12
We are not d. OPTIMISM, 23
Downing the first comic genius…in D. Street DISRAELI, B, 2
downtown beautiful d. Burbank PLACES, 3
dozen a d. are only a chorus BEAUTY, 22; FITZGERALD, F, 9
draft a philandering, pot-smoking d. dodger CLINTON, B, 2
drain you will leave Oxford by the town d. SPOONER, W, 5
drainpipe wrong end of a municipal d. LLOYD GEORGE, D, 5; POLITICIANS, 101

drains to distinguish between the Deity and the D. GOD, 49
Drake D. he's in his hammock NEWBOLT, H, 3; WAR, 120
drama A good d. critic is CRITICS, 23; TYNAN, K, 3
D. is the back-stairs of the intellect THEATRE, 4
D. never changed anybody's mind THEATRE, 11
d. shows people dealing nobly with their misery SUFFERING, 3
dramatic a playwright...void of d. interest SARTRE, J, 2
dramatist Sherard Blaw, the d. who had discovered himself SAKI, 23; WRITERS, 84
draught O, for a d. of vintage ALCOHOL, 46; KEATS, J, 36
draw I d. what I feel in my body ART, 13
it took me a lifetime to learn to d. like them PICASSO, P, 10
drawbacks everything has its d. FAMILY, 31; JEROME, J, 6
One of the d. of Fame FAME, 19; MELBA, N, 3
drawer Somebody leaves a pistol in the d. SUICIDE, 22
drawing back to the old d. board FAILURE, 2
the Suez Canal was flowing through my d. room POLITICS, 36
dread all d. and fear DOCTORS, 35
Doth walk in fear and d. FEAR, 7
The d. of beatings EDUCATION, 13
the d. of doing what has been done before ORIGINALITY, 6
the d. of hostesses on both sides of the Atlantic OBITUARIES, 8
dreadful d. is the check BRONTE, E, 5; IMPRISONMENT, 3
Other people are quite d. MISANTHROPY, 5; WILDE, O, 18
Portions and parcels of the d. Past TENNYSON, 54; TIME, 57
some have called thee /Mighty and d. DEATH, 58; DONNE, J, 14
Dreadnoughts A...Duke costs as much...as two D. ARISTOCRACY, 15; LLOYD GEORGE, D, 10
dream All men d.: but not equally DREAMS, 11; LAWRENCE, T, 8
A sight to d. of COLERIDGE, S, 10; DESIRE, 5
awakened from the d. of life LIFE AND DEATH, 30; SHELLEY, P, 4
Awoke one night from a deep d. of peace DREAMS, 8
behold it was a d. BUNYAN, J, 8; DREAMS, 3
d. of perfect bliss DREAMS, 2
For life is but a d. LIFE, 95
God will cease to d. you DEATH, 91; UNAMUNO, M, 1
Happiness is no vague d. HAPPINESS, 22
hope is...the d. of those that wake HOPE, 20
I d. when I am awake REALITY, 1
I have a d. EQUALITY, 20; KING, M, 4
life is a d. LIFE, 49
Like the empty words of a d. MEMORY, 4
Napoleon – mighty somnambulist of a vanished d. NAPOLEON I, 3
The glory and the freshness of a d. INNOCENCE, 16
The young men's vision, and the old men's d. DREAMS, 5; DRYDEN, J, 14
to d. you gotta still be asleep DYLAN, B, 14
To sleep, perchance to d. SHAKESPEARE, 90; SUICIDE, 35
waking life is a d. controlled MADNESS, 33
warned of God in a d. BIBLE, 352; CHRISTMAS, 11
Where is it now, the glory and the d. METAPHYSICS, 5; WORDSWORTH, W, 26
you d. you are crossing the Channel BOATS, 6; GILBERT, W, 22
dreamer that prophet, or...d. of dreams BIBLE, 56
The poet and the d. are distinct KEATS, J, 16; OPPOSITES, 3
this d. cometh BIBLE, 175
dreamers the d. of the day are dangerous men DREAMS, 11; LAWRENCE, T, 8
dreamin' d....o' Plymouth Hoe NEWBOLT, H, 3; WAR, 120
dreaming after-dinner's sleep, d. on both AGE, 80; SHAKESPEARE, 233
a man d. I was a butterfly DREAMS, 4
City with her d. spires ARNOLD, M, 45; OXFORD, 2
I'm d. of a white Christmas CHRISTMAS, 6
dreams doubtful d. of d. PEACE, 20
do we not live in d. DREAMS, 14; TENNYSON, 16
dream our d. away DREAMS, 7
D. and predictions BACON, F, 41; DREAMS, 1
D. culminating in emission DREAMS, 12
Fanatics have their d. FANATICISM, 3; KEATS, J, 15
For one person who d. of making fifty thousand pounds LAZINESS, 8; MILNE, A, 3
I, being poor, have only my d. POVERTY, 44; YEATS, W, 35
In d. begins responsibility RESPONSIBILITY, 23; YEATS, W, 23
liberal d. of a better world IDEALISM, 11
show life...as we see it in our d. CHEKHOV, A, 8; WRITING, 11
Than this world d. of PRAYER, 27; TENNYSON, 24
the city of perspiring d. CAMBRIDGE, 5; RAPHAEL, F, 1
We are nothing; less than nothing, and d. INSIGNIFICANCE, 4; LAMB, C, 4
We are such stuff /As d. are made on MORTALITY, 17; SHAKESPEARE, 327
what d. may come SHAKESPEARE, 90; SUICIDE, 35
your struggles, your d., your telephone number LOVE, 18
dreamt d. of in your philosophy SHAKESPEARE, 79; SUPERNATURAL, 13
I d. that I was making a speech SPEECHES, 9
dreary d. intercourse of daily life OPTIMISM, 42; WORDSWORTH, W, 15
Dying is a very dull, d. affair DEATH, 108; MAUGHAM, W, 26
If your morals make you d. MORALITY, 22; STEVENSON, R, 3
Once upon a midnight d. SUPERNATURAL, 12
dregs the foul d. of his power, the tools of despotism and corruption POLITICS, 119
dress after-dinner speech should be like a lady's d. CLOTHES, 7
choosing d. material for this uncertain summer WRITING, 40
I have no d. except the one I wear CURIE, M, 6; PRACTICALITY, 1
put on a d. of guilt GUILT, 9
sweet disorder in the d. CLOTHES, 12; HERRICK, R, 2
The Englishman's d. is like a traitor's body FASHION, 6
Those who make their d....themselves CLOTHES, 11; HAZLITT, W, 24
why do you d. me /In borrow'd robes PROMOTION, 4
Women are entitled to d. attractively, even provocatively VIOLENCE, 16
dress'd D. in a little brief authority MANKIND, 57; SHAKESPEARE, 230
dressed All d. up, with nowhere to go FUTILITY, 14
Some fruit for Him that d. me HERBERT, G, 3; SERVICE, 3
Today I d. to meet my father's eyes SUITABILITY, 3
dresses long d....cover a multitude of shins CLOTHES, 27; WEST, M, 10
drink A good d. ALCOHOL, 3; PROVERBS, 22
A little in d. MARRIAGE, 145
Another little d. ALCOHOL, 76
A population sodden with d. ENGLAND, 9
a rule never to d. by daylight ALCOHOL, 56; MENCKEN, H, 18
A taste for d., combined with gout ALCOHOL, 35; GILBERT, W, 3
D. and the devil ALCOHOL, 78; STEVENSON, R, 8
D. deep, or taste not the Pierian spring KNOWLEDGE, 36; POPE, A, 23
D.! for you know not whence you came DESTINY, 10; FITZGERALD, E, 18
d. may be said to be an equivocator with lechery ALCOHOL, 69; SHAKESPEARE, 215
d. not to elevation MODERATION, 7
D. to me only with thine eyes JONSON, B, 7; LOVE, 93
First you take a d....then the d. takes you ALCOHOL, 31; FITZGERALD, F, 14
I commended mirth...to eat...to d., and to be merry BIBLE, 72; PLEASURE, 4
I d. anything I can get my hands on LONGEVITY, 14
If you were my wife, I'd d. it INSULTS, 32
let us eat and d. MISQUOTATIONS, 7
let us eat and d.; for tomorrow we...die BIBLE, 205; TRANSIENCE, 8
never to refuse a d. after dark ALCOHOL, 56; MENCKEN, H, 18
no more able to resist a quotation than...a d. CRITICISM, 47
no one has yet found a way to d. for a living ALCOHOL, 48
Nor any drop to d. COLERIDGE, S, 30; WATER, 2
One more d. and I'd be under the host DRINKS, 16
One reason I don't d. DRUNKENNESS, 7
poured himself a d. and...confessed TREASON, 7
she would never take a d. ABSTINENCE, 11
soft d. at a party ABSTINENCE, 2
strong d. is raging ALCOHOL, 20
that he has taken to d. ALCOHOL, 79
the man takes a d. ALCOHOL, 8
There are five reasons we should d. ALCOHOL, 10
we d. too much tea DRINKS, 19; PRIESTLEY, J, 6
willing to taste any d. once DRINKS, 8
woe unto them that...follow strong d. ALCOHOL, 16; BIBLE, 195
you shall d. twice while I d. once DRUNKENNESS, 28; WALPOLE, H, 10
drinkers written by d. of water HORACE, 23; WATER, 6
drinking D....and making love MANKIND, 7
d. deep of that divinest anguish BRONTE, E, 6
I have been d. it for sixty-five years and I am not dead DRINKS, 22; VOLTAIRE, 35

I wasn't this nervous playing golf when I was d. GOLF, 2
let me die d. in an inn ALCOHOL, 54
no d. after death ALCOHOL, 33
resolve to give up smoking, d. and loving ABSTINENCE, 5
smoking cigars and…d. of alcohol before, after, and… during ALCOHOL, 27; SMOKING, 8
the increase in d. is to be laid mainly to the account of the female sex ALCOHOL, 22
there's nothing like d. ALCOHOL, 29
'Tis not the d.…but the excess EXCESS, 9; SELDEN, J, 8
two reasons for d. PEACOCK, T, 6; THIRST, 1
Work is the curse of the d. classes WILDE, O, 75; WORK, 39
drinks An alcoholic…d. as much as you do ALCOHOL, 80
He who d. a little too much ALCOHOL, 4; PROVERBS, 198
drip dry The only label she wears is 'd.'. FASHION, 12
dripping Constant d. hollows out a stone PERSISTENCE, 10
electricity was d. invisibly SCIENCE, 91; THURBER, J, 10
driver great d. and a great champion loses his life SPORT AND GAMES, 29
driver in the d.'s seat BEAVERBROOK, M, 2; POWER, 6
driving busy d. cabs and cutting hair GOVERNMENT, 9
I would spend my life in d. briskly in a post-chaise JOHNSON, S, 115; PLEASURE, 17
drizzle the blasted English d. DISCONTENT, 6; KIPLING, R, 25
droghte d. of Marche CHAUCER, G, 3; MONTHS, 7
droit *Dieu et mon d.* FAITH, 27
drôle *une d. de guerre* WAR, 53
dromedary Donne, whose muse on d. trots COLERIDGE, S, 21; POETS, 28
droop The day begins to d. DAY, 2
drop Nor any d. to drink COLERIDGE, S, 30; WATER, 2
there are people whom one should like very well to d. HURT, 2; JOHNSON, S, 136
dropping peace comes d. slow PEACE, 22; YEATS, W, 18
dropsies there were people who died of d. INSULTS, 75; JOHNSON, S, 160
dropt Mrs Montagu has d. me HURT, 2; JOHNSON, S, 136
drought As the d. continued, prayer was abandoned LEE, L, 1
drown d. in their own blood WAR, 82
I'll d. my book RENUNCIATION, 4; SHAKESPEARE, 328
what pain it was to d. DROWNING, 2; SHAKESPEARE, 303
When you go to d. yourself SUICIDE, 23
drowning A d. man HOPE, 2; PROVERBS, 14
Being an old maid is like death by d. MARRIAGE, 70
If I rescued a child from d. MEDIA, 4; POLITICIANS, 47
not waving but d. DROWNING, 3
drudge a harmless d. JOHNSON, S, 10; LEXICOGRAPHY, 6
drudgery Learn to innure yourself to d. in science EDUCATION, 72
drug A miracle d. is MEDICINE, 40
d. is that substance which DRUGS, 2
Television – the d. of the nation TELEVISION, 7
Words are…the most powerful d. KIPLING, R, 35; WORDS, 22
drugging Imperative d.…no longer…the chief function DRUGS, 13
drugs Americans use d. as…license' to be an asshole DRUGS, 17
A physician is one who pours d. DOCTORS, 105
Give me…a few d., and simple electrical appliances PSYCHIATRY, 6
Half the modern d. could well be thrown out the window DRUGS, 8
how do d., hygiene and animal magnetism heal REMEDIES, 27
I didn't take d. SPORT AND GAMES, 30
if you're on d. then you're in trouble DRUGS, 4
drugstore The brewery is the best d. ALCOHOL, 9
drum brave Music of a *distant* D. FITZGERALD, E, 6; MONEY, 22
Not a d. was heard FUNERALS, 13
Take my d. to England NEWBOLT, H, 2; PATRIOTISM, 30
drums the beating of war d. WAR, 94
drunk Bowen's Beer Makes You D. DRINKS, 2
D. in charge of a narrative FICTION, 2
If, d. with sight of power, we loose KIPLING, R, 23
I was crazy and…he was d. GRANT, U, 2
I would have d. a lot of Pinot Grigio DRINKS, 15
Lord George-Brown d. is a better man DRUNKENNESS, 6; POLITICIANS, 37
man…must get d. BYRON, 21; DRUNKENNESS, 13
most…either d. too much or womanized too much POLITICIANS, 54
'My mother, d. or sober.' CHESTERTON, G, 8; PATRIOTISM, 8
not so think as you d. DRUNKENNESS, 26
someone who has…d.…a…barrel CHEKHOV, A, 13; EXPERIENCE, 10
this meeting is d. DICKENS, C, 49; DRUNKENNESS, 14
drunkards There are more old d. DRUNKENNESS, 1; DOCTORS, 40; PROVERBS, 405
drunken Better sleep with a sober cannibal than a d. Christian DRUNKENNESS, 21
He uses statistics as a d. man uses lamp-posts STATISTICS, 5
What shall we do with the d. sailor ANONYMOUS, 105; DRUNKENNESS, 4
drunkenness A branch of the sin of d. DRUNKENNESS, 19
D. is never anything but a substitute for happiness DRUNKENNESS, 17
D. is temporary suicide DRUNKENNESS, 24
D.…spoils health DRUNKENNESS, 22
D., the ruin of reason DRUNKENNESS, 9
If…'feeling good' could decide, d. would be…supremely valid DRUNKENNESS, 18
there is more drinking…less d. ALCOHOL, 22
dry old man in a d. month AGE, 38; ELIOT, T, 8
out of these wet clothes and into a d. Martini ALCOHOL, 89
O ye d. bones BIBLE, 128
the midst of the sea upon d. ground BIBLE, 112
Dublin D., though…much worse than London JOHNSON, S, 153; PLACES, 18
In D.'s fair city, where the girls are so pretty ANONYMOUS, 47; IRELAND, 2
ducats My daughter! O my d. LOSS, 7; SHAKESPEARE, 245
Duce The D. is always right FASCISM, 1
duck I forgot to d. REAGAN, R, 11
I just forgot to d. SPORT AND GAMES, 12
looks like a d. COMMUNISM, 10
ducks you go about the country stealing d. THEFT, 3
your precious 'lame d.' GALSWORTHY, J, 6; WEAKNESS, 2
due his fruit in d. season PSALMS, 1
duel war…will be considered as antiquated as a d. WAR, 67
dug If people d. up the remains of this civilization ARTISTS, 19
Duke A…D. costs as much…as two Dreadnoughts ARISTOCRACY, 15; LLOYD GEORGE, D, 10
a naked D. of Windlestraw addressing a naked House of Lords CARLYLE, T, 25; NAKEDNESS, 2
the elegant nonchalance of a d. CHAPLIN, C, 3
dukes a drawing-room full of d. AUDEN, W, 8
dulce *D. et decorum est* HORACE, 34; PATRIOTISM, 20
dull a doctrine so illogical and so d. KEYNES, J, 3; MARXISM, 6
as d. as ditch water DICKENS, C, 41
a very d. Play CONGREVE, W, 11; MARRIAGE, 52
Heaven…is a place so inane, so d. HEAVEN, 14; SHAW, G, 34
He was d. in a new way JOHNSON, S, 92; POETS, 43
if he wasn't as d. as ditch water STUPIDITY, 2
Music-hall songs provide the d. with wit MAUGHAM, W, 23; STUPIDITY, 9
not only d. in himself INSULTS, 50; STUPIDITY, 3
Shakespeare…so intolerably d. SHAKESPEARE, 5
The prospect of a lot /Of d. MPs GILBERT, W, 20; POLITICIANS, 11
To make dictionaries is d. work JOHNSON, S, 8; LEXICOGRAPHY, 5
dullard The d.'s envy of brilliant men BEERBOHM, M, 11; GREATNESS, 2
dullest d. Briton of them all TROLLOPE, A, 1
dullness the cause of d. in others INSULTS, 50
dumb think I'm a d. blonde…then they're dumber APPEARANCE, 54
dumplings I am the emperor, and I want d. PETULANCE, 3
dunces the d. are all in confederacy against him GENIUS, 9; SWIFT, J, 14
dung no grass there groweth, /Only their engines' d. ENGLAND, 8
dunghills picking gold out of the d. of old Roman writers VIRGIL, 3
dupe The d. of friendship, and the fool of love BITTERNESS, 1; HAZLITT, W, 12
dusk In the d., with a light behind her AGE, 47; GILBERT, W, 46; INSULTS, 53
slow d. a drawing-down of blinds OWEN, W, 1; WAR, 124
dusky Midnight brought on the d. hour DAY, 12; MILTON, J, 48
dust A heap of d. alone remains EQUALITY, 43; POPE, A, 7
As chimney-sweepers, come to d. MORTALITY, 16; SHAKESPEARE, 63
d. shalt thou eat SEXES, 4
d. thou art BIBLE, 152
Excuse my d. PARKER, D, 31

fear in a handful of d. ELIOT, T, 28
Film...d. and heat and noise CINEMA, 19
fly...said, what a d. do I raise BACON, F, 58; CONCEIT, 3
he is a disease of the d. MANKIND, 17
his enemies shall lick the d. PSALMS, 41
not worth the d. INSULTS, 112
pride that licks the d. POPE, A, 16; SERVILITY, 5
raised a d. COMPLAINTS, 1
The d. and silence of the upper shelf MACAULAY, T, 6; NEGLECT, 3
the d. beneath thy chariot wheel HUMILITY, 5
The d. of great persons' graves DONNE, J, 15; EQUALITY, 40
this quintessence of d. MANKIND, 56; SHAKESPEARE, 85
Dutch my dear old D. LOVE, 53
duties he devotes to the neglect of his d. NEGLECT, 4
One of the first d. of the physician DOCTORS, 70
Property has its d. CAPITALISM, 5
the d. of a physician DOCTORS, 10
duty absolved from all d. to his country MARRIAGE, 118; PEACOCK, T, 10
a stupid man...always declares that it is his d. DUTY, 7; SHAW, G, 7
A thing of d. is a boy for ever POLICE, 5; PUNS, 18
Do your d. and leave the rest to the Gods DUTY, 2
d. of an opposition OPPOSITION, 2
England expects every man will do his d. DUTY, 5; NELSON, H, 4
give my d. to the Queen VICTORY, 14
It is my d. to warn you that it will be used against you DOYLE, A, 10; JUSTICE, 6
it is our d....to break the law PANKHURST, E, 6
It is the d. of a doctor to prolong life DEATH, 82
more than a moral d. to speak one's mind FRANKNESS, 5; WILDE, O, 28
Nor law, nor d. bade me fight FLYING, 7; YEATS, W, 16
our d. even to/ break the law FEMINISM, 29
Patriotism...is a revolutionary d. PATRIOTISM, 42; TROTSKY, L, 12
right of all...d. of some SEPARATION, 4
the art of pleasing was the first d. in life CHESTERFIELD, P, 3
the d. of being happy HAPPINESS, 29; STEVENSON, R, 20
this is the whole d. of man BIBLE, 79; GOD, 11
What's a man's first d. IBSEN, H, 8; SINCERITY, 5
when constabulary d.'s to be done GILBERT, W, 41; POLICE, 2
Young women have a d. to flirt BROOKNER, A, 3
dwarfs A number of anxious d. POLITICIANS, 21; PRIESTLEY, J, 3
dwell d. among scorpions BIBLE, 123
I will d. in the house of the Lord for ever PSALMS, 11
Let other pens d. on guilt and misery AUSTEN, J, 13; OPTIMISM, 14
dwellings how amiable are thy d. PSALMS, 44
dwelt She d. among the untrodden ways LONELINESS, 16; WORDSWORTH, W, 49
dyin' 'Young man, I think you're d.!' ANONYMOUS, 49; LOVE, 13
dying alike are the groans of love to...d. LOVE AND DEATH, 4
All men are afraid of d. DEATH, 130; ROUSSEAU, J, 2
Death must be distinguished from d. DEATH, 161
Don't cheer, boys; the poor devils are d. WAR, 129
D. for an idea LEWIS, W, 2; MARTYRDOM, 3
d. for their country RUSSELL, B, 31
D. /is an art DEATH, 121; PLATH, S, 3
D. is as natural as living LIFE AND DEATH, 2
D. is a very dull, dreary affair DEATH, 108; MAUGHAM, W, 26
D. is the most hellishly boresome experience in the world DEATH, 110
D. while young is a boon in old age OLD AGE, 6
Ever since d. came into fashion DEATH, 9
Everything is d. of art-attacks ARTS, 2
folly to shrink in fear, if this is d. DEATH, 120
For a priest to turn a man when he lies a-d. PERSUASION, 3; SELDEN, J, 6
good for a writer to think he's d. WRITERS, 29
He had been, he said, a most unconscionable time d. CHARLES II, 7; DEATH, 48; LAST WORDS, 17
Here am I, d. LAST WORDS, 69; POPE, A, 59
I am d., Egypt, d. SHAKESPEARE, 36
I cannot forgive my friends for d. DEATH, 159; SMITH, L, 7
If this is d. LAST WORDS, 86
is it my birthday or am I d. LAST WORDS, 5
it is not death, but d., which is terrible DEATH, 63; FIELDING, H, 1
It is not his duty to prolong the act of d. DEATH, 82
poor honest sex, like d., should be a private matter SEX, 33
she cheats the sick and the d. with illusions NATURE, 18
the d. sun SUN, 1
There is a dignity in d. DEATH, 23
Time held me green and d. THOMAS, D, 9; TIME, 58
'Tis not the d. for a faith FAITH, 29; THACKERAY, W, 3
Truth sits upon the lips of d. men ARNOLD, M, 41; TRUTH, 9
we survive amongst the dead and the d. as on a battlefield OLD AGE, 98; SPARK, M, 6
dyke February, fill the d. MONTHS, 11
there wasn't a d. in the land HOMOSEXUALITY, 17
dynamic class people as static and d. SEXES, 34; WAUGH, E, 27
play is a d. thing NOVELS, 17; PLAYS, 15; TYNAN, K, 1
dyspepsia GLUTTON, n. A person...committing d. GREED, 6

E

ear a pistol let off at the e. LAMB, C, 16; PUNS, 12
he that planted the e., shall he not hear PSALMS, 53
I took the right sow by the e. INFLUENCE, 13
jest's prosperity lies in the e. HUMOUR, 29; SHAKESPEARE, 200
more is meant than meets the e. INNUENDO, 3; MILTON, J, 15
nor e. heard BIBLE, 25
the e. begins to hear BRONTE, E, 5; IMPRISONMENT, 3
Earl As far as the 14th E. is concerned TITLES, 1
Life is much easier, being an E. ARISTOCRACY, 3
the whole process has ground to a halt with a 14th E. TITLES, 13; WILSON, H, 9
early A useless life is an e. death GOETHE, J, 5; PURPOSE, 3
E. to bed BED, 1; PROVERBS, 124
E. to rise and e. to bed HEALTH AND HEALTHY LIVING, 15; THURBER, J, 6
God shall help her, and that right e. PSALMS, 27
good die e. GOOD AND EVIL, 4
nobody who does not rise e. BED, 6; JOHNSON, S, 158
The e. bird ANTICIPATION, 3; PROVERBS, 387
The good die e. DEFOE, D, 1
too e. to form a final judgement on the French Revolution FRENCH REVOLUTION, 9
you have to get up e. if you want to get out of bed BED, 8
earn this is the week I e. my salary KENNEDY, J, 5; MERIT, 5
earned He has e. his thirst HUGHES, T, 2
Old age...gives us what we have e. OLD AGE, 25
earnestly striven long and e. to become a man ANTHONY, S, 1
earning learning, e. and yearning LIFE, 67
earnings regular e. for Ziggy Stardust dolls COMMERCIALISM, 1
ears A hungry stomach has no e. HUNGER, 8; LA FONTAINE, J, 9
can you waggle your e. ACHIEVEMENT, 2;
device to keep the e. from grating MIND, 5
e. to hear, let him hear BIBLE, 388
guard over your eyes and e. BRONTE, A, 6
Romans, countrymen, lend me your e. EVIL, 19; SHAKESPEARE, 155
the seven thin e. BIBLE, 178
earth a covenant between me and the e. BIBLE, 161; PROMISES, 3
a new heaven and a new e. BIBLE, 473
axis of the e. sticks out visibly through...every town or city NATURE, 19
But did thee feel the e. move HEMINGWAY, E, 5; SEX, 50
Cool'd...in the deep-delved e. ALCOHOL, 46; KEATS, J, 36
e. doesn't have a cleaning woman PICASSO, P, 11
E. fills her lap with pleasures NATURE, 36; WORDSWORTH, W, 27
E. has not anything to show more fair LONDON, 24; WORDSWORTH, W, 53
E. is just too small and fragile a basket SPACE, 5
escaped pollution on e. SOUL, 6
from whose face the e. and the heaven fled BIBLE, 472
God called the dry land E. BIBLE, 139; CREATION, 3
God created...the e. BIBLE, 137; CREATION, 2
heaven and e. shall pass away BIBLE, 415; TRANSIENCE, 9
heav'n on e. HEAVEN, 8; MILTON, J, 45
hell upon e....in a melancholy man's heart MELANCHOLY, 3
in his hand are all the corners of the e. PSALMS, 54
I will move the e. TECHNOLOGY, 2
lards the lean e. as he walks OBESITY, 14; SHAKESPEARE, 111
let all the e. keep silence before him BIBLE, 183
mine were princes of the e. JEWS, 3

His English e....preserved his intellect...at the stage of boyhood EDUCATION, 23
if e. is...a mere transmission of knowledge EDUCATION, 65
Medical e. is not completed at the medical school EDUCATION, 99; MEDICINE, 105
Nature has always had more power than e. NATURE, 31
one of the ultimate advantages of an e. EDUCATION, 84
part of English middle-class e. is devoted to the training of servants CLASS, 56; EDUCATION, 101
Soap and e. are not as sudden as a massacre EDUCATION, 91; TWAIN, M, 5
the beginning of e. HONESTY, 8; RUSKIN, J, 12
The e. of the doctor EDUCATION, 15
The first staggering fact about medical e. MEDICINE, 79
The great doctors all got their e. off dirt pavements EDUCATION, 30
the most important part of his e. EDUCATION, 15
'Tis e. forms the common mind EDUCATION, 74; POPE, A, 40
traditions of e. have emphasized knowledge EDUCATION, 16
Travel...is a part of e. BACON, F, 54; TRAVEL, 6
with e. and whisky the price it is CHARACTER, 25; WAUGH, E, 16
woman of e. WOMEN, 137
educations last resort of feeble minds with classical e. EDUCATION, 45; INSULTS, 66
Edward King E....made Lord E....Prince of Wales ROYALTY, 110
Edwardian plants left over from the E. Wilderness CHANGE, 20; OSBORNE, J, 6
Edwardians The E....were nomadic TRAVEL, 49
Eena E., meena, mina, mo NURSERY RHYMES, 11
effect little e. after much labour AUSTEN, J, 32; RESULTS, 2
effervesced She should have waited till it e. ANONYMOUS, 32
efficient be e. if you're going to be lazy LAZINESS, 3
effort What is written without e. JOHNSON, S, 41; WRITING, 23
efforts One is happy as a result of one's own e. HAPPINESS, 22
effrontery e. to kiss me on the lips ETIQUETTE, 3
egalitarianism The majestic e. of the law EQUALITY, 12; FRANCE, A, 9; LAW, 15
égalité *Liberté! É.! Fraternité* ANONYMOUS, 50; HUMAN RIGHTS, 2
egg Better an e. today PROVERBS, 86
Everything from an e. EVOLUTION, 18
hand that lays the golden e. GOLDWYN, S, 13; MIXED METAPHORS, 2
Only as an e....are we all equal EQUALITY, 11
the learned roast an e. FOOD, 59; POPE, A, 53
The vulgar boil...an e. FOOD, 59; POPE, A, 53
throw an e. into an electric fan AMBITION, 10
egghead e. weds hourglass MARRIAGE, 8
eggs all my e. in one bastard PARKER, D, 22
Don't put all your e. in one basket CAUTION, 2; PROVERBS, 119
I've met a lot of hardboiled e. CHARACTER, 26
to cook himself a couple of e. EGOTISM, 4
ways to dress e. FRANCE, 14; MOORE, T, 1
A hen is only an e. way EVOLUTION, 3
eggyellow his nicotine e. weeping walrus Victorian moustache THOMAS, D, 27
ego e. fat on arrogance POLITICIANS, 96
e. locks the muse INSPIRATION, 6
I'd clamp an e. as a lid PSYCHOLOGY, 14
egoistic the emancipation of women is...the greatest e. movement KEY, E, 1; FEMINISM, 15
egotism dilemmas of conscience and e. POWER, 24
his e. was all but second childhood CARROLL, L, 2
egotist E., n. A person...more interested in himself BIERCE, A, 6; EGOTISM, 3
Egypt I am dying, E., dying SHAKESPEARE, 36
Remember you're in E. PRONUNCIATION, 4; TREE, H, 7
We are not at war with E. WAR, 60
Egyptians the E. worshipped an insect DISRAELI, B, 34
eight E. for the e. bold rangers ANONYMOUS, 45; NUMBERS, 1
E. maids a-milking CHRISTMAS, 18; NURSERY RHYMES, 59
Pieces of e. MONEY, 49; STEVENSON, R, 9
eighteen From birth to age e., a girl needs good parents AGE, 95
I knew almost as much at e. as I do now JOHNSON, S, 43; KNOWLEDGE, 27
I've had e. straight whiskies ALCOHOL, 81
she speaks e. languages. And she can't say 'No' in any of them PARKER, D, 27; PROMISCUITY, 10
Ein *E. Reich, E. Volk, E. Führer* NAZISM, 1
There's Gert and there's Epp and there's E. HUMOUR, 36
Einstein E. – the greatest Jew since Jesus EINSTEIN, A, 1
E. – the greatest Jew since Jesus SCIENTISTS, 11
Let E. be SCIENTISTS, 15
The genius of E. leads to Hiroshima EINSTEIN, A, 2
Eisenhower E. proved we don't need a president EISENHOWER, D, 1
elations e. and apprehensions of growth AGE, 60
elderly see it as an e. lady CHURCH, 4
When a distinguished but e. scientist states SCIENCE, 20
elders miss not the discourse of the e. BIBLE, 82; LEARNING, 3
elected audacity of e. persons REVOLUTION, 19; WHITMAN, W, 11
I did not usurp the crown, but was duly e. MONARCHY, 14
election Democracy substitutes e. by the incompetent many DEMOCRACY, 23
government gives us is charity at e. time OPPRESSION, 5
I am certain that we will win the e. with a good majority THATCHER, M, 35
Today in Britain, a fascist has won an e. FASCISM, 13
victory in a general e. THATCHER, M, 40
electorate this formidable Kingdom is...a province of a despicable E. ENGLAND, 41
electric e. light will close with it PROPHECY, 15
the e. display of God the Father LIFE, 71
electrical E. force...causes motion of electrical charge SCIENCE, 30
electricity e. was dripping invisibly SCIENCE, 91; THURBER, J, 10
electrification Communism is Soviet power plus the e. COMMUNISM, 8; LENIN, V, 9
electronic They are e. lice POPULAR MUSIC, 8
elegant English women are e. ENGLISH, 29; STYLE, 8
the e. nonchalance of a duke CHAPLIN, C, 3
element One God, one law, one e. DESTINY, 27; TENNYSON, 38
elementary 'E.,' said he DOYLE, A, 9
elements I tax not you, you e., with unkindness SHAKESPEARE, 179; WEATHER, 20
something that was before the e. BROWNE, T, 11; NOBILITY, 1
elephant an e. like Russia RUSSIA, 9
I shot an e. in my pajamas HUMOUR, 49; MARX, G, 2
Nonsense, they couldn't hit an e. at this distance LAST WORDS, 80
elevate E. them guns a little lower WAR, 84
eleven e. for the e. who went to heaven ANONYMOUS, 45; NUMBERS, 1
E. ladies dancing CHRISTMAS, 18; NURSERY RHYMES, 59
Elijah E. went up by a whirlwind into heaven BIBLE, 301
eliminate I e. my individualism CHINA, 14
Eliot to write like Tennyson...rather than E. or Auden BETJEMAN, J, 2
elms The moans of doves in immemorial e. TENNYSON, 68
eloquence Talking and e. are not the same JONSON, B, 9; SPEECH, 13
eloquent the most e. expressions KEATS, J, 4
else Lord High Everything E. GILBERT, W, 23; TITLES, 4
Suppose it had been someone e. who found you like this ADULTERY, 8
elusive One's prime is e. AGE, 86; SPARK, M, 8
Elysian dead, but in the E. fields DISRAELI, B, 41
emaciated This wild, e. look DIETING, 1
emancipate E. yourselves from mental slavery FREEDOM, 39
emancipated e. from...time and space COLERIDGE, S, 6
emancipation imagine that they are upholding women's e. STOPES, M, 6
results of the e. of women ALCOHOL, 22
the e. of women FEMINISM, 15
embalmer A triumph of the e.'s art INSULTS, 126; REAGAN, R, 4
soft e. of the still midnight KEATS, J, 47; SLEEP, 23
embarras *l'e. des richesses* EXCESS, 2
embarrassment God could cause us considerable e. DISCOVERY, 10; GOETHE, J, 8
embassy We're in the E. residence, subject...to some... discomfiture DIPLOMACY, 2
embittered He was an e. atheist ATHEISM, 10; ORWELL, G, 12
embody I, my lords, e. the Law GILBERT, W, 18; LAW, 18
embrace I e. the purpose of God DESTINY, 28; TENNYSON, 58
none, I think, do there e. DEATH, 105; MARVELL, A, 12
whether I e. your lordship's principles or your mistress REPARTEE, 5
embryo This is a question for an e., not for a man LIFE, 23
Emerson E. is one who lives...on ambrosia EMERSON, R, 2
I could...see in E. a gaping flaw EMERSON, R, 1
emission Dreams culminating in e. DREAMS, 12
emotion Poetry is not a turning loose of e. ELIOT, T, 25; POETRY, 21

Sorrow is tranquillity remembered in e. PARKER, D, 10; SORROW, 20
the degree of my aesthetic e. CRITICISM, 7; CRITICS, 1
emotional a well-bred sort of e. anarchy CLASSIFICATION, 2; LAWRENCE, D, 16
comedy is like e. hang-gliding HUMOUR, 35
emotions a sort of metaphysical brothel for e. SENTIMENTALITY, 3
big e. come from big words HEMINGWAY, E, 9; STYLE, 7
noble grounds for the noble e. POETRY, 52; RUSKIN, J, 5
She ran…e. from A to B CRITICISM, 48; PARKER, D, 30
emperor An e. ought at least to die on his feet LAST WORDS, 92
Be the E. ROYALTY, 1
I am the e., and I want dumplings PETULANCE, 3
the E. has nothing on INNOCENCE, 4
the e. of ice-cream POWER, 26
emperors e. can't do it all by themselves BRECHT, B, 6; SUPPORT, 2
empire a more powerful or a more united e. BRITISH EMPIRE, 1
An e. founded by war MONTESQUIEU, 1; WAR, 111
Great Britain has lost an E. , ACHESON, D, 6; BRITAIN, 1
How is the E. LAST WORDS, 42
Our Eastern E.…*made* the English middle class SCOTT, P, 1
The German E. has become a world empire GERMANY, 8
the Holy Roman Empire was neither holy, nor Roman, nor an e. NATIONS, 5; VOLTAIRE, 16
the man who liquidated the E. MOUNTBATTEN OF BURMA, L, 3
to the French the e. of the land EUROPE, 18
empires The day of E. has come NATIONS, 1
employed innocently e. than in getting money JOHNSON, S, 91; MONEY, 28
The rise in the…e. is governed by Parkinson's Law PARKINSON, C, 2; WORK, 23
employee capitalist society has converted Eros into an e. COMMERCIALISM, 4
every e. tends to rise to his level of incompetence WORK, 25
employer ideal of the e.…production without employees INDUSTRIAL RELATIONS, 4
employers e.…only like ballots so long as you lose them STRIKES, 6
employment E. is nature's physician WORK, 11
I will undoubtedly have to seek…gainful e. ACHESON, D, 5; GOVERNMENT, 1
emptiness Never let success hide its e. DESTINY, 13; DETERMINATION, 16
empty Bring on the e. horses LANGUAGE, 18
E. vessels FOOLISHNESS, 5; PROVERBS, 129
You can't think rationally on an e. stomach THINKING, 12
enchantment distance lends e. to the view PERSPECTIVE, 1
Yeats stood for e. YEATS, W, 1
enclose A vacuum can only exist…by the things which e. it SCIENCE, 41
enclosed Check e. MONEY, 39; PARKER, D, 29
encounter I will e. darkness as a bride DEATH, 149
encourage the right to be consulted,…to e.,…to warn BAGEHOT, W, 7; MONARCHY, 3
to e. the others EXAMPLE, 9; VOLTAIRE, 7
encourager *pour e. les autres* EXAMPLE, 9; VOLTAIRE, 7
encyclopaedia a whole E. behind the rest of the world LAMB, C, 8; SCIENCE, 61
end a beginning, a muddle, and an e. LARKIN, P, 5; NOVELS, 9
an e. to the beginnings of all wars ROOSEVELT, F, 17; WAR, 139
a whole is that which has a beginning, a middle, and an e. ARISTOTLE, 4; PLAYS, 1
beginning of the e. DEFEAT, 16; TALLEYRAND, 3
God be at my e., /And at my departing ANONYMOUS, 20; GOD, 2
Here is my journey's e. DEATH, 151
I like a film to have a beginning, a middle and an e. CINEMA, 12
I move softly towards the e. DEATH, 89
In my beginning is my e. BEGINNING, 9
Keep Right on to the E. of the Road PERSISTENCE, 8
my patience is now at an e. PATIENCE, 11
of making many books there is no e. BIBLE, 78; BOOKS, 9
our minutes hasten to their e. SHAKESPEARE, 365; TIME, 50
the e. is not yet BIBLE, 413; WAR, 20
The *e.* is to build well ARCHITECTURE, 21
The e. justifies the means PROVERBS, 388
the e. of the beginning CHURCHILL, W, 59; WORLD WAR II, 21
The first sign of his approaching e. OLD AGE, 50
Walt Whitman who laid e. to e. LODGE, D, 5; POETS, 50
we're forbidden to know – what e. the gods have in store DESTINY, 15; HORACE, 30
world without e. BOOK OF COMMON PRAYER, 16; ETERNITY, 2
Yes, to the very e. ENDURANCE, 18; ROSSETTI, C, 6
endeavour To e. to forget anyone LA BRUYERE, J, 14; MEMORY, 10
endeavours one of the great human e. SCIENCE, 45
ended My life with girls has e. HORACE, 38; SEX, 52
The day Thou gavest, Lord, is e. DAY, 4
ending beginning and the e. BIBLE, 459
The quickest way of e. a war ORWELL, G, 20; WAR, 123
endless History is an e. repetition DURRELL, L, 3; HISTORY, 11
endorsement government e. of homosexuality HOMOSEXUALITY, 28
ends and it is great /To do that thing that e. all other deeds SUICIDE, 33
divinity that shapes our e. DESTINY, 21; SHAKESPEARE, 107
my family begins…yours e. with you ANCESTRY, 3
endurance patient e. is godlike ENDURANCE, 11; LONGFELLOW, H, 6
endure For his mercies ay e. GOD, 39; MILTON, J, 55
It is flattering some men to e. them HALIFAX, 3; TOLERANCE, 3
Jazz will e. POPULAR MUSIC, 24
Youth's a stuff will not e. PRESENT, 13; SHAKESPEARE, 340
endured Human life is everywhere a state in which much is to be e. JOHNSON, S, 28
Job e. everything – until his friends came ENDURANCE, 10
endures When a man is in love he e. more LOVE, 119; NIETZSCHE, F, 2
endureth blessed is the man that e. temptation BIBLE, 216; TEMPTATION, 4
enemies Better a thousand e. ENEMIES, 1; PROVERBS, 87
designing mausoleums for his e. HATE, 7
do not have to forgive my e. LAST WORDS, 60; RUTHLESSNESS, 4
Even a paranoid can have e. ENEMIES, 4
He could not make e. SHERIDAN, R, 2
his e. shall lick the dust PSALMS, 41
love your e. BIBLE, 365; ENEMIES, 3
mine e. shall be confounded PSALMS, 2
Mountains interposed /Make e. of nations COWPER, W, 28; MOUNTAINS, 1
The e. of Freedom INGE, W, 2; OPPRESSION, 4
we have been mortal e. ever since ENEMIES, 5
enemy Every man is his own worst e. PROVERBS, 139; SELF, 1
hasn't an e. in the world POPULARITY, 9; WILDE, O, 66
I am the e. you killed OWEN, W, 7
I cannot get any sense of an e. WORLD WAR I, 14
in politics to chastise his own side than the e. ORWELL, G, 2
It takes your e. and your friend…, to hurt you HURT, 3; TWAIN, M, 6
no more sombre e. of good art BABIES, 2; CONNOLLY, C, 10
Poverty is a great e. to human happiness JOHNSON, S, 140; POVERTY, 24
We have met the e., and they are ours VICTORY, 18
we must be just to our e. PUBLISHING, 5
enemy-friends Israelis are now what we call the e. WAR AND PEACE, 2
energies quarrel…e. displayed in it are fine KEATS, J, 68
energy E. is Eternal Delight BLAKE, W, 32; EFFORT, 2
exhausted my e. in tirades against fate INJUSTICE, 2
enfants *Allons, e., de la patrie* FRANCE, 13
Les e. terribles YOUTH, 12
engaged one of the nicest girls I was ever e. to MARRIAGE, 174; WODEHOUSE, P, 17
engine indefatigable and unsavoury e. of pollution DOGS, 17
England A grain, which in E. is generally given to horses JOHNSON, S, 12; SCOTLAND, 3
a summary opinion of what I have seen in E. ENGLAND, 47
Be E. what she will PATRIOTISM, 9
but the King of E. cannot enter PITT THE ELDER , 1; PRIVACY, 5
can care intelligently for the future of E. ENGLAND, 26
Christianity is part of the Common Law of E. CHRISTIANITY, 40
close my eyes, open my legs and think of E. SEX, 51
Common Law of E. HERBERT, A, 3; LAW, 22
Damn you, E.. You're rotting ENGLAND, 39
don't say that in E. for…they will surely tax it SWIFT, J, 19; TAXATION, 13
E. elects a Labour Government POLITICS, 87; ROGERS, W, 2
E. expects every man will do his duty DUTY, 5; NELSON, H, 4
E. has saved herself by her exertions SELF-PRESERVATION, 10
E. is a nation of shopkeepers ENGLISH, 32; NAPOLEON I, 13

E. is the mother of parliaments ENGLAND, 10
E. is the paradise of individuality ENGLAND, 44; SANTAYANA, G, 9
E. is the paradise of women ENGLAND, 22
E. mourns for her dead across the sea MOURNING, 3
E.'s green and pleasant land BLAKE, W, 33; ENGLAND, 7; FIGHT, 1
E.'s pleasant pastures BLAKE, W, 33; ENGLAND, 7; FIGHT, 1
E....the envy of less happy lands ENGLAND, 19
E. to be the workshop of the world DISRAELI, B, 21; ENGLAND, 21
E. was too big for him ROYALTY, 44
E.!.../What love I bore to thee HOMESICKNESS, 9; WORDSWORTH, W, 7
E. will have her neck wrung like a chicken WORLD WAR II, 49
E., with all thy faults COWPER, W, 23; PATRIOTISM, 10
For E.'s the one land BROOKE, R, 2
go back to thy stately homes of E. LAWRENCE, D, 18; PARTING, 7
God for Harry! E. and Saint George SHAKESPEARE, 132
great ship...is...the realm of E. ENGLAND, 2
hardly be a town in the South of E. ENGLAND, 38
he bores for E. BORES, 4; INSULTS, 100; MUGGERIDGE, M, 6
in E. people have good table manners MANNERS, 5
In E., pop art and fine art ART, 21
In E. there is only silence or scandal ENGLAND, 33
It was twenty-one years ago that E. and I ENGLAND, 35
King of E., who lacks nothing WEALTH, 33
little ships of E. brought the Army home BOATS, 8; WORLD WAR II, 30
Living in E....like being married to a stupid...wife ENGLAND, 23
no man in E. will take away my life ARROGANCE, 2; CHARLES II, 4
occurred nowhere but in E. CONRAD, J, 9; ENGLAND, 16
Oh, to be in E. BROWNING, R, 25; ENGLAND, 13
Old E. is lost BRITAIN, 11; JOHNSON, S, 113
rather hew wood than be...King of E. MONARCHY, 8
shouldn't be playing for E. CRICKET, 5
should they know of E. who only E. know KIPLING, R, 9
Speak for E. PATRIOTISM, 2
Stately Homes of E. ARISTOCRACY, 11; STATELY HOMES, 4
that is forever E. BROOKE, R, 7; WAR, 30
The best thing I know between France and E. FRANCE, 11; JERROLD, D, 2
the defence of E. BALDWIN, S, 6
the earth of E. is in my two hands VICTORY, 30
the Kings of E., Diamonds, Hearts, Spades and Clubs MONARCHY, 12
The Law of E. is a very strange one LAW, 11
The national sport of E. ENGLISH, 39; TREE, H, 6
the old savage E., whose last blood flows still ENGLAND, 29; LAWRENCE, D, 22
There'll always be an E. ENGLAND, 40
The roast beef of E. FIELDING, H, 6; FOOD, 30
The stately homes of E. STATELY HOMES, 6
this generation...found E. a land of beauty ECOLOGY, 5
this realm, this E. SHAKESPEARE, 297
We are honoured...to play for E. CRICKET, 10
we are the people of E. CHESTERTON, G, 38; ENGLISH, 13
When people say E. ENGLAND, 34
When you think about the defence of E. ENGLAND, 5

English Acting in E....I'm like a blind man describing in E. what he can see ACTING, 10
describing in E. what he can see LANGUAGE, 5
Dr Johnson's morality was as E....as a beefsteak ENGLAND, 25
E. people...are surely the *nicest* people in the world ENGLISH, 24; LAWRENCE, D, 4
E. soldiers fight like lions OFFICERS, 8
E.,...the language of an imaginative race LANGUAGE, 9
E. tongue...hodgepodge of all other speeches LANGUAGE, 44
E. women are elegant ENGLISH, 29; STYLE, 8
especially if he went among the E. BARRIE, J, 9; BRITISH, 2
Every man...is entitled to the protection of the E. law EQUALITY, 23
exterminate...the treacherous E. WAR, 184; WILHELM II, 4
foreigners speak E. FOREIGNERS, 1
forfeited their ancient E. dower DECLINE, 16; WORDSWORTH, W, 56
Has anyone here been raped and speaks E. INSENSITIVITY, 2
hearts at peace, under an E. heaven ENGLAND, 12
He is a writer of something occasionally like E. WHITMAN, W, 2
I do love cricket – it's so very E. CRICKET, 2; FOOTBALL, 3
If the E. language had been properly organized LANGUAGE, 33; MILNE, A, 2
If you get the E. people into the way of making kings MELBOURNE, 5; ROYALTY, 86
my own heart to be entirely E. PATRIOTISM, 3
one of the few E. novels for grown up people CRITICISM, 68; WOOLF, V, 5
on you noblest E. SHAKESPEARE, 131
Opera in E. MENCKEN, H, 17; OPERA, 7
our E. nation, if they have a good thing, to make it too common ENGLAND, 45; SHAKESPEARE, 118
part of E. middle-class education is devoted to the training of servants CLASS, 56; EDUCATION, 101
stones kissed by the E. dead OWEN, W, 5; WAR, 125
The attitude of the E....toward E. history ENGLISH, 19
The baby doesn't understand E. LANGUAGE, 29
The E....are rather a foul-mouthed nation HAZLITT, W, 25
the E. are...the least a nation of pure philosophers BAGEHOT, W, 6; ENGLISH, 5
the E. have hot-water bottles ENGLISH, 27; SEX, 81
The E. have no respect for their language CLASS, 44; ENGLISH, 36; SHAW, G, 36
The E. instinctively admire ENGLISH, 4; TALENT, 1
The E. may not like music BEECHAM, T, 4; MUSIC, 6
The E. nation...has successfully regulated the power of its kings GOVERNMENT, 46
The E. take their pleasures ENGLAND, 49
The E. want *inferiors* PRIDE, 13
ther is so greet diversitee /in E. LANGUAGE, 14
This is the sort of E. CHURCHILL, W, 37; GRAMMAR, 4
To Americans E. manners are...frightening MANNERS, 4
to the E. that of the sea EUROPE, 18
two most beautiful words in the E. language JAMES, H, 15
typically E. characteristic ENGLISH, 3; UNITY, 4
writes like a Pakistani who has learned E. when he was twelve years old SHAW, G, 2

English language He uses the E. like a truncheon INSULTS, 15

Englishman Am I not punished enough in not being born an E. NATIONALITY, 11; VOLTAIRE, 34
An E....forms an orderly queue of one ENGLISH, 26
an E.'s heaven-born privilege of doing as he likes ARNOLD, M, 9; PUBLIC, 2
An E.'s home PROVERBS, 51
An E.'s way of speaking CLASS, 23
An E.'s word ENGLISH, 2; PROVERBS, 52
E....is afraid to feel EDUCATION, 31; FORSTER, E, 2
E. never enjoys himself except for a noble purpose ENGLISH, 22; HERBERT, A, 6
E....weighs up the birth, the rank,...the wealth CLASS, 38
He was born an E. BEHAN, B, 1; NATIONALITY, 2
how a carter...a beggar is still...an E. ENGLAND, 36
If I were an American, as I am an E. PATRIOTISM, 33; PITT THE ELDER, 6
in spite of all temptations...He remains an E. GILBERT, W, 14; NATIONALITY, 7
it takes a great deal to produce ennui in an E. ENGLISH, 18
never find an E. among the underdogs ENGLAND, 52; WAUGH, E, 31
Remember that you are an E. ENGLISH, 35; RHODES, C, 2
some other E. despise him CLASS, 44; ENGLISH, 36; SHAW, G, 36
tale...which would have stirred...E. ENDURANCE, 19; EXPLORATION, 4
there are fifty thousand men slain...and not one E. DIPLOMACY, 30
To be an E. ENGLISH, 33; NASH, O, 3
to behold the E. at his *best* ENGLISH, 16
You may be the most liberal Liberal E. CLASS, 21; LAWRENCE, D, 12
young E. of our upper class ARISTOCRACY, 2; ARNOLD, M, 6

Englishmen E. to be subject to Frenchmen VICTORY, 25
Mad dogs and E. COWARD, N, 12
Our fathers were E. TRAVEL, 11
the future E. must take business as seriously as their grandfathers had done BUSINESS, 20
to create Frenchmen in the image of E. CHURCHILL, W, 61; NATIONALITY, 6
to see the absurd nature of E. ENGLISH, 34; PEPYS, S, 7
When two E. meet, their first talk is of the weather JOHNSON, S, 15; WEATHER, 14

Englishwoman This E. is so refined WOMEN, 124

enigma a riddle wrapped in a mystery inside an e. CHURCHILL, W, 47; RUSSIA, 3
enjoy Better to e. and suffer PRAYER, 22
Certainly, there is nothing else here to e. PARTIES, 8; SHAW, G, 49
He knew everything about literature except how to e. it HELLER, J, 4; LITERATURE, 7
Since God has given us the papacy…e. it CATHOLICISM, 10
to e. the interval LIFE, 80
enjoyment a capacity for e. HEMINGWAY, E, 3
I do not eat for the sake of e. FOOD, 33; GANDHI, M, 6
enlightened in this e. age WOLLSTONECRAFT, M, 3
ennui e. the hypochondriac WORK, 14
Idleness begets e. WORK, 14
it takes a great deal to produce e. in an Englishman ENGLISH, 18
enough It comes soon e. EINSTEIN, A, 13; FUTURE, 7
patriotism is not e. LAST WORDS, 14
enrage e. his antagonists…own impotence to e. him ANGER, 1
entente *La cordiale e.* DIPLOMACY, 24
enter but the King of England cannot e. PITT THE ELDER, 1; PRIVACY, 5
enterprise If E. is afoot, Wealth accumulates WEALTH, 30
enterprises e. that require new clothes THOREAU, H, 13; THRIFT, 13
entertain to e. strangers HOSPITALITY, 9
entertained have e. angels unawares BIBLE, 189
entertainment e. branch of Industry POLITICS, 124
what cats most appreciate…is…e. value CATS, 8
enthusiasm all the e. and perseverance that he withheld from books and ideas EISENHOWER, D, 2
He never…felt any real e. for any subject DRYDEN, J, 1
Nothing great was ever achieved without e. EMERSON, R, 7; ENTHUSIASM, 4
Nothing is so contagious as e. ENTHUSIASM, 3
We were as nearly bored as e. would permit CRITICISM, 23
enthusiastic Latins are tenderly e. PLACES, 14
enthusiasts so few e. can be trusted BALFOUR, A, 5; ENTHUSIASM, 2
entire Feminism is an e. world view FEMINISM, 6
Entities E. should not be multiplied SIMPLICITY, 6
entitled bill of rights is what the people are e. to HUMAN RIGHTS, 4
Women are e. to dress attractively, even provocatively VIOLENCE, 16
entrance all men have one e. into life BIBLE, 520; BIRTH, 4
entrances story of my life is about back e. and side doors PRIVACY, 4
the e. of this world made narrow BIBLE, 98
entuned E. in hir nose CHAUCER, G, 6
envied Better be e. ENVY, 1; PROVERBS, 90
There are two things for which animals are…e. ANIMALS, 24; VOLTAIRE, 28
environment a standing-room-only e. ENVIRONMENT, 12
President Robbins was so well adjusted to his e. ADAPTABILITY, 3
the response of man to his total e. ENVIRONMENT, 7
environmental Population growth…e. damage CONSERVATION, 4
envy 2 percent moral, 48 percent indignation and 50 percent e. MORALITY, 21
e. is a kind of praise ENVY, 6; GAY, J, 9
prisoners of addiction and…prisoners of e. MATERIALISM, 14
real genuine, hard-working e. JEALOUSY, 4
The dullard's e. of brilliant men BEERBOHM, M, 11; GREATNESS, 2
the upbringing a nun would e. INNOCENCE, 10; ORTON, J, 1
Epicurus one of E.' herd of pigs HORACE, 18; PRESENT, 10
epidemic feel snubbed if an e. overlooks them DISEASE, 22
going to go crazy, living this e. every minute DISEASE, 24
epidemics Doctors and undertakers /Fear e. of good health DOCTORS, 18
E. have often been more influential than statesman DISEASE, 15
epigrams long despotism tempered by e. CARLYLE, T, 14; FRANCE, 2
epilogue good play needs no e. PLAYS, 13; SHAKESPEARE, 58
Epipsychidion You understand *E.* best when you are in love LITERATURE, 18
epitaph e. of the British Empire – unless we wake up in time. BRITISH EMPIRE, 4
epitaphs a nice derangement of e. MALAPROPISMS, 8; SHERIDAN, R, 9
epithet *Bourgeois*,…is an e. CLASS, 20; HOPE, A, 6
epitome all Mankind's E. DRYDEN, J, 9; HUMAN NATURE, 11
epoch A great e. has begun LE CORBUSIER, 2
there begins a new e. in the history of the world BEGINNING, 11; GOETHE, J, 9
Epp E.'s statues are junk ANONYMOUS, 89; HUMOUR, 36
There's Gert and there's E. and there's Ein HUMOUR, 36
Epsom Had we but stick to E. salts ANONYMOUS, 25
Epstein If people…a thousand years hence…found E.'s statues LESSING, D, 4
The E. makes me feel physically sick ARTISTS, 16
equal All animals are e. EQUALITY, 26; ORWELL, G, 7
all men are created e. EQUALITY, 20; HUMAN RIGHTS, 3
all men are created e. and independent JEFFERSON, T, 5
All shall e. be CLASS, 15; GILBERT, W, 4
all were created e. by nature SLAVERY, 1
Everybody should have an e. chance EQUALITY, 38
Inferiors revolt…that they may be e. REVOLUTION, 1
some animals are more e. than others EQUALITY, 26; ORWELL, G, 7
That all men are e. is a proposition EQUALITY, 14; HUXLEY, A, 30
When you meet someone better…turn your thoughts to becoming his e. CONFUCIUS, 1; SUPERIORITY, 6
equality E.…is the thing EQUALITY, 27
E. may perhaps be a right, but no…fact BALZAC, H, 1; EQUALITY, 5
E. must yield EQUALITY, 8
e.…with our superiors EQUALITY, 7
Freedom! E.! Brotherhood ANONYMOUS, 50; HUMAN RIGHTS, 2
never be e. in the servants' hall CLASS, 6
pushes for e.…is declared "PC" EQUALITY, 4
The cry of e. pulls everyone down EQUALITY, 24
there never will be complete e. FEMINISM, 4
equally I hate everyone e. HATE, 4; PREJUDICE, 5
It comes e. to us all DONNE, J, 15; EQUALITY, 40
Pale Death kicks his way e. EQUALITY, 42; HORACE, 27
That all who are happy, are e. happy HAPPINESS, 13; JOHNSON, S, 73
equals Marriage…regarded as a partnership of e. MARRIAGE, 94
the Republic of E. FRENCH REVOLUTION, 1
equanimity an e. bordering on indifference GILBERT, W, 47; INDIFFERENCE, 3
equivalent musical e. of…St Pancras CRITICISM, 5
erect he faced the firing squad; e. and motionless EXECUTION, 38; THURBER, J, 11
erection Then we must rate the cost of the e. ARCHITECTURE, 17
ergo *Cogito, e. sum* THINKING, 4
erogenous The mind can also be an e. zone MIND, 34; SEX, 125
Eros capitalist society has converted E. into an employee COMMERCIALISM, 4
Unarm, E. REST, 2; SHAKESPEARE, 35
err The Most may e. as grosly PUBLIC, 12; DRYDEN, J, 12
those /Who e. each other must respect LOVE, 125
To e. is human, to forgive, divine MISTAKES, 16; POPE, A, 28
errand What thy e. here below LAMB, C, 20; PURPOSE, 7
erred We have e., and strayed from thy ways BOOK OF COMMON PRAYER, 14; SIN, 8
error A new maxim is often a brilliant e. SAYINGS, 5
but for a typographical e.,…the story of my life HUMAN CONDITION, 20; SEX, 93
Ignorance is preferable to e. IGNORANCE, 13
It is time for the destruction of e. AUDEN, W, 18
show a man that he is in an e. TRUTH, 34
the e. of his way BIBLE, 220
errors E., like Straws, upon the surface flow DRYDEN, J, 17; TRUTH, 23
few e. they have ever avoided CHURCHILL, W, 63; PLACES, 11
I never approved either the e. of his book, or the trivial truths FREEDOM, 60
the e. of those who think they are strong MISTAKES, 3
The medical e. of one century MISTAKES, 6
Esau E.…a hairy man BIBLE, 171
escape Gluttony is an emotional e. GREED, 8
Let no guilty man e. GRANT, U, 7; JUSTICE, 9
escaped e. from a mad and savage master SEX, 112
escaping fortunate in e. regular education WRITERS, 17
esprit English characteristic…*e. de corps* ENGLISH, 3; UNITY, 4

essay an over-ambitious e. by a second-year student CRITICS, 15; PRIESTLEY, J, 2
essence change is the very e. of life CHANGE, 9
Desire is the very e. of man DESIRE, 16
The poet gives us his e. POETRY AND PROSE, 6; WOOLF, V, 4
essential liberty as an e. condition of excellence OXFORD, 9
Essex Man I think E. will vote for a Conservative government THATCHER, M, 42
establishment Shakespeare was something of an E. creep SHAKESPEARE, 3
to refer to your friend's country e. as a 'cottage' POTTER, S, 3; WORDS, 25
estate a fourth e. of the realm JOURNALISM, 23
at no time stand so highly in our e. royal GOVERNMENT, 16
e. o' th' world were now undone SHAKESPEARE, 228; WORLD-WEARINESS, 8
the Third E. contains…a nation FRENCH REVOLUTION, 8
estates Three E. in Parliament CARLYLE, T, 13
état *L'é. c'est moi* LOUIS XIV, 4; MONARCHY, 17
etchings I'll bring the e. down HUMOUR, 62; THURBER, J, 16
eternal A pulse in the e. mind ENGLAND, 12
Hope springs e. in the human breast HOPE, 19; POPE, A, 32
The e. *not ourselves* that makes for righteousness ARNOLD, M, 24; RIGHTEOUSNESS, 1
to the prejudice of the e. king TREASON, 11
We feel…we are e. IMMORTALITY, 8
eternity All things from e.…come round in a circle HISTORY, 5; MARCUS AURELIUS ANTONINUS, 4
Deserts of vast e. AGE, 61; MARVELL, A, 10
E. by term DEATH, 56
E. in an hour BLAKE, W, 9; WONDER, 2
E.'s a terrible thought ETERNITY, 4; STOPPARD, T, 8
from e. spinning the thread of your being DESTINY, 2; MARCUS AURELIUS ANTONINUS, 12
Its narrow measure spans /Tears of e., and sorrow, /Not mine, but man's HOUSMAN, A, 5
I will burn, but…continue our discussion in e. EXECUTION, 36; MARTYRDOM, 5
made his impress on e. HYPATIA, 3
over the Bridge of Sighs into e. DEATH, 96
Tears of e. and sorrow SORROW, 13
without injuring e. THOREAU, H, 8; TIME, 60
ether dons, whose arguments…populated the e. ACADEMICS, 9
ethereal E. minstrel WORDSWORTH, W, 74
ethics E. and Science need to shake hands PRINCIPLES, 2
the rules of medical e. were meant for young fellows DOCTORS, 31
Ethiopians The E. say that their gods are…black RELIGION, 105
Eton Educated…holidays from E. EDUCATION, 83
every imitation from 'E. and Oxford' PARTIES, 12
I was beaten by almost everyone at E., but never by the headmaster. EDUCATION, 86
the Battle of Waterloo *was* won on the playing-fields of E. ORWELL, G, 13; WAR, 122
the playing fields of E. EDUCATION, 100; WELLINGTON, 19
eunuch a kind of moral e. MORALITY, 20; SHELLEY, P, 20
prerogative of the e. RESPONSIBILITY, 18
eureka *E.* DISCOVERY, 1; SCIENCE, 2
Euripides E. portrays them as they are THEATRE, 13
Europe A historic document…towards entering E. EUROPE, 28
another war in E. WAR, 22
Communism continued to haunt E. as a spectre COMMUNISM, 18; TAYLOR, A, 3
E. is the unfinished negative AMERICA, 31; MCCARTHY, M, 4
glory of E. is extinguished BURKE, E, 9; EUROPE, 2
In Western E. there are now only small countries EUROPE, 15
lamps are going out over all E. PROPHECY, 5
sick man of E. DECLINE, 8
That E.'s nothin' on earth EUROPE, 27; WILLIAMS, T, 3
the community of E. EUROPE, 20
the last territorial claim which I have to make in E. WORLD WAR II, 35
the race of men is almost extinct in E. LAWRENCE, D, 27; MEN, 10
The spacious philanthropy which he exhaled upon E. WILSON, W, 1
This going into E. EUROPE, 25
United States of E. CHURCHILL, W, 65; EUROPE, 6; EUROPE, 6
European the feminization of the white E. and American LEWIS, W, 3
to shoot down a E. is to kill two birds with one stone OPPRESSION, 7; SARTRE, J, 18
trend in Hollywood of taking very good E. films CINEMA, 7
Europeanism Their E. is…imperialism with an inferiority complex POLITICS, 48
Europeans only really materialistic people…E. MATERIALISM, 19; MCCARTHY, M, 3
euthanasia E. is a long, smooth-sounding word BUCK, P, 2
Eva If a woman like E. Peron with no ideals THATCHER, M, 19
evacuations Wars are not won by e. CHURCHILL, W, 28; WORLD WAR II, 23
evah Well, did you e.! What a swell party PARTIES, 7; PORTER, C, 6
Evan the Death E. presses hard FUNERALS, 12
eve from noon to dewy e. DECLINE, 5; MILTON, J, 38
Eve E.…the mother of all living BIBLE, 152
When E. ate this particular apple LAWRENCE, D, 9; SEX, 64
even Deep and crisp and e. CHRISTMAS, 16
Don't get mad, get e. REVENGE, 13
evening e. is spread out against the sky DEPARTURE, 6; ELIOT, T, 11
in the e.…cut down, dried up PSALMS, 49
Now came still E. on DAY, 11; MILTON, J, 46
Soup of the e. CARROLL, L, 18; FOOD, 21
the quiet-coloured end of e. BROWNING, R, 34; DAY, 3
thou art fairer than the e. air MARLOWE, C, 3
event greatest e.…that ever happened FRENCH REVOLUTION, 4
hurries to the main e. HORACE, 7; PLAYS, 7
one far-off divine e. DESTINY, 27; TENNYSON, 38
thinking too precisely on th' e. COWARDICE, 9; SHAKESPEARE, 101
eventide Abide with me; fast falls the e. RELIGION, 64
events all great e. and personalities in…history reappear HISTORY, 21; MARX, K, 6
E. which…never happened HISTORY, 18; INGE, W, 1
many e. in the womb of time SHAKESPEARE, 280
There are only three e. in a man's life LA BRUYERE, J, 6; LIFE AND DEATH, 21
When in the course of human e., it becomes necessary INDEPENDENCE, 3; JEFFERSON, T, 4
ever Are you now or have you e. been a member COMMUNISM, 1
for e. hold his peace BOOK OF COMMON PRAYER, 25; OPPORTUNITY, 11
I go on for e. TENNYSON, 6
Everest skied down Mount E. in the nude LOVE, 115
the summit of E. was hardly the place PHOTOGRAPHY, 5
treating the *mons Veneris* as…Mount E. HUXLEY, A, 16; SEX, 53
everlasting God from e. PSALMS, 48
every E. day in e. way REMEDIES, 25
God bless us, e. one BLESSING, 8; DICKENS, C, 10
everybody E. has got to die.… Now what LAST WORDS, 78
E. is always in favour of general economy THRIFT, 8
E. is sleeping with everybody else POPULAR MUSIC, 16
E. was up to something COWARD, N, 9; INTRIGUE, 2
Everyman E., I will go with thee, and be thy guide ANONYMOUS, 17; GUIDANCE, 1
everyone e. against e. HOBBES, T, 1; HUMAN CONDITION, 12
I hate e. equally HATE, 4; PREJUDICE, 5
stop e. from doing it HERBERT, A, 2; PERVERSITY, 4
everything A place for e. ORDER, 6
destroying nearly e. CHESTERTON, G, 5; CIVILIZATION, 4
E. has been discussed and analysed BOOKS, 2
e. in its place ORDER, 6
E. is funny HUMOUR, 27; ROGERS, W, 4
E. is only for a day MARCUS AURELIUS ANTONINUS, 7; TRANSIENCE, 2
E.'s got a moral CARROLL, L, 13; PURPOSE, 1
e. that lives is holy BLAKE, W, 3; LIFE, 17
God made e. out of nothing CREATION, 16
making e. the concern of all RESPONSIBILITY, 17; SOLZHENITSYN, A, 15
men we like are good for e. HALIFAX, 2; SUBJECTIVITY, 3
One fifth of the people are against e. OPPOSITION, 4
She knows e. and can see through e. PANKHURST, C, 1
Was E. by starts DRYDEN, J, 9; HUMAN NATURE, 11
evidence If ever there was a case of clearer e. NONSENSE, 2
Most men…give e. against their own understanding HALIFAX, 8; SPEECH, 12

Some circumstantial e. is very strong PROOF, 6
evil about the dreadful wood /Of conscious e. AUDEN, W, 14; GUILT, 2
as gods, knowing good and e. BIBLE, 149
a thing may look e. in theory BURKE, E, 28; THEORY, 2
belief in a supernatural source of e. CONRAD, J, 7; EVIL, 9
deliver us from e. BIBLE, 367; PRAYER, 6
E., be thou my Good EVIL, 15; MILTON, J, 44
E. be to him who e. thinks EVIL, 1
E. comes at leisure DISEASE, 12
E. comes...like the disease CHESTERTON, G, 27; GOOD AND EVIL, 3
e. communications corrupt good manners BIBLE, 40
e. is wrought by want of thought EVIL, 13; HOOD, T, 8
e. men and seducers BIBLE, 513; EVIL, 5
first to Touch for the E. according to costome REMEDIES, 29
Good can imagine E. GOOD AND EVIL, 2
Government,...is but a necessary e. GOVERNMENT, 29
He who passively accepts e. EVIL, 14
how can ye, being e., speak good BIBLE, 389
know all the e. he does EVIL, 17; ROCHEFOUCAULD, 21
love of money is the root of all e. BIBLE, 511; MONEY, 11
Man's capacity for e. makes democracy necessary DEMOCRACY, 18
men loved darkness...because their deeds were e. BIBLE, 246; EVIL, 6
Men's e. manners live in brass MEMORIALS, 16; SHAKESPEARE, 143
No man is justified in doing e. EXPEDIENCY, 7; ROOSEVELT, T, 3
Only lies and e. come from letting people off MURDOCH, I, 5
party is a political e. POLITICS, 21
Put off the e. hour PROCRASTINATION, 2; PROVERBS, 345
science is...neither a potential for good nor for e. SCIENCE, 83
Socrates is a doer of e., who corrupts the youth SOCRATES, 3
The e. that men do lives after them EVIL, 19; SHAKESPEARE, 155
the fear of one e. VICE, 4
The fearsome...*banality of e.* EVIL, 3
the love of money is the root of all e. BUTLER, S, 6; MONEY, 14
There is no e. in the atom NUCLEAR WEAPONS, 22; STEVENSON, A, 5
the righteous is taken away from the e. to come BIBLE, 215
Vice itself lost half its e. BURKE, E, 8; VICE, 6
we are the origin of all coming e. HUMAN NATURE, 17; JUNG, C, 11
who hath not seen the e. work under the sun BIBLE, 68; EVIL, 4
woe unto them that call e. good BIBLE, 196; LYING, 7
evils death,...the least of all e. BACON, F, 6; DEATH, 27
He...must expect new e. BACON, F, 30; INNOVATION, 1
There exist some e. so terrible...that we dare not think of them LA BRUYERE, J, 10; MISFORTUNE, 14
To great e. we submit; we resent little provocations HAZLITT, W, 7; TRIVIALITY, 10
We cannot remove the e. of capitalism CAPITALISM, 10; KINNOCK, N, 5
Whenever I'm caught between two e. VICE, 15; WEST, M, 18
Work banishes those three great e. VOLTAIRE, 10; WORK, 37
evolution Coolidge is a better example of e. POLITICIANS, 112; ROGERS, W, 6
E. is far more important than living EVOLUTION, 21
e. of the human race MANKIND, 21
our views on e. would be very different EVOLUTION, 17
sex...must itself be subject...to e. SEXES, 5
Some call it E. EVOLUTION, 4
The tide of e. carries everything before it EVOLUTION, 24
evolve Species do not e. toward perfection SURVIVAL, 6
evolved Both main branches of survival machines e. EVOLUTION, 12
ewe one little e. lamb ANIMALS, 5
exact Politics is not an e. science POLITICS, 19
exaggerate master of the English language...not need to e. LANGUAGE, 24
exaggerated Reports of my death are greatly e. OBITUARIES, 11; TWAIN, M, 18
exalted Every valley shall be e. BIBLE, 210
I will be e. among the heathen PSALMS, 28
examine e. our own 'difficulties with the truth GERMANY, 15
One should e. oneself...before...condemning others MOLIERE, 7; SELF, 14
example E. is the school of mankind BURKE, E, 3; EXAMPLE, 2
George the Third......*may profit by their e.* TREASON, 9
exasperating that the afterlife will be any less e. AFTERLIFE, 3; COWARD, N, 3
excel daring to e. EXCELLENCE, 2
excellence acute limited e. at twenty-one FITZGERALD, F, 7; PRECOCITY, 2
liberty as an essential condition of e. OXFORD, 9
excellences e. carried to an excess COLERIDGE, S, 20
e. carried to an excess WRITERS, 7
excellent everything that's e. GILBERT, W, 18; LAW, 18
very e. things are spoken of thee, thou city of God PSALMS, 47
excelsior A banner with the strange device, /E. AMBITION, 14; LONGFELLOW, H, 7
exception I never forget a face, but I'll make an e. MARX, G, 20; MEMORY, 12
Man is an e. MANKIND, 17
The e. proves the rule PROVERBS, 389; RULES, 1
excess excellences carried to an e. COLERIDGE, S, 20
e. is most exhilarating ANOUILH, J, 6; EXCESS, 3
Give me e. of it MUSIC, 57; SHAKESPEARE, 336
In charity there is no e. BACON, F, 27; CHARITY, 4
Nothing in e. EXCESS, 1
Nothing succeeds like e. WILDE, O, 61
The road of e. BLAKE, W, 25; EXCESS, 4
'Tis not the drinking...but the e. EXCESS, 9; SELDEN, J, 8
exchange conversation must be an e. of thought CONVERSATION, 7
I stopped...to e. ideas HEINE, H, 3; INFERIORITY, 1
exchequer Chancellor of the E. TAXATION, 8
exciting He found it less e. COWARDICE, 4; GILBERT, W, 1
Jam today, and men aren't at their most e. PROMISES, 7
woman can look both moral and e. APPEARANCE, 25
exclude we cannot e. the intellect from...any of our functions INTELLECT, 8
excluded when you have e. the impossible DOYLE, A, 3; TRUTH, 22
exclusive the most e. club there is ENGLISH, 33; NASH, O, 3
excuse bet he's just using that as an e. DEATH, 107; MARX, G, 7
E. my dust PARKER, D, 31
execute ask all Moslems to e. them CENSORSHIP, 8
execution some are daily led to e. EXECUTION, 30; RALEIGH, W, 4
executioner I am mine own E. DONNE, J, 6; SELF, 9
executioners victims who respect their e. RESPECT, 3; SARTRE, J, 4
executive the e. expression of human immaturity BRITTAIN, V, 5; POLITICS, 22
exemplary thoroughgoing and e. JEFFERSON, T, 1
exercise E. is bunk SPORT AND GAMES, 17
I get my e. acting as a pallbearer LAZINESS, 4
Prostitution...provides fresh air and wholesome e. HELLER, J, 7; SEX, 49
The only e. I get is when I take the studs out of one shirt LAZINESS, 5
exertion success depends...upon individual initiative and e. EFFORT, 5; SUCCESS, 23
the e. is too much for me LAUGHTER, 10; PEACOCK, T, 9
exhibitionist he was sincerely shy and naively e. LAWRENCE, T, 5
exile cause of Ovid's sudden e. is not known OVID, 2
his attitude of a king in e. DE GAULLE, C, 1
New York...where every one is an e. AMERICA, 18
exist Facts do not cease to e. FACTS, 3; HUXLEY, A, 32
Failure? – the possibilities do not e. FAILURE, 11
I e. by what I think SARTRE, J, 9; THINKING, 16
I feel...a certain difficulty in continuing to e. LAST WORDS, 36
If God did not e. GOD, 52; VOLTAIRE, 14
liberty cannot long e. BURKE, E, 22; CORRUPTION, 1
No more things should be presumed to e. SIMPLICITY, 6
existence A God who let us prove his e. GOD, 16
disregard for the necessities of e. CIVILIZATION, 10; MAUGHAM, W, 14
experimental reasoning, concerning...e. PHILOSOPHY, 3
doubted the e. of the Deity SCIENTISTS, 6
individual e. goes out in a lonely spasm DEATH, 85
Let us contemplate e. DICKENS, C, 25; EXISTENCE, 2
mere e. is swollen to a horror IDEALISM, 5; LAWRENCE, D, 23
the sole purpose of human e. is to kindle a light EXISTENCE, 3; JUNG, C, 4
the struggle for e. DARWIN, C, 9; EVOLUTION, 9
to deny the e. of an unseen kingdom is bad BUTLER, S, 3; SPECULATION, 1
to do something is to create e. EXISTENCE, 5; SARTRE, J, 10

woman's whole e. BYRON, 20; LOVE, 47
exit E., pursued by a bear SHAKESPEARE, 353
Few men of action have been able to make a graceful e. WORK, 22
exits They have their e. and their entrances SHAKESPEARE, 48
expect all any reasonable child can e. ORTON, J, 2; SEX, 90
I e. a judgment DICKENS, C, 6
people e. me to neigh, grind my teeth HORSES, 1
the audience want to be surprised…by things that they e. PLAYS, 3
you e. other people to be…to your liking TOLERANCE, 4
expectation the distinction between hope and e. REALISM, 3
expectations the difference between our talents and our e. DISAPPOINTMENT, 1
expects Blessed is the man who e. nothing EXPECTATION, 6; POPE, A, 60
England e. every man will do his duty DUTY, 5; NELSON, H, 4
expediency the most useful thing about a principle… sacrificed to e. EXPEDIENCY, 5; MAUGHAM, W, 4
expedient all things are not e. BIBLE, 34
e. that one man should die for the people BIBLE, 264
expendable British Government sees black people as e. RACISM, 30
expenditure annual e. nineteen nineteen six DICKENS, C, 13; ECONOMICS, 8
in favour of…particular e. THRIFT, 8
expense flatterers live at the e. of those who listen FLATTERY, 6; LA FONTAINE, J, 2
who /Would be at the e. of two GOD, 18
expensive The most e. habit in the world is celluloid not heroin CINEMA, 24
experience All e. is an arch EXPERIENCE, 21; TENNYSON, 80
An e. of women DOYLE, A, 14; EXPERIENCE, 12
E. is a good teacher EXPERIENCE, 6
E. is never limited EXPERIENCE, 17; JAMES, H, 11
E. isn't interesting EXPERIENCE, 9
E. is the best teacher PROVERBS, 145
E. is the mother EXPERIENCE, 3; PROVERBS, 146
I can't see that it's wrong to give him a little legal e. KENNEDY, J, 4; NEPOTISM, 2
Language is not simply a reporting device for e. LANGUAGE, 52
love like other arts requires e. LOVE, 98
moment's insight…worth a life's e. EXPERIENCE, 16
my e. of life has been drawn from life itself BEERBOHM, M, 16; EXPERIENCE, 8
Notwithstanding the poverty of my…e. CONTENTMENT, 5
plausible happiness /Of a new e. SPENDER, S, 3
Reason, Observation, and E. SCIENCE, 54
she has written…a few moments of human e. PARKER, D, 1
the light which e. gives COLERIDGE, S, 23; EXPERIENCE, 11
The triumph of hope over e. JOHNSON, S, 81; MARRIAGE, 91
What we call e. MISTAKES, 9
experiences the child should be allowed to meet the real e. of life CHILDREN, 42
experiment a great social and economic e. ALCOHOL, 39
A theory can be proved by e. EINSTEIN, A, 11; THEORY, 3
existence remains a…lamentable e. HAPPINESS, 24; SANTAYANA, G, 5
E. alone crowns the efforts of medicine MEDICINE, 74
no path leads from e. to…theory EINSTEIN, A, 11; THEORY, 3
to desist from the e. in despair LAMB, C, 6; SCOTS, 7
experimental *e. reasoning, concerning matter of fact and existence* PHILOSOPHY, 3
experimented I e. with marijuana CLINTON, B, 4
experiments divers e. in Mr Boyle's Pneumatic Engine SCIENTISTS, 10
expert An e.…has made all the mistakes…in a very narrow field EXPERTS, 2
An e.…knows some of the worst mistakes that can be made EXPERTS, 3
e. is one who knows more KNOWLEDGE, 9
Prince Philip.…a world e. on leisure KINNOCK, N, 6; ROYALTY, 76
experts administration must be entrusted to e. GOVERNMENT, 45
expired It's e. DEATH, 113
explain A mission to e. PURPOSE, 4
If you can't e. it, how can you take credit FOOTBALL, 8
Never complain and never e. EXPLANATIONS, 1
explanation When there is no e., they give it a name WORDS, 11
explanations less hideous than e. EXPLANATIONS, 2
exploitation Capitalism is the e. of man by man CAPITALISM, 1
export I integrate the current e. drive BETJEMAN, J, 5; BUSINESS, 4
to e. revolution is nonsense REVOLUTION, 12
exposes A man who e. himself when he is intoxicated DRUNKENNESS, 20; JOHNSON, S, 129
ex-president No candidate…elected e. by such a large majority DEFEAT, 15
expression supreme e. of the mediocrity RUSSIA, 17; TROTSKY, L, 10
the executive e. of human immaturity BRITTAIN, V, 5; POLITICS, 22
expressions the most eloquent e. KEATS, J, 4
expulsion arbitrary arrest and e. SOLZHENITSYN, A, 1
exquisite e. showman minus the show POUND, E, 1
It is e., and it leaves one unsatisfied SMOKING, 37; WILDE, O, 51
the e. touch…is denied to me SCOTT, W, 5; WRITERS, 85
ex-secretary attacking an e. of state ACHESON, D, 3; REPARTEE, 1
exterminate E. all brutes CONRAD, J, 1; RUTHLESSNESS, 3
e.…the treacherous English WAR, 184; WILHELM II, 4
extinct a convention which says you must not make species e. CONSERVATION, 9
the Tasmanians…are now e. ADULTERY, 5; MAUGHAM, W, 1
extinguished glory of Europe is e. BURKE, E, 9; EUROPE, 2
the flame of French resistance must not…be e. WORLD WAR II, 26
extinguishers those twin e. of science SCIENCE, 11
extraordinary Little minds are interested in the e. TRIVIALITY, 11
the most e. collection of talent TALENT, 7
this is an e. man JOHNSON, S, 148
extravagance e.…thrift and adventure THRIFT, 6
Our love of what is beautiful does not lead to e. RESULTS, 4
extreme E. remedies…for extreme diseases REMEDIES, 32
extremism e. in the defence of liberty is no vice EXCESS, 5
exuberance E. is Beauty BEAUTY, 10; BLAKE, W, 29
e. of his own verbosity DISRAELI, B, 32; VERBOSITY, 3
exultations Thy friends are e., agonies, /And love WORDSWORTH, W, 63
ex-wife no fury like an e. searching for a new lover CONNOLLY, C, 17; WOMEN, 35
eye A custom loathsome to the e., hateful to the nose SMOKING, 16
a limit to what one can listen to with the naked e. SPARK, M, 12
A person may be indebted for a nose or an e.,…to a great-aunt FAMILY, 28; HAZLITT, W, 11
a sober colouring from an e. MORTALITY, 21; WORDSWORTH, W, 33
as the apple of his e. BIBLE, 59; SUPPORT, 1
clapped the glass to his sightless e. BLINDNESS, 12; NEWBOLT, H, 1
Every tear from every e. BLAKE, W, 7; SORROW, 3
e. for e. BIBLE, 116; RETRIBUTION, 3
e. hath not seen BIBLE, 25
He had but one e. APPEARANCE, 23; DICKENS, C, 30
he that made the e., shall he not see PSALMS, 53
his keener e. /The axe's edge did try EXECUTION, 22; MARVELL, A, 4
I have only one e. NELSON, H, 3
keep me as the apple of an e. PSALMS, 6
less in this than meets the e. BANKHEAD, T, 8; CRITICISM, 3
man who looks you…in the e.…hiding something INSINCERITY, 1
nearest thing…to the e. of God SHAKESPEARE, 15
neither e. to see, nor tongue to speak HOUSES OF PARLIAMENT, 14
such beauty as a woman's e. LEARNING, 16; SHAKESPEARE, 199
The e. is bigger GREED, 4; PROVERBS, 390
the e.…shall see me no more BIBLE, 226; EYES, 4
There is a road from the e. to the heart CHESTERTON, G, 9
the sort of e. that can open an oyster at sixty paces APPEARANCE, 75; WODEHOUSE, P, 6
the twinkling of an e. PSALMS, 17
Who formed the curious texture of the e. EYES, 7
with an e. made quiet…/We see into the life of things DEATH, 184; WORDSWORTH, W, 12
with the jaundiced e. PASSION, 11; TENNYSON, 52
eyelashes They have perfect e. WOMEN, 22

eyeless E. in Gaza BLINDNESS, 7; MILTON, J, 57
eyelids tir'd e. upon tir'd eyes MUSIC, 62; TENNYSON, 55
When she raises her e. COLETTE, S, 2; SEX, 29
the opening e. of the morn DAY, 10; MILTON, J, 22
eyes And on his grave, with shining e. ARNOLD, M, 30; DEATH, 26
and throws…sand in their e. SLEEP, 18
close my e., open my legs and think of England SEX, 51
Dead e. and a red beard LAWRENCE, D, 1
Drink to me only with thine e. JONSON, B, 7; LOVE, 93
e. have they, and see not PSALMS, 64
Fear has many e. FEAR, 6
fortune and men's e. DISCONTENT, 8; SHAKESPEARE, 362
God be in my e., /And in my looking ANONYMOUS, 20; GOD, 2
guard over your e. and ears BRONTE, A, 6
I first set my e. on sweet Molly Malone ANONYMOUS, 47; BUSINESS, 1; IRELAND, 2
I was e. to the blind BIBLE, 235
I will lift up mine e. unto the hills PSALMS, 67
Look at that man's e. POLITICIANS, 99
Look not in my e., for fear /They mirror true the sight I see HOUSMAN, A, 9; LOVE, 88
Love looks not with the e. LOVE, 147; SHAKESPEARE, 260
Mine e. have seen the glory of the coming of the Lord GOD, 27
My e. are dim BLINDNESS, 3
Open your e. SATISFACTION, 5
pearls that were his e. DEATH, 154; SHAKESPEARE, 323
That youthful sparkle in his e. EYES, 5
the creature hath a purpose and its e. are bright with it KEATS, J, 69; PURPOSE, 6
The e. are the window EYES, 1; PROVERBS, 391; SOUL, 1
the e. are the windows of the soul BEERBOHM, M, 12; EYES, 3
the e. of the blind shall be opened BIBLE, 209
The e. that shone, /Now dimmed and gone MOORE, T, 7; NOSTALGIA, 17
The night has a thousand e. SUN, 1
the whites of their e. WAR, 131
Thy rapt soul sitting in thine e. MILTON, J, 12; SOUL, 11
Two lovely black e. VIOLENCE, 6
When Byron's e. were shut in death BYRON, 1
you'll wear your e. out STARING, 2; ZOLA, 1
Your e. shine like the pants COMPLIMENTS, 18; MARX, G, 4
eyesight with blinded e. TENNYSON, 53
Eyre I wish you had not sent me Jane E. WRITERS, 89

F

Fabian Britain…F. Society writ large BRITAIN, 8
Fabians A good man fallen among F. LENIN, V, 10; WRITERS, 68
fabric chemical barrage has been hurled against the f. of life CARSON, R, 3; ECOLOGY, 2
the baseless f. of this vision MORTALITY, 17; SHAKESPEARE, 327
face a garden in her f. ADMIRATION, 4; CAMPION, T, 2
A good f. is a letter of recommendation BEAUTY, 2; PROVERBS, 23
And hid his f. amid a crowd of stars LOVE, 179; YEATS, W, 34
At 50, everyone has the f. he deserves AGE, 66; ORWELL, G, 36
everybody's f. but their own SATIRE, 3; SWIFT, J, 3
every man is responsible for his f. APPEARANCE, 14; CAMUS, A, 4
False f. must hide DECEPTION, 7; SHAKESPEARE, 212
from whose f. the earth and the heaven fled BIBLE, 472
he turned his f. to the wall BIBLE, 304
I have looked upon the f. of Agamemnon HISTORY, 25
I never forget a f., but I'll make an exception MARX, G, 20
Look in my f.; my name is Might-have-been DISAPPOINTMENT, 7; ROSSETTI, D, 3
Looks the whole world in the f. LONGFELLOW, H, 18; RIGHTEOUSNESS, 9
My f. is my fortune, sir, she said NURSERY RHYMES, 70
my f. looks like a wedding cake left out in the rain APPEARANCE, 7
painting a f. and not washing APPEARANCE, 27
Socialism with a human f. COMMUNISM, 4; SOCIALISM, 7
the f. that launch'd a thousand ships BEAUTY, 30; MARLOWE, C, 2
the f. that she keeps in a jar by the door COSMETICS, 4
The human f. is…a whole cluster of faces MANKIND, 47
The loveliest f.…will not please APPEARANCES, 10
There is not any book /Or f. DEATH, 175
till my f. falls off OLD AGE, 29
to order a new stamp…with my f. on it TRIVIALITY, 12
whole life shows in your f. AGE, 9; APPEARANCE, 8
faces All, all are gone, the old familiar f. LAMB, C, 19; NOSTALGIA, 13
among so many million of f. APPEARANCE, 13; BROWNE, T, 6
grind the f. of the poor CAPITALISM, 2
facetious You must not think me…foolish because I am f. SERIOUSNESS, 3; SMITH, S, 17
fact the slaying of a beautiful hypothesis by an ugly f. HUXLEY, T, 1; SCIENCE, 52
Womanhood…the great f. in her life FEMINISM, 33
faction f. is the worst of all parties POLITICS, 21
To die for f. DRYDEN, J, 15; EXECUTION, 9
factors rationality…f. governing human behaviour HUMAN NATURE, 13
factory In the f. we make cosmetics COSMETICS, 5
facts Comment is free but f. are sacred FACTS, 6; JOURNALISM, 31
F. alone are wanted in life DICKENS, C, 21; FACTS, 1
F. are not science FACTS, 2
F. are ventriloquists' dummies FACTS, 4
F. do not cease to exist FACTS, 3; HUXLEY, A, 32
F. speak louder than statistics FACTS, 7; STATISTICS, 12
Learn, compare, collect the f. EDUCATION, 72
Once a newspaper touches a story, the f. are lost FACTS, 5; JOURNALISM, 24
phantom beings loaded up with f. SCIENCE, 93
Science is not to be regarded merely as a storehouse of f. SCIENCE, 45
fad They always have some new f. DOCTORS, 47
fade the cheek that doth not f. APPEARANCE, 35; KEATS, J, 18
faded interviewing a f. female in a damp basement INSULTS, 57
fading Why so large cost…upon thy f. mansion spend APPEARANCE, 62
fads passing f. and fancies DIETING, 7
fags Nothing but old f. and cabbage-stumps CRITICISM, 34; WRITING, 30
fail If they succeed, they f. HOMOSEXUALITY, 8
Others must f. RUTHLESSNESS, 7; VIDAL, G, 6
to f. conventionally KEYNES, J, 5; ORTHODOXY, 3
failed Here lies Joseph, who f. in everything he undertook FAILURE, 7
Light that F. KIPLING, R, 20
faileth charity never f. BIBLE, 38; CHARITY, 7
fails If thy heart f. thee AMBITION, 8; ELIZABETH I, 12
Nothing f. like success SUCCESS, 21
failure All political lives…end in f. POLITICIANS, 19; POLITICS, 83
crime…not to avoid f. FAILURE, 12
F. is inevitable FAILURE, 10
F.? – the possibilities do not exist FAILURE, 11
no success like f. DYLAN, B, 8; FAILURE, 4
Shakespeare's so bloody difficult, and I don't like f. FAILURE, 6
utterly unspoiled by f. FAILURE, 3; POLITICIANS, 74
we all contain f. and death within us AGE, 60
women…handicapped by a fear of f. SUCCESS, 26
faint Damn with f. praise CRITICISM, 51; POPE, A, 14
fair All is f. LOVE, 1; PROVERBS, 34
all's f. in love and war JUSTICE, 8
Every man's house will be f. and decent MORRIS, W, 4
Fair is foul, and foul is f. APPEARANCES, 30
F. stood the wind for France BOATS, 5
Grief has turned her f. APPEARANCE, 74; WILDE, O, 74
how f.…art thou, O love, for delights BIBLE, 498
Monday's child is f. of face CHILDREN, 50; NURSERY RHYMES, 35
Serious sport has nothing to do with f. play ORWELL, G, 32; SPORT AND GAMES, 33
So foul and f. a day SHAKESPEARE, 203; WEATHER, 22
That's only f. ASHDOWN, P, 4
the Brave deserves the F. COURAGE, 13; DRYDEN, J, 16
the name of Vanity F. BUNYAN, J, 5; TRIVIALITY, 3
There was a f. maid dwellin' ANONYMOUS, 49; LOVE, 13
Whitehall…our attempts to be f. to everybody BRITAIN, 3; MEMORIALS, 2
fairer I can't say no f. than that DICKENS, C, 18
thou art f. than the evening air MARLOWE, C, 3
fairest the f. things have the worst fate TRANSIENCE, 18
fairies Do you believe in f. FAIRIES, 3
I don't believe in f. BARRIE, J, 4; FAIRIES, 1
the beginning of f. BARRIE, J, 3; FAIRIES, 2

There are f. at the bottom of our garden FAIRIES, 4
fairy A myth is, of course, not a f. story MYTHS, 2
the f. tales of science EXPERIENCE, 20; TENNYSON, 49
fairyland The Fleet's lit up. It is like f. NAVY, 11
faith a life of doubt diversified by f. BROWNING, R, 12; DOUBT, 5
an absolute f. that all things are possible to God EDDY, M, 1; FAITH, 13
And f. shines equal BRONTE, E, 3; COURAGE, 4
by f. the walls of Jericho fell down BIBLE, 188; FAITH, 5
F.…an illogical belief in…the improbable FAITH, 21; MENCKEN, H, 14
F. consists in believing when it is beyond the power of reason to believe FAITH, 32; VOLTAIRE, 25
f., if it hath not works, is dead FAITH, 6
f. is the substance of things hoped for BIBLE, 187; FAITH, 3
f. unfaithful kept him falsely true TENNYSON, 17; UNFAITHFULNESS, 8
F. will move mountains FAITH, 1; PROVERBS, 147
f. without doubt is nothing but death FAITH, 30
future states…left to f. BYRON, 22
Lincoln had f. in time LINCOLN, A, 3
no need for any other f. than…f. in human beings BUCK, P, 7; FAITH, 12
Nothing in life is more wonderful than f. FAITH, 24
now abideth f., hope, charity BIBLE, 38; CHARITY, 7
O thou of little f., wherefore didst thou doubt BIBLE, 395; DOUBT, 3
O ye of little f. BIBLE, 370; BIBLE, 383; FAITH, 9
Reason is itself a matter of f. CHESTERTON, G, 33; REASON, 2
science and f. exclude one another FAITH, 31
the f. and morals hold /Which Milton held FREEDOM, 63; WORDSWORTH, W, 55
the f., prayer and self-dedication of the King ROYALTY, 26
The prayer of f. shall save the sick FAITH, 7
There can be no scientific dispute with respect to f. FAITH, 31
thy f. hath saved thee BIBLE, 322
'Tis not the dying for a f. FAITH, 29; THACKERAY, W, 3
to those who yield it an implicit or even a partial f. FAITH, 16
we walk by f., not by sight BIBLE, 44; FAITH, 2
When your ladyship's f. has removed them CHESTERFIELD, P, 22; RELIGION, 27
whoever is moved by f. to assent to it CHRISTIANITY, 43; HUME, D, 3
'You can't probe for f. with a scalpel.' DOCTORS, 38
faithful f. in love…dauntless in war CHIVALRY, 12; SCOTT, W, 15
f. to thee, Cynara FAITHFULNESS, 3
happiness of man that he be mentally f. INTEGRITY, 5
If this man is not f. to his God LOYALTY, 12
if you had been f. LOVE, 132
my heart shall be /The f. compass FAITHFULNESS, 4; GAY, J, 12
O come all ye f. CHRISTMAS, 19
seldom f. if they are in the least attractive UNFAITHFULNESS, 5
thou good and f. servant BIBLE, 418; SERVICE, 1
Translations (like wives) are seldom f. CAMPBELL, R, 4; TRANSLATION, 2
faithfully those things which we ask f. BOOK OF COMMON PRAYER, 7
faithfulness his f. and truth shall be thy shield and buckler PSALMS, 51
fake a sonorous f. as a writer LAWRENCE, T, 1
If I like it…it's mine. If I don't…it's a f. PAINTING, 12
faking worst crime is f. it SUICIDE, 10
fakir It is nauseating to see Mr Gandhi…posing as a f. GANDHI, M, 2
Falklands F.…a fight between two bald men over a comb WAR, 23
fall and an haughty spirit before a f. BIBLE, 451; PRIDE, 1
a thousand shall f. beside thee PSALMS, 51
Fain would I climb, yet fear I to f. AMBITION, 20; RALEIGH, W, 2
gift of wings, and you learn…that you will not f. WRITERS, 30
The airplane stays up because it doesn't have the time to f. SCIENCE, 100
Whenever you f., pick up something OPPORTUNITY, 8
fallacy great f. is that the game is…about winning FOOTBALL, 4
fallen A good man f. among Fabians LENIN, V, 10; WRITERS, 68
y-f. out of heigh degree. Into miserie CHAUCER, G, 15; MISFORTUNE, 7
falleth woe to him that is alone when he f. BIBLE, 69; FRIENDSHIP, 8
falling The glass is f. hour by hour REALISM, 4
We were f. women LOVE, 19
fallow lie f. for a while REST, 4
false beware of f. prophets BIBLE, 378; DECEPTION, 2
F. face must hide what the f. heart DECEPTION, 7; SHAKESPEARE, 212
f. to his friends…true to the public HONESTY, 3
natural f. teeth TEETH, 4
She wore f. hair and that red ROYALTY, 70
The religions we call f. were once true EMERSON, R, 6; RELIGION, 40
the true and the f. and…extracting the plausible LLOYD GEORGE, D, 2
Thou canst not then be f. INTEGRITY, 6; SHAKESPEARE, 75
thou shalt not bear f. witness BIBLE, 115; GOD, 12
True and F. are attributes of speech, not of things HOBBES, T, 2; TRUTH, 29
Vain wisdom all, and f. philosophy MILTON, J, 41; WISDOM, 22
falsehood Let her and F. grapple MILTON, J, 8; TRUTH, 37
falsely a verb meaning 'to believe f.' BELIEF, 13
falsifying f. this one fact about my life made me feel phoney AGE, 88
Falstaff F. sweats to death OBESITY, 14; SHAKESPEARE, 111
fame blush to find it f. GOOD, 15; POPE, A, 10
F. is a powerful aphrodisiac FAME, 16; GREENE, G, 10
F. is like a river BACON, F, 40; FAME, 4
F. is sometimes like unto a…mushroom FAME, 14
F. is the spur FAME, 20; MILTON, J, 25
Here rests…/A youth to fortune and to f. unknown DEATH, 75; GRAY, T, 8
Love of f. is the last thing…to be parted from FAME, 30; TACITUS, C, 3
One of the drawbacks of F. FAME, 19; MELBA, N, 3
one whom f. has not corrupted CURIE, M, 2
The book written against f.…has the author's name on the title-page EMERSON, R, 20; HYPOCRISY, 11
familiar mine own f. friend PSALMS, 25
old f. faces LAMB, C, 19; NOSTALGIA, 13
familiarity F. breeds contempt FAMILIARITY, 1; PROVERBS, 148
F. breeds contempt – and children SEX, 122; TWAIN, M, 12
I like f. FAMILIARITY, 3
families All happy f. resemble one another FAMILY, 59; TOLSTOY, L, 5
Good f. are generally worse than any others FAMILY, 29; HOPE, A, 8
Murder, like talent, seems…to run in f. MURDER, 9
the best-regulated f. ACCIDENTS, 3; DICKENS, C, 17
There are only two f. in the world CERVANTES, M, 20
family A f. with the wrong members in control ENGLAND, 37; ORWELL, G, 14
as if they took the f. to the laundry CENSORSHIP, 5
a tense and peculiar f., the Oedipuses BEERBOHM, M, 21; CLASSICS, 1
average American loves his f. TWAIN, M, 1
disease in the f. IRELAND, 27
educate a woman you educate a f. EDUCATION, 59; WOMEN, 82
if a f. is held together…it's the woman who's doing it FAMILY, 19
Mother is the dead heart of the f. GREER, G, 3; MOTHERHOOD, 7
my f. begins with me ANCESTRY, 3
streak of madness in the f. MADNESS, 5
the dead heart of the f. FEMINISM, 11
the f. of civilized nations RUSSIA, 14
the f.…source of all our discontents FAMILY, 34
The f. that prays together FAMILY, 4; PROVERBS, 392
there would never be more than *three* in a f. SEXES, 16
The sink is the great symbol of the bloodiness of f. life FAMILY, 40
wasn't even aware of the Year of the F. FAMILY, 18
famine f. was sore in the land BIBLE, 179
They that die by f. die by inches HUNGER, 6
you look as if there were f. in the land APPEARANCE, 64; SHAW, G, 52
famous everyone will be f. for 15 minutes FAME, 36
get rich, get f. and get laid FAME, 15; GELDOF, B, 2
I awoke…found myself f. BYRON, 45; FAME, 8
I haven't made any friends since becoming f. FAME, 27
I'm never going to be f. FAME, 23; PARKER, D, 7
let us now praise f. men BIBLE, 91; PRAISE, 4
People either think I'm f. FAME, 18
so f., that it would permit me…to break wind in society BALZAC, H, 5; FAME, 5
What are you f. *for* FAME, 22; MURDOCH, I, 3

famylyarytie He used towardes every men…f. ROYALTY, 112
fan 'F. vaulting'…belongs to the 'Last-supper-carved-on-a-peach-stone' ARCHITECTURE, 7
throw an egg into an electric f. AMBITION, 10
fanatic f. is a man who FANATICISM, 2
f.…over-compensates a…doubt FANATICISM, 1
fanatics F. have their dreams KEATS, J, 15
when f. are on top there is no limit to oppression GOVERNMENT, 25; MENCKEN, H, 8
fancies All universal moral principles are idle f. MORALITY, 15
passing fads and f. DIETING, 7
fancy a young man's f.…turns to…love TENNYSON, 50
Ever let the f. roam DISCONTENT, 5; KEATS, J, 17
F. is…a mode of memory COLERIDGE, S, 6
f. wit will come POPE, A, 9; STUPIDITY, 13
hopeless f. feign'd NOSTALGIA, 26; TENNYSON, 63
In the Spring a young man's f. SEASONS, 24
Little of What You F. Does You Good PLEASURE, 21
sweetest Shakespeare, F.'s child MILTON, J, 19
fantastic the light f. toe MILTON, J, 16
fantasy live in a f. world REALITY, 6
live in a world of f. IMAGINATION, 6
far a f., f., better thing DICKENS, C, 57; EXECUTION, 8
how f. we may go too f. TACT, 5
The night is dark, and I am f. from home FAITH, 23
Thursday's child has f. to go NURSERY RHYMES, 35
Faraday remain plain Michael F. to the last TITLES, 3
farce But not as hard as f. ACTING, 13; LAST WORDS, 45
F. is the essential theatre THEATRE, 9
Parliament is the longest running f. GOVERNMENT, 37
the f. is over LAST WORDS, 71; RABELAIS, F, 9
the wine was a f. and the food a tragedy FOOD, 61; POWELL, A, 2
You just can't have a leisurely f. HUMOUR, 30
farewell F., a long f., to all my greatness HUMAN CONDITION, 24; SHAKESPEARE, 141
F., my poor hands LAST WORDS, 73; MUSICIANS, 13
F.! thou art too dear for my possessing PARTING, 11; SHAKESPEARE, 367
hail and f. GREETINGS, 2
long journey…must bid the company f. LAST WORDS, 74; RALEIGH, W, 7
farmer This is the f. sowing his corn NURSERY RHYMES, 61
To the average British f., organic farming is…as relevant as caviar ECOLOGY, 10
farmyard the f. world of sex ANIMALISM, 2
nothing to distinguish human society from the f. MANKIND, 60; SHAW, G, 12
far-reaching Life's short span forbids us to enter on f. hopes HORACE, 28; MORTALITY, 13
fart can't f. and chew gum at the same time INSULTS, 70; STUPIDITY, 5
farthing It is burning a f. candle at Dover CRITICISM, 25; JOHNSON, S, 68
steal one poor f. without excuse SIN, 22
fascinates I like work; it f. me IDLENESS, 8; JEROME, J, 7
fascination Philosophy…is a fight against…f. PHILOSOPHY, 24
war…will always have its f. WAR, 182; WILDE, O, 10
Fascism F.…future refusing to be born BEVAN, A, 11
F. is a religion MUSSOLINI, B, 4
F. is not an article for export MUSSOLINI, B, 5
F. means war FASCISM, 15
For F. the State is absolute FASCISM, 11
I believe very strongly in F. FASCISM, 2
the twentieth century will be…the century of F. FASCISM, 9; MUSSOLINI, B, 4
fascist Every communist has a f. frown SPARK, M, 4
Today in Britain, a f. has won an election FASCISM, 13
fashion after the f. of their country ENGLAND, 49
A love of f. makes the economy go round FASHION, 14
as…be…out of the f. FASHION, 5
Every man after his f. DIFFERENCE, 1; PROVERBS, 137
faithful to thee, Cynara! in my f. FAITHFULNESS, 3
F. is architecture CHANEL, C, 6; FASHION, 4
Nothing else holds f. SEX, 110; SHAKESPEARE, 335
simplicity of her approach to…f. CHANEL, C, 1
the unreasoning laws of markets and f. ART, 1
Thou art not for the f. of these times SELFLESSNESS, 6
true to you, darlin', in my f. FAITHFULNESS, 5; PORTER, C, 8
fashionable an idea…to be f. is ominous FASHION, 11; SANTAYANA, G, 13
fashions F. in sin change SIN, 16
F.…only induced epidemics FASHION, 13
I cannot…cut my conscience to fit this year's f. INTEGRITY, 3
Medicine is like a woman who changes with the f. MEDICINE, 12
fast f. till he is well GREED, 1
none so f. as stroke BOATS, 2
they stumble that run f. HASTE, 11; SHAKESPEARE, 315
US has to move very f. AMERICA, 24; KENNEDY, J, 7
faster the world would go round a deal f. CARROLL, L, 7
Will you walk a little f. CARROLL, L, 16; HASTE, 5
fastidious to set a chime of words tinkling in…a few f. people PURPOSE, 10; SMITH, L, 9
fasting F. is a medicine MEDICINE, 48
fat A f. paunch never bred a subtle mind OBESITY, 2
butter will only make us f. POWER POLITICS, 3
Enclosing every thin man, there's a f. man APPEARANCE, 71; WAUGH, E, 33
f. content of an avocado DIETING, 8
f. is sexy APPEARANCE, 11
in every f. man a thin one CONNOLLY, C, 18; OBESITY, 6
Let me have men about me that are f. MISTRUST, 10; SHAKESPEARE, 146
O f. white woman OBESITY, 9
Outside every f. man…an even fatter man OBESITY, 1
the f. of the land BIBLE, 180
The opera isn't over till the f. lady sings OPERA, 4
there's a f. man demanding elbow-room OBESITY, 16
there's a thin man inside every f. man OBESITY, 12; ORWELL, G, 9
Who's your f. friend INSULTS, 23; OBESITY, 3
you will come and find me f. and sleek HORACE, 18; PRESENT, 10
fatal Anno domini…the most f. complaint DEATH, 80
Nature has never put the f. question as to the meaning of their lives JUNG, C, 1; PURPOSE, 5
when he does it is nearly always f. LOVE AND DEATH, 5
fate count as profit every day that F. allows you HORACE, 29; PRESENT, 8
Each man the architect of his own f. RESPONSIBILITY, 3
exhausted my energy in tirades against f. INJUSTICE, 2
F. sits on these dark battlements DESTINY, 20
hostages given to f. FAMILY, 36
How wayward the decrees of F. THACKERAY, W, 8; WISDOM, 32
jeers at F. ENVY, 2
Leave the flesh to the f. it was fit for BROWNING, R, 51; SOUL, 5
master of his f. RESPONSIBILITY, 19; TENNYSON, 19
mortifying f. of most English universities LODGE, D, 2; NOVELTY, 6
Prudence…when one is determining the f. of others LACLOS, P, 2
the fairest things have the worst f. TRANSIENCE, 18
Their f. must always be the same as yours AUDEN, W, 25
the life-sentence which f. carries LAWRENCE, T, 6; LIFE AND DEATH, 23
the master of my f. RESPONSIBILITY, 8
the severity of f. DESTINY, 11
We may become the makers of our f. DESTINY, 18
when F. summons DRYDEN, J, 26; MORTALITY, 5
Wilde performed his life…even after f. had taken the plot out of his hands WILDE, O, 1
father a wise f. that knows his own child FAMILY, 53; SHAKESPEARE, 243
Box about: 'twill come to my f. anon FAMILY, 6
brood of Folly without f. MILTON, J, 11; PLEASURE, 25
Dreading to find its F. AUDEN, W, 14; GUILT, 2
easier for a f. to have children CHILDREN, 39
except to shoot rabbits and hit his f. on the jaw MASEFIELD, J, 1; NASTINESS, 5
F.…come home with me now ALCOHOL, 90
f., Harry, to that thought ACTION, 12
Full fathom five thy f. lies DEATH, 154; SHAKESPEARE, 323
God is…an exalted f. FREUD, S, 5; GOD, 23
have we not all one f. BIBLE, 342
he had rather /Have a turnip than his f. JOHNSON, S, 33; NONSENSE, 15
he loved the stags as…though he had been their f. OBITUARIES, 1
If poverty is the mother of crime, stupidity is its f. CRIME, 6; LA BRUYERE, J, 11
If the child is f. of the man CARTER, A, 11
In illness the physician is a f. DOCTORS, 11
in my F.'s house are many mansions BIBLE, 258; HEAVEN, 3

Compassion is not a sloppy, sentimental f. KINNOCK, N, 7; SOCIALISM, 14
forgetting...womanly f. and propriety VICTORIA, 7
feelings First f....most natural FIRST IMPRESSIONS, 2; LOUIS XIV, 3
feels A really intelligent man f. what other men...know INTELLIGENCE, 9; MONTESQUIEU, 2
fees I suppose that delightful immunity doubles their f. DOCTORS, 65
feet Alan will always land on somebody's f. HUMOUR, 56; PARKER, D, 23
An emperor ought at least to die on his f. LAST WORDS, 92
both f. firmly planted in the air IDEALISM, 8
die on your f. than to live on your knees COURAGE, 20; SELF-RESPECT, 2
Fear lent wings to his f. VIRGIL, 15
On your f. and let them know SOUTH AFRICA, 7
those f. in ancient time BLAKE, W, 33; ENGLAND, 7
feigning truest poetry is the most f. POETRY, 53; SHAKESPEARE, 55
felicity f. on the far side of baldness AGE, 85
likely to mar the general f. BUTLER, S, 19; MARRIAGE, 40
fell by faith the walls of Jericho f. down BIBLE, 188; FAITH, 5
crumbs which f. from the rich man's table BIBLE, 333; POVERTY AND WEALTH, 3
Doctor F. HATE, 1
f. among thieves BIBLE, 324
men f. out BUTLER, S, 1; WAR, 38
felled The poplars are f. COWPER, W, 19; TREES, 3
fellow f. of infinite jest MOURNING, 11; SHAKESPEARE, 106
fellows Boys are capital f. in their own way CHILDREN, 44; LAMB, C, 9
fellowship such a f. of good knights shall never be together LOSS, 3; MALORY, T, 4
felt hat baseball cap is just as valid as a f. FASHION, 9
female image of the f....all boobs GREER, G, 5
male and f. created he them CREATION, 6
the f. character...has no sense of justice SCHOPENHAUER, A, 4; WOMEN, 115
the f. of the species is more deadly than the male KIPLING, R, 10; WOMEN, 71
The fundamental fault of the f. character SCHOPENHAUER, A, 4; WOMEN, 115
the increase in drinking is to be laid mainly to the account of the f. sex ALCOHOL, 22
The seldom f. SEXES, 23
What f. heart can gold despise GRAY, T, 11; MATERIALISM, 12
You can now see the F. Eunuch the world over FEMINISM, 13
females F. get hired along procreative lines WOMAN'S ROLE, 5
human f. become sterile in the forties WOMEN, 68
feminine division of human nature into 'f.' HUMAN NATURE, 30
reflection of a boy too long exposed to f. eyes CARROLL, L, 1
Taste is the f. of genius FITZGERALD, E, 1; TASTE, 3
femininity most lesbians...cultivate the treasures of their f. HOMOSEXUALITY, 2
She is abstract f. WOMEN, 55
feminist best home for a f. FEMINISM, 52
People call me a f. FEMINISM, 36
Womanist is to f. as purple is to lavender WALKER, A, 11
feminists not one of those 'angry f.' ANGER, 7
feminity The female breast has been called 'the badge of f.' WOMEN, 78
feminization the f. of the white European and American is already far advanced LEWIS, W, 3
fence The...gentleman has sat so long on the f. NONCOMMITMENT, 3
fences Good f. NEIGHBOURS, 3; PROVERBS, 179
ferries the snow blind twilight f. THOMAS, D, 29
fertility no good reasons left for exercising one's f. CHILDREN, 32
The management of f. HUMAN CONDITION, 10
fetishism Buttock f. is comparatively rare GREER, G, 6
fettered so f. fast we are BROWNING, R, 3; FREEDOM, 8
fettering To rule by f. the mind HYPATIA, 4
fever F. the eternal reproach DISEASE, 27
hand that signed the treaty bred a f. SIGNATURES, 3; THOMAS, D, 11
starve a f. ILLNESS, 1
The f....has just left me ILLNESS, 59
Février Generals Janvier and F. SEASONS, 15
few err as grosly as the F. DRYDEN, J, 12; PUBLIC, 12
happy f., we band of brothers PATRIOTISM, 37
How f. of his friends' houses ILLNESS, 36; JOHNSON, S, 142
I don't want art for a f. MORRIS, W, 3
owed by so many to so f. CHURCHILL, W, 53; WORLD WAR II, 14
fiat f. lux BIBLE, 138
fickle Woman is always f. and changing VIRGIL, 12; WOMEN, 139
fiction ancient history...is no more than accepted f. HISTORY, 34; VOLTAIRE, 17
an improbable f. REALITY, 8; SHAKESPEARE, 345
Children should acquire...heroes and villains from f. AUDEN, W, 4; HISTORY, 3
Imagination and f. IMAGINATION, 7
one form of continuous f. BEVAN, A, 6; JOURNALISM, 10
Poetry is a comforting piece of f. MENCKEN, H, 12; POETRY, 40
Poetry is the supreme f. POETRY, 63
Science f. is no more written for scientists FICTION, 1
She regarded me as a piece of f. WEST, R, 1
Stranger than f. BYRON, 35; TRUTH, 17
fictitious start their programme with f. quotes QUOTATIONS, 6
fiddle consider your puny little f. when He speaks to me MUSIC, 9
good tune played on an old f. AGE, 23
Hey diddle diddle, /The cat and the f. NURSERY RHYMES, 14
keep it shut up...like a rare, rare f. NAKEDNESS, 5
When I play on my f. in Dooney MUSIC, 67; YEATS, W, 12
fiddlers he called for his f. three NURSERY RHYMES, 38
fidelity f. is...one man in the bed PROMISCUITY, 11
field A cow is a very good animal in the f. JOHNSON, S, 156; SUITABILITY, 2
Behold her, single in the f. SOLITUDE, 18; WORDSWORTH, W, 51
For Vaguery in the F. INCOMPETENCE, 3
Man for the f. and woman for the hearth SEXES, 30; TENNYSON, 66
shepherds abiding in the f. BIBLE, 314; CHRISTMAS, 9
some corner of a foreign f. BROOKE, R, 7; WAR, 30
the physic of the f. COUNTRYSIDE, 8
What though the f. be lost DETERMINATION, 12; MILTON, J, 32
fields babbl'd of green f. DEATH, 144; SHAKESPEARE, 128
East and west on f. forgotten WAR, 81
Now there are f. where Troy once was DECLINE, 9; OVID, 5
We plough the f., and scatter AGRICULTURE, 1
fiend a f. hid in a cloud BIRTH, 5; BLAKE, W, 38
a frightful f. /Doth close behind him tread COLERIDGE, S, 36
forgive the f. for becoming a torrent ROYALTY, 43
fierce f. and bald and short of breath SASSOON, S, 1; WAR, 146
fiercest soil of our country is destined to be the /scene of the f. fight MANDELA, N, 3
fiery Nightingale.../A creature of a 'f. heart' WORDSWORTH, W, 35
fifteen F. men on the dead man's chest ALCOHOL, 78; STEVENSON, R, 8
fifth Beethoven's F. Symphony is the most sublime noise FORSTER, E, 7; MUSIC, 26
One f. of the people are against everything OPPOSITION, 4
The F. Column WAR, 109
fifty At f. everyone has the face he deserves APPEARANCE, 49
For one person who dreams of making f. thousand pounds LAZINESS, 8; MILNE, A, 3
Sit on your arse for f. years INDIFFERENCE, 4; MACNEICE, L, 2
there are f. thousand men slain...and not one Englishman DIPLOMACY, 30
You'll see, when you're f. AGE, 79
fifty-fifty There can be no f. Americanism PATRIOTISM, 35; ROOSEVELT, T, 10
fifty-two refuse to admit that I am more than f. AGE, 8
fight a great cause to f. for PANKHURST, C, 4; PRIDE, 7
do not f. with the world BUDDHA, 3
easier to f. for one's principles PRINCIPLES, 1
f., f., f., and f. again POLITICS, 38
F. fire CONFLICT, 2; PROVERBS, 150
f. in your own cause...committed to winning COMMITMENT, 7
f. the good f. BIBLE, 512; FAITH, 10
Good at a f. SHERIDAN, R, 1
I dare not f. COWARDICE, 10; SHAKESPEARE, 126
I f. to win DETERMINATION, 26
I have not yet begun to f. DETERMINATION, 10
I purpose to f. it out on this line DETERMINATION, 8; GRANT, U, 4
I shall f. before Paris WORLD WAR I, 7
I will not cease from mental f. BLAKE, W, 33; ENGLAND, 7
Nor law, nor duty bade me f. FLYING, 7; YEATS, W, 16
Our cock won't f. BEAVERBROOK, M, 5; ROYALTY, 24
soil of our country is destined to be the /scene of the fiercest f. MANDELA, N, 3

The British won't f. BRITISH, 9
The only time...ever put up a f. INSULTS, 35
To f. and not to heed the wounds SELFLESSNESS, 3
too proud to f. WAR, 186; WILSON, W, 9
Ulster will f. IRELAND, 6
We don't want to f., but, by jingo if we do PATRIOTISM, 21
We'll f. and we'll conquer COURAGE, 17
we shall f. on the beaches CHURCHILL, W, 50; WORLD WAR II, 11
when the f. begins within BROWNING, R, 13; CONFLICT, 5
With our backs to the wall...each...must f. on to the end WAR, 74
You cannot f. against the future PROGRESS, 14
fighting f. for this woman's honour CHIVALRY, 9
F. is like champagne MITCHELL, M, 2; WAR, 108
Most sorts of diversion...are an imitation of f. SWIFT, J, 17; WAR, 168
not conquering but f. well VICTORY, 7
This is against f. ever hereafter ROYALTY, 46
What are we f. for WAR, 157
You know I hate f. VIOLENCE, 1
fights He that f. and runs away PROVERBS, 189; SELF-PRESERVATION, 3
I can't spare this man; he f. LINCOLN, A, 20; OFFICERS, 9
fig leaves they sewed f. together BIBLE, 149
figure an oblong angular f. HUMOUR, 47; LEACOCK, S, 6
f. that out BUSH, G, 12
figures prove anything by f. CARLYLE, T, 4; STATISTICS, 2
film A wide screen...makes a bad f. twice as bad CINEMA, 15; GOLDWYN, S, 9
confidence in seasoned f. crews YOUTH, 32
F....dust and heat and noise CINEMA, 19
I like a f. to have a beginning, a middle and an end CINEMA, 12
My first f. will be a very simple one CINEMA, 32
filmed written or thought, it can be f. CINEMA, 17
films thing I liked about f. was looking at the back of my head CINEMA, 11
Why...pay money to see bad f. CINEMA, 14; GOLDWYN, S, 2
filthy her most f. bargain VICE, 12
final The f. solution FASCISM, 6; JEWS, 9
finality F. is death. Perfection is f. PERFECTION, 11
financial a f. interest in being wrong PSYCHIATRY, 24
find terrible thing for a man to f. out HONESTY, 16; WILDE, O, 36
Where does she f. them INSULTS, 104
your sin will f. you out BIBLE, 439; SIN, 7
finders F. keepers LUCK, 3; PROVERBS, 151
fine another f. mess ACCIDENTS, 5
f. feathers that make f. birds CLOTHES, 2
Give me books, fruit, French wine and f. weather KEATS, J, 66
In England, pop art and f. art ART, 21
not only f. feathers AESOP, 5
The big print giveth and the f. print taketh away BUSINESS, 29
finer every baby...is a f. one BABIES, 3; DICKENS, C, 33
finest their f. hour CHURCHILL, W, 51; WORLD WAR II, 12
finger I will shake my little f. – and there will be no more Tito INFLUENCE, 10
leave contraception on the long f. CONTRACEPTION, 9
Moving F. writes DESTINY, 8; FITZGERALD, E, 14
The least pain in our little f. HAZLITT, W, 3; SELF-INTEREST, 4
fingernails if you don't stop biting your f. ARTISTS, 22; ROGERS, W, 11
fingers about time we pulled our f. out SELF-RELIANCE, 11
f. of a man's hand, and wrote BIBLE, 51
F. were made before forks BEGINNING, 2; PROVERBS, 154
ill cook that cannot lick his own f. SELF-CONFIDENCE, 8; SHAKESPEARE, 319
our f. are circumcised MUSICIANS, 6
thy heavens, even the works of thy f. PSALMS, 3
finger-tips An accomplished man to his f. EXPERTS, 4; HORACE, 46
fings F. Ain't Wot They Used T'Be NOSTALGIA, 18
finished it is f. BIBLE, 271; LAST WORDS, 9
We have f. the job TELEGRAMS, 10
finite Our knowledge can only be f. KNOWLEDGE, 37
fir The f. trees dark and high INNOCENCE, 7
fire a chariot...of f. BIBLE, 301
All things, oh priests, are on f. BUDDHA, 1; FIRE, 1
a pillar of f. BIBLE, 111
bound /Upon a wheel of f. SHAKESPEARE, 193
cloven tongues like as of f. BIBLE, 2
f. and brimstone, storm and tempest PSALMS, 5
F. – without hatred WAR, 138
French Guard, f. first WAR, 76
heap coals of f. upon his head BIBLE, 454; RETRIBUTION, 8
He had a f. in his eye, a fever in his blood POETS, 40
heretic that makes the f. MARTYRDOM, 6
how great a matter a little f. kindleth SPEECH, 6
Ideas that enter the mind under f. INDOCTRINATION, 3; TROTSKY, L, 9
It is with our passions as it is with f. and water PASSION, 6
it is your business, when the wall next door catches f. NEIGHBOURS, 4
I warmed both hands before the f. of life LANDOR, W, 7; LIFE AND DEATH, 22
London burnt by f. in three times twenty plus six PROPHECY, 9
that deplorable f. near Fish Street in London LONDON, 12
the bush burned with f. BIBLE, 105
The f. which in the heart resides ARNOLD, M, 29; SOUL, 2
two irons in the f. BEAUMONT, F, 3; PRUDENCE, 6
what wind is to f. ABSENCE, 6; LOVE, 46
firearms Though loaded f. were strictly forbidden at St Trinian's WEAPONS, 9
fired They f. first above the heads CHINA, 6
fire-folk the f. sitting in the air STARS, 4
fireirons Saint Preux never kicked the f. CARLYLE, J, 2; IMPERFECTION, 5
fires Husbands are like f. MARRIAGE, 77
Keep the Home F. Burning HOME, 9
fireside A man may surely be allowed to take a glass of wine by his own f. SHERIDAN, R, 16
firing he faced the f. squad; erect and motionless EXECUTION, 38; THURBER, J, 11
firm not a family; we're a f. ROYALTY, 69
firmness *Commodity, F.,* and *Delight* ARCHITECTURE, 21
first Because of my title, I was the f. COURAGE, 1
British navy always travels f. class NAVY, 6
F. come HASTE, 2; PROVERBS, 155
F. impressions FIRST IMPRESSIONS, 1; PROVERBS, 156
f. in peace WASHINGTON, G, 1
F. in war WASHINGTON, G, 1
F. things first PATIENCE, 3; PROVERBS, 157
f. time I saw Dylan Thomas THOMAS, D, 1
friends...the people who got there f. FRIENDS, 16
If at f. you don't succeed PERSISTENCE, 5
many that are f. shall be last BIBLE, 406; MERIT, 3
The constitution...f. and second class citizens CLASS, 57
The f. day a guest PROVERBS, 393
The morning after is the f. day MACNEICE, L, 1
there is no last or f. BROWNING, R, 48; EQUALITY, 9
which came f., the Greeks or the Romans DISRAELI, B, 39; IGNORANCE, 9
Who ever loved, that loved not at f. sight MARLOWE, C, 8
first-aid His ideas of f. WODEHOUSE, P, 11
firstborn I...will smite all the f. BIBLE, 110
firstfruits first of the f. BIBLE, 118
first-rate the powers of a f. man and the creed of a second-rate man BAGEHOT, W, 9
to mistake for the f., the fecund rate PARKER, D, 18; WRITERS, 21
fir trees The f. dark and high HOOD, T, 7
fish a great f. to swallow up Jonah BIBLE, 286
a recently dead f. before it has had time to stiffen APPEARANCE, 50; POLITICIANS, 110
F. and guests HOSPITALITY, 2; PROVERBS, 158
F. die belly-upward OPPOSITES, 2
F. fuck in it WATER, 4
I have my own f. to fry CERVANTES, M, 10
like a f. needs a bicycle FEMINISM, 10
No human being,...was ever so free as a f. FREEDOM, 53; RUSKIN, J, 15
Phone for the f. knives Norman BETJEMAN, 5, 6; ETIQUETTE, 1
queen did f. for men's souls ELIZABETH I, 1
This man...is a poor f. MARRIAGE, 60
What cat's averse to f. GRAY, T, 11; MATERIALISM, 12
white wine came up with the f. ETIQUETTE, 5
fishbone The monument sticks like a f. MEMORIALS, 10
fishermen a bite every time for f. HUMOUR, 55
fishers f. of men BIBLE, 359; CHRISTIANITY, 25
fishes f. live in the sea SHAKESPEARE, 292
five barley loaves, and two small f. BIBLE, 249; FOOD, 14
So are the f. CHURCHILL, W, 54; WORLD WAR II, 15

fishing Time is but the stream I go a-f. in THOREAU, H, 17; TIME, 59
fishmonger She was a f., but sure 'twas no wonder BUSINESS, 1; IRELAND, 2
fishy something f. about the French COWARD, N, 5; FRANCE, 5
fist You cannot shake hands with a clenched f. GANDHI, I, 5; INFLEXIBILITY, 2
fit Acting…a good way to keep f. ACTING, 21
a pleasing f. of melancholy MILTON, J, 10
It is not f. that you should sit here CROMWELL, O, 7; DISMISSAL, 4
let the punishment f. the crime GILBERT, W, 30
news that's f. to print NEWSPAPERS, 11
only the F. survive SURVIVAL, 9
fitly no one in the realm…f. to come to me ROYALTY, 96
fits periodical f. of morality MACAULAY, T, 10; MORALITY, 10
Strange f. of passion WORDSWORTH, W, 67
fittest Survival of the F. DARWIN, C, 10; EVOLUTION, 11
Fitzgerald F. was an alcoholic FITZGERALD, F, 1
five child of f. would understand this MARX, G, 6; SIMPLICITY, 5
F. for the symbol at your door ANONYMOUS, 45; NUMBERS, 1
F. gold rings CHRISTMAS, 18; NURSERY RHYMES, 59
If you don't find a God by f. o'clock this afternoon ATHEISM, 8
Mister John Keats f. feet high KEATS, J, 61
practise f. things CONFUCIUS, 9; VIRTUE, 13
The formula 'Two and two make f.' PHILOSOPHY, 2
five-pound get a f. note as…a light for a cigarette JAMES, H, 5
five-year-old real menace in dealing with a f. CHILDREN, 41
fixed I am happy…I do not want to be 'f.' DISABILITY, 3
Nothing to be f. except ACTING, 8; TELEGRAMS, 5
flabbiness The moral f. born of…Success SUCCESS, 13
flag But spare your country's f. PATRIOTISM, 44
keep the red f. flying here SOCIALISM, 6
Tonight the American f. floats from yonder hill WAR, 165
flagons stay me with f. BIBLE, 487; LOVE, 33
flame like a moth, the simple maid /Still plays about the f. GAY, J, 2; WOMEN, 59
flames Commit it then to the f. HUME, D, 2; PHILOSOPHY, 3
Superstition sets the whole world in f. SUPERSTITION, 12; VOLTAIRE, 13
Flanders In F. fields MEMORIALS, 11
You have sent me a F. mare INSULTS, 62
flash the f. cut him, and he lies in the stubble ANONYMOUS, 27
flashing His f. eyes, his floating hair CAUTION, 9; COLERIDGE, S, 17
flat f. road to heaven SANTAYANA, G, 1
Very f., Norfolk COWARD, N, 16; ENGLAND, 17
Vile snub-nose, f.-nosed ass APPEARANCE, 58
flatter not f. me CROMWELL, O, 4; REALISM, 1
We f. those we scarcely know HURT, 4
flattered He that loves to be f. is worthy o' the flatterer FLATTERY, 9
flatterer the brave beast is no f. HORSES, 7; JONSON, B, 8
flatterers f. live at the expense of those who listen FLATTERY, 6; LA FONTAINE, J, 2
Self-love…greatest of all f. CONCEIT, 14; ROCHEFOUCAULD, 1
flattering It is f. some men to endure them HALIFAX, 3; TOLERANCE, 3
the talent of f. with delicacy AUSTEN, J, 22; FLATTERY, 2
flattery consider whether…your f. is worth his having FLATTERY, 5; JOHNSON, S, 31
F. is all right FLATTERY, 10
f.'s the food of fools FLATTERY, 11; SWIFT, J, 4
Imitation is the sincerest form of f. IMITATION, 2
ne'er /Was f. lost POETS, 10; SCOTT, W, 6
woman…to be gained by…f. CHESTERFIELD, P, 17; FLATTERY, 4
flaunt if you've got it, f. it OSTENTATION, 1
flautists f. are most obviously the ones who know something we don't know MUSICIANS, 4
flea English literature's performing f. WRITERS, 74
man's whole frame is obvious to a f. CLARITY, 3; POPE, A, 5
The guerrilla fights the war of the f. WAR, 169
the point of precedency between a louse and a f. INSULTS, 74; JOHNSON, S, 144
fleas dog that has praised his f. PARASITES, 4; YEATS, W, 31
F.…upon the body of a giant LANDOR, W, 6; PERSPECTIVE, 3
the f. in my bed were as good CERVANTES, M, 13; COMPLIMENTS, 8
The f. that tease in the high Pyrenees BELLOC, H, 19; NONSENSE, 3
these have smaller f. to bite 'em PARASITES, 3; SWIFT, J, 9
fled I f. Him, down the nights RELIGION, 88
flee then would I f. away, and be at rest PSALMS, 33
fleece On Wenlock Edge the wood's in trouble; /His forest f. the Wrekin heaves HOUSMAN, A, 13
Fleet The F.'s lit up. It is like fairyland NAVY, 11
flesh all f. is as grass BIBLE, 440; DEATH, 36
a thorn in the f. BIBLE, 47
doesn't seem to be any moral place for f. MORALITY, 5
f. and blood so cheap POVERTY, 20
F. perishes FAMILY, 27
f. to feel the chain BRONTE, E, 5; IMPRISONMENT, 3
Heat, madam!…to take off my f. and sit in my bones SMITH, S, 4; WEATHER, 26
I, born of f. and ghost DEATH, 171; THOMAS, D, 4
I have more f. than another man OBESITY, 15
Ishmaelites…will not publicly eat human f. uncooked in Lent CANNIBALISM, 2; WAUGH, E, 41
I wants to make your f. creep DICKENS, C, 43
Leave the f. to the fate it was fit for BROWNING, R, 51; SOUL, 5
Rehearsing a play is making the word f. PLAYS, 12
she is burnt f. SUPERNATURAL, 7
that which is born of the f. is f. BIBLE, 244
the f. is weak BIBLE, 426; IMPERFECTION, 4
the f. lusteth against the Spirit BIBLE, 134; COMPROMISE, 3
the lust of the f. LUST, 1
the way of all f. CONGREVE, W, 12; DEATH, 51
the way of all f.…towards the kitchen FOOD, 72; WEBSTER, J, 4
world, the f., and the devil TEMPTATION, 5
fleshly The F. School of Poetry POETS, 2
flies As f. to wanton boys DESTINY, 22; SHAKESPEARE, 187
certain, that Life f. FITZGERALD, E, 10; LIFE, 39
dead f. cause the ointment…to send forth a stinking savour REPUTATION, 3
Time f., death urges TIME, 66; YOUNG, E, 7
flight Above the vulgar f. of common souls SUPERIORITY, 12
fling I'll have a f. BEAUMONT, F, 11; FREEDOM, 4
flirt f. with their own husbands LOVE AND MARRIAGE, 8; WILDE, O, 22
Young women have a duty to f. BROOKNER, A, 3
float rather be an opportunist and f. BALDWIN, S, 10; EXPEDIENCY, 3
flock he shall feed his f. BIBLE, 211; CHRISTIANITY, 13
keeping watch over their f. by night BIBLE, 314; CHRISTMAS, 9
flogging There is now less f. in our great schools EDUCATION, 51; JOHNSON, S, 100
flood the f. was forty days upon the earth BIBLE, 158
Which, taken at the f. OPPORTUNITY, 19; SHAKESPEARE, 161
flop You write a hit the same way you write a f. SUCCESS, 18
flowed water f. like champagne ABSTINENCE, 4
flower A lovelier f.…was never sown DEATH, 183; WORDSWORTH, W, 70
I have always plucked a thistle and planted a f. LINCOLN, A, 7; REPUTATION, 6
just miss the prizes at the f. show MEDIOCRITY, 3
many a f. is born to blush unseen GRAY, T, 5; WASTE, 2
The F. that once has blown FITZGERALD, E, 10; LIFE, 39
the meanest f.…can give /Thoughts NATURE, 37; WORDSWORTH, W, 32
flowers a book that is a book f. once BOOKS, 27; LAWRENCE, D, 40
Do spring May f. MONTHS, 12
funerals. All those f. BAINBRIDGE, B, 3
Gather the f., but spare the buds FLOWERS, 9; MARVELL, A, 8
Letting a hundred f. blossom MAO TSE-TUNG, 6
No fruits, no f., no leaves, no birds HOOD, T, 10; MONTHS, 10
Say it with f. FLOWERS, 11
the colours of the f. /Have faded OLD AGE, 62
The f. that bloom in the spring APPEARANCE, 28; GILBERT, W, 34
Their f. the tenderness of patient minds OWEN, W, 1; WAR, 124
Too late for fruit, too soon for f. ILLNESS, 20; LAST WORDS, 24
Where have all the f. gone LOSS, 5
flowery A little thin, f. border GARDENS, 9; LAMB, C, 25
flown I see all the birds are f. HOUSES OF PARLIAMENT, 7
flows Everything f. and nothing stays CHANGE, 12
fluency F. in English BUSH, G, 10
flung he f. himself from the room LEACOCK, S, 10; NONSENSE, 17
flutes Gibbon moved to f. and hautboys GIBBON, E, 2
fluxions Sir Isaac Newton…deep in algebra and f. NEWTON, I, 2
fly A f., Sir, may sting a stately horse CRITICS, 11; JOHNSON, S, 49
Do not remove a f.…with a hatchet FORCE, 1
f.…said, what a dust do I raise BACON, F, 58; CONCEIT, 3

said a spider to a f. INVITATIONS, 3
small gilded f. /Does lecher ANIMALISM, 7; SHAKESPEARE, 189
Who saw him die? /I, said the F. NURSERY RHYMES, 72
flying angel to pass, f. slowly THINKING, 5
Days and moments quickly f. DEATH, 47
He ought to have stuck to his f. machines LEONARDO DA VINCI, 3
interior of a f. saucer ADAMS, D, 3
foam the f. /Of perilous seas KEATS, J, 39
the white f. flew COLERIDGE, S, 28; EXPLORATION, 1
foe Heat not a furnace for your f. EXCESS, 13; SHAKESPEARE, 139
he is the sworn f. of our nation PUBLISHING, 5
He…who never made a f. ENEMIES, 10; TENNYSON, 18
foeman When the f. bares his steel COWARDICE, 5; GILBERT, W, 40
foes judge of a man by his f. CONRAD, J, 4; JUDGMENT, 7
fog a London particular…A f. DICKENS, C, 5; WEATHER, 9
The f. comes WEATHER, 18
Folies-Bergère A psychiatrist is a man who goes to the F. PSYCHIATRY, 27
folk-dancing except incest and f. EXPERIENCE, 7
folklore the f. of abortion as life-long trauma ABORTION, 6
folks for de old f. at home HOMESICKNESS, 3
follies f. as the special evidences of our wisdom PRIDE, 14; TROLLOPE, A, 10
lovers cannot see the pretty f. LOVE, 145; SHAKESPEARE, 244
the f. of the town crept slowly among us GOLDSMITH, O, 20; VICE, 9
The f. which a man regrets REGRET, 17
follow F. up!…/Till the field ring again SPORT AND GAMES, 6
He would rather f. public opinion POLITICIANS, 92
I have to f. them, I am their leader LEADERSHIP, 7
take up his cross, and f. me BIBLE, 398; CHRISTIANITY, 27
folly brood of F. without father MILTON, J, 11; PLEASURE, 25
f. to shrink in fear, if this is dying DEATH, 120
His foe was f. and his weapon wit HOPE, A, 9; HUMOUR, 17
Historians will one day look back and think it a curious f. EUROPE, 24
the slightest f. /That ever love did make thee run into LOVE, 144; SHAKESPEARE, 45
When lovely woman stoops to f. GOLDSMITH, O, 29; GULLIBILITY, 2
where ignorance is bliss, /'Tis f. to be wise GRAY, T, 10; IGNORANCE, 10
fond He is very f. of making things FUTILITY, 9; HOPE, A, 2
fonder Absence makes the heart grow f. ABSENCE, 4
food discovered that alcohol was a f. ALCOHOL, 88
do not draw any distinction between f. and medicine CHINA, 17; FOOD, 47
flattery's the f. of fools FLATTERY, 11; SWIFT, J, 4
f. in music MUSIC, 37
f. is, actually, very beautiful FOOD, 64
F. is an important part of a balanced diet FOOD, 45
f. is not necessarily essential CHILDREN, 62
F. is so fundamental FOOD, 36
f. to one man is bitter poison to others TASTE, 5
if someone throws a stone at you, respond with f. FORGIVENESS, 2
man did eat angels' f. PSALMS, 42
Nothing to eat but f. PESSIMISM, 7
On the Continent people have good f. MANNERS, 5
Spleen can subsist on any kind of f. HAZLITT, W, 31
the neglect of f. and eating in depth psychology FOOD, 36
The perpetual struggle for room and f. SURVIVAL, 5
the wine was a farce and the f. a tragedy FOOD, 61
tinned f. is a deadlier weapon WEAPONS, 5
fool a f. among fools or a f. alone MANKIND, 72; WILDER, T, 4
A f. and his money FOOLISHNESS, 1
A f. at forty FOOLISHNESS, 2
A f. believes everything FOOLISHNESS, 3
A f. bolts pleasure, then complains of…indigestion DEBAUCHERY, 1
A f. sees not the same tree BLAKE, W, 27
a greater f. to admire him ADMIRATION, 3
answer a f. according to his folly BIBLE, 456; FOOLISHNESS, 10
a worm at one end and a f. at the other FISHING, 1; JOHNSON, S, 164
Better be a f. than a knave FOOLISHNESS, 4; PROVERBS, 88
brains enough to make a f. of himself STEVENSON, R, 21
Busy old f., unruly Sun DONNE, J, 16; SUN, 3
f. his whole life long PLEASURE, 22
f. walketh in darkness BIBLE, 66
He who holds hopes…is a f. CAMUS, A, 16; PESSIMISM, 4
it needs a very clever woman to manage a f. KIPLING, R, 22
Love is the wisdom of the f. JOHNSON, S, 42; LOVE, 92
loves boxing is either a liar or a f. SPORT AND GAMES, 15
more of the f. than of the wise BACON, F, 13; HUMAN NATURE, 4
No creature smarts…as a f. FOOLISHNESS, 17; POPE, A, 17
One f.…in every married couple FIELDING, H, 4; MARRIAGE, 72
Send a f. to the market PROVERBS, 361
that f. Dawson of Penn ROYALTY, 20
The dupe of friendship, and the f. of love BITTERNESS, 1; HAZLITT, W, 12
the greatest f. may ask more EXAMINATIONS, 1
the old man who will not laugh is a f. AGE, 78; WISDOM, 24
There's no f. like an old f. FOOLISHNESS, 8
The wisest f. in Christendom FOOLISHNESS, 13
wise enough to play the f. WISDOM, 27
Wise Man or a F. BLAKE, W, 17; WISDOM, 13
You can f. too many of the people DECEPTION, 10; THURBER, J, 5
foolish A f. consistency CONSTANCY, 1; EMERSON, R, 15
a f. man, which built his house upon the sand BIBLE, 380
anything very f. MELBOURNE, 8; MOTIVE, 4
a very f., fond old man OLD AGE, 90
If you are f. enough to be contented, don't show it COMPLAINTS, 3; JEROME, J, 4
I'm not denyin' the women are f. WOMEN, 50
more f. when he had not a pen in his hand GOLDSMITH, O, 1
O f. Galatians BIBLE, 131
the f. things of the world WISDOM AND FOOLISHNESS, 3
These f. things MEMORY, 13
You must not think me…f. because I am facetious SERIOUSNESS, 3; SMITH, S, 17
foolishness a story of amazing f. and amazing intelligence MEDICINE, 101
by the f. of preaching BIBLE, 24
Mix a little f. with your serious plans FOOLISHNESS, 14; HORACE, 44
fools Christianity…says that they are all f. CHESTERTON, G, 23; MANKIND, 18
flattery's the food of f. FLATTERY, 11; SWIFT, J, 4
f. and passengers drink at sea BOATS, 16
F. are in a terrible, overwhelming majority FOOLISHNESS, 15; IBSEN, H, 1
F. build houses FOOLISHNESS, 6
f. decoyed into our condition MARRIAGE, 119
F. give you reasons REASON, 3
F. live poor FOOLISHNESS, 7
f. rush in where angels fear to tread HASTE, 8; POPE, A, 29
Fortune always favours f. GAY, J, 8
Fortune, that favours f. JONSON, B, 3; LUCK, 9
I am two f. DONNE, J, 17; LOVE, 65
Is Pride, the never-failing vice of f. POPE, A, 22; PRIDE, 9
Many have been the wise speeches of f. WISDOM AND FOOLISHNESS, 6
not suffer f. gladly ACHESON, D, 2
suffer f. gladly BIBLE, 46
the greater part of the law is learning to tolerate f. LAW, 25; LESSING, D, 5
Thirty millions, mostly f. CARLYLE, T, 36; ENGLISH, 10
this great stage of f. SHAKESPEARE, 192
To suckle f. and chronicle SHAKESPEARE, 282; TRIVIALITY, 13
what delight we married people have to see…f. decoyed into our condition PEPYS, S, 13
what f. these mortals be SHAKESPEARE, 264
world is made up…of f. and knaves FOOLISHNESS, 11
foot caught my f. in the mat EMBARRASSMENT, 2
noiseless f. of Time SHAKESPEARE, 24; TIME, 46
Now I hold creation in my f. CREATION, 11
football F. isn't a matter of life and death FOOTBALL, 17
Professional f. is no longer a game FOOTBALL, 2
footeball F.…causeth fighting FOOTBALL, 18
footprints F. on the sands of time ACTION, 4; PROVERBS, 161
those f. scare me, all directed your way, none coming back MISTRUST, 5
you can have my f. HUMOUR, 52
footsteps home his f. he hath turn'd HOMESICKNESS, 6; SCOTT, W, 8
foppery excellent f. of the world SHAKESPEARE, 171
for neither f. nor against institutions INDIFFERENCE, 7; WHITMAN, W, 4
forbearance f. ceases to be a virtue BURKE, E, 5
forbid I f. my tears SHAKESPEARE, 105
forbidden F. fruit TEMPTATION, 1

he wanted it only because it was f. PERVERSITY, 6; TWAIN, M, 15
we're f. to know – what end the gods have in store DESTINY, 15; HORACE, 30
Ye are f. to eat that which dieth of itself KORAN, 5
force f. alone is but *temporary* BURKE, E, 15; FORCE, 3
F., if unassisted by judgement HORACE, 35; JUDGMENT, 8
F. is not a remedy FORCE, 2
F. that through the green fuse THOMAS, D, 10
Hence no f. however great POETRY, 69
Other nations use 'f.'; we Britons…use 'Might' BRITISH, 14; WAUGH, E, 42
Who overcomes /By f. MILTON, J, 37; VICTORY, 16
forced f. to commend her highly INSINCERITY, 4; PEPYS, S, 9
force-feeding This universal, obligatory f. with lies INDOCTRINATION, 2
forces one of the f. of nature GREATNESS, 10
Ford Jerry F. is so dumb STUPIDITY, 5
The time of our F. FUTURE, 9; HUXLEY, A, 11
fordoes either makes me or f. me quite DECISION, 5
forefathers Think of your f. POSTERITY, 1
forego My native English, now I must f. LANGUAGE, 40
forehead A burning f., and a parching tongue KEATS, J, 31; PASSION, 5
foreign pronounce f. names as he chooses CHURCHILL, W, 36
wandering on a f. strand HOMESICKNESS, 6; SCOTT, W, 8
foreigner f. should…be wiser than ourselves PRIDE, 14; TROLLOPE, A, 10
foreigners f. speak English when our backs are turned LANGUAGE, 17
f.…spell better than they pronounce PRONUNCIATION, 5; SPELLING, 2
f. take too active a hand in our affairs RUSSIA, 21
Sympathy…for being f. BRADBURY, M, 1; SYMPATHY, 1
the time had passed…merely to teach f. BUSINESS, 20
foreparents His f. came to America EQUALITY, 16
foreskin Ye shall circumcise the flesh of your f. RELIGION, 10
forest His f. fleece the Wrekin heaves HOUSMAN, A, 13; TREES, 4
Wandering in a vast f. at night ATHEISM, 5; GUIDANCE, 2
forests the f. of the night ANIMALS, 6; BLAKE, W, 39
foretaste Every parting gives a f. of death SCHOPENHAUER, A, 3
forever Music goes on f. MUSIC, 39
Nothing is won f. in human affairs HUMAN CONDITION, 17
That is f. England BROOKE, R, 7; WAR, 30
forewarned F. is forearmed PROVERBS, 163; PRUDENCE, 2
forget Abortions will not let you f. ABORTION, 3
Better by far you should f. and smile MEMORY, 19; ROSSETTI, C, 5
Fade far away, dissolve, and…f. HUMAN CONDITION, 14; KEATS, J, 38
I could f. what I have been DESPAIR, 7
I f. what I was taught KNOWLEDGE, 41; WHITE, P, 2
I'll not f. old Ireland HOMESICKNESS, 1
I never f. a face, but I'll make an exception MARX, G, 20; MEMORY, 12
nor f. how much she had to forgive FORGIVENESS, 5
Oh Lord!…if I f. thee, do not thou f. me PRAYER, 3
Old men f. MEMORY, 21; SHAKESPEARE, 136
three things I always f. MEMORY, 23
To endeavour to f. anyone LA BRUYERE, J, 14; MEMORY, 10
Were it not better to f. REGRET, 9
When I f. my sovereign LOYALTY, 13
forgetful He is…decrepit and f.…a bore BELLOC, H, 2
forgivable Few books today are f. BOOKS, 24; LAING, R, 3
forgive do not have to f. my enemies LAST WORDS, 60; RUTHLESSNESS, 4
Father, f. them BIBLE, 339
F. and forget FORGIVENESS, 1; PROVERBS, 164
how oft shall…I f. him BIBLE, 402
Men will f. a man CHURCHILL, W, 38; PROSE, 3
nor forget how much she had to f. FORGIVENESS, 5
To err is human, to f., divine MISTAKES, 16; POPE, A, 28
forgiven her sins, which are many, are f. SIN, 6
man can be f. a lot if he can quote Shakespeare SHAKESPEARE, 16
Your blasphemy…can't be f. CENSORSHIP, 7
forgot all the rest f. for which he toil'd TRANSIENCE, 21
auld acquaintance be f. BURNS, R, 4; FRIENDSHIP, 12
How these curiosities would be quite f. GOSSIP, 9
I have f. my part FAILURE, 9; SHAKESPEARE, 60
forgotten East and west on fields f. HOUSMAN, A, 14
five sparrows…not one of them is f. BIBLE, 328; IMPORTANCE, 1
Has God then f. LOUIS XIV, 2
I am clean f., as a dead man PSALMS, 20
I have f. more law than you ever knew INSULTS, 96
Nobody is f. when it is convenient to remember him DISRAELI, B, 36; EXPEDIENCY, 4
the artist is f. ARTISTS, 18
The f. man POVERTY, 33; ROOSEVELT, F, 8
what has been learnt has been f. EDUCATION, 85
fork he had a f. INSULTS, 84
forks I had a knife and two f. left ETIQUETTE, 8
forlorn faery lands f. KEATS, J, 39
The British postgraduate student is a lonely f. soul EDUCATION, 56; LODGE, D, 3
form significant f. ART, 4
formed not f. by nature to bear ENDURANCE, 4
former there is no remembrance of f. things BIBLE, 63
formidable Examinations are f. EXAMINATIONS, 1
forms from outward f. to win APPEARANCES, 13; COLERIDGE, S, 11
formula Matter…a convenient f. PHILOSOPHY, 13; RUSSELL, B, 18
fornicated f. and read the papers CAMUS, A, 6; MANKIND, 15
fornication F.: but that was in another country MARLOWE, C, 11; SEX, 78
forsaken my God, why hast thou f. me BIBLE, 431; DESPAIR, 2
fortress f. built by Nature ENGLAND, 46; SHAKESPEARE, 297
fortuitous f. concurrence of atoms CHANCE, 5
fortune deficiences of f. GOLDSMITH, O, 28; OPTIMISM, 27
fools of f. MANKIND, 59
F. always favours fools GAY, J, 8
f. and men's eyes DISCONTENT, 8; SHAKESPEARE, 362
F. favours fools PROVERBS, 165
F. favours the brave COURAGE, 35; TERENCE, 3
F., that favours fools JONSON, B, 3; LUCK, 9
greater virtues to sustain good f. LUCK, 12; ROCHEFOUCAULD, 3
Here rests…/A youth to f. and to fame unknown DEATH, 75; GRAY, T, 8
hostages to f. BACON, F, 33; FAMILY, 7
O! I am F.'s fool DESTINY, 26
people of f.…a few delinquencies ELIOT, G, 7; POVERTY AND WEALTH, 6
slings and arrows of outrageous f. SHAKESPEARE, 90; SUICIDE, 35
to make your f.…let people see…it is in their interests to promote yours LA BRUYERE, J, 16; SUCCESS, 15
What is your f., my pretty maid NURSERY RHYMES, 70
Whom F. wishes to destroy she first makes mad MADNESS, 42
fortunes f. sharp adversitee CHAUCER, G, 20; MISFORTUNE, 8
share in the good f. of the mighty BRECHT, B, 1
forty f. days and f. nights BIBLE, 356
F. years on PARTING, 4
I am just turning f. AGE, 59
I have been talking prose for over f. years MOLIERE, 3; PROSE, 6
Life Begins At F. AGE, 69; LIFE, 75
look young till f. AGE, 34; DRYDEN, J, 27
made the difference of f. thousand men OFFICERS, 16; WELLINGTON, 11
Pushing f. AGE, 28; INSULTS, 38
When you are f. ANOUILH, J, 7; OLD AGE, 14
forty-five That should assure us of…f. minutes of undisturbed privacy PARKER, D, 13
Forty-niner Dwelt a miner, F., /And his daughter, Clementine MOURNING, 7
forty-three She may very well pass for f. AGE, 47; GILBERT, W, 46; INSULTS, 53
forty-two F. ADAMS, D, 7
forward looking f. to the past NOSTALGIA, 20; OSBORNE, J, 5
Take a step f., lads COURAGE, 9; LAST WORDS, 19
foster-child f. of silence and slow time KEATS, J, 27; SILENCE, 9
fou I wasna f. BURNS, R, 7; SATISFACTION, 2
fought better to have f. and lost DEFEAT, 3
f. for life FAME, 28
f. with us upon Saint Crispin's day SHAKESPEARE, 137
I have f. a good fight BIBLE, 514; FAITH, 11
Women had always f. for men FEMINISM, 28
foul Fair is f., and f. is fair APPEARANCES, 30
F. deeds will rise SHAKESPEARE, 72
Murder most f. MURDER, 10; SHAKESPEARE, 78
So f. and fair a day SHAKESPEARE, 203; WEATHER, 22
foul-mouthed English…are rather a f. nation ENGLISH, 21; HAZLITT, W, 25
found he f. it brick IMPROVEMENT, 1
I have f. it DISCOVERY, 1; SCIENCE, 2

I have f. my sheep which was lost BIBLE, 330; REGRET, 5
Pleasure is…seldom f. where it is sought JOHNSON, S, 16; PLEASURE, 16
Suppose it had been someone else who f. you like this ADULTERY, 8
they f. no more of her than…the palms of her hands BIBLE, 303
When f., make a note of DICKENS, C, 19
foundation The Church's one f. CHRISTIANITY, 57
the final stone…in the f. of St Petersburg VICTORY, 19
foundations her f. are upon the holy hills PSALMS, 47
fountain a f. of gardens BIBLE, 492
fountains their f. piped an answer LAWRENCE, D, 6
four at the age of f.…we're all Generals USTINOV, P, 7
f. essential human freedoms HUMAN RIGHTS, 6; ROOSEVELT, F, 14
F. for the Gospel makers ANONYMOUS, 45; NUMBERS, 1
F. legs good ORWELL, G, 4
f. seasons in the mind of man KEATS, J, 19
Great God grant that twice two be not f. PRAYER, 28; TURGENEV, I, 4
four-day don't want Labour MPs…fighting for a f. week POLITICIANS, 22
fourth a f. estate of the realm JOURNALISM, 23; MACAULAY, T, 4
Because there's no f. class HUMILITY, 9; SANTAYANA, G, 7
on the f. day they will say 'To hell with you!' KHRUSHCHEV, N, 8; PROMISES, 5
there sat a *F. Estate* CARLYLE, T, 13
four-year-old You've got the brain of a f. boy MARX, G, 12; STUPIDITY, 8
fox a f. from his lair HUNTING, 5
Let me remind you what the wary f. said…to the sick lion HORACE, 16; MISTRUST, 5
The f. came home and he went to ground ANIMALS, 16; MASEFIELD, J, 4
The f. knows many things ANIMALS, 2
You don't set a f. to watching the chickens EXPERIENCE, 22; TRUMAN, H, 11
Fox Charles James F. MORTALITY, 20; WORDSWORTH, W, 16
foxes the little f., that spoil the vines BIBLE, 490
fox-hunting athletics as inferior forms of f. WAUGH, E, 20; WOMEN, 140
fraction Only a residual f. is thought SANTAYANA, G, 2
fractions distinguish proper from improper f. MATHEMATICS, 13
fragrant a thousand f. posies FLOWERS, 8; MARLOWE, C, 14
frail strong corruption /Inhabits our f. blood INGRATITUDE, 6
frailty F., thy name is woman SHAKESPEARE, 69
more flesh…more f. OBESITY, 15
frame all the Human F. requires BELLOC, H, 10; FOOD, 10
change their clime, not their f. of mind, who rush across the sea HORACE, 21; TRAVEL, 22
man's whole f. is obvious to a flea CLARITY, 3; POPE, A, 5
frames The finest collection of f. PHILISTINISM, 3
framework Language is…a defining f. LANGUAGE, 52
France all roads lead to F. WAR, 171
and dare for ever; and thus will F. be saved PATRIOTISM, 11
A revolutionary F.…rather win a war FRANCE, 9
but F. has not lost the war FRANCE, 8
Fair stood the wind for F. BOATS, 5
F. before everything PATRIOTISM, 28
F. has more need of me FRANCE, 15; NAPOLEON I, 10
F. is a country where the money falls apart FRANCE, 20
F.…lost a battle…not lost the war WAR, 56
F. was a long despotism CARLYLE, T, 14; FRANCE, 2
Had we gone the way of F. ECOLOGY, 9
king of F.…would assent to no peace or treaty ROYALTY, 52
Like Brighton pier…inadequate for getting to F. KINNOCK, N, 8; TRAVEL, 27
The best thing I know between F. and England FRANCE, 11; JERROLD, D, 2
Thus we have defeated the king of F. VICTORY, 22
franchise vote for giving women the f. FEMINISM, 44
Francis My cousin F. and I are in perfect accord AGREEMENT, 1
frankincense gold, and f., and myrrh BIBLE, 352; CHRISTMAS, 11
Franklin body of /Benjamin F. FRANKLIN, B, 18
Fraternité *Liberté! Égalité! F.* HUMAN RIGHTS, 2
fraud Bonaparte's whole life…was a f. NAPOLEON I, 4
It was certainly a pious f. REMEDIES, 36
frauds many of the great men of history are f. GREATNESS, 9
pious f. of friendship FIELDING, H, 2; FRIENDSHIP, 18
free a f. society…where it is safe to be unpopular FREEDOM, 56; STEVENSON, A, 6
All f. men…are citizens of Berlin GERMANY, 6
All human beings are born f. HUMAN RIGHTS, 1
all men everywhere could be f. LINCOLN, A, 8
f. as the road HERBERT, G, 1
F. Will and Predestination CHURCHILL, W, 19; DESTINY, 6
Greece might still be f. BYRON, 27; EUROPE, 4
I'm with you on the f. press MEDIA, 14; STOPPARD, T, 7
In a f. society the state…administers justice among men STATE, 3
I was born f. as Caesar; so were you EQUALITY, 33
I was f. born FREEDOM, 6
land of the f., and the home of the brave AMERICA, 25
main thing is that he is f. HOSTAGES, 7
Man is condemned to be f. FREEDOM, 54; SARTRE, J, 6
Man was born f. FREEDOM, 52; ROUSSEAU, J, 1
Napoleon is a dangerous man in a f. country NAPOLEON I, 2
No human being…was ever so f. as a fish FREEDOM, 53; RUSKIN, J, 15
none the less f. than you were ADAPTABILITY, 1
no such thing as a f. lunch FOOD, 7; FRIENDSHIP, 7
Only f. men can negotiate MANDELA, N, 5
order you to hold a f. election CORRUPTION, 5
safer to be in chains than to be f. FREEDOM, 30; KAFKA, F, 3
So f. we seem BROWNING, R, 3; FREEDOM, 8
the truth shall make you f. BIBLE, 254; TRUTH, 11
Thou art f. ARNOLD, M, 40
truth that makes men f. TRUTH, 7
we demand f. access to contraception ABORTION, 1
We have to believe in f. will CHOICE, 4
We must be f. or die FREEDOM, 63; WORDSWORTH, W, 55
Who would be f. BYRON, 12; FREEDOM, 10
freedom a heart…of f.; here's my hand MARRIAGE, 136
but inside, the terrible f. APPEARANCES, 15
enemies of F. INGE, W, 2; OPPRESSION, 4
fit to use their f. FREEDOM, 35; MACAULAY, T, 8
flame of f. in their souls KNOWLEDGE, 39
F.! Equality! Brotherhood HUMAN RIGHTS, 2
F. is an indivisible word HUMAN RIGHTS, 7
F. is Slavery ORWELL, G, 18
F. is the right to tell…do not want to hear FREEDOM, 46
f. of speech FREEDOM, 57; TWAIN, M, 7
F.'s just another word FREEDOM, 31
f. to print…proprietor's prejudices MEDIA, 15
If f. were not so economically efficient ECONOMICS, 9
In solitude alone can he know true f. MONTAIGNE, M, 2; SOLITUDE, 13
Me this unchartered f. tires FREEDOM, 62; WORDSWORTH, W, 34
more f.…where it is not your natural language LANGUAGE, 1
nation refreshed by f. BUSH, G, 9
Necessity is the plea for every infringement of human f. NECESSITY, 4; PITT THE YOUNGER, 1
None can love f. heartily, but good men FREEDOM, 42; MILTON, J, 64
only f. can make security secure FREEDOM, 48
So greatly did she care for f. that she died for it WOMEN, 102
So long as the state exists there is no f. STATE, 2
stand up for f. of the imagination CENSORSHIP, 9; RELIGION, 80
The worst enemy of truth and f. IBSEN, H, 3; MAJORITY, 6
Those who deny f. to others FREEDOM, 34; LINCOLN, A, 12
Until you've lost your reputation, you never realize…what f. really is MITCHELL, M, 1; REPUTATION, 7
we suffragettes aspire to be…ambassadors of f. to women PANKHURST, C, 6
what is F. FREEDOM, 12
While the state exists there can be no f. LENIN, V, 4
wind of nationalism and f. blowing BALDWIN, S, 7; FREEDOM, 2
Your f. and mine cannot be separated FREEDOM, 37; MANDELA, N, 4
You took my f. away a long time ago FREEDOM, 55; SOLZHENITSYN, A, 7
freedoms four essential human f. HUMAN RIGHTS, 6; ROOSEVELT, F, 14
free-loader A f. is a confirmed guest PARASITES, 2; RUNYON, D, 8
freely nothing so f. as advice ROCHEFOUCAULD, 16
freemasonry a kind of bitter f. BEERBOHM, M, 13; LOVE, 25
free-will believe in f.. We've got no choice HUMAN CONDITION, 27
French Bouillabaisse is only good because cooked by the F. FOOD, 27; FRANCE, 6

dislike the F. from…vulgar antipathy FRANCE, 19; WALPOLE, H, 9
everyone would always have spoken F. LANGUAGE, 49; VOLTAIRE, 32
fear that the F. would invade NAVY, 10
F. governments more selfish than most GOVERNMENT, 11
F. Guard, fire first WAR, 76
Give me books, fruit, F. wine and fine weather PLEASURE, 19
I do not say the F. cannot come NAVY, 7
I hate the F. FRANCE, 10; GOLDSMITH, O, 12
Imagine the Lord talking F. LANGUAGE, 20
I speak…Italian to women, F. to men LANGUAGE, 13
My suit is pale yellow. My nationality is F. NORMALITY, 2; WILLIAMS, T, 1
something fishy about the F. COWARD, N, 5; FRANCE, 5
the flame of F. resistance must not…be extinguished WORLD WAR II, 26
the F. STERNE, L, 2
The F. are wiser than they seem NATIONALITY, 1
The F. want no-one to be their *superior* PRIDE, 13
The F. will only be united under the threat of danger DE GAULLE, C, 8; FRANCE, 7
the German text of F. operas OPERA, 13
There's something Vichy about the F. FRANCE, 16
too early to form a final judgement on the F. Revolution FRENCH REVOLUTION, 9
to the F. the empire of the land EUROPE, 18
Frenchman F. must be always talking FRANCE, 12; JOHNSON, S, 133
You must hate a F. ENEMIES, 6; NELSON, H, 2
Frenchmen Englishmen to be subject to F. VICTORY, 25
F. drink wine just like ALCOHOL, 51
to create F. in the image of Englishmen CHURCHILL, W, 61; NATIONALITY, 6
frenzy poet's eye, in a fine f. rolling POETRY, 54; SHAKESPEARE, 266
fresh f. as is the month of May CHARACTER, 4; CHAUCER, G, 5
Gentlemen know that f. air NATURE, 25
the cod's wallop is always f. made COMMUNISM, 11
freshen a mighty storm…to f. us up CHANGE, 3; CHEKHOV, A, 9
fret weariness, the fever, and the f. HUMAN CONDITION, 14; KEATS, J, 38
fretting a moth f. a garment PSALMS, 23
Freud F. is all nonsense NEUROSIS, 9
The ideas of F. were popularized by people who only imperfectly understood them PSYCHIATRY, 32
The trouble with F. PSYCHIATRY, 13
Freudian in analysis with a strict F. SUICIDE, 1
the F., it is a very low, Central European sort of humour HUMOUR, 15
Friday F.'s child is loving and giving CHILDREN, 50; NURSERY RHYMES, 35
I takes my man F. DEFOE, D, 4
Worse on F. NURSERY RHYMES, 53
friend A fav'rite has no f. GRAY, T, 12; LONELINESS, 3
a f. can't take a mother's place FRANK, A, 4
a F. for little children GOD, 37
A f. in need FRIENDSHIP, 1; PROVERBS, 18
A f. in power POWER, 4
A f. should bear his f.'s infirmities FRIENDS, 14; SHAKESPEARE, 160
a good f., but bad acquaintance BYRON, 23; FRIENDS, 3
A good f. is my nearest relation FRIENDSHIP, 2; PROVERBS, 24
a new f. is as new wine BIBLE, 83; FRIENDS, 2
A woman can become a man's f. CHEKHOV, A, 11; FRIENDSHIP, 15
damned good-natured f. FRIENDS, 15; SHERIDAN, R, 3
Every time I paint a portrait I lose a f. PAINTING, 18
forsake not an old f. BIBLE, 83; FRIENDS, 2
F.…masterpiece of Nature EMERSON, R, 8; FRIENDS, 8
f., wherefore art thou come BETRAYAL, 3; BIBLE, 427
He makes no f. ENEMIES, 10; TENNYSON, 18
I might give my life for my f. FRIENDSHIP, 27; SMITH, L, 5
in convalescence a f. DOCTORS, 11
In every f. we lose a part of ourselves DEATH, 125; POPE, A, 61
It takes your enemy and your f.…, to hurt you HURT, 3; TWAIN, M, 6
mine own familiar f. PSALMS, 25
no f. like a sister FAMILY, 51; ROSSETTI, C, 2
save me, from the candid f. FRANKNESS, 1
that a man lay down his wife for a f. FRIENDSHIP, 21; JOYCE, J, 9
the last best f. am I DEATH, 163
The night is your f. WORLD WAR II, 4
trust ye not in a f. BIBLE, 434; TRUST, 1
When a f. dies out on us FRIENDSHIP, 23; MACNEICE, L, 6
Whenever a f. succeeds ENVY, 10; VIDAL, G, 7
woman can become a man's f. LOVE AND FRIENDSHIP, 2
friendly Man is the only animal…on f. terms with the victims…he eats BUTLER, S, 20; HYPOCRISY, 7
so large, /So f., and so rich AMERICA, 2; AUDEN, W, 22
friends Animals are such agreeable f. ANIMALS, 13; ELIOT, G, 9
better to drop thy f. CLASS, 8
false to his f.…true to the public HONESTY, 3
F.…God's apology for relations FRIENDS, 10
F., Romans, countrymen EVIL, 19; SHAKESPEARE, 155
Good thoughts his only f. CAMPION, T, 4; RIGHTEOUSNESS, 7
guessed you were f. BRADBURY, M, 4
Have no f. not equal CONFUCIUS, 7; FRIENDS, 5
His best f. hear no more MARRIAGE, 141; SHELLEY, P, 11
How few of his f.' houses ILLNESS, 36; JOHNSON, S, 142
How to Win F. INFLUENCE, 2
I cannot forgive my f. for dying DEATH, 159; SMITH, L, 7
I don't trust him. We're f. BRECHT, B, 5; FRIENDSHIP, 11
I haven't made any f. since becoming famous FAME, 27
I let down my f. BETRAYAL, 11
In the misfortune of our best f. ROCHEFOUCAULD, 14
Job endured everything – until his f. came ENDURANCE, 10
lay down his f. for his life LOVE, 31
Money can't buy f. MILLIGAN, S, 10; MONEY, 36
No doctor takes pleasure in the health even of his f. DOCTORS, 64
none of his f. like him POPULARITY, 9; WILDE, O, 66
not so much our f.' help that helps us FRIENDSHIP, 17
Once more unto the breach, dear f. SHAKESPEARE, 129
our f. are true and our happiness BIERCE, A, 7; OPTIMISM, 16
shameful to distrust one's f. ROCHEFOUCAULD, 12
the best of f. must part ANONYMOUS, 87; PARTING, 2
The day your descendants, /Outnumber your f. OLD AGE, 76
Thy f. are exultations, agonies, /And love WORDSWORTH, W, 63
troops of unrecording f. LIFE, 93; TENNYSON, 77
we…walked in the house of God as f. PSALMS, 34
with a little help from my f. FRIENDS, 11; LENNON, J, 12
without three good f. MONEY, 42; SHAKESPEARE, 52
you choose your f. FAMILY, 15; FRIENDS, 6
friendship A hedge…keeps f. green PROVERBS, 26
A man, Sir, should keep his f. in constant repair FRIENDS, 9; JOHNSON, S, 54
a sort of f. recognized by the police STEVENSON, R, 13
Business…may bring money,…f. hardly ever does AUSTEN, J, 9; MONEY, 6
f. closes its eyes LOVE AND FRIENDSHIP, 1
F. is a disinterested commerce between equals GOLDSMITH, O, 14; LOVE AND FRIENDSHIP, 4
F. is constant in all other things LOVE AND FRIENDSHIP, 6; SHAKESPEARE, 269
F. is unnecessary FRIENDSHIP, 22; LEWIS, C, 1
In f. or in love LOVE AND FRIENDSHIP, 3
love…looks more like hatred than like f. LOVE AND HATE, 5; ROCHEFOUCAULD, 9
Most f. is feigning INSINCERITY, 5; SHAKESPEARE, 51
Society, f., and love COWPER, W, 33; SOLITUDE, 4
The dupe of f., and the fool of love BITTERNESS, 1; HAZLITT, W, 12
To like…the same things, that is…true f. FRIENDSHIP, 26
true bond of f. FRIENDSHIP, 25
frighten by God, they f. me OFFICERS, 13; WELLINGTON, 15
f. the horses SEX, 21
frightened My father was f. of his mother FAMILY, 24
frightening cling to their own sex because it is less f. HOMOSEXUALITY, 29
frigidity The sole criterion of f. SEX, 41
frittered life is f. away by detail SIMPLICITY, 8; THOREAU, H, 16
frivolity gay without f. ARNOLD, M, 20; FUTURE, 2
frocks f. are built in Paris CLOTHES, 22; FASHION, 10
frog A f. he would a-wooing go NURSERY RHYMES, 1
Eye of newt, and toe of f. SHAKESPEARE, 220
your f. lives in hope MARRIAGE, 142
frogs F. and snails /And puppy-dogs' tails NURSERY RHYMES, 69
front door polished up the handle of the big f. GILBERT, W, 13

rontier We stand today on the edge of a new f. BEGINNING, 14
frontiers hungry hare has no f. WAIESA, L, 3
froth Life is mostly f. and bubble MISFORTUNE, 12
fruit brought forth f., some an hundredfold BIBLE, 391
every good tree bringeth forth good f. BIBLE, 379
his f. in due season PSALMS, 1
Ignorance is like a delicate exotic f. IGNORANCE, 24; WILDE, O, 25
she took of the f. thereof BIBLE, 149
Some f. for Him that dressed me HERBERT, G, 3; SERVICE, 3
the f. /Of that forbidden tree MILTON, J, 30; SIN, 20
the f. of the Spirit is love, joy, peace BIBLE, 135; CHRISTIANITY, 11
Too late for f., too soon for flowers ILLNESS, 20; LAST WORDS, 24
fruitful be f. and multiply BIBLE, 142
The command 'Be f. and multiply CONTRACEPTION, 7
fruitfulness Season of…mellow f. KEATS, J, 45
secret of reaping the greatest f.…from life DANGER, 6; NIETZSCHE, F, 6
fruits by their f. ye shall know them ACHIEVEMENT, 3; BIBLE, 379; RESULTS, 3
No f., no flowers, no leaves, no birds HOOD, T, 10; MONTHS, 10
frumpish F. and banal ROYALTY, 91
frustrate In three sips…Arian f. BROWNING, R, 53; DRINKS, 7
Fry Dear Roger F. whom I love as a man CRITICS, 12
fuck couldn't write f. on a dusty venetian blind INSULTS, 22
Fish f. in it WATER, 4
They f. you up, your mum and dad FAMILY, 33; LARKIN, P, 4
fucking all this cold-hearted f. ANIMALISM, 4; LAWRENCE, D, 17; SEX, 65
too f. busy – or vice versa SEX, 92
fugitive a f. and a vagabond PUNISHMENT, 3
Führer *Ein Reich, Ein Volk, Ein F.* NAZISM, 1
fulfilment Contentment and f. don't make for very good fiction FICTION, 7
full f. of new wine BIBLE, 3; DRUNKENNESS, 11
my cup shall be f. PSALMS, 11
Reading maketh a f. man BACON, F, 51; READING, 1
fulness the earth is the Lord's, and the f. BIBLE, 35
fun f. to be in the same decade AGE, 74; COMPLIMENTS, 24; ROOSEVELT, F, 4
It was great f. PLEASURE, 27
Most people get a fair amount of f. out of their lives LIFE, 74; ORWELL, G, 31
No woman has an abortion for *f.* ABORTION, 12
People must not do things for f. HERBERT, A, 4; PLEASURE, 15
the most f. I ever had without laughing ALLEN, W, 2; SEX, 3
the people have f. MONTESQUIEU, 6; PLEASURE, 26
Work is much more f. than f. COWARD, N, 22; WORK, 8
you feel as if a human being sitting inside were making f. of you ANIMALS, 10
function f. of the critic CRITICISM, 7; CRITICS, 1
functions spend most of our time answering invitations to social f. CATHOLICISM, 6
funeral F. marches to the grave LONGFELLOW, H, 10; MORTALITY, 14
the corpse at every f. ROOSEVELT, T, 2
The reason…people showed up at his f. INSULTS, 55
funerals f.. All those flowers BAINBRIDGE, B, 3
I attended their f. DOCTORS, 102
If you don't go to other men's f. FUNERALS, 4
Many f. discredit a physician FUNERALS, 7
weddings is sadder than f. BEHAN, B, 6; MARRIAGE, 23
funny Everything is f. HUMOUR, 27; ROGERS, W, 4
f. old world THATCHER, M, 41
F. peculiar, or funny ha-ha HUMOUR, 16
F. without being vulgar CRITICISM, 21; GILBERT, W, 49
hard to be f. when you have to be clean HUMOUR, 34; WEST, M, 11
its own animality either objectionable or f. HUMOUR, 20; LEWIS, C, 2
Kings…are just as f. ROOSEVELT, T, 4; ROYALTY, 100
to accuse someone of trying to be f. is highly abusive HUMOUR, 22
furiously sleep f. NONSENSE, 10
furnace a burning fiery f. BIBLE, 48; DOOMSDAY, 1
Heat not a f. for your foe EXCESS, 13; SHAKESPEARE, 139
heat the f. one seven times more BIBLE, 49
furniture brain attic stocked with all the f. that he is likely to use DOYLE, A, 12; KNOWLEDGE, 16
don't bump into the f. ACTING, 7
fury full of sound and f. LIFE, 86; SHAKESPEARE, 227
hell a f. like a woman scorned CONGREVE, W, 9; LOVE AND HATE, 3
no f. like an ex-wife searching for a new lover CONNOLLY, C, 17; WOMEN, 35
nothing but beastly f. and extreme violence FOOTBALL, 7
strength and f. LA FONTAINE, J, 4; PATIENCE, 12
the F. of a Patient Man DRYDEN, J, 13; PATIENCE, 10
fuse force that through the green f. THOMAS, D, 10
fustest f. with the mostest MISQUOTATIONS, 16; WAR, 64
future Fascism…f. refusing to be born BEVAN, A, 11
F., n. That period of time in which BIERCE, A, 7; OPTIMISM, 16
f. states…left to faith BYRON, 22
how pleasant…not to have any f. BURGESS, A, 2; FUTURE, 6
If you want a picture of the f. OPPRESSION, 6; ORWELL, G, 16
if you would divine the f. CONFUCIUS, 4; PAST, 5
I have a vision of the f. BETJEMAN, J, 10; FUTURE, 3
I have seen the f. FUTURE, 11
I mean a F. Life AFTERLIFE, 2
I never think of the f. EINSTEIN, A, 13; FUTURE, 7
people who live in the f. BENNETT, A, 4; PROGRESS, 4
pick today's fruits, not relying on the f. in the slightest HORACE, 31; PRESENT, 9
The f. is…black BALDWIN, J, 4; RACISM, 3
The f. is made of the same stuff FUTURE, 13; WEIL, S, 4
The f. is the only kind of property CAMUS, A, 12; SLAVERY, 2
the f.…makes cowards of us PRESENT, 3
the f. of British football FOOTBALL, 6
The past was nothing…The f. was a mystery PRESENT, 2
What is the f. of my kind of writing WRITING, 40
Who controls the past controls the f. ORWELL, G, 15; POWER, 20
You cannot fight against the f. PROGRESS, 14
Fuzzy-Wuzzy to you, F., at your 'ome in the Soudan KIPLING, R, 11

G

gaiety G.…of the Soviet Union RUSSIA, 16; STALIN, J, 5
the only concession to g. THOMAS, G, 5; WELSH, 2
gain never broke the Sabbath, but for G. DRYDEN, J, 10; SIN, 14
richest g. I count but loss HUMILITY, 14; WATTS, I, 8
gained learning hath g. most BOOKS, 22
gainful I will undoubtedly have to seek…g. employment ACHESON, D, 5; GOVERNMENT, 1
gains no g. without pains STEVENSON, A, 4
gaiters gas and g. DICKENS, C, 34
Galatians a great text in G. BIBLE, 525; BROWNING, R, 54
O foolish G. BIBLE, 131
Galen Did we not believe G. implicitly for 1500 years DOCTORS, 68
Galileo If G. had said in verse that the world moved HARDY, T, 15; POETRY, 27
What G. and Newton were to the seventeenth century DARWIN, C, 3
gall the wormwood and the g. BIBLE, 305
gallant a loyal, a g., and good-temper'd people FRANCE, 18; STERNE, L, 2
He was a braw g. ANONYMOUS, 109
gallantry What men call g. ADULTERY, 1; BYRON, 19
gallery The boy I love is up in the g. LOVE, 173
galloped I g., Dirck g. BROWNING, R, 28; HORSES, 3
gallops g. night by night /Through lovers' brains SHAKESPEARE, 307
gallows You will die either on the g., or of the pox REPARTEE, 5
gallows-maker The g.; for that frame outlives a thousand tenants EXECUTION, 37
gamble Life is a g. LIFE, 90; STOPPARD, T, 10
gambling primary notion back of most g. is the excitement SPECULATION, 3
game an interminable and badly printed g. book STEIN, G, 1
English think cricket is a g. ENGLISH, 28
given myself to the g. CRICKET, 6
great fallacy is that the g. is…about winning FOOTBALL, 4
He no play-a da g. CONTRACEPTION, 4; RELIGION, 22
how you played the g. SPORT AND GAMES, 36; VICTORY, 21
I don't like this g. MILLIGAN, S, 4
It's more than a g.. It's an institution CRICKET, 4
'Play up! play up! and play the g.!' NEWBOLT, H, 7; WAR, 119
serious g. of self-censorship CENSORSHIP, 6

The g. isn't over till it's over SPORT AND GAMES, 4
win this g. and thrash the Spaniards SPORT AND GAMES, 14; WAR, 57
woman is his g. SEXES, 29; TENNYSON, 65
gamekeeper would you allow your g. to read it CENSORSHIP, 1
gamekeeping the book cannot take the place of...*Practical G.* WRITERS, 50
games The British, being brought up on team g. PARKINSON, C, 3
The most important thing in the Olympic G. VICTORY, 7
gamesmanship G. or The Art of Winning Games POTTER, S, 1; SPORT AND GAMES, 35
gaming Man is a g. animal LAMB, C, 7; SPORT AND GAMES, 24
gangsters The great nations have always acted like g. DIPLOMACY, 22
garbage G. in PROVERBS, 170
Garbo G. Talks CINEMA, 3
not another Greta G. BLEASDALE, A, 4
one sees in G. sober COMPLIMENTS, 36; TYNAN, K, 6
garden a g. in her face CAMPION, T, 2
A g. is a lovesome thing GARDENS, 4
Come into the g., Maud INVITATIONS, 5; TENNYSON, 56
cultivate our g. PAROCHIALISM, 3; VOLTAIRE, 9
Don't go into Mr McGregor's g. ANIMALS, 21; CAUTION, 12
God Almighty first planted a g. BACON, F, 26; GARDENS, 2
God the first g. made GARDENS, 6
I have a g. of my own GARDENS, 10; MARVELL, A, 6
My heart shall be thy g. LOVE, 117
nearer God's Heart in a g. GARDENS, 7
The chairs are being brought in from the g. AUDEN, W, 18
the g. of Eden BIBLE, 145; KNOWLEDGE, 8; TREES, 1
There are fairies at the bottom of our g. FAIRIES, 4
gardener Every time I talk to...my g., I'm convinced of the opposite HAPPINESS, 20; RUSSELL, B, 33
Nor does a...g. scent his roses POETS, 4
Oh, Adam was a g. GARDENS, 8; KIPLING, R, 13
supposing him to be the g. BIBLE, 275
gardens a fountain of g. BIBLE, 492
closing time in the g. of the West CAPITALISM, 4; CONNOLLY, C, 3
garland wither'd is the g. of the war MOURNING, 9; SHAKESPEARE, 37
garlands consumptive youth weaving g. of sad flowers STEVENSON, R, 2
gather g. there COUNTRYSIDE, 10; SCOTT, W, 20
garment a moth fretting a g. PSALMS, 23
Garrick G. was pure gold ACTORS, 14
garrulous That g. monk HITLER, A, 5
Garter I like the G. MELBOURNE, 6; TITLES, 5
gas effects of the successful g. attack were horrible WORLD WAR I, 5
g. and gaiters DICKENS, C, 34
If silicon had been a g. WHISTLER, J, 6
gas-masks digging trenches and trying on g. CHAMBERLAIN, N, 5; WORLD WAR II, 5
gate I am here at the g. alone INVITATIONS, 5; TENNYSON, 56
I said to the man who stood at the g. of the year FAITH, 15
matters not how strait the g. RESPONSIBILITY, 8
the g. of heaven HEAVEN, 2
gatekeeper After I die, I shall return to earth as a g. of a bordello THREATS, 5; TOSCANINI, A, 3
gates Battering the g. of heaven EXCESS, 16; TENNYSON, 74
lift up your heads, O ye g. PSALMS, 14
the g. of the day LONELINESS, 17; YEATS, W, 19
the iron g. of life LOVE, 111; MARVELL, A, 11
thou leadest to the g. of hell BIBLE, 522
gateway 'Sex,'...'is the g. to life.' SEX, 13
gather G. the flowers FLOWERS, 9; MARVELL, A, 8
G. ye rosebuds while ye may HERRICK, R, 5; PRESENT, 6
If thou may not continually g. thyself together PRAYER, 21
gathered two or three are g. together BOOK OF COMMON PRAYER, 17; BIBLE, 401
gatling The g.'s jammed and the colonel dead NEWBOLT, H, 7; WAR, 119
gaudy round, neat, not g. GARDENS, 9; LAMB, C, 25
Gaul G. is divided into three CAESAR, J, 1; FRANCE, 1
Gaulle I, General de G., now in London WORLD WAR II, 26
Gaullist I...have become a G....little by little DE GAULLE, C, 5; POLITICIANS, 77
gave God...g. his only begotten Son BIBLE, 245; CHRISTIANITY, 17
the Lord g., and the Lord hath taken away BIBLE, 223
gay g. characters...same footing as the straight HOMOSEXUALITY, 25
g. without frivolity ARNOLD, M, 20; FUTURE, 2
I love the g. Eastertide PLEASURE, 7
gays there have always been g. in the military HOMOSEXUALITY, 6
Gaza Eyeless in G. BLINDNESS, 7; MILTON, J, 57
gazelle never nurs'd a dear g. ANIMALS, 17; MOORE, T, 6
G.B.S G.. looked aged and feeble WRITERS, 42
general caviare to the g. SHAKESPEARE, 87; TASTE, 7
In a civil war, a g. must know REED, H, 5; WAR, 134
was good for G. Motors BUSINESS, 38
generalities Stanislavsky ever said was: 'Avoid g. GENERALIZATIONS, 3
generalizations All g. are dangerous GENERALIZATIONS, 2
Physicians are inclined to engage in hasty g. THEORY, 13
generalize To g. is to be an idiot BLAKE, W, 52; GENERALIZATIONS, 1
generals at the age of four with paper hats and wooden swords we're all G. AUTHORITARIANISM, 9; USTINOV, P, 7
Dead battles, like dead g. WAR, 172
It is not the business of g. to shoot one another OFFICERS, 14; WELLINGTON, 17
that's not against the law for g. OFFICERS, 12; TRUMAN, H, 8
to be left to the g. OFFICERS, 5
wish he would *bite*...my g. REPARTEE, 3
generation a g. that don't spend THRIFT, 12
Each g. imagines itself...more intelligent ORWELL, G, 35
greatest, most truly heroic stories of my time and g. WRITING, 27
he suffered...the neurotic ills of an entire g. NEUROSIS, 4
the neurotic ills of an entire g. LAWRENCE, T, 4
to continue the g. of the species SEX, 74
You are all a lost g. STEIN, G, 8
generations all g. shall call me blessed BIBLE, 309
g....have struggled in poverty to build these altars RELIGION, 82
g....pass in a short time MORTALITY, 15
No hungry g. tread thee down KEATS, J, 39
generosity The poor...their function...is to exercise our g. POVERTY, 34; SARTRE, J, 14
generous a gallant, a g....people FRANCE, 18; STERNE, L, 2
generously paid its debt to her too g. BRONTE, E, 1
Genesis The man who started more creations since G. ROOSEVELT, F, 2
genetics biologists studied g. and natural selection EVOLUTION, 17
genial about as g. as an *auto da fé* of teetotallers CHESTERTON, G, 2
genitalia D.H.L.'s interest in the human g. WRITERS, 70
genius a country full of g., but with absolutely no talent IRELAND, 14
A g.! For thirty-seven years I've practiced...and now they call me a g. GENIUS, 8
a g. that could cut a Colossus MILTON, J, 5
a German and a g. LAST WORDS, 87; SWIFT, J, 22
a man of something occasionally like g. WHITMAN, W, 2
G....capacity of taking trouble CARLYLE, T, 10; GENIUS, 2
G. does what it must TALENT AND GENIUS, 3
G. is an infinite capacity GENIUS, 1; PROVERBS, 171
g. is not transmitted TALENT, 10
G. is one per cent inspiration GENIUS, 5
He identified g. with immunity from...cravings WRITERS, 62
his departure was the eclipse of a g. MOUNTBATTEN OF BURMA, L, 1
His thoughts...borne on the gusts of g. POETS, 39
Milton, Madam, was a g. JOHNSON, S, 150; POETS, 44
Nothing, except my g. CONCEIT, 25; WILDE, O, 76
Only an organizing g. BEVAN, A, 7; INCOMPETENCE, 1
Rules and models destroy g. and art HAZLITT, W, 23; RULES, 2
Since when was g....respectable BROWNING, E, 2; RESPECTABILITY, 1
talent instantly recognizes g. DOYLE, A, 17
Taste is the feminine of g. FITZGERALD, E, 1; TASTE, 3
the difference between talent and g. TALENT AND GENIUS, 1
the first comic g. who ever installed himself in Downing Street DISRAELI, B, 2
The g. of Einstein leads to Hiroshima EINSTEIN, A, 2
the most remarkable and seductive g. BEERBOHM, M, 2
the most *vulgar-minded* g. POETS, 33
The poor little woman of g. WRITERS, 90

true g. is a mind of large general powers GENIUS, 7; JOHNSON, S, 20
True g. walks along a line GENIUS, 6; GOLDSMITH, O, 3
Unless one is a g. COMMUNICATION, 2; HOPE, A, 1
What a commonplace g. he has HARDY, T, 3; WRITERS, 66
When a true g. appears GENIUS, 9; SWIFT, J, 14
geniuses G. don't die GENIUS, 3
One of the greatest g. SHAKESPEARE, 20
genocide turning away from what is clearly g. ETHNIC CLEANSING, 3
genome patents that cover the entire…human g. SCIENCE, 67
gent what a man is to a g. BALDWIN, S, 11; INTELLIGENCE, 3
gentil parfit, g. knyght CHAUCER, G, 4; CHIVALRY, 5
gentiles a light to lighten the G. BIBLE, 317; DEATH, 37
gentleman A g. need not know Latin EDUCATION, 61
a g.…never inflicts pain CHIVALRY, 10
A g. of thirty-two who could calculate an eclipse JEFFERSON, T, 2
A g.…wouldn't hit a woman with his hat on CHIVALRY, 2
a nice old g. CHAMBERLAIN, N, 2
Every other inch a g. INSULTS, 130
g. of leisure MATERIALISM, 25
g.…robbing the poor CLASS, 42
God is a g. GOD, 42; ORTON, J, 6
last g. in Europe WRITERS, 69
Not a g.; dresses too well RUSSELL, B, 27
proved it's not just a g.'s game CRICKET, 7
The Devil is a g. DEVIL, 15; SHELLEY, P, 18
the g. is an *attorney* JOHNSON, S, 80; LAWYERS, 8
what a g. is to a gent BALDWIN, S, 11
Who was then the g. CLASS, 5
gentlemanly secondly, g. conduct EDUCATION, 7
gentlemen by g. for g. NEWSPAPERS, 16; THACKERAY, W, 6
extremely difficult to behave like g. WOMEN, 81
g., let us do something today WAR, 51
G.…remember blondes APPEARANCE, 42
God rest you merry, g. ANONYMOUS, 21; CHRISTMAS, 4
Good-morning, g. both ELIZABETH I, 7; INSULTS, 46
one of Nature's G. CHIVALRY, 8
religion for g. CHARLES II, 2; RELIGION, 25
Scholars and g. HONOUR, 7; WORDSWORTH, W, 40
the British bourgeoisie have spoken of themselves as g. CLASS, 51; WAUGH, E, 15
There were g. and…seamen in the navy of Charles the Second MACAULAY, T, 15; NAVY, 8
gentleness G. was considered 'bourgeois' CHINA, 13
gentlewoman a g. made ready WOMEN, 126
gravest sins it was possible for a g. to commit WAUGH, E, 48
genuine real g., hard-working envy JEALOUSY, 4
genuinely g. bogus APPEARANCES, 20
genuineness G. only thrives in the dark HUXLEY, A, 34; SINCERITY, 4
geographical India is a g. term CHURCHILL, W, 45; PLACES, 10
geography G. is about Maps BIOGRAPHY, 1
geometrical Population…increases in a g. ratio ECONOMICS, 17
geometricians we are g. only by chance JOHNSON, S, 22; PHILOSOPHY, 4
geometry G. is not true MATHEMATICS, 14
Poetry is as exact a science as g. POETRY, 22
There is no 'royal road' to g. MATHEMATICS, 7
George *Death of King G. V* BETJEMAN, J, 4; HUNTING, 2
G., be a King ROYALTY, 21
G. the First knew nothing ROYALTY, 75
G. the Third……*may profit by their example* TREASON, 9
King G. will be able to read that SIGNATURES, 2
George III G. was a kind of 'consecrated obstruction' ROYALTY, 23
Georgie G. Porgie, pudding and pie NURSERY RHYMES, 12
geranium madman shakes a dead g. ELIOT, T, 20
German Ah, a G. and a genius MUSICIANS, 21
I speak…G. to my horse LANGUAGE, 13
Life is too short to learn G. LANGUAGE, 36
The G. army was stabbed in the back DEFEAT, 7
The G. Empire has become a world empire GERMANY, 8
the G. text of French operas OPERA, 13
Germans created to jab the life out of G. WORLD WAR I, 19
Don't let's be beastly to the G. COWARD, N, 7; GERMANY, 2
How…thorough these G. always managed to be GERMANY, 5; HUXLEY, A, 36
The G.…are going to be squeezed, as a lemon RETRIBUTION, 10
to the G. that of the air EUROPE, 18
Germany Defeat of G. means ROOSEVELT, F, 6; WORLD WAR II, 45
G. calling TREASON, 8; WORLD WAR II, 32
G., G. before all else GERMANY, 3
G. was the cause of Hitler HITLER, A, 8; LAST WORDS, 97
G. will be…a world power GERMANY, 4; HITLER, A, 12
If we see that G. is winning TRUMAN, H, 4; WORLD WAR II, 48
In G., the Nazis came for the Communists NAZISM, 6
Nazi G. had become a menace to all mankind NAZISM, 5
Gert G.'s poems are bunk ANONYMOUS, 89
gesture g. by the individual to himself BUSINESS, 15; GALBRAITH, J, 8
get a round of G. the Guests PARTIES, 1
I thought it was a pity to g. up BED, 9
getting a secret way…of g. at a boy EVIL, 10
G. and spending WASTE, 3; WORDSWORTH, W, 65
getting married Writing is like g. MURDOCH, I, 2
get up I thought it was a pity to g. MAUGHAM, W, 16
ghastly kind of g. object SHELLEY, P, 2
ghost I, born of flesh and g. DEATH, 171; THOMAS, D, 4
oh that I had given up the g. BIBLE, 227
the G. in the Machine MIND, 29
The Papacy is not other than the G. of the deceased Roman Empire CATHOLICISM, 7; HOBBES, T, 7
There is a g. /That eats handkerchiefs LOSS, 4
yielded up the g. BIBLE, 432; LAST WORDS, 11
ghoulies From g. and ghosties and long-leggety beasties SUPERNATURAL, 1
giant Fleas…upon the body of a g. LANDOR, W, 6; PERSPECTIVE, 3
like a g. refreshed with wine PSALMS, 43
owner whereof was G. Despair BUNYAN, J, 7; DESPAIR, 4
the sun…rejoiceth as a g. PSALMS, 8
we have only awakened a sleeping g. WORLD WAR II, 50
giants A battle of g. WAR, 179; WELLINGTON, 26
it is by standing on the shoulders of g. NEWTON, I, 7; PROGRESS, 19
not g. but windmills CERVANTES, M, 4; DELUSION, 2
war of the g. is over CHURCHILL, W, 30; WORLD WAR II, 25
gibes a great master of g. POLITICIANS, 78
Gideon Why do they put the G. Bibles SEX, 87
gift Beauty is a g. of God BEAUTY, 19
for this g. I feel blest BLESSING, 6
Never look a g. horse INGRATITUDE, 1; PROVERBS, 303
the timeliness of the g. LA BRUYERE, J, 5; PROMPTNESS, 1
True love's the g. which God has given /To man alone LOVE, 140; SCOTT, W, 7
worth more than the g. GIFTS, 4
gifts God's g. put man's best g. BROWNING, E, 4; GOD, 17
I fear the Greeks even when they bring g. MISTRUST, 12; VIRGIL, 9
The Gods themselves cannot recall their g. IRREVOCABILITY, 2; TENNYSON, 76
who knows how to use the gods' g. wisely HAPPINESS, 10; HORACE, 43
gild To g. refined gold EXCESS, 14; SHAKESPEARE, 167
gilded A best-seller is the g. tomb of a mediocre talent BOOKS, 45; SMITH, L, 1
She's only a bird in a g. cage IMPRISONMENT, 7
Gilpin And G., long live he COWPER, W, 11
gin G. was mother's milk ALCOHOL, 74; SHAW, G, 38
No man is genuinely happy, married, who has to drink worse g. MENCKEN, H, 13
Of all the g. joints in all the towns in all the world CHANCE, 3
she was dead; but my father he kept ladling g. REMEDIES, 53; SHAW, G, 37
The shortest way out of Manchester is…g. DRINKS, 6; PLACES, 5
giraffe a human g., sniffing…at mortals beneath his gaze DE GAULLE, C, 3
giraffes No but I adore g. SOLDIERS, 9
gird g. up now thy loins like a man BIBLE, 236
girded Pavilioned in splendour, and g. with praise GOD, 24
girl Every little g. knows about love LOVE, 138
From birth to age eighteen, a g. needs good parents AGE, 95
g. with brains WOMEN, 80
Give me a g. at an impressionable age SPARK, M, 7
If you were the only g. in the world LOVE, 82
one can…see in a little g. the threat of a woman CHILDREN, 27

One g. can be pretty BEAUTY, 22; FITZGERALD, F, 9
park, a policeman and a pretty g. CHAPLIN, C, 5; HUMOUR, 7
Sex and the Single G. SEX, 19
There was a little g. /Who had a little curl SEX, 83
girlfriend Not every problem someone has with his g. CAPITALISM, 12
girlfriends sleep with a boy...old g. AIDS, 7
girls Boys and g. come out to play NURSERY RHYMES, 6
fallen in love with all sorts of g. LOVE, 51
G. and boys grow up more normally together EDUCATION, 75
g. are so queer WOMEN, 10
g. from being g. HOPE, A, 5; SEXES, 15
g....say No when they mean Yes WOMEN, 10
g. who wear glasses APPEARANCE, 51; PARKER, D, 28
if ever I was to have a dozen g., I'd call 'em all Jane NAMES, 8; WELLS, H, 13
little g....slamming doors CHILDREN, 11
My life with g. has ended HORACE, 38; SEX, 52
one of the nicest g. I was ever engaged to MARRIAGE, 174; WODEHOUSE, P, 17
Thank heaven for little g. WOMEN, 77
the...rift between the sexes is...widened by...teaching...to the g. SEXES, 28; STEVENSON, R, 14
Treaties are like roses and young g. DE GAULLE, C, 12; DIPLOMACY, 10
When you see what some g. marry MARRIAGE, 127
Where...boys plan for what...young g. plan for whom SEXES, 13
young g. plan for whom...achieve FEMINISM, 9
Gitche Gumee By the shore of G. LONGFELLOW, H, 13
give freely ye have received, freely g. BIBLE, 385
g. me liberty or g. me death FREEDOM, 22
G. me your tired...Your huddled masses AMERICA, 26
my peace I g. unto you PEACE, 4
such as I have g. I thee BIBLE, 4; REMEDIES, 11
To g. and not to count the cost SELFLESSNESS, 3
When I g. I g. myself SELF, 25; WHITMAN, W, 8
given All I have, I would have g. REGRET, 8
I wish that God had not g. me what I prayed for DISAPPOINTMENT, 8
I would have g. you another CHIVALRY, 6
oh that I had g. up the ghost BIBLE, 227
unto every one that hath shall be g. BIBLE, 419
gives He g. twice who g. promptly PROMPTNESS, 4
giving The manner of g. GIFTS, 4
gizza G. job BLEASDALE, A, 1
gizzard My wife hath something in her g. PEPYS, S, 16
glad g. that part of my life is over SEX, 43
She had /A heart...too soon made g. BROWNING, R, 35; IMPRESSIONABILITY, 1
with a love like that you know you should be g. LENNON, J, 10; LOVE, 106
you would have been very g. if I had written it PLAYS, 9
gladness the g. of her g. VIRTUE AND VICE, 1
gladsome Let us with a g. mind /Praise the Lord GOD, 39; MILTON, J, 55
Gladstone G. BAGEHOT, W, 10; POLITICIANS, 43
G., like Richelieu, can't write POLITICIANS, 79
Mr G. read Homer for fun CHURCHILL, W, 18; CLASSICS, 2
glamorous g. only in retrospect TRAVEL, 43
glamour G....makes a man ask for your telephone number STYLE, 5
glands determined by the state of our ductless g. and our viscera MIND, 13
Worry affects circulation, the heart and the g. WORRY, 14
Glasgow never played the G. Empire PSYCHIATRY, 13
glass baying for broken g. ARISTOCRACY, 21; WAUGH, E, 7
He liked the sound of broken g. BELLOC, H, 18
on the other side of the g. BENNETT, A, 4; LIFE, 13
Satire is a sort of g. SATIRE, 3; SWIFT, J, 3
The g. is falling hour by hour REALISM, 4
through a g., darkly BIBLE, 38; CHARITY, 7
you won't intoxicate with one g. CHEKHOV, A, 13; EXPERIENCE, 10
glasses girls who wear g. APPEARANCE, 51; PARKER, D, 28
glimpse I...catch a g. of a stoat KEATS, J, 69; PURPOSE, 6
Same old g. of /Paradise MARRIAGE, 98
glisters Nor all that g. gold GRAY, T, 13; TEMPTATION, 6
glittering long grey beard and g. eye COLERIDGE, S, 24
The world continues to offer g. prizes RUTHLESSNESS, 6
glitters All that g. is not gold PROVERBS, 39
gloamin Roamin' in the g.' SCOTLAND, 6
global my wars /Were g. REED, H, 1; WAR, 135
the world in the image of a g. village TECHNOLOGY, 12
globe the great g. itself MORTALITY, 17; SHAKESPEARE, 327
globule I can trace my ancestry back to a...g. ANCESTRY, 2; GILBERT, W, 25
gloire *Le jour de g. est arrivé* FRANCE, 13
gloria *g. mundi* GLORY, 3
glorious G. things of thee are spoken HEAVEN, 9
Happy and g. BRITAIN, 6
her army has had a g. victory VICTORY, 14
glory Another g. awaits us in heaven HEAVEN, 10
because he gave not God the g. BIBLE, 11
But trailing clouds of g. METAPHYSICS, 5; WORDSWORTH, W, 26
give you g. GLORY, 2
G. be to God for dappled things BEAUTY, 25
g., jest, and riddle of the world HUMAN CONDITION, 21; POPE, A, 33
g. to God in the highest BIBLE, 315
greatest g. is not in never falling ACHIEVEMENT, 5
His face when he repeats his verses hath its ancient g. COLERIDGE, S, 2
I g. in the name of Briton PATRIOTISM, 17
I go on to g. LAST WORDS, 27
It is a great g. in a woman WOMEN, 131
Land of Hope and G. BRITAIN, 4
Mine eyes have seen the g. of the coming of the Lord GOD, 27
paths of g. lead but to the grave GRAY, T, 3; MORTALITY, 10
Popularity?...g.'s small change HUGO, V, 7; POPULARITY, 4
So passes the g. of the world TRANSIENCE, 1
the g. of Europe is extinguished for ever BURKE, E, 9; EUROPE, 2
the Son of man coming...with power and great g. BIBLE, 414; DOOMSDAY, 2
To the greater g. of God ANONYMOUS, 2; CATHOLICISM, 2
we left him alone with his g. FUNERALS, 14
Wellington has exhausted nature and...g. WELLINGTON, 2
What price G. GLORY, 1
Where is it now, the g. and the dream METAPHYSICS, 5; WORDSWORTH, W, 26
who is the King of g. PSALMS, 14
Gloucester Doctor Foster went to G. NURSERY RHYMES, 10
glow make the corpuscles of the blood g. JEWS, 11; LAWRENCE, D, 14
glum He is very yellow and g. ELIOT, T, 2
I've examined your son's head, Mr G. STUPIDITY, 12
speed g. heroes...to death SASSOON, S, 1; WAR, 146
glutton G., n. A person...committing dyspepsia GREED, 6
gluttony G. is an emotional escape GREED, 8
gnashing weeping and g. of teeth BIBLE, 381
gnomes the little g. of Zürich MONEY, 54; WILSON, H, 6
go a good cook, as cooks g. HUMOUR, 60; SAKI, 16
g., and do thou likewise BIBLE, 326; MERCY, 1
Hell no, we won't g. WAR, 9
In the name of God, *g.!* DISMISSAL, 1
I shall be the last to g. out COURAGE, 1
I will neither g. nor hang DETERMINATION, 13
Let's g. BECKETT, S, 4
Let us g. then, you and I DEPARTURE, 6; ELIOT, T, 11
not to g. anywhere, but to g. STEVENSON, R, 7; TRAVEL, 42
whither thou goest, I will g. BIBLE, 475; LOYALTY, 5
goal g. is not the conquest of Iraq BUSH, G, 13
The g. stands up FOOTBALL, 9; HOUSMAN, A, 12
goat plucking the wild g. by the beard WOOLF, V, 16
goat-footed This g. bard KEYNES, J, 4
goats as a shepherd divideth his sheep from the g. BIBLE, 420
gob hard for an actor to open his g. ACTORS, 3
God A bit like G. THOMAS, G, 3
Act of G....*something which no reasonable man could have expected* DISASTER, 3
A G. who let us prove his existence GOD, 16
a kind of Providence will...end...the acts of G. DISASTER, 2
A man with G. GOD, 32
America is G.'s Crucible AMERICA, 47
an absolute faith that all things are possible to G. EDDY, M, 1; FAITH, 13
an atheist half believes a G. ATHEISM, 13; YOUNG, E, 4
And this man /Is now become a g. EQUALITY, 33
An honest G. GOD, 30
Any G. I ever felt in church I brought in with me WALKER, A, 2

A physician who is a lover of wisdom is the equal to a g. DOCTORS, 53
a pun made by G. MANKIND, 39
Are G. and Nature then at strife NATURE, 30; TENNYSON, 31
As the low-fat diet unfolded…G. was showing me DIETING, 2
as though you were G. on earth ROYALTY, 65
better to have no opinion of G. BACON, F, 52; GOD, 4
but for the grace of G. goes LUCK, 7
charged with the grandeur of G. GOD, 26
concept of G. has any validity BALDWIN, J, 1; RELIGION, 12
cricket is the greatest thing that G. ever created CRICKET, 9
effect Whose cause is G. COWPER, W, 26; NATURE, 6
Either a beast or a g. ARISTOTLE, 7; MANKIND, 3
either a wild beast or a g. BACON, F, 24; SOLITUDE, 1
Even G. cannot change the past PAST, 1
even G. was born /too late RELIGION, 62
Every man thinks G. is on his side ANOUILH, J, 4; GOD, 3
final proof of G.'s omnipotence GOD, 20
G. alone deserves to be loved LOVE, 139
G. and my right FAITH, 27
G. and the Doctor we alike adore FAITH, 25
G. as a working hypothesis GOD, 15
G. be thanked who has matched us with His hour WAR, 31
G. bless … G. damn LAST WORDS, 89; THURBER, J, 21
G. bless us every one BLESSING, 8; DICKENS, C, 10
G. blew and they were scattered WAR, 2
G. can stand being told GOD, 45; PRIESTLEY, J, 8
G. could cause us considerable embarrassment DISCOVERY, 10; GOETHE, J, 8
G. could not be everywhere WOMAN'S ROLE, 1
G. defend me from my friends FRIENDSHIP, 4; PROVERBS, 176
G. did send me FAITH, 17
G. disposes GOD, 31
G. does not play dice EINSTEIN, A, 6; SCIENCE, 35
G. erects a house of prayer DEFOE, D, 5; DEVIL, 10
G., even our own G. PSALMS, 38
G.…first planted a garden BACON, F, 26; GARDENS, 2
G. from everlasting PSALMS, 48
G. has no religion RELIGION, 44
G. has written all the books BUTLER, S, 13; SUBJECTIVITY, 2
G. hath not given us the spirit of fear FEAR, 4
G. heals DOCTORS, 3
G. helps them PROVERBS, 177; SELF, 2
G. is a gentleman GOD, 42; ORTON, J, 6
G. is always on the side of the big battalions POWER POLITICS, 7
G. is beginning to resemble…the last fading smile of a cosmic Cheshire cat GOD, 28
G. is dead GOD, 41; NIETZSCHE, F, 5
G. /Is distant, difficult HILL, G, 2
G. is forgotten, and the Doctor slighted FAITH, 25
G. is nothing more than an exalted father FREUD, S, 5; GOD, 23
G. is on the side not of the heavy battalions, but of the best shots VOLTAIRE, 23
G. is really only another artist GOD, 44; PICASSO, P, 7
G. is subtle but he is not malicious EINSTEIN, A, 7; GOD, 22; SCIENCE, 37
G. is the immemorial refuge of the incompetent GOD, 36; MENCKEN, H, 9
G. is the only president WEBSTER, D, 2
G.…just had the power to kill her RELIGION, 1
G.-like in our…breeding of…plants and animals EVOLUTION, 25
G. made everything out of nothing CREATION, 16
G. made the country COUNTRYSIDE, 2; COWPER, W, 22
G. said, *Let Newton be* POPE, A, 19
G. save our gracious King BRITAIN, 6
G. sent me down to kiss KISSING, 3
G.'s gifts put man's best gifts BROWNING, E, 4; GOD, 17
G. should go before such villains GOD, 46; SHAKESPEARE, 276
G.'s in His heaven BROWNING, R, 45; PERFECTION, 3
G. tempers the wind MERCY, 3
G. the first garden made GARDENS, 6
G. will cease to dream you DEATH, 91; UNAMUNO, M, 1
G. will grant an end to these too ENDURANCE, 27; VIRGIL, 6
G. will pardon me. It is His trade HEINE, H, 5; LAST WORDS, 49
g. would be hanging around Terminal Two ADAMS, D, 8
going back to G. RELIGION, 17
good of G. to let Carlyle and Mrs Carlyle marry MARRIAGE, 39
Great G. grant that twice two be not four PRAYER, 28; TURGENEV, I, 4
Had I but serv'd my G. with half the zeal /I serv'd my King SHAKESPEARE, 142
Has G. then forgotten LOUIS XIV, 2
have one G. only GOD, 18
her conception of G. was certainly not orthodox GOD, 49
Holy, holy, holy, Lord G. Almighty GOD, 25
How could G. do this to me LOUIS XIV, 1
I am glad…he thanks G. for anything. JOHNSON, S, 14
I believe I am becoming a g. LAST WORDS, 92
I did not write it. G. wrote it. I merely did his dictation STOWE, H, 4
If G. did not exist GOD, 52; VOLTAIRE, 14
if G. had wanted to create slaves SLAVERY, 1
If G. made us in His image GOD, 53; VOLTAIRE, 19
If G. were suddenly condemned to live the life HUMAN CONDITION, 7
If this man is not faithful to his G. LOYALTY, 12
if triangles invented a g., they would make him three-sided MONTESQUIEU, 4; RELIGION, 70
If you don't find a G. by five o'clock this afternoon ATHEISM, 8
If you talk to G., you are praying MADNESS, 43; SZASZ, T, 8
I neglect G. and his angels RELIGION, 32
In the Nineteenth Century men lost their fear of G. FEAR, 1
Isn't G. a shit BIBLE, 526
it pisses G. off if you walk by the color purple WALKER, A, 3
It takes a long while for a…trustful person to reconcile himself to…G. FAITH, 22; MENCKEN, H, 10
I wouldn't give up writing about G. WAUGH, E, 48; WRITERS, 94
I wretch lay wrestling with…my G. SOUL, 8
justify the ways of G. to men GOD, 40; MILTON, J, 31
Just what G. would have done if he had the money WEALTH, 50
Kill everyone, and you are a g. KILLING, 10
Know then thyself, presume not G. to scan POPE, A, 34
Live among men as if G. beheld you RIGHTEOUSNESS, 10
Man…is halfway between an ape and a g. MANKIND, 32
Many people believe that they are attracted by G. INGE, W, 4; RELIGION, 56
May G. deny you peace UNAMUNO, M, 3
nature is the art of G. BROWNE, T, 3; NATURE, 1
Nearer, my G., to thee RELIGION, 2
none deny there is a G. ATHEISM, 3; BACON, F, 10
One does not insult the river g. PRUDENCE, 5
One G., one law, one element DESTINY, 27; TENNYSON, 38
One on G.'s side is a majority GOD, 43
only G. can make a tree TREES, 9
Our G., our help in ages past RELIGION, 95; WATTS, I, 6
People think pleasing G. WALKER, A, 4
poems…for the love of Man and in praise of G. POETRY, 64; THOMAS, D, 5
Praise be to G., the Lord of all creatures KORAN, 1
proof that G. is a bore MENCKEN, H, 7; PROTESTANTISM, 6
prose for G. LANGUAGE, 23
put your hand into the hand of G. FAITH, 15
Resistance to tyranny is obedience to G. ANTHONY, S, 6
Sickness, sin and death…do not originate in G. EDDY, M, 4; RELIGION, 37
Since G. has given us the papacy…enjoy it CATHOLICISM, 10
speak to G. as if men were listening RIGHTEOUSNESS, 10
that G. is interested only…in religion GOD, 50
that great Leviathan, or rather…that *Mortal G.* HOBBES, T, 5; STATE, 1
The Act of G. designation ACCIDENTS, 2
the dear G. who loveth us COLERIDGE, S, 39; PRAYER, 12
the electric display of G. the Father LIFE, 71
the G. of ideas INSPIRATION, 5
the good G. prepare me BLINDNESS, 13; PEPYS, S, 17
the highest praise of G. consists in the denial of Him ATHEISM, 11; PROUST, M, 8
the nearer you are to G. PROTESTANTISM, 8
The noblest work of G.? Man MANKIND, 68
the one G. whose worshippers…still trust in Him LUCK, 8
There, but for the Grace of G., goes G. INSULTS, 93
There once was a man who said G. EXISTENCE, 4
Those who marry G.…can become domesticated too GREENE, G, 1; RELIGION, 48
to obstruct the way of G.…is more grievous than to kill in the sacred months KORAN, 3
to the unknown g. SUPERSTITION, 6
To understand G.'s thoughts STATISTICS, 8

we come /From G., who is our home METAPHYSICS, 5; WORDSWORTH, W, 26
we owe G. a death DEATH, 143; SHAKESPEARE, 124
What G. does, He does well GOD, 33; LA FONTAINE, J, 10
What sort of G. are we portraying GOD, 21
When I composed that, I was…inspired by G. MUSIC, 9
when one has loved a man it is very different to love G. LOVE, 139
Which is, I gather, what G. did PSYCHOLOGY, 14
Whom G. wishes to destroy MADNESS, 1, 13
yearning like a G. in pain KEATS, J, 12
you hardly ever mention G. any more MILLER, A, 1; RELIGION, 67
you must believe in G. FAITH, 18

Goddamm Lhude sing G. POUND, E, 7

godlike patient endurance is g. ENDURANCE, 11; LONGFELLOW, H, 6

Godot waiting for G. BECKETT, S, 4

gods Against stupidity the g.…struggle in vain STUPIDITY, 14
a great king above all g. PSALMS, 54
by force of the g. ENDURANCE, 29; VIRGIL, 5
deserves the name of happy who knows how to use the g.' gifts wisely HAPPINESS, 10; HORACE, 43
for what high cause /This darling of the G. DESTINY, 16; MARVELL, A, 7
g. handing down new commandments SCIENTISTS, 4
g. help them AESOP, 4
g.…/Make instruments to plague us SHAKESPEARE, 195
Kings are earth's g. ROYALTY, 103; SHAKESPEARE, 291
leave the rest to the G. DUTY, 2
Live with the g. MARCUS AURELIUS ANTONINUS, 10
man's ignorance of the g. BUTLER, S, 7; SPONTANEITY, 1
no other g. before me BIBLE, 115; GOD, 12
So many g., so many creeds KINDNESS, 13; RELIGION, 102
The Ethiopians say that their g. are…black RELIGION, 105
The G. themselves cannot recall their gifts IRREVOCABILITY, 2; TENNYSON, 76
we're forbidden to know – what end the g. have in store DESTINY, 15; HORACE, 30
Whom the g. love DEATH, 111; PROVERBS, 465
Whom the g. wish to destroy CONNOLLY, C, 9

goe to morowe longe I to g. to God EXECUTION, 25; FAMILY, 41

Goethe G.'s sage mind and Byron's force WORDSWORTH, W, 1

Gog G. and Magog BIBLE, 471; EVIL, 7

going I am just g. outside LAST WORDS, 63
Men must endure /Their g. hence ENDURANCE, 22; SHAKESPEARE, 194
Stand not upon the order of your g. DISMISSAL, 9; SHAKESPEARE, 217

gold A g. rush is what happens when MATERIALISM, 28
all the g. that the goose could give AESOP, 3; MATERIALISM, 2
An angel writing in a book of g. DREAMS, 8
cursed /craving for g. MATERIALISM, 26; VIRGIL, 11
For g. in phisik is a cordial CHAUCER, G, 11; MATERIALISM, 8
Garrick was pure g. ACTORS, 14
gild refined g. EXCESS, 14; SHAKESPEARE, 167
Good morning to the day: and next my g. JONSON, B, 14
I have seen many a man turn his g. into smoke SMOKING, 11
I stuffed their mouths with g. BEVAN, A, 12; BRIBERY, 2
more to be desired…than g. PSALMS, 9
Nor all that glisters g. GRAY, T, 13; TEMPTATION, 6
Nothing melts a Woman's Heart like g. WEALTH, 16
picking g. out of the dunghills of old Roman writers VIRGIL, 3
silver and g. have I none BIBLE, 4; REMEDIES, 11
Silver threads among the g. OLD AGE, 81
Their idols are silver and g. PSALMS, 64
The ring so worn…is yet of g. APPEARANCE, 21
the sick man hands you g. in return REMEDIES, 8
To a shower of g. BRIBERY, 3; CARLYLE, T, 15
travell'd in the realms of g. KEATS, J, 41; TRAVEL, 24
Were't not for g. and women SIN, 25
What female heart can g. despise GRAY, T, 11; MATERIALISM, 12
When every…thing you hold /Is made of silver, or of g. ECONOMICS, 10; GILBERT, W, 5

golden G. slumbers kiss your eyes SLEEP, 10
In good King Charles's g. days ANONYMOUS, 48; SELF-PRESERVATION, 5
In old time we had treen chalices and g. priests CLERGY, 8
Jerusalem the g. PLACES, 27
on a g. treadmill WEALTH, 4
perhaps, the g. rule STEVENSON, R, 22
silence is g. PROVERBS, 368
The g. apples of the sun DESIRE, 18; YEATS, W, 30
the G. Road to Samarkand KNOWLEDGE, 17
there are no g. rules RULES, 3; SHAW, G, 31

gold rush A g. is what happens when WEST, M, 7

Goldsmith To Oliver G. JOHNSON, S, 114

Goldwyn Mr G.…you are only interested in art ART, 32; MONEY, 46

golf an earnest protest against g. BEERBOHM, M, 19; CRICKET, 1; GOLF, 1
G.…a form of moral effort GOLF, 4; LEACOCK, S, 11
G. is a good walk spoiled GOLF, 6
he bestowed upon the games of g. and bridge EISENHOWER, D, 2
he would rather play g. than have sex any day QUAYLE, D, 2
more satisfying to be a bad player at g. GOLF, 3

golf clubs Give me my g.…and a beautiful partner DESIRE, 1

G.O.M The G., when his life ebbs out POLITICIANS, 33

Gomorrah Sodom and…G. BIBLE, 167; PUNISHMENT, 5

gone g. with the wind MEMORY, 8
G. With the Wind MITCHELL, M, 6; TRANSIENCE, 19

gongs women should be struck…like g. COWARD, N, 18; WOMEN, 36

gonna g. have to serve somebody DYLAN, B, 3

good a gigantic reservoir of g. will AMERICA, 43
a g. friend, but bad acquaintance BYRON, 23
A g. man fallen among Fabians LENIN, V, 10; WRITERS, 68
A g. novel tells us the truth CHESTERTON, G, 24; NOVELS, 2
A G. Time Was Had by All PLEASURE, 33
All g. writing FITZGERALD, F, 16; WRITING, 14
Anybody can be g. in the country COUNTRYSIDE, 13; WILDE, O, 52
as gods, knowing g. and evil BIBLE, 149
Be g., sweet maid, and let who can be clever KINGSLEY, C, 1; VIRTUE, 18
being really g. all the time HYPOCRISY, 23; WILDE, O, 27
dedicate this nation to the policy of the g. neighbor CHARITY, 20; ROOSEVELT, F, 11
Do g. by stealth GOOD, 15; POPE, A, 10
doing g.…professions which are full CHARITY, 27; THOREAU, H, 12
doing g. to base fellows CERVANTES, M, 9; CHARITY, 13
dull prospect of a distant g. DRYDEN, J, 25; PLEASURE, 13
every creature of God is g. BIBLE, 508
every man at the beginning doth set forth g. wine ALCOHOL, 17; BIBLE, 242
Every man loves what he is g. at ENTHUSIASM, 7
Evil, be thou my G. EVIL, 15; MILTON, J, 44
Evil comes…like the disease CHESTERTON, G, 27
Far too g. to waste on children SHAW, G, 50; YOUTH, 29
For the g. are always the merry HAPPINESS, 33
Four legs g. ORWELL, G, 4
General G. is the plea of the scoundrel BLAKE, W, 16; GOOD, 2
God saw that it was g. BIBLE, 139; CREATION, 3
G. at a fight SHERIDAN, R, 1
Good, but not religious-g. HARDY, T, 11; VIRTUE, 15
G. girls go to heaven VIRTUE AND VICE, 2
g. in everything GOOD, 16
G. isn't the word CRITICISM, 22; GILBERT, W, 48
g. shepherd giveth his life for the sheep CHRISTIANITY, 19
G. things, when short, are twice as good BREVITY, 2
g. tidings of great joy BIBLE, 314; CHRISTMAS, 9
g. wine is a g. familiar creature if it be well used ALCOHOL, 71
greatest g. GOOD, 3
happiness makes them g. GOOD, 10; LANDOR, W, 3
He who would do g. to another BLAKE, W, 16; GOOD, 2
hold fast that which is g. BIBLE, 504
how *can* they become g. people PREJUDICE, 15; VICTORIA, 6
how can ye, being evil, speak g. BIBLE, 389
How g. is man's life, the mere living BROWNING, R, 50; LIFE, 19
If…'feeling g.' could decide, drunkenness would be DRUNKENNESS, 18
If to do were as easy as to know what were g. ACTION, 13; SHAKESPEARE, 239
If you can't be g. PROVERBS, 217; TEMPTATION, 2
I have fought a g. fight BIBLE, 514; FAITH, 11
it cannot come to g. PESSIMISM, 11; SHAKESPEARE, 70
It is g. to know what a man is UNDERSTANDING, 2
It is seldom…one parts on g. terms PARTING, 9; PROUST, M, 17
little of what you fancy does you g. PLEASURE, 21
Men have never been g. GOOD, 1
Most g. women are hidden treasures VIRTUE, 22
never was a g. war FRANKLIN, B, 16; WAR AND PEACE, 7

no hint throughout the universe /Of g. or ill NECESSITY, 8
Nothing can harm a g. man GOOD, 18; SOCRATES, 4
nothing either g. or bad SHAKESPEARE, 84; THINKING, 17
nothing g. to be had in the country HAZLITT, W, 15
on earth peace, g. will toward men BIBLE, 315
One man is as g. as another WRITERS, 15
Only g. girls keep diaries BANKHEAD, T, 13; DIARIES, 2
our people have never had it so g. MACMILLAN, H, 5; WEALTH, 35
Roman Conquest…a G. Thing HISTORY, 29; SELLAR, W, 4
science is…neither a potential for g. nor for evil SCIENCE, 83
strong antipathy of g. to bad POPE, A, 11; PROVOCATION, 2
suppose the people g. CORRUPTION, 11; LAW, 29
the g. are always the merry YEATS, W, 13
The g. die early DEFOE, D, 1; GOOD AND EVIL, 4
The g. die first GOOD AND EVIL, 9; WORDSWORTH, W, 5
The g. die young DEATH, 13; PROVERBS, 396
The g. is oft interred with their bones EVIL, 19; SHAKESPEARE, 155
The g. is the beautiful GOOD, 14; PLATO, 1
the g. must associate BURKE, E, 20; UNITY, 7
The g. of the people LAW, 9
The g. old times BYRON, 4; NOSTALGIA, 5
The king has been very g. to me MARTYRDOM, 1
the name of perseverance in a g. cause STERNE, L, 6; STUBBORNNESS, 4
The only g. Indians I ever saw were dead ENEMIES, 9
There is so much g. in the worst of us ANONYMOUS, 88; GOOD AND EVIL, 1
the thing which is g. BIBLE, 94; PUNISHMENT, 2; SIN, 3
they are…surprised at hearing of a g. action and never of a bad one KEATS, J, 70
those who go about doing g. CHARITY, 15
thou g. and faithful servant BIBLE, 418; SERVICE, 1
three ingredients in the g. life LIFE, 67
to write g. prose is an affair of g. manners POETRY AND PROSE, 4
what g. came of it at last SOUTHEY, R, 1; VICTORY, 24
What's the g. of a home ABSENCE, 7; HOME, 6
Whenever two g. people argue over principles PRINCIPLES, 4
When I'm g. I'm very g. SEX, 128; WEST, M, 17
when the great and g. depart MORTALITY, 20; WORDSWORTH, W, 16
Why care for grammar as long as we are g. GRAMMAR, 8
You shouldn't say it is not g. GOOD, 20; WHISTLER, J, 10
good-bye Without a single kiss or a g. PARTING, 8
Good-by-ee G.! – g. PARTING, 12
good knights sorrier for my g.' loss than for…my fair queen MALORY, T, 4
goodly make us love your g. gifts /And snatch them SHAKESPEARE, 293
good manners to write good prose is an affair of g. MAUGHAM, W, 17
goodness Abashed the devil…felt how awful g. is GOOD, 13; MILTON, J, 47
G. does not…make men happy GOOD, 10; LANDOR, W, 3
My g. those diamonds are lovely GOOD, 19; WEST, M, 4
Not to be wronged is to forgo…g. WELLS, H, 4
surely g. and mercy shall follow me PSALMS, 13
the earth is full of the g. of the Lord PSALMS, 21
goodnight G., my darlings LAST WORDS, 21
John Thomas says g. to Lady Jane SEX, 66
goods isn't a bad bit of g., the Queen CERVANTES, M, 13; COMPLIMENTS, 8
Poverty of g. is easily cured MONTAIGNE, M, 10
your wife…is a receiver of stolen g. JOHNSON, S, 134
Good Samaritan No one would have remembered the G. THATCHER, M, 22
good taste G.…an utterly dispensable part JOURNALISM, 19
good-temper'd a loyal, a gallant, a generous, an ingenious, and g. people FRANCE, 18; STERNE, L, 2
goodwill in peace, g. CHURCHILL, W, 26; WAR AND PEACE, 4
goose all the gold that the g. could give AESOP, 3; MATERIALISM, 2
goosey G., goosey gander NURSERY RHYMES, 13
gored you tossed and g. several persons CONVERSATION, 3
gorgeous hold the g. east in fee VENICE, 4; WORDSWORTH, W, 59
gorilla these g. damnifications of humanity DARWIN, C, 1
gormed I'm G. DICKENS, C, 18
Gospels literal adherence to…the G. would mean sudden death BIBLE, 537
We had no use for the policy of the G. KHRUSHCHEV, N, 1; REVENGE, 14
gossamer A trip to the moon on g. wings TRAVEL, 37
gossips No one g. about…secret virtues GOSSIP, 12; RUSSELL, B, 17
got Which in our case we have not g. REED, H, 3; WEAPONS, 8
gout A taste for drink, combined with g. ALCOHOL, 35; GILBERT, W, 3
Drink wine, and have the g. DISEASE, 38; MISFORTUNE, 3
G. is not relieved by a fine shoe WEALTH, 41
G.…physician's name for DISEASE, 10
If gentlemen love the pleasant titillation of the g. DISEASE, 21
I refer to g. INTELLECTUALS, 9
Punch cures the g. ALCOHOL, 13
that old enemy the g. /Had taken him in toe HOOD, T, 9; PUNS, 8
what is a cure for g. DISEASE, 2
you have 'g.' for the result PUNS, 5
we have 'g.' for the taste PUNS, 5
gouty My corns ache, I get g. PREJUDICE, 7
govern Every class is unfit to g. GOVERNMENT, 2
Go out and g. new South Wales DISMISSAL, 3; GOVERNMENT, 7
Grammar, which can g. even kings GRAMMAR, 6; MOLIERE, 9
He that would g. others SELF-CONTROL, 6
I will g. according to the common weal MONARCHY, 15
king reigns, but does not g. MONARCHY, 28
Kings g. by…assemblies only when MONARCHY, 13
Labour is not fit to g. CHURCHILL, W, 43; POLITICS, 28
Let the people think they g. GOVERNMENT, 31
No man is good enough to g. another man DEMOCRACY, 13; LINCOLN, A, 10
Under socialism *all* will g. LENIN, V, 5; SOCIALISM, 17
govern'd g. by a child CHILDREN, 54; SHAKESPEARE, 304
governed g. by those who do not speak their language GOVERNMENT, 40
with how little wisdom the world is g. GOVERNMENT, 28
governing become accustomed to no one g. SOCIALISM, 17
the right of g. was not property but a trust GOVERNMENT, 13
government A g.…big enough to give you all you want GOVERNMENT, 15
All g.…is founded on compromise and barter BURKE, E, 14; COMPROMISE, 4
As to religion…duty of g. to protect all…professors thereof GOVERNMENT, 30
Democracy is only an experiment in g. DEMOCRACY, 10; INGE, W, 7
Do not criticize your g. when out of the country POLITICS, 30
every g.…should have its old speeches burned GOVERNMENT, 38
g. by crony NEPOTISM, 1
g. endorsement of homosexuality HOMOSEXUALITY, 28
g. gives us is charity at election time OPPRESSION, 5
G. has no other end but the preservation of property GOVERNMENT, 22
G.…is but a necessary evil GOVERNMENT, 29
g.…must be built upon the rights of the people GOVERNMENT, 45
g. of the people, by the people, and for the people LINCOLN, A, 17
human face on…g. ROYALTY, 101
I would not give half a guinea to live under one form of g. GOVERNMENT, 18; JOHNSON, S, 83
Monarchy is a strong g. BAGEHOT, W, 3; MONARCHY, 2
no man believes, that want of g., is any new kind of g. GOVERNMENT, 17; HOBBES, T, 6
people's g. GOVERNMENT, 43; WEBSTER, D, 4
prepare for g. POLITICS, 99
The g. burns down whole cities MAO TSE-TUNG, 10
the g. it deserves GOVERNMENT, 24
the President is dead, but the G. lives ASSASSINATION, 4
there was no form of g. common to the peoples REPUBLIC, 2; WAUGH, E, 40
the things which g. does…social progress GOVERNMENT, 42
The worst g. is the most moral GOVERNMENT, 25; MENCKEN, H, 8
We live under a g. of men and…newspapers GOVERNMENT, 32; JOURNALISM, 29
You have no right…to speak on behalf of the G. POLITICIANS, 42
governmental liberty…is to be measured not by the g. machinery SOCIETY, 20
governments all G. are selfish GOVERNMENT, 11
G. needs…shepherds and butchers GOVERNMENT, 41
G. will get out of the way EISENHOWER, D, 9

The Beast stands for strong mutually antagonistic g. WAUGH, E, 35
governors Our supreme g., the mob PUBLIC, 21; WALPOLE, H, 3
Gower moral G. BOOKS, 14
grac'd What comfortable hour canst thou name /That ever g. me in thy company CHILDREN, 55
grace but for the g. of God, goes LUCK, 7
God in his mercy lend her g. BEAUTY, 46; TENNYSON, 47
g. a summer queen COUNTRYSIDE, 10; SCOTT, W, 20
g. of our Lord Jesus Christ be with you BIBLE, 43
grow old with a good g. AGE, 87
He had at least the g. BRIBERY, 1
Lord, I ascribe it to Thy g. RELIGION, 94; WATTS, I, 4
she obtained g. and favour BIBLE, 101; LOVE, 27
Such g. had kings BROWNING, R, 47; ROYALTY, 29
Tuesday's child is full of g. CHILDREN, 50; NURSERY RHYMES, 35
Graces the G. do not seem…natives of Great Britain BRITISH, 5; CHESTERFIELD, P, 13
gracious A life that moves to g. ends LIFE, 93; TENNYSON, 77
gradually Boys do not grow up g. CHILDREN, 25; CONNOLLY, C, 13
Grail What were they going to do with the G. BEERBOHM, M, 22
grain A g., which in England is generally given to horses JOHNSON, S, 12; SCOTLAND, 3
He reaps the bearded g. at a breath DEATH, 101; LONGFELLOW, H, 11
grammar down to posterity talking bad g. DISRAELI, B, 17; GRAMMAR, 5
G., which can govern even kings GRAMMAR, 6; MOLIERE, 9
I am…above g. GRAMMAR, 7
Religious law is like the g. of a language RELIGION, 81
Shakespeare…g. school kids EDUCATION, 38
they went to the g. school little children EDUCATION, 9
Why care for g. as long as we are good GRAMMAR, 8
grammatical I have laboured to refine our language to g. purity JOHNSON, S, 24; LANGUAGE, 26
gramophones waxworks inhabited by g. WORDS, 8
grand A 'G. Old Man' LEACOCK, S, 12
that g. old man POLITICIANS, 109
The g. Perhaps BROWNING, R, 11; POSSIBILITY, 1
the g. style arises in poetry ARNOLD, M, 32; POETRY, 3
to be baith g. and comfortable BARRIE, J, 2; LUXURY, 1
Grand Canyon coming across him at the G. INSULTS, 107
grandeur g. is a dream COWPER, W, 30; WEALTH, 20
g. of God GOD, 26
Many people have delusions of g. DELUSION, 5; INSULTS, 68
grandfather ashamed of having an ape for his g. EVOLUTION, 20; HUXLEY, T, 11
I don't know who my g. was ANCESTRY, 5; LINCOLN, A, 22
pass my declining years saluting…g. clocks NASH, O, 9; OLD AGE, 75
grandfathers the future Englishmen must take business as seriously as their g. had done BUSINESS, 20
grandmother I murdered my g. this morning ROOSEVELT, F, 3
We have become a g. AFFECTATION, 1
grandson I am much more concerned to know what his g. will be ANCESTRY, 5; LINCOLN, A, 22
your g. will…be a Communist COMMUNISM, 6; KHRUSHCHEV, N, 5
Granny G. caught her tit in the mangle PLEASURE, 34
Grant Old Cary G. fine AGE, 48
granted an…infinite capacity for taking things for g. HUMAN NATURE, 16; HUXLEY, A, 33
grape Beulah, peel me a g. LUXURY, 6; WEST, M, 6
grapes I am sure the g. are sour AESOP, 2; ENVY, 4
trampling out the vintage where the g. of wrath GOD, 27
grapeshot A whiff of g. CARLYLE, T, 16
grasp he that dares not g. the thorn BRONTE, A, 3
man's reach should exceed his g. AMBITION, 4; BROWNING, R, 4
grasper I never was any greedy, scraping g. IDEALISM, 1
grass all flesh is as g. BIBLE, 440; DEATH, 36
days of man are but as g. PSALMS, 58
There's a snake hidden in the g. DANGER, 7; VIRGIL, 17
grassgreen down the g. gooseberried double bed SEX, 118; THOMAS, D, 23
gratification I have had no real g.…more than my neighbor…who is worth only half a million LAST WORDS, 91; WEALTH, 48
gratifying It is quite g. to feel guilty GUILT, 1
gratitude g. to most benefactors INGRATITUDE, 3
gratuite *L'acte g.* SPONTANEITY, 2
gratuitous Friendship ought to be a g. joy FRIENDSHIP, 28
grave a-mouldering in the g. MEMORIALS, 7
And digs my g. at each remove DEATH, 79; HERBERT, G, 5
And on his g., with shining eyes ARNOLD, M, 30; DEATH, 26
a woman would rather visit her own g. OLD AGE, 52
Between the cradle and the g. TRANSIENCE, 13
Dig the g. and let me lie DEATH, 166; STEVENSON, R, 12
Funeral marches to the g. LONGFELLOW, H, 10; MORTALITY, 14
G., n. A place…to await the coming of the medical student MEDICINE, 13
her heart in his g. is lying MOORE, T, 4; MOURNING, 8
If Roosevelt were alive he'd turn in his g. GOLDWYN, S, 19
I may dread /The g. as little DEATH, 94
I shall soon be laid in the quiet g. DEATH, 93; KEATS, J, 72
Marriage is a step so g. and decisive MARRIAGE, 147; STEVENSON, R, 23
most still, most secret, and most g. EQUALITY, 30
No g. upon the earth SHAKESPEARE, 40
no work, nor device, nor knowledge…in the g. BIBLE, 73; TRANSIENCE, 7; WORK, 4
O g., where is thy victory BIBLE, 42; POPE, A, 6
paths of glory lead but to the g. GRAY, T, 3; MORTALITY, 10
The g.'s a fine and private place DEATH, 105; MARVELL, A, 12
the g. yawns for him BORES, 7; INSULTS, 123; TREE, H, 3
To that dark inn, the g. DEATH, 134; SCOTT, W, 12
vanity-case…g. of masculine illusions COSMETICS, 6
grave-digger if I were a g., or…a hangman JERROLD, D, 6; OCCUPATIONS, 12
graven any g. image BIBLE, 115
graves Let's talk of g., of worms, and epitaphs DEATH, 153
Six million young men lie in premature g. WORLD WAR I, 2
The bitterest tears shed over g. REGRET, 26; STOWE, H, 1
The dust of great persons' g. DONNE, J, 15; EQUALITY, 40
graveyard A young doctor makes a humpy g. DOCTORS, 1
graveyards G.…people associate them with death DEATH, 32
gravity He rose by g.; I sank by levity SERIOUSNESS, 4; SMITH, S, 18
She was once cool but Mr G.'s been very unkind GREER, G, 1
the uncouth g. and supercilious self-conceit of a physician DOCTORS, 94
Gray Robin G., he was gudeman to me MARRIAGE, 20
When you are old and g. OLD AGE, 113; YEATS, W, 33
grazed He is the richest author that ever g. JOHNSON, S, 60; WRITERS, 65
great All my shows are g. GOLDWYN, S, 28
All things both g. and small COLERIDGE, S, 39; PRAYER, 12
A truly g. man GREATNESS, 1
deep consent of all g. men RUSKIN, J, 14
Everything g. in the world is done by neurotics NEUROSIS, 12; PROUST, M, 20
everything that is g.…done by youth DISRAELI, B, 5; YOUTH, 9
fate of the g. wen LONDON, 8
G. men are but life-sized BEERBOHM, M, 5; GREATNESS, 3
g. men have not commonly been g. scholars GREATNESS, 8
G. oaks BEGINNING, 4; PROVERBS, 182
G. White Way PLACES, 28
History is full of ignominious getaways by the g. COWARDICE, 6; ORWELL, G, 33
how g. a matter a little fire kindleth SPEECH, 6
How very small the very g. THACKERAY, W, 8
If I am a g. man GREATNESS, 9
many of the g. men of history are frauds GREATNESS, 9
No g. man lives in vain CARLYLE, T, 11
On earth there is nothing g. but man MANKIND, 30
Some…born g. SHAKESPEARE, 343
the g. break through LAW, 36
The g. man…walks across his century INFLUENCE, 7; LEACOCK, S, 9
the g. ones eat up the little ones RUTHLESSNESS, 5; SHAKESPEARE, 292
the shade /Of that which once was g. REGRET, 29; WORDSWORTH, W, 62
those who were truly g. HEROISM, 10
To be g. is to be misunderstood EMERSON, R, 16; GREATNESS, 7
when the g. and good depart MORTALITY, 20; WORDSWORTH, W, 16
you…who have made me too g. for my house BACON, F, 66; ROYALTY, 22
great-aunt A person may be indebted for a nose or an eye…to a g. FAMILY, 28; HAZLITT, W, 11
Great Britain G. could say that she supported both sides DIPLOMACY, 26

G. has lost an Empire ACHESON, D, 6; BRITAIN, 1
G. is going to make war on a kindred nation WORLD WAR I, 3
To make a union with G. WORLD WAR II, 41
greater g. love hath no man BIBLE, 260; LOVE, 31
The g. the power BURKE, E, 25; POWER, 8
Thy need is yet g. than mine SELF-DENIAL, 2
greatest great city…has the g. men and women GREATNESS, 15; WHITMAN, W, 12
g., most truly heroic stories of my time and generation WRITING, 27
I'm the g. CONCEIT, 1
One of the g. geniuses SHAKESPEARE, 20
the g. deeds require a certain insensitiveness INSENSITIVITY, 4
The g. happiness of the g. number HAPPINESS, 4
the g. of these is charity BIBLE, 38; CHARITY, 7
great-grandfathers Classicism…the literature that gave…pleasure to their g. LITERATURE, 25
great-heart One G. BUNYAN, J, 9
greatness dignity and g. and peace again DRINKS, 9; HOPE, 9
get out with my g. intact SELF-PRESERVATION, 2
long farewell to all my g. HUMAN CONDITION, 24; SHAKESPEARE, 141
Men who have g.…don't go in for politics CAMUS, A, 10; POLITICIANS, 2
some have g. thrust upon 'em GREATNESS, 12; SHAKESPEARE, 343
Great War A Soldier of the G. KIPLING, R, 34
Greece Athens holds sway over all G. INFLUENCE, 11
G. might still be free BYRON, 27; EUROPE, 4
The isles of G. BYRON, 26; EUROPE, 3
greedy be not g. to add money to money BIBLE, 516
Greek I…impress upon you the study of G. literature CLASSICS, 3
it was G. to me CONFUSION, 10; SHAKESPEARE, 147
neither Jew nor G. BIBLE, 132; CHRISTIANITY, 10
Nobody can say a word against G. CLASSICS, 8; SHAW, G, 15
prefers to describe in G. what he can't LANGUAGE, 5
small Latin and less G. CLASSICS, 5; JONSON, B, 10
the intrigue of a G. of the lower empire DISRAELI, B, 33; INSULTS, 43
We were taught…Latin and G. CLASSICS, 9; WELLS, H, 16
Greeks G. Had a Word LANGUAGE, 2
G. seek after wisdom BIBLE, 24
I fear the G. even when they bring gifts MISTRUST, 12; VIRGIL, 9
The Romans and G. found everything human LAWRENCE, D, 6
To the G. the Muse gave native wit CLASSICS, 4; HORACE, 8
uncertainty: a state unknown to the G. UNCERTAINTY, 2
where the G. had modesty, we have cant PEACOCK, T, 2
which came first, the G. or the Romans DISRAELI, B, 39; IGNORANCE, 9
green a g. thought in a g. shade MARVELL, A, 2; OBLIVION, 3
Anything g. that grew out of the mould NATURE, 24
for the wearin' o' the G. ANONYMOUS, 46; IRELAND, 1
G. grow the rashes O BURNS, R, 11; LOVE, 43
G. politics is not about being far left CONSERVATION, 6
in the morning it is g. PSALMS, 49
I was g. in judgment SHAKESPEARE, 29; YOUTH, 26
not quite so g. INNOCENCE, 2
religious system that produced G. Chartreuse SAKI, 17
There is a g. hill far away CHRISTIANITY, 1
Time held me g. and dying TIME, 58
tree of life is g. GOETHE, J, 2
When the g. woods laugh HAPPINESS, 6
green-ey'd jealousy…g. monster SHAKESPEARE, 285
Greenland From G.'s icy mountains PLACES, 17
green-rob'd g. senators of mighty woods KEATS, J, 21; TREES, 7
Greensleeves G. was all my joy ANONYMOUS, 22; LOVE, 14
greenwood Under the g. tree SHAKESPEARE, 46
green woods When the g. laugh BLAKE, W, 47
greeting the sort of g. a corpse would give to an undertaker BALDWIN, S, 5
greetings g. where no kindness is OPTIMISM, 42; WORDSWORTH, W, 15
perhaps the g. are intended for me POPULARITY, 1
grenadier The healthy bones of a single Pomeranian g. DIPLOMACY, 6
grenadiers With a tow…row for the British G. ANONYMOUS, 73
grew I g. up with a lot of brothers and sisters AMBITION, 17
Three years she g. DEATH, 183; WORDSWORTH, W, 70
grey G. hairs are death's blossoms OLD AGE, 2; PROVERBS, 183
pubic hairs went g. SUFFERING, 2
soccer is a g. game FOOTBALL, 12
theory is all g. GOETHE, J, 2; REALITY, 4; THEORY, 7
There is only one cure for g. hair….the guillotine REMEDIES, 61; WODEHOUSE, P, 16
These little g. cells CHRISTIE, A, 3; INTELLECT, 1
well-belovèd's hair has threads of g. AGE, 103; YEATS, W, 14
grey-hound If one is a g. why try to look like a Pekinese SELF-CONFIDENCE, 10
grief A g. too much to be told VIRGIL, 8
calms one's g. by recounting it SORROW, 7
G. and disappointment give rise to anger EMOTION, 3; HUME, D, 7
G. has turned her fair APPEARANCE, 74; WILDE, O, 74
in much wisdom is much g. BIBLE, 65
it is g. that develops the powers of the mind MIND, 27
My heart burned within me with indignation and g. LINCOLN, A, 2
Should be past g. REGRET, 23; SHAKESPEARE, 351
The heart which g. hath cankered ALCOHOL, 24
grievances redress of the g. of the vanquished CHURCHILL, W, 11; WAR, 45
grieve G. not that I die young DEATH, 77
Men are we, and must g. REGRET, 29; WORDSWORTH, W, 62
grill be careful not to look like a mixed g. APPEARANCE, 20; COWARD, N, 10
grimace only pianist I have ever seen who did not g. MUSICIANS, 19
grin All Nature wears one universal g. FIELDING, H, 14
ending with the g., which remained some time CARROLL, L, 8
grind g. the faces of the poor CAPITALISM, 2
mills of God g. slowly GOD, 35
grinders Writers, like teeth, are divided into incisors and g. BAGEHOT, W, 8
grip took a g. on cowardly Marxism NAZISM, 3
grist All's g. that comes to the mill OPPORTUNITY, 1; PROVERBS, 37
groan men sit and hear each other g. HUMAN CONDITION, 14; KEATS, J, 38
groans How alike are the g. of love to those of the dying LOVE AND DEATH, 4
Gromyko the G. of the Labour party POLITICIANS, 91
grooves specialists…tend to think in g. EXPERTS, 6
grope they g. in the dark BIBLE, 229
gross reconciling my g. habits with my net income DEBAUCHERY, 6
grotesque g. chaos of a Labour council INCOMPETENCE, 2
Groucho had Marx been G. instead of Karl HUMOUR, 4
No, G. is not my real name MARX, G, 24; NAMES, 5
ground closer to the g. as children CHILDREN, 12
group A g. of closely related persons FAMILY, 37
groups g. of people like herself BROOKNER, A, 6
grovelled Whenever he met a great man he g. SERVILITY, 7; THACKERAY, W, 10
groves And seek for truth in the g. of Academe EDUCATION, 43; HORACE, 24
grow Green g. the rashes O BURNS, R, 11; LOVE, 43
make two ears of corn…g.…where only one grew before POLITICIANS, 28; SWIFT, J, 8
make two questions g. where only one RESEARCH, 7
some of us never g. out AUTHORITARIANISM, 9
They shall g. not old MEMORIALS, 6
grow'd 'I 'spect I g..' STOWE, H, 2
groweth no grass there g., /Only their engines' dung ENGLAND, 8
growing Be not afraid of g. slowly ACHIEVEMENT, 4
G. old is like being increasingly penalized POWELL, A, 6
growl I hate a fellow…who does nothing…but sit and *g.* JOHNSON, S, 141; PETULANCE, 4
grown Boys…are unwholesome companions for g. people CHILDREN, 44; LAMB, C, 9
one of the few English novels for g. up people CRITICISM, 68
grown up one of the few English novels for g. people WOOLF, V, 5
grown-ups g.…have forgotten what it is like to be a child CHILDREN, 38
grow out some of us never g. USTINOV, P, 7
grows Nothing g. well in the shade GREATNESS, 5
growth as short a Spring; /As quick a g. to meet decay HERRICK, R, 4; TRANSIENCE, 15
elations and apprehensions of g. AGE, 60
G. is a greater mystery than death AGE, 60

grub it is poor g., poor pay, and easy work AMERICA, 28; ENGLAND, 31
grudge feed fat the ancient g. I bear him BUSINESS, 27
grumblers some g. are to be expected LINCOLN, A, 1
grumbling the muttering grew to a g. ANIMALS, 8; BROWNING, R, 43
gruntled he was far from being g. HUMOUR, 65; WODEHOUSE, P, 5
guarantee No one can g. success in war CHURCHILL, W, 27; WAR, 47
guard That g. our native seas NAVY, 3
guardian As g. of His Majesty's conscience MONARCHY, 26
when health is restored, he is a g. DOCTORS, 11
guards Up, G., and at 'em WAR, 180; WELLINGTON, 18
Who is to guard the g. themselves MISTRUST, 7
gudeman Robin Gray, he was g. to me MARRIAGE, 20
guerre *ce n'est pas la g.* WAR, 24
une drôle de g. WAR, 53
guerrilla The g. fights the war of the flea WAR, 169
The g. wins if he does not lose WAR, 93
guest A free-loader is a confirmed g. PARASITES, 2; RUNYON, D, 8
Earth, receive an honoured g. AUDEN, W, 17; POETS, 18
g. who outstays HOSPITALITY, 4; HOSPITALITY, 7; PROVERBS, 397
guests a round of Get the G. PARTIES, 1
Fish and g. smell HOSPITALITY, 2
the g. must be chosen as carefully as the wine ALCOHOL, 67; SAKI, 1
guide Custom, then, is the great g. of human life CUSTOM, 2; HUME, D, 1
Everyman, I will go with thee, and be thy g. ANONYMOUS, 17; GUIDANCE, 1
I have only a faint light to g. me ATHEISM, 5; GUIDANCE, 2
guiding little onward lend thy g. hand GUIDANCE, 3; MILTON, J, 56
guillotine There is only one cure for grey hair....the g. WODEHOUSE, P, 16
guilt g. of having a nice body DRABBLE, M, 6
I have no sense of g. PANKHURST, E, 5
Let other pens dwell on g. and misery AUSTEN, J, 13; OPTIMISM, 14
Life without industry is g. ART, 30; RUSKIN, J, 4
put on a dress of g. GUILT, 9
guiltless Whose g. heart is free CAMPION, T, 3; RIGHTEOUSNESS, 6
guilty feel just a bit g. about laughing AUDIENCES, 9
g. of Noël Cowardice COWARDICE, 1
I declare myself g. GUILT, 7
It is quite gratifying to feel g. GUILT, 1
Let no g. man escape GRANT, U, 7; JUSTICE, 9
Suspicion always haunts the g. mind GUILT, 15
ten g. persons escape than one innocent suffer BLACKSTONE, W, 5; JUSTICE, 3
tremble like a g. thing surprised DOUBT, 9; WORDSWORTH, W, 30
guinea a round disc of fire somewhat like a g. BLAKE, W, 12; PERCEPTION, 3
I would not give half a g. to live under one form of government GOVERNMENT, 18; JOHNSON, S, 83
there go two-and-forty sixpences...to one g. JOHNSON, S, 34; MERIT, 4
guineas I have only five g. in my pocket GENEROSITY, 5
gulphs whelm'd in deeper g. than he COWPER, W, 6; DEATH, 52
gum Any g., chum WORLD WAR II, 3
can't fart and chew g. at the same time MISQUOTATIONS, 21
gun have a man come through a door with a g. in his hand WRITING, 10
it is necessary to take up the g. MAO TSE-TUNG, 4
looks like he's carrying a g. ACTORS, 16
The difference between a g. and a tree POUND, E, 10; TREES, 13
we have got /The Maxim G. BELLOC, H, 16; POWER POLITICS, 1
gunfire Thanks to the movies, g. has always sounded unreal CINEMA, 28; USTINOV, P, 1
Gunga Din You're a better man than I am, G. KIPLING, R, 16; SUPERIORITY, 8
gunpowder G., Printing, and the Protestant Religion CARLYLE, T, 9
ingredients of g....were known to him SCIENTISTS, 12
guns But it's 'Saviour of 'is country' when the g. KIPLING, R, 30; SOLDIERS, 3
Elevate them g. a little lower WAR, 84
G. will make us powerful POWER POLITICS, 3
In Japan, we live life with no g. VIOLENCE, 11
gutless W. H. Auden, a sort of g. Kipling ORWELL, G, 29; SOCIALISM, 21
guts exploding harpoon in the g. PASSION, 3
gutter We are all in the g. OPTIMISM, 40; WILDE, O, 41
gynecology A determining point in the history of g. SEX, 111
gypsies I never should /Play with the g. in the wood NURSERY RHYMES, 36

H

habit a h. the pleasure of which increases with practise LETTER-WRITING, 1
H. is a great deadener BECKETT, S, 6; HABIT, 2
honour peereth in the meanest h. APPEARANCES, 37; SHAKESPEARE, 322
I must...try hard to control the talking h. FRANK, A, 10
habitation to airy nothing /A local h. POETRY, 54; SHAKESPEARE, 266
habits a man who pulls h. out of rats PSYCHOLOGY, 1
Cultivate only the h. HABIT, 5
Curious things, h. CHRISTIE, A, 5; HABIT, 3
h. that carry them far apart CONFUCIUS, 3; HABIT, 4
Old h. die hard HABIT, 1; PROVERBS, 321
hack Do not h. me EXECUTION, 23
had you h. it in you EXPECTATION, 5; PARKER, D, 25
hae Scots, wha h. BURNS, R, 17
ha-ha Funny peculiar, or funny h. HUMOUR, 16
hail All h., the power of Jesus' name CHRISTIANITY, 52
h. and farewell GREETINGS, 2
H., hail rock'n'roll POPULAR MUSIC, 6
the flail of the lashing h. SHELLEY, P, 5; WEATHER, 24
hair busy driving cabs and cutting h. GOVERNMENT, 9
false h. and that red ELIZABETH I, 2
h. was the most important thing on earth O'BRIEN, E, 3
if a woman have long h. APPEARANCE, 10; BIBLE, 37
I think of women, it is their h. WOMEN, 96
long gray h. on Kevin's jacket SUSPICION, 3
Man can have only a certain number of teeth, h. and ideas OLD AGE, 104
never get on in politics, my dear, with *that* h. POLITICIANS, 41
part my h. behind ELIOT, T, 15; OLD AGE, 45
prison for the colour of his h. IMPRISONMENT, 6
scant as h. /In leprosy BROWNING, R, 16
Take a h. of the dog ALCOHOL, 5; PROVERBS, 373
there shall not one h. of his head fall BIBLE, 479
To Crystal, h. was the most important APPEARANCE, 48
Wash That Man Right Out of My H. DECISION, 1
you have lovely h. BEAUTY, 17; CHEKHOV, A, 12
hairy a small, h. individual ROYALTY, 6
Esau...a h. man BIBLE, 171
half And when they were only h. way up ARMY, 1; WAR, 4
H. a loaf EXPEDIENCY, 1; PROVERBS, 184
h. a loaf is better than a whole CHESTERTON, G, 41; COMPROMISE, 6
I am only h. there when I am ill ILLNESS, 43; LAWRENCE, D, 43
I have not told h. of what I saw LAST WORDS, 68
longest h. of your life SOUTHEY, R, 3; YOUTH, 30
One h....cannot understand...the other AUSTEN, J, 4; PLEASURE, 3
There is an old saying 'well begun is h. done' BEGINNING, 13; KEATS, J, 55
half-a-dozen six of one and h. of the other SIMILARITY, 5
half-developed the working-class which, raw and h. ARNOLD, M, 9; PUBLIC, 2
half-quote Don't h. me to reinforce your own prejudices PREJUDICE, 3
half way And when they were only h. up, /They were neither up nor down NURSERY RHYMES, 37
half-wits a wit out of two h. FOOLISHNESS, 16; KINNOCK, N, 4
halitosis h. of the intellect INSULTS, 67; STUPIDITY, 4
hall one of the sparrows...flew...through the h. LIFE, 11
Hall We met...Dr H. in such very deep mourning AUSTEN, J, 31; MOURNING, 1
Hallelujah Here lies my wife, /...H. ANONYMOUS, 31
hallowed The place of justice is a h. place BACON, F, 31
halo What, after all, /Is a h. GOOD, 6
halt the whole process has ground to a h. with a 14th Earl TITLES, 13; WILSON, H, 9
halters talk of h. in the hanged man's house CERVANTES, M, 12

halves Never do things by h. COMMITMENT, 3; PROVERBS, 301
hamburger British h. thus symbolised…failure to provide its ordinary people with food FOOD, 38
Why have h. out MARRIAGE, 115
Hamelin H. Town's in Brunswick BROWNING, R, 41; GERMANY, 1
hammer Art is not a mirror…but a h. ART, 22
Hampden Some village-H. GRAY, T, 6
hand a little bit by the h. of God FOOTBALL, 11
bite the h. that fed them BURKE, E, 19
educate with the head instead of with the h. EDUCATION, 54; KEY, E, 3
fingers of a man's h., and wrote BIBLE, 51
h. that signed the treaty bred a fever SIGNATURES, 3; THOMAS, D, 11
he wouldn't lay a h. on you DOCTORS, 93
I…will cover thee with my h. BIBLE, 122
little onward lend thy guiding h. GUIDANCE, 3; MILTON, J, 56
No, this right h. shall work it all off SCOTT, W, 22; WRITING, 45
one of those parties which got out of h. CHRISTIANITY, 32
Our h. will not tremble RUSSIAN REVOLUTION, 8
put your h. into the h. of God FAITH, 15
Sit thou on my right h. PSALMS, 61
sweeten this little h. GUILT, 19; SHAKESPEARE, 224
The H. that made us is divine ADDISON, J, 15; CREATION, 1
The h. that rocks the cradle PROVERBS, 398; WOMEN, 4
the sheep of his h. PSALMS, 56
This h. hath offended REGRET, 7
touch his weaknesses with a delicate h. GOLDSMITH, O, 15; IMPERFECTION, 8
handbook have used the Bible as if it was a constable's h. BIBLE, 532; KINGSLEY, C, 3
handful for a h. of silver he left us BETRAYAL, 5; BROWNING, R, 31
handicap disability has not been a serious h. HAWKING, S, 2
handicraft Art is not a h. ART, 35; TOLSTOY, L, 13
handkerchief blow his nose…state of the h. industry ORWELL, G, 1
handkerchiefs There is a ghost /That eats h. LOSS, 4
handle I polished up the h. of the big front door GILBERT, W, 13; OFFICERS, 6
polished up the h. of the big front door OFFICERS, 6
hands don't raise your h. because I am also nearsighted AUDEN, W, 28; DISABILITY, 1
Farewell, my poor h. LAST WORDS, 73; MUSICIANS, 13
He hath shook h. with time DEATH, 66
he shakes h. with people's hearts JOURNALISM, 5
his h. prepared the dry land PSALMS, 54
into thy h. I commend my spirit BIBLE, 340; LAST WORDS, 10; PSALMS, 19
Licence my roving h. DONNE, J, 11; LUST, 3
many brains and many h. are needed DISCOVERY, 14
Many h. make light work HELP, 2; PROVERBS, 283
Pale h. I loved beside the Shalimar LOVE, 87
Pilate…washed his h. BIBLE, 430; GUILT, 3
temples made with h. BIBLE, 12; SUPERSTITION, 6
the earth of England is in my two h. VICTORY, 30
To be played with both h. in the pocket MUSIC, 52
Tomorrow my h. will be bound EXECUTION, 2
We draw the sword…with clean h. WAR, 185
You cannot shake h. with a clenched fist GANDHI, I, 5; INFLEXIBILITY, 2
handsaw I know a hawk from a h. MADNESS, 35; SHAKESPEARE, 86
handsome H. is as handsome does APPEARANCE, 2; PROVERBS, 185
not as h. as his photographs ARNOLD, M, 1
vile ill-favour'd faults /Looks h. in three hundred pounds SHAKESPEARE, 257
handwriting Most people enjoy the sight of their own h. WRITING, 3
hang if you want to kill a picture all you have to do is to h. it beautifully PAINTING, 15; PICASSO, P, 13
I will find something…to h. him EXECUTION, 34
I will neither go nor h. DETERMINATION, 13
I will not h. myself today CHESTERTON, G, 7; SUICIDE, 8
They h. us now in Shrewsbury jail EXECUTION, 16; HOUSMAN, A, 8
We must indeed all h. together FRANKLIN, B, 15; UNITY, 9
wretches h. that jury-men may dine JUSTICE, 20; POPE, A, 51
hanged if the King beat us once we shall all be h. ROYALTY, 84
if they were going to see me h. CROMWELL, O, 9; PUBLIC, 10
I went out to Charing Cross, to see Major-general Harrison h. EXECUTION, 29; PEPYS, S, 6
Men are not h. for stealing HALIFAX, 1
resolved to be h. with the Bible EXECUTION, 1
talk of halters in the h. man's house CERVANTES, M, 12
to be h. for nonsense DRYDEN, J, 15; EXECUTION, 9
when a man knows he is to be h. in a fortnight EXECUTION, 18; JOHNSON, S, 116
hang-gliding comedy is like emotional h. HUMOUR, 35
hangin they're h.' Danny Deever in the mornin' EXECUTION, 20; KIPLING, R, 8
hanging H. and wiving goes by destiny DESTINY, 24; SHAKESPEARE, 246
h. prevents a bad marriage MARRIAGE, 137; SHAKESPEARE, 338
hangman if I were a grave-digger, or…a h. JERROLD, D, 6; OCCUPATIONS, 12
Hansard H. is history's ear GOVERNMENT, 36
happen causes itself to h. ADAMS, D, 10
poetry makes nothing h. AUDEN, W, 16; POETRY, 5
happened most of which had never h. CHURCHILL, W, 29; WORRY, 12
happening h. to somebody else HUMOUR, 27; ROGERS, W, 4
happens Everything that h. h. as it should DESTINY, 3; MARCUS AURELIUS ANTONINUS, 6
I don't give a shit what h. NIXON, R, 9
I just don't want to be there when it h. ALLEN, W, 7; DEATH, 16
life…seems to me preparation for something that never h. LIFE, 98; YEATS, W, 5
Nothing h. BECKETT, S, 2; BOREDOM, 1
these are the conditions, now what h. SCIENCE, 39
happiest h. time of all the glad New-year TENNYSON, 60
Poetry is the record of the best and h. moments POETRY, 57; SHELLEY, P, 7
happiness A lifetime of h.…hell on earth HAPPINESS, 26; SHAW, G, 21
a man is always seeking for h. MARRIAGE, 65
among which are the preservation of life, and liberty, an the pursuit of h. JEFFERSON, T, 5
curiously boring about…h. HUXLEY, A, 22; SYMPATHY, 5
Drunkenness is never anything but a substitute for h. DRUNKENNESS, 17
greatest h. of the greatest number HAPPINESS, 4
h. fails, existence remains…experiment HAPPINESS, 24; SANTAYANA, G, 5
H. in marriage AUSTEN, J, 21; MARRIAGE, 12
H. is a mystery like religion CHESTERTON, G, 21; HAPPINESS, 8
H. is an imaginary condition HAPPINESS, 30; SZASZ, T, 5
H. is beneficial for the body MIND, 27; PROUST, M, 19; SORROW, 24
H. is like a butterfly HAPPINESS, 16
H. is like coke HAPPINESS, 12; HUXLEY, A, 26
H. is no laughing matter HAPPINESS, 32
h. is not an ideal of reason HAPPINESS, 14; KANT, I, 3
H. is not best achieved HAPPINESS, 19
H. is no vague dream HAPPINESS, 22
H. is the only sanction of life HAPPINESS, 24; SANTAYANA, G, 5
h. makes them good GOOD, 10; LANDOR, W, 3
h. of man that he be mentally faithful INTEGRITY, 5
H.? That's nothing more than health HAPPINESS, 25
In Hollywood, if you don't have h. CINEMA, 21
In solitude /What h. MILTON, J, 49; SOLITUDE, 11
I thought that success spelled h. HAPPINESS, 16
It is of no moment to the h. of an individual GOVERNMENT, 18; JOHNSON, S, 83
life, liberty, and the pursuit of h. HUMAN RIGHTS, 3; JEFFERSON, T, 6
nothing…by which so much h. is produced as by a good tavern PUBLIC HOUSES, 2
our friends are true and our h. BIERCE, A, 7; OPTIMISM, 16
Poverty is a great enemy to human h. JOHNSON, S, 140; POVERTY, 24
recall a time of h. when in misery SORROW, 9
result h. DICKENS, C, 13; ECONOMICS, 8
the greatest h. for the greatest numbers HAPPINESS, 11
the greatest h. of the whole PLATO, 2; REPUBLIC, 1
the h. of the common man GOVERNMENT, 8
There is nothing…by which so much h. is produced as by a good tavern JOHNSON, S, 102
where…We find our h. WORDSWORTH, W, 43
Who never knew the price of h. HAPPINESS, 35
you'll give h. and joy MUSICIANS, 2
you take away his h. DELUSION, 4; IBSEN, H, 9
happy an unhappy person who was h. BAINBRIDGE, B, 6

hats H. divide generally into three classes CLOTHES, 28; WHITEHORN, K, 1
hatter 'Not the same thing a bit!' said the H. CARROLL, L, 9; MEANING, 1
haunted e'er beneath a waning moon was h. COLERIDGE, S, 16; SUPERNATURAL, 6
hautboys Gibbon moved to flutes and h. GIBBON, E, 2
have All I h., I would h. given REGRET, 8
To h. and to hold BOOK OF COMMON PRAYER, 27; MARRIAGE, 33
haves *H.* and the *Have-nots* CERVANTES, M, 20; POVERTY AND WEALTH, 4
havoc h. of the German bombs ARCHITECTURE, 18
hawk I know a h. from a handsaw MADNESS, 35; SHAKESPEARE, 86
hay Make h. while the sun shines OPPORTUNITY, 4; PROVERBS, 278
hazard an occupational h. of being a wife ROYALTY, 7
he For every h. has got him a she ANONYMOUS, 13; MERRYMAKING, 1
head anyone who slapped us...would get his h. kicked off REVENGE, 14
call that thing under your hat a h. INSULTS, 63
educate with the h. instead of with the hand EDUCATION, 54; KEY, E, 3
God be in my h., /And in my understanding ANONYMOUS, 20; GOD, 2
Here comes a chopper to chop off your h. LONDON, 2; NURSERY RHYMES, 41
If you can keep your h. KIPLING, R, 17; SELF-CONTROL, 5
I'll hold my h. so high it'll strike the stars HORACE, 26; PRIDE, 6
in politics there is no heart, only h. NAPOLEON I, 5; POLITICS, 80
it shall bruise thy h. SEXES, 4
John Baptist's h. in a charger BIBLE, 393
Lay your sleeping h. AUDEN, W, 20; SLEEP, 6
no matter which way the h. lies EXECUTION, 32; RALEIGH, W, 6
Off with his h. CARROLL, L, 12; EXECUTION, 5
ought to have his h. examined GOLDWYN, S, 12; PSYCHIATRY, 16
Scheherazade...a woman saving her h. SELF-PRESERVATION, 15
shorter by a h. ELIZABETH I, 8; ROYALTY, 55
show my h. to the people EXECUTION, 7
sometimes his brains go to his h. INTELLIGENCE, 1
the greatest asset a h. of state can have SLEEP, 38
there shall not one hair of his h. fall BIBLE, 479
the Son of man hath not where to lay his h. LIFE AND DEATH, 24
thing I liked about films was looking at the back of my h. CINEMA, 11
Uneasy lies the h. that wears a crown MONARCHY, 22; SHAKESPEARE, 122
waters flowed over mine h. BIBLE, 307
We had shown that anyone who slapped us...would get his h. kicked off KHRUSHCHEV, N, 1
you are like a pin, but without...h. or...point JERROLD, D, 8
you incessantly stand on your h. CARROLL, L, 6; OLD AGE, 28
head-in-air Johnny h. CHILDREN, 34; IDEALISM, 7
headmasters H. have powers CHURCHILL, W, 17; EDUCATION, 25
headmistress a h. of a certain age wearing calico knickers THATCHER, M, 8
head of state the greatest asset a h. can have WILSON, H, 12
heads better h. on a mop BLEASDALE, A, 5
H. I win VICTORY, 8
They fired first above the h. CHINA, 6
Two h. are better than one HELP, 6; PROVERBS, 446
head-waiter A pompous woman...complaining that the h. EGOTISM, 9; SITWELL, E, 7
diplomat...is nothing but a h. DIPLOMACY, 29; INSULTS, 125; USTINOV, P, 8
heal I will h. me of my grievous wound AFTERLIFE, 11; TENNYSON, 25
physician, h. thyself BIBLE, 320; DOCTORS, 22
To h. the sick EDUCATION, 62
healers The best of h. is good cheer REMEDIES, 45
healeth h. those that are broken in heart PSALMS, 75
healing H. is a matter of time OPPORTUNITY, 12
The art of h. comes from nature MEDICINE, 73
the leaves...were for the h. of the nations BIBLE, 474
health All h. is better than wealth SCOTT, W, 23
always taking care of their h. HYPOCHONDRIA, 2
Doctors and undertakers /Fear epidemics of good h. DOCTORS, 18
for h. is the second blessing HEALTH AND HEALTHY LIVING, 16
good wife and h. are a man's best wealth WEALTH, 3
h. is all they get for it SMOKING, 34
H. is beauty BEAUTY, 44
H. is better than wealth PROVERBS, 187
h. is his most valuable possession HEALTH AND HEALTHY LIVING, 9
H. is the first muse SLEEP, 12
h. to the bones KINDNESS, 3
he drank my h. with a little speech HUGO, V, 2
Here's a h. unto his Majesty ANONYMOUS, 35
In a disordered mind...soundness of h. is impossible PSYCHIATRY, 12
in sickness and in h. BOOK OF COMMON PRAYER, 26, 27; MARRIAGE, 33
living in h. LIFE, 63
Look to your h. HEALTH AND HEALTHY LIVING, 16
Medicine sometimes snatches away h. MEDICINE, 70
medicines when well used restore h. to the sick REMEDIES, 40
Medicine, to produce h., has to examine disease MEDICINE, 80
No doctor takes pleasure in the h. even of his friends DOCTORS, 64
Only do always in h. what you have often promised to do ILLNESS, 65
selling them in h. food shops HEALTH AND HEALTHY LIVING, 14
Sleep is that golden chaine that ties h. and our bodies together SLEEP, 11
Temperance is the love of h. MODERATION, 10
The beginning of h. is sleep SLEEP, 3
the observations of the body in h. and disease NATURE, 16
There is not a doctor who desires the h. of his friends DOCTORS, 78
They pay this price for h. SMOKING, 34
to fence against the infirmities of ill h....by mirth LAUGHTER, 12
to signalize the inauguration of the National H. service PSYCHIATRY, 10
We are usually the best men when in the worst h. HUMAN NATURE, 1
What have I gained by h. MODERATION, 9
when h. is restored, he is a guardian DOCTORS, 11
When you have both, it's h. WORRY, 13
healthy all h. instinct for it LIFE, 22
eat a h. diet DIETING, 4
h. and wealthy and dead BED, 12; THURBER, J, 6
He that goes to bed thirsty rises h. ALCOHOL, 37
how h....to play Da Do Ron Ron AIDS, 5
Nobody is h. in London AUSTEN, J, 5; LONDON, 3
the h. type that was essentially middle-class CLASS, 14; FITZGERALD, F, 10
The sick are the greatest danger for the h. ILLNESS, 53
think of diseases as isolated disturbances in a h. body DISEASE, 3
You should pray for a h. mind in a h. body MIND, 17
hear any of you at the back who do not h. me AUDEN, W, 28; DISABILITY, 1
ear begins to h. BRONTE, E, 5; IMPRISONMENT, 3
ears to h., and h. not BIBLE, 124
ears to h., let him h. BIBLE, 388
he that planted the ear, shall he not h. PSALMS, 53
make any man sick to h. her INSINCERITY, 4; PEPYS, S, 9
one is always sure to h. of it FRIENDS, 15; SHERIDAN, R, 3
swift to h. BIBLE, 217
to-day if ye will h. his voice PSALMS, 56
truth which men prefer not to h. TRUTH, 7
heard first been vividly h. by an inner ear MUSICIANS, 17
I have already h. it MUSIC, 50
nor ear h. BIBLE, 25
hearsay to replace X-ray by h. GOSSIP, 13; THOMAS, G, 4
heart a broken and contrite h....shalt thou not despise PSALMS, 32
Absence makes the h. grow fonder ABSENCE, 4
A h. flutters, a nation shudders QUAYLE, D, 1
a man after his own h. BIBLE, 478
a step away from the natural h. of man WORRY, 5
A woman's h. always has a burned mark SORROW, 15
Because my h. is pure INTEGRITY, 7; TENNYSON, 72
by want of thought, as well as want of h. HOOD, T, 8
cold untroubled h. of stone SELFISHNESS, 4
cut to the h. BIBLE, 5
Death took him by the h. DEATH, 116; OWEN, W, 2

first come to pass in the h. of America AMERICA, 14; EISENHOWER, D, 5
God be in my h., /And in my thinking ANONYMOUS, 20
Good-night, Dear H. ANONYMOUS, 104
Great thoughts come from the h. THINKING, 19
healeth those that are broken in h. PSALMS, 75
h. and stomach of a King ELIZABETH I, 13; ROYALTY, 53
h. to a dog to tear DOGS, 12
holiness of the h.'s affections KEATS, J, 51; TRUTH, 31
I am sick at h. COMFORT, 4; SHAKESPEARE, 65
If thou didst ever hold me in thy h. MOURNING, 12; SHAKESPEARE, 108
I love thee for a h. that's kind KINDNESS, 5
in politics there is no h., only head NAPOLEON I, 5; POLITICS, 80
let not your h. be troubled PEACE, 4
lonely of h. is withered away LONELINESS, 17; YEATS, W, 19
look in thy h. and write INSPIRATION, 3
Mary...pondered them in her h. BIBLE, 316
Mother is the dead h. of the family GREER, G, 3; WOMAN'S ROLE, 6
My h. aches KEATS, J, 35; MELANCHOLY, 8
My h. is a lonely hunter LONELINESS, 8
my h.'s abhorrence BROWNING, R, 52; HATE, 2
my h. shall be /The faithful compass FAITHFULNESS, 4; GAY, J, 12
My h. shall be thy garden LOVE, 117
My h.'s in the Highlands BURNS, R, 15; SCOTLAND, 2; SCOTT, W, 21
my h. was never set on worldly goods ELIZABETH I, 14
Nothing melts a Woman's H. like gold WEALTH, 16
Once a woman has given you her h. WOMEN, 138
Optimism: A kind of h. stimulant OPTIMISM, 29
our h. is not quiet until it rests in Thee HUMAN CONDITION, 2
She had /A h....too soon made glad BROWNING, R, 35
So the h. be right EXECUTION, 32; RALEIGH, W, 6
spring of love gushed from my h. BLESSING, 7
strings...in the human h. DICKENS, C, 4; EMOTION, 2
take heed...that your h. be not deceived BIBLE, 55; CHRISTIANITY, 9
Take thy beak from out my h. EVIL, 16
that mighty h. is lying still SLEEP, 39; WORDSWORTH, W, 54
the beatings of the lonely h. LONELINESS, 2
The fire which in the h. resides ARNOLD, M, 29; SOUL, 2
The h. has its reasons MOTIVE, 5; PASCAL, B, 7
The h. that loved her NATURE, 35; WORDSWORTH, W, 14
The history of every country begins in the h. HISTORY, 9
The intellect is always fooled by the h. EMOTION, 4; ROCHEFOUCAULD, 15
Their h.'s in the right place MANKIND, 37; MAUGHAM, W, 21
them which are true of h. PSALMS, 4
The nation had the lion's h. CHURCHILL, W, 70
There is a road from the eye to the h. CHESTERTON, G, 9; EMOTION, 1
the waters of the h. /Push in their tides EMOTION, 5; THOMAS, D, 14
The way to a man's h. is through his stomach FOOD, 29
to lose your h.'s desire DESIRE, 15; SHAW, G, 24
What comes from the h. COLERIDGE, S, 43; SINCERITY, 2
With rue my h. is laden HOUSMAN, A, 16; NOSTALGIA, 12
with the palsied h. PASSION, 11; TENNYSON, 52
Worry affects circulation, the h. and the glands WORRY, 14
heartbeat h. of the country BUSH, G, 8
heart beats Counting the slow h. TIME, 25
hearth Man for the field and woman for the h. SEXES, 30; TENNYSON, 66
the cricket on the h. MELANCHOLY, 10; MILTON, J, 14
heartless It is h. and it is mindless PORNOGRAPHY, 5
hearts first in the h. of his countrymen WASHINGTON, G, 1
he shakes hands with people's h. JOURNALISM, 5
if ye will hear his voice, harden not your h. PSALMS, 56
Kind h. are more than coronets ARISTOCRACY, 18; TENNYSON, 40
One equal temper of heroic h. DETERMINATION, 24; TENNYSON, 81
The Queen of H. /She made some tarts NURSERY RHYMES, 55
the song that is sung in our h. MUSIC, 44
The Worldly Hope men set their H. upon FITZGERALD, E, 7
those who have stout h. and sharp swords RUTHLESSNESS, 6
Two h. that beat as one LOVE, 108
well-developed bodies, fairly developed minds, and undeveloped h. EDUCATION, 32; FORSTER, E, 3
heart-throbs We should count time by h. TIME, 10
hearty he is so h., so straightforward, outspoken ROOSEVELT, T, 1
heat Britain...is going to be forged in the white h. of this revolution SOCIALISM, 25; WILSON, H, 8
can't stand the h., get out of the kitchen ENDURANCE, 26; TRUMAN, H, 3
Film...dust and h. and noise CINEMA, 19
H., madam!...to take off my flesh and sit in my bones SMITH, S, 4; WEATHER, 26
If you don't like the h. PROVERBS, 218
Heathcliff My love for H. LOVE, 40
heathen I will be exalted among the h. PSALMS, 28
not a H., or a Jew RELIGION, 94; WATTS, I, 4
the h. make much ado PSALMS, 27
Heaven a H. in Hell's despair BLAKE, W, 36; LOVE, 36
all H. in a rage BLAKE, W, 10; IMPRISONMENT, 2
All place shall be hell that is not h. DOOMSDAY, 5; MARLOWE, C, 1
a new h. and a new earth BIBLE, 473
Another glory awaits us in h. HEAVEN, 10
ascend to h. EXECUTION, 12
between H. and Charing Cross HEAVEN, 15
flat road to h. SANTAYANA, G, 1
from whose face the earth and the h. fled BIBLE, 472
God created the h. BIBLE, 137; CREATION, 2
Good girls go to h. VIRTUE AND VICE, 2
hearts at peace, under an English h. ENGLAND, 12
h. and earth shall pass away BIBLE, 415; TRANSIENCE, 9
H. has granted me no offspring CONCEIT, 24; WHISTLER, J, 13
H. in a wild flower BLAKE, W, 9; WONDER, 2
H....is a place so inane, so dull HEAVEN, 14; SHAW, G, 34
H. was in him, before he was in heaven COMPLIMENTS, 37; WALTON, I, 7
H. without being naturally qualified HEAVEN, 13
Home is h. DEBAUCHERY, 10; NASH, O, 5
house as nigh h. as my own IMPRISONMENT, 9
If it's h. for climate BARRIE, J, 1; PERVERSITY, 1
If Max gets to H. BUSINESS, 36; WELLS, H, 21
If this belief from h. be sent MANKIND, 74; WORDSWORTH, W, 17
In h. an angel is nobody in particular IMPORTANCE, 4; SHAW, G, 25
I shall hear in h. MUSIC, 10
it were better for sun and moon to drop from h. SIN, 22
make a H. of Hell, a Hell of H. MILTON, J, 33; MIND, 21
man is as H. made him CERVANTES, M, 15; CHARACTER, 3
Marriage is...excluded from h. BUTLER, S, 19; MARRIAGE, 40
more things in h. and earth SHAKESPEARE, 79; SUPERNATURAL, 13
Mr Chesterton...to h. might have gone CHESTERTON, G, 3
no invention came more easily to man than H. HEAVEN, 7
Now: h. knows FREEDOM, 49; PORTER, C, 1
Order is h.'s first law ORDER, 3; POPE, A, 37
Parting is all we know of h. DICKINSON, E, 4; PARTING, 5
Pennies do not come from h. THATCHER, M, 24; WORK, 35
Pennies from H. OPTIMISM, 20
so much of earth...of h. IMPETUOSITY, 5; WORDSWORTH, W, 48
steep and thorny way to h. EXAMPLE, 8; SHAKESPEARE, 73
Thank h. for little girls WOMEN, 77
the Hell I suffer seems a H. HELL, 5; MILTON, J, 43
The mind...Can make a H. of Hell MIND, 21
there was war in h. BIBLE, 465; DEVIL, 7
the starry h. above me KANT, I, 1; WONDER, 3
to be young was very h. FRENCH REVOLUTION, 11; WORDSWORTH, W, 41
'Twould ring the bells of H. ANIMALS, 15
We are all going to H. LAST WORDS, 39
We are as near to h. by sea as by land LAST WORDS, 43; SEA, 5
what's a h. for AMBITION, 4; BROWNING, R, 4
What they do in h. MARRIAGE, 152; SWIFT, J, 15
When earth was nigher h. BROWNING, R, 46; PAST, 3
heavenward A homely face...aided many women h. APPEARANCE, 5
heavier O you who have borne even h. things VIRGIL, 6
heaviest nickname is the h. stone that the devil can throw HAZLITT, W, 18; NAMES, 4
heav'n h. on earth HEAVEN, 8; MILTON, J, 45
I'm farther off from h. /Than when...a boy HOOD, T, 7; INNOCENCE, 7
Hebrews See H. 13:8 CRITICISM, 9
hedge A leap over the h. CERVANTES, M, 8; PRAYER, 10
hedgehogs If you start throwing h. under me KHRUSHCHEV, N, 4; THREATS, 3
heed To fight and not to h. the wounds SELFLESSNESS, 3
heel to bring a man to h. BROOKNER, A, 1
heels Time wounds all h. MARX, G, 22; TIME, 36

heesh If John or Mary comes h. will want to play LANGUAGE, 33; MILNE, A, 2
heifer plowed with my h. BIBLE, 295
heights If suffer we must, let's suffer on the h. HUGO, V, 3
heiress American h. wants to buy a man MATERIALISM, 19; MCCARTHY, M, 3
hell a H. in Heaven's despite BLAKE, W, 37; LOVE, 37
A lifetime of happiness…h. on earth HAPPINESS, 26; SHAW, G, 21
All place shall be h. that is not heaven DOOMSDAY, 5; MARLOWE, C, 1
all we need of h. PARTING, 5
Better to reign in H. MILTON, J, 34; POWER, 18
Bloody h., Ma'am ROYALTY, 4
buttered slides to h. SANTAYANA, G, 1
h. a fury like a woman scorned CONGREVE, W, 9; LOVE AND HATE, 3
H. is a city much like London HELL, 8; LONDON, 22; SHELLEY, P, 21
H. is oneself ELIOT, T, 5; HELL, 3
H. is other people HELL, 7
h. upon earth…in a melancholy man's heart MELANCHOLY, 3
Italy…h. for women NATIONALITY, 5
make a Heaven of H., a H. of Heaven MILTON, J, 33; MIND, 21
Old age is woman's h. OLD AGE, 65
on the fourth day they will say 'To h. with you!' KHRUSHCHEV, N, 8; PROMISES, 5
out of h. leads up to light HELL, 4; MILTON, J, 40
Raises from H. a human soul BLAKE, W, 5; HELL, 1
spinach, and I say the h. with it FOOD, 74
the H. I suffer seems a Heaven HELL, 5; MILTON, J, 43
the h. of horses ENGLAND, 22
the little holiday steamers made an excursion to h. PRIESTLEY, J, 10; WORLD WAR II, 42
The mind…Can make a Heaven of H. MIND, 21
The religion of H. is patriotism PATRIOTISM, 7; PATRIOTISM, 7
The road to h. is paved PROCRASTINATION, 3; PROVERBS, 423
though h. should bar the way DETERMINATION, 19
thou leadest to the gates of h. BIBLE, 522
To h. with you TELEGRAMS, 1
Ugly h., gape not DAMNATION, 4; MARLOWE, C, 5
War is h. WAR, 162
way down to H. is easy HELL, 9; VIRGIL, 13
Which way I fly is H.; myself am H. HELL, 5; MILTON, J, 43
hell-broth Like a h. boil and bubble SHAKESPEARE, 220
help God shall h. her, and that right early PSALMS, 27
gods h. them that h. themselves AESOP, 4; SELF-RELIANCE, 2
going in without the h. of Russia LLOYD GEORGE, D, 13; WORLD WAR II, 37
H. me down Cemetery Road SUPPORT, 4; TRAVEL, 28
not so much our friends' h. that helps us FRIENDSHIP, 17
People must h. one another HELP, 7; LA FONTAINE, J, 8
Since there's no h. PARTING, 6
The dead…look on and h. DEATH, 98; LAWRENCE, D, 44
the h. of too many physicians DOCTORS, 9
the will to h. others KINDNESS, 9
what is past my h. is past my care BEAUMONT, F, 2; INDIFFERENCE, 1
with a little h. from my friends FRIENDS, 11; LENNON, J, 12
helpless Help of the h. RELIGION, 64
wealth had rendered her h. BROOKNER, A, 7
help meet I will make him an h. for him MARRIAGE, 29
helps He h. little PROVERBS, 188; SELF, 3
not so much our friends' help that h. us FRIENDSHIP, 17
hem only touch the h. of his garment BIBLE, 396; REMEDIES, 13
hen A h. is only an egg's way EVOLUTION, 3
Two Owls and a H. APPEARANCE, 37; LEAR, E, 1
henpecked I am not going to be h. FEMINISM, 44
Henry He is without strict doubt a Hoorah H. ARISTOCRACY, 17
How H. would have loved it FUNERALS, 11; TERRY, D, 4
Junker H. means to be God ROYALTY, 82
pig of a H. VIII BETRAYAL, 13
Prince H.…something of royalty in his demeanour ROYALTY, 62
Herald Price of H. three cents daily NEWSPAPERS, 4; TELEGRAMS, 4
herb an excellent h. to our fathers of old NATURE, 24
sweetest fragrance from the h.…tread on it and bruise it TROLLOPE, A, 9; WOMEN, 134
herbal tea drink h. HEALTH AND HEALTHY LIVING, 13
herbs all the potency of h. is known to me MEDICINE, 68
He preferred to know the power of h. MEDICINE, 103
nature runs either to h., or to weeds BACON, F, 37; HUMAN NATURE, 3
the powerful grace that lies in h. NATURE, 29
Hercules Some talk of Alexander, and some of H. SOLDIERS, 1
herd the H. of such, /Who think too little DRYDEN, J, 8; VERBOSITY, 4
herd-morality Morality…is h. MORALITY, 12; NIETZSCHE, F, 12
here bet you a hundred bucks he ain't in h. FUNERALS, 5
h. today and gone tomorrow BEHN, A, 8; TRANSIENCE, 4
What you are looking for is h., is at Ulubrae HORACE, 21; TRAVEL, 22
hereditary my case is h. FRANK, A, 10
Talent is h. TALENT, 10
heresies new truths…begin as h. HUXLEY, T, 3; NOVELTY, 4
heresy h. signifies no more than private opinion HOBBES, T, 3; OPINIONS, 4
heretic h. that makes the fire MARTYRDOM, 6
I shall never be a h. PROTESTANTISM, 3
heritage I summon age /To grant youth's h. AGE, 21; BROWNING, R, 49
hero a h. with coward's legs HEROISM, 8
Being a h. HEROISM, 9; ROGERS, W, 5
better to be the widow of a h. than the wife of a coward COURAGE, 19
Every h. becomes a bore EMERSON, R, 22; HEROISM, 6
h. and I will write you a tragedy HEROISM, 7
h. to his valet FAMILIARITY, 2
The h. is strangely akin DEATH, 127; RILKE, R, 3
to his very valet seem'd a h. BYRON, 6
Herod for an hour of H. CHILDREN, 37; PLAYS, 6
It out-h.s H. EXCESS, 12; SHAKESPEARE, 95
heroes Children should acquire…h. and villains from fiction AUDEN, W, 4; HISTORY, 3
fit country for h. to live in GOVERNMENT, 21; LLOYD GEORGE, D, 11
speed glum h.…to death SASSOON, S, 1; WAR, 146
the tragedy of life is that…h. lose their glamour DOYLE, A, 2
Unhappy the land that has no h. BRECHT, B, 2; HEROISM, 4
heroic human beings are h. NOBILITY, 4; ORWELL, G, 8
heroin celluloid not h. CINEMA, 24
heroines fearless, high-spirited, resolute and intelligent h. SHAKESPEARE, 19
heroism Where do all the women…get the h. WAR, 95
hert Myn h. ys set LOYALTY, 10
hesitate A leader who doesn't h.…is not fit to be a leader LEADERSHIP, 10; MEIR, G, 1
hesitates A science which h. to forget SCIENCE, 99; WHITEHEAD, A, 5
He who h. is lost DETERMINATION, 1; PROVERBS, 199
Hesperus the schooner H. BOATS, 12; LONGFELLOW, H, 19
Heterodoxy H. or Thy-doxy CARLYLE, T, 17; ORTHODOXY, 1
heterosexual artificial categories 'h.' and 'homosexual' SEX, 133
lived my entire life with h. hatred PREJUDICE, 6
hewers h. of wood BIBLE, 289
Hickory H., dickory, dock NURSERY RHYMES, 15
hidden Most good women are h. treasures VIRTUE, 22
Nature is often h. BACON, F, 36; HUMAN NATURE, 5
hide h. me under the shadow of thy wings PSALMS, 6
I have a big house – and I h. a lot CHILDREN, 58
Robes and furr'd gowns h. all APPEARANCES, 29; SHAKESPEARE, 190
hideous less h. than explanations EXPLANATIONS, 2
hiding man who looks you…in the eye…h. something INSINCERITY, 1
high civil fury first grew h. BUTLER, S, 1; WAR, 38
not to marry ladies in very h. positions ROYALTY, 3
She's the Broad and I'm the H. ACADEMICS, 8
to put off my hat to…h. or low PRIDE, 5
up in the h. numbers KEYNES, J, 10; NUMBERS, 3
ye'll tak' the h. road ANONYMOUS, 67; SCOTLAND, 1
highbrow What is a h. INTELLECTUALS, 15
higher the rock that is h. than I PSALMS, 37
highest h. type of human nature POLITICS, 96
Highland Yon solitary H. lass SOLITUDE, 18; WORDSWORTH, W, 51
Highlandman taking the breeks aff a wild H. SCOTS, 10; SCOTT, W, 4
Highlands My heart's in the H. BURNS, R, 15; SCOTT, W, 21
Ye H. and ye Lawlands ANONYMOUS, 109
highly at no time stand so h. in our estate royal GOVERNMENT, 16
Highness His Royal H.…prides himself SHERIDAN, R, 13

nobody knew whether...he would be alive the next h. FRANK, A, 8
nothing can bring back the h. REGRET, 28; WORDSWORTH, W, 31
one bare h. to live DAMNATION, 3; MARLOWE, C, 4
One h.'s sleep PROVERBS, 327
Some h. to which you have not been looking forward will prove lovely HORACE, 18
the clocks were striking the h. LONGFELLOW, H, 4
their finest h. CHURCHILL, W, 51
Time and the h. runs through SHAKESPEARE, 205
To one dead deathless h. ROSSETTI, D, 2
wage war until the last quarter of an h. WAR, 50
hourglass egghead weds h. MARRIAGE, 8
the sand in the h. TIME, 38
hours h. will take care of themselves CHESTERFIELD, P, 11; TIME, 17
Three h. a day TROLLOPE, A, 3; WRITING, 49
housbondes H. at chirche-dore CHAUCER, G, 12; MARRIAGE, 45
house A h. is a machine for living in LE CORBUSIER, 1
A H. Is Not a Home HOME, 3
A man in the h. is worth two MEN, 15; WEST, M, 3
Cleaning your h. while your kids are still growing HOUSEWORK, 4
Every man's h. will be fair and decent MORRIS, W, 4
get thee out...from thy father's h. BIBLE, 165; JEWS, 4
h. as nigh heaven as my own IMPRISONMENT, 9
h. we all had in common PAST, 4
I had rather be a door-keeper in the h. of my God PSALMS, 45
in my Father's h. are many mansions BIBLE, 258; HEAVEN, 3
in the last days...the Lord's h. shall be established BIBLE, 193
my h. shall be called the h. of prayer BIBLE, 408; CHRISTIANITY, 28
peace be to this h. BIBLE, 323
set thine h. in order BIBLE, 304
The h. of every one is to him as his castle PRIVACY, 2
The h. where I was born HOOD, T, 6; NOSTALGIA, 10
the sparrow hath found her an h. PSALMS, 44
they all lived together in a little crooked h. NURSERY RHYMES, 56
you...who have made me too great for my h. BACON, F, 66; ROYALTY, 22
house-agents Everybody hates h. OCCUPATIONS, 24; WELLS, H, 15
household Spiro Agnew is not a h. name FAME, 1
housekeep To h., one had to plan ahead HOUSEWORK, 6
housekeeping H. ain't no joke HOUSEWORK, 1
housemaid He was a meticulous h. CHAMBERLAIN, N, 3
housemaids damp souls of the h. ELIOT, T, 17
House of Commons leader of the H. DISRAELI, B, 34; POLITICIANS, 80
that D—d H. HOUSES OF PARLIAMENT, 12
House of Lords Every man has a H. in his own head HOUSES OF PARLIAMENT, 16; LLOYD GEORGE, D, 12
The H., an illusion STOPPARD, T, 4
The H....how to care for the elderly HOUSES OF PARLIAMENT, 11
The H. is a perfect eventide home HOUSES OF PARLIAMENT, 20
The H. is the British Outer Mongolia HOUSES OF PARLIAMENT, 5
The H....kept efficient by...persistent absenteeism HOUSES OF PARLIAMENT, 18
House of Peers The H., throughout the war, /Did nothing in particular GILBERT, W, 21; HOUSES OF PARLIAMENT, 13
Houses H. are built to live in BACON, F, 15; HOUSES, 1
plague o' both your h. CURSES, 2; SHAKESPEARE, 317
Rich men's h. are seldom beautiful WEALTH, 6
housewife don't pretend to be an ordinary h. ACTORS, 27
how Everything he saw made him ask h. and why LEONARDO DA VINCI, 1
H. do I love thee BROWNING, E, 5
h's drop thy 'H.' CLASS, 8
Hubbard Old Mother H. /Went to the cupboard FOOD, 56; NURSERY RHYMES, 39
hue native h. of resolution CONSCIENCE, 7; COWARDICE, 8; SHAKESPEARE, 92
Hugo *H. – hélas!* POETS, 36
human a contribution to the h. condition out of all proportion USTINOV, P, 5
Adam was but h. PERVERSITY, 6; TWAIN, M, 15
aggressive competition is part of the h. make-up SPORT AND GAMES, 27
all h. life is there JAMES, H, 9
All that is h. must retrograde GIBBON, E, 10; PROGRESS, 13
a pleasant smile that it seems rather divine than h. LEONARDO DA VINCI, 4
being alone is a fundamental quality of h. life HUMAN CONDITION, 16
Death is the privilege of h. nature DEATH, 131
every h. creature is...that profound secret and mystery MANKIND, 22
Every man carries the entire form of the h. condition HUMAN CONDITION, 18
evolution of the h. race MANKIND, 21
fathers of h. rights turning away from what is clearly genocide ETHNIC CLEANSING, 3
h....assembly of portable plumbing MANKIND, 40
h. being...is a whispering in the steam pipes MANKIND, 39
h. beings are heroic NOBILITY, 4; ORWELL, G, 8
H. beings are like timid punctuation marks MANKIND, 29
h. beings have an...infinite capacity for taking things for granted HUMAN NATURE, 16; HUXLEY, A, 33
H. beings were invented by water WATER, 8
H. beings, yes, but not surgeons MEDICINE, 102
h. face on...government ROYALTY, 101
H. kind cannot bear ELIOT, T, 7; REALITY, 2
H. life is everywhere a state in which much is to be endured JOHNSON, S, 28
h. nature...more of the fool BACON, F, 13; HUMAN NATURE, 4
H. on my faithless arm AUDEN, W, 20; SLEEP, 6
I am a h. being MANKIND, 2
If h. beings could be propagated...aristocracy would be...sound ARISTOCRACY, 13
I got disappointed in h. nature HUMAN NATURE, 10
I have got lots of h. weaknesses IMPERFECTION, 13; THATCHER, M, 26
imagine a boot stamping on a h. face OPPRESSION, 6; ORWELL, G, 16
in a position to see the h. race stark naked DOCTORS, 36
Ishmaelites...will not publicly eat h. flesh uncooked in Lent CANNIBALISM, 2; WAUGH, E, 41
I wish I loved the H. Race MANKIND, 49
Mercy has a h. heart BLAKE, W, 44; MANKIND, 10
my opinion of the h. race MANKIND, 37; MAUGHAM, W, 21
No h. being...was ever so free as a fish FREEDOM, 53; RUSKIN, J, 15
no need for any other faith than...faith in h. beings BUCK, P, 7; FAITH, 12
nothing h. foreign to me MANKIND, 64; TERENCE, 2
nothing to distinguish h. society from the farm-yard MANKIND, 60; SHAW, G, 12
not linen you're wearing out, /But h. creatures' lives HOOD, T, 11; WOMEN, 66
nuclear warfare...might well destroy the entire h. race MISANTHROPY, 3
than it is to turn one brat into a decent h. being CHILDREN, 43
the city is not a concrete jungle, it is a h. zoo MORRIS, D, 1
the curse of all the h. race NAPOLEON I, 1
the darkest page in h. history FEMINISM, 32
The essence of being h. PERFECTION, 7
the full tide of h. existence is at Charing-Cross JOHNSON, S, 93; LONDON, 17
The h. face is...a whole cluster of faces MANKIND, 47; PROUST, M, 4
The h. race...many of my readers CHESTERTON, G, 30; HUMAN CONDITION, 6
The h. race will be the cancer of the planet MANKIND, 31
the importance of the h. factor CHARLES, PRINCE, 2; INDUSTRIAL RELATIONS, 1
the psychic of h. relationship between the sexes SEX, 58
The Romans and Greeks found everything h. LAWRENCE, D, 6
the vilest specimens of h. nature are...found among demagogues MACAULAY, T, 16; POLITICS, 68
To err is h., to forgive, divine MISTAKES, 16; POPE, A, 28
To kill a h. being JAMES, H, 8; KILLING, 7
When in the course of h. events, it becomes necessary INDEPENDENCE, 3; JEFFERSON, T, 4
women want to live like h....live outside the religion RELIGION, 72
you feel as if a h. being sitting inside were making fun of you ANIMALS, 10
humanity Every year h. takes a step towards Communism COMMUNISM, 6; KHRUSHCHEV, N, 5
H. is just a work in progress MANKIND, 73

Oh wearisome condition of h. HUMAN CONDITION, 11
Our h. rests upon a series of learned behaviors HUMAN NATURE, 22
put the blame for the existence of h. INJUSTICE, 9
That unremitting h. BENNETT, A, 5
the crooked timber of h. HUMAN NATURE, 18; KANT, I, 4
these gorilla damnifications of h. DARWIN, C, 1
The still, sad music of h. EXPERIENCE, 23; WORDSWORTH, W, 13
unremitting h. soon had me cheesed off DICKENS, C, 1
if we think that h. is becoming ever more civilised CHARLES, PRINCE, 5

human race no relation to half of the h. FEMINISM, 20

human rights horrendous h. situation there is in China CHINA, 24

humble for the last time in my life, Your H. Servant WALPOLE, H, 1
He'll h. her MEN, 7
h. and meek are thirsting for blood HUMILITY, 8; ORTON, J, 3
It is difficult to be h. HUMILITY, 4
Sherlock Holmes *is* literature on a h.…level DOYLE, A, 1
women h. in character and submissive BOCCACCIO, G, 1

humiliate His great pleasure was to h. people THOMAS, D, 2

humiliating Corporal punishment is…h. for him who gives it KEY, E, 4; PUNISHMENT, 19

humiliation the last h. of an aged scholar OLD AGE, 37
the moment of greatest h. is…when the spirit is proudest PANKHURST, C, 4; PRIDE, 7

humility H. is only doubt BLAKE, W, 13; HUMILITY, 2

humor we have no sense of h. HUMOUR, 33

humour Cynicism is h. in ill-health CYNICISM, 4; WELLS, H, 17
deficient in a sense of h. COLERIDGE, S, 42; HUMOUR, 11
Freudian…low…sort of h. HUMOUR, 15
God withheld the sense of h. from women WOMEN, 33
His taste lay in…good-natured h. COWPER, W, 1
H.…the first of the gifts to perish TRANSLATION, 5
own up to a lack of h. HUMOUR, 10
Total absence of h. COLETTE, S, 1; HUMOUR, 12

hump A woman…without a positive h., may marry whom she likes MARRIAGE, 156; THACKERAY, W, 9

Humpty Dumpty H. sat on a wall NURSERY RHYMES, 18

hunchback The h. in the park LONELINESS, 15; THOMAS, D, 12

hundred a h. schools of thought contend MAO TSE-TUNG, 6
bet you a h. bucks he ain't in here FUNERALS, 5
it would be all the same a h. years hence DICKENS, C, 32; TRIVIALITY, 4
Letting a h. flowers blossom MAO TSE-TUNG, 6
Lloyd George spoke for a h. and seventeen minutes POLITICIANS, 49; SPEECHES, 2
not one will still be alive in a h. years' time MORTALITY, 22
to trade a h. contemporary readers for POSTERITY, 7

Hungarian It's not enough to be H. EUROPE, 14; TALENT, 8

hunger best sauce…is h. CERVANTES, M, 16; HUNGER, 4
convicted of sickness, h., wretchedness, and want SMOLLETT, T, 3
H. is the best sauce PROVERBS, 210
The war against h. HUNGER, 7
to banish h. by rubbing the belly HUNGER, 5

hungred h., and ye gave me meat BIBLE, 421; VIRTUE, 7

hungry A h. stomach has no ears HUNGER, 8; LA FONTAINE, J, 9
h. as a hunter HUNGER, 9; LAMB, C, 23
h. hare has no frontiers POLITICS, 114; WALESA, L, 3
H. Joe collected lists of fatal diseases ILLNESS, 31
h. sheep look up, and are not fed CORRUPTION, 7; MILTON, J, 26
she makes h. /Where most she satisfies SHAKESPEARE, 31
You cannot feed the h. on statistics LLOYD GEORGE, D, 7; STATISTICS, 6

hunt how much more dogs are animated when they h. in a pack HUME, D, 6; UNITY, 11
motto be:– H. BRONTE, C, 4
people who h. are the right people HUNTING, 9

hunted tell the others by their h. expression CHARITY, 19; INSULTS, 86; LEWIS, C, 6

hunter hungry as a h. HUNGER, 9; LAMB, C, 23
Man is the h. SEXES, 29; TENNYSON, 65
My heart is a lonely h. LONELINESS, 8
Nimrod the mighty h. BIBLE, 162
the snare of the h. PSALMS, 51

hunting H. people tend to be church-goers HUNTING, 8
Memories are h. horns MEMORY, 1
their discourse was about h. PEPYS, S, 10
when his half-civilized ancestors were h. the wild boar JEWS, 3

hurricanoes You cataracts and h. SHAKESPEARE, 178

hurries h. to the main event HORACE, 7; PLAYS, 7

hurry An old man in a h. POLITICIANS, 61
He sows h. and reaps indigestion HASTE, 12
H.! I never h. I have no time to h. HASTE, 13; STRAVINSKY, I, 7
So who's in a h. ALCOHOL, 14

hurrying I see a man h. along – to what KEATS, J, 69; PURPOSE, 6

hurt It doesn't h. to lose my crown FAILURE, 5
it h. too much to laugh DISAPPOINTMENT, 9; STEVENSON, A, 7
It takes your enemy and your friend…to h. you HURT, 3; TWAIN, M, 6
power to h. us that we love LOVE, 24
They say hard work never h. anybody REAGAN, R, 12
Those have most power to h. BEAUMONT, F, 6; HURT, 1
wish to h. BRONOWSKI, J, 4; CRUELTY, 1

hurting Art…can go on mattering once it has stopped h. ART, 5
not h.…not working MAJOR, J, 5

husband An archaeologist is the best h. CHRISTIE, A, 6; MARRIAGE, 46
at all times yr faithful h. MARRIAGE, 145
Being a h. is a whole-time job BENNETT, A, 7; MARRIAGE, 24
easier to be a lover than a h. BALZAC, H, 6; MARRIAGE, 17
happened unawares to look at her h. AUSTEN, J, 29; MARRIAGE, 13
h. render unto the wife due benevolence BIBLE, 29; MARRIAGE, 26
in love with…Her own h. LOVE AND MARRIAGE, 3
light wife doth make a heavy h. MARRIAGE, 132; SHAKESPEARE, 255
My h. and I ROYALTY, 60
My h. is dead DEATH, 107; MARX, G, 7
Never trust a h. too far TRUST, 5
that monstrous animal a h. and wife FIELDING, H, 13; MARRIAGE, 74
The h. frae the wife despises BURNS, R, 20; MARRIAGE, 38
trust my h. not to fall asleep POLITICS, 106
You may have my h., but not my horse LAWRENCE, D, 25; MASCULINITY, 2

husbandry borrowing dulls the edge of h. INTEGRITY, 6; SHAKESPEARE, 75
He was into animal h. SEX, 70

husbands American women expect to find in their h. WOMEN, 85
flirt with their own h. LOVE AND MARRIAGE, 8; WILDE, O, 22
h. and wives…belong to different sexes SEXES, 11
h. and wives make shipwreck of their lives MARRIAGE, 65
H. are like fires MARRIAGE, 77
h., love your wives BIBLE, 21; MARRIAGE, 25
h. remind me of an orangutang BALZAC, H, 3; MARRIAGE, 18
h. to stay at home ELIOT, G, 8; WOMEN, 51
that h. and wives should have children alternatively SEXES, 16
The *divine right* of h. FEMINISM, 39; WOLLSTONECRAFT, M, 3

hush a breathless h. in the Close tonight CRICKET, 8; NEWBOLT, H, 6
somebody ought to have said 'h.' PRECOCITY, 1

husks the h. that the swine did eat BIBLE, 331

hussy a brazen h. of a speech SPEECHES, 8

hut Love in a h. KEATS, J, 24; LOVE, 96
The Arab who builds…a h. out of…a temple FRANCE, A, 4

Hyacinth Children with H.'s temperament…merely know more CHARACTER, 18; SAKI, 5
every H. the Garden wears FITZGERALD, E, 8;

hydrostatics It gives me the h. MALAPROPISMS, 5; SHERIDAN, R, 6

hygiene how do drugs, h. and animal magnetism heal REMEDIES, 27

hymn Aisle. Altar. H. MARRIAGE, 111; PUNS, 17

hymn-book Cassock, band, and h. too CLERGY, 15

hymns My poems are h. of praise POETRY, 58; SITWELL, E, 3

hyper-thyroid Shelley had a h. face APPEARANCE, 68

hyphenated h. Americanism PATRIOTISM, 34; ROOSEVELT, T, 9

hypochondriac ennui the h. WORK, 14

hypocrisy an organized h. DISRAELI, B, 24; POLITICS, 35
H.…is a whole-time job HYPOCRISY, 13; MAUGHAM, W, 2
H. is the homage paid by vice to virtue HYPOCRISY, 16; ROCHEFOUCAULD, 19
H. is the most…nerve-racking vice HYPOCRISY, 13; MAUGHAM, W, 2
neither man nor angel can discern /H. HYPOCRISY, 14; MILTON, J, 42
That would be h. HYPOCRISY, 23; WILDE, O, 27

hypocrite h. in his pleasures CAMUS, A, 8
No man is a h. in his pleasures JOHNSON, S, 152; PLEASURE, 18
see…into a h. CHESTERTON, G, 20; HYPOCRISY, 10
hypocritical Man…learns by being h. HYPOCRISY, 12
hypodermic man who cannot work without his h. needle DRUGS, 7
hypotheses resist the fascination of doctrines and h. MEDICINE, 11
hypothesis discard a pet h. every day before breakfast SCIENCE, 63; THEORY, 11
Factual evidence can never 'prove' a h. THEORY, 6
I have no need of that h. ATHEISM, 9; GOD, 34
the slaying of a beautiful h. by an ugly fact HUXLEY, T, 1; SCIENCE, 52
hyssop purge me with h. PSALMS, 31
hysteria comedy at the moment of deepest h. WRITING, 38
I cultivate my h. with joy and terror MADNESS, 3
hysterical No laborious person was ever yet h. WORK, 14

I

I I also had my hour ANIMALS, 12; CHESTERTON, G, 13
I am for people CHAPLIN, C, 7
I am not what I am APPEARANCES, 32
in the infinite I AM COLERIDGE, S, 5; IMAGINATION, 1
I would have done it differently ARROGANCE, 9; WHISTLER, J, 16
ice A Shape of I. BOATS, 9
skating over thin i. EMERSON, R, 13; HASTE, 6
The i. was all around COLERIDGE, S, 26
iceberg as the smart ship grew…grew the I. too BOATS, 9
ice-cream just enjoy your i. while it's on your plate PHILOSOPHY, 23; WILDER, T, 5
the emperor of i. POWER, 26
iced three parts i. over AGE, 7; ARNOLD, M, 47
icicles When i. hang by the wall SEASONS, 20; SHAKESPEARE, 201
icumen Sumer is i. in SEASONS, 1
id I never saw a person's i. PSYCHOLOGY, 14
put the i. back in yid JEWS, 17
the care of the i. by the odd PSYCHIATRY, 1
idea An i. does not pass from one language TRANSLATION, 4
An i. isn't responsible for the people IDEAS, 8
constant repetition…in imprinting an i. HITLER, A, 10
Dying for an i. LEWIS, W, 2; MARTYRDOM, 3
I think it would be a good i. CIVILIZATION, 6; GANDHI, M, 5
Man is ready to die for an i. IDEAS, 3
no stand can be made against invasion by an i. HUGO, V, 4; IDEAS, 5
Retirement…is not a good i. ROYALTY, 39
That fellow seems to me to possess but one i. JOHNSON, S, 79; STUPIDITY, 6
the i. of death as an individual NUCLEAR WEAPONS, 11
they will end by ruining our i. FASCISM, 8; MUSSOLINI, B, 1
ideal an i. for which I am prepared to die MANDELA, N, 2
at fourteen every boy should be in love with some i woman SEXES, 22
Christian i.…found difficult CHRISTIANITY, 34
i. the life of Jesus NIXON, R, 12
the i. American CHESTERTON, G, 44
the incorporated i. of a man of science. DARWIN, C, 2
idealism an extraordinary mixture of i. and lunacy PANKHURST, E, 1
He had a kind of i. in pleasure PEPYS, S, 4
idealist An i.…on noticing that a rose smells better than a cabbage IDEALISM, 6; MENCKEN, H, 16
i. without being a true realist IDEALISM, 2
people call me an i. AMERICA, 44; WILSON, W, 12
ideals Away with all i. LAWRENCE, D, 33; SPONTANEITY, 3
think how far I can go with all the i. that I have THATCHER, M, 19
ideas all the enthusiasm and perseverance that he withheld from books and i. EISENHOWER, D, 2
Human Stupidity consists in having lots of i. STUPIDITY, 10
i. are of more importance than values INTELLECTUALS, 6
i. simply pass through him STUPIDITY, 1
I. that enter the mind under fire INDOCTRINATION, 3; TROTSKY, L, 9
I stopped…to exchange i. HEINE, H, 3; INFERIORITY, 1
Learn our i., or otherwise get out LESSING, D, 2; RACISM, 17
Man can have only a certain number of teeth, hair and i. OLD AGE, 104
Many i. grow better when transplanted into another mind IDEAS, 4
Morality which is based on i. LAWRENCE, D, 8; MORALITY, 9
she's only got two i. in her head STUPIDITY, 7
the addiction of political groups to the i. GALBRAITH, J, 3
the God of i. INSPIRATION, 5
There are no poetic i. POETRY, 68
Whenever i. fail, men invent words WORDS, 12
ides Beware the i. of March PROPHECY, 12; SHAKESPEARE, 144
idiot An inspired i. GOLDSMITH, O, 2
I. wind, blowing like a circle around my skull DYLAN, B, 5
now I feel like a complete i. HEINE, H, 3; INFERIORITY, 1
tale told by an i. LIFE, 86; SHAKESPEARE, 227
The i. who praises…every country but his own GILBERT, W, 27
To generalize is to be an i. BLAKE, W, 52; GENERALIZATIONS, 1
idiots the English seem…to act with…the fatuity of i. IRELAND, 26; SMITH, S, 2
idle As i. as a painted ship BOATS, 3; COLERIDGE, S, 29
I am happiest when I am i. IDLENESS, 12
Satan finds…mischief…/For i. hands IDLENESS, 13; WATTS, I, 1
thousands of i. persons are within this realm IDLENESS, 6
We would all be i. IDLENESS, 9; JOHNSON, S, 107
Young people ought not to be i. THATCHER, M, 31
idleness compulsory and irreproachable i. ARMY, 4; TOLSTOY, L, 9
i. and indifference CHANGE, 3; CHEKHOV, A, 9
I. begets ennui WORK, 14
I. is the parent of all psychology PSYCHOLOGY, 13
I.…the refuge of weak minds CHESTERFIELD, P, 15; IDLENESS, 3
Research! A mere excuse for i. RESEARCH, 3
idling It is impossible to enjoy i. IDLENESS, 7; JEROME, J, 5
idol one-eyed yellow i. to the north of Khatmandu MOURNING, 5
idolatry There is no i. in the Mass CATHOLICISM, 8; JOHNSON, S, 77
idols Their i. are silver and gold PSALMS, 64
if I. you can keep your head KIPLING, R, 17; SELF-CONTROL, 5
much virtue in I. POSSIBILITY, 3; SHAKESPEARE, 57
ifs If i. and ans PROVERBS, 214; UNCERTAINTY, 1
ignominious History is full of i. getaways by the great COWARDICE, 6; ORWELL, G, 33
ignoramus I.…person unacquainted with…knowledge familiar to yourself IGNORANCE, 5
ignorance for i. is never better than knowledge NATURE, 10
From i. our comfort flows IGNORANCE, 19
His i. was an Empire State Building of i. IGNORANCE, 18
I. is like a delicate exotic fruit IGNORANCE, 24; WILDE, O, 25
I. is preferable to error IGNORANCE, 13
I. is Strength ORWELL, G, 18
Ignorance, madam, pure i. IGNORANCE, 14; JOHNSON, S, 53
I. of the law excuses LAW, 31; SELDEN, J, 3
journalism.…keeps us in touch with the i. of the community JOURNALISM, 35; WILDE, O, 15
keeping women in a state of i. FEMINISM, 16
knowledge increases…i. unfolds KNOWLEDGE, 30
Lawyers are the only persons in whom i.…is not punished LAWYERS, 4
man's i. of the gods BUTLER, S, 7; SPONTANEITY, 1
no sin but i. IGNORANCE, 17; MARLOWE, C, 9
opinion breeds i. OPINIONS, 3
Somebody else's i. is bliss IGNORANCE, 23
where i. is bliss, /'Tis folly to be wise GRAY, T, 10; IGNORANCE, 10
Why therefore fear to confess our i. REMEDIES, 58
Your i. cramps my conversation HOPE, A, 7
ignorant a parlourmaid as i. as Queen Victoria VICTORIA, 4
footballers being i. is rubbish FOOTBALL, 19
Let no one i. of mathematics enter here MATHEMATICS, 15; PLATO, 6
The i. man always adores IGNORANCE, 16
the i. man he pretends to be MELBOURNE, 1
the opinionated, the i., and the boorish ARISTOTLE, 3; STUBBORNNESS, 3
To confess that you are totally I. about the Horse HORSES, 9; SELLAR, W, 2
what may follow it, or what preceded it, we are absolutely i. LIFE, 11
ill being i. as one of the greatest pleasures of life ILLNESS, 16
Cannot be i.; cannot be good SHAKESPEARE, 204

give /The i. he cannot cure a name ILLNESS, 8
human i. does not dawn seem...an alternative HUMAN CONDITION, 31
I am only half there when I am i. ILLNESS, 43; LAWRENCE, D, 43
If...someone is speaking i. of you CRITICISM, 18
I. met by moonlight SHAKESPEARE, 262
means to do i. deeds SHAKESPEARE, 168
no hint throughout the universe /Of good or i. NECESSITY, 8
One who is i. has...the duty to seek medical aid ILLNESS, 46
PHYSICIAN, n. One upon whom we set our hopes when i. DOCTORS, 24
the inferior doctor treats those who are i. DOCTORS, 30
the Prince...is restrained from doing i. GOVERNMENT, 46
very fine country to be acutely i. BRITAIN, 12
When people's i., they comes to I DOCTORS, 59
woman colour'd i. CONFLICT, 7; SHAKESPEARE, 375
you had better be too smart to get i. ILLNESS, 5

illegal not to make sex i. AIDS, 10
the things I really like...are either immoral, i., or fattening PLEASURE, 36

illegitimate no i. children ILLEGITIMACY, 4

ill-health Cynicism is humour in i. CYNICISM, 4; WELLS, H, 17

illiteracy The ratio of literacy to i. LITERACY, 1

illiterate I. him...from your memory MALAPROPISMS, 4; SHERIDAN, R, 5
Violence is the repartee of the i. VIOLENCE, 4

illness A long i. seems to be placed between life and death ILLNESS, 15
Considering how common i. is ILLNESS, 71
I. is in part what the world has done to a victim ILLNESS, 49
I. isn't the only thing that spoils the appetite FOOD, 68
I. is the night-side of life ILLNESS, 66
I. makes a man a scoundrel ILLNESS, 38
I. of any kind is hardly a thing to be encouraged in others ILLNESS, 69
In i. the physician is a father DOCTORS, 11
It is the part that makes the i. worth while REST, 3
Prolonged and costly i. in later years OLD AGE, 61
reborn from a mortal i. every day of his life LAWRENCE, D, 2
strange indeed that i. has not taken its place with love ILLNESS, 71
The most important thing in i. is never to lose heart ILLNESS, 44
To be too conscious is an i. ILLNESS, 22

illnesses Most men die of their remedies, and not of their i. REMEDIES, 42

illogical Faith...an i. belief in...the improbable FAITH, 21; MENCKEN, H, 14

ills sharp remedy...for all i. EXECUTION, 33; RALEIGH, W, 5

ill-spent sign of an i. youth SPORT AND GAMES, 41

ill-tempered short i. megalomaniacs ACTORS, 1

ill-treated all i. fellows /Unborn and unbegot SYMPATHY, 3

illuminate i. our whole country with the bright light of their preaching RELIGION, 49

illumine What in me is dark /I. GOD, 40; MILTON, J, 31

illusion it can contain nothing but sophistry and i. HUME, D, 2; PHILOSOPHY, 3
Religion is an i. FREUD, S, 3; RELIGION, 41
The House of Lords, an i. STOPPARD, T, 4
visible universe was an i. UNIVERSE, 2

illusions dispepsia is the apparatus of i. ILLNESS, 50
It's life's i. I recall LIFE, 66
time for open trust, for innocence and i. GERMANY, 13
vanity-case...grave of masculine i. COSMETICS, 6

illustrious This i. man, the largest and most spacious intellect POETS, 32

image any graven i. BIBLE, 115; GOD, 12
A photograph is not only an i. PHOTOGRAPHY, 8
fall down and worship the golden i. BIBLE, 48; DOOMSDAY, 1
If God made us in His i. GOD, 53; VOLTAIRE, 19
make man in our own i. BIBLE, 142
Why should I consent to the perpetuation of the i. of this i. PAINTING, 16

imagery the loveliest i. KEATS, J, 4

imaginary Happiness is an i. condition HAPPINESS, 30; SZASZ, T, 5
i. complaints HYPOCHONDRIA, 3

imagination A lady's i. is very rapid AUSTEN, J, 20; WOMEN, 15
a new audacity of i. SCIENCE, 26
His novels are marvels of sustained i. TOLSTOY, L, 1
I.!...I put it first years ago ACTING, 22; TERRY, D, 2
I. without skill gives us modern art ART, 34; STOPPARD, T, 1
indebted to his...i. for his facts POLITICIANS, 115; SHERIDAN, R, 20
not an ideal of reason but of i. HAPPINESS, 14; KANT, I, 3
of i. all compact LOVE, 148; POETRY, 55; SHAKESPEARE, 265
stand up for freedom of the i. CENSORSHIP, 9; RELIGION, 80
The primary i. COLERIDGE, S, 5; IMAGINATION, 1
treat your facts with i. is one thing TRUTH, 14
truth of i. KEATS, J, 51; TRUTH, 31

imaginative he possessed an exquisite sensitiveness...and abounding i. power OVID, 1

imagine never so happy...as we i. ROCHEFOUCAULD, 6

imagined What is now proved was...i. BLAKE, W, 24; PROOF, 2

imagining How reconcile this world...with...my i. BLINDNESS, 6

imitate A good composer does not i. MUSICIANS, 9
An original writer is...one whom nobody can i. ORIGINALITY, 2
I i. the Saviour HUXLEY, A, 5
never failed to i. CHILDREN, 7
obliged to i. himself, and to repeat IMITATION, 5
people...usually i. each other IMITATION, 3

imitates Photography can never grow up if it i. PHOTOGRAPHY, 1

imitation An i. rough diamond INSULTS, 5
every i. from 'Eton and Oxford' PARTIES, 12
I. is the sincerest form of flattery FLATTERY, 1; PROVERBS, 222
Man...is an i. MANKIND, 45

Immaculate the I. Conception was spontaneous combustion CATHOLICISM, 13; PARKER, D, 20

Immanuel call his name I. BIBLE, 198; CHRISTIANITY, 12

immature the i. man...wants to die nobly for a cause AGE, 89

immaturity common symptom of i. ORIGINALITY, 6
the executive expression of human i. BRITAIN, V, 5

immediate I call for his i. resignation GORBACHOV, M, 4

immodesty towering i., the enjoyable superbity of his self love VIDAL, G, 1

immoral moral or an i. book BOOKS, 53; WILDE, O, 44
the things I really like...are either i., illegal, or fattening PLEASURE, 36
worse than i. ACHESON, D, 4; MISTAKES, 2

immorality the most rigid code of i. BRADBURY, M, 2; ENGLISH, 7

immortal I have lost the i. part REPUTATION, 9; SHAKESPEARE, 283
make me i. with a kiss BEAUTY, 30; MARLOWE, C, 2
Our souls have sight of that i. sea METAPHYSICS, 6; WORDSWORTH, W, 29
Why are you weeping? Did you imagine that I was i. LAST WORDS, 58; LOUIS XIV, 7

immortality I...want to achieve i....through not dying ALLEN, W, 10; IMMORTALITY, 1
just ourselves /And I. DEATH, 55

immutable Few things are as i. GALBRAITH, J, 3; POLITICS, 40

impassioned the average sensual man i. and grandiloquent HUGO, V, 1

impediment cause, or just i. BOOK OF COMMON PRAYER, 23; OBSTRUCTION, 2

imperative This i. is Categorical KANT, I, 2; MORALITY, 8

imperfect He was i., unfinished, inartistic JAMES, H, 7

imperfection i. itself may have its...perfect state IMPERFECTION, 7

imperial be yourself, i., plain and true BROWNING, R, 8; SINCERITY, 1
on the moon as in I. Russia CHEKHOV, A, 1

imperialism i. is the monopoly stage of capitalism LENIN, V, 1; POLITICS, 67
Their Europeanism is...i. with an inferiority complex POLITICS, 48

impersonal In the philosopher there is nothing whatever i. NIETZSCHE, F, 14; PHILOSOPHERS, 7

impertinent ask an i. question BRONOWSKI, J, 2; SCIENCE, 12

impetuous such i. blood IMPETUOSITY, 5; WORDSWORTH, W, 48

importance Official dignity...in inverse ratio to...i. DIPLOMACY, 17; HUXLEY, A, 10

important Fear is an i. feeling SPORT AND GAMES, 39
more i. things...than appearance APPEARANCE, 12
most i. thing women have to do FEMINISM, 22
One doesn't recognize...the really i. moments...until it's too late CHRISTIE, A, 1; REGRET, 6
that basic weekendmanship should contain...I. Person Play ONE-UPMANSHIP, 2; POTTER, S, 4
the little things are infinitely the most i. DOYLE, A, 6; TRIVIALITY, 7

imposed wish to be i. COWPER, W, 20; EXPLOITATION, 2

impossibility a physical and metaphysical i. CARLYLE, T, 3; POETS, 3
impossible complete sorrow is as i. EMOTION, 6; TOLSTOY, L, 12
I believe because it is i. BELIEF, 11; TERTULLIAN, 3
It's either easy or i. PAINTING, 6
something is i., he is...wrong SCIENCE, 20
when you have excluded the i. DOYLE, A, 3; TRUTH, 22
impostors Doctors are mostly i. DOCTORS, 108
impotent an i. people, /Sick with inbreeding WELSH, 3
He also is i. SEX, 32
impregnator the writer...is the i. READING, 19
impress made his i. on eternity HYPATIA, 3
impression knowledge and wonder...is an i. of pleasure BACON, F, 1; WONDER, 1
impressionable Give me a girl at an i. age IMPRESSIONABILITY, 5; SPARK, M, 7
impressions i....lasting as...an oar upon the water INSIGNIFICANCE, 1
imprisonment honourable i. HOSTAGES, 8
Thirty years' i. is IMPRISONMENT, 4
improbable an i. fiction REALITY, 8; SHAKESPEARE, 345
Faith...an illogical belief in...the i. FAITH, 21; MENCKEN, H, 14
whatever remains, however i., must be the truth DOYLE, A, 3; TRUTH, 22
impromptu Winston...preparing his i. speeches CHURCHILL, W, 6
improper I only hope it is not i. ETIQUETTE, 4
impropriety I. is the soul of wit HUMOUR, 21; MAUGHAM, W, 9
improve i. the international situation GORBACHOV, M, 13
improved enormously i. by death SAKI, 4; WRITERS, 83
Victoria has greatly i. VICTORIA, 1
improvement most schemes of political i. are very laughable JOHNSON, S, 76; POLITICS, 59
improvised A master of i. speech and i. policies POLITICIANS, 120
impulse the i. of the moment AUSTEN, J, 22; FLATTERY, 2
the need to talk is a primary i. CERVANTES, M, 14
impulses Mistrust first i. TALLEYRAND, 7
impure To the Puritan all things are i. LAWRENCE, D, 5
in you had it i. you PARKER, D, 25
inactivity wise and masterly i. GOVERNMENT, 23
inadequate Like Brighton pier...i. for getting to France KINNOCK, N, 8; TRAVEL, 27
inarticulate speak for the i. and the submerged BEAVERBROOK, M, 4; JOURNALISM, 4
inartistic He was imperfect, unfinished, i. JAMES, H, 7
inbreeding an impotent people, /Sick with i. WELSH, 3
incense I. of death PLATH, S, 4
incest except i. and folk-dancing EXPERIENCE, 7
inch every i. a king ROYALTY, 105; SHAKESPEARE, 188
Give him an i. GREED, 2; PROVERBS, 174
women i. forward FEMINISM, 31
inches They that die by famine die by i. HUNGER, 6
incident character but the determination of i. CHARACTER, 13
What is i. but the illustration of character JAMES, H, 12
incisors Writers, like teeth, are divided into i. and grinders BAGEHOT, W, 8; WRITERS, 2
inclination A man ought to read just as i. leads him JOHNSON, S, 63; READING, 8
i. to write BOREDOM, 11
include 'I. me out' GOLDWYN, S, 10
incoherent I'm not i. CONFUSION, 9
plays are suited to i. argument BENNETT, A, 6
income Annual i. twenty pounds DICKENS, C, 13; ECONOMICS, 8
difficult to love mankind...private i. SELF-INTEREST, 5
few sorrows...in which a good i. is of no avail MONEY, 48
hardest thing...to understand is i. tax TAXATION, 2
her Majesty...must not...look upon me as a source of i. TAXATION, 6
live beyond its i. BUTLER, S, 11; EXTRAVAGANCE, 2;
incomes people live beyond their i. EXTRAVAGANCE, 4; SAKI, 9
incomparable The I. Max BEERBOHM, M, 1
incompetence their level of i. INCOMPETENCE, 4
incompetent a tax on pianos for the i. MUSIC, 58
Democracy substitutes election by the i. many DEMOCRACY, 23
God is the immemorial refuge of the i. GOD, 36; MENCKEN, H, 9
i. swine SASSOON, S, 4; WAR, 148
incomplete A man in love is i. until...married MARRIAGE, 78
incomprehensible an old, wild, and i. man POLITICIANS, 126; VICTORIA, 8
inconvenience Change is not made without i. CHANGE, 14
inconveniences A good many i. attend play-going PLAYS, 16; TYNAN, K, 4
inconvenient i. to be poor COWPER, W, 7; POVERTY, 7
No one wants the truth if it is i. TRUTH, 36
incorruptible seagreen I. CARLYLE, T, 18; POLITICIANS, 59
the dead shall be raised i. BIBLE, 42; DEATH, 35
increase from fairest creatures we desire i. BEAUTY, 42; SHAKESPEARE, 359
then shall the earth bring forth her i. PSALMS, 38
increased influence of the Crown has i. MONARCHY, 11
incredible i. feeling, like falling in love SOUTH AFRICA, 10
incredibly I....adorably beautiful BEAUTY, 13; COMPLIMENTS, 5
incurable Not even medicine can master i. diseases MEDICINE, 89
the i. disease of writing WRITING, 26
There are no such things as i. SCIENCE, 3
Ind Outshone the wealth of Ormus and of I. DEVIL, 13; MILTON, J, 39
indecency perfectly ordinary little case of a man charged with i. HOMOSEXUALITY, 13
prejudicial...as a public i. CERVANTES, M, 21; SIN, 11
The older one grows the more one likes i. AGE, 101; WOOLF, V, 11
indecent It requires one to assume such i. postures CRICKET, 13; WILDE, O, 72
much more i....than a good smack LAWRENCE, D, 7; PUNISHMENT, 20
sent down for i. behaviour EDUCATION, 93; WAUGH, E, 6
indecision Nothing is so exhausting as i. INDECISION, 3
indefatigable i. and unsavoury engine of pollution DOGS, 17
indefensible political speech and writing are largely the defence of the i. ORWELL, G, 21; POLITICS, 81
independent all men are created equal and i. JEFFERSON, T, 5
an I. Labour Party PARTIES, 10; WAUGH, E, 46
An i....wants to take the politics out of politics POLITICS, 101
one must do some work seriously and must be i. CURIE, M, 3
to become fully i. FAMILY, 22
To be poor and i. POVERTY, 6
indescribable I., O queen SORROW, 35
India From I.'s coral strand PLACES, 17
I. is a geographical term CHURCHILL, W, 45; PLACES, 10
The loss of I. BRITISH EMPIRE, 2
What have we to say to I. RUSKIN, J, 18
Indian base I., threw a pearl away LOVE, 155; SHAKESPEARE, 290
lay out ten to see a dead I. CHARITY, 21; SHAKESPEARE, 324
Indians shock to see Gary Cooper killing off the I. BALDWIN, J, 7
The only good I. I ever saw were dead ENEMIES, 9
indictment an i. against an whole people ACCUSATION, 2; BURKE, E, 16
indifference and cold i. came INDIFFERENCE, 5
equanimity bordering on i. GILBERT, W, 47; INDIFFERENCE, 3
idleness and i. CHANGE, 3; CHEKHOV, A, 9
i. and a coach and six LOVE, 56
Nothing is so fatal to religion as i. BURKE, E, 23; INDIFFERENCE, 2
veil of i. CLINTON, B, 8
indigestion Don't tell your friends about your i. MANNERS, 3
He sows hurry and reaps i. HASTE, 12
I. is charged by God ILLNESS, 33
I., n. A disease...mistake for deep religious conviction ILLNESS, 14; RELIGION, 13
indignation Moral i. is in most cases 2 percent moral MORALITY, 21
My heart burned within me with i. and grief LINCOLN, A, 2
puritan pours righteous i. CHESTERTON, G, 51; PURITANISM, 1
the mists of righteous i. MUGGERIDGE, M, 1; PRUDERY, 4
Wrongdoing can only be avoided if those who are not wronged feel the same i. VICE, 14
indignity ultimate i. is to be given a bedpan MEDICINE, 51
indiscreet people so i. in appearing to know BOCCACCIO, G, 3
indiscretion A lover without i. is no lover HARDY, T, 8; LOVE, 84
poised between a cliché and an i. POLITICS, 69
indispensables She was one of those i. HUXLEY, A, 25
indistinct and makes it i., /As water is in water CHANGE, 23
indistinguishable in America...picture-painter is i. from... business man AMERICA, 27; ART, 19
individual gesture by the i. to himself BUSINESS, 15; GALBRAITH, J, 8
He was unperfect, unfinished, i. WRITERS, 64
It is of no moment to the happiness of an i. GOVERNMENT, 18; JOHNSON, S, 83
the idea of death as an i. NUCLEAR WEAPONS, 11

The liberty of the i. must be thus far limited FREEDOM, 40
The psychic development of the i. FREUD, S, 2; PSYCHIATRY, 14
individualism American system of rugged i. AMERICA, 21
Art is the most intense mode of i. ART, 41; WILDE, O, 55
I eliminate my i. CHINA, 14
individuality England is the paradise of i. SANTAYANA, G, 9
indolence i....qualified with...bad temper RESPECT, 5
Your daily task of i. LAZINESS, 7
indoors God having given us i. and out-of-doors NATURE, 25
indulgence An only son, sir, might expect more i. FAMILY, 26; GOLDSMITH, O, 16
sign of the cross...an i. for all the sins CHRISTIANITY, 6
industrial I. relations are like sexual relations INDUSTRIAL RELATIONS, 2
industry Captains of i. CARLYLE, T, 22; LEADERSHIP, 5
development of i. has created many new sources of danger DISEASE, 36
entertainment branch of I. POLITICS, 124
i. will supply their deficiency WORK, 30
Life without i. is guilt ART, 30; RUSKIN, J, 4
national i. of Prussia WAR, 107
inebriated i. with...his own verbosity DISRAELI, B, 32; VERBOSITY, 3
ineffectual A weak, diffusive, weltering, i. man COLERIDGE, S, 1
Shelley was indeed 'a beautiful and i. angel' SHELLEY, P, 1
inelegance a continual state of i. AUSTEN, J, 28; WEATHER, 7
ineligible honourably i. for the struggle of life ARISTOCRACY, 10; POLITICIANS, 71
ineptitude i. of M. Sartre's political performance SARTRE, J, 3
inequalities only i. that matter begin in the mind DIFFERENCE, 8
inevitable ACCIDENT n. An i. occurrence ACCIDENTS, 1
Failure is i. FAILURE, 10
inexactitude terminological i. CHURCHILL, W, 39; LYING, 10
inexperience I. is what makes a young man AGE, 71
infallibility illusions of i., which of course brought her downfall POLITICIANS, 70
infallible an i. sign of the second-rate INFERIORITY, 3
No man is i. IMPERFECTION, 2; PROVERBS, 312
The only i. criterion of wisdom BURKE, E, 4; SUCCESS, 9
We are none of us i. IMPERFECTION, 14
infamous I have got an i. army ARMY, 6; WELLINGTON, 16
infamy A date that shall live in i. WORLD WAR II, 44
infancy between i. and adultery YOUTH, 2
Heaven lies about us in our i. WORDSWORTH, W, 26
i., childhood, adolescence and obsolescence AGE, 58
Lo, Hudled up, together Lye /Gray Age, Grene youth, White I. ANONYMOUS, 53
infant a mixed i. BEHAN, B, 4; CHILDREN, 9
An i. crying in the night HUMAN CONDITION, 28; TENNYSON, 30
I doubt that the i. monster KIPLING, R, 1
Sooner murder an i. in its cradle BLAKE, W, 21; DESIRE, 3
infanticide as indefensible as i. WEST, R, 5
infants I. do not cry without some legitimate cause BABIES, 5
infection gazing into that happy future when the i. will be banished ILLNESS, 64
the only man who escaped i. SOCRATES, 2
inferior No one can make you feel i. without your consent INFERIORITY, 6
Switzerland...an i. sort of Scotland SMITH, S, 15; SWITZERLAND, 3
inferiority minds so impatient of i. JOHNSON, S, 23
Their Europeanism is...imperialism with an i. complex POLITICS, 48
Ulysses...gives me an i. complex JOYCE, J, 3
Wherever an i. complex exists, there is...reason INFERIORITY, 2; JUNG, C, 10
inferiors I. revolt in order that they may be equal ARISTOTLE, 9; REVOLUTION, 1
The English want *i.* PRIDE, 13
inferno A man who has not passed through the i. of his passions JUNG, C, 3; PASSION, 4
infidelity I....consists in professing to believe INTEGRITY, 5
Infidels War is enjoined you against the I. KORAN 3
infinite Space is almost i. QUAYLE, D, 5
The Desire of Man being I. BLAKE, W, 50; INFINITY, 1
The sight...gave me i. pleasure EXECUTION, 28
infinitive When I split an i. GRAMMAR, 2
infinity I. in the palm of your hand BLAKE, W, 9; WONDER, 2
infirmities friend should bear his friend's i. FRIENDS, 14; SHAKESPEARE, 160
infirmity last i. of noble mind FAME, 20; MILTON, J, 25
they desire but prolonged i. OLD AGE, 15
inflation a little i. is like being a little pregnant ECONOMICS, 11
I. in the Sixties was a nuisance ECONOMICS, 15
the path of low i. ECONOMICS, 7
unemployment and the recession have been the price...to get i. down ECONOMICS, 14
influence guard against...unwarranted i. INFLUENCE, 3
How to...I. People INFLUENCE, 2
i. of the Crown has increased MONARCHY, 11
proper time to i. the character of a child INGE, W, 9
unable to i. events...do not have the power BRITAIN, 10
influenza call it i. if ye like BENNETT, A, 3; ILLNESS, 11
inform all occasions do i. against me SHAKESPEARE, 100
not to i. the reader ACHESON, D, 7; BUREAUCRACY, 1
informed far better i. WISDOM, 28
infortune The worst kinde of i. is this CHAUCER, G, 20
infringement Necessity is the plea for every i. of human freedom NECESSITY, 4; PITT THE YOUNGER, 1
infusion The i. of a China plant ADDISON, J, 12; DRINKS, 1
ingenious a loyal, a gallant, a generous, an i., and good-temper'd people FRANCE, 18; STERNE, L, 2
inglorious mute i. Milton GRAY, T, 6
the i. arts of peace MARVELL, A, 3; POLITICIANS, 105
ingratitude I hate i. more in a man SHAKESPEARE, 347
I., thou marble-hearted fiend SHAKESPEARE, 172
man's i. SHAKESPEARE, 50
ingress Our i..../Was naked and bare LIFE, 58; LONGFELLOW, H, 15
inherit Russia will certainly i. the future LAWRENCE, D, 34; RUSSIA, 10
inherited as if he had i. it GRANT, U, 1
infinitely fragile and never directly i. HUMAN NATURE, 22
inhumanity Man's i. to man BURNS, R, 14; CRUELTY, 2
initiative success depends...upon individual i. and exertion EFFORT, 5; SUCCESS, 23
injured Never trust the man who...hath i. you FIELDING, H, 7; TRUST, 2
injury An i. is much sooner forgotten CHESTERFIELD, P, 7; INSULTS, 31
Recompense i. with justice CONFUCIUS, 12; KINDNESS, 4
injustice A lawyer has no business with...justice or i. JOHNSON, S, 157; JUSTICE, 13
fear of suffering i. JUSTICE, 21; ROCHEFOUCAULD, 10
threatened with a great i. CARLYLE, J, 1
what a man still plans...shows the...i. in his death DEATH, 46
injustices thought only to justify their i. HUMAN NATURE, 33; VOLTAIRE, 12
ink an optimist...fills up his crossword puzzle in i. OPTIMISM, 37
inn no room for them in the i. BIBLE, 313; CHRISTMAS, 8
To that dark i., the grave DEATH, 134; SCOTT, W, 12
innate i. superiority that the successful parents had SUPERIORITY, 15
inner Conscience is the i. voice CONSCIENCE, 6; MENCKEN, H, 2
first been vividly heard by an i. ear MUSICIANS, 17
Innisfree I will arise and...go to I. SOLITUDE, 19; YEATS, W, 17
innocence I. is no earthly weapon HILL, G, 2
it is...our business to lose i. INNOCENCE, 5
my i. begins to weigh me down INNOCENCE, 3
My knowingness and my i. ACTORS, 25
Ralph wept for the end of i. GOLDING, W, 2; INNOCENCE, 6
time for open trust, for i. and illusions GERMANY, 13
innocent Every one is i. LAW, 3; PROVERBS, 141
ten guilty persons escape than one i. suffer BLACKSTONE, W, 5; JUSTICE, 3
innocently i. employed than in getting money JOHNSON, S, 91; MONEY, 28
innovator time is the greatest i. BACON, F, 30; INNOVATION, 1
inquiry The world is but a school of i. MONTAIGNE, M, 9
inquisitive questions to which the i. mind can...receive no answer JOHNSON, S, 127
the i. mind can...receive no answer PHILOSOPHY, 6
insane Charles Lamb...in some considerable degree i. LAMB, C, 1
if we tried to shut up the i. MADNESS, 45
Man is quite i. MONTAIGNE, M, 6; RELIGION, 69
Ordinarily he is i. MADNESS, 21
insanity I. in individuals is something rare MADNESS, 29
I. is a kind of innocence MADNESS, 20
I. is hereditary MADNESS, 27

I. is often the logic of an accurate mind overtaxed MADNESS, 22
lay interest in ecclesiastical matters…often a prelude to i. RELIGION, 96; WAUGH, E, 19
Where does one go from a world of i. MADNESS, 11
inscriptions In lapidary i. a man is not upon oath JOHNSON, S, 99
inscrutable Dumb, i. and grand ARNOLD, M, 33; CATS, 1
fathom the i. workings of Providence REPARTEE, 4
insect the Egyptians worshipped an i. DISRAELI, B, 34
insemination Surely you don't mean by unartificial i. SEX, 120; THURBER, J, 19
insensitiveness the greatest deeds require a certain i. INSENSITIVITY, 4
inside attention to the i.…contempt for the outside BOOKS, 16; CHESTERFIELD, P, 14
insight moment's i.…worth a life's experience EXPERIENCE, 16
insignificance A man of…the utmost i. INSULTS, 41; POLITICIANS, 76
insignificant as i. men as any in England ARISTOCRACY, 20; WALPOLE, R, 4
utterly i. little blue green planet SCIENCE FICTION, 1
insolence a wretch who supports with i. JOHNSON, S, 13; PATRONAGE, 1
i. is not invective DISRAELI, B, 26
the i. of wealth JOHNSON, S, 124; WEALTH, 28
insolent their i. and unfounded airs of superiority FRANCE, 19; WALPOLE, H, 9
insomnia *Amor vincit i.* FRY, C, 5
every man's i. is as different from his neighbor's SLEEP, 13
I. troubles only those who can sleep any time SLEEP, 20
inspiration Genius is one per cent i. GENIUS, 5
Ninety per cent of i. PROVERBS, 308
inspired An i. idiot GOLDSMITH, O, 2
instinct the i. for being unhappy SAKI, 8; SORROW, 26
instincts diseases…no less natural than the i. which preserve him. DISEASE, 32
institution a bit of an i. THATCHER, M, 37
Any i. which does not suppose the people good LAW, 29
more than a game. It's an i. CRICKET, 4
institutions working of great i. SANTAYANA, G, 2
instructed the worst i. ARISTOCRACY, 6
instruction The most essential part of a student's i. EDUCATION, 42
instrument An i. to tickle human ears MUSIC, 11
there you sit with that magnificent i. between your legs TOSCANINI, A, 5
The state is an i.…of the ruling class STALIN, J, 2; STATE, 5
instruments gods…/Make i. to plague us SHAKESPEARE, 195
i. of control in the Soviet Union RUSSIA, 8
insufferable It is Oxford that has made me i. BEERBOHM, M, 8
insult A man should not i. his wife publicly MARRIAGE, 161; THURBER, J, 12
Marriage is an i. MARRIAGE, 114
One does not i. the river god PRUDENCE, 5
sooner forgotten than an i. CHESTERFIELD, P, 7; INSULTS, 31
insulted anyone here whom I have not i. INSULTS, 21
insured you cannot be i. for the accidents ACCIDENTS, 2
insurrection I. is an art REVOLUTION, 13; TROTSKY, L, 6
intangible great i. machine of commercial tyrrany MORRIS, W, 1
integrate I i. the current export drive BETJEMAN, J, 5; BUSINESS, 4
integrity if I accepted the honour…I would not answer for the i. of my intellect TITLES, 3
I. without knowledge is weak JOHNSON, S, 30
intellect a feather to tickle the i. LAMB, C, 16; PUNS, 12
a road…that does not go through the i. CHESTERTON, G, 9
halitosis of the i. INSULTS, 67
his i. is not replenished SHAKESPEARE, 198
i. is…fooled by the heart ROCHEFOUCAULD, 15
I. is invisible SCHOPENHAUER, A, 2
put on I. BLAKE, W, 17
take care not to make the i. our god EINSTEIN, A, 4; INTELLECT, 4
the soul of a martyr with the i. of an advocate BAGEHOT, W, 10; POLITICIANS, 43
The voice of the i. is a soft one FREUD, S, 1; INTELLECT, 5
we cannot exclude the i. from…any of our functions INTELLECT, 8
intellects highest i., like the tops of mountains INTELLECT, 9; MACAULAY, T, 12
There is a wicked inclination…to suppose an old man decayed in his i. JOHNSON, S, 143; OLD AGE, 58
intellectual an i.…mind watches itself CAMUS, A, 11; INTELLECTUALS, 7
artist who's an i. FITZGERALD, F, 11; INTELLECTUALS, 10
Beware of the artist who's an i. ARTISTS, 4
Every i. attitude is latently political POLITICS, 74
i., but I found it too difficult HUMILITY, 10; INTELLECTUALS, 12
i.…doesn't know how to park a bike INTELLECTUALS, 1
I've been called many things, but never an i. BANKHEAD, T, 6; INTELLECTUALS, 3
Man is an i. animal HAZLITT, W, 5; INTELLECT, 7
The word I. suggests AUDEN, W, 21; INTELLECTUALS, 2
thirdly, i. ability EDUCATION, 7
intellectuals i. chief cause of anguish INTELLECTUALS, 4
Pointy-headed i. INTELLECTUALS, 16
vanishing race.…the i. INTELLECTUALS, 13
intelligence a story of amazing foolishness and amazing i. MEDICINE, 101
I. is quickness to apprehend ABILITY, 2; INTELLIGENCE, 13; WHITEHEAD, A, 2
i. is the great polluter ENVIRONMENT, 11
i. of the American people INTELLIGENCE, 8
The more i.…the more…one finds original INTELLIGENCE, 10; PASCAL, B, 3
intelligent A really i. man feels what other men…know INTELLIGENCE, 9; MONTESQUIEU, 2
Each generation imagines itself…more i. AGE, 67; ORWELL, G, 35
fearless, high-spirited, resolute and i. heroines SHAKESPEARE, 19
i. people…are socialists SOCIALISM, 1
man…more i. than dolphins ADAMS, D, 6
stupid are cocksure…i. full of doubt DOUBT, 8
The i. are to the intelligentsia BALDWIN, S, 11; INTELLIGENCE, 3
the most i. Prime Minister of the century MACMILLAN, H, 4
intelligentsia intelligent are to the i. BALDWIN, S, 11; INTELLIGENCE, 3
intelligible to aim at being i. COMMUNICATION, 2; HOPE, A, 1
intensity excellence of every art is its i. KEATS, J, 54
intent A truth that's told with bad i. TRUTH, 13
prick the sides of my i. AMBITION, 23; SHAKESPEARE, 211
intercourse dreary i. of daily life OPTIMISM, 42; WORDSWORTH, W, 15
i. is…a social act SEX, 34
Sexual i. began /In nineteen sixty-three SEX, 63
interest a playwright…void of dramatic i. SARTRE, J, 2
How can I take an i. in my work ENTHUSIASM, 1
It is not my i. to pay the principal, nor my principle to pay the i. SHERIDAN, R, 19
interested always been i. in people MAUGHAM, W, 28; MISANTHROPY, 2
seldom i. in what he is saying POUND, E, 2
The average man is…i. in a woman who is i. in him SEXES, 9
interests all these great i. entrusted to the shaking hand POLITICIANS, 126; VICTORIA, 8
i. of a few, at the expense of the welfare of the majority SOCIETY, 12
intérieur 'Vive l'i. HISTORY, 30; HUMOUR, 61; SELLAR, W, 6
interior i. of a flying saucer ADAMS, D, 3
intermarriage By i. and by every means in his power DIPLOMACY, 27
intermission Pleasure is…i. of pain PLEASURE, 32; SELDEN, J, 4
international improve the i. situation GORBACHOV, M, 13
I. Woman's Day RUSSIAN REVOLUTION, 9
science is essentially i. CURIE, M, 4; SCIENCE, 23
interns scrub of i. LANGUAGE, 4
interpreter The soul fortunately, has an i. BRONTE, C, 5
interval an opera without an i. OPERA, 8
interviewing i. a faded female in a damp basement INSULTS, 57
intimacy misery…caused by a single dangerous i. LACLOS, P, 4
intimidation Years of i. and violence could not stop us MANDELA, N, 8
intolerably I would grow i. conceited CONCEIT, 21; WHISTLER, J, 8
intolerant what is dangerous about extremists is…that they are i. POLITICS, 62

intoxicate you won't i. with one glass someone who has...drunk...a...barrel CHEKHOV, A, 13; EXPERIENCE, 10
intoxicated A man who exposes himself when he is i. DRUNKENNESS, 20; JOHNSON, S, 129
No, thank you, I was born i. DRUNKENNESS, 25
intoxication best of life is...i. BYRON, 21; DRUNKENNESS, 13
intrigue the i. of a Greek of the lower empire DISRAELI, B, 33; INSULTS, 43
introduce let me i. you to that leg of mutton CARROLL, L, 37; INTRODUCTIONS, 1
introduction I could buy back my i. MARX, G, 15
introspection I....he never achieved WRITERS, 44
intrudes society, where none i. BYRON, 16; NATURE, 3
intuition powers of i. INTELLECT, 2
invade when religion is allowed to i....private life MELBOURNE, 11; RELIGION, 66
invalid an invaluable permanent i. called Bunbury DECEPTION, 11; WILDE, O, 20
Every i. is a physician PATIENTS, 1
invalids the modern sympathy with i. ILLNESS, 69
invasion no stand can be made against i. by an idea HUGO, V, 4; IDEAS, 5
the long-promised i. CHURCHILL, W, 54; WORLD WAR II, 15
invective insolence is not i. DISRAELI, B, 26; IMPERTINENCE, 1
invent it would be necessary to i. Him GOD, 52; VOLTAIRE, 14
inventing Prolonged...reviewing of books involves constantly *i.* reactions CRITICISM, 46; ORWELL, G, 11
invention A long poem is a test of i. KEATS, J, 50; POETRY, 33
He was his own greatest i. COWARD, N, 1
i....arises directly from idleness IDLENESS, 4
Woman's virtue is man's greatest i. SEXES, 26
inventions All one's i. are true POETRY, 22
investment There is no finer i. BABIES, 1; CHURCHILL, W, 62
To bear many children is considered...an i. CHILDREN, 29; GANDHI, I, 3
inviolable the i. shade ARNOLD, M, 38; HOPE, 7
invisible O world i. GOD, 51
the only evil that walks /I. HYPOCRISY, 14; MILTON, J, 42
invisibly electricity was dripping i. SCIENCE, 91; THURBER, J, 10
invitations spend most of our time answering i. to social functions CATHOLICISM, 6
invited People were not i. – they went there FITZGERALD, F, 8; PARTIES, 6
still i. to dinner ELIOT, G, 10
involuntary It was i.. They sank my boat KENNEDY, J, 3
inward They flash upon that i. eye WORDSWORTH, W, 9
truth in the i. parts PSALMS, 31
inwards he looked i., and found her DRYDEN, J, 23
Iowa Hollywood – a place where people from I. CINEMA, 1
IRA I. would think me a worthwhile target MOUNTBATTEN OF BURMA, L, 5
Iraq conquest of I.. It is the liberation of Kuwait WAR, 35
Ireland a picture of a relief map of I. APPEARANCE, 6
delivered I. from plunder and oppression SWIFT, J, 1
English should give I. home rule IRELAND, 24
freely expressed consent of the people of Northern I. IRELAND, 15
'How's poor ould I., and how does she stand?' ANONYMOUS, 46; IRELAND, 1
I'll not forget old I. HOMESICKNESS, 1
I never met anyone in I. who understood the Irish question IRELAND, 9
I. is the old sow IRELAND, 12; JOYCE, J, 6
I would have liked to go to I. IRELAND, 28; WILHELM II, 2
Now I. has her madness AUDEN, W, 16; POETRY, 5
The moment...I. is mentioned IRELAND, 26; SMITH, S, 2
The problem with I. IRELAND, 14
Irish All races have...economists, with the exception of the I. GALBRAITH, J, 5; IRISH, 5
answer to the I. Question IRISH, 9
as I. as Black Americans IRISH, 6
historic inability in Britain to comprehend I. feelings IRELAND, 10
I....devotion to higher arts GALBRAITH, J, 5; IRISH, 5
I. might do very good Service IRISH, 10
That is the I. Question DISRAELI, B, 22; IRELAND, 8
The English and Americans dislike only *some* I. BEHAN, B, 8; IRISH, 3
The enviably attractive nephew who sings an I. ballad KENNEDY, J, 1
The I. and the Jews have a psychosis BEHAN, B, 7
The I. are a fair people IRISH, 7; JOHNSON, S, 90
The I....are needed in this cold age IRISH, 4
The I. don't know what they want IRISH, 8
Irishman Put an I. on the spit IRISH, 1; PROVERBS, 344
iron An i. curtain CHURCHILL, W, 64; COLD WAR, 2
blood and i. POWER POLITICS, 2
he has i. teeth GORBACHOV, M, 1
I also wash and i. them FEMINISM, 54; HOUSEWORK, 8
muscles.../Are strong as i. bands LONGFELLOW, H, 17
rule them with a rod of i. LEADERSHIP, 3
the I. Curtain has been demolished RUSSIA, 2
the i. has entered his soul LLOYD GEORGE, D, 14; STERNE, L, 1
The I. Lady of British politics POLITICIANS, 34
the I. Lady of the Western World POLITICIANS, 123
will wink and hold out mine i. COWARDICE, 10; SHAKESPEARE, 126
ironies Life's Little I. HARDY, T, 9; LIFE, 45
ironing when it comes to i. HOUSEWORK, 9
irons Many i. in the fire PROVERBS, 284
two i. in the fire BEAUMONT, F, 3; PRUDENCE, 6
irony everyone gets i. nowadays HUMOUR, 32
irregular i. side of nature...these have been puzzles to science NATURE, 14
irrelevant sexuality was utterly i. HOMOSEXUALITY, 24
the most i. thing in nature FAMILY, 32; LAMB, C, 15
irreproachable compulsory and i. idleness ARMY, 4; TOLSTOY, L, 9
irresponsible better to be i. and right CHURCHILL, W, 66
irretrievable loss of virtue in a female is i. VIRTUE, 2
irretrievably marriage had i. broken down ROYALTY, 42
Irving I. reminded me of a pig ACTORS, 28
Ishmaelites I....will not publicly eat human flesh uncooked in Lent CANNIBALISM, 2; WAUGH, E, 41
Islam In some remote regions of I. MODESTY, 5
I. unashamedly came with a sword RELIGION, 79
My interpretation of women's rights in I. FEMINISM, 24
island cowering on the very i. BRITISH, 1
No man is an I. DONNE, J, 7; SOCIETY, 8
wealth of our i. may be diminished ENGLISH, 14
Islands less known by the British than these selfsame British I. BRITISH, 3
isle Kelly from the I. of Man ABSENCE, 8
this sceptred i. ENGLAND, 46; SHAKESPEARE, 297
isles The i. of Greece BYRON, 26; EUROPE, 3
isolating by i. him...as if he were a leper IRELAND, 20
isolation At the moment of childbirth, every woman has the same aura of i. LONELINESS, 10
our splendid i. DIPLOMACY, 14
Israel When I. was in Egypt land ANONYMOUS, 107
Israelis I. are now what we call the 'enemy-friends WAR AND PEACE, 2
it 'Tisn't beauty...just I. ATHEISM, 14
Italian as sensible as baseball in I. MENCKEN, H, 17; OPERA, 7
I speak...I. to women, French to men LANGUAGE, 13
The crafty, cold-blooded, black-hearted I. FASCISM, 3
Italians The I. will laugh at me MUSSOLINI, B, 2
italics 'I adore i., don't you?' LITERATURE, 24
Italy A man who has not been in I. JOHNSON, S, 110; TRAVEL, 23
I. a paradise for horses NATIONALITY, 5
itch The i. of disputing...the scab of churches RELIGION, 104
the i. of literature WRITING, 31
The Seven Year I. SEX, 11
What used to be merely an i. is now an allergy PROGRESS, 1
iteration i. of nuptials CONGREVE, W, 16; MARRIAGE, 53
itself Love seeketh not i. to please BLAKE, W, 36; LOVE, 36
Iutae the *Saxones*, *Angli*, and *I.* ENGLISH, 6
ivy The holly and the i. ANONYMOUS, 81

J

jab Man...had been created to j. the life out of Germans SASSOON, S, 5; WAR, 144
J'accuse *J.* ACCUSATION, 4; ZOLA, 2
Jack Damn you, J. – I'm all right SELFISHNESS, 3
J. and Jill went up the hill NURSERY RHYMES, 25
J. of all trades OCCUPATIONS, 3; PROVERBS, 239
J. Sprat could eat no fat NURSERY RHYMES, 26
Little J. Horner /Sat in the corner NURSERY RHYMES, 30
the house that J. built NURSERY RHYMES, 61
jackal This whipped j. WORLD WAR II, 17
jackals J. piss at their foot BOOKS, 20
Jackson J. standing like a stone wall DETERMINATION, 5
Jacob Talk to him of J.'s ladder JERROLD, D, 4; PRACTICALITY, 4
the traffic of J.'s ladder HEAVEN, 15

John Wayne J. is dead ACTORS, 12
join He's gone to j. the majority DEATH, 24
will you j. the dance CARROLL, L, 17
joined what...God hath j. together BIBLE, 403; MARRIAGE, 30
Why haven't you j. WORLD WAR I, 21
joint The time is out of j. SHAKESPEARE, 80
joke A j.'s a very serious thing HUMOUR, 9.
a j. with a double meaning HUMOUR, 3
A rich man's j. is always funny FLATTERY, 3
good deed to forget a poor j. HUMOUR, 5
Housekeeping ain't no j. HOUSEWORK, 1
The coarse j. proclaims HUMOUR, 20; LEWIS, C, 2
jokes different taste in j. is a...strain on the affections ELIOT, G, 6; HUMOUR, 13
Forgive...my little j. on Thee FROST, R, 4; PRAYER, 17
He cannot bear old men's j. OLD AGE, 48
I don't make j. GOVERNMENT, 35; ROGERS, W, 7
Woody Allen or me when we stop doing the j. HUMOUR, 31
joking My way of j. is to tell the truth SHAW, G, 13; TRUTH, 42
jolly There was a j. miller HAPPINESS, 5
Jonah a great fish to swallow up J. BIBLE, 286
and the lot fell upon J. BIBLE, 285
Jonathan my brother J. BIBLE, 483
Joneses drag the J. down to my level ONE-UPMANSHIP, 1
Jonson O Rare Ben J. JONSON, B, 2
Jordan the people were passed clean over J. BIBLE, 287
Joseph Here lies J., who failed in everything he undertook FAILURE, 7
jot one j. or one tittle BIBLE, 362
journal *Punch* – the official j. JOURNALISM, 1
journalism Christianity,...but why j. BALFOUR, A, 2
J. is the only job that requires no degrees JOURNALISM, 12
j.....keeps us in touch with the ignorance of the community JOURNALISM, 35; WILDE, O, 15
J. largely consists of saying 'Lord Jones is dead' JOURNALISM, 13
J....the challenge of filling...space JOURNALISM, 34
j. what will be grasped at once CONNOLLY, C, 6
Rock j....people who can't write JOURNALISM, 37
There is a bias in television j. JOURNALISM, 11; TELEVISION, 2
journalist the functions of the modern j. JOURNALISM, 15
to bribe or twist...the British j. JOURNALISM, 36
journalists j. put theirs on the front page OCCUPATIONS, 9
J. say a thing that they know isn't true BENNETT, A, 8; JOURNALISM, 8
an utterly dispensible part of any j. equipment JOURNALISM, 19
journey I prepare for a j....as though for death TRAVEL, 32
Is your j. really necessary TRAVEL, 3
long j....must bid the company farewell LAST WORDS, 74; RALEIGH, W, 7
One of the pleasantest things in the world is going on a j. HAZLITT, W, 28; TRAVEL, 21
Our j. had advanced DEATH, 56
journeying You cannot imagine how strange it seemed to be j. TRAVEL, 25
journeys The destination of all j. CARTER, A, 5
Jowett First come I; my name is J. ACADEMICS, 2
joy a father's j. EXPECTATION, 7; SCOTT, W, 19
A thing of beauty is a j. for ever BEAUTY, 28; KEATS, J, 7
Black people possess the secret of j. WALKER, A, 7
imagining as one's own the suffering and j. of others KINDNESS, 7
j. cometh in the morning PSALMS, 17
j....in heaven over one sinner that repenteth BIBLE, 330; REGRET, 5
let j. be unconfined BYRON, 14; DANCING, 1
One j. scatters a hundred griefs HAPPINESS, 1; PROVERBS, 328
Silence is the perfectest herald of j. SHAKESPEARE, 270; SILENCE, 12
Strength through j. NAZISM, 4
the Lord...give thee j. for this thy sorrow BIBLE, 517
the noise of the shout of j. BIBLE, 130
The Politics of J. POLITICS, 53
They that sow in tears shall reap in j. PSALMS, 69
'tis little j./ To know I'm father off from heav'n INNOCENCE, 7
we could never learn to be brave...if there were only j. COURAGE, 21; ENDURANCE, 9
joys For present j. DRYDEN, J, 25; PLEASURE, 13
Hence, vain deluding J. MILTON, J, 11; PLEASURE, 25
j. of parents are secret BACON, F, 38; FAMILY, 8
jubilation day of j., a day of remembrance GERMANY, 11
judge A j. is not supposed to know JUSTICE, 19
A j. knows nothing LAW, 1; PROVERBS, 27
in righteousness he doth j. and make war BIBLE, 470; RIGHTEOUSNESS, 4
j. not, that ye be not judged BIBLE, 372
j. of a man by his foes CONRAD, J, 4
Never j. from appearances APPEARANCES, 3; PROVERBS, 302
out of thine own mouth will I j. thee BIBLE, 336
salutary check for a j. LAWYERS, 11
shallow people...do not j. by appearances APPEARANCES, 39; WILDE, O, 48
the j. standeth before the door BIBLE, 219
judged j. on how much sex you've had AIDS, 6
that ye be not j. JUDGMENT, 2
they were j. every man according to their works BIBLE, 472
why is my liberty j. of another man's conscience BIBLE, 36
judgement day of j. BOOK OF COMMON PRAYER, 13; DEATH, 40
Don't wait for the Last J. CAMUS, A, 9; DOOMSDAY, 4
Force, if unassisted by j., collapses HORACE, 35
let my will replace reasoned j. AUTHORITARIANISM, 5
no one complains of his j. MEMORY, 17; ROCHEFOUCAULD, 13
Perhaps your fear in passing j. COURAGE, 5
too early to form a final j. on the French Revolution FRENCH REVOLUTION, 9
Your representative owes you...his j. BURKE, E, 26; JUDGMENT, 6
judging if greater want of skill /Appear in writing or in j. ill POPE, A, 20
judgment A Daniel come to j. SHAKESPEARE, 249
I expect a j. DICKENS, C, 6
That fellow would vulgarize the day of j. JERROLD, D, 3; VULGARITY, 3
the j. of the great whore BIBLE, 468
'Tis the Last J.'s fire DOOMSDAY, 3
judgments the j. of the Lord are true PSALMS, 9
'Tis with our j. as our watches OPINIONS, 6; POPE, A, 21
jug Little brown j., don't I love thee ANONYMOUS, 23; DRUNKENNESS, 5
Julia Whenas in silks my J. goes CLOTHES, 13; HERRICK, R, 7
Juliet J. is the sun SHAKESPEARE, 310
Jumblies far and few, /Are the lands where the J. live LEAR, E, 5; NONSENSE, 21
jump We'd j. the life to come ENDING, 6; SHAKESPEARE, 210
Juno /J.'s never-forgetting anger ENDURANCE, 29; VIRGIL, 5
jury how should you like...to be tried before a j. JOHNSON, S, 106
Trial by j. itself...will be a delusion JUSTICE, 5
jury-men wretches hang that j. may dine JUSTICE, 20; POPE, A, 51
just j. and merciful as Nero ELIZABETH I, 3
rain on the j. and on the unjust BIBLE, 365
the path of the j. is as the shining light VIRTUE, 9
justice A lawyer has no business with...j. or injustice JOHNSON, S, 157
In a free society the state...administers j. among men STATE, 3
J. is open to all JUSTICE, 18
J. is such a fine thing JUSTICE, 16
J. is the means by which established injustices are sanctioned FRANCE, A, 2
J. is the...perpetual wish JUSTICE, 15
j. must be seen to be more or less done JUSTICE, 24; STOPPARD, T, 2
J. should not only be done JUSTICE, 10
Let j. be done JUSTICE, 7
moderation in the pursuit of j. is no virtue EXCESS, 5
Recompense injury with j. CONFUCIUS, 12; KINDNESS, 4
Revenge is a kind of wild j. BACON, F, 43; REVENGE, 6
She's like the old line about j. OSBORNE, J, 7; OSTENTATION, 5
the female character...has no sense of j. SCHOPENHAUER, A, 4; WOMEN, 115
The j. of my quarrel JUSTICE, 17; MARLOWE, C, 12
The love of j. in most men JUSTICE, 21; ROCHEFOUCAULD, 10
The place of j. is a hallowed place BACON, F, 31; JUSTICE, 1
truth, j., and the American way HEROISM, 2
which is the j., which is the thief APPEARANCES, 28
You never expected j. from a company BUSINESS, 31; SMITH, S, 5
justification carry its j. in every line CONRAD, J, 5; LITERATURE, 2
justified life of one man can only be j. HUMAN CONDITION, 22
No man is j. in doing evil EXPEDIENCY, 7; ROOSEVELT, T, 3
justifies something that j. the end JUSTICE, 26

justify thought only to j. their injustices HUMAN NATURE, 33; VOLTAIRE, 12
justifying men are more interested in…j. themselves MOTIVE, 6; SZASZ, T, 1
justly Living well and beautifully and j. LIFE, 89

K

Kaiser Belgium put the kibosh on the K. WORLD WAR I, 1
she took down the signed photograph of the K. WAR, 175; WAUGH, E, 45
kaleidoscope a girl with k. eyes LENNON, J, 7
Karaoke running against the K. Kids CLINTON, B, 1
Karl had Marx been Groucho instead of K. HUMOUR, 4
KBO We must just K. DETERMINATION, 15
Keats Here is Johnny K. piss-a-bed poetry POETS, 22
K.'s vulgarity with a Public School accent CRITICISM, 35
Mister John K. five feet high ADMIRATION, 7; KEATS, J, 61
Shelley and K. were…up to date in…chemical knowledge POETS, 7; SCIENCE, 46
When we read his verse, we think of the verse, not of John K. POETS, 49
keen out of a k. city /in the sky CUMMINGS, 1; MOON, 3
Satire should, like a polished razor k. SATIRE, 2
keep if they k. on saying it…it will be true BENNETT, A, 8; JOURNALISM, 8
I'm going to k. it MAJOR, J, 7
k. me as the apple of an eye PSALMS, 6
K. up appearances APPEARANCES, 12
they should k. who can POWER, 31; WORDSWORTH, W, 47
keeper am I my brother's k. BIBLE, 154; MURDER, 2
a poacher a k. turned inside out KINGSLEY, C, 8; OCCUPATIONS, 13
k. stands up FOOTBALL, 9; HOUSMAN, A, 12
keep going in the midst of personal trials and pain, you can and must k. ENDURANCE, 7
Kelly Has anybody here seen K. ABSENCE, 8
ken When a new planet swims into his k. DISCOVERY, 11; KEATS, J, 42
Kennedy K. promised, Johnson delivered JOHNSON, L, 3
K. the politician exuded that musk odour KENNEDY, J, 2
the kind of nation…President K. died for AMBITION, 12; JOHNSON, L, 6
you're no Jack K. QUAYLE, D, 3
Kennedys I don't feel the attraction of the K. at all INSULTS, 97; MCCARTHY, M, 6
Kent K., sir – everybody knows K. DICKENS, C, 42; ENGLAND, 20
Kentucky For the old K. Home far away HOMESICKNESS, 2
kept He k. us out of war WAR, 65
Married women are k. women MARRIAGE, 143; SMITH, L, 4
kettle Polly put the k. on NURSERY RHYMES, 44
system that produced the k. LODGE, D, 6
this is a pretty k. of fish ROYALTY, 85
Kew I am His Highness' dog at K. DOGS, 16; POPE, A, 62
key anybody know what k. that is MUSIC, 27
lawyers…have taken away the k. of knowledge BIBLE, 327; LAWYERS, 5
turn the k. deftly KEATS, J, 48; SLEEP, 24
keys all the k. should hang from the belt of one woman ROYALTY, 28
don't go around hitting too many white k. MUSIC, 12; RACISM, 4
the k. of the kingdom of heaven BIBLE, 397; CHURCH, 1
khaki One black, and one white, and two k. ANONYMOUS, 95
Khatmandu one-eyed yellow idol to the north of K. MOURNING, 5
kibosh Belgium put the k. on the Kaiser WORLD WAR I, 1
kick Death is the greatest k. of all DEATH, 126
every ass thinks he may k. at him WRITERS, 79
if I were under water I would scarcely k. KEATS, J, 60; MELANCHOLY, 6
I get no k. from champagne COMPLIMENTS, 23
k. you out, but…never let you down EDUCATION, 96; WAUGH, E, 11
to k. against the pricks BIBLE, 6
kicked anyone who slapped us…would get his head k. off REVENGE, 14; KHRUSHCHEV, N, 1
he had known many k. down stairs HALIFAX, 9; PROMOTION, 2
Saint Preux never k. the fireirons CARLYLE, J, 2; IMPERFECTION, 5
kicks Get your k. on Route 66 TRAVEL, 47
kid a k. in his mother's milk BIBLE, 118
Here's looking at you, k. ADMIRATION, 2; COMPLIMENTS, 4
kidder Everyone likes a k. MISTRUST, 9
kiddies k. have crumpled the serviettes BETJEMAN, J, 6
kidnapped my parents finally realize that I'm k. ALLEN, W, 9; EXPEDIENCY, 2
kids Cleaning your house while your k. are still growing HOUSEWORK, 4
K. haven't changed much CHILDREN, 47
nice thing about having relatives' k. CHILDREN, 53
kill a man can't step up and k. a woman CHIVALRY, 3
As soon as one does not k. oneself SUICIDE, 6
churchmen fain would k. their church CLERGY, 14; TENNYSON, 59
God.…just had the power to k. her RELIGION, 1
good to k. an admiral EXAMPLE, 9; VOLTAIRE, 7
He would k. Himself HUMAN CONDITION, 7
How many people have wanted to k. themselves SUICIDE, 28
it is always easy to poison and to k. KILLING, 1
It was not…our intention to k. the king ROYALTY, 13
K. a man, and you are a murderer KILLING, 10
k. a wife with kindness KINDNESS, 12; SHAKESPEARE, 321
K. everyone, and you are a god KILLING, 10
K. not the goose GREED, 3; PROVERBS, 243
K. the other guy before he kills you SELF-PRESERVATION, 6
k. the patient BACON, F, 25; REMEDIES, 9
k. us for their sport DESTINY, 22; SHAKESPEARE, 187
likely to k. you is yourself MURDER, 14
Next week…I'll k. myself RHYS, J, 1; SUICIDE, 29
one gramme of explosive to k. a man WAR, 189
only k. you once CARLYLE, T, 30; COMFORT, 2
The bullet that is to k. me ARROGANCE, 6; NAPOLEON I, 11
The word 'revolution' is a word for which you k. REVOLUTION, 17; WEIL, S, 2
they k. you a new way PROGRESS, 20; ROGERS, W, 1
thou shalt not k. BIBLE, 115; GOD, 12
To k. a human being JAMES, H, 8; KILLING, 7
To k. a man is to merit a woman KILLING, 5
to obstruct the way of God,…is more grievous than to k. in the sacred months KORAN 3
When you have to k. a man CHURCHILL, W, 14; DIPLOMACY, 9
killed he k. himself with purgations REMEDIES, 62
He must have k. a lot of men MOLIERE, 5; WEALTH, 38
I don't mind your being k. ROYALTY, 78
it is better that all of these peasants should be k. REBELLION, 11
The crowd of physicians has k. me DOCTORS, 51
the enemy you k. ENEMIES, 7; OWEN, W, 7
killer Aids is a k. AIDS, 4
the first trained k. to be a party leader THATCHER, M, 1
killers Cigarettes are k. that travel in packs SMOKING, 28
killing k. for their country RUSSELL, B, 31
K. /Is the ultimate KILLING, 8
K. myself to die upon a kiss LOVE AND DEATH, 8
k. time /Is only…another of the multifarious ways /By which Time kills us TIME, 56
More ways of k. a cat CHOICE, 3; KINGSLEY, C, 10
no difference between…k. and making decisions that…kill KILLING, 9; MEIR, G, 3
The man is k. time TIME, 35
To save a man's life against his will is…k. him HORACE, 12; KILLING, 6
kills Time is a great teacher, but…k. all its pupils TIME, 13
time quietly k. them TIME, 15
Who k. a man k. a reasonable creature BOOKS, 32; MILTON, J, 6
Yet each man k. the thing he loves KILLING, 11; WILDE, O, 5
kilt Is anything worn beneath the k. CLOTHES, 17
The k. is an unrivalled garment for fornication SCOTS, 9
kin author of himself /And knew no other k. SELF-RELIANCE, 13
k. and kith /Were more fun FAMILY, 42
more than k., and less than kind SHAKESPEARE, 66
kind a k. parent…or a merciless step-mother NATURE, 27; PLINY THE ELDER, 3
be cruel only to be k. CRUELTY, 5
being k. /Is all the sad world needs KINDNESS, 13
charity suffereth long, and is k. BIBLE, 38; CHARITY, 7
He was a vicious man, but very k. JOHNSON, S, 45
I love thee for a heart that's k. KINDNESS, 5
more than kin, and less than k. SHAKESPEARE, 66
One k. word KINDNESS, 1
Too k., too k. LAST WORDS, 62; NIGHTINGALE, F, 6

try to be *k.* ACADEMICS, 5
kindle the sole purpose of human existence is to k. a light EXISTENCE, 3; JUNG, C, 4
kindly a young person, who...marries or dies, is sure to be k. spoken of AUSTEN, J, 7; HUMAN NATURE, 2
the deities so k. DESTINY, 19; RABELAIS, F, 6
kindness a cup o' k. yet BURNS, R, 5; FRIENDSHIP, 13
A word of k. is better than a fat pie KINDNESS, 2
for his k. they still remain in his debt KINDNESS, 10
full o' th' milk of human k. KINDNESS, 11; SHAKESPEARE, 207
greetings where no k. is OPTIMISM, 42; WORDSWORTH, W, 15
its unembarrassed k., its insight into life KINDNESS, 8
kill a wife with k. KINDNESS, 12; SHAKESPEARE, 321
nothing of the milk of human k. BIERCE, A, 1
recompense k. with k. CONFUCIUS, 12; KINDNESS, 4
set a high value on spontaneous k. JOHNSON, S, 139
the k. of strangers CHARITY, 28; WILLIAMS, T, 6
True k. presupposes the faculty KINDNESS, 7
unremembered acts /Of k. and of love KINDNESS, 14; WORDSWORTH, W, 10
kindred Like k. drops, been mingled COWPER, W, 28; MOUNTAINS, 1
king A constitutional k. must learn to stoop MONARCHY, 16
a great k. above all gods PSALMS, 54
A k. is a thing MONARCHY, 20; SELDEN, J, 1
a k. may make a nobleman BURKE, E, 24; CHIVALRY, 4
A k. of shreds and patches INFERIORITY, 7; SHAKESPEARE, 99
All the k.'s horses, /And all the k.'s men NURSERY RHYMES, 18
an atheist if the k. were SERVILITY, 4
and Northcliffe has sent for the K. EDITORS, 2
a new k. over Egypt BIBLE, 102
An unlettered k. is a crowned ass MONARCHY, 1
A pious man...would be an atheist if the k. were LA BRUYERE, J, 1
Authority forgets a dying k. ROYALTY, 109; TENNYSON, 21
A worse k. never left a realm undone BYRON, 43; ROYALTY, 33
better...a poor and a wise child than an old and foolish k. BIBLE, 71; OLD AGE, 22; YOUTH, 3
better have one K. than five hundred GOVERNMENT, 10
but the K. of England cannot enter PITT THE ELDER , 1; PRIVACY, 5
curse not the k., no not in thy thought SECRECY, 3
every inch a k. ROYALTY, 105; SHAKESPEARE, 188
Every man a k. EQUALITY, 21
Every subject's duty is the K.'s MONARCHY, 23; SHAKESPEARE, 135
George, be a K. ROYALTY, 21
God save our Gracious K. BRITAIN, 6
great k.,...fell all at once REVOLUTION, 2
half the zeal I serv'd my K. REGRET, 19; SHAKESPEARE, 142
harm that cometh of a k.'s poverty TAXATION, 3
heart and stomach of a K. ELIZABETH I, 13; ROYALTY, 53
He played the K. as though CRITICISM, 19
his attitude of a k. in exile DE GAULLE, C, 1
horse was k. LEE, L, 4
if I were not k., I should lose my temper LOUIS XIV, 6; ROYALTY, 81
I'm the k. of the castle NURSERY RHYMES, 23
I think the K. is but a man EQUALITY, 31; SHAKESPEARE, 134
I will that a k. succeed me ROYALTY, 58
k. is always a k. FEMINISM, 41
k. is incompetent to govern ROYALTY, 108
K. of England changes his ministers ROYALTY, 67
K. of Scots was named to succeed her ROYALTY, 34
k. reigns, but does not govern MONARCHY, 28
k.'s council...chosen of the great princes, and of the greatest lords of the land GOVERNMENT, 12
Mrs Simpson's pinched our k. ROYALTY, 18
No Bishop, no K. CHURCH, 6
Old K. Cole /Was a merry old soul NURSERY RHYMES, 38
rather hew wood than be...K. of England MONARCHY, 8
service rendered to the temporal k. to the prejudice of the eternal k. TREASON, 11
such divinity doth hedge a k. MONARCHY, 21; SHAKESPEARE, 103
That whatsoever K. shall reign, /I'll be the Vicar of Bray, Sir ANONYMOUS, 48; SELF-PRESERVATION, 5
the faith, prayer and self-dedication of the K. ROYALTY, 26
the k. can do no wrong BLACKSTONE, W, 4
the K....could see things if he would ROYALTY, 31
The k. has been very good to me MARTYRDOM, 1
The k. never dies BLACKSTONE, W,
The K. of Spain's daughter /Came to visit me NURSERY RHYMES, 20
The K. over the Water ANONYMOUS, 82
The k. reigns, and the people govern themselves MONARCHY, 25
The k. sits in Dunfermline town ANONYMOUS, 83
The k. was in his counting-house, /Counting out his money NURSERY RHYMES, 52
The present life of men on earth, O k. LIFE, 11
this house will in no circumstances fight for its K. and country ANONYMOUS, 77; PATRIOTISM, 4
wash the balm from an anointed k. MONARCHY, 24; SHAKESPEARE, 298
Was not that a dainty dish, /To set before the k. NURSERY RHYMES, 52
who is the K. of glory PSALMS, 14
kingdom Childhood is the k. where nobody dies INNOCENCE, 9
glory of your k. EDUCATION, 3
It is folly...to mistake the echo of a...coffee-house for the...k. OPINIONS, 9; SWIFT, J, 5
k. and the priesthood, are brought together by divine mystery POLITICS, 82
my k. for a horse HORSES, 10; SHAKESPEARE, 305
No k. has...had as many...wars as the k. of Christ CHRISTIANITY, 48; MONTESQUIEU, 5
Our k....we place at your disposal DIPLOMACY, 18
repent: for the k. of heaven is at hand BIBLE, 358
the k. of God is not in word, but in power BIBLE, 26; GOD, 8
the k. of God is within you BIBLE, 334
this formidable K. is...a province of a despicable Electorate ENGLAND, 41
to deny the existence of an unseen k. is bad BUTLER, S, 3
kings Conquering k. their titles take ROYALTY, 37
Grammar, which can govern even k. GRAMMAR, 6; MOLIERE, 9
how to dissimulate is the knowledge of k. ROYALTY, 98
If you get the English people into the way of making k. MELBOURNE, 5; ROYALTY, 86
K. are earth's gods ROYALTY, 103; SHAKESPEARE, 291
K....are just as funny ROOSEVELT, T, 4; ROYALTY, 100
K. are naturally lovers of low company BURKE, E, 17; ROYALTY, 30
k. enough in England HOUSES OF PARLIAMENT, 12
K. govern by...assemblies only when MONARCHY, 13
Or walk with K. IDEALISM, 4; KIPLING, R, 18
Pale Death kicks his way...into...the castles of k. EQUALITY, 42; HORACE, 27
sad stories of the death of k. ROYALTY, 104; SHAKESPEARE, 300
Such grace had k. BROWNING, R, 47; ROYALTY, 29
teeming womb of royal k. ENGLAND, 46; SHAKESPEARE, 297
The English nation...has successfully regulated the power of its k. GOVERNMENT, 46
the K. of England, Diamonds, Hearts, Spades and Clubs MONARCHY, 12
This royal throne of k. ENGLAND, 46; SHAKESPEARE, 297
till philosophers become k. PHILOSOPHY, 11; PLATO, 4
'Twixt k. and tyrants there's this difference HERRICK, R, 3; TYRANNY, 5
kingship k. approaches tyranny it is near its end TYRANNY, 9
kinquering K. Congs their titles take SPOONER, W, 3
Kipling K. has done more...to show...that the British race is sound to the core KIPLING, R, 2
W. H. Auden, a sort of gutless K. ORWELL, G, 29; SOCIALISM, 21
kippers like two old k. in a box OLD AGE, 102; THOMAS, D, 21
kiss A k. without a moustache SARTRE, J, 15
come let us k. and part PARTING, 6
effrontery to k. me on the lips ETIQUETTE, 3
Every time we k. he says 'Murder!' LOVE, 107
God sent me down to k. KISSING, 3
Killing myself to die upon a k. LOVE AND DEATH, 8
K. me, Hardy LAST WORDS, 61; NELSON, H, 6
K. me Kate, we will be married o' Sunday MARRIAGE, 134
make me immortal with a k. BEAUTY, 30; MARLOWE, C, 2
The coward does it with a k. KILLING, 11; WILDE, O, 5
The k. of sun for pardon GARDENS, 7
Then come k. me, sweet and twenty SHAKESPEARE, 340
the rough male k. of blankets BED, 4
Without a single k. or a good-bye PARTING, 8
you must not k. and tell CONGREVE, W, 6; SECRECY, 7
You must remember this; /A k. is just a k. TIME, 26
kissed Being k. by a man who didn't wax his moustache KIPLING, R, 27

hail, master; and k. him BETRAYAL, 3; BIBLE, 427
I k. her little sister UNFAITHFULNESS, 6
k. her once by the pig-sty EXPECTATION, 8; THOMAS, D, 20
K. the girls and made them cry NURSERY RHYMES, 12
Wherever one wants to be k. CHANEL, C, 5; COSMETICS, 2
kisses bread and cheese, and k. MARRIAGE, 151; SWIFT, J, 11
concordance of Nicola Six's k. KISSING, 1
remembered k. after death NOSTALGIA, 26; TENNYSON, 63
Stolen sweets are always sweeter, /Stolen k. much completer THEFT, 7
kissing K. don't last FOOD, 52
The President spends most of his time k. PERSUASION, 4; TRUMAN, H, 6
when the k. had to stop BROWNING, R, 57; KISSING, 2
kit-bag pack up your troubles in your old k. OPTIMISM, 13
kitchen A good K. is a good Apothicaries shop FOOD, 18
can't stand the heat, get out of the k. TRUMAN, H, 3
the way of all flesh…towards the k. FOOD, 72; WEBSTER, J, 4
where two ladies get in the same k. WOMEN, 40
Kitchener If K. was not a great man, he was…a great poster OFFICERS, 2
kith kin and k. /Were more fun FAMILY, 42
K-K-Katy K., beautiful Katy LOVE, 121
knackery end up in the Tory k. KINNOCK, N, 11
Knave The K. of Hearts /He stole the tarts NURSERY RHYMES, 55
knaves world is made up…of fools and k. FOOLISHNESS, 11
knee at the name of Jesus every k. should bow BIBLE, 443; CHRISTIANITY, 30
He insisted that this should be *k.-jerk* WORDS, 16
knee-cap The soul started at the k. ANIMALISM, 5; LEWIS, W, 1
knees die on your feet than to live on your k. COURAGE, 20
knew I k. him, Horatio MOURNING, 11; SHAKESPEARE, 106
much righter than one k. at say 17 or 23 POUND,E, 4; YOUTH, 23
We all k. you had it in you PREGNANCY, 7
what we once k. is of little consequence MATHEMATICS, 22; MEDICINE, 87
knife I had a k. and two forks left ETIQUETTE, 8
it keeps them on the k. ANONYMOUS, 41; FOOD, 6
last twist of the k. ELIOT, T, 21; LIFE, 35
War even to the k. BYRON, 11; WAR, 39
knight a verray parfit gentil k. CHAUCER, G, 4
every chance brought out a noble k. TENNYSON, 22
I never realized that I'd end up being the shortest k. of the year PUNS, 22; TITLES, 9
K. of the Doleful Countenance CERVANTES, M, 6
mounted k. is irresistable SOLDIERS, 2
Poor K.! he really had two periods NABOKOV, V, 5; WRITING, 37
There came a k. to be their wooer ANONYMOUS, 97; LOVE, 15
what can ail thee, k. at arms ILLNESS, 39; KEATS, J, 22
knights gives me great joy to see…k. and horses in battle array PLEASURE, 7
sorrier for my good k.' loss than for…my fair queen LOSS, 3
knitter a beautiful little k. INSULTS, 113; WOOLF, V, 3
knives Night of the Long K. FASCISM, 5
Phone for the fish k. Norman ETIQUETTE, 1
knock Don't k. it ALLEN, W, 3; SEX, 4
k., and it shall be opened unto you BIBLE, 375; SUCCESS, 7
K. as you please POPE, A, 9; STUPIDITY, 13
k. him down first, and pity him afterwards JOHNSON, S, 105; SELF-PRESERVATION, 8
Three, four, /K. at the door NUMBERS, 4; NURSERY RHYMES, 40
knocked we k. the bastard off ACHIEVEMENT, 9
knocker pardoned for mistaking her for its k. ILLNESS, 28
know all /Ye k. on earth KEATS, J, 30
A really intelligent man feels what other men…k. MONTESQUIEU, 2
be still then, and k. that I am God PSALMS, 28
Children with Hyacinth's temperament…merely k. more SAKI, 5
flautists are most obviously the ones who k. something we don't k. MUSICIANS, 4
for they k. not what they do BIBLE, 339
I do not k. myself GOETHE, J, 1; SELF-KNOWLEDGE, 4
I k. as much as God knew MATHEMATICS, 23
I k. myself FITZGERALD, F, 12; SELF-KNOWLEDGE, 3
I k. that my redeemer liveth BIBLE, 233
I k. thee not, old man OLD AGE, 89
I k. what I like BEERBOHM, M, 18; SUBJECTIVITY, 1
K. then thyself, presume not God to scan POPE, A, 34; SELF-KNOWLEDGE, 5
K. thyself PROVERBS, 246
Not many people k. that KNOWLEDGE, 10
scarcely hate any one that we k. HATE, 5; HAZLITT, W, 26
Teach thy tongue to say 'I do not k..' KNOWLEDGE, 34
the gentleman in Whitehall really does k. better POLITICS, 54
the only person…I should like to k. EGOTISM, 11; WILDE, O, 40
the words 'I do not k.' stick in every physician's throat REMEDIES, 58
To k. how to say what others only…think SPEECH, 8
tragedy of the world that no one knows what he doesn't k. IGNORANCE, 7
we k. not where they have laid him BIBLE, 274
we should occupy our minds only with what we continue to k. MATHEMATICS, 22; MEDICINE, 87
What we k. of the past HISTORY, 18; INGE, W, 1
What you don't k. IGNORANCE, 3; PROVERBS, 457
What you don't k. would make a great book IGNORANCE, 22; SMITH, S, 6
You k.…what you are HUXLEY, A, 37; KNOWLEDGE, 23
knowed The clever men at Oxford /Know all that there is to be k. KNOWLEDGE, 21; OXFORD, 10
knowest thou k. all things BIBLE, 280
knowing A woman, especially if she have the misfortune of k. anything AUSTEN, J, 16; WOMEN, 14
knowingness My k. and my innocence ACTORS, 25
knowledge a k. of nothing DICKENS, C, 55; KNOWLEDGE, 15
All k. is of itself of some value KNOWLEDGE, 26
all k. to be my province BACON, F, 67; KNOWLEDGE, 4
all our k. is, ourselves to know POPE, A, 36; SELF-KNOWLEDGE, 6
an age in which useless k. KNOWLEDGE, 25
an intimate k. of its ugly side BALDWIN, J, 3; DISILLUSION, 1
ask it for the k. of a lifetime ARTISTS, 25
civilizations…abandon the quest for k. KNOWLEDGE, 31
Foolish the doctor who despises the k. DOCTORS, 54
for ignorance is never better than k. NATURE, 10
he giveth…k. to them that know understanding GOD, 9
his clear k. of the limits of human understanding VOLTAIRE, 3
how to dissimulate is the k. of kings ROYALTY, 98
If a little k. is dangerous, where is the man…out of danger HUXLEY, T, 8; KNOWLEDGE, 24
if a little k. was a dangerous thing KNOWLEDGE, 38
if education is…a mere transmission of k. EDUCATION, 65
Integrity without k. is weak JOHNSON, S, 30
K. advances by steps KNOWLEDGE, 32; MACAULAY, T, 3
k. and wonder…is an impression of pleasure BACON, F, 1
K. can be communicated but not wisdom WISDOM, 20
K. dwells /In heads replete COWPER, W, 32
K. is Life with wings KNOWLEDGE, 18
K. is of two kinds JOHNSON, S, 97
K. is power PROVERBS, 244
K. is proportionate to being HUXLEY, A, 37
K. is the mother KNOWLEDGE, 2
K. itself is power BACON, F, 64
k. puffeth up BIBLE, 32
lawyers…have taken away the key of k. BIBLE, 327
let him receive the new k. BROWNING, R, 33
light of k. in their eyes KNOWLEDGE, 39
never has a man turned so little k. to such great account ELIOT, T, 4
No, I ask it for the k. of a lifetime WHISTLER, J, 7
Our k. can only be finite KNOWLEDGE, 37
Out-topping k. ARNOLD, M, 40; SHAKESPEARE, 1
province of k. to speak KNOWLEDGE, 22; WISDOM, 21
Science is organized k. SCIENCE, 87
Science is the father of k. OPINIONS, 3
Such k. is too wonderful and excellent for me PSALMS, 71
the river of k. has too often turned back on itself SCIENCE, 57
the search for k. PHILOSOPHERS, 10; RUSSELL, B, 4
the tree of the k. of good and evil BIBLE, 144; GARDENS, 3
traditions of education have emphasized k. EDUCATION, 16
What I don't know isn't k. ACADEMICS, 2
worth a pound of k. KNOWLEDGE, 40; LOVE, 175
you impart k. of it through another's death RESEARCH, 2
known apart from the k. and the unknown PINTER, H, 3
knows a woman who k. all…that can be taught CHANEL, C, 3
He that k. little IGNORANCE, 1; PROVERBS, 193
He that k. nothing IGNORANCE, 2; PROVERBS, 194
he thinks he k. everything POLITICIANS, 24; SHAW, G, 18
He who k. only his own side…k. little SUBJECTIVITY, 4
Only the nose k.… SECRECY, 1
knuckle-end k. of England SCOTLAND, 8; SMITH, S, 7

knyf The smyler with the k. CHAUCER, G, 13; HYPOCRISY, 9
knyght parfit, gentil k. CHIVALRY, 5
Kodak painted...by the great artist K. MILLIGAN, S, 2; PHOTOGRAPHY, 7
Koran They to whom we have given...the K....believe therein KORAN 2
Kubla In Xanadu did K. Khan COLERIDGE, S, 14; PLEASURE, 10
Kurtz Mistah K. – he dead CONRAD, J, 3
Kuwait conquest of Iraq. It is the liberation of K. WAR, 35
democracy in K. WAR, 37
K. is an oil monarchy AMERICANS, 2

L

label Lesbian is a l. invented by the man FEMINISM, 30
The only l. she wears is 'drip dry'. FASHION, 12
labor Medical practice is not knitting and weaving and the l. of the hands MEDICINE, 58
laboratorium *L. est oratorium* SCIENCE, 66
laboratory A first-rate l. is one SCIENCE, 9
All the world is a l. SCIENCE, 40
apt to leave his cultures exposed on the l. table SCIENTISTS, 13
if I may offer advice to the young l. worker FLEMING, A, 3
I see there are l. men here. DOCTORS, 62
We're all of us guinea pigs in the l. of God MANKIND, 73
laboring rights and interests of the l. man STRIKES, 1
labor-saving inventing l. devices...manufactured an abyss of boredom BOREDOM, 8
labour all ye that l. and are heavy laden CHRISTIANITY, 26
A mountain in l. shouted so loud LA FONTAINE, J, 6
an Independent L. Party PARTIES, 10; WAUGH, E, 46
bad book is as much a l. to write as a good one HUXLEY, A, 29
disastrous element in the L. party POLITICS, 31
don't want L. MPs...fighting for a four-day week POLITICIANS, 22
England elects a L. Government POLITICS, 87
genius the L. Party has for cutting itself in half POLITICS, 27
grotesque chaos of a L. council INCOMPETENCE, 2
L. is not fit to govern CHURCHILL, W, 43; POLITICS, 28
l. of love BIBLE, 502
leader for the L. Party is a desiccated calculating machine BEVAN, A, 4
little effect after much l. AUSTEN, J, 32; RESULTS, 2
Macmillan would have been L. Prime Minister MACMILLAN, H, 1
Man...can only find relaxation from one...l. by taking up another CHANGE, 8; FRANCE, A, 3
...model L. voter... KINNOCK, N, 12; POLITICS, 63
pederasts who call themselves the L. Party SOCIALISM, 2
Temperance and l. are the two real physicians of man WORK, 32
the Gromyko of the L. party POLITICIANS, 91
The grotesque chaos of a L. council – a *L.* council KINNOCK, N, 10
the l. having been,..., rather in a circle than in progression MEDICINE, 8
The L. party is like a stage-coach POLITICS, 120
To l. and not ask for any reward SELFLESSNESS, 3
water, honey, and l. REMEDIES, 5
labours absorbs a clay /After his l. SMOKING, 7
Children sweeten l. BACON, F, 39; CHILDREN, 6
labyrinthine I fled Him, down the l. ways RELIGION, 88
lack l. of power corrupts absolutely STEVENSON, A, 3
own up to a l. of humour HUMOUR, 10
therefore can I l. nothing PSALMS, 11
lad many a lightfoot l. HOUSMAN, A, 16; NOSTALGIA, 12
ladder behold a l. set up on earth BIBLE, 172; HEAVEN, 1
Talk to him of Jacob's l. JERROLD, D, 4; PRACTICALITY, 4
the traffic of Jacob's l. HEAVEN, 15
We make ourselves a l. out of our vices VICE, 2
ladder's Now that my l. gone YEATS, W, 6
ladies How sweet are looks that l. bend TENNYSON, 73; WOMEN, 129
lion among l. SHAKESPEARE, 263
several other old l. of both sexes DICKENS, C, 23
where two l. get in the same kitchen WOMEN, 40
lady Dance, dance, dance little l. COWARD, N, 6
I want to talk like a l. SPEECH, 19
L. Bountiful CHARITY, 16
l. doth protest too much EXCESS, 11; SHAKESPEARE, 97
l. of a certain age BYRON, 32
My fair l. NURSERY RHYMES, 33
O lang will his L. /Look owre the Castle Downe ANONYMOUS, 109
Put thy shimmy on, L. Chatterley LAWRENCE, D, 18; PARTING, 7
The Iron L. of British politics POLITICIANS, 34
the Iron L. of the Western World POLITICIANS, 123
the L. Is a Tramp DECLINE, 3
The l.'s not for turning THATCHER, M, 20
there had been a l. in the case BYRON, 29; WOMEN, 32
There is a l. sweet and kind ANONYMOUS, 86
When a l. says no...means perhaps WORDS, 9
young l. named Bright LIMERICKS, 7; SCIENCE, 16
lady barber one l. that made good WEST, M, 5
ladybird L., l., /Fly away home NURSERY RHYMES, 27
Lady Chatterley *L.'s Lover*...all Christians might read with profit PORNOGRAPHY, 7
Lady Macbeth combination of Little Nell and L. PARKER, D, 2
ladyship When your l.'s faith has removed them CHESTERFIELD, P, 22; RELIGION, 27
lag a comfortable time l....between the perception PROGRESS, 25
lag-end entertain the l. of my life /With quiet hours OLD AGE, 88
laid all the young ladies...were l. end to end PARKER, D, 15; SEX, 91
get rich, get famous and get l. FAME, 15; GELDOF, B, 2
l. on with a trowel EXCESS, 10; SHAKESPEARE, 41
we know not where they have l. him BIBLE, 274
laissez *L. faire, laissez passer* FREEDOM, 18
lake An arm /Rose up from...the l. TENNYSON, 20
Marriage may often be a stormy l. MARRIAGE, 117; PEACOCK, T, 5
sedge is wither'd from the l. ILLNESS, 39; KEATS, J, 22
Wordsworth...never was a l. poet WORDSWORTH, W, 3
lamb as a l. to the slaughter BIBLE, 214
Charles L., a clever fellow certainly LAMB, C, 2
Charles L....in some considerable degree insane LAMB, C, 1
Did he who made the L. make thee BLAKE, W, 40; CREATION, 7
l. for a burnt BIBLE, 169
l....without blemish BIBLE, 109
Little L., who made thee BLAKE, W, 46; CREATION, 8
Mary had a little l. ANIMALS, 14
one little ewe l. ANIMALS, 5
Pipe a song about a L. BLAKE, W, 42; MUSIC, 14
the L. of God BIBLE, 240; CHRISTIANITY, 15
to make the lion lie down with the l. HUMAN NATURE, 21; LAWRENCE, D, 32
white in the blood of the L. BIBLE, 463
wolf also shall dwell with the l. BIBLE, 203
worthy is the l. that was slain BIBLE, 461
lambs feed my l. BIBLE, 279
send you forth as l. among wolves BIBLE, 323
We're poor little l. DEBAUCHERY, 8; KIPLING, R, 12
lame help a l. dog over a stile HELP, 9
your precious 'l. ducks' GALSWORTHY, J, 6; WEAKNESS, 2
lament reason to l. /What man has made of man MANKIND, 74; WORDSWORTH, W, 17
lamp my l. burns low and dim ENVY, 3
To keep a l. burning CHARITY, 26; TERESA, 5
lampada *vitai l.* MORTALITY, 15
lamp-post I'm leaning on a l. LOVE, 73
like asking a l....about dogs CRITICS, 7; HAMPTON, C, 5
share a quick pee over a common l. CONNOLLY, C, 14; WRITERS, 9
lamp-posts He uses statistics as a drunken man uses l. STATISTICS, 5
lamps l. are going out all over Europe PROPHECY, 5
new l. for old ones BUSINESS, 3
people are forbidden to light l. MAO TSE-TUNG, 10
trimmed their l. BIBLE, 416
Ye living l. MARVELL, A, 5
Lancelot bold Sir L. CHIVALRY, 15; TENNYSON, 45
lancet The l. was the magician's wand MEDICINE, 45
land a l. flowing with milk and honey BIBLE, 106
a stranger in a strange l. BIBLE, 104
England's green and pleasant l. BLAKE, W, 33
For England's the one l. BROOKE, R, 2; ENGLAND, 11
his hands prepared the dry l. PSALMS, 54
I believe that this l....is very great PLACES, 13
I perish through great grief in a strange l. BIBLE, 341

youth now in England...be set to l. EDUCATION, 4
learned A l. man is an idler EDUCATION, 80
child must say something that he has merely l. LEARNING, 8
He was naturally l. DRYDEN, J, 23
I am...of the opinion with the l. CONGREVE, W, 5
I l. just by going around LEARNING, 1
Misquotation is the pride and privilege of the l. MISQUOTATIONS, 2
people...never have l. anything from history EXPERIENCE, 15
the l. roast an egg FOOD, 59; POPE, A, 53
learning A little l. is a dangerous thing KNOWLEDGE, 36; POPE, A, 23
A progeny of l. MALAPROPISMS, 3; SHERIDAN, R, 4
beauty and the lust for l. BEAUTY, 9; BEERBOHM, M, 15
I have been l. how to die DEATH, 178
I thought that I was l. how to live LEONARDO DA VINCI, 6
l., earning and yearning LIFE, 67
L. hath gained most BOOKS, 22
L. is a treasure KNOWLEDGE, 1; PROVERBS, 250
L. is but an adjunct LEARNING, 16; SHAKESPEARE, 199
L. is good in and of itself BUSH, G, 6; EDUCATION, 19
L. without thought is labour lost CONFUCIUS, 5; KNOWLEDGE, 13
public school, where...l. was painfully beaten into him EDUCATION, 73; PEACOCK, T, 8
Their l. is like bread in a besieged town JOHNSON, S, 96; SCOTS, 6
learnt I only remember what I've l. KNOWLEDGE, 41; WHITE, P, 2
More can be l. from Miss Austen AUSTEN, J, 1
Soon l. EDUCATION, 1; PROVERBS, 365
what has been l. has been forgotten EDUCATION, 85
least death,...the l. of all evils BACON, F, 6; DEATH, 27
L. said soonest mended PROVERBS, 251
Strongest minds /...the noisy world /Hears l. MIND, 36; WORDSWORTH, W, 4
the l. of these my brethren BIBLE, 422
leather Mr Lincoln's soul seems made of l. LINCOLN, A, 4
leave Fare thee well, for I must l. thee ANONYMOUS, 87; PARTING, 2
How I l. my country LAST WORDS, 66; PITT THE YOUNGER, 4
If you l. a thing alone you l. it to a torrent of change CHESTERTON, G, 35; CONSERVATISM, 2
L. well alone PROVERBS, 252; TACT, 1
to l. his country as good as he had found it DUTY, 1
leaves before the l. have fallen WILHELM II, 1
If poetry comes not...as l. to a tree KEATS, J, 57; POETRY, 35
No fruits, no flowers, no l., no birds HOOD, T, 10; MONTHS, 10
the l....were for the healing of the nations BIBLE, 474
Though l. are many, the root is one AGE, 105; YEATS, W, 7
With vine l. in his hair IBSEN, H, 5; RETURN, 3
Words are like l. POPE, A, 30; VERBOSITY, 7
leaving became him like the l. it SHAKESPEARE, 206
She's l. home DEPARTURE, 8; LENNON, J, 11
leavings sacrifice...of the devil's l. POPE, A, 56; VIRTUE, 21
Lebanon people of L. have suffered greatly HOSTAGES, 12
lecher small gilded fly does l. ANIMALISM, 7; SHAKESPEARE, 189
lechery drink...an equivocator with l. ALCOHOL, 69; SHAKESPEARE, 215
Still wars and l. SEX, 110; SHAKESPEARE, 335
lectures l. or a little charity SELF, 25; WHITMAN, W, 8
led l. by the nose with gold BRIBERY, 5; SHAKESPEARE, 356
leech A skilful l. is better far DOCTORS, 26
leeches l. have red blood LAST WORDS, 23
left a handful of silver he l. us BETRAYAL, 5; BROWNING, R, 31
And we are l., or shall be l., alone WORDSWORTH, W, 52
better to be l. than never to have been loved CONGREVE, W, 13
man who l. a wife and six children on the parish ROYALTY, 16
not l. to Spain MARTYRDOM, 7; TENNYSON, 70
You just press the accelerator to the floor and steer l. SPORT AND GAMES, 44
leg here I leave my second l. HOOD, T, 3; PUNS, 11
legality do not let so great an achievement suffer from...l. LAW, 24
legal system the English l. will not support EXPLOITATION, 3
legs apart from having two good l. INTELLIGENCE, 5
cannon-ball took off his l. HOOD, T, 2; PUNS, 10
close my eyes, open my l. and think of England SEX, 51
that magnificent instrument between your l. TOSCANINI, A, 5
You were born with your l. apart ORTON, J, 7; PROMISCUITY, 9
Leicester Square Good-bye Piccadilly, Farewell L. HOMESICKNESS, 8
leisure Evil comes at l. DISEASE, 12
gentleman of l. MATERIALISM, 25
I am interested in l....can't get enough of it LEISURE, 4
Men...detest at l. BYRON, 33; LOVE AND HATE, 1
Prince Philip....a world expert on l. KINNOCK, N, 6; ROYALTY, 76
The secret of being miserable is to have l. SHAW, G, 35; SORROW, 31
Very few people can endure much l. LEISURE, 2
wisdom...cometh by opportunity of l. BIBLE, 90
leisurely You just can't have a l. farce HUMOUR, 30
lemon The Germans,...are going to be squeezed, as a l. RETRIBUTION, 10
lend I would not l. my pony now, /For all the lady's hire NURSERY RHYMES, 21
L. only that PROVERBS, 253
the men who borrow, and the men who l. LAMB, C, 10
lender Neither a borrower nor a l. be SHAKESPEARE, 75
lene As l. was his hors as is a rake CHAUCER, G, 8; HORSES, 4
leniency chivalry...dispenses l. CHIVALRY, 1
Lenin L.'s method leads to this COMMUNISM, 19; TROTSKY, L, 11
L. was the first to discover CAPITALISM, 18; TAYLOR, A, 4
transported L....like a plague bacillus RUSSIAN REVOLUTION, 3
lenses That youthful sparkle in his eyes is caused by his contact l. REAGAN, R, 1
Lent Ishmaelites...eat human flesh uncooked in L. CANNIBALISM, 2; WAUGH, E, 41
Leonardo Disney the most significant figure...since L. ART, 20
leopard or the l. his spots BIBLE, 221; CHANGE, 1
leper by isolating him...as if he were a l. IRELAND, 20
more difficult than bathing a l. MEDIA, 16
press is more difficult than bathing a l. MEDIA, 16
leprosy It is full of l. PRACTICALITY, 2
scant as hair /In l. BROWNING, R, 16
lerne gladly wolde he l. CHARACTER, 5; CHAUCER, G, 9
Lesbian L. is a label invented by the man FEMINISM, 30
lesbians most l....cultivate the treasures of their femininity HOMOSEXUALITY, 2
less found it l. exciting COWARDICE, 4; GILBERT, W, 1
I love not Man the l. BYRON, 16; NATURE, 3
l. in this than meets the eye BANKHEAD, T, 8; CRITICISM, 3
L. is more ARCHITECTURE, 10
Specialist...knows more and more about l. and l. EXPERTS, 5
the l. they have...the more noise they make POPE, A, 55
let kick you out, but...never l. you down EDUCATION, 96; WAUGH, E, 11
let down I l. my friends BETRAYAL, 11; NIXON, R, 4
Lethe go not to L. KEATS, J, 32; OBLIVION, 2
wait upon the tedious shores of L. INSIGNIFICANCE, 4; LAMB, C, 4
letter I have made this l. longer PASCAL, B, 1; VERBOSITY, 6
offensive l. follows INSULTS, 4
Someone...wants a l. from you LETTER-WRITING, 2
thou unnecessary l. INSULTS, 111; SHAKESPEARE, 175
writing a l. and forgetting to sign his name INSULTS, 13
letters His sayings are generally like women's l. HAZLITT, W, 6; LETTER-WRITING, 4
The profession of l. WRITING, 42
the republic of l. ADDISON, J, 3; MANKIND, 1
When I pass my name in such large l. FAME, 34; TREE, H, 8
level their l. of incompetence INCOMPETENCE, 4
level-headed When things are steep, remember to stay l. HORACE, 33; SELF-CONTROL, 4
levellers Your l. wish to level *down* as far as themselves EQUALITY, 18; JOHNSON, S, 66
leviathan canst thou draw out l. with an hook BIBLE, 237
that great L., or rather...that *Mortal God* HOBBES, T, 5; STATE, 1
levity He rose by gravity; I sank by l. SMITH, S, 18
lexicographer L....harmless drudge JOHNSON, S, 10; LEXICOGRAPHY, 6
to wake a l. JOHNSON, S, 5; LEXICOGRAPHY, 4
liaison partly a l. man and partly P.R.O BETJEMAN, J, 5; BUSINESS, 4
liar A l. is worse LYING, 1; PROVERBS, 30
He did not feel a l. LYING, 16; MURDOCH, I, 4
loves boxing is either a l. or a fool SPORT AND GAMES, 15
Mr. Speaker, I said the honorable member was a l. APOLOGIES, 7; SHERIDAN, R, 21
Poor Bonar can't bear being called a l. LLOYD GEORGE, D, 6; POLITICIANS, 100
When I was a little boy they called me a l. WRITERS, 25
you are...the club Bore: I am the club L. SAKI, 3; SUPERIORITY, 16
liars All men are l. PSALMS, 66

It has made more l. LYING, 19; ROGERS, W, 8
l. and swearers enow to beat the honest men GOOD AND EVIL, 7
the Cretians are alway l. BIBLE, 515; NATIONALITY, 4
Liberace Bush…looking like L. BUSH, G, 1
liberal a l. education at the Colleges of Unreason REASON, 1
either a little L. GILBERT, W, 19; POLITICS, 44
Just like an old l. /Between the wars LIBERALISM, 3
l. dreams of a better world IDEALISM, 11
the damned, compact, l. majority IBSEN, H, 3; MAJORITY, 6
When a l. is abused, he says LENIN, V, 8; LIBERALISM, 2
Liberal Democrats L. are a racist party POLITICS, 7
liberal education a l. at the Colleges of Unreason BUTLER, S, 1
liberality L. lies less in giving liberally LA BRUYERE, J, 5; PROMPTNESS, 1
liberal-minded booksellers are generous l. men JOHNSON, S, 55; PUBLISHING, 9
Liberal party task of the L. is to strangle it at birth POLITICS, 94
liberals L. think that goats are just sheep from broken homes LIBERALISM, 1
liberated The affluent, educated, l. women of the First World APPEARANCE, 77
liberation conquest of Iraq. It is the l. of Kuwait WAR, 35
truly mankind's war of l. HUNGER, 7
liberté *L.! Égalité! Fraternité* ANONYMOUS, 50; HUMAN RIGHTS, 2
liberties Freedom, what l. are taken FREEDOM, 16
government will protect all l. but one FREEDOM, 45
libertine Prince was…a l. over head and ears in debt ROYALTY, 72
liberty condition upon which God hath given l. FREEDOM, 13
Corruption…symptom of constitutional l. CORRUPTION, 4; GIBBON, E, 9
don't suppose…a revolution is going to bring l. REVOLUTION, 9
extremism in the defence of l. is no vice EXCESS, 5
give me l. or give me death FREEDOM, 22
If men are to wait for l. FREEDOM, 35; MACAULAY, T, 8
It is true that l. is precious FREEDOM, 32; LENIN, V, 11
King still stands between us and l. FRENCH REVOLUTION, 7
l. as an essential condition of excellence OXFORD, 9
l. cannot long exist BURKE, E, 22; CORRUPTION, 1
l. for one person is constrained only EQUALITY, 15
L. is the hardest test FREEDOM, 58
L. is the right to do everything FREEDOM, 43; MONTESQUIEU, 3
l.…is to be measured not by the governmental machinery SOCIETY, 20
L. means responsibility LIBERTY, 2
L.…not…mere declarations of the rights of man FREEDOM, 61
L. of action FREEDOM, 18
L., too, must be limited BURKE, E, 21; FREEDOM, 9
l.…what on earth would they do COMMUNISM, 9
life, l., and the pursuit of happiness HUMAN RIGHTS, 3; JEFFERSON, T, 5, 6
love of l. is the love of others FREEDOM, 21; HAZLITT, W, 13
new nation, conceived in l. LINCOLN, A, 17
Oh l.!…What crimes are committed in thy name EXECUTION, 35; FREEDOM, 51
Power…and L.…are seldom upon good Terms FREEDOM, 19; HALIFAX, 7; POWER, 13
spirit which prizes l. LINCOLN, A, 13
The hopes and prayers of l.-loving people EISENHOWER, D, 4
The l. of the individual must be thus far limited FREEDOM, 40
The L. of the press FREEDOM, 29; MEDIA, 10
the price of l. ORWELL, G, 24
The tree of l. must be refreshed JEFFERSON, T, 8
thy chosen music, L. WORDSWORTH, W, 64
Venice, the eldest Child of L. WORDSWORTH, W, 60
When the People contend for their L. HALIFAX, 6
why is my l. judged of another man's conscience BIBLE, 36
Wilkes and L. FREEDOM, 1
Liberty-Hall This is L. FREEDOM, 17; GOLDSMITH, O, 22
library A l. is thought in cold storage BOOKS, 43
half a l. to make one book JOHNSON, S, 94; WRITING, 22
Jane Austen's books, too, are absent from this l. AUSTEN, J, 3
put away in the lumber room of his l. DOYLE, A, 12; KNOWLEDGE, 16
lice They are electronic l. POPULAR MUSIC, 8
licence a l. to print your own money BUSINESS, 33
A universal l. to be good FREEDOM, 12
L. my roving hands DONNE, J, 11; LUST, 3
Painters and poets…l. to dare anything FREEDOM, 24; HORACE, 1
the rest love…l. FREEDOM, 42; MILTON, J, 64
license Americans use drugs as…l. to be an asshole DRUGS, 17
lick his enemies shall l. the dust PSALMS, 41
licks pride that l. the dust POPE, A, 16; SERVILITY, 5
lie A l. can be half-way round the world LYING, 9
A l. is…help in trouble LYING, 25
a l. which is part a truth LYING, 26; TENNYSON, 15
A lot of people,…tell a l. with their last gasp LAST WORDS, 1
a man…should never venture to l. LYING, 15; MONTAIGNE, M, 3
an honest man sent to l. abroad for…his country DIPLOMACY, 32
Better a l. that heals PROVERBS, 85; TRUTH, 1
'Cannot come, l. follows' PROUST, M, 18
Father, I cannot tell a l. HONESTY, 14; WASHINGTON, G, 5
he maketh me to l. down in green pastures PSALMS, 12
Here l. I by the chancel door ANONYMOUS, 26
He who does not need to l. is proud LYING, 17; NIETZSCHE, F, 16
if a l. may do thee grace LYING, 22
L. follows by post APOLOGIES, 1
moment a man talks…he begins to l. LYING, 6
more easily fall victim to a big l. HITLER, A, 11; LYING, 12
My love and I would l. COUNTRYSIDE, 7; HOUSMAN, A, 10
Nature admits no l. CARLYLE, T, 21; NATURE, 4
Parliaments are the great l. of our time GOVERNMENT, 33
The camera cannot l.. But… PHOTOGRAPHY, 4
The greater the l. PROPAGANDA, 2
the l. has become…a pillar of the State LYING, 24; SOLZHENITSYN, A, 14
The old L. OWEN, W, 3; PATRIOTISM, 32
the only l. he ever told LYING, 20
Those who live by…a l., and those who live by…the truth HAMPTON, C, 2; HONESTY, 5
too crafty a woman to invent a new l. LYING, 13; MAUGHAM, W, 7
Whoever would l. usefully LYING, 11
you would l. if you were in his place TRUTH, 35
lied because our fathers l. WORLD WAR I, 13
Who l. in the chapel /Now lies in the Abbey BYRON, 39
lies believing their own l. POLITICS, 5
enough white l. to ice a wedding cake LYING, 4
It's easy to make a man confess…l. TRUTH, 30
l., damned l. and statistics DISRAELI, B, 16; TWAIN, M, 4
Matilda told such dreadful l. BELLOC, H, 6; LYING, 5
no longer l. but the norm is the truth TRUTH, 27
Only l. and evil come from letting people off MURDOCH, I, 5
Optimistic l. MEDICINE, 91; SHAW, G, 33
polite by telling l. BRADBURY, M, 7; COURTESY, 3
The cruellest l. are…told in silence SILENCE, 15; STEVENSON, R, 15
This universal, obligatory force-feeding with l. INDOCTRINATION, 2; SOLZHENITSYN, A, 11
which way the head l. EXECUTION, 32; RALEIGH, W, 6
Who lied in the chapel /Now l. in the Abbey BYRON, 39
life a keen observer of l. AUDEN, W, 21; INTELLECTUALS, 2
A l. that moves to gracious ends LIFE, 93; TENNYSON, 77
all human l. is there JAMES, H, 9
A long illness seems to be placed between l. and death ILLNESS, 15
an artist in the here and now of both l. and art CARTER, A, 1
answer to L. ADAMS, D, 7
Anythin' for a quiet l. DICKENS, C, 54; PEACE, 9
a pure river of water of l. BIBLE, 474
As our l. is very short LIFE, 91
A well-written L. CARLYLE, T, 7
Bankrupt of L. DRYDEN, J, 6; WORLD-WEARINESS, 1
because I love this l. DEATH, 168
believe in the l. to come AFTERLIFE, 1; BECKETT, S, 1
Books are…a mighty bloodless substitute for l. BOOKS, 47; STEVENSON, R, 18
brief is l. but love is long LOVE, 164; TENNYSON, 64
but for a typographical error,…the story of my l. HUMAN CONDITION, 20; SEX, 93
chemical barrage has been hurled against the fabric of l. CARSON, R, 3; ECOLOGY, 2
cinema is not a slice of l. CINEMA, 16
death after l. does greatly please DEATH, 164
Death is the price paid by l. DEATH, 176
doctrine of the strenuous l. ROOSEVELT, T, 6; WORK, 31
dreary intercourse of daily l. OPTIMISM, 42; WORDSWORTH, W, 15

the ascertainable laws of the science of l. are approximative MEDICINE, 10
The best part of married l. is the fights MARRIAGE, 169
The Book of L. begins BIBLE, 538; WILDE, O, 60
the child should be allowed to meet the real experiences of l. CHILDREN, 42; KEY, E, 2
the crown of l. BIBLE, 216; TEMPTATION, 4
The essential thing in l. VICTORY, 7
The first rule in opera is the first rule in l. MELBA, N, 1; SELF-RELIANCE, 9
The Leaves of L. keep falling FITZGERALD, E, 4; MORTALITY, 6
The L. and Soul, the man who will never go home PARTIES, 11; WHITEHORN, K, 3
the l. of man, solitary, poor, nasty, brutish, and short HOBBES, T, 4; HUMAN CONDITION, 13
the l.-sentence which fate carries LAWRENCE, T, 6; LIFE AND DEATH, 23
The l. so short, the craft so long to learn MORTALITY, 12
the l. to come shall be better for thee than this present l. KORAN 9
the long littleness of l. LIFE, 30
The love of l. is necessary to…any undertaking ENTHUSIASM, 5; JOHNSON, S, 25
the painted veil which those who live /Call l. SHELLEY, P, 12
the phenomena of l. LIFE AND DEATH, 31
The present l. of men on earth, O king LIFE, 11
the pride of l. LUST, 1
The prime goal is…not to prolong l. MEDICINE, 9
The purpose of human l. is to serve and to show compassion KINDNESS, 9
There are only three events in a man's l. LA BRUYERE, J, 6
therefore choose l. BIBLE, 57
the stuff l. is made of FRANKLIN, B, 9; TIME, 23
the tree of l. BIBLE, 144
The vanity of human l. is like a river POPE, A, 58
the veil which those who live call l. DEATH, 157; SHELLEY, P, 22
The Wine of L. keeps oozing FITZGERALD, E, 4; MORTALITY, 6
they get about ten percent out of l. LIFE, 34
this l. /Is nobler CONTENTMENT, 9; SHAKESPEARE, 61
this long disease, my l. ENDURANCE, 16; POPE, A, 13
three ingredients in the good l. LIFE, 67
Three passions…have governed my l. PHILOSOPHERS, 10; RUSSELL, B, 4
Till l. forget MEMORY, 24
To save a man's l. against his will HORACE, 12
total of such moments is my l. CONNOLLY, C, 12; SELF, 8
veil which those who live /Call l. LIFE, 88
waking l. is a dream controlled MADNESS, 33
We'd jump the l. to come ENDING, 6; SHAKESPEARE, 210
We have discovered the secret of l. DISCOVERY, 8; SCIENCE, 21
We pay the first cost on all human l. WAR, 155
We see into the l. of things DEATH, 184
what a queer thing L. is LIFE, 97; WODEHOUSE, P, 14
When he can keep l. no longer in LIFE AND DEATH, 18
'When in death we are in the midst of l.' LIFE AND DEATH, 4
'When in l. we are in the midst of death' LIFE AND DEATH, 4
when religion is allowed to invade…private l. MELBOURNE, 11; RELIGION, 66
wherever l. is dear he is a demigod MEDICINE, 27
While there is l. GAY, J, 7
who is there…would go into the temple to save his l. BIBLE, 435
whole l. shows in your face APPEARANCE, 8
Who saw l. steadily ARNOLD, M, 42; LIFE, 7
Wilde performed his l.…even after fate had taken the plot out of his hands WILDE, O, 1
with an eye made quiet…/We see into the l. of things WORDSWORTH, W, 12
would be furious if they were suddenly restored to l. DEATH, 119
your whole l. shows in your face AGE, 9
life-blood A good book is the precious l. BOOKS, 33; MILTON, J, 7
lifeboat This is a movie, not a l. EQUALITY, 37
life-insurance I detest l. agents IMMORTALITY, 5; LEACOCK, S, 3
life-lie Take the l. away from the average man DELUSION, 4; IBSEN, H, 9
life-like does not matter that Dickens' world is not l. DICKENS, C, 2
life-sized Great men are but l. BEERBOHM, M, 5; GREATNESS, 3
lifetime ask it for the knowledge of a l. ARTISTS, 25; WHISTLER, J, 7
it took me a l. to learn to draw like them PICASSO, P, 10
lift I will l. up mine eyes unto the hills PSALMS, 67
l. up your heads, O ye gates PSALMS, 14
light a l. form of premature baldness AGE, 41
a l. to lighten the Gentiles BIBLE, 317; DEATH, 37
Are all alive with l. BLINDNESS, 5
armour of l. BOOK OF COMMON PRAYER, 4
By the l. of the moon BYRON, 42; LOVE, 48
Culture is the passion for sweetness and l. ARNOLD, M, 23; CULTURE, 2
Doth God exact day-labour, l. deny'd BLINDNESS, 10
drainless shower of l. KEATS, J, 44
Empty space and points of l. REALITY, 9
Fond Memory brings the l. /Of other days MOORE, T, 7; NOSTALGIA, 17
Forward the L. Brigade OBEDIENCE, 4
Give me a l. that I may tread safely into the unknown FAITH, 15
God shall make my darkness to be l. PSALMS, 7
I am the l. of the world BIBLE, 253; CHRISTIANITY, 18
I can't stand a naked l. bulb VULGARITY, 6
I have only a faint l. to guide me ATHEISM, 5; GUIDANCE, 2
Lead, kindly L. FAITH, 23
let there be l. BIBLE, 137
let your l. so shine before men BIBLE, 361
l. a candle of understanding BIBLE, 100
L. breaks where no sun shines THOMAS, D, 14
l. dwelleth with him GOD, 9
Lolita, l. of my life LUST, 9; NABOKOV, V, 1
one might get a five-pound note as one got a l. for a cigarette GENEROSITY, 4; JAMES, H, 5
Put out the l. SHAKESPEARE, 289
speed was far faster than l. LIMERICKS, 7; SCIENCE, 16
The leaping l. for your delight discovers AUDEN, W, 19; DISCOVERY, 2
the l. fantastic toe MILTON, J, 16
the l. of the living PSALMS, 35
the l. shineth in darkness BIBLE, 238
The L. that Failed KIPLING, R, 20
the l. that led astray BURNS, R, 23; DELUSION, 1
thou…shalt l. my candle PSALMS, 7
we shall this day l. such a candle EXECUTION, 21
what l. through yonder window breaks SHAKESPEARE, 310
When I consider how my l. is spent BLINDNESS, 9; MILTON, J, 60
wisdom excelleth folly, as…l. excelleth darkness WISDOM AND FOOLISHNESS, 2
light bulb I can't stand a naked l. WILLIAMS, T, 5
lighten L. our darkness BOOK OF COMMON PRAYER, 9
lightened brooding tragedy and its dark shadows can be l. GANDHI, I, 6; HISTORY, 14
lightfoot many a l. lad HOUSMAN, A, 16; NOSTALGIA, 12
light-headed l., variable men MARRIAGE, 147; STEVENSON, R, 23
lighthouse sitivation at the l. DICKENS, C, 54; PEACE, 9
lightly Angels…take themselves l. CHESTERTON, G, 36; SERIOUSNESS, 1
lightning beheld Satan as l. fall from heaven DEVIL, 3
Here lies a man who was killed by l. ANONYMOUS, 27
reading Shakespeare by flashes of l. COLERIDGE, S, 45; CRITICISM, 14
snatched the l. shaft from heaven SCIENTISTS, 16
lights God made two great l. BIBLE, 140
Of the two l. of Christendom DEFEAT, 14
the Father of l. GIFTS, 1
Turn up the l., I don't want to go home in the dark LAST WORDS, 50
like I don't l. your Christian name MARRIAGE, 22
If I l. it,…it's mine. If I don't…it's a fake PAINTING, 12
I know what I l. BEERBOHM, M, 18; SUBJECTIVITY, 1
I shall not look upon his l. SHAKESPEARE, 71
L. breeds like PROVERBS, 261; SIMILARITY, 3
L. cures like REMEDIES, 31; REMEDIES, 35
L. doth quit like JUSTICE, 23; SHAKESPEARE, 236
men we l. are good for everything HALIFAX, 2; SUBJECTIVITY, 3
People who l. this sort of thing CRITICISM, 37; LINCOLN, A, 19
To l.…the same things, that is…true friendship FRIENDSHIP, 26
Where wilt thou find their l. agen SCOTT, W, 13
liked He's l., but he's not well l. MILLER, A, 2; POPULARITY, 7
I'm so universally l. POPULARITY, 2
likes I know she l. me LOVE, 160
liking it saves me the trouble of l. them AUSTEN, J, 30; NASTINESS, 2

this l. for war BENNETT, A, 2; WAR, 19
you expect other people to be…to your l. TOLERANCE, 4
lilac the l. is in bloom BROOKE, R, 3; FLOWERS, 2
lilacs l. out of the dead land ELIOT, T, 26; MONTHS, 8
lilies consider the l. of the field BIBLE, 370; WORRY, 8
he feedeth among the l. BIBLE, 491; LOVE, 35
L. that fester CORRUPTION, 13; SHAKESPEARE, 368
The l. and roses were all awake LOVE, 163; TENNYSON, 57
lily paint the l. EXCESS, 14; SHAKESPEARE, 167
limb He'll put himself out on a l. ACTORS, 23
Let them bestow on every airth a l. EXECUTION, 13
perils…of wind and l. BUTLER, S, 5; FAITHFULNESS, 2
limelight backing into the l. FAME, 31; LAWRENCE, T, 2
limericks Whose l. never would scan ANONYMOUS, 94; VERBOSITY, 1
limit In order to draw a l. to thinking THINKING, 21
No one who cannot l. himself SELF-CONTROL, 2
limited Liberty too must be l. BURKE, E, 21; FREEDOM, 9
limits his clear knowledge of the l. of human understanding VOLTAIRE, 3
limousine One perfect l. MATERIALISM, 21; PARKER, D, 9
line cancel half a L. DESTINY, 8; FITZGERALD, E, 14
carved not a l. FUNERALS, 14
draw a l. in the sand BUSH, G, 11
I purpose to fight it out on this l. DETERMINATION, 8; GRANT, U, 4
l. in the sand WAR, 34
l. that fits the music POPULAR MUSIC, 21
l. upon l. BIBLE, 208
thin red l. tipped with steel WAR, 141
True genius walks along a l. GENIUS, 6; GOLDSMITH, O, 3
linen It is not l. you're wearing out HOOD, T, 11; WOMEN, 66
washing one's clean l. in public LOVE AND MARRIAGE, 8; WILDE, O, 22
lines give me six l.…by the most honest man EXECUTION, 34
Pray to God and say the l. ACTING, 9
lingerie Brevity is the soul of l. PARKER, D, 16
lingering He dies every day who lives a l. life ILLNESS, 61
Something l.…I fancy GILBERT, W, 33
linguistics Essay in Sociological L. CLASS, 37
links Nothing l. man to man like…cash MONEY, 47
lion A l. among ladies SHAKESPEARE, 263
beard the l. in his den COURAGE, 26
I hear the l. roar COWPER, W, 16
I should be like a l. in a cave of savage Daniels ENEMIES, 11; WILDE, O, 77
Now that the old l. is dead WRITERS, 79
the…fox said…to the sick l. HORACE, 16; MISTRUST, 5
The l. and the unicorn NURSERY RHYMES, 54
The nation had the l.'s heart CHURCHILL, W, 70
to make the l. lie down with the lamb HUMAN NATURE, 21; LAWRENCE, D, 32
lioness feeds a l. at home MARRIAGE, 153
lionized wasn't spoilt by being l. FAME, 33; TREE, H, 4
lions bears and l. growl and fight ANIMALS, 25; WATTS, I, 3
English soldiers fight like l. OFFICERS, 8
l. led by donkeys SOLDIERS, 5
my soul is among l. PSALMS, 36
two huge l. tearing at my flanks APOLOGIES, 3
lip He bit his l. in a manner HUMOUR, 57
stiff upper l. COURAGE, 6
lips her l. narrow and her teeth black ROYALTY, 70
l. that touch liquor must never touch mine ABSTINENCE, 12
My l. are sealed BALDWIN, S, 8; SECRECY, 2
read my l. BUSH, G, 7; DETERMINATION, 14
Red l. are not so red OWEN, W, 5; WAR, 125
You know how to whistle…just put your l. together and blow WHISTLING, 1
lipstick left l. on every pair of underpants CARTER, A, 10
liquefaction That l. of her clothes CLOTHES, 13; HERRICK, R, 7
liquidated the man who l. the Empire MOUNTBATTEN OF BURMA, L, 3
liquidation the l. of the British Empire BRITISH EMPIRE, 3; CHURCHILL, W, 60
liquor But l. /Is quicker ALCOHOL, 59
If…Orientals…drank a l. ALCOHOL, 50; LA BRUYERE, J, 13
lips that touch l. must never touch mine ABSTINENCE, 12
liquors alcoholic l. have been used by the…best races ALCOHOL, 65
lisp stammer and l. and dribble at the mouth SHYNESS, 4
list victim must be found /I've got a little l. GILBERT, W, 26; PUNISHMENT, 13
listen a limit to what one can l. to with the naked eye SPARK, M, 12
privilege of wisdom to l. KNOWLEDGE, 22; WISDOM, 21
they will l. today, they will l. tomorrow KHRUSHCHEV, N, 8; PROMISES, 5
listener A good l. is a good talker with a sore throat CONVERSATION, 11; WHITEHORN, K, 7
listeners L. never hear good GOSSIP, 8; PROVERBS, 263
literacy The ratio of l. to illiteracy LITERACY, 1
literary Classical quotation is the *parole* of l. men JOHNSON, S, 137; QUOTATIONS, 4
'Joe,'…the first great nonstop l. drinker ALCOHOL, 83; THURBER, J, 2
L. men are…a perpetual priesthood CARLYLE, T, 8; WRITERS, 5
sort of l. Cinderella BRONTE, A, 1
the greatest l. stylist of his time JOYCE, J, 4
literature After twenty years…no longer quoted in the medical l. MEDICINE, 88
all l. is written for the amusement of *men* TOLKIEN, J, 2
All that is l. seeks to communicate power BOOKS, 18
All the rest is l. SCIENCE, 95
American professors like their l.…dead LITERATURE, 15
a statesman of l. GALSWORTHY, J, 2
great deal of history to produce a little l. JAMES, H, 6
He knew everything about l. except how to enjoy it HELLER, J, 4; LITERATURE, 7
His roots were buried deep in early l. TOLKIEN, J, 1
If we can't stamp out l. PHILISTINISM, 7; WAUGH, E, 44
I…impress upon you the study of Greek l. CLASSICS, 3
itch of l. WRITING, 31
Language, man!…it's L. LITERATURE, 27; WELLS, H, 10
L. and butterflies are the two sweetest passions LITERATURE, 21; NABOKOV, V, 8
L. flourishes best INGE, W, 8; LITERATURE, 10
L. is mostly about having sex LODGE, D, 1
L. is news LITERATURE, 22; POUND, E, 5
L. is simply language charged with meaning LITERATURE, 23; POUND, E, 11
L. is strewn with the wreckage of men WOOLF, V, 15; WRITERS, 31
L. is the orchestration of platitudes LITERATURE, 28; WILDER, T, 7
l.…poisoned by its own secretions LANGUAGE, 9
L.…something that will be read twice CONNOLLY, C, 6; JOURNALISM, 14; LITERATURE, 1
no l. can outdo the cynicism of real life CHEKHOV, A, 13; EXPERIENCE, 10
one of the greatest texts in our…l. PEPYS, S, 2
Renaissance is a mere ripple on the surface of l. LITERATURE, 14
Sherlock Holmes *is* l. on a humble…level DOYLE, A, 1
That great Cham of l., Samuel Johnson SMOLLETT, T, 6; WRITERS, 88
The Bible is l. BIBLE, 536; SANTAYANA, G, 4
the chief difference between l. and life LITERATURE, 9
the completion of…l. SOLZHENITSYN, A, 2
the sphinx of l. BRONTE, E, 2
litmus Like a piece of l. paper…take the colour of his times HUXLEY, A, 2
litter social virtues…but the virtue of pigs in a l. SOCIETY, 23; THOREAU, H, 7
little Every l. helps HELP, 1; PROVERBS, 136
He who knows only his own side…knows l. SUBJECTIVITY, 4
L. things affect little minds DISRAELI, B, 13; TRIVIALITY, 5
Man wants but l. GOLDSMITH, O, 8
So l. done, so much to do LAST WORDS, 75; RHODES, C, 4
the death of L. Nell without laughing INSENSITIVITY, 5
the l. things are infinitely the most important DOYLE, A, 6; TRIVIALITY, 7
These l. grey cells CHRISTIE, A, 3; INTELLECT, 1
little girls l.…slamming doors BELLOC, H, 11
Little Nell combination of L. and Lady Macbeth PARKER, D, 2
death of L. without laughing WILDE, O, 64
littleness the l. of those that should carry them out BRECHT, B, 6; SUPPORT, 2
the long l. of life LIFE, 30
liv'd And they that L. and Lov'd Either, /Should Dye and Lye and Sleep together ANONYMOUS, 53
I have l. long enough SHAKESPEARE, 225
live All would l. long, but none would be old OLD AGE, 1
anything but l. for it RELIGION, 29

better to die on your feet than to l. on your knees SELF-RESPECT, 2
can only decide how you're going to l. LIFE, 10
Come l. with me DONNE, J, 4; MARLOWE, C, 13
die on your feet than to l. on your knees COURAGE, 20
Do not try to l. forever LONGEVITY, 13
Do you want to l. for ever WAR, 54
eat to l., not l. to eat FOOD, 53; MOLIERE, 2
from the mouths of people who have had to l. LIFE AND DEATH, 34
he forgets to l. LA BRUYERE, J, 6; LIFE AND DEATH, 21
He that would l. for aye, must eat sage in May LONGEVITY, 1
Houses are built to l. in BACON, F, 15; HOUSES, 1
I eat to l. FOOD, 33; GANDHI, M, 6
If God were suddenly condemned to l. the life HUMAN CONDITION, 7
If you l. long enough, the venerability factor creeps in LONGEVITY, 15
I have learned to l. each day as it comes PRESENT, 3
in him we l., and move, and have our being BIBLE, 13; GOD, 6
in Rome, l. as the Romans CONFORMITY, 2
I thought that I was learning how to l. LEONARDO DA VINCI, 6
I want to love first, and l. incidentally LOVE, 71
known I was gonna l. this long AGE, 18
Like a rose, she has lived as long as roses l. TRANSIENCE, 18
L. all you can; it's a mistake not to JAMES, H, 4; LIFE, 52
L. among men as if God beheld you RIGHTEOUSNESS, 10
L. and learn EXPERIENCE, 4; PROVERBS, 264
l. beyond its income BUTLER, S, 11
l. dangerously DANGER, 6; NIETZSCHE, F, 6
l. for ever or die in the attempt HELLER, J, 2; IMMORTALITY, 4
L. Now, Pay Later FUTURE, 12
L. that thou mayest desire to l. again AFTERLIFE, 8; NIETZSCHE, F, 9
L. this day, as…thy last PRESENT, 12
l. to fight another day ANONYMOUS, 38
L. with the gods MARCUS AURELIUS ANTONINUS, 10
Man that is born of a woman…short time to l. BOOK OF COMMON PRAYER, 2
One can't l. on love alone LOVE, 168; TOLSTOY, S, 1
People do not l. nowadays LIFE, 34
people l. beyond their incomes EXTRAVAGANCE, 4; SAKI, 9
Rascals, would you l. for ever WAR, 69
Science says: 'We must l.,' LIFE AND DEATH, 35
self-willed determination to l. LIFE AND DEATH, 20
Sometimes they l. DOCTORS, 59
Teach me to l. DEATH, 94
than to l. up to them PRINCIPLES, 1
there shall no man see me, and l. BIBLE, 121; GOD, 13
They l. ill LONGEVITY, 16
those who l.…believe…to be the truth HAMPTON, C, 2; HONESTY, 5
Those who l. by…a lie, and those who l. by…the truth HAMPTON, C, 2; HONESTY, 5
To l. is like love LIFE, 22
to l. will be more miserable than to die SUICIDE, 17
To l. with thee, and be thy love LOVE, 133; RALEIGH, W, 1
we l. but to make sport AUSTEN, J, 26; RIDICULE, 1
We l. in stirring times PRESENT, 11
we must l. as though…never going to die ACHIEVEMENT, 14
wish to l.,…first attend your own funeral LIFE AND DEATH, 24
You might as well l. PARKER, D, 3; SUICIDE, 24
you will l. to ninety-nine LONGEVITY, 2

lived Never to have l. is best LIFE, 100; YEATS, W, 22
no man…hath l. better than I ACHIEVEMENT, 12; MALORY, T, 2
She…has never l. GAY, J, 5; LOVE, 76
slimy things L. on COLERIDGE, S, 32; GUILT, 6

livelihood slave for l. ENVY, 3

Liverpool L. is the pool of life PLACES, 19
This god-forsaken city…L. SPEECH, 3

lives carry away…years of our own l. DOGS, 8
He that l. long PROVERBS, 195; SUFFERING, 1
He who l. by the sword CONFLICT, 3; PROVERBS, 200
he who l. more l. than one DEATH, 181; WILDE, O, 8
l. of quiet desperation DESPAIR, 9; THOREAU, H, 9
men devote the greater part of their l. LA BRUYERE, J, 2; MANKIND, 34
no man loses any other life than…he now l. LIFE, 8; MARCUS AURELIUS ANTONINUS, 3
women can live their whole l. and not know the law LAW, 14
You medical people will have more l. to answer for DOCTORS, 25

liveth their name l. for evermore BIBLE, 93; MEMORIALS, 5

living A house is a machine for l. in HOUSES, 3; LE CORBUSIER, 1
A l. is made…by selling something that everybody needs WILDER, T, 1
a proper way of l. be adopted ENVIRONMENT, 1
Civilization is a method of l. CIVILIZATION, 1
Dying is as natural as l. LIFE AND DEATH, 2
Evolution is far more important than l. EVOLUTION, 21
he who lives without tobacco isn't worthy of l. SMOKING, 25
History is…the wrong way of l. DURRELL, L, 3; HISTORY, 11
How good is man's life, the mere l. BROWNING, R, 50; LIFE, 19
I make war on the l. REVENGE, 9
It does not then concern either the l. or the dead DEATH, 61
let the earth bring forth the l. creature BIBLE, 141
let them be wiped out of the book of the l. PSALMS, 39
life had prepared Podduyev for l. DEATH, 162; SOLZHENITSYN, A, 4
L. and partly l. LIFE, 37
L. frugally,…he died early ABSTINENCE, 1
L. is a sickness LIFE, 26
l. need charity CHARITY, 3
L. well and beautifully and justly LIFE, 89
no one has yet found a way to drink for a l. ALCOHOL, 48
search the land of l. men SCOTT, W, 13
the l. are the dead on holiday LIFE AND DEATH, 26
the l. bread FOOD, 15
The noble l. and the noble dead WORDSWORTH, W, 44
two people l. together for 25 years without having a cross word MARRIAGE, 86
Vietnam was lost in the l. rooms of America WAR, 105
We owe respect to the l. RESPECT, 4; VOLTAIRE, 24

Livingstone Dr L., I presume EXPLORATION, 5; GREETINGS, 3

llama a female l. surprised in her bath INSULTS, 33; POLITICIANS, 64

Lloyd George L. could not see a belt…hitting below it INSULTS, 6

loaf half a l. is better than a whole l. CHESTERTON, G, 41; COMPROMISE, 6

loafed It is better to have l. and lost LAZINESS, 10; THURBER, J, 4

loathe I l. the country CONGREVE, W, 15; COUNTRYSIDE, 1

loaves five barley l., and two small fishes BIBLE, 249; FOOD, 14

lobby not a man would go into the L. against us BALDWIN, S, 8; SECRECY, 2

local settle up these little l. difficulties MACMILLAN, H, 6; POLITICS, 70

Lochinvar young L. CHIVALRY, 11; SCOTT, W, 14

locusts l. and wild honey BIBLE, 353

lodge a l. in some vast wilderness COWPER, W, 27; SOLITUDE, 3

log-cabin L. to White House ACHIEVEMENT, 13

logic L. must take care of itself LOGIC, 8
L.,…thinking…with the limitations…of the human understanding LOGIC, 1
people…not dealing with creatures of l. HUMAN NATURE, 9
That's l. CARROLL, L, 26; LOGIC, 2
the l. of our times DECLINE, 4
The principles of l. and metaphysics are true PHILOSOPHY, 1
You can only find truth with l. CHESTERTON, G, 28

logical L. consequences are the scarecrows of fools and the beacons of wise men HUXLEY, T, 9; LOGIC, 6

logik un-to l. hadde longe y-go CHAUCER, G, 7; LOGIC, 3

loitered I l. my life away, reading books DISCONTENT, 3; HAZLITT, W, 9

loitering Alone and palely l. ILLNESS, 39; KEATS, J, 22

Lolita L., light of my life LUST, 9; NABOKOV, V, 1

Lomon On the bonnie,…banks o' Loch L.' ANONYMOUS, 67; SCOTLAND, 1

London dominate a L. dinner-table INFLUENCE, 14; WILDE, O, 68
Dublin, though…much worse than L. JOHNSON, S, 153; PLACES, 18
great city of L. LONDON, 16
Hell is a city much like L. SHELLEY, P, 21
I don't know what L.'s coming to LONDON, 9
I, General de Gaulle, now in L. WORLD WAR II, 26
I've been to L. to look at the queen NURSERY RHYMES, 45
I would sell L. LONDON, 20
L.…Clearing-house of the World ECONOMICS, 5
L. is a splendid place to live in LONDON, 4
L., that great cesspool DOYLE, A, 16; LONDON, 10
L., that great sea LONDON, 21; SHELLEY, P, 10
L., thou art the flour of Cities all LONDON, 11
Nobody is healthy in L. AUSTEN, J, 5; LONDON, 3

the agricultural labourers…commute from L. COUNTRYSIDE, 9; POWELL, A, 4
the best club in L. DICKENS, C, 40; HOUSES OF PARLIAMENT, 9
the lowest and vilest alleys of L. DOYLE, A, 8; SIN, 13
When a man is tired of L. JOHNSON, S, 117; LONDON, 18
you have dined in every house in L. – *once* WILDE, O, 78
You will hear…on…a stagecoach from L. to Oxford HAZLITT, W, 27; INTELLECTUALS, 11
Londoner spirit of the L. stands resolute LONDON, 13
loneliest the l. job in the world OCCUPATIONS, 11
loneliness I grow lean in l. LONELINESS, 9
L.…is the most terrible poverty LONELINESS, 14; TERESA, 4
l. may spur you into finding something LONELINESS, 4
l. of my country and my God LONELINESS, 12
lonely All the l. people LENNON, J, 3; LONELINESS, 6
l. of heart is withered away LONELINESS, 17; YEATS, W, 19
My Dear One is mine as mirrors are l. AUDEN, W, 24
None But the L. Heart LONELINESS, 7
She left l. for ever ARNOLD, M, 17; DEPARTURE, 2
So l. am I LONELINESS, 5
the beatings of the l. heart LONELINESS, 2
the l. sea and the sky MASEFIELD, J, 5; SEA, 10
lonesome A l. man…who does not know how to read FRANKLIN, B, 13; READING, 4
one, that on a l. road COLERIDGE, S, 36
long a l., l. way to Tipperary HOMESICKNESS, 8
It is a l. lane HOPE, 4; PROVERBS, 225
Like German opera, too l. and too loud OPERA, 12; WAR, 176; WAUGH, E, 55
L. is the way /And hard HELL, 4; MILTON, J, 40
make no l. tarrying, O my God PSALMS, 24
Night of the L. Knives FASCISM, 5
Not that the story need be l. THOREAU, H, 20; WRITING, 48
longer I have made this letter l. PASCAL, B, 1; VERBOSITY, 6
Was there ever yet anything written…that was wished l. by its readers JOHNSON, S, 36; LITERATURE, 12
longest chapter of accidents is the l.…in the book ACCIDENTS, 10
l. half of your life SOUTHEY, R, 3; YOUTH, 30
The weariest nights, the l. days ENDURANCE, 14
longeth so l. my soul after thee, O God PSALMS, 26
longevity L. is the revenge of talent LONGEVITY, 7
L., n. Uncommon extension of the fear of death LONGEVITY, 4
The brain is the organ of l. LONGEVITY, 12
There is no short-cut to l. LONGEVITY, 8
longing my soul hath a desire and l. to enter into the courts of the Lord PSALMS, 44
the l. for love PHILOSOPHERS, 10; RUSSELL, B, 4
longitude A l. with no platitude FRY, C, 4; MEANING, 4
longueurs Very good, but it has its *l.* CRITICISM, 53
look a proud l. and a high stomach PSALMS, 57
Cassius has a lean and hungry l. MISTRUST, 10; SHAKESPEARE, 146
l. at him! He might be Stalin DE GAULLE, C, 2
L. before you leap CAUTION, 8; PROVERBS, 267
L., stranger, at this island now AUDEN, W, 19; DISCOVERY, 2
sit and l. at it for hours IDLENESS, 8; JEROME, J, 7
To l. down to Camelot CURSES, 5; TENNYSON, 44
looked better to be l. over than overlooked STARING, 1; WEST, M, 12
looker-on sit thou a patient l. PLAYS, 11
looking Don't go on l. at me STARING, 2; ZOLA, 1
Here's l. at you, kid ADMIRATION, 2; COMPLIMENTS, 4
somebody may be l. CONSCIENCE, 6; MENCKEN, H, 2
looking glass The cracked l. of a servant JOYCE, J, 11
looking-glasses Women have served…as l. FEMINISM, 42; WOMEN, 145; WOOLF, V, 12
looks A woman as old as she l. AGE, 27
l. commercing with the skies MILTON, J, 12; SOUL, 11
man who l. you…in the eye…hiding something INSINCERITY, 1
never had the l. to lose APPEARANCE, 15
Well, he l. like a man HOMOSEXUALITY, 20; LINCOLN, A, 21
loose let l. upon the world with £300 BARRIE, J, 9; BRITISH, 2
lord And I replied, 'My L..' HERBERT, G, 2; RELIGION, 52
drunk as a l. DRUNKENNESS, 23
Let us with a gladsome mind /Praise the L. GOD, 39; MILTON, J, 55
L. High Everything Else GILBERT, W, 23; TITLES, 4
l. of all things, yet a prey to all HUMAN CONDITION, 21; POPE, A, 33
L. shall preserve thy going out PSALMS, 68
Mine eyes have seen the glory of the coming of the L. GOD, 27
Praise be to God, the L. of all creatures KORAN 1
Praise the L. and pass the ammunition WAR, 63
The good L. has only ten POLITICIANS, 69
The L. holds copyright on all songs MUSIC, 23
the L. is a man of war BIBLE, 113
the L. is my shepherd PSALMS, 11
the voice of the L. breaketh the cedar-trees PSALMS, 16
This man I thought had been a L. among wits CRITICISM, 27; JOHNSON, S, 50
Works of the L. BOOK OF COMMON PRAYER, 1
lords addressing a naked House of L. CARLYLE, T, 25; NAKEDNESS, 2
Great l. have their pleasures MONTESQUIEU, 6; PLEASURE, 26
he was a king's son and one of the greatest l. in the kingdom ROYALTY, 74
None ought to be l. or landlords over another HUMAN RIGHTS, 8
the cure for admiring the House of L. BAGEHOT, W, 2; HOUSES OF PARLIAMENT, 3
The House of L., an illusion RESPONSIBILITY, 18
The House of L.…how to care for the elderly HOUSES OF PARLIAMENT, 11
lordships good enough for their l. on a hot summer afternoon HOUSES OF PARLIAMENT, 1
lorgnettes something in her voice that made you think of l. APPEARANCE, 29
lorn a lone l. creetur DICKENS, C, 11; MISFORTUNE, 11
lose A man who does not l. his reason REASON, 7
don't l. it again PEACE, 1
In every friend we l. a part of ourselves DEATH, 125; POPE, A, 61
I shall l. no time in reading it DISRAELI, B, 19; INATTENTION, 1
It doesn't hurt to l. my crown FAILURE, 5
l. the substance AESOP, 1; GREED, 5
never had the looks to l. APPEARANCE, 15
nothing to l. but their chains MARX, K, 2; MARXISM, 10
tails you l. VICTORY, 8
We Don't Want To L. You DISMISSAL, 8
What you l. on the swings PROVERBS, 458
Win or l., I'll be going out in style STYLE, 9
You l. BREVITY, 1
loser good and gracious l. FAILURE, 8; SPORT AND GAMES, 37
losers In war…all are l. CHAMBERLAIN, N, 4; WAR, 43
no place…for good l. VICTORY, 10
loses no man l. any other life than…he now lives MARCUS AURELIUS ANTONINUS, 3
The conventional army l. if it does not win WAR, 93
loss more tragic l. of life than the square ring SPORT AND GAMES, 28
richest gain I count but l. HUMILITY, 14; WATTS, I, 8
The l. of India BRITISH EMPIRE, 2
To suffer the l. they were afraid of AUDEN, W, 25
lost All is l. save honour DEFEAT, 4
All is not l. DETERMINATION, 12; MILTON, J, 32
a l. generation STEIN, G, 8; WAR, 166
better to have fought and l. DEFEAT, 3
better to have loved and l. LOVE, 161; TENNYSON, 28
he was l., and is found BIBLE, 332; PARTIES, 3
Home of l. causes ARNOLD, M, 13; OXFORD, 1
I can't say I was ever l. CONFUSION, 3
I look upon every day to be l. FRIENDSHIP, 20; JOHNSON, S, 154
It is better to have loafed and l. LAZINESS, 10; THURBER, J, 4
I've l. one of my children this week LOSS, 9
l. and gone for ever MOURNING, 7
never to have l. at all BUTLER, S, 27; LOSS, 1
What though the field be l. DETERMINATION, 12; MILTON, J, 32
woman that deliberates is l. ADDISON, J, 6; WOMEN, 8
lot and the l. fell upon Jonah BIBLE, 285
policeman's l. is not a happy one GILBERT, W, 41; POLICE, 2
Lot remember L.'s wife BIBLE, 335
lots they parted his raiment, and cast l. BIBLE, 339
loud A l. noise at one end BABIES, 7
Like German opera, too long and too l. OPERA, 12; WAR, 176; WAUGH, E, 55
Louis Son of Saint L. EXECUTION, 12
louse the point of precedency between a l. and a flea JOHNSON, S, 144
lousy For the love of a l. buck DYLAN, B, 13
It was kind of l. CRITICISM, 60
only one fault. It was kind of l. THURBER, J, 20

lov'd I never writ, nor no man ever l. LOVE, 151; SHAKESPEARE, 371
Of one that l. not wisely, but too well LOVE, 155; SHAKESPEARE, 290
love Absence is to l. ABSENCE, 6; LOVE, 46
a comfort in the strength of l. LOVE, 178; WORDSWORTH, W, 22
a girl likes to be crossed in l. a little now and then AUSTEN, J, 24
Alcohol is like l. ALCOHOL, 25
alike are the groans of l. to...dying LOVE AND DEATH, 4
all for l. LOVE, 157
All mankind l. a lover EMERSON, R, 10; LOVE, 69
all's fair in l. and war JUSTICE, 8
all the world and l. were young LOVE, 133; RALEIGH, W, 1
All You Need Is L. LOVE, 104
a man in l. with a dimple LOVE AND MARRIAGE, 5
And l. to all men GOOD, 8; KIPLING, R, 6
An ounce of l. KNOWLEDGE, 40; LOVE, 175
ashamed of having been in l. LOVE, 134; ROCHEFOUCAULD, 8
As honour, l., obedience SHAKESPEARE, 225
Because women can do nothing except l. MAUGHAM, W, 10
Between women l. is contemplative BEAUVOIR, S, 4
brief is life but l. is long LOVE, 164; TENNYSON, 64
But L. has pitched his mansion LOVE, 180; YEATS, W, 8
cannot fully satisfy their sexual instinct without l. SEX, 104
caution in l. LOVE, 136
Christianity has done a great deal for l. CHRISTIANITY, 38; FRANCE, A, 6
Come live with me, and be my l. LOVE, 110; MARLOWE, C, 13
corner in the thing I l. JEALOUSY, 9; SHAKESPEARE, 286
courage to l....courage to suffer LOVE, 169; TROLLOPE, A, 5
Dear Roger Fry whom I l. as a man CRITICS, 12
Deep as first l. NOSTALGIA, 26; TENNYSON, 63
Do not l. your neighbour as yourself SELF, 17; SHAW, G, 27
Drinking...and making l. MANKIND, 7
England!.../What l. I bore to thee HOMESICKNESS, 9; WORDSWORTH, W, 7
Every little girl knows about l. LOVE, 138
Every l. is the l. before LOVE, 123
fallen in l. with all sorts of girls LOVE, 51
Falling out of l. is very enlightening LOVE, 118
folly...l. did make thee run into LOVE, 144; SHAKESPEARE, 45
For the l. of a lousy buck DYLAN, B, 13
God is l. BIBLE, 282; LOVE, 28
greater l. hath no man BIBLE, 260; LOVE, 31
He fell in l. with himself CONCEIT, 13; POWELL, A, 1
help...of the woman I l. LOVE, 176
he told men to l. their neighbour BRECHT, B, 4; HUNGER, 3
how did you l. my picture GOLDWYN, S, 23
How do I l. thee BROWNING, E, 5
how fair...art thou, O l., for delights BIBLE, 498
husbands, l. your wives BIBLE, 21; MARRIAGE, 25
I do not l. thee HATE, 1; LOVE, 120
if men and women marry those whom they do not l. MARTINEAU, H, 5
If music be the food of l. MUSIC, 57; SHAKESPEARE, 336
I hate and l. LOVE AND HATE, 2
I know nothing about platonic l. LOVE, 89
I l. or I hate BEAUTY, 34; PICASSO, P, 8
I'm tired of L. BELLOC, H, 15; MONEY, 9
In friendship or in l. LOVE AND FRIENDSHIP, 3
In l....the amateur status LOVE, 80
In Switzerland they had brotherly l. SWITZERLAND, 5
I rather suspect her of being in l. LOVE AND MARRIAGE, 3
I shall but l. thee better after death BROWNING, E, 6; LOVE, 41
Is thy l. a plant /Of such weak fibre ABSENCE, 10; WORDSWORTH, W, 23
I think my l. as rare ANALOGY, 5; SHAKESPEARE, 374
It is always ourselves we l. SELF, 6
it jumps from admiration to l. AUSTEN, J, 20; WOMEN, 15
I understand only because I l. TOLSTOY, L, 10
I want to l. first, and live incidentally LOVE, 71
jealousy be produced by l. JEALOUSY, 6
labour of l. BIBLE, 502
law of nature which l. alone can alter LACLOS, P, 3; SEX, 61
let brotherly l. continue BIBLE, 189
Let's Fall in L. LOVE, 129; PORTER, C, 9
let us prove...the sports of l. JONSON, B, 16; LOVE, 94
let us too give in to L. LOVE, 172; VIRGIL, 18
lightly turns to thoughts of l. TENNYSON, 50
live with me, and be my l. DONNE, J, 4; LOVE, 63
longing for l. PHILOSOPHERS, 10; RUSSELL, B, 4
l. – all the wretched cant of it GREER, G, 4; LOVE, 81
L. and all his pleasures CAMPION, T, 5; SEX, 22
l. and marriage LOVE AND MARRIAGE, 2
l. and murder will out CONGREVE, W, 4
l., an...intercourse between tyrants and slaves GOLDSMITH, O, 14
l. a place the less for having suffered AUSTEN, J, 17
L. bade me welcome GUILT, 8; HERBERT, G, 6
L. built on beauty BEAUTY, 20; DONNE, J, 9; LOVE, 64
L. ceases to be a pleasure BEHN, A, 7; LOVE, 26
L. conquers all VIRGIL, 18
l. dwells in gorgeous palaces BOCCACCIO, G, 4; LOVE, 38
L. fled LOVE, 179; YEATS, W, 34
l. flies out of the window PROVERBS, 460
l. God, and hateth his brother BIBLE, 284; LOVE, 30
l....has one arch-enemy – and that is life ANOUILH, J, 1; LOVE, 16
L.? I make it constantly but I never talk about it PROUST, M, 7; SEX, 98
l. in a golden bowl BLAKE, W, 11; WISDOM, 12
L. in a hut KEATS, J, 24; LOVE, 96
L. is above the laws LOVE, 158
L. is a boy BUTLER, S, 4
L. is a sickness LOVE, 61
L. is based on a view of women LOVE, 116
L. is blind LOVE, 145; LOVE AND FRIENDSHIP, 1; SHAKESPEARE, 244
L. is...like a coconut LOVE, 39
L. is like quicksilver LOVE, 124
L. is like the measles JEROME, J, 1; LOVE, 90
L. is moral even without...marriage KEY, E, 5; LOVE AND MARRIAGE, 4
L. is my religion KEATS, J, 67; LOVE AND DEATH, 3
L. is not love /Which alters LOVE, 150; SHAKESPEARE, 370
L. is the wisdom of the fool JOHNSON, S, 42; LOVE, 92
L. is two minutes fifty-two seconds of squishing noises SEX, 102
L. itself shall slumber on MEMORY, 22
L. laughs at locksmiths LOVE, 3; PROVERBS, 271
l., like a running brook, is disregarded LOVE, 77
l. like other arts LOVE, 98
l....looks more like hatred than like friendship LOVE AND HATE, 5; ROCHEFOUCAULD, 9
L. looks not with the eyes LOVE, 147; SHAKESPEARE, 260
L. makes the world LOVE, 4; PROVERBS, 272
L. means never having to say APOLOGIES, 5
L. means the pre-cognitive flow LAWRENCE, D, 45; LOVE, 102
L. me, love my dog LOVE, 5; PROVERBS, 273
l. my umbrella LOVE, 95
L. of honour CHIVALRY, 14
l. of justice in most men JUSTICE, 21; ROCHEFOUCAULD, 10
l. of liberty is the l. of others FREEDOM, 21; HAZLITT, W, 13
l. of money is the root of all evil BIBLE, 511; MONEY, 11
L. one another LOVE, 78
l. robs those who have it of their wit LOVE, 62
L....ruined by the desire...legitimacy of the children SEX, 103
L. seeketh not itself to please BLAKE, W, 36
L. seeketh only Self to please BLAKE, W, 37
L.'s like the measles JERROLD, D, 5; LOVE, 91
L. sought is good LOVE, 154; SHAKESPEARE, 344
L.'s pleasure lasts but a moment LOVE, 72
l. that loves a scarlet coat /Should be more uniform HOOD, T, 4; PUNS, 9
l. that moves the sun DANTE ALIGHIERI, 7
L....the gift of oneself ANOUILH, J, 2; LOVE, 17
L., the human form divine BLAKE, W, 44; MANKIND, 10
l. the Lord thy God with all thy heart BIBLE, 411; LOVE, 32
l. thy neighbour as thyself BIBLE, 411; LOVE, 32
l. until after the first attack SCEPTICISM, 1
l....was not as l. is nowadays MALORY, T, 3; NOSTALGIA, 16
l. we swore...seems deceit TRANSIENCE, 11
L. will find a way LOVE, 6; PROVERBS, 274
l. your enemies BIBLE, 365; ENEMIES, 3
L. your neighbour NEIGHBOURS, 1; PROVERBS, 275
make not a bond of l. LOVE, 78
make us l. your goodly gifts /And snatch them SHAKESPEARE, 293
Making l. is the sovereign remedy for anguish SEX, 68
Man's l....a thing apart LOVE, 47
Many a man has fallen in l. with a girl LOVE, 54
Marriage without l. MARRIAGE, 48
Men l. in haste BYRON, 33; LOVE AND HATE, 1

My l. and I would lie COUNTRYSIDE, 7; HOUSMAN, A, 10
My l. for Heathcliff LOVE, 40
My L. in her attire doth show her wit ANONYMOUS, 58; BEAUTY, 6; NAKEDNESS, 1
My l. is like a red red rose LOVE, 44
My l. she's but a lassie yet LOVE, 86
My only l. sprung from my only hate LOVE AND HATE, 6
No l. like the first l. LOVE, 8; PROVERBS, 310
no man dies for l., but on the stage DRYDEN, J, 29; LOVE AND DEATH, 2
Nuptial l. maketh mankind BACON, F, 32; LOVE, 22
office and affairs of l. LOVE AND FRIENDSHIP, 6; SHAKESPEARE, 269
O Lord, to what a state…those who l. Thee RELIGION, 85
One can l.…vulgarity VULGARITY, 2
One can't live on l. alone LOVE, 168; TOLSTOY, S, 1
only l. sprung from my only hate SHAKESPEARE, 309
O tell me the truth about l. AUDEN, W, 26; LOVE, 20
Our l. of what is beautiful does not lead to extravagance RESULTS, 4
perfect l. casteth out fear BIBLE, 283; FEAR, 3; LOVE, 29
permission to 'talk about l.' CHINA, 12
poet without l. CARLYLE, T, 3; POETS, 3
power to hurt us that we l. LOVE, 24
real truth about his or her l. affairs WEST, R, 9
Religion is l. RELIGION, 99
Saying 'Farewell, blighted l..' ANONYMOUS, 71; POVERTY AND WEALTH, 2
She makes l. just like a woman DYLAN, B, 6; WOMEN, 49
She never told her l. LOVE, 153; SHAKESPEARE, 342
Society, friendship, and l. COWPER, W, 33; SOLITUDE, 4
so many computers…use them in the search for l. CRITICISM, 64
strikes where it doth l. SORROW, 30
Such ever was l.'s way BROWNING, R, 20; LOVE, 42
temperate in l. and wine MILTON, J, 2
The boy I l. is up in the gallery LOVE, 173
The dupe of friendship, and the fool of l. BITTERNESS, 1; HAZLITT, W, 12
The first day of Christmas, /My true l. sent to me CHRISTMAS, 17
The l. of life is necessary to…any undertaking ENTHUSIASM, 5; JOHNSON, S, 25
the L. that dare not speak its name HOMOSEXUALITY, 10
the most intense l. on the mother's side FAMILY, 22
There can be no peace of mind in l. LOVE, 131; PROUST, M, 5
these Christians l. one another CHRISTIANITY, 62; TERTULLIAN, 2
Those have most power to hurt us that we l. BEAUMONT, F, 6; HURT, 1
Though lovers be lost l. shall not THOMAS, D, 3
Thy friends are exultations, agonies, /And l. WORDSWORTH, W, 63
time to l., and a time to hate BIBLE, 67
'Tis said that some have died for l. LOVE AND DEATH, 10; WORDSWORTH, W, 71
To be wise and l. LOVE, 152; SHAKESPEARE, 332
To business that we l. we rise betime ENTHUSIASM, 8; SHAKESPEARE, 34
To fear l. is to fear life LOVE, 137
To live with thee, and be thy l. LOVE, 133; RALEIGH, W, 1
to l. and be loved HAPPINESS, 23
to l. and to cherish BOOK OF COMMON PRAYER, 27; MARRIAGE, 33
To l. oneself is the beginning of a lifelong romance CONCEIT, 26; WILDE, O, 17
trick is to l. somebody BALDWIN, J, 6
True l.'s the gift which God has given /To man alone LOVE, 140; SCOTT, W, 7
Try thinking of l. FRY, C, 5; LOVE, 74; SLEEP, 14
vanity and l.…universal characteristics CHESTERFIELD, P, 16; WOMEN, 34
violence masquerading as l. LAING, R, 4; VIOLENCE, 12
War is like l. BRECHT, B, 9; WAR, 28
We must l. one another or die LOVE, 21
Were you ever in l., Beach LOVE, 177
we two had made such wise provision in all our l. MARRIAGE, 47
what a mischievous devil L. is BUTLER, S, 14; LOVE, 49
What are your views on l. PROUST, M, 7; SEX, 98
What is commonly called l. FIELDING, H, 11; LUST, 4
What is l.? 'Tis not hereafter PRESENT, 13; SHAKESPEARE, 340
What will survive of us is l. LOVE, 99
When a man is in l. he endures more LOVE, 119; NIETZSCHE, F, 2
when l. is grown /To ripeness LOVE, 165; TENNYSON, 78
when one has loved a man it is very different to l. God LOVE, 139
where the course of true l. may be expected to run smooth AMERICA, 30; MARTINEAU, H, 2
whom to look at was to l. LOVE, 162; TENNYSON, 51
Wilt thou l. her, comfort her BOOK OF COMMON PRAYER, 26
with a l. like that you know you should be glad LENNON, J, 10; LOVE, 106
with l. from me to you LENNON, J, 4; LOVE, 105
Without l. you will be merely skilful WORK, 18
Work and l. – these are the basics NEUROSIS, 13
worms have eaten them, but not for l. LOVE AND DEATH, 6; SHAKESPEARE, 56
written for the l. of Man and in praise of God THOMAS, D, 5
yet I l. her till I die ANONYMOUS, 86
you and l. are still my argument LANGUAGE, 41
your l. but not your thoughts CHILDREN, 30
you should l. your enemies ENEMIES, 8
loved And the l. one all together BROWNING, R, 36; PERVERSITY, 2
better to be left than never to have been l. CONGREVE, W, 13; LOVE, 58
better to have l. and lost BUTLER, S, 27
God alone deserves to be l. LOVE, 139
I have l. him too much LOVE AND HATE, 4
It seems to me that he has never l. LOVE, 66
l., to have thought, to have done ARNOLD, M, 12; LIFE, 5
She who has never l. has never lived GAY, J, 5; LOVE, 76
'Tis better to have l. and lost TENNYSON, 28
Who ever l. FIRST IMPRESSIONS, 3; MARLOWE, C, 8
lovelier A l. flower /…was never sown DEATH, 183; WORDSWORTH, W, 70
lovelies Fifty l. in the rude OPPORTUNITY, 22; THOMAS, D, 15
loveliest L. of trees, the cherry HOUSMAN, A, 7; TREES, 5
loveliness A woman of so shining l. BEAUTY, 48; YEATS, W, 29
lovely It's all been rather l. LAST WORDS, 57
It was such a l. day BED, 9; MAUGHAM, W, 16
l. and pleasant in their lives BIBLE, 482; FRIENDSHIP, 9
Some hour to which you have not been looking forward will prove l. HORACE, 18; PRESENT, 10
lover All mankind love a l. EMERSON, R, 10; LOVE, 69
a l. with any other career in view COMMITMENT, 10; WELLS, H, 5
A l. without indiscretion is no l. HARDY, T, 8; LOVE, 84
an ex-wife searching for a new l. CONNOLLY, C, 17; WOMEN, 35
easier to be a l. than a husband BALZAC, H, 6; MARRIAGE, 17
lunatic, the l., and the poet SHAKESPEARE, 265
satisfied with her l.'s mind LOVE, 170; TROLLOPE, A, 14
loverly Oh, wouldn't it be l. DESIRE, 10
lovers gallops night by night /Through l.' brains SHAKESPEARE, 307
Hello, Young L., Wherever You Are LOVE, 83
l. cannot see /The pretty follies LOVE, 145; SHAKESPEARE, 244
l. fled away into the storm DEPARTURE, 7; KEATS, J, 14
make two l. happy LOVE, 126; POPE, A, 3
one makes l. as fast as one pleases CONGREVE, W, 14; LOVE, 59
pair of star-cross'd l. SHAKESPEARE, 306
Paris Loves L. PARIS, 7
those of us meant to be l. LOVE, 55
Though l. be lost love shall not THOMAS, D, 3
two young l. lately wed MARRIAGE, 154; TENNYSON, 43
loves Anyone who l. his country, follow me PATRIOTISM, 15
Every man l. what he is good at ENTHUSIASM, 7
He that l. not his wife and children MARRIAGE, 153
He that l. to be flattered is worthy o' the flatterer FLATTERY, 9
I have reigned with your l. ELIZABETH I, 4; ROYALTY, 54
Two l. I have, of comfort and despair CONFLICT, 7; SHAKESPEARE, 375
lovesome garden is a l. thing GARDENS, 4
loveth God l. a cheerful giver BIBLE, 45; GENEROSITY, 2
He prayeth best who l. best COLERIDGE, S, 39; PRAYER, 12
loving A woman despises a man for l. her LOVE, 159
But if we stop l. animals LOVE, 156; SOLZHENITSYN, A, 5
Friday's child is l. and giving CHILDREN, 50; NURSERY RHYMES, 35
l. himself better than all CHRISTIANITY, 35; COLERIDGE, S, 3
most l. mere folly INSINCERITY, 5; SHAKESPEARE, 51
night was made for l. BYRON, 42; LOVE, 48
loving-kindness thy l. and mercy shall follow me PSALMS, 11
low Caesar! dost thou lie so l. DEATH, 146; SHAKESPEARE, 151
He that is l. BUNYAN, J, 10; PRIDE, 2
Holland…lies so l. they're only saved by being dammed EUROPE, 12; HOOD, T, 13

I'll tak' the l. road ANONYMOUS, 67; SCOTLAND, 1
Kings are naturally lovers of l. company BURKE, E, 17; ROYALTY, 30
my lamp burns l. and dim ENVY, 3
to put off my hat to…high or l. PRIDE, 5
when your powder's runnin' l. NEWBOLT, H, 2; PATRIOTISM, 30
Lowder Here lies the body of Mary Ann L. ANONYMOUS, 32
lower if the l. orders don't set us a good example CLASS, 55; WILDE, O, 19
the l. classes had such white skins CLASS, 11
The l. one's vitality ART, 3; BEERBOHM, M, 9
thou madest him l. than the angels PSALMS, 3
lower-middle No one ever describes himself as belonging to the l. class CLASS, 29
lowly In l. pomp ride on to die CHRISTIANITY, 46
meek and l. in heart CHRISTIANITY, 26
Lowry Malcolm L. /Late of the Bowery EPITAPHS, 19
loyal a l., a gallant, a generous, an ingenious, and good-temper'd people STERNE, L, 2
a l.…and good-temper'd people FRANCE, 18
loyalty Hitler showed surprising l. to Mussolini HITLER, A, 2
Party l. lowers the greatest of men LA BRUYERE, J, 9; POLITICS, 65
unswerving l. to his party POLITICIANS, 104
When l. no harm meant ANONYMOUS, 48; SELF-PRESERVATION, 5
lucid he has l. moments when he is only stupid MADNESS, 21
L. intervals and happy pauses MADNESS, 2
Lucifer come not, L.! /I'll burn my books DAMNATION, 4; MARLOWE, C, 5
that same star, /That fitful, fiery L. STARS, 7
luck A self-made man…believes in l. SELF-MADE MEN, 3
it brings you l. whether you believe…or not SUPERSTITION, 7
l.…the harder I work the more I have LUCK, 10
luckiest People who need people are the l. SOCIETY, 16
lucky I'm feeling l. MAJOR, J, 8
It is better to be born l. LUCK, 4; PROVERBS, 226
I wasn't l.. I deserved it MERIT, 7; THATCHER, M, 14
L. at cards LOVE, 7; PROVERBS, 276
My word, Bunyan, you're a l. fellow HOSTAGES, 10
we have only to be l. once LUCK, 6; THREATS, 1
ludicrous He has no sense of the l. POETS, 37
lumber room put away in the l. of his library DOYLE, A, 12; KNOWLEDGE, 16
luminous Dong with a l. Nose LEAR, E, 3; NONSENSE, 19
lump a crowd like that…brings a l. to my wallet MATERIALISM, 27
lunacy an extraordinary mixture of idealism and l. PANKHURST, E, 1
lunatic l. asylums…the stately homes STATELY HOMES, 7
l., the lover, and the poet LOVE, 148; POETRY, 55; SHAKESPEARE, 265
Those comfortably padded l. asylums…the stately homes WOOLF, V, 7
lunatics All are l. PHILOSOPHERS, 1
The relation between psychiatrists and other kinds of l. PSYCHIATRY, 19
lunch married the Duke…not for l. MARRIAGE, 170
no such thing as a free l. BUSINESS, 14
luncheon to read a novel before l. was one of the gravest sins READING, 18; WAUGH, E, 48
lungs don't keep using your l. LEACOCK, S, 4; LONGEVITY, 11
lust All witchcraft comes from carnal l. LUST, 11
l. in action LUST, 10; SHAKESPEARE, 372
Nonconformity and l. stalking hand in hand LUST, 12; WAUGH, E, 14
the l. of the flesh LUST, 1
lusteth the flesh l. against the Spirit BIBLE, 134; COMPROMISE, 3
Lutheran I have a Catholic soul, but a L. stomach CATHOLICISM, 4
luve My l.'s like a red red rose BURNS, R, 16
lux fiat l. BIBLE, 138
luxuries Give us the l. of life LUXURY, 4
luxury Blesses his stars, and thinks it l. ADDISON, J, 5; PLEASURE, 2
Every l.…atheism, breast-feeding INDULGENCE, 2; ORTON, J, 4
The saddest thing…to get used to l. CHAPLIN, C, 6; LUXURY, 2
lyf That l. so short CHAUCER, G, 19; MORTALITY, 3
lyfe Long quaffing maketh a short l. ALCOHOL, 53
lying how this world is given to l. DECEPTION, 5
One of you is l. LOVE, 122; PARKER, D, 12
the air of someone who is l.…to a policeman POLICE, 8
vice of l. LYING, 23
you say you're his…his passion is /Infinite…One of you is l. LYING, 18
lynching he could have attended a l. every day TOLERANCE, 6
Lyndon L. acts like there was never going to be a tomorrow JOHNSON, L, 2
lyre on this wall hang my weapons and my l. SEX, 52; HORACE, 38
lyric if you include me among the l. poets, I'll hold my head…high HORACE, 26; PRIDE, 6
modifying your l. content CENSORSHIP, 14
lyrics I could…*shit* better l. CRITICISM, 43

M

Ma'am Bloody hell, M. ROYALTY, 4
Mab Queen M. hath been with you SHAKESPEARE, 307
Macaroni And called it M. AMERICA, 3; NURSERY RHYMES, 73
Macaulay apostle of the Philistines, Lord M. ARNOLD, M, 21
Macavity there's no one like M. CATS, 4; ELIOT, T, 16
Macbeth M. doth murder sleep SHAKESPEARE, 214
MacDonald Ramsay M. POLITICIANS, 106
mace that fool's bauble, the m. DISMISSAL, 5
machine a taxing m. TAXATION, 8
cannot endow…m. with initiative IDEAS, 6
great intangible m. of commercial tyrrany MORRIS, W, 1
Man is a beautiful m. MANKIND, 38
One m. can do the work of fifty ordinary men TECHNOLOGY, 8
Our body is a m. for living TOLSTOY, L, 11
that magical m., with its flying white breath TRAVEL, 25
the Ghost in the M. MIND, 29
The m. is running away with *him* WILHELM II, 5
The m. threatens RILKE, R, 2
machine-gun a m. riddling her hostess HUXLEY, A, 23; SYMPATHY, 4
machinery liberty…is to be measured not by the governmental m. SOCIETY, 20
machines He ought to have stuck to his flying m. LEONARDO DA VINCI, 3
I see no reason to suppose that these m. will…into general use TECHNOLOGY, 19; WELLINGTON, 9
M.…keep free men in subjection TECHNOLOGY, 4
machine tools make him sit on a crate of m. ECONOMICS, 19
Mackerel M. sky and mares' tails PROVERBS, 277; WEATHER, 1
Macmillan M. is the best prime minister POLITICIANS, 56
M. seemed…to embody the national decay DECLINE, 6; MUGGERIDGE, M, 3
MacWonder M. one moment and MacBlunder the next POLITICIANS, 103
mad being m. among madmen MADNESS, 9
Cicero /And…Homer were */M. as the mist and snow* YEATS, W, 20
Don't get m., get even REVENGE, 13
escaped from a m. and savage master SEX, 112
Every one is more or less m. on one point MADNESS, 24
half of the nation is m. ENGLISH, 37; SMOLLETT, T, 1
he ceased to be m. he became merely stupid PROUST, M, 11; REMEDIES, 46, 47
he first makes m. MADNESS, 1, 13
I am but m. north-north-west MADNESS, 35; SHAKESPEARE, 86
I feel certain that I am going m. WOOLF, V, 17
I said of laughter, it is m. LAUGHTER, 6
let me not be m. MADNESS, 38; SHAKESPEARE, 174
M. about the boy COWARD, N, 11; LOVE, 60
M. as the Mist and Snow MADNESS, 48
M., bad, and dangerous to know BYRON, 3; POETS, 46
Men are so necessarily m. MADNESS, 30
Men will always be m. MADNESS, 46; VOLTAIRE, 29
The dog…/Went m. and bit the man DOGS, 9; GOLDSMITH, O, 10
There is a pleasure sure /In being m. MADNESS, 10
There is no doubt that this poor man was m. POETS, 60
We all are born m. BECKETT, S, 5; MADNESS, 4
We want a few m. people now MADNESS, 40
When we remember that we are all m. MADNESS, 44
Whom Fortune wishes to destroy she first makes m. MADNESS, 42
who turns m. for a reason CERVANTES, M, 11; MADNESS, 6
Madam M. I may not call you ELIZABETH I, 5; TITLES, 2
madame Call me m. TITLES, 7

Madame Bovary All I could think of...was: *M.* MCCARTHY, M, 5; NOVELS, 12
maddest those who think they can cure them are the m. MADNESS, 46; VOLTAIRE, 29
made Annihilating all that's m. MARVELL, A, 2; OBLIVION, 3
Don't you think I was m. for you LOVE, 70
Do you know who m. you CREATION, 14; STOWE, H, 2
Little Lamb, who m. thee BLAKE, W, 46; CREATION, 8
many a gentle person m. a Jack CLASS, 39
Nothing should be m.... which is not worth making MORRIS, W, 2
we're all m. the same COWARD, N, 4; SIMILARITY, 4
Madeira We're from M. EUROPE, 21; SHAW, G, 42
madeleine The taste was that of the little crumb of m. MEMORY, 15; PROUST, M, 2
mademoiselle A m. from Armenteers FRANCE, 17
Madison How were the receipts today in M. Square Garden LAST WORDS, 6
madman frightens us in a m. MADNESS, 14
If a m. were to come into this room JOHNSON, S, 105; SELF-PRESERVATION, 8
m. shakes a dead geranium ELIOT, T, 20
The m.... has lost everything except his reason CHESTERTON, G, 31; MADNESS, 7
The m. is not the man who has lost his reason MADNESS, 7
The m. thinks the rest of the world crazy MADNESS, 41
Thou call'st me m. BLAKE, W, 51; INSULTS, 20
madmen The world is so full of simpletons and m. MADNESS, 18
madness Brussels is a m. EUROPE, 11
destroyed by m., starving hysterical naked MADNESS, 17
devil's m. – War WAR, 157
every man...and every woman, has a dash of m. MADNESS, 12
Great Wits...to M. near alli'd DRYDEN, J, 5; GENIUS, 4
I felt pass over me a breath of wind from the wings of m. MADNESS, 3
M. and suffering can set themselves no limit MADNESS, 32
M. in great ones MADNESS, 37; SHAKESPEARE, 94
M. is part of all of us MADNESS, 15
M. need not be all breakdown LAING, R, 5; MADNESS, 25
Much M. is divinest Sense MADNESS, 8
Now Ireland has her m. AUDEN, W, 16; POETRY, 5
Our occasional m. is less wonderful MADNESS, 34
Sanity is m. put to good uses MADNESS, 33
streak of m. in the family MADNESS, 5
that way m. lies SHAKESPEARE, 181
The great proof of m. MADNESS, 28
What is m. MADNESS, 16, 47
maestro Music, M., Please MUSIC, 38
maggot how to create a m. MONTAIGNE, M, 6; RELIGION, 69
magic men mistook m. for medicine MEDICINE, 100
That old black m. SUPERNATURAL, 11; SZASZ, T, 3
magical M. Mr Mistoffelees CATS, 5
magicians if the way had not been prepared by m. SCIENCE, 70
magistrate Obscenity...happens to shock some elderly... m. PRUDERY, 5; RUSSELL, B, 25
suppose...the m. corruptible CORRUPTION, 11; LAW, 29
magistrates rather than that the sovereigns and m. should be destroyed REBELLION, 11
Magna Charta M. is such a fellow MONARCHY, 10
magnanimity in victory, m. CHURCHILL, W, 26; WAR AND PEACE, 4
magnetism how do drugs, hygiene and animal m. heal REMEDIES, 27
magnificent more than m.... mediocre GOLDWYN, S, 20
some m. myth PLATO, 3; PROPAGANDA, 3
there you sit with that m. instrument between your legs TOSCANINI, A, 5
magnifique *c'est m., mais* WAR, 24
magnify my soul doth m. the Lord BIBLE, 309
Magog Gog and M. BIBLE, 471; EVIL, 7
Mahomet good a Christian as M. ELIZABETH I, 3
If the hill will not come to M. ADAPTABILITY, 2; BACON, F, 14
maid Being an old m. is like death by drowning MARRIAGE, 70
like a moth, the simple m. GAY, J, 2; WOMEN, 59
The m. was in the garden, /Hanging out the clothes NURSERY RHYMES, 52
Where are you going to, my pretty m. NURSERY RHYMES, 71
maiden A m. at college, named Breeze EDUCATION, 6
A simple m. in her flower PURITY, 3; TENNYSON, 39
How could you use a poor m. so ANONYMOUS, 16
I've a neater, sweeter m. DISCONTENT, 6; KIPLING, R, 25
many a rose-lipt m. HOUSMAN, A, 16; NOSTALGIA, 12
That kissed the m. all forlorn NURSERY RHYMES, 61
maidens M., like moths, are ever caught by glare WEALTH, 15
maids And pretty m. all in a row GARDENS, 1; NURSERY RHYMES, 34
Three little m. from school CHILDREN, 31; GILBERT, W, 28
mail the Night M. crossing the Border TRAVEL, 5
maintenance Zen and the Art of Motorcycle M. PHILOSOPHY, 10
majesty A sight so touching in its m. LONDON, 24; WORDSWORTH, W, 53
Her M. is not a subject DISRAELI, B, 37; ROYALTY, 48
her M.... must not...look upon me as a source of income TAXATION, 6
Her M.'s Opposition BAGEHOT, W, 4; OPPOSITION, 1
His M.'s dominions BRITISH EMPIRE, 5
How can I...dislike a sex to which Your M. belongs MISOGYNY, 2; RHODES, C, 3
If Her M. stood for Parliament POLITICS, 95
Ride on! ride on in m. CHRISTIANITY, 46
This earth of m. ENGLAND, 46; SHAKESPEARE, 297
When I invented the phrase 'His M.'s Opposition' OPPOSITION, 3
Major John M. isn't a Tory MAJOR, J, 1
major-general very model of a modern M. GILBERT, W, 38
majority A m. is always the best repartee DISRAELI, B, 14; MAJORITY, 4
Fools are in a terrible...m. FOOLISHNESS, 15; IBSEN, H, 1
great changes occur in history...the m. are wrong MAJORITY, 2
He's gone to join the m. DEATH, 24
I am certain that we will win the election with a good m. SELF-CONFIDENCE, 11; THATCHER, M, 35
No candidate...elected ex-president by such a large m. DEFEAT, 15
One on God's side is a m. GOD, 43
the damned, compact, liberal m. IBSEN, H, 3; MAJORITY, 6
the great silent m. MAJORITY, 7; NIXON, R, 7
The m. has the might IBSEN, H, 2; MINORITY, 2
the tyranny of the m. MAJORITY, 1
we don't stand for black m. rule MANDELA, N, 7
majors scarlet M. SASSOON, S, 1; WAR, 146
make a Scotsman on the m. BARRIE, J, 11; SCOTS, 2
Love? I m. it constantly PROUST, M, 7; SEX, 98
The white man knows how to m. everything CHARITY, 23
maker he adores his m. DISRAELI, B, 18
Whether my M. is ready for...meeting me DEATH, 49; OLD AGE, 33
makes either m. me or fordoes me quite DECISION, 5
making He is very fond of m. things FUTILITY, 9; HOPE, A, 2
If you get the English people into the way of m. kings MELBOURNE, 5; ROYALTY, 86
Nothing should be made...which is not worth m. MORRIS, W, 2
mal *Honi soit qui m. y pense* ARISTOCRACY, 12
maladies all the m. and miseries CARLYLE, T, 31; WORK, 7
m. often have their origin there MIND, 22
Medical men...call all sorts of m.... by one name CARLYLE, J, 4; MEDICINE, 19
There are m. we must not seek to cure PROUST, M, 11; REMEDIES, 46
malady A reckoning up of the cause often solves the m. REMEDIES, 18
It is the m. of our age YOUTH, 14
malaise Wembley, adj. Suffering from a vague *m.* HUMOUR, 44
male all the usual m. problems BLEASDALE, A, 3
especially the m. of the species LAWRENCE, D, 11; MEN, 9
In the sex-war thoughtlessness is the weapon of the m. CONNOLLY, C, 16; SEXES, 8
m. and female created he them BIBLE, 142
m. can represent Christ CLERGY, 16; RELIGION, 24
more deadly than the m. KIPLING, R, 10; WOMEN, 71
preserve one last m. thing LAWRENCE, D, 25; MASCULINITY, 2
the peculiar situation of the human m. BEAUVOIR, S, 2
malefactions They have proclaim'd their m. GUILT, 12
malevolent the most perverse and m. creature HAZLITT, W, 2
malice M. is like a game of poker NASTINESS, 9
malicious Critics are more m. about poetry CRITICS, 9

God is subtle but he is not m. EINSTEIN, A, 7
malign rather m. oneself EGOTISM, 7; ROCHEFOUCAULD, 17
malignant the only part of Randolph that was not m. INSULTS, 127; WAUGH, E, 54
malignity that peculiar m....characteristic of apostates BETRAYAL, 9; MACAULAY, T, 13
malingering Neurosis has an absolute genius for m. NEUROSIS, 10; PROUST, M, 10
malt M. does more than Milton ALCOHOL, 40; HOUSMAN, A, 17
malvesye drowned in a barrel of m. EXECUTION, 10
mama the m. of dada NONSENSE, 12
Mamas The Last of the Red-Hot M. SINGERS, 3
mammal Like the skins of some small m. APPEARANCE, 9
Mammon M. wins his way where Seraphs might despair BYRON, 8; MATERIALISM, 7
ye cannot serve God and m. BIBLE, 369
mammy do what your m. wouldn't WALKER, A, 5
man A 'Grand Old M.' LEACOCK, S, 12; OLD AGE, 64
all animals were created...for the use of m. ANIMALS, 20; PEACOCK, T, 4
a m. after his own heart BIBLE, 478
a m. can die but once DEATH, 143; SHAKESPEARE, 124
a m....having an ape for his grandfather EVOLUTION, 20
A m. in the house is worth two MEN, 15; WEST, M, 3
a m. is always seeking for happiness MARRIAGE, 65
a m. is a m. for a much longer time SEXES, 2
A m. is as old as he feels PROVERBS, 44
A m. is as old as his arteries OLD AGE, 100
A m. is not completely born LIFE AND DEATH, 17
A m. is only as old as the woman AGE, 62; MARX, G, 26
A m....is *so* in the way MEN, 5
A m. must serve his time to every trade BYRON, 38; CRITICS, 2
A m. of sixty has spent twenty years in bed LIFE, 14
a m. of something occasionally like genius WHITMAN, W, 2
A m. of straw PROVERBS, 45; WOMEN, 1
A m.'s a m. for a' that BURNS, R, 10; MEN, 2
A m. should never put on his best trousers FREEDOM, 26; IBSEN, H, 4
A m. should...own he has been in the wrong MISTAKES, 15; POPE, A, 54
A m. with God GOD, 32
an old m. in a dry month AGE, 38; ELIOT, T, 8
a poor m. for the same disease he giveth a more common name REMEDIES, 57
apparel oft proclaims the m. CLOTHES, 24; SHAKESPEARE, 74
'A was a m., take him for all in all SHAKESPEARE, 71
behold the m. BIBLE, 267
Between m. and woman there is little difference SEXES, 1
big m. has no time FAME, 13; FITZGERALD, F, 13
Brutus is an honourable m. HONOUR, 5; SHAKESPEARE, 156
coming together of m. and wife...should be a fresh adventure STOPES, M, 5
condition of m. is a condition of war HOBBES, T, 1; HUMAN CONDITION, 12
dare do all that may become a m. COURAGE, 28
disguised as a complete M. HUXLEY, A, 6
England expects every m. will do his duty DUTY, 5; NELSON, H, 4
Every m. a king EQUALITY, 21
Every m. carries the entire form of the human condition HUMAN CONDITION, 18
every m. did that which was right in his own eyes BIBLE, 296
Every m. has a wild beast within him MANKIND, 27
Every m. is as Heaven made him CERVANTES, M, 15; CHARACTER, 3
Every m. is wanted EMERSON, R, 12; HUMAN CONDITION, 8
Every m. meets his Waterloo DEFEAT, 13
figure of 'The Reasonable M.' LAW, 22
follies which a m. regrets the most MISTAKES, 17
for m. or beast WEATHER, 10
Glory to M. in the highest MANKIND, 62
God made the woman for the m. TENNYSON, 13; WOMEN, 128
Go West, young m. EXPLORATION, 2
hate ingratitude more in a m. SHAKESPEARE, 347
he asks most insistently is about m. LEONARDO DA VINCI, 2
He is a m. of brick CHARACTER, 24; UPDIKE, J, 4
he must view the m. in his world ENVIRONMENT, 6
he owes not any m. LONGFELLOW, H, 18
He was her m., but he done her wrong UNFAITHFULNESS, 2
I care not whether a m. is Good BLAKE, W, 17; WISDOM, 13
If a m. be gracious and courteous BACON, F, 28; COURTESY, 2
If a m. stays away from his wife MARRIAGE, 59
If every m. would mend a m. MEDICINE, 4
I just want every m., woman, and child in America to see it GOLDWYN, S, 8
I love not M. the less BYRON, 16; NATURE, 3
I myself also am a m. BIBLE, 9
In wit a m. POPE, A, 18
I said to the m. who stood at the gate of the year FAITH, 15
Is a m. a salvage at heart MANKIND, 6
I see a m. hurrying along – to what KEATS, J, 69; PURPOSE, 6
I sing of arms and the m. ENDURANCE, 29; VIRGIL, 5
It is good to know what a m. is UNDERSTANDING, 2
It takes...twenty years to make a m. LOVE, 135
it touches a m. that his blood is sea water ENVIRONMENT, 9
judge of a m. by his foes JUDGMENT, 7
King is but a m. EQUALITY, 31; SHAKESPEARE, 134
let no m. put asunder BOOK OF COMMON PRAYER, 29
little m. wears a shocking bad hat CLOTHES, 29; INSULTS, 139
make m. in our own image BIBLE, 142; CREATION, 6
m. alone leaves traces of what he created BRONOWSKI, J, 1; MANKIND, 12
M. appears to be the missing link MANKIND, 36
M. arrives as a novice at each age of his life AGE, 26
m. being in honour hath no understanding PSALMS, 29
M., being reasonable, must get drunk BYRON, 21; DRUNKENNESS, 13
m., by possessing consciousness, is...animal PSYCHOLOGY, 19; UNAMUNO, M, 2
M. can have only a certain number of teeth, hair and ideas OLD AGE, 104
M....can neither repeat his past nor leave it behind AUDEN, W, 9; HISTORY, 4
M....can only find relaxation from one...labour by taking up another CHANGE, 8; FRANCE, A, 3
M....consumes without producing CAPITALISM, 14; ORWELL, G, 3
M. delights not me MANKIND, 56; SHAKESPEARE, 85
m. did eat angels' food PSALMS, 42
m. fell into his anecdotage DISRAELI, B, 9; OLD AGE, 42
M. for the field and woman for the hearth SEXES, 30; TENNYSON, 66
M....grows beyond his work MANKIND, 61; STEINBECK, J, 2
M. hands on misery to man CHILDREN, 46; HUMAN CONDITION, 15
M. has given a false importance to death HUMAN CONDITION, 30
M. has his will SEXES, 14
M. has in him the silence of the sea MANKIND, 63
m. has stopped moving EVOLUTION, 5
m. hath penance done COLERIDGE, S, 35; PUNISHMENT, 11
M. is a beautiful machine MANKIND, 38
M. is a dupable animal GULLIBILITY, 3
M. is a history-making creature AUDEN, W, 9; HISTORY, 4
M. is a museum of diseases MANKIND, 67
M. is...an everlasting contradiction to himself HAZLITT, W, 5; INTELLECT, 7
M. is an exception MANKIND, 17
M. is an intellectual animal HAZLITT, W, 5; INTELLECT, 7
M. is a noble animal BROWNE, T, 12; MANKIND, 13
M. is...a political animal ARISTOTLE, 6; POLITICS, 6
m. is...a religious animal BURKE, E, 11; RELIGION, 19
M. is a social animal SOCIETY, 21
m. is as old as he's feeling AGE, 27; OLD AGE, 38
M. is...a thing of shreds and patches MANKIND, 26
M. is a tool-making animal FRANKLIN, B, 12; TECHNOLOGY, 6
m. is...a wild animal MANKIND, 21
m. is capable of a certain degree of dignity CAMUS, A, 2
M....is halfway between an ape and a god MANKIND, 32
M. is Heaven's masterpiece MANKIND, 48
M. is like a thing of nought PSALMS, 72
M. is Nature's sole mistake MANKIND, 28
M. is not a solitary animal RUSSELL, B, 11
m. is not m. as yet PROGRESS, 6; PROGRESS, 6
M. is something that is to be surpassed NIETZSCHE, F, 17; SUPERIORITY, 13
M. is the hunter SEXES, 29; TENNYSON, 65
M. is the master of things MANKIND, 62
M. is the only animal...on friendly terms with the victims...he eats BUTLER, S, 20; HYPOCRISY, 7
M..../Laid the crops low AGRICULTURE, 5; THOMAS, D, 17
m. made the town COUNTRYSIDE, 2; COWPER, W, 22
M., n. An animal so lost in rapturous contemplation MANKIND, 9
M. proposes GOD, 31
m. right fair CONFLICT, 7; SHAKESPEARE, 375

M.'s chief goal in life NATURE, 17
m.'s greatest crime BIRTH, 6
M.'s inhumanity to man BURNS, R, 14; CRUELTY, 2
M.'s life is cheap as beast's NECESSITY, 5; SHAKESPEARE, 177
M.'s love is of man's life a thing apart BYRON, 20; SEXES, 6
M.'s main task in life is to give *birth* to himself BIRTH, 10
m. so various DRYDEN, J, 9; HUMAN NATURE, 11
m.'s worth something BROWNING, R, 13; CONFLICT, 5
m. that hath no music in himself MUSIC, 56; SHAKESPEARE, 253
m. that hath not walked in the counsel of the ungodly PSALMS, 1
m. that is born of a woman BIBLE, 230; HUMAN CONDITION, 3
m. that is young in years AGE, 11; BACON, F, 61
M. the bad child of the universe MANKIND, 44
M. to command and woman to obey SEXES, 30; TENNYSON, 66
M. wants but little GOLDSMITH, O, 8; MORTALITY, 9
M. was born free FREEDOM, 52; ROUSSEAU, J, 1
M., when perfected, is the best of animals MANKIND, 4
m. who…had the largest…soul DRYDEN, J, 22
m. who's untrue to his wife AUDEN, W, 21; INTELLECTUALS, 2
m. with all his noble qualities DARWIN, C, 7; EVOLUTION, 8
M. with the head and woman with the heart SEXES, 30; TENNYSON, 66
mean m. is always full of distress CONFUCIUS, 10; SUPERIORITY, 4
Men are men, but M. is a woman MANKIND, 19
more even than the whole m. ENVIRONMENT, 6
My mother said it was simple to keep a m. WOMEN, 63
no m.…hath lived better than I ACHIEVEMENT, 12; MALORY, T, 2
No m. is a hero to his wife's psychiatrist PSYCHIATRY, 8
No m. is a hypocrite in his pleasures CAMUS, A, 8
No m. is an Island DONNE, J, 7; SOCIETY, 8
No m. is good enough to govern another DEMOCRACY, 13; LINCOLN, A, 10
Nor in the critic let the m. be lost CRITICS, 14; POPE, A, 31
Nothing happens to any m. MARCUS AURELIUS ANTONINUS, 9
Nothing links m. to m. like…cash MONEY, 47
Not mine, but m.'s HOUSMAN, A, 5
not to the m. to whom the idea first occurs SCIENCE, 25
Nowhere can m. find a quieter…retreat than in his own soul PRAYER, 24
No young m. believes he shall ever die HAZLITT, W, 30; IMMORTALITY, 3
Of M.'s first disobedience MILTON, J, 30; SIN, 20
On earth there is nothing great but m. MANKIND, 30
One cannot be always laughing at a m. AUSTEN, J, 25; MEN, 1
one m. pick'd out of ten thousand HONESTY, 9; SHAKESPEARE, 82
One m. shall have one vote DEMOCRACY, 4
one small step for m. SPACE, 2
only m. is vile MISANTHROPY, 1
only place where a m. can feel…secure GREER, G, 2; MEN, 6
rarely…one can see in a little boy the promise of a m. CHILDREN, 27
reason to lament /What m. has made of m. MANKIND, 74; WORDSWORTH, W, 17
say to all the world 'This was a m.!' SHAKESPEARE, 163
Science made m. feel small NEUROSIS, 7
Sex between a m. and a woman SEX, 7
She is clearly the best m. among them POLITICIANS, 60
She's more of a m. than I expected VICTORIA, 3
single sentence…for modern m. CAMUS, A, 6; MANKIND, 15
Society, being codified by m. SOCIETY, 5
some meannesses…too mean even for m. SEXES, 31; THACKERAY, W, 7
Style is the m. himself STYLE, 1
superior m. is distressed by his want of ability CONFUCIUS, 13; SUPERIORITY, 5
superior m. is satisfied CONFUCIUS, 10; SUPERIORITY, 4
Tears of eternity, and sorrow, /Not mine, but m.'s SORROW, 13
that grand old m. POLITICIANS, 109
That married the m. all tattered and torn NURSERY RHYMES, 61
That was once a m. OLD AGE, 43
The atrocious crime of being a young m. PITT THE ELDER , 2; YOUTH, 21
the century of the common m. PUBLIC, 20
The Child is Father of the M. AGE, 102; WORDSWORTH, W, 24
the credit goes to the m. who convinces the world SCIENCE, 25
the field of the stars is so vast, but…m. has measured it FRANCE, A, 5
The history of m. for the nine months preceding his birth BIRTH, 8
the honest m. who married GOLDSMITH, O, 27; MARRIAGE, 82
the m. takes a drink ALCOHOL, 8
The m. who makes no mistakes MISTAKES, 13
the m. whose second thoughts are good BARRIE, J, 12
The noblest work of God? M. MANKIND, 68
the only real danger that exists is m. himself HUMAN NATURE, 17; JUNG, C, 11
The proper study of Mankind is M. POPE, A, 34
The really original woman…imitates a m. WOMEN, 127
There must be a m. behind the book EMERSON, R, 18; WRITERS, 10
There once was a m. who said God EXISTENCE, 4
the response of m. to his total environment ENVIRONMENT, 7
The silliest woman can manage a clever m. KIPLING, R, 22
the state…M. is in GOD, 41; NIETZSCHE, F, 5
The true science…of m. is m. MANKIND, 16
This is a question for an embryo, not for a m. LIFE, 23
This is the state of m. HUMAN CONDITION, 24; SHAKESPEARE, 141
this is the whole duty of m. BIBLE, 79; GOD, 11
'Tis strange what a m. may do LOVE, 166; THACKERAY, W, 4
To a physician, each m., each woman MEDICINE, 25
To preserve a m. alive in the midst of so many chances LIFE, 92
To the m.-in-the-street, who AUDEN, W, 21; INTELLECTUALS, 2
True love's the gift which God has given /To m. alone LOVE, 140; SCOTT, W, 7
uneducated m. to read books of quotations CHURCHILL, W, 20; QUOTATIONS, 1
Wash That M. Right Out of My Hair DECISION, 1
We have on our hands a sick m. DECLINE, 8
We know nothing of m., far too little HUMAN NATURE, 17; JUNG, C, 11
Well, he looks like a m. HOMOSEXUALITY, 20; LINCOLN, A, 21
were m. /But constant, he were perfect FAITHFULNESS, 7
what a m. is to a gent INTELLIGENCE, 3
What a piece of work is a m. MANKIND, 56; SHAKESPEARE, 85
what a very singularly deep young m. ARROGANCE, 4; GILBERT, W, 36
What is a m. HUMAN NATURE, 28; SHAKESPEARE, 100
What is m.…but a…machine for turning…wine…into urine MANKIND, 11
what is m., that thou art mindful of him PSALMS, 3
What's a m.'s first duty IBSEN, H, 8; SINCERITY, 5
When a m. is in love he endures more LOVE, 119; NIETZSCHE, F, 2
When a woman behaves like a m. WOMEN, 54
whether he is a Wise M. or a Fool BLAKE, W, 17; WISDOM, 13
Whoso would be a m. CONFORMITY, 4; EMERSON, R, 14
Why can't a woman be more like a m. MEN, 11
Women who love the same m. BEERBOHM, M, 13; LOVE, 25
you asked this m. to die AUDEN, W, 13; WAR, 13
You cannot make a m. by standing a sheep BEERBOHM, M, 17; PUBLIC, 4
you'll be a M. my son IDEALISM, 4; KIPLING, R, 18
young m. not yet BACON, F, 35; MARRIAGE, 15

Man Kelly from the Isle of M. ABSENCE, 8
Manchester The shortest way out of M. is…gin DRINKS, 6; PLACES, 5
Mandalay On the road to M. KIPLING, R, 24; PLACES, 21
mandatory condoms are not only necessary but m. AIDS, 8
Mandela Mr M. has walked a long road MANDELA, N, 1
Manderley I dreamt I went to M. again DREAMS, 6
mandrake Get with child a m. root DONNE, J, 13; NONSENSE, 11
manger In a m. for His bed CHRISTMAS, 2
laid him in a m. BIBLE, 313; CHRISTMAS, 8
mangle Granny caught her tit in the m. PLEASURE, 34
Manhattan I like to walk around M. AMERICA, 37
manhood m. a struggle AGE, 33; DISRAELI, B, 4
No sounder piece of British m. was put together SCOTT, W, 1
The tobacco business is a conspiracy…m. SMOKING, 20
mankind about the dreadful wood…runs a lost m. AUDEN, W, 14; GUILT, 2
a decent respect to the opinions of m. INDEPENDENCE, 3; JEFFERSON, T, 4
all M.'s epitome DRYDEN, J, 9; HUMAN NATURE, 11
As I know more of m. EXPECTATION, 3; JOHNSON, S, 147
difficult to love m.…private income SELF-INTEREST, 5
giant leap for m. SPACE, 2
Human reason won. M. won KHRUSHCHEV, N, 3; VICTORY, 12
I am willing to love all m., *except an American* JOHNSON, S, 123
Ideal m. would abolish death IDEALISM, 5; LAWRENCE, D, 23

I love m. MANKIND, 54; MISANTHROPY, 4
in determining the future destinies of m. BRITISH EMPIRE, 1
M. are always happy for having been happy SMITH, S, 1
M. is a closed society MANKIND, 55
M. is a club CHESTERTON, G, 42; MANKIND, 20
Nazi Germany had become a menace to all m. NAZISM, 5
proper study of m. is books HUXLEY, A, 12; LITERATURE, 8
Spectator of m. ADDISON, J, 10; OBJECTIVITY, 2
the earth is free for every son and daughter of m. HUMAN RIGHTS, 8
The mass of m. is divided into two classes MANKIND, 52
The nations which have put m. and posterity most in their debt INGE, W, 12; NATIONS, 4
The proper study of M. is Man POPE, A, 34; SELF-KNOWLEDGE, 5
There are only two classes of m. in the world MANKIND, 33
truly m.'s war of liberation HUNGER, 7
Upon the whole I dislike m. HUMAN NATURE, 20; KEATS, J, 70
We should expect the best and the worst from m. MANKIND, 69
Whatever Nature has in store for m. NATURE, 10
wished that m. were propagated like trees SEX, 62
man-made countryside is one of the most heavily m. habitats CONSERVATION, 10
manna gave you m.…angels' bread BIBLE, 97
it is m. FOOD, 13
your fathers did eat m.…and are dead FOOD, 15
manner he's got a very good bedside m. DOCTORS, 34
manners in England people have good table m. MANNERS, 5
leave off first for m.' sake BIBLE, 88; MANNERS, 1
M. are…the need of the plain MANNERS, 8; WAUGH, E, 51
M. maketh man MANNERS, 9; PROVERBS, 279
The Japanese have perfected good m. PLACES, 34
the m. of a dancing master CRITICISM, 28; JOHNSON, S, 51
the m. of a Marquis CLASS, 16; GILBERT, W, 42
To Americans English m. are…frightening MANNERS, 4
Tom Jones…picture of human m. GIBBON, E, 5; NOVELS, 5
to write good prose is an affair of good m. POETRY AND PROSE, 4
who are…ordered by different m. POVERTY AND WEALTH, 5
mansion Back to its m. call the fleeting breath GRAY, T, 4
mansions in my Father's house are many m. BIBLE, 258
manure The tree of liberty…It is its natural m. FREEDOM, 27; JEFFERSON, T, 8
many I quite agree with you, sir, but what can two do against so m. SHAW, G, 48
m. men, m. women, and m. children CRITICISM, 29; JOHNSON, S, 58
so much owed by so m. CHURCHILL, W, 53; WORLD WAR II, 14
what are they among so m. BIBLE, 249; FOOD, 14
Mao the degree of acceptance and authority which M. has acquired MAO TSE-TUNG, 1
map a picture of a relief m. of Ireland APPEARANCE, 6
Roll up that m. PEACE, 17; PITT THE YOUNGER, 2
The books…create in one's mind a…false m. BOOKS, 34; ORWELL, G, 22
maps Geography is about M. BIOGRAPHY, 1
mar likely to m. the general felicity BUTLER, S, 19; MARRIAGE, 40
Maradona the head of M. FOOTBALL, 11
Marathon mountains look on M. BYRON, 27; EUROPE, 4
marble he…left it m. IMPROVEMENT, 1
Not m., nor the gilded monuments POETRY, 56; SHAKESPEARE, 364
marble-hearted Ingratitude, thou m. fiend INGRATITUDE, 5
march Napoleon's armies used to m. on their stomachs SELLAR, W, 6
Truth is on the m. TRUTH, 49; ZOLA, 3
March Beware the ides of M. PROPHECY, 12; SHAKESPEARE, 144
M. comes in like a lion MONTHS, 1; PROVERBS, 285
M., whan God first maked man CHAUCER, G, 16; CREATION, 9
M. winds and April showers PROVERBS, 286
months…gloomy in England are M. and April SEASONS, 27; TROLLOPE, A, 7
Marche The droghte of M. CHAUCER, G, 3; MONTHS, 7
marched He m. them up to the top of the hill NURSERY RHYMES, 37
March Hare 'Then you should say what you mean,' the M. went on CARROLL, L, 9; MEANING, 1
mare Though patience be a tired m. PATIENCE, 14; SHAKESPEARE, 127
You have sent me a Flanders m. INSULTS, 62
Margaret Thatcher Blimpish patriotism in the mode of M. KINNOCK, N, 9
M.…David Owen in drag POLITICIANS, 35
M.'s great strength WEST, R, 7
Margery See-saw, M. Daw NURSERY RHYMES, 50
marijuana I experimented with m. CLINTON, B, 4
mariner It is an ancient M. COLERIDGE, S, 24
mariners Ye M. of England NAVY, 3
mark an ever-fixed m. LOVE, 150; SHAKESPEARE, 370
If you would hit the m. AMBITION, 15; LONGFELLOW, H, 5
the Lord set a m. upon Cain BIBLE, 155; REVENGE, 4
the m.…of the beast BIBLE, 466; DEVIL, 8
markets the unreasoning laws of m. and fashion ART, 1
Marlboro our new name should be M. Country RUSSIA, 5
marmalade tangerine trees and m. skies LENNON, J, 7
marquis the manners of a M. CLASS, 16; GILBERT, W, 42
marred young man married…m. SHAKESPEARE, 22
marriage comedies are ended by a m. BYRON, 22; THEATRE, 6
hanging prevents a bad m. MARRIAGE, 137; SHAKESPEARE, 338
Happiness in m. AUSTEN, J, 21; MARRIAGE, 12
If a man avoids M. MARRIAGE, 89
In a happy m. it is the wife who provides the climate MARRIAGE, 37
In no country…are the m. laws so iniquitous as in England MARTINEAU, H, 4
It should be a very happy m. MARRIAGE, 159
It takes two to make a m. MARRIAGE, 130
love and m. LOVE AND MARRIAGE, 2
Love is moral even without…m. KEY, E, 5; LOVE AND MARRIAGE, 4
M.…a community…making in all two BIERCE, A, 8
M.…a woman's best investment MARRIAGE, 165
M. has many pains JOHNSON, S, 29; MARRIAGE, 90
m. in a registry office MARRIAGE, 7
M. is a great institition MARRIAGE, 164
M. is an insult MARRIAGE, 114
M. is a step so grave and decisive MARRIAGE, 147; STEVENSON, R, 23
M. is a wonderful invention MARRIAGE, 54
M. is…but a civil contract MARRIAGE, 131; SELDEN, J, 9
M. is…excluded from heaven BUTLER, S, 19; MARRIAGE, 40
M. is for women the commonest mode of livelihood MARRIAGE, 128
M. is like a cage MARRIAGE, 109; MONTAIGNE, M, 7
M. is like life in this MARRIAGE, 148; STEVENSON, R, 25
M. isn't a process of prolonging the life of love MARRIAGE, 172
M. is popular MARRIAGE, 139
M. is the only adventure open to the cowardly MARRIAGE, 163; VOLTAIRE, 26
M. may often be a stormy lake MARRIAGE, 117; PEACOCK, T, 5
m.…not a public conveyance MARRIAGE, 112
m. of true minds LOVE, 150; SHAKESPEARE, 370
m.…resembles a pair of shears MARRIAGE, 144; SMITH, S, 10
m. that denied me my career MARRIAGE, 43
M. without love MARRIAGE, 48
Private practice and m. SCIENCE, 11
rob a lady of her fortune by way of m. FIELDING, H, 12
The value of m. is…that children produce adults MARRIAGE, 61
they neither marry, nor are given in m. MARRIAGE, 152; SWIFT, J, 15
twenty years of m. make her…like a public building MARRIAGE, 168; WILDE, O, 56
Why should m. bring only tears UNFAITHFULNESS, 10
Women…care fifty times more for a m. than a ministry BAGEHOT, W, 5; WOMEN, 17
marriages M. are made in heaven MARRIAGE, 2; PROVERBS, 287
M. are not normally made CONTRACEPTION, 17
m. don't add two people together MARRIAGE, 75
Nearly all m.…are mistakes MARRIAGE, 162; TOLKIEN, J, 8
the early m. of silly children MARRIAGE, 105; MARTINEAU, H, 3
When widows exclaim loudly against second m. FIELDING, H, 3; MARRIAGE, 71
married a cross between a very severe virus and getting m. ACTORS, 30
A man in love is incomplete until…m. MARRIAGE, 78
A m. couple are well suited MARRIAGE, 125
a woman's business to get m. MARRIAGE, 140; SHAW, G, 23
Christian and you were m., for the first time RELIGION, 5
complacency and satisfaction…in…a new-m. couple LAMB, C, 3; MARRIAGE, 97
don't sleep with m. men ADULTERY, 4

Every night of her m. life she has been late for school THOMAS, D, 24
had she been m. well in early life WOLLSTONECRAFT, M, 1
He m. a woman to stop her getting away MARRIAGE, 99
he that is m. careth…how he may please his wife BIBLE, 31; MARRIAGE, 28
I am…thankful for not having m. MARRIAGE, 104; MARTINEAU, H, 1
I did not think I should live till I were m. MARRIAGE, 133
if ever we had been m. GAY, J, 4; MARRIAGE, 79
I have m. a wife BIBLE, 329
I m. beneath me MARRIAGE, 10
I'm getting m. in the morning MARRIAGE, 101
In m. life three is company MARRIAGE, 167; WILDE, O, 24
Living in England…like being m. to a stupid wife ENGLAND, 23
many forms of misconduct are more fatal to m. happiness ADULTERY, 9
m. a few years…can't help window shopping AYCKBOURN, A, 4
m.…like jumping into a hole in the ice MARRIAGE, 85
m. past redemption DRYDEN, J, 28; MARRIAGE, 68
m. six times shows a degree of optimism MARRIAGE, 103
m. to the only man north of the Tiber…untidier than I am MARRIAGE, 166; WHITEHORN, K, 2
M. women are kept women MARRIAGE, 143; SMITH, L, 4
Most m. couples…arrive at tolerable arrangements for living MARRIAGE, 36
My mother m. a very good man MARRIAGE, 138
No man is genuinely happy, m., who has to drink worse gin MENCKEN, H, 13
no taste when you m. me SHERIDAN, R, 10; TASTE, 9
Reader, I m. him BRONTE, C, 6
that Albert m. beneath him COWARD, N, 24; CRITICISM, 15
The best part of m. life is the fights WILDER, T, 2
the honest man who m. GOLDSMITH, O, 27; MARRIAGE, 82
what delight we m. people have to see PEPYS, S, 13
When m. people don't get on MARRIAGE, 107; MAUGHAM, W, 6
Writing is like getting m. MARRIAGE, 113; WRITING, 36
You are playing it like m. men TOSCANINI, A, 4
young man m.…marred SHAKESPEARE, 22

marries a young person, who…m. or dies, is sure to be kindly spoken of AUSTEN, J, 7; HUMAN NATURE, 2
doesn't much signify whom one m. MARRIAGE, 124
When a man m., dies MARRIAGE, 141; SHELLEY, P, 11

marry as easy to m. a rich woman as a poor woman MARRIAGE, 155; THACKERAY, W, 5
A woman…may m. whom she likes MARRIAGE, 156; THACKERAY, W, 9
better to m. than to burn BIBLE, 30; MARRIAGE, 27
Every woman should m. DISRAELI, B, 10; MARRIAGE, 63
friends chose to m. the people they did MARRIAGE, 175
if men and women m. those whom they do not love LOVE AND MARRIAGE, 6; MARTINEAU, H, 5
if only you could persuade him to m. CHRISTIANITY, 45; LEWIS, C, 4
I m.?…never bring myself to do it ARTISTS, 15
M. in haste MARRIAGE, 3; PROVERBS, 288
M. in Lent MARRIAGE, 4; PROVERBS, 289
M. in May MARRIAGE, 5; PROVERBS, 290
M. those who are single KORAN 6; MARRIAGE, 95
No man should m. MARRIAGE, 19
not to m. ladies in very high positions ROYALTY, 3
no woman should m. a teetotaller STEVENSON, R, 22
only way a woman can m. FEMINISM, 21
Then I can't m. you, my pretty maid NURSERY RHYMES, 70
Those who m. God…can become domesticated too GREENE, G, 1; RELIGION, 48
To m. a man out of pity is folly MARRIAGE, 9
We invite people like that to tea, but we don't m. them BETJEMAN, J, 3
when a man should m. BACON, F, 35; MARRIAGE, 15
When you see what some girls m. MARRIAGE, 127
while ye may, go m. HERRICK, R, 6; MARRIAGE, 88

marry'd M. in haste CONGREVE, W, 10; MARRIAGE, 51

marrying Jesus was not…m. sort MARRIAGE, 110

Mars seat of M. ENGLAND, 46; SHAKESPEARE, 297

marshal We may pick up a m. or two OFFICERS, 15; WELLINGTON, 6

Marston M., dropping it in the grate,/broke his pipe SPENDER, S, 1

Martini out of these wet clothes and into a dry M. ALCOHOL, 89

martyr a m. to music MUSIC, 63; THOMAS, D, 26
Now he will raise me to be a m. MARTYRDOM, 1
the soul of a m. with the intellect of an advocate BAGEHOT, W, 10; POLITICIANS, 43

martyrdom M. is the test FREEDOM, 28; JOHNSON, S, 131

martyrs I look on m. as mistakes MARTYRDOM, 4
The blood of the m. is the seed of the Church CHRISTIANITY, 61; TERTULLIAN, 1

marvel To m. at nothing is just about the one and only thing HAPPINESS, 9; HORACE, 19

Marx had M. been Groucho instead of Karl HUMOUR, 4
M. is a case in point GALBRAITH, J, 6; ILLNESS, 27
not even M. is more precious…than the truth TRUTH, 46; WEIL, S, 3

Marxian M. Socialism must always remain a portent KEYNES, J, 3; MARXISM, 6

Marxism M. is like a classical building that followed the Renaissance MARXISM, 8
took a grip on cowardly M. NAZISM, 3

Marxist I am not a M. MARXISM, 13
The M. analysis…like blaming Jesus Christ for the Inquisition MARXISM, 1
to banish…M. socialism MARXISM, 16; THATCHER, M, 30
wasn't a M. all the time MARXISM, 3

Mary Hail M., full of grace ANONYMOUS, 24; PRAYER, 1
I'm sitting on the stile, M. NOSTALGIA, 8
M. had a little lamb ANIMALS, 14
M., M., quite contrary GARDENS, 1; NURSERY RHYMES, 34
O M., go and call the cattle home AGRICULTURE, 4; KINGSLEY, C, 4

Maryland the hills of M. AMERICA, 41

masculine Fighting is essentially a m. idea WOMEN, 61
It makes me feel m. to tell you MASCULINITY, 1
partly from m. clannishness MEN, 13

Masefield M.'s sonnets?…Yes. Pure M. POETRY, 12

mask hate to compose a m. SIN, 24

mass I am a Catholic.…I go to M. every day BELLOC, H, 21; PREJUDICE, 1
Paris is worth a m. PARIS, 3
There is no idolatry in the M. CATHOLICISM, 8; JOHNSON, S, 77

masses Give me your tired…/Your huddled m. AMERICA, 26
I will back the m. against the classes CLASS, 18
The uprising of the m. REVOLUTION, 5

mast This m. new-shaved, through whom I rive the ropes CAMPBELL, R, 1

master A m. is dead MUSICIANS, 10
commerce between m. and slave is…exercise of…boisterous passions JEFFERSON, T, 3; SLAVERY, 6
Man is the m. of things MANKIND, 62
m., is it I BETRAYAL, 1; BIBLE, 423
m. of himself SELF-CONTROL, 6
m. of his soul, /Is servant to his bladder OLD AGE, 9
Not bound to swear allegiance to any m. FREEDOM, 25; HORACE, 13
One for the m. NURSERY RHYMES, 4
the M. Mistress of my passion LOVE, 149; SHAKESPEARE, 361
the m. of my fate RESPONSIBILITY, 8
the morals of a whore, and the manners of a dancing m. CRITICISM, 28; JOHNSON, S, 51
Thou are my m. and my author VIRGIL, 2

masterpiece Man is Heaven's m. MANKIND, 48
the m. of Nature EMERSON, R, 8; FRIENDS, 8
Who am I to tamper with a m. CONCEIT, 27; WILDE, O, 71

masters an ambitious man has as many m. as…may be useful AMBITION, 13; LA BRUYERE, J, 15
Assistant m.…liked little boys EDUCATION, 98; WAUGH, E, 30
Buy old m. BEAVERBROOK, M, 6; PAINTING, 2
By studying the m. EXPERTS, 1
good servants, but bad m. PASSION, 6
no man can serve two m. BIBLE, 369
people are the m. BURKE, E, 18; PUBLIC, 6
that the m. willingly concede to slaves CAMUS, A, 12; SLAVERY, 2
We are the m. at the moment POWER, 23

mastication EAT, v.i. the functions of m. FOOD, 16

masturbation M. is the thinking man's television SEX, 48
m. of war WAR, 132
M.: the primary sexual activity SEX, 116; SZASZ, T, 9
Such writing is a sort of mental m. KEATS, J, 2

mat caught my foot in the m. EMBARRASSMENT, 2

material Increase of m. comforts…moral growth MATERIALISM, 11
that which was most m. in the postscript BACON, F, 17; LETTER-WRITING, 3
materialistic Christianity is the most m. of all great religions CHRISTIANITY, 59
only really m. people…Europeans MATERIALISM, 19; MCCARTHY, M, 3
materialists books with which m. have pestered the world SOUL, 12; STERNE, L, 3
materials m. of city planning DESIGN, 4
maternity M. is…an unsocial experience MOTHERHOOD, 10
mates moves, and m., and slays DESTINY, 7; FITZGERALD, E, 13
mathematical Russell's beautiful m. mind RUSSELL, B, 2
mathematician m.…highest rung on the ladder MATHEMATICS, 6
the most revolutionary m. NEWTON, I, 3
mathematics All science requires m. MATHEMATICS, 1
Angling may be said to be…like the m. FISHING, 3; WALTON, I, 1
As far as the laws of m. refer to reality EINSTEIN, A, 12; MATHEMATICS, 4
How are you at M. MATHEMATICS, 12; MILLIGAN, S, 6
I like m. because it is *not* human MATHEMATICS, 21
Let no one ignorant of m. enter here MATHEMATICS, 15; PLATO, 6
M. may be defined as the subject MATHEMATICS, 18; RUSSELL, B, 13
m.…most inhuman of all human activities MATHEMATICS, 5
M. possesses not only truth, but supreme beauty MATHEMATICS, 17, 20; RUSSELL, B, 19
M.…sphere of complete abstraction MATHEMATICS, 25
Pure m. consists entirely of assertions MATHEMATICS, 19
quite lawful for a Catholic woman to avoid pregnancy by…m. CONTRACEPTION, 10; MENCKEN, H, 4
spirit of delight…in m. MATHEMATICS, 16
the theoreticians, whose language was m. BUCK, P, 5
maths m. we need to carry out science is pretty straightforward EDUCATION, 17
Matilda M. told such dreadful lies BELLOC, H, 6
You'll come a-waltzing, M. PLACES, 29
matinée Robert Houdin who…invented the…theater m. THEATRE, 15
mating Only in the m. season ANIMALISM, 6; MILLIGAN, S, 3
matriarchy In a m. men should be encouraged to take it easy WOMEN, 111
matrimony critical period in m. is breakfast-time HERBERT, A, 5; MARRIAGE, 87
Even if we take m. at its lowest STEVENSON, R, 13
it jumps from…love to m. AUSTEN, J, 20; WOMEN, 15
m., which I always thought a highly overrated performance MARRIAGE, 69
matter It is not much m. which we say MELBOURNE, 3; UNITY, 12
M.…a convenient formula PHILOSOPHY, 13; RUSSELL, B, 18
Mind over m. MIND, 32
proverb is much m. decorated SAYINGS, 4
We die – does it m. when DEATH, 170; TENNYSON, 71
Women represent…m. over mind SEXES, 36; WILDE, O, 50
mattering Art…can go on m. once it has stopped hurting ART, 5
matters Nothing m. very much BALFOUR, A, 6; TRIVIALITY, 1
Matthew M., Mark, Luke and John BLESSING, 1
maturing Do you think my mind is m. late AGE, 65; NASH, O, 7
maturity m. is only a short break in adolescence AGE, 40
Maud Come into the garden, M. INVITATIONS, 5; TENNYSON, 56
maunder m. and mumble CARLYLE, T, 19; PUBLIC, 8
mausoleums designing m. for his enemies HATE, 7
Max If M. gets to Heaven BUSINESS, 36; WELLS, H, 21
The Incomparable M. BEERBOHM, M, 1
maxim A new m. is often a brilliant error SAYINGS, 5
we have got /The M. Gun BELLOC, H, 16
May And after April, when M. follows BROWNING, R, 26; MONTHS, 6
as fresh as is the month of M. CHARACTER, 4; CHAUCER, G, 5
darling buds of M. COMPLIMENTS, 31; SHAKESPEARE, 360
Do spring M. flowers MONTHS, 12
got through the perils of winter till at least the seventh of M. TROLLOPE, A, 7
Here we come gathering nuts in M. ANONYMOUS, 37
I'm to be Queen o' the M. MERRYMAKING, 5; TENNYSON, 60
the merry month of M. ANONYMOUS, 85; MONTHS, 5
wish a snow in M. SHAKESPEARE, 197; SUITABILITY, 4
maybe I'll give you a definite m. GOLDWYN, S, 14
mayest if 'Thou m.' – it is also true that 'Thou m. not' STEINBECK, J, 1
maze Life is a m. CONNOLLY, C, 15; LIFE, 29
mazes The melting voice through m. running MILTON, J, 20; MUSIC, 42
MCC where M. ends and the Church of England begins CHURCH, 10; PRIESTLEY, J, 7
McCarthyism M. is Americanism POLITICS, 76
McDonald's America has brought us M. and horror movies RUSSIA, 24
McGregor Don't go into Mr M.'s garden ANIMALS, 21; CAUTION, 12
M.D.s Weighed down by B.A.s and M. EDUCATION, 6
me Besides Shakespeare and m., who do you think there is CONCEIT, 15; STEIN, G, 6
between m. and the sun REPARTEE, 2
My thought is m. SARTRE, J, 9; THINKING, 16
never talk about anything except m. TELEGRAMS, 13
What's in it for m. UNIVERSE, 10
Whether my Maker is ready for…meeting m. DEATH, 49; OLD AGE, 33
meal A m. without flesh FOOD, 1; PROVERBS, 46
meals Any two m. at a boarding-house FOOD, 43; LEACOCK, S, 7
mean Down these m. streets COURAGE, 7
He nothing common did or m. EXECUTION, 22; MARVELL, A, 4
He who meanly admires m. things is a Snob SNOBBERY, 9; THACKERAY, W, 1
it means just what I choose it to m. CARROLL, L, 32; MEANING, 3
She was a woman of m. understanding AUSTEN, J, 19; INSULTS, 8
'Then you should say what you m.,' the March Hare went on CARROLL, L, 9; MEANING, 1
whatever that may m. LOVE, 52
meaner A patronizing disposition…has its m. side CHARACTER, 8; ELIOT, G, 3
motives m. than your own BARRIE, J, 13; MOTIVE, 1
meanest the m.…deeds require spirit and talent INSENSITIVITY, 4
the m. of his creatures /Boasts two soul-sides BROWNING, R, 40; HYPOCRISY, 6
meaning birth had no m. LEE, L, 2
Even when poetry has a m. HOUSMAN, A, 6
Literature is simply language charged with m. POUND, E, 11
Nature has never put the fatal question as to the m. of their lives JUNG, C, 1; PURPOSE, 5
The least of things with a m. is worth more…than the greatest JUNG, C, 7; MEANING, 5
meannesses some m.…too mean even for man SEXES, 31; THACKERAY, W, 7
means Errors look so very ugly in persons of small m. ELIOT, G, 7; POVERTY AND WEALTH, 6
I shall have to die beyond my m. EXTRAVAGANCE, 5; WILDE, O, 63
live within our m. BORROWING, 6
m. just what I choose it to mean CARROLL, L, 32; MEANING, 3
Private M. is dead PUNS, 23
We are living beyond our m. CONSERVATION, 7; ECOLOGY, 6
measles Love is like the m. JEROME, J, 1; LOVE, 90
Love's like the m. JERROLD, D, 5; LOVE, 91
measure M. still for M. JUSTICE, 23; SHAKESPEARE, 236
Shrunk to this little m. DEATH, 146; SHAKESPEARE, 151
measured purpose of its own /And m. motion WORDSWORTH, W, 38
the field of the stars is so vast, but…man has m. it FRANCE, A, 5
measureless caverns m. to man COLERIDGE, S, 14; PLEASURE, 10
measurements their m. are being taken GOSSIP, 10
meat A man loves the m. in his youth SHAKESPEARE, 271
one man is appointed to buy the m. MONARCHY, 20; SELDEN, J, 1
One man's m. DIFFERENCE, 3; PROVERBS, 329
out of the eater came forth m. BIBLE, 294
Some hae m., and canna eat BURNS, R, 19; FOOD, 19
The public buys its opinions as it buys its m. BUTLER, S, 15; PUBLIC, 7
meats m. for the belly BIBLE, 27
mechanism body is a magnificently devised…m. HEALTH AND HEALTHY LIVING, 7
m. which you can take apart like a watch LITERATURE, 17
meddling He was m. too much in my private life PSYCHIATRY, 33; WILLIAMS, T, 8

media complexities of poetry are destroyed by the m. THEATRE, 3
The m.…a convention of spiritualists STOPPARD, T, 6
medical A m. revolution has extended the life of our elder citizens OLD AGE, 60
an unfair burden upon the m. profession ILLNESS, 63
if the elite of the m. world would be a little less clever THINKING, 6
m. attention – a dog licked me MEDICINE, 96
M. practice is not knitting and weaving MEDICINE, 58
the cost of m. care MEDICINE, 50
two objects of m. education EDUCATION, 62
We shall not refuse tobacco the credit of being…m. SMOKING, 32
You m. people will have more lives to answer for DOCTORS, 25
medicinal observation on the effects of m. substances on that MEDICINE, 47
medicine Among the arts, m.…must always hold the highest place MEDICINE, 17
art of m. consists of DISEASE, 40
A well chosen anthology is a complete dispensary of m. MEDICINE, 32
a young man entering upon the profession of m. MEDICINE, 11
By m. life may be prolonged MEDICINE, 90
Comedy is m. MEDICINE, 33
Common sense is in m. the master workman INTELLIGENCE, 6
do not draw any distinction between food and m. CHINA, 17; FOOD, 47
Everything's quite different in m. nowadays MEDICINE, 67
Experiment alone crowns the efforts of m. MEDICINE, 74
gets well in spite of the m. REMEDIES, 37
If you want to get out of m.…be students all your lives DOCTORS, 83
It is a distinct art to talk m. DOCTORS, 49
It is m. not scenery, for which a sick man REMEDIES, 50
It is unnecessary…in m. to be too clever MEDICINE, 46
I wasn't driven into m. by a social conscience MEDICINE, 66
M. absorbs the physician's whole being MEDICINE, 31
m. becomes a heroic art MEDICINE, 27
M. can never abdicate the obligation to care for the patient MEDICINE, 98
M. can only cure curable diseases MEDICINE, 2
M. cures the man who is fated not to die DRUGS, 1
M. for the dead is too late MEDICINE, 81
M. heals doubts as well as diseases MEDICINE, 60
M. is a conjectural art MEDICINE, 59
M. is an art MEDICINE, 77
M. is a natural art MEDICINE, 84
M. is a noble profession MEDICINE, 85
M. is an occupation for slaves MEDICINE, 86
M. is a science which hath been…more professed than laboured MEDICINE, 8
M. is as old as the human race MEDICINE, 35
M. is a strange mixture of speculation and action MEDICINE, 52
M. is for the patient MEDICINE, 65
M. is like a woman who changes with the fashions MEDICINE, 12
M. is not a lucrative profession MEDICINE, 56
M. is not only a science MEDICINE, 72
M. is not yet liberated from the medieval idea MEDICINE, 76
M. is the one place where all the show is stripped of the human drama DOCTORS, 36
M. makes people ill MEDICINE, 57
M. makes sick patients ILLNESS, 45
M. may be defined as the art…of keeping a patient quiet MEDICINE, 63
m. may be regarded generally as the knowledge of the loves and desires of the body MEDICINE, 78
m., professedly founded on observation, is as sensitive to outside influences MEDICINE, 43
M. sometimes snatches away health MEDICINE, 70
m. still falls somewhere between trout casting and spook writing MEDICINE, 36
M.…the only profession that labours incessantly MEDICINE, 16
M., to produce health, has to examine disease MEDICINE, 80
m. would be much easier ACADEMICS, 4
M. would be the ideal profession OCCUPATIONS, 7
men mistook magic for m. MEDICINE, 100
miserable have no other m. HOPE, 21; SHAKESPEARE, 232
Murder with jargon where his m. fails DOCTORS, 44
Nothing hinders a cure so much as frequent change of m. REMEDIES, 49
Patience is the best m. MEDICINE, 29
Poisons and m. are oftentimes the same substance REMEDIES, 38
Quacks in m.…know this, and act upon that knowledge GULLIBILITY, 3
Sleep is better than m. SLEEP, 2
Sleep's the only m. that gives ease SLEEP, 30
Such m. was…hopelessly unscientific MEDICINE, 54
Surely every m. is an innovation PROGRESS, 2
The aim of m. is surely not to make men virtuous MEDICINE, 64
The aim of m. is to prevent disease MEDICINE, 62
The art of m. is generally a question of time MEDICINE, 69
The Art of M. is in need really of reasoning MEDICINE, 21
The art of m. is my discovery MEDICINE, 68
The care of the human mind is the most noble branch of m. PSYCHIATRY, 25
The foundation of the study of M. MEDICINE, 34
The history of m. MEDICINE, 101
the ideal of m. is to eliminate the need of a physician MEDICINE, 62
The m. increases the disease ILLNESS, 68
the office of m. is but to tune this curious harp of man's body MEDICINE, 7
The only sure foundations of m. MEDICINE, 47
The poets did well to conjoin Music and M. in Apollo MEDICINE, 7
the qualities of a good teacher of m. MEDICINE, 5
the secrets of m. are revealed MEDICINE, 79
The technology of m. has outrun its sociology TECHNOLOGY, 15
The whole imposing edifice of modern m. MEDICINE, 23
they cannot teach students clinical m. MEDICINE, 99
This basis of m. is sympathy and the desire to help others MEDICINE, 75
to educate the masses not to take m. DOCTORS, 70
Tolstoy…wasn't taken in by…science and m. TOLSTOY, L, 4
Truth in m. is an unattainable goal MEDICINE, 82
two physicians cure you of the m. DOCTORS, 12
Visitors' footfalls are like m. REMEDIES, 3
we cannot instruct women as we do men in the science of m. MEDICINE, 22
when religion was strong…men mistook magic for m. SZASZ, T, 3
worthy of the most flourishing days of the m. man PSYCHOLOGY, 5
You give m. to a sick man REMEDIES, 8
mediciners defy the m. MODERATION, 3
medicines as doctors feel about m., or managers about plays BOOKS, 30
Many m., few cures REMEDIES, 2
M. are only fit for old people REMEDIES, 44
m. when well used restore health to the sick REMEDIES, 40
the best m. for an afflicted mind WORK, 20
The Lord hath created m. out of the earth REMEDIES, 12
The poisons are our principal m. REMEDIES, 28
the worthlessness of the most m. REMEDIES, 1
medieval disillusionments in the lives of the m. saints DECLINE, 10; SAKI, 13
mediocre A best-seller is the gilded tomb of a m. talent BOOKS, 45; SMITH, L, 1
m.…always at their best MEDIOCRITY, 5
more than magnificent…m. GOLDWYN, S, 20
Some men are born m. HELLER, J, 5; MEDIOCRITY, 6
Titles distinguish the m. SHAW, G, 28; TITLES, 11
Women want m. men MEDIOCRITY, 7
mediocrities sanity of any number of artistic m. BLAKE, W, 1
mediocrity It isn't evil…but m. MEDIOCRITY, 9
m.…always at its best MEDIOCRITY, 2
M. knows nothing higher DOYLE, A, 17; TALENT AND GENIUS, 2
supreme expression of the m. RUSSIA, 17; TROTSKY, L, 10
meditation M. is…both the means and the end THINKING, 9
Mediterranean All my wife has ever taken from the M. PHILISTINISM, 6
medium The m. is the message COMMUNICATION, 3
TV…is our latest m. MEDIA, 9; TELEVISION, 6
medley a m. of your hit INSULTS, 83

meek Blessed are the m. HUMILITY, 1
humble and m. are thirsting for blood HUMILITY, 8; ORTON, J, 3
m. and lowly in heart CHRISTIANITY, 26
m. and mild HUMILITY, 15
The m. do not inherit the earth HUMILITY, 6
The m.…not the mineral rights WEALTH, 23
the m. shall inherit the Earth HUMILITY, 12
Wisdom has taught us to be calm and m. REVENGE, 11
meet M. on the stairs PROVERBS, 291; SUPERSTITION, 2
never the twain shall m. KIPLING, R, 4; OPPOSITES, 4
The only way for writers to m. CONNOLLY, C, 14; WRITERS, 9
Two may talk…yet never really m. FRIENDSHIP, 14
We only part to m. again FAITHFULNESS, 4; GAY, J, 12
When shall we three m. again SHAKESPEARE, 202
meeting as if I was a public m. POLITICIANS, 127; VICTORIA, 9
life's been a m. BUREAUCRACY, 8; THOMAS, G, 2
this m. is drunk DICKENS, C, 49; DRUNKENNESS, 14
megalomaniac m. differs from the narcissist RUSSELL, B, 8
m.…seeks to be feared POWER, 22; RUSSELL, B, 8
megalomaniacs short ill-tempered m. ACTORS, 1
megaphone M. diplomacy DIPLOMACY, 16
melancholia little about m. that he didn't know TENNYSON, 1
melancholy a pleasing fit of m. MELANCHOLY, 9; MILTON, J, 10
hell upon earth…in a m. man's heart MELANCHOLY, 3
M. has her sovran shrine KEATS, J, 34; MELANCHOLY, 7
Most musical, most m. MILTON, J, 13
Solitude and m. CARTER, A, 4
so sweet as M. MELANCHOLY, 2
Melba Dame Nellie M. PATRIOTISM, 19
mellows A tart temper never m. with age CHARACTER, 12
melodies Heard m. are sweet KEATS, J, 28; MUSIC, 33
melody m. imposes continuity upon the disjointed MUSIC, 41
The heart of the m. MUSIC, 16
the m. of our sweet isle ENGLISH, 15
melt crown o' the earth doth m. SHAKESPEARE, 37
melting the races of Europe are m. AMERICA, 47
melting-pot America is…the great M. AMERICA, 47
member the tongue is a little m. SPEECH, 6
même *plus c'est la m. chose* CONSTANCY, 3
memorandum A m. is written ACHESON, D, 7; BUREAUCRACY, 1
memorial executed a m. longer lasting than bronze HORACE, 39; MEMORIALS, 8
some there be, which have no m. BIBLE, 92; MEMORIALS, 4
memories M. are hunting horns MEMORY, 1
M. are like mulligatawny soup MEMORY, 29
the burden of one's m. OLD AGE, 69
The nice thing about having m. MEMORY, 28
memory Everyone complains of his m. MEMORY, 17; ROCHEFOUCAULD, 13
Fond M. brings the light /Of other days MOORE, T, 7; NOSTALGIA, 17
For my name and m., I leave it to…the next ages BACON, F, 68; REPUTATION, 1
His m. is going JOHNSON, S, 143; OLD AGE, 58
How sweet their m. still COWPER, W, 14; NOSTALGIA, 7
Illiterate him…from your m. MALAPROPISMS, 4; SHERIDAN, R, 5
I would rather be a brilliant m. than a curiosity RENUNCIATION, 2
m. is a painter MEMORY, 14
Music…/Vibrates in the m. SHELLEY, P, 25
O m., hope, love of finished years NOSTALGIA, 22; ROSSETTI, C, 1
Time whereof the m. of man BLACKSTONE, W, 3; MEMORY, 3
Unless a man feels he has a good enough m. LYING, 15; MONTAIGNE, M, 3
What a strange thing is m., and hope MEMORY, 14
men all m. and women are created equal EQUALITY, 36
all m. are created equal HUMAN RIGHTS, 3
All m. are liars PSALMS, 66
All m. are rapists MARRIAGE, 76
all m. have one entrance into life BIBLE, 520; BIRTH, 4
all m. would be tyrants DEFOE, D, 2; TYRANNY, 4
As m. draw near the common goal OLD AGE, 9
Christ called as his Apostles only m. MEN, 8; SEXES, 17
depict m. as they ought to be THEATRE, 13
don't sleep with married m. ADULTERY, 4
England…purgatory of m. ENGLAND, 22
fishers of m. BIBLE, 359; CHRISTIANITY, 25
For m. may come TENNYSON, 6
give place to better m. CROMWELL, O, 7; DISMISSAL, 4
great city…has the greatest m. and women WHITMAN, W, 12
Great m. are almost always bad m. POWER, 3
great m. have not commonly been great scholars GREATNESS, 8
happy breed of m. ENGLAND, 46; SHAKESPEARE, 297
honour all m. BIBLE, 441
how much m. hate them FEMINISM, 12
I don't think m. and women were meant to live together SEXES, 12
It brings m. together in crowds and mobs in bar-rooms SOCIETY, 23; THOREAU, H, 7
It is m. who face the biggest problems MEN, 3
It's not the m. in my life that count SEX, 127
Many m. would take the death-sentence LAWRENCE, T, 6; LIFE AND DEATH, 23
m. about me that are fat MISTRUST, 10; SHAKESPEARE, 146
m. and sea interpenetrate CONRAD, J, 9; ENGLAND, 16
M. are but children of a larger growth AGE, 35; DRYDEN, J, 18
M. are men, but Man is a woman MANKIND, 19
M. are… more careful of the breed of their horses and dogs FAMILY, 47
M. are not hanged for stealing horses HALIFAX, 1
M. are we, and must grieve REGRET, 29; WORDSWORTH, W, 62
m.…capable of every wickedness CONRAD, J, 7; EVIL, 9
M. come of age at sixty AGE, 90
m. devote the greater part of their lives LA BRUYERE, J, 2; MANKIND, 34
m. everywhere could be free FREEDOM, 33; LINCOLN, A, 8
M. fear death BACON, F, 18; DEATH, 29
M. have broad and large chests SEXES, 20
M. have never been good GOOD, 1
M. of few words are the best men BREVITY, 9; SHAKESPEARE, 133
m. represent…mind over morals SEXES, 36; WILDE, O, 50
m.'s attitude to women BRITTAIN, V, 2
M.'s natures are alike CONFUCIUS, 3; HABIT, 4
M. their rights and nothing more FEMINISM, 3
m. think all m. mortal ARROGANCE, 11; YOUNG, E, 3
M. will always be mad MADNESS, 46; VOLTAIRE, 29
M. will confess HUMOUR, 10
Most m. admire /Virtue MILTON, J, 53; VIRTUE, 20
O! m. with sisters dear HOOD, T, 11; WOMEN, 66
Our Lord chose m. SEXES, 37
power over m. WOLLSTONECRAFT, M, 4
rich m. rule the law GOLDSMITH, O, 24; LAW, 20
schemes o' mice an' m. BURNS, R, 22; DISAPPOINTMENT, 2
Science seldom renders m. amiable SCIENCE, 4
So many m., so many opinions OPINIONS, 10; TERENCE, 4
Such m. are dangerous MISTRUST, 10; SHAKESPEARE, 146
that all m. and women are created equal FEMINISM, 34
That all m. are equal EQUALITY, 14; HUXLEY, A, 30
the hearts of M. should seek beyond the world TOLKIEN, J, 7
The many m., so beautiful COLERIDGE, S, 32; GUILT, 6
The mass of m. lead lives DESPAIR, 9; THOREAU, H, 9
the m. who borrow, and the m. who lend LAMB, C, 10
the only advantage women have over m.…they can cry RHYS, J, 2; SEXES, 25
the race of m. is almost extinct in Europe LAWRENCE, D, 27; MEN, 10
the tongues of m. and of angels BIBLE, 38; CHARITY, 7
The War between M. and Women SEXES, 32; THURBER, J, 14
those m. have their price CORRUPTION, 16; WALPOLE, R, 3
tide in the affairs of m. OPPORTUNITY, 19; SHAKESPEARE, 161
To famous m. all the earth is a sepulchre FAME, 32
to form Christian m. EDUCATION, 8
to have power over m. FEMINISM, 40
We are the hollow m. ELIOT, T, 9; INSIGNIFICANCE, 2
we cannot instruct women as we do m. in the science of medicine MEDICINE, 22
We live under a government of m. and…newspapers GOVERNMENT, 32; JOURNALISM, 29
when m. and mountains meet BLAKE, W, 14; GREATNESS, 4
Why are women…so much more interesting to m. SEXES, 38; WOOLF, V, 13
Women…are either better or worse than m. LA BRUYERE, J, 7; WOMEN, 74
Women had always fought for m. PANKHURST, E, 4
Women have smaller brains than m. SEXES, 24
menace Foreigners fooling about in others' civil wars are a m. FOREIGNERS, 4
Nazi Germany had become a m. to all mankind NAZISM, 5
mend God won't, and we can't m. it CONFUSION, 6
If every man would m. a man MEDICINE, 4
mendacity clergyman whose mendicity is only equalled by their m. CLERGY, 13; INSULTS, 120

mended then all the world would be m. MEDICINE, 4
mental A m. stain can neither be blotted out PSYCHIATRY, 11
Christian Science explains all cause and effect as m. EDDY, M, 2; RELIGION, 36
Emancipate yourselves from m. slavery FREEDOM, 39
every 'm.' symptom is a veiled cry of anguish PSYCHIATRY, 30
now they create m. patients PSYCHIATRY, 29
philosophy ought to…unravel people's m. blocks PHILOSOPHY, 12; RAPHAEL, F, 2
Such writing is a sort of m. masturbation KEATS, J, 2
to infer or guess how the m. apparatus is constructed MIND, 9
mentally happiness of man that he be m. faithful INTEGRITY, 5
mentioning m. some woman whom he knew in the past JEALOUSY, 10
merci La belle Dame sans M. KEATS, J, 23; SUPERNATURAL, 10
mercies For his m. ay endure GOD, 39; MILTON, J, 55
merciful just and m. as Nero ELIZABETH I, 3
merciless a kind parent…or a m. step-mother NATURE, 27; PLINY THE ELDER, 3
mercury 'Twas a chilly day for Willie /When the m. went down ANONYMOUS, 51; HUMOUR, 37
Two minutes with Venus, two years with m. SEX, 86
mercy And that is M.'s door COWPER, W, 16
For M. has a human heart BLAKE, W, 44; MANKIND, 10
God ha' m. on such as we, /Baa! Yah! Bah KIPLING, R, 12
his m. endureth for ever PSALMS, 59
'La belle dame sans m.' KEATS, J, 13
m. and truth are met together PSALMS, 46
m. unto you…be multiplied BIBLE, 290
quality of m. is not strain'd SHAKESPEARE, 248
surely goodness and m. shall follow me PSALMS, 13
thy loving-kindness and m. shall follow me PSALMS, 11
To M., Pity, Peace, and Love BLAKE, W, 43; PRAYER, 8
merely I m. did his dictation INSPIRATION, 4
merit no damned m. in it MELBOURNE, 6; TITLES, 5
Satan exalted sat, by m. raised DEVIL, 13; MILTON, J, 39
To kill a man is to m. a woman KILLING, 5
meritocracy The Rise of the M. MERIT, 8
mermaid Choicer than the M. Tavern KEATS, J, 26
mermaids I have heard the m. singing ELIOT, T, 15; OLD AGE, 45
merry A m. monarch ROYALTY, 99
For the good are always the m. HAPPINESS, 33
For tonight we'll m., m. be ANONYMOUS, 12; DRUNKENNESS, 3
I am never m. when I hear sweet music MUSIC, 55; SHAKESPEARE, 252
I commended mirth…to eat…to drink, and to be m. BIBLE, 72; PLEASURE, 4
Old King Cole /Was a m. old soul NURSERY RHYMES, 38
the good are always the m. YEATS, W, 13
Merryman Doctor Diet, /Doctor Quiet and Doctor M. DOCTORS, 97
It's a song of a m. GILBERT, W, 45; LOVE, 79
Mersey quality of M. ENGLAND, 1
mess another fine m. ACCIDENTS, 5
message ask me to take a m. to Albert DISRAELI, B, 42
the electric m. came ILLNESS, 9
The medium is the m. COMMUNICATION, 3
Messiah He was the M. of the new age POLITICIANS, 117
messing m. about in boats BOATS, 7
Mesurier John Le M.…conked out on November 15th OBITUARIES, 6
met I m. a man who wasn't there NONSENSE, 25
We have m. too late INFLUENCE, 5; JOYCE, J, 14
metaphor all m. is poetry CHESTERTON, G, 11; LANGUAGE, 16
m.…most fertile power possessed by man SPEECH, 10
metaphysical a physical and m. impossibility CARLYLE, T, 3; POETS, 3
a sort of m. brothel for emotions SENTIMENTALITY, 3
metaphysics M. is the finding of bad reasons METAPHYSICS, 2
metaquizzical The great M. poet POETS, 21
meteorites The Academy would not accept the reality of m. SCIENCE, 1
method madness, yet there is m. in't MADNESS, 36; SHAKESPEARE, 83
Traditional scientific m. has always been SCIENCE, 72
You know my m. DOYLE, A, 4; TRIVIALITY, 6
Methuselah all the days of M. AGE, 16; BIBLE, 156
meticulous He was a m. housemaid CHAMBERLAIN, N, 3
metre Poetry is opposed to science…prose to m. COLERIDGE, S, 18; POETRY AND PROSE, 1
without…understanding what m. COLERIDGE, S, 44; POETS, 29
metrical difference between…prose and m. composition POETRY AND PROSE, 7; WORDSWORTH, W, 19
Mexico Poor M. AMERICA, 13
mice schemes o' m. an' men BURNS, R, 22; DISAPPOINTMENT, 2
Three blind m., see how they run NURSERY RHYMES, 63
Michael I'd like to be ripped off like George M.'s been EXPLOITATION, 4
Michelangelo If M. had been straight HOMOSEXUALITY, 30
Talking of M. ELIOT, T, 12; WOMEN, 53
Mickey Mouse I love M. more than any woman WOMEN, 45
mickle Many a m. makes a muckle PROVERBS, 281; THRIFT, 4
microbe The M. is so very small BELLOC, H, 17
microbes acquired a fear of m. FEAR, 1
There are more m. *per person* SCIENCE, 6
microscope It is only in the m. that our life looks so big LIFE, 81
mid-day go out in the m. sun COWARD, N, 12
middle a whole is that which has a beginning, a m., and an end ARISTOTLE, 4; PLAYS, 1
Bow, bow, ye lower m. classes CLASS, 17
I like a film to have a beginning, a m. and an end CINEMA, 12
In a man's m. years there is scarcely a part of the body AGE, 98
M. age is when your age starts to show AGE, 52
M. age is youth without its levity AGE, 30
no m. course between the throne and the scaffold MONARCHY, 9
One of the pleasures of m. age AGE, 70; YOUTH, 23
people who stay in the m. of the road BEVAN, A, 5
Senescence begins /And m. age ends OLD AGE, 76
the dead center of m. age AGE, 3
the ease…move into the m. class CLASS, 49
the right wing of the m. of the road POLITICIANS, 48
middle-aged a m. man…is half dead AGE, 29
British loathe the m. AGE, 92
middle class Our Eastern Empire…*made* the English m. SCOTT, P, 1
part of English m. education is devoted to the training of servants CLASS, 56; EDUCATION, 101
respectable, m.…lady AUDIENCES, 5
the healthy type that was essentially m. CLASS, 14; FITZGERALD, F, 10
middle classes Bow, bow, ye lower m. GILBERT, W, 16
Middle East complex problems that face the M. HOSTAGES, 11
Midland M., bound for Cricklewood BETJEMAN, J, 9; TRAVEL, 9
midnight chimes at m. MERRYMAKING, 3; SHAKESPEARE, 123
I stood on the bridge at m. LONGFELLOW, H, 4; TIME, 34
It came upon the m. clear CHRISTMAS, 20
M. brought on the dusky hour DAY, 12; MILTON, J, 48
m. never come DAMNATION, 3; MARLOWE, C, 4
Not to be abed after m. BED, 11; SHAKESPEARE, 339
Once upon a m. dreary SUPERNATURAL, 12
See her on the bridge at m. ANONYMOUS, 71; POVERTY AND WEALTH, 2
soft embalmer of the still m. KEATS, J, 47; SLEEP, 23
To cease upon the m. with no pain DEATH, 92; KEATS, J, 40
midst God is in the m. of her PSALMS, 27
In the m. of life we are in death BOOK OF COMMON PRAYER, 3
mid-stream best to swap horses in m. CHANGE, 16; LINCOLN, A, 16
midway M. along the path DANTE ALIGHIERI, 1
mid-winter In the bleak m. ROSSETTI, C, 3
In the bleak m. SEASONS, 18
might Fight the good fight with all thy m. CHRISTIANITY, 47
Other nations use 'force'; we Britons…use 'M.' WAUGH, E, 42
The majority has the m. IBSEN, H, 2
We m. have been REGRET, 10
might-have-been Look in my face; my name is M. DISAPPOINTMENT, 7; ROSSETTI, D, 3
mightier pen is m. than the sword WRITING, 7
mighty Another m. empire overthrown DEFEAT, 18; WORDSWORTH, W, 52
How are the m. fallen BIBLE, 483; MOURNING, 2
Napoleon – m. somnambulist of a vanished dream NAPOLEON I, 3
put down the m. BIBLE, 310
share in the good fortunes of the m. BRECHT, B, 1

the weak things of the world to confound the...m. WISDOM AND FOOLISHNESS, 3
migraine nor m. by a tiara WEALTH, 41
mike I'm being amplified by the m. CHESTERTON, G, 47
Milan he wants M., and so do I AGREEMENT, 1
miles m. to go before I sleep FROST, R, 8; TRAVEL, 17
militant I am an optimist, unrepentant and m. OPTIMISM, 38; USTINOV, P, 3
militarism m....is one of the chief bulwarks of capitalism CAPITALISM, 9
military The chief attraction of m. service ARMY, 4; TOLSTOY, L, 9
there have always been gays in the m. HOMOSEXUALITY, 6
milk a kid in his mother's m. BIBLE, 118
a land flowing with m. and honey BIBLE, 106
as when you find a trout in the m. PROOF, 6; THOREAU, H, 6
drunk the m. of Paradise CAUTION, 9; COLERIDGE, S, 17
Gin was mother's m. ALCOHOL, 74; SHAW, G, 38
putting m. into babies CHILDREN, 24; CHURCHILL, W, 62
reform for me will be when the m. isn't sour RUSSIA, 1
too full o' th' m. of human kindness KINDNESS, 11; SHAKESPEARE, 207
milksop He is the bully...ready to twist the m.'s arm HEMINGWAY, E, 1
Mill John Stuart M. /By a mighty effort of will ECONOMICS, 3
miller There was a jolly m. HAPPINESS, 5
Millie My dog M. BUSH, G, 16
million man who has a m. dollars WEALTH, 7
million m. spermatozoa, /All of them alive HUXLEY, A, 18; SEX, 54
my neighbor...who is worth only half a m. LAST WORDS, 91; WEALTH, 48
millionaire He must be a m. WEALTH, 25
I am a m.. That is my religion WEALTH, 43
Who Wants to Be a M. PORTER, C, 10; WEALTH, 42
millions take m. off the caring services KINNOCK, N, 9; PATRIOTISM, 26
unrewarded m. without whom Statistics would be a bankrupt science SMITH, L, 6; STATISTICS, 9
mills m. of God grind slowly GOD, 35
millstone a m....hanged about his neck BIBLE, 400; CHILDREN, 18
Milton Malt does more than M. can ALCOHOL, 40; HOUSMAN, A, 17
M., Madam, was a genius JOHNSON, S, 150; POETS, 44
M.! thou shouldst be living at this hour DECLINE, 16; WORDSWORTH, W, 56
mute inglorious M. GRAY, T, 6
the faith and morals hold /Which M. held FREEDOM, 63; WORDSWORTH, W, 55
the making up of a Shakespeare or a M. COLERIDGE, S, 47; WRITERS, 6
mimsy All m. were the borogoves CARROLL, L, 23; NONSENSE, 7
min' never brought to m. BURNS, R, 4; FRIENDSHIP, 12
mince dined on m., and slices of quince FOOD, 44; LEAR, E, 9
mind A fat paunch never bred a subtle m. OBESITY, 2
After all, a doctor is just to put your m. at rest DOCTORS, 77
A good critic...narrates the adventures of his m. CRITICS, 5; FRANCE, A, 7
an exaggerated stress on not changing one's m. DECISION, 3; MAUGHAM, W, 11
Another great Advantage...that it tends to the Improvement of the M. INTELLECT, 6
an unseemly exposure of the m. HAZLITT, W, 17; NASTINESS, 3
A physician is...a consoler of the m. DOCTORS, 14
A short neck denotes a good m. SPARK, M, 2
A sick m. cannot endure any harshness MIND, 24
a sound m. in a sound body HEALTH AND HEALTHY LIVING, 12
At 83 Shaw's m. MIND, 35
Beauty in things exists in the m. which contemplates them BEAUTY, 26; HUME, D, 4
Body and m....do not always agree to die together OLD AGE, 40
Canst thou not minister to a m. diseas'd MADNESS, 39
change their clime, not their frame of m. TRAVEL, 22
clear your *m.* of cant JOHNSON, S, 146; REASON, 6
Do you think my m. is maturing late AGE, 65; NASH, O, 7
Drama never changed anybody's m. THEATRE, 11
Europe is a state of m. EUROPE, 8
fear clawed at my m. and body FRANK, A, 9
forgotten, as a dead man out of m. PSALMS, 20
her long struggle between m. and body ILLNESS, 51
his m. is in perfect tranquillity VOLTAIRE, 1
If it is for m. that we are seaching the brain MIND, 30
it is grief that develops the powers of the m. MIND, 27
it's all in the m. ILLNESS, 70
making things plain...best means of clearing...one's own m. EDUCATION, 46; HUXLEY, T, 7
man's unconquerable m. WORDSWORTH, W, 63
Many ideas grow better when transplanted into another m. IDEAS, 4
men represent...m. over morals SEXES, 36; WILDE, O, 50
M. is ever the ruler of the universe MIND, 26
M. over matter MIND, 32
m. that makes the body rich APPEARANCES, 37; SHAKESPEARE, 322
M. your own business PROVERBS, 292
natural course of the human m. is...from credulity to scepticism MIND, 14
never to ransack any m. but his own IMITATION, 5
No m. is thoroughly well organized COLERIDGE, S, 42; HUMOUR, 11
not to have a m. is very wasteful QUAYLE, D, 4
only inequalities that matter begin in the m. DIFFERENCE, 8
our love...of the m. does not make us soft RESULTS, 4
prodigious quantity of m. INDECISION, 5; TWAIN, M, 9
Reading is to the m. READING, 15
Russell's beautiful mathematical m. RUSSELL, B, 2
So long as the body is affected through the m. FAITH, 16
someone whose m. watches itself CAMUS, A, 11
That's the classical m. at work MIND, 25
the best medicines for an afflicted m. WORK, 20
The care of the human m. is the most noble branch of medicine PSYCHIATRY, 25
The conscious m. may be compared to a fountain MIND, 8
The highest function of *m.* MIND, 18
the inquisitive m. can...receive no answer PHILOSOPHY, 6
The m. can also be an erogenous zone MIND, 34; SEX, 125
The m....Can make a Heaven of Hell MIND, 21
The m. has great influence over the body MIND, 22
The m. is an iceberg MIND, 7
The m. is its own place MILTON, J, 33; MIND, 21
The m. like a sick body can be healed MIND, 20
The m. longs for certainty CERTAINTY, 2
the m. must sweat a poison MIND, 19
the most abhorrent is body without m. MIND, 15
The pendulum of the m. oscillates between sense and nonsense JUNG, C, 2; MIND, 16
the prison of our m. MIND, 31
The psychiatrist is the obstetrician of the m. PSYCHIATRY, 2
There are innumerable questions to which the inquisitive m. can...receive no answer JOHNSON, S, 127
There is in the British Museum an enormous m. MUSEUMS, 3; WOOLF, V, 9
The remarkable thing about the human m. MIND, 10
The tendency of the casual m. GENERALIZATIONS, 4
'Tis education forms the common m. EDUCATION, 74; POPE, A, 40
to change your m. ADAPTABILITY, 1; MARCUS AURELIUS ANTONINUS, 11
To know the *m.* of a woman LAWRENCE, D, 45; LOVE, 102
true genius is a m. of large general powers GENIUS, 7; JOHNSON, S, 20
unless your m. is in a splint DISABILITY, 4
we consider as nothing the rape of the human m. MIND, 11
Women represent...matter over m. SEXES, 36; WILDE, O, 50
You should pray for a healthy m. in a healthy body MIND, 17
minded If everybody m. their own business CURIOSITY, 4
mindful what is man, that thou art m. of him PSALMS, 3
minds All things can corrupt perverted m. CORRUPTION, 10; OVID, 7
great m. in the commonplace MIND, 12
Great m. think alike PROVERBS, 181; SIMILARITY, 2
Little m. are interested in the extraordinary MIND, 12; TRIVIALITY, 11
many open m. should be closed for repairs MIND, 2
marriage of true m. LOVE, 150; SHAKESPEARE, 370
M. are not ever craving BOOKS, 17
M. like beds always made up INFLEXIBILITY, 4
M. like bodies...fall into a pimpled, ill-conditioned state MIND, 6
m. so impatient of inferiority JOHNSON, S, 23
Old age puts more wrinkles in our m. than on our faces OLD AGE, 72
Our m. are lazier than our bodies MIND, 28

Strongest m. /...the noisy world /Hears least MIND, 36; WORDSWORTH, W, 4
Superstition is the religion of feeble m. BURKE, E, 12; SUPERSTITION, 8
the hobgoblin of little m. CONSTANCY, 1; EMERSON, R, 15
To be alone is the fate of all great m. SCHOPENHAUER, A, 1
to lead ignorant and prejudic'd m. LEARNING, 11
well-developed bodies, fairly developed m. EDUCATION, 32; FORSTER, E, 3
When people will not weed their own m. MIND, 33; WALPOLE, H, 8
miner Dwelt a m., Forty-niner, /And his daughter, Clementine MOURNING, 7
mineral animal or vegetable or m. CARROLL, L, 35
miners it is only because m. sweat their guts out ORWELL, G, 23; SUPERIORITY, 14
the Vatican, the Treasury and the m. BALDWIN, S, 12; DIPLOMACY, 4
mingled Like kindred drops, been m. COWPER, W, 28; MOUNTAINS, 1
minister the Prime M. has to be a butcher POLITICIANS, 57
ministering A m. angel thou COMFORT, 3
ministers I don't mind how much my m. talk THATCHER, M, 38
King of England changes his m. ROYALTY, 67
my actions are my m.' CHARLES II, 3
ministries *The Times* has made many m. BAGEHOT, W, 1; NEWSPAPERS, 2
ministry Women...care...more for a marriage than a m. BAGEHOT, W, 5; WOMEN, 17
minorities M....are almost always in the right MINORITY, 3; SMITH, S, 13
we are all m. now POLITICS, 109
minority not enough people to make a m. MINORITY, 1
The m. is always right IBSEN, H, 2; MAJORITY, 5
minstrel A wandering m. I GILBERT, W, 24; SINGERS, 2
Ethereal m. WORDSWORTH, W, 74
The M. Boy MOORE, T, 3; WAR, 113
minute m. hand of history JOURNALISM, 22
M. Particulars BLAKE, W, 16; GOOD, 2
not a m. on the day STRIKES, 3
sucker born every m. GULLIBILITY, 1
To a philosopher no circumstance...is too m. GOLDSMITH, O, 5; PHILOSOPHERS, 3
minutes at the rate of sixty m. an hour LEWIS, C, 5; TIME, 32
some of them are about ten m. long DYLAN, B, 15
take care of the m. CHESTERFIELD, P, 11; TIME, 17
Yes, about ten m. SERMONS, 4; WELLINGTON, 20
miracle A m. is an event which creates faith FAITH, 28
a m. of rare device COLERIDGE, S, 15; PLEASURE, 11
man prays...for a m. PRAYER, 28; TURGENEV, I, 4
m. cannot fix INSULTS, 138
quiet m. of a normal life CLINTON, B, 7
miracles before we *know* he is a saint, there will have to be m. GREENE, G, 8; PROOF, 4
The Christian religion not only was at first attended with m. HUME, D, 3
There are as many m. RELIGION, 58
mirror A novel is a m. NOVELS, 16
Art is not a m....but a hammer ART, 22
Look not in my eyes, for fear /They m. true the sight I see HOUSMAN, A, 9; LOVE, 88
When a man confronts catastrophe...a woman looks in her m. SEXES, 33
mirrors M. and fatherhood are abominable UNIVERSE, 2
M. are the windows of the devil APPEARANCES, 18
M. should think longer APPEARANCE, 18; THINKING, 3
My Dear One is mine as m. are lonely AUDEN, W, 24
Never believe in m. or newspapers NEWSPAPERS, 12
mirth I commended m....to eat...to drink, and to be merry BIBLE, 72
I love such m. as does not make friends ashamed MERRYMAKING, 6; WALTON, I, 5
to fence against the infirmities of ill health...by m. LAUGHTER, 12
misbeliever You call me m., cut-throat dog SHAKESPEARE, 242
miscarriage success and m. are empty sounds DISILLUSION, 4; JOHNSON, S, 7
miscast George Bernard Shaw is sadly m. CRITICISM, 59
mischief If you want to make m....papers BEAVERBROOK, M, 3; JOURNALISM, 6
Satan finds...m..../For idle hands IDLENESS, 13; WATTS, I, 1
thou little knowest the m. done NEWTON, I, 6
To mourn a m. that is past REGRET, 21; SHAKESPEARE, 278
mischievous what a m. devil Love is BUTLER, S, 14; LOVE, 49
misconduct many forms of m. are more fatal to married happiness ADULTERY, 9
misdeeds put out all my m. PSALMS, 31
miserable m. have no other medicine HOPE, 21; SHAKESPEARE, 232
poring over m. books TENNYSON, 53
The secret of being m. is to have leisure SHAW, G, 35; SORROW, 31
two people m. instead of four CARLYLE, T, 1
miserie y-fallen out of heigh degree. Into m. CHAUCER, G, 15; MISFORTUNE, 7
miseries all the maladies and m. CARLYLE, T, 31; WORK, 7
makes men's m. of alarming brevity LONGEVITY, 6
misery certain amount of m....to distribute as fairly as he can TAXATION, 8
drama shows people dealing nobly with their m. SUFFERING, 3
greatest m. is a battle gained VICTORY, 29; WELLINGTON, 8
he /Who finds himself, loses his m. ARNOLD, M, 39; SELF-KNOWLEDGE, 1
Let other pens dwell on guilt and m. AUSTEN, J, 13; OPTIMISM, 14
Man hands on m. to man CHILDREN, 46; HUMAN CONDITION, 15
M. acquaints a man with strange bedfellows SHAKESPEARE, 325
Thou art so full of m. TENNYSON, 79
misfortune In the m. of our best friends ROCHEFOUCAULD, 14
m. of an old man AGE, 25
next greatest m. to losing a battle VICTORY, 28; WELLINGTON, 12
the most unhappy kind of m. HAPPINESS, 7
worst m. was his birth POLITICIANS, 63
misfortunes any man...who could not bear another's m. MISFORTUNE, 15; POPE, A, 57
a share in their m. INJUSTICE, 3
history...a tableau of crimes and m. HISTORY, 35; VOLTAIRE, 20
history...is...the register of the...m. of mankind GIBBON, E, 8; HISTORY, 16
if a man talks of his m. JOHNSON, S, 135; MISFORTUNE, 13
strong enough to bear the m. of others MISFORTUNE, 16; ROCHEFOUCAULD, 2
The m. of poverty POVERTY, 25
the real m. and pains of others BURKE, E, 6
misguided We have guided missiles and m. men WAR, 92
mislead One to m. the public, another to m. the Cabinet GOVERNMENT, 6
misleading Though analogy is often m. ANALOGY, 1; BUTLER, S, 17
misquotation M. is the pride and privilege of the learned MISQUOTATIONS, 2
misquotations M. are...never misquoted MISQUOTATIONS, 1
miss A m. is as good FAILURE, 1; PROVERBS, 47
to m. the one before it CHESTERTON, G, 49; TRAVEL, 13
missed who never would be m. GILBERT, W, 26; PUNISHMENT, 13
missiles We have guided m. and misguided men WAR, 92
mission A m. to explain PURPOSE, 4
missionaries eaten by m. DEATH, 165; SPOONER, W, 6
nice little m. share Jim Bakker's blessed sexual preferences AIDS, 11
missionary I would eat a m. CLERGY, 15
the last of the great m. superstars TERESA, 1
Mississippi Like the M., it just keeps rolling OPTIMISM, 24
Miss J. Hunter Dunn M., M. BETJEMAN, J, 12
Miss T whatever M. eats FOOD, 25
mist Cicero /And...Homer were /*Mad as the m. and snow* MADNESS, 48; YEATS, W, 20
The rolling m. came down DROWNING, 1; KINGSLEY, C, 5
Mistah M. Kurtz – he dead CONRAD, J, 3
mistake he who never made a m. never made a discovery MISTAKES, 19
Live all you can; it's a m. not to JAMES, H, 4; LIFE, 52
m....to put...creativity first DESIGN, 9
Woman was God's *second* m. NIETZSCHE, F, 3; WOMEN, 95
mistaken think it possible you may be m. CROMWELL, O, 5
mistakes A doctor is...licensed to make grave m. DOCTORS, 60
a dreadful list of ghastly m. MISTAKES, 9
An expert...knows some of the worst m. that can be made EXPERTS, 3
Nearly all marriages...are m. MARRIAGE, 162; TOLKIEN, J, 8

The man who makes no m. MISTAKES, 13
Young men make great m. in life YOUTH, 17
you've made plenty of m. if you've lived your life properly REAGAN, R, 9
mistress a m., and only then a friend CHEKHOV, A, 11; FRIENDSHIP, 15
A m. should be like a…retreat SEX, 132
Art is a jealous m. ART, 10; EMERSON, R, 4
by pointing out to a man the faults of his m. IMPERFECTION, 10; PROUST, M, 3
marry your m.…create a job vacancy MARRIAGE, 81
Master M. of my passion LOVE, 149; SHAKESPEARE, 361
m. I am ashamed to call you ELIZABETH I, 5; TITLES, 2
whether I embrace your lordship's principles or your m. REPARTEE, 5
why and how I became…m. of the Earl of Craven SEX, 129
mistresses a better price than old m. BEAVERBROOK, M, 6; PAINTING, 2
No, I shall have m. MARRIAGE, 80
one wife and hardly any m. MARRIAGE, 129; SAKI, 14
Wives are young men's m. BACON, F, 34; MARRIAGE, 14
mistrust M. first impulses FIRST IMPRESSIONS, 4; TALLEYRAND, 7
mists Season of m. KEATS, J, 45; SEASONS, 12
misunderstood To be great is to be m. EMERSON, R, 16; GREATNESS, 7
Mitty Walter M., the undefeated EXECUTION, 38; THURBER, J, 11
mix I m. them with my brains PAINTING, 10
mixed a m. infant BEHAN, B, 4; CHILDREN, 9
not to look like a m. grill APPEARANCE, 20; COWARD, N, 10
mixer water…a m. ALCOHOL, 68
mob do what the m. do DICKENS, C, 44; MAJORITY, 3
Our supreme governors, the m. PUBLIC, 21; WALPOLE, H, 3
mobilized m. the English language WORDS, 21
mobs It brings men together in crowds and m. in bar-rooms SOCIETY, 23; THOREAU, H, 7
mock Let not Ambition m. GRAY, T, 2; POVERTY, 16
M. on, m. on, Voltaire, Rousseau BLAKE, W, 34; FUTILITY, 5
mockery death itself must be…a m. DEATH, 158; SHELLEY, P, 23
m. to allow women to baptise RELIGION, 23
mocks heaven m. itself DECEPTION, 9
mode Fancy is…a m. of memory COLERIDGE, S, 6
model The idea that there is a m. Labour voter…is patronizing KINNOCK, N, 12; POLITICS, 63
very m. of a modern Major-General GILBERT, W, 38
models Rules and m. destroy genius and art HAZLITT, W, 23
moderation astonished at my own m. MODERATION, 6
M. in all things MODERATION, 1; PROVERBS, 293
m. in the pursuit of justice is no virtue EXCESS, 5
M. is a virtue only in those MODERATION, 8
still for m. and will govern by it MODERATION, 5
modern a m. poet's fate HOOD, T, 14
Imagination without skill gives us m. art ART, 34
invading her own privacy…first of the m. personalities BANKHEAD, T, 3
It is so stupid of m. civilization DEVIL, 11
not as closely in touch with m. life AGE, 49
The m. pantheist not only LAWRENCE, D, 21; PHOTOGRAPHY, 6
modern art Imagination without skill gives us m. STOPPARD, T, 1
modest and is m. about it ENGLISH, 4; TALENT, 1
modester People ought to be m. CARLYLE, T, 33; UNIVERSE, 4
modesty a woman…ought to lay aside…m. with her skirt MONTAIGNE, M, 4; SEX, 85
Enough for m. CLOTHES, 6
His m. amounts to deformity MODESTY, 1
I don't think that m. POLITICS, 49
I have often wished I had time to cultivate m. MODESTY, 9; SITWELL, E, 8
There is false m., but there is no false pride PRIDE, 10
where the Greeks had m., we have cant HYPOCRISY, 15; PEACOCK, T, 2
modifying m. your lyric content CENSORSHIP, 14
Mohamed M. wanted equality for women EQUALITY, 3
Mohammed If the mountain will not come to M. BACON, F, 14
moi *L'État c'est m.* LOUIS XIV, 4; MONARCHY, 17
mole Death is still working like a m. DEATH, 79; HERBERT, G, 5
Molly Tonight the American flag floats…or M. Stark sleeps a widow WAR, 165
moment a m. of time ELIZABETH I, 15; LAST WORDS, 29
A m. of time may make us unhappy for ever GAY, J, 1; SORROW, 11
A piece of each of us died at that m. ASSASSINATION, 6
Every m. one is born LIFE AND DEATH, 32; TENNYSON, 82
in a m. of time BIBLE, 319; DEVIL, 4
moments in life, you get m. AYCKBOURN, A, 6
Mona Lisa A lotta cats copy the M. IMITATION, 1
I have…several original M.s MILLIGAN, S, 2; PHOTOGRAPHY, 7
the portrait of his wife M. LEONARDO DA VINCI, 4
monarch make her husband a cuckold to make him a m. AMBITION, 25
m. of all I survey COWPER, W, 34; SOLITUDE, 5
Retirement, for a m., is not a good idea VICTORIA, 2
monarchy decide the fate of the m. FRENCH REVOLUTION, 6
Helm of this Imperial M. ROYALTY, 47
M. is a strong government BAGEHOT, W, 3; MONARCHY, 2
The m. is a labour-intensive industry MONARCHY, 27; WILSON, H, 5
The m.…oldest profession in the world ROYALTY, 40
The Sovereign has, under a constitutional m.…three rights BAGEHOT, W, 7; MONARCHY, 3
They that are discontented under *m.*, call it *tyranny* GOVERNMENT, 17; HOBBES, T, 6
tourists…take in the M.…with…the pigeons LONDON, 15
monastery bastards at the m. PINTER, H, 2
Monday is going to do on M. CHRISTIANITY, 64; HYPOCRISY, 24
M.'s child is fair of face NURSERY RHYMES, 35
Solomon Grundy, /Born on a M. HUMAN CONDITION, 19; NURSERY RHYMES, 53
monetarist One nanny…was a m. MACMILLAN, H, 9
money a blessing that m. cannot buy HEALTH AND HEALTHY LIVING, 16
a licence to print your own m. BUSINESS, 33
always try to rub up against m. MONEY, 41; RUNYON, D, 2
And when I am king…there shall be no m. LAWYERS, 10
a peer can make a bit of extra m. STATELY HOMES, 1
art…of draining m. SMITH, A, 3; TAXATION, 11
be not greedy to add m. to m. BIBLE, 516
Brigands demand your m. or your life BUTLER, S, 29; WOMEN, 31
Business…may bring m.…friendship hardly ever does AUSTEN, J, 9; MONEY, 6
choose people who offer us m. CORRUPTION, 6
descriptions of m. changing hands MONEY, 19
easiest way for your children to learn about m. MONEY, 52
except for large sums of m. RIDICULE, 2
France is a country where the m. falls apart FRANCE, 20
Good Samaritan…had m. as well MONEY, 51; THATCHER, M, 22
He that wants m., means, and content MONEY, 42; SHAKESPEARE, 52
I don't know how much m. I've got WEALTH, 31
If he didn't need the m. DOCTORS, 93
If possible honestly, if not, somehow, make m. MONEY, 26
If women didn't exist…m.…no meaning WOMEN, 99
If you can…count your m. you are not…rich man WEALTH, 24
innocently employed than in getting m. JOHNSON, S, 91; MONEY, 28
just got more m. than I need WEALTH, 46
Just what God would have done if he had the m. WEALTH, 50
killed a lot of men to have made so much m. MOLIERE, 5; WEALTH, 38
Lack of m. MONEY, 45
leaves m. to charity in his will BEQUESTS, 2
love of m. is the root of all evil BIBLE, 511; BUTLER, S, 6
m. answereth all things BIBLE, 76; MONEY, 10
M. can't buy friends MILLIGAN, S, 10; MONEY, 36
m. can't buy me love LENNON, J, 2; MONEY, 31
M. gives me pleasure BELLOC, H, 15; MONEY, 9
m. has something to do with life LARKIN, P, 1; MONEY, 30
M. is good for bribing yourself MONEY, 40
M. is like a sixth sense MAUGHAM, W, 13; MONEY, 35
M. is like manure MONEY, 37
M. is like muck BACON, F, 45; MONEY, 7
M., it turned out, was exactly like sex BALDWIN, J, 2; SEX, 14
M.…source of anxiety GALBRAITH, J, 7
no m. in rape warrants RAPE, 2
pleasant it is to have m. MONEY, 18
Put m. in thy purse MONEY, 44; SHAKESPEARE, 279
rock musicians make a bunch of m. and stick it up their noses DRUGS, 18
Socialism…age or a little m. will not cure SOCIALISM, 8
Some people's m. is merited MONEY, 38
spiritual snobbery…happy without m. MONEY, 16

It's just hard to get out of bed in the m. SPORT AND GAMES, 32
joy cometh in the m. PSALMS, 17
M. in the Bowl of Night DAY, 5; FITZGERALD, E, 2
Oh, what a beautiful m. DAY, 7
she has lived…the space of one m. TRANSIENCE, 18
straight on till m. TRAVEL, 7
that…turneth the shadow of death into the m. BIBLE, 18; GOD, 7
The m. after is the first day MACNEICE, L, 1
the m. cometh, and also the night BIBLE, 204
'Tis always m. somewhere BEGINNING, 12
Morocco We're M. bound LEXICOGRAPHY, 2; PUNS, 3
morphia have yourself squirted full of m. DEATH, 84
morrow take…no thought for the m. BIBLE, 371; WORRY, 9
mortal All men are m. MORTALITY, 1; PROVERBS, 35
Her last disorder m. DEATH, 73
I was not unaware that I had begotten a m. GOETHE, J, 10; MORTALITY, 8
men think all men m. ARROGANCE, 11; YOUNG, E, 3
'Remember that I too am m.' DOCTORS, 90
that great Leviathan, or rather…that *M. God* HOBBES, T, 5; STATE, 1
The doctor found…/Her last disorder m. DOCTORS, 50; GOLDSMITH, O, 9
we have been m. enemies ever since ENEMIES, 5
mortality kept watch o'er man's m. MORTALITY, 21; WORDSWORTH, W, 33
M., behold and fear BEAUMONT, F, 9; MORTALITY, 2
mortals a human giraffe, sniffing…at m. beneath his gaze DE GAULLE, C, 3
A novelist is, like all m. NABOKOV, V, 7; WRITERS, 19
We m. cross the ocean BROWNING, R, 9; HUMAN CONDITION, 5
what fools these m. be FOOLISHNESS, 20; SHAKESPEARE, 264
Moscow don't march on M. WAR, 112
Moses he saw his role as being that of M. LEADERSHIP, 6
there arose not a prophet…like unto M. BIBLE, 60; PROPHECY, 2
Moslems ask all M. to execute them CENSORSHIP, 8
most The M. may err as grossly DRYDEN, J, 12; PUBLIC, 12
mostest fustest with the m. MISQUOTATIONS, 16; WAR, 64
mote the m. that is in thy brother's eye BIBLE, 373
moth a m. fretting a garment PSALMS, 23
like a m., the simple maid GAY, J, 2; WOMEN, 59
The desire of the m. for the star HUMOUR, 45; JOYCE, J, 12
mother a friend can't take a m.'s place FRANK, A, 4
A m.! What are we worth really MOTHERHOOD, 13
And Her M. Came Too FAMILY, 44
as is the m., so is her daughter BIBLE, 125; FAMILY, 10
behold thy m. BIBLE, 270
Dead! and…never called me m. DEATH, 182
Don't tell my m. I'm in politics POLITICS, 4
English girl hates…her m. FAMILY, 54
Eve…the m. of all living BIBLE, 152
I am old enough to be – in fact am – your m. MILNE, A, 1
If poverty is the m. of crime, stupidity is its father CRIME, 6; LA BRUYERE, J, 11
image of the Jewish woman as a m. WOMAN'S ROLE, 11
I was born…because my m. needed a fourth at meals BIRTH, 12
I wished to be near my m. BIRTH, 16; WHISTLER, J, 18
Jerusalem…the m. of us all BIBLE, 133
lot of tranquillisers and my m. ACTORS, 29
May you be the m. of a bishop BEHAN, B, 11
most automated appliance in a household is the m. MOTHERHOOD, 8
M.…dead heart of the family GREER, G, 3; MOTHERHOOD, 7
M. is far too clever to understand PREJUDICE, 2 7; WOMAN'S ROLE, 6
M. love…is a highly respected and much publicised emotion WOMEN, 37
m. of battles WAR, 83
M. of the Free BRITAIN, 4
'My m., drunk or sober.' CHESTERTON, G, 8; PATRIOTISM, 8
My m. said it was simple to keep a man WOMEN, 63
No matter how old a m. is MOTHERHOOD, 11
the most intense love on the m.'s side FAMILY, 22
The m.-child relationship is paradoxical FAMILY, 22
the m. of parliaments ENGLAND, 10
the perfect couple…a m. and child MOTHERHOOD, 6
this war…not justify the sacrifice of a single m.'s son WAR, 126
watched a m. stroke her child's cheek MOTHERHOOD, 9
worse consequences than…a really affectionate m. FAMILY, 39
motherhood m. is the most important of all the professions MOTHERHOOD, 12
M. meant I have written four fewer books MOTHERHOOD, 4
The best thing that could happen to m. MOTHERHOOD, 1
wifehood and m. are but incidental relations WOMEN, 125
Womanliness means only m. MOTHERHOOD, 3
mother-in-law as the man said when his m. died FAMILY, 31; JEROME, J, 6
The sort of place everyone should send his m. FAMILY, 11; PLACES, 6
What a marvellous place to drop one's m. FAMILY, 21
mothers Come m. and fathers /Throughout the land DYLAN, B, 12
O! men with m. and wives HOOD, T, 11; WOMEN, 66
therefore he made m. WOMAN'S ROLE, 1
unfair not only to the m. and ancestors MEDICINE, 94
women become like their m. SEXES, 35; WILDE, O, 21
Women…the m. of all mischief MOTHERHOOD, 2
mothers-in-law Two m. FAMILY, 52
moths Maidens, like m., are ever caught by glare WEALTH, 15
motives m. meaner than your own BARRIE, J, 13; MOTIVE, 1
motorcycle Zen and the Art of M. Maintenance PHILOSOPHY, 10
motorists M.…were utterly irresponsible in their dealings with each other TRAVEL, 20
motors was good for General M. BUSINESS, 38
motto m. be:– Hunt BRONTE, C, 4
mould Anything green that grew out of the m. NATURE, 24
If you cannot m. yourself TOLERANCE, 4
Nature made him, and then broke the m. COMPLIMENTS, 1
There is…an instrument to m. the minds of the young CENSORSHIP, 10
mountain A m. in labour shouted so loud DISAPPOINTMENT, 5; LA FONTAINE, J, 6
hardly be a beast or a fool alone on a great m. SOLITUDE, 10
I don't…care if I never see another m. POETS, 47
If the m. will not come BACON, F, 14
Land of the m. and the flood SCOTLAND, 7; SCOTT, W, 9
never see another m. LAMB, C, 24; MOUNTAINS, 2
mountains all faith, so that I could remove m. BIBLE, 38; CHARITY, 7
England's m. green BLAKE, W, 33; ENGLAND, 7; FIGHT, 1
highest intellects, like the tops of m. INTELLECT, 9; MACAULAY, T, 12
if the Swiss had designed these m. MOUNTAINS, 4; SWITZERLAND, 4
M. interposed /Make enemies of nations COWPER, W, 28; MOUNTAINS, 1
m. look on Marathon BYRON, 27; EUROPE, 4
m. skipped like rams PSALMS, 63
M.…the beginning and the end of all natural scenery MOUNTAINS, 3; RUSKIN, J, 6
M. will heave in childbirth DISAPPOINTMENT, 4; HORACE, 6
Two voices…one is of the sea, /One of the m. FREEDOM, 64; WORDSWORTH, W, 64
when men and m. meet BLAKE, W, 14; GREATNESS, 4
mourn countless thousands m. BURNS, R, 14; CRUELTY, 2
it is chiefly our own deaths that we m. for FUNERALS, 3
To m. a mischief that is past REGRET, 21; SHAKESPEARE, 278
mourning I'm in m. for my life CHEKHOV, A, 7; MOURNING, 4
in m.…for the world MOURNING, 15; SITWELL, E, 6
tedium is the very basis of m. BOREDOM, 6; HUGO, V, 5
We met…Dr Hall in such very deep m. AUSTEN, J, 31; MOURNING, 1
What we call m. for our dead MOURNING, 6
with my m.…and new periwig APPEARANCE, 56; PEPYS, S, 15
mouse a silly little m. will be born DISAPPOINTMENT, 4; HORACE, 6
He bought a crooked cat, which caught a crooked m. NURSERY RHYMES, 56
leave room for the m. EXCESS, 8; SAKI, 22
she brought forth a m. DISAPPOINTMENT, 5; LA FONTAINE, J, 6
The m. ran up the clock NURSERY RHYMES, 15
mouse-trap If a man make a better m. EMERSON, R, 26; FAME, 11
moustache A kiss without a m. SARTRE, J, 15
a man outside with a big black m. APPEARANCE, 46; MARX, G, 10
Being kissed by a man who didn't wax his m. KIPLING, R, 27
his nicotine eggyellow weeping walrus Victorian m. APPEARANCE, 69; THOMAS, D, 27

mouth A politician is a statesman…with an open m. POLITICIANS, 27; STEVENSON, A, 2
butter wouldn't melt in her m. ACTORS, 24; INSULTS, 80
God be in my m., /And in my speaking ANONYMOUS, 20; GOD, 2
Keep your m. shut and your eyes open CAUTION, 6; PROVERBS, 241
need not look in your m. APPEARANCE, 3
out of the m. of…babes and sucklings PSALMS, 3
out of thine own m. will I judge thee BIBLE, 336
mouth-brothels Great restaurants are…nothing but m. FOOD, 62; RAPHAEL, F, 4
move But did thee feel the earth m. HEMINGWAY, E, 5; SEX, 50
in him we live, and m., and have our being BIBLE, 13; GOD, 6
I will m. the earth TECHNOLOGY, 2
The great affair is to m. STEVENSON, R, 7; TRAVEL, 42
movement I want to be a m. SOLITUDE, 12
We are the true peace m. PEACE, 21; THATCHER, M, 29
moves m., and mates, and slays DESTINY, 7; FITZGERALD, E, 13
Yet it m. ASTRONOMY, 3
movie This is a m., not a lifeboat EQUALITY, 37
movies M. for me are a heightened reality CINEMA, 23
Thanks to the m., gunfire has always sounded unreal CINEMA, 28; USTINOV, P, 1
moving In home-sickness you must keep m. HOMESICKNESS, 7
m. Moon went up the sky COLERIDGE, S, 33; MOON, 2
people under suspicion are better m. KAFKA, F, 4
The M. Finger writes DESTINY, 8; FITZGERALD, E, 14
Mozart The sonatas of M. are unique MUSIC, 53
when M. was my age AGE, 56
MPs The prospect of a lot /Of dull M. GILBERT, W, 20; POLITICIANS, 11
Mr Goldwyn M.…you are only interested in art SHAW, G, 47
Mrs Thatcher in favour of M. visit to the Falklands INSULTS, 99
M.…looking like Queen Victoria POLITICIANS, 121
much m.…said on both sides ADDISON, J, 13; OBJECTIVITY, 1
So little done, so m. to do LAST WORDS, 75; RHODES, C, 4
so m. owed by so many to so few CHURCHILL, W, 53; WORLD WAR II, 14
muchness Much of a m. MEDIOCRITY, 10
muck Money is like m. BACON, F, 45; MONEY, 7
sing 'em m. MELBA, N, 4; PLACES, 24
mud One sees the m., and one the stars OPTIMISM, 31
muddle a beginning, a m., and an end LARKIN, P, 5; NOVELS, 9
muddle-headed He's a m. fool CERVANTES, M, 19
muddy The hunter for aphorisms…has to fish in m. water SAYINGS, 2
Mudirs Their Zaptiehs and their M. VIOLENCE, 8
muesli Many children are suffering from m.-belt malnutrition FOOD, 50
Muffet Little Miss M. /Sat on a tuffet NURSERY RHYMES, 31
multiplied Entities should not be m. SIMPLICITY, 6
mercy unto you…be m. BIBLE, 290
multiply be fruitful and m. BIBLE, 142
multitude a m. of sins BIBLE, 220
long dresses…cover a m. of shins CLOTHES, 27; WEST, M, 10
The m. is always in the wrong PUBLIC, 18
this massed m. of silent witnesses to…war WAR, 71
multitudes I contain m. SELF, 27; WHITMAN, W, 10
mum M.'s the word SECRECY, 6
They fuck you up, your m. and dad FAMILY, 33; LARKIN, P, 4
mumble maunder and m. CARLYLE, T, 19; PUBLIC, 8
mundi *gloria m.* GLORY, 3
Munich Glory to God for M. WORLD WAR II, 38
murder Divorce? Never. But m. often MARRIAGE, 160
Every time we kiss he says 'M.!' LOVE, 107
love and m. will out CONGREVE, W, 4
Macbeth doth m. sleep SHAKESPEARE, 214
m. back into its rightful setting – in the home MURDER, 7
M. considered as one of the Fine Arts MURDER, 6
M.…had a mask like Castlereagh MURDER, 12; SHELLEY, P, 13
M., like talent, seems…to run in families MURDER, 9
M. most foul MURDER, 10; SHAKESPEARE, 78
m. shrieks out MURDER, 13; WEBSTER, J, 1
Never m. a man who is committing suicide SUICIDE, 40; WILSON, W, 3
Olivier had m. in his heart ACTORS, 18
So it was m. DEATH, 107; MARX, G, 7
Sooner m. an infant in its cradle BLAKE, W, 21; DESIRE, 3
murdered I m. my grandmother this morning ROOSEVELT, F, 3
murderer Kill a man, and you are a m. KILLING, 10
strong suspicions that Crippen London cellar m. TECHNOLOGY, 10
murderous at Yuletide men/are the more m. CHRISTMAS, 14; HILL, G, 5
murmur live m. of a summer's day ARNOLD, M, 35
murmuring m. of innumerable bees SEASONS, 23
Murray And the bonny Earl of M., /O he might hae been a king ANONYMOUS, 109
muscular His Christianity was m. CHRISTIANITY, 37; DISRAELI, B, 6
muse ego locks the m. INSPIRATION, 6
The M. prefers the liars POETRY, 74
To the Greeks the M. gave native wit CLASSICS, 4; HORACE, 8
With Donne, whose m. on dromedary trots DONNE, J, 1
mused Lancelot m. a little space BEAUTY, 46; TENNYSON, 47
museum the m. of this world LAWRENCE, D, 25; MASCULINITY, 2
museums more philosophical than…curators of the m. FRANCE, A, 4
mushroom a supramundane m. NUCLEAR WEAPONS, 13
Fame is sometimes like unto a…m. FAME, 14
to stuff a m. HOUSEWORK, 2
music A Dance to the M. of Time LIFE, 77
a martyr to m. MUSIC, 63; THOMAS, D, 26
Architecture…is frozen m. ARCHITECTURE, 15
art constantly aspires towards…m. ART, 26
a young man who would…play his m. and be whistled at for it MUSIC, 22
Canned m. is like audible wallpaper POPULAR MUSIC, 9
capable of being well set to m. ADDISON, J, 11; MUSIC, 2
century of aeroplanes deserves its own m. MUSIC, 20
chord of m. MUSIC, 49
food in m. MUSIC, 37
God tells me how he wants this m. played MUSIC, 65
Having verse set to m. POETRY, 67
how potent cheap m. is COWARD, N, 17; MUSIC, 18
How sour sweet m. is ORDER, 4; SHAKESPEARE, 301
I don't write modern m. MUSIC, 60; STRAVINSKY, I, 6
If all the arts aspire to the condition of m. SANTAYANA, G, 14
If m. be the food of love MUSIC, 57; SHAKESPEARE, 336
I'll set it to m. MUSIC, 51
In m., the punctuation is absolutely strict ACTING, 19
line that fits the m. POPULAR MUSIC, 21
making m. throatily and palpitatingly sexual HUXLEY, A, 4; MUSIC, 31
man that hath no m. in himself MUSIC, 56; SHAKESPEARE, 253
m.…affects your nerves MUSIC, 36
M. and women I cannot but give way to MUSIC, 47; PEPYS, S, 14
M. begins to atrophy POUND, E, 3
M.…confirm human loneliness MUSIC, 24
M. creates order out of chaos MUSIC, 41
m. critics.…small and rodent-like with padlocked ears CRITICS, 20
M. has charms to soothe CONGREVE, W, 8; MUSIC, 17
M. helps not MUSIC, 1; PROVERBS, 296
M. is not written in red, white and blue MELBA, N, 2; MUSIC, 40
M. is the arithmetic of sounds MUSIC, 19
M. is the food of love PROVERBS, 297
M. is your own experience MUSIC, 46
M., Maestro, Please MUSIC, 38
M. owes as much to Bach MUSICIANS, 15
M. that gentlier on the spirit lies MUSIC, 62; TENNYSON, 55
M.…/Vibrates in the memory SHELLEY, P, 25
M., when soft voices die MEMORY, 22
never merry when I hear sweet m. MUSIC, 55; SHAKESPEARE, 252
No one really understood m. unless he was a scientist BUCK, P, 5
Poetry…set to more or less lascivious m. MENCKEN, H, 12; POETRY, 40
popular m.…made giant strides in reverse POPULAR MUSIC, 11
public doesn't want a new m. MUSICIANS, 3
silence sank like m. COLERIDGE, S, 37; SILENCE, 3
sometimes I don't even like m. MUSIC, 66
The English may not like m. BEECHAM, T, 4; MUSIC, 6
The hills are alive with the sound of m. MUSIC, 28
The m. teacher came twice each week MUSIC, 3
thy chosen m., Liberty FREEDOM, 64; WORDSWORTH, W, 64
Van Gogh's ear for m. INSULTS, 134
Wagner is the Puccini of m. MUSICIANS, 12
musical cashiers of the M. Banks BUTLER, S, 2; MONEY, 13

N

the Third Estate contains…a n. FRENCH REVOLUTION, 8
ventured my life in defence of this n. PATRIOTISM, 23
national a n. home for the Jewish people JEWS, 1
as clear as a crystal, the synthesis – German N. Socialism NAZISM, 3
nationalism N. is…the measles of mankind PATRIOTISM, 13
wind of n. and freedom blowing BALDWIN, S, 7; FREEDOM, 2
nationality My n. is French NORMALITY, 2
My suit is pale yellow. My n. is French WILLIAMS, T, 1
Other people have a n. BEHAN, B, 7; IRISH, 2; JEWS, 2
nations Commonwealth of N. BRITISH EMPIRE, 6
extends over many n. and three continents DOYLE, A, 14; EXPERIENCE, 12
If people behaved in the way n. do GOVERNMENT, 44; WILLIAMS, T, 7
languages are the pedigree of n. JOHNSON, S, 159; LANGUAGE, 27
The day of small n. has long passed away NATIONS, 1
The great n. have always acted like gangsters DIPLOMACY, 22
the healing of the n. BIBLE, 474
The n. which have put mankind and posterity most in their debt INGE, W, 12; NATIONS, 4
three very powerful n. of the Germans ENGLISH, 6
Two n.; between whom there is no intercourse DISRAELI, B, 12
native My n. Land – Good Night BYRON, 10; DEPARTURE, 5
my own, my n. land HOMESICKNESS, 6; SCOTT, W, 8
to appear considerable in his n. place FAME, 17; JOHNSON, S, 82
To the Greeks the Muse gave n. wit HORACE, 8
white man…looks into the eyes of a n. LESSING, D, 3
natives Britons were only n. HISTORY, 29; SELLAR, W, 4
natural First feelings…most n. FIRST IMPRESSIONS, 2; LOUIS XIV, 3
It is n. to die BACON, F, 19; BIRTH, 1; DEATH, 30
making so much of n. selection DARWIN, C, 4
more freedom in a country where it is not your n. language LANGUAGE, 1
n. false teeth TEETH, 4
N. Selection DARWIN, C, 8; EVOLUTION, 10
Nothing prevents us from being n. ROCHEFOUCAULD, 25; SPONTANEITY, 4
'twas N. to please CHARACTER, 7; DRYDEN, J, 4
What is wrong with a revolution…n. REVOLUTION, 8
naturally Though I am not n. honest HONESTY, 13; SHAKESPEARE, 355
nature Accuse not N., she hath done her part MILTON, J, 50; RESPONSIBILITY, 11
All N. wears one universal grin FIELDING, H, 14; NATURE, 11
Allow not n. more than n. needs NECESSITY, 5; SHAKESPEARE, 177
a noble n.…treats…a serious subject ARNOLD, M, 32; POETRY, 3
a poet to whom n. has denied the faculty of verse CARLYLE, T, 2
but N. more BYRON, 16; NATURE, 3
can't call yourself a great work of n. WHISTLER, J, 12
Consistency is contrary to n. CONSTANCY, 2; HUXLEY, A, 14
drive out n. with a pitchfork HUMAN NATURE, 15
fortress built by N. ENGLAND, 46; SHAKESPEARE, 297
Friend…masterpiece of N. EMERSON, R, 8; FRIENDS, 8
God and N. then at strife NATURE, 30; TENNYSON, 31
go into partnership with n. NATURE, 12
Human n. is so well disposed AUSTEN, J, 7; HUMAN NATURE, 2
I got disappointed in human n. HUMAN NATURE, 10
I have always respected suicide as a regulator of n. SUICIDE, 20
I have learned /To look on n. WORDSWORTH, W, 13
In n. there are neither rewards nor punishments NATURE, 23
I watched what method N. might take REMEDIES, 55
law of n. which love alone can alter LACLOS, P, 3; SEX, 61
Let N. be your Teacher NATURE, 38; WORDSWORTH, W, 68
Little we see in N. that is ours WASTE, 3; WORDSWORTH, W, 65
Man has wrested from n. NUCLEAR WEAPONS, 22
N. abhors a vacuum NATURE, 28; RABELAIS, F, 4
N. admits no lie CARLYLE, T, 21; NATURE, 4
N. can do more than physicians NATURE, 7
N. has always had more power than education NATURE, 31
N. has left this tincture DEFOE, D, 2; TYRANNY, 4
N. has never put the fatal question as to the meaning of their lives JUNG, C, 1; PURPOSE, 5
N. has no cure for this sort of madness COMMUNISM, 14
N. have fair play FASHION, 1
N. heals, under the auspices of the medical profession MEDICINE, 24
N., in medical language MEDICINE, 44
N. is a benevolent old hypocrite NATURE, 18
n. is a conjugation of the verb to eat NATURE, 22
N. is but a name for an effect COWPER, W, 26; NATURE, 6
N. is creeping up ARROGANCE, 8; WHISTLER, J, 11
N. is often hidden BACON, F, 36; HUMAN NATURE, 5
n. is the art of God BROWNE, T, 3; NATURE, 1
N. is usually wrong NATURE, 32; WHISTLER, J, 4
N. is very consonant and conformable NATURE, 26; NEWTON, I, 4
N. made him, and then broke the mould COMPLIMENTS, 1
N.…must be obeyed BACON, F, 62; HUMAN NATURE, 6
N. never did betray NATURE, 35; WORDSWORTH, W, 14
N. puts upon no man an unbearable burden SUICIDE, 20
N. remains NATURE, 33; WHITMAN, W, 13
N.'s ancient power was lost TENNYSON, 33
N.'s handmaid, art DRYDEN, J, 20; NATURE, 9
n.'s law HELP, 7; LA FONTAINE, J, 8
N.'s laws lay hid in night POPE, A, 19
N., time and patience are the three great physicians MEDICINE, 1
N.…wasteful of promising young men NATURE, 21
new sights of N. made me rejoice CURIE, M, 5; NATURE, 8
not formed by n. to bear MARCUS AURELIUS ANTONINUS, 9
o'erstep not the modesty of n. ACTION, 11; SHAKESPEARE, 96
Of all the soft, delicious functions of n. this is the chiefest SLEEP, 31
one of N.'s Gentlemen CHIVALRY, 8
one of the forces of n. GREATNESS, 10
Our foster nurse of n. is repose SLEEP, 28
rules of the game are what we call the laws of N. GOD, 29
science…is…the interplay between n. and ourselves NATURE, 15
secret of the arts is to correct n. VOLTAIRE, 15
The art of healing comes from n. MEDICINE, 73
the encroachment of n. NATURE, 17
the most irrelevant thing in n. FAMILY, 32; LAMB, C, 15
the physician must start from n. MEDICINE, 73
the spectacles of books to read n. DRYDEN, J, 23
Though you drive away N. NATURE, 20
to see the absurd n. of Englishmen ENGLISH, 34; PEPYS, S, 7
True wit is n. to advantage dress'd HUMOUR, 24; POPE, A, 25
unassuming common-place /Of N. FLOWERS, 14; WORDSWORTH, W, 76
until n. kills him or cures him MEDICINE, 63
vacuum…better…stuff that n. replaces NATURE, 34; WILLIAMS, T, 4
Wellington has exhausted n. and…glory WELLINGTON, 2
We must turn to n. itself NATURE, 16
We need more understanding of human n. HUMAN NATURE, 17; JUNG, C, 11
Whatever N. has in store for mankind NATURE, 10
wonderful case of n. imitating art ACTORS, 31; WILDE, O, 62
you can't call yourself a great work of n. INSULTS, 131
natures Men's n. are alike CONFUCIUS, 3; HABIT, 4
Man is N. sole mistake MANKIND, 28
N. ancient power was lost DECLINE, 12
naught N. so sweet as Melancholy MELANCHOLY, 2
naughty wasn't it n. of Smudges BETJEMAN, J, 8
nauseate I n. walking CONGREVE, W, 15; COUNTRYSIDE, 1
nauseating It is n. to see Mr Gandhi…posing as a fakir GANDHI, M, 2
Navee Ruler of the Queen's N. GILBERT, W, 13; OFFICERS, 6, 7
navy British n. always travels first class NAVY, 6
England's chief defence depends upon the n. NAVY, 9
There were gentlemen and…seamen in the n. of Charles the Second MACAULAY, T, 15; NAVY, 8
The Royal N. of England…its greatest defence NAVY, 2
upon the n.…safety, honour, and welfare…chiefly attend NAVY, 4
We joined the N. to see the world EXPECTATION, 1
Nazi N. Germany had become a menace to all mankind NAZISM, 5
Nazis In Germany, the N. came for the Communists NAZISM, 6
near I wished to be n. my mother BIRTH, 16; WHISTLER, J, 18
nearer N., my God, to thee RELIGION, 2
the n. you are to God PROTESTANTISM, 8
nearest the n. run thing you ever saw WAR, 177; WELLINGTON, 7
nearsighted don't raise your hands because I am also n. AUDEN, W, 28; DISABILITY, 1
neat round, n., not gaudy GARDENS, 9; LAMB, C, 25
Nebuchadnezzar N.…did eat grass as oxen BIBLE, 50

necessary Government...is but a n. evil GOVERNMENT, 29
necessities disregard for the n. of existence CIVILIZATION, 10; MAUGHAM, W, 14
we will dispense with its n. LUXURY, 4
necessity Beauty is a social n. BEAUTY, 23
I find alone N. Supreme NECESSITY, 8
N. is the mother NECESSITY, 2; PROVERBS, 298
N. is the plea for every infringement of human freedom NECESSITY, 4; PITT THE YOUNGER, 1
N. knows no law NECESSITY, 7
no virtue like n. SHAKESPEARE, 296
neck a pain in the n. SPEECHES, 1
A short n. denotes a good mind APPEARANCE, 67; SPARK, M, 2
creator had a purpose in equipping us with a n. COURAGE, 22
England will have her n. wrung like a chicken WORLD WAR II, 49
go to the bottom with my principles round my n. BALDWIN, S, 10; EXPEDIENCY, 3
my n. is very short EXECUTION, 26
short n. denotes a good mind INTELLIGENCE, 12
Some n. CHURCHILL, W, 58; WORLD WAR II, 20
the Roman people had but one n. RUTHLESSNESS, 1
necking Whoever named it n. MARX, G, 25; SEX, 79
neckline did so without even lowering her n. WEST, M, 1
neckties men wore their beards, like they wear their n. APPEARANCE, 36; LAWRENCE, D, 20
Ned no more work for poor old N. DEATH, 68
need All You N. Is Love LOVE, 104
artist is someone who produces things that people don't n. ARTISTS, 9
just got more money than I n. WEALTH, 46
reason not the n. NECESSITY, 5; SHAKESPEARE, 177
Thy n. is yet greater than mine SELF-DENIAL, 2
needle easier for a camel to go through the eye of a n. BIBLE, 405; WEALTH, 13
needs N. must NECESSITY, 3; PROVERBS, 299
to each according to his n. MARX, K, 3; MARXISM, 11
You artists produce something that nobody n. ARTISTS, 10
Your country n. YOU WAR, 5
needy as for me, I am poor and n. PSALMS, 24
negation Capitalist production begets...its own n. MARX, K, 5
negative Europe is the unfinished n. AMERICA, 31; MCCARTHY, M, 4
N. Capability DOUBT, 7; KEATS, J, 53
neglect A little n. may breed mischief FRANKLIN, B, 5; NEGLECT, 1
he devotes to the n. of his duties NEGLECT, 4
negligent Celerity...admired...by the n. IMPETUOSITY, 3; SHAKESPEARE, 33
negligible the work is n. CRITICISM, 1
negotiate never fear to n. DIPLOMACY, 21
Negro makes a N. unpleasant to white folk MENCKEN, H, 6; RACISM, 23
Negroes revenge by the culture of the N. MUSIC, 45
neiges *les n. d'antan* NOSTALGIA, 27
neighbor dedicate this nation to the policy of the good n. ROOSEVELT, F, 11
I have had no real gratification...more than my n. LAST WORDS, 91; WEALTH, 48
neighbour better mouse-trap than his n. EMERSON, R, 26; FAME, 11
death...had been his next-door n. DEATH, 135; SCOTT, W, 10
Death is my n. now DEATH, 62; LAST WORDS, 31
Do not love your n. as yourself SELF, 17; SHAW, G, 27
It's a recession when your n. TRUMAN, H, 7; UNEMPLOYMENT, 6
love thy n. as thyself BIBLE, 411; LOVE, 32
they helped every one his n. BIBLE, 212
told men to love their n. BRECHT, B, 4; HUNGER, 3
neighbours fear of what the n. might say SUICIDE, 12
improper thoughts about n. MORALITY, 4
make sport for our n. AUSTEN, J, 26; RIDICULE, 1
neither better if n. of us had been born NAPOLEON I, 6; REGRET, 13
N. am I WRITING, 13
Nell Pretty witty N. COMPLIMENTS, 21; PEPYS, S, 11
the death of Little N. without laughing INSENSITIVITY, 5
Nelly let not poor N. starve CHARLES II, 6; LAST WORDS, 16
Nelson keep the N. touch NEWBOLT, H, 5; PATRIOTISM, 31
N., born in a fortunate hour OFFICERS, 11
The N. touch NELSON, H, 1; OFFICERS, 10
neo-Keynesian One nanny...was a n. MACMILLAN, H, 9
nephew The enviably attractive n. who sings an Irish ballad KENNEDY, J, 1
Nero just and merciful as N. ELIZABETH I, 3
nerve called a n. specialist because it sounds better PSYCHIATRY, 34
nerves grates on our n. NEUROSIS, 6
It destroys one's n. to be amiable every day DISRAELI, B, 15; MARRIAGE, 64
nervous I wasn't this n. playing golf when I was drinking GOLF, 2
One of the symptoms of approaching n. breakdown RUSSELL, B, 6; WORK, 33
winding up its n. and intellectual system to the utmost point SUICIDE, 15
nest broods a n. of sorrows MARRIAGE, 153
nests Dead birds don't fall out of their n. OLD AGE, 34; SEX, 28
nets Laws are generally found to be n. LAW, 36
nettle Out of this n., danger SHAKESPEARE, 112
stroke a n., /And it stings you for your pains DECISION, 2
nettles apt to be overrun with n. MIND, 33; WALPOLE, H, 8
neurasthenia he is put there with the diagnosis of 'n.' PSYCHIATRY, 18
neurosis by accepting the universal n. he is spared...a personal n. BELIEF, 8; BELIEF, 8
Modern n. began with the discoveries of Copernicus NEUROSIS, 7
N. has an absolute genius for malingering NEUROSIS, 10; PROUST, M, 10
N. is always a substitute for legitimate suffering NEUROSIS, 5
N. is the way of avoiding non-being NEUROSIS, 14
the Age of Anxiety, the age of the n. NEUROSIS, 6
the secret of n. is to be found in the family battle of wills NEUROSIS, 9
Without them there is n. NEUROSIS, 13
neurotic Acting is the expression of a n. impulse ACTING, 5
a highly n. young don NEWTON, I, 3
A n. is the man who builds a castle in the air PSYCHIATRY, 31
N. means he is not as sensible as I am NEUROSIS, 8
Psychiatrists classify a person as n. PSYCHIATRY, 28; SZASZ, T, 7
the n. ills of an entire generation LAWRENCE, T, 4
the n. person knows that two and two make four NEUROSIS, 1
neurotics A mistake which is commonly made about n. NEUROSIS, 2
Everything great in the world is done by n. NEUROSIS, 12; PROUST, M, 20
The 'sensibility' claimed by n. NEUROSIS, 11
neutrality people of this country are overwhelmingly for a policy of n. DEMOCRACY, 2
'positive n.' is a contradiction in terms POLITICS, 77
never Better n. than late PROMPTNESS, 3; SHAW, G, 51
I n. would lay down my arms PATRIOTISM, 33; PITT THE ELDER, 6
let us n., n. doubt DOUBT, 2
Love? I make it constantly but I n. talk about it PROUST, M, 7; SEX, 98
N., n., n., n. MOURNING, 13; SHAKESPEARE, 196
n., n. sick at sea GILBERT, W, 9
our people have n. had it so good MACMILLAN, H, 5; WEALTH, 35
Than n. to have loved at all LOVE, 161; TENNYSON, 28
nevermore Quoth the Raven, N. EVIL, 16
Nevershit like you was Lady N. AFFECTATION, 2
new a n. heaven and a n. earth BIBLE, 473
He that will not apply n. remedies BACON, F, 30; INNOVATION, 1
He was dull in a n. way JOHNSON, S, 92
He was the Messiah of the n. age POLITICIANS, 117
I'm the n. Olivier ACTORS, 2
n. book is published, read an old one BOOKS, 38
n. deal for the American people AMERICA, 34; ROOSEVELT, F, 9
N. roads: n. ruts CHESTERTON, G, 52; PROGRESS, 10
n. wine into old bottles BIBLE, 384
Revolution is...the setting-up of a n. order REVOLUTION, 6
something n. out of Africa NOVELTY, 8; PLINY THE ELDER, 4
There are no n. truths MCCARTHY, M, 2; NOVELTY, 7
there is no n. thing under the sun BIBLE, 62; NOVELTY, 1
we shall find something n. NOVELTY, 10; VOLTAIRE, 6
We stand today on the edge of a n. frontier BEGINNING, 14
You suddenly understand something...in a n. way LEARNING, 12; LESSING, D, 1
Youth is something very n. CHANEL, C, 4; YOUTH, 5
new-found-land my n. DONNE, J, 12
newness Americans have been conditioned to respect n. UPDIKE, J, 3
news Bad n. travels fast DISASTER, 1; PROVERBS, 77

good n. from a far country BIBLE, 455
Literature is n. LITERATURE, 22; POUND, E, 5
n. that's fit to print NEWSPAPERS, 11
No n. is good n. JOURNALISM, 9; PROVERBS, 314
Nothing is n. until it has appeared in *The Times*. NEWSPAPERS, 9
only n. until he's read it. After that it's dead NEWSPAPERS, 18; WAUGH, E, 38
when a man bites a dog that is n. MEDIA, 5
newspaper good n.…is a nation talking to itself JOURNALISM, 25; MILLER, A, 5
I read the n. avidly JOURNALISM, 10
Once a n. touches a story, the facts are lost FACTS, 5; JOURNALISM, 24
Reading someone else's n. BRADBURY, M, 6
With the n. strike on OBITUARIES, 3
newspapers I'm with you on the free press. It's the n. MEDIA, 14; STOPPARD, T, 7
I read the n. avidly BEVAN, A, 6
life…happens almost exclusively in n. JOURNALISM, 2
Never believe in mirrors or n. NEWSPAPERS, 12
N. always excite curiosity LAMB, C, 14; MEDIA, 12
We live under a government of men and…n. GOVERNMENT, 32; JOURNALISM, 29
newt Eye of n., and toe of frog SHAKESPEARE, 220
Newton God said, *Let N. be* POPE, A, 19
What Galileo and N. were to the seventeenth century DARWIN, C, 3
Newtons souls of five hundred Sir Isaac N. COLERIDGE, S, 47
New Woman Chanel epitomised the N. CHANEL, C, 2
New York N. is a small place AMERICA, 46; WODEHOUSE, P, 10
N.…that unnatural city AMERICA, 18
New Zealand I went to N. but it was closed PLACES, 4
Niagara one wouldn't *live* under N. CARLYLE, T, 29; INSULTS, 28
nice Be n. to people on your way up PRUDENCE, 11
how nasty the n. people can be NASTINESS, 6; POWELL, A, 5
I am a n. man BENNETT, A, 2
If you haven't anything n. to say about anyone INVITATIONS, 4
N. guys finish last GOOD, 4
Sugar and spice /And all that's n. NURSERY RHYMES, 69
Nicely-Nicely what N. dies of will be over-feeding GREED, 11; RUNYON, D, 10
nicest English people…are surely the *n.* people in the world ENGLISH, 24; LAWRENCE, D, 4
niche you've not got your n. in creation HOMOSEXUALITY, 15
Nicholas St N. soon would be there CHRISTMAS, 15
Nick Satan, N., or Clootie BURNS, R, 3; DEVIL, 9
nickname n. is the heaviest stone NAMES, 4
nicotine his n. eggyellow weeping walrus Victorian moustache APPEARANCE, 69; THOMAS, D, 27
nicotinic N. acid cures pellagra REMEDIES, 54
Nietzsche N.…was a confirmed Life Force worshipper NIETZSCHE, F, 1
nigger Catch a n. by his toe NURSERY RHYMES, 11
niggers He's gone whar de good n. go DEATH, 68
nigh draw n. to God BIBLE, 218
night afraid for any terror by n. PSALMS, 51
An infant crying in the n. TENNYSON, 30
as a thief in the n. BIBLE, 503
calm passage…across many a bad n. SUICIDE, 21
Come to me in the silence of the n. NOSTALGIA, 22; ROSSETTI, C, 1
Do not go gentle into that good n. DEATH, 173; THOMAS, D, 7
From morn to n., my friend ENDURANCE, 18; ROSSETTI, C, 6
Gwine to run all n. HORSES, 6
ignorant armies clash by n. ARNOLD, M, 11; WAR, 11
It ain't a fit n. out WEATHER, 10
It is spring, moonless n. in the small town THOMAS, D, 18
money in a desk by n. BALZAC, H, 4; THEFT, 4
Morning in the Bowl of N. DAY, 5; FITZGERALD, E, 2
Nature's laws lay hid in n. POPE, A, 19
N. and day LOVE, 128; PORTER, C, 4
N. of the Long Knives FASCISM, 5
n. was made for loving BYRON, 42; LOVE, 48
Oft in the stilly n., /Ere Slumber's chain MOORE, T, 7; NOSTALGIA, 17
only one man…can count on steady work – the n. watchman THEATRE, 2
perils…of this n. DANGER, 3
real dark n. of the soul FITZGERALD, F, 3; SOUL, 7
returned home the previous n. LIMERICKS, 7; SCIENCE, 16
Ships that pass in the n. LONGFELLOW, H, 16; TRANSIENCE, 17
So late into the n. BYRON, 41; DEBAUCHERY, 4
sound of revelry by n. BYRON, 13; MERRYMAKING, 2
such a n. /Troilus methinks mounted the Troyan walls SHAKESPEARE, 250
that is past as a watch in the n. PSALMS, 49
the black bat, n., has flown INVITATIONS, 5; TENNYSON, 56
the darkness he called N. BIBLE, 137; CREATION, 2
The dark n. of the soul SOUL, 9
the honey'd middle of the n. KEATS, J, 11; LOVE, 97
the morning cometh, and also the n. BIBLE, 204
The n. has a thousand eyes SUN, 1
The n. is dark, and I am far from home FAITH, 23
The n. is your friend WORLD WAR II, 4
the N. Mail crossing the Border TRAVEL, 5
The n. was pain SORROW, 2
wish the n. /Had borne my breath away HOOD, T, 6; NOSTALGIA, 10
Nightingale Miss N. did inspire awe NIGHTINGALE, F, 1
nightingale N.…/A creature of a 'fiery heart' WORDSWORTH, W, 35
The n. does sit so late MARVELL, A, 5
nightingales From Wales /Whose n. WALES, 4
The n. are singing ELIOT, T, 23
nightmare 'History…n. from which I am trying to awake' JOYCE, J, 8
nights a Chequer-board of N. and Days DESTINY, 7; FITZGERALD, E, 13
The weariest n.…must…end ENDURANCE, 14
They shorten tedious n. CAMPION, T, 5; SEX, 22
nihilist a part-time n. CAMUS, A, 13; COMMITMENT, 4
Nile dam…the N. with bulrushes FREEDOM, 11
my serpent of old N. SHAKESPEARE, 28
Tallulah Bankhead barged down the N. last night and sank CRITICISM, 11
Nimrod N. the mighty hunter BIBLE, 162
nine N. drummers drumming CHRISTMAS, 18; NURSERY RHYMES, 59
N. for the n. bright shiners ANONYMOUS, 45; NUMBERS, 1
ninepence I have but n. in ready money ADDISON, J, 18; CONVERSATION, 2
Nineveh Quinquireme of N. BOATS, 13; MASEFIELD, J, 2
nip I'll n. him in the bud MIXED METAPHORS, 4
Nixon N. is the kind of politician NIXON, R, 2
N.'s motto was, if two wrongs don't make a right NIXON, R, 1
N.…would cut down a redwood tree POLITICIANS, 118
standing between N. and the White House POLITICIANS, 94
You won't have N. to kick around NIXON, R, 5; RENUNCIATION, 3
no become accustomed to n. one governing SOCIALISM, 17
girls…say N. when they mean Yes WOMEN, 10
It's n. go the picture palace INDIFFERENCE, 4
rebel…man who says n. CAMUS, A, 14; REBELLION, 4
she speaks eighteen languages. And she can't say 'N.' in any of them PARKER, D, 27
why Absurdist plays take place in N. Man's Land THEATRE, 1
Noah Out of their cataclysm but one poor N. HUXLEY, A, 18
nobility N. has its own obligations NOBILITY, 3
Real n. is based on scorn NOBILITY, 2
The n.…snored through the Sermon ARISTOCRACY, 5
noble a n. nature…treats…a serious subject ARNOLD, M, 32; POETRY, 3
Englishman never enjoys himself except for a n. purpose ENGLISH, 22; HERBERT, A, 6
n. grounds for the n. emotions POETRY, 52; RUSKIN, J, 5
Ridicule…smothers that which is n. RIDICULE, 4; SCOTT, W, 17
scarcely a man learned in the laws…who is not n. LAWYERS, 7
The n. living and the n. dead NOBILITY, 8; WORDSWORTH, W, 44
though thy tackle's torn, /Thou show'st a n. vessel NOBILITY, 5
nobleman a king may make a n. BURKE, E, 24; CHIVALRY, 4
nobleness perfect plainness of speech…perfect n. ARNOLD, M, 31; BIBLE, 523
noblesse If the French n. had been capable of playing cricket with their peasants ARISTOCRACY, 19; CRICKET, 12
noblest n. man /That ever lived in the tide of times REGRET, 20; SHAKESPEARE, 152
n. Roman of them all NOBILITY, 6; SHAKESPEARE, 162
on you n. English SHAKESPEARE, 131
nobly the immature man…wants to die n. for a cause AGE, 89

nobody a man is n. unless his biography OBITUARIES, 10; TROLLOPE, A, 6
I care for n. SELFISHNESS, 2
N. asked you, sir, she said NURSERY RHYMES, 70
N. ever tells me anything GALSWORTHY, J, 5
whom n. loves OBESITY, 9
nod A n. is as good as a wink BLINDNESS, 1; PROVERBS, 55
the land of N. BIBLE, 155; REVENGE, 4
nods even excellent Homer n. HORACE, 9; IMPERFECTION, 9
noise A loud n. at one end BABIES, 7
dreadful n. of waters in my ears DROWNING, 2; SHAKESPEARE, 303
Film...dust and heat and n. CINEMA, 19
the less they have...the more n. they make CHARACTER, 17
the n....and the people WAR, 6
the n. of the shout of joy BIBLE, 130
they...love the n. it makes BEECHAM, T, 4; MUSIC, 6
Those people...are making such a n. AUDIENCES, 4
noises Like n. in a swound COLERIDGE, S, 26; SEA, 4
noisome the n. pestilence PSALMS, 51
noisy Strongest minds /...the n. world /Hears least MIND, 36; WORDSWORTH, W, 4
The people would be just as n. CROMWELL, O, 9; PUBLIC, 10
noli n. me tangere BIBLE, 276
nomadic the charm...of a n. existence SACKVILLE-WEST, V, 5
nomenclature even the learned ignorance of a n. LEARNING, 9
nominated I will not accept if n. POLITICIANS, 116
no-more I am also called N. DISAPPOINTMENT, 7; ROSSETTI, D, 3
non-being Neurosis is the way of avoiding n. NEUROSIS, 14
nonchalance the elegant n. of a duke CHAPLIN, C, 3
non-combatant War hath no fury like a n. WAR, 110
nonconformist a N. conscience WILDE, O, 42; WOMEN, 142
man must be a n. CONFORMITY, 4; EMERSON, R, 14
Why do you have to be a n. CONFORMITY, 6; THURBER, J, 18
nonconformity N. and lust stalking hand in hand LUST, 12; WAUGH, E, 14
none N. but the Brave COURAGE, 13; DRYDEN, J, 16
nonsense you intend to talk n. KEYNES, J, 9
non-U U and N. CLASS, 37
non-violence to disagree...about...n. without wanting to kick HAMPTON, C, 4; VIOLENCE, 10
noon From morn /To n. he fell DECLINE, 5; MILTON, J, 38
from n. to dewy eve DECLINE, 5; MILTON, J, 38
O dark, dark, dark, amid the blaze of n. BLINDNESS, 8; MILTON, J, 58
noon-day the sickness that destroyeth in the n. PSALMS, 51
no one become accustomed to n. governing LENIN, V, 5
Norfolk bear him up the N. sky BETJEMAN, J, 4; HUNTING, 2
Very flat, N. COWARD, N, 16; ENGLAND, 17
Norgay Tenzing N. PHOTOGRAPHY, 5
norm no longer lies but the n. is the truth TRUTH, 27
Norma Jean Goodbye N. ACTORS, 26
normal I've had a n. life SPORT AND GAMES, 38
'n.' people...cause no trouble either to themselves TAYLOR, A, 6
quiet miracle of a n. life CLINTON, B, 7
the n. is so...interesting NORMALITY, 1; STEIN, G, 3
Normans The Saxon is not like us N. KIPLING, R, 21; NATIONALITY, 8
north mad n.-n.-west SHAKESPEARE, 86
The n. wind does blow PROVERBS, 403; WEATHER, 6
nose A custom loathsome to the eye, hateful to the n. SMOKING, 16
A person may be indebted for a n. or an eye...to a great-aunt HAZLITT, W, 11
Dong with a luminous N. LEAR, E, 3; NONSENSE, 19
Entuned in hir n. ful semely CHAUCER, G, 6
Had Cleopatra's n. been shorter APPEARANCE, 55; PASCAL, B, 6
led by the n. with gold BRIBERY, 5; SHAKESPEARE, 356
My n. bleeds for you INSINCERITY, 6
My n. is huge APPEARANCE, 58
Only the n. knows SECRECY, 1
This fellow did not see further than his...n. LA FONTAINE, J, 5
will it come without warning /Just as I'm picking my n. AUDEN, W, 26; LOVE, 20
noses rock musicians make a bunch of money and stick it up their n. DRUGS, 18
nostrils God...breathed into his n. BIBLE, 144
not Believe it or n. BELIEF, 10
HOW N. TO DO IT DICKENS, C, 22
I am n. what I am APPEARANCES, 32
note make a n. of DICKENS, C, 19
The world will little n., nor long remember LINCOLN, A, 17
notes the pauses between the n. MUSICIANS, 8
thinks two n. a song BIRDS, 2
nothin' N. Like a Dame WOMEN, 64
You ain't heard n. yet PROPHECY, 6
You ain't n. but a hound dog DOGS, 13
nothing a past master in making n. happen very slowly STEIN, G, 2
Blessed is the man who expects n. EXPECTATION, 6; POPE, A, 60
Certainly, there is n. else here to enjoy PARTIES, 8; SHAW, G, 49
certain we can carry n. out BIBLE, 510; WEALTH, 14
Children aren't happy with n. to ignore FAMILY, 43; NASH, O, 8
Death is n. AFTERLIFE, 6; DEATH, 81
doing n. for each other FRIENDSHIP, 16
from n. to a state of extreme poverty MARX, G, 13; POVERTY, 32
George the First knew n. ROYALTY, 75
God made everything out of n. CREATION, 16
have n. whatever to do with it DEATH, 108; MAUGHAM, W, 26
It is very good, sometimes, to have n. POVERTY, 41
I (Who Have N.) POVERTY, 31
N. can be created out of n. NOTHING, 1
n. can be said to be certain but death and taxes FRANKLIN, B, 17
n. can bring back the hour REGRET, 28; WORDSWORTH, W, 31
n. either good or bad SHAKESPEARE, 84; THINKING, 17
N., except my genius CONCEIT, 25; WILDE, O, 76
N. happens BECKETT, S, 2; BOREDOM, 1
n. if not critical CRITICISM, 57; SHAKESPEARE, 281
n. is /But what is not APPEARANCES, 31
n. is certain but death and taxes TAXATION, 4
n....is greater...than one's self SELF, 26; WHITMAN, W, 9
n. is had for n. EFFORT, 4
n. is law that is not reason LAW, 28
N. is won forever in human affairs HUMAN CONDITION, 17
N. long DRYDEN, J, 9; HUMAN NATURE, 11
N. matters very much BALFOUR, A, 6; TRIVIALITY, 1
N. to do but work PESSIMISM, 7
n. to do with the case APPEARANCE, 28; GILBERT, W, 34
N. will come of n. NOTHING, 3; SHAKESPEARE, 170
opened it only to find – n. AESOP, 3; MATERIALISM, 2
People don't resent having n. WEALTH, 18
people who say n. COURAGE, 30
Signifying n. LIFE, 86; SHAKESPEARE, 227
sooner read a time-table...than n. MAUGHAM, W, 18; NOVELS, 11
take *more* than n. CARROLL, L, 11; LANGUAGE, 10
The House of Peers...Did n. GILBERT, S, 21; HOUSES OF PARLIAMENT, 13
the sort of woman now...one would almost feel disposed to bury for n. DICKENS, C, 29
The temerity to believe in n. SCEPTICISM, 6; TURGENEV, I, 2
those who were up to n. COWARD, N, 9
To marvel at n. is just about the one and only thing HAPPINESS, 9; HORACE, 19
We are n.; less than n., and dreams INSIGNIFICANCE, 4; LAMB, C, 4
When you have n. to say, say n. SILENCE, 4
Where some people are very wealthy and others have n. ARISTOTLE, 8; GOVERNMENT, 5
nothingness the n. shows through CREATION, 16
notice The State, in choosing men...takes no n. of their opinions CROMWELL, O, 8; LOYALTY, 6
notices One never n. what has been done CURIE, M, 7; SCIENCE, 24
nought Man is like a thing of n. PSALMS, 72
N.'s had, all's spent CONTENTMENT, 10; SHAKESPEARE, 216
This great world /Should so wear out to n. TRANSIENCE, 20
nourisher a n. of thine old age BIBLE, 476
Chief n. in life's feast SHAKESPEARE, 214; SLEEP, 29
nourishment n. of the body into a painful attack DIETING, 3
novel Among the many problems...the choice of the moment...to begin his n. SACKVILLE-WEST, V, 1
A n. is a mirror NOVELS, 16
A n. is a static thing NOVELS, 17; PLAYS, 15; TYNAN, K, 1
because a n.'s invented, it isn't true NOVELS, 13; POWELL, A, 7
good n. tells us the truth CHESTERTON, G, 24; NOVELS, 2
I'm going to write the Great Australian N. AMBITION, 28; WHITE, P, 4
not a n. to be tossed aside lightly CRITICISM, 49; PARKER, D, 17
scrofulous French n. BROWNING, R, 55; NOVELS, 1
The detective n. NOVELS, 14

the last fashionable n. on the tables of young ladies MACAULAY, T, 20; WRITING, 32
The n. being dead NOVELS, 18; VIDAL, G, 2
the n. tells a story FORSTER, E, 5; NOVELS, 4
The only obligation to which…we may hold a n. JAMES, H, 10; NOVELS, 7
the sex n. is now normal NOVELS, 15
to read a n. before luncheon was one of the gravest sins READING, 18; WAUGH, E, 48
When I want to read a n. DISRAELI, B, 40; NOVELS, 3
novelist A n. is, like all mortals NABOKOV, V, 7
n. who writes nothing for 10 years PRIESTLEY, J, 9
the most precious gift a n. can possess WRITERS, 72
novelists if a third of all the n.…dropped dead WRITERS, 20
n. the story of the present NOVELS, 6
There are many reasons why n. write FICTION, 4; FOWLES, J, 4
novels characters in one of my n. FICTION, 3; FITZGERALD, F, 15
His n. are marvels of sustained imagination TOLSTOY, L, 1
It is a sad feature…that only women…have time to write n. WRITERS, 27
No one has written worse English than Mr Hardy in…his n. HARDY, T, 4
one of the few English n. for grown up people CRITICISM, 68; WOOLF, V, 5
who have to perpetrate thirty bad n. HUXLEY, A, 1
novelty Novelty, n., n. HOOD, T, 15; NOVELTY, 3
November Please to remember the Fifth of N. ANONYMOUS, 69; TREASON, 1
Thirty days hath N. MONTHS, 9
novice Man arrives as a n. at each age of his life AGE, 26
now Are you n. or have you ever been a member COMMUNISM, 1
The n., the here, through which TIME, 27
We are all Socialists n. SOCIALISM, 13
nowhere All dressed up, with n. to go FUTILITY, 14
He's a real N. Man FUTILITY, 10; LENNON, J, 8
noxious the most n. is a tourist BRITISH, 10; TRAVEL, 26
nuclear adopt n. disarmament NUCLEAR WEAPONS, 19
Wars cannot be fought with n. weapons MOUNTBATTEN OF BURMA, L, 6
nude human body remain n. and uncovered JOHN PAUL II, 3
skied down Mount Everest in the n. LOVE, 115
To keep one from going n. PESSIMISM, 7
nudity you don't need the n. CINEMA, 31
nuisance exchange of one n. for another n. PROGRESS, 12
Inflation in the Sixties was a n. ECONOMICS, 15
Never compose…unless…not composing…becomes a positive n. MUSIC, 30
nuisances a change of n. is as good as a vacation CHANGE, 17; LLOYD GEORGE, D, 17
number *abstract reasoning concerning quantity or n.* PHILOSOPHY, 3
a very interesting n. NUMBERS, 5
Look after n. one PROVERBS, 266; SELF-PRESERVATION, 1
n. 1 n. 2 man ACHESON, D, 1
numbers divinity in odd n. SHAKESPEARE, 258; SUPERSTITION, 11
N.…only universal language MATHEMATICS, 24
N. sanctify CHAPLIN, C, 4
Round n. JOHNSON, S, 119; NUMBERS, 2
the greatest happiness for the greatest n. HAPPINESS, 11
up in the high n. KEYNES, J, 10; NUMBERS, 3
numble We live in a n. abode DICKENS, C, 14; SERVILITY, 2
numbness drowsy n. pains /My sense KEATS, J, 35; MELANCHOLY, 8
nun the upbringing a n. would envy INNOCENCE, 10; ORTON, J, 1
nunnery Get thee to a n. SHAKESPEARE, 93
nuns N. are sexy SEX, 75
the n. who never take a bath MODESTY, 8; RUSSELL, B, 7
nuptials prone to any iteration of n. CONGREVE, W, 16
nurse always keep a hold of N. BELLOC, H, 4; COMFORT, 1
definition of what a n. should be FEMINISM, 25; NIGHTINGALE, F, 4
N. unupblown BREVITY, 10; TELEGRAMS, 12
Our foster n. of nature is repose SLEEP, 28
The trained n. has become one of the great blessings of humanity OCCUPATIONS, 22
The trained n. has given nursing the human…touch OCCUPATIONS, 17
nurseries n. of all vice EDUCATION, 29
nurses a giggle of n. LANGUAGE, 4
old men's n. BACON, F, 34; MARRIAGE, 14
nut I had a little n. tree, /Nothing would it bear NURSERY RHYMES, 20
nut-brown the spicy n. ale ALCOHOL, 58; MILTON, J, 18

O

oak Absalom hanged in an o. BIBLE, 484
Heart of o. are our ships COURAGE, 17
To win the palm, the o., or bays MARVELL, A, 1; VICTORY, 15
oar impressions…lasting as…an o. upon the water INSIGNIFICANCE, 1
oat This bread I break was once the o. THOMAS, D, 17
oat-cakes land of Calvin, o., and sulphur SMITH, S, 7
oath In lapidary inscriptions a man is not upon o. JOHNSON, S, 99
oaths God pardon all o. that are broke FAITHFULNESS, 6
O. are but words BUTLER, S, 6; WORDS, 4
obedience As honour, love, o. SHAKESPEARE, 225
'Resistance to tyranny is o. to God.' ANTHONY, S, 6
The reluctant o. of distant provinces DIPLOMACY, 25; MACAULAY, T, 5
obedient o. unto death CHRISTIANITY, 30
obesity O. is a mental state OBESITY, 7
obey born to o. OBEDIENCE, 2
children, o. your parents BIBLE, 95; OBEDIENCE, 1
one of those born neither to o. nor to command MASEFIELD, J, 1; NASTINESS, 5
safer to o. than to rule OBEDIENCE, 3
obeyed Nature…must be o. BACON, F, 62; HUMAN NATURE, 6
She-who-must-be-o. WOMAN'S ROLE, 7
obituaries read many o. with…pleasure OBITUARIES, 2
were my o. good OBITUARIES, 7
obituary autobiography is an o. BIOGRAPHY, 2
object o. will be, if possible to form Christian men EDUCATION, 8
objectionable its own animality either o. or funny HUMOUR, 20; LEWIS, C, 2
objective live with the o. of being happy FRANK, A, 5
objects pull down an outstanding building, no one o. AMERICA, 10
obligation The only o. to which…we may hold a novel JAMES, H, 10; NOVELS, 7
To the University of Oxford I acknowledge no o. GIBBON, E, 3
obligations hothouse of o., both personal and public HOSTAGES, 4
oblige One should o. everyone to…one's ability ABILITY, 1; LA FONTAINE, J, 3
oblivion alms for o. SHAKESPEARE, 333
o. which awaits the uncreative mind SCIENTISTS, 11
oblong an o. angular figure HUMOUR, 47; LEACOCK, S, 6
obscene would not say that our Press is o. MEDIA, 13
obscenely cosmetics names seemed o. obvious COSMETICS, 3
obscenities people leaning out of car windows and shouting o. FAME, 21
obscenity O.…happens to shock some elderly…magistrate PRUDERY, 5; RUSSELL, B, 25
obscure I strive to be brief, and I become o. BREVITY, 3; HORACE, 2
observance More honour'd in the breach than the o. CUSTOM, 4; SHAKESPEARE, 76
the o. of trifles DOYLE, A, 4; TRIVIALITY, 6
observation medicine, professedly founded on o. MEDICINE, 43
Reason, O., and Experience SCIENCE, 54
the gift of keen o. MEDICINE, 58
observations To o. which ourselves we make POPE, A, 39; SUBJECTIVITY, 6
observe Whenever you o. an animal closely ANIMALS, 10
observed your life being set in concrete…a feeling of being constantly o. CHARLES, PRINCE, 7
obsessed O. with self LAWRENCE, D, 1
obsolescence infancy, childhood, adolescence and o. AGE, 58
obsolete the horse, as a means of locomotion, is o. HORSES, 11
obstetrician The psychiatrist is the o. of the mind PSYCHIATRY, 2
obstinacy the name of…o. in a bad one STERNE, L, 6

obstinate O. people can be divided into ARISTOTLE, 3
through his whole life jealous and o. BURKE, E, 1
obtain so run, that ye may o. BIBLE, 33
occasions all o. do inform against me SHAKESPEARE, 100
occupation for ever apologizing for his o. BUSINESS, 21; MENCKEN, H, 15
occupations There are worse o. in the world DOCTORS, 95
occupies every time Hitler o. a country HITLER, A, 4
occur Accidents will o. ACCIDENTS, 3; DICKENS, C, 17
ocean A life on the o. wave SEA, 13
My Bonnie lies over the o. ANONYMOUS, 57
o. is a place of paradoxes CARSON, R, 1
on the o. of life we pass LONGFELLOW, H, 16
We mortals cross the o. BROWNING, R, 9
whilst the great o. of truth lay all undiscovered before me NEWTON, I, 5
o'clock Three o. is always too late or too early DAY, 13; SARTRE, J, 7
octopus dear o. from whose tentacles we never quite escape FAMILY, 55
odd How o. /Of God JEWS, 6
the care of the id by the o. PSYCHIATRY, 1
This world is very o. we see CONFUSION, 6
odds The o. is gone MOURNING, 9; SHAKESPEARE, 37
Odi *O. et amo* LOVE AND HATE, 2
odious comparisons are o. ANALOGY, 2; DONNE, J, 10
little o. vermin INSULTS, 119; SWIFT, J, 7
One is not superior...because one sees the world in an o. light CYNICISM, 1
odorous Comparisons are o. MALAPROPISMS, 2; SHAKESPEARE, 274
odours O..../Live within the sense they quicken SHELLEY, P, 25
Odysseus Like O., he looked wiser when seated WILSON, W, 2
Oedipuses a tense and peculiar family, the O. BEERBOHM, M, 21; CLASSICS, 1
o'er Returning were as tedious as go o. GUILT, 17; SHAKESPEARE, 219
o'er-leaps Vaulting ambition, which o. itself AMBITION, 23; SHAKESPEARE, 211
off Days o. LEISURE, 6
he gets o. with women because he can't get on SEX, 69
O. with his head CARROLL, L, 12; EXECUTION, 5
offence dire o. from am'rous causes springs POPE, A, 48; RESULTS, 5
greatest o. against virtue HAZLITT, W, 16; VIRTUE, 16
It is a public scandal that gives o. MORALITY, 11
It is public scandal that constitutes o. MOLIERE, 10
rock of o. BIBLE, 199
The only defence is in o. BALDWIN, S, 4; WAR, 15
offend the kind of pride least likely to o. MODESTY, 7
Those who o. us are generally punished REVENGE, 21; TROLLOPE, A, 16
offended This hand hath o. REGRET, 7
This hath not o. the king EXECUTION, 27
When people do not respect us we are sharply o. SELF-RESPECT, 7; TWAIN, M, 13
offender a most notorious o. SMOLLETT, T, 3
offensive o. letter follows INSULTS, 4
You are extremely o. IMPERTINENCE, 4
offer an o. he can't refuse BUSINESS, 23; THREATS, 4
office Every man who takes o. in Washington...grows or swells RESPONSIBILITY, 22
in o. but not in power GOVERNMENT, 19
not describe holding public o. ACHESON, D, 5; GOVERNMENT, 1
o. sanctifies the holder POWER, 3
Written by o. boys for o. boys NEWSPAPERS, 14
officer unbecoming the character of an o. ANONYMOUS, 6; OFFICERS, 1
official O. dignity...in inverse ratio to...importance DIPLOMACY, 17; HUXLEY, A, 10
offspring Heaven has granted me no o. CONCEIT, 24; WHISTLER, J, 13
often Do you come here o. ANIMALISM, 6; MILLIGAN, S, 3
oil Kuwait is an o. monarchy AMERICANS, 2
ointment a good name is better than precious o. VIRTUE, 5
dead flies cause the o....to send forth a stinking savour REPUTATION, 3
Time cures the sick man, not the o. TIME, 7
Oklahoma Okie use' to mean you was from O. INSULTS, 118; STEINBECK, J, 3
old All evil comes from the o. AGE, 6; ANOUILH, J, 3
All would live long, but none would be o. OLD AGE, 1
A man is as o. as he's feeling OLD AGE, 38
An o. man looks permanent OLD AGE, 17
an o., wild, and incomprehensible man POLITICIANS, 126; VICTORIA, 8
a nourisher of thine o. age BIBLE, 476
a sight to make an o. man young BEAUTY, 45; TENNYSON, 14
A woman as o. as she looks OLD AGE, 38
Before we grow o. and die AGE, 106; YEATS, W, 9
being o. is having lighted rooms LARKIN, P, 2; OLD AGE, 63
Better be an o. man's darling MARRIAGE, 1; PROVERBS, 89
Dying while young is a boon in o. age OLD AGE, 6
first sign of o. age AGE, 51
for de o. folks at home HOMESICKNESS, 3
Forty is the o. age of youth OLD AGE, 4
gift of perpetual o. age OLD AGE, 106; WILDE, O, 69
grew o. first...in other people's eyes AGE, 13
Growing o. is a bad habit OLD AGE, 70
Growing o. is like being increasingly penalized OLD AGE, 79
grow o. with a good grace AGE, 87
He cannot bear o. men's jokes OLD AGE, 48
I am o. enough to be – in fact am – your mother AGE, 63; MILNE, A, 1
If you want to be a dear o. lady at seventy OLD AGE, 83
I grow o....I grow o. ELIOT, T, 14; OLD AGE, 44
I love everything that's o. CONSERVATISM, 3; GOLDSMITH, O, 19
inclination...to suppose an o. man decayed in his intellects OLD AGE, 58
in these qualities o. age is usually not only not poorer OLD AGE, 35
I prefer o. age to the alternative OLD AGE, 31
It is so comic to hear oneself called o. OLD AGE, 57
I was born o. AGE, 93; TREE, H, 1
I will never be an o. man OLD AGE, 16
man...as o. as the woman he feels AGE, 62; MARX, G, 26
misfortune of an o. man AGE, 25
new book is published, read an o. one BOOKS, 38
Nobody hears o. people complain OLD AGE, 8
no more work for poor o. Ned DEATH, 68
No skill or art is needed to grow o. OLD AGE, 49
o. age a regret AGE, 33
O. age brings...the comfort that you will soon be out of it EMERSON, R, 21; OLD AGE, 46
O. age is a disease OLD AGE, 86
O. age is an island surrounded by death OLD AGE, 73
O. age is...crossed off names in an address book AGE, 19
o. age is...older than I am OLD AGE, 16
O. age is the out-patients' department OLD AGE, 30
O. age puts more wrinkles in our minds than on our faces OLD AGE, 72
o. age...the fear that it may go on too long OLD AGE, 101
O. men are dangerous OLD AGE, 95
O. men are twice children OLD AGE, 5
O. men forget SHAKESPEARE, 136
O. sins PROVERBS, 322; SIN, 1
one has to be very o. before one learns how to be amused AGE, 22; BUCK, P, 4
Physicians...are best when they are o. DOCTORS, 42
redress the balance of the O. AMERICA, 6
so few who can grow o. with a good grace OLD AGE, 99
so young a body with so o. a head WISDOM, 26
Tell me the o., o. story CHRISTIANITY, 41
terrible thing for an o. woman to outlive her dogs OLD AGE, 107
that grand o. man POLITICIANS, 109
That I may seem, though I die o. OLD AGE, 111
That is no country for o. men MORTALITY, 23; YEATS, W, 27
that o. serpent BIBLE, 465; DEVIL, 7
the misery of an o. man is interesting to nobody HUGO, V, 6; OLD AGE, 55
the o. have reminiscences AGE, 77; SAKI, 12
the o. have rubbed it into the young that they are wiser MAUGHAM, W, 3; OLD AGE, 67
the o. is better AGE, 17; ALCOHOL, 18; BIBLE, 321
The o. man has his death DEATH, 14; PROVERBS, 404
The principal objection to o. age OLD AGE, 11
There are no o. men any more AGE, 96; USTINOV, P, 4
There is a wicked inclination...to suppose an o. man decayed in his intellects JOHNSON, S, 143
They shall grow not o. MEMORIALS, 6
they think he is growing o. AGE, 55; COMPLIMENTS, 14

thought the o. man...had so much blood in him SHAKESPEARE, 223
Tidy the o. into tall flats OLD AGE, 19
To be o. is to be part of a...multitude OLD AGE, 24
too much Asia and she is too o. KIPLING, R, 19; PLACES, 20
too o. to go again to my travels CHARLES II, 1; ROYALTY, 38
We grow o. more through indolence LAZINESS, 2
What makes o. age hard to bear OLD AGE, 69
When men desire o. age OLD AGE, 15
When you are o. and gray OLD AGE, 113; YEATS, W, 33
Where are the boys of the O. Brigade NOSTALGIA, 28
Why does he die of o. age LEONARDO DA VINCI, 2
You are getting o. when the gleam in your eyes OLD AGE, 12
You are o., Father William CARROLL, L, 6; OLD AGE, 28
you grow o. beautifully OLD AGE, 68
'You have lived to be an o. man,' DOCTORS, 74
old age nothing funny or commendable about o. OLD AGE, 105
o. a regret DISRAELI, B, 4
O. is a shipwreck OLD AGE, 41
you will remember till o. OLD AGE, 84
older As we get o. we do not get any younger AGE, 73
As you get o....more boring OLD AGE, 80
I was so much o. then AGE, 36
make way for an o. man DISMISSAL, 7
O. men declare war WAR, 80
one is to grow o., the other not OLD AGE, 10
perceive real beauty in a person...o. BEAUTY, 7
The o. one grows the more one likes indecency AGE, 101; WOOLF, V, 11
to go on getting o. SURVIVAL, 1
old-fashioned o. respect for the young RESPECT, 6; WILDE, O, 23
O. ways FEMINISM, 1; WOMEN, 7
old lady nicest o. I ever met INSULTS, 47
old woman that monster, an o. OLD AGE, 39
olfactory an o. bar WELLS, H, 6
oligarchy displeased with *aristocracy,* call it *o.* GOVERNMENT, 17; HOBBES, T, 6
extreme democracy or absolute o....will come ARISTOTLE, 8; GOVERNMENT, 5
olive a land of oil o., and honey WEALTH, 9
an o. leaf plucked off BIBLE, 159
Oliver O. Twist has asked for more DICKENS, C, 36
To O. Goldsmith JOHNSON, S, 114
Olivier I'm the new O. ACTORS, 2
O. had murder in his heart ACTORS, 18
Olympic The most important thing in the O. Games VICTORY, 7
Omega Alpha and O. BIBLE, 459
omelette You can't make an o. PROVERBS, 474
ominous an idea...to be fashionable is o. FASHION, 11; SANTAYANA, G, 13
omnipotence final proof of God's o. GOD, 20
on he gets off with women because he can't get o. SEX, 69
O. with the dance BYRON, 14; DANCING, 1
they get *o.*, then they get *honour* DOCTORS, 85
Onan O. knew that the seed should not be his BIBLE, 177
Onaway O.! Awake, beloved LONGFELLOW, H, 14
once For Christmas comes but o. a year CHRISTMAS, 23
O. more unto the breach, dear friends COURAGE, 27; SHAKESPEARE, 129
One dies only o. DEATH, 112; MOLIERE, 4
you have dined in every house in London – *o.* BORES, 9; INSULTS, 133; WILDE, O, 78
you shall drink twice while I drink o. DRUNKENNESS, 28; WALPOLE, H, 10
one All for o., and o. for all UNITY, 8
have we not all o. father BIBLE, 342
How to be o. up ONE-UPMANSHIP, 3
if we knew o., we knew two METAPHYSICS, 3
I have only o. eye BLINDNESS, 11; NELSON, H, 3
o. and o. are two METAPHYSICS, 3; METAPHYSICS, 3
One is o. and all alone ANONYMOUS, 45; NUMBERS, 1
o. of us MAJOR, J, 3
O. Realm, O. People, O. Leader NAZISM, 1
The number o. book...was written by a committee BIBLE, 534
one-eyed o. yellow idol to the north of Khatmandu MOURNING, 5
the O. Man is King SUPERIORITY, 17; WELLS, H, 9
one-handed Give me a o. economist ECONOMICS, 22; TRUMAN, H, 9
oneself It is a stupidity...to busy o. with the correction of the world IMPROVEMENT, 3; MOLIERE, 6
One should examine o....before...condemning others MOLIERE, 7; SELF, 14
only possible society is o. MISANTHROPY, 5; WILDE, O, 18
the only person with whom one dares to talk continually of o. DOCTORS, 65
Why not be o. SELF-CONFIDENCE, 10
one up *How to be o.* POTTER, S, 2
onions carry their own o. when cycling abroad FRANCE, 3
onward little o. lend thy guiding hand GUIDANCE, 3; MILTON, J, 56
O., Christian soldiers CHRISTIANITY, 3
O., Christians, onward go ENDURANCE, 30
open I declare this thing o. – whatever it is ARCHITECTURE, 11
O. Sesame SUPERNATURAL, 2
opened the eyes of the blind shall be o. BIBLE, 209
opening o. time in the Sailors Arms PUBLIC HOUSES, 4; THOMAS, D, 22
opera an o. without an interval MUSIC, 43; OPERA, 8
baritones are born villains in o. OPERA, 11
Bed...is the poor man's o. HUXLEY, A, 21; SEX, 55
Like German o., too long and too loud WAUGH, E, 55
No good o. plot can be sensible OPERA, 3
O. in English MENCKEN, H, 17; OPERA, 7
o. isn't what it used to be OPERA, 5
The first rule in o. is the first rule in life MELBA, N, 1; SELF-RELIANCE, 9
The o. isn't over till the fat lady sings OPERA, 4
what language an o. is sung in OPERA, 2
operacy O. is what keeps society going EDUCATION, 16
operas Our mistake...was to write interminable large o. OPERA, 10
the German text of French o. OPERA, 13
operate Our doctor would never really o. unless it was necessary DOCTORS, 93
operation I see but as one sees after an o. BLINDNESS, 4
ophthalmologists eyeful of o. LANGUAGE, 4
opinion A man...must have a very good o. of himself AUSTEN, J, 6; CONCEIT, 2
better to have no o. of God BACON, F, 52; GOD, 4
fact that an o. has been widely held OPINIONS, 8
give him my o. DICKENS, C, 7; MARRIAGE, 62
he is.../Now but a climate of o. AUDEN, W, 15; PSYCHIATRY, 5
heresy signifies no more than private o. HOBBES, T, 3; OPINIONS, 4
He would rather follow public o. POLITICIANS, 92
I agree with no man's o. OPINIONS, 11; TURGENEV, I, 1
I am...of the o. with the learned CONGREVE, W, 5
man's o....on all things does not matter OPINIONS, 2
Nobody holds a good o. of a man who has a low o. of himself SELF-RESPECT, 5; TROLLOPE, A, 12
nothing to admire except his o. CRITICS, 6; FRY, C, 2
of his own o. still BUTLER, S, 8; YIELDING, 2
o. breeds ignorance OPINIONS, 3
so vain...care for the o. of those we don't care for CONCEIT, 8
the English think of an o. as something...to hide ENGLISH, 20
The superiority of one man's o. over another's JAMES, H, 13; OPINIONS, 5
They that approve...call it o. HOBBES, T, 3; OPINIONS, 4
opinionated the o., the ignorant, and the boorish ARISTOTLE, 3; STUBBORNNESS, 3
opinions a decent respect to the o. of mankind INDEPENDENCE, 3; JEFFERSON, T, 4
New o. are always suspected NOVELTY, 5
not a writer's business to hold o. WRITERS, 32; YEATS, W, 36
So many men, so many o. OPINIONS, 10; TERENCE, 4
The average man's o. OPINIONS, 7
The doctors are always changing their o. DOCTORS, 47
the proper o. for the time of year AUDEN, W, 27; PUBLIC, 3
The public buys its o. as it buys its meat BUTLER, S, 15; PUBLIC, 7
There are only o., some of which are preferable TRUTH, 25
the same o. have arisen among men in cycles OPINIONS, 1
The State, in choosing men...takes no notice of their o. CROMWELL, O, 8; LOYALTY, 6
The wish to spread those o. that we hold BUTLER, S, 4; ENGLISH, 8
when o. universally prevail OPINIONS, 12

opium Religion…is the o. of the people MARX, K, 4; RELIGION, 65
opium-dose an o. for keeping beasts of burden BIBLE, 532; KINGSLEY, C, 3
opponent Never ascribe to an o. motives meaner than your own BARRIE, J, 13; MOTIVE, 1
opportunist rather be an o. and float BALDWIN, S, 10; EXPEDIENCY, 3
opportunities A wise man will make more o. BACON, F, 16; OPPORTUNITY, 9
One can present people with o. OPPORTUNITY, 15
O. are usually disguised as hard work OPPORTUNITY, 14
opportunity Equality of o. OPPORTUNITY, 17
follies…he didn't commit when he had the o. REGRET, 17
let slip an o. OPPORTUNITY, 21
O. seldom knocks twice OPPORTUNITY, 6; PROVERBS, 331
the o. to move…upward to the Great Society CIVILIZATION, 8; PROGRESS, 16
There is no security…only o. OPPORTUNITY, 16
oppose duty…to o. OPPOSITION, 2
opposites By o. o. are cured REMEDIES, 34
opposition Her Majesty's O. BAGEHOT, W, 4; OPPOSITION, 1
I have spent many years…in o. OPPOSITION, 5
The duty of an o. OPPOSITION, 2
When I invented the phrase 'His Majesty's O.' OPPOSITION, 3
oppressed The o. speak a million tongues PSYCHIATRY, 30
oppression when fanatics are on top there is no limit to o. GOVERNMENT, 25; MENCKEN, H, 8
Where rumour of o. and deceit COWPER, W, 27; SOLITUDE, 3
oppressive Vatican is an o. regime CHURCH, 3
optimism married six times shows a degree of o. MARRIAGE, 103
O.: A kind of heart stimulant OPTIMISM, 29
O. is the content of small men OPTIMISM, 26
Pessimism…is just as agreeable as o. BENNETT, A, 5; PESSIMISM, 1
The place where o. most flourishes OPTIMISM, 25
optimist an o.…fills up his crossword puzzle in ink OPTIMISM, 37
An o. is a guy that never had much experience OPTIMISM, 32
an o. who carries a raincoat OPTIMISM, 41
I am an o., unrepentant and militant OPTIMISM, 38; USTINOV, P, 3
The o. proclaims OPTIMISM, 21; PESSIMISM, 3
optimistic O. lies MEDICINE, 91; SHAW, G, 33
Oracle I am Sir O. EGOTISM, 8; SHAKESPEARE, 238
oracular the use of my o. tongue MALAPROPISMS, 8; SHERIDAN, R, 9
oral a terrific story about o. contraception ALLEN, W, 11; CONTRACEPTION, 2
oral sex worst thing about o. SEX, 71
orange Oh that I were an o.-tree HERBERT, G, 3; SERVICE, 3
'tis an *O.* ROYALTY, 15
oranges bananas or o., the Americans would not go AMERICANS, 2
O. and lemons, /Say the bell of St Clement's LONDON, 2; NURSERY RHYMES, 41
orangutang an o. trying to play the violin BALZAC, H, 3; MARRIAGE, 18
orator Webster is his o. WEBSTER, D, 2
oratorium *Laboratorium est o.* SCIENCE, 66
orchard Before the cherry o. was sold CHEKHOV, A, 6; WORRY, 11
orchestra a woman…cannot be trusted with a symphony o. MUSIC, 35
two golden rules for an o. BEECHAM, T, 2; MUSIC, 5
orchestration Literature is the o. of platitudes LITERATURE, 28; WILDER, T, 7
ordained o. for the procreation of children BOOK OF COMMON PRAYER, 24
order done decently and in o. BIBLE, 39
O. is heaven's first law ORDER, 3; POPE, A, 37
The old o. changeth CHANGE, 25; TENNYSON, 23
upon the o. of your going SHAKESPEARE, 217
wisdom…sweetly doth…o. all things BIBLE, 521
words in the best o. COLERIDGE, S, 41; POETRY AND PROSE, 2
ordered a side dish he hadn't o. CONTEMPT, 3; INSULTS, 82
ordering the better o. of the universe UNIVERSE, 1
orderly Being o.…can be excessively tiresome ORDER, 1
so o. in his way of life SOCRATES, 2
ordinariness remarkable only for her o. TERESA, 2
ordinary One machine can do the work of fifty o. men TECHNOLOGY, 8
talent for describing the…characters of o. life AUSTEN, J, 2
ordination question of women's o. RELIGION, 103
oread Says she was once an o. of the slopes CAMPBELL, R, 1
organ an amplification of one o. MEDICINE, 25
A physician is obligated to consider more than a diseased o. ENVIRONMENT, 6
my second favourite o. ALLEN, W, 6; ANIMALISM, 1
Seated…at the o. MUSIC, 49
organ-grinder no reason to attack the monkey when the o. is present BEVAN, A, 9
organic O. life…has developed…from the protozoon to the philosopher PROGRESS, 21; RUSSELL, B, 15
organization o. could do it that quickly BUREAUCRACY, 2
organized War is an o. bore WAR, 79
organs he'd have given us all more o. BRADBURY, M, 8; SEX, 18
To be solemn about the o. of generation SEX, 59
orgasm One o. in the bush SEX, 99
stimulation to o. centers upon the clitoris SEX, 44
the absence of the vaginal o. SEX, 41
The o. has replaced the Cross MUGGERIDGE, M, 2; SEX, 88
orgies o. are vile DEBAUCHERY, 10; NASH, O, 5
orgy An o. looks particularly alluring MUGGERIDGE, M, 1; PRUDERY, 4
you need an o., once in a while DEBAUCHERY, 10; NASH, O, 5
Orientals If…O.…drank a liquor which…made them vomit ALCOHOL, 50; LA BRUYERE, J, 13
origin the indelible stamp of his lowly o. DARWIN, C, 7; EVOLUTION, 8
original An o. writer is…one whom nobody can imitate ORIGINALITY, 2
Mona did researches in o. sin SEX, 97
o. is unfaithful to the translation TRANSLATION, 1
The more intelligence…the more…one finds o. PASCAL, B, 3
the only absolutely o. creation…is Don Quixote FICTION, 6; MAUGHAM, W, 22
thought is often o. ORIGINALITY, 3
originality absence of inverted commas guarantees…o. QUOTATIONS, 2
All good things…are the fruits of o. ORIGINALITY, 4
without o. or moral courage CHARACTER, 22; SHAW, G, 8
originator quotes…give us a nodding acquaintance with the o. QUOTATIONS, 16
Ormus Outshone the wealth of O. and of Ind DEVIL, 13; MILTON, J, 39
ornamental not merely…useful and o. PURPOSE, 11
orphan defeat is an o. DEFEAT, 2; VICTORY, 5
orthodoxy 'o.'…no longer means being right CHESTERTON, G, 17; ORTHODOXY, 2
O. or My-doxy CARLYLE, T, 17; ORTHODOXY, 1
Oscar if…O. Wilde had lived into his nineties MUGGERIDGE, M, 4; OLD AGE, 74
We all assume that O. said it QUOTATIONS, 8; WILDE, O, 2
ostrich the wings of an o. CRITICISM, 39; MACAULAY, T, 2
other he is the Absolute – she is the O. BEAUVOIR, S, 5
it did a lot of o. things ADMIRATION, 6
O. people are quite dreadful MISANTHROPY, 5; WILDE, O, 18
you expect o. people to be…to your liking TOLERANCE, 4
others By persuading o. we convince ourselves PERSUASION, 2
delight in…misfortunes…of o. BURKE, E, 6
some more than o. COWARD, N, 4; SIMILARITY, 4
tell the o. by their hunted expression CHARITY, 19; INSULTS, 86; LEWIS, C, 6
to encourage the o. EXAMPLE, 9; VOLTAIRE, 7
otherwise nothing in his long career which those…would wish o. ROYALTY, 19
Some folk…are o. SMOLLETT, T, 4; WISDOM, 29
Otis Miss O. regrets APOLOGIES, 4; PORTER, C, 5
ounce An o. of a man's own wit STERNE, L, 10; WISDOM, 30
ours We have met the enemy, and they are o. VICTORY, 18
ourselves all our knowledge is, o. to know POPE, A, 36; SELF-KNOWLEDGE, 6
By persuading others we convince o. PERSUASION, 2
In every friend we lose a part of o. DEATH, 125; POPE, A, 61
It is always o. we love SELF, 6
remedies oft in o. do lie SHAKESPEARE, 21
'tis in o. that we are thus, or thus HUMAN NATURE, 29
we but praise o. in other men POPE, A, 27; PRAISE, 7
What isn't part of o. doesn't disturb us HATE, 6
'ousemaids I walks with fifty o. outer Chelsea to the Strand DISCONTENT, 6; KIPLING, R, 25
'ouses It's 'aving o. built by men HOUSES, 5; WELLS, H, 14

out Mordre wol o. CHAUCER, G, 17; MURDER, 4
once o., what you've said can't be stopped HORACE, 11; PUBLISHING, 7
O., damned spot GUILT, 18; SHAKESPEARE, 222
out-herods it o. Herod ACTING, 20
outlive o. this powerful rhyme POETRY, 56; SHAKESPEARE, 364
outlook religious o. on life JUNG, C, 6; RELIGION, 59
out-of-doors God having given us indoors and o. NATURE, 25
outrun We may o. EXCESS, 13; SHAKESPEARE, 139
outside I am just going o. LAST WORDS, 63
I support it from the o. MELBOURNE, 10; SUPPORT, 6
live o. the law HONESTY, 4
outspoken he is so hearty, so straightforward, o. ROOSEVELT, T, 1
outstanding pull down an o. building, no one objects AMERICA, 10
outstays guest who o. HOSPITALITY, 4; HOSPITALITY, 7
outward I may not hope from o. forms APPEARANCES, 13; COLERIDGE, S, 11
over Now the day is o. DAY, 1
The game isn't o. till it's o. SPORT AND GAMES, 4
we're coming o., /And we won't come back till it's o., o. there. WORLD WAR I, 8
overboard throw the occasional man o. POLITICS, 43
overcomes Who o. /By force MILTON, J, 37; VICTORY, 16
over-confident Not that I am ever o. SELF-CONFIDENCE, 11; THATCHER, M, 35
overdressed overshadowed by his o., extravagant and idle wife STOPES, M, 6
He was o., pompous...and vain WRITERS, 95
over-educated I've o. myself in all the things COWARD, N, 21
overexposure she should catch a cold on o. BUTLER, S, 18; TRUTH, 15
overfed They're overpaid, o., oversexed and over here SOLDIERS, 16
over-feeding what Nicely-Nicely dies of will be o. GREED, 11; RUNYON, D, 10
overlooked better to be looked over than o. STARING, 1; WEST, M, 12
overlord o. of the M5 HILL, G, 4
overpaid They're o., overfed, oversexed and over here SOLDIERS, 16
overpaying o. him but he's worth it GOLDWYN, S, 4
overrated matrimony, which I always thought a highly o. performance MARRIAGE, 69
overrun apt to be o. with nettles MIND, 33; WALPOLE, H, 8
over-running and lose by o. EXCESS, 13; SHAKESPEARE, 139
oversexed They're overpaid, overfed, o. and over here SOLDIERS, 16
overtakers It is the o. who TRAVEL, 36
overthrown Another mighty empire o. DEFEAT, 18; WORDSWORTH, W, 52
overtures I tried to resist his o. PUNS, 21
ovule Man is developed from an o. EVOLUTION, 7
ovules differs in no respect from the o. of other animals EVOLUTION, 7
owe I don't o. a penny to a single soul SNOBBERY, 15; WODEHOUSE, P, 12
owed so much o. by so many to so few CHURCHILL, W, 53; WORLD WAR II, 14
owes A nation is not in danger...because it o. itself money ECONOMICS, 18
he o. not any man LONGFELLOW, H, 18; RIGHTEOUSNESS, 9
oweth woman o. to her husband MARRIAGE, 135
owl The O. and the Pussy-Cat went to sea LEAR, E, 8; NONSENSE, 23
owls Two O. and a Hen APPEARANCE, 37; LEAR, E, 1
own mine o. Executioner DONNE, J, 6; SELF, 9
ownership its source of power: o. CAPITALISM, 10; KINNOCK, N, 5
spread of personal o. is in harmony BRITISH, 11; MATERIALISM, 17
transform this society without...extension of public o. KINNOCK, N, 1; SOCIALISM, 15
own-goal Aids pandemic is a classic o. AIDS, 2
ox This dumb o. will fill the whole world EXPECTATION, 4
When he stands like an o. in the furrow KIPLING, R, 21; NATIONALITY, 8
Oxenford Clerk...of O. CHAUCER, G, 7; LOGIC, 3
Oxford a secret in the O. sense OXFORD, 7; SECRECY, 10
Cambridge as a little town and O. OXFORD, 16
every imitation from 'Eton and O.' PARTIES, 12
Herr Hitler and Signor Mussolini had been at O. OXFORD, 11
It is O. that has made me insufferable BEERBOHM, M, 8
nice sort of place, O. OXFORD, 13; SHAW, G, 22
O.... full of a particular non-social snobbiness OXFORD, 15
O. is on the whole more attractive than Cambridge CAMBRIDGE, 1; OXFORD, 3
The clever men at O. /Know all that there is to be knowed KNOWLEDGE, 21; OXFORD, 10
The King to O. sent a troop of horse CAMBRIDGE, 3; OXFORD, 6
To O. sent a troop of horse CAMBRIDGE, 6; OXFORD, 14
To the University of O. I acknowledge no obligation EDUCATION, 36; GIBBON, E, 3; OXFORD, 8
You will hear more good things on...a stagecoach from London to O. HAZLITT, W, 27; INTELLECTUALS, 11
you will leave O. by the town drain SPOONER, W, 5
oyster bold man that first eat an o. FOOD, 66; SWIFT, J, 12
sympathetic unselfishness of an o. PERFECTION, 9; SAKI, 10
the sort of eye that can open an o. at sixty paces APPEARANCE, 75; WODEHOUSE, P, 6
world's mine o. OPPORTUNITY, 20; SHAKESPEARE, 256
oysters Poverty and o. DICKENS, C, 46; POVERTY, 8
Ozymandias My name is O. King of Kings SHELLEY, P, 17

P

pace this petty p. from day to day LIFE, 86; SHAKESPEARE, 227
Pacific salutes the Admiral of the P. ARROGANCE, 10; WILHELM II, 3
pacifism My p. is not based on...intellectual theory WAR AND PEACE, 6
pack how much more dogs are animated when they hunt in a p. HUME, D, 6; UNITY, 11
P. your bags OLD AGE, 59
the human p. is shuffled and cut EDUCATION, 56; LODGE, D, 3
paddle every man p. his own canoe INDEPENDENCE, 4
padlocked music critics....small and rodent-like with p. ears CRITICS, 20; STRAVINSKY, I, 3
pagan A P. suckled in a creed outworn DISCONTENT, 10; WORDSWORTH, W, 66
Christian glories in the death of a p. CHRISTIANITY, 5
pageant insubstantial p. faded MORTALITY, 17; SHAKESPEARE, 327
paid I do not answer questions like this without being p. MASCULINITY, 1
pain a gentleman...never inflicts p. CHIVALRY, 10
Although p. isn't real ANONYMOUS, 90
a p. in the neck SPEECHES, 1
critics...desire our blood, not our p. CRITICS, 13; NIETZSCHE, F, 15
disinclination to inflict p. upon oneself GOOD, 12
He that is uneasy at every little p. HYPOCHONDRIA, 1
I feel no p., dear mother, now ANONYMOUS, 43
if it did not involve giving p. OCCUPATIONS, 7
in the midst...p., you can and must keep going ENDURANCE, 7
it entails too much p. REMEDIES, 30
momentary intoxication with p. BRONOWSKI, J, 4; CRUELTY, 1
Neither shame nor physical p. have any...effect KEY, E, 4
No p., no palm; no thorns, no throne SUCCESS, 24
owes its pleasures to another's p. COWPER, W, 31
P. and death are a part of life LIFE, 38
P....cannot recollect DICKINSON, E, 5
P. is life – the sharper, the more evidence of life LIFE, 54
People will not...bear p. unless there is hope HOPE, 10
Pleasure is...intermission of p. PLEASURE, 32; SELDEN, J, 4
Religion was my protection against p. RELIGION, 51
The art of life is the art of avoiding p. LIFE, 53
The first cry of p....was the first call for a physician MEDICINE, 84
The least p. in our little finger HAZLITT, W, 3; SELF-INTEREST, 4
The night was p. SORROW, 2
The p. passes, but the beauty remains ART, 28; ENDURANCE, 17
There is no greater p. DANTE ALIGHIERI, 3
they blest him in their p. MARTYRDOM, 7; TENNYSON, 70
what p. it was to drown DROWNING, 2; SHAKESPEARE, 303
yearning like a God in p. KEATS, J, 12
pained greatly p. at how little he was p. WAUGH, E, 26
painful nourishment of the body into a p. attack DIETING, 3
the one is as p. as the other LIFE AND DEATH, 6
painless cane someone and expect it to be p. PUNISHMENT, 32

pains He therefore was at strenuous p. POLITICIANS, 1
no gains without p. ENDURANCE, 25; STEVENSON, A, 4
suffering her p. in his own proper person and character SEXES, 27
With what shift and p. we come into the World DEATH, 44
paint flinging a pot of p. in the public's face RUSKIN, J, 17; WHISTLER, J, 1
I p. objects as I think them ARTISTS, 20; PAINTING, 13
My business is to p.…what I see PAINTING, 20
not p. a portrait to look like the subject ARTISTS, 14
to p. the lily EXCESS, 14; SHAKESPEARE, 167
painted As idle as a p. ship BOATS, 3; COLERIDGE, S, 29
I am p. as the greatest little dictator THATCHER, M, 28
Most women are not so young as they are p. BEERBOHM, M, 10; COSMETICS, 1
p.…by the great artist Kodak MILLIGAN, S, 2
painter A p. should not paint what he sees ARTISTS, 8
I am married to Beatrice Salkeld, a p. BEHAN, B, 10; CHILDREN, 8
I could have become a real p. LAST WORDS, 52
memory is a p. MEMORY, 14
not a great sculptor or p. can be an architect ARCHITECTURE, 13; RUSKIN, J, 3
painters Good p. imitate nature CERVANTES, M, 23; PAINTING, 4
P. and poets…licence to dare anything FREEDOM, 24; HORACE, 1
Poets and p. are outside the class system ARTISTS, 2; POETS, 1
painting a great difference between p. a face APPEARANCE, 27
If I didn't start p., I would have raised chickens OCCUPATIONS, 19
If people only knew…about p. PAINTING, 9
I just keep p. till I feel like pinching. PAINTING, 17
P. is a blind man's profession PAINTING, 14; PICASSO, P, 6
p. on a square of ivory WRITERS, 52
P.…protecting flat surfaces from the weather PAINTING, 3
paintings the women in his p. PICASSO, P, 4
pair A p. so famous LOVE AND DEATH, 7
pajamas I shot an elephant in my p. HUMOUR, 49; MARX, G, 2
Pakistani writes like a P. who has learned English when he was twelve years old SHAW, G, 2
palace Love in a p. KEATS, J, 24; LOVE, 96
palaces Mid pleasures and p. though we may roam HOME, 10
pale a p. horse BIBLE, 462; DEATH, 38
Palestine establishment in P. of a national home BALFOUR, A, 4
not enough prisons…in P. to hold all the Jews MEIR, G, 7
pall The pallor of girls' brows shall be their p. OWEN, W, 1
Palladium Liberty of the press is the *P.* of…rights FREEDOM, 29; MEDIA, 10
pallor The p. of girls' brows shall be their pall OWEN, W, 1
palm happy state of getting the victor's p. without the dust of racing HORACE, 14; VICTORY, 9
No pain, no p.; no thorns, no throne SUCCESS, 24
To win the p., the oak, or bays MARVELL, A, 1; VICTORY, 15
palms p. before my feet ANIMALS, 12; CHESTERTON, G, 13
they found no more of her than…the p. of her hands BIBLE, 303
palm-tree the righteous shall flourish like a p. PSALMS, 52
palsied with the p. heart PASSION, 11; TENNYSON, 52
pan Forty years ago he was Slightly in Peter P. INSULTS, 124
Put on the p.; /Says Greedy Nan NURSERY RHYMES, 7
Pancras musical equivalent of…St P. CRITICISM, 5
pandemic Aids p. is a classic own-goal AIDS, 2
Pandora open that P.'s Box…Trojan 'orses will jump out MIXED METAPHORS, 1
Panjandrum the grand P. NONSENSE, 13
Pankhurst I heard Christabel P. the other day PANKHURST, C, 2
pantheist The modern p. not only LAWRENCE, D, 21; PHOTOGRAPHY, 6
pants There were times my p. were so thin POVERTY, 42
Your eyes shine like the p. COMPLIMENTS, 18; MARX, G, 4
papacy Since God has given us the p.…enjoy it CATHOLICISM, 10
The P. is not other than the Ghost of the deceased Roman Empire CATHOLICISM, 7; HOBBES, T, 7
paper only a p. moon FAITH, 14
reactionaries are p. tigers MAO TSE-TUNG, 5; POLITICS, 75
The atom bomb is a p. tiger MAO TSE-TUNG, 9; NUCLEAR WEAPONS, 14
This p. will no doubt be found interesting CRITICISM, 17
Where were you fellows when the p. was blank EDITORS, 1
papers a great heap of p. ROYALTY, 32
fornicated and read the p. CAMUS, A, 6; MANKIND, 15
only two posh p. on a Sunday NEWSPAPERS, 13; OSBORNE, J, 2
Papists revenged to the utmost upon all P. ASSASSINATION, 1
papyromania *P.* – compulsive accumulation OBSESSIONS, 2
papyrophobia *P.* – abnormal desire OBSESSIONS, 2
parables great p.…but false art CRITICISM, 33; LAWRENCE, D, 42
parade the chief employment of riches consists in the p. of riches OSTENTATION, 6; SMITH, A, 2
paradise A p. for a sect KEATS, J, 15
drunk the milk of P. CAUTION, 9; COLERIDGE, S, 17
England is the p. of individuality ENGLAND, 44; SANTAYANA, G, 9
England is the p. of women ENGLAND, 22
Grant me p. in this world HEAVEN, 16
If a man could pass through P. COLERIDGE, S, 4; PROOF, 3
Same old glimpse of /P. MARRIAGE, 98
the p. of fools is not an unpleasant abode HEAVEN, 6
to hope for P. is to live in P. HEAVEN, 11; SACKVILLE-WEST, V, 4
we go to P. by way of Kensal Green EXPECTATION, 2; LIFE, 28
Wilderness is P. enow FITZGERALD, E, 5
paradox strange p.…need to be left alone HOSTAGES, 3
paradoxes ocean is a place of p. CARSON, R, 1
P. are useful IDEAS, 1
paragon the p. of animals MANKIND, 56; SHAKESPEARE, 85
parallel We never remark any passion…in others, of which…we may not find a p. HUME, D, 5; SELF, 11
parallelogram The landlady…is a p. HUMOUR, 47; LEACOCK, S, 6
paralyse p. it by encumbering it with remedies REMEDIES, 56; TOLSTOY, L, 11
paranoia vanity and a p. about writers WRITERS, 16
paranoid Even a p. can have enemies ENEMIES, 4
Just because you're p. PSYCHIATRY, 3
parasite A crawling and disgusting p. VIRGIL, 1
save every p. alive SURVIVAL, 4
The sick man is a p. of society PATIENTS, 3
parcels Portions and p. of the dreadful Past TENNYSON, 54; TIME, 57
pardon God may p. you, but I never can ELIZABETH I, 6
God will p. me. It is His trade HEINE, H, 5; LAST WORDS, 49
pardoned The women p. all BYRON, 30
parent a kind p.…or a merciless step-mother NATURE, 27; PLINY THE ELDER, 3
To lose one p.…a misfortune; to lose both looks like carelessness LOSS, 10; WILDE, O, 26
parenthood p.…feeding the mouth that bites you FAMILY, 16
parents A Jewish man with p. alive JEWS, 18
by defying their p. and copying one another YOUTH, 8
children, obey your p. BIBLE, 95; OBEDIENCE, 1
Don't hold your p. up to contempt FAMILY, 63
From birth to age eighteen, a girl needs good p. AGE, 95
innate superiority that the successful p. had SUPERIORITY, 15
joys of p. are secret BACON, F, 38; FAMILY, 8
necessary precautions to avoid having p. FAMILY, 14
P.…a disappointment to their children FAMILY, 48
P. are strange FAMILY, 62
P. are the bones CHILDREN, 59; FAMILY, 61
P. are the last people on earth FAMILY, 12
P. learn a lot from their children CHILDREN, 56; SPARK, M, 3
Possessive p. rarely live long enough to see FAMILY, 23
sort of people our p. warned us about VICE, 11
the way p. obey their children FAMILY, 64
what p. were created for FAMILY, 43; NASH, O, 8
Paris delivered of a city bigger than P. LA FONTAINE, J, 6
Good Americans, when they die, go to P. AMERICANS, 1
Her frocks are built in P. CLOTHES, 22
I love P. PARIS, 6; PORTER, C, 3
Is P. burning HITLER, A, 17; PARIS, 4
no home…save in P. NIETZSCHE, F, 7; PARIS, 5
P. is worth a mass PARIS, 3
P. Loves Lovers PARIS, 7
The last time I saw P. PARIS, 1
when good Americans die they go to P. WILDE, O, 57
parish all the world as my p. RELIGION, 100
He was born, bred, and hanged, all in the same p. ANONYMOUS, 34
man who left a wife and six children on the p. ROYALTY, 16
park The hunchback in the p. LONELINESS, 15; THOMAS, D, 12
Parkinson The rise in the…employed is governed by P.'s Law PARKINSON, C, 2
par-lee-voo Hinky, dinky, p. FRANCE, 17
parliament a regular income from his p. INSINCERITY, 3

build your House of P. upon the river WELLINGTON, 14
He stood twice for P. POLITICS, 116; WAUGH, E, 24
If Her Majesty stood for P. POLITICS, 95
more fit for a grammar school than a Court of P. HOUSES OF PARLIAMENT, 6
nailed up the doors of P. FASCISM, 12
no reference to fun in any Act of P. PLEASURE, 15
P. is the longest running farce GOVERNMENT, 37
The rights of p. should be preserved GOVERNMENT, 27
Three Estates in P. CARLYLE, T, 13
parliaments England…mother of p. ENGLAND, 10
P. are the great lie of our time GOVERNMENT, 33
parlour Will you walk into my p. INVITATIONS, 3
parlourmaid a p. as ignorant as Queen Victoria VICTORIA, 4
parochial worse than provincial – he was p. JAMES, H, 7; WRITERS, 64
parody devil's walking p. ANIMALS, 11; CHESTERTON, G, 12
parole Classical quotation is the *p.* of literary men JOHNSON, S, 137; QUOTATIONS, 4
parrot This p. is no more DEATH, 113
to sell the family p. RESPECTABILITY, 4; ROGERS, W, 12
parsnips fine words butter no p. SCOTT, W, 11; WORDS, 27
parson If P. lost his senses ANIMALS, 15
In arguing too, the p. own'd his skill GOLDSMITH, O, 7; KNOWLEDGE, 20
Once a p. OCCUPATIONS, 5; PROVERBS, 324
p. in a tye-wig ADDISON, J, 2
parsons Our dourest p. PRAYER, 25
part A stage where every man must play a p. LIFE, 87
I have forgot my p. FAILURE, 9; SHAKESPEARE, 60
In every friend we lose a p. of ourselves DEATH, 125; POPE, A, 61
it is a little flesh and breath, and the ruling p. MARCUS AURELIUS ANTONINUS, 1
let us kiss and p. PARTING, 6
p. never calls for it ACTING, 16
read p. of it all the way GOLDWYN, S, 18
till death us do p. BOOK OF COMMON PRAYER, 27; MARRIAGE, 33
We only p. to meet again FAITHFULNESS, 4; GAY, J, 12
particular a London p.…A fog DICKENS, C, 5; WEATHER, 9
did nothing in p. GILBERT, W, 21; HOUSES OF PARLIAMENT, 13
particulars Minute P. BLAKE, W, 16; GOOD, 2
parties it is always like that at p. PROUST, M, 14; REGRET, 15
one of those p. which got out of hand CHRISTIANITY, 32
parting Every p. gives a foretaste of death SCHOPENHAUER, A, 3
P. is all we know of heaven DICKINSON, E, 4; PARTING, 5
P. is such sweet sorrow PARTING, 10; SHAKESPEARE, 314
partisanship P. is our great curse SUBJECTIVITY, 7
partly Man p. is AMBITION, 5; BROWNING, R, 22
partnership Marriage…regarded as a p. of equals MARRIAGE, 94
partridge A p. in a pear tree CHRISTMAS, 17
well-shot woodcock, p., snipe BETJEMAN, J, 4; HUNTING, 2
parts It is seldom…one p. on good terms PARTING, 9; PROUST, M, 17
one man in his time plays many p. SHAKESPEARE, 48
Today we have naming of p. REED, H, 2; WEAPONS, 7
truth in the inward p. PSALMS, 31
part-time p. nihilist CAMUS, A, 13; COMMITMENT, 4
parturition P. is a physiological process BIRTH, 7
party A great p. is not to be brought down POLITICS, 47
Any p. which takes credit for the rain POLITICS, 78
best number for a dinner p. is two FOOD, 35
Englishman has to have a P. POLITICS, 91
Heard there was a p. ACCIDENTS, 6
I always voted at my p.'s call POLITICIANS, 10
No p. has a monopoly GORBACHOV, M, 10; TOLERANCE, 2
p. is a political evil POLITICS, 21
soft drink at a p. ABSTINENCE, 2
the Conservative P. at prayer CHURCH, 11
The p. is the rallying-point for the…working class COMMUNISM, 17; STALIN, J, 4
The sooner every p. breaks up the better AUSTEN, J, 8; PARTIES, 2
unswerving loyalty to his p. POLITICIANS, 104
Well, did you evah! What a swell p. PARTIES, 7; PORTER, C, 6
pass but let it p., let it p. THURBER, J, 17
Horseman, p. by YEATS, W, 32
ideas simply p. through him STUPIDITY, 1
I shall not p. this way again MORTALITY, 11
no delight to p. away the time APPEARANCE, 61
p. for forty-three AGE, 47; GILBERT, W, 46; INSULTS, 53
p. through things temporal BOOK OF COMMON PRAYER, 6
Praise the Lord and p. the ammunition WAR, 63
They shall not p. DETERMINATION, 20
To p. away ere life hath lost its brightness DEATH, 77
passage a fair and easie p. for it to go out LIFE AND DEATH, 18
calm p.…across many a bad night NIETZSCHE, F, 11; SUICIDE, 21
Patience and p. of time LA FONTAINE, J, 4; PATIENCE, 12
passageways smell of steaks in p. ELIOT, T, 19; FOOD, 28
passé Sin…not only ugly but p. SIN, 19
passed p. by on the other side BIBLE, 324
p. from death unto life BIBLE, 248
That p. the time BECKETT, S, 3; TIME, 11
the people were p. clean over Jordan BIBLE, 287
We have all p. a lot of water GOLDWYN, S, 17
passengers fools and p. drink at sea BOATS, 16
passeront *Ils ne p. pas* DETERMINATION, 20
passes Men seldom make p. APPEARANCE, 51; PARKER, D, 28
passeth the peace of God, which p. all understanding BIBLE, 445; BLESSING, 5
passion All breathing human p. far above KEATS, J, 31; PASSION, 5
Asthma is a disease that has practically the same symptoms as p. PASSION, 1
cheated into p., but…reasoned into truth DRYDEN, J, 30; TRUTH, 24
Culture is the p. for sweetness and light ARNOLD, M, 23; CULTURE, 2
desolate and sick of an old p. LOVE, 67
Master Mistress of my p. LOVE, 149; SHAKESPEARE, 361
one master-p.…/swallows up the rest PASSION, 7; POPE, A, 35
p. and party blind our eyes COLERIDGE, S, 23; EXPERIENCE, 11
P.…can be destroyed by a doctor PASSION, 9
p. in the human soul MUSIC, 37
So I triumphed ere my p. PASSION, 11; TENNYSON, 52
Strange fits of p. PASSION, 12; WORDSWORTH, W, 67
The p. and the life, whose fountains are within COLERIDGE, S, 11
The ruling p. conquers reason still PASSION, 8; POPE, A, 45
We never remark any p.…in others, of which,…we may not find a parallel HUME, D, 5; SELF, 11
you say you're his…his p. is /Infinite… LYING, 18
passions A man who has not passed through the inferno of his p. JUNG, C, 3
It is with our p. as it is with fire and water PASSION, 6
Literature and butterflies are the two sweetest p. NABOKOV, V, 8
not his reason, but his p. STERNE, L, 8
The man who is master of his p. CONNOLLY, C, 20
Three p., simple but overwhelmingly strong, have governed my life RUSSELL, B, 4
that man /That is not p. slave PASSION, 10
passover it is the Lord's p. BIBLE, 110
past Even God cannot change the p. PAST, 1
half of you belongs to the p. ANOUILH, J, 7; OLD AGE, 14
his p. shut in him like the leaves PAST, 14
Historians tell the story of the p. NOVELS, 6
I do not…prejudge the p. PREJUDICE, 16
I weep like a child for the p. NOSTALGIA, 14
Keep off your thoughts from things that are p. PAST, 12
looking forward to the p. NOSTALGIA, 20; OSBORNE, J, 5
mentioning some woman whom he knew in the p. JEALOUSY, 10
Nothing recalls the p. so potently as a smell NOSTALGIA, 6
people who live in the p. BENNETT, A, 4; PROGRESS, 4
Portions and parcels of the dreadful P. TENNYSON, 54; TIME, 57
remembrance of things p. REGRET, 24; SHAKESPEARE, 363
something…absurd about the p. BEERBOHM, M, 3; PAST, 2
Study the p. CONFUCIUS, 4; PAST, 5
that is p. as a watch in the night PSALMS, 49
The only thing I regret about my p. life AGE, 12
The p., at least, is secure PAST, 13; WEBSTER, D, 5
The p. is a foreign country PAST, 6
The p. is the only dead thing PAST, 11
The p. was a sleep BEGINNING, 7; BROWNING, R, 56
The p. was nothing…The future was a mystery PRESENT, 2
Those who cannot remember the p. HISTORY, 24; SANTAYANA, G, 6
Time present and time p. ELIOT, T, 6
to know nothing but the present, or nothing but the p. CONSERVATISM, 5; KEYNES, J, 2
what is p. my help is p. my care BEAUMONT, F, 2; INDIFFERENCE, 1

what's p. help /Should be p. grief REGRET, 23; SHAKESPEARE, 351
What we know of the p. is HISTORY, 18; INGE, W, 1
Who can afford to live in the p. NOSTALGIA, 21; PINTER, H, 4
Who controls the p. controls the future ORWELL, G, 15; POWER, 20
Why doesn't the p. decently bury itself PAST, 7
pastime Art is not a p. ART, 7
pastoral Cold P. ETERNITY, 3; KEATS, J, 29
investiture by the gift of the p. staff CORRUPTION, 3
pasture the people of his p. PSALMS, 56
pastures fresh woods, and p. new MILTON, J, 27
he maketh me to lie down in green p. PSALMS, 12
pat P.-a-cake, p.-a-cake, baker's man NURSERY RHYMES, 42
patches king of shreds and p. SHAKESPEARE, 99
Man is…a thing of shreds and p. MANKIND, 26
thing of shreds and p. GILBERT, W, 24; SINGERS, 2
pate You beat your p. POPE, A, 9; STUPIDITY, 13
patent The people – could you p. the sun SCIENCE, 81
patents p. that cover vast stretches of the entire human genome SCIENCE, 67
paternal dear and kindly p. DANTE ALIGHIERI, 4
path Midway along the p. DANTE ALIGHIERI, 1
the p. of the just is as the shining light VIRTUE, 9
the primrose p. of dalliance EXAMPLE, 8; SHAKESPEARE, 73
world will make a…p. to his door EMERSON, R, 26; FAME, 11
pathologist an ulcer is wonderful to a p. APPEARANCES, 23
pathologists there were p. present DOCTORS, 62
patience like P. on a monument LOVE, 153; SHAKESPEARE, 342
my p. is now at an end PATIENCE, 11
Nature, time and p. are the three great physicians MEDICINE, 1
P. and passage of time LA FONTAINE, J, 4; PATIENCE, 12
P. is a virtue PATIENCE, 4; PROVERBS, 334
P. is the best medicine MEDICINE, 29
P., n. A minor form of despair BIERCE, A, 9; PATIENCE, 8
the years teach us p. PATIENCE, 15
Though p. be a tired mare PATIENCE, 14; SHAKESPEARE, 127
patient A doctor…is a p. half-cured OCCUPATIONS, 23; PROUST, M, 9
Always give the p. hope HOPE, 18
amusing the p. while Nature cures the disease MEDICINE, 104
An unruly p. makes a harsh physician DOCTORS, 99
A physician who treats himself has a fool for a p. DOCTORS, 69
cure their p. and lose their fee DOCTORS, 86
Fury of a P. Man DRYDEN, J, 13; PATIENCE, 10
if the p. can keep awake, surely you can DOCTORS, 101
INDIGESTION, n. A disease which the p.…mistake…religious conviction ILLNESS, 14; RELIGION, 13
kill the p. BACON, F, 25; REMEDIES, 9
Like a p. etherized upon a table DEPARTURE, 6; ELIOT, T, 11
Medicine can never abdicate the obligation to care for the p. MEDICINE, 98
Medicine is for the p. MEDICINE, 65
p. endurance is godlike ENDURANCE, 11; LONGFELLOW, H, 6
The consultant's first obligation is to the p. DOCTORS, 52
the disease, the p., and physician MEDICINE, 39
The p. lingers and by inches dies DOCTORS, 45
The p. must co-operate with the physician in combating the disease MEDICINE, 39
The p. never dies MEDICINE, 3
Therein the p. /Must minister to himself MADNESS, 39
The safest thing for a p. LEARNING, 14
to secure the co-operation of the p. MEDICINE, 38
patients all of his p. being willing to steal DOCTORS, 66
doctors and p. MANKIND, 33
He never sees his p. REMEDIES, 26
his p. should be his book DOCTORS, 72
Private p., if they do not like me, can go elsewhere CHARITY, 2
Some p., though conscious that their condition is perilous TRUST, 3
the faults of the p. PATIENTS, 2
the greatest fools? The p. DOCTORS, 104
There are some p. whom we cannot help MEDICINE, 15
you will have no p. to cure REMEDIES, 23
patrie *Allons, enfants, de la p.* FRANCE, 13
patriot A good historian…is a p. HISTORIANS, 1
He was a great p.…provided…that he really is dead ADMIRATION, 19; VOLTAIRE, 36
The summer soldier and the sunshine p. COWARDICE, 7
patriotism attractions of p. – it fulfils our worst wishes PATRIOTISM, 22
Blimpish p. in the mode of Margaret Thatcher KINNOCK, N, 9
knock the p. out of the human race PATRIOTISM, 39
p. had to be proved in blood PATRIOTISM, 5
P.…is a revolutionary duty PATRIOTISM, 42; TROTSKY, L, 12
p. is not enough LAST WORDS, 14
P. is often…real estate above principles PATRIOTISM, 29
P.…looking out for yourself while AMERICA, 11
P.…the last refuge of the scoundrel PATRIOTISM, 6
p. which consists in hating all other nations PATRIOTISM, 16
True p. is of no party SMOLLETT, T, 2
patriots P. always talk of dying for their country RUSSELL, B, 31
patron Is not a P., my Lord, one who looks with unconcern JOHNSON, S, 48
patronise He liked to p. coloured people RACISM, 27
patronizing A p. disposition…has its meaner side CHARACTER, 8; ELIOT, G, 3
The idea that there is a model Labour voter…is p. KINNOCK, N, 12
patter particularly rapid, unintelligible p. NONSENSE, 14
pattern p. of excelling nature MURDER, 11; SHAKESPEARE, 289
paucity the p. of human pleasures HUNTING, 6; JOHNSON, S, 35
the p. of restraints it imposes SOCIETY, 20
Paul One named Peter, /The other named P. NURSERY RHYMES, 67
Paul's I am designing St P. ARCHITECTURE, 1
paunch a p. to give him Dignity DOCTORS, 13
Pause Now I'll have *eine kleine P.* LAST WORDS, 33
pauses the p. between the notes MUSICIANS, 8
pavilion The p. of Heaven is bare SHELLEY, P, 6; WEATHER, 23
pavilioned P. in splendour, and girded with praise GOD, 24
pay better…not vow, than…vow and not p. PROMISES, 2
get someone to p. you for doing it OCCUPATIONS, 25; WHITEHORN, K, 6
it is poor grub, poor p., and easy work AMERICA, 28; ENGLAND, 31
Life is too short to do anything…one can p. others to do MAUGHAM, W, 19; WORK, 21
Not a penny off the p. STRIKES, 3
to die you will have to p. MACNEICE, L, 3
we cannot p. too dearly for it JUSTICE, 16
pays He who p. the piper POWER, 2; PROVERBS, 201
PC pushes for equality…is declared "P." EQUALITY, 4
peace all her paths are p. ENGLAND, 48
And who will bring white p. PEACE, 13
Arms alone are not enough to keep the p. PEACE, 12
Courage is the price…for granting p. COURAGE, 15
depart in p. BIBLE, 317; DEATH, 37
dignity and greatness and p. again DRINKS, 9; HOPE, 9
first in p. WASHINGTON, G, 1
Governments will get out of the way and let them have p. EISENHOWER, D, 9
greatest destroyer of p. is abortion ABORTION, 13
He accepted p. WELLINGTON, 1
hearts at p., under an English heaven ENGLAND, 12
hereafter for ever hold his p. BOOK OF COMMON PRAYER, 25
In Switzerland they had brotherly love…and p. SWITZERLAND, 5
in what p. a Christian can die ADDISON, J, 19; LAST WORDS, 3
it is in the minds of men that the defences of p. must be constructed ANONYMOUS, 72
I will die in p. LAST WORDS, 96
king of France…would assent to no p. or treaty ROYALTY, 52
Let him who desires p., prepare for war WAR AND PEACE, 14
Let us have p. GRANT, U, 5; PEACE, 11
life is more interesting in war than in p. WAR AND PEACE, 11
make a wilderness and call it p. TACITUS, C, 1; WAR, 170
makes a good war makes a good p. HERBERT, G, 8
May God deny you p. UNAMUNO, M, 3
my p. I give unto you PEACE, 4
Nation shall speak p. ANONYMOUS, 61; PEACE, 18
never was a good war or a bad p. FRANKLIN, B, 16; WAR AND PEACE, 7
no p.…unto the wicked BIBLE, 213; PEACE, 3; PUNISHMENT, 6
not to send p., but a sword BIBLE, 387
on earth p., good will toward men BIBLE, 315
P.…a period of cheating PEACE, 5
p. at that price would be a humiliation PEACE, 15
p. be to this house BIBLE, 323
P., Bread and Land RUSSIAN REVOLUTION, 1

p. comes dropping slow PEACE, 22; YEATS, W, 18
p. for our time CHAMBERLAIN, N, 6; PEACE, 8
p. has broken out BRECHT, B, 10; PEACE, 7
P. hath her victories MILTON, J, 63; WAR AND PEACE, 12
p. I hope with honour DISRAELI, B, 31; PEACE, 10
p. in our time PEACE, 6
P. is indivisible PEACE, 14
P. is not only better than war WAR AND PEACE, 13
P. is poor reading HARDY, T, 7; WAR AND PEACE, 8
P., n....a period of cheating BIERCE, A, 10
P., the human dress BLAKE, W, 44; MANKIND, 10
P. took them all prisoner HUGHES, T, 3; WAR AND PEACE, 10
p. with honour CHAMBERLAIN, N, 6; PEACE, 8
price which is too great to pay for p. WORLD WAR I, 28
righteousness and p. have kissed each other PSALMS, 46
Satan comes as a man of p. DYLAN, B, 9
The Bomb brought p. but man alone NUCLEAR WEAPONS, 6
the inglorious arts of p. MARVELL, A, 3; POLITICIANS, 105
the p. of God, which passeth all understanding BIBLE, 445
the Prince of P. BIBLE, 201
There can be no p. of mind in love LOVE, 131; PROUST, M, 5
They made p. between us ENEMIES, 5
those who could make a good p. CHURCHILL, W, 22; WAR AND PEACE, 5
War is P. OPPOSITES, 5; ORWELL, G, 18
weak piping time of p. APPEARANCE, 61
We are the true p. movement PEACE, 21; THATCHER, M, 29
We wanted p. on earth MCCARTNEY, P, 1; PEACE, 16
When p. has been broken anywhere PEACE, 19
When there was p., he was for p. AUDEN, W, 27; PUBLIC, 3
peacekeepers Swiss p. would be the personification NATIONS, 3
peach dare to eat a p. ELIOT, T, 15; OLD AGE, 45
'Fan vaulting'...belongs to the 'Last-supper-carved-on-a-p.-stone' ARCHITECTURE, 7
peaches poetry in p. POETRY, 26
with p. and women, it's...the side next the sun that's tempting TEMPTATION, 8
peak One sees...only small things from the p. CHESTERTON, G, 16; PERSPECTIVE, 2
Silent, upon a p. in Darien DISCOVERY, 11; KEATS, J, 42
peanuts pay p....get monkeys BUSINESS, 16
pear And a golden p. NURSERY RHYMES, 20
pearl base Indian, threw a p. away LOVE, 155; SHAKESPEARE, 290
pearls He who would search for P. DRYDEN, J, 17; TRUTH, 23
p. before swine BIBLE, 374; INSULTS, 102
p. that were his eyes DEATH, 154; SHAKESPEARE, 323
peas I always eat p. with honey ANONYMOUS, 41; FOOD, 6
peasant a hard-handed Scottish p. BURNS, R, 1
peasantry a bold p..../When once destroy'd GOLDSMITH, O, 6; PUBLIC, 13
peasants If the French noblesse had been capable of playing cricket with their p. ARISTOCRACY, 19; CRICKET, 12
it is better that all of these p. should be killed REBELLION, 11
peck Peter Piper picked a p. of pickled pepper NURSERY RHYMES, 43
peculiar a tense and p. family, the Oedipuses BEERBOHM, M, 21; CLASSICS, 1
Funny p., or funny ha-ha HUMOUR, 16
the p. situation of the human male BEAUVOIR, S, 2
pederasts p. who call themselves the Labour Party SOCIALISM, 2
pedestal at fourteen every boy should be in love with some ideal woman...on a p. SEXES, 22
pedigree languages are the p. of nations JOHNSON, S, 159
pee share a quick p. over a common lamp-post CONNOLLY, C, 14; WRITERS, 9
Peel D'ye ken John P. HUNTING, 5
P.'s smile INSULTS, 101
Sir Robert P. BAGEHOT, W, 9
peer A life p. is like a mule HOUSES OF PARLIAMENT, 19
peerage When I want a p., I shall buy one TITLES, 6
peers Fears, prejudices, misconceptions – those are the p. LLOYD GEORGE, D, 12
pelican A fashionable surgeon like a p. DOCTORS, 32
A wonderful bird is the p. LIMERICKS, 11
pellagra Nicotinic acid cures p. REMEDIES, 54
pen how much more cruel the p. WRITING, 8
less brilliant p. than mine BEERBOHM, M, 4; CONCEIT, 4
more foolish when he had not a p. in his hand GOLDSMITH, O, 1
nothing can cure it but the scratching of a p. WRITING, 31
p. is mightier than the sword WRITING, 7
penance The man hath p. done COLERIDGE, S, 35; PUNISHMENT, 11
pence Take care of the p. CHESTERFIELD, P, 10
pendulum politics of the p., but of the ratchet THATCHER, M, 17
The p. of the mind oscillates between sense and nonsense JUNG, C, 2; MIND, 16
penetrable most things are p. BRIBERY, 3; CARLYLE, T, 15
penis he also has the biggest p. MANKIND, 43
pennies P. do not come from heaven THATCHER, M, 24; WORK, 35
P. from Heaven OPTIMISM, 20
penny A p. saved PROVERBS, 58; THRIFT, 1
Hot cross buns! /.../One a p., two a p. NURSERY RHYMES, 16
I don't owe a p. to a single soul SNOBBERY, 15; WODEHOUSE, P, 12
In for a p. COMMITMENT, 1
Not a p. off the pay STRIKES, 3
P. wise PROVERBS, 335; THRIFT, 3
pens Let other p. dwell on guilt and misery AUSTEN, J, 13; OPTIMISM, 14
pense *Honi soit qui mal y p.* ARISTOCRACY, 12
Pentecost when the day of P. was fully come BIBLE, 2
people a loyal, a gallant, a generous, an ingenious, and good-temper'd p. FRANCE, 18; STERNE, L, 2
always been interested in p. MAUGHAM, W, 28; MISANTHROPY, 2
a president without a p. GORBACHOV, M, 2
Be nice to p. on your way up PRUDENCE, 11
bill of rights is what the p. are entitled to HUMAN RIGHTS, 4
Boys...are unwholesome companions for grown p. CHILDREN, 44; LAMB, C, 9
Film p. find it difficult to *place* me CINEMA, 10
friends...the p. who got there first FRIENDS, 16
good of the p. LAW, 9
government...must be built upon the rights of the p. GOVERNMENT, 45
government of the p. by the p. DEMOCRACY, 16; LINCOLN, A, 17; MEMORIALS, 9
Hell is other p. HELL, 7
Hell of Too Many P. HELL, 6
How do p. go to sleep PARKER, D, 6; SLEEP, 25
I am for p. CHAPLIN, C, 7
If p. behaved in the way nations do GOVERNMENT, 44; WILLIAMS, T, 7
if the p....can be reached with the truth DEMOCRACY, 20
indictment against an whole p. ACCUSATION, 2; BURKE, E, 16
It is with...p. as with...bottles CHARACTER, 17; POPE, A, 55
Let's talk sense to the American p. STEVENSON, A, 4
Most of the p....will be children FUNERALS, 1
my p. live in such awful conditions POVERTY, 15
Once the p. begin to reason PUBLIC, 19; VOLTAIRE, 31
One Realm, One P., One Leader NAZISM, 1
p....are attracted by God INGE, W, 4; RELIGION, 56
P. are either charming or tedious WILDE, O, 39
p. are forbidden to light lamps CHINA, 21; INJUSTICE, 8
P. are not fallen angels CRITICISM, 33; LAWRENCE, D, 42
p. are the masters BURKE, E, 18; PUBLIC, 6
P. either think I'm famous FAME, 18
p. may be made to follow a course of action CONFUCIUS, 11
P. must help one another HELP, 7; LA FONTAINE, J, 8
p....not dealing with creatures of logic HUMAN NATURE, 9
p.'s government GOVERNMENT, 43; WEBSTER, D, 4
p. under suspicion are better moving KAFKA, F, 4
p....usually imitate each other IMITATION, 3
P. who like this sort of thing CRITICISM, 37; LINCOLN, A, 19
P. who need people are the luckiest SOCIETY, 16
p. whose company is coveted OSTENTATION, 4
p. who stay in the middle of the road BEVAN, A, 5
Pleasant p. are just as real as horrible p. HUMAN NATURE, 8
Religion...is the opium of the p. MARX, K, 4; RELIGION, 65
show my head to the p. EXECUTION, 7
sort of p. our parents warned us about VICE, 11
the bludgeoning of the p. DEMOCRACY, 28; WILDE, O, 54
The Lord prefers common-looking p. LINCOLN, A, 6
the noise...and the p. WAR, 6
the p. are forbidden to light lamps MAO TSE-TUNG, 10
The p. – could you patent the sun DISCOVERY, 13; SCIENCE, 81
the p. of his pasture PSALMS, 56
the p. we should have been seen dead with SNOBBERY, 12; WEST, R, 8
The p. would be just as noisy CROMWELL, O, 9; PUBLIC, 10
there are no unimportant p. IMPORTANCE, 6

phenomena chess-board is the world; the pieces…the p. of the universe GOD, 29; HUXLEY, T, 6
philandering a p., pot-smoking draft dodger CLINTON, B, 2
philanthropy The spacious p. which he exhaled upon Europe WILSON, W, 1
Philip Prince P.….a world expert on leisure ROYALTY, 76
Philistines apostle of the P., Lord Macaulay ARNOLD, M, 21; PHILISTINISM, 2
For this class we have…the designation of P. ARNOLD, M, 7; PHILISTINISM, 1
society distributes itself into Barbarians, P., and Populace AMERICA, 1; ARNOLD, M, 4
to distinguish…the aristocratic class from the P. ARNOLD, M, 8; CLASS, 4
philosopher Donning the p.'s cloak HYPATIA, 1
he says 'I will', he comes to his own as a p. PHILOSOPHY, 19
he who can analyze his delusion is called a p. PHILOSOPHERS, 1
I doubt if the p. lives…who could know himself HUXLEY, T, 5; PHILOSOPHERS, 5
In the p. there is nothing whatever impersonal NIETZSCHE, F, 14; PHILOSOPHERS, 7
never yet p. /That could endure the toothache PHILOSOPHERS, 12; SHAKESPEARE, 277
Once: a p.; twice: a pervert DEBAUCHERY, 11; VOLTAIRE, 38
Organic life…has developed…from the protozoon to the p. PROGRESS, 21; RUSSELL, B, 15
p.…doesn't think in a vacuum PHILOSOPHERS, 15
some p. has said it PHILOSOPHERS, 2
The p. is Nature's pilot PHILOSOPHERS, 13
To a p. no circumstance…is too minute GOLDSMITH, O, 5; PHILOSOPHERS, 3
When you were ill you behaved like a true p. COMPLIMENTS, 25
philosophers good understanding between the chymists and the mechanical p. SCIENCE, 10
now-a-days professors of philosophy but not p. PHILOSOPHERS, 14; THOREAU, H, 11
P. are as jealous as women PHILOSOPHERS, 11
p. have only interpreted the world PHILOSOPHERS, 6
P. never balance between profit and honesty HUME, D, 8
serious p.…looking forward to the pension PHILOSOPHERS, 9
the English are…the least a nation of pure p. BAGEHOT, W, 6; ENGLISH, 5
till p. become kings PHILOSOPHY, 11; PLATO, 4
philosophical European p. tradition…a series of footnotes to Plato PHILOSOPHY, 21
The Arab who builds…a hut out of…a temple…is more p. than…curators of the museums FRANCE, A, 4; MUSEUMS, 1
philosophy a great advantage for…p. to be…true PHILOSOPHY, 18; SANTAYANA, G, 12
Art and religion first; then p. SCIENCE, 86; SPARK, M, 10
Axioms in p. are not axioms KEATS, J, 59; PHILOSOPHY, 8
collection of prejudices which is called political p. POLITICS, 92; RUSSELL, B, 26
dreamt of in your p. SHAKESPEARE, 79; SUPERNATURAL, 13
History is p.…by examples HISTORY, 10
mere touch of cold p. KEATS, J, 25; PHILOSOPHY, 7
necessary for a superstition to enslave a p. INGE, W, 6; RELIGION, 55
new P. calls all in doubt DONNE, J, 3; SCIENCE, 28
Not to care for p. PASCAL, B, 2; PHILOSOPHERS, 8
now-a-days professors of p. but not philosophers PHILOSOPHERS, 14; THOREAU, H, 11
p. and vain deceit BIBLE, 19; CHRISTIANITY, 7
P.…is a fight against…fascination PHILOSOPHY, 24
P. is not a theory PHILOSOPHY, 25
P. is the product of wonder WHITEHEAD, A, 4
P. is the replacement PHILOSOPHY, 17
p. ought to…unravel people's mental blocks RAPHAEL, F, 2
point of p. is to start with something so simple PHILOSOPHY, 15
Socrates was the first to call p. down SOCRATES, 1
Vain wisdom all, and false p. MILTON, J, 41; WISDOM, 22
Western p. is…a series of footnotes to Plato's p. PHILOSOPHY, 22; WHITEHEAD, A, 6
without certainty…hesitation is…the chief thing that p. PHILOSOPHY, 14
phobias I have three p. which…would make my life as slick as a sonnet BANKHEAD, T, 4
phone Death invented the p. HUGHES, T, 1
if I called the wrong number, why did you answer the p. THURBER, J, 15
the most historic p. call ever made COMMUNICATION, 4
phoney a p. war WAR, 53
falsifying this one fact about my life made me feel p. AGE, 88
to dismiss him as a p. SARTRE, J, 3
You're p.. Everything about you is p. APPEARANCE, 4
phonus is nothing but a p. bolonus APPEARANCES, 24; RUNYON, D, 4
photograph A p. is not only an image PHOTOGRAPHY, 8
she took down the signed p. of the Kaiser WAR, 175; WAUGH, E, 45
photography P. can never grow up if it imitates PHOTOGRAPHY, 1
p. is a…lifetime of pleasure PHOTOGRAPHY, 2
P. is truth CINEMA, 13
phrase Self-determination is not a mere p. SELF, 28
Some doctor full of p. and fame ILLNESS, 8
phthisiologists a chest of p. LANGUAGE, 4
physic Kitchen P. is the best P. FOOD, 67
Take p., pomp HUMILITY, 11; SHAKESPEARE, 183
Temperance is the best p. MODERATION, 4
the god of p. and sender of disease DOCTORS, 98
the p. of the field COUNTRYSIDE, 8
Throw p. to the dogs MADNESS, 39
physical a p. and metaphysical impossibility CARLYLE, T, 3; POETS, 3
Disease makes men more p. ILLNESS, 47
It's altogether…less controversial and more p. SPORT AND GAMES, 8
physical laws no right to assume that any p. exist SCIENCE, 73
physician an experienced and thoughtful p. MEDICINE, 82
An unruly patient makes a harsh p. DOCTORS, 99
A p. can sometimes parry the scythe of death TIME, 38
A p. is…a consoler of the mind DOCTORS, 14
A p. is obligated to consider more than a diseased organ ENVIRONMENT, 6
A p. is one who pours drugs DOCTORS, 105
A p. ought to be extremely watchful against covetousness ENVY, 7
A p. who is a lover of wisdom is the equal to a god DOCTORS, 53
A p. who treats himself has a fool for a patient DOCTORS, 69
a p. will be made fun of DOCTORS, 57
died last night of my p. DISEASE, 30; DOCTORS, 81
Employment is nature's p. WORK, 11
Every invalid is a p. PATIENTS, 1
Every p. must be rich in knowledge DOCTORS, 72
He's the best p. REMEDIES, 1
if the p. had the same disease upon him that I have EXAMPLE, 7; SELDEN, J, 5
In illness the p. is a father DOCTORS, 11
I swear by Apollo the p. MEDICINE, 37
Many funerals discredit a p. FUNERALS, 7
No man is a good p. DOCTORS, 4
One of the first duties of the p. DOCTORS, 70
One p. cures you of the colic DOCTORS, 12
owe your life to any but a regular-bred p. DOCTORS, 92
p., heal thyself BIBLE, 320; DOCTORS, 22
P., n. One upon whom we set our hopes when ill DOCTORS, 24
See, one p., like a sculler plies DOCTORS, 45
so fond of the company of their p. DOCTORS, 65
taking a place beside the p. and the priest OCCUPATIONS, 22
That is because I never employed you as my p. DOCTORS, 74
That p. will hardly be thought very careful DOCTORS, 43
the best p. is he who is able to separate fair love from foul MEDICINE, 78
the disease, the patient, and p. MEDICINE, 39
The first cry of pain…was the first call for a p. MEDICINE, 84
The first qualification for a p. is hopefulness HOPE, 16
the goodness of the p. TRUST, 3
the ideal of medicine is to eliminate the need of a p. MEDICINE, 62
The patient must co-operate with the p. in combating the disease MEDICINE, 39
The p. can bury his mistakes MISTAKES, 23
the p. cutteth off a long disease BIBLE, 84; DEATH, 34
the p.…is the flower…of our civilization DOCTORS, 96
The p. is the servant of the art MEDICINE, 39
The p. must be ready MEDICINE, 38

the p. must start from nature MEDICINE, 73
the uncouth gravity and supercilious self-conceit of a p. DOCTORS, 94
They that be whole need not a p. ILLNESS, 13
Time is the great p. TIME, 19
To a p., each man, each woman MEDICINE, 25
whose governor is a p. DOCTORS, 2
Wonderful is the skill of a p. REMEDIES, 57
young p. fattens the churchyard PROVERBS, 76
physicians and remove the pain his p. cannot cure DEATH, 50
body-snatcher…One who supplies the young p. DOCTORS, 23
But two p., like a pair of oars DOCTORS, 45
English p. kill you DOCTORS, 63
Nature can do more than p. NATURE, 7
Nature, time and patience are the three great p. MEDICINE, 1
One of the most successful p.…has…used more bread pills REMEDIES, 36
Other books…written by men p. FEMINISM, 18
P.… are best when they are old DOCTORS, 42
P. are inclined to engage in hasty generalizations THEORY, 13
P. are like kings DOCTORS, 107; WEBSTER, J, 2
p. are the class of people who kill other men DOCTORS, 88
P. of all men are most happy DOCTORS, 82
P. of the utmost fame ILLNESS, 10
P. who care much for the elderly DOCTORS, 71
Temperance and labour are the two real p. of man WORK, 32
The crowd of p. has killed me DOCTORS, 51
The disease of an evil conscience is beyond…the p. EVIL, 12
the help of too many p. DOCTORS, 9
The most dangerous p. DOCTORS, 67
the old p. have supplied the undertaker DOCTORS, 23
The p. are here, too. DOCTORS, 62
The p. are the natural attorneys of the poor DOCTORS, 103
the p. with their art, know…how to make it still shorter DOCTORS, 76
Three remedies of the p. of Myddfai REMEDIES, 5
two p. cure you of the medicine DOCTORS, 12
The p. best remedy is *Tincture of Time* TIME, 43
physicist The great p. Lavoisier, who knew better than any peasant SCIENCE, 1
physicists p. have known sin SCIENTISTS, 5
to find out anything from the theoretical p. EINSTEIN, A, 5; SCIENTISTS, 3
physics Classical p.…superseded by quantum theory SCIENCE, 97
Modern P. is an instrument of Jewry SCIENCE, 92
The content of p. is the concern SCIENCE, 29
pianist do not shoot the p. EFFORT, 7; WILDE, O, 37
only p. I have ever seen who did not grimace MUSICIANS, 19
piano made such a frightful din on the p. MUSICIANS, 18
Piatigorsky Gregor P. EGOTISM, 6; INSULTS, 61
Picardy Roses are flowering in P. COMPLIMENTS, 38
Picasso Nothing divides them like P. ART, 23
There's no such thing as a bad P. PICASSO, P, 5
Piccadilly Crossing P. Circus LONDON, 23
Good-bye P., Farewell Leicester Square HOMESICKNESS, 8
pick Whenever you fall, p. up something OPPORTUNITY, 8
pickle weaned on a p. APPEARANCE, 40; INSULTS, 91
picnic futile to attempt a p. in Eden INNOCENCE, 5
picture Every p. tells a story PROVERBS, 143
how did you love my p. GOLDWYN, S, 23
If you want a p. of the future OPPRESSION, 6; ORWELL, G, 16
It's no go the p. palace INDIFFERENCE, 4
One p. is worth ten thousand words PAINTING, 1
pictures book…without p. BOOKS, 13; CARROLL, L, 4
dearth of bad p. GOLDWYN, S, 25
make my p. for people CRITICS, 4
would never buy my p. PAINTING, 9
pidgin-English I include 'p.' LANGUAGE, 35
pie Amblongus P. LEAR, E, 6; NONSENSE, 24
A word of kindness is better than a fat p. KINDNESS, 2
p. in the sky when you die AFTERLIFE, 5; MATERIALISM, 3
piece A p. of each of us died at that moment ASSASSINATION, 6
p. of cod passes all understanding FOOD, 49
p. of divinity in us BROWNE, T, 11; NOBILITY, 1
Prologues precede the p. PLAYS, 4
What a p. of work is a man MANKIND, 56; SHAKESPEARE, 85
When a p. gets difficult MUSICIANS, 14
pieces P. of eight MONEY, 49; STEVENSON, R, 9
pie-crust Promises and p. are made to be broken PROMISES, 8; SWIFT, J, 10
pieman Simple Simon met a p. NURSERY RHYMES, 51
pier Like Brighton p. KINNOCK, N, 8; TRAVEL, 27
Pierian Drink deep, or taste not the P. spring KNOWLEDGE, 36; POPE, A, 23
pies I could eat one of Bellamy's veal p. LAST WORDS, 67; PITT THE YOUNGER, 3
pig a sort of p. in clover BENNETT, A, 1
p. of a Henry VIII BETRAYAL, 13
when they see the half p. man PROPHECY, 8
pigeons tourists…take in the Monarchy…with…the p. LONDON, 15
piggy This little p. went to market NURSERY RHYMES, 62
pigmy That shriek and sweat in p. wars TENNYSON, 48; TRIVIALITY, 15
pigs And whether p. have wings CARROLL, L, 28; NONSENSE, 9
one of Epicurus' herd of p. HORACE, 18; PRESENT, 10
P. might fly PROVERBS, 336
What men call social virtues…is…but the virtue of p. in a litter SOCIETY, 23; THOREAU, H, 7
pig-sty kissed her once by the p. EXPECTATION, 8; THOMAS, D, 20
Pilate jesting P. BACON, F, 56; TRUTH, 10
P.…washed his hands BIBLE, 430; GUILT, 3
rather have blood on my hands…P. COMMITMENT, 6; GREENE, G, 3
pile P. it high, sell it cheap BUSINESS, 6
piles p. to give him an Anxious Expression DOCTORS, 13
pilgrim p. of the sky WORDSWORTH, W, 74
pilgrims strangers and p. on the earth FAITH, 4
pill buy a p. and buy peace with it MEDICINE, 55
Protestant women may take the P. CONTRACEPTION, 16
The P. has so much bad press CONTRACEPTION, 12
pillar a p. of a cloud BIBLE, 111
a p. of salt BIBLE, 168
the lie has become…a p. of the State LYING, 24; SOLZHENITSYN, A, 14
triple p. of the world LOVE, 142; SHAKESPEARE, 25
pillars wisdom…hath hewn out her seven p. BIBLE, 448
pillow no-sooner-have-I-touched-the-p. people SLEEP, 27
pills I don't take p. HEALTH AND HEALTHY LIVING, 13
It is an age of p. DRUGS, 11
the most successful physicians…used more bread p. REMEDIES, 36
pilot Dropping the p. DISMISSAL, 10
pimp white man can dress like a black p. GOLF, 7
Pimpernel That damned elusive P. ABSENCE, 9
pin If I sit on a p. /And it punctures my skin ANONYMOUS, 90
See a p. and pick it up PROVERBS, 357; SUPERSTITION, 4
you are like a p., but without…head or…point BORES, 3; JERROLD, D, 8
Pinafore Captain of the *P.* CONCEIT, 9; GILBERT, W, 8
pinch time for me to enjoy another p. of snuff EXECUTION, 2
pinching I just keep painting till I feel like p. PAINTING, 17
pine-apple p. of politeness MALAPROPISMS, 7; SHERIDAN, R, 8
pinko-gray white races are…p. FORSTER, E, 10; RACISM, 11
Pinot Grigio I would have drunk a lot of P. DRINKS, 15
pint cannot put a quart in a p. cup POSSIBILITY, 2
You spend half a p. and flush two gallons WATER, 7
pious A p. man…would be an atheist LA BRUYERE, J, 1; SERVILITY, 4
p. bird with the scarlet breast WORDSWORTH, W, 45
p. frauds of friendship FIELDING, H, 2; FRIENDSHIP, 18
pipe Blow your p. there BROWNING, R, 44; CONTEMPT, 2
He called for his p. NURSERY RHYMES, 38
Marston, dropping it in the grate,/broke his p. SPENDER, S, 1
piped their fountains p. an answer LAWRENCE, D, 6
Piper Peter P. picked a peck of pickled pepper NURSERY RHYMES, 43
piping Helpless, naked, p. loud BIRTH, 5; BLAKE, W, 38
P. down the valleys wild BLAKE, W, 41; MUSIC, 13
pips squeezed – until the p. squeak RETRIBUTION, 10
piss p. us off we'll bomb your cities AMERICA, 42
piss-a-bed Here is Johnny Keats' p. poetry KEATS, J, 3
pissed the last four strikes we've had, it's p. down STRIKES, 8
pissing inside my tent p. out JOHNSON, L, 7; PRUDENCE, 8
making a speech on economics is a lot like p. SPEECHES, 10
pistol a p. let off at the ear LAMB, C, 16; PUNS, 12
Somebody leaves a p. in the drawer SUICIDE, 22
pit And wretched, blind, p. ponies ANIMALS, 15
pitcher a p. of warm spit POLITICS, 41

pitchfork drive out nature with a p. HORACE, 20; HUMAN NATURE, 15
pith all the p. is in the postscript HAZLITT, W, 6; LETTER-WRITING, 4
pitied one has…ceased to be an object of *fear* as soon as one is p. NIETZSCHE, F, 18; SYMPATHY, 6
pitiless slow, sure doom falls p. and dark RUSSELL, B, 16
pits You are the p. INSULTS, 98
Pitt P. is to Addington POLITICIANS, 58
pity A p. beyond all telling LOVE, 181; YEATS, W, 25
I thought it was a p. to get up BED, 9
knock him down first, and p. him afterwards JOHNSON, S, 105; SELF-PRESERVATION, 8
My subject is War, and the p. of War OWEN, W, 6; POETRY, 46
no soul will p. me DESPAIR, 8
P. a human face BLAKE, W, 44; MANKIND, 10
p. for the suffering of mankind PHILOSOPHERS, 10; RUSSELL, B, 4
The Poetry is in the p. OWEN, W, 6; POETRY, 46
To marry a man out of p. is folly MARRIAGE, 9
To show p. is felt as a sign of contempt NIETZSCHE, F, 18; SYMPATHY, 6
place A p. for everything ORDER, 6
everything in its p. ORDER, 6
Film people find it difficult to *p.* me CINEMA, 10
firm p. to stand TECHNOLOGY, 2
give p. to better men CROMWELL, O, 7; DISMISSAL, 4
Home is the p. where FROST, R, 3; HOME, 5
I go to prepare a p. for you BIBLE, 258; HEAVEN, 3
In P. of Fear WEAPONS, 3
Never the time and the p. BROWNING, R, 36; PERVERSITY, 2
our own p. in the sun IMPORTANCE, 2
putting her in her p. INSULTS, 114
running…to keep in the same p. CARROLL, L, 24; NONSENSE, 8
there's no p. like home HOME, 10; PROVERBS, 417
the summit of Everest was hardly the p. PHOTOGRAPHY, 5
the wrong p. at the wrong time under the wrong circumstances JOHNSON, L, 1
this is an awful p. PLACES, 32
Upon the p. beneath MERCY, 2; SHAKESPEARE, 248
plague A p. o' both your houses CURSES, 2; SHAKESPEARE, 317
gods…/Make instruments to p. us SHAKESPEARE, 195
plagues of all p. with which mankind are curst CHURCH, 5; DEFOE, D, 6
plain be p. and simple PROSE, 2
be yourself, imperial, p. and true BROWNING, R, 8; SINCERITY, 1
making things p. to uninstructed people EDUCATION, 46; HUXLEY, T, 7
Manners are…the need of the p. MANNERS, 8; WAUGH, E, 51
plainness perfect p. of speech…perfect nobleness ARNOLD, M, 31; BIBLE, 523
plaisir *P. d'amour* LOVE, 72
plan save the p. NIXON, R, 9
To housekeep, one had to p. ahead HOUSEWORK, 6
plane only two emotions in a p.: boredom and terror FLYING, 6
planet brain the size of a p. ADAMS, D, 5
I have lived some thirty years on this p. THOREAU, H, 10
it fell on the wrong p. WEAPONS, 4
The human race will be the cancer of the p. MANKIND, 31
utterly insignificant little blue green p. SCIENCE FICTION, 1
When a new p. swims into his ken DISCOVERY, 11; KEATS, J, 42
planets felt like the moon, the stars, and all the p. had fallen RESPONSIBILITY, 21
planning materials of city p. DESIGN, 4
plans Life…happens…while you're busy making other p. LENNON, J, 1; LIFE, 57
The finest p. have always been spoiled BRECHT, B, 6; SUPPORT, 2
what a man still p.…shows the…injustice in his death DEATH, 46
plant Is thy love a p. /Of such weak fibre ABSENCE, 10; WORDSWORTH, W, 23
The infusion of a China p. ADDISON, J, 12; DRINKS, 1
Plantagenet the winding ivy of a P. should kill the…tree DESTINY, 4
planted like a tree p. by the water-side PSALMS, 1
plants bottinney means a knowledge of p. DICKENS, C, 31
p. left over from the Edwardian Wilderness CHANGE, 20; OSBORNE, J, 6
tend to make us forget the medicinal value of p. NATURE, 13
plashy p. fen passes the questing vole ANIMALS, 26; WAUGH, E, 34
plate clean your p. POLITICS, 89
the silver p. on a coffin INSULTS, 101
platitude A longitude with no p. FRY, C, 4
A p. is simply a truth repeated BALDWIN, S, 13
platitudes Literature is the orchestration of p. WILDER, T, 7
Plato P. is dear to me ARISTOTLE, 10; TRUTH, 8
Western philosophy is…a series of footnotes to P.'s philosophy PHILOSOPHY, 22; WHITEHEAD, A, 6
platonic I know nothing about p. love LOVE, 89
plausible p. happiness /Of a new experience SPENDER, S, 3
rat-like cunning, a p. manner JOURNALISM, 33
the true and the false and…extracting the p. LLOYD GEORGE, D, 2
play a good p. needs no epilogue PLAYS, 13; SHAKESPEARE, 58
a p. is a dynamic thing NOVELS, 17; PLAYS, 15; TYNAN, K, 1
behold the Englishman…p. tip-and-run ENGLISH, 16
Better than a p. CHARLES II, 5; HOUSES OF PARLIAMENT, 8
how healthy…to p. Da Do Ron Ron AIDS, 5
If you p. with fire DANGER, 2; PROVERBS, 219
Judge not the p. PLAYS, 11
p., I remember, pleas'd not the million SHAKESPEARE, 87; TASTE, 7
p.'s the thing PLAYS, 14; SHAKESPEARE, 89
'P. up! p. up! and p. the game!' NEWBOLT, H, 7; WAR, 119
Rehearsing a p. is making the word flesh PLAYS, 12
The little victims p. GRAY, T, 9; IGNORANCE, 11
this may be p. to you, 'tis death to us SERIOUSNESS, 2
unless the p. is stopped, the child cannot…go on AUDIENCES, 3
writing a good p. is difficult PLAYS, 10
play-actors p.…they're a favoured race ACTORS, 6
playboy p. of the western world LOSS, 8
player poor p., /That struts and frets his hour LIFE, 86; SHAKESPEARE, 227
players men and women merely p. SHAKESPEARE, 48
to conceal the fact that the p. cannot act ACTING, 1
play-going A good many inconveniences attend p. PLAYS, 16; TYNAN, K, 4
playing-cards Let's go out and buy p. OLD AGE, 39
plays p. about rape, sodomy and drug addiction THEATRE, 7
p. are suited to incoherent argument BENNETT, A, 6
Robert Browning, you writer of p. BROWNING, R, 30
Some of my p. peter out BARRIE, J, 14
plaything A book that furnishes no quotations is…a p. PEACOCK, T, 3; QUOTATIONS, 10
A child's a p. for an hour CHILDREN, 45
playwright a p.…void of dramatic interest SARTRE, J, 2
the only sophisticated p. England has produced CONGREVE, W, 1
plead Arise, O Lord, p. Thine own cause PRAYER, 23
pleasant If we do not find anything p. NOVELTY, 10; VOLTAIRE, 6
lovely and p. in their lives BIBLE, 482; FRIENDSHIP, 9
p. it is to have money MONEY, 18
p. to be urged to do something FLATTERY, 7
P. words are as an honeycomb, sweet to the soul KINDNESS, 3
pleas'd p. with what he gets CONTENTMENT, 7
please go anywhere I damn well p. FREEDOM, 5
he that is married careth…how he may p. his wife BIBLE, 31; MARRIAGE, 28
I…do what I p. FREEDOM, 15
Music, Maestro, P. MUSIC, 38
Natural to p. CHARACTER, 7; DRYDEN, J, 4
Nothing can permanently p. COLERIDGE, S, 7; PLEASURE, 12
They…say what they p. FREEDOM, 15
You can't p. everyone PROVERBS, 476
pleases every prospect p. MISANTHROPY, 1
one makes lovers as fast as one p. CONGREVE, W, 14; LOVE, 59
pleasing The art of p. consists in HAZLITT, W, 14
the art of p. was the first duty in life CHESTERFIELD, P, 3
the surest method…of p. CHESTERFIELD, P, 9; EXAMPLE, 3
pleasure A fool bolts p., then complains of…indigestion DEBAUCHERY, 1
a p. in the pathless woods BYRON, 16; NATURE, 3
as much p. as any of our poets CHAUCER, G, 2
as much p. in the reading PLEASURE, 29
breathe the p. of natural freedom COUNTRYSIDE, 4
DEBAUCHEE, n. One who has…pursued p. BIERCE, A, 5; DEBAUCHERY, 3
did p. me in his top-boots SEX, 77
dissipation without p. GIBBON, E, 4; LONDON, 14
eating should be a p. DIETING, 6

Everyone is dragged on by their favourite p. VIRGIL, 16
gave p. to the spectators MACAULAY, T, 14; PURITANISM, 3
give p.…because of you INSPIRATION, 2
greatest p.…to do a good action GOOD, 9; LAMB, C, 18
hatred is by far the longest p. BYRON, 33; LOVE AND HATE, 1
He had a kind of idealism in p. PEPYS, S, 4
He that takes p. to hear sermons PLEASURE, 31; SELDEN, J, 7
His great p. was to humiliate people THOMAS, D, 2
I make poetry and give p.…because of you HORACE, 40
in his p. is life PSALMS, 17
knowledge and wonder…is an impression of p. BACON, F, 1
Love ceases to be a p. BEHN, A, 7; LOVE, 26
Money gives me p. BELLOC, H, 15; MONEY, 9
No p. without pain PLEASURE, 1; PROVERBS, 315
no sterner moralist than P. BYRON, 24; PLEASURE, 9
P. after all is a safer guide BUTLER, S, 25; PLEASURE, 8
P. is…intermission of pain PLEASURE, 32; SELDEN, J, 4
P. is…seldom found where it is sought JOHNSON, S, 16; PLEASURE, 16
P. never is at home DISCONTENT, 5; KEATS, J, 17
p. of your company LAMB, C, 24; MOUNTAINS, 2
p. requires an aristocratic setting PLEASURE, 30
Romanticism is…literary works…affording…the greatest…p. LITERATURE, 25
that p.…the sole motive force behind the union of the sexes LACLOS, P, 3; SEX, 61
The only sensual p. without vice JOHNSON, S, 39
The p. is momentary, the position ridiculous SEX, 27
The p. of criticizing CRITICISM, 32; LA BRUYERE, J, 4
the p. of offering my seat to three ladies CHESTERTON, G, 43; OBESITY, 4
There is a p. sure /In being mad MADNESS, 10
The sight…gave me infinite p. EXECUTION, 28
The ugliest of trades have their moments of p. JERROLD, D, 6; OCCUPATIONS, 12
understanding will…extinguish p. HOUSMAN, A, 6; POETRY, 29
what p.…they have in taking their roguish tobacco JONSON, B, 6; SMOKING, 19
Writers like Connolly gave p. a bad name CONNOLLY, C, 1
Youth is full of p. SHAKESPEARE, 357; YOUTH, 27
pleasure-dome A stately p. decree COLERIDGE, S, 14
sunny p. with caves of ice COLERIDGE, S, 15
pleasures being ill as one of the greatest p. of life ILLNESS, 16
Earth fills her lap with p. WORDSWORTH, W, 27
interfering with the p. of others ABSTINENCE, 9
Love and all his p. CAMPION, T, 5; SEX, 22
Mid p. and palaces though we may roam HOME, 10
No man is a hypocrite in his p. CAMUS, A, 8; JOHNSON, S, 152
One half…cannot understand the p. AUSTEN, J, 4; PLEASURE, 3
One of the p. of middle age is to *find out* that one WAS right POUND, E, 4; YOUTH, 23
P. are all alike PLEASURE, 31; SELDEN, J, 7
p. are their only care COWPER, W, 20
P. newly found are sweet PLEASURE, 37; WORDSWORTH, W, 77
purest of human p. BACON, F, 26; GARDENS, 2
The English take their p. ENGLAND, 49
the paucity of human p. HUNTING, 6; JOHNSON, S, 35
pledges Count not his broken p. as a crime POLITICIANS, 86
plenty but just had p. BURNS, R, 7; SATISFACTION, 2
that p. should attain the poor BYRON, 5; SELF-INTEREST, 2
plods plowman homeward p. his weary way DAY, 6; GRAY, T, 1
plot p. hath many changes PLAYS, 11
p. was to have blown up the King TREASON, 10
the p. thickens INTRIGUE, 1
Wilde performed his life…even after fate had taken the p. out of his hands WILDE, O, 1
plots there are only six basic p. FICTION, 5
plough To get it ready for the p. BETJEMAN, J, 11; ENGLAND, 6
We p. the fields, and scatter AGRICULTURE, 1
ploughing Is my team p. AGRICULTURE, 3; HOUSMAN, A, 11
plowed p. with my heifer BIBLE, 295
plowman The p. homeward plods his weary way DAY, 6; GRAY, T, 1
plowshares beat their swords into p. BIBLE, 194; WAR AND PEACE, 3
pluck if thy right eye offend thee, p. it out BIBLE, 363; RETRIBUTION, 7
p. till time and times are done DESIRE, 18; YEATS, W, 30
plumber try getting a p. on weekends. GOD, 1
plumbing an ingenious assembly of portable p. MANKIND, 39
human…assembly of portable p. MANKIND, 40
plunder delivered Ireland from p. and oppression SWIFT, J, 1
What a place to p. LONDON, 5
plural in the p. and they bounce INSULTS, 92
plus *P. ça change* CONSTANCY, 3
Plymouth dreamin'…o' P. Hoe NEWBOLT, H, 3; WAR, 120
pneumatic a splendid girl. /Wonderfully p. WOMEN, 67
divers experiments in Mr Boyle's P. Engine SCIENTISTS, 10
poacher a p. a keeper turned inside out KINGSLEY, C, 8
Pobble The P. who has no toes NONSENSE, 20
pocket carried a…brick in his p. BUSINESS, 32; SWIFT, J, 6
smile I could feel in my hip p. SEX, 26
To be played with both hands in the p. MUSIC, 52
pockets deepest p. who can risk going to law LAW, 40
the p. of the people SMITH, A, 3; TAXATION, 11
Podduyev life had prepared P. for living SOLZHENITSYN, A, 4
poem A long p. is a test of invention KEATS, J, 50; POETRY, 33
A p. is never finished POETRY, 66
A p. lovely as a tree TREES, 8
don't make a p. with thoughts POETRY, 17
I do not think this p. will reach its destination CRITICISM, 62; VOLTAIRE, 37
P. me no poems POETRY, 39
poems A man does not write p. POETRY, 62
My p. are hymns of praise POETRY, 58; SITWELL, E, 3
p.…for the love of Man and in praise of God POETRY, 64; THOMAS, D, 5
that Anon, who wrote so many p. WOMEN, 144; WOOLF, V, 14
The few bad p.…created during abstinence ABSTINENCE, 8
These p., with all their crudities, doubts, and confusions THOMAS, D, 5
We all write p. FOWLES, J, 3; POETRY, 23
poesy shower of light is p. KEATS, J, 44
poet A fascinating combination of scientist and would-be p. STOPES, M, 1
a modern p.'s fate CRITICS, 8; HOOD, T, 14
a p. to whom nature has denied the faculty of verse CARLYLE, T, 2
As a p., Milton seems…the greatest of eccentrics MILTON, J, 4
A true p. does not bother to be poetical POETS, 4
English love p.…composed of body, soul, and mind POETS, 20
godly p. must be chaste himself POETRY, 16
He might have passed…for anything but a p. BROWNING, R, 2
like a p. woo the moon POETRY, 15
lunatic, the lover, and the p. LOVE, 148; SHAKESPEARE, 265
no person can be a p.…without…unsoundness of mind MACAULAY, T, 8; POETRY, 38
No p., no artist of any sort, has his complete meaning alone ELIOT, T, 24
One dislikes to see a man and p.…proclaim on the streets POETS, 26
p.'s eye, in a fine frenzy SHAKESPEARE, 266
p. without love CARLYLE, T, 3
That maniacal Calvinist and coddled p. COWPER, W, 2
The most original p. now living POETS, 41
The p. and the dreamer are distinct KEATS, J, 16; OPPOSITES, 3
The p. gives us his essence POETRY AND PROSE, 6; WOOLF, V, 4
The P. of Immortal Youth POETS, 58
To be a p. is a condition POETS, 6
unmourned and unknown…because they lack their sacred p. HORACE, 42; OBLIVION, 1
We have one p. of genius in Auden AUDEN, W, 1
Yet obviously a nice man and a great p. ELIOT, T, 2
poetic the laws of p. truth and p. beauty ARNOLD, M, 15
poetical A true poet does not bother to be p. POETS, 4
that werges on the p. DICKENS, C, 50
poetry Angling is somewhat like p. FISHING, 2; WALTON, I, 2
As civilization advances, p.…declines CIVILIZATION, 9; MACAULAY, T, 7
A verbal art like p.…Music is immediate POETRY, 7
complexities of p. are destroyed by the media THEATRE, 3
Critics are more malicious about p. CRITICS, 9
Even when p. has a meaning HOUSMAN, A, 6; POETRY, 29
Here is Johnny Keats' piss-a-bed p. KEATS, J, 3
If p. comes not…as leaves to a tree KEATS, J, 57; POETRY, 35
I make p. and give pleasure…because of you HORACE, 40
Mr Shaw…has never written any p. CHESTERTON, G, 34; WRITERS, 43
no man ever talked p. DICKENS, C, 48; POETRY, 19
no person can…enjoy p., without…unsoundness MACAULAY, T, 8; POETRY, 38
One of the purposes of p. POETRY, 59

P. ennobles the heart POETRY, 60
P. is a comforting piece of fiction MENCKEN, H, 12; POETRY, 40
P. is as exact a science as geometry POETRY, 22
P. is as much a part of the universe POETRY, 11
P. is baroque MAUGHAM, W, 17
P. is essentially an amateur activity POETRY, 8
p. is…more philosophical…than history ARISTOTLE, 5; POETRY, 1
P. is not a turning loose of emotion ELIOT, T, 25; POETRY, 21
P. is opposed to science…prose to metre COLERIDGE, S, 18; POETRY AND PROSE, 1
P. is the monster hiding in a child's dark room POETRY, 47
P. is the record of the best and happiest moments POETRY, 57; SHELLEY, P, 7
P. is the spontaneous overflow of powerful feelings POETRY, 72; WORDSWORTH, W, 20
P. is the supreme fiction POETRY, 63
P. is to prose POETRY AND PROSE, 5
P. is what gets lost in translation FROST, R, 11; TRANSLATION, 3
p. makes nothing happen AUDEN, W, 16; POETRY, 5, 6
P.…man explores his own amazement POETRY, 25
p. reminds him of the richness POETRY, 36
P.…set to more or less lascivious music MENCKEN, H, 12; POETRY, 40
P. should be great and unobtrusive KEATS, J, 56; POETRY, 34
p. sinks and swoons under…prose LANDOR, W, 2; POETRY AND PROSE, 3
P.'s unnatural DICKENS, C, 48; POETRY, 19
p. = the best words in the best order COLERIDGE, S, 41; POETRY AND PROSE, 2
p., 'The Cinderella of the Arts.' POETRY, 45
p.…to me it's the oil of life POETRY, 10
read a little p. sometimes HOPE, A, 7; IGNORANCE, 12; INSULTS, 64
Sculpture to me is like p. ARCHITECTURE, 9
Superstition is the p. of life GOETHE, J, 6; SUPERSTITION, 9
that is p. POETRY, 14
The difference between genuine p. ARNOLD, M, 44; POETRY, 4
the grand style arises in p. ARNOLD, M, 32; POETRY, 3
The one…p.…continually flowing is slang CHESTERTON, G, 10; LANGUAGE, 15
The P. is in the pity OWEN, W, 6; POETRY, 46
there is p. in peaches POETRY, 26
to resuscitate the dead art /Of p. POETRY, 49; POUND, E, 12
truest p. is the most feigning POETRY, 53; SHAKESPEARE, 55
unseeing to ask what is the *use* of p. POETRY, 61
Verse libre; a device for making p. POETRY, 41
What is p. POETRY, 52; RUSKIN, J, 5
poets among the English P. after my death KEATS, J, 62; POSTERITY, 6
as much pleasure as any of our p. CHAUCER, G, 2
excellent p. that have never versified POETS, 11
if you include me among the lyric p. PRIDE, 6
I hate the whole race…your professional p. WELLINGTON, 10
Immature p. imitate POETS, 5
Milton the prince of p. MILTON, J, 2
nor even booksellers have put up with p. being second-rate HORACE, 10; POETS, 8
Painters and p.…licence to dare anything FREEDOM, 24; HORACE, 1
P. and painters are outside the class system POETS, 1
p. are the ones who write in words FOWLES, J, 3; POETRY, 23
Souls of p. dead and gone KEATS, J, 26; PUBLIC HOUSES, 3
what would be theft in other p., is only victory in him JONSON, B, 1
po-faced labelled a p. git ACTORS, 3
point Up to a p., Lord Copper WAUGH, E, 43
you are like a pin, but without…head or…p. BORES, 3; INSULTS, 69; JERROLD, D, 8
pointless Making money is pretty p. MONEY, 21
poison food to one man is bitter p. to others TASTE, 5
it is always easy to p. and to kill KILLING, 1
Neither will I administer a p. to anybody MEDICINE, 37
Psychology is as unnecessary as directions for using p. PSYCHOLOGY, 11
remorse is the p. of life GUILT, 4
strongest p. ever known BLAKE, W, 4; POWER, 7
treatment with p. medicines DRUGS, 14
poisoned atmosphere has been p. SPORT AND GAMES, 26
poisons P. and medicine are oftentimes the same substance REMEDIES, 38
The p. are our principal medicines REMEDIES, 28
two p. are more efficacious than one REMEDIES, 6
poker Malice is like a game of p. NASTINESS, 9
pokers Wreathe iron p. into true-love knots COLERIDGE, S, 21; POETS, 28
pole And see all sights from p. to p. ARNOLD, M, 43; SOUL, 3
Beloved from p. to p. COLERIDGE, S, 34; SLEEP, 9
One step beyond the p. EXPLORATION, 3
polecat A semi-house-trained p. INSULTS, 49
Poles few virtues…the P. do not possess CHURCHILL, W, 63
police a sort of friendship recognized by the p. STEVENSON, R, 13
Reading isn't an occupation we encourage among p. officers ORTON, J, 5; POLICE, 6
The p. are the only 24-hour social service POLICE, 3
policeman A p.'s lot is not a happy one GILBERT, W, 41; POLICE, 2
Ask a P. TIME, 41
park, a p. and a pretty girl CHAPLIN, C, 5; HUMOUR, 7
so dismal that a p. couldn't make it worse POLICE, 1
the air of someone who is lying…to a p. POLICE, 8
The terrorist and the p. CONRAD, J, 6; EQUALITY, 10
policemen how young the p. look AGE, 51
P. are numbered MILLIGAN, S, 9; POLICE, 4
repressed sadists…become p. or butchers CONNOLLY, C, 8
Police State P.…always regards all opposition as a crime OPPOSITION, 6
policy My home p.? I wage war WAR, 50
polished p. up the handle of the big front door OFFICERS, 6
Satire should, like a p. razor keen SATIRE, 2
whole man in himself, p. and well-rounded CHARACTER, 11; HORACE, 47
polite it costs nothing to be p. CHURCHILL, W, 14; DIPLOMACY, 9
p. by telling lies BRADBURY, M, 7; COURTESY, 3
time to be p. ENGLISH, 30; MONTESQUIEU, 7
politeness pine-apple of p. MALAPROPISMS, 7; SHERIDAN, R, 8
P. is organised indifference MANNERS, 7
Punctuality is the p. of kings PROMPTNESS, 2
political addiction of p. groups to ideas GALBRAITH, J, 3; POLITICS, 40
After all, we are not p. whores MUSSOLINI, B, 3; POLITICS, 79
All p. lives…end in failure POLITICS, 83
a man who was lucky enough to have discovered a p. theory MARXISM, 2
Every intellectual attitude is latently p. POLITICS, 74
ineptitude of M. Sartre's p. performance SARTRE, J, 3
Jesus was…a first-rate p. economist CHRISTIANITY, 55; SHAW, G, 3
most schemes of p. improvement are very laughable JOHNSON, S, 76; POLITICS, 59
one of these is the history of p. power HISTORY, 23
p. speech and writing are largely the defence of the indefensible ORWELL, G, 21; POLITICS, 81
That points clearly to a p. career POLITICIANS, 24; SHAW, G, 18
the formation of the p. will of the nation HITLER, A, 14; POLITICS, 51
When…it becomes necessary…to dissolve…p. bonds INDEPENDENCE, 3; JEFFERSON, T, 4
political correctness P. is a really inane concept LANGUAGE, 47
politically split down the middle, p. BAINBRIDGE, B, 5
politician a p. is an arse CUMMINGS, 6; POLITICIANS, 3
A p. is a statesman…with an open mouth STEVENSON, A, 2
A statesman is a p. who's been dead TRUMAN, H, 5
at home you're just a p. MACMILLAN, H, 7; POLITICIANS, 16
Coffee which makes the p. wise DRINKS, 17; POPE, A, 52
every Labour p. feels more at home attacking his own POLITICIANS, 32
Kennedy the p. exuded that musk odour KENNEDY, J, 2
like a scurvy p. POLITICIANS, 23; SHAKESPEARE, 191
Nixon is the kind of p. NIXON, R, 2
p. never believes what he says DE GAULLE, C, 11; POLITICIANS, 5
the p. poses as the servant DE GAULLE, C, 13; POLITICIANS, 6
unfair to expect a p. to live…up to the statements he makes POLITICIANS, 17
politicians All p. have vanity POLITICIANS, 26
all the p.…least significant was Bonar Law POLITICIANS, 46
It is a pity…that more p. are not bastards WHITEHORN, K, 4
more sensible than p. or the press PUBLIC, 9
P. are the same all over KHRUSHCHEV, N, 7
P.…can never forgive being ignored POLITICIANS, 30
P. neither love nor hate DRYDEN, J, 7; POLITICIANS, 8
P.…promise to build bridges POLITICIANS, 13
politics are too serious…to be left to the p. DE GAULLE, C, 15

populi *vox p., vox dei* PUBLIC, 1
populism p. that rejects anything different DEMOCRACY, 6
porcupine like fucking a p. CINEMA, 20
porcupines I shall throw two p. under you THREATS, 3
Porlock by a person on business from P. COLERIDGE, S, 13
pornographers P. are the enemies of women CARTER, A, 8
pornography P. is the attempt to insult sex LAWRENCE, D, 35; PORNOGRAPHY, 4
p.…it is terribly, terribly boring PORNOGRAPHY, 2
p. of war WAR, 132
show that gives p. a bad name PORNOGRAPHY, 1
Women do not believe that men believe…p. PORNOGRAPHY, 3
You don't get any p.…on the telly PORNOGRAPHY, 8
port Any p. in a storm DANGER, 1; PROVERBS, 56
it would be p. if it could ALCOHOL, 15
porter Oh, mister p., what shall I do TRAVEL, 29
portion best p. of a good man's life WORDSWORTH, W, 10
portions P. and parcels of the dreadful Past TENNYSON, 54; TIME, 57
portrait Every man's work…is always a p. of himself ARTS, 1; BUTLER, S, 23
Every time I paint a p. I lose a friend PAINTING, 18
Few persons who ever sat for a p. INFERIORITY, 5
I do not paint a p. to look like the subject PAINTING, 7
not paint a p. to look like the subject ARTISTS, 14
p. is a picture…something wrong with the mouth ART, 33
portraits P. of famous bards and preachers PAINTING, 19; THOMAS, D, 28
portraying What sort of God are we p. GOD, 21
posh only two p. papers on a Sunday NEWSPAPERS, 13; OSBORNE, J, 2
posies a thousand fragrant p. FLOWERS, 8; MARLOWE, C, 14
position only one p. for an artist THOMAS, D, 32; WALES, 3
The pleasure is momentary, the p. ridiculous SEX, 27
Twain and I are in the same p. TWAIN, M, 2
positive Power of P. Thinking OPTIMISM, 33; PHILOSOPHY, 9
possessing too dear for my p. PARTING, 11; SHAKESPEARE, 367
possession No human relation gives one p. in another UNITY, 10
P. is nine points LAW, 4; PROVERBS, 337
The p. of a book BURGESS, A, 6; OSTENTATION, 2
the p. of it is intolerable MATERIALISM, 24
possessions Not the owner of many p. will you be right to call happy HAPPINESS, 10; HORACE, 43
p. for a moment of time ELIZABETH I, 15; LAST WORDS, 29
possibilities Failure? – the p. do not exist FAILURE, 11
possibility How great a p. POETS, 25
too much of a sceptic to deny the p. of anything HUXLEY, T, 10; SCEPTICISM, 2
possible something is p., he is…right SCIENCE, 20
the art of the p. POLITICS, 23
post p. of honour is a private station ADDISON, J, 7; VICE, 1
post-chaise I would spend my life in driving briskly in a p. JOHNSON, S, 115
posterity doing something for p. ADDISON, J, 17; POSTERITY, 2
looked upon by p. as a brave, bad man CROMWELL, O, 2
The nations which have put mankind and p. most in their debt INGE, W, 12; NATIONS, 4
Think of your p. POSTERITY, 1
Thy p. shall sway COWPER, W, 3; ENGLAND, 18
postern Present has latched its p. HARDY, T, 5
postgraduate The British p. student is a lonely forlorn soul EDUCATION, 56; LODGE, D, 3
post-Industrial The Coming of P. Society PROGRESS, 3
post-mortem In the p. room we witness the final result of disease DEATH, 132
post-Natal is it p. depression SOUTH AFRICA, 6
postscript all the pith is in the p. HAZLITT, W, 6
that which was most material in the p. BACON, F, 17
postures It requires one to assume such indecent p. CRICKET, 13; WILDE, O, 72
pot greasy Joan doth keel the p. SHAKESPEARE, 201
potent p. cheap music is COWARD, N, 17; POPULAR MUSIC, 10
pot-smoking a philandering, p. draft dodger CLINTON, B, 2
potter Who *is* the P. CREATION, 10; FITZGERALD, E, 16
poultry A p. matter MARX, G, 3; MONEY, 33; PUNS, 15
pound the p.…in your pocket ECONOMICS, 23; WILSON, H, 10
You can call an ecu a p. in Britain MONEY, 25
pounds My dear fellow…I only ask you for twenty-five p. SHERIDAN, R, 14
the p. will take care of themselves CHESTERFIELD, P, 10
two hundred p. a year BUTLER, S, 7; MONEY, 15
vile ill-favour'd faults /Looks handsome in three hundred p. SHAKESPEARE, 257
pouvait *si vieillesse p.* AGE, 39
poverty achieved p. with distinction POVERTY, 40
a darn is…p. THRIFT, 11
crime so shameful as p. POVERTY, 10
declares unconditional war on p. in America POVERTY, 23
discover why…there continues to be so much p. POVERTY, 5
Disease creates p. POVERTY, 37
Do you call p. a crime POVERTY, 36; SHAW, G, 19
For every talent that p. has stimulated POVERTY, 13
from nothing to a state of extreme p. MARX, G, 13; POVERTY, 32
generations…have struggled in p. to build these altars RELIGION, 82
If p. is the mother of crime, stupidity is its father CRIME, 6; LA BRUYERE, J, 11
It is easy enough to say that p. is no crime JEROME, J, 3; POVERTY, 22
Loneliness…is the most terrible p. LONELINESS, 14; TERESA, 4
Notwithstanding the p. of my…experience CONTENTMENT, 5
P. and oysters DICKENS, C, 46; POVERTY, 8
p.…is a blunder JEROME, J, 3; POVERTY, 22
P. is a great enemy to human happiness JOHNSON, S, 140; POVERTY, 24
P. is an anomaly to rich people BAGEHOT, W, 11; HUNGER, 2
P. is not a crime POVERTY, 2; PROVERBS, 338
P. of goods is easily cured MONTAIGNE, M, 10
p. of soul, impossible MONTAIGNE, M, 10
P., therefore, was comparative DRABBLE, M, 5; POVERTY, 9
The misfortunes of p. POVERTY, 25
three great evils, boredom, vice, and p. VOLTAIRE, 10; WORK, 37
When p. comes in PROVERBS, 460
world p. is primarily a problem of two million villages POVERTY, 35
powder keep your p. dry PRUDENCE, 7
She burst while drinking a seidlitz p. ANONYMOUS, 32
when your p.'s runnin' low NEWBOLT, H, 2
powdered Stratford…suggests p. history ENGLAND, 24
powder's when your p. runnin' low PATRIOTISM, 30
power All P. to the Soviets RUSSIAN REVOLUTION, 2
All that is literature seeks to communicate p. BOOKS, 18
As we make sex less secretive, we may rob it of its p. SZASZ, T, 2
corridors of p. POWER, 24
Germany will be…a world p. GERMANY, 4; HITLER, A, 12
greater the p. BURKE, E, 25; POWER, 8
He aspired to p. POWER, 28; TAYLOR, A, 2
If, drunk with sight of p. KIPLING, R, 23
In a country economically backward, the proletariat can take p. earlier CAPITALISM, 19
in office but not in p. GOVERNMENT, 19
its source of p.: ownership CAPITALISM, 10; KINNOCK, N, 5
Knowledge itself is p. BACON, F, 64; KNOWLEDGE, 3
life depends on your p. to master words WORDS, 26
love of p. is the love of ourselves FREEDOM, 21; HAZLITT, W, 13
Men of p. have not time to read BOOKS, 21; POWER, 12
one of these is the history of political p. HISTORY, 23
potential for…misplaced p. INFLUENCE, 3
P.…and Liberty…are seldom upon good Terms FREEDOM, 19; HALIFAX, 7
p. before his hair turned white was called a whizz-kid POWER, 15
P. corrupts POWER, 27; STEVENSON, A, 3
p. is apt to corrupt PITT THE ELDER, 3
P. is the law of man POWER, 10
P. is the ultimate aphrodisiac POWER, 16
P.…like a dead sea fruit MACMILLAN, H, 12; POWER, 17
p. of life and death BIBLE, 522
P. of Positive Thinking OPTIMISM, 33; PHILOSOPHY, 9
p. over men WOLLSTONECRAFT, M, 4
P. tends to corrupt POWER, 3
p. without responsibility BALDWIN, S, 3; KIPLING, R, 36
self-sufficing p. of Solitude WORDSWORTH, W, 39
The accursed p. which stands on Privilege BELLOC, H, 13
The balance of p. WALPOLE, R, 5
the blacks must oppress them today because they have p. POWER, 19
The English nation…has successfully regulated the p. of its kings GOVERNMENT, 46
the foul dregs of his p., the tools of despotism and corruption POLITICS, 119
the kingdom of God is not in word, but in p. BIBLE, 26; GOD, 8

they...take, who have the p. POWER, 31; WORDSWORTH, W, 47
to have p. over men FEMINISM, 40
unable to influence events...do not have the p. BRITAIN, 10
War knows no p. BROOKE, R, 6; WAR, 32
When p. narrows the areas of man's concern POETRY, 36
wrong sort of people are always in p. POWER, 32
You only have p. over people POWER, 25; SOLZHENITSYN, A, 8
powerful a more p. or a more united empire BRITISH EMPIRE, 1
Guns will make us p. POWER POLITICS, 3
P. men...through the help of their wives SUCCESS, 16
The rich and p. know ANOUILH, J, 4; GOD, 3
powerless Brief and p. HUMAN CONDITION, 23; RUSSELL, B, 16
p. to be born ARNOLD, M, 19
powers a taste for *hidden* and *forbidden* p. NIETZSCHE, F, 10; SCIENCE, 70
Headmasters have p. CHURCHILL, W, 17; EDUCATION, 25
the p. of a first-rate man and the creed of a second-rate man BAGEHOT, W, 9; POLITICIANS, 44
pox P. take him and his wit POPE, A, 2
You will die either on the gallows, or of the p. REPARTEE, 5
practical Compassion is...an absolutely p. belief KINNOCK, N, 7
meddling with any p. part of life ADDISON, J, 10
P. men...are usually the slaves of some defunct economist KEYNES, J, 7
practice a thing may look evil in theory...in p. excellent BURKE, E, 28
I p. a lot when I'm on my own SEX, 5
P. makes perfect EXPERIENCE, 5; PROVERBS, 339
P. should always be based upon a sound knowledge of theory LEONARDO DA VINCI, 7
practiced For thirty-seven years I've p....and now they call me a genius GENIUS, 8
practise P. what you preach EXAMPLE, 1; PROVERBS, 340
two kinds of morality...one which we preach but do not p. MORALITY, 14; RUSSELL, B, 21
praise bury Caesar, not to p. him EVIL, 19; SHAKESPEARE, 155
Damn with faint p. CRITICISM, 51; POPE, A, 14
envy is a kind of p. ENVY, 6; GAY, J, 9
his p. shall ever be in my mouth PSALMS, 22
how a man takes p. PRAISE, 5
if we p. ourselves fearlessly, something will always stick BACON, F, 4; PRAISE, 3
I will p. any man that will p. me FLATTERY, 8; SHAKESPEARE, 32
Let us with a gladsome mind /P. the Lord GOD, 39; MILTON, J, 55
My poems are hymns of p. POETRY, 58; SITWELL, E, 3
Pavilioned in splendour, and girded with p. GOD, 24
People...only want p. CRITICISM, 42; MAUGHAM, W, 12
P. and blame are much the same WRITING, 53
P. him in the cymbals and dances PSALMS, 77
P. the Lord and pass the ammunition WAR, 63
The moment you p. a book BOOKS, 31
this blest man, let his just p. be given COMPLIMENTS, 37; WALTON, I, 7
To refuse p. PRAISE, 8; ROCHEFOUCAULD, 18
we but p. ourselves in other men POPE, A, 27; PRAISE, 7
written for the love of Man and in p. of God THOMAS, D, 5
praises He who p. everybody INSINCERITY, 2; JOHNSON, S, 118
The idiot who p....every country but his own GILBERT, W, 27
yet he p. those who follow different paths HORACE, 45
praising advantage of...p....oneself BUTLER, S, 26; PRAISE, 6
pram sombre enemy of good art than the p. BABIES, 2; CONNOLLY, C, 10
pray Common people do not p. CLASS, 43
p. for you at St Paul's PRAYER, 26; SMITH, S, 14
P. to God and say the lines ACTING, 9
watch and p. BIBLE, 426; IMPERFECTION, 4
when ye p., use not vain repetitions BIBLE, 367; PRAYER, 6
praye Fare well...and p. for me EXECUTION, 25; FAMILY, 41
prayed I wish that God had not given me what I p. for DISAPPOINTMENT, 8
prayer As the drought continued, p. was abandoned LEE, L, 1
Comin' in on a Wing and a P. HOPE, 6
cravings...do not become a p. PRAYER, 18
Does God always answer p. PRAYER, 13
More things are wrought by p. PRAYER, 27; TENNYSON, 24
most odious of...narcissisms – p. FOWLES, J, 1
P. makes the Christian's armour bright COWPER, W, 15; PRAYER, 14
storms of p. EXCESS, 16; TENNYSON, 74
the Conservative Party at p. CHURCH, 11
the faith, p. and self-dedication of the King ROYALTY, 26
The people's p. DREAMS, 5; DRYDEN, J, 14
The p. that...heals the sick EDDY, M, 1; FAITH, 13
prayers better than good men's p. CERVANTES, M, 8; PRAYER, 10
The hopes and p. of liberty-loving people EISENHOWER, D, 4
prayeth He p. well COLERIDGE, S, 38; PRAYER, 11
prays man p....for a miracle PRAYER, 28; TURGENEV, I, 4
preach p. Christ crucified BIBLE, 24
two kinds of morality...one which we p. but do not practise MORALITY, 14; RUSSELL, B, 21
preacher The British churchgoer prefers a severe p. SERMONS, 1
preachers Portraits of famous bards and p. PAINTING, 19; THOMAS, D, 28
P. say, Do as I say, not as I do EXAMPLE, 7; SELDEN, J, 5
preaching A woman's p. is like a dog's walking on his hinder legs JOHNSON, S, 69; WOMEN, 69
by the foolishness of p. BIBLE, 24
illuminate our whole country with the bright light of their p. RELIGION, 49
precedency the point of p. between a louse and a flea INSULTS, 74; JOHNSON, S, 144
precedent A p. embalms a principle DISRAELI, B, 25; EXAMPLE, 6
precept for p. must be upon p. BIBLE, 208
precious Right is more p. RIGHT, 4; WILSON, W, 10
so p. that it must be rationed FREEDOM, 32; LENIN, V, 11
that most p. jewel, the Word of God BIBLE, 531
precisely thinking too p. on th' event COWARDICE, 9; SHAKESPEARE, 101
pre-cognitive Love means the p. flow LAWRENCE, D, 45; LOVE, 102
predestination Free Will and P. CHURCHILL, W, 19; DESTINY, 6
predicament Life...is a p. LIFE, 79; SANTAYANA, G, 8
predictions Dreams and p. BACON, F, 41; DREAMS, 1
prefabricated a better word than p. CHURCHILL, W, 10; WORDS, 6
prefect a priggish schoolgirl, captain of the hockey team, a p. ROYALTY, 2
preferable There are only opinions, some of which are p. TRUTH, 25
preferment P.'s door ARNOLD, M, 36; PROMOTION, 1
preferred he...coming after me is p. before me BIBLE, 239; CHRISTIANITY, 14
pregnancy an unwanted p. destroys two lives ABORTION, 10
people die from p. CONTRACEPTION, 13
quite lawful for a Catholic woman to avoid p. by...mathematics CONTRACEPTION, 10; MENCKEN, H, 4
to imagine that p. was ever intended to be a sickness PREGNANCY, 3
pregnant a little inflation is like being a little p. ECONOMICS, 11
If men could get p. ABORTION, 9
in women nine out of ten abdominal swellings are the p. uterus BIRTH, 13
prejudge I do not...p. the past PREJUDICE, 16
prejudice I am free of all p. HATE, 4; PREJUDICE, 5
P. is planted in childhood BAINBRIDGE, B, 7
skilled appeals to religious p. EVOLUTION, 20; HUXLEY, T, 11
suffer them because of the p. HOMOSEXUALITY, 21
prejudices collection of p. which is called political philosophy RUSSELL, B, 26
Common sense is the collection of p. EINSTEIN, A, 10
Don't half-quote me to reinforce your own p. PREJUDICE, 3
freedom to print...proprietor's p. MEDIA, 15
my p. swell like varicose veins PREJUDICE, 7
premise fundamental p. of a revolution TROTSKY, L, 7
pre-natal the greatness of Russia is only her p. struggling LAWRENCE, D, 34; RUSSIA, 10
preparation life...seems to me p. for something that never happens LIFE, 98; YEATS, W, 5
no p. is thought necessary POLITICS, 102; STEVENSON, R, 4
the suspicion...his life was a p. for elder statesmanship MACMILLAN, H, 2
prepare I go to p. a place for you BIBLE, 258; HEAVEN, 3
I p. for a journey...as though for death TRAVEL, 32
prepared Be P. SELF-RELIANCE, 3
prerogative p. of the eunuch RESPONSIBILITY, 18
Presbyter P. is but old Priest writ large MILTON, J, 62; RELIGION, 68
prescribed the taking of things p. PATIENTS, 2
presence A certain person may have...a wonderful p. CHARACTER, 20

come before his p. with thanksgiving PSALMS, 54
present All p. and correct ANONYMOUS, 4
an un-birthday p. CARROLL, L, 31; GIFTS, 3
novelists the story of the p. NOVELS, 6
P. has latched its postern HARDY, T, 5
P. mirth hath present laughter PRESENT, 13; SHAKESPEARE, 340
The future will one day be the p. FUTURE, 10
Time p. and time past ELIOT, T, 6
to know nothing but the p., or nothing but the past CONSERVATISM, 5; KEYNES, J, 2
preservation Government has no other end but the p. of property GOVERNMENT, 22
the p. of life, and liberty...pursuit of happiness JEFFERSON, T, 5
preserve Lord shall p. thy going out PSALMS, 68
p. one last male thing LAWRENCE, D, 25; MASCULINITY, 2
preserves What destroys one man p. another REMEDIES, 24
presidency cancer...close to the P. CORRUPTION, 2
president American...prepared to run for P. POLITICS, 112
An extraordinarily gifted p. who was the wrong man JOHNSON, L, 1
anybody could become P. POLITICIANS, 4
a p. without a people GORBACHOV, M, 2
Eisenhower proved we don't need a p. EISENHOWER, D, 1
God is the only p. WEBSTER, D, 2
I'd rather be right than p. RIGHT, 3
Mothers all want their sons...to become p. POLITICS, 61
nobody is strongminded around a P. SERVILITY, 6
not choose to run for P. in 1928 POLITICIANS, 72
one thing about being P. EISENHOWER, D, 6; POWER, 11
perfect for television is all a P. has to be REAGAN, R, 3
P. spends...time kissing people PERSUASION, 4; TRUMAN, H, 6
the P. is dead, but the Government lives ASSASSINATION, 4
We are all the P.'s men LOYALTY, 7
When the P. does it...not illegal NIXON, R, 11
press a gentleman of the P. DISRAELI, B, 27; JOURNALISM, 16
don't hate the p. JOURNALISM, 28
Facing the p. MEDIA, 16
more sensible than politicians or the p. PUBLIC, 9
Never lose your temper with the P. PANKHURST, C, 3
p. is more difficult than bathing a leper MEDIA, 16
spiteful to me in the American p. SOLZHENITSYN, A, 16
The Pill has so much bad p. CONTRACEPTION, 12
would not say that our P. is obscene MEDIA, 13
presume Dr Livingstone, I p. EXPLORATION, 5; GREETINGS, 3
Know then thyself, p. not God to scan POPE, A, 34
presumption You'll be Amused by its P. DRINKS, 21
pretending p. to be wicked HYPOCRISY, 23; WILDE, O, 27
pretensions star who had no p. ACTORS, 19
pretty anyone lived in a p. how town CUMMINGS, 2
a p. girl who naked is CUMMINGS, 4; NAKEDNESS, 3
One girl can be p. BEAUTY, 22; FITZGERALD, F, 9
P. witty Nell COMPLIMENTS, 21; PEPYS, S, 11
That's a p. little thing ARTISTS, 15
There's only one p. child CHILDREN, 2; PROVERBS, 421
Preux Saint P. never kicked the fireirons IMPERFECTION, 5
prevent not knowing how to p. them CONTRACEPTION, 14
preventing a means of p. it ILLNESS, 54
Politics is the art of p. people from taking part POLITICS, 110
prevention P. is better than cure PROVERBS, 341; PRUDENCE, 4
P. of disease must become the goal of every physician MEDICINE, 95
The p. of disease today is one of the most important factors MEDICINE, 61
preventive one ultimate and effectual p....is death DEATH, 53
the promotion of it is a branch of p. medicine LONGEVITY, 8
prevents a beefsteak p. it REMEDIES, 54
Nothing p. us from being natural ROCHEFOUCAULD, 25
prey he shall devour the p. BIBLE, 182
lord of all things, yet a p. to all POPE, A, 33
price a better p. than old mistresses BEAVERBROOK, M, 6; PAINTING, 2
Courage is the p....for granting peace COURAGE, 15
her p. is far above rubies BIBLE, 458; WOMEN, 25
P. of Herald three cents daily NEWSPAPERS, 4; TELEGRAMS, 4
p. which is too great to pay for peace WORLD WAR I, 28
The p....for pursuing any profession BALDWIN, J, 3; DISILLUSION, 1
the p. of everything and the value of nothing CYNICISM, 5; WILDE, O, 43
those men have their p. CORRUPTION, 16; WALPOLE, R, 3
Who never knew the p. of happiness HAPPINESS, 35
prick If you p. us, do we not bleed EQUALITY, 34; SHAKESPEARE, 247
p. the sides of my intent AMBITION, 23; SHAKESPEARE, 211
pricks to kick against the p. BIBLE, 6
pride A mother's p. EXPECTATION, 7; SCOTT, W, 19
contempt on all my p. HUMILITY, 14; WATTS, I, 8
Is P., the never-failing vice of fools POPE, A, 22; PRIDE, 9
it is p., but understood in a different way PRIDE, 13
P. and Truth...shake their...sides at youth YEATS, W, 24
p. goeth before destruction BIBLE, 451; MISQUOTATIONS, 10
p. is a word often on women's lips PRIDE, 3
p. that licks the dust POPE, A, 16; SERVILITY, 5
So sleeps the p. of former days IRELAND, 17; MOORE, T, 2
the criminal p. of the German Reich WAR, 7
the kind of p. least likely to offend MODESTY, 7
the p. of life LUST, 1
There is false modesty, but there is no false p. PRIDE, 10
women...addicted to p. PRIDE, 11
Pride and Prejudice I had not seen *P.* WRITERS, 40
prides His Royal Highness...p. himself upon...the excellent harvest ARROGANCE, 7; SHERIDAN, R, 13
priest A p. sees people at their best OCCUPATIONS, 1; PROVERBS, 61
For a p. to turn a man when he lies a-dying PERSUASION, 3; SELDEN, J, 6
Presbyter is but old P. writ large MILTON, J, 62; RELIGION, 68
p. is a man who is called Father CATHOLICISM, 1
rid me of this turbulent p. ASSASSINATION, 5
taking a place beside the physician and the p. OCCUPATIONS, 22
That waked the p. all shaven and shorn NURSERY RHYMES, 61
That whisky p. CLERGY, 7; GREENE, G, 7
priest-craft e'r P. did begin DRYDEN, J, 3; RELIGION, 34
priesthood kingdom and the p., are brought together POLITICS, 82
Literary men are...a perpetual p. CARLYLE, T, 8; WRITERS, 5
women in the p. CLERGY, 17; RELIGION, 76
priests All things, oh p., are on fire BUDDHA, 1; FIRE, 1
I always like to associate with a lot of p. BELLOC, H, 20; CLERGY, 1
In old time we had treen chalices and golden p. CLERGY, 8
prig a bore and a bounder and a p. LAWRENCE, T, 3
prim A p....rather querulous person HOUSMAN, A, 1
prima They are for p. donnas or corpses TOSCANINI, A, 1
prime having lost...your p. HERRICK, R, 6; MARRIAGE, 88
One's p. is elusive AGE, 86; SPARK, M, 8
prime minister a P. has to be...a showman MACMILLAN, H, 3
A towering P. THATCHER, M, 11
Macmillan would have been Labour P. MACMILLAN, H, 1
society...pays a harlot 25 times as much as it pays its P. WILSON, H, 7
that of P. is filled by fluke POLITICIANS, 20
the curse of the present British P. CHAMBERLAIN, N, 1
the most intelligent P. of the century MACMILLAN, H, 4
when a British P. sneezed BRITAIN, 13
prime ministers rogue elephant among British p. POLITICIANS, 107
primitive The classics are only p. literature CLASSICS, 6; LEACOCK, S, 2
primroses smiles, /Wan as p. FLOWERS, 6; KEATS, J, 8
prince Milton the p. of poets MILTON, J, 2
p. of royal courage ROYALTY, 118
P. was...a libertine over head and ears in debt ROYALTY, 72
the P....is restrained from doing ill GOVERNMENT, 46
Prince of Wales who's danced with the P. SNOBBERY, 5
Prince Philip P.. He's a world expert on leisure KINNOCK, N, 6
Prince Regent patronized...by Brummel and the P. SOCIETY, 11
princes mine were p. of the earth JEWS, 3
O put not your trust in p. PSALMS, 73
p. learn no art truly, but...horsemanship HORSES, 7; JONSON, B, 8
princess advantage about marrying a p. MARRIAGE, 44; ROYALTY, 41
principal not my interest to pay the p. SHERIDAN, R, 19
principle an imperative p. which statesmen...ignore at their peril SELF, 28
A precedent embalms a p. DISRAELI, B, 25; EXAMPLE, 6
except from some strong p. MELBOURNE, 8; MOTIVE, 4
the most useful thing about a p....sacrificed to expediency EXPEDIENCY, 5; MAUGHAM, W, 4
the p. seems the same CHURCHILL, W, 8; WATER, 1

you never can tell. That's a p. PRINCIPLES, 5; SHAW, G, 43
principles All universal moral p. are idle fancies MORALITY, 15
And wrote 'P. of Political Economy' ECONOMICS, 3
easier to fight for one's p. PRINCIPLES, 1
If one sticks too rigidly to one's p. CHRISTIE, A, 4; PRINCIPLES, 3
It is often easier to fight for p. PRINCIPLES, 6
subverts all the p. of his understanding CHRISTIANITY, 43
The p. of a free constitution GIBBON, E, 7; GOVERNMENT, 14
The p. of logic and metaphysics are true PHILOSOPHY, 1
Whenever two good people argue over p. PRINCIPLES, 4
whether I embrace your lordship's p. or your mistress REPARTEE, 5
print decomposing in the eternity of p. CRITICISM, 67; WOOLF, V, 6
news that's fit to p. NEWSPAPERS, 11
pleasant, sure, to see one's name in p. BOOKS, 11; BYRON, 37
The big p. giveth and the fine p. taketh away BUSINESS, 29
printers those books by which the p. have lost BOOKS, 22
printing Gunpowder, P., and the Protestant Religion CARLYLE, T, 9; CIVILIZATION, 3
priorities The language of p. is BEVAN, A, 2; SOCIALISM, 3
prison an extraordinarily pleasant p. LEXICOGRAPHY, 1
Anyone who has been to...public school will...feel...at home in p. EDUCATION, 97; WAUGH, E, 25
compare /This p. where I live unto the world IMPRISONMENT, 11
In a wall'd p. IMPRISONMENT, 10
People should not be sent to p. PUNISHMENT, 28
p. for the colour of his hair IMPRISONMENT, 6
P....start sending a better class of people CLASS, 35
ready to receive prizes as I am to be thrown into p. WAIESA, L, 1
Stone walls do not a p. make IMPRISONMENT, 8
The only thing I really mind about going to p. PUNISHMENT, 18
the p. of our mind MIND, 31
the true place for a just man is also a p. JUSTICE, 25; THOREAU, H, 3
The world...is but a large p. EXECUTION, 30; RALEIGH, W, 4
prisoner I object to your being taken p. ROYALTY, 78
Peace took them all p. WAR AND PEACE, 10
P., God has given you good abilities THEFT, 3
p. sees the door of his dungeon open he dashes IMPETUOSITY, 4
prisoners If this is the way Queen Victoria treats her p. IMPRISONMENT, 18; WILDE, O, 73
p. of addiction and...prisoners of envy MATERIALISM, 14
ransom not only their p. but their dead HOSTAGES, 9
prisons not enough p....in Palestine to hold all the Jews MEIR, G, 7
P. are built with stones of Law BLAKE, W, 20
privacy a right to share your p. in a public place PRIVACY, 6; USTINOV, P, 6
invading her own p....first of the modern personalities BANKHEAD, T, 3
That should assure us of...forty-five minutes of undisturbed p. PARKER, D, 13
private heart's ease /Must kings neglect, that p. men enjoy EQUALITY, 32
He was meddling too much in my p. life WILLIAMS, T, 8
I should never be allowed out in p. APOLOGIES, 2
most beautiful in Britain...in p. hands BRITAIN, 14
P. faces in public places PRIVACY, 1
P. Means is dead PUNS, 23
P. practice and marriage SCIENCE, 11
public faces in p. places FAME, 3
Scientific discovery is a p. event SCIENCE, 65
sex...a very p. secretive activity SEX, 117; SZASZ, T, 2
The grave's a fine and p. place DEATH, 105; MARVELL, A, 12
Travel is the most p. of pleasures SACKVILLE-WEST, V, 3; TRAVEL, 39
Whatsoever...the p. calamity...not interfere with the public business SHERIDAN, R, 15
when religion is allowed to invade...p. life MELBOURNE, 11; RELIGION, 66
privatising the process of p. our bread shop RUSSIA, 22
privilege a defender of p. PESSIMISM, 2
an Englishman's heaven-born p. of doing as he likes ARNOLD, M, 9; PUBLIC, 2
The accursed power which stands on P. BELLOC, H, 13; POLITICS, 12
privileges men value...not rights but p. SUPERIORITY, 10
prize in a race run all, but one receiveth the p. BIBLE, 33
Men p. the thing ungain'd DESIRE, 14; SHAKESPEARE, 330
Not all that tempts your wand'ring eyes...is lawful p. GRAY, T, 13; TEMPTATION, 6
prize-fighters p. shaking hands WOMEN, 89
prizes just miss the p. at the flower show BRONOWSKI, J, 5
ready to receive p. as I am to be thrown into prison WAIESA, L, 1
The world continues to offer glittering p. RUTHLESSNESS, 6
P.R.O partly a liaison man and partly P. BETJEMAN, J, 5; BUSINESS, 4
problem Not every p. someone has...is...due to... capitalist...production CAPITALISM, 12
P. children tend to grow up into problem adults SOCIETY, 10
the p. as I see it CHARLES, P, 9; LANGUAGE, 12
problems all the usual male p. BLEASDALE, A, 3
Among the many p....the choice of the moment...to begin his novel SACKVILLE-WEST, V, 1; WRITERS, 24
complex p. that face the Middle East HOSTAGES, 11
There are two p. in my life POLITICIANS, 81
process chaos is a science of p. SCIENCE, 43
procession A torchlight p. ALCOHOL, 60
procrastination P. is the thief of time YOUNG, E, 5
procreation ordained for the p. of children BOOK OF COMMON PRAYER, 24
trivialization of the act of p. ABORTION, 4
procreative Females get hired along p. lines WOMAN'S ROLE, 5
proctologists pile of p. LANGUAGE, 4
prodigal P. of Ease DRYDEN, J, 6; WORLD-WEARINESS, 1
producing Man...consumes without p. CAPITALISM, 14; ORWELL, G, 3
production Capitalist p. begets...its own negation CAPITALISM, 13; MARX, K, 5
profaned from the province they have desolated and p. VIOLENCE, 8
professed Medicine is a science which hath been...more p. than laboured MEDICINE, 8
profession Meek wifehood is no part of my p. BRITTAIN, V, 4
Politics is...the only p. POLITICS, 102; STEVENSON, R, 4
The price...for pursuing any p. BALDWIN, J, 3; DISILLUSION, 1
professional the English legal system will not support...p. slavery EXPLOITATION, 3
professor A p. is a gentleman who has a different opinion ACADEMICS, 3
A p. is one who talks in someone else's sleep ACADEMICS, 1; AUDEN, W, 29
professors American p. like their literature LITERATURE, 15
As to religion...duty of government to protect all...p. thereof GOVERNMENT, 30
Culture is an instrument wielded by p. CULTURE, 3; WEIL, S, 1
If there weren't so many p. ACADEMICS, 4
now-a-days p. of philosophy but not philosophers PHILOSOPHERS, 14; THOREAU, H, 11
profit count as p. every day that Fate allows you HORACE, 29; PRESENT, 8
No p. grows where is no pleasure EDUCATION, 79; SHAKESPEARE, 320
Philosophers never balance between p. and honesty HUME, D, 8; PHILOSOPHERS, 4
trouble with the p. system BUSINESS, 37
profound turbid look the most p. LANDOR, W, 5; WRITING, 28
progeny A p. of learning MALAPROPISMS, 3; SHERIDAN, R, 4
programme start their p. with fictitious quotes QUOTATIONS, 6
progress All p. is based BUTLER, S, 11; PROGRESS, 7
beyond these ancient texts if we want p. RELIGION, 71
deviation from the norm 'p.' INDIVIDUALITY, 7
Man's 'p.' is but a gradual discovery PROGRESS, 22
Our p..../Is trouble and care LIFE, 58; LONGFELLOW, H, 15
P....depends on retentiveness HISTORY, 24; PROGRESS, 23; SANTAYANA, G, 6
'p.' is simply a comparative CHESTERTON, G, 19; PROGRESS, 9
P. is /The law of life PROGRESS, 6
stopped believing in p. PROGRESS, 5
the basic principle of all social p. FEMINISM, 8
the things which government does...social p. GOVERNMENT, 42
thievish p. TIME, 51
What p....In the Middle Ages FREUD, S, 7; PSYCHOLOGY, 8
What we call p. is PROGRESS, 12

progression the labour having been…rather in a circle than in p. MEDICINE, 8
Without Contraries is no p. BLAKE, W, 18; CONFLICT, 4
prohibition Communism is like p. COMMUNISM, 13; ROGERS, W, 3
proletarian substitution of the p. for the bourgeois state RUSSIAN REVOLUTION, 6
you are polite to a p. you…bolster up the capitalist system POLITICS, 117; WAUGH, E, 37
proletariat In a country economically backward, the p. can take power earlier CAPITALISM, 19
The dictatorship of the p. MARX, K, 7; MARXISM, 14
the p. will…wage a class struggle for Socialism CLASS, 22; LENIN, V, 6; MARXISM, 7
prologues P. precede the piece PLAYS, 4
prolonged the War is being deliberately p. SASSOON, S, 7; WAR, 149
Prometheus as old as P. NIETZSCHE, F, 1
promise A p. made is a debt unpaid PROMISES, 6
a young man of p. CHURCHILL, W, 3
rarely…one can see in a little boy the p. of a man CHILDREN, 27
promised Only do always in health what you have often p. to do when you are sick ILLNESS, 65
promises a young man of p. CHURCHILL, W, 3
P. are like pie-crust PROVERBS, 342; SWIFT, J, 10
young man of p. BALFOUR, A, 3; INSULTS, 9
promisin Once you were so p.' FRY, C, 1; SHYNESS, 3
promotion the fashion of these times, /Where none will sweat but for p. SELFLESSNESS, 6
promptly He gives twice who gives p. PROMPTNESS, 4
pronounce foreigners…spell better than they p. PRONUNCIATION, 5
last words which I should p. in this Academy ARTISTS, 21
p. foreign names as he chooses CHURCHILL, W, 36; PRONUNCIATION, 2
spell it Vinci and p. it Vinchy SPELLING, 2; TWAIN, M, 10
pronouncements Science should leave off making p. SCIENCE, 57
pronunciation To correct an Englishman's p. PRONUNCIATION, 3
proof The great p. of madness MADNESS, 28
propaganda If p. worked we'd be straight HOMOSEXUALITY, 23
P.…consists in nearly deceiving your friends PROPAGANDA, 1
propagated If human beings could be p.…aristocracy would be…sound ARISTOCRACY, 13
wished that mankind were p. like trees SEX, 62
propagation we were merely intended for the world's p. WOMAN'S ROLE, 13
Women exist…solely for the p. of the species WOMAN'S ROLE, 12
propensities the silk stockings and white bosoms…excite my amorous p. JOHNSON, S, 46; LUST, 6
proper He never does a p. thing without…an improper reason MORALITY, 18; SHAW, G, 17
The p. study of Mankind is Man POPE, A, 34; SELF-KNOWLEDGE, 5
property Government has no other end but the preservation of p. GOVERNMENT, 22
poor have no right to the p. of the rich POVERTY AND WEALTH, 7; RUSKIN, J, 16
P. has its duties CAPITALISM, 5
P. is organised robbery CAPITALISM, 17
P. is theft CAPITALISM, 16; MARXISM, 15
The future is the only kind of p. CAMUS, A, 12; SLAVERY, 2
the right of governing was not p. but a trust GOVERNMENT, 13
Thieves respect p. CRIME, 3
prophecies bring about the verification of his own p. PROPHECY, 13; TROLLOPE, A, 13
prophet A historian is a p. in reverse HISTORIANS, 7
a p. is not without honour BIBLE, 392; HONOUR, 1
single look at the P.'s face RELIGION, 3
there arose not a p.…like unto Moses BIBLE, 60; PROPHECY, 2
The sons of the p. were brave men and bold ANONYMOUS, 98; COURAGE, 2
proportion strangeness in the p. BACON, F, 12; BEAUTY, 8
proportional P. Representation…fundamentally counter-democratic KINNOCK, N, 2; POLITICS, 64
proposes Man p. GOD, 31; PROVERBS, 280
proposition undesirable to believe a p. RUSSELL, B, 20; SCEPTICISM, 4
propriety forgetting…womanly feeling and p. VICTORIA, 7
The p. of…having improper thoughts about…neighbours MORALITY, 4
prose anything except bad p. CHURCHILL, W, 38; PROSE, 3
architecture like p. ARCHITECTURE, 9
difference between…p. and metrical composition POETRY AND PROSE, 7; WORDSWORTH, W, 19
good p. should resemble the conversation PROSE, 5
I can only write p. today POETRY AND PROSE, 8; YEATS, W, 38
I have been talking p. for over forty years MOLIERE, 3; PROSE, 6
no one hears his own remarks as p. AUDEN, W, 3; PROSE, 1
Poetry is opposed to science…p. to metre COLERIDGE, S, 18; POETRY AND PROSE, 1
Poetry is to p. POETRY AND PROSE, 5
poetry sinks and swoons under…p. LANDOR, W, 2; POETRY AND PROSE, 3
p. = words in their best order COLERIDGE, S, 41; POETRY AND PROSE, 2
the cradle of English p. PROSE, 4
the p. for God LANGUAGE, 23
to write good p. is an affair of good manners MAUGHAM, W, 17; POETRY AND PROSE, 4
prosper Treason doth never p. TREASON, 6
whatsoever he doeth, it shall p. PSALMS, 1
prosperitee A man to have ben in p. CHAUCER, G, 20; MISFORTUNE, 8
him that stood in greet p. CHAUCER, G, 15; MISFORTUNE, 7
prosperity P. doth best discover vice BACON, F, 8; MISFORTUNE, 4
prostate moral equivalent of a p. operation TELEVISION, 10
prostitute I don't think a p. is more moral WOMEN, 105
prostitutes the small nations like p. DIPLOMACY, 22
prostitution P.…keeps her out of trouble HELLER, J, 7; SEX, 49
protect Every man I meet wants to p. me CHIVALRY, 16
p. the writer ACHESON, D, 7; BUREAUCRACY, 1
protection Every man…is entitled to the p. of the English law EQUALITY, 23
life deserves the p. of society ABORTION, 8
Religion was my p. against pain RELIGION, 51
protest doth p. too much GUILT, 13; SHAKESPEARE, 97
Protestant A P. with a horse BEHAN, B, 2; NATIONALITY, 3
Gunpowder, Printing, and the P. Religion CARLYLE, T, 9; CIVILIZATION, 3
I am the P. whore RELIGION, 50
P. women may take the Pill CONTRACEPTION, 16
Too much counterpoint; what is worse, P. counterpoint BEECHAM, T, 6; CRITICISM, 4
Protestantism The chief contribution of P. to human thought MENCKEN, H, 7; PROTESTANTISM, 6
Protestants 'God knows how you P.…have any sense of direction CATHOLICISM, 16
P. protesting against Protestantism CATHOLICISM, 9; LAWRENCE, D, 39
Proteus P. rising from the sea DISCONTENT, 10; WORDSWORTH, W, 66
protozoon Organic life…has developed…from the p. to the philosopher PROGRESS, 21; RUSSELL, B, 15
proud a p. look and a high stomach PSALMS, 57
Death be not p. DEATH, 58; DONNE, J, 14
He who does not need to lie is p. LYING, 17; NIETZSCHE, F, 16
I am p. to have a son PRIDE, 12
no guarantee…you will not be p. of the feat HUMILITY, 4
p. me no prouds SHAKESPEARE, 318
scattered the p. BIBLE, 310
too p. to fight WILSON, W, 9; WORLD WAR I, 26
Yes; I am p. POPE, A, 12; PRIDE, 8
proudest the moment of greatest humiliation is…when the spirit is p. PANKHURST, C, 4; PRIDE, 7
prove p. anything by figures CARLYLE, T, 4; STATISTICS, 2
proved p. upon our pulses KEATS, J, 59; PHILOSOPHY, 8
What is now p. was…imagined BLAKE, W, 24; PROOF, 2
Which was to be p. MATHEMATICS, 8
proverb A p. is much matter SAYINGS, 4
no p. to you till your life has illustrated it EXPERIENCE, 18; KEATS, J, 64
p. is one man's wit and all men's wisdom SAYINGS, 6
proverbs p. provide them with wisdom MAUGHAM, W, 23; STUPIDITY, 9
provided Add: 'p. he is really dead' ADMIRATION, 8; LA BRUYERE, J, 12
providence a kind of P. will…end…the acts of God DISASTER, 2
fathom the inscrutable workings of P. REPARTEE, 4

that P. dictates with the assurance of a sleepwalker DESTINY, 14; HITLER, A, 15
This is the temple of P. LUCK, 8
providential a case /of P. interference LUCK, 13
province all knowledge to be my p. BACON, F, 67; KNOWLEDGE, 4
from the p. they have desolated and profaned VIOLENCE, 8
provinces The reluctant obedience of distant p. DIPLOMACY, 25; MACAULAY, T, 5
provincial worse than p. – he was parochial JAMES, H, 7; WRITERS, 64
provincialism rather be taken in adultery than…p. FASHION, 8; HUXLEY, A, 7
provocations To great evils we submit; we resent little p. HAZLITT, W, 7; TRIVIALITY, 10
provocatively Women are entitled to dress attractively, even p. VIOLENCE, 16
provoke p. not your children BIBLE, 22; FAMILY, 9
P. /The years OLD AGE, 110; WORDSWORTH, W, 28
provoked an opportunity of being p. PEPYS, S, 16; PROVOCATION, 1
provokes No one p. me with impunity ANONYMOUS, 62; RETRIBUTION, 2
prude twenty is no age to be a p. MODESTY, 4; MOLIERE, 8
prudence p. never to practise…them FREEDOM, 57; TWAIN, M, 7
P.…when one is determining the fate of others LACLOS, P, 2
Prussia military domination of P. is…destroyed WAR, 12
prussic acid sooner give…a dose of p. than a copy of it HOMOSEXUALITY, 14
pseudonym use a p. during publication years SALINGER, J, 7
psyche the human p. lives in indissoluble union with the body PSYCHOLOGY, 9
Your mournful P. KEATS, J, 33; SOUL, 10
psychedelics discovery of p. one of the three major scientific break-throughs SCIENCE, 50
psychiatric a person who so obviously needs p. attention PSYCHIATRY, 10
psychiatrist And a p. is the man who collects the rent PSYCHIATRY, 31
Anybody who goes to see a p. GOLDWYN, S, 12; PSYCHIATRY, 16
A p. is a man who goes to the Folies-Bergère PSYCHIATRY, 27
I know that each conversation with a p. PSYCHIATRY, 4
No man is a hero to his wife's p. PSYCHIATRY, 8
One should only see a p. out of boredom PSYCHIATRY, 26
P.: A man who asks you a lot of expensive questions PSYCHIATRY, 7
the century of the p.'s couch PSYCHIATRY, 23
The p. is the obstetrician of the mind PSYCHIATRY, 2
psychiatrists P. classify a person as neurotic PSYCHIATRY, 28; SZASZ, T, 7
The relation between p. and other kinds of lunatics PSYCHIATRY, 19
psychiatry P.'s chief contribution to philosophy PSYCHIATRY, 9
The new definition of p. PSYCHIATRY, 1
psychic p. development of the individual FREUD, S, 2; PSYCHIATRY, 14
the p. of human relationship between the sexes SEX, 58
psychoanalysis Freud is the father of p. PSYCHIATRY, 17
psychological historian fits a man for p. analysis PSYCHOLOGY, 15; SARTRE, J, 11
There is no such thing as p. CHARACTER, 19; SARTRE, J, 17
psychologist An animal p. is a man who pulls habits out of rats PSYCHOLOGY, 1
psychology Behavioural p. is…pulling habits out of rats PSYCHOLOGY, 2
Children…have no use for p.. They detest sociology BOOKS, 44
Idleness is the parent of all p. PSYCHOLOGY, 13
Popular p. is a mass of cant PSYCHOLOGY, 5
P. is as unnecessary as directions for using poison PSYCHOLOGY, 11
P.…long past…short history PSYCHOLOGY, 6
p. should have destroyed…human nature PSYCHOLOGY, 3
P. which explains everything PSYCHOLOGY, 12
the dull craft of experimental p. PSYCHOLOGY, 16
The object of p. is to give us a totally different idea PSYCHOLOGY, 20
the popularity and persuasiveness of p. PSYCHOLOGY, 17
There is no p. PSYCHOLOGY, 18
The separation of p. from the premises of biology PSYCHOLOGY, 9
psychopathologist the p. the unspeakable MAUGHAM, W, 8; PSYCHIATRY, 22
psychotherapist time for the clergyman and the p. to join forces PSYCHOLOGY, 10
psychotic A p. is the man who lives in it PSYCHIATRY, 31
If a patient is poor he is committed…as 'p.' PSYCHIATRY, 18
Psychiatrists classify a person as…p. PSYCHIATRY, 28; SZASZ, T, 7
p. means he's even worse than my brother-in-law NEUROSIS, 8
The p. person knows that two and two make five NEUROSIS, 1
puberty We are all American at p. NATIONALITY, 12; WAUGH, E, 28
pubic P. hair is no substitute for wit PLAYS, 10
p. hairs went grey SUFFERING, 2
public a more mean, stupid…ungrateful animal than the p. HAZLITT, W, 10; PUBLIC, 14
a right to share your privacy in a p. place PRIVACY, 6; USTINOV, P, 6
enjoy a p. school EDUCATION, 26
false to his friends…true to the p. HONESTY, 3
flinging a pot of paint in the p.'s face RUSKIN, J, 17
give the p. what they want to see FUNERALS, 10; INSULTS, 115
hothouse of obligations, both personal and p. HOSTAGES, 4
If the British p. falls for this…it will be…bonkers POLITICS, 46
Never lose your temper with…the p. PANKHURST, C, 3; SELF-CONTROL, 7
not describe holding p. office ACHESON, D, 5; GOVERNMENT, 1
Not even a p. figure INSULTS, 41; POLITICIANS, 76
Private faces in p. places PRIVACY, 1
p. faces in private places FAME, 3
p. school, where…learning was painfully beaten into him EDUCATION, 73
strike against p. safety STRIKES, 4
The p. be damned. I am working for my stockholders CAPITALISM, 20
The p. buys its opinions as it buys its meat BUTLER, S, 15; PUBLIC, 7
The p. doesn't give a damn BEECHAM, T, 2; MUSIC, 5
The P. is an old woman CARLYLE, T, 19; PUBLIC, 8
three things…the p. will always clamour for HOOD, T, 15; NOVELTY, 3
transform this society without a major extension of p. ownership KINNOCK, N, 1; SOCIALISM, 15
twenty years of marriage make her…like a p. building MARRIAGE, 168; WILDE, O, 56
Whatsoever…the private calamity…not interfere with the p. business SHERIDAN, R, 15
publican How like a fawning p. he looks SHAKESPEARE, 240
publication use a pseudonym during p. years SALINGER, J, 7
publicity Any p. PROVERBS, 57
public opinion P.…advance of the law LAW, 16
public's flinging a pot of paint in the p. face CRITICISM, 56; WHISTLER, J, 1
public school Anyone who has been to…p. will…feel…at home in prison EDUCATION, 97; WAUGH, E, 25
enjoy a p. CONNOLLY, C, 5
Keats's vulgarity with a P. accent CRITICISM, 35
p., where…learning was painfully beaten into him PEACOCK, T, 8
the p. system all over EDUCATION, 96; WAUGH, E, 11
public schools p. are the nurseries of all vice EDUCATION, 29; FIELDING, H, 10
publish I'll p., right or wrong BYRON, 36; PUBLISHING, 3
P. and be damned PUBLISHING, 11; WELLINGTON, 23
p. and be sued PUBLISHING, 8
published Being p. by the O.U.P. PUBLISHING, 12
not so much p. as carried screaming NEWSPAPERS, 19
you may destroy whatever you haven't p. HORACE, 11; PUBLISHING, 7
publisher Barabbas was a p. PUBLISHING, 4
publishers those with irrational fear of life become p. CONNOLLY, C, 8; PUBLISHING, 6
publishing I would have done an easier job like p. PUBLISHING, 2
Pucelle a disciple…of the fiend, called the P. ACCUSATION, 1
puffeth knowledge p. up, but charity edifieth BIBLE, 32; CHARITY, 8
pulled about time we p. our fingers out SELF-RELIANCE, 11
pulse A p. in the eternal mind ENGLAND, 12

There are worse occupations...than feeling a woman's p. DOCTORS, 95; MEDICINE, 97
two people with one p. LOVE, 109; MACNEICE, L, 4
pulses proved upon our p. KEATS, J, 59; PHILOSOPHY, 8
pumpkin coach has turned into a p. DISILLUSION, 3
pun A man who could make so vile a p. PUNS, 4
punch I'd p. him in the snoot ROYALTY, 111
P. – the official journal JOURNALISM, 1
punctuality P. is the politeness PROMPTNESS, 2; PROVERBS, 343
P. is the virtue of the bored PROMPTNESS, 5; WAUGH, E, 29
punished Am I not p. enough in not being born an Englishman VOLTAIRE, 34
Men are rewarded and p. not for what they do MOTIVE, 6; SZASZ, T, 1
p. for what I did, not what a tabloid distorted it into MEDIA, 1
Those who offend us are generally p. REVENGE, 21; TROLLOPE, A, 16
punishing p. anyone who comes between them MARRIAGE, 144; SMITH, S, 10
punishment Corporal p. is...humiliating for him who gives it KEY, E, 4; PUNISHMENT, 19
let the p. fit the crime GILBERT, W, 30; PUNISHMENT, 14
P. is not for revenge PUNISHMENT, 12
Virtue is its own p. RIGHTEOUSNESS, 2
punishments In nature there are neither rewards nor p. NATURE, 23
puny Every p. whipster gets my sword VIOLENCE, 17
pupils Time is a great teacher, but...kills all its p. TIME, 13
puppy Frogs and snails /And p.-dogs' tails NURSERY RHYMES, 69
purchasers a pattern to encourage p. BUSINESS, 32; SWIFT, J, 6
pure All those who are not racially p. HITLER, A, 9
a p. river of water of life BIBLE, 474
Because my heart is p. INTEGRITY, 7; TENNYSON, 72
P. and ready DANTE ALIGHIERI, 5
p. as the driven slush BANKHEAD, T, 10; PURITY, 2
pure mathematics P. consists entirely of assertions RUSSELL, B, 14
purest The zipless fuck is the p. thing SEX, 56
purgations he killed himself with p. REMEDIES, 62
purgatory the p. of men ENGLAND, 22
purge p. me with hyssop PSALMS, 31
p. the land of all /Corruption ROYALTY, 25
puritan A p.'s a person who pours righteous indignation CHESTERTON, G, 51; PURITANISM, 1
The P. hated bear-baiting MACAULAY, T, 14; PURITANISM, 3
To the P. all things are impure LAWRENCE, D, 5; PURITANISM, 2
Puritanism P. – The haunting fear that someone...may be happy MENCKEN, H, 1; PURITANISM, 5
purity I have laboured to refine our language to grammatical p. JOHNSON, S, 24; LANGUAGE, 26
purple it pisses God off if you walk by the color p. WALKER, A, 3
purple-stained And p. mouth ALCOHOL, 47; KEATS, J, 37
purpose holding hostages achieves no useful, constructive p. HOSTAGES, 1
I want...art /To speak and p. not DECEPTION, 6
p. of God and the doom assigned DESTINY, 28; TENNYSON, 58
p. of its own /And measured motion WORDSWORTH, W, 38
sense of p....from their archbishop PURPOSE, 9
the creature hath a p. and its eyes are bright with it KEATS, J, 69; PURPOSE, 6
You seem to have no real p. in life AMBITION, 6
purse consumption of the p. MONEY, 43; SHAKESPEARE, 119
Put money in thy p. MONEY, 44; SHAKESPEARE, 279
Sickness soaks the p. ILLNESS, 3
pursuit the preservation of life, and liberty, and the p. of happiness JEFFERSON, T, 5
pushing P. forty AGE, 28; INSULTS, 38
pussy Ding dong, bell, /P.'s in the well NURSERY RHYMES, 9
do what your mammy wouldn't...he push his thing inside my p. WALKER, A, 5
P. cat, p. cat, where have you been NURSERY RHYMES, 45
P. rules the world SEX, 76
put I p. away childish things BIBLE, 38; CHARITY, 7
p. down the mighty BIBLE, 310
p. up with bad things TOLERANCE, 8; TROLLOPE, A, 11
To p. an antic disposition on HYPOCRISY, 18
puzzles irregular side of nature...these have been p. to science NATURE, 14
pygmies wars of the p. will begin CHURCHILL, W, 30
pyjamas I in p. for the heat LAWRENCE, D, 28
pylons P., those pillars /Bare SPENDER, S, 2; TECHNOLOGY, 16
pyramid bottom of the economic p. POVERTY, 33; ROOSEVELT, F, 8
pyramids Books are made...like p. BOOKS, 20
Pyrenees The fleas that tease in the high P. BELLOC, H, 19; NONSENSE, 3

Q

quack By q. I mean imposter DOCTORS, 106
uses his words as a q. uses his remedies VERBOSITY, 5
quackery Q. gives birth to nothing MEDICINE, 20
quacks But modern q. have lost the art DOCTORS, 27
Q. are the greatest liars in the world DOCTORS, 41
Q. in medicine...know this, and act upon that knowledge GULLIBILITY, 3
The practice of physic is jostled by q. on the one side MEDICINE, 53
quad *I* am always about in the Q. EXISTENCE, 1
no one about in the Q. EXISTENCE, 4
quadrupeds Dogs, like horses, are q. ANIMALS, 18
quaffing Long q. maketh a short lyfe ALCOHOL, 53
Quaker A philosophical Q. full of...maxims FRANKLIN, B, 2
Quakers I was beaten up by Q. ALLEN, W, 5; SHYNESS, 1
qualifications actor....q., including no money ACTORS, 9
qualities Almost every man...attempts to display q. which he does not possess DECEPTION, 3; JOHNSON, S, 26
He had...most of the q. that make a great scientist FLEMING, A, 2
q....necessary for success upon the stage ACTING, 22; TERRY, D, 2
quality great society...men are more concerned with the q. of their goods SOCIETY, 14
quantity *abstract reasoning concerning q. or number* PHILOSOPHY, 3
a prodigious q. of mind INDECISION, 5; TWAIN, M, 9
quarks Three q. for Muster Mark JOYCE, J, 5; NONSENSE, 16; SCIENCE, 58
quarrel a q. in a far-away country CHAMBERLAIN, N, 5; WORLD WAR II, 5
a q. in the streets is...to be hated KEATS, J, 68
It takes...one to make a q. INGE, W, 5
Out of the q....we make rhetoric POETRY, 73; YEATS, W, 11
q. at the same time MARRIAGE, 125
q....energies displayed in it are fine KEATS, J, 68
The justice of my q. JUSTICE, 17; MARLOWE, C, 12
quarrelled I did not know that we had ever q. LAST WORDS, 88; THOREAU, H, 22
I have q. with my wife MARRIAGE, 118; PEACOCK, T, 10
quarrels q. which vivify its barrenness GREER, G, 4; LOVE, 81
Q. would not last ROCHEFOUCAULD, 26
quart cannot put a q. in a pint cup POSSIBILITY, 2
quarter wage war until the last q. of an hour WAR, 50
Quayle Anyone who knows Dan Q. QUAYLE, D, 2
Quebec I would rather have written those lines than take Q. POETRY, 71
queen 'Fella belong Mrs Q.' LANGUAGE, 35
give my duty to the Q. VICTORY, 14
he...happened to marry the Q. ROYALTY, 107
how very different from the home life of our own dear Q. ANONYMOUS, 40; ROYALTY, 10
I am your anointed Q. ELIZABETH I, 9; SELF-RELIANCE, 7
If this is the way Q. Victoria treats her prisoners WILDE, O, 73
isn't a bad bit of goods, the Q. CERVANTES, M, 13
I've been to London to look at the q. NURSERY RHYMES, 45
I would not be a q. /For all the world SHAKESPEARE, 140
Move Q. Anne? Most certainly not MEMORIALS, 18
q. did fish for men's souls ELIZABETH I, 1
sorrier for my good knights' loss than for...my fair q. MALORY, T, 4
the British warrior q. COWPER, W, 4
The Q. of Hearts CARROLL, L, 19
the q. of Sheba BIBLE, 299
The q. was in the parlour, /Eating bread and honey NURSERY RHYMES, 52
queenly She keeps on being Q. AFFECTATION, 3
queens for q. I might have enough LOSS, 3; MALORY, T, 4
queer All the world is q. SUBJECTIVITY, 5
girls are so q. WOMEN, 10
the q. down the hall PREJUDICE, 6

the q. old Dean SPOONER, W, 4
There's nowt so q. DIFFERENCE, 6; PROVERBS, 419
thou art a little q. SUBJECTIVITY, 5
queerer the universe is…q. than we *can* suppose UNIVERSE, 11
querulous A prim…rather q. person HOUSMAN, A, 1
questing plashy fen passes the q. vole ANIMALS, 26; WAUGH, E, 34
question a good q. for you to ask DIPLOMACY, 12
answer ought to be to his precious little q. JOURNALISM, 38
A timid q. will…receive a confident answer SHYNESS, 2
man who sees both sides of a q. OBJECTIVITY, 5; WILDE, O, 11
Nature has never put the fatal q. as to the meaning of their lives JUNG, C, 1; PURPOSE, 5
not a wise q. for me to answer DIPLOMACY, 12
q.…which I have not been able to answer FREUD, S, 6; WOMEN, 57
That is the Irish Q. IRELAND, 8
that is the q. LANGUAGE, 12; SHAKESPEARE, 90
That's the sixty-four thousand dollar q. TELEVISION, 1
the q. that we do not know KNOWLEDGE, 33
Whatever q. there may be of his talent THOREAU, H, 1
what is the q. LAST WORDS, 85
questioning Q. is not the mode of conversation CONVERSATION, 4; JOHNSON, S, 103
questionings Those obstinate q. DOUBT, 9; WORDSWORTH, W, 30
questions all q. are open OBJECTIVITY, 3
I do not answer q. like this without being paid MASCULINITY, 1
make two q. grow where only one RESEARCH, 7
queue An Englishman…forms an orderly q. of one ENGLISH, 26
quickly organization could do it that q. BUREAUCRACY, 2
quiet Anythin' for a q. life DICKENS, C, 54; PEACE, 9
Doctor Diet, /Doctor Q. and Doctor Merryman DOCTORS, 97
Here, where the world is q. PEACE, 20
quietness unravish'd bride of q. KEATS, J, 27; SILENCE, 9
quince dined on mince, and slices of q. FOOD, 44; LEAR, E, 9
quintessence this q. of dust MANKIND, 56; SHAKESPEARE, 85
quit I don't believe I ought to q. DETERMINATION, 18
quo q. vadis BIBLE, 262
quod *Q. erat demonstrandum* MATHEMATICS, 8
quotable It's better to be q. than…honest QUOTATIONS, 14; STOPPARD, T, 12
quotation Classical q. is the *parole* of literary men JOHNSON, S, 137; QUOTATIONS, 4
Every q. contributes something JOHNSON, S, 4; QUOTATIONS, 5
no more able to resist a q. than…a drink CRITICISM, 47
q. is a national vice QUOTATIONS, 15; WAUGH, E, 32
the great spring of happy q. QUOTATIONS, 7
To say that anything was a q. QUOTATIONS, 12; SAKI, 7
quotations A book that furnishes no q. is…a plaything PEACOCK, T, 3; QUOTATIONS, 10
a list of q. QUOTATIONS, 9
good thing…to read books of q. CHURCHILL, W, 20
It needs no dictionary of q. BEERBOHM, M, 12
q. from the Bible and the rest JOYCE, J, 1
q. very slightly wrong QUOTATIONS, 11
quote man can be forgiven a lot if he can q. Shakespeare SHAKESPEARE, 16
quotes q.…give us a nodding acquaintance with the originator QUOTATIONS, 16

R

rabbit r.-like in our unplanned breeding of ourselves EVOLUTION, 25
The r. has a charming face ANONYMOUS, 84; RABBITS, 1
rabbits a tale of four little r. RABBITS, 2
except to shoot r. and hit his father on the jaw MASEFIELD, J, 1; NASTINESS, 5
Rabelais R. is the wondrous mask of ancient comedy RABELAIS, F, 1
race A loftier r. KNOWLEDGE, 39
Christians…humanity without r. CHRISTIANITY, 54
in a r. run all, but one receiveth the prize BIBLE, 33
I wish I loved the Human R. MANKIND, 49
my opinion of the human r. MANKIND, 37; MAUGHAM, W, 21
r. is not to the swift BIBLE, 74
Slow and steady wins the r. HASTE, 7
races human species…composed of two distinct r. LAMB, C, 10
the r. of Europe are melting AMERICA, 47
Rachmaninov R.'s immortalizing totality was his scowl MUSICIANS, 20
racially not r. pure are mere chaff RACISM, 13
racing happy state of getting the victor's palm without the dust of r. HORACE, 14; VICTORY, 9
racist Liberal Democrats are a r. party POLITICS, 7
racists makes the r. look like the rebels LANGUAGE, 47
rack Leave not a r. behind MORTALITY, 17; SHAKESPEARE, 327
radical A r. is a man IDEALISM, 8; ROOSEVELT, F, 12
I never dared be r. when young YOUTH, 11
The r. invents the views.…the conservative adopts them CONSERVATISM, 8; TWAIN, M, 11
radicals Few r. have good digestions BUTLER, S, 16; POLITICS, 24
radio I had the r. on NAKEDNESS, 6
Simply a r. personality INSULTS, 128; WAUGH, E, 50
Radio 4 I try to find R. MEDIA, 6
What do we want? R. MEDIA, 2
radioactive The Irish Sea is naturally r. ECOLOGY, 7
rage all Heaven in a r. BLAKE, W, 10
R., r., against the dying of the light THOMAS, D, 7
rages the weight of r. SPOONER, W, 1
rags no scandal like r. POVERTY, 10
only men in r.…./Mistake themselves for carpet bags ETIQUETTE, 7
railing R. at life, and yet afraid of death OLD AGE, 32
railway when they think they are alone in r. carriages HABIT, 6
raiment they parted his r., and cast lots BIBLE, 339
rain A Hard R.'s A-Gonna Fall DYLAN, B, 16; PESSIMISM, 5
a hat that lets the r. in ROYALTY, 66
drop of r. maketh a hole in the stone PERSISTENCE, 7
droppeth as the gentle r. MERCY, 2; SHAKESPEARE, 248
falls not hail, or r., or any snow AFTERLIFE, 11; TENNYSON, 25
He comes in the terrible R. CHRISTIANITY, 56; SITWELL, E, 4
R. before seven PROVERBS, 346; WEATHER, 2
R., r., go away PROVERBS, 347; WEATHER, 3
singing in the r. WEATHER, 11
rainbow A r. in the morning PROVERBS, 62
Somewhere over the r. DESIRE, 8
raineth it r. on the just JUSTICE, 4
rains It never r. but it pours MISFORTUNE, 2; PROVERBS, 230
rainy Keep something for a r. day PROVERBS, 240; THRIFT, 2
when it is not r. BYRON, 7; WEATHER, 8
rake every woman is at heart a r. POPE, A, 42; WOMEN, 108
lene…as is a r. CHAUCER, G, 8; HORSES, 4
rallying-point The party is the r. for the…working class COMMUNISM, 17; STALIN, J, 4
Ralph R. wept for the end of innocence GOLDING, W, 2; INNOCENCE, 6
ram a r. caught in a thicket BIBLE, 170
Ramadan month of R. shall ye fast KORAN 4; RELIGION, 61
Rambo I love *R.* but I think it's potentially a very dangerous movie CINEMA, 25
rams mountains skipped like r. PSALMS, 63
Randolph the only part of R. that was not malignant INSULTS, 127; WAUGH, E, 54
Range Rovers creche…happens between two R. POLITICIANS, 25
rank Englishman…weighs up the birth, the r.…the wealth of the people he meets CLASS, 38
O! my offence is r., it smells to heaven GUILT, 14
ransom r. not only their prisoners but their dead HOSTAGES, 9
raped Has anyone here been r. and speaks English INSENSITIVITY, 2
rapidly but not so r. BECKETT, S, 3; TIME, 11
rapist r. and is subject to the criminal law RAPE, 6
rapists All men are r. MARRIAGE, 76; MEN, 4
rapping r. at my chamber door SUPERNATURAL, 12
rapture a r. on the lonely shore BYRON, 16; NATURE, 3
The first fine careless r. BROWNING, R, 27
rare as r. things will, it vanished BROWNING, R, 39
keep it shut up…like a r., r. fiddle NAKEDNESS, 5
neither r. nor well done MEDIA, 11; TELEVISION, 8
Sanity is very r. MADNESS, 12
rascal Get down you dirty r. NURSERY RHYMES, 23
rascals R., would you live for ever WAR, 69

As to r.…duty of government to protect all…professors thereof GOVERNMENT, 30
brothels with bricks of R. BLAKE, W, 20; HYPOCRISY, 5
Cromwell was a man in whom ambition had…suspended…r. CROMWELL, O, 1
Fascism is a r. FASCISM, 9; MUSSOLINI, B, 4
God has no r. RELIGION, 44
I am of the same r. as all those who are brave and true CONSCIENCE, 5
If you reject me on account of my r. BELLOC, H, 21; PREJUDICE, 1
I have nothing to communicate on the subject of r. WOLLSTONECRAFT, M, 5
Love is my r. KEATS, J, 67; LOVE AND DEATH, 3
Many people think they have r. RELIGION, 57
Men will wrangle for r. RELIGION, 29
monstrous a wickedness…within…their r. TREASON, 2
no reason to bring r. into it RELIGION, 74
Not a r. for gentlemen CHARLES II, 2; RELIGION, 25
Nothing is so fatal to r. as indifference BURKE, E, 23; INDIFFERENCE, 2
One r. is as true as another RELIGION, 20
One's r.…yours is Success BARRIE, J, 7; SUCCESS, 5
R. /Has made an honest woman of the supernatural FRY, C, 3; RELIGION, 42; SUPERNATURAL, 8
R. is an illusion FREUD, S, 3; RELIGION, 41
R. is by no means a proper subject CHESTERFIELD, P, 19; RELIGION, 26
R. is love RELIGION, 99
R.…is the opium of the people MARX, K, 4; RELIGION, 65
r. of feeble minds BURKE, E, 12; SUPERSTITION, 8
r. of Socialism BEVAN, A, 2; SOCIALISM, 3
R.'s in the heart JERROLD, D, 1; PRAYER, 19
Science without r. is lame EINSTEIN, A, 3
Sensible men are all of the same r. DISRAELI, B, 7; RELIGION, 31
talks loudly against r. RELIGION, 83; STERNE, L, 8
that God is interested only…in r. GOD, 50
The Christian r. not only was at first attended with miracles HUME, D, 3
To become a popular r. INGE, W, 6; RELIGION, 55
To die for a r. is easier than to live it absolutely MARTYRDOM, 2
tourism is their r. TRAVEL, 38
when r. is allowed to invade…private life MELBOURNE, 11
when r. was strong…men mistook magic for medicine MEDICINE, 100; SZASZ, T, 3
religions a country with thirty-two r. and only one sauce AMERICA, 38; TALLEYRAND, 1
sixty different r., and only one sauce ENGLAND, 15
The r. we call false were once true EMERSON, R, 6; RELIGION, 40
religious a r. animal BURKE, E, 11; RELIGION, 19
first, r. and moral principles EDUCATION, 7
INDIGESTION, n. A disease…frequently mistake for deep r. conviction ILLNESS, 14
not r.-good HARDY, T, 11; VIRTUE, 15
r. outlook on life JUNG, C, 6; RELIGION, 59
skilled appeals to r. prejudice EVOLUTION, 20; HUXLEY, T, 11
tabloids suddenly find they have a r. affairs correspondent NEWSPAPERS, 10
To be at all is to be r. BUTLER, S, 21; RELIGION, 21
relished the taste by which he is…r. WORDSWORTH, W, 21; WRITING, 54
reluctant The r. obedience of distant provinces DIPLOMACY, 25; MACAULAY, T, 5
remarkable nothing left r. /Beneath the visiting moon MOURNING, 9; SHAKESPEARE, 37
r. thing about Shakespeare SHAKESPEARE, 9
remedies amusing him with r. good or bad MEDICINE, 63
doctors worry over the small number of r. REMEDIES, 21
Extreme r.…for extreme diseases REMEDIES, 32
He that will not apply new r. BACON, F, 30; INNOVATION, 1
If you are too fond of new r. REMEDIES, 23
Most men die of their r., and not of their illnesses REMEDIES, 42
Not even r. can master DISEASE, 35
Our r. oft in ourselves do lie SELF-RELIANCE, 12; SHAKESPEARE, 21
paralyse it by encumbering it with r. REMEDIES, 56; TOLSTOY, L, 11
R.…are our great analysers of disease REMEDIES, 39
r.…suggested for a disease CHEKHOV, A, 5; REMEDIES, 20
We cannot do without palliative r. REMEDIES, 30
We do not know the mode of action of almost all r. REMEDIES, 58
Whiskey is the most popular of…r. that won't cure a cold ALCOHOL, 84
remedy a r. for everything except death CERVANTES, M, 17; REMEDIES, 19
a sovereign r. to all diseases SMOKING, 6
Force is not a r. FORCE, 2
I never think of finding a r. ILLNESS, 54
popular r. often throws the scientific doctor into hysterics REMEDIES, 4
r. is worse than the disease BACON, F, 46
Tis a sharp r., but a sure one EXECUTION, 33; RALEIGH, W, 5
To do nothing is also a good r. REMEDIES, 33
remember I only r. what I've learnt KNOWLEDGE, 41; WHITE, P, 2
I r., I r. HOOD, T, 6
I r. it well MEMORY, 11
Oh! don't you r. sweet Alice, Ben Bolt MEMORY, 9
one man to r. me LAST WORDS, 76
r. and regret REGRET, 9
r. Lot's wife BIBLE, 335
R. me when I am gone away MEMORY, 18; ROSSETTI, C, 4
r. what I must be now DESPAIR, 7
she did not r.…her jewelry PRUDENCE, 10
The world will little note, nor long r. LINCOLN, A, 17
we shall be glad to r. even these hardships VIRGIL, 7
We will r. them MEMORIALS, 6
When I meet a man whose name I can't r. DISRAELI, B, 38
Who will r.…/The unheroic dead MEMORIALS, 14
remembered By this may I r. be /When I should be forgotten ANONYMOUS, 106; MEMORIALS, 1
I r. my God GOD, 48; SOUTHEY, R, 5
we r. thee, O Sion PSALMS, 70
remembers r. /The beauty of fire from…embers OLD AGE, 66
remembrance day of jubilation, a day of r. GERMANY, 11
R. is the secret of reconciliation MEMORIALS, 15
r. of things past REGRET, 24; SHAKESPEARE, 363
there is no r. of former things BIBLE, 63
There's rosemary, that's for r. SHAKESPEARE, 104
reminiscences the old have r. AGE, 77; SAKI, 12
remorse r. for what you have thought about your wife MARRIAGE, 126
r. is the poison of life GUILT, 4
remove all faith, so that I could r. mountains BIBLE, 38; CHARITY, 7
Renaissance R. is a mere ripple on the surface of literature LITERATURE, 14
the R. was…the green end of one of civilization's hardest winters FOWLES, J, 2
render husband r. unto the wife due benevolence BIBLE, 29
r.…unto Caesar BIBLE, 410; MATERIALISM, 5
rendezvous a r. with Death DEATH, 136
renegades Political r. always start their career of treachery KINNOCK, N, 11
renew r. a right spirit within me PSALMS, 31
renewal urban r. in New York City EDUCATION, 47
rent they r. out my room ALLEN, W, 9; EXPEDIENCY, 2
repair the landlord does not intend to r. LAST WORDS, 2
repartee A majority is always the best r. DISRAELI, B, 14
Violence is the r. of the illiterate VIOLENCE, 4
repast A new r., or an untasted spring ADDISON, J, 5
repay whatsoever thou spendest more…I will r. BIBLE, 325; CHARITY, 9
repeal the r. of bad or obnoxious laws GRANT, U, 6; LAW, 21
repeat History does not r. itself HISTORY, 6
obliged to imitate himself, and to r. IMITATION, 5
repeated A platitude is simply a truth r. BALDWIN, S, 13
repellent His sickness has created atrocities that are r. PICASSO, P, 2
repent Do you…my Love,/ r. PARTING, 8
If you trust before you try, you may r. before you die PROVERBS, 220
r. at leisure CONGREVE, W, 10; MARRIAGE, 51
r.: for the kingdom of heaven is at hand BIBLE, 358
truly and earnestly r. you of your sins BOOK OF COMMON PRAYER, 10
repentance A Christian…feels /R. on a Sunday CHRISTIANITY, 64; HYPOCRISY, 24
There's no r. in the grave DEATH, 180; WATTS, I, 5
with the morning cool r. REGRET, 18; SCOTT, W, 18
repented it r. the Lord that he had made man BIBLE, 157
repenteth joy…over one sinner that r. BIBLE, 330; REGRET, 5
repetition constant r. will finally succeed in imprinting an idea HITLER, A, 10; PUBLIC, 15

History is an endless r. DURRELL, L, 3; HISTORY, 11
replace no one can r. him FRANKLIN, B, 1
replenished His intellect is not r. IGNORANCE, 20; SHAKESPEARE, 198
replied And I r., 'My Lord.' HERBERT, G, 2; RELIGION, 52
reporter A r. is a man who has renounced everything JOURNALISM, 27
I am a r. ATHEISM, 7; GREENE, G, 9
reporting Language is not simply a r. device for experience LANGUAGE, 52
repose Our foster nurse of nature is r. SLEEP, 28
reprehend If I r. any thing MALAPROPISMS, 8; SHERIDAN, R, 9
representation In Scotland there is no shadow even of r. REPRESENTATION, 1
Proportional R.…is fundamentally counter-democratic KINNOCK, N, 2
Taxation without r. REPRESENTATION, 2
representative Your r. owes you…his judgement JUDGMENT, 6
repressed Catholicism is a completely sexist, r.…religion CATHOLICISM, 11
reproduce butlers and lady's maids do not r. their kind WELLS, H, 3
reproduction The r. of mankind is a great marvel and mystery SEX, 74
reproductions accurate r. of Anne Hathaway's cottage HOUSES, 2
I've seen colour r. PHILISTINISM, 5
republic An aristocracy in a r. is like a chicken ARISTOCRACY, 16
the r. of letters ADDISON, J, 3; MANKIND, 1
republican sold Ulster to buy off the fiendish r. scum IRELAND, 19
Republican The R. form of Government POLITICS, 96
Republicans Please assure me that you are all R. REAGAN, R, 7
republication Every twenty years one sees a r. of the same ideas MEDICINE, 88
republics Revolts, r., revolutions POLITICS, 104; TENNYSON, 69
repugnant Woman to bear rule…is r. to Nature WOMAN'S ROLE, 10
repulsive Roundheads (Right but R.) SELLAR, W, 5
reputability Conspicuous consumption…is a means of r. MATERIALISM, 25
reputation ever written out of r. but by himself REPUTATION, 2
it is better for the r. KEYNES, J, 5; ORTHODOXY, 3
it wrecks a woman's r. COLETTE, S, 4
O, I have lost my r. REPUTATION, 9; SHAKESPEARE, 283
r. grew with every failure REPUTATION, 14
R. is a bubble REPUTATION, 5
spotless r. REPUTATION, 11; SHAKESPEARE, 294
their r. stands…on a foundation of dead bodies REPUTATION, 13
Until you've lost your r., you never realize…what freedom really is MITCHELL, M, 1
requests thou wilt grant their r. BOOK OF COMMON PRAYER, 17; PRAYER, 9
requires all the Human Frame r. BELLOC, H, 10; FOOD, 10
re-rat rat, but you can't r. BETRAYAL, 6
research R.! A mere excuse for idleness RESEARCH, 3
steal from many, it's r. WRITING, 34
The aim of r. is the discovery of the equations RESEARCH, 4
The outcome of any serious r. RESEARCH, 7
researcher made by a 'specialist' or a 'r.' DISCOVERY, 9
R.. learns more and more about less and less OCCUPATIONS, 10
resent I don't r. his popularity POPULARITY, 8
To great evils we submit; we r. little provocations HAZLITT, W, 7
reservoir a gigantic r. of good will AMERICA, 43
residuum this vast r. we may…give the name of Populace ARNOLD, M, 9
resign The son of a bitch isn't going to r. on me DISMISSAL, 11
resignation I call for his immediate r. GORBACHOV, M, 4
resign'd R. unto the Heavenly will ANONYMOUS, 11
resist r. everything except temptation TEMPTATION, 10; WILDE, O, 38
r. the devil, and he will flee BIBLE, 218
there is almost nothing to r. at all ENGLISH, 24; LAWRENCE, D, 4
resistance 'R. to tyranny is obedience to God.' ANTHONY, S, 6
the flame of French r. must not…be extinguished WORLD WAR II, 26
resisting fond of r. temptation TEMPTATION, 3
resolute Be bloody bold, and r. SHAKESPEARE, 221
resolution In war, r. CHURCHILL, W, 26; WAR AND PEACE, 4
native hue of r. CONSCIENCE, 7; COWARDICE, 8; SHAKESPEARE, 92
resources statistics, born to consume r. HORACE, 17; STATISTICS, 4
respeckt little more r. for husbands HUMILITY, 7
respect A child deserves the maximum r. CHILDREN, 40
Civilization is…equal r. for all men CIVILIZATION, 1
old-fashioned r. for the young RESPECT, 6; WILDE, O, 23
The English have no r. for their language CLASS, 44; ENGLISH, 36; SHAW, G, 36
those /Who err each other must r. LOVE, 125
We must r. the other fellow's religion MENCKEN, H, 3; TOLERANCE, 5
We owe r. to the living RESPECT, 4; VOLTAIRE, 24
When people do not r. us we are sharply offended SELF-RESPECT, 7; TWAIN, M, 13
respectable Dr Marie Stopes made contraceptive devices r. STOPES, M, 3
R. means rich PEACOCK, T, 1; RESPECTABILITY, 3
r., middle-class…lady AUDIENCES, 5
riff-raff apply to what is r. CLASS, 20; HOPE, A, 6
respecter God is no r. of persons BIBLE, 10
respects no man much r. himself SELF-RESPECT, 7; TWAIN, M, 13
respiration He said it was artificial r. SEX, 20
respondent the writer…is the impregnator…the reader…is the r. READING, 19
responsibility In dreams begins r. RESPONSIBILITY, 23; YEATS, W, 23
moral and emotional r. about the remaining hostages HOSTAGES, 5
no sense of r. at the other BABIES, 7
No sex without r. SEX, 73
power without r. BALDWIN, S, 3; KIPLING, R, 36
responsible An idea isn't r. for the people IDEAS, 8
every man is r. for his face APPEARANCE, 14; CAMUS, A, 4
No man is r. for his father FAMILY, 60
r. and the irresponsible classes CLASS, 21; LAWRENCE, D, 12
r. and wrong RESPONSIBILITY, 5; RIGHTEOUSNESS, 8
You are r. for your rose RESPONSIBILITY, 13
rest All the r. have thirty-one NURSERY RHYMES, 60
get rid of the r. of her WOMEN, 138
I have nothing; the r. I leave to the poor LAST WORDS, 70; RABELAIS, F, 8
leave the r. to the Gods DUTY, 2
Mary Ann has gone to r. ANONYMOUS, 55
Seek home for r. HOME, 12
then would I flee away, and be at r. PSALMS, 33
The r. is silence DEATH, 141; SHAKESPEARE, 109
To toil and not to seek for r. SELFLESSNESS, 3
restaurants Great r. are…nothing but mouth-brothels FOOD, 62; RAPHAEL, F, 4
rested God…r. on the seventh day BIBLE, 143; SUNDAY, 1
restless r. who will volunteer for anything SOLDIERS, 10
restore Time may r. us ARNOLD, M, 28; POETS, 17
restrained the Prince…is r. from doing ill GOVERNMENT, 46
restraints the paucity of r. it imposes SOCIETY, 20
rests our heart is not quiet until it r. in Thee HUMAN CONDITION, 2
result the long r. of Time EXPERIENCE, 20; TENNYSON, 49
resurrection Destruction and r. in alternate beats LIFE AND DEATH, 8
I am the r., and the life BIBLE, 256; CHRISTIANITY, 20
retain To expect a man to r. everything that he has ever read MEMORY, 20; SCHOPENHAUER, A, 6
reticulated Anything r. or decussated at equal distances JOHNSON, S, 11
retire can't put off being young until you r. LARKIN, P, 1; MONEY, 30
I want to r. at 50 KINNOCK, N, 3
retirement R.…is not a good idea ROYALTY, 39; VICTORIA, 2
retreat A mistress should be like a…r. SEX, 132
Nowhere can man find a quieter…r. than in his own soul PRAYER, 24
retrograde All that is human must r. GIBBON, E, 10; PROGRESS, 13
return I shall r. DETERMINATION, 11
r., r., O Shulamite BIBLE, 497

returning R. were as tedious as go o'er GUILT, 17; SHAKESPEARE, 219
reveal words…half r. and half conceal TENNYSON, 27; WORDS, 34
revealeth he r. the deep and secret things GOD, 9
Revelations It ends with R. BIBLE, 538; WILDE, O, 60
revelry a sound of r. by night BYRON, 13; MERRYMAKING, 2
revels Our r. now are ended MORTALITY, 17; SHAKESPEARE, 327
revenge A man that studieth r. BACON, F, 44; REVENGE, 7
good, old-fashioned, bloodcurdling r. AYCKBOURN, A, 3
he took his r. by speaking ill ENVY, 11; VOLTAIRE, 27
if you wrong us, shall we not r. EQUALITY, 34; SHAKESPEARE, 247
I will think upon r. REVENGE, 20
R., at first though sweet MILTON, J, 51; REVENGE, 15
R.…back on itself recoils MILTON, J, 51; REVENGE, 15
R. his foul and most unnatural murder REVENGE, 16
R. is a dish PROVERBS, 349; REVENGE, 2
R. is a…wild justice BACON, F, 43; REVENGE, 6
R. is sweet PROVERBS, 350; REVENGE, 3
terrible r. by the culture of the Negroes POPULAR MUSIC, 20
their gratitude is a species of r. GRATITUDE, 2
revenged I'll be r. on the whole pack of you REVENGE, 19
revenue name a virtue that brings in as much r. SMOKING, 27
reverence a little more r.…and not so much astonishment SINGING, 3
reverse popular music…made giant strides in r. POPULAR MUSIC, 11
reviewers R.…would have been poets COLERIDGE, S, 19; CRITICS, 3
reviewing Prolonged…r. of books involves constantly *inventing* reactions CRITICISM, 46; ORWELL, G, 11
revolts R., republics, revolutions POLITICS, 104; TENNYSON, 69
revolution Britain…is going to be forged in the white heat of this r. SOCIALISM, 25; WILSON, H, 8
Britain is not…easily rocked by r. BRITAIN, 8
fundamental premise of a r. REVOLUTION, 15; TROTSKY, L, 7
greet in you the victorious Russian R. RUSSIAN REVOLUTION, 5
he'd go to church, start a r. – *something* MATERIALISM, 20; MILLER, A, 3
Hitler has carried out a r. on our lines FASCISM, 8; MUSSOLINI, B, 1
recognition whatsoever of the social r. SOCIETY, 6
restating our socialism in terms of the scientific r. WILSON, H, 8
R. by its very nature REVOLUTION, 16; TROTSKY, L, 1
R.…delightful in the preliminary stages REVOLUTION, 10
r. is a struggle to the death REVOLUTION, 4
Russia is a collapse, not a r. LAWRENCE, D, 37; RUSSIA, 11
single carrot…, will set off a r. PAINTING, 5
The r. eats POLITICS, 85
the R. may…devour each of her children FRENCH REVOLUTION, 10
The word 'r.' is a word for which you kill REVOLUTION, 17; WEIL, S, 2
to export r. is nonsense REVOLUTION, 12
We invented the R. REVOLUTION, 18
revolutionary If you feed people just with r. slogans KHRUSHCHEV, N, 8
I would be a r. myself POVERTY, 15
Patriotism…is a r. duty PATRIOTISM, 42; TROTSKY, L, 12
r. right DEMOCRACY, 15; LINCOLN, A, 15
R. spirits of my father's generation POLITICS, 90
The r. simpleton LEWIS, W, 6
revolutions All modern r. have ended CAMUS, A, 15
Revolts, republics, r. TENNYSON, 69
R. are always verbose TROTSKY, L, 5
state of mind which creates r. ARISTOTLE, 9
revolver I reach for my r. PHILISTINISM, 4
reward The avoidance of taxes…still carries…r. KEYNES, J, 11; TAXATION, 7
The r. of a thing well done EMERSON, R, 11; SATISFACTION, 3
To labour and not ask for any r. SELFLESSNESS, 3
Vice is its own r. VICE, 8
rewarded Men are r. and punished not for what they do MOTIVE, 6; SZASZ, T, 1
rewards each time of life has its appropriate r. LIFE AND DEATH, 3
In nature there are neither r. nor punishments NATURE, 23
Reynolds When…R. died /All Nature was degraded ARTISTS, 12
rhetoric Out of the quarrel…we make r. POETRY, 73; YEATS, W, 11
rheumatism r. is to the heart DISEASE, 23
Screw up the vise…you have r. DISEASE, 4
to complain of r. COMPLAINTS, 6
rheumatologists cast of orthopedic r. LANGUAGE, 4
Rhine The Watch on the R. RIVERS, 4
You think of the R. BALDWIN, S, 6
rhyme it was neither r. nor reason CRITICISM, 45
outlive this powerful r. POETRY, 56; SHAKESPEARE, 364
R. being no necessary adjunct or true ornament MILTON, J, 28; POETRY, 43
the petty fools of r. TENNYSON, 48; TRIVIALITY, 15
rhyming troublesome…bondage of R. MILTON, J, 29; POETRY, 44
rhythm r. imposes unanimity upon the divergent MUSIC, 41
Soul is the r. o' sex POPULAR MUSIC, 13
rib the r.…made he a woman BIBLE, 147; WOMEN, 23
ribbon The blue r. of the turf HORSES, 5
rich A r. man is one WEALTH, 5
a r. man shall hardly enter into…heaven BIBLE, 405; WEALTH, 13
A r. man's joke is always funny FLATTERY, 3
as easy to marry a r. woman as a poor woman MARRIAGE, 155; THACKERAY, W, 5
as well off as if he were r. WEALTH, 7
Beauty too r. for use SHAKESPEARE, 308
get r., get famous and get laid FAME, 15; GELDOF, B, 2
If you can…count your money you are not…r. man WEALTH, 24
I think people still want to marry r. WEALTH, 26
It's the r. wot gets the pleasure ANONYMOUS, 71
nor a r. society too r. POVERTY AND WEALTH, 9
no sin but to be r. HYPOCRISY, 20; SHAKESPEARE, 164
poor have no right to the property of the r. RUSKIN, J, 16
Poor Little R. Girl COWARD, N, 15; WEALTH, 19
Respectable means r. PEACOCK, T, 1; RESPECTABILITY, 3
r. are different from us FITZGERALD, F, 5; WEALTH, 21
r. beyond the dreams of avarice WEALTH, 39
R. men's houses are seldom beautiful WEALTH, 6
so large, /So friendly, and so r. AMERICA, 2; AUDEN, W, 22
that art most r., being poor APPEARANCES, 27
The r. and powerful know ANOUILH, J, 4; GOD, 3
THE R. AND THE POOR DISRAELI, B, 12
The r. are the scum of the earth CHESTERTON, G, 15; WEALTH, 17
the r. he hath sent empty away BIBLE, 310
The r. man has his motor car ENVY, 2
the wretchedness of being r. SMITH, L, 2; WEALTH, 45
too r. for use BEAUTY, 40
very r. people who are r. because they have talents or vital statistics SCOTT, P, 2
Victim of a r. man's game ANONYMOUS, 71; POVERTY AND WEALTH, 2
whether to be r. in things MATERIALISM, 13
you have to live with r. people SMITH, L, 2; WEALTH, 45
richer for r. for poorer BOOK OF COMMON PRAYER, 27
R. than all his tribe SHAKESPEARE, 290
riches God commonly gives r. to those gross asses WEALTH, 34
Infinite r. in a little room MARLOWE, C, 10; WEALTH, 37
R. are for spending BACON, F, 23; EXTRAVAGANCE, 1
R. have wings COWPER, W, 30; WEALTH, 20
r. to be a valuable thing SWIFT, J, 21; WEALTH, 47
the chief employment of r. consists in the parade of r. OSTENTATION, 6; SMITH, A, 2
richesses *l'embarras des r.* EXCESS, 2
richest He is the r. author that ever grazed JOHNSON, S, 60
Richmond On R. Hill there lives a lass COMPLIMENTS, 16
rid gladly…am I r. of it all SEX, 112
glad to get r. of it MARX, G, 12; STUPIDITY, 8
riddle a r. wrapped in a mystery inside an enigma CHURCHILL, W, 47; RUSSIA, 3
glory, jest, and r. of the world HUMAN CONDITION, 21; POPE, A, 33
R. of destiny LAMB, C, 20; PURPOSE, 7
ride R. on! r. on in majesty CHRISTIANITY, 46
rides He who r. a tiger AMBITION, 1; PROVERBS, 202
we look for happiness in boats and carriage r. TRAVEL, 22
ridicule he who endeavours to r. other people BOCCACCIO, G, 2
R. often checks what is absurd RIDICULE, 4; SCOTT, W, 17
R.…smothers that which is noble RIDICULE, 4; SCOTT, W, 17
ridiculous a fine sense of the r. HUMOUR, 1
a step from the sublime to the r. DECLINE, 7; NAPOLEON I, 9
no spectacle so r. MACAULAY, T, 10; MORALITY, 10

The profession of letters...in which one can make no money without being r. WRITING, 42
This is a r. country RUSSIA, 23
riding Commuter...r. to and from his wife TRAVEL, 48
riff-raff r. apply to what is respectable CLASS, 20; HOPE, A, 6
rifles stuttering r.' rapid rattle WORLD WAR I, 18
rift the...r. between the sexes is...widened by...teaching...to the girls STEVENSON, R, 14
Riga There was a young lady of R. ANIMALS, 1; ANONYMOUS, 93
right All's r. with the world BROWNING, R, 45; PERFECTION, 3
better to be irresponsible and r. CHURCHILL, W, 66
every man did that which was r. in his own eyes BIBLE, 296
Every man has a r. to utter what he thinks truth FREEDOM, 28; JOHNSON, S, 131
God and my r. FAITH, 27
I am not and never have been, a man of the r. POLITICIANS, 108
I disapprove of what you say, but I will defend to the death your r. to say it VOLTAIRE, 39
I'd rather be r. than president RIGHT, 3
I...may not always be r., but I am never wrong GOLDWYN, S, 6
It will all come r. in the wash OPTIMISM, 4; PROVERBS, 237
Keep R. on to the End of the Road PERSISTENCE, 8
Liberty is the r. to do everything FREEDOM, 43; MONTESQUIEU, 3
Minorities...are almost always in the r. MINORITY, 3; SMITH, S, 13
no r. to strike against public safety STRIKES, 4
not clever but I'm always r. SELF-CONFIDENCE, 1
No, this r. hand shall work it all off SCOTT, W, 22; WRITING, 45
One of the pleasures of middle age is to *find out* that one was r. AGE, 70; POUND, E, 4
'orthodoxy'...no longer means being r. CHESTERTON, G, 17; ORTHODOXY, 2
our country, r. or wrong PATRIOTISM, 12
publish, r. or wrong BYRON, 36; PUBLISHING, 3
R. is more precious RIGHT, 4; WILSON, W, 10
r. mindfulness, r. contemplation BUDDHA, 4; RELIGION, 18
r. of all...duty of some SEPARATION, 4
r. to have a child WOMEN, 26
Sit thou on my r. hand PSALMS, 61
something is possible, he is...r. SCIENCE, 20
The customer is always r. BUSINESS, 26
The *divine r.* of husbands WOLLSTONECRAFT, M, 3
The Duce is always r. FASCISM, 1
The English are all r. ENGLISH, 40
The man who gets angry...in the r. way...is commended ARISTOTLE, 2
The minority is always r. IBSEN, H, 2; MAJORITY, 5; MINORITY, 2
The r. divine of kings to govern wrong MONARCHY, 19; POPE, A, 4
The r. people are rude MAUGHAM, W, 15
the r. to be consulted...to encourage...to warn BAGEHOT, W, 7; MONARCHY, 3
the r. to blaspheme FREEDOM, 20
the r. to criticize Shakespeare CRITICISM, 58; SHAW, G, 41
the r. wing of the middle of the road POLITICIANS, 48
Those who believe that they are exclusively in the r. HUXLEY, A, 31; SELF-CONFIDENCE, 3
To do a great r., do a little wrong LAW, 34
Ulster will be r. IRELAND, 6
woman's r. to abortion was constitutionally protected ABORTION, 7
Women would rather be r. than reasonable NASH, O, 4; WOMEN, 94
righteous leave r. ways behind BUDDHA, 5; RIGHTEOUSNESS, 5
let them...not be written among the r. PSALMS, 39
the r. perisheth, and no man layeth it to heart BIBLE, 215
the r. shall flourish like a palm-tree PSALMS, 52
righteousness He made r. readable EDITORS, 3
in r. he doth judge and make war BIBLE, 470; RIGHTEOUSNESS, 4
r. and peace have kissed each other PSALMS, 46
r. hath looked down from heaven PSALMS, 46
The eternal *not ourselves* that makes for r. ARNOLD, M, 24; RIGHTEOUSNESS, 1
the paths of r. PSALMS, 11
the r. of the scribes and Pharisees RETRIBUTION, 6
righter much r. than one knew at say 17 or 23 POUND, E, 4
rights All human beings are born free and equal in dignity and r. ANONYMOUS, 3
bill of r. is what the people are entitled to HUMAN RIGHTS, 4
government...must be built upon the r. of the people GOVERNMENT, 45
human beings are born free...dignity and r. HUMAN RIGHTS, 1
Men their r. and nothing more ANTHONY, S, 3
r. and interests of the laboring man STRIKES, 1
The battle for women's r. THATCHER, M, 23
The extension of women's r. FEMINISM, 8
The Sovereign has, under a constitutional monarchy...three r. BAGEHOT, W, 7; MONARCHY, 3
The women who want women's r. FEMINISM, 49
We are here to claim our r. as women PANKHURST, C, 5
Rimbauds always chasing R. PARKER, D, 8
ring Don't carry away that arm till I have...my r. PRACTICALITY, 5
One R. to rule them all POWER, 29; TOLKIEN, J, 5
R. down the curtain LAST WORDS, 71; RABELAIS, F, 9
r. is worn away by use OVID, 4; PERSISTENCE, 11
The r. so worn...is yet of gold APPEARANCE, 21
They now *r.* the bells WALPOLE, R, 2; WAR, 173
With this R. I thee wed BOOK OF COMMON PRAYER, 28
rings R. on her fingers and bells on her toes NURSERY RHYMES, 46
riot A r. is at bottom KING, M, 1; REBELLION, 10
triumph in putting down the r. CHINA, 9
ripe Cherry r. HERRICK, R, 1
we r. and r. LIFE, 82; SHAKESPEARE, 47
ripeness R. is all ENDURANCE, 22; SHAKESPEARE, 194
ripp'd mother's womb untimely r. BIRTH, 15; SHAKESPEARE, 229
ripped off I'd like to be r. like George Michael's been EXPLOITATION, 4
rise Early to r. and early to bed BED, 12; THURBER, J, 6
in the name of Jesus...r. up and walk BIBLE, 4; REMEDIES, 11
nobody who does not r. early BED, 6; JOHNSON, S, 158
Thanks to words, we have been able to r. above the brutes HUXLEY, A, 3
risk deepest pockets who can r. going to law LAW, 40
risks what r. you take...to find money in a desk BALZAC, H, 4
Rita Lovely R. Meter Maid OCCUPATIONS, 14
Ritz like the R. hotel JUSTICE, 18
river a pure r. of water of life BIBLE, 474
build your House of Parliament upon the r. WELLINGTON, 14
can't step into the same r. twice CHANGE, 13
Fame is like a r. BACON, F, 40; FAME, 4
Ol' man r. RIVERS, 2
One does not insult the r. god PRUDENCE, 5
On either side the r. lie TENNYSON, 41
On the breast of the r. of Time ARNOLD, M, 18
the r. of knowledge has too often turned back on itself SCIENCE, 57
The vanity of human life is like a r. LIFE, 76; POPE, A, 58
They promise to build a bridge even where there's no r. KHRUSHCHEV, N, 7
road All I seek...the r. below me STEVENSON, R, 6; TRAVEL, 41
a r....that does not go through the intellect CHESTERTON, G, 9; EMOTION, 1
Does the r. wind up-hill ENDURANCE, 18; ROSSETTI, C, 6
free as the r. FREEDOM, 23; HERBERT, G, 1
He watched the ads /And not the r. NASH, O, 6
Keep Right on to the End of the R. PERSISTENCE, 8
On the r. to Mandalay KIPLING, R, 24; PLACES, 21
people who stay in the middle of the r. COMPROMISE, 2; POLITICS, 16
tell us of the R. DEATH, 64; FITZGERALD, E, 17
the Golden R. to Samarkand KNOWLEDGE, 17
There is a r. from the eye to the heart CHESTERTON, G, 9; EMOTION, 1
the rolling English r. CHESTERTON, G, 37; TRAVEL, 12
the Yellow Brick R. TRAVEL, 19
They shut the r. through the woods KIPLING, R, 31; TIME, 30
roads all r. lead to France WAR, 171
All r. lead to Rome PLACES, 1; PROVERBS, 36
How many r. must a man walk down DYLAN, B, 1; EXPERIENCE, 13
New r.: new ruts CHESTERTON, G, 52; PROGRESS, 10
Two r. diverged CHOICE, 2; FROST, R, 7
roam Mid pleasures and palaces though we may r. HOME, 10
roamin' R. in the gloamin' SCOTLAND, 6
roast the learned r. an egg FOOD, 59; POPE, A, 53
rob Why r. one to feed the other DEATH, 90; LAST WORDS, 55
robb'd He that is r., not wanting what is stol'n SHAKESPEARE, 287
robbed We wuz r. DEFEAT, 9

when you've r. a man of everything POWER, 25; SOLZHENITSYN, A, 8
robber now Barabbas was a r. BIBLE, 266
Robbins President R. was so well adjusted to his environment ADAPTABILITY, 3
robes R. and furr'd gowns hide all SHAKESPEARE, 190
robin A r. redbreast in a cage BLAKE, W, 10; IMPRISONMENT, 2
Our little English r. WORDSWORTH, W, 45
R. Gray, he was gudeman to me MARRIAGE, 20
Who killed Cock R. NURSERY RHYMES, 72
robot the modern conception of a r. CHURCHILL, W, 23
rock a wise man, which built his house upon a r. BIBLE, 380
he smote the r. twice BIBLE, 437
R. and roll is phony and false POPULAR MUSIC, 23
R. and roll or Christianity POPULARITY, 6
R. Around the Clock POPULAR MUSIC, 15
r. musicians make a bunch of money and stick it up their noses DRUGS, 18
R. of ages, cleft for me RELIGION, 89
r. of offence BIBLE, 199
the r. that is higher than I PSALMS, 37
upon this r. I will build my church BIBLE, 397; CHURCH, 1
With my little stick of Blackpool r. FOOD, 32
rocked R. in the cradle of the deep SEA, 11
rock'n'roll Give me that r. music POPULAR MUSIC, 3
R. is part of a pest POPULAR MUSIC, 1
rocks The hand that r. the cradle INFLUENCE, 12
rod Aaron's r. BIBLE, 108
he that spareth his r. hateth his son BIBLE, 450; CHILDREN, 19; PUNISHMENT, 7
rule them with a r. of iron LEADERSHIP, 3
spare the r. BUTLER, S, 4; INDULGENCE, 1; PUNISHMENT, 8
thy r. and thy staff comfort me PSALMS, 11
We spared the r. PUNISHMENT, 31
rode and r. madly off in all directions LEACOCK, S, 10; NONSENSE, 17
rodent-like music critics....small and r. with padlocked ears CRITICS, 20; STRAVINSKY, I, 3
Roland *Childe R. to the Dark Tower came* BROWNING, R, 18; SUMMONS, 4
role he saw his r. as being that of Moses LEADERSHIP, 6
roll our soul /Had *felt* him like the thunder's r. ARNOLD, M, 26
R. up that map PEACE, 17; PITT THE YOUNGER, 2
rolled bottoms of my trousers r. ELIOT, T, 14; OLD AGE, 44
rolling Like a r. stone DYLAN, B, 7; TRAVEL, 15
Like the Mississippi, it just keeps r. OPTIMISM, 24
The r. English drunkard CHESTERTON, G, 37; TRAVEL, 12
Rolls She has a R. body and a Balham mind STUPIDITY, 11
Rolls Royce always using a small car to drive to the dockyard instead of my R. MOUNTBATTEN OF BURMA, L, 4
Roma *R. locuta est* AUTHORITARIANISM, 1
Roman noblest R. of them all NOBILITY, 6; SHAKESPEARE, 162
the Holy R. Empire was neither holy, nor R., nor an empire NATIONS, 5; VOLTAIRE, 16
The Papacy is not other than the Ghost of the deceased R. Empire HOBBES, T, 7
the R. people had but one neck RUTHLESSNESS, 1
romance There is no r. between us ROYALTY, 5
The r. of *Tom Jones* GIBBON, E, 5; NOVELS, 5
Twenty years of r. makes a woman look like a ruin MARRIAGE, 168; WILDE, O, 56
Romans Friends, R., countrymen, lend me your ears SHAKESPEARE, 155
The R. and Greeks found everything human LAWRENCE, D, 6
which came first, the Greeks or the R. DISRAELI, B, 39; IGNORANCE, 9
romantic The charm is purely r. IDEALISM, 9
romanticism R. is...presenting people with the literary works...affording...the greatest...pleasure LITERATURE, 25
Rome I lov'd R. more PATRIOTISM, 38; SHAKESPEARE, 154
R. has spoken; the case is concluded AUTHORITARIANISM, 1
R.'s gross yoke /Drops off BROWNING, R, 19; INFLUENCE, 1
R. shall perish COWPER, W, 5; REVENGE, 10
R.'s just a city like anywhere else BURGESS, A, 5; EUROPE, 1
R. was not built PATIENCE, 5; PROVERBS, 351
so much bounden to the See of R. OBLIGATION, 2
The farther you go from the church of R. PROTESTANTISM, 8
When in R. CONFORMITY, 2
when R. falls – the World BYRON, 15; EUROPE, 5
Romeo R.! wherefore art thou R. NAMES, 6; SHAKESPEARE, 311
room All I want is a r. somewhere DESIRE, 10
before my little r. BROOKE, R, 3; FLOWERS, 2
I have only slipped away into the next r. DEATH, 81
Infinite riches in a little r. MARLOWE, C, 10
no r. for them in the inn BIBLE, 313; CHRISTMAS, 8
R. at the Top AMBITION, 3
The perpetual struggle for r. and food SURVIVAL, 5
There is always r. at the top AMBITION, 27; WEBSTER, D, 7
who sneaked into my r. at three o'clock this morning MARX, G, 14
rooms being old is having lighted r. LARKIN, P, 2; OLD AGE, 63
Roosevelt If R. were alive he'd turn in his grave GOLDWYN, S, 19
the kind of nation that President R. hoped for JOHNSON, L, 6
roost Curses...always come home to r. CURSES, 3; SOUTHEY, R, 2
root love of money is the r. of all evil BIBLE, 511; MONEY, 11
the r. of all sins DRUNKENNESS, 19
Though leaves are many, the r. is one AGE, 105; YEATS, W, 7
rootless We are not r. vagabonds ASHDOWN, P, 2
roots His r. were buried deep in early literature TOLKIEN, J, 1
rope Give a thief enough r. PROVERBS, 173; RETRIBUTION, 1
the end of your r., tie a knot SURVIVAL, 7
rose An unofficial English r. BROOKE, R, 4; FLOWERS, 3
a r. /By any other name NAMES, 7; SHAKESPEARE, 312
A r. without a thorn ADMIRATION, 9; COMPLIMENTS, 16
At Christmas I no more desire a r. SHAKESPEARE, 197; SUITABILITY, 4
do you call that a r. AYCKBOURN, A, 5
killing as the canker to the r. CORRUPTION, 8; MILTON, J, 23
Like a r., she has lived as long as roses live TRANSIENCE, 18
mighty lak' a r. BABIES, 9
One perfect r. MATERIALISM, 21; PARKER, D, 9
R. is a r. STEIN, G, 5
R....where some buried Caesar bled FITZGERALD, E, 8
That which sets...The budding r. above the r. full blown WORDSWORTH, W, 42
the last r. of summer FLOWERS, 10; MOORE, T, 5
the r. of Sharon BIBLE, 486
You are responsible for your r. RESPONSIBILITY, 13
rosebuds Gather ye r. while ye may HERRICK, R, 5; PRESENT, 6
rosemary There's r., that's for remembrance SHAKESPEARE, 104
roses a wreath of r. FLOWERS, 1
days of wine and r. TRANSIENCE, 12
Everything's Coming Up R. PERFECTION, 10
Flung r., r. riotously MEMORY, 8
hand that gives you r. GENEROSITY, 1
I will make thee beds of r. FLOWERS, 8; MARLOWE, C, 14
I would like my r. to see you COMPLIMENTS, 34; SHERIDAN, R, 18
Nor does a...gardener scent his r. POETS, 4
not a bed of r. MARRIAGE, 148; STEVENSON, R, 25
Plant thou no r. DEATH, 129; ROSSETTI, C, 8
Ring-a-ring o'r. NURSERY RHYMES, 47
R. are flowering in Picardy COMPLIMENTS, 38
Send two dozen r. to Room 424 LOVE, 112; MARX, G, 19
so with r. overgrown GARDENS, 10; MARVELL, A, 6
The lilies and r. were all awake LOVE, 163; TENNYSON, 57
Treaties are like r. and young girls DE GAULLE, C, 12; DIPLOMACY, 10
rot lie in cold obstruction, and to r. DEATH, 150; SHAKESPEARE, 234
we r. and r. LIFE, 82; SHAKESPEARE, 47
Rotarians The astronauts!...R. in outer space VIDAL, G, 4
rotten r. in the state of Denmark SHAKESPEARE, 77
rotting Damn you, England. You're r. ENGLAND, 39
rough r. male kiss of blankets BROOKE, R, 1
rough-hew R. them how we will DESTINY, 21; SHAKESPEARE, 107
round R. and r. the garden /Like a teddy bear NURSERY RHYMES, 48
r., neat, not gaudy GARDENS, 9; LAMB, C, 25
The trivial r., the common task SIMPLICITY, 4
roundabouts What's lost upon the r. LOSS, 2
Roundheads R. (Right but Repulsive) HISTORY, 27; SELLAR, W, 5; WAR, 154
route Get your kicks on R. 66 TRAVEL, 47
roving we'll go no more a r. BYRON, 41; DEBAUCHERY, 4
row Row upon r. with strict impunity DEATH, 169
rowed All r. fast BOATS, 2
Rowley Heigh ho! says R. NURSERY RHYMES, 1
royal at no time stand so highly in our estate r. GOVERNMENT, 16
I still get teased mercilessly about the r. family ROYALTY, 45
Once in r. David's city CHRISTMAS, 2

R. family is worth £6 billion ROYALTY, 51
trying not to be different in the sense of being r. MOUNTBATTEN OF BURMA, L, 4
royalty Prince Henry...something of r. in his demeanour ROYALTY, 62
rub R.-a-dub-dub, /Three men in a tub NURSERY RHYMES, 49
there's the r. SHAKESPEARE, 90; SUICIDE, 35
try to r. up against money MONEY, 41; RUNYON, D, 2
rubbish footballers being ignorant is r. FOOTBALL, 19
rubies her price is far above r. BIBLE, 458; WOMEN, 25
the price of wisdom is above r. BIBLE, 234; WISDOM, 6
Rubinstein Arthur R. EGOTISM, 6; INSULTS, 61
rubs sentimentality...r. you up the wrong way MAUGHAM, W, 25; SENTIMENTALITY, 4
ruddy Thy r. face shall turn lean PREGNANCY, 5
rude Fifty lovelies in the r. OPPORTUNITY, 22; THOMAS, D, 15
The right people are r. IMPERTINENCE, 3; MAUGHAM, W, 15
rue With r. my heart is laden HOUSMAN, A, 16; NOSTALGIA, 12
rug Speak up for yourself, or you'll end up a r. SELF-CONFIDENCE, 13
Stop...those dogs...peeing on my cheapest r. DOGS, 11
Rugby R. Union which is a distillation SPORT AND GAMES, 43
ruin formless r. of oblivion TRANSIENCE, 22
for the r. of our sex MEN, 12; SMOLLETT, T, 5
I am inclined to notice the r. in things EUROPE, 16; MILLER, A, 4
the boy will r. himself ROYALTY, 68
Twenty years of romance makes a woman look like a r. WILDE, O, 56
ruined Such another victory and we are r. VICTORY, 20
ruining they will end by r. our idea FASCISM, 8; MUSSOLINI, B, 1
ruins r. that Cromwell knocked about a bit INNUENDO, 2
rule a good r. in life never to apologize WODEHOUSE, P, 9
A little r., a little sway TRANSIENCE, 13
English should give Ireland home r. IRELAND, 24
I don't believe in black majority r. RACISM, 28
Irish Home R. is conceded IRELAND, 25
One Ring to r. them all POWER, 29; TOLKIEN, J, 5
R. all England under a hog INSULTS, 37
r. them with a rod of iron LEADERSHIP, 3
safer to obey than to r. OBEDIENCE, 3
The first r. in opera is the first r. in life MELBA, N, 1; SELF-RELIANCE, 9
the Reagans will be the r. REAGAN, R, 3
To r. by fettering the mind HYPATIA, 4
ruled Art is r....imagination IMAGINATION, 2
ruler I am the R. of the Queen's Navee GILBERT, W, 13
rulers R. of the Queen's Navee GILBERT, W, 12
We are all Home R. today IRELAND, 4
rules R. and models destroy genius and art HAZLITT, W, 23; RULES, 2
r. of the game are what we call the laws of Nature GOD, 29; HUXLEY, T, 6
the hand that r. the world INFLUENCE, 12
there are no golden r. RULES, 3; SHAW, G, 31
the r. of the universe be annulled PRAYER, 7
two golden r. for an orchestra BEECHAM, T, 2
ruleth the cry of him that r. among fools BIBLE, 75; WISDOM, 3
ruling Britain...where the r. class does not rule CLASS, 28
The state is an instrument...of the r. class STALIN, J, 2; STATE, 5
rum r., sodomy, and the lash CHURCHILL, W, 34; NAVY, 5
Yo-ho-ho, and a bottle of r. ALCOHOL, 78; STEVENSON, R, 8
rumble R. thy bellyful SHAKESPEARE, 179; WEATHER, 20
rumour Where r. of oppression and deceit COWPER, W, 27; SOLITUDE, 3
run Gwine to r. all night HORSES, 6
in a race r. all, but one receiveth the prize BIBLE, 33
so r., that ye may obtain BIBLE, 33
You cannot r. with the hare LOYALTY, 3; PROVERBS, 471
runcible ate with a r. spoon FOOD, 44; LEAR, E, 9
He weareth a r. hat LEAR, E, 7; NONSENSE, 22
runners like r. hand on the torch of life MORTALITY, 15
runneth my cup r. over PSALMS, 13
running drive out nature with a pitchfork...she'll be constantly r. back HUMAN NATURE, 15
it takes all the r. *you* can do, to keep in the same place CARROLL, L, 24; NONSENSE, 8
The machine is r. away with *him* WILHELM II, 5
running back drive out nature with a pitchfork...she'll be constantly r. HORACE, 20
runs He that fights and r. away PROVERBS, 189
rush *R. hour:* that hour when TRAVEL, 35
rushes *Green grow the r. O* ANONYMOUS, 45; BURNS, R, 11
rushing a r. mighty wind BIBLE, 2
Ruskin A certain girlish petulance of style that distinguishes R. RUSKIN, J, 1
I doubt that art needed R. STOPPARD, T, 13
Russell R.'s beautiful mathematical mind RUSSELL, B, 2
Russia an elephant like R. RUSSIA, 9
For us in R. communism is a dead dog SOLZHENITSYN, A, 13
going in without the help of R. LLOYD GEORGE, D, 13; WORLD WAR II, 37
on the moon as in Imperial R. CHEKHOV, A, 1
R. is a collapse, not a revolution LAWRENCE, D, 37; RUSSIA, 11
the greatness of R. is only her pre-natal struggling LAWRENCE, D, 34; RUSSIA, 10
Why will America not reach out...to R. DIPLOMACY, 11
Russian greet in you the victorious R. Revolution RUSSIAN REVOLUTION, 5
Scratch the R. and...find the Tartar RUSSIA, 12
the R. people have become RUSSIA, 18; TROTSKY, L, 8
Russians our decadence and the R.' DECLINE, 13; THURBER, J, 13
test the R., not the bombs NUCLEAR WEAPONS, 8
rustling r. in unpaid-for silk CONTENTMENT, 9; SHAKESPEARE, 61
rut It's not good enough...getting into a state of r. WRITERS, 53
people getting into a state of r. CRITICISM, 20
ruts New roads: new r. CHESTERTON, G, 52; PROGRESS, 10
rye Coming through the r. BURNS, R, 6; LOVE, 45

S

Sabbath never broke the S., but for Gain DRYDEN, J, 10
the child that is born on the S. day NURSERY RHYMES, 35
sabotage All business sagacity reduces itself...to...s. BUSINESS, 34
sack Either back us or s. us SUPPORT, 3
sacred the human body is s. MANKIND, 71; WHITMAN, W, 5
to obstruct the way of God...is more grievous than to kill in the s. months KORAN 3
We hold these truths to be s. and undeniable JEFFERSON, T, 5
Sacred Heart Convent of the S. ELIOT, T, 23
sacrifice A woman will always s. herself MAUGHAM, W, 5; WOMEN, 86
s....of the devil's leavings POPE, A, 56; VIRTUE, 21
this war...which did not justify the s. of a single mother's son WAR, 126
thou desirest no s., else would I give it thee PSALMS, 32
sacrificed the most useful thing about a principle...s. to expediency EXPEDIENCY, 5; MAUGHAM, W, 4
sad Becoming an Anglo-Catholic must...be a s. business CATHOLICISM, 15
being kind /Is all the s. world needs KINDNESS, 13; RELIGION, 102
her s. short, short story BRONTE, A, 2
The s., compassionate, loving, romantic man HOUSMAN, A, 2
when thou art absent I am s. LOVE, 120
sadder A s. and a wiser man COLERIDGE, S, 40; WISDOM, 15
sadists repressed s....become policemen or butchers CONNOLLY, C, 8; PUBLISHING, 6
sadly stars /Regard me s. PLATH, S, 5
sadness Good day s. SORROW, 10
S....a form of fatigue SORROW, 12
safari I want you to accompany me on the s. TRAVEL, 34
safe Better be s. than sorry CAUTION, 1; PROVERBS, 91
He...makes us feel s. and comfortable MELBOURNE, 2
make the world s. for diversity DIFFERENCE, 9
The only way to be absolutely s. CAUTION, 13
thou shalt be s. under his feathers PSALMS, 51
safeguard the s. of the west VENICE, 4; WORDSWORTH, W, 59
safer s. to obey than to rule OBEDIENCE, 3
safest Just when we are s. BROWNING, R, 10; WORRY, 10
safety Safe though all s.'s lost BROOKE, R, 6; WAR, 32
s. is in our speed EMERSON, R, 13; HASTE, 6
There is s. in numbers PROVERBS, 411
sage He that would live for aye, must eat s. in May LONGEVITY, 1
Why should a man die who has s. in his garden REMEDIES, 7
without hardness will be s. ARNOLD, M, 20
said a great deal to be s. /For being dead DEATH, 33
Nothing has yet been s. that's not been s. before TERENCE, 1

the best which has been thought and s. in the world ARNOLD, M, 3
they do not know what they have s. CHURCHILL, W, 41
'Tis s. that some have died for love WORDSWORTH, W, 71
When a thing has been s. and s. well QUOTATIONS, 3
sailor common s., a beggar is still…an Englishman ENGLAND, 36
No man will be a s. BOATS, 10; JOHNSON, S, 56
Tinker, /Tailor, /Soldier, /S. NURSERY RHYMES, 64; OCCUPATIONS, 21
sailors Dear comrades, soldiers, s. and workers RUSSIAN REVOLUTION, 5
opening time in the S. Arms PUBLIC HOUSES, 4; THOMAS, D, 22
S. have a port OCCUPATIONS, 6; PROVERBS, 352
saint before we *know* he is a s., there will have to be miracles GREENE, G, 8; PROOF, 4
being a novelist, I consider myself superior to the s., the scientist LAWRENCE, D, 38
fought with us upon S. Crispin's day SHAKESPEARE, 137
never a s. took pity on /My soul COLERIDGE, S, 31; SOLITUDE, 2
S., n. a dead sinner RELIGION, 14
S. Preux never kicked the fireirons IMPERFECTION, 5
saints All are not s. HYPOCRISY, 1; PROVERBS, 31
many bodies of the s. which slept arose BIBLE, 432; LAST WORDS, 11
sake Art for art's s. ART, 8
sakes king…men have made for their own s. MONARCHY, 20; SELDEN, J, 1
salad My s. days SHAKESPEARE, 29; YOUTH, 26
salary The s. of the chief executive BUSINESS, 15; GALBRAITH, J, 8
this is the week I earn my s. KENNEDY, J, 5; MERIT, 5
sales Today's s. should be better than yesterday's BUSINESS, 2
Salisbury Lord S. constitutes himself the spokesman ARISTOCRACY, 7
Salkeld I am married to Beatrice S., a painter BEHAN, B, 10; CHILDREN, 8
sally a sudden s. RIVERS, 6; TENNYSON, 7
Sally There's none like pretty S. LOVE, 50
salmon cider and tinned s. FOOD, 71; WAUGH, E, 36
serve both cod and s. PUNS, 13
the choice between smoked s. and tinned s. FOOD, 75; WILSON, H, 2
salt a pillar of s. BIBLE, 168
nobody likes having s. rubbed into their wounds WEST, R, 4
S. water and absence LOVE, 9; PROVERBS, 353
speech…seasoned with s. BIBLE, 23; SPEECH, 4
the s. of the earth BIBLE, 361
salvage Is a man a s. at heart MANKIND, 6
salvaged Our ships have been s. WORLD WAR II, 31
salvagery is s. but a faint taint in the natural man's gentility MANKIND, 6
salvation let us heartily rejoice in the strength of our s. PSALMS, 54
S. doesn't do them the same good RELIGION, 98
s.…in the hands of the creatively maladjusted PROGRESS, 17
the Lord is my light, and my s. PSALMS, 15
There is no s. outside the church RELIGION, 6
The s. of mankind RESPONSIBILITY, 17; SOLZHENITSYN, A, 15
Sam Play it, S. MISQUOTATIONS, 11; NOSTALGIA, 2
Samaritan But a certain S.…had compassion on him BIBLE, 325; CHARITY, 9
No one would have remembered the Good S. MONEY, 51
ready enough to do the S. CHARITY, 24; SMITH, S, 9
Samarkand the Golden Road to S. KNOWLEDGE, 17
same he is much the s. ILLNESS, 9
It will be all the s. PROVERBS, 238; WORRY, 3
it would be all the s. a hundred years hence DICKENS, C, 32; TRIVIALITY, 4
never been the s. since God died GOD, 38
principle seems the s. CHURCHILL, W, 8; WATER, 1
the s. is my brother BIBLE, 390
we must all say *the s.* MELBOURNE, 3; UNITY, 12
we're all made the s. COWARD, N, 4; SIMILARITY, 4
samite Clothed in white s. TENNYSON, 20
Samuel When they circumcised Herbert S. INSULTS, 87; LLOYD GEORGE, D, 15
sanctify Numbers s. CHAPLIN, C, 4
sanction Happiness is the only s. of life HAPPINESS, 24; SANTAYANA, G, 5
sanctions S.…way of ending apartheid KINNOCK, N, 14
sand a foolish man, which built his house upon the s. BIBLE, 380
and throws…s. in their eyes SLEEP, 18
draw a line in the s. BUSH, G, 11
The s. of the desert is sodden red NEWBOLT, H, 7; WAR, 119
They wept like anything to see /Such quantities of s. CARROLL, L, 27
throw the s. against the wind BLAKE, W, 34; FUTILITY, 5
World in a grain of s. BLAKE, W, 9; WONDER, 2
sane being s. all by oneself MADNESS, 9
See where the s. ones have landed us MADNESS, 40
Show me a s. man and I will cure him for you JUNG, C, 9; MADNESS, 23
the asylums can hold the s. people MADNESS, 45
sanitarium if he can afford the luxury of a private s. PSYCHIATRY, 18
sanity S. is madness put to good uses MADNESS, 33
S. is very rare MADNESS, 12
s. of any number of artistic mediocrities BLAKE, W, 1
sank Tallulah Bankhead barged down the Nile last night and s. CRITICISM, 11
sans S. teeth, s. eyes, s. taste, s. every thing OLD AGE, 87; SHAKESPEARE, 49
Sappho Where burning S. loved BYRON, 26; EUROPE, 3
sarcasm petulance is not s. DISRAELI, B, 26
S.…the language of the devil CARLYLE, T, 26; SARCASM, 1
sardines Life is…like a tin of s. BENNETT, A, 1; LIFE, 12
You can't ravish a tin of s. DEBAUCHERY, 9
Sargent He's a kind of musical Malcolm S. INSULTS, 12
sat The…gentleman has s. so long on the fence LLOYD GEORGE, D, 14
Satan And S. trembles COWPER, W, 15; PRAYER, 14
beheld S. as lightning fall from heaven DEVIL, 3
S. answered the Lord DEVIL, 5
S. comes as a man of peace DYLAN, B, 9
S. exalted sat, by merit raised DEVIL, 13; MILTON, J, 39
S. finds…mischief…/For idle hands IDLENESS, 13; WATTS, I, 1
S., Nick, or Clootie BURNS, R, 3; DEVIL, 9
satanic author of the S. Verses book…sentenced to death RELIGION, 60
women in the priesthood has come as a result of women's liberation, then I think it/ is s. RELIGION, 76
satire hard not to write s. SATIRE, 1
not quite enough of the superb courage of his s. GALSWORTHY, J, 1
S. is alive and well HUMOUR, 64
S. is a sort of glass SATIRE, 3; SWIFT, J, 3
S. should, like a polished razor keen SATIRE, 2
satirists S. should be heard and not seen CRITICISM, 59
satisfaction complacency and s.…in…a new-married couple LAMB, C, 3; MARRIAGE, 97
I can't get no s. SATISFACTION, 4
In work the greatest s. lies WORK, 3
little more regret and a little less s. BEECHAM, T, 8
the s. of knowing that we are avenged TROLLOPE, A, 16
work *gives* s. FRANK, A, 6
satisfied his soul is s. with what is assigned to him MARCUS AURELIUS ANTONINUS, 10
The superior man is s. CONFUCIUS, 10; SUPERIORITY, 4
Saturday betwixt /A S. and Monday SUNDAY, 3
Died on S. NURSERY RHYMES, 53
S.'s child works hard for his living CHILDREN, 50; NURSERY RHYMES, 35
what he did on S. CHRISTIANITY, 64; HYPOCRISY, 24
satyr man is…either a stoic or a s. AGE, 68
sauce a country with thirty-two religions and only one s. AMERICA, 38; TALLEYRAND, 1
Art is not a special s. ART, 18
sixty different religions, and only one s. ENGLAND, 15
The best s. in the world CERVANTES, M, 16; HUNGER, 4
Saul S. hath slain his thousands BIBLE, 481
savage A s. old Nabob POLITICIANS, 102
a time when Britain had a s. culture CIVILIZATION, 2
s. place! as holy and enchanted COLERIDGE, S, 16
soothe a s. breast CONGREVE, W, 8; MUSIC, 17
The young man who has not wept is a s. AGE, 78; SANTAYANA, G, 3; WISDOM, 24
savaged s. by a dead sheep INSULTS, 58
savait *Si jeunesse s.* AGE, 39
save Christ Jesus came into the world to s. sinners BIBLE, 506
s. the plan NIXON, R, 9

S. your breath PROVERBS, 354; SPEECH, 1
To s. a man's life against his will is...killing him HORACE, 12; KILLING, 6
saved he that endureth to the end shall be s. BIBLE, 386
they only s. the world BELLOC, H, 12; HEROISM, 3
thy faith hath s. thee BIBLE, 322
You might have s. him if you would GUILT, 5
Saviour But it's 'S. of 'is country' when the guns KIPLING, R, 30; SOLDIERS, 3
I imitate the S. HUXLEY, A, 5
savour Filths s. but themselves EVIL, 20
saw I came, I s., God conquered VICTORY, 2, 11
I came, I s., I conquered CAESAR, J, 4; VICTORY, 1
I s. it, but I did not realize it PERCEPTION, 4
Saxon The S. is not like us Normans KIPLING, R, 21; NATIONALITY, 8
Saxones the *S.*, *Angli*, and *Iutae* ENGLISH, 6
say cannot s. what you have to s. in twenty minutes SPEECHES, 4
Do as I s. PROVERBS, 111
if we s. that we have no sin, we deceive BIBLE, 281; SIN, 5
If you haven't anything nice to s. about anyone INVITATIONS, 4
I have nothing to s., I am saying it POETRY, 14
people who s. nothing COURAGE, 30
Preachers s., Do as I s., not as I do EXAMPLE, 7; SELDEN, J, 5
Regardless of what they s. DOGS, 15
S. it with flowers FLOWERS, 11
s. what you have to s., and then sit down SPEECHES, 12; WELLINGTON, 25
The great consolation...is to s. what one thinks FRANKNESS, 4; VOLTAIRE, 30
They are to s. what they please FREEDOM, 15
they do not know what they are going to s. CHURCHILL, W, 41; SPEECHES, 6
What have we to s. to India COMMUNICATION, 5; RUSKIN, J, 18
When you have nothing to s. SILENCE, 4
When you take your family on holiday, do you s. LANGUAGE, 6
saying S. is one thing ACTION, 5; PROVERBS, 355
seldom interested in what he is s. POUND, E, 2
when...speaking, they do not know what they are s. CHURCHILL, W, 41; SPEECHES, 6
sayings Dr Johnson's s. WRITERS, 61
His s. are generally like women's letters HAZLITT, W, 6
scab The itch of disputing...the s. of churches RELIGION, 104
scaffold no middle course between the throne and the s. MONARCHY, 9
scalpel You can't probe for faith with a s. DOCTORS, 38
scandal In England there is only silence or s. ENGLAND, 33
It is a public s. that gives offence MORALITY, 11
s. by a woman...proved liar POLITICS, 47
There's no s. like rags POVERTY, 10
Virtue consisted in avoiding s. HYPOCRISY, 8
scape who shall s. whipping MERIT, 6; SHAKESPEARE, 88
scarce S., sir. Mighty s. TWAIN, M, 20; WOMEN, 135
scare A good s. is worth more ADVICE, 1; PROVERBS, 25
scarecrow We must not make a s. of the law LAW, 32
scarecrows Logical consequences are the s. of fools HUXLEY, T, 9; LOGIC, 6
scared s. to go to the brink COWARDICE, 2
scarlet His sins were s. BELLOC, H, 14; BOOKS, 7
pious bird with the s. breast WORDSWORTH, W, 45
though your sins be as s. BIBLE, 191
scars He jests at s. SHAKESPEARE, 310
scatter We plough the fields, and s. AGRICULTURE, 1
scattered God blew and they were s. WAR, 2
s. the proud BIBLE, 310
scenery Mountains...the beginning and the end of all natural s. MOUNTAINS, 3; RUSKIN, J, 6
S. is fine HUMAN NATURE, 19; KEATS, J, 58
scenes I'll come no more behind your s., David JOHNSON, S, 46; LUST, 6
sceptic too much of a s. to deny the possibility of anything HUXLEY, T, 10; SCEPTICISM, 2
scepticism natural course of the human mind is...from credulity to s. MIND, 14
only her s. kept her from being an atheist SARTRE, J, 16
sceptred this s. isle ENGLAND, 46; SHAKESPEARE, 297
Scheherazade S....a woman saving her head SELF-PRESERVATION, 15
schemes best laid s. o' mice an' men BURNS, R, 22; DISAPPOINTMENT, 2
schizophrenia if God talks to you, you have s. MADNESS, 43; SZASZ, T, 8
S. cannot be understood LAING, R, 2; PSYCHIATRY, 21
schizophrenic if God talks to you, you are a s. SZASZ, T, 8
S. behaviour...a special strategy PSYCHIATRY, 20
Schoenberg people who do Brahms without knowing S. MUSIC, 21
scholar ills the s.'s life assail EDUCATION, 52
the last humiliation of an aged s. OLD AGE, 37
scholars great men have not commonly been great s. GREATNESS, 8
S. and gentlemen WORDSWORTH, W, 40
S. dispute HORACE, 5
school A good clinical teacher is himself a Medical S. EDUCATION, 40
enjoy a public s. EDUCATION, 26
Every night of her married life she has been late for s. THOMAS, D, 24
Example is the s. of mankind BURKE, E, 3; EXAMPLE, 2
fleshly s. of Poetry POETS, 2
If every day in the life of a s. EDUCATION, 55; LEACOCK, S, 1
more fit for a grammar s. than a Court of Parliament HOUSES OF PARLIAMENT, 6
never gone to s. may steal from a freight car CRIME, 8; EDUCATION, 76
nothing on earth...so horrible as a s. EDUCATION, 81
public s., where...learning was painfully beaten into him EDUCATION, 73
The Stealthy S. of Criticism CRITICISM, 54; ROSSETTI, D, 5
The world is but a s. of inquiry CURIOSITY, 6; MONTAIGNE, M, 9
Three little maids from s. CHILDREN, 31; GILBERT, W, 28
till he's been to a good s. EDUCATION, 77; SAKI, 15
schoolboy a s.'s barring out TENNYSON, 69
every s. repeating my words POSTERITY, 9
I see a s. when I think of him KEATS, J, 5
schoolboys 'tis the s. that educate my son EDUCATION, 28; EMERSON, R, 19
schoolgirl a priggish s., captain of the hockey team, a prefect ROYALTY, 2
schoolmaster Every s. after the age of 49 EDUCATION, 68
Nothing is more hideous than an old s. EDUCATION, 58
schoolmasters Let s. puzzle their brain GOLDSMITH, O, 21
schoolroom in the s....does the difference of sex...need to be forgotten ANTHONY, S, 5
schools a hundred s. of thought contend MAO TSE-TUNG, 6
Public s. are the nurseries of all vice EDUCATION, 29
There is now less flogging in our great s. EDUCATION, 51; JOHNSON, S, 100
We class s....into four grades EDUCATION, 94; WAUGH, E, 8
schoolteacher The s....ludicrously overpaid as an educator EDUCATION, 69
science All s. requires mathematics MATHEMATICS, 1
A man of true s....uses but few hard words LANGUAGE, 32
A s. which hesitates to forget WHITEHEAD, A, 5
Christian S. explains all cause and effect as mental RELIGION, 36
drawback that s....invented after I left school SCIENCE, 19
Ethics and S. need to shake hands PRINCIPLES, 2
Facts are not s. FACTS, 2
god of s....has given us the atomic bomb SCIENCE, 60
great grey holy book of s. fiction SCIENCE FICTION, 3
great tragedy of S. HUXLEY, T, 1; SCIENCE, 52
guy in a s. fiction movie INSULTS, 51
In everything that relates to s. LAMB, C, 8; SCIENCE, 61
invoke the wonders of s. instead of its terrors SCIENCE, 59
irregular side of nature...these have been puzzles to s. NATURE, 14
its hold on s. KINDNESS, 8
Language is only the instrument of s. JOHNSON, S, 6; LANGUAGE, 28
lastly s. IMPORTANCE, 5; SPARK, M, 10
Learn to innure yourself to drudgery in s. EDUCATION, 72
maths we need to carry out s. is pretty straightforward EDUCATION, 17
Medical s. is...imperfectly differentiated from...witchcraft MEDICINE, 92
men only care for s. so far as they get a living by it SCIENCE, 44
No one should approach the temple of s. SCIENCE, 15

grow a little crazy...like all men at s. MADNESS, 19
Jesus...walking on the s. BIBLE, 394
kings of the s. ARNOLD, M, 17; DEPARTURE, 2
Learn the secret of the s. LONGFELLOW, H, 12; SEA, 9
like throwing water into the s. CERVANTES, M, 9; CHARITY, 13
Man has in him the silence of the s. MANKIND, 63
men and s. interpenetrate CONRAD, J, 9; ENGLAND, 16
Out of the s. came he COLERIDGE, S, 25; SUN, 2
Over the s. to Skye ROYALTY, 27
Owl and the Pussy-Cat went to s. LEAR, E, 8; NONSENSE, 23
precious stone set in the silver s. ENGLAND, 46; SHAKESPEARE, 297
s., trembling with a long line of radiance SEA, 12
Stick...to your desks and never go to s. GILBERT, W, 12
that gong-tormented s. SEA, 16
the midst of the s. upon dry ground BIBLE, 112
The s. is calm to-night ARNOLD, M, 10; SEA, 1
the s. is his PSALMS, 54
The s.! the s. SEA, 15
The voice of the s. speaks to the soul SEA, 3
They went to s. in a sieve LEAR, E, 4
to the English that of the s. EUROPE, 18
Two voices...one is of the s., /One of the mountains WORDSWORTH, W, 64
We are as near to heaven by s. as by land LAST WORDS, 43; SEA, 5
when they can see nothing but s. BACON, F, 3; DISCOVERY, 4
why the s. is boiling hot CARROLL, L, 28; NONSENSE, 9
sea-change doth suffer a s. DEATH, 154; SHAKESPEARE, 323
seagreen The s. Incorruptible CARLYLE, T, 18; POLITICIANS, 59
seal you heard a s. bark BELIEF, 12
sealed My lips are s. BALDWIN, S, 8; SECRECY, 2
sea-life When men come to like a s. JOHNSON, S, 101; SEA, 6
seals sealed with seven s. BIBLE, 460
seam And sew a fine s. NURSERY RHYMES, 8
seamen There were gentlemen and...s. in the navy of Charles the Second MACAULAY, T, 15
sear My way of life /Is fall'n into the s. SHAKESPEARE, 225
search in s. of a great perhaps LAST WORDS, 72; RABELAIS, F, 10
s. for knowledge PHILOSOPHERS, 10; RUSSELL, B, 4
s. the land of living men ADMIRATION, 14; SCOTT, W, 13
seas I must down to the s. again MASEFIELD, J, 5; SEA, 10
That guard our native s. NAVY, 3
the waters called he S. BIBLE, 139; CREATION, 3
seaside Beside the S. SEASIDE, 4
the drawback of all s. places SEASIDE, 3
season a perfectly ghastly s....for you Spanish dancers BANKHEAD, T, 9; CHARITY, 6
Only in the mating s. ANIMALISM, 6; MILLIGAN, S, 3
S. of mists and mellow fruitfulness SEASONS, 12
s. with lots of accidents SPORT AND GAMES, 40
to every thing there is a s. BIBLE, 67; TIME, 14
seasoned speech...s. with salt BIBLE, 23; SPEECH, 4
seasons a man for all s. ADAPTABILITY, 4
Four s. fill the measure SEASONS, 10
seat the pleasure of offering my s. to three ladies CHESTERTON, G, 43; OBESITY, 4
seated S....at the organ MUSIC, 49
sea-water Wealth is like s. GREED, 12; SCHOPENHAUER, A, 8
second The constitution...first and s. class citizens CLASS, 57
second-hand Would you buy a s. car TRUST, 6
second-rate an infallible sign of the s. INFERIORITY, 3
nor even booksellers have put up with poets being s. HORACE, 10
the powers of a first-rate man and the creed of a s. man BAGEHOT, W, 9
secrecy S. is the first essential GOVERNMENT, 34
secret a s. in the Oxford sense OXFORD, 7; SECRECY, 10
a s. way...of getting at a boy EVIL, 10
bread eaten in s. is pleasant BIBLE, 449; SECRECY, 5
I know that's a s. CONGREVE, W, 7; SECRECY, 8
it is no sin to sin in s. MORALITY, 11
joys of parents are s. BACON, F, 38; FAMILY, 8
Learn the s. of the sea LONGFELLOW, H, 12; SEA, 9
s. of reaping the greatest fruitfulness...from life DANGER, 6; NIETZSCHE, F, 6
Three may keep a s. FRANKLIN, B, 7; SECRECY, 9
We have discovered the s. of life SCIENCE, 21
when it ceases to be a s. BEHN, A, 7; LOVE, 26
secreted Not in Utopia.../Or some s. island FRENCH REVOLUTION, 13
secretive As we make sex less s., we may rob it of its power SZASZ, T, 2
secrets Conversation...elicits s. from us CONVERSATION, 8
sect paradise for a s. KEATS, J, 15
sedate, sober, silent, serious, sad-coloured s. HOOD, T, 1
secure only place where a man can feel...s. GREER, G, 2; MEN, 6
The past, at least, is s. PAST, 13; WEBSTER, D, 5
security only freedom can make s. secure FREEDOM, 48
Sedan in a flood of tears and a S. chair HUMOUR, 42
sedentary Henry has always led...a s. life LAZINESS, 9
sedge s. has wither'd from the lake ILLNESS, 39; KEATS, J, 22
seditious s. person is an outlaw before God PROTESTANTISM, 5
seduce s. each other by their articulateness WRITING, 4
seducers evil men and s. BIBLE, 513; EVIL, 5
seductive the most remarkable and s. genius BEERBOHM, M, 2
see change we think we s. FROST, R, 1; NOVELTY, 2
Come up and s. me some time MISQUOTATIONS, 23
complain we cannot s. COMPLAINTS, 1
eyes have they, and s. not PSALMS, 64
eyes to s., and s. not BIBLE, 124; REBELLION, 3
he that made the eye, shall he not s. PSALMS, 53
I s. but as one sees after an operation BLINDNESS, 4
I s. none coming out AESOP, 6; MISTRUST, 2
It is...at my age I now begin to s. things as they really are LAST WORDS, 35
My business is to paint...what I s. PAINTING, 20
s....into a hypocrite CHESTERTON, G, 20; HYPOCRISY, 10
seem to s. things thou dost not SHAKESPEARE, 191
the day I was meant not to s. THATCHER, M, 33
there shall no man s. me, and live BIBLE, 121
we received from that S. our Crown OBLIGATION, 2
whereas I was blind, now I s. BIBLE, 255
Why don't you come up sometime and s. me INVITATIONS, 6; WEST, M, 8
seed Fair s.-time had my soul SOUL, 13; WORDSWORTH, W, 36
I do not want to die...until I have...cultivated the s. ACHIEVEMENT, 11
In s. time learn, in harvest teach BLAKE, W, 22; SUITABILITY, 1
Onan knew that the s. should not be his BIBLE, 177
seeing S. is believing BELIEF, 2; PROVERBS, 358
seek I will undoubtedly have to s....gainful employment ACHESON, D, 5; GOVERNMENT, 1
s., and ye shall find BIBLE, 375; SUCCESS, 7
the hearts of Men should s. beyond the world TOLKIEN, J, 7
To toil and not to s. for rest SELFLESSNESS, 3
We s. him here, we s. him there ABSENCE, 9
We s....In every cranny but the right COWPER, W, 21
We s. it, ere it comes to light PERVERSITY, 3
seem s. a saint when most I play the devil APPEARANCES, 34
Things are not always what they s. APPEARANCES, 5; PROVERBS, 429
thinks men honest that but s. to be so INNOCENCE, 11
seeming beguile /The thing I am by s. otherwise APPEARANCES, 33
The s. truth...entrap the wisest APPEARANCES, 36
seen blessed are they that have not s., and yet have believed BIBLE, 278
eye hath not s. BIBLE, 25
I have s. Voltaire VOLTAIRE, 4
Who has s. the wind ROSSETTI, C, 9; WEATHER, 17
sees fool s. not the same tree BLAKE, W, 27
What, when drunk, one s. in other women COMPLIMENTS, 36; TYNAN, K, 6
Seine Today I spat in the S. WORLD WAR II, 40
seize S. the day HORACE, 32; PRESENT, 7
S. today OPPORTUNITY, 13
seldom s. attribute common sense ROCHEFOUCAULD, 24
selection biologists studied genetics and natural s. EVOLUTION, 17
making so much of natural s. DARWIN, C, 4
Natural S. DARWIN, C, 8; EVOLUTION, 10
self All censure of a man's s. JOHNSON, S, 125; SELF, 13
met with anything that was dearer to anyone than his own s. BUDDHA, 2
nothing...is greater...than one's s. SELF, 26; WHITMAN, W, 9
Obsessed with s. LAWRENCE, D, 1
sickness enlarges the dimensions of a man's s. ILLNESS, 40; LAMB, C, 17
to thine own s. be true INTEGRITY, 6; SHAKESPEARE, 75

part of English middle-class education is devoted to the training of s. CLASS, 56; EDUCATION, 101
S. should not be ill CLASS, 10
Socialists treat their s. with respect POLITICS, 103; STOPPARD, T, 3
We teachers can only help…as s. EDUCATION, 66
serve capacity to permit his ministers to s. him ROYALTY, 97
gonna have to s. somebody DYLAN, B, 3
if thou…s. the Lord, prepare…for temptation BIBLE, 80
Mr. Lincoln…cannot s. them all at once LINCOLN, A, 1
They also s. who only stand and wait MILTON, J, 61; SERVICE, 5
served I must have things daintily s. BETJEMAN, J, 6; ETIQUETTE, 1
Youth will be s. SATISFACTION, 1
service I will see you in the vestry after s. CLERGY, 11; SMITH, S, 8
life goes in the s. of the nation GANDHI, I, 7
Small s. is true s. SERVICE, 6; WORDSWORTH, W, 73
serviettes kiddies have crumpled the s. BETJEMAN, J, 6; ETIQUETTE, 1
servitude delivered them from s. to other lands ROYALTY, 12
Sesame Open S. SUPERNATURAL, 2
sessions s. of sweet silent thought REGRET, 24; SHAKESPEARE, 363
set all, except their sun, is s. BYRON, 26; EUROPE, 3
best plain s. BACON, F, 11; VIRTUE, 3
s. thine house in order BIBLE, 304
setter up Proud s. and puller down of kings INFLUENCE, 9
setting clouds that gather round the s. sun WORDSWORTH, W, 33
settled Thank God, that's s. SHERIDAN, R, 17
Settlement coach and six horses through the Act of S. IRELAND, 23
seven his acts being s. ages HUMAN CONDITION, 25; SHAKESPEARE, 48
sealed with s. seals BIBLE, 460
Seven for the s. stars in the sky ANONYMOUS, 45; NUMBERS, 1
S. swans a-swimming CHRISTMAS, 18; NURSERY RHYMES, 59
the s. pillared worthy house LOVE, 103
The S. Year Itch SEX, 11
wisdom…hath hewn out her s. pillars BIBLE, 448; WISDOM, 9
seventh God…rested on the s. day BIBLE, 143; SUNDAY, 1
seventy Being over s. is like being engaged in a war OLD AGE, 98; SPARK, M, 6
Being s. is not a sin MEIR, G, 5; OLD AGE, 71
Oh, to be s. again LUST, 7; OLD AGE, 36
sever a tie that only death can s. MARRIAGE, 107; MAUGHAM, W, 6
severity Summer has set in with its usual s. COLERIDGE, S, 46
sewage piped growing volumes of s. into the sea ENVIRONMENT, 4
sewer s. in a glass-bottomed boat CORRUPTION, 15
sex As we make s. less secretive, we may rob it of its power SZASZ, T, 2
both of them were extremely interested in s. SEX, 72
Christian view of s. SEX, 101
Continental people have s. life ENGLISH, 27; SEX, 81
Everything…Wanted to Know About S. SEX, 100
farmyard world of s. ANIMALISM, 2
For all the pseudo-sophistication of twentieth-century s. theory SEX, 46
Freud found s. an outcast in the outhouse SEX, 131
Gandhi was very keen on s. GANDHI, M, 3
have s. or appear on television OPPORTUNITY, 23
His excessive emphasis on s. SEX, 105
How can I…dislike a s. to which Your Majesty belongs RHODES, C, 3
If s. is such a natural phenomenon SEX, 80
if there was a third s. MEN, 14
in the schoolroom…does the difference of s.…need to be forgotten ANTHONY, S, 5
In the s.-war thoughtlessness is the weapon of the male CONNOLLY, C, 16; SEXES, 8
Is s. dirty ALLEN, W, 1; SEX, 2
Is S. Necessary SEX, 121
it's s. with someone you love ALLEN, W, 3; SEX, 4
judged on how much s. you've had AIDS, 6
Literature is mostly about having s. CHILDREN, 48; LITERATURE, 16; LODGE, D, 1
make s. funny SEX, 10
meant us to have group s. BRADBURY, M, 8; SEX, 18
Money, it turned out, was exactly like s. BALDWIN, J, 2; MONEY, 8; SEX, 14
much more fundamental than s. MONEY, 19
No more about s. DURRELL, L, 2; SEX, 33
no more weakness than is natural to her s. WOMEN, 131
No s. is better than bad s. SEX, 47
No s. without responsibility SEX, 73
Nothing nauseates me more than promiscuous s. PROMISCUITY, 8
not to make s. illegal AIDS, 10
People should be very free with s. HOMOSEXUALITY, 16
Personally I know nothing about s. SEX, 42
poor honest s., like dying, should be a private matter SEX, 33
Pornography is the attempt to insult s. LAWRENCE, D, 35; PORNOGRAPHY, 4
professed tyrant to their s. MISOGYNY, 3; SHAKESPEARE, 268
promiscuous s. in and out of season SEX, 67
S. and the Single Girl SEX, 19
S. between a man and a woman SEX, 7
S.…Every bit as interesting as agriculture SEX, 113
s. has been a very private, secretive activity SZASZ, T, 2
S. is one of the nine reasons for reincarnation SEX, 82
S. is on the up AIDS, 9
S. is something I really don't understand SALINGER, J, 4; SEX, 106
S. is the biggest nothing SEX, 123
'S.,'…'is the gateway to life.' SEX, 13
S. is the tabasco sauce SEX, 130
s.…must itself be subject…to evolution SEXES, 5
s. plays a more important part in the life of woman SEX, 111
Soul is the rhythm o' s. POPULAR MUSIC, 13
system…to call you darling after s. LOVE, 23
the condition of our s. is so deplorable that it is our duty…to break the law PANKHURST, E, 6
the difference of s., if there is any ANTHONY, S, 5
the s. novel is now normal NOVELS, 15; SHAW, G, 40
To defend society from s. is no one's business CENSORSHIP, 2
we English have s. on the brain ENGLISH, 31; SEX, 89
we have had s. BUSH, G, 4
You mustn't think I advocate perpetual s. PROMISCUITY, 8
if S. ever rears its ugly head AYCKBOURN, A, 2
sexes husbands and wives…belong to different s. SEXES, 11
more difference within the s. than between them SEXES, 7
several other old ladies of both s. DICKENS, C, 23
that pleasure, which is undeniably the sole motive force behind the union of the s. LACLOS, P, 3
the psychic of human relationship between the s. SEX, 58
the…rift between the s. is…widened SEXES, 28
sexist Catholicism is a completely s., repressed…religion CATHOLICISM, 11
sexton went and told the s. HOOD, T, 5; PUNS, 7
sexual avowed purpose is to excite s. desire MUGGERIDGE, M, 5; PORNOGRAPHY, 6
Civilized people cannot fully satisfy their s. instinct without love SEX, 104
Ignorance of the necessity for s. intercourse SEX, 31
In an uncorrupted woman the s. impulse SEX, 38
Industrial relations are like s. relations INDUSTRIAL RELATIONS, 2
many females…never feel…s. excitement SEX, 1
Masturbation: the primary s. activity SZASZ, T, 9
music throatily…s. HUXLEY, A, 4; MUSIC, 31
nice little missionaries share Jim Bakker's blessed s. preferences AIDS, 11
The discussion of the s. problem SEX, 58
sexuality difficulties with their s. HOMOSEXUALITY, 21
protect virginity or otherwise to control female s. VIRGINITY, 6
S. is the lyricism of the masses SEX, 16
s. was utterly irrelevant HOMOSEXUALITY, 24
sexy fat is s. APPEARANCE, 11
Nuns are s. SEX, 75
shabby For tamed and s. tigers ANIMALS, 15
shackles women freed of their political s. FEMINISM, 27
shade a green thought in a green s. MARVELL, A, 2; OBLIVION, 3
inviolable s. ARNOLD, M, 38; HOPE, 7
No s., no shine, no butterflies, no bees HOOD, T, 10; MONTHS, 10
Nothing grows well in the s. GREATNESS, 5
the s. /Of that which once was great REGRET, 29; WORDSWORTH, W, 62
shadow be caves…in which his s. will be shown GOD, 41; NIETZSCHE, F, 5

hide me under the s. of thy wings PSALMS, 6
I am no s.…I am a wife PLATH, S, 7
lose the substance by grasping at the s. AESOP, 1; GREED, 5
the valley of the s. of death PSALMS, 11
unhappy s. CAMPION, T, 1; SORROW, 5
Who live under the s. of a war SPENDER, S, 5; WAR, 163
Your s. at morning ELIOT, T, 28
shadows brooding tragedy and its dark s. can be lightened GANDHI, I, 6; HISTORY, 14
half sick of s. MARRIAGE, 154; TENNYSON, 43
If we s. have offended SHAKESPEARE, 267
s. of our history give us cause to reflect GERMANY, 12
The s. that I feared so long BLINDNESS, 5
shak'd when degree is s. ORDER, 5; SHAKESPEARE, 331
shake I will s. my little finger – and there will be no more Tito INFLUENCE, 10
Shakespeare after S. and Milton are fogotten POETS, 51
A strange, horrible business…good enough for S.'s day VICTORIA, 10
Besides S. and me, who do you think there is STEIN, G, 6
he had read S. and found him weak in chemistry WELLS, H, 18
I despise S. SHAW, G, 11
I don't *really* like words by S. MCCARTNEY, P, 2
myriad-minded S. COLERIDGE, S, 9
reading S. by flashes of lightning COLERIDGE, S, 45; CRITICISM, 14
S.…grammar school kids EDUCATION, 38
S., I come LAST WORDS, 26
S. never had six lines together without a fault JOHNSON, S, 75
S.'s so bloody difficult, and I don't like failure FAILURE, 6
S., undoubtedly wanted taste WALPOLE, H, 4
sweetest S., Fancy's child MILTON, J, 19
the making up of a S. or a Milton COLERIDGE, S, 47
the right to criticize S. CRITICISM, 58; SHAW, G, 41
tried lately to read S. DARWIN, C, 5
We can say of S. ELIOT, T, 4
When I read S. I am struck LAWRENCE, D, 30
who speak the tongue /That S. spake FREEDOM, 63
Wodehouse, whose works I place a little below S.'s WODEHOUSE, P, 1
Wonderful women!…how much we…owe to S. TERRY, D, 1
shaking After s. hands with a Greek MISTRUST, 1; PROVERBS, 20
all these great interests entrusted to the s. hand VICTORIA, 8
Shakspeare who speak the tongue /That S. spake WORDSWORTH, W, 55
Shalimar Pale hands I loved beside the S. LOVE, 87
shambles Our civilization is founded on the s. DEATH, 85
shame expense of spirit in a waste of s. SHAKESPEARE, 372
Neither s. nor physical pain have any…effect KEY, E, 4; PUNISHMENT, 19
Put off your s. with your clothes MODESTY, 10
put to s. suddenly PSALMS, 2
shamefaced Perjury…is truth that is s. TRUTH, 20
shape hearts of Men…should have a virtue to s. their life MANKIND, 65
S. of Things to Come FUTURE, 14
shapely it's…more important for a theory to be s., than…true HAMPTON, C, 1
shapen I was s. in wickedness PSALMS, 31
shapes A Catalan wizard who fools with s. PICASSO, P, 1
share a s. in their misfortunes INJUSTICE, 3
s. in the good fortunes of the mighty BRECHT, B, 1
shares Fair S. for All EQUALITY, 17; POLITICS, 55
Sharon the rose of S. BIBLE, 486
sharp those who have stout hearts and s. swords RUTHLESSNESS, 6
sharper the word of God is…s. than any two-edged sword BIBLE, 185
shaves man who s. and takes a train TRAVEL, 48
Shaw Bernard S. LENIN, V, 10
G. B. S. POPULARITY, 9; WILDE, O, 66
George Bernard S. is sadly miscast CRITICISM, 59
George Too S. To Be Good WRITERS, 91
Mr S.…has never written any poetry CHESTERTON, G, 34
S. has no enemies…disliked by…friends WRITERS, 96
S. relished every opportunity WRITERS, 46
S. replied 'I'll wait for you to grow up' WRITERS, 41
S.'s judgements are often scatterbrained WRITERS, 35
she s. is my country still PATRIOTISM, 9
S.-who-must-be-obeyed WOMAN'S ROLE, 7
shears marriage…resembles a pair of s. MARRIAGE, 144; SMITH, S, 10
sheathe never s. the sword WAR, 12
Sheba the queen of S. BIBLE, 299
shed s.…for the remission of sins BIBLE, 424; CHRISTIANITY, 29
shedding without s. of blood is no remission BIBLE, 186; EXECUTION, 3
sheep an old half-witted s. WORDSWORTH, W, 2
as a shepherd divideth his s. from the goats BIBLE, 420
A s. in s.'s clothing WEAKNESS, 3
Baa, baa, black s. NURSERY RHYMES, 4
feed my s. BIBLE, 280
good shepherd giveth his life for the s. CHRISTIANITY, 19
hungry s. look up, and are not fed MILTON, J, 26
I have found my s. which was lost BIBLE, 330
like lost s. BOOK OF COMMON PRAYER, 14
make a man by standing a s. BEERBOHM, M, 17
not armies…but flocks of s. CERVANTES, M, 5; DELUSION, 3
savaged by a dead s. INSULTS, 58
s.'s clothing BIBLE, 378; DECEPTION, 2
The mountain s. are sweeter GREED, 10; PEACOCK, T, 7
the s. of his hand PSALMS, 56
The s.'s in the meadow NURSERY RHYMES, 29
the wolf in the s.'s clothing AESOP, 10; APPEARANCES, 8
useless for the s. to pass resolutions in favour of vegetarianism INGE, W, 5
shelf The dust and silence of the upper s. MACAULAY, T, 6
Shelley S. and Keats were…up to date in…chemical knowledge POETS, 7; SCIENCE, 46
S. had a hyper-thyroid face APPEARANCE, 68
S.'s nature is utterly womanish POETS, 45
S. was indeed 'a beautiful and ineffectual angel' SHELLEY, P, 1
the right sphere for S.'s genius ARNOLD, M, 25
shells shrill demented choirs of wailing s. MEMORIALS, 12
With silver bells and cockle s. NURSERY RHYMES, 34
shelter Our s. from the stormy blast RELIGION, 95
Shenandoah O, S., I long to hear you ANONYMOUS, 66
shepherd Go, for they call you, S., from the hill ARNOLD, M, 34; SUMMONS, 1
I am the good s. CHRISTIANITY, 19
the Lord is my s. PSALMS, 11
This is the weather the s. shuns HARDY, T, 14; WEATHER, 13
shepherds Governments needs to have both s. and butchers GOVERNMENT, 41; VOLTAIRE, 22
s. abiding in the field BIBLE, 314; CHRISTMAS, 9
s. watch'd their flocks CHRISTMAS, 22
Sherard S. Blaw, the dramatist who had discovered himself SAKI, 23
sherry With first-rate s. flowing into second-rate whores MEDIOCRITY, 8
shield his faithfulness and truth shall be thy s. and buckler PSALMS, 51
shift for coming down let me s. for myself EXECUTION, 24
shimmy Put thy s. on, Lady Chatterley LAWRENCE, D, 18
shine s. on, s. on, harvest moon MOON, 6
shining A woman of so s. loveliness BEAUTY, 48; YEATS, W, 29
shins long dresses…cover a multitude of s. WEST, M, 10
ship all I ask is a tall s. MASEFIELD, J, 5
as the smart s. grew…grew the Iceberg too BOATS, 9
A whale s. was my Yale College EDUCATION, 63
being in a s. is being in a jail BOATS, 10; JOHNSON, S, 56
Don't give up the s. LAST WORDS, 56
I have not been on a s.…they still call me 'Admiral' INSULTS, 3
places his s. alongside that of an enemy NELSON, H, 5; WAR, 118
S. me somewheres east of Suez DESIRE, 9; KIPLING, R, 26
The s. follows Soviet custom CLASS, 50
They did not…so much as sink…one s. WAR, 3
ships go down to the sea in s. PSALMS, 60
Heart of oak are our s. COURAGE, 17
I spied three s. come sailing by ANONYMOUS, 8; CHRISTMAS, 3
little s. of England brought the Army home BOATS, 8; WORLD WAR II, 30
My experience of s.…one makes an interesting discovery about the world TRAVEL, 10
S. that pass in the night LONGFELLOW, H, 16; TRANSIENCE, 17
something wrong with our bloody s. BOATS, 1
Spare your s. SUPERIORITY, 2
stately s. go on NOSTALGIA, 24; TENNYSON, 5
the face that launch'd a thousand s. BEAUTY, 30; MARLOWE, C, 2
We've got the s., we've got the men, we've got the money too PATRIOTISM, 21

Study s. while you are well MEDICINE, 30
the greatest misery of s. is *solitude* SOLITUDE, 6
The problem of economic loss due to s. ILLNESS, 63
the s. that destroyeth in the noon-day PSALMS, 51
The superior doctor prevents s. DOCTORS, 7
weary thing is s. ILLNESS, 26
Sidcup If only I could get down to S. PINTER, H, 1; PROOF, 5
side A door is what a dog is...on the wrong s. of DOGS, 14; NASH, O, 2
a s. dish he hadn't ordered CONTEMPT, 3; INSULTS, 82
He who knows only his own s....knows little SUBJECTIVITY, 4
passed by on the other s. BIBLE, 324
Time is on our s. PROGRESS, 14
sides Do not...write on both s. of the paper EXAMINATIONS, 2; SELLAR, W, 8
said on both s. ADDISON, J, 13; OBJECTIVITY, 1
We...assume that everything has two s. SUBJECTIVITY, 7
sieve They went to sea in a s. LEAR, E, 4
sighed They s. for the dawn and thee LOVE, 163; TENNYSON, 57
sighs S. are the natural language of the heart SPEECH, 18
Sighs over the Bridge of S. into eternity DEATH, 96
sight a s. to make an old man young BEAUTY, 45; TENNYSON, 14
keep death in my line of s. DEATH, 57
Lord giveth s. to the blind PSALMS, 74
Out of s. ABSENCE, 2; PROVERBS, 333
s. is the most perfect and most delightful of all our senses EYES, 2
we walk by faith, not by s. BIBLE, 44; FAITH, 2
sightless clapped the glass to his s. eye BLINDNESS, 12; NEWBOLT, H, 1
When I was s. I cared for nothing BLINDNESS, 4
sights And see all s. from pole to pole ARNOLD, M, 43; SOUL, 3
few more impressive s. in the world BARRIE, J, 11; SCOTS, 2
sign Jews require a s. BIBLE, 24
Never s. a walentine DICKENS, C, 51
s. a piece of paper at the beginning of your career BUSINESS, 22
S. language is the equal of speech LANGUAGE, 37
s. of an ill-spent youth SPORT AND GAMES, 41
the s. 'Members Only' SEX, 84
writing a letter and forgetting to s. his name INSULTS, 13
signal I really do not see the s. BLINDNESS, 11; NELSON, H, 3
signed s. with their honour FAME, 29
universe was dictated but not s. UNIVERSE, 16
significance profoundly moral and packed with deep spiritual s. NOVELS, 8
significant s. form ART, 4
signifying S. nothing LIFE, 86; SHAKESPEARE, 227
signing I am s. my death warrant PROPHECY, 3
silence a period of s. on your part would be welcome POLITICIANS, 42
Come to me in the s. of the night ROSSETTI, C, 1
foster-child of s. and slow time KEATS, J, 27
God is the friend of s. SILENCE, 16
In England there is only s. or scandal ENGLAND, 33
let all the earth keep s. before him BIBLE, 183
looking for the s. in somebody PHOTOGRAPHY, 3
Make him a bishop, and you will s. him CHESTERFIELD, P, 21
My personal hobbies...s. SILENCE, 14
occasional flashes of s. INSULTS, 116; SMITH, S, 11
s. can be taken as consent GERMANY, 14
S. is as full of potential wisdom HUXLEY, A, 28; SILENCE, 8
S. is become his mother tongue GOLDSMITH, O, 18; SILENCE, 6
s. is golden PROVERBS, 368
S. is the best tactic ROCHEFOUCAULD, 11; SILENCE, 10
S. is the perfectest herald of joy SHAKESPEARE, 270; SILENCE, 12
S. is the...perfect expression of scorn SHAW, G, 6; SILENCE, 13
s. sank /Like music COLERIDGE, S, 37; SILENCE, 3
Sorrow and s. are strong ENDURANCE, 11; LONGFELLOW, H, 6
That man's s. is wonderful to listen to HARDY, T, 12; SILENCE, 7
The cruellest lies are...told in s. SILENCE, 15; STEVENSON, R, 15
The dust and s. of the upper shelf MACAULAY, T, 6; NEGLECT, 3
the impression that their normal condition is s. SARTRE, J, 13; SILENCE, 11
the more absolute s. of America ENGLAND, 30; LAWRENCE, D, 24
the rest is s. DEATH, 141; SHAKESPEARE, 109
the s. of astounded souls PLATH, S, 2
With s. and tears BYRON, 44; SEPARATION, 2
silences There are two s. PINTER, H, 7
silent burst /Into that s. sea COLERIDGE, S, 28; EXPLORATION, 1
His thoughts...lay s. THINKING, 11
the great s. majority MAJORITY, 7; NIXON, R, 7
the man who can be s. in several languages DIPLOMACY, 15
thereon one must remain s. SILENCE, 17
The 't' is s. – as in 'Harlow' INSULTS, 7
silicon If s. had been a gas SCIENCE, 98
silk rustling in unpaid-for s. CONTENTMENT, 9; SHAKESPEARE, 61
s., too often hides eczema CAMUS, A, 5; STYLE, 2
the s. stockings and white bosoms...excite my amorous propensities JOHNSON, S, 46
silks Whenas in s. my Julia goes CLOTHES, 13; HERRICK, R, 7
silly A s. remark can be made in Latin CERVANTES, M, 3
it's lovely to be s. at the right moment FOOLISHNESS, 14; HORACE, 44
S. Billy INSULTS, 60
some damned s. thing in the Balkans WAR, 22
You s. twisted boy MILLIGAN, S, 7
silver First of...Georgian s. goes POLITICS, 72
for a handful of s. BETRAYAL, 5; BROWNING, R, 31
no s. linings without a cloud OPTIMISM, 22
s. and gold have I none BIBLE, 4
S. buckles on his knee NURSERY RHYMES, 5
S. threads among the gold OLD AGE, 81
Their idols are s. and gold PSALMS, 64
The s. apples of the moon DESIRE, 18; YEATS, W, 30
thirty pieces of s. BETRAYAL, 4; BIBLE, 429
When every...thing you hold /Is made of s., or of gold GILBERT, W, 5
silvery the s. adamant walls of life's exclusive city LAWRENCE, D, 10
Silvia Who is S.? What is she SHAKESPEARE, 350
Simon Simple S. met a pieman NURSERY RHYMES, 51
simple A s. race POETS, 10; SCOTT, W, 6
Everything should be made as s. as possible SCIENCE, 38
My first film will be a very s. one CINEMA, 32
short and s. annals of the poor GRAY, T, 2; POVERTY, 16
Teach us delight in s. things GOOD, 8; KIPLING, R, 6
simpleton The revolutionary s. LEWIS, W, 6
simpletons The world is so full of s. and madmen MADNESS, 18
simplicity football...the s. of its laws FOOTBALL, 5
O holy s. EXECUTION, 17
s. a child POPE, A, 18
s. of her approach to...fashion CHANEL, C, 1
simplify ability to s. means SIMPLICITY, 2
S., simplify SIMPLICITY, 8; THOREAU, H, 16
simplifying s. something by destroying nearly everything CHESTERTON, G, 5; CIVILIZATION, 4
Simpson Mrs S.'s pinched our king ROYALTY, 18
sin A branch of the s. of drunkenness DRUNKENNESS, 19
All s. tends to be addictive AUDEN, W, 5; SIN, 2
a more dreadful record of s. than...countryside DOYLE, A, 8; SIN, 13
A private s. is not so prejudicial CERVANTES, M, 21; SIN, 11
Be a sinner and s. strongly FAITH, 20
beauty is only s. deep BEAUTY, 39; SAKI, 21
Being seventy is not a s. MEIR, G, 5; OLD AGE, 71
disease is the result of s. MEDICINE, 76
Don't tell my mother I'm living in s. SIN, 17
fall into no s. BOOK OF COMMON PRAYER, 18
Fashions in s. change SIN, 16
go, and s. no more BIBLE, 252
He that is without s. among you MISQUOTATIONS, 8
he that is without s....let him first cast a stone BIBLE, 251; SIN, 4
if we say that we have no s., we deceive BIBLE, 281; SIN, 5
it is no s. to s. in secret MORALITY, 11
my s. is ever before me PSALMS, 30
nicest boy who ever committed the s. of whisky ALCOHOL, 77; SPARK, M, 5
no s. but to be rich HYPOCRISY, 20; SHAKESPEARE, 164
no s. except stupidity STUPIDITY, 15; WILDE, O, 14
orders men to triumph over s....But...'Thou mayest'...that gives a choice STEINBECK, J, 1
people who can s. with a grin SIN, 21
Sickness, s. and death...do not originate in God EDDY, M, 4; RELIGION, 37
S. brought death DEATH, 60; EDDY, M, 3; SIN, 15
s. no more, lest a worse thing come unto thee BIBLE, 247
S....not only ugly but passé SIN, 19
than that one soul...should commit one single venial s. SIN, 22
They are written as if s. were to be taken out...by...sleep SERMONS, 2; SMITH, S, 3

Wealth covers s. WEALTH, 29
which taketh away the s. of the world BIBLE, 240; CHRISTIANITY, 15
your s. will find you out BIBLE, 439; SIN, 7
Sinai S. was...on a smoke BIBLE, 114
Sinatra that's for S. POPULAR MUSIC, 2
sincere for the moment, so absolutely s. ROOSEVELT, T, 1
Some of the worst men in the world are s. SINCERITY, 3
sincerest Imitation...s. of flattery IMITATION, 2
sincerity A little s. is a dangerous thing SINCERITY, 6; WILDE, O, 12
style, not s., is the vital thing STYLE, 11; WILDE, O, 31
sinecure a widow...is a kind of s. EXPEDIENCY, 8
sinews Stiffen the s. SHAKESPEARE, 130
sing Can't act. Can't s. ACTING, 3; ACTORS, 11
Did certain persons die before they s. COLERIDGE, S, 12; SINGERS, 1
I will s. of the sun POUND, E, 9; WOMEN, 110
O come, let us s. unto the Lord PSALMS, 54
s. the Lord's song in a strange land PSALMS, 70
The Welsh...just s. WAUGH, E, 17; WELSH, 4
singed s. the Spanish king's beard WAR, 59
singing nightingales are s. near ELIOT, T, 23
s. in the rain WEATHER, 11
To hear the lark...s..../From his watch-tower in the skies MILTON, J, 17
when you shit? S., it's the same thing SINGING, 1
single a s. man...must be in want of a wife AUSTEN, J, 18; MARRIAGE, 11
begins with a s. step BEGINNING, 1
Behold her, s. in the field SOLITUDE, 18; WORDSWORTH, W, 51
Living s. LONELINESS, 13
singular Ball...how very s. NAMES, 1
sink The s. is the great symbol of...family life FAMILY, 40; NEUROSIS, 9
sinn'd More s. against than sinning INJUSTICE, 10; SHAKESPEARE, 180
sinned father, I have s. against heaven BIBLE, 331
sinner one s. that repenteth BIBLE, 330; REGRET, 5
sinners At such an hour the s. are still in bed RUNYON, D, 6; SIN, 23
breeder of s. SHAKESPEARE, 93
Christ Jesus came into the world to save s. BIBLE, 506
Get thee to a nunnery: why wouldst thou be a breeder of s. HUMAN NATURE, 27
It's your combination s....who dishonour the vices VICE, 16; WILDER, T, 3
the way of s. PSALMS, 1
sinning I delight in s. SIN, 24
nothing so artificial as s. nowadays LAWRENCE, D, 26; SIN, 18
sins atone for the s. of your fathers HORACE, 36; INJUSTICE, 6
bloody old s. washed white SASSOON, S, 6
from Expensive S. refrain DRYDEN, J, 10; SIN, 14
gravest s. it was possible for a gentlewoman to commit READING, 18; WAUGH, E, 48
her s., which are many, are forgiven SIN, 6
hide a multitude of s. BIBLE, 220
His s. were scarlet BELLOC, H, 14; BOOKS, 7; PUNS, 1
must not reheat his s. for breakfast FORGIVENESS, 3
One of the unpardonable s.... is...to go about unlabelled CLASSIFICATION, 1; HUXLEY, T, 4
shed...for the remission of s. BIBLE, 424; CHRISTIANITY, 29
though your s. be as scarlet BIBLE, 191
to read a novel before luncheon was one of the gravest s. WAUGH, E, 48
truly and earnestly repent you of your s. BOOK OF COMMON PRAYER, 10
Sion the Lord loveth the gates of S. PSALMS, 47
we remembered thee, O S. PSALMS, 70
Sir I am S. Oracle EGOTISM, 8; SHAKESPEARE, 238
Sirens Blest pair of S. MILTON, J, 9; POETRY, 42
Sisera the stars...fought against S. BIBLE, 292
sister I kissed her little s. UNFAITHFULNESS, 6
no friend like a s. FAMILY, 51; ROSSETTI, C, 2
sisters And so do his s. FAMILY, 25; GILBERT, W, 10
little s. to all the world WOMEN, 46
O! men with s. dear HOOD, T, 11; WOMEN, 66
sit I will s. down now PROPHECY, 4
men s. and hear each other groan HUMAN CONDITION, 14; KEATS, J, 38
nobody can tell you when to s. down EISENHOWER, D, 6
say what you have to say, and then s. down SPEECHES, 12; WELLINGTON, 25
So I did s. and eat HERBERT, G, 7; LOVE, 85
Though I s. down now DISRAELI, B, 20
sitting Are you s. comfortably? Then I'll begin BEGINNING, 15
by s. down round you WELLINGTON, 14
I do most of my work s. down HUMOUR, 39
situation s. excellent. I shall attack WAR, 62
six Candidates should not attempt more than s. BELLOC, H, 22; BIBLE, 524
S. for the s. proud walkers ANONYMOUS, 45; NUMBERS, 1
S. geese a-laying CHRISTMAS, 18; NURSERY RHYMES, 59
s. of one and half-a-dozen of the other SIMILARITY, 5
two and two do not make s. LAST WORDS, 90; TOLSTOY, L, 16
sixpence He found a crooked s. against a crooked stile NURSERY RHYMES, 56
I love s., jolly little s. NURSERY RHYMES, 22
Sing a song of s. NURSERY RHYMES, 52
sixpences there go two-and-forty s....to one guinea JOHNSON, S, 34; MERIT, 4
sixth Money is like a s. sense MAUGHAM, W, 13; MONEY, 35
sixty at the rate of s. minutes an hour LEWIS, C, 5; TIME, 32
close-up of a woman past s. APPEARANCE, 6
Men come of age at s. AGE, 90
S. HORSES WEDGED IN A /CHIMNEY JOURNALISM, 26
sixty-five drinking it for s. years and I am not dead DRINKS, 22; VOLTAIRE, 35
sixty-four That's the s. thousand dollar question TELEVISION, 1
When I'm s. AGE, 57
sixty-three Sexual intercourse began /In nineteen s. SEX, 63
size I am not this s., really CHESTERTON, G, 47
skating s. over thin ice EMERSON, R, 13
skeleton Every family has a s. in the cupboard PROVERBS, 135
ski unbecoming for a cardinal to s. badly JOHN PAUL II, 1
skied s. down Mount Everest in the nude LOVE, 115
skies looks commercing with the s. MILTON, J, 12; SOUL, 11
look up at the s. STARS, 4
skill if greater want of s. POPE, A, 20
In arguing too, the parson own'd his s. GOLDSMITH, O, 7; KNOWLEDGE, 20
S. without imagination is craftsmanship ART, 34; STOPPARD, T, 1
Wonderful is the s. of a physician REMEDIES, 57
skin I've Got You Under My S. LOVE, 127; PORTER, C, 2
my s. bristles so that the razor ceases to act POETRY, 30
never...sell the bear's s. ANTICIPATION, 6; LA FONTAINE, J, 7
There is more than one way to s. a cat DIFFERENCE, 4; PROVERBS, 409
Woollen clothing keeps the s. healthy CLOTHES, 1
skinning When you are s. your customers BUSINESS, 19; KHRUSHCHEV, N, 2
skins beauty of their s. SEXES, 29; TENNYSON, 65
Like the s. of some small mammal APPEARANCE, 9
skipper s. had taken his little daughter BOATS, 12; LONGFELLOW, H, 19
skirt a woman...ought to lay aside...modesty with her s. MONTAIGNE, M, 4; SEX, 85
skittles Life isn't all beer and s. LIFE, 51
skull Idiot wind, blowing like a circle around my s. DYLAN, B, 5
skunk what a guilty s. she made me feel GUILT, 10
sky a Friend for little children /Above the bright blue s. GOD, 37
inverted Bowl we call The S. DESTINY, 9; FITZGERALD, E, 15
pie in the s. when you die AFTERLIFE, 5; HEAVEN, 5; MATERIALISM, 3
Which prisoners call the s. IMPRISONMENT, 14; WILDE, O, 4
Skye Over the sea to S. ROYALTY, 27
slack a man becomes s. and selfish MARRIAGE, 149; STEVENSON, R, 24
slain Saul hath s. his thousands BIBLE, 481
there are fifty thousand men s....and not one Englishman DIPLOMACY, 30
slamming little girls...s. doors BELLOC, H, 11; CHILDREN, 11
slander it is always said of s. that something always sticks BACON, F, 4; PRAISE, 3
slang All s. is metaphor CHESTERTON, G, 11; LANGUAGE, 16
The one...poetry...continually flowing is s. CHESTERTON, G, 10; LANGUAGE, 15
slapped anyone who s. us...would get his head kicked off KHRUSHCHEV, N, 1; REVENGE, 14
slaughter as a lamb to the s. BIBLE, 214

slave Be not the s. of Words CARLYLE, T, 24; WORDS, 5
came to America in s. ships EQUALITY, 16
commerce between master and s. is...exercise of... boisterous passions JEFFERSON, T, 3; SLAVERY, 6
man...is Reason's s. CONNOLLY, C, 20; PASSION, 2
s. for livelihood ENVY, 3
The s. begins by demanding justice SUPERIORITY, 3
slavery Emancipate yourselves from mental s. FREEDOM, 39
Freedom is S. ORWELL, G, 18
the English legal system will not support...professional s. EXPLOITATION, 3
The prolonged s. of women FEMINISM, 32
slaves if God had wanted to create s. SLAVERY, 1
In a consumer society there are...two kinds of s. MATERIALISM, 14
love, an...intercourse between tyrants and s. GOLDSMITH, O, 14; LOVE AND FRIENDSHIP, 4
Practical men...are usually the s. of some defunct economist INFLUENCE, 6; KEYNES, J, 7
S. cannot breathe in England COWPER, W, 29; SLAVERY, 4
that the masters willingly concede to s. CAMUS, A, 12; SLAVERY, 2
slaying the s. of a beautiful hypothesis by an ugly fact HUXLEY, T, 1
slays moves, and mates, and s. FITZGERALD, E, 13
sleave ravell'd s. of care SHAKESPEARE, 214; SLEEP, 29
sleek you will come and find me fat and s. HORACE, 18
sleep A good laugh and a long s. are the best cures LAUGHTER, 4
amount of s. required SLEEP, 22
A professor is one who talks in someone else's s. AUDEN, W, 29
Better s. with a sober cannibal than a drunken Christian DRUNKENNESS, 21
Can s. so soundly as the wretched slave RESPONSIBILITY, 15
haven't been to s. for over a year SLEEP, 37; WAUGH, E, 21
How do people go to s. PARKER, D, 6; SLEEP, 25
I have come to the borders of s. SLEEP, 33
Let me s. the s. of the earth SOLITUDE, 16
Let us s. now OWEN, W, 7
Now I lay me down to s. ANONYMOUS, 64; SLEEP, 4
Our birth is but a s. METAPHYSICS, 5; WORDSWORTH, W, 26
our little life /Is rounded with a s. SHAKESPEARE, 327
S. and watchfulness...when immoderate, constitute disease SLEEP, 17
s. begins for weary /mortals SLEEP, 35; VIRGIL, 10
S. is better than medicine SLEEP, 2
S. is good, death is better HEINE, H, 2; PESSIMISM, 6
S. is gross SLEEP, 16
S. is that golden chaine that ties health and our bodies together SLEEP, 11
s. is the condition to produce it SLEEP, 12
S. is when all the unsorted stuff comes flying out SLEEP, 15
s.! it is a gentle thing COLERIDGE, S, 34; SLEEP, 9
S....knows not Death SLEEP, 32; TENNYSON, 32
S. that knits up the ravell'd sleave SHAKESPEARE, 214; SLEEP, 29
s. with a boy...old girlfriends AIDS, 7; PROMISCUITY, 1
That sweet, deep s., so close to tranquil death SLEEP, 36
The amount of s. required by the average person SLEEP, 5
The beginning of health is s. SLEEP, 3
The past was a s. BEGINNING, 7; BROWNING, R, 56
they are even as a s. PSALMS, 49
They are written as if sin were to be taken out...by...s. SERMONS, 2; SMITH, S, 3
To s., perchance to dream SHAKESPEARE, 90; SUICIDE, 35
we must s. REST, 2; SHAKESPEARE, 35
youth would s. out the rest SHAKESPEARE, 352; YOUTH, 28
sleepin' Capten, art tha s. there below NEWBOLT, H, 3; WAR, 120
sleeping Everybody is s. with everybody else POPULAR MUSIC, 16
fuss about s. together...sooner go to my dentist SEX, 124; WAUGH, E, 47
Let s. dogs lie PROVERBS, 255; TACT, 2
like s. with someone else's wife BRADBURY, M, 6; UNFAITHFULNESS, 3
S. as quiet as death OLD AGE, 102; THOMAS, D, 21
There will be s. enough DEATH, 15; PROVERBS, 422
we have only awakened a s. giant WORLD WAR II, 50
sleeps eats, s. and watches the television GREER, G, 3; WOMAN'S ROLE, 6
She s. alone at last EPITAPHS, 1
S. the only medicine that gives ease SLEEP, 30

sleepwalker that Providence dictates with the assurance of a s. DESTINY, 14; HITLER, A, 15
sleepy Come, let's to bed /Says S.-head NURSERY RHYMES, 7
sleeve let the last man...brush the Channel with his s. WAR, 151
slepe S. is the nouryshment SLEEP, 26
slept David s. with his fathers BIBLE, 297
Splendid couple – s. with both MARRIAGE, 34
slick make my life as s. as a sonnet BANKHEAD, T, 4; OBSESSIONS, 1
slides buttered s. to hell SANTAYANA, G, 1
Slightly Forty years ago he was S. in Peter Pan INSULTS, 124
slimy thousand thousand s. things COLERIDGE, S, 32; GUILT, 6
sling his s. was in his hand BIBLE, 480
slings s. and arrows of outrageous fortune SHAKESPEARE, 90; SUICIDE, 35
slip he gave us all the s. ABSENCE, 5; BROWNING, R, 58
There's many a s. ALCOHOL, 6; PROVERBS, 415
slipped I have only s. away into the next room AFTERLIFE, 6; DEATH, 81
slippers Same old s. MARRIAGE, 98
slipping Time is s. underneath FITZGERALD, E, 12; TIME, 22
slitty If you stay much longer you will go back with s. eyes RACISM, 25
slob just a lucky s. from Ohio ACTORS, 17
slogan democracy is just a s. DEMOCRACY, 8; GORBACHOV, M, 5
slogans If you feed people just with revolutionary s. KHRUSHCHEV, N, 8
slough the s. was Despond BUNYAN, J, 2; DESPAIR, 3
Slough Come, friendly bombs, and fall on S. BETJEMAN, J, 11
slow I am s. of study SHAKESPEARE, 261
On a s. boat to China BOATS, 11
S. and steady wins the race HASTE, 7
S. but sure PERSISTENCE, 3; PROVERBS, 363
s. to wrath BIBLE, 217
Tarry a while, says S. NURSERY RHYMES, 7
too swift arrives as tardy as too s. SHAKESPEARE, 316
with a s. deliberate carelessness LAWRENCE, T, 10; READING, 10
slug-horn the s. to my lips I set BROWNING, R, 18; SUMMONS, 4
slum if you've seen one city s. POVERTY, 4
slumber A s. did my spirit seal IMMORTALITY, 9; WORDSWORTH, W, 50
Love itself shall s. on MEMORY, 22
Oft in the stilly night, /Ere S.'s chain MOORE, T, 7; NOSTALGIA, 17
slumber'd s. here While these visions did appear SHAKESPEARE, 267
slumbers Golden s. kiss your eyes SLEEP, 10
slush pure as the driven s. BANKHEAD, T, 10; PURITY, 2
smack much more indecent...than a good s. LAWRENCE, D, 7; PUNISHMENT, 20
small Errors look so very ugly in persons of s. means ELIOT, G, 7; POVERTY AND WEALTH, 6
From s. beginnings BEGINNING, 3; PROVERBS, 168
In Western Europe there are now only s. countries EUROPE, 15
It's a s. world PROVERBS, 232
Microbe is so very s. BELLOC, H, 17; SMALLNESS, 2
Popularity?...glory's s. change POPULARITY, 4
S. is beautiful BEAUTY, 5; CONSERVATION, 11; PROVERBS, 364
The best things come in s. parcels PROVERBS, 379; SMALLNESS, 1
virtue's still far too s. COLETTE, S, 3; VIRTUE, 12
smaller accepts a s. as a favour CARLYLE, J, 1
someone s. than oneself LA FONTAINE, J, 3
these have s. fleas to bite 'em PARASITES, 3; SWIFT, J, 9
small-talking Where in this s. world FRY, C, 4; MEANING, 4
smart you had better be too s. to get ill ILLNESS, 5
smartness the s. of an attorney's clerk DISRAELI, B, 33; INSULTS, 43
smarts No creature s....as a fool FOOLISHNESS, 17; POPE, A, 17
smattering A s. of everything DICKENS, C, 55; KNOWLEDGE, 15
smell rose...would s. as sweet NAMES, 7; SHAKESPEARE, 312
Sweet S. of Success SUCCESS, 17
their s. brings on my migraine CLASS, 7
smells O! my offence is rank, it s. to heaven GUILT, 14
the only dead thing that s. sweet PAST, 11
smile A dear old man with his...somewhat toothless s. GANDHI, M, 1
a pleasant s. that it seems rather divine than human LEONARDO DA VINCI, 4
a s. I could feel in my hip pocket SEX, 26
a s. like a razor-blade INSULTS, 110

A s. that floated without support APPEARANCE, 57
A s. that snapped back after using APPEARANCE, 38
Cambridge people rarely s. CAMBRIDGE, 2; PLACES, 7
nice s., but…iron teeth POLITICIANS, 89
Oh, good gigantic s. BROWNING, R, 29
s. at perils past PAST, 10; SCOTT, W, 3
S. at us, pay us, pass us CHESTERTON, G, 38; ENGLISH, 13
s. of a woman…dined off her husband ANALOGY, 3
s., s., s. OPTIMISM, 13
the vain tribute of a s. POETS, 10; SCOTT, W, 6
Under the s. of safety HYPOCRISY, 19

smiled He s. bunching his fat cheeks APPEARANCE, 72
the soldiers he s. at SASSOON, S, 4; WAR, 148

smiles A Scout s. and whistles OPTIMISM, 15
She is Venus when she s. COMPLIMENTS, 15; JONSON, B, 13
s., /Wan as primroses FLOWERS, 6; KEATS, J, 8
The s., the tears, /Of boyhood's years MOORE, T, 7; NOSTALGIA, 17

smiling O villain, villain, s., damned villain HYPOCRISY, 17
S. encouragement APPEARANCE, 45

smite whosoever shall s. thee on thy right cheek BIBLE, 364; ENEMIES, 2

Smith Chuck it, S. CHESTERTON, G, 6; RELIGION, 28
if…it's only wind, I'll call it F. E. S. APPEARANCE, 31
The s., a mighty man is he LONGFELLOW, H, 17; OCCUPATIONS, 16

smoke A woman is only a woman, but a good cigar is a s. SMOKING, 21
Don't screw around, and don't s. HEALTH AND HEALTHY LIVING, 5
I have seen many a man turn his gold into s. SMOKING, 11
I s. almost constantly LONGEVITY, 14
no woman should marry…a man who does not s. STEVENSON, R, 22
resembling the horrible Stygian s. of the pit SMOKING, 16
Sinai was…on a s. BIBLE, 114
S., my friend SMOKING, 29
s. of their foul dens /Broodeth on Thy Earth ENGLAND, 8
There's no s. without fire GOSSIP, 5; PROVERBS, 418

smokers S., male and female, inject and excuse idleness SMOKING, 9

smoking he had read of the effects of s. SMOKING, 30
resolve to give up s., drinking and loving ABSTINENCE, 5
s. at such a rate LAMB, C, 22; SMOKING, 24
s. can play a valuable role in a society SMOKING, 26
s. cigars and…drinking of alcohol before, after, and… during CHURCHILL, W, 24
S.…is a shocking thing SMOKING, 17
s. is one of the leading causes of statistics SMOKING, 22
the beginning of the s. era SMOKING, 4
To cease s. is the easiest thing I ever did TWAIN, M, 21
What a blessing this s. is SMOKING, 14
why he doesn't stop s. SMOKING, 31

smooth course of true love never did run s. LOVE, 146; SHAKESPEARE, 259
many cities had rubbed him s. GREENE, G, 4; TRAVEL, 18

smote I took by the throat…And s. him thus REVENGE, 17
they s. the city with the edge of the sword BIBLE, 291

Smudges wasn't it naughty of S. BETJEMAN, J, 8

smyler The s. with the knyf CHAUCER, G, 13; HYPOCRISY, 9

snail said a whiting to a s. CARROLL, L, 16; HASTE, 5
s.'s on the thorn BROWNING, R, 45; PERFECTION, 3

snails Frogs and s. /And puppy-dogs' tails NURSERY RHYMES, 69

snake A s. came to my water-trough LAWRENCE, D, 28; WEATHER, 15
There's a s. hidden in the grass DANGER, 7; VIRGIL, 17

snapper-up s. of unconsidered trifles BUSINESS, 28; SHAKESPEARE, 354

snare a s. in which…women have always become readily entangled FEMINISM, 1; WOMEN, 7
the s. of the hunter PSALMS, 51

snares s. of death compassed me round PSALMS, 65

Snark For the S. *was* a Boojum CARROLL, L, 22; NONSENSE, 6

snatch make us love your goodly gifts /And s. them SHAKESPEARE, 293

sneezed Not to be s. at IMPORTANCE, 3
when a British Prime Minister s. BRITAIN, 13

snipe well-shot woodcock, partridge, s. BETJEMAN, J, 4

snob He who meanly admires…is a S. SNOBBERY, 9; THACKERAY, W, 1
impossible, in our condition of society, not to be sometimes a S. SNOBBERY, 10; THACKERAY, W, 2
Indian s. reasons, like calling an English person by his Christian name SCOTT, P, 3
Mr. Waugh…is…a s. in search of a class WAUGH, E, 2
no s. welcomes another SNOBBERY, 2

snobbery that school of S. with Violence WRITING, 6

snobbish Don't be s., we seek to abolish CLASS, 25
He was… s., sentimental and vain WILDE, O, 3

snobs His hatred of s. PROUST, M, 12; SNOBBERY, 6

snoot I'd punch him in the s. ROYALTY, 111

snore s. and you sleep alone BURGESS, A, 3; SLEEP, 8
snorer can't hear himself s. SLEEP, 34; TWAIN, M, 16

snotgreen The s. sea JOYCE, J, 10; SEA, 7

snow both its national products, s. and chocolate, melt SWITZERLAND, 1
I used to be S. White PURITY, 6
Like an army defeated /The s. hath retreated WORDSWORTH, W, 78
S. had fallen, s. on s. ROSSETTI, C, 3
the s. blind twilight ferries THOMAS, D, 29
The s. hath retreated SEASONS, 28
the wrong kind of s. WEATHER, 28
wish a s. in May SHAKESPEARE, 197; SUITABILITY, 4

snows the s. of yesteryear NOSTALGIA, 27

Snow White I used to be S. WEST, M, 13

snub Vile s.-nose, flat-nosed ass APPEARANCE, 58
weapon is the s. GANDHI, I, 1

snuff time for me to enjoy another pinch of s. EXECUTION, 2

snug s. /As a bug /In a rug FRANKLIN, B, 14

so It is s.. It is not s. FRANKLIN, B, 10

soap S. and education…are more deadly EDUCATION, 91; TWAIN, M, 5

soapboxes They keep getting up on s. FEMINISM, 19

soar to run, though not to s. CRITICISM, 39; MACAULAY, T, 2

sobbing Lying alone and s. SORROW, 18

sober a s. colouring from an eye WORDSWORTH, W, 33
as s. as a Judge DRUNKENNESS, 15; FIELDING, H, 5
Better sleep with a s. cannibal than a drunken Christian DRUNKENNESS, 21
England should be compulsorily s. FREEDOM, 36
he that will go to bed s. ALCOHOL, 34
How do you look when I'm s. CLOTHES, 16
'My mother, drunk or s..' CHESTERTON, G, 8; PATRIOTISM, 8
one sees in Garbo s. COMPLIMENTS, 36; TYNAN, K, 6
sedate, s., silent, serious, sad-coloured sect HOOD, T, 1; RELIGION, 53
Tomorrow we'll be s. ANONYMOUS, 12; DRUNKENNESS, 3

soccer s. is a grey game FOOTBALL, 12

sociable I am a s. worker BEHAN, B, 5; SOCIETY, 2
Society is no comfort to one not s. SHAKESPEARE, 62; SOCIETY, 19

social a great s. and economic experiment ALCOHOL, 39
At s. gatherings he was liable to engage in…arguments OBITUARIES, 8
Beauty is a s. necessity BEAUTY, 23
Man is a s. animal SOCIETY, 21
our s. spheres have been widely different WILDE, O, 29
recognition whatsoever of the s. revolution SOCIETY, 6
the things which government does…s. progress GOVERNMENT, 42
the…world was stumbling…in s. blindness BLINDNESS, 6
true self-love and s. are the same POPE, A, 36; SELF-KNOWLEDGE, 6

socialising I'm not very good at ordinary s. WRITERS, 4

socialism as clear as a crystal…German National S. NAZISM, 3
Communism is in fact the completion of S. COMMUNISM, 12
Marxian S. must always remain a portent KEYNES, J, 3; MARXISM, 6
one word…to identify modern s., it was 'Science' SOCIALISM, 26
Only s. would put up with it SOCIALISM, 10
religion of S. BEVAN, A, 2; SOCIALISM, 3
restating our s. in terms of the scientific revolution SOCIALISM, 25; WILSON, H, 8
S.…age or a little money will not cure SOCIALISM, 8
s.…alien to the British character SOCIALISM, 24; THATCHER, M, 27
s.…as a whole is threatened SOCIALISM, 5
S. can only arrive by bicycle SOCIALISM, 9
S.…the conquest of the…economy SOCIALISM, 4
S. with a human face COMMUNISM, 4; SOCIALISM, 7
S. would put up with it GORBACHOV, M, 14

the proletariat will…wage a class struggle for S. LENIN, V, 6
the worst advertisement for S. is its adherents ORWELL, G, 27
to banish…the dark divisive clouds of Marxist s. MARXISM, 16; THATCHER, M, 30
To the ordinary working man…S. ORWELL, G, 28; SOCIALISM, 20
Under s. *all* will govern LENIN, V, 5; SOCIALISM, 17
unites s. with democracy SOCIALISM, 12
socialist construct the s. order SOCIALISM, 16
I am a s.…wish the Labour Party was SOCIALISM, 22
socialists For s., going to bed with the Liberals is POLITICS, 125
intelligent people…are s. SOCIALISM, 1
S. treat their servants with respect POLITICS, 103; STOPPARD, T, 3
We are all S. now SOCIALISM, 13
what are you s. going to do about me SOCIALISM, 11
social science dark mass of s. BRADBURY, M, 5
societies range of human s. in time, the other in space MANKIND, 35
society a free s.…where it is safe to be unpopular FREEDOM, 56
a poor s. cannot be too poor POVERTY AND WEALTH, 9
A s.…of individuals…capable of original thought IDEAS, 9; MENCKEN, H, 11
Comedy, we may say, is s. HUMOUR, 25; PRIESTLEY, J, 1
great s.…men are more concerned with the quality of their goods SOCIETY, 14
if it be our clothes alone which fit us for s. CLOTHES, 9
impossible, in our condition of s., not to be sometimes a Snob SNOBBERY, 10; THACKERAY, W, 2
In a consumer s. there are…two kinds of slaves MATERIALISM, 14
it proved that I was in a civilized s. EXECUTION, 28
Mankind is a closed s. MANKIND, 55
Man was formed for s. BLACKSTONE, W, 1; SOCIETY, 3
nation is a s. united by a delusion about its ancestry INGE, W, 10
Never speak disrespectfully of S. SNOBBERY, 14; WILDE, O, 33
no intellectual s. can flourish where a Jew feels…uneasy JEWS, 10
no new baby in the womb of our s. LAWRENCE, D, 37; RUSSIA, 11
nothing to distinguish human s. from the farm-yard MANKIND, 60; SHAW, G, 12
only possible s. is oneself MISANTHROPY, 5; WILDE, O, 18
Operacy is what keeps s. going EDUCATION, 16
S., being codified by man SOCIETY, 5
S., friendship, and love COWPER, W, 33; SOLITUDE, 4
S. goes on and on and on IDEAS, 7
S. is no comfort /To one not sociable SHAKESPEARE, 62; SOCIETY, 19
S. is now one polish'd horde BORES, 2; BYRON, 34
s.…pays a harlot 25 times as much as it pays its Prime Minister WILSON, H, 7
s., where none intrudes BYRON, 16; NATURE, 3
so famous, that it would permit me…to break wind in s. BALZAC, H, 5; FAME, 5
The history of all…s. is the history of class struggles MARX, K, 1
the ideal of a democratic and free s. RACISM, 22
the opportunity to move…upward to the Great S. CIVILIZATION, 8
There are two classes in good s. CLASS, 40
There is no such thing as S. THATCHER, M, 36
The sick man is a parasite of s. PATIENTS, 3
the transition from the…'closed s.'…to the 'open s.' SOCIETY, 17
to change s. and to define its finer values POLITICS, 10
transform this s. without a major extension of public ownership KINNOCK, N, 1; SOCIALISM, 15
Women…the real architects of s. SOCIETY, 22
sociology Children…detest s. BOOKS, 44
The technology of medicine has outrun its s. TECHNOLOGY, 15
sockets The candles burn their s. HOUSMAN, A, 4
socks His s. compelled one's attention CLOTHES, 21; SAKI, 11
sod off I don't want you here – now s. INSULTS, 2
Sodom S. and…Gomorrah BIBLE, 167; PUNISHMENT, 5
the men of S. were wicked BIBLE, 166; HOMOSEXUALITY, 4
sodomite s. had been a temporary aberration HOMOSEXUALITY, 12
sodomy Comedy, like s., is an unnatural act HUMOUR, 14
rum, s., and the lash CHURCHILL, W, 34
sofa rather lie on a s. than sweep beneath it LAZINESS, 3
soft I'm not hard – I'm frightfully s. CHARACTER, 23; THATCHER, M, 15
our love…of the mind does not make us s. RESULTS, 4
soft drink someone asks for a s.…think he is a wimp DRINKS, 11
softened subjects are s. and sentimentalised too much ARTISTS, 17
solar the whole s. and stellar systems CARLYLE, T, 30; COMFORT, 2
sold never hate a song that has s. half a million copies POPULAR MUSIC, 4
soldier a chocolate cream s. SHAW, G, 5; SOLDIERS, 14
A S. of the Great War KIPLING, R, 34
Ben Battle was a s. bold HOOD, T, 2; PUNS, 10
Every French s. carries in his cartridge-pouch SOLDIERS, 8
I never expect a s. to think SHAW, G, 10; SOLDIERS, 15
in the s. is flat blasphemy SHAKESPEARE, 231
strength and majesty the British s. fights SOLDIERS, 7
The s.'s body…a stock of accessories SOLDIERS, 11
The summer s. and the sunshine patriot COWARDICE, 7
Tinker, /Tailor, /S., /Sailor NURSERY RHYMES, 64; OCCUPATIONS, 21
soldiers Dear comrades, s., sailors and workers RUSSIAN REVOLUTION, 5
English s. fight like lions OFFICERS, 8
Old s. never die OCCUPATIONS, 4; PROVERBS, 323
S. are citizens of death's grey land SASSOON, S, 3; SOLDIERS, 12
when staring at our s. drilling in Berlin ENGLAND, 36
soliciting supernatural s. SHAKESPEARE, 204
Solidarity S. was born…when the shipyard strike evolved WAŁESA, L, 2
solitary heard among the s. hills /Low breathings WORDSWORTH, W, 37
He lived the life of a s. NEWTON, I, 1
Life is for each man a s. cell LIFE, 72
Man is not a s. animal MANKIND, 51; RUSSELL, B, 11; SOCIETY, 18
solitude In s. alone can he know true freedom MONTAIGNE, M, 2; SOLITUDE, 13
In s. /What happiness MILTON, J, 49; SOLITUDE, 11
self-sufficing power of S. WORDSWORTH, W, 39
so companionable as s. SOLITUDE, 15; THOREAU, H, 14
S. and melancholy CARTER, A, 4
S. is the playfield of Satan SOLITUDE, 14
s.! where are the charms COWPER, W, 34; SOLITUDE, 5
the bliss of s. SOLITUDE, 17; WORDSWORTH, W, 9
the greatest misery of sickness is *s.* SOLITUDE, 6
Whosoever is delighted in s. BACON, F, 24; SOLITUDE, 1
Solomon S. Grundy, /Born on a Monday HUMAN CONDITION, 19; NURSERY RHYMES, 53
solution difficulty for every s. BUREAUCRACY, 6
Life itself is a mystery which defies s. LIFE, 69
The final s. FASCISM, 6; JEWS, 9
total s. of the Jewish question NAZISM, 2
sombrero the sunbonnet as well as the s. has helped COURAGE, 16
some I…may be s. time LAST WORDS, 63
s. more than others COWARD, N, 4; SIMILARITY, 4
You can fool s. of the people all the time DECEPTION, 4; LINCOLN, A, 18
somebody looking for the silence in s. PHOTOGRAPHY, 3
s. may be looking CONSCIENCE, 6; MENCKEN, H, 2
someone I wouldn't be…talking to s. like you SNOBBERY, 4
like sleeping with s. else's wife NEWSPAPERS, 5
Somerset corroboration…in the records of S. House HUMILITY, 12
something Everybody was up to s. COWARD, N, 9; INTRIGUE, 2
I too hope to become 's.' AMBITION, 11; FASCISM, 4
S. must be done UNEMPLOYMENT, 7
S. nasty in the woodshed EVIL, 11
Time for a little s. MILNE, A, 7
sometime Why don't you come up s. and see me WEST, M, 8
somewhat More than s. RUNYON, D, 3
somewhere 'Tis always morning s. BEGINNING, 12
son An only s., sir, might expect more indulgence GOLDSMITH, O, 16
I've examined your s.'s head, Mr Glum STUPIDITY, 12
O Absalom, my s. BIBLE, 485
the earth is free for every s. and daughter of mankind HUMAN RIGHTS, 8
the S. of man coming…with power BIBLE, 414; DOOMSDAY, 2
the S. of man hath not where to lay his head LIFE AND DEATH, 24

woman, behold thy s. BIBLE, 270
sonatas The s. of Mozart are unique MUSIC, 53
song I have a s. to sing O GILBERT, W, 44; SINGING, 2
the s. that is sung in our hearts MUSIC, 44
they shall not drink wine with a s. BIBLE, 206
thinks two notes a s. BIRDS, 2
Who loves not wine, woman and s. PLEASURE, 22
songs all our pretty s. IGNORANCE, 8
Sing no sad s. DEATH, 129; ROSSETTI, C, 8
The Lord holds copyright on all s. MUSIC, 23
Where are the s. of Spring KEATS, J, 46; SEASONS, 11
sonne soft was the s. SEASONS, 14
sonnet s. is a moment's monument ROSSETTI, D, 2
would make my life as slick as a s. BANKHEAD, T, 4
son-of-a-bitch The poor s. FITZGERALD, F, 2; PARKER, D, 14
sons I have a wife, I have s. FAMILY, 36
my four s. who cease not to persecute me CHILDREN, 33
Now we are all s. of bitches NUCLEAR WEAPONS, 3
S. of Belial had a Glorious Time DRYDEN, J, 11
soon day returns too s. BYRON, 42
sophisticated the only s. playwright England has produced CONGREVE, W, 1
sophistry it can contain nothing but s. and illusion HUME, D, 2
Universities incline wits to s. and affectation BACON, F, 65
sorcery false enchantments and s. ACCUSATION, 1
sores Lazarus…laid at his gate, full of s. BIBLE, 333
sorrow Down, thou climbing s. SHAKESPEARE, 176; SORROW, 28
in s. thou shalt bring forth children CHILDREN, 15; SEXES, 4
Its narrow measure spans /Tears of eternity, and s. HOUSMAN, A, 5
Much in s., oft in woe ENDURANCE, 30
One for s. BIRDS, 1; PROVERBS, 325; SUPERSTITION, 3
Parting is such sweet s. PARTING, 10; SHAKESPEARE, 314
Pure and complete s. is as impossible EMOTION, 6; TOLSTOY, L, 12
S. and silence are strong ENDURANCE, 11; LONGFELLOW, H, 6
S. is tranquillity remembered in emotion PARKER, D, 10; SORROW, 20
s. makes us wise SORROW, 32; TENNYSON, 36
Tears of eternity and s. SORROW, 13
the Lord…give thee joy for this thy s. BIBLE, 517
There is no greater s. SORROW, 9
Through the night of doubt and s. ENDURANCE, 5
sorrows few s.…in which a good income is of no avail MONEY, 48
When s. come, they come not single spies SHAKESPEARE, 102
sort that like that s. of place OXFORD, 13; SHAW, G, 22
Soudan to you, Fuzzy-Wuzzy, at your 'ome in the S. KIPLING, R, 11
soufflé can't make a s. rise twice FOOD, 48
sought Love s. is good LOVE, 154; SHAKESPEARE, 344
Pleasure is…seldom found where it is s. JOHNSON, S, 16; PLEASURE, 16
soul And never once possess our s. ARNOLD, M, 43; SOUL, 3
animated with the s. of a Briton VOLTAIRE, 2
Artists are not engineers of the s. ART, 15
a…s. like season'd timber HERBERT, G, 10; VIRTUE, 17
become a living s. DEATH, 184; WORDSWORTH, W, 12
company…have neither a s. to lose nor a body to kick BUSINESS, 31; SMITH, S, 5
education is a leading out of what is…in the pupil's s. EDUCATION, 88; SPARK, M, 11
Education is…the s. of a society CHESTERTON, G, 46; EDUCATION, 24
Fair seed-time had my s. SOUL, 13; WORDSWORTH, W, 36
he shall convert my s. PSALMS, 11
His s. is marching on MEMORIALS, 7
his s. is satisfied with what is assigned to him MARCUS AURELIUS ANTONINUS, 10
I am positive I have a s. SOUL, 12; STERNE, L, 3
I am the captain of my s. RESPONSIBILITY, 8
Impropriety is the s. of wit HUMOUR, 21; MAUGHAM, W, 9
In mystery our s. abides ARNOLD, M, 29; SOUL, 2
I pray the Lord my s. to keep ANONYMOUS, 64; SLEEP, 4
it must be inspired with s. MEDICINE, 58
Man has no Body distinct from his S. BLAKE, W, 31; SOUL, 4
Mr Lincoln's s. seems made of leather LINCOLN, A, 4
my s. doth magnify the Lord BIBLE, 309
my s. hath a desire PSALMS, 44
My s. in agony COLERIDGE, S, 31; SOLITUDE, 2
my s. is among lions PSALMS, 36
my s. is athirst for God PSALMS, 26
My s. is full of whispered song BLINDNESS, 5
my s. is white BLAKE, W, 48; RACISM, 5
my s.…should flee as a bird PSALMS, 4
Never mind about my s.…get my tie right JOYCE, J, 13; PAINTING, 8
Nobody can have the s. of me WOMEN, 76
No coward s. is mine BRONTE, E, 3; COURAGE, 4
Nowhere can man find a quieter…retreat than in his own s. PRAYER, 24
Our Language…was unequal to that greatness of s. MILTON, J, 1
passion in the human s. MUSIC, 37
possessive outrage done to a free solitary human s. FAMILY, 50
poverty of s., impossible MONTAIGNE, M, 10
Raises from Hell a human s. BLAKE, W, 5; HELL, 1
real dark night of the s. FITZGERALD, F, 3; SOUL, 7
seal the hushed casket of my s. KEATS, J, 48; SLEEP, 24
S. is the rhythm o' sex POPULAR MUSIC, 13
than that one s.…should commit one single venial sin SIN, 22
The British postgraduate student is a lonely forlorn s. LODGE, D, 3
the…essence of a human s. BOOKS, 12; CARLYLE, T, 27
the eyes are the windows of the s. BEERBOHM, M, 12; EYES, 3
the iron enter into his s. STERNE, L, 1
the iron has entered his s. LLOYD GEORGE, D, 14
the largest and most comprehensive s. DRYDEN, J, 22
The Life and S., the man who will never go home PARTIES, 11; WHITEHORN, K, 3
The s. fortunately, has an interpreter BRONTE, C, 5
The s. hath not her generous aspirings LAMB, C, 26
the s. is not more than the body SELF, 26; WHITMAN, W, 9
the s. of a martyr with the intellect of an advocate BAGEHOT, W, 10
The s. started at the knee-cap ANIMALISM, 5; LEWIS, W, 1
The S. that rises with us, our life's Star WORDSWORTH, W, 26
The voice of the sea speaks to the s. SEA, 3
Thy rapt s. sitting in thine eyes MILTON, J, 12
Thy s. was like a star, and dwelt apart WORDSWORTH, W, 57
souls Above the vulgar flight of common s. SUPERIORITY, 12
damp s. of the housemaids ELIOT, T, 17; MELANCHOLY, 5
Our s. have sight of that immortal sea WORDSWORTH, W, 29
queen did fish for men's s. ELIZABETH I, 1
S. of poets dead and gone KEATS, J, 26; PUBLIC HOUSES, 3
Stars…robbed men of their s. STARS, 1
their s. dwell in the house of tomorrow CHILDREN, 30
the silence of astounded s. PLATH, S, 2
The s. of women are so small BUTLER, S, 9; WOMEN, 30
Two s. dwell, alas! in my breast CONFLICT, 6; GOETHE, J, 3
Two s. with but a single thought LOVE, 108
You may house their bodies but not their s. CHILDREN, 30
soul-sides the meanest of his creatures /Boasts two s. BROWNING, R, 40
sound full of s. and fury LIFE, 86; SHAKESPEARE, 227
s. of a great Amen MUSIC, 49
The hills are alive with the s. of music MUSIC, 28
The most persistent s.…through men's history WAR, 94
The s. must seem an echo to the sense POPE, A, 26
The s. of the English county families ARISTOCRACY, 21; WAUGH, E, 7
the trumpet shall s. BIBLE, 42; DEATH, 35
whispering s. of the cool colonnade COWPER, W, 19; TREES, 3
sounding s. brass BIBLE, 38; CHARITY, 7
sounds Music is the arithmetic of s. MUSIC, 19
the s. will take care of themselves CARROLL, L, 14; MEANING, 2
soup concludes that it will…make better s. MENCKEN, H, 16
S. of the evening, beautiful S. CARROLL, L, 18; FOOD, 21
Take the s. away FOOD, 37
sour How s. sweet music is ORDER, 4; SHAKESPEARE, 301
I am sure the grapes are s. AESOP, 2; ENVY, 4
source her Majesty…must not…look upon me as a s. of income TAXATION, 6
sourest sweetest things turn s. CORRUPTION, 13; SHAKESPEARE, 368
south beaker full of the warm S. ALCOHOL, 47; KEATS, J, 37
go s. in the winter ELIOT, T, 27; READING, 3; TRAVEL, 16
hardly be a town in the S. of England ENGLAND, 38
South Africa Our Own S. SOUTH AFRICA, 7
S., renowned both far and wide SOUTH AFRICA, 4
S. will not allow the double standards SOUTH AFRICA, 1
you have mandated us to change S. SOUTH AFRICA, 8

South African I was ashamed of being S. SOUTH AFRICA, 9
South Africans You won't force S. SOUTH AFRICA, 2
southern mother bore me in the s. wild BLAKE, W, 48
South of England hardly be a town in the S. ORWELL, G, 26
souvenir give him my autograph as a s. WORLD WAR II, 36
sovereign A Subject and a S. are clean different things LAST WORDS, 15
he will have no s. MONARCHY, 10
That s. of insufferables WRITERS, 38
The S. has, under a constitutional monarchy...three rights BAGEHOT, W, 7; MONARCHY, 3
The s. is absolute ROYALTY, 36
When I forget my s. LOYALTY, 13
sovereigns s. and magistrates should be destroyed REBELLION, 11
Soviet as spiteful to me in the American press as the S. press NEWSPAPERS, 15
Communism is S. power plus the electrification COMMUNISM, 8; LENIN, V, 9
S. people want full-blooded...democracy GORBACHOV, M, 11
The ship follows S. custom CLASS, 50
Soviets All Power to the S. RUSSIAN REVOLUTION, 2
Soviet Union instruments of control in the S. RUSSIA, 8
sow Ireland is the old s. IRELAND, 12; JOYCE, J, 6
I took the right s. by the ear INFLUENCE, 13
like a s. that hath overwhelm'd all her litter SHAKESPEARE, 117
s. not, neither do they reap BIBLE, 370
They that s. in tears shall reap in joy PSALMS, 69
soweth whatsoever a man s., that shall he also reap BIBLE, 136
sown A lovelier flower /...was never s. WORDSWORTH, W, 70
soya workers' flats in fields of s. beans FUTURE, 3
space annihilate but s. and time LOVE, 126; POPE, A, 3
Empty s. and points of light REALITY, 9
In the United States there is more s. AMERICA, 36; STEIN, G, 4
Outer s. is no place SPACE, 3
range of human societies in time, the other in s. MANKIND, 35
S. is almost infinite QUAYLE, D, 5; SPACE, 8
S....is big. Really big SPACE, 1
S. isn't remote at all SPACE, 6
S. is out of this world SPACE, 9
there are no breasts in s. CINEMA, 8
spaceship s., Earth ENVIRONMENT, 8; SPACE, 4
spade never so merely a s. as the word WORDS, 15
When I see a s. I call it a s. SNOBBERY, 13; WILDE, O, 29
Spain Farewell and adieu to you, Ladies of S. ANONYMOUS, 18; PARTING, 3
not left to S. MARTYRDOM, 7; TENNYSON, 70
spam he wanted steak and they offered s. DISAPPOINTMENT, 6
span Life's short s. forbids us...far-reaching hopes HORACE, 28
Spaniards the S. seem wiser than they are BACON, F, 47
time to win this game, and to thrash the S. SPORT AND GAMES, 14; WAR, 57
spaniel the cur dog of Britain and s. of Spain POLITICIANS, 119
Spanish I speak S. to God LANGUAGE, 13
singed the S. king's beard WAR, 59
spare bread enough and to s. BIBLE, 331
I can't s. this man; he fights LINCOLN, A, 20; OFFICERS, 9
S. all I have WORLD-WEARINESS, 2
s. the rod BUTLER, S, 4
S. your ships SUPERIORITY, 2
Woodman, s. that tree TREES, 11
spareth he that s. his rod hateth his son BIBLE, 450; CHILDREN, 19; PUNISHMENT, 7
sparkle That youthful s....is caused by his contact lenses REAGAN, R, 1
sparkling pair of s. eyes GILBERT, W, 6
sparrow a s. alight upon my shoulder HONOUR, 6; THOREAU, H, 18
I, said the S., /With my bow and arrow NURSERY RHYMES, 72
It is a city where you can see a s. fall IRELAND, 18
the s. hath found her an house PSALMS, 44
sparrowhawks S., Ma'am REMEDIES, 60; WELLINGTON, 27
sparrows five s....not one of them is forgotten BIBLE, 328
one of the s....flew...through the hall LIFE, 11
spasm a lonely s. of helpless agony DEATH, 85
statesmanship. I call it an emotional s. POLITICS, 18
spat So he stood up and s. on the ceiling ANONYMOUS, 91
Today I s. in the Seine WORLD WAR II, 40
spats Buster Jones in white s. CATS, 3
speak I didn't s. up NAZISM, 6
I only s. right on SHAKESPEARE, 159; SPEECHES, 11
I want...art /To s. and purpose not DECEPTION, 6
Let him now s. BOOK OF COMMON PRAYER, 25
more than a moral duty to s. one's mind WILDE, O, 28
Never s. ill of the dead DEATH, 11; PROVERBS, 306
province of knowledge to s. KNOWLEDGE, 22; WISDOM, 21
some...s....before they think IMPETUOSITY, 2; LA BRUYERE, J, 3
s., Lord; for thy servant heareth BIBLE, 477
S. softly and carry a big stick ROOSEVELT, T, 7
s. to God as if men were listening RIGHTEOUSNESS, 10
S. up for yourself, or you'll end up a rug SELF-CONFIDENCE, 13
S. when you are spoken to CARROLL, L, 36
time to think before I s. SPEECH, 9
When I think, I must s. SHAKESPEARE, 53; WOMEN, 118
Whereof one cannot s. SILENCE, 17
women.../Forgiveness but to s. FORGIVENESS, 4
speaking An Englishman's way of s. CLASS, 23
People talking without s. FUTILITY, 13
when...s., they do not know what they are saying CHURCHILL, W, 41
special a s. relationship POLITICS, 29
specialist called a nerve s. because it sounds better PSYCHIATRY, 34
S. – A man who knows more and more about less and less EXPERTS, 5
specialists s....tend to think in grooves EXPERTS, 6
species S. do not evolve toward perfection SURVIVAL, 6
the idea of its death as a s. NUCLEAR WEAPONS, 11
their gratitude is a s. of revenge GRATITUDE, 2
the one s. I wouldn't mind seeing vanish BENNETT, A, 3
Women exist...solely for the propagation of the s. WOMAN'S ROLE, 12
spectacle Life is not a s. LIFE, 79; SANTAYANA, G, 8
spectacles Putting on the s. of science SCIENCE, 27
spectator a S. of mankind ADDISON, J, 10; OBJECTIVITY, 2
spectre Communism continued to haunt Europe as a s. TAYLOR, A, 3
speculation If the world were good for...s. HAZLITT, W, 4; SPECULATION, 2
Medicine is a strange mixture of s. and action MEDICINE, 52
speech a brazen hussy of a s. SPEECHES, 8
An after-dinner s. should be like a lady's dress SPEECHES, 5
a s. by Chamberlain is like...Woolworths INSULTS, 18; SPEECHES, 3
freedom of s. ROOSEVELT, F, 14; TWAIN, M, 7
freedom of s., freedom of conscience FREEDOM, 57
he drank my health with a little s. HUGO, V, 2
I dreamt that I was making a s. SPEECHES, 9
let thy s. be short BIBLE, 89; SPEECH, 5
making a s. on economics is a lot like pissing SPEECHES, 10
perfect plainness of s....perfect nobleness ARNOLD, M, 31; BIBLE, 523
Sign language is the equal of s. LANGUAGE, 37
S. is civilisation itself SPEECH, 14
S. is silver PROVERBS, 368; SILENCE, 2
s. only to conceal their thoughts HUMAN NATURE, 33; VOLTAIRE, 12
s....seasoned with salt BIBLE, 23; SPEECH, 4
S. was given to man to disguise his thoughts SPEECH, 20; TALLEYRAND, 4
The most precious things in s. SPEECH, 16
The true use of s. GOLDSMITH, O, 13; SPEECH, 11
the whole earth was...of one s. BIBLE, 163; UNITY, 6
True and False are attributes of s., not of things HOBBES, T, 2; TRUTH, 29
speeches every government...should have its old s. burned GOVERNMENT, 38
he tries on s. like a man trying on ties POLITICIANS, 75
Many have been the wise s. of fools WISDOM AND FOOLISHNESS, 6
more than whisky into my s. SPEECHES, 7
solved by s. and majority votes POWER POLITICS, 2
Statesmen are far too busy making s. RUSSELL, B, 23; THINKING, 14
Winston...preparing his impromptu s. CHURCHILL, W, 6
speechless *The Times* is s. CHURCHILL, W, 40; NEWSPAPERS, 6
speed safety is in our s. EMERSON, R, 13; HASTE, 6
s. was faster than light LIMERICKS, 7; SCIENCE, 16
spell as long as you s. my name right FAME, 9
s. it Vinci and pronounce it Vinchy TWAIN, M, 10
spend s. a single day really well GOOD, 7

spurts They move forward in s. CHILDREN, 25; CONNOLLY, C, 13
squandermania The Happy Warrior of S. POLITICIANS, 65
square Shed his blood...given a s. deal ROOSEVELT, T, 8
square ring more tragic loss of life than the s. SPORT AND GAMES, 28
squares city is arrayed in s. just like a chess-board PLACES, 30
walk on the lines or s. MILNE, A, 5; SUPERSTITION, 10
squeezed The Germans...are going to be s., as a lemon RETRIBUTION, 10
squire Bless the s. and his relations CLASS, 13; DICKENS, C, 9
stabbed The German army was s. in the back DEFEAT, 7
stability anything conducive to our national s. CHINA, 10
stable It's too late to shut the s. door PROVERBS, 233; REGRET, 2
staff I'll break my s. RENUNCIATION, 4; SHAKESPEARE, 328
stage All the world's a s. SHAKESPEARE, 48
A s. where every man must play a part LIFE, 87
Don't put your daughter on the s. COWARD, N, 8; THEATRE, 8
great s. of fools BIRTH, 14
If this were play'd upon a s. REALITY, 8; SHAKESPEARE, 345
no man dies for love, but on the s. DRYDEN, J, 29
qualities...necessary for success upon the s. TERRY, D, 2
the Attic s. ARNOLD, M, 42; LIFE, 7
this great s. of fools SHAKESPEARE, 192
we go quite off this s. POPE, A, 61
stagecoach You will hear more good things on...a s. from London to Oxford HAZLITT, W, 27
stages The four s. of man AGE, 58
St Agnes S.' Eve – Ah, bitter chill it was KEATS, J, 9
stags he loved the s. as...though he had been their father OBITUARIES, 1
stair As I was going up the s. NONSENSE, 25
stairs he had known many kicked down s. HALIFAX, 9; PROMOTION, 2
walks up the s. of his concepts MANKIND, 61; STEINBECK, J, 2
stake To the thumbscrew and the s. MARTYRDOM, 7; TENNYSON, 70
Stalin If Mr S. dies DIPLOMACY, 12
I like old Joe S. POLITICIANS, 124
look at him! He might be S. DE GAULLE, C, 2
S. hates the guts of POLITICIANS, 113; ROOSEVELT, F, 5
stammer s. and lisp and dribble at the mouth SHYNESS, 4
You persisted...like a s. LEWIS, W, 5; PERSISTENCE, 9
stamp If we can't s. out literature PHILISTINISM, 7; WAUGH, E, 44
the indelible s. of his lowly origin DARWIN, C, 7; EVOLUTION, 8
to order a new s....with my face on it TRIVIALITY, 12
stand a firm place to s. TECHNOLOGY, 2
at no time s. so highly in our estate royal GOVERNMENT, 16
no time to s. and stare IDLENESS, 5
s. not upon the order of...going DISMISSAL, 9; SHAKESPEARE, 217
s. the course ENDURANCE, 20
S. your ground...if they mean to have a war, let it begin here WAR, 127
They also serve who only s. and wait MILTON, J, 61; SERVICE, 5
We s. today on the edge of a new frontier BEGINNING, 14
standard a s. of rebellion REBELLION, 8
standards South Africa will not allow the double s. SOUTH AFRICA, 1
stands S. the Church clock BROOKE, R, 5; NOSTALGIA, 3
Stanislavsky S. ever said was: Avoid generalities GENERALIZATIONS, 3
star a s. or two beside COLERIDGE, S, 33; MOON, 2
Being a s. has made it possible FAME, 10
Bright s., would I were steadfast KEATS, J, 6; STARS, 5
Go, and catch a falling s. DONNE, J, 13; NONSENSE, 11
Hitch your wagon to a s. AMBITION, 9; EMERSON, R, 23
one s. differeth from another...in glory ASTRONOMY, 1; BIBLE, 41
Remember you are a s. ACTORS, 7
She was always a s....intermittently a good actress BANKHEAD, T, 2
Someday I'll wish upon a s. DESIRE, 7
s. who had no pretensions ACTORS, 19
Sunset and evening s. DUTY, 8; TENNYSON, 12
that same s., /That fitful, fiery Lucifer STARS, 7
The desire of the moth for the s. HUMOUR, 45; JOYCE, J, 12
The Soul that rises with us, our life's S. METAPHYSICS, 5; WORDSWORTH, W, 26
Thy soul was like a s., and dwelt apart NOBILITY, 9; WORDSWORTH, W, 57
Twinkle, twinkle, little s. STARS, 6
we have seen his s. in the east BIBLE, 351; CHRISTMAS, 10
star-cross'd pair of s. lovers SHAKESPEARE, 306
stare no time to stand and s. IDLENESS, 5
Stark Tonight the American flag floats from yonder hill or Molly S. sleeps a widow WAR, 165
Starkie There was a young woman called S. ANONYMOUS, 95; RACISM, 1
starry the s. heaven above me KANT, I, 1; WONDER, 3
Under the wide and s. sky DEATH, 166; STEVENSON, R, 12
stars Clad in the beauty of a thousand s. COMPLIMENTS, 17; MARLOWE, C, 3
felt like the moon, the s., and all the planets had fallen RESPONSIBILITY, 21
he made the s. also BIBLE, 140; CREATION, 4; STARS, 2
I am greater than the s. SELF, 20
I'll hold my head so high it'll strike the s. HORACE, 26; PRIDE, 6
Look at the s. STARS, 4
My eyes were blind with s. and still /I stared into the sky. STARS, 3
One sees the mud, and one the s. OPTIMISM, 31
some of us are looking at the s. OPTIMISM, 40; WILDE, O, 41
Some s....Fell like a falling tear STARS, 8
s. /Regard me sadly PLATH, S, 5
S....robbed men of their souls STARS, 1
strives to touch the s. AMBITION, 26
Tempt not the s. DESTINY, 11
The fault, dear Brutus, is not in our s. SELF, 16; SHAKESPEARE, 145
the field of the s. is so vast, but...man has measured it FRANCE, A, 5
The s. grew bright in the winter sky ANIMALS, 16; MASEFIELD, J, 4
the s. in their courses BIBLE, 292
the Stone that puts the S. to Flight DAY, 5; FITZGERALD, E, 2
The Syrian s. look down ARNOLD, M, 30; DEATH, 26
Through endeavour to the s. AMBITION, 2; ANONYMOUS, 68
We are merely the s.' tennis-balls DESTINY, 29; WEBSTER, J, 3
what is the s. CURIOSITY, 7
star-spangled 'Tis the s. banner AMERICA, 25
start Wrong from the s. POETRY, 49; POUND, E, 12
star treatment s....I was just as good when I was poor WEALTH, 36
starts make certain it never s. NUCLEAR WEAPONS, 5
starve Let not poor Nelly s. CHARLES II, 6; LAST WORDS, 16
starving all around you people are s. CAPITALISM, 15
state a s. in the proper sense of the word CAPITALISM, 11; LENIN, V, 3
attacking an ex-secretary of s. ACHESON, D, 3; REPARTEE, 1
For Fascism the S. is absolute FASCISM, 11
I am the S. LOUIS XIV, 4; MONARCHY, 17
In a free society the s....administers justice among men STATE, 3
O Lord, to what a s....those who love Thee RELIGION, 85
Our object in the construction of the s. PLATO, 2; REPUBLIC, 1
reinforcement of the power of the S. CAMUS, A, 15; REVOLUTION, 3
s. exists...no freedom LENIN, V, 4; STATE, 2
s. can simply be removed from the economy SOCIETY, 7
S. socialism is totally alien SOCIALISM, 24; THATCHER, M, 27
the lie has become...a pillar of the S. LYING, 24; SOLZHENITSYN, A, 14
The S., in choosing men...takes no notice of their opinions CROMWELL, O, 8; LOYALTY, 6
The s. is an instrument...of the ruling class STALIN, J, 2; STATE, 5
The s. is not 'abolished', it withers away COMMUNISM, 5
the s....Man is in GOD, 41; NIETZSCHE, F, 5
The worth of a S. STATE, 4
stately go back to thy s. homes of England LAWRENCE, D, 18; PARTING, 7
lunatic asylums...the s. homes STATELY HOMES, 7
S. Homes of England ope their doors STATELY HOMES, 3
The S. Homes of England ARISTOCRACY, 11
statement Any general s. is like a cheque GENERALIZATIONS, 5; POUND, E, 6
states S., like men, have their growth...their decay LANDOR, W, 4; POLITICS, 66
statesman abroad you're a s. MACMILLAN, H, 7; POLITICIANS, 16
agree with him he was a s. LLOYD GEORGE, D, 20
A politician is a s....with an open mouth POLITICIANS, 27; STEVENSON, A, 2
A s. is a politician who POLITICIANS, 18

A s. is a politician who's been dead POLITICIANS, 29; TRUMAN, H, 5
a s. of literature GALSWORTHY, J, 2
definition of a constitutional s. BAGEHOT, W, 9; POLITICIANS, 44
if you agree with him he is a s. POLITICIANS, 15
statesmanship s.. I call it an emotional spasm POLITICS, 18
the suspicion…his life was a preparation for elder s. MACMILLAN, H, 2
statesmen an imperative principle which s.…ignore at their peril SELF, 28
Most British s.…drunk too much or womanized too much POLITICIANS, 54
S. are far too busy making speeches RUSSELL, B, 23; THINKING, 14
s.…estranged from reality LAING, R, 1; NUCLEAR WEAPONS, 12
static class people as s. and dynamic SEXES, 34; WAUGH, E, 27
novel is a s. thing NOVELS, 17; PLAYS, 15; TYNAN, K, 1
stating power of *s.* an argument ELIOT, G, 2
station honour is a private s. ADDISON, J, 7; VICE, 1
stationmaster The s.'s whiskers are of a Victorian bushiness APPEARANCE, 76; WODEHOUSE, P, 19
stations always know our proper s. CLASS, 13; DICKENS, C, 9
statistics Facts speak louder than s. FACTS, 7; STATISTICS, 12
He uses s. as a drunken man uses lamp-posts STATISTICS, 5
lies, damned lies and s. DISRAELI, B, 16; STATISTICS, 3; TWAIN, M, 4
Medical s. are like a bikini STATISTICS, 1
smoking is one of the leading causes of s. SMOKING, 22
s., born to consume resources HORACE, 17; STATISTICS, 4
S. will prove anything STATISTICS, 7
There are two kinds of s. STATISTICS, 11
unrewarded millions without whom S. would be a bankrupt science SMITH, L, 6
we must study s. STATISTICS, 8
You cannot feed the hungry on s. LLOYD GEORGE, D, 7
statue no s.…put up to a critic CRITICS, 17
that *my* s. should be moved, which I should much dislike VICTORIA, 11
there's a s. inside every block of stone OBESITY, 12; ORWELL, G, 9
statues worth a million s. CUMMINGS, 4; NAKEDNESS, 3
stature man of giant s. OBITUARIES, 9
stay s. me with flagons BIBLE, 487; LOVE, 33
S., s., /Until the hasting day /Has run HERRICK, R, 4; TRANSIENCE, 15
stay-at-home Sweet S. CONTENTMENT, 2
steak he wanted s. and they offered spam DISAPPOINTMENT, 6
when you've got s. at home MARRIAGE, 115
steaks smell of s. in passageways ELIOT, T, 19; FOOD, 28
steal A lawyer with his briefcase can s. more LAWYERS, 9
all of his patients being willing to s. DOCTORS, 66
A man who will s. *for* me will s. *from* me LOYALTY, 8; ROOSEVELT, T, 5
thou shalt not s. BIBLE, 115; GOD, 12
stealing hanged for s. horses EXAMPLE, 5; HALIFAX, 1; PUNISHMENT, 21
steals A good composer…s. STRAVINSKY, I, 5
Who s. a common from a goose ANONYMOUS, 80; THEFT, 1
Who s. my purse s. trash REPUTATION, 10; SHAKESPEARE, 284
stealth Do good by s. GOOD, 15; POPE, A, 10
greatest pleasure I know, is to do a good action by s. LAMB, C, 18
stealthy The S. School of Criticism ROSSETTI, D, 5
steamer tossing about in a s. from Harwich BOATS, 6; GILBERT, W, 22
steel arm'd with more than complete s. JUSTICE, 17; MARLOWE, C, 12
the cold s. WAR, 10
thin red line tipped with s. COURAGE, 24
When the foeman bares his s. COWARDICE, 5; GILBERT, W, 40
steep When things are s., remember to stay level-headed HORACE, 33; SELF-CONTROL, 4
steeple clock in the s. strikes one ALCOHOL, 90
steeples Talk about the pews and s. CHESTERTON, G, 6
Till you have drench'd our s. SHAKESPEARE, 178; WEATHER, 19
steer You just press the accelerator to the floor and s. left SPORT AND GAMES, 44
Stein There's a wonderful family called S. ANONYMOUS, 89; HUMOUR, 36
stellar the whole solar and s. systems CARLYLE, T, 30; COMFORT, 2
stem a rod out of the s. of Jesse BIBLE, 202
stench he begins as dirt and departs as s. MANKIND, 67
step a s. from the sublime to the ridiculous DECLINE, 7; NAPOLEON I, 9
one small s. for man MISQUOTATIONS, 5; SPACE, 2
One s. forward, two steps back LENIN, V, 2; PROGRESS, 18
only the first s.…is difficult BEGINNING, 8
Take a s. forward, lads COURAGE, 9; LAST WORDS, 19
The first s. BEGINNING, 5; PROVERBS, 394
step-mother a kind parent…or a merciless s. NATURE, 27; PLINY THE ELDER, 3
Stepney When will that be? /Say the bells of S. NURSERY RHYMES, 41
stepp'd in blood s. in so far SHAKESPEARE, 219
stereotypes abandon established s. GORBACHOV, M, 12
sterile human females become s. in the forties WOMEN, 68
sterility The desert, the abode of enforced s. CARTER, A, 3
Stevenson S.…like a man playing spillikins STEVENSON, R, 1
stick if we praise ourselves fearlessly, something will always s. BACON, F, 4
kind of burr; I shall s. SHAKESPEARE, 235
Speak softly and carry a big s. ROOSEVELT, T, 7
sticks it is always said of slander that something always s. BACON, F, 4
S. and stones INSULTS, 1; PROVERBS, 369
stiff a s. upper lip COURAGE, 6
stiffen a recently dead fish before it has had time to s. APPEARANCE, 50; POLITICIANS, 110
S. the sinews SHAKESPEARE, 130
stigma Any s.…to beat a dogma PUNS, 6
stile He found a crooked sixpence against a crooked s. NURSERY RHYMES, 56
help a lame dog over a s. HELP, 9
I'm sitting on the s., Mary NOSTALGIA, 8
still And if she's not gone /She lives there s. NURSERY RHYMES, 57
a s. small voice BIBLE, 300; GOD, 14; SUICIDE, 36; TENNYSON, 79
A s. tongue PROVERBS, 67; SILENCE, 1
be s. then, and know that I am God PSALMS, 28
Even when conversing he could not keep s. WRITERS, 80
of his own opinion s. BUTLER, S, 8; YIELDING, 2
S. waters run deep APPEARANCES, 4; PROVERBS, 370
stilly Oft in the s. night, /Ere Slumber's chain MOORE, T, 7; NOSTALGIA, 17
stimulated perverse nature can be s. by anything BURGESS, A, 1
sting O death, where is thy s. BIBLE, 42; DEATH, 35, 123; POPE, A, 6
stings stroke a nettle, /And it s. you for your pains DECISION, 2
stingy Gimme a viskey….don't be s., baby DRINKS, 12
stirrup I sprang to the s. BROWNING, R, 28; HORSES, 3
stitch A s. in time ANTICIPATION, 1; PROVERBS, 68
St Ives As I was going to S. NURSERY RHYMES, 3
stoat I…catch a glimpse of a s. KEATS, J, 69; PURPOSE, 6
stock the public s. of harmless pleasure JOHNSON, S, 21
stockholders The public be damned. I am working for my s. CAPITALISM, 20
stocking silk s.'s hanging down LANGUAGE, 39
stockings the silk s. and white bosoms…excite my amorous propensities JOHNSON, S, 46
stoic man is…either a s. or a satyr AGE, 68
stole She s. everything but the cameras WEST, M, 2
That title from a better man I s. IMITATION, 6; STEVENSON, R, 11
stolen not wanting what is s. SHAKESPEARE, 287
S. sweets are always sweeter, /S. kisses much completer THEFT, 7
S. sweets are best THEFT, 5
s. waters are sweet BIBLE, 449
your wife…is a receiver of s. goods JOHNSON, S, 134
stomach A hungry s. has no ears HUNGER, 8; LA FONTAINE, J, 9
a little wine for thy s.'s sake DRINKS, 5
An army marches on its s. FOOD, 55; NAPOLEON I, 14
a proud look and a high s. PSALMS, 57
Do I have a clitoris halfway up my s. SEX, 39
my s. must just digest in its waistcoat ALCOHOL, 75
No one can worship God…on an empty s. BUSINESS, 39; WILSON, W, 7
The way to a man's heart is through his s. FOOD, 29
use a little wine for thy s.'s sake ALCOHOL, 21; BIBLE, 509
Well, then, my s. must just digest in its waistcoat SHERIDAN, R, 12
with enforcing morality on the s. ILLNESS, 33
You can't think rationally on an empty s. THINKING, 12

stomachs Napoleon's armies used to march on their s. SELLAR, W, 6
stone and youth s. dead SASSOON, S, 2
Constant dripping hollows out a s. PERSISTENCE, 10
draw in their horns or…bomb them into the S. Age WAR, 100
Dripping water hollows out a s. OVID, 4; PERSISTENCE, 11
he that is without sin…let him first cast a s. BIBLE, 251
if his son ask bread, will he give him a s. BIBLE, 376
if someone throws a s. at you, respond with food FORGIVENESS, 2
Jackson standing like a s. wall DETERMINATION, 5
Like a rolling s. DYLAN, B, 7; TRAVEL, 15
precious s. set in the silver sea ENGLAND, 46; SHAKESPEARE, 297
raised not a s. FUNERALS, 14
tables of s., and a law AUTHORITARIANISM, 3; BIBLE, 119
the final s.…in the foundation of St Petersburg VICTORY, 19
the s. taken away from the sepulchre BIBLE, 274
Virtue is like a rich s. BACON, F, 11; VIRTUE, 3
Stonehenge bring S. to Nyasaland CIVILIZATION, 2
stones He found in s. the sermons…hidden there POETS, 59
Sermons in s. SHAKESPEARE, 43
s. kissed by the English dead OWEN, W, 5; WAR, 125
the s. would immediately cry out BIBLE, 337
stony fell upon s. places BIBLE, 391
stood We should have s. in bed DEFEAT, 9
stoop A constitutional king must learn to s. MONARCHY, 16
stoops When lovely woman s. to folly GOLDSMITH, O, 29; GULLIBILITY, 2
stop come to the end: then s. CARROLL, L, 20; ORDER, 2
s. everyone from doing it HERBERT, A, 2; PERVERSITY, 4
S. the World, I Want to Get Off WORLD-WEARINESS, 5
time…must have a s. DEATH, 142; SHAKESPEARE, 115
when the kissing had to s. BROWNING, R, 57; KISSING, 2
stopped man has s. moving EVOLUTION, 5
stoppeth he s. one of three COLERIDGE, S, 24
stops The buck s. here RESPONSIBILITY, 20; TRUMAN, H, 10
storage A library is thought in cold s. BOOKS, 43
stories She likes s. that make her cry SENTIMENTALITY, 5
s. of mystery and crime LITERATURE, 20
storm After a s. comes a calm OPTIMISM, 1; PROVERBS, 19
a mighty s.…to freshen us up CHANGE, 3; CHEKHOV, A, 9
fire and brimstone, s. and tempest PSALMS, 5
lovers fled away into the s. DEPARTURE, 7; KEATS, J, 14
S. in a Teacup TRIVIALITY, 2
storms greater s. in politics than you'll ever find at sea OCCUPATIONS, 15
s. of prayer EXCESS, 16; TENNYSON, 74
The summer talk stopped…/Before the s. AUDEN, W, 18
story A cruel s. runs on wheels CRUELTY, 4
a s. that starts with an earthquake and…a climax GOLDWYN, S, 5
brother-in-law wrote an unusal murder s. BOOKS, 48
her sad short, short s. BRONTE, A, 2
Not that the s. need be long THOREAU, H, 20; WRITING, 48
novel tells a s. FORSTER, E, 5; NOVELS, 4
snowy summits old in s. TENNYSON, 61
Tell me the old, old s. CHRISTIANITY, 41
the most interesting thing about any s. is…that he has arrived to cover it STOPPARD, T, 5
The s. is like the wind SENSATION, 2
stout those who have s. hearts and sharp swords RUTHLESSNESS, 6
stoutness I see no objection to s. GILBERT, W, 15; OBESITY, 11
Stowe S., Harriet Beecher INFLUENCE, 8; LINCOLN, A, 5
straight gay characters…same footing as the s. HOMOSEXUALITY, 25
If Michelangelo had been s. HOMOSEXUALITY, 30
If propaganda worked we'd be s. HOMOSEXUALITY, 23
I tell them s. DISEASE, 5
the street which is called S. BIBLE, 7
where Beauty was, nothing ever ran quite s. GALSWORTHY, J, 4
straightforward he is so hearty, so s., outspoken ROOSEVELT, T, 1
straight-jacket the discredited s. of the past POLITICS, 100
strain'd quality of mercy is not s. MERCY, 2; SHAKESPEARE, 248
strait matters not how s. the gate RESPONSIBILITY, 8
s. is the gate BIBLE, 377; VIRTUE, 6
straitened to face s. circumstances at home POVERTY, 26
strand wandering on a foreign s. HOMESICKNESS, 6; SCOTT, W, 8
Strand I walk down the S. FASHION, 7
Let's all go down the S. LONDON, 7
strange A s., horrible business…good enough for Shakespeare's day CRITICISM, 61; VICTORIA, 10
I perish through great grief in a s. land BIBLE, 341
it's a jolly s. world BENNETT, A, 6; CONFUSION, 2
laughing and jeering at everything…s. ENGLISH, 34; PEPYS, S, 7
pass my declining years saluting s. women OLD AGE, 75
sing the Lord's song in a s. land PSALMS, 70
The Law of England is a very s. one LAW, 11
truth is always s. BYRON, 35; TRUTH, 17
wrinkles…s. and exciting AGE, 91
strangely he acted s. NEWTON, I, 1
strangeness s. in the proportion BACON, F, 12; BEAUTY, 8
stranger a s. in a strange land BIBLE, 104
Look, s., at this island now AUDEN, W, 19; DISCOVERY, 2
S. than fiction BYRON, 35; TRUTH, 17
strangers better s. SEPARATION, 6; SHAKESPEARE, 54
s. and pilgrims on the earth FAITH, 4
the kindness of s. CHARITY, 28; WILLIAMS, T, 6
to entertain s. HOSPITALITY, 9
strangle task of the Liberal party is to s. it at birth POLITICS, 94
Stratford S.…suggests powdered history ENGLAND, 24
S. trades on Shakespeare BURGESS, A, 5; EUROPE, 1
straw Headpiece filled with s. ELIOT, T, 9; INSIGNIFICANCE, 2
strawberries innocent as s. INNOCENCE, 14; THOMAS, D, 13
We may say of angling as Dr Boteler said of s. FISHING, 4; WALTON, I, 4
strawberry My good man, I'm not a s. ACCIDENTS, 4
will teach you how to make s. jam TOLSTOY, L, 3
straws Errors, like S. DRYDEN, J, 17; TRUTH, 23
strayed s. from thy ways BOOK OF COMMON PRAYER, 14; SIN, 8
straying s. away from the church RELIGION, 17
stream Still glides the S. CONSTANCY, 5; WORDSWORTH, W, 46
Time is but the s. I go a-fishing in THOREAU, H, 17; TIME, 59
despised by a s. boy HUXLEY, T, 5; PHILOSOPHERS, 5;
street don't do it in the s. SEX, 21
she could walk down the middle of the s. THATCHER, M, 9
the s. which is called Straight BIBLE, 7
streets a quarrel in the s. is…to be hated KEATS, J, 68
S. full of water VENICE, 1
The s. of London LONDON, 1; PROVERBS, 425
strength Credulity is…the child's s. INNOCENCE, 8; LAMB, C, 12
Ignorance is S. ORWELL, G, 18
My s. is as the s. of ten INTEGRITY, 7; TENNYSON, 72
O Lord, my s. PSALMS, 10
s. and fury LA FONTAINE, J, 4; PATIENCE, 12
S. through joy NAZISM, 4
their s. then but labour and sorrow PSALMS, 50
the Lord is the s. of my life PSALMS, 15
We are not now that s. DETERMINATION, 24; TENNYSON, 81
strenuous doctrine of the s. life ROOSEVELT, T, 6; WORK, 31
stress s. and the violence is worse at home VIOLENCE, 19
stretched things which he s. LYING, 27; TWAIN, M, 3
stretch marks clothes have s. CLOTHES, 23
strides popular music…made giant s. in reverse POPULAR MUSIC, 11
strife God and Nature then at s. NATURE, 30; TENNYSON, 31
With phantoms an unprofitable s. LIFE AND DEATH, 30; SHELLEY, P, 4
strike difficult to go on s. STRIKES, 5
If you s. a child SHAW, G, 30; VIOLENCE, 18
no right to s. against the public safety STRIKES, 4
SOLIDARITY was born…when the shipyard s. evolved WAŁESA, L, 2
S. while the iron is hot OPPORTUNITY, 7; PROVERBS, 371
The general s.…is the road to anarchy STRIKES, 2
themselves must s. the blow BYRON, 12; FREEDOM, 10
the twenty-four-hour s. STRIKES, 7
where ever you meet with a passage…s. it out JOHNSON, S, 88; WRITING, 24
strikes the last four s. we've had, it's pissed down STRIKES, 8
Strindberg S. when you have a temperature LITERATURE, 18
string chewing little bits of S. BELLOC, H, 9; FOOD, 11
strings There are s.…in the human heart DICKENS, C, 4; EMOTION, 2
stripling yon pale s. EXPECTATION, 7; SCOTT, W, 19
strive I s. to be brief, and I become obscure BREVITY, 3; HORACE, 2
men should s. to learn HUMAN CONDITION, 29
needst not s. /…to keep alive KILLING, 4

To s., to seek, to find, and not to yield DETERMINATION, 24; TENNYSON, 81
strives s. to touch the stars AMBITION, 26
stroke man fears…only the s. of death BACON, F, 7; DEATH, 28
none so fast as s. BOATS, 2
strong a s. ass BIBLE, 181
battle to the s. BIBLE, 74
be s. and of a good courage BIBLE, 58; GOD, 10
be s. in the Lord BIBLE, 96
disarm the s. and arm the weak FRANCE, A, 2; INJUSTICE, 5
how sublime…/To suffer and be s. ENDURANCE, 12; LONGFELLOW, H, 8
Sorrow and silence are s. ENDURANCE, 11; LONGFELLOW, H, 6
S. enough to answer back to desires CHARACTER, 11; HORACE, 47
s. enough to bear the misfortunes of others MISFORTUNE, 16; ROCHEFOUCAULD, 2
the errors of those who think they are s. MISTAKES, 3
the s. shall thrive SURVIVAL, 9
the wall is s. IMPRISONMENT, 17; WILDE, O, 9
The weak…always prevail over the s. SURVIVAL, 6
thou…hast made my hill so s. PSALMS, 17
waxed s. in spirit BIBLE, 311
woe unto them that…follow s. drink ALCOHOL, 16; BIBLE, 195
strongest S. minds /…the noisy world /Hears least WORDSWORTH, W, 4
strongminded nobody is s. around a President SERVILITY, 6
strove I s. with none LANDOR, W, 7; LIFE AND DEATH, 22
struck Certain women should be s. regularly COWARD, N, 18
structure s. of the…British sentence CHURCHILL, W, 16; GRAMMAR, 3
struggle each man must s., lest the moral law become…separated MORALITY, 1
I believe in the armed s. as the only solution REVOLUTION, 7
manhood a s. AGE, 33; DISRAELI, B, 4
The perpetual s. for room and food SURVIVAL, 5
the s. for existence DARWIN, C, 9; EVOLUTION, 9
struggles The history of all…society is the history of class s. CLASS, 26; MARX, K, 1; MARXISM, 9
your s., your dreams, your telephone number LOVE, 18
struggling the greatness of Russia is only her pre-natal s. LAWRENCE, D, 34; RUSSIA, 10
strumpet a s.'s fool LOVE, 142; SHAKESPEARE, 25
struts player that s. and frets LIFE, 86; SHAKESPEARE, 227
stubborn s. spear-men COURAGE, 25; SCOTT, W, 16
student an over-ambitious essay by a second-year s. CRITICS, 15; PRIESTLEY, J, 2
a s. to the end of my days CHEKHOV, A, 4; LEARNING, 6
GRAVE, n. A place…to await the coming of the medical s. MEDICINE, 13
He was…a s. of history EXPERIENCE, 19; TAYLOR, A, 7
I have learned since to be a better s. EDUCATION, 71
In teaching the medical s. EDUCATION, 48
students Half of what you are taught as medical s. EDUCATION, 18
If you want to get out of medicine…be s. all your lives DOCTORS, 83
I taught medical s. in the wards EDUCATION, 70
s. had tanks run over them CHINA, 4
studies S. serve for delight BACON, F, 49; EDUCATION, 11
study I am slow of s. SHAKESPEARE, 261
much s. is a weariness of the flesh BIBLE, 78; BOOKS, 9
s. at small cost and short wayfaring EDUCATION, 34
s. what you most affect EDUCATION, 79; SHAKESPEARE, 320
The proper s. of Mankind is Man POPE, A, 34
the result of previous s. AUSTEN, J, 22
studying By s. the masters EXPERTS, 1
stuff Ambition should be made of sterner s. AMBITION, 22; SHAKESPEARE, 157
such s. as dreams are made on MORTALITY, 17; SHAKESPEARE, 327
The future is made of the same s. FUTURE, 13; WEIL, S, 4
the s. of which tyrants are made TYRANNY, 1
to s. a mushroom HOUSEWORK, 2
stuffed We are the s. men ELIOT, T, 9; INSIGNIFICANCE, 2
stumble they s. that run fast HASTE, 11; SHAKESPEARE, 315
stumbled s. when I saw SHAKESPEARE, 185
stumbling the…world was s.…in social blindness BLINDNESS, 6
stupid clever man…came of…s. people CARLYLE, T, 32; INTELLIGENCE, 4
he ceased to be mad he became merely s. PROUST, M, 11
Living in England…must be like being married to a s.…wife ENGLAND, 23
s. are cocksure…intelligent full of doubt DOUBT, 8
The s. neither forgive SZASZ, T, 6
To be clever enough to get…money, one must be s. CHESTERTON, G, 26; MATERIALISM, 9
stupidity Against s. the gods…struggle in vain STUPIDITY, 14
Human S. consists in having lots of ideas STUPIDITY, 10
If poverty is the mother of crime, s. is its father CRIME, 6; LA BRUYERE, J, 11
It is a s.…to busy oneself with the correction of the world IMPROVEMENT, 3; MOLIERE, 6
no sin except s. STUPIDITY, 15; WILDE, O, 14
Nothing…more dangerous…conscientious s. IGNORANCE, 15
Stygian resembling the horrible S. smoke of the pit SMOKING, 16
ye S. set LANDOR, W, 1; LUST, 8
style change in musical s.…change in clothing s. POPULAR MUSIC, 26
killed a calf he would do it in a high s. SHAKESPEARE, 2
s. is the man himself STYLE, 1
s., not sincerity, is the vital thing STYLE, 11; WILDE, O, 31
s.…often hides eczema CAMUS, A, 5; STYLE, 2
the grand s. arises in poetry ARNOLD, M, 32; POETRY, 3
The s. is the man PROVERBS, 426; WRITING, 2
styles All s. are good except the tiresome sort STYLE, 10; VOLTAIRE, 18
stylist the greatest literary s. of his time JOYCE, J, 4
subconscious American women know far more about the s. WOMEN, 88
subject a noble nature…treats…a serious s. ARNOLD, M, 32; POETRY, 3
A S. and a Sovereign are clean different things LAST WORDS, 15
Every s.'s duty is the King's MONARCHY, 23; SHAKESPEARE, 135
Her Majesty is not a s. DISRAELI, B, 37; ROYALTY, 48
the individual s.…'has nothing to do with the laws but to obey them.' LAW, 23
there's no s. you can't tackle on television CENSORSHIP, 11
subjective 'primitive' is clearly a highly s. SOCIETY, 9
subjects Although there exist many thousand s. CONVERSATION, 1; PROVERBS, 42
my heart was never set on worldly goods, but/ only for my s.' good ELIZABETH I, 14
subjunctive S. to the last, he preferred GRAMMAR, 9
sublime Beethoven's Fifth Symphony is the most s. noise FORSTER, E, 7; MUSIC, 26
From the s. to the ridiculous DECLINE, 7; NAPOLEON I, 9; PROVERBS, 169
how s.…/To suffer and be strong ENDURANCE, 12; LONGFELLOW, H, 8
The s. and the ridiculous OPPOSITES, 7
sublimity When young…still aspire to s. BROOKNER, A, 2
submerged speak for the inarticulate and the s. BEAVERBROOK, M, 4
speak for the inarticulate and the s. JOURNALISM, 4
submissive women humble in character and s. BOCCACCIO, G, 1
submit To great evils we s.; we resent little provocations HAZLITT, W, 7; TRIVIALITY, 10
subscribers reasons for not printing any list of s. FRANKNESS, 2; JOHNSON, S, 138
subsequence It is incident to physicians…to mistake s. for consequence JOHNSON, S, 44
physicians…mistake s. for consequence DOCTORS, 56
substance faith is the s. of things hoped for BIBLE, 187; FAITH, 3
lose the s. by grasping at the shadow AESOP, 1; GREED, 5
substantial he that chiefly owes himself…is the s. Man BROWNE, T, 2
substantives tell the s. from the adjectives POLITICS, 73
substitute a s. for reading it BURGESS, A, 6
no s. for talent HUXLEY, A, 27
substitutes and finally a single dictator s. himself TROTSKY, L, 11
subtil the serpent was more s. ANIMALS, 4; BIBLE, 148
subtle Time, the s. thief of youth AGE, 64; MILTON, J, 59
subtlety one-dimensional s. of a comic-strip THATCHER, M, 6
suburbia I come from s. RAPHAEL, F, 3; SUBURBIA, 1
subverts which s. all the principles of his understanding CHRISTIANITY, 43

succeed don't s., try, try again. PERSISTENCE, 5; PROVERBS, 213; REALISM, 2
If they s., they fail HOMOSEXUALITY, 8
I'm...ugly enough to s. on my own ALLEN, W, 4; INDEPENDENCE, 1
It is not enough to s. RUTHLESSNESS, 7; SUCCESS, 30; VIDAL, G, 6
Never having been able to s. in the world ENVY, 11; VOLTAIRE, 27
those who ne'er s. SUCCESS, 10
to s. unconventionally KEYNES, J, 5; ORTHODOXY, 3
way to s. is to make people hate you SUCCESS, 28
succeeds Nothing s. PROVERBS, 318; SUCCESS, 1
Whenever a friend s. ENVY, 10; VIDAL, G, 7
success a self-made man who owed his lack of s. to nobody HELLER, J, 1; SELF-MADE MEN, 2
A woman who is loved always has s. SUCCESS, 6
I don't think s. is harmful SUCCESS, 22
I thought that s. spelled happiness HAPPINESS, 16
I was never affected by the question of the s. MEIR, G, 2; SELF-CONFIDENCE, 4
Never let s. hide its emptiness DESTINY, 13; DETERMINATION, 16
no s. like failure DYLAN, B, 8; FAILURE, 4
Nothing fails like s. SUCCESS, 21
not in mortals to command s. ADDISON, J, 4; SUCCESS, 3
no very lively hope of s. PRAYER, 26; SMITH, S, 14
only place where s. comes before work SUCCESS, 27; WORK, 34
religion...yours is S. BARRIE, J, 7; SUCCESS, 5
secret of my s. JEALOUSY, 7; SUCCESS, 20
s. and miscarriage are empty sounds DISILLUSION, 4; JOHNSON, S, 7
s....by dint of hard work EFFORT, 5; SUCCESS, 23
s. depends...upon individual initiative and exertion EFFORT, 5; SUCCESS, 23
S. is counted sweetest DICKINSON, E, 6; SUCCESS, 10
S. is relative SUCCESS, 11
Sweet Smell of S. SUCCESS, 17
The moral flabbiness born of...S. SUCCESS, 13
The penalty of s. SUCCESS, 4
two to make a marriage a s. MARRIAGE, 130
what s....they have, the world proclaimeth DOCTORS, 82
successful It was very s. WEAPONS, 4
two reasons why I am s. in show business SUCCESS, 12
we do everything we can to appear s. ROCHEFOUCAULD, 7; SUCCESS, 25
sucker a s. born every minute GULLIBILITY, 1
suckle To s. fools SHAKESPEARE, 282; TRIVIALITY, 13
sucklings out of the mouth of...babes and s. PSALMS, 3
sucks s. the nurse asleep SHAKESPEARE, 39; SUICIDE, 32
suddenly No one...s. became depraved DEBAUCHERY, 7
sued publish and be s. PUBLISHING, 8
Suez Ship me somewheres east of S. DESIRE, 9; KIPLING, R, 26
the S. Canal was flowing through my drawing room POLITICS, 36
suffer courage to love...courage to s. LOVE, 169; TROLLOPE, A, 5
how sublime.../To s. and be strong LONGFELLOW, H, 8
If s. we must, let's s. on the heights HUGO, V, 3
Rather s. than die LA FONTAINE, J, 1
s. fools gladly BIBLE, 46
sufferance s. is the badge of all our tribe ENDURANCE, 23
suffered he s....the neurotic ills of an entire generation NEUROSIS, 4
love a place the less for having s. AUSTEN, J, 17
people of Lebanon have s. greatly HOSTAGES, 12
suffering A man who fears s. MONTAIGNE, M, 11
imagining as one's own the s. and joy of others KINDNESS, 7
Madness and s. can set themselves no limit MADNESS, 32
Neurosis is always a substitute for legitimate s. NEUROSIS, 5
pity for the s. of mankind PHILOSOPHERS, 10; RUSSELL, B, 4
sympathize with everything, except s. SYMPATHY, 7; WILDE, O, 49
The prime goal is to alleviate s., and not to prolong life MEDICINE, 9
we cannot be created for this sort of s. AFTERLIFE, 7; KEATS, J, 71
sufficient s. unto the day is the evil thereof BIBLE, 371; WORRY, 9
suffragettes s....ambassadors of freedom to women PANKHURST, C, 6
sugar like sulphuric acid and s. VIRTUE AND VICE, 7
S. and spice /And all that's nice NURSERY RHYMES, 69
suggestion They'll take s. IMPRESSIONABILITY, 3
suicide committed s. 25 years after his death DIARIES, 3
if her limits be exceeded, man responds by s. SUICIDE, 20
If you must commit s. SUICIDE, 4
I have always respected s. as a regulator of nature SUICIDE, 20
it is true that the s. braves death SUICIDE, 2
Never murder a man who is committing s. WILSON, W, 3
No one ever lacks a good reason for s. SUICIDE, 25
Not only is s. a sin SUICIDE, 9
Not that s. always comes from madness SUICIDE, 38
one truly serious philosophical problem...s. SUICIDE, 5
s. in this man's town SUICIDE, 30
s. is God's best gift to man PLINY THE ELDER, 2; SUICIDE, 26
S. is not a remedy SUICIDE, 16
S. is the worst form of murder SUICIDE, 11
s. remains the courageous act SUICIDE, 17
the only man...who cannot commit s. SUICIDE, 37
The prevalence of s. is a test of height in civilization SUICIDE, 15
There is no refuge from confession but s. SUICIDE, 39
The statistics of s. show SUICIDE, 18
thought of s. is a great...comfort NIETZSCHE, F, 11; SUICIDE, 21
To attempt s. is a criminal offense SUICIDE, 7
who has never dallied with the thought of s. SUICIDE, 19
suit in a light so dim he would not have chosen a s. by it LOVE, 54
My s. is pale yellow. My nationality is French WILLIAMS, T, 1
suitable no s. material to work on OBEDIENCE, 2
Sukey S. take it off again NURSERY RHYMES, 44
sulphur land of Calvin, oat-cakes, and s. SCOTLAND, 8; SMITH, S, 7
Puffed its s. to the sunset BETJEMAN, J, 9; TRAVEL, 9
sulphuric like s. acid and sugar VIRTUE AND VICE, 7
sultry common where the climate's s. ADULTERY, 1; BYRON, 19
sum *Cogito, ergo s.* THINKING, 4
sumer S. is icumen in ANONYMOUS, 75; SEASONS, 1
summer after many a s. dies the swan MORTALITY, 19; TENNYSON, 75
All on a s. day CARROLL, L, 19; FOOD, 20
Beauty sat with me all the s. day BEAUTY, 12
Before the war...it was s. all the year round NOSTALGIA, 19; ORWELL, G, 10
choosing dress material for this uncertain s. WRITING, 40
Made glorious s. OPTIMISM, 35; SHAKESPEARE, 302
murmur of a s.'s day SEASONS, 3
Now the peak of s.'s past TRANSIENCE, 11
Spring and s. did happen in Cambridge CAMBRIDGE, 4; NABOKOV, V, 6
S. afternoon – s. afternoon JAMES, H, 15
S. has set in COLERIDGE, S, 46; SEASONS, 7
the last rose of s. FLOWERS, 10; MOORE, T, 5
The s. talk stopped SEASONS, 4
Warm s. sun shine kindly here ANONYMOUS, 104
summit the s. of Everest was hardly the place PHOTOGRAPHY, 5
summits snowy s. old in story TENNYSON, 61
summons when Fate s. DRYDEN, J, 26; MORTALITY, 5
summum *S. bonum* GOOD, 3
sun all, except their s. is set BYRON, 26; EUROPE, 3
aweary of the s. SHAKESPEARE, 228; WORLD-WEARINESS, 8
before you let the s. in, mind it wipes its shoes THOMAS, D, 19
better is he...who hath not seen the evil work under the s. BIBLE, 68; EVIL, 4
between me and the s. REPARTEE, 2
Busy old fool, unruly S. DONNE, J, 16; SUN, 3
Fear no more the heat o' th' s. MORTALITY, 16; SHAKESPEARE, 63
Follow thy fair s. CAMPION, T, 1; SORROW, 5
Furnish'd and burnish'd by Aldershot s. BETJEMAN, J, 12
go out in the mid-day s. COWARD, N, 12
Hath Britain all the s. that shines SUN, 7
If they had said the s. and the moon was gone CARLYLE, J, 3
it were better for s. and moon to drop from heaven SIN, 22
I will sing of the s. POUND, E, 9; WOMEN, 110
Juliet is the s. SHAKESPEARE, 310
let not the s. go down upon your wrath BIBLE, 94
Light breaks where no s. shines EMOTION, 5; THOMAS, D, 14
love that moves the s. DANTE ALIGHIERI, 7
millions of people who sit out in the s. to become darker APPEARANCE, 33
Mother, give me the s. SUN, 4
My s. sets BROWNING, R, 7; OPTIMISM, 17
nothing like the s. ANALOGY, 4; SHAKESPEARE, 373
our own place in the s. IMPORTANCE, 2

So sicken waning moons too near the s. DRYDEN, J, 19; MOON, 4
Spring...stipple leaves with s. SEASONS, 19
s. and the moon was gone out of the heavens POETS, 23
s. came dazzling thro' the leaves CHIVALRY, 15; TENNYSON, 45
s. had risen to hear him crow ELIOT, G, 5
S. remains fixed in the centre ASTRONOMY, 2
s. shall not burn thee by day PSALMS, 68
Thank heavens the s. has gone in LAST WORDS, 82; SMITH, L, 8
The kiss of s. for pardon GARDENS, 7
The people – could you patent the s. DISCOVERY, 13; SCIENCE, 81
there is no new thing under the s. BIBLE, 62; NOVELTY, 1
There rises the s. of Austerlitz NAPOLEON I, 7; WAR, 116
The S. came up upon the left COLERIDGE, S, 25; SUN, 2
the s....cometh forth as a bridegroom PSALMS, 8
The s. does not set in my dominions ROYALTY, 102
the s....rejoiceth as a giant PSALMS, 8
the s. shining ten days a year and shit in the streets ENGLAND, 27
this s. of York OPTIMISM, 35; SHAKESPEARE, 302
To have enjoy'd the s. ARNOLD, M, 12; LIFE, 5
we cannot make our s. /Stand still LOVE, 111; MARVELL, A, 11
with peaches and women, it's...the side next the s. that's tempting TEMPTATION, 8

sunbonnet the s. as well as the sombrero has helped COURAGE, 16
sunburn S. is very becoming APPEARANCE, 20; COWARD, N, 10
Sunday A Christian...feels /Repentance on a S. CHRISTIANITY, 64; HYPOCRISY, 24
Buried on S. HUMAN CONDITION, 19; NURSERY RHYMES, 53
only two posh papers on a S. NEWSPAPERS, 13; OSBORNE, J, 2
S. morning, Fate's great bazaar MACNEICE, L, 5
The feeling of S. is the same everywhere RHYS, J, 3; SUNDAY, 5
sundial s., and I make a botch BELLOC, H, 7
sung I have s. women in three cities POUND, E, 9; WOMEN, 110
sunk thanks to words, we have often s. to the level of the demons HUXLEY, A, 3; WORDS, 19
sunless Down to a s. sea COLERIDGE, S, 14; PLEASURE, 10
sunlight s. as a kind of cosmetic effulgence SUN, 8
sunlit broad, s. uplands WORLD WAR II, 10
sunset a s.-touch BROWNING, R, 10; WORRY, 10
Puffed its sulphur to the s. BETJEMAN, J, 9; TRAVEL, 9
S. and evening star DUTY, 8; TENNYSON, 12
s. breezes shiver BOATS, 15; NEWBOLT, H, 4
sunsets I have a horror of s. PROUST, M, 16; SUN, 5
superbity towering immodesty, the enjoyable s. of his self love VIDAL, G, 1
superior being a novelist, I consider myself s. to the saint, the scientist LAWRENCE, D, 38
One is not s....because one sees the world in an odious light CYNICISM, 1
The French want no-one to be their *s.* PRIDE, 13
young man with so s. a voice OXFORD, 4
superiority their insolent and unfounded airs of s. FRANCE, 19; WALPOLE, H, 9
The s. of one man's opinion over another's JAMES, H, 13; OPINIONS, 5
superiors equality...with our s. EQUALITY, 7
everybody is of the opinion that he has no social s. EQUALITY, 28; RUSSELL, B, 22
Super-jew I'm S. JEWS, 5
superlative we have not settled the s. CHESTERTON, G, 19; PROGRESS, 9
Super-Mac Introducing S. POLITICIANS, 125
Superman he...raked up the S. NIETZSCHE, F, 1
I teach you the S. NIETZSCHE, F, 17
supernatural Religion /Has made an honest woman of the s. FRY, C, 3
This s. soliciting SHAKESPEARE, 204; SUPERNATURAL, 14
supersititious vouched for by...human beings...must be benighted and s. SCIENCE, 55
superstition necessary for a s. to enslave a philosophy INGE, W, 6; RELIGION, 55
S. is the poetry of life GOETHE, J, 6; SUPERSTITION, 9
S. is the religion of feeble minds BURKE, E, 12; SUPERSTITION, 8
S. sets the whole world in flames SUPERSTITION, 12; VOLTAIRE, 13
superstitions new truths...end as s. HUXLEY, T, 3; NOVELTY, 4
s. of the human mind PURITY, 4; VOLTAIRE, 21
superstitious men of Athens...ye are too s. SUPERSTITION, 6
superstructure Sentimentality is a s. covering brutality JUNG, C, 8; SENTIMENTALITY, 2
supp'd I have s. full with horrors SHAKESPEARE, 226; WORLD-WEARINESS, 7
support atheist...no invisible means of s. ATHEISM, 6
my fellow Americans – I ask for your s. SUPPORT, 7
s. me when I am...wrong MELBOURNE, 4; SUPPORT, 5
supposing s. him to be the gardener BIBLE, 275
suppressed must be s. CHINA, 8
supreme Our s. governors, the mob PUBLIC, 21; WALPOLE, H, 3
sups He who s. with the devil CAUTION, 4; PROVERBS, 203
surgeon A fashionable s. like a pelican DOCTORS, 32
one little touch of a s.'s lancet REMEDIES, 43
surgeons Human beings, yes, but not s. MEDICINE, 102
start with the s....and work *up* to the gutter THOMAS, D, 6
There is no counting the names, that s. and anatomists give KNOWLEDGE, 35
'The s. have arrived.' DOCTORS, 62
surmise with a wild s. DISCOVERY, 11; KEATS, J, 42
surpassed Man is something that is to be s. NIETZSCHE, F, 17; SUPERIORITY, 13
surprise Life is a great s. NABOKOV, V, 2
surprised it is *I* who am s.; you are merely astonished WORDS, 36
the audience want to be s....by things that they expect PLAYS, 3
they are...s. at hearing of a good action KEATS, J, 70
surrender never s. to what is right QUAYLE, D, 6
No terms except...s. GRANT, U, 3; WAR, 73
we shall never s. CHURCHILL, W, 50; WORLD WAR II, 11
survey When I s. the wondrous Cross HUMILITY, 14; WATTS, I, 8
survival Both main branches of s. machines evolved EVOLUTION, 12
S. of the fittest DARWIN, C, 10; EVOLUTION, 11
without victory there is no s. CHURCHILL, W, 49; VICTORY, 3
survive always be some that s. SURVIVAL, 3
as fitted to s....as a tapeworm GOLDING, W, 1; INSULTS, 54
only the Fit s. SURVIVAL, 9
Out of their cataclysm but one poor Noah /Dare hope to s. HUXLEY, A, 18; SEX, 54
that far down you have to struggle to s. FAMILY, 30
What will s. of us is love LOVE, 99
survived I s. SELF-PRESERVATION, 12
survives Education is what s. EDUCATION, 85
suspect I rather s. her of being in love LOVE AND MARRIAGE, 3
suspected New opinions are always s. NOVELTY, 5
suspense This s. is terrible EXPECTATION, 9; WILDE, O, 35
suspension Bible demands s. of belief BIBLE, 529
willing s. of disbelief COLERIDGE, S, 8; POETRY, 18
suspicion Caesar's wife must be above s. CAESAR, J, 2; INTEGRITY, 2
people under s. are better moving KAFKA, F, 4
S. always haunts the guilty mind GUILT, 15
the s....his life was a preparation for elder statesmanship MACMILLAN, H, 2
suspicions strong s. that Crippen London cellar murderer TELEGRAMS, 9
S. amongst thoughts BACON, F, 53; SUSPICION, 1
swagman Once a jolly s. camped by a billy-bong PLACES, 29
swains all our s. commend her ADMIRATION, 18; COMPLIMENTS, 32; SHAKESPEARE, 350
swallow One s. does not make a summer PROOF, 1; PROVERBS, 330
the s. a nest where she may lay her young PSALMS, 44
swallowed death is s. up in victory BIBLE, 42; DEATH, 35
swallows I hate a man who s. it FOOD, 42; LAMB, C, 5
one master-passion.../s. up the rest PASSION, 7; POPE, A, 35
swan after many a summer dies the s. MORTALITY, 19; TENNYSON, 75
Sweet S. of Avon JONSON, B, 12; SHAKESPEARE, 12
What time is the next s. MISTAKES, 18
Swanee 'Way down upon de S. Ribber HOMESICKNESS, 3
swans S. sing before they die COLERIDGE, S, 12; SINGERS, 1
sway A little rule, a little s. TRANSIENCE, 13
swear Not bound to s. allegiance to any master HORACE, 13
s. not by the moon SHAKESPEARE, 313; UNFAITHFULNESS, 7
swearing S. at the polo club SPORT AND GAMES, 16
swear-word A foreign s. is LANGUAGE, 46
sweat blood, toil, tears and s. CHURCHILL, W, 48; EFFORT, 3
it is only because miners s. their guts out ORWELL, G, 23; SUPERIORITY, 14
That shriek and s. in pigmy wars TENNYSON, 48; TRIVIALITY, 15

sweats Falstaff s. to death OBESITY, 14; SHAKESPEARE, 111
sweet Heard melodies are s. KEATS, J, 28; MUSIC, 33
How s. are looks that ladies bend TENNYSON, 73; WOMEN, 129
How s. the moonlight SHAKESPEARE, 251
if TODAY be s. FITZGERALD, E, 12; TIME, 22
Is trifle sufficient for s. BETJEMAN, J, 7; FOOD, 12
Pleasures newly found are s. PLEASURE, 37; WORDSWORTH, W, 77
Revenge, at first though s. MILTON, J, 51; REVENGE, 15
so s. as Melancholy MELANCHOLY, 2
S. childish days NOSTALGIA, 29; WORDSWORTH, W, 72
S. day, so cool, so calm DAY, 8; HERBERT, G, 9
S. Smell of Success SUCCESS, 17
s. will be the flower COWPER, W, 18; PATIENCE, 9
that bitter beer that tastes s. IMMORTALITY, 6; RILKE, R, 4
sweeter s. also than honey PSALMS, 9
The mountain sheep are s. GREED, 10; PEACOCK, T, 7
what is s. than honey BIBLE, 295
sweetes S.' li'l' feller BABIES, 9
sweetest Success is counted s. SUCCESS, 10
s. things turn sourest CORRUPTION, 13; SHAKESPEARE, 368
s. thing that ever grew /Beside a human door ADMIRATION, 20; COMPLIMENTS, 39; WORDSWORTH, W, 18
sweetness Culture is the passion for s. and light ARNOLD, M, 23; CULTURE, 2
He who works for s. and light ARNOLD, M, 5; PERFECTION, 1
waste its s. on the desert air GRAY, T, 5; WASTE, 2
sweets Stolen s. are always sweeter, /Stolen kisses much completer THEFT, 7
Stolen s. are best THEFT, 5
swept away often we support change, and then are s. CHANGE, 11
swift Irish dolphin, s. and single ANIMALS, 22
race is not to the s. BIBLE, 74
s. to hear BIBLE, 217
Too s. arrives as tardy as too slow SHAKESPEARE, 316
swimming s. under water FITZGERALD, F, 16; WRITING, 14
swine a s. to show you where the truffles are VULGARITY, 1
Come in, you Anglo-Saxon s. BEHAN, B, 9; INSULTS, 16
pearls before s. BIBLE, 374; FOOLISHNESS, 9; INSULTS, 102
the husks that the s. did eat BIBLE, 331
swines Curse the blasted, jelly-boned s. PUBLISHING, 10
swing S., s. together BOATS, 4
swings we pulls up on the s. LOSS, 2
Swiss if the S. had designed these mountains SWITZERLAND, 4
S. peacekeepers would be the personification NATIONS, 3
The S.…are not a people so much as a…business SWITZERLAND, 2
Swithin St. S.'s Day, if thou dost rain WEATHER, 5
Switzerland Austria is S.…with history added EUROPE, 17
In S. they had brotherly love SWITZERLAND, 5
S.…an inferior sort of Scotland SMITH, S, 15; SWITZERLAND, 3
swollen mere existence is s. to a horror IDEALISM, 5; LAWRENCE, D, 23
sword for all they that take the s. MISQUOTATIONS, 9
his sore and great and strong s. BIBLE, 207
Islam unashamedly came with a s. RELIGION, 79
longing for justice is the s. I carry JUSTICE, 14
more cruel…the pen than the s. WRITING, 8
nation shall not lift up s. against nation BIBLE, 194
not to send peace, but a s. BIBLE, 387
pen is mightier than the s. WRITING, 7
s. sleep in my hand BLAKE, W, 33; ENGLAND, 7; FIGHT, 1
the bank was mightier than the s. LIBERALISM, 3
the word of God is…sharper than any two-edged s. BIBLE, 185
they smote the city with the edge of the s. BIBLE, 291
they that take the s. shall perish with the s. BIBLE, 428
two-edged s. in their hands PSALMS, 76
We draw the s. with a clear conscience WAR, 185
swords beat their s. into plowshares BIBLE, 194
those who have stout hearts and sharp s. RUTHLESSNESS, 6
swound Like noises in a s. COLERIDGE, S, 26; SEA, 4
Sydney There was the vast town of S. LAWRENCE, D, 13; PLACES, 22
symbol vivid and poignant s. of Jewish suffering FRANK, A, 2
symmetry S. is tedious BOREDOM, 6; HUGO, V, 5
thy fearful s. ANIMALS, 6; BLAKE, W, 39
sympathetic To be s. without discrimination SYMPATHY, 2
sympathize s. with everything, except suffering SYMPATHY, 7; WILDE, O, 49
sympathy failed to inspire s. in men BEERBOHM, M, 14; WOMEN, 21
machine-gun riddling her hostess with s. HUXLEY, A, 23
S.…lay over the gathering like a woolly blanket BRADBURY, M, 1
hers MEDICINE, 75
symptom common s. of immaturity ORIGINALITY, 6
symptoms Here am I dying of a hundred good s. ILLNESS, 60
One of the s. of approaching nervous breakdown RUSSELL, B, 6; WORK, 33
syne For auld lang s. BURNS, R, 5; FRIENDSHIP, 13
synthesis as clear as a crystal, the s. – German National Socialism NAZISM, 3
Syrian The S. stars look down ARNOLD, M, 30
system Christianity accepted…a metaphysical s. HUXLEY, A, 19
I'm not interested in the bloody s. GELDOF, B, 1
s. that produced the kettle LODGE, D, 6
s.…to call you darling after sex LOVE, 23
The true s. of the World has been recognized BOOKS, 2
systems Our little s. have their day TENNYSON, 26; TRANSIENCE, 23
Simple s. give rise to complex behavior SCIENCE, 42
the whole solar and stellar s. CARLYLE, T, 30; COMFORT, 2

T

tabasco Sex is the t. sauce SEX, 130
table A man is…better pleased…a good dinner upon his t. JOHNSON, S, 37; WOMAN'S ROLE, 9
crumbs which fell from the rich man's t. BIBLE, 333; POVERTY AND WEALTH, 3
patient etherized upon a t. DEPARTURE, 6; ELIOT, T, 11
put them at a t. together CHURCHILL, W, 33
tableau history…a t. of crimes and misfortunes HISTORY, 35; VOLTAIRE, 20
tables It is not your trade to make t. CRITICISM, 26; JOHNSON, S, 59
t. of stone, and a law AUTHORITARIANISM, 3; BIBLE, 119
tabloid punished for what I did, not what a t. distorted it into MEDIA, 1
tabloids t. suddenly find they have a religious affairs correspondent NEWSPAPERS, 10
taboos Her frontal attacks on old t. STOPES, M, 2
tact Social t. is TACT, 3
T. consists in knowing TACT, 5
tactic Silence is the best t. ROCHEFOUCAULD, 11; SILENCE, 10
tae Here's t. us wha's like us ANONYMOUS, 36; INDIVIDUALITY, 1
tail A case of the t. dogging the wag HUMOUR, 59
The only man who really needs a t. coat CLOTHES, 26
tailor I go to a better t. than any of you CLOTHES, 8
Tinker, /T., /Soldier, /Sailor NURSERY RHYMES, 64; OCCUPATIONS, 21
tails t. you lose VICTORY, 8
'taint That's right. 't. yours, and 't. mine PUNS, 24
tainted the supply is not t. FACTS, 6; JOURNALISM, 31
take T. care of the sense CARROLL, L, 14; MEANING, 2
T. things as they come PROVERBS, 375; WORRY, 4
They have to t. you in FROST, R, 3; HOME, 5
they…t., who have the power POWER, 31; WORDSWORTH, W, 47
You can't t. it with you PROVERBS, 477; WEALTH, 2
taken from him that hath not shall be t. away BIBLE, 419
the Lord gave, and the Lord hath t. away BIBLE, 223
takes It t. all sorts OPPOSITES, 1; PROVERBS, 234
taking not winning but t. part VICTORY, 7
tale A t. never loses GOSSIP, 2; PROVERBS, 69
a t. that is told PSALMS, 50
a t. /Told by an idiot LIFE, 86; SHAKESPEARE, 227
Life is as tedious as a twice-told t. LIFE, 85; SHAKESPEARE, 166
t. to tell of the hardihood, endurance, and courage of my companions ENDURANCE, 19; EXPLORATION, 4
thereby hangs a t. LIFE, 82; SHAKESPEARE, 47
talent A best-seller is the gilded tomb of a mediocre t. BOOKS, 45; SMITH, L, 1
a country full of genius, but with absolutely no t. IRELAND, 14
any man who has no t. ENGLISH, 4; TALENT, 1
A t. to amuse TALENT, 3
Like Tolstoy, he is a man of great t. SOLZHENITSYN, A, 3
Middle age snuffs out more t. TALENT, 5

T. alone cannot make a writer EMERSON, R, 18
T. alone cannot make a writer WRITERS, 10
T. develops in quiet places GOETHE, J, 7
T. does what it can TALENT AND GENIUS, 3
t. for describing the...characters of ordinary life AUSTEN, J, 2
t. instantly recognizes genius DOYLE, A, 17
t. is in coming up with good stories about lawyers WRITING, 18
the difference between t. and genius TALENT AND GENIUS, 1
the meanest...deeds require spirit and t. INSENSITIVITY, 4
the most extraordinary collection of t. TALENT, 7
There is no substitute for t. HUXLEY, A, 27; TALENT, 6
There is no such thing as a great t. without great will-power BALZAC, H, 2
the t. of flattering with delicacy AUSTEN, J, 22
Whatever question there may be of his t. THOREAU, H, 1
talents A vain...coxcomb without...solid t. PEPYS, S, 1
If you have great t., industry will improve them WORK, 30
the difference between our t. and our expectations DISAPPOINTMENT, 1
very rich people who are rich because they have t. or vital statistics SCOTT, P, 2
talk If you can t. with crowds and keep your virtue IDEALISM, 4; KIPLING, R, 18
If you want me to t. for ten minutes SPEECHES, 13
my ministers t. – as long as they do what I say THATCHER, M, 38
never t. about anything except me TELEGRAMS, 13
T. of the devil DEVIL, 2; PROVERBS, 376
Teas, /Where small t. dies CONVERSATION, 9; SHELLEY, P, 19
the need to t. is a primary impulse CERVANTES, M, 14; IMPETUOSITY, 1
think too little...t. too much DRYDEN, J, 8; VERBOSITY, 4
Two may t....yet never really meet FRIENDSHIP, 14
We have ways of making men t. MISQUOTATIONS, 4
we never t. about anything except me CONCEIT, 23; WHISTLER, J, 5
when I hear anyone t. of Culture PHILISTINISM, 4
When two Englishmen meet, their first t. is of the weather JOHNSON, S, 15
women should t. an hour BEAUMONT, F, 10; SEXES, 3
you wished him to t. on for ever POETS, 38
talked He t. on for ever HAZLITT, W, 8
The more you are t. about, the more you...wish to be t. about RUSSELL, B, 12
There is only one thing...worse than being t. about WILDE, O, 46
talker A good listener is a good t. with a sore throat WHITEHORN, K, 7
a non-stop t. to whom someone has given a typewriter WRITERS, 39
Nothing is more despicable than a professional t. VERBOSITY, 5
talkers fluent t. HAZLITT, W, 20; THINKING, 7
talking for thirty-five years he had not stopped t. SCIENTISTS, 17
Frenchman must be always t. FRANCE, 12; JOHNSON, S, 133
good newspaper...is a nation t. to itself JOURNALISM, 25; MILLER, A, 5
I must...try hard to control the t. habit, but...my case is hereditary FRANK, A, 10
I wouldn't be...t. to someone like you SNOBBERY, 4
People t. without speaking FUTILITY, 13
T. and eloquence are not the same JONSON, B, 9; SPEECH, 13
T. of Michelangelo ELIOT, T, 12; WOMEN, 53
While we're t., time will have meanly run on HORACE, 31; PRESENT, 9
talks Garbo T. CINEMA, 3
tall all I ask is a t. ship MASEFIELD, J, 5
Let our children grow t. TALENT, 9; THATCHER, M, 16
Tallulah T. Bankhead barged down the Nile last night and sank CRITICISM, 11
tally-ho Maybe it's that t. lads attitude INSULTS, 121
tambourine Hey! Mr T. Man DYLAN, B, 10; LEISURE, 3
tame the tongue can no man t. SPEECH, 7
tamper Who am I to t. with a masterpiece CONCEIT, 27; WILDE, O, 71
tangere noli me t. BIBLE, 276
tangerine t. trees and marmalade skies LENNON, J, 7
tankard heart which grief hath cankered /...remedy – the T. ALCOHOL, 24
tanks students had t. run over them CHINA, 4
tanned getting more t. and more tired ROYALTY, 94
tapeworm as fitted to survive...as a t. GOLDING, W, 1
Tara through T.'s halls MOORE, T, 2; IRELAND, 17
target IRA would think me a worthwhile t. MOUNTBATTEN OF BURMA, L, 5
tarmac t. over the whole of England CONSERVATION, 3
tarnished neither t. nor afraid COURAGE, 7
tarry having lost...your prime, /You may for ever t. HERRICK, R, 6; MARRIAGE, 88
tarrying make no long t., O my God PSALMS, 24
tart no Joan Bakewell, but you're fairly t. HUMOUR, 48
Tartar Scratch the Russian and...find the T. RUSSIA, 12
tarts He's lost us the t.' vote MEDIA, 7; RESPONSIBILITY, 6
she made some t. CARROLL, L, 19; FOOD, 20; NURSERY RHYMES, 55
Tarzan Me? T. CINEMA, 30
task No t. is a long one but the t. on which one dare not start BEGINNING, 6
The trivial round, the common t. SIMPLICITY, 4
tasks best ways of avoiding necessary and even urgent t. WORK, 12
Tasmanians the T....are now extinct ADULTERY, 5
the T., who never committed adultery, are now extinct MAUGHAM, W, 1
taste bad t. is better than no t. BENNETT, A, 9; TASTE, 2
Between friends differences in t. TASTE, 1
different t. in jokes is a...strain on the affections HUMOUR, 13
Drink deep, or t. not the Pierian spring POPE, A, 23
Every one to his t. DIFFERENCE, 2; PROVERBS, 142
great common sense and good t. CHARACTER, 22; SHAW, G, 8
If you want to see bad t. LE CORBUSIER, 3
I suspect his t. in higher matters FOOD, 42; LAMB, C, 5
no t. when you married me SHERIDAN, R, 10; TASTE, 9
people who always go on about...good t. TASTE, 6
Shakespeare, undoubtedly wanted t. WALPOLE, H, 4
T. is the feminine of genius FITZGERALD, E, 1; TASTE, 3
the bouquet is better than the t. ALCOHOL, 64; POTTER, S, 7
the t. by which he is...relished WORDSWORTH, W, 21
The t. was that of the little crumb of madeleine PROUST, M, 2
Things sweet to t. prove...sour REGRET, 22; SHAKESPEARE, 295
willing to t. any drink once DRINKS, 8
tasted Sir, you have t. two whole worms SPOONER, W, 5
Some books are to be t. BACON, F, 50; BOOKS, 4
tastes It is like a cigar....it never t. quite the same LOVE, 174
Our t. greatly alter JOHNSON, S, 74; TASTE, 4
t. may not be the same TASTE, 8
There is no accounting for t. DIFFERENCE, 5; PROVERBS, 410
taught all the things that can be t. STYLE, 3
a woman who knows all...that can be t. CHANEL, C, 3; INSULTS, 30; KNOWLEDGE, 11
I forget what I was t. KNOWLEDGE, 41; WHITE, P, 2
tavern A t. chair is the throne JOHNSON, S, 38; PUBLIC HOUSES, 1
he has...opened a t. for his friends PARASITES, 1
jangled in every ale-house and t. BIBLE, 531
nothing...so much happiness is produced as by a good t. JOHNSON, S, 102; PUBLIC HOUSES, 2
There is a t. in the town ANONYMOUS, 87; PARTING, 2
tawney that t. weed tobacco JONSON, B, 4; SMOKING, 18
tax a crushing t. on bachelors FEMINISM, 50
A hateful t. JOHNSON, S, 9; TAXATION, 5
don't say that in England for...they will surely t. it SWIFT, J, 19; TAXATION, 13
hardest thing...to understand is income t. TAXATION, 2
has to get her husband to sign her t. form TAXATION, 9
outrageous act to t. me because I am living in Holy matrimony TAXATION, 12
year dead for t. reasons ADAMS, D, 12
taxation T. without representation REPRESENTATION, 2
taxed all the world should be t. BIBLE, 312
taxes Death and t. and childbirth EXPEDIENCY, 6; MITCHELL, M, 3
nothing can be said to be certain but death and t. FRANKLIN, B, 17
people overlaid with t. TAXATION, 1
read my lips, no new t. BUSH, G, 7
The avoidance of t....still carries...reward KEYNES, J, 11; TAXATION, 7
taxi done almost every human activity inside a t. BOASTS, 1
taxis hiring t....handing out redundancy notices to its own workers KINNOCK, N, 10
I don't take whores in t. PROMISCUITY, 11
taxpayer The t. is someone who works for the federal government TAXATION, 10

Tay Beautiful Railway Bridge of the Silv'ry T. DISASTER, 4
tea Dinner, Lunch and T. BELLOC, H, 10; FOOD, 10
honey still for t. BROOKE, R, 5; NOSTALGIA, 3
If I had known there was no Latin word for t. DRINKS, 4
if this is coffee, I want t. DRINKS, 3
it is just like having a cup of t. SEX, 94
sometimes counsel take – and sometimes T. DRINKS, 18; POPE, A, 49
Take some more t. CARROLL, L, 11; LANGUAGE, 10
T. for Two, and Two for T. DRINKS, 13
we drink too much t. DRINKS, 19; PRIESTLEY, J, 6
We invite people like that to t., but we don't marry them BETJEMAN, J, 3
When I makes t. I makes t. HUMOUR, 46; JOYCE, J, 7
teach Don't t. your grandmother PROVERBS, 121
For every person wishing to t. SELLAR, W, 1
He who shall t. the child to doubt BLAKE, W, 8; DOUBT, 4
It is no matter what you t. them first JOHNSON, S, 67
the time had passed…merely to t. foreigners BUSINESS, 20
they cannot t. students clinical medicine MEDICINE, 99
You can't t. an old dog OLD AGE, 7; PROVERBS, 478
teacher A good clinical t. is himself a Medical School EDUCATION, 40
A t. is paid to teach EDUCATION, 35
Experience is a good t. EXPERIENCE, 6
the qualities of a good t. of medicine MEDICINE, 5
Time is a great t., but…kills all its pupils TIME, 13
teachers We t. can only help…as servants EDUCATION, 66
teaches He who cannot, t. EDUCATION, 82; SHAW, G, 32
teaching it is easily possible for t. to be too 'up to date' EDUCATION, 44
the true center of medical t. EDUCATION, 41
teacup Storm in a T. TRIVIALITY, 2
team Is my t. ploughing AGRICULTURE, 3; HOUSMAN, A, 11
The British, being brought up on t. games PARKINSON, C, 3
women…are better t. members than men SPORT AND GAMES, 13
team games The British, being brought up on t. HOUSES OF PARLIAMENT, 17
tear Every t. from every eye BLAKE, W, 7; SORROW, 3
heart to a dog to t. DOGS, 12
Some stars…Fell like a falling t. STARS, 8
tears blood, toil, t. and sweat CHURCHILL, W, 48; EFFORT, 3
foolish t. upon my grave HYPOCRISY, 21; TENNYSON, 11
He spoke, and loos'd our heart in t. ARNOLD, M, 27; POETS, 16
his t. are salt ENVIRONMENT, 9
I forbid my t. SHAKESPEARE, 105
If you have t., prepare to shed them SHAKESPEARE, 158; SORROW, 27
in a flood of t. and a Sedan chair DICKENS, C, 53; HUMOUR, 42
mine own t. /Do scald SHAKESPEARE, 193
No more t. now REVENGE, 20
No t. in the writer FROST, R, 2; WRITING, 15
our t. /Thaw not the frost MOURNING, 14; SHELLEY, P, 3
shed t. when they would devour BACON, F, 60; HYPOCRISY, 2
T., idle tears SORROW, 34; TENNYSON, 62
T. such as angels weep MILTON, J, 36; SORROW, 17
T. were to me SORROW, 8
The bitterest t.…are for words…unsaid REGRET, 26; STOWE, H, 1
The bitterest t. shed over graves STOWE, H, 1
the land of t. SORROW, 25
The smiles, the t., /Of boyhood's years MOORE, T, 7; NOSTALGIA, 17
the women whose eyes have been washed…with t. WOMEN, 46
They that sow in t. shall reap in joy PSALMS, 69
Violet Elizabeth dried her t. THREATS, 2
With silence and t. BYRON, 44; SEPARATION, 2
teas T., /Where small talk dies SHELLEY, P, 19
tease The fleas that t. in the high Pyrenees BELLOC, H, 19; NONSENSE, 3
teased I still get t. mercilessly about the royal family ROYALTY, 45
tea-stirring t. times PRESENT, 11
teatray Like a t. in the sky CARROLL, L, 10; NONSENSE, 5
teche gladly wolde he lerne, and gladly t. CHARACTER, 5; CHAUCER, G, 9
technological For t. man it is time TECHNOLOGY, 13
technology t.…indistinguishable from magic TECHNOLOGY, 5
The t. of medicine has outrun its sociology TECHNOLOGY, 15
Teddy Bear T. to the Nation BETJEMAN, J, 1
tedious People are either charming or t. WILDE, O, 39
They shorten t. nights CAMPION, T, 5; SEX, 22
tedium t. is the very basis of mourning BOREDOM, 6; HUGO, V, 5
teeth he has iron t. GORBACHOV, M, 1
her lips narrow and her t. black ROYALTY, 70
I had braces on my t. and got high marks APPEARANCE, 43
I have let dentists ride roughshod over my t. TEETH, 2
I'll dispose of my t. as I see fit TEETH, 3
It is necessary to clean the t. frequently ETIQUETTE, 2
Man can have only a certain number of t., hair and ideas OLD AGE, 104
natural false t. TEETH, 4
nice smile, but…iron t. POLITICIANS, 89
removing the t. TEETH, 1
take the bull between the t. GOLDWYN, S, 16
taking out his false t. and hurling them at his wife DOYLE, A, 5
They will steal the very t. out of your mouth THEFT, 2
to lose one's t. is a catastrophe TEETH, 6
white sharp t. SUPERNATURAL, 16
whose t. are spears and arrows PSALMS, 36
teething they escaped t. TEETH, 5
teetotaller a beer t., not a champagne t. ALCOHOL, 72
no woman should marry a t. STEVENSON, R, 22
teetotallers about as genial as an *auto da fé* of t. CHESTERTON, G, 2
T. lack the sympathy ABSTINENCE, 3
telephone Glamour…makes a man ask for your t. number STYLE, 5
I don't know his t. number KEYNES, J, 10
your struggles, your dreams, your t. number LOVE, 18
telephone-exchange we are supposing the brain…more than a t. MIND, 30
television eats, sleeps and watches the t. GREER, G, 3
have sex or appear on t. OPPORTUNITY, 23
Masturbation is the thinking man's t. SEX, 48
perfect for t. is all a President has to be REAGAN, R, 3
stay at home and see bad t. GOLDWYN, S, 2
T. brought the brutality of war WAR, 105
T. is for appearing on TELEVISION, 4
t. programs are so much chewing gum TELEVISION, 3
There is a bias in t. journalism JOURNALISM, 11; TELEVISION, 2
there's no subject you can't tackle on t. CENSORSHIP, 11
tell do not t. them so CHESTERFIELD, P, 5; WISDOM, 14
How could they t. POLITICIANS, 111
people who love to t. us what to do ENGLISH, 25
T. the truth PROVERBS, 377; TRUTH, 3
you must not kiss and t. CONGREVE, W, 6; SECRECY, 7
you never can t.. That's a principle PRINCIPLES, 5; SHAW, G, 43
telly You don't get any pornography…on the t. PORNOGRAPHY, 8
Téméraire She's the Fighting T. BOATS, 15; NEWBOLT, H, 4
temper A tart t. never mellows with age CHARACTER, 12
if I were not king, I should lose my t. LOUIS XIV, 6
Never lose your t. with the Press PANKHURST, C, 3; SELF-CONTROL, 7
temperament artistic t. is a disease CHESTERTON, G, 25
temperance by t. they all mean the opposite ABSTINENCE, 11
I prefer t. hotels ALCOHOL, 85
She belongs to a T. Society ABSTINENCE, 11
T. is the love of health MODERATION, 10
tempests On whom Thy t. fell all night HERBERT, G, 4; OLD AGE, 53
That looks on t. LOVE, 150; SHAKESPEARE, 370
temple in the very t. of delight KEATS, J, 34; MELANCHOLY, 7
The Arab who builds…a hut out of…a t. FRANCE, A, 4; PRACTICALITY, 3
the veil of the t. was rent in twain BIBLE, 432; LAST WORDS, 11
This is the t. of Providence LUCK, 8
who is there…would go into the t. to save his life BIBLE, 435
your body is the t. of the Holy Ghost BIBLE, 28
temples t. made with hands BIBLE, 12; SUPERSTITION, 6
tempora *O t.! O mores* CUSTOM, 1
temporal pass through things t. BOOK OF COMMON PRAYER, 6
rendered to the t. king to the prejudice of the eternal king TREASON, 11
temporary force alone is but *t.* BURKE, E, 15; FORCE, 3
tempt thou shalt not t. the Lord thy God BIBLE, 357
temptation blessed is the man that endureth t. BIBLE, 216
I never resist t. TEMPTATION, 9
lead us not into t. BIBLE, 367
over-fond of resisting t. TEMPTATION, 3

prepare thy soul for t. BIBLE, 80
resist everything except t. TEMPTATION, 10; WILDE, O, 38
the day of t. in the wilderness PSALMS, 56
The last t. ELIOT, T, 18; MOTIVE, 2
The only way to get rid of a t. TEMPTATION, 11; WILDE, O, 47
virtue is only elicited by t. BRONTE, A, 4
'You oughtn't to yield to t..' HOPE, A, 4; TEMPTATION, 7
temptations in spite of all t.…He remains an Englishman GILBERT, W, 14
tempting the devil did not play in t. of me PROSE, 2
with peaches and women, it's…the side next the sun that's t. TEMPTATION, 8
ten only t. PUBLIC, 17
T. Days that Shook the World RUSSIAN REVOLUTION, 7
Ten for the t. commandments ANONYMOUS, 45; NUMBERS, 1
T. pipers piping CHRISTMAS, 18; NURSERY RHYMES, 59
The good Lord has only t. POLITICIANS, 69
Where there aren't no T. Commandments KIPLING, R, 26
Yes, about t. minutes SERMONS, 4; WELLINGTON, 20
tender Leah was t. eyed BIBLE, 173
tenderness Their flowers the t. of patient minds OWEN, W, 1
ten-dollar He thinks I don't know the t. words HEMINGWAY, E, 9
tenement I inhabit a weak, frail, decayed t. LAST WORDS, 2
tennis Anyone for t. INVITATIONS, 1; SPORT AND GAMES, 2
playing t. with the net down FROST, R, 9; POETRY, 24
tennis-balls We are merely the stars' t. DESTINY, 29; WEBSTER, J, 3
Tennyson T. was not Tennysonian TENNYSON, 4
to write like T.…rather than Eliot or Auden BETJEMAN, J, 2
tenses Hopi, an Indian tribe, have…no t. for past, present and future TIME, 63
tent inside my t. pissing out JOHNSON, L, 7; PRUDENCE, 8
tentacles dear octopus from whose t. we never quite escape FAMILY, 55
tents the t. of ungodliness PSALMS, 45
Those who have never dwelt in t. SACKVILLE-WEST, V, 5
term Is a t. that will bolster my thesis WORDS, 10
terminal god would be hanging around T. Two ADAMS, D, 8
terminological t. inexactitude CHURCHILL, W, 39; LYING, 10
terminology The jargon of scientific t. LANGUAGE, 22
terms No t. except…surrender GRANT, U, 3; WAR, 73
terrible It is well that war is so t. WAR, 99
t. as an army with banners BIBLE, 496
t. thing for a man to find out HONESTY, 16; WILDE, O, 36
This suspense is t. WILDE, O, 35
terribles *Les enfants t.* YOUTH, 12
territorial the last t. claim which I have to make in Europe WORLD WAR II, 35
terror afraid for any t. by night PSALMS, 51
Christianity has made of death a t. CHRISTIANITY, 51; DEATH, 115
new t. to life TECHNOLOGY, 18
terrorist The t. and the policeman CONRAD, J, 6; EQUALITY, 10
terrorists All t.…end up with drinks at the Dorchester POLITICS, 37
test Martyrdom is the t. FREEDOM, 28; JOHNSON, S, 131
text great t. in Galatians BIBLE, 525; BROWNING, R, 54
texts one of the greatest t. in our…literature PEPYS, S, 2
Thackeray W. M. T. CLERGY, 15
Thames Sweet T.! run softly RIVERS, 5
the T. is liquid history RIVERS, 1
What is there to make so much of in the T. RIVERS, 3
thank Don't bother to t. me BANKHEAD, T, 9
T. me no thankings SHAKESPEARE, 318
thankful I am…t. for not having married MARRIAGE, 104; MARTINEAU, H, 1
thankings Thank me no t. GRATITUDE, 3
thankless To have a t. child! SHAKESPEARE, 173
thanks For this relief much t. COMFORT, 4; SHAKESPEARE, 65
'I am glad…he t. God for anything.' JOHNSON, S, 14
thanksgiving come before his presence with t. PSALMS, 54
With proud t. MOURNING, 3
that 1066 And All T. HISTORY, 28; SELLAR, W, 3
Thatcher Blimpish patriotism in the mode of Margaret T. PATRIOTISM, 26
Margaret T.'s great strength CLASS, 54; THATCHER, M, 13
Thatcherism characteristic of T. SOCIETY, 1
the term 'T.' will be seen as a compliment THATCHER, M, 34
thcream I'll t., an' t.…till I'm thick THREATS, 2
theatre Farce is the essential t. THEATRE, 9
For the t. one needs long arms ACTING, 6
nobody goes to the t. unless he…has bronchitis AUDIENCES, 1
T. director: a person ACTING, 1
the t. of events MEDICINE, 28
theft Property is t. CAPITALISM, 16; MARXISM, 15
what would be t. in other poets, is only victory in him JONSON, B, 1
themselves power…over t. WOLLSTONECRAFT, M, 4
theologian This stranger is a t. ATHEISM, 5; GUIDANCE, 2
theologians cathedral is worth a hundred t. RELIGION, 8
theorems About binomial t. GILBERT, W, 39
the world can be expressed in…arguments…axioms and t. THEORY, 5
theories In making t. always keep a window open THEORY, 14
Medical t. are most of the time even more peculiar THEORY, 1
the bewitching delusions of their t. EDUCATION, 49
theorist I'm not a t. PINTER, H, 6
theory A t. can be proved by experiment EINSTEIN, A, 11
a thing may look evil in t. BURKE, E, 28; THEORY, 2
Don't confuse *hypothesis* and *t.* THEORY, 4
it's…more important for a t. to be shapely, than…true HAMPTON, C, 1
no path leads from experiment to…t. EINSTEIN, A, 11
Philosophy is not a t. PHILOSOPHY, 25
Practice should always be based upon a sound knowledge of t. LEONARDO DA VINCI, 7; THEORY, 10
The establishment of t. is the very purpose of science THEORY, 4
t. is all grey GOETHE, J, 2
the scream is sometimes a t. STEVENSON, R, 16; THEORY, 15
therapeutic have such immense t. value SHAW, G, 33
therapy how much valuable t.…cast on the dump PRAYER, 16
I go to t. ROYALTY, 119
there, there brought to shame, that cry over me, t. PSALMS, 40
thesis Is a term that will bolster my t. WORDS, 10
thick Through t. and thin BUTLER, S, 5; FAITHFULNESS, 2
thicken other things than dissipation…t. the features APPEARANCE, 73; WEST, R, 2
thickens plot t. INTRIGUE, 1
thief as a t. in the night BIBLE, 503
I come as a t. BIBLE, 467
Procrastination is the t. of time YOUNG, E, 5
Time, the subtle t. of youth AGE, 64; MILTON, J, 59
which is the justice, which is the t. APPEARANCES, 28
thieves a den of t. BIBLE, 408; CHRISTIANITY, 28
fell among t. BIBLE, 324
T. respect property CRIME, 3
thin Enclosing every t. man OBESITY, 16
Enclosing every t. man, there's a fat man APPEARANCE, 71; WAUGH, E, 33
in every fat man a t. one CONNOLLY, C, 18; OBESITY, 6
One can never be too t. WEALTH, 49
Outside every t. girl LUST, 13; OBESITY, 17
The one way to get t. OBESITY, 8
there's a t. man inside every fat man OBESITY, 12; ORWELL, G, 9
There were times my pants were so t. POVERTY, 42
t. red line tipped with steel COURAGE, 24; WAR, 141
Through thick and t. BUTLER, S, 5; FAITHFULNESS, 2
thing call that t. under your hat a head INSULTS, 63
good t., to make it too common ENGLAND, 45; SHAKESPEARE, 118
It is a far, far, better t. that I do DICKENS, C, 57; EXECUTION, 8
only t. we have to fear is fear itself FEAR, 8
something between a t. and a thought PAINTING, 11
sooty bosom /Of such a t. as thou PREJUDICE, 14
That's a pretty little t. ARTISTS, 15
The play's the t. PLAYS, 14; SHAKESPEARE, 89
the t. which is good BIBLE, 94; PUNISHMENT, 2; SIN, 3
thing-in-itself The t., the will-to-live SCHOPENHAUER, A, 5; SURVIVAL, 8
things all t. were made by him BIBLE, 238
be without some of the t. you want HAPPINESS, 21
Glorious t. of thee are spoken HEAVEN, 9
T. are entirely what they appear to be APPEARANCES, 25; REALITY, 7; SARTRE, J, 8
To talk of many t. CARROLL, L, 28; NONSENSE, 9
think apparatus with which we t. BIERCE, A, 4; MIND, 1
He can't t. without his hat THINKING, 2
I cannot sit and t. LAMB, C, 13; READING, 9
I exist by what I t. SARTRE, J, 9; THINKING, 16

who sneaked into my room at t. o'clock this morning COMPLAINTS, 5; MARX, G, 14
threefold a t. cord is not quickly broken BIBLE, 70; UNITY, 5
three-piece first t. suit, first lawsuit SUCCESS, 31
three-pipe a t. problem DOYLE, A, 13; SMOKING, 10
threescore years the days of our age are t. and ten PSALMS, 50
three-sided if triangles invented a god, they would make him t. MONTESQUIEU, 4
thrice before the cock crow, thou shalt deny me t. BIBLE, 425
thrift extravagance…t. and adventure THRIFT, 6
T. has nearly killed her THRIFT, 7
thriller bolt down a cheap t. LITERATURE, 5
thrive strong shall t. SURVIVAL, 9
throat A good listener is a good talker with a sore t. WHITEHORN, K, 7
man holds you round the t. APOLOGIES, 6
the second act and the child's t. CRITICISM, 16
throats cutting each other's t. CARLYLE, T, 34; SLAVERY, 3
throne A man may build…a t. of bayonets INGE, W, 11
A tavern chair is the t. JOHNSON, S, 38
barge…like a burnished t. SHAKESPEARE, 30
High on a t. of royal state DEVIL, 13; MILTON, J, 39
It helps…to remind your bride that you gave up a t. for her MARRIAGE, 171
no middle course between the t. and the scaffold MONARCHY, 9
No pain, no palm; no thorns, no t. SUCCESS, 24
royal t. of kings ENGLAND, 46; SHAKESPEARE, 297
something behind the t. MONARCHY, 18; PITT THE ELDER, 5
through part of it all the way t. GOLDWYN, S, 18
throve that on which it t. /Falls off LOVE, 165; TENNYSON, 78
throw t. an egg into an electric fan AMBITION, 10
t. away the dearest thing he ow'd DEATH, 147; SHAKESPEARE, 206
thrush That's the wise t. BROWNING, R, 27
Thucydides the historical works of T. NEWSPAPERS, 7
thumbscrew To the t. and the stake TENNYSON, 70
thunder laugh as I pass in t. SHELLEY, P, 5; WEATHER, 24
our soul /Had *felt* him like the t.'s roll ARNOLD, M, 26
trivial people…t. /In such lovely language SHAKESPEARE, 13
Thurlow No man…so wise as T. looked APPEARANCES, 16
Thursday T.'s child has far to go CHILDREN, 50; NURSERY RHYMES, 35
Took ill on T. HUMAN CONDITION, 19; NURSERY RHYMES, 53
'Twas on a Holy T. CHILDREN, 21
thyself Be so true to t. BACON, F, 59; INTEGRITY, 1
Know then t., presume not God to scan POPE, A, 34
Resolve to be t. ARNOLD, M, 39
Tiananmen demonstrations from Chengdu to T. Square CHINA, 5
Tiber married to the only man north of the T.…untidier than I am WHITEHORN, K, 2
the River T. foaming with much blood PROPHECY, 11; RACISM, 26
the T. foaming with /much blood PROPHECY, 14; VIRGIL, 14
Tiberius Had T. been a cat ARNOLD, M, 33; CATS, 1
tickle a feather to t. the intellect LAMB, C, 16; PUNS, 12
ticky-tacky They're all made out of t. HOUSES, 4
tide a t. in the affairs of men OPPORTUNITY, 19; SHAKESPEARE, 161
a t. in the affairs of women BYRON, 31; FEMINISM, 43
ever lived in the t. of times REGRET, 20; SHAKESPEARE, 152
the full t. of human existence is at Charing-Cross JOHNSON, S, 93; LONDON, 17
The t. is full ARNOLD, M, 10; SEA, 1
The western t. crept up DROWNING, 1; KINGSLEY, C, 5
tides the waters of the heart /Push in their t. EMOTION, 5; THOMAS, D, 14
tidings good t. of great joy BIBLE, 314; CHRISTMAS, 9
tie Never mind about my soul…get my t. right JOYCE, J, 13; PAINTING, 8
tied t. to the stake ENDURANCE, 20
tiger It is not the ape, nor the t. HUMAN NATURE, 32
The atom bomb is a paper t. MAO TSE-TUNG, 9; NUCLEAR WEAPONS, 14
T.! T.! burning bright ANIMALS, 6; BLAKE, W, 39
tigers Dictators ride to and fro upon t. AUTHORITARIANISM, 4; CHURCHILL, W, 31
For tamed and shabby t. ANIMALS, 15
reactionaries are paper t. MAO TSE-TUNG, 5; POLITICS, 75
tightrope You may reasonably expect a man to walk a t. safely NUCLEAR WEAPONS, 21; RUSSELL, B, 29
tile it's not even red brick, but white t. CLASS, 34; OSBORNE, J, 4
tiller a t. of the ground BIBLE, 153
timber a…soul like season'd t. HERBERT, G, 10; VIRTUE, 17
replacing some of the t. used up by my books TREES, 6
Timbuctoo On the plains of T. CLERGY, 15
time a book to kill t. CRITICISM, 40
a comfortable t. lag…between the perception PROGRESS, 25
A Dance to the Music of T. LIFE, 77
advantage of t. and place…is half a victory WAR, 58
Ageing…the only…way to live a long t. LONGEVITY, 3
A Good T. Was Had by All PLEASURE, 33
And t., that takes survey of all the world, /Must have a stop SHAKESPEARE, 115
annihilate but space and t. LOVE, 126; POPE, A, 3
are subjects all /To envious and calumniating t. TIME, 53
Art is long, and T. is fleeting LONGFELLOW, H, 10; MORTALITY, 14
As if you could kill t. THOREAU, H, 8; TIME, 60
Ask him the t. REAGAN, R, 6
As t. goes by NOSTALGIA, 2; TIME, 26
a t. to be born, and a t. to die BIBLE, 67; TIME, 14
bid t. return REGRET, 25
big man has no t. FAME, 13; FITZGERALD, F, 13
But get me to the church on t. MARRIAGE, 101
But t. is too large SARTRE, J, 12
chronicle of wasted t. SHAKESPEARE, 369
do not squander t. FRANKLIN, B, 9
Even such is T. RALEIGH, W, 3
For technological man it is t. TECHNOLOGY, 13
Had we but world enough, and t. MARVELL, A, 9
He hath shook hands with t. DEATH, 66
Hurry! I never hurry. I have no t. to hurry STRAVINSKY, I, 7
If your t. hasn't come DOCTORS, 75
I haven't got t. to be tired LAST WORDS, 95; WORK, 40
I…may be some t. LAST WORDS, 63
in a moment of t. BIBLE, 319; DEVIL, 4
inaudible and noiseless foot of T. SHAKESPEARE, 24; TIME, 46
irretrievable t. is flying TIME, 61; VIRGIL, 19
I shall lose no t. in reading it DISRAELI, B, 19; INATTENTION, 1
It is only t. that weighs TIME, 39
it's for such a long t. DEATH, 112; MOLIERE, 4
killing t.…T. kills us TIME, 56
Lincoln had faith in t. LINCOLN, A, 3
make the beat keep t. with short steps FUNERALS, 1
many events in the womb of t. SHAKESPEARE, 280
Men talk of killing t. TIME, 15
moment of t. ELIZABETH I, 15; LAST WORDS, 29
My t. has not yet come NIETZSCHE, F, 8; POSTERITY, 10
Nature, t. and patience are the three great physicians MEDICINE, 1
Never before have we had so little t. HASTE, 9; ROOSEVELT, F, 15
Never the t. and the place BROWNING, R, 36; PERVERSITY, 2
no delight to pass away the t. APPEARANCE, 61
not had the t. to make it shorter PASCAL, B, 1; VERBOSITY, 6
No t. like the present PRESENT, 1; PROVERBS, 320
no t. to stand and stare IDLENESS, 5
not of an age, but for all t. JONSON, B, 11
now doth t. waste me TIME, 49
O aching t. KEATS, J, 20; TIME, 28
On the breast of the river of T. ARNOLD, M, 18
peace for our t. CHAMBERLAIN, N, 6
peace in our t., O Lord PEACE, 6
pluck till t. and times are done DESIRE, 18; YEATS, W, 30
Procrastination is the thief of t. YOUNG, E, 5
range of human societies in t. MANKIND, 35
Redeem thy mis-spent t. PRESENT, 12
such a t. must inevitably…arrive will cheer my dying hour ILLNESS, 64
that old common arbitrator, T. SHAKESPEARE, 334
That passed the t. BECKETT, S, 3; TIME, 11
The art of medicine is generally a question of t. MEDICINE, 69
The Bird of T.…little way /To fly FITZGERALD, E, 3; TIME, 21
the long result of T. EXPERIENCE, 20; TENNYSON, 49
The man is killing t. TIME, 35
the original good t. that was had by all PROMISCUITY, 2
The physician's best remedy is *Tincture of T.* TIME, 43
There is a t. and place PROVERBS, 407; TIME, 3
There was a t. when meadow INNOCENCE, 16
the t. had passed…merely to teach foreigners BUSINESS, 20
'The t. has come,' the Walrus said CARROLL, L, 28; NONSENSE, 9
The t. is out of joint SHAKESPEARE, 80
the t. of my departure is at hand BIBLE, 514; FAITH, 11
the t. will come when you will hear me DISRAELI, B, 20

the wrong place at the wrong t. under the wrong circumstances JOHNSON, L, 1
this bank and shoal of t. ENDING, 6; SHAKESPEARE, 210
those feet in ancient t. BLAKE, W, 33; ENGLAND, 7; FIGHT, 1
Thus the whirligig of t. brings in his revenges TIME, 55
t. and chance happeneth to them all BIBLE, 74; CHANCE, 2
T. and the hour runs through SHAKESPEARE, 205; TIME, 47
T. and tide PROVERBS, 433; TIME, 4
t. as a tool not as a couch KENNEDY, J, 6; TIME, 29
T. cures the sick man, not the ointment TIME, 7
T. driveth onward fast TENNYSON, 54; TIME, 57
T. drops in decay TIME, 64; YEATS, W, 21
T. flies, death urges TIME, 66; YOUNG, E, 7
T. for a little something MILNE, A, 7
T. goes by: reputation increases OLD AGE, 51
T. had robbed her of her personal charms DISEASE, 18
T. hath, my lord, a wallet at his back SHAKESPEARE, 333; TIME, 52
T. heals what reason cannot TIME, 44
T. held me green and dying THOMAS, D, 9; TIME, 58
T. is a great healer PROVERBS, 434; TIME, 5
T. is a great teacher, but...kills all its pupils TIME, 13
T. is a physician TIME, 18
T. is but the stream I go a-fishing in THOREAU, H, 17; TIME, 59
T. is like a river made up of the events which happen MARCUS AURELIUS ANTONINUS, 8; TRANSIENCE, 3
t. is money BUSINESS, 13; FRANKLIN, B, 3
T. is on our side PROGRESS, 14
T. is slipping underneath our Feet FITZGERALD, E, 12; TIME, 22
T....is something you're only given when...you don't need it TIME, 16
T. is the creator TIME, 8
t. is the greatest innovator BACON, F, 30; INNOVATION, 1
T. is the great physician TIME, 19
T. is too large TIME, 42
T. may restore us ARNOLD, M, 28; POETS, 17
t. of life is short LIFE, 84
T. present and t. past ELIOT, T, 6; TIME, 20
t. quietly kills them TIME, 15
T.'s up for Sir John, an' for little Lady Jane LAWRENCE, D, 18
T.'s winged chariot AGE, 61; MARVELL, A, 10
T., the subtle thief of youth AGE, 64; MILTON, J, 59
t. to love, and a t. to hate BIBLE, 67
T. was away and somewhere else LOVE, 109; MACNEICE, L, 4
T. whereof the memory of man BLACKSTONE, W, 3; MEMORY, 3
T., /Will one day end it TIME, 54
T. will tell PROVERBS, 435; TIME, 6
T. wounds all heels MARX, G, 22; TIME, 36
To choose t. is to save t. BACON, F, 20; TIME, 9
to waste my t. making money MONEY, 4
We have short t. to stay, as you TRANSIENCE, 15
We take no note of t. TIME, 65; YOUNG, E, 6
What do the ravages of t. not injure AGE, 53; HORACE, 37
While we're talking, t. will have meanly run on HORACE, 31; PRESENT, 9
Work expands so as to fill the t. PARKINSON, C, 1; WORK, 24
timeliness the t. of the gift LA BRUYERE, J, 5; PROMPTNESS, 1
times chronicler of her t. BRITTAIN, V, 1
It was the best of t. DICKENS, C, 56; FRENCH REVOLUTION, 3
Like a piece of litmus paper...take the colour of his t. HUXLEY, A, 2
logic of our t. DECLINE, 4
one copy of *The T.* NEWSPAPERS, 7
The 'good old t.' BYRON, 4; NOSTALGIA, 5
The T. has made many ministries BAGEHOT, W, 1; NEWSPAPERS, 2
The T. is speechless CHURCHILL, W, 40; NEWSPAPERS, 6
The T. They Are A-Changin' CHANGE, 6
the true old t. are dead NOSTALGIA, 25; TENNYSON, 22
T. carries all things TIME, 62
Top people take *The T.* NEWSPAPERS, 1
We live in stirring t. PRESENT, 11
times table Once I had learnt my twelve t. MATHEMATICS, 11
time-table I would sooner read a t. MAUGHAM, W, 18; NOVELS, 11
Timor T.'s petroleum smells better than Timorese blood OPPRESSION, 2
tim'rous Wee...t. beastie ANIMALS, 9; BURNS, R, 21
timshel Hebrew word...*t.*...gives a choice CHOICE, 5
tinker heart expands to t. with his car MACNEICE, L, 5
T., /Tailor, /Soldier, /Sailor NURSERY RHYMES, 64; OCCUPATIONS, 21
tinkling a t. cymbal BIBLE, 38; CHARITY, 7
to set a chime of words t. in...a few fastidious people PURPOSE, 10; SMITH, L, 9
tinned t. food is a deadlier weapon ORWELL, G, 25; WEAPONS, 5
tinsel Strip the phoney t. off Hollywood APPEARANCES, 22; CINEMA, 18
tip-and-run watch him play t. ENGLISH, 16
Tipperary a long, long way to T. HOMESICKNESS, 8
tipping Do they allow t. on the boat MARX, G, 17; MONEY, 34
tipster A racing t....Hitler's level of accuracy HITLER, A, 7; TAYLOR, A, 5
tiptoe T. through the tulips FLOWERS, 4
tired getting more tanned and more t. ROYALTY, 94
Give me your t..../Your huddled masses AMERICA, 26
I haven't got time to be t. LAST WORDS, 95; WORK, 40
I'm t. of Love BELLOC, H, 15; MONEY, 9
Life...process of getting t. BUTLER, S, 9; LIFE, 20
tiresome All styles are good except the t. sort STYLE, 10; VOLTAIRE, 18
Being orderly...can be excessively t. ORDER, 1
tit caught her t. in the mangle PLEASURE, 34
Titanic furniture...of the *T.* FUTILITY, 11
Titian Nobody cares much at heart about T. ARTISTS, 23; RUSKIN, J, 14
title Because of my t., I was the first COURAGE, 1
does he feel his t. /Hang loose about him LOYALTY, 9
my t. as Defender of Faith CHARLES, PRINCE, 6
quiet life is greatly helped by not having a t. TITLES, 8
That t. from a better man I stole STEVENSON, R, 11
title-page The book written against fame...has the author's name on the t. EMERSON, R, 20; HYPOCRISY, 11
titles I've been offered t....get one into disreputable company SHAW, G, 44; TITLES, 12
Kinquering Congs their t. take SPOONER, W, 3
T. distinguish the mediocre SHAW, G, 28; TITLES, 11
Tito I will shake my little finger – and there will be no more T. INFLUENCE, 10
tittle one jot or one t. BIBLE, 362
toad Why should I let the t. *work* WORK, 17
toast never had a piece of t....But fell...on the buttered side PERVERSITY, 5
toasted cheese – t., mostly DREAMS, 13; FOOD, 65; STEVENSON, R, 10
tobacco he who lives without t. isn't worthy of living SMOKING, 25
leave off t. LAMB, C, 26; SMOKING, 23
never since have I wasted any more time on t. SMOKING, 33
than without t. for an hour SMOKING, 1
that tawney weed t. JONSON, B, 4
there's nothing like t. SMOKING, 25
The t. business is a conspiracy against womanhood and manhood SMOKING, 20
T., divine, rare, superexcellent SMOKING, 6
T. drieth the brain SMOKING, 36
T. hic, /Will make a man well if he be sick SMOKING, 2
T. is a dirty weed. I like it SMOKING, 15
T. surely was designed /To poison SMOKING, 13
We shall not refuse t. the credit of being...medical SMOKING, 32
what pleasure...they have in taking their roguish t. JONSON, B, 6
who lives without t. MOLIERE, 1
tocsin The t. you hear today is not an alarm but an alert PATRIOTISM, 11
today here t., and gone tomorrow BEHN, A, 8; TRANSIENCE, 4
He who can call t. his own DRYDEN, J, 31; PRESENT, 4
if T. be sweet FITZGERALD, E, 12; TIME, 22
Its history dates from t. ROYALTY, 115; WHISTLER, J, 14
the Cup that clears /T. of past Regrets FITZGERALD, E, 9; PRESENT, 5
they will listen t., they will listen tomorrow KHRUSHCHEV, N, 8; PROMISES, 5
wiser t. than...yesterday MISTAKES, 15; POPE, A, 54
toddle I'd t. safely home SASSOON, S, 2; WAR, 147
toe that old enemy the gout /Had taken him in t. HOOD, T, 9
the light fantastic t. MILTON, J, 16
together And the loved one all t. BROWNING, R, 36; PERVERSITY, 2
two people living t. for 25 years without having a cros word MARRIAGE, 86
We must...all hang t. FRANKLIN, B, 15; UNITY, 9
toil as some men t. after virtue LAMB, C, 22; SMOKING, 24
blood, t., tears and sweat CHURCHILL, W, 48; EFFORT, 3
Horny-handed sons of t. WORK, 16

they t. not BIBLE, 370; WORRY, 8
To t. and not to seek for rest SELFLESSNESS, 3
toilet *Ulysses*...can be read only in the t. JOYCE, J, 2
tolerance lead this people into war and they'll forget...t. WILSON, W, 4
magnificent t. and broadmindedness of the English SHAW, G, 1
tolerant Eddy was a tremendously t. person WELSH, 1
tolerate the greater part of the law is learning to t. fools LAW, 25; LESSING, D, 5
toleration t. produced...religious concord GIBBON, E, 6
toll'd The sexton t. the bell HOOD, T, 5; PUNS, 7
tolls for whom the bell t. DEATH, 59; DONNE, J, 8; MANKIND, 24
Tolstoy Like T., he is a man of great talent SOLZHENITSYN, A, 3
Their teacher had advised them not to read T. novels SOLZHENITSYN, A, 9
Tom Old Uncle T. Cobbleigh and all ANONYMOUS, 103
The romance of *T. Jones* GIBBON, E, 5
T., he was a piper's son NURSERY RHYMES, 65
T., T., the piper's son NURSERY RHYMES, 66
tomb A best-seller is the gilded t. of a mediocre talent SMITH, L, 1
drink a dozen of Claret on my T. KEATS, J, 65
Tom Jones The romance of *T.* NOVELS, 5
Tommy Little T. Tucker, /Sings for his supper NURSERY RHYMES, 32
Oh, it's T. this, an' T. that KIPLING, R, 29; SOLDIERS, 4
tomorrow assure him that he'd live t. DESTINY, 19; RABELAIS, F, 6
Drop...what t. may bring PRESENT, 8
here today and gone t. BEHN, A, 8; TRANSIENCE, 4
I'll see you t. LAST WORDS, 21
jam t. CARROLL, L, 30; PROMISES, 4
let us eat and drink; for t. we...die BIBLE, 40, 205; TRANSIENCE, 8
Lyndon acts like there was never going to be a t. JOHNSON, L, 2
Never put off till t. PROCRASTINATION, 1; PROVERBS, 304
T., and t. and t. LIFE, 86; SHAKESPEARE, 227
t. is another day HOPE, 17; MITCHELL, M, 4
T. never comes FUTURE, 1; PROVERBS, 439
tom-tit little t. sang Willow GILBERT, W, 35
tone Take the t. of the company CHESTERFIELD, P, 8
tongue A burning forehead, and a parching t. KEATS, J, 31
a sharp t. is the only edged tool CHARACTER, 12
him whose strenuous t. /Can burst Joy's grape KEATS, J, 34
hold your t. and let me love DONNE, J, 5; SILENCE, 5
neither eye to see, nor t. to speak HOUSES OF PARLIAMENT, 14
One t. is sufficient for a woman MILTON, J, 65
saying right off what comes to my t. CERVANTES, M, 14; IMPETUOSITY, 1
Silence is become his mother t. GOLDSMITH, O, 18; SILENCE, 6
their t. a sharp sword PSALMS, 36
the t. can no man tame SPEECH, 7
the t. is a little member SPEECH, 6
the use of my oracular t. MALAPROPISMS, 8; SHERIDAN, R, 9
who speak the t. /That Shakespeare spake FREEDOM, 63; WORDSWORTH, W, 55
tongues cloven t. like as of fire BIBLE, 2
flick of their t. GOSSIP, 11
Self-interest speaks all sorts of t. ROCHEFOUCAULD, 5; SELF-INTEREST, 6
Tony T....he immatures with age INSULTS, 135
too You can have t. much MODERATION, 2; PROVERBS, 469
took I t. thee for thy better DISILLUSION, 6
tool a sharp tongue is the only edged t. CHARACTER, 12
time as a t., not as a couch KENNEDY, J, 6; TIME, 29
tools Give us the t. CHURCHILL, W, 55; WORLD WAR II, 16
the foul dregs of his power, the t. of despotism and corruption POLITICS, 119
tool-using Man is a t. animal TECHNOLOGY, 3
tooth sharper than a serpent's t. DICKENS, C, 41
t. for t. BIBLE, 116; RETRIBUTION, 3
toothache man with t....teeth are sound ENVY, 8
philosopher that could endure the t. PHILOSOPHERS, 12; SHAKESPEARE, 277
top I shall be like that tree; I shall die from the t. DECLINE, 11; SWIFT, J, 20
I started at the t. and worked my way down DECLINE, 14
looking at the men at the t. AMBITION, 7
People at the t. of the tree EDUCATION, 92; USTINOV, P, 10
Room at the T. AMBITION, 3, 27; WEBSTER, D, 7
top-boots did pleasure me in his t. SEX, 77
torch like runners hand on the t. of life MORTALITY, 15
Truth, like a t. TRUTH, 28
torches she doth teach the t. to burn bright SHAKESPEARE, 308
Tories All T. are monsters MAJOR, J, 1
the difference between the T. and the Alfred Chicken Party POLITICS, 45
tormentor it is I who am my t. SELF, 21; TOLSTOY, L, 7
torrent When the t. sweeps a man against a boulder STEVENSON, R, 16; THEORY, 15
Tory a deep burning hatred for the T. Party BEVAN, A, 8; POLITICS, 15
end up in the T. knackery KINNOCK, N, 11; POLITICIANS, 14
Every Briton is at heart a T. POLITICS, 13
to what is called the T....called the Conservative, party POLITICS, 33
tossed you t. and gored several persons CONVERSATION, 3
total *t. solution* of the Jewish question NAZISM, 2
totter t. towards the tomb OLD AGE, 85
touch facility to do such things at the t. of a button TECHNOLOGY, 11
keep the Nelson t. NEWBOLT, H, 5; PATRIOTISM, 31
mere t. of cold philosophy KEATS, J, 25; PHILOSOPHY, 7
not as closely in t. with modern life AGE, 49
only t. the hem of his garment BIBLE, 396; REMEDIES, 13
sunset t. BROWNING, R, 10; WORRY, 10
t. me not BIBLE, 275
t. of a vanish'd hand NOSTALGIA, 24; TENNYSON, 5
We t. our caps ANTHONY, S, 2
Wound with a t. SATIRE, 2
tour The time to enjoy a European t. TRAVEL, 2
tourist Only on the third class t. class passengers' deck CLASS, 30
the most vulgar...is the British t. BRITISH, 10; TRAVEL, 26
tourists people were t. because of their religion TRAVEL, 38
t....take in the Monarchy...with...the pigeons LONDON, 15
toves slithy t. did gyre CARROLL, L, 23; NONSENSE, 7
towels never darken my t. again DISMISSAL, 6; MARX, G, 8
tower Childe Roland to the Dark T. BROWNING, R, 18; SUMMONS, 4
towered Tolstoy t. above his age TOLSTOY, L, 1
towering the height of his own t. style CHESTERTON, G, 40; POETS, 27
towers The cloud-capp'd t. MORTALITY, 17; SHAKESPEARE, 327
town anyone lived in a pretty how t. CUMMINGS, 2
axis of the earth sticks out visibly through...every t. or city NATURE, 19
man made the t. COUNTRYSIDE, 2; COWPER, W, 22
This t. was made to make money in COMMERCIALISM, 3
towns Of all the gin joints in all the t. in all the world CHANCE, 3
toy but a childish t. IGNORANCE, 17; MARLOWE, C, 9
tracks wrong side of the t. CARTER, A, 9
trade a king that...could not endure to have t. sick WEALTH, 8
Every man to his t. OCCUPATIONS, 2; PROVERBS, 140
God will pardon me. It is His t. HEINE, H, 5; LAST WORDS, 49
half a t. and half an art INGE, W, 8; LITERATURE, 10
It is not your t. to make tables CRITICISM, 26; JOHNSON, S, 59
man must serve his time to every t. BYRON, 38; CRITICS, 2
no nation was ever ruined by t. BUSINESS, 12; FRANKLIN, B, 4
Two of a t. can ne'er agree GAY, J, 6
trades The ugliest of t. have their moments of pleasure JERROLD, D, 6
tradition deadly weight of the terrible t. of a dialogue MANDELA, N, 6
the dead hand of medical t. MEDICINE, 42
We don't want t. HISTORY, 13
traffic the t. of Jacob's ladder HEAVEN, 15
tragedie go litel myn t. BOOKS, 14
T. is to seyn a certeyn storie CHAUCER, G, 15; MISFORTUNE, 7
tragedies There are two t. in life DESIRE, 15; SHAW, G, 24
t. are finish'd by a death BYRON, 22; THEATRE, 6
tragedy a t. and therefore not worth reading AUSTEN, J, 11; PLAYS, 2
brooding t. and its dark shadows can be lightened GANDHI, I, 6; HISTORY, 14
Comedy is t. HUMOUR, 6
farce brutalized becomes t. THEATRE, 9
great t. of Science HUXLEY, T, 1
hero and I will write you a t. HEROISM, 7
That is their t. SEXES, 35; WILDE, O, 21

The greatest t.…except a defeat WELLINGTON, 13
the t. of life is that…heroes lose their glamour DOYLE, A, 2
the wine was a farce and the food a t. POWELL, A, 2
T. is if I cut my finger THEATRE, 5
we have conceived life as a t. LIFE, 99
We participate in a t. HUXLEY, A, 13; THEATRE, 10
what t. means STOPPARD, T, 9; THEATRE, 14
world is a comedy…a t. to those that feel LIFE, 96; WALPOLE, H, 6
You *may* abuse a t. CRITICISM, 26; JOHNSON, S, 59
You're a bloody t. POLITICIANS, 106
tragically Everything must be taken seriously, nothing t. PERSPECTIVE, 4
train I have seldom heard a t. go by and not wished TRAVEL, 44
in charge of the clattering t. JOURNALISM, 7
man who shaves and takes a t. TRAVEL, 48
The only way…of catching a t. CHESTERTON, G, 49; TRAVEL, 13
trained t. and organized common sense HUXLEY, T, 2; SCIENCE, 51
trains t. all night groan on the rail /To men that die at morn EXECUTION, 16; HOUSMAN, A, 8
trait Death is an acquired t. DEATH, 17
traitor grieves me that I should be noted a t. LAST WORDS, 22
I find myself a t. with the rest TREASON, 14
traitors t. rose against him REBELLION, 1
tramp He began to think the t. a fine…fellow WELLS, H, 6
the Lady Is a T. DECLINE, 3
the t. of the twenty-two men SPORT AND GAMES, 6
t. a fine, brotherly, generous fellow FAMILIARITY, 4
trampling t. out the vintage where the grapes of wrath GOD, 27
tranquility being well-dressed gives a sense of t. CLOTHES, 5
tranquilizer The t. of greatest value ALCOHOL, 55
tranquillisers lot of t. and my mother ACTORS, 29
tranquillity his mind is in perfect t. VOLTAIRE, 1
Sorrow is t. remembered in emotion PARKER, D, 10; SORROW, 20
T. comes with years OLD AGE, 20
tranquillizer What is dangerous about the t. DRUGS, 10
tranquillizers if t. could be bought DRUGS, 9
transform t. this society without…extension of public ownership KINNOCK, N, 1; SOCIALISM, 15
transformation The universe is t. LIFE, 9; MARCUS AURELIUS ANTONINUS, 5
transition I expect no very violent t. HEAVEN, 12
translation original is unfaithful to the t. TRANSLATION, 1
Poetry is what gets lost in t. FROST, R, 11; TRANSLATION, 3
translations T. (like wives) are seldom faithful CAMPBELL, R, 4; TRANSLATION, 2
transplanted Many ideas grow better when t. into another mind IDEAS, 4
trapeze daring young man on the flying t. SPORT AND GAMES, 25
trappings the t. and the suits of woe MOURNING, 10; SHAKESPEARE, 67
trash *Paradise Lost*, is such barbarous t. MILTON, J, 3
Who steals my purse steals t. REPUTATION, 10; SHAKESPEARE, 284
trauma the folklore of abortion as life-long t. ABORTION, 6
travel he must fly rather than t. WONDER, 4
To t. hopefully is…better…than to arrive ANTICIPATION, 7; STEVENSON, R, 26
T. broadens the mind PROVERBS, 441; TRAVEL, 1
t. for t.'s sake STEVENSON, R, 7; TRAVEL, 42
T., in the younger sort BACON, F, 54; TRAVEL, 6
T. is the most private of pleasures SACKVILLE-WEST, V, 3; TRAVEL, 39
T. light THEFT, 6
wherever the wind takes me I t. as a visitor FREEDOM, 25; HORACE, 13
travelled He t. in order to come home TRAVEL, 46
I t. among unknown men HOMESICKNESS, 9; WORDSWORTH, W, 7
traveller a t. from an antique land MEMORIALS, 17; SHELLEY, P, 16
A t. would sit down MANDELA, N, 1
from whose bourn no t. returns AFTERLIFE, 10; SHAKESPEARE, 91
travelling in which direction the car was t. LLOYD GEORGE, D, 3
The grand object of t. JOHNSON, S, 110; TRAVEL, 23
T. is…like talking with men of other centuries TRAVEL, 14
travels A man t. the world over HOME, 8
He t. fastest PROVERBS, 196; SELF, 4
too old to go again to my t. CHARLES II, 1; ROYALTY, 38
treachery Political renegades always start their career of t. KINNOCK, N, 11; POLITICIANS, 14
To kings that fear their subjects' t. TREASON, 12
Weakness is not t. ROYALTY, 116
tread fools rush in where angels fear to t. HASTE, 8; POPE, A, 29
frightful fiend…behind him t. COLERIDGE, S, 36
Where'er you t. ADMIRATION, 13; COMPLIMENTS, 22; POPE, A, 47
treadmill on a golden t. WEALTH, 4
treason If *this* be t., make the most of it TREASON, 9
in trust I have found t. EXPERIENCE, 14
T. doth never prosper TREASON, 6
T. was no Crime DRYDEN, J, 11; TREASON, 3
treasure Preserve it as your chiefest t. BELLOC, H, 3; BOOKS, 8
purest t. mortal times afford REPUTATION, 11; SHAKESPEARE, 294
treasures lay not up…t. upon earth BIBLE, 368; WEALTH, 12
treasury the Vatican, the T. and the miners BALDWIN, S, 12; DIPLOMACY, 4
treaties T. are like roses and young girls DE GAULLE, C, 12; DIPLOMACY, 10
treating In t. a patient MEDICINE, 83
treatment I will use t. to help the sick MEDICINE, 37
remind those responsible for the t. of tuberculosis DISEASE, 41
treaty hand that signed the t. bred a fever SIGNATURES, 3; THOMAS, D, 11
tree A billboard lovely as a t. NASH, O, 10; TREES, 12
A poem lovely as a t. TREES, 8
as the twig is bent, the t.'s inclined POPE, A, 40
first violated the forbidden t. RELIGION, 86
gave me of the t., and I did eat BIBLE, 151
If poetry comes not…as leaves to a t. KEATS, J, 57
I shall be like that t.; I shall die from the top DECLINE, 11; SWIFT, J, 20
like a t. planted by the water-side PSALMS, 1
only God can make a t. TREES, 9
Rock-a-bye baby on the t. top SLEEP, 7
same t. that a wise man sees BLAKE, W, 27
soon think of taking the arm of an elm t. THOREAU, H, 2
spare the beechen t. TREES, 2
The difference between a gun and a t. POUND, E, 10; TREES, 13
the fruit /Of that forbidden t. MILTON, J, 30; SIN, 20
the oak t. and the cypress LOVE, 78
The t. of liberty must be refreshed FREEDOM, 27; JEFFERSON, T, 8
the t. of life BIBLE, 144; GARDENS, 3
t. of life is green GOETHE, J, 2; REALITY, 4; THEORY, 7
treen In old time we had t. chalices and golden priests CLERGY, 8
trees Loveliest of t., the cherry HOUSMAN, A, 7; TREES, 5
T. are poems CONSERVATION, 5
Trelawny shall T. die EXECUTION, 15
tremble Our hand will not t. RUSSIAN REVOLUTION, 8
t. like a guilty thing surprised DOUBT, 9; WORDSWORTH, W, 30
trembled And t. with fear at your frown MEMORY, 9
trembles And Satan t. COWPER, W, 15; PRAYER, 14
trenches boys who were killed in the t. WAR, 68
digging t. and trying on gas-masks CHAMBERLAIN, N, 5
trial T. by jury…a delusion JUSTICE, 5
trials in the midst of personal t. and pain ENDURANCE, 7
triangles if t. invented a god, they would make him three-sided MONTESQUIEU, 4; RELIGION, 70
tribe Abou Ben Adhem (may his t. increase!) DREAMS, 8
Mankind is not a t. CHESTERTON, G, 42; MANKIND, 20
Richer than all his t. LOVE, 155; SHAKESPEARE, 290
tribute the vain t. of a smile POETS, 10; SCOTT, W, 6
trick t. is to love somebody BALDWIN, J, 6
When in doubt, win the t. SPORT AND GAMES, 19
trifle Is t. sufficient for sweet BETJEMAN, J, 7; FOOD, 12
trifles observance of t. DOYLE, A, 4; TRIVIALITY, 6
snapper-up of unconsidered t. BUSINESS, 28; SHAKESPEARE, 354
trigger Whose Finger do you want on the T. ANONYMOUS, 108; GOVERNMENT, 4
Trinian's firearms were strictly forbidden at St T. WEAPONS, 9
Trinity I the T. illustrate BROWNING, R, 53; DRINKS, 7
the Holy T. of Science SCIENCE, 54
trip A t. to the moon on gossamer wings TRAVEL, 37
Triton Old T. blow his wreathed horn WORDSWORTH, W, 66
triumph meet with T. and Disaster KIPLING, R, 17
One more devils'-t. and sorrow for angels BROWNING, R, 32
t. in putting down the riot CHINA, 9
We t. without glory VICTORY, 6

Pride and T....shake their...sides at youth YEATS, W, 24
Pride and T....That long to give themselves for wage AGE, 104
put him in possession of t. TRUTH, 34
Some men love t. so much BUTLER, S, 18; TRUTH, 15
speaking nothing but the t. HONESTY, 16; WILDE, O, 36
the laws of poetic t. and poetic beauty ARNOLD, M, 15; POETRY, 2
the t. is not in us BIBLE, 281; SIN, 5
the t. of imagination KEATS, J, 51; TRUTH, 31
the t. shall make you free BIBLE, 254; TRUTH, 11
the unclouded face of t. suffer wrong FACTS, 6; JOURNALISM, 31
The worst enemy of t. and freedom IBSEN, H, 3; MAJORITY, 6
those who live...believe...to be the t. HAMPTON, C, 2; HONESTY, 5
to the dead we owe only t. RESPECT, 4; VOLTAIRE, 24
T. be veiled OPTIMISM, 36; SHELLEY, P, 8
T. comes out in wine ALCOHOL, 62; PLINY THE ELDER, 5
T. fears no trial PROVERBS, 443; TRUTH, 4
T. has no special time of its own TRUTH, 40
T. in medicine is an unattainable goal MEDICINE, 82
t. in the inward parts PSALMS, 31
t. is always strange BYRON, 35; TRUTH, 17
t. is a point of view HYPATIA, 2
T. is on the march TRUTH, 49; ZOLA, 3
T. is stranger PROVERBS, 444; TRUTH, 5
T. is...the test of experience TRUTH, 26
t., justice, and the American way HEROISM, 2
T., like a torch TRUTH, 28
t. shall flourish out of the earth PSALMS, 46
T., Sir, is a cow JOHNSON, S, 65; SCEPTICISM, 3
T. sits upon the lips of dying men ARNOLD, M, 41; TRUTH, 9
T. telling is not compatible with the defence of the realm TRUTH, 41
t. that makes men free TRUTH, 7
T. will out PROVERBS, 445; TRUTH, 6
Two half-truths do not make a t. HALF MEASURES, 1
whatever remains, however improbable, must be the t. DOYLE, A, 3; TRUTH, 22
what is t. BACON, F, 56; BIBLE, 265; TRUTH, 10, 12
When t. is discovered by someone else SOLZHENITSYN, A, 6; TRUTH, 43
whilst the great ocean of t. lay all undiscovered before me DISCOVERY, 12; NEWTON, I, 5; SCIENCE, 68
who ever knew T. put to the worse MILTON, J, 8; TRUTH, 37
you are to tell the t. FRANKNESS, 3
You can only find t. with logic CHESTERTON, G, 28
truths All great t. begin as blasphemies SHAW, G, 4
all t. are half-t. TRUTH, 47; WHITEHEAD, A, 1
commonplaces are the great poetic t. STEVENSON, R, 27
He was a man of two t. MURDOCH, I, 4
new t....begin as heresies HUXLEY, T, 3; NOVELTY, 4
The only t. which are universal TRUTH, 45
There are no new t. MCCARTHY, M, 2; NOVELTY, 7
The...schoolboy is now familiar with t. for which Archimedes SCIENCE, 79
those three fundamental t. OBJECTIVITY, 3
t. being in and out of favour FROST, R, 1; NOVELTY, 2
We hold these t. to be sacred and undeniable JEFFERSON, T, 5
We hold these t. to be self-evident JEFFERSON, T, 6
while easy t. were told HILL, G, 1
try t. everything once EXPERIENCE, 7
T., t. again PERSISTENCE, 5
tu *Et t., Brute* SHAKESPEARE, 149
tub Rub-a-dub-dub, /Three men in a t. NURSERY RHYMES, 49
tubby a t. little chap WODEHOUSE, P, 18
tuberculosis remind those responsible for the treatment of t. DISEASE, 41
Tudor Owen T....was beheaded at the market place EXECUTION, 14
Tuesday Christened on T. NURSERY RHYMES, 53
If It's T. TRAVEL, 4
T.'s child is full of grace NURSERY RHYMES, 35
tulips Tiptoe through the t. FLOWERS, 4
tumbler He who drinks a t. of London water SMITH, S, 16
tumors In men nine out of ten abdominal t. are malignant BIRTH, 13
tune good t. played on an old fiddle AGE, 23
There's many a good t. AGE, 2; PROVERBS, 414
Whistle a Happy T. WHISTLING, 3
tunes why the devil should have all the good t. MUSIC, 29
tunnel Calais should have done more...once the t. opens FRANCE, 4
light at the end of the t....of an oncoming train PESSIMISM, 8
turban the royal t. of the Turks RELIGION, 35
turbot would give the price of a large t. for it BOOKS, 42; RUSKIN, J, 9
turbulent rid me of this t. priest ASSASSINATION, 5
turf The blue ribbon of the t. DISRAELI, B, 8; HORSES, 5
Turks the royal turban of the T. RELIGION, 35
turn I do not hope to t. ELIOT, T, 3
I wouldn't have left a t. unstoned CRITICISM, 65
One good t. deserves another HELP, 3; PROVERBS, 326
You t. if you want to THATCHER, M, 20
turned mine enemies...shall be t. back PSALMS, 2
turning Life is a maze in which we take the wrong t. CONNOLLY, C, 15; LIFE, 29
The lady's not for t. INFLEXIBILITY, 3; THATCHER, M, 20
turnip he had rather /Have a t. than his father JOHNSON, S, 33; NONSENSE, 15
turtle the voice of the t. is heard BIBLE, 489
tu-whit T., Tu-who SHAKESPEARE, 201
TV T....is our latest medium MEDIA, 9; TELEVISION, 6
twain never the t. shall meet KIPLING, R, 4; OPPOSITES, 4
Twain T. and I are in the same position TWAIN, M, 2
twang the triumphant t. of a bedspring SEX, 95
Tweedledee Tweedledum said T. /Had spoiled his nic new rattle CARROLL, L, 25; WAR, 41
Tweedledum T. and Tweedledee /Agreed to have a battle CARROLL, L, 25; WAR, 41
twelve I was born at the age of t. CINEMA, 9
T. for the t. apostles ANONYMOUS, 45; NUMBERS, 1
T. lords a-leaping CHRISTMAS, 18; NURSERY RHYMES, 59
'Why only t.?...get thousands.' GOLDWYN, S, 21
twentieth the t. century will be...the century of Fascism FASCISM, 9; MUSSOLINI, B, 4
T. Century Blues COWARD, N, 20; MELANCHOLY, 4
twenty the first t. years SOUTHEY, R, 3; YOUTH, 30
The United States...are t. years in advance of this country AMERICA, 20
twenty-five My dear fellow...I only ask you for t. pounds SHERIDAN, R, 14
twenty-four There are only t. hours in the day PROVERBS, 406; TIME, 2
the t. hour day BEERBOHM, M, 6; TIME, 12
the t.-hour strike STRIKES, 7
twenty-nine t. distinct damnations BIBLE, 525; BROWNING, R, 54
twenty-two the tramp of the t. men SPORT AND GAMES, 6
twice can't make a soufflé rise t. FOOD, 48
can't step into the same river t. CHANGE, 13
desire to be praised t. over PRAISE, 8; ROCHEFOUCAULD, 18
Literature...something that will be read t. CONNOLLY, C, 6
no shirt or collar ever comes back t. LEACOCK, S, 13
t. as natural CARROLL, L, 34
will bear to be read t....was thought t. THOREAU, H, 5; WRITING, 47
you shall drink t. while I drink once DRUNKENNESS, 28; WALPOLE, H, 10
Twickenham wicked asp of T. POPE, A, 1
twig as the t. is bent, the tree's inclined EDUCATION, 74; POPE, A, 40
twilight T. grey DAY, 11; MILTON, J, 46
twinkle T., t., little bat CARROLL, L, 10
T., t., little star STARS, 6
twinkling his wrath endureth but the t. of an eye PSALMS, 17
in the t. of an eye BIBLE, 42
twist last t. of the knife ELIOT, T, 21
Twist Oliver T. has asked for more DICKENS, C, 36
twisted You silly t. boy MILLIGAN, S, 7
two Great God grant that twice t. be not four PRAYER, 28; TURGENEV, I, 4
if we knew one, we knew t. METAPHYSICS, 3
into the ark, t. and t. BIBLE, 158
It takes t. ARGUMENTS, 1; PROVERBS, 235
It takes t. to speak the truth THOREAU, H, 19; TRUTH, 44
It takes t. to tango COMPROMISE, 1; PROVERBS, 236
make t. questions grow where only one RESEARCH, 7
Of the t. lights of Christendom DEFEAT, 14
One step forward, t. steps back LENIN, V, 2; PROGRESS, 18
Tea for T., and T. for Tea DRINKS, 13
The formula 'T. and t. make five' PHILOSOPHY, 2
t. and t. do not make six LAST WORDS, 90; TOLSTOY, L, 16
t. legs bad ORWELL, G, 4
T. nations POVERTY AND WEALTH, 5
T. of a trade can ne'er agree GAY, J, 6

U

We need more u. of human nature HUMAN NATURE, 17; JUNG, C, 11
understood Only one man ever u. me LAST WORDS, 48; UNDERSTANDING, 4
undertaker the sort of greeting a corpse would give to an u. BALDWIN, S, 5
undertakers Doctors and u. /Fear epidemics of good health DOCTORS, 18
I have nothing against u. personally OCCUPATIONS, 18
undertaking no such u. has been received WORLD WAR II, 7
The love of life is necessary to...any u. ENTHUSIASM, 5; JOHNSON, S, 25
under water if I were u. I would scarcely kick KEATS, J, 60
Undine something as unique and remote as U. DICKINSON, E, 1
undiscovered the great ocean of truth lay all u. before me DISCOVERY, 12; NEWTON, I, 5
undone estate o' th' world were now u. SHAKESPEARE, 228; WORLD-WEARINESS, 8
left u. those things BOOK OF COMMON PRAYER, 15; SIN, 9
Things hitherto u. should be given...a wide berth BEERBOHM, M, 7; ORIGINALITY, 1
uneasy U. lies the head that wears a crown MONARCHY, 22; SHAKESPEARE, 122
uneatable the unspeakable in full pursuit of the u. HUNTING, 11; WILDE, O, 58
uneducated Democracy...government by the u. ARISTOCRACY, 9; CHESTERTON, G, 45
unemployment more than attack the scourge of u. UNEMPLOYMENT, 1
u. and the recession ECONOMICS, 14; UNEMPLOYMENT, 4
When a great many people...u. results UNEMPLOYMENT, 3
unendurable individuals...capable of original thought would probably be u. IDEAS, 9; MENCKEN, H, 11
unequal Men are made by nature u. EQUALITY, 13
Our Language...was u. to that greatness of soul MILTON, J, 1
unexamined The u. life SELF, 19; SOCRATES, 5
unexpected Old age is the most u. OLD AGE, 103; TROTSKY, L, 2
unexplained number of u. cures has dropped REMEDIES, 48
unfaithful better to be u. FAITHFULNESS, 1
original is u. to the translation TRANSLATION, 1
unfortunates one of those u. to whom death is EXPLANATIONS, 2
ungain'd Men prize the thing u. more DESIRE, 14; SHAKESPEARE, 330
ungodliness the tents of u. PSALMS, 45
ungodly the u....privily shoot at them which are true of heart PSALMS, 4
ungrateful one u. person and a hundred with a grievance PROMOTION, 3
unhappily The bad end u. STOPPARD, T, 9; THEATRE, 14
unhappy A moment of time may make us u. for ever GAY, J, 1; SORROW, 11
an u. person who was happy BAINBRIDGE, B, 6
don't believe one can ever be u. for long SELF, 23; WAUGH, E, 13
each u. family is u. in its own way FAMILY, 59; TOLSTOY, L, 5
It is better that some should be u. EQUALITY, 19; JOHNSON, S, 109
making their remaining years u. LA BRUYERE, J, 2; MANKIND, 34
most u. kind of misfortune HAPPINESS, 7
one is u. one becomes moral PROUST, M, 6; SORROW, 23
only when I am unbearably u. KAFKA, F, 2
the instinct for being u. SAKI, 8; SORROW, 26
Today you're u.?...Go shopping MATERIALISM, 20; MILLER, A, 3
U. the land that has no heroes BRECHT, B, 2; HEROISM, 4
unheralded spring now comes u. by the return of the birds CARSON, R, 4; ECOLOGY, 1
unicorn The lion and the u. NURSERY RHYMES, 54
uniform love that loves a scarlet coat /Should be more u. HOOD, T, 4; PUNS, 9
The u. 'e wore CLOTHES, 15; KIPLING, R, 14
uniformity let use be preferred before u. BACON, F, 15; HOUSES, 1
unimportant We are u. WOMAN'S ROLE, 3
uninstructed making things plain to u. people EDUCATION, 46; HUXLEY, T, 7
uninterested exist is an u. person KNOWLEDGE, 12
uninteresting no...u. subject CHESTERTON, G, 18; CURIOSITY, 5
union the sole motive force behind the u. of the sexes LACLOS, P, 3; SEX, 61
To make a u. with Great Britain WORLD WAR II, 41
U. is strength PROVERBS, 448; UNITY, 2
unionist most conservative man...is the British Trade U. CONSERVATISM, 1
unique something as u. and remote as Undine DICKINSON, E, 1
unite u. in some holy confederacy CHRISTIANITY, 36
Workers of the world, u. MARX, K, 2; MARXISM, 10
united U. we stand PROVERBS, 449; UNITY, 3
United Nations U. is not...equivalent of our own legal system LAW, 13
United States In the U. there is more space AMERICA, 36; STEIN, G, 4
so near to the U. AMERICA, 13
The best immediate defence of the U. ROOSEVELT, F, 7; WORLD WAR II, 43
The U....are twenty years in advance of this country AMERICA, 20
The U. has to move very fast AMERICA, 24; KENNEDY, J, 7
The U. is like a gigantic boiler AMERICA, 19
The U....six hours behind AMERICA, 20
U. is the best and fairest...nation BUSH, G, 5
U. of Europe CHURCHILL, W, 65; EUROPE, 6
unites Nothing u. the English like war PICASSO, P, 3
unity u. of the party and the prospects of victory THATCHER, M, 40
universal Aunt Edna is u. AUDIENCES, 5
There is no u. law LAWRENCE, D, 33; SPONTANEITY, 3
universals Myth deals in false u. CARTER, A, 7
universe a hell of a good u. next door UNIVERSE, 9
chess-board is the world; the pieces...the phenomena of the u. GOD, 29; HUXLEY, T, 6
I accept the u. CARLYLE, T, 35; UNIVERSE, 5
I don't pretend to understand the U. CARLYLE, T, 33; UNIVERSE, 4
In this unbelievable u....no absolutes UNIVERSE, 3
I regarded the u. as an open book UNIVERSE, 14
Life exists in the u. SCIENCE, 56
Man's the bad child of the u. MANKIND, 44
Mind is ever the ruler of the u. MIND, 26
no hint throughout the u. /Of good or ill NECESSITY, 8
no reason to assume that the u. has the slightest interest UNIVERSE, 7
Perish the U. REVENGE, 8
take his attention away from the u. PRAYER, 15
the better ordering of the u. UNIVERSE, 1
the u. and all that surrounds it UNIVERSE, 8
the u. is expanding and contracting SELF-INTEREST, 3
The u. is not hostile UNIVERSE, 12
the u. is...queerer than we *can* suppose UNIVERSE, 11
The u. is transformation MARCUS AURELIUS ANTONINUS, 5
The u....more like a great thought UNIVERSE, 13
The u. ought to be presumed too vast UNIVERSE, 17
the u., the reflection of the structure of the brain MIND, 4
The visible u. was an illusion UNIVERSE, 2
unbelievable u....there are no absolutes BUCK, P, 1
universes Out of all possible u., the only one which can exist UNIVERSE, 15
universities mortifying fate of most English u. LODGE, D, 2
The King, observing...the state of both his u. CAMBRIDGE, 6; OXFORD, 14
U. are the cathedrals of the modern age EDUCATION, 57
U. incline wits to sophistry and affectation BACON, F, 65
university Any attempt to reform the u. EDUCATION, 47
it is necessary to go to a u....to become a successful writer BRITTAIN, V, 3; WRITERS, 3
true U....collection of books CARLYLE, T, 12
u., where it was carefully taken out EDUCATION, 73; PEACOCK, T, 8
unjust The u. steals the just's umbrella JUSTICE, 4
unkind Thou art not so u. SHAKESPEARE, 50
unkindness I tax not you, you elements, with u. SHAKESPEARE, 179; WEATHER, 20
unknown apart from the known and the u. METAPHYSICS, 4; PINTER, H, 3
Give me a light that I may tread safely into the u. FAITH, 15
I travelled among u. men WORDSWORTH, W, 7
Many brave men...before Agamemnon's time...are all, unmourned and u....because they lack their sacred poet HORACE, 42
the U. Prime Minister POLITICIANS, 38
To go into the u. DEATH, 175
to the u. god SUPERSTITION, 6
unmourned and u. OBLIVION, 1

unlabelled One of the unpardonable sins...to go about u. CLASSIFICATION, 1; HUXLEY, T, 4
unlettered An u. king is a crowned ass MONARCHY, 1
unlike the Jews bring the u. into the heart of *every milieu* JEWS, 20
The law of dislike for the u. JEWS, 20
unluckily the good u. STOPPARD, T, 9; THEATRE, 14
unlucky person born /who is so u. ACCIDENTS, 7
unmarried to keep u. MARRIAGE, 140; SHAW, G, 23
unmotivated The u. action SPONTANEITY, 2
unmuzzled The world regards such a person as...an u. dog CLASSIFICATION, 1; HUXLEY, T, 4
unnatural so u. as the commonplace DOYLE, A, 7; TRIVIALITY, 8
unobtrusive Poetry should be great and u. KEATS, J, 56; POETRY, 34
unofficial An u. English rose BROOKE, R, 4; FLOWERS, 3
unpaid A promise made is a debt u. PROMISES, 6
unpardonable One of the u. sins... is...to go about unlabelled CLASSIFICATION, 1; HUXLEY, T, 4
unperfect He was u., unfinished, inartistic WRITERS, 64
unpleasant Cynicism is an u. way of saying the truth CYNICISM, 2
without mentioning a single book, or *in fact anything u.* BOOKS, 37; REED, H, 7
unpopular a free society...where it is safe to be u. FREEDOM, 56; STEVENSON, A, 6
unprofitable How weary, stale, flat, and u. SHAKESPEARE, 68; WORLD-WEARINESS, 6
unpronouncables unspellables killing the u. AMERICANS, 3
unreason a liberal education at the Colleges of U. REASON, 1
unrecording troops of u. friends LIFE, 93; TENNYSON, 77
unremembered u. acts /Of kindness and of love KINDNESS, 14; WORDSWORTH, W, 10
unremitting That u. humanity BENNETT, A, 5
unrequited Self-love seems so often u. CONCEIT, 13; POWELL, A, 1
unsaid The bitterest tears...are for words...u. REGRET, 26; STOWE, H, 1
unsatisfied It is exquisite, and it leaves one u. SMOKING, 37; WILDE, O, 51
unsavoury indefatigable and u. engine of pollution DOGS, 17
unsealed my lips are not yet u. BALDWIN, S, 8; SECRECY, 2
unseemly an u. exposure of the mind HAZLITT, W, 17; NASTINESS, 3
unseen to deny the existence of an u. kingdom is bad BUTLER, S, 3; SPECULATION, 1
unselfishness sympathetic u. of an oyster PERFECTION, 9; SELFLESSNESS, 5
unsex u. me here, /And fill me...full /Of direst cruelty EVIL, 22
unsexed she must be a woman pretty nearly u. BRONTE, C, 1
unshriven curious to see what happens...to one who dies u. LAST WORDS, 65
unsoundness no person can be a poet...without...u. of mind MACAULAY, T, 8; POETRY, 38
no person can...enjoy poetry, without...u. MACAULAY, T, 8
unspeakable the psychopathologist the u. MAUGHAM, W, 8; PSYCHIATRY, 22
the u. in full pursuit of the uneatable HUNTING, 11; WILDE, O, 58
unspellables u. killing the unpronouncables AMERICANS, 3
unspoiled utterly u. by failure FAILURE, 3; POLITICIANS, 74
unstoned I wouldn't have left a turn u. CRITICISM, 65
untidier the only man north of the Tiber...u. than I am WHITEHORN, K, 2
untravelled Gleams that u. world EXPERIENCE, 21; TENNYSON, 80
untruth The camera...an accessory to u. PHOTOGRAPHY, 4
unupblown Nurse u. BREVITY, 10; WAUGH, E, 53
unvaccinated let his children go u. ILLNESS, 34
unwashed The great U. PUBLIC, 5
unwholesome Boys...are u. companions for grown people CHILDREN, 44; LAMB, C, 9
up *How to be one u.* ONE-UPMANSHIP, 3
I saw it at a disadvantage – the curtain was u. CRITICISM, 66
u. with which I will not put CHURCHILL, W, 37; GRAMMAR, 4
What's u., Doc CINEMA, 4
upbringing the u. a nun would envy INNOCENCE, 10; ORTON, J, 1
uplands broad, sunlit u. WORLD WAR II, 10
upper Like many of the u. class ARISTOCRACY, 4; BELLOC, H, 18
the person that...has the u. hand CHARACTER, 16
the u. classes /Have still the u. hand COWARD, N, 14
upper-middle class Shirley Williams...a member of the u. CLASS, 54; WEST, R, 7
upright man of life u. CAMPION, T, 3; RIGHTEOUSNESS, 6
upstaging learnt the art of u. ACTING, 15
upstairs U. and downstairs /And in my lady's chamber NURSERY RHYMES, 13
Uriah U....made a ghastly writhe DICKENS, C, 16; SERVILITY, 3
urine machine for turning...the red wine of Shiraz into u. MANKIND, 11
nose-painting, sleep, and u. ALCOHOL, 70
urn Can storied u. DEATH, 74; GRAY, T, 4
urologists flood of u. LANGUAGE, 4
US U. is a truly monstrous force AMERICA, 32
usage if u. so choose, with whom resides the decision HORACE, 4; WORDS, 18
use force themselves into general u. WELLINGTON, 9
let u. be preferred before uniformity BACON, F, 15
what is the u. of a book BOOKS, 13; CARROLL, L, 4
What is the u. of a new-born child FRANKLIN, B, 11; PURPOSE, 2
useful not merely...u. and ornamental PURPOSE, 11
the most u. thing about a principle...sacrificed to expediency EXPEDIENCY, 5; MAUGHAM, W, 4
useless All Art is quite u. ART, 40; WILDE, O, 45
A u. life is an early death GOETHE, J, 5; PURPOSE, 3
most beautiful things...are the most u. BEAUTY, 38; RUSKIN, J, 11
uses all the u. of this world SHAKESPEARE, 68; WORLD-WEARINESS, 6
usual Business as u. BRITISH, 6; CHURCHILL, W, 42
usurp I did not u. the crown, but was duly elected MONARCHY, 14
Utopia Not in U..../Or some secreted island WORDSWORTH, W, 43
U-turn U. if you want to INFLEXIBILITY, 3

V

V The 'V' is your sign WORLD WAR II, 4
vacancy marry your mistress...create a job v. MARRIAGE, 81
vacant In v. or in pensive mood SOLITUDE, 17; WORDSWORTH, W, 9
vacation a change of nuisances is as good as a v. CHANGE, 17; LLOYD GEORGE, D, 17
vaccination V. is the medical sacrament corresponding to baptism MEDICINE, 18
vacuum A v. can only exist...by the things which enclose it SCIENCE, 41
v....better...stuff that nature replaces NATURE, 34; WILLIAMS, T, 4
vadis quo v. BIBLE, 262
vagabond a fugitive and a v. PUNISHMENT, 3
vagabonds We are not rootless v. ASHDOWN, P, 2
vagina incapacitated by cramps...sides of Tashi's v. with a couple of thorns WALKER, A, 10
The v. walls are quite insensitive SEX, 60
vaguery For V. in the Field INCOMPETENCE, 3; OSBORNE, J, 3
vain A v....coxcomb without...solid talents PEPYS, S, 1
generous aspirings implanted in her in v. SMOKING, 23
He was...snobbish, sentimental and v. WILDE, O, 3
things that were but v. OLD AGE, 62
thou shalt not take the name of...God in v. BIBLE, 115; GOD, 12
V. are the thousand creeds BELIEF, 4; BRONTE, E, 4
v. babblings SCIENCE, 8
V. man is apt to think WOMAN'S ROLE, 13
V. wisdom all, and false philosophy MILTON, J, 41; WISDOM, 22
vales the cup of the v. THOMAS, D, 29
valet hero to his v. FAMILIARITY, 2
valiant v. never taste of death but once COWARDICE, 11; SHAKESPEARE, 148
valid drunkenness would be...supremely v. DRUNKENNESS, 18
valley Every v. shall be exalted BIBLE, 210
One sees great things from the v. CHESTERTON, G, 16; PERSPECTIVE, 2
the v. of the shadow of death PSALMS, 11
valleys Piping down the v. wild BLAKE, W, 41; MUSIC, 13
valour The better part of v. is discretion SELF-PRESERVATION, 11; SHAKESPEARE, 116
valuable decide...how we are v. SELF, 10
riches to be a v. thing SWIFT, J, 21; WEALTH, 47
value All knowledge is of itself of some v. KNOWLEDGE, 26
Friendship...has no survival v. FRIENDSHIP, 22; LEWIS, C, 1

the price of everything and the v. of nothing CYNICISM, 5; WILDE, O, 43
values ideas are of more importance than v. INTELLECTUALS, 6
to change society and to define its finer v. POLITICS, 10
Victorian v....were the v. when our country THATCHER, M, 25
Van Gogh V.'s ear for music INSULTS, 134
vanished as rare things will, it v. BROWNING, R, 39; TRANSIENCE, 10
vanity all is v. and vexation of spirit BIBLE, 64; TRANSIENCE, 6
it doesn't do to upset one's own v. SELF-RESPECT, 4
name of V. Fair BUNYAN, J, 5; TRIVIALITY, 3
The v. of human life is like a river LIFE, 76; POPE, A, 58
v. and a paranoia about writers WRITERS, 16
v. and love...universal characteristics CHESTERFIELD, P, 16
V. dies hard CONCEIT, 17; STEVENSON, R, 5
v. of vanities BIBLE, 61
V. plays lurid tricks CONCEIT, 6
vanquished a Roman by a Roman /Valiantly v. SUICIDE, 31
redress of the grievances of the v. CHURCHILL, W, 11; WAR, 45
variable light-headed, v. men MARRIAGE, 147; STEVENSON, R, 23
varies quality of moral behaviour v. HUXLEY, A, 20; MORALITY, 7
variety a sad v. of woe POPE, A, 8; SORROW, 21
custom stale her infinite v. SHAKESPEARE, 31
V.'s the very spice of life COWPER, W, 24
various man so v., that he seem'd to be HUMAN NATURE, 11
man so v., that he seemed to be DRYDEN, J, 9
vary money appears to v. MONEY, 27
vasectomies American males must...have v. ABORTION, 2
vasectomy V. means not ever having to say you're sorry CONTRACEPTION, 1
vast The universe ought to be presumed too v. UNIVERSE, 17
Vatican One of the best warehouses I ever see was the V. EUROPE, 26
the V., the Treasury and the miners BALDWIN, S, 12; DIPLOMACY, 4
V. is an oppressive regime CHURCH, 3
vaulting 'Fan v.'...belongs to the 'Last-supper-carved-on-a-peach-stone' ARCHITECTURE, 7
veal I could eat one of Bellamy's v. pies FOOD, 58; PITT THE YOUNGER, 3
vegetable animal or v. or mineral CARROLL, L, 35
vegetables you must talk to your v. GARDENS, 5
vegetarianism useless for the sheep to pass resolutions in favour of v. INGE, W, 5
V. is harmless enough HEALTH AND HEALTHY LIVING, 11
v. is the only road to salvation of some HEALTH AND HEALTHY LIVING, 10
vegetarians V. have wicked, shifty eyes PREJUDICE, 9
vegetate When I am in the country I wish to v. COUNTRYSIDE, 6; HAZLITT, W, 29
veil Death is the v. SHELLEY, P, 22
the painted v. which those who live /Call life SHELLEY, P, 12
the v. of the temple was rent in twain BIBLE, 432; LAST WORDS, 11
the v. which those who live call life DEATH, 157; SHELLEY, P, 22
v. of indifference CLINTON, B, 8
veils v. of the morning PEACE, 22; YEATS, W, 18
Velasquez Why drag in V. CONCEIT, 22; WHISTLER, J, 9
vellicated v. by some sharp serosity ILLNESS, 37
velvet like black v. on sandpaper POPULAR MUSIC, 25
venerability the v. factor creeps in LONGEVITY, 15
venereal Despite a lifetime of service...v. disease SEX, 45
venetian couldn't write fuck on a dusty v. blind INSULTS, 22
vengeance No one delights more in v. than a woman REVENGE, 12; WOMEN, 70
venial than that one soul...should commit one single v. sin SIN, 22
Venice She only went to V. INSULTS, 79; THATCHER, M, 9
V. is like eating...chocolate liqueurs VENICE, 2
V., the eldest Child of Liberty VENICE, 3; WORDSWORTH, W, 60
venite v., exultemus PSALMS, 55
ventured Nothing v. OPPORTUNITY, 5; PROVERBS, 319
Venus She is V. when she smiles COMPLIMENTS, 15; JONSON, B, 13
Two minutes with V., two years with mercury SEX, 86
verb a v. meaning 'to believe falsely' BELIEF, 13
verbal v. contract isn't worth the paper GOLDWYN, S, 15
verbose Revolutions are always v. REVOLUTION, 14; TROTSKY, L, 5
verbosity inebriated with...his own v. DISRAELI, B, 32; VERBOSITY, 3
Verdi strains of V. will come back to you tonight HUMOUR, 53; MARX, G, 18
verdict Sentence first – v. afterwards CARROLL, L, 21
verification bring about the v. of his own prophecies PROPHECY, 13; TROLLOPE, A, 13
verify Always v. your references RESEARCH, 5
veritas *In vino v.* ALCOHOL, 62; PLINY THE ELDER, 5
Verlaine I'll stay off V. too PARKER, D, 8
vermin lower than v. BEVAN, A, 8; POLITICS, 15
vernal One impulse from a v. wood WORDSWORTH, W, 69
versa too fucking busy – or vice v. SEX, 92
Versailles a lady at the court of V. LANGUAGE, 49; VOLTAIRE, 32
That bastard of the V. treaty PLACES, 26
yardstick of V. PLACES, 12
verse a poet to whom nature has denied the faculty of v. CARLYLE, T, 2
Curst be the v. POETRY, 48; POPE, A, 15
Having v. set to music POETRY, 67
If Galileo had said in v. that the world moved HARDY, T, 15; POETRY, 27
no v. can give pleasure for long...is written by drinkers of water HORACE, 23; WATER, 6
the keynote of Burns' v. BURNS, R, 2
Writing free v. FROST, R, 9; POETRY, 24
writing v. /Should terminate in drink POETRY, 28
verses His face when he repeats his v. hath its ancient glory COLERIDGE, S, 2
v....as a literary performance POETRY, 70; WHITMAN, W, 3
versified excellent poets that have never v. POETS, 11
versifiers now swarm many v. POETS, 11
vertebrate he is the highest v. PHILOSOPHY, 19
vertical The v. man AUDEN, W, 12; POSTERITY, 3
vessel a chosen v. BIBLE, 8
the weaker v. BIBLE, 442; MARRIAGE, 31
vestry I will see you in the v. after service CLERGY, 11; SMITH, S, 8
vet At the v.'s with hard pad INSULTS, 136
veterinarian The best doctor in the world is the V. DOCTORS, 84
vex they die to v. me CLERGY, 10; MELBOURNE, 9
with no deep researches v. the brain CLARITY, 1
vexation all is vanity and v. of spirit BIBLE, 64; TRANSIENCE, 6
viable I'm v. from ten o'clock till five BETJEMAN, J, 5; BUSINESS, 4
vice Art is v....you ravish it ART, 9
extremism in the defence of liberty is no v. EXCESS, 5
Hypocrisy is the most...nerve-racking v. MAUGHAM, W, 2
Is Pride, the never-failing v. of fools POPE, A, 22; PRIDE, 9
no v. but beggary SHAKESPEARE, 164
Prosperity doth best discover v. BACON, F, 8
public schools are the nurseries of all v. FIELDING,H,10
quotation is a national v. QUOTATIONS, 15; WAUGH, E, 32
restrictions placed on v. by our social code VICE, 10
That v. pays homage to virtue BUTLER, S, 24
the function of v. to keep virtue VIRTUE AND VICE, 3
The only sensual pleasure without v. JOHNSON, S, 39; MUSIC, 32
there is no distinction between virtue and v. JOHNSON, S, 64; MISTRUST, 6
This v. brings in one hundred million francs...every year SMOKING, 27
three great evils, boredom, v., and poverty VOLTAIRE, 10; WORK, 37
too fucking busy – or v. versa SEX, 92
V. and virtues are products VIRTUE AND VICE, 7
V. is its own reward VICE, 8
V. is often clothed APPEARANCES, 6; PROVERBS, 450
V. is waste of life VICE, 13
V. itself lost half its evil BURKE, E, 8; VICE, 6
When v. prevails ADDISON, J, 7; VICE, 1
vices It's your combination sinners...who dishonour the v. VICE, 16; WILDER, T, 3
one of the v. of our age ARMY, 5
small v. do appear APPEARANCES, 29; SHAKESPEARE, 190
That I abandon all my v. DOCTORS, 17
virtues and v. couple with one another HALIFAX, 4; VIRTUE AND VICE, 4
virtues are...v. in disguise ROCHEFOUCAULD, 27; VIRTUE AND VICE, 6
We make ourselves a ladder out of our v. VICE, 2
Vichy There's something V. about the French FRANCE, 16
vicious can't expect a boy to be v. EDUCATION, 77; SAKI, 15
He was a v. man, but very kind CHARACTER, 14; JOHNSON, S, 45

woman...so v., or so feeble-minded BRONTE, A, 4
victim a v. of any kind ACTORS, 13
more easily fall v. to a big lie HITLER, A, 11; LYING, 12
subtle and effective way of blaming the v. FEMINISM, 35
v. must be found /I've got a little list GILBERT, W, 26
victims Every reformation must have its v. SAKI, 19
Man is the only animal...on friendly terms with the v....he eats BUTLER, S, 20; HYPOCRISY, 7
The little v. play GRAY, T, 9; IGNORANCE, 11
There are born v. MURDER, 8
v. who respect their executioners RESPECT, 3; SARTRE, J, 4
victor getting the v.'s palm without the dust of racing HORACE, 14; VICTORY, 9
Victoria If this is the way Queen V. treats her prisoners IMPRISONMENT, 18
Mrs Thatcher...looking like Queen V. POLITICIANS, 121
take a ticket at V. Station FREEDOM, 5
Victorian the most antagonistic to the V. age WRITERS, 97
the V. Era when asterisks were followed...by a baby PRUDERY, 2
V. values...were the values when our country MORALITY, 23; THATCHER, M, 25
Victorians consent to live in the houses the V. built TRANSIENCE, 24
The V. had not been anxious to go away TRAVEL, 49
victories Peace hath her v. MILTON, J, 63; WAR AND PEACE, 12
victorious Send him v. BRITAIN, 6
victors bursting with the dead bodies of the v. VICTORY, 23
victory Before Alamein we never had a v. CHURCHILL, W, 15; WORLD WAR II, 24
death is swallowed up in v. BIBLE, 42; DEATH, 35
every v. turns into a defeat BEAUVOIR, S, 6; DISILLUSION, 2
in v. unbearable CHURCHILL, W, 32; OFFICERS, 3
In...war it is not right that matters, but v. HITLER, A, 13; WAR, 78
let there be v. WORLD WAR I, 11
no substitute for v. WAR, 102
O grave! where is thy v. DEATH, 123; POPE, A, 6
Such another v. and we are ruined VICTORY, 20
This is *your* v. VICTORY, 4; WORLD WAR II, 22
to gain such a v. as this VICTORY, 28; WELLINGTON, 12
'twas a famous v. SOUTHEY, R, 1; VICTORY, 24
V. at all costs CHURCHILL, W, 49; VICTORY, 3
v. finds a hundred fathers DEFEAT, 2; VICTORY, 5
v. for all the people of South Africa MANDELA, N, 9
V. has a thousand fathers SUCCESS, 14
v. under the belly of a Cossack's horse RUSSIAN REVOLUTION, 10; TROTSKY, L, 4
without v. there is no survival CHURCHILL, W, 49; VICTORY, 3
vidders be very careful o' v. CAUTION, 11; DICKENS, C, 45
vieillesse si v. pouvait AGE, 39
Vietnam To win in V. WAR, 164
V. was lost in the living rooms of America WAR, 105
view modern v. of life is always to seek what is more convenient DISEASE, 37
truth is a point of v. HYPATIA, 2
vigilance eternal v. FREEDOM, 13
vile Chesterton is like a v. scum on a pond CHESTERTON, G, 1
only man is v. MISANTHROPY, 1
orgies are v. DEBAUCHERY, 10; NASH, O, 5
vilest the v. specimens of human nature are...found among demagogues MACAULAY, T, 16; POLITICS, 68
village the world in the image of a global v. TECHNOLOGY, 12
villages world poverty is primarily a problem of two million v. POVERTY, 35
villain Bloody, bawdy v.!...lecherous, kindless v. INDECISION, 4
I am determined to prove a v. EVIL, 23
That one may smile, and smile, and be a v. HYPOCRISY, 17
v. of the earth GUILT, 11
villains Children should acquire...heroes and v. from fiction AUDEN, W, 4; HISTORY, 3
God should go before such v. GOD, 46; SHAKESPEARE, 276
vine With v. leaves in his hair IBSEN, H, 5; RETURN, 3
vines the little foxes, that spoil the v. BIBLE, 490
vino *In v. veritas* ALCOHOL, 62; PLINY THE ELDER, 5
vintage O, for a draught of v. ALCOHOL, 46; KEATS, J, 36
trampling out the v. where the grapes of wrath GOD, 27
violate men never v. the laws of God without...consequences RETRIBUTION, 9
violated first v. the forbidden tree RELIGION, 86
violence nothing but beastly fury and extreme v. FOOTBALL, 7
Remove your pants before resorting to v. VIOLENCE, 14
that school of Snobbery with V. WRITING, 6
used words with the v. of a horse-breaker BROWNING, R, 1
V. is the repartee of the illiterate VIOLENCE, 4
v. is the rhetoric VIOLENCE, 15
v. masquerading as love LAING, R, 4; VIOLENCE, 12
Years of intimidation and v. could not stop us MANDELA, N, 8
violent better to be v....than...cover impotence GANDHI, M, 4; VIOLENCE, 7
I expect no very v. transition HEAVEN, 12
virtue in ambition is v. BACON, F, 29; VIRTUE, 4
violet My regret /Becomes an April v. SORROW, 33; TENNYSON, 37
violets Good God, I forgot the v. FLOWERS, 7; LANDOR, W, 8
violin an orangutang trying to play the v. BALZAC, H, 3; MARRIAGE, 18
If the Almighty himself played the v. EGOTISM, 6; INSULTS, 61
vipers O generation of v. BIBLE, 354; HYPOCRISY, 3
virgin a v. shall conceive BIBLE, 198; CHRISTIANITY, 12
Elizabeth, who reigned a v. ELIZABETH I, 10
fashionable...to be a v. SEX, 23
Lillian, you should have stayed a v. CHILDREN, 23
v. territory for whorehouses AMERICA, 7
virginity Age...nor custom stale her infinite v. WEBSTER, D, 3
a little more v., if you don't mind ACTING, 23; TREE, H, 10
lost my v. as a career move AMBITION, 18
that v. could be a virtue PURITY, 4; VOLTAIRE, 21
V. is rather a state of mind SEX, 8
virgins everyone is back to v. again SEX, 25
those v. arose, and trimmed their lamps BIBLE, 416
virtue adversity doth best discover v. BACON, F, 8
a man of much wit...void of v. CHESTERFIELD, P, 4
as some men toil after v. LAMB, C, 22; SMOKING, 24
Crime, like v., has its degrees CRIME, 7
fair woman without v. VIRTUE, 1
Fine words...seldom associated with v. CONFUCIUS, 6
forbearance ceases to be a v. BURKE, E, 5
greatest offence against v. HAZLITT, W, 16
hearts of Men...should have a v. to shape their life MANKIND, 65
kindled his fire but extinguished his v. LUST, 5
Let the blessing...be...upon all that are lovers of v. FISHING, 5; WALTON, I, 6
loss of v. in a female is irretrievable VIRTUE, 2
moderation in the pursuit of justice is no v. EXCESS, 5
Most men admire /V. MILTON, J, 53
much v. in If SHAKESPEARE, 57
My v.'s still far too small COLETTE, S, 3; VIRTUE, 12
name a v. that brings in as much revenue SMOKING, 27
next to impossible is the exercise of v. VIRTUE, 14
no v. like necessity SHAKESPEARE, 296
Our king does not desire gold...but v. ROYALTY, 90
Self-denial is not a v. SELF-DENIAL, 1; SHAW, G, 29
That vice pays homage to v. BUTLER, S, 24
there is no distinction between v. and vice JOHNSON, S, 64; MISTRUST, 6
to practise five things...constitutes perfect v. CONFUCIUS, 9; VIRTUE, 13
V. consisted in HYPOCRISY, 8; VIRTUE, 11
v. in ambition is violent BACON, F, 29; VIRTUE, 4
v. in the creator is not the same as v. in the creature CREATION, 13
V. is its own punishment RIGHTEOUSNESS, 2
V. is like a rich stone BACON, F, 11; VIRTUE, 3
v. is only elicited by temptation BRONTE, A, 4
What is it that constitutes v. BRONTE, A, 5
Woman's v. is man's greatest invention SEXES, 26
virtues ape-like v. without which CONNOLLY, C, 5; EDUCATION, 26
few v....the Poles do not possess CHURCHILL, W, 63; PLACES, 11
greater v. to sustain good fortune LUCK, 12; ROCHEFOUCAULD, 3
No one gossips about...secret v. GOSSIP, 12; RUSSELL, B, 17
Vice and v. are products VIRTUE AND VICE, 7
v. and vices couple with one another HALIFAX, 4; VIRTUE AND VICE, 4
v. are...vices in disguise ROCHEFOUCAULD, 27; VIRTUE AND VICE, 6
v. /We write in water MEMORIALS, 16; SHAKESPEARE, 143
What men call social v....is...but the virtue of pigs in a litter SOCIETY, 23; THOREAU, H, 7
Whenever there are tremendous v. VIRTUE, 10

world to hide v. in SHAKESPEARE, 337
you meet Winston...you spend in discovering his v. CHURCHILL, W, 5
virtuous more v. man...does not exist ROYALTY, 73
the v. poor WILDE, O, 53
When men grow v. in their old age POPE, A, 56; VIRTUE, 21
who can find a v. woman BIBLE, 458
virus a cross between a very severe v. and getting married ACTORS, 30
visage He was of v. louelye ROYALTY, 87
Sir Launcelot saw her v., but he wept not greatly MALORY, T, 5; SORROW, 16
viscera determined by the state of our ductless glands and our v. MIND, 13
vise Screw up the v....you have rheumatism DISEASE, 4
vision I have a v. of the future BETJEMAN, J, 10; FUTURE, 3
The young men's v., and the old men's dream DREAMS, 5; DRYDEN, J, 14
turn to the wider v. of the Commonwealth MACMILLAN, H, 6; POLITICS, 70
visionary Whither is fled the v. gleam METAPHYSICS, 5; WORDSWORTH, W, 26
visions slumber'd here While these v. did appear SHAKESPEARE, 267
visit Be not slow to v. the sick ILLNESS, 12
visiting like v. another country BAINBRIDGE, B, 4
visitors V.' footfalls are like medicine REMEDIES, 3
visits Its v., /Like those of angels DEATH, 39
viskey Gimme a v.....don't be stingy, baby DRINKS, 12
vitai *v. lampada* MORTALITY, 15
vitalism As long as v. and spiritualism are open questions SCIENCE, 96
the desire, rarely actually expressed, to refute v. SCIENCE, 22
vitality a symptom of deficient v. EXCESS, 15; STEVENSON, R, 19
The lower one's v. ART, 3; BEERBOHM, M, 9
vitamins the right proteins and v. HEALTH AND HEALTHY LIVING, 4
they are crazy about v. or about roughage HEALTH AND HEALTHY LIVING, 10
vivify quarrels which v. its barrenness GREER, G, 4; LOVE, 81
vivisect We v. the nightingale RESEARCH, 1
vocabulary A v. that would take the feathers off a hoody crow LANGUAGE, 7
v. needs constant fertilisation WORDS, 35
vocal His v. cords were kissed by God COMPLIMENTS, 26; OPERA, 9
vodka Communists used to bring v. RUSSIA, 4
vogue It is charming to totter into v. AGE, 97; WALPOLE, H, 5
voice a bird of the air shall carry the v. SECRECY, 3
a still small v. BIBLE, 300; TENNYSON, 79
Conscience is the inner v. CONSCIENCE, 6; MENCKEN, H, 2
His v. was intimate as APPEARANCE, 53
If you'll be my v. today CLINTON, B, 6
something in her v. that made you think of lorgnettes APPEARANCE, 29
the dead shall hear the v. of the Son of God BIBLE, 248
The higher the v. INTELLECT, 11
The melting v. through mazes running MILTON, J, 20; MUSIC, 42
the v. of my beloved BIBLE, 488; LOVE, 34
The v. of the intellect is a soft one FREUD, S, 1; INTELLECT, 5
the v. of the Lord breaketh the cedar-trees PSALMS, 16
the v. of the turtle is heard BIBLE, 489
to-day if ye will hear his v. PSALMS, 56
v. of the people is the v. of God PUBLIC, 1
voices Music, when soft v. die MEMORY, 22
Two v....one is of the sea, /One of the mountains FREEDOM, 64; WORDSWORTH, W, 64
volcano dancing on a v. REVOLUTION, 11
explode at last in a fiery v. in one's great toe DISEASE, 17
vole plashy fen passes the questing v. ANIMALS, 26; WAUGH, E, 34
Volk *Ein Reich, Ein V., Ein Führer* NAZISM, 1
Voltaire I have seen V. VOLTAIRE, 4
One does not arrest V. DE GAULLE, C, 10; RESPECT, 2
volunteer restless who will v. for anything SOLDIERS, 10
vomit a liquor which...made them v. ALCOHOL, 50; LA BRUYERE, J, 13
To write a diary...returning to one's own v. DIARIES, 4
vote Give women the v. SHAW, G, 20
He's lost us the tarts' v. MEDIA, 7; RESPONSIBILITY, 6
in the same boat...not a chance of recording the v. WOMEN, 39
I shall not v....I do not aspire to advise DEMOCRACY, 27
One man shall have one v. DEMOCRACY, 4
The v....means nothing to women FEMINISM, 26; O'BRIEN, E, 4
v. is the most powerful instrument DEMOCRACY, 11
voted I always v. at my party's call GILBERT, W, 11; POLITICIANS, 10
voter appeal to 'Every intelligent v.' POLITICS, 1
The idea that there is a model Labour v....is patronizing KINNOCK, N, 12; POLITICS, 63
votes Democrats only come here when they want v. RUSSIA, 4
disadvantage of merely counting v. DEMOCRACY, 10; INGE, W, 7
solved by speeches and majority v. POWER POLITICS, 2
V. for Women WOMEN, 11
vow better...not v., than...v. and not pay PROMISES, 2
I v. to thee, my country PATRIOTISM, 41
vows God keep all v. unbroke FAITHFULNESS, 6
vox *Vox populi, v. dei* PUBLIC, 1
vulgar Above the v. flight of common souls SUPERIORITY, 12
dislike the French from...v. antipathy FRANCE, 19; WALPOLE, H, 9
Funny without being v. CRITICISM, 21; GILBERT, W, 49
the most v....is the British tourist BRITISH, 10; TRAVEL, 26
the sign of a v. mind ARROGANCE, 1
The v. boil...an egg FOOD, 59; POPE, A, 53
v. is to use a gold toothpick VULGARITY, 4
war...is looked upon as v. WAR, 182; WILDE, O, 10
vulgarity One can love a certain kind of v. for its own sake VULGARITY, 2
v. begins at home VULGARITY, 5; WILDE, O, 67
vulgarize That fellow would v. the day of judgment JERROLD, D, 3; VULGARITY, 3
vulgarizing the only thing we haven't succeeded in completely v. DEATH, 83; HUXLEY, A, 17
vulture I eat like a v. APPEARANCE, 47
vulva To the Blameless V. WALKER, A, 6

W

wabe gyre and gimble in the w. CARROLL, L, 23; NONSENSE, 7
wag A case of the tail dogging the w. HUMOUR, 59
Every man has...an ambition to be a w. HUMOUR, 18; JOHNSON, S, 32
wage One man's w. rise is another man's price increase ECONOMICS, 24; WILSON, H, 4
waggle can you w. your ears ACHIEVEMENT, 2; BOOKS, 6
Wagner W. has lovely moments CRITICISM, 55
W. is the Puccini of music MUSICIANS, 12
wagon Hitch your w. to a star AMBITION, 9; EMERSON, R, 23
Wagstaff a disgrace to our family name of W. FAMILY, 38; MARX, G, 11
waist his arm round your w. and his eye on the clock POLITICIANS, 39
waistcoat my stomach must just digest in its w. ALCOHOL, 75; SHERIDAN, R, 12
wait I can w. PATIENCE, 13
I thought I told you to w. in the car BANKHEAD, T, 12
They also serve who only stand and w. MILTON, J, 61; SERVICE, 5
W. and see PATIENCE, 7
waiting people w. for you stand out far less clearly CLARITY, 2
There was I, w. at the church MARRIAGE, 100
w. for the cock to crow BETRAYAL, 8
We're w. for Godot BECKETT, S, 4
wake hope is...the dream of those that w. HOPE, 20
I w. up...and remember I am the Pope RESPONSIBILITY, 9
waking w. from a troubled dream AFTERLIFE, 4
walentine Never sign a w. DICKENS, C, 51; SIGNATURES, 1
Wales From W. /Whose nightingales WALES, 4
Go out and govern new South W. GOVERNMENT, 7
King Edward...made Lord Edward...Prince of W. ROYALTY, 110
trace...the disasters of English history to...W. WALES, 5; WAUGH, E, 18
W....genuinely more classless WALES, 1
walk Doth w. in fear and dread FEAR, 7
Golf is a good w. spoiled GOLF, 6
How does he w. LEONARDO DA VINCI, 2
in the name of Jesus...rise up and w. BIBLE, 4; REMEDIES, 11

I w. down the Strand FASHION, 7
not once in all my life have I gone out for a w. HEALTH AND HEALTHY LIVING, 3
Or w. with Kings IDEALISM, 4; KIPLING, R, 18
w. before God in the light of the living PSALMS, 35
w. on the lines or the squares MILNE, A, 5; SUPERSTITION, 10
We must learn to w. before we can run PROVERBS, 453
Where'er you w. POPE, A, 47
walked He w. by himself CATS, 10
man that hath not w. in the counsel of the ungodly PSALMS, 1
walking idea of w. through walls ADAMS, D, 2
I'm w. backwards till Christmas MILLIGAN, S, 5; NONSENSE, 26
I nauseate w. CONGREVE, W, 15; COUNTRYSIDE, 1
I were w. with destiny CHURCHILL, W, 12; DESTINY, 5
Jesus...w. on the sea BIBLE, 394
W. My Baby Back Home LOVE, 171
w. round him has always tired me BEERBOHM, M, 20
When I am not w., I am reading LAMB, C, 13; READING, 9
walks She w. in beauty BEAUTY, 16; BYRON, 40
wall he turned his face to the w. BIBLE, 304
Humpty Dumpty sat on a w. NURSERY RHYMES, 18
I shall leap over the w. PSALMS, 7
it is your business, when the w. next door catches fire HORACE, 22
Something...doesn't love a w. FROST, R, 5
the w. fell down flat BIBLE, 288
thou whited w. BIBLE, 16
W. is the name – Max W. HUMOUR, 63
With our backs to the w. WAR, 74; WORLD WAR I, 12
wallet a crowd like that...brings a lump to my w. MATERIALISM, 27
Time hath...a w. at his back SHAKESPEARE, 333
wallop the cod's w. is always fresh made COMMUNISM, 11
wallpaper Either that w. goes, or I do LAST WORDS, 93; WILDE, O, 79
walls by faith the w. of Jericho fell down BIBLE, 188; FAITH, 5
idea of walking through w. ADAMS, D, 2
No part of the w. is left undecorated EXCESS, 7
splendour falls on castle w. TENNYSON, 61
Stone w. do not a prison make IMPRISONMENT, 8
W. have ears GOSSIP, 7; PROVERBS, 451
walrus The W. and the Carpenter CARROLL, L, 27; SEASIDE, 2
walruses you damned w. INSULTS, 11
Walt Disney centres of strong Christian presence...kind of W. Theme Park COMMERCIALISM, 2
waltzing You'll come a-w., Matilda PLACES, 29
wandered I w. lonely as a cloud FLOWERS, 15; WORDSWORTH, W, 8
wanderer A w. is man from his birth ARNOLD, M, 18; HUMAN CONDITION, 1
wandering Poor w. one GILBERT, W, 37; RETURN, 2
W. in a vast forest at night ATHEISM, 5; GUIDANCE, 2
w. minstrel I GILBERT, W, 24; SINGERS, 2
wankers We're all w. underneath SEX, 35
want be without some of the things you w. HAPPINESS, 21
convicted of sickness, hunger, wretchedness, and w. SMOLLETT, T, 3
Economy is going without something you do w. HOPE, A, 3; THRIFT, 9
evil is wrought by w. of thought EVIL, 13; HOOD, T, 8
for w. of a nail FRANKLIN, B, 5; PROVERBS, 166
freedom from w. HUMAN RIGHTS, 6; ROOSEVELT, F, 14
give the public what they w. to see and they'll come out for it FUNERALS, 10; INSULTS, 115
If you w. a thing well done PROVERBS, 221; SELF-RELIANCE, 1
I w. to be alone.' MISQUOTATIONS, 17
the Lord is my shepherd; I shall not w. PSALMS, 12
The w. of a thing is perplexing enough MATERIALISM, 24
What does a woman w. FREUD, S, 6; WOMEN, 57
What do we w.? Radio 4 MEDIA, 2
wanted bought things because she w. 'em WOMEN, 137
Every man is w. EMERSON, R, 12; HUMAN CONDITION, 8
I have w. only one thing to make me happy HAZLITT, W, 9
wanting stop w. something you get it DESIRE, 17
wants Man w. but little MORTALITY, 24
war after the w. he should be publicly castrated LLOYD GEORGE, D, 4
Against the beautiful...one can wage a pitiless w. GREENE, G, 5
All diplomacy is a continuation of w. DIPLOMACY, 23
all's fair in love and w. JUSTICE, 8
An empire founded by w. MONTESQUIEU, 1; WAR, 111
a phoney w. WAR, 53
As a woman I can't go to w. WAR, 133
As long as w. is regarded as wicked WAR, 182; WILDE, O, 10
average men and women were delighted at...w. WAR, 140
Before the w....it was summer all the year round NOSTALGIA, 19; ORWELL, G, 10
Being over seventy is like being engaged in a w. OLD AGE, 98; SPARK, M, 6
blast of w. SHAKESPEARE, 130
but France has not lost the w. FRANCE, 8
consequently this country is at w. with Germany WORLD WAR II, 7
could lose the w. in an afternoon CHURCHILL, W, 35; OFFICERS, 4
defeat without a w. CHURCHILL, W, 46; WORLD WAR II, 9
desire of our two peoples never to go to w. WORLD WAR II, 6
do in the Great W., Daddy WORLD WAR I, 6
done very well out of the w. BALDWIN, S, 1; HOUSES OF PARLIAMENT, 4
except the British W. Office WAR, 160
First in w. WASHINGTON, G, 1
France...lost a battle...not lost the w. WAR, 56
Great Britain is going to make w. on a kindred nation WORLD WAR I, 3
Grim-visag'd w. hath smooth'd his wrinkl'd front APPEARANCE, 61
he came hiccupping to the w. EXCESS, 6
He kept us out of w. WAR, 65
him who desires peace, prepare for w. WAR AND PEACE, 14
I could have lost the w. in an afternoon WAR, 85
I'd like to see the government get out of w. altogether WAR, 77
I don't care for w. WAR, 117
If we lose this w. WAR, 55
I make w. on the living REVENGE, 9
In a civil w., a general must know WAR, 134
in righteousness he doth judge and make w. BIBLE, 470; RIGHTEOUSNESS, 4
In starting and waging a w. it is not right that matters, but victory HITLER, A, 13; WAR, 78
In w....there are no winners CHAMBERLAIN, N, 4; WAR, 43
is a w. to end w. WORLD WAR I, 15
It is well that w. is so terrible WAR, 99
I wage w. POLITICS, 32
lead this people into w. and they'll forget...tolerance WAR, 188; WILSON, W, 4
Lenin was the first to discover that capitalism 'inevitably' caused w. CAPITALISM, 18; TAYLOR, A, 4
let slip the dogs of w. SHAKESPEARE, 153; WAR, 158
life is more interesting in w. than in peace WAR AND PEACE, 11
little woman who wrote the book that made this great w. LINCOLN, A, 5
makes a good w. makes a good peace HERBERT, G, 8; WAR AND PEACE, 9
My home policy? I wage w. WAR, 50
My subject is W., and the pity of W. OWEN, W, 6; POETRY, 46
never was a good w. FRANKLIN, B, 16; WAR AND PEACE, 7
No one can guarantee success in w. CHURCHILL, W, 27; WAR, 47
nothing that w. has ever achieved WAR, 61
Now w. has a bad conscience KEY, E, 6; WAR, 90
Older men declare w. WAR, 80
only twenty seconds of w. to destroy him WAR, 18
on this wall will hang my weapons and my lyre, discharged from the w. HORACE, 38
Stand your ground...if they mean to have a w., let it begin here WAR, 127
Television brought the brutality of w. WAR, 105
that devil's madness – W. WAR, 157
the...barbarity of w....forces men...to commit acts KEY, E, 7; WAR, 91
The first casualty when w. comes WAR, 88
the Lord is a man of w. BIBLE, 113
The quickest way of ending a w. ORWELL, G, 20; WAR, 123
there was w. in heaven BIBLE, 465; DEVIL, 7
the second rule of w. WAR, 112
The W. between Men and Women SEXES, 32; THURBER, J, 14
the W. is being deliberately prolonged SASSOON, S, 7; WAR, 149
the w. of the giants is over CHURCHILL, W, 30; WORLD WAR II, 25
The W. that will End W. WELLS, H, 20
The w. we have just been through...is not to be compared WAR, 187; WILSON, W, 6
the women's lib movement came from the w. FEMINISM, 37

The wrong w., at the wrong place WAR, 25
they'll give a w. and nobody will come WAR, 143
This is how w. is begun WAR, 128
this liking for w. BENNETT, A, 2; WAR, 19
this massed multitude of silent witnesses to…w. WAR, 71
This w.…is a w. to end w. LLOYD GEORGE, D, 18; WAR, 101
This w. is not as in the past WORLD WAR II, 47
this w.…which did not justify the sacrifice of a single mother's son WAR, 126
Those who can win a w. well CHURCHILL, W, 22; WAR AND PEACE, 5
W. alone brings up to their highest tension all human energies WAR, 114
w. can only be abolished through w. MAO TSE-TUNG, 4
w. ended, the explosions stopped WAR AND PEACE, 10
W. even to the knife BYRON, 11; WAR, 39
W. hath no fury like a non-combatant WAR, 110
W. is, after all, the universal perversion WAR, 132
W. is an organized bore WAR, 79
W. is capitalism WAR, 167
W. is enjoined you against the Infidels KORAN 3
W. is hell WAR, 162
W. is like love BRECHT, B, 9
W. is much too serious a thing to be left to military men TALLEYRAND, 6
W. is never cheap BUSH, G, 14
W. is not an adventure WAR, 142
W. is Peace OPPOSITES, 5; ORWELL, G, 18
W. is the continuation of politics MAO TSE-TUNG, 3
W. is too important OFFICERS, 5
W. is war ORWELL, G, 5; WAR, 121
W. knows no power BROOKE, R, 6; WAR, 32
W. makes rattling good history HARDY, T, 7; WAR AND PEACE, 8
w. minus the shooting ORWELL, G, 32; SPORT AND GAMES, 33
W. should belong to the tragic past JOHN PAUL II, 4; WAR, 87
w. which…left nothing to be desired BRECHT, B, 7; WAR, 27
w.…will be considered as antiquated as a duel WAR, 67
W. will never cease until babies MENCKEN, H, 5; WAR, 106
we are…in the midst of a cold w. COLD WAR, 1
We are not at w. with Egypt WAR, 60
We have all lost the w. LAWRENCE, D, 15; WAR, 98
What they could do with round here is a good w. BRECHT, B, 3; WAR, 26
when there was w., he went AUDEN, W, 27; PUBLIC, 3
When the rich wage w. POVERTY AND WEALTH, 8
when they learn how we began this w. PRIESTLEY, J, 10; WORLD WAR II, 42
When was a w. not a w. WAR, 40
When you're at w. you think about a better life WAR AND PEACE, 15; WILDER, T, 6
Who live under the shadow of a w. SPENDER, S, 5; WAR, 163
World W. II began last week WORLD WAR II, 1

ward as if I were locked up in a w. too CHEKHOV, A, 3

wards I taught medical students in the w. EDUCATION, 70
key deftly in the oiled w. KEATS, J, 48; SLEEP, 24

Ware And I should dine at W. COWPER, W, 13; MARRIAGE, 56

warehouses One of the best w. I ever see was the Vatican EUROPE, 26

Waring What's become of W. ABSENCE, 5; BROWNING, R, 58

warmongers w. who…pull the chestnuts out of the fire STALIN, J, 3

warmth No w., no cheerfulness, no healthful ease HOOD, T, 10

warn the right to be consulted…to encourage…to w. BAGEHOT, W, 7; MONARCHY, 3

warned my Friends, be w. by me BELLOC, H, 10; FOOD, 10

warning will it come without w. AUDEN, W, 26; LOVE, 20

War Office except the British W. SHAW, G, 9

warrants no money in rape w. RAPE, 2

warrior Here lies a valiant w. ANONYMOUS, 28
the British w. queen BRITAIN, 7; COWPER, W, 4

wars All w. are planned by old men WAR, 137
All w. are popular for the first thirty days WAR, 150
end to the beginnings of all w. ROOSEVELT, F, 17; WAR, 139
he maketh w. to cease in all the world PSALMS, 28
Just like an old liberal /Between the w. LIBERALISM, 3
military don't start w. WAR, 181
my w. /Were global REED, H, 1; WAR, 135
No kingdom has…had as many…w. as the kingdom of Christ MONTESQUIEU, 5
Still w. and lechery SHAKESPEARE, 335
the men who conduct their w. WAR, 66
W. are not won by evacuations CHURCHILL, W, 28; WORLD WAR II, 23
W. cannot be fought with nuclear weapons MOUNTBATTEN OF BURMA, L, 6; NUCLEAR WEAPONS, 15
W. come because WAR, 152
W., conflict, it's all business CHAPLIN, C, 4; WAR, 44
w., horrible w. PROPHECY, 14; VIRGIL, 14

warts pimples, w., and everything as you see me CROMWELL, O, 4; REALISM, 1

war-war To jaw-jaw is better than to w. CHURCHILL, W, 67; DIPLOMACY, 7

wary the w. fox said…to the sick lion HORACE, 16; MISTRUST, 5

wash Don't w. your dirty linen GOSSIP, 3; PROVERBS, 123
I do, and I also w. and iron them HOUSEWORK, 8
w. me throughly from my wickedness PSALMS, 30
W. That Man Right Out of My Hair DECISION, 1

washed Pilate…w. his hands BIBLE, 430; GUILT, 3
w. their robes…in the blood of the lamb BIBLE, 463

washing painting a face and not w. APPEARANCE, 27

wasps w. and hornets break through LAW, 38; SWIFT, J, 18

waste biggest w. of water in the country CONSERVATION, 8
Far too good to w. on children SHAW, G, 50; YOUTH, 29
The years to come seemed w. of breath FLYING, 7; YEATS, W, 16
W. not, want not PROVERBS, 452; WASTE, 1

wasted most w. of all days LAUGHTER, 7

wasting she did not believe in w. her effects THREATS, 2

watch Either he's dead or my w. has stopped MARX, G, 5
keeping w. over their flock by night BIBLE, 314
mechanism which you can take apart like a w. LITERATURE, 17
The W. on the Rhine RIVERS, 4
w. and pray BIBLE, 426; IMPERFECTION, 4
why not carry a w. TREE, H, 2

watch-dog to hear the w.'s honest bark BYRON, 18; DOGS, 5

watched A w. pot PROVERBS, 73

watches 'Tis with our judgments as our w. POPE, A, 21

watchmaker I should have become a w. EINSTEIN, A, 9

watchman only one man…can count on steady work – the night w. THEATRE, 2

watch-tower From his w. in the skies MILTON, J, 17

water a pure river of w. of life BIBLE, 474
better deeds /Shall be in w. writ BEAUMONT, F, 8
biggest waste of w. in the country WATER, 7
Dripping w. hollows out a stone OVID, 4; PERSISTENCE, 11
half the landscape is…covered by useless w. SEASIDE, 3
Here lies one whose name was writ in w. KEATS, J, 49
He who drinks a tumbler of London w. SMITH, S, 16; WATER, 9
Human beings were invented by w. WATER, 8
I came like W. FITZGERALD, E, 11; LIFE AND DEATH, 15
if I were under w. I would scarcely kick MELANCHOLY, 6
impressions…lasting as…an oar upon the w. INSIGNIFICANCE, 1
It is with our passions as it is with fire and w. PASSION, 6
Like a bridge over troubled w. COMFORT, 6
like throwing w. into the sea CERVANTES, M, 9; CHARITY, 13
no verse can give pleasure…that is written by drinkers of w. HORACE, 23; WATER, 6
rural cleanliness lies in *w. supply* NIGHTINGALE, F, 5
Streets full of w. TELEGRAMS, 3; VENICE, 1
the w. that was made wine ALCOHOL, 17; BIBLE, 242
Too much of w. hast thou SHAKESPEARE, 105
virtues we write in w. MEMORIALS, 16; SHAKESPEARE, 143
w.…a mixer ALCOHOL, 68
w. flowed like champagne ABSTINENCE, 4
w., honey, and labour REMEDIES, 5
W. is H_2O, hydrogen two parts, oxygen one LAWRENCE, D, 19
w., is unsuitable in colour HERBERT, A, 7; WATER, 5
w. still keeps falling over CHURCHILL, W, 8; WATER, 1
W., w., every where COLERIDGE, S, 30; WATER, 2
We have all passed a lot of w. GOLDWYN, S, 17
when I makes w. I makes w. HUMOUR, 46; JOYCE, J, 7
when I touch wine, it turns into w. ALCOHOL, 49

watering a-w. the last year's crop ELIOT, G, 4; FUTILITY, 7

Waterloo Battle of W. WAR, 179; WELLINGTON, 26
Every man meets his W. DEFEAT, 13
the Battle of W. *was* won on the playing-fields of Eton WAR, 122

watermark high w.…of Socialist literature is W. H. Auden AUDEN, W, 2

waters By the w. of Babylon PSALMS, 70
dreadful noise of w. in mine ears DROWNING, 2; SHAKESPEARE, 303

he leadeth me beside the still w. PSALMS, 12
stolen w. are sweet BIBLE, 449; SECRECY, 5
the earth shall be full...as the w. cover the sea BIBLE, 203; PEACE, 2
the Spirit of God moved upon...the w. BIBLE, 137; CREATION, 2
the w. of comfort PSALMS, 11
the w. of the heart EMOTION, 5; THOMAS, D, 14
w. flowed over mine head BIBLE, 307

water-trough A snake came to my w. LAWRENCE, D, 28
Watson Mr W., come here; I want you SUMMONS, 3
Waugh Evelyn W....is a Roman Catholic WAUGH, E, 1
Mr. W....is...a snob in search of a class WAUGH, E, 2
wave Churchill on top of the w. TYRANNY, 1
waves the w. make towards the pebbled shore SHAKESPEARE, 365; TIME, 50
waxworks w. inhabited by gramophones WORDS, 8
way A man...is *so* in the w. MEN, 5
blow out your candle...to find your w. ATHEISM, 5; GUIDANCE, 2
catch the nearest w. KINDNESS, 11; SHAKESPEARE, 207
Great White W. PLACES, 28
I am the w., the truth, and the life BIBLE, 259; CHRISTIANITY, 21
I did it my w. SELF, 5
I go my w. to him that sent me BIBLE, 261
in every war they kill you a new w. PROGRESS, 20; ROGERS, W, 1
plowman homeward plods his weary w. DAY, 6; GRAY, T, 1
the error of his w. BIBLE, 220
The w. to a man's heart LOVE, 10; PROVERBS, 427
The w. to dusty death LIFE, 86; SHAKESPEARE, 227
though hell should bar the w. DETERMINATION, 19
Through Eden took their solitary w. MILTON, J, 52
w. of all flesh CONGREVE, W, 12
which w. the wind blows DYLAN, B, 11
woman has her w. SEXES, 14

wayfaring study at small cost and short w. EDUCATION, 34
ways consider your w. BIBLE, 184
Let me count the w. BROWNING, E, 5
She dwelt among the untrodden w. WORDSWORTH, W, 49
We have w. of making men talk MISQUOTATIONS, 4
wayside If you see anybody fallen by the w. CHARITY, 22
we put it down a w. DICKENS, C, 52; SPELLING, 1
weak A w., diffusive, weltering, ineffectual man COLERIDGE, S, 1; POETS, 24
Beauty stands /In the admiration...of w. minds BEAUTY, 33; MILTON, J, 54
concessions of the w. BURKE, E, 13; YIELDING, 1
disarm the strong and arm the w. FRANCE, A, 2; INJUSTICE, 5
Idleness...the refuge of w. minds CHESTERFIELD, P, 15; IDLENESS, 3
I inhabit a w., frail, decayed tenement LAST WORDS, 2
Is thy love a plant /Of such w. fibre ABSENCE, 10; WORDSWORTH, W, 23
Like all w. men...an exaggerated stress DECISION, 3; MAUGHAM, W, 11
surely the w. shall perish SURVIVAL, 9
The concessions of the w. are the concessions of fear BURKE, E, 13
The w....always prevail over the strong SURVIVAL, 6
The w. have one weapon MISTAKES, 3

weaker the w. vessel BIBLE, 442; MARRIAGE, 31
weakest The w. goes to the wall PROVERBS, 428; WEAKNESS, 1
weakness no act of w. can be tolerated WAR, 86
no more w. than is natural to her sex WOMEN, 131
private universe of physical w. and mental decay OLD AGE, 56
rail at w. themselves create INJUSTICE, 11
weaknesses I have got lots of human w. IMPERFECTION, 13; THATCHER, M, 26
Never support two w. VICE, 16; WILDER, T, 3
touch his w. with a delicate hand GOLDSMITH, O, 15; IMPERFECTION, 8
weal I will govern according to the common w. MONARCHY, 15
wealth All health is better than w. SCOTT, W, 23
God shows his contempt for w. WEALTH, 40
His w. a well-spent age CAMPION, T, 4; RIGHTEOUSNESS, 7
If Enterprise is afoot, W. accumulates WEALTH, 30
Outshone the w. of Ormus and of Ind DEVIL, 13; MILTON, J, 39
the insolence of w. JOHNSON, S, 124; WEALTH, 28
W. covers sin WEALTH, 29
w. had rendered her helpless BROOKNER, A, 7
W. has never been a sufficient source of honour GALBRAITH, J, 2
W. I ask not TRAVEL, 41
W. I seek not STEVENSON, R, 6
W. is like sea-water GREED, 12; SCHOPENHAUER, A, 8
W. is not without its advantages GALBRAITH, J, 1; WEALTH, 22
when the nation depended on agriculture for its w. ECONOMICS, 19
Where w. and freedom reign, contentment fails GOLDSMITH, O, 23

wealthy Where some people are very w. and others have nothing ARISTOTLE, 8; GOVERNMENT, 5
weaned w. on a pickle APPEARANCE, 40; INSULTS, 91
weapon art is not a w. ART, 15
Innocence is no earthly w. HILL, G, 2
In the sex-war thoughtlessness is the w. of the male CONNOLLY, C, 16; SEXES, 8
The weak have one w. MISTAKES, 3
tinned food is a deadlier w. ORWELL, G, 25; WEAPONS, 5
w. is the snub GANDHI, I, 1
weapons books are w. BOOKS, 39; ROOSEVELT, F, 16
If sunbeams were w. ENVIRONMENT, 10; WAR, 130
on this wall will hang my w. and my lyre HORACE, 38; SEX, 52
wear I...chose my wife...not for...such qualities as would w. well GOLDSMITH, O, 26; MARRIAGE, 83
I want you to w. me LOVE, 70
you'll w. your eyes out STARING, 2; ZOLA, 1
weariest The w. nights...must...end ENDURANCE, 14
weariness much study is a w. of the flesh BIBLE, 78; BOOKS, 9
The w., the fever, and the fret KEATS, J, 38
weary Art thou w. SORROW, 19
let us not be w. in well doing RETRIBUTION, 4
weasel w. under the cocktail cabinet PINTER, H, 5; PLAYS, 8
weather even the w. forecast seemed to be some kind of spoof LODGE, D, 4; WEATHER, 16
Give me books, fruit, French wine and fine w. PLEASURE, 19
I like the w. BYRON, 7; WEATHER, 8
This is the w. the cuckoo likes HARDY, T, 13; WEATHER, 12
This is the w. the shepherd shuns HARDY, T, 14; WEATHER, 13
When two Englishmen meet, their first talk is of the w. ENGLISH, 23; JOHNSON, S, 15
won't hold up the w. REALISM, 4
You don't need a w. man DYLAN, B, 11
weather-eye Keep your w. open CAUTION, 7; PROVERBS, 242
weather-wise Some are w. FRANKLIN, B, 6; WISDOM, 18
web The w. of our life is of a mingled yarn GOOD AND EVIL, 6; SHAKESPEARE, 23
what a tangled w. we weave LYING, 21
webs Laws are like spider's w. LAW, 37
Webster W. is his orator WEBSTER, D, 2
W. struck me much like a steam engine in trousers WEBSTER, D, 1
wed With this Ring I thee w. BOOK OF COMMON PRAYER, 28
wedding the bride at every w. ROOSEVELT, T, 2
weddings w. is sadder than funerals BEHAN, B, 6; MARRIAGE, 23
Wednesday Married on W. NURSERY RHYMES, 53
W.'s child is full of woe CHILDREN, 50; NURSERY RHYMES, 35
wee W....tim'rous beastie ANIMALS, 9; BURNS, R, 21
weed that tawney w. tobacco JONSON, B, 4; SMOKING, 18
What is a w. EMERSON, R, 17; GOOD, 5
weeds Lilies that fester smell far worse than w. SHAKESPEARE, 368
nature runs either to herbs, or to w. BACON, F, 37
Worthless as wither'd w. BELIEF, 4; BRONTE, E, 4
week A w. is a long time in politics WILSON, H, 11
greatest w....since the creation NIXON, R, 8
Of all the days that's in the w. SUNDAY, 3
see what can be accomplished in a w. DETERMINATION, 23
the greatest w. in the history of the world NIXON, R, 8; SPACE, 7
World War II began last w. WORLD WAR II, 1
weekendmanship that basic w. should contain...Important Person Play ONE-UPMANSHIP, 2; POTTER, S, 4
weekends try getting a plumber on w.. GOD, 1
weep By the waters of Babylon we sit down and w. AMERICA, 40; WALPOLE, H, 7
Fair daffodils, we w. to see HERRICK, R, 4; TRANSIENCE, 15
For men must work, and women must w. KINGSLEY, C, 7; SEXES, 18
not to w. at them, nor to hate them, but to understand them UNDERSTANDING, 9
She must w. or she will die MOURNING, 16; TENNYSON, 67
so that I do not w. LAUGHTER, 5
Tears such as angels w. MILTON, J, 36; SORROW, 17
w. for her sins at the other ADULTERY, 3
W. no more, my lady HOMESICKNESS, 2

weeping Do you hear the children w. BROWNING, E, 3
w. and gnashing of teeth BIBLE, 381
Why are you w.? Did you imagine that I was immortal LAST WORDS, 58; LOUIS XIV, 7
weigh my innocence begins to w. me down INNOCENCE, 3
weighed thou art w. in the balances, and art found wanting BIBLE, 52; JUDGMENT, 1
weight deadly w. of the terrible tradition of a dialogue MANDELA, N, 6
the w. of rages SPOONER, W, 1
weight loss dieters will regain all the w. DIETING, 5
welcome Advice is seldom w. CHESTERFIELD, P, 12
a period of silence on your part would be w. POLITICIANS, 42
Love bade me w. GUILT, 8; HERBERT, G, 6
Thrice w., darling of the spring WORDSWORTH, W, 75
welfare a few, at the expense of the w. of the majority SOCIETY, 12
Welfare-State led to that of the W. SOCIALISM, 23
well as w. off as if he were rich WEALTH, 7
At last I am going to be w. LAST WORDS, 79
do not speak w. of yourself MODESTY, 6; PASCAL, B, 4
eat wisely but not too w. ETIQUETTE, 6
Every man who feels w. is a sick man ILLNESS, 62
fast till he is w. GREED, 1
I am not w.; pray get me…brandy INSULTS, 52
Is getting w. ever an art REMEDIES, 41
Living w. and beautifully and justly LIFE, 89
lov'd not wisely, but too w. LOVE, 155; SHAKESPEARE, 290
nothing…and did it very w. GILBERT, W, 21; HOUSES OF PARLIAMENT, 13
reward of a thing w. done EMERSON, R, 11; SATISFACTION, 3
There are two things…I can do very w. CRITICISM, 24; JOHNSON, S, 52
The skilful doctor treats those who are w. DOCTORS, 30
the world's work…is done by men who do not feel…w. GALBRAITH, J, 6
We never do anything w. HAZLITT, W, 19
worth doing w. CHESTERFIELD, P, 6
well-bred a w. sort of emotional anarchy LAWRENCE, D, 16
well-dressed being w. gives a sense of tranquility CLOTHES, 5
Wellington Lord W. was at the ball WAR, 52
W. has exhausted nature and…glory WELLINGTON, 2
well-knownness The celebrity…known for his w. FAME, 6
well-rounded whole man in himself, polished and w. CHARACTER, 11
Wells Whatever W. writes is not only alive WELLS, H, 1
well-spent as rare as a w. one CARLYLE, T, 7
well-written A w. Life CARLYLE, T, 7
Welsh but he wouldn't put up with the W. WELSH, 1
The W.…just sing WAUGH, E, 17; WELSH, 4
whole of the W. nation REBELLION, 6
Wembley W., adj. Suffering from a vague *malaise* HUMOUR, 44
wen the fate of the great w. LONDON, 8
Wenceslas Good King W. looked out CHRISTMAS, 16
wench beside the w. is dead MARLOWE, C, 11; SEX, 78
Wenlock Edge On W. the wood's in trouble HOUSMAN, A, 13; TREES, 4
went as cooks go she w. HUMOUR, 60; SAKI, 16
wept Jesus w. BIBLE, 257
They w. like anything to see CARROLL, L, 27; SEASIDE, 2
young man who has not w. AGE, 78; SANTAYANA, G, 3
West Amid the applause of the W. GORBACHOV, M, 3
closing time in the gardens of the W. CAPITALISM, 4; CONNOLLY, C, 3
East is East, and W. is W. KIPLING, R, 4; OPPOSITES, 4
Go W., young man EXPLORATION, 2
the safeguard of the w. VENICE, 4; WORDSWORTH, W, 59
Western W. philosophy is…a series of footnotes to Plato's philosophy PHILOSOPHY, 22; WHITEHEAD, A, 6
Westerns W. are closer to art CINEMA, 29
wet joly whistle wel y-w. ALCOHOL, 26; CHAUCER, G, 18
out of these w. clothes and into a dry Martini ALCOHOL, 89
whale A w. ship was my Yale College EDUCATION, 63
Very like a w. SHAKESPEARE, 98
what Aye, and w. then COLERIDGE, S, 4; PROOF, 3
Their names are W. and Why HONESTY, 6
W. is truth BACON, F, 56; TRUTH, 10
W.'s in it for me UNIVERSE, 10
wheat An editor…separates the w. from the chaff STEVENSON, A, 1
wheel bound upon a w. of fire SHAKESPEARE, 193
wheels A cruel story runs on w. CRUELTY, 4
spoke among your w. BEAUMONT, F, 5; OBSTRUCTION, 1
when have they fixed the where and w. EXECUTION, 15
w. a man should marry BACON, F, 35; MARRIAGE, 15
where have they fixed the w. and when EXECUTION, 15
to die, and go we know not w. DEATH, 150; SHAKESPEARE, 234
W. are you now LOVE, 87
W. does she find them INSULTS, 104
W. were you fellows when the paper was blank EDITORS, 1
where'er W. you tread COMPLIMENTS, 22; POPE, A, 47
wherefore There is occasions and causes why and w. SHAKESPEARE, 138
w. art thou Romeo SHAKESPEARE, 311
why and w. in all things REASON, 8
whey Eating her curds and w. NURSERY RHYMES, 31
whiff w. of grapeshot CARLYLE, T, 16
Whig Sir, I perceive you are a vile W. JOHNSON, S, 84
Whigs caught the W. bathing DISRAELI, B, 23; POLITICS, 34
whim The strangest w. CHESTERTON, G, 7; SUICIDE, 8
whimper not with a bang but a w. ELIOT, T, 10; ENDING, 3
whipping W. and abuse are like laudanum STOWE, H, 3
who shall scape w. MERIT, 6; SHAKESPEARE, 88
whirlwind Elijah went up by a w. into heaven BIBLE, 301
sown the wind…reap the w. BIBLE, 190; RETRIBUTION, 5
whisker can't speak above a w. PUNS, 14
whiskey W. is the most popular of…remedies ALCOHOL, 84
whiskies I've had eighteen straight w. ALCOHOL, 81
whisky A good gulp of hot w. at bedtime ALCOHOL, 32; FLEMING, A, 4
nicest boy who ever committed the sin of w. ALCOHOL, 77; SPARK, M, 5
That w. priest CLERGY, 7; GREENE, G, 7
with education and w. the price it is CHARACTER, 25; WAUGH, E, 16
whispered it's w. every where CONGREVE, W, 7; SECRECY, 8
whispering w. sound of the cool colonnade COWPER, W, 19; TREES, 3
whisperings Foul w. are abroad CONSCIENCE, 9
It keeps eternal w. around KEATS, J, 43; SEA, 8
whistle a shrimp learns to w. COMMUNISM, 7
I heard the bullets w.…charming in the sound WAR, 174; WASHINGTON, G, 4
So was hir joly w. wel y-wet ALCOHOL, 26; CHAUCER, G, 18
W. a Happy Tune WHISTLING, 3
W. and she'll come to you BEAUMONT, F, 13; SUMMONS, 2
You know how to w. WHISTLING, 1
whistled who would…play his music and be w. at for it MUSIC, 22
Whistler James W. WILDE, O, 67
W. himself entirely concurs WHISTLER, J, 2
whistles A Scout smiles and w. OPTIMISM, 15
They hang us now in Shrewsbury jail: /The w. blow forlorn EXECUTION, 16; HOUSMAN, A, 8
whistling W. aloud to bear his courage up WHISTLING, 2
white an old black ram /Is tupping your w. ewe SEX, 108
architecture…who can contemplate it…are those…with a w. stick ARCHITECTURE, 8
avarice and oppression of the w. man OPPRESSION, 8
bloody old sins washed w. SASSOON, S, 6
Britain…is going to be forged in the w. heat of this revolution SOCIALISM, 25; WILSON, H, 8
'E was w., clear w., inside APPEARANCES, 21; KIPLING, R, 15
Great W. Way PLACES, 28
If the w. man *says* he does RACISM, 19
it's not even red brick, but w. tile CLASS, 34; OSBORNE, J, 4
I used to be Snow W. PURITY, 6
I want to be the w. man's brother KING, M, 2; RACISM, 14
makes a Negro unpleasant to w. folk RACISM, 23
my soul is w. BLAKE, W, 48; RACISM, 5
One black, and one w., and two khaki ANONYMOUS, 95; RACISM, 1
so-called w. races FORSTER, E, 10; RACISM, 11
Take up the W. Man's burden KIPLING, R, 32; RACISM, 15
the lower classes had such w. skins CLASS, 11
the silk stockings and w. bosoms…excite my amorous propensities JOHNSON, S, 46
The w. man knows how to make everything CHARITY, 23
When a w. man in Africa LESSING, D, 3; RACISM, 18
When the w. man came we had the land RACISM, 12
w. man can dress like a black pimp GOLF, 7
whited thou w. wall BIBLE, 16

the voice of one crying in the w. BIBLE, 353
the w. of this world BUNYAN, J, 1; WORLD, 2
W. is Paradise enow COMPLIMENTS, 11; FITZGERALD, E, 5
wild-fowl more fearful w. than your lion SHAKESPEARE, 263
Wilkes W. and Liberty FREEDOM, 1
will complies against his w. BUTLER, S, 8; YIELDING, 2
Do what you w. FREEDOM, 50; RABELAIS, F, 5
formation of the political w. of the nation HITLER, A, 14; POLITICS, 51
he says 'I w.', he comes to his own as a philosopher PHILOSOPHY, 19
His right was clear, his w. was strong ANONYMOUS, 102; RIGHT, 1
His W.'s the law EXECUTION, 11
In His w. DANTE ALIGHIERI, 6
John Stuart Mill /By a mighty effort of w. ECONOMICS, 3
leaves money to charity in his w. BEQUESTS, 2
let my w. replace reasoned judgement AUTHORITARIANISM, 5
Man has his w. SEXES, 14
The man who leaves money to charity in his w. VOLTAIRE, 33
We have to believe in free w. CHOICE, 4
Where there's a w. DETERMINATION, 2; PROVERBS, 463
W. ye no come back again RETURN, 4
You w., Oscar, you w. IMITATION, 7; WHISTLER, J, 17
William You are old, Father W. CARROLL, L, 6
William Blake That W. /Who beat upon the wall YEATS, W, 3
Williams Shirley W.…a member of the upper-middle class CLASS, 54
Willie Wee W. Winkie runs through the town NURSERY RHYMES, 68
Willie Michie Here lie W.'s banes BURNS, R, 9
willin Barkis is w.' DICKENS, C, 12
willow a little tom-tit /Sang 'W., titwillow GILBERT, W, 35
willows W. whiten, aspens quiver TENNYSON, 42; WEATHER, 27
will-power There is no such thing as a great talent without great w. BALZAC, H, 2; DETERMINATION, 4
will-to-live the w., exists…in every being SCHOPENHAUER, A, 5; SURVIVAL, 8
Wilson Mr W.…is the 14th Mr W. TITLES, 1
wimp someone asks for a soft drink…think he is a w. DRINKS, 11
win Heads I w. VICTORY, 8
high sentiments always w. in the end NOBILITY, 4; ORWELL, G, 8
I am certain that we will w. the election SELF-CONFIDENCE, 11; THATCHER, M, 35
I fight to w. DETERMINATION, 26
The conventional army loses if it does not w. WAR, 93
Those who can w. a war well CHURCHILL, W, 22; WAR AND PEACE, 5
W. or lose, I'll be going out in style STYLE, 9
wind a rushing mighty w. BIBLE, 2
Blow, blow, thou winter w. SHAKESPEARE, 50
God tempers the w. MERCY, 3
gone with the w. MEMORY, 8
Gone With the W. MITCHELL, M, 6; TRANSIENCE, 19
if…it's only w., I'll call it F. E. Smith APPEARANCE, 31
It's an ill w. OPTIMISM, 3; PROVERBS, 231
like W. I go FITZGERALD, E, 11; LIFE AND DEATH, 15
of w. and limb BUTLER, S, 5; FAITHFULNESS, 2
O Wild West W. SHELLEY, P, 14; WEATHER, 25
so famous, that it would permit me…to break w. in society BALZAC, H, 5; FAME, 5
The answer…is blowin' in the w. DYLAN, B, 2; FREEDOM, 14
The story is like the w. SENSATION, 2
throw the sand against the w. BLAKE, W, 34; FUTILITY, 5
what w. is to fire ABSENCE, 6; LOVE, 46
wherever the w. takes me I travel as a visitor FREEDOM, 25; HORACE, 13
which way the w. blows DYLAN, B, 11
Who has seen the w. ROSSETTI, C, 9; WEATHER, 17
w. of nationalism and freedom blowing BALDWIN, S, 7; FREEDOM, 2
words but w. BUTLER, S, 6; WORDS, 4
windmills not giants but w. CERVANTES, M, 4
window married a few years…can't help w. shopping AYCKBOURN, A, 4
Serve up…and throw…out of the w. LEAR, E, 6; NONSENSE, 24
what light through yonder w. breaks SHAKESPEARE, 310
windows Mirrors are the w. of the devil APPEARANCES, 18
Windsor Walk wide o' the Widow at W. ROYALTY, 77
wine A Flask of W. FITZGERALD, E, 5
a little w. for thy stomach's sake DRINKS, 5
A man may surely be allowed to take a glass of w. SHERIDAN, R, 16
And drink of my Algerian w. BEHAN, B, 9; INSULTS, 16
days of w. and roses TRANSIENCE, 12
drinks his w. 'mid laughter free ANONYMOUS, 87; PARTING, 2
Drink w., and have the gout DISEASE, 38; MISFORTUNE, 3
for its poisonous w. KEATS, J, 32; OBLIVION, 2
Frenchmen drink w. just like ALCOHOL, 51
full of new w. BIBLE, 3
Give me books, fruit, French w. and fine weather PLEASURE, 19
good w. needs no bush PLAYS, 13; SHAKESPEARE, 58
like a giant refreshed with w. PSALMS, 43
look not thou upon the w. when it is red ALCOHOL, 19
new w. into old bottles BIBLE, 384
no man…having drunk old w. straightway desireth new ALCOHOL, 18; BIBLE, 321
temperate in love and w. MILTON, J, 2
that w. could derange its functions ALCOHOL, 38
the guests must be chosen as carefully as the w. ALCOHOL, 67; SAKI, 1
the water that was made w. ALCOHOL, 17; BIBLE, 242
the w. is in, the wit is out DRUNKENNESS, 10
the w. was a farce and the food a tragedy POWELL, A, 2
they shall not drink w. with a song BIBLE, 206
This w. is too good for toast-drinking DRINKS, 14
This w. upon a foreign tree THOMAS, D, 17
Truth comes out in w. PLINY THE ELDER, 5
use a little w. for thy stomach's sake ALCOHOL, 21; BIBLE, 509
What is man…a…machine for turning…the red w. of Shiraz into urine MANKIND, 11
when I touch w., it turns into water ALCOHOL, 49
When the w. is in ALCOHOL, 7; PROVERBS, 462
white w. came up with the fish ETIQUETTE, 5
Who loves not w., woman and song PLEASURE, 22
W. comes in at the mouth AGE, 106; YEATS, W, 9
W. is a mocker BIBLE, 453; DRUNKENNESS, 12
W. is the most healthful ALCOHOL, 61
wing Comin' in on a W. and a Prayer HOPE, 6
winged Time's w. chariot AGE, 61; MARVELL, A, 10
Doth the w. life destroy BLAKE, W, 15; PLEASURE, 5
wings Fear lent w. FEAR, 9; VIRGIL, 15
gift of w., and you learn…that you will not fall WRITERS, 30
hide me under the shadow of thy w. PSALMS, 6
man with w.…might…overcome the resistance of the air FLYING, 5; LEONARDO DA VINCI, 5
my trust shall be under the covering of thy w. PSALMS, 37
O that I had w. like a dove PSALMS, 33
shall…arise with healing in his w. BIBLE, 343; CHRISTIANITY, 22
the seraphims: each one had six w. BIBLE, 197
the w. of a dove COWPER, W, 33; SOLITUDE, 4
whether pigs have w. CARROLL, L, 28; NONSENSE, 9
wink I will w. and hold out mine iron SHAKESPEARE, 126
never came a w. too soon HOOD, T, 6; NOSTALGIA, 10
winners In war…there are no w. CHAMBERLAIN, N, 4; WAR, 43
winning All I think about is w. that bleedin' title SUCCESS, 8
great fallacy is that the game is…about w. FOOTBALL, 4
not w. but taking part VICTORY, 7
W. isn't everything FOOTBALL, 10; VICTORY, 13
wins Who dares, w. COURAGE, 3
Winston It hasn't taken W. long to get used to American ways ACHESON, D, 3
W.…preparing his impromptu speeches CHURCHILL, W, 6
W.'s back RETURN, 1; TELEGRAMS, 2
W. with his hundred-horse-power mind BALDWIN, S, 2
you meet W.…you spend in discovering his virtues CHURCHILL, W, 5
winter Blow, blow, thou w. wind INGRATITUDE, 4
got through the perils of w. till at least the seventh of May TROLLOPE, A, 7
human beings say that they enjoy the w. SEASONS, 2
It is a w.'s tale SEASONS, 25; THOMAS, D, 29
No one thinks of w. KIPLING, R, 28; SEASONS, 13
the furious w.'s rages MORTALITY, 16; SHAKESPEARE, 63
The stars grew bright in the w. sky ANIMALS, 16; MASEFIELD, J, 4
the w. is past SEASONS, 5
W. is icummen in POUND, E, 7; SEASONS, 16
w. of our discontent OPTIMISM, 35; SHAKESPEARE, 302
wintry sailed the w. sea BOATS, 12; LONGFELLOW, H, 19
wiped let them be w. out of the book of the living PSALMS, 39
wisdom fear of the Lord is the beginning of w. PSALMS, 62

follies as the special evidences of our w. PRIDE, 14; TROLLOPE, A, 10
Greeks seek after w. BIBLE, 24
If one is too lazy to think…never attain w. WISDOM, 16
in much w. is much grief BIBLE, 65; KNOWLEDGE, 7; WISDOM, 2
Knowledge can be communicated but not w. WISDOM, 20
Love is the w. of the fool JOHNSON, S, 42; LOVE, 92
privilege of w. to listen KNOWLEDGE, 22; WISDOM, 21
proverb is one man's wit and all men's w. SAYINGS, 6
proverbs provide them with w. MAUGHAM, W, 23; STUPIDITY, 9
Self-reflection is the school of w. WISDOM, 19
Silence is…full of potential w. HUXLEY, A, 28; SILENCE, 8
The highest w. has but one science TOLSTOY, L, 8
The only infallible criterion of w. BURKE, E, 4
the palace of W. BLAKE, W, 25
the price of w. is above rubies BIBLE, 234
therefore get w. WISDOM, 8
There is more w. in your body WISDOM, 23
Vain w. all, and false philosophy MILTON, J, 41; WISDOM, 22
want of human w. WAR, 97
w.…a pure influence flowing from the glory of the WISDOM, 11
W. be put in a silver rod BLAKE, W, 11; WISDOM, 12
w.…cometh by opportunity of leisure BIBLE, 90; LEISURE, 1
w. excelleth folly, as…light excelleth darkness WISDOM AND FOOLISHNESS, 2
W. has taught us to be calm and meek REVENGE, 11
w.…hath hewn out her seven pillars BIBLE, 448; WISDOM, 9
W. in minds attentive COWPER, W, 32; KNOWLEDGE, 14
w. is more moving than any motion WISDOM, 11
W. is not additive DEMOCRACY, 9
W. not WISDOM, 31
w. of the crocodiles BACON, F, 60; HYPOCRISY, 2
w. says: 'We must die,' LIFE AND DEATH, 35
w.…sweetly doth…order all things BIBLE, 521; WISDOM, 10
with how little w. the world is governed GOVERNMENT, 28
with the ancient is w. BIBLE, 228; WISDOM, 5
Women…the guardians of w. FEMINISM, 38

wise a w. man, which built his house upon a rock BIBLE, 380
A w. man will make more opportunities BACON, F, 16; OPPORTUNITY, 9
Coffee which makes the politician w. DRINKS, 17; POPE, A, 52
How very weak the very w. THACKERAY, W, 8
Many have been the w. speeches of fools WISDOM AND FOOLISHNESS, 6
more of the fool than of the w. BACON, F, 13; HUMAN NATURE, 4
No man…so w. as Thurlow looked APPEARANCES, 16
sorrow makes us w. SORROW, 32; TENNYSON, 36
So w. so young PRECOCITY, 5
The only wretched are the w. IGNORANCE, 19
the w. forgive SZASZ, T, 6
To be w. and love SHAKESPEARE, 332
where ignorance is bliss, /'Tis folly to be w. GRAY, T, 10
w. enough to play the fool WISDOM, 27
w. man makes his own decisions WISDOM AND FOOLISHNESS, 1

wisely deserves the name of happy who knows how to use the gods' gifts w. HAPPINESS, 10; HORACE, 43
eat w. but not too well ETIQUETTE, 6
lov'd not w., but too well LOVE, 155; SHAKESPEARE, 290

Wiseman Mr Worldly W. BUNYAN, J, 3; MATERIALISM, 6

wiser Be w. than other people CHESTERFIELD, P, 5; WISDOM, 14
foreigner should…be w. than ourselves TROLLOPE, A, 10
Like Odysseus, he looked w. when seated WILSON, W, 2
sadder and a w. man COLERIDGE, S, 40
The French are w. than they seem BACON, F, 47; NATIONALITY, 1
the old have rubbed it into the young that they are w. MAUGHAM, W, 3; OLD AGE, 67
w. than thou art ware of WISDOM, 25
w. to-day than…yesterday MISTAKES, 15; POPE, A, 54

wisest The most attractive sentences are not perhaps the w. LANGUAGE, 48; THOREAU, H, 4

wish Conscience is…rejection of a…w. CONSCIENCE, 3; FREUD, S, 4
Justice is the…perpetual w. JUSTICE, 15
most…w. they were the only one alive AUDEN, W, 11; EGOTISM, 2
quite a number fondly believe their w.…granted AUDEN, W, 11
Someday I'll w. upon a star DESIRE, 7
The w. to hurt BRONOWSKI, J, 4; CRUELTY, 1
The w. to spread those opinions that we hold BUTLER, S, 4; ENGLISH, 8
w. to be imposed EXPLOITATION, 2

wished consummation devoutly to be w. SHAKESPEARE, 90; SUICIDE, 35

wishes If w. were horses PROVERBS, 216

wishful There is w. thinking in Hell as well as on earth DESIRE, 11; LEWIS, C, 3

wit a man of much w.…void of virtue CHESTERFIELD, P, 4
An ounce of a man's own w. STERNE, L, 10; WISDOM, 30
Attic w. PLINY THE ELDER, 1
a w. out of two half-wits FOOLISHNESS, 16; KINNOCK, N, 4
Brevity is the soul of w. BREVITY, 8; SHAKESPEARE, 81
cause that w. is in other men SHAKESPEARE, 117
fancy w. will come POPE, A, 9; STUPIDITY, 13
His foe was folly and his weapon w. HOPE, A, 9; HUMOUR, 17
I have neither w., nor words, nor worth SHAKESPEARE, 159
Impropriety is the soul of w. MAUGHAM, W, 9
In w. a man POPE, A, 18
love robs those who have it of their w. LOVE, 62
men of w. can so hardly use that gift INTELLECTUALS, 8
Music-hall songs provide the dull with w. MAUGHAM, W, 23
Pox take him and his w. POPE, A, 2
proverb is one man's w. and all men's wisdom SAYINGS, 6
To the Greeks the Muse gave native w. CLASSICS, 4
True w. is nature to advantage dress'd HUMOUR, 24; POPE, A, 25
wine is in, the w. is out DRUNKENNESS, 10
W. that can creep POPE, A, 16; SERVILITY, 5

witch thou shalt not suffer a w. to live BIBLE, 117; SUPERNATURAL, 3

witchcraft All w. comes from carnal lust LUST, 11
Medical science is…imperfectly differentiated from…w. MEDICINE, 92

witches I have ever believed…that there are w. BROWNE, T, 5; SUPERNATURAL, 4
In the past, men created w. PSYCHIATRY, 29
they think we're burning w. CHESTERTON, G, 29

wither Age cannot w. her COMPLIMENTS, 29; SHAKESPEARE, 31
his leaf also shall not w. PSALMS, 1

wither'd w. is the garland of the war SHAKESPEARE, 37

withered lonely of heart is w. away LONELINESS, 17; YEATS, W, 19

withers The state is not 'abolished', it w. away COMMUNISM, 5

within that w. which passes show MOURNING, 10; SHAKESPEARE, 67
the kingdom of God is w. you BIBLE, 334
when the fight begins w. himself BROWNING, R, 13; CONFLICT, 5

without I can do w. LUXURY, 5; SOCRATES, 7

witness I am a w. BALDWIN, J, 5
thou shalt not bear false w. BIBLE, 115; GOD, 12

witnesses this massed multitude of silent w. to…war WAR, 71

wits Great W.…to Madness near alli'd DRYDEN, J, 5; GENIUS, 4
homely w. HOME, 11; SHAKESPEARE, 348
their poetry is conceived and composed in their w. ARNOLD, M, 44; POETRY, 4
This man I thought had been a Lord among w. CRITICISM, 27; JOHNSON, S, 50

witty a very w. prologue CONGREVE, W, 11; MARRIAGE, 52
I am not only w. in myself HUMOUR, 28; SHAKESPEARE, 117
Pretty w. Nell COMPLIMENTS, 21; PEPYS, S, 11
stumbling on something w. AUSTEN, J, 25; MEN, 1

wives Bricklayers kick their w. to death CLASS, 53; WELLS, H, 19
husbands and w.…belong to different sexes SEXES, 11
husbands and w. make shipwreck of their lives MARRIAGE, 65
husbands, love your w. BIBLE, 21; MARRIAGE, 25
I met a man with seven w. NURSERY RHYMES, 3
O! men with mothers and w. HOOD, T, 11; WOMEN, 66
Powerful men…through the help of their w. SUCCESS, 16
The others were only my w. JEALOUSY, 5
Translations (like w.) are seldom faithful CAMPBELL, R, 4; TRANSLATION, 2
W. are young men's mistresses BACON, F, 34; MARRIAGE, 14
you do not make the laws but…are the w.…of those who do WOMEN, 62

wiving Hanging and w. goes by destiny DESTINY, 24; SHAKESPEARE, 246

wizard A Catalan w. who fools with shapes PICASSO, P, 1
Is a w. when he enjoys your confidence DOCTORS, 38

Wodehouse like P. G. W. dropping Jeeves WAUGH, E, 48; WRITERS, 94
W., whose works I place a little below Shakespeare's WODEHOUSE, P, 1

woe And who can blame my w. SORROW, 14

a sad variety of w. POPE, A, 8; SORROW, 21
Life protracted is protracted w. LONGEVITY, 10
Much in sorrow, oft in w. ENDURANCE, 30
suits of w. MOURNING, 10; SHAKESPEARE, 67
Wednesday's child is full of w. CHILDREN, 50; NURSERY RHYMES, 35
W. is me REGRET, 4
w. to him that is alone when he falleth BIBLE, 69; FRIENDSHIP, 8
W. to the land that's govern'd by a child SHAKESPEARE, 304
W. to the vanquished DEFEAT, 10
w. unto them that call evil good BIBLE, 196; LYING, 7
w. unto them that...follow strong drink ALCOHOL, 16; BIBLE, 195

wolf The boy cried 'W., w.!' AESOP, 9; LYING, 2
the w. in the sheep's clothing AESOP, 10; APPEARANCES, 8
w. also shall dwell with the lamb BIBLE, 203

Wolf's-bane neither twist /W. KEATS, J, 32; OBLIVION, 2

Wollstonecraft the name of Mary W. has obtained a lamentable distinction WOLLSTONECRAFT, M, 2

wolves people being thrown to the w. POLITICIANS, 98
send you forth as lambs among w. BIBLE, 323

woman A diplomat...always remembers a w.'s birthday DIPLOMACY, 13; FROST, R, 10
Alas! a w. that attempts the pen WRITERS, 11
all the keys should hang from the belt of one w. ROYALTY, 28
A man is only as old as the w. AGE, 62; MARX, G, 26
An ailing w. lives forever WOMEN, 6
And a w. is only a w. KIPLING, R, 5; WOMEN, 72
an ugly *w.* is a blot on the fair face of creation BRONTE, C, 4
Any w. who understands the problems of running a home POLITICS, 105
As a w. I can't go to war WAR, 133
A w....anxious to get children PSYCHOLOGY, 7
A w. as old as she looks OLD AGE, 38
a w....cannot be trusted with a symphony orchestra MUSIC, 35
a w. is a w. SEXES, 2
a w. is on a...hunt for trouble MARRIAGE, 65
A w. is only a w., but a good cigar is a smoke SMOKING, 21
a w. of resolute character FEMINISM, 7
a w....ought to lay aside...modesty with her skirt MONTAIGNE, M, 4; SEX, 85
A w. should be an illusion WOMEN, 56
A w. should open everything WOMEN, 83
A w.'s place is in the home PROVERBS, 74; WOMEN, 2
a w.'s reason SHAKESPEARE, 349; WOMEN, 123
A w.'s work PROVERBS, 75; WOMEN, 3
A w. who is loved always has success SUCCESS, 6
A w. will always sacrifice herself MAUGHAM, W, 5; WOMEN, 86
a w. would rather visit her own grave OLD AGE, 52
a w. yet think him an angel LOVE, 166; THACKERAY, W, 4
Between man and w. there is little difference SEXES, 1
body of a weak and feeble w. ELIZABETH I, 13; ROYALTY, 53
Christ-like heroes and w.-worshipping Don Juans LAWRENCE, D, 27; MEN, 10
close-up of a w. past sixty APPEARANCE, 6
educate a w. you educate a family EDUCATION, 59; WOMEN, 82
every w. is at heart a rake POPE, A, 42; WOMEN, 108
Every w. is infallibly to be gained CHESTERFIELD, P, 17; FLATTERY, 4
Every w. knows ACHIEVEMENT, 1; WOMEN, 18
Every w. should marry DISRAELI, B, 10; MARRIAGE, 63
fair w. without virtue VIRTUE, 1
Frailty, thy name is w. SHAKESPEARE, 69; WOMEN, 119
God made the w. for the man TENNYSON, 13; WOMEN, 128
good w. if I had five thousand MONEY, 50; THACKERAY, W, 12
he has studied anatomy and dissected at least one w. MARRIAGE, 19
hell a fury like a w. scorned CONGREVE, W, 9; LOVE AND HATE, 3
I am a...*w.* – nothing more TOLSTOY, S, 2; WOMEN, 133
I am a w.? When I think, I must speak SHAKESPEARE, 53; WOMEN, 118
I don't care...I just want every man, w., and child...to see it GOLDWYN, S, 8
if a family is held together...it's the w. who's doing it FAMILY, 19
if a w. have long hair APPEARANCE, 10; BIBLE, 37
If a w. like Eva Peron with no ideals IDEALISM, 10; THATCHER, M, 19
I had become a w. of...character CHARACTER, 6
I have nothing /Of w. in me DETERMINATION, 21
I love Mickey Mouse more than any w. WOMEN, 45
In an uncorrupted w. the sexual impulse SEX, 38
International W.'s Day RUSSIAN REVOLUTION, 9
It is a great glory in a w. WOMEN, 131
It is almost a pity that a w. has a womb WOMEN, 12
It's a sort of bloom on a w. BARRIE, J, 8; CHARM, 3
I would...guess that Anon...was often a w. WOMEN, 144
little w. who wrote the book that made this great war LINCOLN, A, 5
Man for the field and w. for the hearth TENNYSON, 66
Medicine is like a w. who changes with the fashions MEDICINE, 12
Men are men, but Man is a w. MANKIND, 19
none of w. born /Shall harm Macbeth SHAKESPEARE, 221
No one delights more in vengeance than a w. REVENGE, 12; WOMEN, 70
no one ever speaks of 'a beautiful old w.' OLD AGE, 18
nor w. neither MANKIND, 56; SHAKESPEARE, 85
No w. has an abortion for *fun* ABORTION, 12
No w. should ever be quite accurate about her age AGE, 99; WILDE, O, 34
No w. so naked as...underneath her clothes NAKEDNESS, 4
Old age is w.'s hell OLD AGE, 65
Once a w. has given you her heart WOMEN, 138
one can...see in a little girl the threat of a w. CHILDREN, 27
One is not born a w. BEAUVOIR, S, 3; WOMEN, 19
one of w. born BIRTH, 15; SHAKESPEARE, 229
One tongue is sufficient for a w. EDUCATION, 64; MILTON, J, 65
only three things to be done with a w. WOMEN, 47
put back the chance of another w. becoming PM THATCHER, M, 3
Sex between a man and a w. SEX, 7
sex plays a more important part in the life of w. SEX, 111
She makes love just like a w. DYLAN, B, 6; WOMEN, 49
she must be a w. pretty nearly unsexed BRONTE, C, 1
She really is a w. just like my mum WOMEN, 113
She was a w. of mean understanding AUSTEN, J, 19; INSULTS, 8
Six men give a doctor less to do than one w. WOMEN, 5
such beauty as a w.'s eye LEARNING, 16; SHAKESPEARE, 199
Than to ever let a w. in my life MISOGYNY, 1
the anxiety of being a w. WOMEN, 20
the help and support of the w. I love LOVE, 176
the mind of a w. is easily disturbed and misled WOMEN, 28
the most beautiful w. I've ever seen BEAUTY, 32; MARX, G, 1
The really original w....imitates a man WOMEN, 127
There was an old w. /Lived under a hill NURSERY RHYMES, 57
There was an old w. who lived in a shoe NURSERY RHYMES, 58
the rib...made he a w. BIBLE, 147; WOMEN, 23
The silliest w. can manage a clever man KIPLING, R, 22
the sort of w. now...one would...bury for nothing DICKENS, C, 29; WOMEN, 43
the sort of w. who lives for others LEWIS, C, 6
The surgical cycle in w. WOMEN, 100
The w.'s a whore JOHNSON, S, 89; PROMISCUITY, 6
The w. that deliberates is lost ADDISON, J, 6; WOMEN, 8
the w. who is really kind to dogs BEERBOHM, M, 14; WOMEN, 21
The years that a w. subtracts AGE, 32
To a physician, each man, each w. MEDICINE, 25
To know the *mind* of a w. LAWRENCE, D, 45
Twenty years of romance makes a w. look like a ruin WILDE, O, 56
What does a w. want FEMINISM, 45; FREUD, S, 6
What is w. WOMEN, 38
When a w. becomes a scholar WOMEN, 97
When a w. behaves like a man WOMEN, 54
when a w. is strong, she is strident THATCHER, M, 39
When lovely w. stoops to folly GOLDSMITH, O, 29; GULLIBILITY, 2
who can find a virtuous w. BIBLE, 458; WOMEN, 25
Who loves not wine, w. and song PLEASURE, 22
Why can't a w. be more like a man MEN, 11
Why...was I born a w. WOMEN, 98
will not stand...being called a w. in my own house WAUGH, E, 39
w. alone, can...commit them THACKERAY, W, 7
w. as old as she looks AGE, 27
w., behold thy son BIBLE, 270
w. governs America AMERICA, 29
w. has her way SEXES, 14
w. is a dish for the gods WOMEN, 117
W. is always fickle and changing VIRGIL, 12; WOMEN, 139
w. is an animal that WOMEN, 84
w. is his game SEXES, 29; TENNYSON, 65
W. is unrivaled as a wet nurse WOMEN, 136

w....knowing anything AUSTEN, J, 16; WOMEN, 14
w. of education WOMEN, 137
W.'s at best a contradiction POPE, A, 43; WOMEN, 109
w. seldom asks advice ADDISON, J, 16; WOMEN, 9
w....so vicious, or so feeble-minded BRONTE, A, 4
W.'s virtue SEXES, 26; VIRTUE, 23
w.'s weapon is her tongue WOMEN, 61
w.'s whole existence BYRON, 20; SEXES, 6
W. to bear rule...is repugnant to Nature WOMAN'S ROLE, 10
W. was God's *second* mistake NIETZSCHE, F, 3; WOMEN, 95
w. who...locked in alone in the National Gallery WOMEN, 13
W. will be the last thing civilized by Man WOMEN, 90
wrecks a w.'s reputation COLETTE, S, 4
You're a fine w., Lou WEST, M, 9

womanhood tobacco...conspiracy against w. and manhood SMOKING, 20
W. is the great fact in her life FEMINISM, 33; WOMEN, 125

womanized Most British statesmen have either drunk too much or w. too much POLITICIANS, 54

woman-kind whole race of w. is...made subject to man BOCCACCIO, G, 5; WOMAN'S ROLE, 2

woman's A w. heart always has a burned mark SORROW, 15

Woman's Rights mad, wicked folly of 'W.' FEMINISM, 51; VICTORIA, 7

womb How does a child live in the w. LEONARDO DA VINCI, 2
It is almost a pity that a woman has a w. WOMEN, 12
many events in the w. of time SHAKESPEARE, 280
mother's w. /Untimely ripp'd BIRTH, 15; SHAKESPEARE, 229
no new baby in the w. of our society LAWRENCE, D, 37
teeming w. of royal kings SHAKESPEARE, 297
think with our w. INTELLIGENCE, 7
this rifled and bleeding w. ABORTION, 5

women A homely face...aided many w. heavenward APPEARANCE, 5
All Berkshire w. are very silly WOMEN, 48
all men and w. are created equal EQUALITY, 36
all w. do MARRIAGE, 10
American w. expect to find in their husbands WOMEN, 85
An experience of w. DOYLE, A, 14
a snare in which the feet of w. FEMINISM, 1
a tide in the affairs of w. FEMINISM, 43
Because w. can do nothing except love MAUGHAM, W, 10
Between w. love is contemplative HOMOSEXUALITY, 3
comely to w. to nourish their hair WOMEN, 112
Does anybody wonder so many w. die SORROW, 6
Few w. care to be laughed at RIDICULE, 2
Give w. the vote SHAW, G, 20
God withheld the sense of humour from w. WOMEN, 33
gossip of two w. GOSSIP, 1
great city...has the greatest men and w. WHITMAN, W, 12
he gets off with w. because he can't get on SEX, 69
I don't think men and w. were meant to live together SEXES, 12
if civilisation is to advance...it must be through...w. PANKHURST, E, 3
If men knew how w. pass their time WOMEN, 65
If w. be proud PRIDE, 11
If w. didn't exist...money...no meaning WOMEN, 99
I have sung w. in three cities POUND, E, 9; WOMEN, 110
imagine that they are upholding w.'s emancipation STOPES, M, 6
I'm not denyin' the w. are foolish WOMEN, 50
Intimacies between w. WOMEN, 27
in w. nine out of ten abdominal swellings BIRTH, 13
I think of w., it is their hair WOMEN, 96
It is a sad feature...that only w....have time to write novels WRITERS, 27
keeping w. in a state of ignorance FEMINISM, 16
made love to ten thousand w. PROMISCUITY, 12
men's attitude to w. FEMINISM, 5
Mohamed wanted equality for w. EQUALITY, 3
Monstrous Regiment of W. WOMEN, 73
Most good w. are hidden treasures WOMEN, 103
Most w. have no characters POPE, A, 41; WOMEN, 107
Most w. set out to try to change a man CHANGE, 5; SEXES, 10
Music and w. I cannot but give way to PEPYS, S, 14
no one ever asks the w. and children what they think WAR, 156
Older w. are best SEX, 37
Pornographers are the enemies of w. CARTER, A, 8
pride is a word often on w.'s lips PRIDE, 3
proper function of w. ELIOT, G, 8
several young w....would render the Christian life intensely difficult LEWIS, C, 4
some w. who...should only be caressed WOMEN, 41
souls of w. are so small BUTLER, S, 9; WOMEN, 30
stir up the zeal of w. FEMINISM, 22
Suffer the w. whom ye divorce KORAN 8; MARRIAGE, 96
surest signs of his genius...w. dislike his books PRECOCITY, 4
that all men and w. are created equal FEMINISM, 34
The battle for w.'s rights... THATCHER, M, 23
the emancipation of w. FEMINISM, 15; KEY, E, 1
The happiest w....have no history WOMEN, 52
the largest scope for change still lies in men's attitude to w. BRITTAIN, V, 2
the man who does not know sick w. does not know w. WOMEN, 93
the only advantage w. have over men...they can cry RHYS, J, 2
The prolonged slavery of w. FEMINISM, 32
The question of the rights of w. WOMEN, 143
There are two kinds of w. WOMEN, 106
there never will be...equality until w....make laws ANTHONY, S, 4
the vote means nothing to w. O'BRIEN, E, 4
The War between Men and W. THURBER, J, 14
the w. come and go ELIOT, T, 12
the w. in his paintings PICASSO, P, 4
the w. whose eyes have been washed...with tears WOMEN, 46
The w. who want w.'s rights FEMINISM, 49
tide in the affairs of w. BYRON, 31
Votes for W. WOMEN, 11
We are here to claim our rights as w. PANKHURST, C, 5
we cannot instruct w. as we do men in the science of medicine MEDICINE, 22
Were't not for gold and w. SIN, 25
we suffragettes aspire to be...ambassadors of freedom to w. PANKHURST, C, 6
We were falling w. LOVE, 19
Whatever w. do, they must do it twice as well EQUALITY, 39
what most w. think about anything AYCKBOURN, A, 1
When w. go wrong SEX, 126; WEST, M, 14
Where do all the w....get the heroism WAR, 95
Why are w....so much more interesting to men SEXES, 38; WOOLF, V, 13
Why need...w. know so much BROWNING, R, 5; WOMEN, 29
with peaches and w., it's...the side next the sun that's tempting TEMPTATION, 8
w....are better team members than men SPORT AND GAMES, 13
W....are either better or worse than men LA BRUYERE, J, 7; WOMEN, 74
W. are equal because...not different WOMEN, 58
W. are most fascinating between the ages of thirty-five and forty WOMEN, 44
W. are much more like each other CHESTERFIELD, P, 16
W. are so opinionated WOMEN, 114
w. become like their mothers SEXES, 35; WILDE, O, 21
W. can be great athletes SPORT AND GAMES, 23
w. can live their whole lives and not know the law LAW, 14
W. cannot be part of the Institute of France CURIE, M, 1
W....care fifty times more for a marriage than a ministry BAGEHOT, W, 5
w. defend themselves so poorly LACLOS, P, 1
w. dislike his books ORWELL, G, 34
W. do not believe that men believe...pornography PORNOGRAPHY, 3
W. exist...solely for the propagation of the species WOMAN'S ROLE, 12
W. fail to understand FEMINISM, 12
w. freed of their political shackles FEMINISM, 27
W. had always fought for men PANKHURST, E, 4
W. have served...as looking-glasses WOOLF, V, 12
W. have smaller brains than men SEXES, 24
w....help to make laws FEMINISM, 4
w....ill-using them and then confessing it TROLLOPE, A, 9
w. in the priesthood CLERGY, 17
w., never SCIENCE, 4
W. never have young minds WOMEN, 42
w....not so young as...painted BEERBOHM, M, 10
W. represent...matter over mind WILDE, O, 50
w. require both BUTLER, S, 29
w.'s attitude to themselves FEMINISM, 5

Clear w.…do not seem so deep as they are LANDOR, W, 5; WRITING, 28
Creative w. are…greater than the causes…they represent FORSTER, E, 6; WRITERS, 12
Irish w. – the ones that *think.* BEHAN, B, 8; IRISH, 3
No regime has ever loved great w. SOLZHENITSYN, A, 10; WRITERS, 26
picking gold out of the dunghills of old Roman w. VIRGIL, 3
The only way for w. to meet CONNOLLY, C, 14; WRITERS, 9
W. like Connolly gave pleasure a bad name CONNOLLY, C, 1
W., like teeth, are divided into incisors and grinders BAGEHOT, W, 8; WRITERS, 2

writes He w. as fast as they can read HAZLITT, W, 21; WRITERS, 60
Moving Finger w. DESTINY, 8; FITZGERALD, E, 14

writhe Uriah…made a ghastly w. DICKENS, C, 16; SERVILITY, 3

writhing Reeling and W. CARROLL, L, 15; EDUCATION, 21

writing All good w. is swimming under water FITZGERALD, F, 16; WRITING, 14
as I had in the w. PLEASURE, 29
give up w. today – read Pepys instead PEPYS, S, 3
it was a woman's w. ELIOT, G, 1
I wouldn't give up w. about God WAUGH, E, 48; WRITERS, 94
That's not w., that's typing INSULTS, 27; WRITING, 9
the disease of w. books MONTESQUIEU, 8
the incurable disease of w. WRITING, 26
the worst…is w. about w. CRITICISM, 8
True ease in w. comes from art POPE, A, 26
What is the future of my kind of w. WRITING, 40
When a man is in doubt about…his w. BUTLER, S, 12
w. an exact man BACON, F, 51; READING, 1
W.…is but a different name for conversation STERNE, L, 7; WRITING, 46
W. is like getting married MARRIAGE, 113; MURDOCH, I, 2

writings historians left blanks in their w. HISTORIANS, 6; POUND, E, 8

written Books are well w., or badly w. BOOKS, 53; WILDE, O, 44
books…w. by people who don't understand them BOOKS, 29
No one has w. worse English than Mr Hardy in…his novels HARDY, T, 4
she has w.…a few moments of human experience PARKER, D, 1
what I have w. I have w. BIBLE, 269
w.…for the sake of 'self-expression' HARDY, T, 2
w. or thought, it can be filmed CINEMA, 17
you would have been very glad if I had w. it PLAYS, 9

Wromantic Cavaliers (Wrong but W.) HISTORY, 27; SELLAR, W, 5

wrong A door is what a dog is…on the w. side of DOGS, 14; NASH, O, 2
a financial interest in being w. PSYCHIATRY, 24
A man should…own he has been in the w. MISTAKES, 15; POPE, A, 54
An extraordinarily gifted president who was the w. man JOHNSON, L, 1
anxious to do the w. thing correctly ETIQUETTE, 9; SAKI, 20
doing no w. INNOCENCE, 12
History is…the w. way of living DURRELL, L, 3; HISTORY, 11
Holders of one position, w. for years AUDEN, W, 25
If anything can go w. PROVERBS, 212
I…may not always be right, but I am never w. GOLDWYN, S, 6
Of course not…I may be w. RUSSELL, B, 32; UNCERTAINTY, 4
orthodoxy…practically means being w. CHESTERTON, G, 17; ORTHODOXY, 2
our country, right or w. PATRIOTISM, 12
responsible and w. RESPONSIBILITY, 5; RIGHTEOUSNESS, 8
right deed for the w. reason ELIOT, T, 18; MOTIVE, 2
Science is always w. SCIENCE, 84
sentimentality…rubs you up the w. way MAUGHAM, W, 25; SENTIMENTALITY, 4
something is impossible, he is…w. SCIENCE, 20
something w. with our bloody ships BOATS, 1
support me when I am…w. MELBOURNE, 4; SUPPORT, 5
their authors could not endure being w. CAMUS, A, 7; CRIME, 2
The multitude is always in the w. PUBLIC, 18
The right divine of kings to govern w. MONARCHY, 19; POPE, A, 4
the unclouded face of truth suffer w. FACTS, 6; JOURNALISM, 31
the w. place at the w. time under the w. circumstances JOHNSON, L, 1
The w. war, at the w. place WAR, 25
they've shot the w. person INSULTS, 108
To do a great right, do a little w. LAW, 34
When a doctor does go w. DOCTORS, 33
When women go w. SEX, 126; WEST, M, 14
W. from the start POETRY, 49; POUND, E, 12
w. side of the tracks CARTER, A, 9
Yes, once…I thought I had made a w. decision MISTAKES, 10

wrongdoing W. can only be avoided VICE, 14

wronged Not to be w. is to forgo…goodness WELLS, H, 4

wrong number if I called the w., why did you answer the phone THURBER, J, 15

wrongs for one class to appreciate the w. of another CLASS, 48
if two w. don't make a right NIXON, R, 1; POLITICIANS, 73
Two w. do not make a right MISTAKES, 1; PROVERBS, 447

Wykehamist A rather dirty W. EDUCATION, 14

XYZ

Xanadu In X. did Kubla Khan COLERIDGE, S, 14; PLEASURE, 10

x-ray to replace X. by hearsay GOSSIP, 13; THOMAS, G, 4

x-rays X.: Their moral is this SCIENCE, 17

yacht I had to sink my y. to make my guests go home FITZGERALD, F, 6; PARTIES, 5

yaks a lot of y. jumping about CRITICISM, 6

Yale all the young ladies who attended the Y. promenade dance were laid end to end PARKER, D, 15; SEX, 91
A whale ship was my Y. College EDUCATION, 63

yang Y. – positive cosmic force MARRIAGE, 50

Yank another Y. half a step behind CLINTON, B, 5

Yankee Y. Doodle came to town AMERICA, 3; NURSERY RHYMES, 73

yard a y.…3.37 inches longer than other people's FRANCE, 3
let a bully come into your front y. DIPLOMACY, 20

yarn web of our life is of a mingled y. GOOD AND EVIL, 6; SHAKESPEARE, 23

yawn When a book is boring, they y. openly BOOKS, 44

yawns grave y. for him BORES, 7; INSULTS, 123; TREE, H, 3

ye that y. be not judged JUDGMENT, 2

year all the y. were playing holidays LEISURE, 5; SHAKESPEARE, 110
Another y.! – another deadly blow DEFEAT, 18; WORDSWORTH, W, 52
each day is like a y. IMPRISONMENT, 17; WILDE, O, 9
Even if the doctor does not give you a y. DETERMINATION, 23
I said to the man who stood at the gate of the y. FAITH, 15
Let it be kept till the ninth y. HORACE, 11; PUBLISHING, 7
Not to hope for things to last for ever, is what the y. teaches HORACE, 41; TRANSIENCE, 16
That time of y. thou mayst in me behold OLD AGE, 94; SHAKESPEARE, 366
two months of every y. BYRON, 7; WEATHER, 8
y.'s at the spring BROWNING, R, 45; PERFECTION, 3

yearning a y. for all that is wide AMERICA, 22
learning, earning and y. LIFE, 67

years After long y. BYRON, 44; SEPARATION, 2
a thousand y.…are but as yesterday PSALMS, 49
carry away…y. of our own lives DOGS, 8
he that cuts off twenty y. of life DEATH, 145; SHAKESPEARE, 150
how many y. can some people exist DYLAN, B, 2; FREEDOM, 14
I have been talking prose for over forty y. MOLIERE, 3; PROSE, 6
It will keep for y. LEACOCK, S, 4; LONGEVITY, 11
One thousand y. more…*Homo sapiens* has before him MANKIND, 70; WELLS, H, 22
The y. that a woman subtracts AGE, 32
world must be made safe for…fifty y. CHURCHILL, W, 9; WAR, 46
Y. hence, perhaps, may dawn an age ARNOLD, M, 20; FUTURE, 2
y. of discretion AGE, 20; BOOK OF COMMON PRAYER, 19

Yeats In Drumcliff churchyard Y. is laid YEATS, W, 32
William Y. is laid to rest POETS, 18
Y. is not a man of this world YEATS, W, 2
Y. stood for enchantment YEATS, W, 1

yellow He is very y. and glum ELIOT, T, 2
the Y. Brick Road TRAVEL, 19

Yeltsin Bill Clinton, Boris Y. and François Mitterand; we all like to eat POLITICIANS, 97

yes girls…say No when they mean Y. WOMEN, 10
She didn't say y. INDECISION, 2

yes-men I don't want any y. GOLDWYN, S, 24

yesterday a thousand years…are but as y. PSALMS, 49

NAMES INDEX

11; GOVERNMENT, 7; HEROISM, 3; ILLNESS, 10; LYING, 5, 6; MONEY, 9; NONSENSE, 3; POLITICIANS, 1, 46; POLITICS, 12; POWER POLITICS, 1; PREJUDICE, 1; PUNS, 1; SCIENCE, 5; SMALLNESS, 2
Bellow, Saul LIFE AND DEATH, 8
Benchley, Robert ALCOHOL, 14; CHIVALRY, 3; CRITICISM, 9; DEBAUCHERY, 2; DOCTORS, 20; EPITAPHS, 1; HUMOUR, 39; SMALLNESS, 3; TELEGRAMS, 3; VENICE, 1; WRITERS, 36
Benda, Julien INTELLECTUALS, 5
Benét, William CAMUS, 1, 2
Benjamin, Judah Philip JEWS, 3
Benn, Tony HOUSES OF PARLIAMENT, 5; MARXISM, 1; MEDIA, 4; PHOTOGRAPHY, 2; POLITICIANS, 47, 48; POLITICS, 10
Bennett, Alan CHILDREN, 12; DICKENS, 1; DOCTORS, 21; DOGS, 3; INSULTS, 17; LIFE, 12, 13; NOSTALGIA, 1; OLD AGE, 19; SCIENCE, 6; SOCIALISM, 1, 2; THEATRE, 4; WAR, 19; WRITING, 6
Bennett, Arnold BELIEF, 3; CONFUSION, 2; ILLNESS, 11; JOURNALISM, 8; LIFE, 14; MARRIAGE, 24; PESSIMISM, 1; POLITICIANS, 49; POLITICS, 13; PREJUDICE, 2; PROGRESS, 4; SPEECHES, 2; TASTE, 2
Bennett, James Gordon NEWSPAPERS, 3, 4; TELEGRAMS, 4
Bennett, Rodney GANDHI, M, 1
Benny, Jack DESIRE, 1; MERIT, 2
Benson, A. C. BRITAIN, 4; HOUSMAN, 1
Benson, E. F. HUMAN NATURE, 7; OLD AGE, 20
Bentham, Jeremy EQUALITY, 8; HAPPINESS, 4; LAW, 8; LAWYERS, 4
Bentley, Edmund Clerihew ARCHITECTURE, 1; BIOGRAPHY, 1; BRIBERY, 1; DEATH, 33; DISRAELI, 1; ECONOMICS, 3; SCIENTISTS, 7
Bentley, Nicolas JOURNALISM, 9; LIFE, 15
Bentley, Richard ALCOHOL, 15; POETRY, 9; REPUTATION, 2
Bentsen, Lloyd QUAYLE, 3
Berenson, Bernhard PICASSO, 1
Beresford, Charles APOLOGIES, 1
Berger, John ARTISTS, 11; WOMEN, 22
Bergerac, Cyrano de REVENGE, 8
Bergman, Ingrid ACTING, 4
Berkeley, Bishop COMPLAINTS, 1; HONESTY, 3
Berksted, Roger de ROYALTY, 25
Berlin, Irving CHRISTMAS, 6; EXPECTATION, 1; HUMOUR, 4; NAVY, 1; POPULAR MUSIC, 4
Berlioz, Hector TIME, 13
Bernal, John Desmond LIFE, 16
Bernard, St CHRISTIANITY, 5, 6
Bernard, Tristan PLAYS, 3
Bernard, W. B. TRIVIALITY, 2
Berne, Eric LIFE AND DEATH, 9; PSYCHIATRY, 8
Berners, Gerald Hugh Tyrwhitt-Wilson LAWRENCE, T, 2
Bernhardt, Sarah ACTING, 6; CRICKET, 2; FOOTBALL, 3
Berra, Yogi SPORT AND GAMES, 4
Berry, Chuck POPULAR MUSIC, 5, 6
Bertolucci, Bernardo CHILDREN, 13
Bethmann-Hollweg, Theobald von WORLD WAR I, 3
Betjeman, Sir John ADMIRATION, 1; BUSINESS, 4; COMPLIMENTS, 3; EDUCATION, 13, 14; ENGLAND, 6; ENVIRONMENT, 3; ETIQUETTE, 1; FOOD, 12; FUTURE, 3; HUNTING, 2; OLD AGE, 21; POETRY, 10; TRAVEL, 9; WRITERS, 37
Bevan, Aneurin BRIBERY, 2; CHURCHILL, 4; COMMUNISM, 3; COMPROMISE, 2; INCOMPETENCE, 1; INSULTS, 18, 19; JOURNALISM, 10; LEADERSHIP, 1; NONCOMMITMENT, 1; NUCLEAR WEAPONS, 4; POLITICIANS, 50, 51; POLITICS, 14, 15, 16, 17, 18; RIGHTEOUSNESS, 2; SOCIALISM, 3, 4; SPEECHES, 3; WEAPONS, 2, 3
Beveridge, Lord GOVERNMENT, 8; LEADERSHIP, 2; PESSIMISM, 2
Bevin, Ernest CONSERVATISM, 1; FREEDOM, 5; MIXED METAPHORS, 1; POLITICIANS, 52
Bickerstaffe, Isaac HAPPINESS, 5; SELFISHNESS, 2
Bidault, Georges MISTAKES, 3
Bier, August ACADEMICS, 3, 4; MEDICINE, 12; SCIENCE, 7; THEORY, 1
Bierce, Ambrose ACCIDENTS, 1; BORES, 1; DEBAUCHERY, 3; DISEASE, 10; DOCTORS, 23, 24; EGOTISM, 3; FOOD, 16; FUTURE, 5; GREED, 6; IGNORANCE, 5; ILLNESS, 14; LOGIC, 1; LONGEVITY, 4; MANKIND, 9; MARRIAGE, 32; MEDICINE, 13, 14; MIND, 1; MISFORTUNE, 5; MUSIC, 11; OPTIMISM, 16; PAINTING, 3; PATIENCE, 8; PEACE, 5; PHILOSOPHERS, 1; PRAYER, 7; RELIGION, 13, 14; WRITERS, 38
Billings, John Shaw EDUCATION, 15
Billings, Victoria MOTHERHOOD, 1
Binding, Rudolph WORLD WAR I, 4, 5
Binyon, Laurence MEMORIALS, 6; MOURNING, 3
Birt, John JOURNALISM, 11; TELEVISION, 2
Bismarck CHILDREN, 20; DETERMINATION, 6; DIPLOMACY, 5, 6; POLITICS, 19, 20; POWER POLITICS, 2; WAR, 22
Blacker, Valentine PRUDENCE, 7
Blackett, Patrick Maynard Stuart SCIENCE, 9
Blackmore, R. D. MOTHERHOOD, 2
Blackstone, Sir William JUSTICE, 3; MEMORY, 3; MONARCHY, 5; NAVY, 2; SOCIETY, 3
Blackwell, Antoinette Brown SEXES, 5
Blackwood, Helen Selina HOMESICKNESS, 1
Blade, Toledo MIND, 2
Blair, Robert DEATH, 39; WHISTLING, 2
Blair, Tony UNEMPLOYMENT, 1
Blake, Charles Dupee SLEEP, 7
Blake, Eubie AGE, 18; MUSIC, 12; RACISM, 4
Blake, Lord MOUNTBATTEN, 1
Blake, William ACTION, 7; ANIMALS, 6; ARTISTS, 12; BEAUTY, 10; BIRTH, 5; CHILDREN, 21; CONFLICT, 4; CREATION, 7, 8; DESIRE, 2, 3, 4; DOUBT, 4; EFFORT, 2; ENGLAND, 7; EPITAPHS, 7; EXCESS, 4; FIGHT, 1; FUTILITY, 5; GENERALIZATIONS, 1; GOOD, 2; GREATNESS, 4; HAPPINESS, 6; HELL, 1; HUMILITY, 2; HYPOCRISY, 5; IMPRISONMENT, 2; INFINITY, 1; INSULTS, 20; LIFE, 17; LOVE, 36, 37; MANKIND, 10; MUSIC, 13, 14; PERCEPTION, 1, 2, 3; PLEASURE, 5; POWER, 7; PRAYER, 8; PROOF, 2; RACISM, 5; SORROW, 3; SOUL, 4; SUITABILITY, 1; TRUTH, 13; WISDOM, 12, 13; WISDOM AND FOOLISHNESS, 5; WONDER, 2
Blanchflower, Danny FOOTBALL, 4
Blank, Joost de OPPRESSION, 3; RACISM, 9
Blatter, Joseph FOOTBALL, 5
Bleasdale, Alan UNEMPLOYMENT, 2
Blixen, Karen MANKIND, 11
Blok, Aleksandr MIND, 3
Bloomfield, Arthur L. MEDICINE, 15
Bloomingdale, Judith CARROLL, 1
Blücher, Gebhard LONDON, 5
Blunden, Edmund POETRY, 11
Blunt, Alfred ROYALTY, 26
Blunt, Wilfred Scawen ENGLAND, 8
Blythe, Ronald AGE, 19; CLERGY, 3; OLD AGE, 24; RELIGION, 15
Boccaccio, Giovanni LOVE, 38; RIDICULE, 3; WOMAN'S ROLE, 2
Boethius HAPPINESS, 7
Boff, Leonardo CHURCH, 3
Bogarde, Dirk ORDER, 1
Bogart, Humphrey ADMIRATION, 2; CHANCE, 3; COMPLIMENTS, 4; MISQUOTATIONS, 11; NOSTALGIA, 2
Bogart, John B. MEDIA, 5
Bohr, Niels EXPERTS, 2; SUPERSTITION, 7
Boileau, Nicolas ADMIRATION, 3; IDLENESS, 2; SELF-CONTROL, 2; VICE, 4
Boleyn, Anne MARTYRDOM, 1
Bolingbroke, Henry St John, Viscount, POLITICS, 21
Bolitho, William DRINKS, 6; PLACES, 5
Bolt, Robert ARISTOCRACY, 5; MORALITY, 3
Bonaparte, Lucien NAPOLEON, 2; TYRANNY, 3
Bone, David SELFISHNESS, 3
Bone, James EDITORS, 3
Bonhoeffer, Dietrich GOD, 15, 16
Bono, Edward de DISAPPOINTMENT, 1; EDUCATION, 16, 17
Boone, Daniel CONFUSION, 3
Boorstin, Daniel J. BOOKS, 15; FAME, 6, 7
Booth, Charles ALCOHOL, 22
Booth, William ENGLAND, 9
Borah, Mrs Mary LONGEVITY, 5
Borah, William Edgar DEMOCRACY, 2
Borge, Victor REMEDIES, 14
Borges, Jorge Luis MARTYRDOM, 2; PROGRESS, 5; TRANSLATION, 1; UNCERTAINTY, 2; UNIVERSE, 2; WAR, 23
Born, Bertrand le PLEASURE, 7
Borrow, George BRITISH, 3; SATISFACTION, 1; SUICIDE, 4
Bosquet, Pierre WAR, 24
Bossidy, John Collins SNOBBERY, 3
Boswell, James ACTORS, 14; CONVERSATION, 3; GIBBON, 1; VOLTAIRE, 1, 2
Botha, Elize RACISM, 6
Botha, P. W. SOUTH AFRICA, 1, 2, 3
Botham, Ian FAMILY, 11; PLACES, 6; SPORT AND GAMES, 5
Bottomley, Horatio William PUNS, 2
Bottomley, Virginia WOMEN, 26
Boucicault, Dion TIME, 15
Boulay de la Meurthe, Antoine MISTAKES, 4
Boulton, H. E. ROYALTY, 27
Boulton, Canon Peter RELIGION, 16
Bourdillon, Francis William SUN, 1
Bowen, Charles JUSTICE, 4
Bowen, E. E. PARTING, 4; SPORT AND GAMES, 6
Bowen, Elizabeth ART, 5; EXPERIENCE, 9; INNOCENCE, 5; JEALOUSY, 3; LYING, 8; WOMEN, 27
Bowen, Lord METAPHYSICS, 1
Bowie, David ART, 6; COMMERCIALISM, 1; FASCISM, 2; MADNESS, 5
Bowra, Maurice DEATH, 41; FOOD, 17; MARRIAGE, 34
Boyer, Charles INVITATIONS, 2
Boyle, Robert SCIENCE, 10
Brabazon of Tara, Lord SPEECHES, 4
Bracken, Brendan HUMOUR, 5
Bracken, Peg DIETING, 1
Bradbury, Malcolm COURTESY, 3; ENGLISH, 7; FRIENDSHIP, 10; LIBERALISM, 1; MARRIAGE, 35; NEWSPAPERS, 5; SEX, 18; SYMPATHY, 1; TRAVEL, 10; UNFAITHFULNESS, 3
Bradford, John LUCK, 7
Bradford, William TRAVEL, 11
Bradley, F. H. LUCK, 8; METAPHYSICS, 2; MORALITY, 4; SAYINGS, 2; STUPIDITY, 1; UNDERSTANDING, 2
Bradley, Omar Nelson NUCLEAR WEAPONS, 5; WAR, 25
Bragg, Melvyn PATRIOTISM, 6
Brahms, Johannes INSULTS, 21; MUSICIANS, 10
Braine, John AMBITION, 3; HUMAN NATURE, 8; MARRIAGE, 36; TIME, 16; UNFAITHFULNESS, 4

Bramah, Ernest IMMORTALITY, 2; SOCIETY, 4
Bramston, James LONDON, 6
Branagh, Kenneth ACTORS, 1, 2, 3
Brancusi, Constantin GREATNESS, 5
Brand, Jo APPEARANCE, 11, 12; VIOLENCE, 2
Brando, Marlon ACTING, 5; ACTORS, 4
Brandy, Leo SALINGER, 1
Branson, Richard LEADERSHIP, 4
Braude, Jacob M. ENVY, 5
Braun, Wernher von WEAPONS, 4
Brecht, Bertolt CLASS, 7; FRIENDSHIP, 11; HEROISM, 4; HUNGER, 3; INJUSTICE, 3; LOVE, 39; NONSENSE, 4; PEACE, 7; SUPPORT, 2; SURVIVAL, 2; VICE, 5; VIRTUE, 10; WAR, 26, 27, 28
Brenan, Gerald ARTISTS, 2; FUNERALS, 3; INTELLECTUALS, 6; LANGUAGE, 9; LEISURE, 2; MARRIAGE, 37; OLD AGE, 25; POETS, 1; SELF-KNOWLEDGE, 2; WRITERS, 39
Brenton, Howard SHAKESPEARE, 3
Brezhnev, Leonid POLITICIANS, 53; SOCIALISM, 5
Briant, Keith STOPES, 1
Bridgeman, Richard STEIN, 1
Bridges, Robert BEAUTY, 11, 12; DAY, 2; MEMORY, 4; POETRY, 12
Brien, Alan BOASTS, 1; VIOLENCE, 4
Bright, John ENGLAND, 10; FORCE, 2; LINCOLN, 1; WAR, 29
Brinton, Thomas ROYALTY, 28
Brittain, Vera FEMINISM, 5; POLITICS, 22; WRITERS, 3
Britton, Colonel WORLD WAR II, 4
Broca, Paul SCIENCE, 11
Bronowski, Jacob CRUELTY, 1; MANKIND, 12; MEDIOCRITY, 3; SCIENCE, 12, 13, 14
Brontë, Anne
Brontë, Charlotte GUILT, 4; WRITERS, 40
Brontë, Emily BELIEF, 4; COURAGE, 4; IMPRISONMENT, 3; LOVE, 40
Brook, Peter ENDURANCE, 6
Brooke, Rupert BEAUTY, 13; BED, 4; CAMBRIDGE, 2; COMPLIMENTS, 5; ENGLAND, 11, 12; FLOWERS, 2, 3; NOSTALGIA, 3; PLACES, 7; POETS, 20; WAR, 30, 31, 32
Brookner, Anita HUMAN CONDITION, 4
Brooks, Gwendolyn ABORTION, 3
Brooks, Mel OSTENTATION, 1; THEATRE, 5
Brooks, Phillips CHRISTMAS, 12
Brophy, Brigid CENSORSHIP, 2
Brougham, Henry Peter PUBLIC, 5
Brown, Coral INSULTS, 22
Brown, Helen Gurley SEX, 19; VIRTUE AND VICE, 2
Brown, Heywood POSTERITY, 4
Brown, John Mason CRITICISM, 11; TELEVISION, 3
Brown, Thomas FLATTERY, 3; GARDENS, 4; HATE, 1
Browne, Cecil JEWS, 7
Browne, Sir Thomas APPEARANCE, 13; CHARITY, 12; CRITICISM, 12; DEATH, 42, 43, 44; EXPLOITATION, 1; INDIVIDUALITY, 3; JUDGMENT, 5; LIFE AND DEATH, 12; MANKIND, 13, 14; NATURE, 1; NOBILITY, 1; REMEDIES, 15; SCIENCE, 15; SELF, 7; SELF-RELIANCE, 5; SUPERNATURAL, 4; WORLD, 1
Browne, William CAMBRIDGE, 3; OXFORD, 6
Browner, Professor J. M. V. RAPE, 3
Browning, Elizabeth Barrett GOD, 17; LOVE, 41; RESPECTABILITY, 1; SORROW, 4
Browning, Robert ABSENCE, 5; AGE, 21; AMBITION, 4, 5; ANIMALS, 7, 8; BEGINNING, 7; BETRAYAL, 5; BIBLE, 525; CHRISTIANITY, 31; CONFLICT, 5; CONTEMPT, 2; DAMNATION, 1; DAY, 3; DEATH, 45; DOOMSDAY, 3; DOUBT, 5; DRINKS, 7; ENGLAND, 13; EQUALITY, 9; EVIL, 8; FREEDOM, 8; GERMANY, 1; HATE, 2; HEAVEN, 4; HORSES, 3; HUMAN CONDITION, 5; HYPOCRISY, 6; IMPRESSIONABILITY, 1; INFLUENCE, 1; KISSING, 2; LIFE, 18, 19; LOVE, 42; MISFORTUNE, 6; MONTHS, 6; MOTHERHOOD, 3; NOVELS, 1; OPTIMISM, 17, 18; PAST, 3; PERFECTION, 3, 4; PERVERSITY, 2; POSSIBILITY, 1; PROGRESS, 6; ROYALTY, 29; SINCERITY, 1; SOUL, 5; SUMMONS, 4; TRANSIENCE, 10; WOMEN, 29; WORDS, 3; WORRY, 10
Bruce, Lenny CHRISTIANITY, 32; JEWS, 5; RELIGION, 17
Brummell, 'Beau' FASHION, 2; INSULTS, 23; OBESITY, 3
Bruno, Frank SUCCESS, 8
Bruno, Giordano COURAGE, 5
Bryant, Anita HOMOSEXUALITY, 5
Bryce, Sir James MEDICINE, 16
Brydges, E. COWPER, 1
Buchanan, Robert Williams CLOTHES, 6; POETS, 2
Buck, Pearl S. AGE, 22; BEAUTY, 14; CHINA, 1; FAITH, 12; FEAR, 5; KILLING, 3; MUSIC, 15; UNIVERSE, 3
Buckingham, Duke of FOOLISHNESS, 11; ILLEGITIMACY, 2; INTRIGUE, 1
Buckle, Henry Thomas MEDICINE, 17
Buckle, Richard POPULAR MUSIC, 7
Buddha FIRE, 1; RELIGION, 18; RIGHTEOUSNESS, 5
Buffon, Comte de STYLE, 1
Bukovsky, Vladimir OPTIMISM, 19
Bullein, William FOOD, 18
Buller, Arthur Henry Reginald LIMERICKS, 7; SCIENCE, 16
Bullock, Alan HITLER, 1, 2
Bulmer-Thomas, Ivor CONCEIT, 5; INSULTS, 24
Bülow, Bernhard, Prince von IMPORTANCE, 2
Bulwer-Lytton, Edward ENTHUSIASM, 3; TENNYSON, 2; WRITING, 7
Bunch, Charlotte FEMINISM, 6
Bunner, Henry Cuyler REPUTATION, 4
Buñuel, Luis ATHEISM, 4
Bunyan, John ARCHITECTURE, 2; DESPAIR, 3, 4; DREAMS, 3; MATERIALISM, 6; PRIDE, 2; PROSE, 2; TRIVIALITY, 3; VIOLENCE, 5; WORLD, 2
Burchfield, Robert LEXICOGRAPHY, 1
Burgess, Anthony BEHN, 2; CLEANNESS, 2; ENGLAND, 14; EUROPE, 1; FITZGERALD,F, 1; FUTURE, 6; OSTENTATION, 2; POPULAR MUSIC, 8; SEX, 20; SLEEP, 8
Burke, Edmund ACCUSATION, 2; BEAUTY, 15; CHIVALRY, 4; COMPROMISE, 4; CORRUPTION, 1; CROMWELL, 1; DANGER, 4; EUROPE, 2; EXAMPLE, 2; FORCE, 3; FREEDOM, 9; HONOUR, 2; INDIFFERENCE, 2; INGRATITUDE, 2; JUDGMENT, 6; POLITICIANS, 55; POWER, 8; PUBLIC, 6; RELIGION, 19; ROYALTY, 30; SUCCESS, 9; SUPERSTITION, 8; THEORY, 2; TOLERANCE, 1; UNITY, 7; VICE, 6; YIELDING, 1
Burke, Johnny LEXICOGRAPHY, 2; OPTIMISM, 20; PUNS, 3
Burke, Thomas PRAISE, 5
Burleigh, Lord Balfour of LONDON, 4
Burnet, Gilbert ARISTOCRACY, 6; PLEASURE, 6; REVOLUTION, 2; ROYALTY, 31, 32
Burney, Fanny INNOCENCE, 1; SEASIDE, 1
Burns, George GOVERNMENT, 9; MONEY, 12; OLD AGE, 26
Burns, John RIVERS, 1
Burns, Robert ACTION, 8; ANIMALS, 9; CRUELTY, 2; DELUSION, 1; DEVIL, 9; DISAPPOINTMENT, 2; FOOD, 19; FRIENDSHIP, 12, 13; LOVE, 43, 44, 45; MARRIAGE, 38; MEN, 2; NATURE, 2; NOSTALGIA, 4; RESPECTABILITY, 2; SATISFACTION, 2; SCOTLAND, 2; WAR, 33
Burroughs, John TRUTH, 14
Burton, Richard ACTORS, 5
Burton, Robert DISEASE, 11; MELANCHOLY, 2, 3; NATIONALITY, 5; RELIGION, 20; SMOKING, 6; WRITING, 8
Burwell, C. Sidney EDUCATION, 18
Busch, Douglas PSYCHOLOGY, 2
Bush, George AMERICA, 5; CLINTON, 1; DETERMINATION, 14; EDUCATION, 19; WAR, 34, 35, 36, 37
Bussy-Rabutin ABSENCE, 6; LOVE, 46
Butcher, Terry FOOTBALL, 6
Butler, Alban HOSTAGES, 2
Butler, Joseph AFTERLIFE, 2
Butler, Nicholas Murray KNOWLEDGE, 9
Butler, R. A. CLOTHES, 7; POLITICIANS, 56, 57; POLITICS, 23; SPEECHES, 5
Butler, Samuel AGE, 23; ANALOGY, 1; ANTICIPATION, 5; ARTS, 1; BEQUESTS, 1; BOOKS, 10; CARLYLE, T, 1; DOCTORS, 26; DOGS, 4; ENGLISH, 8; EVOLUTION, 3; EXTRAVAGANCE, 2; FAITHFULNESS, 2; FAMILY, 12; HATE, 3; HYPOCRISY, 7; ILLNESS, 16; INDULGENCE, 1; LAWYERS, 6; LEARNING, 5; LIFE, 20, 21, 22, 23; LOSS, 1; LOVE, 49; MARRIAGE, 39, 40; MEDICINE, 18; MONEY, 13, 14, 15; PLEASURE, 8; POLITICS, 24; POSTERITY, 5; PRAISE, 6; PROGRESS, 7; PUBLIC, 7; PUNISHMENT, 8; REASON, 1; RELIGION, 21; REMEDIES, 16; SCIENCE, 17; SPECULATION, 1; SPONTANEITY, 1; SUBJECTIVITY, 2; TRUTH, 15; VICE, 7; VIRTUE AND VICE, 3; WAR, 38; WOMEN, 30, 31; WORDS, 4; YIELDING, 2
Butz, Earl CONTRACEPTION, 4; RELIGION, 22
Buxbaume, Martin POWER, 9
Byatt, A. S. MOTHERHOOD, 4; WRITERS, 4
Byrom, John CHRISTMAS, 13
Byron, Henry James SPORT AND GAMES, 7
Byron, Lord ADULTERY, 1; AGE, 24; ALCOHOL, 23; BEAUTY, 16; BOOKS, 11; BORES, 2; CHAUCER, 1; COMPLIMENTS, 6; COWPER, 2; CRITICS, 2; DANCING, 1; DEBAUCHERY, 4; DEPARTURE, 4, 5; DETERMINATION, 7; DOGS, 5; DRUNKENNESS, 13; EPITAPHS, 8; EUROPE, 3, 4, 5; FAME, 8; FEMINISM, 43; FREEDOM, 10; FRIENDS, 3; HEROISM, 5; INSULTS, 25; KEATS, 2, 3; LONGEVITY, 6; LOVE, 47, 48; LOVE AND HATE, 1; MATERIALISM, 7; MERRYMAKING, 2; MILTON, 2; NATURE, 3; NOSTALGIA, 5; PLEASURE, 9; POETRY, 13; POETS, 21, 22; PUBLISHING, 3; PUNISHMENT, 9; ROYALTY, 33; SELF-INTEREST, 2; SEPARATION, 2; SEXES, 6; SHERIDAN, 1; THEATRE, 6; TRUTH, 16, 17; WAR, 39; WEALTH, 15; WEATHER, 8; WOMEN, 32
Cabell, James DRINKS, 8; OPTIMISM, 21; PATRIOTISM, 7; PESSIMISM, 3
Cabot, Richard Clarke PRINCIPLES, 2
Caesar, Julius FRANCE, 1; INTEGRITY, 2; IRREVOCABILITY, 1; LAST WORDS, 12; VICTORY, 1
Cage, John POETRY, 14
Cagney, James INSULTS, 26; MISQUOTATIONS, 12
Cahn, Sammy LOVE AND MARRIAGE, 2
Caine, Michael KNOWLEDGE, 10
Caird, Edward POVERTY, 5
Cajal, Santiago Ramón y MIND, 4
Calder, Ritchie SCIENCE, 18
Caligula RUTHLESSNESS, 1
Callaghan, James BRITAIN, 5; LYING, 9; SUPPORT, 3
Calverley, C. S. ALCOHOL, 24; CLASS, 8; SMOKING, 7
Calvin, John RELIGION, 23
Campbell, Jane Montgomery AGRICULTURE, 1
Campbell, Joseph OLD AGE, 27
Campbell, Mrs Patrick MARRIAGE, 41; PRECOCITY, 1; SEX, 21; WOMEN, 33
Campbell, Patrick JOURNALISM, 12
Campbell, Roy LIFE, 24; POETRY, 15;

Mirren, Helen ACTING, 16; HUMAN CONDITION, 16
Mitchell, Adrian SOLITUDE, 12
Mitchell, Joni LIFE, 66
Mitchell, Julian FAMILY, 40; NEUROSIS, 9; TOLSTOY, 3
Mitchell, Margaret EXPEDIENCY, 6; HOPE, 17; REPUTATION, 7; TRANSIENCE, 19; WAR, 108
Mitchell, S. Weir WOMEN, 93
Mitford, Jessica OCCUPATIONS, 18
Mitford, Mary Russell WRITERS, 73
Mitford, Nancy ARISTOCRACY, 16; ENGLISH, 29; FOREIGNERS, 2; READING, 12; STYLE, 8; TIME, 37
Mitterrand, François HUMAN CONDITION, 17
Mizner, Wilson CINEMA, 20; PRUDENCE, 11; WRITING, 34
Mohamed, Mahathir bin CORRUPTION, 6
Mola, Emilio WAR, 109
Molière DEATH, 112; FOOD, 53; GRAMMAR, 6; IMPROVEMENT, 3; MEDICINE, 67; MIND, 22; MODESTY, 4; MORALITY, 11; PROSE, 6; PRUDERY, 3; REMEDIES, 42; SELF, 14; SMOKING, 25; WEALTH, 38
Molotov, Vyacheslav Mikhailovich PLACES, 26
Molyneux, William GOVERNMENT, 27
Monmouth, Duke of EXECUTION, 23
Monroe, Harriet POETRY, 45
Monroe, Marilyn NAKEDNESS, 6
Monsell, John CHRISTIANITY, 47
Montague, C. E. QUOTATIONS, 7; WAR, 110
Montague, Lady Mary Wortley POPE, 1; SATIRE, 2
Montaigne, Michel de ADMIRATION, 10; CATS, 12; CURIOSITY, 6; DOCTORS, 64; HUMAN CONDITION, 18; LYING, 15; MARRIAGE, 109; MIND, 23; OLD AGE, 72; RELIGION, 69; REMEDIES, 43; SELF-RELIANCE, 10; SEX, 85; SOLITUDE, 13
Montalvo, Juan OLD AGE, 73
Montefiore, Hugh MARRIAGE, 110
Montesquieu, Baron de CHRISTIANITY, 48; ENGLISH, 30; FREEDOM, 43; INTELLIGENCE, 9; PLEASURE, 26; RELIGION, 70; WAR, 111; WRITING, 35
Montessori, Maria EDUCATION, 65, 66
Montgomery, Lord HOMOSEXUALITY, 26; WAR, 112
Montherlant, Henry de LAST WORDS, 1; STUPIDITY, 10
Montolieu, Baronne de VOLTAIRE, 5
Montrose, Percy MOURNING, 7; UNFAITHFULNESS, 6
Moore, Clement Clarke CHRISTMAS, 15
Moore, Edward WEALTH, 39
Moore, George ACTING, 17; ART, 24; BRONTE, A, 1; HOME, 8; STEVENSON, R, 2
Moore, J. Earle SEX, 86
Moore, Marianne PSYCHOLOGY, 12
Moore, Thomas ANIMALS, 17; FLOWERS, 10; FRANCE, 14; IRELAND, 17; LAMB, 2; MOURNING, 8; NOSTALGIA, 17; WAR, 113
Moore, T. Sturge FRIENDSHIP, 24
Moravia, Alberto LITERACY, 1
More, Hannah DOCTORS, 65
More, Thomas CRITICISM, 45; EXECUTION, 24, 25, 26, 27; FAMILY, 41; IMPRISONMENT, 9; ROYALTY, 87, 88
Moreau, Jeanne SUCCESS, 22
Morell, Thomas VICTORY, 17
Morgan, Elaine EXPERTS, 6; FEMINISM, 23
Morgan, Dr Kenneth POLITICIANS, 107
Morgan, Robin COMMITMENT, 7
Morgenstern, Christian LOSS, 4
Morison, Rutherford BIRTH, 13; PREGNANCY, 6
Moritz, Karl Philipp ENGLAND, 36
Morley, Christopher LIFE, 67, 68; MANKIND, 39; SEX, 87; UNIVERSE, 16
Morley, Robert COMMUNISM, 11; CONVERSATION, 6; MANKIND, 40
Morpurgo, J. E. EUROPE, 17
Morrell, Jill HOSTAGES, 7
Morris, Desmond FRIENDSHIP, 25; HUMAN NATURE, 23; MANKIND, 41, 42, 43; SMOKING, 26
Morris, George Pope TREES, 11
Morris, Robert Tuttle DOCTORS, 66
Morris, William COMMUNISM, 12; DESIGN, 5, 6, 7
Morrison, Rutherford EVOLUTION, 23
Morrison, Toni GOSSIP, 11
Morrow, Dwight W. POLITICS, 78
Mortimer, John CLASS, 31; INSULTS, 99; LAW, 26; LIFE, 69; LITERATURE, 20; WELSH, 1
Mortimer, Raymond MODESTY, 5
Morton, J. B. HUMOUR, 55; JOURNALISM, 26; MISTAKES, 12; MUSICIANS, 12; PREJUDICE, 9; STUPIDITY, 11; TRAVEL, 35
Morton, Rogers FUTILITY, 11
Moses, Grandma ARTISTS, 5; MEMORY, 14; OCCUPATIONS, 19
Mosley, Oswald BRITISH EMPIRE, 4; FASCISM, 7; FREEDOM, 44; POLITICIANS, 108
Motley, John Lothrop LUXURY, 4
Mountbatten, Lord CLASS, 32; NUCLEAR WEAPONS, 15; ROYALTY, 89
Mountjoy, Lord ROYALTY, 90
Moynihan, Noël STATISTICS, 7
Mugabe, Robert POWER, 19
Muggeridge, Malcolm BORES, 4; DECLINE, 6; DRUGS, 11; ENGLISH, 31; HUMOUR, 22; INSULTS, 100; MISANTHROPY, 3; OBITUARIES, 8; OLD AGE, 74; PORNOGRAPHY, 6; PRUDERY, 4; ROYALTY, 91; SEX, 88, 89; TELEVISION, 10; WAUGH, 2; WELLS, 2; WORK, 22
Muir, Frank ANIMALS, 18; BEHN, 3; FOOD, 54; HEALTH AND HEALTHY LIVING, 14; MARRIAGE, 111; PUNS, 17; STRIKES, 7; STUPIDITY, 12
Mumford, Lewis BOREDOM, 8
Münster, Ernst Friedrich Herbert RUSSIA, 13
Murchison Jnr, Clint MONEY, 37
Murdoch, Dame Iris ART, 25; EQUALITY, 24; FAME, 22; LOVE, 118; LYING, 16; MARRIAGE, 112, 113; REALITY, 6; WRITING, 36
Murphy, Arthur SUPERIORITY, 12
Murphy, C. W. ABSENCE, 8
Murray, David JOURNALISM, 27
Murray, Jenni MARRIAGE, 114
Musset, Alfred de NATIONALITY, 9
Mussolini, Benito FASCISM, 8, 9, 10, 11, 12; HITLER, 4, 5; POLITICS, 79; WAR, 114; WORLD WAR II, 39; YOUTH, 19
Nabokov, Vladimir ACADEMICS, 6; CAMBRIDGE, 4; EDUCATION, 67; LIFE AND DEATH, 25; LITERATURE, 21; LUST, 9; SOLITUDE, 14; WRITERS, 19; WRITING, 37
Naipaul, V. S. WRITING, 38
Nairne, Carolina ADMIRATION, 11; COMPLIMENTS, 20; RETURN, 4
Namier, Lewis B. LAWRENCE, T, 5
Nannakaiyar, Kaccipettu LONELINESS, 9
Napier, Sir William SOLDIERS, 7
Napoleon I ARROGANCE, 6; DEATH, 114; DECLINE, 7; DOCTORS, 25; ENGLISH, 32; FOOD, 55; FRANCE, 15; LAST WORDS, 59; MADNESS, 28; PATRIOTISM, 28; POLITICS, 80; REGRET, 13; SOLDIERS, 8; WAR, 115, 116
Napoleon III SMOKING, 27; WAR, 117
Narváez, Ramón Maria LAST WORDS, 60; RUTHLESSNESS, 4
Nash, Ogden AGE, 65; ALCOHOL, 59; ANIMALS, 19; DEBAUCHERY, 10; DOGS, 14; ENGLISH, 33; EPITAPHS, 20; FAMILY, 42, 43; MATHEMATICS, 13; MONEY, 38; OLD AGE, 75, 76; SIN, 21; TREES, 12; WOMEN, 94
Nasreen, Taslima FEMINISM, 24; RELIGION, 71, 72
Nathan, G. J. PATRIOTISM, 29
Nation, Terry LIFE AND DEATH, 26
Navratilova, Martina DRINKS, 15; SPORT AND GAMES, 32; STYLE, 9
Neale, John Mason CHRISTMAS, 16; PLACES, 27; SORROW, 19
Needham, Joseph SCIENCE, 66
Needham, Richard THATCHER, 12
Needler, Henry EYES, 7
Nehru, Jawaharlal OBITUARIES, 9
Nelson, Horatio BLINDNESS, 11; DUTY, 5; ENEMIES, 6; LAST WORDS, 61; OFFICERS, 10; WAR, 118
Nevins, Allan NAZISM, 5
Newbolt, Sir Henry BLINDNESS, 12; BOATS, 15; CRICKET, 8; PATRIOTISM, 30, 31; WAR, 119, 120
Newcastle, Margaret, Duchess of EPITAPHS, 21
Newley, Anthony WORLD-WEARINESS, 5
Newman, Cardinal ARGUMENTS, 5; CHIVALRY, 10; FAITH, 23; RESPONSIBILITY, 12; SIN, 22
Newman, Ernest HELP, 9; INTELLECT, 11; MUSIC, 43; OPERA, 8
Newman, Paul MARRIAGE, 115
Newton, Howard W. SPEECH, 15
Newton, Sir Isaac ACCIDENTS, 8; DISCOVERY, 12; NATURE, 26; PROGRESS, 19; SCIENCE, 68, 69
Newton, John HEAVEN, 9
Nicholas I DECLINE, 8
Nicholas II ROYALTY, 92
Nicholas of Oresme TYRANNY, 9
Nichols, John Beverley SOLDIERS, 9
Nickson, Delbert H. ILLNESS, 52
Nicoll, W. Robertson BRONTE, E, 2
Nicolson, Harold EDUCATION, 68; ELIOT, T, 2; MACMILLAN, 4; MOUNTBATTEN, 3; TRUMAN, 2
Niebuhr, Reinhold DEMOCRACY, 18
Niemöller, Martin NAZISM, 6
Nietzsche, Friedrich AFTERLIFE, 8; BOREDOM, 9; CHRISTIANITY, 49; CRITICS, 13; DANGER, 6; DOCTORS, 67; DRUGS, 12; EMERSON, 2; GOD, 41; ILLNESS, 53; LOVE, 119; LYING, 17; MADNESS, 29; MORALITY, 12; PARIS, 5; PATIENTS, 3; PHILOSOPHERS, 7; POSTERITY, 10; PSYCHOLOGY, 13; RELIGION, 73; SCIENCE, 70; SUICIDE, 21; SUPERIORITY, 13; SURVIVAL, 6; SYMPATHY, 6; WISDOM, 23; WOMEN, 95, 96, 97
Nightingale, Florence FEMINISM, 25; LAST WORDS, 62; OCCUPATIONS, 20; STATISTICS, 8
Niven, David SOLDIERS, 10
Niven, Larry ADVICE, 4; FEMINISM, 48
Nixon, Richard Milhous BETRAYAL, 11; COMMUNICATION, 4; CORRUPTION, 9; DEFEAT, 12; DETERMINATION, 18; DOGS, 15; EQUALITY, 25; MAJORITY, 7; MOON, 5; RENUNCIATION, 3; SPACE, 7; SUICIDE, 22; SUPPORT, 7; TRUTH, 38, 39
Nogarola, Isotta WOMEN, 98
Norfolk, Roger Bigod, Earl of DETERMINATION, 13
Norman, Barry SEXES, 22
Norman, Frank NOSTALGIA, 18
North, Christopher BRITISH EMPIRE, 5; LAW, 27
Northcliffe, Lord PUBLIC, 17; TITLES, 6
Northcote, Lord POLITICIANS, 109
Norton, Caroline Elizabeth Sarah LOVE, 120
Norworth, Jack MOON, 6
Nostradamus PROPHECY, 7, 8, 9
Novello, Ivor FAMILY, 44; FRANCE, 16; HOME, 9
Noyes, Alfred DETERMINATION, 19